THE EUROPA
INTERNATIONAL
FOUNDATION
DIRECTORY 2012

THE EUROPA INTERNATIONAL FOUNDATION DIRECTORY 2012

Routledge
Taylor & Francis Group
LONDON AND NEW YORK

Twenty-first edition published 2012
by Routledge
2 Park Square, Milton Park, Abingdon, OX14 4RN, United Kingdom
Simultaneously published in the USA and Canada
by Routledge
711 Third Avenue, New York, NY 10017
Routledge is an imprint of the Taylor & Francis Group, an informa business

First published 1974

ISBN 978-185743-647-1
ISSN 1366-8048

Typeset in Century Schoolbook 9/10 (essays), 8½/9 (directory)
by AMA DataSet Limited, Preston

Europa Commissioning Editor: Cathy Hartley

Printed and bound in the United States of America by Edwards Brothers Malloy

Foreword

Since it was first published in 1974, when it was known as *The International Foundation Directory*, this book has undergone many revisions. Now in its 21st edition, *The Europa International Foundation Directory* includes, as well as some 2,500 directory entries, a section of introductory essays, a bibliography and comprehensive indexes, and aims to provide a thorough and up-to-date overview of civil society and the third sector world-wide.

The distinction between foundations, trusts and foundation-type organizations and other non-governmental organizations (NGOs) is, to some extent, unclear; thus, since its 10th edition, the Directory has formally included grant- and non-grant-making NGOs and similar civil society organizations. Hence, the Directory includes not only foundations and trusts (private, operating, grant-making and corporate), but also charities and other NGOs, some of which make grants to organizations and individuals, while others carry out their own programmes and projects.

To gain entry to the publication, an organization must be international, or, where operating on a purely national basis, must be important enough to have a widespread impact; it must have charitable or public benefit status; and must have significant funds available, or make significant charitable donations, or run its own projects of importance (however, the Editors have no pre-determined figure to establish inclusion, as the importance of an organization's funds is relative, depending on the wealth of the country in which it is located). The Editors have excluded foundations established purely for the benefit of a particular named hospital or school; moreover, governmental bodies may only be included if they are independent of political control.

The Directory contains introductory essays, a directory section and three indexes. The essays offer an overview of the development, and current state, of foundations and the third sector in a global context; foundations and NGOs and disaster management; and foundations and NGOs and the current financial crisis. The directory section is organized by country, with organizations arranged alphabetically under the appropriate heading: Foundation Centres and Co-ordinating Bodies, or Foundations, Trusts and Non-Profit Organizations. A bibliography is followed by three indexes: a full index of organizations, an index by main activity (where organizations are listed under headings including conservation and the environment, education, medicine and health, and social welfare), and an index by geographical area of activity. This latter index allows the reader to find organizations active in, for example, South America, Central America and the Caribbean, Central and South-Eastern Europe, or South Asia.

April 2012

Acknowledgements

The Editor and publishers of *The Europa International Foundation Directory* are greatly indebted to the many people who advised and helped with its compilation, and offer their sincere thanks.

They gratefully acknowledge the assistance of those foundations, trusts, NGOs and other non-profit organizations that updated their entries to ensure accuracy, and would like to thank the governmental bodies and other national and international institutions, foundation centres and co-ordinating bodies that have helped provide information on foundations and NGOs in all parts of the world.

Contents

Abbreviations	ix
International Telephone Codes	xi
Currencies and Exchange Rates	xii

Essays

Foundations and the Third Sector in International
Perspective—an Overview
HELMUT K. ANHEIER AND MARCUS LAM   3

Non-Governmental Organizations, Foundations and
Disaster Management
MICHELLE KECK   14

Non-profits during Times of Crisis: Organizational
Behaviour and Policy Responses
HELMUT K. ANHEIER, ANNELIE BELLER AND NORMAN
SPENGLER   20

Directory

Albania	29
Algeria	30
Argentina	31
Armenia	35
Australia	36
Austria	46
Azerbaijan	50
Bahamas	51
Bangladesh	52
Barbados	53
Belarus	54
Belgium	55
Benin	65
Bermuda	66
Bolivia	67
Bosnia and Herzegovina	68
Botswana	69
Brazil	70
Bulgaria	74
Burkina Faso	78
Cambodia	79
Canada	80
Chile	100
China (People's Republic)	102
Colombia	104
Costa Rica	106
Croatia	109
Curaçao	110
Cyprus	111
Czech Republic	112
Denmark	117
Dominican Republic	123
Ecuador	124
Egypt	127
El Salvador	128
Estonia	129
Ethiopia	130
Finland	131
France	135
The Gambia	156
Georgia	157
Germany	159
Ghana	185
Greece	186
Guatemala	190
Haiti	192
Honduras	193
Hong Kong	194
Hungary	195
Iceland	197
India	198
Indonesia	207
Iran	209
Ireland	210
Israel	214
Italy	216
Jamaica	229
Japan	230
Jordan	241
Kazakhstan	243
Kenya	244
Korea (Republic)	246
Kosovo	248
Kuwait	249
Kyrgyzstan	250
Latvia	251
Lebanon	252
Lesotho	254
Liechtenstein	255
Lithuania	256
Luxembourg	257
Macedonia	258
Malawi	259
Malaysia	260
Malta	261
Mexico	262
Moldova	264
Monaco	265
Mongolia	266
Montenegro	267
Morocco	268
Mozambique	269
Namibia	270
Nepal	271
Netherlands	272
New Zealand	284
Nicaragua	288
Nigeria	289
Norway	291
Pakistan	294
Palestinian Autonomous Areas	296
Panama	297
Paraguay	298
Peru	299
Philippines	301
Poland	305
Portugal	310
Puerto Rico	314
Qatar	315
Romania	316

CONTENTS

Russian Federation	318	Ukraine	393
Saudi Arabia	321	United Arab Emirates	395
Senegal	322	United Kingdom	396
Serbia	324	United States of America	458
Singapore	326	Uruguay	560
Slovakia	327	Uzbekistan	561
Slovenia	330	Vatican City	562
South Africa	331	Venezuela	563
Spain	337	Viet Nam	565
Sri Lanka	350	Zambia	566
Sweden	352	Zimbabwe	567
Switzerland	359		
Taiwan	379	Select Bibliography	568
Tajikistan	381		
Tanzania	382		
Thailand	383	**Indexes**	
Timor-Leste	386	Index of Foundations	573
Turkey	387	Index of Main Activities	595
Uganda	392	Index by Area of Activity	639

Abbreviations

AB	Alberta	EU	European Union
AC	Companion of the Order of Australia	eV	eingetragener Verein
ACT	Australian Capital Territory	Exec.	Executive
Admin	Administration	Fax	facsimile
Admin.	Administrative, Administrator	FL	Florida
AG	Aktiengesellschaft (Joint Stock Company)	Fr	Father
AIDS	Acquired Immune Deficiency Syndrome	GA	Georgia
al.	aleja (alley, avenue, Spanish)	Gdns	Gardens
Amb.	Ambassador	Gen.	General
Apdo	Apartado (apartment, Spanish)	GmbH	Gesellschaft mit beschränkter Haftung
Approx.	approximately	h.c.	honoris causa (honorary)
Apt	Apartment	HE	His (Her) Excellency
AR	Arkansas	HI	Hawaii
Assoc.	associate	HIV	Human immunodeficiency virus
Asst	assistant	HM	His (Her) Majesty
Aug.	August	Hon.	Honourable; honorary
Av.	Avenida (Portuguese)	HRH	His (Her) Royal Highness
Avda	Avenida (Spanish)	IA	Iowa
Ave	Avenue	ICT	Information and communication technology
AZ	Arizona	i.e.	id est (that is to say)
BC	British Columbia	IL	Illinois
Bldg	Building	IN	Indiana
Blvd	Boulevard	Inc	Incorporated
BP	Boîte Postale	Ing.	Engineer (German, Spanish)
Bte	Boîte (P.O. Box)	Int.	International
bul.	bulvar (boulevard)	Ir	Engineer (Dutch)
CA	California	Izq.	Izquierda (left, Spanish)
CEO	Chief Executive Officer	Jan.	January
Chair.	Chairman/woman, Chairmen/women	Jr	Junior
CIS	Commonwealth of Independent States	km	kilometre
Cnr	Corner	Lic.	Licenciado (Spanish)
CO	Colorado	Lt	Lieutenant
Co.	Company, County	Ltd	Limited
Col	Colonel	m.	million
Col.	Colonia	MA	Massachusetts
COO	Chief Operating Officer	Maj.	Major
Corpn	Corporation	Man.	Manager, Managing
CP	Case (Casa) Postale	MB	Manitoba
Cres.	Crescent	MBA	Master of Business Administration
CT	Connecticut	MD	Maryland
Ct	Court	Mgr	Monseigneur, Monsignor
Cttee	Committee	MI	Michigan
DC	District of Columbia	MN	Minnesota
DE	Delaware	MO	Missouri
Dec.	December	MP	Member of Parliament
Dept	Department	MS	Mississippi
DF	Distrito Federal	n.a.	not available
Dir(s)	Director(s)	Nat.	National
DNA	deoxyribonucleic acid	NC	North Carolina
Dott.	Dottore	NGO	non-governmental organization
Dr	Doctor	NH	New Hampshire
Dr.	Drive	NJ	New Jersey
Drs	Doctorandus	No(.)	Numéro, Número, Number
ECOSOC	Economic and Social Council (United Nations)	Nov.	November
Edif.	Edificio (building)	NSW	New South Wales
e-mail	electronic mail	NV	Naamloze Vennootschap
Emer.	Emeritus	NW	North West
Eng.	Engineer	NY	New York
etc.	et cetera	Of.	Oficina (Spanish)

ABBREVIATIONS

OH	Ohio		Sept.	September
On.	Honourable (Italian)		Sq.	Square
ON	Ontario		Sr	Senior
PA	Pennsylvania		St	Saint, Street
per.	pereulok (lane, alley, Russian)		Str.	Strasse (street, German)
Pl.	Place		Treas.	Treasurer
PLC	Public Limited Company		TX	Texas
POB	Post Office Box		u./út	utca (street, Hungarian)
PR	Public Relations		UK	United Kingdom (of Great Britain and Northern Ireland)
Preb.	Prebendal, Prebendary			
Pres(.)	President, Presidents		ul.	ulitsa (street, Polish, Russian)
Prof.	Professor		UN	United Nations
Pty	Proprietary		UNESCO	United Nations Educational, Scientific and Cultural Organization
QC	Québec			
QC	Queen's Counsel		UNHCR	United Nations High Commissioner for Refugees
Qld	Queensland			
qq.v.	quae vide (see—plural)		UNICEF	United Nations Children's Fund
q.v.	quod vide (see)		USA	United States of America
Rd	Road		USSR	Union of Soviet Socialist Republics
Rep.	Representative		UT	Utah
Retd	Retired		VA	Virginia
Rev.	Reverend		Vic	Victoria
RI	Rhode Island		vul.	vulitsa (street, Ukrainian)
Rm	Room		WA	Washington (state), Western Australia
Rt	Hon. Right Honourable		WHO	World Health Organization
Rt	Rev. Right Reverend		WI	Wisconsin
SA	South Australia		YMCA	Young Men's Christian Association
Sec.	Secretary		YWCA	Young Women's Christian Association
Sec.-Gen.	Secretary-General			

International Telephone Codes

The following codes should be added to the relevant telephone and fax numbers listed in *The Europa International Foundation Directory*.

The code and number must be preceded by the International Dialling Code of the country from which you are calling.

Albania	355	Kyrgyzstan	996
Algeria	213	Latvia	371
Argentina	54	Lebanon	961
Armenia	374	Liechtenstein	423
Australia	61	Lithuania	370
Austria	43	Luxembourg	352
Azerbaijan	994	Macedonia	389
Bahamas	1 242	Malawi	265
Bangladesh	880	Malaysia	60
Barbados	1 246	Malta	356
Belarus	375	Mexico	52
Belgium	32	Moldova	373
Benin	229	Monaco	377
Bermuda	1 441	Mongolia	976
Bolivia	591	Montenegro	382
Bosnia and Herzegovina	387	Morocco	212
Botswana	267	Mozambique	258
Brazil	55	Namibia	264
Bulgaria	359	Nepal	977
Burkina Faso	226	Netherlands	31
Cambodia	855	New Zealand	64
Canada	1	Nicaragua	505
Chile	56	Nigeria	234
China (People's Republic)	86	Norway	47
Colombia	57	Pakistan	92
Costa Rica	506	Palestinian Autonomous Areas	970 or 972
Côte d'Ivoire	225	Panama	507
Croatia	385	Paraguay	595
Curaçao	599	Peru	51
Cyprus	357	Philippines	63
Czech Republic	420	Poland	48
Denmark	45	Portugal	351
Dominican Republic	1 809	Puerto Rico	1 787
Ecuador	593	Romania	40
Egypt	20	Russian Federation	7
El Salvador	503	Saudi Arabia	966
Estonia	372	Senegal	221
Finland	358	Serbia	381
France	33	Singapore	65
Gambia	220	Slovakia	421
Georgia	995	Slovenia	386
Germany	49	South Africa	27
Ghana	233	Spain	34
Greece	30	Sri Lanka	94
Guatemala	502	Sweden	46
Haiti	509	Switzerland	41
Honduras	504	Taiwan	886
Hong Kong	852	Tajikistan	992
Hungary	36	Tanzania	255
Iceland	354	Thailand	66
India	91	Timor-Leste	670
Indonesia	62	Turkey	90
Iran	98	Uganda	256
Ireland	353	Ukraine	380
Israel	972	United Arab Emirates	971
Italy	39	United Kingdom	44
Jamaica	1 876	United States of America	1
Japan	81	Uruguay	598
Jordan	962	Uzbekistan	998
Kazakhstan	7	Vatican City	39
Kenya	254	Venezuela	58
Korea (Republic)	82	Viet Nam	84
Kosovo	381	Zambia	260
Kuwait	965	Zimbabwe	263

Currencies and Exchange Rates

(as at 31 December 2011 unless otherwise indicated)

Country	Unit	Value (1,000 units)		
		£ sterling	US $	Euro €
Albania *(30 November 2011)*	lek	6.089	9.503	7.082
Algeria *(30 November 2011)*	dinar (AD)	8.424	13.148	9.799
Argentina	new peso	150.978	233.427	180.406
Armenia	dram	1.677	2.592	2.003
Australia	Australian dollar ($A)	656.879	1,015.600	784.914
Austria	euro (€)	836.880	1,293.900	1,000.000
Azerbaijan	new manat	822.363	1,271.456	982.654
Bahamas	Bahamas dollar	646.789	1,000.000	772.857
Bangladesh	taka	7.902	12.217	9.442
Barbados	Barbados dollar	323.394	500.000	386.429
Belarus	rouble	0.077	0.120	0.093
Belgium	euro (€)	836.880	1,293.900	1,000.000
Benin	CFA franc	1.276	1.973	1.524
Bermuda	Bermuda dollar (B$)	646.789	1,000.000	772.857
Bolivia	boliviano	93.602	144.718	111.846
Bosnia and Herzegovina	convertible marka	427.890	661.561	511.292
Botswana	pula	85.941	132.873	102.692
Brazil	real	344.936	533.305	412.169
Brunei	Brunei dollar	497.262	768.817	594.186
Bulgaria	lev	427.883	661.551	511.284
Burkina Faso	CFA franc	1.276	1.973	1.524
Cambodia *(30 November 2011)*	riel	0.159	0.248	0.185
Canada	Canadian dollar (C $)	633.485	979.432	756.961
Chile	peso	1.240	1.918	1.482
China, People's Republic	yuan	102.650	158.707	122.658
Colombia	peso	0.333	0.515	0.398
Costa Rica	colón	1.264	1.954	1.510
Côte d'Ivoire	CFA franc	1.276	1.973	1.524
Croatia	kuna	111.133	171.823	132.795
Cuba	peso	698.551	1,080.030	834.709
Curaçao	guilder (NA Fl.)	361.334	558.659	431.764
Cyprus	euro (€)	836.880	1,293.900	1,000.000
Czech Republic	koruna	32.437	50.150	38.759
Denmark	krone	112.571	174.046	134.513
Dominican Republic	peso	16.673	25.779	19.923
Ecuador	US dollar ($)	646.789	1,000.000	772.857
Egypt *(31 October 2011)*	Egyptian pound	104.777	167.895	119.917
El Salvador	colón	73.919	114.286	88.327
Estonia	euro (€)	836.880	1,293.900	1,000.000
Ethiopia	birr	49.247	58.113	55.352
Finland	euro (€)	836.880	1,293.900	1,000.000
France	euro (€)	836.880	1,293.900	1,000.000
Gambia *(31 October 2011)*	dalasi	20.719	33.200	23.713
Georgia *(30 November 2011)*	lari	386.358	603.027	449.417
Germany	euro (€)	836.880	1,293.900	1,000.000
Ghana *(30 September 2011)*	Ghana cedi	421.198	656.858	486.453
Greece	euro (€)	836.880	1,293.900	1,000.000
Guatemala	quetzal	82.851	128.097	99.000
Haiti	gourde	15.784	24.404	18.861
Honduras	lempira	34.230	52.924	40.903
Hong Kong	Hong Kong dollar (HK $)	83.290	128.775	99.524
Hungary	forint	2.687	4.155	3.211
Iceland	króna	5.271	8.149	6.298
India	Indian rupee	12.144	18.776	14.511
Indonesia	rupiah	0.071	0.110	0.085
Iran	rial	0.058	0.090	0.069
Ireland	euro (€)	836.880	1,293.900	1,000.000
Israel	new shekel	169.272	261.712	202.266
Italy	euro (€)	836.880	1,293.900	1,000.000
Jamaica	Jamaican dollar (J $)	7.489	11.578	8.948
Japan	yen	8.322	12.867	9.944
Jordan	dinar (JD)	910.970	1,408.451	1,088.531
Kazakhstan	tenge	4.358	6.739	5.208

Country	Unit	Value (1,000 units)		
		£ sterling	US $	Euro €
Kenya	Kenya shilling	7.603	11.755	9.085
Korea, Republic	won	0.561	0.867	0.670
Kosovo	euro (€)	836.880	1,293.900	1,000.000
Kuwait	dinar (KD)	2,321.984	3,590.020	2,774.573
Kyrgyzstan	som	13.914	21.512	16.626
Latvia	lats	1,188.950	1,838.235	1,420.693
Lebanon	Lebanese pound	0.429	0.663	0.513
Liechtenstein	Swiss franc	687.415	1,062.812	821.402
Lithuania	litas	242.297	374.616	289.620
Luxembourg	euro (€)	836.880	1,293.900	1,000.000
Macedonia, fmr Yugoslav Repub.	new denar	13.607	21.037	16.259
Malawi *(30 September 2011)*	kwacha	3.864	6.025	4.462
Malaysia	ringgit	203.585	314.762	243.266
Malta	euro (€)	836.880	1,293.900	1,000.000
Mexico	peso	46.231	71.478	55.242
Moldova *(30 November 2011)*	leu	53.939	84.189	62.743
Monaco	euro (€)	836.880	1,293.900	1,000.000
Mongolia	tögrög (tugrik)	0.463	0.716	0.553
Montenegro	euro (€)	836.880	1,293.900	1,000.000
Morocco *(30 November 2011)*	dirham	77.344	120.719	89.968
Mozambique *(30 November 2011)*	metical	23.835	37.202	27.726
Namibia	Namibian dollar (N $)	79.430	122.806	94.912
Nepal	Nepalese rupee	8.011	12.385	9.572
Netherlands	euro (€)	836.880	1,293.900	1,000.000
New Zealand	New Zealand dollar ($NZ)	498.868	771.300	596.105
Nicaragua	gold córdoba	28.150	43.522	33.637
Nigeria *(30 November 2011)*	naira	4.112	6.418	4.783
Norway	krone	107.929	166.870	128.966
Pakistan	Pakistani rupee	7.189	11.115	8.590
Palestinian Autonomous Areas	n.a.	n.a.	n.a.	n.a.
Panama	balboa	646.789	1,000.000	772.857
Paraguay	guaraní	0.144	0.223	0.172
Peru *(30 November 2011)*	new sol	237.339	370.439	276.076
Philippines	peso	14.724	22.765	17.594
Poland	new złoty	189.263	292.620	226.154
Portugal	euro (€)	836.880	1,293.900	1,000.000
Puerto Rico	US dollar ($)	646.789	1,000.000	772.857
Romania	leu	193.690	299.464	231.443
Russian Federation	new rouble	20.089	31.060	24.005
Saudi Arabia	Saudi riyal	172.477	266.667	206.095
Senegal	CFA franc	1.276	1.973	1.524
Serbia	Serbian dinar	7.998	12.366	9.557
Singapore	Singapore dollar (S $)	497.262	768.817	594.186
Slovakia	euro (€)	836.880	1,293.900	1,000.000
Slovenia	euro (€)	836.880	1,293.900	1,000.000
South Africa	rand	79.430	122.806	94.912
Spain	euro (€)	836.880	1,293.900	1,000.000
Sweden	krona	93.905	145.186	112.208
Switzerland	Swiss franc	687.415	1,062.812	821.402
Taiwan	New Taiwan dollar (NT $)	21.353	33.014	25.515
Tajikistan	somoni	135.917	210.141	162.409
Tanzania *(31 October 2011)*	Tanzanian shilling	0.375	0.602	0.430
Thailand	baht	20.409	31.555	24.387
Timor-Leste	US dollar ($)	646.789	1,000.000	772.857
Trinidad and Tobago	Trinidad and Tobago dollar (TT $)	100.815	155.870	120.465
Turkey	new Turkish lira	338.438	523.259	404.404
Uganda	new Uganda shilling	0.260	0.401	0.310
Ukraine	hryvnya	80.952	125.160	96.730
United Arab Emirates	UAE dirham	176.117	272.294	210.444
United Kingdom	pound sterling (£)	1,000.000	1,546.100	1,194.915
United States of America	US dollar ($)	646.789	1,000.000	772.857
Uruguay	peso uruguayo	32.505	50.256	38.841
Uzbekistan	som	0.361	0.558	0.432
Vatican City	euro (€)	836.880	1,293.900	1,000.000
Venezuela	bolívar fuerte	150.791	233.138	180.183
Viet Nam *(30 June 2011)*	new dông	0.030	0.049	0.034
Zambia	kwacha	0.126	0.195	0.151
Zimbabwe *(31 December 2008)*	Zimbabwe dollar (Z.$)	0.000	0.000	0.000

PART ONE

Introductory Essays

Foundations and the Third Sector in International Perspective—an Overview

HELMUT K. ANHEIER AND MARCUS LAM

Introduction

In recent years, there has been a renewed interest in the broad range of philanthropic institutions that operate outside the confines of the market and the state (Salamon et al., 1999). Referred to as the 'voluntary', 'non-profit', 'non-governmental', or 'third' sector, this set of institutions includes a vast array of entities—charities and social service providers, interest and lobby organizations of all kinds, universities, social clubs, professional organizations, museums, human rights organizations, environmental groups, international development and relief organizations, sports clubs, marriage counselling centres, art history societies, and many more.

Foundations are part of this third sector, but are none the less seen as a separate category. As with the third sector, foundations seem to have experienced a veritable renaissance and increased attention from policy-makers (Anheier, 2001). Already by the mid-1980s, and in countries as different as the United Kingdom, the USA, Japan, Italy, Germany, Sweden, Turkey and Brazil, observers had begun to report the end of the relative decline in the overall size and importance of the foundation sector—a trend that had characterized the previous two decades (Leat, 1992; Odendahl, 1987; Boris, 1987; Biermann, Cannon and Klainberg, 1992; Arias Foundation, 1992). Some analysts suggested the possibility of a new, third 'foundation wave', after a first growth period in the late middle ages, alongside the rise of commerce and finance, and a second period of growth in the late 19th century, following the industrial revolution.

What are the reasons behind the growth in the importance and scale of foundations, and the third sector more generally? Political stability, an increase in demand for social, educational and cultural services of all kinds, and economic prosperity are certainly significant factors behind this growth. Yet a more immediate reason is the way in which foundations and voluntary organizations have been suggesting themselves as alternatives to, or instruments of, the modern welfare state. In this context, foundations have become more attractive options in recent years. Politically, they appear more acceptable tools to governments that are less certain about their own roles and ambitions, and willing to have institutions like foundations occupy more 'institutional space'. In contrast to previous historical periods, foundations seem to pose less of a challenge to the state—on the contrary, national governments and international organizations alike welcome foundation involvement in a broad range of activities and fields.

Economically, foundations seem an appropriate vehicle to solve a number of corporate challenges. For the German, Austrian or Swiss *Mittelstand* (middle class), foundations are one way to solve the succession problem for owner-managers of medium-scale enterprises, and to help provide stability in terms of ownership and control. For large international corporations, foundations are a tool to express corporate citizenship and concern for the public good. For government and corporations alike, foundations may be a more neutral way to handle specific problems, e.g. the issue of how to deal with assets of Holocaust victims, which have been held in Swiss banks for many decades.

Culturally, foundations are an expression of what could be called 'bourgeois confidence', particularly among private citizens. The vastly expanded middle class in most developed countries seems to have regained the self-confidence and institutional trust it lost during the first half of the 20th century, particularly in Europe. There appears to be a greater acceptance of private actors in the provision of public services and quasi-public services. At the same time, the state is no longer expected to be the sole provider of social security and many other areas that previously have been lodged with the public sector.

Thus, policy-makers, corporations and private citizens alike have discovered and rediscovered foundations and third sector institutions more generally. For the state, non-profit organizations and foundations tend to be vehicles either for privatizing certain tasks that are not as easily or as efficiently accomplished within the bounds of the regular state administration, or to leverage private money for public purposes. Accordingly, some countries have begun to enact legislation to encourage the establishment of foundations. At the European level, the European Commission of the European Union (EU) supports the establishment and operations of foundations in fostering a 'New Europe' (European Commission, 1997). Moreover, the European Commission calls for the introduction of the European Foundation and Association Statute as a legal instrument that would allow foundations to operate at a European-wide level (Kendall and Anheier, 1999).

Yet, it is not only national and international government agencies that have discovered foundations. Local communities and municipalities in Europe are increasingly turning to the idea of foundations to deliver services. Indeed, community foundations have been among the fastest growing segments of US philanthropy over the past two decades (Renz et al., 1997), and are spreading in most European countries as well (Walkenhorst, 2000). Corporations, too, are making more frequent use of foundations. They may establish foundations as part of their corporate giving and outreach strategy. Less frequently, foundations may assume legal ownership of significant parts of corporate assets and, in some cases, even officially become owner of the profit-making enterprise.

Of course, the most frequent founders of foundations are private citizens. In the USA and the United Kingdom, individuals set up virtually all foundations; in Switzerland, individuals founded 95% of foundations under federal jurisdiction, of which 5% are primarily grant-making, with the great majority either operating or of a mixed type. Similarly, in Germany individuals set up the great majority of foundations, followed by those that public authorities and corporations establish.

The Modern Foundation: A US Phenomenon?

Historically, foundations are among the oldest existing social institutions and show great longevity. However, it is difficult to point to the precise moment when the first foundation was established, or which of the existing foundations today can look back farthest in time. Scholars do not see the origin of foundations in early medieval times, but trace the 'genealogy' of foundations back to antiquity (Coing, 1981). These roots include Plato's Academy in Greece (Whitaker, 1974, p. 31), and the library of Alexandria in Egypt (Coon, 1938, p. 20).

THE EUROPEAN EXPERIENCE

Throughout the Middle Ages, foundations were largely synonymous with religious institutions operating in the fields of health and education, and operating as orphanages, hospitals, schools, colleges and the like. An integral part of feudal social structures, the governance and operations of foundation boards frequently combined both aristocracy and clergy. Indeed, foundations were the prototypical institutional mechanism for the delivery of educational, health and social services under the feudal order. However, from the High Middle Ages on founders of foundations, which were often linked—and dedicated—to particular trades or crafts guilds, were an increasing presence in the emerging urban middle class (Schiller, 1969). Gradually, the emerging bourgeoisie began to replace gentry and clergy as the dominant founder group—a trend the process of industrialization amplified throughout the 19th century.

As Smith and Borgmann (2001) suggest, the role and *raison d'être* of foundations in Europe underwent several dramatic changes between the 16th and the 20th centuries. The Reformation era did away with the medieval ideal of community and triggered the complex process of state-building, in which foundations were no longer part of a *res publica christiania*.[1] Instead, foundations had to compete for space in an increasingly secular public sphere. Only some foundations succeeded in this task and many, if not most, became victims of secularization and state expansion. At the same time, new foundations emerged, fuelled by the interests of the crown, landed élite and the emerging middle class, particularly urban merchants and craftsmen.

As the nation state developed, the role of foundations changed from that of a traditional, religion-based charitable institution to a somewhat more pluralist provider of quasi-public services, used by special groups and for particular interests. The numerous guild-based and trade-related foundations in the growing cities of the 17th and 18th centuries are perhaps the best example to illustrate how foundations became a private tool for serving public needs. However, this re-positioning had the result that, throughout the 19th and early 20th centuries, the role of foundations continued to be challenged to the extent that the consolidated nation state assumed responsibility for and over other parts and groups of society.

During much of the 19th century, the development of foundations depended on the political solution, if any, that could be found between the aspirations of an expanding, and frequently struggling, nation state on the one hand, and the interests of a more pluralist civil society on the other. The latter included, in particular, the new economic élite, the urban middle class and the professions as the major force in the establishment of foundations. From a supply-side perspective, the development of foundations also depended on the extent to which the proceeds of market transactions could be transformed into philanthropic assets. In other words, even where public 'space' for foundations existed, countries and regions differed in terms of philanthropic entrepreneurship, whereby public-minded merchants, industrialists or professionals set up foundations.

While the potential supply of founders is difficult to estimate, the 19th century growth of foundations in Britain, Scandinavia and the Netherlands, and even in countries with autocratic regimes like Germany, the Austro-Hungarian Empire and Italy, suggest that the supply-side considerations were much less of a constraint than restrictive state policies. The urban middle class at the local level supported much of the growth in the number of foundations under aristocratic and autocratic regimes. Most foundations remained local in character, often with well-defined circles of beneficiaries. For example, the foundation directory for the city of Vienna from the late 19th century lists 2,148 foundations, the great majority of which served highly specialized and localized needs ranging from welfare provisions to education support (Markhoff, 1895).

However, in other countries, such as France, the state succeeded in establishing itself as the primary representative of the public will *and* in keeping foundations at bay through the use of anti-clerical, anti-liberal policies (Archambault, 1996). Yet not all nation states were as successful as France in establishing a hegemonic regime across and against diverse political and cultural interests. More frequently, the emerging nation state remained weak, failed in its attempt to consolidate power, and had to forge political compromises with existing power bases and their institutions. As a result, traditional foundations remained strong (for example in Italy and Spain) and many new ones emerged (for example in Switzerland and Germany).

In other cases, early forms of private-public partnerships began to emerge between state and foundations, with Sweden and the Netherlands as prime examples, leading to a general expansion and consolidation. Only in Britain did the formation of a relatively independent set of foundations develop without too much state interference. The 19th-century philanthropists and industrialists provided welfare services, supported the arts and even championed causes overseas, for example the Anti-Slavery Society (Leat, 1992).

Two key insights emerge from this tour through European foundation history. First, at least since the reformation period, foundations have operated at or close to the major 'fault lines' of society: secularization in the 17th century, republicanism and political liberalization in the 18th century, industrialization and the social upheavals of the 19th and early 20th centuries. Depending on the sustainability and extent of the political compromises that were

---

[1] The history of foundations in the Islamic world is substantially different and shows more continuity from the Middle Ages to the early modern period.

found or that emerged, foundations occupied more or less public space, either flourished or declined in numbers and importance, and either helped shape the social order or moved to more marginal positions.

Second, throughout this historical development, certain patterns or path dependencies emerged that accounted for more or less distinct national or regional traditions. Britain and France offer perhaps the best examples for the extreme range of persistent policy patterns across Europe. In the British case, the Statute of Charitable Uses of 1601 has functioned for 400 years to delineate the purpose and limitations of charity even though prevailing practices and common law traditions continue to shape its actual definition and legal application. The Protestant gentry of the 17th century found the Statute appealing for its philanthropic aspirations, as did the industrialists of the 19th century who wanted to support educational institutions to improve the living standards of the poor. In France, we find a different pattern that essentially sought to prevent the development of foundations as a modern tool of civil society. The *Loi de Chapelier* of 1791 established state monopoly over the public interest, which meant that foundations lost their legal status altogether; it was only at the end of the 19th century that foundations regained some ground, albeit under strict state supervision (Archambault et al., 1999).

In most European countries, foundations were caught in a complicated political conundrum, from which few foundation sectors managed to escape unharmed. It would have taken a consolidated state, a self-confident middle class and enlightened élite, in addition to the increasing economic prosperity of the 19th century, to bring about a full renaissance of foundations. Concerns over the *main morte* remained (France, Belgium, Luxembourg), as did social-democratic reservations that saw foundations as undemocratic (Finland, Sweden), or as paternalistic instruments of the Victorian age (Ireland, Britain). Yet whatever patterns and path dependencies had developed until the early 20th century, nothing could have prepared European foundations for the upheavals that two world wars, economic crises, the Holocaust, and the establishment of communist regimes in the central and eastern parts of the continent would bring to most countries.

Of course, foundations in some countries such as Switzerland or Sweden were spared the devastation, but unknown numbers of foundations across the continent did not manage to survive confiscation, destruction, capital depletion or loss of property, and many faced legal and frequently illegal dissolution. In other words, the variations of foundation sector size reflect not only long-term developments, but significantly also the impact of the two major wars in the last century. It is no historical accident that, of the countries with large foundation sectors, most escaped the destructive force of the Second World War (e.g. Sweden, Switzerland and Liechtenstein).

The impact of war was perhaps nowhere greater than in the central and eastern parts of the continent. The philanthropic élite and much of the middle class that had been central in building and maintaining foundations in the late 19th and early 20th centuries were displaced and often killed. The Stalinist and state socialist regimes that followed saw no need for foundations and, with few exceptions, confiscated the remaining foundation property that war and Nazism had not yet destroyed. It is, therefore, not surprising that much of the current impetus to create and re-establish foundation communities in this part of Europe relies on external support, capital and know-how, at least initially, and perhaps for some time to come.

THE US EXPERIENCE

By contrast, the US experience has been very different. Significantly, while Europe's foundations faced great uncertainty and frequent decline, the US foundation moved to the forefront of organized philanthropy. While foundations in various forms have existed throughout US history, perhaps the most important development occurred in the USA at the beginning of the 20th century, with the emergence of large-scale philanthropic foundations associated with names like Carnegie and Rockefeller. Historians like Karl and Katz (1981; 1987) have shown that the first of these new foundations did not adopt the more traditional charity approach of directly addressing social and other public problems, but aimed at exploring the causes of such problems systematically, with the aim of generating long-term solutions rather than just alleviating them (see Bulmer, 1999; McCarthy, 1989). Given the significance of this new orientation of foundation work and the large amount of resources that went into it, the first of these foundations came to symbolize a new era of institutional philanthropy pushing the more traditional aspects of foundation work to the background.

Perhaps because of the importance of these developments, the modern foundation is often perceived as a genuinely US invention, as a 'unique American answer' to the problem of excess wealth in a society with limited income redistribution. Although foundations existed before, it was suggested that 'in no other civilization have such instruments been utilized so widely as in the United States. It may even be said that the foundation had become the ascendant American device for disposing of large accumulations of surplus wealth' (Lindeman, 1988, p.8).

It becomes clear that the rise of the US foundation in the early part of the 20th century highlights their financial redistributive function, and neglects, if not outright discards, the service delivery function that was, and indeed remains, one of the major *raisons d'être* of the European foundations. It would indeed appear that Americans in the past have shown a high propensity to transfer excess wealth to private foundations serving public purposes; moreover, against the backdrop of low government social spending and a rudimentary social welfare system, foundations in the USA occupy a more prominent role in public life than in other countries. In addition, the international presence of such philanthropic giants as the Ford and Rockefeller Foundations has further emphasized this particular variant of 'American Exceptionalism' not only in the USA, but all over the globe.

However, public and scholarly concentration on a limited number of large grant-makers as the 'prototypical' US foundations has led to a monolithic view of the foundation community in the USA, and may have contributed to a certain mystification of the US foundation phenomenon. In this still widespread view, there are numerous large-scale foundations in the USA that are professionally organized, and which thrive in the absence of competition from an activist state. Compared to the perceived lack of proper incentives and the administrative barriers that foundations face in other parts of the world (see van der Ploeg, 1999), the USA appears to be the *El Dorado* of foundation activity.

The tendency to emphasize the US foundation experience holds two potential dangers. First, the actual economic importance of foundations relative to government spending may be over-estimated. Although US foundations held nearly US $583,400m. in assets in 2009 (Foundation Center, 2010), total foundation assets none the less represent only a very small fraction of the national wealth (see

Margo, 1992). Against this background, Salamon (1992a, p. 17) observed that 'although the overall scale of foundation assets seems quite large, it pales in comparison to the assets of other institutions in American society'. The second potential danger lies in downplaying other philanthropic traditions and styles. Other countries have developed a rich tapestry of foundation types and can look back to a long history of philanthropic traditions, as is the case of Europe. How then does the US experience compare internationally? The following sections will attempt to summarize what is known about foundations internationally in terms of size, prevailing types and relationship with the state. To do this, a brief look at the different forms foundations and related organizations can take needs to be taken.

Definitions and Types

A highly complex, sometimes confusing, terminology complicates our understanding of foundations: what is defined as a foundation in one country may not qualify as such in another (Anheier, 2001). Moreover, not all organizations labelled 'foundation' are in fact foundations. In Central and Eastern Europe, many foundations are either membership associations or corporations. The German political foundations such as the Friedrich-Ebert-Stiftung or the Konrad-Adenauer-Stiftung are registered associations with no significant assets of their own; annual subventions from the German government largely cover their operating budgets (Beise, 1998). In the Netherlands, the distinction between foundation (asset-based) and association (membership-based) has become largely indistinguishable in the field of education and social services. In Switzerland, some foundations are primarily investment trusts for families, pension schemes for corporations, or local sickness funds.

The definition of foundations varies from one country to another (Anheier, 2001; Anheier and Toepler, 1999), not along one primary axis, but frequently in several dimensions. There are legal definitions that reflect either common law traditions with an emphasis on trusteeship (e.g. the USA, the United Kingdom), or civil law traditions (e.g. Switzerland and Germany), with the important distinction between legal personalities based on either membership or assets (Van der Ploeg, 1999). Other definitions bring in additional aspects, such as type of founder (private or public), purpose (charitable or other), activities (grant-making or operating), revenue structure (single or multiple funding sources), asset type (own endowment or regular allocations), and the degree of independence from either the state, business or family interest.

To cut across this terminological tangle, Anheier (2001) proposed a modification of the structural/operational definition that Salamon and Anheier (1997) had developed for non-profit organizations generally. Accordingly, a foundation has the following characteristics:

1. It must be an asset-based entity, financial or otherwise. The foundation must rest on an original deed, typically a charter that gives the entity both intent of purpose and relative permanence as an organization.

2. It must be a private entity. Foundations are institutionally separate from government, and are 'non-governmental' in the sense of being structurally separate from public agencies. Therefore, foundations do not exercise governmental authority and are outside direct majoritarian control.

3. It must be a self-governing entity. Foundations are equipped to control their own activities. Some private foundations are tightly controlled either by governmental agencies or corporations, and function as parts of these other institutions, even though they are structurally separate.

4. It must be a non-profit-distributing entity. Foundations are not to return profits generated by either use of assets or commercial activities to their owners, members, trustees or directors. In this sense, commercial goals neither principally nor primarily guide foundations.

5. It must serve a public purpose. Foundations should do more than serve the needs of a narrowly defined social group or category, such as members of a family, or a closed circle of beneficiaries. Foundations are private assets that serve a public purpose.[2]

Grant-making foundations are usually regarded as the prototype of the modern foundation, which is largely a reflection of the US experience and its post-war dominance in the field of philanthropy (Toepler, 1999). Whereas in the USA more than 99% of the existing 50,000 foundations are grant-making, the majority of foundations in Europe are either operating, or pursue their objectives by combining grant-making activities with the running of their own institutions, programmes and projects. Historically, of course, foundations were operating institutions primarily (e.g. hospitals, orphanages, schools and universities), although many did distribute money (alms-giving) and contributions in kind (food or wood, for example). By contrast, the sharp distinction between grant-making and operating foundations emerged much later historically, and is for both the USA and Europe largely a product of the 19th and early 20th centuries (Karl and Katz, 1987; Bulmer, 1999). Behind the complexity of forms are, none the less, several basic categories:

First, grant-making foundations, i.e. endowed organizations that primarily engage in grant-making for specified purposes. Examples include the Ford Foundation in the USA, the Leverhulme Trust in the United Kingdom, the Volkswagen Stiftung in Germany, the Bernard van Leer Foundation in the Netherlands and the Carlsbergfondet in Denmark.

Second, operating foundations, i.e. foundations that primarily operate their own programmes and projects. Examples include the Institut Pasteur in France, the Pescatore Foundation in Luxembourg, which runs a home for senior citizens, and the Calouste Gulbenkian Foundation in Portugal (although this could also fall into the mixed category—see below).

Third, mixed foundations, i.e. foundations that operate their own programmes and projects and engage in grant-making on a significant scale. Examples include the Fundación BBV in Spain and the Robert Bosch Stiftung in Germany.

Non-governmental organizations (NGOs) would differ from a foundation in the sense that no asset base or original deed would be required. They would be either based on

---

2 Of course, as with any comparative definition, some problems remain. Specifically, there are three major areas where the definition proposed here encounters difficulties: firstly, where foundations engage with a market economy and change into primarily economic actors; secondly, where foundations become instruments of the state; and thirdly, where they become a dynastic means of asset protection and control (see Anheier, 2001, pp. 42–47).

membership, i.e. associations, or some other corporate form such as limited liability corporation or co-operative. However, like foundations NGOs have no owners as such (see Salamon and Anheier, 1997). Operating foundations are closer to the NGO form than they are to grant-making foundations.

A Profile of Foundations

There is great variation in the number of foundations (see Figure 1), ranging from a high of 76,545 in the USA, 15,000 in Germany, around 14,000 in Denmark, 13,553 in Japan, approximately 10,000 in Switzerland, 6,000 in Spain, 3,008 in Italy to lows of 600 in Austria, 601 in Estonia, some 400–600 foundations in Portugal (excluding foundations registered under canonical law), around 500 in Greece, and 107 in Ireland. In some countries, such as the Netherlands, there is no clear estimate of the total number of foundations. The data suggest that there are between 80,000 and 110,000 foundations in Europe (including Greece and Turkey), or an average of around 4,500 per country. Figures for the countries of Central and Eastern Europe tended to fluctuate in the 1990s due to changes and reforms to the laws governing foundations. In the Czech Republic, for example, 5,238 foundations were listed in 1997 whereas this number had fallen to 969 in 1999, a year after a new foundation law came into effect, with an estimate of approximately 360 in 2004.[3]

Among European foundations, the economic weight of running institutions, programmes and projects tends to be more important than the actual grant-making activities. For example, in Spain foundations employ approximately 64,332 full-time staff, which accounts for 13.5% of all employment in the country's non-profit sector. Estimates of employment in German grant-making foundations in 1995 ranged between 3,000–5,000 employees, whereas operating foundations employed more than 90,000. However, the majority of German foundations employ no staff at all: nine out of 10 foundations are run and managed by volunteers only. In Scandinavia, similar results can be found: only a few of Denmark's 14,000 foundations have paid employment at all, and only eight of the more than 2,500 Finnish foundations have more than 10 full-time staff. Similarly, in Italy, more than 85% of foundations have fewer than 10 employees, while fewer than 1% of foundations employ more than 250 people. In Poland,

---

[3] The data reported in this section draw on a comparative analysis by Anheier (2001), which itself uses data from individual country reports in Schlüter, Then and Walkenhorst (2001). The authors of the country studies are W. Bachstein and C. Badlet (Austria), M. Maree and S. Mousny (Belgium), G. Hellman and J. Parving (Denmark), K. Herbets (Finland), E. Archambault (France), R. Strachwitz (Germany), S. Tsakraklides (Greece), F. Donoghue (Ireland), G. Barbetta and M. Demarie (Italy), M. Wanger (Liechtenstein), A. Bonn and A. Schmitt (Luxembourg), A. Burger, P. Dekker and V. Veldheer (the Netherlands), H. Lorentzen (Norway), C. Monjardino (Portugal), J. Olabuenaga (Spain), F. Wijkstroem (Sweden), M. Steinert (Switzerland), D. Aydin (Turkey), Diana Leat (United Kingdom) and Francis Pinter (Central and Eastern Europe). These reports are in Schlüter et al. (2001, pp. 83–317). Data for Canada are from the Canadian Centre for Philanthropy; for Japan from the Japan Foundation Center; for the USA from the Foundation Center, New York. The data are updated and expanded by information provided by the project 'The Politics of Foundations' by Anheier and Daly (Eds), 2007.

Figure 1: Number and Types of Foundations

Country	Number	Relative share of grant-making foundation	Relative share of operating foundations	Mixed type
Austria	600			Majority
Belgium	310	Few		Majority
Great Britain	~ 8800	100	0	
Canada	1,353	Great majority		Very few
Denmark	~14,000			
Estonia	601			
Finland	2,522	50%	30%	20%
France	404		Majority	
Germany	15,000	~50%	~25 %	~25 %
Greece	~500	Few	Majority	Few
Ireland	107	27%	70%	3%
Italy	~3,008	15%	39%	43%
Japan	13,553	Not known		
Liechtenstein	~600		Majority	
Luxembourg	143		Majority	
Netherlands	~1,000	Majority		
Norway	2,989			Majority
Portugal	~400-600		Majority	
Spain	~6,000	5%	95%	
Sweden	~20,000-30,000			
Switzerland	~10,000	5%	Majority	
Turkey	9,326			Majority
USA	76,545	Majority	6.3%	

~ = approximately

Source: Anheier 2001; Anheier and Daly, 2007; Foundation Center, 2011

foundations employ more than 13,000 people, although full-time employees can only be found in one in three foundations. In 2000, fewer than 10% of private and public foundations in Hungary had full-time employees, making foundations particularly dependent on part-time employees and volunteers.

In the USA, the impact of the terrorist attacks on the country on 11 September 2001, along with the economic recession in 2008, with resulting uncertainties about economic performance and political stability, meant a decline in foundation assets in 2001 and 2002—and the first decreases reported since 1981, as well as a sharp decrease from 2007–08. While foundation assets of US $467,000m. in 2001 were almost 4% lower than the year before, assets have been steadily rising, with $510,000m. in 2004, a 5% increase since 2000. Foundation assets peaked in 2007, with close to $700,00m., but declined to $565,000m. in 2008 and increased slightly (3.3%) to $583,400m. in 2009. Accordingly, between 2001 and 2003 grants paid declined by nearly $200m. to just over $30,000m.; and between 2008 and 2009 grants paid declined by 8% from $46,800m. to $42,900m (Foundation Center, 2010). Even with these losses, asset values and grant dollars paid out by US foundations remain at much higher levels than a decade earlier.

Asset estimates are the most difficult data to obtain on foundations, especially cross-nationally, given the influence of different valuation measures and techniques. Irrespective of these difficulties, available estimates reveal significant cross-national variations. For example, the assets that the 20 largest Japanese foundations hold amount to ¥4,980m., whereas the 20 largest US foundations are, with an equivalent yen value of ¥154,177, about 31 times larger (Japan Foundation Center, 2005). The assets of German foundations are €354 per head. However, only 17% have assets exceeding €2,500,000 (Adloff et al., 2007); the figure is higher for foundations in the United Kingdom (€536) or €44,000m. (Leat, 2007), and more than €1,000 for foundations in Italy, Sweden and Switzerland. Finally, the highest per head assets are reported for Liechtenstein, with a figure that exceeds €12,000 because of offshore foundation assets. The high amount of assets per head for Italian foundations is a function of the privatization of the banking sector in Italy (Law 218/1990, or Amato law).

Most public savings banks were previously quasi-public, 'nationalized' non-profit organizations, and became stock corporations as a result of the 1990 reforms (see Barbetta, 1999). The shares in the privatized banks became the endowment for the new 'foundations of banking origin', which, not surprisingly, have significant assets, of €50,000m.–€75,000m. combined. (In Austria, the total assets of all charitable foundations are estimated to be €7,000,000–€7,100,000.) Portugal represents a rather unusual case whereby assets are concentrated in the largest foundations. Indeed, the Gulbenkian Foundation has 10 times as many assets as the next largest foundation, while the majority of foundations are set up with a capital of less than €100,000 (Anheier and Daly, 2007). In Belgium, the Ministry for Justice estimates that the assets of foundations vary between €3,000 and €40,000,000. Estimates from Norway suggest that a typically large foundation will have assets of €12,000,000–€16,000,000, but fewer than 5% or 30–50 foundations belong to this category (Anheier and Daly, 2004). In Switzerland estimates of foundation assets are 30,000m. Swiss francs (€19,000m.), with payouts equivalent to 2% of the federal government's budget (Anheier and Daly, 2007).

Foundation sectors by country can be grouped into three classes: small, medium and large, with the middle group further divided into subcategories. Given the data situation, it is not possible to construct a strict and consistent ranking of countries in terms of foundation sector size. Yet, taken together, the various size indicators suggest three groups or clusters, and even such an admittedly crude classification involves some qualitative judgements. The relative size of the foundation sectors of European countries can be classified as follows:

1. Countries with a small foundation sector: Austria, Belgium, France, Greece, Ireland, Luxembourg, and countries of Central and Eastern Europe.

2. Countries with a small–medium foundation sector: Portugal, Spain and Turkey; and countries with a medium–large foundation sector: Denmark, Finland, Germany, the Netherlands, Norway, Japan, Canada and the United Kingdom.

3. Countries with a large foundation sector: the USA, Italy, Liechtenstein, Sweden and Switzerland.

Foundation Areas of Activity

Yet, what do foundations do? Two fields clearly dominate the profile of foundation activity: education and research, with an average of 30% of foundation activity, and social service (25%). Together, both fields account for more than one-half of foundation activities so measured. In fact, education and research, and social services are the main categories of foundation activity in eight of the 15 countries studied. Adding health care, with an average of 17% of foundation activity, pushes the total share up to 71%. In other words, two-thirds of foundations operate in just three fields, the same fields that also dominate the non-profit sector at large (Salamon et al., 1999).

The field of art and culture accounts for the next largest share of foundation activities. It is the most important area of activity of foundations in Spain, with 44% of all foundations involved in this field, and is relatively prominent in Finland, Germany, Italy, Portugal and Switzerland. Some countries show clear concentration in one field in particular: this is the case for health-care foundations in France,

housing foundations in Ireland, international activities in the Netherlands, and cultural foundations in Spain. Such concentrations are the result of specific historical developments, e.g. urgent demand for affordable housing in early 20th-century Ireland, or institutional effect, such as the prominence of large health-care research foundations in France, e.g. the Institut Pasteur and Institut Curie (Archambault et al., 1999).

Growth Patterns of Foundations

Foundations are largely a product of the period following the Second World War, and a veritable foundation 'boom' seems to have set in, beginning in the late 1980s. More foundations were created in the 1980s and 1990s than in the three preceding decades, and more of the foundations existing in the early 2000s were established after 1950 than prior to that date. However, this growth is not evenly spread across countries.

- *High-growth countries, such as the USA, Italy, Spain, Turkey and Portugal.* From 1980 onwards, the USA experienced one of the most sustained expansions in the growth in the number of foundations as well as the amounts of assets held. In Europe, with the exception of Turkey, high-growth countries are those in which foundation law underwent a major reform: in Italy, Law 218/1990 (or Amato law), in Spain, the Foundation Act, 1994, and in Portugal, Law 460/1977, with the proven effect that foundations increased sharply in number. In Portugal, where 56% of all foundations were established after 1980, and Spain (over 90% of cultural foundations and 70% of educational foundations), the rapid growth could also be a delayed effect of the democratization in the 1970s, when both countries shed their autocratic regimes. The high growth is also a reflection of the rapid economic development of the countries of Europe's south, in particular Portugal, Spain and Turkey (see Baloglu, 1996).

- *Medium-growth countries, such as Finland, Germany, Greece, Switzerland and the United Kingdom.* In Finland, for example, the economic boom of the 1990s was marked with the registration of 663 new foundations. (However, in 2001 alone some 200 foundations related to savings banks were dissolved due to crises in the financial sector.) With the exception of Belgium and Greece, these are countries with already sizeable foundation sectors, and recent growth rates of 20–30 per decade add to a relatively high base. Finland, Germany, Switzerland and the United Kingdom are high-income countries with stable political systems. We can assume that the foundation boom of recent years is in large measure a function of political stability and economic prosperity, which a more self-confident middle class has amplified. Greece has a small foundation sector, and the expansion is probably the result of increased economic prosperity and greater political stability. The 1990s in particular witnessed a period of substantial activity in the establishment of foundations, which can be attributed to factors such as the stabilization of the Greek economy; a growing immigrant population and preparations for the Olympic Games (Anheier and Daly, 2004).

Some countries in Central and Eastern Europe enjoyed moderate growth in the late 1990s. The Czech Republic saw a €7,000,000 increase in endowment size between 1999 and 2002. In Poland, the number of foundations increased from 288 in 1989 to 6,065 in 2000. The problem with such high growth figures, however, is that many of these foundations may be inactive, and not foundations according to the definition suggested above.

- *Low-growth Countries, such as Austria, Belgium and France.* All three of these countries have relatively small foundation sectors. Japanese foundations grew significantly between 1980 and the early 1990s, but they have largely stagnated since, due to difficult economic conditions. At the same time, however, the regulatory environment has become more encouraging for foundations in Japan generally. The same cannot be said for countries like France. The country's relatively few foundations are, on average, older, with one-half pre-dating the post-war period, and with fewer foundations being established during the expansion period that began in the 1980s. Similarly, growth rates have changed little in Austria and Belgium over the last four decades, even though a slight upward trend is discernible. In Austria, the 1994 Private Foundations Act (PSG) encouraged some public welfare organizations to adopt the form of the foundation, which is perceived more flexible and less bureaucratic. However, this law has also attracted criticism and controversy as a useful tool for the capital market as it does not stipulate that a foundation must have a public purpose. The reasons for the slow growth in some countries are largely legal and procedural. For example, the establishment of foundations in France or Belgium is highly regulated and complicated, providing relatively few incentives for potential founders.

New Political Developments

In Europe, the international dimension of the work of foundations has become more and more relevant for the political system on all levels in recent years, and particularly so for the European Union (EU). The European Court of Justice (ECJ) has ruled in a series of landmark decisions (the most recent being Persche, ECJ, Case C-318/07) in favour of cross-border activities by foundations. The European Commission has been evaluating options for a new legal instrument, the European Foundation Statute, which would further foster international activities of foundations across member states. A growing awareness of the limitations of current regulatory frameworks for philanthropy has prompted this development. Indeed, the fragmentation of Europe's foundations in terms of grant-making as well as in terms of fund acquisition and management is perceived as a barrier to potentially greater philanthropic impact. Regardless of the chances of such a foundation statute becoming EU law, the foundation sector is seen as an option to enhance the competitiveness of member states and to boost flexibility in a range of fields from social services to research and education.

The Third Sector

How do the profile and growth patterns of foundations compare to those of the third sector at large?[4] Of particular interest were four critical dimensions of such organizations: paid full-time equivalent employment, volunteer employment converted to full-time equivalent, operating expenditures and revenue sources (government payments,

Figure 2. Non-profit workforce as a share of the economically active population, by country

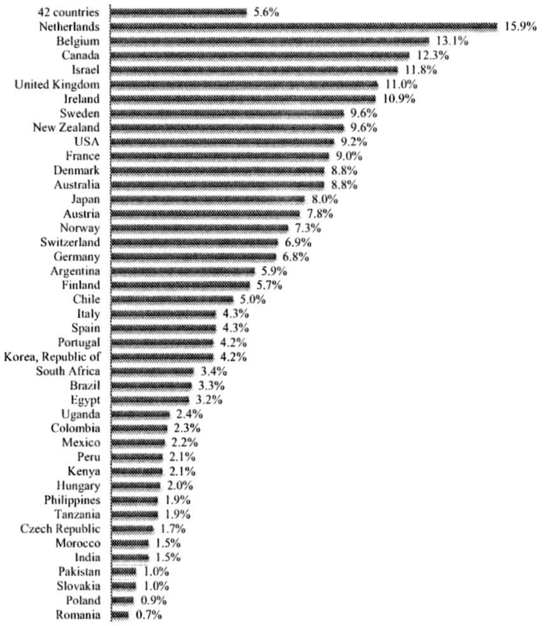

Source: Salamon, 2010

private fees and charges, and private philanthropy). There are a number of major conclusions about the scope, structure and financing of non-profit activity in the more than 42 countries covered by the Johns Hopkins Comparative Nonprofit Sector Project (see Salamon, 2010).

In the first place, the third sector was found to be a major economic force. In the 40 countries for which financial data are available, as estimated by the Johns Hopkins Project, the sector constitutes a US $2,200,000m. industry (Salamon, 2010). In the 42 countries for which employment data are available, the Johns Hopkins Project estimates that the sector employs close to 56m. full-time equivalent employees (Salamon, 2010). Moreover, the sector attracts a considerable amount of volunteer effort and constitutes a significant percentage of the non-profit workforce. Indeed, within the countries studied, volunteers accounted for some 41% of the total non-profit workforce (Salamon, 2010).

As shown in Figure 2, the third sector is larger in the more developed countries and much less in evidence in Central and South America and Central Europe. Perhaps one of the most surprising outcomes is that the USA, commonly thought to be the seedbed of non-profit activity, ranks only ninth in terms of paid employment as a share of the economically active population, after countries including the Netherlands, Belgium, Ireland and Canada. The developed Western European countries have the largest third sectors among all project countries, surpassing many of their Eastern European neighbours (note: the definition of Eastern European countries used includes Norway, Finland, Austria, the Czech Republic, Hungary,

---

[4] The data reported in this section are from the Johns Hopkins Comparative Nonprofit Sector Project, Salamon et al. (2004), and the following paragraphs draw from the overview chapter by Salamon et al. in *Global Civil Society: Dimensions of the Nonprofit Sector* (2004), Anheier (2003), Sanders et al., 2008, and Salamon, 2010.

Slovakia, Poland and Romania). In fact, the size of the third sectors in former communist countries turns out to be surprisingly low, accounting for a mere 1% of the economically active population. By comparison, Central and South American as well as African and Asian countries are located in-between, as far as the size of their third sectors is concerned, but there is also substantial variability among them. For example, Argentina has a third sector that is only slightly smaller than that of many Western European countries on the employment measure, and on a par with Western Europe on the value added measure. On the other hand, Mexico is above the Eastern European level on both measures.

When we take a closer look at the non-profit workforce, however, we see that in all countries, the non-profit sector relies heavily on volunteers. In 'social democratic' (i.e. Finland, Norway, Sweden, Austria, etc.) and 'traditional' (i.e. Pakistan, Kenya, Tanzania, Uganda, the Philippines) country clusters, volunteers make up more than 50% of the respective countries' non-profit workforce (Helmig et al, 2011), while in all other countries in the study, volunteers comprise one-third to nearly one-half of the non-profit workforce with a 42-country average of 41% (Salamon et al, 2010). Two-thirds of all non-profit employment is concentrated in the three traditional fields of welfare services, or what Salamon et al. refer to as 'service functions'[5]: education (accounting for 21% of total non-profit employment), health (12%) and social services (19%). While, on average, education and research is the largest field (on a par with membership associations), it is larger in Latin American and Eastern European countries. Eastern European and Nordic countries also have a larger culture and recreation sector (35% and 26%, respectively) and Asian countries have the largest health sector (24%). (Sanders et al., 2008.)

More specifically, Western Europe in particular displays a significant concentration of non-profit employment in welfare services, in large part a reflection of the historic prominence organized religion traditionally maintained in this particular field. In Central and Eastern Europe, on the other hand, the recreation and culture field plays a much more important part in the employment base of the third sector, constituting one-third of all full-time equivalent workers employed in non-profit associations in the region. In Central and South America the education field dominates the employment base of the third sector, again an indication of the strong influence the Catholic Church historically maintained in the field. Finally, in the USA, Japan, Australia and Israel, a major area of non-profit employment is in the health field, which accounts, on average, for 35% of total non-profit employment in these countries, followed closely by education (accounting for 29% of total non-profit employment).

The major sources of non-profit income in the 42 countries of the Johns Hopkins Project are fees and government support. In fact, fees and other commercial income alone account for between 35% and 58%, across all country clusters, of all non-profit revenue, while public-sector payments amount to 18%–56% of the total (Helmig, 2011). By contrast, private philanthropy—from individuals, corporations and foundations combined—constitutes only between 9%–24% of total non-profit income across all country clusters (Helmig, 2011). Revenue from public sources is almost twice as much in 'welfare partnership' countries (i.e. Belgium, France, Germany, Ireland, the Netherlands, Israel, etc.) as in 'deferred democratization' (i.e. Brazil, Colombia, Poland, Slovakia, etc.) countries (56% and 30% respectively), while revenue from fees is greater in 'traditional' countries (i.e. Pakistan, Kenya, Tanzania, Uganda, the Philippines) (58%). Revenue from philanthropy in 'traditional' (24%), 'deferred democratization' (13%), and 'liberal' (13%) countries is also greater than 'welfare partnership' and 'social democratic' countries (9%) (Helmig, 2011). However, this pattern varies somewhat by country and region. Whereas fee income is predominant in Central and South America and Central and Eastern Europe, as well as in the USA, Australia and Japan, public grants and third-party payments, primarily from public social insurance funds, are the most important sources of income for the third sector in the Western European region (Sanders et al., 2008.)

Not only is the non-profit sector a major economic force, but it was also an unusually dynamic one in the 1990s, surpassing the general economies in most of the Johns Hopkins Project countries in generating employment growth. Non-profit employment in Belgium, France, Germany and the United Kingdom grew by an average of 24%, or by more than 4% a year, between 1990 and 1995. In comparison, overall employment in these same countries grew at a considerably slower rate during this same period: 6%, or barely 1% a year. The non-profit sector therefore outpaced the overall growth of employment in these countries by a ratio of almost 4:1. Social services accounted for the largest share of non-profit employment growth in Western Europe.

More generally, a substantial increase in fee income has chiefly made the growth in non-profit employment evident in these figures possible, not a surge in private philanthropy or public sector support. In the eight countries for which Salamon et al. (1999) report revenue data going back to 1990, fees accounted for 58% of the real growth in non-profit revenue between 1990 and 1995. In comparison, the public sector accounted for 34%, and private giving, which includes foundation grants, 8% of the growth in non-profit income. Thus, while both non-profit and foundation sectors increased in size and number, the relative importance of foundation revenue for voluntary associations declined, relative to more 'commercial' forms of revenue.

Non-governmental Organizations and Globalization

Next to the national third sectors in the various countries covered above, a somewhat different phenomenon took place, particularly in the 1990s: the rise of international NGOs, or INGOs. This led to the emergence of a supranational sphere of social and political participation in which NGOs, groups and individuals engage in dialogue, debate, confrontation and negotiation with each other and with various governmental bodies—international, national and local—as well as with the business world. Many INGOs employ staff and are professional organizations. They can include campaigning groups like Amnesty

---

[5] Salamon et al. (2004) group non-profit sector activity into two categories: organizations primarily engaged in service functions, and those primarily engaged in advocacy/expressive functions. Service functions involve the delivery of direct services such as education, health, housing, economic development promotion and the like; expressive functions involve activities that provide avenues for the expression of cultural, religious, professional or policy values, interests and beliefs. Included here are cultural institutions, recreation, religious worship organizations, professional associations, advocacy groups, community organizations, environmental organizations and human rights groups.

International or Greenpeace, the famous 'brand names' of global civil society; professional societies like international employers' federations or trades unions; charities like Christian Aid or CARE International; and 'think tanks' and international commissions.

Historically, of course, elements of a supra-national non-governmental sphere have existed: INGOs are not new. They date back to the 19th century, but the term itself is of more recent origins, coined during the League of Nations period. The earliest INGO is generally said to be the Anti-Slavery Society, formed as the British and Foreign Anti-Slavery Society in 1839, although there was a transnational social movement against slavery much earlier. Henri Dunant founded the International Committee of the Red Cross (ICRC) in 1863 after his experiences at the battle of Solferino.

What seems new, however, is the sheer scale and scope that international and supra-national institutions and organizations of many kinds have achieved in recent years. The number of organizations and individuals that are part of global civil society has probably never been bigger, and the range and type of fields in which they operate never been wider: from United Nations (UN) conferences about social welfare or the environment to conflict situations in Kosovo, and from media corporations spanning the globe to indigenous peoples' campaigns over the internet.

By 1874, there were 32 registered INGOs and this number had increased to 1,083 by 1914 (Chatfield, 1997). INGOs grew steadily after the Second World War, but there was an acceleration in the 1990s. Around one-quarter of the 13,000 INGOs in existence in 2000 were created after 1990. Moreover, membership by individuals or national bodies of INGOs has increased even faster; well over one-third of the membership of INGOs joined after 1990. (These figures include only NGOs narrowly defined as 'international'; they do not include national NGOs with an international orientation.)

Moreover, during the 1990s INGOs became much more interconnected, both to each other and to international institutions such as the UN or the International Bank for Reconstruction and Development (World Bank). Thus, not only did the global range of INGO presence grow during the 1990s and early 2000s, but the networks linking these organizations became denser as well. In Held's terms (Held et al., 1999), the data suggest that networking of INGOs is becoming 'thicker' and is increasingly becoming part of globalization more generally.

The growth of resources available, i.e. technology and money, has facilitated the growth of INGOs. Increases in internet usage and in both mobile or cell phones and land-lines have greatly facilitated the construction of networks and have allowed greater access for groups outside the main centres of international power. Thus, even just taking membership of INGOs, that of low- and middle-income regions (70% and 98%, respectively) increased faster between 1990 and 2000 than membership in high-income regions (56%). The biggest increases were for Eastern Europe and Asia.

Likewise, during the 1990s and early 2000s there was a big increase in the economic importance of NGOs. Specifically, governments and international institutions greatly increased the amount of development funds channelled through NGOs (OECD, 1997). In addition, private giving also increased from both foundations and corporations. Pinter (2001) estimates that global civil society receives approximately US $7,000m. in development funds and $2,000m. in funds from US foundations. Salamon et al. (1999) show that the number of full-time equivalent employees in INGOs for France, Germany, Japan, the Netherlands, Spain and the United Kingdom alone amounts to more than 100,000 and that volunteers in INGOs represent an additional 1.2m. full-time jobs in these countries. Even without precise and comprehensive figures, available data suggest the significant economic scale of INGO activities.

Conclusion

The political stability and economic prosperity of the USA, Japan, Europe and other parts of the developed world are closely related to the renaissance of foundations in recent decades. The rise of the third sector and INGOs is closely related to this process, which an opening of institutional space for private activities and self-organization among citizens have additionally fuelled. These expansions are fairly recent phenomena, and their continued growth and sustainability by no means a foregone conclusion. At the very least such pronounced and prolonged growth brings policy options and dilemmas to the political agenda. For instance, to what extent can governments, national as well as international, allow private actors, be they foundations or NGOs, to influence the political agenda? Who is responsible for delivering public and quasi-public good? If governments no longer see themselves as the party primarily responsible for social security, welfare, education, culture, etc., who has legitimacy to act in the public interest? Should the fate of fortunes, large and small, be left primarily to individuals, or can government express some moral or political priority? Ultimately, foundations and NGOs, unlike democratic governments, are not answerable to the electorate, which creates profound accountability problems. Moreover, unlike interest and lobby groups, foundations are typically not answerable to specific members and stakeholders who might control or own them.

Of course, to some extent, the answers to these dilemmas and questions depend on the relevant policies and laws in place, but the prevailing political climate also shapes them. Across much of the developed world, this climate currently favours a reduced role for government and greater responsibility lodged with individuals—yet, what theoretical case can be made for foundations and NGOs more generally? Why do they exist, and why are they expanding? While a fuller answer to these questions is beyond the scope of this chapter, it may be useful, in conclusion, to examine briefly some of the answers suggested in the literature (see Anheier and Toepler, 1999, for an overview).

Foundations and NGOs, like all non-profit institutions, exist for several basic reasons. More specifically, foundations and non-profit organizations exist because markets and government may fail, as Hansmann (1996) and Weisbrod (1988) have pointed out. Under conditions of demand heterogeneity and information asymmetries, because of the moral hazard inherent in such transactions, markets fail to supply some public and quasi-public goods in efficient and equitable ways (Anheier and Ben-Ner, 1997). Moreover, the state cannot supply such goods because of government failure, i.e. the inability of the state to meet and safeguard minority demands. Correcting for such failures would otherwise run into conflict with the inherent constitutional doctrine of limited state interference in liberal democracies.

This reasoning implies that diverse societies have needs that neither market nor state can provide at reasonable economic costs and acceptable political risks. And it is in this context, that, according to Prewitt (1999), foundations make their truly distinct contribution to modern society: pluralism. By promoting diversity and differentiation in thought, approaches and practice of advocacy and service provision, foundations create and preserve pluralism, and thereby increase the problem-solving capacity of societies. In other words, modern societies both require and reflect the pluralism that foundations and NGOs generate.

References

Addloff, F., P. Schwertmann, R. Sprengeland and R. G. Strachwitz. 'Germany', in Anheier, H., and Daly, S., *The Politics of Foundation: A Comparative Analysis*. Routledge, Abingdon and New York, 2007.

Anheier, H. 'Foundations in Europe: A Comparative Perspective', in Schlüter, A. et al. (Eds), *Foundations in Europe*, pp. 35–81. Directory of Social Change, London and Bertelsmann Foundation, Gütersloh, 2001.

Anheier, H. 'Das Stiftungswesen in Zahlen: Eine sozial-ökonomische Strukturebeschreibung deutscher Stiftungen', in Bertelsmann Foundation (Ed.), *Handbuch Stiftungen*, pp. 47–82. Gabler, Wiesbaden, 1998.

Anheier, H. and Ben-Ner, A. 'The Shifting Boundaries: Long-term Changes in the Size of the For-profit, Non-profit, Co-operative and Government Sectors', in *Annals of Public and Cooperative Economics*, 68 (3), 1997, pp. 335–354.

Anheier, H. and S. Daly. *The Politics of Foundation: A Comparative Analysis*. Routledge, Abingdon and New York, 2007.

Anheier, H. and S. Daly. *The Roles and Visions of Foundations in Europe*. London School of Economics, London, 2004.

Anheier, H., M. Glasius and M. Kaldor (Eds). *Global Civil Society 2001*. Oxford University Press, Oxford, 2001.

Anheier, H. and S. Toepler. 'Philanthropic Foundations: An International Perspective', in Anheier, H. and S. Toepler (Eds), *Private Funds, Public Purpose: Philanthropic Foundations in International Perspective*, pp. 3–23. Kluwer Academic/Plenum Publishers, New York, 1999.

Archambault, E., J. Bournendil and S. Tsyboula. 'Foundations in France', in Anheier, H. and S. Toepler (Eds), *Private Funds, Public Purpose: Philanthropic Foundations in International Perspective*, pp. 185–198, as above.

Arias Foundation For Peace And Human Progress. *The State of Philanthropy in Central America*. San José, 1992.

Baloglu, Z. (Ed.). *The Foundations of Turkey*. TÜSEV, Istanbul, 1996.

Barbetta, G. 'Foundations in Italy', in Anheier, H. and S. Toepler (Eds), *Private Funds, Public Purpose: Philanthropic Foundations in International Perspective*, pp. 199–218, as above.

Beise, M. 'Politische Stiftungen', in Bertelsmann Foundation (Ed.), *Handbuch Stiftungen*. Gabler, Wiesbaden, 1998.

Bertelsmann Foundation (Ed.). *Handbuch Bürgerstiftungen*. Bertelsmann Foundation, Gütersloh, 2000.

Biermann, B., L. Cannon and D. Klainberg. *A Survey of Endowed Grantmaking Development Foundations in Africa, Asia, Eastern Europe, Latin America, and the Caribbean*. Synergos Institute, New York, 1992 (mimeo).

Boris, E. 'Creation and Growth: A Survey of Private Foundations', in Odendahl, T. (Ed.), *America's Wealthy and the Future of Foundations*, pp. 65–126. Foundation Center, New York, 1987.

Bulmer, M. 'The History of Foundations in the United Kingdom and the United States: Philanthropic Foundations in Industrial Society', in Anheier, H. and S. Toepler (Eds), *Private Funds, Public Purpose: Philanthropic Foundations in International Perspective*, pp. 27–53, as above.

Coing, H. (1981). 'Remarks on the History of Foundations and their Role in the Promotion of Learning', in *Minerva*, XIX (2), pp. 271–181.

European Commission. *Communication from the Commission on Promoting the Role of Voluntary Organizations and Foundations in Europe* (COM 97/241). EUR-OP, Luxembourg, 1997.

Foundation Center. *Foundation Growth and Giving Estimates*. Foundation Center, New York, 2003.

Foundation Center. *Foundation Yearbook: Facts and Figures on Private and Community Foundations*. Foundation Center, New York, 2010.

Hansmann, H. *The Ownership of Enterprise*. Harvard University Press, Cambridge, MA, 1996.

Held, D., A. McGrew, D. Goldblatt and J. Perraton. *Global Transformations*. Polity Press, Cambridge, 1999.

Helmig et al, 2011 (http://ccss.jhu.edu/wp-content/uploads/downloads/2011/10/Switzerland.cnp.NationalReport2011.pdf)

Karl, B. and S. Katz. 'Foundations and the Ruling Class', in *Daedalus*, 116 (1), 1987, pp. 1–40.

Kendall, J. and H. Anheier. 'The third sector and the European Union policy process: an initial evaluation', in *Journal of European Public Policy*, 6 (2), 1999, pp. 283–307.

Leat, D. 'United Kingdom' in Anheier, H. and S. Daly. *The Politics of Foundation: A Comparative Analysis,* Routledge, Abingdon and New York, 2007.

Leat, D. *Trusts in Transition: The Policy and Practice of Grant-making Trusts*. Joseph Rowntree Foundation, York, 1992.

Lindeman, Eduard C. *Wealth and Culture*. Reprint, Society and Philanthropy Series. Transaction Books, New Brunswick and Oxford, 1988 [1936].

Margo, R., 'Foundations', in Clotfelter, C. T. (Ed.), *Who Benefits from the Nonprofit Sector?*, pp. 207–234. University of Chicago Press, Chicago, 1992.

Neuhoff, K. *Kommentar zum bürgerlichen Gesetzbuch*, (11th edn), *Band 1: Allgemeiner Teil*. Sonderdruck aus SOERGEL, Stifterverband für die Deutsche Wissenschaft, Essen, 1978.

Odendahl, T. 'Independent Foundations and the Wealthy Donors: An Overview', in Odendahl, T. (Ed.), *America's Wealthy and the Future of Foundations*, pp. 1–26. Foundation Center, New York, 1987.

Pharoah, C. 'The growth of community trusts and foundations', in CAF (Ed.), *Dimensions of the Voluntary Sector*, pp. 70–73. CAF Publications, West Malling, 1996.

Pinter, F. 'Funding Global Civil Society', in Anheier, H. K., M. Glasius and M. Kaldor (Eds) *Global Civil Society 2001*. Oxford University Press, Oxford, 2001.

Prewitt, K. 'The Importance of Foundations in an Open Society', in Bertelsmann Foundation (Ed.), *The Future of Foundations in an Open Society*, pp. 17–29. Bertelsmann Foundation, Gütersloh, 1999.

Renz, L., C. Mandler and T. Tran. *Foundation Giving. Yearbook of Facts and Figures on Private, Corporate and Community Foundations.* Foundation Center, New York, 1997.

Salamon, L. M. *America's Nonprofit Sector: A Primer.* Foundation Center, New York, 1992a.

Salamon, L. M. http://ccss.jhu.edu/wp-content/uploads/downloads/2011/10/Annals-June-2010.pdf, 2010

Salamon, L., and H. Anheier. *The Emerging Nonprofit Sector: An Overview.* Manchester University Press, Manchester, 1996.

Salamon, L., and H. Anheier (Eds). *Defining the Nonprofit Sector: A Cross-National Analysis.* Manchester University Press, Manchester, 1997.

Salamon, L., H. Anheier, R. List, S. Toepler and W. Sokolowski (Eds). *Global Civil Society: Dimensions of the Nonprofit Sector.* Johns Hopkins Institute for Policy Studies, Baltimore, MD, 1999.

Salamon, L. M., S. Sokolowski and R. List. 'Global Civil Society: An Overview'. Johns Hopkins Center for Civil Society Studies, Baltimore, MD, 2003.

Sanders, J., M. O'Brien, M. Tennant, W. Sokolowski and L. M. Salamon. *The New Zealand Nonprofit Sector in Comparative Perspective.* Office for the Community and Voluntary Sector, New Zealand. (See www.ccss.jhu.edu/pdfs/cnp/cnp.newzealandnationalreport2008.pdf.) 2008.

Schiller, T. *Stiftungen im gesellschaftlichen Prozeß.* Nomos, Baden-Baden, 1969.

Schlüter, A., V. Then and P. Walkenhorst (Eds). *Foundations in Europe: Society, Management and Law.* Directory of Social Change, London, 2001.

Smith, J. and K. Borgmann. 'Foundations in Europe: the Historical Context', in Schlüter, A., V. Then and P. Walkenhorst (Eds), *Foundations in Europe: Society, Management and Law.* Directory of Social Change, London, 2001.

Smith, J., C. Chatfield and R. Pagnucco (Eds). *Transnational social movements and global politics: solidarity beyond the state.* Syracuse University Press, Syracuse, NY, 1997.

Strachwitz, R. 'Foundations in Germany and Their Revival in East Germany after 1989', in Anheier, H., and S. Toepler (Eds), *Private Funds, Public Purpose: Philanthropic Foundations in International Perspective*, pp. 219–233, as above.

Strachwitz, R., and S. Toepler. 'Traditional Methods of Funding: Endowments and Foundations', in Doyle, L. (Ed.), *Funding Europe's Solidarity*, pp. 100–108. AICE, Brussels, 1996.

Toepler, S. 'Operating in a Grantmaking World: Reassessing the Role of Operating Foundations', in Anheier, H., and S. Toepler (Eds), *Private Funds, Public Purpose: Philanthropic Foundations in International Perspective*, pp. 163–185, as above.

UIA (Union of International Associations). *Yearbook of International Organizations: Guide to civil society networks.* K. G. Saur, Munich, 1905–1999/2000.

Van der Ploeg, T. 'A Comparative Legal Analysis of Foundations: Aspects of Supervision and Transparency', in Anheier, H., and S. Toepler (Eds), *Private Funds, Public Purpose: Philanthropic Foundations in International Perspective*, pp. 55–78, as above.

Walkenhorst, P. (Ed.). *Building Philanthropic and Social Capital: The Work of Community Foundations.* Bertelsmann Foundation, Gütersloh, 2001.

Weisbrod, B. *The Nonprofit Economy.* Harvard University Press, Cambridge, MA, 1988.

Whitaker, Benjamin. *The Philanthropoids.* William Morrow, New York, 1974.

Ylvesaker, P. 'Foundations and Nonprofit Organizations', in Powell, W. (Ed.), *The Nonprofit Sector: A Research Handbook*, pp. 360–379. Yale University Press, New Haven, CT, 1987.

Helmut Anheier is Chair of Sociology at Heidelberg University, and Academic Director of the Centre for Social Investment. He is also Professor of Sociology at the Hertie School of Governance, Berlin. From 2001–09 he was professor at the School of Public Affairs and Director of the UCLA Center for Civil Society. From 1998–2002 he was the founding Director of the Centre for Civil Society at the London School of Economics (LSE), where he now holds the title of Centennial Professor. Prior to this he was a Senior Research Associate and Project Co-Director at the Johns Hopkins University Institute for Policy Studies, Associate Professor of Sociology at Rutgers University, and a Social Affairs Officer with the United Nations.

Marcus Lam is an Assistant Professor at Columbia University School of Social Work.

Non-Governmental Organizations, Foundations and Disaster Management

MICHELLE KECK

Introduction

Non-governmental organizations (NGOs) and foundations have a long history of providing assistance in response to man-made emergencies and natural disasters, including food distribution, shelter, water, sanitation and medical care. Many international NGOs, particularly those in the USA and Europe, have roots in the work of Christian missionaries that date back to the 16th century. The International Committee of the Red Cross (ICRC), created in 1863 by Henri Dunant as a result of his experiences in the Battle of Solferino, is considered the forerunner of modern-day secular NGOs. In addition to the ICRC, several other prominent NGOs were created in response to war, including Oxfam, Save the Children and CARE (Ahmed and Potter, 2006). The ICRC established the humanitarian principles that guide NGO work in disaster and relief aid today, including impartiality, which refers to basing the provision of aid solely upon the need of the recipients and not discriminating on the basis of nationality, race, religion, gender or political opinions; independence, which means that aid should not be connected to any parties directly involved in the conflict or who have a stake in the outcome of conflict; and neutrality, which involves refraining from taking action that benefits or disadvantages either party to a conflict.

NGOs and foundations involved in providing relief have greatly expanded in number, particularly since the end of the cold war. Currently it is estimated that there are approximately 37,000 NGOs and foundations involved in relief work and the ICRC notes that every major disaster attracts about a thousand national and international aid organizations (Polman, 2010). High-profile emergencies, such as the 2010 Haitian earthquake, attracted 12,000 NGOs and foundations (Betancur, 2011). The increasing number of NGOs and foundations active in states experiencing armed conflict illustrates this trend. For example, in 1980 there were 37 NGOs and foundations providing relief in a Cambodian refugee camp on the Thailand border; by contrast, in 1995 there were 200 active in Goma, Congo (Democratic Repub.), and a year later 240 NGOs and foundations were present in Bosnia (Smillie, 1999).

Reimann (2006) attributes the growth of citizen groups such as foundations and NGOs to an increase in resources in the form of grants, contracts and other kinds of institutional support from states and international organizations (IOs) as well as to greater political access granted to NGOs by country and IO decision-making and agenda-setting bodies. Monetary resources that states and international organizations give to NGOs and foundations have grown sharply, increasingly in the form of short-term contracts reserved for disaster and relief aid. Barnett (2005:5) notes that disaster and relief aid as a percentage of official development assistance rose from 5.8% between 1989 and 1993 to 10.5% in 2000. Money available to NGOs and foundations for disaster and relief aid from states and international organizations rose from $2,000m. in 1990 to $6,000m. by 2000 and to $11,200m. in 2008 (Polman, 2010:10). Barnett (2005:5) indicates that the USA is the lead state donor to assist with disasters by a factor of three, followed by the European Community Humanitarian Organization (ECHO), the United Kingdom, several European countries, Canada and Japan.

Intense media coverage of natural and man-made disasters also leads to an increase in NGO and foundation relief activities. Rosenblatt (1996:139-140) argues: 'In a narrowly focused situation such as humanitarian emergencies, the media play a decisive role in informing the public and stimulating action'. Research by Robinson (1999) found evidence of a strong 'CNN effect' (Cable News Network, offering 24-hour televised news updates), with humanitarian emergencies garnering large responses from domestic audiences and global élites. For example, estimates of private contributions given to NGOs responding to the 2004 tsunamis in the Indian Ocean range from US $5,000m.— $7,000m. (Canny, 2005:3). A study by Olsen, Carstensen and Hoyen (2003) found that the amount of disaster and relief aid given by the private sector is positively related to how much media coverage the event receives. Several scholars have also found that media coverage motivates political action from states and IOs in response to disasters and humanitarian crises (Robinson 1999; Minear et al. 1996).

Man-made emergencies and natural disasters bring together many different actors. This raises questions regarding how NGOs and foundations interact with states, IOs and one another, and how these relations affect NGO and foundation responses to disasters. An examination of the 2001 military intervention in Afghanistan and the 2004 Indian Ocean tsunamis will explore the interactions between NGOs, states and IOs to assess NGO activities in man-made crises and natural disasters.

States and NGOs

By and large, literature regarding NGOs treats relations between NGOs and states as one-dimensional. NGOs are typically portrayed as actors that have 'private foreign policies that may deliberately oppose or impinge on state policies' (Nye and Keohane 1971:337). NGOs are conceptualized as autonomous actors that stand apart from states, with scholars perceiving the relationship as a unilateral one in which NGOs influence states' foreign policies to realize their normative goals (Finnemore 1996; Keck and Sikkink 1998).

A major weakness of the above studies involves the failure to consider the reality of NGO and state relations. States are active supporters of NGOs and several scholars attribute NGOs' increased role in international relations to their popularity with states, particularly the willingness of states to make funds available to them (Reimann 2006; Smillie 1999). Edwards and Hulme (1997) note that the sudden upsurge in the number of NGOs occurred exactly at the same time as the overall level of state funding of NGOs increased in the 1970s and 1990s. OECD data detail that state funding increases with the percentage of total OECD members' official aid channelled through NGOs, increasing from 0.2% in 1970 to 17% in 1996 (Nancy and Yontcheva, 2006:5). Several states including the USA, Canada, Germany, the Netherlands and Switzerland channel between 10% and 25% of their total annual foreign aid through NGOs (Smillie, 1999). As a result, many NGOs have switched from being primarily funded by private donors to being mostly funded by states (Nancy and Yontcheva). Evidence suggests that some NGOs are aware of the risks of accepting too much state funding as a portion of their overall budget. For example, Stoddard (2003) indicates that the NGO Médecins Sans Frontières (MSF) purposely limits the amount of state funding to no more than 50% of its total funds to maintain its independence. Additionally, a small number of NGOs refuse to accept any public-sector funding.

The reality of state and NGO relations has garnered the attention of a number of scholars, who have raised questions regarding how state funding affects NGO behaviour (Edwards and Hulme 1997; Smillie 1999; Mingst 2008; Ahmed and Potter 2006; O'Neill, Balsiger and VanDeveer 2004). NGOs involved in humanitarian and disaster activities have received special consideration from scholars because they are considered the 'workhorses' of disaster aid, with approximately two-thirds of all governmental humanitarian spending funnelled through them (Smillie and Minear 2004). In addition, NGOs involved in humanitarian activities are often studied because they are thought to adhere to humanitarian principles, which include impartiality, independence and neutrality. The increased funding of NGOs by states has raised doubts of NGOs' ability to adhere to humanitarian principles, and led to concerns that their activities have become politicized and dictated by the interests of the funding states.

As the relations between states and NGOs have increased, a number of studies have been conducted utilizing various theories better to understand these relations, including a study that employs game theory (Heins 2005), as well as studies that apply institutional theories from the sociological institutionalism (Barnett 2005) and rational choice (Cooley and Ron 2000; Mingst 2008) traditions.

Heins applies an analytical framework based on game theory, which explains why states and NGOs—both assumed to be rational and to have given preferences and perceptions—interact and how this interaction affects NGOs' activities. Utilizing popular games, including 'Battle of the Sexes' and the 'Stag Hunt', Heins classifies different types of NGOs and how these differences influence NGO-state relations. Heins contends that there is diversity among NGOs: some respect the sovereign role of states within the international system and refraining from questioning governments' policies; others question states' sovereignty claims as well as their policies; and a third group supports government policies and helps to implement them.

Applying sociological institutional theory, Barnett (2005) seeks to determine why NGOs have taken on specific sets of institutional forms and procedures and how that has influenced their activities. According to sociological institutionalism, the environment in which NGOs exist helps to shape the organizations. Essentially, NGOs are embedded in an environment, which is defined by a culture containing acceptable models, standards of action, goals, requirements and rules. To gain resources and legitimacy, NGOs must conform to the rules and requirements of their environment. According to Barnett, the pressure on NGOs to conform, which he argues has resulted in the professionalization, bureaucratization and politicization of the organizations, arose from state funders that began to question NGO effectiveness and legitimacy. To ensure that state funding continued, NGOs responded to states' demands and adopted behaviours that Barnett argues has acted to transform NGOs' structure and purpose, resulting in a situation in which interests in self-preservation and survival override concerns about their principal commitments.

While Barnett relies on sociological institutional theory to explain state and NGO relations, scholars such as Cooley and Ron (2002) and Mingst (2008) apply a principal agent framework from rational choice institutional theory to describe the relationship between states and NGOs. Principal agency theory examines why principals (states) delegate to agents (NGOs) and what mechanisms states use to try and control NGOs. States act as principals that provide a temporary transfer of authority to NGOs as agents. States delegate authority to NGOs to deliver public services, including relief and development aid, due to their perceived expertise and efficiency.

In their study, Cooley and Ron also focus on how the use of contracts by states (and IOs) to provide funding to NGOs may negatively influence NGO activities. The authors contend that contractual relations between states and NGOs create a market environment in which states are concerned with effective project implementation and NGOs are preoccupied with survival. Faced with the uncertainty that a market environment creates, the authors argue that NGOs' interests come to be shaped, often unintentionally, by material incentives. According to Cooley and Ron, the more reliant NGOs are on contracts, the more likely that NGOs will attempt to acquire and maintain contracts, particularly under market-generated pressure. Cooley and Ron argue that the need to acquire contracts compels NGOs to replicate the structures and procedures of for-profit organizations, resulting in a situation in which material interests typically become more important to NGOs than normative concerns. As a result, NGOs come to resemble and act like for-profit organizations.

Cooley and Ron also illustrate how the use of competitive contracts by states constrains and alters NGO activities. The authors undertake a case study of NGOs involved in relief work during the Rwandan civil war and find that competitive contracting resulted in NGOs acting counter to their normative objectives. Cooley and Ron argue that a highly competitive environment among NGOs acts to increase survival concerns, resulting in a situation in which concerns of securing contracts outweighed ethical considerations. In their study, the authors find that a highly competitive atmosphere among NGOs to secure contracts from official donors leads NGOs to permit relief aid diversion by militants and suspected war criminals. Cooley and Ron indicate that state-funded NGOs were hesitant to speak out about the abuse of aid because of fears that their contracts would be revoked or offered to other NGOs, highlighting how the need for state funding causes NGOs to act in ways counter to their normative intentions.

While scholars such as Barnett and Cooley and Ron emphasize how state funding modifies NGOs and their activities, other scholars (Minsgt 2008; O'Neill, Balsiger and VanDeveer 2004; Ahmed and Potter 2006) argue that state-funded NGOs can maintain autonomy and influence states. In her study, Mingst applies principal agent theory to explain the relationship between NGOs and states. Although Mingst acknowledges that states, as principals, have controls that they exert over NGOs as agents, through funding, earmarking and the monitoring of their behaviour, she asserts that NGOs have power in their relationship with states that they can utilize to maintain their autonomy. According to Mingst, NGOs often have specialized expertise that principals such as states need because of their closeness to aid recipients. This results in a situation in which NGOs have more local information than states and their ability to exploit the information gives them power over states. NGOs can also gain autonomy as a result of having multiple principals (states, IOs, individual donors). Mingst argues that having multiple principals gives NGOs more power by allowing them to select and adapt to one principal over the other and to frame arguments to specific audiences.

O'Neill, Balsiger and VanDeer (2004:155) also assert that state-funded NGOs have agency independent of states, which they define as the 'ability to choose among different courses of action, to learn from previous experience, and to effect change'. The authors argue that NGOs often have agency in areas of issue definition and agenda-setting. As a result, NGOs play an important role in issue-framing to convince states to alter their positions or modify their policies. NGOs also demonstrate agency from states as a result of their ideational methods of influence in which they pursue normative change by reframing problems as global rather than the sole interest of states.

In their study, Ahmed and Potter (2006) indicate how NGOs can pursue their private interests and increase their autonomy in their relations with state funders. As constituents of state funders, NGOs can act to influence state policy. According to Ahmed and Potter, state funding of NGOs has created a constituency that can be called on by states to support aid programmes through public education efforts as well as lobbying during budgetary hearings. However, the authors note that NGOs are interested in the substance as well as in the implementation of states' aid policies, which can involve costs to states. NGOs often undertake advocacy and monitoring roles in their relations with states, which leads them to seek changes in state policy.

Ahmed and Potter specify two strategies that NGOs can utilize to influence states to pursue their private interests and increase their autonomy. The first is at the project level, in which NGOs attempt to stop or change the conditions of a particular project. In this case, NGOs will accept a contract from states to carry out a specific project and attempt to halt or change the conditions of the project once contracted. The second level of influence occurs at the policy-making level. States often give NGOs an advisory role and invite them to participate in project and programme reviews, in which NGOs provide advice and policy recommendations. Ahmed and Potter indicate that the two strategies often overlap, with NGOs first accepting funding from a state to carry out a project, which in turn leads to a debate within the NGO about the state's policies, resulting in the NGO engaging the state in a discussion about the assumptions that underlie the project.

International Organizations and NGOs

Relations between NGOs and IOs first developed in 1919 upon the founding of the League of Nations, which maintained informal relations with relief NGOs. The UN is considered to be the IO with the longest working relationship with NGOs, a relationship that was solidified in Article 71 of the UN Charter. Article 71 gives NGOs a political presence in the UN by granting them formal international recognition and accreditation for participating in UN conferences. Some of the first NGO interactions with the UN involved agencies concerned with relief and disaster assistance. In areas of refugee and relief aid, NGOs began working with the UN Relief and Rehabilitation Administration (UNRRA) and the UN Relief and Works Agency (UNRWA) in the 1940s, and with the Office of the UN High Commissioner for Refugees (UNHCR) when it began operating in 1951 (Smith 1990). This close relationship has persisted, and UN support of NGOs continues to grow. Reimann (2006:49) indicates that the UN gives the largest amount of direct aid to NGOs involved in humanitarian and relief efforts, and by the 1990s NGOs implemented $2,200m. in UNHCR and World Food Programme aid.

The European Union (EU) also provides considerable support to NGOs. EU funding of NGOs began with a small co-financing program of US $3.2m. in the 1970s; by 1995 it approached $1,000m., representing 15%–20% of all EU foreign aid (Randel and German 1999). As of 1998, 31 budget lines of EU programmes representing approximately $1,700m. was reported by the European Commission. Reimann (2006:52) notes that recent estimates of EU funding to NGOs is between $2,000m.—$3,000m. Humanitarian aid has experienced the largest increase in funding to NGOs. Randel and German (1999:267) indicate that by the 1990s around one-half of all funding originating from the European Community Humanitarian Office (ECHO) was implemented by NGOs.

In their interactions with IOs, NGOs have been granted considerable political access, and Reimann argues that this has expanded NGO presence and activities in world politics. This increased access has given NGOs the opportunity to participate in policy-making and implementation processes in conjunction with IOs. NGOs have a number of political roles in their relations with IOs, including advocacy and lobbying, public education and consciousness-raising, and agenda-setting. Ahmed and Potter (2006) note that NGOs were engaged in agenda setting with IOs from the beginning, with the ICRC and other NGOs taking up the question of refugees at the founding of the League of Nations.

A significant amount of attention by scholars has involved examining relations between the UN and NGOs. Ahmed and Potter indicate several factors have given NGOs unprecedented access in the UN policy-making process including the UN's organizational structure, UN-sponsored conferences and NGO forums, and unofficial conferences organized by NGOs through the Conference of NGOs in Consultative Relationship with the United Nations (CONGO). Regarding UN structure, Ahmed and Potter note that UN relief agencies' missions tend to coincide with NGO activities, which makes it worthwhile for the agencies to co-operate with NGOs involved in relief and gives NGOs an opportunity to implement projects and influence UN objectives. UN-sponsored conferences give NGOs the chance to set the agenda by submitting information and preparing reports at the request of the UN Secretariat and governments as well as lobbying delegates and putting forward draft resolutions. NGO forums include panels and seminars and are designed to air the disagreements of stakeholders. Ahmed and Potter note that the most important aspect of the NGO-sponsored forums is that they bring NGOs and diplomats together, which provides NGOs with additional opportunities to advocate and lobby to get their issues and concerns heard by member states.

The access granted to NGOs by the UN has allowed them to become involved in all three stages of the policy-making process. NGOs help to set the agenda by promoting issues that are not being considered by UN member states or to contest member states' positions on issues (Willetts 1996). For example, NGOs often have a presence in a number of countries and can provide the UN with information regarding conditions in particular areas to get the attention of member states and elicit an official UN relief response.

NGOs also help to formulate UN policy by providing ideas, information and advice as well as assisting in the drafting of policies and resolutions. To encourage policy adoption, NGOs can rally public opinion and pressure member states to support resolutions. NGOs also have unparalleled access to major UN decision-making bodies. Ahmed and Potter note that in 1990 the ICRC was the first NGO to be granted observer status in the General Assembly. NGOs also have gained access to the Security Council; CARE and MSF have provided information to Security Council committees regarding global disaster and relief needs. For example, in 1997 CARE provided information to the Security Council regarding the situation in the Great Lakes region in Africa, which was mired in civil war creating a refugee crisis that garnered UN-sponsored relief NGO assistance.

NGOs are also actively involved in UN policy implementation. NGOs work closely with UN relief agencies such as UNHCR. Ahmed and Potter indicate that UNHCR funnels 20% of its operating budget to NGOs. These agencies act for the UN on the ground and are responsible for co-ordinating relief operations and channelling money to NGOs that carry out relief projects on the UN's behalf (Beigbeder, 1991). As a result, NGOs are frequently involved in implementing UN relief projects and take on co-ordination and consultation roles in their relationships with UN disaster relief agencies.

Ahmed and Potter note that relations between NGOs and IOs are often less complicated than those between NGOs and states, because IOs cannot force NGOs to obey laws and regulations in the same way as states can, and NGOs can avoid working with those IOs they perceive as too restrictive. Nevertheless, many scholars have raised concerns about how IO funding influences NGO behaviour. Cooley and Ron (2002) argue that the use of competitive short-term relief contracts by UN agencies such as UNHCR often creates incentives that result in negative outcomes, such as NGOs ignoring the misuse and diversion of relief aid. Barnett (2005) also expresses concern about NGO dependence on funding from IOs, arguing that it often leads to NGOs putting survival concerns ahead of their principled commitments.

NGO Interactions with NGOs

NGOs have taken a number of steps to facilitate co-operation with one another. USA-based NGOs have organized an alliance, known as InterAction, which comprises some 190 NGOs involved in relief and development activities as members (see www.interaction.org). InterAction helps to increase NGOs' efficiency by tracking where its members work and plotting specific projects to avoid duplication. InterAction also establishes standards for NGOs, including term limits for board members, diversity in hiring practices, rules regarding nepotism, and limitations on the number of senior staff who serve on their boards. European NGOs, along with those in the global South, have organized a similar alliance known as the International Council of Voluntary Agencies (ICVA), which has more than 70 members that are committed to humanitarian relief issues and activities (see www.icva.ch). As with its US counterpart, ICVA also sets standards for its members. Natosis (1995) indicates that the majority of relief NGOs are members of one of these two alliances and most attempt to adhere to their standards.

NGOs involved in relief activities have also taken a number of steps to facilitate co-operation and adopt standards that dictate their activities in the field of operations. In 1994, the NGO community developed the NGO Code of Conduct in Disaster Relief, which provides guidelines for NGOs responding to man-made and natural disasters. The code emphasizes a number of principles, including the humanitarian nature of NGOs' response, the commitment not to act as tools of donor governments' foreign policy, and neutrality when delivering aid.

The adoption of the code was in part a response to problems observed by a number of NGOs regarding relief activities, characterized by Nicholas Stockton, a former executive director of Oxfam as, 'The deterioration of humanitarian space, with a proliferation of agencies and a high degree of amateurism' (Rieff, 2008:1). The attention that some disasters and man-made crises garner results in large sums of money available to NGOs because of donor and state interest. This can lead to increased competition among NGOs for funding, which can result in redundancy, inefficiency, neglect of other disasters and crises in need of aid, a lack of NGO co-ordination, and in cases of man-made disasters, aid diversion (Rieff, 2002; 2008; Cooley and Ron, 2002; Polman, 2010). Additionally, a number of NGOs have expressed concerns about dependence on state funding, and suggested that in a number of cases NGOs have acted as state contractors.

Case Studies

Recent responses to the military intervention in Afghanistan since 2001 and the 2004 tsunamis in the Indian Ocean reveal the difficulties that humanitarian activities often create among NGOs, states and IOs. The intervention in Afghanistan, which started shortly after the terrorist attacks in the USA in September 2001, immediately garnered attention and relief funding from European countries, member states of the OECD, in addition to the USA. Rieff (2002) indicates that the USA insisted that NGOs co-ordinate their activities, arguing that it would result in more efficiency. However, in reality the USA utilized NGOs in its counter-insurgency efforts. The USA made its expectations of US-funded NGOs clear by utilizing them as force multipliers, which can be defined as factors that significantly increase the effectiveness of military forces (Lischer 2007). Former US Secretary of State Colin Powell emphasized the importance of NGOs to US military efforts in Afghanistan when he noted that he and his colleagues were 'serious about making sure we have the best relationship with the NGOs who are such a force multiplier for us, such an important part of our combat team' (Powell 2001). Furthermore, Polman (2010) argues that by working with the UN Assistance Mission in Afghanistan (UNAMA) and the interim government, and by accepting funds from governments involved in military intervention, NGOs (as well as UN agencies) were seen by Afghans as actors working on behalf of the opposing forces rather than as neutral humanitarians.

This close co-ordination violates the neutrality and independence principles that guide NGOs' humanitarian relief in addition to article 4 in the NGO Code of Conduct, which discourages NGOs from becoming tools of states. In Afghanistan, violation of these principles created a situation in which NGOs became associated with states' foreign policy. As a result, humanitarian workers in Afghanistan became targets of violence, which was highlighted by the death in 2004 of five staff members of MSF Holland, demonstrating the confusion and lack of separation of the military and humanitarian missions (Polman, 2010).

The earthquake and resulting tsunamis in the Indian Ocean in 2004 affected a number of countries and resulted in the deaths of more than 227,000 people and the displacement of 1.7m. (Inderfurth, Fabrycky and Cohen, 2005). The disaster response garnered relief donations totalling US $13,000m., which was heralded as 'The most generous and immediately funded international response ever' (Flint and Goyder, 2006). Official government pledges of $5,900m. represented 44% of relief aid, with private donations to NGOs amounting to $5,000m. or 37% of the total (Telford and Cosgrave, 2007). Rieff (2008) notes that this massive response resulted in the involvement of nearly every relief NGO capable of deploying personnel and supplies long-distance.

In his study on the NGOs community response to the disaster, Rieff indicates that initial calls regarding widespread epidemics and food shortages in Aceh, Indonesia proved to be unfounded, yet NGOs did not withdraw or lobby for government funding to be redirected to countries or areas in more need, such as Sudan's Darfur region and Angola; instead, competition among NGOs for funding and market share determined NGO behavior, rather than humanitarian principles. The scale of the NGO response revealed many problems that the NGO community has since attempted to address through the NGO Code of Conduct in Disaster Relief, including NGO co-ordination, which is often missing because of competition among NGOs for funding. In his study, Stirrat (2006:16) highlights the competitive environment within the Sri Lankan NGO community in which 'Continued funding depended not only on being effective but being seen as effective'. This competitive environment can often result in negative outcomes. For example, Telford and Cosgrave (2007) argue that the presence of too many NGOs in Indonesia resulted in poor quality aid, because it did not match the needs of the people, which was in part because of the competitive need of NGOs to spend the money visibly rather than efficiently.

Conclusion

These cases highlight the complex relations that exist between states, NGOs and IOs involved in relief and disaster aid. Attempts have been made by all parties to improve humanitarian responses to avoid future mistakes. In 2003, 200 aid practitioners from NGOs, governments and IOs participated in a series of consultations organized by the Feinstein International Famine Center concerning issues regarding the state funding of NGOs, the politicization of NGO activities and solutions to improve NGO co-ordination. Ultimately, the participants concluded that a reinvigoration of humanitarian aid was needed, with NGOs leading the way. The discussions resulted in a number of specific steps that NGOs could take to improve humanitarian responses, including agreeing on measures to insulate NGO humanitarian activities from manipulation by states and IOs and to launch an effort to reform the way in which official relief activities are funded (Donini et al. 2004). To address NGO co-ordination problems, the discussions suggest that the NGO community explore competitive advantages among one another in the delivery of relief aid. Ultimately, the authors conclude that the future of NGO relief activities depends on the ability of NGOs to find consensus on what role they should have in the delivery of humanitarian aid.

References

'About ICVA'. http://www.icva.ch/about.html accessed 26 January 2012.

'About Interaction'. http://www.interaction.org/about-interaction accessed 26 January 2012.

Ahmed, S. and David Potter. *NGOs in International Politics*. Kumarian Press, Bloomfield, CT, 2006.

Barnett, M. 'Humanitarianism Transformed'. in *Perspectives on Politics*, 3: 723-740, 2005.

Beigbeder, Y. *The Role and Status of International Humanitarian Volunteers and Organizations*. Martinus Nijhoff Publishers, Dordrecht, 1991.

Betancur, K. (January 9, 2011). A year on, hubris and debris clog Haiti quake recovery. *Reuters*. http://www.trust.org/alertnet/news/a-year-on-hubris-and-debris-clog-haiti-quake-recovery accessed 10 January 2012.

Canny, B. 8 April 2005. A Review of NGO Coordination in Aceh Post Earthquake/Tsunami. *International Council of Voluntary Agencies*. http://reliefweb.int/sites/reliefweb.int/files/resources/FEA7B9C91F77119949257021001C-FEC0-icva-idn-8apr.pdf accessed 10 January 2012.

Cooley, A. and J. Ron. 'The NGO Scramble: Organizational Insecurity and the Political Economy of Transnational Action'. In *International Security*, 27: 1-33, 2002.

Donini, A., L. Minear, P. Walker. 'The Future of Humanitarian Action: Mapping the Implications of Iraq and Other Recent Crises', in *Disasters*, 28: 190-204, 2004.

Edwards, M. and D. Hulme. 'NGOs, States, and Donors: An Overview', in *NGOs, States, and Donors,* David Hulme and Michael Edwards (Eds), 3–22. St. Martin's Press, New York, 1997.

Finnemore, M. *National Interests and International Society*. Cornell University Press, Ithaca, NY, 1996.

Flint, M. and H. Goyder. *Funding the Tsunami Response*. Tsunami Evaluation Coalition, London, 2006.

Heins, V. 'Democratic States, Aid Agencies and World Society: What's the Name of the Game?', in *Global Society*, 19: 361–384, 2005.

Inderfurth, K., D. Fabrycky, and S. Cohen. 2005. 'The Tsunami Report Card', in *Foreign Policy Magazine*. http://www2.gwu.edu/~elliott/assets/docs/research/report-card.pdf accessed 10 January 2012.

Keck, M. and K. Sikkink. *Activists Beyond Borders: Advocacy Networks in International Society*. University of Cornell Press, Ithaca, NY, 1998.

Lischer, S. K. 'Military Intervention and Humanitarian "Force Multiplier"', in *Global Governance*, 13: 99-118, 2007.

Minear, L., C. Scott, and T.G. Weiss. *The News Media, Civil War, and Humanitarian Action.* Lynne Rienner, Boulder, CO, 1996.

Mingst, K. 'Humanitarian NGOs: Principals and Agents'. Paper presented at the Annual International Studies Association, San Francisco, 2008.

Nancy, G. and B. Yontcheva. 'Does NGO Aid Go to the Poor? Empirical Evidence from Europe'. International Monetary Fund Working Paper 06/39. International Monetary Fund, Washington, DC, 2006.

Natsios, A. 'NGOs and the UN System in Complex Humanitarian Emergencies: Conflict or Cooperation?', in *Third World Quarterly*, 16: 405-419, 1995.

Nye, J. and R. Keohane. 'Transnational Relations and World Politics: An Introduction', in *Transnational Relations and World Politics*. Keohane, Robert and Joseph Nye (Eds). Harvard University Press, Cambridge, MA, 1971.

Olsen, G. R., N. Cartensen, and K. Hoyen. 'Humanitarian Crises: What Determines the Level of Emergency Assistance? Media Coverage, Donor Interests, and the Aid Business', in *Disasters*, 27: 109-126, 2003.

O'Neill, K., J. Balsiger and S. D. VanDeveer. 'Actors, Norms, and Impact: Recent International Theory and the Influence of the Agent-Structure Debate', in *Annual Review of Political Science* 7: 149-175, 2004.

Polman, L. *The Crisis Caravan.* Metropolitan Books, New York, 2010.

Powell, C. 2001. 'Remarks by Secretary of State Colin L. Powell to the National Foreign Policy Conference For Leaders of Non-Governmental Organizations'. http://usinfo.state.gov/topical/pol/terror/01102606.htm accessed 10 January 2012.

Randel, J. and T. German. 'European Union', in Smillie, Ian and Henny Helmich (Eds) *Stakeholders*, 263–277. Earthscan, London, 1999.

Reimann, K. 'A View from the Top: International Politics, Norms and the Worldwide Growth of NGOs', in *International Studies Quarterly*, 50: 45-67, 2006.

Rieff, D. *A Bed for the Night: Humanitarianism in Crisis.* New York: Simon and Schuster, 2002.

Rieff, D. August 18, 2008. Tsunamis, Accountability, and the Humanitarian Circus. Humanitarian Practice Network. http://www.hapinternational.org/pool/files/tsunamis,-accountability-and-the-humanitarian-circus.pdf accessed 10 January 2012.

Robinson, P. 'The CNN Effect: Can the News Media Drive Foreign Policy?', in *Review of International Studies*, 25: 301-309, 1999.

Rosenblatt, L. 'The Media and the Refugee', in R. I. and T. G. Weiss (Eds) *From Massacres to Genocide, The Media, Public Policy, and Humanitarian Crises.* The Brookings Institute, Washington, DC, 1996.

Smillie, I. 'At Sea in a Sieve? Trends and Issues in the Relationship Between Northern NGOs and Northern Governments', in Smillie, Ian and Henny Helmich (Eds) *Stakeholders*, 7–38. Earthscan, London, 1999.

Smillie, Ian and Larry Minear. *The Charity of Nations. Humanitarian Action in a Calculating World.* Kumarian Press, Bloomfield, CT, 2004.

Smith, B. *More Than Altruism.* Princeton University Press, Princeton, NJ, 1990.

Stirrat, J. 'Competitive Humanitarianism: Relief and the Tsunami in Sri Lanka'. *Anthropology Today*, 22: 11-16, 2006.

Stoddard, A. 'Humanitarian NGOs: Challenges and Trends', in J. Macrae and A. Harmer (Eds) 'Humanitarian Action and "The Global War of Terror": A Review of Trends and Issues', HPG Report no. 14, ODI, London, 25-36, 2003.

Telford, J. and J. Cosgrave. 'The International Humanitarian System and the 2004 Indian Ocean Earthquake and Tsunamis', in *Disasters*, 31: 1-28, 2007.

Willetts, P. 'The Conscience of the World: The Influence of Non Governmental Organizations in World Politics'. The Brookings Institute, Washington, DC, 1996.

Michelle Keck is Assistant Professor of Government at The University of Texas at Brownsville. Her research interests include NGOs, IOs, border studies and foreign policy.

Non-profits during Times of Crisis: Organizational Behaviour and Policy Responses

HELMUT K. ANHEIER, ANNELIE BELLER AND NORMAN SPENGLER

Introduction

This discursive essay takes a wide ranging, long-term view of the impact of the financial and economic crisis that occurred from the late 2000s onwards on non-profit organizations, and the strategic management and policy implications involved. Borrowing from organizational theory and policy analysis, we explore the organizational and policy responses in the non-profit sector to guide future research and policy initiatives. In so doing, we show that organizational behaviour and policy responses for and from non-profit organizations are dependent on their encompassing institutional settings. The aftermath of the economic crisis may restrict the options open to non-profits, but it also enables new forms of significant change that might otherwise be unlikely during stable situations.

Challenges for Non-profits: What would have happened anyway?

That the political and economic changes triggered by the global financial crisis are negatively affecting foundations and non-profits is clear to everyone who follows frequent reports of cancellations and closings of programmes, or learns about economic troubles, even bankruptcies, of one organization or another. It is also clear that the global financial crisis is still having serious and often time-lagged implications. Less clear is for how long the crisis and its fallout will last; and especially unclear is what the crisis will ultimately mean for non-profit managers and policymakers in the field. How could they respond to growing uncertainty in the sector itself as well as in the various fields in which non-profits and philanthropies operate?

A closer look at this question requires separating what would have most probably happened anyway from what is happening additionally, sooner, or more forcefully because of the crisis in the medium term. Of course, one can only imagine alternative futures by extrapolating from developments that have taken place over the past two decades, and identifying a number of patterns and trends. Among these are (see Gidron and Bar, 2009; Boris and Steuerle, 2006; Kendall, 2009; Young, 2007; Anheier, 2005):

- Greater demand for non-profit goods and services combined with less, and more competitive, public funding.
- Competition models developed elsewhere (health, social services, education) being applied to many

other fields where non-profits operate, with an emphasis on cost control rather than outcome quality.
- The search for new business models for non-profits in many fields, from health to arts and culture, and from higher education to social services, to compensate for lower levels of government support.
- Professionalization of finance, management and service delivery, often combined with a certain tameness—even timidity—in terms of advocacy.

What these developments would have meant is more than a rhetorical question, and for the simple reason that these very trends are continuing. Above all, according to economic theory (Hansmann, 1996; Ben-Ner and Gui, 2003; Steinberg, 2003) between non-profits and businesses. As supply and demand conditions for non-profits and businesses continue to converge, such processes would have become more frequent in regulated quasi-markets (health, social services), as would have, in particular, conversions of public to private institutions (education, culture). In other words, many organizations would have changed form, many non-profits would have become more like businesses, many public institutions more private, and public-private partnerships more frequent and more complex.

This in turn would have brought about fierce and long drawn-out debates (Hopt et al., 2005; Billis, 2010): about the right revenue structure for non-profits and the optimal mix of earned income, public funds and private donations, including foundation grants; about asset management and acquisition policies; about barriers of exit and (re)entry for donors and recipients alike; about stakeholder involvement (consumer, client, member, funder, staff, the general public, etc.); about professional control over mission and operations, and the role of the board; about social entrepreneurship and non-profit management and leadership styles; and, very prominently, about the role of the state.

The Global Financial Crisis: What is New Now for Non-profits?

All of these topics were common in non-profit-related, future-looking discussions, even before the global financial crisis surfaced. Now, these debates continue, albeit in the context of a profound crisis, and a potent mix of new challenges has been added:

- At the societal level, there is a loss of trust in the 'system', a general sense of insecurity among populations and opportunism among political actors on the left and the right. Growing parts of the population look more critically at their economic system and call for a repression of the market liberalization that has gained almost uncontrollable global complexity since the breakdown of the former competing system at the end of the 1980s. It seems that there is another story after 'the end of history' (Fukuyama, 1992). As a result, new opinion patterns and political movements have been formed with different faces in different countries (e.g. the rise of populism in the USA and of right-wing governments in Hungary, or the formation of a new left party in Germany).

- Governments, some fiscally sounder than the USA and with more room to manoeuvre, rediscover Keynesianism and interpret it to their own political advantage, which typically results in massive public spending programmes another (of which only a rather small portion is likely to reach non-profits or help philanthropy). Increases in public investments combine with reductions in current budgets and create shortfalls, some of which—especially in those countries characterized by close liaison between state and non-profit organizations in terms of welfare provision—are passed on to non-profits. Non-profits in countries with high public governmental spending (see Salamon and Anheier, 1998) are expected to suffer most from governmental shortfalls as the delayed impact on the budget takes effect.

- One would expect businesses to engage in 'short-termism' to calm shareholders by cutting expenses outside their original value chain, among them corporate social responsibility and giving programmes, including funding aimed at non-profits. Indeed, empirical evidence shows divergent paths of corporate giving since the economic downturn: when comparing giving from 2007 with 2010, 50% of companies gave more, 45% gave less and 5% remained about the same. More remarkable is a large increase in non-cash giving of 39% since 2007 (Committee Encouraging Corporate Philanthropy, 2011).

- The policy of financial market liberalizations that was meant to reduce the economic and organizational size of the public sector is, at least in the short-to-medium term, having the opposite effect: the financial stake governments have in business is now greater than at any time before the neo-liberal policies and the now-defunct Washington Consensus took hold. Government and business, in particular in the areas of finance, energy and key technologies, have rarely been closer to each other.

- Philanthropic foundations have seen drops in asset values at a scale not seen in decades: in the USA, in 2008 foundation assets dropped by an unprecedented 17%. The relative stabilization (2.1% decline in 2009; 0.2% decline in 2010) that has been seen in the two subsequent years is the result of bold foundation behaviour. Nevertheless, in total numbers, recovery remains shaky and the outlook for the next years is uncertain (Foundation Center, 2011).

- While most economies recover, the latest Nonprofit Fundraising Study shows that the US non-profit sector has not seen improvement in fundraising yet. This provides evidence that the financial crisis of the late 2000s, as with previous economic crises, is having a delayed impact on the sector. While not all types of organizations (depending on activity area and size— smaller organizations, those with expenditures below US $3m. are more likely to be at risk) are affected the same way, for 65% of responding organizations demand for services continues to increase (Nonprofit Research Collaborative, 2011).

- Many households have been and are facing both greater financial uncertainty and declining net worth. According to numbers of a recent European Union (EU) survey (Eurobarometer, 2010), one-fifth of European citizens claimed to be having difficulties in keeping up with credit commitments and bills; one-quarter indicated that they expected their financial situation to worsen within the following year. This is leading to drops in donations: in Germany the number of donors is at a historical low since 1995 (TNS Infratest, 2011); in the United Kingdom (UK) charitable giving declined by 11% and in the USA by 6% in 2007/08 (Charities Aid Foundation and National Council for Voluntary Organisations, 2009).

For non-profits, the current crisis means fewer resources in terms of current expenditures for ongoing and planned programmes. However, in some cases and depending on public spending priorities, it may also yield some additional funding for investment programmes as part of stimulus packages; but first and foremost, it means greater financial instability, more uncertainty for management and staff, possibilities of unfulfilled contracts and obligations, and unmet demand. These uncertainties clearly pose diverse challenges to non-profits.

Organizational Behaviour and Policy Responses: Leads from Organizational Theory

How then do non-profits respond to these challenges? What is a possible range of organizational behaviour? And which different kinds of policy responses support non-profit organizations in dealing with the crisis? Here, organizational theory points to some useful answers.

Neo-institutionalism assumes that organizations form themselves according to the requirements of their environment to gain legitimacy (DiMaggio and Powell, 1983). In times of crisis not only do these requirements turn out to be unclear and uncertain, but legitimacy can also become the central commodity deciding the survival or failure of organizations. Faced with high levels of uncertainty, organizations may model themselves on organizations that are perceived to be successful. Those mimetic processes can either be intended or unintended. According to neo-institutionalism, copycat behaviour, as well as the increased incorporation of stakeholders, may be one possible reaction of non-profits during the crisis to secure legitimacy. From a policy perspective, one possible response would be to present and expose viable organizational as well as business models to non-profit organizations.

Also dealing with relations between organizations and their environments, contingency theory proposes another possible form of organizational crisis behaviour (Burns and Stalker, 1961). In contrast with neo-institutionalism, this approach focuses on efficiency requirements and argues that the efficiency of an organization's structure depends on the fit to its environment. It therefore suggests that there is more than one 'best way' to manage. According to Burns and Stalker (1961), for an environment with changing conditions, such as the financial crisis, organic or flexible organizational structures are appropriate. Hence, organizations have to adapt to the volatile environments implied by the crisis to guarantee future efficiency. Therefore organizations are loosening their structures to reflect the environment, and to be able to react in more flexible ways. With this in mind, policy makers could take the precaution of reducing barriers for re-organization as well as transaction costs for contingent mergers and acquisitions.

In common with these two approaches, the resource-dependency approach also recognizes the open system and contingent nature of organizations, and focuses on context to understand organizations' behaviour (Pfeffer and Salancik, 1978). Pfeffer and Salancik assume that all organizations in some way depend on external resources. Organizations must address environmental changes, otherwise they cannot survive. In times of crisis resource dependencies can increase and organizations may primarily seek to secure especially critical resources, such as funding. Attempts to safeguard this can be seen in the search for new business models, as well as intensification of public-private partnerships. The capacity to diversify the business models available to non-profits depends also on the state, more precisely, on legislation.

Studying the question of how organizations evolve, Romanelli and Tushman (1994) introduce the notion of 'punctuated equilibrium' to refer to discontinuous transformation. They assume that organizations pass through relatively long periods of stability in terms of structure and activity. These are punctuated by short bursts of fundamental changes, which are triggered when several key organizational domains are threatened or become critically uncertain, particularly in terms of available resources. In response, some organizations seek to adapt by modifying strategy, structure, incentive and control systems, as well as power relations that are more far-reaching than would have been the case without the pressures resulting from the crisis.

Organizational theorists such as Gersick (1991) suggest that revolutionary periods are times of greater innovation in organizations that manage to break the structural and cultural inertia of embedded routines. Specifically, such periods involve changes in the 'deep structure' of organizations (i.e., a set network of fundamental, interdependent choices about rationales, activities and the environment). They come about when two types of disruption occur simultaneously: internal changes that misalign the deep structure with its environment, and environmental changes that threaten the system's overall ability to obtain resources. It may well be that the current crisis offers this 'rare' combination of external and internal disruptions to the deep structure.

These disruptions and changes can also lead to new forms or speciation. Romanelli (1991) highlights the processes of re-combination and 're-functionality', which either involve the introduction of new elements into an existing form, such as corporate management tools, which include benchmarking in non-profits, or the relocation of one form into a new context (e.g. the migration of for-profit providers into social services).

We also owe the notion of niches (Hannan and Freeman, 1989; Aldrich, 1999) to this theoretical school. Organizational niches are recognized as comparatively distinct combinations of resources that organizations use. Finding, defending and optimizing niches, on the demand as well as the supply side, can become a key task for organizational survival, especially in times of crisis. Operating within a niche makes organizations less vulnerable to competition.

The concept of inertia (Hannan and Freeman, 1977) is another essential insight. Inertia results from different factors that constrain the organization's capacity to adapt to environmental changes. These can be internal (e.g. resistance to change) or external (e.g. market entry barriers).

From the field of evolutionary organizational theory, therefore, we can conclude that radical organizational change is one possible response to a crisis by which organizations try to adapt to the changed environment. Policymakers can respond to those radical shifts and changes by easing exit and entry regulations for organizations and, more specifically, minimizing the costs of founding and dissolving an organization.

One other well-known hypothesis in the field of organizational crisis research is 'threat rigidity', by which an organization becomes rigid when faced with a perceived threat (Staw et al., 1981), such as the global economic crisis. Rigid behaviour manifests itself in a tightening of control, as well as restriction of information, and entails mechanization of the organizational structure. Rigid reactions can partly be prevented through management education and crisis management, in particular.

A brief examination of these different theoretical approaches shows that through the presumption of interdependency, environmental change triggered by the financial crisis will influence non-profit organizations. The changed framework demands a different course of action, particularly because new policy windows will open. Why then is there so little response by non-profits at the policy level and scant policy attention? Even if policy opportunities emerge, they are unlikely to be seized because of the sector's own inertia. Why does such inertia and path dependency exist?

The answer may well be found in a version of the 'principal-agent' problem as it applies to the third sector. The standard problem asks how can owners (i.e., the principals) ensure that managers (i.e., the agents) run an organization to the owners' benefit. In the business world, owners/shareholders delegate oversight to a board of directors charged with ensuring that management acts in accordance with the principals' goals and interests. In the public sector, voters elect politicians to exercise oversight over public sector performance; the media, regulatory agencies and interest organizations monitor the government's performance.

However, in the third sector the situation is undetermined, and it is unclear who should be regarded as or function as the owner. Trustees are not owners in the sense of shareholders, and while different parties could assume or usurp the role of principal, such a position would not rest on property rights.

The key to understanding the relationship between the characteristics of third sector organizations, their governance and accountability requirements is to recognize the special importance of multiple stakeholders rather than owners. Critically, because of the limited application of the principal-agent problem in non-market situations, information about performance is not as clearly and keenly demanded or analyzed to the same extent as in the for-profit and public sectors. In other words, the third sector suffers from chronic signal and incentive weaknesses (see Anheier and Hawkes, 2007)—a constellation inviting inertia because of a preference for the status quo.

While the weak signal-weak incentive syndrome may well be the reason for greater inertia in the third sector than in other sectors, a second characteristic of non-profit organizations may be the reason for pronounced path dependencies: the presence of values and deep-seated dispositions that guard the organization and often provide its very *raison d'être*. Values are, if anything, organizationally conservative, not in the political sense, but as more or less

Table 1 A summary of the range of organization-level hypotheses and suggested corresponding policy measures.

Approach	What crisis means for organizations	How organizations could react and find a solution	Policy responses or reactions
Neo-institutionalism	Because legitimacy bases may dwindle in times of crisis, organizations face high levels of uncertainty.	Organizations seek to regain legitimacy either by copycat behaviour or increased stakeholder incorporation to secure legitimacy.	Present viable organizational and business models.
Contingency Theory	Crisis implies volatile environments to which organizations have to adapt to guarantee future efficiency.	Organizations modify their structure to ensure efficiency and adapt to their environment.	Reduce barriers to re-organization and transaction costs for mergers and acquisitions.
Resource Dependency	Because resource dependencies may increase in times of crisis, organizations must take action to influence their environment.	Organizations primarily seek to secure resources by taking action to reduce dependency.	Diversify business models available for non-profits; encourage public-private partnerships.
Evolutionary Theory	Crisis increases selection pressures and incentives for organizations to adapt to changing environments.	Organizations try to adapt to changed environments through niche-building, re-functionality and re-combination.	Allow for ease of exit and entry; minimize cost of founding and dissolving organizations.
Threat Rigidity	Crisis is perceived as an external threat to organizations.	Organizations behave rigidly faced with the threat that the crisis presents.	Advocate management education and crisis management.

permanent fixtures or principles. We could then suggest that these combined factors may account for higher degrees of inertia and path dependency.

Responses and Actors Embedded in Institutional Settings

The general characteristics of an organization's relationship with its environment appear to be significant when examining policy responses and behaviours. Although a much broader array of useful theories exists, we have explored those mentioned above because they address not only the relationship itself, but also the processes within this relationship by making a case for the embeddedness of organizations in changing contexts. These theoretical approaches also introduced the ideas of inertia and path dependency. By recognizing these mechanisms, policy-makers and non-profit managers may consider various options in times of crisis. This is not only a question of reactive adaptation and active initiative, but is also related to changes in their surrounding institutional settings. Generally, an answer to the question of how actors should react seems very complicated and an overarching solution too simplistic or not sensible, when the variety of civil society organizations worldwide is taken into consideration.

As pointed out, there have been ongoing debates about a stronger market orientation of non-profits, mainly focusing on aspects of cost-efficiency, resource management, structure, processes and strategies. These often-discussed internal responses to a more business-orientated environment

are not new. But to what extent do these have an internal impact on the organizations that take into account external rationalities that have been changed by the current crisis?

The answer seems to be located within the organizational environment and also responds to the question of which reactions are perceived as legitimate and rational. Based on this insight, we believe that internal organizational responses differ not only between countries, but also within different national non-profit sectors, as different claims from varying stakeholders take effect. We should expect organizations to cope with uncertainty by taking over structures, tasks and strategies that their stakeholders perceive as 'rational'. The more organizations are embedded within given welfare service delivery systems and the liberal variety of capitalism, the higher the pressure on non-profit organizations to behave according to the market by streamlining internal processes and acting more efficiently. Other contexts, such as greater distance from service delivery fields and less dependency on economic resources may result in a more sophisticated focus on values and social mission. It would be interesting to examine more closely the extent to which, and under what circumstances, the economic crisis has shifted the well-known organizational trade-offs between efficiency and effectiveness in civil society organizations.

The economic crisis has affected not only the internal realm of non-profit organizations, but at a macro-level state-civil society relations. There have been as many different national reactions to the crisis and its consequences as there were differences manifested within the varieties of capitalism affected. So far, policy-orientated responses have been mixed, varying from country to country and underlining the power relations between the actors involved. Whereas in some countries the third sector has been relatively mute, in others it has undertaken initial crisis management.

The third sector in the UK, as one example, has been among the most active by directly calling on the Government to step in to help minimize the impact of the financial crisis. The National Council for Voluntary Organisations (NCVO) proposed a support package in response to consultations on the recession. Subsequently, the government released an action plan (see Office of the Third Sector, 2009) that allocates financial support for third-sector organizations that are experiencing difficulties because of the recession. By contrast, German non-profits have remained more silent and cautious. They mostly reacted to topics the government presented to them, rather than presenting their own. Direct governmental responses to the financial crisis, such as the various economic stimulus packages in 2008–09, as well as the Growth Acceleration Act of 2009, largely ignored the sector. However, instead of putting forward concrete demands, the main third sector actors—the so-called Free Welfare Organizations—decided to advocate for themselves and the client bases they serve.

A brief look at other countries shows that collective responses, as in the UK example above, still remain an exception. Some of the reasons can again be traced to the third sector's peculiarities and characteristics: the great diversity and richness of organizational forms, the multiplicity and mix of financial resources, as well as the plurality of operational fields and embeddedness of civil society actors in public governance structures. This existing dissimilarity not only means that third sector organizations are affected by the 2008–10 economic downturn in very different and varying ways, but also that lobbying for the sector's needs and interests becomes a very challenging task. This again is because most organizations are mainly concerned with their own survival, which in this instance can be equated with weathering the storm, rather than collective action.

A consequence of this absence collective action is that power and responsibility are shifted over to the political arena, demanding a resurgence of the state. However, the state's new role is neither as the welfare or provider state of the past, nor the enabling state of recent decades (see Schuppert, 2005). Private debt was replaced by sovereign indebtedness that requires public sector retrenchment and cuts. It is a reluctant state forced into expansion mode by the current crisis, and the need to bail out defaulting banks and failing businesses, incurring significant debt as a consequence and responding by imposing severe spending cuts.

Tentative Conclusions

What potential does the crisis have for threatening the deep structures of the third sector, given its inertia and path dependency? This is, of course, an open question, but organizational theory again offers some leads: co-ordinated market economies such as Japan and Germany have developed institutions that encourage long-term institutional relations for facilitating the development of distinctive organizational competences that are conducive to continuous but incremental innovation (Lam, 2004). Such policy settings will seek reform from within. By contrast, the liberal market economies develop institutional structures that encourage 'adhocracy' and more radical innovations. We might hypothesize that the institutional

environments in the USA or the UK reveal a greater propensity for system-wide policy changes, whereas the co-ordinated market economies prefer gradual policy approaches.

Every crisis makes the restriction of older frameworks for action obvious and brings them into question: to ensure future survival, current organizational patterns have to be revised and often adapted, whether towards more managerialist approaches or bringing the focus back to the value base. However, at the same time, every crisis enables the emergence of new opportunities because other societal systems often have to review assumptions that were taken for granted, standard operating procedures and governance structures. The insight that 'business-as-usual' principles have caused problems in the past and therefore meant no option for the future may lead to a greater consensus that framing conditions need to be questioned and changed.

The mechanisms of interaction between civil society and the political system, and within civil society, seem to depend on institutional settings: among them, the variety of capitalism applied, the welfare state, and established governance structures. As we have argued, these factors are framing the nature of responses by non-profit organizations during the current financial crisis. But it would be wrong to portray non-profit organizations as victims without any potential for action. Given differing contexts, non-profits have huge capacities to create and 'enact' (Weick, 1979). The question is, how can non-profit organizations expand their creative power?

Given these developments, new policy opportunities for non-profit organizations pave the way for de-institutionalization processes of former systemic conditions (state-civil society relations, governance, societal division of labour, financial/idealistic support, etc.) towards structures that fit better with the global situation. As we see, uncertainty need not be bad at all. Uncertainty, especially in times of crisis, forces actors to revise current patterns, and allows the emergence of new alliances and co-operation within and beyond sectoral and national borders.

In conclusion, we suggest that the capacity for third sector policy innovations—and the possibility of overcoming inertia and path dependency—is located within existing institutional arrangements in co-ordinated market economies, and between—as well as outside—given structures in liberal market economies. Overall, the stability of the third sector implies less volatility in times of crisis. Interestingly, this also seems to suggest a certain paradox: what can be regarded as a liability during periods of stability can become an asset when deep structures are put in question.

If we assume that the current crisis will not be the last and forecast that global crises will occur more often than before, these environmental changes could encourage the emergence of new civil society infrastructures, not only within nation states but also for strengthening global civil society. By considering the above-mentioned effects of organizational and systemic inertia and path dependency, we can hypothesize that these policy windows during the current economic crisis will certainly trigger innovations of many kinds that allow new structures that themselves are to be understood as junctions and bases for future path dependencies in the face of future crises.

References

Aldrich H. E. *Organizations Evolving*. Sage, London 1999.

Anheier, H. K. *Non-profit Organizations. Theory, Management, Policy*. Routledge, London and New York, 2005.

Anheier, H. K. and A. Hawkes. 'Accountability in a Globalizing World', in Albrow, M., H. K. Anheier M. Glasius and M. Kaldor (Eds) *Global Civil Society 2007/08*, pp. 124–143. Sage, London, 2007.

Charities Aid Foundation and National Council of Voluntary Organisations 'The impact of the recession on charitable giving in the UK.', available online via https://www.cafonline.org/pdf/UKGivingrecessionreport2009.pdf, 2009.

Committee Encouraging Corporate Philanthropy 'Giving in Numbers: 2011 Edition'. Available online via CorporatePhilanthropy.org/research.

Ben-Ner, A. and B. Gui. 'The Theory of Non-profit Organizations Revisited', in Anheier, H. K. and A. Ben-Ner (Eds) *The Study of the Non-profit Enterprise. Theories and Approaches.* Kluwer Academic, New York, 2003.

Billis, D. (Ed.). *Hybrid Organizations and the Third Sector: Challenges for Practice, Theory and Policy.* Palgrave Macmillan, 2010.

Boris, E. T. and C. E. Steuerle (Eds). *Non-profits and Government. Collaboration and Conflict*, 2nd edn. Urban Institute Press, Washington, DC 2006.

Burns, T. and G. M. Stalker. *The Management of Innovation.* Tavistock, London 1961.

DiMaggio, P. J. and W. W. Powell. 'The Iron Cage Revisited: Institutional Isomorphism and Collective Rationality in Organizational Fields', in *American Sociological Review*, 48 (2), pp. 147-160, 1983.

Eurobarometer. 'Monitoring the Social Impact of the Crisis: Public Perceptions in the European Union', Wave 2, Analytical Report, 2010.

Foundation Center. *Highlights of Foundation Yearbook, 2011 Edition.* Available online via www.foundationcenter.org. New York, 2011.

Fukuyama, F. *The End of History and the Last Man.* Harper, New York, 1992.

Gersick, C. J. G. 'Revolutionary Change Theories: A Multi-Level Exploration of the Punctuated Equilibrium Paradigm', in *Academy of Management Review,* 16 (1), pp. 10-36, 1991.

Gidron, B. and M. Bar (Eds) *Policy Initiatives Towards the Third Sector in International Perspective.* Non-profit and Civil Society Studies Series. Springer, New York, 2009.

Giving USA. *The Annual Report on Philanthropy for the year 2008–09.* Available online via www.givingusa.org. 2010.

Hannan M. T. and J. Freeman. 'The population ecology of organizations', in *American Journal of Sociology, 82*, pp. 929-964, 1977.

Hannan M. T. and J. Freeman. *Organizational Ecology.* Harvard University Press, Cambridge, MA, 1989.

Hansmann, H. *The Ownership of Enterprise.* Harvard University Press, Cambridge, MA, 1996.

Hopt, K. J., von Hippel, T. and W. R. Walz (Eds). 'Non-profit-Organisationen', in *Recht, Wirtschaft und Gesellschaft: Theorien, Analysen, Corporate Governance.* Mohr Siebeck, Tübingen, 2005.

Kendall, J. (Ed.). *Handbook on Third Sector Policy in Europe: Multi-level Processes and Organized Civil Society.* Edward Elgar, Cheltenham, 2009.

Lam, A. *Organizational Innovation. Brunel Research in Enterprise, Innovation, Sustainability, and Ethics,* Working Paper No. 1. Brunel University, London 2004.

Nonprofit Research Collaborative 'Late Fall 2011 Nonprofit Fundraising Study'. Available online via http://www2.guidestar.org/ViewCmsFile.aspx?ContentID=4050, December 2011.

Office of the Third Sector. *Real Help for Communities: Volunteers, Charities and Social Enterprises.* London, 2009.

Pfeffer, J. and G. Salancik. *The External Control of Organizations. A Resource Dependence Perspective.* Harper & Row, New York, 1978.

Romanelli, E. 'The Evolution of New Organizational Forms', in *Annual Review of Sociology*, 17, pp. 79-103, 1991.

Romanelli, E. and M. L. Tushman. 'Organizational Transformation as Punctuated Equilibrium: An Empirical Test', *in The Academy of Management Journal*, 37 (5), pp. 1141-1166, 1994.

Salamon, L. M. and H. K. Anheier. 'Social Origins of Civil Society: Explaining the Non-profit-Sector Cross-Nationally', *in Voluntas* 9 (3), pp. 213-248, 1998.

Schuppert, G. F. 'Der Gewährleistungsstaat—modisches Label oder Leitbild sich wandelnder Staatlichkeit?', in Schuppert, G. F. (Ed.) *Der Gewährleistungsstaat—ein Leitbild auf dem Prüfstand*, pp. 11–52. Nomos, Baden Baden, 2005.

Staw, B. M., Sandelands, L. E. and J. E. Dutton. 'Threat Rigidity Effects in Organizational Behavior: A Multilevel Analysis', *in Administrative Science Quarterly*, 26 (4), pp. 501-524, 1981.

Steinberg, R. 'Economic Theories of Non-profit Organizations: An Evaluation', in Anheier H. K. and A. Ben-Ner (Eds) *The Study of the Non-profit Enterprise.* Kluwer Academic/Plenum, New York, 2003.

TNS Infratest '17 Jahre Deutscher Spendenmonitor. Fakten und Trends im Zeitverlauf'. December 2011. Available online via www.tnsinfra-test.com

Weick, K. E. *The Social Psychology of Organizing.* McGraw-Hill, New York, 1979.

Young, D. R. (Ed.). *Financing Non-profits: Putting Theory into Practice.* Altamira, Plymouth, 2007.

Helmut Anheier is Chair of Sociology at Heidelberg University, and Academic Director of the Centre for Social Investment. He is also Professor of Sociology at the Hertie School of Governance, Berlin. From 2001–09 he was professor at the School of Public Affairs and Director of the UCLA Center for Civil Society. From 1998–2002 he was the founding Director of the Centre for Civil Society at the London School of Economics (LSE), where he held the title of Centennial Professor from 2001–008. Prior to this he was a Senior Research Associate and Project Co-Director at the Johns Hopkins University Institute for Policy Studies, Associate Professor of Sociology at Rutgers University, and a Social Affairs Officer with the United Nations.

Annelie Beller, M.A. is a Research Associate at the Berlin Office of the Centre for Social Investment, Heidelberg University.

Norman Spengler, Dipl. Soz. was member of the Centre for Social Investment, Heidelberg University.

PART TWO

Directory

Albania

FOUNDATION CENTRE AND CO-ORDINATING BODY

Albanian Civil Society Foundation

Established in 1995 to support the development of civil society, through offering support to Albanian NGOs.

Activities: Provides grants, fellowships, information, assistance and training to NGOs and their staff. Maintains a database of NGOs in Albania, and Citizens' and Information centres.

Geographical Area of Activity: Albania.

Restrictions: No funding for individuals for social assistance or medical requirements, nor for political parties or foreign non-profit organizations operating in Albania.

Publications: Annual Report; directories of Albanian NGOs; newsletter (6 a year); study brochures on inter-ethnic understanding.

Trustees: Violanda Thedhori (Chair.).

Principal Staff: Exec. Dir Pandeli Theodhori.

Address: POB 1537, Tirana, Shqiperi.

Telephone: (4) 238056; **Fax:** (4) 238056; **Internet:** www.a-csf .org; **e-mail:** acsf@a-csf.org.

FOUNDATIONS, TRUSTS AND NON-PROFIT ORGANIZATIONS

Fondacioni Shqiptar per te Drejtat e Paaftesise (Albanian Disability Rights Foundation)

Initially established as an Oxfam (q.v.) disability programme in Albania in 1994, and subsequently established as an independent local NGO in 1996. Aims to empower disabled people by improving their capacities to support their integration into society.

Activities: The work of the Foundation benefits people with disabilities, their families, disability NGOs, and professionals who work directly with the disabled. The foundation works in the areas of information and documentation services; running a training and technical assistance centre; providing a counselling service; organizing lobbying initiatives; and awareness-raising.

Geographical Area of Activity: Albania.

Publications: Information brochures; monographs; *Challenge* magazine; Annual Report.

Finance: Annual revenue €417,495, expenditure €408,713 (2007).

Governing Body: Arjana Haxhiu (Pres.).

Principal Staff: Exec. Dir Blerta Çani.

Address: Rr. Mujo Ulqinaku, 26, Tirana.

Telephone: (4) 266892; **Fax:** (4) 266892; **Internet:** www.adrf .org.al; **e-mail:** adrf@albmail.com.

International Humanitarian Assistance—IHA

Established to provide humanitarian aid and assistance.

Activities: Operates in the fields of health, education and human rights. Health programmes include: basic preventative and curative services; maternal and child health care; training for midwives and traditional birth attendants; health education and training in the medical and managerial skills needed to serve local communities suffering from a breakdown in health services; information about HIV/AIDS, prevention of sexually transmitted diseases and opportunistic infections, as well as training for HIV/AIDS carers, distribution of appropriate informative materials, and public education; reproductive health care; nutrition services, including supplemental and therapeutic feeding programmes for populations affected by famine and shortages, particularly small children; microfinance community-based initiatives to help restore economic self-sufficiency and help finance local health programmes; and training courses for local health care workers and community organizations to increase awareness of gender-based violence and establish treatment protocols. Education programmes include: support for education systems through public awareness, legislative lobbying and training programmes, through the development of partnerships with universities, policy makers and organizations, which focus on helping students from developing countries to complete their public education; raising funds for humanitarian education programmes, increasing support for teacher quality programmes to recruit, train, and retain highly qualified educators in developing countries and areas in need; and encouraging parents' involvement in their children's education. Also aims to promote peace and understanding throughout the world, through designing and implementing new initiatives that focus on ethical dilemmas in the field of human rights.

Geographical Area of Activity: Albania and international.

Publications: *Teens Sexually Transmitted Diseases and HIV/ AIDS*; *Young Gay Men Talking*; *Euro-Atlantic Rift*; *Public Health Care Report for Albania 2002*; and other reports and publications.

Board: Alba Fishta (Chair.); Flora Bejko (Treas.).

Principal Staff: Law Programmes Dir Jorida Fishta.

Address: L.2 Rruga Shefqet Beja Nr. 823, Durres.

Telephone: (52) 25319; **Fax:** (52) 25319; **Internet:** www.iha -info.org; **e-mail:** mail@iha-info.org.

Open Society Foundation for Albania—OSFA (Fondacioni Shoqeria e Hapur per Shqiperine)

Established in January 1992 as an independent foundation, and part of the Soros foundations network, aiming to foster political and cultural pluralism, and to reform economic structures to encourage private enterprise and a market economy.

Activities: Operates mainly in the areas of economic reform, education (including a fellowship programme), information and youth, and strengthening public institutions, although grants are also made in the areas of the arts and culture, women's programmes, public health, ethnic minorities and civil society. Co-operates with other foundations in the Soros network on international programmes, and aims to assist with the integration of Albania into the European Union.

Geographical Area of Activity: Albania.

Finance: Total assets US $1,589,572 (2009); expenditure $1,627,023 (2010).

Principal Staff: Exec. Andi Dobrushi.

Address: Rruga Qemal Stafa, P.120/2, Tirana.

Telephone: (4) 234621; **Fax:** (4) 235855; **Internet:** www.soros .al; **e-mail:** info@osfa.soros.al.

Algeria

FOUNDATIONS, TRUSTS AND NON-PROFIT ORGANIZATIONS

Réseau Africain de la Jeunesse pour le Développement Durable (African Youth Network for Sustainable Development)

Established in 1997 to work towards sustainable development.

Activities: Operates in the field of the environment, particularly where it relates to children and young people, through networking and representation at international level at conferences and symposia. Also organizes media campaigns in Algeria and throughout Africa, volunteer programmes to support elderly people and environmental clean-up activities.

Geographical Area of Activity: Algeria and throughout Africa.

Publications: Electronic periodicals.

Address: 22 rue Dr Matiben, El-Mouradia, Algiers 16000.

Telephone: (61) 505-368; **Fax:** (21) 936-929; **e-mail:** aynsd@ hotmail.com.

Argentina

FOUNDATION CENTRES AND CO-ORDINATING BODIES

Fundación José María Aragón (José María Aragón Foundation)

Founded in 1962 by Ing. José María Aragón to promote university education and scientific and technological research, and to make available information on professional training opportunities throughout the world.

Activities: Provides information about Argentine foundations, postgraduate studies, international courses and scholarships (national and international), and Argentine social sciences publications.

Geographical Area of Activity: International.

Publications: Annual Report and financial statement; monthly reports on scholarships and international courses.

Finance: Annual grant disbursements approx. US $30,000,000.

Directors: Roberto Aguirre (Pres.).

Principal Staff: Exec. Dir Guillermo Battro; Admin. Officer F. Aragón.

Address: Casilla de Correo 2870, 1000 Buenos Aires.

Telephone: (11) 4331-6300; **Fax:** (11) 4331-6300; **Internet:** www.aragon.com.ar; **e-mail:** info@aragon.org.ar.

Grupo de Fundaciones y Empresas (Association of Foundations and Businesses)

Established in 1995 to promote the development of foundations in Argentina.

Activities: Promotes the development of philanthropy; offers information to foundations about philanthropy in Argentina, including news on foundations' activities. There were 29 member organizations in 2011. Also maintains online databases on foundations and projects operated by not-for-profit organizations.

Geographical Area of Activity: Argentina.

Publications: Newsletter (monthly); *Proyectos Aprobados* (quarterly publication on projects funded by foundations).

Board of Directors: Enrique Morad (Pres.); Matilde Grobocopatel (Vice-Pres.); Constanza Goleri (Treas.); Silvio Schlosser (Sec.).

Principal Staff: Exec. Dir Carolina Langan.

Address: Maipú 696, Piso 1'B', (C1006ACH) Buenos Aires.

Telephone: (11) 5272-0513; **Fax:** (11) 5272-0513; **Internet:** www.gdfe.org.ar; **e-mail:** gdfe@gdfe.org.ar.

FOUNDATIONS, TRUSTS AND NON-PROFIT ORGANIZATIONS

Federación Argentina de Apoyo Familiar—FAAF (International Confederation of Family Support)

Founded in 1986 by Dr Ana Mon to support families in need and to help children living on the streets.

Activities: Operates internationally in the field of social welfare. Supports children, women and families in need through a network of day-care centres. Children are given education and training, including craft workshops and micro-enterprise training, and women are offered programmes in literacy, self-esteem and skills training, as well as support for drug and alcohol problems. Support is also offered to older members of the family. Currently operates 167 support centres in Argentina, and a further eight in Haiti, India, Mexico, Peru, South Africa, Uruguay and Venezuela.

Geographical Area of Activity: Mainly Argentina, but also Haiti, India, Mexico, Peru, South Africa, Uruguay and Venezuela.

Restrictions: No grants for individuals and only to organizations working in the area of social promotion among children and young people, women and families in need.

Publications: Various reports and publications.

Finance: Each National Federation has its own budget.

Board of Trustees: Dr Ana Mon (Pres.); Sabina Carranza (Sec.); Ma. del Carmen Gibert (Treas.).

Address: Calle 33, No. 1118, 1900 La Plata.

Telephone: (221) 422-3734; **Fax:** (221) 422-3734; **Internet:** www.apoyofamiliar.org.ar; **e-mail:** apoyofamiliar@ciudad.com.ar.

Fundación Acíndar (Acíndar Foundation)

Founded in 1962 by Arturo Acevedo, J. M. Aragón, J. E. Acevedo, A. F. A. Acevedo, M. Ezcurra, Rogelio A. Galarce, R. S. Pujals, J. José Ré, Thomas Jefferson Williams and C. A. Acevedo to provide social, cultural, educational and philanthropic assistance, and to promote scientific investigation and professional and technical training in Central and South America and the Caribbean.

Activities: Operates mainly in the areas of education, health, social welfare and the environment, including grants to hospitals, multimedia education projects and training schemes.

Geographical Area of Activity: Central and South America and the Caribbean.

Publications: Annual Report.

Administrative Council: Arturo T. Acevedo (Pres.).

Principal Staff: Exec. Dir Cecilia Barbón.

Address: Estanislas Zeballos 2739, 1643 Beccar, Buenos Aires.

Telephone: (11) 4719-8311; **Fax:** (11) 4719-8501; **Internet:** www.fundacionacindar.org.ar; **e-mail:** fundacion@acindar.com.ar.

Fundación Ambiente y Recursos Naturales—FARN (Environment and Natural Resources Foundation)

Founded in 1985 by Guillermo J. Cano to promote the conservation of natural resources and the environment, and sustainable development in South America.

Activities: Operates in the fields of agriculture, energy, conservation and forestry, through campaigning on environmental policy and law, public participation and the promotion of public debate. Maintains a library and database. Awards the annual Adriana Schiffrin Essay Prize on sustainable development.

Geographical Area of Activity: South America (mainly Argentina).

Publications: Annual Report; *Suplemento de Derecho Ambiental* (quarterly, in Spanish); articles, reports, papers and other publications.

Finance: Financed through public donations. Annual income 659,342 pesos (2008–09).

Administrative Council: Daniel Sabsay (Pres.); Aída Kemelmajer de Carlucci (Vice-Pres.); Pedro Tarak (Sec.); Juan Manuel Velasco (Treas.).

Principal Staff: Exec. Dir María Eugenia di Paola.

Address: Tucumán 255, 6° A, 1049 Buenos Aires.

Telephone: (11) 4312-0788; **Fax:** (11) 4893-0718; **Internet:** www.farn.org.ar; **e-mail:** info@farn.org.ar.

Fundación Bariloche (Bariloche Foundation)

Founded in March 1963 to improve the quality of life in Central and South America; to stimulate creative thinking in these areas; to conduct research and teaching programmes; and to offer activities of a similar type to leaders of social groups and to promote the exchange of ideas and information among them, as well as among scientists and intellectuals.

Activities: In 1978, as a result of changed socio-political conditions in Argentina, the Foundation changed its style of operation to become primarily a promotional rather than an executive institution for teaching and research. Since then, it has concentrated on four main fields of interest: energy economics and planning, with an emphasis on developing countries; environmental policy and sustainable development; quality of life; and philosophy. Assists with the planning of government programmes relating to these areas. The Foundation promotes scientific meetings and the publication of a series of books in various languages to give world-wide diffusion to Central and South American intellectual activity; and maintains a library.

Geographical Area of Activity: Argentina.

Publications: *Boletín Bibliográfico* (2 a year); *Revista Desarrollo y Energía* (2 a year); *Revista Patagónica de Filosofía* (journal); *AEDH—Aspectos Económicos del Desarrollo Humano/Economic Aspects of Human Development; LAWM—Modelo Mundial Latinoamericano/The Latin American World Model;* publications relating to foundation programmes.

Finance: Budget of Fundación Bariloche and its associated groups approx. US $1,100,000.

Board of Directors: Héctor Pistonesi (Pres.); Daniel Bouille (Vice-Pres.).

Principal Staff: Exec. Pres. Héctor Pistonesi.

Address: Avda Bustillo 9500, R8402AGP, San Carlos de Bariloche, Prov. de Río Negro.

Telephone: (29) 4446-2500; **Fax:** (29) 4446-1186; **Internet:** www.fundacionbariloche.org.ar; **e-mail:** fb@fundacionbariloche.org.ar.

Fundación Bunge y Born (Bunge y Born Foundation)

Founded in 1963 by the Bunge group of companies to promote and facilitate studies and investigations that will be of benefit to the community as a whole, through financial aid in the broad fields of social welfare, culture and science; and to award prizes to those who have best distinguished themselves in the field of scientific investigation.

Activities: Operates nationally in the fields of education, research, health and culture, chiefly through grants to institutions and the allocation of prizes and scholarships for research, or to attend conferences. Also provides emergency disaster aid and provides medical equipment.

Geographical Area of Activity: Argentina.

Publications: *Memoria* (Annual Report and financial statement); *Humor in Rural Argentine Schools; 25 Years with Rural Argentine Schools; The Art of Juan Manuel Blanes.*

Finance: Receives contributions from the Bunge Group, private donations and bequests. Annual budget 10,132,366 pesos (2010).

Governing Board: Jorge Born (Pres.); Alejandro de La Tour d'Auvergne (Vice-Pres.); Jenefer Féraud (Second Vice-Pres.); Alix Born (Third Vice-Pres.).

Principal Staff: Exec. Dir Ludovico Videla; Project Dir Asunción Zumárraga.

Address: 25 de Mayo 501, 6°, C1002ABK, 1002 Buenos Aires.

Telephone: (11) 4318-6600; **Fax:** (11) 4318-6610; **Internet:** www.fundacionbyb.org; **e-mail:** info@fundacionbyb.org.

Fundación Ecológica Universal—FEU (Universal Ecological Foundation)

Founded in Buenos Aires in 1990 to disseminate information and link fields of ecological information, and to promote sustainable development.

Activities: Operates in the field of conservation and the environment in Bolivia, Brazil, Chile, Mexico, Paraguay and Uruguay. Organizes environmental education projects in conjunction with schools, training workshops and conferences, and conducts research. Works in partnership with international organizations, and co-operates at government level for the dissemination of environmental policy information.

Geographical Area of Activity: Central and South America.

Publications: Reports and bulletins.

Board: Dr Gabriel Juricich (Founder-Pres.); Emilio Hisas (Treas.).

Principal Staff: Exec. Dir Rodolfo Cisterna.

Address: Avda Corrientes 1584, 4°, Buenos Aires (C1043ABA).

Telephone: (11) 4373-1243; **Fax:** (11) 4373-0552; **Internet:** www.feu999.org; **e-mail:** info@feu999.org.

Fundación para Estudio e Investigación de la Mujer—FEIM (Foundation for Women's Research and Studies)

Established in 1989 to promote the rights of women and the enhancement of their social and economic position in society.

Activities: Operates in Argentina in the area of women's rights, through providing services such as health care and health education (especially AIDS and reproductive health); promotes the development of small enterprises; conducts research; maintains a library. Also operates in the area of the environment, promoting recycling, solar energy and the development of environmental organizations in Argentina.

Geographical Area of Activity: Argentina.

Publications: *DeSidamos* (quarterly, in Spanish); *Safe Motherhood* (in Spanish); books and information on various health issues.

Finance: Annual budget approx. US $120,000.

Advisory Committee: Carmen Barroso; Julia Constenla; Esther Corona; Guillermo Jaim Echeverri; Eva Giberti; Telma Luzzani; Federico Polack; Graciela Rommers; Eugenia Trumper; Catalina Wainerman.

Principal Staff: Pres. Dr Mabel Bianco; Sec. Cecilia Correa; Treas. Catalina Abifadel.

Address: Paraná 135, 3°, Of. 13, 1017 Buenos Aires.

Telephone: (11) 4372-2763; **Internet:** www.feim.org.ar; **e-mail:** feim@feim.org.ar.

Fundación de Investigaciones Económicas Latinoamericanas—FIEL (Foundation for Latin American Economic Research)

Founded in 1964 by the Chamber of Commerce of Argentina, the Stock Exchange of Buenos Aires, the Argentine Industrial Union and the Cattle Breeders' Association to analyse economic problems.

Activities: Operates in the field of economic affairs, by conducting research on business trends and structural problems of the Argentine and Central and South American economies. Co-operates with similar Central and South American organizations; runs a computerized data bank and maintains a library.

Geographical Area of Activity: Central and South America (mainly Argentina).

Publications: *Indicadores de Coyuntura* (monthly); *Documentos de Trabajo* (quarterly); *Indicadores de Actividad y Precios* (monthly); surveys and studies.

Finance: Receives regular donations from its associated companies, and revenue from sales of publications and services.

Board of Directors: Dr Juan P. Munro (Pres.); Juan C. Masjoan (Vice-Pres.); Manuel Sacerdote (Vice-Pres.); Vicor L.

Savanti (Vice-Pres.); Franco Livini (Sec.); Dr Mario E. Vázquez (Treas.).

Principal Staff: Chief Economists Daniel Artana, Juan Luis Bour, Fernando Navajes, Santiago Urbiztondo.

Address: Córdoba 637, 4°, C1054AAF Buenos Aires.

Telephone: (11) 4314-1990; **Fax:** (11) 4314-8648; **Internet:** www.fiel.org; **e-mail:** postmaster@fiel.org.ar.

Fundación Mediterránea—IERAL (Mediterranean Foundation)

Founded in 1977 by a number of industrial concerns to promote national economic research and to contribute to a better understanding of and solution to Central and South American economic problems.

Activities: Sponsors a regional economic research institute, the Instituto de Estudios Económicos sobre la Realidad Argentina y Latinoamericana (IEERAL); organizes conferences and publishes the results of investigations.

Geographical Area of Activity: Central and South America.

Publications: *Estudios* (quarterly); *Novedades Económicas* (monthly); newsletter (quarterly).

Board: Martín Amengual (Pres.); Maria Pia Astori (First Vice-Pres.); Dr Fulvio Rafael Pagani (Second Vice-Pres.); Sergio Oscar Roggio (Treas.).

Principal Staff: Gen. Man. José A. Santanoceto; Exec. Dir Myrian R. Martínez.

Address: Viamonte 610, 2°, C1053ABN Buenos Aires.

Telephone: (11) 4393-0375; **Internet:** www.fundmediterranea.org.ar; **e-mail:** joses@fundmediterranea.org.ar.

Fundación Mujeres en Igualdad (Women in Equality Foundation)

Established in March 1990 to fight gender violence and discrimination, and for the promotion of the social, economic, cultural and political development of women.

Activities: Aims to support women's empowerment, mainly in Argentina, with a focus on human rights, political and civil rights. Raises awareness about gender issues, such as human-trafficking prevention, through advocacy campaigns, networking, coalition building and training; organizes international women's forums against corruption. Its project 'Organizing women against corruption' has been funded by UNIFEM/UNDEF.

Geographical Area of Activity: Mainly Argentina.

Publications: *Gender and Corruption* (2010); *Mujeres en Política* (magazine); handbooks, bulletins, brochures.

Finance: Multi-stakeholders.

Board of Trustees: Zita C. Montes de Oca (Founder); Hebe Molinuevo (Pres.); Elisabeth Rapela (Vice-Pres.); Silvia Ferraro (Sec.); María Inés Rodríguez (Treas.).

Principal Staff: Exec. Dir Monique Thiteux-Altschul; Admin. Asst Maiten Strazzaboschi.

Address: Urquiza 1835, 1602 Florida, Buenos Aires.

Telephone: (11) 4791-0821; **Fax:** (11) 4791-0821; **Internet:** www.mujeresenigualdad.org.ar; **e-mail:** mujeresenigualdad@infovia.com.ar.

Fundación Paz, Ecología y Arte—Fundación PEA (Foundation for Peace, Ecology and the Arts)

Established in 1997 for the promotion of peace throughout the world.

Activities: Promotes the peaceful resolution of war, and works towards world peace and a culture of peace through supporting ecology and the arts, and peace education.

Geographical Area of Activity: International.

Administrative Council: Nancy B. Ducuing de Martorelli (Pres.); Prof. Elsa Peña (Sec.); Prof. Isabel Susana Guzzo (Treas.).

Principal Staff: Dir-Gen. Prof. Marcelo G. Martorelli.

Address: Córdoba 2069, 13°, Dpto A, 1120 Buenos Aires.

Telephone: (11) 4961-7941; **Fax:** (11) 4961-7941; **Internet:** www.fundacionpea.org; **e-mail:** contacto@fundacionpea.org.

Fundación Schcolnik (Schcolnik Foundation)

Founded in 1964 by Dr Enrique Schcolnik, Dr Manuel Schcolnik, José Schcolnik and Juan Schcolnik.

Activities: Operates nationally in the fields of education and social welfare, through self-conducted programmes, grants to individuals and institutions, scholarships, publications and lectures.

Geographical Area of Activity: Argentina.

Publications: List of schools and libraries assisted by the Schcolnik Foundation.

Board: Dr Enrique Schcolnik (Pres.); Dr Alejandro Carlos Piazza (Vice-Pres.); Dr Horacio della Rocca (Sec.); Jorge Acevedo (Treas.).

Address: Avda Jujuy 425, C1083AAE Buenos Aires.

Telephone: (11) 4931-0188; **Fax:** (11) 4956-1368; **Internet:** www.fundacionschcolnik.org.ar; **e-mail:** secretaria@fundacionschcolnik.org.ar.

Fundación SES—Sustentabilidad, Educación, Solidaridad (SES Foundation—Sustainability, Education, Solidarity)

Established in 1999 to support disadvantaged youth in Argentina, promote enhancement of the education system, and extend support to other NGOs undertaking similar activities.

Activities: Aims to promote educative strategies towards the social inclusion of disadvantaged adolescents; funds projects in schools and higher education establishments; extends technological and financial assistance to other community organizations and NGOs operating in similar fields.

Geographical Area of Activity: Argentina.

Restrictions: No grants to individuals; grants only to partner organizations.

Publications: Report of innovative educational experiences; *Boletín* (electronic newsletter); *Construyendo con los Jóvenes Desde Organizaciones Comunitarias*; *Estrategias Educativas de Trabajo con Adolescentes y Jóvenes con Menos Oportunidades*; *Experiencias de Construyendo Vinculos*; *Herramientas para el trabajo con jóvenes*; *Prevención del fracaso escolar en el MERCOSUR—Las experiencias de las organizaciones de la sociedad civil*.

Administrative Council: Alberto César Croce (Pres.); Alejandra Esther Solla (Treas.); Luisa Cerar (Sec.).

Principal Staff: Exec. Dir Alberto Croce.

Address: Avda de Mayo 1156, 2°, 1085 Buenos Aires.

Telephone: (11) 4381-4225; **Fax:** (11) 4381-3842; **Internet:** www.fundses.org.ar; **e-mail:** info@fundses.org.ar.

Fundación Dr J. Roberto Villavicencio (Dr J. R. Villavicencio Foundation)

Established in 1982 by Dr Roberto L. Villavicencio and his family to promote teaching and research on medical sciences, and medical assistance to deprived people.

Activities: Operates in Rosario and its surrounding area in the fields of education, medicine and health, and science and technology, through self-conducted programmes, research, grants to institutions and individuals, scholarships and fellowships, prizes, conferences, training courses and publications.

Geographical Area of Activity: Argentina (Rosario).

Publications: Annual Report; *Artículos de información médica*; *Trabajos de actualización médica*; *Trabajos científicos*; *Presentación de casos*.

Trustees: Susana Toncich (Pres.); Lisandro José Villavicencio (Vice-Pres.); Ivonne Villavicencio (Sec.); Roberto Villavicencio (Treas.).

Principal Staff: Dir Fernando Amelong; Exec. Sec. Claudia Miranda.

Address: Alvear 854, S2000QGB Rosario, Santa Fe.

Telephone: (341) 449-0152; **Fax:** (341) 449-0152; **Internet:** www.villavicencio.org.ar; **e-mail:** info@villavicencio.org.ar.

Instituto para la Integración de América Latina y el Caribe—BID-INTAL (Institute for Latin American and Caribbean Integration)

Founded in 1965 as a result of an agreement between the Inter-American Development Bank and the Government of Argentina to promote regional integration.

Activities: A unit of the Inter-American Development Bank. Its activities are mainly focused on trade issues; regional integration and co-operation; technical assistance, especially institutional strengthening and dialogue with civil society, including the private sector. Also contributes to the exchange of background knowledge in the areas of regional integration and physical infrastructure, and provides capacity building tools to governments of Latin America. Active in four principal areas: regional and national technical co-operation projects on integration; policy forums; integration forums; and the REDINT Integration Research Centres Network. The INTAL Documentation Center (CDI) identifies, compiles, organizes and disseminates information on integration, trade, infrastructure, development and related topics. It holds 40,000 documents, 11,500 books and 600 periodicals. A digitization process has begun for those publications made only on paper in the 1965–95 period to make their contents accessible online, in a full-text and open-access format, in a digital library model.

Geographical Area of Activity: North, Central and South America, Europe and the Asia-Pacific region.

Publications: *Integration and Trade* (2 a year, in English and Spanish); *INTAL Monthly Newsletter* (monthly, in English and Spanish); and *Sub-regional Integration Reports Series*.

Principal Staff: Dir Ricardo Carciofi.

Address: Esmeralda 130, 16°, 1035 Buenos Aires.

Telephone: (11) 4323-2350; **Fax:** (11) 4323-2365; **Internet:** www.iadb.org/intal; **e-mail:** intal@iadb.org.

Instituto Torcuato di Tella (Torcuato di Tella Institute)

Founded in 1958 by the Fundación Torcuato di Tella, Siam di Tella Ltda, María Robiola di Tella, Torcuato di Tella, Guido di Tella, Guido Clutterbuck, Antonio Sudiero, Torcuato Sozio, Mario Robiola and Arturo Uriarte, as an entity of public benefit with the purpose of serving the community, promoting educational and intellectual activities in general, and scientific research in particular.

Activities: Operates nationally and internationally in the fields of economics, sociology, epistemology and methodology of the social sciences, political science, history and educational science, through self-conducted research, fellowships, scholarships, conferences, courses, seminars, publications and lectures. The Institute creates, directs and administers centres of investigation such as the Centro de Investigaciones Económicas and the Centro de Investigaciones Sociales. It also supports an associated centre: the Centro de Investigaciones en Ciencias de la Educación. Training courses are held for graduate students, in economics, public policy and history. Maintains a library.

Geographical Area of Activity: International.

Publications: Annual Report and Financial Statement; each Centre publishes the results of its research work in the form of books, papers and articles in specialized journals. The Institute Press publishes books and working-papers.

Principal Staff: Pres Torcuato di Tella; Andres Lautaro di Tella.

Address: Miñones 2159/77, 1 Piso, 1428 Buenos Aires.

Telephone: (11) 4783-8680; **Fax:** (11) 4783-3061; **Internet:** www.itdt.edu.

Red de Acción en Plaguicidas y sus Alternativas de América Latina—RAP-AL

Part of the Pesticide Action Network (PAN) group of organizations (qq.v.) working towards reducing levels of pesticides. RAP-AL is the Regional Center for Latin America for PAN, and is co-ordinated by Centro de Estudios sobre Tecnologías Apropiadas de la Argentina (CETAAR)/Pesticide Action Network.

Geographical Area of Activity: Central and South America.

Principal Staff: Co-ordinator Southern Cone Region Javier Souza.

Address: Centro de Estudios sobre Tecnologías Apropiadas de la Argentina, Rivadavia 4097, POB 89 (1727), Marcos Paz, Buenos Aires.

Internet: www.rap-al.org; **e-mail:** javierrapal@yahoo.com .ar.

Armenia

FOUNDATION CENTRES AND CO-ORDINATING BODIES

Centre for the Development of Civil Society—CDCS

The Centre, formerly the Ghevond Alishan Cultural-Educational Association, was established during Perestroika in 1988 by a group of well-known scholars from Yerevan State University and the Institute of Linguistics of the National Academy of Sciences of the Republic of Armenia. It was registered as an NGO when Armenia became independent of the USSR in 1991.

Activities: Works to promote peace and human rights and the development of civil society in Armenia, through its own projects and as a partner with other international networking organizations. Activities include project implementation, networking, training, information dissemination, advocacy, education, research, and publishing. Operates programmes for refugees and educational programmes; organizes conferences; funds support centres; and provides leadership training. Includes the following sub-divisions: the Women Scholars Council, the Refugee Women's Council, the Youth Council, and the Elderly Women's League.

Geographical Area of Activity: Armenia.

Publications: *Multilingual Illustrated Dictionary* (1995); *Encouraging Women's Political Participation in National Elections* (1996); *Warning to Women: Did someone promise you a better life by going to Europe?* (1997); *Russian-Armenian Tutorial Word-Forming Dictionary* (1999); *Introduction to Gender: History, Culture and Society* (2000); *Women, Culture and Society* (2002); *Healthy Lifestyle* (2004); *Personal Leadership* (2004); *English Language tutorial materials* (2004); *Civic Education* (2005); *Computer Skills* (2005); *Human Rights* (2005); *Interactive Teaching Methods* (2005); *NGO Management* (2005); *Local Action, Global Change: Learning About the Human Rights of Women and Girls* (2006); *Go to Vote* (2007); *Know Your Rights* (2007); *Civil Society in Armenia: from a theoretical framework to reality* (2007); *Gender Analysis of the European Union: Developmental Aid for Armenia* (2008); and others.

Finance: Raises funds from grant-making international development agencies and other donors. Activities are supported by individual or business donations.

Trustees: Svetlana Aslanyan (Pres.).

Principal Staff: Exec. Dir Anahit Abrahamyan.

Address: 0025 Yerevan, 49 Nalbandian St, No. 7.

Telephone: (10) 56-05-44; **Fax:** (10) 58-56-77; **Internet:** www.cdcs.am; **e-mail:** info@cdcs.am, s.aslanyan@cdcs.am.

NGO Centre—NGOC

Founded in 1997 to provide training and technical assistance on advocacy and public policy advocacy.

Activities: Supports NGOs aiming to influence decision-making bodies. Since 2001 the NGOC has promoted social partnership, offering training and technical assistance to NGOs, representatives of national and local government, and establishing two social partnership mechanisms.

Geographical Area of Activity: Armenia.

Publications: *Armenian NGO News in Brief* (annual); *NGOC Gazette* (annual).

Board Members: Margarit Piliposyan (Pres.).

Principal Staff: Co-ordinator Arpine Hakobyan.

Address: c/o Gayane Martirosyan, NGO Centre Northern Branch, Garegin Njdeh 14, Vanadzor.

Telephone: (322) 43315; **Internet:** www.ngoc.am; **e-mail:** ngoc@ngoc.am.

FOUNDATIONS, TRUSTS AND NON-PROFIT ORGANIZATIONS

AREGAK—Sun/Soleil

Established in 1996 (officially registered in 1998) to assist in the social development of orphaned Armenian children.

Activities: Operates in the fields of social welfare, education and health, offering assistance to needy orphan children and to the elderly, refugees and those living in poverty. Also offers training.

Geographical Area of Activity: Armenia.

Principal Staff: Pres. Varduhi Khatchikyan; Accountant Armine Stepanyan.

Address: 0008 Yerevan, 15 Suvorov.

Telephone: (10) 52-15-64; **Internet:** www.childrensun.narod.ru; **e-mail:** vkhatchikyan@yahoo.com.

Open Society Institute Assistance Foundation, Armenia—OSIAFA

Established in 1996; an independent foundation, part of the Soros foundations network.

Activities: Promotes reform in the fields of education, information and the media, social welfare, public health, law and human rights, ethnic minorities and the arts and culture. Collaborates with other Armenian NGOs. Also operates on a regional level through the East-East programme.

Geographical Area of Activity: Armenia.

Finance: Annual expenditure US $1,477,637 (2008).

Board: Hrayr Ghukasyan (Chair.).

Principal Staff: Exec. Dir Larisa Minasyan; Deputy Dir, Programmes David Amiryan; Dir of Finance Kristina Danielyan.

Address: 375002 Yerevan, 7/1 Tumanyan St, 2nd cul-de-sac.

Telephone: (10) 53-38-62; **Fax:** (10) 53-67-58; **Internet:** www.osi.am; **e-mail:** info@osi.am.

Australia

FOUNDATION CENTRES AND CO-ORDINATING BODIES

AMP Foundation

Established in 1992 by the AMP Group, a financial services company, for general charitable purposes in the areas of capacity building and community involvement.

Activities: Invests in two key areas: Capacity Building and Community Involvement. The Capacity Building programmes focus on the education and employment of young people and the sustainability of the non-profit sector; the Community Involvement programmes focus on supporting the work of AMP employees and financial planners in the community, including an employee volunteering programme. Operates in long-term partnerships, not on a grant-giving basis.

Geographical Area of Activity: Australia, New Zealand.

Restrictions: No unsolicited applications for funding are accepted.

Publications: Annual Report.

Finance: Total assets $A91,750,264 (Dec. 2010).

Board of Directors: Peter Hunt (Chair.).

Principal Staff: Man. Helen Liondos.

Address: 33 Alfred St, Sydney, NSW 2000.

Telephone: (2) 9257 5334; **Fax:** (2) 9257 2864; **Internet:** www.amp.com.au; **e-mail:** amp_foundation@amp.com.au.

Philanthropy Australia

Established in 1975, and formerly known as the Australian Association of Philanthropy. National peak body for philanthropy and is a non-profit membership organization. Its members are trusts, foundations, families and individuals who want to make a difference through their own philanthropy and to encourage others to become philanthropists.

Activities: Represents the philanthropic sector; promotes philanthropy by the community, business and government sectors; inspires and supports new philanthropists; increases the effectiveness of philanthropy through the provision of information, resources and networking opportunities; promotes strong and transparent governance standards in the philanthropic sector.

Geographical Area of Activity: Australia.

Restrictions: A grant-maker support organization only; does not make grants itself.

Publications: *Australian Philanthropy* journal (3 a year); *The Australian Directory of Philanthropy* (online and print version); *A Guide to Giving for Australians*; *The Community Foundation Kit*; *Trustee Handbook*; *Private Ancillary Funds (PAF) Trustee Handbook*; *A Grantseeker's Guide to Trusts and Foundations*.

Finance: Total assets $A542,464 (Dec. 2010).

Council: Bruce Bonyhady (Pres.); Dur-e Dara (Vice-Pres.); Sam Meers (Vice-Pres.); David Ward (Treas.).

Principal Staff: Chief Exec. Dr Deborah Seifert.

Address: Level 2, 55 Collins St, Melbourne, Vic 3000.

Telephone: (3) 9662 9299; **Fax:** (3) 9662 2655; **Internet:** www.philanthropy.org.au; **e-mail:** info@philanthropy.org.au.

FOUNDATIONS, TRUSTS AND NON-PROFIT ORGANIZATIONS

Activ Foundation

Established in 1951 by a group of parents to provide support services for people with intellectual disability and their families.

Activities: Provides accommodation, recreation, respite, employment, training and skills-development to 2,300 people with a disability, and to their families. Employs some 1,070 people with a disability.

Geographical Area of Activity: Western Australia.

Publications: *Activ News* (quarterly newsletter); Annual Report.

Board of Directors: Andrew Edwards (Pres.); Tina Thomas (Deputy Pres.).

Principal Staff: CEO Tony Vis.

Address: POB 446, Wembley, WA 6913.

Telephone: (8) 9387 0555; **Fax:** (8) 9387 0599; **Internet:** www.activ.asn.au; **e-mail:** records@activ.asn.au.

APACE Village First Electrification Group—APACE VFEG

Established in 1976 by Dr Robert Waddell and other senior academics from Sydney-based universities to promote renewable energy in rural communities in less-developed countries.

Activities: Operated in more than 150 rural communities in South and South-East Asia and the island states of the Pacific region, in the fields of aid to less-developed countries, and conservation of the environment, providing technical assistance, research facilities, project design, and management and evaluation services in the areas of appropriate technology, micro-hydro-electricity and sustainable agriculture. Now only involved in support of existing hydro installations in the Pacific and the dissemination of information.

Geographical Area of Activity: Pacific and South-East Asia.

Publications: Annual Report; *APACE Newsletter* (quarterly to 2001); *Replanting the Banana Tree: a study in ecologically sustainable development*; *SAPA: the natural way of growing food*; *Rural Electrification: assessing the impacts*; *Micro-hydro Systems for Small Communities*; *Community-based Electrification Models*; and others.

Trustees: Prof. Paul Bryce (Pres.).

Principal Staff: Admin. Officer Peter Vail.

Address: c/o UTS, POB 123, Broadway, NSW 2007.

Telephone: (2) 9514 2547; **Internet:** www.apace.uts.edu.au; **e-mail:** apacevfeg@gmail.com.

Apex Foundation

Founded by the Association of Apex Clubs to improve the quality of life for young Australians with special needs.

Activities: Manages a number of trusts, including the Cranio Facial Surgery Trust, Autism Trust, Children's Cancer and Leukaemia Trust, Diabetes Trust, Melanoma Trust, Underprivileged Children's Trust, Destiny Youth Trust, Fine Arts Trust.

Geographical Area of Activity: Australia.

Restrictions: Researchers may be of any nationality but research must be undertaken in Australia.

Publications: Annual Report; *Apex in Action*.

Trustees: Jim Hughes (Chair.); Graham Henry (Deputy Chair.); Mike Fitze (Sec.).

Principal Staff: Admin. Man. Braddley Hayes; Nat. Man. Noel Hadjimichael.

Address: Level 5 AON Tower, 201 Kent St, Sydney, NSW 2000.

Telephone: (2) 9253 7775; **Fax:** (2) 9253 7117; **Internet:** www .apexfoundation.org.au; **e-mail:** info@apexfoundation.org .au.

Arthritis Australia

Established to provide information and support to people with arthritis and related conditions, and promote medical and scientific research in the field. Acts as the national secretariat for affiliated foundations throughout Australia.

Activities: Operates in Australia, the United Kingdom and the USA in the field of medicine and health, in particular arthritis research and education; provides assistance to the medical, scientific and allied health professions in the form of research grants, fellowships and scholarships.

Geographical Area of Activity: Australia, United Kingdom and USA.

Publications: Annual Report; books.

Finance: Total assets $A6,536,725; annual income $A2,277,114 expenditure $A2,259,541 (2010/11).

Trustees: Prof. Patrick McNeil (Pres.); David Motteram (Vice-Pres.); Wayne Jarman (Treas.); Kristine Riethmiller (Sec.).

Principal Staff: Chief Exec. Ainslie Cahill.

Address: POB 550, Broadway NSW 2007.

Telephone: (2) 9518 4441; **Fax:** (2) 9518 4011; **Internet:** www .arthritisaustralia.com.au; **e-mail:** info@arthritisaustralia .com.au.

ATSE Clunies Ross Foundation

Founded in 1959 in memory of Sir Clunies Ross to promote the development of science and technology to the benefit of Australia.

Activities: Runs *ATSE Clunies Ross Award* for the application of science and technology to benefit Australia economically, socially or environmentally.

Governors: Bruce Kean (Chair.).

Address: POB 4055, Melbourne, VIC 3001.

Telephone: (3) 9864 0900; **Fax:** (3) 9864 0930; **Internet:** www .cluniesross.org.au; **e-mail:** cluniesross@atse.org.au.

Australia Business Arts Foundation—AbaF

Established in 2000 by the Department of Communication, Information Technology and the Arts, which aims to increase the level of private-sector resources available to the arts, culture and humanities, and encourage reflection on what it is to be Australian. The Foundation is an Australian Government company directed by an independent board.

Activities: Encourages and promotes private-sector support for the arts and humanities in Australia and develops partnerships between the arts and business. Initiatives include Art-support Australia, which assists the cultural sector, particularly small and medium-sized arts organizations and individual artists, to build capacity to better secure and manage philanthropic funding and encourages and helps donors to find and connect with arts organizations and practitioners, and the Australia Cultural Fund, which channels corporate donations to arts practitioners and organizations.

Geographical Area of Activity: Australia.

Publications: *Partnerships News* (quarterly newsletter); *AbaF E-News* (online newsletter); *The Gold Book of Business Arts Partnerships*; *Business Arts Partnerships—a Guide to the Business Case Approach for the Cultural Sector*; *Connect* (magazine).

Board of Directors: Terry Campbell (Chair.).

Principal Staff: CEO Jane Haley; Chief Fin. Officer Joanne Simon; Gen. Man. Damien Hodgkinson.

Address: Level 2, 405 Collins St, Melbourne, VIC 3000.

Telephone: (3) 9616 0300; **Fax:** (3) 9614 2550; **Internet:** www .abaf.org.au; **e-mail:** info@abaf.org.au.

Australia-Japan Foundation

Founded in 1976 by the Australian Government as an independent statutory body to strengthen relations between Australia and Japan.

Activities: Operates in Australia and Japan in the fields of education, science and the arts, by developing projects that enhance understanding. Projects include a Japanese-language website and a public access Australian Resource Centre, as well as support for Australian community groups to gain access to a Japanese audience. The Sir Neil Currie Memorial Australian Studies Awards offer funding to Japanese post-graduate scholars and academics.

Geographical Area of Activity: Australia and Japan.

Publications: Annual Report; occasional papers; *Science Communication in Theory and Practice; Nourishing Terrains: Australian Aboriginal Views of Landscape and Wilderness.*

Advisory Board: Peter Corish (Chair.).

Principal Staff: Chief Exec. Catherine Harris; Dir, Canberra Office Don Smith; Dir, Tokyo Office Leonie Boxtel.

Address: RG Casey Bldg, John McEwen Crescent, Barton, ACT 0221; Australian Embassy, 2-1-14 Mita, Minato-Ku, Tokyo 108-8361, Japan.

Telephone: (2) 6261 3898 (Australia); (3) 5232-4063 (Japan); **Fax:** (2) 6261 2143 (Australia); (3) 5232-4064 (Japan); **Internet:** http://ajf.australia.or.jp; **e-mail:** ajf.australia@ dfat.gov.au.

Australian Academy of the Humanities

Established in 1969 by the Australian Humanities Research Council to grant scholarships and further research in the field of humanities.

Activities: Aims to advance knowledge in the field of humanities, in particular archeology; European languages and cultures; classical studies; history; the arts; Asian studies; English; linguistics; philosophy, religion and the history of ideas; cultural and communication studies.

Geographical Area of Activity: Australia.

Publications: *Proceedings* (Annual Report); symposium papers; monographs; occasional papers; edited collections.

Finance: Maximum grant disbursed $A4,000.

Council Members: Prof. Lesley Johnson (Pres.); Prof. Anna Haebich (Vice-Pres.); Prof. Pam Sharpe (Treas.).

Principal Staff: Exec. Dir Dr Christina Parolin.

Address: GPO Box 93, Canberra, ACT 2601.

Telephone: (2) 6125 9860; **Fax:** (2) 6248 6287; **Internet:** www .humanities.org.au; **e-mail:** enquiries@humanities.org.au.

Australian Academy of Science

Geographical Area of Activity: Mainly Australia.

Principal Staff: Chief Exec. Dr Sue Meek.

Address: POB 783, Canberra, ACT 2601.

Telephone: (2) 6201 9400; **Fax:** (2) 6201 9494; **Internet:** www .science.org.au; **e-mail:** aas@science.org.au.

Australian-American Fulbright Commission

Founded in 1949 by the governments of Australia and of the USA to further mutual understanding between the people of the two nations through educational and cultural exchanges.

Activities: Operates in the field of education by operating the Fulbright Scholarship programme for Americans and Australians to undertake research, study or lecturing assignments in Australia or the USA respectively. Awards cover all academic disciplines and professions.

Geographical Area of Activity: USA and Australia.

Restrictions: Scholarships are open to Australian and US citizens only.

Publications: Annual Report; *The Fulbrighter* (newsletter).

Board of Directors: Julia Gillard (Hon. Co-Chair.); Jeffrey Bleich (Hon. Co-Chair.).

Principal Staff: Exec. Dir Dr Tangerine Holt.

Address: POB 9541, Deakin, ACT 2600.

Telephone: (2) 6260 4460; **Fax:** (2) 6260 4461; **Internet:** www.fulbright.com.au; **e-mail:** fulbright@fulbright.com.au.

Australian Cancer Research Foundation

Established in 1984 by Sir Peter Abeles and Lady Sonia McMahon, the Foundation is committed to national excellence in cancer research.

Activities: Operates nationally in the field of cancer research. Provides funding for capital projects and equipment, research and seed grants. Raises funds through corporate sponsorship, donations, bequests and committee fundraising activities.

Geographical Area of Activity: Australia.

Publications: Newsletter (annual).

Finance: Total grants $A9,000,000 (2011).

Board of Trustees: Tom S. Dery (Chair.).

Principal Staff: Chief Exec. David Brettell.

Address: Suite 409, The Strand Arcade, 412 George St, Sydney 2000.

Telephone: (2) 9223 7833; **Fax:** (2) 9223 1800; **Internet:** www.acrf.com.au; **e-mail:** info@acrf.com.au.

Australian Conservation Foundation

Founded in 1965 to promote the understanding and practice of conservation throughout Australia and its territories.

Activities: Operates in the field of conservation and the environment through campaigning, research, policy development, enterprises, membership services and promotion of public awareness. Operates campaign offices in South Australia and New South Wales, and a national lobby office in Canberra.

Geographical Area of Activity: Australia and the Asia-Pacific region.

Restrictions: Not a grant-making organization.

Publications: Annual Report; *Habitat* (6 a year); *Sustainability Report*; monthly online newsletter; reports, policy statements and discussion papers; financial report.

Finance: Provided by membership subscriptions, donations and government grants. Total assets $16,339,771 (2011).

Council Members: Prof. Ian Lowe (Pres.); Dr Rosemary Hill (Vice-Pres.); Dr Peter Christoff (Vice-Pres.); Todd Davies (Treas.).

Principal Staff: Exec. Dir Don Henry.

Address: 1st Floor, 60 Leicester St, Carlton, VIC 3053.

Telephone: (3) 9345 1111; **Fax:** (3) 9345 1166; **Internet:** www.acfonline.org.au; **e-mail:** acf@acfonline.org.au.

Australian Council for International Development

Founded in 1965 to provide for consultation and co-operation between member organizations concerning their work at home and abroad, with the federal and state governments, the UN and its specialized agencies, and in the field of overseas aid nationally and internationally; to bring the needs for, and the purposes and results of, overseas aid before member organizations, the Australian community and governments and the UN and its agencies; to prepare and disseminate information on aid activities and issues of development, including refugee and migrant services; and to promote research into aid activities. Formerly known as the Australian Council for Overseas Aid—ACFOA.

Activities: Co-ordinates the activities of its numerous member organizations during international disasters or emergencies through the International Disaster Emergencies Committee, and has sub-committees co-ordinating activities in areas such as North-South relations, the Pacific, Indo-China and regional human rights. A development education programme co-ordinates the educational activities of member agencies, and informs and educates particular groups in the community that have a special opportunity to promote international development and co-operation, such as teachers, students and those engaged in voluntary aid administration. The Council holds specialized conferences and consultations and, in addition, promotes more stringent self-regulation by the aid sector, particularly through its development of a Code of Conduct for NGOs.

Geographical Area of Activity: International.

Publications: *Beyond the Horizon: a guide for managing projects from a distance*; *Reality of Aid 2004*; *How ethical is Australia?*; campaign brochures; other publications related to research and development, fact sheets and papers.

Finance: Total assets $A1,402,206; total income $A2,487,431, expenditure $A2,424,918 (June 2011).

Executive Committee: Meredith Burgmann (Pres.); Betty Hounslow, Jack de Groot, Andrew Hewett (Vice-Pres).

Principal Staff: Exec. Dir Marc Purcell.

Address: 14 Napier Close, Private Bag 3, Deakin, ACT 2600.

Telephone: (2) 6285 1816; **Fax:** (2) 6285 1720; **Internet:** www.acfid.asn.au; **e-mail:** main@acfid.asn.au.

The Australian Elizabethan Theatre Trust

Founded in 1954 to promote independent drama, opera, ballet and the performing arts in general.

Activities: Sponsors national tours for Australian and overseas works. Conducts research, training courses and conferences, and awards prizes and grants within Australia. Also awards grants and scholarships for international programmes. Prizes include the A$20,000 Opera Award, which must be used exclusively for overseas study.

Geographical Area of Activity: Mainly Australia.

Publications: *Trust News* (6 a year).

Finance: Total assets $A5,681,844 (Dec. 2010).

Board of Directors: Justice Lloyd D. S. Waddy (Chair.).

Address: 269 Miller St, North Sydney NSW 2060.

Telephone: (2) 9955 6580; **Fax:** (2) 9929 6964; **Internet:** theindependent.org.au/history-aett; **e-mail:** sales@theindependent.org.au.

Australian Foundation for the Peoples of Asia and the Pacific—AFAP

Established in 1968, originally to co-ordinate philanthropic programmes in the Pacific region, now expanded to include Africa and Asia; formerly known as the Foundation for the Peoples of the South Pacific.

Activities: Supports the economic and social development of communities in Africa, Asia and the Pacific Islands, through grants to projects in the fields of health, education, rural development and the environment. Funded initiatives include HIV awareness, water and sanitation projects, literacy programmes, and training of health-care workers. Funding is currently directed towards projects in Afghanistan, Cambodia, Timor Leste, Fiji, India, Iran, Kazakhstan, Kenya, Kyrgyzstan, Laos, Malawi, Mozambique, Nepal, Philippines, Papua New Guinea, Samoa, Sri Lanka, Tajikistan, Tonga, Turkmenistan, Uzbekistan, Viet Nam, Zambia and Zimbabwe. Also donates medical equipment and supplies.

Geographical Area of Activity: Africa, Asia and the Pacific.

Publications: Reports; newsletter.

Finance: Total assets $A2,750,518; annual revenue $A6,583,016, expenditure $A6,413,886 (mid-2011).

Board of Directors: John Rock (Chair.); Prof. Jock Harkness (Co Sec.).

Principal Staff: International Programs Dir Christine Murphy.

Address: POB 12, Crows Nest, NSW 1585; 536 Pacific Highway, St Leonards NSW 2065.

Telephone: (2) 9906 3792; **Fax:** (2) 9436 4637; **Internet:** www .afap.org; **e-mail:** info@afap.org.

Australian Institute of International Affairs

Founded in 1933 to stimulate interest in, and provide a forum for, the discussion of international affairs and foreign policy, both among its members and the general public. Provides a wide range of opportunities for the dissemination of information and the free exchange of views in this field; it does not itself hold or express any opinions.

Activities: Work covers international relations, economics, trade, strategic and defence studies, and international law, through research, publications, lectures and national and international conferences. There are branches in all States and Territories.

Geographical Area of Activity: Australia.

Publications: *Australian Journal of International Affairs— (AJIA)* (journal, five issues a year); *Australia in World Affairs* (series); occasional papers and conference proceedings.

Finance: Financed mainly through membership subscriptions, a modest government subvention, private benefactions and rental income.

National Executive Board: John McCarthy (Pres.); Zara Kimpton (Vice-Pres.); Dayle Redden (Treas.).

Principal Staff: Exec. Dir Melissa H. Conley Tyler.

Address: Stephen House, 32 Thesiger Ct, Deakin, ACT 2600.

Telephone: (2) 6282 2133; **Fax:** (2) 6285 2334; **Internet:** www .aiia.asn.au; **e-mail:** ceo@aiia.asn.au.

Australian Multicultural Foundation—AMF

Established in 1988 to foster commitment in Australians towards Australia.

Activities: Operates in Australia, with a focus on education, medicine and health, arts and humanities, law and human rights, and social welfare and studies. Works towards its objective by conducting research, organizing programmes, training courses, conferences, and providing grants to institutions, and issuing publications. Other significant activities include creating and promoting an awareness of different cultures through literacy programmes; improving cultural tolerance through improved community relations, social links and overseas links; and promoting the participation of Australians in organizations significant for community responsibility and citizenship.

Geographical Area of Activity: Australia, with ties to the People's Republic of China, Europe and the United Kingdom.

Restrictions: No grants to individuals or outside Australia.

Publications: Annual Report; newsletter; project reports; research and projects archive.

Board of Directors: Sir James Gobbo (Chair.).

Principal Staff: Exec. Dir B. (Hass) Dellal.

Address: POB 538, Carlton South, VIC 3053.

Telephone: (3) 9347 6622; **Fax:** (3) 9347 2218; **Internet:** www .amf.net.au; **e-mail:** info@amf.net.au.

Australian Spinal Research Foundation

Established in 1976 to work towards the betterment of health of Australians through research on spinal health care.

Activities: Supports research on the causes, diagnosis, cure and prevention of spinal syndromes and diseases. Offers grants for research pertaining to the principles and practices of chiropractic care. The Dynamic Growth (DG) Congress, a fundraising activity, is conducted annually by the Foundation on the Gold Coast in Queensland.

Geographical Area of Activity: Australia.

Restrictions: Priority is given to applicants from Australia.

Publications: Annual Report; newsletters; brochures.

Governors: Dr Martin Harvey (Pres.); Dr Ray Hayek (Deputy Pres.); Dr Mark Uren (Treas.); Dr Tony Rose (Sec.).

Principal Staff: CEO Roley Cook.

Address: POB 1047, Springwood, QLD 4127.

Telephone: (7) 3808 4098; **Fax:** (7) 3808 8109; **Internet:** www .spinalresearch.com.au; **e-mail:** info@spinalresearch.com .au.

Australian Volunteers International

Founded in 1961 and previously known as the Overseas Service Bureau to encourage the transference of technical expertise from Australia to people of the developing world, particularly countries of Africa, Asia and the Pacific.

Activities: Promotes exchanges between experts in international development; recruits, prepares and sends volunteers to work in less-developed countries, in partnership with local communities. The organization has placed approximately 6,000 Australian volunteers in more than 50 countries of Africa, Asia, the Pacific and Central and South America, and in Australian Aboriginal communities.

Geographical Area of Activity: Africa, Asia and the Pacific, and Central and South America.

Publications: *Australian Volunteers* (newsletter, 3 a year); Annual Report.

Finance: $A14,654,083 (June 2006).

Board of Directors: Richard Refshauge (Chair.); Alison Crook, Robert McLean (Deputy Chair.).

Principal Staff: CEO Dimity Fifer.

Address: 71 Argyle St, POB 350, Fitzroy, VIC 3065.

Telephone: (3) 9279 1788; **Fax:** (3) 9419 4280; **Internet:** www .australianvolunteers.com; **e-mail:** info@ australianvolunteers.com.

Baker IDI Heart & Diabetes Institute

Created in 2008 after the merger of the Baker Heart Research Institute and the International Diabetes Institute (IDI). The Institute provides important medical research and patient care, in Australia and internationally.

Activities: Endeavours to fight against one of the greatest threats to the health and productivity of Australia, namely the increasing rate of obesity and its complications, especially diabetes and heart disease. Aims to dramatically reduce death and disability caused by these serious health issues through state-of-the-art research, clinical care, education and advocacy.

Geographical Area of Activity: Australia.

Publications: *Baker IDI Research Update* (annually); *Baker IDI Magazine* (quarterly).

Finance: Independently funded by donations, grants, etc. Total assets $A102,729,587 (2010).

Board of Directors: Robert Stewart (Pres.); Paula Dwyer (Vice-Pres.); Lindsay Maxstead (Hon. Treas.).

Principal Staff: Dir Prof. Garry Jennings.

Address: POB 6492, St Kilda Rd Central, Melbourne VIC 8008; 75 Commercial Rd, Melbourne VIC 3004.

Telephone: (3) 8532 1111; **Fax:** (3) 8532 1100; **Internet:** www .bakeridi.edu.au; **e-mail:** reception@bakeridi.edu.au.

Jack Brockhoff Foundation—JBF

Established in 1979 by the late Sir Jack Brockhoff to provide philanthropic support to organizations that aim to have a positive and enduring impact on the health and well-being of communities. Particularly assists young people by providing opportunities to enable them to improve their circumstances and future livelihoods.

Activities: Grants funds to hospitals, research institutions, community groups, youth support and charitable organizations in Victoria. Funds are offered to assist those with disabilities, severely disadvantaged families, elderly people, children, people with debilitating diseases and unsheltered young people at risk.

Geographical Area of Activity: Victoria, Australia only.

Restrictions: No funding for budget deficits, general operating expenses, core programmes funded from other sources, attendance at conferences and seminars, travel, bodies that are themselves grant-making agencies, bequest programmes, contribution to the corpus of another trust, general fund-raising campaigns/annual appeals. The Foundation only considers applications from organizations endorsed by the Australian Taxation Office as a Deductible Gift Recipient and a Tax Concession Charity.

Publications: *Biscuits & Beyond* (Robert Murray, 2006).

Finance: Annual disbursements approx. $A5,700,000.

Trustees: Robert H. N. Symons (Chair.).

Principal Staff: Exec. Officer Jan Robins.

Address: Level 1, 150 Queen St, Melbourne, Vic 3000.

Telephone: (3) 9670 5686; **Fax:** (3) 9670 0150; **Internet:** www.brockhoff.info; **e-mail:** info@brockhoff.info.

Cancer Council Australia

Established, as the Australian Cancer Society, as the national non-governmental cancer control organization with the aim of preventing cancer, and the illness, disability and death caused by cancer.

Activities: Operates in the field of health and welfare. The Council and its eight member organizations, operating in each state and territory of Australia, work in partnership to undertake and fund cancer research, cancer prevention and control, and information and support services. Maintains a telephone helpline.

Geographical Area of Activity: Australia.

Publications: Annual Report; *National Cancer Prevention Policy*; *Research Highlights*; *Cancer Forum*.

Finance: Total assets $A5,738,000; annual income $A6,744,000 (2009/10).

Board of Directors: Hendy Cowan (Pres.); Stephen Foster (Vice-Pres.).

Principal Staff: CEO Prof. Ian Olver.

Address: POB 4708, Sydney NSW 2001; Level 1, 120 Chalmers St, Surry Hills, NSW 2010.

Telephone: (2) 8063 4100; **Fax:** (2) 8063 4101; **Internet:** www.cancer.org.au; **e-mail:** info@cancer.org.au.

Children's Medical Research Institute

Established in 1958 to undertake and carry out pediatric research; to assess the findings of the research and disseminate such information to the medical field as well as those involved in child care. The Institute is affiliated with the Children's Hospital Westmead and the University of Sydney.

Activities: Operates in the field of medical research. Grants funds to students carrying out research, in particular research into childhood diseases, especially cancer, genetic disorders, leukaemia, neurosciences, and to those utilizing recombinant DNA technology. Also offers grants for post-doctoral research to Australian residents, and fellowships to postgraduates from outside Australia.

Geographical Area of Activity: Australia.

Restrictions: Grants to students who are Australian residents and internationally to postgraduate students.

Publications: Annual Report; newsletters.

Finance: Total assets $A85,487,444; annual income $A21,065,839, expenditure $A20,951,638 (2010).

Board of Directors: Dr Frank J. Martin (Pres.); Carolyn Forster (Vice-Pres.); Rod Atfield (Treas.).

Principal Staff: Dir Prof. Roger Reddel.

Address: Locked Bag 23, Wentworthville, NSW 2145; 214 Hawkesbury Rd, Westmead NSW 2145.

Telephone: (2) 9687 2800; **Fax:** (2) 9687 2120; **Internet:** www.cmri.org.au; **e-mail:** info@cmri.org.au.

Winston Churchill Memorial Trust

Founded in 1965 to perpetuate and honour the memory of Sir Winston Churchill, who died that year, by the award of Memorial Fellowships, known as 'Churchill Fellowships'.

Activities: Churchill Fellowships are awarded each year to Australian citizens to undertake an overseas investigative project of a kind not available in Australia. There are no prescribed qualifications, academic or otherwise, for the award of a Churchill Fellowship. Merit is the primary test, whether based on past achievements or on demonstrated ability for future achievement in any field. The value of an applicant's work to the community and the extent to which it will be enhanced by the applicant's overseas study project are also important criteria.

Geographical Area of Activity: Fellowships can be completed anywhere in the world.

Restrictions: Australian citizens only.

Publications: Annual Report.

Finance: Total assets approx. $A68m. (Jan. 2011).

Board of Directors: Elizabeth Alexander (National Pres.); Justice Margaret White (National Chair.).

Principal Staff: CEO Paul Tys.

Address: POB 1536, Canberra, ACT 2601; Churchill House, 30 Balmain Cresc., Acton, ACT 2601.

Telephone: (2) 6247 8333; **Fax:** (2) 6249 8944; **Internet:** www.churchilltrust.com.au; **e-mail:** info@churchilltrust.com.au.

Clean Up the World Pty Ltd

Founded by Ian Kiernan in 1993 as a global outreach programme of Clean Up Australia to help communities make a positive impact on the health of their environment.

Activities: Operates internationally in the field of conservation and the environment, through supporting community-based environmental projects. The emphasis is on simple activities, such as rubbish collection and removal, tree-planting, education initiatives such as schools-focused lectures and activities, worm-farming and composting. Clean Up events are currently held in 130 countries.

Geographical Area of Activity: International.

Restrictions: Acts as a sponsorship facilitator; no direct grants.

Publications: Factsheets.

Board of Directors: Ian Kiernan (Chair. and Founder).

Principal Staff: Chief Exec. Terrie-Ann Johnson.

Address: POB R725, Royal Exchange NSW 1225.

Telephone: (2) 8197 3420; **Fax:** (2) 9251 6249; **Internet:** www.cleanuptheworld.org; **e-mail:** info@cleanuptheworld.org.

Collier Charitable Fund

Established in February 1954 by the wills of three sisters, Alice, Annette and Edith Collier, to support charitable activities in Australia.

Activities: Operates in the fields of health, welfare and education through making grants to hospitals, institutions helping the sick and aged, for poverty relief, public education, to the Australian Red Cross, and for causes of significance in Australia.

Geographical Area of Activity: Australia.

Restrictions: Grants made within Australia only.

Publications: Annual Report.

Finance: Total assets $A59,546,745; Expenditure $A1,865,279 (mid-2010).

Trustees: C. M. Beeny (Chair.).

Principal Staff: Sec. G. I. Linton.

Address: 31/570 Bourke St, Melbourne, VIC 3000.

Telephone: (3) 9670 1647; **Fax:** (3) 9670 1647; **Internet:** www.colliercharitable.org; **e-mail:** glinton@colliercharitable.org.

Credit Union Foundation Australia—CUFA

Established to support the development of credit unions in less-developed countries to assist in the empowerment of communities.

Activities: Operates in the field of aid to less-developed countries and economic affairs through supporting the development of credit unions in disadvantaged countries of South-East Asia and the Pacific. Also operates in Australia in community advocacy and education.

Geographical Area of Activity: Australia, South-East Asia and the Pacific.

Publications: Newsletters.

Board of Directors: Margot Sweeny (Chair.).

Principal Staff: Exec. Officer Peter Mason.

Address: POB 4720, Sydney, NSW 2001; 1 Margaret St, Level 1, Sydney, NSW 2001.

Telephone: (2) 8299 9031; **Fax:** (2) 8299 9606; **Internet:** www .cufa.com.au; **e-mail:** info@cuscal.com.au.

Foundation for Young Australians

Established in June 2000 following the merger of the Queen's Trust for Young Australians and the Australian Youth Foundation; aims to create positive opportunities and outcomes for children and youth by leading the development of innovative strategies that enable young people to reach their potential and participate fully in society.

Activities: Some 50% of funding is spent on programmes to benefit disadvantaged young people in the fields of education, law and human rights, employment, health and mental health, housing and homelessness, and civic and youth participation. The remaining 50% is spent on programmes to develop leadership potential and promote the pursuit of excellence. The Foundation is an affiliated partner of the International Youth Foundation (USA, q.v.) and a member of the International Youth Foundation Global Network of Partners.

Geographical Area of Activity: Australia.

Restrictions: Funding is only provided to benefit young Australians.

Publications: *Social Marketing for the New Millennium* (2000); *Young People and Police Powers*; reports and evaluations; Annual Report.

Finance: Total assets $A52,526,900; annual revenue $A2,033,417, expenditure $A4,894,969 (2010).

Board of Directors: Mark Paton (Chair.); Peter Williams (Treas.).

Principal Staff: CEO Jan Owen.

Address: POB 239, Melbourne, Vic 3001; 21–27 Somerset Pl., Melbourne, Vic 3000.

Telephone: (3) 9670 5436; **Fax:** (3) 9670 2272; **Internet:** www .fya.org.au; **e-mail:** info@fya.org.au.

The Fred Hollows Foundation

Established in 1992 to prevent unnecessary and avoidable blindness.

Activities: Operates world-wide in the field of medicine and health, providing funding, training and expertise to assist with the treatment of the cataract blind in developing countries; and working with local agencies to develop programmes to provide modern cataract surgery and support local health infrastructure relating to eye health in these countries. The Foundation is active in Australia, Africa, Asia and the Pacific and has links with various international blindness-prevention programmes, including Vision 2020: The Right to Sight. Maintains local programme offices in Australia, Cambodia, China, New Zealand, Pakistan, South Africa and Viet Nam.

Geographical Area of Activity: Africa, Asia and the Pacific and Australia.

Restrictions: No grants or scholarships available.

Publications: *Sharing the Vision* (quarterly newsletter); *Strategic Framework: Seeing is Believing* (monthly electronic newsletter); Annual Report.

Finance: Funded through public donations, government grants, corporate and foundation support, bequests, research and development and merchandise proceeds; total assets $A25,321,569, revenue $A38,643,254, expenditure $A35,557,596 (Dec. 2010).

Board of Directors: Les Fallick (Chair.); Robert Dalziel (Sec.); Graham Skeates (Treas.).

Principal Staff: CEO Brian Doolan.

Address: Locked Bag 5021, Alexandria, NSW 2015; Level 2, 61 Dunning Ave, Rosebery, NSW 2018.

Telephone: (2) 8741 1900; **Fax:** (2) 8741 1999; **Internet:** www .hollows.org; **e-mail:** fhf@hollows.org.

Law and Justice Foundation of New South Wales

Founded in 1967, seeks to improve access to justice, particularly for socially- and economically-disadvantaged people.

Activities: Identifies the needs, in particular of socially and economicallydisadvantaged people with regard to access to justice; conducts rigorous, independent research to inform policy development; contributes to the availability of understandable legal information; and supports organizations and projects that improve access to justice.

Geographical Area of Activity: Australia.

Restrictions: Grants only in New South Wales.

Publications: *e-Bulletin* (6 a year); Annual Report; electronic newsletters on Plain Language Law and JARA (Justice Access Research Alert).

Finance: Publicly funded. Annual disbursements vary.

Board of Governors: Paul Stein (Chair.).

Principal Staff: Dir Geoff Mulherin; Finance Man. Richard Wood.

Address: POB 4264, Sydney, NSW 2001; Level 14, 130 Pitt St, Sydney, NSW 2000.

Telephone: (2) 8227 3200; **Fax:** (2) 9221 6280; **Internet:** www .lawfoundation.net.au; **e-mail:** lf@lawfoundation.net.au.

Macquarie Group Foundation

Established in 1984 by the Macquarie Group to demonstrate the organization's commitment to the society in which it operates and to contribute toward the betterment of society.

Activities: Focuses on five main areas: the arts; education; the environment; welfare; and health. It is also committed to supporting indigenous communities, and supports the philanthropic endeavours of Macquarie staff and businesses.

Geographical Area of Activity: International.

Publications: Annual Review; application guidelines.

Board: Richard Sheppard (Chair.).

Principal Staff: Global Head Julie White.

Address: Level 17, 1 Martin Pl., Sydney, NSW 2000.

Telephone: (2) 8232 6951; **Fax:** (2) 8232 0019; **Internet:** www .macquarie.com/foundation; **e-mail:** foundation@macquarie .com.

The Sir Robert Menzies Memorial Foundation Ltd

Founded in 1979 by the Sir Robert Menzies Memorial Trust using funds raised in memory of Sir Robert Menzies.

Activities: Provides funding for postgraduate scholarships in the discipline of law, engineering and the allied health sciences. Applicants must be Australian citizens. Also provides funds for three health research centres: the Menzies School of Health Research (Darwin); the Menzies Research Institute (Hobart); and the Menzies Centre for Health Policy (Canberra and Sydney).

Geographical Area of Activity: Australia.

Restrictions: Scholarship applicants must be Australian citizens.

Publications: Annual Report.

Finance: Total assets $A17,342,050 (Dec. 2010).

Board of Directors: Sir Guy Green (Chair.); Brian J. Doyle (Deputy Chair.); Brian Jamieson (Treas.).

Principal Staff: Exec. Dir Prof. John Mathews; Gen. Man. Sandra Mackenzie.

Address: Clarendon Terrace, 210 Clarendon St, East Melbourne, VIC 3002.

Telephone: (3) 9419 5699; **Fax:** (3) 9417 7049; **Internet:** menziesfoundation.org.au; **e-mail:** menzies@vicnet.net.au.

R. G. Menzies Scholarship Fund

Inaugurated in 1967 by prominent Australian alumni of Harvard to honour the Australian statesman and former Prime Minister.

Activities: The Menzies Scholarship grants at least one annual award to talented Australians who have gained admission to a Harvard graduate school. Sponsored by The Harvard Club of Australia, The Menzies Foundation and The Australian National University.

Geographical Area of Activity: Australia and the USA.

Restrictions: To be considered for a Menzies Scholarship, applicants must be Honours graduates (or equivalent) of an Australian university or other recognized Australian tertiary institution; be Australian citizens or have permanent residential status, and normally reside in Australia; intend to return to Australia after completing their studies or directly represent Australia overseas; have not previously undertaken a postgraduate degree course at a US university; and have not accepted another major scholarship. Applicants must also have either been accepted to Harvard graduate school, or be confident about meeting its admission requirements and deadlines.

Finance: In 2011, the selection Committee awarded three Menzies Scholarships, each valued at US $60,000.

Principal Staff: Scholarship Admin. Karen Holt.

Address: Rm 1.09, Chancelry Bldg 10, The Australian National University, Canberra, ACT 0200.

Telephone: (2) 6125 2825; **Fax:** (2) 6125 8524; **Internet:** info .anu.edu.au/ovc/Committees/120PP_Scholarships/Menzies; **e-mail:** cabs.admin@anu.edu.au.

Murdoch Children's Research Institute

Established originally as the Royal Children's Hospital Research Foundation in 1960, merged with the Murdoch Institute (established in 1984) in 2000, the Institute conducts, supports and promotes research to improve the health of children and adolescents.

Activities: Operates in the field of medicine and health, nationally and internationally through carrying out and funding research in a number of themed areas, including bone disorders, addiction, cerebral palsy and chromosome abnormalities, each area encompassing biomedical and public health research and community education. All research is carried out at the Institute; however, the Institute maintains strong international links and encourages visits by overseas students.

Restrictions: No outside grants available.

Publications: Annual Report.

Board of Directors: Leigh Clifford (Chair.).

Principal Staff: Dir Prof. Terry Dwyer; COO Brent Dankesreither.

Address: Royal Children's Hospital, Flemington Rd, Parkville, Vic 3052.

Telephone: (3) 8341 6200; **Fax:** (3) 9348 1391; **Internet:** www .mcri.edu.au; **e-mail:** mcri@mcri.edu.au.

The Myer Foundation

Founded in 1959 by Kenneth B. Myer and S. Baillieu Myer to support programmes responding to community needs.

Activities: Works nationally through self-conducted programmes and grants to institutions, particularly in the five following areas selected for specific focus: the arts and humanities, developing Australian and Aboriginal cultural identity; 'beyond Australia' projects, supporting Australian organizations that work in the Asia-Pacific region, and assisting refugees and asylum seekers; social justice, funding research and organizations in the field; water and the environment, empowering communities to engage actively in environmental protection, and improving water resources; and the development of Australian philanthropy. Also supports special projects, including the annual Sydney Myer Performing Arts Awards, collectively worth $A105,000, and research into the future needs of elderly people in Australia. The Foundation also manages the grant programme of the Sidney Myer Fund (q.v.).

Geographical Area of Activity: Australia and the Asia-Pacific region.

Restrictions: No support is given for medical research, scholarships, travel, film or video, nor to individuals.

Publications: Annual Report; *Aged Care: 2020 A Vision for Aged Care in Australia; Sidney Myer Centenary Celebration.*

Finance: Total grants disbursed A$11,519,441 (2010/11).

Board of Directors: Martyn Myer (Pres.) Carillo Gantner (Chair.).

Principal Staff: CEO Christine Edwards.

Address: 8 Exhibition St, Level 18, Melbourne, Vic 3000.

Telephone: (3) 9207 3040; **Fax:** (3) 9207 3070; **Internet:** www .myerfoundation.org.au; **e-mail:** enquiries@myerfoundation .org.au.

Sidney Myer Fund

Founded by Sidney Myer in 1934 to support programmes that respond to community needs.

Activities: Operates nationally in all areas relating to community needs, including the fields of human rights, law, welfare, the environment and personal services. Emphasis is placed on social development and innovation. Limited support is available for building programmes and general appeals. The Fund is managed by the Myer Foundation (q.v.).

Geographical Area of Activity: Australia.

Restrictions: No support is given for scholarships, travel, films or videos, nor for individuals.

Publications: Annual Report.

Finance: Total grants disbursed $A11,519,441 (2010/11).

Board of Trustees: Carrillo Gantner (Chair.).

Principal Staff: CEO Leonard Vary.

Address: 8 Exhibition St, Level 18, Melbourne, Vic 3000.

Telephone: (3) 9207 3040; **Fax:** (3) 9207 3070; **Internet:** www .myerfoundation.org.au; **e-mail:** enquiries@myerfoundation .org.au.

National Heart Foundation of Australia

Established in 1961 to support individuals and organizations pursuing efforts into the causes, diagnosis, cure and prevention of cardiac diseases so as to arrest the resulting disability and increased mortality rate in Australia; and to promote public awareness on treating and preventing cardiac diseases.

Activities: Focuses on medicine, community education and science nationally through research, self-conducted programmes, scholarships, fellowships, lectures, publications, courses, conferences and grants to institutions and individuals. Also works in collaboration with institutions aiming at similar activities in the USA and Europe. Offers scientific and medical research scholarships to permanent residents and nationals of Australia, and travel grants for Australian residents. The Warren McDonald International Fellowship is offered to bring individuals conducting research on the Foundation's areas of interest to Australia. The Overseas Research Fellowship, aimed at Australian permanent residents and nationals, is offered for carrying out research within and outside Australia.

Geographical Area of Activity: Australia.

Publications: Report of operations and financial statement; research reports; Annual Report.

Finance: Annual income $55,522,000, expenditure $A63,002,000 (2008).

Board of Directors: Dr Peter T. Sexton (Pres.); Dr Jennifer A. Johns (Vice-Pres.); Barry J. Davies (Treas.).

Principal Staff: Chief Exec. Dr Lyn M. Roberts.

Address: 15 Denison St, Deakin, ACT 2600.

Telephone: (2) 6282 5744; **Fax:** (2) 6282 5877; **Internet:** www.heartfoundation.org.au; **e-mail:** act@heartfoundation.org.au.

Oxfam Australia

Began in Melbourne in 1953 as a church-affiliated group, Food for Peace Campaign, sending weekly donations to a small health project in India. Food for Peace Campaign groups were later established throughout Victoria. In 1962, a full-time Director of the Campaign was appointed and the name was changed to Community Aid Abroad, reflecting an aim to assist communities more broadly. In 1995, Community Aid Abroad became part of Oxfam International (q.v.), changing its name to Oxfam Australia in 2005. The agency is now a secular, independent, non-governmental, non-profit organization working in 27 countries around the world.

Activities: Activities include: long-term development projects, helping poor communities in 27 countries around the world create their own lasting solutions to poverty; responding to humanitarian emergencies and crises, then staying with communities over the longer term, helping them to rebuild their communities and livelihoods; campaigning for a just world without poverty, seeking to address the root causes of poverty and injustice; involving the Australian community through events such as Trailwalker; Oxfam Australia Shops, selling handcrafts from around the world to support people who live with poverty and injustice; promoting economic and social justice through selling fairtrade goods through Oxfam shops.

Geographical Area of Activity: Southern Africa, East Asia and South Asia.

Publications: *Oxfam News* (quarterly magazine); policy papers, reports and books.

Finance: Total assets $A24,723,000 (2010/11).

Board of Directors: Dr Michael Henry (Chair.); Ann Byrne (Treas.).

Principal Staff: Exec. Dir Andrew Hewett.

Address: 132 Leicester St, Carlton, Vic 3053.

Telephone: (3) 9289 9444; **Fax:** (3) 9347 1983; **Internet:** www.oxfam.org.au; **e-mail:** enquire@oxfam.org.au.

OzChild

Established in 1993, through the merger of Family Action (established 1851), Family Focus (established 1893) and the National Children's Bureau of Australia (established 1971), for the protection of children.

Activities: Operates primarily in Victoria in the areas of children's welfare, including the protection of children from abuse, disability, out of home care, family support, youth pathways and educational support, with some national outreach services.

Geographical Area of Activity: Australia.

Publications: Newsletter; Annual Report.

Finance: Total assets $A25,497,858 (June 2011).

Board of Directors: Chris Ralph (Pres.); Nader Gayed (Vice-Pres.); Michael Bugelly (Vice-Pres.); David Fraser (Treas.).

Principal Staff: CEO Tony Pitman.

Address: 150 Albert Rd, Level 3, South Melbourne, Vic 3205.

Telephone: (3) 9695 2200; **Fax:** (3) 9695 0507; **Internet:** www.ozchild.org.au; **e-mail:** ozchild@ozchild.org.au.

Perpetual Foundation

The Foundation was established by Perpetual Trustees Australia, a trustee company operating throughout Australia.

Activities: Administers more than 400 charitable trusts and foundations operating in Australia. Income generated from the capital of these foundations is distributed annually to charitable organizations, in accordance with the wishes of the founders of the managed trusts, supporting initiatives in the areas of social and community welfare, education, medical and scientific research, arts and culture and the environment.

Geographical Area of Activity: Australia.

Restrictions: No grants are made to individuals.

Principal Staff: Chair. Chris Ryan.

Address: POB 4171, Sydney, NSW 2001.

Telephone: (2) 9229 9633; **Fax:** (2) 8256 1471; **Internet:** www.perpetual.com.au/philanthropy; **e-mail:** philanthropy@perpetual.com.au.

Ian Potter Foundation

Established in 1964, provides grants to enable organizations to advance knowledge and develop ideas and programmes that contribute to a healthy, vibrant and progressive nation.

Activities: Awards grants for general charitable purposes in the areas of the arts, community well-being, education, environment & conservation, health & disability, medical research and science. Also operates a travel grants programme that enables outstanding individuals to attend an international conference in their field of growing expertise. Conference grants support symposia and conferences of international status to be held within Australia. Since inception, has contributed more than $A160M to many thousands of projects, both large and small.

Established the Ian Potter Cultural Trust in 1993 to encourage and support the diversity and excellence of emerging Australian artists. The Trust offers grants to assist early career artists of exceptional talent to undertake professional development, usually overseas.

Geographical Area of Activity: Australia.

Restrictions: No grants to individuals (except through The Ian Potter Cultural Trust). Organisations must have approved tax status (DGR and TCC).

Publications: Annual Distribution Report; e-newsletter (3 a year).

Finance: Annual disbursements $A12,400,000 (2010/11).

Board of Governors: Charles B. Goode (Chair.).

Principal Staff: CEO Janet Hirst.

Address: 3/111 Collins St, Melbourne, VIC 3000.

Telephone: (3) 9650 3188; **Fax:** (3) 9650 7986; **Internet:** www.ianpotter.org.au; www.ianpotterculturaltrust.org.au; **e-mail:** admin@ianpotter.org.au.

Pratt Foundation

Established by Richard and Jeanne Pratt in 1978 for the support of philanthropic organizations.

Activities: Focuses on Aboriginal health programmes, offering training to Aboriginal health workers; and offers Pratt Family Scholarships through Victorian College of the Arts to students pursuing full-time postgraduate studies in the fields of dance, drama, visual arts, music, television, film and production. The scholarships are offered to students in three categories: children of Aboriginal heritage, financially challenged students, and refugees or offspring of refugees. The Foundation works in collaboration with other welfare organizations focusing on conservation, family welfare, education, international relief, including developmental assistance and emergency relief, immigrant development, medical advancement, mental health and rural life development and promoting philanthropy.

Board: Heloise Waislitz (Chair.).

Principal Staff: Chief Exec. Sam Lipski.

Address: 55 Collins St, 39th Floor, Melbourne, VIC 3000.

Telephone: (3) 9921 7143; **Fax:** (3) 9921 7177; **Internet:** www.prattfoundation.com.au.

Clive and Vera Ramaciotti Foundations

Established in 1970 by Vera Ramaciotti to support biomedical research.

Activities: Operates in the field of medical resarch, in particular molecular biology, immunology and genetics, offering grants to research initiatives and biomedical institutions. Also awards the annual Clive and Vera Ramaciotti Major Medical Research Initiative, worth $A1,000,000, to a single major medical research initiative in New South Wales. A Scientific Advisory Committee advises Perpetual Trustees on the grants to be awarded each year.

Geographical Area of Activity: Australia.

Finance: The combined capital of the Foundation is $A65,000,000, managed by Perpetual Trustees.

Address: c/o Perpetual Trustee Co Ltd, GPO Box 4171, Sydney, NSW 2001.

Telephone: (2) 9229 9633; **Fax:** (2) 8256 1471; **Internet:** www.perpetual.com.au/ramaciotti; **e-mail:** philanthopy@perpetual.com.au.

Reichstein Foundation

Established with the aim of facilitating structural change in society and community development.

Activities: Aims to support community development and facilitate structural change in society in Australia, through grants to community organizations, within the priority areas of indigenous peoples, people with disabilities, and refugees and asylum seekers. Support is also available for community organizations working in the field of human rights and social justice-related causes, for projects concerning violence against women, criminal justice, the environment, rural communities. Also organizes workshops and training sessions aimed at raising awareness and understanding.

Geographical Area of Activity: Australia.

Restrictions: No grants for direct service provision, unless it facilitates community development; only Australian not-for-profit organizations are eligible to apply.

Publications: *Reichstein News* (quarterly newsletter).

Finance: Annual grant distributions approx. $A700,000.

Board of Trustees: Jill Reichstein (Chair.).

Principal Staff: Exec. Officer Christa Momot.

Address: 172 Flinders St, 2nd Floor, Melbourne, VIC 3000.

Telephone: (3) 9650 4400; **Fax:** (3) 9650 7501; **Internet:** www.reichstein.org.au; **e-mail:** info@reichstein.org.au.

R. E. Ross Trust

Founded in 1970 under the terms of the will of the late R. E. Ross.

Activities: Operates through awarding grants for projects in the fields of the arts, social welfare, health, nature conservation and the education of foreign students, through a teacher exchange programme, with particular regard to students from Timor Leste and the South-Pacific Islands. Makes several major grants each year and funds an annual travel scholarship awarded by the Royal Australasian College of Physicians. Grants are restricted to charitable organizations based within the State of Victoria.

Geographical Area of Activity: South-East Asia and the South Pacific, Australia.

Restrictions: Grants are only made in the Victoria area. Generally no funding for projects deemed to be the responsibility of government, general appeals, long-term support, travel expenses or conferences, or for projects too rigid in application to groups defined by religion or ethnic origin, social surveys or social research. No grants for individuals.

Publications: Annual Report and financial statement.

Finance: Total assets $A39,853,000 (June 2010).

Board of Trustees: Alix Bradfield; John McInnes; Ian A. Renard; Eda N. Ritchie; Ian M. Vaughan (position of Chair. rotates annually).

Principal Staff: Chief Exec. Sylvia Admans.

Address: 24 Albert Rd, 7th Floor, South Melbourne, VIC 3205.

Telephone: (3) 9690 6255; **Fax:** (3) 9690 5497; **Internet:** www.rosstrust.org.au; **e-mail:** information@rosstrust.org.au.

The Royal Australasian College of Physicians— RACP

Founded in 1938 to promote the study of the science and art of medicine; to encourage research in clinical science and the institutes of medicine; to bring together physicians for their common benefit and for scientific discussions and clinical demonstrations; and to disseminate knowledge of the principles and practice of medicine. Established the Research and Education Foundation in 1991 to increase funding to its medical research awards programme.

Activities: Presents the views of physicians and paediatricians on questions of medical importance to the Government and other bodies; it encourages continuing education for qualified physicians; conducts a training and examination programme for admission of trainees to Fellowship; makes grants for research and overseas study through its Research and Education Fund; provides lecturers for medical teaching in the Asia-Pacific region; maintains a library on the history of medicine; and publishes the results of research and study. There are 70 Honorary Fellows and more than 9,000 Fellows and Trainees. Maintains a library of 30,000 volumes, including the Ford Collection. Awards more than 40 fellowships and awards annually.

Geographical Area of Activity: Asia-Pacific and Australia.

Publications: Annual Report; *Internal Medicine Journal*; *The Journal of Paediatrics and Child Health*; research reports; magazine.

Board: Dr Leslie Bolitho (Pres.-elect); Prof. Michael Hooper (Treas.).

Principal Staff: CEO Craig G. Patterson.

Address: 145 Macquarie St, Sydney, NSW 2000.

Telephone: (2) 9256 5444; **Fax:** (2) 9252 3310; **Internet:** www.racp.edu.au; **e-mail:** racp@racp.edu.au.

Royal Flying Doctor Service of Australia—RFDS

Established in 1928 by the Very Rev. John Flynn as a charitable service to provide emergency medical care, primary health-care services and education assistance by air to people in remote areas of Australia.

Activities: Provides 24-hour emergency health services; primary health-care clinics at remote sites; tele-health radio and telephone consultations; medical chests to be stored in isolated areas; inter-hospital transfers; and female health clinics. Currently operates from 21 bases throughout Australia.

Geographical Area of Activity: Australia.

Restrictions: Not a grant-making organization.

Publications: Annual Report.

Finance: Total assets $A32,275,572 (2011).

Board of Directors: Maj.-Gen. Michael Jeffery (Chair.).

Principal Staff: CEO Greg Rochford.

Address: 15–17 Young St, Level 8, Sydney, NSW 2000.

Telephone: (2) 8259-8100; **Fax:** (2) 9247-3351; **Internet:** www.flyingdoctor.net; **e-mail:** health@rfdsno.com.

SpinalCure Australia

Established in 1994 with the aim of finding a cure for the paralysis caused by spinal cord injury. Formerly known as the Australasian Spinal Research Trust.

Activities: Operates in the field of health, through funding and promoting research into curing spinal cord injury, fostering co-operation between all disciplines involved in central nervous system research, disseminating information about research progress, and co-operating with international efforts in the same field.

Geographical Area of Activity: Australia.

Publications: Annual Report; newsletters; e-newsletters.

Finance: Total assets $A1,234,216; annual income $A532,830; annual expenditure $A242,673 (2010).

Board of Directors: Stewart Yesner, Co-founder Joanna Knott, Co-founder and Chair. Prof. Perry Bartlett, Scientific Chair. Gary Allsop, Dr Stella Engel, Gabriel McDowell.

Principal Staff: Exec. Dir Duncan Wallace, Man. Leah Mayne.

Address: POB 393, Summer Hill, NSW 2130.

Telephone: (2) 9356 8321; **Fax:** (2) 9356 1135; **Internet:** www .spinalcure.org.au; **e-mail:** research@spinalcure.org.au.

TEAR Australia

In 1971, TEAR Australia was set up to support Christian non-profit organizations in less developed countries involved in relief and development work.

Activities: Operates internationally in the field of aid to less developed countries. Supports indigenous Christian development projects that aim for long-term, sustainable change in the life circumstances of communities living with poverty, in the fields of agriculture and livestock, fisheries and aquaculture, forestry, water resources, income generation, health, children's care and education, community organization, non-formal education, vocational training, and relief and rehabilitation. Also provides emergency relief assistance.

Geographical Area of Activity: World-wide.

Publications: *Target Magazine* (2 a year); *TEAR News* (quarterly); Annual Report.

Finance: Total assets $8,183,089; annual revenue $A15,502,614 (2009).

Board of Trustees: E. Moncrieff-Philp (Chair); Matthew Maury (Sec.).

Principal Staff: Nat. Dir Matthew Maury.

Address: POB 164, Blackburn, VIC 3130
U1 4 Solwood Lane, Blackburn, VIC 3130.

Telephone: (3) 9264 7000; **Fax:** (3) 9877 7944; **Internet:** www .tear.org.au; **e-mail:** info@tear.org.au.

Union Aid Abroad—APHEDA

Established in 1984 by the ACTU (the Australian Council of Trade Unions) as its humanitarian overseas aid agency.

Activities: Operates in 16 countries in the Asia Pacific, the Middle East, Southern Africa, South-East Asia and Cuba, in partnership with local communities and trade unions to promote skills development, better employment opportunities, education, sustainable agriculture, health care and workers' rights.

Geographical Area of Activity: Asia, Middle East, Southern Africa and Cuba.

Publications: *Solidarity Partnerships* (quarterly newsletter); Annual Report; monthly e-bulletin, reports and submissions.

Finance: Annual income $A7,739,004, expenditure $A5,989,719 (2010/11).

Management Committee: Angelo Gavrielatos (Chair.); Paul Bastian (Hon. Treas.).

Principal Staff: Exec. Officer Peter Jennings; Int. Projects Man. Ken Davis.

Address: 377–383 Sussex St, Level 3, Sydney NSW 2000.

Telephone: (2) 9264 9343; **Fax:** (2) 9261 1118; **Internet:** www .unionaidabroad.org.au; **e-mail:** office@apheda.org.au.

Sylvia and Charles Viertel Charitable Foundation

Charles Viertel established the Foundation in his will. The Foundation was established to benefit organizations or institutions involved in medical research into diseases, and the alleviation of hardship of the aged and infirm. Money is also given to charities with low administrative expenses, and to three Queensland organizations: The Salvation Army (Queensland) Property Trust, Cancer Council Queensland and Prevention of Blindness Foundation.

Activities: As well as long-term partnerships with three organizations, supports medical research, the disadvantaged, the homeless and the elderly. Has invested in young medical researchers, particularly through its medical research grant programmes. Flagship programme is the Senior Medical Research Fellowships worth $A195,000 a year, for five years, helping outstanding researchers to establish a research career in Australia. There is also the Clinical Investigatorship programme for younger clinicians starting their careers. Recipients are selected with the assistance of the Foundation's Medical Advisory Board.

Geographical Area of Activity: Australia.

Trustees: George Curphey OAM (Chair.); **Medical Advisory Board:** Prof. Peter Leedman (Chair.).

Address: C/o Philanthropy, ANZ Trustees, POB 389, Melbourne, Vic 3001.

Telephone: (1) 800 011 047; **Internet:** www.anz.com/ anztrustees; **e-mail:** charitabletrusts@anz.com.

Austria

FOUNDATION CENTRE AND CO-ORDINATING BODY

The World of NGOs

Founded in 1997 by Christiana Weidel and Christian Pichler-Stainern to promote and support the non-profit sector in Austria.

Activities: Operates nationally and internationally in the fields of education, law and human rights, social welfare and social studies and the provision of information, through self-conducted programmes, research, conferences, training courses and publications.

Geographical Area of Activity: Austria and Europe.

Restrictions: No grants made.

Publications: Annual Report; annual brochure about the development of the Third Sector; and other publications.

Finance: Funded through membership fees, public funds and project finance.

Principal Staff: Man. Dir Christiana Weidel.

Address: Nibelungengasse 7/7, 1010 Vienna.

Telephone: (676) 3359715; **Internet:** www.ngo.at; **e-mail:** office@ngo.at.

FOUNDATIONS, TRUSTS AND NON-PROFIT ORGANIZATIONS

Afro-Asiatisches Institut in Wien (Afro-Asian Institute in Vienna)

Founded in 1959 by Cardinal Dr. Franz König, former Archbishop of Vienna, to provide a place for intercultural and interreligious dialogue.

Activities: Offers financial support for students of development countries in Africa and Asia, as well as other foreign students in Austria; it is a centre for encounter and adult education in development issues, intercultural topics and interreligious dialogue. Houses prayer rooms of three world religions—a Muslim prayer room, a Hindu temple and a Christian chapel—and invites people to meet representatives of these religions. In-house publishing company aa-infohouse publishes books in various fields by migrant authors in Austria.

Geographical Area of Activity: Africa, Asia, Central and South America and Austria.

Publications: Newsletter, annual report, books.

Supervisory Board: Josef Mayer (Chair.).

Principal Staff: Mans Dr Rainer Porstner, Nikolaus Heger.

Address: Türkenstr. 3, 1090 Vienna.

Telephone: (1) 3105145311; **Fax:** (1) 3105145312; **Internet:** www.aai-wien.at; **e-mail:** office@aai-wien.at.

AMURT International

Founded in Switzerland in 1985. In 2002, it joined other regional teams to form an international network of AMURT organizations, originally founded in India, which works in the fields of disaster relief, rehabilitation and development co-operation, aiming to help people regardless of race, religion or nationality.

Activities: AMURT works with and assists poor, underprivileged and marginalized communities to improve their quality of life. Also concerned with improving the lives of victims of natural and man-made disasters. All projects supported and implemented by AMURT are community-based, emphasizing and encouraging maximum participation from local communities in determining their own future.

Geographical Area of Activity: World-wide.

Restrictions: Exclusively charitable.

Address: Sterngasse 3/2/6, 1010 Vienna.

Telephone: (1) 201-80209; **Fax:** (1) 201-80609; **Internet:** www.amurt.org; **e-mail:** info@amurt.org.

Ludwig Boltzmann Gesellschaft

Non-profit association of research institutes.

Activities: Institutes carry out research, mainly in two areas (human medicine and humanities, social sciences and cultural sciences) in collaboration with companies and institutions. Most institutes are located in Vienna; outside Austria, institutes are located in Germany, Sweden and Switzerland.

Principal Staff: Gen. Man. Claudia Lingner.

Address: Nußdorferstr. 64, 6th Floor, 1090 Vienna.

Telephone: (1) 5132750; **Fax:** (1) 5132310; **Internet:** www.lbg.ac.at; **e-mail:** office@lbg.ac.at.

Entwicklungshilfe-Klub (Aid for Development Club)

Supports community development initiatives in the developing world.

Activities: Supports community development initiatives in less-developed countries, through grants to small grassroots projects and work with partner organizations in Africa, Asia, Central and South America, Eastern Europe and North Africa.

Geographical Area of Activity: Africa, Asia, Central and South America, Eastern Europe and North Africa.

Publications: Annual Report.

Principal Staff: Dir Gabriele Tabatabai.

Address: Böcklinstr. 44, 1020 Vienna.

Telephone: (1) 7205150; **Fax:** (1) 7283793; **Internet:** www.eh-klub.at; **e-mail:** office@eh-klub.at.

ERSTE Stiftung—Die ERSTE Österreichische Spar-Casse Privatstiftung (ERSTE Foundation)

Established in 2005 (as a successor to a savings association originally established in 1819) to assist in social change in Central and South-Eastern Europe. The Foundation is the major shareholder in the ERSTE Bank Group, which operates in the region.

Activities: Operates in Central and South-Eastern Europe within three programme areas: Social Affairs, Culture and Europe, specifically working towards social integration in co-operation with local organizations in the field of culture.

Geographical Area of Activity: Central and South-Eastern Europe in areas where ERSTE Bank Group operates (Austria, Croatia, Czech Republic, Hungary, Romania, Serbia, Slovakia, Slovenia and Ukraine).

Board of Trustees: Andreas Treichl (Chair.).

Principal Staff: Man. Dir Boris Marte.

Address: Friedrichstr. 10, 4. OG, 1010 Vienna.

Telephone: (501) 0015100; **Fax:** (501) 0011094; **Internet:** www.erstestiftung.org; **e-mail:** office@erstestiftung.org.

European Centre for Social Welfare Policy and Research

Established as the European Centre for Social Welfare Training and Research in 1974 in Vienna, based on an Agreement between the UN and Austria. Subsequent agreements in 1978 and 1981 reconfirmed the European Centre as an autonomous, UN-affiliated intergovernmental organization. Present name adopted in 1989.

Activities: Provides expertise in the fields of welfare and social policy development in a broad sense, particularly in areas where multi- or interdisciplinary approaches, integrated policies and inter-sectoral action are required. Expertise includes issues of demographic development, work and employment, incomes, poverty and social exclusion, social security, migration and social integration, human security, care, health and well-being through the provision of public goods and personal services. The focus is on the interplay of socio-economic developments with institutions, public policies, monetary transfers and in-kind benefits, population needs and the balance of rights and obligations.

Geographical Area of Activity: Europe, USA, Canada and Israel.

Publications: Book; reports; policy briefs.

Board of Directors: Yury Fedotov (Chair.).

Principal Staff: Exec. Dir Prof. Dr Bernd Marin.

Address: Berggasse 17, 1090 Vienna.

Telephone: (1) 31945050; **Fax:** (1) 319450519; **Internet:** www.euro.centre.org; **e-mail:** ec@euro.centre.org.

European Institute of Progressive Cultural Policies

Aims to promote the development of innovative cultural policies in the European Union and Central and Eastern Europe.

Activities: Encourages co-operation across Europe between arts organizations and cultural networks, carries out transnational research projects, organizes workshops, maintains a database of European art networks and issues publications.

Geographical Area of Activity: European Union and Central and Eastern Europe.

Publications: Publications in the field of art and culture and networking.

Address: Gumpendorfer Str. 63B, 1060 Vienna.

Telephone: (1) 5856478; **Internet:** www.eipcp.net; **e-mail:** contact@eipcp.net.

Fonds zur Förderung der Wissenschaftlichen Forschung—FWF (Austrian Science Fund)

Founded in 1967 with the aim of supporting scientific research.

Activities: Provides finance for basic research in all fields of science, including the humanities. Also responsible for assisting in the formulation and implementation of national science policy, for public relations work relating to science, and for the promotion of the internationalization (in particular Europeanization) of the scientific sector in Austria. Awards include support for non-Austrian scientists working at Austrian science institutes and for Austrian postgraduate students wishing to carry out scientific research abroad.

Geographical Area of Activity: Austria.

Publications: Annual Report; *Info* (magazine in German); statistical publications.

Supervisory Board: Wilhelm Krull (Chair.); Horst Seidler (Deputy Chair.).

Principal Staff: Pres. Dr Christoph Kratky.

Address: Sensengasse 1, 1090 Vienna.

Telephone: (1) 5056740; **Fax:** (1) 5056739; **Internet:** www.fwf.ac.at; **e-mail:** office@fwf.ac.at.

International Institute for Applied Systems Analysis—IIASA

Founded in 1972 as a non-governmental interdisciplinary research institute by the Academies of Sciences or equivalent institutions in 12 countries in both East and West. Membership has meanwhile increased to 18 countries.

Activities: Researches global environmental, economic, technological, and social change in the twenty-first century. Develops assessment and decision-support methodologies, global databases, and analytical tools to study these issues. Concentrates efforts within three research themes: Energy and Climate Change; Food and Water; Poverty and Equity. Awards a number of fellowships and scholarships.

Geographical Area of Activity: International.

Publications: Annual Report; *Options* (quarterly); Research Reports; *Interim Reports* (approx. 75 a year); and others.

Finance: Annual income €15,832,317; expenditure €15,204,456 (2010).

Advisory Committee: Prof. Arild Underdal (Chair.).

Principal Staff: Dir Prof. Pavel Kabat; Deputy Dir Prof. Nebojsa Nakicenovic.

Address: Schlossplatz 1, 2361 Laxenburg.

Telephone: (2) 2368070; **Fax:** (2) 23671313; **Internet:** www.iiasa.ac.at; **e-mail:** web@iiasa.ac.at.

International Press Institute—IPI

Founded in New York in 1950 to promote and safeguard the freedom of the press.

Activities: Main objectives are to defend and promote freedom of the press; to publish studies of governmental pressure on the media; to ensure the safety of journalists and allow them to work without interference; to improve the practice of journalism; to promote the free exchange of news and the free flow of information; and to encourage co-operation and communication between its members. Organizes congresses, seminars and workshops world-wide, as well as missions to countries where press freedom is under threat; conducts editorial research; arranges conferences; and disseminates information. Support is given to journalists and editors in developing countries through the Press Freedom Fund and the Emergency Response Fund. Has members in more than 120 countries.

Geographical Area of Activity: World-wide.

Publications: *IPI World Press Freedom Review* (annually); *The Kosovo News and Propaganda War*; *Ten Years IPI Headquarters in Vienna*; *Caught in the Crossfire: The Iraq War and the Media (A Diary of Claims and Counterclaims)*; IPI Annual World Congress Reports.

Executive Board: Carl-Eugen Eberle (Chair.); Pavol Mudry, Galina Sidorova, Simon Li (Vice-Chairs).

Principal Staff: Exec. Dir Alison Bethel McKenzie.

Address: Spiegelgasse 2, 1010 Vienna.

Telephone: (1) 5129011; **Fax:** (1) 5129014; **Internet:** www.freemedia.at; **e-mail:** ipi@freemedia.at.

Bruno Kreisky Forum für internationalen Dialog (Bruno Kreisky Forum for International Dialogue)

Aims to bring together politicians, academics, businesspeople and others from all over the world to create international dialogue.

Activities: Operates in five areas: the Middle East, Unemployment and the Global Economy, New Europe, North-South Dialogue and Human Rights, through research projects, discussions, symposia, lectures and seminars. Maintains the Bruno Kreisky Archives, established the Bruno Kreisky Foundation for Outstanding Achievements in Human Rights, and awards the Bruno Kreisky European Scholarship.

Geographical Area of Activity: Austria.

Publications: Annual Report; newsletter; Dialogue Series; *Le rôle de la Social-Démocratie dans la Nouvelle Europe*; *From Cancún to Vienna. International Development in a New World*; *The Social Left: The Present and the Prospect*; and others.

Board of Directors: Franz Vranitzky (Hon. Pres.); Rudolf Scholten (Pres.); Brigitte Ederer (Vice-Pres.); Max Kothbauer

(Vice-Pres. and Dep. Treas.); Margit Schmidt (Treas.); Eva Nowotny (Sec.).

Principal Staff: Sec.-Gen. Gertraud Auer Borea d'Olmo.

Address: Armbrustergasse 15, 1190 Vienna.

Telephone: (1) 3188260; **Fax:** (1) 3188260-10; **Internet:** www.kreisky.org; **e-mail:** kreiskyforum@kreisky.org.

KulturKontakt Austria–KKA

Founded in 1989 to support cultural and art projects that are related both to the democratization processes in Central and Eastern Europe as well as European integration.

Activities: Promotes the development of the arts in Eastern Europe and Austria, and collaborative activities between Austria and countries in Eastern Europe. Activities include the sponsoring of individual artists, start-up funding for innovative initiatives, participation in infrastructure programmes, and pan-European co-operation programmes in the fine arts, film, media, literature, music, theatre and dance. Distributes awards including the Henkel CEE Art Award for experimental design, and the Henkel Young Artists' Award. Also promotes educational co-operation and sponsorship support for art projects. On behalf of the Austrian Federal Ministry of Education, Science and Culture, KulturKontakt maintains and supports an educational network of project offices in 11 Eastern European countries.

Geographical Area of Activity: Austria and Central, Eastern and South-Eastern Europe.

Publications: *KulturKontakt* (quarterly magazine).

Board: Anton Dobart (Chair.), Wolfgang Stelzmüller (Treas.).

Principal Staff: Dir Gerhard Kowar.

Address: Universitätsstr. 5, 1010 Vienna.

Telephone: (1) 52387650; **Fax:** (1) 523876520; **Internet:** www.kulturkontakt.or.at; **e-mail:** office@kulturkontakt.or.at.

MEDIACULT—International Research Institute for Media, Communication and Cultural Development

Founded in 1969, on the initiative of the International Music Council under the auspices of UNESCO, for research in the field of cultural development, with special reference to the audio-visual media.

Activities: Operates in the fields of the arts and humanities, and science and technology, especially in the areas of the digital technologies of production and distribution, and the globalization of culture and culture industries. Carries out research in three main areas: new communication technologies, art and culture; the global music market and music in Austria; and social policy and cultural development. Publishes the results of its research; advises on cultural policy; and holds congresses, symposia and workshops.

Geographical Area of Activity: International.

Publications: *MEDIACULT Newsletter* (2 a year); books and research reports.

Finance: Regular subsidies are provided by the Austrian Government and the City of Vienna; the Institute also receives donations and grants from other sources, and income is also derived from payment for research services.

Board of Directors: Prof. Raymond Weber (Pres.); Prof. Dr Josef Trappel (Vice-Pres.); Prof. Dr Roman Hummel (Treas.).

Principal Staff: Hon. Sec.-Gen. Prof. Dr Alfred Smudits; Dir Dr Andreas Gebesmair.

Address: Marxergasse 48/8, 1030 Vienna.

Telephone: (1) 2363923; **Fax:** (1) 2363923-99; **Internet:** www.mediacult.at; **e-mail:** office@mediacult.at.

Österreichische Forschungsstiftung für Internationale Entwicklung—ÖFSE (Austrian Research Foundation for International Development)

Founded in 1967 by the Afro-Asiatisches Institut in Wien (q.v.) and the Österreichischer Auslandsstudentendienst to support research in connection with developing countries.

Activities: Operates in the field of aid to less-developed countries, through grants to individuals and institutions, and issuing publications. Provides documentation and information on development aid and policy, developing countries and international development, particularly relating to Austria. Maintains a library of approximately 45,000 volumes, of which 30,000 are monographs and 10,000 periodicals, as well as 130 subscription magazines.

Publications: *Österreichische Entwicklungspolitik*; *ÖFSE—Forum*; *ÖFSE—Edition*; newsletter; publications on Austrian development politics and collaboration, country and statistical information.

Trustees: Dr Andreas Novy (Chair.); Heinz Hödl (Deputy Chair.).

Principal Staff: Man. Werner Raza.

Address: Sensengasse 3, 1090 Vienna.

Telephone: (1) 3174010; **Fax:** (1) 3174010–150; **Internet:** www.oefse.at; **e-mail:** office@oefse.at.

Österreichische Gesellschaft für Außenpolitik und Internationale Beziehungen (Foreign Policy and United Nations Association of Austria—UNA-AUSTRIA)

Founded in 1945 to increase and widen interest in, and knowledge of, foreign policy, particularly Austrian foreign policy and the UN.

Activities: Operates internationally in the fields of foreign affairs and international relations, through international conferences, lectures, panel discussions and publications on foreign policy.

Geographical Area of Activity: Austria.

Publications: *GLOBAL VIEW* (quarterly magazine).

Principal Staff: Pres. Dr Wolfgang Schüssel; Sec.-Gen. Michael F. Pfeifer.

Address: Hofburg–Stallburg, Reitschulgasse 2, 1010 Vienna.

Telephone: (1) 5354627; **Internet:** www.oegavn.org; **e-mail:** office@oegavn.org.

Österreichische Gesellschaft für Umwelt und Technik—ÖGUT (Austrian Society for Environment and Technology)

Established in 1985 to support communication and co-operation between its members.

Activities: Focuses on problems in the field of environment and technology, aiming for the avoidance or handling of environmental conflicts, strengthening the balance of interests between all relevant protagonists in environmental politics (especially environmental associations and organizations, businesses, interest groups and public administration), supporting Central and Eastern European countries in the solving of environmental problems, evaluating and developing the basic legal, social and economic conditions necessary for the implementation of environmental technologies, informing the public about possibilities and risks in the field of environmental technology, and tackling environmental and technological topics in the interests of its members. Works through supporting networking and communication between members, providing information, and promoting development and innovation in the environmental sphere. An annual award is given to projects presenting innovative ecological ideas, which serve ecological demands as well as economic aims.

Geographical Area of Activity: European Union and Central and Eastern Europe.

Publications: *Environmental Technology Markets in South-Eastern Europe*; *Environmental Policies, Strategies and Programmes of the EU Accession Countries in Central and Eastern Europe*; *Electricity liberalization*; *Long Term Trends and Options in the Austrian Building Sector*; *Tagungsband des 1st European Symposium Environmental Mediation in Europe—New Methods in Conflict Resolution and Participation*; *Bauen, Energie & Innovation*; *Energie-Contracting*; *Gender & Soziale Nachhaltigkeit*; *Nachhaltiger Finanzmarkt*; and other publications.

Board of Directors: Dr Rene Alfons Haiden (Pres.); Dr Stephan Schwarzer (Vice-Pres.); Elisabeth Freytag (Vice-Pres.); Gertrud Körbler (Vice-Pres.).

Principal Staff: Sec.-Gen. Gerlinde Wimmer.

Address: Hollandstr. 10/46, 1020 Vienna.

Telephone: (1) 3156393; **Fax:** (1) 315639322; **Internet:** www.oegut.at; **e-mail:** office@oegut.at.

South East Europe Media Organisation—SEEMO—IPI (South East Europe Media Organisation)

Established in Zagreb in 2000 to promote and safeguard the freedom of the press in South-Eastern Europe, and as a leading media organization in the region.

Activities: Seeks to promote and safeguard press freedom, including freedom of access to news, freedom of transmission of news, freedom of publication of newspapers and freedom of expression. Its activities include fostering understanding between journalists and other media professionals; improving standards and practices; ensuring safety of journalists; and promoting co-operation. Programmes include a Media Aid Programme, Media Law Programme and a Media in Transition Programme. Through the SEEMO South-East Europe Media Foundation for Emergency Help, the organization offers support for projects in the region. The Organization maintains national offices in all countries in the region. It also awards the annual SEEMO Award for Better Understanding, a prize of € 3,000, made to a journalist, editor or media executive in South-Eastern Europe, who, through the media, has promoted a climate of better understanding among peoples and worked toward ending minority problems, ethnic divisions, racism and xenophobia. Additional Awards are CEI-SEEMO Award for investigative journalism (€ 5,000), SEEMO Human Rights Award and SEEMO Human Rights Award. Also makes awards from the SEEMO Emergency Fund to provide direct help to journalists in need in South-Eastern Europe.

Geographical Area of Activity: South-Eastern and Central Europe.

Publications: *SEEMO Media Handbook* (annually, in English); *SEEMO Review*; *DeScripto* (quarterly journal); *SEEMO Investigative Journalism Handbook*; publications in local languages.

Board of Directors: Boris Bergant (Pres.); Radomir Licina (Deputy Pres.).

Principal Staff: Sec.-Gen. Oliver Vujovic.

Address: Spiegelgasse 2/29, 1010 Vienna.

Telephone: (1) 5133940; **Fax:** (1) 5129015; **Internet:** www.seemo.org; **e-mail:** info@seemo.org.

Wiener Institut für Internationalen Dialog und Zusammenarbeit (Vienna Institute for International Dialogue and Co-operation)

Founded in 1987 as successor to the Vienna Institute for Development (founded in 1962 by Bruno Kreisky); aims to disseminate information on the cultural, social and economic life of the countries of Asia, Africa and Central and South America to increase public awareness of the problems of economic development and international co-operation.

Activities: The Institute conducts research programmes, holds conferences, seminars and workshops on development policy and developing countries, and issues publications relating to international development. Operates a cultural exchange programme with the countries of the South, and is the lead agency of a European-wide network of sports organizations concerned with anti-racism and anti-discrimination both within and outside sport. Members come from 20 countries.

Geographical Area of Activity: World-wide.

Publications: *Report Series* (in English and German).

Advisory Board: Barbara Prammer (Pres.).

Principal Staff: Dir Walter Posch; Deputy Dir Franz Schmidjell.

Address: Möllwaldplatz 5/3, 1040 Vienna.

Telephone: (1) 7133594; **Fax:** (1) 7133573; **Internet:** www.vidc.org; **e-mail:** office@vidc.org.

Azerbaijan

FOUNDATIONS, TRUSTS AND NON-PROFIT ORGANIZATIONS

Heydar Aliyev Foundation

Established to honour the late Heydar Aliyev and his philosophy.

Activities: Operates in the areas of education, public health, the environment, science and technology, culture and sport.

Geographical Area of Activity: Azerbaijan.

Publications: *Ekhlagi-Nasiri* (2009); *Gala Archeological-Ethnographic Museum Complex* (2008); *Photoalbum 'Mir Jalal – 100'* (2008); *Mugham Encyclopedia* (2008); *World of Uzeyir* (2008); *New Revivers of Mugham* (2008).

Trustees: Aliyeva Mehriban Arif gyzy (Pres.).

Address: Niyazi Str. 5, Baku 1000.

Telephone: (12) 435-12-93; **Fax:** (12) 435-12-96; **Internet:** www.heydar-aliyev-foundation.org; **e-mail:** office@heydar-aliyev-foundation.org.

Open Society Institute—Assistance Foundation (Azerbaijan)

Established in 1996; an independent foundation, part of the Soros foundations network.

Activities: Promotes the development of an open society by supporting programmes in the fields of education, information and the media, women, the arts and culture, law and human rights, and public health. Encourages the creation and development of NGOs in Azerbaijan as well as developing community information centres in regional public libraries.

Geographical Area of Activity: Azerbaijan.

Finance: Grants disbursed US $3,180,021 (2006).

Board of Trustees: Zardusht Alizade (Chair.).

Principal Staff: Exec. Dir Farda Asadov.

Address: AZ1110 Baku, Akademik Hasan Aliyev Str. 117a.

Telephone: (12) 564-34-65; **Fax:** (12) 564-34-66; **Internet:** www.osi-az.org; **e-mail:** office@osi-az.org.

Bahamas

FOUNDATIONS, TRUSTS AND NON-PROFIT ORGANIZATIONS

TK Foundation

Established in 2002.

Activities: Aims to advance knowledge of oceanography, marine biology, marine engineering, naval architecture, seamanship and other maritime sciences. Also aims to relieve poverty and promote the welfare of impoverished, sick or injured seamen.

Geographical Area of Activity: World-wide.

Board of Directors: Arthur F. Coady (Chair.).

Principal Staff: Admin. Esther Blair.

Address: 1st Floor Bayside House, Bayside Executive Park, West Bay St and Blake Rd, POB AP 59214, Nassau.

Telephone: (502) 8935; **Fax:** (502) 8840; **Internet:** www .thetkfoundation.com; **e-mail:** info@tkfoundation.bs.

Bangladesh

FOUNDATIONS, TRUSTS AND NON-PROFIT ORGANIZATIONS

Action in Development—AID

Founded by Tarikul Islam Palash in 1992 to promote development.

Activities: Operates in the fields of education, law and human rights, good governance, agriculture, community health care and social welfare through self-conducted programmes including the Disabled programme, Human Development programme and Income-Generating programme, and through conferences and seminars. Collaborates internationally with similar organizations.

Geographical Area of Activity: Bangladesh.

Finance: Financed by the Bangladesh Government and by grants from the European Commission and SLF-Netherlands.

Executive Committee: Shahidul Islam Latu (Pres.); Israel Hossain Shanti (Vice-Pres.); Nurun Nahar Kusum (Treas.).

Principal Staff: Exec. Dir Aminul Islam Bakul.

Address: AID Complex, Shatbaria, Jhenaidah 7300.

Telephone: (451) 61188-9; **Fax:** (451) 61189-105; **Internet:** www.aid-bd.org; **e-mail:** aid@btcl.net.bd.

Bangladesh Freedom Foundation

Established in May 1997 to make grants to not-for-profit organizations concerned with problems of fundamental freedoms of the citizens of Bangladesh, and to promote and strengthen indigenous philanthropy in Bangladesh.

Activities: Provides funding support to programmes promoting three fundamental freedoms: freedom from poverty, freedom from ignorance and freedom from oppression. Other areas of interest include freedom of expression, freedom of the press and media, human rights and equality before the law. Groups prioritized for funding under these interest areas include those working with women, children and minority groups in poverty and disadvantage; and habitable and sustainable ecology and environment.

Geographical Area of Activity: Bangladesh.

Restrictions: Preference is given to small-scale initiatives in Bangladesh.

Publications: Annual Report; *An Introduction to the Non-Profit Sector in Bangladesh*; *Neither Freedom Nor Choice: A Study of Wife Abuse in Bangladesh*; *Security of Marginalized Women*; *The Bangladesh Context*.

Finance: Total assets 249,422,000 taka (2008).

Board of Trustees: Syed Manzur Elahi (Chair.).

Principal Staff: Exec. Dir Sazzadur Rahman Chowdhury.

Address: Level 5, 6/5A Sir Syed Rd, Mohammadpur, Dhaka 1207.

Telephone: (2) 8113258; **Fax:** (2) 8113258; **Internet:** www.freedomfound.org; **e-mail:** info@freedomfound.org.

BRAC—Building Resources Across Communities

Established in 1972, originally as a relief organization, and formerly known as the Bangladesh Rural Advancement Committee. Currently a development NGO working for the relief of poverty and empowerment of the poor.

Activities: Operates in the field of development aid, mainly through microfinance, education and health services, especially targeting those not reached by government-administered programmes. Runs the BRAC University, BRAC Bank, craft shops and food projects. Has established offices in Afghanistan and Sri Lanka, and in Africa.

Geographical Area of Activity: Afghanistan, Bangladesh and Sri Lanka.

Governing Body: Fazle Hasan Abed (Chair. and Founder).

Principal Staff: Exec. Dir Mahabub Hossain.

Address: BRAC Centre, 75 Mohakhali, Dhaka 1212.

Telephone: (2) 988126572; **Fax:** (2) 8823542; **Internet:** www.brac.net; **e-mail:** info@brac.net.

Mukti Lawrence Foundation

Founded in 1990 by Dr A. A. Quoreshi to establish a voluntary social welfare organization to help in the formation of a drug-free generation of people and to campaign for justice for women.

Activities: Operates in the fields of social welfare and health care, particularly the reduction of drug abuse and the treatment of mental health problems related to drug abuse. Established *Mukti*, a centre for the treatment of drug addicts in Bangladesh, in 1988. This currently holds 100 beds and provides treatment and rehabilitation for drugs users, as well as a number of other services, including psychiatric treatment, advice and counselling, a drug help-line, and research and campaigns for drugs prevention and education. Also runs projects, conferences and produces a number of publications. In the field of women's justice, the Foundation recently campaigned for government action on the sexual abuse of garment workers.

Geographical Area of Activity: Asia and Europe.

Publications: Publications on human rights, and awareness, prevention and treatment of drug addiction.

Executive Committee: Fahima Nasrin (Chair.).

Principal Staff: Man. Dir Dr Ali Asker Quoreshi.

Address: House No. 2, Rd 49, Gulshan-2, Dhaka 1212.

Telephone: (2) 9983991; **Fax:** (2) 8827147; **Internet:** muktidrughelpline.com; **e-mail:** info@muktidrughelpline.com.

Barbados

FOUNDATION CENTRE AND CO-ORDINATING BODY

Caribbean Policy Development Centre
Established in 1991; it is the leading umbrella body representing the major national and regional NGO networks in the Caribbean.

Activities: Represents Caribbean NGOs in both regional and international forums.

Geographical Area of Activity: The Caribbean.

Address: POB 284 Bridgetown.

Telephone: (246) 437 6055; **Fax:** (246) 437 3381; **Internet:** www.cpdcngo.org; **e-mail:** cpdc@caribnet.net.

Belarus

FOUNDATION CENTRES AND CO-ORDINATING BODIES

Assembly of Belarusian Pro-democratic Non-governmental Organizations

Established in 1996 by a group of Belarusian NGOs to facilitate their development and ability to move forward in a democratic and open fashion.

Activities: Aims to establish co-operation among NGOs in the informal exchange of information and experience; to build a system of mutual assistance and service-rendering; to expand the influence of the civil sector in Belarusian society; to build a collective system for the protection of rights of NGOs; and to promote the Assembly among other NGOs. Activities include maintenance of a database of more than 700 Belarusian NGOs, facilitation of regional co-operation among NGOs, and holding annual congresses and other conferences to discuss relevant issues.

Geographical Area of Activity: Belarus.

Publications: *The Bulletin of Belarusian NGOs* (monthly).

Principal Staff: Chair. Siarhiej Mackievic.

Address: POB 196, 220036 Minsk.

Telephone: (17) 225-51-10; **Fax:** (17) 206-59-09; **Internet:** belngo.info/cgi-bin/indextesten.pl; **e-mail:** international@belngo.info.

Support Centre for Associations and Foundations—SCAF

Founded in 1996, a member of the European Foundation Centre (q.v.) network of NGO resource centres under the EFC Orpheus Programme and a think tank focusing on education, peace-building and civil society development.

Activities: Acts as an education and information support centre and think tank for NGOs in Belarus. Maintains a database of Belarusian NGOs; provides advisory services and workshops for representatives of organizations, relating to grant management, proposal writing, leadership and staff development; promotes the exchange of knowledge and information between NGOs. Along with 27 other internationally known Belarusian organizations, SCAF is represented at the Public Advisory Council under the aegis of the Belarus Presidential Administration; civil society platform for strategy development in the areas of society, economy and politics.

Geographical Area of Activity: Belarus.

Publications: *Grantsmanship* (journal); *Belarus Civil Society: In Need of a Dialogue*; *The State of Civil Society in Belarus*; *Index on Civil Society in Belarus*; *Fundraising and Grantsmanship*; *Organizational Management and Development of NGOs*; *Partnership Building Between NGOs and Local Government*; and others.

Principal Staff: Dir Dr Iouri Zagoumennov; Asst Dirs Tatsiana Puchkouskaya, Ihar Zahumionau.

Address: 4-13 Korolia St, 220004 Minsk.

Telephone: (17) 2849216; **Fax:** (17) 2849216; **Internet:** www.scaf.int.by; **e-mail:** scaf@tut.by; scaf_belarus@yahoo.com.

United Way—Belarus/NGO Development Centre

Established in 1995, aims to provide an overview of NGOs in Belarus and assist in their development.

Activities: Operates as an information portal, disseminating information on the Belarusian third sector; promotes capacity building through collaboration, consultation and organizing training programmes; maintains databases of Belarusian NGOs; offers legislative and NGO management services; and monitors the Belarusian press.

Geographical Area of Activity: Belarus.

Publications: Directories of Belarusian NGOs; legal handbooks on Belarus.

Principal Staff: Exec. Dir Alitsyia Shybitskaya.

Address: 9 Masherov Ave, 220000 Minsk.

Telephone: (17) 295-10-96; **Internet:** www.ngo.by; **e-mail:** uwb@ngo.by.

FOUNDATIONS, TRUSTS AND NON-PROFIT ORGANIZATIONS

Belarusian Charitable Fund 'For the Children of Chornobyl'

Established in 1990 by Gennady V. Grushevoy as a charitable fund to aid the victims of the Chornobyl (Chernobyl) disaster.

Activities: Operates in the fields of ecology, research into the consequences of the Chornobyl nuclear disaster, social and humanitarian aid, medical aid, rebuilding of community, cultural and educational exchanges, information, youth policy and alternative power supplies, through the following main programmes: Medical Programme (including co-operation with hospitals and research institutes); Charitable Recuperation Programme (for the recuperation of mothers and children in families and rest homes abroad); Educational Programme (projects include arranging postgraduate medical education or further training for Belarusian doctors, nurses and medical specialists abroad); Resettlement (the development of partnership between regions, towns and institutions with institutions abroad, and construction and economic projects); Information and Cultural Programme (publishing, international congresses, seminars and conferences, cultural projects and cultural exchanges); Youth Programmes (creation of regional youth centres and educational, informational, international exchanges); and Social Programmes (legal aid, assistance for 'street children', orphanages, 'weekend clubs' for elderly people, social rehabilitation of under-age delinquents). The Foundation has also established the Social Medical Consulting Centre. The Foundation collaborates with organizations and institutions in 26 countries and maintains local branches in more than 70 cities and districts in Belarus.

Geographical Area of Activity: International.

Publications: *DEMOS* (magazine); *World after Chernobyl*; *Chernobyl Digest*.

Finance: The Foundation is financed through charitable donations and subscriptions.

Board of Directors: Prof. Dr Gennady V. Grushevoy (Chair.).

Principal Staff: Technical Secs Olga Dashkevich, Irina Pobyazhina.

Address: Staravilenskaya 14, 220029 Minsk.

Telephone: (17) 234-12-15; **Fax:** (17) 234-34-58; **Internet:** bbfchernobyl.iatp.by; **e-mail:** bbf@charity.belpak.minsk.by.

Belgium

FOUNDATION CENTRES AND CO-ORDINATING BODIES

Belgian Foundation Network

Established in February 2004 by the Centre Européen pour Enfants Disparus et Sexuellement Exploités, Cera Holding, Fondation Belge de la Vocation, Fondation Bernheim, Fondation Charcot, Fondation Evens, Fondation Francqui, Fondation pour les Générations Futures, Fondation Roi Baudouin and Fortis Foundation Belgium, and administered by the Köning Boudewijnstichting/Fondation Roi Baudouin (q.v.). Aims to make the sector of Belgian foundations more transparent by creating a meeting forum where foundations can exchange good practices, as well as defending common interests of its members, informing the public and giving advice.

Activities: Operates three main working parties: law and finance, communication and governance, through which the organization defends the interests of its members, provides information to the public and promotes transparency.

Geographical Area of Activity: Belgium.

Administrative Council: Isabelle Bloem (Pres.); Micheline Mardulyn (Vice-Pres.); Franky Depickere (Treas.); Dominique Allard (Sec.).

Principal Staff: Co-ordinator Diletta Brignoli.

Address: (correspondence) Ave Huart Hamoir, 48–1030, Bruxelles.

Telephone: (2) 788-21-06; **Internet:** www.reseaufondations .be; **e-mail:** info@reseaufondations.be.

European Foundation Centre—EFC

Established in 1989 by seven of Europe's leading foundations, a knowledge-based membership association dedicated to strengthening organized philanthropy, which is embedded in and supports civil society, in Europe and internationally. Helps nurture efforts aimed at supporting independent, accountable and sustainable funders throughout Europe, particularly when this fundamental human right to associate private capital for public benefit needs fostering. Has more than 200 members.

Activities: Develops and pursues activities in line with its four key objectives: creating an enabling legal and fiscal environment; documenting the foundation landscape; building the capacity of foundation professionals; and promoting collaboration among foundations, and between foundations and other actors. Emphasising transparency and best practice, all members sign up to and uphold the EFC Principles of Good Practice.

Geographical Area of Activity: Europe and international.

Restrictions: Not a grant-making organization.

Publications: *Laying the foundations: 20 years of the EFC* (2010); *European Forum on Philanthropy and Research Funding – Evaluation Guidelines on Research Funding* (2010); *The Case for a Long Overdue European Foundation Statute* (2010); *Understanding European Research Foundations – Findings from the FOREMAP project* (2009); *Championing Diversity – Opportunities for the European Foundation Sector* (2009); *EFC Membership Synopsis* (2009); *Foundations in the European Union – Facts and figures* (2008); *Foundations' Legal and Fiscal Environments – Mapping the European Union of 27* (2007); *Comparative Highlights of Foundation Laws: The European Union of 27* (2007); *Principles of Good Practice* (2007); *Principles of Accountability for International Philanthropy* (2007); *Disaster Grantmaking: A Practical Guide for Foundations and Corporations* (2007); *Foundations' Support for European Citizenship – A Snapshot Results of a European Foundation Centre Survey* (2006); *European Perspectives on Global Health: A Policy Glossary* (2006), *Foundations for Europe: Rethinking our Legal and Fiscal Environments* (2003); *Funding Vocational Training and Employment for People with Disabilities in Europe* (2002); *Effect magazine* (2 a year); *EFC Update* (monthly e-newsletter).

Finance: Total assets €3,421,972; annual revenue €3,568,798, expenditure €3,564,727 (2010).

Management Committee: Erik Rudeng (Chair.); Ingrid Hamm (Vice-Chair.); Luc Tayart de Borms (Treas.).

Principal Staff: CEO Gerry Salole; COO Leticia Ruiz-Capillas.

Address: 78 ave de la Toison d'Or, 1060 Brussels.

Telephone: (2) 512-89-38; **Fax:** (2) 512-32-65; **Internet:** www .efc.be; **e-mail:** efc@efc.be.

EVPA—European Venture Philanthropy Association

Established in 2004, a membership association for organizations and individuals involved in venture philanthropy.

Activities: Promotes venture philanthropy through research publications and events. Member organizations include foundations and trusts, private equity firms, law firms and educational institutions.

Geographical Area of Activity: primarily Europe.

Publications: Newsletter; *European Venture Philanthropy Directory of Members*; *Praxis: European Venture Philanthropy in Practice*; *Establishing a Venture Philanthropy Fund in Europe*; *Distance Learning: Managing Investments Overseas*.

Trustees: Serge Raicher (Chair.).

Principal Staff: Man. Dir Beate Trueck.

Address: 78 ave de la Toison d'Or, 1060 Brussels.

Telephone: (2) 513- 21- 31; **Internet:** www.evpa.eu.com; **e-mail:** info@evpa.eu.com.

Fédération Européenne des Associations Nationales Travaillant avec les Sans-Abri—FEANTSA (European Federation of National Organizations Working with the Homeless)

An umbrella of not-for-profit organizations that participate in or contribute to the fight against homelessness in Europe. Aims to prevent and alleviate the poverty and social exclusion of people threatened by or living with homelessness. Encourages and facilitates the co-operation of all those fighting homelessness in Europe. Established in 1989, currently has more than 100 member organizations working in almost all European Union member states.

Activities: Committed to: engage in constant dialogue with the European institutions and national and regional governments to promote the development and implementation of effective measures to fight homelessness; conduct and promote research and data collection better to understand the nature, extent, causes of, and solutions for homelessness; promote and facilitate the exchange of information, experience and good practice between member organizations and relevant stakeholders, with a view to improving policies and practices addressing homelessness; raise public awareness about the complexity of homelessness and the multi-dimensional nature of the problems faced by homeless people.

Geographical Area of Activity: Europe.

Publications: *Homeless in Europe* (magazine, 3 a year); *Flash* (monthly newsletter); *Health and Homelessness* (quarterly newsletter); *European Observatory on Homelessness*; national and international research reports; European Journal on Homelessness (2 a year); books; toolkits; glossaries.

Finance: European Commission funding through PROGRESS programme.

Executive Committee: Rene Kneip (Pres.); André Gachet (Vice-Pres.); Thomas Specht (Vice-Pres.); Hannu Puttonen (Treas.); Danny Lescrauwaet (Sec.).

Principal Staff: Dir Freek Spinnewijn.

Address: 194 chaussée de Louvain, 1210 Brussels.

Telephone: (2) 538-66-69; **Fax:** (2) 539-41-74; **Internet:** www .feantsa.org; **e-mail:** information@feantsa.org.

Network of European Foundations—NEF

Formerly known as the Association for Innovative Co-operation in Europe, name changed in 2002. In 2012, a total of 13 European foundations were actively involved in the NEF.

Activities: Promotes co-operation between European foundations.

Publications: Quarterly newsletter; Annual Report.

Finance: Total assets €8,617,868 (2008).

Board of Directors: Dieter Berg (Chair.); Boris Marte (Vice-Chair.); Luc Tayart de Borms (Treas.); Dominique Lemaistre (Sec.).

Principal Staff: Exec. Dir Lisa Jordan.

Address: Résidence Palace, Block C, 4th Floor, Office 4221, rue de la Loi 155, 1040 Brussels.

Telephone: (2) 235 2416; **Fax:** (2) 230 2209; **Internet:** www .nefic.org; **e-mail:** info@nefic.org.

Pôle européen des fondations de l'économie sociale
(European Network of Foundations for Social Economy)

Established in January 1999, an international non-profit association governed by Belgian law, with its head office in Brussels. Links numerous foundations keen to bring about a process of social transformation within the European Union. .

Activities: Supports members' best practices and develops new cross-border synergy opportunities to promote social innovation, active citizenship and social entrepreneurship among young people in Europe. .

Geographical Area of Activity: European Union.

Publications: White paper on *Social Economy and integration of first and second generation immigrant youth within European society* (2003);
White paper on *Work for integration* (2007);
European guide on *Citizenship, Interculturality, Dialogue* (2009);.

Principal Staff: Co-ordinator Sophie Chiha.

Address: Rue Royale 151, 1210 Brussels.

Telephone: (2) 250-96-67; **Internet:** www.pedondes.eu; **e-mail:** pefondes@pv.be.

Union des associations internationales—UAI (Union of International Associations—UIA/Unie van de Internationale Verenigingen—UIV)

Founded 1907 as the Central Office of International Associations by Henri La Fontaine, Nobel Peace Prize winner in 1913, and Paul Otlet, Sec.-Gen.of the then International Institute of Bibliography, which subsequently became the International Federation for Information and Documentation (FID), and with which UIA activities were closely associated. Officially founded under patronage of the Belgian Government in 1908, and became a federation under its present name in 1910 at the First World Congress of International Organizations. Registered as an international association with scientific aims under the Belgian law of 25 October 1919.

Activities: Facilitates the evolution of the world-wide network of non-profit organizations; collects and disseminates information on these bodies and their inter-relationships; presents this information in both established and experimental ways to promote understanding of the role of non-profit organizations in global society; and promotes research on the legal and administrative problems common to these bodies. It maintains a database on more than 65,000 international organizations and more than 330,000 of their meetings. Also documents complementary information on international associations, including: biographies of their officers; logotypes and emblems; problems perceived and strategies adopted by international associations, and values and approaches that animate them.

Geographical Area of Activity: International.

Publications: *International Congress Calendar* (quarterly); *Yearbook of International Organizations*; *Encyclopaedia of World Problems and Human Potential*; and others.

Finance: Budget €621,000 (2009).

Trustees: Anne-Marie (Pres.); Bernard Miche (Treas.).

Principal Staff: Sec.-Gen. Jacques De Mévius.

Address: Rue Washington 40, 1050 Brussels.

Telephone: (2) 640-18-08; **Fax:** (2) 643-61-99; **Internet:** www .uia.org; **e-mail:** uia@uia.be.

FOUNDATIONS, TRUSTS AND NON-PROFIT ORGANIZATIONS

Alamire Foundation

Founded in July 1991 by the Catholic University of Leuven and Musica (the Flemish Early Music Centre) to stimulate research in the musical history of Belgium, southern Netherlands and northern France before 1800.

Activities: Organizes conferences and exhibitions, carries out research, publishes books, and has created a database of publications relevant to the Foundation's research.

Geographical Area of Activity: Europe and the USA.

Restrictions: Grants made to specific international research projects only.

Publications: *Journal of the Alamire Foundation*; facsimile editions, monographs, books, repertories and encyclopedias.

Finance: Receives funding from the government of the Flemish region, from the University of Leuven and the Belgian National Lottery.

Board of Directors: Herman Vanden Berghe (Pres.); Herman Baeten (Treas.).

Principal Staff: Dir Bart Demuyt.

Address: Mgr Ladeuzeplein 21, POB 5591, 3000 Leuven.

Telephone: (16) 32-87-50; **Fax:** (16) 32-87-49; **Internet:** www .alamirefoundation.org; **e-mail:** info@alamirefoundation.be.

ARGUS

Founded in 1970 as Stichting Leefmilieu (Environment Foundation); name changed in 2002.

Activities: Promotes the environment and urban and rural sustainable development through providing information and awarding prizes. Also acts as a forum, mostly via publications, on environmental problems and solutions; informs on environmental issues and is involved in educational programmes. Maintains a documentation centre and information databases.

Geographical Area of Activity: Europe.

Publications: Magazine, e-newsletters.

Principal Staff: Dir Helga Van der Veken.

Address: Eiermarkt 8, 2000 Antwerp.

Telephone: (3) 202-90-70; **Fax:** (3) 202-90-88; **Internet:** www .argusmilieu.be; **e-mail:** info@argusmilieu.be.

ASMAE—Association de coopération et d'éducation aux développements (Association for Development Co-operation and Education)

Established in 1981 to promote an equality of exchange between countries in the Northern and Southern hemispheres, in particular in the areas of action and education.

Activities: Operates in the fields of aid to less-developed countries and education, working in partnership with local organizations in Djibouti, Egypt, and Senegal to give financial and material aid. Operates volunteer-exchange programmes for young people from Belgium to work in less-developed countries. Also promotes the establishment of links between partner associations for North-South and South-North co-operation.

Geographical Area of Activity: Mainly Djibouti, Egypt, Senegal, Romania, Rwanda, Kenya and Morocco.

Restrictions: No grants for medical activities.

Publications: *Passerelles* (quarterly); *Les Cahiers asmae*; *Passe-Partout*; *Oops* (newspaper).

Council of Administration: Julie Rijpens (Pres.); Francois van Rooten (Treas.); Benoit Lietaer (Sec.).

Principal Staff: Dir Gery de Broqueville.

Address: 14 ave de Woluwé-St-Lambert, 1200 Brussels.

Telephone: (2) 742-03-01; **Fax:** (2) 742-03-13; **Internet:** www .asmae.org; **e-mail:** info@asmae.org.

Association Égyptologique Reine Elisabeth (Queen Elisabeth Egyptological Association)

Founded in 1923 by Jean Capart to promote studies in the fields of Egyptology and papyrology. Formerly known as Fondation Egyptologique Reine Elisabeth.

Activities: Operates nationally and internationally through research, conferences, lectures and publications; sponsors study trips to Egypt. Holds an extensive papyrus archive.

Geographical Area of Activity: International.

Publications: *Chronique d'Egypte* (2 a year); more than 100 books.

Board of Directors: Comte Arnoul D'arschot Schoonhoven (Chair.).

Principal Staff: Sec.-Gen. Dr Luc Limme.

Address: 10 parc du Cinquantenaire, 1000 Brussels.

Telephone: (2) 741-73-64; **Fax:** (2) 733-77-35; **Internet:** www .aere-egke.be; **e-mail:** aere.egke@kmkg-mrah.be.

Association Internationale des Charités—AIC (International Association of Charities)

Founded by Saint Vincent de Paul in 1617, as Confraternity of Ladies of Charity. Re-established under Belgian law in 1986.

Activities: Operates internationally in the field of welfare. Works with 52 member organizations to eliminate poverty and sustain the promotion and development of the underprivileged in 52 countries. Encourages voluntary work for, with, and of the poor. Develops various kinds of social work, mainly to fight poverty of women. Also support for drug addicts and alcoholics; care for the elderly and the sick; help to single mothers; assistance to the lonely; defence of human rights; and working towards a culture of solidarity, respect and peace. Runs literacy and other forms of educational workshops, provides technical training, as well as making loans to individuals in need.

Geographical Area of Activity: International.

Restrictions: No grants available.

Publications: *Initiation to Associative Life*; *AIC Volunteers Today*; activity report; booklets.

Principal Staff: Int. Pres. Laurence de la Brosse; Treas. Elisabeth Gindre; Sec.-Gen. Natalie Monteza.

Address: 23 rampe des Ardennais, 1348 Louvain La Neuve.

Telephone: (10) 45-63-53; **Fax:** (10) 45-80-63; **Internet:** www .aic-international.org; **e-mail:** info@aic-international.org.

Association of Voluntary Service Organisations— AVSO

Established in 1996 to promote voluntary service at European level.

Activities: Promotes voluntary service through lobbying European Union institutions and national authorities. Provides information to organizations; carries out research, including surveys and country reports; and develops partnerships to organize training events in the field of full-time or long-term voluntary service.

Geographical Area of Activity: Europe and international.

Restrictions: Does not make grants.

Publications: Monthly electronic newsletter; Annual Report; manuals; research studies.

Finance: Financed by European Commission, membership fees, foundations and private donations.

Board of Directors: Massimiliano Viatore (Pres.); Renate Lange (Vice-Pres.); Steve Egan (Treas.); Karin Wimmer (Sec.).

Principal Staff: Dir Agnes Uhereczky.

Address: Rue Henri Stacquet 61, 1030 Brussels.

Telephone: (2) 230-68-13; **Fax:** (2) 245-62-97; **Internet:** www .avso.org; **e-mail:** linden@avso.org.

Cera

Established in 1998 as the Cera Foundation, a division of Cera Holding, a co-operative financial group, following the merger of CERA Bank with Kreditbank and ABB Insurance in 1998. As from June 2004 Cera Foundation changed its operating name to Cera.

Activities: The Foundation supports projects that promote co-operative principles for the development of society and that are consistent with a pluralist view of society. Funding is provided within the areas of: poverty alleviation; medical and social aid; art and culture; agriculture, horticulture and the environment; and education, training and entrepreneurship. International operations are carried out by the affiliated Belgische Raiffeisenstichting.

Geographical Area of Activity: Belgium.

Restrictions: No funding for projects that receive substantial financial support from other financial institutions. No direct support for individuals, with the exception of art and culture grants, which requires prior selection by a small committee of experts; and there is no support for associations and enterprises where the submitted project has a commercial interest.

Publications: Annual Report; *To build our future together*; *Collection of the works of art of Cera*; *The marble smile of cosmos*.

Executive Committee: Rik Donckels (Pres.).

Principal Staff: Man. Matthieu Vanhove.

Address: Philipssite 5, bus 10, 3001 Leuven.

Telephone: (70) 69-52-42; **Fax:** (70) 69-52-41; **Internet:** www .cera.be; **e-mail:** info@cera.be.

Churches' Commission for Migrants in Europe (Commission des Eglises auprès des Migrants en Europe/Kommission der Kirchen für Migranten in Europa)

A network of churches and ecumenical groups in Europe established in 1964 to protect and defend the rights of migrants in Europe. Includes churches and ecumenical councils from Austria, Belgium, Cyprus, Czech Republic, Finland, France, Germany, Greece, Hungary, Ireland, Italy, the Netherlands, Norway, Romania, Slovakia, Spain, Sweden, Switzerland and the United Kingdom.

Activities: Operates in Europe in the area of human rights. Raises awareness of migration problems in Europe and develops the role of religious organizations in solving these problems. Aims to defend the rights of migrants and asylum seekers in Europe, and lobbies various European institutions. Conducts studies on problems relating to European migration policies and racial discrimination and anti-trafficking; and organizes seminars and conferences on migration and related legal issues. Participates in a network of NGOs throughout Europe and has launched the Migration News Sheet and the Migration Policy Group.

Geographical Area of Activity: Europe.

Publications: *Towards a Right of Permanent Residence for Long-Term Migrants*; *Combating Trafficking for forced Labour* *in Europe; Migrants' Experiences in Active Participation in Churches in Europe;Trafficking for Forced Labour in Europe: Emerging Challenges – Emerging Responses; Mapping migration – Mapping Churches responses*; newsletters; leaflets; workshop modules; guides; reports.

Exec. Committee: Moderator Prof. Dr Victoria Kamondji (France); Vice-Moderators Kristina Hellqvist (Sweden) Dr. Antonios K. Papantoniou (Greece); Treas. Apostle Adejare Oyewole (United Kingdom); Members Rev. Alfredo Abad (Spain); Rev. Thorsten Leisser (Germany); Ms Elena Timofticiuc (Romania); Rep. of the World Council of Churches Prof Dr. Amélé Ekué (Switzerland); Rep. of the Conference of European Churches Father Cristian Popescu (Czech Republic)

.

Principal Staff: Sec.-Gen. Doris Peschke; Office Man. Emmanuel Kabalisa; Exec. Sec. Dr Torsten Moritz.

Address: 174 rue Joseph II, 1000 Brussels.

Telephone: (2) 234-68-00; **Fax:** (2) 231-14-13; **Internet:** www .ccme.be; ccme.ceceurope.org; **e-mail:** info@ccme.be.

CIDSE—Together for Global Justice

Established in September 1967 (formerly known as International Co-operation for Development and Solidarity) to promote and provide aid to developing nations; to enable enhanced communication through information exchange, and co-ordination between Catholic development organizations in North America and Europe; and to empower people in these countries through attainment of social, economic and political rights.

Activities: Operates in the field of aid to less-developed countries through advocating and campaigning for the reform of current policy-making. Promotes and facilitates the social justice agenda of its members and partners, targeting major events at European, North American and international level to influence policy-making and thereby improve the lives of the world's most vulnerable people. Advocacy priorities are: resources for development; food, agriculture and sustainable trade; climate justice; and business and human rights.

Geographical Area of Activity: International.

Restrictions: Not a grant-making organization.

Publications: *Advocacy Newsletter* (quarterly, in English); Annual Report (in English and French), EU News (monthly, in collaboration with Aprodev and Caritas Europa); policy papers.

Finance: Annual expediture €1,020,700 (2008).

Executive Committee: Chris Bain (Pres.); Heinz Hödl (Vice-Pres.); Hilde Demoor (Treas.).

Principal Staff: Sec.-Gen. Bernd Nilles.

Address: 16 rue Stévin, 1000 Brussels.

Telephone: (2) 230-77-22; **Fax:** (2) 230-70-82; **Internet:** www .cidse.org; **e-mail:** postmaster@cidse.org.

CONCAWE—Oil Companies' European Association for Environment, Health and Safety in Refining and Distribution

Founded in 1963 as the Oil Companies' International Study Group for Conservation of Clean Air and Water in Europe. It aims to collect and disseminate scientific, technical and economic information on all aspects of environmental and health protection related to the petroleum-refining industry (including pollution control, safety advice for workers and customers, and legislation).

Activities: Collects, exchanges and evaluates environmental and health data; initiates and evaluates research; assesses the consequences of proposed environmental legislation in terms of economic feasibility and cost/benefit; promotes co-operation between petroleum companies, industry and governments on all environmental issues concerning the oil-refining industry; publishes reports and other information. Work areas comprise: industrial atmospheric emissions; water protection; packaging, labelling and safe handling of petroleum products; health protection; automotive fuels and vehicle emissions; oil-

spill cleaning technology; pipeline integrity; and refinery safety management. Has 39 members in 19 Organisation for Economic Co-operation and Development (OECD) European countries and one associate member in Eastern Europe.

Geographical Area of Activity: Europe.

Publications: *CONCAWE Review* (2 a year); *CONCAWE Reports.*

Principal Staff: Sec.-Gen. Michael Lane.

Address: 165 blvd du Souverain, 1160 Brussels.

Telephone: (2) 566-91-60; **Fax:** (2) 566-91-81; **Internet:** www .concawe.org; **e-mail:** info@concawe.org.

Damien Foundation

Founded in 1964 to promote the eradication of leprosy and tuberculosis in developing countries.

Activities: Operates in developing countries to provide specialist medical assistance, aiming to eradicate leprosy and tuberculosis, through long-term projects, research and international co-operation. The Foundation also supports field training and formal training in specialized institutions; operates charitable programmes; supports local people in developing countries both medically and morally; and maintains a library.

Geographical Area of Activity: Africa, America, Asia, Bangladesh, Burundi, People's Republic of China, Comoros, Democratic Republic of the Congo, Egypt, Guatemala, India, Laos, Nicaragua, Nigeria, Panama, Peru, Rwanda and Viet Nam.

Publications: *Perspectives* (quarterly, in Dutch and French); Annual Report.

Finance: Total assets €18,309,343; annual revenue €13,981,037, expenditure €15,779,891 (2007).

Trustees: M. De Doncker (Pres.).

Principal Staff: Pres. Paul Jolie; Gen. Sec. Rigo Peeters.

Address: 263 blvd Léopold II, 1081 Brussels.

Telephone: (2) 422-59-11; **Fax:** (2) 422-59-00; **Internet:** www .damienfoundation.org; **e-mail:** info.projects@damien -foundation.be.

EGMONT—Institut royal des relations internationales (Royal Institute of International Relations)

Founded in 1947 to further studies into foreign politics, international law and economics, in particular in relation to the foreign policies of Belgium, Luxembourg and the Netherlands. The foundation expresses no official opinion on national or international affairs.

Activities: Operates internationally through self-conducted programmes, including research projects, carried out on an international basis. The main research programmes are: Central Africa; European Affairs; Security and Global Governance; Youth and Europe; and Visitor Programmes. Also organizes national and international conferences and lectures, hosts working groups, and issues publications. Maintains a library.

Geographical Area of Activity: International.

Publications: *Studia Diplomatica* (quarterly, in English); *Egmont Papers*; publications on European affairs; conference notes; working papers.

Board of Directors: Étienne Davignon (Pres.).

Principal Staff: Dir-Gen. Marc Trenteseau; Exec. Dir M. Cruysmans.

Address: 69 rue de Namur, 1000 Brussels.

Telephone: (2) 223-41-14; **Fax:** (2) 223-41-16; **Internet:** www .egmontinstitute.be; **e-mail:** info@egmontinstitute.be.

EMonument

Offers quality-assurance management networking tools and programme planning for strengthening sustainable development into community co-operation policies and international research areas.

Activities: Actively assists the development of communities through the promotion of technology transfer, commercialization of research results for scientific and sustainable programmes. The non-profit resource group consists of material evaluations and associations, dissemination, news and training aimed at sustainable quality assurance management for the e-learning environment, and external co-operation programmes.

Geographical Area of Activity: International.

Restrictions: Not a grant-making organization.

Principal Staff: Exec. Dir Ian Muse.

Address: Goedmoedstraat 18, 8310 Assebroek, Bruges.

Telephone: (4) 88646265; **Internet:** www.environmonument .com; **e-mail:** contact@environmonument.com.

EURODAD—European Network on Debt and Development

A network of 54 NGOs from 18 European countries working on issues related to debt, development finance and poverty reduction. The EURODAD network offers a platform for exploring issues, collecting intelligence and ideas, and undertaking collective advocacy.

Activities: Co-ordinates the activities of member organizations working in the areas of debt cancellation, aid effectiveness, World Bank/IMF policy conditionality, and capital flight and financial regulation. Work is continuing on the promotion of responsible finance principles and practices and the redesign of the financial architecture. The network is analysing and influencing European governments' policy responses to the financial crisis of 2007–08. The main institutions targeted by the network are European governments, the World Bank, IMF and OECD.

Geographical Area of Activity: International.

Publications: Annual Report, newsletter and other reports (available online).

Finance: Funded by EURODAD members, the European Commission and private foundations. Annual revenue and expenditures of approx. €700,000.

Board of Directors: Emma Seery (Chair.); Antonio Gambini (Treas.).

Principal Staff: Dir Nuria Molina.

Address: 18–26 rue d'Edimbourg, 1050 Ixelles, Brussels.

Telephone: (2) 894-46-40; **Fax:** (2) 791-98-09; **Internet:** www .eurodad.org; **e-mail:** assistant@eurodad.org.

European Anti-Poverty Network—EAPN

Independent coalition of national and international NGOs established in 1990; aims to eliminate poverty and social exclusion in the member states of the European Union (EU).

Activities: Works in the countries of the EU and in Norway, combating poverty through campaigning for the issue to be dealt with by the institutions of the EU, promoting action against poverty and supporting existing campaigns against social exclusion; and providing advocacy services for people and groups affected by poverty. There are national secretariats in 26 European countries.

Geographical Area of Activity: Europe.

Publications: Annual Report; *Network News* (newsletter in Danish, Dutch, English, French, German, Hungarian, Italian and Spanish); *European Manual on the Management of the Structural Funds*; position papers and reports.

Principal Staff: Dir Fintan Farrell.

Address: Sq. de Meeûs 18, 1050 Brussels.

Telephone: (2) 226-58-50; **Fax:** (2) 226-58-69; **Internet:** www .eapn.eu; **e-mail:** team@eapn.eu.

European Coalition for Just and Effective Drug Policies—ENCOD

Established in 1993 by NGOs from more than 20 European countries to provide information on the causes of the international traffic in illegal drugs and the consequences of current anti-drugs policies, and formerly known as the European NGO Council Drugs Development. Operates as a network of European NGOs and citizens concerned with the impact of current international drugs policies on the lives of the people who are most affected by this issue. Aims to improve understanding of the causes and effects of the drugs trade; contribute to the elaboration of just and effective drugs control policies; and to bring about greater consistency between drugs control efforts and economic and social policies.

Activities: Operates in Europe facilitating co-ordination, information exchange and joint analysis between its members; carrying out joint information campaigns aimed at the general public; and pursuing joint advocacy activities, aimed at policy-makers and the media.

Geographical Area of Activity: Europe.

Restrictions: Not a grant-making organization.

Publications: Reports and articles.

Board: Fredrick Polak (Chair.); Joep Oomen (Treas.).

Principal Staff: Sec. Marisa Felicissimo.

Address: Lange Lozanastraat 14, 2018 Antwerp.

Telephone: (3) 293-08-86; **Internet:** www.encod.org; **e-mail:** office@encod.org.

European Environmental Bureau

Established in 1974, a federation of around 150 environmental citizens' organizations based in 31 countries across the enlarged European Union (EU) and beyond, which aims to protect the environment in Europe and to enable European citizens to play a part in its defence.

Activities: Operates in Europe in the area of conservation and the environment, through providing member organizations with information, producing reports, representing member organizations in relations with European Union institutions, and organizing working groups and conferences. Works as an advocate for improved environment and conservation protection policies, and co-ordinates workshops and seminars. Operates in several environmental areas, including agriculture, air pollution, global warming, noise pollution, waste and tourism.

Geographical Area of Activity: Europe.

Restrictions: Not a fund-issuing organization.

Publications: *Metamorphosis* (quarterly newsletter, also available online); *EU Environmental Policy Handbook*; Annual Report; conference reports; memoranda; position papers.

Executive Committee: Mikael Karlsson (Pres.); Axel Jansen (Treas.).

Principal Staff: Sec.-Gen. Jeremy Wates.

Address: 34 blvd de Waterloo, 1000 Brussels.

Telephone: (2) 289-10-90; **Fax:** (2) 289-10-99; **Internet:** www .eeb.org; **e-mail:** eeb@eeb.org.

European Foundation for Management Development

Founded in 1971 to provide an international network of private and public organizations, educational institutions and individuals for promoting management development.

Activities: Organizes annual activities for particular sections of its membership, and an annual conference on a subject of current and prospective importance for all categories; initiates special studies, meetings, seminars, workshops and projects on selected topics; brings relevant issues in the field of management development and education to the attention of national or international representative bodies; sponsors professional associations in specific fields; publishes or sponsors publications for its members. In 2007 the Foundation had more than 600 member organizations, located in more than 70 countries. Members include major European business schools and management centres, and a large number of companies and consultancy organizations. The Foundation promotes the creation of national networks of members to facilitate the exchange of information on a national basis and the development of transnational activities, and co-operates with management development associations in Central and Eastern

Europe, North, Central and South-East Asia and Africa. The Foundation administers management training programmes in the People's Republic of China, India, Algeria, Russia and the Commonwealth of Independent States.

Geographical Area of Activity: World-wide.

Publications: *Forum* (magazine, 3 a year); *Bulletin* (newsletter, 3 a year); *Guide to the EC*; *Lobbying in the EU*; *European Directory on Executive Education*; Annual Report.

Finance: Total assets €8,512,683 (Dec. 2010).

Board Members: Alain Dominique Perrin (Pres.); Thomas Sattelberger (Vice-Pres.).

Principal Staff: Dir-Gen. and CEO Eric Cornuel.

Address: 88 rue Gachard, bte 3, 1050 Brussels.

Telephone: (2) 629-08-10; **Fax:** (2) 629-08-11; **Internet:** www .efmd.org; **e-mail:** info@efmd.org.

European Foundation for Quality Management— EFQM

Founded in 1988 by 14 of Europe's largest companies to promote management in Europe.

Activities: EFQM is a non-profit membership foundation that shares information and methodologies to help its members – private and public organizations of every size and in many sectors – to implement strategies.

Geographical Area of Activity: World-wide.

Publications: Various print publications on management, training and similar issues.

Board of Directors: Marc Duhem (Chair.).

Principal Staff: Chief Exec. Pierre Cachet.

Address: Ave des Olympiades 2, 1140 Brussels.

Telephone: (2) 775-35-11; **Fax:** (2) 775-35-35; **Internet:** www .efqm.org; **e-mail:** info@efqm.org.

Eurostep—European Solidarity Towards Equal Participation of People

Established in 1990 as an association of NGOs involved in development. Seeks to influence development policies of national governments and of the European Union and other international organizations, and to improve the quality and effectiveness of development initiatives taken by NGOs.

Activities: A group of 18 development NGOs from 14 European countries, which seeks to lobby national governments and international organizations in areas such as the eradication of poverty, social development, trade and international trade agreements, and the quality of aid. Also aims to improve the quality and effectiveness of initiatives taken by NGOs in support of people-centred development. Issues numerous position papers on development issues.

Geographical Area of Activity: Europe.

Restrictions: No grants available.

Publications: Briefing papers; *Eurostep Weekly (e-bulletin)*.

Principal Staff: Dir Simon Stocker.

Address: 115 rue Stévin, 1000 Brussels.

Telephone: (2) 231-16-59; **Fax:** (2) 230-37-80; **Internet:** www .eurostep.org; **e-mail:** admin@eurostep.org.

Fondation pour l'Architecture (Fondation pour l'Architecture)

Founded in 1986, a private cultural institution that supports the interaction of different areas of contemporary design and promotes architectural excellence.

Activities: Operates internationally through self-conducted programmes. It has established a system of cultural and financial partnership between Belgian and foreign public authorities and private businesses, and also works closely with museums, galleries, publishers and cultural centres. Stages exhibitions, conferences and public events devoted to all aspects of the built environment—contemporary architecture, history, current affairs, urban planning and design. Maintains

two exhibition halls and awards the Prix Philippe Rotthier every three years.

Geographical Area of Activity: International.

Publications: Numerous catalogues.

Board of Trustees: Maurice Culot (Pres.); Philippe Rotthier (Founder).

Principal Staff: Bertille Amaudric.

Address: 55 rue de l'Ermitage, 1050 Brussels.

Telephone: (2) 644-24-80; **Fax:** (2) 642-24-82; **Internet:** www .fondationpourlarchitecture.be; **e-mail:** info@ fondationpourlarchitecture.be.

Fondation Auschwitz (Auschwitz Foundation)

Founded in 1980 by Amicale des Ex-Prisonniers Belge as a study and documentation centre to preserve the memory of the prisoners of Auschwitz.

Activities: Operates nationally and internationally in the fields of education, the arts, law and human rights, and holocaust studies, through self-conducted programmes, awarding prizes, conferences and issuing publications. Awards the annual Auschwitz Foundation Prize of €2,500 for an original and unpublished text that makes an important contribution to the political, economic, social or historical analysis of the world of the Nazi concentration camps and the processes leading to its creation.

Geographical Area of Activity: Europe.

Publications: *Bulletin Trimestriel de la Fondation Auschwitz/ Driemaandelijks Tijdschrift*; *International Journal*; *Quarterly Bulletin*; *Sporen*; teaching materials.

Board of Directors: Baron Paul Halter (Pres.).

Principal Staff: Sec.-Gen. Henri Goldberg.

Address: 65 rue des Tanneurs, 1000 Brussels.

Telephone: (2) 512-79-98; **Fax:** (2) 512-58-84; **Internet:** www .auschwitz.be; **e-mail:** fondation@auschwitz.be.

Fondation Bernheim (Bernheim Foundation)

Established in 1974 for general charitable purposes.

Activities: Operates in the fields of education, culture, peace, and economic and social issues, through offering grants, awarding prizes, including a biennial literature prize worth €5,000, holding conferences and seminars, publications, scholarships and student assistance. Also supports entrepreneurial initiatives and medical research, including a chair in entrepreneurial studies at the Université Libre de Bruxelles.

Geographical Area of Activity: Belgium.

Publications: Information brochures; Annual Report.

Finance: Annual grant disbursement more than €2,000,000 (2008).

Board of Directors: Françoise Thys-Clément (Pres.); Baron Raymond Vaxelaire (Vice-Pres. and Treas.); Baron Robert Tollet (Vice-Pres.).

Principal Staff: Gen. Delegate Micheline Mardulyn;.

Address: 2 pl. de l'Albertine, 1000 Brussels.

Telephone: (2) 213-14-99; **Fax:** (2) 213-14-95; **Internet:** www .fondationbernheim.be; **e-mail:** fondationbernheim@online .be.

Fondation Boghossian (Boghossian Foundation)

Established in 1992 by Robert Boghossian and his sons to support a better life for young people in Armenia and Lebanon.

Activities: Operates projects for young people in Armenia and Lebanon in the areas of welfare, education, art and culture, and medicine. Also offers the President of Armenia Prizes for young people in the arts and sciences.

Geographical Area of Activity: Armenia and Lebanon.

Advisory Committee: Jean Boghossian (Chair.); Albert Boghossian (Treas.).

Principal Staff: Dir Diane Hennebert.

Address: Villa Empain, 67 ave Franklin Roosevelt, 1000 Brussels.

Telephone: (2) 534-60-85; **Fax:** (2) 537-43-24; **Internet:** www
.fondationboghossian.com; **e-mail:** hennebert@skynet.be.

Fondation Evens Stichting (Evens Foundation)

Active since 1996; founded by late diamond trader and philanthropist Georges Evens.

Activities: Initiates, develops and supports projects that encourage citizens and states to live together harmoniously in a peaceful Europe. Promotes respect for diversity, individual and collective, and seeks to uphold physical, psychological and ethical integrity.

Geographical Area of Activity: European Union countries, particularly Belgium, France and Poland.

Restrictions: does not support unsolicited applications.

Publications: *Learning for Change in a Multicultural Society; Europe's New Racism? Causes, Manifestations and Solutions; Catalogue 'Community Art Collaboration 2002', Floating Territories – a journal.*

Board of Directors: Corinne Evens (founder and Hon. Pres.); Luc Luyten (Chair.).

Principal Staff: Gen. Prog. Man. Guido Knops.

Address: Stoopstraat 1, 2000 Antwerp.

Telephone: (3) 231-39-70; **Fax:** (3) 233-94-32; **Internet:** www
.evensfoundation.be; **e-mail:** ef@evensfoundation.be.

Fondation Francqui (Francqui Foundation)

Founded in 1932 by Emile Francqui and Herbert Hoover to promote the development of higher education and scientific research in Belgium.

Activities: Operates in the field of higher education. Confers the annual Prix Francqui on a Belgian under 50 years of age, who has made a notable advance in the fields of science, humanities or medicine. Also awards Francqui Professorships each year, inviting two scholars from each Belgian university and three foreign professors to teach in Belgium under the Foundation's auspices. Provides annual fellowships to selected young Belgian academics to enable them to study abroad, mainly in the USA.

Geographical Area of Activity: Belgium.

Restrictions: Grants only available to Belgian nationals.

Board of Directors: Mark Eyskens (Chair.); Herman Balthazar (Vice-Chair.); Viscount Étienne Davignon (Vice-Chair.).

Principal Staff: Exec. Dir Prof. Dr Pierre van Moerbeke.

Address: 1B rue Defacqz, 1000 Brussels.

Telephone: (2) 539-33-94; **Fax:** (2) 537-29-21; **Internet:** www
.francquifoundation.be; **e-mail:** francquifoundation@skynet
.be.

Fondation Marcel Hicter (Marcel Hicter Foundation)

Established in 1980 to promote and carry out activities contributing to the socio-cultural development of the French community in Belgium, and to promote co-operation at a European and international level in the area of culture.

Activities: Operates in the field of the arts and culture, formerly through organizing the European Diploma in Cultural Project Management, which operates in three countries; training cultural managers from 36 countries; and managing, on behalf of the Council of Europe, mobility grants for cultural management experts and trainees. Also organizes conferences, carries out research and issues publications.

Geographical Area of Activity: Central, Eastern and Western Europe, the Russian Federation and Central Africa.

Publications: *Citoyens et Pouvoirs en Europe; Another brick in the wall, A critical review of cultural management education in Europe; Arts management in turbulent times: Adaptable quality management; Survey on Funding opportunities for international cultural co-operation in and with South-eastern Europe; The arts, politics and change. Participative cultural policymaking in South-Eastern Europe;* guidance on heritage assessment.

Board of Directors: Xavier Mabille (Pres.); E. Grosjean (Sec.); J. P. Braine (Treas.).

Principal Staff: Dir Jean-Pierre Deru.

Address: Association Marcel Hicter pour la Démocratie culturelle, 27 rue du Belvédère, 1050 Brussels.

Telephone: (2) 641-89-80; **Fax:** (2) 641-89-81; **Internet:** www
.fondation-hicter.org; **e-mail:** contact@fondation-hicter.org.

Fondation P&V

Established in 2000 by the company P&V Assurances to work with young people.

Activities: Works with and for young people.

Board: Mark Elchardus (Chair.).

Principal Staff: Exec. Dir Marnic Speltdoorn.

Address: Rue Royale 151, 1210 Brussels.

Telephone: (2) 250-91-24; **Fax:** (2) 250-91-45; **Internet:** www
.fondationpv.be; **e-mail:** fondation@pv.be.

Fondation Paul-Henri Spaak—Stichting Paul-Henri Spaak (Paul-Henri Spaak Foundation)

Founded in 1973 by Vicomte Étienne Davignon, Fernand Dehousse, Auguste Edmond De Schryver, André de Staercke, Walter Ganshof van der Meersch, Marcel Grégoire, André Jaumotte, Comte Georges Moens de Fernig, Jean Rey, Paul Smets and Fernand Spaak to constitute a centre of thought and action to prolong the European work of Paul-Henri Spaak, particularly in the field of the external relations of the European Community (now the EU); to promote any activity contributing to a better understanding of the European ideal and associating new generations with the construction of Europe.

Activities: Established to operate nationally, internationally and on a European level in the field of international relations and economic affairs, through self-conducted programmes, research, conferences and publications. It encourages education and scientific research related to its aims, through creating specialized professorships in European Union external affairs to be occupied by distinguished foreigners; international fellowships and scholarships; and the sponsoring of publications and diffusion of documentation and information. Lectures and seminars as well as regional, national and international congresses are organized. Also awards a science prize.

Geographical Area of Activity: International.

Administrative Council: Vicomte Étienne Davignon (Pres.).

Principal Staff: Sec.-Gen. François Danis.

Address: 62 ave George Bergmann, bte 4, 1050 Brussels.

Telephone: (2) 672-08-05; **Internet:** www.fondationspaak
.org; **e-mail:** fond.spaak@skynet.be.

Fonds InBev-Baillet Latour (InBev-Baillet Latour Fund)

Created by Count Alfred de Baillet Latour in 1974.

Activities: The Fund encourages human accomplishments in the scientific, educational or artistic fields, and awards prizes, research grants, travel and gifts. Activities are in four fields: clinical research, training, Belgian heritage and Olympic spirit.

Geographical Area of Activity: World-wide.

Board of Directors: Baron Jan Huyghebaert (Pres.).

Principal Staff: Gen. Sec. Sir Alain De Waele.

Address: Brouwerijplein 1, 3000 Leuven.

Telephone: (16) 27-61-59; **Fax:** (16) 50-61-59; **Internet:** www
.inbevbailletlatour.com.

Fonds National de la Recherche Scientifique—FNRS (National Fund for Scientific Research)

Founded in 1928 by King Albert I to promote scientific research in Belgium.

Activities: Provides subsidies each year to scientists or research workers to enable them to continue their investigations, and awards about 800 grants annually to university students in the field of science. Also provides more than 200 research posts of limited duration to qualified research workers and supports the attendance at scientific meetings and conferences of Belgian researchers. Enables qualified research workers to undertake short visits abroad to familiarize themselves with new developments and techniques in scientific research. Awards prizes for achievement in the field of research. Also administers the Fund for Medical Scientific Research, the Fund for Fundamental Collective Research, the Inter-University Institute for Nuclear Sciences and the Industry and Agriculture Research Training Fund.

Geographical Area of Activity: Belgium.

Publications: Annual Report; *La Lettre du FNRS*.

Administrative Council: Bernard Rentier (Pres.); Philippe Vincke (Vice-Pres.).

Principal Staff: Sec.-Gen. Dr Véronique Halloin.

Address: 5 rue d'Egmont, 1000 Brussels.

Telephone: (2) 504-92-11; **Fax:** (2) 504-92-92; **Internet:** www .frs-fnrs.be; **e-mail:** veronique.pirsoul@frs-fnrs.be.

Fonds Wetenschappelijk Onderzoek—Vlaanderen
(Research Foundation—Flanders)

Established in 1928 at the initiative of King Albert I to encourage and support fundamental scientific research.

Activities: Promotes and finances fundamental scientific research in the universities and in research institutions in Flanders (Belgium) in all fields of science, including medicine, technology, environmental studies, social sciences and the humanities, including law. Provides pre- and postdoctoral fellowships and grants for national and international research projects, contacts and co-operation.

Geographical Area of Activity: Flanders (Belgium).

Publications: Yearbook; newsletter; brochure; *Founders of Knowledge: 80 years of FWO; FWO Excellence Prizes*.

Finance: Annual expenditure €192,000,000 (2009).

Trustees: Prof. Mark Waer (Pres.) Alain Verschoren (Vice-Pres.).

Principal Staff: Sec.-Gen. Elisabeth Monard.

Address: Egmontstraat 5, 1000 Brussels.

Telephone: (2) 512-91-10; **Fax:** (2) 512-58-90; **Internet:** www .fwo.be; **e-mail:** fwo@fwo.be.

GAIA—Groupe d'Action dans l'Intérêt des Animaux
(Global Action in the Interest of Animals)

Established in 1992 by Ann de Greef and Michel Vandenbosch, for the support of animal rights.

Activities: Works for the cause of animal rights, through education, active campaigns, lobbying and the publication of informative materials. Promotes vegetarianism, campaigns against experimentation on animals for the production of cosmetics and for medical research and against maltreatment of animals in farming.

Geographical Area of Activity: Belgium.

Publications: *Animalibre*; *Vrijdier*; educational material.

Board: Michel Vandenbosch (Founder).

Principal Staff: Gen. Dir Ann De Greef.

Address: Ravensteingalerij 27, 1000 Brussels.

Telephone: (2) 245-29-50; **Fax:** (2) 215-09-43; **Internet:** www .gaia.be; **e-mail:** info@gaia.be.

Îles de Paix (Islands of Peace)

Founded in 1965 by Father Dominique Pire to ameliorate conditions for people living in the Southern regions of the world through food security and infrastructure development; and to educate people in more developed countries about life in the Southern hemisphere.

Activities: Operates internationally in the field of aid to less-developed countries, through self-conducted programmes carried out with partner organizations in West Africa (including Benin, Burkina Faso, Mali, Niger, and Togo) and South America (Bolivia and Ecuador). Also educates the public in Belgium about life in less-developed countries.

Geographical Area of Activity: West Africa and South America.

Publications: *Transitions* (quarterly); Annual Report; financial statements; reports and news-sheets.

Finance: Annual revenue and expenditure €2,857,943 (2009).

Trustees: Eric Tilman (Pres.).

Principal Staff: Sec.-Gen. Laurence Albert.

Address: 37 rue du Marché, 4500 Huy.

Telephone: (85) 23-02-54; **Fax:** (85) 23-42-64; **Internet:** www .ilesdepaix.org; **e-mail:** info@ilesdepaix.org.

Institut Européen Interuniversitaire de l'Action Sociale—IEIAS

Founded in 1970 to provide the study of social welfare and to encourage a uniform social welfare policy for all European countries.

Activities: Finances and conducts research into methods of supplying the needs (physical and psychological) of individuals in society; assesses the effect of different methods; maintains a library of approximately 67,000 articles and publications and a database; organizes seminars and courses; and issues publications.

Geographical Area of Activity: Europe.

Publications: *COMM* (English and French, 3 a year); seminar papers and other publications.

Finance: Annual budget approx. US $400,000.

Directors: Joseph Gillain (Pres.).

Principal Staff: CEO Bernard Kennes.

Address: 179 rue du Débarcadère, 6001 Marcinelle.

Telephone: (71) 44-72-11; **Fax:** (71) 47-11-04; **Internet:** www .ieias.be; **e-mail:** info@ieias.be.

International Yehudi Menuhin Foundation—IYMF

Founded byYehudi Menuhin in 1991. Aims to remind political, cultural and educational institutions of the central role of art and creativity in the whole personal and societal development process.

Activities: Maintains a network of 11 national structures based in Europe and Israel. Activities concentrate on promoting the arts at school (MUS-E programme); arts on stage (multicultural concerts and international artist residencies); arts and intercultural dialogue (ACE/Assembly of Culture of Europe). Also promotes music and the arts internationally; encourages exchanges and encounters between different cultures through the organization of events; promotes the representation of those cultures that are under threat by organizing a forum (the Assembly of Cultures of Europe); and co-ordinates cultural projects initiated by Yehudi Menuhin, and disseminates them throughout the world.

Geographical Area of Activity: World-wide.

Restrictions: Funds are dedicated only to the development of the Foundation's programmes and the training of MUS-E artists and co-ordinators.

Publications: Online newsletter; CDs; DVDs; books.

Finance: Mainly supported by public subsidies, event sponsors and donations.

Board of Administration: Enrique Baron Crespo (Pres.).

Principal Staff: Exec. Vice-Pres. Marianne Poncelet.

Address: 61 chaussée de la Hulpe, 1180 Brussels.

Telephone: (2) 673-35-04; **Fax:** (2) 672-52-99; **Internet:** www .menuhin-foundation.com; **e-mail:** marianne.poncelet@ menuhin-foundation.com.

Köning Boudewijnstichting/Fondation Roi Baudouin
(King Baudouin Foundation)

Founded in 1976 to commemorate the 25th anniversary of King Baudouin's coronation, the Foundation is an independent public welfare institution, which aims 'to carry out initiatives to improve the life of the population, including measures of an economic, social, scientific and cultural nature'; to stimulate solidarity and generosity; and to act as a catalyst for sustainable change.

Activities: Operates in Belgium and internationally, supporting projects in the areas of justice, democracy and diversity. Current themes include migration and a multicultural society; poverty and social justice; civil society and social commitment; health; philanthropy; the Balkans; and Central Africa. Also organizes round tables, forums and seminars, works in partnership with governmental and non-governmental organizations, and issues publications.

Geographical Area of Activity: International.

Publications: Annual Report and financial statement; newsletter; reports and studies.

Finance: Receives a grant from the Belgian National Lottery.

Board of Governors: Francoise Tulkens (Chair.); Clarisse Albert (Vice-Chair.); Luc Coen (Vice-Chair.).

Principal Staff: Man. Dir Luc Tayart de Borms.

Address: 21 rue Bréderode, 1000 Brussels.

Telephone: (2) 511-18-40; **Fax:** (2) 511-52-21; **Internet:** www.kbs-frb.be; **e-mail:** info@kbs-frb.be.

Fernand Lazard Stichting (Fernand Lazard Foundation)

Founded in 1949 and administered by representatives of seven Belgian universities; promotes continuing education.

Activities: Makes awards to university students from the European member states for study in Belgium to fund relocation costs and to finance study at universities or research centres in Belgium and other European Union countries.

Geographical Area of Activity: Europe.

Administrative Council: Alain Siaens (Pres.); Pierre Lefebvre (Vice-Pres.).

Principal Staff: Chair. Alain Siaens.

Address: 100 ave de Merode, 1330 Rixensart.

Telephone: (2) 687-21-40; **Fax:** (2) 687-21-40; **Internet:** www.redweb.be/lazard/index.html; **e-mail:** fernandlazard@hotmail.com.

Madariaga European Foundation

Established to work towards prosperity, peace and solidarity through strengthening European union.

Activities: Operates two main project areas, conflict prevention, and health, organizing conferences on the European Union and other relevant issues. Issues books and papers.

Geographical Area of Activity: Europe.

Publications: Books and papers.

Finance: Total assets €757,762 (2007); income €646,960, expenditure €664,236 (2007).

Administrative Council: Javier Solana (Pres.); Jean-Luc Dehaene (Vice-Pres.); Jean Courtin (Treas.).

Principal Staff: Man. Dir Pierre Defraigne.

Address: Ave de la Joyeuse Entrée 14/2, 1040 Brussels.

Telephone: (2) 209-62-10; **Fax:** (2) 209-62-11; **Internet:** www.madariaga.org; **e-mail:** info@madariaga.org.

Open Society Institute—Brussels

Established in 1997 as the representative office of the Open Society Foundations to the European Union (EU) and West European partner countries.

Activities: Works to advocate open society values (transparency and rule of law, human rights and fundamental freedoms, and democratic principles) with regard to EU policies; also assists in collaboration between the Open Society Foundations network (qq.v.) and the EU and other intergovernmental agencies.

Principal Staff: Dir Heather Grabbe.

Address: 9-13 rue d'Idalie, Brussels 1050.

Telephone: (2) 505-46-46; **Fax:** (2) 502-46-46; **Internet:** www.soros.org/initiatives/brussels; **e-mail:** osi-brussels@osi-eu.org.

Oxfam-en-Belgique

Part of the Oxfam confederation of organizations (qq.v.).

Activities: Operates internationally in the areas of sustainability, health and welfare, aid to less-developed countries and education.

Geographical Area of Activity: International.

Address: 60 rue des Quatre Vents, 1080 Brussels.

Telephone: (2) 501-67-00; **Internet:** www.oxfam.be; **e-mail:** oxfamsol@oxfamsol.be.

Pesticide Action Network—Europe

Established in 1987. Brings together consumer, public health, and environmental organizations, trade unions, women groups and farmers. Main purpose is to reduce, and where possible eliminate, dependency on chemical pesticides and to support safe sustainable pest control methods.

Activities: Operates in the field of the environment, with projects in the areas of biodiversity, pesticides, agriculture, chemicals and testing levels of pesticides in supermarket produce.

Geographical Area of Activity: Europe.

Address: 1 rue de la Pépinière, 1000 Brussels.

Telephone: (2) 503 08 37; **Fax:** (2) 402 30 42; **Internet:** www.pan-europe.info; **e-mail:** henriette@pan-europe.info; hans@pan-europe.info.

Ruralité Environnement Développement—RED (Rurality Environment Development)

Founded in 1980 to encourage communication between those involved in rural development throughout Europe.

Activities: Organizes conferences and seminars in the fields of economic development, planning and cultural heritage in rural areas. The organization chairs and co-ordinates the European Countryside Movement, and is President of the Advisory Committee on Rural Development of the European Commission of the European Union. The organization has members in 15 countries.

Geographical Area of Activity: Europe.

Restrictions: No grants are made.

Publications: *RED Dossier* (2 a year); *Eurobrèves* (newsletter); seminar papers.

Board of Directors: Gérard Peltre (Pres.); Felipe González de Canales, Alfons Hausen, Camilo Mortagua, Patrick Senault (Vice-Pres); Alain Delchef (Treas.).

Principal Staff: Dir Patrice Collignon.

Address: 304 rue des Potiers, 6717 Attert.

Telephone: (63) 23-04-90; **Fax:** (63) 23-04-99; **Internet:** www.ruraleurope.org; **e-mail:** infored@ruraleurope.org.

Service Civil International—SCI

Founded in 1920 by Pierre Ceresole to provide opportunities for men and women, young and old, irrespective of their race, nationality, creed or politics to join together in giving useful voluntary service to the community in a spirit of friendship and international understanding, with the aim of promoting peace, international understanding and solidarity, social justice, sustainable development and concern for the environment.

Activities: Operates internationally by providing volunteers for community service and work-camp exchanges world-wide. Projects include the East-West Working Group. Has more than 40 branches and groups in Europe, Asia, Africa and North America, plus an affiliate in Australia. A second International Secretariat, serving Asia, is based in Sri Lanka. Has consultative status with UNESCO and the Council of Europe.

Geographical Area of Activity: International.

Restrictions: Not a grant-making organization.

Publications: Newsletter.

International Executive Committee: Mihai Crisan (Pres.); Heinz Gabathuler (Vice-Pres. and Treas.).

Principal Staff: Int. Co-ordinator Margherita Serafina; Finance and Admin Officer Ossi Lemstrom.

Address: St Jacobsmarkt 82, 2000 Antwerp.

Telephone: (3) 266-57-27; **Fax:** (3) 232-03-44; **Internet:** www .sciint.org; **e-mail:** iec@scimail.org.

Solidar

Established in 1948 as International Workers Aid.

Activities: *A European network of 56 NGOs based in 25 countries working to advance social justice in Europe and world-wide. Voices the concerns of its member organizations to the European Union (EU) and international institutions across the policy sectors of social affairs, international co-operation and lifelong learning.*

Geographical Area of Activity: Europe.

Publications: *Weekly Round Up (e-news bulletin); Activity Report; 60 years of SOLIDAR* book; Decent Work and Quality Jobs in Europe – series of case studies on different aspects and recommendations for EU decision makers; report on Global Social Protection; *Global Network Report on Decent Work and Millennium Development Goals; Decent Work Decent Life* case studies.

Board of Directors: Josef Weidenholzer (Pres.); Francisca Sauquillo (Vice-Pres.); Jean-Marc Roirant (Treas.).

Principal Staff: Sec.-Gen. Conny Reuter.

Address: 22 rue du Commerce, 1000 Brussels.

Telephone: (2) 500-10-20; **Fax:** (2) 500-10-30; **Internet:** www .solidar.org; **e-mail:** solidar@solidar.org.

Universitaire Stichting (University Foundation)

Founded in 1920 to promote scientific progress.

Activities: Operates in the field of higher education, through grants to associations and individuals and for the publication of scientific works and periodicals. Participates in the awarding of the Emile Bernheim European Prizes and the Fernand Collin Prize for Law. The Foundation also maintains a university club with lecture room.

Geographical Area of Activity: Europe.

Publications: *Annual University Statistics for Belgium; Akkadica; Analecta Bollandiana; Annales d'histoire d'art et d'archéologie; Anthropologie et Préhistoire; Antiquité Classique; Augustiniana; Belgian Journal of Botany; Belgian Journal of English Language and Literature; Belgian Journal of Entomology; Belgian Journal of Linguistics; Belgian Journal of Zoology.*

Board of Directors: Prof. Jacques Willems (Pres.).

Principal Staff: Exec. Dir Eric de Keuleneer.

Address: 11 rue d'Egmont, 1000 Brussels.

Telephone: (2) 545-04-00; **Fax:** (2) 513-64-11; **Internet:** www .universitairestichting.be; **e-mail:** fu.us@ universityfoundation.be.

World Animal Handicap Foundation—WAHF

Founded in 1992 to care for disabled animals using adapted orthopaedic therapy.

Activities: Works with veterinary surgeons, pet clinics and hospitals, animal protection associations, pet owners and others to further its aims.

Geographical Area of Activity: International.

Publications: *WAHF News* (quarterly).

Finance: Funded by charities, gifts and membership fees.

Principal Staff: Chair. G. de Beauffort; Vice-Chair. M. Mommer-Horikoshi; Sec. P. Vanhamme.

Address: 40 square Marie-Louise, bte 22, 1000 Brussels.

Telephone: (2) 230-76-46; **Internet:** wahf.over-blog.com; **e-mail:** asbl.wahf@chello.be.

Benin

FOUNDATIONS, TRUSTS AND NON-PROFIT ORGANIZATIONS

Centre Pan-Africain de Prospective Sociale (Pan-African Centre for Social Prospects)

Founded in 1987 by Association Mondiale de Prospective Sociale.

Activities: Undertakes research and training programmes linked to social and development issues; trains young professionals as future leaders in Africa in the areas of social policy, economics, communication, consumer protection, environmental protection and management; facilitates the exchange of business and technological information; and supports NGOs involved in development projects and programmes, and socio-economic projects. The Centre also helped found the African Humanitarian Initiative to assist refugees with food and medicines.

Geographical Area of Activity: Africa.

Publications: *Actes des Colloques et Séminaires*; Annual Report.

Principal Staff: Pres. Prof. Albert Tevoedjre.

Address: BP 1501, Porto Novo.

Telephone: 21-44-36; **Fax:** 21-44-36; **Internet:** www.tevoedjre.com; **e-mail:** cppsamps@intnet.bj.

Fondation de l'Entrepreneurship du Bénin (Enterprise Foundation of Benin)

Aims to help establish and promote new businesses and private companies in Benin.

Activities: Provides assistance and support to entrepreneurs (both nationals and foreigners) who wish to invest in Benin. Organizes seminars, offers advice on marketing and management skills and strategies, training, and the opportunity to contact other suppliers and potential customers around the world. Runs an annual entrepreneurial competition for young people, funded by the Benin National Lottery and the Canadian International Development Agency. Manages the Place du Québec socio-cultural centre.

Geographical Area of Activity: Benin.

Principal Staff: Dir Pierre Dovonou Lokossou.

Address: Pl. du Québec, 08 BP 1155, Cotonou.

Telephone: 30-53-52; **Fax:** 31-37-26; **e-mail:** dovonoupierre@yahoo.fr.

Groupe d'Action pour la Justice et l'Egalité Sociale—GAJES (Action Group for Justice and Social Equality)

Founded in 1990, a pressure group dedicated to achieving equality for all women in society.

Activities: Operates in the field of social justice, primarily in the field of social justice for women. Programmes include education of girls in the Mono department; the development and support of parent-teacher associations; and the Unité Documentaire Femmes et Développement, a documentation centre providing information sources for women on sustainable development and empowerment.

Geographical Area of Activity: Benin.

Council of Administration: Thècla Midiohouan Gbikpi (Founding Pres.); Marie-Odile Comlanvi-Hountondji (Pres.); Victoire Idossou Atihou Kegue (Vice-Pres.); Anne-Marie Falade Gandji (Treas.).

Principal Staff: Sec.-Gen. Gisèle Agboton.

Address: Immeuble OKETOKOUN, face Église Protestante Béthanie, Quartier Missessin Akpakpa, 04 BP 778, Cotonou.

Telephone: (229) 33-61-05; **Internet:** www.bj.refer.org/benin_ct/cop/gajes/accueil.htm; **e-mail:** ongajes_99@yahoo.com.

Bermuda

FOUNDATION CENTRE AND CO-ORDINATING BODY

Centre on Philanthropy

Membership organization set up in 1991 to promote a philanthropic philosophy in the community, and an attitude of giving, through information, seminars and dialogue with charities, the public, government and the business sector.

Activities: Acts as a resource and advocacy centre for Bermuda's charities and volunteers, promoting a philosophy of philanthropy in the community, through information, seminars and dialogue with its member charities, the public, the government and the corporate sector. Provides information, training workshops and seminars for its members. Resources include databases of charities and volunteers and a library of educational and reference materials.

Geographical Area of Activity: Bermuda.

Publications: Newsletter; guides for charities; town hall meeting; rotary speech (annually).

Board of Directors: Brian Madeiros (Chair.); Graham Pewter (Dep. Chair); Kathleen Moniz (Sec.); Jane Edgett (Treas.).

Principal Staff: Exec. Dir Pamela Barit Nolan.

Address: POB HM 3217, Hamilton HM NX; Sterling House, 16 Wesley St, Hamilton.

Telephone: 236-7706; **Fax:** 236-7693; **Internet:** www.centreonphilanthropy.org; **e-mail:** info@centreonphilanthropy.org.

FOUNDATIONS, TRUSTS AND NON-PROFIT ORGANIZATIONS

International Charitable Fund of Bermuda—ICFB

Formed in 1994 and co-sponsored by the Centre on Philanthropy (q.v.) and PricewaterhouseCoopers (formerly Price Waterhouse) to promote and support the purposes and activities of not-for-profit charitable organizations in Bermuda through tax-deductible gifts from US taxpayers.

Activities: Makes grants to non-profit organizations in Bermuda operating exclusively for charitable, scientific or educational purposes.

Geographical Area of Activity: Bermuda.

Board of Trustees: David Lang (Pres. and Treas.); Mairi Redmond (Sec.).

Principal Staff: Capital G Private Banking Relationship Man. Suzanne Martin.

Address: c/o Capital G Private Banking, POB HM 1322, Hamilton HM FX.

Telephone: 294-2570; **Fax:** 294-3165; **Internet:** www.centreonphilanthropy.org/icfb; **e-mail:** ICFB@capitalg.bm.

Bolivia

FOUNDATIONS, TRUSTS AND NON-PROFIT ORGANIZATIONS

Fundación Amigos de la Naturaleza (Friends of Nature Foundation)

Founded in November 1988 by a small group of naturalists located in Santa Cruz for the conservation of biodiversity in Bolivia.

Activities: A private non-profit organization aiming to protect biodiversity in Bolivia and countries bordering Bolivia, through self-conducted programmes, research, offering scholarships and fellowships, and through conferences.

Geographical Area of Activity: South America.

Publications: *Flora de la region del Parque Nacional Amboro, Bolivia; Biodiversidad la riqueza de Bolivia.*

Trustees: Hermes Justiniano Suárez (Pres.); León Merlot (Vice-Pres.).

Principal Staff: Exec. Dir Karin Columba.

Address: Km 7 1/2 Doble Via la Guardia, Casilla 2241.

Telephone: (3) 3556800; **Fax:** (3) 3547383; **Internet:** www.fan-bo.org; **e-mail:** fan@fan-bo.org.

Fundación Sartawi (Sartawi Foundation)

Founded in 1989 by the Lutheran Church, and part of Oikocredit, the Ecumenical Development Co-operative Society; aims to help the rural population of Bolivia.

Activities: Provides technical assistance to groups of people with little access to resources, with an emphasis on rural areas, facilitating economic initiatives and strengthening the artisan industry to increase job opportunities for women. Runs programmes relating to agricultural forestation in valleys and areas of the *altiplano*, micro-enterprises and providing easier access to credit for those in need.

Geographical Area of Activity: Bolivia.

Publications: Annual Report.

Finance: Annual revenue US $2,863,895, expenditure $2,531,260 (2007).

Board of Directors: Dr Maria Elena Soruco Vidal (Pres.); Claudia Kuruner (Sec.); Gonzalo Endara de Ugarte (Treas.).

Principal Staff: Man. Dir Marcio Oblitas Fernández; Finance Dir Gustavo Velásquez Bejarano.

Address: Héroes del Acre No. 1734, esq. Capitán Castrillo, Zona San Pedro, La Paz.

Telephone: (2) 420341; **Fax:** (2) 419598; **Internet:** www.sartawisayariy.org; **e-mail:** moblitas@sembrarsartawi.org.

Bosnia and Herzegovina

FOUNDATIONS, TRUSTS AND NON-PROFIT ORGANIZATIONS

Open Society Fund—Bosnia-Herzegovina

Founded in November 1992 to restore a belief in the values of an open society; encourage individuals important to the preservation of an open society to remain in the country; foster an atmosphere in which the prospect of a new and valuable society remains viable; and offer hope and a sense of perspective to younger generations. An independent foundation, part of the Soros foundations network, which aims to foster political pluralism and reform economic structures to encourage private enterprise and a market economy.

Activities: Provides financial support to assist institutions working towards the development of an open society. Funds educational programmes, including the printing of textbooks, awarding scholarships to university students and initiating alternative educational programmes. Supports media institutions, and has established an e-mail network. Humanitarian programme provides medical assistance, food parcels and employment opportunities. In the field of the arts and culture, supports local artists, and promotes visits to Sarajevo by famous foreign artists. Also operates grant programmes within the fields of women's rights and empowerment and the development of the Roma community. Collaborates with other Soros institutions on projects such as the Open Society City of Sarajevo Project to restore damaged schools and cultural institutions.

Geographical Area of Activity: Bosnia and Herzegovina.

Publications: Reports.

Board of Trustees: Mirza Kusljugić (Chair.).

Principal Staff: Exec. Dir Dobrila Govedarica; Prog. Coordinator Bogdan Popovic.

Address: Marsala Tita 19/III, 71000 Sarajevo.

Telephone: (33) 444488; **Fax:** (33) 444488; **Internet:** www .soros.org.ba; **e-mail:** osf@soros.org.ba.

Botswana

FOUNDATION CENTRE AND CO-ORDINATING BODY

Botswana Council of Non-Governmental Organisations—BOCONGO

Established in 1995. Aims to assist and support NGOs in Botswana to further the development process.

Activities: Facilitates the development of NGOs, and works to ensure their participation in the ongoing development process in Botswana; enables NGOs, the Government, the private sector and other development partners to network effectively, and promotes improved communication and the dissemination of information; aims to take on a leading role in policy advocacy and lobbying to allow NGOs to work as a united body on issues of national interest.

Geographical Area of Activity: Botswana.

Publications: programme reports (online); quarterly newsletters.

Executive Committee: Rev. Biggie Butale (Chair.); David Mbulawa (Treas.).

Principal Staff: Exec. Sec. Rev. Mosewen Simane.

Address: Bonokopila House, Plot 53957, Machel Dr., Gaborone; Private Bag 00418, Gaborone.

Telephone: 3911319; **Fax:** 3912935; **Internet:** www.bocongo.org.bw; **e-mail:** bocongo@bocongo.org.bw.

FOUNDATIONS, TRUSTS AND NON-PROFIT ORGANIZATIONS

Chobe Wildlife Trust

Founded in 1988 to assist in the conservation of the Chobe National Park and its immediate surroundings.

Activities: Works to achieve a local response to global sustainability as described at the Rio 1992 summit by way of environmental education, community-based natural resources management and conservation research and management, including the protection of the rhinoceros; assists the Botswana Department of Wildlife; campaigns against poaching.

Geographical Area of Activity: Chobe District (north-eastern Botswana).

Publications: *Serondella News* (newsletter).

Trustees: S. Griesel (Chair.).

Principal Staff: CEO Machana Shamukuni.

Address: POB 55, Kasane, Chobe District.

Telephone: 6250516; **Fax:** 6250223; **Internet:** www.envngo.co.bw/pages/cwt.html; **e-mail:** cwt@info.bw.

Brazil

FOUNDATION CENTRES AND CO-ORDINATING BODIES

GIFE—Grupo de Institutos, Fundações e Empresas
(Group of Institutes, Foundations and Enterprises)

Established in 1995 as a membership organization representing companies and foundations in Brazil. Aims to improve and disseminate the concepts and practical means of using private funds for the good of the community.

Activities: Composed of institutes, foundations and corporations that are active within the third sector in Brazil. Provides member organizations with information, and a centre where they can exchange knowledge and experience through meetings, seminars, courses and forums. Establishes links between similar local and national organizations, aiming to create an environment to enable private businesses to invest in community development. Maintains a national reference centre, which contains materials on philanthropic knowledge and practices.

Geographical Area of Activity: Brazil.

Publications: *Censo GIFE* (biennial); others.

Governing Board: Denise Aguiar Álvarez (Pres.).

Principal Staff: Sec.-Gen. Fernando Rossetti.

Address: Av. Brigadeiro Faria Lima 2413, 1° andar, Conjunto 11, Jardim America, 01.452-000 São Paulo, SP.

Telephone: (11) 3816-1209; **Fax:** (11) 3816-1209; **Internet:** www.gife.org.br; **e-mail:** redegife@gife.org.br.

WINGS—Worldwide Initiatives for Grantmaker Support

Established in 2000 to support world-wide network between, and development of, associations of grant-making organizations and to support organizations serving philanthropy.

Activities: Peer-learning events for members; regional meetings; global forum; knowledge generation and dissemination; e-library. Has 147 network participants in 54 countries on every continent except Antarctica.

Geographical Area of Activity: International.

Publications: *WINGS* (newsletter); case studies of grantmaker associations (2003); *Community Foundation Global Status Report* (biennially); *Global Institutional Philanthropy-Preliminary Report*; *WINGS Strategic Plan 2011-2014*; *Wings Global Status Report on Community Foundations* (biannually).

Principal Staff: CEO/Exec. Dir Helena Monteiro.

Address: Av. 9 de Julho 5143, Conjunto 61, Jardim Paulistano, 01407-7300 São Paulo, SP.

Telephone: (11) 3078-7299; **Internet:** www.wingsweb.org; **e-mail:** info@wingsweb.org.

FOUNDATIONS, TRUSTS AND NON-PROFIT ORGANIZATIONS

Brazil Foundation

Established by Leona Forman in 2000; focuses on generating resources for projects that enable improvement of social and economic conditions of Brazilians.

Activities: Operates in the fields of social welfare, culture, medicine and health, education, and human rights, working in partnership with other charitable organizations. Maintains an office in New York, USA.

Geographical Area of Activity: Brazil.

Restrictions: Grants are made only in Brazil.

Publications: Annual Report; newsletter archives.

Finance: Total assets US $1,251,422 (2008).

Board of Directors: Leona Forman (Pres.); Marcello Hallake (Gen. Counsel); Roberta Mazzariol (Treas.).

Principal Staff: CEO Patricia Lobaccaro.

Address: Av. Calógeras, 15°–13° andar, 20.030-070 Rio de Janeiro, RJ.

Telephone: (21) 2532-3029; **Fax:** (21) 2532-2998; **Internet:** www.brazilfoundation.org; **e-mail:** info@brazilfoundation.org.

ChildHope Brasil

Founded in 1986 in Guatemala to provide information about the problems of 'street children'—homeless young people living and working in the streets—and previously known as the Childhope International Foundation. Now a network of independent regional and national groups operating in the United Kingdom and Europe, Asia and Central and South America.

Activities: Provides support to other agencies involved in the provision of services and the operation of programmes, such as AIDS prevention, which cater for children in their own communities. Projects include support for pre-school care facilities.

Geographical Area of Activity: Brazil.

Publications: *Let Us Speak* (2 a year); *Our Child-Our Hope* (2 a year); *Study Ideas* (2 a year); numerous books.

Board of Directors: Dayse Tozzato (Pres.).

Principal Staff: Sec. Grace Bürguer.

Address: Av. General Justo 275, Sala 202, Bloco A, Palácio das ONGS, Centro, 20021-130 Rio de Janeiro, RJ.

Telephone: (21) 2544-7784; **Fax:** (21) 2240-7399; **Internet:** www.childhope.org.br; **e-mail:** childhope@childhope.org.br.

Federação Democrática Internacional de Mulheres
(Women's International Democratic Federation)

Founded in 1945 to prevent the recurrence of war and the resurgence of fascism for the sake of the well-being of women and children.

Activities: Defends women's rights in every area of life and every region of the world. Works for equal rights in society and in the workplace, and for women's rights to adequate health care and education. Also promotes world peace and democracy, and campaigns against racial inequality and discrimination. Organizes congresses. Has 126 affiliated organizations in 99 countries world-wide.

Geographical Area of Activity: International.

Publications: Bulletin.

Principal Staff: Pres. Marcia Campos.

Address: Rua Gulmarães Passos 422, Via Martana, 04.107-031 São Paulo, SP.

Telephone: (11) 5082-4418; **Internet:** www.fdim-widf.com.br; **e-mail:** fdimpresidencia@terra.com.br.

Fundação Abrinq pelos Direitos da Criança e do Adolescente (Abrinq Foundation for the Rights of Children and Adolescents)

Established in 1990 to support the fundamental rights of children and adolescents.

Activities: Extends support to projects that work to defend the basic rights of children and young people; promotes inter-sector co-operation and offers technical assistance; and equips NGOs, government agencies and community groups with information and documentation.

Geographical Area of Activity: Brazil.

Publications: Annual Report; *A History of Action 1990–97.*

Executive Board: Synésio Batista da Costa (Pres.); Carlos Antonio Tilkian (Vice-Pres.); Bento José Goncalves Alcoforado (Sec.).

Principal Staff: Exec. Admin. Heloisa Helena Silva de Oliveira.

Address: Av. Santo Amaro 1386, Vila Nova Conceição, 04.506-001 São Paulo, SP.

Telephone: (11) 3848-8799; **Internet:** www.fundabrinq.org.br; **e-mail:** amkt8@fundabrinq.org.br.

Fundação Armando Alvares Penteado—FAAP (Armando Alvares Penteado Foundation)

Founded in 1947 by Armando Alvares Penteado and Annie Alvares Penteado for exclusively pedagogical purposes. It aims to contribute, through teaching and related activities, to Brazil's cultural expansion and integration in the technological world of today.

Activities: Operates through the maintenance of a University, a Museum of Fine Arts and various Centres and Institutes. Courses are offered in science and technology, the arts and humanities, economics, business management and international relations. Awards scholarships.

Geographical Area of Activity: Brazil.

Publications: Magazine.

Board of Trustees: Celita Procopio de Carvalho (Pres.).

Principal Staff: Man. Dir Dr Antonio Bias Bueno Guillon.

Address: Rua Alagoas 903, Higienópolis, 01.242-902 São Paulo, SP.

Telephone: (11) 3662-1662; **Fax:** (11) 3662-7000; **Internet:** www.faap.br; **e-mail:** rel.internacional@faap.br.

Fundação ArcelorMittal Acesita (ArcelorMittal Acesita Foundation)

Established in 1944 as a private, non-profit organization by Acesita SA as Fundação Acesita para o Desenvolvimento Social; aims to promote local relevance, develop know-how, create innovative methods and strategies for local development, and share knowledge.

Activities: Operates in the Vale do Aço and Timóteo areas, funding social and economic development projects, including educational, cultural, environmental and community work. Created a Cultural Centre in Timóteo.

Geographical Area of Activity: Brazil (Vale do Aço).

Publications: Annual Report.

Board of Directors: Jean-Yves André Aimé Gilet (Chair.); José Armando de Figueiredo Campos (Vice-Chair.).

Principal Staff: CEO Jean-Philippe André Demaël; Sales and Logistics Dir Sérgio Augusto Cardoso Mendes; Technical and Development Dir Benoît Pierre Marie Carrier.

Address: Alameda 31 de Outubro 500, Centro Timóteo, 35180-014 Timóteo, MG.

Telephone: (31) 3849-7002; **Fax:** (31) 3849-7294; **Internet:** www.acesita.com.br/ing/fundacao/index.asp; **e-mail:** inox.fundacao@arcelormittal.com.br.

Fundação Banco do Brasil (Bank of Brazil Foundation)

Founded in 1985, dedicated to social community work in Brazil.

Activities: Promotes, assists and financially supports initiatives in a number of areas within urban and rural communities, including education, culture, health, social welfare, recreation and sports, and science and technology. Provides credit and technical support to other non-profit organizations and grassroots groups in Brazil, and promotes volunteerism and philanthropy.

Geographical Area of Activity: Brazil.

Publications: News articles; reports.

Board of Directors: Jorge Alfredo Streit (Pres.).

Principal Staff: Exec. Dir Eder Melo.

Address: SCN Quadra 1, Bloco A, 9 e 10 andares, Asa Norte, 70.711-900 Brasília, DF.

Telephone: (61) 3310-1900; **Fax:** (61) 3310-1966; **Internet:** www.fundacaobancodobrasil.org.br; **e-mail:** fbb@fbb.org.br.

Fundação O Boticário de Proteção à Natureza (Boticário Group Foundation)

Established in 1990 by Miguel Gellert Krigsner, founder of O Boticário, a cosmetics company, to conserve nature.

Activities: Protects natural areas and supports to projects by other organizations. Raises awareness about and mobilizes support for for nature conservation. Through its nature preserves, protects more than 11,000 hectares of natural Atlantic Forest and Cerrado remnants, and surrounding areas. In addition, encourages people to conserve natural areas, either via the Oásis Project or by supporting other organizations' projects, thereby protecting Brazilian biodiversity. Also promotes events such as the Brazilian Congress on Protected Areas. Created interactive Nature Station exhibitions, presenting the beauty and importance of Brazilian nature to urban populations.

Geographical Area of Activity: Brazil.

Council: Miguel Gellert Krigsner (Pres.).

Principal Staff: Pres. Dir Artur Noemio Grynbaum; Exec. Dir Maria de Lourdes Nunes; Man. Leide Yassuco Takahashi; Man. Ceres Loise Bertelli Gabardo.

Address: St Gonçalves Dias 225, Batel, 80240-340 Curitiba, PR.

Telephone: (41) 3340 2636; **Fax:** (41) 3340 2635; **Internet:** www.fundacaogrupoboticario.org.br; **e-mail:** contato@fundacaogrupoboticario.org.br.

Fundação Brasileira para a Conservação da Natureza (Brazilian Foundation for Nature Conservation)

Founded in 1958 by José Cândido de Melo Carvalho to promote management and conservation of natural areas and endangered species; environmental education; reforestation and aforestation projects; sustainable development projects; and scientific research applied to conservation.

Activities: Operates nationally, through self-conducted programmes, research, awarding prizes and offering training courses. Carries out projects in conjunction with national and international organizations; executes management plans for various national parks and ecological stations; co-ordinates campaigns for the preservation of endangered species, such as whales, turtles, Amazon manatees, the golden lion tamarin and woolly spider monkeys; and maintains an extensive library. Has about 5,000 members nationally and internationally.

Geographical Area of Activity: Brazil.

Publications: *Informativo FBCN* (newsletter); *Boletim FBCN* (annually).

Board of Trustees: Adm. Ibsen de Gusmão Câmara (Chair.).

Principal Staff: Pres. Jairo Cortes Costa.

Address: Rua Miranda Valverde 103, Botafogo, 22.281-020 Rio de Janeiro, RJ.

Telephone: (21) 2537-7565; **Fax:** (21) 2537-1343; **Internet:** www.fbcn.org.br; **e-mail:** fbcn@fbcn.org.br.

Fundação Gaia (Gaia Foundation)

Established in June 1987 by the environmentalist José A. Lutzenberger to promote sustainable development.

Activities: Operates in the Brazilian state of Rio Grande do Sul in the field of protection of the environment, by providing advisory services, participating in conferences, offering training courses and issuing publications. Promotes sustainable development, working with regenerative agriculture, environmental education, protection of biodiversity, conservation of the cultural identity of minorities, and the use of 'soft' technologies.

Geographical Area of Activity: Brazil.

Restrictions: No grants available.

Publications: *Ecológica*; *Fruticultura*; *Sanidade Animal na Agroecologia*; *A Teoria da Trofobiose*; publications in English, German and other languages; Annual Reports.

Finance: Financed by private donations, consultancies, projects, courses and sale of products.

Trustees: Lara Josette W. Lutzenberger (Pres.); Franco A. Werlang (Vice-Pres.).

Address: Rua Jacinto Gomes 39, Barrio Santana, 90.040-270 Porto Alegre, Rio Grande do Sul.

Telephone: (51) 3331-3105; **Fax:** (51) 3330-3567; **Internet:** www.fgaia.org.br; **e-mail:** sede@fgaia.org.br.

Fundação Iochpe

Established in 1989 by Iochpe-Maxion SA.

Activities: Aims to promote the development of people's full potential and improve the quality of life of the people and communities in which the founding company operates, including funding not-for-profit organizations active in the areas of education, culture and social welfare, with a specific focus on the education of at-risk children and young people. Also provides information and documentation to not-for-profit organizations, grassroots groups, international organizations and government agencies, as well as technical assistance and training for grassroots groups and other not-for-profit organizations.

Geographical Area of Activity: Argentina and Brazil.

Finance: Annual grants approx. US $1,000,000.

Board of Advisers: Ivoncy Ioschpe (Pres.); Mauro Knijnik (Vice-Pres.).

Principal Staff: Dir Pres. Evelyn Berg Ioschpe.

Address: Al. Tiete 618, Casa 1, Cerqueira César, 01.417-020 São Paulo, SP.

Telephone: (11) 3060-8388; **Fax:** (11) 3060-8388; **Internet:** www.fiochpe.org.br; **e-mail:** fundacao.iochpe@fiochpe.org.br.

Fundação Roberto Marinho (Robert Marinho Foundation)

Established in 1977 by journalist Roberto Marinho to provide quality education to Brazilians.

Activities: Undertakes activities on a national as well as an international level primarily focusing on the field of education, and several other areas including national heritage, and ecology and conservation. Operates in partnership with other organizations focusing on similar issues to fund and execute projects such as literacy programmes for adults and children. Offers funds for music, dance and national museums; awards annual prizes for young scientists; and devises ecological campaigns for environment protection.

Geographical Area of Activity: Brazil.

Board of Directors: José Roberto Marinho (Pres.).

Principal Staff: Sec.-Gen. Hugo Barreto.

Address: Rua Santa Alexandrina 336, Rio Comprido, 20.261-232 Rio de Janeiro, RJ.

Telephone: (21) 2502-3233; **Internet:** www.frm.org.br; **e-mail:** imprensa@frm.org.br.

Fundação Museu do Homem Americano—FUMDHAM (Foundation Museum of American Man)

Established in 1986 to encourage scientific research, ecology conservation and sustainable development.

Activities: Operates nationally and internationally, with a focus on supporting less-developed regions in Brazil; other areas of focus are environment and conservation, sustainable development studies, education, economic and international affairs, science and technology, and medicine and health. Carries out self-conducted programmes, prizes, training courses and conferences. Also protects Serra da Capivara National Park and the Environmental Protection Area.

Geographical Area of Activity: Brazil.

Publications: *Fumdhamentos*; articles.

Board of Directors: Niéde Guidon (Pres.).

Principal Staff: Scientific Dir Maria Gabriela Martin Avila; Finance Dir Dorath Pinto Uchoa.

Address: Centro Cultural Sérgio Motta s/n, Bairro Campestre, 64.770-000 São Raimundo Nonato, PI.

Telephone: (89) 3582-1612; **Fax:** (89) 3582-1612; **Internet:** www.fumdham.org.br; **e-mail:** contato@fumdham.org.br.

Fundação Romi (Romi Foundation)

Established in 1957 in Santa Bárbara d'Oeste, São Paulo to promote educational and cultural development to ensure the development of society.

Activities: Supports cultural, social and educational initiatives, such as computer training, to advance Brazilian development.

Geographical Area of Activity: Brazil.

Publications: *Arquivos*.

Principal Staff: Pres. Dr André Luis Romi; Vice-Pres. Patrícia Romi Cervone.

Address: Av. Monte Castelo 1095, Jd. Primavera, CEP 13.450-285, Santa Bárbara d'Oeste, SP.

Telephone: (19) 3455-1055; **Fax:** (19) 3455-1345; **Internet:** www.fundacaoromi.org.br; **e-mail:** fundacaoromi@fundacaoromi.org.br.

Fundação Maurício Sirotsky Sobrinho (Maurício Sirotsky Nephew Foundation)

Established in 1987 to defend the rights of children and young people.

Activities: Promotes sustainable self-development aimed at building citizenship and respecting fundamental social rights, with a particular focus on the defence of the rights of children and adolescents, primarily in the states of Rio Grande do Sul, Santa Catarina and Paraná. Also provides information resources to not-for-profit organizations.

Geographical Area of Activity: Brazil.

Publications: Articles.

Finance: Annual grants approx. US $2,000,000.

Board of Trustees: Jayme Sirotsky (Pres.).

Principal Staff: Pres. Nelson Pacheco Sirotsky; Exec. Dir Lucia Ritzel.

Address: Rua Rádio e TV Gaúcha 189, 2° andar, 90.850-080 Porto Alegre, RS.

Telephone: (51) 3218-5002; **Fax:** (51) 3218-5035; **Internet:** www.fmss.org.br; **e-mail:** fundacao@fmss.org.br.

Fundação SOS Mata Atlântica (Foundation for the Conservation of the Atlantic Rainforest)

Founded in 1986 to work towards the protection of the forests of Brazil's Atlantic region, the preservation of the communities inhabiting them and their cultural heritage, and the sustained development of these areas.

Activities: Operates in Brazil in the area of conservation and the environment.

Geographical Area of Activity: Brazil.

Finance: Revenue 20,497,000 reais; expenditure 12,845,000 reais (2007).

Board of Directors: Roberto Luiz Leme Klabin (Pres.); Pedro Luiz Barreiros Passos (Vice-Pres.).

Principal Staff: Dir of Communications Ana Ligia Scachetti; Finance Dir Olavo Garrido.

Address: Rua Manoel dâ Nóbrega 456, Paraíso, 04.001-001 São Paulo, SP.

Telephone: (11) 3055-7888; **Fax:** (11) 3885-1680; **Internet:** www.sosmatatlantica.org.br; **e-mail:** info@sosma.org.br.

Fundação Hélio Augusto de Souza—Fundhas (Hélio Augusto de Souza Foundation)

Established in 1987, a non-profit institution aiming to assist children and young people.

Activities: Operates three basic programmes in education, welfare and training: the Child Programme, for children between the ages of seven and 14; the Adolescent Programme, for young people 14–18 years old; and the Supporting/Partnership Programmes. Currently assists around 5,000 children and young people through its programmes.

Geographical Area of Activity: São José dos Campos (Brazil).

Publications: *Notícias*.

Principal Staff: Pres. Roniel T. Soeiro de Faria.

Address: Rua Santarém 560, Parque Industrial, 12.235-550 São José dos Campos, SP.

Telephone: (12) 3932-0540; **Fax:** (12) 3931-8416; **Internet:** www.fundhas.org.br.

Fundação Maria Cecilia Souto Vidigal

Established in 1965 to develop increased research into leukamia in Brazil.

Activities: Improved treatment and understanding of leukamia led the founders of the organization to review its mission in 2001. It currently supports a number of programmes that focus on early childhood development.

Geographical Area of Activity: Brazil.

Principal Staff: CEO Eduardo Queiroz.

Address: Avda Brigadeiro Faria Lima 3015, Conjunto 81, Jardim Paulistano, 01452-000 São Paulo, SP.

Telephone: (11) 3330 2888; **Fax:** (11) 3079 2746; **Internet:** www.fmcsv.org.br; **e-mail:** fmcsv@fmcsv.org.br.

GRUMIN—Grupo Mulher-Educação Indigena (Indigenous Women's Education Group)

Established in 1987 in north-east Brazil by Eliane Potiguara to aid native women's social, economic and political development by eradicating social discrimination and improving women's self-determination through seminars, conferences and vocational training.

Activities: Operates nationally through a wide network of offices. GRUMIN finances several projects such as the creation of community gardens where landless families can grow food; organizes training courses to provide an insight into indigenous history and handicrafts; organizes vocational training, seminars and conferences for native women; and presents a forum to facilitate online debates.

Geographical Area of Activity: Brazil.

Publications: Journal; bulletin; and other publications.

Principal Staff: Gen. Co-ordinator Eliane Potiguara.

Address: Daline Braga, Av. Heitor Beltrao 71, Sala 301, Tijuca, 20.550-000 Rio de Janeiro, RJ.

Telephone: (21) 567-2675; **Fax:** (21) 567-2675; **Internet:** www .elianepotiguara.org.br/organizacao.html; **e-mail:** grumin@ elianepotiguara.org.br.

Instituto Ayrton Senna (Ayrton Senna Institute)

Established in 1995 to commemorate late Brazilian racing-car driver Ayrton Senna and achieve his ideals: assisting child welfare and other welfare activities in the areas of education and health.

Activities: Activities focus nationally on: providing direct assistance to safeguard the rights of Brazilian adolescents and children, and advocating development activities that are of help to future generations; health and medicine, and education, supporting small-scale projects in the areas of education, poverty relief, health, nutrition, culture and sports; anti-poverty programmes in support of 'street children' in Brazil. International activities carried out through the United Kingdom-based Ayrton Senna Foundation.

Geographical Area of Activity: Brazil.

Restrictions: Grants are not made to individuals.

Finance: Receives 100% of the profits obtained from the licensing of the Senna brand and image, and is also financed through alliances with the Brazilian and multinational business community.

Board of Directors: Viviane Senna (Pres.).

Principal Staff: Pres. Viviane Senna.

Address: Rua Dr Olavo Egídio 287, 16º andar, 02.037-000 São Paulo, SP.

Telephone: (11) 2974-3000; **Fax:** (11) 2950-8007; **Internet:** www.senna.globo.com/institutoarytonsenna; **e-mail:** ias@ ias.org.br.

REDEH—Rede de Desenvolvimento Humano (Network for Human Development)

Established in 1990, REDEH works towards creating awareness among women on issues of health, education, environment, and sexual and reproductive rights.

Activities: A forum for women to exchange their views and voice their concerns in different forms, such as Fala Mulher (Speak Women), a daily one-hour radio broadcast. Conducts training programmes for activists; runs projects to contain desertification; undertakes sustainable development initiatives, health and prevention initiatives, and programmes to better efforts undertaken to induct women in the local governing bodies in towns and cities.

Geographical Area of Activity: Brazil.

Publications: Numerous publications and videos.

Finance: Annual budget approx. 661,000 reais.

Principal Staff: Gen. Co-ordinator Thais Corral; Exec. Co-ordinator Schuma Schumaher.

Address: Rua Alvaro Alvim 21, 16º andar, Centro, 20.031-010 Rio de Janeiro, RJ.

Telephone: (21) 2262-1704; **Fax:** (21) 2262-6454; **Internet:** www.redeh.org.br; **e-mail:** redeh@redeh.org.br.

Bulgaria

FOUNDATION CENTRES AND CO-ORDINATING BODIES

BCAF—Bulgarian Charities Aid Foundation

Founded by CAF—Charities Aid Foundation (q.v.) in 1995 to help design and build the framework for a robust voluntary sector in Bulgaria.

Activities: Runs grant-making programmes; promotes corporate giving, providing information to companies and helping them organize their giving schemes effectively; has developed Bulgaria's first payroll giving scheme; runs financial and legal management training courses; manages an emergency fund providing support for the medical treatment of children (up to the age of 18) from disadvantaged families; and issues publications.

Geographical Area of Activity: Bulgaria.

Publications: *Businesses and their Charitable Attitudes–research on corporate giving in Bulgaria*; *Financial Management, Legal and Tax Regulations of NGOs*; *Donations and Tax Relief*; *Corporate Social Responsibility–whys and hows in Bulgaria and world-wide*; *Partners Bulletin*; Annual Report.

Finance: Assets 269,000 lev (2007).

Board of Directors: Michael Tachev (Chair.).

Principal Staff: Exec. Dir Elitza Barakova.

Address: 1000 Sofia, Vitosha Blvd 65, 2nd Floor.

Telephone: (2) 981-1901; **Fax:** (2) 987-1574; **Internet:** www.bcaf.bg.

Bulgarian Donors' Forum

Established in September 2003 to promote the development of civil society and the sustainable development of the non-governmental sector in Bulgaria by improvement of the framework for its operation, recognition of self-regulation mechanisms, and co-ordination of donors' policies. Membership is open to donor organizations that provide annual grants in excess of €5,000 and accept the Forum's Code of Ethics.

Activities: The Forum represents the interests of its members as well as aiming to build the financial sustainability of the Bulgarian non-profit sector, including encouraging new donors. Also carries out research, lobbies government and provides information and advice to members and NGOs.

Geographical Area of Activity: Bulgaria.

Publications: *Developing local grantmaking in Bulgaria*.

Principal Staff: Dir Krassimir Velichkova.

Address: 1000 Sofia, Solunska St 56.

Telephone: (2) 951-5978; **Fax:** (2) 954-9847; **Internet:** www.dfbulgaria.org; **e-mail:** info@dfbulgaria.org.

Civil Society Development Foundation

Established in 1995 to support the development of Bulgarian civil society by assisting the non-profit sector; creating a favourable environment for its operation; and extending its capacity, the types of activity, and the participation of NGOs at local, regional and national level.

Activities: Provides financial assistance to Bulgarian NGOs for the protection and development of minorities; to combat crime and corruption; to protect nature and the environment; to promote social entrepreneurship in marginalized groups; and to inform and train civil society organizations. Also works to promote effective donor dialogue and collaboration, improving information exchange, networking and research on the Bulgarian NGO sector and bridging private and state resources in community development partnerships.

Geographical Area of Activity: Bulgaria.

Restrictions: No grants to individuals; grants are made depending on programme priorities to NGOs and civic associations registered under Bulgarian law.

Publications: Annual Report; brochures, newsletters.

Board of Directors: Georgi Lipovanski (Chair.).

Principal Staff: Exec. Dir Bouryana Konaklieva.

Address: 1000 Sofia, Ivan Vazov St 42.

Telephone: (2) 877-724; **Fax:** (2) 819-134; **e-mail:** csdf@cserv.mgu.bg.

Resource Center Foundation

Founded in 1998 to contribute to the process of democratization in Bulgaria by promoting sustainable development in all spheres of social and political life and through the establishment of mechanisms and structures of civil society.

Activities: Aims to develop civil society in Bulgaria through the provision of information on activities conducted by Bulgarian NGOs, lobbying on legal and fiscal issues, adaptation of business practices, stimulation of citizens' involvement and participation in Bulgaria's European Union accession process, developing social entrepreneurship development, and creating innovative alternatives for dealing with the problems arising as a result of the economic and social restructuring of society.

Geographical Area of Activity: Bulgaria.

Publications: Annual Report; Financial Report; bulletin; articles.

Board of Trustees: Valeri Rousanov (Chair.).

Principal Staff: Head Man. Marieta Tsvetkova.

Address: 1000 Sofia, Serdika St 20.

Telephone: (2) 915-4810; **Fax:** (2) 915-4811; **Internet:** www.ngorc.net; **e-mail:** info@ngorc.net.

Union of Bulgarian Foundations and Associations

Established in 1992 to lend assistance to Bulgarian NGOs and foundations, working nationally and internationally.

Activities: Facilitates co-operation among non-profit organizations; supports NGOs in their development and work; protects the interests of its member organizations; encourages good practices and high standards in the activities of NGOs; provides information services and issues publications.

Geographical Area of Activity: Bulgaria.

Publications: Annual Report; list of funders; strategic plan.

Principal Staff: Exec. Dir Ognian Lipovski.

Address: 1000 Sofia, POB 615, Central Post.

Telephone: (2) 943-3456; **Fax:** (2) 946-1684; **e-mail:** ubfa@cserv.mgu.bg.

Manfred Woerner Foundation

Founded by the Atlantic Club of Bulgaria in October 1994 to foster and promote Atlantic values, solidarity and co-operation, promote the trans-Atlantic link, help advance the global role and enlargement of NATO, and uphold the vision of the late NATO Sec.-Gen. Manfred Woerner.

Activities: Operates nationally and internationally in the fields of education and international affairs, through self-conducted programmes, research, scholarships and fellowships, conferences and publications. Has established an Atlantic

Solidarity Award, which was first awarded to NATO Sec.-Gen. Lord George Robertson.

Geographical Area of Activity: Europe, USA and Canada, South Atlantic and Pacific Region, Eurasia, Middle East and South Asia.

Publications: *The Future of the Falkland Islands and Its People* (2003); *Immigrants and Refugees in Bulgaria and Their Integration: Guidelines for New Immigration Policies* (2003); *Bulgarian Policies on the Republic of Macedonia: Recommendations on the development of good neighbourly relations following Bulgaria's accession to the EU and in the context of NATO and EU enlargement in the Western Balkans* (2008).

Trustees: Lyubomir Ivanov (Founding Pres.).

Principal Staff: CEO Lyubomir Ivanov; Programme Dir Nadezhda Stoyanova.

Address: 1000 Sofia, Slavyanska St 29.

Telephone: (2) 987-2729; **Fax:** (2) 981-5782; **Internet:** www .mwfbg.org; **e-mail:** mwfbg@yahoo.com.

FOUNDATIONS, TRUSTS AND NON-PROFIT ORGANIZATIONS

America for Bulgaria Foundation

Geographical Area of Activity: Bulgaria.

Finance: Total assets US $389,393,000 (2010).

Principal Staff: Pres. Frank L. Bauer.

Address: Prof. Asen Zlatarov St 5, Sofia 1504.

Telephone: (2) 806-3800; **Fax:** (2) 843-5123; **Internet:** www .americaforbulgaria.org; **e-mail:** applications@ americaforbulgaria.org.

Black Sea NGO Network—BSNN

Established in 1998, and registered in 1999, to operate as a regional association of NGOs from all Black Sea countries (Bulgaria, Georgia, Romania, Russian Federation, Turkey and Ukraine) brought together by the common concern for the decreasing environmental quality of the Black Sea and the need for the adoption of democratic values and practices in the Black Sea countries that follow the ideals of sustainability.

Activities: Aims to facilitate the free flow and exchange of information, resources and experience for the accomplishment of its aims of the protection and rehabilitation of the Black Sea, including the Azov Sea, and the sustainable development of the Black Sea countries, through increased participation of NGOs, governments, businesses and other institutions, as well as the general public. Operates through lobbying and advocacy for environmentally sound national legislation, for development and adoption of National Strategic Action Plans for rehabilitation and protection of the Black Sea environment, and for international conventions' appliance in the Black Sea countries; encouraging sustainable practices in the Black Sea coastal area; raising environmental awareness for acute Black Sea environmental issues through environmental education and information; facilitating public participation in the decision-making processes concerning acute Black Sea environmental issues; promoting activities for solving Black Sea acute environmental problems and specific environmental issues; and building the capacity and self-sustainability of the Black Sea NGO community.

Geographical Area of Activity: Black Sea countries (Bulgaria, Georgia, Romania, Russian Federation, Turkey and Ukraine).

Publications: Newsletter; topical items; regional directories on Bulgaria, Georgia, Romania, Russian Federation, Turkey and Ukraine; numerous project publications.

Network Board: Dan Manoleli Romania (Chair.).

Principal Staff: Emma Gileva.

Address: 9000 Varna, POB 91; Varna, Dr L. Zamenhof St 2.

Telephone: (52) 615856; **Fax:** (52) 602047; **Internet:** www .bsnn.org; **e-mail:** bsnn@bsnn.org.

Bulgarian Fund for Women

Established in September 2004 by the Gender Project for Bulgaria Foundation to support Bulgarian women and girls for the recognition of women's rights as human rights; to strengthen their capacity and skills for their active involvement in social, cultural, economic, political and professional life.

Activities: Provides financial and development support to NGOs for projects aiming to combat all forms of violence against women; to promote women's economic independence and to reduce poverty and unemployment; to encourage women's more active participation in public and political life for their promotion in decision-making positions; to achieve equal rights and equal opportunities for marginalized groups of women and those with different sexual orientation; and facilitate women's access to information technology. Also seeks to improve the quality of services provided by trainers, consultants and facilitators who work with NGOs on gender equality, and participates in international networks of women's funds.

Geographical Area of Activity: Bulgaria.

Publications: *Identification of the Inner Gender Resources of the Roma Community for Enhancing their Integration with Bulgarian Society* (2007).

Board of Trustees: Stanimira Hadjimitova (Pres.).

Principal Staff: Chief Exec. Stoila Bongalova.

Address: 1000 Sofia, Parchevich St 37B.

Telephone: (2) 986-4710; **Fax:** (2) 981-5604; **Internet:** www .bgfundforwomen.org; **e-mail:** gender@fastbg.net.

Creating Effective Grassroots Alternatives—CEGA

Established in 1995; aims towards sustainable democratic development through stimulating citizens' involvement in the community decision-making process and local self-governance.

Activities: Promotes sustainable democratic development through providing support to disadvantaged minority groups and provides for their participation in the transformation of their communities. Provides funding and technical support to grassroots groups and organizations to increase their effectiveness and impact in resolving social problems; disseminates democratic practices that work and supports effective community-based initiatives; and engages in advocacy, coalition-building and public campaigns, based on lessons learned at the community level. Operates through two main programmes: Youth in Action and Initiative for Local Changes.

Geographical Area of Activity: Bulgaria.

Restrictions: No grants to individuals.

Publications: *Why Not* (newsletter).

Board of Directors: Dr Yvonne Kojouharova (Chair.).

Principal Staff: Exec. Man. Rumian Sechkov.

Address: 1000 Sofia, G. S. Rakovsky St 96, 2nd Floor.

Telephone: (2) 981-0913; **Fax:** (2) 988-9696; **Internet:** www .cega.bg; **e-mail:** cega@cega.bg.

Evrika Foundation

Founded in 1990 to encourage and educate young people in the fields of science, economics, technology and management.

Activities: The Foundation operates nationally and internationally in the fields of economic and international affairs, education, medicine and health, and science and technology, through self-conducted programmes, grants to individuals and institutions, scholarships and fellowships, and conferences. It supports the education of talented young people; works towards implementing scientific and technological ideas and projects; provides equipment and material for creative work; encourages international co-operation in the fields of science, technology and management; disseminates information; organizes events; provides financial support for scientific research undertaken by talented young scholars; awards for innovative young farmers; and credit and loans to young inventors developing research and technological products and new products and services.

Geographical Area of Activity: Bulgaria.

Publications: Annual Report; *Computer*; *Do-it-Yourself*; *EVRIKA* (monthly bulletin); *Andromeda* (magazine); *Telescope*.

Governing Council: Jachko Ivanov (Chair.); Georgi Ivanov (Vice-Chair.).

Principal Staff: Exec. Dir Boryana Kadmonova; Programme Dir Grigor Tzankov.

Address: 1000 Sofia, Patriarh Evtimii 1 blvd.

Telephone: (2) 981-5181; **Fax:** (2) 981-5483; **Internet:** www.evrika.org; **e-mail:** office@evrika.org.

Elizabeth Kostova Foundation for Creative Writing

The Foundation was established in 2007 by US author Elizabeth Kostova.

Activities: Supports creative writing in Bulgaria, especially in the field of translation. Offers translation awards and fellowships for Bulgarian literary translators working from Bulgarian into English, international creative writing seminar (www.ekf.bg/sozopol), and runs a contest for contemporary Bulgarian writers and translators. Established the first website for contemporary Bulgarian literature in English language: www.contemporarybulgarianwriters.com.

Geographical Area of Activity: Bulgaria and English-speaking countries.

Trustees: Julian Popov (Chair.).

Principal Staff: Man. Dir Milena Deleva.

Address: 1142 Sofia, Ljuben Karavelov Str. 15.

Telephone: (2) 9888188; **Internet:** http://ekf.bg; **e-mail:** info@ekf.bg.

National Trust EcoFund

Established in 1995 to manage funds provided under debt-for-nature and debt-for-environment swaps, as well as funds provided under other types of agreements with international, foreign or Bulgarian sources aimed at environmental protection in Bulgaria.

Activities: Operates within the priority areas of pollution clearing, including hazardous waste and hazardous substances disposal; sources of drinking water or food contamination (by heavy metals, toxic organic compounds or other harmful chemicals); reduction of air pollution, including pollutants of health concern; clean water protection; and the protection of biodiversity, including the development of infrastructure in protected areas for species protection and habitat preservation, and biodiversity inventory and monitoring and sustainable utilization of components for creating social alternatives.

Geographical Area of Activity: Bulgaria.

Principal Staff: Exec. Dir Prof. Demeter Nenkov.

Address: 1574 Sofia, Shipchenski Prohod Blvd 67 B.

Telephone: (2) 973-3637; **Internet:** www.ecofund-bg.org; **e-mail:** ecofund@ecofund-bg.org.

Open Society Institute—Sofia (Bulgaria)

Founded in April 1990 as the Open Society Foundation to support education and culture and the development of Bulgarian society. An independent foundation, part of the Soros foundations network, which aims to foster political and cultural pluralism and reform economic structures to encourage private enterprise and a market economy.

Activities: Supports projects under the programme areas of economic integration and regional stability; public life and civil participation; democracy and rule of law; education policies; and public health. Initiatives include support for electoral reform and accession to the European Union. Also runs a nation-wide network of 17 information centres offering consultation and funding advice.

Geographical Area of Activity: Bulgaria; some aid to Kosovo and Metohija.

Publications: *Wide Awake* (newsletter, 6 a year); fortnightly newsletter.

Finance: Total assets €5,300,000 (2010).

Trustees: Nelly Ognyanova (Chair.).

Principal Staff: Exec. Dir George Stoytchev; Financial Dir Veliko Sherbanov.

Address: 1000 Sofia, Solunska St 56.

Telephone: (2) 930-6619; **Fax:** (2) 951-6348; **Internet:** www.osf.bg; **e-mail:** info@osf.bg.

Roma Lom Foundation

Established in 1996 with the aim of enhancing the social development and integration of the Roma community.

Activities: Aims to support the development of the Roma community in the areas of education, employment, social services, work with youth and women, crime prevention, sport, media, and agriculture, through encouraging participation of the Roma community in foundation-initiated projects. The Foundation also established a Self-Help Bureau in 1996.

Geographical Area of Activity: Bulgaria.

Board Members: Nikolay Kirilov (Chair.).

Principal Staff: Programme Dir Asen Slavchev.

Address: 3600 Lom, Neofit Bozveli St 4.

Telephone: (9) 716-6751; **Fax:** (9) 716-6751; **Internet:** www.roma-lom.org; **e-mail:** roma-lom@roma-lom.org.

Saint Cyril and Saint Methodius International Foundation

Founded in 1982 as the Lyudmila Zhivkova International Foundation, dedicated to preserving and popularizing the spiritual heritage of St Cyril and St Methodius; the Foundation aims to encourage cultural co-operation and the creative and educational development of young people, and to assist in the integration of Bulgaria into the 'New Europe' and the world.

Activities: Operates internationally in the fields of the arts and humanities and cultural education; arranges cultural and educational exchanges; promotes cultural exchange, international understanding and the creative development of young people; awards prizes and scholarships; organizes conferences and exhibitions; supports publishing projects; organizes events and seminars; and maintains an art gallery.

Geographical Area of Activity: International.

Publications: Annual Report; brochure; financial report.

Executive Board: Petar Kenderov (Pres.); Prof. Svetlin Russev (Vice-Pres.); Boyko Vassilev (Vice-Pres.); Prof. Dimo Platikanov (Vice-Pres.); Dr Roumen Hristov (Vice-Pres.).

Principal Staff: Chief Exec. Michael Tachev.

Address: 1504 Sofia, Vassil Aprilov St 3.

Telephone: (2) 943-4185; **Fax:** (2) 944-6027; **Internet:** www.cmfnd.org; **e-mail:** cmfnd@cmfnd.org.

Trust for Civil Society in Central and Eastern Europe

Founded in 2001 by a group of private US foundations, Atlantic Philanthropies, Charles Stewart Mott Foundation, Ford Foundation, German Marshall Fund of the United States, Open Society Institute and Rockefeller Brothers Fund.

Activities: Supports the long-term, sustainable development of civil society and NGOs in Central and Eastern Europe.

Geographical Area of Activity: Central and Eastern Europe.

Restrictions: No grants to political organizations, trade unions or businesses.

Finance: Total assets US $16,606,174 (2010).

Board of Trustees: Heike MacKerron (Chair.); Haki Abazi (Sec. and Treas.).

Principal Staff: Exec. Dir Lidia Zolucka.

Address: 1000 Sofia, 22A San Stefano St.

Telephone: (2) 944-2350; **Fax:** (2) 944-2350; **Internet:** www.ceetrust.org; **e-mail:** trust@ceetrust.org.

Values Foundation

Founded in 1998 by Antonina Stoyanova to address the issue of sustainable development through culture.

Activities: Promoting and supports the development of Bulgarian science, education and culture. Concerned with the integration of Bulgaria into Europe, while also preserving the cultural values and cultural diversity of the nation. Works to strengthen projects that work on social integration and communication. Also concentrates on secondary school and university education, awarding prizes and promoting exchanges. Works in collaboration with other Bulgarian organizations.

Geographical Area of Activity: Bulgaria.

Managing Board: Antonina Stoyanova (Chair.).

Principal Staff: Contacts Liliana Panova, Petya Georgieva.

Address: 1000 Sofia, POB 1302.

Telephone: (2) 988-1204; **Fax:** (2) 988-4047; **Internet:** www.values.bg; **e-mail:** eustory_bg@yahoo.com.

Burkina Faso

FOUNDATIONS, TRUSTS AND NON-PROFIT ORGANIZATIONS

Fédération Panafricaine des Cinéastes—FEPACI (Pan-African Federation of Film-makers)

Founded in 1970 by African film-makers for the development and promotion of African cinema.

Activities: Operates in almost all African countries to defend democracy in communications as a basic human right, through self-conducted programmes, conferences, training courses and publications. Organizes cinema festivals and campaigns in conjunction with other organizations, for government funding for cultural organizations.

Geographical Area of Activity: Africa.

Publications: *FEPACI-Infos* (quarterly); *Ecrans d'Afrique* (quarterly).

Board: Charles Mensah (Pres.); Albert Egbe (Treas.).

Principal Staff: Sec.-Gen. Seipati Bulane-Hopa.

Address: BP 2524, Ouagadougou 01.

Telephone: 31-02-58; **Fax:** 31-18-59; **Internet:** www.fepaci-film.org; **e-mail:** info@fepaci-film.org.

Fondation Jean-Paul II pour le sahel (John Paul II Foundation for the Sahel)

Established in February 1984 by Pope John Paul II, for the training of local leaders, who place themselves at the service of their country, for the purpose of fighting desertification and its causes and the purpose of aiding victims of drought in the nine countries of the Sahel region.

Activities: Supports the professional training of local leaders to carry out micro-projects relating to agriculture, water and the environment.

Geographical Area of Activity: Sahelian region of Africa (Burkina Faso, Cape Verde, Chad, Gambia, Guinea-Bissau, Mali, Mauritania, Niger and Senegal).

Restrictions: Grants only made within the nine Sahelian countries.

Finance: Receives donations from Catholics in Germany and Italy, through their Episcopal conferences. Total annual grants approx. US $3,000,000.

Council of Administration: Jean-Pierre Bassene (Pres.); Michel Cartateguy (Vice-Pres.).

Address: BP 4890, Ouagadougou 01.

Telephone: 50-36-53-14; **Fax:** 50-36-53-93; **Internet:** fondationjeanpaul2.org; **e-mail:** info@fjp2-sahel.org.

Fondation Nationale pour le Développement et la Solidarité—FONADES (National Foundation for Solidarity and Development)

Established in 1973 to promote economic development designed to meet the needs of local populations and their capabilities.

Activities: Promotes sustainable economic development, through supporting locally administered development programmes. Types of projects include building anti-erosion structures to protect fragile areas; organization of local communities in the management and production of manure as a fertilizer; assisting in the production of seeds and tree-planting programmes; well-building in different villages; and the organization of micro-credit programmes among indigenous women to help them start commercial activities.

Geographical Area of Activity: Burkina Faso.

Publications: Annual Report; manuals.

Principal Staff: Dir Maurice Oudet.

Address: BP 523, Ouagadougou 01.

Telephone: 36-37-68; **Fax:** 36-10-79; **Internet:** www.abcburkina.net/content/view/307/51/lang,fr; **e-mail:** fonades@fasonet.bf.

Cambodia

FOUNDATION CENTRE AND CO-ORDINATING BODY

Co-operation Committee for Cambodia

A professional association of NGOs in Cambodia with a total of 114 member organizations in 2009.

Activities: Promotes the development of civil society in Cambodia.

Principal Staff: Exec. Dir Lun Borithy; Programme Dir Soeung Saroeun.

Address: House #9–11, St 476, POB 885, Sangkat Toul Tom Poung I, Phnom Penh.

Internet: www.ccc-cambodia.org; **e-mail:** info@ccc-cambodia.org.

FOUNDATIONS, TRUSTS AND NON-PROFIT ORGANIZATIONS

Don Bosco Foundation of Cambodia—DBFC

Established in May 1991 to support the development of young people in Cambodia.

Activities: Focuses on supporting education and training initiatives in Cambodia, with a particular emphasis on helping orphans and economically disadvantaged young people. Since its establishment, the DBFC has funded the construction of seven technical schools in Phnom Penh, Sihanoukville, Battambang, Poipet and Kep. DBFC also provides scholarships to young people aged 6–12 years, and organizes literacy projects through the Don Bosco Children Fund (DBCF).

Geographical Area of Activity: Cambodia.

Publications: Technical books for education (in Khmer language) about mechanic, automotive, welding, electricity, hotel management, secretarial, audiovisual edition, web development; *Don Bosco Sihanoukville 2007: Visit of HM Norodom Sihamoni*; Khmer Grammar for Spanish speakers.

Finance: International donations, from countries including the Netherlands, Italy, USA, UK and Germany.

Principal Staff: Country Rep. Fr John Visser; Dep. Country Rep. Fr Leonard Ochoa; Communications Albeiro Rodas; Admin. Roberto Panetto.

Address: POB 47, 67 St 315 Sankat Boeng Kak 2, Khan Toul Kouk, Phnom Penh.

Telephone: (23) 23986344; **Fax:** (23) 23986407; **Internet:** www.donboscokhmer.org; **e-mail:** management@donboscokhmer.org.

Canada

FOUNDATION CENTRES AND CO-ORDINATING BODIES

Canadian Co-operative Association

Established in 1987 by the merger of the Co-operative College of Canada and the Co-operative Union of Canada, as a co-ordinating organization for co-operatives in Canada.

Activities: Provides leadership and support to its membership organizations in maintaining and improving the co-operative presence in Canada, which works to improve the quality of life of those in all parts of Canada and abroad. Member organizations work in the areas of finance, insurance, agri-food, wholesale and retail, housing, health and day-care. Its international development programme provides technical and financial assistance to credit unions and co-operatives in more than 20 countries. Has offices in eight countries other than Canada. Funded by member dues for its activities in Canada and by the Canadian International Development Agency (CIDA) and the affiliated Co-operative Development Foundation of Canada (CDF) for its international development activities. CCA is a member of the International Co-operative Alliance (ICA).

Geographical Area of Activity: Mainly Canada, but has development projects in Africa, Asia and Latin America.

Publications: *International Development Digest* (3 a year); *Co-operative News Briefs* (fortnightly electronic newsletter); *Governance Matters*; *International Dispatch* (monthly e-newsletter); Annual Report; research papers and reports; videos.

Finance: Assets C $7,293,703 (March 2009); annual revenue $17,640,488, expenditure $16,895,516 (March 2009).

Board of Directors (executive): Claude Gauthier (Pres.); Beryl Bauer, Jill Kelly (Vice-Pres); Nick Sidor (Exec. Member).

Principal Staff: Exec. Dir Denyse Guy.

Address: Co-operative House, 275 Bank St, Suite 400, Ottawa, ON K2P 2L6.

Telephone: (613) 238-6711; **Fax:** (613) 567-0658; **Internet:** www.coopscanada.coop; **e-mail:** info@coopscanada.coop.

Canadian Council for International Co-operation—CCIC/Conseil canadien pour la coopération internationale—CCCI

Established in 1968, a coalition of more than 100 Canadian development organizations, which aim to change human development for the better.

Activities: Conducts research, disseminates information, and co-ordinates the efforts of its members to work in the field of human development world-wide, to promote national and international policies that serve the public interest, and to build a social movement for global citizenship in Canada. In the international field, CCIC members aim to ensure that all people have the basic necessities for living: food, shelter, education, health and sanitation. Other members actively campaign for human rights, fair trade and corporate social responsibility. Its International Co-operation Award recognizes organizations' innovative work to combat poverty.

Geographical Area of Activity: Canada.

Publications: *Corporate Social Responsibility/Engagement with the Private Sector*; *Ethics*; *Gender Issues and Diversity*; general information documents on CCIC.

Finance: Total assets C $963,205; annual revenue $1,686,097, expenditure $1,321,575 (March 2011).

Board of Directors: Jim Cornelius (Chair.); June Webber (Vice-Chair.); Shams Alibhai (Treas.).

Principal Staff: Pres. and CEO Julia Sanchez.

Address: 450 Rideau St, Suite 200, Ottawa, ON K1N 5Z4.

Telephone: (613) 241-7007; **Fax:** (613) 241-5302; **Internet:** www.ccic.ca; **e-mail:** info@ccic.ca.

Imagine Canada

Established in January 2005 following the merger of the Canadian Centre for Philanthropy (CCP) and the Coalition of National Voluntary Organizations (NVO); aims to assist Canadian charitable and voluntary organizations through research, public affairs, information products and professional development.

Activities: The Centre operates through research into the charitable and voluntary sector and the environment in which they function; issuing publications; and organizing conferences and seminars. It is involved in communicating with government, the media and the public on the voluntary sector, and informs its affiliates on legislative and regulatory initiatives proposed by government. Operates through a family of sub-sites, providing statistics and information on giving and volunteering, information on the non-profit sector in Canada, grants for research on volunteerism, and Imagine, which promotes corporate citizenship and community investment.

Geographical Area of Activity: Canada.

Publications: *Canadian Directory to Foundations and Grants*; *Building Foundation Partnerships*; *Portrait of Canada's Charities*; *Give and Take: a resource manual for Canadian Fundraisers*; *Connecting Companies to Communities*; *Promoting Corporate Citizenship*; *Charities and Not-for-Profits Fundraising Handbook*; *Front and Centre* (newspaper); Annual Report; publications on foundations and fundraising; resource guides, brochures, pamphlets and special papers.

Board of Directors: Faye Wightman (Chair.).

Principal Staff: Pres. and CEO Marcel Lauzière.

Address: 2 Carlton St, Suite 600, Toronto, ON M5B 1J3.

Telephone: (416) 597-2293; **Fax:** (416) 597-2294; **Internet:** www.imaginecanada.ca; **e-mail:** info@imaginecanada.ca.

FOUNDATIONS, TRUSTS AND NON-PROFIT ORGANIZATIONS

Aga Khan Foundation Canada

Established in 1980, and part of the network of foundations established by HH Prince Karim Aga Khan, aiming to support social development projects in Africa and Asia to benefit the poor, regardless of race, religion or political affiliation.

Activities: Works to address the root causes of poverty: finding and sharing solutions that help improve the quality of life for poor communities. Programmes focus on four core areas: health, education, rural development and building the capacity of NGOs, with considerations for gender equity and protecting the environment integrated into every programme. Major initiatives include: the Pakistan-Canada Social Institutions Development Program; the Aga Khan Rural Support Program in Pakistan; the Tajikistan Institutional Support Program; the Coastal Rural Support Program in Mozambique and the Non-Formal Education Program of the Bangladesh Rural Advancement Committee. Supports several school improvement projects carried out with Aga Khan Education Services and primary health care projects implemented with Aga Khan Health Services. Sectors receiving support include microfinance, the improvement of livelihoods and micro-enterprise development, as well as rural development, health and education.

Geographical Area of Activity: Canada, East Africa, and South and Central Asia.

Principal Staff: CEO Nazeer Aziz Ladhani.

Address: The Delegation of the Ismaili Imamat, 199 Sussex Dr., Ottawa, ON K1N 1K6.

Telephone: (613) 237-2532; **Fax:** (613) 567-2532; **Internet:** www.akfc.ca; **e-mail:** info@akfc.ca.

Alberta Innovates Health Solutions

Founded in 1980 as the Alberta Heritage Foundation for Medical Research, by an act of legislation to support biomedical and health research, principally in the province of Alberta. Changed its name in 2009.

Activities: The Foundation supports biomedical and health research, by offering awards based on international standards of excellence to researchers and researchers-in-training.

Geographical Area of Activity: Alberta, Canada and international.

Restrictions: Awards only for salary support, equipment costs, student support, renovation costs, construction costs and partnership initiatives.

Publications: *AHFMR Research News* (quarterly); Annual Report; community reports (annually); triennial reports.

Finance: Total assets C $13,703,000 (March 2010); annual revenue $83,274,000, expenditure $81,114,000 (March 2010).

Trustees: Robert Seidel (Chair.); Dr Raymond Rajotte (Vice-Chair.).

Principal Staff: CEO Dr Jaques Magnan.

Address: 10104 103 Ave, Suite 1500, Edmonton, AB T5J 4A7.

Telephone: (780) 423-5727; **Fax:** (780) 429-3509; **Internet:** www.ahfmr.ab.ca; **e-mail:** health@albertainnovates.ca.

The Alva Foundation

Established in 1965 to support Canadian not-for-profit organizations helping children at risk.

Activities: Aims to help Canadian children at risk, through funding organizations conducting research and/or developing services that address significant risk factors in early childhood development.

Geographical Area of Activity: Canada.

Restrictions: Grants will not be made to individuals, nor for emergency or deficit funding.

Finance: Annual grants C $30,000–$50,000.

Board of Directors: Graham F. Hallward (Pres.); Derek Fisher (Vice-Pres. and Treas.).

Address: c/o Graham Hallward, 199 Albertus Ave, Toronto, ON M4R 1J6.

Internet: www.alva.ca; **e-mail:** donations@alva.ca.

Arctic Institute of North America—AINA (Institut Arctique de l'Amérique du Nord—IAAN)

Founded in 1945 by Act of Parliament in Canada; incorporated concurrently in the USA under the laws of the state of New York. The Canadian Corporation became an integral part of the University of Calgary in 1979.

Activities: The Institute's aims are to advance the study of Arctic and sub-Arctic conditions and problems; to collect material relating to these regions and to make it available for scientific use; to arrange for the publication of relevant material; and to maintain contact with organizations engaged in similar studies. The physical, natural and social sciences and the humanities are all represented in AINA's work. Although mainly concerned with the North, its interests also extend to Antarctica and to Alpine environments. Programmes investigating the ecology of the Arctic and the physiology of high altitude and expeditions are typical of the work supported by AINA. The Institute maintains a major library and an automated bibliographic database, the Arctic Science and Technology Information System (ASTIS). The Institute administers a small grants fund to assist student researchers on field projects, makes travel awards to enable researchers to travel to conferences, and awards scholarships.

Geographical Area of Activity: Canada, Alaska and Greenland.

Publications: *Arctic* (quarterly); *Northern Lights Series*; Annual Report; research papers, technical papers, monographs and other occasional publications.

Finance: Budget C $1,000,000.

Board of Directors: Henry Sykes (Chair.).

Principal Staff: Exec. Dir Benoît Beauchamp.

Address: University of Calgary, 2500 University Dr. NW, Calgary, AB T2N 1N4.

Telephone: (403) 220-7515; **Fax:** (403) 282-4609; **Internet:** www.arctic.ucalgary.ca; **e-mail:** arctic@ucalgary.ca.

Asia Pacific Foundation of Canada

Founded in 1984 to enhance economic, social and cultural relations and networks between Canada and the countries of the Asia-Pacific Region.

Activities: The Foundation is a Canadian leading authority on Canada-Asia relations. It is the site of the Asia-Pacific Economic Co-operation (APEC) Study Centre in Canada, which promotes collaborative research and disseminates information; it also acts as the secretariat for the Asia Pacific Business Network, the Pacific Economic Co-operation Council, the Pacific Basin Economic Council and the APEC Business Advisory Council. It is developing, in partnership with the Federal Government, a network of Canadian Education Centres in Asian cities, including Seoul, Taipei, Kuala Lumpur, Jakarta, Bangkok, Singapore, Hong Kong and New Delhi. The Foundation maintains databases. Further Foundation offices are located in Québec. Through its subsidiary, the GLOBE Foundation, the Foundation manages the GLOBE Series of conferences and trade exhibitions on business and the environment.

Geographical Area of Activity: Canada and the Asia-Pacific region.

Publications: *Canada/Asia Review*; *Canada Asia Commentary*; and other publications.

Finance: Receives more than 50% of its financial support from the Federal Government, the provinces of British Columbia, Alberta, Saskatchewan, Manitoba and Québec, and from a number of private companies; the balance of its revenues are made up of fees paid for Foundation programmes. Annual revenue C $2,399,045, expenditure $1,817,858 (March 2009).

Board of Directors: John H. McArthur (Chair.).

Principal Staff: Pres. and CEO Yuen Pau Woo; Exec. Dir Jill Price.

Address: Suite 220, 890 West Pender St, Vancouver, BC V6C 1J9.

Telephone: (604) 684-5986; **Fax:** (604) 681-1370; **Internet:** www.asiapacific.ca; **e-mail:** info@asiapacific.ca.

Max Bell Foundation

Founded in 1965 by George Maxwell Bell for general charitable purposes, particularly in the fields of health, medical education and veterinary sciences in Canada and the Asia-Pacific region.

Activities: Operates in Canada and the Asia-Pacific region through research and grants to institutions; currently the Foundation is focusing on health, education and communications in society, especially in relation to public policy and responsible journalism.

Geographical Area of Activity: Canada and the Asia-Pacific region.

Publications: Programme Report.

Board of Directors: Carolyn Hursh (Chair.); Ken Marra (Vice-Chair.).

Principal Staff: Pres. David Elton; Sr Programme Officers Ralph Strother, Allan Northcott.

Address: 1201 5th St SW, Suite 380, Calgary, AB T2R 0Y6.

Telephone: (403) 215-7310; **Fax:** (403) 215-7319; **Internet:** www.maxbell.org; **e-mail:** northcott@maxbell.org.

Samuel and Saidye Bronfman Family Foundation

Established in 1952 by the estate of Samuel Bronfman and family members to promote initiative and enterprise in Canada, and the development of new ideas and innovative projects aiming to find solutions to emerging problems in Canada.

Activities: Operates throughout Canada in the fields of the arts and humanities, conservation and the environment, education, human rights and social welfare, through grants to charitable organizations in Canada. The main funding priorities are: Urban Issues, supporting projects that unite urban conservation with community development, to protect and enhance community life inside city neighbourhoods; Futures, making grants for projects that exhibit potential for lasting national benefit; and Cultural Management Development, promoting, in particular, the concept of arts stabilization requiring multi-sector partnerships. Awards the C $25,000 Saidye Bronfman Award for craftwork and funds the Saidye Bronfman Centre for the Arts in Montréal and the Federation CJA of Montréal (formerly the Combined Jewish Appeal of Montréal).

Geographical Area of Activity: Canada.

Restrictions: Grants are currently restricted to existing commitments.

Publications: Brochure.

Officers and Directors: Phyllis Lambert (Hon. Pres.); Stephen R. Bronfman (Pres.); Zeno Santache (Treas.); Robert Vineberg (Sec.).

Principal Staff: Exec. Dir Nancy Rosenfeld.

Address: 1170 Peel St, Suite 800, Montréal, QC H3B 4P2.

Telephone: (514) 878-5270; **Fax:** (514) 878-5299; **Internet:** www.bronfmanfoundation.org.

The Canada Council for the Arts/Conseil des Arts du Canada

An independent agency created by the Parliament of Canada in 1957 to provide grants and services to professional Canadian artists and arts organizations in dance, media arts, music, theatre, writing and publishing, visual arts and integrated arts.

Activities: Provides a wide range of grants, prizes and services to professional Canadian artists and arts organizations in accordance with its aims. Its Art Bank rents contemporary Canadian art to the public and private sectors in Canada. Maintains the secretariat for the Canadian Commission for UNESCO, administers the Killam Program of awards and prizes, and offers other awards. Operates the Public Lending Right Commission to administer payments to Canadian writers for their books held in Canadian libraries.

Geographical Area of Activity: Canada.

Publications: Annual Report; publications describing programmes of assistance; grant lists.

Finance: Funded by and reports to Parliament through the Minister of Canadian Heritage; its annual appropriation from Parliament is supplemented by endowment income, donations and bequests; grants disbursed C $158,390 (March 2010).

Board of Directors: Joseph L. Rotman (Chair.); Simon Brault (Vice-Chair.).

Principal Staff: Dir and CEO Robert Sirman.

Address: 350 Albert St, POB 1047, Ottawa, ON K1P 5V8.

Telephone: (613) 566-4414; **Fax:** (613) 566-4390; **Internet:** www.canadacouncil.ca; **e-mail:** info@canadacouncil.ca.

Canada Foundation for Innovation/Fondation canadienne pour l'innovation

Established in 1997 by the Federal Government to strengthen Canadian capability for research, ultimately contributing to economic growth and improvements in employment, health and the environment.

Activities: Invests in research infrastructure to encourage innovation in universities, colleges, hospitals and other non-profit institutions, including funding the acquisition of state-of-the-art equipment, buildings, laboratories, and databases required to conduct research. Promotes the training of young Canadians for research and other careers, attracts and retains able research workers, and works to ensure the best results in innovation by promoting sharing of information and resources among institutions. Also occasionally launches calls for proposals for international research projects.

Geographical Area of Activity: Canada and international.

Publications: Annual Report; other reports on activities.

Finance: Total assets C $1,726,400,902; annual income and expenditure $472,624.015 (March 2011).

Board of Directors: Kevin P. D. Smith (Chair.).

Principal Staff: Pres. and CEO Gilles G. Patry.

Address: 230 Queen St, Suite 450, Ottawa, ON K1P 5E4.

Telephone: (613) 947-6496; **Fax:** (613) 943-0923; **Internet:** www.innovation.ca; **e-mail:** feedback@innovation.ca.

Canada Israel Cultural Foundation

Established in 1963 to promote intercultural exchange between Canada and Israel.

Activities: Operates in the field of the arts and humanities, through the organization of cultural, artistic, musical and social events and support for Israeli performers to travel to Canada.

Geographical Area of Activity: Canada and Israel.

Board: Ron Bresler (Pres.), Murray B. Koffler (Hon. Chair.); Karen Green, Sara Riesman (Vice-Pres); Sydney Frankford (Sec., Treas.).

Principal Staff: Exec. Dir Cheryl Wetstein.

Address: 4700 Bathurst St, 2nd Floor, Toronto, ON M2R 1W8.

Telephone: (416) 932-2260; **Fax:** (416) 398-5780; **Internet:** www.cicfweb.ca; **e-mail:** cicf@bellnet.ca.

Canada World Youth/Jeunesse Canada Monde

Founded in 1971 by the late Hon. Jacques Hébert (1923–2007), its continuing mission is to provide young people from Canada and overseas with an opportunity to participate in an educational international programme that helps foster informed and involved global citizens.

Activities: Core programme is the Youth Leaders in Action programme, where groups of 18 young people (nine Canadians and nine from overseas) from different cultures live with host families and work together on voluntary projects for six months (three in a Canadian community and three in a community abroad). The Global Learners programme is designed for educators, sending youths to an overseas community for a period of two weeks up to three months. The InterAction programme offers an opportunity for youths to have an international volunteer experience in an overseas host country for two to six weeks. Youth participants will volunteer in local projects dealing with health issues, eco-tourism or work with indigenous communities while living with a host family and learning about and from another culture.

Geographical Area of Activity: Africa, Asia, North, Central and South America and the Caribbean, and Central and Eastern Europe.

Publications: Newsletter (2 a year); annual Report.

Finance: Funded by the Canadian International Development Agency and by Canadian donors.

Directors: Prof. Charles J. McMillan (Chair.).

Principal Staff: Pres. and CEO Iris Almeida-Côté.

Address: 2330 Notre-Dame St West, 3rd Floor, Montréal, QC H3J 1N4.

Telephone: (514) 931-3526; **Fax:** (514) 939-2621; **Internet:** www.cwy-jcm.org; **e-mail:** communication@cwy-jcm.org.

Canadian Cancer Society

Founded in 1938 with the mandate to disseminate important information about the early warning signs of cancer to the Canadian public; from 1947 it also funded research through its research partner, the National Cancer Institute of Canada, and more recently through the Canadian Cancer Society Research Institute. It is a national, community-based organization of volunteers whose mission is the eradication of cancer and the enhancement of the quality of life of people living with cancer.

Activities: Operates nationally through funding and carrying out research on all types of cancer; providing comprehensive information about cancer care and treatment; giving support to people living with cancer; promoting healthy lifestyles and strategies for reducing cancer risk; and advocating public policy to prevent cancer and to help those living with it.

Geographical Area of Activity: Canada.

Publications: Annual Report; information on specific cancers, treatment, risk reduction, supportive care and tobacco control.

Finance: Assets C $194,413,000; annual revenue C $212,707,000, expenditure $222,283,000 (2011).

Board of Directors: Elizabeth Newson (Chair.).

Principal Staff: Pres. and CEO Peter Goodhand.

Address: 55 St Clair Ave West, Suite 300, Toronto, ON M4V 2Y7.

Telephone: (416) 961-7223; **Fax:** (416) 961-4189; **Internet:** www.cancer.ca; **e-mail:** info@cancer.ca.

Canadian Catholic Organization for Development and Peace

Established in 1967, aiming to improve living and working conditions world-wide, support initiatives by people in less-developed countries to take control of their future, and to educate Canadians about North-South issues.

Activities: Supports local organizations in less-developed countries, in the fields of human rights, women's rights, community development, housing, education and employment opportunities, and agrarian reform. Provides emergency relief for the victims of natural and man-made disasters, and humanitarian aid for those who need it. Works to inform Canadians about the causes of poverty, and to enlighten them of the alternatives to unjust social, political and economic systems and offering support for democratization.

Geographical Area of Activity: Africa, Asia, Eastern and Western Europe, North, Central and South America, and the Middle East.

Publications: *Global Village Voice* (quarterly newsletter); Annual Report; general information leaflet.

Finance: Total assets C $20,329,373; annual revenue $29,826,259, expenditure $31,386,530 (2009).

Board: Pat Hogan (Pres.).

Principal Staff: Exec. Dir Michael Casey.

Address: 10 St Mary St, Suite 420, Toronto, ON M4Y 1P9.

Telephone: (416) 922-1592; **Fax:** (416) 922-0957; **Internet:** www.devp.org; **e-mail:** ccodp@devp.org.

Canadian Centre for International Studies and Co-operation/Centre d'études et de coopération internationale—CECI

Originally founded in 1958, the Centre was officially incorporated under its current name as a non-profit NGO in 1968, with the aim of fighting poverty and injustice in the developing world.

Activities: Works to strengthen the opportunities for development in disadvantaged communities around the world, operating in the fields of human rights and democracy, the environment, humanitarian aid, socio-economic rehabilitation, and supporting peace initiatives.

Geographical Area of Activity: Asia and the Far East, Africa, North, Central and South America and the Caribbean.

Publications: *Capacity Building: a Manual for NGOs and Field Workers*; Annual Report; other publications in French and Spanish.

Finance: Annual revenue C $48,914,598, expenditure $48,611,105 (March 2011).

Board of Directors: Suzanne Laporte (Chair.); Danielle Sauvage (Exec. Vice-Chair.); Patricia Borlace (Treas.).

Principal Staff: Exec. Dir Mario Renaud; Deputy Exec. Dir Chantal-Sylvie Imbeault.

Address: 3000 rue Omer-Lavallée, Montréal, QC H1Y 3R8.

Telephone: (514) 875-9911; **Fax:** (514) 875-6469; **Internet:** www.ceci.ca; **e-mail:** info@ceci.ca.

Canadian Crossroads International/Carrefour Canadien International—CCI

Canadian Crossroads International (CCI) grew out of its American counterpart, Operation Crossroads Africa, founded by Dr James H. Robinson in the 1950s. The first Canadian volunteers went overseas in 1958.

Activities: CCI brings individuals, organizations and communities in Canada and the Global South together to reduce poverty, prevent the spread of HIV/AIDS and defend the rights of women. The organization offers people and organizations a space to collaborate across borders on pressing global issues. By supporting the development of international partnerships and facilitating staff exchanges and volunteer placements, CCI helps community-based organizations find the skills, expertise and resources they need to strengthen their communities. CCI works with organizations in West Africa, Southern Africa and the Andean region of South America, and facilitates the development of partnerships with Canadian organizations working on similar issues. The partnerships enable organizations to share strategies, knowledge and resources, while fostering a sense of international solidarity. The exchange of skilled volunteers and staff is central to the partnerships: each year CCI brings partners from the global south to work in Canada, sends Canadians to work with partners in the South and facilitates staff and volunteer exchanges between Southern partner organizations. Placements vary in length from several weeks to a year depending on the needs of the project.

Geographical Area of Activity: West Africa, Southern Africa, South America.

Restrictions: Programmes are available only to Canadian citizens and to volunteers from partner organizations.

Publications: *Sankofa* (newsletter, 2 a year); Annual Report.

Finance: Total assets C $2,057,309 (2010); annual income $4,851,002, expenditure $4,848,560.

Board of Directors: Darlene Bessey (Chair.); Jonathan Carlzon (Treas.).

Principal Staff: Exec. Dir Karen Takacs.

Address: 49 Bathurst St, Suite 201, Toronto, ON M5V 2P2.

Telephone: (416) 967-1611; **Fax:** (416) 967-9078; **Internet:** www.cciorg.ca; **e-mail:** info@cciorg.ca.

Canadian Executive Service Organization—CESO/Service d'assistance canadienne aux organismes—SACO

Founded in 1967, CESO is a non-profit volunteer-sending organization that works with clients in Canada, in Aboriginal and non-Aboriginal communities, and overseas in countries in the Americas, Africa, Asia and Eastern Europe. Its mission is to build capacity in governance and economic development through the transfer of knowledge and skills by volunteer advisers.

Activities: CESO volunteer advisers work on short-term assignments to transfer their skills and knowledge.

Geographical Area of Activity: International.

Publications: *FOCUS issues* (quarterly newsletter); Annual Report.

Finance: Total assets C $4,733,716; annual revenue $13,940,295, expenditure $14,138,643 (2009).

Board of Directors: Peter Chiddy (Chair.).

Principal Staff: Pres. and CEO Wendy Harris.

Address: 700 Bay St, Suite 700, Box 328, Toronto, ON, M5G 1Z6.

Telephone: (416) 961-2376; **Fax:** (416) 961-1096; **Internet:** www.ceso-saco.com; **e-mail:** information@ceso-saco.com.

Canadian Feed the Children

Aims to relieve the effects of hunger, poverty and suffering in Canada and around the world, and to help communities to achieve self-sufficiency successfully.

Activities: Focuses on both long-term solutions to poverty and hunger, and immediate aid to those who are suffering. Works nationally, running and supporting food supply and nutrition programmes in schools, community centres, refugee centres, women's shelters and subsidized housing projects, as well as supporting other programmes throughout the country that work to mitigate the effects of hunger and poverty. Internationally, the organization operates a number of programmes that work with communities to ensure that children have their basic needs fulfilled in terms of food, water, sanitation and education; train and support child-focused charities around the world; provide vegetable seeds to refugees and displaced families to provide them with a self-sufficient lifestyle; provide credit and training to families so that they can begin to break out of the poverty cycle; and provide emergency materials for communities and families in times of crisis.

Geographical Area of Activity: International.

Restrictions: Does not make grants.

Publications: Annual Report; newsletters.

Finance: Annual revenue C $16,018,956, expenditure $15,694,983 (2010).

Board of Directors: Rob King (Chair.); Derek Briffett (Vice-Chair.).

Principal Staff: Exec. Dir Debra Kerby.

Address: 174 Bartley Dr., Toronto, ON M4A 1E1.

Telephone: (416) 757-1220; **Fax:** (416) 757-3318; **Internet:** www.canadianfeedthechildren.ca; **e-mail:** contact@canadianfeedthechildren.ca.

Canadian Foodgrains Bank

Established in 1983 to allow farmers in Canada share their yield with hunger victims in less-developed countries, helping thereby to alleviate world hunger.

Activities: Operates in partnership with 13 Canadian churches. Collects contributions in the form of money and agricultural produce including grains, to distribute them to hunger victims in developing countries. Other activities include: providing services and advice on food programming and related aspects; encouraging policy development; and educating people about hunger and food security.

Geographical Area of Activity: Less-developed countries.

Publications: Annual Report; *End Hunger*; *Myths About Hunger*; *Hungry Farmers*; *HIV/AIDS and Hunger*; *Bulletin Covers and Inserts*.

Finance: Total assets C $45,201,539; annual revenue $34,476,159, expenditure $31,798,531 (March 2011).

Board of Directors: Don Peters (Chair.); Bob Granke (Vice-Chair.).

Principal Staff: Exec. Dir Jim Cornelius.

Address: POB 767, Winnipeg, MB R3C 2L4; 400-393 Portage Ave, Winnipeg, MB R3B 3H6.

Telephone: (204) 944-1993; **Fax:** (204) 943-2597; **Internet:** www.foodgrainsbank.ca; **e-mail:** cfgb@foodgrainsbank.ca.

Canadian Friends of the Hebrew University

Founded in 1944 to identify and maintain the interest of Canadian Jewish communities in Jewish and Hebrew studies, traditions and culture.

Activities: Operates nationally and internationally in the field of education, through speaker-orientated programmes, conferences, publications, and by awarding grants for study at the Hebrew University in Jerusalem.

Geographical Area of Activity: Canada.

Restrictions: Grants only to students studying at the Hebrew University of Jerusalem.

Publications: Newsletter (monthly).

Board of Directors: Ronnie Appleby (Pres.).

Principal Staff: Nat. Dir Rami Kleinmann.

Address: 3080 Yonge St, Suite 5024, Toronto, ON M4N 3N1.

Telephone: (416) 485-8000; **Fax:** (416) 485-8565; **Internet:** www.cfhu.org; **e-mail:** inquiry@cfhu.org.

Canadian Hunger Foundation

Founded in 1961 under the auspices of FAO to enable people in poor communities to attain sustainable, healthy livelihoods. Formerly known as the Canadian Hunger Foundation/Fondation canadienne contre la faim—Partners in Rural Development.

Activities: Works with NGOs in 38 countries in Africa, Asia, Central and South America and the Caribbean to strengthen the capacity of community-based organizations and support self-help projects. Promotes policies that reduce poverty, and programmes that raise public understanding of development issues. Priorities are: subsistence food production and income generation; self-help initiatives—rural infrastructure and services; community-based organization building; NGO partners—institutional capacity development; long-term sustainability; participation of women; ecological practices; and Canadian development education. Projects focus on agriculture (food production and processing), water and sanitation, energy (alternative and renewable), nutrition and health, and capacity building and networking.

Geographical Area of Activity: Africa, Asia, Central and South America and the Caribbean.

Publications: Annual Report; technical papers; HIV/AIDS information; newsletter; e-bulletin.

Finance: Total assets C$9,979,111; Annual revenue $10,926,803, expenditure $11,971,014 (March 2010).

Board of Directors: Hon. Mitchell Sharp (Founder); Louise Bergeron (Chair.); Erica Mongiat (Treas.); Tony Breuer (Sec.).

Principal Staff: Exec. Dir Tony Breuer.

Address: 323 Chapel St, Ottawa, ON K1N 7Z2.

Telephone: (613) 237-0180; **Fax:** (613) 237-5969; **Internet:** www.chf-partners.ca; **e-mail:** info@chf-partners.ca.

Canadian International Council/Conseil International du Canada—CIC

Founded in 1928 as an independent, non-partisan organization with the aim of providing a nationwide forum for discussion and analysis of international affairs. Formerly known as the Canadian Institute of International Affairs.

Activities: Operates briefing missions, conferences, lectures and a research and publications programme. There are 1,400 members in 16 branches across Canada.

Geographical Area of Activity: Mainly Canada.

Publications: Annual Report and financial statement; research reports; *International Journal* (quarterly); *International Security Series*; *International Insights*.

Board of Directors: Jim Balsillie (Chair.); Bill Graham (Vice-Chair.); Perrin Beatty (Vice-Chair.).

Principal Staff: Pres. Dr. Jennifer A. Jeffs.

Address: 45 Willcocks St, Suite 210, Toronto, ON M5S 1C7.

Telephone: (416) 977-9000; **Fax:** (416) 946-7319; **Internet:** www.opencanada.org; **e-mail:** info@opencanada.org.

Canadian Liver Foundation/Fondation Canadienne du Foie

Established in 1969 by a group of business leaders and doctors in response to the increasing rate of liver diseases to support education and research on the cause, diagnosis, treatment and prevention of all liver diseases.

Activities: Provides studentships and operating grants to qualified individuals researching the causes, diagnosis, treatment and prevention of liver and biliary tract diseases.

Geographical Area of Activity: Canada.

Restrictions: Organizations must be registered in Canada.

Publications: Pamphlets and information sheets on all forms of liver disease; Annual Report.

Finance: Total assets C $3,699,734; annual revenue $6,708,338, expenditure $5,461,756 (2010).

Board of Directors: Morris Sherman (Chair.); Elliot Jacobson (Sec. and Treas.).

Principal Staff: Pres. and COO Gary A. Fagan.

Address: 2235 Sheppard Ave East, Suite 1500, Toronto, ON M2J 5B5.

Telephone: (416) 491-3353; **Fax:** (416) 491-4952; **Internet:** www.liver.ca; **e-mail:** clf@liver.ca.

Canadian Organization for Development through Education—CODE

Founded in 1959, CODE encourages self-sufficiency through literacy in the developing world.

Activities: Supports literacy and education by distributing books from Canadian and US sources (usually new books from publishers) to countries in the developing world, primarily in Africa, although shipments are also made to the Caribbean and the Pacific region. Also funds training of librarians, writers, illustrators and literacy workers.

Geographical Area of Activity: Mainly Africa and Guyana.

Publications: *NGOMA* (bi-annual newsletter); Annual Report.

Finance: Annual income C $12,240,037, expenditure $12,180,092 (March 2010).

Board of Directors: Judy Hauserman (Chair.); Lynn Beauregard (Vice-Chair.); Jacque Bérubé (Treas.).

Principal Staff: Exec. Dir Scott Walter.

Address: 321 Chapel St, Ottawa, ON K1N 7Z2.

Telephone: (613) 232-3569; **Fax:** (613) 232-7435; **Internet:** www.codecan.org; **e-mail:** codehq@codecan.org.

Canadian Urban Institute (Institut urbain du Canada)

Launched by the Municipality of Metropolitan Toronto and the City of Toronto in 1990, CUI is a not-for-profit organization focusing on improvement of urban life in Canada and abroad.

Activities: Operates nationally and internationally towards the betterment of management and policy-making in urban areas, by elevating the understanding of government, businesses and other significant institutions regarding urban issues. Conducts conferences and seminars; takes part in applied research and training; produces publications; and recognizes emerging social and economic issues that can influence the urban sector in areas of social development, urban infrastructure, sustainability, housing, environment and economic development. Awards annual Brownie Awards in recognition of leadership, environmental sustainability and innovation, and its Urban Leadership Awards are conferred on individuals and organizations that have contributed to the urban environment.

Geographical Area of Activity: Canada and internationally.

Publications: *Smart Growth in North America: New Ways to Create Liveable Communities*; *The Urban Century* (quarterly newsletter); and other publications.

Board of Directors: John Farrow (Chair.).

Principal Staff: Pres. and CEO Fred Eisenberger.

Address: 555 Richmond St West, Suite 402, POB 612, Toronto, ON M5V 3B1.

Telephone: 416-365-0817; **Fax:** 416-365-0650; **Internet:** www.canurb.org; **e-mail:** cui@canurb.org.

Lucie and André Chagnon Foundation/Fondation Lucie et André Chagnon

Established in 2000 by André Chagnon.

Activities: Aims to contribute to the development and improvement of health through the prevention of poverty and disease, by intervening primarily with children and their parents; and to ensure that young people succeed in school, by taking notable action among those who live in poverty.

Geographical Area of Activity: Québec, Canada.

Restrictions: Not currently soliciting outside requests for project funding.

Finance: Total assets C $1,274,941 (2009); annual expenditure $218,147,000 (2009).

Board of Directors: André Chagnon (Pres. and CEO).

Principal Staff: Pres. Claude Chagnon.

Address: 2001 McGill College Ave, Suite 1000, Montréal, QC H3A 1G1.

Telephone: (514) 380-2001; **Fax:** (514) 380-8434; **Internet:** www.fondationchagnon.org; **e-mail:** info@fondationchagnon.org.

Chastell Foundation

Established in 1987 for general charitable purposes.

Activities: Donations are made in the areas of social, educational and health services. In 2001 established the Andrea and Charles Bronfman Ontario Graduate Scholarship to fund graduate students at McMaster University as part of an Ontario Graduate Scholarship in the Faculty of Humanities.

Geographical Area of Activity: Canada.

Restrictions: Moratorium on new funding because of fiscal constraints.

Officers and Directors: Charles R. Bronfman (Pres.); Andrew J. Parsons (Vice-Pres. and Treas.); Richard P. Doyle (Vice-Pres.); Arnold M. Ludwick (Sec.).

Address: 1170 Peel St, 8th Floor, Montréal, QC H3B 4P2.

Telephone: (514) 878-5248; **Fax:** (514) 878-5293.

Club 2/3

Founded in 1970 by students concerned about the poverty and injustice that affects around two-thirds of the world's population. Now a divison of Oxfam in Quebec.

Activities: Works in the field of international development and international solidarity in co-operation with Oxfam Québec, through supporting projects, mostly concerned with drinking-water, education and training, initiated by partner organizations in 10 less-developed countries in Africa, Asia and Central and South America. Particularly focuses on young people between the ages of 12 and 17 years.

Geographical Area of Activity: Brazil, Burkina Faso, El Salvador, Haiti, Nepal, Paraguay, Peru, the Philippines, Senegal and Togo.

Publications: Project reports; Annual Report; *Courrier Sud* (quarterly).

Finance: Revenue C $1,515,929, expenditure $1,236,577 (2008).

Principal Staff: Dir-Gen. Pierre Verroneau.

Address: 1259 rue Berri, bureau 510, Montréal, QC H2L 4C7.

Telephone: (514) 937-1614; **Fax:** (514) 937-9452; **Internet:** http://oxfam.qc.ca/fr/secondaire; **e-mail:** info@oxfam.qc.ca.

CNIB/INCA

Founded in 1918 as the Canadian National Institute for the Blind—CNIB, the institute is the primary source of support and information for all Canadians affected by vision loss.

Activities: Provides vital programmes and services, innovative consumer products, research, peer support and one of the world's largest libraries for the visually impaired. Focuses on protection and prevention, as well as on treatments and cures.

Geographical Area of Activity: Canada.

Publications: Vision health resources; _You and Your Vision Health: Yes! Something More CAN be Done; Tape Measure/Success Facilitators; Circles of Light; An Unequal Playing Field; Clear Print Accessibility Guidelines; Connecting to the World: Early Intervention with Young Children who are Blind or Visually Impaired; Living with Vision Loss: Guidance for Parents of Young Children who are Visually Impaired or Blind; Step by Step: A How-to Manual for Guiding Someone with Vision Loss; A Strong Beginning: A Sourcebook for Health and Education Professionals Working with Young Children who are Visually Impaired or Blind._

Finance: Total assets C $95,440,000; annual revenue $75,549,000, expenditure $56,965,000 (March 2009).

Board of Directors: Jane Beaumont (Chair.).

Principal Staff: Pres. and CEO John M. Rafferty.

Address: 1929 Bayview Ave, Toronto, ON M4G 3E8.

Telephone: (416) 486-2500; **Fax:** (416) 480-7677; **Internet:** www.cnib.ca; **e-mail:** info@cnib.ca.

Coady International Institute

Founded by the St Francis Xavier University in 1959 to improve the lives of disadvantaged people by empowering them with knowledge and skills.

Activities: Action research for community-driven development. Offers diploma, certificate and graduate programmes that are driven by the immediacy of students' direct work on the ground. Coady also works with partners throughout the world. The Institute offers Canadian youth fellowships to promote community development.

Geographical Area of Activity: International.

Restrictions: An educational facility, not a grant-making organization.

Publications: _From Clients to Citizens: Communities changing the course of their own development_ (2009); _Reaching the Hard to Reach: A global comparative study on member owned microfinance in Ecuador & Mexico_ (2008); 'ITC Choupal Fresh', in _Inclusive Value Chains in India_; occasional papers, journal articles and conference presentations (available online).

Finance: Annual revenue and expenditure C $4,429,988 (March 2011).

Advisory Committee: Harold Redekopp (Chair.).

Principal Staff: Dir Dr John Gaventa; Programme Man. Pauline Achola.

Address: St Francis Xavier University, POB 5000, Antigonish, NS B2G 2W5.

Telephone: (902) 867-3960; **Fax:** (902) 867-3907; **Internet:** www.coady.stfx.ca; **e-mail:** coady@stfx.ca.

Columbia Foundation

Established by Working Enterprises, a group of companies owned by the labour movement, to invest in human and social capital for the benefit of all Canadians.

Activities: Aims to fund innovative social research, to develop and fund new scholarships that promote retraining and life-long learning, and promote the inclusive involvement of citizens in decision-making and community building.

Geographical Area of Activity: Canada.

Board of Directors: David Levi (Chair.).

Principal Staff: Exec. Dir Charley Beresford.

Address: 1166 Alberni St, Suite 1200, Vancouver, BC V6E 3Z3.

Telephone: (604) 408-2500; **Fax:** (604) 408-2525; **Internet:** www.columbiainstitute.ca/about-us/columbia-foundation; **e-mail:** info@columbiafoundation.ca.

CPAR—Canadian Physicians for Aid and Relief

Established in 1984 in response to famine and poor health conditions suffered by Ethiopian refugees in Sudan. The organization now aims to build health communities for vulnerable people in parts of rural Africa.

Activities: Works to improve the quality of life of people living in Ethiopia, Malawi, Tanzania and Uganda, by operating long- and short-term programmes that focus on primary health care, water and sanitation, food security, community agro-forestry, agricultural rehabilitation, environmental protection, rural feeder road construction, adult training, credit programmes for small-scale enterprises, and peace-building. CPAR is also committed to informing Canadians about these causes, engaging them in the global effort for health and development. Has offices in Ethiopia, Malawi, Tanzania and Uganda.

Geographical Area of Activity: Africa.

Publications: Annual Report; _CPA Report_ (quarterly); _Global Perspectives_ (annually); _Global Kidz._

Finance: Funded by government grants and funding, the Canadian public, foundations and other organizations.

Board of Directors: Diane Lacaille (Chair.); Andrew Williamson (Treas.).

Principal Staff: Exec. Dir Kevin O'Brien.

Address: 1425 Bloor St West, Toronto, ON M6P 3L6.

Telephone: (416) 369-0865; **Fax:** (416) 369-0294; **Internet:** www.cpar.ca; **e-mail:** info@cpar.ca.

The CRB Foundation/La Fondation CRB

Founded in 1988 by Charles R. Bronfman to support major initiatives contributing to the enhancement of 'Canadianism' and to strengthening the unity of the Jewish people.

Activities: Operates at national and international levels, running programmes that the Foundation has conceptualized, incubated and nurtured, including the Canadian heritage programme, which became Historica, Project Involvement, a major educational reform programme running in Israel, and Birthright Israel, a programme that provides adults with their first living and learning experience in Israel. Currently prioritises 'incubator' programmes in the areas of Jewish identity; relations between Israel and Jewish people world-wide; the quality of life in Israel, especially in the area of educational reform; general and Jewish strategic philanthropy; and building diverse networks of young Jewish people examining their identity, community and/or philanthropy.

Geographical Area of Activity: USA, Canada and Israel.

Restrictions: Does not support annual health, welfare or education campaigns; building campaigns or capital projects; equipment; general operating expenses; deficit funding or endowment funds; academic chairs or scholarship programmes.

Publications: Information booklet.

Officers and Directors: Charles R. Bronfman (Chair.); Andrea M. Bronfman (Deputy Chair.); Jeffrey R. Solomon (Sec.); Karen Adler (Treas.).

Principal Staff: Exec. Dir Thomas S. Axworthy.

Address: 1170 Peel St, 8th Floor, Montréal, QC H3B 4P2.

Telephone: (514) 878-5250; **Fax:** (514) 878-5299; **e-mail:** taxworthy@rogers.com.

CUSO-VSO

CUSO was established in 1961, aiming to support alliances that work for global social justice, the elimination of poverty and international development. Merged with VSO Canada in 2008.

Activities: Operates in the fields of development, human rights, the environment and international development, mainly through placing Canadian volunteers in less-developed countries of Asia and the Pacific region, Africa, and Central and South America and the Caribbean; also by disseminating information, human and material resources and promoting policies for developing long-term sustainability.

Geographical Area of Activity: Asia and the Pacific, Africa, Central and South America and the Caribbean, Canada.

Publications: *CUSO News*; *Sustainable Times*; *Kébek News*; *Health Advice for Living Overseas*; *A Healthy Stay in Canada*; Annual Report; and other publications.

Finance: Financed by the Canadian International Development Agency and other donors. Total assets C $12,433,916; annual income $9,806,029, expenditure $9,326,496 (2009).

Board of Directors: Cameron Charlebois (Chair.); Laurie Wein (Vice-Chair.); Dan Wright (Treas.).

Principal Staff: Exec. Dir Derek Evans.

Address: 44 Eccles St, Ottawa, ON K1R 6S4.

Telephone: (613) 829-7445; **Fax:** (613) 829-7996; **Internet:** www.cuso-vso.org; **e-mail:** questions@cuso-vso.org.

Cystic Fibrosis Canada

Founded as the Canadian Cystic Fibrosis Foundation in 1960, a non-profit voluntary health organization. Works through more than 50 chapters throughout Canada; raises and allocates funds to promote public awareness of cystic fibrosis; conducts research into improved care and treatment; and seeks a cure or control for this disorder. Name changed to Cystic Fibrosis Canada in 2011.

Activities: Promotes research on cystic fibrosis in Canadian universities and hospitals; funds research grants and major research development programmes; and gives special grants for training and research to students, fellows, scholars and visiting scientists skilled in such areas as respirology, paediatrics and the behavioural sciences.

Geographical Area of Activity: Canada.

Publications: *Candid Facts* (newsletter 2 a year, in English and French); *Circle of Friends* (newsletter, 2 a year, in English and French); *Report of the Canadian cystic fibrosis patient data registry;* Annual Report; brochures and reports. All available on-line at www.cysticfibrosis.ca.

Board of Directors: Debra Berlet (Pres.); Art Parons (Vice-Pres.); René Coutu (Vice-Pres.); Doug Ingersoll (Sec.); Miles Nagamatsu (Treas.).

Principal Staff: CEO Maureen Adamson.

Address: 2221 Yonge St, Suite 601, Toronto, ON M4S 2B4.

Telephone: (416) 485-9149; **Fax:** (416) 485-0960; **Internet:** www.cysticfibrosis.ca; **e-mail:** info@cysticfibrosis.ca.

Disabled People's International

A network of national organizations or assemblies of disabled people, established to promote human rights of disabled people through full participation, equalization of opportunity and development.

Activities: Promotes the human rights of disabled persons; promotes the economic and social integration of disabled persons; works to develop and support organizations of disabled persons. There are currently 133 National Assemblies (member organizations), and five Regional Development Offices in Italy (Europe), Mauritania (Africa), Thailand (Asia/Pacific), Peru (Latin America) and Antigua and Barbuda (North America/Caribbean).

Geographical Area of Activity: International.

Publications: Position papers; newsletters.

Executive Council: Javed Abidi (Chair.); Micheal Fraser and Rachel Kachaje (Deputy Chairs); Samuel Kabue (Sec.); Wilfredo Juzman Jara (Treas.).

Principal Staff: Elizabeth da Silva.

Address: 38 Pearson St, Suite 188, St. John's, NL A1A 3R1.

Telephone: (709) 747-7600; **Fax:** (709) 747-7603; **Internet:** www.dpi.org; **e-mail:** info@dpi.org.

EJLB Foundation

Established in 1983 to fund scientific research in all areas of neuroscience pertaining to mental illness, and to promote the protection of the environment.

Activities: Operates in two main areas: a Canadian Scholar Research Programme in neuroscience, particularly aimed at research that pertains directly or indirectly to schizophrenia and mental illness, which offers three awards of C $350,000 annually; and grants to support environmental projects in Canada that are working for the preservation of natural areas, and for environmental scientific research. Funds the EJLB–CIHR Michael Smith Chair in Neurosciences and Mental Health, in conjunction with the Canadian Institute of Health Research (CIHR), to be awarded every five years to a Canadian university, or affiliated research institute, for a scientist in neurosciences and mental health. Also provides funding to community organizations, mainly those providing assistance to sufferers of mental health problems.

Geographical Area of Activity: Canada, with limited international grant-making.

Restrictions: Grants will be made for building funds, capital funds, endowment funds or equipment funds, laboratory renovations, but not for the applicant's salary or that of other faculty members who may be participating in the research project.

Finance: Awarded community grants totalling C $2,676,000 and environmental grants worth $1,589,000 in 2011.

Scientific Advisory Committee: Dr Michel Chrétien (Chair.).

Principal Staff: Exec. Dir Kevin Leonard.

Address: 1350 Sherbrooke St West, Suite 1050, Montréal, QC H3G 1J1.

Telephone: (514) 843-5112; **Fax:** (514) 843-4080; **Internet:** www.ejlb.qc.ca; **e-mail:** general@ejlb.qc.ca.

Eldee Foundation

Founded in 1961 for the support of Canadian organizations and charitable institutions.

Activities: Operates nationally in the fields of medicine and health, the environment, and Jewish causes in Canada and Israel, especially medical research and hospital development where it pertains directly or indirectly to schizophrenia and mental illness, and acquiring and preserving natural areas of significance to the urban landscape and funding Canada-based environmental research.

Geographical Area of Activity: Canada and Israel.

Restrictions: No grants are made to individuals for awards, fellowships, scholarships, bursaries or research grants.

Board: Harry J. F. Bloomfield (Pres.); David A. Johnson (Sec. and Treas.).

Address: 1080 côte du Beaver Hill, Suite 1720, Montréal, QC H2Z 1S8.

Telephone: (514) 871-9261; **Fax:** (514) 397-0816; **Internet:** www.eldeefoundation.ca.

EnerGreen Foundation

Founded in 1994 and supported by companies and individuals active in the independent power industry, specifically renewable and clean energy technologies.

Activities: Aims to promote renewable energy and sustainable development in Canada and around the world through support of projects, including reforestation initiatives, micro-hydro and solar projects and renewable energy education programmes.

Geographical Area of Activity: International.

Publications: Newsletter.

Board of Directors: Jeff W. Arsenych (Pres.).

Principal Staff: Projects Co-ordinator Maryann Lester; Treas. Pat MacDonald.

Address: 700 Fourth Ave SW, Suite 1210, Calgary, AB T2P 3J4.

Telephone: (403) 210-9552; **Fax:** (403) 266-1462; **e-mail:** energreen@energreen.org.

ETC Group—Action Group on Erosion, Technology and Concentration

Founded as the Rural Advancement Foundation International in 1985 and reformed as the ETC Group in 2001 to protect ecological diversity.

Activities: We address the socioeconomic and ecological issues surrounding new technologies that could have an impact on the world's poorest and most vulnerable. We investigate ecological erosion (including the erosion of cultures and human rights); the development of new technologies (especially agricultural but also new technologies that work with genomics and matter); and we monitor global governance issues including corporate concentration and trade in technologies. We operate at the global political level. We work closely with partner civil society organizations (CSOs) and social movements, especially in Africa, Asia and Latin America.

Geographical Area of Activity: World-wide.

Restrictions: Not a grant-making organization.

Publications: *Submission: ETC Group Submission to Rio+20– Tackling Technology: Three Proposals for Rio.* (2011);*Earth Grab!– Geoengineering, biomass and climate-ready crops* (2011); *Road to Rio Countdown Map of Key Events* (2011); *The New Biomasters, Geopiracy: The case against Geoengineering, The Big Downturn? Nanogeopolitics* (2010);*Communiqué* (research journal published 4–6 times a year);*ETC Century: Erosion, Technological Transformation, and Corporate Concentration in the 21st Century* (2001);*The Seed Giants: Who Owns Whom?;* reports and financial statements; other specialist publications and occasional papers.

Finance: Annual revenue C $ 1,210,679 (2010) Annual expenditure $ 1,184,665 (2010).

Board of Directors: Tim Brodhead (Pres.), Michael Hansen (Sec. and Treas.).

Principal Staff: Exec. Dir Pat Roy Mooney.

Address: 180 Metcalfe St, Suite 206, Ottawa, ON K2P 1P5.

Telephone: (613) 241-2267; **Fax:** (613) 241-2506; **Internet:** www.etcgroup.org; **e-mail:** etc@etcgroup.org.

Focus Humanitarian Assistance

Founded in 1994 by the Ismaili Muslim community in Europe and North America; a network of agencies providing emergency humanitarian assistance in less-developed countries. The organization is an affiliate of the Aga Khan foundations network (q.v.).

Activities: Operates in less-developed countries of Africa, and Central and Southern Asia, providing humanitarian assistance to areas stricken by natural disasters or by conflict. Maintains liaison offices in Afghanistan, the United Kingdom, India, Pakistan and the USA.

Geographical Area of Activity: World-wide.

Board of Directors: HH the Aga Khan (Chair.).

Address: International Co-ordinating Committee, Suite 201, 789 Don Mills Rd, Don Mills, ON M3C 1T5.

Telephone: (416) 422-0177; **Fax:** (416) 422-5032; **Internet:** www.akdn.org/focus; **e-mail:** ficc@focushumanitarian.org.

Fondation Marcelle et Jean Coutu (Marcelle et Jean Coutu Foundation)

Established in 1990 by the Groupe Jean Coutu to assist those in less-developed countries and the disadvantaged in Canada.

Activities: Operates in Canada, especially Québec, in the field of social welfare, in particular disadvantaged women and children, and drug abuse.

Geographical Area of Activity: Mainly Canada.

Board of Directors: Marie-Josée Coutu (Pres.).

Principal Staff: Admins Read Bastarache, Nicolle Forget.

Address: 1374 Mont-Royal est, bureau 101, Montréal, QC H2V 4P3.

Internet: www.jeancoutu.com; **e-mail:** hbisson@jeancoutu .com.

Fondation Armand-Frappier (Armand-Frappier Foundation)

Established in 1978 to support scholarship programmes and the purchase of scientific equipment, as well as the Institut Armand-Frappier, which aims to promote the pursuit of excellence and innovative research.

Activities: Operates in the fields of education and science and technology, offering scholarships to pre- and post-doctoral students studying at the Institut Armand-Frappier, and scholarships to students at Québec universities aiming to continue their studies at the Institut Armand-Frappier. Also offers Armand-Frappier prizes in the areas of Health, Innovation and Emerging Businesses in Québec working in relevant areas.

Geographical Area of Activity: Canada.

Publications: Annual Report.

Finance: Assets C$8,226,831; annual expenditure $516,081 (June 2010).

Board of Directors: Pierre-Yves Châtillon (Pres.); Daniel Hudon, Luc Reny, Guy Lord, Serge Paquette (Vice-Pres); Guylaine Legault (Treas.); Louis-François Hogue (Sec.).

Principal Staff: Gen. Man. Michael Pecho.

Address: 531 blvd des Prairies, Ville de Laval, QC H7V 1B7.

Telephone: (450) 686-5360; **Fax:** (450) 686-5361; **Internet:** www.fondation-afrappier.qc.ca; **e-mail:** fondation.armand -frappier@iaf.inrs.ca.

Fondation Jean-Louis Lévesque (Jean-Louis Lévesque Foundation)

Established in 1961 by Jean-Louis Lévesque to promote the development of universities, research institutes and charitable organizations.

Activities: Operates in Québec, Ontario and the Atlantic Provinces of Canada in the fields of education, medical research and social welfare, through making grants for research and special projects.

Geographical Area of Activity: Canada.

Restrictions: All funds are currently committed.

Board: Suzanne Lévesque (Pres.).

Principal Staff: Vice-Rector Patrick Robert, Dr Patrick Vinay; Vice-Chancellor Robert Lacroix.

Address: 2000 ave McGill College, Suite 2340, Montréal, QC H3A 3H3.

Fondation Baxter and Alma Ricard

Established by Baxter and Alma Ricard in 1999 to offer French Canadians living in a linguistic minority situation the opportunity to pursue graduate studies in the best schools in the world without having to go into debt.

Activities: The Foundation offers annual graduate and post-graduate scholarships to young French Canadians, for a period of up to three years. Candidates are evaluated on the basis of academic excellence, leadership, civic pride and their commitment to the community.

Geographical Area of Activity: Canada.

Finance: Total assets approx. C $35,000,000.

Board of Trustees: Paul Desmarais (Pres.).

Principal Staff: Exec. Dir Alain Landry; Asst Sylvie Lebel.

Address: 225 rue Metcalfe, Suite 407, Ottawa, ON K2P 1P9.

Telephone: (613) 236-7065; **Fax:** (613) 236-3718; **Internet:** www.fondationricard.com; **e-mail:** fonricar@rogers.com.

Foundation for International Training—FIT

Founded in 1976 to enhance self-reliance in developing countries by providing training.

Activities: Operates internationally in providing training and consultancy services and materials. The Foundation works with both private and public sectors, collaborating with local institutions; it concentrates on strengthening the capabilities of those who can then offer training to others. The three main programme areas are: social development, economic development and environmental management.

Geographical Area of Activity: World-wide.

Publications: Annual Report; training materials, and policy and background papers.

Board of Directors: Richard Beattie (Chair.).

Principal Staff: Exec. Dir Mirabelle Rodrigues.

Address: 7181 Woodbine Ave, Suite 110, Markham, ON L3R 1A3.

Telephone: (905) 305-8680; **Fax:** (905) 305-8681; **Internet:** www.ffit.org; **e-mail:** info@ffit.org.

Frontiers Foundation Inc/Fondation Frontière Inc

Established in 1968 by the Rev. Charles R. Catto to contribute to the relief of poverty by supporting tangible community development projects that have enduring significance. The Operation Beaver Program began in 1964; the Frontiers Foundation assumed responsibility for its administration in Canada in 1968 and overseas in 1969.

Activities: Operates through the Operation Beaver Program in Canada, Haiti and Bolivia in the areas of aid to less-developed countries, education and housing, through self-conducted programmes for community development, grants to individuals and institutions, training courses and publications.

Geographical Area of Activity: Canada, Bolivia and Haiti.

Publications: Annual Report; *Beaver Tales*; films, video documentaries, slides.

Finance: Annual budget C $1,500,000 (2006).

Board of Directors: Lawrence Gladue (Pres.); Rhonda Dickemous (Vice-Pres.); Glen Jennings (Sec. and Treas.).

Principal Staff: Exec. Dir Marco A. Guzman.

Address: 419 Coxwell Ave, Toronto, ON M4L 3B9.

Telephone: (416) 690-3930; **Fax:** (416) 690-3934; **Internet:** www.frontiersfoundation.ca; **e-mail:** marcoguzman@frontiersfoundation.ca.

Gairdner Foundation

Founded in 1957 by James A. Gairdner for the recognition of individuals who have made outstanding contributions through research in the field of medical science.

Activities: Operates internationally in the fields of medicine, biomedical science, and global health through awards to individuals.

Geographical Area of Activity: International.

Restrictions: Awards are only made on the basis of nominations and peer review.

Publications: News reports.

Finance: Total assets C $27,583,850 (2010).

Board of Directors: Lorne Tyrrell (Chair.); Kevin Lynch (Vice-Chair.).

Principal Staff: Pres. and Scientific Dir Dr John H. Dirks.

Address: 4 Devonshire Pl., Toronto, Ontario M5S2E1.

Telephone: (416) 596-9996; **Fax:** (416) 596-9992; **Internet:** www.gairdner.org; **e-mail:** john.dirks@gairdner.org.

Mahatma Gandhi Canadian Foundation for World Peace

Established in 1988, aims to share the beliefs and philosophies of Mahatma Gandhi to promote international understanding and world peace.

Activities: Conducts and supports research and scholarship to promote Gandhian philosophy in a contemporary context, through supporting exchanges, lectureships and other academic posts; organizing conferences and lectures on the life and thoughts of Gandhi; and other educational projects.

Geographical Area of Activity: Canada.

Publications: *Declaration Towards a Global Ethic*; newsletter.

Board of Directors: Jitendra A. Shah (Chair.); Harchand Grewal (Treas.); Dr Prem Kharbanda (Sec.).

Principal Staff: Co-ordinator Jaime Beck.

Address: POB 60002, University of Alberta Postal Outlet, Edmonton, AB T6G 2S4.

Telephone: (780) 492-5504; **Fax:** (780) 492-0113; **Internet:** www.gandhi.ca; **e-mail:** sonia.houle@ualberta.ca.

Impact First International

Founded in 1982 as Gems of Hope; changed to present name in April 2010. Non-sectarian and non-political not-for-profit organization. Works with local partners, with a focus on women, to promote the well-being and self-sufficiency of communities in the developing world, by supporting capacity building initiatives in local enterprise, health and basic education.

Activities: Works with local partners to support grassroots community development initiatives in the areas of micro-credit, gender awareness, basic healthcare services and education.

Geographical Area of Activity: Latin America and the Caribbean, Asia.

Restrictions: Works with local NGOs.

Publications: Newsletter.

Finance: Supported by the Canadian International Development Agency, local companies, foundations and individuals.

Board of Directors: Joy Bews (Chair.); Dororthy Nyambi (Treas.); Lynda Bell (Sec.).

Principal Staff: CEO Thierry Zomahoun.

Address: 720 Spadina Ave, Suite 205, Toronto, ON, M5S 2T9.

Telephone: (416) 362-4367; **Fax:** (416) 362-4170; **Internet:** www.impactfirst.net.

Globe Foundation of Canada—GLOBE

Founded in 1993 to promote the development of eco-business throughout the world.

Activities: Not-for-profit organization dedicated to finding practical business-orientated solutions to the world's environmental problems. Helps companies and individuals realize the value of economically viable environmental business opportunities through conferences and events, research and consulting, project management, communications and awards. Champions green initiatives and sustainable ventures.

Geographical Area of Activity: Canada, Asia and Eastern Europe.

Publications: *British Columbia's Green Economy: Securing the Workforce of Tomorrow.*

Finance: Annual budget approx. C $1,850,000.

Board of Directors: Michael E. J. Phelps (Chair.).

Principal Staff: Pres. and CEO Dr John D. Wiebe.

Address: World Trade Center, 999 Canada Pl., Suite 578, Vancouver, BC V6C 3E1.

Telephone: (604) 695-5001; **Fax:** (604) 695-5019; **Internet:** www.globe.ca; **e-mail:** info@globe.ca.

Walter and Duncan Gordon Charitable Foundation

Established in 1965 by Walter L. Gordon, his wife Elizabeth, and brother, Duncan L. Gordon, to support programmes that strengthen Canada and enhance the well-being of Canadians.

Activities: Operates in three main areas: the Canadian North (Northwest Territories, Nunavut and Yukon); Fresh Water Resources Protection (national), and Art Acquisitions (Ontario).

Geographical Area of Activity: Canada.

Restrictions: Does not offer scholarships, nor does it offer bursaries or make grants to individuals.

Publications: E-Newsletter; Annual Report; *The Canadian North*; *Fresh Water Resources Protection*; *Global Citizenship*.

Finance: Total assets C \$51,506,602; annual income \$3,911,037, expenditure \$4,081,333 (Dec. 2010).

Board of Trustees: Karen Hanna (Chair.); Dr Janice G Ross Stein (Vice-Chair.); Jonathan Wilkinson (Treas.).

Principal Staff: Pres. and CEO Dr Thomas S. Axworthy.

Address: 11 Church St, Suite 400, Toronto, ON M5E 1W1.

Telephone: (416) 601-4776; **Fax:** (416) 601-1689; **Internet:** www.gordonfoundation.ca; **e-mail:** info@gordonfn.org.

The Lotte and John Hecht Memorial Foundation

Lotte and John Hecht Memorial Foundation was set up in 1962 as the 1945 Foundation on the returns obtained from the sale of shares of one of its proprietary companies.

Activities: Operates in two main areas: research and support of alternative and complementary medicine, specifically for the treatment of cancer; and economic education that furthers the principles of free market, through offering grants to non-profit organizations.

Geographical Area of Activity: Canada.

Finance: Annual disbursements approx. C \$5,000,000 (2010).

Principal Staff: Exec. Dir A. Webster.

Address: 325 Howe St, Suite 502, Vancouver, BC V6C 1Z7.

Telephone: (604) 683-7575; **Fax:** (604) 683-7580; **Internet:** www.hecht.org/index.htm; **e-mail:** info@hecht.org.

HOPE International Development Agency—HOPE

Established in 1974, HOPE aims to provide support to developing countries where environmental, economic or social circumstances have interfered with communities' abilities to sustain themselves.

Activities: Provides help less-developed countries in crisis in a number of ways: by providing emergency aid, including clean water and sanitation, shelter, medicine and food, as well as more long-term solutions, such as technological and educational support, training in food production and nutrition, and health-care and community development programmes. Aims to assist communities to learn the skills necessary to sustain themselves in the long term. Also maintains offices in Afghanistan, Australia, Cambodia, Ethiopia, Japan, Myanmar, New Zealand, United Kingdom and the USA.

Geographical Area of Activity: International.

Publications: Annual Report.

Finance: Annual income and expenditure C \$26,636,695 (2010).

Board of Directors: David S. McKenzie (Pres.).

Principal Staff: Exec. Dir Aklilu Mulat (acting).

Address: 214 Sixth St, New Westminster, BC V3L 3A2.

Telephone: (604) 525-5481; **Fax:** (604) 525-3471; **Internet:** www.hope-international.com; **e-mail:** hope@hope-international.com.

Horizons of Friendship

Established in 1973 by Tim Coughlan and Christine and David Stewart, with the aim of eliminating poverty in Mexico and Central America.

Activities: Works with people living with the effects of poverty in rural and urban communities. Runs development projects to provide clean water and sanitation, health care, housing and skills training. Horizons has given humanitarian assistance to victims of war and political oppression, aided refugees in need of rehabilitation and provided aid to those affected by natural disasters.

Geographical Area of Activity: Mexico and Central America.

Publications: Newsletter; Annual Report.

Finance: Total assets C \$1,219,740 (March 2010); annual revenue \$1,333,675, expenditure \$1,333,603 (2010).

Board of Directors: Dr David Morrison (Pres.); Linda Seppanen (Vice-Pres.); Rev. Timothy Coughlan (Hon. Pres.); Mike Dupuis (Treas.).

Principal Staff: Exec. Dir Patricia Rebolledo Klogies.

Address: 50 Covert St, POB 402, Cobourg, ON K9A 4L1.

Telephone: (905) 372-5483; **Fax:** (905) 372-7095; **Internet:** www.horizons.ca; **e-mail:** info@horizons.ca.

Imperial Oil Foundation

Established in 1994 for general charitable purposes in Canada that are compatible with the company's business objectives and activities.

Activities: Operates nationally in the fields of arts and humanities, education, medicine and health, and social welfare (in particular community and social services and sport and recreation), through grants to Canadian charitable organizations for existing facilities and programmes.

Geographical Area of Activity: Canada.

Restrictions: No grants are made to individuals; grants are limited to communities in which the company has employees; no finance for research projects, fellowships or scholarships.

Publications: *Tradition of Giving*; Annual Report.

Finance: Grant expenditure C \$12,100,000 (2008).

Officers and Directors: Barbara Hejduk (Pres.); Susan E. Young (Treas.); John Zych (Sec.).

Principal Staff: Corporate Citizenship Catherine Teasdale.

Address: POB 2480, Station M, Calgary, AB T2P 3M9.

Telephone: (416) 968-4111; **Internet:** www.imperialoil.ca.

Institute of Cultural Affairs International

Established in 1977 to campaign for the fundamental right of all peoples to define and shape their own futures, with the ultimate goal of achieving sustainable, just solutions to human challenges.

Activities: Operates in the fields of development, health, welfare and human rights, seeking to influence international development policies and co-ordinating and supporting projects run by its member organizations. A global network of national member organizations located in Australia, Bangladesh, Belgium, Benin, Bosnia and Herzegovina, Canada, Chile, Côte d'Ivoire, Egypt, Ghana, Guatemala, India, Japan, Kenya, Malaysia, Nepal, the Netherlands, Nigeria, Peru, South Africa, Spain, Taiwan, Tajikistan, Tanzania, Togo, Uganda, the United Kingdom, the USA, Zambia and Zimbabwe.

Geographical Area of Activity: International.

Restrictions: Not a grant-making organization.

Publications: Annual Report; *Network Exchange* (newsletter).

Board of Directors: Lawrence Philbrook (Pres.); Shankar Jadhav (Treas.); Gerald Gomani (Sec.).

Principal Staff: Sec.-Gen. Lambert Okrah.

Address: 417 St-Pierre St, Suite 804, Montréal, QC H2Y 2M4.

Telephone: (514) 875-7111; **Fax:** (514) 875-0702; **Internet:** www.ica-international.org; **e-mail:** info@ica-international.org.

Inter Pares

Founded in 1975 by Timothy Brodhead and Ian Smiley to support the efforts of self-help groups in developing countries in gaining control over their lives, create economic alternatives and find sustainable solutions to poverty.

Activities: Inter Pares ('among equals'), supports local groups in 20 countries in Asia, Africa, Central America and the Caribbean to establish co-operatives and credit schemes; reclaim land for food production; promote reproductive rights; protect the environment; provide community-based health care, education and training; and organize women, farmers and urban poor to improve their lives. In Canada Inter Pares promotes understanding of the causes of poverty and powerlessness, and encourages groups in Canada and developing countries to learn from and support each other in strategies for change.

Inter Pares works with local and regional organizations in Canada to support community development and social change.

Geographical Area of Activity: Africa, Asia, Central and South America, and Canada.

Publications: *Inter Pares Bulletin* (5 a year); Annual Report; occasional papers; photo essays; collaborative works; co-publications.

Finance: Total assets C $3,666,682; annual revenue $7,162,249, expenditure $6,998,657 (2009).

Board of Directors: Tamara Levine (Chair.); Bill Van Iterson (Treas.).

Principal Staff: Exec. Dir Rita Morbia.

Address: 221 Laurier Ave East, Ottawa, ON K1N 6P1.

Telephone: (613) 563-4801; **Fax:** (613) 594-4704; **Internet:** www.interpares.ca; **e-mail:** info@interpares.ca.

International Development and Relief Foundation

Founded in 1984 by a group of Canadian Muslims aiming to empower the world's disadvantaged people.

Activities: Aims to empower the world's disadvantaged people of the world through emergency relief and participatory development programmes based on the Islamic principles of human dignity, self-reliance and social justice. For more than 27 years, IDRF has successfully implemented relief and development projects in Asia, Africa, the Middle East, Eastern Europe, and the Americas.

Geographical Area of Activity: International.

Publications: *IDRF Reporter* (annually); financial statements; newsletter.

Board of Directors: Winston Kassim (Chair.); Javed Akbar (Vice-Chair.); Zeib Jeeva (Vice-Chair. and Treas.).

Principal Staff: Gen. Sec. Yasmeen Siddiqui.

Address: 2 Berkeley St, Suite 210, Toronto, ON M5A 4J5.

Telephone: (416) 497-0818; **Fax:** (416) 497-0686; **Internet:** www.idrf.ca; **e-mail:** office@idrf.ca.

International Institute for Sustainable Development—IISD

Founded in 1990 to promote sustainable social and economic development world-wide and to promote innovation.

Activities: Collates and disseminates information on economic development; serves, in an advisory capacity, government agencies and national and international organizations involved in development work; devises business strategies and trade principles; promotes community living and the creation of sustainable economies. Also conducts research, produces educational materials and maintains a library. Maintains offices in Ottawa, Geneva and New York.

Geographical Area of Activity: International.

Publications: *IISD News*; Annual Report; various books, brochures and handbooks.

Finance: Total assets C $19,364,970; annual revenue $16,312802, expenditure $13,571,781 (March 2011).

Board of Directors: Daniel Gagnier (Chair.).

Principal Staff: Pres. and CEO Franz Tattenbach; Vice-Pres. and COO William H. Glanville; Sec.-Treas. and CFO Ian Seymour; Dir Janice Gair.

Address: 161 Portage Ave East, 6th Floor, Winnipeg, MB R3B 0Y4.

Telephone: (204) 958-7700; **Fax:** (204) 958-7710; **Internet:** www.iisd.org; **e-mail:** info@iisd.ca.

Ivey Foundation

A private charitable foundation established in 1947 by Richard G. and Richard M. Ivey.

Activities: Supports three programmes: Conserving Canada's Forests, Strategic Opportunities and Director-Initiated.

Geographical Area of Activity: Canada.

Restrictions: Grants only to registered Canadian charities. Grants not normally made for the following: building campaigns; scholarships or student aid; sabbaticals or academic leaves; land acquisitions; seminars, workshops, conferences, tours, competitions or special events; costs of performances; publication of studies and research; operating expenditures, except temporarily for new undertakings; deficits; private foundations or other grant-making organizations; production of films, videos, CD-ROMs or websites.

Publications: Annual Report; programme brochures.

Finance: Total assets C $71,869,316 (Dec. 2010); total income $5,502,240, annual expenditure $4,164,607 (Dec. 2010).

Board of Directors: Rosamond A. Ivey (Chair.); Suzanne E. Ivey Cook (Vice-Pres.); Richard W. Ivey (Sec. and Treas.).

Principal Staff: Pres. Bruce Lourie.

Address: 11 Church St, Suite 400, Toronto, ON M5E 1W1.

Telephone: (416) 867-9229; **Fax:** (416) 601-1689; **Internet:** www.ivey.org; **e-mail:** info@ivey.org.

Kahanoff Foundation

Established in 1979 by the estate of Sydney Kahanoff for general charitable purposes, in particular innovative projects.

Activities: Operates throughout Canada, with an emphasis on projects in Alberta, and in Israel, in the areas of education, the arts and humanities, medicine and health, research, social welfare, philanthropy and community development, through grants to non-profits in Canada and partner organizations carrying out Foundation projects in Israel.

Geographical Area of Activity: Canada and Israel.

Restrictions: Grants are not given to individuals, for conferences, fellowships, bursaries, scholarships, tours, exhibitions or conferences, public works, non-applied research, nor for operating or endowment funds.

Finance: Funded by the estate of Sydney Kahanoff; total assets in excess of C $100,000,000.

Board of Directors: James B. Hume (Pres.); Cynthia P. Moore (Vice-Pres.).

Principal Staff: Exec. Vice-Pres. Shira Herzog; Dir Alan C. Moon.

Address: 101 Six St SW, Suite 105, Calgary, AB T2P 5K7.

Telephone: (403) 237-7896; **Fax:** (403) 261-9614; **Internet:** www.kahanoff.com; **e-mail:** info@kahanoff.com.

Laidlaw Foundation

Established in 1949 by W. C. Laidlaw, R. A. Laidlaw, R. W. L. Laidlaw and Dr R. G. N. Laidlaw to strengthen the environment for children, young people and families, to promote opportunities for human development and creativity, and to support healthy communities and ecosystems.

Activities: Operates in the fields of the arts and humanities, conservation and the environment, and social welfare. The Foundation's main programmes are: Contaminants and Child Health; Youth Arts; Youth Engagement, which promotes leadership and decision-making skills; and a pilot project, Inclusive Communities for Children, Youth and Families.

Geographical Area of Activity: Mainly Ontario, Canada.

Publications: Annual Report; information brochures; occasional papers.

Finance: Total assets C $54,715,471; annual income $7,123,241 expenditure $3,819,479 (Dec. 2010).

Board of Directors: Alina Chatterjee (Chair.).

Principal Staff: Exec. Dir Nathan Gilbert.

Address: 365 Bloor St East, Suite 2000, Toronto, ON M4W 3L4.

Telephone: (416) 964-3614; **Fax:** (416) 975-1428; **Internet:** www.laidlawfdn.org; **e-mail:** mail@laidlawfdn.org.

Daniel Langlois Foundation/Fondation Daniel Langlois

Established in 1997 by Daniel Langlois to further artistic and scientific knowledge by promoting the meeting of science and art in the field of technology internationally.

Activities: Operates internationally in the fields of the arts, science, technology and the environement. Supports interdisciplinary research that encourages the co-operation of people from a variety of fields; funds projects by high-level artists and scientists; makes the results of its research public and encourages public exhibition of projects in galleries, museums and other public institutions; promotes the integration of different cultures by providing scholarships to individuals and organizations from less-developed countries, so that they can immerse themselves in technological contexts not usually available to them; and provides research grants to individual artists or scientists.

Geographical Area of Activity: International.

Restrictions: No grants to projects that entertain a commercial approach.

Publications: *Images du Futur Past* by Hervé Fischer; *A Meditation on the Vasulka Archive* by Gene Youngblood; *Experiments in Art and Technology*; *The Body of the Line: Eisenstein's Drawings*; *anarchive 2: Digital Snow*; and numerous other publications.

Board: Daniel Langlois (Pres.).

Principal Staff: Dir Alain Depocas.

Address: 3530 blvd St-Laurent, Suite 500, Montréal, QC H2X 2V1.

Telephone: (514) 987-7177; **Fax:** (514) 987-7492; **Internet:** www.fondation-langlois.org; **e-mail:** info@fondation-langlois.org.

The Lawson Foundation

Established in 1956 by the Hon. Ray Lawson to enrich the quality of life of Canadians.

Activities: Aims to enrich the quality of life of Canadians, with a particular focus on early childhood competencies and the strengthening of communities, through support of projects targeting young children, their families and caregivers, and the delivery of community-based, patient-centred health care services.

Geographical Area of Activity: Canada.

Publications: Annual Report; *The Science of Early Child Development*; *The Motherisk Guide to Cancer in Pregnancy and Lactation*; *Parenting in the Beginning Years: Priorities for Investment*; *Parent Education*; *Toward the Development of a 'Know-How' Knowledge Diffusion and Utilization Model for Social and Health Programs*.

Finance: Total grants C $3,900,000 (2010).

Board of Directors: Evan Wood (Pres.); G. A. Irving (Vice-Pres.); L. E. Lawson (Sec. and Treas.).

Principal Staff: Exec. Dir Angie Killoran.

Address: 200 Queens Ave, Suite 511, London, ON N6A 1J3.

Telephone: (519) 667-5114; **Fax:** (519) 667-5118; **Internet:** www.lawson.on.ca; **e-mail:** akilloran@lawson.ca.

Lifeforce Foundation

Founded in 1981 by Peter Hamilton as the first ecological organization to protect people, animals and the environment. Lifeforce is promoting the harmonious co-existence of humans and animals.

Activities: Operates internationally in the fields of human, animal and environmental problems, promoting vegetarianism and the cessation of animals being used for entertainment and research purposes. The Foundation also conducts marine life programmes (education, conservation and research) to further the protection of marine habitats; develops public education programmes; compiles statistics; conducts symposia; provides educational packages and materials; and maintains a library and image gallery. Wildlife and various types of campaign photos are available for a donation.

Geographical Area of Activity: International.

Restrictions: Not a grant-making organization; seeks grants for its programmes.

Publications: *Lifeforce News* (newsletter); *Orca: A Family Story*; *Orca Field Guide*; *Whale Watch Guidelines*; *Respect Life with Lifeforce*; brochures, booklets and educational materials (including photos and videos).

Principal Staff: Dir Peter Hamilton.

Address: POB 3117, Main Post Office, Vancouver, BC V6B 3X6.

Telephone: (604) 649-5258; **Internet:** www.lifeforcefoundation.org; **e-mail:** lifeforcesociety@hotmail.com.

Samuel Lunenfeld Charitable Foundation

Established in 1954 and funded by the estate of the late Samuel Lunenfeld to support religious, educational and general charitable activities.

Activities: Operates, principally in Ontario, in the fields of medicine and health, and social welfare, through funding medical research projects, the Baycrest Hospital for sufferers of Alzheimer's disease (with the Ontario government), the Samuel Lunenfeld Research Foundation at the Mount Sinai Hospital and the Samuel Lunenfeld Summer Research Programme at the Hospital for Sick Children, Toronto. Makes grants for research projects, emergency funds, endowment funds, awards, seed money, fellowships and scholarships. Also operates a scholarship scheme for international students at the Raphael Recanati International School in Israel.

Geographical Area of Activity: Canada.

Restrictions: No grants to individuals.

Officers and Directors: Sybil Kunin (Pres.); William Andrew (Sec.).

Principal Staff: Dirs Barbara Hania, Helen Tater.

Address: 8 King St East, Suite 705, Toronto, ON M5C 1B5.

Telephone: (416) 363-9191.

The J. W. McConnell Family Foundation

Private foundation established in 1937 by J. W. McConnell, helping Canadians to build a more inclusive and sustainable society.

Activities: Grants to federally registered Canadian charities only.

Geographical Area of Activity: Canada.

Restrictions: No grants for conferences, seminars, scholarships, fellowships, bursaries, research, nor to individuals nor to projects oriented towards Third World development.

Principal Staff: Pres. and CEO Stephen Huddard.

Address: Suite 1800, 1002 Sherbrooke St West, Montréal, QC H3A 3L6.

Telephone: (514) 288-2133; **Fax:** (514) 288-1479; **Internet:** www.mcconnellfoundation.ca; **e-mail:** information@mcconnellfoundation.ca.

Macdonald Stewart Foundation

Established in 1973 by David Macdonald Stewart for general charitable purposes in the areas of the humanities, education and medicine.

Activities: Operates throughout Canada in the fields of the arts and humanities, in particular assisting museums, including the Stewart Museum; education, promoting new and innovative ideas; and medicine and health, supporting projects, short-term research and medical services. Projects supported must be Canadian or have Canadian content, and be carried out by registered charitable organizations.

Geographical Area of Activity: Canada.

Restrictions: Grants are not made to individuals.

Finance: Total grants approximately C $6,500,000.

Officers and Directors: Liliane Stewart (Pres.); L. Jacques Ménard, Jean Monet (Vice-Pres); Bruce D. Bolton (Vice-Pres. and Exec. Dir).

Principal Staff: Exec. Dir Bruce D. Bolton.

Address: POB 1200, Stn A, Montréal, QC H3C 2Y9.

Telephone: (514) 284-0723; **Fax:** (514) 284-0123.

The McLean Foundation

Established in 1945 by J. S. McLean.

Activities: Aims to support projects showing promise of general social benefit, but which may initially lack broad public appeal, within the fields of the arts, education, conservation, health and social welfare.

Geographical Area of Activity: Canada.

Restrictions: Grants only to registered Canadian charities; no grants to individuals.

Finance: Total assets C $43,231,108 (Dec. 2010); annual income $1,433,434, annual expenditure $1,787,187 (2010).

Principal Staff: Pres. Paul S. McLean; Vice-Pres. Timothy C. Stewart.

Address: 2 St Clair Ave West, Suite 1008, Toronto, ON M4V 1L5.

Telephone: (416) 964-6802; **Fax:** (416) 964-2804; **Internet:** mcleanfoundation.ca; **e-mail:** info@mcleanfoundation.ca.

Nelson Mandela Children's Fund—Canada

Established in 1998 by former South African President Nelson Mandela.

Activities: Funds the Nelson Mandela Children's Fund in South Africa in support of non-profit organizations working with disadvantaged children in South Africa affected by poverty, disability, HIV and AIDS. The projects funded are in four main programme areas: Well-being of the Child, Children and Youth with Disabilities; Goelama (HIV/AIDS); Leadership and Excellence; and Skills Development. The Fund also campaigns to raise public awareness in Canada of the plight of disadvantaged children and youth in South Africa and the importance of international development and volunteering. This is done through youth-targeted events such as an annual youth conference in Ottawa.

Geographical Area of Activity: Canada and South Africa.

Publications: *Ubuntu!* (newsletter, 2 a year).

Board of Directors: Michael Eubanks (Chair.); Yola Grant (Treas.).

Principal Staff: Pres. and CEO Diane O'Reggio.

Address: 2 Berkeley St, Suite 210, Toronto, ON M5A 4J5.

Telephone: (416) 496-8403; **Fax:** (416) 496-8824; **Internet:** www.mandela-children.ca; **e-mail:** info@mandela-children.ca.

The Ernest C. Manning Awards Foundation

Established in 1982 to encourage innovation in Canada.

Activities: Makes awards to Canadian resident citizens who have demonstrated recent innovative talent in developing and successfully marketing a new concept, process or procedure. Awards are made under the categories of the Principal Award, worth C $100,000; Award of Distinction, worth $25,000; Innovation Awards, two awards of $10,000 each; and the Young Canadian programme, which makes eight awards totalling $20,000.

Geographical Area of Activity: Canada.

Publications: Newsletter.

Finance: Total annual awards C $165,000.

Principal Staff: Exec. Dir D. K. Bruce Fenwick.

Address: POB 2850, Calgary, AB T2P 2S5.

Telephone: (403) 645-8277; **Fax:** (403) 645-8320; **Internet:** www.manningawards.ca; **e-mail:** manning@encana.com.

The MasterCard Foundation

Established in 2006.

Activities: The MasterCard Foundation advances microfinance and youth learning to promote financial inclusion and prosperity. Through collaboration with committed partners in more than 45 countries, helps people living in poverty to access opportunities to learn and prosper.

Geographical Area of Activity: World-wide.

Board of Directors: Lois Juliber (Chair.)

.

Principal Staff: Pres. and CEO Reeta Roy.

Address: 2 St Clair Ave East, Suite 301, Toronto, ON M4T 2T5.

Telephone: 416-214-2857; **Internet:** www.mastercardfdn.org; **e-mail:** info@mastercardfdn.org.

Match International Centre

International development NGO established in 1976 to promote equal rights for women world-wide, through international solidarity.

Activities: Operates in the fields of gender equality, human rights and sustainable development, working with partner groups in Africa, Asia, South America and the Caribbean to improve conditions and quality of life for women. Runs campaigns, awareness training and carries out research to work towards the elimination of violence against women in Canada and abroad. Seeks to empower women in developing countries by giving them the opportunities to improve their lives and enhance their roles, through training, community work and networking initiatives.

Geographical Area of Activity: Canada, Africa, Asia, South America and the Caribbean.

Publications: Annual Report; *MATCH International Centre's Review of the New Partnership for Africa's Development (NEPAD)*; *An UnMatched Partnership: 25 Years of Working with Women*; *Two Halves Make a Whole: Balancing Gender Relations in Development.*

Board of Directors: Patricia Harewood (Pres.); Sharmini Fernando (Vice-Pres. North); Mita Meyers (Sec. and Treas.).

Principal Staff: Exec. Dir Kim Bulger.

Address: 310-411 Roosevelt Ave, Ottawa, ON K2A 3X9.

Telephone: (613) 238-1312; **Fax:** (613) 238-6867; **Internet:** www.matchinternational.org; **e-mail:** info@matchinternational.org.

The Maytree Foundation

Established in 1982 for social welfare purposes; the organization is committed to the reduction of poverty and inequality in Canada and to building strong civic communities; seeks to identify, support and fund ideas, leaders and organizations with the capacity to achieve change and advance the common good.

Activities: Activities include grants to community leaders and to community organizations to support and sustain important solution-seeking efforts for community issues and problems, and the provision of scholarships to protected persons for post-secondary pursuits. Also supports and operates learning and leadership opportunities that empower communities to solve their problems and funds convening and collaboration opportunities to bring together people with knowledge and differing perspectives to find effective solutions.

Geographical Area of Activity: Canada, primarily large urban areas.

Restrictions: No funding for deficit reduction, equipment purchases, building or renovation costs, capital campaigns or endowments, partisan political activities, religious activities, legal challenges, conferences or workshops.

Publications: Annual policy insights; programme brochures; policy and research papers.

Board of Directors: Alan Broadbent (Chair.); Judy Broadbent (Vice-Chair.); Colin Robertson (Treas.); Vali Bennett (Sec.).

Principal Staff: Pres. Ratna Omidvar.

Address: 170 Bloor St West, Suite 804, Toronto, ON M5S 1T9.

Telephone: (416) 944-2627; **Fax:** (416) 944-8915; **Internet:** www.maytree.com; **e-mail:** info@maytree.com.

Medical Women's International Association—MWIA

Established in 1919, a non-profit-making, non-political, non-sectarian organization that aims to assist communication between female doctors world-wide, encourage women into medicine, and overcome gender-related inequalities in the medical profession.

Activities: Operates in the field of medicine, encouraging women to enter the profession and to undertake postgraduate study, through regional and international scientific meetings and congresses, collaborating with the World Health Organization and running local health and women's projects. Also sponsors a scholarship programme for postgraduate education, open to its members. There are national associations in 43 countries, and individual members in a further 45 countries.

Geographical Area of Activity: World-wide.

Publications: *Congress Report* (every 3 years); *Training Manual on Gender Mainstreaming in Health*; *Training Manual for Adolescent Sexuality*; newsletter; annual reports.

Executives: Prof Afua Hesse (Pres.); Dr Kyung Ah Park (Pres.-elect), Dr Eleanor Nwadinobi (Finance Chair.).

Principal Staff: Sec.-Gen. Dr Shelley Ross; Treas. Dr Gail Beck.

Address: 7555 Morley Dr., Burnaby, BC V5E 3Y2.

Telephone: (604) 439-8993; **Fax:** (604) 439-8994; **Internet:** www.mwia.net; **e-mail:** secretariat@mwia.net.

George Cedric Metcalf Charitable Foundation

Established in 1960 by George Cedric Metcalf for general charitable purposes.

Activities: Operates in Canada and less-developed countries in three programme areas: the performing arts, the environment and community development initiatives.

Geographical Area of Activity: International (through Canadian organizations).

Restrictions: Grants only available to registered charitable organizations in Canada; no grants to individuals or for-profit organizations.

Publications: Annual Report.

Finance: Total assets C $131,418,087; annual revenue $21,320,319 (2009).

Board of Directors: Kirsten Hanson (Chair.); Johanna Metcalf (Vice-Chair.); Peter Hanson (Treas.); William T. Pashby (Sec.).

Principal Staff: Pres. and CEO Sandy Houston.

Address: 174 Avenue Rd, Toronto, ON M5R 2J1.

Telephone: (416) 926-0366; **Fax:** (416) 926-0370; **Internet:** www.metcalffoundation.com; **e-mail:** info@metcalffoundation.com.

Molson Donations Fund/Fonds de bienfaisance Molson

Established in 1973 to channel the charitable giving for Molson to give back to the communities it serves.

Activities: Operates throughout Canada. As a manufacturer of alcohol operating in a highly regulated environment, Molson targets its donations and sponsorships to programmes that benefit adult audiences. Primary areas for funding consideration are: healthy communities (food banks, hunger programmes, community hospitals); active lifestyles (arenas, baseball diamonds, soccer pitches, etc.); skills development; and United Way chapters in select Canadian communities where Molson has a presence.

Geographical Area of Activity: Canada.

Restrictions: Grants made only to registered Canadian charities.

Publications: Annual Report.

Address: 33 Carlingview Dr., Etobicoke, ON M9W 5E4.

Telephone: (416) 679-1786; **Fax:** (416) 679-1494; **Internet:** www.molsoncoorscanada.com.

Molson Foundation

Established in 1958 by T. H. P. Molson, Hartland de Montarville Molson, E. H. Molson and S. T. Molson to support innovative projects in the fields of the humanities, education, health and welfare, and social and national development; formerly known as the Molson Family Foundation.

Activities: Operates throughout Canada in the fields of health and welfare, education, social development, national development, and the humanities, through grants to charitable organizations for special projects. Funds the Molson Award for the Arts, comprising two prizes of C $50,000 each awarded annually to distinguished Canadians, in the fields of the arts and the social sciences and humanities, and administered by the Canada Council for the Arts (q.v.) and the Social Sciences and Humanities Research Council.

Geographical Area of Activity: Canada.

Restrictions: Grants are not made for conferences, seminars, publications, fellowships or scholarships. Only rgistered Canadian charities are eligible.

Publications: Annual Report.

Address: 1555 Notre Dame St East, Montréal, QC H2L 2R5.

Telephone: (514) 521-1786; **Fax:** (514) 599-5396.

The F. K. Morrow Foundation

Established in 1944 in Ontario.

Activities: The Foundation works to promote religion, education and charity for public welfare. It funds projects promoting the arts and culture; offers grants in the fields of education, special education, universities, native peoples culture, film and video, to Christian and religious institutions, libraries, hospitals, for community services, special needs groups, sports and recreation, and helps promote science and environmental conservation.

Geographical Area of Activity: Mainly Canada.

Finance: Total assets approx. C $70,000,000.

Principal Staff: Sec. and Treas. Fern Densem.

Address: 3377 Bayview Ave, North York, ON M2M 3S4.

Telephone: (416) 229-2009.

The Muttart Foundation

Founded in 1953 by Merrill Muttart and Gladys Muttart.

Activities: Aims to support the development of not-for-profit organizations in Canada, through grants for infrastructure development. Also provides grants for technological development of not-for-profit organizations, community development, fellowships, training grants and bursaries, and a grant programme for young people, that makes grants to not-for-profit organizations working with young people.

Geographical Area of Activity: Canada.

Publications: Research reports and surveys.

Finance: Total assets approx. C $58,000,000.

Board: Marion Gracey (Pres.); Dr Ruth Collins-Nakai (Vice-Pres.); W. Laird Hunter (Treas.).

Principal Staff: Exec. Dir Bob Wyatt; Asst Exec. Dir Dr Christopher Smith.

Address: 1150 Scotia Pl., 10060 Jasper Ave, Edmonton, AB T5J 3R8.

Telephone: (780) 425-9616; **Fax:** (780) 425-0282; **Internet:** www.muttart.org; **e-mail:** lbeairsto@muttart.org.

North-South Institute/Institut Nord-Sud

Founded in 1976, it is Canada's first independent, non-profit and non-partisan research institute, focusing on international development.

Activities: NSI provides research and analysis on foreign policy and international development issues for policy-makers, educators, business, the media and the general public; examines the role of the public and private sectors, and of civil society in Canada's relations with developing countries; supports global efforts to increase aid effectiveness; strengthen governance and accountability; prevent conflicts, promote equitable trade and commercial relations; improve international financial systems and institutions; and enhance gender equality.

Geographical Area of Activity: Africa, Asia and the Americas.

Publications: *Canadian Development Report*; Annual Report; Briefing Papers.

Finance: Total assets C $1,520,777; annual revenue $3,329,645 expenditure $3,351,518 (2010).

Executive Committee: Arpi Hamalian (Chair.); Colin Cooke (Deputy Chair.); Ron Salole (Treas.).

Principal Staff: Pres. and CEO Joseph K. Ingram.

Address: 55 Murray St, Suite 500, Ottawa, ON K1N 5M3.

Telephone: (613) 241-3535; **Fax:** (613) 241-7435; **Internet:** www.nsi-ins.ca; **e-mail:** nsi@nsi-ins.ca.

Operation Eyesight Universal/Action universelle de la vue

Founded in 1963 to promote the prevention of blindness and the restoration of sight to people in developing countries.

Activities: works to eliminate avoidable blindness focusing on India and the African countries of Ghana, Kenya, Rwanda and Zambia – places where blindness can be deadly, especially to those who are very young, old or poor; works in partnership with local medical professionals and community development teams, building resources for all people, especially the poor; focused on high-quality, comprehensive eye care ensuring a sustainable service for entire communities, with long-lasting results.

Geographical Area of Activity: South Asia and Sub-Saharan Africa.

Publications: Annual Report; *Strategic Plan*; *SightLines* newsletter (3 a year).

Board of Directors: Raju Paul (Chair.).

Principal Staff: Pres. and CEO Pat Ferguson.

Address: 4 Parkdale Cres. NW, Calgary, AB T2N 3T8.

Telephone: (403) 283-6323; **Fax:** (403) 270-1899; **Internet:** www.operationeyesight.com; **e-mail:** info@ operationeyesight.com.

Oxfam Canada

Part of the Oxfam confederation of organizations (qq.v.).

Activities: Supports long-term development, advocacy and emergency programmes in 28 countries world-wide, with core programmes in the Americas, East and Southern Africa and South Asia.

Geographical Area of Activity: International.

Trustees: Margaret Hancock (Chair.); Blair Redlin (vice-Chair.); Don MacMillan (Treas.).

Principal Staff: Exec. Dir Robert Fox.

Address: 39 McArthur Ave, Ottawa, ON, K1L 8L7.

Telephone: (613) 237-5236; **Internet:** www.oxfam.ca/; **e-mail:** info@oxfam.ca.

Oxfam-Québec

Part of the Oxfam confederation of organizations (qq.v.).

Activities: Operates in Africa, Central and South America and the Caribbean, South-East Asia and the Middle East in the areas of literacy and education, water and sanitation, the environment, women's economic development, disaster relief, health, food security and civil society.

Geographical Area of Activity: Benin, Bolivia, Burkina Faso, Cambodia, Congo (Dem. Repub.), Dominican Republic, Haiti, Honduras, Jordan, Lebanon, Niger, Palestinian Autonomous Areas, Peru, Sudan, Vietnam.

Trustees: Monique Letourneau (Chair.).

Principal Staff: Exec. Dir Pierre Veronneau.

Address: 2330 rue Notre-Dame Ouest, Montréal, QC H3J 2Y2.

Internet: www.oxfam.qc.ca; **e-mail:** info@oxfam.qc.ca.

Pacific Peoples' Partnership

Pacific Peoples' Partnership (PPP) – previously known as the South Pacific Peoples' Foundation of Canada – was founded in 1975. It promotes rights-based sustainable development initiatives that enable communities to harness their own creativity to address poverty, environmental degradation and loss of culture.

Activities: The PPP mission is to support the aspirations of Pacific islanders for peace, justice, environmental sustainability and development; and to raise the profile of the Pacific island nations and territories internationally. It provides and supports educational programmes and print and audio-visual materials on Pacific island issues; encourages links between Canadian and Pacific island organizations working in similar areas, and between indigenous peoples in Canada and the Pacific; holds conferences and training courses; and provides direct and indirect support to projects in the Pacific.

Geographical Area of Activity: Canada and the Pacific islands.

Restrictions: Grants only to specific organizations.

Publications: *Tok Blong Pasifik* (quarterly); videos.

Finance: Budget approx. C $200,000.

Board of Directors: Dr James Boutilier (Emer. Pres.); Eugene Lee (Pres.); Vance Gardner (Vice-Pres.).

Principal Staff: Exec. Dir April Ingham.

Address: 620 View St, Suite 407, Victoria, BC V8W 1J6.

Telephone: (250) 381-4131; **Fax:** (888) 581-8987; **Internet:** www.pacificpeoplespartnership.org; **e-mail:** info@ pacificpeoplespartnership.org.

Partnership Africa Canada—PAC

Established in 1986 with support from Canadian and African NGOs and the Canadian International Development Agency.

Activities: Operates in the field of sustainable human development in Africa, in partnership with NGOs in Canada.

Geographical Area of Activity: Africa.

Restrictions: No grants available.

Publications: Annual Report; *Insights*; *Diamonds and Human Security*; *APRM Monitor*; *Sierra Leone Conference Report*; *Sudan Symposium Report*.

Finance: Annual revenue C $889,391, expenditure $874,456 (2010/11).

Board of Directors: David Kalete (Pres.); Hon. Flora MacDonald (Hon. Pres.); Susan Cote-Freeman (Vice-Pres.); Alex Neve (Sec.).

Principal Staff: Exec. Dir Bernard Taylor.

Address: 600-331 Cooper St, Ottawa, ON K2P 0G5.

Telephone: (613) 237-6768; **Fax:** (613) 237-6530; **Internet:** www.pacweb.org; **e-mail:** info@pacweb.org.

Pearson Peacekeeping Centre—PPC

Established in 1994 by the Canadian Government; formerly known as the Lester B. Pearson Canadian International Peacekeeping Centre. A division of the Canadian Institute of Strategic Studies. Aims to support and increase the Canadian contribution to international peace and stability.

Activities: Provides research, education and training in international peace-keeping. Conducts seminars and courses on the subjects of world peace, produces a number of related publications each year through its publishing arm The Canadian Peacekeeping Press, and funds mobile training teams in Canada and abroad. Awards scholarships to university students and NGOs, and takes an active role in the New Peacekeeping Partnership (consisting of those organizations and individuals in Canada that work to improve peace-keeping operations).

Geographical Area of Activity: International.

Publications: Annual Report; *The Pearson Papers*.

Board of Directors: Philip Murray (Chair.).

Principal Staff: Pres. and CEO Kevin McGarr.

Address: HCI Building, 1125 Colonel By Dr., Suite 5110, Ottawa, ON K1S 5B6.

Telephone: (613) 520-5617; **Fax:** (613) 520-3787; **Internet:** www.peaceoperations.org; **e-mail:** info@peaceoperations .org.

Presbyterian World Service and Development

Established as the development and relief agency of the Presbyterian Church in Canada. Works to make positive changes in the world through partnerships supporting those affected by poverty, injustice, disease and disaster in Central America, Africa and Asia.

Activities: Programmes focus on empowering communities to address poverty by providing nutrition and agriculture training for farmers; literacy training and small business initiatives for women; education for vulnerable children; care and support for people living with and affected by HIV and AIDS; and clean-water wells and sanitation training for communities. Assists in overcoming natural disasters and emergencies through relief efforts that meet both physical and emotional needs, and helps refugees to Canada. Also works to educate and promote awareness of development issues within Canada.

Geographical Area of Activity: International.

Publications: PWS Developments (quarterly newsletter); PWS&D Spotlight (monthly e-newsletter); Annual Report.

Address: 50 Wynford Dr., Toronto, ON M3C 1J7.

Telephone: (416) 441-1111; **Fax:** (416) 441-2825; **Internet:** www .presbyterian.ca/pwsd; **e-mail:** pwsd@presbyterian.ca.

Primate's World Relief and Development Fund

Established in 1959 by the General Synod of the Anglican Church of Canada as the official relief and development agency of the Anglican Church of Canada. The fund is committed to international development work.

Activities: Operates in the fields of justice, human rights and political advocacy (non-partisan), as well as community development. Helps local partners in developing countries to provide long-term solutions to the causes of suffering and disaster. Also provides emergency relief to victims of crisis, and to protect refugees. A percentage of funds is reserved for work with Canada's indigenous population for land claims, self-determination and Aboriginal rights. Works to educate and advocate for change.

Geographical Area of Activity: International.

Publications: Annual Report; *Under the Sun* (quarterly).

Finance: Total revenue C $7,286,585, expenditure $7,538,876 (March 2010).

Board of Directors: The Most Rev. Archbishop Fred Hiltz (Pres.); Rev. David Pritchard (Vice-Pres.); Rev. Laura Marie Piotrowicz (Sec.); Jim Cullen (Treas.).

Principal Staff: Exec. Dir Adele Finney.

Address: 80 Hayden St, Toronto, ON M4Y 3G2.

Telephone: (416) 924-9192; **Fax:** (416) 924-3483; **Internet:** www.pwrdf.org; **e-mail:** pwrdf@pwrdf.org.

RBC Foundation

Established in 1993 by the Royal Bank of Canada for general charitable purposes. Formerly known as the Royal Bank of Canada Charitable Foundation.

Activities: Operates throughout Canada in the fields of education, health, arts and culture, social services and civic activities, through grants to organizations for programmes, projects, awards, fellowships and scholarships, operating funds, etc. RBC Financial Group is committed to contributing at least 1% of net income before tax.

Geographical Area of Activity: Canada.

Restrictions: Grants are not made for conferences or seminars, nor to individuals.

Publications: *Corporate Social Responsibility Report*.

Finance: Contributed approx. C $130,000,000 to community causes world-wide (2010).

Officers and Directors: Elizabeth Bigsby (Chair.).

Principal Staff: Exec. Dir Stephen Voisin.

Address: Royal Bank Plaza, South Tower, 9th Floor, Toronto, ON M5J 2J5.

Telephone: (416) 974-3113; **Fax:** (416) 974-0624; **Internet:** www.rbc.com/donations; **e-mail:** donations@rbc.com.

Richelieu International

Founded in 1944 by Horace Viau to promote the social and cultural needs of the francophone population of Canada. The Richelieu International Foundation was created in 1977.

Activities: Operates in the French-speaking regions of the world in the fields of the arts and humanities, education, and medicine and health, through self-conducted programmes, grants to individuals and institutions, scholarships and fellowships, and prizes.

Geographical Area of Activity: French-speaking communities in North America, Europe, Africa and the Caribbean.

Publications: *Le P'tit Bulletin* (online newsletter); and downloadable reports and information leaflets.

Board of Directors: Rene Martin (Pres.).

Principal Staff: Dir-Gen. Laurier Thériault.

Address: 1010 rue Polytek, bureau 25, Ottawa, ON K1J 9J1.

Telephone: (613) 742-6911; **Fax:** (613) 742-6916; **Internet:** www.richelieu.org; **e-mail:** international@richelieu.org.

Rights and Democracy/Droits et Démocratie

Established in 1988 by the Canadian Parliament; formerly known as the International Centre for Human Rights and Democratic Development. An independent and non-partisan non-profit organization, which aims to promote the universal values of human rights and democracy world-wide.

Activities: Operates internationally, principally in Guatemala, Haiti, Indonesia, Kenya, Mexico, Myanmar, Nigeria, Pakistan, Peru, Rwanda, Thailand and Togo, in the fields of human rights, in four principal areas: democratic development and justice; women's rights; the rights of indigenous peoples; and globalization and human rights, with two additional focus points, International Human Rights Advocacy and Urgent Action and Important Opportunities. Works in collaboration with Canadian and foreign NGOs and governments to support advocacy and capacity building initiatives. Aims to increase public awareness of human rights issues, and sponsors research, conferences and publications. Makes grants as well as managing its own projects and awarding prizes, including the annual John Humphrey Freedom Award, worth C $25,000.

Geographical Area of Activity: International.

Publications: *Libertas* (newsletter); *Strengthening Democracy in Asia, Conference Report* (2006); *The Human Right to Food in Malawi: Report of an International Fact-Finding Mission* (2006); *Documenting Women's Rights Violations by Non-state Actors* (2006); *Indigenous Women of the Americas* (2nd edn, 2006); *Behind Closed Doors* (2006); *Where Are the Girls?* (2006); Annual Report; occasional papers.

Finance: Total assets C \$3,561,870 (2009).

Board of Directors: Aurel Braun (Chair.).

Principal Staff: Pres. Gerard Latulippe.

Address: 1001 blvd de Maisonneuve est, bureau 1100, Montréal, QC H2L 4P9.

Telephone: (514) 283-6073; **Fax:** (514) 283-3792; **Internet:** www.dd-rd.ca; **e-mail:** dd-rd@dd-rd.ca.

Rooftops Canada Foundation

Established in 1984 to support community housing projects in developing countries.

Activities: Provides technical assistance to community-based and co-operative housing organizations in less-developed countries; training and capacity building for NGOs; conducts educational programmes; and maintains a library.

Geographical Area of Activity: Africa, Asia, Central and South America, the Caribbean and Eastern Europe.

Restrictions: Grants only to community-based housing organizations.

Publications: *Program Report* (annually).

Finance: Budget C \$1,000,000.

Board: Jo Ferris-Davies (Acting Pres.); Kit Hickey (Sec. and Treas.).

Principal Staff: Exec. Dir Barry Pinsky.

Address: 720 Spadina Ave, Suite 313, Toronto, ON M5S 2T9.

Telephone: (416) 366-1445; **Fax:** (416) 366-3876; **Internet:** www.rooftops.ca; **e-mail:** info@rooftops.ca.

Salamander Foundation

Established in 1965 by Richard G. Ivey; originally known as the Richard and Jean Ivey Fund.

Activities: Makes grants to Canadian registered charities within the fields of arts and culture and the environment, with particular emphasis on resource management, pollution, environmental degradation and their impacts on ecosystems and human health.

Geographical Area of Activity: Great Lakes–St Lawrence River Basins, east to the Atlantic. Regional issues in the Yukon, Northwest Territories and Nunavut.

Restrictions: No grants for annual appeals, capital campaigns, conferences or seminars, deficit financing, emergency funds, festivals, seed funding, bursaries, scholarships, individuals, sponsorship, public education or film projects.

Finance: Total grants (approx.) C \$400,00 (2011).

Board of Directors: Nan Shuttleworth (Pres.); Paul O. Gratias (Sec. and Treas.).

Address: 180 Bloor St W, Suite 1201, Toronto, ON M5S 2V6.

Telephone: (416) 972-9200; **Fax:** (416) 972-9203; **Internet:** www.salamanderfoundation.org; **e-mail:** info@ salamanderfoundation.org.

The Sharing Way

Established as the relief and development arm of Canadian Baptist Ministries; aims to promote self-reliance, social justice and peace in grassroots communities in the developing world.

Activities: Provides relief to victims of natural and man-made disasters around the world. Mainly supports long-term development projects in Central and South America, Africa, Asia and Europe, including Bolivia, Brazil, El Salvador, Ethiopia, Ghana, India, Kenya and Rwanda. Programmes include a partnership with the Canadian Foodgrains Bank (CFGB) distributing cash and crops received from farmers, churches and other groups.

Geographical Area of Activity: International.

Publications: Newsletter; *Mosaic* (magazine, quarterly); *Meet the Neighbours*; *Food for All*.

Board of Directors: Brenda Halk (Pres.); Norm Hubley (Treas.).

Principal Staff: Gen. Sec. Rev. Dr Gary V. Nelson.

Address: c/o Canadian Baptist Ministries, 7185 Millcreek Dr., Mississauga, ON L5N 5R4.

Telephone: (905) 821-3533; **Fax:** (905) 826-3441; **Internet:** www.cbmin.org/cbm/the-sharing-way; **e-mail:** info@cbmin .org.

Shastri Indo-Canadian Institute

Founded in 1968 by the Governments of Canada and India to enhance mutual understanding between the two countries.

Activities: Operates internationally in the fields of development studies, the humanities and social sciences, management and law. Fellowships for research and study, and language training in India, are offered to junior and senior scholars in Canada. The Institute's Library Programme acquires Indian documents and publications for scholarly use in Canada, and Canadian publications are presented to Indian institutions. Also organizes international academic conferences; runs an educational resources programme for Canadian schools and a summer programme, when funding is available; co-ordinates a visiting lecturer programme for Canadian universities; and supports the growth of Canadian studies at Indian universities and of development studies at Canadian universities. Members of the Institute include 21 Canadian universities and the Canadian Museum of Civilization.

Geographical Area of Activity: South Asia and Canada.

Restrictions: Grants only for Canadians or landed immigrants to go to India, or for Indians from India to go to Canada.

Publications: *Shastri News* (newsletter).

Finance: Total assets C \$692,371 (2010/11).

Executive Council: Dr Braj Sinha (Pres.); Dr Rabir Singh (Vice-Pres.); Dr Shanthi Johnson (Sec. and Treas.).

Principal Staff: Exec. Dir Michelle Neider.

Address: 1402 Education Tower, 2500 University Dr. NW, Calgary, AB T2N 1N4.

Telephone: (403) 220-7467; **Fax:** (403) 289-0100; **Internet:** www.sici.org; **e-mail:** sici@ucalgary.ca.

SickKids Foundation

Founded in 1972 by, among others, Duncan L. Gordon and John T. Law to provide funds for research, special programmes and public health education at the Hospital for Sick Children, Toronto and throughout Canada.

Activities: Organizes educational and research programmes in two main areas: developing research skills, and knowledge generation and community action. Provides grants to Canadian institutions and individuals; awards fellowships and scholarships (including the Duncan L. Gordon Fellowships for post-doctoral study in child health, and the Visiting Scientists and Foreign Research Fellowship Program for researchers from Canada and abroad); National Grants Program funds research, conferences, scholarships and fellowships nationally; runs a grants programme in youth and child home care; and also maintains a Research Institute.

Geographical Area of Activity: Canada.

Publications: *Handbooks for Parents* (various); *Child Safety*; *Planning for Kids* (newsletter, 2006); Annual Report; conference proceedings; *Reasons to Believe* (e-newsletter, monthly).

Finance: Total Assets C \$939,872,000 (March 2011); annual revenue \$698,647,000, annual expenditure \$697,486,000.

Board of Trustees: Robert Harding (Chair.); John Thompson (Vice-Chair.); Rose Patten (Vice-Chair.).

Principal Staff: Pres. and CEO Mary Jo Haddad.

Address: The Hospital for Sick Children, 555 University Ave, Toronto, ON M5G 1X8.

Telephone: (416) 813-1500; **Fax:** (416) 813-5024; **Internet:** www.sickkids.ca.

Steelworkers Humanity Fund

Labour-based NGO, established in 1985 by the United Steelworkers of America, to support development, relief and social justice issues, nationally and internationally.

Activities: Four broad main areas of interest: project support, education, exchange, and policy and advocacy. Involved in social and development issues in Canada, setting up health clinics, credit unions, day-care centres and housing co-operatives for its members and others in the community. Works internationally in the fields of workers' rights, food self-sufficiency, structural adjustment and North-South relations, as well as providing emergency relief. An active member of NGO coalitions with policy and advocacy objectives worldwide.

Geographical Area of Activity: Africa, Central and South America and Canada.

Publications: *Global Solidarity Humanity Fund Bulletin*; *Our Union and the Environment*; 'The Global Class War'; *Current Contract Summaries*; *Building Power*; *Steel Resource Publications*; *Securing Our Children's World*; *USW@Work*; *Contract Summaries*; *Archived Publications*; policy papers and fact sheets; newletter.

Board of Directors: Ken Neumann (Pres.); Carolyn Egan (Vice-Pres.); Paula Turtle (Sec.); Doug Olthuis (Treas.).

Principal Staff: Pres. Ken Neumann; Dir Wayne Fraser.

Address: 234 Eglington Ave East, 8th Floor, Toronto, ON M4P 1K7.

Telephone: (416) 487-1571; **Fax:** (416) 482-5548; **Internet:** www.uswa.ca/union/humanity; **e-mail:** usw@usw.ca.

Nathan Steinberg Family Foundation

Established in 1967 for general charitable purposes.

Activities: Operates in Canada, Israel and the USA in the fields of the arts and humanities, education, medicine and health (including cancer research and services), and social services (in particular Jewish organizations).

Geographical Area of Activity: Canada, Israel and the USA.

Restrictions: The Foundation does not currently accept applications.

Officers and Directors: Lewis Steinberg (Pres.); Murray Steinberg (Vice-Pres.); H. Arnold Steinberg (Sec. and Treas.).

Address: 3500 blvd de Maisonneuve West, Suite 900, Montréal, QC H3Z 3C1.

Telephone: (514) 931-7500.

Street Kids International

Founded in 1988 by Peter Dalglish; Street Kids International aims to help street kids internationally become healthy, self-sufficient and respected.

Activities: Advocates and delivers innovative programmes that are adopted, adapted and shared by its world-wide network of partners. Programmes build on the resilience of street kids to improve their quality of life. Trains youth workers and educators to help youth realize their potential through entrepreneurship and health education.

Geographical Area of Activity: Africa, Europe, South America, Canada, Central Asia, South Asia, Haiti, Middle East.

Publications: Newsletter; reports and articles; curriculum units.

Finance: Total assets C $275,120 (June 2007); annual revenue $754,865, expenditure $748,052 (June 2007).

Board of Directors: Bindu Dhaliwal (Chair.); Paul Pathak (Vice-Chair.); Steve Yuzpe (Treas.).

Principal Staff: Exec. Dir David Pell.

Address: 20 Toronto St, 9th Floor, Suite 960, Toronto, ON M5C 2B8.

Telephone: (416) 504-8994; **Fax:** (416) 504-8977; **Internet:** www.streetkids.org; **e-mail:** info@streetkids.org.

Joseph Tanenbaum Charitable Foundation

Established in 1967 by Joseph Tanenbaum for general charitable purposes.

Activities: Operates in the fields of aid to less-developed countries, the arts and humanities, education, health and welfare, and social welfare, through grants to organizations involved in the areas of education (including international education and community colleges), disabled children, international relief (including medical services), Jewish social services and medical research.

Geographical Area of Activity: International.

Restrictions: Grants are primarily given to Jewish organizations.

Finance: Total assets approx. C $10,000,000; annual grants approx. $2,000,000.

Officers and Directors: Kurt Rothschild (Pres.).

Principal Staff: Pres. Kurt Rothschild.

Address: 1051 Tapscott Rd, Scarborough, ON M1X 1A1.

Terre Sans Frontières—TSF

Established as Prodeva FIC by the Brothers of Christian Instruction in 1980; became Prodeva Tiers-Monde in 1986; known as Terre Sans Frontières since 1994.

Activities: Operates in the field of sustainable development and self-sufficiency. Works in partnership with associated organizations to conducts programmes for individuals in developing countries, especially in Africa, Haiti and Honduras. Provides grants and micro-credit to institutions, and also provides skilled volunteers. Also works towards creating awareness among Canadians of development issues.

Geographical Area of Activity: Africa, Central America and the Caribbean.

Publications: Newsletter.

Finance: Annual budget approx. C $6,000,000.

Board of Trustees: Joseph Bourgeois (Pres.); Linda Bambonye (Vice-Pres.); Guy Mercier (Sec.); Denis Majeau (Treas.).

Principal Staff: CEO Robert Gonnevile.

Address: 399 rue des Conseillers, Suite 23, La Prairie, QC J5R 4H6.

Telephone: (450) 659-7717; **Fax:** (450) 659-2276; **Internet:** www.terresansfrontieres.ca; **e-mail:** tsf@terresansfrontieres.ca.

USC Canada

Established in 1945, an international development organization that works in partnership with people in Africa and Asia to break the pattern of poverty.

Activities: Operates in collaboration with local organizations in less-developed countries of Africa and Asia (Bangladesh, Lesotho, Timor Leste, Indonesia, Mali and Nepal) and in Honduras in the fields of water, health, income generation, training and education, savings and credit, the environment and food security. One of the main programmes is Seeds of Survival, a sustainable agriculture initiative, which works to provide a long-term solution to hunger in developing countries through the preservation, utilization and enhancement of farmers' indigenous seeds and traditional practices. USC Canada also works nationally in outreach and community projects, and education to improve awareness of global issues. Maintains offices in Bangladesh, Nepal, East Timor and Mali.

Geographical Area of Activity: Central America (Honduras), Africa, Asia and Canada.

Publications: Newsletter; *Jottings*; Annual Report; posters.

Finance: Total assets C $1,340,917; annual income $4,566,895, expenditure $4,566,454 (April 2011).

Board of Directors: Mark Austin (Chair.); Rev. Allison Barrett (Sec.).

Principal Staff: Exec. Dir Susan Walsh.

Address: 56 Sparks St, Suite 705, Ottawa, ON K1P 5B1.

Telephone: (613) 234-6827; **Fax:** (613) 234-6842; **Internet:** www.usc-canada.org; **e-mail:** info@usc-canada.org.

Vancouver Foundation

Founded in 1943.

Activities: Canada's largest community foundation, which aims to make a lasting impact on communities in British Columbia through philanthropy and grants.

Geographical Area of Activity: Mainly British Columbia, Canada.

Publications: *Vancouver Foundation Magazine*; *Vital Signs*; *Moving Foundations*.

Finance: Annual disbursements C $60,000,000 (2010).

Board of Directors: Gordon MacDougall (Chair.); John McLernon (Vice-Chair.).

Principal Staff: Pres. and CEO Faye Wightman.

Address: 555 West Hastings St, Suite 1200, POB 12132, Harbour Centre, Vancouver, BC V6B 4N6.

Telephone: (604) 688-2204; **Fax:** (604) 688-4170; **Internet:** www.vancouverfoundation.bc.ca; **e-mail:** info@vancouverfoundation.ca.

R. Howard Webster Foundation

Established in 1967 to make grants to hospitals, universities and for general charitable purposes.

Activities: Operates throughout Canada in the fields of the arts and humanities, education, medicine and health, and social welfare, funding scholarships and fellowships.

Geographical Area of Activity: Canada.

Board of Directors: Lorne C. Webster (Chair.); W. Ronald Shaw (Sec.); Howard W. Davidson (Treas.).

Principal Staff: Pres. Norman E. Webster.

Address: 1155 René-Lévesque blvd ouest, Suite 2912, Montréal, QC H3B 2L5.

Telephone: (514) 866-2424; **Fax:** (514) 866-9918.

World Accord

Established in 1980 to provide development assistance in less-developed countries.

Activities: Works in less-developed countries of Asia and Central America, in collaboration with partners in Canada and overseas, to improve the quality of life of individuals and communities in the developing world in the long term, through the building of local institutional and human capacities and encouraging participation in civil society. Funds educational self-help programmes to create a better future for disadvantaged people. Runs development education projects in Canada.

Geographical Area of Activity: Central America, Asia and Canada.

Publications: *Global Voice* (newsletter); Annual Report.

Finance: Total assets C $891,003; annual revenue $1,051,001, expenditure $1,036,025 (March 2009).

Board of Directors: Rosilyn Coulsoun (Pres.); Mary D. Pearson (Treas.).

Principal Staff: Exec. Dir David Barth.

Address: 1c 185 Frobisher Dr., Waterloo, ON N2V 2E6.

Telephone: (519) 747-2215; **Fax:** (519) 747-2644; **Internet:** www.worldaccord.org; **e-mail:** dbarth@worldaccord.org.

World Literacy of Canada—WLC

Founded in 1955, non-profit charitable organization. Aims to promote adult literacy in Canada and abroad, raise public awareness, and to fund community literacy development programmes in Southern Asia.

Activities: Operates internationally, aiming to improve general adult literacy world-wideto improve social, cultural and economic conditions. In Canada, the organization has initiated presentations, forums and national tours; supported the formation of the Movement for Canadian Literacy; and provided resources for schools and literacy groups on effective and innovative strategies. Overseas, it provides financial support for literacy programmes that integrate health, housing, vocational training, and credit and savings programmes; offers funding for teacher training, educational supplies and development of literary resources; and also arranges a variety of capacity building programmes for human resource development at a grassroots level. Has a particular focus on the literacy needs of poor women. Also maintains an office in India.

Geographical Area of Activity: Southern Asia and Canada.

Publications: WLC Engagement calender; *Askshar* (annual magazine); *The Kama Cookbook*; *Storytelling Soup*.

Finance: Total assets C $356,493; annual revenue $971,160; annual expenditure $863,214 (March 2011).

Board of Directors: Sandra Onufryk (Pres.); Marguerite Piggott (Vice-Pres.); Doug Shrigley (Treas.); Jamie Zeppa (Sec.).

Principal Staff: Exec. Dir Mamta Mishra.

Address: 401 Richmond St West, Studio 236, Toronto, ON M5V 3A8.

Telephone: (416) 977-0008; **Fax:** (416) 977-1112; **Internet:** www.worldlit.ca; **e-mail:** info@worldlit.ca.

World University Service of Canada/Entraide universitaire mondiale du Canada

Founded in 1939 to involve the Canadian community in social and academic development in Canada and overseas.

Activities: The organization operates nationally in development studies and education, and internationally in the fields of aid to less-developed countries, conservation, education, medicine, and science and technology, through self-conducted programmes, annual seminars and publications.

Geographical Area of Activity: International.

Publications: Annual Report; E-*Communiqué* (2 a year); *Fifty Years of Seminars*; general brochure; videos; fact sheets; project-related documents.

Finance: Total assets C $8,253,826; revenue $30,086,718, expenditure $30,063,148 (March 2011).

Board of Directors: Dr Amit Chakma (Chair.); David Turpin (Vice-Chair.); Rani Dhaliwal (Treas.).

Principal Staff: Exec. Dir Chris Eaton.

Address: 1404 Scott St, Ottawa, ON K1Y 4M8.

Telephone: (613) 798-7477; **Fax:** (613) 798-0990; **Internet:** www.wusc.ca; **e-mail:** wusc@wusc.ca.

Chile

FOUNDATIONS, TRUSTS AND NON-PROFIT ORGANIZATIONS

Fundación Chile (Chile Foundation)

Established in 1976 by the Chilean government and ITT Corporation of the USA; with BHP Billiton Escondida Mine becoming a new member in 2004, it aims to support scientific and technological research and development and the application of the scientific and technological advances made in the production and service areas.

Activities: Aims to contribute to development of innovation and the use of technology to develop the Chilean economy, through support for projects in the fields of education, human capital, the environment, small business development, agribusiness, forestry and marine resources.

Geographical Area of Activity: Chile.

Restrictions: No grants to individuals.

Publications: *Lignum*; *Aqua* (trade magazines); monographs.

Board of Directors: Álvaro Fischer (Pres.).

Principal Staff: Dir-Gen. and CEO Marcos Kulka Kuperman.

Address: Avda Parque Antonio Rabat Sur 6165, Vitacura, Santiago.

Telephone: (2) 240-0300; **Fax:** (2) 242-6900; **Internet:** www.fundacionchile.cl; **e-mail:** info@fundacionchile.cl.

Fundación para el Desarrollo Regional de Aysen (Regional Development Foundation of Aysen)

Established in 1976.

Activities: Aims to support integrated development activities for people with few resources in the Aysen region of Chile.

Geographical Area of Activity: Primarily the Aysen region of Chile.

Finance: Annual grants approx. US $500,000.

Board of Directors: Santiago Bessone Barolo (Pres.).

Principal Staff: Exec. Dir Jorge Reyes Gonzales.

Address: Pedro Dussen 360, Casilla 340, Coyhaique, XI Región de Aysen.

Telephone: (67) 23-11-27; **Fax:** (67) 23-20-50; **e-mail:** funda@ctcinternet.cl.

Fundación Invica (Invica Foundation)

Founded in 1959 to promote co-operation among housing projects; founded the Cooperativa Abierta de Vivienda—PROVI-COOP in 1977 to operate in the area of housing.

Activities: Works in the fields of urban planning, housing finance, development assistance, co-operatives and community development; sponsors exhibitions; conducts research programmes and training courses; operates a database.

Geographical Area of Activity: Chile.

Publications: *Boletín Construyendo*.

Board of Directors: Diego Vidal Sánchez (Pres.); Nicolas Parot Boragk (Vice-Pres.); Manuel Castillo Lea-Plaza (Sec.).

Principal Staff: Dir-Gen. Felipe Arteaga.

Address: Cienfuegos 67, Clasificador 900, Santiago.

Telephone: (2) 690-04-00; **Fax:** (2) 696-78-22; **Internet:** www.invica.cl; **e-mail:** casapropia@invica.cl.

Fundación Pablo Neruda (Pablo Neruda Foundation)

Established in June 1986, named after the Chilean poet Pablo Neruda, to promote and cultivate the arts.

Activities: Operates in the field of education and culture, offering scholarships and fellowships, awarding prizes, organizing conferences, organizing cultural activities and issuing publications.

Geographical Area of Activity: Chile.

Publications: *Federico García Lorca*; *Neruda's Objects*; *Pablo Neruda's Houses*; *At the Table with Neruda*; *My Friend Pablo*.

Trustees: Juan Agustín Figueroa (Pres.); Raúl Bulnes Calderón (Vice-Pres.).

Principal Staff: Exec. Dir Fernando Sáez García.

Address: Fernando Márquez de la Plata 0192, POB 6640152, Santiago.

Telephone: (2) 777-8741; **Fax:** (2) 737-8712; **Internet:** www.fundacionneruda.org; **e-mail:** info@fundacionneruda.org.

Hogar de Cristo (Home of Christ)

Founded in 1944 (Fundación de Viviendas Hogar de Cristo established in 1958) by Fr Alberto Hurtado Ianza to assist the poor through the provision of shelter.

Activities: Operates in the fields of social welfare, and medicine and health, particularly in the areas of housing, education, poverty, young people, the aged and the disabled. The Foundation evaluates and improves housing conditions and is particularly concerned with low-cost housing and the use of wooden building materials. Also established five foundations serving specific community and social welfare needs for disadvantaged people in Chile.

Geographical Area of Activity: Chile.

Finance: Annual income US $18,474,640, expenditure $21,025,310 (July 2011).

Board of Directors: Padre Pablo Walker S.J. (Chaplain-Gen.); Cirilo Córdova de Pablo (Pres.); Juan Pablo Armas M. (First Vice-Pres); José Musalem Sarquis (Second Vice-Pres.); Carolina dell'Oro Crespo (Sec.).

Principal Staff: Exec. Dir Susana Tonda M.

Address: Las Uvas y el Viento 0316, Parador 27 1/2, Santa Rosa, La Granja, Santiago, Casilla 871, Correo Central.

Telephone: (2) 541-6456; **Fax:** (2) 541-6463; **Internet:** www.hogardecristo.com; **e-mail:** vivienda@hcvivienda.cl.

Isis Internacional (Isis International)

Founded in 1988 to empower women through sharing information, communication and networking.

Activities: Operates in the field of women's rights, through resource centres, information-sharing, publications, conferences, international multimedia communication and research. Co-ordinates the Latin American and Caribbean Women's Health Network (q.v.), and maintains a documentation centre. Also maintains an office in Manila, which focuses specifically on issues facing women in the Asia-Pacific region; and works in conjunction with Isis–Women's International Cross-Cultural Exchange (Isis-WICCE) in Kampala, Uganda.

Geographical Area of Activity: Central and South America and the Asia-Pacific region.

Publications: *Ediciones de las Mujeres*; *Perspectivas*; *Agenda Salud*; *Boletín de la Red Feminista contra la Violencia*; *Boletines impresos y electrónicos*; *Directorio de instituciones y grupos*; electronic publications (catalogue available online).

Address: Esmeralda 636, 2º, Santiago.

Telephone: (2) 633-4582; **Internet:** www.isis.cl; **e-mail:** isis@isis.cl.

Nonprofit Enterprise and Self-sustainability Team— NESsT

Founded in 1997 to solve critical social problems in emerging market countries, by developing and supporting social enterprises that strengthen the financial sustainability of civil society organizations to maximize their social impact.

Activities: NESsT works in three main areas: applied research; capacity building; and policy and outreach. It aims to increase awareness, critical analysis and understanding of non-profit enterprise, and to attract new leaders to the emerging field. Operates in a variety of areas, including offering internships to young and mid-career professionals, and encouraging the integration of the teaching of non-profit enterprise into the formal curricula of graduate-level non-profit management and business schools. NESsT has launched initiatives promoting self-financing for non-profits in both South America and Central Europe, as well as the NESsT Venture Fund providing targeted finance and capacity building support to non-profits in Central Europe and Central and South America. Maintains offices in Chile, Hungary and the USA.

Geographical Area of Activity: Central and South America and Central Europe.

Publications: *All in the Same Boat: An Introduction to Engaged Philanthropy*; *Commitment to Integrity: Guiding Principles for Nonprofits in the Marketplace*; *Enterprising Mentality: A Social Enterprise Guide for Mental Health and Intellectual Disabilities Organizations*; *Get Ready, Get Set: Starting Down the Road to Self-Financing*; *Hit the Ground Running: Getting a Head Start with Local Lessons for Sustainable Social Enterprise*; *Legal Guides* (Chile, Colombia, Croatia, Peru, Romania); *Risky Business: The Impacts of Merging Mission and Market*.

Finance: Financed by private foundations, corporations, individuals and self-financing initiatives.

Board of Directors: Steve Smith (Chair.); Richard Surrey (Sec.); Robert Line (Treas.).

Principal Staff: Co-Founders and CEOs Nicole Etchart and Lee Davis.

Address: José Arrieta 89, Providencia, 7500900 Santiago.

Telephone: (2) 222-5190; **Fax:** (2) 634-2599; **Internet:** www.nesst.org; **e-mail:** nesst@nesst.org.

Red de Salud de las Mujeres Latinoamericanas y del Caribe (Latin American and Caribbean Women's Health Network—LACWHN)

Established in 1984, during the first Regional Women and Health meeting in Colombia, to promote women's health, women's civil and human rights, and women's citizenship through the cultural, political and social transformation of the Central and South America and the Caribbean region.

Activities: Operates in Central and South America and the Caribbean, through linking regional organizations that work in the area of women's health to provide common objectives and strategies. Promotes health and rights for women of all ages throughout Central and South America and the Caribbean, particularly focusing on sexual and reproductive health rights. Incorporates human resource training, strengthens regional co-ordination among organizations and individuals working in this area, supports and organizes regional and international events and runs international campaigns focused on priority issues in women's health. Also acts as an information network through its publications.

Geographical Area of Activity: Central and South America and the Caribbean.

Publications: *Women's Health Journal* (magazine, quarterly); *Women's Health Collection* (annually).

Principal Staff: Gen. Co-ordinator Nirvana González Rosa.

Address: CP 6850892, Casilla 50610, Santiago 1, Santiago.

Telephone: (2) 223-7077; **Fax:** (2) 223-1066; **Internet:** www.reddesalud.org; **e-mail:** secretaria@reddesalud.org.

SELAVIP International—Service de Promotion de l'Habitation Populaire en Amérique Latine, Afrique et Asie (Latin American, African and Asian Social Housing Service)

Founded in 1976 by Fr Josse van der Rest to assist local urban communities, families and NGOs in cities of less-developed regions. Focuses on providing shelter to the urban poor and/ or promoting and empowering organizations to initiate community-driven processes that will improve their shelter.

Activities: After a Call for Projects each year in July–August, proposals are selected from among those that are sent by organizations such as NGOs, CBOs or social services. The target is very poor people in need of basic shelter (max. US $1,000 per unit). Permanent supervision by Internet and visits to the projects in the field by the executive staff make possible the exchange of experience and lessons learned. SELAVIP also shares knowledge gained over four decades through lectures in academic, professional and technical centres when visiting the projects.

Geographical Area of Activity: Africa, Asia, Latin America and the Caribbean.

Restrictions: Does not work in developed countries, with families or groups that are not in social emergency, or in rural areas.

Finance: Private donations from Fondation Caritative Van der Rest-Emsens, Liechtenstein.

Board of Directors: Joan MacDonald (Chair.).

Principal Staff: Co-ordinator for Latin America Erika Carmona.

Address: Hogar de Cristo 3812, Estación Central, Santiago.

Telephone: (2) 5409341; (2) 5409335; **Fax:** (2) 7762292; **Internet:** www.selavip.org; **e-mail:** selavip@hogardecristo.cl.

China (People's Republic)

FOUNDATION CENTRES AND CO-ORDINATING BODIES

China Foundation Center

Established in 2010 to support foundations in China.

Activities: Informs on foundtions in China; holds an archive of information on China's foundation sector.

Geographical Area of Activity: People's Republic of China.

Trustees: Xu Yongguang (Chair.).

Principal Staff: Exec. Pres. Cheng Gang.

Telephone: (10) 65691231; **Fax:** (10) 65691231-612; **Internet:** www.foundationcenter.org.cn; **e-mail:** cfc@foundationcenter.org.cn.

China NPO Network

Established in 1998 by a number of NGOs, including the China Youth Development Foundation, China Association of Science Foundations, China Charity Federation, Amity Foundation, China Foundation for Poverty Alleviation, and the Social Policy Research Center under Chinese Academy of Social Sciences to promote the healthy development of civil society in China.

Activities: Aims to advance the development of not-for-profit organizations in China, through providing information and resources and acting as an information co-ordinator. Supports the capacity building of NGOs, provides training in accountability, develops networks, carries out research, and issues publications.

Geographical Area of Activity: People's Republic of China.

Publications: *NPO Exploration* (newsletter, 2 a year, in Chinese); *Training* (newsletter, in Chinese); *Research Report* (in Chinese, 20 issues 1999–2003); *Study on NPO Capacity Building in China* (in Chinese and English); *The Rules of the Road— A Guide to the Law of Charities in the United States* (in Chinese); *Philanthropy and Law in Asia* (in Chinese); *Taiwan Foundations Entering the 21 Century* (in Chinese); *The Rules of the Road – A Guide to the Law of Charities in the United States* (in Chinese); *Philanthropy and Law in Asia* (in Chinese); Annual Report; volunteer service journal; periodicals.

Principal Staff: Pres. Shang Yusheng; Dirs Cui Yu, Prof. Liqing Zhao.

Address: Rm 303, Unit 7, Bldg 2, New Era Garden, Wan Liu Zhong Lu, Haidian District, Beijing 100089.

Telephone: (10) 82573870; **Fax:** (10) 82573850; **e-mail:** npo@npo.com.cn.

FOUNDATIONS, TRUSTS AND NON-PROFIT ORGANIZATIONS

China Environmental Protection Foundation

Established by Qu Geping in April 1993 to serve the cause of environmental conservation.

Activities: Operates in the area of conservation and the environment. Encourages the development of eco-friendly manufacturing by aiding in the development of eco-friendly products. Supports training, research, academic exchange and education in the field of environmental protection. Also sponsors eco-friendly businesses, organizations and individuals; issues publications; and implements environmental conservation projects.

Geographical Area of Activity: People's Republic of China.

Publications: Financial audit reports.

Board of Directors: Qu Geping (Pres.); Wang Jirong (Vice-Pres.); Xie Qihua (Vice-Pres.); Wang Tao (Vice-Pres.).

Principal Staff: Sec.-Gen. Li Wei.

Address: No. 16 Guang Qu Men Nei St, Chongwen District, Beijing 100062.

Telephone: (10) 67130419; **Fax:** (10) 67118190; **Internet:** www.cepf.org.cn; **e-mail:** luying@cepf.org.cn.

China Foundation for Poverty Alleviation—CFPA

Established in March 1989 to help disadvantaged people improve their production conditions, upgrade their quality of life and promote sustainable development.

Activities: Aims to help people living below the poverty line, through grants to organizations and collaboration with foreign charities and relief organizations. Poverty relief projects are operated within three categories: improving farmers' independence, raising social security and co-ordinating emergency aid to disaster-stricken regions. Also provides hospitals with computer equipment and software, as well as providing management training. Makes loans under its Micro-Finance Poverty Reduction Project to improve farmers' skills.

Geographical Area of Activity: People's Republic of China.

Publications: Financial reports.

Principal Staff: Pres. Wang Yuzhao; Vice-Pres. Duan Yingbi; Exec. Dir He Daofeng.

Address: South Bldg, 4th and 5th Floors, 36 Shuangyushu Xili, Haidian District, Beijing 100086.

Telephone: (10) 82872688; **Fax:** (10) 62526268; **Internet:** www.fupin.org.cn; **e-mail:** fupin@fupin.org.cn.

China Soong Ching Ling Foundation (Children's Foundation of China)

Founded in 1982 in memory of Soong Ching Ling (Madame Sun Yat-sen, 1893–1981), former Chinese Honorary Chairman, to support the welfare, education and cultural advancement of Chinese children, and to promote international friendship and world peace.

Activities: Operates in the areas of children's education and culture. The Foundation provides training for kindergarten teachers and scholarships for girls to receive further education. It has established a Children's Science and Technology Pavilion that provides activities for children; the Tianjin Bohai Children's World, an education and recreation centre; and the Huayin Music School. Sponsored the Red Apple Child Development Center in 2000, and promotes children's sporting activities and exchanges. It awards various prizes, including a literary prize given biennially for children's literature in China and a Children's Invention Prize; and sponsors an electric organ competition. Works in co-operation with the UN Children s Fund (UNICEF). Sister foundations have been established in Canada, Japan and the USA.

Geographical Area of Activity: People's Republic of China.

Publications: Books for children on a variety of subjects and documents about the life of Soong Ching Ling.

Executive Council: Hu Qili (Chair.).

Principal Staff: Sec.-Gen. Li Ning.

Address: A12F Zhejiang Plaza, No. 29 Anzhen Xili, Chaoyang District, Beijing 100009.

Telephone: (10) 64253192; **Fax:** (10) 64011354; **Internet:** www.sclf.org; **e-mail:** sclf@ht.rol.cn.net.

China Youth Development Foundation

Established in 1989 by the All-China Youth Federation.

Activities: Enlists the support of organizations in China and abroad to engage in development work with Chinese young people and children. Promotes the work, education, culture and social welfare of Chinese youth through projects and awarding prizes to outstanding young people; seeks to enhance relations between young people around the world with a view to safe-guarding world peace. Main focus is Project Hope, a programme providing underprivileged children with improved educational opportunities, and financial aid to help children who do not attend school return to education. Through the programme, funds the construction of Hope Schools in remote rural areas, with more than 8,890 schools built to date. Has established a Stars of Hope Award Fund to support Project Hope students in further studies and a Hope Primary School Teacher-Training Fund to allow teachers to sharpen their skills and expand their knowledge. Also operates a river and wetland protection programme. Conducts joint programmes with the company Nokia.

Geographical Area of Activity: People's Republic of China.

Publications: *Hope Journal*; *News of CYDF*; *The Project Hope Public Announcement* (annually); Auditing Reports.

Finance: Total Assets 20,000,000 yuan (2009).

Board of Directors: He Junke (Chair.); Gu Xiaojin, Xu Yongguang, Xi Jieying, Chen Yueguang, Kang Xiaoguang (Vice-Chairs).

Principal Staff: Sec.-Gen. Tu Meng.

Address: 51 Wangjing West Rd, Chaoyang District Beijing 100102, PRC.

Telephone: (10) 64033904; **Fax:** (10) 64790600; **Internet:** www.cydf.org.cn; **e-mail:** info@cydf.org.cn.

Colombia

FOUNDATIONS, TRUSTS AND NON-PROFIT ORGANIZATIONS

Centro Internacional de Agricultura Tropical—CIAT (International Centre for Tropical Agriculture)

Established in 1967 by the Rockefeller Foundation and the Ford Foundation (qq.v.) to contribute to the alleviation of hunger and poverty in tropical developing countries by applying science to the generation of technology that will lead to lasting increases in agricultural output, while preserving the natural resource base.

Activities: Conducts research in five main areas: crop improvement; conservation of biological diversity; pest and disease management; soil quality and production systems; and land management. It carries out this work in collaboration with a wide range of national partner organizations. While concentrating mainly on tropical America (especially the Andean zone, the Amazon and Central America), the Centre also conducts projects in South-East Asia and Eastern, Central and Southern Africa. Scientists work on a global scale in crop improvement, and in research on soil quality. Focuses on three major agro-ecosystems of tropical America: forest margins, hillsides and savannahs.

Geographical Area of Activity: Central and South America, South-East Asia, and Eastern, Central and Southern Africa.

Publications: *Growing Affinities* (2 a year); *CIAT in Perspective* (annual report); *Pasturas Tropicales* (tropical pastures newsletter, 3 a year); Publications Catalogue; research reports.

Finance: Core budget is provided by about 23 donor countries and organizations that are members of the Consultative Group for International Agricultural Research—CGIAR (q.v.). Additional funds for specific projects are provided by some of these and other donors.

Board of Trustees: Wanda Collins (Chair.).

Principal Staff: Dir-Gen. Ruben G. Echeverría; Exec. Dir Juan Lucas Restrepo.

Address: Apdo Aéreo 6713, Cali.

Telephone: (2) 4450000; **Fax:** (2) 4450073; **Internet:** www.ciat.cgiar.org; **e-mail:** ciat@cgiar.org.

Fundación Amanecer

Established in 1994.

Activities: Provides grants and financial support, including loans, to not-for-profit organizations in Colombia. Also provides technical support in the field of agriculture and agricultural technology to co-operative enterprises and grassroots organizations.

Geographical Area of Activity: Colombia.

Finance: Annual grants approx. US $1,000,000.

Principal Staff: Exec. Dir Cesar Ivan Velosa Proveda.

Address: Calle 24 No. 20A-27, Yopal, Casanare.

Telephone: (8) 6354739; **Internet:** www.amanecer.org.co.

Fundación Antonio Restrepo Barco

Aims to foster the educational, cultural, and technical development of children and young people.

Activities: Supports projects in the fields of health, family, social participation and income improvement, and publishes books.

Geographical Area of Activity: Colombia.

Publications: *Niños, niñas y conflicto armado en Colombia*; *Cartilla Prácticas culturales para la educación de la niñez*; and other related publications.

Principal Staff: María Paula Ballesteros.

Address: Carrera 7, No. 73-55, Piso 12, Bogotá.

Telephone: (2) 3121511; **Fax:** (2) 3121182; **Internet:** www.funrestrepobarco.org.co; **e-mail:** frb@funrestrepobarco.org.co.

Fundación Corona

Fundación Corona was established in 1963 by the Echavarría Olózaga family, Colombian entrepreneurs who have participated in the industrial development of the country through the establishment and operation of Corona, an entrepreneurial organization mainly dedicated to the manufacture and commercialization of ceramic products.

Activities: Aims to contribute to the social development of Colombia by improving the management of social processes and through innovative programmes and projects that help the poorest members of the population have access to the benefits of development. Makes grants in the fields of health, education, the environment and the development of microenterprises at both local and national levels. Strategies comprise: development of management models useful to social organizations and groups, such as schools, hospitals, microenterprises and community organizations with the objective of working more efficiently (organizational effectiveness); development of knowledge in specific sectors and promotion of public debate in topics of interest to improve the design and development of public policies; promotion of citizenship participation to allow community problem solving and stimulate the follow up and control of local governments; development of programmes for the generation of job and income opportunities for the vulnerable population.

Geographical Area of Activity: Colombia.

Restrictions: Only supports development projects in Colombia.

Publications: Education: *Una Mirada a las Cifras de la Educación en Colombia 2002–2009*; *La gratuidad en la educación en los planes de desarrollo de los departamentos y los municipios de Colombia, 2008–2011*; *Lecturas complementarias para maestros: leer y escribir con niños y niñas* (2008). Local and community development: *Informe de calidad de vida de Cartagena* (2009); *Premio cívico por una Bogotá Mejor* (2009). Health: *Seguridad del paciente, un modelo organizacional para el control sistemático de los riesgos en la atención en salud*; *Aportes al bienestar de la vejez*. Entrepreneurial Development: *Retos y desafíos del sector de la microempresa en Colombia*; *Micro finanzas en Colombia*; *Mejoramiento de las condiciones de acceso al crédito para microempresarios*.

Finance: Project expenditure US $8,552,330 (2009).

Board of Directors: Daniel Echavarría Arango (Pres.).

Principal Staff: Exec. Dir Ana Mercedes Botero Arboleda.

Address: Calle 90, No 13A-20, Oficina 503, Bogotá.

Telephone: (1) 4000031; **Fax:** (1) 4010540; **Internet:** www.fundacioncorona.org.co; **e-mail:** fundacion@fcorona.org.

Fundación para la Educación Superior y el Desarrollo—Fedesarrollo (Foundation for Higher Education and Development)

Founded in 1970 by Manuel Carvajal Sinisterra, Rodrigo Botero Montoya and Alberto Vargas Martínez to promote cultural and scientific advancement and to stimulate research into Colombia's social, economic and political problems.

Activities: Operates nationally in the fields of social welfare and political science and administration, and nationally and internationally in the fields of economic affairs and international relations, through research, surveys, publications and lectures on an international level and through conferences and courses conducted in Colombia.

Geographical Area of Activity: Colombia.

Publications: *Coyuntura Económica* (quarterly); *Coyuntura Social* (quarterly); economic and employment statistics; more than 50 social science publications and working papers.

Principal Staff: Exec. Dir Roberto Steiner; Sec.-Gen. Marcela Pombo.

Address: Calle 78, No 9–91, Bogotá.

Telephone: (1) 3259777; **Fax:** (1) 3259770; **Internet:** www .fedesarrollo.org.co; **e-mail:** comercial@fedesarrollo.org.co.

Fundación Hábitat Colombia—FHC (Colombian Habitat Foundation)

Established in 1991. Specializes in knowledge management on urban best practices, research, communication, technical assistance and co-operation for urban and regional development.

Activities: Operates in Colombia, promoting a better quality of life for urban dwellers in collaboration with the Government, the private sector and social organizations. Supports initiatives that encourage environmental development, the exchange of experience and information, the establishment of strategic alliances and promote sustainability.

Geographical Area of Activity: Colombia.

Publications: *Hábitat Colombia* (magazine); *Intercambios/Exchanges; Best Practices Transfer; Locals Demands/Offers Globals.*

Principal Staff: Dir. Lucelena Betancur Salazar.

Address: Carretera 7 BisA 123-33, Bogotá.

Telephone: (1) 2147974; **Fax:** (1) 4931121; **Internet:** www .fundacionhabitatcolombia.org; **e-mail:** informacion@fundacionhabitatcolombia.org.

Fundación Herencia Verde (Green Heritage Foundation)

Founded in September 1983 by a group of 30 people to protect Colombia's natural resources.

Activities: The Foundation operates nationally in the Andean and Pacific coast regions in the fields of biodiversity, conservation and the environment, through self-conducted programmes, research and publications. Proprietor of the Natural Reserve of Alto Quindio in the central Andes.

Geographical Area of Activity: Colombia.

Publications: Research findings.

Principal Staff: Exec. Dir Juan Carlos Riascos.

Address: Calle 4a, Oeste No 3a–32, Barrio el Peñón.

Telephone: (92) 8933052; **e-mail:** fhv-adm@cali.cetcol.net .co.

Fundación SERVIVIENDA (Housing Services Foundation)

Founded in 1972 by the Society of Jesus to develop housing programmes for low-income families.

Activities: Operates nationally and internationally. Produces, sells, finances and erects more than 4,000 concrete pre-fabricated houses a year; built more than 100,000 houses in 2005.

Finance: Financed from sale of houses: approx. US $8,000,000 annually.

Principal Staff: Dir-Gen. María Margarita Ruíz Rodgers.

Address: Avda Caracas 46-47, Bogotá.

Telephone: (1) 2879666; **Fax:** (1) 2887605; **Internet:** www .servivienda.org.co; **e-mail:** direccion@servivienda.org.co.

Grupo Latinoamericano para la Participación, la Integración y la Inclusión de Personas con Discapacidad—GLARP-IIPD (Latin American Group for the Participation, Integration and Inclusion of People with Disability)

Founded in 1977 by a group of 10 national rehabilitation institutions and nine individuals to co-ordinate rehabilitation services in Central and South America and the Caribbean and to create new centres to reinstate as active members of the community those incapacitated by illness or other disadvantages.

Activities: Encourages co-operation among its members and acts as a centre for the exchange of information. It Internationally promotes the development of rehabilitation programmes, in co-operation with private and governmental bodies. It offers advisory and training services, and finance for specific projects.

Geographical Area of Activity: Central and South America and the Caribbean.

Publications: *Boletín GLARP-CEDIR* (monthly); reports; bibliographies.

Finance: Provided by subscriptions and donations; annual budget approx. US $450,000.

Board of Directors: Soledad Fernández Malagarriga (Pres.); Soledad Murrillo Galindo (Vice-Pres.); Libia Elvira Henríquez (Sec.).

Principal Staff: Exec. Dir Dr Martha Aristizábal Gómez.

Address: Carretera 13 77-22, Bogotá.

Telephone: (1) 6082255; **Fax:** (1) 6082255; **Internet:** www .glarp-iipd.org; **e-mail:** glarp@etb.net.co.

Costa Rica

FOUNDATIONS, TRUSTS AND NON-PROFIT ORGANIZATIONS

DEMUCA—Fundación para el Desarrollo Local y el Fortalecimiento Municipal e Institucional de Centroamérica y el Caribe (Foundation for Local Development and the Municipal and Institutional Support of Central America and the Caribbean)

Founded in 1990; aims to strengthen the capacity of local governments in Central America and the Caribbean to promote human development.

Activities: Promotes the exchange of experience and information, and international co-operation between Spain, Central America and the Caribbeanto improve human development work in the latter two regions. Works to improve municipal finances, and raise the level of efficiency in grant-making and of basic public services in local governments, including clean water supplies and sanitation, rubbish disposal, and public transport. Also provides general support for local and regional governments.

Geographical Area of Activity: Central America and the Caribbean.

Publications: *El Régimen Municipal de Nicaragua; Organización, Funciones y Prácticas Generales de Gestión Pública; La Basura; El Agua como Servicio Público Municipal; La Gestión de los Servicios Públicos Municipales; ¿Qué es una Municipalidad?; Memoria del Seminario Taller 'Municipio, Turismo y Desarrollo' Contabilidad Municipal; Recolección y Disposición Final de la Basura: Un Servico Público Municipal; Los 10 Años de DEMUCA.*

Principal Staff: Exec. Dir Mercedes Peñas Domingo.

Address: Apdo 697-1005, San José; Barrio Escalante, del Parque Francia 25m Sur, San José.

Telephone: 258-1813; **Fax:** 248-0297; **Internet:** www.demuca .org.

Fondo Latinoamericano de Desarrollo (Latin American Fund for Development)

Created in 1993 to bring development groups together to work on projects across Latin America.

Activities: Aims to provide microfinance to create self-sufficiency and encourage development.

Geographical Area of Activity: South and Central America.

Board of Directors: Luis Pedro Errazúriz (Pres.); José Ernesto Mancía (Vice-Pres.); José Alberto Tejada E. (Sec.); Marcelo Mayorga (Treas.).

Principal Staff: Exec. Dir Edgar Zurita Pozo.

Address: Bario Escalante, 300m norte y 175m oeste de la Iglesia Santa Teresita, Apdo 1783-2050, San José.

Internet: www.folade.org; **e-mail:** folade@folade.org.

Fundación Acceso (Access Foundation)

A non-profit, technical assistance organization, which aims to provide training, technical assistance and institution-building services to organizations working towards sustainable development in Central and South America.

Activities: Lends support and assistance to grassroots development organizations, and regional, national and international institutions, NGOs, private firms and individuals in Central and South America that work in the field of sustainable development. Areas covered include programme planning, human resource development, fundraising, strategic Internet use and other related areas.

Geographical Area of Activity: Central and South America.

Publications: Reports, booklets and directories.

Principal Staff: Co-ordinator Tanya Lockwood Fallas.

Address: Apdo 288-2050, San José.

Telephone: 2226-0145; **Fax:** 2226-0308; **Internet:** www .acceso.or.cr; **e-mail:** info@acceso.or.cr.

Fundación Arias para la Paz y el Progreso Humano (Arias Foundation for Peace and Human Progress)

Established in 1988 by Dr Oscar Arias Sánchez, former president of Costa Rica, to work to build just and peaceful societies in Central America.

Activities: Operates in Central America in the fields of education, law and human rights, and social welfare and social studies, through self-conducted programmes, research, workshops, training courses and publications through three main centres: the Center for Human Progress, which carries out work on gender equality; the Center for Peace and Reconciliation, working in the field of demilitarization and conflict prevention; and the Center for Organized Participation, working in the field of civil society and democracy. Also administers the Museum of Peace.

Geographical Area of Activity: Central America.

Publications: *Genero y Tecnologia Agropecuaria; Memoria Taller Hagamos las Cuentas: Politicas Publicas, ciudadania, y presupuestas; Capacitacion en Incidencia*; and many other publications.

Finance: Annual budget approx. US $1,000,000.

Board of Governors: Rodrigo Aria Sánchez (Pres.).

Principal Staff: Exec. Dir Luis Alberto Cordero; Admin. Dir Marco Soto; Finance Dir Catalina Flores.

Address: Apdo 8-6410-100, San José.

Telephone: 2222-9191; **Fax:** 2257-5011; **Internet:** www.arias .or.cr; **e-mail:** info@arias.or.cr.

Fundación Costarricense de Desarrollo—FUCODES (Costa Rican Foundation for Development)

Established in 1973 to improve the quality of life of the underprivileged.

Activities: Operates nationally in the areas of social welfare and economic affairs, promoting the creation of small businesses, collective effort and supporting education through technical and financial assistance, and conferences and training programmes; co-operates with other national and international organizations.

Geographical Area of Activity: Costa Rica.

Publications: *Correo Gráfico* (monthly); *Últimas Notícias* (monthly).

Finance: Annual budget approx. US $2,500.

Principal Staff: Dir William Flores.

Address: Calle 7, Avda 0 y 1, 75m norte del Hotel Balmoral, Apdo 71270-1000 San José.

Telephone: 223-5735; **Fax:** 222-5770; **e-mail:** fucodes@racsa .co.cr.

Fundación para el Desarrollo de Base—FUNDE-BASE (Foundation for Basic Development)

Founded in 1995 to offer alternative finance to NGOs and micro-enterprises in both rural and urban areas of the country.

Activities: Offers micro-credit under three programme areas: finance for microenterprise, finance for rural groups, and finance for NGOs.

Geographical Area of Activity: South and Central America.

Board of Trustees: Tarcisio Mora Ulloa (Pres.); Carlos Gamboa Leiva (Sec.).

Principal Staff: Exec. Dir José Roberto Jiménez Barletta.

Address: Edificio Galerías del Este, local #11, 150m al este de Plaza del Sol, Curridabat, Apdo 714-1011 La y Griega, San José.

Telephone: 234-8534, 281-2760; **Fax:** 234-0393; **Internet:** www.fundebasecr.org; **e-mail:** fundeba@racsa.co.cr.

Fundación para el Desarrollo Sostenible de la Pequeña y Mediana Empresa—FUNDES Internacional (Foundation for the Sustainable Development of Small and Medium-sized Enterprises—FUNDES International)

Founded in 1984 to develop the region's private sector.

Activities: Seeks to improve the competitiveness of small and medium-sized enterprises (SMEs), resulting in better market access, higher profitability and improved efficiency. Conducts research into the the sector, as well as the environment in which these businesses operate and the strategies that make their growth and development viable. Projects use complementary tools (training, business consulting, access to financing, and information technologies) to deal with businesses as a whole, and are based on the premise that businesses are not islands, but rather interact with other businesses and supporting organizations. Areas of intervention are: development at a business level; value chain development; sectoral/ territorial development; and improving the business environment. Regional offices in Argentina, Bolivia, Chile, Colombia, Costa Rica, Guatemala, El Salvador, Mexico, Panama, Venezuela.

Geographical Area of Activity: Latin America.

Publications: 2009 publications: *Improvement in Strategic Management and Productivity of the MSMEs through Information and Communication Technologies Project; Growing with Tourism; Supplier Development: Huachipato Iron and Steel; Retail Trade Program; Camelid Chain Development; Forestry Service Associativity; Situation on MSME Business Social Responsibility in Bolivia; Fostering Entrepreneurship; Dynamics of the MSME Family Business 'Exploratory Study in Colombia'; Research on the Value Chain of Iron as Scrap Metal in Argentina; Successful Exporting, Innovation, and Social Impact: An exploratory Study on Exporting SMEs in Latin America; Business Dynamics in Chile (1999–2006).*

Finance: Non-profit.

Principal Staff: Exec. Dir Ulrich Frei; Int. Strategy Man. Elfid Torres.

Address: La Asunción de Belén, Heredia, Apdo 798 – 4005, San Antonio de Belén.

Telephone: 2209-8300; **Fax:** 2209-8399; **Internet:** www.fundes.org; **e-mail:** internacional@fundes.org.

Fundación para la Economía Popular—FUNDECO (Foundation for the People's Economy)

Founded in 1991.

Activities: Offers technical, professional and financial advice to help implement social development schemes aiming to improve the quality of life for people in Latin American countries.

Principal Staff: CEO Roinel Vargas.

Address: Barrio Francisco Peralta, 100m este y 75m sur y 50 mtrs oeste de KFC, San José.

Telephone: 2281-3107, 2281-3150; **Fax:** 2253-6270; **e-mail:** funepo@ice.co.cr.

Fundación Integral Campesina—FINCA (Comprehensive Rural Foundation)

Founded in 1984 by Maria Marta Padilla.

Activities: Aims to aid rural communities by offering micro-credit for development projects.

Geographical Area of Activity: Costa Rica.

Principal Staff: Exec. Dir Luis Jiménez Padilla.

Address: 200m norte y 15m este del parqueo del Hotel San José Palacio, La Uruca, San José.

Telephone: 2520-2076; **Fax:** 2520-2075; **Internet:** www.fincacostarica.org; **e-mail:** info@fic.or.cr.

Fundación Mujer (Women's Foundation)

Founded in 1988 to finance women in business.

Activities: Offers micro-finance to businesses run by women.

Geographical Area of Activity: Costa Rica.

Principal Staff: Exec. Dir Licda Zobeida Moya Lacayo.

Telephone: 2253-1661; **Fax:** 2253-1613; **Internet:** www.fundacionmujer.org; **e-mail:** fundacionmujer@racsa.co.cr.

Fundación Unión y Desarrollo de Comunidades Campesinas (Foundation for the Unity and Development of Rural Communities)

Founded in 1990 as a CARE International project, later becoming an independent foundation.

Activities: Community credit scheme for rural communities.

Geographical Area of Activity: Costa Rica.

Address: 400m al norte y 75m oeste del Mercado Municipal, Ciudad Quesada, San Carlos.

Telephone: 460-6035; **Fax:** 460-0412; **Internet:** www.fundecoca.org; **e-mail:** fundecoc@racsa.co.cr.

Instituto Interamericano de Derechos Humanos—IIHR (Inter-American Institute of Human Rights)

Founded in 1980, dedicated to the promotion of, and investigation into, human rights in Central and South America.

Activities: Operates in the fields of education and human rights. Promotes human rights and social justice, and works to consolidate democracy through investigation, education, political mediation, technical assistance and the dissemination of relevant information through specialized publications. Organizes conferences, issues publications, and works with a number of other organizations and local governments. Maintains an online documentation centre.

Geographical Area of Activity: Central and South America.

Publications: *Boletín Infomativo* (3 a year, in Spanish; published in English as *IIHR Newsletter*); *Boletín Electoral Latinoamericano* (weekly); *Revista IIDH* (weekly); *The Current Outlook for Human Rights and Democracy 2003*; *Estudios Básicos en Derechos Humanos*; *Estudios Especializados en Derechos Humanos*; *Exodos en América Latina*; *Iudicum et Vita*; and more than 250 other titles including books, magazines, manuals, videos and CD-ROMs.

Board of Directors: Thomas Buergenthal (Hon. Pres.); Sonia Picado Sotela (Pres.); Mónica Pinto (Vice-Pres.); Margaret Crahan (Vice-Pres.).

Principal Staff: Exec. Dir Roberto Cuéllar M.

Address: Apdo 10081-1000, San José.

Telephone: 234-0404; **Fax:** 234-0955; **Internet:** www.iidh.ed.cr; **e-mail:** direccionejecutiva@iidh.ed.cr.

Red de Mujeres para el Desarrollo (Women's Development Network)

Established in 1998 as a strategic alliance among grassroots women's groups, NGOs, churches, development professionals, and international agencies, concerned for the economic development of excluded women in Central and South America and the Caribbean.

Activities: Operates in the field of women's rights by representing women at risk of exclusion in Central and South America and the Caribbean. Promotes communication and collaboration and the development and empowerment of women. Activities include publication of a quarterly newsletter; access to a database providing information on economic projects, bibliographic material and sources of financing and training; support for not-for-profit organizations searching for funding and training; and the formation of local support networks. Maintains offices in Brazil, Colombia, Curaçao (Netherlands Antilles), Dominica, Haiti, Honduras, Puerto Rico, Trinidad and Tobago and the USA.

Geographical Area of Activity: Central and South America and the Caribbean, and the USA.

Publications: Newsletter (quarterly).

Principal Staff: Co-ordinators Nancy Boye, Noemi Barquero, Olga Parrado.

Address: Apdo 692-2070, Sabanilla, San José.

Telephone: 2225-0248; **Fax:** 2253-9128; **Internet:** www.redmujeres.org; **e-mail:** info@redmujeres.org.

Croatia

FOUNDATION CENTRES AND CO-ORDINATING BODIES

Association for Civil Society Development—SMART

Aims to strengthen and support the development of the non-profit sector in Croatia.

Activities: Promotes capacity building of civil society organizations in Croatia, through organizing training workshops, providing technical assistance and consultancy services to non-formal groups and non-profit organizations on the principles of strengthening, self-assistance, active involvement, maintenance of positive initiatives, stimulation of co-operation, mutual evaluation and respect of differences, carries out research, and funds capacity building initiatives.

Geographical Area of Activity: Croatia.

Governing Board: Igor Bajok; Sanja Baric; Sonja Grozc Zivolic; Zelimir Grzancic; Maja Halvaks Gericic; Neven Santic; Mira Shalabi.

Principal Staff: Executive team Gordana Forcic, Sladjana Novota, Zvijezdana Schulz Vugrin.

Address: 51000 Rijeka, Blaza Polića 2/IV.

Telephone: (51) 332-750; **Fax:** (51) 330-792; **Internet:** www .smart.hr; **e-mail:** smart@smart.hr.

Centar za razvoj neprofitnih organizacija—CERANEO (Centre for Development of Non-Profit Organizations)

Activities: Think tank dedicated to collecting, analysing and researching social policy problems, promoting development of civil society organizations and foundations in Croatia through debates, lobbying, organizing conferences and networking with similar organizations. Programme activities include: analysing different drafts of laws or policy programmes on public policies, organizing debates (workshops, round tables, seminars, conferences) to influence decisions in Parliament; initiating changes of existing legislation and policies; building a bridge between academics, researchers, decision-makers in government and practitioners; publishing results of projects and briefing articles in the media. Supports new initiatives and advocates a more important role for civil society. Researches civil society in Croatia; contributes to public debate about foundation law; offers resources to Croatian civil society organizations and promotes the organizations to potential international donors.

Geographical Area of Activity: Croatia.

Publications: Newsletter, books, articles, translations, publications, research reports.

Governing Board: Gojko Bezovan (Pres.); Sinisa Zrinscak (Vice-Pres.).

Principal Staff: Project Man. Marina Dimic Vugec; Sec. Vesela Grabovac.

Address: 10000 Zagreb, Nazorova 51.

Telephone: (1) 4812-384; **Fax:** (1) 4812-384; **Internet:** www .ceraneo.hr; **e-mail:** ceraneo@zg.t-com.hr.

Nacionalne Zaklade za Razvoj Civilnoga Drustva (National Foundation for Civil Society Development)

Founded on 16 October 2003 by an act of the Croatian Parliament, to promote and support civil society development in Croatia.

Activities: The Foundation provides expert and financial support to innovative programmes that encourage the sustainability of the non-profit sector, inter-sector co-operation, civil initiatives, philanthropy, voluntary work and the improvement of democratic institutions in society. Aims to achieve active citizenship for the development of a modern, democratic and inclusive society in Croatia.

Geographical Area of Activity: Croatia.

Publications: *Guide to EU Funding, 50 Questions and Answers on the Treaty Establishing a Constitution for Europe, Guide to EU Associations* (translations of ECAS publications); *Assessment of Development of the NGO Sector in Croatia; The Legal Framework for the Activity of Public Benefit Organizations in the Republic of Croatia/Public Benefit Status: A Comparative Overview; A Survey of Tax Laws Affecting NGOs in Central and Eastern Europe* (collaboration with ICNL); *Awards for Examples of Good Practice in Collaboration of Towns and Associations in the Republic of Croatia; Catalogue of Programmes for Informal Education on Human Rights and Democratic Citizenship Implemented by Civil Society Organizations in the Republic of Croatia; The Partnering Toolbook* (by Ros Tennyson, IBLF and GAIN, Croatian translation); *Volunteer Stories; Social Capital in Croatia; Public Position on Volunteering;* Annual Report.

Finance: Financed by state lottery funds, donations, and EU funds.

Management Board: Boris Hajoš (Pres.); Zrinka Kovacevic (Vice-Pres.).

Principal Staff: Dir Cvjetana Plavša-Matić; Sec. Iva Grgić.

Address: Štrigina 1a, 10000 Zagreb.

Telephone: (1) 2399-100; **Fax:** (1) 2399-111; **Internet:** zaklada .civilnodrustvo.hr; **e-mail:** zaklada@civilnodrustvo.hr.

FOUNDATIONS, TRUSTS AND NON-PROFIT ORGANIZATIONS

Budi aktivna, Budi emancipiran—BaBe! (Be Active, Be Emancipated)

Founded in 1994 by Vesna Kesic and nine activists to promote women's human rights. Came out of the Center for Women War Victims. Since then, more than 100 women have been working either as full or part time employees and activists or volunteers together with experts in different field.

Activities: Operates in the field of human rights, through advocacy and lobbying for the affirmation and implementation of women's rights and gender equality. At the very beginning supported activities aiming at elimination and protection of women from violence in the domestic and public spheres; promotes the right to freedom of choice and other reproductive rights, and adequate health-care protection; and the right to equal and full participation in all areas of society. Priorities and specific objectives change in response to the needs of women who are marginalized and discriminated against. Since 2008, has created projects within three main programmes: Gender equality; Prevention and protection against gender-based violence; and Human rights.

Geographical Area of Activity: Croatia and South-Eastern Europe.

Restrictions: Not a grant-making organization.

Publications: Books, documentaries, musical videos, social advertisements, installations, brochures, posters, leaflets.

Finance: project-based financing.

Principal Staff: Pres. Sanja Sarnavka; Programme co-ordinators Zdravka Sadakov,Senka Rebić, Korana Radman; Finance Man. Tanja Repalust.

Address: 10000 Zagreb, Human Rights House, Selska 112.

Telephone: (1) 46 63 666; **Fax:** (1) 46 62 606; **Internet:** www .babe.hr; **e-mail:** babe@babe.hr.

Curaçao

FOUNDATIONS, TRUSTS AND NON-PROFIT ORGANIZATIONS

CARMABI Foundation

Established in 1955 as the Caribbean Marine Biological Institute; currently involved in applied marine natural resource research.

Activities: Operates in the area of conservation of the environment and research. Conducts marine biological research and conservation research (has established nature sanctuaries and parks in the Netherlands Antilles); provides advice to local government; and carries out an education programme for schoolchildren. Visiting scientists from the Netherlands and the USA carry out research.

Geographical Area of Activity: Netherlands Dependencies.

Publications: Numerous scientific reports and publications; *Caribbean Journal of Science* (journal); *Bina* (newsletter); Annual Report.

Board: Dito Abbad (Chair.); Jeffrey Sybesma (Sec.); Peter Bongers (Treas.).

Principal Staff: Dir Paul G. C. Stokkermans; Scientific Dir Dr Mark Vermeij.

Address: POB 2090, Piscaderabaai z/n, Willemstad.

Telephone: (9) 462-42-42; **Fax:** (9) 462-76-80; **Internet:** www .carmabi.org; **e-mail:** info@carmabi.org.

Cyprus

FOUNDATIONS, TRUSTS AND NON-PROFIT ORGANIZATIONS

Bank of Cyprus Cultural Foundation

Founded in 1994 by the Bank of Cyprus Group, promotes studies on Cyprus at a professional and scholarly level. All projects are aimed at extending the study of the history and culture of Cyprus as an island of the wider Hellenic world.

Activities: Operates four major collections: coins, maps, rare historical documents and contemporary Cypriot art. Each of the collections is linked to a long-term project involving research, publications, lectures, seminars, educational programmes, and temporary and permanent exhibitions. Opened the Museum of the History of Cypriot Coinage in 1995, and the Museum of the Archaeological Collection of George and Nefeli Tziapra Rierides was inaugurated in 2002.

Geographical Area of Activity: Cyprus and Greece.

Publications: Newsletters; information brochures; monographs; multi-year report; publications catalogue/list. Publications programme includes publications in the following areas: Cypriot cartography; Cypriot coinage; archaeology and history of Cyprus; guides to archaeological and historical monuments; Cypriot literature; CDs and video publications.

Board of Trustees: Yiannis Kypri (Chair.).

Principal Staff: Dir Lefki Michaelidou; Curators Christodoulos Hadjichristodoulou, Eleni Zapiti.

Address: POB 21995, 1515 Nicosia.

Telephone: (22) 128157; **Fax:** (22) 662898; **Internet:** www.boccf.org; **e-mail:** info@cultural.bankofcyprus.com.

Christos Stelios Ioannou Foundation

Established in 1983 by Stelios and Elli Ioannou; aims to improve the quality of life of people with mental disabilities.

Activities: Operates in Cyprus in the field of medicine and health, and welfare. Promotes the treatment of people with mental disabilities as individuals, the development of their full potential, and the provision of opportunities for a fully active and fulfilling life within society. Increases public awareness and acceptance of mental disabilities, and provides support for people with such disabilities in a rehabilitation group for students and former students of the Foundation. Provides accommodation services, and a variety of events and activities outside its basic services, including trips, foreign exchanges, music, dance and drama. Organizes staff training programmes for those who work for the Foundation, and in schools and institutions elsewhere in Cyprus. Maintains links with similar organizations throughout Europe.

Geographical Area of Activity: Cyprus.

Board of Directors: Dakis Joannou (Chair.); Christakis K. Stefani (Vice-Chair.).

Principal Staff: Dir Andreas R. Georgiou.

Address: POB 590, 1660 Nicosia.

Telephone: (22) 481666; **Fax:** (22) 485331; **Internet:** www.ioannoufoundation.org; **e-mail:** csjfound@spidernet.com.cy.

A. G. Leventis Foundation

Established in May 1979 by the will of Anastasios G. Leventis to support artistic, cultural, educational and charitable activities in Greece, Cyprus and other areas.

Activities: The Foundation operates to promote and preserve Cyprus' cultural heritage, including supporting the establishment of new museums. Promotes environmental conservation; offers grants for study at the University of Cyprus and for postgraduate study abroad, especially in the fields of science and education; funds publications; and promotes social welfare.

Geographical Area of Activity: Greece, Cyprus, the Balkans, West Africa, Central and Western Europe.

Restrictions: No support for projects outside of the geographic focus.

Publications: Numerous publications in English, French and Greek on Cypriot and Greek art and civilization; archaeological reports and studies; Byzantine art; cartography; children's books; collections of essays; conference proceedings; coroplastic art of Cyprus; lecture series; proceedings of symposiums.

Governing Board: Anastasios P. Leventis (Chair.).

Principal Staff: Dir Dr Vassos Karageorghis.

Address: 40 Gladstonos St, POB 2543, 1095 Nicosia.

Telephone: (22) 667706; **Fax:** (22) 675002; **Internet:** www.leventisfoundation.org; **e-mail:** leventcy@zenon.logos.cy.net.

George and Thelma Paraskevaides Foundation

Founded in 1980 by George and Thelma Paraskevaides for medical, educational and cultural purposes.

Activities: The Foundation assists indigent Cypriots who need to go abroad for medical treatment, as well as making grants to medical institutions; awarding scholarships for higher studies abroad; and providing grants for cultural purposes in Cyprus (particularly conservation). Also funds the Annual Prize for Journalism and Democracy awarded by the Organization for Security and Co-operation in Europe (OSCE).

Geographical Area of Activity: Cyprus.

Address: Paraskevaides Foundation Bldg, 36 Griva Dighenis Ave, POB 2200, 1518 Nicosia.

Telephone: (22) 463798.

Czech Republic

FOUNDATION CENTRES AND CO-ORDINATING BODIES

AGNES—Vzdělávací Organizace (Agency for the Non-profit Sector)

Established in 1998 to support the NGO sector in the Czech Republic.

Activities: Activities include training programmes for NGO staff; research and publishing on the NGO sector; and the promotion and development of NGOs in the Czech Republic. Aims to aid the development of NGOs across the country, increase bilateral activities, and foster international co-operation. Established the Jeleni Club in 2000 for NGOs' staff, clients, volunteers and supporters.

Geographical Area of Activity: Czech Republic.

Publications: *Non-profit Organizations and Influencing Public Policy; Philanthropy and Volunteerism in the Czech Republic.*

Principal Staff: Dir Jiri Jezek; Project Man. Irena Pekova.

Address: Jeleni 196/15, 118 00 Prague 1.

Telephone: 233350120; **Fax:** 233350120; **Internet:** www .agnes.cz; **e-mail:** agnes@agnes.cz.

Council of Humanitarian Associations

Founded in 1990 as the Czechoslovak Council for Humanitarian Co-operation—an independent non-governmental voluntary association of 154 organizations aimed at relieving human suffering which. After the division of Czechoslovakia into the Czech Republic and Slovakia, became the Czech Council for Humanitarian Co-operation and the Slovak Humanitarian Council (q.v.).

Activities: Work focuses on minority groups, the underprivileged and the disabled; it provides a database of humanitarian organizations, training for members, and organizes seminars and workshops. Operates mainly in the Czech Republic, but has worked in Armenia and with organizations active internationally. Has around 180 member organizations.

Geographical Area of Activity: Mainly Czech Republic.

Publications: Monthly review; bulletin; newsletter; conference reports.

Principal Staff: Pres. Pavel Dušek; Vice-Pres. Jiří Lodr.

Address: Ceskobratrská 9, 130 00 Prague 3.

Telephone: 222587455; **Fax:** 222960962; **Internet:** www.crho .org; **e-mail:** kancelar@crho.org.

Czech Donors Forum

An association of grant-makers that was established as a non-profit membership initiative in October 1995 and became a registered civic association in July 1997. It is a national association of grant-makers providing support and leadership to the donor community. Associates both foundations with and without endowments and also unites corporate donors in the Donator, a club of corporate donors. The Forum's mission is to support the development of organized philanthropy and to serve the Czech foundation community.

Activities: Operates as a support organization for grant-making organizations in the Czech Republic focusing on the cultivation and development of the foundation sector and philanthropy, strengthening the co-operation and development of the foundation and private sectors, and playing an infrastructural role. Main programmes are the Educational Training Programme, the Programme for the Development of Corporate Philanthropy and the 1% of tax designation project.

Geographical Area of Activity: Western, Central and Eastern Europe.

Restrictions: Not a grant-making organization.

Publications: Newsletter (quarterly); *Directory of Foundations; The Economic Development of the Civil and Not-for-Profit Sector in the Czech Republic: Foundations and Assets; Foundations in the Czech Republic; Strategy for the Development of the Non-Profit Sector in the Czech Republic; Manual for Foundations without an Endowment; Cookbook* (manual for communication agencies); Annual Report.

Executive Board: Hana Silhanova (Chair.).

Principal Staff: Exec. Dir Klara Splichalova.

Address: Palac Lucerna, 5. patro, Stepanska 61, 116 02 Prague 1.

Telephone: 224216544; **Fax:** 224216544; **Internet:** www .donorsforum.cz; **e-mail:** donorsforum@donorsforum.cz.

ICN—Information Centre for Non-profit Organizations

A non-profit organization; raises public awareness about the non-profit sector and to strengthen its role in civic society in the Czech Republic and internationally.

Activities: Aims to provide access to information on government regulations and training for organization personnel; to facilitate national and international co-operation; to encourage greater public involvement in the non-profit sector; and to influence government policy with regard to the development of the non-profit sector in the Czech Republic. ICN maintains a library and information centre, a database of financial resources for non-profits, and a database of non-profit organizations in the Czech Republic, comprising more than 2,600 entries. Also provides consultancy services to non-profit organizations; and information, educational and publishing services.

Geographical Area of Activity: Czech Republic.

Publications: *GRANTIS—Non-Profit Sector Monthly* (monthly in Czech, annually in English); *Directory of Czech NGOs; Compendium of Financial Resources in the Czech Republic; Guide to the Law for Not-for-Profit Organizations;* Annual Report.

Board of Directors: Dana Berova (Chair.).

Principal Staff: Exec. Dir Marek Sedivy.

Address: Malé námesti 12, 110 00 Prague 1.

Telephone: 224239876; **Fax:** 224239875; **Internet:** www .neziskovky.cz; **e-mail:** neziskovky@neziskovky.cz.

Nadace Auxilia (Auxilia Foundation)

Founded in 1992 to provide information, training and co-ordination services to support the development of non-profit organizations in the Czech Republic. In 1998 the organization split into two: Auxilia Foundation (ICN Foundation until 2005), a grant-making foundation that supports co-operation between NGOs, networking and partnership with public administration at regional level; and ICN—Information Centre for Non-profit Organizations (q.v.), providing information, training and co-ordination services to the third sector in the Czech Republic.

Activities: Offers educational training, consultancy, networking, publication services and support to the non-profit sector to support the development of non-profit activities.

Geographical Area of Activity: Czech Republic.

Restrictions: No grants are made to individuals; limited grants are made to state-run organizations.

Board of Directors: Marek Sedivy (Chair.).

Address: Malé nám. 12, 110 00 Prague 1.

Telephone: 224239876; **Fax:** 224239875; **Internet:** www
.auxilia.cz; **e-mail:** prchalova@auxilia.cz.

PASOS—Policy Association for an Open Society

Established in 2004.

Activities: Supports civil society development in Central and
Eastern Europe through: organizing conferences, seminars,
workshops, etc.; supporting joint projects in public policy formulation; providing training in public policy; disseminating
information including publishing information. Has 50 member
organizations.

Geographical Area of Activity: Central and Eastern Europe.

Principal Staff: Exec. Dir Jeff Lovitt.

Address: Tesnov 3, 110 00 Prague 1.

Telephone: (420) 2223 1644; **Fax:** (420) 2223 1644; **Internet:**
www.pasos.org; **e-mail:** info@pasos.org.

FOUNDATIONS, TRUSTS AND NON-PROFIT ORGANIZATIONS

Cindi Foundation

Established in 1993 by the National Institute of Public Health.

Activities: Supports the Institute's Cindi Programme, which
aims to promote preventative action in the field of public
health, focusing on lifestyle and environmental risk factors.
Funds conferences, meetings, educational activities, information dissemination and training, and fellowships.

Geographical Area of Activity: Czech Republic.

Board of Directors: Dr Kamil Provaznik (Chair.).

Address: Srobarova 48, 100 42 Prague 10.

Telephone: 267310819; **Fax:** 267311188; **e-mail:** kprov@szu
.cz.

Civic Forum Foundation

Founded in 1990 by the Civic Forum to revive educational, cultural and humanistic ideals in the Czech Republic.

Activities: The Foundation's Board of Directors decided that
from 1996 the Foundation's resources would be focused on cultural heritage issues, and that its mission would be to endeavour to aid in the protection and conservation of the Czech
Republic's cultural heritage through awareness-building and
the promotion of partnerships between the business, non-
profit and governmental sectors, with specific attention paid
to neglected monuments. The Foundation operates through
self-conducted projects, grants to organizations within the
Czech Republic and conservation awards. It collaborates with
international organizations on several projects. Maintains a
cultural heritage database.

Geographical Area of Activity: Czech Republic.

Publications: Newsletter (3 a year); *Children's Guide Book to
Třeboň Chateau*; *Cultural Programme Information Sheet*;
Annual Report.

Board of Directors: Dasa Havel (Chair.).

Principal Staff: Exec. Dir Sunny A. Stastny.

Address: Hálkova 2, 120 00 Prague 2.

Telephone: 224941305; **Fax:** 224941306; **e-mail:** info@
nadaceof.cz.

Clovek v tisni—spolecnost pri Ceske televizi, o.p.s. (People in Need)

Established in 1992 to provide relief and development assistance and to defend human rights and democratic freedom.

Activities: Operates in the areas of human rights, relief and
development assistance. Relief and development assistance
programmes operate in 12 countries in Asia, Europe and
Africa. Also delivered aid to thousands of families affected by
floods in 1997, 2002 and 2006 in the Czech Republic. A development education and development awareness project also forms
an integral part of PIN relief and development department.
Offers support for democratization processes and human
rights protection in Belarus, Cuba, Moldova, Myanmar and
Ukraine. Also runs the annual human rights documentary
film festival, One World. Social integration programmes
address poverty and social exclusion problems in the Czech
Republic and Slovakia. Educational and informative programmes raise awareness on issues such as global problems
and development co-operation, migration and multiculturalism among the public, the state administration and the media.

Geographical Area of Activity: International.

Finance: Annual revenue €13,732,379, expenditure
€13,606,883 (2008).

Executive Board: Vlasta Lajčaková; Jan Urban; Kristina
Taberyová; Jan Pergler.

Principal Staff: Exec. Dir Šimon Pánek.

Address: Sokolska 18, 120 00 Prague 2.

Telephone: 226200400; **Fax:** 226200401; **Internet:** www
.clovekvtisni.cz; www.peopleinneed.cz; **e-mail:** mail@
clovekvtisni.cz.

Czech Literary Fund

Aims to promote literature in the Czech Republic.

Activities: Presents awards for prose, poetry, literary essays
and literary research, including the Josef Hlavka Prize for an
original piece of academic or specialist literature published in
book form in the Czech Republic. Supports cultural organizations through subsidies in the fields of translation, film and television, theatre, science and journalism.

Geographical Area of Activity: Czech Republic.

Restrictions: Grants only to specific organizations in the
Czech Republic.

Finance: Annual budget 10,000,000 koruny (2008).

Trustees: Tomas Jezek (Chair.); John Lukes (Vice-Chair.).

Principal Staff: Dir Michal Novotny.

Address: Pod Nuselskymi schody 3, 120 00 Prague 2.

Telephone: 222560081; **Fax:** 222560083; **Internet:** www.nclf
.cz; **e-mail:** nadace@nclf.cz.

Czech Music Fund Foundation (Nadace cesky hudebni fond)

Founded by the Czech Music Fund in 1994. Aims to support
and encourage the development of Czech musical culture.

Activities: Provides grants and scholarships to talented
Czech musicians; supports musical activities, such as competitions for composers and performers, workshops and music education; holds public composition competitions to stimulate
new works. Has set up two beneficial institutions—the Music
Information Centre and the Czech Music Fund, which runs an
instrument hire service with branches throughout the Czech
Republic, and hires out musical scores and parts from other
institutions all over the world.

Geographical Area of Activity: Czech Republic.

Publications: Annual Report.

Finance: Annual expenditure approx. 6,000,000 koruny.

Principal Staff: Dir Miroslav Drozd.

Address: Besedni 3, 118 00 Prague 1.

Telephone: 257320008; **Fax:** 257312834; **Internet:** www.nchf
.cz; **e-mail:** nadace@nchf.cz.

Deutsch-Tschechischer Zukunftsfonds (Czech-German Fund for the Future)

Established in 1998, as an NGO based in the Czech Republic,
by the Governments of the Czech Republic and Germany to
compensate Czech victims of Nazism.

Activities: The Fund operates in the field of social welfare,
funding social projects for Czech survivors of atrocities committed during the country's occupation by German forces

before and during the Second World War, including Jewish and Roma (Gypsy) people, Catholics, Jehovah's Witnesses, homosexuals and political prisoners. The Fund received €84,900,000 between 1998 and 2002, with Germany contributing 84.3% of this amount. Of these funds, approximately €46m. of the Fund was expended on humanitarian aid to victims of National Socialist (Nazi) violence, while the remainder of approximately €38m. was designated for support of Czech–German projects focused on the future and for the work of the Czech–German discussion forum. In addition the Fund provides 10-month scholarships for Czech and German students in the fields of the humanities and social sciences who plan to work on a project with a Czech–German theme while studying in the partner country.

Geographical Area of Activity: Czech Republic.

Principal Staff: Dir Tomas Jelinek.

Address: Na Kazance 634/7, 171 00 Prague 7.

Telephone: 283850512; **Fax:** 283850503; **Internet:** www.fb .cz; **e-mail:** info@fb.cz.

Euronisa Foundation

Founded in 1995 by the Moravian church in Liberec, aims to support cultural pursuits, education and to solve social problems prevalent in the Czech Republic.

Activities: Operates in the fields of health and social welfare, culture and education. Provides support services to the elderly and the infirm; funds projects working to solve health and social problems such as drug abuse, AIDS, abandoned children and alcoholism. Operates mainly in the Czech area of the Neisse-Nisa-Nysa Euroregion.

Geographical Area of Activity: Czech Republic (mainly the Czech sectors of the Nisa Euroregion).

Restrictions: No grants to individuals.

Publications: Annual Report; electronic/online information.

Principal Staff: Dir Aleš Rozkovec; Grant Man. Peter Kuntosova.

Address: Rumjancevova 3, 460 01 Liberec 1.

Telephone: 485251953; **Fax:** 485102753; **Internet:** www .euronisa.cz; **e-mail:** nadace@euronisa.cz.

Foundation Czech Art Fund

Aims to support artists and art projects through awarding grants as well as managing exhibition spaces in Prague.

Activities: Provides support to the fine arts in the Czech Republic, through making grants to individuals and organizations and organizing and hosting exhibitions, including the biennial Salons, bringing together a group of artists and individual exhibitions. The Fund's exhibition spaces in Prague include the Mánes Exhibition Hall, the Gallery of Václav Spála, and the Golden Lily Gallery, and the Fund also owns the newly renovated recreational building the Staré Splavy 'farmhouse'.

Geographical Area of Activity: Czech Republic.

Publications: Annual Report.

Board of Directors: Petr Kuthan (Chair.); Jan Tatousek (Vice-Chair.).

Principal Staff: Dir Dagmar Baberadová.

Address: Masarykovo nábrezí 250, 110 00 Prague 1.

Telephone: 224932938; **Fax:** 224934318; **Internet:** www.ncvu .cz; **e-mail:** info@ncvu.cz.

Global Ethic Foundation Czech Republic

Established in 1993 by Karel Floss as an educational and ecological centre with the Global Ethic Foundation in Tübingen, Germany, and the Stiftung für Gesellschaftliche Lebensqualität in Basle, Switzerland, to promote human rights, health protection and public participation. Founded in 1999 in the Czech Republic.

Activities: Provides grants to NGOs in the Czech Republic carrying out educational activities, practical project implementation, exhibitions, heritage reconstruction, natural area protection, and for innovative approaches to sustainable rural development. Also provides consultancy services to NGOs and offers training.

Geographical Area of Activity: Czech Republic.

Trustees: Dr Hans Kung (Pres.).

Principal Staff: Sec.-Gen. Stephan Schlensog.

Address: Benesovska 441, 285 06 Sazava by Prague.

Telephone: 328490171; **Fax:** 328490604; **Internet:** www .weltethos.org; **e-mail:** svetetos@mestosazava.cz.

Hestia—The National Volunteer Centre

Established in 1993 to Promote, develop and support volunteering.

Activities: Co-ordinates voluntary work in the Czech Republic. Raises awareness of the voluntary opportunities available to the public, offers training programmes for volunteers, co-ordinators and organizations, and acts as an advice and information source for volunteers. Also helps supervise all existing regional voluntary centres throughout the Czech Republic, and organizes the national Five Ps/Pet P programme, a mentoring volunteer programme to help children who encounter social or health problems in life and need support.

Geographical Area of Activity: Czech Republic.

Publications: Books and articles on volunteer management.

Board: Jiri Tosner (Chair.).

Principal Staff: Dir Olga Sozanska.

Address: Na Porici 12, 110 00 Prague 1.

Telephone: 224872075; **Fax:** 224872076; **Internet:** www.hest .cz; **e-mail:** info@hest.cz.

Nadace Charty 77 (Charter 77 Foundation)

Established in 1989 on the initiative of František Janouch, Karel Jan Schwarzenberg and George Soros. It is a non-profit organization, an autonomous branch of the Swedish Charta 77 Foundation, promoting open society, civil society, democracy, and the development of culture, science, technology, education and international co-operation.

Activities: Operates in the Czech Republic in the fields of education, law and human rights, medicine and health, and social welfare (especially for disabled citizens). Annual awards are the literary Jaroslav Seifert and Tom Stoppard prizes; the František Kriegel prize for civil courage; and the Josef Vavroušek environmental prize.

Geographical Area of Activity: Czech Republic and Europe.

Publications: Annual Report.

Board of Trustees: František Janouch (Pres.); Gita Tučná (Vice-Pres.); Evžen Hart (Vice-Pres.).

Principal Staff: Exec. Dir Boena Jirku.

Address: Melantrichova 5, 110 00 Prague 1.

Telephone: 224214452; **Fax:** 224213647; **Internet:** www .bariery.cz; **e-mail:** nadace77@bariery.cz.

Nadace SLUNÍČKO (Slunicko Foundation)

Established in 1991 with the support of the Swedish NGO Secretariat on Acid Rain (q.v.). Aims to provide assistance to NGOs in the Czech Republic that focus on issues such as alternative and renewable energy sources, reduction of harmful emissions, energy savings and nature conservation.

Activities: Promotes environmental activities, both through its own projects and through providing funding for a variety of environmental activities carried out by NGOs in the Czech Republic, including advisory services, awareness-raising campaigns, clean-up activities, educational camps, conferences, meetings, information dissemination, lobbying and campaigning, monitoring, publishing, research and demonstration projects.

Geographical Area of Activity: Czech Republic.

Finance: Principally sponsored by the Swedish NGO Secretariat on Acid Rain.

Principal Staff: Dir Pavel Cincera.

Address: c/o BEZK, Malirska 6, 170 00 Prague 7.

Telephone: 33381546; **Fax:** 33382252; **Internet:** www
.slunicko.ecn.cz; **e-mail:** slunicko@ecn.cz.

Nadace Táta a Máma (Mum and Dad Foundation)

Founded by Tereza Maxová in 1997 as the Tereza Maxová Foundation to address the social issues that lead to the abandonment of children, and to provide assistance to children's homes.

Activities: Operates in the Czech Republic in the field of social welfare, specifically that of abandoned children. Works to prevent abandonment through education; provides assistance to adoptive families, thus shortening the time that children must stay in institutions; and raises public awareness of the plight of children who have been abandoned. Also provides material support to children's homes.

Geographical Area of Activity: Czech Republic.

Finance: Total grants approx. €6,600,000 (1997–2009).

Principal Staff: Admin. Jana Vacenovská.

Address: Klimentská 1246/1, 110 00 Prague 1.

Telephone: 226222050; **Fax:** 226222049; **Internet:** www
.nadacetm.cz; **e-mail:** info@nadacetm.cz.

Open Society Fund Prague—OSF Prague

Founded in 1992 to support the building of civil society, the development of educational and cultural activities, and the promotion of intellectual co-operation between Central and Eastern European countries. The Fund is an independent foundation, part of the Soros foundations network, which aims to foster political and cultural pluralism and reform economic structures to encourage private enterprise and a market economy.

Activities: Supports the development of civic society, education and culture, and law reform in the Czech Republic; co-operates with non-governmental and non-profit organizations; offers educational programmes; contributes to the promotion of intellectual co-operation between Central and Eastern European countries; issues publications; and supports other non-profit activities.

Geographical Area of Activity: Czech Republic.

Publications: Annual Report (in Czech).

Board of Directors: Monika Ladmanova (Chair.).

Principal Staff: Exec. Dir Robert Basch; Fin. Dir Zdenka Almerova.

Address: 130 00 Prague 3, Seifertova 47.

Telephone: 222540979; **Fax:** 222540978; **Internet:** www.osf
.cz; **e-mail:** osf@osf.cz.

Preciosa Foundation

Founded in 1996 by the Preciosa company to raise funds to support non-profit and publicly beneficial activities in the Czech Republic.

Activities: Funds projects in the fields of health care, education, the arts and culture, science and research, sports, and humanitarian work. Projects are mainly carried out in the region of northern Bohemia, but some activities are carried out throughout the Czech Republic, often in co-operation with Prague-based organizations. The Foundation has set up seven funds, to support each operational area in which it works, including the Health Fund, the Ecology and Environment Fund and the Education and Retraining Fund. These funds then distribute money to sponsor projects within that particular sphere.

Geographical Area of Activity: Czech Republic.

Finance: Total assets approx. 50,000,000 koruny.

Administrative Board: Prof. Víníkilhán (Chair.); Stanislav Vohlídal (Vice-Chair.).

Principal Staff: Dir Ivo Schotta; Sec. Marcela Vojtíšková.

Address: Opletalova 3197, 466 67 Jablonec nad Nisou.

Telephone: 488115555; **Fax:** 488115665; **Internet:** www
.preciosa.com/en/company/preciosa-foundation; **e-mail:**
info@preciosa.com.

Slovak-Czech Women's Fund

Founded in 2004 by the Open Society Fund Prague and the Open Society Foundation Bratislava (qq.v.) to support the development of women in Slovakia and the Czech Republic.

Activities: Provides funding to NGOs and community organizations, targeting marginalized populations, including Roma women in Slovakia, young women who exceed the age for foster care in the Czech Republic and young women who can benefit from leadership skills. A sister office operates in Bratislava.

Geographical Area of Activity: Slovakia and the Czech Republic.

Board of Directors: Andrea Vadkerti (Chair.).

Principal Staff: Dir Markéta Hronková.

Address: Bořivojova 105, 130 00 Prague 3.

Telephone: 222716823; **Fax:** 222716823; **Internet:** www
.womensfund.cz; **e-mail:** hronkova@womensfund.cz.

VIA Foundation

Established in October 1997 as the successor to the USA-based Foundation for a Civil Society's Prague office to promote and strengthen active public participation in democratic society in the Czech Republic.

Activities: Operates in the Czech Republic in the fields of community development, the development of philanthropy, and institutional support for NGOs. The Foundation makes grants to institutions, offers prizes (the Via Bona awards to philanthropic donors, businesses and individuals), organizes training courses and issues publications. Programmes include the Community Development Fund, The T-Mobile Fund, Cultural Heritage Fund, Accelerator—The Academy of Social Enterpreneurship and many more. It co-operates with other organizations in Central and Eastern Europe.

Geographical Area of Activity: Czech Republic.

Publications: *Místo pro zivot* (A Place for Life, 1999); Annual Report; newsletter.

Finance: Total assets 55,311,953 koruny (Dec. 2009); annual revenue 22,828,205 koruny, expenditure 22,633,755 koruny (2009).

Board of Directors: Ivan Dvorak (Chair.).

Principal Staff: Exec. Dir Jiří Bárta.

Address: Jelení 195/9, 118 00 Prague 1.

Telephone: 233113370; **Fax:** 233113380; **Internet:** www
.nadacevia.cz; **e-mail:** via@nadacevia.cz.

Výbor dobré vule—Nadace Olgy Havlové (Committee of Good Will—Olga Havel Foundation)

Founded by the late Olga Havel in 1990 to alleviate suffering caused by disability and chronic illness, and to assist with social problems in society. Originally a clearing-house for health-related aid from the West, but has now expanded to invest in public health and social assistance with long-term grants and projects.

Activities: Aims to raise awareness of the problems and challenges faced by people with disabilities and chronic illnesses, particularly in the areas of employment, education and housing; to provide organizational and financial support to humanitarian projects and for disaster relief; and to help create an integrated society. Operates the following programmes: Salzburg Medical Cornell Seminars; Sasakawa Asthma Fund, established to address the growing problem of asthma-related diseases; Ordinary Life, supporting civic associations in their programmes for homeless, excluded communities, mothers in difficult situations and the Education Fund, which awards scholarships to students with social problems and disabilities. The Sasakawa Asthma Fund operates in both the Czech Republic and Slovakia, the other programmes operate only in the Czech Republic. Also distributes the annual Olga Havel

Award to people who are engaged in helping others despite disability.

Geographical Area of Activity: Czech Republic.

Publications: Annual Report; *Ten Letters to Olga*; *Life in Black and White*.

Finance: Receives funding from domestic and foreign donors, bequests, interest from the foundation's assets and benefit events. Annual income 9,753,943 koruny, expenditure 12,973,202 koruny (2008).

Board of Directors: Dana Nemcová (Pres.); Franziska Sternbergova (Vice-Pres.).

Principal Staff: Dir Dr Milena Černá.

Address: POB 240, 111 21 Prague 1.

Telephone: 224217331; **Fax:** 224217082; **Internet:** www.vdv .cz; **e-mail:** vdv@vdv.cz.

Vzdělávací nadace Jana Husa (Jan Hus Educational Foundation)

Founded in 1990 by Miroslav Pospíil, Jana Kuchtová and Julie Tastná to support the development of higher education in the arts, humanities and law in the Czech Republic and Slovakia.

Since 1993, the former branch office in Bratislava has operated as a sister foundation in Slovakia.

Activities: Operates in the Czech Republic in the fields of the development of education, and the development of civil society, through self-conducted programmes, training courses, grants to institutions and publication awards.

Geographical Area of Activity: Czech Republic and Slovakia.

Restrictions: Only open to applicants from the Czech Republic and Slovakia.

Publications: Annual Reports for both the Czech Republic and Slovakia; *Going Abroad to Study*; *The Velvet Philosophers*; *Granting—a Process of Grant-Giving in Foundations*; *Ethical Principles in Foundations*; *Work*; *The Management of Foundation Assets, a Way to Self-Sustainability of the Foundation Sector*.

Board of Trustees: Jí Müller (Chair.); Krístina Korená (Deputy Chair.); Tomáš Holecek (Deputy Chair. for Programmes).

Principal Staff: Exec. Dir Jana Švábová.

Address: Zerotinovo nám. 9, 602 00 Brno.

Telephone: 549491049; **Fax:** 549491050; **Internet:** www.vnjh .cz; **e-mail:** vnjh@ics.muni.cz.

Denmark

FOUNDATIONS, TRUSTS AND NON-PROFIT ORGANIZATIONS

Aktion Børnehjælp (Action Children Aid)

Founded in 1965 to help children in need in India. Part of Emmaüs International (q.v.).

Activities: Provides funding to children's aid projects in India, as well as food and equipment, including powdered milk, blankets and children's clothes. Also distributes handicrafts manufactured in India, as well as disseminating information about the area.

Geographical Area of Activity: India.

Publications: *Aktion Børnehjælp Nyt* (quarterly magazine).

Board of Trustees: Jacob Moller (Chair.); Rune-Christoffer Dragsdahl (Vice-Chair.).

Principal Staff: Sec. Naja Kastanje.

Address: Hermodsgade 8, st. K67, 2200 Copenhagen N.

Telephone: 35-85-03-15; **Fax:** 35-85-03-15; **Internet:** www.aktionb.dk; **e-mail:** children-aid@vip.cybercity.dk.

Alfred Benzons Fond (Alfred Benzon Foundation)

Founded by Dr Bøje Benzon in 1952 in memory of his paternal grandfather Alfred Nicolai Benzon, founder of the first pharmaceutical company in Denmark, to promote biomedical research.

Activities: The main activity of the Alfred Benzon Foundation is the organization of the Benzon Symposia, which concentrate on medicine and pharmacy and related sciences. It also offers fellowships to Danish research scientists undertaking study at foreign institutions, and to a limited number of foreign scientists wishing to conduct their research in Denmark. Applications for these latter fellowships must be forwarded by a Danish scientist. Grants are also made to the Copenhagen Zoological Garden.

Geographical Area of Activity: Denmark.

Restrictions: No grants to non-Danish individuals.

Publications: *The Alfred Benzon Foundation 1952–2002.*

Board of Trustees: Prof. Mads Bryde Andersen (Chair.); Prof. Povl Krogsgaard-Larsen (Vice-Chair.); Prof. Niels Borregaard (Vice-Chair.).

Principal Staff: Admin Man. Jette Buur, Ph.D.

Address: Dantes Plads 3, II.t.v, 1556 Copenhagen V.

Telephone: 39-62-09-37; **Fax:** 39-62-09-33; **Internet:** www.benzon-foundation.dk; **e-mail:** benzon@post1.tele.dk.

Carlsbergfondet (Carlsberg Foundation)

Founded in 1876 by Jacob Christian Jacobsen to contribute to the growth of science in Denmark; to continue and extend the work of the chemical-physiological Carlsberg Laboratory; to further the various natural sciences, together with mathematics, philosophy, history, linguistics and social sciences; and to set up and develop the Museum of National History at Frederiksborg Castle. Tuborgfondet (the Tuborg Foundation), established in 1931, merged with Carlsbergfondet in 1991; it works for socially beneficial purposes, especially those which foster Danish economic life.

Activities: Operates in the fields of science and the arts and humanities, through self-conducted programmes, research, grants to institutions and individuals, fellowships, scholarships, publications and lectures. Activities are carried out through three departments and the New Carlsberg Foundation (q.v., founded in 1902 by Carl Jacobsen) as follows: Department A, the Carlsberg Laboratory, studies science with a view to improvements in malting, brewing and fermentation; Department B awards grants to support Danish scholars and various activities including archaeological research, the Academy of Sciences and Letters, and publication of books and papers; Department C supports the Museum of National History; and the New Carlsberg Foundation supports the visual arts and architecture, chiefly through the purchase of works for art galleries and public buildings.

Geographical Area of Activity: Denmark.

Publications: Annual Report; financial statement.

Board of Directors: Prof. Flemming Besenbacher (Chair.).

Principal Staff: Dir Lene Bisgaard Kyhse.

Address: H. C. Andersens Blvd 35, 1553 Copenhagen V.

Telephone: 33-43-53-63; **Fax:** 33-43-53-64; **Internet:** www.carlsbergfondet.dk; **e-mail:** carlsbergfondet@carlsbergfondet.dk.

Danmark-Amerika Fondet (Denmark-America Foundation)

Founded in 1914 to encourage understanding between the peoples of Denmark and the USA.

Activities: Encourages educational exchange between Denmark and the USA through the provision of grants to Danes; organizes programmes; assists Danish academics in finding appointments in US institutions of higher education; awards prizes to Danish citizens. It works in conjunction with the Danish Fulbright Commission, sharing an administration and a secretariat.

Geographical Area of Activity: USA, Denmark.

Restrictions: Grants only to Danish citizens.

Publications: Reports (annually, in Danish).

Board of Directors: Sten Scheibye (Chair.); Caroline Pontoppidan (Deputy Chair.); Peter Højland (Treas.).

Principal Staff: Exec. Dir Marie Mønsted; Sr Programme Co-ordinator Anders Folkmann.

Address: Nørregade 7A, 1.tv., 1165 Copenhagen K.

Telephone: 35-32-45-45; **Internet:** www.wemakeithappen.dk; **e-mail:** advising@daf-fulb.dk.

Danske Kulturinstitut (The Danish Cultural Institute)

Founded in 1940 (originally as Danske Selskab—The Danish Institute) to stimulate cultural relations between Denmark and other countries.

Activities: Operates internationally, providing information about prominent Danish cultural, social and educational organizations, in the fields of education, social welfare, architecture, and the arts and humanities, through self-conducted programmes, lectures, conferences, professional study tours, exchange programmes, reference services and publication of books and pamphlets, all of which are organized on an international basis. The Institute's activities are based on the principle of mutuality and its information work is seen as a comparative study of cultural traditions and development. It has offices in Edinburgh, Brussels, Bonn, Warsaw, Kecskemét, Riga, Tallinn, Vilnius, St Petersburg, Beijing and Rio de Janeiro.

Geographical Area of Activity: Western Europe, Estonia, People's Republic of China, Hungary, Latvia, Lithuania, Poland, Russia, South America.

Publications: *From the Golden Age to the Present Day; Flora Danica; Discover Denmark; Learning in Denmark; Songs from Denmark; Kierkegaard's Universe; Søren Kierkegaard; The*

Welfare Society in Transition; Danish Literature; Danish Painting and Sculpture.

Finance: Receives a grant from the Danish Ministry of Culture, which is supplemented by donations from foundations, business sponsors and local government organizations.

Principal Staff: Sec.-Gen. Finn Andersen.

Address: Vartov, Farvergade 27L, 2nd Floor, 1463 Copenhagen K.

Telephone: 33-13-54-48; **Fax:** 33-15-10-91; **Internet:** www.dankultur.dk; **e-mail:** dankultur@dankultur.dk.

Egmont Fonden (Egmont Foundation)

Founded in 1920 in accordance with the wishes of Egmont Harald Petersen, printer to the Royal Danish Court, to operate the businesses established by him, so as to raise funds for charitable purposes.

Activities: The Foundation is the owner of the Egmont Group, one of Scandinavia's leading media groups, operating in the fields of publishing, radio, television, children's games, etc., in more than 20 countries, including countries in Western and Eastern Europe and the USA. The charitable activities of the Foundation are concentrated on initiatives that can help provide lasting improvements for children and young people. In the social welfare and health area priority is given to initiatives that seek to reduce, and if possible prevent, the marginalization of disadvantaged children. In the field of education and leisure efforts are concentrated on initiatives that address and develop curiosity, imagination and creativity, stimulating a broad range of learning and strengthening new ways of acquiring knowledge, and developing the communication skills of children and young people. Examples of the Foundation's work include the modernization of the Danish National Museum, a children's art gallery in the Royal Museum of Fine Art, a science centre 'Experimentarium', the establishment of the Children's Centre for Rehabilitation of Brain Injury, the 'Music as Medicine' Music Programme for Intensive Care and Recovery Patients and the Centre for the Prevention of Congenital Malformations. Since 1992 the Foundation has been involved in the 'Democratization of Pre-school Education' project in co-operation with the Open Society Fund (q.v.) in Lithuania.

Geographical Area of Activity: Denmark.

Restrictions: No grants to individuals.

Publications: Annual Report.

Trustees: Mikael O. Olufsen (Chair.); Steen Riisgaard (Deputy Chair.).

Principal Staff: Dir Henriette Christiansen.

Address: Møntergade 1, 1., 1116 Copenhagen K.

Telephone: 33-91-36-44; **Fax:** 33-91-37-36; **Internet:** www.egmontfonden.dk; **e-mail:** mail@egmontfonden.dk.

Foundation for Environmental Education—FEE

Founded in 1981 as the Foundation for Environmental Education in Europe to raise awareness of environmental issues and effect change through education, as a means of achieving sustainability. In 2001, became the Foundation for Environmental Education—FEE, with the addition of South Africa as the first non-European member country.

Activities: The Foundation co-ordinates international campaigns and creates an awareness of the concept of environmental education; its three main programmes are: the Blue Flag Campaign, Eco-Schools, Learning About Forests—LeAF, Young Reporters for the Environment network. The Foundation has members in 59 countries world-wide.

Geographical Area of Activity: World-wide.

Publications: Newsletters; Annual Report.

Executive Board: Jan Eriksen (Pres.); Lourdes Díaz (Vice-Pres.); Malcolm Powell (Treas.).

Principal Staff: Dir Finn Bolding Thomsen.

Address: c/o The Danish Outdoor Council, Scandiagade 13, 2450 Copenhagen SV.

Telephone: 33-28-04-11; **Fax:** 33-79-01-79; **Internet:** www.fee-international.org; **e-mail:** secretariat@fee-international.org.

Fredsfonden (Danish Peace Foundation)

Founded in 1981 by Lise and Niels Munk Plum to support activities intended to promote peace and disarmament mainly in Denmark but also world-wide.

Activities: Operates in the fields of international affairs and human rights, through the provision of grants and prizes to NGOs, individuals and institutions in Denmark and other countries. Activities include awarding a bi-annual international peace prize.

Geographical Area of Activity: Mainly Denmark.

Restrictions: No scholarships.

Trustees: Jens Vedsted-Hansen (Chair.).

Principal Staff: Admin. Sec. Mille Rode.

Address: Dronningensgade 14, 1420 Copenhagen K.

Telephone: 32-95-44-17; **Fax:** 32-95-44-18; **Internet:** www.fredsfonden.dk; **e-mail:** info@fredsfonden.dk.

Friluftsraadet (Danish Outdoor Council)

Founded in 1942 as a membership organization; the Council now has 94 individual member organizations.

Activities: Works in all areas of outdoor recreational facilities and conservation. Lobbies on relevant issues, including sustainable tourism and develops environmental education projects. Operates a small-grants programme for environmental work involving Danish organizations and indigenous organizations in Eastern and Southern Europe.

Geographical Area of Activity: Scandinavia, the Baltic region and Eastern and Southern Europe.

Finance: Small grants available of up to 250,000 Danish kroner.

Board of Trustees: Lars Mortensen (Chair.); Kirsten Nielsen (Vice-Chair.).

Principal Staff: Dir Jan Eriksen.

Address: Scandiagade 13, 2450 Copenhagen SV.

Telephone: 33-79-00-79; **Fax:** 33-79-01-79; **Internet:** www.friluftsraadet.dk; **e-mail:** fr@friluftsraadet.dk.

IBIS

Established in 1966 to provide assistance to people in developing countries.

Activities: Supports development and capacity building projects in less-developed countries in Central and South America, and Africa; raises awareness in Denmark of problems suffered by people living in developing countries, including HIV and AIDS programmes; promotes ecologically sustainable growth; and campaigns for positive change in Denmark's foreign aid policy. Supports 200 large and small-scale projects in Angola, Bolivia, Ecuador, El Salvador, Ghana, Guatemala, Honduras, Mozambique, Namibia, Nicaragua, Peru and South Africa.

Geographical Area of Activity: Central and South America, and Africa.

Publications: *Zig Zag*; Annual Report.

Finance: Expenditure 213,600,000 Danish kroner, revenue 217,400,000 Danish kroner (2009).

Trustees: Mette Muller (Chair.).

Principal Staff: Sec.-Gen. Vagn Berthelsen.

Address: Nørrebrogade 68b, 2200 Copenhagen N.

Telephone: 35-35-87-88; **Fax:** 35-35-06-96; **Internet:** www.ibis.dk; **e-mail:** ibis@ibis.dk.

Institut for Menneskerettigheder (Danish Institute for Human Rights)

Founded in 1987. Aims to gain and disseminate human rights information, with a particular focus on sexual and reproductive rights.

Activities: Operates in the field of human rights, engaging in research, education and disseminating information and documentation regionally, nationally and internationally. Co-operates with a number of other human rights organizations, in Denmark and abroad. Established a student internship programme in collaboration with private companies and the Danish Industrialization Foundation for Developing Countries.

Geographical Area of Activity: International.

Publications: *As If Peoples Mattered: Critical Appraisal of 'Peoples' and 'Minorities' from the International Human Rights Perspective and Beyond; The Declaration* (CD-ROM); *Let's be Careful Out There* (video); *Human Rights Education in a European Perspective; Between Culture and Constitution—The Cultural Legitimacy of Human Rights in Nigeria; Substantive Equality and Pregnancy (UN) Defined: Some Repercussions; An Analysis of Human Rights and Politics; The Universal Declaration of Human Rights—A Common Standard of Achievement; Political Development and Human Rights in China: Report from Five Seminars at the Danish Centre for Human Rights; UPDATE* (newsletter); Annual Report.

Finance: Annual expenditure 92,800,000 Danish kroner (2007).

Council: Leo Bjørnskov (Chair.).

Principal Staff: Exec. Dir Jonas Christoffersen.

Address: 56 Strandgade, 1401 Copenhagen K.

Telephone: 32-69-88-88; **Fax:** 32-69-88-00; **Internet:** www .humanrights.dk; **e-mail:** center@humanrights.dk.

International Work Group for Indigenous Affairs— IWGIA

Established in 1968; aims to support and assist indigenous peoples around the world.

Activities: Operates in the field of human rights, specifically the rights of indigenous peoples. Supports their land rights, self-governance and independence, cultural integrity and the right to control their own futures. Works in collaboration with a number of indigenous peoples' organizations; runs development projects all over the world (especially in Africa, Central and South America, Asia and the Pacific, and the Arctic); holds conferences; engages in research; and produces related publications and documentation, which it disseminates internationally.

Geographical Area of Activity: International.

Publications: *Indigenous Affairs* (periodical, 2 a year); *The Indigenous World* (annually); books each year (mainly in English and Spanish).

Finance: Total assets 7,232,442 Danish kroner; annual income 4,997,695 Danish kroner, annual expenditure 27,381,347 Danish kroner (2009).

Board of Directors: Espen Wæhle (Chair.).

Principal Staff: Dir Lola García-Alix.

Address: Classengade 11 E, 2100 Copenhagen.

Telephone: 35-27-05-00; **Fax:** 35-27-05-07; **Internet:** www .iwgia.org; **e-mail:** iwgia@iwgia.org.

IUC-Europe Internationalt Uddanneless Center (IUC-Europe International Education Centre)

Founded in 1985 (reorganized in 1991) by Frits Korsgaard, Dr Jacob Christensen, Dr Tom Høyem, Dr Knud Overø, Bent le Févre and Ingolf Knudsen to promote international understanding and co-operation through a variety of interdisciplinary and intercultural programmes that emphasize experiential education.

Activities: The Foundation develops and implements numerous educational programmes, including study missions for students, teachers and businesspeople to the capitals of the member states and the institutions of the European Union, and for North American students and teachers to Europe and European students and teachers to the USA; exchanges with Central, Eastern and Western Europe, Scandinavia and the Baltic republics; Holocaust study; and international conferences and seminars. The IUC network includes affiliate offices in Hungary, Poland, Canada, the United Kingdom and the USA; the organization also has partners in most European countries. IUC-Europe has an International Board of Advisers.

Geographical Area of Activity: Western, Central and Eastern Europe, and North America.

Restrictions: Does not sponsor individuals, groups or programmes outside the IUC network.

Publications: *IUC-News* (newsletter, 2 a year); *Waves of Democracy* (2007).

Board: Nina Nørgaard (Chair.); Jette Petersen (Vice-Chair.).

Principal Staff: Man. Kirsten Stribley.

Address: A. P. Moellersvej 31, 5700 Svendborg.

Telephone: 62-21-68-92; **Fax:** 62-20-28-92; **Internet:** www .iuc-europe.dk; **e-mail:** iuc@iuc-europe.dk.

Lauritzen Fonden (Lauritzen Foundation)

Established in 1945 by two brothers, Ivar and Knud Lauritzen, and their sister, Anna Lønberg-Holm, to mark the 50th anniversary of Dampskibsselskabet Vesterhavet, the shipping company founded in 1895 by their father, Ditlev Lauritzen. Supports projects in shipping, agriculture, the arts, and trade and industry, together with humanitarian work of both a Nordic and an international nature. Particular focus on education and training of young people in Denmark and abroad. Originally the J. L. Fondet, it was renamed in 2009 as the Lauritzen Fonden.

Activities: Makes large and small grants to institutions, associations and individuals over a broad spectrum of activities. Supports studies and projects of a technical, commercial or other nature in shipping, trade and industry, agriculture and other sectors; and the education or training of young people in Denmark and abroad. Promotes healthy, bright and well-maintained workplaces and company housing, organized so as best to promote job satisfaction, and assists personnel and institutions working for such purposes, especially in the shipping sector and companies associated with the Foundation and Group comanies. Supports institutions, associations and people who work in and look after the interests of the shipping sector, particularly institutions and associations set up by the Lauritzen Group or its companies, or those with an interest in other humanitarian institutions. Aids Foundation or Lauritzen Group employees and their families. Supports institutions, associations and people working to encourage awareness and esteem of Danish cultural activities, including corporate culture, education/training, self-improvement and character training of the young, and studies into disease prevention, especially preventative medicine. Also supports institutions, associations and people working to promote Nordic and international relations of a purely humanitarian nature.

Geographical Area of Activity: Mainly Denmark.

Publications: Annual Report; prize essays.

Finance: Total grants 27,700,000 Danish kroner (2010).

Board: Jens Ditlev Lauritzen (Chair.); Michael Fiorni (Vice-Chair.).

Principal Staff: Gen. Man. Inge Grønvold; Admin. Linda Sparrevohn.

Address: Sankt Annæ Plads 28, 1291 Copenhagen K.

Telephone: 33-96-84-25; **Fax:** 33-96-84-35; **Internet:** www .lauritzenfonden.com; **e-mail:** lf@lauritzenfonden.com.

Lego Fonden (The Lego Foundation)

Established in 2009 with the aim of inspiring children through learning and play.

Activities: Donates Lego products world-wide; promotes children's education through new learning materials, research programmes and training of teachers in less-developed countries.

Geographical Area of Activity: International.

Principal Staff: Sec. Rita Nielsen.

Address: Koldingvej 2, 7190 Billund.

Internet: www.lego-fonden.dk; **e-mail:** ole.kirks.fond@lego.com.

Lundbeckfonden (Lundbeck Foundation)

Established in 1954 by Grete Lundbeck, whose late husband founded H. Lundbeck A/S company, to fund the Lundbeck Group of companies and to make grants for scientific research.

Activities: Operates in the field of science and technology through offering grants for research projects in the specific areas of health and natural sciences. Also offers the Nordic Research Award for a young scientist along with other awards. Research within Denmark is prioritized.

Geographical Area of Activity: Mainly Denmark.

Finance: Grants budget approx 384,000,000 Danish kroner (2010).

Board of Trustees: Mikael Rorth (Chair.); Jorgen Huno Rasmussen (Vice-Chair.).

Principal Staff: CEO Christian Dyvig.

Address: Vestagervej 17, 2900 Hellerup.

Telephone: 39-12-80-00; **Fax:** 39-12-80-08; **Internet:** www.lundbeckfonden.dk; **e-mail:** mail@lundbeckfonden.dk.

A. P. Møller og Hustru Chastine Mc-Kinney Møllers Fond til almene Formaal (The A. P. Møller and Chastine Mc-Kinney Møller Foundation)

Founded in 1953 by shipowner A. P. Møller.

Activities: Supports Danish culture and heritage, Danish shipping and medical science. Grants are only occasionally made to non-Danish projects. Major institutions established with foundation funding include a new opera house in Copenhagen.

Geographical Area of Activity: Denmark.

Restrictions: No grants are made to individuals.

Finance: Net assets in excess of 10,000,000,000 Danish kroner (Dec. 2007); annual revenue in excess of 500,000,000 Danish kroner (2007).

Trustees: Mærsk Mc-Kinney Møller (Chair.); Ane Mærsk Mc-Kinney Uggla (Vice-Chair.).

Principal Staff: Exec. Pres. Henrik Tvarnø.

Address: Esplanaden 50, 1098 Copenhagen K.

Telephone: 33-63-34-00; **Fax:** 33-63-34-10; **Internet:** www.apmollerfonde.dk; **e-mail:** cphapmfond@maersk.com.

Otto Mønsteds Fond (Otto Mønsteds Foundation)

Founded in 1934 by Otto Mønsted to further the development of Danish trade and industry, and in particular, to assist in the education of young commercial workers and polytechnic students and graduates; to train teachers at commercial or technical universities; and to promote and sponsor plans or enterprises that might advance Danish commerce or industry.

Activities: Awards grants to teachers and students at commercial and technical universities for study and participation in congresses abroad.

Geographical Area of Activity: Denmark.

Publications: Annual Report.

Board of Directors: Prof. Knut Conradsen (Chair.).

Principal Staff: Man. Dir Bo Staernose; Admin. Annette Bergmann.

Address: Tingskiftevej 5, 2900 Hellerup.

Telephone: 39-62-08-11; **Internet:** www.ottomoensted.dk; **e-mail:** omf@omfonden.dk.

MS ActionAid Denmark

Established in January 1944 as Mellemfolkeligt Samvirke (Danish Association for International Co-operation) to promote solidarity and understanding through co-operation beyond geographical and cultural boundaries, and contribute to sustainable global development and fair distribution of resources.

Activities: Membership organization consisting of 100 institutional members and about 6,000 individuals. Carries out grassroots activism, political lobbying and provides development assistance. Maintains a searchable online database with information on partner organizations in the global South.

Geographical Area of Activity: International, including Kenya, Mozambique, Nepal, Southern Africa, Tanzania, Uganda, Zambia, Zimbabwe and Central America.

Publications: Annual Report; *Kontakt* (magazine).

Finance: Annual income 234,000,000 Danish kroner, expenditure 233,000,000 Danish kroner (2008/09).

Board: Elsebeth Kroghe (acting Chair.); Niss Ben (Vice-Chair.).

Principal Staff: Int. Dir Birte Hald.

Address: Fælledvej 12, 2200 Copenhagen N.

Telephone: 77-31-00-00; **Fax:** 77-31-01-01; **Internet:** www.ms.dk; **e-mail:** ms@ms.dk.

Nordisk Kulturfond (Nordic Culture Fund)

Founded in 1966 by the Nordic Council to encourage cultural co-operation in all its aspects by the Nordic countries (Denmark, Finland, Iceland, Norway and Sweden, including Greenland, Faroe Islands and Åland Islands.).

Activities: Aims to further cultural co-operation between the Nordic countries. Concerned with a wide range of artistic and cultural areas, involving professionals and amateurs. Supports activities characterized by quality, vision, accessibility and variety, where both traditional and new ways of working can be developed. Contributions can be granted to conferences, concerts, tours, exhibitions and festivals, for example. A project may be completed both within and outside the Nordic countries.

Geographical Area of Activity: Nordic countries and the rest of the world.

Restrictions: A project is conidered 'Nordic' if a minimum of three Nordic countries or self-governing areas are involved, either as participants, organizers, or as subject areas. Funding is not awarded for: activities already started before the Fund has made its decision; technical equipment; repairs; construction work; running expenses of institutions; production of records/CDs, computer games, feature films, short films, documentaries, TV drama or series; ordering of music compositions; translation of fiction or non-fiction literature; personal studies, further education, or research work; student exchange and school trips; or sports events.

Finance: Total expenditure 37,017,000 Danish kroner (2011).

Governing Board: Olemic Thommessen (Chair.); Kjell Myhren (Vice-Chair.).

Principal Staff: Dir Karen Bue; Sr Adviser Thomas Heikkilä; Sr Adviser Maria Tsakiris; Adviser Peter Larsen; Sec. Co-ordinator Helena Kaarina Karhu; Press and Communication Adviser Gitte Merrlid.

Address: Ved Stranden 18, 1061 Copenhagen K.

Telephone: 33-96-02-00; **Fax:** 33-32-56-36; **Internet:** www.nordiskkulturfond.dk; **e-mail:** kulturfonden@norden.org.

Novo Nordisk Foundation

Founded in January 1989 following the merger of the Novo Foundation (established in 1951), the Nordisk Insulinfond (Nordic Insulin Foundation, established in 1926) and the Nordisk Insulinlaboratorium (Nordic Insulin Laboratory). A commercial foundation, aims to provide a stable basis for the commercial and research activities of Novo Nordisk A/S, which is engaged in the development, production and sale of pharmaceuticals and related products and services; of Novozymes A/S, which is engaged in the development, production and trade in biological solutions; and of any future public or private limited companies in which the Foundation's subsidiary, Novo A/S, may hold a material equity interest or over which Novo A/S may have material influence.

Activities: Operates in the Nordic countries, supporting research in physiology, endocrinology, metabolism and other medical areas. It provides a base for the commercial and research activities conducted by the companies within the Novo Group, and supports various scientific, humanitarian and social programmes. Awards the Novo Nordisk Prize to a Danish scientist for a contribution in the field of medical science.

Geographical Area of Activity: Scandinavia.

Finance: Annual disbursements 194,000,000 Danish kroner (2008).

Trustees: Ulf J. Johansson (Chair.); Jørgen Boe (Vice-Chair.).

Principal Staff: Dir Birgitte Nauntofte.

Address: Tuborg Havnevej 19, 2900 Hellerup.

Telephone: 35-27-66-00; **Fax:** 35-27-66-01; **Internet:** www .novonordiskfonden.dk; **e-mail:** nnfond@novo.dk.

Ny Carlsbergfondet (New Carlsberg Foundation)

Established in 1902 by Carl and Ottilia Jacobsen to promote the arts in Denmark. Part of the Carlsbergfondet (q.v.).

Activities: Operates in the field of the arts and culture, supporting the New Carlsberg Glypotek and other museums in Denmark, and promoting the study of art and art history through offering grants for travel and for publications on art.

Geographical Area of Activity: Denmark.

Finance: Annual grants budget approx. 60,000,000 Danish kroner.

Board of Management: Hans Edvard Nørregård-Nielsen (Chair.).

Principal Staff: Anne Krøigaard; Elsebet Tvede.

Address: Brolæggerstræde 5, 1211 Copenhagen K.

Telephone: 33-11-37-65; **Internet:** www.ny-carlsbergfondet .dk; **e-mail:** sekretariatet@nycarlsbergfondet.dk.

Realdania

Established in 2000 following a merger between two large financial institutions; it is a strategic foundation that aims to initiate and support projects that improve the built environment so as to improve quality of life for the common good.

Activities: Operates in Denmark in the field of the built environment. Currently involved in around 54 strategic flagship projects and 255 focus projects.

Geographical Area of Activity: Denmark.

Finance: Grants disbursed approx. €121,000,000 (2010).

Supervisory Board: Jesper Nygard (Chair.); Carsten With Thygesen (Deputy Chair.).

Principal Staff: Chief Exec. Flemming Borreskov.

Address: Jarmers Plads 2, 1551 Copenhagen V.

Telephone: 70-11-66-66; **Fax:** 32-88-52-99; **Internet:** www .realdania.dk; **e-mail:** realdania@realdania.dk.

Rockwool Fonden (Rockwool Foundation)

Founded in 1981 by the children of the late Gustav Kähler to support scientific, social and humanitarian goals, and contribute to the improvement of the environment and social development.

Activities: Provides funding for a wide range of projects, including research on the labour market, immigrants and their living conditions, politicians and credibility, the shadow economy and environmental problems. Supports numerous social and humanitarian projects carried out by small organizations or by individuals; practical self-help projects in the third world; and social capacity building projects in Denmark.

Geographical Area of Activity: Denmark; some grants are made internationally, via Danish organizations.

Publications: Numerous publications; Annual Report.

Finance: Assets 5,960,583,000 Danish kroner (2007); total income 13,662,000 Danish kroner (2007).

Board: Tom Kähler (Chair.); Lars Nørby Johansen (Deputy Chair.).

Principal Staff: Pres. Elin Schmidt.

Address: Hovedgaden 584, 2640 Hedehusene.

Telephone: 46-55-80-06; **Fax:** 46-59-10-92; **Internet:** www .rockwoolfonden.dk; **e-mail:** rockwool.fonden@rockwool .org.

Sonnings-Fonden (Sonning Foundation)

Founded in 1949 by the late writer and editor C. J. Sonning to award a prize biennially for meritorious work in the promotion of European civilization.

Activities: The Sonning Prize, awarded biennially, amounts to 1m. Danish kroner; European universities have the right to propose candidates, and the winner is selected by a committee established by the Rector of the University of Copenhagen. Former prize-winners include Sir Winston Churchill (extraordinary award, 1950), Albert Schweitzer (1959), Bertrand Russell (1960), Dominique Pire (1964), Sir Laurence Olivier (1966), Arthur Koestler (1968), Karl Popper (1973), Dario Fo (1981), Simone de Beauvoir (1983), William Heinesen (1985), Ingmar Bergman (1989), Václav Havel (1991), Krzysztof Kieslowski (1994), Günter Grass (1996), Jørn Utzon (1998), Eugenio Barba (2000), Mary Robinson (2002), Mona Hatoum (2004), Agnes Heller (2006).

Geographical Area of Activity: Europe.

Publications: Books.

Sonning Prize Committee: Prof. Ralf Hemmingsen (Chair.).

Principal Staff: Contact Anna Christine Schmidt.

Address: University of Copenhagen, Communications Division, Nørregade 10, POB 2177, 1017 Copenhagen K.

Telephone: 35-32-42-64; **Internet:** www.ku.dk/english/ sonning_prize; **e-mail:** ansch@adm.ku.dk.

Léonie Sonnings Musikfond (Léonie Sonning Music Foundation)

Established in 1959.

Activities: Operates in the field of the arts and culture. Offers an annual prize of 600,000 Danish kroner to an internationally acknowledged composer, conductor, singer or musician; also offers grants to support young musicians, composers, conductors and singers in the Nordic countries. Prize-winners include Anne-Sophie Mutter (2001), Alfred Brendel (2002), Keith Jarrett (2004), John Eliot Gardiner (2005), Yo-Yo Ma (2006), Lars Ulrik Mortensen (2007).

Geographical Area of Activity: International.

Restrictions: Applications for grants not accepted.

Board of Directors: Steen Frederiksen (Chair.); Torsten Hoffmeyer (Sec.).

Principal Staff: Sec. Bente Legarth.

Address: Advokatselskabet Horten, Philip Heymans Allé 7, 2900 Hellerup.

Telephone: 33-34-42-32; **Internet:** www.sonningmusik.dk; **e-mail:** bl@horten.dk.

Thomas B. Thriges Fond (Thomas B. Thrige Foundation)

Founded in 1934 by Thomas B. Thrige to benefit Danish business, particularly industry and the trades.

Activities: Promotes scientific and educational projects that the Board of Trustees believe are of importance to the wellbeing of Danish business and industry. Provides grants to Danish universities and research institutes for specialized equipment, and finances study tours abroad for Danish researchers and participation in international conferences by Danish experts; it also gives grants to visiting professors from abroad.

Geographical Area of Activity: Denmark.

Publications: Annual Report and accounts.

Board of Trustees: Poul Svanholm (Chair.).

Principal Staff: Man. Claus Ehlers.

Address: Vasekær 10, 2730 Herlev.

Telephone: 39-61-50-30; **Fax:** 39-61-50-31; **Internet:** www .thrigesfond.dk; **e-mail:** ehlers@thrigesfond.dk.

Folmer Wisti Fonden (Folmer Wisti Foundation)

Founded in 1974 by Folmer Wisti to contribute to international understanding and co-operation on issues of importance in daily life at local and regional level, the support of decentralization and regionalism, and the exchange of experience and ideas primarily in the fields of culture and general education.

Activities: Operates in Europe. The Foundation has sponsored the 'Europe of Regions' conferences on decentralization and regional autonomy; and supports activities of the Danske Kulturinstitut (q.v.). Institutions eligible for support must be independent of party politics, non-profit-making and non-governmental.

Geographical Area of Activity: Europe.

Restrictions: No grants to individual students.

Publications: *Industrial Life in Denmark, The Faroe Islands and Greenland*; *Danish Foundations*; *Regional Contact* (vols 1–16, journal for the exchange of ideas and experiences in regionalism).

Finance: Assets 12,000,000 Danish kroner (2009).

Principal Staff: Chair. Helle Wisti; Deputy Chair. Finn Andersen.

Address: Gammel Vallerødvej 26, 2960 Rungsted Kyst.

Telephone: 45-86-13-36.

Dominican Republic

FOUNDATION CENTRE AND CO-ORDINATING BODY

Solidarios—Consejo de Fundaciones Americanas de Desarrollo (Council of American Development Foundations)

Founded in 1972 by representatives of national development foundations in Central and South American and Caribbean countries to exercise multinational representation of its members; to assist and support the individual and collective work of its members; to co-ordinate joint programmes; to stimulate the participation of the private sector in social development activities; to make available the necessary information to extend and improve the work of its members; and to administer funds for development programmes carried out by its members.

Activities: Provides technical assistance, training services and preferential loans to members carrying out social and economic development programmes in their own countries. Consists of 17 member organizations based in 10 Central and South American countries.

Geographical Area of Activity: Central and South America and the Caribbean.

Publications: *SOLIDARIOS* (quarterly); Newsletters (3 or 4 a year); Annual Report.

Finance: Budget approx. US $300,000.

Executive Committee: César Alarcón Costta (Pres.); Francisco Abate (Vice-Pres.).

Principal Staff: Finance and Admin. Dir Zulema Brea de Villaman.

Address: Apdo 620, Calle 6, No 10, Ensanche Paraíso, Santo Domingo.

Telephone: 549-5111; **Fax:** 544-0550; **Internet:** www.redsolidarios.org; **e-mail:** solidarios@codetel.net.do.

FOUNDATIONS, TRUSTS AND NON-PROFIT ORGANIZATIONS

Fundación Dominicana de Desarrollo—FDD (Dominican Development Foundation)

Founded in 1962 to stimulate private sector participation in finding solutions to the basic problems encountered by the low-income sector, particularly those problems experienced in rural areas. Promotes the participation of individuals in the process of their own development.

Activities: Operates nationally in the fields of education, social welfare and economic affairs through research and capacity building programmes. Also involved in funding environmental programmes and providing support to micro-enterprises.

Geographical Area of Activity: Dominican Republic.

Publications: Report of operations and financial statement; *Notas de Desarrollo*; *Catálogo de Organizaciones Voluntarias de Acción Social*.

Board of Directors: Pedro Gamundi (Pres.); Ernesto Armenteros Calac (Vice-Pres.); Elias Julia (Treas.).

Principal Staff: Exec. Dir Maribel Perez.

Address: Calle Mercedes No 4, Casa de Las Gárgolas, Apdo 857, Santo Domingo.

Telephone: 688-8101; **Fax:** 686-0430; **Internet:** www.fdd.org.do; **e-mail:** fdd@codetel.net.do.

Fundación Solidaridad (Solidarity Foundation)

Established in 1991 to promote sustainable development in urban and rural communities, and to promote democracy.

Activities: Offers education, capacity building and development services to non-profits in the Dominican Republic. Supports the structural development of community organizations, as well as co-ordinating networking activities between community organizations and the private sector and providing information and resources. Also supports the development of democracy and youth education projects.

Geographical Area of Activity: Dominican Republic.

Publications: Numerous publications on democracy and development issues; *Democracia Local* (bulletin).

Board of Directors: Denis Mota Álvarez (Pres.); Leandro Matínez (Sec.); Guillermina Peña (Treas.).

Principal Staff: Exec. Dir Juan Castillo.

Address: Avda Francia 40, Apdo 129-2, Santiago.

Telephone: 971-5400; **Fax:** 587-3656; **Internet:** www.solidaridad.org.do; **e-mail:** fsolidaridad@gmail.com.

Ecuador

FOUNDATION CENTRE AND CO-ORDINATING BODY

CERES—Ecuadorean Consortium for Social Responsibility

Established in 2002, an association of Ecuadorean private, independent organizations that aim to promote and develop social responsibility in Ecuador.

Activities: Comprised 30 member organizations in 2009, including corporate, private and community foundations from throughout Ecuador. Aims to promote civil society in Ecuador by: promoting social responsibility; fostering dialogue between foundations and government agencies, the media and the private sector; and increasing the institutional capacity and skills of Ecuadorean foundations.

Geographical Area of Activity: Ecuador.

Publications: *Boletín Cero* (newsletter); *ABC de la responsibilidad social empresarial* (2008); *RSE: Mis primeros pasos* (2008); *Memoria CERES 2007*; *VIH-SIDA en el lugar de trabajo* (2007).

Board of Directors: Carlos Andretta (Pres.).

Principal Staff: Exec. Dir Fabrice Hanse; Institutional Relations Laura Fahndrich.

Address: Avda Colón 1346 y Foch, Edif. Torres de la Colón, Of. 8, Quito.

Telephone: (2) 252-4911; **Fax:** (2) 252-5833; **Internet:** www.redceres.org; **e-mail:** comunicacion@redceres.org.

FOUNDATIONS, TRUSTS AND NON-PROFIT ORGANIZATIONS

EcoCiencia—Fundación Ecuatoriana de Estudios Ecologicos (Ecuadorian Foundation of Ecological Studies)

Founded in November 1989 by Danilo Silva, Patricio Mena, Roberto Ulloa, Mario Garcia, Luis Suarez, Juan Manuel Carrión and Miguel Vazquez to promote wildlife and biodiversity conservation and environmental education.

Activities: Operates in the field of conservation and the environment, in particular the conservation of biodiversity, through research, environmental education, training programmes and natural resources management; maintains a GIS Laboratory, an Aquatic Ecology Laboratory and a Biodiversity Economics Department; runs a University scholarship programme for Ecuadorian students; current programmes include: Bioandes; Paramo Andino; Fortalecimiento a Gobiernos Locales (Strengthening of Local Governments); Ecosistemas del Cuaternario en el Parque Nacional Podocarpus (Quaternary Ecosystems in National Park Podocarpus), the platform Grupo Nacional de Trabajo en Páramos (National Páramo Working Group), Conservation Program for Endangered Species in Ecuador among others.

Geographical Area of Activity: Ecuador.

Publications: Books on conservation and sustainable development, ethnobiology; technical reports and papers; maps; Páramo Series (dissemination of Grupo de Trabajo en Páramos sessions).

Finance: Total income US $1,100,000 (2009).

Principal Staff: Exec. Dir Janett Ulloa Sosa.

Address: Pasaje Estocolmo E2-166 y Avda. Amazonas (Sector El Labrador), Quito.

Telephone: (2) 2410-781/791; **Fax:** (2) 2410-489; **Internet:** www.ecociencia.org; **e-mail:** direccion@ecociencia.org.

FEPP—Fondo Ecuatoriano Populorum Progressio

Established in 1970 to promote the development of marginalized rural and urban groups.

Activities: Aims to support the development of marginalized groups in rural and urban areas of Ecuador, through the provision of grants and technical assistance, and by raising awareness. Target groups include children and young people, with grants made to projects in the fields of health, social services, development, civil and human rights, and conflict resolution.

Geographical Area of Activity: Ecuador.

Publications: Pamphlets; books.

Finance: Annual grants approx. US $12,000,000.

Principal Staff: Exec. Dir José Tonello Foscarini.

Address: Mallorca N24-275 y Coruña, La Floresta, Casilla 17-110-5202, Quito.

Telephone: (2) 2520408; (2) 2554727; **Fax:** (2) 2504978; **Internet:** www.fepp.org.ec; **e-mail:** fepp@fepp.org.ec.

Fundación Alternativas para el Desarrollo (Alternatives for Development Foundation)

Established in 1991 by Mónica Hernández de Phillips and Santiago Ribadeneira to promote alternatives for development.

Activities: Promotes small and micro entrepreneurship by providing financial and non-financial sustainable services to foster local economic development. It aims to contribute to the improved quality of life of vulnerable people, their families and their communities. Specialises in micro-credit, training, technical assistance, entrepreneurship and local economic development through innovative projects in rural and urban areas. Beneficiaries are entrepreneurs, communitarian businesses, associations, migrants, artisans and peasants as well as private organizations with social responsibility.

Geographical Area of Activity: Ecuador.

Publications: *Directorio de Organizaciones Sociales de Desarrollo 2004* (5th ed.).

Finance: Externally financed by financial corporations, public, private and international organizations, and through the commercialization of its services and products.

Principal Staff: Exec. Dir Mónica Hernández de Phillips.

Address: Pablo Claudel N41-61 e Isla Pinzón, Quito.

Telephone: (593) 2226-4484; **Fax:** (593) 2226-4500; **Internet:** www.fundacionalternativa.org.ec; **e-mail:** aperez@fundacionalternativa.org.ec.

Fundación Charles Darwin para las Islas Galápagos—FCD (Charles Darwin Foundation for the Galapagos Islands—CDF)

Founded in 1959 under the auspices of the Government of Ecuador, UNESCO and the World Conservation Union (IUCN, q.v.) to administer the Charles Darwin Research Station on the Galapagos Islands, and to provide facilities for research and conservation measures.

Activities: Operates internationally in the fields of science and the conservation of natural resources. The Charles Darwin Research Station, with its research vessel, *Beagle*, provides research facilities to visiting scientists of many nationalities, and undertakes conservation measures for the unique fauna, flora and habitat of the archipelago, including a breeding programme for tortoises and iguanas and the protection of endangered plants and animals. Supports the

Galapagos National Park Service and assists in the management for a marine reserve. Also holds courses in field ecology, offers training to Ecuadorean university students, and publishes the results of research. Maintains a library of books, maps and photographs of the Galapagos Islands. Has fundraising offices in the USA and Europe.

Geographical Area of Activity: Galapagos Islands, Ecuador.

Publications: *Noticias de Galápagos*; Annual Report; e-newsletter; and numerous specialist publications.

Finance: Assets US $1,663,028; revenue $4,415,599, expenditure $3,991,562 (2009).

Board of Directors: Pablo Iturralde Barba (Pres.); Peter Kramer (Vice-Pres.); Barbara West (Treas.).

Principal Staff: Exec. Dir Swen Lorenz.

Address: Charles Darwin Research Station, Puerto Ayora, Santa Cruz Island, Galapagos.

Telephone: (5) 2526-146; **Fax:** (5) 2526-147; **Internet:** www .darwinfoundation.org; **e-mail:** cdrs@fcdarwin.org.ec.

Fundación para el Desarrollo Agropecuario—FUNDAGRO (Foundation for Agricultural Development)

Founded in 1987 to support the modernization of agriculture and to improve the standard of living of those working in agriculture.

Activities: The Foundation designs and manages projects in the fields of sustainable development, agricultural research and education. Supports innovations in agricultural technology, marketing, financing and organizational schemes. FUNDAGRO is a member of the Consortium for the Sustainable Development of the Andean Ecoregion (CONDESCAN).

Geographical Area of Activity: Ecuador.

Publications: Annual Report; manuals; working papers.

Board of Directors: Jorge Muñoz Torres (Pres.); Nicolás Gillén (Vice-Pres.).

Principal Staff: Exec. Dir Jorge Chang Gomez.

Address: Moreno Bellido E6-168 y Avda Amazonas, Apdo 16-17-219 CEQ, Quito.

Telephone: (2) 2507-361; **Fax:** (2) 2507-422; **e-mail:** quito@ fundagro.org.

Fundación Ecuatoriana de Desarrollo—FED (Ecuadorean Development Foundation)

Established in 1968 to improve the standard of living for the disadvantaged in Ecuador.

Activities: Operates in the fields of aid to less-developed countries, economic affairs and social welfare, through supporting business, economic and social development in microenterprise programmes, giving loans to individual borrowers, the majority of whom are women. Also offers training programmes.

Geographical Area of Activity: Ecuador.

Publications: *Fedinforma* (monthly); training materials.

Finance: Loans disbursed US $40,668,000 (2008).

Principal Staff: Exec. Dir Anibal Baño.

Address: 9 de Octubre 1212 entre Colón y Orellana, Apdo 2529, Quito.

Telephone: (2) 547-864; **Fax:** (2) 509-084; **e-mail:** fed@ ecuanex.net.ec.

Fundación Eugenio Espejo (Eugenio Espejo Foundation)

Established in 1978 to work in social welfare and the development of civil society, particularly promoting development in rural and urban communities.

Activities: The Foundation supports small enterprises, education and training, special education, health and welfare. Also operates a private health clinic in southern Quito serving disadvantaged people, with plans for a network of similar clinics across Ecuador.

Geographical Area of Activity: Ecuador.

Principal Staff: Pres. Dr F. Huerta Montalvo; Exec. Dir Patricia Salvador de Dossman.

Address: Samanes 2°, Mz. 204, Solar P21, Apdo 09014557, Guayaquil.

Telephone: (4) 2210-813; **Fax:** (4) 2210-813; **e-mail:** fespejo@ ecua.net.ec.

Fundación General Ecuatoriana (General Ecuadorean Foundation)

Established in 1980 to assist the disabled in areas such as education, health, housing and culture.

Activities: Operates nationally in the areas of education, medicine and health, and social welfare for disabled people, through conferences and training courses for mentally disabled young people.

Geographical Area of Activity: Ecuador.

Publications: Directory of institutes for people with mental disability, autism, cerebral palsy and Down's Syndrome; diagnostic of the occupational situation of disabled persons.

Finance: Total income US $69,391; total expenditure $321,481 (2007).

Board of Directors: Dr Esteban Pérez Arteta (Pres.); Dr Antonio Terán Salazar (Vice-Pres.); Dr Luis Ponce Palacios (Sec.).

Principal Staff: Pres. Exec. Council Dr Jorge Luna Maldonado.

Address: San Javier N26-63 y Orellana, Casilla 17-17-282, Quito.

Telephone: (2) 222-1929; **Fax:** (2) 250-0781; **Internet:** www .fge.org.ec; **e-mail:** fge1@fge.org.ec.

Fundación Grupo Esquel—Ecuador (Esquel Group Foundation—Ecuador)

Established in 1990 to contribute to the sustainable human development of Ecuador, improve the quality of life of disadvantaged people and build a democratic society.

Activities: Operates through the following programmes: the Programme for Children and Youth Development, which aims to improve the quality of life of children and young people; the Programme for Sustainable Human Development, which aims to improve the quality of life of the rural and low-income urban populations of the coastal region, the highlands and the Amazon region; the Programme for Economic and Social Community Development, which aims to improve the quality of life of low-income groups that have alternative business ideas but cannot access traditional financing sources; the Social Responsibility Programme, which promotes social responsibility through establishing the concept and value of citizenship, building solidarity and forming a new culture of dialogue; the Civic Education Programme, which works through training and the encouragement of civic education; and the Programme for Community Development, which carries out socially orientated projects emerging from community initiatives and aims to strengthen small NGOs. Other Group foundations operate in Brazil and the USA.

Geographical Area of Activity: Ecuador.

Publications: Annual Report; *Esquela* (quarterly newsletter); *Con los sueños sobre la tierra*; *Responsabilidad Social: Una empresa de Todos*; *La Aventura de lo Alternativo*; *Publicaciones sobre Corrupción*; *Temas para una sociedad en crisis*; books; handbooks; working papers; monographs.

Board of Directors: Pablo Better (Pres.); Walter Spurrier (Vice-Pres.).

Principal Staff: Exec. Pres. Cornelio Marchán.

Address: República de El Salvador N34-229 y Moscú, Edificio San Salvador, Piso 7 y 8, Quito.

Telephone: (2) 245-3800; **Fax:** (2) 245-3777; **Internet:** www .esquel.org.ec; **e-mail:** fesquel@esquel.org.ec.

Fundación Natura (Nature Foundation)

A non-profit volunteer organization established in 1978 for the conservation of the environment in Ecuador to promote the conservation of biodiversity, sustainable management of natural resources, control and prevention of environmental pollution, and improve the standard of living.

Activities: Promotes environmental management and education; its projects aim to: promote conservation of biodiversity and sustainable management of natural resources; contribute to the control and prevention of environmental pollution; promote responsible attitudes and behaviour towards the environment; strengthen the capacity of individuals and organizations for environmental management.

Geographical Area of Activity: Ecuador.

Publications: *Environmental Agenda for Local Governments* (2009); *Atlas of the Territory of Shuar Arutam People* (2010); *Municipal Environmental Management and the New Constitution* (2010); publications on waste managment, environmental education and environmental management.

Finance: Annual budget approx. US $6,000,000.

Board of Directors: Adolfo Brinkmann (Pres.); José María Pérez (Vice-Pres.).

Principal Staff: Project Dir Ruth Elena Ruiz; Fin. Dir Adriana Arauz.

Address: Calle Elia Liut N45-10 y el Telégrafo 1, Quito.

Telephone: (2) 2272-863; **Fax:** (2) 2503-219; **Internet:** www.fnatura.org; **e-mail:** natura@fnatura.org.ec.

Egypt

FOUNDATIONS, TRUSTS AND NON-PROFIT ORGANIZATIONS

Arab Fund for Technical Assistance to African Countries—AFTAAC

Founded in 1974 (known until 1992 as the Arab Fund for Technical Assistance) to benefit African and Arab countries through the promotion of human resources development initiatives. The Fund is considered to be one of the organs of the League of Arab States but has an independent budget.

Activities: Provides technical assistance to African countries mainly through the dispatch of Arab experts and consultants, the financing and organizing of training programmes for African candidates in Arab and African countries, the granting of scholarships to African students to study at Arab universities and institutes, and the preparation of feasibility studies in the economic and scientific fields. AFTAAC co-operates with international, regional and national institutions sharing similar development goals in Africa.

Geographical Area of Activity: Africa.

Finance: Annual budget US $5,000,000.

Board of Directors: Amr Mousa (Chair.).

Principal Staff: Dir-Gen. Amb. Nouri Beitelmal.

Address: 33 Sakanat el-Maadi St, Cairo.

Telephone: (2) 3590322; **Fax:** (2) 3592099; **Internet:** www.aftaac.org.eg; **e-mail:** info@aftaac.org.eg.

Arab Office for Youth and Environment—AOYE

Established in 1978. Aims to encourage environmental protection.

Activities: Works to raise awareness, particularly among young people, of environmental issues and the need for sustainable development in Egypt. Co-operates with other environmental NGOs, the government, and the UN to develop and carry out programmes and projects and to educate young people to produce future leaders with an increased awareness of the need to protect the environment and natural resources, as well as collaborating to establish environmental networks. Founded the Arab Union for Youth and Environment in 1983 and is the Secretariat for the Arab Network for Environment and Development (RAED). Also participates in international conferences and networks.

Geographical Area of Activity: Egypt.

Publications: *Montada Elbiah* (RAED monthly newsletter).

Board: Dr Emad Adly (Pres.); El Nagdy Hagar (Vice-Pres.); Dr Ahmed esh-Shazly (Treas.).

Principal Staff: Sec.-Gen. Daliah Lotayef.

Address: POB 2 Magless esh-Shaab, Cairo.

Telephone: (2) 3041634; **Fax:** (2) 3041635; **Internet:** www.aoye.org; **e-mail:** aoye@link.net.

Arab Organization for Human Rights

Founded in 1983 to defend human rights.

Activities: Works to protect the human rights of those living in Arab countries, and to defend anyone whose rights have been violated. Provides legal assistance and campaigns for people convicted without fair trial, as well as financial assistance to their families; supports improvements in conditions for prisoners of conscience; and fights for amnesty for people sentenced for political reasons.

Geographical Area of Activity: North Africa and the Middle East.

Publications: *Al-monazzama al-arabiya lihoqouq al-insan–nashra ikhbariya* (monthly newsletter); *Arab Organization for Human Rights Newsletter* (monthly); *Hoqouq al-insan filwatan al-arabi* (quarterly); *Al-kitab as-senaoui lihoqouq al-insan filwatan al-arabi* (annual); Annual Report; special bulletins.

Finance: Funded by members' dues and contributions.

Address: 91 al-Marghany St, Heliopolis, Cairo.

Telephone: (2) 4181396; **Fax:** (2) 4185346; **Internet:** www.aohr.net; **e-mail:** AOHR@Link.net.

Anna Lindh Euro-Mediterranean Foundation for Dialogue between Cultures

Established as a partnership between the European Union (EU) and its partners in the southern Mediterranean region, and launched at a conference in Barcelona in 1995. The Foundation is the first common institution jointly established and financed by all 35 members of the Euro-Mediterranean Partnership, and aims to promote regional co-operation in the economic, social and cultural fields.

Activities: Operates to support young people in the areas of culture, education, science and technology, human rights, development and women's empowerment, and funds projects which involve at least two EU and two non-EU Mediterranean partner countries. Programmes for 2007–09 included the Network of National Networks programme to develop diverse and active networks at national and international levels so as to promote the dialogue between cultures; Our Common Future, which provides opportunities for cultural collaboration and a Euro-Mediterranean teacher training programme; Our Creative Diversity, which explores ways of cultural creation; Science without Frontiers, which invites young researchers to work together; Information Society to promote educational and cultural journalism, women as promoters of dialogue in the media, children's literature and reading; and Strategies for Revitalising the Dialogue between Cultures, which aims to cope with critical moments in cultural relations between North and South.

Geographical Area of Activity: The European Union countries and 10 southern Mediterranean countries.

Restrictions: Applicants for funds under the Call for Proposals Scheme must be members of one of the 35 National Networks; partners can be from outside.

Publications: *Unity in Diversity–Implications of the international debate on cultural diversity of the Euro-Mediterranean Co-operation*; *Culture and Communication–Key Factors for Changing Mentalities and Societies*; brochures.

Finance: Funded by the 37 member states of the Euro-Mediterranean Partnership, and the European Commission.

Board of Governors: Veronica Stabej (Chair.).

Principal Staff: Exec. Dir Andreu Claret.

Address: Bibliotheca Alexandrina, POB 732, el-Mansheia, Alexandria 21111.

Telephone: (3) 4820342; **Fax:** (3) 4820471; **Internet:** www.euromedalex.org; **e-mail:** info@euromedalex.org.

El Salvador

FOUNDATIONS, TRUSTS AND NON-PROFIT ORGANIZATIONS

Fundación de Capacitación y Asesoría en Microfinanzas (Foundation for the Qualification and Consultancy in Microfinance)

Founded in 2000 as part of a joint project by the European Union and Banco Multisectorial de Inversiones.

Activities: Provides specialist technical services for micro-enterprises.

Geographical Area of Activity: El Salvador and Central America.

Board of Directors: Sigfredo Figueroa (Pres.); Mercedes Llort (Vice-Pres.); Ana Menjivar de Carazo (Sec.).

Address: Edif. Century Plaza, Alameda Manuel Enrique Araujo, Km 4 Carretera a Santa Tecla, San Salvador.

Telephone: 2265-2177; **Fax:** 2265-2173; **Internet:** www.fundamicro.com; **e-mail:** fundamicro@fundamicro.com.

Fundación Nacional para el Desarrollo (National Foundation for Development)

A research institution that formulates socioeconomic policies, advocates and promotes development, with its target group being the most disadvantaged sectors of society.

Activities: Works in the areas of Macroeconomics and Development, Territorial Development and Transparency, through providing funding for development, integration and development, employment and growth construction and development of territories, national public policies for territorial development, environmental management and transparency.

Geographical Area of Activity: El Salvador and Central America.

Finance: Revenue US $2,841,755; expenditure $2,755,722 (2010).

Principal Staff: Exec. Dir Dr Roberto Rubio-Fabian.

Address: Calle Arturo Ambrogi 411, Col. Escalón, San Salvador.

Telephone: 2209-5300; **Fax:** 2263-0454; **Internet:** www.funde.org; **e-mail:** funde@funde.org.

Fundación Salvadoreña para el Desarrollo Económico y Social (El Salvador Foundation for Economic and Social Development)

Think tank and research centre founded in 1983.

Activities: The research centre studies economics, society, the environment and institutionsto formulate and influence public policies. The aim is for social advancement and through sustainable development.

Geographical Area of Activity: El Salvador.

Publications: Bulletins; numerous reports from the Research Centre, Development Centre, and the Economic and Legal Information System.

Board of Directors: Francisco de Sola (Pres.); Miguel Angel Simán (Vice-Pres.); Freddie Frech (Treas.).

Principal Staff: Exec. Dir Álvaro Ernesto Guatemala.

Address: Edif. FUSADES, Apdo 01-278, Blvd y urbanización Santa Elena, Antiguo Cuscatlán, La Libertad.

Telephone: 2248-5600; **Fax:** 2278-3356; **Internet:** www.fusades.org; **e-mail:** fusades@fusades.org.

Estonia

FOUNDATION CENTRE AND CO-ORDINATING BODY

Eesti Mittetulundusühingute ja Sihtasutuste Liit (Network of Estonian Non-profit Organizations)

Established in October 1991 by representatives of 26 Estonian foundations to promote co-operation between charitable, non-governmental and not-for-profit organizations. Currently has 108 member NGOs and foundations. Previously known as the Estonian Foundation Centre.

Activities: Operates nationally and internationally in the fields of education, international affairs, law and human rights, and information dissemination, through conducting research, organizing training courses and conferences and issuing publications.

Geographical Area of Activity: Estonia, Central and Eastern Europe.

Restrictions: Not a grant-making organization.

Principal Staff: Exec. Dir Urmo Kübar; Head of Policy Alari Rammo.

Address: Rotermanni 8, 10111 Tallinn.

Telephone: 664 5077; **Fax:** 664 5078; **Internet:** www.ngo.ee; **e-mail:** info@ngo.ee.

FOUNDATIONS, TRUSTS AND NON-PROFIT ORGANIZATIONS

Eestimaa Looduse Fond—ELF (Estonian Fund for Nature)

Established in February 1991 to protect Estonia's rich biodiversity through the development, funding and implementation of nature conservation projects, to offer expertise in the formation of public policy, and to work towards increased public environmental awareness through education.

Activities: The Foundation operates in Estonia in the fields of conservation and the environment, and education, through self-conducted programmes, research, conferences, training courses and publications; it provides financial support for conservation and environmental projects such as scientific research, the application of practical conservation measures, and public information and education.

Geographical Area of Activity: Estonia.

Publications: *Orchid Ecology and Protection in Estonia* (1994); *Estonian Coastal and Flood Plain Meadows* (1996); *Minu mets (My forest)* (1999); *Action plan for Grey Seals in Estonia 2001–2005* (2001); *Naturewatch Baltic Report 2003*; *Baltic Forest Mapping: Keskkonna õigus (Environmental Justice)* (2003); *Keskkonnasõbra taskuraamat (Activist Handbook)* (2003); *Genetically modified organisms and their risks to the environment* (2006); *Overview Estonian forestry 2005–2008* (2009); *Environmental impacts of Forestry Drainage* (2009); Annual Report.

Principal Staff: Exec. Dir Jüri-Ott Salm.

Address: PK 245, 51002 Tartu; Magasini 3, POB PK245, 50002 Tartu.

Telephone: 7428-443; **Fax:** 7428-166; **Internet:** www.elfond.ee; **e-mail:** elf@elfond.ee.

Open Estonia Foundation

Founded in 1990 to support the development of open society through supporting democratic principles, the creation of non-profit organizations and assisting those working in the areas of human rights and economic and legal reform; it is an independent foundation, part of the Soros foundations network (q.v.).

Activities: Operates in the areas of open governance, human rights and social justice, youth and active citizenship, civil society capacity building and cross-border co-operation through making grants as well as initiating its own projects. Previously has operated in education, information and the media, public health, youth, law and criminal justice, the arts and culture, and many more areas. Involved in the CIVICUS Index on Civil Society.

Geographical Area of Activity: Estonia.

Publications: Annual Report; special reports.

Finance: Annual expenditure US $3,800,000 (2009).

Board of Directors: Linnar Viik (Chair.).

Principal Staff: Exec. Dir Mall Hellam.

Address: Estonia Ave 5A, 10143 Tallinn.

Telephone: 631-3791; **Fax:** 631-3796; **Internet:** www.oef.org.ee; **e-mail:** info@oef.org.ee.

Sihtasutus Eesti Rahvuskultuuri Fond (Estonian National Culture Foundation)

Founded in 1991 to promote and preserve Estonian national culture.

Activities: Operates in the area of the arts and humanities. Offers scholarships and grants to individuals and projects dedicated to developing aspects of Estonian culture; presents Lifetime Achievement Awards to people who have made significant contributions to national culture; and works in co-operation with a number of institutions and individuals that support Estonian culture. Administers 150 special foundations.

Geographical Area of Activity: Estonia.

Finance: Total income 5,380,416 Estonian kroons, expenditure 3,875,652 Estonian kroons (June 2010).

Council: Eri Klas (Chair.).

Principal Staff: Man. Dir Toivo Toomemets.

Address: A. Weizenbergi 20, A-13, 10150 Tallinn.

Telephone: 601-3428; **Fax:** 601-3429; **Internet:** www.erkf.ee; **e-mail:** post@erkf.ee.

Ethiopia

FOUNDATIONS, TRUSTS AND NON-PROFIT ORGANIZATIONS

Africa Humanitarian Action

Established in 1994 by Dr Dawit Zawde in response to the ethnic cleansing in Rwanda.

Activities: Offers humanitarian assistance to refugees, internally displaced persons and to local communities in Africa. Maintains a Europe office in Geneva, Switzerland, and an office in the USA; there are country offices in Burundi, Democratic Republic of Congo, Liberia, Namibia, Rwanda, Sudan, Uganda and Zambia.

Geographical Area of Activity: Africa.

Trustees: Dr Salim Ahmed Salim (Chair.).

Principal Staff: Pres. Dr Dawit Zawde.

Address: Guinea-Conakry Rd, POB 110, code 1250, Addis Ababa.

Telephone: (11) 551-1224; **Fax:** (11) 551 3851; **Internet:** www .africahumanitarian.org/; **e-mail:** info@africahumanitarian .org.

Finland

FOUNDATION CENTRE AND CO-ORDINATING BODY

Säätiöiden ja rahastojen neuvottelukunta ry (Council of Finnish Foundations)

Established in 1970, an association of Finnish grant-making foundations and associations.

Activities: Assists its more than 135 member foundations and associations to exchange information and ideas; represents its members; advises members and grant seekers through its Foundation Service (Säätiöpalvelu), which also provides information on grants and foundations; and issues publications.

Geographical Area of Activity: Finland.

Publications: Good Governance in Foundations.

Finance: Grants disbursed by represented organizations €290,000,000 (2010).

Board of Directors: T. Lähdesmäki (Chair.).

Principal Staff: Coordinator Kai Kilpinen; Man. Dir Prof. Paavo Hohti.

Address: Fredrikinkatu 61 A, 00100 Helsinki.

Telephone: (9) 6818949; **Internet:** www.saatiopalvelu.fi; **e-mail:** info@saatiopalvelu.fi.

FOUNDATIONS, TRUSTS AND NON-PROFIT ORGANIZATIONS

Baltic Sea Foundation

Founded in 1989 by Anders Wiklöf to support activities for the protection of the Baltic Sea environment.

Activities: Grants scholarships, prizes and financial support for relevant scientific research, technology, published material and other activities in the Baltic Sea region. Aims to establish new economic relations between countries.

Geographical Area of Activity: The Baltic region.

Finance: Net assets €800,000 (2010).

Board of Trustees: Henrik Beckman (Chair.); Lotta Wickstrom-Johansson (Vice-Chair.).

Principal Staff: Man. Dir Edgar Öhberg.

Address: Strandgatan 7, 22100 Mariehamn.

Telephone: (18) 15270; **Internet:** www.ostersjofonden.org; **e-mail:** info@ostersjofonden.org.

Foundation for Commercial and Technical Sciences—KAUTE

Founded in 1956 to support study in the fields of commercial and technical sciences, and to support teaching and research activities in these fields.

Activities: Operates nationally in the fields of economic affairs, education and science and technology, through grants to individuals and granting scholarships and fellowships. Member of the Säätiöiden ja rahastojen neuvottelukunta ry (Council of Finnish Foundations, q.v.).

Geographical Area of Activity: Finland.

Principal Staff: Officer Sirkku Kuoppamäki.

Address: Ratavartijankatu 2, 00520 Helsinki.

Telephone: (9) 47677217; **Internet:** www.kaute.net; **e-mail:** hannu.raulo@kaute.net.

Signe och Ane Gyllenbergs stiftelse (Signe and Ane Gyllenberg Foundation)

Established in 1948 to support medical and scientific research, especially in the area of psychosomatic illness, and research in the field of medicine following the ideas of Rudolf Steiner.

Activities: Operates internationally. Supports medical and scientific research, especially in the area of psychosomatic illness and blood disorders, through awarding grants; also maintains the Villa Gyllenberg Art Museum in Helsinki.

Geographical Area of Activity: International.

Restrictions: Grants are not given for research that involves painful experiments on animals.

Finance: Grants disbursed €2,000,000 (2008–09).

Trustees: Prof. Per-Henrik Groop (Pres.); Magnus Bargum (Vice-Pres. and Treas.).

Principal Staff: Man. Dir Jannica Fagerholm.

Address: Yrjönkatu 4A, 5, 00120 Helsinki.

Telephone: (9) 647390; **Fax:** (9) 607119; **Internet:** www.gyllenberg-foundation.fi; **e-mail:** stiftelsen@gyllenberg-foundation.fi.

Helsingin Sanomain Säätiö (Helsingin Sanomat Foundation)

To advance and support excellence in research as a means of insuring the broad base, independence and continuity of Finnish scientific work. The fields of particular interest for the Foundation are communications, the communications industry and futures research. Also promotes and supports freedom of expression, including research into the history of freedom of expression, and it fosters educational and cultural activities in Finland.

Activities: Operates in the areas of communications, the communications industry and futures research, awarding grants for research.

Geographical Area of Activity: Finland.

Finance: Grants budget approx. €5,000,000.

Board of Trustees: Reetta Meriläinen; Matti Sintonen; Janne Virkkunen; Kaius Niemy; Paavo Hohti; Matti Sintonen; Liisa Välikangas.

Principal Staff: Pres. Heleena Savela.

Address: POB 35, 00089 Sanoma.

Telephone: (9) 1221; **Internet:** www.hssaatio.fi; **e-mail:** saatio@hssaatio.fi.

Yrjö Jahnssonin säätiö (Yrjö Jahnsson Foundation)

Founded in 1954 by Hilma Jahnsson to sponsor Finnish research in economics and medicine, as well as to support Finnish educational and research institutes.

Activities: Operates nationally in the field of education, and internationally in economic affairs, and science and medicine, through grants to Finnish institutions and individuals, and fellowships and scholarships for Finnish citizens, and through international research, conferences, courses, publications and lectures. Distributes the Yrjö Jahnsson Award in Economics to a young European economist who has significantly advanced the field of economics research.

Geographical Area of Activity: Finland and Europe.

Publications: Report of operations and financial statement.

Principal Staff: Man. Dir Elli Dahl; Research Dir Ari Hyytinen.

Address: Yrjönkatu 11 D 19, 00120 Helsinki.

Telephone: (9) 6869100; **Fax:** (9) 605002; **Internet:** www.yjs .fi; **e-mail:** toimisto@yjs.fi.

Sigrid Jusélius Säätiö (Sigrid Jusélius Foundation)

Founded in 1930 by the terms of the will of Fritz Arthur Jusélius to promote and support medical research, independently of language and nationality, with the aim of fighting diseases particularly harmful to humanity.

Activities: Operates in the fields of medicine, pharmacology, biochemistry and genetics. Supports research in those fields and awards grants to individuals and institutions. Organizes occasional symposia and workshops. Grants are made to medical research projects, conducted by senior researchers in Finland and to foreign nationals carrying out research in Finland, and can cover living costs, equipment, materials and consumables.

Geographical Area of Activity: Finland.

Restrictions: No direct grants for foreign medical research, or for studies or doctoral theses.

Publications: Annual Report (in Finnish and Swedish).

Board: Leif Sevón (Chair.).

Principal Staff: Man. Dir Christian Elfving.

Address: Aleksanterinkatu 48 B, 00100 Helsinki.

Telephone: (20) 7109083; **Fax:** (20) 7109089; **Internet:** www .sigridjuselius.fi; **e-mail:** info@sigridjuselius.fi.

Kansainvälinen solidaarisuussäätiö (International Solidarity Foundation—ISF)

Founded in 1970 to encourage co-operation between Finland and less-developed countries.

Activities: Through long-term projects in the partner countries, ISF improves the living conditions of the poorest sectors of society, particularly women and children. The main objective is to strengthen women's social, economic and political status and to provide the poorest people with opportunities to decent work. ISF operates in Nicaragua, Somalia, Uganda and Russian Karelia.

Geographical Area of Activity: International.

Finance: Annual budget approx. €2,500,000 (2011).

Principal Staff: Exec. Dir Miia Nuikka.

Address: Agricolankatu 4, 00530 Helsinki.

Telephone: (9) 7599730; **Fax:** (9) 75997320; **Internet:** www .solidaarisuus.fi; **e-mail:** solidaarisuus@solidaarisuus.fi.

KIOS—Finnish NGO Foundation for Human Rights

Founded in September 1998 by 11 Finnish NGOs working with human rights and development issues; aims to promote the awareness and realization of human rights in developing countries.

Activities: Operates in the field of human rights in developing countries by providing financial support to local civil society organizations that work to promote or protect human rights. KIOS thematic priorities are: democratic rights, the right to education, and gender equality. Support is focused primarily on East Africa and South Asia. Post-conflict countries and countries, where the mechanisms for protecting human rights are weak, are prioritized. Special attention is given to the promotion of human rights of the most vulnerable members of society.

Geographical Area of Activity: East Africa and South Asia, and developing countries elsewhere.

Restrictions: No funding for individuals, international NGOs, or governmental bodies. Nor are projects targeted at development work, humanitarian aid, or socio-economic support for marginalized groups granted funding. No funding is granted for scholarships, fellowships, conference participation or travel.

Finance: Receives financial support for its activities from the Department for Development Policy at the Ministry for Foreign Affairs of Finland. Budget €1,400,000 (2010).

Principal Staff: Acting Exec. Dir Ulla Anttila; Project Co-ordinators Katja Ilppola, Kristiina Vainio, Elina Vuola.

Address: Haapaniemenkatu 7-9 B, 00530 Helsinki.

Telephone: (9) 68131534; **Fax:** (9) 68131531; **Internet:** www .kios.fi; **e-mail:** kios@kios.fi.

Maj and Tor Nessling Foundation

Established by Maj and Tor Nessling in 1972 for the promotion of Finnish science and culture, especially in the field of environmental protection.

Activities: Operates in the field of environmental protection, through awarding grants for scientific research projects in all areas of environmental protection; organizes and funds scientific symposia; supports dissemination of research findings.

Geographical Area of Activity: Finland and the countries nearby.

Finance: Annual grants €2,300,000.

Governing Board: Felix Björklund (Chair.); Prof. Timo Kairesalo (Vice-Chair.).

Principal Staff: Office Man. Leena Pentikäinen.

Address: Fredrikinkatu 20 B 16, 00120 Helsinki, Finland.

Telephone: (9) 4342550; **Fax:** (9) 43425555; **Internet:** www .nessling.fi; **e-mail:** toimisto@nessling.fi.

Paavo Nurmen Säätiö (Paavo Nurmi Foundation)

Established in 1968; aims to contribute to research into heart and vascular disease and to promote public welfare in Finland.

Activities: Provides funding to talented Finnish medical researchers for sabbatical research terms of between two and six months, for cardiovascular disease research. Also provides some support to Estonian cardiologists for visiting research tenures in Finland, and to Finnish scientists for visits to foreign research institutions. Awards the annual International Paavo Nurmi Foundation Award in recognition of an individual's outstanding work in the field of medical research. Also runs an annual symposia programme, and is a co-founding sponsor of the *Tiede 2000* (Science 2000) journal, which aims to make the latest research findings accessible to the public.

Geographical Area of Activity: Finland.

Restrictions: No grants for assistants or equipment.

Trustees: Antti Louhija; Vesa Manninen.

Address: PL 330, 00121 Helsinki.

Internet: www.paavonurmensaatio.fi; **e-mail:** petri .manninen@paavonurmensaatio.fi.

Paulon Säätiö (Paulo Foundation)

Founded in 1966 by Hulda and Marja Paulo to support research in the fields of medicine and the economy, and to promote music and fine art.

Activities: Operates in the areas of the arts and humanities, economic affairs, medicine and health, and science and technology, nationally through research, grants to individuals and awarding prizes, and nationally and internationally through awarding scholarships and fellowships. Main sponsor for The International Paulo Cello Competition.

Geographical Area of Activity: Finland.

Restrictions: Grants and prizes are awarded to Finns and permanent residents of Finland.

Publications: *Why Finland is so Expensive* (1991).

Finance: Grants disbursed some €600,000 (1999–2008).

Trustees: Yrjö Palotie (Chair.); Erkki Hämäläinen (Vice-Chair.).

Address: Lönnrotinkatu 11 A, 3. krs, 00120 Helsinki.

Telephone: (10) 2399290; **Fax:** (10) 2399293; **Internet:** www .paulo.fi; **e-mail:** toimisto@paulo.fi.

Suomen Kulttuurirahasto (Finnish Cultural Foundation)

Founded in 1939 by Suomen Kulttuurirahaston Kannatusyhdistys to promote the development of cultural life in Finland.

Activities: The Foundation provides grants and scholarships for individuals, work groups and communities in the fields of arts and science. It operates primarily within Finland but also internationally through travel and research grants. Large-scale, long-term projects, especially relating to Finnish culture, which require major support are also encouraged. The Foundation's own cultural activities include annual events and other special projects. The Mirjam Helin International Singing Competition, inaugurated in 1984, is held every fifth year. Its purpose is to support young, gifted singers. The Kirpilä Art Collection is a collection of Finnish art donated to the Foundation by Dr Juhani Kirpilä. Some 17 regional funds have been established to support cultural life throughout the country.

Geographical Area of Activity: Primarily Finland, with some international activity.

Publications: *Cultura* (series of publications); Annual Report; reports and brochures.

Finance: Current assets €952,000,000 (Sept. 2010).

Trustees: Ms Pirjo Ståhle (Chair.); Mr Timo Viherkenttä (Vice-Chair.).

Principal Staff: Sec.-Gen. Antti Arjava; Dir of Cultural Affairs Juhana Lassila; Finance Man. Tuula Mäenpää; Dir of Legal Affairs Kristiina Rintala.

Address: Bulevardi 5 A, POB 203, 00121 Helsinki.

Telephone: (9) 612810; **Fax:** (9) 640474; **Internet:** www.skr.fi; **e-mail:** yleisinfo@skr.fi.

Svenska Kulturfonden (Foundation for Swedish Culture in Finland)

Founded in 1908 by the Svenska Folkpartiet to support educational institutions; associations, unions and institutions with cultural interests and purposes; individual scientific, literary and artistic activities; and other purposes serving Swedish culture in Finland.

Activities: Operates nationally in the fields of education, the arts and humanities, social studies, science and medicine, through grants to institutions and individuals, conferences and courses. Maintains an art collection comprising works by contemporary Finno-Swedish artists and operates regional grant offices.

Geographical Area of Activity: Finland.

Restrictions: Support is given only to projects serving Swedish culture in Finland.

Publications: Annual and conference reports; catalogues.

Finance: Budget approx. €36,000,000 (2011).

Principal Staff: Dir Berndt Arell.

Address: POB 439, 00101 Helsingfors.

Telephone: (9) 69307300; **Internet:** www.kulturfonden.fi; **e-mail:** kansliet@kulturfonden.fi.

Taiga Rescue Network—TRN

Established in 1992 to give a voice to those wanting to see sensitive development in the boreal region, through the linking and publicizing of local campaigns on behalf of the boreal forests and peoples. Around 200 organizations participate in the network, which is the only international network of NGOs, indigenous peoples and individuals working to defend the world's boreal forests.

Activities: Operates internationally in the field of forest conservation. Projects include forest mapping, supporting the rights of indigenous peoples, youth activities, monitoring of trade flows, international forest policy, forest certification and combating illegal logging activities in Russian forests.

Geographical Area of Activity: Europe, North America and the Russian Federation.

Restrictions: Grants only to participating organizations to finance joint projects.

Publications: *Taiga News; Boreal Bulletin* (6 a year); reports; fact sheets; brochures; Annual Report.

Board: Jonas Rudberg (Chair.).

Principal Staff: Co-ordinator Sini Eräjää.

Address: c/o Finnish Association for Nature Conservation, Kotkankatu 9, 00510 Helsinki.

Internet: www.taigarescue.org; **e-mail:** sini@taigarescue.org.

Tekniikan Edistämissäätiö–Stiftelsen för teknikens främjande—TES (Finnish Foundation for Technology Promotion)

Founded in 1949 by 63 industrial or business institutions and persons to further technology in Finland by supporting relevant education and research, and generally to improve the conditions of technical activities in the various sectors of economic life, with special emphasis on essential tasks.

Activities: Operates nationally in the fields of technology, education, international relations and the conservation of natural resources. Programmes are carried out nationally, through research, grants to institutions, fellowships and scholarships, and nationally and internationally through grants to individuals, conferences, courses, publications and lectures. Awards are made chiefly to advanced technical students and in support of technical research, training and education.

Geographical Area of Activity: Finland.

Publications: Report of operations and financial statement.

Principal Staff: Pres. Harri Hintikka; Sec.-Gen. Onni Juva.

Address: PL 32, Aleksanterinkatu 4, 00023 Valtioneuvosto.

Telephone: (9) 16063722; **Fax:** (9) 16063705; **Internet:** www.tekniikanedistamissaatio.fi; **e-mail:** etunimi.sukunimi@tem.fi.

Väestöliitto (The Family Federation of Finland)

Founded in February 1941. The Foundation acts in the social and health fields, promoting, according to its rules, the welfare, health, safety, and happy and balanced life of families, young people, and the population in general. The Foundation's activities also have an international element.

Activities: The Foundation carries out advocacy work in society, conducts research, is a developer and a service provider. It distributes information, and educational and publishing materials in its field. It treats infertility, supports sexual health and people's responsible sexual well-being, as well as providing counseling. Development projects are currently under way in Africa, Asia and the eastern border areas of Finland.

Geographical Area of Activity: Finland, Africa, Asia, Baltic states and Russia.

Publications: Publishes materials on the focus areas of family, sexual and reproductive health, sexuality, and family and population policy. The Global Development Unit publishes materials on global development questions and especially on sexual and reproductive health and rights. Annual publications include a translation from the UNFPA's State of World Population into Finnish, a monthly electronic newsletter, and booklets on topical population themes. The Unit has also produced videos for global education. The clinics, the Population Research Institute and other departments publish studies, reports and educational materials on their fields of activity. *Pari ja perhe* (quarterly).

Board of Trustees: Reino T. Hjerppe (Chair.).

Principal Staff: Man. Dir Helena Hiila.

Address: POB 849, 00101 Helsinki; Kalevankatu 16, 00101 Helsinki.

Telephone: (9) 228050; **Fax:** (9) 6121211; **Internet:** www.vaestoliitto.fi; **e-mail:** helena.hiila@vaestoliitto.fi.

Wihurin kansainvälisten palkintojen rahasto (Wihuri Foundation for International Prizes)

Founded in 1953 by Antti Wihuri to promote and sustain the cultural and economic development of society by distributing international prizes, in particular the Wihuri Sibelius Prize; shares administration with the Jenny ja Antti Wihurin Rahasto (q.v.).

Trustees: S. Palokangas (Chair.); E. K. M. Leppävuori (Vice-Chair.).

Principal Staff: Exec. Dir Arto Mäenmaa.

Address: Arkadiankatu 21 A 14, 00100 Helsinki.

Telephone: (9) 4542400; **Fax:** (9) 444590; **Internet:** www
.wihurinrahasto.fi; **e-mail:** toimisto@wihurinrahasto.fi.

Jenny ja Antti Wihurin Rahasto (Jenny and Antti
Wihuri Foundation)

Founded in 1942 by Jenny and Antti Wihuri to promote and
sustain Finnish cultural and economic development.

Activities: Awards grants and prizes for science, art and
other activities in a variety of fields.

Geographical Area of Activity: Finland.

Restrictions: Grants are available to Finnish nationals.

Finance: Grants and awards disbursed €9,700,000 (2011).

Trustees: S. Palokangas (Chair.); E. K. M. Leppävuori (Vice-Chair.).

Principal Staff: Exec. Dir Arto Mäenmaa.

Address: Arkadiankatu 21 A 14, 00100 Helsinki.

Telephone: (9) 4542400; **Fax:** (9) 444590; **Internet:** www
.wihurinrahasto.fi; **e-mail:** toimisto@wihurinrahasto.fi.

France

FOUNDATION CENTRES AND CO-ORDINATING BODIES

Centre Français des Fondations—CFF (French Foundation Centre)

Founded in 2002, the Centre aims to develop the exchange of information among foundations in France, and the development of new foundations. There were approximately 170 member organizations in 2010.

Activities: Dedicated to promoting the development of foundations in France and to enhancing their international representation by improving the knowledge of their status and action and supporting their developing projects. Aims to represent the interests of French foundations vis-à-vis public authorities whether national, European or international institutions; to advise individuals and corporations intending to create a foundation; to be a source of information (database, research, studies and directories); to constitute a network of expertise servicing all foundations by sharing and exchanging experiences.

Geographical Area of Activity: France and Europe.

Publications: e-newsletter.

Board of Directors: Francis Charhon (Pres.).

Principal Staff: Delegate-Gen. Béatrice de Durfort.

Address: 40 ave Hoche, 75008 Paris.

Telephone: 1-44-21-31-27; **Fax:** 1-44-21-31-01; **Internet:** www.centre-francais-fondations.org; **e-mail:** info@centre-francais-fondations.org.

Fédération Internationale des Ligues des Droits de L'Homme—FIDH (International Federation of Human Rights)

Established in 1922, a non-profit NGO, to fight for international justice and defend human rights as contained in the Universal Declaration of Human Rights.

Activities: Operates internationally, representing more than140 national human rights organizations, that are working in nearly 100 countries to defend human rights. Organizes campaigns, lobbies internationally, co-ordinates a human rights network, provides information services, and works to protect people suffering from human rights abuses. Issues publications.

Geographical Area of Activity: International.

Publications: *La Lettre* (newsletter, 10 a year); *Mission Reports* (15 a year); Annual Report.

Finance: Annual revenue €4,615,623; expenditure €4,600,499 (2009).

International Board: Souhayr Belhassen (Pres.); Jean-Francois Plantin (Treas.).

Principal Staff: Exec. Dir Antoine Bernard.

Address: 17 passage de la Main d'Or, 75011 Paris.

Telephone: 1-43-55-25-18; **Fax:** 1-43-55-18-80; **Internet:** www.fidh.org; **e-mail:** ggrilhot@fidh.org.

Fondation de France

Founded in 1969 with an initial endowment made by the Caisse des Dépôts et Consignations (Bank of Security Deposits) and 17 major French banks. The Foundation aims to encourage and develop the practice of making charitable donations, and is the only foundation in France empowered to support actions in all areas of general interest.

Activities: The Foundation operates in three main areas: financial contributions to projects carried out by organizations acting in the fields of social welfare, scientific and medical research, culture and the environment; assistance to individuals or companies in the creation of a foundation under the aegis of the Fondation de France; and the development of associations, through helping them to raise funds. In 2005 the Foundation managed 543 individual foundations, and maintained seven regional delegations.

Geographical Area of Activity: France and Europe.

Publications: Annual Report; newsletter; publications on social welfare, social work, and philanthropy in France.

Administrative Council: Philippe Lagayette (Pres.); Yves Sabouret (Hon. Pres.); Bertrand Duforcq (Hon. Pres.); Olivier Philip (Hon. Pres.); Jean Huet (Treas.).

Principal Staff: Dir-Gen. Francis Charhon.

Address: 40 ave Hoche, 75008 Paris.

Telephone: 1-44-21-31-00; **Fax:** 1-44-21-31-01; **Internet:** www.fondationdefrance.org; **e-mail:** webmaster@fdf.org.

Open Society Institute—Paris (Soros Foundations)

Established as the Open Society Institute's Paris branch, part of the Soros foundations network, which aims to foster political and cultural pluralism and reform economic structures to encourage private enterprise and a market economy.

Activities: Acts as a networking and resource centre to assist Soros foundations and affiliated organizations in Central and Eastern Europe in fostering cultural and educational exchange programmes with international donor organizations in Western European countries. Since 1997 has focused primarily on the Belarus Project, which was initiated when the Belarus Soros Foundation closed, supporting the development of open society in Belarus through a number of projects focusing on independent media, non-partisan voter information and mobilization campaigns, human rights, and civil society resource centres. With the exception of this project, all other Open Society Institute–Paris operational and grant-giving programmes are being phased out.

Geographical Area of Activity: Central and Eastern Europe.

Publications: Press releases; newsletters; *Open Society News: Working to Break the Chains of Injustice; Closed to Reason: The International Narcotics Board and HIV/AIDS; Towards a People-Driven African Union: Current Obstacles & New Opportunities; Confronting a Hidden Disease: TB in Roma Communities; Monitoring Education for Roma; Civil Society Perspectives on TB Policy in Bangladesh, Brazil, Nigeria, Tanzania, and Thailand; Bureaucratic Politics and Foreign Policy; Dismantling a Community; Keeping America Open: OSI US Programs Tenth Anniversary Report.*

Principal Staff: Vice-Pres. Annette Laborey; Deputy Dir Julia Jurys.

Address: 38 blvd Beaumarchais, 75011 Paris.

Telephone: 1-48-05-24-74; **Fax:** 1-40-21-65-41; **Internet:** www.soros.org/about/locations/paris; **e-mail:** osi-paris@osi-eu.org.

Réseau d'ONG Européennes sur l'Agro-alimentaire, le Commerce, l'Environnement et le Développement—RONGEAD (European NGOs on Agriculture, Food, Trade and Development)

Founded in 1983 to support professional and non-governmental development organizations in Europe and less-developed countries.

Activities: Acts as a co-ordinating body for European NGOs, and NGOs and professional organizations in less-developed countries concerned with agriculture, food and trade issues in the developing world. Organizes an information exchange network, and education programmes in Europe, and runs training seminars for local groups in developing countries.

Geographical Area of Activity: Europe, Africa, Pacific region, Caribbean, North America.

Publications: Articles, briefings, training and educational materials.

Board of Trustees: Maurice Perroux (Pres.); Patrick Mundler (Sec.); Marion Beyard (Treas.).

Principal Staff: Dir Cedric Rabany.

Address: 21 rue Longue, 69001 Lyon.

Telephone: 4-72-00-36-03; **Fax:** 4-72-00-35-98; **Internet:** www.rongead.org; **e-mail:** rongead@rongead.org.

FOUNDATIONS, TRUSTS AND NON-PROFIT ORGANIZATIONS

Académie Goncourt—Société des Gens de Lettres
(Goncourt Academy—Literary Society)

Founded in 1896 by a legacy of Edmond de Goncourt, to support literature, to give material assistance to a certain number of writers and to strengthen the links between them.

Activities: Awards the annual Prix Goncourt for the best prose work of the year published in French, as well as scholarships in different fields of literature. The Academy has 10 members. Since 1973 the Academy has aimed to encourage francophone literature throughout the world, and to support international cultural exchanges; it organizes conferences and lectures.

Geographical Area of Activity: France and francophone countries.

Principal Staff: Pres. Edmonde Charles-Roux; Sec.-Gen. Didier Decoin.

Address: c/o Drouant, pl. Gaillon, 75002 Paris.

Telephone: 1-40-46-88-11; **Internet:** www.academie -goncourt.fr; **e-mail:** bruit.de.lire@wanadoo.fr.

Acting for Life

Established in 1981 as Groupe Développement. Changed its name in 2009.

Activities: Operates in the field of aid to less-developed countries. Promotes local action in developing countries, supporting social and rural development projects; facilitates information exchange between development organizations; campaigns for human rights and social justice for all, and against the sexual exploitation of women.

Geographical Area of Activity: Africa, Asia, the Middle East, and Central and South America.

Publications: *Transfaire* (newsletter); Annual Report.

Board: René Lapautre (Pres.); Olivier Mondot (Treas.); Jean-Marie Joly (Sec.-Gen.).

Principal Staff: Dir-Gen. Christophe Paquette.

Address: 1050 Avenue de l'Europe, Bâtiment 106, BP 07, 93352 Le Bourget Cedex.

Telephone: 1-49-34-83-13; **Fax:** 1-49-34-83-10; **Internet:** www.acting-for-life.com; **e-mail:** amborges@acting-for-life .org.

Action contre la Faim (Action against Hunger)

Established in 1979 to combat hunger world-wide.

Activities: Operates emergency and post-emergency programmes to combat hunger; programmes include nutrition, health, water and food security, and agricultural development projects; sister organizations operate in Spain, the United Kingdom and the USA.

Geographical Area of Activity: Central and South America, Africa, Eastern Europe, Asia and the Far East.

Publications: *Géopolitique de la Faim*; *Alimentation en eau*; *La Faim dans le Monde*; *Souffles du Monde*; *La Malnutrition en Situation de Crise*; newsletter (monthly).

Finance: Annual income €72,861,997, expenditure €71,423,960 (2008).

Board of Directors: Benoit Miribel (Pres.); Christophe Le Houedec (Treas.).

Principal Staff: Sec.-Gen. Louis Guerre.

Address: 4 rue Niepce, 75662 Paris Cedex 14.

Telephone: 1-43-35-88-88; **Fax:** 1-45-35-88-00; **Internet:** www.actioncontrelafaim.org; **e-mail:** info@ actioncontrelafaim.org.

Action d'Urgence Internationale—AUI (International Emergency Action)

Founded in 1977 with the aim of co-ordinating organizations and volunteers to provide aid during times of natural disaster.

Activities: Intervenes in areas of natural disaster through prevention (training local populations), through intervention (sending trained volunteers to carry out rescue and clearing tasks), and through reconstruction (developing long-term reconstruction projects adjusted to local customs and needs).

Geographical Area of Activity: International.

Publications: *La Déferlante* (bulletin, 3 a year); Annual Report.

Principal Staff: Joint Pres. and Chair. Christian Herbette, Fréderique Bonneaud.

Address: Terrasses de Montcalm, 1401 rue de Fontcouverte, 34070 Montpellier.

Telephone: 4-67-27-06-09; **Fax:** 4-67-27-03-59; **Internet:** www.aui-ong.org; **e-mail:** aui-ong@tiscali.fr.

Agriculteurs Français et Développement International—AFDI (French Agriculturalists and International Development)

Founded in 1975 to mobilize the French farming community and agricultural organizations to promote rural development in the countries of the South.

Activities: Promotes sustainable rural development throughout the world; supports farm workers internationally; arranges international exchanges; campaigns against the exploitation of agricultural workers; works directly in rural areas of Africa, South America and Asia. Maintains representative offices throughout France and in Benin, Burkina Faso, Cameroon, Côte d'Ivoire, Madagascar, Mali and Senegal.

Geographical Area of Activity: Central and West Africa, South America, Asia.

Publications: Annual Report.

Finance: Annual income €3,317,000, expenditure €3,288,000 (2008).

Board of Directors: Gerard Renouard (Pres.); Henry Jouve (Vice-Pres.); Jean-François Cesbron (Treas.).

Principal Staff: Dir Laure Hamdi.

Address: 11 rue de la Baume, 75008 Paris.

Telephone: 1-45-62-25-54; **Fax:** 1-42-89-58-16; **Internet:** www.afdi-opa.org; **e-mail:** afdi@afdi-opa.org.

Agronomes et vétérinaires sans frontières—AVSF

Established in 1977 by Bertrand Naegelen, Jean-Marie Abbès and Jean-Marie Lechevallier, as the Centre International de Coopération pour le Développement Agricole—CICDA to provide agricultural development aid. Merged with Vétérinaires sans frontières—VSF in 2004.

Activities: Operates in the field of aid to less-developed countries, through supporting agricultural development, to improve the quality of life of people living in rural areas. Provides technical and financial support, exchange of knowledge and information, and training for land-workers; and funds local development projects and publications focusing on local aid.

Geographical Area of Activity: Central and South America and the Caribbean, Africa, Asia and Eastern Europe.

Restrictions: Grants only to specific countries and agricultural organizations.

Publications: *Revue Habbanae*; *Editions Ruralter* (technical manuals); *Collection Traverses*.

Finance: Funded by the European Union, the French Ministry of Foreign Affairs and various grants.

Principal Staff: Dir-Gen. Jean-Jacques Boutrou.

Address: 18 rue de Gerland, 69007 Lyon.

Telephone: 4-78-69-79-59; **Fax:** 4-78-69-79-56; **Internet:** www.avsf.org.

Aide et Action

Established in 1981 by Pierre-Bernard Le Bas to improve standards of education in less-developed countries.

Activities: The organization is active in less-developed countries in the fields of education, development, training and solidarity, through defending children's right to education, particularly the most disadvantaged children; contributing to children's basic education in developing countries where there are low levels of schooling (with the help of partner organizations, parents, teachers, local education authorities, NGOs, etc.); promoting self-development within communities; teacher training; and creating solidarity between the northern and southern hemispheres through sponsorship.

Geographical Area of Activity: Africa, India, South-East Asia and the Caribbean.

Publications: *Aide et Action* (quarterly); e-newsletter on various issues.

Finance: Total expenditure €25,200,000 (2010).

Board of Directors: Francois Colas (Pres.); Dominique Saintier (Sec.); Gerard Neveu (Treas.).

Principal Staff: Dir-Gen. Claire Calosci.

Address: 53 blvd de Charonne, 75545 Paris Cedex 11.

Telephone: 1-55-25-70-00; **Fax:** 1-55-25-70-29; **Internet:** www.aide-et-action.org; **e-mail:** info@aide-et-action.org.

Aide Médicale Internationale

Established in 1979 to give the most underprivileged populations access to health care.

Activities: Aims to give the world's most underprivileged populations access to health care through training local staff to promote the assumption of responsibility for the health care system by the individuals directly concerned with its operation, as well as providing training in project management. Targets the representative organizations of the local population, including women's groups, dignitaries, teachers, traditional doctors/healers, contributing to the labour force during rehabilitation work, organizing health education meetings, contributing to the cost of the operation of the health care system by creating income-generating activities, and organizing community funds.

Geographical Area of Activity: Afghanistan, Democratic Republic of the Congo, Haiti, Thailand, Myanmar, Yemen, Central African Republic, Pakistan.

Publications: Financial information; magazines.

Finance: Annual income €16,083,282, expenditure €16,083,282 (2008).

Board of Directors: Dr Philippe Augoyard (Pres.); Geoffroy Malcor (Vice-Pres.); Dr Omolade Alao (Sec.-Gen.); Benoit Lagente (Treas.).

Principal Staff: Dir-Gen. Erwan Le Grand.

Address: 1 rue du Pré Saint Gervais, 93500 Pantin.

Telephone: 1-46-36-04-04; **Fax:** 1-46-36-66-10; **Internet:** www.amifrance.org; **e-mail:** info@amifrance.org.

Alliance Israélite Universelle (Universal Jewish Alliance)

Founded in 1860 by Narcisse Leven, Charles Netter, Isidore Cahen, Eugène Manuel, Aristide Astruc and Jules Carvallo, to work for the emancipation and moral progress of Jewish people.

Activities: Operates internationally in the fields of education and religion through self-conducted programmes, publications and lectures. Maintains a network of schools in Belgium, Canada, France, Israel, Morocco and Spain, and a Hebrew teacher-training college in Casablanca, Morocco, the Ecole Normale Hebraique. The Alliance holds a Jewish library of more than 120,000 volumes and runs the College des études juives and the Nadir publishing house. Through the Consultative Council of Jewish Organizations, the Alliance contributes to the defence of international human rights.

Geographical Area of Activity: International.

Publications: *Les Cahiers de l'Alliance*; *Les Cahiers du judaisme*; *Traces* collection; *The Basics*.

Governing Board: Prof. Ady Steg (Hon Pres.); Marc Eisenberg (Pres.).

Principal Staff: Dir-Gen. Jo Toledano.

Address: 45 rue La Bruyère, 75428 Paris Cedex 09.

Telephone: 1-53-32-88-55; **Fax:** 1-48-74-51-33; **Internet:** www.aiu.org; **e-mail:** info@aiu.org.

ATD Quart-Monde (ATD Fourth World)

Founded in 1957 by Father Joseph Wresinksi as Aide à Toute Détresse (ATD); aims to eliminate extreme poverty and exclusion all over the world, and is open to people of all religious or political convictions. Since 2009 ATD has stood for All Together In Dignity.

Activities: Operates in Europe, Africa, North, Central and south America and Asia in the fields of human rights and social development. Runs education and training programmes in the areas of nursery schools, family centres, literacy and basic skills training, regular Fourth World University gatherings and artistic and cultural programmes with children and young people are undertaken by members of ATD's Volunteer Corps. Raises awareness about the poverty affecting many of the world's population, carries out research into poverty in partnership with the people affected, and works to combat these problems. Holds consultative status with the UN Economic and Social Council (ECOSOC), the UN Children s Fund (UNICEF), the International Labour Organization and the Council of Europe.

Geographical Area of Activity: Europe, Africa, North, Central and South America and Asia.

Publications: *Artisans of Democracy*; *The Human Face of Poverty*; *Talk With Us, Not At Us*; *This is How We Live: Listening to the Poorest Families*; and other publications.

Principal Staff: Dir-Gen. Eugen Brand; Deputy Dirs-Gen. Isabelle Perrin, Diana Skelton.

Address: 114 ave du Général Leclerc, 95480 Pierrelaye.

Telephone: 1-34-30-46-10; **Fax:** 1-34-30-46-21; **Internet:** www.atd-fourthworld.org; **e-mail:** information@atd-fourthworld.asso.org.

Aviation Sans Frontières—ASF (Aviation Without Frontiers)

Established in 1980 by André Gréard, Gérald Similowski and Alain Yout to make air transport available for humanitarian relief.

Activities: Operates in France and internationally, providing humanitarian relief through volunteer air services, transporting people in less-developed countries in need of medical aid, dispatching medical supplies and transporting medical personnel, offering emergency assistance following natural disasters, and assisting other NGOs in their activities; volunteers accompany children on flights to countries where they can be treated.

Geographical Area of Activity: International.

Publications: Bulletin (quarterly, in French).

Directors: Jean Claude Gérin (Pres.); André Fournerat (Vice-Pres.); Gérald Sévignac (Gen. Sec.); Christian Tirobois (Treas.).

Address: Orly Fret 768, 94398 Orly Aérogares Cedex.

Telephone: 1-49-75-74-37; **Fax:** 1-49-75-74-33; **Internet:** www.asf-fr.org; **e-mail:** asfparis@asf-fr.org.

The Camargo Foundation

Founded in 1967 by Jerome Hill to promote the arts and education related to French and Francophone studies for scholars pursuing studies in the humanities and social sciences related to French and francophone cultures as well as for composers, writers, and visual artists (painters, sculptors, photographers, filmmakers, video artists, and new media artists) pursuing creative projects.

Activities: Based in the Mediterranean town of Cassis and includes a reference library and three art/music studios. .

Geographical Area of Activity: France.

Restrictions: Not accepting applications for the 2012–13 academic year.

Board of Trustees: Ann Folliott (Chair.).

Address: 1 ave Jermini, 13260 Cassis.

Telephone: 4-42-01-11-57; **Fax:** 4-42-01-36-57; **Internet:** www.camargofoundation.org; **e-mail:** apply@camargofoundation.org.

Centre d'Études, de Documentation, d'Information et d'Action Sociales—CÉDIAS—Musée Social (Centre for Social Studies, Documentation, Information and Action)

Founded in 1963 through the merger of the Office Central des Oeuvres de Bienfaisance and the Musée Social, which was founded in 1894.

Activities: Operates nationally in the field of education, and nationally and internationally in the fields of social welfare and studies, economic affairs, law and other professions, through conferences, courses, publications and lectures organized and sponsored in France. Maintains a library containing documentation compiled in France and abroad on subjects in the social field.

Geographical Area of Activity: France.

Publications: *Revue Vie Sociale* (quarterly); *Les implicites de la politique familiale*; postcards; reports and other publications.

Administrative Council: Dr Pierre Charbonneau (Hon. Pres.); Simone Crapuchet (Hon. Vice-Pres.); Marc de Montalembert (Pres.); Edouard Secretan (Vice-Pres.); Guy Courtois (Treas.).

Principal Staff: Sec.-Gen. Jacques Ladsous.

Address: 5 rue Las Cases, 75007 Paris.

Telephone: 1-45-51-66-10; **Fax:** 1-44-18-01-81; **Internet:** www.cedias.org; **e-mail:** webmaster@musee-social.org.

Centre Français de Droit Comparé (French Centre of Comparative Law)

Founded in 1951 to co-ordinate research and publication in the fields of international and comparative law within France; to co-ordinate libraries of comparative law and develop conformity of documentation in the field; to organize meetings on an international level; and to encourage exchange of scholars in the field.

Activities: Operates nationally and internationally in the field of international comparative law, through self-conducted programmes, research, conferences, courses, publications and lectures. Awards prizes annually for theses in comparative law.

Geographical Area of Activity: International.

Publications: *Revue Internationale de Droit Comparé* (quarterly); series of monographs; La présomption d'innocence en droit comparé; L'Europe des moyens de paiement à l'heure de l'euro et de l'internet; Les médiateurs en France et à l'étranger.

Administrative Council: Prof. Jacques Robert (Pres.).

Principal Staff: Sec.-Gen. Didier Lamèthe.

Address: 28 rue Saint-Guillaume, 75007 Paris.

Telephone: 1-44-39-86-29; **Fax:** 1-44-39-86-28; **Internet:** www.centrefdc.org; **e-mail:** cfdc@legiscompare.com.

Centre International de Développement et de Recherche—CIDR (International Centre for Development and Research)

Established in 1982 to support less-developed countries.

Activities: Operates in Africa, including Benin, Burkina Faso, Cameroon, Mali, Tanzania and Togo, in the field of aid to less-developed countries, through providing assistance in areas such as agricultural development, health, community development, micro-enterprise and food security. Raises awareness of development issues in France and abroad.

Geographical Area of Activity: Africa.

Publications: Annual Report.

Trustees: Isabelle Hoyaux (Pres.).

Principal Staff: Exec. Dir Cecile Fruman.

Address: 17 rue de l'Hermitage, 60350 Autrèches.

Telephone: 3-44-42-71-40; **Fax:** 3-44-42-94-52; **Internet:** www.groupecidr.org; **e-mail:** webmaster@groupecidr.org.

Centre International de Recherche sur le Cancer—CIRC (International Agency for Research on Cancer—IARC)

Founded in 1965 as a self-governing body within the framework of the World Health Organization to generate and disseminate information useful for the primary prevention of cancer, through intra- and extra-mural activities.

Activities: Operates internationally in the field of medical research, through self-conducted programmes and collaboration with other agencies, as well as with national institutions and laboratories. Has developed programmes that represent an integrated approach to the identification of causative factors in human cancer, and of individuals and population groups at different risks of developing cancer. Topics of research include: studies on geographical incidence and time trends; determination of environmental and occupational hazards; site-orientated studies; childhood cancer; nutrition and cancer; genetics and cancer; mechanisms of carcinogenesis; and host susceptibility in chemical carcinogenesis. Studies for the improvement of data collection and of research methods are also conducted. Provides technical support in the form of computing services and statistical support, library and bibliographical services, banks of human biological material, and common laboratory services. Research training fellowships and a visiting scientist award are awarded annually, and training courses on cancer epidemiology are held in various countries.

Geographical Area of Activity: World-wide.

Publications: Biennial Report; *IARC Monographs on the Evaluation of Carcinogenic Risks to Humans*; *Directory of Ongoing Research in Cancer Epidemiology*; *Cancer Incidence in Five Continents*; *IARC Scientific Publications* (symposia proceedings, manuals, monographs); *Cancer Epidemiology*; *Social Inequalities and Cancer*.

Finance: Budget US $44,751,000 (2008–09).

Governing Council: Dr P. Puska (Chair.).

Principal Staff: Dir Dr Christopher Wild.

Address: 150 cours Albert-Thomas, 69372 Lyon Cedex 08.

Telephone: 4-72-73-84-85; **Fax:** 4-72-73-85-75; **Internet:** www.iarc.fr; **e-mail:** www@iarc.fr.

CIMADE—Service Oecuménique d'Entraide (Ecumenical Service for Mutual Help)

Founded in 1939 by French Protestant youth movements under the presidency of the Rev. Marc Boegner for work among refugees and immigrants.

Activities: Supports work among refugees and migrant workers in France, with emphasis on the defence of human rights. La Cimade also attempts to raise public awareness of these groups in France and the rest of Europe. Internationally, the organization works in partnership with local organizations supporting projects in the field of human rights.

Geographical Area of Activity: Africa, Middle East and Europe.

Publications: Annual Reports about migration and detention centres; *Causes Communes* (quarterly journal).

Finance: Annual budget €8,795,709 (2008).

Advisory Council: Patrick Peugeot (Pres.); Jean-Charles Tenreiro (Vice-Pres.); Lionel Sautter (Treas.).

Principal Staff: Sec.-Gen. Jerome Martínez.

Address: 64 rue Clisson, 75013 Paris.

Telephone: 1-44-18-60-50; **Fax:** 1-45-56-08-59; **Internet:** www.lacimade.org; **e-mail:** infos@lacimade.org.

Cité Internationale des Arts (International Centre for the Arts)

Founded in 1957 by Félix Brunau, Paul Léon and Eero de Snellman to gather the necessary funds for, and to ensure the construction and maintenance of, community buildings and installations at the Cité Internationale des Arts, as well as artists' studios and houses in the estate.

Activities: Operates internationally in the field of the arts, through the construction and management of studios, which may be purchased by individuals or institutions of any nation, to enable an artist of their choice to reside at the Cité. Programmes are also carried out through the organization of concerts and exhibitions, and through the Association of Friends of the Cité Internationale des Arts.

Geographical Area of Activity: International.

Board of Directors: André Larquié (Pres.).

Principal Staff: Dir-Gen. Sidney Peyroles.

Address: 18 rue de l'Hôtel de Ville, 75180 Paris Cedex 4.

Telephone: 1-42-78-71-72; **Fax:** 1-42-78-40-54; **Internet:** www.citedesartsparis.net; **e-mail:** citedesarts@citedesartsparis.net.

Cité Internationale Universitaire de Paris (International University Centre of Paris)

Created during the inter-war period of the 1920s to restore France's international role in higher education, and promote exchanges and friendships between students and researchers from across the globe.

Activities: Accommodates 10,000 students and researchers each year within its 40 houses. Set in a 34-hectare park, it provides dedicated premises for international students.

Geographical Area of Activity: France.

Publications: Annual Report; Citescope cultural programme (monthly); periodicals.

Finance: Total assets €173,745,827 (2008).

Trustees: Marcel Pochard (Pres.); Patrick Gerard (Vice-Pres.); Marie-Hélène Berard (Vice-Pres.); Jacques Sallois (Sec.); Patrice Henri (Treas.).

Principal Staff: Dir-Gen. Carine Camby.

Address: 17 blvd Jourdan, 75014 Paris.

Telephone: 1-44-16-64-00; **Internet:** www.ciup.fr; **e-mail:** claire.genevray@ciup.fr.

Écoles Sans Frontières—ESF (Schools Without Frontiers)

Founded in 1980 to provide education to refugees in South-East Asia (Laos and Viet Nam), and Albania.

Activities: Researches into the educational needs of refugees; finances training courses for teachers; organizes programmes in basic learning skills for refugees, in their own language where possible; and participates in resettlement projects. Volunteers participate in two-year programmes in target countries.

Geographical Area of Activity: Albania, Guatemala, Haiti, Laos, Thailand and Viet Nam.

Publications: Annual Report; educational books.

Finance: Annual budget approx. €600,000.

Principal Staff: Exec. Officers A. L. Jubert, N. Seywert.

Address: 1023 route de Janas, 83500 La Seyne Sur Mer.

Telephone: 4-94-34-47-27; **Fax:** 4-94-30-10-25; **Internet:** ecolessansfrontieres.pagesperso-orange.fr; **e-mail:** esf.siege@wanadoo.fr.

Emmaüs International

Established internationally in 1971 (Emmaüs founded in 1949 by Abbé Pierre), an international movement promoting solidarity, combating the causes of exclusion and injustice.

Activities: Operates nationally and internationally in the areas of social welfare, development and conservation of the environment, assisting people with disabilities, those with addictions, ex-prisoners, refugees and other underprivileged people, through the creation of communities for marginalized people; promoting fair trade; developing networking between groups in less-developed countries; and supporting recycling activities. The international office acts as a liaison centre for member organizations world-wide.

Geographical Area of Activity: International.

Publications: *Emmaus International Newsletter* (quarterly); *Tam-Tam* (6 a year).

Finance: Annual income €3,699,627, expenditure €3,461,255 (2009).

Executive Committee: Jean Rousseau (Pres.).

Principal Staff: Exec. Dir Alain Fontaine.

Address: 47 avenue de la Résistance, 93100 Montreuil.

Telephone: 1-41-58-25-50; **Fax:** 1-48-18-79-88; **Internet:** www.emmaus-international.org; **e-mail:** contact@emmaus-international.org.

Enfance et Partage (Children and Sharing)

Established in 1977, involved in assisting and safeguarding children subjected to neglect, and physical, psychological as well as sexual abuse.

Activities: Intervenes to protect child victims of negligence, ill-treatment, and/or sexual abuse. Abroad, it helps tackle emergencies, and invests in programmes of development.

Geographical Area of Activity: France, Africa, South America and the Caribbean, and the Far East.

Restrictions: No public grants.

Publications: *Enfance et Partage* (quarterly).

Board of Directors: Christiane Ruel (Pres.); Marie-Pierre Colombel (Vice-Pres.); André Genay (Treas.).

Principal Staff: Sec.-Gen. Isabelle Guillemet.

Address: 2–4 Cité Ameublement, 75011 Paris.

Telephone: 1-55-25-65-65; **Fax:** 1-55-25-65-66; **Internet:** www.enfance-et-partage.org; **e-mail:** contacts@enfance-et-partage.org.

Enfants du Mekong (Children of the Mekong)

Established in Laos in 1958 by René Péchard to assist children and families in South-East Asia.

Activities: Operates in Cambodia, Laos, Nepal, the Philippines, Thailand, Tibet and Viet Nam, as well as in France, constructing schools and medical centres, supporting individual children and their families, housing children from South-East Asia in France, supporting the French South-East Asian community, and issuing publications. Was awarded the French Prix des Droits de l'Homme (human rights prize) in 1990.

Geographical Area of Activity: Cambodia, France, Laos, Nepal, The Philippines, Thailand, Tibet and Viet Nam.

Publications: *Revue Enfants du Mekong* (magazine).

Finance: Total reserves €1,713,184 (2010).

Administrative Council: François Foucart (Hon. Pres.); Christin Lotholary Nguyen (Pres.); Alain Deblock (Vice-Pres.); Didier Rochard (Sec.-Gen.); Tristan de Bodman (Treas.).

Principal Staff: Dir-Gen. Yves Meaudre.

Address: 5 rue de la Comète, 92600 Asnières.

Telephone: 1-47-91-00-84; **Fax:** 1-47-33-40-44; **Internet:** www.enfantsdumekong.com; **e-mail:** contact@enfantsdumekong.com.

Enfants Réfugiés du Monde—ERM

Founded in 1981 to rehabilitate refugees and homeless children in the developing world.

Activities: Assists children in distress the world-over, providing them with food and shelter, and fulfilling their health-care and educational needs. It also extends psychological support to trauma victims and conducts training courses for local personnel.

Geographical Area of Activity: Africa, the Middle East, South-Eastern Europe and Central America.

Publications: Newsletter (quarterly); articles.

Principal Staff: Pres. Phillipe Vals; Treas. Denis Wetzel; Sec.-Gen. Muriel Roque; Dir Nicole Dagnino.

Address: 34 rue Gaston Lauriau, 93512 Montreuil Cedex.

Telephone: 1-48-59-60-29; **Fax:** 1-48-59-64-88; **e-mail:** erm@erm.asso.org.

Fédération des Agences Internationales pour le Développement—AIDE (Federation of International Agencies for International Development)

Founded in 1986 with the aim of helping developing countries to resolve their economic problems caused through increased industrialization. In 1998 formed the Federation of International Agencies for Development, represented in 18 countries and including 341 NGO members.

Activities: Operates educational programmes with an emphasis on self-help; provides training for industrial work; promotes agricultural projects; works towards improving the quality of life of people in developing countries by improving sanitation conditions, children's services and humanitarian aid; conducts research; organizes seminars and symposia; operates a documentation centre and reference library. Holds General Consultative Status with the UN Economic and Social Council.

Geographical Area of Activity: International.

Publications: *Journal* (quarterly).

Finance: Annual budget approx. US $4,600,000.

Principal Staff: Pres. and CEO Abdelkbir el-Hakkaoui; Chief Admin Officer Abdellatif Kerkeni.

Address: 29 rue Traversière, 75012 Paris.

Telephone: 1-40-19-91-51; **Fax:** 1-43-44-38-40; **Internet:** www.aide-federation.org; **e-mail:** aide@aide-federation.org.

Fondation Abbé Pierre pour le logement des défavorisés

Established in 1988 to assist homeless people; part of the Emmaüs network (q.v.).

Activities: Assists the homeless through offering counselling and support. Maintains regional offices in France.

Geographical Area of Activity: Mainly France; some international aid.

Finance: Annual revenue and expenditure €40,663,000 (2009/10).

Trustees: Raymond Étienne (Pres.); Jacques Oudot, François Chaillou (Vice-Pres.); Bernard Zuber (Treas.).

Principal Staff: Man. Dir Patrick Doutreligne.

Address: 3 and 5 rue de Romainville, 75019 Paris.

Telephone: 01-55-56-37-00; **Internet:** www.fondation-abbe-pierre.fr; **e-mail:** contact@fondation-abbe-pierre.fr.

Fondation Agir Contre l'Exclusion—FACE (Campaign Against Exclusion Foundation)

Founded in 1993 on the initiative of Martine Aubry, by 13 French companies, including Casino, Club Méditerranée, Crédit Lyonnais, Renault and Péchiney, with the aim of mobilizing companies to develop, in collaboration with local authorities and local partners, campaigns against social exclusion. The Foundation is a network of enterprise clubs, created in partnership with local communities, contributing to the economic and social development of disadvantaged areas and encouraging social inclusion.

Activities: Aims to reduce social exclusion in employment and local enterprise, through research and activities aimed locally and nationally. Enterprise centres in many different sectors, such as the environment, recreation, tourism, goods and services, aim to support the local community and rejuvenate training and employment facilities. Encourages the enterprises in its network to take diversity into account in their policy of foreign affairs, in their human resources process and in their development.

Geographical Area of Activity: France.

Publications: *Les Journaux de Face*; *Temoignages*.

Finance: Receives funding from a number of French companies. Assets approx. €7,000,000.

Governing Board: Gérard Mestrallet (Pres.); Antoine Guichard (Hon. Pres.); Pierre Mognan (Vice-Pres.); Philippe Aziz (Treas.); Jean Jacques Rey (Sec.).

Principal Staff: Dir-Gen. Vincent Baholet.

Address: 24 pl. Raoul Follerau, 75010 Paris.

Telephone: 1-49-23-77-77; **Fax:** 1-42-23-77-94; **Internet:** www.fondationface.org; **e-mail:** l.aurouet@fondationface.org.

Fondation Auchan pour la Jeunesse (Auchan Foundation for Youth)

Established in 1996 by Auchan France retail group, under the aegis of the Fondation de France (q.v.).

Activities: Supports projects orientated towards young people, in the fields of job creation, health and prevention, and community development. Priority is given to projects in close proximity to an Auchan hypermarket.

Geographical Area of Activity: France, particularly in areas of company operation.

Restrictions: Does not give money for sponsorship.

Publications: Annual Report.

Board of Directors: Arnaud Mulliez (Pres.); Marie-Hélène Boidin-Dubrule (Vice-Pres.).

Principal Staff: Dir-Gen. Philippe Baroukh; Delegate Gen. Alain Reners.

Address: Bâtiment Le Colibri, 200 rue de la Recherche, 59650 Villeneuve d'Ascq.

Telephone: 3-20-67-55-05; **Internet:** www.auchan.fr; **e-mail:** fondationauchan@auchan.fr.

Fondation de l'Avenir (Foundation of the Future)

Established in 1987 by the Mutualité Fonction Publique and the Association Française de Cautionnement Mutuel.

Activities: Operates nationally in the area of medicine and health, through supporting applied medical research into new surgical techniques, and training.

Geographical Area of Activity: France.

Publications: Newsletter (monthly).

Administrative Council: Étienne Caniard (Pres.); Jackie Fonfria (Vice-Pres.); Michel Montaut (Vice-Pres.); Serge Brichet (Treas.).

Principal Staff: Sec.-Gen. Jean-Claude Simon.

Address: 255 rue Vaugirard, 75719 Paris Cedex 15.

Telephone: 1-40-43-23-80; **Fax:** 1-40-43-23-90; **Internet:** www.fondationdelavenir.org.

Fondation Brigitte Bardot (Brigitte Bardot Foundation)

Established in 1986 for the protection of wild and domestic animals world-wide; supported by around 40,000 members.

Activities: Operates in France and world-wide in the area of conservation and the environment, promoting the defence of the rights of wild and domestic animals. Also runs a retirement home for animals in Normandy, France.

Geographical Area of Activity: International.

Publications: *Info Journal*.

Finance: Reserves €10.5m. (2010).

Principal Staff: Pres. Brigitte Bardot.

Address: 28 rue Vineuse, 75116 Paris.

Telephone: 1-45-05-14-60; **Fax:** 1-45-05-14-80; **Internet:** www.fondationbrigittebardot.fr; **e-mail:** communication@fondationbrigittebardot.fr.

Fondation Bettencourt-Schueller (Bettencourt Schueller Foundation)

Founded in 1987 by Liliane Bettencourt to help to initiate, support and develop projects in the humanitarian, cultural and medical fields.

Activities: Active in the fields of medical research, culture and social and humanitarian relief. Devotes more than one-half of its budget to support medical research and health programmes including: the Young Researchers' Award, comprising up to 14 prizes of €21,000 annually to young researchers in life sciences for doctoral training courses abroad; the Liliane Bettencourt Life Sciences Award, awarded to a European researcher under 45 years of age, who is known in the scientific community and carrying out a particularly promising research project; and the Prix 'Coups d'Elan' pour la Recherche Française awarded annually to two or three French laboratories engaged in biomedical research. In the field of culture, the Foundation supports talented artists or craftsmen and the development of new projects of exceptional quality, as well as awarding the annual Prix Liliane Bettencourt pour le Chant Choral and the Prix Liliane Bettencourt pour l'Intelligence de la Main. In the field of social and humanitarian relief, funds associations engaged in social and humanitarian work, including co-financing the building of a hospital in Phnom Penh, Cambodia.

Geographical Area of Activity: France and developing countries.

Finance: Funds disbursed €13,200,000 (2009).

Board of Trustees: Liliane Schueller Bettencourt (Pres.).

Principal Staff: Dir-Gen. Patrice de Maistre.

Address: 27–29 rue des Poissonniers, 92522 Neuilly-sur-Seine Cedex.

Internet: www.fondationbs.org; **e-mail:** ibf@alchimia-communication.fr.

Fondation Marcel Bleustein-Blanchet pour la Vocation (Marcel Bleustein-Blanchet Vocation Foundation)

Founded in 1960 by Marcel Bleustein-Blanchet to encourage young people to achieve their chosen vocation.

Activities: The Foundation gives financial and practical help to young people aged between 18 and 30 years: it awards 20 scholarships ('Bourses de la Vocation') annually to provide training for young French and European people in numerous branches of science, technology, medicine, the arts and sports. Two prizes, the Prix Littéraire de la Vocation and the Prix de Poésie, are awarded annually for literary work in the French language. 'Sister' foundations have been established in Belgium, Brazil, Israel, Spain and Switzerland.

Geographical Area of Activity: Europe.

Restrictions: No grants for pursuing religious or political vocations.

Board: Elisabeth Badinter (Pres.).

Address: 104 rue de Rennes, 75006 Paris.

Telephone: 1-53-63-25-93; **Fax:** 1-42-22-16-66; **Internet:** www.fondationvocation.org; **e-mail:** secretariat@fondationvocation.org.

Fondation BNP Paribas (BNP Paribas Foundation)

Established in 1984 to fund cultural and humanitarian projects, operating under the aegis of the Fondation de France (q.v.).

Activities: Operating under the aegis of the Fondation de France, the Foundation is a vehicle for dialogue between the world of banking and the broader cultural and social environment. Through its multiple programmes, the Foundation strives to promote the cultural wealth of museums to encourage creative talent to aid specialized medical research, and to support initiatives that promote education, social inclusion and overcoming disabilities. The Foundation is also responsible for developing and guiding the Group's corporate patronage policy; providing oversight, advice and control to the corporate patronage policies deployed by the business; and guaranteeing the consistency of messages communicated via the Group's corporate patronage activities targeting international and external public.

Geographical Area of Activity: World-wide.

Publications: *Sustainable Development Report*; Annual Report; press releases.

Board of Directors: Michel Pébereau (Chair.).

Principal Staff: Pres. Alain Papiasse; Man. Dir Martine Tridde.

Address: 3 rue d'Antin, 75002 Paris.

Telephone: 1-42-98-12-34; **Fax:** 1-42-98-14-11; **Internet:** mecenat.bnpparibas.com.

Fondation Caisses d'Epargne pour la solidarité—FCES (Caisses d'Epargne Foundation for Social Solidarity)

Created in 1994 by the Groupe Caisse d'Epargne, under the aegis of the Fondation de France (q.v.), with the aim of preventing social exclusion of those people in difficult situations when they have not had the ability or resources to put aside any savings.

Activities: Operates nationally in the fields of education and social welfare, and in three areas in particular: working against illiteracy, and the risks of marginalization of the long-term unemployed and the aged, through offering grants to organizations in need. Funds are awarded for conferences and seminars, equipment, programme development and research.

Geographical Area of Activity: France.

Publications: Annual Report; guides and reports; *The Caisse d'Epargne Observatoire* (annually); economic trend reports; *Epargne et Finance* (magazine).

Finance: Total assets €594,132 (Dec. 2005).

Administrative Council: Astrid Boos (Pres.).

Principal Staff: Dir-Gen. Andre Aoun.

Address: 9 ave René Coty, 75014 Paris.

Telephone: 1-58-40-41-42; **Fax:** 1-58-40-48-00; **Internet:** www.fces.fr; **e-mail:** communication@fondation.caisse-epargne.fr.

Fondation Cartier pour l'Art Contemporain (Cartier Foundation for Contemporary Art)

Founded in 1984 by Alain-Dominique Perrin to promote creative arts and to establish direct dialogue between artists and the general public.

Activities: The Foundation commissions works of art to exhibit at home and abroad; it collects and exhibits the works of young artists and stages exhibitions of its collection of contemporary art (it maintains a collection of more than 1,000 works of art by around 250 French and international artists). The Foundation commissions transitory or performance art for evening performances. The Foundation also organizes travelling exhibitions and promotes artistic exchange with foreign institutions, organizes conferences and issues publications.

Geographical Area of Activity: Asia, South America, Europe and the USA.

Publications: Artists' books and exhibition catalogues.

Finance: Financed by the Cartier Group.

Trustees: Alain-Dominique Perrin (Pres.).

Principal Staff: Dir Hervé Chandès.

Address: 261 blvd Raspail, 75014 Paris.

Telephone: 1-42-18-56-50; **Fax:** 1-42-18-56-52; **Internet:** www.fondation.cartier.com; **e-mail:** herve.chandes@fondation.cartier.com.

Fondation Henri Cartier-Bresson (Henri Cartier-Bresson Foundation)

Established in 2003 to promote photography in general, as well as the work of Henri Cartier-Bresson.

Activities: Promotes the work of Henri Cartier-Bresson, through the establishment of a studio to house the photographer's works, books, films and designs, which is open to researchers. Every two years the Foundation awards the €30,000 HCB Award, launched in June 2003. Also organizes films, screenings and exhibitions of Cartier-Bresson's work and the work of other photographers.

Geographical Area of Activity: Mainly Paris area.

Restrictions: No grants are made, apart from the HCB Award.

Publications: *Le Scrapbook d'Henri Cartier-Bresson* (exhibition catalogue); *Joan Colom – Les Gens du Raval* (exhibition catalogue); *Le silence intérieur d'une victime consentante* (exhibition catalogue); *Documentary and Anti-Graphic Photographs* (exhibition catalogue); *Les Choix d'Henri* (exhibition catalogue); *Walker Evans / Henri Cartier Bresson, photographier l'Amérique* (exhibition catalogue); *Robert Doisneau, Du metier à l'oeuvre* (exhibition catalogue); *Saul Leiter* (exhibition catalogue); *Jim Goldberg, Open see* (exhibition catalogue), Harry Callahan, Variations (exhibition catalogue).

Finance: Budget approx. €500,000.

Board of Directors: Martine Franck (Pres.); Kirsten Van Riel (Vice-Pres.); Mélanie Cartier-Bresson (Sec.); François Voss (Treas.).

Principal Staff: Dir Agnès Sire.

Address: 2 impasse Lebouis, 75014 Paris.

Telephone: 1-56-80-27-03; **Fax:** 1-56-80-27-01; **Internet:** www.henricartierbresson.org; **e-mail:** contact@henricartierbresson.org.

Fondation Casip-Cojasor

Formed on 29 December 1999, Foundation CASIP-COJASOR is a recognized public utility. The foundation began its activities on 1 January 2000.

Activities: Aims to help children, the handicapped and the elderly.

Geographical Area of Activity: France.

Board of Directors: Eric of Rothschild (Pres.); Jean-Claude Picard (Vice-Pres.); George Koltein (Treas.).

Principal Staff: Sec.-Gen. Julien Roitman.

Address: 8 rue Pali-Kao, 75020 Paris.

Telephone: 1-44-62-13-13; **Fax:** 1-44-62-13-14; **Internet:** www.casip-cojasor.fr; **e-mail:** fondation@casip-cojasor.fr.

Fondation Chirac (Chirac Foundation)

Established in 2007 by the former President of France, Jacques Chirac, to help build a peaceful international society.

Activities: Operates in the areas of development, health, safeguarding languages and cultures threatened with extinction and the environment, through its projects: access to medicines; access to water; combatting desertification; and support for endangered languages and cultures.

Geographical Area of Activity: International.

Trustees: Jacques Chirac (Pres.); Jean-Pierre Lafon (Vice-Pres.); Valérie Terranova (Sec.); Marie-Hélène Bérard (Treas.); Bernard Vatier (Vice-Pres. and Legal Adviser).

Principal Staff: Dir-Gen. Catherine Joubert.

Address: 14 rue d'Anjou, 75008 Paris.

Telephone: 1-47-42-87-60; **Fax:** 1-47-42-87-78; **Internet:** www.fondationchirac.eu; **e-mail:** contact@fondationchirac.eu.

Fondation Le Corbusier—FLC (Le Corbusier Foundation)

Founded in 1968 according to the wish of Charles Edouard Jeanneret, known as 'Le Corbusier', to maintain a museum in the Villa La Roche in Paris displaying his works, and to encourage research in the spirit defined by his own written and architectural work.

Activities: Operates internationally in the field of the arts and humanities. Maintains a permanent exhibition in the Villa La Roche of Le Corbusier's works: furniture, paintings and sculptures. Loans original works for exhibitions. Advises and supervises the preservation of buildings designed by Le Corbusier. Publishes an information bulletin. Maintains a library. Also awards research scholarships.

Geographical Area of Activity: France.

Publications: Guidebooks; *informations* (monthly newsletter).

Administration Council: Jean-Pierre Duport (Pres.); Claude Prelorenzo (Sec.-Gen.); Jean-Marc Blanchecotte (Treas.).

Principal Staff: Dir Michel Richard; Admin. Christine Mongin.

Address: 8–10 sq. du Docteur Blanche, 75016 Paris.

Telephone: 1-42-88-41-53; **Fax:** 1-42-88-33-17; **Internet:** www.fondationlecorbusier.fr; **e-mail:** info@fondationlecorbusier.fr.

Fondation de Coubertin (Coubertin Foundation)

Established in 1973 by Yvonne de Coubertin and Jean Bernard for the further training of young craft workers, and for the conservation of and research into craft techniques.

Activities: Operates in the area of education and training, offering courses of 11 months for some 30 young craft workers annually, from France or abroad, between the ages of 20 and 25. Courses involve general courses and crafts such as joinery, decorative metal, fine-art foundry and stone masonry. Also organizes concerts open to the public, and seminars for professionals.

Geographical Area of Activity: International.

Publications: *Le Compagnonnage de l'an 2000; Jean-Paul le Forézien Compagnon Menuisier du Devoir; Dodeigne; Etienne-Martin; Etienne Hajdu; Genèse d'une sculpture: Le monument à Michel Servet à Vienne; Jean Chauvin; Sculpture en taille directe en France de 1900 à 1950; Pierres et marbres de Joseph Bernard; Aux grands hommes.*

Board of Trustees: Alice W. Handy (Vice-Pres.).

Address: Domaine de Coubertin, 78470 Saint-Rémy les Chevreuse.

Telephone: 1-30-85-69-60; **Fax:** 1-30-85-69-69; **Internet:** www.coubertin.fr; **e-mail:** info@coubertin.fr.

Fondation Jean Dausset—Centre d'Étude du Polymorphisme Humain—CEPH

The Centre was founded in 1983 by Prof. Daniel Cohen and Prof. Jean Dausset to promote and conduct research into the human genome.

Activities: Operates nationally and internationally in the fields of medicine and health, and science and technology, through self-conducted programmes, research and publications. It conducts genetic research and produced the first 'map' of the genetic constitution of human beings (genome map). Research is also carried out at its 'daughter' laboratory, Généthon, which is now an independent organization. The

Centre maintains a database and the online Human BAC Library.

Publications: *A first generation physical map of the human genome*; *A YAC contig map of the human genome*.

Finance: The Centre was founded using a US $10,000,000 bequest from a French art collector.

Principal Staff: Pres. Pierre Tambourin.

Address: 27 rue Juliette Dodu, 75010 Paris.

Telephone: 1-53-72-50-00; **Fax:** 1-53-72-51-28; **Internet:** www .cephb.fr; **e-mail:** cephdbm@cephb.fr.

Fondation Simone et Cino del Duca (Simone and Cino del Duca Foundation)

Founded in 1975 by Simone del Duca to maintain, develop and improve the natural and cultural heritage, and to promote scientific research, especially biomedical research. Administered by the Institut de France.

Activities: Operates internationally in the fields of science and medicine, and the arts and humanities, through making grants to organizations, awarding prizes and awarding a number of maintenance and travel grants for French research workers wishing to study abroad, and for foreign research workers to spend a period of time in a French laboratory. Grants are exclusively made to research workers whose scientific activity is in the following areas: the cardiovascular system (molecular and cellular biology, pathology, pharmacology and epidemiology), and the nervous system, behaviour and mental health (molecular and cellular biology, pathology, pharmacology and epidemiology), and are made to research workers provided that they have obtained a doctorate before applying for the grant. In the arts and humanities, the Foundation awards the Prix Mondial Cino del Duca and music, painting and sculpture prizes, makes two literary grants for published and unpublished authors, and organizes Medici conference weeks in Rome and conferences in Paris.

Geographical Area of Activity: World-wide.

Publications: Report of operations.

Trustees: Jean Baechler (Pres.).

Principal Staff: Pres. Jacques de Larosiere.

Address: 10 rue Alfred-de-Vigny, 75008 Paris.

Telephone: 1-47-66-01-21; **Fax:** 1-46-22-45-02; **Internet:** www.institut-de-france.fr.

Fondation Eisai (Eisai Foundation)

Established in 2002 by the Eisai company to promote health.

Activities: Provides support to sick people and their families, through funding public-awareness activities and health projects, organizing symposia to disseminate medical knowledge, and the creation of support centres. Also provides study scholarships to nurses and awards three annual prizes worth €6,000 each to projects organized by nurses or health-care workers, which aim to preserve the dignity of elderly people and increase their autonomy.

Geographical Area of Activity: Mainly France.

Board of Directors: Dr Paul Cadre (Pres.).

Principal Staff: Pres. Dr Paul Cadre.

Address: 231 rue Saint Honoré, 75001 Paris.

Telephone: 1-47-67-00-05; **Fax:** 1-47-67-00-15; **Internet:** www .fondation-eisai.org; **e-mail:** info@eisai-fondation.org.

Fondation Electricité de France (EDF Foundation)

Established in 1987 to fund projects in the fields of the environment, culture, health, sport and solidarity.

Activities: Operates in France in the fields of the arts and humanities, scientific and medical research, solidarity, sport, and conservation and the environment, principally working in the areas of cultural heritage and conservation, and contemporary creative initiatives. Created an exhibition area, Espace EDF Electra, in Paris for exhibitions of contemporary art, concerts, conferences, etc. Collaborates with national institutions on cultural and environmental projects. Awards an annual

medical research prize worth €45,000 and five post-doctoral research scholarships of €15,000 each. Assisted in the restoration of, and supports the cultural activities of, the Villa Medici in Rome. There are regional delegations throughout France.

Geographical Area of Activity: International.

Restrictions: Individual artists are not supported.

Publications: Reports; catalogues; brochures.

Administrative Council: Henri Proglio (Pres.).

Principal Staff: Sec.-Gen. Corinne Chouraqui.

Address: 22–30 ave de Wagram, 75008 Paris.

Telephone: 1-40-42-22-22; **Fax:** 1-40-42-48-62; **Internet:** foundation.edf.com.

Fondation Énergies pour le Monde (Energies for the World Foundation)

Founded in 1990 by Alain Liebard to assist developing countries by providing energy sources that do not damage the environment.

Activities: Operates internationally in the field of aid to less-developed countries, through self-conducted programmes.

Geographical Area of Activity: Sub-Saharan Africa, Madagascar, Cambodia, Lao.

Publications: *Fondation Energies pour le Monde Infos* (2 a year).

Board of Directors: Alain Liebard (Pres.); Catherine Becquaert (Vice-Pres.); Cedric Philibert (Sec.); Didier Moret (Treas.).

Principal Staff: Dir-Gen. Yves-Bruno Civel, Dir Yves Maigne.

Address: 146 rue de l'Université, 75007 Paris.

Telephone: 1-44-18-00-36; **Fax:** 1-44-18-00-36; **Internet:** www.energies-renouvelables.org; **e-mail:** energiespourlemonde@energies-renouvelables.org.

Fondation Ensemble (Together Foundation)

Established in 2004 by Gérard Brémond and his wife Jacqueline Délia-Brémond.

Activities: Private foundation working to alleviate poverty while protecting the environment, through water and sanitation projects, renewable energy forms, the protection of biodiversity, and sustainable agriculture.

Geographical Area of Activity: Bangladesh, Burkina Faso, Cambodia, France, India, Madagascar, Malawi, Mali, Morocco, Peru, Romania, Senegal and Ukraine.

Publications: Newsletters; technical sheets available online; Annual Report.

Finance: Programme fund (€50,000 to €300,000); small grants fund (up to €30,000). Annual project disbursements €385,377 (2009).

Administrative Council: Gérard Brémond (Pres.); Jacqueline Délia-Brémond (Vice-Pres.).

Principal Staff: Dir Olivier Braunsteffer; Sec.-Gen. Barry Windsor.

Address: 45 rue de Babylone, 75007 Paris.

Telephone: 1-45-51-18-82; **Fax:** 1-45-51-18-90; **Internet:** www .fondationensemble.org; **e-mail:** contact@fondationensemble .org.

Fondation 'Entente Franco-Allemande' (Foundation for Franco-German Co-operation)

Established in 1981 to receive the funds offered by the German Government in settlement for the forced enrolment of French nationals in the German army during the Second World War and to distribute these funds to alleviate the social problems and uphold the human rights of these former soldiers, as well as to develop Franco-German co-operation through other projects.

Activities: Aims to develop Franco-German co-operation through funding projects in the fields of culture, science, sports, economics and social welfare.

Geographical Area of Activity: France and Germany.

Board of Directors: André Bord (Pres.); Louis Harig (Vice-Pres.); Paul Minges (Treas.).

Principal Staff: Sec.-Gen. Yves Muller.

Address: 1 rue St-Léon, 67000 Strasbourg.

Telephone: 3-88-32-18-00; **Fax:** 3-88-22-48-14; **Internet:** www.fefa.fr; **e-mail:** info@fefa.fr.

Fondation d'Entreprise Air France (Air France Corporate Foundation)

Established in 1992 by the Air France Group.

Activities: Operates nationally and internationally to promote education, which is realized through grants to institutions and self-conducted programmes. Focuses on the care of child refugees, children from underprivileged rural or urban areas, and sick and disabled children.

Geographical Area of Activity: International.

Publications: Press releases; fact sheets; news bulletins.

Finance: Total project expenditure €195,600 (2009).

Board of Directors: Jean-Cyril Spinetta (Chair.).

Principal Staff: Pres. François Brousse; Delegate-gen. Cecile Vic.

Address: 45 rue de Paris, 95747 Roissy CDG Cedex.

Telephone: 1-41-56-57-27; **Fax:** 1-41-75-71-97; **Internet:** http://fondation.airfrance.com; **e-mail:** mail.fondationaf@airfrance.fr.

Fondation d'Entreprise Gaz de France (Gaz de France Foundation)

Founded in 1992 to pursue charitable works related to society, the environment and cultural heritage.

Activities: Operates nationally and internationally in the fields of the environment, cultural heritage and solidarity, especially relating to young people. Also supports relief projects, sporting activities, literacy initiatives and employee volunteering.

Geographical Area of Activity: France and international, including Viet Nam.

Finance: Funded solely by Gaz de France.

Officers and Directors: Gerard Mestrallet (Chair. and CEO); Jean-Francois Cirelli (Vice-Chair. and Pres.).

Principal Staff: Gen. Sec. Patrick Marcel; Exec. Dir Philippe Peyrat.

Address: 22 rue du Docteur Lancereaux, Paris.

Telephone: 1-47-54-28-02; **Fax:** 1-47-54-30-45; **Internet:** www.gdfsuez.com.

Fondation d'Entreprise La Poste (Post Office Foundation)

Established in 1995 under the aegis of the Fondation de France (q.v.), principally to promote literature.

Activities: Operates nationally and in francophone countries in the area of the arts and culture, through financing festivals and literary prizes such as the Prix Wepler, promoting French song writing through the Prix Timbres de Voix prize, and supporting publishing initiatives.

Geographical Area of Activity: France.

Publications: *Flori Lettre* (online newsletter).

Executive Committee: Jean-Paul Bailly (Pres.).

Principal Staff: Head Patricia Huby.

Address: 44 blvd de Vaugirard, Case Postale F603, 75757 Paris Cedex 15.

Telephone: 1-41-41-62-07; **Fax:** 1-41-41-62-60; **Internet:** www.fondationlaposte.org; **e-mail:** fondation.laposte@laposte.fr.

Fondation d'Entreprise Renault (Renault Foundation)

Established in 2001 to promote the French language and French and European culture world-wide.

Activities: Operates in the field of education, offering to fund a period of study in France for around 70 non-French postgraduate students each year. There are three postgraduate training programmes, located in Paris, Bordeaux and Strasbourg (Programme Renault, MBA IP Fondation Renault and Master ParisTech Fondation Renault). Also promotes collaboration between business and tertiary-level educational establishments in France and abroad.

Geographical Area of Activity: International.

Publications: *The Mediterranean Directory.*

Finance: Annual income €3,376,681, expenditure €3,376,681 (2008).

Administrative Council: Carlos Ghosn (Chair.).

Principal Staff: Dir Claire Martin.

Address: 13–15 quai Alphonse le Gallo, FQLG V 15140, 92513 Boulogne-Billancourt Cedex.

Telephone: 1-76-84-96-82; **Fax:** 1-76-84-25-00; **Internet:** www.fondation.renault.com; **e-mail:** fondation.renault@renault.com.

Fondation d'Entreprise VINCI pour la Cité (VINCI Corporate Foundation for the City)

Established in May 2002 by the VINCI construction company to help disadvantaged people gain access to employment.

Activities: Grant programmes aim to help people who find themselves excluded to gain access to employment, and to encourage citizens' initiatives aimed at sustainable development and quality of life. Priority is given to projects developing social responsibility, or helping the socially excluded get back to work.

Geographical Area of Activity: France and several countries where the company operates in Western Europe (United Kingdom, Germany, Belgium, Czech Republic).

Restrictions: Projects from a country other than France must be submitted to the foundation by a company employee.

Finance: Annual budget €2,000,000.

Administrative Council: Xavier Huillard (Pres.).

Address: 1 cours Ferdinand de Lesseps, 92851 Rueil-Malmaison Cedex.

Telephone: 1-47-16-30-63; **Fax:** 1-47-16-49-45; **Internet:** www.vinci.com/fondation; **e-mail:** fondation@vinci.com.

Fondation Euris (Euris Foundation)

Founded in June 2000 by Jean-Charles Naouri, chairman of the Euris company located in Paris, to promote the education of disadvantaged young French people.

Activities: Provides annual scholarships to French students from high schools classified as ZEP (Zones d'Education Prioritaire), REP (Réseaux d'Education Prioritaire) and ZS (Zone Sensible) in need of financial support to acquire a university education. Scholarships are renewable one time only. Under the aegis of Fondation de France.

Geographical Area of Activity: France.

Board of Trustees: Jean-Charles Naouri (Chair.).

Principal Staff: Sec-Gen. Sara Briolin.

Address: 83 rue du Faubourg-Saint-Honoré, 75008 Paris.

Telephone: 1-44-71-14-70; **Fax:** 1-44-71-14-53; **Internet:** www.fondationdefrance.org.

Fondation Européenne de la Science (European Science Foundation)

Founded in 1974, assists its member organizations by bringing scientists together in its activities to work on topics of common concern; and through the joint study of issues of strategic importance in European science policy.

Activities: Sponsors basic research in natural and technical sciences, medical and bio-sciences, humanities and social sciences. The Foundation maintains close relations with other scientific institutions within and outside Europe. Through its activities, adds value by co-operation and co-ordination across national frontiers and endeavours, offers expert scientific advice on strategic issues, and provides the European forum for fundamental science. Has 72 member organizations in 30 countries. Awards the annual European Latsis Prize, funded by the Latsis Foundation (q.v.), made in recognition of an individual or organization's contribution to research in a particular scientific field. Supports around 30 exploratory workshops each year across all scientific domains.

Geographical Area of Activity: Europe.

Publications: Annual Report (in English); Science Policy Briefings; Policy Papers; other specialized publications, studies and reports.

Finance: Member Organizations and EC contracts.

Principal Staff: Chief Exec. Martin Hynes.

Address: 1 quai Lezay-Marnésia, BP 90015, 67080 Strasbourg Cedex.

Telephone: 3-88-76-71-00; **Fax:** 3-88-37-05-32; **Internet:** www.esf.org; **e-mail:** communications@esf.org.

Fondation FARM—Fondation pour l'Agriculture et la Ruralité dans le Monde (FARM Foundation— Foundation for World Agriculture and Rural Life)

Established in 2006.

Activities: Operates in developing countries to improve agriculture and to help introduce new techniques of sustainable development.

Geographical Area of Activity: Developing countries.

Publications: Reports on cotton, water, microfinance and agricultural policies. Studies on price volatility and its impact on Subsaharan farmers.

Board of Directors: Rene Carron (Chair.); Jean-Louis Blanc (Treas.); Jean-Paul Betbeze (Sec.).

Principal Staff: Dir Jean-Christophe Debar.

Address: 91–93 blvd Pasteur, 75710 Paris Cedex 15.

Telephone: 1-57-72-07-19; **Internet:** www.fondation-farm.org; **e-mail:** contact@fondation-farm.org.

Fondation France-Israel (France-Israel Foundation)

Launched in 2005 by the French and Israeli governments to reinforce links and relations between France and Israel at all levels.

Activities: Activities include combating anti-Semitism in France. Promotes the development of relations between the two countries through supporting educational, cultural, economic, scientific and technological projects.

Geographical Area of Activity: France and Israel.

Administrative Council: Nicole Guedj (Pres.); Dina Sorek (Vice-Pres.); Michael Zaoui (Vice-Pres.); Cyril Benoit (Treas.).

Principal Staff: Sec.-Gen. Hervé Bercovier; Deputy Sec.-Gen. Dov Zérah.

Address: 2 rue Alfred de Vigny, 75008 Paris.

Telephone: 1-82-28-95-85; **Fax:** 1-82-28-95-21; **Internet:** www.fondation-france-israel.org; **e-mail:** contact@fondationfranceisrael.org.

Fondation Franco-Japonaise Sasakawa (Franco-Japanese Sasakawa Foundation)

Founded in 1990 by the Sasakawa Foundation (Japan, q.v.) to promote cultural awareness and harmony between France and Japan.

Activities: Operates in France and Japan in the fields of the arts and humanities, education, and science and technology, by awarding scholarships, research grants and travel grants in several areas, including education, the teaching of French and Japanese, translation and publication of works, art, scientific research, promoting exchanges of people and of knowledge, journalism, exhibitions, etc. Also organizes conferences, operates self-conducted programmes and issues publications. In particular, aims to encourage projects dealing with contemporary rather than historical issues, and which favour the long-term development of Franco-Japanese relations.

Geographical Area of Activity: France and Japan.

Publications: *Cent Objets—Produits Artisanaux Traditionnels Japonais Commentés; Guide pour la promotion des objets d'artisanat traditionnel japonais*; cultural register of Japanese institutions located in France.

Finance: Received an initial grant of 132,000,000 francs from the Foundation for the Japanese Naval Construction Industry, and is financed by the Sasakawa Foundation. Annual budget €403,000.

Trustees: Shigeatsu Tominaga (Pres.); Jean-Bernard Ouvrieu (Vice-Pres.); Yves Rousset-Rouard (Sec.); Georges-Christian Chazot (Treas.).

Principal Staff: Dir-Gen. Claire Gallian; Communication Dir Eric Mollet.

Address: 27 rue du Cherche-Midi, 75006 Paris.

Telephone: 1-44-39-30-40; **Fax:** 1-44-39-30-45; **Internet:** www.ffjs.org; **e-mail:** siegeparis@ffjs.org.

Fondation Fyssen (Fyssen Foundation)

Established in 1979 by A. H. Fyssen; aims to encourage all forms of scientific research into cognitive mechanisms, including thought and reasoning, that underlie animal and human behaviour, their biological and cultural bases, and phylogenetic and ontogenetic development.

Activities: Operates a research programme, awarding post-doctoral study grants and research grants to French scientists going abroad and to foreign scientists wishing to work in French research centres. Organizes symposia and publishes research results, and awards an annual international scientific prize worth €50,000.

Geographical Area of Activity: World-wide.

Restrictions: Grants are made only for a first post-doctorate, less than two years after a PhD thesis on 1 September of the year of application.

Publications: *Annales de la Fondation Fyssen.*

Board of Directors: Daniel Lallier (Pres.).

Principal Staff: Man. Dir Genevieve Chertier.

Address: 194 rue de Rivoli, 75001 Paris.

Telephone: 1-42-97-53-16; **Fax:** 1-42-60-17-95; **Internet:** www.fondationfyssen.fr; **e-mail:** secretariat@fondation-fyssen.org.

Fondation Groupama Gan pour le Cinéma (Groupama Gan Foundation for the Cinema)

Established in 1987 to safeguard the cinematographic heritage and promote the production of full-length feature films by new cinematographers.

Activities: Operates in France and internationally, including Hungary, Italy and Portugal, to promote cinema and the audio-visual arts through film restoration, supporting the work of new film-makers, offering financial assistance for the distribution of films, sponsoring French film festivals and awarding prizes. Also provides financial support to the Max Linder Panorama cinema in Paris.

Geographical Area of Activity: Mainly France.

Publications: Newsletter.

Principal Staff: Delegates-Gen. Gilles Duval, Dominique Hoff.

Address: 8–10 rue d'Astorg, 75383 Paris Cedex 08.

Telephone: 1-44-56-32-06; **Fax:** 1-44-56-86-39; **Internet:** www.fondation-groupama-gan.com.

Fondation Hugot du Collège de France (Hugot Foundation of the Collège of France)

Founded in 1979 by the Collège de France to foster scientific and cultural exchange.

Activities: Operates internationally in the fields of science and medicine, the arts and humanities, religious studies, international relations and the conservation of natural resources, through grants to institutions, research,

FRANCE

conferences and publications, and by arranging for scholars from abroad to teach at the Collège de France.

Geographical Area of Activity: International.

Governing Board: André Miquel (Pres.); J. Thuillier (Vice-Pres.); J. Bachelot (Sec.); François Bloch-Lainé (Treas.).

Principal Staff: Dir Jean-Pierre de Morant.

Address: 11 rue de l'Université, 75007 Paris.

Telephone: 1-42-96-04-22; **Internet:** www.college-de-france .fr; **e-mail:** f.terrasse-riou@college-de-france.fr.

Fondation Nicolas Hulot pour la Nature et l'Homme
(Foundation Nicolas Hulot for Nature and Humankind)

Since its creation in 1990, the Foundation has devoted itself to educating people to change individual and collective behaviours, with the objective of preserving the planet. A member of the International Union for Conservation of Nature and acts as a non-governmental adviser to the Economic and Social Council of the UN.

Activities: Aims to encourage citizens to adopt eco-friendly habits on a daily basis; have an influence on the political and economic decision-makers and encourage them to take action; support projects in France and around the world. Also aims to bring about changes in daily behaviour to develop a new way of thinking and a culture based on sustainable development.

Geographical Area of Activity: France, Madagascar, Morocco, Romania, Senegal.

Finance: Receives funding from EDF, IBIS, L'Oréal and TF1.

Board: Nicolas Hulot (Pres.); Henri Rouille d'Orfeuil (Vice-Pres.); André Jean Guérin (Treas.).

Principal Staff: Dir-Gen. Cécile Ostria.

Address: 6 rue de l'Est, 92100 Boulogne-Billancourt.

Telephone: 1-41-22-10-70; **Fax:** 1-41-22-10-99; **Internet:** www .fondation-nicolas-hulot.org.

Fondation Internationale pour la Gestion de la Faune—IGF (International Foundation for the Conservation of Wildlife)

Founded in 1976, and known until 1990 as the Fondation Internationale pour la Sauvegarde du Gibier, to contribute throughout the world towards conservation of wildlife and of nature in all its forms and aspects, and to help to promote the rational and reasonable harvesting of national and international game populations to ensure their survival and their development for the benefit of humanity.

Activities: Operates internationally in the field of conservation of natural resources, through self-conducted programmes, research, grants to institutions and individuals, fellowships, scholarships, conferences, courses, publications and lectures. The Foundation co-operates in particular with the International Council for Game and Wildlife Conservation (CIC) and puts itself at the disposal of governments to study ways of improving legislation pertaining to hunting and wildlife conservation. The Foundation has a 'sister' Foundation in Switzerland that shares the same title, President, Director and Treasurer, but has a different Board of Directors. In practice it is the French Foundation that decides on action, while the Swiss Foundation is mainly a financial body, trustee of the majority of the French body's funds. The following details refer to the French Foundation.

Geographical Area of Activity: International.

Publications: *African Wildlife: the Forgotten Resource; Proceedings of the International Symposium and Conference on Wildlife Management in Sub-Saharan Africa and Sustainable economic benefits and contribution towards rural development;* and numerous other reports and publications.

Finance: Annual budget approx. US $300,000.

Board of Directors: Yves Burrus (Pres.); Eric Turquin (Sec.); Charles de Bagneux (Treas.).

Principal Staff: Dirs Phillipe Chardonnet, Herbert Boulet.

Address: 15 rue de Téhéran, 75008 Paris.

Telephone: 1-45-63-51-33; **Fax:** 1-45-63-32-94; **Internet:** www.wildlife-conservation.org; **e-mail:** igf@fondation-igf.fr.

Fondation Internationale Léon Mba—Institut de Médecine et d'Epidémiologie Appliquée (International Foundation Léon Mba—Institute of Applied Medicine and Epidemiology)

Founded in 1967 by the Governments of France and Gabon, according to the wishes of Léon Mba, then President of Gabon, to promote, within the framework of the activities of the Hôpital Claude-Bernard, the progress of tropical medicine for the benefit of the populations of Black Africa.

Activities: Operates internationally in the fields of education, and science and medicine, through self-conducted programmes, research, grants to individuals, fellowships and scholarships, conferences, courses, publications and lectures. Organizes annual courses in tropical medicine and epidemiology, and related disciplines, conducted by a specialized staff of French and foreign professors.

Geographical Area of Activity: France, Africa.

Administrative Council: Prof. Pierre-Marie Girard (Pres.).

Principal Staff: Dir-Gen. Prof. Jacques Le Bras.

Address: Faculté de Médecine Paris 7 – site Xavier Bichat, Département de Santé Tropicale, 16 rue Henri Huchard, 75018 Paris.

Telephone: 1-57-27-78-12; **Internet:** www.imea.fr; **e-mail:** imea@univ-paris-diderot.fr.

Fondation de Lourmarin Laurent-Vibert (Foundation Robert Laurent-Vibert)

Founded in 1927 by the Académie des Sciences, Agriculture, Arts et Belles Lettres d'Aix, according to the will of Robert Laurent-Vibert, with the aim of promoting literature and the arts.

Activities: Provides grants in the field of the arts and humanities, and invites annually six to eight artists and scholars of French and other nationalities to spend one month as guests at the Castle of Lourmarin. Conducts seminars on the national and international aspects of education, social welfare, the arts and conservation. Programmes are also carried out through lectures, concerts, plays and exhibitions, including the 'Musiques d'été à Lourmarin' music festival. More recently, has widened its areas of interest to include the natural and social sciences, and collaborates in this field with the Académie des Sciences, Agriculture, Arts et Belles Lettres d'Aix.

Geographical Area of Activity: France.

Restrictions: Artists must be younger than 35 years of age.

Publications: Annual Report.

Principal Staff: Curator D. Antonelli; Man. J. Mead.

Address: Château de Lourmarin, BP 23, 84160 Lourmarin.

Telephone: 4-90-68-15-23; **Fax:** 4-90-68-25-19; **Internet:** www.chateau-de-lourmarin.com; **e-mail:** contact@chateau -de-lourmarin.com.

Fondation MACIF (MACIF Foundation)

Established in 1993 by the MACIF non-profit insurance company to support organizations working to better the social economy in France and the rest of Europe.

Activities: Supports the creation of social economy initiatives, including co-operatives and mutual associations, which are independent of the state and not for personal profit.

Geographical Area of Activity: France and Western Europe.

Board: Alain Philippe (Pres.).

Principal Staff: Sec.-Gen. Serge Bonnet.

Address: 64 rue René Boulanger, 75010 Paris.

Telephone: 1-40-40-53-75; **Fax:** 1-40-40-35-14; **Internet:** www.fondation-macif.fr.

Fondation Marguerite et Aimé Maeght (Marguerite and Aimé Maeght Foundation)

Founded in 1964 by Marguerite and Aimé Maeght to acquire, preserve and exhibit contemporary art.

Activities: Operates nationally and internationally in the field of modern art, through exhibitions, permanent collections, conferences and publications. Presents exhibitions of contemporary art in its museum in Saint-Paul and exhibits its collections, including works by Braque, Giacometti, Kandinsky, Bonnard, Chagall, Calder, Miró, etc., abroad. Operates a library with documentation on various aspects of modern art, and a bookshop.

Geographical Area of Activity: Europe, the USA, Africa and Asia.

Publications: Catalogue and posters published to coincide with exhibitions.

Finance: Financed privately.

Trustees: A. Maeght (Chair.); P. Laffitte (Treas.).

Principal Staff: Dir Michel Enrici.

Address: 06570 Saint-Paul.

Telephone: 4-93-32-81-63; **Fax:** 4-93-32-53-22; **Internet:** www.fondation-maeght.com; **e-mail:** contact@fondation-maeght.com.

Fondation MAIF (MAIF Foundation)

Established in 1989 by the Mutuelle Assurance des Instituteurs de France (mutual insurance company for primary school teachers) to promote technological improvements working towards an improved quality of life and an increase in safety.

Activities: Operates internationally in safety and risk prevention, promoting collaboration between local government, universities and research institutions, NGOs and industry, focusing on young people at risk and on traffic safety. Supports research, the establishment of a research institute and a database, offers prizes and research grants, issues publications and promotes conferences, meetings and the dissemination of information.

Geographical Area of Activity: International.

Finance: Annual income €14,562,822, expenditure €14,562,822 (2009).

Administrative Council: Pierre Guillot (Pres.); Christophe Lafond (Sec.); Alain Isambert (Treas.).

Principal Staff: Sec.-Gen. Bernard Benoist.

Address: Le Pavois, 50 ave Salvador Allende, 79000 Niort.

Telephone: 5-49-73-87-04; **Fax:** 5-49-73-87-03; **Internet:** www.fondation.maif.fr; **e-mail:** contact@fondation.maif.fr.

Fondation de la Maison de la Chimie (Chemistry Centre Foundation)

Founded in 1927 on the occasion of the centenary of the birth of Marcelin Berthelot to contribute to the advancement of chemical science in the widest sense and the development of its applications, by promoting exchanges among scholars, technicians and industrialists of all countries.

Activities: The Centre makes available its lecture rooms, technical facilities and professional staff to French, foreign and international organizations to enable them to expand their mutual relations. It accommodates permanently institutions operating in the field of chemistry and provides lodging facilities for participants in the meetings and conferences it sponsors. The Foundation co-operates with other institutions in arranging scientific, cultural, professional and educational events. Also makes a biennial award of €30,000 to recognize original work in chemistry of benefit to society, mankind or nature.

Geographical Area of Activity: France.

Administrative Council: Bernard Bigot (Pres.); Danièle Olivier (Vice-Pres.); Jean-Bernard Borfiga (Vice-Pres.); Henri Dugert (Sec.); Henri Baquiast (Treas.).

Principal Staff: Gen. Sec. Jacques Hui.

Address: 28 rue Saint Dominique, 75007 Paris.

Telephone: 1-40-62-27-18; **Fax:** 1-40-62-95-21; **Internet:** www.maisondelachimie.asso.fr; **e-mail:** presidence@maisondelachimie.com.

Fondation Maison des Sciences de l'Homme—FMSH (Foundation House of the Social Sciences)

Founded in 1963 to promote the study of human societies.

Activities: Operates internationally in the fields of the humanities and social sciences, through research, publications, exchange of scientific information and a library (of 140,000 volumes and 1,800 current periodicals).

Geographical Area of Activity: International.

Finance: Financed through public and private donations.

Board of Directors: Ronan Stephan (Dir-Gen.).

Principal Staff: Admin. Michel Wieviorka; Sec.-Gen. Nicolas Catzaras.

Address: 54 blvd Raspail, 75270 Paris Cedex 06.

Telephone: 1-49-54-20-30; **Fax:** 1-49-54-21-33; **Internet:** www.msh-paris.fr; **e-mail:** andriap@msh-paris.fr.

Fondation Méditerranéenne d'Etudes Stratégiques—FMES (Mediterranean Foundation of Strategic Studies)

Established in 1989 to promote strategic studies in all areas of Mediterranean affairs.

Activities: Operates in the areas of education, scientific research and information, organizing conferences, seminars and international meetings, conducting research, organizing training, and publishing and disseminating information. Also participates in international networking activities.

Geographical Area of Activity: Mediterranean area.

Publications: *La Collection Stradedem*; *Memoires des Auditeurs des Sessions Méditeranénnes*.

Board of Directors: Jacques Lanxade (Pres.); André Added; Roger Peiffer (Vice-Pres.); Jean Banivello (Sec.); Gérard Masurel (Treas.).

Principal Staff: Dir-Gen. Pierre Lasserre.

Address: Maison des technologies, pl. Georges Pompidou, 83000 Toulon.

Telephone: 4-94-05-55-55; **Fax:** 4-94-03-89-45; **Internet:** www.fmes-france.org; **e-mail:** info@fmes-france.org.

Fondation Mérieux (Mérieux Foundation)

Founded in 1967 by Dr Charles Merieux to promote research and education in biology, immunology, epidemiology and individual and collective prevention.

Activities: Operates nationally and internationally in the fields of medical and veterinary research, education, social welfare and aid to less-developed countries, through self-conducted programmes of research, grants to institutions and individuals, scholarships to overseas candidates, conferences and publications. The Foundation is closely involved with the Institut pour le Développement de l'Epidémiologie Appliquée (Annecy), the Association pour la Médecine Préventive (in conjunction with the Pasteur Foundation), and Bioforce (a training programme for polyvalent health auxiliaries).

Geographical Area of Activity: International.

Publications: *Collection fondation Mérieux*.

Board of Directors: Alain Mérieux (Pres.); Dr David Heymann (Vice-Pres.); Sophie Mérieux (Sec.); Didier Cherpitel (Treas.).

Principal Staff: Dir-Gen. Benoît Miribel.

Address: 17 rue Bourgelat, 69002 Lyon.

Telephone: 4-72-40-79-79; **Fax:** 4-72-40-79-50; **Internet:** www.fondation-merieux.org; **e-mail:** fondation.lyon@fondation-merieux.org.

Fondation Mondiale Recherche et Prévention SIDA
(World Foundation for AIDS Research and Prevention)

Established in 1993 by Luc Montagnier and Federico Mayor, UNESCO Dir-Gen., to assist in efforts to combat AIDS and to mobilize the private sector. Also known as the Fondation mondiale pour la recherche contre le SIDA—World Foundation for AIDS Research and Prevention.

Activities: Operates internationally, in close co-operation with UNESCO, in the area of AIDS research and prevention, to promote global awareness and humanitarian concern; to develop research by opening four research centres in Europe, Africa, Asia and the USA; to help developing countries acquire indigenous capacities in building national AIDS programmes (including preventative education and assistance to AIDS orphans); and to promote networking among scientists and the twinning of universities within developing countries and between developed and developing countries.

Geographical Area of Activity: International.

Principal Staff: Pres. Prof. Luc Montagnier.

Address: c/o UNESCO, 1 rue Miollis, 75732 Paris Cedex 15.

Telephone: 1-45-68-38-41; **Fax:** 1-42-73-37-45; **Internet:** erc .unesco.org/ong/fr/directory/ong_desc .asp?mode=gn&code=1459
e-mail: c.restif@unesco.org; .

Fondation Marc de Montalembert
(Marc de Montalembert Foundation)

Established in 1994 in memory of Marc de Montalembert; operates under the aegis of the Fondation de France (q.v.).

Activities: Aims to provide opportunities to young people from Mediterranean countries to experience other cultures, through scholarships and grants in the fields of literature, architecture, music, photography and singing, and through the organization of discussion forums on themes relating to peace and tolerance among Mediterranean countries. Maintains a dialogue centre in Rhodes, Greece.

Geographical Area of Activity: Mediterranean countries.

Address: c/o Fondation de France, 40 ave Hoche, 75008 Paris.

Internet: www.fondationmdm.com; **e-mail:** montalembert@ foundationmdm.com.

Fondation Nationale pour l'Enseignement de la Gestion des Entreprises (French National Foundation for Management Education)

Founded in 1968 by the Conseil National du Patronat Français, the Assemblée Permanente des Chambres de Commerce et d'Industrie and the State to promote management education in France.

Activities: Operates nationally and internationally in the field of management education, in five basic areas: promotion of stronger ties between education and industry; training and improvement of management teachers; updating of the curricula of management training institutions; development of management institutions; and promotion of French management education abroad. Operates through research, grants both to institutions and individuals, scholarships, conferences, courses, seminars and publications.

Geographical Area of Activity: International.

Finance: Financed by French public authorities and businesses.

Administrative Council: Michel Bon (Pres.).

Principal Staff: Delegate-Gen. Pierre-Louis Dubois.

Address: 2 ave Hoche, 75008 Paris.

Telephone: 1-44-29-93-60; **Fax:** 1-47-54-05-99; **Internet:** www.fnege.org; **e-mail:** info@fnege.fr.

Fondation Nationale des Sciences Politiques (National Foundation for Political Sciences)

Founded in 1945 by government ordinance to succeed the École Libre des Sciences Politiques (founded in 1872), to foster the progress and diffusion of the political, economic and social sciences in France and abroad.

Activities: Operates internationally in the fields of political, economic and social sciences, and international relations, through research, teaching, publications and documentation services. Conducts research into: international relations; political life in France; economic activity; social affairs; contemporary European history; economic conditions; American studies; and social change. Documentation services comprise a social science library of more than 620,000 books and 6,000 periodicals, and compiling and keeping a documentation centre maintaining around 16,000 press-cuttings files since 1945. The Foundation also administers the Institut d'Études Politiques de Paris, assists the research and documentation activities of the Institutes of Political Studies at Grenoble and Bordeaux and owns publisher Presses de Sciences Po.

Geographical Area of Activity: France.

Publications: *Revue française de science politique* (6 a year, jointly with the Association Française de Science Politique); *Critique Internationale* (quarterly); *Raisons Politique* (quarterly); *Revue économique* (6 a year); *Vingtième Siècle—Histoire* (quarterly); *Revue de l'OFCE* (quarterly); books and research monographs in the social sciences and history published by the Presses de Sciences Politiques.

Board of Directors: Jean-Claude Casanova (Pres.).

Principal Staff: Dir Richard Descoings.

Address: 27 rue Saint-Guillaume, 75007 Paris Cedex 07.

Telephone: 1-45-49-50-50; **Fax:** 1-42-22-31-26; **Internet:** www.sciences-po.fr; **e-mail:** cyril.delhay@sciences-po.fr.

Fondation Orange (Orange Foundation)

Established in 1987 as Fondation d'Entreprise France Telecom.

Activities: Operates in France and internationally in emerging countries. Supports music (particularly singing), through sponsoring training, concerts, and festivals for talented vocalists; finances specialized development and training for professional staff to care for people suffering from autism; supports projects aimed at promoting socially relevant uses of the Internet; and in emerging countries supports literacy projects for girls.

Geographical Area of Activity: France and international.

Principal Staff: Chair. Didier Lombard.

Address: 6 pl. d'Alleray, 75505 Paris Cedex 15.

Telephone: 1-44-44-89-63; **Fax:** 1-44-44-00-96; **Internet:** www.francetelecom.com/en_EN/corporate_philanthropy/ foundation; **e-mail:** la.fondation@francetelecom.com.

Fondation du Patrimoine (Heritage Foundation)

Created in 1996 with the mission to defend and value threatened heritage sites not protected by the State.

Activities: Acts as an umbrella organization bringing together private and corporate funders to protect heritage sites in France, including unprotected heritage, natural or landscaped areas of interest, and architectural sites, and funding the restoration of buildings not covered by State subsidies.

Geographical Area of Activity: France.

Board of Directors: Charles de Croisset (Chair.); Bertrand de Feydeau (Vice-Pres.); Dominique Leger (Vice-Pres.).

Principal Staff: Dir-Gen. Frederic Neraud.

Address: 23–25 rue Charles Fourier, 75013 Paris.

Telephone: 1-53-67-76-00; **Fax:** 1-40-70-11-70; **Internet:** www .fondation-patrimoine.com; **e-mail:** info@fondation -patrimoine.com.

Fondation Claude Pompidou (Claude Pompidou Foundation)

Established in 1970 at the instigation of Claude Pompidou to help children with disabilities, elderly people and people in hospital.

Activities: The Foundation supports projects helping children with disabilities, elderly people and people in hospital, as well as establishing residential homes and centres. Other current Foundation projects include an initiative to help elderly hospitalized people return home.

Geographical Area of Activity: France.

Administrative Council: Bernadette Chirac (Pres.); Jocelin de Rohan (Sec.); Bernard Esambert (Treas.).

Principal Staff: Dir-Gen. Richard Hutin.

Address: 42 rue de Louvre, 75001 Paris.

Telephone: 1-40-13-75-00; **Fax:** 1-40-13-75-19; **Internet:** www.fondationclaudepompidou.asso.fr; **e-mail:** direction.fcp@club-internet.fr.

Fondation 'Pour la Science'—Centre International de Synthèse (Foundation for International Scientific Co-ordination)

Founded in 1924 by Henri Berr to encourage liaison between different scientific disciplines, and to develop and co-ordinate research and contacts among experts and researchers.

Activities: The Centre holds international conferences for scientists of different disciplines, and issues scientific publications.

Geographical Area of Activity: France.

Publications: *Revue de Synthèse; Revue d'Histoire des Sciences; Semaines de Synthèse; L'Evolution de l'Humanité* (series).

Administrative Council: Jochen Hoock (Pres.).

Principal Staff: Dir Éric Brian.

Address: 45 rue d'Ulm, 75005 Paris.

Telephone: 1-55-42-83-11; **Fax:** 1-55-42-83-19; **Internet:** www.revue-de-synthese.eu; **e-mail:** eric.brian@ens.fr.

Fondation pour la Recherche Médicale (Foundation for Medical Research)

Founded by Prof. Jean Hamburger, Prof. Jean Bernard and Dr C. Escoffier-Lambiotte in 1947 to promote all forms of scientific medical research, in particular research connected with the basic biological sciences related to medicine, and to co-ordinate these endeavours.

Activities: Operates exclusively in the field of medicine and the biological sciences on a national and international basis. Awards grants to individuals and institutions especially in France, through grants to young researchers and to laboratories. Subsidizes study abroad and assists the purchase of scientific equipment. Also publishes *Recherche & Santé* (mainly for its donors), organizes conferences, lectures and exhibitions, and maintains regional committees. Major annual awards include the Rosen Prize for Cancer Research, and a number of other prizes for research in molecular biology, endocrinology, immunology, infectiology, clinical investigation, neurobiology, nephrology and cancer. Awards special prizes in the field of scientific communication.

Geographical Area of Activity: France.

Publications: Report of activities; *Recherche & Santé* (quarterly).

Board of Directors: Jacques Bourrier (Pres.).

Principal Staff: Pres. Denis Le Squer.

Address: 54 rue de Varenne, 75335 Paris Cedex 07.

Telephone: 1-44-39-75-75; **Fax:** 1-44-39-75-99; **Internet:** www.frm.org; **e-mail:** cnil@frm.org.

Fondation pour la Recherche Stratégique (Foundation for Strategic Research)

Established by a number of French companies and by the merger of the Fondation pour les Études de Défense and the Centre de Recherche sur les Stratégies et les Technologies to conduct politico-military research.

Activities: Conducts research into strategic issues, essentially in three areas: the politics of defence, technological and security issues, and the nature of crises and conflicts. Maintains a documentation centre and library.

Geographical Area of Activity: France.

Publications: Essays and occasional papers.

Administrative Council: Bruno Racine (Pres.); Alain Coldefy (Vice-Pres.); Bernard Zeller (Treas.).

Principal Staff: Dir Camille Grand; Sec.-Gen. Alexandre Houdayer.

Address: 27 rue Damesme, 75013 Paris.

Telephone: 1-43-13-77-77; **Fax:** 1-43-13-77-78; **Internet:** www.frstrategie.org; **e-mail:** webmaster@frstrategie.org.

Fondation Ripaille (Ripaille Foundation)

Founded in 1976 by Mrs Harold Necker to promote the use of the Château de Ripaille, ancient residence of Duke Amédée VIII of Savoy, as a centre for study, meditation, work, training and cultural exchange in ecology, human and physical geography, and the conscientious development of resources and the environment, particularly in the most underprivileged areas and countries.

Activities: Lakes, inland waterways and coastlines are studied, as well as the problems of mountainous regions, with particular attention being paid to Lake Geneva. The centre organizes exchanges between the institutions and associations concerned at regional, national and international levels. It also organizes colloquia, seminars and congresses, exhibitions, tours and conferences; and holds cultural, artistic, historical or scientific events or meetings. The centre offers facilities for receptions.

Geographical Area of Activity: International.

Address: Château de Ripaille, 74200 Thonon-les-Bains.

Telephone: 4-50-26-64-44; **Fax:** 4-50-26-54-74; **Internet:** www.ripaille.fr/fondation.html; **e-mail:** fondation@ripaille.fr.

Fondation Scelles (Scelles Foundation)

Established in 1993 by Jean and Jeanne Scelles to campaign against all forms of sexual exploitation and assist the victims of sexual violence.

Activities: Operates nationally and internationally in the field of human rights in three areas: collecting information for the Centre of International Research and Documentation on Sexual Exploitation database; giving grants to organizations assisting victims of sexual violence; and providing information to the public and the media on sexual exploitation through its publications.

Geographical Area of Activity: World-wide.

Publications: Newsletter; Annual Report.

Trustees: Philippe Scelles (Hon. Pres.); Yves Charpenell (Pres.).

Principal Staff: Sec.-Gen. Hubert de Roux.

Address: 14 rue Mondétour, 75001 Paris.

Telephone: 1-40-26-04-45; **Fax:** 1-40-26-04-58; **Internet:** www.fondationscelles.org; **e-mail:** fondationscelles@wanadoo.fr.

Fondation Schneider Electric (Schneider Electric Foundation)

Created by Schneider Electric SA in 1998 under the aegis of the Fondation de France (q.v.) to help the development of young people. Formerly known as Fondation Schneider Electric pour l'Insertion des Jeunes.

Activities: In partnership with local NGOs, supports projects involving young people (under 30 years old) in the areas of culture, society, sport, the environment and creative enterprise. Helps young people to find employment by supporting Schneider Electric employees who wish to donate their time to training and imparting advice. Works internationally, helping orphans, improving health care access, providing education and training for under-achieving young people, rewards young entrepreneurs, supporting disabled children and working to eliminate violence against young people. Particularly focuses on projects in areas around Schneider Electric's sites, as well as operating international campaigns to promote the development of young people. Awarded the Oscar Admical du Mécénat d'entreprise in 2003.

Geographical Area of Activity: World-wide.

Principal Staff: Chair. Jean-Pascal Tricoire.

Address: c/o Schneider Electric SA, 35 rue Joseph Monier, 92500 Rueil Malmaison.

Telephone: 1-41-29-70-00; **Fax:** 1-41-29-71-00; **Internet:** www.schneider-electric.fr; **e-mail:** fr-webmaster-info@schneider-electric.com.

Fondation Robert Schuman (Robert Schuman Foundation)

Founded in 1991 after the fall of the Berlin Wall, works to promote the construction of Europe. A reference research centre, it develops studies on the European Union and its policies promoting their findings in France, Europe and internationall. Encourages, contributes to and stimulates European debate thanks to the wealth of its research, publications and the organization of conferences. Based in Paris and Brussels.

Activities: Produces high-level studies on European policies. Organizes and participates in numerous European and international meetings and conferences. Develops research programmes in co-operation with university centres and think-tanks.

Geographical Area of Activity: Europe.

Publications: *La Lettre de la Fondation Robert Schuman* (weekly electronic newsletter); *Notes de la Fondation Robert Schuman* (hard copy); *Observatoire des Elections en Europe* (electronic publication); *The State of the Union, Schuman Report on Europe* (annual); *The European Opinion* (annual); *EUscope* (app. for iPhone/iPad).

Trustees: Jean-Dominique Giuliani (Chair.); **Multinational Scientific Committee:** Alain Lancelot (Chair.).

Principal Staff: Gen. Man. Pascale Joannin; Studies Dir Thierry Chopin.

Address: 29 blvd Raspail, 75007 Paris.

Telephone: 1-53-63-83-00; **Fax:** 1-53-63-83-01; **Internet:** www.robert-schuman.eu; **e-mail:** info@robert-schuman.eu.

Fondation René Seydoux pour le Monde Méditerranéen (René Seydoux Foundation for the Mediterranean World)

Founded in 1978 by Geneviève René Seydoux with the aim of perpetuating René Seydoux's conviction that the Mediterranean countries share a common culture, and that dialogue between all peoples is vital.

Activities: The Foundation aims to help unite countries on both sides of the Mediterranean by organizing, encouraging and facilitating actions that bring people together. The Foundation supports several partnership projects with other independent organizations working towards the same goal. It collects information on the Mediterranean and it manages a database of organizations and journals in this field. It also offers advice and support to those developing cultural projects.

Geographical Area of Activity: European and Mediterranean countries.

Publications: *Mediterranean Directory* (online database).

Board: Jérôme Seydoux (Pres.).

Principal Staff: Delegate-Gen. Giovanna Tanzarella.

Address: 21 rue du Sommerard, 75005 Paris.

Telephone: 1-53-10-24-34; **Fax:** 1-53-10-87-12; **Internet:** www.fondation-seydoux.org; **e-mail:** fondation-seydoux@fondation-seydoux.org.

Fondation Singer-Polignac (Singer-Polignac Foundation)

Founded in 1928 by Princess Edmond de Polignac (née Singer) to promote science, literature, art and general culture in France.

Activities: Operates in the fields of science, the arts, humanities and the conservation of natural resources, awarding grants, scholarships and prizes to individuals and institutions in France. Also publishes reports on works undertaken under its auspices and organizes lectures, conferences and concerts.

Geographical Area of Activity: France.

Publications: Letters.

Board of Directors: Yves Pouliquen (Pres.); Yves Laporte (Vice-Pres.).

Principal Staff: Admin. and Finance Dir Olivier Le Gal.

Address: 43 ave Georges-Mandel, 75116 Paris.

Telephone: 1-47-27-38-66; **Fax:** 1-53-70-99-60; **Internet:** www.singer-polignac.org; **e-mail:** infos@singer-polignac.org.

Fondation Teilhard de Chardin (Teilhard de Chardin Foundation)

Founded in 1964 by Jeanne Mortier to preserve and disseminate the thought of Pierre Teilhard de Chardin (1881–1955) by the conservation and classification of his manuscripts and writings; the publication of his unpublished works; the defence of his thought against misinterpretation and of his texts against misuse; the collection of all documents and studies about him; the provision of facilities for the study of his works; the running of seminars, discussions and conferences; and the publication of accounts of these activities.

Activities: Operates internationally in those fields covered by the thought of Teilhard de Chardin, especially religion and science, philosophy and education, but also social welfare and studies, humanities and international relations. The Association des Amis de P. Teilhard de Chardin, under the Foundation, runs study centres in many countries throughout the world; these centres have their own meetings, publications, courses and lectures.

Geographical Area of Activity: International.

Publications: Annual Report; the complete works of Teilhard de Chardin (in progress); *Cahiers*.

Board of Directors: Henry de Lumley (Pres.); Maurice Ernst (Treas.).

Principal Staff: Admin. Delegate Maurice Ernst; Sec.-Gen. Anne Dambricourt-Malasse.

Address: 38 rue Geoffroy-Saint-Hilaire, 75005 Paris.

Telephone: 1-43-31-18-55; **Fax:** 1-43-31-01-15; **Internet:** www.mnhn.fr/teilhard; **e-mail:** teilhard@mnhn.fr.

Fondation Total (Total Foundation)

Founded in 1992 by TOTAL, an international oil and gas company.

Activities: Funds research, organizes campaigns, and provides support to further the preservation of marine biodiversity, particularly within the areas of islands, coral reefs and wetlands. The Foundation's actions include partnerships with Port-Cros National Park and Porquerolles Botanical Conservation Centre, WWF Indonesia, a world-wide long-term programme on coral reefs, and several others. Includes the Atlantic Coast Fund, set up by the Foundation as part of a programme to restore the ecosystems on the French Atlantic coast.

Geographical Area of Activity: International.

Publications: Activités Report; *Le corail et les récifs coralliens* (book); *La France Marine* (book); *Ecological maps of the French coast* (maps); leaflets.

Finance: Annual disbursements €12,000,000 (2010).

Board of Directors: Thierry Desmarest (Pres.); Jean-François Minster (Sr Vice-Pres.).

Principal Staff: Delegate-Gen. Catherine Ferrant.

Address: 2 place Jean Millier, 92400 Courbevoie.

Internet: www.fondation.total.com; **e-mail:** fondation.total@total.com.

Fondation 30 Millions d'Amis (30 Million Friends Foundation)

Established in 1995 by Jean-Pierre Hutin to promote respect for and protection of animals.

Activities: Operates nationally and internationally to protect animals. Makes grants to centres for abandoned animals, provides food supplies and veterinary support for the treatment, vaccination and sterilization of animals. Campaigns against experimentation on animals, and for the protection of animals close to extinction. Runs an online animal adoption service and database of animal protection organizations.

Geographical Area of Activity: International.

Publications: Newsletter; magazine.

Principal Staff: Pres. Reha Hutin.

Address: 40 cours Albert 1er, 75402 Paris Cedex 08.

Telephone: 1-56-59-04-44; **Fax:** 1-58-56-33-55; **Internet:** www.30millionsdamis.fr; **e-mail:** mabrouk@30millionsdamis.fr.

Fonds Européen pour la Jeunesse—FEJ (European Youth Foundation—EYF)

Founded in 1972 by the Council of Europe to provide financial support to international youth activities undertaken by non-governmental national or international youth organizations and networks.

Activities: Funds youth meetings (category A), youth activities other than meetings (category B), administrative costs of international youth organizations and networks (category C) and pilot projects (category D). The Foundation has contributed financially towards activities connected with the European youth campaign against racism, xenophobia, anti-Semitism and intolerance. A special Solidarity Fund for Youth Mobility has been created, a joint venture by the International Union of Railways and the Council of Europe, to assist disadvantaged young people with the cost of rail travel when attending international activities.

Geographical Area of Activity: Europe.

Restrictions: No grants to individuals.

Finance: Finance provided by the Foundation's 46 member governments. Annual budget €3,000,000.

Principal Staff: Principal Admin. Jean-Claude Lazaro; Admin. Karen Palisser.

Address: 30 rue Pierre de Coubertin, 67000 Strasbourg.

Telephone: 3-88-41-20-19; **Fax:** 3-90-21-49-64; **Internet:** www.eyf.coe.int/fej; **e-mail:** eyf@coe.int.

Forum International de l'Innovation Sociale—FIIS (International Forum for Social Innovation—IFSI)

Founded in 1976 to promote social innovation and institutional transformation in private and public institutions.

Activities: Encourages meetings, studies and exchange of information, and the implementation of projects; disseminates information; organizes workshops and seminars; organizes international working conferences on institutional transformation; maintains an information centre on social innovation projects.

Geographical Area of Activity: International.

Publications: *FIIS-IFSI Annual Agenda.*

Board of Directors: ÉLouise Edberg (Pres.); Leonardo Veneziani (Treas.).

Principal Staff: Exec. Vice-Pres. David Gutmann.

Address: 60 rue de Bellechasse, 75007 Paris.

Telephone: 1-45-41-39-49; **Fax:** 1-45-41-39-42; **Internet:** www.ifsi-fiis-conferences.com; **e-mail:** ifsi.fiis@wanadoo.fr.

France Amérique Latine—FAL (Latin America France)

Established in 1970 to support and provide aid to Central and South America.

Activities: Works to protect the cultural heritage of and support the people of Central and South America. Defends human rights by condemning violations of the rights of indigenous peoples and children within the region, and fighting discrimination regarding the image of the region throughout the rest of the world by holding conferences, debates, exhibitions and exchanges. Works to improve literacy and education, health care and sanitation, and provides emergency aid in Central and South America.

Geographical Area of Activity: Central and South America, France.

Publications: Newsletter; *FAL Magazine* (quarterly); *One Culture.*

Principal Staff: Pres. Sophie Thono-Wesfreid.

Address: 37 blvd Saint Jacques, 75014 Paris.

Telephone: 1-45-88-20-00; **Fax:** 1-45-65-20-87; **Internet:** www.franceameriquelatine.org; **e-mail:** falnationale@franceameriquelatine.fr.

France-Libertés Fondation Danielle Mitterrand (Danielle Mitterrand France-Liberty Foundation)

Founded in 1986 by Danielle Mitterrand to improve living standards for the less affluent in society, and to protect their human rights.

Activities: Operates internationally in the fields of human rights, the environment, racial discrimination, apartheid, AIDS, poverty and hunger. The Foundation supports numerous projects including the construction of housing for 'street children' and orphans in Peru, providing humanitarian aid for landless people in Brazil and equipment for a clinic working to prevent deafness in children in Senegal; it works to combat the marginalization of the disabled in Mauritania, organizes an AIDS information campaign and provides disposable syringes in Africa, and runs several education programmes in Cambodia and Bangladesh.

Geographical Area of Activity: International.

Publications: Annual Report; newsletter; *Olivier Unchained* (article).

Board of Directors: Danielle Mitterrand (Pres.); Claude Vercoutere (Vice-Pres); Alain Souvreneau (Treas.); Michel Joli (Sec.-Gen.).

Principal Staff: Dir Emmanuel Poilane.

Address: 22 rue de Milan, 75009 Paris.

Telephone: 1-53-25-10-40; **Fax:** 1-48-74-01-26; **Internet:** www.france-libertes.fr; **e-mail:** contact@france-libertes.fr.

France Nature Environnement

Established in 1968 to co-ordinate environmental protection and conservation nationally and internationally; operates as a national federation of around 3,000 associations for the protection of nature and the environment.

Activities: Operates in France and internationally in the field of conservation and the environment, through the dissemination of information on the state of the environment in the areas of scientific research, the conservation of fauna and flora and the protection of biodiversity. Established national networks concerned with biodiversity, agriculture, forestry, water, industrial production cycles, power, waste, development, transport and health.

Geographical Area of Activity: International.

Publications: Newsletter; *Lettre du Hérisson*; *La Lettre Eau*; *La Lettre des Sylves*; *La Voie du Loup*; *Le Blaireau et l'homme*; *Mettons les toxiques hors la loi*; *Les emballages utiles et inutiles*; *Dès aujourd'hui moins d'ordures pour les générations futures*; *Faites une fleur à votre environnement*; *Changement climatique: la nature menacée en France?*.

Finance: Annual income €1,634,987, expenditure €1,634,987 (2010).

Board of Directors: Bruno Genty (Pres.); Jean-Claude Bevillard, Michel Dubromel, Marc-William Millereau (Vice-Pres); Gael Virlouver (Treas.).

Address: 6 rue Dupanloup, 45000 Orléans.

Telephone: 2-38-62-44-48; **Fax:** 2-38-52-11-57; **Internet:** www.fne.asso.fr; **e-mail:** information@fne-asso.fr.

Frères des Hommes—FDH

Created in 1965, Frères des Hommes is an organization for international solidarity, working in the area of global development. It supports development projects that have been initiated and implemented by local populations in Africa, Asia, Latin America and the Caribbean to build long-term solutions to world poverty.

Activities: Operates world-wide to bring together local and international solidarity organizations to help combat global poverty. Intervenes mainly in favour of community-supported farming, community-based economy and civil democracy. In France, raises public awareness about the international issues of sustainable development.

Geographical Area of Activity: Africa, Asia, Latin America and the Caribbean.

Restrictions: Grants only made in partnership with specific organizations.

Publications: *Agir*; *Témoignages et Dossiers* (quarterly); *Résonances* (newsletter).

Finance: Annual budget approx. €2,900,000.

Board: Luc Michelon (Pres.); Anne-Marie Auvergne (Vice-Pres.); Claude Perseval (Sec.); Guy Chevreau (Treas.).

Principal Staff: Dir Yves Altazin.

Address: 9 rue de Savoie, 75006 Paris.

Telephone: 1-55-42-62-62; **Fax:** 1-43-29-99-77; **Internet:** www.fdh.org; **e-mail:** fdh@fdh.org.

Handicap International

Founded in 1982 in response to the needs of people with disabilities and war victims, seeking solutions adapted to the context using local resources.

Activities: Operates internationally in 60 countries. Supports programmes to meet the needs and defend the rights of people with disabilities. In countries affected by poverty, disasters and conflicts, Handicap International implements prevention, emergency relief and mine action projects, and provides long-term development support. Co-founder of the International Campaign to Ban Landmines, Handicap International is Co-Winner of the 1997 Nobel Peace Prize. It has consultative status with the the UN Economic and Social Council (ECOSOC). National sections operate in Belgium, Canada, France, Germany, Luxembourg, Switzerland, United Kingdom and USA.

Geographical Area of Activity: World-wide.

Publications: Newsletter (quarterly); technical publications; financial report; videos.

Principal Staff: Pres. Jacques Tassi; Gen. Man. and Co-Founder Jean-Baptiste Richardier.

Address: 14 ave Berthelot, 69361 Lyon Cedex 07.

Telephone: 4-78-69-79-79; **Fax:** 4-78-69-79-94; **Internet:** www.handicap-international.org; **e-mail:** contact@handicap-international.org.

Institut Néerlandais (Netherlands Institute)

Founded in 1956 by Frits and Jacoba Lugt to develop cultural relations between France and the Netherlands.

Activities: Organizes exhibitions, lectures, concerts and film/video presentations to present the culture of the Netherlands in France; study visits, language courses and exchanges are also arranged. Also mediates between French and Dutch cultural institutions and artists. The Institute has a library containing approximately 200,000 publications, mainly related to the arts.

Geographical Area of Activity: France and the Netherlands.

Trustees: H. H. Siblesz (Pres.); P. J. A. M. Nijnens (Vice-Pres.); J. Gielen (Treas.).

Principal Staff: Dir Rudi Wester; Deputy Dir Bas Berends.

Address: Centre culturel des Pays-Bas, 121 rue de Lille, 75007 Paris.

Telephone: 1-53-59-12-40; **Fax:** 1-45-56-00-77; **Internet:** www.institutneerlandais.com; **e-mail:** info@institutneerlandais.com.

Institut Océanographique—Fondation Albert 1er, Prince de Monaco (Oceanographic Institute—Albert 1st, Prince of Monaco Foundation)

Established in 1906 by Albert 1st, Prince of Monaco for the study and teaching of oceanographic science, and for knowledge of marine science to be transmitted to as many people as possible.

Activities: The Foundation comprises two institutions: the Institut Océanographique in Paris (also the headquarters of the Foundation); and the Musée Océanographique in Monaco. Supports exhibitions and maintains libraries at both centres.

Geographical Area of Activity: France and Monaco.

Publications: Books on marine science.

Trustees: Michel Petit (Pres.); Pierre Bordy (Vice-Pres.); Gerard Riou (Sec.-Treas.).

Principal Staff: Dir-Gen. Robert Calcagno.

Address: 195 rue Saint-Jacques, 75005 Paris.

Telephone: 1-44-32-10-70; **Fax:** 1-40-51-73-16; **Internet:** www.oceano.org; **e-mail:** institut@oceano.org.

Institut Pasteur (Pasteur Institute)

Founded in 1886 by Louis Pasteur and incorporated as a foundation in 1887 to promote research into infectious and parasitic diseases, including their prevention and treatment, and into immunity from disease; to further the study of microorganisms, including their role in natural processes, both normal and pathological, and the reactions they provoke; to further the study and teaching of all aspects of microbiology, as well as the training of scientific and technical staff in view of the growth of study into basic and applied microbiology; and to study all the theoretical and practical problems connected with microbiology and immunology or, more generally, with basic and applied biology.

Activities: Operates essentially in the field of microbiology and its related disciplines, through research, teaching, prevention and diagnosis of infectious and parasitic diseases. Maintains a large library at its headquarters and operates through 21 branches throughout the world. The work of several of its laboratories has been recognized as of great importance by the World Health Organization and they have accordingly been granted the status of regional, national or international centres. Has its own medical centre providing international vaccinations as well as specialized consultations (including allergies, tropical diseases and HIV).

Geographical Area of Activity: World-wide.

Publications: Annual Report; *Research in Microbiology* (10 a year); *Lettre de l'Institut Pasteur* (quarterly); *Annales de l'Institut Pasteur: Actualités* (quarterly); *Microbes and Infection* (15 a year); *Collections des Laboratoires de Références et d'expertise* (11-title series of technical publications).

Finance: Total income €250,400,000 (2010).

Board of Directors: Jean-Pierre Jouyet (Chair.); Daniel Louvard (Vice-Chair.); Bernard Guirkinger (Vice-Chair.); Guillaume Gaubert (Treas.); Alain Jacquier (Sec.).

Principal Staff: Pres. Alice Dautry; Sr Vice-Pres Anthony Pugsley, Christophe Mauriet.

Address: 25–28 rue du Docteur Roux, 75724 Paris Cedex 15.

Telephone: 1-45-68-80-00; **Fax:** 1-43-06-98-35; **Internet:** www.pasteur.fr; **e-mail:** info@pasteur.fr.

Institut Pasteur de Lille (Pasteur Institute of Lille)

Founded in 1899 by the City of Lille for biological and medical research, training and analysis.

Activities: The four main areas are biological research (developing vaccinations against diseases caused by parasites, particularly tropical diseases; molecular oncology); public health, including providing information; training; and medical analysis and toxicology. Awards are available for French and non-French researchers.

Geographical Area of Activity: France.

Board: Martine Aubry (Pres.); Jacques Richir (Vice-Pres.).

Principal Staff: Dir of Scientific Affairs Dr Camille Locht.

Address: 1 rue du Professeur Calmette, BP 245, 59019 Lille Cedex.

Telephone: 3-20-87-78-00; **Fax:** 3-20-87-79-06; **Internet:** www.pasteur-lille.fr; **e-mail:** webmaster@pasteur-lille.fr.

International Union for Health Promotion and Education—IUHPE

Founded in 1951 as an independent global association of professionals and organizations committed to world-wide health promotion and education.

Activities: The Union aims to promote global health and contribute to the achievement of equity in health, through advocacy, professional development, networking, partnership building and strengthening capacity. The Union has members in more than 90 countries, and works through seven decentralized regional offices (in Africa, Europe, North America, Northern part of the Western Pacific, South-West Pacific, and Central and South America and South-East Asia). It works closely with international organizations such as the World Health Organization, UNESCO and the UN Children s Fund (UNICEF) to influence and facilitate the development of health promotion strategies and projects. It organizes a World Conference on Health Promotion and Health Education every three years, and also regional conferences, seminars and workshops.

Geographical Area of Activity: World-wide.

Restrictions: This is not a grant-making organization.

Publications: *Promotion and Education* (quarterly, in English, French and Spanish); *Health Education Research* (official research journal of the IUHPE); *Health Promotion International* (an official journal of the IUHPE); research reports; electronic newsletter; conference reports, academic research and studies and information manuals.

Finance: Annual income €1,196,341, expenditure €1,193,332 (2009).

Board of Directors: Michael Sparks (Pres.).

Principal Staff: Exec. Dir Marie-Claude Lamarre; Programme Dir Catherine Jones.

Address: 42 blvd de la Libération, 93203 St-Denis Cedex.

Telephone: 1-48-13-71-20; **Fax:** 1-48-09-17-67; **Internet:** www.iuhpe.org; **e-mail:** iuhpe@iuhpe.org.

Médecins du Monde International (Doctors of the World International)

Established in 1980; aims to promote international solidarity through providing emergency health care and medical support internationally.

Activities: Operates in the field of medicine and health, sending voluntary doctors and other medical staff into areas of crisis and disaster to administer emergency aid and to provide necessary medical support. Also works to develop new approaches to health care in developing countries based on the principles of dignity and respect, works to improve standards and accessibility of public health facilities in less-developed regions, and promotes human rights and social justice.

Geographical Area of Activity: World-wide.

Publications: *Médecins du Monde* (journal); newletters; *Revue humanitaire*; rapport; film, documentaire; bulletins.

Trustees: Dr Olivier Bernard (Pres.); Dr Frederic Jacquet Dr Christophe Adam (Vice-Pres); Dr Patrick Beauverie (Sec-Gen.); Dr Thierry Brigaud (Treas.).

Principal Staff: Dir Int. Secretariat Alexandre Kamarotos.

Address: 62 rue Marcadet, 75018 Paris.

Telephone: 1-44-92-15-15; **Fax:** 1-44-92-14-55; **Internet:** www.medecinsdumonde.org; **e-mail:** international@medecinsdumonde.net.

Office International de l'Eau (International Office for Water)

Non-profit organization established in 1991 to promote improved water management throughout the world.

Activities: Operates internationally in the area of water conservation and the environment. Has established a International network of Basin organizations and other institutions involved in water resources management and protection. Also holds international conferences, trainning courses, exhibitions and symposia and produces a number of water-related publications and manage water data. In 2010 had 145 member organizations and may mobilize their expert to support project all around the world. develop a international Web portal in English, french, Spanish and Russian.

Geographical Area of Activity: World-wide.

Publications: *Information d'Eaux* (quarterly); *Newsletter* (annually); *Water International News* (annually).

Directors: Pierre Roussel (Pres.);.

Principal Staff: Man. Dir Jean-Francois Donzier.

Address: 21 rue de Madrid, 75008 Paris.

Telephone: 1-44-90-88-60; **Fax:** 1-40-08-01-45; **Internet:** www.iowater.org; **e-mail:** dg@oieau.fr.

Organisation Panafricaine de Lutte Contre le SIDA—OPALS (Pan-African Organization for AIDS Prevention)

Founded in 1988 to provide an information service and training for medical practitioners and scientists involved in trying to prevent the spread of AIDS, and caring for AIDS patients.

Activities: Assists the establishment of mobile day-care centres for the provision of care and support in Africa; encourages the adaptation of European preventive campaigns to suit different ways of life in Africa; provides assistance for the training of specialists, including those involved in community development; organizes workshops; supports media prevention campaigns. Works in collaboration with other international organizations.

Geographical Area of Activity: Africa and Europe.

Finance: The Foundation is financed by government grants, fundraising activities and private grants.

Administration Council: Prof. Marc Gentilini (Pres.); Prof. Dominique Richard-Lenoble (Sec.-Gen.).

Principal Staff: Exec. Dir Dr Claude Moncorgé.

Address: 15–21 rue de l'Ecole de Médecine, 75006 Paris.

Fax: 1-42-21-04-35; **Internet:** www.opals.asso.fr; **e-mail:** contact@opals.asso.fr.

Oxfam France

Oxfam France, created under the name Agir ici (Act here) in 1988, is a non-profit organization registered and based in France that works on the causes of poverty and injustice through advocacy and citizen mobilization campaigns. Part of the international confederation Oxfam International (q.v.).

Activities: Activities include campaigning, advocacy and mobilization comprising: high-level research and advocacy targeting economic and political decision-makers, towards respect of fundamental human rights; information and mobilization of the general public, through opinion campaigns, by highlighting the causes of global inequalities and by giving each citizen opportunities to act against injustice; proposal of concrete recommendations, such as new public policies or regulations, budget priorities and policies, signature of international agreements or the adoption of fair commercial rules.

Geographical Area of Activity: International.

Finance: Total budget €2,078,863 (2010/11).

Administrative Council: Françoise Toutain (Pres.); Véronique Rioufol (Vice-Pres.); Johanne Ruyssen (Treas.); Nathalie Héraud (Sec.).

Principal Staff: Dir-Gen. Luc Lamprière.

Address: 104 rue Oberkampf, 75011 Paris.

Telephone: 1-56-98-24-40; **Fax:** 1-56-98-24-09; **Internet:** www.oxfamfrance.org; **e-mail:** info@oxfamfrance.org.

Partage (Share)

Established in 1973, as Comité de Soutien aux Orphelins du Viêtnam, by Pierre Marchand to help orphans of the Viet Nam war; registered in 1976 as Partage avec les enfants du Tiers-Monde, renamed Partage in 1998.

Activities: Operates nationally and internationally in the fields of aid to less-developed countries, education, health and social welfare, through assisting individual sponsors help children to access all that is vital for their development, i.e. food and shelter, care, clothing and education.

Geographical Area of Activity: Albania, Bangladesh, Benin, Bosnia and Herzegovina, Brazil, Burkina Faso, Cambodia, Chile, Comoros, Croatia, Ecuador, Ethiopia, France, Haiti, Honduras, India, Lebanon, Madagascar, Nepal, Thailand, Viet Nam and other countries.

Publications: Annual Report.

Administrative Council: Pascal Ponty (Pres.); Christian Renoux (Vice-Pres.); Hubert Loesch (Treas.); Danièle Chagnon (Sec.).

Principal Staff: Dir Erik Jorgensen.

Address: 40 rue Vivenel, 60203 Compiègne.

Telephone: 3-44-20-92-92; **Fax:** 3-44-20-94-95; **Internet:** www.partage.org; **e-mail:** info@partage.org.

Patrimoine mondial (World Heritage)

Established in 1972 by the Convention Concerning the Protection of the World Cultural and Natural Heritage to protect world cultural and natural heritage.

Activities: The Fund assists in identifying and preserving World Heritage sites through providing international assistance in five specific areas: preparatory assistance; promotion and education, technical co-operation; emergency assistance; and training.

Geographical Area of Activity: International.

Publications: *World Heritage Review* (quarterly magazine); *World Heritage Newsletter* (2 a month); books, manuals and reports.

Finance: The Fund receives its income essentially from compulsory contributions from states party to the Convention (amounting to 1% of their UNESCO dues) and from voluntary contributions.

Governing Committee: João Luiz Silva Ferreira (Chair.).

Principal Staff: Dir Kishore Rao.

Address: c/o UNESCO, 7 pl. de Fontenoy, 75352 Paris.

Telephone: 1-45-68-15-71; **Fax:** 1-45-68-55-70; **Internet:** whc .unesco.org; **e-mail:** wh-info@unesco.org.

Santé Sud (Southern Health)

Founded in 1986 to improve the quality of care provided to people living in underprivileged areas, by supporting its partners in their efforts to take their development into their own hands.

Activities: Operates in the field of assistance to less-developed countries, through long-term projects providing financial, technical and material aid, especially in the area of health care. Consists of 150 members who contribute their skills as experts on the organization's projects. Works in co-operation with local grassroots organizations in Africa, the Middle East and Asia and has delegations in Madagascar, Mali, Mongolia and Tunisia.

Geographical Area of Activity: Africa, Asia, and the Middle East.

Publications: *Santé Sud* (quarterly newsletter); reviews; articles; films.

Board of Directors: Paul Benos (Pres.); Guy Farnarier (Vice-Pres.); Pascal Faucher (Treas.).

Principal Staff: Dir Nicole Hanssen.

Address: 200 blvd National, le Gyptis Bt N, 13003 Marseille.

Telephone: 4-91-95-63-45; **Fax:** 4-91-95-68-05; **Internet:** www.santesud.org; **e-mail:** santesud@wanadoo.fr.

Schlumberger Foundation

Established in 1956 to generate conditions that result in more women pursuing scientific disciplines.

Activities: Operates in the field of education, in recognition of the role of education in realizing people's potential, and of the link between science, technology and socio-economic development. Focus is on strengthening university faculties and mitigating obstacles faced by women scientists through the Faculty for the Future Programme, which offers fellowships to women from developing and emerging economies preparing for PhD or post-doctoral study in the physical sciences, engineering or related disciplines to pursue study at top universities abroad. Grant recipients are selected as much for their leadership capabilities as for their scientific talents, and they are expected to return to their home countries to continue their academic careers and inspire other young women.

Geographical Area of Activity: World-wide.

Restrictions: The Foundation does not accept unsolicited grant requests.

Publications: Faculty for the Future 2008 conference proceedings; DVD material.

Board of Directors: Jean-Marc Perraud (Chair. and Pres.); Jesus Grande (Vice-Pres.); Jean Chevallier (Vice-Pres.); Ranaa Riyamy (Vice-Pres.); Hatem Soliman (Vice-Pres.); Sola Oyinlola (Vice-Pres., Treas. and Sec.).

Principal Staff: Exec Dir Sola Oyinlola.

Address: 42 rue Saint Dominique, 75007 Paris.

Internet: www.foundation.slb.com/fftf; **e-mail:** foundation@paris.sl.slb.com.

Secours Catholique—Caritas de France (Catholic Help—Caritas France)

Founded in 1946 by Mgr Jean Rodhain as part of Caritas Internationalis (q.v.) with the aim of helping poor people throughout the world.

Activities: The organization provides aid to developing countries and operates its own programmes in the fields of education, human rights, health care and social welfare. It also provides grants to institutions and finances scholarships and fellowships. Also publishes annual statistical surveys of the extent of poverty in France.

Geographical Area of Activity: World-wide.

Publications: *Messages* (monthly); *Paix et réconciliation*.

Board of Directors: Francois Soulage (Pres.); Catherine Soublin, Gaston Vandecandelaere (Vice-Pres); Claudine Berland (Sec.); Gerard Raulin (Treas.).

Principal Staff: Sec.-Gen. Bernard Thibaud.

Address: 106 rue du Bac, 75341 Paris Cedex 7.

Telephone: 1-45-49-73-00; **Fax:** 1-45-49-94-50; **Internet:** www.secours-catholique.asso.fr; **e-mail:** info@secours -catholique.org.

Service d'Entraide et de Liaison—SEL (Mutual Aid and Liaison Service)

Christian (Protestant) organization for international solidarity founded in 1980 by the French Evangelical Alliance.

Activities: Operates internationally in the field of aid to less-developed countries through local partners. Provides aid and assistance in developing countries, particularly to children. Supports child sponsorship programmes and development projects in the areas of health, nutrition, agriculture, micro-credit, water, sanitation and other social concerns, and offers emergency relief to areas in crisis. Involved in raising public awareness about poverty and aid to developing countries.

Geographical Area of Activity: World-wide through local partners (with a focus on French-speaking African countries and Madagascar).

Publications: *SEL–Informations* (periodical).

Finance: Annual income €4,366,350 (2010/11).

Principal Staff: Dir-Gen. Patrick Guiborat.

Address: 157 rue des Blains, 92220 Bagneux.

Telephone: 1-45-36-41-51; **Fax:** 1-46-16-20-86; **Internet:** www.selfrance.org; **e-mail:** info@selfrance.org.

Solidarité (Solidarity)

Founded in 1980. Aims to reduce unemployment in rural areas and to improve the quality of life of people living in developing countries.

Activities: Promotes sustainable rural development in Africa, Central and South America and Asia. Supports local organizations financially, technically or physically to carry out development projects to encourage and enable rural people to become more independent. Creates small industries by using local resources; carries out research into suitable technologies; promotes improved medical and sanitary systems and environmental awareness. There is a particular focus on the development and empowerment of women and children, and tribal peoples' rights. Also disseminates information about the projects, runs training courses and liaises with local and international NGOs.

Geographical Area of Activity: Africa, Central and South America, Asia and Europe.

Publications: *Solidarité* (quarterly magazine); Annual Report.

Governing Board: Francine Cueille; Marie-Hélène Delon; Sylvio Pensantez; Guilhem Bato.

Principal Staff: Exec. Dir Clotilde Bato.

Address: 14 rue Lafon, 31000 Toulouse.

Telephone: 5-61-13-66-95; **Fax:** 5-61-13-66-95; **Internet:** www.solidarite.asso.fr; **e-mail:** contact@solidarite.asso.fr.

Universal Education Foundation—UEF

Founded in 2004 to promote learning for well-being.

Activities: A partnership initiative dedicated to creating a global movement towards learning for well-being, through the improvement of learning environments. Promotes the idea that education of children and young people does not happen only within the school setting; and that systems of education, health, information and communications technologies, and media, as well as society at large, need to foster the unique and holistic development of every child, while supporting their desire for joy in learning.

Geographical Area of Activity: International.

Publications: *Elham Palestine 2009 (UEF)*; *Developing instruments to capture young people's perceptions of how school as a learning environment affects their well-being* (M. Awartani, V. C. Whitman and J. Gordon, in European Journal of Education 43 (1), 2008); *Lessons from the Voice of Children initiative: A sense of belonging as part of children's well-being* (J. Gordon, L. O'Toole and C. V. Whitman, in Early Childhood Matters, No. 111, Nov. 2008); *The Voice of Children: Student Well-Being and the School Environment* (report, M. Awartani, V. C. Whitman and J. Gordon, 2007).

Board: Raymond Georis (Chair.).

Principal Staff: Co-founder and Exec. Dir Daniel Kropf; Co-Founder and Sec.-Gen. Marwan Awartani; Learning for Well-being Youth Movement Co-ordinator Jean Anne Kennedy.

Address: c/o EIESP, Université de Paris Dauphine, place du Maréchal de Lattre de Tassigny, 75775 Paris Cedex 16.

Telephone: 6-19-69-68-02; **Internet:** www.learningforwellbeing.org; **e-mail:** uef-learningforwellbeing@orange.fr.

The Gambia

FOUNDATION CENTRE AND CO-ORDINATING BODY

Association of Non-Governmental Organizations in The Gambia—TANGO

Established in 1983.

Activities: Co-ordinates activities of member organizations to ensure that resources are used efficiently to further social development in The Gambia. Works as an information forum and as a meeting place for NGOs to exchange information, knowledge and expertise. Also co-ordinates the National Poverty Alleviation Programme and works on voter education programmes to increase female participation in elections and to raise issues of agrarian concern.

Geographical Area of Activity: The Gambia.

Principal Staff: Dir Ousman M. S. Yabo.

Address: c/o Fajara 'M' Section, PMB 392, Serekunda.

Telephone: 390525; **Fax:** 390521; **Internet:** www.tango.gm; **e-mail:** tango@qanet.gm.

FOUNDATIONS, TRUSTS AND NON-PROFIT ORGANIZATIONS

Foundation for Research on Women's Health, Productivity and the Environment—BAFROW

Established in 1991 by nine individuals to assist in and contribute to the development of a conceptual framework regarding gender and development, and to facilitate dialogue on empowerment, focusing on major factors significant to the development and sustainability of women and female children.

Activities: Operates in the fields of conservation and the environment, economic affairs, education, and medicine and health, nationally through self-conducted programmes, conferences and training courses, and internationally through research. Projects include research into genital mutilation, and a series of public education campaigns to end its practice, as well as the promotion of access to schooling for girls and research into the implications of polygamy for women. Works in association with other international organizations, including the American Jewish World Service (q.v.).

Geographical Area of Activity: Mainly The Gambia.

Publications: *Curriculum for Initiation Rites in Madinka, Fula and Jola*; *Needs Assessment Study for Skills Development for Circumcisers*; *Female Genital Mutilation (FGM)*.

Governing Board: M. G. Bala-Gaye (Chair.); Veronic Wright (Vice-Chair.); Fatou Waggeh (Sec.); Mariam Thomasi (Treas.).

Principal Staff: Dir Fatou Waggeh.

Address: 214 Tafsir Demba Mbye St, Tobacco Rd, Banjul.

Telephone: 225270; **Fax:** 226739; **e-mail:** bafrow@gamtel.gm.

Georgia

FOUNDATION CENTRES AND CO-ORDINATING BODIES

Centre for Training and Consultancy

Established in December 1999.

Activities: Provides support to non-profit organizations in Georgia, for the institutional development of the not-for-profit sector. Offers training and consultancy services in institutional development, capacity building and strategic planning and provides support through its resource centre. Promotes co-operation between Georgian NGOs and organizations from other Eastern and Western European countries. A regional partner of the Management for Development Foundation based in the Netherlands; maintains an office in Azerbaijan, with links to Armenia and Kyrgyzstan.

Geographical Area of Activity: Armenia, Azerbaijan, Georgia and Kyrgyzstan.

Publications: *Directory of non-government organizations of Tbilisi working on public policy* (2005); *European Institute of Public Administration* (2005); *The Role in System Education in Civil Integration of Ethnic Minorities: The vision of interested bodies in civil and governmental sectors* (2005); *Basic Competances for life-long learning European framework* (2006); *An Assessment of Georgian Civil Society* (2006); *European Studies* (series, 2006); Annual Report.

Finance: Total assets 4,355,911 GEL (2010).

Principal Staff: Exec. Dir Irina Khantadze; Financial Man. Julia Shendrikova.

Address: 0177, Tbilisi, 5 Otar Chkheidze Str.

Telephone: (32) 20-67-74; (32) 20-67-75; **e-mail:** ctc@ctc.org.ge.

Civil Society Support Centre

Founded in 2000.

Activities: Launched the Business Incubator Initiative (BII) in 2002 to provide expertise in knowledge-orientated business development. Currently managing IT business incubator in Tbilisi, Georgia.

Geographical Area of Activity: Georgia.

Principal Staff: Contact Vazha Goginashvili.

Address: 0105 Tbilisi, 11/23 Atoneli St.

Telephone: (32) 251-42-42; **Fax:** (32) 298-37-78; **Internet:** www.bii.ge; **e-mail:** info@bii.ge.

Horizonti, the Foundation for the Third Sector

Founded in 1997 by Michael Clayton and Nino Saakashvili. Aims to support the development of a civil society in Georgia.

Activities: Assists in the development of foundations and similar organizations in Georgia by providing technical and financial assistance. Also offers grants, training, consulting and information. Operates five main programmes: Cross-Sectoral Partnership; Citizens Activation, Community Development and Constituency Building; Organizational Development; Constituency Awareness Raising; and Sustainable Development Support.

Geographical Area of Activity: Caucasus, Georgia.

Restrictions: No grants to individuals; grants are for Georgian NGOs.

Publications: Annual Report; NGO databases; NGO news bulletin (2 a month), and books on NGO organization and development (in Georgian).

Finance: Funded by the US Agency for International Aid (USAID) and by private donations.

Governing Board: Lancelot R. Fletcher (Chair.).

Principal Staff: Co-ordinator Rezo Zedgenidze.

Address: Tbilisi, 2 Dolidze St, 6th Floor.

Telephone: (32) 33-28-16; **Fax:** (32) 98-75-04; **e-mail:** adm@horizonti.org.

FOUNDATIONS, TRUSTS AND NON-PROFIT ORGANIZATIONS

Caucasus Institute for Peace, Democracy and Development—CIPDD

Set up in 1992 as an independent policy research organization.

Activities: Primary areas of research are regional security, state-building, democratization and civil integration. Main activities include public policy research, publishing research results, and organizing debates and round-table discussions. Hosts an online discussion forum and services for journalists and researchers.

Geographical Area of Activity: Mainly Georgia, but co-operates with organizations in the South Caucasus and Black Sea regions.

Publications: *Effects/impacts of media* (research paper); *After August 2008: Consequences of the Russian–Georgian War* (analytical paper); *Security sector reform in Georgia 2004–2007* (research paper); *Political Forum: 10 questions on Georgia's political development; Feasibility of Construction of a Nuclear Power Plant in Georgia; The President's New Initiative for South Ossetia: what will it bring for Georgia in the future?; Urban Development and Private Property in Tbilisi; Civil Society Development in Georgia: Achievements and Challenges; Constitutional/Political Reforms in Armenia, Azerbaijan and Georgia: Political Elite and Voices of the People; The Political Landscape of Georgia; Taking Stock: small arms and human security in Georgia; Ethnic-confessional Groups and Challenges to Civic Integration in Georgia; Society and Politics.*

Finance: Total budget US $74,300 (2009).

Board: Emzar Jgerenaia (Chair.).

Principal Staff: Exec. Dir Avtandil Jokhadze.

Address: 0154 Tbilisi, 72 Tsereteli Ave, 2nd floor.

Telephone: (32) 35-51-54; **Fax:** (32) 35-51-54; **Internet:** www.cipdd.org; **e-mail:** info@cipdd.org.

OSGF—Open Society Georgia Foundation

Established in May 1994, an independent foundation, part of the Soros foundations network, which aims to foster political and cultural pluralism and reform economic structures to encourage private enterprise and a market economy.

Activities: Operates mainly in the fields of education, higher education, civil society, the arts and humanities, law, and information and the media, through supporting 26 national and regional programmes. Also supports other NGOs in Georgia, as well as regional projects in collaboration with the Soros foundations of Armenia and Azerbaijan.

Geographical Area of Activity: Georgia.

Publications: Annual Report.

Finance: Annual expenditure US $892,379 (2009).

Executive Board: George Nizharadze (Chair.).

Principal Staff: Exec. Dir Keti Khutsishvili; Deputy Exec. Dir Tamar Kaldani.

Address: 0108 Tbilisi, Chovelidze St 10.

Telephone: (32) 25-05-92; **Fax:** (32) 29-10-52; **Internet:** www
.osgf.ge; **e-mail:** contact@osgf.ge.

People's Harmonious Development Society

Founded in December 1996.

Activities: Works for and with people on issues of human
rights and sustainable development, through education, training and research. The organization conducts research on
migration issues and people-trafficking, environmental security, and disseminates results through seminars, training, conferences and mass-media campaigns.

Geographical Area of Activity: World-wide, particularly in
the South Caucasus and Black Sea regions.

Publications: Training manuals, research materials, booklets.

Finance: Support from European Union and others.

Trustees: Tsovinar Nazarova (Chair.).

Principal Staff: Programme coordinator Tsovinar Nazarova.

Address: 16, Abashidze St, app.3, Tbilisi.

Telephone: (32) 18-21-82; **Fax:** (32) 22-23-47; **Internet:** www
.phds.ge; **e-mail:** phds@phds.ge.

Germany

FOUNDATION CENTRES AND CO-ORDINATING BODIES

Bundesverband Deutscher Stiftungen eV (Association of German Foundations)

Founded in 1948 to represent the interests of German foundations.

Activities: Provides information about German foundations; publishes directories, books, reports, brochures and leaflets; organizes conferences, exhibitions and training for foundation staff. Maintains a database with more than 12,000 entries for foundations and works internationally with similar national and international organizations.

Geographical Area of Activity: Germany.

Restrictions: Does not make grants.

Publications: *Verzeichnis Deutscher Stiftungen*; *Schriftenreihen*; *Deutsches Stiftungswesen, Lebensbilder Deutscher Stiftungen*; *Ratgeber für Stifter*; *Die Verwaltung einer Stiftung*; *Tagungsberichte*; *Deutsche Stiftungen—Mitteilungen* (quarterly).

Governing Board: Dr Wilhelm Krull (Chair.); Jurgen Regge (Vice-Chair.).

Principal Staff: Sec.-Gen. Prof. Dr Hans Fleisch.

Address: Mauerstr. 93, Haus Deutscher Stiftungen, 10117 Berlin.

Telephone: (30) 897947-0; **Fax:** (30) 897947-11; **Internet:** www.stiftungen.org; **e-mail:** post@stiftungen.org.

Initiative Bürgerstiftungen (Community Foundations Initiative)

Established in 2001 to support new community foundations and professionalize existing ones, offer a platform for all community foundations in Germany and promote the idea of community foundations in Germany.

Activities: Promotes the development of community foundations in Germany, through mentoring, coaching, and providing consultancy and advice to community foundations; an annual grants programme to support operating costs for selected community foundations; a travel fund for community foundation practitioners; regional meetings, seminars and workshops; information and communication; and research, including an annual survey of the community foundation sector in Germany.

Geographical Area of Activity: Germany.

Publications: Electronic newsletter (monthly); information resources; books.

Trustees: Prof. Dr Werner J. Bauer (Chair.).

Principal Staff: CEO Prof. Gunter Thielen.

Address: Bertelsmann Stiftung, Carl-Bertelsmann-Str. 256, 33311 Gütersloh.

Telephone: (5241) 8181128; **Fax:** (5241) 81681396; **Internet:** www.buergerstiftungen.de; **e-mail:** info@buergerstiftungen.de.

Maecenata Management GmbH

Founded in 1989 by Count Rupert Strachwitz to provide management assistance to and for non-governmental, non-profit-making institutions (foundations in particular).

Activities: Operates internationally, in the fields of the arts and humanities, conservation and the environment, international affairs, education, and social welfare and social studies, through self-conducted programmes, research, conferences, training courses and publications. Maintains an office in Berlin. A subsidiary, Maecenata International, is the German partner in the Transnational Giving Europe Network specializing in facilitating cross-border donations.

Geographical Area of Activity: Germany, countries of the European Union, Central and Eastern Europe and the USA.

Restrictions: Does not make grants.

Publications: Reports on foundations in Germany and Europe.

Finance: Holds 60 foundations in trust; total capital approx. €75,000,000.

Principal Staff: Dir Dr Count Rupert Strachwitz.

Address: Herzogstr. 60, 80803 Munich.

Telephone: (89) 284452; **Fax:** (89) 283774; **Internet:** www.maecenata.eu; **e-mail:** info@dsz-maecenata.de.

Maecenata Stiftung (Maecenata Foundation)

Established in 2010 to incorporate 2 previously independent not-for-profit activities: the Maecenata Institute and Maecenata International.

Activities: The Maecenata Institute operates in the field of research into civil society and philanthropy, through collecting and publishing information on foundations and other third-sector organizations; maintaining a database on around 15,000 German foundations and trusts; carrying out research; academic teaching; organizing conferences; promoting research in the field through academic exchange. Maecenata International, the German partner to the Transnational Giving Europe Network (TGE) facilitates cross-border giving world-wide by enabling donors to obtain a tax deductable receipt in their country of residence. The Foundation acts as a policy think tank in the field of civil society, civic engagement, and philanthropy.

Geographical Area of Activity: Germany, Europe and world-wide.

Publications: *Maecenata Schriften* (8 vols. to date); *Opuscula series; Maecenata Notizen* (3 a year).

Finance: Voluntary donations, grants.

Board: Christian Petry (Chair.).

Principal Staff: Dirs Dr Rupert Graf Strachwitz, Dr Veronika Hofmann.

Address: Albrechtstr. 22, 10117 Berlin.

Telephone: (30) 28387909; **Fax:** (30) 28387910; **Internet:** www.maecenata.eu; **e-mail:** mst@maecenata.eu.

Stifterverband für die Deutsche Wissenschaft eV (Donors' Association for the Promotion of Sciences and Humanities)

Founded in 1920 and re-established in 1949 by 61 national industrial and commercial organizations to support the sciences and humanities in research and teaching, as well as the rising scientific and technical generation; to undertake measures that might be helpful in bringing support to science and technology.

Activities: Operates nationally in the fields of education, the arts and humanities, and nationally and internationally in the fields of science, medicine and international relations, through self-conducted programmes. The Association has around 4,000 members, comprising companies, associations and individuals making donations on an annual basis; administers more than 250 trusts and foundations (German Foundation Centre).

Geographical Area of Activity: Germany and international.

Publications: Annual Report; *Wirtschaft und Wissenschaft* (quarterly); *Materialien aus dem Stiftungszentrum*; *Materialien zur Wissenschaftsstatistik*; *Beiträge zu Statistiken über Forschung und Entwicklung*; *Schriftenreihe zum Stiftungswesen*.

Board of Trustees: Dr Arend Oetker (Pres.); Dr Kurt Bock (Vice-Pres.); Dr Johannes Teyssen (Vice-Pres.); Prof. Dr Wolfgang Reitzle (Treas.).

Principal Staff: Gen. Sec. Prof. Dr Andreas Schlüter.

Address: Barkhovenallee 1, 45239 Essen.

Telephone: (201) 84010; **Fax:** (201) 8401301; **Internet:** www.stifterverband.de; **e-mail:** mail@stifterverband.de.

FOUNDATIONS, TRUSTS AND NON-PROFIT ORGANIZATIONS

Konrad-Adenauer-Stiftung eV—KAS (Konrad Adenauer Foundation)

Founded in 1964, emerging from the Society for Christian Democratic Education (founded in 1956), and named after the first Chancellor of the Federal Republic, Konrad Adenauer. The Foundation is guided by the same principles that inspired Adenauer's work.

Activities: Operates in the field of the humanities, development and international relations, through: granting scholarships to gifted individuals; organizing public events; and supporting projects in the field of international understanding (approx. 200 projects and programmes are organized in more than 100 countries). Offers political education and research for political projects; researches the history of Christian Democracy; supports and encourages European unification, operates a think-tank on domestic policy and the social market economy, international understanding and co-operation on development policy. Maintains two education centres and 21 education institutes.

Geographical Area of Activity: World-wide.

Publications: Annual Report; *Die Frau in unserer Zeit* (quarterly); *Eichholz Brief* (quarterly); *Einblicke* (6 a year); *German Comments* (monthly); *KAS-Auslandsinformationen* (monthly); *Watch Series* (2 a year); *Development policy*; *Education and Research*; *European Policy*; *Local Government Policy*; *Social Market Economy*; *women and Family Policy*; *Overseas Information*; books.

Finance: Total annual expenditure and revenue €63,380,034 (Dec. 2010).

Board of Trustees: Prof. Dr Roman Herzog (Chair.).

Principal Staff: Chair. Board of Dirs Dr Hans-Gert Poettering; Sec.-Gen. Michael Thielen; Treas. Dr Franz Schoser.

Address: Klingelhöferstr. 23, 10785 Berlin.

Telephone: (30) 269960; **Internet:** www.kas.de; **e-mail:** zentrale-berlin@kas.de.

Aid to the Church in Need—ACN

Founded in 1947 by Fr Werenfried van Straaten to promote Christianity and support and provide pastoral relief to Catholics in need.

Activities: Operates in around 144 less-developed countries of Africa, Asia, Central and South America and the Caribbean, and Eastern Europe, through providing grants towards church-building and transport funds, for students, seminarians, novices and clergy, and in the area of the press, radio and religious literature; it also supports persecuted, oppressed and poor Catholics, Russian Orthodox, and refugees, regardless of religion. The organization's international office is located in Germany, and national offices operate in 16 countries in Europe, North and South America and Australia.

Geographical Area of Activity: International.

Publications: *Fifty Years of the Church in Need*; and other publications.

Finance: Annual budget approx. US $75,000,000 (2010).

Trustees: Joaquin Alliende Luca (Pres.).

Principal Staff: Exec. Dir Susanne Zeidler.

Address: Bischof-Kindermann-Str. 23, 61462 Königstein im Taunus.

Telephone: (6174) 2910; **Fax:** (6174) 3423; **Internet:** www.acn-intl.org; **e-mail:** info@acn-intl.org.

Allianz Kulturstiftung (Allianz Cultural Foundation)

Established in 2000 by the former Allianz AG, now Allianz SE, for the promotion of culture, especially with regard to young people, and European integration with an emphasis on South-Eastern Europe.

Activities: Operates in Europe in its broadest sense, primarily supporting multinational and intercultural co-operation projects that effectively promote the European integration process with a lasting influence. Innovativeness and European dynamism are essential criteria for selecting the projects as well as an outstanding artistic and academic quality or a special relevance with regard to conveying European cultural history. Operative projects concerning the Eastern European and South-Eastern European countries forge the basis of the Foundation's philanthropic activity.

Geographical Area of Activity: Europe.

Restrictions: No grants to individuals.

Publications: Publications on the foundation.

Finance: Initial capital €50,000,000.

Board of Trustees: Dr Henning Schulte-Noelle (Chair.); Prof. Dr Christina Weiss (Assoc. Chair.); **Advisory Board:** Prof. Dr Christina Weiss (Chair.).

Principal Staff: Man. Dir Michael M. Thoss.

Address: Maria-Theresia-Str. 4A, 81675 Munich.

Telephone: (89) 4107303; **Fax:** (89) 41073040; **Internet:** www.allianz-kulturstiftung.de; **e-mail:** kulturstiftung@allianz.de.

Allianz Umweltstiftung (Allianz Foundation for Sustainability)

Established in 1990 by Allianz Versicherung to work towards ensuring a safe future.

Activities: Operates in Germany in the field of environmental conservation, focusing on the protection and development of the countryside, land planning and sustainable development. Supports innovative and inspirational projects. Sponsors the Benediktbeurer Talks, a forum for debating environmental protection issues.

Geographical Area of Activity: Germany.

Publications: *10 Jahre Allianz Umweltstiftung*; various project reports; video.

Finance: Assets €50,000,000.

Principal Staff: Dr Lutz Spandau; Peter Wilde; Susanne Luberstetter; Monika Schäfer.

Address: Maria-Theresia-Str. 4A, 81675 Munich.

Telephone: (89) 410733-6; **Fax:** (89) 410733-70; **Internet:** www.allianz-umweltstiftung.de; **e-mail:** info@allianz-umweltstiftung.de.

Arbeiterwohlfahrt Bundesverband eV—AWO (Federal Association of Social Welfare Organizations)

Founded in 1919, the organization aims to improve the social welfare of those in need in Germany, particularly the young and the sick.

Activities: Organizes and finances social welfare programmes in Germany, including the operation of sheltered accommodation, day centres and counselling centres; runs training courses for social workers; operates educational programmes for adults; and co-operates with other social welfare organizations at both national and international levels, including development, aid and disaster relief projects in Eastern Europe, Asia and Central and South America.

Geographical Area of Activity: Mainly Germany, some work carried out internationally.

Publications: *Theorie und Praxis* (monthly); *Sozialprism* (monthly); *directory*; *yearbook*; monographs and handbooks.

Finance: Annual budget approx. €1,000m.

Trustees: Wolfgang Stadler (Chair.).

Principal Staff: Sec.-Gen. Rainer Bruckers; Head of Communications Berit Grundler.

Address: Heinrich-Albertz-Haus, Blücherstr. 62–63, 10961 Berlin.

Telephone: (30) 26309-0; **Fax:** (30) 32599; **Internet:** www.awo .org; **e-mail:** info@awo.org.

ASKO Europa-Stiftung (ASKO Europe Foundation)

Established in 1990 by the ASKO Deutsche Kaufhaus AG company to promote academic research and education, especially in the area of European integration on a federal basis. In 1996, when ASKO Deutsche Kaufhaus AG merged with METRO AG, the Foundation became an independent entity.

Activities: Promotes study in the area of European integration. Special emphasis is given to Franco-German relations and their significance for the European integration process. Committed to the development of the European region spanning Saarland, Lorraine and Luxembourg.

Geographical Area of Activity: Europe.

Restrictions: No scholarships to individuals.

Publications: Denkart Europa; activity reports; discussion report; AES-News; *Dialogue in dialogue*; newsletter.

Board of Trustees: Klaus-Peter Beck (Chair.); Klaus Wiegandt (Vice-Chair.).

Principal Staff: Sec. Barbara Dony.

Address: Pestelstr. 2, 66119 Saarbrücken.

Telephone: (681) 92674-0; **Fax:** (681) 92674-99; **Internet:** www.asko-europa-stiftung.de; **e-mail:** info@asko-europa -stiftung.de.

Aventis Foundation

Established in 1996 by Hoechst AG, and formerly known as the Hoechst Foundation, for the promotion of projects in the areas of culture, civil society and science.

Activities: Operates internationally, promoting projects in areas such as the fine arts, civil society and science, through making grants to organizations. Special funds operate in the field of education, offering grants to gifted students in need, and for scientific research.

Geographical Area of Activity: International.

Restrictions: Individual scholarship applications not accepted.

Publications: Annual Report.

Finance: Total assets €58,400,000 (2010).

Board of Trustees: Jürgen Dormann (Chair.).

Principal Staff: Chair. Dieter Kohl; Man. Dir Eugen Müller.

Address: Industriepark Höchst, Bldg F 821, 65926 Frankfurt am Main.

Telephone: (69) 3057256; **Fax:** (69) 30580554; **Internet:** www .aventis-foundation.org; **e-mail:** eugen.mueller@aventis -foundation.org.

Professor Otto Beisheim Stiftung (Professor Otto Beisheim Foundation)

Founded by Prof. Otto Beisheim.

Activities: Promotes education, entrepreneurship and culture, particularly in Germany, through funding symposia and colloquia, donating art exhibits and funding chairs in entrepreneurship at German universities. Also established the Otto Beisheim Graduate School of Management in Vallendar, Germany. Promotes the use of new technologies, including funding the first Swiss Internet House.

Geographical Area of Activity: Germany and Europe.

Principal Staff: Prof. Dr Erich Greipl; Prof. Dr Stefan Muller; Sandra Baumanns.

Address: Fakultät Wirtschaftswissenschaften, Technische Universität Dresden, 01062 Dresden.

Telephone: (351) 46333138; **Fax:** (351) 46337176; **e-mail:** beisheim-stiftung@mailbox.tu-dresden.de.

Bellagio Forum for Sustainable Development

Founded in 1996 by a group of international donor organizations and initiated by the Compagnia di San Paolo di Torino and the Rockefeller Foundation (qq.v.) to fund and provide expertise for activities that influence policy and thinking in the area of sustainable development.

Activities: The Forum's members provide funding and expertise for a wide range of activities that influence policy and thinking on sustainable development issues, as well as providing practical improvements towards environmental sustainability, within the broad categories of sustainable livelihoods, the media, policy and research. Initiatives include the Environmental Communications Award, launched in 2001; an annual environmental studies award at Oxford University in the United Kingdom; the Cooking Stove Project, a pilot initiative aiming to reduce the use of wood as fuel under way in Guatemala, India and the Philippines; a protection programme for the Mediterranean sea; and the development of a nature reserve in Lebanon. In 2004 the Forum had 29 member organizations based in Europe and the USA.

Geographical Area of Activity: International.

Restrictions: Does not accept outside requests for financial support.

Publications: Newsletter; Annual Report; Status Report; *BFSD Magazine* (3–4 times a year).

Board of Trustees: Ola Engelmark (Chair.); Jan-Olaf Willums (Vice-Chair.); Ulrich Witte (Vice-Chair.); Charles Buchanan (Treas.).

Principal Staff: Exec. Dir Per Rosenberg.

Address: An der Bornau 2, 49090 Osnabrück.

Telephone: (541) 9633490; **Fax:** (541) 9633491; **Internet:** bfsd .server.enovum.com/en; **e-mail:** info@bellagio-forum.org.

Otto-Benecke-Stiftung eV (Otto Benecke Foundation)

Founded in 1965 by the Verband Deutscher Studentenschaften (Association of German Student Bodies) to provide assistance for refugee students and students from developing countries.

Activities: Operates internationally in the field of education, by providing a counselling and scholarship programme enabling students from less-developed countries (particularly refugees from Southern Africa) to study at universities, polytechnics and vocational schools in Germany and less-developed countries; it also runs a programme for training in manual and industrial occupations in African countries of asylum. International conferences are held, in collaboration with other organizations, on basic questions concerning the right to asylum.

Geographical Area of Activity: International.

Restrictions: Grants are made only to immigrants, refugees and asylum-seekers.

Publications: Conference Reports; Report of Operations.

Finance: Total expenditure approx. €37,000,000.

Trustees: Eberhard Diepgens (Chair.).

Principal Staff: Exec. Pres. Dr Lothar Theodor Lemper; Man. Dir Harwig Möbes.

Address: Kennedyallee 105–107, 53175 Bonn.

Telephone: (228) 81630; **Fax:** (228) 8163300; **Internet:** www .obs-ev.de; **e-mail:** post@obs-ev.de.

Berghof Stiftung für Konfliktforschung GmbH (Berghof Foundation for Conflict Research)

Founded in 1971 by Prof. Dr Georg Zundel, deriving its name from the Berghof Estate, the home of the founder, with an aim to perform research in peace-related conflict studies.

Activities: Supports research in constructive conflict management and significant issues in ethics and natural sciences. Maintains the Berghof Centre for Constructive Conflict Management in Berlin. Also awards the annual Hans Götzelmann Prize in conflict studies.

Geographical Area of Activity: Europe; Germany; Sri Lanka.

Restrictions: Grants restricted to Western, Southern, Central and Eastern Europe, for a three-year period of support only.

Publications: Specialist publications detailing the foundation's work; reports; occasional papers; *Berghof Handbook for Conflict Transformation*; other publications.

Board of Trustees: Prof. Dr Horst Fischer (Chair.).

Principal Staff: CEO Johannes S. Zundel; Dir Prof. Dr Hans J. Giessmann; Deputy Dir Martina Fischer.

Address: Altensteinstr. 48A, 14195 Berlin.

Telephone: (30) 844154-0; **Fax:** (30) 844154-99; **Internet:** www.berghof-center.org; **e-mail:** info@berghof-center.org.

Bertelsmann Stiftung (Bertelsmann Foundation)

Founded in 1977 by Reinhard Mohn to support projects in education, economic and social issues, democracy and civil society, international co-operation and health.

Activities: Operates internationally in the following main areas: the annual Carl Bertelsmann Prize for innovative approaches to problem-solving; Education, focusing on developing ideas for expanding the network within the education system; Economic and Social Affairs, developing approaches toward a sustainable social market economy; Democracy and Civil Society, supporting citizen-orientated discussion and decision-making processes in communities and calls for public accountability and transparency; International Relations, dedicated to settling conflict through international change management for a peaceful balance of interests and constructive cultural co-existence; and Health, working towards a fundamental reform of the German health-care sector, also supporting the Academy of Manual Medicine, CKM Centre for Hospital Management, and the German Stroke Foundation; and Foundations, to assist in the improvement of the management, strategies and methods of foundations. Since 1999 the Stiftung has co-operated in a joint initiative with the C. S. Mott Foundation (q.v.), aiming to facilitate the exchange of experience among community foundations from Europe, North America and Mexico.

Geographical Area of Activity: Germany, Europe and USA.

Restrictions: Operating foundation; no grants on application.

Publications: Annual Report; newsletter (3–4 a year); publications related to projects undertaken; *Effectiveness, Efficiency and Accountability in Philanthropy*; *Violence, Extremism and Transformation* (2006); *Cultures in Globalization* (2006); *Active Aging in Economy and Society* (2006); *Assessment, Evaluation, Improvement: Success through Corporate Culture* (2006); *Health Policy Developments* (2006); *Bertelsmann Transformation Index* (2006); *The Strategy of Politics* (2007).

Finance: Annual expenditure €60,315,000 (2010).

Board of Trustees: Prof. Dr Werner J. Bauer (Chair.); Liz Mohn (Deputy Chair.).

Principal Staff: Chief Exec. Dr Gunter Thielen.

Address: Carl-Bertelsmann-Str. 256, 33311 Gütersloh.

Telephone: (5241) 810; **Fax:** (5241) 8181999; **Internet:** www.bertelsmann-stiftung.de; **e-mail:** info@bertelsmann-stiftung.de.

Bischöfliches Hilfswerk Misereor eV (German Catholic Bishops' Organization for Development Co-operation)

Founded in 1958 by the Catholic Church in the Federal Republic of Germany with the aim of combating world hunger and injustice.

Activities: Promotes long-term solutions to the problems of developing countries by organizing and financing education and training programmes that emphasize self-help.

Geographical Area of Activity: International.

Publications: Annual Report; pamphlets.

Board of Directors: Dr Josef Sayer (Dir-Gen.); Martin Bröckelmann-Simon; Thomas Antkowiak (Man. Dir).

Principal Staff: Prelate Prof. Dr Joseph Sayer; Man. Dirs Martin Bröckelmann-Simon, Thomas Antkowiak.

Address: Postfach 101545, 52015 Aachen; Mozartstr. 9, 52064 Aachen.

Telephone: (241) 4420; **Fax:** (241) 442188; **Internet:** www.misereor.org; **e-mail:** postmaster@misereor.de.

BMW Stiftung Herbert Quandt (BMW Foundation Herbert Quandt)

Founded in June 1970 by BMW AG, on the 60th birthday of Herbert Quandt, to foster international dialogue.

Activities: The foundation seeks to foster national and international dialogue and mutual understanding between business, politics and society. Organizes a range of events bringing together leaders of industry and society, which aim to demonstrate the importance of co-operation between social institutions to ensure industrial nations have stable and successful economies. International events are often organized in co-operation with other organizations.

Geographical Area of Activity: International.

Restrictions: Unsolicited applications are not accepted: no scholarships or any other kind of financial support are provided.

Publications: Texts of lectures and conference documentation.

Trustees: Dr Joachim Milberg (Chair.).

Principal Staff: Chair. Jürgen Chrobog; Exec. Dir Markus Hipp.

Address: Reinhardtstr. 58, 10117 Berlin.

Telephone: (30) 33963500; **Fax:** (30) 33963530; **Internet:** www.bmw-stiftung.de; **e-mail:** info@bmw-stiftung.de.

Boehringer Ingelheim Fonds—Stiftung für Medizinische Grundlagenforschung (Foundation for Basic Research in Biomedicine)

Established in January 1983 by the companies C. H. Boehringer Sohn and Boehringer Ingelheim International as an independent foundation for the exclusive and direct promotion of basic research in biomedicine.

Activities: The Foundation operates nationally and internationally, offering long-term fellowships for doctoral students, travel grants for doctoral students and post-doctoral scientists, research fellowships for medical students studying in Germany, and organizing the International Titisee Conferences for established scientists.

Geographical Area of Activity: Europe and overseas (supports Europeans in Europe and overseas; scientists from overseas working in Europe).

Restrictions: No grants to scientific institutions; no grants for the payment of staff or for overheads, equipment or materials.

Publications: *B.I.F.—FUTURA* (quarterly).

Finance: Annual budget €4,880,000 (2011).

Board of Trustees: Prof. Andreas Barner (Chair.); Prof. U. Benjamin Kaupp (Deputy Chair.).

Principal Staff: Man. Dir Dr Claudia Walther.

Address: Grabenstr. 46, Schlossmühle, 55262 Heidesheim.

Telephone: (6132) 8985-0; **Fax:** (6132) 8985-11; **Internet:** www.bifonds.de; **e-mail:** secretariat@bifonds.de.

Heinrich-Böll-Stiftung (Heinrich Böll Foundation)

Established in 1987 and associated with the German Green Party, to promote political education in the areas of ecology, solidarity, democracy, arms control and sexual equality; and preserve the works and thoughts of the writer Heinrich Böll.

Activities: Operates nationally and internationally in the fields of the arts and humanities, conservation and the environment, international affairs, economic sustainability, and law and human rights; co-operates with NGOs working in 60 countries. Maintains 28 offices in Europe, North America, South America, Africa, Asia and the Middle East. Also founded the Feminist Institute and the Green Academy. Operates a fellowship study programme open to students and postgraduates in all fields and of all nationalities.

Geographical Area of Activity: International.

Publications: Annual Report.

Finance: Annual budget €46,433,011 (2010).

Board of Directors: Ralf Fücks (Pres.); Barbara Unmüssig (Pres.).

Principal Staff: CEO Dr Birgit Laubach.

Address: Schumannstr. 8, 10117 Berlin-Mitte.

Telephone: (30) 28534-0; **Fax:** (30) 28534-109; **Internet:** www.boell.de; **e-mail:** info@boell.de.

Robert-Bosch-Stiftung GmbH (Robert Bosch Foundation)

Founded in 1964 by the Bosch organization to embody the philanthropic and social endeavours of its founder, Robert Bosch (1861–1942).

Activities: The Foundation supports and promotes public health, international relations (especially with France, the USA, Central and Eastern Europe, and Turkey), education, civic society, arts and culture, the humanities, and social and natural sciences. It develops innovative programmes, competitions and prizes, and supports promising pilot projects within these objectives. In Stuttgart, the foundation operates three public health and research facilities: the Robert Bosch Hospital, the Dr Margarete Fischer-Bosch Institute for Clinical Pharmacology and the Institute for the History of Medicine. The foundation also operates an office in Berlin.

Geographical Area of Activity: Europe, Turkey, Japan, India, USA, People's Republic of China.

Restrictions: Grants only given in defined areas of interest and for limited periods.

Publications: Annual Report; magazine.

Finance: Net assets 92% of the common stock capital of Robert Bosch GmbH. Total assets €5,155,282,000 (2010); annual expenditure €78,815,000 (2010).

Board of Trustees: Dr Kurt W. Liedtke (Chair.).

Principal Staff: Chief Exec. Dieter Berg; Exec. Dir Dr Ingrid Hamm.

Address: Heidehofstr. 31, 70184 Stuttgart.

Telephone: (711) 46084-0; **Fax:** (711) 46084-1094; **Internet:** www.bosch-stiftung.de; **e-mail:** info@bosch-stiftung.de.

Bundeskanzler-Willy-Brandt-Stiftung (Federal Chancellor Willy Brandt Foundation)

Established in 1994 by the German Bundestag to further the aims of the former Chancellor Willy Brandt. Aims to contribute to an understanding of the history of the 20th century, and of the development of the Federal Republic of Germany.

Activities: Promotes the ideals of Willy Brandt in the areas of the peace, freedom and unity of the German people; the safeguarding of democracy; and understanding and reconciliation between nations. Operates in the areas of the arts and humanities, education, international affairs, law and human rights, and social welfare, nationally and internationally, through self-conducted programmes, research, conferences, training courses and publications. Only provides external financial support to college students and rising young scholars, through awarding the Willy Brandt Prize for the Advancement of Rising Young Scholars and granting internships to students of political science and/or modern history.

Geographical Area of Activity: International.

Restrictions: No grants. Conducts only its own projects.

Publications: *Schriftenreihe der Bundeskanzler-Willy-Brandt-Stiftung*; *Edition Willy Brandt—Berliner Ausgabe*; Annual Newsletter.

Finance: Annual expenditure €1,543,000 (2010).

Board of Governors: Dr Wolfgang Thierse (Pres.); Dr Jürgen Burckhardt (Vice-Pres.).

Principal Staff: Exec. Dir Dr Wolfram Hoppenstedt.

Address: Unter den Linden 62–68, 10117 Berlin.

Telephone: (30) 787707-0; **Fax:** (30) 787707-50; **Internet:** www.willy-brandt.de; **e-mail:** info@bwbs.de.

Brot für die Welt (Bread for the World)

Founded in 1959 by protestant churches in Germany to help people living in need and misery.

Activities: Operates more than 700 self-help projects each year in around 80 developing countries, including countries of Central and South America, Africa and South-East Asia, in collaboration with partner organizations. Projects operate in the areas of education, advice and practical assistance, health and welfare, and emergency relief.

Geographical Area of Activity: Developing countries in Central and South America, Africa, South-East Asia and the Far East; Germany.

Restrictions: Does not conduct own projects in the countries of the Southern hemisphere, but supports local partners in their work.

Principal Staff: Dir Cornelia Füllkrug-Weitzel.

Address: Stafflenbergstr. 76, 70184 Stuttgart.

Telephone: (711) 2159-0; **Fax:** (711) 2159-110; **Internet:** www.brot-fuer-die-welt.de; **e-mail:** kontakt@brot-fuer-die-welt.de.

CBM

Founded in 1908 by Pastor Ernst Jakob Christoffel and formerly known as Christoffel Blindenmission, CBM is an international Christian disability and inclusive development organization, committed to improving the quality of life of persons with disabilities in the poorest countries of the world.

Activities: Along with its partner organizations, CBM takes part in 700 projects in 70 countries in Africa, Asia and Central and South America. CBM works with people with disabilities, their families, local partner organizations, alliance partners including UN agencies, global organizations, and disabled persons' organizations. It is involved with 'VISION 2020: the Right to Sight', a global initiative with the World Health Organization and the International Agency for the Prevention of Blindness (IAPB). Also collaborates with international organizations. Ten CBM member associations (in Australia, Canada, Germany, Ireland, Italy, Kenya, New Zealand, Switzerland, UK and the USA) support a joint programme of work.

Geographical Area of Activity: World-wide.

Publications: Annual Reports.

Finance: Annual programme expenditure approx. €60,000,000.

Presiding Board: Wolfgang Fischer (Chair.).

Principal Staff: Pres. Prof. Allen Foster.

Address: Nibelungenstr. 124, 64625 Bensheim.

Telephone: (6251) 1310; **Fax:** (6251) 131309; **Internet:** www.cbm.org; **e-mail:** contact@cbm.org.

Sergiu-Celibidache-Stiftung (Sergiu Celibidache Foundation)

Founded in December 1999 by Serge Ioan and Joana Celibidache.

Activities: The Foundation aims to promote the musical work of Sergiu Celibidache, through documentation, continuation and discussion of his music through seminars and publications. Activities include supporting young musicians, organizing master classes, discussions, and conducting courses and concerts. Organized the first Sergiu Celibidache Festival in October 2002 in Munich.

Geographical Area of Activity: International.

Trustees: Dr Richard von Weizsacker (Pres.).

Principal Staff: Pres. Serge Celebidachi; Intendant Mark Mast.

Address: Bäckerstr. 46, 81241 Munich.

Telephone: (89) 836606; **Fax:** (89) 8204232; **Internet:** www .celibidache.net; **e-mail:** info@celibidache.net.

Daimler und Benz Stiftung (Daimler and Benz Foundation)

Founded in 1986 by Daimler-Benz AG (now Daimler AG) to support research relating to the inter-relationships between human beings, the environment, and technology.

Activities: Provides funds for research undertaken by groups working on special topics within the frame of defined research programmes; research activities are co-ordinated and the results published. Grants are also awarded to individuals and institutions.

Geographical Area of Activity: Germany and international.

Publications: Annual Reports; *Bertha Benz Lectures* series; additional and recent publications are on the website.

Finance: Annual expenditure €2,200,000 (2009).

Board of Trustees: Dr Thomas Weber (Chair.).

Principal Staff: Man. Dir Dr Jörg Klein.

Address: Dr.-Carl-Benz-Platz 2, 68526 Ladenburg, Germany.

Telephone: (6203) 10920; **Fax:** (6203) 10925; **Internet:** www .daimler-benz-stiftung.de; **e-mail:** info@daimler-benz -stiftung.de.

Deutsch-Russischer Austausch eV—DRA (German-Russian Exchange)

Established in 1992 to assist the democratic process of Russia through co-operative projects.

Activities: Operates in Germany, Russia, Ukraine and Belarus through local activities in large cities, including St Petersburg and Berlin. Provides support to citizens' initiatives, human rights organizations and non-governmental social organizations, as well as running programmes in the fields of continuing education and exchange initiatives as well as facilitating the search for contacts with Western partners.

Geographical Area of Activity: Germany, Belarus, Ukraine and the Russian Federation.

Publications: Newsletter.

Board of Directors: Sabine Erdmann-Kutnevic; Elfie Siegl; Hanno Gundert; Jörg Albinsky; Tim Bohse.

Principal Staff: Exec. Dir Stefan Melle.

Address: Badstr. 44, 13357 Berlin.

Telephone: (30) 4466800; **Fax:** (30) 44668010; **Internet:** www .austausch.org; **e-mail:** info@austausch.org.

Deutsche AIDS-Stiftung (German AIDS Foundation)

Established in 1987 to help HIV-positive individuals. Also supports projects to assist those affected and has received more than 70,000 project proposals. Has provided assistance to individuals and funded projects to the value of almost €30m.

Activities: Main spheres of activity include financial assistance and improved care for the HIV-affected, and promotion of the Foundation's objectives. Also assists best-practice projects in Sub-Saharan Africa.

Geographical Area of Activity: Germany and Sub-Saharan Africa.

Publications: Annual Report; electronic newsletter; additional material for events; *Stiftung konkret* and other publications.

Supervisory Board: Rainer Jarchow (Chair.); Dr Jurgen Stechel (Vice-Chair.); **Board of Trustees:** Dr Christophe Uleer (Chair.).

Principal Staff: Man. Dir. Dr Ulrich Heide.

Address: Markt 26, 53111 Bonn.

Telephone: (228) 6046910; **Fax:** (228) 6046969; **Internet:** www.aids-stiftung.de; **e-mail:** info@aids-stiftung.de.

Deutsche Bank Stiftung (Deutsche Bank Foundation)

Established in 1986 by Deutsche Bank AG.

Activities: Spheres of activity include the humanities, social welfare and economic affairs. Aims to assist people in attaining self-reliance in social spheres through self-conducted programmes. Provides grants to individuals, as well as to projects that help achieve the Foundation's goals.

Geographical Area of Activity: Germany and Europe.

Publications: Annual Report (in German and English).

Finance: Annual income €5,624,000; expenditure €5,200,000 (2009) Total reserves €136,400,000 (2011).

Trustees: Dr Tessen von Heydebreck (Chair.); Michael Münch (Deputy Chair.).

Principal Staff: Man. Dir Joerg Eduard Krumsiek.

Address: Rossmarkt 18, 60262 Frankfurt.

Telephone: (69) 91034999; **Fax:** (69) 91038371; **Internet:** www .deutsche-bank-stiftung.de; **e-mail:** office.dbstiftung@db .com.

Deutsche Bundesstiftung Umwelt—DBU (German Federal Foundation for the Environment)

Established in 1990 by the German Government for research, development and innovation in the field of the environment.

Activities: Encourages research, development and innovation in the field of environmentally- and health-friendly products, especially by small and medium-sized companies; promotes the exchange of information on the environment between the scientific and business communities; and aims to safeguard national natural and cultural heritage from environmental damage. Also awards an annual environmental prize worth €500,000.

Geographical Area of Activity: Germany, with occasional grants to other countries in Central and Eastern European countries and beyond.

Restrictions: No grants to state organizations.

Publications: see website.

Finance: Assets €1,800,000,000; annual budget approx. €50,000,000.

Board of Advisers: Hubert Weinzierl (Chair.); Jürgen Becker (Vice-Chair.); Helmut Jäger (Vice-Chair.);.

Principal Staff: Gen. Sec. Dr Fritz Brickwedde.

Address: An der Bornau 2, 49090 Osnabrück.

Telephone: (541) 9633-0; **Fax:** (541) 9633-190; **Internet:** www .dbu.de; **e-mail:** info@dbu.de.

Deutsche Gesellschaft für Auswärtige Politik— DGAP (German Council on Foreign Relations)

Founded in 1955, a national foreign-policy network. As an independent, non-partisan and non-profit organization, it actively takes part in the political decision-making process, and aims to improve the understanding of German foreign policy and international relations. It promotes research in these areas and provides documentation regarding problems of international relations.

Activities: Operates in the field of international relations through research and advises decision-makers in politics, business and society. It informs both the public and the media. Operations include a research institute, documentation, conferences and study groups, courses, publications and lectures. Maintains a research library specializing in foreign affairs.

Geographical Area of Activity: Europe, USA, Russia, Eurasia and China.

Publications: *Jahrbuch Internationale Politik* (annually); *Internationale Politik* (bimonthly); *Internationale Politik* (global edition, bimonthly).

Finance: The DGAP is funded by the German Federal Foreign Office, private corporations, foundations and others, as well as through the financial support of its more than 2,000 members.

Board: Dr Arend Oetker (Pres.); Christopher Freiherr von Oppenheim (Treas.).

Principal Staff: Exec. Vice-Pres. Paul Freiherr von Maltzahn.

Address: Rauchstr. 17–18, 10787 Berlin.

Telephone: (30) 2542310; **Fax:** (30) 25423116; **Internet:** www.dgap.org; **e-mail:** info@dgap.org.

Deutsche Krebshilfe eV (German Cancer Assistance)

Founded in September 1974 by Dr Mildred Scheel, Dr Helmut Geiger, D. Kühn, Bechtold Freiherr von Massenbach, F. L. Müller, Prof. Hermann Schardt, Heinz Schmidt and Martin Virchow to support the welfare of cancer patients, and to fight against cancer.

Activities: Operates in the fields of education, research and medicine and health, nationally through research and training courses, and nationally and internationally through self-conducted programmes and conferences. Makes grants to institutions to support research into cancer diagnosis, therapy, after-care and self-help, organizes and supports medical education projects, further education courses and information events. Also provides advice, help and financial support to people suffering from cancer. Administers the Dr Mildred Scheel Stiftung für Krebforschung.

Geographical Area of Activity: Germany.

Publications: Booklets on cancer; videos; CD-ROM; newsletter and other publications.

Board of Directors: Dr Fritz Pleitgen (Pres.).

Principal Staff: Gen. Man. Gert Nettekoven.

Address: Buschstr. 32, 53113 Bonn.

Telephone: (228) 72990-0; **Fax:** (228) 72990-11; **Internet:** www.krebshilfe.de; **e-mail:** deutsche@krebshilfe.de.

Deutsche Nationalstiftung (German National Trust)

Established in 1993 by former Chancellor Helmut Schmidt and a group of his friends, including Herman J. Abs, Gerd Bucerius, Kurt Körber and Michael Otto, to bring to the public consciousness the mutual relationship between science, art and literature, law, politics and commerce, and to influence the values of the nation with respect to domestic and international concerns so as to contribute to the common good; to promote and strengthen the process of German unity and promote German cultural identity within a European cultural mosaic; and to comment on the pressing questions facing Germany at present and in the future.

Activities: Organizes annual meetings to consider urgent problems and discuss questions of national and European relevance; Bestows an annual National Prize of approximately €75,000; organizes forums; and publishes theses on issues affecting Germany and Europe.

Geographical Area of Activity: Germany and European Union countries.

Publications: Annual Report.

Board of Trustees: Dr Ulrich Cartellieri (Chair.).

Principal Staff: Exec. Pres. Dirk Reimers.

Address: Feldbrunnenstr. 56, 20148 Hamburg.

Telephone: (40) 413367-53; **Fax:** (40) 413367-55; **Internet:** www.nationalstiftung.de; **e-mail:** info@nationalstiftung.de.

Deutsche Orient-Stiftung (German Orient Foundation)

Established in 1960 by the German Near and Middle East Association to promote relations between Germany and the lands of the Orient. It is the oldest private scientific institute in Germany.

Activities: Operates in the field of science, culture, general knowledge and modern history, promoting dialogue between Germany and the countries of the Orient. Carries out research into local political and social developments in the Near and Middle East.

Geographical Area of Activity: Germany and the Middle East.

Restrictions: Does not make grants to individuals.

Publications: *ORIENT* (magazine).

Board Members: Martin Bay (Chair.); Henry Hasselbarth, Dr Michael Luders (Deputy Chairs).

Principal Staff: Exec. Dir Dr Gunter Mulack.

Address: Jägerstr. 63A, 10117 Berlin.

Telephone: (30) 20641021; **Fax:** (30) 20641029; **Internet:** www.deutsche-orient-stiftung.de.

Deutsche Stiftung für internationale rechtliche Zusammenarbeit eV (German Foundation for International Legal Co-operation)

Established in 1992 as a non-profit-making association at the initiative of the then Federal Minister of Justice Dr Klaus Kinkel. In the early years, the work of the Foundation was largely promoted within the framework of the TRANSFORM consultation programme, and after this additionally by the Stability Pact for South Eastern Europe, and primarily from the budget of the Federal Ministry of Justice.

Activities: The Foundation supports partner states on behalf or the German Federal Government in reforming their legal systems and judiciary. In providing legislative consultation, the Foundation undertakes discussions with experts, draft expert reports and assists in drawing up draft Bills; promotes the implementation of reform statutes, in particular through basic and further training of judges, public prosecutors, attorneys, notaries, academics and young lawyers, including within the framework of the EU's IPA and ENPI programmes; arranges seminars, workshops, lecture events and symposia in the partner states, as well as working visits, training periods and guest visits, primarily to Germany but also to other European Union States; focus on German and European law, supplemented by a cross-border exchange of experience.

Geographical Area of Activity: Bulgaria, the Czech Republic, Hungary, Poland, Romania and the Slovak Republic, the countries of the former USSR (Azerbaijan, Belarus, Estonia, Georgia, Latvia, Lithuania, the Russian Federation, Ukraine), and the partner states of the Stability Pact for South-Eastern Europe (Albania, Bosnia-Herzegovina, Croatia, Kosovo, Macedonia, Moldova, Montenegro, Serbia). Also carries out projects with Algeria, Iraq, Jordan, Lebanon, Saudi Arabia, Syria, Turkey, Tunisia, Uzbekistan, Kazakhstan and Vietnam, as well as with states in Latin America.

Restrictions: No unsolicited applications for grants are accepted.

Publications: Annual Report.

Finance: Funded by the German Federal Government and the European Union.

Board of Trustees: Dr Jörg Freiherr Frank von Fürstenwerth (Chair.); Dr Bernhard Dombek and Dr. Max Stadler (Deputy Chair.).

Principal Staff: Dir Dirk Mirow.

Address: Ubierstr. 92, 53173 Bonn.

Telephone: (228) 9555-0; **Fax:** (228) 9555-100; **Internet:** www.irz.de; **e-mail:** info@irz.de.

Deutsche Stiftung Weltbevölkerung—DSW (German Foundation for World Population)

Established in 1991 by Dirk Rossmann and Erhard Schreiber, the foundation operates as a development co-operation organization working at international level, focusing on demographic development and reproductive health.

Activities: Promotes development, especially in the areas of family planning, prevention of HIV and AIDS, and population studies in Ethiopia, Kenya and Uganda. Carries out development projects with local non-profit organizations, carries out information and advocacy campaigns in Germany and Europe, and awards a limited number of fellowships. Maintains country offices in Ethiopia, Kenya, Tanzania and Uganda and a Liaison Office in Brussels.

Geographical Area of Activity: Ethiopia, Kenya, Tanzania, Uganda.

Publications: *DSW Update* (monthly); *The Guide to European Population Assistance; Tips and Tricks: How to Apply for the European Commission's Budget Lines for Sustainable Development;* reports; factsheets; newsletters and data reports; posters; online newsletter; Annual Report.

Finance: Assets €6,718,969; annual revenue €6,086,592, expenditure €4,759,400 (2010).

Board of Directors: Erhard Schreiber (Chair.); Helmut Heinen (Co-Chair.).

Principal Staff: Exec. Dir Renate Bähr; Vice-Exec. Dir Karen Hoehn.

Address: Göttinger Chaussee 115, 30459 Hanover.

Telephone: (511) 943730; **Fax:** (511) 9437373; **Internet:** www.weltbevoelkerung.de; **e-mail:** info@dsw-hannover.de.

Deutsche Telekom Stiftung (Deutsche Telekom Foundation)

Established in 1993 to further education in science and technology in Germany.

Activities: Operates in Germany in the field of education, specifically in the areas of natural science, technology and mathematics, through funding projects in all sectors of education, including pre-schools, primary and secondary schools, and universities. Also offers prizes for innovation in new technology.

Geographical Area of Activity: Germany.

Restrictions: Does not accept unsolicited applications for grants.

Finance: Grants disbursed €5,700,000 (2010).

Board: Dr Klaus Kinkel (Chair.).

Principal Staff: Dir Dr Ekkehard Winter.

Address: Postfach 2000, 53105 Bonn.

Internet: www.telekom-stiftung.de; **e-mail:** stiftung@telekom.de.

Deutscher Akademischer Austauschdienst—DAAD (German Academic Exchange Service)

Founded in 1925, (re-established in 1950), the DAAD is a joint organization of institutions of higher education that aims to promote academic exchanges between Germany and other countries.

Activities: Awards long- and short-term scholarships in all fields of study to foreign students and young research workers, including 'sur place' scholarships tenable at some universities in developing countries, and to students from European countries for university summer vacation and language courses. The Foundation has bilateral agreements with German and foreign institutions and promotes student exchange in connection with specific research projects. Supports a programme of exchanges of university teachers for short-term teaching and research visits on a reciprocal basis.

Geographical Area of Activity: International.

Publications: Newsletter; Annual Report.

Board of Trustees: Prof. Dr Margret Wintermantel (Pres.); Prof. Dr Joybrato Mukherjee (Vice-Pres.).

Principal Staff: Sec.-Gen. Dr Dorothea Rüland.

Address: Kennedyallee 50, 53175 Bonn.

Telephone: (228) 882-0; **Fax:** (228) 882-444; **Internet:** www.daad.de; **e-mail:** postmaster@daad.de.

Deutsches Institut für Internationale Pädagogische Forschung (German Institute for International Educational Research)

Incorporated in 1951 as a foundation under public law to support international and intercultural comparative and historical educational research as well as educational planning.

Activities: The Institute consists of five units, focusing on two themes: educational information and history of education, and the quality of education. The Educational Information Centre comprises the office of the German Educational Server, the Information System for Education, Information and Documentation, and the Frankfurt Research Library, including the Frankfurt Teacher Library. The Centre for History of Education incorporates the Bibliothek für Bildungsgeschichtliche Forschung (Library for Research on Educational History) in Berlin and the Research Office, Berlin. Other units are the Centre for Educational Quality and Evaluation, the Centre for Financing and Planning in Education and the Centre for Education and Culture. The Institute also collaborates with universities and educational research institutes in Germany and abroad.

Geographical Area of Activity: Germany.

Restrictions: Applications for grants are not accepted.

Publications: *Archives DIPF in the press* (annual report).

Governing Board: Prof. Dr Marc Rittberger (Dir); Prof. Dr Marcus Hasselhorn (Deputy Dir).

Principal Staff: Man. Dir Susanne Boomkamp-Dahmen.

Address: Schloss-Str. 29, 60486 Frankfurt am Main.

Telephone: (69) 24708-0; **Fax:** (69) 24708-444; **Internet:** www.dipf.de; **e-mail:** dipf@dipf.de.

Deutsches Rheuma-Forschungszentrum Berlin (German Rheumatism Research Centre Berlin)

Founded in December 1988 by the City of Berlin and Immanuel Hospital to promote research into rheumatic diseases.

Activities: Operates in the fields of medicine and health, and science and technology, nationally and internationally through self-conducted programmes and research, and internationally through conferences, training courses and publications.

Geographical Area of Activity: Mainly Germany.

Publications: Annual Scientific Report.

Finance: The Foundation is financed by the City of Berlin and other sources; annual expenditure approx. €3,000,000.

Board of Trustees: Prof. Dr Reinhard Kurth (Pres.).

Principal Staff: Admin. Dir Petra Starke.

Address: Charitéplatz 1, 10117 Berlin.

Telephone: (30) 28460-280; **Fax:** (30) 28460-603; **Internet:** www.drfz.de; **e-mail:** info@drfz.de.

Dräger-Stiftung (Dräger Foundation)

Established in 1974 by Dr Heinrich Dräger as a non-profit foundation for the promotion of science and research in the field of economic and social order.

Activities: Operates nationally and internationally in the fields of economic and social affairs, international affairs, and medicine and health, through self-conducted programmes, conferences and publications; national (regional) activities in the areas of conservation and the environment.

Geographical Area of Activity: Europe and USA.

Restrictions: No grants are made to individuals; no postgraduate scholarships.

Publications: *Edition 'Zukunft', Series* (Vols 1-17, 1980-2001); *Conference Documentations Malente Symposia* (2001-2008).

Finance: Total assets approx. €6,100,000.

Board of Trustees: Dr Christian Dräger; Prof. Dr Dieter Feddersen.

Principal Staff: Dir Petra Pissulla.

Address: Moislinger Allee 53-55, 23558 Lübeck.

Telephone: (451) 8822151; **Fax:** (451) 8823050; **Internet:** www
.draeger-stiftung.de; **e-mail:** draeger-stiftung@draeger.com.

Friedrich-Ebert-Stiftung eV (Friedrich Ebert Foundation)

Founded in 1925 as a political legacy of Friedrich Ebert, the
first President of the Weimar Republic, and re-established
after the Second World War, to further the democratic education of the German people, and international co-operation
towards democracy.

Activities: Operates internationally through developing its
own projects in the field of aid to less-developed countries,
and nationally and internationally in the fields of education,
the arts and humanities, social welfare and studies, economic
affairs and international relations, through self-conducted
programmes, research, fellowships, scholarships, conferences,
courses, publications and lectures. Maintains offices in Bonn
and Berlin, four academies and 13 regional offices in Germany,
as well as maintaining its own representations in 70 countries
of Africa, Asia, the Middle East, and Central and South America, and offices in 33 countries of Western Europe, Central and
South-Eastern Europe, the CIS countries and the USA and
Japan. Maintains a specialized library of approximately
700,000 volumes on the German and international labour
movement, the archive of social democracy, which is the largest collection of documents on the history of the labour movement in Germany.

Geographical Area of Activity: Africa, Asia, CIS countries,
Central and South-Eastern Europe, Central and South America, Japan, Middle East, USA, Western Europe.

Restrictions: Does not provide financial assistance of any
sort.

Publications: Report of operations; publications on economic
policy, labour and social research, technology and society,
social and contemporary history, and foreign policy research
(nearly 600 titles a year in German, in addition 500 approx.
world-wide); political reviews: *Neue Gesellschaft/Frankfurter
Hefte*; *International Politics and Society, Nueva Sociedad*.

Finance: Funded mainly from public sources; annual budget
approx. €137,000,000 (2010).

Trustees: Dr Peter Struck (Chair.); Kurt Beck (Vice-Chair.).

Principal Staff: Exec. Dir Dr Roland Schmidt.

Address: Godesberger Allee 149, 53175 Bonn.

Telephone: (228) 883-0; **Fax:** (228) 833-9207; **Internet:** www
.fes.de; **e-mail:** presse@fes.de.

Erinnerung, Verantwortung und Zukunft (Remembrance, Responsibility and the Future)

Established in 2000 by an Act of the German Federal Government and German companies to mark their historical and
moral responsibility for the forced labour perpetrated under
the National Socialist regime, particularly during the Second
World War, through assisting former forced labourers and
other victims of the Nazis, and keeping alive the memories of
the Holocaust to prevent a resurgence of a totalitarian system.
More than 6,500 German companies had contributed to the
fund by the end of 2001.

Activities: Operates through partner organizations in countries of Western, Central and Eastern Europe, Israel and the
USA to make payments to former forced labourers who were
detained in a concentration camp or ghetto and were subjected
to forced labour, or who were deported from their native country to the German Reich or countries occupied by the German
Reich (apart from Austria) and who were subjected to forced
labour and harsh living conditions. Those affected by other
injustices from the period (e.g. personal injury or loss of property) may also apply for compensation. A Remembrance and
Future Fund fosters international understanding, social justice, remembrance and future-orientated projects, and promotes projects in the interest of the heirs of those who did not
survive the National Socialist regime. Grants are currently
directed primarily to projects in the interests of the victims
and their heirs, as well as work with witnesses. Future grant

programmes will focus on projects that promote youth
exchange, reconciliation, international understanding,
respect of human rights and social justice.

Geographical Area of Activity: International.

Restrictions: No funding for institutions.

Finance: The capital fund is financed by German companies
(the Foundation Initiative of German Industry) and the German Federal Government; total assets approx.
€5,000,000,000. The Remembrance and the Future Fund had
an initial endowment of approx. €350,000,000.

Trustees: Dr Michael Jansen (Chair.); Dr Jorg Freiherr Frank
von Furstenwerth (Vice-Chair.).

Principal Staff: Chair. Dr Martin Salm; Dir Gunther
Saathoff.

Address: Lindenstr. 20–25, 10969 Berlin.

Telephone: (30) 20616776; **Fax:** (30) 20282473; **Internet:** www
.stiftung-evz.de; **e-mail:** info@stiftungsinitiative.de.

Europäische Rechtsakademie—ERA (Academy of European Law)

Established on the initiative of the European Parliament in
1992 by the governments of Luxembourg and Rhineland-Pala-
tinate, the City of Trier and the Association for the Promotion
of the Academy.

Activities: Provides legal training and a forum for debate for
lawyers throughout Europe. Activities include the organization of conferences, seminars, language courses, e-learning
courses and the implementation of legal training projects, as
well as publishing activities and the rental of congress facilities. Runs a scholarship programme to enable lawyers from
new and future European Union member states to attend its
training courses in Trier.

Geographical Area of Activity: Austria, Bulgaria, Croatia,
Cyprus, Czech Republic, Finland, France, Germany, Greece,
Hungary, Ireland, Italy, Luxembourg, Malta, the Netherlands,
Poland, Portugal, Romania, Slovakia, Slovenia, Spain, Swe-
den, United Kingdom.

Restrictions: Unsolicited applications for grants outside the
framework of the Peter Caesar Scholarship Programme are
not accepted.

Publications: *ERA Forum* (quarterly review of European law,
published in co-operation with Springer).

Finance: Operating budget €6,000,000 (2010).

Board of Trustees: Dr. Pauliine Koskelo (Chair.); Prof. Josef
Azizi (Deputy Chair.); Dr Péter Köves (Deputy Chair.).

Principal Staff: Pres. Dr Jacques Santer; Vice-Pres. Joachim
Mertes.

Address: Metzer Allee 4, 54295 Trier.

Telephone: (651) 937370; **Fax:** (651) 93737773; **Internet:** www
.era.int; **e-mail:** info@era.int.

Evangelisches Studienwerk eV (Protestant Study Foundation)

Founded in 1948 by several Protestant Churches to bring
together and promote Protestant students of any faculty; to
provide for their advanced training and to give advice, also
beyond the limits of their studies, regarding their evangelical
responsibilities in their profession, community and society.
The organization is now supported by all Protestant Churches
in Germany.

Activities: Operates nationally in the fields of religion, education and research, social welfare and studies, economic
affairs, science and medicine, the arts and humanities, law
and other professions, through self-conducted programmes,
grants to individuals, fellowships, scholarships, seminars,
conferences, courses and advisory services. Support is given
to German Protestant university students and graduates in
Germany and in other European Union countries.

Geographical Area of Activity: Europe.

Publications: *Villigst Profile; Oriens Christianus: History and
Presence of Middle East Christianity; Individuality in Russia*

and Germany; The Uneasiness in the 'Third generation': Reflections of the Holocaust, Antisemitism and National Socialism; Challenge Development: Newer contributions for theoretical and practice-oriented development research.

Board of Directors: Bishop Dr Johannes Friedrich (Chair.); Albert Henz (Vice-Chair.).

Principal Staff: Dir Friederike Faß.

Address: Iserlohner Str. 25, 58239 Schwerte.

Telephone: (2304) 755196; **Fax:** (2304) 755250; **Internet:** www .evstudienwerk.de; **e-mail:** info@evstudienwerk.de.

filia.die frauenstiftung (filia—the Women's Foundation)

Established in 2001 to promote women playing a decisive role in all areas of society.

Activities: Offers grants to women's NGOs, community and grassroots organizations in Central and Eastern Europe (45% of budget), Germany (20%), global South (20%), international networking (10%) and rapid response (5%). filia works on behalf of women who are dicriminated against, not only because of their gender, but also because of the colour of their skin, their origin, or their sexual orientation.

Geographical Area of Activity: Central and Eastern Europe, Germany and the global south.

Restrictions: filia funds global South region projects only in co-operation with the International Network of Women's Funds (INWF). Does not fund the fields of art and science or on an individual basis.

Publications: Business reports; *filianews*; Annual Report.

Finance: Total grants expenditure €320,000 (2010).

Board of Trustees: comprises seven members, elected every three years.

Principal Staff: Contact Sonja Schelper.

Address: Alte Königstr. 18, 22767 Hamburg.

Telephone: (40) 380381990; **Fax:** (40) 380381999; **Internet:** www.filia-frauenstiftung.de; **e-mail:** info@filia -frauenstiftung.de.

F. C. Flick-Stiftung gegen Fremdenfeindlichkeit, Rassismus und Intoleranz (F. C. Flick Foundation against Xenophobia, Racism and Intolerance)

Established by Dr Friedrich Christian Flick to fight against xenophobia, intolerance and racism and to encourage international open-mindedness.

Activities: Supports projects that focus on developing ways of combating xenophobia, racism and intolerance, in the focus areas of culture, sport and young people, aged between five and 15. Focuses on work with children and young people in the eastern states of Germany, supporting existing projects, youth exchanges with Eastern Europe, assisting initiatives linking artistic ideas with political and contemporary enlightenment and promoting sport projects. Long-term projects include the German-Polish student exchange programme, Kopernikus; the Lindenstrasse Workshop for Youth in Potsdam; and the Rosa Luxemburg Elementary School in Potsdam.

Geographical Area of Activity: Germany.

Publications: Annual report; Funding guidelines.

Board of Trustees: Dr Friedrich Christian Flick (Chair.); Monika Griefahn (Deputy Chair.).

Principal Staff: Exec. Dir Christiane Fetscher.

Address: Am Neuen Markt 8, 14467 Potsdam.

Telephone: (331) 2007770; **Fax:** (331) 2007771; **Internet:** www .stiftung-toleranz.de; **e-mail:** fetscher@stiftung-toleranz.de.

Forschungsgesellschaft für das Weltflüchtlingsproblem—AWR (Association for the Study of the World Refugee Problem)

Founded in 1951 (merged in October 1961 with the European Association for the Study of Refugee Problems) to promote, examine thoroughly and co-ordinate the scientific study of refugee problems to give competent organs throughout the world the scientific basis to solve these problems.

Activities: Operates internationally as an independent association in which scholars from all fields of knowledge co-operate with experts from national and international organizations to investigate refugee problems and to provide theoretical bases of possible solutions. The field of study has also been extended to the problems of migrant workers. The Association is a consultative body of the UN and the Council of Europe. National sections exist in most Western European countries and are connected by the International General Assembly; there are observers in many other countries. The scientific investigations are carried out by international committees of experts, each dealing with a particular aspect such as population and health, international refugees, cultural questions, legal questions, sociology, economic integration, housing and employment. Their findings are co-ordinated by the International Curatorium. The results of the Association's comparative research work are communicated to specialists from countries with refugee problems and also, often with recommendations, to governments and the appropriate organizations. Congresses are held annually in one of the member countries. The Association has members in 21 countries.

Geographical Area of Activity: International.

Publications: *AWR Bulletin* (quarterly); reports are published regularly in four languages.

Board of Trustees: Prof. Dr Andrzej Sakson (Pres.); Prof. Dr Peter Van Krieken (Vice-Pres.).

Principal Staff: Sec.-Gen. Prof. Dr Markus Babo.

Address: Postfach 1241, 97201 Höchberg.

Telephone: (931) 3511486; **Internet:** www.awr-int.de; **e-mail:** awr_int_forschungsg@yahoo.de.

Frankfurter Stiftung für Deutsch-Italienische Studien (Frankfurt Foundation for German-Italian Studies)

Established in 1992 by the Deutsch-Italienische Vereinigung eV for the promotion of international understanding through the cultivation of academic, cultural and human relations between Germany and Italy.

Activities: Operates in the fields of the arts and humanities and education, nationally and internationally through self-conducted programmes and publications and funding of other publications, and nationally through conferences.

Geographical Area of Activity: Europe.

Publications: *Italienisch* (magazine of Italian language and literature).

Trustees: Dietrich Herbst (Hon. Chair.); Cristof Reiser (Chair.); Cristina Herbst (Vice-Chair.).

Principal Staff: Salvatore A. Sanna.

Address: Arndtstr. 12, 60325 Frankfurt am Main.

Telephone: (69) 746752; **Fax:** (69) 7411453; **Internet:** www.div -web.de; **e-mail:** div@div-web.de.

Freudenberg Stiftung

Founded in 1984 as a not-for-profit limited company to support the cause of peace and helping the needy. Returns on company capital are used to advance science, education and humanities, and to promote peace.

Activities: Operates nationally. Main spheres of activity include education and social welfare, which are promoted through self-conducted programmes, grants to institutions, training courses and prizes. Also supports youngsters at risk, the mentally-challenged, and cultural minorities. Social, economic or cultural projects that help surmount disadvantage and exclusion, strengthen democracy are favoured. Functions at grassroots level; allows inter-organizational co-operation and promotes self-help, as well as managing other foundations.

Geographical Area of Activity: Germany.

Restrictions: No grants are made to individuals, for scholarships, research or construction.

Publications: Reports.

Board of Trustees: Dr Reinhart Freudenberg (Chair.).

Principal Staff: Exec. Dir Dr Pia Gerber.

Address: Freudenbergstr. 2, 69469 Weinheim.

Telephone: (6201) 17498; **Fax:** (6201) 13262; **Internet:** www .freudenbergstiftung.de; **e-mail:** info@freudenbergstiftung .de.

Friedensdorf International (Peace Village International)

Established in 1967 as a citizens' initiative to provide assistance to children in areas of war and crisis and to campaign for peace.

Activities: Operates world-wide in the areas of medicine, health and social welfare. Children are brought to Europe for short-term medical care and rehabilitation, although projects for the improvement of medical care have also been established in the native countries of the children, and where possible children are treated there. The organization also promotes peace and carries out educational work, including the Peace Village Bildungswerk educational centre, which promotes peace.

Geographical Area of Activity: International.

Publications: *Peace Village Report* (2 a year).

Address: Lanterstr. 21, 46539 Dinslaken.

Telephone: (2064) 4974; **Fax:** (2064) 4974; **Internet:** www .friedensdorf.de; **e-mail:** info@friedensdorf.de.

Gemeinnützige Hertie-Stiftung (Gemeinnützige Hertie Foundation)

Established in 1974 by Georg Karg as a charity for the promotion of science and education.

Activities: Operates in the fields of preschool and school, higher education, neurosciences as well as the compatibility of job and family.

Geographical Area of Activity: Germany and the rest of Europe.

Restrictions: Preference is given to projects that are innovative, with a broad span of application.

Finance: Total assets €800,000,000 (2010); annual expenditure €20,000,000 (2010).

Governing Board: Dr Michael Endres (Chair.); Dr Bernhard Wunderlin (Vice-Chair.).

Principal Staff: Man. Dir Dr Antje Becker.

Address: Grüneburgweg 105, 60323 Frankfurt am Main.

Telephone: (69) 6607560; **Fax:** (69) 660756999; **Internet:** www.ghst.de; **e-mail:** info@ghst.de.

GIGA—German Institute of Global and Area Studies (Leibniz-Institut für Globale und Regionale Studien)

Founded in 1964 for research and documentation on political, economic and social developments in overseas countries, especially in the countries of Africa, Asia, Latin America, and the Middle East. Known as the Deutsches Übersee-Institut until 2005.

Activities: Through a combination of area and comparative area studies, the GIGA examines not only the issues and challenges facing Africa, Asia, Latin America and the Middle East but also new developments in North–South and South–South relationships. The GIGA is the largest German research institute for area and comparative area studies, also among the largest in Europe. The GIGA's main priority is research. In addition, the Institute supports the advancement of junior researchers; provides consultation services to the media, the government and civil society organizations; and makes information available to the public through its Information Centre. The GIGA defines itself as a think tank serving the academic, political and economic communities as well as the general public.

Restrictions: Applications for grants are not accepted.

Publications: Publishes four academic open access journals: *Africa Spectrum, Journal of Current Chinese Affairs, Journal of Politics in Latin America, Journal of Current Southeast Asian Affairs* (all available online); GIGA Working Papers; *GIGA Focus.*

Finance: Finance provided by the Government of Germany (Ministry of Foreign Affairs) and the City of Hamburg.

Principal Staff: Acting Pres. Prof. Dr D. Nolte; Acting Vice-Pres. Prof. Dr H. Fürtig.

Address: Neuer Jungfernstieg 21, 20354 Hamburg.

Telephone: (40) 42825593; **Fax:** (40) 42825547; **Internet:** www .giga-hamburg.de; **e-mail:** info@giga-hamburg.de.

Goethe-Institut Inter Nationes

Founded in 1951 for the promotion of the German language abroad and for the fostering of international cultural relations.

Activities: Operates internationally in the fields of the arts and humanities, international relations, language teaching and information brokerage, through self-conducted programmes, partnership programmes, grants to institutions and individuals, fellowships, scholarships, conferences, courses, publications and lectures. The Institute is particularly concerned with the teaching and promotion of the German language abroad and provides professional assistance to foreign teachers of German and students of German philology, and for the development and improvement of teaching methods and materials. It also provides information abroad about the cultural life of Germany and co-operates with cultural organizations abroad. There are 16 branches of the Institute in Germany and 126 abroad in 77 countries.

Geographical Area of Activity: World-wide.

Publications: Annual Report; *Goethe Institut Aktuell; Markt; Legal Principles;* and other publications.

Board of Trustees: Prof. Dr Klaus-Dieter Lehmann (Pres.).

Principal Staff: Sec.-Gen. Dr Hans-Georg Knopp; Business Dir Bruno Gross.

Address: Dachauerstr. 122, 80637 Munich.

Telephone: (89) 159210; **Fax:** (89) 15921450; **Internet:** www .goethe.de; **e-mail:** info@goethe.de.

Haniel-Stiftung (Haniel Foundation)

Founded in 1988 by Franz Haniel & Cie GmbH to encourage the European business community to support humanitarian causes to promote the image of business in educational establishments, and to further the development of management techniques and training.

Activities: The Foundation pursues the aim of promoting achievement and the courage to make entrepreneurial decisions in a socially responsible manner. In conrete terms this means: strengthening entrepreneurs' commitment to public welfare, positively shaping the entrepreneurial image in society, and supporting the training and further education of young leaders on a national and international scale.

Geographical Area of Activity: International, especially Europe.

Publications: Project and conference reports; Annual reports; *Stippvisite; Building bridges.*

Finance: Net assets €45,000,000; annual grants expenditure approx. €2,000,000 (2009).

Trustees: Franz M. Haniel (Chair.); Christoph Böninger (Deputy Chair.).

Principal Staff: Exec. Dir Dr Rupert Antes.

Address: Franz-Haniel-Platz 6–8, 47119 Duisburg.

Telephone: (203) 806367/368; **Fax:** (203) 806720; **Internet:** www.haniel-stiftung.de; **e-mail:** stiftung@haniel.de.

H. W. und J. Hector-Stiftung (H. W. and J. Hector Foundation)

Established by Hans-Werner Hector in 1995.

Activities: Promotes medical research, especially in the areas of cancer and AIDS, as well as art and historical preservation.

Geographical Area of Activity: Europe.

Finance: Annual expenditure approx. €1,000,000.

Principal Staff: Contact Dr Ernstlothar Keiper.

Address: Elizabethstr. 9, 68165 Mannheim.

Telephone: (621) 410980; **Fax:** (621) 4109858; **Internet:** www
.hector-stiftung.de.

Heinrich-Heine-Stiftung für Philosophie und Kritische Wissenschaft (Heinrich Heine Foundation for Philosophy and Critical Theory)

Founded in 1970 by Charlotte A. Morat to promote philosophy and critical theory in research and teaching; to promote pure theory in the classical tradition; and to support any activity that is aimed at improving social relations through constructive criticism.

Activities: Operates nationally and internationally in the field of the arts and humanities, by providing grants to individuals, fellowships and scholarships to promote philosophy and critical knowledge, and research.

Geographical Area of Activity: Germany and international.

Address: Egonstr. 28, 79106 Freiburg Breisgau.

Telephone: (761) 31031.

Minna-James-Heineman-Stiftung (Minna James Heineman Foundation)

Founded in 1928 (to provide care for elderly Jewish women in Hanover) and re-established in 1951 by Dannie N. Heineman for the promotion of scientific research, education and international co-operation; and for the support of charitable institutions. The Foundation is administered by the Stifterverband für die Deutsche Wissenschaft (q.v.).

Activities: Makes grants to scientific institutions in Germany, the USA and Israel, in particular the Max-Planck-Gesellschaft (q.v.), the Weizmann Institute of Science (Israel) and the Heineman Medical Research Centre (USA), preferably for research in the life sciences. The Dannie Heineman Prize is conferred biennially by the Academy of Sciences at Göttingen for an outstanding work, mainly in the field of natural and life sciences. Dannie Heineman scholarships are awarded to students and doctoral students. The Foundation also offers the James Heineman Research Award.

Geographical Area of Activity: Germany, Israel and the USA.

Restrictions: No grants to individuals.

Publications: *People Can No Longer Escape People.*

Finance: Assets approx. €5,000,000.

Board of Directors: Anders Bergendahl (Chair.); Dr Lorenz C. Stech (Sec.); Dr Agnes Gautier (Treas.).

Principal Staff: Gen. Man. Dr Kai de Weldige.

Address: c/o Deutsches Stiftungszentrum (DSZ), Barkhovenallee 1, 45239 Essen.

Telephone: (201) 8401154; **Fax:** (201) 8401255; **Internet:** www
.heineman-stiftung.de; **e-mail:** harald.schaaf@
stifterverband.de.

Gerda Henkel Stiftung (Gerda Henkel Foundation)

Founded in June 1976 by Lisa Maskell in memory of her mother Gerda Henkel as a private, non-profit, grant-making organization dedicated to foster research in the humanities. Focuses on the support of academic projects and PhD fellowships, primarily in the fields of history, art history, archaeology and history of Islam.

Activities: Active in Germany and abroad. Seeks to advance academic research, primarily by supporting projects in the humanities and their publication. In particular, by: supporting research projects by national and international scholars as well as academic conferences on clearly defined, humanities-based topics; awarding research and doctoral scholarships to national and international scholars; supporting measures in the field of historic preservation based on

scholarly grounds; undertaking and supporting all measures that serve the purpose of the Foundation; implementing measures to raise public awareness of the above-mentioned objectives. Focuses particularly on the advancement of young scholars. When awarding scholarships, special consideration is given to research projects that provide young scholars with the opportunity to be involved in research and to improve their professional qualification.

Geographical Area of Activity: International.

Restrictions: Only supports research projects with a clearly defined scope and timeframe. Priority is given to research projects that are outstanding because of the nature of their results and which promise to make the greatest use of the funds available.

Publications: Annual Report; lecture series.

Trustees: Julia Schulz-Dornburg (Chair.); Prof. Dr Meinhard Miegel (Deputy Chair.).

Principal Staff: Exec. Dir Dr Michael Hanssler; Deputy Exec. Dir Dr Angela Kühnen.

Address: Malkastenstr. 15, 40211 Düsseldorf.

Telephone: (211) 9365240; **Fax:** (211) 93652444; **Internet:** www.gerda-henkel-stiftung.de; **e-mail:** info@gerda-henkel
-stiftung.de.

Hirschfeld-Eddy-Stiftung (Hirschfeld-Eddy Foundation)

Established in 2007 to uphold the rights of homosexual, bisexual and transgender people world-wide.

Activities: Aims to encourage respect for the human rights of homosexual, bisexual and transgender people, actively support human rights defenders and remove prejudice.

Geographical Area of Activity: World-wide.

Address: Postfach 040165, 10061 Berlin.

Telephone: (30) 78954778; **Fax:** (30) 78954779; **Internet:** www
.hirschfeld-eddy-stiftung.de; **e-mail:** info@hirschfeld-eddy
-stiftung.de.

Dietmar-Hopp-Stiftung (Dietmar Hopp Foundation)

Established by Dietmar Hopp, a founder member of the computer software company SAP AG, in 1995, with a shareholding in the company.

Activities: Operates nationally and internationally in the fields of science, sport, education and medical research; realizes its objectives by making grants to educational institutions, organizations and companies carrying out medical research.

Geographical Area of Activity: International.

Finance: The Foundation holds more than 15% of SAP AG shares.

Principal Staff: Chair. Dietmar Hopp; Dir Dietrich Lutat.

Address: Raiffeisenring 51, 68789 St Leon-Rot.

Telephone: (6227) 8608560; **Fax:** (6227) 8608591; **Internet:** www.dietmar-hopp-stiftung.de; **e-mail:** info@dietmar-hopp
-stiftung.de.

Alexander von Humboldt Stiftung (Alexander von Humboldt Foundation)

Established in 1860 as a private foundation in memory of the naturalist Alexander von Humboldt, and re-established as a public foundation under private law in 1925 and again in 1953. The Foundation promotes academic co-operation between excellent scientists and scholars from abroad and from Germany. It maintains a network of well over 23,000 Humboldtians from all disciplines in more than 130 countries worldwide, including 43 Nobel Prize winners.

Activities: Every year the Foundation awards more than 800 research fellowships and awards. These allow scientists and scholars from abroad to go to Germany to work on a research project with a host and collaborative partner. Scientists and scholars from Germany can carry out a research project abroad as a guest of one of the alumni of the foundation.

Programmes include the Humboldt Research Fellowship (for postdoctoral and experienced researchers); Georg Forster Research Fellowship (for postdoctoral and experienced researchers from developing countries); Feodor Lynen Research Fellowship (for postdoctoral and experienced researchers in Germany going abroad); Humboldt Research Award (for foreign researchers at the peak of their academic career); Alexander von Humboldt Professorship (for internationally recognized cutting-edge researchers); Sofja Kovalevskaja Award (for outstanding junior researchers); Friedrich Wilhelm Bessel Research Award (for internationally renowned scientists and scholars).

Geographical Area of Activity: World-wide.

Publications: Annual Report; *Bibliographia Humboldtiana* (online); *Humboldt Kosmos* (magazine); *Profile and Services* (brochure); *Alexander von Humboldt Professorship* (brochure); *EURAXESS Germany—National Co-ordination Point at the Alexander von Humboldt Foundation* (flyer).

Finance: Budget approx. €68m.

Board of Governors: Prof. Helmut Schwarz (Pres.); Prof. Dr Matthias Kleiner (Vice-Pres.); Prof. Wolfgang Frühwald (Hon. Pres.); Prof. Reimar Lüst (Hon. Pres.).

Principal Staff: Sec.-Gen. Dr Wolfgang Holl; Deputy Sec.-Gen. Dr Gisela Janetzke.

Address: Jean-Paul-Str. 12, 53173 Bonn.

Telephone: (228) 833-0; **Fax:** (228) 833-199; **Internet:** www.avh.de; **e-mail:** info@avh.de.

Indienhilfe eV (India Assistance)

An NGO established in 1980 offering financial assistance to Indian partner NGOs in West Bengal for projects aimed at improving the situation of children (access to education, reduction of infant mortality, proper nutrition, protection from exploitation and abuse, combating child labour in hazardous jobs).

Activities: Operates in the areas of sustainable agriculture, environment, health, women's self-help groups, education (formal and informal), promotion of fair trade, education for sustainability and intercultural dialogue between Bengal and Bavaria (school partnerships, town twinning between Chatra near Kolkata and Herrsching near Munich). Grants are made to Indian partner NGOs.

Geographical Area of Activity: West Bengal, India.

Restrictions: Operates in co-operation with NGOs and organizations in India with which it already has a partnership.

Publications: Brochures; books; magazines.

Principal Staff: Dr Dirk Provoost; Elisabeth Kreuz; Udo Kirkamp.

Address: Luitpoldstr. 20, 82211 Herrsching.

Telephone: (8152) 1231; **Fax:** (8152) 48278; **Internet:** www.indienhilfe-herrsching.de; **e-mail:** info@indienhilfe-herrsching.de.

Initiative und Leistung, Stiftung der Nassauischen Sparkasse für Kultur, Sport und Gesellschaft (Initiative and Achievement, Foundation of the Nassauische Sparkasse for Culture, Sport and Society)

Established in 1989 by the Nassauische Sparkasse (savings bank).

Activities: Operates in the areas of culture and the arts, sport, conservation and the environment, health care and the support of young people.

Geographical Area of Activity: Germany.

Publications: Newsletter.

Board of Trustees: Helmut Müller (Chair.).

Principal Staff: Man. Winfrid W. Rogge.

Address: Adolfstr. 1, 65185 Wiesbaden.

Telephone: (611) 36406601; **Fax:** (611) 36406699; **Internet:** www.naspa-stiftung.de; **e-mail:** naspa-stiftung@naspa-mail.de.

Institut für Agrarentwicklung in Mittel- und Osteuropa—IAMO (Institute for Agricultural Development in Central and Eastern Europe)

Established in 1994 by the Federal State of Saxony-Anhalt as a public foundation, a non-affiliated research institute to promote knowledge and research in the field of international agricultural development.

Activities: Supports basic and applied research in international agricultural development, especially in the former communist countries of Central and Eastern Europe, with projects in the areas of studying the economic and social implications of changing agricultural processes, providing advice to those involved in changing agricultural systems, and training for new academics; shares research findings through publications, conferences and international co-operation. Maintains a library containing approximately 18,000 publications.

Geographical Area of Activity: Central and Eastern Europe.

Restrictions: Unsolicited applications are not accepted.

Publications: Magazines; discussion papers; Annual Report; *Monographien*; series of studies.

Board of Trustees: Dr Joachim Welz (Chair.); Dr Rudolf Wendt (Vice-Chair.).

Principal Staff: Man. Dir Prof. Dr Thomas Herzfeld.

Address: Theodor-Lieser-Str. 2, 06120 Halle/Saale.

Telephone: (345) 2928-325; **Fax:** (345) 2928-199; **Internet:** www.iamo.de; **e-mail:** iamo@iamo.de.

INTEGRATA—Stiftung für Humane Nutzung der Informationstechnologie (INTEGRATA Foundation)

Founded in September 1999 by Prof. Dr Wolfgang Heilmann.

Activities: Aims to sponsor and implement research, and fund longer-term projects and academic institutions engaged in the pursuit of the humane use of information technology in the fields of work, education, health, art and culture, in particular in working and professional life. Awards the annual Wolfgang Heilmann-Preis in recognition of work in the social uses of information technology.

Geographical Area of Activity: International.

Publications: *Thesis and Objectives on the Management of Tele-Processes*.

Trustees: Prof. Dr Wolfgang Heilmann (Pres.).

Principal Staff: Sec. Renate Hellak.

Address: Schleifmühleweg 70, 72070 Tübingen.

Telephone: (7071) 408698; **Fax:** (7071) 408699; **Internet:** www.integrata-stiftung.de; **e-mail:** info@integrata-stiftung.de.

International Arctic Science Committee—IASC

Founded in August 1990. Aims to encourage and facilitate co-operation in all aspects of arctic research, in all countries engaged in arctic research and in all areas of the arctic region. Member organizations are national science organizations covering all fields of arctic research.

Activities: Acts as an information and communication forum for the arctic science community, with 19 member countries (2012). Promotes arctic research and develops research projects that necessitate international and multi-disciplinary co-operation.

Geographical Area of Activity: Arctic countries.

Publications: *IASC-Progress* (newsletter).

Executive Committee: David Hik (Pres.); Naja Mikkelsen; Susan Barr; Jackie Grebmeier; Byong-Kwon Park (Vice-Pres.).

Principal Staff: Exec. Sec. Dr Volker Rachold.

Address: Telegrafenberg A43, 14473 Potsdam.

Telephone: (331) 2882214; **Internet:** web.arcticportal.org/iasc; **e-mail:** iasc@iasc.se.

International Environmental Foundation of the Kommunale Umwelt-AktioN UAN—IntEF-UAN

Established in February 2001 by the Kommunale Umwelt-AktioN UAN.

Activities: Promotes environmental protection activities in Germany and in other European countries, in particular the promotion of international waste-water partnerships.

Geographical Area of Activity: Germany and Europe.

Restrictions: Grants only to communities which take part in international waste-water partnerships.

Publications: Comprehensive manuals; informative materials.

Board of Trustees: Rainier Timmermann (Chair.); Uwe-Peter Lestin (Vice-Pres.); Hans-Georg Niesel (Vice-Pres.).

Principal Staff: Man. Dir Joachim Vollmer.

Address: Arnswaldtstr. 28, 30159 Hannover.

Telephone: (511) 3028560; **Fax:** (511) 3028556; **Internet:** www .umweltaktion.de; **e-mail:** flasche@uan.de.

International Society for Human Rights—ISHR

Established in 1972 to uphold the UN Universal Declaration of Human Rights; the organization operates independently of state institutions, religious bodies and politics.

Activities: Operates world-wide in the field of law and human rights. National sections operate in 27 countries, with working groups in an additional four countries, and the organization has more than 30,000 members. Projects include strengthening civil society in Central and Eastern Europe and the countries of the former USSR, promoting the International Criminal Court, and providing democracy and human rights training to the Ukrainian military. ISHR holds consultative status with the Council of Europe.

Geographical Area of Activity: World-wide.

Restrictions: No grants available directly, except through co-financed international projects.

International Board: Alexander Freiherr von Bischoffshausen (Pres.); Vu Quoc Dung (Sec.-Gen.); Karl Hafen (Treas.).

Address: Borsigalle 9, 60388 Frankfurt am Main.

Telephone: (69) 42010-8; **Fax:** (69) 42010-833; **Internet:** www .ishr.org; **e-mail:** is@ishr.org.

Internationale Bachakademie Stuttgart (Stuttgart International Bach Academy)

Established in 1981 by the Stuttgarter Konzertvereinigung eV for the development and management of a research and further education institute for German and foreign music researchers and musicians to carry out research into the theoretical and practical interpretation of the works of Johann Sebastian Bach.

Activities: Operates in the field of music through co-ordinating international research into Bach, and co-operating in the promotion of Bach's music. Organizes conferences and seminars, concerts and exhibitions in Germany and abroad. Organizes the Music Fest Stuttgart. Maintains a specialized library and documentation centre.

Geographical Area of Activity: International.

Restrictions: Unsolicited applications are not accepted.

Publications: *Series of the Stuttgart International Bach Academy; Forum Bachakademie* (both in German).

Finance: Assets €6,084,643 (2009); annual expenditure €6,047,835 (2009).

Principal Staff: Man. Dir Christian Lorenz; Artistic Dir Prof. Dr Helmuth Rilling.

Address: Johann-Sebastian-Bach-Platz, 70178 Stuttgart.

Telephone: (711) 61921-0; **Fax:** (711) 61921-23; **Internet:** www .bachakademie.de; **e-mail:** musikfest@bachakademie.de.

Internationale Jugendbibliothek (International Youth Library Foundation)

The International Youth Library has evolved a range of programmes for schools since 1994.

Activities: The Foundation's main spheres of activity include arts and humanities, education and international affairs. It functions nationally as well as internationally through research and self-conducted programmes. Operates nationally, providing training courses and issuing publications, and internationally, granting scholarships and fellowships. Other activities include: creating awareness among adults and educationists on the importance of books for children and youngsters by providing information to organizations involved in composing children's literature and their distribution; contributing to advanced training of the personnel involved; advising illustrators, publishers, writers, translators, etc; extending support to organizations with similar objectives in Germany and abroad; promoting inter-cultural and international understanding through aquisition and distribution of children's literature from Germany and abroad; furthering research on international literature for children, particularly within the scope of the International Youth Library, which has an approximate 530,000-volume collection. The Foundation also offers study fellowships.

Geographical Area of Activity: International.

Restrictions: Applications for grants are not accepted; grants are made only to professionals working in the area of children's and youth literature.

Publications: *IJB Report* (2 a year); *The White Ravens* (annually); books; *Children Between Worlds; Children's Books from Canada; Cold World; Hello, dear Enemy; Young and Old; Paddington, Pu und Baloo; Pinocchio; Waterworlds in books for children and pictures made by children; Ivan Gantschev; From Robinson to Lummerland.*

Finance: Sources of finance include the Federal Ministry for Family and Youth, and the Federal Ministry of Foreign Affairs, City of Munich, and the Bavarian state government.

Board of Trustees: Dr Sabine Solf (Chair.).

Principal Staff: Dir Christiane Raabe.

Address: Schloss Blutenburg, 81247 Munich.

Telephone: (89) 8912110; **Fax:** (89) 8117553; **Internet:** www.ijb .de; **e-mail:** info@ijb.de.

Internationale Stiftung zur Förderung von Kultur und Zivilisation (International Foundation for Culture and Civilization)

Established in 1995 by Erich Fischer.

Activities: Supports cultural and humanitarian projects in Germany and internationally, principally musical activities, including festivals, and partnerships with Amnesty International (q.v.).

Geographical Area of Activity: Germany and international.

Publications: Newsletter report.

Principal Staff: Gabriele Mantaj; Inge Weber Kummert; Johannes Erkes.

Address: Dr Carl von Linde Str. 9, 81479 Munich.

Telephone: (89) 54041180; **Fax:** (89) 540411819; **Internet:** www.internationalestiftung.de; **e-mail:** ulrichrueger@web .de.

InWEnt—Internationale Weiterbildung und Entwicklung gemeinnützige GmbH (Capacity Building International)

Founded in 2002 through a merger of Carl Duisberg Gesellschaft eV and the Deutsche Stiftung für Internationale Entwicklung (German Foundation for International Development) to promote international human resources development, advanced training and dialogue.

Activities: Promotes international human resources development, advanced training and dialogue, through structured long-term training programmes, practice-orientated training, conferences, seminars and workshops, policy dialogue and individual internships. Approximately 55,000 people participate in the organization's programmes each year.

Geographical Area of Activity: International.

Restrictions: Applications for grants are not accepted.

Publications: *Entwicklung und Zusammenarbeit* (monthly); *Development and Cooperation* (monthly); *Rural 21* (6 a year); catalogues; directories; Annual Report.

Finance: The organization is funded by the Federal Government, Länder governments, the European Union and other multilateral bodies, and foundations.

Board of Trustees: Manfred Grund (Chair.).

Principal Staff: Chief Exec. Dr Sebastian Paust; Man. Dir Bernd Schleich.

Address: Friedrich-Ebert-Allee 40, 53113 Bonn.

Telephone: (228) 44600; **Fax:** (228) 44601766; **Internet:** www.inwent.org; **e-mail:** presse@inwent.org.

Japanisch-Deutsches Zentrum Berlin (Japanese-German Center Berlin)

Founded in 1985 to promote and strengthen JapaneseGerman and international co-operation in the fields of science and culture.

Activities: Organizes academic conferences, seminars and workshops with a wide range of topics, and joint exhibitions and concerts of German, Japanese and international artists. Offers Japanese language courses. Manages the German side of the German-Japanese Forum, and co-ordinates several programmes for German-Japanese Peoples Exchange. Maintains a library of more than 10,000 volumes.

Geographical Area of Activity: The work covers Germany and Japan, Europe, Asia and North America.

Restrictions: Unsolicited applications are not accepted.

Publications: *jdzb echo* (quarterly newsletter); documents and proceedings of the Foundation's events; Directory of German-Japanese Co-operation.

Finance: Annual expenditure approx. €2,300,000 (2010).

Council: Prof. Dr Bernhard Scheuble (Chair.); Kojima Akira (Vice-Chair.).

Principal Staff: Exec. Pres. Kume Kunisada; Sec.-Gen. Dr Friederike Bosse.

Address: Saargemünder Str. 2, 14195 Berlin.

Telephone: (30) 839070; **Fax:** (30) 83907220; **Internet:** www.jdzb.de; **e-mail:** jdzb@jdzb.de.

Klassik Stiftung Weimar (Foundation of Weimar Classics)

Founded in October 1991 (becoming an independent foundation in 1994), the legal successor to the former non-independent National Research and Memorial Centre of Classical German Literature in Weimar, to preserve and expand the sites and collections of classical German literature in Weimar; to make them available to the public; to encourage the communication, research and dissemination of this cultural heritage; and to maintain the sites and collections of the former National Research and Memorial Centre, as well as the collections of 19th- and 20th-century works. Formerly known as the Stiftung Weimarer Klassik, merged with the Kunstsammlungen zu Weimar on 1 January 2003.

Activities: Maintains the Goethe National Museum, the Schiller House, the Palace Museum, the Bauhaus Museum, the New Museum, Belvedere Palace, and 18 other literary museums, palaces and memorials, the Duchess Anna Amalia Library, the Goethe-Schiller Archives, five parks in and around Weimar, and several other properties. Carries out research, organizes exhibitions and events, issues numerous publications and holds conferences.

Geographical Area of Activity: Europe and USA.

Restrictions: Applications for grants are not accepted.

Publications: *Johann Wolfgang Goethe: Geschichte des Hauses*; *Bestandsübersicht*; *Inventare des Goethe- und Schiller-Archivs*; *Erschienene Publikationen*; *Reineke Fuchs*; *Goethe-Briefrepertorium*; *Goethe Autographensammlung*; *Goethes Tagebücher*; *Nietzsche*; *Büchner*.

Finance: The Foundation is financed by the Federal Government, the State of Thuringia and the City of Weimar.

Principal Staff: Pres. Hellmut Seemann; Dir-Gen. Prof. Dr Wolfgang Holler.

Address: Burgplatz 4, 99423 Weimar.

Telephone: (3643) 545401/-402/-403; **Fax:** (3643) 419816; **Internet:** www.klassik-stiftung.de; **e-mail:** info@klassik-stiftung.de.

Körber-Stiftung (Körber Foundation)

Founded in 1959 by the entrepreneur Kurt A. Körber in Hamburg-Bergedorf, the Foundation runs national and international projects and events.

Activities: The Foundation is active in the fields of international affairs, education, science, civil society and youth culture. It offers people the opportunity to participate actively, and provides them with ideas and initiative.

Geographical Area of Activity: World-wide.

Restrictions: The Foundation finances and runs its own projects; it does not make grants to individuals.

Publications: *Reflexion und Initiative* (report, 2 a year); information brochure; annual list; books; newsletter.

Finance: Total assets €510,000,000 (2009).

Board of Trustees: Prof. Dr Thomas Straubhaar (Chair.); Dr Sabine Bergmann-Pohl (Deputy Chair.).

Principal Staff: Chair. Christian Wriedt; Deputy Chair. Dr Klaus Wehmeier.

Address: Kehrwieder 12, 20457 Hamburg.

Telephone: (40) 808192-0; **Fax:** (40) 808192-300; **Internet:** www.koerber-stiftung.de; **e-mail:** info@koerber-stiftung.de.

Else Kröner-Fresenius-Stiftung (Else Kröner-Fresenius Foundation)

Established by Else Kröner in 1983 to extend support to medical and scientific research.

Activities: The Foundation focuses on medicine, health and science and technology by providing grants for research projects, in particular novel research in nutritional medicine, clinical research, infections and dialysis; and finances humanitarian and educational initiatives, especially if they are conducive to development.

Geographical Area of Activity: International.

Restrictions: Basic research is not funded.

Publications: Annual reports.

Finance: Total grants disbursed €21,600,000 (2011).

Administrative Board: Dr Dieter Schenk (Chair.); Dr Karl Schneider (Vice-Chair.).

Principal Staff: CEO Rainer Baule; Chief Financial Officer Stephan Sturm.

Address: Postfach 1852, 61288 Bad Homburg.

Telephone: (6172) 8975-0; **Fax:** (6172) 8975-15; **Internet:** www.ekfs.de; **e-mail:** kontakt@eksf.de.

Alfried Krupp von Bohlen und Halbach-Stiftung (Alfried Krupp von Bohlen und Halbach Foundation)

Founded in 1967 by Dr Alfried Krupp von Bohlen und Halbach for philanthropic aims of benefit to the community.

Activities: Operates nationally and internationally through support of Foundation projects in the fields of scientific research and teaching (including the fostering of young scientific talent), education, health services, sport, literature, music and the fine arts, through offering grants and fellowships (including an Internship Programme for students of Stanford University, CA, USA to train in Germany, and a China Studies Programme for German students to spend a year of study in the People's Republic of China). Awards an annual environmental prize.

Geographical Area of Activity: International.

Finance: Total grants expenditure since 1968 €442,000,000.

Governing Board: Prof. Dr B. Beitz (Chair.); Prof. Dr H. Leussink (Deputy Chair.).

Principal Staff: Pres. Prof. Dr B. Beitz.

Address: Hügel 15, 45133 Essen.

Telephone: (201) 188-1; **Fax:** (201) 412587; **Internet:** www .krupp-stiftung.de; **e-mail:** info@krupp-stiftung.de.

Karl-Kübel-Stiftung für Kind und Familie (Karl Kübel Foundation for Child and Family)

Founded in 1972 by Karl Kübel to support family-orientated programmes.

Activities: Operates nationally and internationally, mainly in German-speaking countries, Kosovo and Metohija, India and the Philippines, through self-conducted programmes, grants to institutions, prizes, training courses, publications and the implementation of development projects. The Foundation's four main programmes are: the Karl Kübel Award and the support of family-centred self-help activities; family-centred housing projects; education through the Foundation's institutes in Germany and India; supporting development projects and training development personnel. Also provides humanitarian relief.

Geographical Area of Activity: Germany, Kosovo, India and the Philippines.

Publications: Annual Report; documentation; *Against Trafficking of Children and Women in Commercial Sexual Exploitation.*

Finance: Annual income and expenditure €15,609,672 (2008).

Council: Matthias Wilkes (Chair.); Dr Klaus-Volker Schutz, Dietmar Heeg (Vice-Pres.).

Address: Postfach 1563, 64605 Bensheim.

Telephone: (6251) 7005-0; **Fax:** (6251) 7005-55; **Internet:** www.kkstiftung.de; **e-mail:** info@kkstiftung.de.

Kulturstiftung Haus Europa (House of Europe Cultural Foundation)

Founded in September 1990 by the Government of the German Democratic Republic (became an autonomous private foundation in 1992); it aims to promote the German effort for European understanding, European cultural networking, private initiative and funding for the arts and cultural affairs; to represent German interests in European cultural bodies; and to distribute European cultural information in Germany. The Foundation is managed by Maecenata Management GmbH (q.v.).

Activities: Promotes and manages cultural projects; holds conferences on international cultural matters; and issues publications.

Geographical Area of Activity: Europe.

Restrictions: Does not make grants.

Publications: *Heritage and the Building of Europe*; conference reports.

Finance: Total assets €260,323 (2008).

Council: Christian Petry (Chair.).

Principal Staff: Chair. Rupert Graf Strachwitz.

Address: c/o Maecenata Management GmbH, Albrechtstr. 22, 10117 Berlin.

Telephone: (30) 28387900; **Fax:** (30) 28387901; **Internet:** www.maecenata.eu; **e-mail:** khe@maecenata.eu.

Kulturstiftung der Länder—KSL (Cultural Foundation of the German Länder)

Established in 1988 to promote and preserve national art and culture.

Activities: Operates nationally and internationally in the field of the arts, promoting and preserving cultural heritage of national importance.

Geographical Area of Activity: Germany.

Publications: *Patrimonia, Arsprototo.*

Finance: Annual expenditure €9,700,000 (2010).

Trustees: Dr Heribald Narger (Chair.); Prof. Dr Reinhold Würth (Deputy Chair.); Prof. Dr Klaus-Dieter Lehmann (Deputy Chair.); Prof Dr Rolf-E. Breuer (Vice-Chair.).

Principal Staff: Sec.-Gen. Isabel Pfeiffer-Poensgen; Deputy Sec.-Gen. Dr Martin Hoernes.

Address: Lützowpl. 9, 10785 Berlin.

Telephone: (30) 8936350; **Fax:** (30) 8914251; **Internet:** www .kulturstiftung.de; **e-mail:** kontakt@kulturstiftung.de.

Lateinamerika-Zentrum eV—LAZ (Latin America Centre)

Established in 1961 by Prof. Hermann M. Görgen to help alleviate suffering in Latin America.

Activities: Operates in Central and South America, mainly in Brazil, supporting local organizations that develop projects to suit local needs; projects include schooling and training for disadvantaged children and young people, combating the abandonment of the countryside, promotion of women, basic health care, protection of the environment and the promotion and protection of indigenous peoples. Also publishes books on the politics of development and hosts exhibitions and workshops.

Geographical Area of Activity: Central and South America, with an emphasis on Brazil.

Restrictions: Operates in collaboration with local partner organizations. No grants to individuals.

Publications: *Tópicos* (German/Brazilian pamphlets); Annual Report; brochures on the promotion of women in Mexico, and rural development in Brazil.

Finance: Funding from Ministry of Co-operation and Development and the European Commission. Annual budget approx. €1,200,000.

Board: Dr Helmut Hoffmann (Pres.); Dr Hans Thomas, Dr Claudio Zettel (Vice-Pres).

Address: Dr Werner-Schuster-Haus, Kaiserstr. 201, 53113 Bonn.

Telephone: (228) 210788; **Fax:** (228) 241658; **Internet:** www .lateinamerikazentrum.de; **e-mail:** info@ lateinamerikazentrum.de.

The Ronald S. Lauder Foundation

Founded in 1987 by Ronald S. Lauder for the support of Central and Eastern Europe and the former USSR to promote Jewish education, and for the preservation of Jewish monuments and buildings.

Activities: Operates primarily in Central and Eastern Europe, in Austria, Belarus, Bulgaria, Czech Republic, Estonia, Germany, Hungary, Latvia, Lithuania, Moldova, Poland, Romania, Russia, Slovakia and Ukraine, making grants in the areas of Jewish welfare, religion, cultural programmes, conservation and education. Also supports a non-sectarian international student exchange.

Geographical Area of Activity: Central and Eastern Europe, and the former USSR.

Restrictions: No applications for grants accepted.

Publications: Financial statement; information brochure; newsletter.

Trustees: Ronald S. Lauder (Chair.).

Principal Staff: Exec. Vice-Pres. and CEO Joshua I. Spinner.

Address: Rykestrasse 53, 10405 Berlin.

Telephone: (30) 440131610; **Fax:** (30) 440131619; **Internet:** www.lauderfoundation.com; **e-mail:** info@lauderfoundation .com.

Rosa-Luxemburg-Stiftung (Rosa Luxemburg Foundation)

Established in 1991 for the promotion of political education (associated with the Social Democratic Party—SPD), knowledge and research, culture and the arts, and international understanding.

Activities: Operates in the fields of the arts and humanities, economic affairs, education, international affairs, and law and human rights, through promoting research; publications; awarding scholarships and the annual Rosa Luxemburg Prize; maintaining archives and a library; and national and international projects, in particular in countries of Africa, Asia and Central and South America. Maintains regional offices in the Russian Federation, Brazil, Poland and South Africa.

Geographical Area of Activity: International, in particular Central and Eastern Europe and the Russian Federation, Africa, Asia and Central and South America.

Publications: *Utopie kreativ* (magazine).

Finance: Annual expenditure approx. €1,000,000.

Managing Board: Dr Florian Weis (Dir).

Principal Staff: Sec. Viola Siebeck.

Address: Franz-Mehring-Platz 1, 10243 Berlin.

Telephone: (30) 44310221; **Fax:** (30) 44310222; **Internet:** www.rosalux.de; **e-mail:** info@rosalux.de.

medica mondiale e.V.

Established in 2004 for the support of women and girls in areas of conflict and natural disasters.

Activities: Operates in the areas of human rights, and medicine and health, to assist women and girls in areas of crisis.

Geographical Area of Activity: Areas of conflict and natural disasters, including Africa, Central and South America, the Middle East and South Asia.

Trustees: Dr Monika Hauser (Pres.).

Principal Staff: Man. Dir Christiane Overkamp.

Address: Hülchrather Str. 4, 50670 Cologne.

Telephone: (221) 9318980; **Fax:** (221) 9318981; **Internet:** www.medicamondiale.org; **e-mail:** info@medicamondiale.org.

Medico International

Established in 1968 to send medical supplies to countries in need.

Activities: Operates world-wide, in particular in less-developed countries or in countries where emergency relief is necessary, in the field of medicine and health, offering medicines and medical equipment, medical personnel, ambulances and other equipment. Runs campaigns against landmines, and various projects in the areas of asylum, rehabilitation, AIDS, human rights and basic health care. Long-term projects have been instituted in Central and South America, North, Central and Southern Africa, the Middle and Far East, and Central Asia (Kurdistan).

Geographical Area of Activity: International.

Publications: *Rethinking the Power of Aid—Humanitarianism in Crisis* (report, 2003).

Finance: Annual budget approx. €5,100,000.

Supervisory Board: Brigitte Kühn (Chair.); Prof. Dr Alexander Wittkowsky (Deputy Chair.); Prof. Dr Joachim Hirsch (Deputy Chair.).

Principal Staff: Exec. Dir Thomas Gebauer.

Address: Burgstr. 106, 60389 Frankfurt/Main.

Telephone: (69) 944380; **Fax:** (69) 436002; **Internet:** www.medico.de; **e-mail:** info@medico.de.

Messerschmitt-Stiftung (Messerschmitt Foundation)

Established in 1976 by Prof. Willy Messerschmitt.

Activities: Operates in the fields of conservation of heritage, and science and technology; promotes science and research, especially in the area of aero- and space technology; also promotes the conservation of German art and cultural memorials nationally and internationally. Owns several historically important Messerschmitt aircraft.

Geographical Area of Activity: Europe.

Finance: Annual expenditure approx. €11,000,000.

Trustees: Prof. Gero Madelung (Chair.).

Principal Staff: Chair. Dr Hans Heinrich von Srbik.

Address: Pienzenauerstr. 17, 81679 Munich.

Telephone: (89) 981830; **Fax:** (89) 98290126.

Friedrich-Naumann-Stiftung (Friedrich Naumann Foundation)

Founded in 1958 by Dr Theodor Heuss (former President of the Federal Republic of Germany) with the objective of promoting a liberal foundation for political and civic education, improving the dialogue between Eastern and Western industrial countries, and developed and developing countries, and giving advisory and vocational assistance to developing countries.

Activities: Operates nationally and internationally, primarily in the field of civic education, but also in the areas of aid to less-developed countries, economic and international affairs, and law and human rights, through self-conducted programmes, research, scholarships and fellowships, prizes, conferences, training courses and publications. In developing countries assistance is given to co-operative associations, training institutes for journalism and organizations in the field of adult education. The Foundation has projects in around 45 countries and maintains offices in approximately 47 countries outside Germany.

Geographical Area of Activity: International.

Publications: Annual Report; *liberal* (quarterly); *Classical author of liberty*; *Philosopher of liberty*; *Arguments of liberty*; *Concepts of Liberty*; occasional papers; *Political principles*; *Tasks and activities*; *Friedrich Naumann*.

Finance: Assets €40,000,000 (2009).

Board of Trustees: Walter Scheel (Hon. Chair.); Dr Jürgen Morlok (Chair.); Peter Menke-Glückert (Vice-Chair.); Prof. Dr Karl-Hans Laermann (Vice-Chair.).

Principal Staff: Pres. Dr Wolfgang Gerhardt; Vice-Pres. Dr Wolf-Dieter Zumpfort, Alex Hoffmann.

Address: Karl-Marx-Str. 2, 14482 Potsdam.

Telephone: (331) 70190; **Fax:** (331) 7019188; **Internet:** www.freiheit.org; **e-mail:** fnst@fnst.org.

Niedersächsische Sparkassenstiftung (Lower Saxony Savings Bank Foundation)

Established in 1984 by the Niedersächsischer Sparkassen und Giroverband savings bank.

Activities: Operates in the Federal State of Lower Saxony in the field of the arts, with an emphasis on fine art, music, conservation of monuments and museums. Supports projects carried out by other organizations, carries out its own activities, awards prizes and scholarships, and maintains an art collection.

Geographical Area of Activity: The Federal State of Lower Saxony, Germany.

Restrictions: Grants are made only to organizations in Lower Saxony.

Finance: Total assets approx. €24,000,000 (2010).

Trustees: Kai-Uwe Bielefeld (Pres., Board of Trustees); Thomas Mang (Pres. of Board).

Principal Staff: Man. Dir Dr Sabine Schormann; Deputy Man. Dir Michael Heinrich Schormann.

Address: Schiffgraben 6–8, 30159 Hannover.

Telephone: (511) 3603489; **Fax:** (511) 3603684; **Internet:** www.nsks.de; **e-mail:** martina.fragge@svn.de.

Novartis-Stiftung für therapeutische Forschung (Novartis Foundation for Therapeutical Research)

Established in 1969 by Sandoz AG Nuremberg to further therapeutical research, and to carry out other research in the field of medicine.

Activities: Operates in the field of medical research, including awarding an annual prize in the field of pharmaceutical research.

Geographical Area of Activity: Germany.

Restrictions: Grants only made in specific areas.

Publications: *Ecomed*; *'ME-TOO'-preparations*; *Bases of the Measurement of Quality of Life* (book).

Trustees: Ludwig Hantson (Chair.).

Principal Staff: Dir Almut Richter; Sec. Susanne Schaller.

Address: Roonstr. 25, 90429 Nuremberg.

Telephone: (911) 27312796; **Fax:** (911) 27312056; **Internet:** www.novartis.de/forschung_entwicklung/stiftung_fuer_therap_forschung/index.shtml; **e-mail:** susanne.schaller@pharma.novartis.com.

Michael-Otto-Stiftung für Umweltschutz (Michael Otto Foundation for Environmental Protection)

Established in 1993 by Dr Michael Otto.

Activities: The Foundation develops strategies and supports projects for future-orientated initiatives in the conservation of nature and the environment. The Foundation aims to set signs and create motivation for other trailblazing initiatives, conserving the environment for future generations. Its three fields of action are funding, education and dialogue. The Foundation provides funding for innovative environmental projects. This is done by financing major nature conservation projects, and by helping young people to implement their own 'Aqua Projects'. Its current funding focus is on the protection of flowing water and sustainable treatment of rivers and streams. Education and awareness raising are essential for action to improve the environment. The Foundation contributes to this by setting up academic chairs such as 'The Economics of Climate Change' (Berlin Technical University), and by supporting research and educational institutions. In early 2010 the Foundation launched its own educational project, 'Aqua Agents', aimed at primary schools in Hamburg. Alongside its educational and funding work, the Foundation works as a mediator, getting different interest groups within society around a table, initiating dialogue between influential players from business, nature conservation, government and academia. Its goal is to work with policy-makers to develop pragmatic solutions for current environmental issues.

Geographical Area of Activity: Mainly Germany.

Publications: Regularly published documentations on the annually held Hamburg Nature Conservation Forum, a discussion series intended to enliven the debate within society on important environmental issues, to raise awareness for the concerns of nature conservation, and to develop integrated national and international approaches to problem solving.

Finance: Annual budget approx. €650,000.

Board of Trustees: Dr Michael Otto (Chair.).

Principal Staff: Exec. Dir Dr Johannes Merck.

Address: Wandsbeker Str. 3–7, 22179 Hamburg.

Telephone: (40) 64616452; **Fax:** (40) 64646452; **Internet:** www.michaelottostiftung.org; **e-mail:** info@michaelottostiftung.de.

Oxfam Deutschland e.V.

Part of the Oxfam confederation of organizations (qq.v.).

Activities: Operates in the areas of aid to less-developed countries and social welfare in Africa and South Asia.

Geographical Area of Activity: Africa and South Asia.

Trustees: Dr Matthias von Bismark (Chair.); Babette Neumann (Vice-Chair.).

Principal Staff: Man. Dir Marion Leiser.

Address: Greifswalder Str. 33A, 10405 Berlin.

Telephone: (30) 4285 0621; **Fax:** (30) 4285 0622; **Internet:** www.oxfam.de; **e-mail:** info@oxfam.de.

Pesticides Action Network Europe—PAN Europe

Established in 1983 and facilitated by PAN Germany and Pesticide Action Network UK—PAN UK (q.v.); a network of European environmental NGOs promoting a sustainable alternative to the use of pesticides.

Activities: Operates in Europe in the area of conservation and the environment, promoting alternatives to the use of pesticides, through pesticide reduction programmes, lobbying, networking, publications and conferences.

Geographical Area of Activity: Europe.

Publications: *PAN Europe Monthly* (monthly e-mail newsletter); policy papers.

Principal Staff: Co-ordinators Carina Weber, Susanne Smolka.

Address: Nernstweg 32, 22767 Hamburg.

Telephone: (40) 3991910-0; **Fax:** (40) 3907520; **Internet:** www.pan-germany.org; **e-mail:** info@pan-germany.org.

Max-Planck-Gesellschaft zur Förderung der Wissenschaften eV (Max Planck Society for the Advancement of Science)

Founded in 1948 to succeed the Kaiser-Wilhelm-Gesellschaft (founded 1911) with the object of promoting basic research in the sciences.

Activities: Operates nationally and internationally in the fields of science, medicine, social sciences and humanities, and law and other professions. Maintains international relations through self-conducted projects, research, conferences, prizes, publications and lectures. Basic research, particularly in the fields of biology, medicine, chemistry, physics and the humanities, is carried out in 80 institutes and research facilities belonging to the Society, with the aim of complementing research conducted at the universities.

Geographical Area of Activity: International, centered in Germany.

Restrictions: Not a funding organization.

Publications: *Max-Planck-Forschung* (research journal in German); *Max Planck Research* (research journal in English); information booklets; *Research perspectives 2000, 2005 and 2010*; Annual Report including Yearbook (online).

Finance: Financed through public funds (95%). Annual budget €1,400,000,000 (2011).

Principal Staff: Pres. Prof. Dr Peter Gruss.

Address: Hofgartenstr. 8, 80539 Munich.

Telephone: (89) 21080; **Fax:** (89) 21081111; **Internet:** www.mpg.de; **e-mail:** post@gv.mpg.de.

Prix Jeunesse Foundation

Established in 1964 by the Government of Bavaria, the City of Munich and Bayerischer Rundfunk to improve the quality of television world-wide for young people, deepen understanding, promote communication between nations and increase programme exchange.

Activities: Operates internationally in the field of children's and youth television, awarding the Prix Jeunesse International Prizes for children's and youth television programmes, organizing conferences, training courses and issuing publications. Maintains a video library covering four decades of children's and youth television and organizes a bi-annual festival, the Prix Jeunesse International Festival.

Geographical Area of Activity: International.

Publications: *WATCHwords Online*.

Finance: The Foundation is financed by annual contributions from its founders.

Trustees: Dr Ludwig Spaenle (Chair.).

Principal Staff: Head Dr Maya Goetz; Co-ordinator Kirsten Schneid.

Address: c/o Bayerischer Rundfunk, Rudfunkpl. 1, 80335 Munich.

Telephone: (89) 59002058; **Fax:** (89) 59003053; **Internet:** www.prixjeunesse.de; **e-mail:** info@prixjeunesse.de.

Johanna-Quandt-Stiftung

Founded in 1995 by Johanna Quandt.

Activities: The foundation aims to promote the importance of private entrepreneurship as a contributor to economic development in the public and the media.

Geographical Area of Activity: Germany.

Principal Staff: Chair. Johanna Quandt; Chair. Stefan Quandt; Dir Helmut Reitze.

Address: Günther-Quandt-Haus, Seedammweg 55, 61352 Bad Homburg v.d. Hohe.

Telephone: (6172) 404342; **Fax:** (6172) 404420; **Internet:** www.johanna-quandt-stiftung.de; **e-mail:** info@johanna-quandt-stiftung.de.

Werner-Reimers-Stiftung (Werner Reimers Foundation)

Founded in 1963 by Werner Reimers to contribute towards explaining the development of human society and its institutions, to analyse its present problems, to recognize tendencies of its further development and to open for it ways into the future.

Activities: Operates nationally and internationally in the fields of social welfare and studies, the physical and social sciences, medicine and the humanities. Interdisciplinary study groups organized by the Foundation form the focal point of its activities. The groups devote several years to the study of well-defined problems, meet regularly to exchange information and publish the results of their work. Meetings take place at the Foundation's conference centre and the Foundation provides travelling expenses and accommodation.

Restrictions: Does not award scholarships.

Publications: Report of operations.

Finance: Annual expenditure approx. €700,000.

Trustees: Ruth Wagner (Chair.).

Principal Staff: Pres. Wolfgang R. Assmann.

Address: Am Wingertsberg 4, 61348 Bad Homburg.

Telephone: (6172) 24058; **Fax:** (6172) 21408; **Internet:** www.reimers-stiftung.de; **e-mail:** reimers.stiftung@t-online.de.

Hedwig und Robert Samuel-Stiftung (Hedwig and Robert Samuel Foundation)

Established in 1932 to support education, primarily in Central America and Asia.

Activities: Aims to provide occupational qualifications for the poor, focusing on children and teenagers to improve their quality of life in the future. Runs projects in Costa Rica, Cuba, Germany, India, Nicaragua and Thailand.

Geographical Area of Activity: Central America and Asia.

Finance: Funded through the Foundation's own capital, donations and co-financing.

Board of Directors: Martin Barth (Pres.).

Principal Staff: Supervisory Board Karin Reuter, Martin Barth.

Address: Königsallee 14, 40212 Düsseldorf.

Telephone: (211) 1386666; **Fax:** (211) 1386611; **Internet:** www.samuel.de; **e-mail:** info@samuel.de.

Wilhelm-Sander-Stiftung (Wilhelm Sander Foundation)

Founded in 1974 to support medical research.

Activities: Operates in the field of medicine and health, through sponsoring medical research and supporting the fight against ill health, especially cancer, by means of grants to institutions and individuals.

Geographical Area of Activity: Germany and Switzerland.

Publications: Report of operations and financial statement.

Finance: Annual grants expenditure €10,000,000 (2009).

Supervisory Board: Dr Jörg Koppenhöfer (Pres.); Prof. Dr Udo Lohrs (Vice-Pres.).

Principal Staff: Chair. Bernhard Knappe.

Address: Goethestr. 74, 80336 Munich.

Telephone: (89) 5441870; **Fax:** (89) 54418720; **Internet:** www.wilhelm-sander-stiftung.de; **e-mail:** sekretariat@sanst.de.

Save Our Future Umweltstiftung—SOF (Save Our Future Environmental Foundation)

Founded in 1989 by Jürgen Oppermann to create environmental awareness and encourage environmental protection.

Activities: Operates nationally and internationally in the field of environmental education and sustainability, mainly through projects in education for children, pre-school children and young people. Develops model projects such as 'richtig Leben', an agenda of 21 climate protection projects for kindergartens, providing play activities for children, as well as training for educators, as well as building up an Internet-communication system for environmental education activities in Hamburg. Has also established the first two mobile environmental education vehicles as a model for China, in collaboration with Friends of Nature Beijing and the Shanghai Education Centre. Also organizes environmental round tables for young people in Germany, carried out a Sport and Environment campaign and established a Chair for water economy and water supply at the Technical University of Hamburg.

Geographical Area of Activity: International, mainly Germany and the People's Republic of China.

Restrictions: Only supports its own projects.

Publications: *Die Sonne und ihre Kinder* (children's publication); *Umweltschutz im Sportverein—Ein Praxisleitfaden* (video and brochures).

Finance: Total assets approx. €5,000,000.

Board of Trustees: Jürgen Oppermann (Chair.); Johan Lorenzen (Deputy Chair.).

Principal Staff: Chief Exec. Dr Jorg von Bargen; Man. Ralf Thielebein-Pohl.

Address: Bahnhof Klein Flottbek, Jürgensalle 51–53, 22609 Hamburg.

Telephone: (40) 240600; **Fax:** (40) 240640; **Internet:** www.save-our-future.de; **e-mail:** info@save-our-future.de.

Ernst-Schering-Stiftung (Ernst Schering Foundation)

Independent, non-profit Foundation, established in 2002 by Schering AG, Berlin to promote science and the arts.

Activities: The Foundation aims to promote science, with a focus on the natural sciences, and the arts, with a focus on the contemporary visual and performing arts, including dance and music. The Foundation promotes the scientific and cultural education of children and youth and dialogue between science and society. Particular emphasis is on projects in frontier areas, especially at the interface of art and science. This interface is also the focus of the Foundation's project space, where it puts on shows by young, experimental artists as well as lectures and workshops, thus serving as a platform for interdisciplinary dialogue among science, culture and society.

Geographical Area of Activity: Germany and international.

Publications: Image Brochure; exhibition catalogues; publications of scientific symposia; others.

Finance: Endowment of €35,000,000.

Council: Prof. Dr Reinhard Kurth (Chair.); Dr Hubertus Erlen (Deputy Chair.).

Principal Staff: Dir of Science Dr Sonja Kießling; Dir of Arts and Culture Heike Catherina Mertens.

Address: Unter den Linden 32–34, 10117 Berlin.

Telephone: (30) 206229-65; **Fax:** (30) 206229-61; **Internet:** www.scheringstiftung.de; **e-mail:** info@scheringstiftung.de.

Eberhard-Schöck-Stiftung (Eberhard Schöck Foundation)

Established in 1992 by Eberhard Schöck to promote the building trade in the former communist countries of Central and Eastern Europe.

Activities: Operates internationally in Eastern and Central Europe in the areas of aid, economic affairs and education, through self-conducted programmes, grants, scholarships and fellowships, conferences, training courses and publications. The Foundation runs practical programmes to train young building workers from the former communist countries of Europe to become self-employed builders in their own countries; it thus aims to contribute to stability and the principles of democracy and the market economy. It also runs practical programmes to train vocational teachers and managers of small and medium-sized enterprises in the building trade. Two prizes are offered by the Foundation: the Schoeck Building Innovation Prize and the German Language Cultural Prize (in co-operation with the Dortmund Verein Deutsche Sprache). Since 1998 the Foundation has run pilot projects to modernize vocational training in Russia, Ukraine and, since 2010, in Moldova.

Geographical Area of Activity: Central and Eastern Europe.

Restrictions: Grants are made only within the Foundation's own projects.

Publications: Annual Report; conference documentation; and commemorative publication.

Finance: Assets approx. €15,000,000.

Board of Trustees: Eberhard Schöck (Chair.); Dr J. D. Wickert (Deputy Chair.).

Principal Staff: Man. Dir Peter Möller; Asst to Man. Heike Esper-Frietsch.

Address: Vimbucher Str. 2, 76534 Baden-Baden.

Telephone: (7223) 967-371; **Fax:** (7223) 967-373; **Internet:** www.eberhard-schoeck-stiftung.de; **e-mail:** kontakt@eberhard-schoeck-stiftung.de.

Schwarzkopf-Stiftung Junges Europa (Schwarzkopf Foundation Young Europe)

Founded in 1971 as the Heinz-Schwarzkopf-Foundation to promote political awareness and social responsibility in young people aged 16–28, thus building on and strengthening European integration.

Activities: Operates across Europe in the fields of international relations, culture, political and economic affairs, science and education, through international youth conferences and travel scholarships. Annually awards the Young European of the Year prize and Schwarzkopf-Europe-Prize. It is the international umbrella organization of the European Youth Parliament.

Geographical Area of Activity: Western, Central and Eastern Europe.

Publications: Travel reports on areas of Europe, with an emphasis on young people.

Board of Trustees: Dr André Schmitz-Schwarzkopf (Chair.).

Principal Staff: Man. Dir Philipp Scharff.

Address: Sophienstr. 28–29, 10178 Berlin.

Telephone: (30) 28095146; **Fax:** (30) 28095150; **Internet:** www.schwarzkopf-stiftung.de; **e-mail:** info@schwarzkopf-stiftung.de.

Schweisfurth-Stiftung (Schweisfurth Foundation)

The Schweisfurth Foundation was founded in 1985 by the entrepreneur Karl Ludwig Schweisfurth as an 'ideas business'. It promotes innovative approaches, visions and concrete models relating to the future of agriculture, science, education, and society.

Activities: The Foundation works towards identifying environmentally-friendly methods of agriculture and the improvement of the living standards of livestock. Other focal points are; heightened food safety, the safeguarding of food quality, innovative means of organic food processing and novel marketing methods. The Foundation also proposes new forms of education and training in the artesian aspects of food processing. It works closely with government agencies in these areas, and has published guidelines for sustainable agriculture and food production.

Geographical Area of Activity: Germany, Europe and China.

Restrictions: The Foundation runs its own projects; no funds or scholarships are given.

Publications: Project results; books; flyers.

Finance: Total assets €15,000,000 (2009); annual expenditure €600,000–€700,000 (2009).

Trustees: Karl Ludwig Schweisfurth (Founder, Hon. member); Josef Jacobi (Chair.); Anna Schweisfurth (Deputy Chair.).

Principal Staff: Dir Prof. Dr Franz-Theo Gottwald; Sec. Christa Thomas.

Address: Südliches Schlossrondell 1, 80638 Munich.

Telephone: (89) 17959510; **Fax:** (89) 17959519; **Internet:** www.schweisfurth-stiftung.de; **e-mail:** info@schweisfurth.de.

Hanns-Seidel-Stiftung eV (Hanns Seidel Foundation)

Founded in 1967 to promote the democratic and civic development of the German people on a Christian basis; to foster the academic sector; to foster international attitudes and understanding between peoples; and to promote the process of European unification.

Activities: The Foundation operates nationally in the fields of the arts and humanities and education; internationally it works in the fields of education, international affairs, health and social welfare, through promoting self-sufficiency and individual initiatives, and through scholarships, travel grants, conferences and publications. Works through five departments: Academy for Politics and Current Affairs; Institute for Political Education; Institute for International Co-operation; and Scholarship Organization. Maintains three liaison offices and more than 50 project offices.

Geographical Area of Activity: International.

Publications: Infobrief; Annual Report; Political Studies.

Finance: Annual expenditure approx. €48,000,000 (2010).

Board of Directors: Dr Hans Zehetmair (Chair.); Alois Glück (Deputy Chair.); Prof. Ursula Männle (Deputy Chair.); Dr Wolfgang Piller (Treas.); Michael Glos (Sec.).

Principal Staff: CEO Dr Peter Witterauf.

Address: Lazarettstr. 33, 80636 Munich.

Telephone: (89) 1258-0; **Fax:** (89) 1258-356; **Internet:** www.hss.de; **e-mail:** info@hss.de.

Software AG Foundation

Established in 1992 by Peter M. Schnell and Software AG.

Activities: Provides funding and technical support to non-profit organizations operating in the areas of education, support for young people, care for people with disabilities, science and research, and environmental protection.

Geographical Area of Activity: Europe and Brazil.

Finance: Total assets €1,282,000,000 (Dec. 2010).

Supervisory Board: Dr Peter M. Schnell (Chair.).

Principal Staff: Man. Dir Prof. Dr Horst Philipp Bauer.

Address: Am Eichwäldchen 6, 64297 Darmstadt.

Telephone: (6151) 916650; **Fax:** (6151) 91665129; **Internet:** www.software-ag-stiftung.de; **e-mail:** stiftung@sagst.de.

Sparkassen-Kulturstiftung Hessen-Thüringen (Hesse and Thuringia Savings Banks Cultural Foundation)

Established in 1989 by the Sparkassen- und Giroverband Hessen-Thüringen savings banks for the promotion of culture and the arts in the Federal States of Hesse and Thuringia.

Activities: Operates in Hesse and Thuringia in the fields of the arts and humanities, and conservation and the environment, through conservation of cultural heritage, research, and care for the environment; and in the fields of health and welfare, in particular with relation to young people, the aged, and public health care.

Geographical Area of Activity: Hesse and Thuringia, Germany.

Finance: Annual expenditure €1,800,000 (2008).

Principal Staff: Man. Dr Thomas Wurzel; Sec. Nicole Schlabach.

Address: Alte Rothofstr. 9, 60313 Frankfurt.

Telephone: (69) 2175-511; **Fax:** (69) 2175-499; **Internet:** www.sparkassen-finanzgruppe-ht.de; **e-mail:** sgvht@sgvht.de.

Sparkassenstiftung für internationale Kooperation eV (Savings Banks Foundation for International Cooperation)

Established in 1992 for the promotion of economic and social development in developing and transition countries and areas.

Activities: Operates internationally, especially in Central and Eastern Europe, Central America, Asia and Africa, in the field of aid to developing countries, supporting retail banks and microfinance institutions through providing technical assistance in the areas of internal organization, human resource development and product development (especially lending to micro- and small entrepreneurs and attracting deposits).

Geographical Area of Activity: International, especially Central and Eastern Europe, Central America, Asia and Africa.

Restrictions: Unsolicited applications for grants are not accepted.

Publications: Annual Report.

Finance: Total assets €12,000,000 (Dec. 2010).

Trustees: Heinrich Haasis (Chair.); Michael Breuer (Deputy Chair.).

Principal Staff: Chair. Dr Holger Berndt.

Address: Simrockstr. 4, 53113 Bonn.

Telephone: (228) 9703-0; **Fax:** (228) 9703-613; **Internet:** www.sbfic.de; **e-mail:** office@sbfic.de.

Friede Springer Herz Stiftung (Friede Springer Heart Foundation)

Founded in 2004, the aim of the foundation is to aid research in cardiac and vascular diseases.

Activities: Supports publications in professioal journals and other media, organizes scientific seminars and lectures, and supports non-profit institutions.

Trustees: Dr Roland Hetzer (Chair.); Prof. Dr Steffen Behrens (Vice-Chair.).

Principal Staff: CEO Dr Erik Lindner.

Address: Axel-Springer-Straße 65, 10969 Berlin.

Telephone: (30) 259172204; **Fax:** (30) 259172202; **Internet:** www.friede-springer-herz-stiftung.de; **e-mail:** info@friede-springer-herz-stiftung.de.

Axel-Springer-Stiftung (Axel Springer Foundation)

Founded in 1953 by Axel Springer to support scholarly and philanthropic activities within the country and abroad.

Activities: The Foundation supports all branches of learning through grants for research work, publications, conferences and courses of further education. Support is also given to elderly journalists and actors in need as a result of sickness; for preventative health and fitness activities; for youth welfare; for refugees; for artistic events; and for the restoration of religious buildings. The Foundation also encourages good relations between Germany and Israel by supporting youth exchange.

Geographical Area of Activity: Germany, Eastern Europe and Israel.

Restrictions: New projects are only occasionally supported.

Board of Directors: Friede Springer, Gerhard Menzel, Prof. Dr Dieter Stolte.

Principal Staff: Dr Erik Lindner, Ulrike Bach, Ute Schweitzer.

Address: Axel-Springer-Str. 65, 10969 Berlin.

Telephone: (30) 2591 72203; **Fax:** (30) 2591 72202; **Internet:** www.axelspringerstiftung.de; **e-mail:** mail@axelspringerstiftung.de.

Friede Springer Stiftung (Friede Springer Foundation)

Founded in 2010 as an organization independent of politics and religion to promote and support philanthropic goals on an economic, spiritual and cultural basis.

Activities: supports scientific, artistic and cultural projects, meetings and symposia in scientific, artistic, cultural and educational areas; funds scholarships and endowments; promotes scientific publications and research projects.

Geographical Area of Activity: Germany.

Principal Staff: Chief Exec. Friede Springer.

Telephone: (30) 259172203; **Fax:** (30) 259172202; **Internet:** www.friedespringerstiftung.de; **e-mail:** info@friedespringerstiftung.de.

Stiftung CAESAR (Centre of Advanced European Studies and Research)

Established in 1995 by the German Government and the Federal State of North-Rhine-Westphalia to support science and research.

Activities: Operates nationally and internationally in the fields of education, science and technology, through self-conducted programmes and training courses. Operates the CAESAR Centre. Current research priorities are: nanotechnology/materials science; coupling of biological and electronic systems; and ergonomics in communications. Maintains a library.

Geographical Area of Activity: International.

Restrictions: No grants are made.

Publications: *Smart Materials*; *Proceedings of the First Caesarium* (1999); annual reports; research materials and publications.

Board of Trustees: Prof. Dr Peter Gruss (Chair.).

Principal Staff: Admin. and Scientific Man. Prof. Dr Ulrich Benjamin Kaupp; Admin. Dir Heike Krause.

Address: Ludwig-Erhard-Allee 2, 53175 Bonn.

Telephone: (228) 9656-0; **Fax:** (228) 9656-111; **Internet:** www.caesar.de; **e-mail:** office@caesar.de.

Stiftung Deutsche Geisteswissenschaftliche Institute im Ausland—DGIA (Foundation for German Humanities Institutes Abroad)

This incorporated foundation, directly accountable to the Federal Government, was established on 1 July 2002.

Activities: The Foundation's objective is to promote research, particularly in the fields of history, cultural studies, economics and the social sciences, in selected countries; and mutual understanding between Germany and these countries. It is an umbrella organization including various institutes worldwide, which carry out research and promote co-operation between scholars and institutions within their own spheres by means of publications and academic conferences, providing academic information and advice, facilitating contacts between scholars, supporting the future generation of scholars, as well as setting up and maintaining libraries and collections of other media.

Geographical Area of Activity: International.

Publications: Series of monographs; journals; bulletins.

Finance: Annual budget approx. €35,000,000 (2010).

Board of Trustees: Prof. Dr Heinz Duchhardt (Chair.).

Principal Staff: Exec. Dir Dr Harald Rosenbach.

Address: Rheinallee 6, 53173 Bonn.

Telephone: (228) 377860; **Fax:** (228) 3778619; **Internet:** www
.stiftung-dgia.de; **e-mail:** geschaeftsstelle@stiftung-dgia.de.

Stiftung Entwicklung und Frieden—SEF (Development and Peace Foundation)

Established in 1986 by the Federal States of North Rhine-West-
phalia, Berlin, Brandenburg and Saxony on the initiative of
the former Chancellor of the Federal Republic of Germany
(Bundesrepublik Deutschland) Willy Brandt.

Activities: A cross-party, not-for-profit organization, which
argues for a new political order in a world marked by globalization. The Foundation's work is based on three principles: global responsibility, cross-party and cross-cultural dialogue,
and an interdisciplinary approach to understanding interde-
pendencies. It carries out its work through conferences,
including symposia, expert workshops and dialogues, and publications.

Geographical Area of Activity: Germany and international.

Restrictions: Does not make grants.

Publications: *Global Trends* (biennially); *Series ONE
WORLD*; *SEF Policy Papers*; *SEF News* (3 a year, in German
and English); *World Politics*; *UN Peacekeeping Operations in
Africa*; *Una mirada desde América Latina*.

Finance: Annual expenditure approx. €650,000.

Board of Trustees: Hannelore Kraft (Chair.); Matthias Plat-
zeck (Deputy Chair.); Klaus Wowereit (Deputy Chair.); Stanis-
law Tillich (Deputy Chair.).

Principal Staff: Exec. Dir Dr Michèle Roth.

Address: Dechenstr. 2, 53115 Bonn.

Telephone: (228) 95925-0; **Fax:** (228) 95925-99; **Internet:**
www.sef-bonn.org; **e-mail:** sef@sef-bonn.org.

Stiftung Ettersberg

Established in Spring 2002 by the Government of the Federal
State of Thuringia to promote the comparative study of European dictatorships in the 20th century as well as their democratic transition. Through this the foundation strives to
contribute to the historical coming to terms with and the comparative analysis of dictatorships of fascist, national socialist
and communist provenance as well as authoritarian regimes;
to elucidate their mechanisms of rule and their driving forces;
to reveal the significance of opposition and resistance against
authoritarian and totalitarian suppression and to keep alive
the memory of the victims of dictatorial violence. In addition,
it confronts the problems of coping with the past and questions
of transition from dictatorship to democracy, as well as the stability conditions of liberal democracies.

Activities: The foundation carries out historical research
and attempts to foster international and interdisciplinary dialogue between political scholars, historians, and researchers
in the field of social and cultural studies in Europe, through
disseminating the research results. Organizes international
symposia, scientific conferences and colloquia, of which the
results are issued in the foundation's dedicated series of publications. Also promotes dialogue between universities, scientific and pedagogical institutions and other initiatives that
operate in the field of dictatorship research and democratic
transition processes. It organizes exhibitions and initiates
competitions for students on issues such as experience of dictatorship, stabilization and endangering of democracy and
awards scholarships to junior academics.

Geographical Area of Activity: Germany.

Executive Board: Prof. Dr Hans-Joachim Veen (Chair.); Prof.
Dr Volkhard Knigge (Vice-Chair.).

Principal Staff: Man. Dir Michael Siegel.

Address: Jenaer Str. 4, 99425 Weimar.

Telephone: (3643) 49750; **Fax:** (3643) 497522; **Internet:** www
.stiftung-ettersberg.de; **e-mail:** weimar@stiftung-ettersberg
.de.

Stiftung Europäisches Naturerbe—EURONATUR
(European Nature Heritage Fund)

Established in 1987 by German environmental organizations
for nature and environmental protection.

Activities: Operates in Europe, the Middle East, North
Africa and the Philippines in the fields of conservation and
the environment and environmental policies, on an international level, through self-conducted programmes, grants to
NGOs and other institutions, conferences, training courses
and issuing publications. Awards the prizes 'Euronatur Environmental Award' (unendowed) and 'European Stork Village'.

Geographical Area of Activity: Mainly Europe, Middle
East, North Africa and the Philippines.

Restrictions: Grants only for measures supporting self-conducted programmes.

Publications: *Euronatur* (quarterly journal); papers on scientific and environmental issues.

Presiding Committee: Christel Schroeder (Pres.).

Principal Staff: Exec. Dir Gabriel Schwaderer.

Address: Konstanzer Str. 22, 78315 Radolfzell.

Telephone: (7732) 92720; **Fax:** (7732) 927222; **Internet:** www
.euronatur.de; **e-mail:** info@euronatur.org.

**Stiftung zur Förderung der Hochschulrektorenkon-
ferenz** (Foundation for the Promotion of the German Rectors' Conference)

Founded in 1965 by Prof. Dr Julius Speer, Prof. Dr Rudolf Sie-
verts, Prof. Dr Helmut Witte, Prof. Dr Gerhard Kielwein and
Prof. Dr Hans Leussink to provide personnel and appropriate
facilities for the accomplishment of the tasks of the Conference of Rectors of higher/further education institutes in Germany.

Activities: Operates within the spheres of activity of the German Rectors' Conference, a voluntary association of universities and other institutions of higher education, which aims to
find a common solution to problems of higher education, and
publicizes those problems; makes recommendations to the
appropriate authorities; aims to promote co-operation among
state, scientific and academic bodies, etc.; provides information services to member institutions and all other interested
parties; and generally concerns itself with developments in
higher education. Staff put at the disposal of the conference
by the Foundation are mainly active in the field of education,
nationally and internationally, and in the fields of social welfare and studies and international relations. Programmes are
carried out through conferences, courses, publications and
reports.

Geographical Area of Activity: Mainly Germany.

Publications: Annual Report; statements.

Executive Board: Prof. Dr Margret Wintermantel (Pres.).

Principal Staff: Sec.-Gen. Dr Thomas Kathofer.

Address: Ahrstr. 39, 53175 Bonn.

Telephone: (228) 887-0; **Fax:** (228) 887-110; **Internet:** www
.hrk.de/de/home/index.php; **e-mail:** serk@hkr.de.

Stiftung Jugend forscht e. V. (Foundation for Youth
Research)

Founded in 1965 by Henri Nannen to promote competitions for
young scientists under the age of 21 to encourage the research
work of students, trainees and other young people.

Activities: Organizes competitions in Germany; also makes
grants, and awards scholarships and fellowships.

Geographical Area of Activity: Germany.

Restrictions: Applications for grants are not accepted.

Publications: Commemorative volumes and brochures concerning the competitions; *Jugend forscht*; *Schüler experiment-
ieren*.

Finance: Financed by the German Government, Stern, and other companies. Annual expenditure approx. €900,000.

Trustees: Prof. Dr Annette Schavan (Pres.).

Principal Staff: Dir Dr Sven Baszio; Deputy Dir Dr Nico P. Kock.

Address: Baumwall 5, 20459 Hamburg.

Telephone: (40) 374709-0; **Fax:** (40) 374709-99; **Internet:** www .jugend-forscht.de; **e-mail:** info@jugend-forscht.de.

Stiftung für Kinder (Foundation for Children)

Established in 1986 to help children in less-developed countries learn and experience new forms of living together after their basic needs have been met, and to set an example of sharing in developed countries.

Activities: Operates in Germany and the Philippines in the areas of development aid, education, law and human rights, and medicine and health, through research, grants to organizations and individuals, and issuing publications. Its main concern is to use its resources for the elimination of misery, to overcome social, economic, political and cultural domination and power structures through co-operation with project partners on a reciprocal basis. Maintains a database of more than 6,000 German child-related foundations and associations.

Geographical Area of Activity: Germany and the Philippines.

Restrictions: Grants are not normally made to individuals.

Publications: *Children—War and Persecution: Proceedings of the Congress, Hamburg, Sept. 26–29 1993* (in Romanian, 2001); *Migrating on the Edges: Migration Theory, Discussion and Philippine Case Study; Lesezeichen Philippinen: Insulare Streifzüge durch Geschichte, Politik, Gesellschaft, Wirtschaft und Kultur; Documents of the European Forum for Child Welfare; Focus Philippines* (journal); *Ziel- oder Prozessorientierte Zusammenarbeit mit Projektpartnern im Süden?; Eliminating Racist Discrimination in Germany* (from the UN Committee on the Elimination of All Forms of Racial Discrimination, 2008).

Principal Staff: Exec. Dir Ekkehard Arnsperger.

Address: c/o RA. Ekkehard Arnsperger, Schwaighofstr. 14, 79100 Freiburg im Breisgau.

Telephone: (761) 71015; **Fax:** (761) 77306; **Internet:** www .stiftung-fuer-kinder.org; **e-mail:** stiftung.fuer.kinder@t -online.de.

Stiftung Kinder in Afrika (Children in Africa Foundation)

Founded in December 1984 by Horst W. Zillmer to grant aid and assistance to children in Africa.

Activities: Operates in Africa in the fields of education, and medicine and health, through grants to individuals and institutions. Projects since 1985 have taken place in Burkina Faso, Cameroon, Equatorial Guinea, Ghana, Kenya, Madagascar, Morocco, Mozambique, Namibia, South Africa, Sudan, Tanzania, Togo and Zambia.

Geographical Area of Activity: Africa (Burkina Faso, Cameroon, Equatorial Guinea, Ghana, Kenya, Madagascar, Morocco, Mozambique, Namibia, South Africa, Sudan, Tanzania, Togo and Zambia).

Trustees: Dr Hans-Dieter Hohnke (Chair.).

Principal Staff: Dir Horst W. Zillmer; Man. Klaus Dieter.

Address: Holsteiner Str. 12c, 21465 Reinbek.

Telephone: (40) 7221105; **Fax:** (40) 7221105; **Internet:** www .kinder-in-afrika.de; **e-mail:** info@kinder-in-afrika.de.

Stiftung Lesen (Foundation for Reading)

Established in 1988 to promote reading.

Activities: Operates in the fields of the arts and humanities, and education for young people and adults, promoting the reading of books, newspapers and magazines; supporting a reading and oral culture; and supporting research into reading, communication and the media.

Restrictions: Applications for grants are not accepted.

Finance: Total assets approx. €5,000,000.

Board of Trustees: Prof. Dr Markus Schachter (Chair.).

Principal Staff: Man. Dir Dr Joerg Pfuhl; Deputy Man. Dir Monica Ziller.

Address: Römerwall 40, 55131 Mainz.

Telephone: (6131) 28890-20; **Fax:** (6131) 230333; **Internet:** www.stiftunglesen.de; **e-mail:** mail@stiftunglesen.de.

Stiftung Nord-Süd-Brücken (North-South-Bridge Foundation)

Established in 1994 to assist development in less-developed regions, and to promote an understanding of the necessity of co-operation in development and international understanding.

Activities: Operates in the field of aid to less-developed countries, through promoting partnerships for development projects in less-developed regions of the world; informing the public about the necessity of co-operation in development, especially through promoting tolerance and international understanding. The Foundation supports only NGOs based in the former German Democratic Republic (East Germany) and East Berlin.

Geographical Area of Activity: Asia, Africa and Latin America.

Principal Staff: Dir Walter Hättig; Finance Dir Ingrid Rosenburg.

Address: Greifswalder Str. 33a, 10405 Berlin.

Telephone: (30) 42851385; **Fax:** (30) 42851386; **Internet:** www .nord-sued-bruecken.de; **e-mail:** info@nord-sued-bruecken .de.

Stiftung Ökologie & Landbau (Ecology and Agriculture Foundation)

Founded in 1962 by Karl Werner Kieffer to promote scientific research into the cultivation of agricultural produce with a view towards saving natural resources, preserving the ecological equilibrium and producing high-quality foodstuffs free of noxious substances.

Activities: Operates through the encouragement and support of the ecological schools of thought developing in agricultural science and practice; the co-ordination of exchange of knowledge and experience; support for active initiatives in training practice and science; and the organization of meetings and other events.

Geographical Area of Activity: Western Europe.

Publications: *Ökologie & Landbau; Ökologische Konzepte* (series); *SÖL-Sonderausgaben* (series); report on operations and activities.

Finance: Annual revenue and expenditure approx. €500,000.

Board of Trustees: Dagi Kieffer (Chair.); Edda Knief (Deputy Chair.).

Principal Staff: Exec. Dir Peter Kieffer.

Address: Weinstr. Süd 51, Postfach 1516, 67089 Bad Dürkheim.

Telephone: (6322) 989700; **Fax:** (6322) 989701; **Internet:** www .soel.de; **e-mail:** info@soel.de.

Stiftung Weltethos (Global Ethic Foundation)

Established in 1995 by Count K. K. von der Groeben for intercultural and inter-religious research, education and encounter, for the dissemination of the idea of a global ethic, with the basic conviction that there can be no peace among nations without peace between religions, that there can be no peace among religions without dialogue between religions, and that there can be no dialogue between religions without research into the foundations of religions.

Activities: Operates nationally and internationally in the areas of the humanities, inter-cultural and inter-religious dialogue, education, international affairs, and human rights, through self-conducted programmes, research, lectures, conferences, training courses and publications. A small research team engages in long-term work to further a global ethic, and the Foundation also supports wider initiatives and projects. The basis of the Foundation's programme is the Declaration toward a Global Ethic endorsed by the Parliament of the World's Religions in 1993 (i.e. a commitment to a culture of non-violence and respect for life, to a culture of solidarity and a just economic order, to a culture of tolerance and a life of truthfulness, and to a culture of equal rights and partnership between men and women).

Geographical Area of Activity: International.

Publications: *Global Responsibility: In Search of a New World Ethic*; *Yes to a Global Ethic*; *A Global Ethic for Global Politics and Economics*; *A Global Ethic and Global Responsibilities*; and other publications.

Board: Prof. Dr Hans Küng (Pres.).

Principal Staff: Sec.-Gen. Dr Stephan Schlensog.

Address: Waldhäuser Str. 23, 72076 Tübingen.

Telephone: (7071) 62646; **Fax:** (7071) 610140; **Internet:** www .global-ethic.org; **e-mail:** office@weltethos.org.

Stiftung West-Östliche Begegnungen (West-East Foundation)

Established in 1994 to promote contact between the peoples of Germany and the countries of the former USSR to promote friendship, international peace and understanding.

Activities: Operates in the areas of the arts and culture, education and international affairs, through projects of exchanges of information and of pupils, other young people and professionals.

Geographical Area of Activity: Azerbaijan, Belarus, Georgia, Kazakhstan, Lithuania, Moldova, Russia, Tajikistan, Turkmenistan and Ukraine.

Restrictions: Grants only to German institutions (e.g. registered NGOs, schools, institutes, etc.). No grants to individuals.

Publications: Activity Report; financial statement; information brochures.

Finance: Financed by an endowment consisting of the remaining assets of the former East German Society for German-Soviet Friendship; assets approx. €12,500,000; annual expenditure approx. €600,000.

Governing Board: Prof. Dr Hans-Peter Fussel (Chair.); Fritz Tangermann (Deputy Chair.).

Principal Staff: Man. Dir Dr Helmut Domke; Deputy Man. Dir Klaus D. Schickhaus.

Address: Mauerstr. 93, 10117 Berlin.

Telephone: (30) 2044840; **Fax:** (30) 20647646; **Internet:** www .stiftung-woeb.de; **e-mail:** info@stiftung-woeb.de.

Stiftung Wissenschaft und Politik—Deutsches Institut für internationale Politik und Sicherheit—SWP (German Institute for International and Security Affairs)

Founded in 1962, an independent research centre that advises the German parliament and the German federal government on all matters relevant to German foreign and security policy.

Activities: Organized into eight research units, currently consisting of approximately 50 researchers; organizes conferences and workshops; maintains a library of approximately 85,000 volumes and a computerized information system with more than 300,000 bibliographical references in international relations and area studies.

Geographical Area of Activity: Germany.

Restrictions: Applications for grants are not accepted.

Publications: *Internationale Politik und Sicherheit*; *Aktuelle Materialien zur Internationalen Politik*; SWP Comments; SWP Research Papers; SWP Newsletter.

Advisory Council: Prof. Dr Hans-Peter Keitel (Pres.); Ronald Pofalla (Deputy Pres.); Hans-Ulrich Klose (Deputy Pres.).

Principal Staff: Dir Prof. Dr Volker Perthes; Deputy Dir Christoph Geisler.

Address: Ludwigkirch Platz 3–4, 10719 Berlin.

Telephone: (30) 88007-0; **Fax:** (30) 88007-100; **Internet:** www .swp-berlin.org; **e-mail:** swp@swp-berlin.org.

Stiftungsfonds Deutsche Bank zur Förderung der Wissenschaft in Forschung und Lehre (Deutsche Bank Endowment Fund for the Promotion of Science in Research and Teaching)

Established in 1970 by Deutsche Bank AG for the promotion of science and research.

Activities: Operates in the field of science and technology, mainly through funding programmes at universities and other institutions.

Geographical Area of Activity: Europe.

Publications: Study courses.

Board: Prof. Dr Horst Köhler (Chair.); Dr Arend Oetker (Pres.); Dr Wulf Bernotat, Dr Jürgen Hambrecht (Vice-Pres.).

Principal Staff: Gen. Sec. Dr Andreas Schlüter.

Address: c/o Stifterverband für die Deutsche Wissenschaft eV, Barkhovenallee 1, 45239 Essen.

Telephone: (201) 8401-0; **Fax:** (201) 8401-301; **Internet:** www .stifterverband.de; **e-mail:** mail@stifterverband.de.

Studienstiftung des deutschen Volkes (German National Academic Foundation)

Refounded in 1948 to give grants and scholarships to particularly gifted students and to aid them in their university studies.

Activities: Operates in the fields of science and medicine, the arts and humanities, law and other professions, through grants to individuals. Scholars may participate in summer schools arranged by the Foundation, receive special research grants or special tuition at any German and many foreign universities. Awards around 2,000 scholarships each year.

Geographical Area of Activity: Germany.

Publications: Annual Report of operations and financial statement.

Finance: Annual expenditure approx. €38,000,000.

Board of Directors: Prof. Dr Reinhard Zimmermann (Pres.); Prof. Dr Stefan Matuschek (Vice-Pres.); Prof. Dr Eva Haberfellner (Treas.).

Principal Staff: Sec.-Gen. Dr Gerhard Teufel.

Address: Ahrstr. 41, 53175 Bonn.

Telephone: (228) 820960; **Fax:** (228) 82096103; **Internet:** www.studienstiftung.de; **e-mail:** info@studienstiftung.de.

Südost-Institut—Stiftung für wissenschaftliche Südosteuropaforschung (South-East Institute—Foundation for Academic Research into South-Eastern Europe)

Founded in 1930 by the German Government to carry out research into the history, societies and politics of South-Eastern Europe.

Activities: Operates nationally and internationally in the fields of the history and current affairs of South-Eastern Europe, through research, conferences and publications; hosts guest researchers; public research library of approximately 130,000 items.

Geographical Area of Activity: Europe.

Restrictions: No grants are made.

Publications: Journals: *Südost-Forschungen* (history); *Südosteuropa* (current affairs); Series: *Südosteuropäische Arbeiten*; *Südosteuropa Bibliographie – Ergänzungsbände*.

Finance: Annual expenditure €670,000 (2010).

Principal Staff: Dirs Prof. Dr Ulf Brunnbauer, Dr Konrad Clewing.

Address: Landshuter Str. 4, D – 93047 Regensburg.

Telephone: (941) 9435470; **Fax:** (941) 9435485; **Internet:** www .suedost-institut.de; **e-mail:** info@suedost-institut.de.

Fritz Thyssen Stiftung (Fritz Thyssen Foundation)

Founded in 1959 by Amélie Thyssen and her daughter, Anita Countess Zichy-Thyssen, to promote research and scholarships in universities and research institutes, particularly in Germany. Special consideration is given to the rising generation of scientists and scholars.

Activities: Supports particular research projects of limited duration, mainly in basic research in the humanities; international relations; state, economy and society; and medicine.

Geographical Area of Activity: Mainly Germany.

Publications: Annual Report; *Publications of the Foundation*; *The Establishment the Fritz Thyssen Foundation*; *Historia Scientiarum*; *Tradition and Tasks of National and Private Science Promotion*; *The Fritz Thyssen Foundation 1960–1970*; *Fritz Thyssen Foundation*; *Thyssen lectures*.

Finance: Annual expenditure €15,500,000 (2009).

Board of Trustees: Dr Manfred Schneider (Chair.); Dr Arend Oetker (Deputy Chair.).

Principal Staff: Exec. Dir Jürgen Chr. Regge.

Address: Apostelnkloster 13-15, 50672 Cologne.

Telephone: (221) 2774960; **Fax:** (221) 27749629; **Internet:** www.fritz-thyssen-stiftung.de; **e-mail:** fts@fritz-thyssen-stiftung.de.

Alfred Toepfer Stiftung F.V.S. (Alfred Toepfer Foundation F.V.S.)

Founded in 1931 by Dr h.c. Alfred Toepfer to promote European unity and understanding between nations. The Foundation was formerly known as Stiftung F.V.S.

Activities: Operates in Europe in the fields of the arts, science, humanities, young people, European relations and the conservation of natural resources, through self-conducted programmes, scholarships, grants to institutions and the awarding of prizes. Four awards are made annually for achievements in the field of European relations. The Foundation also operates an extensive scholarship programme for students from Central and Eastern Europe.

Geographical Area of Activity: Europe.

Publications: Annual Report and a variety of books on the foundation's history and prizes; *Jahrbuch Alfred Toepfer Stiftung F.V.S.* (year book); articles, essays, speeches.

Finance: Assets €85,938,812 (2009); expenditure €5,387,917 (2009).

Foundation Supervisory Council: Prof. Jurgen Schlaeger (Chair.); Dr Ulrich Bopp (Vice-Chair.).

Principal Staff: Chair. Ansgar Wimmer; Andreas Holz.

Address: Georgplatz 10, 20099 Hamburg.

Telephone: (40) 33402-10; **Fax:** (40) 335860; **Internet:** www.toepfer-fvs.de; **e-mail:** benecke@toepfer-fvs.de.

Transparency International—TI

Established to combat corruption at national and international level; operates as a coalition of civil society, business and governmental organizations.

Activities: Anti-corruption organization operating in more than 90 countries world-wide, through national chapters that work in collaboration with relevant players from civil society organizations, government, business and the media to promote transparency in elections, in public administration, in procurement and in business. Involved in regional as well as national programmes. TI also uses advocacy campaigns to lobby governments to implement anti-corruption reforms.

Geographical Area of Activity: International.

Publications: Annual Report; financial report; *Global Corruption Report*; working papers; *Policy Positions*; *Progress Reports*.

Finance: Annual income €18,027,000, expenditure €17,790,000 (2010).

Board of Directors: Huguette Labelle (Chair.); Akere T. Muna (Vice-Chair.).

Principal Staff: Man. Dir Cobus de Swardt.

Address: Alt Moabit 96, 10559 Berlin.

Telephone: (30) 3438200; **Fax:** (30) 34703912; **Internet:** www.transparency.org; **e-mail:** ti@transparency.org.

Klaus Tschira Stiftung GmbH (Klaus Tschira Foundation)

Established in 1995 by Dr Klaus Tschira, co-founder of oftware company SAP AG.

Activities: Operates in the fields of promoting science and international scientific co-operation, with a current focus on information science and related fields and pure and applied research, as well as funding educational projects at universities. The Foundation spends 51% of its annual budget on its own projects, particularly the European Media Laboratory, founded by Klaus Tschira in 1997. Invites applications for project funding, provided that the projects in questions are in line with the central concerns of the Foundation.

Geographical Area of Activity: International.

Restrictions: Grants not normally made to individuals.

Finance: Capital consists of approx. 11.5% of shares in SAP AG.

Board of Directors: Konrad Muller (Chair.).

Principal Staff: Founder and Man. Dir Dr Klaus Tschira; Office Man. Beate Spiegel.

Address: Villa Bosch, Schloss-Wolfsbrunnenweg 33, 69118 Heidelberg.

Telephone: (6221) 533101; **Fax:** (6221) 533199; **Internet:** www.kts.villa-bosch.de; **e-mail:** beate.spiegel@kts.villa-bosch.de.

Kurt-Tucholsky-Stiftung (Kurt Tucholsky Foundation)

Founded 1969 by Mary Gerold-Tucholsky to promote international communication and understanding.

Activities: The Foundation promotes international student exchanges through scholarships in the fields of German studies, journalism, sociology or political sciences, awarding scholarships to German students to study abroad, and to foreign students to study in Germany for one year. The foundation also administers the Tucholsky literary legacy at the German literature archives in Marbach on the Neckar.

Geographical Area of Activity: International.

Trustees: Dr Ian King (Chair.); Frank-Burkhard Habel (Vice-Chair.).

Principal Staff: Sec. Renate Bokenkamp.

Address: Tornberg 14, 22337 Hamburg.

Telephone: (40) 331819; **Fax:** (40) 30392000; **Internet:** www.tucholsky-gesellschaft.de; **e-mail:** ktstiftung@aol.com.

Vodafone Stiftung Deutschland (Vodafone Foundation Germany)

One of the largest company foundations in Germany.

Activities: Operates in the fields of education, social welfare, medicine and health, and culture and the arts.

Geographical Area of Activity: Germany.

Restrictions: No new projects are currently being taken on for funding.

Publications: Newsletter.

Trustees: Thomas Ellerbeck (Chair.).

Principal Staff: Dirs Thomas Holtmanns, Dr Mark Speich.

Address: Am Seestern 1, 40547 Düsseldorf.

Telephone: (211) 5335579; **Fax:** (211) 5331898; **Internet:** www.vodafone-stiftung.de; **e-mail:** info@vodafone-stiftung.de.

VolkswagenStiftung (Volkswagen Foundation)

Founded in 1961 by the Federal Republic of Germany and the State of Lower Saxony for the promotion of science, technology and the humanities in research and university teaching.

Activities: Operates nationally and internationally, through grants for specific purposes to academic and technical institutions engaged in research and teaching. The Foundation is free to support any area of science, as well as the humanities, but has limited its funding programme to a range of specific fields; special programmes operate for Sub-Saharan Africa and Central Asia/Caucasus.

Geographical Area of Activity: International.

Restrictions: In the case of applications from abroad, cooperation with German research workers or scholars is usually essential.

Publications: Annual Report; *Crossing Borders* (information in English); *Impulse für die Wissenschaft*; brochures.

Finance: Total grants expenditure since 1962 approx. €3,600m.; total assets €2,300,000,000 (2009); annual grants expenditure €101,400,000 (2009).

Board of Trustees: Lutz Stratmann (Chair.); Dr Annette Schavan (Vice-Chair.); Prof. Dr Wolf Singer (Vice-Chair.).

Principal Staff: Sec.-Gen. Dr Wilhelm Krull.

Address: Kastanienallee 35, 30519 Hannover.

Telephone: (511) 8381-0; **Fax:** (511) 8381-344; **Internet:** www.volkswagenstiftung.de; **e-mail:** info@volkswagenstiftung.de.

WasserStiftung (Water Foundation)

Established in 2000 to support those in regions with too little, or polluted, drinking water, helping them to help themselves.

Activities: Operates in the areas of development aid, health and welfare, and environmental conservation. Supports water projects in Afghanistan, Bolivia, Chile, Eritrea, Ethiopia and the Palestinian Autonomous Areas.

Geographical Area of Activity: Afghanistan, Bolivia, Chile, Eritrea, Ethiopia and Palestinian Autonomous Areas.

Board of Directors: Ernst Frost (Founder and Chair.); Henner Lang (Co-Founder).

Principal Staff: Dir Wolf-Dietrich Pfaelzer; Deputy Dir Wolfgang A. Schaal.

Address: Lechnerstr. 23, 82067 Ebenhausen.

Telephone: (8178) 998418; **Fax:** (8178) 998419; **Internet:** www.wasserstiftung.de; **e-mail:** wasserstiftung@t-online.de.

Dr Rainer Wild-Stiftung—Stiftung für gesunde Ernährung (Dr Rainer Wild Foundation for Healthy Nutrition)

Established in 1991 by Dr Rainer Wild, and accorded full legal status by the governing council of Karlsruhe in 1993, to organize actively, on an international basis, scientific research, public education, occupational training and scientific and cultural events aimed at advancing the area of healthy human nutrition.

Activities: Operates in the fields of nutritional education, consumer behavior, food and culture, food sensory science; through networking, conventions and awarding prizes. Target groups are food scientists, nutritionists, dieticians, social scientists and educationalists. It hosts conventions, publishes books and journals, awards the Dr Rainer Wild Prize for outstanding accomplishments in the field of healthy nutrition, initiates research projects and provides scholarships to young scientists.

Geographical Area of Activity: International.

Restrictions: No grants are made to individuals or organizations.

Publications: *Healthy Nutrition* (book series); *Mitteilungen* (journal); textbooks; articles; lectures.

Board or Trustees: Prof. Dr Klaus Landfried (Chair.).

Principal Staff: CEO Prof. Dr Rainer Wild.

Address: Mittelgewannweg 10, 69123 Heidelberg.

Telephone: (6221) 7511-200; **Fax:** (6221) 7511-240; **Internet:** www.gesunde-ernaehrung.org; **e-mail:** info@gesunde-ernaehrung.org.

Carl-Zeiss-Stiftung (Carl-Zeiss Foundation)

Founded in 1889 by Dr Ernst Abbe with the following objectives: to develop the precision technical industry, at the Optical Works and the Glass Works, Jena; to fulfil higher social obligations than individual owners could permanently guarantee towards all the employees to improve their situation with regard to their personal and economic rights; outside the works, to promote the general interests of the branches of precision technical industry as mentioned above, to participate in organizations and measures designed for the public good of the working population in Jena and its immediate neighbourhood; to promote study in natural and mathematical sciences in research as well as teaching. After the expropriation of the Carl-Zeiss-Stiftung in June 1948, the legal seat of the Foundation was transferred to the Federal Republic of Germany (Bundesrepublik Deutschland).

Activities: The Foundation's main interest is the operation of the two companies Carl Zeiss AG, Oberkochen and SCHOTT AG, Mainz; as well as these commercial ventures the Foundation supports research in the field of science and technology. Operates through self-conducted programmes, research, conferences, courses, publications and lectures, and through grants to German institutions and individuals.

Geographical Area of Activity: Germany.

Restrictions: Religious or political institutions are not supported.

Publications: Annual Report and financial statement.

Board of Trustees: Theresia Bauer (Chair.).

Principal Staff: Man. Dir Dr Klaus Herberger; Deputy Man. Dir Dennys Klein.

Address: Ministerium für Wissenschaft, Forschung und Kunst Baden-Württemberg, Königstr. 46, 70173 Stuttgart.

Telephone: (711) 2793253; **Internet:** www.carl-zeiss-stiftung.de; **e-mail:** klaus.herberger@mwk.bwl.de.

ZEIT-Stiftung Ebelin und Gerd Bucerius (Ebelin and Gerd Bucerius ZEIT Foundation)

Gerd Bucerius founded the weekly newspaper *Die Zeit* in Hamburg in 1946 and created the non-profit ZEIT-Stiftung in 1971. Bucerius liked active involvement in civic affairs; *Die Zeit* benefited greatly from his passionate interest in politics, business and culture. His thinking continues to influence the ZEIT-Stiftung that carries his name and the name of his wife.

Activities: Operates in three areas: science and scholarships (including innovation in higher education, scholarship in the field of history, and research); education and training (including press and journalism, dialogue in society, development of the Hamburg secondary school system); and art and culture (including literature, art and museums, cultural heritage, and music and theatre), through research centres, scholarships and prizes. In 2000 the Foundation established the first private German law school, Bucerius Law School, and in 2002 it founded its own arts forum, the Bucerius Kunst Forum, in Hamburg.

Geographical Area of Activity: Germany, Central, Eastern and Western Europe, and Israel.

Publications: Report (biennially); variety of brochures.

Board of Directors: Prof. Manfred Lahnstein (Pres.).

Principal Staff: Man. Dir Prof. Michael Goring.

Address: Feldbrunnenstr. 56, 20148 Hamburg.

Telephone: (40) 413366; **Fax:** (40) 41336700; **Internet:** www.zeit-stiftung.de; **e-mail:** zeit-stiftung@zeit-stiftung.de.

Ghana

FOUNDATIONS, TRUSTS AND NON-PROFIT ORGANIZATIONS

African Women's Development Fund—AWDF

The Fund was established in June 2000 by Bisi Adeleye-Fayemi, Hilda Tadria and Joana Foster to support organizations promoting women's rights in Africa.

Activities: The Fund finances sub-regional, regional, local and national organizations working in Africa towards empowering women; extends technical support to projects aiming at women's development in Africa; disseminates information pertaining to the work and achievements of organizations working for upliftment of African women.

Geographical Area of Activity: Africa.

Publications: Annual Report.

Executive Board: Dr Hilda Tadria (Co-Founder and Chair.); Bisi Adeleye-Fayemi (Pres. and Co-Founder); Joana Foster (Co-Founder).

Principal Staff: Intermin CEO Theo Sowa.

Address: Plot Number 78, AWDF House, Ambassadorial Enclave, East Legon, Accra.

Telephone: (30) 2521257; **Internet:** www.awdf.org; **e-mail:** awdf@adwf.org.

The Bridge Foundation—TBF

Set up in 1996 to support the development of disadvantaged children living in distressed non-formal urban settlements and rural communities.

Activities: Operates in the fields of social welfare and education for disadvantaged children, through the support of sports and literacy programmes, and vocational training initiatives. Runs a youth development resource centre for the promotion and channelling of the talents and energies of disadvantaged young people; also operates sports clubs and runs literacy programmes for out-of-school children, particularly homeless street children living in deprived urban areas.

Geographical Area of Activity: Ghana.

Restrictions: Partners only European and American NGOs working with children in West Africa.

Board of Trustees: E. Ray Quarcoo (Founder and Pres.).

Principal Staff: Admin. Officer Christable Harwey-Ewusi; Sec. Agatha Ntiakoh; Asst Anita Agbenyegah.

Address: Planet House, 8 Third Ringway, Ringway Estates, POB 13463, Accra.

Internet: www.thebridgefoundationghana.org; **e-mail:** tbfghana@yahoo.com.

Greece

FOUNDATIONS, TRUSTS AND NON-PROFIT ORGANIZATIONS

Bodossaki Foundation

Founded in 1972 by Prodromos Bodossakis Athanassiades to promote education, health care and the environment.

Activities: Operates nationally in the fields of conservation and the environment, education, and medicine and health, through self-conducted programmes, grants to institutions and individuals, scholarships and fellowships, and awarding prizes. Greek citizens are also eligible to apply for the Bodossaki Graduate Scholarships at Oxford University, United Kingdom (in science), London School of Economics, Hellenic Observatory, United Kingdom (in economics), and Tufts University, Fletcher School of Law and Diplomacy, USA (in economics).

Geographical Area of Activity: Mainly Greece.

Restrictions: Benefits are restricted to persons of Greek origin.

Publications: Information brochures; co-publishing of special editions; electronic/online information; newsletters; reports.

Finance: Total Assets €130,000,000; annual expenditure €3,000,000.

Trustees: Dimitris Vlastos (Pres.); Ioannis Detsis (Vice-Pres.).

Principal Staff: Sec. Sotiris Laganopoulos.

Address: 23A Vassilissis Sofias Ave, 106 74 Athens.

Telephone: (21) 03237973; **Fax:** (21) 03237976; **Internet:** www .bodossaki.gr; **e-mail:** secr@bodossaki.gr.

The J. F. Costopoulos Foundation

Established in 1979 by endowment of the late Spyros and Eurydice Costopoulos, for the promotion of Greek culture and civilization in Greece and internationally.

Activities: Aims to support the promotion of Hellenic culture, through the funding of scientific, educational and cultural activities. The Foundation focuses on the fields of cultural heritage and tradition, society, science and research, education and studies, and arts, funding museums, libraries, holy metropolises and churches, public welfare societies, associations and unions, foundations and schools, research projects, seminars and conferences, publications, studies, Chairs of Greek studies abroad, archaeological excavations and publications, theatre and dance companies, musical productions, and visual arts projects.

Geographical Area of Activity: Mainly Greece and Europe; some activity in the USA.

Restrictions: Activities supported focus on the promotion of Hellenic Culture, and are non-profit and for public benefit. This forms part of the Foundation's policy to subsidize important initiatives that would not be otherwise funded. Priority is given to Greek researchers or researchers of Greek origin. The Board of Trustees has temporarily suspended the provision of financial support for doctoral and post-doctoral programmes. In the field of holy dioceses and churches, grants are given for the restoration of Byzantine monuments but not contemporary churches. In the field of films, grants are given mainly for short films and documentaries.

Publications: Annual Report; Anniversary Report (1979-2009); catalogues of visual arts exhibitions organised by the Foundation.

Finance: Assets €100,724,914; annual income €1,431,222, expenditure €1,431,222 (2010).

Trustees: Yannis S. Costopoulos (Chair.); Anastasia S. Costopoulos (Vice-Chair. and Sec.); Demetrios P. Mantzounis (Treas.); Thanos M. Veremis (Trustee); Theodoros N. Filaretos (Trustee).

Principal Staff: Dir Hector P. Verykios; Artistic Dir Katerina H. Koskina.

Address: 9 Ploutarchou St, 106 75 Athens.

Telephone: (210) 7293503; **Fax:** (210) 7293508; **Internet:** www .costopoulosfoundation.org; **e-mail:** info@ costopoulosfoundation.org.

Foundation of the Hellenic World

Established in 1993 by Lazaros D. Efaimoglou and his family. Aims to raise awareness of the importance of Hellenic culture and history throughout the world.

Activities: Runs the cultural centre 'Hellenic Cosmos', which holds exhibitions, educational programmes and an Internet café providing access to the Foundation's online projects. Participates in a number of technological and historical projects, a genealogy programme, made available to the public through cultural events, and produces publications, films, documentaries and DVDs.

Geographical Area of Activity: Mainly Greece.

Publications: Annual Report; *Olympia: A Journey to Four Dimensions* (2004); *History of Perge Political and Ecclesiastical* (2004); *Tales of Olympic Games: A unique exhibition*; *Ancient Athens* (2003); *Is there an answer to everything: a journey to the world of Greek mathematics* (2004); *Plato's Rhapsody and Homer's Music: the Poetics of the Panathenaic Festival in Classical Athens* (2002); *Greek Ritual Poetics* (2004); *Towards a Ritual Poetics* (2003).

Finance: Established with an initial endowment of €1,200,000.

Board of Trustees: Lazaros D. Efraimoglou (Pres.); Elias G. Klis (Vice-Pres.); Ourania L. Efraimoglou (Sec.); Sophia Kounenaki-Efaimoglou (Treas.).

Principal Staff: Man. Dir Dimitris Efraimoglou.

Address: 38 Poulopoulou St, 118 51 Athens.

Telephone: (212) 2548000; **Fax:** (212) 2543838; **Internet:** www.fhw.gr; **e-mail:** info@fhw.gr.

Hellenic Foundation for Culture

Established in 1992, has branches and offices in Europe, North Africa, Australia and the USA.

Activities: Promotes Greek language and culture through developing and implementing exhibitions, concerts, lectures, dramas and other major cultural events in Greece and in other countries, as well as organizing events devoted to Greek culture that promote Greek artists and writers abroad, including cultural months and weeks, anniversary celebrations, film festivals and concerts. Plans and co-ordinates the participation and representation of Greece in international cultural events, and participates in international cultural networks. Also collaborates with museums, universities, cultural centres and organizations, in Greece and abroad, to plan and develop cultural programmes.

Geographical Area of Activity: Europe, Middle East, the USA, Australia.

Restrictions: Institutions applying for sponsorship must come within the scope of the Foundation's interests and offer guarantees of quality.

Publications: Bulletin (2 a year); brochures; exhibition catalogues, newsletter.

Executive Board: Georgios Babiniotis (Pres.); Konstantinos Svolopoulos (Vice-Pres.); Michael Dermitzakis (Treas.).

Address: 50 Stratigou Kallari, 154 52 Palaio Psychico, Athens.

Telephone: (21) 06776540; **Fax:** (21) 06725826; **Internet:** www .hfc.gr; **e-mail:** hfc-centre@hfc.gr.

Hellenic Foundation for European and Foreign Policy—ELIAMEP

Established in 1988 as an independent, policy-orientated, non-profit research and training institute for the study European integration, transatlantic relations as well as the Mediterranean, South-Eastern Europe, the Black Sea and other regions of particular interest to Greece.

Activities: Operates in Europe, South-Eastern Europe, the Black Sea region and the Mediterranean Middle East in the area of international affairs, through self-conducted programmes, research, scholarships and fellowships, conferences, training courses and publications.

Geographical Area of Activity: Europe, South-Eastern Europe, the Black Sea region, the Mediterranean and the Middle East.

Publications: *Journal of South-East European and Black Sea Studies*; ELIAMEP Thesis; books; policy papers; working papers.

Finance: The Foundation's main sources of funding include research and training contracts with public- and private-sector entities, and grants from international institutions and foundations.

Board of Directors: Prof. Loukas Tsoukalis (Pres.); Thanos Veremis (Vice-Pres.); Theodore Couloumbis (Vice-Pres.), Alexis Papahelas (Sec.-Gen.); Panagis Vourloumis (Treas.).

Principal Staff: Dir-Gen. Thanos Dokos; Deputy Dir-Gen. Elizabeth Phocas.

Address: 49 Vasilissis Sofias Ave, 106 76 Athens.

Telephone: (21) 07257110; **Fax:** (21) 07257114; **Internet:** www .eliamep.gr; **e-mail:** eliamep@eliamep.gr.

Hellenic Society for Disabled Children

Founded in 1937 to prevent and treat physical disability in children.

Activities: Operates nationally in the fields of medicine, social welfare and education. Maintains six centres in Greece, which provide rehabilitation for disabled children up to the age of 16 through physical, occupational and speech therapy and computer training. The centres also provide vocational training for people with disabilities aged between 15 and 30 years. Conferences and lectures are organized for medical staff to follow recent developments in their fields. Also extended to parents. Since 2008, an innovative Neuropsychological Rehabilitation Programme has been implemented for people with brain injuries, in co-operation with the Rusk Institute of Rehabilitation Medicine of New York Medical Center and a donation from Eurobank EFG. This includes an extensive neuropsychological evaluation and a 20-week rehabilitation programme, which addresses in a systematic and specialized manner the cognitive, behavioural, psychosocial and interpersonal difficulties of people with brain injuries.

Geographical Area of Activity: Greece and Europe.

Restrictions: No grants outside Greece.

Publications: Report of operations and financial statement.

Finance: Total revenue €6,864,607; expenditure €6,890,967 (2010).

Trustees: Mary Carella (Pres.); Agathie Dourmousoglou (Vice-Pres.); Iro Covas (Vice-Pres.); Eta Pagidas-Samaras (Treas.).

Principal Staff: Sec.-Gen. Marianna A. Moschou; Dir Athina Paliggini.

Address: 16 Kononos St, 116 34 Athens.

Telephone: (21) 07254726; **Fax:** (21) 07228380; **Internet:** www .elepap.gr; **e-mail:** elepap@otenet.gr.

Kokkalis Foundation

Established in 1998, a non-profit organization based in Athens, Greece. The Foundation honours the vision of Socrates Kokkalis, an international business leader in information technology and telecommunications, and his father Petros Kokkalis, an eminent surgeon and professor of medicine at the University of Athens. The Foundation's central mission is the promotion of a peaceful, democratic and prosperous South-eastern Europe through the development of public, cultural and scientific life in the region.

Activities: The promotion of education in South-Eastern Europe through the Kokkalis fellowship programme at Harvard University and education programmes organized in strategic collaboration with Harvard University, AIT and Carnegie Mellon University. The advancement of knowledge through a research and publications programme, with emphasis on the fields of innovation and entrepreneurship; medicine and medical research; social policies; geopolitics and international relations; sports and athletics. Supports public dialogue through public fora and an event series. Runs a sponsorship programme in the areas of education and human capital; medical research and human development; culture and athletics. Promotes the development of South-Eastern Europe through the creation of human networks for regional co-operation and effective democratic governance.

Geographical Area of Activity: South-Eastern Europe, Western Europe, USA and international.

Publications: Research publications (in English and Greek) in the areas of innovation and entrepreneurship, medicine and medical research, social policies, geopolitics and international relations, sports and athletics; monographs; newsletters; information brochures; electronic/online information.

Board of Directors: Socrates P. Kokkalis (Pres.); Petros S. Kokkalis (Vice-Pres.); Eleni S. Kokkali (Treas. and Sec.).

Principal Staff: Exec. Dir Dr Chrysostomos Sfatos.

Address: 2 Adrianiou St, 115 25 Athens.

Telephone: (213) 0004901; **Fax:** (213) 0004905; **Internet:** www.kokkalisfoundation.gr; **e-mail:** kf@ kokkalisfoundation.gr.

Lambrakis Foundation

Established in 1991 by Christos D. Lambrakis to promote the introduction of technological innovations in the Greek education system, the dissemination of Greek and European cultural heritage through the use of new technologies, and research into social and environmental issues and regional development within the framework of the European Union. Formerly known as the Lambrakis Research Foundation.

Activities: Operates in Greece and countries of the European Union in the areas of education, the arts and humanities, science and technology, and conservation of the environment, by undertaking studies, projects and awareness activities and addressing the increasing needs for human resources policies and human capital development, through self-conducted programmes, research, scholarships, conferences, training courses and publications (books, videos and CD-ROM multimedia publications on ancient and Byzantine history, astronomy, biology and chemistry). Offers Manolis Andronikos scholarships for archaeologists wishing to pursue postgraduate studies in archaeological computing. Maintains a specialist website addressed to schools in Greece, offering educational and cultural material in digital form, suggestions for using modern technological tools and educational software in schools as well as information on current educational issues in Greece and the world.

Geographical Area of Activity: Europe.

Restrictions: Grants only to specific organizations.

Publications: *Teaching Greek as a Second (Foreign) Language*; *Teachers Training on ICT*; *ICT Policies in School Education, in*

Europe and the World; electronic multimedia publications; educational videos with accompanying printed material; conference proceedings.

Board of Directors: Christos Lambrakis (Pres.); Stavros Psycharis (Vice-Pres.); Tryphon Koutalidis (Treas.).

Principal Staff: Dir Dr Nikitas Kastis.

Address: 3 Christou Lada St, 102 37 Athens.

Telephone: (21) 03333900; **Fax:** (21) 03333901; **Internet:** www.lrf.gr; **e-mail:** lrf@lrf.gr.

A. G. Leventis Foundation

Established in 1979 to preserve the cultural heritage of Greece and Cyprus.

Activities: Operates in a number of areas in Cyprus and Greece as well as internationally, protecting and promoting the cultural heritage of Cyprus and Greece; working to preserve the environment; granting scholarships for postgraduate study abroad and at the University of Cyprus (particularly in the fields of education and science); financing publications; working in the field of social welfare; and funding agricultural and technical education in West Africa. Has branch foundations in Cyprus (the Anastasios G. Leventis Foundation, q.v.) and Nigeria.

Geographical Area of Activity: West Africa, Cyprus, Greece, Europe.

Publications: *The A. G. Leventis Collection: 19th and 20th Century Greek Paintings*; *The A. G. Leventis Foundation and the Cultural Heritage of Cyprus*; *Ancient Cypriot Art in Berlin*; *Ancient Cypriot Art in Copenhagen*; and other publications on the arts and culture.

Governing Board: A. P. Leventis (Chair.).

Address: 9 Fragoklissias St, 151 25 Maroussi.

Telephone: (21) 06165232; **Fax:** (21) 06165235; **Internet:** www.leventisfoundation.org; **e-mail:** foundation@leventis.net.

Marangopoulos Foundation for Human Rights

Established in 1977 by the bequest of George M. Marangopoulos, President of the Supreme Administrative Court of Greece. Aims to promote the research, study, defence, protection and promotion of generally recognized fundamental human rights and freedoms. Within this framework, the Foundation takes a special interest in the advancement of human rights education and training and the raising of public awareness in all matters affecting human rights, peace and the development of democratic institutions.

Activities: Promotes human rights, focusing on the advancement of human rights education, through organizing courses, lectures, seminars, symposia and conferences in Greece and representing Greece in similar events abroad. Also awards scholarships, provides financial support and sponsorship for specialized studies in human rights, particularly for young scholars and human rights activists, funds research and awards prizes. Also lobbies governments and public authorities on general human rights issues, as well as specific instances of human rights violations including providing free legal aid to people whose fundamental rights have allegedly been violated, and the dispatch or funding of fact-finding missions in Greece and abroad. Disseminates information and maintains a library open to the public, containing collections of case-law, series of the major human rights periodicals, specialized books and other relevant material, mainly in Greek, English, French, Italian and German.

Geographical Area of Activity: Greece.

Publications: *Criminology in the Face of Contemporary Challenges* (2011); *Le patrimoine culturel en droit international* (2011); *1st Anniversary of the Universal Declaration of Human Rights: Poverty, a Challenge to Human Rights* (2010); *Une approche de la notion de principe dans le système de la Convention européenne des droits de l'homme* (2010); *Les droits fondamentaux: charnières entre ordres et systèmes juridiques* (2010); *Trafficking in Human Beings* (2010); *Le génocide révisité-Genocide Revisited* (2010); *Collective Violence and Aggressiveness at School* (2010); *International, European and National Law on Forest Protection, and the Forest Fires in Greece* (2010).

Governing Board: Alice Yotopoulos-Marangopoulos (Pres.); Sotirios Mousouris; Gerasimos Arsenis; Dimitrios Gourgourakis; Antonios Bredimas.

Address: 1 Lycavittou St, 106 72 Athens.

Telephone: (210) 3637455; **Fax:** (210) 3622454; **Internet:** www.mfhr.gr; **e-mail:** info@mfhr.gr.

National Bank of Greece Cultural Foundation

Established in 1966 by the National Bank of Greece to support fine art, humanities and sciences in Greece.

Activities: Houses a collection of works of art and organizes exhibitions; manages three cultural centres in Athens; maintains an archive of maps and a paper conservation laboratory; organizes seminars; issues publications that cannot be published commercially.

Geographical Area of Activity: Greece.

Publications: Numerous publications in the field of history, archaeology, anthropology, classical studies, art theory, law, philosophy, etc.

Board of Directors: Vasileios Rapanos (Chair.); Dimosthenis Kokkinidis (Vice-Chair.); Victor Th. Melas (Sec.); Michalis A. Tiverios (Treas.).

Principal Staff: Dir Dionysis Kapsalis.

Address: 13 Thukydidou St, 105 58 Athens.

Telephone: (21) 3221335; **Fax:** (21) 03245089; **Internet:** www.miet.gr; **e-mail:** miet2@otenet.gr.

National Youth Foundation

Founded in 1947 by King Paul as the Royal National Foundation to improve the educational and cultural standard of living of the Greek people, especially young people.

Activities: Operates nationally in running student hostels for residence and cultural activities, the Anavryta Model School and the National Hostel, a centre for seminars and hospitality. Adult education courses, congresses, lectures and publications are also undertaken. The Foundation promotes international cultural and educational exchanges for young people and adults, and since 1995 has run the Centre of Vocational Training, which offers professional training to young people with the aid of several European Union programmes.

Geographical Area of Activity: Greece.

Publications: Reports of operations; press bulletins; books, etc.

Address: An. Tsoha 36, 11521 Athens.

Telephone: (21) 06424923; **Fax:** (21) 07299972; **Internet:** www.ein.gr; **e-mail:** web_ein@ein.gr.

Stavros Niarchos Foundation

Established as an international philanthropic organization to make grants to non-profit organizations, in support of education, health and medicine, social welfare, and arts and culture.

Activities: Operates world-wide in the areas of arts and culture, education, health and medicine, and social welfare. Also supports projects within Greece and world-wide that promote and/or maintain Greek heritage and culture. In January 2012 the foundation announced a three-year programme committing US $130m. of funds to projects aimed at easing the adverse effects of the socio-economic crisis in Greece. Maintains offices in Athens, Monte Carlo and New York.

Geographical Area of Activity: World-wide.

Restrictions: No grants are made to individuals.

Finance: Total grants disbursed US $1,146,000,000 (1996–2010).

Board of Directors: Philip Niarchos (Co-Pres.); Spyros Niarchos (Co-Pres.); Andreas Dracopoulos (Co-Pres.).

Principal Staff: COO Vasili Tsamis; CFO Christina Lambropoulou.

Address: POB 13607, 103 10 Athens.

Telephone: (210) 8778 300; **Fax:** (210) 6838 304; **Internet:** www.snf.org; **e-mail:** info@snf.org.

Alexander S. Onassis Public Benefit Foundation

Established according to the will of the late Aristotle Onassis, as a public benefit foundation with numerous cultural and public benefit projects. The main purpose of the Foundation's activities is to promote Hellenic culture in Greece and abroad.

Activities: The Foundation operates in the fields of education, medicine, social welfare, the arts and humanities. The Foundation's areas of activities include: scholarship programmes for Hellenes for postgraduate and doctoral studies in Greece or abroad, and for foreigners for research and postgraduate studies in Greece; the promotion of Greek culture and Greek studies abroad through subsidized programmes in the USA, Canada, South America, Europe and Asia; the donation of teaching material and technical equipment to primary and secondary schools for children with special needs, and to Greek communities abroad; the funding of the annual Onassis Foundation Science Lecture Series, in association with the Foundation for Research and Technology in Heraklion, Crete, given on the applied sciences by Nobel Prize winners and other internationally acclaimed scientists from Greece and elsewhere; and the awarding of the Onassis International Prizes. The Onassis Prize in Shipping, Trade and Finance, in co-operation with the City of London and Cass Business School of the City University London, is awarded biennially to recognize lifetime achievement of an academic of international stature, rotating between shipping, trade and finance. The first prize in Finance was awarded in 2008 to Prof. Eugene Fama, the Robert R. McCormick Distinguished Service Professor of Finance at the University of Chicago Graduate School of Business, who is recognised as the father of empirical finance and is credited with being the inventor of the 'efficient market hypothesis'. The Onassis Prize in Law and Humanities, in collaboration with the French Institute, is awarded biennially in rotation to academics, thinkers or distinguished personalities. The prize in law will be awarded to an individual who has contributed to improved understanding between states and cultures and to the protection of human rights, while the prize in humanities will be bestowed on those who have concentrated their studies on Greek culture and the promotion of Greek cultural heritage in the fields of archaeology, history and literature. The Foundation has established the affiliated Alexander S. Onassis Public Benefit Foundation in the USA to promote Greek culture. It sponsors seminar and lecture programmes of visiting professors to universities in the USA, Canada and South America, and organizes diverse cultural events in the Olympic Tower on Fifth Avenue, New York. The events are based on Classical, Byzantine and contemporary Greek culture and include exhibitions of archaeology, contemporary art and sculpture, lectures, concerts and drama. It has also constructed the Onassis House of Arts and Letters, a cultural centre to encourage the development of modern Greek culture, as well as promoting it outside Greece, and to provide Greek artists with a fully equipped venue from which to present their work.

Geographical Area of Activity: International.

Publications: Brochure; newsletter of the Onassis Foundation Scholars' Association; catalogues of the exhibitions at the Onassis Cultural Center, New York.

Finance: The Foundation is the sole beneficiary of an endowment bequeathed to it by Aristotle Onassis.

Board of Directors: Anthony S. Papadimitriou (Pres. and Treas.); Ioannis P. Ioannidis (Vice-Pres.); Peter Marxer (Vice-Pres.); Marianna Moschou (Sec.).

Principal Staff: Dir Effie Tsiotsiou.

Address: 56 Amalias Ave, 105 58 Athens.

Telephone: (21) 03713000; **Fax:** (21) 03713013; **Internet:** www.onassis.gr; **e-mail:** contact@onassis.gr.

State Scholarships Foundation

Founded to grant scholarships to foreigners for postgraduate or post-doctoral studies in Greece.

Activities: The Foundation offers scholarships annually for postgraduate and post-doctoral studies in Greece to nationals of any other country world-wide and to non-Greek nationals of Greek origin. Awards scholarships to teachers or researchers (foreigners or foreign nationals of Greek origin) working in Greek centres of studies abroad for further education in language, literature, philosophy, history and art. In 2004–05 the Foundation offered up to 90 scholarships for study in Greece for nationals (foreigners or of Greek origin) from the Balkans, Central and Eastern Europe, Asia, Africa and Central and South America, and up to 40 scholarships for study in Greece for nationals (foreigners or of Greek origin) from Western Europe, Australia, Canada, Japan or the USA for postgraduate doctoral studies (from one to four years); for post-doctoral research (six months to one year); for further education in Greek language, literature, philosophy, history and art for professors of Greek language in foreign universities (six months to one year); or for further study in fine arts (one to two years); for collection of research data for applicants who are conducting doctoral studies in their country (one year).

Geographical Area of Activity: International.

Principal Staff: Head of Section M. Mikedaki-Drakaki.

Address: 1 Makri and Dionisiou Areopagitou (Makrigianni), 117 42 Athens.

Telephone: (210) 3726300; **Fax:** (210) 3221863; **Internet:** www.iky.gr; **e-mail:** iky@hol.gr.

Swedish Institute at Athens

Founded in 1946 by King Gustaf VI Adolf and others to promote the study of the ancient culture of Greece and to stimulate and support cultural exchange between Sweden and Greece and to further education.

Activities: Operates internationally in the fields of the arts and humanities (mainly archaeology) and Greek-Swedish relations, through research, conferences, courses, publications and lectures.

Geographical Area of Activity: Greece.

Restrictions: Grants only to students at Swedish universities.

Publications: *Skrifter utgivna av Svenska institutet i Athen* (monographs); collections of articles in *Opuscula Atheniensia*.

Principal Staff: Dir Arto Penttinen; Asst Dir Monica Nilsson.

Address: 9 Mitseon, 117 42 Athens; Stiftelsen Svenska institutet i Athen, Skeppargatan 8, 114 52 Stockholm, Sweden.

Telephone: (21) 09232102; **Fax:** (21) 09220925; **Internet:** www.sia.gr; **e-mail:** swedinst@sia.gr.

Guatemala

FOUNDATION CENTRE AND CO-ORDINATING BODY

Consejo de Fundaciones Privadas de Guatemala—CFPG (Council of Private Foundations of Guatemala)

Founded in 1996, as one association to represent the many foundations that seek social improvements in Guatemala.

Activities: Aims to facilitate and co-ordinate organizations in Guatemala whose aims comprise social development, economic development, and industrial development. Its members include private foundations and governmental organizations.

Geographical Area of Activity: Guatemala.

Publications: *Conceptos Básicos de la RSE; Alianzas RSE; Empresas Privadas de RSE, los Indicadores Ethos de Responsabilidad Social de la Empresa.*

Principal Staff: Exec. Dir Miguel Antonio Gaitan.

Address: 6 Diagonal 10-31, Zona 10, Centro Gerencial Las Margaritas, 01010 Guatemala City.

Telephone: (2) 2277-5131; **Fax:** (2) 2277-5132; **e-mail:** mgaitan@pantaleon.com.

FOUNDATIONS, TRUSTS AND NON-PROFIT ORGANIZATIONS

Fundación de Asesoría Financiera a Instituciones de Desarrollo y Servicio Social—FAFIDESS (Foundation for the Financial Assessment of Social Service and Development Institutions)

Established in 1986 by members of the Rotary Club of Guatemala City.

Activities: Aims to support the economic and social development of Guatemala by offering sustainable microfinance, technical advice and support to small and medium-sized enterprises, particularly those run by women.

Geographical Area of Activity: Guatemala.

Finance: Total assets US $6,942,957 (2007).

Board of Directors: José Francisco Monroy Galindo (Pres.); Leonel Fernando González Cifuentes (Vice-Pres.); Arturo Melville Aguirre (Sec.); Eduardo Sebastian Aballi Coto (Treas.).

Principal Staff: Exec. Dir Reynold O. Walter.

Address: 5a Avda 16–68, zona 10, 01010 Guatemala City.

Telephone: (2) 311-5800; **Fax:** (2) 311-5807; **Internet:** www.fafidess.org; **e-mail:** admin@fafidess.org.

Fundación de Asistencia para la Pequeña Empresa (Small Business Assistance Foundation)

Founded in 1986.

Activities: Encourages the development of small and medium-sized enterprises through microfinance, community support and advice.

Geographical Area of Activity: Guatemala.

Finance: Total assets US $617,974 (2007).

Principal Staff: CEO Sergio Roberto González Ayala.

Address: 37 Avda 2-29, Colonia El Rodeo, Zona 7, Guatemala City.

Telephone: (2) 439-3113; **Fax:** (2) 439-3113; **e-mail:** fape@c.net.gt.

Fundación para el Desarrollo—FUNDAP (Development Foundation)

Established in August 1982 by a group of businesspeople to develop the western part of Guatemala by supporting small businesses.

Activities: Aims to develop the low-income areas of western Guatemala through innovative projects that improve the quality of life of those communities.

Geographical Area of Activity: Guatemala.

Finance: Annual expenditure 188,524 quetzals (2010).

Board: Francisco Roberto Gutiérrez Martín (Pres.).

Principal Staff: Exec. Dir Jorge A. Gándara G.

Address: 17 Avda 4-25, Zona 3, Quetzaltenango.

Telephone: (7) 767-4538; **Fax:** (7) 767-5831; **Internet:** www.fundap.com.gt; **e-mail:** info@fundap.com.gt.

Fundación Esperanza de los Niños (Hope for the Children Foundation)

Founded in 1986 in Guatemala to provide information about the problems of 'street children'—homeless young people living and working in the streets—and previously known as the Childhope International Foundation. Now a network of independent regional and national ChildHope (q.v.) groups operating in the United Kingdom and Europe, Asia and Central and South America.

Activities: Operates in the fields of human rights and social welfare, with the aim of upholding the Convention on the Rights of Children, which the Government of Guatemala ratified in 1990. Operates programmes in the areas of mental health, children's rights, and research into various issues including child labour and violence against children.

Geographical Area of Activity: Guatemala.

Principal Staff: Dir Dr Elizabeth Porras, Dir Lucas Ventura.

Address: 37 Calle Manzana X Lote 16, 5-89, Villas Club El Dorado, Ciudad San Cristóbal, Zona 8, Guatemala City.

Telephone: (2) 443-5321; **Fax:** (2) 443-5321; **e-mail:** childhope@itelgua.com.

Fundación Génesis Empresarial (Business Formation Foundation)

Founded in 1988 as a non-governmental, non-profit Private Development Organization–PDO.

Activities: The Foundation's aim is to promote the social and economic strengthening and development of micro-enterprises and small businesses as well as communal banks located in urban, marginal and rural areas of Guatemala, offering credit, training and advice. Also aims to help poor communities in rural areas with dwelling improvement and the introduction of basic services. The Foundation also deals with remittances from abroad. It has 59 branches throughout Guatemala.

Geographical Area of Activity: Guatemala.

Publications: *ACCION International Annual Reports; Gènesis Annual Work Memory.*

Finance: Annual average of loans disbursement US $85,500,000.

Principal Staff: Gen. Man. Carlos Herrera, Planning and Marketing Man. Adela de Rizzo, Human Resources and Administrative Man. Cirsa Lòpez, Finance Dir Francisco Pacheco, Mircofinance Man. Wagner Curup, Technology Man. Mauricio Pèrez.

Address: 13 Calle 5-51, Zona 9, Guatemala City.

Telephone: (2) 383-9000; **Fax:** (2) 334-4474; **Internet:** www .genesisempresarial.com; **e-mail:** genesis@ genesisempresarial.com.

Fundación MICROS—Fundación para el Desarrollo de la Microempresa (Microenterprise Development Foundation)

Founded 1987.

Activities: The Foundation helps poor communities to sustain themselves through micro-enterprise, by providing advice,training and financing, through the granting of credit on an individual basis.

Geographical Area of Activity: Guatemala.

Principal Staff: Exec. Dir Otto Mauricio González Molina.

Address: 20 Calle 6-37, Zona 11, Col. Mariscal, Guatemala City.

Telephone: (502) 2476-6361; **Fax:** (502) 2442-3366; **e-mail:** fundacionmicros@gmail.com; info@fundacionmicros.org.

Fundación Soros Guatemala (Soros Foundation Guatemala)

Established in 1997, an independent foundation, part of the Soros foundations network.

Activities: Operates in the fields of civil society, economic reform, law and criminal justice, rural development and public administration. Supports the Guatemala Clarification Commission, which was established to determine the extent and nature of human rights violations during the civil war. Other programmes are concerned with promoting improved relations between ethnic and linguistic groups. Also approved the establishment of justice, public policy and rural development institutes.

Geographical Area of Activity: Guatemala.

Board of Directors: Helen Mack Chang (Pres.); Maria Caba Mateo (Vice-Pres.); Arnolod Ortiz Mosoco (Sec.); Enma Chirix Garcia (Treas.).

Principal Staff: Exec. Dir Mario Marroquin.

Address: Edif. Plaza Maritima, 6 Nivel, 6A Avda 20–25, Zona 10, 01010 Guatemala City.

Telephone: (2) 466-4647; **Fax:** (2) 337-1472; **Internet:** www .soros.org.gt; **e-mail:** fsg@soros.org.gt.

PRODESSA—Proyecto de Desarrollo Santiago (Santiago Development Project)

Established in 1989 to promote development in rural communities in Guatemala and to help build a just and multicultural society.

Activities: Operates programmes in the fields of education, the environment and development, providing loans, grants and technical assistance.

Geographical Area of Activity: Guatemala.

Publications: Bulletin; educational materials; research papers.

Finance: Annual grants expenditure approx. US $1,000,000.

Board of Directors: Oscar Azmitia Barranco (Pres.); Otto René Armas Bonilla (Treas.); Felipe Antonio Casellán Gonzáles (Sec.).

Principal Staff: Dirs Federico Roncal, Edgar García Tax.

Address: Km 15, Carretera Roosevelt, Zona 7, Mixco, Apdo 13-B, 19103 Guatemala City.

Telephone: (2) 435-3911; **Fax:** (2) 435-3913; **Internet:** www .prodessa.net; **e-mail:** direccion@prodessa.net.

Haiti

FOUNDATIONS, TRUSTS AND NON-PROFIT ORGANIZATIONS

Fondation Connaissance et Liberté (Haiti)—FOKAL (Foundation for Knowledge and Liberty)

Established in 1995 to promote the development of open society in Haiti; an independent foundation, part of the Soros foundations network.

Activities: Operates in the fields of education, culture and strengthening of civil society organizations, especially landworkers' and women's organizations. Operates programmes promoting debate, libraries, the Internet, early childhood education, local production and water facilities in rural areas. Through the community library project the Foundation supports 35 community libraries, as well as providing training in library management, finance and computers. In 2007 FOKAL signed a contract with the Government of Haiti for the creation and management of an urban park that was to include the first botanical garden in the country.

Geographical Area of Activity: Haiti.

Publications: *Beyond Mountains More Mountains.*

Finance: Total expenditure US $4,200,000 (2010).

Board of Trustees: Michele D. Pierre-Louis (Pres.); Daniele Magloire (Chair.); Nicole Magloire (Vice-Chair.).

Principal Staff: Exec. Dir Lorraine Mangones; Finance Dir Vanessa Goscinny.

Address: 143 ave Christophe, BP 2720, Port-au-Prince.

Telephone: 2813-1694; **Fax:** 2510-9814; **Internet:** www.fokal .org; **e-mail:** mpierrelouis@fokal.org.

Haitian Economic Development Foundation

Established in 2009 to foster economic growth throughout Haiti, and comprising some of Haiti's most influential enterprises; its goal is to foster business in Haiti.

Activities: Fosters the development of business in Haiti.

Geographical Area of Activity: Haiti.

Principal Staff: Pres. Youri Mevs; Press Contact Vladimir Laborde.

Telephone: 3729-4325; **Internet:** www .haitianeconomicdevelopment.org.

Honduras

FOUNDATIONS, TRUSTS AND NON-PROFIT ORGANIZATIONS

Fundación BANHCAFE—FUNBANHCAFE (BANHCAFE Foundation)

Established in 1985, under the initiative of Banco Hondureño del Café (BANHCAFE) and the Ministry of Home Affairs and Justice, to aid the development of coffee-producing communities in Honduras.

Activities: Aims to develop social, cultural, economic and environmental elements of coffee-producing communities, through non-profit organizations in the local area.

Geographical Area of Activity: Honduras.

Publications: Guides; strategic reports; manuals; reports on different agricultural products.

Board of Directors: Miguel Alfonso Fernández Rápalo (Pres.); Guillermo Sagastume Perdomo (Sec.).

Principal Staff: Exec. Dir Arnold Sabillón Ortega.

Address: Colonia Rubén Dario, Avda Las Minitas, Calle Cervantes 319, Apdo 3814, Tegucigalpa.

Telephone: 239-5211; **Fax:** 239-9171; **Internet:** www.funbanhcafe.hn; **e-mail:** direccion@funbanhcafe.hn.

Fundación para la Inversión y Desarrollo de Exportaciones—FIDE (Foundation for the Investment and Development of Exports)

FIDE, Investment and Exports is a private non-profit organization created in 1984 to promote investment in Honduras, support export development and work closely with the government and other private organizations to promote and design new legislation aimed at improving the country's business climate.

Activities: FIDE promotes sustainable development in Honduras through strengthening investment and export by seeking to improve the international competitiveness of the country and its business sector. FIDE runs a series of programmes and activities to offer investors and business owners, both local and foreign, a wide range of services to develop new exports or expand existing ones, forge strategic alliances and take advantage of emerging business opportunities.

Geographical Area of Activity: Honduras.

Publications: *Export Directory*; Annual Report; promotional brochures.

Board of Directors: Arturo Alvarado (Pres.).

Principal Staff: Exec. Pres. Vilma Sierra de Fonseca; Exec. Dir Arturo Chavez.

Address: Colonia La Estancia, costado sur/este de Plaza Marte, final del Blvd Morazán, Apdo 2029, Tegucigalpa.

Telephone: 221-6303; **Fax:** 221-6318; **Internet:** www.hondurasinfo.hn; **e-mail:** nturcios@fidehonduras.com; lsanchez@fidehonduras.com.

Fundación Nacional para el Desarrollo de Honduras—FUNADEH (National Foundation for the Development of Honduras)

Founded in 1983.

Activities: Aims to provide community development through education and training, and through microfinance.

Geographical Area of Activity: Honduras.

Principal Staff: Pres. José Manuel Pineda Silva; Vice-Pres. John Rodgers.

Address: Colonia Lomas del Guijarro, calle principal contiguo al Ministerio Público, Edificio Plaza Güijarros, 4º Piso, Tegucigalpa.

Telephone: 221-3691/3693; **Fax:** 221-3695; **Internet:** www.funadeh.org; **e-mail:** funadeh@funadeh.org.

Hong Kong

FOUNDATIONS, TRUSTS AND NON-PROFIT ORGANIZATIONS

Croucher Foundation

Founded to promote education, learning and research in the areas of natural science, technology and medicine.

Activities: The Foundation operates a scholarship and fellowship scheme for individual applicants who wish to pursue doctoral or post-doctoral research outside Hong Kong. This scheme is limited to individual permanent residents of Hong Kong. The Foundation also makes grants to institutions: it offers senior research fellowships to universities in Hong Kong to promote research; contributes to international scientific conferences held in Hong Kong; supports advanced study institutes; funds international exchanges between scientific institutions in Hong Kong and other countries; and provides funds for a scheme to enable scientists in mainland China to undertake attachments at Hong Kong institutions.

Geographical Area of Activity: Hong Kong.

Restrictions: Individual fellowships and scholarships scheme for overseas studies limited to permanent Hong Kong residents; annual closing date for applications in mid-November.

Trustees: Prof. Tak Wah Mak (Chair.); I. R. A. MacCallum (Vice-Chair.).

Principal Staff: David Foster.

Address: Suite 501, Nine Queens Rd Central, Hong Kong.

Telephone: 27366337; **Fax:** 27300742; **Internet:** www .croucher.org.hk; **e-mail:** cfadmin@croucher.org.hk.

HER Fund

Established to promote the development of women's rights in Hong Kong through fundraising, grant-making and gender educational activities.

Activities: Operates in the fields of education, fundraising and make small grants to women and girls' rights projects, promoting the development of philanthropy that recognizes the status of women. Funding is directed towards projects and rights initiatives, with particular attention paid to economic justice, grassroots women's initiatives and the rights of young girls. Also supports women's efforts to instigate social change.

Geographical Area of Activity: Hong Kong.

Publications: Research reports; Annual Report; *HER Voice* (newsletter and e-news).

Finance: Annual income HK $1,316,690, expenditure $1,164,290 (March 2010).

Executive Committee: Mary Ann King (Chair.); Fong Man-ying (Vice-Chair. and Sec.); Lam Ying Hing (Treas.).

Principal Staff: Exec. Dir Linda To Kit Lai.

Address: Flat C01, 13/F, Hang Cheong Factory Building, 1 Wing Ming St, Cheung Sha Wan, Kowloon.

Telephone: 27941100; **Fax:** 23967488; **Internet:** www .herfund.org.hk; **e-mail:** info@herfund.org.hk.

Hong Kong Society for the Blind

Founded in 1981 by K. L. Stumpf, Dr Arthur Lim, Thomas Clydesdale, John Holmes, D. D. B. McLeod, Q. W. Lee and John Boyer to investigate blindness and advance the science of ophthalmology.

Activities: The Foundation operates in South-East Asia, conducting and supporting research in ophthalmology, through grants to institutions and individuals; and assists in the training of all kinds of ophthalmic and multidisciplinary staff. The Foundation places special emphasis on cataract operations, the prevention of blindness and services that will benefit the blind directly. It also organizes conferences and co-operates with governmental and other organizations working for the prevention and cure of blindness, and is a member of the Vision 2020 Right to Sight campaign.

Geographical Area of Activity: South-East Asia.

Publications: training manuals.

Council: Nancy Law Tak Yin (Chair.); Michael Szeto Chak Wah (Vice-Chair.); Patrick Ng Wing Hang (Hon. Treas.).

Principal Staff: Exec. Dir Maureen Tam.

Address: East Wing, 248 Nam Cheong St, Samshuipo, Kowloon.

Telephone: 27788332; **Fax:** 27881336; **Internet:** www.hksb .org.hk; **e-mail:** enquiry@hksb.org.hk.

Li Ka-shing Foundation

Established in 1980 by Li Ka-shing to provide support in the fields of education, medical care and research, and poverty relief, and to nurture a culture of giving.

Activities: Operates in the fields of education, and medicine and health through grants and sponsorships. The Foundation's most notable project is the founding and continuing development of Shantou University in mainland China to engineer reforms in the higher education sector. The Foundation also makes significant contributions to medical research at leading institutions world-wide, particularly in the area of cancer research. In mainland China, the Foundation has pioneered a number of innovative programmes to improve rural health care and to provide free hospice care services.

Geographical Area of Activity: International.

Publications: *Sphere* bulletin.

Finance: Grants, sponsorships and commitments of US $1,550,000 to date.

Address: Cheung Kong Center, 7th Floor, 2 Queen's Rd, Central.

Internet: www.lksf.org; **e-mail:** general@lksf.org.

Oxfam Hong Kong

Established in 1976. Part of the Oxfam confederation of organizations (qq.v.).

Activities: Operates in Southern Africa, and South and South-East Asia, offering assistance in emergencies and natural disasters, advocacy and development education, and development programmes.

Geographical Area of Activity: Southern Africa, South and South-East Asia.

Finance: Revenue US $230m., expenditure $260,000,000 (2010/11).

Trustees: Dr Lo Chi Kin (Chair.); Bernard Chan (Vice-Chair.); David Hodson (Vice-Chair.); Prof. Japhet Law (Vice-Chair.); May Tan (Treas.).

Principal Staff: Programme Man. Aman Yee.

Address: 17/F China United Centre, 28 Marble Rd, North Point, Hong Kong.

Telephone: (852) 2520 2525; **Fax:** (852) 2527 6307; **Internet:** www.oxfam.org.hk; **e-mail:** info@oxfam.org.hk.

Hungary

FOUNDATION CENTRES AND CO-ORDINATING BODIES

Civil Society Development Foundation–Hungary

Established in 1994 to enhance the growth of civil organizations and grassroots networks in Hungary, by providing non-profit management and development assistance, and to contribute to the expansion of dynamic, effective and self-sustaining non-profit sectors in Hungary and Central and Eastern Europe.

Activities: The Foundation provides a number of services to NGOs in Hungary, including non-profit management training, consultancy support to individuals and specific organizations, publications on non-profit management and development, and organizing forums for networking and dialogue among non-profit organizations and building links with the business and the government sectors.

Geographical Area of Activity: Hungary and Central and Eastern Europe.

Publications: Annual Report.

Principal Staff: Chair. Tibor Kálmán; Exec. Dir Balázs Sátor.

Address: 1117 Budapest, Mészöly u. 4. III. 3.

Telephone: (1) 385-2966; **Fax:** (1) 381-0011; **Internet:** www.ctf.hu; **e-mail:** ctf@ctf.hu.

Hungarian Foundation for Self-Reliance—HFSR

Founded in 1990 to promote the development of civil society and the not-for-profit sector in Hungary.

Activities: Aims to improve employment opportunities for Roma people by providing assistance to develop their civil organizations.

Geographical Area of Activity: Hungary, Bulgaria, Romania, Serbia, Slovakia.

Publications: Annual Report.

Finance: Financed mainly on an individual project basis by the European Union. Total assets €523,583 (2008).

Board of Trustees: Zsuzsa Foltanyi (Chair.).

Principal Staff: Exec. Dir Anna Csongor.

Address: 1137 Budapest, Pozsonyi út 14, II/9.

Telephone: (361) 237-6020; **Fax:** (361) 237-6029; **Internet:** www.autonomia.hu; **e-mail:** autonomia@autonomia.hu.

Nonprofit Információs és Oktató Központ Alapítvány—NIOK (Non-Profit Information and Training Centre Foundation)

Established in 1994 by the Nonprofit Research Association to promote the development of civil society in Hungary.

Activities: Promotes the development of the third sector in Hungary, through the provision of capacity building services to NGOs, and by supporting NGOs; maintains a Civil Service Centre, a library and a database of more than 12,000 Hungarian NGOs. Also campaigns on behalf of Hungarian NGOs, including organizing the 1% Campaign ('Give your 1% to a civil society organization'), promoting philanthropic giving in Hungary, and social dialogue.

Geographical Area of Activity: Hungary.

Publications: *Citizen's Votes for Nonprofit Activities in Hungary*; *International Fund-Raising Techniques*; *Effective Management for Voluntary Organizations and Community Groups*; Annual Report.

Principal Staff: Pres. Kornél Jellen; Dir Balázs Gerencsér.

Address: 1122 Budapest, Maros utca 23–25. mfszt. 2.

Telephone: (1) 315-3151; **Fax:** (1) 315-3366; **Internet:** www.niok.hu; **e-mail:** contact@niok.hu.

Semmelweis Alapítvány Magyarországi Ortopédia Fejlesztéséért (Semmelweis Foundation for the Development of Orthopaedics in Hungary)

Founded in 1988 by Prof. T. Vizkelety and Dr A. Rényi-Vámos to assist with the development of all aspects of orthopaedics in Hungary.

Activities: The Foundation operates nationally in the fields of education, medicine, and health and social welfare through self-conducted programmes, and operates internationally in the field of aid to less-developed countries.

Geographical Area of Activity: Hungary.

Trustees: Prof. T. Vizkelety (Pres.); Prof. M. Szendroi.

Address: SE Ortopédiai Klinika, 1113 Budapest, Karolina út 27.

Telephone: (1) 466-6611; **Fax:** (1) 466-8747; **Internet:** www.sote.hu; **e-mail:** titkarsag@orto.sote.hu.

FOUNDATIONS, TRUSTS AND NON-PROFIT ORGANIZATIONS

Carpathian Foundation

Founded in 1994 by the Institute for East–West Studies to support projects to improve the quality of life and the community in rural areas of the Carpathian mountains, through integrated community development.

Activities: A cross-border regional foundation that provides grants and technical assistance to NGOs and local governments, focusing primarily on inter-regional, economic development and transfrontier activities. It encourages the development of public/private/NGO partnerships, including cross-border and inter-ethnic approaches to promote regional and community development and to help prevent conflicts. The Foundation promotes good relations, social stability and economic progress in the border regions of Hungary, Poland, Romania, Slovakia and Ukraine. It does so by providing financial and technical assistance to projects that will result in tangible benefits to the communities on both sides of national borders, and will improve the quality of life of the people in the cities and small towns of the Carpathian Mountains.

Geographical Area of Activity: The Carpathian region, bordering areas of Hungary, Poland, Romania, Slovakia and Ukraine. In Slovakia the Foundation concentrates its activities on the Košice and Presov regions situated in Eastern Slovakia.

Restrictions: No grants for investment activities, nor to businesses, state organizations or churches.

Publications: *Research and Analysis of Community Economic Development in the Carpathian Euroregion*; *The Potential of Regional Co-operation in Overcoming Social Marginality Within the Hungarian–Romanian–Ukrainian Border Area*; Annual Report.

Principal Staff: Chair. Millet Alexander; Exec. Dir Bata Boglarka.

Address: 3300 Eger, Mekcsey u. 1.

Telephone: (36) 516-750; **Fax:** (36) 516-751; **Internet:** www.carpathianfoundation.org; **e-mail:** cfhu@cfoundation.org.

Czegei Wass Foundation

Established in 1996 by the five sons of the late Albert Wass de Czege, the noted Transylvanian-Hungarian novelist, to provide economic and humanitarian aid to that region.

Activities: Promotes economic and social development, primarily in small villages of the Transylvanian area of Hungary, in a variety of areas. Support is given for the repair and maintenance of school buildings and churches; sponsorship of scout troops; provision of agricultural equipment; the establishment of orphanages for homeless children; provision of scholarships for high school graduates to attend college; financial assistant for creation of local businesses; and emergency relief to families in need. Maintains sister foundations in Romania and the USA.

Geographical Area of Activity: Hungary.

Board of Directors: Vid Wass de Czege (Chair.); Geza Wass de Czege (Treas.).

Principal Staff: Pres. Huba Wass de Czege; Vice-Pres. Miklos Wass de Czege.

Address: 1112 Budapest, Brasso útca 6A.

Telephone: (1) 319-3540.

Demokratikus Átalakulásért Intézet (International Centre for Democratic Transition—ICDT)

Established in 2005.

Activities: Collects and shares information on countries that have experienced recent democratic transition. Aims to facilitate the smooth and peaceful process of democratic transition on the basis of participatory principles. It records the political, economic, legal, cultural and civil societal aspects of transformation, and the socio-cultural context of regions and countries where the process takes place. Also promotes inter-regional co-operation between governments and civil societies of neighbouring countries to enable democratic transition and to ensure regional stability; it provides assistance and learning opportunities to new and fragile democracies, concentrating on practical elements of democracy, such as elections and freedom of speech; and it strengthens the involvement of marginalized groups, such as ethnic minorities, women and similar social groups in both the transition process and the functioning of democracy.

Geographical Area of Activity: North Africa, the Middle East, Latin America, Asia, Central, Eastern and South-Eastern Europe.

Publications: *Minorities in Transition in South, Eastern and Central Europe* (ICDT Papers No. 1, 2008); *Democratic Change and Gender: The Foremother Exercise* (2008); *A European Alternative for Belarus—Report of the Belarus Task Force of the International Centre for Democratic Transition* (2008).

Executive Board: Sonja Licht (Chair.).

Principal Staff: Pres. and CEO Laszlo Varkonyi; Dir Prof. Dr István Gyarmati.

Address: 1022 Budapest, Árvácska u. 12.

Telephone: (1) 438-0820; **Fax:** (1) 438-0821; **Internet:** www .icdt.hu; **e-mail:** info@icdt.hu.

Europako Rromano Čačimasko Centro—ERRC (European Roma Rights Centre)

Established in 1996 to increase awareness on issues of human rights of Roma people.

Activities: Operates internationally, extending legal support in cases of human rights to Roma people, and carrying out research into human rights. It disseminates legal findings and issues publications; advocates Roma rights; maintains a documentation centre consisting of legal material; awards scholarships to Roma students pursuing law and public administration studies; and offers internships for Roma people to study human rights law.

Geographical Area of Activity: Europe.

Publications: *Roma Rights Quarterly* (quarterly newsletter); *Knowing Your Rights and Fighting for Them: A Guide for Romani Activists* (2004); thematic and country reports; fact sheets; position papers; Romani language translations; pamphlets.

Principal Staff: Chair. Robert A. Kushen; Exec. Dir Dezideriu Gergely.

Address: 1074 Budapest, Madach Tér 4-H.

Telephone: (1) 413-2200; **Fax:** (1) 413-2201; **Internet:** www .errc.org; **e-mail:** office@errc.org.

Magyar Ökumenikus Segélyszervezet (Hungarian Interchurch Aid—HIA)

Established in 1991 by a multi-faith coalition.

Activities: Provides international aid and emergency relief in Central and Eastern Europe and Africa; helps refugees and displaced people; supports programmes relating to social welfare issues in Hungary through a network of 17 social institutions with 100 staff members, in particular focusing on finding solutions for families facing crisis situations, drug addicts, endangered and disadvantaged children and homeless people. Also operates a home nursing service for sick people and promotes the integration of Roma minorities.

Geographical Area of Activity: Africa, Central and Eastern Europe.

Publications: Annual Report; newsletter; *HIA activity in Uzbekistan*.

Finance: Total assets 1,022,147 forint (Dec. 2010); annual revenue 1,508,351 forint, expenditure 2,222,556 forint (2009).

Supervisory Board: Szent-Iványi Ilona (Pres.).

Principal Staff: Dir Rev. László Lehel.

Address: 1116 Budapest, Tomaj u. 4.

Telephone: (1) 208-4932; **Fax:** (1) 208-4934; **Internet:** www .segelyszervezet.hu; **e-mail:** info@hia.hu.

Regional Environmental Center for Central and Eastern Europe—REC

Established in 1990, the REC is legally based on a Charter signed by the governments of 30 countries and the European Commission.

Activities: An international organization with a mission to assist in solving environmental problems. The Center fulfils this mission by promoting co-operation among governments, NGOs, businesses and other environmental stakeholders, and by supporting the free exchange of information and public participation in environmental decision making. The REC has its head office in Szentendre, Hungary, and country offices and field offices in 17 beneficiary countries: Albania, Bosnia and Herzegovina, Bulgaria, Croatia, the Czech Republic, Estonia, Hungary, Latvia, Lithuania, Macedonia, Montenegro, Poland, Romania, Serbia, Slovakia, Slovenia and Turkey. The REC actively participates in key global, regional and local processes and contributes to environmental and sustainability solutions within and beyond its country office network, transferring transitional knowledge and experience to countries and regions.

Geographical Area of Activity: Central and Eastern Europe.

Publications: *Developing a Priority Environmental Investment Programme for South Eastern Europe; Assessing Environmental Law Drafting Needs in South Eastern Europe; Developing and Implementing Integrated National Pollutant Release and Transfer Registers; Advising Citizens: Grants for Public Participation Advisory Services; Investing in the Local Environment: Assisting Municipalities in South Eastern Europe to Access Environmental Financing;* and others.

Board of Directors: Jaakko Henttonen (Chair.).

Principal Staff: Exec. Dir Marta Szigeti Bonifert; Deputy Exec. Dirs Radoje Lausevic, Zoltan Erdelyi.

Address: 2000 Szentendre, Ady Endre út 9–11.

Telephone: (26) 504-000; **Fax:** (26) 311-294; **Internet:** www .rec.org.

Iceland

FOUNDATIONS, TRUSTS AND NON-PROFIT ORGANIZATIONS

Mannréttindaskrifstofa Íslands (Icelandic Human Rights Centre)

The Centre was set up in 1994 by the Bishops Office of the Lutheran Church, the Icelandic Red Cross Society, Icelandic Church Aid, the Icelandic Section of Amnesty International, the Office for Gender Equality, the National Federation for the Aid of the Disabled, Save the Children in Iceland, the Women's Rights Association and Association of '78, and the United Nations Development Fund for Women (UNIFEM) in Iceland. The Centre operates by acquiring information on issues of human rights in Iceland and abroad, and to provide general public access to such information.

Activities: The Centre aims to promote human rights by creating awareness and acquiring information on issues of human rights in Iceland and abroad; works towards disseminating information on human rights issues and making such information accessible to general public through organizing seminars on issues of human rights and imparting education on human rights; promotes research and legal reforms in the sphere of human rights issues, and has been responsible for the establishment of a specialized library on human rights in Iceland; issues comments on bills of law, and equips treaty bodies working on human rights issues in Iceland with pertinent information.

Geographical Area of Activity: Iceland.

Publications: Research Reports; *The Human Rights Reference Handbook*; *Universal and Regional Human Rights Protection: Cases and Commentaries*; *Human Rights Instruments* and *Human Rights Ideas, Concepts and Fora*; *Réttarstaða fatalaðra*; *Nordic Journal of Human Rights*; *Yearbook of Human Rights in Development; Ragnarsbók; a tribute to Supreme Court Attorney Ragnar Aðalsteinsson, an avid advocate for human rights; brochures on CEDAW, The UN Declaration on Human Rights, on National Human Rights Institutions.*

Board of Trustees: Oddny Mjoll Arnardottir (Chair.); Halldor Gunnarsson (Vice-Chair.); Bjarni Jonsson (Treas.).

Principal Staff: Dir Margrét Steinarsdóttir.

Address: Túngata 14, 101 Reykjavík.

Telephone: 552-2720; **Fax:** 552-2721; **Internet:** www.humanrights.is; **e-mail:** info@humanrights.is.

West-Nordic Foundation

Founded in August 1986 as a result of an agreement signed by the Governments of Denmark, Finland, Iceland, Norway and Sweden, along with the autonomous governments of the Faeroe Islands and Greenland to provide funding for small and medium-sized business enterprises in the Faeroe Islands, Greenland and Iceland; and to encourage industrial and technical co-operation between Nordic countries.

Activities: Makes loans to businesses in the Faeroe Islands and Greenland, financing new and existing fishing businesses, expanding the Greenland tourist industry as well as developing co-operative projects to include the participation of Icelandic businesses.

Geographical Area of Activity: The Faeroe Islands, Greenland and Iceland.

Directors: Jørn Birk Olsen (Chair.); Sigurd Poulsen (Vice-Chair.).

Principal Staff: Dir Sverri Hansen.

Address: POB 8096, 128 Reykjavík.

Telephone: 530-2100; **Fax:** 530-2109; **Internet:** www.vestnorden.is; **e-mail:** vestnorden@vestnorden.is.

India

FOUNDATION CENTRES AND CO-ORDINATING BODIES

Association of Voluntary Agencies for Rural Development—AVARD

A network of organizations established in 1958 to strengthen voluntary action and capacity building of Indian NGOs.

Activities: Works in the fields of conservation and the environment, economic affairs, education, law and human rights, international affairs, medicine and health, science and technology, social welfare, and self-governance and empowerment of the disadvantaged, through research, conferences, workshops, seminars and projects (particularly in the areas of poverty reduction, food security, women's empowerment and self-governance).

Geographical Area of Activity: India.

Restrictions: Works in association with other NGOs; is not a funding agency.

Publications: *Voluntary Action* (6 a year); planning studies.

Finance: Annual revenue and expenditure Rs 6,000,000.

Trustees: P. M. Tripathi (Pres.); Narain Bhai (Vice-Pres.); K. D. Gangrade (Treas.).

Principal Staff: Gen. Sec. Ram Kumar Singh.

Address: 5 (FF) Institutional Area, Deen Dayal Upadhyay Marg, New Delhi 110 002.

Telephone: (11) 23234690; 23236782; **Fax:** (11) 23232501; **Internet:** www.avard.in; **e-mail:** avard@bol.net.in; avard@del3.vsnl.net.in.

Centre for Advancement of Philanthropy—CAP

Founded in 1986 to provide philanthropic organizations with information, advice and assistance in the areas of charity law, taxation, investments, financial planning, management, good governance and resources.

Activities: Organizes training courses, seminars, conferences and workshops. Provides consultancy services; conducts research; publishes books and journals. Established the Bombay Community Public Trust in 1991 (which is now run independently). Has around 500 members, including corporate bodies, grant-making foundations, NGOs and professionals involved in the field of philanthropy.

Geographical Area of Activity: India.

Publications: *Management of Philanthropic Organizations*; *Art of Fundraising*; *Merchants of Philanthropy*; *FAQ*; *Profile 500*; *Philanthropy* (journal, 6 a year); and other publications.

Finance: Funded by grants from local foundations and companies and membership fees.

Board of Directors: D. M. Forbes (Chair.).

Principal Staff: CEO Noshir H. Dadrawala.

Address: Mulla House, 4th Floor, 51 M. G. Rd, Fort, Mumbai 400 001.

Telephone: (22) 22846534; **Fax:** (22) 22029945; **Internet:** www.capindia.in; **e-mail:** info@capindia.in.

Centre for Civil Society

An independent, non-profit, research and educational organization aiming to improving the quality of life for all citizens of India by reviving and reinvigorating civil society.

Finance: Total assets Rs 29,668,129 (2011).

Board of Trustees: Gurcharan Das (Chair.).

Principal Staff: Exec. Dir Dr Parth J. Shah.

Address: K-36 Hauz Khas Enclave, New Delhi 110 016.

Telephone: (11) 2653-7456; **Fax:** (11) 2651-2347; **Internet:** www.ccs.in; **e-mail:** ccs@ccs.in.

Dasra

Established in 1999 to assist in the development of the non-profit sector in India.

Activities: Provides support to non-profit organizations. Organizes the Indian Philanthropy Forum. Maintains offices in the United Kingdom and the USA.

Geographical Area of Activity: India.

Board: Matthew Spacie (Chair.).

Principal Staff: CEO Deva Sanghavi.

Address: M.R. Co-op Housing Society, 1st Floor, Bldg No. J/18, opp. Raheja College of Arts and Commerce, Relief Rd, off Juhu Tara Rd, Juhu, Santa Cruz (West), Mumbai 400 054.

Telephone: (22) 3240-3453; **Internet:** www.dasra.org; **e-mail:** info@dasra.org.

IndianNGOs.com Pvt Ltd

Founded in 1999 by Sanjay Bapat as a social enterprise established to provide Internet-based information on the social and development sector in India, to build the capacity of NGOs, donors, development professionals and students and to promote corporate social responsibility.

Activities: Provides Internet-based information on the not-for-profit social and development sector in India, examples of good corporate giving practice internationally and in India, background information on issues facing NGOs and a searchable database of approximately 35,000 NGOs.

Geographical Area of Activity: India.

Address: 6c, Devendra Apartments, next to Sahayog Mandir, Ghantali, Naupada, Thane 400 602.

Telephone: (22) 25348905; **Fax:** (22) 25342379; **Internet:** www.indianngos.com; **e-mail:** info@indianngos.com.

Sampradaan Indian Centre for Philanthropy

Founded in 1996 as a national support organization to promote the development of the non-profit sector, particularly the philanthropy sector, in India.

Activities: A foundation centre aiming to foster co-operation between the state, corporations and civil society; encourage networking between donors and between donors and NGOs; and to carry out advocacy in support of philanthropy. Carries out its objectives through conducting conferences, seminars and workshops; carrying out research and providing documentation; conducting campaigns; offering advice and supporting the third sector; institution building, establishment of Local Funds and Foundations; and maintaining a resource centre.

Geographical Area of Activity: India.

Restrictions: Does not give grants, nor does it collect funds for other organizations.

Publications: *Sampradaan* (newsletter, 6 a year); *Directory of Indian Donor Organisations*; *For God's Sake: Religious Charity and Social Development in India*; *Giving and Fund-Raising in India;* occasional papers, monographs, information leaflets and case studies.

Finance: Annual revenue Rs 1,006,168, expenditure Rs 1,923,140 (2008–09).

Governing Council: Jyoti Sagar (Pres.); Dr Mrithyunjay Athreya (Chief Mentor).

Principal Staff: Exec. Dir Dr Pradeepta Kumar Nayak.

Address: C-8/8704, Vasant Kunj, New Delhi 110 070.

Telephone: (11) 26899368; **Fax:** (11) 46594573; **Internet:** www .sampradaan.org; **e-mail:** info@sampradaan.org.

FOUNDATIONS, TRUSTS AND NON-PROFIT ORGANIZATIONS

Afro-Asian Rural Development Organization— AARDO (Organisation Afro-Asiatique Pour Le Developpement Rural)

Founded in Cairo in 1962 to act as catalyst to restructure the economy of the rural populations of Africa and Asia, and to explore, collectively, opportunities for promoting welfare and eradicating malnutrition, disease, illiteracy and poverty among rural people in Africa and Asia. Formerly known as the Afro-Asian Rural Reconstruction Organization.

Activities: Conducts collaborative research on development issues; gives financial assistance for development projects and disseminates information; organizes international conferences and seminars; facilitates pilot projects; and awards more than 200 individual training fellowships at nine institutes in India, China (Taiwan), Republic of Korea, Japan, Malaysia, Nigeria and Egypt. Membership comprises 15 African and 14 Asian countries, and the Institute of Rural Development, Kenya.

Geographical Area of Activity: Africa and Asia.

Publications: *Afro-Asian Journal of Rural Development* (2 a year); *AARDO Newsletter* (2 a year, in Arabic and English); Annual Report; workshop and seminar reports.

Finance: Receives membership contributions from member countries. Annual revenue US $1,003,685, expenditure $1,071,210 (2009).

Principal Staff: Sec.-Gen. Wassfi Hassan El-Sheihin.

Address: 2 State Guest Houses Complex, Chanakypuri, New Delhi 110 021.

Telephone: (11) 26877783; **Fax:** (11) 24672045; **Internet:** www .aardo.org; **e-mail:** aardohq@nde.vsnl.net.in.

All India Disaster Mitigation Institute

NGO founded in 1995 by Mihir R. Bhatt to mitigate the effects of natural disasters on the poor in India.

Activities: The Institute runs four sector programmes concerned with disaster mitigation: food security; water security; habitat security; and livelihood security. Also runs 11 activity centres, including: Action Review and Research Services, Bhuj Reconstruction Project, Building Peace and Protection, DMI–AMA Joint Research Centre, Emergency Food Security Network, Emergency Health Unit, Learning Resources, Livelihood Relief Fund, Organizational Resources, Sphere Resource Centre, and the Water Security Programme. The Institute is also expanding its work on risk transfer and long-term recovery, based on the joint efforts of action and learning.

Geographical Area of Activity: India and South Asia.

Restrictions: Supported efforts must reduce risks.

Publications: *Afat Nivaran* (monthly journal); *Vipada Nivaran* (quarterly journal); *Pocket Book Series*; *Jal Sankal* (in Gujarati); *Anubhav Pustika Shreni (Experience Learning Series)*; *Preparedness Pocketbook Series*; promoting awareness material; and other material.

Trustees: Sunita Narain (Chair.); Mihir R. Bhatt (Man. Trustee).

Principal Staff: Co-ordinators Tejal Dave, Himanshu Kikani, Girija Makwana, Mehul Pandya, K. K. Prakash, Hasmukh Sadhu, Arpana Shah, Deepesh Sinha, Jikesh Thakkar, Niraj Trivedi.

Address: 411 Sakar Five, Near Natraj Cinema, Ashram Rd, Ahmedabad 380 009.

Telephone: (79) 26583607; **Fax:** (79) 26582962; **Internet:** www.aidmi.org; **e-mail:** bestteam@aidmi.org.

Ambuja Cement Foundation

Established in 1993 by Ambuja Cements Ltd. The Foundation is a developmental organization committed to engaging the rural communities in and around Ambuja Cements Ltd manufacturing locations. The Foundation undertakes programmes and projects on developmental issues in line with needs of people in partnership with them. These developmental initiatives are undertaken through meaningful involvement either with like-minded NGOs or with the Government. The Foundation has a team of more than 250 professionals and works in collaboration with local, national and international development agencies.

Activities: The Foundation's mission statement mentions 'energize, involve and enable communities to realise their potential'. Its overarching vision is to make people prosperous where they are. Managing human and natural resources for sustainable development, the Foundation aims to make people in India both productive and prosperous and to improve their quality of life, through technical and financial support, as well as serving as a catalyst for appropriate planning, implementation and post-implementation care. Operates in the areas of livelihoods (agricultural and skill-based), natural resource management (water and energy), human development (health, education, women's empowerment and training), and rural infrastructure. Also provides disaster relief and long-term reconstruction support.

Geographical Area of Activity: India.

Publications: Annual Report; *The story of an NGO Network, Kutch Nav Nirman Abhiyan; Sealing Salinity, An Innovative Drinking Water Project in Salinity Affected Coastal Areas; A Year of People Centred Development; A Unique Case Study of Ground Water Recharge through Check Dam; Enriching Experience – A step forward by women farmers to sustain traditional agriculture wisdom; Impact of Watershed Development Project in Jafrabad Taluka, Dist. Amreli; Impact of Water Resource Development Programme in Kodinar and surrounding areas, Dist. Junagadh; Impact of ACF's drinking water programme in Kodinar; Interlinking Water Harvesting Structures through Link Water Channels – A viable alternative at micro level; Sandhanidhar Women's Dairy Co-operative Society – Women's Empowerment & Socio-Economic Development through Collective Action; Salinity Prevention and Mitigation Initiative – agriculture and water resource development in salinity ingress affected coastal areas; Integrated Development of the village Valadar through Wasteland Development Initiative – managing CPRs (Common Property Resources) through community participation; Health Services at Rural Doorsteps – Creating a cadre of village health functionaries; Village Education Committees: Recharging School Education Systems; Water Resource Management in Junagadh: Transforming Lives* (all in English); *Ocha Pani ane Vadhu Utpadan; Krishima Bio Technology; Krishi Adharit Udyog ane Mulyavruddhi; Jal Sanchay ane Teno Karyasham Upyog; Sajeev Kheti Uttam Kheti; Mishra Kheti Kariye, Jokham Ghatadiye* (all in Gujarati).

Finance: Total expenditure Rs 3,755,500 (2008–09).

Board of Directors: Suresh Neotia (Chair.).

Principal Staff: Dir Pearl Tiwari; Regional Programme Mans Ravi Nayse, Chandrakant Kumbhani, Anagha Mahajani.

Address: 5th Floor, Elegant Business Park, MIDC Cross Road 'B', Off Andheri Kurla Rd, Andheri (East), Mumbai 400059.

Telephone: (22) 66167000; **Fax:** (22) 30827794; **Internet:** www.ambujacement foundation.org; **e-mail:** admin.acf@ ambujacement.com.

Angaja Foundation

Founded in 1998 to help improve the lives of underprivileged people.

Activities: Works to protect children's rights, focusing on: promoting creative non-formal education for children living in slum areas; increasing school admissions for children in need; improving government schools; providing health checkups for children from slum areas; and health education for adult men and women and adolescents living in slum areas.

Operates training and sensitization workshops for judges, public prosecutors of the lower courts, police, doctors, NGOs and the media on child rape, child sexual abuse, crimes against women and street children. Also runs a Child Sexual Abuse and Child Rape Programme that provides counselling, legal, financial and educational services.

Geographical Area of Activity: Delhi, India.

Restrictions: No grants made.

Publications: *Child Rape and Child Sexual Abuse—Sensitization for Lawyers, Police, Doctors and NGOs* (workshop report).

Finance: Funding from ActionAid (q.v.) and Siddartha's Intent. Annual revenue Rs 3,000,000, annual expenditure Rs 2,000,000.

Board of Trustees: Tarkeshwari (Pres.).

Principal Staff: Gen. Sec. Raka Sinha Bal; Admin. and Accounts Officer C. V. Daniel.

Address: A-7, Amrit Nagar, Behind South Extention Part-I, New Delhi 110 003.

Telephone: (11) 224616717; **Fax:** (11) 224617414; **Internet:** www.angaja.org.

Asian Development Research Institute—ADRI

Established in 1991 by a group of social scientists in the eastern Indian state of Bihar.

Activities: The Institute is active in development and social science research, in the Bihar region and internationally, particularly concentrating on promoting literacy development and education. Also active in the area of cultural regeneration, including documenting Bihar's folk art tradition. The Institute has established two financially independent research centres in Ranchi and New Delhi, and works in collaboration with foreign universities and development organizations. Also holds conferences and the annual ADRI Foundation Lecture.

Geographical Area of Activity: Mainly India.

Trustees: Prof. Muchkund Dubey (Chair.); Sunita Lall (Treas.).

Principal Staff: Dir Dr Shaibal Gupta.

Address: B.S.I.D.C. Colony, Off-Boring Patliputra Rd, Patna 800 013.

Telephone: (612) 2265649; **Fax:** (612) 2267102; **Internet:** www.adriindia.org; **e-mail:** adri_patna@hotmail.com.

Asian Institute for Rural Development

A national and regional NGO established in 1976 by Dr A. T. Ariyaratne, Dr K. C. Naik, M. V. Rajasekharan and others to undertake scientific research, training and field action in the area of rural development.

Activities: Operates in Asia and Africa in the fields of conservation and the environment, science and technology, and social welfare, through promoting networking among NGOs, running training programmes and field projects, carrying out research, working to develop public policy and issuing publications. Founding member of the Asian NGO Coalition for Agrarian Reform and Rural Development.

Geographical Area of Activity: Asia and Africa.

Restrictions: Does not make grants.

Publications: *AIRD News.*

Board of Trustees: Dr A. T. Ariyaratne (Patron); M.V. Rajasekharan (Chair.); N. Ariyaratne, Prof. G. Agarwal (Vice-Chair.).

Principal Staff: Exec. Dir and Coordinator M. V. Rajasekharan.

Address: No. 7/1, Ratnavilasa Rd, Basavangudi, Bangalore 560 004.

Telephone: (80) 26604091.

AWHRC—Asian Women's Human Rights Council

Established in 1990 to foster solidarity among women's groups in the Asia region and to promote a feminist and critical perspective on human rights, including focusing on violence against women.

Activities: Pursues human rights for women in Asia through campaigns, lobbying, organizing workshops and conferences, networking, participating in regional and international meetings, conducting fact-finding missions, Women in Black protest actions, and organizing Courts of Women public hearings, as well as through issuing publications and producing and disseminating audio-visual material. AWHRC also maintains a regional office in Bangalore, India and the secretariat rotates between the Philippines and India every five years.

Geographical Area of Activity: Asia.

Publications: *Asia Womenews* (newsletter, 2 a year); *Quilt* (journal); *War and Crimes on Asian Women*; and other publications.

Finance: Funding from foundations and international funding agencies.

Principal Staff: Regional Co-ordinator Corinne Kumar.

Address: 33/1-9 Thyagaraj Layout, Jaibharathnagar, M S Nagar Post, Bangalore, 560 033.

Telephone: (80) 25492782; **Internet:** www.awhrd.in; **e-mail:** awhrc@yahoo.com.

The Bridge Foundation

Established in August 1984 by Dr Vinay Samuel to work with the economically disadvantaged in their struggle to attain economic security and social justice with dignity and self-worth. Affiliated with Opportunity International (q.v.).

Activities: Operates in Southern India in the field of microenterprise development, extending credit to people too poor to borrow from the traditional banking system, through self-conducted programmes and training courses. Loans are made to individuals and to groups from village communities wishing to acquire skills or equipment, and the Foundation offers training in basic accounting and group leadership. The Foundation is currently particularly interested in assisting marginalized women in rural areas, encouraging them to form self-help groups.

Geographical Area of Activity: Southern India.

Publications: Annual Report; newsletter.

Finance: Net assets approx. Rs 20,203,153.

Trustees: Rev. Dr Vinay Samuel; Jagadish Devadasen; Collin R. Timms.

Principal Staff: Dir Albin Pinto.

Address: 139 Infantry Rd, 1st Floor, Bangalore 560 001.

Telephone: (80) 25581869; **Fax:** (80) 25466485; **Internet:** www.bridgefoundation.org.in; **e-mail:** tbfindia@vsnl.com.

Chandana Art Foundation International

A charitable trust established in 1999 by K. Venkatesh for the preservation and promotion of the art and cultural heritage of India, in particular aiming to foster an intellectual and artistic environment for children, women and disabled people and socially and economically disadvantaged people.

Activities: Promotes various forms of art, including traditional and folk art, puppetry, photography and tribal art, through research and documentation, education, exhibitions, workshops, scholarships, competitions, and cultural exchange programmes. Runs programmes for the visually impaired and physically challenged, especially women and children.

Geographical Area of Activity: India, Germany, USA, Republic of Korea, United Arab Emirates.

Principal Staff: Man. Trustee K. Venkatesh.

Address: No. 784, 10th Main, II Block, BSK I Stage, Bangalore 560 050, Karnataka.

Telephone: (80) 22424820; **Internet:** www.chandanaartfoundation.org; **e-mail:** cafivenkatesh@gmail.com; chandanaartfoundation@gmail.com.

Chemtech Foundation

Established in 1975, an industry association promoting industrial growth in India, the development of strategic alliances and encouraging foreign investment in India.

Activities: The Foundation addresses environmental issues faced by industries by organizing conferences, trade fairs and workshops, providing thereby a marketing base for companies involved in pollution control; sponsors visits by foreign delegates to India as well as visits of Indian delegates to foreign countries; and confers the CHEMTECH-CEW award in recognition of corporate, institutional and individual initiative in economic and scientific achievement. Maintains regional offices throughout India and an international office in Abu Dhabi.

Geographical Area of Activity: India.

Publications: *Chemical Engineering World, Offshore World, Pharma Bio World, Shipping Marine & Ports World, Chemical Product Finder* (magazines).

Advisory Board: Jasu Shah (Chair.).

Principal Staff: Sec.-Gen. Tarun Hukku.

Address: 26 Maker Chambers VI, Nariman Point, Mumbai 400 021.

Telephone: (22) 40373737; **Fax:** (22) 22870502; **Internet:** www.chemtech-online.com.

Concern India Foundation

Founded in 1991 to support development-orientated organizations working with the most vulnerable people of society in the areas of education, health and community development.

Activities: Through financial and non-financial support, helps bring about a positive change in the lives of destitute children, youth, the differently abled people, women and the aged. Supports more than 170 programmes through its offices in Mumbai, Delhi, Bangalore, Chennai, Hyderabad, Kolkata and Pune.

Geographical Area of Activity: India.

Publications: Annual Report.

Finance: Annual income Rs 923,130,000, expenditure Rs 798,640,000 (2010).

Board of Trustees: Ardeshir B. K. Dubash (Chair. and Man. Trustee).

Principal Staff: Chief Exec. Kavita Shah.

Address: Ador House, 3rd Floor, 6 K. Dubash Marg, Mumbai 400 001.

Telephone: (22) 22029708; **Fax:** (22) 22818128; **Internet:** www.concernindia.org; **e-mail:** concern@concernindia.org.

Dignity, Education, Vision International—DEVI

Established in 1992 by Dr Sunita Gandhi to promote education and development in India.

Activities: Provides education for the poor in India and encourages self-help through learning and development. Particular focus on empowering poor women from both rural and urban areas.

Geographical Area of Activity: India.

Principal Staff: Convenor Dr Sunita Gandhi.

Address: DEVI Sansthan, 12 Station Rd, Lucknow 226 001.

Telephone: (522) 2638606; **Fax:** (522) 2838008.

Environmental Protection Research Foundation

Founded in 1982 by Dr B. Subba Rao, Dr S. V. Ranade and Prof. J. M. Gadgil to promote research in the field of environmental engineering.

Activities: Operates in the fields of conservation and the environment. Helps companies, pollution control boards, local bodies and governmental agencies carry out effective implementation of pollution control programmes. Also runs development activities in agro-based industries, environmental degradation and watershed management.

Geographical Area of Activity: India.

Publications: *Souvenirs*; laboratory manuals.

Council of Management: Dr B. Subba Rao (Pres.); Dr S. V. Ranade (Vice-Pres.).

Principal Staff: Chief Development Officer Sushilkumar Bhandare.

Address: Arundhati, nr MSEB, Vishrambag, Sangli 416 415, Maharashtra.

Telephone: (233) 2300924; **Fax:** (233) 2301857; **e-mail:** eprf@vsnl.com.

Foundation of Occupational Development—FOOD

Established in 1979 by Ms Rajeswari S. and Loyola Joseph with an objective of implementing welfare programmes and carrying out research on social development.

Activities: Focuses on energy conservation, clean energy, solar and wind energy and LED lighting for villages.

Geographical Area of Activity: India.

Finance: Total assets Rs 8,450,842.

Principal Staff: Exec. Dir Loyola Joseph.

Address: Bharathiar Complex, C-Block, 1st Floor, 100 Feet Rd, Vadapalani, Chennai 600 026.

Telephone: (44) 24848201; **Fax:** (44) 24838826; **Internet:** www.foodindia.org.in; **e-mail:** food@foodindia.org.in.

Foundation for Revitalization of Local Health Traditions—FRLHT

Established in 1991.

Activities: Operates in the field of health care by encouraging the use of traditional medicine as part of public health programmes. Maintains medicinal plant database and promotes their conservation. The Foundation is committed to international co-operation in the field of complementary medicine. Engages in trans-disciplinary research, education and training in the use of medicinal plants and traditional health care.

Geographical Area of Activity: India.

Restrictions: Research grants only.

Publications: *Challenging Indian Medical Heritage* (2004); books on conservation of medicinal plants; *Amruth* (traditional health care magazine, 6 a year); educational material, such as CD-ROMs and posters; *Ksemakutuhalam* (medicinal plant guide).

Finance: Annual budget approx. US $2,000,000.

Governing Council: Sam G. Pitroda (Chair.).

Principal Staff: Dir Padma Venkat.

Address: Attur, Via Yelahanka, Bangalore 560 064.

Telephone: (80) 28568000; **Fax:** (80) 28568007; **Internet:** envis.frlht.org.in; **e-mail:** info@frlht.org.in.

Rajiv Gandhi Foundation

Established in 1991 by Sonia Gandhi to promote the ideals of her late husband Rajiv Gandhi. The Foundation is independent of party or political affiliation and gives particular attention to providing enlarged opportunities to the underprivileged and deprived, and to promoting diversity and pluralism in human societies, the empowerment of women, the alleviation of poverty, and the regeneration of India's environment.

Activities: Operates mainly in the areas of natural resource management, libraries and education, health, welfare of the disabled, women and child development, applied science and technology in rural areas, and the promotion of grassroots democracy through local self-government. Its largest programmes include the establishment of village libraries throughout India; implementing schemes for rainwater harvesting and environmental regeneration in rural India through its own corps of volunteers; supporting the education of child victims of terrorism; projects for the economic and educational empowerment of women; and AIDS control and awareness campaigns. These are implemented through self-conducted programmes, grants to institutions, scholarships, research, conferences, and publications. The attached Rajiv Gandhi Institute for Contemporary Studies is a centre for interdisciplinary studies, including economic and legal reform, social issues and international relations; it also conducts seminars and workshops, and issues publications. Following a tsunami in late 2004 the Foundation announced plans to support all children in India orphaned by the disaster.

Geographical Area of Activity: India.

Publications: *Challenges of Globalization*; *Economic Reforms for the Poor*; *Salvaging the WTO's Future: Doha and Beyond*; *Reinventing the Public Sector*; *District Level Deprivation in the New Millennium*.

Finance: Funded by income from its corpus of approx. UK £4,600,000 and donor contributions for projects.

Board of Trustees: Sonia Gandhi (Chair.).

Principal Staff: Exec. Trustee Priyanka Gandhi Vadra.

Address: Jawahar Bhawan, Dr Rajendra Prasad Rd, New Delhi 110 001.

Telephone: (11) 23755117; **Fax:** (11) 23755119; **Internet:** www .rgfindia.com; **e-mail:** info@rgfindia.org.

Gandhi Peace Foundation

Founded in 1958 to promote the beliefs and practices of Mohandas Karamchand Gandhi; registered in 1964.

Activities: The Foundation works towards helping people attain and maintain peaceful, happy and harmonious social relations, encourages the principles of truth and non-violence in national and international affairs, and promotes the teaching of the practices of Gandhi. Also active in environmental affairs, including forest preservation and support for environmental activists. Awards the annual Pranavanand Peace Award.

Geographical Area of Activity: India.

Publications: *Gandhi Marg* (quarterly in English, 6 a year in Hindi); several books.

Finance: Funded by the Gandhi Memorial Trust. Annual budget approx. Rs 47,79,500.

Trustees: Radha Bhatt (Chair.); Shri Rajagopal (Vice-Chair.).

Principal Staff: Sec. Shri Surender Kumar.

Address: 221–223 Deen Dayal, Upadhyaya Marg, New Delhi 110 002.

Telephone: (11) 23237491; **Fax:** (11) 23236734; **Internet:** www .gandhibookhouse.com; **e-mail:** gpf18@rediffmail.com.

IIEE—Indian Institute of Ecology and Environment

IIEE is a not-for-profit autonomous institution decreed as a public charitable trust.

Activities: Focuses on environmental protection, sustainable development, disaster mitigation, study of meteorological phenomena, population control, energy and resource management, and other issues pertaining to environment and ecology; conducts consultancy, research and training, and issues several publications on research results.

Geographical Area of Activity: India.

Publications: *International Encyclopaedia of Ecology and Environment*; *Encyclopaedia of International Environmental Laws*; *Concise Encyclopaedia of Indian Environment*; *Global Environmental Education: World Ecology and Environment Directory*; and other publications.

Principal Staff: Chair. Prof. Dr Priya Ranjan Trivedi.

Address: A-15, Paryavaran Complex, Saket-Ignou Rd, New Delhi 110 030.

Telephone: (11) 29535081; **Fax:** (11) 29533514; **Internet:** www .ecology.edu; **e-mail:** info@ecology.edu.

Indian Council for Child Welfare

Established in 1952 to promote development services for children in India.

Activities: Promotes development services for children, particularly focusing on welfare and education. Runs educational programmes, childcare centres and creches for young children; operates childcare and education centres; disseminates information throughout India, enhancing awareness of children's needs; acts as an advocate for children's rights and benefits; funds training centres and organizes seminars, conferences and workshops on issues relating to child development. Maintains a library. There are 31 State or Union Territory Councils throughout India.

Geographical Area of Activity: India.

Board of Trustees: Gita Siddhartha (Pres.); Kasturi Mahapatra (Vice-Pres.); Chandra Devi Thanikachalam (Vice-Pres.); T. Phanbuh (Vice-Pres. and Sec.-Gen.); Asha Gupta (Treas.).

Principal Staff: Contact Sunita Gadgil.

Address: 4 Deen Dayal Upadhayay Marg, New Delhi 110 002.

Telephone: (11) 23236616; **Internet:** www.iccw.in; **e-mail:** iccw.delhi@gmail.com.

Indian Council for Cultural Relations

Founded in 1950 to establish and strengthen cultural relations between India and other countries.

Activities: Operates nationally and internationally through the reciprocal development of studies in Indian and foreign universities; publications in English and other languages on different aspects of Indian culture; the exchange and presentation of cultural material with libraries and museums abroad; and the promotion of exchange visits of cultural delegations, scholars and artists. Organizes the Azad Memorial Lectures, international seminars, symposia and conferences; establishes chairs and centres of Indian studies abroad; looks after the welfare of foreign students in India; compiles select bibliographies and publishes books and journals in English, French, Spanish and Arabic. Also administers the Jawaharlal Nehru Award for international understanding, instituted by the Government of India in 1964. The Council has regional offices in Bangalore, Calcutta, Chandigarh, Chennai, Hyderabad, Lucknow, Mumbai and Trivandrum, and cultural centres in Almaty, Berlin, Cairo, Colombo, Durban, Georgetown, Jakarta, Johannesburg, London, Moscow, Paramaribo, Port Louis, Port of Spain and Tashkent.

Geographical Area of Activity: International.

Publications: *Indian Horizons* (periodic, in English); *Africa Quarterly* (in English); *Thaqafat-ul-Hind* (quarterly, in Arabic); *Papeles de la India* (quarterly, in Spanish); *Rencontre avec l'Inde* (quarterly, in French); *Gagananchal* (quarterly, in Hindi).

Finance: Annual income Rs 7,763,620, expenditure Rs 7,741,980 (2007/08).

Principal Staff: Pres. Dr Karan Singh; Dir-Gen. Virendra Gupta.

Address: Azad Bhavan, Indraprastha Estate, New Delhi 110 002.

Telephone: (11) 23379309; **Fax:** (11) 23378639; **Internet:** www .iccrindia.org; **e-mail:** dgiccr@iccrindia.org.

Indian Council of Social Science Research—ICSSR

Founded in 1969 by the government of India as an autonomous organization to promote and co-ordinate research in social sciences.

Activities: The ICSSR funds research projects in social sciences proposed by scholars, and sponsors projects on its own initiative (e.g. research on the North-Eastern region of India, women's studies and entrepreneurship); conducts surveys of research in the social sciences and publishes them periodically; awards research fellowships, contingency grants and grants for study and publications; gives financial support for conferences and seminars, and organizes or supports training courses in research methodology; provides guidance and consultancy services in data-processing, and has a documentation centre that provides information support to social scientists; collaborates in research and exchange programmes with a number of countries, and evaluates research proposals submitted by foreign nationals intending to undertake research in India; part-finances 27 other research institutes and has six regional offices throughout the country.

Geographical Area of Activity: India.

Publications: *ICSSR Journal of Abstracts and Reviews: Economics* (2 a year); *ICSSR Journal of Abstracts and Reviews: Geography* (2 a year); *ICSSR Journal of Abstracts and Reviews: Political Science* (2 a year); *ICSSR Newsletter* (quarterly); *ICSSR Research Abstracts* (quarterly); *Indian Psychological Abstracts and Reviews* (2 a year); Annual Report; NASSDOC research information series; ICSSR surveys of research; and various other publications of research reports, monographs, national and international seminar proceedings.

Finance: Total expenditure Rs 524,384,000 (2009–10).

Council: Prof. Sukhadeo Thorat (Chair.).

Principal Staff: Member Sec. Dr Ranjit Sinha.

Address: Aruna Asaf Ali Marg, JNU Institutional Area, New Delhi 110 067.

Telephone: (11) 26741849; **Fax:** (11) 26749836; **Internet:** www .icssr.org; **e-mail:** info@icssr.org.

Indian National Trust for Art and Cultural Heritage—INTACH

Established in 1984 for the conservation and promotion of Indian heritage: architectural, natural, cultural, environmental, heritage. Promotes heritage awareness.

Activities: The Foundation supports the preservation of man-made and natural heritage of India, including places of archaeological, historical, artistic and scientific value. It also promotes public awareness of cultural issues and preservation of Indian heritage and acts as a pressure group when necessary. Works through eight divisions: Art Conservation; Heritage Education and Communication Services; Architectural Heritage; Natural Heritage; Cultural Affairs; Intangible Heritage; Heritage Tourism; and Chapters. There are 140 Chapters in various states and territories of India and three Chapters in Belgium, the United Kingdom and the USA. The INTACH UK Trust offers scholarships and funding for British nationals to carry out research on India, and exchanges for young architects and planners in association with the Charles Wallace India Trust and the British Council (qq.v.).

Geographical Area of Activity: India, United Kingdom, USA and Belgium.

Publications: *Virasat* (quarterly newsletter); Young INTACH (newsletter); environmental series; studies in ecology and sustainable development; science in public policy series; INTACH Southern Western Ghats environment series; documentation on heritage properties; and other series.

Governing Council: L. K. Gupta (Chair.); Tasneem Mehta (Vice-Chair.).

Principal Staff: Mem. Sec. Dr C. T. Misra.

Address: 71 Lodi Estate, New Delhi 110 003.

Telephone: (11) 24631818; **Fax:** (11) 24611290; **Internet:** www .intach.org; **e-mail:** intach@del3.vsnl.net.in.

Inlaks Foundation

Founded in 1976 by Indoo Shivdasani to give education and medical assistance, mainly in India.

Activities: The Foundation's main activity is to award scholarships in any subject to exceptionally talented young Indians for study or research at any reputed university or institution, including the universities of Oxford, Cambridge and London (United Kingdom), Harvard and Columbia (USA), and universities in Europe and elsewhere. It also assists young Indians through Take-Off Grants in India, which aim to develop individual talent, and offers Inlaks Fine Arts Awards to help artists under 35 years of age in India to develop their talent. Also funds and operates social and health projects.

Geographical Area of Activity: International.

Restrictions: Candidates for scholarships abroad must have been accepted for a course before applying for a scholarship, and must be under 30 years of age.

Publications: Annual Report.

Board of Trustees: Lakshmi Shivdasani (Chair.).

Principal Staff: Asst Krishna Kumar; Admin. Amita Malkani.

Address: POB 2108, Delhi 110007.

Telephone: (11) 27666539; **Fax:** (11) 27667965; **Internet:** www .inlaksfoundation.org; **e-mail:** inlaksindia@gmail.com.

International Foundation for Human Development—IFHD

Founded in 1993 to improve quality of life through development.

Activities: Promotes self-help, self-employment and long-term development programmes in collaboration with other national and international organizations. Works to improve education systems, and offers a number of scholarships and grants for students; promotes volunteerism and social justice; runs a documentation centre and library with reference to development studies and voluntary service. Runs conferences and workshops. Co-operates with NGOs in Asia and the Pacific, Africa and the Middle East.

Geographical Area of Activity: Africa, Asia and the Middle East.

Publications: *Asia Pacific Link*; Annual Report.

Trustees: Dr Rao V. B. J. Chelikani (Chair.).

Principal Staff: Sec. Rajeswara Rao.

Address: Balaji Residency 106, 12-13–705/10/A&B, Gokulnagar, Tarnaka, Hyderabad 500 017.

Telephone: (40) 55214993; **Fax:** (40) 27154118; **Internet:** www .ifhd.org; **e-mail:** ifhd@sify.com.

Nand and Jeet Khemka Foundation

Established in 2005.

Activities: The Foundation seeks to develop multi-stakeholder, strategic, long-term initiatives in areas including leadership and ethics, media and awareness, civic engagement, social entrepreneurship, development and philanthropy infrastructure, and climate change.

Geographical Area of Activity: Mainly in India.

Restrictions: No unsolicited grant proposals.

Trustees: Uday Nabha Khemka (Man. Trustee).

Principal Staff: Pres. and CEO Don Mohanlal.

Address: Khemka House, 1st Floor, 11 Community Centre, Saket, New Delhi 110 017.

Telephone: (11) 46034800; **Fax:** (11) 46034823; **Internet:** www .khemkafoundation.org; **e-mail:** info@khemkafoundation .org.

Naandi Foundation—A New Beginning

Established in 1998 by four businesses (Dr Reddy's Laboratories Ltd, Global Trust Bank, Satyam Computer Services Ltd and the Nagarjuna Group of companies) and a state government as a unique non-profit autonomous development organization.

Activities: Supports development initiatives in the fields of children's rights, sustainable livelihood of marginal and small farmers, and safe drinking water, through working directly with communities in partnership with the government and civil society organizations.

Geographical Area of Activity: Nine states in India: Andhra Pradesh, Madhya Pradesh, Chhattisgarh, Nagaland, Rajasthan, Punjab, Haryana, Andaman and Nicobar Islands.

Publications: Annual Report.

Finance: Total assets Rs 548,971,234; annual income Rs 905,893,130, expenditure Rs 891,209,931 (2010).

Board of Trustees: Dr K. Anji Reddy (Chair.).

Principal Staff: CEO Manoj Kumar.

Address: 502 Trendset Towers, Rd No. 2, Banjara Hills, Hyderabad 500 034.

Telephone: (40) 23556491; **Fax:** (40) 23556537; **Internet:** www .naandi.org; **e-mail:** info@naandi.org.

National Institute for Sustainable Development—NISD

A non-profit, secular, voluntary organization established in 1991 by Prakash Palande to work to improve the lives of rural poor masses, especially *bidi* (cigarette) workers and people displaced by irrigation projects. Current project activities are concentrated in the rural areas of Ahmednagar and Pune districts in Maharashtra state, India.

Activities: Works to improve the quality of life of bidi rollers and people affected by the Pimpalgoan Joge and Dimbhe irrigation projects. NISD implements programmes such as organizing a strong network of self-help groups, youth and children groups. The Foundation runs programmes including pre-school centres, training for teachers, youth development, support to school children to encourage attendance at school. It also assists with building houses, toilets and other hygiene and sanitation facilities; and has started a programme on reproduction, children's health, rights and protection, HIV awareness, and youth development. The Foundation undertakes land-levelling and land development activities for tribal and marginal farmers and supports them to create small income generating activities so that they can earn/supplement their income.

Geographical Area of Activity: India, Pune and Ahmednagar districts of Maharashtra state.

Restrictions: Does not award grants.

Finance: Supported by government and national and international funding organizations. Annual budget Rs 10,000,000.

Trustees: Prakash Palande (Pres.); Dr Chandrashekhar Divekar (Sec.).

Principal Staff: Admin. Officer Smita Pawar.

Address: 'Sunder', House No. 560, Survey No. 21/1, Sainikwadi, Wadgaonsheri, Pune 411 014, Maharashtra.

Telephone: (20) 27033020; **Fax:** (20) 2707517; **e-mail:** nisdpune@nisd.org.in.

NFI—National Foundation for India

The Foundation was launched under the aegis of Ford Foundation, USA (q.v.) to fund and provide grants in support of social development.

Activities: Focuses on gender equity, child and health issues pertaining to adolescent reproduction, urban environment, urban management, poverty, illiteracy, health and hygiene, and communication-building between communities. The Foundation funds initiatives involving children and youngsters; awards annual media fellowships in recognition of young journalists working on issues of development; recognizes NGOs through good governance awards to encourage efficacious multi-sectoral partnership between the corporate sector, the state, and civil society.

Geographical Area of Activity: India.

Restrictions: No grants to groups and organizations affiliated to political or religious organizations.

Publications: *Status of the Girl Child in India*; *Accountablility and Decentralization in Urban Governance*; *Women's Empowerment: Role of Women's Universities and Women's Studies Centre*; *Assignment—Giving Voices to the Unheard*; and booklets.

Board of Trustees: Dr M. S. Swaminathan (Chair.).

Principal Staff: Exec. Dir Ajay S. Mehta.

Address: India Habitat Centre, Zone IV-A, Upper Ground Floor, Lodhi Rd, New Delhi 110 003.

Telephone: (11) 24648491; **Fax:** (11) 24641867; **Internet:** nfidel.tripod.com; **e-mail:** root@nfi.ren.nic.in.

Nirnaya

Established in 1998 by Mini Nair, Uma Maheshwari and Indira Jena to empower marginalized women in rural and urban regions.

Activities: Aims to develop the position of women in India. Assists in the formation of self-help groups promoting social and economic empowerment; encourages entrepreneurship and other means of subsistence; works to improve women's skills base; extends support to organizations working to promote literacy and education among women and girls; supports individual efforts, as well as organizations run by women.

Geographical Area of Activity: India.

Restrictions: Funds are provided only to women who are working in India.

Board of Trustees: Gitanjali Mishra; Lalita Missal; B. Rajamani; Sujatha Rita; Syeda Faizunnisa.

Address: 11 Deepti Apartments, S. P. Rd, Secunderbad 26, AP.

Telephone: (40) 27805089; **Fax:** (40) 27717305; **Internet:** www.nirnaya.org; **e-mail:** info@nirnaya.org.

Oxfam India

Part of the Oxfam confederation of organizations (qq.v.).

Activities: Operates in India in the areas of poverty reduction, humanitarian relief, gender justice and economic justice. Maintains a number of offices in India.

Geographical Area of Activity: India.

Finance: Total income Rs 805,726,000; Total expenditure Rs Mridula Bajaj (Vice-Chair.).

Principal Staff: Chief Exec. Nisha Agrawal.

Address: 2nd Floor, 1 Community Centre, New Friends Colony, New Delhi 110 025.

Telephone: (11) 4653 8000; **Fax:** (11) 4653 8099; **Internet:** www.oxfamindia.org; **e-mail:** delhi@oxfamindia.org.

Azim Premji Foundation

Established by Azim Premji, Chair. of the Wipro Corporation; aims to transform the lives of children in India through acting as a catalyst to universalize elementary education.

Activities: Aims to develop elementary education for all children in India, through funding training, development of the education system and innovative utilization of technology, creating models to promote orientated learning, building capacity through local planning processes, and effectively using research, academic, advocacy and communication tools to augment these efforts.

Geographical Area of Activity: India.

Publications: *Learning Curve* (newsletter).

Board of Trustees: Azim Premji (Chair.).

Principal Staff: Dir Yasmeen Premji.

Address: 134 Doddakannelli, next to Wipro Corporate Office, Sarjapur Rd, Bangalore 560 035.

Telephone: (80) 55144900; **Fax:** (80) 55144903; **Internet:** www.azimpremjifoundation.org; **e-mail:** info@azimpremjifoundation.org.

C. P. Ramaswami Aiyar Foundation

Established in 1966 in remembrance of the work of statesman and educationist Dr C. P. Ramaswami Aiyar.

Activities: Funds projects and institutions to advance Indian community development, including the C. P. Ramaswami Aiyar Institute of Indological Research, which carries out research, and holds seminars, courses and lectures on subjects relating to Indian culture and society; the C. P. Art Centre, an exhibition centre, which displays the work of Indian artists and holds workshops and demonstrations; and the Saraswathi Kendra Centre for Children, which provides aid for children suffering from behavioural and learning difficulties. Works in association with the Indian Government through the C. P. R. Environmental Education Centre, established in 1989 to promote environmental awareness, produce and disseminate basic educational and reference material on environment and to support environmental education projects.

Geographical Area of Activity: India.

Publications: Reports and Prospects.

Council of Management: Dr Sarojini Varadappan (Pres.); V. K. Rajamani (Vice-Pres.); M. Bargavi Devendra (Hon. Sec.); K. Krishnan (Hon. Treas.); Dr Nanditha Krishna (Hon. Dir).

Address: The Grove, 1 Eldams Rd, Chennai 600 018.

Telephone: (44) 24341778; **Fax:** (44) 24341022; **Internet:** cprfoundation.org; **e-mail:** cpraf@vsnl.com.

Ryan Foundation International

Founded in 1982 to promote the use of appropriate technologies in rural areas, and to provide safe water for those without it, through the use of renewable energy and minimal investment.

Activities: Organizes training programmes for government organizations and NGOs from all over the world, and income-generating programmes for women in rural areas; disseminates information; conducts research; promotes community development organizations and co-operatives. The Foundation's main area of interest is a sea-water distillation programme that uses solar energy and reflectors. It also conducts research into plants that grow well in sea water and looks at ways of exploiting their potential.

Geographical Area of Activity: International.

Publications: *Better Life Technologies for the Poor* (3 vols); *RYFO Handout*; *RYFO Income Generation Series*; *Drought Trees for Dry Villages*; *Water Management in Homes and Villages*; *How to Convert Sea Water into Drinking Water*; *Survival by Sea Water*; *Sea water canals*; *Sea water for cooking*; *Water a basic human right*; and other publications.

Finance: Funded by founders' endowment, publication sales, membership fees, consultation fees and donations. Annual revenue Rs 500,000.

Principal Staff: Pres. Dr Felix Ryan; Man. Trustee A. Veethoose.

Address: 8 West Mada St, Srinagar Colony, Saidapet, Chennai 600 015.

Telephone: (44) 22351993; **Internet:** www.felixryanh2o.com; **e-mail:** info@felixryanh2o.com.

Sabera Foundation India

Created in 1999 by Spanish pop singer and songwriter Nacho Cano to support development projects in India, with a particular emphasis on women.

Activities: The Foundation works towards the social transformation of women in India, through support for integration and education projects, the creation of safe shelter, health care, nutrition and self-employment/microfinance programmes. Also launched a branch in the USA in 2002.

Geographical Area of Activity: India.

Publications: Bulletin (monthly).

Finance: Funded through private donations and sponsorship.

Board of Trustees: Nacho Cano (Hon. Pres.); José Herrero de Egaña y López del Hierro (Pres.); José Manuel Lapeña Casamayor (Vice-Pres.); Pablo Lago Bornstein (Sec.).

Principal Staff: Press Officer José Domingo.

Address: Village Gazipur, PO Kangaberria, P. S. Bishnupur, 24 Parganas South, West Bengal.

Telephone: (33) 4957186; **Internet:** http://sabera-foundation.org; **e-mail:** saberafoundationindia@gmail.com.

M. S. Swaminathan Research Foundation—MSSRF

Founded in May 1988 by Dr M. S. Swaminathan, Prof. V. L. Chopra, Dr V. K. Ramachandran and Mina Swaminathan to support research and training in the application of modern science and technology, and to apply contemporary development experience to the problems of ecologically sustainable agricultural production and the distribution and consumption of agricultural commodities; to ensure a reasonable standard of living; and to secure the livelihood of poor people in rural areas.

Activities: Operates in the fields of rural development and science and technology through research, conferences, publications and training courses. The Foundation collaborates with individuals and other institutions to realize its aims and objectives. Programmes include the Every Child a

Scientist project, Coastal Systems Research, Information Village Research Project, Farmers' Rights Information Service, and Eco-Technology and Eco-Jobs. Also operates four field centres across India.

Geographical Area of Activity: India.

Restrictions: Not a grant-making organization.

Publications: Annual Report; numerous books.

Finance: Total assets Rs 948,215,838; annual income Rs 92,146,290, expenditure Rs 92,146,290 (2010/11).

Trustees: Prof. M. S. Swaminathan (Chair.).

Principal Staff: Exec. Dir Dr Ajay K. Parida.

Address: 3rd Cross St, Institutional Area, Taramani, Chennai 600 113.

Telephone: (44) 22541229; **Fax:** (44) 22541319; **Internet:** www.mssrf.org; **e-mail:** swami@mssrf.res.in.

Lady Tata Memorial Trust—LTMT

Founded in 1932 by Sir Dorabji Jamsetji Tata to encourage and advance original research in medical science, in relation to the diseases of the blood, especially leukaemia, and related diseases.

Activities: Operates in the field of science and medicine: four-fifths of the Trust's annual income is allocated to international awards for study and research into leukaemia, with special reference to leukaemogenic viruses, the epidemiology, pathogenesis and immunology of leukaemia. One-fifth is allocated to Indian nationals working in India for scientific investigation into the alleviation of human suffering from the disease. International awards are made on the recommendation of a Scientific Advisory Committee, based in London.

Geographical Area of Activity: International.

Finance: Total income US $61.81m.; total expenditure $61,810,000 (2010/11).

Board of Trustees: Ratan N. Tata (Chair.).

Principal Staff: Sec. and Chief Accountant S. N. Batliwalla.

Address: Bombay House, 24 Homi Mody St, Fort, Mumbai 400 001.

Telephone: (22) 66658282; **Fax:** (22) 22826092; **Internet:** www.dorabjitatatrust.org/about/allied_trust.aspx; **e-mail:** fjguard@sdtatatrust.com.

Sir Dorabji Tata Trust

Founded in 1932 by Sir Dorabji Jamsetji Tata to relieve distress, and advance learning, especially research work in connection with medical and industrial problems; provision of scholarships in any branch of science or the arts; and to give aid to charitable institutions.

Activities: Operates nationally in the fields of the management of natural resources, livelihood, education, health, and social development initiatives, covering community development, human rights, family welfare, the physically and mentally challenged, civil society, art and culture, and relief. Projects are carried out through self-conducted programmes, research, grants to national institutions, grants to individuals, fellowships and scholarships. The Trust has established pioneering institutions in India, including the Tata Institute of Social Sciences (1936), the Tata Memorial Hospital (for cancer, 1941), the Tata Institute of Fundamental Research (1945, now known as the National Centre for Nuclear Science and Mathematics) and the National Centre for the Performing Arts (1966). In association with the UN, the Trust started the first Demographic Research Institute in 1956 (now the International Institute for Population Studies, Mumbai). The Foundation established the National Institute for Advanced Studies, Bangalore in 1988, the J. R. D. Tata Centre for Ecotechnology, Chennai in 1998 and the Sir Dorabji Tata Centre for Research in Tropical Diseases, Bangalore in 2000.

Geographical Area of Activity: India.

Restrictions: Currently only funding to projects within India because of exchange restrictions.

Publications: Annual Report; Strategy Papers.

Finance: Annual disbursements Rs 3,298,300,000 (2010/11).

Board of Trustees: Ratan N. Tata (Chair.).

Principal Staff: Sec. and Chief Accountant S. N. Batliwalla; Programme Co-ordinator Nayantara Sabavala; Programme Officers Jasmine Pavri.

Address: Bombay House, 24 Homi Mody St, Fort, Mumbai 400 001.

Telephone: (22) 66658282; **Fax:** (22) 22045427; **Internet:** www.dorabjitatatrust.org; **e-mail:** sdtt@sdtatatrust.com.

Vanarai

Founded in 1986 by Mohan Dharia to promote use of natural resources and sustainable development throughout India.

Activities: The Trust implements sustainable development initiatives in villages in co-operation with villagers, schools, co-operatives, community leaders, etc. Villages taking part in Vanarai projects must adhere to certain conditions. Promotes the greening of rural and urban areas through tree-planting schemes run in co-operation with other organizations. Programmes include: training for farmers in integrated rural development, watershed management, new agricultural techniques, improved seeds, cattle breeding, nurseries, harvesting technologies, etc.; wasteland development, including lobbying local and central governments; empowerment of women and young people; sanitation and energy; and the Latur Project, which promotes integrated rural development in 21 villages in the Latur district—this project is implemented in conjunction with local and central governments and partially funded by the Sir Dorabji Tata Trust (q.v.).

Geographical Area of Activity: India.

Publications: *Vanarai* (magazine, monthly, in Marathi); booklets; videos; slides.

Board of Trustees: Dr Mohan Dharia (Pres.); Shriram Gomarkar (Sec.).

Principal Staff: Chief Project Dir Jaywant Deshmukh.

Address: 498 Aditya Residency, Parvati Mitra, Pune 411 009.

Telephone: (20) 24440351; **Fax:** (20) 24445299; **Internet:** www.vanarai-trust.org; **e-mail:** vanaraitrust@rediffmail.com.

M. Venkatarangaiya Foundation

Established in 1981 in memory of Prof. Mamidipudi Venkatarangaiya; aims to empower women and abolish child labour through the universalization of education.

Activities: The Foundation aims to abolish child labour through campaigning for a universal education system in India, enrolling children at school and providing support, and running summer camps and extra courses. Also works to empower women through action on issues such as livelihood and natural resource management. The foundation is now actively involved in the implementation of the RTE Act 2009 through empowerment of the local elected bodies. Maintains an office in the USA.

Geographical Area of Activity: India.

Board of Trustees: Dr M. Krishnamurthi (Chair. and Managing Trustee); M. Ravindra Vikram (Sec.).

Address: 201 Narayan Apartments, Marredpalli (West), Secunderabad, 500 026, AP.

Telephone: (40) 27801320; **Fax:** (40) 27808808; **Internet:** www.mvfindia.in; **e-mail:** mvfindia@gmail.com.

Voluntary Action Network India—VANI

Established in 1990 as a platform for research, advocacy, capacity building and information exchange on issues relating to voluntarism and voluntary agencies.

Geographical Area of Activity: India.

Trustees: Jayant Kumar (Chair.); Ashok Singh (Treas.).

Principal Staff: CEO Harsh Jaitli.

Address: BB-5, First Floor, Greater Kailash Enclave-II, New Delhi 110 048.

Internet: www.vaniindia.org; **e-mail:** info@vaniindia.org.

World Teacher Trust

Founded in 1971 by Dr Ekkirala E. Krishnamacharya to promote health and hygiene; to establish and maintain hospitals and clinics; to distribute free medicines to the public; to promote homeopathic medicine; to establish and maintain educational institutions; and to organize seminars and conferences.

Activities: The Foundation promotes family life, human rights, social harmony, education, and health and welfare, and has members in Belgium, Denmark, Germany, Nigeria, Poland and Spain.

Geographical Area of Activity: North and South America, Europe and India.

Restrictions: Does not support financial schemes, only those related to human values.

Publications: *Vaisakh* (newsletter); numerous books, articles, leaflets and pamphlets.

Executive Committee: Dr K. Parvathi Kumar (Pres.); Ludger Philips (Sec.); Sabine Mrosek (Treas.).

Principal Staff: Sec. Ludger Philips.

Address: 45-40-36/1, Akkayya palem, Visakhapatham 530 016, Andhra Pradesh.

Telephone: (891) 2565291; **Fax:** (891) 2755834; **Internet:** www.worldteachertrust.org; **e-mail:** info@worldteachertrust.org.

Indonesia

FOUNDATION CENTRE AND CO-ORDINATING BODY

International NGO Forum on Indonesian Development—INFID

Established in June 1985. Aims to give a voice to the concerns of the people represented by NGOs involved in Indonesia and to facilitate communication between NGOs inside and outside Indonesia.

Activities: Network of more than 100 NGOs from Indonesia, member countries of the Consultative Group for Indonesia and international organizations with a commitment to Indonesia. Works to alleviate poverty in Indonesia by addressing its root causes. Acts as an advocate for the creation and implementation of new policies relating to development aid, investment and trade to ensure that they are in the interests of the underprivileged and are based on principles of peace and justice. Also creates an environment in which democracy can develop and be strengthened, particularly placing an emphasis on human rights. Member organizations assemble twice a year, and the INFID Conference is held biennially. Maintains a liaison office in Belgium.

Geographical Area of Activity: Indonesia, international.

Publications: Publishes books, leaflets, booklets, fact sheets, etc., on issues related to INFID advocacy priorities.

Board: Farah Sofa (Chair.); Antarini Pratiwi Arna (Vice-Chair.); J. Danang Widoyoko (Treas.).

Principal Staff: Exec. Sec. Don K. Marut; Deputy Exec. Sec. Dian Kartika Sari.

Address: Jl. Mampang Prapatan XI No. 23, Jakarta 12790.

Telephone: (21) 7919 6721; **Fax:** (21) 7941 577; **Internet:** www.infid.org; **e-mail:** infid@infid.org.

FOUNDATIONS, TRUSTS AND NON-PROFIT ORGANIZATIONS

ASEAN Foundation

Established in 1997 at the Association of Southeast Asian Nations' (ASEAN) 30th Anniversary Summit to help bring about shared prosperity and a sustainable future to the countries of ASEAN (Brunei, Cambodia, Indonesia, Laos, Malaysia, Myanmar, the Philippines, Singapore, Thailand and Viet Nam).

Activities: Operates in the fields of social and economic development, and poverty reduction, promoting access to information and communication technologies in particular to disadvantaged groups, young people, women, the disabled and rural communities. Also promotes awareness of ASEAN, and volunteer exchanges for young people.

Geographical Area of Activity: ASEAN countries.

Publications: *Gazette*.

Board of Trustees: Pengiran Hajjah Basmillah Pengiran Haji Abbas (Chair.); Kan Pharidh (Vice-Chair.).

Principal Staff: Exec. Dir Dr Makarim Wibisono.

Address: Jl. Sam Ratulangi No. 2, Menteng, Jakarta 10350.

Telephone: (21) 31924828; **Fax:** (21) 31926078; **Internet:** www.aseanfoundation.org; **e-mail:** secretariat@aseanfoundation.org.

Tifa Foundation—Indonesia

Part of the Soros foundation network.

Activities: Promotes democratic development in Indonesia based on the rule of law, good governance and support for the rights of all citizens, including women, minority groups, and marginalized populations. Focuses its activities on human rights and access to justice; equality and citizenship; civil society and democracy; local governance; and information and media.

Geographical Area of Activity: Indonesia.

Address: Jl. Jaya Mandala II No. 14E, Menteng Dalam, Jakarta 12870.

Telephone: 021 829 2776; **Fax:** 021 837 83648; **Internet:** www.tifafoundation.org.

WALHI—Wahana Lingkungan Hidup Indonesia (Indonesian Forum for the Environment—Friends of the Earth Indonesia)

Established in 1980 by a number of individuals to pursue justice, social equity, control of people over resources management, and fair governance.

Activities: Operates in Indonesia in the areas of conservation of natural resources, and civil and human rights, through advocacy, community empowerment, assisting community development and self-organization, and networking. Had more than 438 member organizations in 2004.

Geographical Area of Activity: Indonesia.

Restrictions: Grants made only to member organizations.

Publications: *Tanah Air* (quarterly magazine); *Simpul Jaringan* (monthly magazine); *Walhi Updates* (electronic newsletter, 2 a month).

Board of Directors: Yani Sagaroa (Chair.); Irsyad Thamrin (Vice-Chair.); Khalisah Khalid (Sec.).

Principal Staff: Exec. Dir Berry Nahdian Forqan.

Address: Jl. Tegal Parang Utara No. 14, Jakarta 12790.

Telephone: (21) 79193363; **Fax:** (21) 7941673; **Internet:** www.walhi.or.id; **e-mail:** info@walhi.or.id.

Yayasan Dian Desa (Dian Desa Foundation)

Founded in 1972 to improve the welfare of rural communities by making use of effective and efficient technologies.

Activities: Aims to improve the welfare of rural communities in Indonesia, through acting as a catalyst, introducing new ideas, which are then implemented and popularized by village communities. Provides guidance, support and training to help people help themselves. Active in the fields of education and training, environmental conservation, public health and community development. Also supports the development of small businesses through the provision of micro-credit. Maintains branch offices in Kupang and Maumere.

Geographical Area of Activity: Indonesia.

Publications: *The Kotakatikotakita Urban Bulletin*; *ASAP* (magazine); *SODIS* (magazine).

Principal Staff: Exec. Dir Anton Soedjarwo.

Address: Jl. Kaliurang Gg Jurug Sari IV/19, POB 19, Yogyakarta.

Telephone: (27) 4885247; **Fax:** (27) 4885423; **e-mail:** christina@arecop.org.

Yayasan Indonesia untuk Kemajuan Desa (YASIKA) (Indonesian Foundation for Rural Progress)

Founded in 1985 to reform socio-economic patterns of inequality to achieve a more equitable distribution of income and to develop initiatives in poor rural areas.

Activities: Operates in the areas of environmental conservation, community development and the development of small businesses, through grants and micro-credit loans. Also provides training and technical assistance to NGOs.

Geographical Area of Activity: Indonesia.

Principal Staff: Exec. Dir Surya Dharma.

Address: Jalan Airlangga No. 16B, Medan 20112.

Telephone: (61) 4535016; **Fax:** (21) 4564794; **e-mail:** laras@indosat.net.id.

Yayasan Indonesia Sejahtera (Indonesian Prosperity Foundation)

Founded in 1974 to promote national self-reliance and sustainable development.

Activities: Operates through supporting development activities in Indonesia in the fields of education and training, institution building, community development and publications, and providing public information. Operates training courses, provides technical assistance to NGOs, carries out research and collaborates with other organizations. Also provides emergency and disaster relief.

Geographical Area of Activity: Indonesia.

Publications: Books; bulletins; *Vibro* (newsletter); *Bergetar*.

Board of Trustees: Joseph Gustama (Pres.).

Principal Staff: Chair. Muki Reksoprojo; Sec. Sri Djoewarini; Treas. Lanny Hendrata.

Address: Jl. Kramat VI No. 11, Jakarta 10430.

Telephone: (21) 3902973; **Fax:** (21) 326914; **Internet:** www.yis.or.id; **e-mail:** yisjkt@indosat.net.id.

Yayasan Keanekaragaman Hayati Indonesia—KEHATI (Indonesia Biodiversity Foundation)

Founded in 1994 to promote biological diversity conservation and the sustainable use of natural resources, and to empower local communities.

Activities: Promotes biodiversity and the conservation of natural resources in local communities, through grants to projects in the fields of education and training, organizational development, environmental conservation, community development and research. Also runs training courses and workshops, publishes information for public use, lobbies government and provides technical assistance to NGOs.

Geographical Area of Activity: Indonesia.

Publications: Annual Report; *Warta KEHATI* (newsletter).

Finance: Total endowment US $22,500,000.

Executive Board: Hariadi Kartodihardjo (Chair.).

Principal Staff: Exec. Dir Damayanti Buchori.

Address: Jl. Bangka VIII No. 3B, Pela Mampang, 12720, Jakarta.

Telephone: (21) 7183185; **Fax:** (21) 7196131; **Internet:** www.kehati.or.id; **e-mail:** kehati@kehati.or.id.

Yayasan Pengembangan Masyarakat Desa—YADESA (Foundation of Village Community Development)

Established in 1987 to run activities in the fields of education and training, home industry, rural development, co-operation, guidance and counselling.

Activities: Operates within the above areas, providing funding and technical support to NGOs, generating resources, organizing co-operatives and running micro-credit activities, and channelling funding distributed by international NGOs.

Geographical Area of Activity: South-East Asia, Indonesia.

Restrictions: No grants to individuals.

Publications: Publications on micro-credit and development issues.

Board of Trustees: H. Abdul Gani Nurdin (Chair.); Edy Marsudi (Vice-Chair.).

Principal Staff: Exec. Dir Dr Martunis Yahya.

Address: Jalan Kuta Alam No. 71; POB 137, 23000, Banda Aceh.

Telephone: (651) 32112.

Iran

FOUNDATIONS, TRUSTS AND NON-PROFIT ORGANIZATIONS

Islamic Thought Foundation

Founded in 1984 to promote Islam internationally and to introduce Islamic teachings to all people of the world.

Activities: The Foundation operates in the fields of development studies, the arts and humanities, conservation, economic affairs, education, international affairs, human rights, medicine and health, science and technology, and social welfare.

Geographical Area of Activity: Iran.

Publications: *Echo of Islam*; *Mahjubah*; *Sauti ya Ummah*; *Message del'Islam*; *Al-Tahira-Ashra-Al-Wahda*; *Sakon Musulurci*; *ZamZam* (all monthly); and numerous books, including *A Jug of Love*; *Abdullah—Ibn Saba & Other Myths*; *Velaa and Vilayat*; *Imam Ali AS's Letter*; *Wahabiya in Mizan*; *The Role of Divine Assistance in Human Life*; *Ethical Aspects of Power in Islam*; *Sexual Ethics in Islam and the West*; *The Glory of Martyrdom*; *Footprint of Blood*; *Everlasting Life*; *The Collector of Felicities*; *Imam Ali AS's Hadiths*; *Equality*; *The Marriage Portion of Blood*; *Midnight Call to Prayer*; *Islamic Morals in Wav*; *The Answered Prayer*; *Juibar and Zulfa*; *The Cancelled Immunity*; *Hatam's Son*; *In Rustam's Court*; *The Possessors of the Elephant*; *The Candle of the Dawn*; *India Bird on the Branch of Art of Iran*; *Poetry in Pre-Islamic Iran*; *Angular Kufic*; *Migration to Habasheh*; *Night but the Light*; *Religious Instructions for Young People*; *Message of Imam Khomeini RA on the Occasion of Hajj (1408–1988)*; *Spirit of Monotheism*; *The Enchanted Necklace*; *When He Comes*; *The Tale of Two Palm Trees*.

Principal Staff: Man. Dir Ali Akbar Ziaee.

Address: 766, Valiy-e Asr Ave, POB 14155-3899, Teheran, 14155.

Telephone: (21) 88897662; **Fax:** (21) 88902725; **Internet:** www.itf.org.ir; **e-mail:** info@itf.org.ir.

Ireland

FOUNDATION CENTRES AND CO-ORDINATING BODIES

Dóchas

Established in 1993 as a co-ordinating body for development NGOs in Ireland, following the merger between CONGOOD, which represented the common interests of Irish development NGOs since 1974, and the Irish National Assembly.

Activities: Promotes co-operation between development organizations in Irelandncrease the efficiency and effectiveness of programmes carried out in less-developed countries. Disseminates information and research findings to its 44 members and promotes development education, as well as providing a forum for member agencies to meet together.

Geographical Area of Activity: Ireland.

Restrictions: Not a funding agency.

Publications: *DOCHAS Wednesday News* (weekly e-mail news bulletin); Annual Report.

Finance: Annual income €409,108 (2010).

Board: Jim Clarken (Chair.); Colman Farrell (Vice-Chair); Alan Moore (Treas.).

Principal Staff: Dir Hans Zomer.

Address: 1–2 Baggot Ct, Lower Baggot St, Dublin 2.

Telephone: (1) 4053801; **Fax:** (1) 4053802; **Internet:** www .dochas.ie; **e-mail:** anna@dochas.ie.

Philanthropy Ireland

Philianthropy Ireland is the association of independent philanthropic organizations in Ireland. Its mission is to increase the level of philanthropy in Ireland and to expand the community of engaged donors who are regular, strategic, long-term contributors to good causes.

Activities: Philanthropy Ireland contributes to the growth of philanthropy by supporting quality research on giving, advocating for tax and policies that encourage philanthropy, and by providing a range of membership services.

Geographical Area of Activity: Ireland.

Publications: *Philanthropy Scope* (journal, 2 a year); Guide to Effective Giving (2010); Guide to Setting up a Foundation in Ireland (2008); Guide to Giving (2007).

Board of Directors: John R. Healy (Chair); Colin McCrea; Sheila Nordon; Mary Higgins; Deirdre Mortell; Maurice A. Healy; Orla O'Neill.

Principal Staff: Jordan Campbell, Membership & Communications Manager.

Address: 18 Merrion Sq. South, Dublin 2.

Telephone: 353 (0)16768751; **Internet:** www.philanthropy.ie; **e-mail:** info@philanthropy.ie.

FOUNDATIONS, TRUSTS AND NON-PROFIT ORGANIZATIONS

The Barretstown Camp Fund Ltd

The Fund was launched in 1994 by the late US actor Paul Newman following the success of his first Hole In The Wall Camp in Connecticut, USA, which is a camp for children who have life-threatening conditions and serious illnesses.

Activities: The Fund presents European children suffering from life-threatening illnesses, such as cancer or other serious illnesses, with an opportunity to enjoy 'serious fun'. The medically endorsed programme of therapeutic recreation presents children with 'challenge by choice'. Success is followed by reflection, leading children to discover that they can achieve much more than they previously imagined. This rebuilds their self esteem and confidence. Sibling camps are also offered, recognizing the negative impact that childhood cancer has on siblings' lives. Special autumn and spring family camps are also organized for the children as well as their carers and families; programmes are also included for bereaved families.

Geographical Area of Activity: Europe.

Trustees: Maurice Pratt (Chair.).

Principal Staff: CEO Dee Ahearn.

Address: Barretstown Castle, Ballymore Eustace, Co Kildare.

Telephone: (45) 864115; **Fax:** (45) 864197; **Internet:** www .barretstown.org; **e-mail:** info@barretstown.org.

Bóthar

Established in 1991 by a group of farmers, businesspeople and community and church leaders under the chairmanship of the late T. J. Maher. Aims to help families in need to overcome hunger and malnutrition in a sustainable manner through the use of livestock in development aid.

Activities: Operates internationally in the field of aid to less-developed countries. Establishes livestock development projects for families in need, providing a sustainable solution to the problems of poverty and hunger. Each family receives a farm animal or animals, such as a dairy cow, a dairy goat, a flock of laying hens or three hives of bees, as well as the training and support necessary to establish a micro-farming enterprise. Nutrition is improved by the consumption of the resulting produce and income is generated by the sale of the surplus produce. Recipients pass on a gift of offspring, similar to that which they receive, to other families chosen by the community. Maintains four additional offices in Ireland and Northern Ireland.

Geographical Area of Activity: Africa, South America, Asia and Eastern Europe.

Publications: *The Bó Vine* (quarterly newsletter).

Finance: Funded by public subscription, grants from government agencies, NGOs and foundations. Total assets €3,763,183.

Board: John Finucane (Chair.).

Principal Staff: CEO Peter Ireton; Deputy CEO David Moloney, Dir of Donor Care Maureen Purcell.

Address: Old Clare St, Limerick.

Telephone: (61) 414142; **Fax:** (61) 315833; **Internet:** www .bothar.org; **e-mail:** info@bothar.org.

Concern Worldwide

Established in 1968; aims to eliminate poverty in developing countries.

Activities: Operates in the fields of development aid, emergency relief and advocacy and development education, working to alleviate the effects of severe poverty in the developing world, particularly in Africa and Asia. Projects involving volunteers include improving health care and sanitation, and providing clean water, food, shelter and education. Also works to eliminate poverty through advocacy, and funds development education on issues such as third-world debt, human rights, fair trade and refugees. Maintains offices in Belfast, Glasgow and London, and an affiliate organization in the USA.

Geographical Area of Activity: World-wide.

Publications: Newsletter; Annual Review.

Finance: Total assets £4,203,698; annual income £24,728,803, expenditure £21,923,956 (2010).

Board of Trustees: Myles A. Wickstead (Chair.).

Principal Staff: CEO Tom Arnold; Exec. Dir Rose Caldwell.

Address: 52–55 Lower Camden St, Dublin 2.

Telephone: (1) 4177700; **Fax:** (1) 4757362; **Internet:** www.concern.net; **e-mail:** info@concern.net.

European Foundation for the Improvement of Living and Working Conditions

Founded in 1975 by the Council of Ministers of the European Community (now the European Union—EU) to contribute to the formulation of policies that would improve living and working conditions in Member States.

Activities: Operates in the Member States of the EU in the field of social issues, by conducting research and publishing the results. The Foundation provides the EU with a scientific basis against which medium- and long-term policies for the improvement of social and work-related matters can be developed. In particular, the Foundation carries out research in the following areas: employment and competitiveness; industrial relations and the workplace; and living conditions and quality of life.

Geographical Area of Activity: Europe (Member States of the European Union and candidate countries).

Restrictions: Does not make grants.

Publications: *Eurofound News* (newsletter); research reports and infosheets; information brochures and booklets; electronic publications online.

Governing Board: Stefania Rossi (Chair.); Jerzy Ciechanski (Vice-Chair.); Herman Fonck (Vice-Chair.); Armindo Silva (Vice-Chair.).

Principal Staff: Dir Juan Menéndez-Valdes; Deputy Dir Erika Mezger.

Address: Wyattville Rd, Loughlinstown, Dublin 18.

Telephone: (1) 2043100; **Fax:** (1) 2826456; **Internet:** www.eurofound.europa.eu; **e-mail:** postmaster@eurofound.europa.eu.

GOAL

Founded in 1977 by Irish sports journalist John O'Shea to relieve suffering in the developing world caused by war, disaster and catastrophe regardless of race, religion or nationality.

Activities: Operates in 12 countries of Africa, Asia, Central America, in the areas of aid to less-developed countries, nursery and primary education, medicine and health, and social welfare, through direct implementation of relief and development projects, and grants to missionary and indigenous organizations. Runs programmes that provide rehabilitation, emergency aid, housing, health care, clean water and education to those who need it, as well as a number of projects working with 'street children' around the world. It also runs training programmes for local people in less-developed countries to help precipitate long-term improvements. Also maintains offices in the United Kingdom and the USA.

Geographical Area of Activity: World-wide.

Publications: Newsletter.

Trustees: Michael Spellman (Chair.); Jerry Sheehan (Sec.); Sean Dunne (Treas.).

Principal Staff: Chief Exec. John O'Shea.

Address: 12 Cumberland St, Dun Laoghaire, Co Dublin.

Telephone: (1) 2809779; **Fax:** (1) 2809215; **Internet:** www.goal.ie; **e-mail:** info@goal.ie.

Gorta—Freedom from Hunger Council of Ireland

Established in 1965 by the Department of Agriculture; since 1979 the Department of Foreign Affairs has had responsibility for the organization, which aims to eliminate world hunger, and to initiate and support long-term development programmes in less-developed countries world-wide.

Activities: Co-operates with local NGOs to support development projects in Africa, Asia and South America. Works to prevent famine through long-term projects encouraging self-sufficient community work that mitigates the effects of natural famine. Emphasizes the importance of local resources and trains local people so that they can manage their own projects. Raises funds through running charity shops throughout Ireland. Also hosts the annual World Food Day Conference.

Geographical Area of Activity: Africa, South America and Asia.

Publications: Newsletter.

Board: Prof. Denis Lucey (Chair.).

Principal Staff: CEO Brian Hanratty.

Address: 12 Herbert St, Dublin 2.

Telephone: (1) 6615522; **Fax:** (1) 6612627; **Internet:** www.gorta.org; **e-mail:** info@gorta.org.

Katharine Howard Foundation

Founded in 1979 by Katharine Howard, the Foundation is an independent Irish grant-making Foundation with a particular emphasis on the support of community projects and initiatives in areas that are socially disadvantaged.

Activities: Operates through the provision of small grants to community organizations across the 32 counties of Ireland. The Foundation places special emphasis on projects that help disadvantaged people, the elderly, young people, refugees and asylum seekers, and people with disabilities, provided that these projects are community-based and involve the targeted group in their design and management.

Geographical Area of Activity: Ireland.

Restrictions: Grant schemes have not been run since 2009 because of difficult financial conditions.

Publications: Young Men on the Margins: Suicidal Behaviour amongst Young Men; The Whitaker Committee Report 20 Years On, Lessons Learned or Lessons Forgotten?; Community Matters No. 5: Tallaght West Small Grants Programme (in partnership with Atlantic Philanthropies); Community Matters No. 6: Parent & Toddler Group Initiative 2006–2008 (in partnership with the Office of the Minister for Children and Youth Affairs); newsletters; interim reports.

Trustees: David Kingston (Chair.).

Principal Staff: Development Dir Noelle Spring.

Address: ISFC, 10 Grattan Cresc., Inchicore, Dublin 8.

Telephone: (1) 4002107; **Fax:** (1) 4531862; **Internet:** www.khf.ie; **e-mail:** info@khf.ie.

International Fund for Ireland

Founded in 1986 by the Governments of Ireland and the United Kingdom to promote economic and social advance and to encourage contact, dialogue and reconciliation between nationalists and unionists throughout the island of Ireland.

Activities: Operates in Northern Ireland and the six border counties of the Republic of Ireland. The Fund's programmes are: the Business Enterprise Programme, which promotes the development of local businesses through training schemes, marketing, business accommodation and revolving loan funds; the Rural Development Programme, which promotes the regeneration of disadvantaged rural areas; the Community Leadership Programme, which provides the resources and support necessary to initiate community-led development programmes; the Community Bridges Programme, which is designed to bring people from different communities to work together on joint projects for mutual benefit, while encouraging the participants to address issues of difference and division; the Wider Horizons Programme, which promotes improved relations between communities in Northern Ireland and on a cross-border basis through training and work experience schemes for young people abroad; the Key Programme, which works to develop the personal and entrepreneurial skills of young people while facilitating contact and dialogue; the Newradiane Programme, a pilot programme aimed at helping local companies undertake product and process development projects in partnership with a company located in the USA, Canada, Australia, and New Zealand or in a European Union member state; and the Tourism Programme, which encourages economic regeneration by stimulating private sector investment in the provision and upgrading of tourist accommodation and amenities and by supporting tourism marketing and human resource development initiatives. Maintains an office in Belfast.

Geographical Area of Activity: Northern Ireland and the border counties of the Republic of Ireland.

Publications: Annual Report; Accounts.

Finance: Committed financial contribution €60,000,000 (2007–10).

Governing Board: Dennis Rooney (Chair.).

Principal Staff: Joint Dirs-Gen. Orla O'Hanrahan, Sandy Smith.

Address: POB 2000, Dublin 2.

Telephone: (1) 4780655; **Fax:** (1) 4751351; **Internet:** www .internationalfundforireland.com.

Irish Youth Foundation

Established in 1985 as an independent development trust to support projects and programmes making a positive difference in the lives of marginalized and socially excluded children and young people.

Activities: Operates in Ireland and the United Kingdom in the area of children and young people between the ages of five and 20, through research, grants to voluntary and community groups, and in partnership with statutory and state agencies. Supports projects tackling problems of poverty, unemployment, drugs, alcohol abuse, crime, violence and vandalism; AIDS preventative programmes that promote personal growth and development; and facilities and amenities for education and recreation. Promotes standards of excellence in service providers and in programmes, and seeks to identify, strengthen and expand existing programmes for Irish children and young people. There are Boards of Trustees in the United Kingdom and the USA, where the Foundation raises funds. Works in partnership with the International Youth Foundation (q.v.).

Geographical Area of Activity: Ireland and United Kingdom.

Publications: Annual Report; various papers and studies on youth and children's sector issues.

Board: Ursula Murphy (Chair.).

Principal Staff: Chief Exec. Liam O'Dwyer.

Address: 56 Fitzwilliam Sq., Dublin 2.

Telephone: (1) 6766535; **Fax:** (1) 6769893; **Internet:** www.iyf .ie; **e-mail:** info@iyf.ie.

The One Foundation

Founded by Declan Ryan and Deidre Mortell in 2004 to support philanthropic causes in Ireland and the developing world. The Foundation aimed to distribute all its resources within 10 years.

Activities: Funds programmes in Viet Nam and the Republic of Ireland. During its initial phase, funding focuses on: helping disadvantaged children, funding organizations that help disadvantaged children in Ireland to overcome the barriers they face in life; capacity building of social change organizations in Ireland; supporting new social entrepreneurs in Ireland; and funding anti-poverty work in Viet Nam, particularly on programmes that identify areas where the adverse effects of poverty and human rights overlap.

Geographical Area of Activity: Ireland and Viet Nam.

Restrictions: No unsolicited proposals currently accepted.

Trustees: Declan Ryan (Co-Founder and Chair.).

Principal Staff: Co-Founder and CEO Deirdre Mortell.

Address: 4th Floor, Research Bldg, National College of Ireland, Mayor St, Dublin 1.

Telephone: (1) 8088800; **Fax:** (1) 8088850; **Internet:** www .onefoundation.ie; **e-mail:** ozadmin@global-ethics.com.

Oxfam Ireland

Part of the Oxfam confederation of organizations (qq.v.).

Activities: Works in less-developed countries of Africa in the areas of sustainable livelihood, emergency relief, campaigning, equal rights and status, and fair trade. Its head offices are located in Dublin and Belfast; maintains an office in Tanzania.

Geographical Area of Activity: Congo (Dem. Repub.), Kenya, Malawi, Rwanda, South Africa, Sudan, Tanzania, Uganda, Zimbabwe.

Principal Staff: CEO Jim Clarken.

Address: 9 Burgh Quay, Dublin 2; 115 North St, Belfast BT1 1ND, UK.

Internet: www.oxfamireland.org; **e-mail:** info@ oxfamireland.org.

Plan Ireland

Plan Ireland was established in 1937 during the Spanish Civil War, and was opened in 2003 in Ireland. Plan carries out welfare activities for children.

Activities: Plan currently functions in 46 developing countries, working in collaboration with its regional partners on long-term projects in the fields of education, health, habitat, building relationships and livelihood; handles anti-child-trafficking projects, support programmes for orphans and susceptible children, assistance programmes for street children, and child media projects; sponsors a child through its Sponsor a Child programme; promotes and protects child rights; also focuses on promoting awareness on HIV/AIDS and its prevention, and birth registration.

Geographical Area of Activity: Africa, South America, Asia and Europe.

Finance: Total assets €2,260,596; annual income €3,026,692, expenditure €3,080,696 (2011).

Board of Trustees: Jane Clare (Chair.).

Principal Staff: Chief Exec. David Dalton.

Address: 126 Lower Baggot St, Dublin 2.

Telephone: (1) 6599601; **Fax:** (1) 6599602; **Internet:** plan.ie; **e-mail:** info@plan.ie.

RIA—Royal Irish Academy

Founded in 1785 for the promotion of study in the sciences, humanities and social sciences.

Activities: Operates in the fields of the humanities, pure sciences and social sciences, through research programmes, a library, publications, conferences and around 30 mobility grants each year. The Academy is actively involved in the development of many academic and scientific disciplines in Ireland and provides international academic links including membership of the International Council of Scientific Unions.

Geographical Area of Activity: Ireland.

Publications: *The Proceedings of the RIA*—three sections (mathematical and physical sciences; biology and environmental sciences; archaeology, Celtic studies, history, linguistics and literature); *Ériu* (Irish philology and literature); *Irish Journal of Earth Sciences; Irish Studies in International Affairs;* conference proceedings; books on Irish archaeology, history, folklore, science and arts.

Finance: Total assets €4,018,789; annual income €5,222,643, expenditure €5,025,003.

Council: Nicholas P. Canny (Pres.); David J. Fegan (Sr Vice-Pres.); John Corish (Treas.); Thomas J. Brazil (Sec.); Jane Conroy (Sec., Polite Literature and Antiquities); Peter I. Mitchell (Sec., Science); Marie Therese Flanagan (Sec., International Relations).

Principal Staff: Exec. Sec. Patrick Buckley.

Address: 19 Dawson St, Dublin 2.

Telephone: (1) 6762570; **Fax:** (1) 6762346; **Internet:** www.ria .ie; **e-mail:** webmaster@ria.ie.

Self Help Development International

Founded in 1984, following the famine in Ethiopia, to provide long-term development solutions to the challenges facing communities in Africa.

Activities: Implements integrated rural development programmes in Eritrea, Ethiopia, Kenya, Malawi and Uganda. Employs no ex-patriate staff, and implements sustainable development programmes that promote self-sufficiency and seek to build the capacity of local communities. The primary focus of work is on improving agricultural productivity and farm household incomes, improving access to social services such as health and education, together with measures that are designed to combat deteriorating natural resources, gender inequality and HIV/AIDS.

Geographical Area of Activity: Africa.

Publications: Newsletter; Annual Review.

Finance: Annual income €7,077,046, expenditure €7,849,265 (2010).

Board of Directors: Nigel Clarke (Chair.).

Principal Staff: Chief Exec. Ray Jordan.

Address: Annefield House, Dublin Rd, Portlaoise, Co Laois.

Telephone: (57) 8694034; **Fax:** (57) 8694038; **Internet:** changeherlife.org/selfhelp.

Trócaire—Catholic Agency for World Development

Established in 1973 by the Catholic Bishops of Ireland to provide funding to developing countries in need, and to raise awareness in Ireland of development issues.

Activities: Operates internationally to relieve the suffering of people in need around the world, including those suffering the effects of poverty, conflict and oppression, through projects, grants, publications and conferences. Actively supports programmes in a number of areas including food security, education, health, human rights, community development of agriculture and microfinance. Funds emergency relief in man-made and natural disaster areas, engaging in food assistance, construction of new homes and providing emergency water, clothing and medical supplies. Also works to raise awareness within Ireland of development issues and problems suffered by people in other parts of the world.

Geographical Area of Activity: Africa, Latin America, Asia, Middle East and Europe.

Restrictions: No grants to individuals.

Publications: *Trócaire Development Review*; *Trócaire World*; *Campaigns Update;* Annual Report*; Mwangaza Newsletter* (2006)*; Dóchas Presentation to the Joint Committee on Foreign Affairs* (2004); *Voices for Peace: Changing perspectives on the Israel–Palestine conflict* (2006); *Response to Irish Government's 2003 Report on Participation in the IMF and World Bank 2004*; *Trócaire Annual Report In Brief 2003/04* (2004)*; Trócaire World 2004/05* (2005).

Finance: Total assets €35,991,000; annual income €63,061,000, expenditure €51,939,000 (2011).

Board of Trustees: Cardinal Sean Brady (Chair.).

Principal Staff: Dir Justin Kilcullen; Chair. of Exec. Board Bishop John Kirby.

Address: Maynooth, Co Kildare.

Telephone: (1) 6293333; **Fax:** (1) 6290661; **Internet:** www .trocaire.org; **e-mail:** webmaster@trocaire.ie.

Vita

Founded in 1989, Vita's vision is to forge long-term international partnerships that bring an end to extreme poverty, reduce the vulnerability of poor people in Africa by building sustainable livelihoods.

Activities: Vita aims to bring about lasting positive change in the living conditions of poor and marginalized people in Ethiopia, Eritrea and Kenya, by developing and supporting income generation activities with marginalized and deprived communities. Goals include eradicating extreme poverty and hunger; promoting gender equality; reducing child mortality; combating HIV/AIDS, malaria and other diseases; and creating a global partnership for development.

Geographical Area of Activity: Africa.

Board of Directors: Larry O'Loughlin (Chair.).

Principal Staff: Chief Exec. John Weakliam.

Address: 73A Blessington St, Dublin 7.

Telephone: (1) 8820108; **Fax:** (1) 8820633; **Internet:** www.vita .ie; **e-mail:** info@vita.ie.

Women's Aid

Founded in 1974, Women's Aid is a feminist, service-based political and campaigning voluntary organization that aims to eliminate violence against women through effecting political, cultural and social change.

Activities: Responds to some 12,000 calls annually. Services include a national telephone helpline; a one-to-one support service from a centrally located service and five outreach clinics; and a court accompaniment service for women accessing the legal system. Also provides an Arts Programme for women and children living in refugee accommodation in Dublin. Works with community groups country-wide on the issue of violence against women. Provides training on the issue of domestic violence to a range of voluntary and statutory agencies and service providers, including health professionals, refuge workers, An Garda Síochána, community and social services, and community groups. Provides research, statistics and vital information to the media and public. Influences policy and lobbies for improved legislation.

Geographical Area of Activity: Ireland.

Publications: *Vision Action Change: Feminist Principles and Practice of Working on Violence Against Women* (2002); *Responding to Violence Against Women With Disabilities* (2003); *Child Custody and Access in the Context of Domestic Violence: Women's Experiences and the Response of the Legal System* (2003); *Women's Aid National Freephone Helpline Statistics* (annual).

Finance: Funded from various sources, including the Irish Government, private donors, fundraising and philanthropic organizations.

Trustees: Catherine Heaney (Chair.).

Principal Staff: Dir Margaret Martin.

Address: 5 Wilton Pl., Dublin 2.

Telephone: (1) 8684721; **Fax:** (1) 8684722; **Internet:** www .womensaid.ie; **e-mail:** info@womensaid.ie.

World Mercy Fund (Ireland) Ltd

Established in 1969 by Fr Thomas Rooney to fund health-care projects in Africa; has now expanded its operations internationally.

Activities: Works internationally to improve health-care facilities and support community development in less-developed countries, establishing clinics and hospitals and providing clean water and basic education. Provides funding to small community development projects. Branches of the Fund exist in Austria, Germany, Italy, Switzerland and the USA.

Geographical Area of Activity: International.

Publications: Regional reports; Annual Report.

Board of Directors: Fr Walter McNamara (Pres.).

Address: TRC House, Dundrum Rd, Dublin 14.

Telephone: (1) 2961360; **Fax:** (1) 2961372; **Internet:** www .worldmercyfund.ie; **e-mail:** info@worldmercyfund.ie.

Israel

FOUNDATIONS, TRUSTS AND NON-PROFIT ORGANIZATIONS

Lady Davis Fellowship Trust

Founded in 1973 in the name of the late Lady Davis of Montréal, Canada to make the cultural heritage of ancient and modern Israel, and its achievements in development, state-building, scholarship, science and education, widely available and known to people from both technologically advanced and evolving societies; and to advance the interests of international scholarship and of higher education in Israel.

Activities: Operates through providing fellowships to visiting professors, post-doctoral researchers and doctoral students at the Hebrew University of Jerusalem and at the Technion—Israel Institute of Technology in Haifa. Since its establishment the Trust has supported more than 1,400 scholars, who have spent between three months and one year at these institutions. The fellowship programme is open to scholars of any age, from any region and in any field of study.

Geographical Area of Activity: International.

Publications: Report of operations; newsletter.

Principal Staff: Chair. Neri Bloomfield; Gen. Sec. Prof. Alexander Solan; Exec. Sec. M. Mark Sopher; Sec. Debbie Yakobian.

Address: Hebrew University, Givat Ram, Jerusalem 91904.

Telephone: (2) 6512306; **Fax:** (2) 5663848; **Internet:** ldft.huji .ac.il; **e-mail:** ldft@vms.huji.ac.il.

Joseph S. and Caroline Gruss Life Monument Fund

Established in 1968 by Joseph S. Gruss to assist ex-servicemen and -women on completion of service in the Israeli defence force to integrate into civilian society.

Activities: The Gruss Life Monument Fund provides scholarships to ex-servicemen and -women from the Israeli defence force, as well as providing assistance to projects that further the personal development of ex-servicemen and -women in the fields of education and employment.

Geographical Area of Activity: Israel.

Finance: Receives interest from the Life Monument Fund.

Principal Staff: Chair. Jacob Turkel; Exec. Dir Naomi Freund.

Address: 8 Hatzfirah St, POB 8052, Jerusalem 93102.

Telephone: (2) 5617176; **Fax:** (2) 5660549; **Internet:** www .gruss.org.il; **e-mail:** gruss@gruss.org.il.

Guttman Center of Applied Social Research

Founded in 1948 by Prof. Louis Guttman and others to plan and carry out research projects in the fields of social psychology, sociology, psychology and related disciplines; to supply government offices and other public and private institutions with research material and advice in these areas; to co-operate with organizations in Israel and abroad that are engaged in these fields and in related fields; to raise the level of research in Israel in these areas and to maintain its professional standards.

Activities: The Center carries out research projects initiated by its own staff and conducts research commissioned by government departments, public and academic institutions in Israel and abroad, and by private commercial and industrial organizations in a wide variety of theoretical and applied fields of social science. Projects include methodological and theoretical research; a continuing survey of social problem indicators; research on political attitudes, conflict resolution, demographic problems, the mass media, cultural activities, immigration and emigration, health and the quality of life; and market research. The Center puts the use of its technical equipment and facilities at the disposal of other research organizations and provides advisory technical services. The Center is affiliated to the Israel Democracy Institute.

Geographical Area of Activity: Israel.

Publications: Annual research report; Israeli democracy index; a portrait of Israeli jewry; occasional brochures in English, books, research papers and reports.

Principal Staff: Chair. Shlomo Dovrat; Pres. Dr Arye Carmon.

Address: c/o The Israel Democracy Institute, 4 Pinsker St, Jerusalem 91046.

Telephone: (2) 5300888; **Fax:** (2) 5300837; **Internet:** www.idi .org.il; **e-mail:** info@idi.org.il.

Jerusalem Foundation

Founded in 1966 by the former Mayor of Jerusalem, Teddy Kollek.

Activities: The Foundation's mission is to strengthen and enrich Jerusalem's cultural life and communities. Capital projects include community centres, sports facilities and parks, libraries, theatres, museums, schools, neighbourhood and community facilities, and educational centres. It also funds social and educational activities for the benefits of all the city's residents.

Geographical Area of Activity: Jerusalem.

Board of Directors: Sallai Meridor (Int. Chair.); Mark Sofer (Pres.); Mayor Nir Barkat (Chair.).

Principal Staff: Gen. Dir Daniel Mimran.

Address: 11 Rivka St, POB 10185, Jerusalem 91101.

Telephone: (2) 6751711; **Fax:** (2) 5651014, 6722384; **Internet:** www.jerusalemfoundation.org; **e-mail:** info@jerusalem -foundation.org.

Jewish Agency for Israel Allocations Program

Founded in 1986 by the Jewish Agency for Israel; aims to improve the quality of life in Israel by supporting innovative and creative social and environmental projects implemented by NGOs.

Activities: Funds projects that promote the strengthening of Jewish identity, mutual respect and unity of the Jewish people, within the fields of education and social welfare.

Geographical Area of Activity: Israel.

Restrictions: Only funds NGOs in Israel.

Publications: *Mapping Programs*; Annual Report.

Finance: Funded by the Jewish Agency for Israel.

Board of Governors: James S. Tisch (Chair).

Principal Staff: Exec. Chair. Natan Sharansky; Dir Rachel Schilo.

Address: 48 King George St, POB 92, Jerusalem 99000.

Telephone: (2) 6202727; **Fax:** (2) 6204116; **Internet:** ww.jafi .org.il; **e-mail:** frd@jafi.org.

KIEDF—Koret Israel Economic Development Funds

Established in 1994 to promote the deployment of philanthropy in the private sector to stimulate economic development and job creation via support to small businesses.

Activities: The Funds operate as revolving loan funds offered through commercial banks, providing bank guarantees and subsidizing interest rates to small business borrowers, offering micro-enterprise lending to home-based businesses, and operating a loan facility for not-for-profit organizations.

Geographical Area of Activity: Israel.

Restrictions: Only operates through granting loans.

Publications: Annual Report.

Finance: Provided financing worth US $27,857,583 (2010).

Board of Directors: Brig.-Gen. (res.) Eival Giladi (Chair.); Dr Michael Reiner (Sec.).

Principal Staff: Man. Dir Carl. H. Kaplan.

Address: POB 33406, Tel Aviv 61333.

Telephone: (3) 691 6827; **Fax:** (3) 685 0029; **Internet:** www .kiedf.org; **e-mail:** koret-il@zahav.net.il.

Van Leer Jerusalem Institute

The Institute was founded by the late Polly van Leer in 1959 with the aim of providing a platform for studying cultural, social and educational issues, as well as to voice a wide range of opinions existing on these subjects in Israel.

Activities: The Institute focuses on research and practical activities in the fields of social policies, education and Jewish-Arab coexistence; projects are so considered that they deliver lessons of universal value including their repercussions on Israeli society; discussions and debates on key social and cultural topics are initiated through workshops, lectures and conferences, held on local and international levels.

Geographical Area of Activity: Israel.

Restrictions: The Institute does not make grants.

Publications: Books; journals; policy papers.

Trustees: Tom de Swaan (Chair.); Sir Zelman Cowen (Hon. Chair.).

Principal Staff: Dir Prof. Gabriel Motzkin; COO Shimon Alon.

Address: POB 4070, Jerusalem 91040.

Telephone: (2) 5605222; **Fax:** (2) 5619293; **Internet:** www .vanleer.org.il; **e-mail:** vanleer@vanleer.org.il.

PEF Israel Endowment Funds, Inc

Established in 1922 by Judge Louis D. Brandeis and others with the aim of promoting social services, health, public advocacy, scientific, educational and religious institutions, immigrant absorption and other services of philanthropy in Eretz Yisrael.

Activities: Funds organizations working in areas of health, social services, public advocacy, and immigrant absorption; also funds educational, scientific and religious organizations; maintains a fund-generating office in the USA.

Geographical Area of Activity: Mainly Israel.

Finance: Total assets approx. US $76,000,000.

Principal Staff: Pres. Geoffrey Stern.

Address: 1 Shimoni St, Jerusalem 92623.

Telephone: (2) 5631193; **Internet:** www.pefisrael.org; **e-mail:** pefisrael@aol.com.

Peres Center for Peace

Established in 1996 by Nobel Peace Laureate Shimon Peres, with the aim of furthering his vision in which people of the Middle East region work together to build peace through socio-economic co-operation, science and research activities and people-to-people interaction. Aims to break through the constraints of misconception and suspicion to trigger a process of conciliation and arrive at authentic co-operation.

Activities: The Center's activities focus on common Arab and Israeli economic and social interests, with particular emphasis on Palestinian-Israeli relations. Peace-building projects are developed to address these interests, through partnerships with regional and international players. Fields of activity include agriculture, academia and research, civil society co-operation, peace education and culture, economics and business, medicine and health care, sports and youth.

Geographical Area of Activity: Middle East.

Publications: *Peace in Progress* (newsletter); e-bulletins (monthly); newsletter (2 a year).

Executive Board: Lt-Gen. (res.) Amnon Lipkin-Shahak (Chair.).

Principal Staff: Dir-Gen. Dr Ron Pundak; Deputy Dir-Gen. Amnon Vidan.

Address: The Peres Peace House, 132 Kedem St, Jaffa 68066.

Telephone: (3) 5680680; **Fax:** (3) 5627265; **Internet:** www .peres-center.org; **e-mail:** info@peres-center.org.

Arthur Rubinstein International Music Society

Founded by Jan Jacob Bistritzky in 1980 in tribute to the artistry of Arthur Rubinstein (1887–1982) and to maintain his spiritual and artistic heritage in the art of the piano.

Activities: Organizes and finances the Arthur Rubinstein International Piano Master Competition; runs master classes, world-wide concert series, film shows and memorial festivals.

Geographical Area of Activity: International.

Principal Staff: Artistic Dir Idith Zvi; Music Adviser Prof. Arie Vardi.

Address: 12 Huberman St, Tel-Aviv 64075.

Telephone: (3) 6856684; **Fax:** (3) 6854924; **Internet:** www .arims.org.il; **e-mail:** competition@arims.org.il.

Henrietta Szold Institute—National Institute for Research in the Behavioural Sciences

Founded in 1941 by Henrietta Szold to undertake research in human behaviour, policy evaluation and experimentation, with special emphasis on children and youth.

Activities: Conducts research and experiments in the fields of education, psychometrics, sociology and psychology; operates an information retrieval centre for Israeli research in the social sciences; provides a measurement and evaluation service for the Israeli education system; organizes workshops and training courses; and maintains databases for researchers.

Geographical Area of Activity: Israel.

Publications: *Megamot* (quarterly); research reports; bibiliographies; monographs; literature reviews and publications.

Principal Staff: Dir Dr Rachel Zorman.

Address: 9 Colombia St, Jerusalem 96583.

Telephone: (2) 6494444; **Fax:** (2) 6437698; **Internet:** www .szold.org.il; **e-mail:** szold@szold.org.il.

USIEF—United States-Israel Educational Foundation

Founded in 1956 to administer the Fulbright Program between the USA and Israel.

Activities: The Foundation enables outstanding Israeli and American scholars and students to pursue research, lectures and study at leading institutes of higher learning in the USA and Israel.

Geographical Area of Activity: USA and Israel.

Restrictions: No grants to institutions or organizations.

Publications: News events.

Finance: Financed by the Governments of the USA and Israel. Annual budget approx. US $1,600,000.

Board of Directors: H.E. Richard H. Jones (Hon. Chair.); Dan Vilenski (Chair.).

Principal Staff: Exec. Dir Dr Neal Sherman; Deputy Dir Judy Stavsky.

Address: 1 Ben Yehuda St, POB 26160, Tel-Aviv 61261.

Telephone: (3) 5172392; **Fax:** (3) 5162016; **Internet:** www .fulbright.org.il; **e-mail:** info@fulbright.org.il.

Italy

FOUNDATION CENTRE AND CO-ORDINATING BODY

Associazione di Fondazioni e di Casse di Risparmio Spa—ACRI (Association of Italian Foundations and Savings Banks)

Established in 1912 to represent and support the development of Italian savings banks and since 1990 to represent and support Italian banking foundations.

Activities: Provides support to Italian banking foundations, representing their interests in Italy and abroad. Maintains and develops the relationships with other non-profit organizations and foundation networks. Provides support to Italian savings banks representing their interests. Publishes reports and studies.

Geographical Area of Activity: Italy.

Publications: *Il Risparmio*; *Fondazioni*; *ACRI Notizie* (online); *Acres News* (Weekly); Annual Report and yearbooks.

Board of Directors: Giuseppe Guzzetti (Chair.); Gabriello Mancini, Antonio Miglio, Antonio Patuelli (Deputy Chairs).

Principal Staff: Gen. Man. Giorgio Righetti.

Address: Piazza Mattei 10, 00186 Rome.

Telephone: (06) 681841; **Fax:** (06) 68184269; **Internet:** www .acri.it; **e-mail:** info@acri.it.

FOUNDATIONS, TRUSTS AND NON-PROFIT ORGANIZATIONS

Accademia Musicale Chigiana

Founded in 1932 by Count Guido Chigi Saracini to provide courses in advanced musical studies.

Activities: Operates internationally in the fields of education and the arts and humanities, through publications and courses, and scholarships and fellowships organized on an international basis.

Geographical Area of Activity: International.

Publications: *Chigiana* (annual magazine); music recordings; *Quaderni dell'Accademia Musicale Chigiana*; *Numeri Unici delle 'Settimane Musicali Senesi'*.

Board of Advisers: Gabriello Mancini (Pres.); Vittorio Carnesecchi (Vice-Pres.).

Principal Staff: Artistic Dir Aldo Bennici; Admin. Dir Lauro Mariani.

Address: Via di Città 89, 53100 Siena.

Telephone: (0577) 22091; **Fax:** (0577) 288124; **Internet:** www .chigiana.it; **e-mail:** accademia.chigiana@chigiana.it.

Biblioteca dell'Accademia Nazionale dei Lincei (Library of the National Academy of Lincei)

Founded in 1924 by Leone Caetani di Sermoneta, Prince of Teano, and formerly known as the Fondazione Leone Caetani, to promote knowledge of the ancient and contemporary Muslim world and Islamic culture, by means of conferences, lectures and publications.

Activities: Has organized a series of conferences on the Muslim world. Maintains a specialized library of 23,000 volumes, 350 manuscripts (Arabic, Persian and Ethiopian) and 350 periodicals on Arab-Islamic classical civilization, which constitutes the Oriental Section of the Biblioteca dell'Accademia Nazionale dei Lincei e Corsiniana.

Geographical Area of Activity: Italy.

Publications: *Giuseppe Montalenti*; *Biotecnologie e Produzione Vegetale*; *Norberto Bobbio*; *Allosteric Proteins*.

President's Council: Lamberto Maffei (Pres.); Prof. Alberto Quadrio Curzio (Vice-Pres.).

Principal Staff: Dir-Gen. Dr Ada Baccari.

Address: Palazzo Corsini, Via della Lungara 10, 00165 Rome.

Telephone: (06) 6861983; **Fax:** (06) 68027343; **Internet:** www .lincei.it; **e-mail:** segreteria@lincei.it.

CENSIS—Fondazione Centro Studi Investimenti Sociali (Foundation Centre for the Study of Social Investment)

A research institute established in 1964, became a foundation in 1973. Aims to research all aspects of Italian society.

Activities: Operates in the fields of the arts and culture, economic affairs, social welfare, employment and the environment. Provides training and advice, and engages in research commissioned by exterior groups and institutions, including the European Union, chambers of commerce and private businesses. Publishes an annual report on the social situation in Italy.

Geographical Area of Activity: Italy and Europe.

Restrictions: No grants available.

Publications: Annual Report; *Italy Today*; *Censis – Materiali di Ricerca*; *Censis – Note e Commenti* (monthly); *Censis and the Forum per la Ricerca Biomedica (FBM)*.

Finance: Funding from contracts. Annual budget US $5,000,000.

Board of Directors: Giorgio Cigliana (Pres.).

Principal Staff: Sec.-Gen. Giuseppe de Rita; Dir Giuseppe Roma.

Address: Piazza di Novella 2, 00199 Rome.

Telephone: (06) 860911; **Fax:** (06) 86211367; **Internet:** www .censis.it; **e-mail:** censis@censis.it.

Centro di Cultura e Civiltà Contadina (Rural Culture and Civilization Centre)

Founded in 1955 by the Giorgio Cini Foundation (q.v.) to promote and facilitate activities and initiatives contributing to the arts and sciences.

Activities: Awards scholarships and organizes meetings, national and international conferences, lectures and advanced international courses in the field of culture. The Centre administers the School of San Giorgio for the Study of Venetian Civilization, which comprises five institutes: the Institute of the History of Art; the Institute of the History of Society and the State; the Institute of Letters, Theatre and Opera; the Institute of Music; and the Venice and the East Institute. Also organizes exhibitions, concerts and theatrical performances and sponsors the publication of studies on Venetian art and civilization.

Geographical Area of Activity: Italy.

Publications: Publications on culture and traditions.

Administrative Council: Mario Bagnara (Pres.); Luigino Curti (Vice-Pres.).

Principal Staff: Gen. Sec. Massimo Carta.

Address: Palazzo Brusarosco Zaccaria, Contrà Porta Santa Croce 3, 36100 Venice.

Telephone: (0444) 543000; **Fax:** (0444) 321167; **Internet:** www.lavigna.it; **e-mail:** info@lavigna.it.

Centro Studi e Ricerca Sociale Fondazione Emanuela Zancan Onlus (Emanuela Zancan Onlus Foundation Centre for Social Studies and Research)

Founded in 1964, works in the field of research, in particular educational, social and health services.

Activities: Operates nationally and internationally in the fields of education, health and social welfare and studies, through self-conducted programmes, research, conferences, publications and lectures. Works in collaboration with other institutions as well as with foreign experts.

Geographical Area of Activity: International.

Publications: *Studi Zancan* (journal, 2 a month); *La valutazione di efficacia nei servizi alle persone; La continuità assistenziale nei rapporti tra ospedale e territorio; La valutazione di efficacia degli interventi con le persone anziane; Solidarietà; Improving outcomes for children and families; Rapporto su povertà ed esclusione sociale; La valutazione di impatto della progettazione sociale del volontariato; Le risposte domiciliari; Forme di convivenza; Disabiliità, famiglia e servizi; L'integrazione sociosanitaria;* and others.

Board: Giuseppe Benvegnù-Pasini (Pres.).

Principal Staff: Dir Dr Tiziano Vecchiato.

Address: Via Vescovado 66, 35141 Padova.

Telephone: (049) 663800; **Fax:** (049) 663013; **Internet:** www .fondazionezancan.it; **e-mail:** fz@fondazionezancan.it.

Compagnia di San Paolo

Established in 1563 as a brotherhood to help the poor and fight usury; now an independent grant-making foundation, aiming to foster civic, cultural and economic development.

Activities: Operates in the following areas in particular: scientific, economic and legal research; education; the arts and humanities; preservation of cultural heritage and activities, and of environmental assets; and health and welfare. The following permanent organizations also come under the remit of the Compagnia's institutional activities: the Istituto Superiore Mario Boella, which operates in the field of Information and Communication Technologies, in co-operation with Turin Polytechnic; the Consorzio Collegio Carlo Alberto, for setting up a Centre for Advanced Training in Finance and Economics, also in association with Turin University; the Ufficio Pio, which operates in co-operation with a strong network of volunteers and acts as a crisis centre for people most in need and gives training-as-you-study grants for the vocational training of socially at risk young people; and the Educatorio Duchessa Isabella, which during 2001 became the Fondazione per la Scuola (the Foundation for Schools) with the aim of becoming a centre for education able to support self-governing schools. Also maintains a searchable grants database.

Geographical Area of Activity: World-wide.

Restrictions: Operates exclusively to the benefit of non-profit-making organizations. No grants are made to individuals.

Publications: Annual Report; newsletter (3 a year); *Quaderni della Compagnia; Quaderni dell'Archivio Storico* (monograph series, in Italian); reports; press releases and other publications.

Management Committee: Angelo Benessia (Chair.); Elsa Fornero (Vice-Chair.); Luca Remmert (Vice-Chair.).

Principal Staff: Sec.-Gen. Piero Gastaldo.

Address: Corso Vittorio Emanuele II 75, 10128 Turin.

Telephone: (011) 5596911; **Fax:** (011) 5596976; **Internet:** www .compagnia.torino.it; **e-mail:** info@compagnia.torino.it.

Cooperazione Internazionale—COOPI (International Co-operation)

Founded in 1965 by Vincenzo Barbieri, an independent and lay NGO legally recognized by the Italian Ministry of Foreign Affairs that campaigns against poverty of all kinds to make the world a better place.

Activities: Operates in the following main areas: agriculture, education, health, water and sanitation, socio-economical services, humanitarian assistance, governance, civil society and human rights. Assist populations struck by natural disasters and promotes their civil, economic and social development; carries out development projects and emergency interventions abroad; and in Italy has been working towards eliminating the cause of the existent vast and grave economic gap between emerging countries of the southern hemisphere and those of the north.

Geographical Area of Activity: Sub-Saharan Africa; Central and South-Eastern Europe; Middle East and North Africa; South America, Central America and the Caribbean.

Publications: Newsletter; Annual Report.

Finance: Total net fixed assets €515,713 (Dec. 2008); annual revenue €34,691,621 (2008).

Board of Directors: Fr Vincenzo Barbieri (Pres. and Legal Rep.); Claudio Ceravolo (Vice-Pres.).

Principal Staff: Dir Ennio Miccoli.

Address: Via De Lemene 50, 20151 Milan.

Telephone: (02) 3085057; **Fax:** (02) 33403570; **Internet:** www .coopi.org; **e-mail:** coopi@coopi.org.

EMERGENCY

Established in 1994 by Italian surgeon Gino Strada.

Activities: Provides medical and surgical care to the victims of war, through the provision of medical and technical personnel. Constructs and rehabilitates health clinics and hospitals, supports educational institutions and distributes medical and first aid supplies. Currently operates relief projects in Afghanistan, Cambodia, Iraq, Sierra Leone, and has supported humanitarian activities in Algeria, Chechnya, Eritrea and Rwanda. Also organizes cultural activities designed to promote awareness about development and humanitarian needs.

Geographical Area of Activity: World-wide.

Publications: *Magazine* (quarterly); newsletter.

Trustees: Cecilia Strada (Pres.); Alessandrao Bertani (Vice-Pres.); Mariangela Borella (Treas.).

Principal Staff: Exec. Dir Gino Strada.

Address: Via Gerolamo Vida 11, 20127 Milan.

Telephone: (02) 881881; **Fax:** (02) 86316336; **Internet:** www .emergency.it; **e-mail:** info@emergency.it.

Eni Foundation

Established in 2006 to apply business efficiency criteria to philanthropy.

Activities: The Foundation aims to protect the rights of children and the elderly through social initiatives that encourage their overall well-being and development.

Geographical Area of Activity: World-wide.

Board of Directors: Paolo Scaroni (Chair.); Raffaella Leone (Deputy Chair.).

Principal Staff: Sec.-Gen. Vicenzo Boffi.

Address: Piazzale Enrico Mattei 1, 00144 Rome.

Telephone: (06) 59824108; **Fax:** (06) 59822106; **Internet:** www .eni.it/enifoundation/eng-home.shtml; **e-mail:** enifoundation@eni.it.

Ente Cassa di Risparmio di Firenze (Florence Savings Bank Foundation)

Founded in 1992 to promote social and economic development and to continue the tradition of Cassa di Risparmio di Firenze (a fund established in 1829 to encourage saving among poorer people and to promote socio-economic development through the distribution of banking profits).

Activities: The Foundation supports the arts and humanities, scientific research and technological innovation, medicine and health, social welfare and restoration projects, through self-conducted programmes and grants in Tuscany. Also administers three smaller foundations.

Geographical Area of Activity: Italy.

Publications: Newsletter; electronic/online information; grants list.

Administrative Council: Edoardo Speranza (Hon. Pres.); Dr Jacopo Mazzei (Pres.); Prof. Gian Piero Maracchi (Vice-Pres.).

Principal Staff: Dir-Gen. Renato Gordini.

Address: Via Bufalini 6, 50122 Florence.

Telephone: (055) 2612214; **Fax:** (055) 2612756; **Internet:** www.entecarifirenze.it; **e-mail:** info@entecarifirenze.it.

European Training Foundation—ETF

Established in 1990 by the Council of Ministers of the European Community (now the European Union—EU); began its activities in 1995.

Activities: The Foundation is an EU agency and part of the family of decentralized bodies. It is the EU's centre of expertise supporting vocational education and training reform in third countries (partner countries) within the context of the EU external relations programme. It also provides technical assistance to the European Commission for the implementation of the Tempus programme in the field of higher education. Provides expertise in the areas of human resources, vocational training reform policies, skills development for enterprises, management and entrepreneurial training, and active labour market policies. Supports the European Commission's project cycle and contributes to the development and design of country strategy papers and indicative and action programmes, including country analyses; sector analyses; analyses of needs and feasibility studies; training needs assessment methodologies; key indicators and benchmarking; impact assessment, evaluation and peer reviews; and examples of good practice. From January 2009 the Foundation has been able to work world-wide in the area of human capital development.

Geographical Area of Activity: World-wide.

Restrictions: Not a training provider, nor a provider of financial assistance for individual students.

Publications: *Live & Learn*; *Albania Stabilisation and Association report —European Commission*; *Adult learning strategy papers and action plans*; *Assessment and certification of vocational training in Kosovo*; yearbook.

Governing Board: Jan Truszczyński (Chair.).

Principal Staff: Dir Serban Madlen.

Address: Villa Gualino, Viale Settimio Severo 65, 10133 Turin.

Telephone: (011) 6302222; **Fax:** (011) 6302200; **Internet:** www.etf.europa.eu; **e-mail:** info@etf.europa.eu.

FEEM—Fondazione ENI Enrico Mattei (Enrico Mattei Eni Foundation)

Fondazione Eni Enrico Mattei (FEEM) is a non-profit, non-partisan research institution devoted to the study of sustainable development and global governance. Officially recognized by the President of the Italian Republic in 1989 and in full operation since 1990, FEEM has grown to become a major research centre, providing timely and objective analysis on a wide range of environmental, energy and global economic issues.

Activities: FEEM's mission is to improve through research the quality of decision-making in public and private spheres. This goal is achieved by creating an international and multidisciplinary network of researchers working on several innovative programmes, by providing and promoting training in specialized areas of research, by disseminating research results through a wide range of outreach activities, and by delivering directly to policy makers via participation in various institutional fora. FEEM conducts research on a wide range of economic, environmental, and energy issue. The starting point of FEEM research is the realization of the high level of complexity of the problems emerging in international energy markets, and more particularly the need to foster awareness on the interaction between the firm and the environment, the economy and energy scenarios, corporate responsibility and social conflict, and cultural responsibility.

Geographical Area of Activity: International.

Publications: FEEM working papers series 'Note di Lavoro'; Policy briefs; Books; *Equilibri* Journal; FEEM News (digital newsletter, 2 a month); annual report.

Board of Directors: Paolo Scaroni (Chair.).

Principal Staff: Exec. Dir Giuseppe Sammarco.

Address: Palazzo delle Stelline, Corso Magenta 63, 20123 Milan.

Telephone: (02) 52036934; **Fax:** (02) 52036946; **Internet:** www.feem.it; **e-mail:** letter@feem.it.

Fondation Emile Chanoux—Institut d'Etudes Fédéralistes et Régionalistes (Emile Chanoux Foundation—Institute for Federalist and Regionalist Studies)

Established in 1995, a university-level institute for the study and defence of federalism and regionalism, including linguistic minorities.

Activities: Operates in the fields of economic affairs, education, international affairs, law and human rights, and social welfare and social studies, through research, awarding prizes, grants to individuals, conferences, training courses and publications.

Geographical Area of Activity: Europe.

Publications: *L'Ordre nouveau*; *Une Vallée d'Aoste bilingue dans une Europe plurilingue*; *Contre l'Etat totalitaire*; *Tra baita e bunker*.

Finance: Annual revenue approx. €150,000.

Council of Administration: Alessandro Celi (Pres.); Nicolas Schmitt (Vice-Pres.).

Principal Staff: Dirs Étienne Andrione; Patrick Perrier; Alberto Bertin.

Address: 1 passage du Verger, 11100 Aoste.

Telephone: (0165) 40777; **Fax:** (0165) 234819; **Internet:** www.fondchanoux.org; **e-mail:** pp@fondchanoux.org.

Fondazione Giovanni Agnelli (Giovanni Agnelli Foundation)

Founded in 1966 on the 100th anniversary of Senator Giovanni Agnelli's birth by Fiat SpA and the Istituto Finanziario Industriale to carry out research in social, cultural, political and economic problems in Italy and elsewhere. Aims to spread knowledge of the conditions on which Italy's progress in economic, scientific, social and cultural fields depends, as well as supporting research.

Activities: Main research area focuses on education (schools, universities, adult training systems and lifelong learning) as an asset for economic and social growth. The Foundation also offers a limited number of scholarships in various research fields.

Geographical Area of Activity: Italy.

Finance: Total assets €63,000,000 (2010); total expenditure €2,700,000 (2010).

Board of Directors: Maria Sole Agnelli Teodorani Fabbri (Chair.); John Philip Elkann (Vice-Chair.).

Principal Staff: Dir Andrea Gavosto.

Address: Via Giacosa 38, 10125 Turin.

Telephone: (011) 6500500; **Fax:** (011) 6502777; **Internet:** www.fondazione-agnelli.it; **e-mail:** segreteria@fga.it.

Fondazione Ambrosiana Paolo VI (Ambrosiana Paolo VI Foundation)

Founded 1976 to promote research into religion.

Activities: Funds research, conferences and studies primarily in the fields of faith and religion, including a collection of studies on the religious history of Ireland.

Geographical Area of Activity: Europe.

Publications: *Quaderni della Gazzada*; *Storia religiosa della Lombardia*; *Europa ricerche*.

Principal Staff: Pres. Luigi Stucchi; Dir Prof. Luigi Mistò; Sec.-Gen. Luciano Vaccaro.

Address: Villa Cagnola, 21045 Gazzada Schianno.

Telephone: (0332) 462104; **Fax:** (0332) 463463; **e-mail:** fapgazzada@tin.it.

Fondazione per l'Arte (Foundation for the Arts)

Founded in 1985 at the initiative of the Istituto Bancario San Paolo di Torino to promote the arts and science; formerly known as the Fondazione San Paolo di Torino, and established by the Compagnia di San Paolo (q.v.).

Activities: Operates in the fields of arts and culture, through grants for the performing arts, exhibitions and restoration projects. Works in association with the Compagni di San Paolo, programmes focusing on the safeguarding, enrichment and enhancement of artistic heritage. The Foundation also focuses on training and research projects in the fields of history, art and restoration, as well as implementing new models for managing and enhancing museums and cultural heritage, through a number of different initiatives.

Geographical Area of Activity: Italy and Europe.

Publications: Information brochures; books on art.

Board of Directors: Angelo Benessia (Chair.); Luca Remmert (Vice-Chair.); Guiliana Galli (Vice-Chair.).

Principal Staff: Sec.-Gen. Piero Gastaldo.

Address: Via Lagrange 35, 10123 Turin.

Telephone: (011) 5118799; **Fax:** (011) 5118740; **Internet:** www.fondazionearte.it; **e-mail:** info@fondazionearte.it.

Fondazione Lelio e Lisli Basso Issoco—Sezione Internazionale (Lelio and Lisli Basso Issoco Foundation—International Section)

Founded in 1976 by Senator Lelio Basso to promote research into human rights issues in developing countries.

Activities: Operates in the fields of the environment, development studies and human rights. Promotes information exchange between politicians, academics and lawyers concerned with human rights issues; offers grants to individuals for research; operates training courses and workshops; and organizes seminars and conferences. In the 1990s the work of the Foundation concentrated on the environment and development, industrial hazards and human rights, and the rights of children, young people and refugees.

Geographical Area of Activity: World-wide.

Publications: Newsletter (quarterly); numerous publications on human rights issues.

Finance: Financed by private funds.

Principal Staff: Sec.-Gen. Linda Bimbi.

Address: Via della Dogana Vecchia 5, 00186 Rome.

Telephone: (06) 68801468; **Fax:** (06) 6877774; **Internet:** www.internazionaleleliobasso.it; **e-mail:** filb@iol.it.

Fondazione Benetton Studi Ricerche (Benetton Foundation for Study and Research)

Founded in 1981, under present name since 1987. Research activities focus on the knowledge and stewardship of landscapes, with special reference to Europe and the Mediterranean basin. A secondary branch of research concerns the history of games and sports.

Activities: Operates nationally and internationally in the above quoted research fields, through self-conducted programmes, research, prizes, conferences, training courses and publications, with the general aim to improve the knowledge, protection and promotion of the natural and built heritage. Awards the annual International Carlo Scarpa Prize for Gardens to promote the conservation of sites that are particularly rich in natural and historical values. The Foundation has a documentation centre, open to the public, with a library, archives, and map and image collections.

Geographical Area of Activity: Mainly Europe.

Restrictions: No grants or sponsorship.

Publications: *Bollettino* (irregular); annual booklet on Premio Internazionale Carlo Scarpa per il Giardino; *Ludica* (annual review of games and sport); *Studi veneti*.

Trustees: Luciano Benetton (Chair.); Gilberto Benetton (Vice-Chair.).

Principal Staff: Dir. Marco Tamaro.

Address: Via Cornarotta 7–9, 31100 Treviso.

Telephone: (0422) 5121; **Fax:** (0422) 579483; **Internet:** www.fbsr.it; **e-mail:** fbsr@fbsr.it.

Fondazione Ugo Bordoni (Ugo Bordoni Foundation)

Founded in 1952 by Cesare Albanese, Albino Antinori, Felice Calvanese, Antonio Carrelli, Romolo De Caterini, Andrea Ferrara-Toniolo, Alberto Fornò, Vittorio Gori, Ernesto Lensi, Algeri Marino, Enrico Medi, Michele Paris, Giuseppe Spataro and Scipione Treves to facilitate and promote research and scientific studies applicable to the postal system, telecommunications and electronics; and to facilitate initiatives to further technical-scientific development in the same field. The Foundation was reconstituted in 2000.

Activities: Operates in the fields of electronics and communications, through research and publications, mainly in co-operation with the Istituto Superiore delle Comunicazioni e delle Tecnologie dell' Informazione (Advanced Institute for Communications and Information Technology). Collaborates with national and international bodies.

Geographical Area of Activity: Italy.

Publications: Report of operations; various scientific and technical publications.

Board of Directors: Alessandro Luciano (Pres.).

Principal Staff: Exec. Dir Antonio Sassano.

Address: Via B. Castiglione 59, 00142 Rome.

Telephone: (06) 54801; **Fax:** (06) 54804400; **Internet:** www.fub.it; **e-mail:** info@fub.it.

Fondazione Cariplo (Cariplo Foundation)

The Foundation was established in December 1991 as part of the reorganization process resulting from the implementation of the Amato-Carli Act for the rationalization and privatization of Italian banks, with a mission to continue the philanthropic activities previously carried out by the Cassa di Risparmio delle Provincie Lombarde (Savings Bank of the Lombard Provinces, founded in 1823). It aims to foster the growth of the local economy, culture and civil society.

Activities: The Foundation aims to help social and civil organizations better serve their community, to anticipate emerging needs, try new solutions or attempt to respond to problems more effectively and in a less costly fashion, and ultimately to disseminate successful solutions.

Geographical Area of Activity: Italy.

Restrictions: No grants to individuals; trade union or patronage organizations; political parties and trade associations.

Publications: annual report; monographs; conference reports; financial statements.

Finance: Total assets €7,465,264,933 (2009), total expenditure €11,432,939 (2009).

Directors: Giuseppe Guzzetti (Pres.); Carlo Sangalli, Mariella Enoc (Vice-Pres.).

Principal Staff: Sec.-Gen. Dr Pier Mario Vello.

Address: Via Manin 23, 20121 Milan.

Telephone: (02) 6239285; **Fax:** (02) 623928202; **Internet:** www.fondazionecariplo.it; **e-mail:** comunicazione@fondazionecariplo.it.

Fondazione Cassa di Risparmio di Padova e Rovigo (Foundation Cassa di Risparmio di Padova e Rovigo)

Established in 1991 as the continuation of Cassa di Risparmio di Padova e Rovigo, which was founded in 1822 to support economic development of local communities.

Activities: Works to promote quality of life and sustainable development in the regions of Padova and Rovigo in Italy. It is inspired by a vision of an open, co-operative community aiming at innovation. Supports and plans projects in the fields of scientific research; education; art and cultural activities; health and the environment; assistance and protection of minorities; other sectors (sport, civil protection, food safety, quality agriculture).

Geographical Area of Activity: Italian provinces of Padova and Rovigo.

Restrictions: No grants are made to individuals, profit-seeking organizations, parties, political movements, trade unions or charitable institutions and trade associations.

Publications: Corporate Annual Report; information brochures.

Finance: Total assets €1,700,000,000.

Board of Directors: Antonio Finotti (Pres.).

Principal Staff: Sec.-Gen. Roberto Saro.

Address: Piazza Duomo 14, 35141 Padova.

Telephone: (49) 8234800; **Fax:** (49) 657335; **Internet:** www .fondazionecariparo.it; **e-mail:** info@fondazionecariparo.it.

Fondazione Cassa di Risparmio di Torino (Turin Savings Bank Foundation)

Established following the Amato law in 1991.

Activities: Operates principally, but not exclusively, in the regions of Piemonte and Valle d'Aosta in Italy, promoting the economic and social development of those regions. Grants are made within the following sectors: scientific research, education, art, culture and conservation of artistic heritage, health, assistance to socially-disadvantaged groups, and the general social and economic development of the regions.

Geographical Area of Activity: Regions of Piemonte and Valle d'Aosta, Italy.

Restrictions: No grants are made to individuals.

Publications: annual report; books; monographs; press releases; online magazine.

Board of Directors: Andrea Comba (Pres.); Giovanni Quaglia (Vice-Pres.); Giovanni Ferrero (Vice-Pres.).

Principal Staff: Sec.-Gen. Angelo Miglietta.

Address: Via XX Settembre 31, 10121 Turin.

Telephone: (011) 6622491; **Fax:** (011) 6622432; **Internet:** www .fondazionecrt.it; **e-mail:** relazioniesterne@fondazionecrt.it.

Fondazione Giorgio Cini (Giorgio Cini Foundation)

Founded in 1951 by Count Vittorio Cini in memory of his son Giorgio. The island of San Giorgio Maggiore, Venice, was entrusted to the Foundation for the purpose of restoring the area's historic buildings and supporting the development of social, cultural and artistic institutions in this area.

Activities: Operates through eight advanced-study institutes: the Institute for the History of Art; the Institute for the History of the Venetian State and Society; the Institute for Music; the Institute for Literature and Theatre; the Venice and the East Institute; the Venice and Europe Institute; the Intercultural Institute of Comparative Music Studies; and an institute devoted to the study and illustration of the works of Antonio Vivaldi. The institutes each have their own director, possess a library, undertake research, organize study-encounters and seminars, and promote publications, concerts and artistic exhibitions. The Foundation works nationally and internationally organizing postgraduate courses, conferences and seminars on topics of historic, scientific, social or cultural interest.

Geographical Area of Activity: Italy.

Publications: Numerous publications.

Principal Staff: Pres. Prof. Giovanni Bazoli; Sec.-Gen. Pasquale Gagliardi.

Address: Palazzo Cini, Dorsoduro (San Vio) 864, 30123 Venice.

Telephone: (041) 2710402; **Fax:** (041) 5238540; **Internet:** www .cini.it; **e-mail:** marketing@cini.it.

Fondazione CittàItalia (CittàItalia Foundation)

CittàItalia Foundation was founded on 30 June 2003 by Mecenate 90 Association, banking foundations and several art cities to address and support the cause of arts and restore cultural and artistic heritage.

Activities: Creates, promotes and spreads art and culture symbolic of Italian cultural heritage, as well as artistic, historic and monumental works. Extends support to art through awareness- and fund-raising campaigns aimed to protect, conserve and recover cultural heritage. Designs and implements projects to restore, recover and enhance Italy's artistic and cultural heritage as a step towards protection of heritage.

Geographical Area of Activity: Italy.

Board of Directors: Prof. Giuseppe De Rita (Hon. Pres.); Alain Elkann (Pres.).

Principal Staff: Gen. Sec. Dr Ledo Prato.

Address: Corso Vittorio Emanuele II, 21, 00186 Rome.

Telephone: (06) 36006206; **Fax:** (06) 3208396; **Internet:** www .fondazionecittaitalia.it; **e-mail:** info@fondazionecittaitalia .it.

Fondazione Rodolfo Debenedetti—FRDB (Foundation Rodolfo Debenedetti)

Established by Carlo de Benedetti.

Activities: The Foundation promotes applied and policy-orientated research on the following main topics: the reform of public pension systems in light of demographic trends and the ongoing transformation of capital markets and of the political economy limits of the reforms; the causes of European unemployment, its social costs and the political feasibility of strategies aimed at liberalizing European Union (EU) labour markets; the harmonization and co-ordination of social and immigration policies in the European Union as a precondition for effective labour mobility across EU countries; and the dynamics of poverty and inequalities and the role played in this respect by the welfare systems. Also organizes conferences and maintains a public documentation centre on social policy reforms and EU labour markets.

Geographical Area of Activity: Europe.

Publications: *Note Rapide* (online newsletter); conference proceeds.

Board: Carlo de Benedetti (Pres.).

Principal Staff: Scientific Dir Tito Boeri.

Address: Via Roentgen 1, Room 5.C1-11, 20136 Milan.

Telephone: (02) 58363341; **Fax:** (02) 58363309; **Internet:** www.frdb.org; **e-mail:** info@frdb.org.

Fondazione Giordano Dell'Amore (Giordano Dell'Amore Foundation)

Founded in 1977 as Finafrica Foundation by Cassa di Risparmio delle Province Lombarde bank. The Foundation is member of RITMI-the Italian microfinance network and of Comitato Nazionale Italiano Permanente per il Microcredito; it is associated with the European Microfinance Network and the European Microfinance Platform.

Activities: The mission of the Foundation is to activate and catalyze the skills and resources of Italian agents to develop projects and methods of intervention in the microfinance sector, in industrialized and developing countries, in compliance with consolidated best practice. It aims to contribute significantly to the development and innovation of the microfinance sector. The Foundation sponsors the annual Microfinance Best Practices Awards.

Geographical Area of Activity: World-wide.

Trustees: Federico Manzoni (Pres.).

Principal Staff: Sec.-Gen. Maria Cristina Negro.

Address: Via Monte di Pietà 12, 20121, Milan.

Telephone: (02) 32168401; **Fax:** (02) 32168430; **Internet:** www .fgda.org; **e-mail:** info@fgda.org.

Fondazione Angelo Della Riccia (Angelo Della Riccia Foundation)

Founded in 1939 by Angelo Della Riccia to encourage, support and reward Italian students of micro-physics; and to promote research in nuclear, atomic and molecular physics, including collective and cosmic radiation.

Activities: Awards prizes and scholarships for study in Italy and Switzerland. Supports research in nuclear physics. Awards in Switzerland are made through the Foundation's sister foundation in Glarus.

Geographical Area of Activity: Italy and Switzerland.

Finance: Grants available in 2010/11 €240,000.

Principal Staff: Pres. Prof. Roberto Casalbuoni; Chair. B. Bosco.

Address: Casella Postale 38, 50123 Florence.

Telephone: (05) 52476650; **Internet:** theory.fi.infn.it/casalbuoni/dellariccia; **e-mail:** casalbuoni@fi.infn.it.

Fondazione Guido Donegani (Guido Donegani Foundation)

Founded in 1951 by Ing. Guido Donegani to further the study of chemistry in Italy.

Activities: Operates internationally in the field of science. The Foundation awards study grants to Italian and foreign students and graduates in the field of chemistry, and has created special prizes for Italian scientists and technicians who have made an outstanding contribution towards the investigation or solution of problems in chemistry. It has also established courses of higher education and grants for research and experiment in the field of chemistry.

Geographical Area of Activity: Europe.

Publications: A series of publications regarding the activities of the Foundation, published by the Accademia Nazionale dei Lincei.

Finance: Source of finance is income from property and investments. Annual revenue approx. €77,000, expenditure approx. €72,000.

Principal Staff: Vice-Chair. Marco Fortis.

Address: Accademia Nazionale dei Lincei, Via della Lungara 10, 00165 Rome.

Telephone: (06) 6838831; **Fax:** (06) 6893616.

Fondazione Luigi Einaudi (Luigi Einaudi Foundation)

Founded in 1964 by the family of Luigi Einaudi, former President of Italy, with the help of local financial institutions and the Italian Government, to train young scholars in economics and political and historical studies, and to maintain a library in the social sciences open to all scholars.

Activities: Maintains the Luigi Einaudi Library, which currently contains more than 230,000 volumes and 2,700 periodicals; awards fellowships and research grants, organizes seminars and conferences, and sponsors publications in the fields of economics, politics and history. Also operates internationally, collaborating with the Colegio de México in Mexico and Cornell University in the USA; carrying out research into the effect of property on agricultural productivity in Europe and Central and South America; as well as developing projects dealing with regional integration, conflict resolution, comparative models of employment and social policy, and contemporary political thought.

Geographical Area of Activity: Mainly Italy.

Publications: *Annali della Fondazione Luigi Einaudi*; *Scrittori italiani di politica, economia e storia* (collection of classics); *Studi* (collection of monographs).

Board of Directors: Prof. Enrico Filippi (Pres.); Prof. Terenzio Cozzi.

Principal Staff: Dr Emanuele Bellavia.

Address: Palazzo d'Azeglio, Via Principe Amedeo 34, 10123 Turin.

Telephone: (011) 835656; **Fax:** (011) 8179093; **Internet:** www.fondazioneeinaudi.it; **e-mail:** segreteria@fondazioneeinaudi.it.

Fondazione Europa Occupazione—Impresa e Solidarietà (Europa Employment Foundation—Enterprise and Solidarity)

Founded in 1995 by the banking foundation, Fondazione Cassa di Risparmio di Roma to promote social enterprise for the improvement of the welfare system.

Activities: Funds and supports social development enterprise projects by making grants, holding seminars and producing publications. Also works to better relations within Europe to increase the opportunities for co-ordinating employment policies in the non-profit sector. Works in collaboration with Compagnia Sviluppo Imprese Sociali S.p.A. (COSIS) to foster the growth and development of social enterprises. Also maintains an office in Brussels.

Geographical Area of Activity: Italy.

Restrictions: Only makes grants within Italy.

Publications: annual report.

Principal Staff: Pres. Stefano Zapponini; Silvana Torquati.

Address: Via Nazionale 39, 00184 Rome.

Telephone: (06) 489291; **Fax:** (06) 4892932; **Internet:** www.feo.it; **e-mail:** fondazionefeo@feo.it.

Fondazione Giangiacomo Feltrinelli (Giangiacomo Feltrinelli Foundation)

The Giangiacomo Feltrinelli Foundation was established in 1949 to collect, preserve and make available to scholars and interested members of the public diverse materials documenting the history of ideas, in particular those related to the development of the international labour and socialist movements.

Activities: The Foundation makes available for consultation library and archival holdings consisting of some 200,000 books, extensive newspaper and periodical collections, and more than 1m. primary source materials. It also promotes scholarly research initiatives, organizes seminars, conferences and exhibitions exploring both historical and contemporary subjects, and produces a range of printed and online publications. A long-term digitization project is underway to enable online access to reproductions of thousands of the most significant materials in the holdings.

Geographical Area of Activity: Italy.

Restrictions: The Foundation is not a grant-making organization.

Publications: *Movimento Operaio; Annali* (annual series featuring original research by international scholars within the fields of modern social history and historiography); *Biblioteca Europea* (collection of anastatic reprints of significant 17th- to 19th-century works); *Quaderni*; catalogues and other library finding aids (both printed and online) to the principal thematic sections and archives; an online eBook collection of hard-to-find texts held at the Foundation.

Board of Directors: Carlo Feltrinelli (Pres.).

Principal Staff: Dir Chiara Daniele.

Address: Via Gian Domenico Romagnosi 3, 20121 Milan.

Telephone: (02) 874175; **Fax:** (02) 86461855; **Internet:** www.fondazionefeltrinelli.it; **e-mail:** segreteria@fondazionefeltrinelli.it.

Fondazione Piera, Pietro e Giovanni Ferrero—ONLUS (Piera, Pietro and Giovanni Ferrero Foundation)

Established in 1983 by Michele Ferrero for the welfare of pensioners of Ferrero companies, and to make grants for cultural activities and medical research.

Activities: Operates nationally, carrying out cultural activities in Alba, including conferences and publications; funding and organizing activities for Ferrero pensioners; and supporting medical research, especially in relation to the aged.

Geographical Area of Activity: Italy.

Publications: *Filodiretto* (magazine); and other publications.

Board of Administration: Maria Franca Ferrero (Pres.); Gian Luigi Viglino (Vice-Pres.).

Principal Staff: Gen. Sec. Mario Strola.

Address: Via Vivaro 49, 12051 Alba.

Telephone: (0173) 295259; **Fax:** (0173) 363274; **Internet:** www .fondazioneferrero.it; **e-mail:** info@fondazioneferrero.it.

Fondazione Edoardo Garrone

Established in 2004 to support and implement new models and instruments of social and cultural management.

Activities: Support and promotion of art and culture; social integration and development; education; sustainable cultural development of the province of Siracusa, Sicily. The foundation is in the process of creating an excellence centre and a school for international studies in tourism economy in Siracusa, Sicily.

Geographical Area of Activity: Italy.

Board of Directors: Riccardo Garrone (Pres.); Carla Garrone Mondini (Vice-Pres.).

Principal Staff: Sec.-Gen. Paolo Corradi.

Address: Via S. Luca 2, 16124 Genova.

Telephone: (010) 868-1530; **Fax:** (010) 868-1539; **Internet:** www.fondazionegarrone.it; **e-mail:** info@fondazionegarrone .it.

Fondazione Internazionale Menarini (Menarini International Foundation)

Founded in 1976 to promote research and knowledge in the fields of biology, pharmacology and medicine but also, though more implicitly, of economic and human sciences.

Activities: Promotes biomedical and economic and human sciences research, primarily through the organization of conferences and symposia. Also produces art and scientific publications.

Geographical Area of Activity: Italy.

Publications: *Minuti Menarini* (monthly journal).

Principal Staff: Pres. Sergio Gorini.

Address: Via W. Tobagi 8, 20068 Peschiera Borromeo, Milan.

Telephone: (02) 55308110; **Internet:** www.fondazione -menarini.it; **e-mail:** milan@fondazione-menarini.it.

Fondazione ISMU—Iniziative e Studi sulla Multietnicità (ISMU Foundation—Initiatives and Studies on Multiethnicity)

Established in 1991; aims to promote internationalism and multiculturalism, particularly within Europe.

Activities: Promotes study and research, especially in the field of immigration issues; holds seminars and produces publications promoting multi-ethnicity; funds training and owns a document archive consisting of national and international informative material.

Geographical Area of Activity: Mainly Europe.

Publications: *ISMU informa* (newsletter); *Multicultural Policies and Modes of Citizenship;* annual report.

Board of Directors: Mariell Enoc (Pres.).

Principal Staff: Sec.-Gen. Vincenzo Cesareo.

Address: Via Copernico 1, 20125 Milan.

Telephone: (02) 6787791; **Fax:** (02) 66877979; **Internet:** www .ismu.org; **e-mail:** ismu@ismu.org.

Fondazione per l'Istituto Svizzero di Roma (Foundation for the Swiss Institute of Rome)

Founded in 1947 to provide an opportunity for young Swiss scholars and artists to pursue their activities in the 'classical' environment of Rome, the Swiss Institute of Rome (ISR) now also organizes regular events in both the artistic and the scholarly field to contribute to the mutual understanding and to deepen further artistic and intellectual relations between Switzerland and Italy. The ISR also has branch offices in Milan and Venice.

Activities: The Swiss Institute operates internationally in the field of the arts and humanities, providing a high-level programme of various activities.

Geographical Area of Activity: International, with a special focus on the Swiss–Italian relations.

Publications: *Bibliotheca Helvetica Romana*; and others.

Finance: Funded by the Swiss Confederation, Pro Helvetia, BSI, Swiss National Foundation, others.

Governing Board: Charles Kleiber (Pres.).

Principal Staff: Dir Prof. Dr Christoph Riedweg; Head of Arts Programme Salvatore Lacagnina; Head of Scholarly Programme Dr Henri de Riedmatten.

Address: Istituto Svizzero di Roma, Via Ludovisi 48, 00187 Rome.

Telephone: (06) 420421; **Fax:** (06) 42042420; **Internet:** www .istitutosvizzero.it; **e-mail:** info@istitutosvizzero.it.

Fondazione Italcementi Cavaliere del Lavoro Carlo Presenti (Italcementi Carlo Presenti Foundation)

Established in 2004 by Italcementi and Italmobiliare, in honour of industrialist Carlo Presenti.

Activities: Promotes education and scientific research, and sustainable economic and social development of enterprises. The Foundation also undertakes humanitarian projects, helping those affected by natural disasters and in similar emergency situations.

Geographical Area of Activity: World-wide.

Board of Directors: Giovanni Giavazzi (Pres.); Giampiero Pesenti (Vice-Pres.).

Address: Via Gabriele Camozzi 124, 24121 Bergamo.

Telephone: (035) 219774; **Fax:** (035) 210509; **Internet:** www .fondazioneitalcementi.it; **e-mail:** info@ fondazioneitalcementi.it.

Fondazione Ing. Carlo M. Lerici—FL (Ing. Carlo M. Lerici Foundation)

Founded in 1947 by Carlo Maurilio Lerici to promote, develop and co-ordinate initiatives and activities concerned with archaeological prospecting both within Italy and abroad. Fondazione Ing. Carlo M. Lerici is a founder member of the European Consortium for Asian Field Study (ECAF).

Activities: Carries out archaeological prospecting campaigns in Italy and abroad, including experimental surveys independently and in collaboration with other institutions. Conducts research for the development of new instruments and of new methods of treatment, interpretation and representation of surveying results. Operates its own archaeological researches and restoration of monuments in Laos, Viet Nam, Myanmar and Brazil.

Geographical Area of Activity: Italy, Asia and South America.

Restrictions: Does not make grants.

Publications: Occasional reports on specific research; *Prospezioni Archeologiche* (in Italian and English); monographic volumes and reviews of geophysical prospectings and archaeology; *Filtering Optimisation and Modelling of Geophysical Given in Archaeological Prospecting.*

Governing Board: Prof. Giulio Ballio (Chair.).

Principal Staff: Dir Mauro Cucarzi.

Address: Politecnico di Milano, Via Vittorio Veneto 108, 00187 Rome.

Telephone: (06) 4880083; **Fax:** (06) 4827085; **Internet:** www .lerici.polimi.it; **e-mail:** folerici@tin.it.

Fondazione Giovanni Lorenzini (Giovanni Lorenzini Foundation)

The Foundation was launched in 1969 as a non-profit scientific organization as per a decree passed by the President of Italy.

Activities: The Foundation consists of two not-for-profit scientific organizations, one based in Milan (established in 1969) and the second in Houston, USA (established in 1984). Both are committed to international scientific exchange and education in basic and medical research. The Foundation aims to transfer the most recent developments and results in experimental science to clinical and applied research to be used for both the single patient and for the community. Activities include the organization of international conferences and courses, and the development of guidelines, position papers, proceedings, highlights, websites and CD-ROMs. The Foundation also promotes public educational campaigns mainly focused on the prevention of CVD and on women's health.

Geographical Area of Activity: International.

Publications: Proceedings; position papers; websites: e-newsletters.

Principal Staff: Pres. Rodolfo Paoletti; Vice-Pres. Andrea Peracino; Sec.-Gen. Emanuela Folco.

Address: Via Andrea Appiani 7, 20121 Milan.

Telephone: (02) 29006267; **Fax:** (02) 29007018; **Internet:** www.lorenzinifoundation.org; **e-mail:** info@lorenzinifoundation.org.

Fondazione Salvatore Maugeri—Clinica del Lavoro e della Riabilitazione (Salvatore Maugeri Foundation—Occupational Health and Rehabilitation Clinic)

Founded in 1965 by Prof. Salvatore Maugeri for health assistance and medical research in occupational health.

Activities: Supports clinics and institutes of occupational medicine, which carry out research of international significance in the field of occupational diseases. Support is also given to five medical centres for cardio-respiratory and neurological rehabilitation.

Geographical Area of Activity: Italy.

Administrative Council: Prof. Umberto Maugeri (Pres.); Erasmo Pierro (Vice-Pres.).

Principal Staff: Sec. Costantino Passerino.

Address: Via Salvatore Maugeri 4, 27100 Pavia.

Telephone: (0382) 592504; **Fax:** (0382) 592576; **Internet:** www.fsm.it; **e-mail:** segreteria.scientifica@fsm.it.

Fondazione Nazionale Carlo Collodi (Carlo Collodi National Foundation)

Founded in 1952 for the diffusion of the works of Carlo Lorenzini (Collodi), particularly 'The Adventures of Pinocchio'; for the collection and exhibition of national and international publications regarding Carlo Collodi and his works; for the promotion of children's literature and establishment of a centre for the study of children's literature; and for the conservation and enlargement of the Monumental Park of Pinocchio in the village of Collodi.

Activities: Operates nationally through self-conducted programmes and grants to individuals, and nationally and internationally through conferences, courses, publications and lectures. Maintains a library of works by Collodi, including translations; the Monumental Park of Pinocchio; and the International Study Centre for Young People's Literature. Awards the Rolando Anzilotti prize for a critical or historical monograph on children's or young people's literature.

Geographical Area of Activity: World-wide.

Publications: *Quaderni della Fondazione Nazionale Carlo Collodi.*

Trustees: Vincenzo Cappelletti (Chair.).

Principal Staff: Man. Daniele Narducci.

Address: Villa Arcangeli, Via Pasquinelli 6/8, 51014 Collodi.

Telephone: (057) 2429613; **Fax:** (057) 2429614; **Internet:** www.pinocchio.it/fondazionecollodi; **e-mail:** fondazione@pinocchio.it.

Fondazione Adriano Olivetti (Adriano Olivetti Foundation)

Founded in 1962 by Maria Luisa Lizier Galardi, Dino Olivetti, Magda Olivetti Jaksic, Roberto Olivetti and Silvia Olivetti Marxer. Promote, develops and co-ordinates research on: constitutional and federalist studies; the international organization of economic structures; city planning; local government; labour problems; the sociology of co-operation; cultural services and social work; and studies aimed at increasing knowledge of the conditions that affect social progress.

Activities: Operates nationally and internationally, through self-conducted programmes, grants, research and publicationsmprove the social and cultural basis of the community, through offering support in four main areas: Institutional and Public Policies; Processes of Economic and Social Development; Cultural and Social Policies; and Art, Architecture and Urban Studies.

Geographical Area of Activity: Europe and USA.

Publications: *Esiste un Diritto di Ingerenza? L'Europa di fronte alla guerra; Mol013tepliCittà;* archive; annual report; and numerous other publications.

Board of Directors: Laura Olivetti (Pres.); Davide Olivetti (Vice-Pres.).

Principal Staff: Gen. Sec. Melina Decaro.

Address: Via Guiseppe Zanardelli 34, 00186 Rome.

Telephone: (06) 6877054; **Fax:** (06) 6896193; **Internet:** www.fondazioneadrianolivetti.it; **e-mail:** info@fondazioneadrianolivetti.it.

Fondazione Giulio Pastore—FGP (Giulio Pastore Foundation)

Founded in 1971 by the Associazioni Cristiane Lavoratori Italiani, Confederazione Italiana Sindacati dei Lavoratori, Democrazia Cristiana, Prof. Mario Romani, Prof. Vincenzo Saba, Vincenzo Scotti, Don Pierfranco Pastore and Idolo Marcone to promote research and study concerning the problems of labour and the trade union experience of workers, both as a single relevant discipline and in interdisciplinary terms; and to promote the diffusion and application of the results.

Activities: Operates in the fields of education, social welfare and studies, and economic affairs, nationally through self-conducted programmes, and nationally and internationally through research, grants to individuals, fellowships, scholarships, conferences, courses, publications and lectures.

Geographical Area of Activity: World-wide.

Publications: *Annali* (annual report of operations); yearbooks; *Lavoro e Sindacato* (6 a year); *Quaderni della Fondazione Giulio Pastore 01; Quaderni della Fondazione Giulio Pastore 02; Quaderni della Fondazione Giulio Pastore 03; Quaderni della Fondazione Giulio Pastore 04; Quaderni della Fondazione Giulio Pastore 05.*

Board of Directors: Prof. Michele Colasanto (Pres.).

Principal Staff: Sec.-Gen. Prof. Gustavo De Santis.

Address: Via del Viminale 43, 00184 Rome.

Telephone: (06) 48905258; **Fax:** (06) 48906642; **Internet:** www.fondazionepastore.it; **e-mail:** info@fondazionepastore.it.

Fondazione Alessio Pezcoller (Alessio Pezcoller Foundation)

Founded in 1980 by Prof. Alessio Pezcoller to promote biomedical research.

Activities: The Foundation operates nationally and internationally in the field of medicine and health, by awarding prizes: the Pezcoller Foundation-AACR International Award for Cancer Research, worth €75,000 and presented annually to a scientist who has made a major scientific discovery in the field of cancer, and the Pezcoller Foundation-ECCO Recognition for Contribution to Oncology, worth €30,000 and presented biennially to an individual for his or her unique contribution to oncology, and for dedication of his or her professional life to cancer. The Foundation organizes an annual symposium promoting interaction between international scientists working in basic oncological sciences, and a series of educational meetings for local medical doctors.

Geographical Area of Activity: International.

Restrictions: No grants to individuals.

Publications: *The Pezcoller Foundation Journal* (2 a year).

Trustee: Davide Bassi (Pres.); Gios Bernardi (Hon. Pres.).

Principal Staff: Secretariat Admin. Giorgio Pederzolli.

Address: Via Dordi 8, 38100 Trento.

Telephone: (0461) 980250; **Fax:** (0461) 980350; **Internet:** www.pezcoller.it; **e-mail:** pezcoller@pezcoller.it.

Fondazione Prada (Prada Foundation)

Established in 1993 by Miuccia Prada and Patrizio Bertelli.

Activities: Curates exhibitions and organizes cultural symposia; also produces visual art exhibitions. Holds a collection of catalogues, monographs and artists' books.

Geographical Area of Activity: Italy and Europe.

Board of Trustees: Miuccia Prada, Patrizio Bertelli (co-Pres).

Principal Staff: Artistic Dir Germano Celant.

Address: Largo Isarco 2, 20139 Milan.

Telephone: (02) 535709200; **Fax:** (02) 535709213; **Internet:** www.fondazioneprada.org; **e-mail:** info@fondazioneprada.org.

Fondazione Querini Stampalia (Querini Stampalia Foundation)

Founded in May 1869 by Count Giovanni Querini to support university studies in Venice and Padua, and to promote the diffusion of culture through library and museum services, and cultural activities, particularly in and around Venice.

Activities: Operates in the field of the arts and humanities, through seminars and conferences, training courses, concerts and publications. Maintains a library of 300,000 volumes and a museum.

Geographical Area of Activity: Italy.

Publications: Numerous historical and cultural publications.

Trustees: Marino Cortese (Pres.); Antonio Foscari (Vice-Pres.).

Principal Staff: Dir Marigusta Lazzari.

Address: Santa Maria Formosa, Castello 5252, 30122 Venice.

Telephone: (041) 2711411; **Fax:** (041) 2711445; **Internet:** www.querinistampalia.it; **e-mail:** fondazione@querinistampalia.org.

Fondazione Ricci Onlus (Ricci Onlus Foundation)

Established in 1990 by da Giovanni Mario Ricci, a non-profit corporation aiming to promote initiatives of a social and humanitarian nature, and to encourage the restoration and protection of the environmental, cultural and historical heritage of the middle and upper valley of the Serchio river.

Activities: Operates in di Lucca province in the areas of the arts and humanities, and conservation and the environment, through self-conducted programmes, conferences and publications. Aims to acquire an art collection to exhibit to the public.

Geographical Area of Activity: Italia.

Publications: Mino Maccari *I Selvaggi della Lucchesia: Mino Maccari a Barga* (2000); G. Siccardi *OmaggioUNO Giovanni Pascoli* (2001); *John Bellany Nella Valle del Serchio: a new provence* (2002); Angelo Roberto Fiori *Phatosformel* (2003); Nicholas Swietlan Kraczyna *40 anni di Icaro 1962–2002* (2003); *Cesare Puccinelli* (2004); Antonio Possenti *Lo zoo dell'anima. Gli animali Nella poesia di Giovanni Pascoli* (2005); *Adolfo Balduini nel Novecento Toscano* (2006); *Il Sentimento della natura nell'opera di Alfredo Meschi* (2008); L'Armonia della terra. Immagini della Valle del Serchio nella pittura toscana del Novecento (2010); *Barga cartolina* a cura di Antonio Nardini (2003); *Le ricette di Marilena. I sapori della Garfagnana* di Marilena Bonugli (2004); *Garfagnana. Vita nelle Valli incantate* di

Giancarlo Cerri (2005); *Briciole Fra e ricordi* di Tedice Santini (2006); *Venti ricette di una cucina povera, anzi poverissima* di Tista Meschi (2009); *Inventario Storico risorgimentale Antonio Mordini* (2009).

Administrative Council: Ettore Ricci (Pres.); Dr Rolando Notini (Vice-Pres.); Daniela Papi, Antonio Ricci (co-Treas).

Principal Staff: Dir Cristiana Ricci.

Address: Via Roma 20, 55051 Barga, Lucca.

Telephone: (0583) 724357; **Fax:** (0583) 724921; **Internet:** www.fondazionericcionlus.it; **e-mail:** fondricci@iol.it.

Fondazione Roma (Rome Foundation)

The Foundation is the perpetuation of the Cassa di Risparmio di Roma, established in 1836; aims to provide social benefit and to promote economic development in the fields of health, fine arts and cultural heritage, education, scientific research, aid to the underprivileged, and also to support activities in the voluntary service sector.

Activities: The Foundation operates its own programmes and co-operates on initiatives proposed by non-profit organizations in the areas of health, fine arts and cultural heritage, education, scientific research, and aid to the underprivileged. Funds hospitals and health centres, operates an exhibition space and has established a youth orchestra, supports a Master's Course in International Studies on Philanthropy, sponsors the Centre for the Dissemination of the Results of Agricultural Research—CEDRA, and operates through the Fondazione Italiana per il Volontariato, operative since 1991, and the Fondazione Europa Occupazione: Impresa e Solidarietà established in 1995. The former promotes, encourages and supports voluntary service, and the latter fosters occupational opportunities, through training activities for young people, the disabled and the socially disadvantaged.

Geographical Area of Activity: Italy, with focus on the province of Rome and the region of Lazio.

Restrictions: No funding for profit-making organizations, individuals and enterprises.

Publications: *NOTIZIARIO*; financial statement; newsletter.

Board of Directors: Prof. Emmanuele Francesco Maria Emanuele (Chair.); Serafino Gatti (Vice-Chair.).

Principal Staff: CEO Franco Parasassi.

Address: Palazzo Sciarra, Via M. Minghetti 17, 00187 Rome.

Telephone: (06) 6976450; **Fax:** (06) 697645300; **Internet:** www.fondazioneroma.it; **e-mail:** info@fondazioneroma.it.

Fondazione Roma-Mediterraneo

Established in 2008 by Fondazione Roma (q.v.) for the encouragement of economic, cultural and social development in the Mediterranean region; and to help establish a network of cultural relationships between Mediterranean countries.

Activities: Operates in the areas of economic and social development, culture and the arts, and education.

Board of Trustees: Prof. Emmanuele Francesco Maria Emanuele (Pres.); Ercole Pietro Pellicano (Vice-Pres.).

Principal Staff: Contact Carla Capocasale.

Address: Via Marco Minghetti 17, 00187 Rome.

Telephone: (06) 697645117; **Fax:** (06) 697645301; **Internet:** www.fondazioneroma-mediterraneo.it.

Fondazione Romaeuropa (Romaeuropa Foundation)

Founded in February 1990 to promote the arts between European countries.

Activities: Non-profit organization that administers and promotes the Romaeuropa Festival for contemporary culture.

Geographical Area of Activity: Italy.

Board of Directors: Giovanni Pieraccini (Hon. Pres.); Monique Veaute (Pres.).

Principal Staff: Gen. and Artistic Dir Fabrizio Grifasi.

Address: Via dei Magazzini Generali 20/A, 00187 Rome.

Telephone: (06) 422961; **Fax:** (06) 48904030; **Internet:** www
.romaeuropa.net; **e-mail:** comunicazione@romaeuropa.net.

Fondazione RUI (RUI Foundation)

Founded in 1959 by university teachers, professional workers
and parents concerned with studying and resolving problems
facing young people. The Foundation's activities are aimed at
promoting the further training of university students and
intellectuals, and promoting cultural activities for youth;
awarding scholarships to Italian and foreign students, and
acclimatizing the latter to the Italian way of life; and collaborating with national and international organizations to these
ends.

Activities: Operates nationally in the field of the arts and
humanities, and nationally and internationally in the fields of
education, social welfare and studies. Also active in the fields
of international relations and aid to less-developed countries.
Programmes are carried out internationally through self-conducted projects, and nationally and internationally through
research, fellowships and scholarships, conferences, courses,
publications and lectures. Also maintains an office in Milan.

Geographical Area of Activity: Europe.

Publications: *Fondazione Rui* (magazine); *Universitas* (magazine); guides on higher education in Italy.

Principal Staff: Pres. Prof. Cristiano Ciappei; Dir Dott.
Alfredo Razzano.

Address: Via Domenichino 16, 20149 Milan.

Telephone: (02) 48010813; **Fax:** (02) 4819286; **Internet:** www
.fondazionerui.it; **e-mail:** sede.milano@fondazionerui.it.

Fondazione di Studi di Storia dell'Arte 'Roberto Longhi' (Roberto Longhi Foundation for the Study of the History of Art)

Founded in 1971 by Prof. Roberto Longhi to promote and
develop, with suitable scientific principles and critical severity, the study of the history of art among young Italian and foreign students.

Activities: Operates internationally in the field of the arts
and humanities, through research and study courses. A number of grants, fellowships and prizes are available to both Italian and non-Italian students studying at the Foundation's own
institute. The Foundation maintains a library of 35,000 art
publications and 60,000 photographs of Italian art, and also a
collection of pictures of some 200 important artists.

Geographical Area of Activity: International.

Publications: *Proporzioni* (art magazine); *Annali della Fondazione Roberto Longhi* (art magazine); catalogues.

Board of Trustees: Mina Gregori (Pres.).

Principal Staff: Dir Maria Cristina Bandera.

Address: Via Benedetto Fortini 30, 50125 Florence.

Telephone: (055) 6580794; **Fax:** (055) 6580794; **Internet:**
www.fondazionelonghi.it; **e-mail:** longhi@fondazionelonghi
.it.

Fondazione Umana Mente (Umana Mente Foundation)

Established in September 2001 by Allianz Group S.p.A. to support disadvantaged people.

Activities: The Foundation's mission is to provide valid and
effective solutions for people with social and behavioural problems. Activities are mainly focused on children with social
and behavioural problems or people affected by congenital
mental disabilities, by supporting and financing projects promoted by non-profit organizations throughout Italy. The Foundation offers financial and managerial support to non-profit
organizations through a structured operating model based on
an evaluation process and continuous monitoring of supported
projects.

Geographical Area of Activity: Italy.

Publications: *Polinrete: Il lavoro in rete tra servizi per persone
disabili* (2007); *Sestante: un'esperienza di counselling per il benessere dei minori*; *Attivare risorse nelle periferie: Guida alla
promozione di interventi nei quartieri difficili di alcune città italiane* (2009).

Trustees: Maurizio Devescovi (Pres.); Paola di Lieto (Vice-Pres.).

Principal Staff: Gen. Sec. Nicola Corti.

Address: Corso Italia 23, 20122 Milan.

Telephone: (02) 72162669; **Fax:** (02) 72162793; **Internet:** www
.umana-mente.it; **e-mail:** info@umana-mente.it.

Fondazione Unipolis

Established in 2007 by Unipol Gruppo Financiario.

Activities: Operates through grants to non-profit organizations in the areas of the arts and culture, social welfare and
research.

Principal Staff: Man. Dir Walter Dondi.

Address: Via Marconi 1, 40122 Bologna.

Telephone: (051) 6437601; **Fax:** 051 6437600; **Internet:** www
.fondazioneunipolis.org; **e-mail:** info@fondazioneunipolis
.org.

Fondazione di Venezia (Venice Foundation)

Established in 1992 by the Cassa di Risparmio di Venezia.

Activities: Active in the areas of education, training, scientific research, conservation and culture, through its own programmes and projects, direct grants and co-operation with
other organizations.

Geographical Area of Activity: Mainly Venice, Italy.

Publications: Annual Report; conference reports.

Finance: Total assets €417,382,049 (Dec. 2008).

Board of Trustees: Prof. Giuliano Segre (Pres.); Prof. Cesare
Mirabelli (Vice-Pres.).

Principal Staff: Dir Massimo Lanza; Deputy Dir Fabio
Achilli.

Address: Dorsoduro 3488/U, 30123 Venice.

Telephone: (041) 2201211; **Fax:** (041) 2201219; **Internet:** www
.fondazionedivenezia.org; **e-mail:** segretaria@
fondazionedivenezia.org.

Fondo per l'Ambiente Italiano—FAI (Fund for the Italian Environment)

Founded in 1975 to increase awareness of environmental protection and the preservation of Italy's cultural heritage.

Activities: Operates nationally, acquiring historically, culturally or environmentally valuable sites and opening them to
the public, and also running educational conferences and exhibitions.

Geographical Area of Activity: Italy.

Publications: Annual Report.

Board of Directors: Giulia Maria Mozzoni Crespi (Hon.
Pres.); Ilaria Borletti Buitoni (Pres.); Paolo Baratta, Guido
Roberto Vitale (Vice-Pres.).

Principal Staff: Dir-Gen. Angelo Maramai.

Address: Viale Coni Zugna 5, 20144 Milan.

Telephone: (02) 4676151; **Fax:** (02) 48193631; **Internet:** www
.fondoambiente.it; **e-mail:** internet@fondoambiente.it.

Institute for Scientific Interchange Foundation—ISI

Aims to provide an accessible scientific environment, while
also funding research to perpetuate scientific discovery.

Activities: Operates internationally in the field of science and
technology, through funding scientific programmes, and
recruiting scientists to lecture and carry out research to
encourage and support science. Proposals for research projects are considered by a Science Board within the Foundation,
and carried out by research co-ordinators from more than 15
countries at the Institute's premises in Turin. Also administers European Union-funded activities.

Geographical Area of Activity: International.

Board of Trustees: Mario Rasetti (Pres.).

Principal Staff: Exec. Dir Tiziana Bertoletti.

Address: Viale S. Severo 65, 10133 Turin.

Telephone: (011) 6603090; **Fax:** (011) 6600049; **Internet:** www.isi.it; **e-mail:** isi@isi.it.

International Balzan Foundation—Prize

Founded in 1956 by Angela Lina Balzan to honour the memory of her father, Eugenio Balzan, a famous Italian journalist, who died in 1953. The Foundation acts jointly through two foundations, the International Balzan Foundation-Fund under Swiss jurisdiction, and the International Balzan Foundation-Prize under Italian jurisdiction.

Activities: The International Balzan Foundation—Prize awards the Balzan Prizes. Four prizes are awarded annually: two within the humanities, and two within the sciences on subjects chosen each year. The 2012 prizes are worth 750,000 Swiss francs each and one-half of this amount must be reserved by the winner for research projects preferably involving young scholars and scientists. In 2011 prizes were awarded in the areas of Enlightenment Studies, Ancient History (The Graeco-Roman World), Theoretical Biology or Bioinformatics and The Early Universe (From the Planck Time to the First Galaxies). In addition, a Prize for Humanity, Peace and Brotherhood among Peoples is awarded at intervals of not less than three years. The General Prize Committee, responsible for the selection of the candidates, is made up of about 20 European academics and scientists. The candidates are submitted by universities and learned societies from all over the world, following an invitation by the Chairman of the Balzan General Prize Committee to presidents of academies and universities, and other similar institutions to submit nominations for the awards.

Geographical Area of Activity: World-wide.

Restrictions: Personal applications not accepted.

Publications:
Balzan Prizes (information on the Prizewinners and the Foundation, annually, in English, French, German and Italian); *Balzan Prizes Interdisciplinary Forum* (includes Prizewinners' research projects, annually); *The Annual Balzan Lecture* (annual); *The Balzan Prizewinners' Research Projects: An Overview* (2 a year) .

Board: Bruno Bottai (Chair.); Carlo Fontana (Vice-Chair.).

Principal Staff: Sec.-Gen. Suzanne Werder.

Address: Piazzetta Umberto Giordano 4, 20122 Milan.

Telephone: (02) 76002212; **Fax:** (02) 76009457; **Internet:** www.balzan.org; **e-mail:** balzan@balzan.it.

International Development Law Organization—IDLO (Organisation internationale de droit du développement—OIDD)

Founded in 1983 by L. Michael Hager, Gilles Blanchi and William Loris to improve the deployment of legal resources in the development process and the negotiating capability of developing countries.

Activities: IDLO trains development lawyers, mostly from developing and transitioning countries. It provides practical training for mid-career legal advisers in government ministries, government organizations, banks, private companies and law firms. The Organization runs three programmes at its Rome headquarters: a 10-week Development Lawyers' Course (DLC), two-week International Business Transactions (IBT) Seminars, the five-week Enterprise and Investment Lawyers' Course (EILC), and the three-week Public International Trade Law Course (PITLC) on a regional basis—all courses are conducted in English and French. The DLC focuses on development lawyer skills (advising, planning, negotiating, drafting, monitoring performance and resolving disputes) in the context of project financing, international contracting and foreign investment. IBT seminars address specialized legal topics related to economic development. The EILC is intended for lawyers who act as advisers in the economic reform process. In addition, IDLO organizes in-country training workshops on special request. IDLO's members are the governments of 17 countries in Africa, Europe, Asia, Australasia and the USA.

Geographical Area of Activity: International.

Publications: annual report.

Finance: Governments, multilateral development organizations, foundations and private companies contribute towards IDLO's budget, programme and fellowship requirements. Total assets €14,781,575; annual income €11,133,628, expenditure €14,600,222 (2010).

Board of Advisers: Prof. Alfredo F. Tadiar (Chair.); Prof. Jan Michiel Otto (Deputy Chair.).

Principal Staff: Dir-Gen. Irene Khan.

Address: Viale Vaticano 106, 00165 Rome.

Telephone: (06) 40403200; **Fax:** (06) 40403232; **Internet:** www.idlo.int; **e-mail:** idlo@idlo.int.

International Fund for Agricultural Development—IFAD

Founded in 1977, a specialized agency of the UN, to improve food production in developed countries and to assist developing countries in establishing productive farming methods and better standards of nutrition.

Activities: IFAD works with poor rural people to enable them to grow and sell more food, increase their incomes and determine the direction of their own lives. More than US $1,000m. has been invested since 1978 in grants and low-interest loans to developing countries. Operates as a partnership of 165 member countries.

Geographical Area of Activity: Asia, Central and South America and the Caribbean, the Middle East and North Africa, and Sub-Saharan Africa.

Publications: *Governing Council Report* (annually, in Arabic, English, French and Spanish); *IFAD Annual Report* (in Arabic, English, French and Spanish); also publishes books, electronic newsletters and thematic publications.

Finance: Total assets US $7,801,075,000; annual revenue $409,168,000, expenditure $514,300,000 (2009).

Principal Staff: Pres. Kanayo F. Nwanze.

Address: Via Paolo di Dono 44, 00142 Rome.

Telephone: (06) 54591; **Fax:** (06) 5043463; **Internet:** www.ifad.org; **e-mail:** ifad@ifad.org.

Istituto Affari Internazionali—IAI (Institute of International Affairs)

Founded in 1965 by Altiero Spinelli to promote the study of international relations, in particular Europe's position in world affairs.

Activities: Promotes research, often in collaboration with research institutes of other countries, and belongs to a number of international networks of research centres. Organizes national and international conferences in international relations. The Institute's main fields of interest are: Italian integration and international competition; the evolution of European integration and European policy; new issues in the security and defence field; transatlantic relations; international relations (particularly with the countries on the southern shore of the Mediterranean); and relations between Europe and Asia. The Institute has an extensive library containing more than 25,000 publications in book and periodical form, in the major European languages, on international relations, especially of a politico-cultural nature.

Geographical Area of Activity: International.

Publications: *The International Spectator* (quarterly English language review); *IAI Quaderni* (series, irregular); *La politica estera dell'Italia* (yearbook); *AffarInternazionali* (webzine); numerous books and pamphlets, some in collaboration with other publishers.

Board of Trustees: Cesare Merlini (Pres.); Carlo Azeglio Ciampi (Hon. Pres.).

Principal Staff: Pres. Stefano Silvestri; Dir Ettore Greco; Deputy Dir Nathalie Tocci.

Address: Via Angelo Brunetti 9, 00186 Rome.

Telephone: (06) 3224360; **Fax:** (06) 3224363; **Internet:** www .iai.it; **e-mail:** iai@iai.it.

Istituto Auxologico Italiano (Italian Institute for Auxology)

Founded in 1963 as a scientific institute for biomedical research focusing on the treatment of diseases that undermine physical and psychological development. The scope of the Institute has broadened since, to encompass prevention, treatment and rehabilitation of endocrine, metabolic and cardiovascular diseases. In 1972 it was recognized by the Ministries of Health and for Universities and Scientific and Technological Research as a Scientific Institute for Research and Care.

Activities: Operates in the area of medicine and health, and in particular endocrinology and metabolism, cardiovascular disease and neuroscience. The Institute operates in three health-care centres: the Istituto Scientifico San Michele (Milan), the Istituto Scientifico San Luca (Milan) and the Istituto Scientifico San Giuseppe (Verbania); these centres care for approx. 165,000 patients each year. The diagnostic and clinical activities of the Institute are supported by the continuous research activity of several experimental laboratories.

Geographical Area of Activity: Mainly Italy.

Publications: Report of operations; *Acta Medica Auxologica* (scientific review).

Principal Staff: Pres. Prof. Giovanni Ancarani; Dir-Gen. Mario Colombo; Scientific Dir Prof. Alberto Zanchetti.

Address: Via Ariosto 13, 20145 Milan.

Telephone: (02) 582111; **Fax:** (02) 58211480; **Internet:** www .auxologico.it; **e-mail:** info@auxologico.it.

Istituto Carlo Cattaneo (Carlo Cattaneo Institute)

Founded in 1965 by a group of academic scientific publishers, the Foundation was granted foundation status in 1986. Aims to promote democratic values through the dissemination of research findings on politics and social science.

Activities: Conducts research, studies and activities relating to culture and education, particularly in the fields of social and political science. Spreads knowledge of Italian society, especially regarding its political system.

Geographical Area of Activity: Italy.

Publications: *Polis. Ricerche e studi su società e politica in Italia* (journal); *Politica in Italia/Italian Politics* (annually); *Ricerche e studi dell-Istituto Cattaneo; Stranieri in Italia; Elezioni, Governi, democrazia;Cultura in Italia; Misure e Materiali di Ricerca dell'Istituto Cattaneo;* papers.

Board of Directors: Elisabetta Gualmini (Pres.).

Principal Staff: Sec.-Gen. Andrea Cerino.

Address: Via Santo Stefano 11, 40125 Bologna.

Telephone: (051) 239766; **Fax:** (051) 262959; **Internet:** www .cattaneo.org; **e-mail:** istitutocattaneo@cattaneo.org.

Istituto di Ricerche Farmacologiche Mario Negri (Mario Negri Pharmacological Research Institute)

Founded in April 1961 by Mario Negri to promote technical and scientific research in pharmacology and in the biomedical sciences, and prevent and cure human and animal diseases.

Activities: Operates nationally and internationally in the fields of education, science and medicine, through self-conducted biomedical research programmes, research fellowships, scholarships, conferences, courses, publications and lectures. Research institutes are situated also in Bergamo and in Ranica (Bergamo) and Santa Maria Imbaro (Chieti), and the friends of the Institute have established the Mario Negri Institute Foundation in New York.

Geographical Area of Activity: International.

Restrictions: The Institute does not apply for patents.

Publications: *Negri News* (monthly); *Research and Practice* (6 a year); scientific reports; books; journals; annual list of publications.

Board of Directors: Franco Russo (Hon. Chair.); Dr Paolo Martelli (Chair.); Dr Mario Russo (Deputy Chair.); Dr Federico Guasti (Sec.).

Principal Staff: Dir Prof. Silvio Garattini.

Address: Via Giuseppe La Masa 19, 20156 Milan.

Telephone: (02) 390141; **Fax:** (02) 3546277; **Internet:** www .marionegri.it; **e-mail:** mnegri@marionegri.it.

Istituto Luigi Sturzo (Luigi Sturzo Institute)

Founded in 1951 by a committee in honour of Luigi Sturzo to promote the social sciences, in particular sociology, in Italy and abroad.

Activities: Operates in the fields of history and the social sciences, through research, conferences and discussions, scholarships and publications. Prizes are awarded to Italian and foreign scholars. Also maintains a library.

Publications: *Sociologia* (3 a year); scientific studies.

Board of Directors: Roberto Mazzotta (Pres.); Andrea Bixio (Vice-Pres.).

Principal Staff: Sec.-Gen. Flavia Piccoli Nardelli.

Address: Palazzo Baldassini, Via delle Coppelle 35, 00186 Rome.

Telephone: (06) 6840421; **Fax:** (06) 68404244; **Internet:** www .sturzo.it; **e-mail:** segretariogenerale@sturzo.it.

Lama Gangchen World Peace Foundation

Founded in 1992 by TYS Lama Gangchen to develop a culture of peace, through non-formal education and funding projects in support of UN Humanitarian programmes. NGO with Special UN Economic and Social Council (ECOSOC) status.

Activities: Works on international humanitarian projects and promotes world peace in the fields of the arts and humanities, conservation and the environment, non-formal education, and medicine and health, and provides aid to less-developed countries. Also operates cultural exchanges and promotes inter-religious dialogue.

Geographical Area of Activity: Europe, Asia and South America.

Restrictions: Grants only to specific organizations.

Publications: *Peace Times Quarterly*; books.

Principal Staff: CEO and UN Representative Isthar D. Adler.

Address: Via Zara 20, Albagnano di Bèe.

Telephone: (335) 6140584; **Fax:** (0323) 569608; **Internet:** www.lgpt.net; **e-mail:** lgwpf@lgpt.net.

Mani Tese (Stretched Hands)

Founded in 1964 with the aim of awakening the Italian public to the problems of developing countries and financing development projects.

Activities: Operates self-conducted programmes, in conjunction with local partners in the areas of education, agriculture, infrastructure development, humanitarian aid and preventive health programmes, as well as organizing training courses in development studies; lobbies and campaigns on related issues, organizes conferences; maintains a reference library of 20,000 publications.

Geographical Area of Activity: Africa, Asia, and Central and South America.

Publications: *Mani Tese* (monthly newspaper); books, educational materials, audiovisual aids, pamphlets and brochures.

Finance: Financed by its local groups and members, the operation of two co-operatives, the European Commission, the Italian Ministry of Foreign Affairs and several city councils.

Principal Staff: Pres. Luigi Idili; Co-ordinator Angela Comelli.

Address: Piazza Gambara 7–9, 20146 Milan.

Telephone: (02) 4075165; **Fax:** (02) 4046890; **Internet:** www .manitese.it; **e-mail:** manitese@manitese.it.

SID—Society for International Development

Established in 1957, a global network of individuals and institutions concerned with development that is participative, pluralistic and sustainable.

Activities: The Society comprises approximately 3,000 individual members, 65 local chapters and 55 institutional members, as well as more than 100 partner institutions from a variety of fields, in more than 125 countries. Its purpose is to support development innovation at all levels; to encourage and facilitate the creation of a sense of community among individuals and organizations committed to social justice at local, national, regional and international levels; and to promote dialogue, understanding and co-operation for social and economic development that furthers the well-being of all peoples. Activities focus on five areas: sustainable livelihoods; democratic approaches to national governance; women's empowerment; international relations and global governance; and strengthening civil society in post-conflict situations. Projects are implemented at global, national and local level, and include networking and advocacy, cross-sectorial dialogues, research, publications and online debates. Also maintains an office in Nairobi, Kenya.

Geographical Area of Activity: International.

Publications: Annual Report; *Development* (quarterly journal); *Bridges* (newsletter, 6 a year); programme reports and other publications.

Governing Council: Jan Pronk (Pres.); Juma Volter Mwapachu (Vice-Pres.); Jacqueline Pitanguy (Vice-Pres.); Stephen F. Moseley (Treas.).

Principal Staff: Man. Dir Stefano Prato.

Address: Via Panisperna 207, 00184 Rome.

Telephone: (06) 4872172; **Fax:** (06) 4872170; **Internet:** www.sidint.org; **e-mail:** info@sidint.org.

Svenska Institutet i Rom/Istituto Svedese di Studi Classici a Roma (Swedish Institute in Rome)

Founded in 1926 by Crown Prince Gustaf Adolf and others to further, within the framework of Swedish cultural activity, the knowledge of classical culture in the Mediterranean area; to act as a medium for Swedish humanist research and education primarily in the field of classical antiquity and history of art and architecture.

Activities: Operates internationally in the fields of education and the arts and humanities, through research, fellowships, scholarships, conferences, courses, publications and lectures.

Geographical Area of Activity: International.

Publications: *Skrifter utgivna av Svenska Institutet i Rom*; *Opuscula: Annual of the Swedish Institutes at Athens and Rome*; *Suecoromana: Studia artis historiae Instituti Romani Regni Sueciae.*

Principal Staff: Dir Prof. Barbro Santillo Frizell.

Address: Via Omero 14, Valle Giulia, 00197 Rome.

Telephone: (06) 3201596; **Fax:** (06) 3230265; **Internet:** www.isvroma.it; **e-mail:** info@isvroma.org.

UniCredit Foundation—Unidea

Established in 2003 by UniCredito Italiano to operate in the areas of development and co-operation through humanitarian intervention.

Activities: Operates in less-developed countries and in countries of Central and South-Eastern Europe that need to develop to join the European Union, in the fields of medicine and health, education, and conservation and the environment, through the creation and management of projects.

Geographical Area of Activity: Developing countries and Central and South-Eastern Europe.

Board of Directors: Maurizio Carrara (Chair.); Maria Antonella Massari, Paolo Cornetta (Deputy Chair.).

Address: Via San Protaso 3, 20121 Milan.

Telephone: (02) 88623071; **Fax:** (02) 88623937; **Internet:** www.unicreditfoundation.org; **e-mail:** info@unicreditfoundation.org.

Jamaica

FOUNDATIONS, TRUSTS AND NON-PROFIT ORGANIZATIONS

Environmental Foundation of Jamaica

Established in 1993 under a formal agreement between the Governments of Jamaica and the USA as an independent foundation. Uses the proceeds from a debt-swap arrangement to promote sustainable development in Jamaica.

Activities: Aims to promote, support and implement activities designed to conserve the natural resources and the environment of Jamaica and fosters the well-being of the country's children, through funding projects that address issues of the environment and child welfare and development.

Geographical Area of Activity: Jamaica.

Publications: Annual Report; public lecture booklets (annually); brochures.

Board of Directors: Prof. Dale Webber (Chair.); Albert Walker (Treas.).

Principal Staff: Chief Exec. Karen McDonald Gayle; Finance Man. Barrington Lewis; Exec. Sec. Sydonnie Rothery.

Address: 1B Norwood Ave, Kingston 5.

Telephone: 960-6744; **Fax:** 920-8999; **Internet:** www.efj.org .jm; **e-mail:** srothery@efj.org.jm; kmcdonaldgayle@efj.org .jm.

Japan

FOUNDATION CENTRES AND CO-ORDINATING BODIES

JANIC—Japanese NGO Center for International Co-operation

A non-profit, non-partisan networking NGO established in 1987 to foster closer relations among Japanese NGOs working in international co-operation; to provide services for the development of NGOs; to encourage networking between domestic and international NGOs and related organizations; to encourage dialogue between NGOs and other sectors of society; to deepen Japanese public understanding of and support for the activities of NGOs; and to conduct research on NGOs and international co-operation.

Activities: Runs courses and training programmes; carries out research; hosts meetings; offers advisory services; conducts lobbying and networking activities aimed at Japanese Government and business; promotes educational activities, including the 'Global Citizenship Education Caravan' held throughout Japan; and issues publications. Maintains a library and database on NGOs. In 2011 there were 96 member organizations.

Geographical Area of Activity: Japan.

Restrictions: Does not make grants.

Publications: *Directory of Japanese NGOs Concerned with International Co-operation*; *NGO Correspondence: Global Citizens* (newsletter in Japanese, 10 a year); *Kokoro* (quarterly newsletter, in English); *Directory of Non-governmental Organizations in Japan 1994*; *Creating Together a New Partnership—NGO Support Schemes Contributing to People's Self-Reliance*; other publications on NGOs, conference and symposia reports.

Finance: Five major sources of income: membership fees, individual and corporate contributions, income from publication sales, seminar fees, etc., private foundations and subsidies; Total income ¥116,350,333 (2009).

Board of Trustees: Masaaki Ohashi (Chair.); Kazuo Tsurumi (Vice-Chair.); Yuka Iwatsuki (Vice-Chair.); Hiroshi Taniyama (Vice-Chair.).

Principal Staff: Sec.-Gen. Masashi Yamaguchi.

Address: Avaco Bldg, 2-3-18 Nishiwaseda, 5th Floor, Shinjuku-ku, Tokyo 169-0051.

Telephone: (3) 5292-2911; **Fax:** (3) 5292-2912; **Internet:** www.janic.org; **e-mail:** global-citizen@janic.org.

Japan Association of Charitable Organizations—JACO

Established in 1972 by Masao Watanabe to represent the charity sector in Japan.

Activities: JACO offers information, advice and support to the charity sector in Japan. It represents around 1,500 organizations. Major activities include: consulting services, training programmes, public relations and publications, exchange of information, study and research, and advocacy.

Geographical Area of Activity: Japan.

Publications: *Koueki Houjin* (monthly magazine, in Japanese); books on management, commentaries on accounting standards, tax theories and practice, glossary of technical terms.

Finance: Annual income ¥192,859,471, expenditure ¥191,544,631 (2006/07).

Board of Directors: Tatsuo Ohta (Pres. and CEO).

Principal Staff: Exec. Dir and Sec.-Gen. Toshihiro Kanazawa.

Address: 2-27-15 Hon-komagome Bunkyo-ku, Tokyo 113-0021.

Telephone: (3) 3945-1017; **Fax:** (3) 3945-1267; **Internet:** www.kohokyo.or.jp; **e-mail:** info@kohokyo.or.jp.

Japan Foundation Center

Founded in November 1985 to disseminate information on foundations in Japan, provide assistance to member foundations, and publicize the role and activities of grant-making foundations.

Activities: The Center compiles and publishes information on the activities of grant-making foundations in Japan; conducts research and publishes the results; maintains a library of publications relating to Japanese and overseas foundations; and sponsors seminars, lectures and symposia.

Geographical Area of Activity: Japan.

Restrictions: No direct grant-making to individuals or organizations.

Publications: *JFC Views* (in Japanese); *Directory of Grant-making Foundations* (Japanese and English); *Summary of Current Grant Awards* (in Japanese); *Guide to Private Grant Sources* (in Japanese).

Principal Staff: Pres. Kazuo Kumagai; Exec. Dir Seitaro Horiuchi; Dir Programmes and Overseas Morihisa Miyakawa.

Address: 1-26-9 Shinjuku, Believe Shinjuku Bldg 4F, Tokyo 160-0022.

Telephone: (3) 3350-1857; **Fax:** (3) 3350-1858; **Internet:** www.jfc.or.jp; **e-mail:** pref@jfc.or.jp.

FOUNDATIONS, TRUSTS AND NON-PROFIT ORGANIZATIONS

Asahi Beer Arts Foundation (Asahi Biiru Geijutsu Bunka Zaidan)

Founded in 1989 by Asahi Breweries Ltd to contribute to the enhancement of Japanese culture by awarding grants for artistic and cultural activities, including fine arts and music, and by extending financial support for international exchange in artistic and cultural activities.

Activities: Grants-in-aid are made towards fine arts exhibitions and music concerts in Japan, sponsorship and scholarships are awarded to foreign students studying the arts at higher education institutions in Japan, and scholarships are awarded to Japanese students studying the arts abroad (sponsorship is only provided for exhibitions and concerts organized in Japan on their return). Also awards prizes.

Geographical Area of Activity: Japan.

Restrictions: Grants are only given for events held in Japan.

Publications: *Guide to the Foundation*.

Board of Directors: Hitoshi Ogita (Pres.).

Address: 23-1 Azumabashi 1-chome, Sumida-ku, Tokyo 130-8602.

Telephone: (3) 5608-5202; **Fax:** (3) 5608-5152; **Internet:** www.asahibeer.co.jp/culture/zaidan/geijutu/body_gei.htm.

Asahi Glass Foundation

Established in 1933 as the Asahi Foundation for Chemical Industry Promotion, by the Asahi Glass Company Ltd; under current name since 1990. Supports research in scientific, technological and environmental areas.

Activities: Funds for research and commendation programmes aimed at contributing to solving the major issues facing mankind. Research grants are made in the fields of life sciences, information sciences, the environment, energy, humanity and the global environment. The Foundation also provides funding for overseas research at Chulalongkorn University, Thailand, and the Institut Teknologi Bandung, Indonesia. As part of its commendation programmes, the Foundation has presented the Blue Planet Prize, an international environmental prize, since 1992; an annual award given in recognition of individuals and organizations that have made major contributions to solving global environmental problems. Each year two recipients are chosen from a list of candidates put forward by nominators from Japan and overseas; each winner receives a certificate of merit, a commemorative trophy, and a supplementary award of ¥50,000,000.

Geographical Area of Activity: International.

Restrictions: Research grants generally made to university researchers in Japan.

Publications: *Results of the Questionnaire on Environmental Problems and the Survival of Humankind* (annually); *af News* (newsletter, 2 a year); *Blue Planet Prize Commemorative Lectures* (annually); Annual Report; research reports; brochure (updated annually).

Finance: Total assets ¥37,468,788,418; annual income ¥516,910,364, expenditure ¥773,401,051 (2010/11).

Board of Directors and Councillors: Tetsuji Tanaka (Chair.); Shunichi Samejima (Sr Exec. Dir).

Principal Staff: Sec.-Gen. Tetsuro Yasuda.

Address: 2nd Floor, Science Plaza, 5-3 Yonbancho, Chiyoda-ku, Tokyo 102-0081.

Telephone: (3) 5275-0620; **Fax:** (3) 5275-0871; **Internet:** www .af-info.or.jp; **e-mail:** post@af-info.or.jp.

Asia-Africa International Voluntary Foundation— AIV

Founded in 1989.

Activities: Operates in the fields of aid to less-developed countries, education, and medicine and health, through the provision of technical and financial assistance to encourage appropriate and sustainable development in less-developed countries. Promotes co-operation between Japan and developing countries.

Geographical Area of Activity: Asia and Africa.

Finance: Annual budget approx. US $159,000.

Principal Staff: Masuhisa Oka.

Address: 3 Tsubosaka Takatori-cho, Takaichi-gun, Nara 635-0102.

Telephone: (7) 4452-3172; **Fax:** (7) 4452-3835; **Internet:** www .tsubosaka1300.or.jp/aiv/; **e-mail:** tbsk2@tsubosaka1300.or .jp.

Asia Crime Prevention Foundation—ACPF

Founded in 1982 by Atsushi Nagashima with the purpose of promoting effective measures for the prevention of crime and for the treatment of offenders in the Asian, Pacific, African, and Central and South American regions.

Activities: Organizes lectures on crime prevention and the treatment of offenders; carries out research; provides grants to institutions and individuals for relevant study programmes. The Foundation has members in 93 countries, and has general consultative status with the UN. Maintains nine offices in Japan and international offices in Bangladesh, the People's Republic of China, Fiji, India, Indonesia, Kenya, Republic of Korea, Malaysia, Mongolia, Nepal, Pakistan, the Philippines, the Solomon Islands, Sri Lanka, Thailand, Tonga and Uganda.

Geographical Area of Activity: International.

Publications: *ACPF Today*; newsletter.

Finance: The Foundation is financed by interest on capital, membership fees and donations from public and private sources.

Board of Directors: Taichi Sakaiya (Pres.).

Principal Staff: Chair. Minoru Shikita; Sec.-Gen. Kunihiro Horiuchi.

Address: Akasaka Belgo, Suite 1007, 3-11-14 Akasaka, Minato-ku, Tokyo 107-0052.

Telephone: (3) 3433-2124; **Fax:** (3) 3433-2125; **Internet:** www .acpf.org; **e-mail:** info@acpf.org.

Asia/Pacific Cultural Centre for UNESCO—ACCU

Founded in 1971 to promote mutual understanding and cultural co-operation among peoples in the Asia-Pacific region through the implementation of various programmes in the fields of culture, book development and literacy promotion.

Activities: Operates regionally in Asia and the Pacific in the fields of culture, book development and literacy, through joint programmes of UNESCO member states in the region for production of low-priced quality books for children, materials such as posters, booklets and video cassettes for literates in rural areas, audiovisual materials; training of cultural and book personnel in the region; publications (see below); special programmes (annual photography contest and travelling exhibition, biennial Noma Concours for illustrators of children's picture books in developing countries); Asia/Pacific Programme for Regional Co-operation in Protection of Cultural Heritage and the International Exchange Programme for the Promotion of International Co-operation and Mutual Understanding); and maintenance of the ACCU Library, with emphasis on children's books and school textbooks from Asian countries, as well as UNESCO publications.

Geographical Area of Activity: Asia and the Pacific.

Restrictions: UNESCO member states in Asia-Pacific region.

Publications: *Asian/Pacific Book Development (ABD)* (quarterly); reference materials; meeting reports.

Finance: Annual income ¥230,476,000, expenditure ¥820,783,000 (2008).

Board of Directors: Fujio Cho (Pres.); Tetsuo Tamura (Dir-Gen.).

Principal Staff: Pres. Shiraishi Masaru.

Address: Japan Publishers Bldg, 6 Fukuromachi, Shinjuku-ku, Tokyo 162-8484.

Telephone: (3) 3269-4435; **Fax:** (3) 3269-4510; **Internet:** www .accu.or.jp; **e-mail:** general@accu.or.jp.

Asian Community Trust—ACT

Founded in November 1979 to promote social and economic development in Asian communities, and mutual understanding between people in Japan and in neighbouring Asian countries, by assisting activities that contribute to development. Since 2005 the Asian Community Centre 21 (ACC21) has acted as the ACT steering committee and secretariat.

Activities: Provides financial assistance to institutions in South-East and South Asia for specific activities in rural development, education and youth development, health, environment and conservation, and the institutional development of NGOs; also administers a number of semi-independent trust funds. Operates two resource desks in Indonesia and the Philippines. In 2011 the ACT contributed to relief work and funding in the aftermath of the devastating tsunami in Japan in March.

Geographical Area of Activity: South-East Asia and South Asia.

Publications: *ACT Now* (2 a year); Annual Report.

Finance: Grant expenditure approx. ¥8,000,000.

Principal Staff: Chair. Taroichi Yoshida; Exec. Sec. Toshihiro Menju.

Address: Asian Community Center 21, ABK Bldg 2-12-13 Hon-komagome, Bunkyo-ku Tokyo 113-8642.

Telephone: (3) 3945-2615; **Fax:** (3) 3945-2692; **Internet:** www .acc21.org/act; **e-mail:** act-info@acc21.org.

Asian Health Institute—AHI

An NGO established in 1980 by Dr Hiromi Kawahara, member of the Japan Christian Medical Doctors Association, to promote accessible and affordable health care for marginalized people in Asia through human resource development among NGOs throughout Asia.

Activities: Encourages the formation and maintenance of effective community health-care organizations through training. Courses funded by the Institute aim to enhance leadership skills so that more community-based health workers take the initiative to develop their own organizations, and work to combat curable diseases in less-developed parts of Asia.

Geographical Area of Activity: Asia.

Restrictions: No grants to individuals or to organizations.

Publications: *Asian Health Institute* (newsletter, 3–4 a year); Annual Report; *Children of Asia* (newsletter for children, 1–2 a year);.

Finance: Funded by membership fees and donations. Total assets ¥676,212,267 (2010); annual revenue ¥133,356,288, expenditure ¥92,428,000 (2011).

Board of Directors: Hisafumi Saito (Chair.).

Principal Staff: Gen. Sec. Kagumi Hayashi.

Address: 987-30, Komenoki, Minamiyama, Nisshin, Aichi, 470-0111.

Telephone: (561) 73-1950; **Fax:** (561) 73-1990; **Internet:** www .ahi-japan.jp/english/english.html; **e-mail:** info@ahi-japan .jp.

Bridge Asia Japan—BAJ

Established in 1993, as Indochina Co-operation Centre Japan, renamed in 1994, to undertake projects in Myanmar and Viet Nam.

Activities: Operates in the areas of aid to less-developed countries, and conservation and the environment, in Myanmar and Viet Nam, through self-conducted projects, especially to assist vulnerable people, including refugees, disabled people, and women and children. Projects include supporting education and school construction, water and sanitation, afforestation and training. Nationally, the organization supports exchanges and study tours, and issues publications. Maintains offices in Myanmar and Viet Nam.

Geographical Area of Activity: Myanmar and Viet Nam.

Publications: *BAJ Newsletter* (2 a month); Annual Report.

Finance: Receives funding from donations, grants, public funding and membership fees; Total liabilities and net assets ¥97,590,753, annual revenue ¥186,706,603, annual expenditure ¥288,958,425 (2010).

Principal Staff: Pres. Etsuko Nemoto.

Address: 4F Business Tower, 3-39-3 Honmachi, Shibuya-ku, Tokyo 151-0071.

Telephone: (3) 3372-9777; **Fax:** (3) 5351-2395; **Internet:** www .baj-npo.org/english/; **e-mail:** info@baj-npo.org.

Defense of Green Earth Foundation—DGEF

Founded in 1982 to promote the protection of the environment.

Activities: Supports projects to protect the environment, including afforestation projects, the protection of the Oze swamp, and attempts to reduce desertification; sponsors environmental research and surveys; aims to increase awareness of environmental issues.

Geographical Area of Activity: Japan, Tanzania, People's Republic of China.

Publications: *Green Earth* (quarterly newspaper); *Environmental Issues Research Report* (annually).

Finance: Annual budget approx. US $620,000; Total revenue ¥36,762,000,000 ,total expenditure ¥41,759,000,000 (2010).

Principal Staff: Chair. Oishi Masamitsu.

Address: 2-6-16 Shinkawa, Chuo-ku, Tokyo 104-0033.

Telephone: (3) 3297-5505; **Fax:** (3) 3297-5507; **Internet:** http://green-earth-japan.net; **e-mail:** defense@green.email .ne.jp.

GEA—Global Environmental Action

Established in 1991 to promote sustainable development and help solve global environmental problems.

Activities: Operates internationally in the field of conservation and the environment, through organizing conferences and disseminating the results of conferences. Initiatives include an information resource for environmental NGOs in developing countries. In 2003 launched the Virtual Globe Project, which supports NGOs that are engaged in environmental conservation activities.

Geographical Area of Activity: International.

Advisory Committee: Toshiki Kaifu (Chair.).

Principal Staff: Chair. Juro Saito; Dir-Gen. Hiroshi Ohki.

Address: 404C Tokyo Sakurada Bldg, 1-1-3 Nishishinbashi, Minato-ku, Tokyo 105-0003.

Telephone: (3) 3503-7484; **Fax:** (3) 3503-6953; **Internet:** www .gea.or.jp; **e-mail:** gea@gea.or.jp.

Global Voluntary Service—GVS

Established in 1992 by Teiko Inabata to foster volunteer activity in developing nations, for the improvement of living conditions, expertise and for the protection of the environment.

Activities: Operates in less-developed countries, mainly Kenya, Peru and the Philippines, in the areas of rural and agricultural development, education, training, medical assistance, environmental protection and welfare for underprivileged women, through developmental education, medical missions, health programmes, vocational training, information provision, exchange of personnel, collaboration with other NGOs, exhibitions, study tours, work camps and seminars. Maintains an office in Tokyo, and overseas offices in Manila, Nairobi and Lima.

Geographical Area of Activity: Japan, and less-developed countries, in particular Kenya, Peru and the Philippines.

Publications: Annual Report; brochures and audiovisual materials.

Trustees: Teiko Inabata (Chair.).

Principal Staff: Exec. Dir Seizo Inahata.

Address: 3-25-501, 12–6 Funado-cho, Ashia City, Hyogo 659-0093.

Telephone: (7) 9734-0078; **Fax:** (7) 9734-1061; **Internet:** www .32.ocn.ne.jp/~gvs/; **e-mail:** gvs@cc.mbn.or.jp.

The Hitachi Scholarship Foundation

The Foundation was set up under the aegis of electrical goods manufacturer, Hitachi Ltd, in 1984 to promote cultural, academic and educational exchange between Japan and the South-East Asian countries. The Foundation aims to develop human resources in South-East Asian universities, thus helping to advance education, co-operation and collaboration among the universities in Japan and South-East Asia. It also aims to develop a co-operative network among university personnel in Japan and South-East Asian countries and better cultural understanding.

Activities: Supports and finances promising research in Japan carried out by successful young faculty members and graduates from universities of Singapore, Indonesia, Malaysia, Thailand and the Philippines. Awards scholarships, fellowships and grants.

Geographical Area of Activity: South-East Asia.

Restrictions: No grants to individuals.

Finance: Assets ¥2,300,000,000 (March 2009).

Board of Trustees: Kazuo Kumagai (Chair.).

Principal Staff: Man. Dir T. Gomibuchi; Sec.-Gen. H. Sugai; Programme Officers M. Homma, M. Nunokami.

Address: 21F Akihabara UDX Bldg, 14-1, Soto-Kanda 4-chome, Chiyoda-ku, Tokyo 101-8010.

Telephone: (3) 3257-0853; **Fax:** (3) 3257-0854; **Internet:** www .hitachi-zaidan.org/global/scholarship; **e-mail:** scholarship@hdg.hitachi.co.jp.

Honda Foundation

Founded in 1977 by Soichiro Honda to support the development of technology that is in harmony with the environment ('eco-technology').

Activities: Supports annual international symposia, seminars and workshops at which experts from all countries gathe rto discuss scientific and technological problems inherent in modern civilization with a view to creating a better society. Awards the annual Honda Prize of ¥10m. to an individual or organization, irrespective of nationality, for a distinguished achievement in 'eco-technology'. Launched the YES Award programme in Viet Nam in 2006 to foster students who are helping to develop science and eco-technology for the future; the programme was subsequently extended to India, Cambodia and Laos.

Geographical Area of Activity: International.

Publications: Annual Report.

Finance: Total assets ¥5,566,234,012 (March 2011).

Board of Directors: Hiroto Ishida (Pres.); Kunio Nakajima (Vice-Pres.).

Principal Staff: Man. Dir Yoichi Harada.

Address: 2nd Floor, Honda Yaesu Bldg, 6-20 Yaesu 2-chome, Chuo-ku, Tokyo 104-0028.

Telephone: (3) 3274-5125; **Fax:** (3) 3274-5103; **Internet:** www .hondafoundation.jp; **e-mail:** h_info@hondafoundation.jp.

Hoso Bunka Foundation, Inc—HBF

Founded in 1974 by the Japan Broadcasting Corpn—NHK to contribute to the advancement of broadcasting and the dissemination of culture through broadcasting.

Activities: The Foundation provides financial assistance for research in broadcasting technology; for the development of receiving equipment; for international co-operation in broadcasting; and for legal, socio-economic and cultural studies related to broadcasting. Awards the annual HBF Prizes for outstanding domestic television and radio programmes and broadcasting technology development.

Geographical Area of Activity: International.

Restrictions: Grants only to professional projects related to broadcasting culture.

Publications: *HBF* (annually, in Japanese); Annual Research Report (in Japanese); activity report (3 a year, in Japanese); activity report in English available on website.

Finance: Net assets approx. ¥15,000,000,000.

Board of Directors: Hiroshi Shiono (Pres.).

Principal Staff: Gen. Man. Dir Susumu Tanimura.

Address: Kyodo Bldg, 5th Floor, 41-1 Udagawa-cho, Shibuya-ku, Tokyo 150-0042.

Telephone: (3) 3464-3131; **Fax:** (3) 3770-7239; **Internet:** www .hbf.or.jp; **e-mail:** inform@hbf.or.jp.

IATSS—International Association of Traffic and Safety Sciences

Founded in 1974 by Soichiro Honda and Takeo Fujisawa with the purpose of promoting the development of the ideal transportation system by the prompt undertaking of traffic and safety-related research activities, hosting of research conferences, active support of publicity and publication activities, and bestowing awards for transportation-related research, education and other activities.

Activities: Operates nationally and internationally in conducting research; collecting and applying data; sponsoring domestic and international conferences and meetings; publishing the results of research; and giving annual IATSS Dissertation, Literature and Achievement Awards to (respectively) the author of the best paper appearing in the *IATSS Review and IATSS Research,* for outstanding literary works concerning the realization of an ideal mobile society, and the individual and organization making the most useful contribution to mobile society. The IATSS Forum provides the opportunity for young people from the countries of South-East Asia to learn together.

Geographical Area of Activity: International.

Publications: *IATSS Forum Reviews and Reports* (2 a year); *IATSS Research* (2 a year, in English); *IATSS Review* (quarterly, in Japanese); *Statistics-Road Accidents Japan* (abridged edn, annually, in English).

Principal Staff: Chair. Yasuhei Oguchi; Exec. Sec. Koji Suzuki.

Address: 2-6-20, Yaesu, Chuo-ku, Tokyo 104-0028.

Telephone: (3) 3273-7884; **Fax:** (3) 3272-7054; **Internet:** www .iatss.or.jp; **e-mail:** mail@iatss.or.jp.

Institute of Developing Economies/Japan External Trade Organization—IDE-JETRO

The Institute of Developing Economies was established in 1958 (reorganized in 1960 as a semi-governmental body) for basic and comprehensive research on economic and related affairs in developing countries to contribute to the improvement of economic co-operation and trade relations between Japan and these countries. The Institute merged with the Japan External Trade Organization (JETRO) in July 1998. The new organization is an integral unit of the Japan External Trade Organization, an Incorporated Administrative Agency under the supervision of the Ministry of Economy, Trade and Industry.

Activities: The Institute operates in Asia, Middle East, Africa and Latin America with various regional organizations. It conducts its own research projects on about 50 topics annually, covering various aspects of development, economic co-operation and statistical analysis; research is carried out by the Institute's own staff, with the co-operation of outside experts. It also runs a Joint Research Programme for joint studies with scholars in developing countries, and a Visiting Research Fellows Programme, under which foreign researchers or experts are invited to work at the Institute. Every year about 150 researchers are sent overseas for up to 30 days to conduct field surveys, and 34 research staff are sent abroad for two years. The Institute also collects and compiles statistical data, and maintains a library. Makes awards in recognition of outstanding publications. It holds international symposia, and conducts about 50 seminars and lectures a year in various parts of Japan to inform the public on development issues.

Geographical Area of Activity: Asia, Middle East, Central Asia, Africa and Latin America.

Publications: *The Developing Economies* (quarterly, in English); *Ajia Keizai* (Asian Economies, monthly); *Ajiken warudo torendo* (Asian World Trends, monthly); *Yearbook of Asian Affairs* (in Japanese); *The Contemporary Middle East* (in Japanese); *Latin America Report* (2 a year, in Japanese); *Africa Report* (2 a year, in Japanese); *Development Perspective Series;* Annual Report; occasional papers, symposium proceedings, statistical data, bibliographies and research reports.

Finance: Total income ¥40,220,000,000 (2009), total expenditure ¥40,220,000,000 (2009).

Governing Body: The organization is an integral unit of JETRO, an Incorporated Administrative Agency under the supervision of the Ministry of Economy, Trade and Industry.

Principal Staff: Pres. Takashi Shiraishi.

Address: 3-2-2 Wakaba, Mihama-ku, Chiba-shi, Chiba 261-8545.

Telephone: (4) 3299-9500; **Fax:** (4) 3299-9724; **Internet:** www .ide.go.jp; **e-mail:** info@ide.go.jp.

The Institute of Energy Economics, Japan—IEEJ

Founded in 1966 by the energy industry to conduct research and studies that will contribute towards the framing of Japan's energy policy and towards the business activities of the energy industries, through an extensive collection of information and data on the world energy situation and the energy policy in major countries, and through their objective and positive analysis.

Activities: Operates nationally and internationally in the fields of economic affairs, the conservation of natural resources and climate change, through self-conducted programmes, research, conferences, courses, publications and lectures. Current projects include a long- and mid-term forecast of the demand and supply of energy in Japan; an analysis of the flow of world and Asia's crude petroleum and natural gas market, and an evaluation of crude petroleum and natural gas in the Japanese market; an analysis of energy-related technologies, including nuclear, renewable energy and clean coal technology; an analysis of the relationship between economic activity and energy. A number of researchers are sent abroad each year to obtain first-hand information on energy and the environment, or to attend international conferences; several others are also sent to research institutes abroad under exchange programmes. The Institute established the affiliated Oil Information Centre in 1981, the Asia Pacific Energy Resource Centre in 1996 and The Green Energy Certification Centre in 2008, all of which carry out research into energy and environmental issues.

Geographical Area of Activity: Japan.

Publications: *IEEJ Energy Journal* (quarterly, in English); *EDMC Handbook of Energy & Economic Statistics in Japan*; *EDMC Energy Trend* (monthly, in Japanese); *Energy Economics* (6 a year, in Japanese);.

Principal Staff: Chair. and CEO Masakazu Toyoda, Sr Man. Dir Masaki Chiba.

Address: Inui Bldg, Kachidoki, 13-1, Kachidoki 1-Chome, Chuo-ku, Tokyo 104-0054.

Telephone: (3) 5547-0211; **Fax:** (3) 5547-0223; **Internet:** eneken.ieej.or.jp/en; **e-mail:** otoiawase@tky.ieej.or.jp.

International Development Center of Japan

Founded in 1971 by Toshiwo Doko and Saburo Okita to assist the advancement of the economic growth of developing countries by promoting Japanese development co-operation, and by contributing to the efforts of national and international organizations.

Activities: The Center organizes development training programmes (some of which are open to participants from developing nations) in, for example, development economics, project analysis, project leaders' training and language and cultural orientation. It conducts basic research on problems of economic development, and undertakes research and surveys commissioned by other organizations. It sponsors international conferences, accepts overseas research associates, and sends Japanese scholars (five or six a year) abroad for study connected with development problems.

Geographical Area of Activity: International.

Publications: Annual Report; *IDC Forum* (2 a year); regular series of working papers; occasional publications.

Finance: Fund ¥1,227,684,500 (1 April 2010).

Board of Directors: Masaji Shinagawa (Chair.).

Principal Staff: Pres. Masaoki Takeuchi.

Address: Hitachi Solutions Tower B, 22nd Floor, 4-12-6 Higashi-Shinagawa, Shinagawa-ku, Tokyo 140-0002.

Telephone: (3) 6718-5931; **Fax:** (3) 6718-1651; **Internet:** www.idcj.or.jp; **e-mail:** general_dep@idcj.or.jp.

International Lake Environment Committee Foundation

Founded in 1986 by the Shiga Prefectural Government to promote the environmentally sound management of the world's lakes and reservoirs; given legal status in 1987.

Activities: Operates nationally and internationally in the fields of aid to less-developed countries and conservation and the environment, through self-conducted programmes, research, conferences, training courses and publications. The Foundation's major activities include collecting and organizing data on the condition of lakes throughout the world; organizing training seminars and workshops on development issues and lake environment conservation in developing countries; promoting lake environment management; and providing support for the UN Environment Programme's International Environmental Technology Centre. Also maintains a database surveying the condition of the world's lakes and awards the annual Biwako Prize for Ecology.

Geographical Area of Activity: International.

Publications: *ILEC Newsletter* (3 a year, in Japanese and English); *Lakes and Reservoirs: Research and Management* (quarterly journal); surveys and guidelines on lake management and workshop reports; *Lake Basin Management Initiative*; *World Lake Vision*.

Board of Directors: Hironori Hamanaka (Dir-Gen.).

Principal Staff: Sec.-Gen. Toshiaki Kagatsume.

Address: 1091 Oroshimo-cho, Kusatsu-shi, Shiga 525-0001.

Telephone: (7) 7568-4567; **Fax:** (7) 7568-4568; **Internet:** www.ilec.or.jp; **e-mail:** infoilec@ilec.or.jp.

The International Movement against All Forms of Discrimination and Racism—IMADR

An international, not-for-profit NGO founded in 1988 by the Burakumin in Japan, one of Japan's largest minority groups, to serve the cause of human rights through elimination of racism and discrimination, establishing international solidarity among minorities subjected to discrimination, and enhancing the international human rights system.

Activities: The organization focuses on eliminating discrimination based on both race and gender. Activities include developing grassroots movements; building links between minority groups to promote solidarity and support; building awareness of the adverse effects of discrimination on society through participation in and organization of regional, local and international events. Also carries out research to assist national and international advocacy against discrimination; partners with academic institutions and NGOs to sponsor joint action/research projects on exploitative migration and trafficking of women and children; promotes networking among minority groups through the Internet and publications; conducts campaigns advocating against discrimination; and addresses discrimination issues at major world conferences and UN meetings. IMADR has regional committees and partners in Europe, North, Central and South America, and Asia, and maintains a UN liaison office in Geneva, Switzerland.

Geographical Area of Activity: World-wide.

Restrictions: Grants only to specific organizations which are in partnership with IMADR.

Publications: *Connect* (quarterly newsletter); *Peoples for Human Rights Series* (journal); *ICERD: A Guide for NGOs*.

Board of Directors: Nimalka Fernando (Pres.); Bernadette Hétier, Kinhide Mushakoji, Mario Jorge Yutzis (Vice-Pres).

Principal Staff: Sec.-Gen. Yuriko Hara; Under-Sec.-Gen. Megumi Komori.

Address: 6th Floor, 1-7-1, Irifune, Chuo-ku, Tokyo 104-0042.

Telephone: (3) 6280-3100; **Fax:** (3) 6280-3102; **Internet:** www.imadr.org; **e-mail:** imadr@imadr.org.

Ishizaka Foundation

Founded in 1976 to further mutual understanding and friendship between Japan and other countries by cultural and educational interchange.

Activities: Provides scholarships for Japanese undergraduate and graduate students to study abroad, and for foreign (Asian) students enrolled at Japanese universities. The Foundation also sponsors lectures and symposia that contribute to international cultural and educational interchange, and disseminates the proceedings.

Geographical Area of Activity: Brunei, Cambodia, Indonesia, Japan, Laos, Malaysia, Myanmar, Philippines, Singapore, Thailand and Viet Nam.

Finance: Net assets ¥79,100,000,000 (31 Dec. 2010).

Principal Staff: Chair. Takashi Imai; Sec.-Gen. Yoshio Nakamura.

Address: c/o Keidanren, 1-3-2 Otemachi, Chiyoda-ku, Tokyo 100-8188.

Telephone: (3) 6741-0162; **Fax:** (3) 5255-6233; **Internet:** www .keidanren.or.jp/japanese/profile/ishizaka/; **e-mail:** kyoikuzaidan@keidanren.or.jp.

Iwatani Naoji Foundation

Founded in 1973 by Naoji Iwatani, President of Iwatani & Co, Ltd, to improve national welfare and promote international mutual understanding by providing assistance for research, development and international exchange in the fields of science and technology.

Activities: Operates nationally through providing grants for research and development projects in science and technology that will result in the improvement of the national welfare, and through giving recognition to those whose work in these fields will make a lasting contribution to Japan. The Foundation also provides aid for the promotion of international exchange of information in science and technology. It presents the Iwatani Naoji Memorial Prize each year for research into gas and energy; and the Iwatani International Scholarships, which are awarded to foreign students from East or South-East Asian countries, for postgraduate study in natural science and technology.

Geographical Area of Activity: Grants for East and South-East Asian students (mainly from Japan).

Publications: Annual Report; *Kenkyu Hokokusho* (report on the research results funded by the Foundation, annually, in Japanese).

Finance: Net assets ¥5,139,747,352 (31 Dec. 2010).

Councillors: Fumio Kitamura (Chair.).

Principal Staff: Chair. Mitsuru Ohba; Exec. Dir Yukio Komatsu.

Address: 3rd Floor, Building 5, 13-4, Hatchobori 2-chome, Chuo-ku, Tokyo 104-0032.

Telephone: (3) 3552-9960; **Fax:** (3) 3552-9961; **Internet:** www .iwatani-foundation.or.jp; **e-mail:** information@iwatani -foundation.or.jp.

Japan Center for Economic Research—JCER

Founded in 1963 to conduct studies and research on various problems of government finance, money and credit, economy, industry, management and other related subjects at home and abroad; and to promote mutual study and training of its members with the aim of contributing to the economic growth of Japan.

Activities: Conducts research on Japan's economy with particular emphasis on economic forecasting; organizes joint economic research; and undertakes research projects on a contractual basis. The Center sponsors economic study courses, seminars, lectures and symposia, and provides training for junior businesspeople in advanced economics and research; it publishes the results of its research projects and operates a specialized library of 37,500 volumes, 861 periodicals and 1,280 statistics. At international level, the Center conducts joint research on specific problems with foreign institutions, organizes lectures and seminars for foreign economists, and sponsors an annual conference to which leading economists from both advanced and developing countries are invited. Study facilities are made available to a limited number of foreign researchers, particularly from Asia. There are approximately 700 institutional and 300 individual members.

Geographical Area of Activity: International.

Publications: Annual Report and financial statement; *Bulletin* (monthly); *Short-term Economic Forecast Series* (quarterly); *International Conference Series*; *Japan Financial Report* (2 a year, in Japanese); *Asia Research Report* (annually, in English); *China Research Report* (annually, in English); *Asian Economic Policy Review* (2 a year, in English).

Board of Directors: Junichi Arai (Chair.).

Principal Staff: Pres. Kazumasa Iwata.

Address: Nikkei Inc. Bldg. 11F, 1-3-7 Otemachi, Chiyoda-ku, Tokyo 100-8066.

Telephone: (3) 6256-7710; **Fax:** (3) 6256-7924; **Internet:** www .jcer.or.jp; **e-mail:** jcernet@jcer.or.jp.

Japan Economic Research Institute Inc—JERI

Founded in 1962 to promote the overall development of Japan's economy and to contribute to interchange between nations in economic research and to the making of economic policy at industrial, national and international levels.

Activities: Operates nationally and internationally in the fields of economic affairs and management, including urban and regional development, social infrastructure, energy, and industry, through research, international co-operation and dissemination of material. Economic research is carried out by research committees involving experts from industry, government agencies and the academic world. The resulting reports, as well as other up-to-date information on national and international economics, are distributed to members of the Institute and other organizations. Other activities include the organization of conferences, lectures and seminars, as well as playing an advisory role on private finance initiative (PFI) projects.

Geographical Area of Activity: International.

Finance: Derived from annual contributions by Japanese business corporations; Paid-in capital ¥480,000,000.

Principal Staff: Pres. Takashi Ando.

Address: 3-3-4 Kandasurugadai, Chiyoda-ku, Tokyo 101-0062.

Telephone: (3) 5280-6105; **Fax:** (3) 5280-6106; **Internet:** www .jeri.co.jp; **e-mail:** info@jeri.co.jp.

The Japan Foundation

Founded in 1972 to further international mutual understanding through the promotion of cultural exchange; reorganized in 2003.

Activities: Operates internationally by offering fellowships to overseas scholars, enabling them to conduct research in Japan. Dissertation fellowships are offered to scholars in the social sciences and humanities, and professional fellowships to scholars engaged in studies on Japanese society and culture. Visiting professorships abroad are offered to Japanese professors, enabling them to teach in institutions overseas or to take part in research or conferences connected with Japan. Promotes Japanese language studies abroad and produces, collects and distributes materials that introduce Japanese culture abroad. Provides funding for cultural exhibitions and the performing arts, organizes lectures and seminars, and supports arts-related and media exchanges (including Special Programs for Japan-Europe Cultural Exchange). The Japan Foundation Information Center, which is based at the Foundation's headquarters in Tokyo, incorporates a library. The Japan Foundation Centre for Global Partnership was established in 1991 to promote relations between Japan and the USA through intellectual exchange and the promotion of mutual understanding. The Foundation maintains overseas offices in Australasia, North, Central and South America, Asia, Africa and Europe, and Japanese Language Centers/Centres for Global Partnership in Australia, Brazil, Indonesia, South Korea, Malaysia, Thailand, the United Kingdom and the USA; information may also be obtained from Japanese diplomatic missions.

Geographical Area of Activity: World-wide.

Publications: Annual Report; *Japanese Book News* (quarterly); *Wochi Kochi* (online, 6 a year); *CGP Newsletter* (quarterly); bibliographical series; *Nihongo Kyoiku Tsushin* (journal, online); *Asia Center News* (quarterly); *Japanese-Language Education around the World* (journal); *Bunka Jigyo Tsushin* (newsletter).

Finance: Annual revenue ¥17,833,466,204, expenditure ¥15,202,271,611 (2009/10).

Governing Board: Hiroyasu Ando (Pres.); Sohei Yoshino, Toru Kodaki, Hideya Taida (Exec. Vice-Pres.).

Address: 4-4-1 Yotsuya, Shinjuku-ku, Tokyo 160-0004.

Telephone: (3) 5369-6051; **Fax:** (3) 5369-6031; **Internet:** www
.jpf.go.jp; **e-mail:** webmaster@jpf.go.jp.

The Japan Foundation Centre for Global Partnership—CGP

Established in April 1991 inside the Japan Foundation, an
independent administrative institution, to promote collaboration between Japan and the USA with the goal of fulfilling
shared global responsibilities and contributing to improvements in the world's welfare, and to enhance dialogue and
interchange between Japanese and US citizens on a wide
range of issues, thereby strengthening mutual understanding
and improving bilateral relations.

Activities: CGP makes institutional grants in three programme areas: intellectual exchange, grassroots exchange
and education. In addition, CGP operates the Abe Fellowship
for scholars and researchers of the humanities and social
sciences, and the NPO Fellowship for mid-career staff members working in Japan's non-profit sector.

Geographical Area of Activity: Japan and the USA.

Restrictions: Only supports projects from Japan or the USA.

Publications: Annual Report (in Japanese and English);
newsletter; *NewsOnline*; symposia reports; field surveys; conference papers.

Finance: Funded by investment income and other sources.

Advisory Committee: Kazuo Ogoura (Pres.).

Principal Staff: Exec. Dir Sadaaki Numata; Man. Dir
Tadashi Ogawa.

Address: 4-4-1 Yotsuya, Shinjuku-ku, Tokyo 160-0004.

Telephone: (3) 5369-6072; **Fax:** (3) 5369-6042; **Internet:** www
.cgp.org; **e-mail:** info@cgp.org.

Japan Heart Foundation

Founded in 1970 to contribute to the improvement of national
welfare by providing financial aid for research on heart and
blood vessel diseases by educating the public about heart disease prevention, and by co-operating with counterpart organizations in foreign countries.

Activities: Operates nationally and in South-East Asia
through providing grants to individuals, groups and research
institutes engaged in research into heart and blood vessel diseases and providing finance for the publication of research
findings; and internationally through maintaining contact
and exchanging information with foreign institutions with
similar interests.

Geographical Area of Activity: International, mainly
South-East Asia and Japan.

Publications: *Kenko Heart* (monthly).

Finance: Grants of up to ¥800,000.

Principal Staff: Chair. Takuji Shidachi; Vice-Chair. Dr
Tsuneaki Sugimoto; Pres. Yoshio Yazaki.

Address: 835-A New Kokusai Bldg, 3-4-1 Marunouchi,
Chiyoda-ku, Tokyo 100-0005.

Telephone: (3) 3201-0810; **Fax:** (3) 3213-3920; **Internet:** www
.jhf.or.jp; **e-mail:** info@jhf.or.jp.

Japan International Volunteer Center—JVC

Established in 1980, originally to assist refugees from Indo-
china, now an international NGO supporting development.

Activities: Currently operates in nine countries of Asia,
Africa and the Middle East (Afghanistan, Cambodia, Palestinian Autonomous Areas, Iraq, Sudan, Laos, North Korea,
South Africa and Thailand), as well as in Japan, in the fields
of aid to less-developed countries, education and agricultural
development, through projects in collaboration with local people; also involved in disaster relief operations in Africa and
Asia.

Geographical Area of Activity: Africa, Asia and the Middle
East.

Finance: Annual budget ¥269,000,000 (2009).

Board of Directors: Hiroshi Taniyama (Pres.).

Principal Staff: Sec.-Gen. Toshihiro Shimizu.

Address: Maruko Bldg 6F, 1-20-6 Higashiueno, Taito-ku,
Tokyo 110-8605.

Telephone: (3) 3834-2388; **Fax:** (3) 3835-0519; **Internet:** www
.ngo-jvc.net; **e-mail:** info@ngo-jvc.net.

Japan Society for the Promotion of Science—JSPS

Founded in 1932 through an endowment granted by Emperor
Showa, re-established in 1967 by the Japanese Government to
contribute to the advancement of science.

Activities: Operates nationally through providing research
fellowships and giving grants for joint research activities
among Japanese scientists belonging to different institutions;
promoting joint research by industrial concerns and universities; providing information services; publishing scientific
works and producing films; and organizing lectures. The
Society awards the International Prize for Biology annually
to a person judged to have made outstanding scientific
achievements in the field of biology. The Society operates internationally in providing research fellowships for overseas
scientists, and grants to Japanese scientists for travel abroad;
it supports international joint research projects, international
research workshops and seminars. It also administers a number of bilateral programmes for scientific co-operation and
exchange with various foreign academic institutions. Maintains overseas liaison offices in China, Egypt, France, Germany, Kenya, Sweden, Thailand, the United Kingdom and the
USA.

Geographical Area of Activity: International.

Publications: *Gakujutsu Geppo (Japanese Science Monthly)*
(magazine); information resources; scientific publications.

Finance: Approx. 99.7% of funds are provided by the Japanese Government, the rest by private sources; Total budget
¥334,700,000,000 (direct funding ¥291,700,000,000 , indirect
funding ¥43,000,000,000) in 2011.

Advisory Board: Hiroyuki Yoshikawa (Chair.).

Principal Staff: Pres. Yuichiro Anzai; Exec. Dirs Makoto
Asashima, Hayashi Towatari.

Address: Sumitomo-Ichibancho Bldg, 6 Ichibancho, Chiyoda-
ku, Tokyo 102-8471.

Telephone: (3) 3263-1722; **Fax:** (3) 3221-2470; **Internet:** www
.jsps.go.jp; **e-mail:** enquire@jsps.org.

JCIE—Japan Center for International Exchange

Founded in 1970 by Tadashi Yamamoto to promote Japan's role
in international affairs.

Activities: The Foundation operates internationally, specifically in the USA, Europe and the Asia-Pacific region. It sponsors exchange and study programmes, conducts comparative
studies of public policy in Japan and the USA, organizes seminars and conferences, conducts research into all areas of policy development and international relations, examines
relations between Japan and the Association of South-East
Asian Nations (ASEAN), and encourages philanthropic
works through the Asian Community Trust (q.v.). New initiatives include Global ThinkNet, the basis of the Center's
research programmes, and CivilNet, a programme to
strengthen civil society and philanthropy. In addition, the
Center administers a donor advised fund on behalf of Levi
Strauss & Co.

Geographical Area of Activity: USA, Europe and the Asia-
Pacific region.

Publications: Annual Report; *Civil Society Monitor* (annual
newsletter); *GrassNet* (online magazine); *Pacific Asia 2022:
Sketching Futures of a Region; Asian Reflections on a New
World after 9–11; A Gender Agenda: Asia-Europe Dialogue;
JCIE Papers Series; Major Power Relations in Northeast Asia;
Guidance for Governance; Asia Pacific Security Outlook 2005;
The Third Force: the Rise of Transnational Civil Society; Gov-
ernance and Civil Society in a Global Age; New Perspectives on
US-Japan Relations; Philanthropy and Reconciliation; East*

Asian Regional Response to HIV/AIDS, Tuberculosis, and Malaria; Fighting a Rising Tide; ASEM in Its Tenth Year; New Challenges, New Approaches: Regional Security Cooperation in East Asia; A Pacific Nation: Perspectives on the US Role in an East Asia Community; Report on the New Shimoda Conference: Revitalizing Japan-US Strategic Partnership for a Changing World; Reinvigorating US-Japan Policy Dialogue and Study.

Board of Directors: Tadashi Yamamoto (Pres.).

Principal Staff: Man. Dir and Exec. Sec. Hideko Katsumata.

Address: 4-9-17 Minami Azabu, Minato-ku, Tokyo 106-0047.

Telephone: (3) 3446-7781; **Fax:** (3) 3443-7580; **Internet:** www.jcie.or.jp; **e-mail:** admin@jcie.or.jp.

JEN

Established in 1994 as Japan Emergency NGOs, a network of Japanese relief organizations operating internationally to give emergency relief.

Activities: Operates internationally in the fields of assistance to less-developed countries, especially in the area of disaster relief. Projects cover emergency supplies, reconstruction and rehabilitation, education, health and social welfare. Programmes currently operate in Afghanistan, Iraq, Eritrea, Sudan, Myanmar, Indonesia, Haiti, Sri Lanka, Pakistan and Niigata (Japan); 434 members (2010).

Geographical Area of Activity: Current Operations in Afghanistan, Iraq, Eritrea, Sudan, Myanmar, Indonesia, Haiti, Sri Lanka, Pakistan and Niigata (Japan).

Publications: Newsletter; Annual Report.

Finance: Total assets ¥631,110,000, annual income ¥782,397,000, annual expenditure ¥829,828,000 (2010).

Trustees: Keichi Akagawa (Co-Pres.); Kenji Yoshioka (Co-Pres.).

Principal Staff: Sec.-Gen. Keiko Kiyama.

Address: 2-16, Agebacho, Daini Tobundo Bldg 7F, Shinjuku-ku, Tokyo 162-0824.

Telephone: (3) 5225-9352; **Fax:** (3) 5225-9357; **Internet:** www.jen-npo.org; **e-mail:** info@jen-npo.org.

JIIA—Japan Institute of International Affairs
(Nihon Kokusai Mondai Kenkyusho)

Founded in 1959 by Shigeru Yoshida, the late Prime Minister, as a national institution authorized by the Ministry of Foreign Affairs to promote studies on international affairs and foreign policy; to encourage new thinking on major foreign policy issues; to give information on international affairs and foreign policy to its members; to promote wider public understanding of international affairs and foreign policy issues; and to provide a forum for discussion on these subjects and to exchange information with institutions abroad.

Activities: Operates in the field of international affairs mainly through research and publications, and through international conferences and seminars. Studies are conducted on the former USSR and Eastern European countries (by the Center for Soviet Studies, established within the Institute in 1984), arms control and disarmament, international organizations, South-East Asia and the People's Republic of China. The Center for Asia-Pacific Studies, founded in 1987, conducts research relating to Japan's Asia-Pacific neighbours. Research at the Center for American Studies, set up in 1989, concentrates on US current affairs. In 1993 two centres were established: the European Studies Center, which conducts research on Western Europe and the Middle East, and the Global Issue Section, which is responsible for research on human rights, nuclear proliferation, the UN and environmental issues. The Center for the Promotion of Disarmament and Non-Proliferation was established in 1996. Maintains a library of 6,200 books and more than 600 periodicals, and an online database of organizations working for conflict prevention in the Asia-Pacific region. Currently has around 150 corporate members and 800 individual members.

Geographical Area of Activity: Japan.

Publications: *Kokusai Mondai* (International Affairs) (monthly, in Japanese); *Shoten (Focus)* (newsletter, 10 times a year); books; policy reports.

Finance: Primary funding sources are public and private research contracts, corporate and individual membership fees, donations and publication sales. Annual income ¥731,049,000, annual expenditure ¥768,399,000 (2010).

Board of Trustees: Taizo Nishimuro (Chair.); Sigemitsu Miki, Akishige Okada, Yukio Satoh (Vice-Chairs).

Principal Staff: Pres. Yoshiji Nogami; Exec. Dir Yutaka Endo.

Address: Toranomon Mitsui Bldg, 3rd Floor, 3-8-1 Kasumigaseki, Chiyoda-ku, Tokyo 100-0013.

Telephone: (3) 3503-7261; **Fax:** (3) 3503-7292; **Internet:** www.jiia.or.jp; **e-mail:** jiiajojho@jiia.or.jp.

Kajima Foundation

The Foundation was established in 1976 to promote research in science and to encourage international co-operation in science.

Activities: Provides grants to students, who are selected by their university or educational institution, to undertake research, especially in the fields of science and technology; finances visits by overseas researchers as well as long-term (spanning 1 year) and short-term (spanning 3 months) studies abroad for Japanese researchers; supports international scientific conferences held in Japan, and supports joint co-operative research carried out by Japanese and foreign scholars. In 2009 the Foundation provided ¥57m. to a total of 46 projects (including 12 international academic conferences held in Japan).

Geographical Area of Activity: Mainly Japan.

Publications: Annual Report.

Board: Sadao Umeda (Chair. and Representative Dir); Mitsuyoshi Nakamura (Pres. and Representative Dir).

Principal Staff: Chair. and Representative Dir Sadao Umeda; Pres. and Representative Dir Mitsuyoshi Nakamura.

Address: 2-7 1-chome, Minato-ku, Tokyo 107.

Telephone: (3) 3404-3311; **Fax:** (3) 3474-1444; **Internet:** www.kajima.co.jp; **e-mail:** webmaster@kajima.co.jp.

KDDI Foundation

Established in 2009 by merging the resources of International Communications Foundation (ICF, founded by Kokusai Denshin Denwa Co Ltd—KDD Corpn—in 1988) and KDDI Engineering and Consulting, Inc (KEC, founded in 1974). Aims to contribute to a peaceful, healthy global society using some of the profits from information and communications technology to achieve social, economic and cultural progress.

Activities: Operates internationally in the area of information, communications, science and technology, by supporting a range of projects relating to international telecommunications, including grants for research and conferences, social support and cultural activities, and educational programmes. Fellowships are also available for foreign students.

Geographical Area of Activity: World-wide.

Principal Staff: Pres. Yasuhiko Ito.

Address: Bunkyo Green Ct, Center Office, 2-28-8 Hon-komagome, Bunkyo-ku, Tokyo.

Telephone: (3) 5978-1031; **Fax:** (3) 5978-1050; **Internet:** www.kddi-foundation.or.jp; **e-mail:** office@kddi-foundation.or.jp.

Maison Franco-Japonaise

Founded in 1924 by Paul Claudel and Eiichi Shibusawa for the development of French and Japanese cultural and scientific research activities and exchanges.

Activities: To achieve its objective, the Foundation conducts simultaneous studies of the French and Japanese cultures, organizes collections and exhibitions of study materials, meetings and conferences and publishes works relating to these studies. The Foundation operates research exchanges between France and Japan.

Geographical Area of Activity: France, Japan and Asia.

Publications: *Ebisu*; *Nichifutsu Bunka;* monographs on diverse subjects.

Finance: Activities are funded by private Japanese sources and by the French Ministry of Foreign Affairs. Annual income ¥139,966,000, annual expenditure ¥186,252,000 (2011/12).

Board of Directors: Matsuura Koichiro (Chair.); Mario Mizukami, Koji Suzuki (Vice-Chairs).

Principal Staff: Sec.-Gen. Noriaki Ida.

Address: 3-9-25 Ebisu Shibuya-ku, Tokyo 150-0013.

Telephone: (3) 5424-1141; **Fax:** (3) 5424-1200; **Internet:** www .mfj.gr.jp; **e-mail:** bjmfj@mfjtokyo.or.jp.

The Matsumae International Foundation

Established in 1979 by Dr Shigeyoshi Matsumae to make a real contribution to permanent peace world-wide, by deepening the understanding of Japan, and establishing links with other countries through inviting to Japan young research workers of outstanding character, without regard to sex, race, religion, ideology or nationality.

Activities: Operates world-wide in the fields of medicine and health and science and technology, through offering grants to individuals, and scholarships and fellowships, tenable for three to six months. Applicants, who must apply from outside Japan, must be under 49 years old, and be post-doctoral researchers, or be recognized by the Foundation as possessing equivalent academic qualifications. Fields of study in the areas of natural science, engineering and medicine are prioritized.

Geographical Area of Activity: International.

Restrictions: Non-Japanese applicants must have a doctorate degree, be under 49 years old, have not been to Japan previously and have established professions or positions in their home country.

Publications: *Fellowship Announcement*; newsletter; *Fellowship Directory*; *Fellowship Research Report*.

Board of Directors: Dr Hirohisa Uchida (Chair.).

Address: 4-14-46 Kamiogi, Suginami-ku, Tokyo 167-0043.

Telephone: (3) 3301-7600; **Fax:** (3) 3301-7601; **Internet:** www .mars.dti.ne.jp/mif; **e-mail:** contact2mif@mist.dti.ne.jp.

Moriya Foundation

Founded in March 1982 by Kimio Moriya to provide scholarships.

Activities: Offers two-year scholarships to students from Asia who are in postgraduate courses at designated universities in Tokyo, Japan. The designated universities choose and recommend candidates to the Foundation every April. Fields of study are limited to geography, history, education and related cultural sciences.

Geographical Area of Activity: Asia.

Principal Staff: Chair. Misao Mariya; Chief Sec. Takahide Nishioka.

Address: c/o Teikoku-Shoin Co Ltd, 3-29 Kanda Jimbo-cho, Chiyoda-ku, Tokyo 101-0051.

Telephone: (3) 3263-7952; **Fax:** (3) 3262-7770; **Internet:** www .teikokushoin.co.jp; **e-mail:** somu@teikokushoin.co.jp.

Naito Foundation

Founded in 1969 by Toyoji Naito to extend financial aid to researchers engaged in basic studies on the life sciences, particularly medical, biological, chemical and pharmaceutical studies for the prevention and treatment of human diseases.

Activities: Operates nationally in the fields of education, science and medicine. Extends support to researchers in universities and public institutions to Japanese researchers who wish to study abroad and to domestic research institutions. Sponsors educational visits to Japan by foreign research workers and supports the publication of reading materials in the life sciences. Arranges exhibitions for the promotion of studies and research in the life sciences, particularly pharmacy. Also awards prizes in recognition of outstanding contributions to the advancement of the life sciences.

Geographical Area of Activity: mainly Japan.

Publications: Report of operations and financial statement; various books; newsletter.

Finance: Total assets ¥16,102,399,781, total revenue ¥652,073,424, total expenditure ¥555,290,079 (2010/11).

Council: Hiroo Imura (Chair.).

Principal Staff: Chair. Haruo Naito; Man. Dir H. Mitsui.

Address: NKD Bldg, 42-6 Hongo 3, Bunkyo-ku, Tokyo 113-0033.

Telephone: (3) 3813-3005; **Fax:** (3) 3811-2917; **Internet:** www .naito-f.or.jp; **e-mail:** info@naito-f.or.jp.

Nippon Foundation

Founded in 1962 by Ryoichi Sasakawa for general philanthropic purposes. Initially focused on the maritime and shipping sectors, but subsequently expanded to cover the areas of education, social welfare, public health, etc.

Activities: Operates nationally in supporting the development of shipbuilding technology, the prevention of marine disasters, and promotion of physical training and social welfare. The Foundation also provides international humanitarian assistance, particularly through the agencies of the UN—e.g. for programmes conducted by the World Health Organization, the UN High Commissioner for Refugees (UNHCR), the UN Children's Fund (UNICEF) and the UN Environment Programme (UNEP). It also supports the treatment of leprosy in a number of countries (through the Sasakawa Memorial Health Foundation); training in shipbuilding technology in developing countries; planning of ports, railway modernization and other transport improvements in developing countries; and activities aimed at strengthening links between Japan and the USA, the United Kingdom and Scandinavia. In Africa, the Foundation is conducting a project aimed at solving the food-shortage crisis through improved agricultural methods, and in Asia and Central and South America it supports agricultural, crop-research and training programmes. The Foundation has also established various other national and international foundations.

Geographical Area of Activity: International.

Publications: Newsletter; articles.

Finance: The Foundation draws the funds required to finance its many projects from the proceeds of Japanese motorboat racing. Annual revenue and expenditure ¥31,155,034,000 (2010/11).

Board of Trustees: Yohei Sasakawa (Chair.).

Principal Staff: Pres. Takeju Ogata.

Address: The Nippon Zaidan Bldg, 1-2-2 Akasaka, Minato-ku, Tokyo 107-8404.

Telephone: (3) 6229-5111; **Fax:** (3) 6229-5110; **Internet:** www .nippon-foundation.or.jp; **e-mail:** cc@ps.nippon-foundation .or.jp.

Niwano Peace Foundation

Established in 1978 to work towards the attainment of world peace and the betterment of culture through promotion of research and other constructive actions, based on religious spirit and serving to promote world peace, in such fields as culture, thought, education and science.

Activities: Offers annual grants for activities on religion, ethics and peace; sponsors symposia and lectures throughout Japan; supports counterparts in South Asia in improving human well-being by alleviating poverty in the region; and awards the Niwano Peace Prize annually to an organization or individual contributing to the cause of peace through promotion of inter-religious tolerance.

Geographical Area of Activity: International.

Finance: Total grants ¥68,400,000 (2008).

Principal Staff: Pres. Nichiko Niwano; Chair. Kinjiro Niwano; Exec. Dir Shin'ichi Noguchi.

Address: Shamvilla Catherina 5F 1-16-9 Shinjuku, Shinjuku-ku, Tokyo 160-0022.

Telephone: (3) 3226-4371; **Fax:** (3) 3226-1835; **Internet:** www .npf.or.jp; **e-mail:** info@npf.or.jp.

OISCA International

Established in October 1961 by Dr Yonosuke Nakano to carry out development and reforestation projects in less-developed countries.

Activities: Operates internationally, with an emphasis on the Asia-Pacific region, in the areas of aid to less-developed countries, and conservation and the environment, through sending volunteers to assist indigenous organizations to carry out projects such as the tree-planting, the development of agriculture, and the Children's Forest Programme. Co-operates with local NGOs and indigenous populations. Holds consultative status with the UN Economic and Social Committee (ECOSOC). Maintains four training centres in Japan. Affiliated organizations exist in more than 100 countries world-wide.

Geographical Area of Activity: World-wide, but mainly in Asia-Pacific region.

Publications: Annual Report.

Administrative Board: Dr Yoshiko Y. Nakano (Pres.); Toshihiro Nakano (Exec. Vice-Pres.); Etsuko Nakano (Vice-Pres.).

Principal Staff: Sec.-Gen. Yasuaki Nagaishi; Deputy Sec.-Gen. Fumio Kitsuki; Asst Sec.-Gen. Aravind Babu.

Address: 3-6-12 Izumi, Suginami, Tokyo 168-0063.

Telephone: (3) 3322-5161; **Fax:** (3) 3324-7111; **Internet:** www .oisca.org; **e-mail:** oisca@oisca.org.

Peace Winds Japan—PWJ

Established in 1996 to assist people internationally who are victims of political circumstances, conflict, poverty or natural disasters; a non-political, non-religious organization.

Activities: Operates internationally, assisting those in need in collaboration with local organizations, offering emergency relief, medical assistance, scholarships, social services, promoting equal rights for women, and supporting education, agriculture, and housing and sanitation. Projects operate in many countries, including Afghanistan, Timor-Leste, Indonesia, Iran, Iraq, Kosovo and Metohija, Liberia, Mongolia, Sudan and Sierra Leone. Nationally, the organization promotes its work through symposia and lectures, and through fair trade activities.

Geographical Area of Activity: International.

Publications: Annual Report; newsletter.

Finance: Total income and expenditure ¥1,193,332,736 (2010/11).

Board: Masaru Ishibashi (Chair.).

Principal Staff: Vice-Pres. and Rep. Dir Ken Susumu Onishi.

Address: Ichigaya-KT I Bldg, 5th Floor, 4-7-16, Kudanminami, Chiyoda-ku, Tokyo 102-0074.

Telephone: (3) 5213-4070; **Fax:** (3) 3556-5771; **Internet:** www .peace-winds.org; **e-mail:** meet@peace-winds.org.

The PHD Foundation—Peace, Health and Human Development Foundation

Established in 1981 by Dr Noboru Iwamura, aims to promote activities that would help bring about peace and health through human development among people in Asia and the South Pacific.

Activities: Promotes the sharing of values, knowledge and skillsmprove the quality of life of those living in poverty in Asia and the South Pacific. Runs training programmes in Japan to provide long-term solutions for people suffering the effects of poverty, as well as follow-up programmes to consolidate technical and leadership skills. Also aims to build stronger links between the Japanese people and their less-wealthy neighbours.

Geographical Area of Activity: Asia and the South Pacific.

Publications: *Irebun Nepal* (study tour reports, 1983); *Kobe Hatsu Asia* (1986); *Asia No Kusanone Kokusaikoryu* (1993); *PHD Letter* (quarterly newsletter); project reports and other publications.

Finance: Financed by membership fees, private contributions, income from publications sales, etc.

Trustees: Shizuo Imai (Chair.).

Principal Staff: Dir-Gen. Tatsuya Fujino (acting); Gen. Affairs/Financial Affairs Sasaki Jiro.

Address: 202 Motomach Urban Life, 5-4-3 Motomachi-dori, Chuo-ku, Kobe-shi, Hyogo 650-0022.

Telephone: (78) 351-4892; **Fax:** (78) 351-4867; **Internet:** www .kisweb.ne.jp/phd; **e-mail:** phd@mb1.kisweb.ne.jp.

Refugees International Japan—RIJ

Established in 1979 to assist in the restoration of the physical well-being and dignity of refugees throughout the world.

Activities: Raises funds to assist refugees who have lost everything as a result of war and conflict. RIJ funds projects for emergency situations, provides assistance to meet basic survival needs, supports pilot schemes and distributes grants for training and education. Countries and regions supported over the past 30 years include Burma (Myanmar), Cambodia, Caucasus, Congo, Ethiopia, Guinea, Kenya, Palestinian Autonomous Areas, Sierra Leone, Sri Lanka, Sudan, Tanzania, Thailand and Timor-Leste.

Geographical Area of Activity: International.

Publications: Annual Review; regular e-newsletters to members.

Finance: Funded through donations, membership and annual fund-raising events and activities. Total grant disbursements ¥21,589,000 (2010/11).

Trustees: Haruyuki Niimi (Chair.).

Principal Staff: Pres. and CEO Jane Best; Sec. to the Board Sarah Cockerill; Finance Dir Takaaki Fukunaga.

Address: c/o Showa Shell Sekiyu K. K. Daiba Frontier Bldg, 12F 2-3-2 Daiba, Minato-ku, Tokyo 135-8074.

Telephone: (3) 5500-3093; **Fax:** (3) 5500-3094; **Internet:** www .refugeesinternationaljapan.org; **e-mail:** enquiries@ refugeesinternationaljapan.org.

Rohm Music Foundation

Established on 19 February 1991 for the promotion of music in Japan and throughout the world.

Activities: Operates in the field of the arts and humanities, through supporting young Japanese musicians, organizing international music exchange activities, offering grants for music research, awarding scholarships, disseminating information and carrying out research. Organizes the Kyoto International Music Students' Festival for the promotion of young musicians from around the world.

Geographical Area of Activity: Japan.

Finance: Net assets ¥48,383,691,976 (31 Mar. 2011), projected annual income ¥1,083,970,000 (2011/12), projected annual expenditure ¥1,308,443,000 (2011/12).

Principal Staff: Chair. Ken Sato; Man. Dir Hiroshi Watanabe; Sec.-Gen. Susumu Taniguchi.

Address: 1 Nishinakamizu-cho, Saiin, Ukiyo-ku, Kyoto 615-0044.

Telephone: (75) 311-7710; **Fax:** (75) 311-0089; **Internet:** www .rohm.com/rmf/index.html.

Rotary Yoneyama Memorial Foundation, Inc

The Foundation was founded in 1967, an endeavour by Rotarians in Japan to promote international relations by granting scholarships to foreigners aspiring to study or pursue research at Japanese higher education institutions (including universities, junior colleges, colleges of technology and specialized training colleges).

Activities: Supported by 90,000 Rotarians. Functions at an international level, focusing on education; grants scholarships and fellowships to foreign students; stipulations for grants include the enrolment of the applicant in the designated Japanese college or university as an undergraduate or graduate on a full-time basis.

Geographical Area of Activity: World-wide.

Board of Trustees: Toshio Itabashi (Chair.).

Principal Staff: Sec.-Gen. Hiroyasu Sakashita.

Address: Kokuryu-Shibakoen Bldg 3F, 2-6-15, Shibakoen, Minato-ku, Tokyo.

Telephone: (3) 3434-8681; **Fax:** (3) 3578-8281; **Internet:** www .rotary-yoneyama.or.jp; **e-mail:** mail@rotary-yoneyama.or .jp.

The Saison Foundation

Established in 1987 by Seiji Tsutsumi to carry out activities conducive to the stimulation of creativity among individuals or organizations engaged in the arts, especially contemporary Japanese theatre and dance, and to expedite international cultural exchanges.

Activities: Operates nationally and internationally in the field of the performing arts. The Foundation operates through two main grant programmes: Direct Support to Artists, which supports the activities and projects by individual artists (e.g. playwrights, directors, choreographers) as well as their sabbatical (overseas travel/vacation) projects; and Partnership Programmes, which support individuals and organizations as partners working to improve the infrastructure of contemporary performing arts in Japan or to enhance international artistic exchange. The Foundation also allows grantees to use its Morishita Studio in Tokyo.

Geographical Area of Activity: World-wide.

Publications: Annual Report; *Viewpoint* (quarterly newsletter).

Finance: Assets ¥7,359,315,150 (March 2010).

Principal Staff: Pres. Seiji Tsutsumi; Man. Dir Masao Katayama.

Address: Toka Bldg, 8th Floor, 16-1, Ginza, 1-chome, Chuo-ku, Tokyo 104-0061.

Telephone: (3) 3535-5566; **Fax:** (3) 3535-5565; **Internet:** www .saison.or.jp; **e-mail:** foundation@saison.or.jp.

Sasakawa Peace Foundation—SPF

Founded in September 1986, seeks to contribute to general human welfare and the substantial development of the international community, thereby to world peace, through programmes promoting international communication, understanding and co-operation.

Activities: The Foundation functions at an international level organizing programmes and issuing grants to institutions. Activities include: development of human resources; undertaking research and surveys; organizing international forums and conferences; conducting other activities to strengthen international understanding and co-operation; and publishing information in support of the Foundation's objectives. Implemented a total of 56 projects in 2010/11 at a cost of ¥1,161,370,000.

Geographical Area of Activity: World-wide.

Restrictions: No grants are made to individuals and business corporations.

Publications: Annual Report; newsletter; brochures; survey reports; conference transcripts/minutes; books.

Finance: Total assets 76,977,749,000 (March 2011); annual income ¥1,737,569,000 (2009/10), expenditure ¥511,167,000 (2009/10).

Board of Trustees: Jiro Hanyu (Chair.); Yuji Takagi (Pres.).

Principal Staff: Exec. Dirs Akinori Sugai, Junko Chano.

Address: Nippon Foundation Bldg, 4th Floor, 1-2-2, Akasaka, Minato-ku, Tokyo 107-8523.

Telephone: (3) 6229-5400; **Fax:** (3) 6229-5470; **Internet:** www .spf.org; **e-mail:** spfpr@spf.or.jp.

Tokyu Foundation for Inbound Students

Established in 1975 by the Tokyu Corporation and other companies to promote international exchanges; and to promote communication between students, and between students and the Japanese people; to foster the development of international goodwill between Japan and other Asia-Pacific countries to contribute to international co-operation and cultural exchange.

Activities: Offers 24 scholarships a year to non-Japanese postgraduate students from the Asia-Pacific region to enable them to study in Japan. Scholarships are normally awarded for up to two years.

Geographical Area of Activity: Asia and Pacific areas.

Restrictions: Scholarships for doctoral degrees are available only to those aged under 34 years old; scholarships for Masters degrees are available only to those aged under 29.

Principal Staff: Gen.-Sec. Yasushi Teranaka.

Address: 1-21-6 Dogenzaka, Shibuya-ku, Tokyo 150.

Telephone: (3) 3461-0844; **Fax:** (3) 5458-1696; **Internet:** www .tokyu-f.jp; **e-mail:** info@tokyu-f.jp.

Toshiba International Foundation—TIFO

Founded in 1989 by the Toshiba Corp to promote international exchange activities and a better understanding of Japan.

Activities: Operates in the fields of the arts and humanities, education, international affairs and science and technology, through its own international programmes and the provision of grants to institutions. The Foundation also awards scholarships to overseas nationals to promote international understanding of Japan.

Geographical Area of Activity: World-wide.

Publications: *Japan's Role in the 1990s*; *Proceedings of Toshiba International Foundation Symposium*; *TIFO News*.

Finance: Total assets ¥3,000,000,000 (2008).

Board of Trustees: Taizo Nishimuro (Chair.); Shigeji Ueshima, Shinji Fukukawa (Vice-Chairs).

Principal Staff: Pres. Fumihiko Namekawa.

Address: 3rd Floor, Toshiba Bldg, 1-1 Shibaura 1-chome, Minato-ku, Tokyo 105-8001.

Telephone: (3) 3457-2733; **Fax:** (3) 3457-4389; **Internet:** www .toshiba.co.jp/about/tifo/index_j.html; **e-mail:** tifo@toshiba .co.jp.

The Toyota Foundation

Founded in 1974 by Toyota Motor Corpn to contribute towards creating a human-orientated society by providing grants for research and projects related to the human and natural environments, social welfare, education, culture and other fields.

Activities: The Foundation's publicly solicited grant programmes are: the Asian Neighbors Programme, which supports practical projects in Asia; the Research Grant Programme, which supports research reflecting original thinking and with broad social significance; and the Grant Programme for Community Activities in Japan. The Foundation sets 'realizing a sustainable society' and 'community revitalization and coexistence' as common goals of these programmes.

Geographical Area of Activity: Mainly Japan and Asian countries.

Restrictions: In general, the Foundation does not approve grants for capital investment, plant or equipment; endowments; museum or library acquisitions; annual budgets of organizations or institutions, or of established programmes; propaganda or lobbying activities; religious activities; nor for unsponsored individuals.

Publications: *The Toyota Foundation Occasional Report* (annually); *JOINT* (3 a year).

Finance: Total grants budget ¥533,000,000 (2011).

Principal Staff: Chair. Hiroshi Okuda; Pres. Atsuko Toyama; Man. Dir Hiroshi Ito.

Address: 37F Shinjuku Mitsui Bldg, 2-1-1 Nishi Shinjuku, Shinjuku-ku, Tokyo 163-0437.

Telephone: (3) 3344-1701; **Fax:** (3) 3342-6911; **Internet:** www .toyotafound.or.jp; **e-mail:** admin@toyotafound.or.jp.

Jordan

FOUNDATIONS, TRUSTS AND NON-PROFIT ORGANIZATIONS

King Hussein Foundation—KHF

Established by Royal Decree in 1999 as a national and international NGO dedicated to the humanitarian vision of the late King Hussein of Jordan.

Activities: Operates nationally and internationally in the fields of peace and democracy, sustainable community development, education and leadership, the environment, and health. Has established a number of institutes in Jordan: the Jubilee Institute (teacher training), the Information and Research Centre, the National Centre for Culture and the Performing Arts, the National Music Conservatory and the Institute for Family Health. In 2001 the Foundation launched the King Hussein Foundation International (KHFI) in Washington, DC, USA, to raise endowment funds for the Foundation. KHFI programmes include the King Hussein Leadership Prize and the Media and Humanity Program.

Geographical Area of Activity: Jordan and the USA.

Board: HM Queen Noor al-Hussein (Chair.).

Address: POB 926687, Amman 11110.

Telephone: (6) 5607460; **Fax:** (6) 5606994; **Internet:** www.kinghusseinfoundation.org; **e-mail:** khf-nhf@khf.org.jo.

JOHUD—Jordanian Hashemite Fund for Human Development

Established in 1977 to advance comprehensive and sustainable human development through the enhanced participation of Jordanian people.

Activities: Through its network of 50 community development centres, the Fund focuses on developing a model of integrated development activities, through support for projects working in a range of areas, including child development, family health and nutrition, education and awareness, leadership skills for women, young people, income generation and enterprise development.

Geographical Area of Activity: Jordan.

Publications: *Humanity* (quarterly newsletter); *Jordan National Human Development Report.*

Trustee: HRH Princess Basma bint Talal (Chair.).

Principal Staff: Exec. Dir Farah Daghistani.

Address: POB 5118, Amman 11183.

Telephone: (6) 5560741; **Fax:** (6) 5515950; **Internet:** www.johud.org.jo; **e-mail:** info@johud.org.jo.

Jordan River Foundation

Established in 1995 by HM Queen Rania al-Abdullah to empower local community members, help to combat poverty and ensure sustainable development.

Activities: The Foundation aims to promote the development of Jordanian society through sustainable social, economic and cultural programmes. It works to protect the rights and needs of children, and to empower individuals and communities; projects include the Community Empowerment Programme, the Child Safety Programme and the Capacity Building and Business Development Programme.

Geographical Area of Activity: Jordan.

Publications: *Jordan in Bloom – Wildflowers of the Holy Land; Crossing the River Jordan; Historical Trees of Jordan*; newsletter; *Paths to Success* (Jordan River Foundation Success Stories); Annual Report; Sustainability Report 2007; Sustainability Report 2008.

Board of Trustees: HM Queen Rania al-Abdullah (Chair.); Maysa Jalbout (Vice-Chair.).

Principal Staff: Dir-Gen. Valentina Qussisiya; Dep. Dir-Gen. Ghaleb al-Qudah.

Address: POB 2943, 11181 Amman.

Telephone: (6) 5933211; **Fax:** (6) 5933210; **Internet:** www.jordanriver.jo; **e-mail:** info@jrf.org.jo.

Noor al-Hussein Foundation—NHF

NHF is a non-profit, NGO that works to create a lasting, positive impact on the lives of disadvantaged people in Jordan and the Middle East. Established to initiate and support projects nationally and internationally in the fields of integrated community development, microfinance, child and family health, women and enterprise development. Operates as an independent entity under the umbrella of the King Hussein Foundation (q.v.).

Activities: Operates nationally and regionally, through projects that promote self-help and participation in decision-making and project management. Initiated and owns the Jordan Micro Credit Company, Tamweelcom, now a financially independent company, to disburse loans to low-income entrepreneurs to enable them to set up micro-enterprises or expand existing ones. Provides comprehensive health care services for children and families, and refugees through its Institute for Family Health. The NHF Community Development Programme provides capacity building, business development services, loans and grants to establish income-generating projects (IGPs), as well as the creation of job opportunities at the grassroots level, assisting in reducing poverty and unemployment.

Geographical Area of Activity: Jordan.

Principal Staff: Chair. HM Queen Noor al-Hussein.

Address: POB 926687, Amman 11110.

Telephone: (6) 5607460; **Fax:** (6) 5606994; **Internet:** www.nooralhusseinfoundation.org; **e-mail:** khf-nhf@khf.org.jo.

Scientific Foundation of Hisham Adeeb Hijjawi

Established in 1981 by Hisham Hijjawi to support education in the field of technical and applied sciences.

Activities: Operates in Jordan and Palestinian Autonomous Areas in the field of education, and in particular in the area of research in technical and applied sciences at universities and colleges; also supports scientific conferences and workshops, funds the purchase of scientific equipment, and makes three awards annually for research projects in the applied sciences. The Foundation funds a technical college in the Palestinian Autonomous Areas. It also operates in the field of social welfare and is a founding member of the Welfare Association, providing development assistance in human resource development, institutional building and the promotion of culture and identity for Palestinians, in the Palestinian Autonomous Areas and elsewhere.

Geographical Area of Activity: Jordan and Palestinian Autonomous Areas.

Finance: Funded by investment portfolio of founder, the late Hisham Hijjawi.

Board of Directors: Ayman Hisham Hijjawi (Chair.); Jaafar Hisham Hijjawi (Vice-Chair.).

Address: 190 Zhran St, POB 1944, Amman 11821.

Telephone: (6) 5500999; **Fax:** (6) 5500998; **Internet:** www .hijjawi.org/The-Foundation.html; **e-mail:** info@hijjawi.org.

Abdul Hameed Shoman Foundation

A non-profit cultural institution established in 1978 by the Arab Bank PLC, to embody and perpetuate the legacy of the Bank's founder, the late Abdul Hameed Shoman, to support and enhance scientific research and Arab humanistic creativity; build bridges of dialogue and cultural communication; and collect and disseminate general knowledge by all feasible means.

Activities: Awards annual prizes in 12 fields to 'Young Arab Researchers' whose works demonstrate exceptional scientific value. Also grants prizes biennially to teachers in Jordanian preparatory and secondary schools who demonstrate original approaches to the teaching of science. Also grants annual prizes for children's literature. In 1986 established the Abdul Hameed Shoman Public Library, and the Abdul Hameed Shoman Cultural Forum, which hosts lectures made by prominent Jordanian or Arab lecturers, and tackles important public issues; and the Dialogue of the Month, where prominent intellectuals present their viewpoints and opinions, as well as organizing seminars and workshops. In 1989 the Forum established a cinema, which offers weekly screenings of modern and classical films. In 1999 established the Abdul Hameed Shoman Fund for the Support and Encouragement of Scientific Research, which funds research at Jordanian universities.

Geographical Area of Activity: Jordan.

Publications: Proceedings from lectures, seminars and workshops; numerous works in Arabic and English.

Finance: Endowment based on 3% of net annual profits of the Arab Bank PLC.

Board of Directors: Mohamed Abdel Hamid Shoman (Chair.); Ibrahim Izzeddine (Dep. Chair.); Basem Ali al-Imam (Sec. of the Board).

Principal Staff: Dir-Gen. Thabet al-Taher.

Address: POB 940255, Amman 11194.

Telephone: (6) 5679166; **Fax:** (6) 5679182; **Internet:** www .shoman.org; **e-mail:** ahsf@shoman.org.jo.

Kazakhstan

FOUNDATIONS, TRUSTS AND NON-PROFIT ORGANIZATIONS

BOTA Foundation

Established in 2008 to improve the lives of children and young people suffering from poverty in Kazakhstan through improvements in health, education and social welfare; the Foundation was established under the terms of a trilateral agreement between the governments of the USA, Kazakhstan and Switzerland to invest approximately US $100m. funds from Kazakhstan frozen in Switzerland in 1999.

Activities: Projects are undertaken through the Conditional Cash Transfer Programme, the Social Service Programme, and the Tuition Assistance Programme.

Geographical Area of Activity: Kazakhstan.

Publications: *BOTAzhan* (quarterly).

Board of Directors: Evgeniy Zhovtis (Chair.).

Principal Staff: Exec. Dir Aaron Bornstein.

Address: 3rd Floor, 160 Dostyk Ave, 050051 Almaty.

Telephone: (727) 2641269; **Fax:** (727) 2643614; **Internet:** www.bota.kz; **e-mail:** mail@bota.kz.

Soros Foundation—Kazakhstan

Founded in September 1995 to promote open society; it is an independent foundation, part of the Soros foundations network, which aims to foster political and cultural pluralism and reform economic structures to encourage free enterprise and a market economy.

Activities: The Foundation operates in the fields of economic affairs, health and statistics, law and juvenile justice, media and information, and civil society. It provides support for innovative projects focused on budget and extractive industries transparency at all levels, supports Kazakhstan's NGOs and the independent mass media, economic and law reform projects, including policy-making, dissemination of information and exchange of experties.

Geographical Area of Activity: Kazakhstan.

Publications: Annual Report; policy papers; books.

Finance: Total funds allocated 490,484,367 tenge (2010).

Board of Trustees: Kasenova Nargis Umirserikovna (Chair.).

Principal Staff: Chair. Exec. Council (vacant); Deputy Chair. Exec. Council Irina V. Koshkina.

Address: 050000 Almaty, ul. Zheltoksan 111A-9.

Telephone: (727) 2503811; **Fax:** (727) 2503814; **Internet:** www.soros.kz/en.html; **e-mail:** sfk@soros.kz.

Kenya

FOUNDATION CENTRES AND CO-ORDINATING BODIES

African NGOs Environment Network—ANEN

Founded in Nairobi in 1982 by 21 African NGOs to strengthen co-operation between African NGOs and their governments, and similar organizations abroad; to support the involvement of NGOs in environmental and development projects; and to provide information on African development and environment projects.

Activities: The Foundation operates in the fields of conservation and the environment by supporting several projects, including: water management, renewable energy, forestry, agriculture, health, desertification, soil conservation and the use of science and technology for development purposes; it also produces educational materials, organizes training workshops, disseminates information and maintains a database. The Network liaises with organizations in 47 African countries.

Geographical Area of Activity: Africa.

Publications: *EcoAfrica* (6 a year, in English and French); *News Elert*; Annual Report; numerous directories, papers and manuals.

Principal Staff: Dir Simon M. Muchiru.

Address: POB 53844, Nairobi.

Telephone: (2) 228138; **Fax:** (2) 335108.

Allavida—Alliances for Voluntary Initiatives and Development

Founded in 2001 by the merger of Charity Know How and Alliance magazine, both of which were formerly part of CAF—Charities Aid Foundation (q.v.).

Activities: Allavida works in Africa mobilizing financial resources, building local grant-making and grant management capacity, enhancing skills in community organizations for local development, encouraging local philanthropy, and facilitating learning in and between organizations. Concentrates on five key themes: organizational development, individual learning, grant-making, promoting philanthropy, and influencing. Operates small grants programmes, training programmes, provides consultancy support, and carries out research and development activities in the areas of capacity building of non-profit organizations and the development of local and regional philanthropy.

Geographical Area of Activity: East Africa.

Publications: *An Introduction to the Non-Profit Sector in Kenya; An Introduction to the Non-Profit Sector in Uganda; An Introduction to the Non-Profit Sector in Tanzania; Philanthropy in East Africa; In Trust for Tomorrow; Promoting Philanthropy in Kenya—The Case for Tax Law Reform; One Woman at a Time; A Legacy of Giving; Allavida* (newsletter); Annual Report.

Finance: Funded by a variety of trusts and foundations.

Board of Directors: Aleke Dondo (Chair.).

Principal Staff: Chief Exec. Andrew Kingman.

Address: 3rd Floor, Rattansi Educational Trust Building, Koinange St, POB 10434, 0100 Nairobi.

Telephone: (20) 310526; **Internet:** www.allavida.org; **e-mail:** info@allavida.or.ke.

East African Association of Grantmakers

Incorporated in 2003 to develop a culture of local philanthropy to improve the lives of the people of East Africa.

Activities: Aims to develop local philanthropy in East Africa, through demonstrating and promoting philanthropy in East Africa as an integral strategy for permanent wealth-creation for social development. Also promotes ethical grant-making practices as a tool for development; supports members with learning and capacity building opportunities for effective asset development, management, governance and grant-making; strengthens the individual and collective voice of member organizations; and enters into dialogue with governments, the private sector and civil society partners in an effort to influence policy. Organizes conferences and seminars.

Geographical Area of Activity: East Africa.

Publications: Newsletter; Annual Report.

Board of Directors: Frederick Bwire Ouma (Chair.); Olive Luena (Vice-Chair.); Rene Kiamba (Treas.); Nicanor Sabula (CEO/Secretary.).

Principal Staff: CEO Nicanor Sabula.

Address: 4th Floor, Rattansi Educational Trust Bldg, Koinange St, POB 49626 00100, Nairobi.

Telephone: (020) 315773; **Fax:** (020) 2244470; **Internet:** www.eaag.org; **e-mail:** info@eaag.org.

ELCI—Environment Liaison Centre International

Established in 1974. Aims to ensure good communication between NGOs and local communities, and increase the capacity of environmental organizations.

Activities: Works internationally as a networking body between organizations and communities, and between NGOs and international organizationsto improve co-operation between these groups and the effectiveness of the environmental work carried out. Aims to strengthen NGOs by assisting them through providing information, training workers in communication skills, and project and resource management. Has more than 850 member organizations. A sister organization exists in Costa Rica. Co-ordinator of the Regional Network of Women and Sustainable Energy in Africa.

Geographical Area of Activity: International.

Publications: *Ecoforum* (quarterly magazine); *ELCI News; Directory of Francophone NGOs*.

Board: Cyril Ritchie (Chair.); Rajen Awotar (Treas.).

Principal Staff: Exec. Dir Tanveer Arif.

Address: POB 72461-00200, Nairobi.

Telephone: (20) 8566172; **Fax:** (20) 8566175; **Internet:** www.elci.org; **e-mail:** info@elci.org.

Ufadhili Trust

Established in 2000, acts as a resource organization for philanthropy, corporate social responsibility and volunteerism in East Africa. Champions the cause of local resource mobilization for social development and a reduction in dependence on foreign aid.

Activities: Acts as a resource for the non-profit sector in Kenya and East Africa to facilitate strategic and effective partnerships between business, non-profit organizations, individuals and government towards sustainable development. Maintains a resource centre; provides technical assistance to East African foundations; operates community development pilot projects; and lobbies on issues relating to the legal and fiscal status of NGOs and foundations. Has advisory boards in Uganda and Tanzania.

Geographical Area of Activity: East Africa.

Publications: *Corporate Concern* (quarterly newsletter).

Board of Trustees: John H. Mramba (Chair.).

Principal Staff: Exec. Dir Mumo Kivuitu.

Address: Rattansi Educational Trust Bldg, 1st Floor, Koinange St, POB 14041-00100, Nairobi.

Telephone: (2) 343061; **Fax:** (2) 343067; **Internet:** www.ufadhilitrust.org; **e-mail:** info@ufadhilitrust.org.

FOUNDATIONS, TRUSTS AND NON-PROFIT ORGANIZATIONS

ACORD—Agency for Co-operation and Research in Development

Founded in 1976 as a consortium of international agencies with headquarters in the North to empower its members with operational capacity to tackle poverty issues ensuant to droughts in Sub-Saharan Africa; became Africa-led in 2006.

Activities: ACORD is active in 18 African countries. It promotes aid and social welfare through grants and research into long-term development. Programmes around five core themes are undertaken: conflict prevention and peacebuilding, strengthening civil society, women's rights, HIV/AIDS and livelihoods within a global programme to promote social activism. Maintains offices in London, United Kingdom, and country offices throughout Africa.

Geographical Area of Activity: Africa.

Publications: Annual Report; ACORD policies; reports; newsletter.

Finance: Net assets £1,044,000, annual income £8,426,000; annual expenditure £8,674,000 (2010).

Board of Trustees: Ibrahim Ouedraogo (Chair.); Maggie Pankhurst (Hon. Treas.).

Principal Staff: Exec. Dir and Company Sec. Ousainou Ngum.

Address: ACK Garden House, 1st Ngong Ave, First Floor, Wing C, POB 61216, 00200 Nairobi.

Telephone: (20) 2721172; **Fax:** (20) 2721166; **Internet:** www.acordinternational.org; **e-mail:** info@acordinternational.org.

The African Agricultural Technology Foundation—AATF

A non-profit organization established in 2002. Aims to facilitate and promote public-private partnerships for the access and delivery of appropriate proprietary agricultural technologies for use by resource-poor smallholder farmers in Sub-Saharan Africa.

Activities: Provides advice and expertise in the area of agricultural technologies, working towards food security and poverty reduction.

Geographical Area of Activity: Sub-Saharan Africa.

Publications: Annual Report; newsletters.

Finance: Total assets US $4,997,357 (2010); annual income $12,261,299, annual expenditure $11,747,439 (2010).

Board of Trustees: Idah Sithole-Niang (Chair.); Josephine Ayugi Okot (Dep. Chair.).

Principal Staff: Exec. Dir Denis Tumwesigye Kyetere.

Address: POB 30709, Nairobi 00100.

Telephone: (20) 422-3700; **Fax:** (20) 422-3701; **Internet:** www.aatf-africa.org; **e-mail:** aatf@aatf-africa.org.

African Medical and Research Foundation—AMREF

Established in 1957 to provide health-care services in East Africa; originally known as the Flying Doctors Service of East Africa.

Activities: Operates in Africa in the fields of aid to less-developed countries, and medicine and health, through five main projects: Child and Adolescent Health and Development; Sexual and Reproductive Health; Clinical Services and Emergency Response; Health Policy and Systems Reform; and Environmental Health. Runs a Flying Doctor Service in East Africa, which carries out emergency medical evacuations. Maintains country offices in Kenya, South Africa, Tanzania and Uganda, and field offices in Ethiopia, Mozambique, Rwanda, Somalia and Sudan. There are also offices in European countries, the USA and Canada. The organization won the 1999 Conrad Hilton Humanitarian Award and the 2005 Gates Award for Global Health.

Geographical Area of Activity: Africa.

Publications: Annual Report; books and manuals on health care; reports (technical and medical); *AMREF News* (quarterly newspaper).

Finance: Total assets US $46,929,000, annual income $67,530,000, annual expenditure $68,043,000 (2010).

Board of Directors: Dr Pascoal Manuel Mocumbi (Chair.); Dr Noerina Kaleeba (Deputy Chair.).

Principal Staff: Dir-Gen. Dr Teguest Guerma, Chief Operations Officer Jenny Panow.

Address: Langata Rd, POB 27691-00506, Nairobi.

Telephone: (20) 6993000; **Fax:** (20) 609518; **Internet:** www.amref.org; **e-mail:** info@amref.org.

EABL Foundation

Established in 2005 by East African Breweries Limited to lead community investment efforts.

Activities: A corporate community development foundation operating in East Africa with an emphasis on water, environment and education. Offers scholarships to universities in East Africa to students in need for study in the areas of business, information technology, engineering and food science.

Geographical Area of Activity: East Africa.

Publications: Newsletter; reports.

Principal Staff: Man. Keith Obure.

Address: Office of the Dir of Corporate Affairs, East African Breweries Ltd, POB 30161, 00100 Nairobi.

Internet: www.eablfoundation.com; **e-mail:** eablfoundation@eabl.com.

KCDF—Kenya Community Development Foundation

Established in 1997 to mobilize resources effectively for building permanent funds for grant-making in the area of community development.

Activities: Active in the area of grant-making to community-based and civil society organizations, and NGOs working with communities in need at grassroots level in community capacity building and endowment fund building (in areas including food security, gender equality, youth development and educational scholarships) as a basis for building permanent assets for sustainable community development.

Geographical Area of Activity: Kenya.

Restrictions: Grants only to community-based, civil society and NGOs working mainly with communities in need.

Publications: *Endowment Challenge Booklet*; Annual Report; booklets on local philanthropy.

Board of Trustees: Isaac Wanjohi (Chair.).

Principal Staff: Chair. of Bd of Dirs Atia Yahya, CEO Janet Mawiyoo, Deputy CEO Tom Were.

Address: Cnr Pamba and Chai Rd, Pangani, POB 10501-00100, Nairobi.

Telephone: (20) 3540239; **Fax:** (20) 8067440; **Internet:** www.kcdf.or.ke; **e-mail:** info@kcdf.or.ke.

Korea (Republic)

FOUNDATIONS, TRUSTS AND NON-PROFIT ORGANIZATIONS

Arts Council Korea

Founded in 1973 as the Korean Culture and Arts Foundation to promote Korean culture and art and to encourage its development; became Arts Council Korea in 2005.

Activities: Promotes Korean culture abroad and encourages international cultural exchange; awards fellowships; finances research into aspects of Korean culture through institutions in the Republic of Korea and in other countries; runs courses; maintains a library. Nationally invests in Korean artistic and cultural infrastructures.

Geographical Area of Activity: World-wide.

Publications: *Promotion of Arts and Culture* (monthly); *Almanac of Culture and Arts* (annually); financial statements.

Council: Oh Kwang-su (Chair.).

Principal Staff: CEO Sim Jai-chan.

Address: 1-130 Dongsoong-Dong, Jongno-gu, Seoul 110-766.

Telephone: (2) 7604-500; **Fax:** (2) 7604-700; **Internet:** www .arko.or.kr; **e-mail:** arko@arko.or.kr.

The Beautiful Foundation

Established in 2000.

Activities: Aims to create a world filled with 'affluent beauty' in which extremes of wealth and poverty are eradicated. Holds an annual international symposium entitled 'Giving Korea'. Conducts research on philanthropy and corporate social responsibility.

Geographical Area of Activity: Republic of Korea.

Publications: Books on philanthropy.

Finance: Total income 17,401,258,074 Korean won; total expenditure 12,965,816,270 Korean won (2009).

Address: 16-3 Gahoe-dong, Jongno-gu, Seoul 110-260.

Telephone: (2) 766-1004; **Fax:** (2) 730-1243; **Internet:** www .beautifulfund.org; **e-mail:** give@beautifulfund.org.

ChildFund Korea

Founded in 1948 as a non-governmental social welfare organization aiming to improve the lives of less-privileged children. Renamed Korea Children's Foundation in 1979 and Korea Welfare Foundation in 1994. Renamed ChildFund Korea in 2008.

Activities: The Foundation helps needy children, with programmes to prevent child abuse, support severely ill children, protect children in local society, and prevent child loss. It also runs a foster family programme. Operates in South Korea, North Korea, Cambodia, Ethiopia, Senegal, Sierra Leone, Sri Lanka, Uganda, Viet Nam, Bolivia, China, etc.

Geographical Area of Activity: South-East Asia, South Asia, South America and Africa.

Publications: *Danbee* (newsletter, 6 a year); *Apple Tree* (monthly magazine); books.

Finance: Total income 100,852,846,919 Korean won, expenditure 96,414,642,977 Korean won (2010); total projected income and expenditure 105,690,478,795 Korean won (2012).

Board of Directors: Lee Je-Hun (Chair.).

Principal Staff: Pres. Kim Seok-San.

Address: 95 Mugyo-Dong, ChildFund Bldg, 11th Floor, Jung-Gu, Seoul 100-170.

Telephone: (2) 775-9121; **Fax:** (2) 756-4256; **Internet:** eng .childfund.or.kr; **e-mail:** kwf@kwf.or.kr.

Good Neighbors International

Established in 1991, a non-profit NGO, originally known as Good Neighbors, Inc Korea, which aims to provide humanitarian aid to people in developing countries and Korea. Re-established in 1996 as Good Neighbors International working in the areas of nutrition and sanitation, education and training, community development, promoting the equal rights and self-determination of marginalized people and pursuing world peace and security.

Activities: Operates humanitarian and development projects throughout the world, providing relief for the suffering, and funding long-term development projects in poor communities. Focuses particularly on teaching young people to be self-sufficient, thus providing a lasting solution to poverty and hunger. Involved in the Rwandan refugee crisis, providing medical teams and setting up schools in refugee camps. Also played a role in relief operations in Haiti following an earthquake in 2010. Type of activities supported include child abuse prevention and counselling centres, training in vocational skills, dam construction and well drilling, soup kitchens, dairy farms, latrine construction, refugee medical teams, rural community development and agricultural training for young people and women. Maintains some 21 field offices world-wide.

Geographical Area of Activity: Asia, Africa and Central and South America.

Publications: *Partnership* (newsletter, 6 a year).

Finance: Receives funding from membership dues, the Government and gifts-in-kind.

Principal Staff: Pres. Lee Il-Ha.

Address: 101-4,Cheongpa-dong 2ga, Yongsan-gu, Seoul 140-132.

Telephone: (2) 6717-4000; **Fax:** (2) 6717-4293; **Internet:** www .goodneighbors.org; **e-mail:** gni@gni.kr.

IACD—Institute of Asian Culture and Development

Established in 1983, offers long-term assistance mainly to developing countries in Asia in the areas of education and training, community development and medical services in its endeavour to build peaceful and fair communities.

Activities: IACD actively participates in founding and managing educational institutions; dispatches experts to oversee social and economic development projects; provides medical relief services; organizes academic, sports and cultural exchange programmes; hosts international academic conferences; provides training opportunities and scholarships; operates welfare programmes for children, women and the disabled; provides international peace volunteers; provides business/investment consultancy services.

Geographical Area of Activity: Asia, Central Asia and Middle East and North Africa.

Publications: *International Journal of Central Asian Studies*.

Board of Directors: Lee Jun (Pres.).

Principal Staff: Sec.-Gen. Kang Sung-Han.

Address: POB 180, Seoul 100-601.

Telephone: (2) 795-9410; **Fax:** (2) 077-8819; **Internet:** www .iacd.or.kr; **e-mail:** iacd@chol.com.

The Korea Foundation

Established on 14 December 1991 to promote understanding of the Republic of Korea world-wide, and to enhance international goodwill and friendship through international exchange programmes.

Activities: Operates internationally to promote Korean studies overseas, cultural exchange activities, and exchange and publication programmes, through grants to individuals and institutions, sponsorship of international forums, awarding scholarships and fellowships, and supporting overseas organizations, including museums and art galleries, and international conferences. Maintains six overseas offices (two in the USA, and one in China, Russia, Germany and Viet Nam respectively).

Geographical Area of Activity: World-wide.

Publications: *Koreana* (quarterly, in Arabic, German, English, French, Chinese, Russian, Spanish and Japanese); *Korea Focus* (monthly web magazine, in English); newsletter (quarterly, in English and Korean); Annual Report.

Finance: Annual revenue 78,120,190,114 Korean won, expenditure 78,120,190,114 Korean won (2010).

Board of Directors: Kim Byung-Kook (Pres.); Zeon Nam-Jin (Exec. Vice-Pres.); Cha Du-Hyeogn (Exec. Vice-Pres.).

Principal Staff: Dir Gen. Affairs Park Mi-Sook.

Address: Diplomatic Center Bldg, 10th Floor, 2558 Nambu-sunhwanno, Seocho-gu, Seoul 137-863.

Telephone: (2) 2046-8500; **Fax:** (2) 3463-6076; **Internet:** www .kf.or.kr; **e-mail:** general@kf.or.kr.

Seoam Scholarship Foundation

Established in 1989 by Taeyoung Group. Aims to improve education and to contribute to the education of students who will go on to have a positive effect on the development of the Republic of Korea.

Activities: Provides scholarships to promising secondary school and university students in various fields. Established the Seoam Library; engages in fundraising activities; and supports a number of activities. Also awards the Seoam Scholarship Education Prize.

Geographical Area of Activity: Republic of Korea.

Principal Staff: Dir Yoon Se-Young.

Address: 923-14, Mok-dong, Yangchun-gu, Seoul.

Telephone: (2) 3660-1761; **Fax:** (2) 3270-6920; **Internet:** www .taeyoung.co.kr/group/seoam/seoam.html; **e-mail:** seoam@ sbs.co.kr.

Kosovo

FOUNDATIONS, TRUSTS AND NON-PROFIT ORGANIZATIONS

Fondaccioni per Iniciative Demokratike (Foundation for Democratic Initiatives—FDI)

Founded in 2001.

Activities: The Foundation aims to strengthen civic participation in communities across Kosovo and among all ethnic groups, by providing grants and advice to NGOs and informal groups. Activities include the Community Development Grants Programme, the Cultural Heritage Grants Programme, the Minority Integration and Reconciliation Grants Programme, the Institutional Support Grants Programme, the Learning and Support Activities Programme, and the Place-Making Programme.

Geographical Area of Activity: Kosovo.

Publications: Reports; analysis; research.

Finance: The Foundation is supported by the Charles Stewart Mott Foundation, East-West Management Institute, Rockefeller Brothers Fund, Balkan Trust for Democracy, Kosovo Foundation for Open Society, Norwegian Embassy, Freedom House/USAID, People in Peril/Slovak Aid.

Board: Fitnete Dula (Chair.).

Principal Staff: Exec. Dir Bashkim Rrahmani; Programme Man. Bujar Nura; Programme Man. Dafina Bakija; Finance Man. Nora Soba.

Address: 10000 Prishtina, Rr. Nëna Terezë 49B Nr 2.

Telephone: (38) 220364; **Fax:** (38) 220364; **Internet:** fdi-ks.com; **e-mail:** info@fdi-kosovo.org.

Kosovar Civil Society Foundation

Established in 1998 to assist in the development of civil society.

Activities: Provides information on European integration. Launched 'Democratic Society Promotion' project in June 2011.

Geographical Area of Activity: Kosovo.

Publications: Various research documents and manuals.

Board Members: Xheraldina Vula (Pres.).

Principal Staff: Exec. Dir Venera Hajrullahu, Finance and Admin. Dir Vjolica Sllamniku.

Address: 10000 Prishtina, Fazli Grajqevci 4A.

Internet: www.kcsfoundation.org.

Kosovo Foundation for Open Society—KFOS

An independent foundation, formerly the Prishtina office of the Fund for an Open Society—Yugoslavia, established in 1999; part of the Soros foundations network, which aims to foster political and cultural pluralism and reform economic structures to encourage free enterprise and a market economy.

Activities: Operates in the areas of humanitarian aid to refugees, as well as supporting small-scale projects in the fields of education, culture and the arts, information and the media, democratic institutions and human rights. Internationally the Foundation co-operates with the East-East programme, collaborating regionally on democracy programmes. Other programmes cover the areas of : Civil Society, European Integration, and Minorities and Roma.

Geographical Area of Activity: Kosovo and Metohija.

Publications: Annual Report; *European Magazine*; books.

Finance: Annual income €3,208,706.4, annual expenditure €3,073,272.4 (2010).

Board: Aliraza Arënliu (Chair.).

Principal Staff: Exec. Dir Luan Shllaku, Finance Dir Dukagjin Hyseni.

Address: Prishtina, Ulpiana, Imzot Nike Prela Vila 13.

Telephone: (38) 542157; **Fax:** (38) 542157; **Internet:** kfos.org; **e-mail:** info@kfos.org.

Kuwait

FOUNDATIONS, TRUSTS AND NON-PROFIT ORGANIZATIONS

IOMS—Islamic Organization for Medical Sciences

Founded in 1984 to raise awareness of Islamic medicinal practices.

Activities: Promotes Islamic methods of treatment for physical and psychological afflictions; supports research carried out by Muslim physicians, especially studies to find common ground between traditional Islamic medicine and modern technological medical advances, and to find alternatives to drugs prohibited by Islam; provides health centres for Muslims in need around the world; publishes Islamic scientific and medical journals; and holds seminars and international conferences on Islamic medicine.

Geographical Area of Activity: Mainly North African and Middle Eastern countries.

Publications: *The Law of Herbal Drugs; The Islamic Guide to Medical Jurisprudence; Topics in Islamic Medicine; Islamic Perspectives in Obstetrics and Gynaecology*; conference and seminar proceedings in Arabic and English.

Finance: Funded by Government of Kuwait and through donations from individuals. Annual budget of more than US $1,000,000.

Principal Staff: Pres. Dr Abdul Rahman al-Awadi; Sec.-Gen. Dr Ahmed Regai el-Gendy.

Address: POB 31280, 90803 Sulaibekhat.

Telephone: 4834984; **Fax:** 4837854; **Internet:** www.islamset .org/ioms/main.html; **e-mail:** conference@islamset.org.

Kuwait Awqaf Public Foundation

Established in 1993 as a *waqf,* or community fund to support private sector organizations in the promotion and development of society.

Activities: Operates nationally in the areas of religion and culture, the environment, community development, health and social welfare, science and technology, and Islamic co-operation.

Geographical Area of Activity: Kuwait.

Publications: *Journal of Endowments* (online); books.

Principal Staff: Chair. Mohamed Dhaifallah Sharar; Sec.-Gen. Abdul Mohsen Abdullah al-Kharafi.

Address: Sharq, Dasman Complex, POB 482, 13005 Safat.

Telephone: 2418008; **Fax:** 2418011; **Internet:** www.awqaf .org; **e-mail:** webmaster@islamic-council.org.

Kuwait Foundation for the Advancement of Sciences—KFAS

A private, non-profit scientific organization established in 1976 by HH Sheikh Jaber al-Ahmad al-Sabah.

Activities: Supports pure and applied research of national importance in all disciplines and promotes collaborative studies and deliberations with scientists from the international scientific community through conferences and symposia. Annual prizes are awarded in various disciplines for meritorious contributions by scientists and researchers in Kuwait and other Arab and Islamic countries. Also awards scholarships and fellowships to Kuwaiti nationals. The Foundation has established the Scientific Center, the Dasman Diabetes Institute and the Sabah Al-Ahmad Center for Giftedness and Creativity. It also hosts the Kuwaiti branch of the Arab School for Science and Technology.

Geographical Area of Activity: Mainly Kuwait.

Publications: *Atlas of the State of Kuwait from Satellite Images; The Golden Jubilee of the Independence of the State of Kuwait 1961–2011; Majallat Al-Oloom* (monthly magazine—the Arabic language edition of Scientific American); *Al-Taqaddum Al-Ilmi Magazine* (quarterly); technical reports, scientific books and encyclopedias.

Finance: Funds are given by public Kuwaiti corporations (1% of their annual profits) and by other organizations and individuals.

Board of Directors: HH The Amir Sheikh Sabah al-Ahmed al-Jaber al-Sabah (Chair.); Suleiman A. al-Awadi (Sec.).

Principal Staff: Dir-Gen. Dr Adnan A. Shihab-Eldin.

Address: POB 25263, Safat, Kuwait City.

Telephone: 22425898; **Fax:** 22415365; **Internet:** www.kfas .org; **e-mail:** publicr@kfas.org.kw.

Kuwait Institute for Scientific Research—KISR

Founded in 1967 by the Arabian Oil Company Ltd (Japan) to promote and conduct applied scientific research related to national industrial development and environmental protection.

Activities: Conducts research in environmental science, earth science, food and water resources, engineering, petroleum, petrochemicals, urban development, infrastructure services and techno-economics. Research is also carried out into ways of using technology to help people with special needs. Provides documentation and information services, and training schemes for scientific research workers.

Geographical Area of Activity: Kuwait.

Publications: Annual Reports; *Environmental Characteristics and the Natural Resources of Kuwait; Vegetation in Kuwait; The Effects of Insecticides on the Human and the Environment; New Technologies for Soil Reclamation and Desert Greenery; The Scientific Guide for Food Safety: The Fundamentals of Production, Preparation, and Usage of Safe and Healthy Food; Plankton of the Arabian Gulf*; and others.

Principal Staff: Dir-Gen. Dr Naji Mohamed al-Mutairi.

Address: POB 24885, 13109 Safat, Kuwait City.

Telephone: 24836100; **Fax:** 24830643; **Internet:** www.kisr .edu.kw; **e-mail:** public_relations@kisr.edu.kw.

Zakat House

Founded in 1982 with the aim of implementing the Islamic practice of *zakat* (giving a fixed proportion of one's wealth to charity), and collecting and distributing *zakat* by implementing the most sophisticated technology and management.

Activities: Funds numerous Islamic humanitarian programmes in Kuwait and abroad. Its major project is an orphan sponsorship programme, which supports more than 17,000 orphans all over the world (although the majority are from Asia). Also supports a number of other charitable projects, aiming to alleviate suffering and improve the quality of life for people world-wide. Organizes symposia.

Geographical Area of Activity: Mainly Asia.

Principal Staff: Dir Adel al-Jery, Dir of External Activity Abdullah al-Haider.

Address: Salmiya Qater St, Block 6, POB 23865, 13099 Safat, Kuwait City.

Telephone: 2241911; **Fax:** 2241888; **Internet:** www .zakathouse.org.kw; **e-mail:** info@zakathouse.org.kw.

Kyrgyzstan

FOUNDATIONS, TRUSTS AND NON-PROFIT ORGANIZATIONS

Soros Foundation–Kyrgyzstan

Founded in September 1993 to promote open society; the Foundation is part of the Soros Foundations network, which aims to foster the development of open societies around the world, particularly in the post-communist countries. The Soros Foundations help to build the infrastructure and institutions necessary for open societies by supporting a broad array of programmes in education, media and communications, human rights and humanitarian aid, science and medicine, arts and culture, economic restructuring and legal reform; the Foundation's specific mission is to promote the development of an open society in Kyrgyzstan.

Activities: The Foundation operates in the fields of civil society, legal reform, education, mass media, budget transparency, public health, development of youth initiatives, and other areas.

Geographical Area of Activity: Kyrgyzstan.

Publications: Annual Report; books.

Finance: Annual expenditure US $3,373,000 (2009); Annual budget $4,310,987 (2010).

Advisory Board: Ulan Asanovich Ryskeldiev (Chair.).

Principal Staff: Exec. Dir Kumar Bekbolotov.

Address: Bishkek 720040, ul. Logvinenko 55A.

Telephone: (312) 66-34-75; **Fax:** (312) 66-34-48; **Internet:** www.soros.kg; **e-mail:** office@soros.kg.

Latvia

FOUNDATIONS, TRUSTS AND NON-PROFIT ORGANIZATIONS

Latvijas Bērnu fonds (Latvia Children's Fund)

Founded in 1988 to protect children's rights in Latvia. Since 1991 it is the official representative of the Christian Children's Fund International in Latvia. In 2003 the Fund became a member of the UN Children s Fund (UNICEF) regional network for children in Central Europe, Eastern Europe, Russia and the Baltic States.

Activities: Activities of the Latvia Children's Fund are organized within four activity programmes: Family, Orphans, Health, and Development-Sport-Culture-Talent. Several larger and smaller projects are being developed within these programmes that provide practical support to the groups of children and individual children who have no parents, who are in crisis situations or are severely ill, as well as talented children who lack assets for the development of their talent. Currently, the main activities of Latvia Children's Fund are: development of a rehabilitation centre for children with cerebral palsy; implementation of the projects financed by the European Union and other funds; organization of summer camps for children with special needs; treatment of severely ill children, support for low-income large families; grants for large families, grants for high school students from large families and for orphans; grants for winners of the competition 'Talent for Latvia' from children's music schools; support of rehabilitation and crisis centres; organization of the Christmas charity campaign 'Don't Pass By!' and charity concert; collection and distribution of humanitarian aid.

Geographical Area of Activity: Latvia.

Board: Andris Bērzinš (Pres.); Vaira Vucāne (Vice-Pres.).

Address: Brīvības Ave 310-75, 1006 Rīga.

Telephone: 6754-2072; **Fax:** 6754-1814; **Internet:** www.lbf.lv; **e-mail:** bernufonds@latnet.lv.

Latvijas Kultūras Fonds—LKF (Latvian Cultural Foundation)

Founded in 1987 to promote Latvian culture.

Activities: Promotes the development of culture in Latvia, through providing scholarships for cultural studies and events. Also organizes conferences and exhibitions, and issues publications.

Geographical Area of Activity: Latvia.

Executive Board: Peter Bankovsky (Chair.).

Address: Peldu iela 21, 1050 Rīga.

Telephone: 722-7230; **Fax:** 721-2545; **Internet:** www.lkf.lv; **e-mail:** lkf@lkf.lv.

Soros Foundation Latvia

Founded in June 1992 to promote the development of open society; the Foundation is part of the Soros foundations network, which aims to foster political and cultural pluralism and reform economic structures to encourage free enterprise and a market economy.

Activities: The Foundation funds a variety of projects in Latvia in its priority areas: education, criminal justice, civil society, health-care reform, legal reform and public policy. It also promotes scholarship exchanges.

Geographical Area of Activity: Latvia.

Publications: *Know Your Rights* (booklet).

Finance: Total expenditure US $4,013,000 (2009).

Board of Directors: Sarmite Elerte (Chair.); Guntars Catlaks (Deputy Chair.).

Principal Staff: Exec. Dir Andris Aukmanis; Dep. Dir Pēteris Vinķelis; Admin. Dir Egita Prāma.

Address: Alberta iela 13, 1010 Rīga.

Telephone: 6703-9241; **Fax:** 6703-9242; **Internet:** www.sfl.lv; **e-mail:** sfl@sfl.lv.

Lebanon

FOUNDATION CENTRE AND CO-ORDINATING BODY

ANND—Arab NGO Network for Development

Established in 1997; a network of NGOs operating in 11 countries of the Middle East.

Activities: Aims to strengthen the role of civil society, enhance the values of democracy, respect for human rights and sustainable development. Advocates more sound and effective socio-economic reforms in the region. Organizes conferences, workshops and seminars.

Geographical Area of Activity: Middle East.

Publications: Annual Report; monthly newsletter (online, in Arabic and English); papers and conference reports.

Finance: Total income US $452,043, total expenditure $447,710 (2009).

Principal Staff: Exec. Dir Ziad Abdel Samad, Programmes Dir Kinda Mohamedieh.

Address: Wata Museitbeh, Boustani St, Quantz II Blgd, 4th Floor, POB 5792/14, Mazraa, 1105-2070, Beirut.

Telephone: (1) 319366; **Fax:** (1) 815636; **Internet:** www.annd .org; **e-mail:** annd@annd.org.

FOUNDATIONS, TRUSTS AND NON-PROFIT ORGANIZATIONS

Arab Thought Foundation

Established in 2000.

Activities: Offers the Arab Creativity Award, the Pioneers Award, the Innovators Award, the Talented Award and the Arabic Book Award; publishes the 'One Civilization' series of translated books; undertakes educational projects, youth programmes and organizes annual Fikr Conference.

Geographical Area of Activity: Middle East.

Principal Staff: Gen. Dir Dr Suleiman Abdel Muneim; Asst Sec.-Gen. Dr Munira Riser.

Address: Al-Maarad St behind al-Oumary Mosque, Arab Thought Foundation Bldg, Down Town, POB 524-11, Beirut.

Telephone: (1) 997100; **Fax:** (1) 997101; **Internet:** www .arabthought.org; **e-mail:** info@arabthought.org.

Fondation Arabe pour l'Image (Arab Image Foundation)

Established in 1997 to preserve and promote the photographic heritage in the Middle East, North Africa and the Arab Diaspora.

Activities: Locates, collects, preserves, interprets and presents the photographic heritage of the Middle East, North Africa and the Arab Diaspora from the mid-19th century to the present. The ongoing research and acquisition of photographs covers Lebanon, Syria, Palestine, Jordan, Egypt, Morocco, Iraq, Iran, Mexico, Argentina and Senegal. The collection comprises more than 300,000 photographs, and the Foundation aims to make its collection accessible to the public through exhibitions, publications, videos, a website and an online image database. It also seeks further to encourage critical approaches to reading and interpreting photographs. Maintains a library, a laboratory and a research centre. Organizes exhibitions and runs a residency programme for artists and scholars.

Geographical Area of Activity: The Middle East and North Africa.

Restrictions: No grants to individuals.

Publications: *Histoires Intimes: 1900-1960*; *Portraits du Caire*; *The Vehicle*; *Mapping Sitting: On Portraiture and Photography*; *Hashem el-Madani, Studio Practices*; *Hashem el-Madani, Promenades*.

Finance: Receives grants from the Ford Foundation, the Open Society Institute and the Prince Claus Fund (q.v.). Receives donations from the Audi Bank in Lebanon and a committee of private donors.

Principal Staff: Dir Zeina Arida; Pres. Nigol Bezjian; Collection Man. Tamara Sawaya.

Address: Zoghbi Bldg, 4th Floor, 337 Gouraud St, Gemmayzeh (opposite Byblos Bank), Beirut.

Telephone: (1) 569373; **Fax:** (1) 569374; **Internet:** www.fai.org .lb; **e-mail:** info@fai.org.lb.

Rafik Hariri Foundation

Founded in 1979 by former Prime Minister of Lebanon Rafik Hariri as the Islamic Institute for Culture and Higher Education to promote education as a means of development for children and young people.

Activities: Operates in the fields of education, arts and humanities, and health sector (38 branches throughout Lebanon), through language programmes designed to enable students to attend university. Makes loans and scholarships to students, and provides support for academic institutions affected by conflict in the Middle East. Offers career guidance and support for educational organizations and programmes. Promotes Lebanese heritage through the renovation and care of old buildings. Fosters relations with international organizations. The Foundation also supports five schools, two of which are in Sidon and the others in Beirut and the Hariri Canadian University, which was founded in 1999.

Geographical Area of Activity: Lebanon and other countries of the Middle East.

Publications: *Lebanon: Its History and Heritage*; *Lebanon at Present: Its Needs for Development*; *The Arabs*; *Islam in Western Europe*; *Islam and the Moslems in the World*; *The Generations of Hariri Foundation*; *The Educational Evaluation Process*; *Proceedings: Seminar on the Teaching of the Arts in Universities and Higher Institutes*; *Sidon: The Old City*; *Dialogue on Coexistence Among All Denominations and Religions: The Lebanese Model*; *Civic Education and the Rights of Citizens*.

Executive Board: Nazek Rafik Hariri (Pres.).

Principal Staff: Office Dir Rubina Abu Zeinab Chahine.

Address: Rafik Hariri Foundation Bldg, Adnan Hakim St, Bir Hasan Area, Beirut.

Telephone: (1) 1853055; **Fax:** (1) 1853006; **Internet:** www.rhf .org.lb; **e-mail:** infolb@rhf.org.lb.

Institute for Palestine Studies, Publishing and Research Organization—IPS ()

Founded in 1963 by Najla Abou Izzedin, Maurice Gemayel, Said Himadeh, Burhan Dajani, Edmond Rabbath, Constantine Zurayk, Fuad Sarrouf, Nabih Amin Faris, Wadad Cortas and Walid Khalidi to encourage research into all aspects of the Palestine problem.

Activities: Specializes in research into the history and development of Palestine, the Palestinian problem and the Arab–Israeli conflict, and possible ways of arriving at a peaceful resolution. The Institute publishes books, quarterly journals, documentaries, studies and opinion polls; conducts occasional seminars and makes grants; serves as a repository for documents, manuscripts, periodicals, books and other publications on Palestine and the Palestinian problem. Maintains offices in Beirut, Jerusalem, Paris, and Washington, DC.

Geographical Area of Activity: Middle East.

Publications: *Journal of Palestine Studies* (quarterly, in English); *Revue d'études palestiniennes* (quarterly, in French); *Jerusalem Quarterly* (in English); *Majallat al-Dirasat al-Filistiniyah* (quarterly, in Arabic); *IPS Papers*; monographs.

Board of Trustees: Hisham Nashabe (Chair.); Said T. Khoury (Hon. Chair.); Mazen Dajani (Treas.); Walid Khalidi (Sec.).

Principal Staff: Dirs Mahmoud Soueid, Mona Nsouli.

Address: Nsouli-Verdun St, POB 11-7164, 1107-2230 Beirut.

Telephone: (1) 804959; **Fax:** (1) 814193; **Internet:** www .palestine-studies.org; **e-mail:** ipsbrt@palestine-studies.org.

René Moawad Foundation

Established in 1990, in memory of President René Moawad, to promote social, economic and rural development, and to assist in the development of civil society in Lebanon.

Activities: Operates in Lebanon in the fields of human rights, education, health and welfare, economic affairs and agriculture, in particular to assist disadvantaged people. Operates centres, including the Agricultural Centre of the North, centres for working children and for youth, and medical and business development centres.

Geographical Area of Activity: Lebanon.

Principal Staff: Pres. Nayla René Moawad.

Address: 844 rue Alfred Naccache, BP 468, Achrafieh, Beirut.

Telephone: (1) 613367; **Fax:** (1) 613370; **Internet:** www.rmf .org.lb; **e-mail:** rmf@rmf.org.lb.

Lesotho

FOUNDATION CENTRE AND CO-ORDINATING BODY

Lesotho Council of Non-Governmental Organisations

Established in 1990 to provide support services to the NGO community in Lesotho.

Activities: Operates through networking and leadership training and development, providing information, capacity building, co-ordination, advocacy and representation when dealing with the Government and the international community.

Geographical Area of Activity: Lesotho.

Board of Directors: Lira Theko (Pres.).

Address: House No. 544 Hoohlo Extension, Private Bag A445, Maseru 100.

Telephone: 22317205; **Fax:** 22310412; **Internet:** www.lecongo .org.ls; **e-mail:** admin@lcn.org.ls.

Liechtenstein

FOUNDATIONS, TRUSTS AND NON-PROFIT ORGANIZATIONS

IHCF—Stiftung zur Förderung der Gesundheit (Foundation to Promote Health)

International non-profit organization established in 1991 by a group of dentists to promote improved oral health care worldwide.

Activities: Operates internationally in the field of health care. Raises public awareness of the importance of dental health care; disseminates information and research results to dentists through lectures and conferences; carries out programmes to improve the quality of dental material and care in Europe and Asia; and offers accreditation to dental health-care products of benefit to patients. Operates in collaboration with international partner organizations in Europe and the Far East.

Geographical Area of Activity: Western Europe and Asia.

Publications: Newsletter.

Finance: non-profit organization.

Principal Staff: Hon. Sec. Dr Volker Scholz.

Address: Austrasse 15, POB 1117, 9490 Vaduz.

Telephone: 237 28 50; **Fax:** 237 28 51; **Internet:** www.ihcf.org; **e-mail:** info@ihcf.org.

International Music and Art Foundation

Established in 1988 to promote art and cultural activities.

Activities: The Foundation aims to preserve, facilitate the study of, and disseminate information on ancient art and culture. Provides grants to a variety of arts and cultural organizations, including chamber music groups, museums, opera and ballet companies, symphony orchestras, and organizations involved in art conservation and architectural restoration, and for research into and issuing publications on the history of art.

Geographical Area of Activity: International.

Restrictions: Does not generally respond to unsolicited applications. No grants are made to individuals, for start-up costs of new organizations, nor for meetings and discussions.

Finance: Total assets 40,783,176 Swiss francs (Dec. 2010).

Address: POB 39, 9490 Vaduz.

Telephone: 237 4545; **Fax:** 237 4546; **Internet:** www .imafoundation.homestead.com; **e-mail:** trustees@imaf.li.

Lithuania

FOUNDATION CENTRE AND CO-ORDINATING BODY

NGO Information and Support Centre—NISC

Founded by the Open Society Fund—Lithuania in 1995 to develop the NGO sector in Lithuania.

Activities: The Centre is sponsored by the UN Development Programme; it operates in the fields of information dissemination, consultancy, training and support for NGOs and their development. Promotes co-operation between NGOs and other institutions and provides information on the legal constitution of NGOs in Lithuania. Maintains an online database of funding sources for Lithuanian NGOs and a library of more than 1,000 publications.

Geographical Area of Activity: Lithuania.

Publications: *Partnership among NGOs and local governments*; *The Third Sector* (occasional newsletter); and other research publications.

Board: Ricardas Dirzys (Chair.).

Principal Staff: Dir Martinas Zaltauskas; Project Man. Olia Zuravliova, Viktorija Daujotyte.

Address: Odminiu g. 12, 01122 Vilnius.

Telephone: (5) 2618782; **Fax:** (5) 2126045; **Internet:** www.nisc.lt; **e-mail:** info@nisc.lt.

FOUNDATIONS, TRUSTS AND NON-PROFIT ORGANIZATIONS

Lietuvos vaikų fondas (Lithuanian Children's Fund)

Founded in 1988 to protect the interests of children in Lithuania.

Activities: Operates nationally, providing financial support to foster families, for housing and scholarships to gifted students. Also operates literacy and other educational programmes, as well as funding activities that aim to improve access to social, economic and health care services for Roma people.

Geographical Area of Activity: Lithuania.

Finance: Partly financed by the European Union and the European Social Fund.

Principal Staff: Dir Romualda Navikaitė.

Address: Vilnius, Laisvės pr. 125.

Telephone: (2) 628836; **Fax:** (2) 627180; **Internet:** www.lvf.lt; **e-mail:** info@lvf.lt.

Pilietinės Atsakomybés Fondas (Civic Responsibility Foundation)

Established in 2006 to strengthen civic responsibility by fostering philanthropy and empowering the people of Lithuania.

Activities: Works through capacity building to advance democracy, voluntary activity and awareness of NGOs, especially community-based activities.

Geographical Area of Activity: Lithuania.

Restrictions: No support to organizations that foment hatred, discrimination, inequality, social exclusion, violence, are established by public institutions or dependent on public authorities, are of a political or religious nature.

Founder-Dirs: Mindaugas Danys; Birutė Jatautaitė; Danutė Jokubėnienė; Skirma Kondratienė.

Principal Staff: Chief Exec. Mindaugas Danys.

Address: 01128 Vilnius, Didzioji Str. 5.

Telephone: (5) 266-1208; **Fax:** (5) 266-1221; **Internet:** www.paf.lt; **e-mail:** info@paf.lt.

Luxembourg

FOUNDATION CENTRE AND CO-ORDINATING BODY

European Foundation for Street Children—EFSC

Founded in Amsterdam in 1995; a network of European organizations, which aims to improve the rights and living conditions of children at risk, particularly street children at a national, European and international level.

Activities: A networking organization with member organizations in Europe and world-wide that works to improve living conditions for street children and provide better opportunities for them by addressing the causes of their homelessness and poverty; raising public awareness of the existence of homeless children and of their rights and needs; promoting strategies to eliminate this phenomenon; lobbying and advocacy on behalf of homeless children; seeking financial and technical support for member organizations; and facilitating the exchange of information through workshops and conferences.

Geographical Area of Activity: World-wide.

Publications: Annual Report; Newsletter.

Executive Board: Anthony Simpson (Treas.).

Principal Staff: Dir Reinhold Müller.

Address: 15 route d'Esch, 1470 Luxembourg.

Telephone: 2744-51; **Fax:** 2744-5170; **Internet:** www.efsc-eu .org; **e-mail:** info@efsc-eu.org.

FOUNDATIONS, TRUSTS AND NON-PROFIT ORGANIZATIONS

Action Solidarité Tiers Monde—ASTM (Third World Solidarity Action)

Established in 1969 to support the political, economic and social emancipation of the people of the developing world and to address the global economic issues affecting this emancipation.

Activities: Works in partnership with indigenous organizations in the developing world, in the areas of education and sustainable development, concentrating on programmes in the areas of access to land, commercialization of the agricultural production, micro-credit, health rights and women's rights. Also provides information on the cultures of the developing world, generates support for cultural activities and develops cultural exchanges between the developed and the developing world, initially through a pilot programme linking Luxembourg with Algeria, India and Senegal.

Geographical Area of Activity: Africa, Asia, Central and South America and the Middle East.

Publications: *Brennpunkt Drëtt Welt* (newsletter); reports and brochures.

Finance: Financed by private donations and state subsidies.

Principal Staff: Pres. Richard Graf; Vice-Pres. Monique Langevin; Treas. Pierre Schmit.

Address: 55 ave de la Liberté, 1931 Luxembourg.

Telephone: 400-42725; **Fax:** 400-42727; **Internet:** www.astm .lu; **e-mail:** astm@astm.lu.

Fondation Follereau Luxembourg—FFL (Follereau Foundation Luxembourg)

Established in 1966 by Raoul Follereau to promote international solidarity, and to combat leprosy.

Activities: Operates mainly in Africa in the fields of aid to less-developed countries, medicine and health, and social welfare. Its main aims are to combat leprosy, Buruli ulcer and tuberculosis, and assist those who have been cured of these diseases, through projects. The Foundation is also involved with helping underprivileged children, through the Follereau-Children project. Also aims to increase awareness in Luxembourg on these issues. Operates in collaboration with other organizations and members of the International Federation of Anti Leprosy Associations.

Geographical Area of Activity: Mainly Africa.

Publications: *Solidarité Follereau* (newsletter).

Principal Staff: Pres. Jean Hilger; Vice-Pres. Emile Rossler; Admin. Dir Robert Kohll.

Address: 151 ave du X Septembre, 2551 Luxembourg.

Telephone: 44-66-061; **Fax:** 45-96-53; **Internet:** www.ffl.lu; **e-mail:** info@ffl.lu.

Unity Foundation

The Foundation was launched in 1980 as the Organization of Public Utility.

Activities: The Foundation focuses on developmental activities in education, health care and sustainable development in developing countries by providing grants (to elevate the status of women in particular), enhancing global health and hygiene, improving literacy standards and promoting world peace. The Foundation extends financial assistance to projects in Central and South America, Asia and Africa; it has set up a not-for-profit print shop and publishing house in the Democratic Republic of the Congo. The Foundation also works as a partner in the capacity of a co-financer, with the Ministère des Affaires Etrangères of Luxembourg.

Geographical Area of Activity: Africa, Asia, and Central and South America.

Publications: Activity Report (annually).

Administrative Council: Fernand Schaber (Pres.); Abbas Rafii (Vice-Pres.); Mahvash Ahmadzadeh (Treas.).

Principal Staff: Secs Claudine Winkel, Christiane Wolff.

Address: 17 allée Léopold Goebel, 1635 Luxembourg.

Telephone: 25-26-20; **Internet:** www.unityfoundation.lu; **e-mail:** info@unityfoundation.lu.

Macedonia

FOUNDATION CENTRES AND CO-ORDINATING BODIES

Association for Democratic Initiatives—ADI

Membership organization established in 1994 with the aim of building a civil society in Macedonia.

Activities: Promotes the development of civil society in Macedonia, through conducting voter education activities and a range of other civic initiatives throughout the country; currently operating in 32 towns and villages. Operates programmes in the fields of human rights, refugees, youth, election monitoring and the media, including a Civic and Voter Education Programme; Election Monitoring Programme; Civic Education Programme; Promotion of Inter-Ethnic Co-operation and Intercultural Learning Programme; Local Government Programme; Youth Programme; and Human Rights. Has also established three NGO Resource Centres in Gostivar, Stip and Tetovo, which offer individuals and organizations interested in developing civic initiatives advice and technical support. ADI is a member of numerous national and international networks and NGO coalitions and is a founding member of the Steering Committee of the Balkan Human Rights Network—BHRN (q.v.). Also maintains Country Offices in Prishtina, Kosovo and Metohija, Sarajevo, Bosnia and Herzegovina, Tirana, Albania, and New York, USA.

Geographical Area of Activity: Macedonia.

Publications: *Social integration of refugees and stateless people in Macedonia*; *Conflict and the Media*; *Arms in Macedonia*; publications in the areas of human rights, refugees and migrants, democracy and civil society, and education and youth; Annual Report.

Board: Shpend Imeri (Pres.).

Principal Staff: Exec. Dir Albert Musliu; Admin. Dir Bekim Abdullai; Sec. Natasha Tancevska.

Address: Braka Ginovski Bul. 61, 3rd Entrance, 3rd Floor, 1230 Gostivar.

Telephone: (42) 221100; **Fax:** (42) 221102; **Internet:** www.adi.org.mk; **e-mail:** albert@adi.org.mk.

Macedonian Centre for International Co-operation—MCIC

Established in 1993, active in the fields of development, rehabilitation and humanitarian assistance in Macedonia, with the aims of promoting peace and developing civil society.

Activities: Provides funding to organizations active in the fields of civic society, peace, human rights, education, arts and culture, democratization, health, economics, refugees and returnees, water and sanitation, and tolerance. Supports numerous activities carried out by NGOs, principally in Macedonia, including the stimulation of education of young people, especially in rural and suburban areas, as well as among different nationalities, emergency assistance, civil society and democracy development, cultural understanding and tolerance. In 1999 also began operating in Kosovo. The Centre is also the founder and manager of the Macedonian Enterprise Development Foundation—MEDF, which provides loans for small and micro-enterprises.

Geographical Area of Activity: Macedonia, and Kosovo and Metohija.

Publications: *NGO-Bulletin*; *NGO-Address Book*; *Ten Years of MCIC*; Annual Report.

Board: Sulejmani Rizvan (Chair.); Angjušev Kočo (Vice-Chair.).

Principal Staff: First CEO Alexander Krzalovski; CEO Dime Mitreski.

Address: Ul. Nikola Parapunov bb, POB 55, 1060 Skopje.

Telephone: (2) 3065381; **Fax:** (2) 3065298; **Internet:** www.mcms.org.mk; **e-mail:** mcms@mcms.org.uk.

South East European Environmental NGOs Network—SEEENN

Established following the Conference for Sustainable Development in the Balkans, held in Struga, Macedonia, June 2000. Aims to develop and co-ordinate environmental NGOs on a regional level, both by creating a forum that will initiate long-term processes and by organizing and facilitating the implementation of specific tasks placed on it by its members and broader public in the region. As of 2009, the network had eight partners.

Activities: Activities include strengthening networks and contacts between environmental NGOs in the Balkan region, organizing conferences and eco-summer camps for young people interested in environmental issues, co-ordinating Task Force meetings for member organizations, and running online discussion forums. Also maintains offices in Belgrade and Zagreb.

Geographical Area of Activity: Balkans.

Address: Vasil Gjorgov 39, baraka 6, 1000 Skopje.

Telephone: (2) 3290118; **Fax:** (2) 3290119; **e-mail:** seeenn@seeenn.org.mk.

FOUNDATIONS, TRUSTS AND NON-PROFIT ORGANIZATIONS

Foundation Open Society Institute Macedonia—FOSIM

Founded in October 1992 (previously known as the Open Society Fund of Macedonia) to support the development of Macedonia as an independent and democratic state respectful of multi-ethnic cultural traditions, and to encourage the development of Western standards in the country. An independent foundation, part of the Soros foundations network.

Activities: Operates in the fields of education, information and the media, publishing, Roma people and ethnic minorities, youth and women's programmes, public health, law and criminal justice, the arts and culture, civil society and economic reform. Supported initiatives to assist refugees from Kosovo in 1999. Advocates the speedy accession of Macedonia to the European Union. Finances and operates the Soros International House—Skopje, the Soros Centre for Contemporary Arts, the SOS Centre (which provides counselling to teenagers), the Civil Society Resource Centre and Student Resource Centres.

Geographical Area of Activity: Macedonia.

Publications: Annual Report and other publications.

Finance: Annual expenditure US $7,046,000 (2009).

Executive Board: Gordana Duvnjak (Chair.).

Principal Staff: Exec. Dir Vladimir Milcin; Deputy Exec. Dir Slavica Inzdevska.

Address: Bul. Jane Sandanski 111, POB 378, 1000 Skopje.

Telephone: (2) 2444488; **Fax:** (2) 2444499; **Internet:** www.soros.org.mk; **e-mail:** osi@soros.org.mk.

Malawi

FOUNDATIONS, TRUSTS AND NON-PROFIT ORGANIZATIONS

Tea Research Foundation of Central Africa

Founded in 1966 to conduct research into Central African tea and coffee production.

Activities: Conducts research into aspects of tea and coffee production in southern and central Africa, with an emphasis on plant breeding, plant propagation and crop management. Maintains two research stations in Malawi and one on-farm research centre in Chipinge, Zimbabwe. Runs a training programme for tea estate workers and managers.

Geographical Area of Activity: Malawi, Zimbabwe, Mozambique and Zambia.

Publications: Annual Report; newsletter (2 a year); *Tea Planter's Handbook*; *Coffee Manual for Malawi, Clonal Catalogue, Code of Practice Handbook on the use of Pesticides in Tea in Malawi and Zimbabwe.*

Finance: Funded by members; budget approx. US $800,000 (2011).

Board of Management: Sam Magombedze (Chair.).

Principal Staff: Dir Dr Albert Changaya; Chief Research Officer Dr H. E. Nyirenda.

Address: POB 51, Mulanje, Malawi.

Telephone: (1) 467250; **Fax:** (1) 467209; **Internet:** www.trfca .org; **e-mail:** trfdirector@trfca.org.

Malaysia

FOUNDATIONS, TRUSTS AND NON-PROFIT ORGANIZATIONS

Pesticide Action Network Asia and the Pacific—PAN AP

Co-ordinating regional branch of PAN International, which aims to promote sustainable agricultural methods without the need for pesticides.

Activities: Co-ordinates agricultural programmes and projects in the Asia-Pacific region, particularly focusing on sustainable, pesticide-free farming methods, the empowerment of women and peasants in agriculture, and food security. This is done through disseminating information, campaigning, holding workshops and conferences, training and practical field work.

Geographical Area of Activity: The Asia-Pacific region.

Publications: *Pesticide Monitor* (quarterly newsletter); *Bilateral Free Trade and Investment Agreements and the US Corporate Biotech Agenda*; *Women's Wisdom*; *Appetite for Destruction: The Real Issues Behind Bird Flu and Other Outbreaks*.

Principal Staff: Exec. Dir Sarojeni V. Rengam; Admin. and Finance Dir Rosmah Ismail.

Address: POB 1170, 10850 Penang.

Telephone: (4) 6560381/6570271; **Fax:** (4) 6583960; **Internet:** www.panap.net; **e-mail:** panap@panap.net.

Third World Network—TWN

Non-profit international network of organizations and individuals, founded in November 1984.

Activities: Carries out research on cultural, social, environmental and economic issues affecting less-developed countries and regions, and raises awareness of these issues by publishing a number of books and magazines. Also organizes seminars and articulates the interests of developing countries at international conferences. Has offices in Ghana, India, Switzerland and Uruguay, and affiliated organizations in Africa, Asia, the Far East, and Central and South America.

Geographical Area of Activity: Asia, Africa, Latin America, Western Europe.

Publications: *Third World Resurgence* (magazine, monthly); *Third World Economics* (magazine, 2 a month); *SUNS bulletin* (bulletin, daily); *TWN Features Service* (media service, 3 a week); other books on environment, technology, economics and trade issues.

Finance: Funded by magazine subscription fees and sale of publications.

Principal Staff: Co-Dirs Chee Yoke Ling, T. Rajamoorthy.

Address: 131 Jalan Macalister, 10400 Penang.

Telephone: (4) 2266728; **Fax:** (4) 2264505; **Internet:** www.twnside.org.sg; **e-mail:** twnet@po.jaring.my.

Women's Aid Organisation—WAO (Pertubuhan Pertolongan Wanita)

Established in 1982 to promote women's rights in Malaysia, originally through the provision of women's refuges.

Activities: Works as an advocate for women suffering domestic violence in Malaysia by monitoring the implementation of laws to protect them. Lends support to women suffering violence by helping them with legal advocacy, loans, and giving refuge to them and their children. Also raises awareness of the problem through research, conferences and disseminating information.

Geographical Area of Activity: Malaysia.

Publications: *Inroads* (quarterly newsletter); Annual Report.

Finance: Total annual expenditure approx. 1,000,000 ringgit Malaysia.

Executive Committee: Meera Samanther (Pres.); Vivienne Lee Iskander (Vice-Pres.); Chin Oy Sim (Sec.); Carol Chin (Treas.).

Principal Staff: Exec. Dir Ivy Josiah; Finance and Admin. Man. Sharmini Kanesamoorthy.

Address: POB 493, Jalan Sultan, 46760 Petaling Jaya, Selangor Darul Ehsan.

Telephone: (3) 79575636; **Fax:** (3) 79563237; **Internet:** www.wao.org.my; **e-mail:** wao@po.jaring.my.

The WorldFish Center

Previously known as the International Center for Living Aquatic Resources Management (ICLARM), the Center was conceived by the Rockefeller Foundation (q.v.) in 1973, became a small programme of the University of Hawaii in 1975, and was incorporated in Manila in March 1977. It became a member of the Consultative Group on International Agricultural Research (CGIAR) in May 1992.

Activities: The WorldFish Center is an autonomous, non-governmental, non-profit-making, international scientific and technical centre established to conduct, stimulate and accelerate research on all aspects of fisheries and other living aquatic resources. Main areas of research are: improving productivity; protecting the environment; improving policies; saving biodiversity and strengthening national programmes. The Center operates through research, conferences, publications, scholarships and awarding prizes (the Naga Award is given annually to a nominated scientific paper or book by an author from a developing country in any area of fisheries science). Maintains project offices in nine countries (Bangladesh, Cameroon, Caribbean/Eastern Pacific, Egypt, Malawi, New Caledonia, the Philippines, the Solomon Islands and Cambodia) and is currently conducting research projects with collaborators in 50 countries and 39 regional and international organizations.

Geographical Area of Activity: Asia, Africa and the Pacific.

Publications: *NAGA* (quarterly); Operation Plan; Annual Reports; conference proceedings, reviews, studies, technical reports, education and software series.

Finance: Total budget US $17,700,000 (2010).

Board of Trustees: Remo Gautschi (Chair.); Dr Wendy Craik (Vice-Chair.).

Principal Staff: Dir-Gen. Dr Stephen J. Hall; Deputy Dir-Gen. Dr Patrick Dugan.

Address: POB 500, GPO 10670, Penang; Jalan Batu Maung, Batu Maung, 11960 Bayan Lepas, Penang.

Telephone: (4) 6261606; **Fax:** (4) 6265530; **Internet:** www.worldfishcenter.org; **e-mail:** worldfishcenter@cgiar.org.

Malta

FOUNDATION CENTRE AND CO-ORDINATING BODY

Solidarity Overseas Service Malta—SOS Malta

Established in 1991, aiming to help people in times of crisis and empower them by providing support services and opportunities to implement development and change in their country to ensure a better quality of life.

Activities: Operates internationally through encouraging advocacy on behalf of social causes, research and training, promoting models of good care and practice, volunteering and sustainable development; maintains the Malta Resource Centre for Civil Society NGOs.

Geographical Area of Activity: International.

Publications: *Social Affairs Committee Reports; SOS Malta Final Reports; SOS Malta Activity Reports; Handbook – INTI; The Structural Funds Training Technical Assistance Programme for NGOs and Civil Society Organisations* (2007); *Attaining the Millennium Development Goals: The need for increased international cooperation; Malta's Overseas Development Priorities; Annual Report.*

Board: Philip Calleja (Dir); Lilian Miceli Farrugia (Chair.); Claudia Taylor-East (Sec.); Francis Frendo (Treas.).

Principal Staff: Man. Dir Claudia Taylor-East; Project Mans Nicola Critien, Monique Falzon.

Address: Dar L-Emigrant, Castille Pl., Valletta VLT1062.

Telephone: 21244123; **Fax:** 21224742; **Internet:** www.sosmalta.org; **e-mail:** info@sosmalta.org.

FOUNDATIONS, TRUSTS AND NON-PROFIT ORGANIZATIONS

Fondazzjoni Patrimonju Malti (Maltese Heritage Foundation)

Set up in 1992 by a small group of Maltese cultural heritage enthusiasts with the backing of government. Its aim is to spread awareness of the island's cultural heritage, through exhibitions, study, research and publications. It strives to ensure that the Maltese world-class heritage is enjoyed both by the Maltese and visitors to the country.

Activities: Activities aim to advance and enrich the understanding of Maltese cultural heritage through exhibitions that display artefacts from private collections and public and non-profit institutions and organizations, which would otherwise not be accessible to the public. Over the last few years, the Foundation restored Palazzo Falson in the medieval city of Mdina. This 13th-century palazzo, together with all its extensive collections, has been open to the public as a state-of-the-art Historic House Museum since May 2007.

Geographical Area of Activity: Malta.

Publications: *Treasures of Malta* (3 a year); various publications about Melitensia.

Principal Staff: Chair. Maurice de Giorgio.

Address: Palazzo Bonici, 115 Triq tat-Teatru l-Qadim, Valletta VLT 1426.

Telephone: 21231515; **Fax:** 21250118; **Internet:** www.patrimonju.org; **e-mail:** info@patrimonju.org.

Foundation for International Studies—FIS

Founded in 1986 by the Government of Malta to promote research and training in the fields of the arts, the environment, economic and international affairs, and law and human rights. The Foundation, which is attached to the University of Malta, concerns itself largely with the Mediterranean region.

Activities: Organizes international conferences; operates its own international programmes and training courses. Initiatives include the Islands and Small States Institute, the International Environment Institute, the Future Generations Programme, and the Euro-Mediterranean Centre on Insular Coastal Dynamics.

Geographical Area of Activity: Europe, the Mediterranean region and the Middle East.

Restrictions: No grants to individuals.

Publications: *The Future of the Mediterranean; Med in the Law of the Sea; Journal of Mediterranean Studies.*

Board of Trustees: Rector of the University of Malta; Dir-Gen. UNESCO; Exec. Dir UNEP.

Principal Staff: CEO Josef N. Grech.

Address: Old University Bldg, St Paul's St, Valletta VLT 1216.

Telephone: 21234121; **Fax:** 21230551; **Internet:** www.um.edu.mt/intoff/fis.html; **e-mail:** conferences@fis.org.mt.

Malta Ecological Foundation

Founded in 1992 as the Malta Ecological Society to promote education on environmental issues and to study and protect the environment.

Activities: The Foundation organizes numerous environmental campaigns in Malta on land use, public transport, ecological tourism, human and animal rights, and smoking; organizes the Ecological Summit of Malta; conducts research; and provides consultancy services to national and local government, independent organizations, businesses and schools, as well as organizing the annual Ecological Generational Award.

Geographical Area of Activity: Malta.

Publications: *Making One World; The Caught Hedgehog; Ecological Stories; What You Can Do to Help the Environment; Rozina's Secret Cave; The Stakeholder* (newsletter); Annual Report; tourist leaflets.

Finance: Annual budget approx. €20,000.

Principal Staff: Pres. Dunstan Hamilton; Sec. Josephine Aquilina.

Address: POB 322, Valletta CMR 01.

Telephone: 21611486; **Fax:** 21338780; **Internet:** www.ecomalta.org; **e-mail:** eco@ecomalta.org.

Strickland Foundation

Established in 1979 to promote cultural heritage and human rights in Malta.

Activities: Promotes Maltese cultural heritage through organizing and hosting seminars and conferences, supporting awards for Maltese journalists through the Malta-EU Information Centre, and funding publications, including *The Mediterranean Journal of Human Rights*, which is published by the University of Malta.

Geographical Area of Activity: Malta.

Principal Staff: Sec. Frank Bonello.

Address: Villa Parisio 36, Mabel Strickland St, Lija.

Telephone: 21435890.

Mexico

FOUNDATION CENTRES AND CO-ORDINATING BODIES

Asociación Latinoamericana de Organizaciones de Promoción al Desarrollo—ALOP (Latin American Association of Development Organizations)

Established in 1979 by 11 Central and South American organizations.

Activities: Works to develop communication and co-operation between members. Promotes the rights of native peoples affected by development projects; supports the use of appropriate technology in development projects; collates and distributes information on projects world-wide. Also awards prizes, and organizes conferences and training courses.

Geographical Area of Activity: Central and South America and the Caribbean.

Publications: *El Mercosur ciudadano: Retos para una nueva institucionalidad; Mito y Realidad de la Ayuda Externa: América Latina; La negociación del Acuerdo de Asociación Centroamérica y la Unión Europea: Balance y Alternativas;* newsletter.

Executive Committee: Oscar Azmitia (Pres.); Maria Pia Matta (Attorney).

Principal Staff: Exec. Sec. Jorge Balbis Pérez; Asst Sec. Norma Bustamente Castañeda; Administrator Balbuena Adolfo Maya.

Address: Benjamín Franklin 186, Col. Escandón, M. Hidalgo, 11800 México, DF.

Telephone: (55) 5273-3400; **Fax:** (55) 5273-3449; **Internet:** www.alop.org.mx; **e-mail:** info@alop.org.mx.

Centro Mexicano para la Filantropía—CEMEFI (Mexican Centre for Philanthropy)

Founded in December 1988 to obtain and disseminate information on organizations and groups committed to philanthropic activities; to establish communications between associations involved in philanthropic activities; and to promote relations with philanthropic organizations world-wide.

Activities: Operates through self-conducted programmes, research, conferences, training courses and publications to promote philanthropy. Lobbies government on fiscal and legal issues and represents the Mexican third sector at international level.

Geographical Area of Activity: Mexico.

Publications: *Directorio de Instituciones Filantrópicas; Mexican Civil Society Index; Vision con Futuro* (newsletter); *Cemefi Informa* (newsletter); guides to strengthening the internal organs of government and on legal aspects for non-profit organizations; publications on philanthropy, civil society, business social responsibility, fund procurement, volunteering.

Board of Directors: Mercedes C. Aragones Ruipérez (Pres.); Jorge Aguilar Valenzuela (Treas.); Mario González Cos Garciadiego (Sec.).

Principal Staff: Chief Exec. Jorge V. Villalobos Grzybowicz.

Address: Col. Escandón, Cerrada de Salvador Alvarado 7, 11800 México, DF.

Telephone: (55) 5276-8530; **Fax:** (55) 5515-5448; **Internet:** www.cemefi.org; **e-mail:** cemefi@cemefi.org.

FOUNDATIONS, TRUSTS AND NON-PROFIT ORGANIZATIONS

Centro Internacional de Mejoramiento de Maíz y Trigo—CIMMYT (The International Maize and Wheat Improvement Center)

Founded in 1966 by the Government of Mexico and the Rockefeller Foundation (q.v.), CIMMYT is an international, non-profit, agricultural research and training centre, working towards assisting the poor in developing countries through increasing the profitability, productivity and sustainability of maize and wheat farming systems.

Activities: Operates internationally through self-conducted programmes, research, fellowships, scholarships, conferences, courses, publications and lectures. Supports the development and distribution world-wide of higher-yielding maize and wheat with in-built genetic resistance to diseases and insects; the conservation and distribution of maize and wheat genetic resources; research on natural resource management in maize- and wheat-based cropping systems; documentation of new knowledge in the area of wheat and maize; development of more effective research methods; training; and technical consultation. Maintains regional offices in Afghanistan, Bangladesh, the People's Republic of China, Colombia, Ethiopia, India, Iran, Kazakhstan, Kenya, Nepal, Pakistan, Turkey and Zimbabwe.

Geographical Area of Activity: World-wide.

Publications: CIMMYT Annual Report; *Literature Update on Wheat, Barley and Triticale;* newsletter.

Finance: Funding comes from overseas development assistance agencies; total assets US $50,082,000 (2007).

Board of Trustees: Dr Sara Boettiger (Chair.); Dr Usha Barwale Zehr (Vice-Chair.); Dr Pedro Brajcich Gallegos (Vice-Chair.).

Address: Apdo 6-641, 06600 México, DF.

Telephone: (55) 5804-2004; **Fax:** (55) 5804-7558; **Internet:** www.cimmyt.org; **e-mail:** cimmyt@cgiar.org.

Fundación Miguel Alemán AC (Miguel Alemán Foundation)

Founded in 1984 by Miguel Alemán Valdés to promote and support humanitarian activities, tourism development, health and ecological issues, and technological advances in agriculture.

Activities: The Foundation operates nationally in the fields of conservation and the environment, gender equality, agricultural productivity, tourism, the arts and humanities, economic affairs, education, international affairs, medicine and health, science and technology, and social welfare, through self-conducted programmes, research, grants to institutions, prizes, conferences, training courses and publications.

Geographical Area of Activity: Mexico.

Publications: *Inform* (annually); several other publications.

Finance: Financed by private donors; net assets approx. US $1,600,000; total expenditure $324,587 (2007).

Executive Committee: Miguel Alemán Velazco (Pres.); Beatriz Alemán de Girón (Treas.); Francisco Javier Mondragón (Sec.).

Principal Staff: Dir-Gen. Dr Alejandro Carrillo Castro.

Address: Col. Chapultepec Morales, Ruben Darío 187, 11570 México, DF.

Telephone: (55) 1946-2200; **Internet:** www.miguelaleman .org; **e-mail:** fundacionmiguelaleman@fma.org.mx.

Fundación México Unido—FMU (United Mexico Foundation)

Established in 1995 by a group of young people who wanted to help promote the appreciation and development of authentic Mexican values and culture, and to promote human values.

Activities: Programmes operated by the Foundation include a 'Telethon', which funds rehabilitation centres for children with disabilities, and Lazos, which provides financial support to schools and to poor children to ensure they receive an education. Awards the annual Premio Fundación México Unido a la Excelencia de lo Nuestro.

Geographical Area of Activity: Mexico and South America.

Publications: *Friends of Teleton* (6 a year); publications promoting Mexican values and history.

Principal Staff: Pres. Dr Fernando Landeros Verdugo; Dir Public Relations José Antonio Dorbecker; Chief Financial Officer Rossana Corona.

Address: Copérnico 51, Col. Anzures, 11590 México, DF.

Telephone: (55) 5531-2255; **Fax:** (55) 5531-1498; **Internet:** www.mexicounido.org.mx; **e-mail:** info@participacion.org .mx.

Oxfam Mexico

Part of the Oxfam confederation of organizations (qq.v.).

Activities: Operates in the areas of humanitarian assistance, climate change, migration, and health and education.

Geographical Area of Activity: South America, Central America,the Caribbean and Africa.

Finance: Total income US $57,092,247, total expenditure $58,471,999 (2010).

Board of Directors: Jesus Cantu Escalante (Pres.).

Principal Staff: Exec. Dir Carlos Zarco Mera; Dir of Development and Advocacy Elena Aguilar; Dir of Finance Gilberto Centeno.

Address: Alabama 105 Col. Nápoles, Del. Benito Juárez, 03810 México, DF.

Telephone: (55) 5687-3002; **Internet:** www.oxfammexico.org; **e-mail:** contacto@oxfammexico.org.

Moldova

FOUNDATION CENTRES AND CO-ORDINATING BODIES

National Assistance and Information Centre for NGOs in Moldova—CONTACT (Centrul Naţional de Asistenţă şi Informare a Organizaţiilor Neguvernamentale din Republica Moldova)

Established in 1995, at the initiative of the Soros Foundation—Moldova (q.v.), in collaboration with the International Foundation for Electoral Systems and Centras, Romania (q.v.). Aims to support democratic processes in civil society through the encouragement of civic initiatives and the promotion and implementation of open society ideas.

Activities: Promotes the development of civil society in Moldova, principally through its NGO Development Department, which aims to respond to the needs of the developing non-governmental sector in Moldova, particularly in rural areas, through provision of a broad spectrum of services for NGOs, including information, training, consultancy and technical assistance and an online database. Provides additional help through a support network of NGOs, which lobbies government and serves to develop dialogue between the non-governmental sector and state institutions, and promotes information exchange.

Geographical Area of Activity: Moldova.

Publications: *Study: Community Participation and Development in the Republic Moldova*; *The White Book II*; *Non-Governmental Organizations in the Republic of Moldova: Their evolution and future* (1998); *Catalogue of Non-governmental Organizations from the Republic of Moldova* (1998).

Principal Staff: Exec. Dir Serghei Neicovcen; Dep. Dir Pavel Cernocan.

Address: Bucuresti str. 83, 2012 Chişinău.

Telephone: (2) 233946; **Fax:** (2) 233948; **Internet:** www.contact.md; **e-mail:** info@contact.md.

NGO Rural and Social Initiative

Established in November 2000 to consolidate democracy in Moldova through the development of civil society, poverty alleviation and specific services for vulnerable categories of people.

Activities: Operates in the fields of project management and provider of expertise to authorities to develop specific projects/programmes, capacity building for grassroots civil society organizations in rural areas to promote human rights, democracy and community development.

Geographical Area of Activity: Moldova.

Publications: *Dialog* (bulletin); *Work Participative Methods in the Community*; guide for public servants, posters and booklets, leaflets and other publications.

Finance: Annual budget approx. US $190,000.

Principal Staff: Exec. Dir. Maria Brodesco.

Address: 9 Decebal str., 6811, Bardar, Ialoveni.

Telephone: 79471568; **Fax:** 26837361; **Internet:** www.ngorural.org; **e-mail:** office@ngorural.org.

Resource Centre for the Human Rights Nongovernmental Organizations of Moldova—CReDO

CReDO, though constituted in 1999, became operational as an organization in 2000, working towards promoting development of the civil society in Moldova in the area of human rights. CReDO was the result of an initiative taken by three prominent human rights NGOs in Moldova: League for Defence of Human Rights of Moldova, Moldovan Helsinki Committee for Human Rights and Independent Society for Education and Human Rights. A generous contribution from CordAid (the Netherlands), and technical support extended by the Netherlands Helsinki Committee, also helped in the establishment of CReDO.

Activities: CReDO operates by providing assistance to community groups and NGOs working in Moldova in support of human rights so as ultimately to strengthen organizational and institutional capacities.

Geographical Area of Activity: Moldova.

Principal Staff: Exec. Dir Serghei Ostaf.

Address: Alexandru Hasdeu str. 95A, 2005 Chişinău.

Telephone: (22) 212816; **Fax:** (22) 225257; **Internet:** www.credo.md; **e-mail:** credo@credo.md.

FOUNDATIONS, TRUSTS AND NON-PROFIT ORGANIZATIONS

Soros Foundation—Moldova

Established in 1992 to promote the development of open society; it is part of the Soros foundations network, which aims to foster political and cultural pluralism and reform the economy so as to encourage free enterprise and a market economy.

Activities: Principal areas of concern are: supporting independent media by providing training and access to information; civil society, promoting human rights and the rights of ethnic minorities; and providing grants for NGOs and training for NGO workers through the contact centres for NGOs. Also works in the areas of public administration and good governance, law and criminal justice, public health and European integration.

Geographical Area of Activity: Moldova.

Publications: Annual Report; newsletter (monthly).

Finance: Annual expenditure US $10,730,722 (2010).

Board of Directors: Arcadie Barbarosie (Chair.).

Principal Staff: Exec. Dir Victor Ursu; Dep. Dir Varvara Colibaba; Financial Dir Elena Vacarciuc.

Address: Bulgara str. 32, 2001 Chişinău.

Telephone: (22) 270031; **Fax:** (22) 270507; **Internet:** www.soros.md; **e-mail:** foundation@soros.md.

Monaco

FOUNDATIONS, TRUSTS AND NON-PROFIT ORGANIZATIONS

AMADE Mondiale—Association Mondiale des Amis de l'Enfance (World Association of Children's Friends)

Funded in 1963 by Princess Grace of Monaco, the World Association of Children's Friends strives to contribute to the well-being of the most vulnerable children in this world.

Activities: In compliance with these core beliefs, AMADE dedicates its action to the following objectives: to contribute to providing access to education and health care for every child world-wide; to promote the defence of children's essential rights; to raise public awareness of the place of the child in our society; maintains network of 11 local organizations (in Belgium, Burundi, Cambodia, Chad, Chile, Cyprus, Congo, Guinea, Italy, Lithuania and Monaco).

Geographical Area of Activity: Europe, Asia, South America and Africa.

Finance: Funds disbursed €599,622 (2009).

Board of Directors: HRH The Princess of Hanover (Chair.); Jean-Claude Michel (Vice-Chair.); Jean-Paul Samba (Treas.).

Principal Staff: Sec.-Gen. Francis Kasasa; Projects Co-ordinator Ana-Maria Hahn.

Address: 4 rue des Iris, 98000 Monaco.

Telephone: 97-70-52-60; **Fax:** 97-70-52-72; **Internet:** www.amade-mondiale.org; **e-mail:** info@amade-mondiale.org.

Fondation Prince Albert II de Monaco (Prince Albert II of Monaco Foundation)

Established in 2006.

Activities: Aims to protect the environment and to encourage sustainable development. Programmes cover three environmental issues: climate change, biodiversity and water resources. A total of 43 projects were approved by the Board of Directors in 2010. By 2010 the Foundation had supported a total of 154 projects at a cost of €15.7m.

Geographical Area of Activity: World-wide (with particular emphasis on the Arctic and Antarctic, the Mediterranean and the least-developed countries of the world).

Publications: Annual Report; brochures and bulletins.

Board of Directors: HSH Prince Albert II (Pres.); Bernard Fautrier (Vice-Pres. and CEO).

Principal Staff: Gen. Sec. Pascal Granero.

Address: Villa Girasole, 16 blvd de Suisse, 98000 Monaco.

Telephone: 98-98-44-44; **Fax:** 98-98-44-45; **Internet:** www.fpa2.mc; **e-mail:** contact@fpa2.mc.

Fondation Princesse Grace (Princess Grace Foundation)

Founded in 1964 to carry out general charitable activities.

Activities: Engaged in the following ongoing projects: the Boutiques du Rocher, which supports local craftspeople, the Université Médicale Virtuelle de Monaco (an online educational facility for paediatric medicine), the Académie de Danse, which funds training for talented young dancers, and the Princess Grace Irish Library. Also contributes to humanitarian projects related to children's health care, including some international work, and to cultural activities, providing scholarships to students of the arts. The Princess Grace Foundation—USA operates in the USA.

Geographical Area of Activity: Mainly Monaco and France.

Restrictions: No grants directly to students or children.

Finance: Total expenditure €1,447,699 (2008).

Board of Trustees: HRH Princess of Hanover (Pres.); HSH Prince Albert (Vice-Pres.); Jean-Claude Riey (Treas.).

Address: 9 rue Princesse Marie de Lorraine, BP 520, 98015 Monte Carlo.

Telephone: 97-70-86-86; **Fax:** 97-70-79-99; **Internet:** www.fondation-psse-grace.mc; **e-mail:** fpg@meditnet.com.

Mongolia

FOUNDATION CENTRE AND CO-ORDINATING BODY

Mongolian Women's Fund—MONES

Established in 2000, MONES is a non-partisan, not-for-profit, NGO, which financially supports public projects by women's NGOs and grassroots women's groups, as well as female-led NGOs and civic groups working towards women's human rights.

Activities: MONES raises funds and provides financial support to women's organizations and groups that are committed to issues such as gender-based discrimination and violence; increasing the income capacity of women; increasing women's participation in civic life; and the capacity building of women's organizations and groups.

Geographical Area of Activity: Mongolia.

Restrictions: No support for religious or political activities.

Finance: Project disbursement 166,500,000 Mongolian tugriks (2007).

Board of Trustees: Sh. Tsevelmaa (Chair.).

Principal Staff: Founder and Exec. Dir Chinchuluun Naidandorj.

Address: 4, Bldg 44, Small Ring Rd, Sukhbaatar District, Ulaanbaatar; POB 280, Ulaanbaatar 210646A.

Telephone: (11) 317904; **Fax:** (11) 317904; **Internet:** www .mones.org.mn; **e-mail:** mones@mongol.net.

FOUNDATIONS, TRUSTS AND NON-PROFIT ORGANIZATIONS

Open Society Forum (Mongolia)

Established in 1996 as the Mongolian Foundation for Open Society—MFOS to promote the development of open society in Mongolia. It is an independent foundation, part of the Soros foundations network. The Foundation changed its name in 2009.

Activities: Operates in the areas of education, information and the media, arts and culture, civil society, law and criminal justice, public health, economic development, women and youth. Also runs an extensive scholarship programme and an online grant database.

Geographical Area of Activity: Mongolia.

Publications: Annual Report; *Freedom in the world 2007: Freedom stagnation amid pushback against democracy*; *Conceptions of Democracy*; *Social Protection Index for Committed Poverty Reduction*; *Politbarometer*.

Finance: Annual expenditure US $1,346,023, grants disbursed $559,686 (2008); annual expenditure $1,340,000 (2009); funded by the Open Society Forum, Soros Foundation Network Programmes, World Bank, Revenue Watch Institute, and other donor organizations.

Board of Directors: Purevjav Tsenguun (Chair.).

Principal Staff: Exec. Dir P. Erdenejargal; Man. Dorjdari Namkhaijantsan.

Address: Silk Rd Building, Jamiyan Gun St 5/1, Sukhbaatar District, Ulaanbaatar 48.

Telephone: (11) 313207; **Fax:** (11) 324857; **Internet:** www .forum.mn; **e-mail:** osf@forum.mn.

Zorig Foundation

A non-profit NGO established in October 1998 in memory of the late Sanjaasürengiin Zorig; aims to advance the formation of democratic society and support political reforms in Mongolia.

Activities: Promotes democracy through organizing workshops, conferences, lectures and seminars in areas such as anti-corruption and the free media. Other initiatives include an essay competition for students in the social sciences, scholarships for students from families with low incomes, and a project to help families develop sustainable livelihoods through the provision of livestock and help with their upkeep.

Geographical Area of Activity: Mongolia.

Board of Directors: Dr Sanjaasürengiin Oyun (Chair.).

Principal Staff: Exec. Dir B. Oyundari.

Address: Central Post Office, POB 357, Ulaanbaatar.

Telephone: (11) 315444; **Fax:** (11) 315444; **Internet:** www .zorigfoundation.org.mn; **e-mail:** zorigfoundation@hotmail .com.

Montenegro

FOUNDATION CENTRE AND CO-ORDINATING BODY

Centre for the Development of Non-Governmental Organizations (Centar za Razvoj Nevladinih Organizacija—CRNVO)

Established in 1999 to provide support to development of NGOs in Montenegro and contribute to the creation of a favourable environment for citizens' participation in public policy issues and civil society development.

Activities: The Centre aims to build capacity of NGOs, improve co-operation between the State, NGOs and the commercial sector, increase understanding of the importance of the role that NGOs play in society, and contribute to the development of democracy, the rule of law and human rights. Provides training and technical assistance to NGOs, acts as a policy advocate to government, organizes discussion meetings between donors and NGOs, and trains NGO leaders in policy advocacy and human-rights issues.

Geographical Area of Activity: Montenegro.

Publications: *Tax and Financial Guidebook for NGOs*; *Learning Through Work*; *Co-operation Between State and NGOs*; *Strategic Planning*; *Volunteers*; *Grassroots Fundraising*; *Report on the Readiness of Serbia and Montenegro to Negotiate on a Stabilization and Association Agreement with the European Union*; *Basic Terms of Non-Governmental Sector; Citizen* (newsletter).

Principal Staff: Exec. Dir Ana Novakovic; Financial Man. Mary Ivancevic.

Address: 81000 Podgorica, Dalmatinska St 78.

Telephone: and fax (81) 20219122; **Internet:** www.crnvo.co.me; **e-mail:** crnvo@crnvo.me.

FOUNDATIONS, TRUSTS AND NON-PROFIT ORGANIZATIONS

Foundation Open Society Institute—Representative Office Montenegro—FOSI ROM

Independent, non-profit institute founded in March 2002 after the reorganization of the Open Society Institute, Montenegro.

The Institute aims to extend assistance to reform programmes and the development of civil society in Montenegro. Its mission is to contribute to the strengthening of democracy and democratic institutions, as well as to the sustainable social development of Montenegro, in line with European Union (EU) standards and policies, and with respect to universal human values. Part of the Open Society Institute network founded by George Soros.

Activities: Through its education programme, the Institute offers expertise on reform and supports initiatives aimed at providing an open and participatory reform process. The European Programme focuses on issues pertinent to European integration; on training and preparing NGOs to produce reform policies and implement international standards; and on supporting the collaboration of NGOs with state and local government, creating awareness regarding the European Union integration process and reforms. The Institute works towards successful implementation of European standards with regard to human and minority rights; it also extends support to monitoring political party funding led by NGOs, and supports initiatives aimed at improved implementation of the free access to information law. In addition, the Institute operates programmes related to local government and public administration institution building, child education, women and Roma.

Geographical Area of Activity: Montenegro.

Publications: *Law on Training in Judicial Authorities* (2006); *Instruments for Improvement of Inter-ethnic Relations* (2007); *Action Plan for the Introduction of Sustainable Development in the Education System 2007–2009*; *Reform Proposal for the Appointment of Judges in Montenegro* (2007); *Financing of political parties in Montenegro*; *Understanding NATO* (2007); and other reports.

Finance: Total programme budget €847,406.5 (2009).

Board of Directors: Srdjan Darmanovic (Pres.).

Principal Staff: Regional Dir Beka Vuco.

Address: 81000 Podgorica, Vuka Karadzica 2.

Telephone: and fax (20) 232111; **Internet:** www.osim.org.me; **e-mail:** montenegro@osim.org.me.

Morocco

FOUNDATIONS, TRUSTS AND NON-PROFIT ORGANIZATIONS

Fondation Orient-Occident (The Orient-Occident Foundation)

Created in 1994 by Yasmine Filali.

Activities: Aims to contribute to enhancing dialogue between cultures and promoting mutual understanding. Has established socio-educational and professional training centres in six centres in Morocco and has built bridges between North and South by means of actions geared towards Moroccan and immigrant youth. The Foundation's mission is to listen to the needs of the country's youth in five main fields: educational reinforcement, psychological listening, vocational training, solidarity economy, and human rights.

Geographical Area of Activity: Morocco.

Publications: Newsletter.

Finance: Financed by the Government, European Union grants and a number of private sponsors.

Board of Directors: Yasmine Filali (Founding Pres. and CEO); Abdou Filali-Ansary, Patrick Guerrand Hermes (Vice-Pres); Rachid Badouli (Sec.-Gen.); Said Lamrani (Treas.).

Address: Avenue des F.A.R, Commune de Yacoub el Mansour, BP 3210,Rabat.

Telephone: (53) 7793637; **Fax:** (53) 7291543; **Internet:** fondation.orient-occident.org; **e-mail:** yf_foo@menara.ma.

Fondation du Roi Abdul-Aziz al-Saoud pour les Etudes Islamiques et les Sciences Humaines (King Abdul-Aziz al-Saoud Foundation for Islamic Study and the Humanities)

Established in 1985 to offer library and database services to researchers working in the field of Islamic culture and in the humanities.

Activities: Maintains a research library of approximately 287,000 volumes and 1,992 periodicals, mainly in Arabic, English and French, but other languages are represented. The Foundation also maintains three databases: the Ibn Rushd database of more than 78,000 bibliographical references, with information on the Maghreb, Western European and West African Islamic communities; the Fahras database of approximately 58,000 references, with information covering the rest of the Arab world and general Islamic research; and the Mawsu'a database of more than 241,000 entries containing bibliographical information on the human and social sciences, regarding their methodological and theoretical aspects. There is also a multimedia service. In addition the Foundation organizes, in collaboration with other research and documentation institutions, international conferences and seminars.

Geographical Area of Activity: Morocco.

Publications: *Études maghrébines; Ethique et entreprises: perspectives maghrébines* (books); *Le droit international privé dans les pays maghrébins; La Méditerranée en question: conflits et interdépendance; Renouveau de la pensée islamique; Renouveau des études sur l'Islam et le Monde arabe; Droit et environnement social;* newsletter (twice a year).

Address: BP 12585, Casablanca 20052; blvd de la Corniche, Ain Diab, Anfa, Casablanca 20050.

Telephone: (52) 2391027; **Fax:** (52) 2391031; **Internet:** www.fondation.org.ma; **e-mail:** secretariat@fondation.org.ma.

Mozambique

FOUNDATIONS, TRUSTS AND NON-PROFIT ORGANIZATIONS

FDC—Fundação para o Desenvolvimento da Comunidade (Community Development Foundation)

Established in 1994 by Graça Machel, wife of Nelson Mandela and a former Minister of Education in Mozambique, to bring health care, education, economic development, access to technology and peace to the African continent. Originally constituted in 1990 as the Association for the Development of the Community.

Activities: The Foundation promotes economic development, health care and related programmes in disadvantaged communities in Mozambique and other parts of Africa, aiming to increase human and financial resources for development at the community level. Priority is given to education, health, water and training projects, which develop human potential, generate income, and put in place necessary infrastructure. The Foundation has financed the construction of hospitals and schools, and skills training, and has provided microcredit funds. Also acts as an advocate in the areas of land tenure, promotes a landmine ban, supports education for girls and works in the areas of external debt and development issues.

Geographical Area of Activity: Mozambique and Africa.

Publications: newsletter, manuals, reports.

Administrative Council: Graça Simbine Machel (Chair.).

Principal Staff: Exec. Dir Narciso Matos; Dir of Programmes Jacinto Uqueio; Dir of Admin. and Finance Eunica Zunguza.

Address: Av. 25 de Setembro, Edificio Times Square, Bloco 2, 2–3º andar, CP 4206, Maputo.

Telephone: (21) 355300; **Fax:** (21) 355355; **Internet:** www.fdc .org.mz; **e-mail:** info@fdc.org.mz.

Namibia

FOUNDATIONS, TRUSTS AND NON-PROFIT ORGANIZATIONS

DRFN—Desert Research Foundation of Namibia

Dedicated to furthering understanding and competence appropriately to manage arid environments for sustainable development. Incorporates the Desert Ecological Research Unit, which was founded by Dr Charles Koch in 1963 to promote ecological education and research training.

Activities: The Foundation works collaboratively in all sectors involved in management and use of natural resources, concentrating on the agriculture, water and energy sectors, with government, commercial, non-governmental and community-based organizations. Carries out its mission at a number of levels: by involving communities in participatory learning to develop sustainable management practices; engaging managers and policy-makers in dialogue to improve the policy and regulatory framework for sustainable development; building a body of knowledge to improve understanding of arid and semi-arid lands; building the capacity and commitment to manage natural resources sustainably. The Foundation is a co-partner, together with the Ministry of Environment and Tourism, in guiding the Gobabeb Training and Research Centre in the Namib Desert, on the banks of the ephemeral Kuiseb River. Also undertakes commercial environmental work through its consulting arm, Environmental Evaluation Associates of Namibia (Pty) Ltd.

Geographical Area of Activity: Southern Africa, particularly Namibia.

Publications: 2008 publications: *Age and dynamics of linear dunes in the Namib Desert; Dynamics of flood water infiltration and ground water recharge in hyperarid desert; Ecophysiology of atmospheric moisture in the Namib Desert; Community-driven local level monitoring: recording environmental change to support multi-level decision-making in Namibia; Water points and their influence on grazing resources in central northern Namibia; Recovery of lichen-dominated soil crusts in a hyper-arid desert; Infection of the cones and seeds of Welwitschia mirabilis by Aspergillus niger var. phoenicis in the Namib-Naukluft Park.*

Finance: The Foundation is funded by grants, donations and a trust fund. Implements donor funds, annual budget approx N $10,000,000.

Board of Trustees: Cornelius Tangeni Erkana (Chair.).

Principal Staff: Exec. Dir Viviane Kinyaga.

Address: POB 20232, Windhoek; 7 Rossini St, Windhoek West.

Telephone: (61) 377500; **Fax:** (61) 230172; **Internet:** www.drfn.org.na; **e-mail:** drfn@drfn.org.na.

Gobabeb Training and Research Centre

Established in 1962 as the Namib Desert Research Station to carry out research on desert climate, ecology, geology and geomorphology of the desert landscape. Since 1990 the Centre is a Southern African Development Community (SADC) Centre of Excellence, promoting sustainable lifestyles and practices through wise management of natural resources within Namibia and the SADC region, with an emphasis on desertification, land degradation and sustainable natural resource management.

Activities: The Centre is located in the Namib Naukluft Park in the Central Namib Desert. The Centre is the only arid land training facility in Sub-Saharan Africa and one of only a few facilities available for arid land research. Offers training at all levels to Namibian institutions and environmental groups, and conducts long-term ecological research, and, through the Gobabeb Environmental Observatories Network, is linked world-wide.

Geographical Area of Activity: Namibia and southern Africa.

Publications: *Gobabeb Times* (newsletter); *Management of alluvial aquifers in two Southern African ephemeral rivers; The impacts of an invasive species and hydrological change in an aquifer-dependent ecosystem; Home range and seasonal movements of* Giraffa camelopardalis angolensis *in the norther Namib Desert;* and others.

Finance: Annual budget N $10,000,000.

Board of Trustees: Dr Kalumbi Shangula (Chair.); Tangeni Erkana (Deputy-Chair.); Dr Joh Henschel (Exec. Dir).

Principal Staff: Exec. Dir Dr Joh Henschel.

Address: POB 953, Walvis Bay.

Telephone: (64) 694199; **Fax:** (64) 694197; **Internet:** www.gobabeb.org; **e-mail:** gobabeb@gobabeb.org.

Rössing Foundation

Established in 1978 by Rössing Uranium Ltd, Namibia and Rio Tinto Zinc, London (UK) to promote research and education in Namibia.

Activities: The Foundation carries out research, grants scholarships, and conducts training courses and conferences in the areas of social welfare and studies and education; runs four education centres, at Lüderitz, Ondangwa, Omaruru and Khomasdal, offering courses in vehicle maintenance, textile design, needlework, technical skills, commercial practice, art, office practice, typing, mathematics and English, and a Teachers' Programme. Also runs libraries at the Khomasdal centre and Katutura; encourages the pursuit of science in high schools by extending support to Namibian Young Scientists National Exhibition, which is conducted at the Khomasdal centre; conducts workshops on skills training for the self-employed; and offers support to rural women craft workers. The Foundation receives support from several national and international organizations.

Geographical Area of Activity: Southern Africa.

Finance: The Foundation has been funded almost entirely by Rössing Uranium Ltd. Total expenditure N $23,168,286 (2010).

Board of Directors: Rehabeam Hoveka (Chair.); Job Tjiho (Dir); Cornell Meeks (Sec.).

Address: 360 Sam Nujoma Dr., Windhoek; POB 22391, Windhoek.

Telephone: (61) 211721; **Fax:** (61) 233637; **Internet:** www.rossing.com/rossing_foundation.htm; **e-mail:** jtjiho@rossing.com.na.

Nepal

FOUNDATIONS, TRUSTS AND NON-PROFIT ORGANIZATIONS

Asia-Pacific Mountain Network—APMN

Established in 1995, a network of organizations and individuals concerned with sustainable mountain development in the Asia-Pacific region. Managed by the International Centre for Integrated Mountain Development (ICIMOD). Acts as the Asia-Pacific node of the Mountain Forum.

Activities: Operates in the area of conservation and development in mountainous areas of the Asia-Pacific region, promoting the idea of a sustainable ecosystem in these areas. Disseminates information on this subject, encouraging information exchange among members; works on capacity building, especially relating to technological advances and electronic communications; acts as an advocate for improved legislation in the field of sustainable mountain development; and supports the alleviation of poverty among mountain populations. New initiatives include grassroots outreach activities targeting young people and the development of a subsidiary office in Central Asia.

Geographical Area of Activity: The Asia-Pacific region.

Publications: *Asia Pacific Mountain Courier* (2 a year); *Tough Terrain: Media Reports on Mountain Issues;* occasional reports and briefs.

Principal Staff: Man. Tek Jung Mahat.

Address: c/o ICIMOD, POB 3226, Khumaltar Lalitpur.

Telephone: (1) 5003222; **Fax:** (1) 5003277.

Himalayan Light Foundation—HLF

Founded to support the use of environmentally friendly energy technology to improve the quality of life of people living in remote Himalayan communities.

Activities: Operates in the fields of conservation and the environment, education and social welfare, through self-conducted programmes, research and dissemination of information. The Foundation operates the Solar Sisters and Home Employment and Lighting Programme (HELP); it also provides solar lighting systems to remote monasteries (which, in turn, provide education for children and support for communities). The establishment of rural energy extension centres in rural areas also provides education and employment for local villagers. Maintains office in Leonia, USA.

Geographical Area of Activity: Nepal.

Publications: *The Solar Siblings Manual; The Solar Sisters and Home Employment and Lighting Package Manual; Charged Newsletter.*

Board of Directors: Adam Friedensohn (Founder and Chief Adviser).

Principal Staff: Pres. and Dir Sapana Shakya; Prog. Man. Yadav Gurung.

Address: POB 12191, Kathmandu.

Telephone: (1) 4425393; **Fax:** (1) 4412924; **Internet:** www.hlf.org.np; **e-mail:** info@hlf.org.np.

INHURED International—International Institute for Human Rights, Environment and Development

Founded in 1991 to defend human rights in the Asia-Pacific region, particularly in South Asia.

Activities: Works to advance human rights and gender equality and to promote democracy in Asia, by strengthening existing human rights bodies; monitoring international institutions for signs of human and environmental rights abuses; observing elections; funding training; co-ordinating international conferences and workshops; and disseminating information. Offers internship and fellowship programmes for international and university students and scholars in the areas of human rights, environment, development and the democratization process. Also promotes environmental conservation.

Geographical Area of Activity: Asia-Pacific region.

Finance: Funded by membership fees, donations, sale of publications and grants.

Board: Dr Gopal Krishna Siwakoti (Pres.); Hemanta Raj Dahal (Gen. Sec.); Shree Krishna Subedi (Sec.); B. P. Adhikari (Treas.).

Principal Staff: Programme Dir Anjana Shakya.

Address: Ceasefire House, Jhamsikhel, Lalitpur 2; POB 12684, Kathmandu.

Telephone: (1) 5520054; **Fax:** (1) 5520042; **Internet:** www.inhuredinternational.org; **e-mail:** inhured@ntc.net.np.

Nepal Forward Foundation

Founded in 1996 to provide assistance in Nepal.

Activities: Operates in the fields of economic development, conservation and the environment, education and youth, and cultural preservation. Projects include installing solar panels in remote villages of Nepal in conjunction with the Himalayan Light Foundation (q.v.), promoting the export of organic tea from Nepal to Europe and the USA, and eco-tourism initiatives. Also organizes cultural exchanges between Nepal and the USA, where it maintains an office. Launched an initiative to end discrimination against Nepalese Gurkhas who had served in the British army.

Geographical Area of Activity: Nepal.

Principal Staff: Founder and Chair. Eric J. Urbani; Exec. Dir Kamal Z. El-Wattar.

Address: Murxana House, Lal Durbar, Durbar Marg, Kathmandu.

Telephone: (1) 426850; **Fax:** (1) 428844; **Internet:** www.nepalforward.org; **e-mail:** nepal.forward@ibm.net.

Tewa

Established by Rita Thapa in 1996 to promote the advancement of women through grant-making to women's groups in Nepal.

Activities: Operates in three principal areas: grant-making; fundraising; and training of fundraising volunteers. Community children's programme launched in 2007 and the Tewa Model Adaptation Initiative in 2008.

Geographical Area of Activity: Nepal.

Publications: *Tewa Times* (annual report); newsletter.

Finance: Total assets NRs 85,538,233.4 (2010); Total grants disbursed NRs 1,756,710 (2009/10).

Principal Staff: Chair. Sadhana Shrestha; Pres. Draupadi Rokaya; Gen. Sec. Amita Adhikary; Treas. Rama Laxmi Shrestha.

Address: Dhapakhel, Laltipur; POB 11, Lalitpur.

Telephone: (1) 5572654; **Fax:** (1) 5572659; **Internet:** www.tewa.org.np; **e-mail:** info@tewa.org.np.

Netherlands

FOUNDATION CENTRE AND CO-ORDINATING BODY

Vereniging van Fondsen in Nederland—FIN (Association of Foundations in the Netherlands)

Established in 1988, the Association's membership is comprised of private foundations established in the Netherlands. Its aim is to promote the interests of its members and enable them to function effectively.

Activities: Promotes the interests of its member foundations and assists them to function in the most effective way by: organizing meetings, workshops and symposia for its members; providing information concerning foundations operating in the Netherlands; maintaining contact with public authorities, social organizations and the media; and providing advice on matters of management and donations policy. Also promotes the establishment of new foundations and the exchange of information between members. The Association has approximately 300 members.

Geographical Area of Activity: Netherlands.

Publications: *Fondsenboek*; *Fondsendisk* (annually); informative publications including *Het besturen van een fonds* (*Managing a Foundation*) and *Fiscaliteit* (*Tax Law*); publications are only available in Dutch.

Finance: Financed by subscriptions from its members.

Board: Dr M. C. E. van Gendt (Chair.); K. W. Sluyterman van Loo (Vice-Chair.); J. W. Pieterson (Treas.).

Principal Staff: Dir H. Wagenvoort; Sec. V. A. L. M. Theewen.

Address: Jan van Nassaustraat 102, 2596 BW The Hague.

Telephone: (70) 3262753; **Fax:** (70) 3262229; **Internet:** www.verenigingvanfondsen.nl; **e-mail:** info@verenigingvanfondsen.nl.

FOUNDATIONS, TRUSTS AND NON-PROFIT ORGANIZATIONS

Adessium Foundation

Established in 2005 by the van Vliet family.

Activities: Funds initiatives that benefit people and society; and projects promoting sustainable exploitation, production and certification of natural resources.

Geographical Area of Activity: World-wide, mainly in the Netherlands.

Restrictions: Projects must have a scientific basis, self-sustaining capacity; a focus on innovative and practical solutions; aim for structural and sustainable change; have visible and quantifiable results. The Foundation does not accept unsolicited project proposals.

Board of Directors: Roger D. van Vliet (Chair.).

Principal Staff: Man. Dir Pieter M. Stemerding; Dir of Progs Rogier van der Weerd.

Address: POB 76, 2810 AB Reeuwijk.

Telephone: (182) 308450; **Fax:** (182) 308499; **Internet:** www.adessium.org; **e-mail:** info@adessium.org.

Eduard Van Beinum Stichting (Eduard Van Beinum Foundation)

Founded in 1960 by harpist Phia Berghout for the stimulation of musical life in general and particularly the promotion of the artistic and social interests of musicians, all in the broadest sense.

Activities: Operates nationally and internationally in the arts; provides sums annually for commissions in the field of contemporary classical music, including operatic works.

Geographical Area of Activity: International.

Publications: *Eduard van Beinum Over zijn leven en werk*; *Eduard van Beinum 1900–1959, Musicus Tussen Musici*.

Governing Board: F. A. W. Bannier (Pres.); Yvonne van Baarle (Sec.); A. W. J. van der Heijden (Treas.).

Principal Staff: Man. Aleida Hamel.

Address: Tafelbergweg 6, 1251 AE Laren.

Telephone: (35) 624-57-88; **Internet:** www.eduardvanbeinumstichting.nl; **e-mail:** info@eduardvanbeinumstichting.nl.

Evert Willem Beth Foundation

Founded in 1978 under the terms of the will of Cornelia P. C. Beth-Pastoor to promote interest in logic, the philosophy of the exact sciences, and research into the foundations of the sciences.

Activities: Operates nationally and internationally in education and the humanities, through publications, teaching and organizing symposia; it conducts research in logic, the origins and philosophy of the exact sciences, and any philosophical activity that is conceptually connected with these subjects. Also funds an endowed chair of study and research and scientific gatherings. Regular series of E. W. Beth Lectures are given by philosophers and scientists of international repute.

Finance: Provides annual funding of approx. €32,000.

Executive Committee: Prof. Dr Henk Visser (Pres.); J. F. A. K. van Benthem (Treas.).

Principal Staff: Secretariat Prof. Dr Henk Visser.

Address: Kleverlaan 172, 2023 JM Haarlem.

Telephone: (20) 5510746; **Internet:** www.knaw.nl/beth; **e-mail:** henkxvisser@gmail.com.

Canon Foundation in Europe

Founded in December 1987 by Canon Europa NV to facilitate mutual understanding and the development of scientific expertise, in particular between Europe and Japan.

Activities: The Foundation offers up to 15 Research Fellowships every year to individuals in all fields of interest, in order for Europeans to carry out research in Japan, and to enable Japanese people to carry out research in Europe.

Geographical Area of Activity: Europe and Japan.

Publications: *Bulletin* (annually).

Board of Directors: James Leipnik (Chair.); Willem R. van Gulik (Treas. and Sec.); Andreas van Agt (Hon. Chair.).

Principal Staff: Sec. Suzy Cohen.

Address: Bovenkerkerweg 59–61, 1185 XB Amstelveen; POB 2262, 1180 EG Amstelveen.

Telephone: (20) 5458934; **Fax:** (20) 7128934; **Internet:** www.canonfoundation.org; **e-mail:** foundation@canon-europe.com.

Carnegie-Stichting, Watelerfonds (Carnegie Foundation, Wateler Fund)

Founded in 1927 by J. G. D. Wateler for the awarding of an annual peace prize.

Activities: Awards the Wateler Peace Prize biennially to the person or institution having rendered the most valuable service in the cause of peace, or having contributed to finding the means of preventing war. The prize is given alternately to a person of Dutch and foreign nationality. In 2010 the non-profit organization Peace One Day and its founder, Jeremy Gilley, were awarded the prize.

Geographical Area of Activity: International.

Publications: *The Peace Palace* (annual); *The Trusteeship of an Ideal.*

Trustees: Dr Bernard R. Bot (Chair.).

Principal Staff: Gen. Dir S. van Hoogstraten; Sec. Ch. van der Linden; Head of Internal Services J. H. Endlich.

Address: Carnegieplein 2, 2517 KJ The Hague.

Telephone: (70) 3024242; **Fax:** (70) 3024234; **Internet:** www .vredespaleis.nl; **e-mail:** carnegie@carnegie-stichting.nl.

Europa Nostra (Pan-European Federation for Cultural Heritage)

Established in 1963 in response to the threat to Venice caused by rising floodwaters. Since then, Europa Nostra has become a leading European NGO bringing together representatives of the growing European movement to safeguard cultural heritage in all its forms. Its specific objectives are to promote high standards of quality in the fields of heritage conservation, architecture, urban and rural planning, and to advocate balanced and sustainable development of the built and natural environment. Through its various activities, Europa Nostra seeks to illustrate the importance of cultural heritage as a building block of European identity and as a contribution to the strengthening of the sense of European citizenship.

Activities: Europa Nostra, an umbrella network of heritage organizations, both large and small, which act at local, regional, national or European levels, is considered to be the voice of Europe's organized civil society committed to cultural heritage. The network is composed of 250 member NGOs, 210 associate members and 1,500 individual members from 53 countries, of which 45 are in Europe. Europa Nostra's activities aim to increase public awareness of cultural heritage; to campaign at local, national and international levels for the preservation and rescue of Europe's endangered heritage; to highlight the multiple benefits that cultural heritage provides for society; and to make cultural heritage a priority for public policy both at European and national levels. In 2002 the European Union (EU) selected Europa Nostra to run the EU Prize for Cultural Heritage/Europa Nostra Awards, which promote exemplary restorations and initiatives of the many facets of Europe's cultural heritage in various categories, including the restoration of monuments and buildings, urban and rural landscape rehabilitation, archaeological site interpretation, care for art collections, research and education, and dedicated service to heritage conservation. Every year, up to six monetary awards of €10,000 each are awarded to the top laureates in the various categories. Convenes a General Assembly every year (in Amsterdam in 2011 and in Lisbon in 2012).

Geographical Area of Activity: Europe (greater Europe as defined by the Council of Europe).

Restrictions: Member organizations must be approved by the Council. Europa Nostra has no funding available for restorations, etc.

Publications: Annual Report; electronic newsletter; *European Cultural Heritage Review* (including themed *Dossiers* issues, annually); issues dedicated to the laureates of the EU Prize for Cultural Heritage/Europa Nostra Awards (annually); *Scientific Bulletin* (annually).

Finance: Total assets €573,434; annual income €1,088,224, expenditure €1,184,129 (2010).

Board: Denis de Kergorlay (Exec. Pres.); John Sell (Exec. Vice-Pres.); Roelf E. Rogaar (Treas.).

Principal Staff: Sec.-Gen. Sneska Quaedvlieg-Mihailovic.

Address: Lange Voorhout 35, 2514 EC The Hague.

Telephone: (70) 3024050; **Fax:** (70) 3617865; **Internet:** www .europanostra.org; **e-mail:** info@europanostra.org.

European Climate Foundation

Established in 2008 to promote climate and energy policies that greatly reduce Europe's greenhouse gas emissions and help Europe play a strong international leadership role in mitigating climate change.

Activities: The Foundation is dedicated to developing and implementing climate and energy policies to reduce Europe's global greenhouse gas emissions through five priority programmes: Energy Efficiency; Climate Diplomacy; Low-Carbon Power Generation; Transportation; and EU Climate Policies. Maintains offices in Berlin and Brussels.

Geographical Area of Activity: European Union.

Restrictions: Does not accept unsolicited proposals.

Publications: Newsletter.

Supervisory Board: John McCall MacBain (Chair.).

Principal Staff: Chief Exec. Officer Dr Johannes Meier.

Address: Tournooiveld 4, 2511 CX The Hague.

Telephone: (70) 711 9600; **Fax:** (70) 711 9601; **Internet:** www .europeanclimate.org; **e-mail:** info@europeanclimate.org.

European Cultural Foundation—ECF (Fondation Européenne de la Culture/Europese Culturele Stichting)

Founded in Geneva in 1954 as an NGO, supported by Dutch charity lotteries and private sources to promote cross-cultural co-operation on a multilateral European level.

Activities: The Foundation initiates and manages its own programmes and projects, and gives grants to other bodies for European-level cultural activities. The ECF initiates and supports cultural expression and interaction that empower people to realize a shared future in Europe. The Foundation aims to be a catalyst of cultural expression and interaction that makes the diverse societies of Europe more open and inclusive. The Foundation supports high-quality artistic activities and cultural co-operation across different countries, borders and boundaries. It advocates for culture, helping to create better conditions for the arts and campaigning to change political attitudes towards culture at European Union level. It helps provide better access to cultural information. Commitment is to the whole of Europe and its neighbouring regions, targetting those places believed to be in most need of support. The ECF has a special commitment to the new generation of Europeans, with many activities geared towards bringing out the creativity in young people of all backgrounds.

Geographical Area of Activity: Europe.

Restrictions: ECF programmes are initiated, developed and run in partnership with other organizations. Grants are made only to non-profit organizations for a cultural co-operation project; grants are made only in Europe. All pertinent information on the different programmes and grants schemes can be found on the ECF website.

Publications: Annual Report; e-zine.

Finance: Annual income €6,000,000; total grants budget €1,250,000 (2008).

Board: Wolfgang Petritsch (Chair.); Rien van Gendt (Dep. Chair.); Arent A. Foch (Treas.).

Principal Staff: Pres. HRH Princess Laurentien of the Netherlands; Dir Katherine Watson; Sec. Mariette Verhaar.

Address: Jan van Goyenkade 5, 1075 HN Amsterdam.

Telephone: (20) 5733868; **Fax:** (20) 6752231; **Internet:** www .eurocult.org; **e-mail:** eurocult@eurocult.org.

European Youth For Action—EYFA

Founded in 1986 (as European Youth For Action) as an activist network to encourage young people to work towards the prevention of environmental pollution and the decimation of forests.

Activities: The organization works in Europe in the field of conservation and the environment, through promoting sustainable ways of living and working, non-violent campaigns against ecologically and socially unsustainable systems, cultural activism and alternative media. Helps other organizations with their fundraising, as well as providing financial services, including book-keeping assistance and the legal status to receive funds on behalf of other organizations. Particular focus on youth-initiated activities and projects. Opposed to 'car culture', nuclear power and coal-fired power plants. Organizes annual Ecotopia gathering, which is a training camp involving political and environmental activists from across Europe. Maintains office in Berlin and has partner organizations in 18 European countries.

Geographical Area of Activity: Europe.

Publications: *Green Pepper;* newsletter.

Finance: Receives funding from various organizations, including the European Union. Annual budget approx. €114,00.

Principal Staff: Financial Co-ordinator Katrin McGauran.

Address: Plantage Doklaan 12A, 1018 CM Amsterdam; POB 49115, 1090 GC Amsterdam.

Telephone: (20) 6682236; **Fax:** (20) 6928757; **Internet:** www .eyfa.org; **e-mail:** eyfa@eyfa.org.

Eurotransplant International Foundation

Founded in 1967 with the aim of facilitating the exchange of human organs to save lives.

Activities: Supports co-operation between transplant centres, donor hospitals, tissue typing laboratories and national authorities; aims to maximize the outcome of organ transplants and minimize the risks by making the best possible match between donor organ and transplant candidate; assists in the organization of organ transplants; works to ensure an optimal use of available donor organs in Austria, Belgium, Croatia, Germany, Luxembourg, the Netherlands, and Slovenia. The Foundation provides finance for programmes intended to improve the system whereby human organs may be transplanted. Maintains a database of patients.

Geographical Area of Activity: Europe.

Publications: Annual Report; *Eurotransplant Newsletter;* articles and brochures.

Finance: Total assets €5,203,000 (2010).

Board of Management: Dr Bruno Meiser (Pres.); Prof. Dr Ferdinand Mühlbacher (Vice-Pres.); Prof. Dr A. van Montfort (Sec. and Treas.).

Principal Staff: Gen. Dir Arie Oosterlee MD; Medical Dir Dr Axel O. Rahmel.

Address: POB 2304, 2301 CH Leiden.

Telephone: (71) 5795700; **Fax:** (71) 5790057; **Internet:** www .eurotransplant.org; **e-mail:** contact.et@eurotransplant.org.

De Faunabescherming (Wildlife Protection)

Founded in December 1975 to work toward scientific and ethical wildlife management.

Activities: Operates nationally in the field of conservation and wildlife management; issues publications, legal procedures, actions.

Geographical Area of Activity: Netherlands.

Publications: *Argus* (quarterly); online newsletter.

Principal Staff: H. Niesen; I. van den Abeele; P. de Jong.

Address: Amsteldijk Noord 135, 1183 TJ Amstelveen.

Telephone: (20) 6410798; **Fax:** (20) 6473700; **Internet:** www .faunabescherming.nl; **e-mail:** info@faunabescherming.nl.

FEMCONSULT (Consultants on Gender and Development)

Founded in 1985 as a non-profit organization, a multidisciplinary group of professionals applying a gender perspective in programmes and projects in developing countries.

Activities: Offers technical expertise with a focus on gender-based constraints and opportunities for the development of programmes and projects aimed at the reduction of poverty. In particular, promotes the participation of women in development programmes; implements projects in developing countries focusing on women, in areas such as agriculture and rural development, education and communication; democracy and good governance; human resources development; nutrition and food aid; natural resources and the environment; small businesses; and public and reproductive health. Also offers a range of consultancy services concerning development programmes and projects, including participatory planning; project identification and appraisal; pre-investment studies; project design, planning, management, monitoring and evaluation; institutional strengthening and training; social, poverty and gender assessment studies; and preparation of tender documents.

Geographical Area of Activity: International.

Publications: *FEMCONSULT* (newsletter, in English); *Project Report*; *Skills Bank* (2 a year, in Dutch and English); *Symposium Report*.

Principal Staff: Man. Dir Catharina M. G. van Heel; Deputy Dir and Project Man. Patricia Tesselhoff.

Address: Nassaulaan 5, 2514 JS The Hague.

Telephone: (70) 3655744; **Fax:** (70) 3623100; **Internet:** www .femconsult.org; **e-mail:** info@femconsult.org.

FONDAD—Forum on Debt and Development

Independent policy research centre and forum for international discussion established in the Netherlands in 1987.

Activities: Supported by a world-wide network of experts, FONDAD provides policy-orientated research on a range of North-South issues, with particular emphasis on international financial issues. Through research, seminars and publications, it aims to provide factual background information and practical strategies for policy-makers and other interested groups in industrial, developing and transition countries.

Geographical Area of Activity: International.

Restrictions: No grants are available.

Publications: Recent publications: *Global Imbalances and Developing Countries: Remedies for a Failing International Financial System; Global Imbalances and the US Debt Problem: Should Developing Countries Support the US Dollar?; Africa in the World Economy: The National, Regional and International Challenges; Protecting the Poor: Global Financial Institutions and the Vulnerability of Low-Income Countries;* and many others.

Principal Staff: Dir Jan Joost Teunissen.

Address: Nieuwendammerdijk 421, 1023 BM Amsterdam.

Telephone: (20) 6371954; **Fax:** (20) 6371954; **Internet:** www .fondad.org; **e-mail:** jj.teunissen@fondad.org.

Anne Frank Stichting (Anne Frank Foundation)

Founded in 1957 to preserve the Anne Frank House and to propagate the ideals left to the world in Anne Frank's diary; and to fight against prejudice and discrimination in the world.

Activities: Operates nationally and internationally in the fields of education and international relations; runs a museum in the house where Anne Frank and her family lived in hiding, providing visitors with information on the developments and events of the Second World War, and regular exhibitions on contemporary subjects, such as its Free2choose programme, about fundamental rights that clash with the safeguarding of the democratic rule of law. The education department organizes study programmes in collaboration with teachers. The Foundation also maintains archives, develops educational material on the Second World War for schools, and investigates neo-Nazi groups.

Geographical Area of Activity: Netherlands and international.

Publications: Newsletter; Annual Report; numerous reports and books.

Trustees: W. Kok (Chair.); R. C. Musaph-Andriesse (Vice-Chair.).

Principal Staff: Exec. Dir Ronald Leopold; Man. Dir Garance Reus-Deelder.

Address: Postbus 730, 1000 AS Amsterdam.

Telephone: (20) 5567100; **Fax:** (20) 6207999; **Internet:** www
.annefrank.org; **e-mail:** press@annefrank.nl.

Friends of the Earth International

A federation of environmental organizations and groups active
throughout the world with more than 2m. members and supporters around the world. Aims to campaign on today's most
urgent environmental and social issues; to challenge the current model of economic and corporate globalization; and to
promote solutions that will help to create environmentally
sustainable and socially just societies.

Activities: Operates internationally in the area of the environment, by campaigning on issues such as genetically-modi-
fied crops, climate change, trade and sustainability, human
rights and natural resources. Also issues publications on sustainable use of the environment. The International Secretariat
supports its member network, by raising funds, co-ordinating
campaigns, organizing workshops, disseminating information
and maintaining databases. There are currently 76 national
member groups.

Geographical Area of Activity: International.

Publications: Annual Report; electronic bulletins.

Finance: Total assets €1,422,370; annual income €2,751,958,
expenditure €2,703,794 (2010).

Executive Committee: Nnimmo Bassey (Chair.); Jagoda
Munic (Treas.).

Principal Staff: Communications Co-ordinator Ann Doherty.

Address: POB 19199, 1000 GD Amsterdam.

Telephone: (20) 6221369; **Fax:** (20) 6392181; **Internet:** www
.foei.org; **e-mail:** foei@foei.org.

Health Action International

Founded in May 1981.

Activities: An international network of over 200 health, consumer and development groups operating in more than 70
countries, working to increase access to essential medicines
and improve their rational use through research excellence
and evidence-based advocacy.

Geographical Area of Activity: Africa, Asia and the Pacific, Europe, and North, Central and South America.

Publications: reports; briefing papers; press releases; fact
sheets.

Finance: Total income €1,463,709; total expenditure
€1,356,663 (2010).

Principal Staff: Global Dir Dr Tim Reed; Europe Co-ordinator Teresa Alves.

Address: Overtoom 60/II, 1054 HK Amsterdam.

Telephone: (20) 4124523; **Fax:** (20) 6855002; **Internet:** www
.haiweb.org; **e-mail:** info@haiweb.org.

Dr H. P. Heineken Stichting (Dr H. P. Heineken Founda-
tion)

Founded in 1963 by Heineken's Bierbrouwerij Maatschappij
NV to promote science and culture.

Activities: Awards a prize amounting to approximately
US $150,000 biennially to a person or team of any nationality,
which has made an outstanding contribution in the fields of
biochemistry or biophysics (including microbiology and the
physiology of seed germination). The award is made on the
basis of recommendations of a special commission of the Physics Department of the Royal Netherlands Academy of Arts
and Sciences. In 2010 the prize was awarded to Prof. Franz-
Ulrich Hartl, the Man. Dir of the Max Planck Institute for Biochemistry in Martinsried, Germany.

Geographical Area of Activity: International.

Principal Staff: Chair. Charlene L. de Carvalho-Heineken.

Address: Tweede Weteringplantsoen 5, 1017 ZD Amsterdam.

Telephone: (20) 5510759; **Fax:** (20) 6204941; **Internet:** www
.heinekenprizes.com; **e-mail:** heinekenprizes@bureau.knaw
.nl.

Humanistisch Instituut voor Ontwikkelings Samen-
werking—HIVOS (Humanistic Institute for Co-operation with Developing Countries)

Founded in 1968, a development organization working towards
emancipation, democratization and the alleviation of poverty
in developing countries.

Activities: Financial support is given to more than 700 organizations in Africa, Asia and Central and South America, as
well as to organizations in the Netherlands, with projects in
the areas of economic self-reliance, arts and culture, human
rights and AIDS, environment and sustainable development,
gender, and information and communication technology. Operates the North-South Plan, which issues loans to microfinance
institutions and organic or fair trade importers, the HIVOS
Culture Fund, which stimulates cultural diversity through
financial support to the arts and culture sector in developing
countries, and the ICT policy programme, which helps organizations in developing countries utilize the opportunities provided by information technology. The organization also
provides information on development issues and promotes the
interests of developing countries; and collaborates with
related organizations. Manages the Fund for Sustainable Biodiversity Management, in association with the Stichting
NOVIB (q.v.), launched in 2000. Maintains regional offices in
Costa Rica, India, Indonesia and Zimbabwe.

Geographical Area of Activity: Africa, Asia, Central and
South America, South and South-East Europe, the Middle
East, and the Netherlands.

Restrictions: Grants only made in specific countries.

Publications: Annual Review; *Hivos International* (newsletter).

Finance: Funded by the Government of the Netherlands and
by institutional funds. Total fixed assets €5,512,000, annual
income €75.2m., expenditure €73,700,000 (2010).

Supervisory Board: F. Ch. Giskes (Chair.); H. F. Hoekzema
(Vice-Chair.); M. H. A. Kortekaas (Sec.).

Principal Staff: Exec. Dir Manuela Monteiro; Dir of
Programmes and Projects Ben Witjes.

Address: Raamweg 16, 2596 HL The Hague; POB 85565, 2508
CG The Hague.

Telephone: (70) 3765500; **Fax:** (70) 3624600; **Internet:** www
.hivos.nl; **e-mail:** info@hivos.nl.

IKEA Foundation

Established in 1982, originally to work in the areas of architecture and interior design; since 2009 the Foundation works to
improve opportunities for children and young people in less-
developed countries.

Activities: Operates to support children in four main project
areas: a place to call home; a healthy start in life; a quality education; and a sustainable family income. As part of the Foundation's partnership with the Office of the UN High
Commissioner for Refugees (UNHCR), it was announced in
2011 that the Foundation was to give US $62,000,000 over
three years to the UNHCR, for the assistance of refugees
from Somalia in Kenya.

Geographical Area of Activity: International, with a focus
on the Caribbean (Haiti), South and South-East Asia (particularly India) and Africa.

Finance: Donations of €5,000,000 (2010).

Principal Staff: CEO Per Heggenes; Programme Mans Petra
Hans, Arnold Roozenbeek.

Address: Crown Business Centre, Schipholweg 103, 2316 XC
Leiden.

Internet: http://ikeafoundation.org; **e-mail:** info@
ikeafoundation.org.

Institute of Social Studies—ISS (International Institute of Social Studies (ISS))

Founded in 1952 and part of Erasmus University Rotterdam since 2009.

Activities: ISS is an international university institute focusing on research and education in the area of development studies and international co-operation. It brings together students and teachers from the Global South and the North in a European environment. ISS is located in The Hague.

Geographical Area of Activity: All continents, focusing on developing countries and countries in transition.

Publications: *Development and Change* (quarterly); *Development Issues* (magazine, 2 a year); *ISS at a glance; Prospectus*; research reports; books; newsletters.

Finance: Total income €24,500,000 (2010).

Institute Board: Prof. Dr Leo de Haan (Rector); Renée de Louw; Prof. Mohamed Salih; Dr Jos Mooij.

Principal Staff: Exec. Sec. Linda Johnson.

Address: POB 29776, 2502 LT The Hague.

Telephone: (70) 4260460; **Fax:** (70) 4260799; **Internet:** www.iss.nl; **e-mail:** information@iss.nl.

Internationaal Instituut voor Sociale Geschiedenis—IISG (International Institute of Social History—IISH)

Founded in 1935 by Dr N. W. Posthumus and the Central Workers' Insurance Company to preserve and make available for study material of importance for social history, especially in the field of socialism and the international labour movement.

Activities: Operates internationally in the field of social history, through the maintenance of a library and archives, and the publication of monographs, reviews and source material. Acquisitions include the archives of many socialist organizations and trade unions, and original documents, books, letters, pamphlets, posters, photographs, etc., relating to political events and leading Marxist, anarchist and socialist figures of the 19th and 20th centuries.

Geographical Area of Activity: International.

Publications: Annual Report; *International Review of Social History* (3 a year); *Sources for a History of the German and Austrian Working-class Movements* (series); *Studies in Social History* (series); *Contributions to the History of Labour and Society* (series); *Archives Michael Bakounine* (series); *Household Strategies for Survival, 1600–2000: Fission, Faction and Co-operation*; books; journals and various other publications.

Finance: The Institute is subsidized by an annual grant from the Netherlands Ministry of Education and Science, and by contributions from various institutions and organizations. Total income €9,381,122, total expenditure €9,381,122 (2010).

Governing Board: Hans van de Kar (Chair.).

Principal Staff: Gen. Dir Eric-Jan Zürcher; Dir of Research Marcel van der Linden; Exec. Sec. Monique Kruithof.

Address: POB 2169, 1000 CD Amsterdam; Cruquiusweg 31, 1019 AT Amsterdam.

Telephone: (20) 6685866; **Fax:** (20) 6654181; **Internet:** www.iisg.nl; **e-mail:** info@iisg.nl.

International Penal and Penitentiary Foundation—IPPF (Fondation Internationale Pénale et Pénitentiaire—FIPP)

Founded in 1951 as successor to the Commission Internationale Pénale et Pénitentiaire.

Activities: Promotes studies in the field of crime prevention and treatment of offenders, especially by scientific research, publications and teaching. The IPPF has consultative status with the UN Commission on Crime Prevention and Criminal Justice, the UN Economic and Social Council (ECOSOC) and the Council of Europe.

Geographical Area of Activity: International.

Publications: Report of operations; reports of sessions and meetings (in French and English).

Executive Committee: Georges Kellens (Pres.); Pierre-Henri Bolle (Treas.); Prof. Dr Piet Hein van Kempen (Sec.-Gen.).

Address: c/o Prof. Dr Piet Hein van Kempen, Radboud University of Nijmegen, BP 9049, 6500 KK Nijmegen.

Telephone: (24) 3615538; **Fax:** (24) 3616145; **Internet:** http://fondationinternationalepenaleetpenitentiaire.org; **e-mail:** info@internationalpenalandpenitentiaryfoundation.org.

Koninklijke Hollandsche Maatschappij der Wetenschappen (Royal Holland Society of Sciences and Humanities)

Founded in 1752 by seven leading citizens of Haarlem for the promotion of science.

Activities: Operates nationally in the field of science through grants to institutions and individuals, conferences and courses, publications and lectures. Awards annual prizes and subsidies for research and publication of scientific work. The Society has 350 directors and more than 350 members.

Geographical Area of Activity: Netherlands.

Publications: *Oeuvres complètes the Christiaan Huygens; Martinus of Marum, life and Work; Geleerden and Leken; The Future or the Sciences and Humanities; Mappae Mundi; Haarlemse Voordrachten; De challenge the Vergrijzing.*

Finance: The Society manages three funds: the Pieter Langer Houses Lambert Son Fund, the Fund Van der Knaap and Jan Brouwer Fund.

Board: Dr Alexander H. G. Rinnooy Kan (Chair.); M. E. Bierman-Beukema toe Waters (Vice-Chair.); R. E. Rogaar (Treas.).

Principal Staff: Secs Dr G. van Dijk, A. Soeteman, Dr S. van Manen.

Address: Spaarne 17, 2011 CD Haarlem; POB 9698, 2003 LR Haarlem.

Telephone: (23) 5321773; **Fax:** (23) 5362713; **Internet:** www.hollmij.nl; **e-mail:** secretaris@khmw.nl.

KWF Kankerbestrijding (Dutch Cancer Society)

Founded in 1949 by Queen Wilhelmina to fight cancer.

Activities: Operates nationally in the field of cancer control, through subsidizing programmes at major specialized cancer hospitals, and providing grants for projects on fundamental, epidemiological, clinical and psychosocial cancer research, research on methods for cancer prevention, fellowships, scholarships, conferences, courses and publications. Promotes international scientific co-operation. The Foundation also runs a cancer information centre, a free telephone helpline, publishes information brochures for patients and the general public, and subsidizes national support groups for cancer patients. The Foundation is a member of the International Union Against Cancer.

Geographical Area of Activity: Netherlands, its dependencies and former colonies.

Restrictions: There are limited funds for financial support of individual cancer patients.

Publications: Annual Report and financial statement; *Current Cancer Research in the Netherlands* (annually); *KWF Journal* (11 a year); *Kracht* (quarterly); progress reports and brochures.

Finance: Funding is provided by individual and corporate donations, legacies and various lotteries. Annual income €109,400,000, expenditure €125,400,000 (2010).

Foundation Board: Harm Bruins Slot (Chair.); Prof. Jaap Verweij (Vice-Chair.); Philippe Creijghton (Sec.); Dr Paul Dirken (Treas.).

Principal Staff: Gen. Man. Dr Michel T. Rudolphie; Head of Research Programme Dr Gijs Boerrigter.

Address: Delflandlaan 17, 1062 EA Amsterdam; POB 75508, 1070 AM Amsterdam.

Telephone: (20) 5700500; **Fax:** (20) 6750302; **Internet:** www.kwfkankerbestrijding.nl; **e-mail:** info@kwfkankerbestrijding.nl.

Bernard van Leer Foundation

Established in 1949 by industrialist and philanthropist Bernard van Leer (1883–1958) as a charitable foundation with broad humanitarian goals. After van Leer's death in 1958, his son Oscar van Leer reorganized the Foundation. From 1964 the Foundation focused on young children, primary education and youth, and since 1980 has concentrated exclusively on disadvantaged young children. It funded its first international project in Jamaica in 1966.

Activities: Seeks to improve opportunities for children up to the age of eight who are growing up in socially and economically difficult circumstances. Grant-making works primarily through supporting programmes implemented by local partners in selected countries. Partners include public, private and community-based organizations. Aims to build local capacity through partnerships, promote innovation and flexibility, and help to ensure that the work funded is culturally and contextually appropriate. Through its publications and advocacy, the Foundation aims to inform and influence policy and practice.

Geographical Area of Activity: International.

Restrictions: Unsolicited applications are not considered. Grants are the result of extensive consultations with organizations known by the Foundation.

Publications: *Early Childhood Matters* (journal, twice a year); *Early Childhood in Focus*; *Working Papers in Early Childhood Development* (series); *Practice and Reflections* (series); Annual Report; and other publications.

Finance: Funding derived from the bequest of Bernard van Leer, which is managed by a holding foundation, the Van Leer Group Foundation, Netherlands. Total assets €19,457,400, annual expenditure €16,293,442 (2010).

Board of Trustees: Peter Bell (Chair.).

Principal Staff: Exec. Dir Lisa Jordan; Sec. Jane Hartman; Progs Dir Michael Feigelson.

Address: Lange Houtstraat 2, 2511 CW The Hague; POB 82334, 2508 EH The Hague.

Telephone: (70) 3312210; **Fax:** (70) 3502373; **Internet:** www .bernardvanleer.org; **e-mail:** info@bvleerf.nl.

Mama Cash

Founded in 1983 by Marjan Sax, Dorelies Kraakman, Tania Leon, Patti Slegers and Lida van den Broek to work for social transformation and the advancement of women's rights worldwide. Mama Cash is the oldest international women's fund in the world and is one of only two women's funds working globally to support innovative local women's and girls' human rights organizations engaged in promoting and defending women's and girls' human rights.

Activities: Core areas of activity are strategic grant-making and resource mobilization. Mama Cash makes grants and provides accompaniment support to women's and girls' rights groups internationally. Mama Cash aims to promote the human rights of women and girls by funding women-led organizations working in the thematic areas of body (safety from violence, sexual and reproductive rights, challenging harmful traditional practices), money (economic justice, workers' rights, property and inheritance rights) and voice (representation and participation, decision-making and leadership, and being seen and heard). Mama Cash also provides support to local and regional women's funds around the world, which in turn raise money locally, regionally and internationally to support women's rights initiatives in their own communities. Mama Cash mobilizes resources from institutional and individual donors to increase the scale, influence and collective power of women's and girls' rights groups; Mama Cash also works actively to engage more donors in the social justice philanthropy movement.

Geographical Area of Activity: Europe (including the Commonwealth of Independent States), Latin America and the Caribbean, Asia, Africa and the Middle East.

Restrictions: Does not fund: organizations whose mission and primary focus are not the promotion of women or girls' human rights; organizations that are led by men or based in the United States and Canada; organizations whose primary focus is development work, humanitarian assistance, poverty alleviation, or basic charity (e.g. income-generating activities and credit programmes, formal education, literacy programmes and traditional skills training, providing social services or regular medical care); organizations founded by, or structurally or economically dependent on, political parties government agencies, or religious institutions; businesses; individuals; academic research; scholarships; stand-alone travel grants.

Publications: Annual Report; *she has news* (newsletter); *she has e-news* (electronic newsletter).

Finance: Total expenditure €6,073,252 (2010).

Board of Directors: Marjo Meijer and Geetanjali Misra (Co-Chair.); Eveline de Jong (Treas.).

Principal Staff: Exec. Dir Nicky McIntyre; Dir of Programmes Annie Hillar; Dir of Finance and Operations Janet Zeegers.

Address: POB 15686, 1001 ND Amsterdam; Eerste Helmersstraat 17, 1054 CX Amsterdam.

Telephone: (20) 5158700; **Fax:** (20) 5158799; **Internet:** www .mamacash.nl; **e-mail:** info@mamacash.nl.

MDF Training & Consultancy

Founded in 1984 in Ede, the Netherlands, MDF Training & Consultancy is a training and consultancy agency operating world-wide, which aims to enhance management capacities of professionals and organizations in the development sector.

Activities: MDF has more than 25 years' experience in helping collaboration between policies and practice. MDF organizes training courses and workshops and provides consultancy services for individuals and organizations, designed to strengthen the managerial and organizational capacity required to perform effectively and efficiently. The head office is located in the Netherlands; there are branch offices in Sri Lanka, Tanzania, Viet Nam, Belgium, Democratic Republic of the Congo, Ghana, Colombia and Indonesia. There is also a special office to serve the Dutch market.

Geographical Area of Activity: International.

Publications: Monthly digital NewsLetter; Annual programme and brochure; *Break the Ice Energise!; Tango Toolkit for Organizations*.

Finance: Annual revenue €10,800,000 (2010).

Board of Directors: Herman Snelder (Dir); Mike Zuyderduyn (Dir).

Principal Staff: Man. Dir Herman Snelder.

Address: Bosrand 28, 6718 ZN Ede; Postbus 430, 6710 BK Ede.

Telephone: (318) 650060; **Fax:** (318) 614503; **Internet:** www .mdf.nl; **e-mail:** mdf@mdf.nl.

Milieukontakt International

Founded in 1988 as Milieukontakt Oost-Europa, by a group of foundations, including Friends of the Earth International (q.v.) and Stichting Natuur en Milieu, to strengthen the environmental movement in Europe and Asia.

Activities: The Foundation operates by giving training and advice to NGOs in Europe and Asia, particularly at a local level, and by encouraging partnerships between Eastern and Western environmental groups. Encourages projects in the areas of the environment, sustainable agriculture, citizen participation, new technologies and NGO development. Maintains offices in Albania, Macedonia and Moldova.

Geographical Area of Activity: World-wide.

Publications: Annual Report; factsheets; *Manual Green Agenda* (2005); *Almanac Participation; Public participation in Central Asia; Report on the evaluation of Milieukontakt projects; Open Book on Green Agenda in Romania; Handouts Public Participation training; Our Ecological Rights and Their Defense; Access to Justice in Environmental Matters; Building National Co-operation between Environmental NGOs*.

Finance: Annual income €2,092,013, expenditure €2,090,520 (2010).

Governing Board: Peter van de Veer (Chair.); Peter van Drunen (Treas.).

Principal Staff: Dir Jerphaas Donner; Financial Man. Farnosh Forozesh.

Address: Postbus 18185, 1001 ZB Amsterdam; Plantage Middenlaan 2D, 1018 DD Amsterdam.

Telephone: (20) 5318930; **Fax:** (20) 5318940; **Internet:** milieukontakt.net; **e-mail:** info@milieukontakt.nl.

Nederlands instituut voor Zuidelijk Afrika—NiZA (Netherlands Institute for Southern Africa)

Established in 1997 as a result of the merger of the Eduardo Mondlane Foundation, the Anti-Apartheid Movement Netherlands and the Dutch Committee on Southern Africa. It is an independent NGO devoted to human rights, democracy and reconstruction in Southern Africa, and the dissemination of information on the region.

Activities: Operates in the Netherlands, Southern Africa and the European Union member states. Operates within three main programmes—Media and Freedom of Expression; Human Rights and Peace-Building; and Economic Development—which the Institute supports through technical assistance and grants for small projects. Also organizes campaigns, conferences, lectures, including the Mandela Lecture, debates and exchange programmes to stimulate mutual contact between Southern Africa and the Netherlands; and aims to influence Dutch and European policy towards Southern Africa through lobbying. Issues publications and disseminates information. Maintains a library and information and resource centre, which the Institute plans to make available through the Internet.

Geographical Area of Activity: Netherlands, Southern Africa and European Union member states.

Publications: *Zuidelijk Afrika* (quarterly); *MediaNews*; *NiZA Informatie* (quarterly magazine, in Dutch); Annual Report; conference reports and proceedings; *State of Media Report 2006*.

Finance: Total assets €1,558,111, annual income €2,949,315, annual expenditure €3,021,247 (2010).

Board: Lucille Hegger (Chair.); Bastiaan de Gaay Fortman (Vice-Chair.); Niek van der Linden (Sec.); Venda Sykora (Treas.).

Principal Staff: Exec. Dir Ruud van den Hurk.

Address: POB 10707, 1001 ES Amsterdam; Van Diemen St 186, 1013 CP Amsterdam.

Telephone: (20) 5206210; **Fax:** (20) 5206249; **Internet:** www.niza.nl; **e-mail:** niza@niza.nl.

Nederlandsche Maatschappij voor Nijverheid en Handel—NMNH (Netherlands Society for Industry and Trade)

Founded in 1777 by the Hollandsche Maatschappij der Wetenschappen (Netherlands Society of Sciences) for the furtherance of common welfare by promoting industry, commerce, transport and communications, mining, agriculture and fisheries in the Netherlands and its overseas possessions.

Activities: Operates nationally and internationally in the fields of social welfare and studies, economic affairs and the conservation of natural resources, through self-conducted programmes, conferences, publications and lectures. The Society comprises 32 regional departments which, although responsible to the head office in The Haague, operate on an autonomous basis in their own area.

Geographical Area of Activity: Mainly the Netherlands and its overseas dependencies.

Publications: Annual Report; *Maatschappijbelangen* (monthly magazine).

Board: Jan Mengelers (Chair.).

Principal Staff: Dir Geert van der Tang; Sec. Patricia Punter.

Address: Jan van Nassaustraat 75, 2596 BP The Hague.

Telephone: (70) 3141940; **Fax:** (70) 3247515; **Internet:** www.de-maatschappij.nl; **e-mail:** info@de-maatschappij.nl.

Nederlandse organisatie voor internationale samenwerking in het hoger onderwijs (Netherlands Organization for International Co-operation in Higher Education—NUFFIC)

Founded in 1952 by the boards of governors of all Netherlands universities to foster international co-operation in higher education and scientific research in the widest sense of the term, with special attention to those forms of international co-operation directed towards developing countries.

Activities: Operates nationally and internationally in the field of education. NUFFIC's main activity areas are development co-operation, internationalization of higher education, international recognition and certification, and marketing of Dutch higher education.

Geographical Area of Activity: World-wide.

Publications: Annual Report and financial statement; *Living in Holland*; *A practical guide to living in Holland*; *Higher education in the Netherlands: is it for me?*; *Higher Education in the Netherlands: the system, institutions and degrees*; *Huygens scholarship programme*; *Indigenous Knowledge WorldWide*; *Best Practices of Indigenous Knowledge*; *Brain Drain and Brain Gain*; *Conference a Changing Landscape*; *Foreign students and part-time jobs*; *Guide to Nuffic*.

Finance: Funded by the Ministries of Foreign Affairs and of Education, Culture and Science of the Netherlands, and the European Commission. Total grants/funding €151,000,000 (2010).

Board of Trustees: Jan Veldhuis (Chair.); Arie Nieuwenhuijzen (Vice-Chair.).

Principal Staff: Dir-Gen. Sander van den Eijnden.

Address: POB 29777, 2502 LT The Hague; Kortenaerkade 11, 2518 AX The Hague.

Telephone: (70) 4260260; **Fax:** (70) 4260399; **Internet:** www.nuffic.nl.

Oranje Fonds

Founded in 1948 to support social welfare at home and, in exceptional cases, abroad. Formerly known as the Juliana Welzijn Fonds (Juliana Welfare Fund); assumed current name in 2002.

Activities: The Foundation operates in the fields of social services, community work and socio-cultural work, self-help groups, development programmes and experiments. Maintains an operational section that deals with projects abroad. Supports projects that are experimental and are aimed at improving existing ways and means, and show an original approach or represent a new activity; makes grants to self-help groups and organizations.

Geographical Area of Activity: Central and Eastern Europe, Netherlands.

Restrictions: No grants are made to individuals, health, arts, education, environment or for development aid.

Publications: Annual Report; brochure; *Oranje fund reported*; *Appeltjes of oranje* (newsletter); Digital newsletter.

Finance: Annual income €35,906,000, total expenditure €34,502,000 (2010).

Board of Directors: Dr J. G. Wijn (Chair.); R. R. Latenstein van Voorst (Treas.).

Principal Staff: Dir R. C. van der Giessen; Deputy Dir Theo van Oosten.

Address: POB 90, 3500 AB Utrecht; Maliebaan 18, 3581 CP Utrecht.

Telephone: (30) 6564524; **Fax:** (30) 6562204; **Internet:** www.oranjefonds.nl; **e-mail:** info@oranjefonds.nl.

Oxfam NOVIB—Nederlandse Organisatie voor Internationale Ontwikkelingssamenwerking (Oxfam NOVIB—Netherlands Organization for International Development Co-operation)

Founded in 1956 as NOVIB to promote sustainable development by supporting the efforts of poor people in developing countries; since 1994 part of the Oxfam confederation of 14 development agencies (qq.v.).

Activities: The Foundation works to ensure that poor people have access to basic rights, through: support for local development projects initiated by private organizations in developing countries; advocacy through lobbying national governments, the European Union, and international organizations, including the World Bank, World Trade Organization and the UN. Work is done in co-operation with the sister organizations of Oxfam International and with around 3,000 local organizations across the world and in the Netherlands.

Geographical Area of Activity: Africa, Asia, Central and South America, Eastern Europe and the countries of the former USSR.

Publications: *Onze Wereld* (monthly magazine); *Novib Network;* Annual Report; series of novels from developing countries; newsletter.

Finance: Total assets €210,607,000 (2009); annual income €198,307,000, expenditure €189,063,000 (2010).

Board of Supervision: J. J. C. Voorhoeve (Chair.).

Principal Staff: Exec. Dir Farah Karimi; Dir Projects Theo Bouma.

Address: Postbus 30919, 2500 GX The Hague; Mauritskade 9, 2514 HD The Hague.

Telephone: (70) 3421777; **Fax:** (70) 3614461; **Internet:** www .oxfamnovib.nl; **e-mail:** info@oxfamnovib.nl.

Prins Claus Fonds Voor Cultuur en Ontwikkeling (Prince Claus Fund for Culture and Development)

Established to mark the 70th birthday of HRH Prince Claus of the Netherlands on 6 September 1996 to expand insight into cultures and promoting interaction between culture and development.

Activities: Stimulates and supports activities in the field of culture and development by granting awards, funding and producing publications, and financing and promoting networks and innovative cultural activities. Gives support to people and organizations in Africa, Asia, Central and South America and the Caribbean. Supports intercultural networks and the organization of conferences or meetings, primarily in Africa, Asia and Central and South America, as well as funding innovative cultural activities and initiatives of people and organizations that involve creative processes leading to productions in the realm of theatre, music, art, architecture, design and audio-visual media. The Cultural Emergency Response Programme of the Prince Claus Fund provides aid for cultural heritage damaged by man or nature. There is also a Prince Claus Prize awarded every year.

Geographical Area of Activity: Africa, Central and South America, Asia and the Caribbean.

Publications: *The Prince Claus Fund Library*; *The Prince Claus Fund Journal*; *The Prince Claus Awards Book*; Annual Report.

Finance: Total budget €4,500,000 (2010).

Board of Trustees: Prince Johan Friso, Prince Constantijn (Hon. Chairs); Lilian Gonçalves-Ho Kang You (Chair.); Judith Belinfante (Vice-Chair.); Marcel Smits (Treas.).

Principal Staff: Dir Christa Meindersma.

Address: Herengracht 603, 1017 CE Amsterdam.

Telephone: (20) 3449160; **Fax:** (20) 3449166; **Internet:** www .princeclausfund.org; **e-mail:** info@princeclausfund.nl.

Rabobank Foundation

Established in 1973 by the Dutch Rabobank Group to help improve the position of socio-economic underprivileged people in society.

Activities: Operates nationally in the Netherlands and internationally in 25 countries in Africa, Central and South America, and South-East Asia, offering financial support and advice in two fields: Microfinance (and micro insurance); and developing sustainable supply chains in coffee, cocoa, fruit, cotton, nuts and sugar. Works in partnership with local, national and international NGOs.

Geographical Area of Activity: Africa, Central and South America, and South-East Asia.

Publications: numerous publications (see website for list).

Finance: Rabobank Nederland and its branches donate a percentage of their profit annually to the Foundation.

Principal Staff: Dir Pierre Van Hedel.

Address: POB 17100, 3500 HG Utrecht.

Telephone: (30) 2163346; **Fax:** (30) 2161937; **Internet:** www .rabobank.com/content/csr/rabobank_foundation; **e-mail:** rabobankfoundation@rn.rabobank.nl.

Rutgers WPF

Founded in 1987, as the World Population Foundation (WPF), the Foundation aims to encourage sexual and reproductive health and rights throughout the world. The Foundation strongly believes that the ability to break out of the circle of poverty starts with the freedom of choice. The Foundation merged with the Rutgers Nisso Group in 2010 and was renamed Rutgers WPF.

Activities: Operates in less-developed countries of South and South-East Asia, and East and Southern Africa, through supporting local NGOs and governmental organizations in setting up and managing sexual and reproductive health projects. Rutgers WPF provides information and training services and has developed an interactive CD-rom to educate the youth from the age of 10 years old. Rutgers WPF also disseminates information and campaigns at national and international level and provides support to the youth organizations CHOICE and YouAct. Maintains three field offices in Asia.

Geographical Area of Activity: Europe (especially the Netherlands), South and South-East Asia, and East and Southern Africa.

Publications: Annual Report.

Finance: Total assets €6,677,063; annual income €12,697,926, expenditure €12,497,578 (2010).

Supervisory Board: Bert Koenders (Chair.).

Principal Staff: Man. Dir Dianda Veldman.

Address: Oudenoord 176–178, 3513 EV, Utrecht.

Telephone: (30) 2313431; **Internet:** www.rutgerswpf.org; **e-mail:** office@rutgerswpf.org.

Safe Internet Foundation—SIF

Founded in 1999 to promote a secure and responsible Internet.

Activities: Acts as a forum for Internet service organizations to encourage and promote systems and software to create a safe Internet for everyone. Organizes conferences and activities.

Geographical Area of Activity: Netherlands.

Publications: Newsletter.

Directors: C. A. G. D'Agnolo (Pres.); F. D. van den Dool (Sec.); D. G. Blom (Treas.).

Principal Staff: Dir Peter van der Wel.

Address: Zeestr. 80–82, 2518 AD The Hague.

Telephone: (70) 3307591; **Fax:** (70) 3650598; **Internet:** www .sif.nl; **e-mail:** info@sif.nl.

ScriptumLibre Foundation

The international branch of Stichting Vrijschrift.org in the Netherlands, established to raise awareness of freedom of information issues, promoting the sharing of software information.

Activities: The Foundation encourages and protects the freedom of digital creations.

Geographical Area of Activity: World-wide.

Board of Directors: Wiebe Van Der Worp (Chair.); Jeroen Dekkers (Treas.); Jeroen Hellingman (Sec.).

Address: Trekwei 7, 8711 GR Workum.

Telephone: (515) 543434; **Internet:** scriptumlibre.org; **e-mail:** office@scriptumlibre.org.

SIW Internationale Vrijwilligersprojecten (SIW International Volunteer Projects)

Established in 1953, a youth exchange organization aiming to promote international contact, personal growth and voluntary service.

Activities: The Foundation operates world-wide, in the fields of the arts and humanities, conservation and the environment, and social welfare, through voluntary work. About 250 young Dutch volunteers work abroad annually, with projects operating in more than 50 countries. A number of projects operate in the Netherlands for around 200 overseas participants.

Geographical Area of Activity: World-wide.

Restrictions: No direct applications from outside the Netherlands are accepted.

Finance: Financed through subsidies and an application fee.

Board: Frank Wagemans (Chair.); Jacqy Cleijne (Sec.); Maarten Bruna (Treas.).

Address: Willemstraat 7, 3511 RJ Utrecht.

Telephone: (30) 2317721; **Fax:** (30) 2343465; **Internet:** www .siw.nl; **e-mail:** info@siw.nl.

SOTA—Research Centre for Turkestan and Azerbaijan

Established in 1991 by Mehmet Tutuncu as a centre of research and study into the Turkic peoples of the former USSR, as the Foundation for the Research of Turkestan, Azerbaijan, Crimea, Caucasus and Siberia. Changed to the Research Centre for Turkestan and Azerbaijan in 2009.

Activities: Carries out research and analysis relating to Turkey and the Central Asian countries of the former USSR, also organizes conferences and symposia. Promotes human rights and peace through democratic governance. Also aims to inform public opinion in Western Europe and the USA. Maintains an archive and library containing more than 4,000 books and periodicals, and more than 10,000 pamphlets and newspaper articles.

Geographical Area of Activity: Turkey and the republics of Central Asia.

Publications: *BITIG* (quarterly journal); *Reform Movements and Revolution in Turkistan* (1900–1924); *Sefika Gaspirali and Turkic Women's Movement in Russia* (1893–1920); *Caucasus: War and Peace*; *Turkey and Ataturk's Legacy*; *Geopolitical Importance of Central Asia*; *Pax Ottomana*; and other publications.

Principal Staff: Chair. Mehmet Tutuncu.

Address: Postbus 9642, 2003 LP Haarlem.

Telephone: (23) 5292883; **Fax:** (23) 5292883; **Internet:** www .turkiye.net/sota/sotainfo.html; **e-mail:** sota@turkiye.net.

Stichting Agromisa (Agromisa Foundation)

Founded in 1934 to improve the lives of people in developing countries through providing information on small-scale sustainable agriculture. The Foundation also aims to raise awareness of development problems among the Dutch people.

Activities: Gives advice in the fields of nutrition, food processing, biogas, plant and animal husbandry, water and soil management, agricultural engineering, etc.; provides an Internet database on natural resource management; and maintains a library of books pertaining to small-scale agriculture.

Geographical Area of Activity: Africa, Asia, and Central and South America.

Restrictions: This is not a grant-making organization.

Publications: *Agrodok Series*; *AgroSpecials Series*; *Agro-Source: Educational Materials for agriculture & animal husbandry in warm climate zones*; Annual Report.

Finance: Total assets €225,187 (2009).

Board: R. Keijzer (Chair.); Ruud Ludemann (Treas.).

Principal Staff: Office Mans Connie Campbell, Lineke van Dongen.

Address: Postbus 41, 6700 AA Wageningen; Duivendaal 8, Bldg 401, 6701 AR Wageningen.

Telephone: (31) 7412217; **Fax:** (31) 7419178; **Internet:** www .agromisa.org; **e-mail:** agromisa@agromisa.org.

Stichting DOEN (DOEN Foundation)

Established in 1991 by the Dutch Postcode Lottery to pursue the same objectives as the lottery (people and nature) and to complement the lottery's work. To promote its entrepreneurial aims, DOEN not only grants subsidies, but also issues participations, loans and guarantees. Since 1998 DOEN Foundation has received an annual contribution from the FriendsLottery. With this it finances initiatives focusing on welfare issues. In September 2004 DOEN Foundation also became a beneficiary of the BankGiro Lottery; with this lottery funding DOEN finances cultural initiatives. In 2006 the National Postcode Lottery decided to add Social Cohesion to Development Cooperation and Human Rights, and Nature and the Environment in the distribution of its funds.

Activities: DOEN promotes sustainable, cultural and socially-minded pioneers. Pioneers are defined as people who: take risks; have a creative or innovative approach; can transform pioneering concepts into concrete projects; can serve as an inspiring example to others; run sustainable and social business operations; put social and/or ecological objectives first and foremost, and/or create resourceful connections between sustainable, social and cultural interests. From 2010 DOEN Foundation is active in three principal areas: climate change, the new economy, and culture and cohesion.

Geographical Area of Activity: International.

Restrictions: Grants made only to organizations.

Publications: Annual Report.

Finance: Receives funding from Dutch Postcode Lottery, FriendsLottery and the BankGiro Lottery. Annual income €46,106,854, annual expenditure €29,458,360 (2010).

Supervisory Board: Kick van der Pol (Chair.).

Principal Staff: CEO Nina Tellegen; CFO Jasper Snoek; Office Man. Yvette Konjanan de Jesus.

Address: Postbus 75621, 1070 AP Amsterdam; Van Eeghenstraat 70, 1071 GK Amsterdam.

Telephone: (20) 5737333; **Fax:** (20) 5737370; **Internet:** www .doen.nl; **e-mail:** doen@doen.nl.

Stichting Fonds 1818 (1818 Fund Foundation)

Founded in 1990 as the VSB Fonds Den Haag by the VSB Bank to provide financial support to social, cultural and educational projects; name changed to Stichting Fonds 1818 in 2001.

Activities: The Foundation supports projects in The Hague, Netherlands and surrounding areas in the fields of the arts and culture, economic affairs, conservation and the environment, medicine and health, sport and recreation, animal welfare and social welfare.

Geographical Area of Activity: Principally The Hague, Netherlands.

Restrictions: No grants to individuals and only donates money to projects that focus on the region in which the fund is established.

Publications: Annual Report; information brochure; *Fonds 1818* (quarterly magazine).

Finance: Total assets €394,578,880; annual income €33,653,392, annual expenditure €13,085,627 (2010).

Trustees: Dr G. Lycklama à Nijeholt (Chair.).

Principal Staff: Dir Boudewijn de Blij.

Address: Riviervismarkt 4, Postbus 895, 2513 AM The Hague.

Telephone: (70) 3641141; **Fax:** (70) 3641891; **Internet:** www .fonds1818.nl; **e-mail:** info@fonds1818.nl.

Stichting voor Fundamenteel Onderzoek der Materie—FOM (Foundation for Fundamental Research on Matter)

Founded in 1946 by Dr H. Bruining, Prof. Dr H. J. Clay, Prof. Dr H. A. Kramers, Prof. Dr J. M. W. Milatz, Dr H. J. Reinink and Prof. G. van der Leeuw, for the advancement of fundamental scientific research on matter in the Netherlands for the general interest, higher education and industry.

Activities: Operates internationally in the field of physics through research, publications and lectures. The Foundation assists in the co-ordination of existing research projects and carries out its own work through research working groups (of which there are currently 182, spanning 11 Dutch universities). Research interests include: subatomic physics, atomic physics, optical physics, molecular physics, condensed matter physics, nanophysics, physical biology, thermonuclear research and plasma physics, applied and phenomenological physics. In addition, research is carried out in four institutes, which are financed completely or partly by FOM: the FOM Institute for Atomic and Molecular Physics; the FOM Institute for Plasma Physics; the Nuclear Accelerator Institute KVI; and the FOM Institute for Subatomic Physics.

Geographical Area of Activity: Europe.

Restrictions: Grants only to researchers with a working address in the Netherlands.

Publications: *FOM-jaarboek* (annual).

Finance: Funded by Government, European Union, and industry and university contracts. Total assets €99,694,000; annual income €91,174,000, annual expenditure €103,581,000 (2010).

Board: Prof. N. J. Lopes Cardozo (Chair.); Prof. D. Lohse (Vice-Chair.).

Principal Staff: Dir Dr Wim van Saarloos; Sec. Petra M. W. van Luling.

Address: POB 3021, 3502 GA Utrecht; Van Vollenhoven Ave 659, 3527 JP Utrecht.

Telephone: (30) 6001211; **Fax:** (30) 6014406; **Internet:** www .fom.nl; **e-mail:** info@fom.nl.

Stichting Gaudeamus (Gaudeamus Foundation)

Founded in 1945 by Walter Alfred Friedrich Maas for the purpose of assisting young composers, promoting contemporary music in general and stimulating young musicians in performing contemporary music.

Activities: Operates internationally in the field of contemporary music, through the sponsoring of annual competitions, such as the Gaudeamus Composers and Interpreters Competition. In 2008 the Foundation helped to establish the Muziek Centrum Nederland. Organizes annual Gaudeamus Music Week.

Geographical Area of Activity: International.

Publications: *Dijkdoorbraak, de promotie van Nederlandse muziek in het buitenland* (Peter van Amstel); *Eeuwige jeugd, Een halve eeuw Stichting Gaudeamus* (Peter Peters); composer essays.

Board of Directors: G. C. van der Does (Chair.); C. A. A. Cook (Treas.).

Principal Staff: Exec. Dir Leo Pot; Exec. Sec. Marloes Reus.

Address: c/o Muziek Centrum Nederland, Contemporary Music Dept. Rokin 111, 1012 KN Amsterdam.

Telephone: (20) 3446060; **Internet:** www.mcn.nl; **e-mail:** hedendaags@mcn.nl.

Stichting Max Havelaar (Max Havelaar Foundation)

Established in 1988 for fair and direct trade with small producers from developing countries.

Activities: Operates in developing countries in the areas of conservation and the environment, and international affairs. Promotes fair trade, co-operating with small-scale producers in developing countries, Dutch importers and consumers, and maintains a register of producers and checks on importers to insure fair trade principles are adhered to.

Geographical Area of Activity: Africa, Asia, and Central and South America; Netherlands.

Publications: *Handel onder Voorwaarden*; *Sinds maart* (yearly).

Finance: Total assets €2,194,275; annual income €3,681,539, annual expenditure €3,053,211 (2010).

Principal Staff: Man. Dir Peter d'Angremond; Sec. Jonne van Eck.

Address: Lucasbolwerk 7, 3512 EG Utrecht.

Telephone: (30) 2337070; **Fax:** (30) 2332992; **Internet:** www .maxhavelaar.nl; **e-mail:** info@maxhavelaar.nl.

Stichting Alfred Heineken Fondsen (Alfred Heineken Fondsen Foundation)

Established to award prizes in various fields.

Activities: The Foundation awards the Dr A. H. Heineken Prizes (known as the Amsterdam Prizes until 1994), which were first awarded in 1988. Prizes are given in the areas of art, history, medicine, environmental sciences and cognitive science. The prize for art is open to artists living and working in the Netherlands; prizes for medicine, history, environmental sciences and cognitive science are open to candidates internationally. The awards are made on the basis of recommendations of a special commission of the Royal Netherlands Academy for Arts and Sciences.

Geographical Area of Activity: International.

Restrictions: The prize for art is open only to artists living and working in the Netherlands; prizes in the fields of medicine, history, environmental science and cognitive science are open internationally.

Principal Staff: Chair. Charlene L. de Carvalho-Heineken.

Address: Tweede Weteringplantsoen 5, 1017 Amsterdam.

Telephone: (20) 6263349; **Fax:** (20) 6252213; **Internet:** www .heinekenprizes.com; **e-mail:** heinekenprizes@bureau.knaw .nl.

Stichting Liliane Fonds (Liliane Foundation)

Founded in March 1980 by Liliane Brekelmans to provide aid for disabled children and youth (up to the age of 25 years) in developing countries.

Activities: The Foundation operates in Africa, Asia and Central and South America; it offers grants to individuals in the field of medical and social rehabilitation. Maintains office in Brussels, Belgium.

Geographical Area of Activity: Africa, Asia, and Central and South America.

Publications: Newsletter (quarterly); *International* (newsletter); Newsflash; Annual Report; *Meedoen* (practical guidebook); various brochures.

Finance: The Foundation is funded by donations. Total assets €12,942,294; annual income €22,243,280, annual expenditure €16,305,683 (2010).

Board of Trustees: J.H. (Jack) van Ham (Chair.).

Principal Staff: Dir Kees van den Broek.

Address: Havensingel 26, 5211 TX 's-Hertogenbosch.

Telephone: (73) 5189420; **Fax:** (73) 5189421; **Internet:** www .lilianefonds.nl; **e-mail:** voorlichting@lilianefonds.nl.

Stichting Mondiaal Alternatief (Foundation for Ecodevelopment)

Founded in 1972 by Ernst Bartels and Fanny Rosenzweig to increase awareness of the dangers of pollution and deforestation, especially in developing countries.

Activities: Operates primarily in the fields of aid to less-developed countries and environmental conservation. The Foundation emphasizes the dependence of humans on the ecosystem; encourages respect for all life; lobbies governments on environmental issues; promotes ecologically sound pest-control techniques, pesticide production and export; works to slow the rate of deforestation and encourages small communities to use alternative fuel sources; compiles statistics; maintains a reference library; and conducts international research programmes and conferences.

Geographical Area of Activity: International.

Publications: *Ecoscripts* (in English); brochures; research reports.

Principal Staff: R. Gerrits.

Address: Postbus 151, 2130 AD Hoofddorp.

Telephone: (23) 5632305; **Fax:** (23) 5641359; **Internet:** www.mondiaalalternatief.nl; **e-mail:** mondiaal@freemail.nl.

Stichting Praemium Erasmianum (Praemium Erasmianum Foundation)

Founded in 1958 by HRH Prince Bernhard of the Netherlands to award one or more monetary prizes, if possible annually, to individuals or institutions that have made a particularly important contribution to Europe in the cultural, social or socio-scientific sphere.

Activities: Operates internationally in the fields of education, social welfare and studies, the arts and humanities, law and other professions, through the awarding of the 'Erasmus Prize'. The prize amounts to €150,000. The Erasmus Prize 2012 was awarded to the US philosopher Daniel C. Dennett.

Geographical Area of Activity: International.

Restrictions: No applications for grants are considered.

Publications: Yearbook (including report of prize-giving ceremony); series of publications in connection with the laureates or theme of the prize.

Finance: Funded by private sources.

Governing Board: HRH the Prince of Orange (Patron); Dr M. Sanders (Chair.); M. Dijkgraaf (Vice-Chair.); T. de Swaan (Treas.).

Principal Staff: Dir Dr M. Sparreboom; Sec. L. J. Aalbers; Asst R. J. Duinker.

Address: Jan van Goyenkade 5, 1075 HN Amsterdam.

Telephone: (20) 6752753; **Fax:** (20) 6752231; **Internet:** www.erasmusprijs.org; **e-mail:** spe@erasmusprijs.org.

Stichting Prins Bernhard Cultuurfonds (Prince Bernhard Cultural Foundation)

Established in London in 1940 to raise money to buy war material for the British and Dutch Governments. After the Second World War it was decided to continue the fund to rebuild cultural life in the Netherlands.

Activities: Operates in the Netherlands, the Netherlands Antilles and Aruba. Emphasis is placed on self-generated activity, private initiative and non-professional work. The Foundation currently supports initiatives in the fields of the visual arts; dance; theatre; literature; music; conservation of historic buildings and monuments; research in the humanities; cultural education; and nature conservation. Promotes Dutch culture abroad, by providing financial support.

Geographical Area of Activity: Netherlands, Netherlands Antilles and Aruba.

Publications: Annual Report; newsletter.

Finance: The Foundation receives a share of the revenue of national lotteries, income from its own collections, and from assets and gifts. Total assets €205,973,545; annual income €45,459,145, annual expenditure €24,712,045 (2010).

Board of Trustees: Dr A. H. G. Rinnooy Kan (Chair.); I. H. J. M. van Waesberghe (Vice-Chair.); J. M. de Jong (Treas.).

Principal Staff: Dir Dr Adriana Esmeijer.

Address: POB 19750, 1000 GT Amsterdam; Herengracht 476, 1017 CB Amsterdam.

Telephone: (20) 5206130; **Fax:** (20) 6238499; **Internet:** www.cultuurfonds.nl; **e-mail:** info@cultuurfonds.nl.

Stichting Reinwater (Clean Water Foundation)

Founded in September 1974 by D. M. J. Lasonder, E. de Bloeme and J. G. W. Bolomey to combat the pollution of European freshwater sources.

Activities: The Foundation operates nationally and internationally in the fields of environmental conservation, education, diffusing information and international affairs, through various self-conducted programmes, research and publications. It is concerned in particular with the water systems of the Rhine, Maas and Schelde rivers. Maintains two research and education ships. In 2009 the Foundation combined some administrative responsibilities with Triple E Water en Samenleving, although it remained an independent foundation.

Geographical Area of Activity: Netherlands.

Publications: Press bulletins; reports; brochures; illustrated magazines; *Meuse* (newsletter); teaching packages; Annual Report.

Finance: Funding is provided by the Government of the Netherlands, the European Union, regional and local governments, and private bequests.

Board: Annemarie Moons (Chair.).

Principal Staff: Dir Jan van Dijk.

Address: c/o Kantoor Arnhem, Oude Kraan 8, 6811 LJ Arnhem.

Telephone: (26) 3701481; **Fax:** (26) 3701482; **Internet:** www.reinwater.nl; **e-mail:** info@reinwater.nl.

Stichting Triodos Foundation (Triodos Foundation)

Established in 1971 to mobilize gifts and loans for promising new social initiatives and enterprises. After the establishment of Triodos Bank in 1980, Triodos Foundation limited its role to granting gifts to institutions.

Activities: Triodos Foundation has three fields of activity: nature and environment, people and society, and international co-operation. Organic farming, renewable energy and solidarity with developing countries are given priority within these fields. The aim is to stimulate both national and international projects that initiate innovation. Branches of Triodos Bank in Belgium, Spain and the United Kingdom each have a similar foundation.

Geographical Area of Activity: World-wide.

Finance: Total assets €8,444,973; annual income €5,700,801, annual expenditure €1,683,016 (2010).

Board of Directors: P. Blom (Chair.); Mrs. G. van Wijk Treas.); C. H. Middendorp (Sec.).

Principal Staff: Man Dir. Ted van den Bergh.

Address: POB 55, 3700 AB Zeist.

Telephone: (30) 6936535; **Internet:** www.triodosfoundation.nl; **e-mail:** triodos.foundation@triodos.nl.

Stichting Vluchteling (Refugee Foundation)

Founded in 1976 (restructured 1982) by various churches and other groups in the Netherlands to provide assistance for refugees outside the Netherlands.

Activities: Provides assistance to refugees through grants to various organizations active overseas, providing both emergency aid and long-term self-reliance projects; it has no fieldworkers of its own, but attempts to co-ordinate assistance and to inform the public of the plight of refugees.

Geographical Area of Activity: International.

Restrictions: No assistance provided to refugees in the Netherlands.

Publications: *Jaarverslag* (annual report).

Finance: Total assets €8,588,615; annual income €13,315,487, annual expenditure €13,203,213 (2010).

Board: Femke Halsema (Chair.); Frank Bluiminck (Vice-Chair.); Guido Visser (Treas.).

Principal Staff: Dir Tineke Ceelen.

Address: Stadhouderslaan 28, 2517 HZ The Hague.

Telephone: (70) 3468946; **Fax:** (70) 3615740; **Internet:** www .vluchteling.org; **e-mail:** info@vluchteling.org.

Technologiestichting—STW (Technology Foundation)

Founded in 1981 by Prof. W. A. Koumans and Dr C. le Pair to promote research in technology. Formerly known as Stichting voor de Technische Wetenschappen.

Activities: Operates nationally in the field of applied science and engineering, through research, travel grants, lectures and publications. The Foundation subsidizes research projects at universities and technological institutes in the Netherlands: projects may be drawn from all technological fields, and are selected on the basis of both high scientific quality and applicability in industry.

Geographical Area of Activity: Netherlands.

Publications: Annual Utilization Report; Annual Report; project reports and others.

Finance: Total assets €263,471,000; annual revenue €89,556,000, expenditure €94,453,000 (2010).

Principal Staff: Dir Dr E. E. W. Bruins; Dep. Dir Chris Mombers.

Address: POB 3021, 3502 GA Utrecht; Van Vollenhoven Ave 661, 3527 JP Utrecht.

Telephone: (30) 2116001; **Fax:** (30) 6014408; **Internet:** www .stw.nl; **e-mail:** info@stw.nl.

Tilapia International Foundation

Founded in 1952 by J. D. F. Heine to encourage the breeding of the tilapia fish to relieve malnutrition in developing countries.

Activities: Organizes training programmes designed to educate people in the breeding of tilapia; provides financial assistance for the establishment of fish farms; disseminates information; active internationally.

Geographical Area of Activity: International.

Publications: Brochures.

Finance: Annual budget approx. €318,000.

Board: B. Heijne (Pres.); M. J. H. P. Pinkers (Sec.-Gen. and Treas.).

Address: Postbus 2375, 3500 GJ Utrecht.

Telephone: (30) 2948700; **Fax:** (30) 2936810; **Internet:** www .tilapiastichting.nl; **e-mail:** tif@tilapiastichting.nl.

XminusY Solidarity Fund

Established in 1968, aims to promote self-determination and social change world-wide.

Activities: Provides financial support to small local groups in Africa, Asia, Central and South America, and Eastern Europe that would otherwise not be able to exist. Funded groups operate in the areas of human rights and social and political justice. The Fund also works in Western Europe as an advocate for these goals, and for international solidarity. The maximum grant awarded is approximately US $3,000.

Geographical Area of Activity: World-wide.

Restrictions: Does not usually finance conferences, research projects, educational trips, travel expenses or general office expenses. No grants for children's projects, health programmes or projects that are income-generating.

Publications: Brochures; video documentary; reports; CD ROM on direct action; newsletter.

Principal Staff: Spokesperson Rutger van den Dool; Sec. Cees Sies; Projects Denise Grobben, Ruby van Leyenhorst.

Address: De Wittenstr. 43–45, 1052 AL Amsterdam.

Telephone: (20) 6279661; **Fax:** (20) 6228229; **Internet:** www .xminy.nl; **e-mail:** info@xminy.nl.

Youth for Development and Co-operation—YDC

Established in Switzerland in 1947 as World Federalist Youth, a network of youth organizations; present name adopted in 1986 when YDC became an independent youth development organization.

Activities: Promotes communication between young people in the West, and those in developing countries. Works to strengthen opportunities for young people to participate in projects in the areas of sustainable development, human rights and the environment. Organizes international workshops, conferences, disseminates information and provides youth training.

Geographical Area of Activity: Europe, Africa, Central and South America, and Asia.

Address: Delflandplein 24, 1062 NL Amsterdam.

Telephone: (20) 6142510; **Fax:** (20) 6175545; **e-mail:** ydc@ xs4all.nl.

Zero-Kap Foundation

Established as a foundation in 1989 by private individuals who set up a fund to advance interest-free loans to groups and organizations of the least-privileged in developing countries to develop income-generating activities and home ownership. Merged with Stichting FEMI in Aug. 2011.

Activities: Operates in the fields of income generation (mainly in the area of primary production and the processing and trading of the resulting produce) and the construction of facilities to encourage income-generating activities and private housing. Loans are between €10,000 and €50,000. They are paid back from five years (income generation) up to nine years (private homes).

Geographical Area of Activity: Asia, Africa, and Central and South America.

Restrictions: No grants to individuals, and only to groups with a legal status, such as co-operatives and village communities.

Publications: Annual Report; newsletter.

Finance: Funded by private individuals or organizations which supply capital funding through donations. Total assets €1,165,473; annual income €101,303, annual expenditure €18,294 (2010).

Board: Ton Cools (Chair.); Erika van Scheijndel-Eelderink (Treas.); Dr Dik Stroband (Sec.).

Address: p/a Hooge Raedt, Torenlaan 15, 3742 CR Baarn.

Telephone: (35) 5488422; **Fax:** (35) 5488412; **Internet:** www .zero-kap.nl; **e-mail:** info@zero-kap.nl.

ZOA

Founded in 1973 to provide assistance to people in need, as a sign of Christian compassion, through emergency relief, rehabilitation and reintegration programmes. ZOA's mission can be summarized in three words: Relief, Hope, Recovery.

Activities: ZOA supports people who suffer as a result of armed conflict or natural disasters, in helping them to rebuild their livelihoods. Currently operates in 14 countries worldwide. Helped approx. 1.9m. people through its programmes in 2010.

Geographical Area of Activity: Africa, Asia, Central America.

Publications: *ZOA Magazine* (7 a year); *ZieZOA* (children's magazine, quarterly); Annual Report (Dutch and English).

Finance: Receives funding from more than 50,000 private donors, governments, the EU and the UN. Total assets €17,416,430; annual income €28,761,380, annual expenditure €26,764,229 (2010); Annual budget €28,000,000 (2011).

Supervisory Board: Dr H. Paul (Chair.).

Principal Staff: CEO Johan Mooij.

Address: POB 4130, 7320 AC Apeldoorn.

Telephone: (55) 3663339; **Fax:** (55) 3668799; **Internet:** www .zoa.nl; www.zoa-international.com; **e-mail:** info@zoa.nl.

New Zealand

FOUNDATION CENTRE AND CO-ORDINATING BODY

Philanthropy New Zealand

Established in 1990 by patron Sir Roy McKenzie.

Activities: Operates projects in the areas of taxation, research and education, through working with other organizations in the voluntary and not-for-profit sector, networking with government departments, including lobbying for tax concessions for New Zealand foundations, supporting research, organizing seminars and conferences and issuing publications. Currently has 98 members.

Geographical Area of Activity: Asia-Pacific region.

Publications: Newsletter; *Philanthropy News.*

Finance: Financed by membership subscriptions.

Board: Kate Frykberg (Chair.); Helena Francis (Deputy Chair.).

Principal Staff: Exec. Dir Robyn Scott.

Address: POB 1521, Wellington; Level 4, Civic Assurance House, 114 Lambton Quay, Wellington.

Telephone: (4) 499-4090; **Fax:** (4) 472-5367; **Internet:** www.philanthropy.org.nz; **e-mail:** info@philanthropy.org.nz.

FOUNDATIONS, TRUSTS AND NON-PROFIT ORGANIZATIONS

Cancer Society of New Zealand, Inc

Founded in 1929 by the British Empire Cancer Campaign Society, for the alleviation, prevention and cure of cancer.

Activities: The Society supports cancer research through grants to institutions and individuals in New Zealand, and through travelling fellowships enabling New Zealand graduates to travel abroad for study; it holds conferences with international participation, and disseminates the results of research. Also provides information and support services (including Living Well Programme and online forum, CancerChatNZ) to people affected by cancer.

Geographical Area of Activity: New Zealand.

Publications: Research Report; *Present State and Future Needs of Cancer Research in New Zealand;* press releases; information sheets.

Finance: Total assets NZ $7,904,000 (31 March 2011); annual income $5,352,000, expenditure $5,266,000 (2010/11).

National Board: Clive Cleland (Pres.).

Principal Staff: Chief Exec. Dalton Kelly.

Address: POB 12700, Wellington 6144; Red Cross House, Level 2, 69 Molesworth St, Wellington 6011.

Telephone: (4) 4947270; **Fax:** (4) 4947271; **Internet:** www.cancernz.org.nz; **e-mail:** admin@cancer.org.nz.

Family Planning

Family Planning began in 1936 to help women choose the size of their families and the spacing of their children.

Activities: Family Planning works to promote a positive view of sexuality and to enable people to make informed choices about their sexual and reproductive health and well-being. Clinical services include contraception, sexually-transmitted infection checks and treatment, advice around menopause, cervical screening, vasectomy, pregnancy testing and advice, etc. Health promotion services include parenting programmes, producing educational resources and workshops on adolescent sexuality. Family Planning also has an advocacy function to ensure sexual and reproductive health are well understood and supported in the community, makes submissions on proposed government legislation and works closely with appropriate government departments.

Geographical Area of Activity: New Zealand, South-East Asia and the Pacific region.

Publications: Annual Report; newsletter (3 a year).

Finance: Annual revenue NZ $12,987,000, expenditure $12,695,000 (2007).

Council: Dr Tammy Steeves (Pres.); Dr Marie Bismark (Deputy Pres.).

Principal Staff: Chief Exec. Jackie Edmond.

Address: POB 11515, Wellington; 203–209 Willis St, Wellington 6142.

Telephone: (4) 384-4349; **Fax:** (4) 382-8356; **Internet:** www.familyplanning.org.nz; **e-mail:** national@familyplanning.org.nz.

Norman Kirk Memorial Trust

Founded in 1976 to promote the welfare and progress of the people of New Zealand and the South Pacific who have the ability to benefit from further education, study or training, but who need financial assistance in realizing their potential.

Activities: Within New Zealand, the Trust accepts direct applications from mature individuals who are either disadvantaged or disabled, and who are committed to taking advantage of education or training opportunities; or from mature applicants who are seeking a qualification or training that will enable them to assume a fuller role in the community, as well as supporting organizations helping people achieve these aims. The Trust also funds a number of scholarships through other trusts focusing on education. Programme funding in the South Pacific region is made following the advice of other NGOs operating in the field; direct applications for these funds are not accepted.

Geographical Area of Activity: New Zealand and the South Pacific.

Restrictions: Does not consider direct applications from individuals or organizations based outside New Zealand. Grants to the South Pacific are allocated in co-operation with a partner agency working in the area.

Publications: Annual Report.

Finance: Funding from individual donations and from governments of New Zealand, Australia and several South Pacific nations. Total assets NZ $364,261; annual income $88,024, expenditure $85,710 (2009).

Trustees: Ian Johnstone (Chair.).

Address: POB 805, Wellington 6140; 46 Waring Taylor St, Wellington 6011.

Fax: (4) 495-9444; **Internet:** www.communitymatters.govt.nz; **e-mail:** community.matters@dia.govt.nz.

J. R. McKenzie Trust

Founded in 1940 by Sir John Robert McKenzie to assist national organizations and local community groups in New Zealand.

Activities: The Trust supports those organizations working with people with special needs, especially children and young people, people 'at risk' or at significant social disadvantage. Focuses on social, health and developmental needs supporting project-related costs, training of paid and unpaid staff, equipment, publications, administration, salaries, volunteer expenses and organizational development. Also supports new and innovative approaches to social problems and organizations seeking to make their services more effective and empowering.

Geographical Area of Activity: New Zealand.

Restrictions: No grants are made to individuals, sports groups, schools and early childhood centres, out-of-school care programmes, rest homes and hospitals, environmental groups or religious and campaigning groups.

Publications: Annual Report.

Finance: Total funds NZ $60,600,000 (31 March 2011); total grants paid out NZ $1.8m., total expenditure NZ $509,000 (2010/11).

Board: Radha Balakrishnan (Chair.).

Principal Staff: Exec. Dir Iain Hines; Administrator Alison Glen.

Address: POB 10-006, Wellington 6143; Level 4, 114–118 Lambton Quay, Wellington.

Telephone: (4) 472-8876; **Fax:** (4) 472-5367; **Internet:** www .jrmckenzie.org.nz; **e-mail:** info@jrmckenzie.org.nz.

National Heart Foundation of New Zealand

Established in 1968, the Foundation is dedicated to the reduction of premature death and suffering from diseases of the heart and circulation.

Activities: The Foundation operates in the area of medicine and health, through research, providing grants for research projects, training fellowships for cardiology trainees to study overseas, senior fellowships and a Chair in Cardiovascular Studies; health promotion, through programmes to promote good health for all and reduce underlying causes of the disease; and medical care to prevent people at high risk from developing heart and blood vessel disease and to improve the care and rehabilitation of people with heart disease. Operates around 20 branches throughout New Zealand.

Geographical Area of Activity: New Zealand.

Publications: Annual Report; newsletter.

Finance: Net assets NZ $31,105,000 (June 2011); income $23,269,000, expenditure $12,391,000 (2010/11).

Board of Directors: Michael Tomlinson (Chair.); Michael Benjamin (Dep. Chair.); Russell Wood (Pres.).

Principal Staff: Chief Exec. Tony Duncan; medical Dir Norman Sharpe.

Address: POB 17160, Greenlane, 9 Kalmia St, Ellerslie, Auckland 1546.

Telephone: (9) 571-9191; **Fax:** (9) 571-9190; **Internet:** www .heartfoundation.org.nz; **e-mail:** info@heartfoundation.org .nz.

New Zealand Winston Churchill Memorial Trust

Founded in 1965 by Act of the New Zealand Parliament to give fellowships to New Zealand residents, for the advancement of any vocation carried out in New Zealand, or to the benefit in general of New Zealand.

Activities: Operates nationally in the fields of education, social welfare, economic affairs, science and medicine, the arts and humanities, and conservation of natural resources, and internationally in the field of international relations, through the award of up to 25 international fellowships each year. New Zealand residents may undertake an activity anywhere. Fellowships amount to as much as 80% of costs for short-term travel and activity followed by publication of a report within six months. Assistance is not renewable or extendable and is only available for travel outside New Zealand. Trust is administered by the Department of Internal Affairs.

Geographical Area of Activity: New Zealand.

Restrictions: Fellowships are not granted for the gaining of academic or professional qualifications and funding is not normally granted for attending academic or professional

conferences. Applications must be for travel between 1 January and 31 December in the year immediately after the year of application.

Publications: Annual Report and financial statement; Fellows' reports; bibliography reports.

Finance: Maximum individual grant disbursed NZ $10,000.

Board of Trustees: Rachael Selby (Chair.); A. Graeme Hall (Deputy Chair.).

Address: POB 805, Wellington 6140; 46 Waring Taylor St, Wellington 6011.

Telephone: (4) 495-9431; **Fax:** (4) 495-9444; **Internet:** www .communitymatters.govt.nz; **e-mail:** community.matters@ dia.govt.nz.

NZIIA—New Zealand Institute of International Affairs

Founded in 1934 to promote an understanding of international questions and problems particularly in so far as these may relate to New Zealand, the Commonwealth, and the countries of South-East Asia and the Pacific.

Activities: Operates internationally in the fields of economic affairs, law and other professions, international relations and aid to less-developed countries, through self-conducted programmes, research, conferences, publications and lectures. Maintains eight branches throughout New Zealand.

Geographical Area of Activity: International.

Publications: *New Zealand International Review* (6 a year); pamphlet series; occasional papers and books.

Standing Committee: Sir Douglas Kidd (Pres.); Prof. Roberto Rabel (Vice-Pres.); Prof. Athol Mann (Hon. Treas.).

Principal Staff: Dir Brian Lynch; Exec. Officer Ngaire Flynn.

Address: c/o Victoria University of Wellington, POB 600, Wellington 6140; Room 507, Level 5, Railway West Wing, Victoria University of Wellington, Pipitea Campus, Wellington.

Telephone: (4) 463-5356; **Fax:** (4) 463-5437; **Internet:** www .vuw.ac.nz/nziia; **e-mail:** nziia@vuw.ac.nz.

Oxfam New Zealand

Established in 1991 as part of the Oxfam confederation of organizations (qq.v.).

Activities: Works in partnership with local communities in the Pacific and South-East Asia, supporting long-term development and campaigning for economic and political change to combat poverty. Maintains offices in Wellington and in Papua New Guinea.

Geographical Area of Activity: Pacific and South-East Asia.

Finance: Annual income NZ $7,884,309, annual expenditure $7,543,673 (2010/11).

Board of Trustees: Peter Conway (Chair.); Nicki Wrighton (Dep. Chair.).

Principal Staff: Exec. Dir Barry Coates.

Address: POB 68357, Newton, Auckland 1145; Level 1, 14 West St.

Telephone: (9) 355-6500; **Fax:** (9) 355-6505; **Internet:** www .oxfam.org.nz/; **e-mail:** oxfam@oxfam.org.nz.

Pacific Development and Conservation Trust

Established in 1989 by the Government of New Zealand with funds from the French Government in recognition of the events surrounding the destruction of the Greenpeace ship the *Rainbow Warrior,* which was blown up and sunk in Auckland Harbour by French secret service agents in 1985.

Activities: Operates in New Zealand and the South Pacific through self-conducted programmes, research and grants; grants are available for groups to use for charitable purposes to promote the enhancement and conservation of the environment, natural and historic resources and cultural heritage, and the peaceful, economic, physical and social development of the South Pacific and of its peoples, providing such development is consistent with sound conservation and resource management policies. Administered by Department of Internal Affairs.

Geographical Area of Activity: New Zealand and the South Pacific.

Restrictions: Projects must be charitable and promote the objectives of the Trust. The purchase of land and buildings will be funded only in exceptional circumstances. Applicants must be New Zealand or South Pacific citizens.

Publications: Annual Report and financial statements.

Finance: Total assets NZ $3,200,000m.; average annual grant disbursements of $250,000.

Advisory Trustees: Peter Kiely (Chair.).

Address: POB 805, Wellington 6140; 46 Waring Taylor St, Wellington 6011.

Telephone: 0800 824 824 (freephone, New Zealand only); **Internet:** www.communitymatters.govt.nz; **e-mail:** community.matters@dia.govt.nz.

Pacific Leprosy Foundation

Founded in 1939 to help people with leprosy; formerly known as the Makogai NZ Lepers' Trust Board.

Activities: Operates in the areas of medicine, health and social welfare, working to eliminate leprosy as a threat to public health, through research and attention to sanitation and health issues, and providing medical and social assistance to those affected by leprosy and their families.

Geographical Area of Activity: Australasia and the Pacific.

Publications: Newsletter; Annual Report.

Board: Richard C. Gray (Chair.); Dr Brian T. McMahon (Deputy Chair.); Andrew Tomlin (Treas.).

Principal Staff: Gen. Man. Jill Tomlinson; Relations Man. Lala Gittoes.

Address: Freepost Authority Number 204, Private Bag 4730, Christchurch Mail Centre, Christchurch 8140.

Telephone: (3) 343-3685; **Fax:** (3) 343-5525; **Internet:** www.leprosy.org.nz; **e-mail:** admin@leprosy.org.nz.

Peace and Disarmament Education Trust—PADET

Established in 1988 by the Government of New Zealand with funds from the French Government in recognition of the events surrounding the destruction of the Greenpeace ship the *Rainbow Warrior,* which was blown up and sunk in Auckland Harbour by French secret service agents in 1985.

Activities: Operates in New Zealand in the fields of education, international affairs, law and human rights, social studies and disarmament and arms control, through self-conducted programmes, research, grants to individuals and institutions, scholarships, conferences and training courses. The Trust aims to promote international peace, arms control and disarmament. It also offers scholarships for higher educational study in two categories: up to NZ $14,000 for a year's work towards a Masters thesis, and up to $21,000 (plus up to $5,000 for tuition fees) each year for up to three years' work towards a PhD doctoral thesis. Grants administered by the Department of Internal Affairs.

Geographical Area of Activity: New Zealand.

Restrictions: Will not fund the purchase of land, buildings, furniture or fittings, general running costs or day-to-day administration expenses; scholarship research topic must be relevant to current New Zealand disarmament and arms control policy.

Publications: Annual Report; theses.

Finance: Established with an initial capital donation of NZ $1,500,000 from the French Government.

Advisory Trustees: Graham Fortune (Deputy Chair.).

Principal Staff: Co-ordinator Dalpat Nana.

Address: Trust and Fellowships Office, Department of Internal Affairs, POB 805, Wellington 6140; 46 Waring Taylor St, Wellington 6011.

Telephone: 0800 824 824 (freephone, New Zealand only); **Fax:** (4) 495-9444; **Internet:** www.communitymatters.govt.nz; **e-mail:** community.matters@dia.govt.nz.

Royal Forest and Bird Protection Society of New Zealand

Established in 1923.

Activities: Operates nationally in the field of nature conservation, protecting natural areas, and plants and animals native to New Zealand. Promotes sustainability in farming and land management; works as an advocate for conservation by lobbying the Government on environmental issues; and supports the protection of Antarctica. Runs the Kiwi Conservation Club for young people. Has more than 50 branches.

Geographical Area of Activity: New Zealand and Antarctica.

Publications: *Forest and Bird Magazine* (quarterly); Annual Report; *Best Fish Guide* (biennial consumer booklet); Kiwi Conservation Club magazine (5 a year); newsletters and e-newsletters; fact sheets.

Executive: Andrew Cutler (Pres.); Mark Hanger (Deputy Pres.); Graham Bellamy (Treas.).

Principal Staff: Gen. Man. Mike Britton.

Address: Level 1, 90 Ghuznee St, POB 631, Wellington 6140.

Telephone: (4) 385-7374; **Fax:** (4) 385-7373; **Internet:** www.forestandbird.org.nz; **e-mail:** office@forestandbird.org.nz.

Sutherland Self Help Trust

Founded in 1941 with funds donated by Arthur F. H. Sutherland; the Trust's purpose is to help people in need through gifts to relevant charities and organizations in New Zealand.

Activities: Provides capital and training/equipment grants to institutions in New Zealand operating in the fields of education, science and technology, medicine and health, and social welfare. Particular focus on the care and advancement of physically disabled and disadvantaged children, community youth work, care of the sick and elderly people, and the alleviation of social problems, including alcohol and drug abuse and sexual abuse.

Geographical Area of Activity: New Zealand.

Restrictions: No grants to individuals, nor for administration costs, vehicles or overseas travel nor for environmental, artistic, cultural or sporting purposes.

Board of Trustees: John B. Sutherland (Chair.).

Principal Staff: Hon. Sec. David H. Gibbons.

Address: POB 193, Wellington 6140; 7 Kenwyn Terrace, Newtown, Wellington 6021.

Telephone: (4) 385-1563; **Fax:** (4) 384-9515; **Internet:** ssht.co.nz; **e-mail:** ssht@ssht.co.nz.

Tindall Foundation

Established in 1994 by Stephen and Margaret Tindall with the aim of helping New Zealanders reach their full potential.

Activities: Active in five funding programme areas: family and social services; enterprise and employment; care of the environment and preservation of biodiversity; strengthening the community sector; and promoting philanthropy. A sizeable proportion of the Foundation's resources is allocated directly by appointed Fund Managers.

Geographical Area of Activity: New Zealand.

Publications: Annual Report.

Finance: Total assets NZ $148,505,494 (31 March 2011); annual expenditure $8,450,230 (2010/11).

Principal Staff: Man. Trevor Gray; Administration and Donations Man. Evelyn Gauntlett.

Address: POB 33 181, Takapuna, North Shore City 0740.

Telephone: (9) 488-0170; **Fax:** (9) 486-2365; **Internet:** www.tindall.org.nz; **e-mail:** admin.ttf@tindall.org.nz.

The Todd Foundation

Established by the Todd family's corporate interests in 1972, for charitable purposes within New Zealand.

Activities: The General Fund awards major grants within a theme. The current theme is youth, and grants are offered for substantial projects supporting children and young people. The Centenary Fund funds two or three large grants each year for significant projects in conservation, environment, the arts, culture, education and health facilities. The Awards for Excellence are for postgraduate research projects within categories of science, technology, engineering, manufacturing, business and commerce. The Awards are administered through the New Zealand Universities' Vice-Chancellors' Committee.

Geographical Area of Activity: New Zealand.

Publications: Annual Report.

Finance: Total funds disbursed NZ $3,762,036 (2010).

Administration Board: John Todd (Chair.).

Principal Staff: Exec. Dir Kate Frykberg; Grants Co-ordinator Wainui Bedford.

Address: POB 3142, Wellington; L14, Todd Building, 95 Customhouse Quay, Wellington.

Telephone: (4) 931-6189; **Fax:** (4) 931-6049; **Internet:** www.toddfoundation.org.nz; **e-mail:** info@toddfoundation.org.nz.

Trade Aid NZ Inc—TANZ

Established in 1973 to encourage sustainable development through fair trade.

Activities: Operates in 30 developing countries in the area of aid to less-developed countries and economic affairs, by promoting self-reliance through fair trade. Trade Aid imports products made by people from poor communities, offering a fair price for goods so as to provide a sustainable income. Also campaigns for a solution to the problem of 'third-world debt'.

Geographical Area of Activity: Africa, Asia and Australasia, and Central and South America.

Publications: *Vital Magazine* (approx. 4 a year); Annual Report; *Pick of the Crop* (coffee-focused newsletter).

Board of Trustees: Lyn Jackson (Chair.).

Principal Staff: Gen. Man. Geoff White.

Address: POB 35 049, Christchurch 8640; 174 Gayhurst Rd, Christchurch.

Telephone: (3) 385-3535; **Fax:** (3) 385-3536; **Internet:** www.tradeaid.org.nz; **e-mail:** customerservice@tradeaid.org.nz.

Volunteer Service Abroad—VSA

Established in 1962, a non-profit development agency that recruits skilled New Zealanders to work overseas.

Activities: Provides volunteers for local partner organizations in developing regions to assist local communities. Volunteers share knowledge and experience in a range of areas, including health, education and training, community development, economic development, enterprise, conservation and agriculture.

Geographical Area of Activity: Africa, Asia and Pacific.

Publications: *VISTA* (magazine, 2 a year); *Talk Talk* (bimonthly e-newsletter); media releases; Annual Review.

Council: Gavin Kerr (Pres.); Farib Sos (Chair.); Don Higgins (Deputy Chair.).

Principal Staff: CEO Deborah Snelson.

Address: Level 3, 32 Waring Taylor St, POB 12246, Wellington 6144.

Telephone: (4) 472-5759; **Fax:** (4) 472-5052; **Internet:** www.vsa.org.nz; **e-mail:** vsa@vsa.org.nz.

Nicaragua

FOUNDATIONS, TRUSTS AND NON-PROFIT ORGANIZATIONS

Financiera FAMA

Founded in 1991 (as Fundación para el Apoyo a la Microempresa) as a non-profit foundation to help small enterprises. FAMA is an affiliate of ACCION Network and the Network Micro Finance Network.

Activities: Supports small businesses (particularly those run by women) through micro-credit and training. Credit sources include the Foundation's own resources, commercial credit and funds from international organizations. Maintains 25 branches throughout Nicaragua.

Geographical Area of Activity: Nicaragua.

Finance: Assets US $26,590,729 (Dec. 2010); Total funds disbursed $9,779,000 (2010).

Board of Directors: Mario José Rosales Pasquier (Pres.); Leana María Lovo de Vidaurre (Vice-Pres.); Roberto Harding Zamora (Sec.).

Principal Staff: Gen. Man. Víctor Tellería Gabuardi; Operations Man. Salvador Zambrano; Chief Financial Officer Álvaro Rocha.

Address: Apdo 3695, 3.5 cuadras al oeste de Montoya, sobre Carretera Sur, Managua.

Telephone: 268-4826; **Fax:** 266-5292; **Internet:** www.financierafama.com.ni; **e-mail:** fama@fama.org.ni.

Fundación Augusto César Sandino—FACS (Augusto César Sandino Foundation)

Founded in 1980 by Fr Ernesto Cardenal, Silvia McEvans, Fr Uriel Molina and Dr Mariano Fiallos O. to support community and grassroots self-help social and economic projects nationally.

Activities: The Foundation operates nationally in the fields of economic affairs, education, international affairs, medicine and health, and conservation and the environment, through self-conducted programmes, research, training courses and publications. Maintains a library and database and provides information services.

Geographical Area of Activity: Nicaragua.

Publications: *Con Vos* (3 a year, in English and Spanish).

Finance: Annual budget approx. C $2,000,000.

Principal Staff: Sec.-Gen. Edwin Zablah.

Address: Apdo 2458, Zona Postal 5, Managua.

Telephone: 277-4773; **Fax:** 267-5670; **Internet:** www.facs.org.ni; **e-mail:** facs@facs.org.ni.

Nigeria

FOUNDATIONS, TRUSTS AND NON-PROFIT ORGANIZATIONS

African Refugees Foundation—AREF

Established in 1993 by Chief Segun Olusola to assist refugees in Africa.

Activities: Offers assistance to refugees and displaced people in Africa, as well as organizing workshops on peace initiatives and conflict mediation, seminars on conflict prevention and management, and working to develop policy for governments. Offers voluntary medical corps services. Sister organizations exist in the United Kingdom and the USA. Has UN accreditation.

Geographical Area of Activity: Africa.

Publications: Multimedia documentaries and periodic publications.

Board of Trustees: Segun Olusola (Pres.).

Principal Staff: Exec. Dir Olujimi Olusola.

Address: Lagos State Old Secretariat Rd, off Oba Akinjobi St, Ikeja, PMB 5051, Lagos.

Telephone: (1) 2622795; **Fax:** (1) 5850962; **e-mail:** jolusola@yahoo.com.

Sir Ahmadu Bello Foundation (Sir Ahmadu Bello Memorial Foundation)

Established in 2009 to promote the legacies of the late Sir Ahmadu Bello, especially with regard to leadership, good governance and accountability.

Activities: Operates in the areas of human rights, conflict resolution, alleviation of poverty, health, education and conservation through research, financial aid, conferences, advocacy and workshops.

Geographical Area of Activity: Nigeria.

Finance: Mainly funded by the Northern Governors' Forum, donations and independently generated through investments.

Board of Trustees: Dr Muazu Babangida Aliyu, OON (Chair.); Gabriel T. Suswam (Deputy Chair.).

Principal Staff: Man. Dir/Chief Exec. Officer Dr Shettima A. Ali.

Address: 13A Belel Close, off Ohinoyi St, Unguwan Rimi, Kaduna.

Telephone: (813) 500-0001-4; **e-mail:** ahmadubellofoundation@gmail.com.

Fate Foundation

Founded by Fola Adeola in 2000 to tackle the high rate of unemployment and poverty in Nigeria; aims to foster wealth creation among Nigerian young people.

Activities: The Foundation aims to promote wealth creation in Nigeria through providing Nigerian young people with the skills, tools, networks and financing needed to create successful businesses that will in turn offer employment to other people. Makes annual awards to successful entrepreneurs.

Geographical Area of Activity: Nigeria.

Publications: *Impact Report* (annually); newsletter.

Board: Fola Adeola (Chair.).

Principal Staff: Exec. Dir Osayi Alile Oruene.

Address: Water House, 1st Floor, Lagos State Water Corpn, Ijora Causeway, PMB 54495, Ikoyi, Lagos 101010.

Telephone: 07098123371 (mobile); **Internet:** www.fatefoundation.com; **e-mail:** info@fatefoundation.com.

Institute of Human Rights and Humanitarian Law

A non-governmental, non-political, community-based human rights and education research network generating and sharing knowledge about law. Established in 1988.

Activities: Operates in the field of human rights and humanitarian law, through education and training, advocacy, lobbying, dissemination of information, creating rural advice offices, research, and workshops, seminars and symposia. Maintains a Human Rights Documentation Centre.

Geographical Area of Activity: Nigeria and Western Africa.

Publications: *Human Rights Defender* (quarterly journal) and other publications.

Int. Advisory Board: Prof. Akin Oyebode (Chair.).

Principal Staff: Exec. Dir Anyakwee S. Nsirimovu.

Address: 2B, Railway Close, behind NITEL Garrison, PMB 2292, Port Harcourt.

Telephone: (84) 231716; **Fax:** (84) 231716; **Internet:** ihrhl-ng.org; **e-mail:** ihrhl@ihrhl.org.

International Institute of Tropical Agriculture—IITA

Founded in 1967 by the Ford and Rockefeller Foundations (qq.v.) to contribute to the improvement of tropical farming techniques.

Activities: The Institute conducts research, at its own stations and in collaboration with institutions in other countries. The Resource and Crop Management Programme aims to develop methods of land use and cropping systems that will enable efficient, economical and sustained production of food crops for the humid and sub-humid tropics, with particular emphasis on the problems of small farmers: co-operating programmes have been established in Cameroon and Ghana. Crop improvement programmes aim to bring about genetic improvements and control pests: the Root and Tuber Improvement Programme covers cassava and yams, and includes co-operation with similar programmes in Cameroon and the Democratic Republic of the Congo; the Cereals Improvement Programme (maize and rice) involves co-operation with the West Africa Rice Development Association (Côte d'Ivoire), the International Rice Research Institute (Philippines), the International Maize and Wheat Improvement Centre in Mexico (q.v.) and African regional organizations; and the Grain Legume Improvement Programme (cowpeas and soybeans) is linked with projects in Brazil, Tanzania and Burkina Faso. The Institute's Genetic Resources Unit collects and stores germplasm for genetic research in collaboration with donors and recipients all over the world, and the Virology Unit studies virus diseases affecting crops. The Training Programme involves about 550 participants a year from African and other countries. Conferences and seminars are organized and the Institute also maintains a library and documentation centre.

Geographical Area of Activity: International.

Publications: Annual Report (in French and English); *IITA Research* (2 a year, in French and English); brochures, conference proceedings, technical papers, training manuals; newsletter (monthly).

Finance: Total income US $51,090,000, expenditure $50,747,000 (2008).

Board of Trustees: Dr Bryan Harvey (Chair.).

Principal Staff: Dir-Gen. Dr Nteranya E. Sanginga.

Address: Oyo Rd, PMB 5320, Ibadan, Oyo State.

Telephone: (2) 2412626; **Fax:** (2) 2412221; **Internet:** www.iita .org; **e-mail:** iita@cgiar.org.

A. G. Leventis Foundation Nigeria

Established in 1988; a subsidiary foundation of the A. G. Leventis Foundation (q.v.) in Greece.

Activities: Active in the fields of education, the environment, health care and culture, although principal support has been given to training young farmers in modern agricultural methods through the establishment of five schools in Ghana and Nigeria. The Foundation has also established an Environmental Resource Centre, in collaboration with the Nigerian Conservation Foundation, as well as developing an agro-forestry conservation programme, and donating equipment to technical colleges for vocational training of young Nigerians.

Geographical Area of Activity: Ghana and Nigeria.

Principal Staff: Exec. Dir Dr Abimbola Shafau Adewumi.

Address: 4th Floor, Iddo House, Ebute-Metta, POB 26, Lagos.

Telephone: (1) 08023003980; **Fax:** (1) 4730968; **Internet:** www.leventisfoundation.org; **e-mail:** leventisfoundation@ gmail.com.

Nigerian Conservation Foundation—NCF

Established in 1980 by Chief S. L. Edu, and registered as a Charitable Trust in 1982. Its purpose is to conserve natural resources through conservation projects, environmental education and awareness, and advocacy.

Activities: Pursues the conservation of nature and its resources with the aim of improving the quality of human life by: preserving the full range of Nigeria's biodiversity, which includes species, ecosystems and genetic diversity; promoting the sustainable use of natural resources for the benefit of the present and future generations; and advocating actions that minimize pollution and wasteful utilization of renewable and non-renewable resources. Runs participatory community-based projects, conducts research, organizes workshops, seminars, conferences and various other training courses. NCF is an affiliate of the WWF—World Wide Fund for Nature (WWF), and a partner of Birdlife International.

Geographical Area of Activity: Nigeria, West Africa.

Publications: Monthly newsletter.

Finance: Funded by donations, membership subscriptions and investment income. Annual income 83,653,000 Naira, expenditure 82,418,000 Naira (2008).

Trustees: Izoma Philip C. Asiodu (Pres.).

Principal Staff: Exec. Dir Prof. Emmanuel Obot; Technical Programmes Dir Alade Adeleke; Dir of Finance and Administration Adeyombo Oyesola; Hon. Treas. Ede Dafinone.

Address: Km 19, Lagos-Epe Expressway, POB 74638, Victoria Island, Lagos.

Telephone: (1) 8160091; **Fax:** (1) 2642497; **Internet:** www .ncfnigeria.org; **e-mail:** info@ncfnigeria.org.

Nigerian Institute of International Affairs—NIIA

Established in 1961 to provide direction for Nigeria in international affairs.

Activities: Provides advice and guidance for foreign policy development. Organizes conferences, workshops and lectures.

Geographical Area of Activity: Nigeria.

Publications: Address: Nigerian Journal of International Affairs; Nigerian Forum; Nigerian Bulletin on Foreign Affairs; niianews (newsletter).

Governing Council: Dr Wahab Dosunmu (Chair.).

Principal Staff: Dir-Gen. Prof. Bola A. Akinterinwa.

Address: 13–15 Kofo Abayomi Rd, Victoria Island, POB 1727, Lagos.

Telephone: (1) 9500983; **Fax:** (1) 2611360; **Internet:** www .niianet.org; **e-mail:** info@niianet.org.

Norway

FOUNDATIONS, TRUSTS AND NON-PROFIT ORGANIZATIONS

Environmental Foundation Bellona

Established in 1986 to raise awareness of environmental issues.

Activities: Operates in the field of the environment, especially in the areas of nuclear energy, fossil fuels and renewable energy. Maintains offices in Russia (Murmansk and St Petersburg), USA and Belgium.

Geographical Area of Activity: World-wide.

Publications: Numerous reports and papers.

Principal Staff: Pres. Frederic Hauge; Man. Nils Bøhmer; Sec. Marianne Pfeffer Gjengedal.

Address: Postboks 2141, Grünerløkka, 0505 Oslo; Maridalsveien 17B, Oslo.

Telephone: 23-23-46-00; **Fax:** 22-38-38-62; **Internet:** www .bellona.org; **e-mail:** info@bellona.no.

Janson Johan Helmich og Marcia Jansons Legat (Janson Johan Helmich and Marcia Jansons Foundation)

Founded in 1949.

Activities: Operates in the field of education. Awards scholarships to Norwegian postgraduate students for advanced study abroad in any field, including doctoral or postgraduate study, and professional development.

Geographical Area of Activity: World-wide.

Finance: 66 grants offered; maximum value of grant 100,000 NOK (2011).

Board: Gudmund Knudsen (Chair.).

Principal Staff: Reidun Haugen.

Address: Blommeseter, Norderhov, 3512 Hönefoss.

Telephone: 32-13-54-65; **Fax:** 32-13-56-26; **Internet:** www .jansonslegat.no; **e-mail:** post@jansonslegat.no.

Institusjonen Fritt Ord (Freedom of Expression Foundation)

Established in 1974 to promote freedom of speech in Norway and internationally.

Activities: Operates in the field of the arts and culture; supports the Norwegian Institute of Journalism and offers the annual Freedom of Expression Prize. Internationally, the Foundation offers the Gerd Bucerius Free Press of Eastern Europe Award (with the ZEIT-Stiftung, q.v.) and the Press Prize for Russia.

Geographical Area of Activity: Norway and international.

Board of Trustees: Georg Fr Rieber-Mohn (Chair.); Prof. Grete Brochmann (Vice-Chair.).

Principal Staff: Dir Erik Rudeng; Project Dir Bente Roalsvig.

Address: Uranienborgveien 2, 0258 Oslo.

Telephone: 23-01-46-46; **Fax:** 23-01-46-47; **Internet:** www .fritt-ord.no; **e-mail:** post@fritt-ord.no.

Anders Jahres Humanitære Stiftelse (Anders Jahre's Foundation for Humanitarian Purposes)

Established in 1966 by Anders Jahre; the Foundation is managed by UNIFOR at the University of Oslo.

Activities: Operates in the area of the arts and humanities to promote Norwegian culture. Awards the Anders Jahre Prize for Culture every year.

Geographical Area of Activity: Norway.

Finance: Disburses approx. £7,000,000 every year.

Board: Svein Aaser (Chair.); Ellen Gjerpe Hansen (Vice-Chair.).

Principal Staff: Dir Anne-Lie Merethe Solberg.

Address: Postboks 440, Sentrum, 3201 Sandefjord.

Telephone: 33-46-02-90; **Fax:** 33-46-48-60; **Internet:** www .ajhs.no; **e-mail:** post@ajhs.no.

Chr. Michelsen Institute—CMI

CMI was founded in 1930.

Activities: The CMI is an independent centre for research on international development and policy. CMI conducts both applied and theoretical research, and has a multidisciplinary profile anchored in 10 thematic research groups: aid, culture and politics of faith, gender politics, global health and development, governance and corruption, natural resources, peace and conflict, poverty dynamics, public finance management, and rights and legal institutions.

Geographical Area of Activity: Sub-Saharan Africa, Southern and Central Asia, the Middle East and Latin America.

Publications: CMI Report; CMI Working Paper; CMI Brief.

Finance: Annual revenue 70,000,000 NOK.

Board: Jan Fridthjof Bernt (Chair.).

Principal Staff: Dir Dr Ottar Mæstad; Dep. Dir Dr Arne Strand; Administration and Finance Dir Vigdis Anita Gåskjenn.

Address: Postboks 6033, Bedriftssenteret, 5892 Bergen; Jekteviksbakken 31, Bergen.

Telephone: 47-93-80-00; **Fax:** 47-93-80-01; **Internet:** www .cmi.no; **e-mail:** cmi@cmi.no.

Minor Foundation for Major Challenges

Established in February 2000 by Peter Opsvik and members of his family.

Activities: The Foundation provides support to information projects that aim to limit human-created climate changes, through influencing public opinion and changing attitudes to these problems. Priority is given to projects that are innovative, experimental and untested, look likely to have the greatest impact, and would be difficult to realize without the Foundation's assistance.

Geographical Area of Activity: Norway.

Finance: Total grant expenditure approx. 1,500,000 NOK per year.

Board: Tore Killingland (Chair.).

Principal Staff: Sec. Tore Braend.

Address: c/o Grette DA, Postboks 1397, Vika, 0114 Oslo.

Internet: www.minor-foundation.no; **e-mail:** tore.braend@ minor-foundation.no.

Fridtjof Nansen Institute—FNI

Founded in May 1958 to conduct applied social science research on international issues in the fields of resource management, the environment and energy.

Activities: The Institute is an independent foundation engaged in research on international environmental, energy and resource-management politics. Within this framework the institute's research is mainly grouped around six focal points: Global Governance and Sustainable Development; Marine Affairs and Law of the Sea; Biodiversity and Biosafety; Polar and Russian Politics; European Energy and Environmental Politics; and Chinese Energy and Environmental Politics. The main discipline is political science, but FNI researchers also hold degrees in law, economics, history, human geography, social anthropology, development studies and biology, and have special language and regional competence on Russia and China. Activities include academic studies, contract research, investigations and evaluations.

Geographical Area of Activity: International.

Restrictions: No grants to other organizations.

Publications: Books; peer-reviewed articles and chapters; FNI reports; *The FNI Newsletter* (2 a year); Annual Report.

Finance: Total assets 22,200,000 NOK; annual revenue 30,700,000 NOK; expenditure 31,000,000 NOK (2010).

Board: Sven Ullring (Chair.); Sissel Rogne (Deputy Chair.).

Principal Staff: Dir Peter Johan Schei; Man. Dir Paul Chaffey; Sec.-Gen. Rasmus Hansson.

Address: POB 326, 1326 Lysaker; Fridtjof Nansens vei 17, 1366 Lysaker.

Telephone: 67-11-19-00; **Fax:** 67-11-19-10; **Internet:** www.fni.no; **e-mail:** post@fni.no.

Norsk Utenrikspolitisk Institutt—NUPI (Norwegian Institute of International Affairs—NUPI)

Founded in 1959 by the Stortinget (Parliament) to increase insight into questions concerning international relations by disseminating information, and to encourage the study of international problems of co-operation and the causes of international conflicts.

Activities: Operates nationally in the field of information and research, and nationally and internationally in the fields of foreign affairs and international relations, through self-conducted programmes, research, conferences, courses, publications and lectures.

Geographical Area of Activity: Norway and the Russian Federation.

Publications: Conference proceedings; *Internasjonal politikk* (quarterly journal); *Forum for Development Studies* (journal, 2 a year); *NUPI-notat* (20–30 a year); *NUPI-rapport* (10–15 a year); *Nordisk Østforum* (quarterly); *Caspian Energy Politics*; and other articles, papers and books.

Board: Elsbeth S. Tronstad (Chair.).

Principal Staff: Dir Jan Egeland.

Address: POB 8159, 0033 Oslo; C.J. Hambros pl. 2D, Oslo.

Telephone: 22-99-40-00; **Fax:** 22-36-21-82; **Internet:** www.nupi.no; **e-mail:** info@nupi.no.

Henie Onstad kunstsenter (Henie Onstad Art Centre)

Founded in 1968 by Sonja Henie and Niels Onstad to support and present international modern art in Norway.

Activities: Arranges exhibitions of modern and contemporary art; maintains a library and an art centre, which houses a collection of modern and contemporary paintings; engages international artists for concerts and performances.

Geographical Area of Activity: Norway.

Publications: Catalogues; Annual Report.

Principal Staff: Dir Tone Hansen; Head of Admin. Anna-Maija Isachsen.

Address: Sonja Henie vei 31, 1311 Høvikodden.

Telephone: 67-80-48-80; **Fax:** 67-54-32-70; **Internet:** www.hok.no; **e-mail:** post@hok.no.

Peace Research Institute Oslo—PRIO

Founded in 1959, an independent research institution known for its effective synergy of basic and policy-relevant research.

Activities: Research at the Institute is multidisciplinary and concentrates both on the driving forces behind violent conflict and on ways in which peace can be built, maintained and spread. Projects carried out at the Institute are organized within three programmes and one centre: the Security Programme; the Ethics, Norms and Identities Programme; the Conflict Resolution and Peacebuilding Programme; and the Centre for the Study of Civil War (CSCW). The latter is a long-term, interdisciplinary initiative that was awarded Centre of Excellence status and core funding (for the period 2002–2011) by the Research Council of Norway. Cutting across the Institute's programmes are research teams with particular expertise in three priority areas: migration, gender and energy. The diversity of disciplines at PRIO creates a thriving research community that attracts both scholars and funding from around the world. In addition to such research, PRIO conducts graduate training and is engaged in the promotion of peace through conflict resolution, dialogue and reconciliation, public information and policymaking activities.

In collaboration with the University of Oslo and the Norwegian University of Science and Technology, PRIO runs the Research School in Peace and Conflict, which offers advanced research training for the next generation of peace and conflict scholars. The collaboration is characterized by multidisciplinary approaches to peace and conflict issues, international profile and outlook, and research excellence.

Geographical Area of Activity: Norway.

Publications: *Journal of Peace Research*; *Security Dialogue*; reports; working papers; policy briefs.

Finance: Total assets 85,107,000 NOK; annual revenue 81,947,000 NOK, expenditure 75,616,000 NOK (2010).

Board of Directors: Bernt Aardal (Chair.); Mette Halskov Hansen (Deputy Chair.).

Principal Staff: Dir Kristian Berg Harpviken; Admin. Dir Lene K. Borg.

Address: POB 9229, Grønland, 0134 Oslo; Hausmanns Gate 7, 0186 Oslo.

Telephone: 22-54-77-00; **Fax:** 22-54-77-01; **Internet:** www.prio.no; **e-mail:** info@prio.no.

The Rafto Foundation

Established in 1986 to commemorate the life of Professor Thorolf Rafto.

Activities: The Foundation's principal activity is the annual award of the Rafto Prize, to encourage and honour individuals and organizations fighting for human rights, freedom and democracy around the world. Previous winners include Aung San Suu Kyi (1990), José Ramos-Horta (1993), Leyla Zana (1994), the Romani People (1997), ECPAT (1998), Gennady Grushevoy (1999), Kim Dae-Jung (2000), Shirin Ebadi (2001), Sidi Mohammed Daddach (2002), Paulos Tesfagiorgis (2003), Rebiya Kadeer (2004), Lidia Yusupova (2005), Thich Quang Do (2006), The National Campaign on Dalit Human Rights (2007), Bulambo Lembelembe Josué (2008), Malahat Nasibova (2009), José Raúl Vera López (2010) and Sexual Minorities Uganda (2011).

Geographical Area of Activity: International.

Restrictions: A candidate should be active in the struggle for the ideals and principles underlying the Human Rights Charter; a candidate's struggle for human rights should represent a non-violent perspective; and a candidate may be a person or an organization, and two or more candidates may share the prize.

Publications: Newsletter.

Board of Directors: Anne Kloster Holst (Chair.); Eva Tamber (Vice-Chair.).

Principal Staff: Exec. Dir Therese Jebsen; Head of Admin. Gunta Venge; Sec. Rea Parashar.

Address: Rafto House, Menneskerettighetenes plass 1, 5007 Bergen.

Telephone: 55-21-09-50; **Fax:** 55-21-09-59; **Internet:** www.rafto.no; **e-mail:** rafto@rafto.no.

Regnskogfondet (Rainforest Foundation Norway)

Established in 1989 as part of the Rainforest Foundation network (qq.v.) to combat rainforest destruction and to support indigenous peoples of the world's rainforests in their effort to protect their forests; aims to strengthen national and international public awareness and action.

Activities: Operates in the area of conservation in rainforest areas of South America, Africa and South-East Asia to combat rainforest destruction.

Geographical Area of Activity: Rainforest areas of South America, Africa and South-East Asia, including Bolivia, Brazil, Democratic Republic of Congo, Ecuador, Indonesia, Malaysia, Papua New Guinea, Paraguay, Peru, Venezuela.

Publications: *News Magazine* (quarterly newsletter).

Finance: Projects funded NOK 100,500,000 (2009).

Principal Staff: Dir Lars Løvold.

Address: Grensen 9B, 0159 Oslo.

Telephone: 23 10 95 00; **Fax:** 23 10 95 01; **Internet:** www.regnskog.no; **e-mail:** rainforest@rainforest.no.

Sparebankstiftelsen DnB NOR (Savings Bank Foundation DnB NOR)

Established in 2002 to contribute to charitable causes in Norway, thereby continuing the traditions pursued by Norwegian savings banks of donating their profits to the local communities in which they have operated. Second-largest shareholder in Norway's largest financial group, DnB.

Activities: Makes grants to not-for-profit organizations in Norway in fields including the arts and culture, environment and heritage.

Geographical Area of Activity: Norway.

Finance: Total assets 8,880,116,155 NOK (2010); annual expenditure 45,137,893 NOK (2010).

Board: Randi Eek Thorsen (Chair.); Elsbeth Tronstad Sande (Deputy Chair.).

Principal Staff: CEO Frode Helgerud; Admin. Man. Lisbet Stenseth.

Address: Postboks 555 Sentrum, Øvre Slottsgt. 3, 0105 Oslo.

Telephone: 90-24-41-00; **Internet:** www.sparebankstiftelsen.no; **e-mail:** post@sparebankstiftelsen.no.

Pakistan

FOUNDATION CENTRE AND CO-ORDINATING BODY

Pakistan Centre for Philanthropy—PCP

Established in December 2001 as a membership organization serving grant-makers in Pakistan.

Activities: Provides a range of support services to foundations, philanthropists and corporate donors in Pakistan, as well as promoting the development of philanthropy. Work includes the Enabling Environment Initiative, aiming to establish dialogue between government and civil society organizations; Creating Linkages, which boosts corporate support for the education sector; and the NPO Certification System, which sets sector-wide standards of good internal governance, transparent financial management and effective programme delivery. Also carries out research into the nature and scope of diaspora and corporate philanthropy.

Geographical Area of Activity: Pakistan.

Publications: Reports and studies on philanthropy in Pakistan; Annual Report.

Board of Directors: Dr Shamsh Kassim-Lakha (Chair.).

Principal Staff: Exec. Dir Tanwir Ali Agha; Sr Man. (Finance and Admin.) Syed Mohammad Ahmad.

Address: 1A, St 14, F-8/3, Islamabad.

Telephone: (51) 2855903; **Fax:** (51) 2287073; **Internet:** www.pcp.org.pk; **e-mail:** mail@pcp.org.pk.

FOUNDATIONS, TRUSTS AND NON-PROFIT ORGANIZATIONS

Foundation Open Society Institute—Pakistan

Established in 2003 as part of the Soros network of foundations.

Activities: Promotes the development of an open, democratic and rights-based society. Operates in the areas of education, media, government transparency and accountability, justice and human rights, and economic policy.

Geographical Area of Activity: Pakistan.

Principal Staff: Country Dir Absar Alam.

Address: N Wing, L3, Serena Office Complex, Plot 17, Islamabad G-5/1 Ramna 5.

Telephone: (51) 2600192; **Internet:** www.soros.org/about/locations/pakistan.

Hamdard Foundation Pakistan

Founded in 1969 to administer and control the charitable and philanthropic works arising from the financial support of Hamdard Laboratories (Waqf) Pakistan; to advance learning and education, health and medical care, and emergency relief; to develop an indigenous or Eastern system of medicine and medical science; and to support general welfare and charitable purposes.

Activities: Supports the Pakistan Association of Eastern Medicine, Hamdard al-Majeed College of Eastern Medicine; established the Madinat al-Hikmah (City of Education, Science and Culture) in Karachi, comprising a library (Bait-al-Hikmah), institutes for education, medicine, science, Islamic studies and comparative religion, etc.; also provides medicine and health-care services in its clinics and through free mobile dispensaries. Initiated the Shura Hamdard (Hamdard Thinkers' Forum) a medico-scientific, educational and cultural service for the exchange of views on matters of national interest by leading intellectuals and business people, and the Naunehal Assembly for children and youth. Grants are made to individuals and institutions for research and education, particularly in the fields of medicine and pharmacy, and for general charitable purposes. Awards fellowships and scholarships, and sponsors publication of books.

Geographical Area of Activity: Pakistan.

Publications: Report of operations and financial statement; *Hamdard-i-Sehat*(monthly); *Hamdard Naunehal* (monthly); *Khaber Nama Hamdard* (monthly); *Hamdard Islamicus* (quarterly); *Hamdard Medicus* (quarterly); and other publications.

Board of Trustees: Sadia Rashid (Pres.); Dr Navaid-ul-Zafar (Vice-Pres.).

Principal Staff: Dir-Gen. Furqan Ahmad Shamsi.

Address: Hamdard Centre, Nazimabad No. 3, Karachi 74600.

Telephone: (21) 6616001; **Fax:** (21) 6620945; **Internet:** www.hamdardfoundation.org; **e-mail:** hfp@hamdardfoundation.org.

Pakistan Institute of International Affairs—PIIA

Founded in 1947 with the aim of promoting interest and research in international affairs in Pakistan.

Activities: Operates internationally through research, publications, seminars, lectures and conferences. The Institute has a specialized library with more than 33,500 books and monographs. It assists the Institute's members and research staff, and helps Pakistani and foreign scholars in the field of international affairs and Pakistani foreign policy.

Geographical Area of Activity: South Asia.

Publications: *Pakistan Horizon* (quarterly).

Finance: Independent organization, funded by publication sales, rental income and membership fees.

Council: Dr Masuma Hasan (Chair.); Syed Mohammad Fazal (Hon. Treas.); Syed Abdul Minam Jafri (Hon. Sec.).

Address: Aiwan-e-Sadar Rd, POB 1447, Karachi 74200.

Telephone: (21) 35682891; **Fax:** (21) 35686069; **Internet:** www.piia.org.pk; **e-mail:** info@piia.org.pk.

Quaid-i-Azam Academy

Founded in 1976 by the Federal Government of Pakistan to undertake research on Quaid-i-Azam Mohammad Ali Jinnah (Founder of the Nation) and on the history of Pakistan.

Activities: Conducts and supports research on political, economic, social, religious and cultural aspects of the history of Pakistan; grants scholarships and professorships; sponsors and participates in lectures, conferences and seminars; awards seven prizes every three years to Pakistani or foreign scholars for work of academic merit on Quaid-i-Azam or on any aspects of modern Indo-Muslim history. The Academy maintains a library and collection of research materials and archives, and publishes the results of research.

Geographical Area of Activity: International.

Publications: Studies, translations and bibliographies.

Board of Governors: Minister for Inter-Provincial Co-ordination (Chair.).

Principal Staff: Acting Dir Dr Shehla Kazmi.

Address: 297 M. A. Jinnah Rd, Karachi 74800.

Telephone: (21) 99215234; **Fax:** (21) 99215236; **Internet:** www.quaidiazamacademy.com; **e-mail:** qaak@quaidiazamacademy.com.

Zuleikhabai Valy Mohammad Gany (Z. V. M. G.) Rangoonwala Trust

Founded in 1967 by M. A. Rangoonwala to improve the life of indigent and deserving persons without any discrimination of caste, creed and colour, through the advancement of education and vocational training, the advancement of health and the prevention and relief of sickness, and through the care and comfort of the needy.

Activities: Operates nationally in the fields of education, social welfare, science and medicine, and the arts and humanities, and internationally in the fields of education, science and medicine, religion and the conservation of natural resources. Operates through self-conducted programmes, grants to institutions both at home and abroad, grants to individuals, fellowships, scholarships, conferences, courses, publications and lectures. Establishes, aids and maintains community centres, educational institutions, hospitals, dispensaries, maternity homes, nursing homes, clinics, sanatoria and medical research centres.

Geographical Area of Activity: International.

Publications: Report of operations and financial statement; Annual Report.

Finance: Funded by the Rangoonwala family.

Board of Trustees: Asif M. A. Rangoonwala (Man. Trustee); Mohammad Afzal Nagaria (Hon. Sec.).

Principal Staff: Dir Saeed A. B. Mirza; Deputy Dir Arshad Jamil Bhatti.

Address: Plot No. 4 and 5, K.D.A. Scheme No. 7, Block-4, Dhoraji Colony, Karachi 74800.

Telephone: (21) 34935168; **Fax:** (21) 34930534; **Internet:** www.rcc.com.pk; **e-mail:** zvmgrcc@super.net.pk.

Palestinian Autonomous Areas

FOUNDATIONS, TRUSTS AND NON-PROFIT ORGANIZATIONS

Center for Human Research and Social Development—CHRSD

Founded in 1994 by Dr Sufian Abu Nijaila, Dr Yousef S. Abu Maila, Dr Ehsan Khalil al-Agha, Dr Mohammad Joma Abd al-Aziz and Dr Adnan M. Abu Nijela as a non-profit-making organization to contribute to the construction of civil society, the development of the Palestinian Society and in support of the peace process.

Activities: The Center's objectives are to publicize awareness of the problems concerning Palestinian society; to carry out research projects dealing with the needs of Palestinian society; to advance the status of Palestinian women; to organize and conduct training courses and programmes in the areas of education, the development of society and welfare of local inhabitants; to set up a library in the humanities and social and economic development; to participate in mutual co-operation and understanding at local, regional and international level; to consolidate and create means of co-operation and co-ordination with scientific and other institutes and research centres nationally and internationally; and to prepare and conduct cultural studies and research projects, in addition to joint research projects that contribute to the construction of peace. The Center also organizes training courses and symposia, provides advisory services and issues publications.

Geographical Area of Activity: Palestinian Autonomous Areas.

Publications: *Characteristics of Palestinians' Personality: A Comparative Psychological Study among Generations of Palestinian Society*; *Democracy and Education*; *Alleged Palestinian Collaborators with Israel and their Families: A study of victims of internal political violence*; *Collected Papers on Personality and Mental Health*; *Principles of Developmental Psychology*; *Coping Strategies with Stressful Life Events and Mental Health*; *Knowledge, Attitude and Practice of Palestinian Women towards Family Planning in the Gaza Strip*; *Level and Aspects of Wife Abuse and its Relationship with Some Social and Political Variables*; *Relationship between Acceptance of Domestic Violence, Aggressiveness, Masculinity-Femininity and Violence against Wives in Gaza*; *Coping Strategies of Marital Violence among Palestinian Women Recipients of Domestic Violence Intervention Services*; studies and reports.

Finance: Projects financed by international foundations and NGOs, research institutes, etc.

Administrative and Supervisory Board: Dr Sufian Abu Nijaila (Chair.); Dr Yousef S. Abu Maila (Deputy Chair.); Dr Mohammad-Joma Abd al-Aziz (Treas.).

Principal Staff: Dir Dr Sufian Abu Nijaila.

Address: Zein Ed-deen Bldg, Thalatheeny St Remal, POB 1073, Gaza City.

Telephone: (8) 2867903; **Fax:** (8) 2848702; **e-mail:** chrsd@palnet.com.

Panama

FOUNDATION CENTRE AND CO-ORDINATING BODY

Fundación AVINA (AVINA Foundation)

Founded by Stephen Schmidheiny in 1994 to build partnerships with the corporate sector and the leaders of civil society to promote sustainable development in Central and South America and parts of Europe.

Activities: Funds activities that promote relations between civil society and private sector leaders, principally change-orientated projects in the fields of formal and non-formal education and training, citizen participation and grassroots social involvement, eco-efficiency and effective management of natural resources, economic and community development, and corporate social responsibility.

Geographical Area of Activity: Argentina, Bolivia, Brazil, Chile, Colombia, Costa Rica, Ecuador, Guatemala, Nicaragua, Peru, Paraguay, Uruguay, Venezuela;Portugal, Spain; and the USA.

Publications: Annual Report; books; *VIVA Publications*; *Informe de Odecu detectó altos niveles de caloría en leches saborizadas*; *Los Secretos del Eclipse*; *Informe de ODECU sobre los CFT de Chile*; *Revista Surcos; Conexion AVINA*.

Finance: Total disbursements US $36.5m. (2010).

Board of Directors: Brizio Biondi-Morra (Pres.).

Principal Staff: Exec. Dir Sean McKaughan.

Address: Local 131B, Calle Evelio Lara, Ciudad del Saber, Clayton, POB 0832-0390 WTC, Panama City.

Telephone: 317-0657; **Fax:** 317-0239; **Internet:** www.avina .net; **e-mail:** comunicaciones@avina.net.

FOUNDATIONS, TRUSTS AND NON-PROFIT ORGANIZATIONS

Consejo de Educación de Adultos de América Latina—CEAAL (Council for the Education of Adults in Latin America)

Established in 1982, an association of 195 civil organizations (located across 21 countries), aiming to improve adult literacy and advance social development throughout Central and South America and the Caribbean.

Activities: Operates in the field of education, consolidating the training and abilities of teaching staff in Central and South America and the Caribbean, promoting socio-cultural advancements in society, peace, human rights and democracy through education and raising adult literacy levels. Holds a General Assembly meeting every four years.

Geographical Area of Activity: Central and South America and the Caribbean.

Publications: *La Piragua; La Carta* (weekly); other books and texts.

Council: Nélida Céspedes (Pres.).

Principal Staff: Sec.-Gen. Raúl Leis.

Address: Apdo 0831-00817, Paitilla, Panama City.

Telephone: 270-1085; **Fax:** 270-1084; **Internet:** www.ceaal .org; **e-mail:** info@ceaal.org.

Fundación Dobbo Yala (Dobbo Yala Foundation)

Founded in 1990 to promote sustainable development for indigenous development and environmental conservation.

Activities: Provides administrative, technical and management support for environmental projects. Programmes include environmental education, training and extension of sustainable agriculture, socio-economic and environmental education, management of native forests projects, and training and support for indigenous micro-enterprises.

Geographical Area of Activity: Central America.

Publications: *Territorios Indigenas, Biodiversidad y Turismo; El valor del ambiente en los kunas desde una perspectiva de género; Minería en territorio indígena: Proyecto Cerro Colorado* (case study); *Diagnóstico Socio-Ambiental de la Actividad Minera en Panamá; Conflicto Socio-Ambiental en Panamá: Caso de Arimae y Emberá Puru; Aspecto legal sobre la protección de los Recursos Naturales; We Napa Nega Ibi Nuedi, Anmar Nue Sabgumala (Esta Tierra es Nuestra, Cuidémosla)*; and other publications.

Principal Staff: Pres. Aurelio Chiari; Dir Finance Rubén Pinzón; Exec. Dir Eligio Alvarado P.; Technical Dir Heraclio Herrera.

Address: Apdo 83-0308, Zona 3, Panama.

Telephone: 261-7229; **Fax:** 261-6347; **e-mail:** dobbo@ cableonda.net.

Paraguay

FOUNDATIONS, TRUSTS AND NON-PROFIT ORGANIZATIONS

Fundación Moisés Bertoni—FMB (Moisés Bertoni Foundation)

Established in 1988 to protect animals and plants in Paraguay.

Activities: The Foundation promotes the conservation of nature and biodiversity; management of protected areas; sustainable use of resources; and education and training in environmental management. Also runs eco-tourism projects in managed private game reserves.

Geographical Area of Activity: Paraguay.

Publications: *Plantas Comunes del Mbaracayo; Helechos del Mbaracayo; Maniteros de la Reserva de Mbaracayo; Plantas Medicinales de la Comunidad Guarani; Membresías;* agreements of technical cooperation with numerous national and international organizations.

Principal Staff: Exec. Dir Yan Speranza.

Address: Prócer Carlos Argüello 208, POB 714, Asunción.

Telephone: (21) 60-8740; **Fax:** (21) 60-8741; **Internet:** www.mbertoni.org.py; **e-mail:** mbertoni@mbertoni.org.py.

Peru

FOUNDATION CENTRE AND CO-ORDINATING BODY

Asociación Latinoamericana de Instituciones Financieras para el Desarrollo—ALIDE (Latin American Association of Development Financing Institutions)

Founded in 1968 to promote the participation of financial institutions in the social and economic progress of countries in Central and South America and the Caribbean.

Activities: The Association is made up of public and private development financing institutions; it encourages members to co-operate and contribute to the development and integration of Central and South American economies. The organization disseminates information; reports on investment projects; supports the collaboration of members on projects; organizes training projects and seminars; works to strengthen banking institutions in Central and South America; and maintains an information network, documentation centre and database. Also acts as an executive institution for projects and programmes being funded by international co-operation organizations and agencies.

Geographical Area of Activity: Central and South America and the Caribbean.

Restrictions: Only works with member organizations and institutions.

Publications: *ALIDE Bulletin* (6 a year, in English and Spanish); *Memoria de ALIDE* (annually); *Anales Asamblea General* (annually); Alide Noticias (monthly); *Directorio de Instituciones de Desarrollo* (biennially); *Revista ALIDE* (Bimonthly); *Boletín ALIDENOTICIAS* (monthly); *E-Banca* (monthly); *ALIDE E-News* (online bulletin, every four months); numerous technical papers and publications.

Finance: Funded by grants from international organizations and foundations, and membership fees. Total assets US $2,394,820 (31 Dec. 2009); annual income $795,337, annual expenditure $768,556 (2009).

Board of Directors: Rodrigo Mújica Sánchez (Pres.); Calloia Fernando Raffo (Vice-Pres.).

Principal Staff: Sec.-Gen. Rommel Acevedo.

Address: POB 3988, Lima 100; Avda Paseo de la República 3211, San Isidro, Lima 27.

Telephone: (1) 4422400; **Fax:** (1) 4428105; **Internet:** www.alide.org.pe; **e-mail:** sg@alide.org.pe.

FOUNDATIONS, TRUSTS AND NON-PROFIT ORGANIZATIONS

CEDRO—Centro de Información y Educación para la Prevención del Abuso de Drogas (Information and Education Centre for the Prevention of Drug Abuse)

Founded in 1986. Aims to raise awareness of drug abuse in Peru, and to help people afflicted by drug addiction.

Activities: Disseminates information about the impact of drug use, production and commercialization, and works to overcome problems in society that are drug-related. Funds community development projects in Peru, including working with 'street children' to overcome drug abuse through education and rehousing, where possible. Also provides vocational training and support, and funds research.

Geographical Area of Activity: Mainly Peru.

Publications: *Psychoactive Journal*.

Principal Staff: Exec. Dir Alejandro Vassilaqui; Dep. Dir Carmen Masías.

Address: Roca y Bologna 271, San Antonio–Miraflores, Lima 18.

Telephone: (1) 4467046; **Fax:** (1) 4460751; **Internet:** www.cedro.org.pe; **e-mail:** postmaster@cedro.org.pe.

CLADEM—Comité de América Latina y el Caribe para la Defensa de los Derechos de la Mujer (Latin American Committee for the Defence of Women's Rights)

A network of individual women and women's organizations, established in 1987, aiming to defend the rights of women in Central and South America and the Caribbean.

Activities: Operates in the field of women's rights, through education and information, proposals for legislative change and campaigning, solidarity activities, and through prizes awarded in recognition of women's achievements. Maintains offices in 17 countries of Central and South America and the Caribbean, and a regional office in Peru.

Geographical Area of Activity: Central and South America and the Caribbean.

Publications: Books; reports; pamphlets; videos.

Principal Staff: Dir Roxana Vásquez.

Address: Apdo 11-0470, Lima.

Telephone: (1) 4639237; **Fax:** (1) 4635898; **Internet:** www.cladem.org; **e-mail:** oficina@cladem.org.

ProNaturaleza—Fundación Peruana para la Conservación de la Naturaleza (Pro Nature—Peruvian Foundation for Nature Conservation)

Founded in 1984, a not-for-profit private organization dedicated to the conservation and protection of the environment in Peru.

Activities: Supports the conservation of soils, water resources, flora, fauna and other renewable natural resources in Peru, and promotes the development of a conservation culture. Works in conjunction with the Tropical Rainforest Coalition.

Geographical Area of Activity: Peru.

Publications: *Diagnóstico Rural Participativo en las cuencas altas de los ríos Tambopata e Inambari; Estudio Etnobotánico en las cuencas altas de los ríos Tambopata e Inambari; Áreas de Conservación Privada en el Perú; Dos décadas de conservación en el Perú;* various documents and papers.

Board of Administration: Manuel Ríos Rodríguez (Pres.); Enrique Agois Banchero (Vice-Pres.).

Principal Staff: Exec. Dir Martín Alcalde.

Address: Calle Doña Juana 137, Urb. Los Rosales, Santiago de Surco, Lima.

Telephone: (1) 2712662; **Fax:** (1) 4480947; **Internet:** www.pronaturaleza.org; **e-mail:** comunicaciones@pronaturaleza.org.

PROTERRA

Established in 1983, a non-profit organization and centre of investigation and promotion of environmental and development issues, which aims to improve the quality of life through achieving sustainable development.

Activities: Operates nationally and internationally, throughout Central and South America, in the fields of environmental policies and law, and sustainable development, through research, projects, training, publications, information dissemination, conferences, workshops, seminars and lobbying; co-operates with environmental workers and other national and international organizations; and supports projects in Peru and Central and South America, especially in the Andes and Amazonia regions. Participated in the drafting of the Peruvian Environment and Natural Resources Code. Maintains a library of books, magazines, documents, photographs, videos, etc. on the environment, and a databank of environmental legislation.

Geographical Area of Activity: Central and South America.

Publications: books on environmental law and the environment.

Principal Staff: Exec. Pres. Dr Carlos Andaluz Westreicher.

Address: Calle Ayacucho 176, Miraflores, Lima 18.

Telephone: (1) 4466363; **Fax:** (1) 2420238; **Internet:** www .proterra.org.pe; **e-mail:** proterra@proterra.org.pe.

Philippines

FOUNDATION CENTRES AND CO-ORDINATING BODIES

AF—Association of Foundations

Founded in 1972 to foster broader public understanding of the nature of foundations as institutions in nation-building, to promote co-ordination and co-operation among member foundations with a view to the optimum use of available resources, to represent members whenever necessary, and to serve as a clearing house for information, establishing and maintaining a central file of foundation materials, and preparing and updating a directory of Philippine foundations.

Activities: Operates nationally through the dissemination of information, organization of conferences and workshops, liaison among members and between members and government agencies, maintenance of an information centre, and through various publications. Operates as a host to four major databanks, providing information on all indigenous and international grant-makers operating in the Philippines as well as on 941 social development organizations. Has approximately 135 member foundations and is one of six founding members of the Philippines Council for NGO Certification.

Geographical Area of Activity: Philippines.

Publications: Annual Report and financial statement; *AF Brochure*; *Foundation Bulletin*; *Directory of Philippine Foundations*; *Donor Trends: A Resource Book of Development Assistance in the Philippines*; *Philippines NGOs: A Resource Book of Social Development NGOs*.

Executive Committee: Judy A. Roxas (Chair.); Fely C. Rixhon (Pres.); Marichu R. López (Vice-Pres.); Rose J. Depra (Vice-Pres.); Joemil S. Montebon (Vice-Pres.); Mario A. Deriquito (Treas.); Menchu A. Sarmiento (Sec.).

Principal Staff: Exec. Dir Oman Q. Jiao; Programme Officer Joey A. Alegre.

Address: Rm 1102, 11th Floor, Aurora Tower, Aurora Blvd, Cubao, 1109 Quezon City.

Telephone: (2) 9137231; **Fax:** (2) 9119792; **Internet:** www.afonline.org; **e-mail:** afonline@info.com.ph.

Asian NGO Coalition for Agrarian Reform and Rural Development—ANGOC

Founded in Bangkok (Thailand) in February 1979.

Activities: Has three major programme areas covering the topic of food security: sustainable agriculture and resource management; agrarian reform and access to land; and participatory local governance. Member organizations operate in Bangladesh, Cambodia, China, India, Indonesia, Nepal, Pakistan, the Philippines and Sri Lanka.

Geographical Area of Activity: South-East, East and South Asia.

Publications: Conference Reports; *Policy and Institutional Priorities for Sustainable Agriculture and Rural Development: Results of a Regional Workshop of the SARD-FSE Project*; *Highlights and Proceedings of the Third Country Training Program (TCTP) on Building Capacities of Asian NGOs in Poverty Eradication through Community Action: Enhancing Access to Land for the Rural Poor*; *Strengthening Capacities of Organizations of the Poor: IFAD's Experience in Building and Strengthening Rural Poor Organizations in Asia*; *Sustainable Agriculture: A Viable Alternative for Resource-Poor Farmers*; *Sustainable Agriculture in Asia: Prospects for Marketing and Promotion of Organic Products*.

Board: Francis Lucas (Chair.); Rohini Reddy (Vice-Chair.); Nathaniel Don E. Marquez (Treas.).

Principal Staff: Exec. Dir Nathaniel Don E. Marquez; Sr Prog. Officer Maricel Almojuela-Tolentino.

Address: POB 3107, QCCPO 1103, Quezon City; 73-K Dr Lazcano St, Barangay Laging Handa, 1103 Quezon City.

Telephone: (2) 3510581; **Fax:** (2) 3510011; **Internet:** www.angoc.org.

Asian Philanthropy Advisory Network—APAN

Established in 2011 following the acquisition of the Asia Pacific Philanthropy Consortium (founded 1994) by Give2Asia (founded 2001).

Activities: Assists foundations and corporate donors in the Asia-Pacific region, through technical support, training, research, information services, networking, exchanges and conferences. Currently developing a network of Internet-linked information centres in Asian societies, including Australia, China, Hong Kong, Republic of Korea, Japan, Philippines, Taiwan, and Thailand, with additional links being established in Bangladesh, India, Indonesia and Malaysia.

Geographical Area of Activity: Asia-Pacific region.

Publications: *Philanthropy and Law in Asia*; *Evolving Patterns of Asia Pacific Philanthropy*; *Emerging Civil Society in the Asia Pacific Community*; *Civil Society Response to Asian Crisis: Thailand, Indonesia and Korea*; *Investing in Ourselves: Giving and Fundraising in Asia*.

Address: 2nd Floor, Lexington Condominium, 65 Xavierville Ave, Loyola Heights, 1108 Quezon City.

Telephone: (2) 4351990; **Fax:** (2) 4351990; **Internet:** www.asianphilanthropy.org; **e-mail:** info@asianphilanthropy.org.

Philippine Foundation Center—PFC

Established by the Association of Foundations to act as a resource and information centre on non-government organizations, foundations and the civil society sector in general.

Activities: The Center provides up-to-date information on NGOs, foundations and donors, including information on their programmes and projects, scope of operations, partners and beneficiaries, and issues and concerns. Also carries out research on trends in the civil society sector, on areas such as philanthropy, impact assessment, governance and regulation, and carries out training and education sessions in financial management, fundraising, proposal writing, board governance and similar topics of interest to the non-profit sector.

Geographical Area of Activity: Philippines.

Publications: Research reports; Annual Report; audiovisual materials; books; magazines; articles; newspapers.

Address: Rm 1101, 11/F Aurora Tower, Aurora Blvd, Cubao, Quezon City.

Telephone: (2) 9119792; **Fax:** (2) 9137231; **Internet:** www.pfconline.org; **e-mail:** info@pfconline.org.

FOUNDATIONS, TRUSTS AND NON-PROFIT ORGANIZATIONS

Ayala Foundation, Inc—AFI

Founded in 1961 by Col Joseph McMicking and his wife Mercedes Zobel to fund projects related to the arts, technology, social sciences and education. Formerly known as the Filipinas Foundation; now the socio-cultural development section of the Ayala Group of companies, one of the largest conglomerates in the Philippines.

Activities: Promotes and advances social development in the Philippines, including providing vocational training for disabled people, and funding environmental projects; technological development; funds cultural programmes, and runs the Ayala Museum. Also owns the Filipinas Heritage Library, the Center for Social Development and the Center of Excellence in Public Elementary Education.

Geographical Area of Activity: Philippines.

Publications: Annual Report.

Finance: Assets 1,513,437,993 Philippine pesos (Dec. 2010); annual revenue 513,750,005 pesos, expenditure 262,567,920 pesos (Dec. 2010).

Board of Trustees: Jaime Zobel de Ayala (Chair.); Jaime Augusto Zobel de Ayala II (Co-Vice Chair.); Fernando Zobel de Ayala (Co-Vice Chair.); Maria Lourdes Heras-de Leon (Pres.).

Principal Staff: Pres. Victoria Garchitorena; Exec. Vice-Pres. and COO Guillermo Manuel Luz; Corporate Sec. Solomon Hermosura; Treas. Ramon Opulencia; CFO Wilma Zapata.

Address: 10th Floor Ayala Wing, BPI Building, 6768 Ayala Ave cnr Paseo de Roxas, Makati City.

Telephone: (2) 7521101; **Fax:** (2) 8134488; **Internet:** www.ayalafoundation.org; **e-mail:** info@ayalafoundation.org.

Center for the Development of Human Resources in Rural Asia—CenDHRRA

Founded in 1975 to promote the establishment of rural development projects for rural communities in Asia.

Activities: Organizes research into matters concerning rural development; operates training programmes and workshops in conjunction with NGOs; provides information to and encourages communication between those concerned with development projects; maintains a library of about 1,000 volumes.

Geographical Area of Activity: Asia.

Publications: *CenDHRRA Network News*; *CenDHRRA Development Memo* (10 a year); *Dialogue with Asia's Rural Man and Woman* (series); *CenDHRRA Directory of Development Partners*; *Solicitudo* (development information for church leaders); *Priests Forum for Development Newsletter*; monographs and occasional papers.

Executive Committee: Marimuthu Nadason (Chair.); Sil Vineth (Deputy Chair., Mejong Region); Jaybee Garganera (Deputy Chair., South-East Asia); Sung Lee (Deputy Chair., North Asia).

Principal Staff: Sec.-Gen. Marlene D. Ramirez.

Address: Room 201 Partnership Center, 59 C. Salvador St, Loyola Heights, 1108 Quezon City.

Telephone: (2) 4364706; **Fax:** (2) 4266739; **Internet:** asiadhrra.org; **e-mail:** asiadhrra@asiadhrra.org.

ChildHope Asia Philippines, Inc

Founded in 1986 by representatives from international children's agencies and individuals working directly with street children.

Activities: Among the functions of ChildHope Asia Philippines are advocacy, capacity building and technical assistance, networking, databanking, and programme development and implementation.

Publications: Newsletter; narrative reports; directories; research series; guidebooks; workshop proceedings; manuals.

Principal Staff: Pres. and Exec. Dir Teresita Silva.

Address: 1210 Peñafrancia St, Paco 1007, Manila.

Telephone: (2) 5634647; **Fax:** (2) 5632242; **Internet:** www.childhope.org.ph; **e-mail:** chap@childhope.org.ph.

Communication Foundation for Asia

The Communication Foundation for Asia (CFA) was established in 1973 as a non-stock, non-profit organization, but its origins go back to 1960, with the launch of the Philippine

Catholic Digest, and the eventual establishment of the Social Communication Cente (SCC) in 1965. Both CFA and SCC were founded by the Dutch missionary Fr Cornelio Lagerwey, in collaboration with a young journalist, Genaro V. Ong, and other lay Filipino communicators. Together, they pursued a mission to use media for the spiritual upliftment and empowerment of people.

Activities: CFA has evolved into a multi-media centre with around 100 staff, producing video documentries and TV programmes, publishing educational comics and magazines that reach an estimated readership of more than 1m. nationwide, conducting training workshops on communication skills and media education, organizing media events such as film festivals, peace communication camps, environmental forums and travelling exhibits.

Geographical Area of Activity: Asia.

Publications: *Baby Jesus* (for pre-school and early elementary readers, 5 a year); *Jesus (Gospel Komiks Edition for Young Readers)* (for early elementary readers, 5 a year; *Gospel Komiks* (for intermediate readers, 5 a year, in English and Filipino); *Gospel K Magazine for High School* (5 a year); *Pambata* (for elementary school readers, 5 a year).

Board of Trustees: Fr Tito Y. Maratas, MSC (Chair.); Fr Filoteo C. Pelingon, MSC (Pres.); Fr Leonardo Cabrera, MSC (Vice-Chair. and Treas.).

Principal Staff: Exec. Dir Teresita Z. Hermano.

Address: 4427 Old Santa Mesa St, Santa Mesa, 1016 Manila.

Telephone: (2) 7132981; **Fax:** (2) 7132974; **Internet:** www.cfamedia.org; **e-mail:** info@cfamedia.org.

Cultural Center of the Philippines—CCP

Founded in 1966, the Center is mandated by Philippine Laws to preserve, promote and enhance the Filipino people's cultural heritage, and to encourage the evolution of the national culture of the Philippines.

Activities: Operates as a national centre for the performing arts; encourages, conserves and disseminates Filipino creativity and artistic experience, through providing artistic programmes, services and facilities. Maintains a library and organizes international exchanges.

Geographical Area of Activity: Philippines.

Publications: Catalogues on dance, theatre and music, and various monographs.

Board of Trustees: Emily Abrera (Chair.).

Principal Staff: Pres. Dr Raul M. Sunico.

Address: CCP Complex, Roxas Blvd, Pasay City 1300, Manila.

Telephone: (2) 8321125; **Fax:** (2) 8323683; **Internet:** www.culturalcenter.gov.ph; **e-mail:** ccp.publicrelations@gmail.com.

Haribon Foundation for the Conservation of Natural Resources, Inc

Established in 1972 by Alicia Busser, Dr Robert Kennedy and Pedro Gonzales to promote sustainable development for the Philippines, through community-based, socially equitable and scientifically-sound management of natural resources.

Activities: Operates nationally in the field of conservation and the environment, through self-conducted programmes, research, scholarships, conferences, training courses and community-based projects. Key programmes include the Marine Ecosystems Programme, the Institutional Partnership Development Programme and the Terrestrial Ecosystems Programme. Maintains links with local and international organizations.

Geographical Area of Activity: Asia-Pacific.

Publications: Books on biodiversity; policy papers; research and educational materials; digital media; *Haring Ibon* magazine.

Finance: Total assets 34,063,156 Philippine pesos (31 Dec. 2010).

Board of Directors: John Lesaca (Chair.); Archimedes E. King (Vice-Chair. and Treas.); Himerio Ll. Garcia, IV (Sec.).

Principal Staff: COO Anabelle E. Plantilla.

Address: 2F Santos and Sons Bldg, 973 Aurora Blvd, Cubao, Quezon City.

Telephone: (2) 4344642; **Fax:** (2) 4344696; **Internet:** www .haribon.org.ph; **e-mail:** act@haribon.org.ph.

IBON Foundation

Established in 1978 to provide advocacy, research, education and information.

Activities: Operates in the Philippines and abroad providing research, education, publications, information and advocacy. Also involved in the education sector, providing non-formal education to people's organizations; conducting in-depth research and information services to various sectors; media education; and international networking. The international arm of the organization maintains an office in Belgium.

Geographical Area of Activity: Mainly the Philippines.

Board of Directors: Mary Soledad Perpiñan (Hon. Chair.); Dr Edberto Villegas (Chair.); Prof. Judy Taguiwalo (Vice-Chair.); Prof. Roland Simbulan (Sec.); Reynaldo Oliveros (Treas.).

Address: IBON Center, 114 Timog Ave., Quezon City 1103.

Telephone: 9277060; **Fax:** 9292496; **Internet:** www.ibon.org; **e-mail:** admin@ibon.org.

Integrated Rural Development Foundation

Established to promote sustainable development in the Philippines, especially with regard to the rural poor.

Activities: Operates nationally in the area of sustainable development through local community-based projects in natural resource management and food security. There are four main programmes: Sustainable Farming; Sustainable Community-based Resource Management; Rural Livelihood and Development; and Policy Research, Advocacy and Campaigns.

Geographical Area of Activity: Philippines.

Principal Staff: Admin. Officer Art Francisco.

Address: POB 741, Araneta Center Post Office, Cubao, Quezon City; 87 Malakas St, Pinyahan, Quezon City 1100.

Telephone: (2) 4265518; **Fax:** (2) 9250987; **Internet:** www .irdfphil.org; **e-mail:** irdf@irdfphil.com.

International Institute of Rural Reconstruction— IIRR

Established in 1960 to bring about integrated community-based development and to generate models for reducing poverty based on participatory approaches to development.

Activities: Promotes people-centered development through capacity building for poor people and their communities, development organizations and agencies. The Institute shares its experiences and knowledge through training programmes and publications. Main themes of operation are: Education for Pastoralists and other Marginalized Communities; Food Security and Wealth Creation; Disaster Risk Reduction and Climate Change Adaptation; and Applied Learning. Maintains Africa Regional Center in Kenya, a liaison office in New York, USA, and country offices in Ethiopia, Kenya, South Sudan and Uganda.

Geographical Area of Activity: Africa and Asia.

Publications: Annual Report, newsletters; publications relating to sustainable development.

Finance: Total assets US $5,124,157 (2010); annual income $4,989,526, annual expenditure $2,977,684 (2010).

Board of Trustees: Isaac B. Bekalo (Pres.); James F. Kelly (Chair. and Treas.); Ricardo A. Anzaldúa-Montoya (Sec.).

Principal Staff: Pres. Isaac B. Bekalo.

Address: Y. C. James Yen Center, Km. 39 Aguinaldo Highway, Silang, Cavite 4118.

Telephone: (46) 4143216; **Fax:** (46) 4143216; **Internet:** www .iirr.org; **e-mail:** information@iirr.org.

Ramon Magsaysay Award Foundation

Founded in 1957 by Belen H. Abreu, Paz Marquez Benitez, Jaime N. Ferrer, Jesus Magsaysay, Francisco Ortigas, Jr, Pedro Tuason and Leopoldo Uichanco, in memory of former President of the Philippines Ramon Magsaysay.

Activities: Confers the Ramon Magsaysay Award: six annual awards of US $50,000 each are offered in the fields of government service; public service; community leadership; journalism, literature and creative communication arts; international understanding; and since 2001, emergency leadership. Also operates the Programme for Asian Projects to enable awardees to develop their projects and runs an essay writing competition. The Foundation maintains an Asian Library, housing an extensive collection of reference materials on contemporary Asia, as well as the Magsaysay Papers. Also organizes international seminars on issues affecting the Asian region, and offers film and slide presentations on the peoples and cultures of the region to secondary school pupils.

Geographical Area of Activity: Asia.

Restrictions: Grants are made only to people or institutions that work in Asia.

Publications: Newsletter; *Awardee*Links (e-newsletter).

Finance: Funded by the Rockefeller Brothers Fund (q.v.) from 1958 to 1968, the Foundation is now supported by the income from the Ramon Magsaysay Center, which it owns. The Rockefeller Brothers Fund grants approx. US $150,000 annually to support the awards.

Board of Trustees: Maria Cynthia Rose B. Bautista (Chair.); Emily A. Abrera (Vice-Chair.); Federico M. Macaranas (Treas.).

Principal Staff: Pres. and CEO Carmencita T. Abella.

Address: POB 3350, Manila; Ground Floor, Ramon Magsaysay Center, 1680 Roxas Blvd, 1073 Manila.

Telephone: (2) 5213166; **Fax:** (2) 5218105; **Internet:** www.rmaf .org.ph; **e-mail:** rmaf@rmaf.org.ph.

Philippine-American Educational Foundation— PAEF

Founded in 1948 (as the US Educational Foundation in the Philippines, present name 1969) by the Governments of the USA and the Philippines to promote further mutual understanding by a wider exchange of knowledge and professional talents through educational contacts.

Activities: Operates nationally and internationally in sponsoring research, educational conferences, lectures, seminars and scholarship and fellowship programmes, notably educational exchanges between students from the USA and the Philippines, the Philippine Fulbright Programme for study in the USA, the Hubert H. Humphrey North-South Fellowship Program for professional candidates, and the East-West Center student degree awards providing financial assistance to students from the Philippines studying at the University of Hawaii. Also provides information and counselling services, and maintains an information resource library on US universities.

Geographical Area of Activity: USA and the Philippines.

Finance: Income is derived from the Governments of the USA and the Philippines, from private agencies and individuals.

Board of Directors: Kristie Anne Kenney (Hon. Chair.); Richard W. Nelson (Chair.).

Principal Staff: Exec. Dir Dr Esmeralda S. Cunanan.

Address: 10/F Ayala Life–FGU Center-Makati, 6811 Ayala Ave, 1226 Makati City.

Telephone: (2) 8120919; **Fax:** (2) 8120822; **Internet:** www.paef .org.ph; **e-mail:** fulbright@paef.org.ph.

Press Foundation of Asia—PFA

Founded on 31 August 1967 by a group of Asian publishers and editors concerned about the failure of newspapers to relate fully to the needs and aspirations of the fast-developing Asian nations; the Foundation aims to improve editorial, production and management techniques, and to instil in journalists and publishers an awareness of their role and responsibilities.

Activities: The Foundation's training programme comprises intensive courses, seminars and workshops for journalists, dealing with coverage of different topics such as development economics, energy, science and the environment; it also provides training in new printing technology, design and marketing. The Foundation collaborates with national press institutions throughout the region, provides consultancy and information services, and operates a scheme whereby Western journalists are invited to participate in the Foundation's work and gain Asian experience. A databank is maintained and training manuals are published. Members are newspapers in 24 countries and territories of Asia and Australasia.

Geographical Area of Activity: Philippines.

Publications: *Environment Folio* (quarterly); *PFA Newsletter* (quarterly); *Asian Women and Children* (quarterly); *Presses* (quarterly); *Asia Press and Media Directory* (annual); *Data Asia* (weekly reference bulletin); *Detail* (on Philippine economics, 2 a week); *Media* (monthly).

Finance: The Foundation was established with an endowment of US $600,000, and receives grants from other foundations, funds and newspapers, and donations.

Board of Directors: Mazlan bin Nordin (Exec. Chair.); Tsuneo Watanabe (Vice-Chair.).

Principal Staff: Editorial Dir Juan L. Mercado.

Address: POB 1843, Manila.

Telephone: (2) 591478; **Fax:** (2) 5224365.

Tebtebba Foundation

Established in 1996; aims to resolve conflicts and promote sustainable development in indigenous communities.

Activities: Works internationally in the field of law and human rights, as an advocate to attain peace and social justice in indigenous territories around the world, and to promote indigenous rights. Provides training for indigenous leaders and acts as a consultant to indigenous organizations. Also disseminates information about issues affecting indigenous people, carries out research and holds conferences.

Geographical Area of Activity: World-wide.

Publications: *Tebtebba* (magazine); *UN Declaration on the Rights of Indigenous Peoples and the Programme of the 2nd Decade of the World's Indigenous People; Capacity Building and Advocacy Report; Extracting Promises; Celebrating Diversity, Heightening Solidarity; Beyond the Silencing of the Guns; Engaging the UN Special Representative on Indigenous People: Opportunities and Challenges; The Kimberley Declaration and the Indigenous Peoples' Plan of Implementation on Sustainable Development; Indigenous Perspectives* (magazine).

Principal Staff: Exec. Dir Victoria Tauli-Corpuz.

Address: 1 Roman Ayson Rd, 2600 Baguio City.

Telephone: (74) 4447703; **Fax:** (74) 4439459; **Internet:** www.tebtebba.org; **e-mail:** tebtebba@tebtebba.org.

Villar Foundation, Inc.

Established by Manuel B. Villar, Jr and others in 1995 to initiate, undertake, support or otherwise foster educational, cultural, scientific, charitable and civic activities aimed at benefiting the Filipino people, in particular the poor and needy.

Activities: Operates financial assistance or incentive programmes for young people, aimed at skills development and livelihood assistance; socio-civic, cultural, educational, religious, scientific and technological projects for the social or economic amelioration of poor and needy Filipino people; social welfare and relief services for the poor; tree-planting and other conservation programmes including historical preservation.

Geographical Area of Activity: Philippines.

Publications: Annual Report; books.

Board of Trustees: Manuel B. Villar, Jr (Chair.); Mark A. Villar (Sec. and Treas.).

Principal Staff: Man. Dir Cynthia A. Villar.

Address: C. Masibay St, BF Resort Village, Talon, 1740 Las Pinas City.

Telephone: (632) 8728540; **Fax:** (632) 8725488; **Internet:** www.villarfoundation.org; **e-mail:** villarfoundationinc@gmail.com.

Poland

FOUNDATION CENTRES AND CO-ORDINATING BODIES

Akademia Rozwoju Filantropii w Polsce (Academy for the Development of Philanthropy in Poland)

Established in 1998; aims to support philanthropy in Poland and to promote its development and the long-term sustainability of Poland's third sector.

Activities: Promotes philanthropy in Poland and supports the development of the third sector, through a local grants programme, a grant programme for organizations promoting Polish-Jewish dialogue, a local youth fund, senior citizen programmes, scholarships for young gifted people and participation in international philanthropy networks. Also operates the Benefactor of the Year competition, recognizing corporate philanthropists in Poland.

Geographical Area of Activity: Poland.

Publications: *The White Book of Philanthropy—Coalition for Better Law*; Annual Report; other publications.

Finance: Annual income US $2,466,453 (2008).

Board: Paweł Łukasiak (Pres.).

Principal Staff: Dir Paweł Łukasiak; Finance Dir Tomasz Bruski.

Address: 00-590 Warsaw, ul. Marszalkowska 6/6.

Telephone: (22) 6220122; **Fax:** (22) 6220211; **Internet:** www.filantropia.org.pl; **e-mail:** arfp@filantropia.org.pl.

Forum Inicjatyw Pozarzadowych—FIP (Forum for Non-Governmental Initiatives)

Established in 1993 to promote civil society.

Activities: Supports the development of civil society and non-profit organizations in Poland, and co-operation with governmental and private-sector organizations through meetings and the exchange of information. These meetings contribute to co-operation among all three sectors as well as an apparent growth in community involvement in Poland.

Geographical Area of Activity: Poland.

Publications: Bulletins and papers.

Board of Directors: Jan Jakub Wygnański (Pres.).

Address: 00-031 Warsaw, ul. Szpitalna 5/5.

Telephone: (22) 8289128; **Fax:** (22) 8289129; **Internet:** www.fip.ngo.pl; **e-mail:** ofip@ofip.org.pl.

Grupa Zagranica (Zagranica Group)

A coalition of Polish NGOs operating outside Poland founded in 2001, originating from a conference held by the Stefan Batory Foundation (q.v.) in co-operation with the Ministry of Foreign Affairs.

Activities: Supports the exchange of information, experiences and common standards between Polish NGOs working abroad; fosters co-operation between the NGOs and other sectors; lobbies government on Polish foreign and development aid policy in countries where the NGOs are engaged; facilitates contacts between NGOs and potential partners; establishes contacts and co-operation with similar groups of NGOs in other countries and with European Union (EU) institutions, to exert influence on EU development aid policy and take part in its implementation; and disseminates information concerning the activities of Polish NGOs working abroad and campaigning for public support for their activities. Five working groups are currently active: Global Education, Polish AidWatch, Belarus, Eastern Partnership and Caucasus+.

Geographical Area of Activity: Poland.

Publications: *Guiding Principles of Polish Non-governmental Organisations Working Abroad.*

Principal Staff: Exec. Sec. Marta Pejda.

Address: 00-589 Warsaw, ul. Litewska 11/13.

Telephone: (22) 2990105; **Fax:** (22) 2072560; **Internet:** www.zagranica.org.pl; **e-mail:** grupa@zagranica.org.pl.

OPUS—Centre for Promotion and Development of Civil Initiatives

Created in June 1999 to support the development of civil society in Poland.

Activities: Supports civil society development in Poland through providing advice and consultancy services to NGOs, co-operating internationally in networks and with other organizations and channelling European Union programme funds to local Polish NGOs.

Geographical Area of Activity: Poland.

Publications: Annual Report.

Board of Directors: Lukasz Waszak (Pres.); Aleksandra Wasik (Sec.).

Principal Staff: Pres. Jolanta Woźnicka.

Address: 91-415 Łódź, pl. Wolności 2.

Telephone: (42) 2313101; **Fax:** (42) 2313102; **Internet:** www.opus.org.pl; **e-mail:** opus@opus.org.pl.

Polsko-Amerykańska Fundacja Wolności (Polish-American Freedom Foundation)

Established by the Polish-American Enterprise Fund in the USA in 1999; opened a Representative Office in Warsaw in 2000, and began its operating activity in 2000. Aims to support the development of civil society, democracy and a market economy in Poland.

Activities: The Foundation's goal is to support the development of civil society, democracy and market economy in Poland, including efforts to equalize opportunities for personal and social development, as well as to support the transformation processes in other countries of Central and Eastern Europe. Runs programmes the following areas: Initiatives in Education; Development of Local Communities; Citizen in a Democratic State of Law; and Sharing the Polish Experiences in Transformation. In Poland, the Foundation currently focuses on initiatives that help level the playing field in education, as well as release and reinforce citizens' potential, particularly in villages and small cities.

Geographical Area of Activity: Poland.

Restrictions: No grants for commercial projects and grants only for Polish NGOs.

Publications: *10 years of the Polish-American Freedom Foundation*; Annual Report; general information brochures.

Finance: Financed through revenues generated by its endowment, the source of which is the Polish-American Enterprise Fund. Total assets US $297,978,780 (Dec. 2010); annual income $2,999,701, annual expenditure $2,025,548 (2010).

Board of Directors: John P. Birkelund (Chair.).

Principal Staff: Pres. and CEO Jerzy Kozminski.

Address: Warsaw, ul. Królowej Marysienki 48.

Telephone: (22) 5502800; **Fax:** (22) 5502801; **Internet:** www.pafw.pl.

Sieć Wspierania Organizacji Pozarządowych—SPLOT (Network of Information and Support for Non-Governmental Organizations)

Established in 1994, comprises 14 independent NGOs aiming to promote the development of civil society in Poland.

Activities: Aims to support the development of civil society in Poland through providing funding and advisory services to associations, foundations, support groups and other civil initiatives, training and information.

Geographical Area of Activity: Poland.

Publications: Various manuals and studies.

Board: Lukasz Domagala (Pres.); Izabela Dembicka-Starska (Vice-Pres.).

Principal Staff: Contact Izabela Jarocka.

Address: 00-098 Warsaw, ul. Niecała 6/42.

Telephone: (22) 8275211; **Internet:** www.siecsplot.pl; **e-mail:** biuro@siecsplot.pl.

Stowarzyszenie Klon/Jawor (Klon/Jawor Association)

Established in 1990 as part of the Regardless of the Weather Foundation to provide access to information so as to promote the development of civil society; became independent in 2000.

Activities: Promotes the development of civil society through maintaining a database of Polish NGOs (JAWOR); conducting research, especially on the third sector in the European Union and local government and NGOs; supporting NGOs; issuing publications; promoting European networking; an Internet programme; and generally assisting NGOs in their operations.

Geographical Area of Activity: Poland.

Publications: *JAWOR; KLON; Citizen Information Center; Warsaw Information Guide for Senior; The Third Sector in the European Union; Know Your Rights* (series); *Know More* (series); and other publications on NGOs in Poland.

Board: Ula Krasnodębska-Maciula (Pres.); Alina Galazka (Sec.); Renata Niecikowska (Treas.).

Principal Staff: Dir Ula Krasnodębska-Maciula.

Address: 00-031 Warszawa, ul. Szpitalna 5/5.

Telephone: (22) 8289128; **Fax:** (22) 8289129; **Internet:** www.klon.org.pl; **e-mail:** klon@klon.org.pl.

Trust for Civil Society in Central and Eastern Europe

Established in 2001, a consortium of grant-making organizations, including the Charles Stewart Mott Foundation, the Ford Foundation, the Open Society Institute (q.v.), the German Marshall Fund of the USA and the Rockefeller Brothers Fund, formed to promote the development of civil society in Central and Eastern Europe.

Activities: Operates in seven countries of Central and Eastern Europe, promoting the development of indigenous third-sector organizations, through making grants to local intermediary non-profit organizations, for distribution to local NGOs.

Geographical Area of Activity: Bulgaria, the Czech Republic, Hungary, Poland, Romania, Slovakia and Slovenia.

Restrictions: The following are not eligible for grants: political organizations, trade unions, business organizations and businesses.

Finance: Total assets US $16,606,174 (31 Dec. 2010); annual income $1,203,580, expenditure $6,745,363 (2010).

Board of Trustees: Heike MacKerron (Chair.); Haki Abazi (Sec. and Treas.).

Principal Staff: Exec. Dir Lidia Kolucka-Zuk.

Address: 00-020 Warsaw, ul. Szpitalna 1 lok. 54/55.

Telephone: (22) 5768090; **Fax:** (22) 5768099; **Internet:** www.ceetrust.org; **e-mail:** trust@ceetrust.org.

FOUNDATIONS, TRUSTS AND NON-PROFIT ORGANIZATIONS

Atlas Charity Foundation

Established in 1996 by the Atlas Group for the alleviation of poverty.

Activities: Operates in the area of social welfare in Poland and Central and Eastern Europe, particularly children's welfare and Polish communities in Belarus, Kazakhstan, Lithuania, Russia and Ukraine.

Geographical Area of Activity: Eastern Europe and Poland.

Principal Staff: Chair. Jolanta Rojek.

Address: 80-126 Gdańsk, ul. Jaśkowa Dolina 21.

Telephone: (58) 3421122; **Fax:** (58) 3430619; **Internet:** www.atlas.com.pl/en/fundacja; **e-mail:** atlas@atlas.com.pl.

Fundacja Agory (Agora Foundation)

Established in 2004 to manage all charitable and social initiatives of the Agora and Agora Holding companies.

Activities: Provides support to educational and cultural initiatives, with the aim of promoting and shaping good attitudes, providing funding to disadvantaged individuals and families, health-care development and initiatives to save people's lives, and for the development of entrepreneurship, professionalism and active living. Also sponsors *Zeszyty Literackie* (a literary periodical) and awards scholarships and a literary prize.

Geographical Area of Activity: Poland.

Publications: Annual Report.

Board of Directors: Wojciech Kaminski (Pres.); Joanna Kosmal, Maciej Gamrot, Grzegorz Piechota (Deputy Pres.).

Address: 00-732 Warsaw, ul. Czerska 8/10.

Telephone: (22) 5555263; **Fax:** (22) 5558263; **Internet:** www.fundacjaagory.com; **e-mail:** fundacja@agora.pl.

Fundacja Auschwitz-Birkenau (Auschwitz-Birkenau Foundation)

Established in 2009 by Prof. Władysław Bartoszewski to finance the upkeep and conservation work on the Auschwitz-Birkenau Memorial.

Activities: The Foundation was established to raise €120m., the interest on which would be used to protect the remains of the Auschwitz concentration camp and their maintenance as a memorial and museum. The Foundation has been given funding by a number of governments, including Austria, Belgium, Germany, Israel, the Netherlands, New Zealand, Poland and the USA.

Geographical Area of Activity: Poland.

Principal Staff: Council Chair. Prof. Władysław Bartoszewski; Pres. Piotr M. A. Cywiński; Dir-Gen. Jacek Kastelaniec.

Address: 00-105 Warsaw, ul. Twarda 6.

Telephone: (22) 608 300 627; **Fax:** (22) 620 48 99.

Fundacja Bankowa im. Leopolda Kronenberga (Leopold Kronenberg Foundation)

Established in 1996 to mark the 125th anniversary of Bank Handlowy Warszawie SA to support general charitable work in Poland.

Activities: Operates in the areas of education, science, the arts and humanities, health care and social welfare, by supporting organizations and projects engaged in work in these areas. Also presents prizes for entrepreneurship.

Geographical Area of Activity: Poland.

Restrictions: Grants only to non-profit organizations in Poland.

Advisory Council: Prof. Daria Nałęcz (Pres.); Alan Okada (Vice-Pres.).

Principal Staff: Dir Krzysztof Kaczmar.

Address: 00-067 Warsaw, ul. R. Traugutta 7/9.

Telephone: (22) 8268324; **Fax:** (22) 6925094; **Internet:** www
.citibank.pl/poland/homepage/english/3498.htm; **e-mail:**
poczta@kronenberg.org.pl.

Fundacja im. Stefana Batorego (Stefan Batory Foundation)

Founded by George Soros in May 1988 to support the development of Polish society in the areas of science, culture, education, information and civil society to strengthen democracy and a free market, and to encourage co-operation between the countries of Central and Eastern Europe. The Foundation is part of the Soros foundations network.

Activities: The Foundation supports the development of a democratic and open society in Poland and other Central and Eastern European countries. Through its grant-making and operating programmes, the Foundation aims to enhance the role and involvement of civil society, promote civil liberties and the rule of law, and develop international co-operation and solidarity.

Geographical Area of Activity: Central and Eastern Europe, Poland.

Restrictions: Grants to organizations based in Poland. In some programmes also to organizations based in Ukraine, Belarus and in Kaliningrad District.

Publications: Annual Report; *Stefan Batory Foundation E-newsletter;* film on the Stefan Batory Foundation; numerous thematic publications.

Finance: Total assets 182,537,425 new złotys (31 Dec. 2010); Total annual expenditure 19,064,108 new złotys (2010).

Board of Directors: Aleksander Smolar (Pres.).

Principal Staff: Exec. Dir. Ewa Kulik-Bielinska; Programme Dir Anna Rozicka.

Address: 00 215 Warsaw, ul. Sapiezynska 10A.

Telephone: (22) 5360200; **Fax:** (22) 5360220; **Internet:** www
.batory.org.pl; **e-mail:** batory@batory.org.pl.

Fundacja Biblioteka Ekologiczna (Ecological Library Foundation)

Founded in November 1988 by Jacek Purat.

Activities: The Foundation operates in the fields of conservation and the environment and economic affairs, through research, conferences, publications and a library. It distributes books; conducts research; organizes conferences; presents films; has established an ecological library; and organizes projects for the protection of endangered species in Poland.

Geographical Area of Activity: Poland.

Board of Directors: Ryszard Gołdyn (Pres.); Zbigniew Krysiński (Vice-Pres.); Halina Szyper (Treas.).

Principal Staff: Chair. Jan Śmiełowski.

Address: 61-715 Poznań, ul. Kościuszki 79.

Telephone: (61) 8521325; **Fax:** (61) 8528276; **Internet:** www
.bibliotekaekologiczna.prv.pl; **e-mail:** rceebepz@free.ngo.pl.

Fundacja Centrum Prasowe (Central and Eastern European Media Centre Foundation)

Founded in Warsaw in December 1990 by the Polish Journalist Association to support the development of an independent media in former communist countries.

Activities: The Foundation promotes the exchange of ideas and experiences between journalists; monitors and documents changes within the media and the social communication systems; lobbies governments with regard to media legislation and policies; organizes training courses for journalists and publishers; maintains a database; and conducts seminars and conferences. Also makes awards and distributes prizes.

Geographical Area of Activity: Belarus, Poland, Russia and Ukraine.

Board of Trustees: Elizabeth Skotnicka-Illasiewicz (Chair.).

Principal Staff: Pres. Stefan Bratkowski; Dirs Joanna Kaczerska, Margorzata Wójcik.

Address: 00-363 Warsaw, ul. Nowy Swiat 58 III p.

Telephone: (22) 8264557; **Fax:** (22) 8263002; **Internet:** www
.fcp.edu.pl; **e-mail:** biuro@fcp.edu.pl.

Fundacja Gospodarcza (Economic Foundation)

Established in March 1990 by the National Commission (NSZZ) of Solidarność (Solidarity) to confront the problems of unemployment and education.

Activities: Organizes programmes in Poland in the fields of trade union education and economic affairs. Projects include establishing an international system of exchange for economic information, promoting small businesses, programmes to reduce unemployment, and social activities programmes. The Foundation holds conferences; organizes consultancy programmes, providing information for people intending to start in business; and runs an occupational information centre for secondary-school students.

Geographical Area of Activity: Poland.

Publications: *Economics; Career Skills; Labour Code;* publications of interest to the unemployed and people in business.

Board of Trustees: Ewa Zydorek (Chair.); Bogdan Olszewski (Vice-Chair.).

Principal Staff: Dir-Gen. Irena Muszkiewicz-Herok; Dir Małgorzata Makiewicz.

Address: 81-538 Gdynia, ul. Olimpijska 2.

Telephone: (58) 6226017; **Fax:** (58) 6225985; **Internet:** www
.fungo.com.pl; **e-mail:** fungos@fungo.com.pl.

Fundacja Partnerstwo dla Środowiska (Polish Environmental Partnership Foundation)

Established in 1992 as a Programme Office of the German Marshall Fund of the USA; present name and status since 1997, when it was registered as a foundation in Poland. It aims to promote and support non-profit organizations and communities that implement environmental projects, where these contribute to the development of democracy in Poland. Currently, the Foundation operates as part of the Environmental Partnership Consortium (q.v.), which supports grassroots environmental action in Central Europe. Sister foundations operate within the framework of the Consortium in the Czech Republic, Slovakia and Hungary.

Activities: Helps NGOs and local communities to solve environmental problems by supporting partnership action with the Government, businesses, universities and individuals. Provides direct financial support and technical assistance for community development. Maintains an Environmental Information Centre, disseminating information through weekly and monthly bulletins, providing a helpline for members and access to information resources.

Geographical Area of Activity: Poland.

Restrictions: Grants made only to NGOs registered in, and operating in, Poland.

Publications: Annual Report; *International Trails & Greenways Directory; Caring for the Land; A Decade of Nurturing the Grassroots; A frog, a wooden house, a stream and a trail; Ten Years of Community Revitalization in Central Europe.*

Management Board: Rafał Serafin (Pres.); Joanna Wegrzycka (Vice-Pres.).

Principal Staff: Office Man. Mariola Kontykiewicz-Biel.

Address: 31-028 Kraków, sw. Krzyża St 5/6.

Telephone: (12) 4302443; **Fax:** (12) 4302465; **Internet:** www
.fpds.pl; **e-mail:** biuro@fpds.pl.

Fundacja Pogranicze (Borderland Foundation)

Established in 1990 to carry out cultural activities in Central and Eastern Europe.

Activities: Operates in the countries of Central and Eastern Europe in the fields of the arts and humanities, education, and law and human rights, through self-conducted programmes, conferences, training courses and publications. Maintains a library and an arts and cultural centre.

Geographical Area of Activity: Central and Eastern Europe.

Publications: *Krasnogruda* (quarterly, in Polish and English); also history books, literary criticism, poetry; newsletters.

Finance: Annual budget approx. 1,500,000 new złotys.

Management Board: Krzysztof Czyżewski (Pres.).

Principal Staff: Dir Małgorzata Sporek-Czyżewska.

Address: 16-500 Sejny, ul. Piłsudskiego 37.

Telephone: (87) 5162189; **Fax:** (87) 5162765; **Internet:** www .pogranicze.sejny.pl; **e-mail:** kris@pogranicze.sejny.pl.

Fundacja Pomocy Wzajemnej Barka (Barka Foundation)

Founded in 1989 by Tomasz Sadowski, Maria Garwolińska and Barbara Sadowska to promote improved living and working conditions.

Activities: Operates in Poland, France, Germany the United Kingdom and the Netherlands in the field of social welfare, through self-conducted programmes, scholarships, prizes, conferences, training courses and publications; assists the homeless through self-help projects throughout Poland; encourages co-operation and communication between NGOs. Operates four programmes in the fields of the community, social education, employment opportunity and housing. The Foundation also established the Poland-wide Confederation for Social Employment, which provides support to the long-term unemployed and homeless people.

Geographical Area of Activity: France, Germany, the Netherlands, the United Kingdom, Poland.

Publications: *Citizens' Initiatives of Greater Poland*; *Barka Bulletin*; Financial Report.

Finance: The Government of Poland provides 5% of the Foundation's funds.

Trustees: Tomasz Sadowski (Pres.); Barbara Sadowska (Vice-Pres.).

Principal Staff: Teresa Belter.

Address: 61-003 Poznań, ul. sw. Wincentego 6/9.

Telephone: (61) 6682300; **Fax:** (61) 8729050; **Internet:** www .barka.org.pl; **e-mail:** barka@barka.org.pl.

Fundacja Pro Bono II (Pro Bono Foundation)

Established in 1993 by a group of people connected with the pastoral services for the universities affiliated with the Rectory of St Ann's Academic Church in Warsaw.

Activities: Supports NGOs in Poland active in the areas of charity, cultural and educational work, as well as funding Catholic organizations, the conservation of works of art and the promotion of the Catholic press. Funded projects include orphanages, symposia and scholarships, medical costs and community centres. The Foundation has also established an art gallery to promote the work of young artists.

Geographical Area of Activity: Poland.

Principal Staff: Pres. Bogdan Bartold.

Address: 00-322 Warsaw, ul. Krakowskie Przedmieście 68, Kościół Akademicki św. Anny.

Telephone: (22) 8269977; **Fax:** (22) 8269977; **Internet:** www .probono.art.pl; **e-mail:** fundacja@probono.org.pl.

Fundacja Rozwoju Demokracji Loaklnej (Foundation in Support of Local Democracy)

Founded in September 1989 by Prof. Jerzy Regulski, Andrzej Celićski, Aleksander Paszyński, Walerian Paćko and Jerzy Stępień to promote civic self-government at local level.

Activities: Operates in the fields of education, and law and human rights, through self-conducted programmes, grants to institutions, conferences, training courses, publications, Internet information systems and offering technical assistance. The Foundation's main activities are training and education programmes for local government officers, councillors, NGOs, community leaders and local businesspeople; and consulting services in the technical areas of local government. Also involved in sharing the Polish experience in building democracy with other countries of Central, Eastern and Southern Europe and Kazakhstan. Maintains national network of 16 regional centres and branches and three Colleges of Public Administration.

Geographical Area of Activity: Central, Eastern and Southern Europe, Kazakhstan and Poland.

Publications: Publications on local government, management, legal and economic issues.

Finance: Finance is provided by national and foreign sponsors, the Foundation's own income and programmes. Total assets 10,489,474 new złotys (31 Dec. 2009).

Supervisory Board: Adam Kowalewski (Chair.); Jan Król (Vice-Chair.).

Principal Staff: Pres. Prof. Jerzy Regulski.

Address: 01-552 Warsaw, plac Inwalidów 10.

Telephone: (22) 3228400; **Fax:** (22) 3228410; **Internet:** www .frdl.org.pl; **e-mail:** biuro@frdl.org.pl.

Fundacja Solidarności Polsko-Czesko-Słowackiej (Polish-Czech-Slovak Solidarity Foundation)

Established in 1990 by J. Broda, Z. Janas, M. Jasiński and M. Piotrowski 'Ducina' for the support of Polish-Czech-Slovak solidarity activities.

Activities: Operates in Central and Eastern Europe in the areas of aid to less-developed countries, the arts and humanities, education, independent media, international affairs, through self-conducted programmes, grants to institutions, conferences, training courses and publications.

Geographical Area of Activity: Central and Eastern Europe.

Board: Jarosław Szostakowski (Pres.).

Address: 00-031 Warsaw, ul. Szpitalna 5/5.

Telephone: (22) 8289128; **Fax:** (22) 8289129; **Internet:** www .spczs.engo.pl; **e-mail:** fundacja@spczs.engo.pl.

Fundacja Współpracy Polsko-Niemieckiej/Stiftung für Deutsch–Polnische Zusammenarbeit (Foundation for German–Polish Co-operation)

Established in 1991 by the Governments of Poland and Germany to sponsor non-commercial projects of German-Polish interest.

Activities: Operates in Poland in the fields of the arts and humanities, conservation and the environment, education, international affairs, medicine and health, science and technology, and social welfare and social studies, through research, grants to institutions, scholarships and fellowships, conferences, training courses and publications. Maintains office in Berlin. Allocated 15,437,115 new złotys to a total of 657 projects in 2010.

Geographical Area of Activity: Germany and Poland.

Publications: Annual Report; Polish foundation traditions.

Board of Trustees: Markus Meckel (Co-Pres.); Edmund Wnuk-Lipinski (Co-Pres.).

Principal Staff: Dirs Albrecht Lempp, Margaret Lawrowska.

Address: 00-108 Warszawa, ul. Zielna 37.

Telephone: (22) 3386200; **Fax:** (22) 3386200; **Internet:** www .fwpn.org.pl; **e-mail:** sekretariat@fwpn.org.pl.

Fundacja Wspomagania Wsi (Rural Development Foundation)

Established in 1999 as a result of the merger of the Water Supply Foundation and the Agricultural Foundation. Aims to support economic, social, cultural, educational and pro-environmental initiatives of rural and small town inhabitants, so as to contribute to the comprehensive, sustainable development of rural Poland.

Activities: Aims to support economic, social, cultural, educational and pro-environmental initiatives in rural Poland, through providing loans and credits to businesses, local governments, public benefit agencies and individuals. Also makes grants for infrastructural development, including funding the construction of village clubs, and offers training and runs programmes for local youth. Programme themes are: microloans; development of ICT use in rural areas of Poland; training for local NGO leaders; support of children and young people in education; and local cultural heritage preservation. The Foundation also operates an exchange or partnership programme with organizations in other countries of Europe.

Geographical Area of Activity: Poland.

Publications: Annual Report; information brochures; manuals.

Finance: Total assets 165,210,058 new złotys (Dec. 2008).

Council: Prof. Aleksander Szeptycki (Chair.); Adam Tanski; Andrzej Wasowicz.

Principal Staff: Pres. Piotr Szczepanski.

Address: 01-022 Warsaw, ul. Bellottiego 1.

Telephone: (22) 6362570; **Fax:** (22) 6366270; **Internet:** www .fundacjawspomaganiawsi.com; **e-mail:** fww@fww.org.pl.

Institute for Private Enterprise and Democracy—IPED

Established in 1993 by the Polish Chamber of Commerce to carry out research into the Polish private sector and economic policy, and to support the development of the private sector.

Activities: Operates in Poland in the areas of economic affairs and social welfare, through research, conferences and the publication of policy and economic reports. Major projects include: a report on the state of the private sector in Poland; a study on the reform of the Polish tax system; business ethics and social responsibility; Polish women in private business; regional development and the promotion of entrepreneurship; legislative monitoring; and monitoring barriers to the development of small- and medium-sized enterprises and their financing in Poland. Supports the network of Chambers of Commerce in Poland.

Geographical Area of Activity: Poland.

Publications: *Influence of Justice on SME Development in Poland*; *Capital Investment Funding in Poland*; *Co-operation of NGOs with Local Self-Government*; *Economic Reform Today*; *Development of Entrepreneurship in Rural Areas*; *Sources of Inflation in Poland*; *Informal Labour Market*; *Dilemmas and Chances of Rural Development*; numerous other reports.

Board: Mieczysław Bak (Pres.); Prof. Tomasz Mroczkowski (Vice-Pres.).

Principal Staff: CEO Mieczysław Bak.

Address: 00-074 Warsaw, ul. Trebacka 4, Room 319.

Telephone: (22) 6309801; **Fax:** (22) 8262596; **Internet:** www .iped.pl; **e-mail:** iped@kig.pl.

J&S Pro Bono Poloniae Foundation

Established by the J&S Group in 2001 to support initiatives that help active and ambitious people and that hold a promise of success, as well as ideas and proposals designed to support the development of culture and combat all forms of social pathology, including intolerance and discrimination.

Activities: The Foundation makes donations to NGOs running programmes in the areas of children and young people and culture, as well as funding educational scholarships for gifted young people.

Geographical Area of Activity: Poland.

Publications: Annual Reports.

Principal Staff: Chair. Ryszard Romanowski.

Address: 00-722 Warsaw, ul. Podchorążych 83/4.

Telephone: (22) 8408340; **Fax:** (22) 8516093; **Internet:** www .jsprobono.pl; **e-mail:** fundacja@jsprobono.pl.

Microfinance Centre—MFC

Established in 1997, a grass-root network of 105 member institutions that play an active role in shaping the microfinance sector, to advance economic development, improve employment, and alleviate poverty through microfinance in Europe and Central Asia.

Activities: MFC plays an important role in delivering microfinance services, offering support and development to a wide range of financial institutions, promoting microfinance among policy-makers, regulators, the formal banking sector and investors. Maintains office in Kyrgyzstan.

Geographical Area of Activity: Europe and Central Asia.

Publications: *MFC Newsletter.*

Finance: Total assets 8,502,063 złotys (2008); annual revenue 6,518,461 złotys, expenditure 5,076,184 złotys (2008).

Board of Directors: Jhale Hajiyeva (Chair.); Emmanuel de Lutzel (Vice-Chair.); Cristian Jurma (Treas.).

Principal Staff: Exec. Dir Grzegorz Galusek; Deputy Dir Katarzyna Pawlak.

Address: 00-666 Warsaw, ul. Noakowskiego 10/38.

Telephone: (22) 6223465; **Fax:** (22) 6223485; **Internet:** www .mfc.org.pl; **e-mail:** microfinance@mfc.org.pl.

POLSAT Foundation

Established by POLSAT, a television company.

Activities: Operates in the areas of education and medicine and health, in particular for the benefit of children and young people.

Geographical Area of Activity: Poland.

Publications: Newsletter.

Principal Staff: Exec. Pres. Malgorzata Zak; Vice-Pres. Elzbieta Zajacowna.

Address: 04-175 Warsaw, ul. Ostrobramska 77.

Telephone: (22) 5145555; **Fax:** (22) 5144730; **Internet:** www .fundacjapolsat.pl; **e-mail:** fundacja@polsat.com.pl.

Polska Fundacja Upowszechniania Nauki—PFUN
(Polish Foundation for Science Advancement—PFSA)

Established in 1990 by the Polish Academy of Sciences, the Society for the Advancement of Sciences and Arts, the Society of the Polish Free University, the Scientific Publications Distribution Centre and the Polish Scientific Film Association. The PFSA is a leading non-profit organization working for the dissemination of Polish science in Poland and abroad, and for the diffusion of foreign science in Poland.

Activities: Operates nationally and internationally in the fields of education and science and technology, through conducting research and promoting public understanding of science; publishing books and producing films and audio-visual materials for teaching and study; organizing courses, seminars and competitions; supporting the activities of Polish institutions and scientific associations in Poland and abroad in the advancement of science; granting aid to foreign organizations seeking to promote knowledge in Poland of the scientific achievements of their respective countries. Three major achievements of the Foundation are Internet at Schools, a programme initiated by the President of the Polish Republic; the Postgraduate Science Communication and Media Studies programme undertaken jointly with the Institute for Literary Research of the Polish Academy of Sciences; and establishing the Open Television University in Poland.

Geographical Area of Activity: International.

Publications: Brochures and books; annual reports.

Principal Staff: Dir Wojciech Wiśniewski.

Address: 00-901 Warsaw, Pałac Kultury i Nauki, skr.poczt.27, pok. 2104, 2105, 2107.

Telephone: (22) 6209174; **Fax:** (22) 6209174; **Internet:** pfun .pan.pl; **e-mail:** pfun@pan.pl.

Portugal

FOUNDATION CENTRE AND CO-ORDINATING BODY

Centro Português de Fundações—CPF (Portuguese Foundation Centre)

Established in 1993 by the Fundação Oriente (q.v.) in association with the Fundação Eng. António de Almeida and the Fundação Calouste Gulbenkian (qq.v.).

Activities: A membership organization of more than 100 foundations and trusts, which operates to promote the interests of foundations in Portugal through co-operation and support. Organizes meetings and conferences.

Geographical Area of Activity: Portugal.

Publications: *Portuguese Foundation Centre Directory*; Annual Report.

Board of Directors: Emílio Rui Vilar (Chair.).

Principal Staff: Gen. Sec. Mário Curveira Santos.

Address: Rua Rodrigo da Fonseca 178, 6° Esq., 1070-239 Lisbon.

Telephone: (21) 3538280; **Fax:** (21) 3538285; **Internet:** www .cpf.org.pt; **e-mail:** cpf@cpf.org.pt.

FOUNDATIONS, TRUSTS AND NON-PROFIT ORGANIZATIONS

Fundação Eng. António de Almeida (Eng. António de Almeida Foundation)

Founded in 1969 at the bequest of Eng. António de Almeida to promote art, culture and education for all people.

Activities: The Foundation sponsors art exhibitions and musical recitals; makes grants to cultural institutions in Portugal and to Portuguese graduates for research work; awards the Eng. António de Almeida Prize annually to students from six universities, who have excelled in dedication to their studies; holds international conferences; and issues cultural publications. The Foundation also maintains a museum of art to exhibit items collected by the founder, which include furniture, textiles, porcelain, paintings, time-pieces and an important numismatic collection.

Publications: Annual Report; periodical magazines in the spheres of literature, philosophy, ethnography and museums, art, culture and science.

Board of Directors: Dr Fernando Aguiar-Branco (Pres.).

Principal Staff: Exec. Dir. Eugénia Aguiar-Branco.

Address: Rua Tenente Valadim 231–325, 4100-479 Porto.

Telephone: (22) 6067418; **Fax:** (22) 6004314; **Internet:** www .feaa.pt; **e-mail:** fundacao@feaa.pt.

Fundação Assistência Médica International—AMI (International Medical Assistance Foundation)

Established in December 1984 by Dr Fernando de la Vieter Nobre to provide humanitarian aid world-wide.

Activities: Operates internationally in the fields of humanitarian aid to less-developed countries, education, medicine and health, and social welfare, through self-conducted programmes, grants to institutions, conferences, training courses and publications. AMI's activities are organized in four pillars: Medical Assistance; Social Action; Environmental Care; and Raising Awareness. Awards the AMI Journalism Against Indifference prize.

Geographical Area of Activity: Portugal and international.

Publications: *AMI Notícias* (quarterly).

Finance: Total assets €34,312,980 (31 Dec. 2009); annual income €13,551,150, annual expenditure €13,551,150 (2009).

Trustees: Fernando José de La Vieter Ribeiro Nobre (Pres.); Maria Leonor de La Vieter Ribeiro Nobre (Vice-Pres.).

Principal Staff: Sec.-Gen. Maria Luísa Nemésio.

Address: Rua José do Patrocínio, 49, 1959-003 Lisbon.

Telephone: (21) 8362100; **Fax:** (21) 8362199; **Internet:** www .ami.org.pt; **e-mail:** fundacao.ami@ami.org.pt.

Fundação da Casa de Mateus (Mateus House Foundation)

Established in 1970 by Francisco de Sousa Botelho de Albuquerque, Count of Mangualde, Vila Real and Melo to maintain the Casa de Mateus, study and publish its archives, and promote scientific, cultural and pedagogical activities.

Activities: The Foundation operates in the fields of the arts and humanities, including music, history and literature; and science. Part of the House is maintained as a museum. The Foundation awards the Prémio D. Diniz and the Prémio Morgado de Mateus in the field of literature. Courses in theatre, sculpture, drawing and painting are also held at the Foundation, as are exhibitions and seminars. The Foundation chairs the International Institute Casa de Mateus, established in 1986 by Portuguese public universities, academies and scientific institutes, which organizes meetings of national and foreign scientists. Has set up an artists' residence for artists from any country.

Geographical Area of Activity: Portugal.

Board of Directors: Fernando de Albuquerque (Chair.); Adriano Jordão (Artistic Dir).

Principal Staff: Chief Exec. Fernando de Albuquerque.

Address: 5000-291 Vila Real.

Telephone: (25) 9323121; **Fax:** (25) 9326553; **Internet:** www .casademateus.com; **e-mail:** casademateus@casademateus .pt.

Fundação Centro Cultural de Belém (Belém Cultural Centre Foundation)

Established in 1991 by the Government of Portugal and several Portuguese companies to promote culture and the arts, especially Portuguese culture. Formerly known as Fundação das Descobertas.

Activities: The Foundation's main aims are to manage the Belém Cultural Centre, run a permanent museum and a document centre, and facilitate exchanges with similar Portuguese and foreign institutions.

Geographical Area of Activity: Portugal.

Board of Directors: Vasco Graça Moura (Chair.).

Principal Staff: Fiscal Council Pres. Pedro Matos Silva.

Address: Praça do Império, 1449-003 Lisbon.

Telephone: (21) 3612400; **Fax:** (21) 3612500; **Internet:** www .ccb.pt; **e-mail:** ccb@ccb.pt.

Fundação Champalimaud (Champalimaud Foundation)

The Champalimaud Foundation was created in 2004 in accordance with the will of the late Portuguese industrialist and entrepreneur, António de Sommer Champalimaud.

Activities: The Champalimaud Foundation primarily supports work in the areas of cancer and neuroscience. It is one of the Foundation's primary concerns that breakthroughs in research laboratories should bring benefits to those most in need—patients receiving clinical treatment. For this reason, the Champalimaud Foundation supports translational cancer research, linking the 'bench to the bedside', and bringing the most up-to-date scientific advances to those most in need. A particular focus of this work is the prevention, diagnosis and treatment of metastatic diseases. The Champalimaud Cancer Clinic, housed in the Champalimaud Centre for the Unknown, Lisbon, began receiving patients in 2011. The Champalimaud Foundation is also committed to driving forward advances in the area of neuroscience research. The Champalimaud Neuroscience Programme aims to unravel the neural basis of behaviour and currently comprises 15 research groups. In addition to its in-house activities, the Foundation supports an outreach programme to aid the fight against global blindness. The €1m.-Antonio Champalimaud Vision Award was launched in 2006 to support this fight from two angles—blindness prevention interventions in the developing world and outstanding vision research. This Award is the world's largest in the field and has already added €5m. to organizations working to alleviate the burden of vision disorders. In laboratory-based research, clinical treatment, and support of public health initiatives, the Champalimaud Foundation strives to bring the benefits of biomedical science to those most in need.

Geographical Area of Activity: World-wide.

Scientific Committee: James Watson (Chair.).

Principal Staff: Pres. Leonor Beleza; Dir of Champalimaud Centre for the Unknown Zvi Fuks; Clinical Dir António Parreira; Dir of Champalimaud Neuroscience Programme Zachary Mainen.

Address: Champalimaud Centre for the Unknown, Av. Brasilia s/n, 1400-038 Lisbon.

Internet: www.fchampalimaud.org; **e-mail:** info@fundacaochampalimaud.pt.

Fundação Cidade de Lisboa (City of Lisbon Foundation)
Founded in 1989.

Activities: Operates nationally and in Angola, Cape Verde, Mozambique and São Tomé and Príncipe, in the fields of aid to less-developed countries and education, through self-conducted programmes, grants to individuals and institutions, scholarships and prizes, and conferences.

Geographical Area of Activity: Portugal, Angola, Cape Verde, Mozambique and São Tomé and Príncipe.

Publications: Several books.

Board of Trustees: Eugénio Anacoreta Correia (Pres.).

Principal Staff: Pres. of Board of Dirs Álvaro João Duarte Pinto Correia; Sec.-Gen. José Filipe Nogueira.

Address: Campo Grande 380, 1700-097 Lisbon.

Telephone: (21) 7568241; **Fax:** (21) 7568248; **Internet:** www.fundacaocidadedelisboa.pt; **e-mail:** fclisboa@mail.telepac.pt.

Fundação Dom Manuel II (Dom Manuel II Foundation)
Established in August 1966 by Dona Augusta Viktoria, Duchess of Bragança, widow of King Dom Manuel II of Portugal, to help Portuguese emigrants.

Activities: Operates in the areas of aid to less-developed countries, conservation and the environment, education and social welfare, through self-conducted programmes, awarding prizes, and organizing conferences and training courses. Provides help in the areas of housing, integration of Portuguese emigrants into local communities, and education. Has established a subsidiary in Timor-Leste, the Timorese Cultural Foundation, which operates a printing factory.

Geographical Area of Activity: Europe, Portuguese-speaking Africa, Timor-Leste and Brazil.

Publications: *Futuro Real* (Bulletin).

Finance: Funded by donations and income from rented property.

Trustees: The Duke of Bragança (Pres.).

Principal Staff: Man. Nelson Figueiredo; Sec. Rosa Pratas; Contact Francisco de Mendia.

Address: Rua Duques de Bragança 10, 1200-162 Lisbon.

Telephone: (21) 3423705; **Fax:** (21) 3420225; **Internet:** www.fdommanuel.org; **e-mail:** fdommanuel@portugalmail.pt.

Fundação EDP (EDP Foundation)
Established in 2004, a corporate foundation, to foster knowledge of science and technology in the areas of energy and the environment, preservation of historical heritage, and to promote culture and the arts.

Activities: Operates in the areas of culture and the arts, preservation of historical heritage and the environment; runs an Electricity Museum, Study Centre (Energy and Environment) and Documentation Centre. Aims to convert the campus at the Tejo Power Station into a scientific and cultural unit.

Geographical Area of Activity: Portugal (except the Azores and Madeira islands).

Principal Staff: Dir, Corporate Social Responsibility Guilherme Collares Pereira.

Address: Av. de Brasília, Central Tejo, 1300-598 Lisbon.

Telephone: (210) 028130; **Fax:** (210) 028104; **Internet:** www.fundacao.edp.pt; **e-mail:** fundacaoedp@edp.pt.

Fundação Ricardo do Espírito Santo Silva (Ricardo do Espírito Santo Silva Foundation)
Founded in 1953 by Ricardo do Espírito Santo Silva to preserve the tradition of decorative arts and crafts threatened by modern industrial development.

Activities: Maintains 18 workshops devoted to producing reproductions and to restoration in 21 traditional crafts, including cabinet-making, marquetry, decorative and enamel paintings, Arraiolos carpets, bookbinding, book decoration, chiselling, hand-made gold leaf, etc. Also runs workshops and restoration projects in Brazil, and collaborates with other organizations to form cultural associations and run exhibitions. The Foundation runs the Portuguese Museum-School for Decorative Arts, the High School of Decorative Arts and the Arts and Crafts Institute.

Geographical Area of Activity: Portugal.

Board of Directors: Dr Luís Ferreira Calado (Pres.).

Principal Staff: Sec. of the Bd Ana Mafalda Machado da Cruz.

Address: Rua de S. Tomé 90, 1100-564 Lisbon.

Telephone: (21) 8814600; **Fax:** (21) 8814637; **Internet:** www.fress.pt; **e-mail:** geral@fress.pt.

Fundação Calouste Gulbenkian (Calouste Gulbenkian Foundation)
Founded in 1956 by Calouste Sarkis Gulbenkian as a perpetual foundation to operate in the general fields of charity, art, education and science, in Portugal and abroad.

Activities: Provides grants on public health and social exclusion issues, focusing on a spectrum of activities, which includes healthcare, hospital services and equipment, preventive and palliative medicine, childcare and welfare of the elderly, and migrants, among other strategic priorities periodically reassessed. In the arts, the Foundation maintains a museum, containing the founder's private collection, and a Modern Art Centre, which comprises and exhibits the Foundation's collection of contemporary art works. The Foundation also supports the creation, dissemination and research on plastic arts architecture and design; history of art; archaeology and heritage; cinema and theatre. The Foundation's Music Department manages two artistic groups, an orchestra and a choir, and annually promotes a music season. In education, the Foundation promotes educational development in Portugal, in particular through projects and activities in the area of lifetime training; the use of new technologies in education; the acquisition of new skills and know-how to increase the educational/training system effectiveness; the development of basic training areas; and all activities contributing to the full development of children, young people and adults, in emotional, cognitive, social and cultural terms. The Foundation also houses an art library with more than 220,000 documents, including books, audiovisual and multimedia records. In science, the Foundation provides grants for the stimulation of creativity and scientific research; supports the promotion of links between science and culture; supports the strengthening of interaction between science and society. The Instituto Gulbenkian de Ciência (IGC) undertakes scientific research and postgraduate training in biomedicine, helping to train new national scientific community leadership. It operates as a host institution, providing an intellectual environment in addition to premises and services to young Portuguese and overseas researchers for setting up autonomous research groups and developing their projects over specific time periods.

Geographical Area of Activity: International.

Publications: Annual Report and accounts; *Newsletter* (monthly); *Colóquio-Letras* (periodical).

Finance: Total assets €2,930,800 (2010).

Board of Trustees: Emílio Rui Vilar (Pres.).

Principal Staff: Sec. to the Board of Trustees Rui Esgaio.

Address: Av. de Berna 45A, 1067-001 Lisbon.

Telephone: (21) 7823000; **Fax:** (21) 7823021; **Internet:** www .gulbenkian.pt; **e-mail:** info@gulbenkian.pt.

Fundação Luso-Americana para o Desenvolvimento (Luso-American Development Foundation)

Founded in 1985 to assist Portugal in its development, mainly by building strong ties with the USA.

Activities: Operates in the fields of business, technology and science, education and culture. Provides funding for scholarships, internships, exchanges, conferences, publications, medical, scientific and technological research, business and trade development. The Foundation aims to implement projects in the following areas: research programmes and co-operation with US universities and other institutions; modernization of national and regional administration; environmental protection; cultural programmes; and co-operation with Portuguese-speaking African countries. Also maintains a documentation centre, housing around 6,000 items.

Geographical Area of Activity: Portugal, the USA and Portuguese-speaking countries in Africa.

Publications: Annual Report; brochures; newsletter; monographs; *Parallel Magazine* (in Portugese and English).

Finance: An initial fund of €85,000,000 was provided by the Government of Portugal. Annual funds disbursed €3,611,053 (2010). Annual income €17,321,254, annual expenditure €15,055,816 (2010).

Board of Trustees: Maria Teodora Osório Pereira Cardoso (Chair.).

Principal Staff: Pres. of Exec. Council Maria de Lurdes Rodrigues; Sec.-Gen. José Sá Carneiro.

Address: Rua do Sacramento à Lapa 21, 1249-090 Lisbon.

Telephone: (21) 3935800; **Fax:** (21) 3963358; **Internet:** www .flad.pt; **e-mail:** fladport@flad.pt.

Fundação Oriente (Orient Foundation)

Established in 1988, a private institution that aims to encourage the maintenance and strengthening of historical and cultural ties between Portugal and Asia, particularly Macau, so as to bring the Macanese communities around the world into closer contact.

Activities: The Foundation carries out and supports cultural, educational, artistic and philanthropic activities. It awards funding to the following activities: exhibitions, cinema/video, theatre, music, dance, publications, conferences, festivals, health, philanthropic and social activities, and heritage recovery. Also provides support for Macau communities; conducts research; awards scholarships and prizes; and co-operates with other organizations. Established the Documentation

Centre which works to strengthen historical, cultural, scientific and artistic links between Portugal and countries and territories in the Far East. Operates primarily in Portugal but also in Macau, the People's Republic of China, India, East Timor, Japan, Thailand, Malaysia, and territories of the Far East which have cultural and historic links with Portugal and where Macanese communities exist. Also a founding member of the European Foundation Centre and the Portuguese Foundation Centre (qq.v.), which was established in 1993. Opened the Museu do Oriente in 2008.

Geographical Area of Activity: Europe, South-East Asia and the Far East.

Publications: Annual Report; publications relating to historical and cultural relations between Portugal and Asia; *Oriente Magazine*.

Finance: Total assets €300,482,740 (2009); annual expenditure €16,083,715 (2009).

Board of Trustees: Prof. Dr João José Fraústo da Silva (Chair.).

Principal Staff: Chair. Bd of Dirs Dr Carlos Augusto Pulido Valente Monjardino.

Address: Rua do Salitre 66, 1269-065 Lisbon.

Telephone: (21) 3585200; **Fax:** (21) 3527042; **Internet:** www .foriente.pt; **e-mail:** info@foriente.pt.

Fundação Eça de Queiroz (Eça de Queiroz Foundation)

Established in September 1990 by the estate of Maria de Graça Salema de Castro, widow of the grandson of the novelist José Maria de Eça de Queiroz, and the J. P. Vinhos company. The Foundation operates as a cultural organization that promotes the works of the novelist Eça de Queiroz nationally and internationally, maintains the Casa de Tormes museum and promotes the culture of the Tormes region.

Activities: Promotes Portuguese culture, education, tourism and agriculture; summer courses for Portuguese and foreign university students and teachers; conferences about Eça de Queiroz in Portugal and abroad; chamber concerts and educational activities.

Geographical Area of Activity: Portugal, Europe, USA and Brazil.

Publications: *Queirosiana* (literary magazine, 2 a year).

Finance: Funded through entrance fees to the museum, sales of wine and books, government subsidies and corporate donations.

Administration Board: Maria da Graça Almeida Salema de Castro (Pres.).

Principal Staff: Finance Sec. Anabela Rodrigues Cardoso; Cultural Sec. Sandra Melo.

Address: Caminho de Jacinto, 3110 Quinta de Tormes, Santa Cruz do Douro, 4640-424 Baiao.

Telephone: (25) 4882120; **Fax:** (25) 4885205; **Internet:** www .feq.pt; **e-mail:** info@feq.pt.

Fundação de Serralves (Serralves Foundation)

Established in 1989 as a partnership between the Government of Portugal and a group of companies and other institutions (now numbering around 170) to promote contemporary art and to raise public awareness of environmental issues.

Activities: The Foundation operates nationally and internationally in the areas of the contemporary art and humanities, and conservation and the environment, through self-conducted programmes, conferences, environmental education programmes and publications. It organizes environmental conferences, seminars on the management of urban green areas and open-air classes and nature clubs; and promotes the arts through sponsorship of art exhibitions, conferences, dance, music and video production. The Foundation established a Museum of Contemporary Art in Porto in 1999.

Geographical Area of Activity: International.

Publications: Information brochures, exhibition catalogues; e-newsletter.

Board of Directors: Dr António Gomes de Pinho (Chair.); Vergílio Folhadela Moreira (Deputy Chair.); Dr António Lobo Xavier (Deputy Chair.).

Principal Staff: Man. Dir Odete Patrício; Museum Dir João Fernandes; Admin. and Financial Dir Sofia Castro.

Address: Rua D. João de Castro 210 4150-417 Porto.

Telephone: (22) 6156500; **Fax:** (22) 6156533; **Internet:** www.serralves.pt; **e-mail:** serralves@serralves.pt.

Fundação Mário Soares (Mário Soares Foundation)

Founded in 1991 by Dr Mário Soares, the former President of Portugal.

Activities: Promotes and sponsors cultural, scientific and educational projects in the fields of political science, international relations and human rights. Awards the Mário Soares Foundation Prize annually, maintains an archive and funds the João Soares Museum-House. Holds conferences and seminars in the areas of political science and contemporary history.

Geographical Area of Activity: Portugal.

Finance: Initial fund US $100,000,000.

Board of Directors: Mário Alberto Nobre Lopes Soares (Pres.); Maria Isabel Barroso Lopes Soares (Vice-Pres.).

Principal Staff: Sec.-Gen. Dr Carlos Barroso.

Address: Rua de S. Bento 176, 1200-821 Lisbon.

Telephone: (21) 3964179; **Fax:** (21) 3964156; **Internet:** www.fmsoares.pt; **e-mail:** fms@fmsoares.pt.

Fundação Arpad Szenes–Vieira da Silva (Arpad Szenes–Vieira da Silva Foundation)

Established in 1994 by the Portuguese Government, Lisbon Municipal Council, the Luso-American Development Foundation (q.v.), the Fundação Cidade de Lisboa (q.v.) and the Calouste Gulbenkian Foundation (q.v.) to promote and study the work of Arpad Szenes and Maria Helena Vieira da Silva.

Activities: Operates in the field of the arts and humanities, nationally through training courses, and nationally and internationally through research and conferences. The Foundation comprises a museum of the artists' works and works of other contemporary artists, and a study and documentation centre; it organizes exhibitions and conferences on modern art and cultural development, issues publications in the field of art criticism and 20th-century art history, and promotes exchanges with similar national and international institutions.

Geographical Area of Activity: Mainly Portugal and South America.

Publications: Catalogues of temporary exhibitions.

Finance: The Foundation is financed by the Ministry of Culture and other sponsors.

Board of Trustees: Manuel Pinho (Pres.).

Principal Staff: Dir Marina Bairrão Ruivo ; Deputy Dir Ivonne Felman Cunha Rego.

Address: Praça das Amoreiras 56/58, 1250-020 Lisbon.

Telephone: (21) 3880044; **Fax:** (21) 3880039; **Internet:** www.fasvs.pt; **e-mail:** fasvs@fasvs.pt.

Puerto Rico

FOUNDATIONS, TRUSTS AND NON-PROFIT ORGANIZATIONS

Fundación Comunitaria de Puerto Rico—FCPR (Puerto Rico Community Foundation)

Established in 1984; aims to promote community development, funding and philanthropy, so as to improve the socio-economic development of Puerto Rico.

Activities: Operates nationally, through community development programmes in areas including the arts, business–community relations and youth. More than 27% of its annual expenditure is directed towards youth programmes, including a programme to provide alternative education to adolescents who have dropped out of formal education and a university-based programme of youth volunteer service. Supports other non-profit organizations in Puerto Rico, promoting charitable work to solve social problems on the island. Also operates a regional Institute for the Development of Philanthropy (IDEFI), which provides training and technical assistance to philanthropic initiatives in other Caribbean countries.

Geographical Area of Activity: Latin America, the Caribbean, Puerto Rico.

Publications: Annual Report; educational newsletter; community newsletter; donor service newsletter.

Finance: Total assets US $26,086,517 (Dec. 2009); annual revenue $2,519,168, annual expenditure $3,154,496 (2009).

Board of Directors: René Pinto-Lugo (Pres.); César A. Rey-Hernández (Vice-Pres.); Aida Torres-Cruz (Sec.); Manuel Cidre (Treas.).

Principal Staff: Chief Exec. Dir Dr Nelson I. Colón Tarrats; Admin. Dir Juan J. Reyes Rivera; Finance Dir Noelia Marín Oquendo.

Address: POB 70362, San Juan, PR 00936-8362.

Telephone: 721-1037; **Fax:** 982-1673; **Internet:** www.fcpr.org; **e-mail:** fcpr@fcpr.org.

Qatar

FOUNDATIONS, TRUSTS AND NON-PROFIT ORGANIZATIONS

Qatar Foundation

Established in 1995 by HH Sheikh Hamad bin Khalifa ath-Thani, Emir of Qatar, to help convert the country's mineral wealth into durable human capital.

Activities: Operates in the fields of education, scientific research and community development. Aims to change Qatar into an advanced knowledge-based society, as a major research base, with some commercialization, helping to diversify the economy. The Foundation also addresses social issues to accelerate the human development process. Programmes are split into Education, Science and Research, and Community Development. Established a publishing house in partnership with Bloomsbury Publishing in 2008.

Geographical Area of Activity: Qatar.

Publications: *The Foundation* (magazine); radio channel QF Radio (93.7FM).

Board of Trustees: HH Sheikha Mozah bint Nasser al-Missned (Chair.); HH Sheikh Tamim bin Hamad al-Thani (Vice-Chair.).

Principal Staff: Pres. Dr Mohammad Fathy Saoud.

Address: POB 5825, Doha.

Telephone: 4540000; **Fax:** 4806117; **Internet:** www.qf.org.qa; **e-mail:** info@qf.org.qa.

Romania

FOUNDATION CENTRES AND CO-ORDINATING BODIES

CENTRAS—Assistance Centre for NGOs

Established in April 1995 to promote freedom of thought and creativity, education and free exchange of opinion and information based on democratic and humanitarian principles, through the development of Romania's non-profit sector.

Activities: Operates in the fields of NGO development, conservation and the environment, economic affairs, education, law and human rights, and social welfare, nationally through projects, research, conferences, training courses and publications, and internationally through projects and training courses.

Geographical Area of Activity: Romania.

Publications: *Attitudini* (magazine); *White Papers of the Romanian NGOs FORUM*.

Board of Trustees: Dorin Tudoran (Pres.).

Principal Staff: Exec. Dir. Viorel Micescu; Programmes Dir Ioana Olteanu.

Address: 011454 Bucharest, blvd Maresal Averescu 17, Pavilion 7, Et. 3, Sector 1.

Telephone: (21) 2230010; **Fax:** (21) 2230012; **Internet:** www.centras.ro; **e-mail:** office@centras.ro.

CIVITAS Foundation for Civil Society

Founded in October 1992 to stimulate local and regional development.

Activities: Works through developing and implementing local and regional development programmes; supporting local initiatives that seek to develop relations between local governments and the local population; providing specialist consultancy services in various fields for local governments; running training courses for local public officials; and supporting the establishment and functioning of NGOs. Maintains offices in Cluj-Napoca and Odorheiu Secuiesc.

Geographical Area of Activity: Romania.

Publications: Annual Report; *Civil Forum* (twice a year, magazine); books.

Finance: Annual income 2,405,057 lei, expenditure 2,198,283 lei (2010).

Board of Trustees: Gábor Kolumbán (Pres.).

Principal Staff: Regional Dirs Márton Balogh, Árpád Orbán.

Address: 400124 Cluj-Napoca, blvd 21 Decembrie 1989 108/22.

Telephone: (264) 590554; **Fax:** (264) 590555; **Internet:** www.civitas.ro; **e-mail:** office@civitas.ro.

Fundatia pentru Dezvoltarea Societatii Civile—FDSC (Civil Society Development Foundation)

Established in 1994 with a mission to offer information, financing, training and advocacy to develop the capacity of civil society organizations and communities and improve people's lives.

Activities: Supports the development of civil society through consultancy and lobbying (adopting and amending those regulating acts regarding the way in which NGOs run their activity); information (NGO database, *Voluntar* publication); training and consultancy (Foundation trainers provide courses covering 30 topics); research (surveys on civil society, needs assessment, NGO sustainability, etc.); and technical assistance in European Union Phare programmes and structural funds.

Geographical Area of Activity: Romania.

Publications: *Voluntar* (weekly magazine for volunteers); studies, including *Civicus Index on Civil Society, Social Watch World Report*.

Finance: Receives funding from a number of governmental and non-governmental sources, including the European Union, Central and East European Trust, World Learning Romania, Netherlands Governement, USAID, Concorde and Eurostep.

Board of Directors: Catalin Cretu (Pres.).

Principal Staff: Exec. Dir Ionut Sibian; Financial Dir Lucian Ionita; Communications Co-ordinator Ileana Timofte.

Address: Bucharest, Str. Orzari 86a, Sector 2.

Telephone: (21) 3100181; **Fax:** (21) 3100180; **Internet:** www.fdsc.ro; **e-mail:** office@fdsc.ro.

Romanian Donors' Forum (Forumul Donatorilor din România)

Established in November 1999 to offer grant-making instruments and services—the communication, co-ordination and advocacy means necessary for the development of foundations' capacity to act to support NGOs and the community; as of 2009 comprised 12 members.

Activities: The Forum's activities include: facilitating the exchange of information between grant-makers about their individual programmes and strategies; providing services to member foundations and promoting their interests; creating a framework for co-ordination and co-operation between grant-makers; promoting best practices in grant-making; providing information about the NGO and donor community to existing and potential grant-makers; disseminating information about foreign grant-makers and their changing priorities; raising awareness of possible new sources of funding available to the NGO sector; raising public awareness about grant-makers and the general concept of philanthropy; creating a common platform for the protection and promotion of organized philanthropy; gathering and disseminating information about the problems and priorities of organized philanthropy; and promoting and assisting the development of corporate philanthropy in Romania.

Geographical Area of Activity: Romania.

Publications: *Review of Donor Support for Non-Profit Sector in Romania*; *Nine Steps towards a Successful Annual Report: A Guide to Writing an Annual Report*; *The 2001 Review of the Romanian NGO Sector*; *Tendencies in the Dynamic of the Romanian NGO Sector*; Annual Report.

Governing Board: Tincuta Baltag (Pres.); Adriana Stoica (Vice-Pres.).

Principal Staff: Exec. Dir Magdalena Ciobanu Stoian.

Address: 010101 Bucharest, Str. Stirbei Voda 29, 3rd Floor, Apt 5, Sector 1.

Telephone: (21) 3118811; **Fax:** (21) 3118811; **Internet:** www.forumuldonatorilor.ro; **e-mail:** contact@donorsforum.ro.

FOUNDATIONS, TRUSTS AND NON-PROFIT ORGANIZATIONS

Black Sea University Foundation—BSUF

Established in 1992 by 21 members of the Romanian scientific and cultural community to develop better professional skills and increase knowledge through regional and international co-operation.

Activities: Operates internationally in the field of education, through training courses and workshops run by the Black Sea University, on topics in areas such as Peace Diplomacy, Ecology and Sea Resources, Economy and Management, Advanced and Applied Science, and Culture, Contemporary Problems and Future Studies. Courses are attended by scholars, professionals, government experts, etc. from around the world. The Foundation, in co-operation with national and international institutions, has established a number of permanent institutions, including a Conflict Prevention Studies Centre, a Laboratory for Information Technologies in Education an Applied Economy Centre and a Black Sea Universities Network. It also collaborates with universities in other countries, and with international organizations. The BSUF became the Head of Network of the Anna Lindh Foundation for Romania in 2007.

Geographical Area of Activity: Romania.

Publications: *Letter from the Black Sea University* (quarterly newsletter); *Millennium III* (quarterly, in English); papers and brochures.

Board: Prof. Mircea Malitza (Founding Pres.); Liviu Aurelian Bota (Pres.).

Principal Staff: Exec. Dir Cosmin Dugan.

Address: 761172 Bucharest 5, Calea 13 Septembrie 13, Casa Academiei Romane.

Telephone: (21) 2224118; **Fax:** (21) 2339125; **Internet:** www.bsuf.ro; **e-mail:** office@bsuf.ro.

Institutul Cultural Român (Romanian Cultural Institute)

Established in August 2003 following the restructuring of the Romanian Cultural Foundation and of the Romanian Cultural Foundation Publishing House.

Activities: The Foundation operates in the fields of the arts and humanities, education and science, through self-conducted programmes, grants, research, scholarships and fellowships, prizes, training courses and publications. It organizes several programmes, including grants to overseas students wishing to study in Romania; supports Romanian cultural institutes abroad; promotes relations with those interested in Romanian culture and civilization, and with Romanians living abroad; organizes international symposia, conferences and exhibitions; edits and distributes books, information bulletins, magazines, audio and video materials; encourages cultural exchange; and co-operates with similar institutions in other countries. The Institute also runs its own publishing concern.

Geographical Area of Activity: Romania.

Publications: *Curierul Românesc* (monthly); *Lettre Internationale* (quarterly); *Dilema* (weekly newspaper); *Transylvanian Review* (quarterly); *Contrafort* (monthly); *Destin Românesc* (quarterly); *Glasul Bucovinei* (quarterly); newsletter.

Finance: Partly self-financing, also receives government subsidies and.

Board of Directors: Horia-Roman Patapievici (Pres.); Tania Radu (Vice-Pres.); Mircea Mihăieș (Vice-Pres.).

Principal Staff: Sec.-Gen. Dan Croitoru; Dep. Sec.-Gen. Valentin Sandulescu.

Address: 011824 Bucharest, Aleea Alexandru 38, Sector 1.

Telephone: (31) 7100627; **Fax:** (31) 7100607; **Internet:** www.icr.ro; **e-mail:** icr@icr.ro.

Dinu Patriciu Foundation (Fundatia Dinu Patriciu)

Established in 2007 to promote education in Romania.

Activities: Supports Romanian education by implementing two of the largest private scholarship programmes in the country, awarding excellence in the field.

Geographical Area of Activity: Romania.

Publications: *Stiinta & Tehnica* (monthly science and technology magazine).

Finance: Annual revenue 28,460,934 new lei, expenditure 27,932,913 new lei (2010).

Board: Dinu Patriciu (Pres.).

Principal Staff: Gen. Man. Tincuta Apateanu.

Address: 020276 Bucharest, Bd Barbu Vacarescu 301–311, Sector 2.

Telephone: (31) 4254120; **Fax:** (31) 4254127; **Internet:** www.fundatiadinupatriciu.ro/en; **e-mail:** office@fundatiadinupatriciu.ro.

Soros Foundation Romania

Established in 1990 as the Soros Foundation for an Open Society Association, an independent foundation, part of the Soros foundations network.

Activities: The Foundation started with a clear mandate of developing programmes promptly and efficiently to fill the lack of civic initiatives and educational alternatives. In 1994–95 the Foundation's main role became creating opportunities and opening paths, instead of entirely building them. The main fields of activity continued to revolve around education, civil society, communication, culture and health. In 1997 the Foundation reflected the changes within Romanian society, being renamed Open Society Foundation, and focusing on four prior domains: public administration, legislative and judiciary reform, education, and public health. In 2000, in response to a need for expertise concentrated on key domains of reform, the Open Society Foundation restructured its most important programmes as 13 independent organizations, which now function as centres of expertise and public policies development, all united within a network: SON (Soros Open Network–Romania). Since 2003 the Foundation has chosen to intervene in the institutional reform and democratization process through advocacy activities, both directly and supporting other NGOs in their public initiatives. In March 2007 the SON changed its name to Soros Foundation Romania. Current projects include the Migration and Development programme, which started in 2006, studying work migration of Romanians in 1990–2006 and now the Romanian migration legislative framework; the Foreign Affairs Initiative; and the Decade of Roma Inclusion (2005–2015). The Foundation also runs two European structural projects: Rures—dedicated to social economy in Romanian rural areas—and EU Inclusive—dedicated to best practices experience on Roma work integration issues between Romania, Bulgaria, Spain and Italy.

Geographical Area of Activity: Romania.

Restrictions: Grants only to Romanian organizations or individuals.

Publications: *The Beneficial Regularisation of Immigration in Romania; Commentaries on the Romanian Constitution; Local Authorities face to face with the European Funds; Moldova: At the Crossroads; A Comparative Analysis of the Mining Fiscal Regime in Romania; Attitudes Towards Work in Romania; Political Culture in Romania; Immigrants in Romania: Perspectives and Risks; Enhancing the Contribution of Mining to Sustainable Development; Integrated Strategies for Natural Resource Exploitation; Roma: Life Stories; Effects of Migration: Children left at home – Risks and solutions.*

Finance: Annual budget US $2,458,125 (2009).

Council of Directors: Mircea Vasilescu (Pres.).

Principal Staff: Exec. Dir Gabriel Petrescu; Programmes Dir Radu Motoc; Finance Dir Ileana Musetescu.

Address: 010613 Bucharest, Sector 1, Str. Caderea Bastiliei 33.

Telephone: (21) 2121101; **Fax:** (21) 2121032; **Internet:** www.soros.ro; **e-mail:** info@soros.ro.

Russian Federation

FOUNDATION CENTRES AND CO-ORDINATING BODIES

CAF Russia—Charities Aid Foundation Russia

Established in 1993 by CAF—Charities Aid Foundation (q.v.).

Activities: Distributes grants provided by Russian and international donors, as well as providing support to companies and private philanthropists in the areas of planning of charitable and social projects that take into account the demands and interests of the donors, and the demands of the non-profit organizations in the regions where the projects are being carried out, and legal and financial advice in management of the projects. Also aims to develop new forms of philanthropy, including developing corporate giving, providing support to community foundations, and promoting payroll giving. Also carries out research work aimed at the study and development of different aspects of charitable activity in the Russian Federation, and promotes the development of civil society in the Russian Federation campaigning for improvement to Russian legislation regarding philanthropy and non-profit organizations and consultancy and training support for civil initiatives.

Geographical Area of Activity: Russian Federation.

Publications: *Money and Charity* (magazine, 6 a year).

Principal Staff: Dir Maria Chertok; Dir, Programmes and Donor Relations Polina Filippova; Dir, Legal and Policy Julia Chekmaryova; Dir, Finance Elena Orlova; Head of Communication Kirill Ezhov.

Address: 101000 Moscow, ul. Myasnitskaya 24/7, Bldg 1, Entrance 10, Floor 4, Office 102.

Telephone: (495) 792-59-29; **Fax:** (495) 792-59-86; **Internet:** www.cafrussia.ru; **e-mail:** nakramovskaya@cafrussia.ru.

International Bank of Ideas

Founded in 1988 to register and develop ideas and projects relevant to Russian society.

Activities: The organization provides ideas for projects in all areas: cultural, political, commercial, scientific and ecological. Develops ideas that are registered in a database and have received scientific and public support; has established the Moscow Business Library, a joint project with the 22nd Century Foundation in the USA; and provides business literature, reference books, a database, fax and e-mail services to enable organizations to make contacts abroad. The Enterprise Development Programme is carried out in conjunction with the Center for Citizen Initiatives, providing training for participants from small businesses; and the Center of International Foundations project aims to set up an information centre on charity organizations world-wide, in co-operation with the Soros foundations and the Open Society Institute—Moscow, now the Open Society Institute—Russia (q.v.).

Geographical Area of Activity: World-wide.

Principal Staff: Chair. Sergei N. Agapitov.

Address: 129301 Moscow, Boris Galushkina ul. 19, Bldg 1.

Telephone: (495) 283-09-19; **Fax:** (495) 283-09-19; **Internet:** www.bankideas.ru; **e-mail:** acn@aha.ru.

NGO Development Centre

Formerly the Russian-German Exchange Society; established in 1994.

Activities: Works as an information centre for the non-profit sector in the Russian Federation. Supports the development of a strong civil society in the Russian Federation through providing advice on forming an NGO, education, sector information exchange and organizational development, including advice on management, fundraising, relations with the public and media, accountancy, taxation and legal matters. Also sponsors international, national and regional conferences on issues concerning non-profit sector development in the Russian Federation.

Geographical Area of Activity: Russian Federation.

Publications: *Pchela* (magazine); bulletins, brochures and booklets; Annual Report.

Principal Staff: Exec. Dir Anna Skvortsova; Finance Man. Daria Shubin; Dir of Development Anna Kletsina.

Address: 191040 St Petersburg, 87 Ligovsky pr., office 300.

Telephone: (812) 718-37-94; **Fax:** (812) 118-37-94; **Internet:** www.crno.ru; **e-mail:** crno@crno.ru.

Russian Donors Forum

Founded in 1996 as a membership organization of around 25 Russian and non-Russian grant-making organizations; aims to enhance the effectiveness of organized grant-making to support the development of a democratic civil society in the Russian Federation.

Activities: Organizes the exchange of information between grant-makers and facilitating networks; provides information on the grant-making operating environment; provides services to support the development of member organizations; carries out research; organizes the Top Corporate Philanthropist Award.

Geographical Area of Activity: Russian Federation.

Publications: Annual Report.

Finance: Total grant revenue US $350,000, total grant expenditure $350,000 (2007/08).

Principal Staff: Exec. Sec. Natalya Kaminarskaya.

Address: 127055 Moscow, ul. Sushevskaya 9, Bldg 4, Office 311.

Telephone: (499) 978-59-93; **Fax:** (499) 973-34-78; **Internet:** www.donorsforum.ru; **e-mail:** dfinfo@donorsforum.ru.

Union of Charitable Organizations of Russia

Established in November 2000 as a membership organization to strengthen and develop philanthropy in the Russian Federation by establishing an efficient general system of charitable activity in Russia.

Activities: Aims to unite efforts of its members for the most efficient realization of charitable activity; supports members with legal, informational, financial and other kinds of support and protects interests of its members in relation to federal, regional and local authorities. Also promotes members' interaction with public associations, commercial and non-profit organizations in the Russian Federation, with the countries of the Commonwealth of Independent States and also with Russian communities. Its website contains the whole register of the Russian Federation charitable organizations. Also campaigns on fiscal issues and laws on charities' regulation.

Geographical Area of Activity: Russian Federation and the Commonwealth of Independent States.

Board of Directors: Pyotr Anatolyevich Ishchenko (Pres.); Yevgeny Vladislavovich Vodopianov (Sr Vice-Pres.).

Principal Staff: Dir-Gen. Vladimir Erikovich Riabtsev; Dep. Dir-Gen. Renat Salavatovich Shayakhmetov.

Address: 127299 Moscow, ul. Kosmonavta Volkova 10.

Telephone: (495) 225-13-16; **Fax:** (495) 490-96-78; **Internet:** www.sbornet.ru; **e-mail:** sbor@sbornet.ru.

FOUNDATIONS, TRUSTS AND NON-PROFIT ORGANIZATIONS

Dmitry Zimin Dynasty Foundation

Established in 2002 by Dr Dmitry Zimin, president emeritus of Vimpelkom, Inc., to support young and talented people in Russia and Russian research in the area of fundamental science.

Activities: A private foundation operating in the fields of education, science and youth through science and education support programmes, and community and cultural programmes. Educational projects include support for tertiary-level science students, for the teaching of physics and mathematics, and for scientific research.

Geographical Area of Activity: Russian Federation.

Finance: Annual budget US $10,268,147 (2010).

Board of Directors: Sergey Guriev (Chair.).

Principal Staff: Exec. Dir Anna Piotrovskaya; Dep. Exec. Dir Roza Khatskelevich; Financial Dir Natalia Shustova.

Address: 127006 Moscow, ul. First Tverskaya-Yamskaya 2, Bldg 1, Office 400.

Telephone: (495) 969-28-83; **Fax:** (495) 969-28-84; **Internet:** www.dynastyfdn.ru; **e-mail:** apiotrovskaya@dynastyfdn.ru.

Glasnost Defence Foundation—GDF

Established in 1991 to provide legal support to the media in Russia, and to monitor censorship.

Activities: Operates in the areas of the arts and humanities, and law and human rights, through providing legal and advocacy services to the media, and conducts day-to-day monitoring of abuses of media rights in the Russian Federation and the Commonwealth of Independent States (CIS). Carries out research and analysis, runs projects and organizes seminars for journalists, lawyers and human rights activists. Maintains 10 Legal Defence Centres throughout the Russian Federation, and a monitoring network in the CIS.

Geographical Area of Activity: Russian Federation and the Commonwealth of Independent States.

Publications: *Digest* (online, weekly).

Principal Staff: Pres. Alexey Simonov; CEO Nataliya Y. Maksimova.

Address: 119021 Moscow, 4 Zubovsky Blvd, Rm 432, POB 536.

Telephone: (095) 637-44-20; **Fax:** (095) 637-49-47; **Internet:** www.gdf.ru; **e-mail:** fond@gdf.ru.

Gorbachev Foundation (The International Foundation for Socio-Economic and Political Studies)

Founded by M. S. Gorbachev, G. I. Revenko and A. N. Yakovlev in December 1991 to conduct socio-economic and political studies.

Activities: Operates in the fields of education, international affairs, medicine and health, welfare and social studies, through self-conducted programmes, research, conferences, training courses and publications. Research programmes include: the Twenty-First Century—a Century of Challenges and Responses (the principal international research project), Building a New Russia's Statehood, Russia, Greater Europe, the Asian Flank of the Commonwealth of Independent States (CIS), and Russia and Europe in a New World Order. The Foundation also undertakes humanitarian work, providing funds for medicines and equipment to treat children with blood diseases. Assists foreign business people in finding business partners in the countries of the former USSR. Maintains offices and has partner organizations in the Russian Federation, Canada, Germany, Switzerland and the USA.

Geographical Area of Activity: World-wide.

Publications: Numerous books and information bulletins.

Executive Board: Mikhail Gorbachev (Pres.); Irina Mikhailovna Gorbacheva-Virganskaya (Vice-Pres.); Olga Zdravomyslova (Exec. Dir).

Address: 125167 Moscow, Leningradsky Prospect 39, Bldg 14.

Telephone: (495) 945-38-20; **Fax:** (495) 945-78-99; **Internet:** www.gorby.ru; **e-mail:** gf@gorby.ru.

New Eurasia Foundation

The New Eurasia Foundation, a Russian NGO, was founded in April 2004 by the USA-based Eurasia Foundation, the Brussels-based European Madariaga Foundation and Russia's Dynasty Foundation.

Activities: The Foundation implements territorial development projects; supports the modernization of regional education systems at all levels; supports the development of local self-governance and housing reform; supports the development of small and medium-sized businesses; creates programmes for young people; encourages the effective utilization of migrant workers; and improves the efficiency of the mass media.

Geographical Area of Activity: Russian Federation.

Restrictions: The New Eurasia Foundation does not accept grant applications, nor does it issue grants on the basis of the 'open door' principle. All grant programmes are only administered on the basis of competition and as part of the Foundation's current projects and programmes.

Publications: Newsletter and numerous reports; Annual Report.

Finance: Total assets 42,500,000 rubles; annual income 187,919,000 rubles, expenditure 191,996,000 rubles (2008).

Principal Staff: Pres. Andrey V. Kortunov; Assistant to the Pres. Elena Timofeeva; Dir of Financial and Analytical Dept Natalia Shuranova.

Address: 105120 Moscow, Third Syromyatnichesky per. 3/9, Bldg 1, 5th Floor.

Telephone: (495) 970-15-67; **Fax:** (495) 970-15-68; **Internet:** www.neweurasia.ru; **e-mail:** reception@neweurasia.ru.

New Perspectives Foundation

Established in 1995 by Nadia Seryakova to promote youth-leadership development, introduce democratic ideas, maintain stability and understanding in society, and carry out cultural, educational and philanthropic activities.

Activities: The goal of the Foundation is to develop and strengthen civil society by means of consolidated efforts of NGOs, business and government institutions of Russia. Operates in the fields of youth policy, business, culture, education, and developing leadership and life skills in young people; runs projects for children and young people; promotes human rights issues and democracy; supports social welfare projects in the regions of the Russian Federation; and runs cultural and educational programmes. Activities and initiatives include human rights teaching programmes, a youth service project, a connection programme (which makes small grants to community-based organizations), teaching new technologies to youth, life skills development, computers world-wide, millennium of information reality and other ICT projects.

Geographical Area of Activity: 75 regions of the Russian Federation.

Publications: More than 70 publications, including methodological materials; *Volunteerism Development Training Guidebook*; *Youth Life Skills Development through Volunteer Projects Implementation*; *Volunteer Project Design Training Guidebook*; *Teaching Human Rights*; *Life Skills Development* ; *Review of Russian Financial Education Programmes*; *Register of Methodologies and Programmes of Financial, Economic and Entrepreneurial Education used in Russian Schools and other Materials on Financial Literacy*.

Finance: Annual revenue and expenditure US $1,870,000 (2010).

Trustees: Nadia Seryakova (Founder and Pres.); V. Laschevsky (Dir-Gen.).

Principal Staff: Ekaterina Afonyushkina.

Address: 101000 Moscow, ul. 3/13 Maroseyka.

Telephone: (495) 621-11-85; **Fax:** (495) 621-14-73; **Internet:** www.npf.ru; **e-mail:** npf@npf.ru.

Non-Governmental Ecological Vernadsky Foundation

Established in 1995 by the OAO Gazprom Company, OAO UKOIL Oil Company, RAO EES Russii, Russian Federation Savings Bank, the Ministry of Public Health of the Russian Federation and the Russian Academy of Medical Sciences.

Activities: The Foundation supports environmentally orientated educational projects and represents the interests of people in Russia who are concerned about the environment, as well as socially responsible businesses. Has initiated and participates in environmental protection programmes in Russia. In 2000 the Foundation launched the idea of the Blue Corridor Project, the objective of which was to establish transport corridors for heavy-duty transport vehicles in central and eastern Europe using compressed natural gas as fuel rather than diesel. Each year, the Foundation supports events held in Russia and abroad, including conferences, forums and round tables on issues of sustainable development, with participation by scientists, representatives of government agencies and leaders of industry. A scholarship programme introduces talented young people to the scientific heritage of Academician V. I. Vernadsky, and encourages their interest in issues of environmental protection and balanced economic development. The Foundation has established 14 regional competition committees at leading universities in Russia, Ukraine, Belarus and Bulgaria. It also awards the V. I. Vernadsky Medal for Contributions to Sustainable Development, given for outstanding service in the area of sustainable economic, social and environmental development. The Foundation supports professional environmental experts, and efforts to bring them together to enhance the effectiveness of environmental protection in Russia. It also sponsors international exhibitions and promotes partnerships established with major foreign and domestic organizations.

Geographical Area of Activity: Russian Federation, Europe.

Restrictions: No grants to individuals.

Publications: *Noosphere* (journal); *The Ecological Encyclopedia*; *On the Way to Sustainable Development*; *Ecological Aspects of the Sustainable Development of Thermal Power Engineering in Russia*; Annual Report; scientific, educational, environmental and sustainable development literature.

Principal Staff: Pres. and Dir-Gen. Kirill Alexandrovich Stepanov; Academic Sec. Reviakin Alexander Ivanovich.

Address: 119019 Moscow, Gogolevsky blvd 17, office 517.

Telephone: (495) 740-01-00; **Fax:** (495) 290-47-92; **Internet:** www.vernadsky.ru; **e-mail:** info@vernadsky.ru.

The Vladimir Potanin Foundation

Established in 1999 by Vladimir Potanin, president of the Interros Company, to promote education and culture in the Russian Federation.

Activities: Through the grant-making process, the Foundation fosters the development of knowledge and professionalism, encourages volunteer activity and individual creativity, strengthens institutions, and elevates the development of philanthropy. The Foundation supports a number of programmes providing scholarships, promoting teacher training and awarding grants to socio-cultural projects. Federal scholarships are awarded to the best students from the leading state educational institutions in the Russian Federation who possess strong organizing skills and the ability to think creatively. Foundation promotes the development of young teachers who successfully combine pedagogical and scientific activities and provides grants to the most innovative museum projects.

Geographical Area of Activity: Russian Federation.

Finance: Annual expenditure US $6,786,000 (2010).

Board of Trustees: Vladimir Potanin (Pres.).

Principal Staff: Dir-Gen. Zelkova G. Larisa; Exec. Dir Natalia Samoilenko.

Address: 119180 Moscow, ul. Bolshaya Yakimanka 9.

Telephone: (495) 726-57-64; **Fax:** (495) 726-57-54; **Internet:** www.fondpotanin.ru; **e-mail:** info@fondpotanin.ru.

Russian Cultural Foundation

Founded in 1986, as the Cultural Foundation of the USSR, by prominent Soviet artists and scientists and by more than 50 public and government organizations, including unions of creative workers, major museums, research and education institutions, and ministries. Since 1996 the Foundation has operated as an NGO, and aims to enable all citizens to participate directly in the cultural development of the Russian Federation.

Activities: Engages in activities to preserve, assimilate and augment the cultural heritage of the past, and to promote the continuity of culture in the present and the future. The Foundation is particularly concerned with history, architecture, literature, music and education. Co-operates with government, business, NGOs and the public to finance its numerous cultural programmes. Main programmes are: the church and culture; culture and society; culture and the state; culture and creativity; the nation and culture; culture, education and science; cultural ambassadorships; the return of Russian culture from abroad; cultural policies; and culture and publishing activities. It supports cultural activities through making grants in all these areas. It also offers a variety of scholarships, including the D. S. Likhachev Award, made to students at institutions of higher musical education in Russia. Runs the Pari-Parizh lottery, and the Prestizh-Tur agency for the development of cultural tourism. Maintains 52 regional offices within and outside the Russian Federation.

Geographical Area of Activity: Russian Federation.

Publications: *Our Heritage* (6 a year); *The Russian Archive* (20 vols completed by 2011).

Finance: The Foundation is financed by voluntary donations from citizens, by the founding organizations and from the proceeds of its publishing and exhibition activities.

Board of Directors: Nikita S. Mikhalkov (Chair.).

Principal Staff: Gen. Man. Dmitry Levtchuk; Press Officer Dennis Artsibashev.

Address: 119019 Moscow, Gogolevskii bul 6/7.

Telephone: (495) 739-20-65; **Fax:** (495) 690-05-73; **Internet:** www.culture.ru; **e-mail:** info@culture.ru.

Victoria Children Foundation

Established in 2004 to ensure the well-being, equal opportunities and sustainable future of disadvantaged children in Russia and the former USSR.

Activities: Operates in the following programme areas: prevention of abandonment of children; support and family placement services for abandoned children; life skills development for children in care; advancing volunteerism and a supportive social environment for disadvantaged children.

Geographical Area of Activity: Russian Federation.

Principal Staff: Communications Officer Tatiana Babanova.

Address: 119002 Moscow, ul. Arbat 36/2 Stroenie 6.

Telephone: (495) 705-92-66; **Fax:** (495) 960-29-11; **Internet:** www.victoriacf.ru; **e-mail:** info@victoria-foundation.ru.

Saudi Arabia

FOUNDATIONS, TRUSTS AND NON-PROFIT ORGANIZATIONS

International Islamic Relief Organization of Saudi Arabia—IIROSA

Established in 1978 to alleviate suffering world-wide.

Activities: Aids victims of natural disasters and war, and other displaced persons, on an international scale. Runs programmes to provide education, medical aid and social support; and sponsors projects and small businesses whose work contributes to the objectives of the Organization. Maintains more than 100 offices in Saudi Arabia and world-wide.

Geographical Area of Activity: World-wide.

Publications: *Bulletin* (quarterly); newsletter (monthly); Annual Report (in Arabic, English and French); *Igatha* (magazine in Arabic); *Yanabie al-Khair* (newsletter in Arabic).

Principal Staff: Sec.-Gen. Dr Adnan Khalil Basha.

Address: POB 14843, Jeddah 21434.

Telephone: (2) 651-2333; **Fax:** (2) 651-8491/651-2997; **Internet:** www.iirosa.org; **e-mail:** relief@iirosa.org.

King Faisal Foundation—KFF

Founded in 1976 to use the estate of the late King Faisal bin Abdulaziz al-Saud for charitable purposes.

Activities: Operates nationally and internationally in the fields of science and medicine, and the arts and humanities, chiefly by awarding the King Faisal International Prizes (for Arabic Literature, Islamic Studies, Service to Islam, Science and Medicine), with prizes totalling approx. US $1,000,000, and academic scholarships. The Foundation finances the King Faisal Centre for Research and Islamic Studies, the King Faisal School, the Effat University and the Alfaisal University (a private university established in partnership with a US technology institute).

Geographical Area of Activity: World-wide.

Restrictions: Nominations for the King Faisal International Prize are not acceptable from political institutes.

Publications: *Al-Faisal.*

Finance: Total assets approx. 1,441,000,000 Saudi riyal.

Principal Staff: Man. Dir HRH Prince Khalid al-Faisal; Deputy Man. Dir HH Prince Bandar bin Saud bin Khalid al-Saud; Vice-Sec.-Gen. HE Yousef A. al-Hamdan; Asst Sec.-Gen. Musaed A. as-Said.

Address: POB 352, Riyadh 11411.

Telephone: (1) 465-2255; **Fax:** (1) 465-6524; **Internet:** www.kff.com; **e-mail:** info@kff.com.

Sultan bin Abdulaziz al-Saud Foundation

A private non-profit organization established by HRH Prince Sultan bin Abdulaziz al-Saud in 1995 to provide humanitarian, social and cultural services, and to empower Saudi Arabia to participate in the spread of knowledge through modern means of communication.

Activities: Operates in the fields of social welfare and education through four principal programmes: the City for Humanitarian Services, the Science and Technology Centre, the Programme for Medical and Educational Telecommunications (Medunet) and the Special Education Programme.

Geographical Area of Activity: Saudi Arabia.

Board of Trustees: HRH Prince Khalid bin Sultan bin Abdulaziz (Chair.).

Principal Staff: Dir-Gen. Dr Majed al-Qasabi; Deputy Dir-Gen. Abdul Aziz al-Magushi.

Address: POB 64400, Riyadh 11536.

Telephone: (1) 482-7663; **Fax:** (1) 482-2617; **Internet:** www.sultanfoundation.org; **e-mail:** question@sultanfoundation.org.

Senegal

FOUNDATION CENTRE AND CO-ORDINATING BODY

FAVDO—Forum for African Voluntary Development Organizations

International association of approximately 450 African development organizations, which aims to provide mutual support and co-operation services, and to assist development organizations so as to aid the general development of people in Africa.

Activities: Operates in the field of aid to less-developed countries, through establishing links and communication networks between NGOs and governments and governmental organizations in Africa and internationally.

Geographical Area of Activity: Africa.

Principal Staff: Pres. and CEO Mazide Ndiaye.

Address: Rue 4, Zone-B, BP 12093, Dakar.

Telephone: 22-125-5547; **Fax:** 22-125-5564; **e-mail:** mazide@sonatel.senet.net.

FOUNDATIONS, TRUSTS AND NON-PROFIT ORGANIZATIONS

Enda Tiers Monde—Environnement et Développement du Tiers-Monde (Enda Third World—Environment and Development Action in the Third World)

Established in 1972 as an international associative organization active in combating poverty, and in the field of environmental development.

Activities: Operates in the fields of aid to less-developed countries and environmental development, through assisting local community organizations operating in areas such as cultural protection, urban economy, youth and energy. There are decentralized branches of the organization in Africa, South America and Asia, and representative offices in Europe.

Geographical Area of Activity: Africa, South America, Asia, the Caribbean and Europe.

Publications: Reports; *Trade Liberalisation and Sustainable Management of Fishery's Sector in West Africa: Case study of Gambia; Reconciling Countries throuth Culture; Contes seereer; Plantes médicinales du Sahel; Une Afrique s'invente.*

Board: Fatou Sow Sarr (Pres.).

Principal Staff: Exec. Sec. Masse Lô.

Address: Complexe Sicap Point E, Bâtiment B, 1er étage, ave Cheikh Anta Diop, BP 3370, Dakar.

Telephone: (33) 869-99-48; **Fax:** (33) 860-51-33; **Internet:** www.enda.sn; **e-mail:** se@endatiersmonde.org.

Fondation des Organisations Rurales pour l'Agriculture et la Gestion Ecologique—FORAGE (Foundation of Rural Organizations for Agriculture and Economic Management)

Principal Staff: Chief Exec. Tamba Yancouba; Treas. Amadou Manga; Fin. Co-ordinator Ansoumana Sané.

Address: BP 01, Marsassoum, Kolda.

Telephone: 95-31-46; **Fax:** 95-27-06; **e-mail:** sudinfo@telecomplus.sn.

Fondation Rurale pour l'Afrique de l'Ouest (West African Rural Foundation)

Established in 1993 to promote rural development.

Activities: Operates internationally, supporting community organizations working in the fields of rural development, the environment and human rights, through promoting research and collaboration between researchers in the area of agricultural and rural development research, providing training materials, offering technical and management advice, promoting links between organizations involved in rural development, and lobbying on behalf of rural organizations and individuals.

Geographical Area of Activity: West Africa.

Publications: *WARF Newsletter.*

Finance: Annual budget approx. US $1,500,000.

Council of Governors: Dr Dominique Hounkonnou (Chair.).

Principal Staff: Exec. Dir Ndèye Coumba Fall; Sec. Saran Thiam Kourouma.

Address: Sacré Coeur 3, VDN Villa 10075, CP 13 Dakar-Fann.

Telephone: 33-865-0060; **Fax:** 33-860-6689; **Internet:** www.frao.info; **e-mail:** warf@frao.org.

Fondation Léopold Sédar Senghor (Léopold Sédar Senghor Foundation)

Founded in 1974 by Léopold Sédar Senghor, former President of Senegal, to preserve national heritage and support training and research, especially in the areas of culture and international co-operation.

Activities: Operates nationally and internationally in the fields of the arts and humanities, education, law and human rights, and science and technology, through self-conducted programmes, research, grants, literary prizes, conferences, training courses and publications. Maintains a library comprising approximately 2,500 volumes. Has membership organizations in Brazil, Côte d'Ivoire, France, Switzerland and the USA.

Geographical Area of Activity: World-wide.

Publications: *Éthiopiques* (2 a year); *Lettres Majeures* (bulletin).

Principal Staff: Exec. Dir Basile Senghor.

Address: Rue Alpha Hachamiyou Tall et René Ndiaye, BP 2035, 2035 Dakar.

Telephone: 33-821-5355; **Fax:** 33-821-5355; **e-mail:** senghorf@syfed.refer.sn.

OSIWA—Open Society Initiative for West Africa

Established in 2000; part of the global network of autonomous Soros foundations.

Activities: Provides funding to organizations working in the areas of human rights (including women's political and economic empowerment), democracy and governance, media and technology (including information and communications technologies), legal reform and transitional justice, and HIV/AIDS. Supports national projects and projects involving more than one country in West Africa. Maintains offices in Nigeria, Liberia and Sierra Leone. Established West Africa Civil Society Institute (WACSI) in Ghana in 2005 to reinforce the capacities of civil society in the sub-region. WACSI, which became operational in 2007, serves as a resource centre for training, research, experience-sharing and dialogue for civil society organizations in West Africa.

Geographical Area of Activity: West Africa.

Publications: Annual Report; *Osiwa News* (newsletter).

Finance: Total expenditure US $20,207,000 (2008).

Board of Directors: Akwasi Aidoo (Chair.).

Principal Staff: Exec. Dir Dr Nana Tanko.

Address: BP 008, Dakar-Fann; Stèle Mermoz, rue El Hadj Ibrahima Niasse, Dakar.

Telephone: (33) 869-10-24; **Fax:** (33) 824-09-42; **Internet:** www.osiwa.org; **e-mail:** osiwa-dakar@osiwa.org.

PAALAE—Pan African Association for Literacy and Adult Education

Established to promote adult education and literacy in Africa. Originally known as the African Association for Literacy and Adult Education, which was founded in 1984 (combining the former African Adult Education Association and the Afrolit Society, both founded in 1968).

Activities: Promotes literacy and adult education, and aims to increase understanding of the concept of life-long learning within Africa. Conducts studies on educational problems and literacy, holds conferences and disseminates information. Educators form networks to develop programmes concerned with such issues as literacy, women in adult education and development, environmental education, training of trainers, artists for development, participatory research, and university, adult and continuing education. Provides professional training to educators. Maintains a reference library and pool of expert educators to act as consultants.

Geographical Area of Activity: Africa.

Finance: Funded through membership fees and grants and donations from sister organizations.

Principal Staff: Co-ordinators of Steering Cttee Lamine Kane, Yacine Diagne, Joseph Pokawa; Rep. Charles Owens Ndiaye.

Address: Bldg 306, rue 10, BP 10358, Dakar.

Telephone: (33) 855-94-50; **Fax:** (33) 855-94-60; **e-mail:** anafa@sentoo.sn.

PAN Africa—Pesticide Action Network Africa

Founded in 1996, PAN Africa works as one of the regional arms of PAN International (founded in Malaysia in 1982). It aims to promote protection of the environment and pesticide-free sustainable agriculture, raise awareness of the problems and dangers related to pesticide use in agriculture, and work towards promoting an understanding of the issues surrounding the indiscriminate use of pesticides.

Activities: Works to disseminate information regarding the use of pesticides and their alternatives, through the publication of journals, leaflets and audiovisual material, and a Regional Documentation Centre. PAN Africa organizes workshops and training sessions, and has set up a databank on pesticides, sustainable agriculture and agro-ecology, and works to strengthen legislation in Africa regarding the use of toxic pesticides.

Geographical Area of Activity: Africa.

Publications: *Pesticides and Alternatives* (newsletter in French and English, 3 a year); brochures; Annual Report; Journal; *PAN Africa* bulletin.

Principal Staff: Regional Co-ordinator Dr Abou Thiam; Project Officer Marie Suzanne Traore, Mourtada Thiam.

Address: POB 15938, Dakar-Fann.

Telephone: 33-825-4914; **Fax:** 33-825-1443; **Internet:** www.pan-afrique.org; **e-mail:** panafrica@pan-afrique.org.

Serbia

FOUNDATION CENTRES AND CO-ORDINATING BODIES

Centre for Development of Non-Profit Sector

Established in 1996 to aid in building and renewing the non-profit sector in Serbia and Montenegro and to promote the development of autonomous civil initiatives and civil society.

Activities: The Centre's initiatives include an information and documentation programme, including the development of a database of non-profit organizations in Serbia; publishing bulletins, brochures and books; operating a training and education programme to advance the development of NGOs; the provision of aid to NGOs in the form of counselling and information; helping NGOs find suitable volunteers; and a research programme. Operates a regional network that aims to develop NGOs in Serbia.

Geographical Area of Activity: Serbia.

Publications: *Third Sector in Serbia: Status and Prospects* (2001); *Civil Society Driving Development: An Assembly of Non-Governmental Organizations from Central Europe, Former Soviet Union and Turkey* (2002); *Saradnja Nevladinog Sektora I Vlade* (2004).

Finance: Funded by donations.

Board of Directors: Danilo Milic (Pres.).

Principal Staff: Dir Jasna Filipovic; Admin. Sec. Darko Grubic.

Address: 11000 Belgrade, 47A Jevremova/2.

Telephone: (11) 2626113; **Fax:** (11) 3240128; **Internet:** www.crnps.org.rs; **e-mail:** info@crnps.org.rs.

Gradjanske inicijative—GI (Civic Initiatives)

Established in 1996 by a team of NGO activists that had contributed to non-nationalist democratic opposition and anti-war movements since 1990. GI works towards strengthening civil society in Serbia through promotion of democracy, education and supporting active citizenship.

Activities: Provides development, training and relevant information to NGOs to enable them to develop the third sector in Serbia with enhanced sustainability. Activities carried out include providing education, professional advice, technical assistance and information pertinent to the areas of interest of NGOs.

Geographical Area of Activity: Serbia.

Publications: *NGO sector in Serbia; Civil Society and Democracy; Human Rights Monitoring; Little Dictionary of Parliamentary Terms; Market Democracy; Financing of the Political Parties in Europe; Membership in the Council of Europe; The Dictionary of Democracy; Trade Unions in Europe;* and other materials.

Principal Staff: Exec. Dir Miljenko Dereta; Co-ordinator of Financial Services Kemal Gegić.

Address: POB 35-27, 11120 Belgrade; Cara Dušana 70, 11000 Belgrade.

Telephone: (11) 3284164; **Internet:** www.gradjanske.org; **e-mail:** civin@gradjanske.org.

FOUNDATIONS, TRUSTS AND NON-PROFIT ORGANIZATIONS

European Centre for Peace and Development—ECPD

Established in 1985 following an agreement between the UN University for Peace and the Government of Yugoslavia to contribute to peace and development in Europe and to international co-operation in the transfer of knowledge.

Activities: Works towards finding solutions for acute and chronic problems of development and the quality of life in specific regions of Europe, particularly South-Eastern Europe, with an emphasis on countries in transition. Runs a series of inter-connected programmes: development of human resources; development of natural resources; economic development; scientific and technological development; social development; integrated development; development of international relations and co-operation; and management. Organizes and conducts postgraduate studies; research projects; international scientific meetings, conferences, symposia and seminars; provides consulting services; and publishes materials and papers relevant to its studies. Has been involved in science and research in numerous areas including sustainable development, environmental protection, banking, finance and international trade, and the promotion of small and medium-sized enterprises, the integration of modern and traditional medicine to preserve human resources for development. Runs projects in co-operation with universities and institutions in host countries, and with international organizations.

Geographical Area of Activity: Europe, with a current emphasis on South-Eastern Europe, and in the USA and Canada.

Publications: In 2008: *Inter-ethnic Reconciliation, Religious Tolerance and Human Security in the Balkans; Organomatika i Sinergetika—Osnove društvenog Inženjerstva; Ekspertizna Medicina, Ekspertizna analiza; National Reconciliation, Religious Tolerance and Human Security in the Balkans.*

Finance: Funded through donations from national and international organizations, tuition and registration fees.

Council of Trustees: Dr Takehiro Togo (Pres.) ; Prof. Dr Don Wallace (Vice-Pres.); Prof. Dr Albert Maes (Vice-Pres.).

Principal Staff: Exec. Dir Dr Negoslav P. Ostojić.

Address: 11000 Belgrade, Terazije 41.

Telephone: (11) 3246041; **Fax:** (11) 3240673; **Internet:** www.ecpd.org.rs; **e-mail:** ecpd@eunet.rs.

Fund for an Open Society—Serbia

Founded in June 1991. An independent foundation, part of the Soros foundations network, which aims to foster political and cultural pluralism and reform economic structures to encourage free enterprise and a market economy.

Activities: Operates in the fields of information and the independent media, education, economic reform, civil society, the arts and culture, science, law and criminal justice, public health, Roma and ethnic minorities, local government and public administration, and women's and youth programmes.

Geographical Area of Activity: Serbia.

Publications: *Open News.*

Finance: Annual expenditure US $5,159,000 (2009).

Governing Board: Srdjan Bogosavljević (Pres.).

Principal Staff: Exec. Dir Jadranka Jelinčić.

Address: 11000 Belgrade, Kneginje Ljubice 14.

Telephone: (11) 3025800; **Fax:** (11) 3283602; **Internet:** www
.fosserbia.org; **e-mail:** office@fosserbia.org.

Karić Foundation (Karić fondacija)

Established in 1979 by the Karić family with the goal of helping others, and the promotion of Serbian national culture and
tradition. Originally known as the BK Foundation.

Activities: Operates in Serbia and Montenegro, Europe and
the USA in the areas of the arts and humanities, education,
international affairs, law and human rights, medicine and
health, and social welfare, through awarding prizes (the
Karić Brothers Awards), humanitarian projects, publishing,
international co-operation and family development. Also
maintains branches in Austria, Canada, Cyprus, the United
Kingdom and the USA.

Geographical Area of Activity: USA, Europe, Montenegro
and Serbia.

Publications: *Bulletin* (newsletter).

Board of Management: Milanka Karić (Pres.).

Principal Staff: Dir Jasmina Mitrović Marić.

Address: Belgrade, Terazije 28.

Telephone: (11) 3629193; **Internet:** www.karicfoundation
.com; **e-mail:** kf@karicfoundation.com.

Singapore

FOUNDATIONS, TRUSTS AND NON-PROFIT ORGANIZATIONS

Singapore International Foundation—SIF

Established in 1991 with the aim to enable Singaporeans in Singapore and resident in other countries to think globally, feel Singaporean, be responsible world citizens and foster friendships for Singapore.

Activities: Foundation programmes seek to connect Singaporeans at home and abroad with international communities in a range of areas, including volunteerism, business development, arts, culture and academia. SIF operates various programmes focusing on international volunteerism and international networking, including Singapore Internationale, Ideas for a Better World Forum, Young Social Entrepreneurs, Friends of Singapore and Young Business Ambassadors. In May 2011 the SIF and the British Council (q.v.) entered into a two-year partnership to promote cross-cultural understanding between the people of Singapore and the United Kingdom through arts and cultural exchanges.

Geographical Area of Activity: Singapore.

Publications: Annual Report; *Singapore Kopitiam*; *Singapore Magazine* (quarterly); research papers.

Finance: Total assets S $32,581,942 (2008); total income S $7,612,908, expenditure S $6,734,669 (2008).

Board of Governors: Euleen Goh (Chair.).

Principal Staff: Exec. Dir Jean Tan.

Address: 9 Bishan Pl., Level 9, Junction 8, Singapore 579837.

Telephone: 68378700; **Fax:** 68378710; **Internet:** www.sif.org .sg; **e-mail:** sifnet@sif.org.sg.

Slovakia

FOUNDATION CENTRES AND CO-ORDINATING BODIES

Asociácia komunitných nadácií Slovenska—AKNS
(Association of Slovakian Community Foundations)

Established by eight Slovakian community foundations in 2003 to promote the activities of its members and the concept of community philanthropy in Slovakia.

Activities: Promotes the community foundation movement in Slovakia, representing its members, informing the public about the activities of community foundations in Slovakia. Also lobbies government for legislation favourable to the development of philanthropy in Slovakia. Co-operates with similar organizations internationally.

Geographical Area of Activity: Slovakia.

Principal Staff: Pres. Jozef Jarina; Co-ordinator Katarína Minárová.

Address: 811 03 Bratislava, Partizánska 2.

Telephone: (2) 5441-9998; **Fax:** (2) 5441-9998; **Internet:** www .asociaciakns.sk; **e-mail:** nkn@nkn.sk.

Nadácia Ekopolis (Ekopolis Foundation)

Established in 1991 to promote sustainable development, civil society development and public participation.

Activities: Operates in Central Europe making grants in the areas of civil society development, rural development, environmental protection, community foundation development and women's rights. 'Sister' foundations operate in the Czech Republic, Hungary, Poland and Romania.

Geographical Area of Activity: Central Europe.

Publications: Annual Report.

Finance: Annual income €669,680, expenditure €663,757 (2011).

Principal Staff: Dir Peter Medved; Finance Man. Lívia Haringová.

Address: 974 01 Banska Bystrica, Komenskeho 21.

Telephone: (48) 414-5478; **Fax:** (48) 414-5259; **Internet:** www .ekopolis.sk; **e-mail:** ekopolis@ekopolis.sk.

Nadácia Pontis (Pontis Foundation)

Established in 1997 as the successor to the Foundation for a Civil Society.

Activities: The Foundation encourages and supports the development and long-term financial sustainability of non-profit organizations in Slovakia and a number of other countries world-wide through the provision of grants and consultancy. It supports development of corporate philanthropy and social responsibility, provides consultancy for creating philanthropic strategies, undertakes research projects and organizes educational events. Awards the Via Bona Slovakia Award for philanthropic activity, and administers the Business Leaders Forum, an association of 21 businesses that promotes corporate social responsibility in Slovakia. In November 2009 launched new programme of individual giving called Dobrá Krajina (Great Country).

Geographical Area of Activity: Mainly Slovakia, but also Belarus, Western Balkans, Moldova, Kenya, Egypt, Georgia and Cuba.

Restrictions: Grants are only open to registered NGOs in Slovakia. Restricted support available for individuals, travel grants and internships abroad.

Publications: Annual Report; reports; information brochures; e-newsletter.

Board of Directors: Luboš Vančo (Chair.).

Principal Staff: Dir Lenka Surotchak; Financial Dir Gabriela Zúbriková.

Address: 821 08 Bratislava, Zelinárska 2.

Telephone: (2) 5710-8111; **Fax:** (2) 5710-8125; **Internet:** www .nadaciapontis.sk; www.pontisfoundation.sk; **e-mail:** pontis@pontisfoundation.sk.

NGDO—Non-Governmental Development Organizations Platform (Platforma Mimovládnych Rozvojovych Organizáchií—MVRO)

An umbrella organization of non-profit organizations (23 full members and eight observers) focused on foreign development and humanitarian assistance based in Slovakia; represents the NGOs with major governmental and inter-governmental institutions.

Activities: Aims to contribute to public awareness in the field of solidarity, mutual assistance and to contribute to resolving the problem of global poverty and humanitarian crises, through supporting its member NGOs. Represents its members' common interests in the field of international development co-operation and humanitarian aid, provides information to member organizations on developments within the field of international development co-operation and humanitarian aid and on co-operation possibilities, co-ordinates the common activities and projects of the Platform members; co-operates with national government and local governments; develops relations with foreign organizations; and issues publications.

Geographical Area of Activity: Slovakia.

Publications: Annual report.

Board: Nora Beňáková (Chair.); Ján Mihálik (Vice-Chair.).

Principal Staff: Exec. Sec. Lenka Nemcová; Financial Officer Veronika Kurinova.

Address: 821 08 Bratislava, Mileticova 7.

Telephone: (2) 2044-5255; **Fax:** (2) 2044-5255; **Internet:** www .mvro.sk; **e-mail:** info@mvro.sk.

SAIA—Slovak Academic Information Agency

Established in 1990 to assist in the development of the education system and civil society in general.

Activities: Provides services for NGOs in Slovakia, including training and advisory services, a library on the third sector and an NGO database with approximately 3,000 entries. Also issues publications; organizes conferences and seminars; runs volunteer projects and grants the Heart on Palm volunteer awards; and collaborates regionally and internationally with other similar organizations on programmes. Its educational services include providing information, scholarship competitions, seminars and workshops for those wishing to study abroad. Maintains five branch offices throughout Slovakia.

Geographical Area of Activity: Slovakia.

Publications: SAIA Bulletin (monthly information journal); NonProfit (monthly magazine); Annual Report; International Students' Guide to the Slovak Republic.

Finance: Total assets €796,736 (Dec. 2010); Annual income €2,544,252, expenditure €2,539,924 (2010).

Board of Directors: Milan Zalman (Chair.); Stanislav Cekovský (Vice-Chair.).

Principal Staff: Exec. Dir Katarína Kostálová; Deputy Dirs Michal Fedák, Karla Zimanová.

Address: Námestie slobody 23,
812 20 Bratislava 1,.

Telephone: (2) 5441-1426; **Fax:** (2) 5441-1429; **Internet:** www
.saia.sk; **e-mail:** saia@saia.sk.

Slovak Donors' Forum—SDF

Established in 1996 as an association of Slovak and foreign
grant-making organizations to promote effective grant-making and support not-for-profit organizations in Slovakia.

Activities: Carries out research, promotes the work and effectiveness of its member foundations and implements outreach
initiatives focused on development of corporate and individual
philanthropy in Slovakia.

Geographical Area of Activity: Slovakia.

Publications: Annual report; newsletter; expert manuals.

Executive Board: Laura Dittel (Chair.).

Principal Staff: Project Man. Katarína Podracká.

Address: 821 08 Bratislava, Páričkova 24.

Telephone: (2) 5441-7917; **Fax:** (2) 5441-7917; **Internet:** www
.donorsforum.sk; **e-mail:** donorsforum@donorsforum.sk.

Slovenská Humanitná Rada (Slovak Humanitarian Council)

Established in 1990 as the Czechoslovak Council for Humanitarian Co-operation—an independent non-governmental
voluntary association of 169 organizations aiming to relieve
human suffering, which, after the division of Czechoslovakia
into the Czech Republic and Slovakia, became the Czech Council for Humanitarian Co-operation (now the Council of Humanitarian Associations, q.v.) and the Slovak Humanitarian
Council. The Council comprises numerous voluntary organizations and aims to promote the interests of the voluntary sector,
and to provide humanitarian aid in collaboration with the
State.

Activities: Supports the projects of its member organizations; offers advice on management and fund distribution;
organizes training courses; disseminates information; provides consultancy services; and issues publications.

Geographical Area of Activity: Slovakia.

Restrictions: Only provides financial support, aid in kind
and technical assistance for projects in the social field.

Publications: *Humanita* (newsletter, monthly); Annual
Report; electronic/online information; information brochures.

Governing Board: Ivan Sykora (Pres.); Jaroslav Hinšt (Vice-
Pres.).

Principal Staff: Dir Eva Lysicanová.

Address: 821 08 Bratislava, Páričkova 24.

Telephone: (2) 5020-0517; **Fax:** (2) 5020-0522; **Internet:** www
.shr.sk; **e-mail:** shr@changenet.sk.

FOUNDATIONS, TRUSTS AND NON-PROFIT ORGANIZATIONS

Children of Slovakia Foundation (Nadácia pre deti Slovenska)

Established in December 1995 by the International Youth
Foundation (q.v.) as independent nongovernmental organization to support the positive development of children and
young people in Slovakia.

Activities: Operates in the fields of education and social welfare, specifically in the area of children and young people,
through self-conducted programmes, grants to institutions
and training courses.

Geographical Area of Activity: Slovakia.

Restrictions: Projects are limited to Slovakia.

Publications: *Novo vynárajúce sa potreby detí na slovensku—
prieskumná štúdia (newly emerging needs of children in Slovakia—exploratory study).*

Finance: Annual revenue approx. €1,000,000.

Board: Matej Ribanský (Chair.).

Principal Staff: Exec. Dir Dana Rusinová; Office Man. Oľga
Hátasová.

Address: 811 08 Bratislava, Heydukova 3.

Telephone: (2) 5263-6461; **Fax:** (2) 5263-6462; **Internet:** www
.nds.sk; **e-mail:** nds@nds.sk.

International Visegrad Fund—IVF

Established on 9 June 2000 by the countries of the Visegrad
Group: Czech Republic, Hungary, Poland and Slovakia.

Activities: Aims to promote regional co-operation among the
Visegrad countries of the Czech Republic, Hungary, Poland
and Slovakia, by supporting the development of common cultural and scientific research projects, educational projects,
exchanges between young people and cross-border co-operation. In 2002 the Visegrad Scholarship Programme was
launched for doctoral studies. Supports more than 30 scholarships each year. The annual International Visegrad Prize
(worth €20,000) was launched in 2005 and is awarded in appreciation of support given to and the development of cultural co-
operation between the Visegrad countries.

Geographical Area of Activity: Czech Republic, Hungary,
Poland and Slovakia.

Restrictions: Organizational grantees must be from at least
three countries of the Visegrad Group; scholarship grantees
must be resident in one of the Visegrad Group countries.

Publications: Newsletter; Annual Report; factsheet.

Finance: Receives equal annual contributions from the member states; total budget €6,598,510 (2011).

Principal Staff: Exec. Dir Petr Vagner; Deputy Exec. Dir
Zbigniew Machej; Head Sec. Miroslava Nosálova Fekiacová.

Address: 811 02 Bratislava, Kralovske udolie 4570/8.

Telephone: (2) 5920-3811; **Fax:** (2) 5920-3805; **Internet:** www
.visegradfund.org; **e-mail:** visegradfund@visegradfund.org.

Nadácia Zelená Nádej (Green Perspective Foundation)

Founded in April 1991 by Juraj Lukáč, Dagmar Balažováand
Radoslav Potončý to support environmental protection, primarily focusing on protection and regeneration of natural forests within a philosophy of deep ecology.

Activities: The Foundation supports the activities of individuals, public initiatives and NGOs working in the above fields
and education, through advisory, publishing, cultural, social
and specific activities. The Foundation's main programmes
include an annual award to the best forest protection activity
open to applicants from the Czech Republic, Hungary, Poland
and Slovakia, donations of books to rural libraries, financial
help to students whose career goals are in accordance with
the aims of the Foundation, and a small grant initiative for forest protection activities.

Geographical Area of Activity: Czech Republic, Hungary,
Poland and Slovakia.

Publications: Several books.

Principal Staff: Exec. Dir Mária Hudáková.

Address: 082 13 Tulčík, Slovensko 27.

Telephone: (5) 1778-9138; **Fax:** (5) 1778-9138; **Internet:** www
.gpf.sk; **e-mail:** maria@gpf.sk.

Open Society Foundation—Bratislava

Founded in June 1992, an independent foundation, part of the
Soros foundations network, which aims to support, develop,
protect and strengthen democratic and liberal values of open
society through the implementation of programmes and projects.

Activities: The Foundation's programme priorities include
public administration, law and judiciary, Roma people, social
integration, educational reform, education, co-operation
between European countries, library support, Internet, publishing, public health, media, criminal justice, women, civil
society and European integration. Also operates as a partner
within the NGO sector, at governmental and donor level, and

with individuals in Slovakia, as well as with international partners. In 2010 the Foundation awarded 142 grants worth more than €840,000 in total.

Geographical Area of Activity: Slovakia.

Publications: Annual Report; *Manual for Foundations*; *Free Access to Information Law*; *Prevention of HIV Epidemics in CEE and NIS*; *A Reader for Non-Profit Organizations*; and other publications.

Finance: Total assets 136,843,288 SKK (2008).

Board of Directors: Zuzana Kušová (Chair.).

Principal Staff: Exec. Dir Alena Pániková; Chief Financial Officer Magdalena Feniková.

Address: 811 03 Bratislava, Baštová 5.

Telephone: (2) 5441-6913; **Fax:** (2) 5441-8867; **Internet:** www .osf.sk; **e-mail:** osf@osf.sk.

Milan Simecka Foundation (Nadácia Milana Šimečku)

Founded in 1991 in memory of the Slovak philosopher, author, and democratic activist Milan Simecka; aims to initiate and promote activities leading to the development of democracy, culture, humanity and civil society.

Activities: Supports those educational, publishing, training, and counselling activities that help to disseminate and strengthen democratic values in society and to apply ethical approaches in politics. Also funds activities focusing on mutual understanding and co-operation between states, nationalities, and ethnic groups, with special emphasis on the development of Czech and Slovak relations. The Foundation has initiated major projects in the field of human rights and civic education, community development, independent media support, and oral history research, and has established a Holocaust Documentation Centre.

Geographical Area of Activity: Czech Republic and Slovakia.

Publications: books; Annual Report; training manuals and handbooks.

Board: Ingrid Vagacová-Antalová (Pres.).

Principal Staff: Exec. Dir Martina Mazenská; Programme Dir Laco Oravec.

Address: 811 03 Bratislava, Panenska 4.

Telephone: (2) 5443-3552; **Fax:** (2) 5443-3552; **Internet:** www .nadaciamilanasimecku.sk; **e-mail:** nms@nadaciams.sk.

SOSNA Foundation

Founded in 1992 to help the environment in Košice and its surroundings. Aims to encourage people to support and achieve alternative methods of solving environmental problems primarily at local and regional level.

Activities: Operates programmes in the areas of environmental education, the sustainable development of the Košice region of Slovakia, and organic agriculture, through organizing campaigns for solving environmental problems, funding pilot projects on principles of sustainable life, organizing educational programmes, workshops, lectures and exhibitions, and producing publications. Opened Eco Centre in the village of Družstevná pri Hornáde in 2010.

Geographical Area of Activity: Slovakia.

Principal Staff: Chair. Stefan Szabó; Man. Silvia Szabóová.

Address: 044 31 Drustevná pri Hornáde, ul. Okruzná.

Telephone: (5) 5625-1903; **Fax:** (9) 0495-1139; **Internet:** www .sosna.sk; **e-mail:** omar.sosna@gmail.com.

Vzdelávacia nadácia Jana Husa (Jan Hus Educational Foundation)

Founded in 1990 to support civil society and the development of higher education in the arts, humanities and law in the Czech Republic and Slovakia. Until 1993, the Foundation was a branch office of the Vzdělávací Nadace Jana Husa (q.v.). Since 1993, two sister organizations have been in operation, one in Slovakia and one in the Czech Republic.

Activities: Aims to contribute to the integration of Slovak civilization, science and arts into European culture. The Foundation's main project areas are to: support higher and continuing education, with a particular emphasis on the humanities, social sciences and civic-democratic education; initiate a fundamental transformation in the education system through the training and preparation of university teachers; and initiate and support permanent international academic co-operation.

Geographical Area of Activity: Slovakia and the Czech Republic.

Restrictions: Grants are made within Slovakia and the Czech Republic only.

Publications: Annual Report; *Velvet Philosophers*; *Jaromír Adamec*.

Board of Trustees: Jircaroní Müller (Chair.); Krístina Korená (Deputy Chair.); Tomáš Holeček (Deputy Chair. for Programmes).

Principal Staff: Programme Man. Olga Pestuková.

Address: 831 04 Bratislava, Kalinciakova 114/25.

Telephone: (2) 5564-8787; **Fax:** (2) 5564-8788; **Internet:** www .vnjh.sk; **e-mail:** vnjh@vnjh.sk.

Slovenia

FOUNDATION CENTRE AND CO-ORDINATING BODY

Zavod Center za Informiranje, Sodelovanje in Razvoj Nevladnih Organizacije—CNVOS (Centre for the Information Service, Co-operation and Development of NGOs)

Established in 2001 by 27 NGOs to promote the development of civil society in Slovenia. More than 200 member organizations.

Activities: Offers services to NGOs and develops NGOs' ability to take on activities carried out by public sector bodies. Provides networking opportunities for Slovenian NGOs with European institutions and NGOs from other European countries. Also provides legal assistance to NGOs.

Geographical Area of Activity: Slovenia.

Publications: *NGO-ZINE = SEKTOR* (newsletter); *How to Write a Good Project; Ethical Code; Relations with Media: Handbook for NGOs; Actor in the Decision-making Process?; How to Use Smart EU Funding; NGO Networks in Slovenia; Strategic Planning for NGOs: Communication Tools.*

Principal Staff: Dir Goran Forbici; Deputy Dir Tina Divjak.

Address: 1000 Ljubljana, Povsetova 37.

Telephone: (1) 542 14 22; **Fax:** (1) 542 14 24; **Internet:** www.cnvos.si; **e-mail:** info@cnvos.si.

FOUNDATIONS, TRUSTS AND NON-PROFIT ORGANIZATIONS

Slovenian Science Foundation

Set up in 1994 by the Slovenian Government and prominent Slovenian organizations in the fields of education, research, economy, finance and the media to work towards the promotion of science in Slovenia.

Activities: Operates in the areas of science and technology and education, through offering professional training to develop existing as well as future research; conducting basic and applied research; extending scientific co-operation, such as synergizing with national science foundations including the European Science Foundation (q.v.); and organizing programmes to deepen public understanding of technology and science, including the Slovene Park of Science and Technology and the Slovene Science Festival. The Foundation also extends support to scientific training by providing scholarships and fellowships; makes research grants; issues publications; conducts conferences; and promotes joint research projects and interchange of scientific knowledge.

Geographical Area of Activity: Slovenia.

Publications: *Glasnik ustanove Slovenske znanstvene fundacije* (Slovenian Science Foundation Courier).

Trustees: Prof. Dr Andrej Umek (Pres.); Prof. Dr Rado Bohinc (Pres., Foundation Council); Prof. Dr Venčeslav Kaučič; (Pres., Science Council).

Principal Staff: Dir Dr Edvard Kobal.

Address: 1000 Ljubljana, Štefanova 15.

Telephone: (1) 426 35 90; **Fax:** (1) 426 35 91; **Internet:** www.szf.si; **e-mail:** info@szf.si.

South Africa

FOUNDATION CENTRES AND CO-ORDINATING BODIES

Association for Progressive Communications—APC

An Internet network established in 1990 by a group of seven computer networks from around the world to promote and facilitate ICT use by groups and individuals working in the areas of human rights, environmental protection and peace, and use of the Internet to further the development of civil society.

Activities: APC operates in various areas: the promotion of non-commercial Internet space for NGOs; network development, aiding existing communication service providers to expand; women, promoting gender-aware web design and use; improving networking capabilities in Africa; information dissemination; and special projects, including the APC Betinho Prize of US $7,500 awarded to groups or NGOs in any country that have used information and communication technology significantly and successfully in development work. APC has member Internet networks world-wide and the directorate is based in South Africa.

Geographical Area of Activity: International.

Restrictions: Not a grant-making organization.

Publications: *APCNews* (monthly newsletter); numerous other publications.

Finance: Annual revenue US $3,002,926, expenditure $2,981,945 (Dec. 2009).

Board of Directors: Danijela Babic (Chair.); Valentina Pellizzer (Vice-Chair.); Andrew Garton (Sec.); Julian Casasbuenas Gallo (Treas.).

Principal Staff: Exec. Dir Anriette Esterhuysen.

Address: POB 29755, Melville 2109.

Telephone: (11) 726 1692; **Fax:** (11) 726 1692; **Internet:** www.apc.org; **e-mail:** info@apc.org.

CIVICUS—World Alliance for Citizen Participation

Established in 1993, an international alliance dedicated to strengthening citizen action and civil society world-wide, in particular in areas where participatory democracy, freedom of association of citizens and their funds for public benefit are threatened.

Activities: Operates world-wide in the areas of the arts and humanities, conservation and the environment, international affairs and social welfare, through self-conducted programmes, research, conferences and publications. Through its programmes and actions the organization seeks an increased understanding and promotion of the nature and contributions of civil society; a political, legal and fiscal environment that enables freedom and autonomy of association; innovative forms of funding and partnership to enhance the resource base of civil society organizations; the strengthening of the institutional, leadership, networking and advocacy capacities of the sector; and increased partnerships among business, government and civil society institutions. Holds a World Assembly biennially, and sponsors regional meetings. Current main focus is the CIVICUS Index on Civil Society project mapping the development of civil society world-wide.

Geographical Area of Activity: World-wide.

Publications: *e-Civicus* (weekly bulletin); *Civil Society at the Millennium* (1999); *Promoting Corporate Citizenship: Opportunities for Business and Civil Society Engagement* (1999); *Sustaining Civil Society: Strategies for Resource Mobilization* (1997); *Legal Principles for Citizen Participation: Toward a Legal Framework for Civil Society Organizations* (1997); *Building Civil Society Worldwide: Strategies for Successful Communications* (1997); *The New Civic Atlas: Profiles of Civil Society in 60 Countries* (1997); *Cutting the Diamonds: Civil Society Index 2008–2011; CIVICUS World* (6 a year); and others.

Finance: Total assets US $2,657,157 (2007); expenditure $2,925,428 (2007).

International Board: David Bonbright (Chair.); Nyaradzayi Gumbonzvanda (Vice-Chair.); Martin Sime (Treas.); Dr Uygar Ozesmi (Sec.).

Principal Staff: Sec.-Gen. Ingrid Srinath; Deputy Sec.-Gen. Katsuji Imata; Finance Man. Joyce Tshabalala.

Address: POB 933, Southdale, Johannesburg 2135; 24 Gwigwi Mrwebi St, Newtown 2001, Johannesburg.

Telephone: (11) 8335959; **Fax:** (11) 8337997; **Internet:** www.civicus.org; **e-mail:** info@civicus.org.

Global Fund for Community Foundations—GFCF

Established in 2006, with funding from the World Bank, the Ford Foundation, Mott Foundation and other US and European funders (qq.v.) to support the development of community foundations world-wide (with particular focus on the global South and the emerging economies of Central and Eastern Europe).

Activities: The Fund provides grants and technical support to community foundations and other local philanthropy institutions and support organizations in low- and middle-income countries.

Geographical Area of Activity: Low- and middle-income countries and occasionally in disadvantaged communities in the global North.

Restrictions: Does not make grants to NGOs for direct implementation of projects.

Board of Trustees: Barry D. Gaberman (Chair.); Avila Kilmurray (Sec.); Bongi Mkhabela (Treas.).

Principal Staff: Exec. Dir Jenny Hodgson; Programme Consultant Halima Mahomed; Financial and Office Administrator Julia Maishoane.

Address: PostNet Suite 135, Private Bag X2600, Houghton, Johannesburg 2041; 4th Floor, 158 Jan Smuts Ave, Rosebank, Johannesburg 2196.

Telephone: (11) 4474396; **Internet:** www.globalfundcommunityfoundations.org; **e-mail:** info@globalfundcf.org.

FOUNDATIONS, TRUSTS AND NON-PROFIT ORGANIZATIONS

ActionAid

Founded in 1972 by Cecil Jackson Cole, ActionAid works in partnership with poor people to eradicate poverty by overcoming the injustice and inequity that cause it. In December 2003, ActionAid moved its head office from the United Kingdom to South Africa.

Activities: Works directly with poor communities and through local partner organizations in more than 40 countries of Africa, Asia, Central and South America and the Caribbean to improve access to food, water, education, health care, shelter and a livelihood. These programmes are designed to address the underlying causes of poverty by helping poor people to recognize, promote and secure their basic rights. ActionAid runs three major international campaigns: food; education; and HIV/AIDS. There are regional offices in Brazil,

Thailand and Kenya, and offices in Washington, DC, and Brussels. ActionAid and its sister organizations in France, Greece, Ireland, Italy and Spain form the ActionAid Alliance.

Geographical Area of Activity: World-wide.

Restrictions: Grants only to approved partner organizations.

Publications: *Global Progress Report*; *Common Cause* (supporters' magazine, 2 a year); Annual Report; numerous books.

Finance: Total assets €90,959,000 (31 Dec. 2010); Total income €231,216,000, expenditure €223,011,000 (2010).

International Board: Irene Ovonji-Odida (Chair.); Patrick Dowling (Treas.).

Principal Staff: International Chief Exec. Joanna Kerr.

Address: PostNet Suite No. 248, Private bag X31, Saxonwold 2132, Johannesburg.

Telephone: (11) 7314500; **Fax:** (11) 8808082; **Internet:** www.actionaid.org; **e-mail:** mail.jhb@actionaid.org.

AISA—Africa Institute of South Africa

Founded in 1960 by the South African Academy of Arts and Science and the University of South Africa, the Institute is the principal nationally based centre for the study of African affairs, whose role is to inform South African society about trends and events in Africa.

Activities: The Institute collects, interprets and disseminates information and analyses on African, and especially Southern African, affairs. Information is disseminated through periodicals and other publications, commentary to the media, and through seminars, workshops and conferences. It conducts research, and maintains a specialized reference library of around 60,000 volumes and about 480 journals and a monitoring service. The Institute collaborates with other institutions and with researchers and academics in the field of African studies world-wide, and has co-operation agreements with centres of African studies abroad (including joint research projects). African studies seminar programmes are conducted. The Institute focuses primarily on the political, socio-economic, international and developmental issues facing Africa. While the geographical scope of its interest covers the entire continent, the Institute's main concern is with Sub-Saharan Africa, and Southern Africa in particular.

Geographical Area of Activity: Africa.

Publications: Annual Report; *Political Reforms in the Arab World*; *South Africa's Foreign Direct Investment in Africa*; *Somalia Peace Process*; *Elite Conflict in Botswana*; *Exploring Islamic Fundamentalist Ideologies in Africa*; *The New Partnership for Africa's Development*; *Defence, Militarism, Peace Building and Human Security in Africa*; *The Nature of the Conflict in Sudan*; *The Mazruiana Collection Revisited*; *The Social Sciences in South Africa Since 1994*; *Africa at a Glance 2006/ 2007*; *AISA Focus* (monthly newsletter).

Finance: Total assets 17,761,940 rand (March 2007); annual revenue 24,251,889 rand, expenditure 23,709,141 rand (March 2007).

Council: Dr Bekumuzi Hlatshwayo (Chair.).

Principal Staff: CEO Dr Matlotleng Patrick Matlou.

Address: POB 630, Pretoria 0001; Embassy House, 1 Bailey Lane, cnr Edmond St, Arcadia, Pretoria.

Telephone: (12) 3049700; **Fax:** (12) 3213164; **Internet:** www.ai.org.za; **e-mail:** balangs@ai.org.za.

Eskom Development Foundation

Established in December 1998; aims to contribute to the well-being of disadvantaged South Africans through the evolvement and implementation of integrated and efficient social investment programmes.

Activities: The Foundation focuses on poverty alleviation, income generation, job creation and social well-being. It is active in underdeveloped locales, particularly rural regions and new urban settlements, in all the provinces of South Africa. Supports social projects by offering donations and providing grants to enable economic development.

Geographical Area of Activity: South Africa.

Board of Directors: Linda J. Mngomezulu (Chair.).

Principal Staff: CEO Mabel Makibelo; Finance Man. Wayne Hempe.

Address: POB 1091, Johannesburg 2001.

Telephone: (11) 8002758; **Fax:** (11) 8002246; **Internet:** www.eskom.co.za/esdef/content.html; **e-mail:** paia@eskom.co.za.

EWT—Endangered Wildlife Trust

Founded in October 1973, a non-profit NGO that aims to conserve the diversity of species in Southern Africa. It is a fully-accredited NGO member of the IUCN—World Conservation Union (q.v.).

Activities: Founded to promote the conservation of biological diversity in Southern Africa; conducts research; organizes practical conservation campaigns; aims to raise public awareness of conservation and environmental issues; issues publications.

Geographical Area of Activity: Southern Africa.

Publications: *Vision* (annually); *EWT* (magazine); *Environment—people and conservation in Africa* (quarterly magazine); *Vulture News* (twice a year); *The Grus Grapevine*; *Indwa*; *Gabar*.

Trustees: Dirk Ackermann (Chair.).

Principal Staff: CEO Yolan Friedmann; COO Mandy Poole; Financial Man. Abbas Moolla.

Address: Private Bag X11, Modderfontein, 1645, Gauteng; Pinelands Office Park, Ardeer Rd, Modderfontein, 1609, Gauteng.

Telephone: (11) 3723600; **Fax:** (11) 6084682; **Internet:** www.ewt.org.za; **e-mail:** ewt@ewt.org.za.

FirstRand Foundation

Established in 1998 to support social causes and initiatives conducive to development, including educational as well as HIV/AIDS-combative initiatives. The Foundation receives an annual contribution of 1% from the after-tax profits of the FirstRand group companies (First National Bank—FNB, Momentum, FirstRand, Wesbank and Rand Merchant Bank—RMB).

Activities: The Foundation's funding is categorized into four sections with each section focusing on specific areas. The Discovery Fund focuses on primary health care; the FNB Fund is concerned with safe community initiatives, education, hospice programmes, development of skill base and job creation; the Momentum Fund assists support programmes for those with AIDS, disabled people and early childhood issues; and the RMB Fund is aimed at conservation and the environment, community care projects, and art, music and culture.

Geographical Area of Activity: South Africa.

Publications: Annual Report.

Board of Trustees: Sizwe Nxasana (Chair.); Adrian Arnott (Sec.).

Address: POB 61713, Marshalltown 2107.

Telephone: (11) 3777360; **Fax:** (11) 8343682; **Internet:** www.firstrandfoundation.org.za; **e-mail:** firstrandfoundation@tsi.org.za.

Gift of the Givers Foundation

Established in 1992; aims to build bridges between peoples of different cultures and religions engendering goodwill, harmonious co-existence, tolerance and mutual respect; the largest disaster response NGO of African origin on the African continent.

Activities: Active nationally and internationally, through operating education, health-care and humanitarian programmes and providing support for a range of different projects, including bursaries for international study, HIV/AIDS workshops and anti-drug campaigns in South Africa. Has also funded projects in Afghanistan, Bosnia and Herzegovina, Chechnya, Haiti, India, Iran, Malawi, Mozambique,

Palestinian Autonomous Areas, Rwanda, Somalia, Sudan and Turkey. In 2002 the Foundation launched the Millions for Africa Campaign. Other campaigns include South Africans Helping South Africans, which promotes corporate social responsibility in South Africa. Maintains branches in Johannesburg, Cape Town and Durban and an additional country office in Malawi.

Geographical Area of Activity: World-wide.

Principal Staff: Chair. and Founder Dr Imtiaz Suliman.

Address: 290 Prince Alfred St, Pietermaritzburg.

Telephone: (33) 3450175; **Fax:** (33) 3427489; **Internet:** www.giftofthegivers.org; **e-mail:** info@giftofthegivers.org.

Global Water Foundation

Founded by Johan Kriek and Minnie Hildebrand to provide technical assistance, facilitate the sharing of information and support technical innovation to provide humanitarian aid to the developing world.

Activities: Operates in the area of aid and development to help provide sources of safe drinking water and sanitation. Maintains offices in Florida and North Carolina, USA.

Geographical Area of Activity: Africa.

Restrictions: Grants strictly limited to water and sanitation-related programmes and projects.

Principal Staff: Contact Minnie Hildebrand.

Address: Chedza House, 95 Jan Smuts Ave, Saxonwold 2196, Johannesburg.

Telephone: (11) 4772441; **Internet:** www.globalwaterfoundation.org.

Nelson Mandela Children's Fund

Established by Nelson Mandela in 1994, who contributed one-third of his salary to the Fund for five years. The Fund works towards the empowerment and well-being of children and youth.

Activities: Supports children to combat poor economic and social circumstances, abuse and exploitation; supports the disadvantaged by providing education, counselling and care; focuses on initiatives pertaining to child welfare, leadership, disability, and education and development; works in partnership with similar organizations to implement projects empowering and bettering the lives of children and youth; advocates children and youth rights through awareness programmes and utilizing influence of public policies; supports HIV/AIDS-affected children and families coping with debilitating illnesses. The Fund has offices in several countries including the USA and the United Kingdom. It also operates in association with Nelson Mandela Children's Fund—in Canada, an independently-registered welfare organization.

Geographical Area of Activity: South Africa.

Publications: Annual Report; newsletter.

Finance: Total assets 507,714,000 rand; annual income 114,298,000 rand (2009).

Principal Staff: CEO and Programmes Dir Moipone Buda-Ramatlo; Finance Dir Victor Songelwa.

Address: 21 Eastwold Way, Saxonwold, POB 797, Highlands North, Johannesburg 2037.

Telephone: (11) 2745600; **Fax:** (11) 4863914; **Internet:** www.nelsonmandelachildrensfund.com; **e-mail:** bridgetm@nmcf.co.za.

Nelson Mandela Foundation

The Foundation was established following Nelson Mandela's retirement on 19 August 1999 and leads the development of a living legacy that captures the vision and values of his life and work. The Foundation embodies the spirit of reconciliation, *ubuntu*, and social justice. The Foundation's work is a celebration of Nelson Mandela's life.

Activities: The Foundation's core business is memory and dialogue work, with the key institutional vehicle being the Nelson Mandela Centre of Memory and Dialogue. In 2009 the Foundation, together with its sister charities, initiated Mandela Day, which takes place on 18 July every year, as a way of galvanizing members of the public towards community service. The UN has since declared it Nelson Mandela Internatonal Day.

Geographical Area of Activity: South Africa.

Publications: Financial reports; news; educational publications on the life and times of Nelson Mandela; publications on ongoing memory and dialogue work.

Finance: Total assets 227,442,678 rand (Feb. 2011); annual income 64,100,487 rand, annual expenditure 49,802,797 rand (2011).

Board of Trustees: Prof. G. J. Gerwel (Chair.).

Principal Staff: CEO Achmat E. Dangor.

Address: Private Bag X70000, Houghton 2041; 107 Central St, Houghton 2198.

Telephone: (11) 547-5600; **Fax:** (11) 728-1111; **Internet:** www.nelsonmandela.org; **e-mail:** nmf@nelsonmandela.org.

The Mandela Rhodes Foundation

Established by Nelson Mandela in February 2002, in Cape Town, in partnership with the Rhodes Trust (q.v.) to build exceptional leadership capacity in Africa.

Activities: Operating in the field of education, specifically postgraduate study in Africa, the Foundation awards scholarships on academic and leadership merit for Masters and Honours degrees at accredited South African tertiary education institutions. The Mandela Rhodes scholarship is open to applicants of any gender, race, culture, religion, class and field of academic study, aged 19–30 years old and a citizen of an African country. Leadership development is promoted and supported by four supplementary residential courses annually and a mentor system.

Geographical Area of Activity: Africa.

Publications: Annual Yearbook.

Finance: Fundraising toward a full endowment structure. Also Black Economic Empowerment partnership with Oxford University Press. Total income 24,945,609 rand, total expenditure 15,437,531 rand (2010).

Board of Trustees: Nelson Rolihlahla Mandela (Patron); Prof. G. J. Gerwel (Chair.).

Principal Staff: Chief Exec. Shaun Johnson; Dep. CEO and Scholarships Man. Theresa Laaka-Daniels.

Address: The Mandela Rhodes Bldg, 150 St George's Mall, Cape Town 8001, POB 15897, Vlaeberg 8018.

Telephone: (21) 4243346; **Fax:** (21) 4249617; **Internet:** www.mandelarhodes.org; **e-mail:** info@mandelarhodes.org.za.

NRF—National Research Foundation

Established in April 1999 by the South African Government, replacing the former Foundation for Research Development, to support and promote research through funding, human resource development and the provision of the necessary research facilities to facilitate the creation of knowledge, innovation and development in all fields of science and technology, including indigenous knowledge, and thereby to contribute to the improvement of the quality of life of all the people of South Africa.

Activities: The Foundation offers research grants, scholarships and bursaries to researchers and students at the country's higher education institutions. All support programmes give high priority to the development of black and female researchers and building research capacity at previously disadvantaged institutions. The Foundation aims to focus on the development of skills and research related to South Africa's indigenous knowledge systems. Research and research skills are promoted across many disciplines; including natural sciences and engineering, agricultural and environmental sciences, health sciences, and social sciences and the humanities. Seven national research facilities also offer opportunities for research, advanced training and international collaboration. The Foundation also promotes collaboration between disciplines and institutions through international agreements and exchange programmes. Several research-related databases are maintained.

Geographical Area of Activity: South Africa.

Restrictions: Training of human resources through grants essential.

Publications: Annual Report; newsletter; research publications of national facilities; and register of grants.

Finance: Total assets 1,884,976,000 rand (31 March 2011); annual revenue 2,039,216,000 rand, annual expenditure 1,944,692,000 rand (2010/11).

Board of Directors: Dr Kgotso Mokhele (Chair.).

Principal Staff: Pres. and CEO Dr Albert S. van Jaarsveld; Vice-Pres Dr G. Mazithulela, Dr D. Pillay.

Address: Meiring Naudé Rd,
Brummeria,
POB 2600,
Pretoria 0001.

Telephone: (12) 4814000; **Fax:** (12) 3491179; **Internet:** www .nrf.ac.za; **e-mail:** info@nrf.ac.za.

Open Society Foundation for South Africa—OSF-SA

Founded in July 1993 by George Soros to support the promotion and protection of human rights and open, democratic society. The Foundation is an independent foundation, part of the Soros foundations network.

Activities: The Foundation operates in the fields of civil society, law and criminal justice, public health, youth and women, democracy building, economic reform, and information and the media.

Geographical Area of Activity: South Africa.

Publications: Annual Report; *Economic Justice and Development Programme*; *Criminal Justice Initiative*; *Human Rights and Governance Programme*; *Media Programme*; *Sentencing in South Africa—Conference Report* (2006); *The Effect of Sentencing on the Size of the South African Prison Population* (2006); *The Impact of Minimum Sentencing in South Africa* (2006).

Board of Directors: Zyda Rylands (Chair.).

Principal Staff: Exec. Dir Zohra Dawood.

Address: POB 143, Howard Pl., Pinelands 7450.

Telephone: (21) 5111679; **Fax:** (21) 5115058; **Internet:** www.osf .org.za; **e-mail:** admin@ct.osf.org.za.

Open Society Initiative for Southern Africa—OSISA

Founded in 1997, OSISA is an African institution committed to deepening democracy and human rights in southern Africa. OSISA's vision is to promote and sustain the ideals, values, institutions and practice of open society, with the aim of establishing a vibrant southern African society in which people, free from material and other deprivation, understand their rights and responsibilities and participate democratically in all spheres of life. While it is part of the Open Society network, OSISA is an independent foundation whose Board and staff all come from southern Africa.

Activities: OSISA operates in 10 countries in southern Africa funding civil society projects and advocacy activities in the areas education, human rights, democracy, HIV/AIDS, women's rights, media, economic justice, law, language rights and ICTs. OSISA provides support to a wide-range of civil society organizations across southern Africa.

Geographical Area of Activity: Southern Africa (Angola, Botswana, Democratic Republic of the Congo, Lesotho, Malawi, Mozambique, Namibia, Swaziland, Zambia and Zimbabwe).

Publications: *Openspace* (3 a year); *Buwa* (2 a year).

Finance: Annual expenditure US $25,000,000 (2010).

Board of Trustees: Alice Mogwe (Chair.); Thuli Brilliance Makama (Deputy Chair.).

Principal Staff: Exec. Dir Sisonke Msimang; Deputy Dir Deprose Muchena.

Address: 148 Jan Smuts Ave, Rosebank, Johannesburg 2196.

Telephone: (11) 5875000; **Fax:** (11) 5875099; **Internet:** www .osisa.org; **e-mail:** info@osisa.org.

Pitseng Trust

Established in 1998 by a group of disadvantaged women; aims to facilitate, through funding, the work of autonomous women's organizations and groups striving to transform the subordinate condition of women in the socio-economic, political and cultural life of South Africa society.

Activities: Provides funding to women's community organizations, NGOs and grassroots organizations working in South Africa's most disadvantaged areas. Also gives seed funding to new women's groups that adopt innovative approaches to projects that take a comprehensive approach to development.

Geographical Area of Activity: South Africa.

Board of Trustees: Syriana Maesela (Chair.).

Principal Staff: Contact Fikile Dlamini; Programme Officer Mamotshidisi Mohapi.

Address: 55 Empire Rd, Block C, 1st Floor, Office 11, Parktown Ext. 1, Johannesburg 2193.

Telephone: (11) 5447928; **Fax:** (11) 4869580; **Internet:** www .pitsengtrust.co.za; **e-mail:** pitseng@tiscali.co.za.

SAASTA—South African Agency for Science and Technology Advancement

Established in 1955 to increase knowledge and understanding of the sciences; up until 2002 known as the Foundation for Education, Science and Technology—FEST.

Activities: The Agency promotes education in mathematics, biology, geography and science and technology; promotes the study of mathematics and science in schools, and culture among the whole population; organizes the Annual National Science Olympiad; disseminates information; holds annual conferences and seminars; sponsors competitions and awards; runs the Bureau for Scientific Publications, a science and technology museum, and resource centres.

Geographical Area of Activity: South Africa.

Publications: *Archimedes* (quarterly, in Afrikaans and English); *Easy Science; Young Science Writers winners announced* (newsletter); *Science Communication Workshops* (newsletter); *ASCC—looking to the future* (newsletter); and other newsletters and leaflets.

Principal Staff: Exec. Dir Beverley Damonse; Finance Man. Lucy Coetsee.

Address: POB 1758, Pretoria 0001; Didacta Bldg, 211 Skinner St, Pretoria.

Telephone: (12) 3929300; **Fax:** (12) 3207803; **Internet:** www .saasta.ac.za; **e-mail:** info@saasta.ac.za.

Shuttleworth Foundation

Set up in 2001 by Mark Shuttleworth to serve the cause of social development through grant of funds to social upliftment projects and educational institutions. The Foundation prides itself on investing in initiatives and individuals who challenge the status quo and positively contribute to change.

Activities: The Foundation is an innovative non-profit organization that provides funding for dynamic leaders who are at the forefront of social change. Fellowship grants are awarded to social innovators who are helping to change the world for the better. The Foundation is an experiment in open philanthropy and uses alternative funding methodologies, new technologies and collaborative ways of working to ensure that every initiative receives the best exposure and resources to succeed.

Geographical Area of Activity: World-wide.

Publications: Annual Report.

Finance: Total assets 15,606,965 rand (Feb. 2010).

Trustees: Mark Shuttleworth (Founder).

Principal Staff: Chief Exec. Helen Turvey; CFO Karen Gabriels; COO Karien Bezuidenhout.

Address: POB 4615, Durbanville, Cape Town 7551.

Telephone: (21) 9701204; **Fax:** (21) 86 609 9205; **Internet:** www.shuttleworthfoundation.org; **e-mail:** info@shuttleworthfoundation.org.

South African Institute of International Affairs

Founded in 1934 as an independent NGO to perform a public educational role by promoting an understanding of international questions, especially South Africa's foreign relations.

Activities: Key research areas are: South African foreign policy and African driver countries; governance and the African Peer Review Mechanism; governance of Africa's resources; economic diplomacy; relations of existing and emerging powers to Africa; current global challenges. Activities include programmes of empirical research in-country, fellowships and awards, study and discussion groups, lectures, public addresses, conferences, symposia and publications. Maintains a library and information service, as well as a vibrant youth development programme. Maintains branches in East London, Pietermaritzburg and the Western Cape.

Geographical Area of Activity: majority of research work conducted across Africa.

Publications: *South African Journal of International Affairs* (2 a year); occasional papers, special studies, reports and publications.

Finance: Total assets 23,347,948 rand (June 2010); annual revenue 27,844,406 rand, annual expenditure 28,019,042 rand (2009/10).

Council: Fred Phaswana (Chair.); Moeletsi Mbeki (Deputy Chair.); John Buchanan (Hon. Treas.).

Principal Staff: Nat. Dir Elizabeth Sidiropoulos; Man. Rosemary Vingerling.

Address: POB 31596, Braamfontein 2017; Jan Smuts House, East Campus, University of the Witwatersrand, Johannesburg.

Telephone: (11) 339-2021; **Fax:** (11) 339-2154; **Internet:** www.saiia.org.za; **e-mail:** info@saiia.org.za.

South African Institute of Race Relations

Founded in 1929 to encourage peace, goodwill and practical co-operation between the various races in South Africa, and to promote a free and open society based on liberal democratic values.

Activities: The Institute conducts research on macro-economic, socio-economic, labour, constitutional and political trends, as well as on race relations in South Africa. Also administers a large bursary programme for students at universities and technikons, and provides a consultancy service.

Geographical Area of Activity: South Africa.

Publications: *South Africa Survey* (annually); *Fast Facts* (monthly); *Spotlight Series* (occasional); news releases, *South Africa Mirror* (briefing).

Finance: Total assets 49,860,000 rand (Dec. 2010); annual income 9,860,000 rand, annual expenditure 11,270,000 rand (2010).

Council: Charles E. W. Simkins (Chair.); Prof. Jonathan Jansen; (Pres.); Prof. Hermann Giliomee, Prof. Lawrence Schlemmer, Dr Musa Shezi (Vice-Pres).

Principal Staff: Chief Exec. John Kane-Berman; Dep. Chief Exec. Frans Cronje.

Address: POB 291722, Melville 2109; 2 Clamart Rd, Richmond, Johannesburg 2092.

Telephone: (11) 4827221; **Fax:** (11) 4827690; **Internet:** www.sairr.org.za; **e-mail:** prisca@sairr.org.za.

The Helen Suzman Foundation

Established in 1995 to promote liberal constitutional democracy and human rights in South Africa and other Southern African countries.

Activities: The Foundation's mission is to defend the values that underpin the liberal constitutional democracy and to promote respect for human rights. The work of the Foundation is driven by the principles that were exemplified throughout Helen Suzman's public life, focusing on public service in all its constituent parts. Research focus areas: education, health, economic policy and wealth creation, institutional governance and South Africa's regional impact.

Geographical Area of Activity: Southern Africa.

Restrictions: Not a grant-making organization.

Publications: *Focus* (quarterly); various monographs based on roundtables and conferences.

Trustees: Richard Steyn (Chair.).

Principal Staff: Dir and Ed.-in-Chief Francis Antonie; Gen. Man. Rob Hewitt.

Address: Postnet Suite 130, Private Bag X2600, Houghton 2041; 2 Sherborne Rd, Parktown 2193.

Telephone: (11) 4822872; **Fax:** (11) 4828468; **Internet:** www.hsf.org.za; **e-mail:** info@hsf.org.za.

Transnet Foundation

Established in 1994 by Transnet, South Africa's government-owned transport and logistics organization, to promote initiatives conducive to organizational and national sustainability and development.

Activities: The goals of the Foundation are concomitant with the Government's integrated sustainable rural development (ISRDP) programme, which focuses on job creation, socio-economic development, transport heritage preservation, economic empowerment of black people, human capital development and expanded public works programmes. The Foundation also supports projects in the areas of health, arts and culture, education, sports and under-utilized assets.

Geographical Area of Activity: South Africa.

Restrictions: No grants are made to individuals, or small groups in their personal capacity, political parties or groups with partisan political affiliations, professional fundraising institutions, religious organizations for sectarian activities, institutions or bodies that are racially exclusive, profit-making concerns, trade unions, research projects, or for travel.

Principal Staff: Foundation Head Cynthia Mgijima.

Address: Postnet Suite 244, Private Bag X2226, Johannesburg 2000; 24th Floor, Carlton Centre, 150 Commissioner St, Johannesburg 2001.

Telephone: (11) 3082488; **Fax:** (11) 3082573; **Internet:** www.transnetfoundation.co.za; **e-mail:** eleanor.mthethwa@transnet.net.

The Desmond Tutu Educational Trust

Established in 1990 by Archbishop Desmond Tutu and Professor Jakes Gerwel, aiming to transform tertiary education in South Africa.

Activities: The Trust works to provide opportunities to historically disadvantaged students to develop knowledge and skills that are market orientated; contributes towards the restructuring of a non-racial education system; promotes participation by black students in leadership programmes and develops the leadership capabilities of black students; reflects a curriculum responsive to the socio-economic needs of South Africa; facilitates dialogue, co-operation and institutional sharing among tertiary institutions; assists students to improve their academic and social performance; and facilitates involvement in community work. Operates through two main programmes: the Tertiary Education Linkages Programme (TELP), through which the Trust provides academic development services; and the Support to Tertiary Education Programmes (STEP), through which it distributes grants. Also offers the Desmond Tutu Footprints of Legends Leadership Awards, including the Award for Promoting Social Justice and Equity, and runs a Work Study Programme.

Geographical Area of Activity: South Africa.

Principal Staff: Founders Desmond Tutu, Prof. Jakes Gerwel; Contact George Van Der Ross.

Address: POB 394, Kasselvlei 7533.

Telephone: (21) 9517544; **Fax:** (21) 9517668; **Internet:** www
.tututrust.org.za; **e-mail:** dtetvdross@xsinet.co.za.

WHEAT Trust—Women's Hope Education and Training Trust

Established on Women's Day in 1988 with the aim of identifying
and assisting women whose initiatives within their communities have a clear potential to transform, and promoting a culture of giving towards women's development initiatives.

Activities: The Trust operates through sourcing donations to
an endowment fund to pay for the training and education of
individual women leaders or group members of viable community groups led by women, as well as supporting projects for
women operating at grassroots level. Target areas for support
are projects in the fields of health and social services, education, promotion of small, medium and micro enterprises,
human rights and housing, and domestic violence.

Geographical Area of Activity: South Africa.

Publications: Newsletter.

Finance: Total assets 3,090,498 rand (Feb. 2011); annual
income 2,187,118 rand, annual expenditure 2,094,299 rand
(2010/11).

Trustees: Freda Daniels (Chair.); Ferose Oaten (Deputy
Chair.).

Principal Staff: Exec. Dir Soraya Matthews; Deputy Dir
Bregje Wijsenbeek.

Address: POB 18046, Wynberg, 7824 Western Cape; 4 Devonshire Ct, 20 Devonshire Rd, Wynberg, 7800 Western Cape.

Telephone: (21) 7626214; **Fax:** (21) 7972876; **Internet:** www
.wheattrust.co.za; **e-mail:** communications@wheattrust.co
.za.

WWF South Africa

A national organization of the WWF (q.v.), and until 1995
known as the Southern African Nature Foundation, which
aims to assist in the protection and conservation of nature;
raise awareness among the general public of nature conservation; and distribute and raise funds for urgent nature conservation projects in Southern Africa.

Activities: WWF works in South Africa to promote the conservation of natural resources to preserve species, and genetic
and ecosystem diversity, through encouraging sustainable
resource utilization; lowering pollution; supporting projects
on freshwater, grasslands, flora and marine conservation.
WWF has assisted in the creation or development of 23 protected areas and 11 national parks; and has managed or
funded more than 1,000 conservation projects, which include
plant conservation projects and projects devised to save more
than 70 species of endangered animals.

Geographical Area of Activity: South Africa.

Restrictions: Funding is restricted to South African conservation activities that fall within WWF South Africa's strategic
focus.

Publications: Annual Report; *Panda Bulletin* (3 a year); *Living Planet Report* (2006); *State of Marine Protected Area Management in South Africa*; *Stock Assessment of Reef Fish Species along the Coast of the Cape Peninsula National Park*; *Status of Swordfish report in South Africa*; *Business Plan for the proposed Kogelberg Marine Park*; *Education in Africa Booklet*; *Coal & Water Futures in South Africa.*

Finance: Funded by membership fees, donations and sponsorship. Total assets 201,398,000 rand (March 2007).

Board: Valli Moosa (Chair.).

Principal Staff: CEO Dr Moré du Plessis; Finance Dir Ian
Goodwin.

Address: POB 23273, Claremont 7735; 1st Floor, Bridge House,
Boundary Terraces, Mariendahl Lane, Newlands, Cape Town.

Telephone: (11) 4471213; **Fax:** (11) 4470365; **Internet:** www
.wwf.org.za; **e-mail:** info@wwf.org.za.

Spain

FOUNDATION CENTRES AND CO-ORDINATING BODIES

Asociación Española de Fundaciones (Spanish Association of Foundations)

Established in 2003 following merger of the Confederación Española de Fundaciones with the Centro de Fundaciones, to form a collective association of 1,050 member foundations.

Activities: Provides a forum for foundations and represents their common interests and needs to society, the media and the Government; co-ordinates initiatives and resolves problems. Promotes co-operation between foundations nationally and internationally, sharing experience and allowing co-ordinated work. Gives advice to foundations on a range of legal, fiscal, economic, financial and telecommunication issues; operates training courses, conferences and seminars; and maintains a database of foundations and other funding sources. Represents the foundation sector in Spanish society, aiming to portray Spanish non-profit entities in a transparent and accurate manner.

Geographical Area of Activity: Spain.

Publications: *Cuadernos de la Asociación Española de Fundaciones* (quarterly); *Tribuna de las Fundaciones* (monthly bulletin); monographs; electronic bulletin; Annual Report.

Board of Directors: SAR Don Carlos de Borbón (Hon. Pres.); Javier Nadal Arino (Pres.); Amadeo Petitbò Juan, Patricia Moreira Sanchez, Carlos Álvarez Jiménez (Vice-Pres); Adolfo Menedez Menedez (Sec.); Inigo Saenz de Miera Cardenas (Treas.).

Principal Staff: Dir-Gen. Silverio Agea Rodríguez.

Address: Calle General Castaños, 4-4A Planta, 28004 Madrid.

Telephone: 91- 310-63-09; **Fax:** 91- 578-36-23; **Internet:** www.fundaciones.org; **e-mail:** info@fundaciones.org.

Fundación Lealtad (Loyalty Foundation)

Established in February 2001 by a group of civic-minded businesspeople in Spain to promote trust among private donors and companies in NGOs active in the areas of social services, international development, humanitarian aid and environmental protection. The purpose of the Foundation is to promote donations and volunteer participation on the part of individuals and the business world in such organizations.

Activities: The Foundation monitors the compliance of NGOs with nine standards of transparency and best practices. In addition, the Foundation provides self-assessment and improvement workshops for NGOs that are not yet being monitored. The Foundation works with companies and corporate foundations with an interest in financing or working with NGOs in the framework of their social commitment strategy, and has developed several tools that help companies in the execution of their strategy. Also offers private donors specific knowledge and insight into charitable entities that have been monitored. Fundación Lealtad is supporting a project in Mexico involving the adaptation of the Spanish NGO analysis methodology in that country. The Foundation is a member of the International Committee on Fundraising Organizations (ICFO).

Geographical Area of Activity: Spain and Mexico.

Publications: *Solidarity Transparency*; *Transparency and Best Practices Guide to Spanish NGOs* (online).

Finance: Total assets €172,592 (2010); annual budget €546,653 (2010).

Board of Trustees: Salvador García-Atance Lafuente (Chair.); Ignacio Garralda Ruiz de Velasco (Vice-Chair.); Patricia de Roda Garcia (Sec.).

Principal Staff: Man. Dir Patricia de Roda García.

Address: Calle Velazquez 100, 1° dcha., 28006 Madrid.

Telephone: 91-789-01-23; **Fax:** 91-789-01-13; **Internet:** www.fundacionlealtad.org; **e-mail:** fundacion@fundacionlealtad.org.

World Forum of Civil Society Networks—UBUNTU

Constituted in 2001 within the UNESCO Chair in Technology, Sustainable Development, Imbalances and Global Change at the Technical University of Catalonia. Aims to unite and federate efforts, build bridges of dialogue and communication among national and international institutions that are focused on promoting peace, development, dignity and human rights. Operates as a network of networks, forming structures and forums of opinion aimed at promoting the principles and values that sustain democratic life and attain real human development on a world-wide scale, in harmony with nature and cultural diversity.

Activities: Promotes peace and human development in line with the principles established in the Universal Declaration of Human Rights; holds forums annually or biennially, and publishes a quarterly newsletter.

Geographical Area of Activity: World-wide.

Restrictions: No grants available.

Publications: Newsletter (quarterly); International Conference reports; Secretariat Position Document (2006); and other reports.

Finance: Funded by the Catalan Government, Barcelona City Council, Technical University of Catalonia and the Foundation for a Culture of Peace.

Principal Staff: Chair. Prof. Federico Mayor; Dir Manuel Manonelles.

Address: c/o Josep Xercavins i Valls, Technical University of Catalonia, Ed. Nexus II, Jordi Girona 29, 08034 Barcelona.

Telephone: 93-413-77-73; **Fax:** 93-413-77-77; **Internet:** www.ubuntu.upc.edu; **e-mail:** info@ubuntu.upc.edu.

FOUNDATIONS, TRUSTS AND NON-PROFIT ORGANIZATIONS

ANESVAD

Founded in 1968 by José Luis Gamarra Aranoa to undertake health-care and social development projects in less-developed countries.

Activities: The Foundation's initiatives aim to balance the inequities between South and North and to promote sustainable development in less favoured countries and sectors. Works in the area of development co-operation, primarily in the health-care field, in particular those activities aimed at eliminating leprosy, Buruli's ulcer and other diseases that affect the most vulnerable groups of poor societies. Also considers social and educational projects related to children facing sexual exploitation or in emergency situations. ANESVAD also carries out various development education and sensibilization activities. Maintains office in Madrid.

Geographical Area of Activity: Africa, Central and South America, Asia and Europe.

Publications: Magazines; leaflets; brochures; annual report.

Finance: Annual revenue €25,635,000, expenditure €17,170,000 (2007).

Principal Staff: Dir Bernardo Garcia; Dir of Administration and Finance Alberto Fernandez.

Address: Henao 29, 48099 Bilbao.

Telephone: (902) 11-88-00; **Fax:** (94) 441-07-39; **Internet:** www.anesvad.org; **e-mail:** anesvad@anesvad.org.

Centro de Investigación para la Paz, CIP—FUHEM (Peace Research Center)

A private NGO set up in 1984 by FUHEM, involved in conducting research in the fields of peace, ecology and education, and publishing the results of research. It is an active participant in national as well as international forums and networks.

Activities: Conducts research; publishes research findings; organizes conferences and seminars, and training courses for educating school teachers on peace; co-operates with international peace centres; maintains a documentation centre comprising 5,000 publications, and a press and communications office. In 1988 the Centre was awarded the Messengers of Peace award by the UN.

Geographical Area of Activity: Spain.

Publications: *Guerra y Paz en el comienzo del siglo XXI*; *De Nueva York a Kabul*; *Políticas mundiales, tendencias peligrosas*; *Anuario sobre paz, militarización y conflictos*; *Papeles para la Paz*; *Colección de Economía Crítica* (series); *Ecología Política*; *CIP Reports on Peace and Ecology*; Annual Report; numerous books on peace studies and ecology.

Board of Directors: Enrique Benedicto Mamblona (Pres.); Francisco Seco (Dir-Gen.); Francisco José Montiel Lara (Sec.); Adolfo Nunez Astray (Treas.).

Principal Staff: Dir Santiago Álvarez Cantalapiedra.

Address: Calle Duque de Sesto 40, 28009 Madrid.

Telephone: 91-576-32-99; **Fax:** 91-577-47-26; **e-mail:** fuhem@fuhem.es.

FRIDE—Fundación para las Relaciones Internacionales y el Diálogo Exterior (FRIDE—A European Think Tank for Global Action)

Established in 1999.

Activities: FRIDE is a think tank based in Madrid that aims to provide the best and most innovative thinking on Europe's role in the international arena. It strives to break new ground in its core research interests of peace and security, human rights, democracy promotion, and development and humanitarian aid, and mould debate in governmental and non-governmental bodies through rigorous analysis, rooted in the values of justice, equality and democracy. FRIDE concentrates its work in the following areas: development co-operation security and conflict; Europe and the international system; democracy and human rights policies.

Geographical Area of Activity: World-wide.

Publications: *Foreign Policy en Español* (online journal); *Challenges for European Foreign Policy in 2012*; *What kind of geo-economic Europe?*; numerous reports on international affairs; policy brief series; working papers series.

Board of Trustees: Diego Hidalgo (Founder and Hon. Pres.); Pedro Solbes (Pres.); José Manuel Romero (Vice-Pres.); Belén Galindo (Sec.).

Principal Staff: Dir-Gen. Richard Youngs; Dep. Dir-Gen. Cristina Manzano.

Address: Calle Felipe IV 9, 1º derecha, 28014 Madrid.

Telephone: 91-244-47-40; **Fax:** 91-244-47-41; **Internet:** www.fride.org; **e-mail:** fride@fride.org.

Fundació Agrupació Mútua (Agrupació Mutual Foundation)

Established in 1993 to promote social welfare.

Activities: Offers support to the elderly, children, young people and disabled people; promotes healthy living and personal autonomy; social and humanist programmes.

Geographical Area of Activity: Spain.

Address: Gran Via de les Corts Catalans 619, 08010 Barcelona.

Telephone: 93 482 67 01; **Fax:** 93 482 67 00; **Internet:** www.fundacioagrupacio.es; **e-mail:** fundacio@agrupaciomutua.es.

Fundació Jaume Bofill (Jaume Bofill Foundation)

Founded in 1969 by Teresa Roca Formosa and Josep Maria Vilaseca Marcet to encourage initiatives in the social sciences that seek to achieve a deeper understanding of society and to contribute in some tangible way towards its betterment. Merged with the Fundació Serveis de Cultura Popular in December 2000.

Activities: Promotes initiatives that work towards a better understanding of society and improving it by eliminating all forms of inequality and discrimination and extending culture and education to those who are socially deprived. Awards scholarships and individual research grants in sociology, political science, demography, city planning, etc.; makes grants to research teams and centres to further the development of research in these areas; supports meetings and discussions between social science researchers and co-operates with similar organizations, including those of international scope. Its activities come from the fields selected as a priority for successive four-year periods.

Geographical Area of Activity: Catalonia.

Publications: Newsletter (quarterly, in Catalan); books containing research projects of major contemporary relevance (also in Catalan).

Board: Teresa Roca i Formosa (Founder-Pres.); Isabel Vilaseca i Roca (Pres.) Joan Majó i Cruzate, Ángel Castiñeira i Fernández (Vice-Pres); Xavier Aragay i Tusell (Sec.).

Principal Staff: Dir Ismael Palacín i Giner; Man. Eva Queralt.

Address: Provença 324, 08037 Barcelona.

Telephone: 93-458-87-00; **Fax:** 93-458-87-08; **Internet:** www.fbofill.cat; **e-mail:** fbofill@fbofill.cat.

Fundació 'La Caixa' ('La Caixa' Foundation)

The Foundation came into existence in 1991 after the merger of Fundació Caixa de Barcelona and Fundació Caixa de Pensions.

Activities: The Foundation aims to address social needs unaddressed by other organizations in the areas of social aid, education, health care, science and culture, through self-devised programmes as well as through programmes carried out in collaboration with other organizations in Spain as well as in other countries where La Caixa savings bank operates. It manages funds allotted for social welfare by Caja de Ahorros y Pensiones de Barcelona; runs two proprietary science museums, an art gallery exhibiting a collection of contemporary art, and a school of nursing.

Geographical Area of Activity: Spain and international, in countries where La Caixa operates.

Publications: *Estrella* (6 a year); Annual Report; brochures.

Finance: Funded by the Caixa d'Estalvis i Pensions de Barcelona. Welfare projects expenditure €462,629,000 (2010); welfare projects budget €500,000,000 (2011).

Board of Trustees: Josep Vilarasau Salat (Hon. Chair.); Isidre Fainé Casas (Chair.); Alejandro García-Bragado Dalmau (Sec.).

Principal Staff: CEO Jaume Lanaspa Gatnau.

Address: Avda Diagonal 621–629, 08028 Barcelona.

Telephone: 93-404-60-00; **Fax:** 93-404-61-16; **Internet:** www.fundacio.lacaixa.es; **e-mail:** info.fundacio@lacaixa.es.

Fundació CIDOB (CIDOB Foundation)

Established in 1973 as a not-for-profit organization, became a private foundation in 1979.

Activities: Operates in the areas of development studies, education and international affairs, through self-conducted programmes, research, conferences, training courses and publications. Fields of interest are international politics, strategic studies, development and co-operation, intercultural relations, migrations and population and development, with a geographical focus on the Arab world, Asia, Sub-Saharan Africa, Central and South America, Central and Eastern Europe, countries of the former USSR, and the Mediterranean region. Also maintains a documentation centre.

Geographical Area of Activity: Spain, Latin America, the Mediterranean and Arab world, Europe and Asia.

Publications: *Anuario Internacional; Afers Internationals; CIDOB News* (monthly newsletter); Annual Report; monographs; yearbooks; books and special reports.

Board of Directors: Narcís Serra i Serra (Chair.); Javier Solana Madariaga (Hon. Chair.).

Principal Staff: Dir Dr Jordi Vaquer i Fanés.

Address: Calle Elisabets 12, 08001 Barcelona.

Telephone: 93-302-64-95; **Fax:** 93-302-21-18; **Internet:** www .cidob.org; **e-mail:** cidob@cidob.org.

Fundación Actilibre

Established in 1976.

Activities: Promotes cultural and social activities, including funding festivals, conferences, seminars and training courses. Also grants a number of annual awards.

Geographical Area of Activity: Spain.

Publications: *Coleccíon Bricolage; Coleccíon Expolingua; Coleccíon Medios de Comunicacíon; Coleccíon Ocio Y Arte; Coleccíon Turismo; Expolingua Congreso-Muestra Internacional*; and other publications.

Board of Directors: Florencio Arnán y Lombarte (Pres.); Camilo José Vizoso López (Vice-Pres.); José Luis Alemany López (Treas.).

Principal Staff: Pres. D. Florencio Arnán y Lombarte.

Address: Guzmán el Bueno 99, 1º, 28015 Madrid.

Telephone: 91-543-17-02; **Fax:** 91-543-25-19; **Internet:** www .fundacionactilibre.com; **e-mail:** info@fundacionactilibre .com.

Fundación AFIM—Ayuda, Formación e Integración del Minusválido (Foundation for Assistance, Training and Integration of Disadvantaged People)

Established in 1992 to support the integration of people disadvantaged in society, whether through mental disability or their economic circumstances.

Activities: Promotes the reintegration in society of economically disadvantaged people or people with mental disabilities through self-conducted and funded programmes in the fields of training, rehabilitation and cultural visits.

Geographical Area of Activity: Spain.

Publications: Newsletter (quarterly); magazine.

Principal Staff: Dir Patricia Lacasa.

Address: Ctra de La Coruña km 18,200, Edif. D, 1º, 28231 Las Rozas, Madrid.

Telephone: 91-710-58-58; **Fax:** 91-637-66-49; **Internet:** www .fundacionafim.org.

Fundación de los Agentes Comerciales de España (Foundation of Spanish Commercial Agents)

Established in 1989 for cultural and social purposes.

Activities: Operates in the areas of economic affairs, education, international affairs and social welfare, nationally and internationally through self-conducted programmes and conferences, and nationally through grants to individuals and institutions, prizes and publications. Maintains a database.

Geographical Area of Activity: World-wide.

Publications: *La Gaceta del Agente Comercial* (journal, 6 a year).

Board of Trustees: Manuel Francisco Maestre Barrajón (Pres.); Galerón Lorenzo González (Vice-Pres.); Joaquin Pago Torrén (Treas.); José Alejandro Blanco de Lara (Sec.).

Address: Calle Goya 55, 5º piso, 28001 Madrid.

Telephone: 90-236-69-56; **Fax:** 91-577-00-84; **Internet:** www .cgac.es; **e-mail:** fundacion@cgac.es.

Fundación Albéniz (Albéniz Foundation)

Established in November 1986 by Federico Sopeña, Paloma O'Shea, Elena G. Botín, J. L. Martínez Marauri, Pedro Robles and Luis Revenga to support the arts and humanities and education.

Activities: Operates in the areas of the arts and humanities and education, through self-conducted programmes, research, scholarships and fellowships, publications and training courses. Principal activities are the Concurso Internacional de Piano de Santander Paloma O'Shea, supporting a music school, maintaining an archive and documentation centre and funding a music academy in Santander.

Geographical Area of Activity: Spain.

Publications: *Rubinstein y España; Albénez; Imágenes de la Música Iberoamericana; Imágenes de Isaac Albéniz.*

Board of Trustees: HH Infanta Doña Margarita Duquesa de Soria (Hon. Pres.); Alicia de Larrocha (Hon. Vice-Pres.); Paloma O'Shea (Pres.); Enrique Franco (Vice-Pres.); José Luis Zambade (Sec.).

Principal Staff: Dir-Gen. Vicente Ferrer y Pérez de León.

Address: Plaza de Oriente s/n, 28013 Madrid.

Telephone: 91-523-04-19; **Fax:** 91-532-96-61; **Internet:** www .fundacionalbeniz.com; **e-mail:** fundacion@albeniz.com.

Fundación Alzheimer España—FAE (Alzheimer Spain Foundation)

Founded in 1991 to inform, assess, support and train families and carers of those suffering from Alzheimer's Disease, increase the possibilities of early diagnosis and disseminate information about the disease.

Activities: Operates in the fields of medicine and health and social welfare and social studies, through training courses, consultancy, publications and international conferences. A founding member of Alzheimer Europe.

Geographical Area of Activity: Spain.

Publications: *Vivir con la enfermedad de Alzheimer; Vivencias Familiares; Como cuidarse de sí mismo-Cuidador principal; Cómo elegir la residencia adecuada al momento de institucionalizar al paciente con EA; Proceedings of the European Conference on Alzheimer's Disease and Public Health*; Bulletin (quarterly).

Governing Board: Micheline Antoine Selmes (Pres.); Ana Arribas (Sec.).

Address: Calle Pedro Muguruza 1, 6C, 28036 Madrid.

Telephone: 91-343-11-65; **Fax:** 91-359-54-50; **Internet:** www .alzfae.org; **e-mail:** fae@alzfae.org.

Fundación Carlos de Amberes (Carlos de Amberes Foundation)

Established in 1594 by Carlos de Amberes, a Flemish merchant living in Madrid, to support pilgrims from the then Spanish Low Countries. In 1988 the Foundation adapted its aims from acts of charity to cultural activities, aiming to build a united Europe.

Activities: Operates in the field of the arts and humanities, acting as a cultural link between Spain, Belgium, Luxembourg, France and the Netherlands, through organizing exhibitions, courses, seminars, conferences and music concerts, held at the Foundation's headquarters. Maintains a library specializing in European Union issues and organizes seminars on the construction of a new Europe.

Geographical Area of Activity: Spain.

Publications: *Man Ray Lights and dreams; Monograph Felipe I the Beautiful one; 1506: European chronicles; Verse music;*

Madrid, mayo 1955 Cas Oorthuys; Anton van Dyck y el arte del grabado; Signos febriles y frágiles: Obra sobre papel de Henri Michaux; Paul Delvaux: Dibujos de una vida; Ceci n' est pas une pomme: Arte contemporáneo en Bélgica.

Trustees: HH King Juan Carlos (Pres.).

Principal Staff: Pres. Miguel Ángel Aguilar; Sec. Daniel de Busturia; Dir Catherine Geens.

Address: Claudio Coello 99, 28006 Madrid.

Telephone: 91-435-22-01; **Fax:** 91-578-10-92; **Internet:** www .fcamberes.org; **e-mail:** fca@fcamberes.org.

Fundación Ramón Areces (Ramón Areces Foundation)

Founded in March 1976 by Ramón Areces Rodríguez to support scientific and technical research.

Activities: The Foundation co-operates with other organizations interested in the promotion and preservation of Spanish culture and scientific research. Awards research grants for scientific and technical projects, and scholarships to universities and research centres abroad. The cultural programme includes lectures, symposia, conferences and inter-university courses.

Geographical Area of Activity: Spain.

Finance: Annual expenditure approx. US $11,000,000.

Board of Directors: Isidoro Álvarez Álvarez (Chair.); Juan Manuel de Mingo y Contreras (Sec.).

Principal Staff: Dir Raimundo Pérez-Hernández y Torra.

Address: Calle Vitruvio 5, 28006 Madrid.

Telephone: 91-515-89-80; **Fax:** 91-564-52-43; **Internet:** www .fundacionareces.es; **e-mail:** info@fundacionareces.es.

Fundación Banco Bilbao Vizcaya Argentaria—Fundación BBVA (BBVA Foundation)

Founded in 1988 to create conditions that support discussion on the problems and challenges faced by society. Merged with the Fundación Argentaria in 2000.

Activities: Operates internationally and devotes a special interest to promoting scientific research in the areas of social science, biomedicine and the environment. Promotes knowledge as the most effective means to address the challenges facing contemporary society (environmental protection, sustainable development, health care, demographic change, globalization, social integration and innovation at the service of expanding opportunities for all members of society). Also seeks to promote analysis, reflection and debate in the areas of economic and international affairs, social science, and science and technology through programmes, conferences, publications and courses in collaboration with other groups and organizations. A series of major awards was launched in 2005, focusing on biodiversity conservation. Prizes are given in Spain and Central and South America to recognize achievement in excellence in scientific research, innovative action in nature conservation, and dissemination of knowledge in the area of environmental preservation.

Geographical Area of Activity: Spain, Europe, the USA, and Central and South America.

Restrictions: Research grants are open to Spanish organizations, but with an emphasis on international co-operation.

Publications: Working papers; Annual Report; books; newsletter.

Board of Trustees: Francisco González Rodríguez (Pres.); Domingo Armengol Calvo (Sec.).

Principal Staff: Dir Rafael Pardo Avellaneda.

Address: Plaza de San Nicolás 4, 48005 Bilbao.

Telephone: 94-487-52-52; **Fax:** 94-424-46-21; **Internet:** www .fbbva.es; **e-mail:** informacion@fbbva.es.

Fundación José Miguel de Barandiarán (José Miguel de Barandiaran Foundation)

Established in June 1988 by the Sociedad de Estudios Vascos–Eusko Ikaskuntza in conjunction with José Miguel de Barandiaran Ayerbe to promote science and culture.

Activities: The Foundation operates through organizing and funding programmes and awarding research grants in the fields of prehistory, archaeology, anthropology and ethnology. Also organizes courses, seminars, conferences and other related activities, and disseminates their results.

Geographical Area of Activity: Spain.

Publications: *Collection Sara; Yearbook of Eusko Folklore; Collection Barandiar;* catalogues.

Board of Trustees: Josemari Velez de Mendizabal Azkarraga (Pres.); Beatriz Akizu Aizpiri (Sec.).

Address: General Alava 5, 1°, 01005 Vitoria-Gasteiz.

Telephone: 94-514-30-66; **Fax:** 94-514-13-64; **Internet:** www .barandiaranfundazioa.com; **e-mail:** gasteiz@ barandiaranfundazioa.com.

Fundación Barceló (Barceló Foundation)

A non-profit institution set up in October 1989 by the Barceló Oliver family.

Activities: Focuses on Central America but also provides some grants in Africa and South America. Operates in the areas of health, research, education, culture and art, aiming to contribute to the upliftment of people and society through its projects and resources. Offers micro-loans; provides medical equipment and assistance for medical training; extends financial support to housing projects and initiatives conducive to agricultural development; hosts art exhibitions; and extends support to educational projects aimed at developing countries.

Geographical Area of Activity: Central America and South America, Africa, and Mallorca, Spain.

Finance: Total assets €23,072,105 (2010).

Principal Staff: Dir-Gen. Rafael Torra Torreguitart.

Address: Casa del Marqués de Reguer, Calle San Jaime 4, 07012 Palma de Mallorca.

Telephone: 97-172-24-67; **Fax:** 97-172-03-80; **Internet:** www .barcelo.com/BarceloHotels/en-GB/Foundation/Presentacion .htm; **e-mail:** fundacion@barcelo.com.

Fundación Barenboim-Said (Barenboim-Said Foundation)

Established in 2004 by the Andalusian regional government to develop a broad project promoting intercultural conciliation through music.

Activities: The Foundation promotes peace and reconciliation through music; promotes music education; and operates and promotes music education projects in Andalusia, Israel, Palestinian areas and Arab countries. Initiatives include the West-Eastern Divan Orchestra of musicians from Israel, the Middle East and Spain; the Academy of Orchestral Studies; a music education project in Palestinian Autonomous Areas; and an early childhood music education project that operates in Andalusian primary schools. Maintains represenatative offices in Berlin and Ramallah.

Geographical Area of Activity: Israel, Spain and the Middle East.

Publications: newsletter; *Parallels and Paradoxes; Humanism and Democratic Criticism; Musical Elaborations; Representations of the Intellectual; Music and Literature against the grain;* dvds.

Board of Trustees: Mariam C. Said (Hon. Pres.).

Principal Staff: Pres. Daniel Barenboim Schuster; Man. Dir Muriel Páez Rasmussen.

Address: Calle Cardenal Bueno Monreal 58, 2°, 41013 Seville.

Telephone: 95-503-73-85; **Fax:** 95-503-73-84; **Internet:** www .barenboim-said.org; **e-mail:** info.fbs@juntadeandalucia.es.

Fundación Pedro Barrié de la Maza (Pedro Barrié de la Maza Foundation)

Founded in 1966 by Pedro Barrié de la Maza, Conde de Fenosa, to promote research in the sciences and in the field of arts and letters; to support deserving Spanish students; to promote the industrialization and prosperity of Spain in general and the Galicia region in particular; and to support charitable, educational and social institutions, with priority to those in Galicia.

Activities: Operates mainly in Galicia in the fields of education, social welfare and studies, science, medicine and the arts and humanities, through self-conducted programmes, research, grants to individuals and institutions, conferences, courses and publications. The Foundation awards scholarships, prizes and research grants, and has financed the construction and equipment of technical schools and cultural and social institutions. Established the Galician Institute of Economic Studies in 1994.

Geographical Area of Activity: Galicia, Spain.

Publications: Annual Report; books on humanities and economics; dictionaries.

Finance: Annual expenditure €10,946,341 (2010).

Board of Trustees: José María Arias Mosquera (Pres.); Pilar Romero Vázquez-Gulías (Vice-Pres.); Vicente Arias Mosquera (Sec.).

Principal Staff: Gen. Dir Javier López Martínez.

Address: Cantón Grande 9, 15003 A Coruña.

Telephone: 98-122-15-25; **Fax:** 98-122-44-48; **Internet:** www .fundacionbarrie.org; **e-mail:** info@fundacionbarrie.org.

Fundación José María Blanc (José María Blanc Foundation)

Established in 1982 by José María Blanc.

Activities: Operates in the field of conservation and the environment, through the study, conservation and promotion of wild fauna and game and their natural habitat. In 1988 the Foundation created the Cañada Real environmental centre in Peralejo, dedicated to the preservation of wildlife and the promotion of environmental education.

Geographical Area of Activity: Spain.

Principal Staff: Founding Pres. José María Blanc Díaz.

Address: Ctra. MV-533, km 16, 28211 Peralejo, Madrid.

Telephone: 91-890-69-80; **Fax:** 91-890-04-51; **Internet:** www .opennature.com; **e-mail:** contacto@opennature.com.

Fundación Marcelino Botín (Marcelino Botín Foundation)

Established in 1964 by Marcelino Botín to 'mitigate the needs and promote the social development' of the Cantabria region.

Activities: Operates in the fields of education, technological transfer, social sciences, arts and creativity, heritage and sustainable development, through innovative projects, grants, awarding prizes (such as the Manuel Valcárcel International Piano Composition Competition with a first prize of €12,000) and organizing conferences, training courses, concerts and exhibitions.

Geographical Area of Activity: Europe.

Publications: Library includes section on Cantabria in historical documents, art, environment and sustainable development; *Science and Economy Collection*; *Literature Collection*.

Finance: Approx. budget €25,000,000 (2008).

Board of Trustees: Emilio Botín Ríos (Chair.).

Principal Staff: Dir-Gen. Iñigo Saenz de Miera Cárdenas.

Address: Calle Pedrueca 1, 39003 Santander.

Telephone: 94-222-60-72; **Fax:** 94-236-04-94; **Internet:** www .fundacionmbotin.org; **e-mail:** info@fundacionbotin.org.

Fundación Caja Madrid (Caja Madrid Foundation)

Established in 1991 by the Caja Madrid savings bank to operate in the fields of the arts and humanities.

Activities: Operates mainly in Spain in the fields of the arts and conservation, through various programmes, grants for research, scholarships and bursaries. The Music Programme promotes music through concerts, operatic productions and television programmes; the Madrid Programme publishes information about the history and culture of Madrid. The Foundation is also currently funding the restoration of two monasteries at Yuste (Cáceres) and Sijena (Huesca), and other monuments. It works in collaboration with other public and private sector organizations.

Geographical Area of Activity: Spain.

Publications: Annual Report; *Música y Educación* (quarterly); books and brochures; *Vanguardias Rusas*; *Gauguin y los Orígenes del Simbolismo*; *Willi Baumeister*; *Museo Thyssen-Bornemisza*; *Exposiciones Sobre Arte y Cultura*; *Pensadores Españoles Contemporáneos*; *Real Academia de Medicina*; *Boletín Instituto Libre de Enseñanza*.

Finance: Total income €132,916,172, expenditure €132,916,172 (2010).

Board of Trustees: Rodrigo de Rato Figaredo (Pres.); Miguel Crespo Rodríguez (Sec.).

Principal Staff: Dir Rafael Spottorno Díaz-Caro.

Address: Plaza de San Martin 1, 28013 Madrid.

Telephone: 90-224-68-10; **Fax:** 91-379-20-20; **Internet:** www .fundacioncajamadrid.es; **e-mail:** consultasfundacion@ bankia.com.

Fundación de las Cajas de Ahorros—FUNCAS (Foundation of Savings Banks)

Founded in 1968 by the Confederación Española de Cajas de Ahorros to study all scientific matters related to savings and savings banks; its research has been extended to include economics and financial systems, fiscal and taxation law, contemporary history and statistics, with special emphasis on their relation to the field of savings, and to similar European institutions.

Activities: Maintains close links with economic ministries and financial centres. The Foundation has an extensive library, a publishing fund that has produced more than 300 titles and a small grants fund for sustainable development projects in Spain. Awards annual Enrique Fuentes Quintana Prize (€4,000) for doctoral thesis.

Geographical Area of Activity: Spain.

Publications: *Papeles de Economía Española*; *Perspectivas del Sistema Financiero*; *Cuadernos de Información Económica*; *Panorama Social*; *Documentos de Trabajo*; *Economía de las Comunidades Autónomas*; *Estudios de la Fundación*; *El futuro del sector bancario;* and other publications.

Trustees: Isidro Faine Casas (Pres.); José Maria Méndez Álvarez-Cedrón (Vice-Pres.); Fernando Conlledo Lantero (Sec.).

Principal Staff: Dir-Gen. Carlos Ocana Pérez de Tudela.

Address: Edificio Foro, Calle Caballero de Gracia 28, 28013 Madrid.

Telephone: 91-596-57-18; **Fax:** 91-596-57-96; **Internet:** www .funcas.es; **e-mail:** funcas@funcas.es.

Fundación Eduardo Capa (Eduardo Capa Foundation)

Established in December 1998 by Eduardo Capa Sacristán and Julia Sanz Vaca to house the Eduardo Capa sculpture collection.

Activities: Operates in the areas of the arts and humanities, and education, through self-conducted programmes, conferences, training courses and publications; also holds a summer university of sculpture and organizes temporary sculpture exhibitions.

Geographical Area of Activity: Spain.

Publications: Catalogues of temporary exhibitions; newsletter.

Finance: Financed by local government.

Trustees: Eduardo Capa Sacristán (Founder and Pres.); Luis Díaz Alperi (Pres.); Manuel Tarancón Fandós (First Vice-Pres.).

Principal Staff: Dir Fernando Capa Sanz; Man. José García Gomez; Museum Dir Aurora Martín Nájera.

Address: Calle Gorrión 7, 28500 Arganda del Rey, Madrid.

Telephone: 91-871-04-63; **Fax:** 91-870-20-16; **Internet:** www
.fundacioncapa.com; **e-mail:** fundacion@capaesculturas
.com.

Fundación Científica de la Asociación Española Contra el Cáncer—AECC (Scientific Foundation of the Spanish Cancer Association)

Established in 1971 to channel and manage the funds that the
Spanish Cancer Association devotes to cancer research, with
two fundamental objectives: to promote and advance oncological research; and to link research and society through the
spreading of scientific advances about cancer and involving
society in research.

Activities: The Spanish Cancer Association has delegations
in all Spanish provinces, and co-operates with health authorities, scientific institutions and similar organizations. The
Foundation offers funding for cancer research under the following programmes: Stable research groups; Child cancer
research project; Advanced cancer training programme;
Assistance for researchers.

Geographical Area of Activity: Mainly Spain.

Publications: *Estadística* (annually); information and monographs; *Cuidados Estéticos*; *Cómo ayudar tras el fallecimiento
de un ser querido*; *InfoCáncer*; *Cómo hacer frente a la pérdida
de un ser querido*.

Executive Council: Isabel Oriol Díaz de Bustamante (Pres.);
Pilar Perote Mendizábal, Antonio González-Adalid García-
Zozaya (Vice-Pres); José Luis Sáenz de Miera Alonso (Treas.);
Enrique García-Romeu Fleta (Sec.).

Principal Staff: Dir-Gen. Iñaki Martín-Gromaz Hernández.

Address: Amador de los Ríos 5, 28010 Madrid.

Telephone: 91-319-41-38; **Fax:** 91-319-09-66; **Internet:** www
.todocancer.com; **e-mail:** sedecentral@aecc.es.

Fundación CODESPA—Futuro en Marcha (Co-operation for the Promotion and Development of Welfare Activities)

Established in 1985 to promote the economic and social development of the countries of Central and South America, the
Mediterranean, Asia and Africa.

Activities: Operates nationally and internationally, in Central and South America, Africa, the Middle East and the Philippines and Viet Nam, in the fields of aid to less-developed
countries, economic affairs, education and social welfare,
through awarding grants to institutions, conferences, training
courses and issuing publications. Maintains offices in Peru,
Honduras, Philippines, the Maghreb countries, Colombia,
Dominican Republic and the USA.

Geographical Area of Activity: Asia, Central and South
America, Africa, the Middle East, the Philippines, Viet Nam
and Spain.

Publications: *CODESPA Foundation Bulletin*; Annual
Report.

Finance: Annual income €27,694,239, annual expenditure
€27,694,239 (2010).

Trustees: HH Don Felipe de Borbón y Grecia, Príncipe de
Asturias (Hon. Pres.); Laura Castán Visa (Pres.); Enrique Sendagorta Gomendio (Vice-Pres.); Pablo de la Esperanza Rodríguez (Sec.).

Principal Staff: Dir-Gen. José Ignacio González-Aller.

Address: Rafael Bergamín 12, Bajo, 28043 Madrid.

Telephone: 91-744-42-40; **Fax:** 91-744-42-41; **Internet:** www
.codespa.org; **e-mail:** codespa@codespa.org.

Fundación EAES

Established in 2002 by the Confederación de Entidades para la
Economía Social de Andalucía and the Federación Andaluza
de Empresas Cooperativas de Trabajo Asociado to support education, research, corporate development, innovation and international co-operation.

Activities: Runs a lifelong education centre and discussion
groups.

Geographical Area of Activity: Spain.

Board: Antonio Romero Moreno (Pres.); Manuel Mariscal
Sigüenza (Vice-Pres.); Francisco Moreno Navajas (Sec.); Teresa
Páez Moreno (Treas.).

Address: Plaza de La Merced s/n, CP 41640, Osuna, Seville.

Telephone: 95-481-21-15; **Fax:** 95-582-05-63; **Internet:** www
.eaes.es; **e-mail:** info@feaes.es.

Fundación EFE

Established in 1987 by the Agencia EFE, a Spanish-language
news agency, as a cultural organization principally concerned
with the preservation and dissemination of the Spanish language.

Activities: The Foundation is active in the fields of art and
culture, information technology, education and science; it collaborates with other organizations to hold exhibitions, funds
postgraduate courses at universities, provides student bursaries and organizes seminars and conferences.

Geographical Area of Activity: Spain.

Principal Staff: Pres. Paloma Rupérez; Programme Co-ordinator Marisa Mendívil.

Address: Calle Espronceda 32, 3º, 28003 Madrid.

Telephone: 91-346-71-72; **Fax:** 91-346-71-75; **Internet:** www
.fundacionefe.es; **e-mail:** fundacion@efe.es.

Fundación Empresa y Sociedad (Business and Society Foundation)

Established in 1995 to encourage Spanish and foreign companies working in Spain to improve their corporate community
involvement through social innovation.

Activities: Operates in the areas of research, debate and
advice, promoting discussion on corporate community involvement in Spain. Carries out research on issues relevant to business, and acts as a source of information on community
commitment, practice and experience. Links companies,
NGOs and government agencies. Advises companies on corporate community involvement and establishing community
involvement initiatives, and manages projects. Produces a
database on community programmes and the voluntary sector.

Geographical Area of Activity: Spain.

Publications: Annual Report; Best Practices; Guidelines.

Finance: Total income €362,521, total expenditure €419,797
(2010).

Board: María Aparicio (Pres.); Antonio Fernández (Vice-Pres.).

Principal Staff: Dir Estela Fernández.

Address: Orense 29, 6º, 28020 Madrid.

Telephone: 91-435-89-97; **Fax:** 91-435-39-74; **Internet:** www
.empresaysociedad.org; **e-mail:** info@empresaysociedad.org.

Fundación Empresa-Universidad de Zaragoza— FEUZ (University of Zaragoza Business Foundation)

Founded in 1982 by the Universidad y Cámara de Comercio e
Industria de Zaragoza to promote business research and training.

Activities: Operates nationally and internationally, in the
fields of aid to less-developed countries, arts and humanities,
conservation and the environment, economic affairs, education, international affairs, law and human rights, medicine
and health, science and technology, and social welfare and
social studies, through research, grants to individuals, scholarships and fellowships, prizes, conferences and training
courses.

Geographical Area of Activity: International, with an
emphasis on Central and South America and Europe.

Publications: Newsletter.

Trustees: Manuel Teruel Izquierdo (Pres.); Manuel López
Pérez (Vice-Pres.); María Dolores Roche Gil (Treas.); José
Miguel Sánchez Muñoz (Sec.).

Address: Paseo Fernando el Católico 2, 50005 Zaragoza.

Telephone: 97-635-15-08; **Fax:** 97-655-85-49; **Internet:** www
.feuz.es; **e-mail:** feuz@feuz.es.

Fundación Entorno, Empresara y Desarrollo Sostenible

Established in 1995, as Fundación Teneo para la Mejora del
Medio Ambiente y la Conservación de la Naturaleza, with the
support of 16 companies to advise businesses on environmental matters.

Activities: Operates in Spain and in Central and South American countries in three main programme areas: information
and training; research and education; and nature conservation. Organizes training programmes, workshops, conferences
and seminars; supports research into environmental issues;
and offers scholarships for environmental research carried
out abroad. Maintains an online corporate database.

Geographical Area of Activity: Central and South America, Spain.

Publications: *Environmental Magazine*; conference reports
and technical publications.

Finance: Total income €2,395,874. total expenditure
€2,395,874 (2010).

Trustees: Javier Salas Collantes (Pres.); Miguel Cuenca Valdivia (Vice-Pres.); Félix Benítez de Lugo Guillén (Sec.).

Principal Staff: Man. Dir Cristina García-Orcoyen Tormo.

Address: Calle Monte Esquinza 30, 6º derecha, 28010 Madrid.

Telephone: 91-575-63-94; **Fax:** 91-575-77-13; **Internet:** www
.fundacionentorno.org; **e-mail:** info@fundacionentorno.org.

Fundación Dr Antonio Esteve (Dr Antonio Esteve Foundation)

The Foundation was set up in 1983 primarily to promote
advancement in pharmacotherapy through scientific communication and discussion.

Activities: Organizes multidisciplinary meetings on an international level where discussions are carried by groups of
researchers about their findings, which are broadcast through
the Esteve Foundation Symposia collection; provides grants in
support to pharmaceutical, biological and medical sciences;
bestows a number of research awards on a biennial basis;
arranges conferences for Spanish researchers where they discuss their findings, which are disseminated through Dr Antonio Esteve Monographs.

Geographical Area of Activity: Spain.

Publications: Monographs; booklets; articles; Foundation
symposia; *Pharmacotherapy Revisited* (series); and other publications.

Board of Trustees: Josep Esteve Soler (Pres.); Joan Esteve
Soler (First Vice-Pres.); Montserrat Esteve Soler (Second
Vice-Pres.).

Principal Staff: Pres. Josep Esteve Soler; Dir Sergio Erill
Sáez; Sec. Josep Maria Ràfols Ferrer.

Address: Llobet i Vall-Llosera 2, 08032 Barcelona.

Telephone: 93-433-53-20; **Fax:** 93-450-48-99; **Internet:** www
.esteve.org; **e-mail:** fundacion@esteve.org.

Fundación Gala–Salvador Dalí (Salvador Dalí Foundation)

Created on 23 December 1983 at the express wish of the artist
Salvador Dalí to promote, lend prestige to, protect and defend
in Spain and in any other country the artistic, cultural and
intellectual oeuvre of the painter, his goods and rights of any
nature; his life experience, his thoughts, his projects and ideas
and artistic, intellectual and cultural works; his memory and
the universal recognition of his contribution to the fine arts,
culture and contemporary thought.

Activities: Promotes the work of the Spanish artist Salvador
Dalí through the study and dissemination of the most diverse
aspects of his works, publishing books and articles and staging conferences. Also provides research grants and organizes
international events such as the International Salvador Dalí
Symposium, and temporary exhibitions. The Foundation also

holds and conserves the collections that the painter
bequeathed to the Spanish Government on his death, including manuscripts, letters, photographs, books and films, which
are made available to students and researchers from all over
the world for academic purposes. The Foundation also administers four museums dedicated to the artist's work.

Geographical Area of Activity: Spain.

Publications: Annual Report; *Catalogue Raisonné of paintings*; *Dalí Theatre-Museum, Figueres*; *Dalí: Joyas/Jewels*; *Dalí
versus Schaal*; *Dallibres*; *Dalí Gaudí: The Revolution of the Feeling of Originality*; *Cadaqués, Scenario of Antoni Pitxot*; *Dalí:
Elective Affinities*; *The Secret Life of Salvador Dalí*; *Dalí: Mass
Culture*.

Finance: Total assets €200,000,000 (2010).

Board of Trustees: Rámon Boixadós Malé (Chair.); Santi
Vila Vicente (Sr Vice-Chair.).

Principal Staff: Man. Dir Joan Manuel Sevillano.

Address: Torre Galatea, Pujada del Castell 28, 17600 Figueres.

Telephone: 97-267-75-05; **Fax:** 97-250-16-66; **Internet:** www
.salvador-dali.org.

Fundación Hogar del Empleado—FUHEM (Workers' Centre Foundation)

Founded in 1965 (existed as an association since 1949) to promote solidarity, peace and justice.

Activities: The Foundation operates through editing magazines and other publications; creating educational and professional centres; organizing courses and conferences for
professionals; and other activities directed at fostering
employment and social participation, promoting tolerance,
respect for human rights, peace, issues of co-operation for
development, and humanitarian assistance initiatives. It
owns seven schools, and established the Centro de Investigación para la Paz (q.v.) in 1984, which carries out research in
the fields of international relations, environmental issues and
economics, and the Centro de Innovación Educativa, which
conducts educational programmes aimed at young people at
risk of exclusion.

Geographical Area of Activity: Spain.

Publications: *Papeles de cuestiones internacionales*; *Ecología
política*; *La situación del mundo (World Watch Institute Report)*;
Anuario CIP; *Observatorio de conflictors*; *Guias didacticas de
educación para el desarrollo*; *Colección de Economía Critica* (2
a year); *Centro de Investigación para la Paz*; *Repensar, reorientar el CIP*.

Board of Trustees: Angel Martínez González-Tablas (Pres.);
Javier Gutiérrez Hurtado (Vice-Pres.); Maria Luisa Rodríguez
Garcia-Robes (Sec.).

Principal Staff: Dir Yayo López Herrero; Gen. Man. José
García del Pozo.

Address: Calle Duque de Sesto 40, 28009 Madrid.

Telephone: 91-431-02-80; **Fax:** 91-578-33-13; **Internet:** www
.fuhem.es; **e-mail:** fuhem@fuhem.es.

Fundación Innovación de la Economía Social—INNOVES

Established in 2006 to promote innovation among social economy companies in the Andalusia region.

Activities: Carries out research and training; promotes
social development and innovation; promotes international
co-operation.

Geographical Area of Activity: Spain.

Principal Staff: Man. José Carlos Rodrigo.

Address: Parque Tecnológico de Andalucía, Calle Ivan Pavlov
8, Bloque 3, Bajo E, 29590 Campanillas.

Telephone: 952-27-22-53; **Fax:** 952-02-83-92; **Internet:** www
.innoves.es; **e-mail:** info@innoves.es.

Fundación Instituto de Empresa (Business Institute Foundation)

Established in 1997 to promote the training and involvement of young people in the business sector, and their continual training in relevant corporate areas.

Activities: Operates in the field of education. Awards aid and scholarships to Spanish and foreign students who wish to undertake studies at Instituto de Empresa or in other training centres; and to professors and researchers to undertake training or research work. Also finances research interns, seminars and conferences. Maintains a library; issues publications.

Geographical Area of Activity: Primarily Spain, but also North and South America, South-East Asia, the Middle East, North Africa and Europe.

Publications: *IDEAS* (quarterly magazine).

Finance: Annual revenue €3,804,931, annual expenditure €3,239,679 (2010).

Board of Governors: Diego del Alcázar (Pres.); Rafael Puyol (Vice-Pres.); Macarena Rosado (Sec.).

Principal Staff: Dir Margarita Alonso.

Address: María de Molina 6, 1°, 28006 Madrid.

Telephone: 91-787-01-00; **Fax:** 91-564-76-91; **Internet:** www .ie.edu/IE/php/en/fundacion_ie.php; **e-mail:** info@ie.edu.

Fundación Intervida (Intervida Foundation)

Established in 1995 to assist vulnerable children and their families in the developing world.

Activities: Works in the area of capacity building, education and development in less-developed countries, focusing on children in need and their families.

Geographical Area of Activity: Central and South America, West Africa, South Asia and South-East Asia.

Publications: *Contigo* (newsletter); magazine and other publications.

Finance: Total income €44,664,054, expenditure €24,209,612 (2009).

Trustees: Guillermo Mejía Valenzuela (Pres.); José Antonio García (Vice-Pres.); Francisca Ruiz Perez (Sec.).

Address: Calle Pujades 77–79, 4°, 08005 Barcelona.

Telephone: 90-219-19-19; **Fax:** 93-309-68-68; **Internet:** www .intervida.org; **e-mail:** intervida@intervida.org.

Fundación para la Investigación Agraria de la Provincia de Almería—FIAPA (Foundation for Agricultural Research in the Province of Almería)

Established in 1988 to operate in the field of teaching, financing and promotion of research and development.

Activities: Operates in Almería (Andalusia region), North Africa and South America in the field of science and technology, and specifically agricultural research, through research, grants, scholarships and fellowships, conferences, training courses and issuing publications. Also acts as an information and co-ordination centre for the development of the agricultural economy.

Geographical Area of Activity: Almería, Spain; North Africa and South America.

Publications: Numerous agricultural publications; books; and research reports.

Principal Staff: Man. Dir Isabel M. Cuadrado Gómez.

Address: Carretera de la playa s/n, La Cañada de San Urbano, 04120 Almería.

Telephone: 95-029-19-81; **Fax:** 95-029-00-92; **Internet:** www .fiapa.es; **e-mail:** info@fiapa.es.

Fundación Yannick y Ben Jakober (Yannick and Ben Jakober Foundation)

Established in 1993 by Yannick Vu, Ben Jakober and Georges Coulon Karlweis, this private cultural foundation aims to conserve and restore Spanish heritage and promote the arts in general and painting and sculpture in particular,

through the exhibition of the pictures and works in its collection, and the exchange of cultural and artistic ideas and material.

Activities: Operates in the field of the arts, through self-conducted programmes, conferences, publications and art exhibitions, which are open to the public. Operates mostly in Spain, but parts of the collection of portraits travel each year to museums in other countries: in the past they have appeared at the Kunst und Austellungshalle (Bonn), Frist Center for the Arts (Tennessee), Museum of Brazilian Art (Sao Paulo), the State Historical Museum (Moscow), a tour of the USA and Kunst Halle Krems.

Geographical Area of Activity: Mainly Mallorca.

Restrictions: No grants available.

Publications: *Piccoli Principi Nella Grande Pittura Europea*; *Domenico Gnoli*; *Ben Jakober, Yannick Vu*; *I Love Mallorca*; *Sa Bassa Blanca*.

Board of Trustees: Marie-Claire Yannick Jakober (Pres.); Firoz Ladak (First Vice-Pres.); Anthonie Stal (Second Vice-Pres.); Benedict P. Jakober (Sec.).

Principal Staff: Admin. Dir Xanthe Jeffries; Conservation Dir Solange Artiles; Technical Dir Edgar Da Cunha.

Address: Finca Sa Bassa Blanca, Apdo 10, camino del Coll Baix, Malpas, 07400 Alcudia, Mallorca.

Telephone: 97-154-69-15; **Fax:** 97-189-71-63; **Internet:** www .fundacionjakober.com; **e-mail:** mail@fundacionjakober.org.

Fundación Jiménez Díaz (Jiménez Díaz Foundation)

Founded in 1963 by Dr Carlos Jiménez Díaz for the education of students, postgraduates, nurses and laboratory technicians in medical and paramedical fields and techniques; for clinical and basic investigation in existing departments of biochemistry, physiology, pathology and immunology, as well as in the laboratories of other services; for the study of all kinds of patients, both hospitalized and in out-patient departments.

Activities: Operates nationally in the fields of education, science and medicine through funding research and awarding prizes.

Geographical Area of Activity: Spain.

Publications: Annual Report.

Trustees: Julio R. Villanueva (Pres.); Eugenio Martínez Jiménez (Vice-Pres.); Celso González García (Sec.).

Principal Staff: Man. Juan Antonio Álvaro de la Parra; Assistant Man. Jesús María Rodríguez Alejandre.

Address: Avda Reyes Católicos 2, 28040 Madrid.

Telephone: 91-550-48-00; **Fax:** 91-544-26-36; **Internet:** www .fjd.es; **e-mail:** fjd@fjd.es.

Fundación Laboral Sonsoles Ballvé Lantero (Sonsoles Ballvé Lantero Labour Foundation)

Established in 1974 by José Luis Ballvé and Eulalia Lantero for the protection of mentally and physically disabled children, and for the protection of pensioners and workers of food producer Campofrío Alimentación, and to support their children's education in the arts, humanities, science, technology and social welfare by offering scholarships, courses and seminars.

Activities: Operates nationally and internationally in the fields of social welfare, training, education, the arts and humanities and recreational activities. Maintains library of more than 6,000 volumes.

Geographical Area of Activity: Europe.

Publications: *ECOS* (monthly); Annual Report.

Executive Board: Miguel Ángel Ortega Bernal (Pres.); Alfredo Sanféliz Mezquita (Vice-Pres.); Francisco Alonso de la Iglesia (Sec.).

Principal Staff: Dir Manuel Ortega Porras.

Address: Calle Fundación Sonsoles Ballvé 2, 1°, 09007 Burgos.

Telephone: 94-728-31-03; **Internet:** www.campofrio.es/portal/page?_pageid=35,48830dad=portalschema=PORTAL; **e-mail:** fsballvc@adcnlc.cs.

Fundación Loewe (Loewe Foundation)

Established in 1988 to promote culture.

Activities: Promotes culture and education of young people, through awarding an international poetry prize, organizing a piano competition, and promoting dance and design in Spain.

Geographical Area of Activity: Spain.

Board of Trustees: Enrique Loewe (Pres.); Lisa Montague (Vice-Pres.); Juan Vázquez-Guillén (Sec.).

Principal Staff: Gen. Co-ordinator Carla Fernández-Shaw.

Address: Carrera de San Jerónimo 15, 28014 Madrid.

Telephone: 91-204-13-00; **Internet:** www.loewe.com; **e-mail:** fundacion@loewe.es.

Fundación MAPFRE (MAPFRE Foundation)

Founded in 1975 by the MAPFRE insurance company to promote safety at work, on the road and in the home. In 2006 the Foundation expanded into areas previously covered by separate foundations.

Activities: Operates in Europe and Central and South America. Its main activities cover fields such as civil society, insurance, culture, the prevention of environmental pollution, health and security. Provides scholarships, awards research grants and promotes the dissemination of technical and scientific knowledge through publications.

Geographical Area of Activity: Central and South America, Portugal and Spain.

Publications: *MAPFRE Seguridad*; *Libros de la Fundación*; *Proyectos de Investigación*; *LaFundación* (quarterly review); books; brochures; newsletter; Annual report.

Trustees: José Manuel Martínez Martínez (Pres.); Alberto Manzano Martos, Carlos Álvarez Jiménez, Filomeno Mira Candel, Francisco Ruiz Risueño, Santiago Gayarre Bermejo (Vice-Pres); José Manuel González Porro (Sec.).

Principal Staff: Dir José Luis Catalinas Calleja.

Address: Paseo de Recoletos, 2328004 Madrid.

Telephone: 91-581-11-31; **Fax:** 91-581-17-95; **Internet:** www.fundacionmapfre.com; **e-mail:** informacion.fundacion@mapfre.com.

Fundación Juan March (Juan March Foundation)

Founded in 1955 by Juan March Ordinas to stimulate studies of direct relevance and utility to Spanish scientific and cultural life; and to assist social institutions.

Activities: The Foundation's headquarters in Madrid serve as a cultural centre. The Foundation organizes science courses and workshops, awards prizes, and makes grants for fellowships and group research programmes in the fields of scientific and technical research. The Centre for International Meetings on Biology, established in 1991 within the Juan March Institute for Study and Research, promotes collaboration between Spanish and foreign scientists working in the field of biology. A Centre for Advanced Study in the Social Sciences opened in 1987, within the Juan March Institute, to promote and conduct research, and offer postgraduate courses. Cultural activities include the organization of art exhibitions, music concerts, lectures, film projections, etc. The Programme for Cultural Advancement in Spanish Provinces operates with central, regional and local governments. Grants are made to institutions devoted to social welfare. The Foundation awards scholarships to artists and researchers in the visual arts undertaking work nationally and abroad. Maintains a library, research and documentation centre, including a specialized collection in Spanish contemporary theatre and music.

Geographical Area of Activity: International.

Publications: *Anales* (annual report); *Revista de la Fundación Juan March* (monthly); *Calendario de actos* (monthly); *Center for Advanced Study in the Social Sciences*; brochures; catalogues and other publications.

Trustees: Juan March Delgado (Pres.); Carlos March Delgado (Vice-Pres.).

Principal Staff: Dir Javier Gomá Lanzón.

Address: Castelló 77, 28006 Madrid.

Telephone: 91-435-42-40; **Fax:** 91-576-34-20; **Internet:** www.march.es; **e-mail:** info@march.es.

Fundación Ana Mata Manzanedo (Ana Mata Manzanedo Foundation)

Established in 1977 by Ana Mata Manzanedo to provide assistance to those in need.

Activities: Operates mostly in Spain, particularly in the Burgos area, in the areas of education, social welfare and conservation of historic heritage, through grants to institutions and individuals, and through providing scholarships and fellowships.

Geographical Area of Activity: Mainly Spain.

Trustees: Moises Arroyo Alcalde (Pres.); Fernando Dancausa Treviño (Vice-Pres.).

Principal Staff: Sec. Gustavo Adolfo Burgos Peña.

Address: Off 603, Calle Vitoria 4, 6°, 09004 Burgos.

Telephone: 94-727-67-16; **Fax:** 94-727-67-16; **e-mail:** fanamata@teleline.es.

Fundación Mujeres (Foundation for Women)

Established in June 1994 to support women's participation in political and social affairs, to promote women in business and education and to promote co-operation between women in Spain and those in developing countries.

Activities: Operates nationally and internationally in the areas of international co-operation with less-developed countries, international affairs, social welfare and social studies, with an emphasis on promoting equal opportunities between men and women and preventing violence against women. The Foundation operates through self-conducted programmes, research, conferences, training courses and publications.

Geographical Area of Activity: International.

Publications: *Fundación Mujeres Bulletin* (2 a year); *El Libro del Buen Hablar: Una Apuesta por un Lenguaje no Sexista*; and others (see website).

Board: Carlota Bustelo García del Real (Hon. Pres.); Elena Valenciano Martínez Orozco (Chair); Florentina Alarcón Hita (Vice-Pres.); María Luisa Soleto Ávila (Exec. Vice-Pres.).

Principal Staff: Gen. Sec. Cristina García Comas.

Address: Calle Francisco de Rojas 2, 1° izquierda, 28010 Madrid.

Telephone: 91-591-24-20; **Fax:** 91-447-24-61; **Internet:** www.fundacionmujeres.es; **e-mail:** mujeres@fundacionmujeres.es.

Fundación Nantik Lum (Nantik Lum Foundation)

Established in 2003 by a group of Spanish businesspeople who wished to develop solutions for the world's poorest people through the promotion and research of micro-enterprise development and microfinance solutions.

Activities: The Foundation operates its own projects, and assists the development of activities of other organizations in Spain, Europe and the developing world that seek to achieve similar goals. The Foundation supports projects in areas of micro-enterprise, microfinance, research and training. It also funds projects that create self-employment, employment and income-generating opportunities for society's most underprivileged groups—particularly women, young people, farmers and immigrants—by supporting the development of microfinance systems that generate economic resources. The Foundation also operates a forum on microfinance, Foro Nantik Lum de Microfinanzas, which encourages open debate and the ongoing study of microfinance as a tool to fight poverty and the social exclusion of disadvantaged groups. The forum is an initiative in association with Universidad Pontificia Comillas (Madrid), the Spanish Red Cross and Fundación ONCE (q.v.).

Geographical Area of Activity: Spain and developing countries, including Dominican Republic, Haiti and Mexico.

Publications: Research reports on microfinance (in Spanish and English); monographs; books; European micro-credit sector overviews.

Board of Trustees: Juan Riva de Aldama (Pres.); Linda Facchinetti (Sec.).

Principal Staff: Man. Dir Linda Facchinetti; Founder and Deputy Dir Silvia Rico Garrido.

Address: Calle Manuel Silvela 1, 1°, Madrid.

Telephone: 91- 593-34-14; **Fax:** 91- 411-46-59; **Internet:** www.nantiklum.org; **e-mail:** nantiklum@nantiklum.com.

Fundación ONCE (ONCE—Spanish National Organization for the Blind—Foundation)

Founded in 1988 by ONCE, the Spanish National Organization for the Blind, the Foundation aims to assist people with disabilities and their integration in society.

Activities: Operates primarily in Spain co-operating with government agencies to help the disabled; makes grants and low-interest loans for employment creation, education, rehabilitation, training and to assist in the breaking down of communication and social barriers; and promotes sport for its role in the personal and social development of people with disabilities. Maintains an online information resource.

Geographical Area of Activity: Mainly Spain.

Publications: Annual Report; *Manual de Accesibilidad Global para la Formacion;* information brochures; books concerning disability and social issues.

Finance: Receives 3% of revenue from the lottery tickets sold by ONCE, equivalent to 20% of ONCE's operating revenue. Total project grants disbursed €70,906,853 (2008).

Board of Trustees: HH Margarita de Borbón y Borbón (Hon. Chair.); Miguel Carballeda Piñeiro (Chair.); Alberto Durán López (Exec. Vice-Chair.).

Principal Staff: Dir-Gen. Luis Crespo Asenjo.

Address: Calle Sebastián Herrera 15, 28012 Madrid.

Telephone: 91-506-88-88; **Fax:** 91-539-34-87; **Internet:** www.fundaciononce.es; **e-mail:** dae@fundaciononce.es.

Fundación Amancio Ortega (Amancio Ortega Foundation)

Founded in July 2001 by Amancio Ortega Gaona to promote all types of activities in the fields of culture, education, society, welfare research and science.

Activities: The Foundation designs, manages and evaluates its own initiatives, supporting pilot projects orientated towards the modernization of civil society, through public and private co-operation.

Geographical Area of Activity: Galicia, Spain.

Restrictions: No grants available.

Publications: Press releases.

Board of Trustees: Amancio Ortega Gaona (Chair.); Flora Pérez Marcote (Vice-Pres.); Antonio Abril Abadin (Sec.).

Principal Staff: Gen. Dir. Oscar Ortega Chávez.

Address: Avda Diputación s/n Arteixo, 15142 La Coruña.

Telephone: (981) 18-55-96; **Fax:** (981) 18-55-95; **Internet:** www.faortega.org; **e-mail:** contacto@faortega.org.

Fundación José Ortega y Gasset (José Ortega y Gasset Foundation)

Established in December 1978 as a private, non-profit-making academic research institute to further the cultural legacy of the philosopher and essayist José Ortega y Gasset (1883–1955).

Activities: Operates in the fields of the humanities and social sciences, through research and study activities, including postgraduate and doctoral research projects, seminars, lectures, exhibitions, and cultural and scientific meetings that cover unlimited topics. Emphasis is placed on subjects covering Iberia, Europe and Central and South America. The Foundation runs an International Programme of Spanish Language, Latin American and European Studies at its centre in Toledo, providing study opportunities for undergraduate and graduate students, as well as the annual Young Hispanic Leaders Programme, providing young US citizens of Hispanic origin with the opportunity to familiarize themselves with Spain's political, economic, social and cultural environment. It has links with universities in the United Kingdom, USA, Argentina, Colombia, Puerto Rico and Israel. Maintains the private library and archives of José Ortega y Gasset.

Geographical Area of Activity: Spain.

Publications: *Revista de Occidente* (monthly); papers and series.

Trustees: HH King Juan Carlos I (Hon. Pres.); José Varela Ortega (Pres.); Gregorio Marañón Bertrán de Lis (Vice-Pres.).

Principal Staff: Dir-Gen. Jesús Sánchez Lambás.

Address: Calle Fortuny 53, 28010 Madrid.

Telephone: 91-700-41-00; **Fax:** 91-700-35-30; **Internet:** www.ortegaygasset.edu; **e-mail:** comunicacion@fog.es.

Fundación Paideia Galiza (Paideia Galiza Foundation)

Founded by Rosalía Mera Goyenechea in April 1986 to undertake initiatives orientated towards training, investigation and intervention in the field of social sciences; to implement programmes and dynamic tasks that are responsive to social issues; and to search for excellence in services and professional practices, from an inter-disciplinary, transversal and integrated point of view to promote social and scientific development.

Activities: Develops integrated training for a variety of professional sectors (in-service training); promotes projects and initiatives aimed at integration, both socially and in the workplace, for society's most vulnerable groups; and undertakes initiatives aimed at local, economic, cultural and environmental development of areas with little access to resources. The Foundation works in the following areas: social exclusion, disability, the social economy and development of rural and semiurban zones, ethics and values, ongoing training and research, and inter-institutional co-operation. Maintains office in Padrón.

Geographical Area of Activity: Spain.

Publications: *Código de Derecho Internacional Público en Materia de Discapacidad; Jurisprudencia de la Personas con Discapacidad (constitucional, civil, penal y laboral); El Mayor Interés en la Esfera Personal del Incapaz; Normativa Jurídica Básica de las Personas con Discapacidad; Derecho y Retraso Mental; Hacia un Estatuto Jurídico de la Persona con Retraso Mental; Discursos Profesionales de las Ciencias de la Salud; Educación y Trabajo Social sobre la Discapacidad Psíquica; Antear un Modelo Integral.*

Board of Directors: Rosalía Mera Goyenechea (Pres.); Sandra Ortega Mera (Vice-Pres.); María Cotón (Sec.).

Principal Staff: Pres. Rosalía Mera Goyenechea.

Address: Plaza de María Pita 17, 15001 A Coruña.

Telephone: 98-122-39-27; **Fax:** 98-122-46-59; **Internet:** www.paideia.es; **e-mail:** paideia@paideia.es.

Fundación Paz y Solidaridad Serafín Aliaga—FPyS (Serafín Aliaga Foundation for Peace and Solidarity)

Founded in 1989 to promote peace and solidarity world-wide; to support democratic freedom, especially in the area of labour and trade union rights; to promote the strengthening of labour and social organizations, and support social and economic development; and to promote international co-operation.

Activities: Provides resources to contribute to the social, cultural, economic and scientific and technical development of developing countries. Organizes training and educational activities, conferences and symposia on subjects related to peace and solidarity world-wide. Also publishes and distributes leaflets, essays and other publications relating to international co-operation, peace and solidarity.

Geographical Area of Activity: Central and South America, Western Africa, the Mediterranean region, the Middle East.

Publications: Annual Report; education and development publications.

Finance: Total assets €9,752,860 (Dec. 2009).

Board: Marisol Pardo Ruiz (Pres.); Javier Doz Orrit (Vice-Pres.); Maria Engracia Cardeñosa Peñas (Treas.); Félix A. Ovejero Torres (Sec.).

Principal Staff: Dir Juan Ramón Ortega Alborch.

Address: Calle Julián Gayarre 18, 28014 Madrid.

Telephone: (914) 44-09-50; **Fax:** (914) 46-19-77; **Internet:** www.pazysolidaridad.ccoo.es; **e-mail:** fps@fps.ccoo.es.

Fundación Rafael del Pino (Rafael del Pino Foundation)

Established in 1999 by Rafael del Pino y Moreno. Aims to contribute towards improving the knowledge of future Spanish, promote private initiative and foster free market and free enterprise principles.

Activities: Operates in the fields of training, providing scholarships to Spanish students, funding research programmes and management training for NGOs, and organizing seminars, lectures and meetings, including the Free Enterprise Forum; Spanish cultural heritage, including lectures and conferences and grants to projects aiming to protect and develop Spain's cultural heritage; and a series of awards and prizes, recognizing Spanish literature, dissertations in the fields of economy, law, business, politics, international relations, mass media and education, and initiatives aiming to eliminate inefficient regulations or foster competition within the goods and services markets.

Geographical Area of Activity: Spain.

Publications: Extensive publications on economics, business, law, history and other subjects.

Finance: Total assets €124,252,130 (31 Dec. 2010); annual income €12,010,780, annual expenditure €11,860,800 (2010).

Board of Trustees: Rafael del Pino y Moreno (Founder); María del Pino y Calvo-Sotelo (Pres.); Ricardo López Moráis (Sec.); José Ignacio Ysasi-Ysasmendi y Pemán (Deputy Sec.).

Principal Staff: Dir Amadeo Petitbò Juan; Deputy Dir Vicente José Montes Gan.

Address: Rafael Calvo 39, 28010 Madrid.

Telephone: 91-396-86-00; **Fax:** 91-396-86-19; **Internet:** www.frdelpino.es; **e-mail:** info@frdelpino.es.

Fundación Príncipe de Asturias (Prince of Asturias Foundation)

Founded in Oviedo, Asturias, on 24 September 1980 at a formal ceremony presided over by HRH the Prince of Asturias. The essential aims of the Foundation are to consolidate links between the Principality and the Prince of Asturias, and to contribute to encouraging and promoting scientific, cultural and humanistic values that form part of mankind's universal heritage.

Activities: Distributes the annual Prince of Asturias Awards, in Communication and Humanities, Social Sciences, Arts, Letters, Technical and Scientific Research, International Co-operation, Concord, and Sports. They are intended to acknowledge scientific, technical, cultural, social and humanistic work performed by individuals, institutions, groups of individuals or institutions at an international level. Nominees for any of the Awards should be outstandingly exemplary, and their work should be of acknowledged international standing. As part of its endeavours to contribute to fostering culture at its highest levels, the Prince of Asturias Foundation created a Music Department in 1983, the honorary conductors of which are Jesús López Cobos and Krzysztof Penderecki. The Department boasts three choirs and an International Music School.

Geographical Area of Activity: International.

Finance: Total assets €29,800,000 (31 Dec. 2010); annual income €5,490,084, annual expenditure €5,090,000 (2010).

Board of Trustees: HRH Felipe de Borbón, Prince of Asturias (Hon. Pres); Francisco Álvarez-Cascos Fernández (Hon. Vice-Pres.); Matías Rodríguez Inciarte (Pres.).

Principal Staff: Gen. Sec. Adolfo Menéndez Menéndez; Dir Teresa Sanjurjo González.

Address: General Yague 2, 33004 Oviedo.

Telephone: 98-525-87-55; **Fax:** 98-524-21-04; **Internet:** www.fpa.es; **e-mail:** info@fpa.es.

Fundación Promi (Promi Foundation)

Founded in 1998, aims to uphold the rights of mentally disabled people.

Activities: Works to improve the quality of life of mentally disabled people throughout Europe, through projects, conferences and training programmes, concentrating on integration in work and society, and the rehabilitation of people with mental disabilities. Promotes and helps NGOs and other organizations with similar aims and lends its support to businesses employing people with mental disabilities. Maintains two research and information centres.

Geographical Area of Activity: Europe.

Publications: *Deficiencia, Enfermedad Mental y Senilidad: Mecanismos Legales de Protección*; and numerous other publications relating to disability.

Board: Juan Perez Marin (Pres.); Eduardo de Bordóns Piqueras (Vice-Pres.); José María Castilla Martínez (Sec.).

Principal Staff: Dir-Gen. Cristina Ruiz Castillo.

Address: Ctra Madrid-Cádiz, km 396 (P.T. Rabanales), 14014 Córdoba.

Telephone: 95-732-53-80; **Internet:** www.promi.es; **e-mail:** fundación@promi.es.

Fundación Fernando Rielo (Fernando Rielo Foundation)

Founded in 1982 by Fernando Rielo, Spanish poet and philosopher, to promote understanding between different cultures and traditions.

Activities: The Foundation operates internationally, organizing conferences, seminars and concerts, and poetry, music, education and philosophy courses. Awards prizes, scholarships and grants to foster cultural activity, and in particular literature, including the annual Fernando Rielo World Mystical Poetry Prize. Maintains close ties with foundations and universities abroad, including establishing the Fernando Rielo Chair in Spanish Literature and Thought at the University of the Philippines, and operates exchange programmes with foreign universities for Spanish university teachers. The Foundation has 53 delegations world-wide.

Geographical Area of Activity: World-wide.

Publications: *Equivalencias/Equivalences* (3 a year, in English and Spanish); several poetry collections and books on philosophy and education; *Dios y arbol*; *Lianto azul*; *Paisaje desnudo*; *Noche clara*; *Pasion y muerte*; *Transfiguration*; *Via lueis*.

Principal Staff: Dir-Gen. Dr Jesús María González.

Address: Jorge Juan 82, 1º6, 28009 Madrid.

Telephone: 91-575-40-91; **Fax:** 91-578-07-72; **Internet:** www.rielo.com; **e-mail:** fundacion@rielo.com.

Fundación María Francisca de Roviralta (María Francisca de Roviralta Foundation)

Established in 1959 by José María Roviralta and Manuel Roviralta for general charitable purposes.

Activities: Operates in Spain and internationally in the fields of aid to less-developed countries, education, medicine and health, science and technology, and social welfare, through making grants to institutions. Four programmes are run by the Foundation: social development; medicine and health; education and science; and other activities. Awarded Medal of Honour by Asociación Española de Fundaciones in 2009.

Geographical Area of Activity: Spain and international.

Publications: Annual Report.

Board of Trustees: Gerardo Salvador (Pres.); Augusto Testor (Vice-Pres. and Sec.).

Principal Staff: Dir Javier Serra; Sec.-Gen. Tomás Testor.

Address: Av. Bruselas 15, 4º, 2810 Alcobendas, Madrid.

Telephone: 91-556-02-28; **Fax:** 91-556-37-36; **Internet:** www .roviralta.org; **e-mail:** fundacion@roviralta.org.

Fundación Santa María (Santa María Foundation)

Founded in 1977 by a religious order to provide the disadvantaged in society with access to education and culture, and to promote the development of pedagogic sciences and specialist training for teaching staff.

Activities: The Foundation operates programmes in four main areas. The Special Programmes aim to integrate marginalized groups at a social and cultural level; provide training for volunteers working in prisons; promote women; organize occupational workshops; and provide financial support for the construction of libraries, houses, etc. The Literature Programme organizes competitions for teenagers and children to stimulate artistic and literary creativity. The Social Research Programmes provide a platform for discussing the problems facing society from a Christian perspective. The Pedagogical Programmes organize training courses for teachers; provide research grants to centres whose interests are similar to those of the Foundation; and operate the Foundation's prize programme.

Geographical Area of Activity: Europe and South America.

Restrictions: Grants only to people who work or study in Spain.

Publications: Annual Report; brochures; grants list; monographs.

Finance: The Foundation is funded by annual contributions from Ediciones SM. Annual project expenditure €2,422,759 (2008).

Board of Trustees: Ramón Iceta Olaizola (Pres.); Francisco Canseco Llera (Vice-Pres.); Miguel Agustí Martínez-Arcos (Sec.).

Principal Staff: Dir José Joaquin Cerezo.

Address: Calle Joaquín Turina 39, 28044 Madrid.

Telephone: 91-535-96-00; **Fax:** 91-535-96-01; **Internet:** www .fundacio-sm.com; **e-mail:** fsm@fundacion-sm.com.

Fundación Santillana (Santillana Foundation)

Founded in July 1979 to promote co-operation in education, the media and culture.

Activities: The Foundation supports experimental educational projects; conducts conferences and studies on educational policies; organizes cultural exhibitions; publishes educational materials; and conducts projects on the mass media. Operates nationally and in Central and South America, with a sister Fundación Santillana active in Colombia, and co-operates with organizations in other European countries.

Geographical Area of Activity: Central and South America, Spain.

Publications: Catalogues; conference and symposia proceedings and results; *Documento Básico*; *Ponencias y Conclusiones*; *Seminario de Primavera*; *La Educación en España; La Educación que Queremos*; *Novedades de la Ocde*; *I Foro Latinoamericano de Educación*.

Board of Trustees: Ignacio Polanco Moreno (Pres.); Francisco Pérez González (Vice-Pres.); José María Aranaz Cortezo (Sec.).

Principal Staff: Dir Basilio Baltasar.

Address: Calle Gran Vía 32, 6º, 28013 Madrid.

Telephone: 91-330-10-28; **Internet:** www .fundacionsantillana.org; **e-mail:** secretaria@ fundacionsantillana.com.

Fundación Juanelo Turriano (Juanelo Turriano Foundation)

Established in 1987 by José Antonio García-Diego.

Activities: Dedicated to studies of history of science, technology and engineering. For this purpose the Foundation publishes books, gives study grants and organizes exhibitions and courses, among other activities.

Geographical Area of Activity: Spain.

Finance: Annual budget €700,000.

Trustees: Victoriano Muñoz Cava (Pres.); Javier Goicolea Zala (Vice-Pres.); Pedro Navascués Palacio (Sec.).

Principal Staff: Dir-Gen. Bernardo Revuelta Pol.

Address: Calle Zurbano 41, 1º, 28010 Madrid.

Telephone: 91-531-30-05; **Fax:** 91-531-30-03; **Internet:** www .juaneloturriano.com; **e-mail:** fundacion@juaneloturriano .com.

Fundación Universidad-Empresa—UE (University-Industry Foundation)

Founded in 1973 by the Universities of Madrid and the Chamber of Commerce and Industry to promote co-operation between the universities and industries of Madrid.

Activities: The Foundation is the first Spanish institution designed to address the challenges and opportunities generated in the framework of university-business relations, with a special focus on: education; job market and career development; entrepreneurship; research and innovation.

Geographical Area of Activity: All regions, with a special focus on Europe.

Publications: *Guía de Empresas que Ofrecen Empleo* (annual job opportunities guide); books and reports in the field of university-business co-operation.

Board of Governors: Arturo Fernández (Pres.); Arsenio Huergo Fernández (Vice-Pres.); Javier Cuadrado de Vicente (Sec.).

Principal Staff: Gen. Dir Fernando Martínez Gómez.

Address: Calle Pedro Salinas 11, Edificio Anexo, 2º, 28043 Madrid.

Telephone: 91-548-98-60; **Fax:** 91-547-06-52; **Internet:** www .fue.es; **e-mail:** info@fue.es.

Fundación Luis Vives (Luis Vives Foundation)

Established in 1987 by the merger of 11 private foundations. Currently under the supervision of the Ministry of Social Affairs, the Foundation works towards assisting individuals plagued by social problems, and towards furtherance of social services through support to not-for-profit organizations.

Activities: Offers consulting services and technical support to foundations involved in social services, especially pertaining to programme design, management and evaluation; works in collaboration with similar foundations to support projects promoting social welfare; encourages the development of new trusts and foundations; provides grants to organizations to enable participation in international forums and for promoting international liaison; promotes exchange of research at international level in social welfare projects.

Geographical Area of Activity: Spain.

Publications: Annual Report; brochures.

Trustees: Óscar Alzaga Villaamil (Pres.); Virgilio Zapatero Gómez (Vice-Pres.); Paula Cisneros del Prado (Sec.).

Principal Staff: Dir-Gen. José Manuel Fresno García.

Address: Doctor Zamenhof St 36, 28027 Madrid.

Telephone: 91-540-08-78; **Fax:** 91-541-90-52; **Internet:** www .fundacionluisvives.org; **e-mail:** luisvives@ fundacionluisvives.org.

FUNDESO—Fundación Desarrollo Sostenido (Foundation for Sustainable Development)

Established in December 1995 by Rafael Guardans Cambó to promote socio-economic programmes in developing countries.

Activities: Operates nationally and internationally, especially in Central and South America, in the areas of aid to less-developed countries, education and social welfare, through self-conducted programmes, scholarships and fellowships, and conferences. Maintains nine regional offices in Spain.

Geographical Area of Activity: Latin America, Africa and Asia.

Publications: Annual Report; *Guía Turística de Timor Este*; *Microcréditos y Desarrollo, Siete Experiencias en América Latina*; *Manual de ecoturismo en Vietnam*; *Manual para el Marqueting y la promoción del Turismo sostenible en Vietnam*.

Finance: Total assets €4,187,416 (2005); total revenue €3,143,712, expenditure €3,005,424 (2005).

Board of Directors: Rafael Guardans Cambó (Exec. Pres.); Blanca Herrero Muñoz-Cobo (Sec.).

Principal Staff: Gen. Dir Blanca Herrero Muñoz-Cobo; Dir of International Co-operation Projects Raquel Martí Lezana.

Address: Calle Gran Vía 16, 4° izquierda, 28013 Madrid.

Telephone: 91-701-47-00; **Fax:** 91-701-47-01; **Internet:** www .fundeso.org; **e-mail:** fundeso@fundeso.org.

Institut Europeu de la Mediterrània—IEMed (European Mediterranean Institute)

The European Institute of the Mediterranean (IEMed), founded in 1989, is a consortium comprising the Catalan Government, the Spanish Ministry of Foreign Affairs and Co-operation and Barcelona City Council.

Activities: In accordance with the principles of the Euro-Mediterranean Partnership's Barcelona Process, and today with the objectives of the European Union for the Mediterranean, the aim of IEMed is to foster actions and projects that contribute to mutual understanding, exchange and co-operation between the different Mediterranean countries, societies and cultures as well as to promote the progressive construction of a space of peace and stability, shared prosperity and dialogue between cultures and civilizations in the Mediterranean. As a think tank specializing in Mediterranean relations based on a multidisciplinary and networking approach, the IEMed encourages analysis, understanding and co-operation through the organization of seminars, research projects, debates, conferences and publications, in addition to a broad cultural programme.

Geographical Area of Activity: The Mediterranean region.

Publications: Newsletter; *Mediterranean Yearbook; Afkar/ Ideas; Quaderns de la Mediterrània; Mediterranean Monographies; Euromed Surveys; afkar/ideas* (quarterly journal).

Board of Trustees: Francisco González (Chair.).

Principal Staff: Pres. Senén Florensa; Dir-Gen. Andreu Bassols.

Address: Calle Girona 20, 5°, 08010 Barcelona.

Telephone: 93-244-98-50; **Fax:** 93-247-01-65; **Internet:** www .iemed.org; **e-mail:** info@iemed.org.

Instituto Europeo de Salud y Bienestar Social (European Institute of Health and Social Welfare)

Founded to encourage health, social health and environmental protection through multiple co-operation.

Activities: The Institute focuses its activities on environmental protection, health and safety at work, health management and social protocol. It organizes congresses, conferences and seminars and supports research in the area of environment and social issues.

Geographical Area of Activity: Europe.

Publications: Books include: *Obligaciones del empresario en prevención; Calidad en la asistencia sanitaria; La satisfacción de los Pacientes.*

Principal Staff: Pres. Dr Manuel Peña Castiñeira; Dir-Gen. Sonia Fernández-Duran; Exec. Dir Francisco Álvarez.

Address: Calle Joaquín Costa 16, El Viso, 28002 Madrid.

Telephone: 91-411-80-90; **Fax:** 91-411-80-80; **Internet:** www .institutoeuropeo.es; **e-mail:** infcursos@institutoeuropeo.es.

Intermón Oxfam

Part of the Oxfam confederation of organizations (qq.v.).

Activities: Operates in 44 countries world-wide, in the areas of development, humanitarian assistance, fair trade and campaigning.

Geographical Area of Activity: International.

Publications: monthly newsletter.

Board: Xavier Torra Balcells (Chair.); Oriol Tuni Vancells (Sec.); Ramon Casals (Treas.).

Principal Staff: Dir Ariane Arpa.

Address: Roger de Lluria 15, 08010 Barcelona.

Telephone: (902) 330331; **Fax:** 93-482-07-07; **Internet:** www .intermonoxfam.org; **e-mail:** info@intermonoxfam.org.

Paz y Cooperación (Peace and Co-operation)

Founded in 1982 by Joaquin Antuña with the aim of promoting disarmament, sustainable development in developing countries and human rights world-wide.

Activities: Organizes and manages co-operative projects in 27 countries around the world, which operate in the fields of human rights, co-operative development, children and young people, women and development, micro-credit, education, health, agriculture and the environment, and integral development with local communities and authorities. Also funds the International Peace and Co-operation School Award, an annual event that promotes education for peace and global solidarity.

Geographical Area of Activity: World-wide, with an emphasis on Africa, Central and South America, Asia and the Middle East.

Publications: *Education and Solidarity; Another Mankind: Third Millennium* (weekly television debate show on issues including the peace culture, non-violence and solidarity); *Breaking Through* (20-year foundation review); *Verso Verso il Duemila* (in Italian); *The Strategy of Hope.*

Governing Board: Joaquín Antuña (Pres. and Founder); María del Pino Monzón (Vice-Pres.); Milagros González (Sec.-Gen.).

Principal Staff: Project Man. Elisa Franceschinis.

Address: Calle Meléndez Valdes 68, 4° izquierda, 28015 Madrid.

Telephone: 91-549-61-56; **Fax:** 91-543-52-82; **Internet:** www .peaceandcooperation.org; **e-mail:** pazycooperacion@ hotmail.com.

Sri Lanka

FOUNDATIONS, TRUSTS AND NON-PROFIT ORGANIZATIONS

Agromart Foundation

Established in 1989 to train women in rural areas to be entrepreneurs and to empower them to participate in the socio-economic and political process.

Activities: Works in the areas of agriculture, small industry group training, providing micro-credit and transfer of technologies and skills. Focus is on empowering women in rural areas to acquire the skills necessary for their chosen field of self-employment; developing female entrepreneurship in rural areas; facilitating access to credit for agriculture and industry and promoting rural savings and self-help groups for non-bank funding through Agromart Production Societies; and promoting environmental awareness among rural entrepreneurs. Operates nine regional offices in Sri Lanka and has training office at the Northern Illinois University in the USA.

Geographical Area of Activity: Sri Lanka and USA.

Publications: *Agro News* (quarterly journal); *Poverty to Prosperity—Success Stories of Entrepreneurs*; Annual Report.

Board of Trustees: Beulah Moonesinghe (Chair.); C. Goonetilleke (Treas.); A. C. B. Pethiyagoda (Sec.); R. M. Pillai (Asst Sec.).

Address: 38 Iswari Rd, Colombo 6.

Telephone: (11) 587823; **Fax:** (11) 596804; **Internet:** www.niu.edu/srilankaproj/agromart.html; **e-mail:** agromart@slt.lk.

International Water Management Institute—IWMI

Founded in 1985, and formerly known as the International Irrigation Management Institute, to improve water resources management and irrigated agriculture in developing countries, through research.

Activities: The International Water Management Institute (IWMI) is a non-profit profit research organization working towards the sustainable management of land and water resources for food, livelihoods and the environment. IWMI's vision is to improve water productivity in agriculture and ensure future food security. In recent years, the Institute has also been studying the implications of climate change and its impacts on water and land resources. IWMI has four research themes, which cover the following: water availability and access to water; productive use of water; water quality health and environment; water and society. IWMI works with partners form the North and South. This includes international research institutes, national research institutes, government departments, universities and development organizations. In recent years IWMI has also established links with private sector organizations.

Geographical Area of Activity: Africa and Asia.

Publications: scientific and corporate material; research report series; working papers; policy and issue briefs, brochures and newsletters.

Finance: Total assets US $34,229,000 (31 Dec. 2010); Annual grant income $30,883,127 (2010).

Board of Governors: Prof. John Skerritt (Chair.); Asger Kej (Vice-Chair.); Shanthi Weerasekera (Sec.).

Principal Staff: Dir-Gen. Colin Chartres; Deputy Dir-Gen. Dr David Molden.

Address: 127 Sunil Mawatha, Pelawatte, Battaramulla; POB 2075, Colombo.

Telephone: (11) 2880000; **Fax:** (11) 2786854; **Internet:** www.iwmi.org; **e-mail:** iwmi@cgiar.org.

Regional Centre for Strategic Studies—RCSS

Established in 1993 as an NGO to carry out collaborative research on international issues relating to Southern Asia, and to network and interact with similar organizations.

Activities: Operates in the field of international affairs, through carrying out research into issues relating to Southern Asia, including regional security, conflict and co-operation. Promotes communication exchange between organizations and individuals; organizes seminars and workshops; promotes research; and disseminates information through its publications. Also distributes the Kodikara Awards to scholars from Bangladesh, Bhutan, India, Maldives, Nepal, Pakistan and Sri Lanka, and the Mahbub ul Haq Research Awards for Non-Traditional Security Issues in South Asia, sponsoring collaborative research projects in the fields of governance in plural societies and security, environment and security, globalization and security, and conflict resolution; and the Mahbub ul Haq Award for collaborative research on non-traditional security issues that are relevant to contemporary South Asia, within the themes of Governance in Plural Societies and Security, Environment and Security, Globalization and Security, and Conflict Resolution.

Geographical Area of Activity: Southern Asia.

Publications: *Documents on Sri Lanka's Foreign Policy 1947–1965*; *Defence, Technology and Cooperative Security in South Asia*; *Terrorism in South Asia: Impact on Development and Democratic Process*; *Environment, Development and Human Security: Perspectives from South Asia*; *South Asia and the War on Terrorism: Analysing the Implications of 11 September*; policy papers; RCSS newsletter.

Finance: Funded through grants from donor organizations.

Principal Staff: Exec. Dir Prof. Mallika Joseph; Associate Dir Chaminda Hettiarachchi; Sec. Dharshani Dias.

Address: 68/1 Saravasi Lane (off Castle St), Colombo 8.

Telephone: (11) 2690913; **Fax:** (11) 2690769; **Internet:** www.rcss.org; **e-mail:** rcss@rcss.org.

A. M. M. Sahabdeen Trust Foundation

Founded in 1991 by Dr A. M. M. Sahabdeen to advance knowledge, social development and to promote inter-cultural and international understanding through awards to outstanding scientists, scholars and community leaders.

Activities: Operates in the fields of education and social development by awarding educational scholarships, particularly to students in need. Makes grants to organizations in a variety of educational and social welfare fields including hostels, libraries, educational institutions, rehabilitation and refugee centres. In 1991 the Foundation established the Sri Lankan International Awards to honour scholars and scientists in the Asian region, and others who have made outstanding contributions to human progress in the fields of International Understanding, Science, Literature and Human Development. In 1998 the Foundation established the Mohamed Sahabdeen Institute for Advanced Studies and Research at Pahamune in the Kurunegala District. The Foundation established Pahamune House in January 2005 to assist in the rehabilitation of destitute children affected by the tsunamis in December 2004.

Geographical Area of Activity: Asia.

Publications: *The Sufi Doctrine in Tamil Literature*; *Iraivanum Pirapanjamum*; *God and the Universe*; *The Circle of Lives*.

Finance: Net assets 14,900,000 rupees; annual expenditure 1,100,000 rupees.

Board of Trustees: Dr A. M. M. Sahabdeen (Chair.).

Principal Staff: Dirs Rizvan Sahabdeen, S. R. Sahabdeen.

Address: 4th Floor, 86 Galle Rd, Colombo 03.

Telephone: (11) 2399601; **Fax:** (11) 2399603; **Internet:** www .ammstrustfoundation.org; **e-mail:** ammstrust@gmail.com.

Sweden

FOUNDATIONS, TRUSTS AND NON-PROFIT ORGANIZATIONS

Air Pollution and Climate Secretariat—AirClim

Established in 1982 as a collaborative venture between four Swedish environmental organizations, as the Swedish NGO Secretariat on Acid Rain; aims to promote awareness of, and reduction of, air pollution, including greenhouse gases. Name changed in 2008.

Activities: Operates primarily in the European Union and Central and Eastern Europe in the field of the environment, specifically seeking to lower emissions of air pollutants (including greenhouse gases), through campaigns, offering information, lobbying, supporting environmental organizations in other countries, and issuing publications.

Geographical Area of Activity: World-wide (primarily in the European Union and Central and Eastern Europe).

Publications: *Air and the Environment*; *Acid News* (newsletter); fact sheets; leaflets; reports (in the Air Pollution & Climate series).

Address: POB 7005, 402 31 Gothenburg.

Telephone: (31) 711 45 15; **Fax:** (31) 711 46 20; **Internet:** www.airclim.org; **e-mail:** info@airclim.org.

Folke Bernadottes Minnesfond (Folke Bernadotte Memorial Foundation)

Founded in 1948 by the Swedish Relief Committee for Europe, in memory of Count Folke Bernadotte, to promote understanding between nations, particularly through enabling young persons to become acquainted with the culture, ideals and social conditions of other countries, and to bring aid to those in need. To the extent that organizations commemorating Count Folke Bernadotte, and having largely similar aims, are formed in other countries, the Foundation seeks to co-ordinate the activities of these organizations.

Activities: Offers scholarships to people living in Sweden, and under the age of 35, who want to travel outside Scandinavia to experience other cultural conditions. Some kind of exchange must be included, and the social aspect is important. Scholarships are also given to those taking part in camps and volunteering.

Geographical Area of Activity: World-wide.

Restrictions: No scholarships for study.

Principal Staff: Dir Bernt Rehn; Dir Nelson de Macedo; Sec. Helga Ponzio.

Address: POB 24009, 104 50 Stockholm.

Telephone: (8) 662 25 05; **Internet:** www.folkebernadottesminnesfond.se.

Cancerfonden (Swedish Cancer Society)

Founded in 1951 to support, organize and co-ordinate cancer research that is primarily concerned with basic medical and scientific research tasks; to promote the development of new research and treatment methods in cancer cases and to lend support to other measures in the interest of cancer patients; and to support educational activities concerned with the aims and means of cancer research and with the prevention, symptoms and treatment of cancer diseases.

Activities: Awards grants to individuals of any nationality to carry out cancer research, or research in a related science, including biochemistry, cell biology, pathology, virology, immunology, etc. The Society also disseminates information on cancer for public education purposes.

Geographical Area of Activity: Sweden.

Restrictions: No grants to individuals. Awards for Swedish researchers are tenable in countries outside Sweden; foreign recipients must carry out their research in Sweden.

Publications: Annual Report; *Rädda Livet* (quarterly).

Board of Directors: Bengt Holgersson (Pres.); Birgitta Lindholm (Vice-Pres.).

Principal Staff: Sec.-Gen. Stefan Bergh; Asst to Sec.-Gen. Kiki Nordstrom.

Address: David Bagares gata 5, 101 55 Stockholm.

Telephone: (8) 677 10 00; **Fax:** (8) 677 10 01; **Internet:** www.cancerfonden.se; **e-mail:** info@cancerfonden.se.

Crafoordska stiftelsen (The Crafoord Foundation)

The Foundation was set up in 1980 by Holger Crafoord to support basic scientific research at a national and international level.

Activities: Focuses on geosciences, mathematics and astronomy, biosciences (particularly ecology), and medicine (rheumatoid arthritis); awards grants to individuals and organizations in Sweden pursuing scientific research; awards Nobel prizes in Chemistry and Physics totalling 9m. kronor each; and may also support education of, and assistance to, disadvantaged children and youngsters.

Geographical Area of Activity: World-wide.

Restrictions: Capital 1,530,000 kronor (31 Dec. 2010); Total disbursements 66,500,000 kronor (2010).

Publications: Annual Report.

Board of Trustees: Ebba Fischer (Chair.).

Principal Staff: Chief Exec. Lennart Nilsson.

Address: POB 137, 221 00 Lund; Malmövägen 8, 222 25 Lund.

Telephone: (46) 38 58 80; **Fax:** (46) 38 58 85; **Internet:** www.crafoord.se; **e-mail:** crafoord@crafoord.se.

Diakonia

An NGO-supporting organization established in 1966 by five swedish churches to promote equality for all people.

Activities: Operates in South-East Asia, Central and South America, Africa and the Middle East in the areas of aid to less-developed countries, conservation and the environment, international affairs, and law and human rights, through making grants to organizations.

Geographical Area of Activity: Africa, Central, Latin and South America, South-East Asia and the Middle East.

Restrictions: Grants are not made to individuals, nor are they given to organizations in Europe or in the countries of the former USSR.

Publications: Annual Report.

Finance: 90% of the budget comes from the Swedish Government (through the Swedish Development Agency), the rest from private donors. Total assets 149,345 kronor (31 Dec. 2010). Annual revenue 388,462 kronor; expenditure 354,029 kronor (2010).

Board: Oskar Permvall (Chair.); Louise Alm (First Vice-Chair.); Marcus Bernström (Second Vice-Chair.).

Principal Staff: Sec.-Gen. Bo Forsberg.

Address: Gustavslundsvägen 18, Alviks torg, Bromma; POB 14038, 167 14 Bromma.

Telephone: (8) 453 69 00; **Fax:** (8) 453 69 29; **Internet:** www.diakonia.se; **e-mail:** diakonia@diakonia.se.

Eden Foundation

Established in 1985 to show how the enormous number of underexploited plant species can be used to reverse desertification and bring welfare to the poorest people. The Foundation works on the premise that natural plants are fully capable of feeding the world's population in a way that is constructive for the environment, and pioneers this practice in drylands.

Activities: Operates in the field of conservation and the environment, and aid to less-developed countries. Runs a research project in Niger on how to combat desertification. Researches how to establish drought-tolerant perennial plants through rainfall only. Disseminates research results to local farmers and gives them seeds to establish plants on their own. Once established, these plants improve food security by stabilizing the environment and providing a supplemental, reliable food source. Projects are long term. Eden teaches villagers basic principles in preventive health, covering issues such as malaria, diarrhoea and HIV/AIDS.

Geographical Area of Activity: Niger.

Board: Staffan Göranson (Chair.).

Principal Staff: Exec. Dir Arne Victor Garvi.

Address: Skreavagen 45в, 311 72 Falkenberg.

Telephone: (346) 53 157; **Fax:** (346) 53 171; **Internet:** www .edenfoundation.com; **e-mail:** project@edenfoundation.org.

Ekhagastiftelsen (Ekhaga Foundation)

Founded in 1944 by Gösta Videgård, an engineer, to support research into improvement and further development of ecological agriculture (ecologically well-suited agricultural systems where chemical compounds for fertilization and other uses are replaced with ecological and biological measures of promoting production) and research relating to the improvement and further development of such methods of healing that are natural and suited to promote the inherent human ability of self-healing.

Activities: Operates nationally and internationally in the fields of science and medicine, through grants to Scandinavian institutions and individuals, and the provision of fellowships and scholarships.

Geographical Area of Activity: World-wide.

Restrictions: Applicants from outside Europe must be in cooperation with a European institution. No sponsorship of basic education at university level.

Board: Jan-Erik Lindstedt (Chair.).

Address: POB 34012, 100 26 Stockholm.

Telephone: (70) 240 81 81; **Internet:** www.ekhagastiftelsen .se; **e-mail:** info@ekhagastiftelsen.se.

Föreningen Svenska Atheninstitutets Vänner (Association of the Friends of the Swedish Institute at Athens)

Founded in 1976 by Anders Sundberg and 13 others with the aim of supporting the Swedish Institute at Athens (q.v.) and promoting cultural contacts between Sweden and Greece.

Activities: Provides grants to institutions and individuals, and awards prizes and scholarships within Scandinavia; organizes conferences and training courses.

Geographical Area of Activity: Scandinavia.

Publications: *Hellenika* (quarterly).

Board of Directors: Krister Kumlin (Chair.).

Principal Staff: Sec. Ebba Engström.

Address: POB 14124, 104 41 Stockholm.

Telephone: (8) 667 64 55; **Fax:** (8) 25 95 91; **Internet:** www .athenvannerna.se; **e-mail:** info@athenvannerna.se.

Globetree Association

Founded in November 1982 by Kajsa B. Dahlström and Ben van Bronckhorst to support the education of children, with particular emphasis on the environment with an international perspective.

Activities: The Foundation operates nationally and internationally in the fields of aid to less-developed countries, the arts and humanities, conservation and the environment, education, medicine and health; it operates self-conducted programmes, organizes training courses, conferences and research programmes, offers grants to individuals, and awards scholarships and fellowships.

Geographical Area of Activity: International.

Restrictions: No grants made.

Publications: *Meeting in the Globetree*; books and teaching aids.

Principal Staff: Chair. Kajsa B. Dahström; Vice-Chair. Jan-Åke Samuelsson; Treas. Sam Samuelsson.

Address: POB 2048, 103 11 Stockholm.

Telephone: (8) 652 35 27; **Fax:** (8) 653 21 67; **Internet:** www .globetree.org; **e-mail:** sam@globetree.org.

Hjärt-Lungfonden (The Swedish Heart-Lung Foundation)

The Swedish Heart-Lung Foundation is a charitable fundraising organization. The Foundation was established in 1904 during the fight against tuberculosis (TB), and was then called Svenska Nationalföreningen mot Tuberkulos (the Swedish National Anti-tuberculosis Association). The fight against TB in Sweden was successful then and, now, the Heart-Lung Foundation is aiming to conquer the major national diseases of today: heart, lung and vascular diseases.

Activities: The Foundation collects and distributes money for heart, lung and vascular research, and provides information about heart-lung disease. The Swedish Heart-Lung Foundation obtains no state subsidies and its activities are completely dependent on donations from private individuals and companies.

Geographical Area of Activity: Mainly Sweden.

Publications: Report of operations and financial statement; annual review on heart disease in Sweden; information brochures on heart and lung diseases.

Board: Anna-Karin Lundin (Chair.); Anders Westerberg (Vice-Chair.); Lars Lundquist (Treas.).

Principal Staff: Sec.-Gen. Staffan Josephson; CEO Maj-Charlotte Wallin.

Address: POB 5413, Biblioteksgatan 29, 114 84 Stockholm.

Telephone: (8) 566 242 00; **Fax:** (8) 566 242 29; **Internet:** www .hjart-lungfonden.se; **e-mail:** info@hjart-lungfonden.se.

Institut Mittag-Leffler (Mittag-Leffler Foundation of the Royal Swedish Academy of Sciences)

Founded in 1916 by Gösta Mittag-Leffler and Signe Lindfors Mittag-Leffler to promote pure mathematics in Sweden and Scandinavia with international co-operation.

Activities: Conducts research in pure mathematics; awards grants and scholarships open to researchers who have recently obtained a doctorate, and to advanced graduate students researching within the topic of the year.

Geographical Area of Activity: International.

Restrictions: Grants restricted to the annual theme.

Publications: *Acta Mathematica*; *Arkiv för matematik* (journals).

Finance: Funded by the research councils of Denmark, Norway and Sweden, the Ministry of Education of Finland, the Icelandic Mathematical Society and foundations. Annual income 9,148,000 kronor, annual expenditure 9,148,000 kronor (2010).

Board: Anders Björner (Chair.); Björn Jahren (Vice-Chair.) .

Principal Staff: Dir Prof. Ari Laptev; Dep. Dir Tobias Ekholm; Head of Admin. Margareta Wiberg Roland.

Address: Auravägen 17, 182 60 Djursholm.

Telephone: (8) 622 05 60; **Fax:** (8) 622 05 89; **Internet:** www .mittag-leffler.se; **e-mail:** info@mittag-leffler.se.

International Foundation for Science—IFS

Founded in 1972 by the national academies or research councils of 12 countries to encourage scientific work in developing countries.

Activities: Provides young scientists and technologists of outstanding merit from developing countries with financial and other support in their work. The sharing of scientific information between researchers and advisers is encouraged by regional meetings and visits to project sites. As of 2011 there were 135 member organizations (scientific academies, research councils and national and international organizations) in 86 countries (mainly in the developing world).

Geographical Area of Activity: International.

Restrictions: Researchers must carry out the work in their own country, and research is restricted to biological and agricultural sciences, and the chemistry of natural resources.

Publications: Report of operations and financial statement; electronic newsletter; Annual Reports; *IFS Impact Studies (MESIA)*; *External Evaluations of IFS*; *IFS Strategic Plans*; *IFS Work Plans*.

Finance: Core contributions to the budget come from France, Germany, the Netherlands, Norway, Sweden, Switzerland and the USA; restricted contributions are made by several other organizations. Total assets 33,964,000 (31 Dec. 2010); annual income 43,558,000 kronor, expenditure 39,900,000 kronor (2010).

Board of Trustees: Dr Jürg Pfister (Chair.); Prof. Olanrewaju Babatunde Smith (Vice-Chair.).

Principal Staff: Dir Dr Graham Haylor.

Address: Karlavägen 108, 5th Floor, 115 26 Stockholm.

Telephone: (8) 545 818 00; **Fax:** (8) 545 818 01; **Internet:** www.ifs.se; **e-mail:** info@ifs.se.

KK-stiftelsen (Knowledge Foundation)

The Foundation was set up in 1994 to improve the potential of business sectors and higher education to enable healthy cooperation in pursuing common goals.

Activities: Increases communication between academic and business sectors by developing research in Sweden's universities and colleges; invests resources in postgraduate programmes to promote competence in business; supports advancement in Swedish schools; works towards improving health care by utilizing new technologies.

Geographical Area of Activity: Sweden.

Finance: Capital 6,700,000,000 kronor (31 Jan. 2012); Total disbursements approx. 311,000,000 kronor (2011).

Board of Directors: Christina Ullenius (Acting Chair.).

Principal Staff: Chief Exec. Madelene Sandström; Sec. and Gen. Man. Eva Högström.

Address: POB 3222, 103 64 Stockholm; Mäster Samuelsgatan 60, 9 tr, Stockholm.

Telephone: (8) 566 481 00; **Fax:** (8) 24 75 09; **Internet:** www.kks.se; **e-mail:** info@kks.se.

Konstnärsnämnden (The Arts Grants Committee)

Founded in 1976 to administer state grants in the arts. Incorporates IASPIS, the International Artists' Studio Programme in Sweden.

Activities: The Foundation operates nationally and internationally in the area of the arts; it awards grants to individuals in all areas of the arts with the exception of literature.

Geographical Area of Activity: International.

Restrictions: Grants open to Swedish residents and artists working in Sweden.

Finance: Funded by the Swedish Government; annual grants disbursed approx. 100,000,000 kronor.

Board Trustees: Dean Ingrid Elam (Chair.).

Principal Staff: Admin. Dir Ann Larsson.

Address: Maria skolgata 83, 2 tr, 118 53 Stockholm.

Telephone: (8) 506 550 00; **Fax:** (8) 506 550 90; **Internet:** www.konstnarsnamnden.se; **e-mail:** info@konstnarsnamnden.se.

Konung Gustaf V's 90-Årsfond (King Gustaf V 90th Birthday Foundation)

Founded in 1949 by the Swedish people, in honour of King Gustaf's 90th birthday, to support voluntary youth activities.

Activities: Awards grants to Swedish youth organizations for their international exchange programmes with focus on leadership training. There is a particular emphasis on promoting leadership training programmes in Europe. Awards the annual Ernst Killander Scholarship, recognized as the foremost award to a voluntary Swedish youth leader.

Geographical Area of Activity: Mainly Europe.

Restrictions: No grants to individuals.

Finance: Total disbursements 4,947,000 kronor (2007).

Board of Trustees: Gunnar Brodin (Pres.).

Principal Staff: Gen. Sec. Lennart Elbe.

Address: Kungliga Slottet, 111 30 Stockholm.

Telephone: (8) 108 433; **Fax:** (8) 108 433; **Internet:** www.gv90.a.se; **e-mail:** suzanne.fredborg@gv90.a.se.

Kulturfonder for Sverige och Finland (Swedish and Finnish Cultural Foundation)

Established in 1960.

Activities: Grants are provided for a broad range of activities that aim to increase contact and understanding between the people of Sweden and Finland, especially in the fields of culture, the environment and industry. Also works to promote the Finnish language in Sweden.

Geographical Area of Activity: Sweden and Finland.

Restrictions: No grants made to municipalities, counties or state agencies.

Finance: Assets 200,000,000 kronor (2009).

Board: Anders Björck (Chair.); Jan-Erik Enestam (Vice-Pres.).

Principal Staff: Dir Gunvor Kronman (Finland); Dir Mats Wallenius (Sweden).

Address: Föreningen Norden, POB 12707, 112 94 Stockholm; Hanaholmens kulturcentrum, 2100 Esbo, Finland.

Telephone: (8) 506 113 00; **Fax:** (8) 506 113 20; **Internet:** www.kulturfonden.net; www.nordiskafonder.se; **e-mail:** foreningen@norden.se.

Kvinna till Kvinna Foundation

Founded in 1993 in response to the war in the Balkans and the atrocities committed against women; supports women's empowerment projects in armed conflict and post-conflict societies.

Activities: The Foundation supports a range of projects targeting women living in conflict or post-conflict areas. The projects cover areas such as women's participation in peace processes and crisis mangagement, sexual and reproductive health and rights, psychological health care, training for empowerment and employment, addressing domestic violence and trafficking, legal advice and other issues that arise in conflict and post-conflict situations. The Foundation also seeks to build networks among women's groups across conflict borders and raise awareness on developing issues. maintains regional offices in the Balkans, South Caucasus and the Middle East.

Geographical Area of Activity: Albania, Bosnia and Herzegovina, Kosovo, Macedonia, Montenegro, Serbia, Georgia, Armenia, Azerbaijan, Israel, Palestinian Autonomous Areas, Iraq, Lebanon, Jordan, Egypt, Democratic Republic of the Congo, Liberia.

Restrictions: No unsolicited proposals accepted.

Publications: Annual Report; thematic reports.

Finance: Funding from the Swedish International Development Agency and other trusts and foundations. Public fundraising activities. Total assets 40,735,000 kronor (31 Dec. 2010); annual revenue 81,579,000 kronor, total project funds disbursed 67,493,000 kronor (2010).

Board of Directors: Birgit Hansson (Pres.); Mari Mörth (Vice-Pres.) ; Lennart Lindgren (Sec.).

Principal Staff: Sec.-Gen. Lena Ag; Man. Dir Anna Lidén.

Address: Slakthusplan 3, 121 62 Johanneshov.

Telephone: (8) 588 891 00; **Fax:** (8) 588 891 01; **Internet:** www.kvinnatillkvinna.se; **e-mail:** info@kvinnatillkvinna.se.

Nobelstiftelsen (Nobel Foundation)

Founded in 1900 in accordance with the will of Alfred Nobel to award annual prizes to those who, during the preceding year, are judged to have conferred the greatest benefit on mankind in each of the following fields: physics, chemistry, physiology or medicine, literature and peace.

Activities: Operates internationally in the fields of science and medicine, literature and peace promotion, through the prizes to individuals, a peace prize to institutions or individuals, conferences and publications. Prize-winners are chosen by the Royal Academy of Sciences, Stockholm (Physics, Chemistry), the Nobel Assembly at the Karolinska Institutet, Stockholm (Physiology or Medicine), the Swedish Academy, Stockholm (Literature) and the Norwegian Nobel Committee (Peace). In 1968 the Central Bank of Sweden instituted an Alfred Nobel Memorial Prize in Economic Sciences of the same value as the Nobel Prize—the prize-winner of this award is chosen by the Royal Swedish Academy of Sciences.

Geographical Area of Activity: International.

Publications: Annual Report and financial statement; *Les Prix Nobel*; *Nobel Lectures;* books and journals.

Finance: Total assets 134,170,000 kronor, total operating expenses 66,180,000 kronor (2010).

Board of Directors: Marcus Storch (Chair.); Göran K. Hansson (Vice-Chair.).

Principal Staff: Exec. Dir Lars Heikensten.

Address: POB 5232, 102 45 Stockholm; Sturegatan 14, Stockholm.

Telephone: (8) 663 09 20; **Fax:** (8) 660 38 47; **Internet:** nobelprize.org/nobelfoundation/index.html; **e-mail:** info@nobel.se.

Nordiska Afrikainstitutets Stipendier (Nordic Africa Institute Scholarships)

Founded in 1962 to provide funds for researchers associated with universities and other research institutions in the Nordic countries (Denmark, Finland, Iceland, Norway and Sweden) to conduct fieldwork in Africa.

Activities: Provides grants for those preparing and conducting research projects concerned with development issues in Africa, and emphasis is placed on the social sciences and closely related fields.

Geographical Area of Activity: The Nordic countries (Denmark, Finland, Iceland, Norway and Sweden) and Africa.

Restrictions: Grants only to researchers associated with institutions in the Nordic countries.

Publications: Published more than 600 academic titles on African politics, economics, social issues and modern history.

Principal Staff: Dir Carin Norberg; Chief Assistant Annika Franklin.

Address: POB 1703, 751 47 Uppsala.

Telephone: (18) 56 22 00; **Fax:** (18) 56 22 90; **Internet:** www.nai.uu.se/scholarships; **e-mail:** nai@nai.uu.se.

NORDITA—Nordisk Institut for Teoretisk Fysik (Nordic Institute for Theoretical Physics)

Founded in 1957 by the Governments of Denmark, Finland, Iceland, Norway and Sweden to undertake research, provide training to young physicists from the Nordic countries, and promote co-operation between institutes in member countries. The Institute is run jointly by the Royal Institute of Technology (KTH) and Stockholm University and is located on the premises of AlbaNova University Center in Stockholm.

Activities: NORDITA's purpose is to carry out research and strengthen Nordic collaboration within the basic areas of theoretical physics. The main research areas are: Astrophysics and Astrobiology; Condensed Matter and Statistical and Biological Physics; and Subatomic Physics.

Geographical Area of Activity: Scandinavia.

Publications: *Nordita News* (newsletter, approx. six a year); research reports; science news.

Finance: Funded by the Nordic Council of Ministers together with the Swedish Research Council, KTH and Stockholm University. Annual budget approx. 19,800,000 Swedish kronor.

Board: Prof. Thordur Jonsson (Chair.).

Principal Staff: Dir Prof. Lárus Thorlacius; Dep. Dir Prof. Axel Brandenburg.

Address: Roslagstullsbacken 23, 106 91 Stockholm.

Telephone: (5) 537 84 44; **Fax:** (5) 537 84 04; **Internet:** www.nordita.org; **e-mail:** info@nordita.org.

Olof Palmes Minnesfond (Olof Palme Memorial Foundation)

Established by Olof Palme's family and by the Social Democratic Party to honour his memory. The Fund's purpose is, through scholarships and grants, to give opportunities to young people for international exchange and for studies of peace and disarmament, to support work against racism and against hostility toward foreigners, and to foster in other ways work for international understanding and common security.

Activities: The Fund awards the annual Olof Palme prize for an outstanding achievement, as well as awarding scholarships in the fields of peace and disarmament, anti-racism and hostility to foreigners and supporting projects ranging from advanced research to simple individual projects, including trade union and cultural exchanges between young people in different countries, and studies and research, principally for young people in Sweden. The Fund also supports initiatives by schools and youth organizations, both at a national and a local level. Also works to promote international understanding in other ways, by actively seeking out and supporting suitable projects in Sweden and elsewhere.

Geographical Area of Activity: Sweden and international.

Board: Pierre Schori (Chair.); Joakim Palme (Vice-Chair.); Björn Wall (Treas.).

Address: POB 836, 101 36 Stockholm.

Telephone: (8) 677 57 90; **Fax:** (8) 677 57 71; **Internet:** www.palmefonden.se; **e-mail:** palmefonden@palmecenter.se.

Reumatikerförbundet (Swedish Rheumatism Association)

Founded in 1945 by the Swedish Confederation of Trade Unions, the Co-operative Union and Wholesale Society, the Federation of Swedish Farmers' Associations, the Federation of Swedish Trade Unions, and different associations of workers in social welfare to combat rheumatic diseases in Sweden.

Activities: Operates nationally running a hospital for rheumatic patients; enables information to be exchanged among members and others interested; makes grants for research in rheumatology, and participates in international conferences; has approx. 60,000 members.

Geographical Area of Activity: Sweden.

Publications: *Reumatikertidningen* (periodical); Annual Report and financial statement.

Board: Anne Carlsson (Chair.); David Magnusson (Vice-Chair.); Bo Jonsson (Vice-Chair.).

Principal Staff: Gen. Sec. Magdalena Olsson; Deputy Gen. Sec. Lena Ridemar.

Address: Alströmergatan 39, POB 12851, 112 98 Stockholm.

Telephone: (8) 505 805 00; **Fax:** (8) 505 805 50; **Internet:** www.reumatikerforbundet.org; **e-mail:** info@ reumatikerforbundet.org.

Right Livelihood Awards Foundation
Established in 1980 by Jakob von Uexkull.

Activities: The purpose of the Foundation is to present the Right Livelihood Awards annually, and through them promote scientific research, education, public understanding and practical activities that contribute to a global ecological balance; the Awards are aimed at eliminating material and spiritual poverty and contributing to lasting peace and justice in the world. The Foundation also supports and reports on the projects for which the Awards are presented.

Geographical Area of Activity: International.

Restrictions: Anyone—except Right Livelihood Award jury and staff members—can propose anyone else (individuals or organizations) for an award, with the exception of themselves, close relatives or their own organization.

Publications: brochures; bibliographies of Laureates (mainly online); DVDs and CDs.

Finance: Funded by private donations.

Board of Trustees: Jakob von Uexkull (Co-Chair.); Monika Griefahn (Co-Chair.); Paul Ekins (Vice-Chair.).

Principal Staff: Exec. Dir Ole von Uexkull; Foundation Man. Kajsa Övergaard.

Address: POB 15072, 104 65 Stockholm; Nutidshuset, Hornsgatan 15, 5th Floor, 118 46 Stockholm.

Telephone: (8) 702 03 40; **Fax:** (8) 702 03 38; **Internet:** www.rightlivelihood.org; **e-mail:** info@rightlivelihood.org.

SNF—Swedish Nutrition Foundation
Founded in 1961 by 14 food and related industries and associations to further scientific nutrition research of interest to the food industry and other allied producers, and the practical utilization of advances in nutritional science. Has around 40 member organizations.

Activities: Operates nationally in the field of education, and nationally and internationally in the fields of science and medicine and international relations. Awards scholarships and supports research in basic and applied nutrition through grants to Swedish students. Travel grants enable researchers to participate in congresses and conferences and to visit laboratories abroad. International symposia are organized, and extracts of the proceedings are published. Information and advice is provided to sponsors enabling them to profit from the results of nutrition research.

Geographical Area of Activity: Sweden.

Publications: Report of operations and financial statement; *Symposia of the Swedish Nutrition Foundation* (series); *Food & Nutrition Research* (open access journal); *Nordisk Nutrition* (quarterly).

Board: Annika Ahnberg (Chair.).

Principal Staff: Pres. Susanne Bryngelsson; Sec. and Finance Asst Agneta Hartlén.

Address: Ideon Science Park, Beta, Bldg 1, 2v, Scheelevägen 17, 223 70 Lund.

Telephone: (46) 286 22 82; **Fax:** (46) 286 22 81; **Internet:** www.snf.ideon.se; **e-mail:** info@snf.ideon.se.

Erik Philip-Sörensens Stiftelse (Erik Philip-Sörensen Foundation)
Founded in 1976 to promote research into genetic science and the humanities.

Activities: In the field of genetic science, research grants are made to individuals or groups regardless of the institute where they choose to operate. Both basic research and specialized research are supported. Grants in the field of the humanities are awarded on the recommendation of Lund University.

Geographical Area of Activity: Sweden.

Restrictions: The Foundation does not give grants for research work outside Sweden; only accepts applications from Swedish universities.

Address: SEB, Kapitalförvaltning, Institutioner & Stiftelser, 205 20 Malmö.

Internet: www.epss.se.

Stiftelsen Blanceflor Boncompagni-Ludovisi, född Bildt (Blanceflor Boncompagni-Ludovisi, née Bildt Foundation)
Founded in 1955 to promote scientific and education research for Swedish and Italian citizens under the age of 35.

Activities: Grants are provided to individuals under the age of 35 for study in scientific fields (for example, chemistry, physics, medicine, dentistry and engineering) where study abroad is seen to be of specific value. Grants are awarded for higher education (at university or the equivalent) to those not eligible for state or community grants. The preferred host countries are Canada, Germany, Italy, Japan, Sweden, Switzerland, the United Kingdom and the USA.

Geographical Area of Activity: International.

Restrictions: No grants to groups or associations, nor for undergraduate study. Grants are made for study in certain disciplines only.

Finance: Total annual grants 3,000,000–4,000,000 kronor.

Principal Staff: Treas. Dag Wersén.

Address: c/o Advokaterna Wersén & Partners, Grev Turegatan 13B, 114 46 Stockholm.

Telephone: (8) 678 01 65; **Fax:** (8) 679 84 98; **Internet:** www.blanceflor.se.

Stiftelsen Dag Hammarskjölds Minnesfond (Dag Hammarskjöld Foundation)
Established in 1962 in memory of the second Secretary-General of the UN.

Activities: The Dag Hammarskjöld Foundation is an autonomous organization that provides a forum for free and frank debate, stimulating Another Development for the future. The Foundation does not give grants. Activities focus on UN-related issues. The Foundation promotes the values of Dag Hammarskjöld, the second UN Secretary-General, within the current global development discourse.

Geographical Area of Activity: International.

Restrictions: The Foundation is an operating and not a grant-making foundation; its work programmes are carried out under its own auspices.

Publications: Two series: *Development Dialogue* (2 a year) and *Critical Currents*. Occasionally other publications.

Board of Trustees: Prof. Göran Bexell (Chair.).

Principal Staff: Exec. Dir. Henning Melber; Sr Coordinator (Admin.) Karin Andersson Schiebe.

Address: Övre Slottsgatan 2, 753 10 Uppsala.

Telephone: (18) 410 10 00; **Fax:** (18) 12 20 72; **Internet:** www.dhf.uu.se; **e-mail:** secretariat@dhf.uu.se.

Stiftelsen för Miljöstrategisk Forskning—Mistra (Swedish Foundation for Strategic Environmental Research)
Founded in 1994 to encourage research, especially in the field of the environment.

Activities: The Foundation supports environmental research programmes in the area of sustainable development, and promotes co-operation between universities, industry and international centres of research.

Geographical Area of Activity: International.

Publications: Annual Report; brochures; conference and reports.

Finance: Total assets 2,670,076,779 kronor (31 Dec. 2010); annual income 50,302,101 kronor, expenditure 24,860,094 kronor (2010).

Board: Lena Treschow Torell (Chair.); Stefan Nyström (Vice-Chair.).

Principal Staff: Exec. Dir Lars-Erik Liljelund; Admin. Chief Fredrik Gunnarsson.

Address: Gamla Brogatan 36–38, 111 20 Stockholm.

Telephone: (8) 791 10 20; **Fax:** (8) 791 10 29; **Internet:** www .mistra.org; **e-mail:** mail@mistra.org.

Stiftelsen Riksbankens Jubileumsfond

Established in 1964 by the Swedish Parliament and the Bank of Sweden to commemorate the tercentenary of the bank, and to support scientific research.

Activities: Aims to support research in the humanities and social sciences through grants and scholarships. Programmes include the Nils-Eric Svensson Fund, which promotes educational exchanges between young researchers in Sweden and the rest of Europe, and several grants that support research projects and programmes in the humanities and social sciences. Internationally, the Foundation funds the Swedish–German Research Awards for Scientific Co-operation programme in conjunction with the Alexander-von-Humboldt-Stiftung, and is one of a number of foundations funding the Collegium Budapest for Advanced Study. The Foundation is also involved in several projects with VolkswagenStiftung, Compagnia di San Paolo, Bosch Stiftung, European Cultural Foundation and the European Foundation Centre.

Geographical Area of Activity: Sweden and world-wide.

Restrictions: No grants to undergraduate students, nor to doctoral students.

Publications: Annual Report and financial statement; conference reports; Yearbook.

Finance: Total assets 8,501,014,000 kronor (31 Dec. 2010); Grants disbursed approx. 350,000,000 kronor (2010).

Board of Directors: Prof. Daniel Tarschys (Chair.); Per Bill (Vice-Chair.).

Principal Staff: Chief Exec. Göran Blomqvist.

Address: Kungsträdgårdsgatan 18, POB 5675, 114 86 Stockholm.

Telephone: (8) 506 264 00; **Fax:** (8) 506 264 31; **Internet:** www .rj.se; **e-mail:** rj@rj.se.

Stockholm Environment Institute

Founded in 1989 by the Swedish Parliament to unite scientific research and policy development, particularly in the areas of environment and development.

Activities: The Institute has centres in Stockholm, Tallinn (Estonia), Bangkok (Thailand), Dar es Salaam (Tanzania), Boston (USA), Oxford (United Kingdom) and York (United Kingdom). Research is carried out in four main programme areas: reducing climate risk; managing environmental systems; transforming governance; and rethinking development. Maintains regional offices in Belgium and Thailand, and work is carried out in more than 20 countries world-wide.

Geographical Area of Activity: International.

Publications: Newsletters; fact sheets; *Renewable Energy for Development; Urban Air Pollution in Asian Cities: Status Challenge and Management; Sun, Sea, Sand and Tsunamis: Examining Disaster Vulnerability in the Tourism Community of Khao Lak, Thailand; Greening the Greys: Climate Change and the Over 50s; Sustainable Energy for All: from Basic Access to a Shared Development Agenda; Climate Policy in India: What Shapes International, National and State Policy?; The Baltic-Climate toolkit: Bringing data and resources to key actors in the public and private sectors.*

Finance: Total research funding approx. 149,000,000 kronor (2010).

Board: Kerstin Niblaeus (Chair.).

Principal Staff: Exec. Dir Dr Johan Rockström; Dir (Stockholm) Johan Kuylenstierna.

Address: Kräftriket 2B, 106 91 Stockholm.

Telephone: (8) 674 70 70; **Fax:** (8) 723 03 48; **Internet:** www.sei .se; **e-mail:** info@sei-international.org.

Stockholm International Peace Research Institute—SIPRI

SIPRI is an independent international institute dedicated to research into conflict, armaments, arms control and disarmament. Established in 1966, SIPRI provides data, analysis and recommendations, based on open sources, to policy-makers, researchers, media and the interested public. SIPRI was recently named as one of the world's leading think tanks in the 'Think Tank Index' issued by the journal Foreign Policy.

Activities: Operates internationally in the fields of regional and global security, armed conflict and conflict management, military spending and armaments and arms control, disarmament and non-proliferation. Recently established programmes include China and Global Security as well as Global Health and Security. SIPRI maintains a number of databases on international arms transfers, military expenditure, multilateral peace operations, and international arms embargoes. Further activities include seminars and conferences as well as advice and consulting.

Geographical Area of Activity: International.

Publications: *SIPRI Yearbook*; monographs and research reports; policy papers; insights on peace and security' policy briefs; fact sheets; special reports and handbooks.

Finance: SIPRI receives a substantial part of its funding through an annual grant from the Swedish Government. The Institute also seeks financial support from other organizations. Total annual budget US $6,000,000 (2010).

Governing Board: Göran Lennmarker (Chair.).

Principal Staff: Dir Dr Bates Gill; Deputy Dir Daniel Nord; Chief Financial Officer Elisabet Isacson Rendert.

Address: Signalistgatan 9, 169 70 Solna.

Telephone: (8) 655 97 00; **Fax:** (8) 655 97 33; **Internet:** www .sipri.org; **e-mail:** sipri@sipri.org.

Sverige-Amerika Stiftelsen (Sweden-America Foundation)

Founded in 1919 by representatives of private business and industry, with the aim of developing understanding between Sweden and the USA and Canada by promoting the exchange of scientific, cultural and practical experiences between the countries.

Activities: Provides scholarships to Swedish citizens for advanced study and research in the USA or Canada. Supports an internship programme for Swedes in the USA.

Geographical Area of Activity: Sweden, the USA and Canada.

Publications: Annual Report.

Trustees: HM Crown Princess Victoria (Hon. Chair.); Mariana Burenstam Linder (Chair.); Magnus Sjöqvist (Vice-Chair.); Harald Mix (Vice-Chair.).

Principal Staff: Exec. Dir Anna Rosvall Stuart; Contact Michelle Jacobson.

Address: Grev Turegatan 14, POB 5280, 102 46 Stockholm.

Telephone: (8) 611 46 11; **Fax:** (8) 611 40 04; **Internet:** www .sweamfo.se; **e-mail:** info@sweamfo.se.

Sweden-Japan Foundation—SJF

Founded in 1971 with the purpose of increasing understanding between the people of Sweden and Japan.

Activities: Operates in the fields of research and development, industry, science, commerce and culture, through the provision of scholarships for undergraduate students, organizing courses, seminars and study trips, and the publication of relevant documentation. The Foundation encourages cultural exchange and co-operation between the two countries.

Geographical Area of Activity: Sweden and Japan.

Publications: *Japan-Nytt* (monthly newsletter); papers.

Board of Directors: Bo Dankis (Chair.); Robert Stenram (Deputy Chair.).

Principal Staff: Exec. Chair. Carl Eric Stålberg.

Address: Grev Turegatan 14, 114 46 Stockholm.

Telephone: (8) 611 68 73; **Fax:** (8) 611 73 44; **Internet:** www .swejap.a.se; **e-mail:** info@swejap.a.se.

Transnationella Stiftelsen för Freds- och Framtids-forskning—TFF (Transnational Foundation for Peace and Future Research)

Founded in 1986 by Christina Spännar and Jan Øberg, to promote conflict mitigation, peace research and education; to improve conflict understanding; and to promote alternative security and global development based on non-violent politics and economics.

Activities: The Foundation has established the following programmes: world images and peace thinking; European orders of peace and co-operation; reconciliation and forgiveness; Gandhi's relevance in the contemporary world; conflict mitigation—theory and practice in the former Yugoslavia, Iraq, Burundi and Greenland, and the roles of the UN in the emerging world order.

Geographical Area of Activity: International.

Restrictions: Not a grant-making organization.

Publications: Books, research reports, occasional papers and annual reports and three free mail services: *TFF Press-Info* (analyses and debate articles); *TFF PeaceTips*; *TFF Peace-Browser*.

Board of Directors: Jan Øberg (Chair.).

Principal Staff: Dir Jan Øberg.

Address: Vegagatan 25, 224 57 Lund.

Telephone: 738 525200; **Internet:** www.transnational.org; **e-mail:** tff@transnational.org.

Knut och Alice Wallenbergs Stiftelse (Knut and Alice Wallenberg Foundation)

Founded in 1917 by Knut Agathon Wallenberg and Alice O. Wallenberg to promote research and education of value to Sweden.

Activities: Operates primarily nationally in the fields of education, medicine, the natural sciences and the arts and humanities, through grants to institutions, particularly for high-value equipment and laboratories.

Geographical Area of Activity: Sweden.

Restrictions: Grants are not made to private individuals without connection to a research institution, with the exception of scholarship programmes established by or supported by the Foundation. Only Swedish applications are considered.

Finance: Net assets 49,679,000,000 kronor (2010); total grants disbursed 959,000 kronor (2010).

Board of Directors: Peter Wallenberg (Chair.); Peter Wallenberg, Jr (Vice-Chair.).

Principal Staff: Exec. Dir Göran Sandberg.

Address: Knut och Alice Wallenberg Stiftelse, POB 16066, 103 22 Stockholm.

Telephone: (8) 545 017 80; **Fax:** (8) 545 017 85; **Internet:** www .wallenberg.com/kaw; **e-mail:** kaw@kaw.se.

Dr Marcus Wallenbergs Stiftelse för Utbildning i Internationellt Industriellt Företagande (Dr Marcus Wallenberg Foundation for Further Education in International Industry)

Founded in 1982 with the aim of providing financial assistance for education in industry and business.

Activities: The Foundation awards grants to Swedish citizens for study abroad. Grants are also made to educational institutions.

Geographical Area of Activity: Sweden.

Restrictions: Grants are available to Swedish citizens with a university degree and two years' experience in business or public administration.

Board of Directors: Peter Wallenberg (Chair.); Peter Wallenberg Jr (Vice-Chair.).

Principal Staff: Exec. Dir Erna Möller.

Address: POB 16066, 103 22 Stockholm.

Telephone: (8) 54 50 17 77; **Fax:** (8) 54 50 17 85; **Internet:** www .wallenberg.com/tmw; **e-mail:** tmw@tmw.se.

Wenner-Gren Foundations

The Wenner-Gren Foundations comprise the Wenner-Gren Centre Foundation for Scientific Research and the Axel-Wenner-Gren Foundation for International Exchange of Scientists. The Foundations were established to promote international co-operation in scientific research in Sweden, and organize symposia and conferences in the sciences.

Activities: The Foundations supply guest apartments for foreign researchers in Stockholm; award fellowships to Swedish researchers wanting to go abroad, and to guest scientists who wish to visit Sweden; support the invitation of foreign guest lecturers; organize international symposia; and support the exchange of knowledge between researchers in different countries.

Geographical Area of Activity: International.

Restrictions: All applications for fellowships must come through Swedish institutions.

Publications: *Eye Movements in Reading*; *Active Hearing*; *Challenges and Perspectives in Neuroscience*; *Life and Death in the Nervous System*; *Molecular mechanisms of Neuronal Communication*; *Goals and Purposes of Higher Education in the 21st Century*; *Politics and Culture in the Age of Christina*; *Genetics and Psychiatric Disorders*; *Basic Sensory Mechanisms in Cognition and Language*; *Connective Tissue Biology: Integration and Reductionism*; *The Chemistry, Biology and Medical Applications of Hyaluronan and its Derivatives*; *The Impact of Electronic Publishing on the Academic Community*.

Principal Staff: Science Sec. Prof. Bertil Daneholt; Admin. Dir Kristina Lindstedt.

Address: Sveavägen 166, 23rd Floor, 113 46 Stockholm.

Telephone: (8) 736 98 00; **Fax:** (8) 31 86 32; **Internet:** www .swgc.org; **e-mail:** maria.helgostam@swgc.org.

Switzerland

FOUNDATION CENTRES AND CO-ORDINATING BODIES

Alliance Sud—Swiss Alliance of Development Organisations

Established in 1971 to pursue development projects common to the six member organizations; SWISSAID (q.v.), the Catholic Lenten Fund, Bread for All, Swiss Interchurch Aid, Helvetas (q.v.) and Caritas (q.v.). Formerly known as the Swiss Coalition of Development Organisations.

Activities: The Swiss Coalition focuses on development policy, acting as an advocate within Switzerland for disadvantaged social classes in the Global South. It works through a combination of lobbying, public relations works and grassroots mobilization in activities designed to be politically effective. Maintains information and documentation centres in Berne and Lausanne.

Geographical Area of Activity: World-wide.

Restrictions: No grants available.

Publications: Annual Report; newsletters.

Finance: Funded by member organizations; annual budget approx. US $3,200,000.

Principal Staff: Dir Peter Niggli; Asst to the Dir Kathrin Spichiger.

Address: Monbijoustr. 31, POB 6735, 3001 Berne.

Telephone: 313909330; **Fax:** 313909331; **Internet:** www.alliancesud.ch; **e-mail:** mail@alliancesud.ch.

Fondation Philias (Philias Foundation)

Established in 1997 by Bettina Ferdman Guerrier to promote Corporate Social Responsibility (CSR) in Switzerland and help companies to put CSR into practice.

Activities: The Foundation provides information about CSR to its members, organizes workshops, and provides consultancy services on corporate community involvement and CSR strategy. By running the Philias corporate network, Philias also acts as a catalyst and unifying force on various CSR projects and issues. Philias organizes an annual conference, CSR events and releases publications on corporate social responsibility. The Foundation is a member of CSR Europe (q.v.) network.

Geographical Area of Activity: Switzerland.

Publications: *Philgood* (quarterly newsletter).

Finance: Annual revenue 972,883 Swiss francs, expenditure 966,163 Swiss francs (2010).

Board of Trustees: Philippe Nordmann (Chair.); Claude Bébéar (Hon. Chair.); Charles Firmenich (Vice-Chair. and Treas.).

Principal Staff: Founder and Dir Bettina Ferdman Guerrier; Finance and Admin. Man. Heidi Frei.

Address: 17 clos de la Fonderie, 1227 Carouge.

Telephone: 223084650; **Fax:** 223084656; **Internet:** www.philias.org; **e-mail:** info@philias.org.

International Council of Voluntary Agencies—ICVA

Founded in 1962, the Council functions as an advocacy network adding value to the work of the NGOs that form its membership. It aims to facilitate a successful partnership between NGOs and international agencies, and to act as a catalyst and a tool for the accurate, timely and effective exchange of information, concerns and issues among member NGOs, international humanitarian agencies and governments working towards common objectives. These objectives include the alleviation of human suffering in disaster areas, protection and promotion of human rights.

Activities: The Council facilitates access and NGO input to the Standing and Executive Committees of the UN High Commissioner for Refugees (UNHCR). As one of the three NGO networks on the UN Inter-Agency Standing Committee, ICVA facilitates dialogue between NGOs and the main international body for humanitarian co-ordination. ICVA is also actively involved in the Sphere Project. ICVA has more than 75 member agencies world-wide.

Geographical Area of Activity: International.

Restrictions: Not a grant-making agency.

Publications: *Talk Back* (newsletter, e-mail or online); Annual Report.

Executive Committee: Paul O'Brien (Chair.); Dr Misikir Tilahun (Vice-Chair.); Dale Buscher (Treas.).

Principal Staff: Exec. Dir Ed Schenkenberg van Mierop.

Address: 26–28 ave Giuseppe-Motta, 1202 Geneva.

Telephone: 229509600; **Fax:** 229509609; **Internet:** www.icva.ch; **e-mail:** secretariat@icva.ch.

Interphil—International Standing Conference on Philanthropy

Founded in 1969 by CAF—the Charities Aid Foundation (q.v.), the European Cultural Foundation (q.v.), Fomento de entitades beneficias and Stifterverband für die deutsche Wissenschaft (q.v.) to promote the principles and the practices of philanthropy; it is a voluntary, non-governmental, non-profit association working for the good of the community.

Activities: The Conference works internationally towards the advancement of the non-profit sector, in the fields of education, research, the arts, conservation and social welfare and social studies, through self-conducted programmes, prizes, conferences, lectures, advisory services and publications. Interphil is committed to the strengthening of civil society in Central and Eastern Europe, as well as in other parts of the world.

Geographical Area of Activity: International.

Restrictions: No grants are made to individuals.

Publications: *Philanthropy International*; conference reports.

Finance: Funded through membership contributions.

Board of Directors: Countess Anne Sforza (Pres.); Rena Sha'shua-Hasson, Colin Graham (Vice-Pres); Cyril Ritchie (Exec. Dir and Treas.).

Principal Staff: Exec. Dir Cyril Ritchie.

Address: CIC Case 20, 1211 Geneva 20.

Telephone: 227336717; **Fax:** 227347082.

proFonds

Established in 1990 to support the development and activities of foundations and associations in Switzerland.

Activities: Promotes the rights and activities of foundations and associations in Switzerland, through networking at national and international level, lobbying government on legal and fiscal issues relating to the non-profit sector, and promoting and facilitating the exchange of information between non-profit organizations. Also issues publications and carries out research.

Geographical Area of Activity: Switzerland.

Publications: *Stiftungsland Schweiz*; *Aufgaben und Verantwortlichkeit von Stiftungsorganen*; *Gemeinnützige Stiftungen* *und Steuern: Steuerbefreiung, Spendenabzug und MWST*; *pro-Fonds-Info* (quarterly newsletter); and other publications.

Committee: Bernhard Hahnloser (Pres.); Dr Harold Grüninger (Vice-Pres.).

Principal Staff: Dir Dr Christoph Degen.

Address: Dufourstr. 49, 4052 Basel.

Telephone: 612721080; **Fax:** 612721081; **Internet:** www.profonds.org; **e-mail:** info@profonds.org.

SwissFoundations—Verband der Schweizer Förderstiftungen/Association des fondations donatrices suisses (Association of Grantmaking Foundations in Switzerland)

Established in May 2001, an initiative of 11 large Swiss grantmaking foundations.

Activities: SwissFoundations represents its member foundations in Switzerland, imparts technical expertise and experience, promotes transparency, presents a platform for interfoundation interaction where experiences of foundations can be exchanged, and encourages involvement of new foundations. In 2011 there were 83 member organizations.

Geographical Area of Activity: Switzerland.

Publications: *Swiss Foundation Code 2009* (in German); Annual Report (in German).

Finance: Total assets 130,785 Swiss francs (31 Dec. 2010); annual income 402,295 Swiss francs, annual expenditure 386,305 Swiss francs (2010).

Executive Board: Dr Beat von Wartburg (Pres.).

Principal Staff: Gen. Man. Beate Eckhardt.

Address: Kirchgasse 42,8001 Zürich.

Telephone: 444400010; **Fax:** 444400011; **Internet:** www.swissfoundations.ch; **e-mail:** info@swissfoundations.ch.

FOUNDATIONS, TRUSTS AND NON-PROFIT ORGANIZATIONS

Abegg-Stiftung (Abegg Foundation)

Founded in 1961 by Werner Abegg for the collection and restoration of ancient woven fabrics dating up to the 18th century; the collection and display of works of minor arts, sculptures and paintings from the Near East, Byzantium, the European Middle Ages and the Renaissance and Baroque periods; the education of textile restorers; research in the fields of textiles and minor arts.

Activities: The Foundation supports textile restoration projects and students of textile restoration, through creating and running a degree course in textile art at the University of Applied Science, Berne. Maintains a library and a museum. Promotes scientific exchange in textile art by founding a research institute, organizing conferences and issuing publications.

Geographical Area of Activity: Switzerland.

Publications: Collection catalogues and other specialist publications; *Riggisberger Berichte*; *Schriften*.

Principal Staff: Dir Dr Regula Schorta.

Address: Werner Abegg-Str. 67, 3132 Riggisberg.

Telephone: 318081201; **Fax:** 318081200; **Internet:** www.abegg-stiftung.ch; **e-mail:** info@abegg-stiftung.ch.

Aga Khan Agency for Microfinance

The Aga Khan Angency for Microfinance was established in November 2004 in Geneva, Switzerland. Under Swiss law, it is a private, not-for-profit, non-denominational international development agency.

Activities: The Aga Khan Angency for Microfinance's mandate is to alleviate poverty, diminish the vulnerability of poor populations and reduce economic and social exclusion. It aims to accomplish the following: help people become self-reliant and eventually gain the skills needed to graduate into the mainstream financial sector; realize long-term sustainability

covering costs and contributing to expansion; reach out as broadly as possible, in terms of geographical coverage and range of services offered; and maximize impact on intended beneficiaries by ensuring that resources flow primarily to the poor and the excluded.

Geographical Area of Activity: Asia, Africa and the Middle East.

Publications: brochures; Annual Report.

Finance: Loans disbursed US $205,168,000 (2009).

Board of Directors: HH the Aga Khan (Chair.).

Address: Aga Khan Development Network, POB 2049, 1–3 Ave de la Paix, 1211 Geneva 2.

Telephone: 229097200; **Fax:** 229097292; **Internet:** www.akdn.org/akam.asp; **e-mail:** akam@akdn.org.

Aga Khan Development Network—AKDN

AKDN, launched by HH Prince Karim Aga Khan, is a body of development agencies working together to execute welfare activities mainly in the poorest Asian and African regions.

Activities: Focuses on promoting education, health and welfare, economic development, culture and NGO development, mainly in Asia and Africa. The Network comprises the Aga Khan Foundation (q.v.), Aga Khan Education Services, Agha Khan Academies, Focus Humanitarian Assistance, Aga Khan Health Services, Aga Khan Trust for Culture (qq.v.), Aga Khan University and University of Central Asia, Aga Khan Fund for Economic Development, Aga Khan Planning and Building Services, and Aga Khan Agency for Microfinance (q.v.).

Geographical Area of Activity: World-wide, but primarily Africa and Asia.

Restrictions: No grants to individuals or for research; grants made in specific countries or regions only; no grants for construction.

Publications: Press releases; calendars; bulletins.

Finance: Funded by individual agencies.

Board of Directors: HH the Aga Khan (Chair.).

Address: 1–3 ave de la Paix, POB 2049, 1211 Geneva 2.

Telephone: 229097200; **Fax:** 229097292; **Internet:** www.akdn.org; **e-mail:** afk@akdn.org.

Aga Khan Foundation—AKF

Founded in 1967 by HH Prince Karim Aga Khan to promote new and effective solutions to certain well-defined problems that impede social development in developing countries. The Bellerive Foundation merged with the Foundation in 2006 to become the Prince Sadruddin Aga Khan Fund for the Environment within the AKF. An agency of the Aga Khan Development Network.

Activities: The Foundation operates nationally and internationally in the fields of health, education, rural development, the strengthening of civil society and related concerns, including community participation, gender and the environment, through grants to institutions, fellowships and scholarships, and publications. Prefers to fund innovative solutions to generic problems. With few exceptions, the Foundation provides funding for programmes in countries where it has branch offices and local professional staff to monitor implementation. Travel and study awards are made only to sponsored staff directly involved in programme implementation. The Foundation has offices in Afghanistan, Bangladesh, Canada, India, Kenya, Kyrgyzstan, Mozambique, Pakistan, Portugal, Syria, Tajikistan, Tanzania, Uganda, the United Kingdom and the USA.

Geographical Area of Activity: Afghanistan, USA, Bangladesh, Canada, India, Kenya, Kyrgyzstan, Mozambique, Pakistan, Portugal, Syria, Tajikistan, Tanzania, Uganda and United Kingdom.

Restrictions: No grants to individuals or for research; grants made in specific countries or regions only; no grants for construction.

Publications: Annual Report; numerous reports and evaluations.

Board of Directors: HH the Aga Khan (Chair.).

Principal Staff: Gen. Man. Thomas G. Kessinger; Finance Man. Christopher Beck.

Address: 1–3 ave de la Paix, 1202 Geneva 2.

Telephone: 229097200; **Fax:** 229097291; **Internet:** www .akdn.org/akf; **e-mail:** akf@akdn.ch.

Aga Khan Fund for Economic Development

Activities: An international development agency promoting entrepreneurship and economically sound enterprise in the developing world, with more than 90 project companies in areas including banking, electricity, agricultural processing, tourism, airlines and telecommunications. Additionally runs social programmes in microfinance, education and health.

Geographical Area of Activity: Afghanistan, Bangladesh, Burkina Faso, the Democratic Republic of the Congo, Côte d'Ivoire, India, Kenya, Kyrgyzstan, Mali, Mozambique, Pakistan, Senegal, Syria, Tajikistan, Tanzania and Uganda.

Finance: Revenue US $2,300,000,000 (2010).

Board of Directors: HH the Aga Khan (Chair.).

Address: Aga Khan Development Network, POB 2049, 211 Geneva 2.

Telephone: 229097200; **Fax:** 229097200; **Internet:** www .akdn.org/akfed.asp; **e-mail:** afk@akdn.org.

Aga Khan Trust for Culture—AKTC

Founded by HH Prince Karim Aga Khan in June 1988 to promote a deeper understanding of the role of the built environment in society, and the development of Muslim societies.

Activities: The main activities of the Trust focus on architecture and its importance in cultural and social development; it supports enterprises that it expects to become self-sustaining in time. The Trust supports the Aga Khan Program for Islamic Architecture at Harvard University and Massachusetts Institute of Technology (MIT), USA, and the Historic Cities Support Program; operates a Music Initiative in Central Asia; offers the Aga Khan Award for Architecture; and maintains a documentation centre.

Geographical Area of Activity: International, in countries where Muslims have a significant presence, with an emphasis on Asia and Africa.

Publications: The Trust publishes international and regional seminar proceedings.

Finance: Funds are provided by private donations and international development organizations.

Trustees: HH Prince Karim Aga Khan (Chair.).

Principal Staff: Dir Nicholas Bulloch; Dir-Gen. Luis Monreal; Sec-Gen. Suha Özkan.

Address: 1–3 ave de la Paix, 1202 Geneva 2.

Telephone: 229097200; **Fax:** 229097292; **Internet:** www .akdn.org/agency/aktc.html; **e-mail:** aktc@akdn.ch.

Kofi Annan Foundation

Established in 2010 to promote peace and conflict resolution.

Activities: Aims to promote better global governance and strengthen the capacities of people and countries to achieve a fairer, more secure world. To this end, the Foundation has developed programmes and partnerships in three main focus areas: Sustainable Development, Human Rights and the Rule of Law, and Peace and Security.

Geographical Area of Activity: International.

Restrictions: Not a grant-making organization.

Publications: Newsletter (quarterly).

Finance: Funded by public and private donors.

Principal Staff: Exec. Dir Ruth McCoy; Admin. and Finance Officer Li Ling Low.

Address: CP 157, 1211 Geneva 20.

Telephone: 229197520; **Fax:** 229197529; **Internet:** www .kofiannanfoundation.org; **e-mail:** info@ kofiannanfoundation.org.

Associazione Donatella Flick

Set up by Donatella Flick.

Activities: Promotes the arts, including sponsoring concerts of contemporary music, exhibitions, opera, etc., and supports the European Union-wide Donatella Flick International Conducting Competition, begun in 1991. Has also funded research into genetic disease.

Geographical Area of Activity: Europe.

Address: c/o ribo Treuhand AG, Chalet Litzi, 3780 Gstaad.

Sophie und Karl Binding-Stiftung (Sophie and Karl Binding Foundation)

Sophie and Karl Binding Foundation was set up in 1963 to extend support to projects concerned with the environmental, social and cultural development of Switzerland.

Activities: The Foundation extends financial and technical support to projects aimed at achieving social welfare, as well as environmental, educational, art and cultural development. The Foundation extends holiday accommodation for the challenged and their families; awards Prix Binding pour la Forêt annually; grants educational scholarships; and supports inter-ethnic cultural exchanges in Switzerland.

Geographical Area of Activity: Switzerland.

Restrictions: Grants for Swiss-based organizations only.

Publications: Annual reports; *Medienmitteilung 'Binding Sélection d'Artistes' – ein neues Förderprogramm für Schweizer Künstler* (2004); *Die Konferenz Schweizer Kunstmuseen (KSK)* (2004); *Kurzportrait der Stiftung*; *Portrait der Stiftung*; *Fakten zur Stiftung*; *Stiftungsflyer.*

Board of Trustees: Dr Bernhard Christian (Pres.); Dr Carl Binding (Vice-Pres.).

Principal Staff: Man. Dir Dr Benno Schubiger.

Address: Rennweg 50, 4020 Basel.

Telephone: 613171239; **Fax:** 613131200; **Internet:** www .binding-stiftung.ch; **e-mail:** contact@binding-stiftung.ch.

Ludwig-Borchardt-Stiftung (Ludwig Borchardt Foundation)

Founded in 1931 by Ludwig Borchardt and Emily Borchardt-Cohen to promote architectural research in Ancient Egypt; to maintain the Swiss Institute for Architectural and Archaeological Research of Ancient Egypt in Cairo; and to assist similar institutes as well as researchers. Originally known as the Borchardt-Cohen'sche Stiftung.

Activities: Supports the Institute's excavations and research in Egypt, which are partly undertaken in collaboration with other archaeological institutes in Egypt.

Geographical Area of Activity: Egypt.

Publications: *Beiträge zur Aegyptischen Bauforschung und Altertumskunde* (Contributions on Ancient Egyptian Architecture and Archaeology); reports and articles.

Finance: Funded through privately-held assets of the Foundation.

Principal Staff: Dir Dr Cornelius von Pilgrim.

Address: c/o Office-Alder Peyer Keiser Laemmli, Pestalozzistr. 2, Postfach 395, 8200 Schaffhausen.

Telephone: 526300620; **Fax:** 526256240; **e-mail:** info@ peyerlaw.ch.

CARE International—CI

Founded in November 1945 in Washington, DC, as Co-operative for American Remittances to Europe, registered under present name in 1981. An association of 12 national member organizations, it provides disaster relief and aims to improve social and economic conditions in developing countries.

Activities: The organization promotes the use of indigenous resources, and provides disaster relief and rehabilitation support. Development activities include: agriculture and environment; small business development; health, including immunization, water and sanitation, family planning services and AIDS education; and food security.

Geographical Area of Activity: Africa, Central and South America, Asia, Eastern Europe, Middle East.

Restrictions: Does not normally award grants; funds its own programmes.

Publications: annual reports and other member publications.

Finance: The organization is financed through: donations from individuals and the private sector; grants from CARE member governments and multilateral agencies; host government support; donations-in-kind. Total expenditure €580,000,000 (2010).

International Board: Ralph Martens (Chair.).

Principal Staff: Sec.-Gen. Dr Robert Glasser.

Address: Chemin de Balexert 7–9, 1219 Chatelaine Geneva.

Telephone: 227951020; **Fax:** 227951029; **Internet:** www.care-international.org; **e-mail:** cisecretariat@careinternational.org.

Centre Ecologique Albert Schweitzer—CEAS (Albert Schweitzer Ecological Centre)

Founded in 1980 to promote ecological solutions to agricultural problems.

Activities: Encourages ecologically sound practices in agriculture through the application of appropriate technology. Projects include: promoting solar energy; the reduction of desertification; and the production and distribution of water pumps, solar heaters and dryers, in collaboration with African organizations. The Centre also organizes training, compiles documentation and maintains a library, and an office in Burkina Faso.

Geographical Area of Activity: Burkina Faso, Senegal and Madagascar.

Publications: *L'Avenir est entre vos mains* (periodic, in French and German); *Tropical Fruits Processing Manual* (in English and French).

Finance: Annual budget approx. 1,500,000 Swiss francs.

Principal Staff: Dir Daniel Schneider.

Address: 2 rue de la Côte, 2000 Neuchâtel.

Telephone: 327250836; **Fax:** 327251507; **Internet:** www.ceas.ch; **e-mail:** info@ceas.ch.

Centre Européen de la Culture—CEC (European Centre of Culture)

Founded in 1950 by Denis de Rougemont and Salvador de Madariaga to contribute to the unification of Europe by encouraging cultural pursuits.

Activities: Conducts training programmes for young people through its Euroateliers programme. Previously the Centre housed a number of other cultural events, workshops and festivals, but in 2001 these activities were curtailed. Members of the Centre are national and international cultural institutions established by the Centre, and other individuals and organizations.

Geographical Area of Activity: Europe.

Publications: *Newsletter* (periodic, in English, French and German); *Temps Européens*; various books.

Finance: Annual budget approx. 800,000 Swiss francs.

Principal Staff: Pres. Prof. Charles Méla; Gen. Sec. Claus Hassig.

Address: Villa du Chateau, 1296 Coppet.

Telephone: 227106603; **Fax:** 227880449; **Internet:** www.ceculture.org; **e-mail:** contact@ceculture.org.

the cogito foundation

Established in 2001 to encourage a dialogue between science and technology on the one hand and humanities and the social sciences on the other hand. It also strives to make scientific thinking better known and understood by the public at large.

Activities: Aims to bridge the gap between science and technology, and the humanities and social sciences, through funding of research projects, scholarships for post-doctorate researchers, fellowships, conferences, seminars and publications, which are in line with the mission statement of the Foundation. Every two years the cogito foundation awards the cogito prize to a distinguished scientist for acting as a role model in fulfilling the goals of the foundation.

Geographical Area of Activity: Switzerland and international.

Publications: Annual reports; press releases, articles.

Finance: Annual budget 650,000 Swiss francs.

Council: Dr Simon Aegerter (Pres.); Dr Irene Aegerter (Vice-Pres.).

Address: Säumerstr. 26, 8832 Wollerau.

Telephone: 447877676; **Fax:** 447877677; **Internet:** www.cogitofoundation.ch; **e-mail:** info@cogitofoundation.ch.

Defence for Children International—DCI

Independent NGO, founded in 1979 to provide practical help to children internationally, and to promote and protect the rights of the child.

Activities: Works in the field of children's human rights, promoting issues involving children that are inadequately documented. Initiates world-wide action in response to abuses of children's human rights, and generally seeks to improve children's rights internationally, taking up specific cases regarding violations of human rights. Publishes information about children's rights, and monitors the implementation of laws that should protect children. There are 60 sections and associate members world-wide.

Geographical Area of Activity: International.

Publications: *DCI Monitor* (quarterly magazine); newsletter; reports; *The World of the Defenseless*; *The Monitor, The Child Labour Problem*; *Regional Analysis on Child Labor in Western and Eastern Europe*; *Can there be a life during and after detention?*; *STOP for political abuse of children during the electoral campaign*; *Children's rights and juvenile justice*; *The World of Working Children*.

Executive Council: Rifat Odeh Kassis (Pres.); Benoît Van Keirsbilck (Treas.); Abdul Manaff Kemokai (Vice-Pres. Africa); Marcos Guillén (Vice-Pres. Americas); Jean-Luc Rongé (Vice-Pres. Europe).

Principal Staff: Exec. Dir Ileana Bello.

Address: 1 rue de Varembé, POB 88, 1211 Geneva 20.

Telephone: 227340558; **Fax:** 227401145; **Internet:** www.defenceforchildren.org; **e-mail:** info@dci-is.org.

Earthwatch—United Nations System-wide Earthwatch

Founded in June 1972 within the framework of the UN Environment Programme (UNEP) at the UN Conference on Human Environment. Restructured in 1994, when it became the joint responsibility of all relevant UN agencies, it is currently organized through the UN System-wide Earthwatch Co-ordination United within UNEP/DEWA–Europe.

Activities: The UN System-wide Earthwatch mechanism is a broad UN initiative to co-ordinate, harmonize and integrate observing, assessment and reporting activities across the UN system to provide environmental and appropriate socio-economic information for national and international decision-making on sustainable development and for warning of emerging problems requiring international action. Provides up-to-date information on: environmental resources; assessment; reporting; data; observation and indicators; and organizes regular Working Party meetings. Every year an Inter-Agency Earthwatch Working Party, supported by Earthwatch, is organized.

Geographical Area of Activity: World-wide.

Publications: *Earthwatch Bulletin*; news reports; books.

Principal Staff: Co-ordinators Ivar Baste, Jaap van Woerden.

Address: UN System-wide Earthwatch Support Unit, UNEP, International Environment House, chemin des Anémones 11, 1219 Châtelaine.

Telephone: 229178176; **Fax:** 229178029; **Internet:** www.un .org/earthwatch; **e-mail:** earthwatch@grid.unep.ch.

European Foundation for the Sustainable Development of the Regions—FEDRE

Established in 1996 as a network for the promotion of exchanges and economic, environmental and social partnerships to promote the regions of Europe.

Activities: Works in the area of conservation and the environment through operating three main programmes: Local and regional democracy in the Balkans; Energy and sustainable development; and Cities and nature ('Salève in another way'), which promotes public transport around Mt Salève. Organizes annual Economic Forums of the Regions of Europe.

Geographical Area of Activity: Eastern, Central and Western Europe.

Publications: Articles and magazines.

Board of Directors: Claude Haegi (Pres.); Yves Berthelot (Vice-Pres.); Daniel Goeudevert (Vice-Pres.).

Principal Staff: Sec.-Gen. François Saint-Ouen.

Address: 12 rue de l'Arquebuse, 1204 Geneva.

Telephone: 228071717; **Fax:** 228071718; **Internet:** www.fedre .org; **e-mail:** info@fedre.org.

The Evian Group at IMD

Founded in 1995 by the late Katsuo Seiki, founding Executive Director of the Tokyo-based Global Industrial and Social Progress Research Institute (GISPRI) and Jean-Pierre Lehmann, Professor of International Political Economy at IMD (International Institute for Management Development).

Activities: The Evian Group at IMD activities are aimed at building confidence and creating knowledge among its members, stakeholders and constituents; establishing vision and direction by formulating agendas for action; enhancing global leadership and business statesmanship; influencing policymakers; promoting its ideas. To achieve these goals, the Evian Group annually convenes a plenary meeting in Europe and roundtable meetings in the Arab Region, Greater China and South Asia, in addition to ad hoc meetings, forums and symposia.

Geographical Area of Activity: The Middle East, Europe, South Asia, China.

Publications: Policy briefs; position papers, reports and communiqués; web-based newsletter.

Finance: Relies on a pool of corporate and institutional members, as well as ad hoc sponsorships.

Executive Committee: Victor K. Fung, Michael W. Garrett, Dhruv Sawhney (Co-Chairs).

Principal Staff: Founding Dir Jean-Pierre Lehmann; Deputy Dir Michelle Barbeau Noguchi.

Address: c/o IMD, chemin de Bellerive 23, POB 915, 1001 Lausanne.

Telephone: 216180551; **Fax:** 216180619; **Internet:** www .eviangroup.org; **e-mail:** info@eviangroup.org.

Focus on Hope—Nana Mouskouri Foundation

Established by Nana Mouskouri in 1994.

Activities: Set up to support cultural and arts projects, particularly in the areas of cinema and music, to provide advice and financial help to young artists, and to award cultural prizes including the Nana Mouskouri Foundation Prix 'Focus Hope'. Also sponsors exhibitions and cultural events, including a travelling exhibition on the Parthenon Marbles.

Geographical Area of Activity: International.

Principal Staff: Founder and Pres. Nana Mouskouri.

Address: rue de Candolle 20, 1205 Geneva.

Telephone: 223113644; **Fax:** 223114588.

Fondation pour le Développement de la Psychothérapie Médicale, spécialement de la psychothérapie de groupe (Foundation for the Development of Medical Psychotherapy, especially Group Psychotherapy)

Founded in 1982 with the aim of promoting the development of medical psychotherapy.

Activities: Finances and organizes activities aiming to help people who are mentally ill; particularly interested in supporting projects involving group therapy; awards prizes; holds conferences and seminars.

Principal Staff: Pres. Dr Edouard de Perrot; Sec. Dr D. Peter.

Address: Chemin des Noisetiers 2, 1271 Givrins.

Telephone: 223691295; **Fax:** 223691295; **e-mail:** edep@ bluewin.ch.

Fondation Hindemith (Hindemith Foundation)

Founded in 1968 in execution of the will of Johanna-Gertrud Hindemith, widow of the composer Paul Hindemith, to maintain his musical and literary heritage; to encourage interest and research in the field of music, in particular contemporary music; and to disseminate the results of this research.

Activities: Operates internationally in the field of music, through self-conducted programmes, research, publications, courses, lectures and concerts. Maintains a course centre, the Hindemith Music Center Blonay, near Vevey, Switzerland; and a centre of archives, documentation and publication, the Hindemith-Institut Frankfurt, Germany.

Geographical Area of Activity: International.

Restrictions: No grants to outside organizations currently available.

Publications: *Hindemith General Original Edition*; *Les Annales Hindemith*; *Hindemith-Forum*.

Foundation Council: Prof. Dr Andreas Eckhardt (Pres.); M. F. Margot (Vice-Pres.).

Principal Staff: Dir Hindemith Music Center Blonay Marcel M. Lachat; Dir Hindemith-Institut Frankfurt Prof. Dr Giselher Schubert; Secs Admin. Silvia Rumo, Georges Rosset.

Address: 41 champ Belluet, 1807 Blonay.

Telephone: 219430528; **Fax:** 219430529; **Internet:** www .hindemith.org; **e-mail:** administration@hindemith.org.

Fondation Hirondelle: Media for Peace and Human Dignity

Established in 1995 to establish and support information media in war zones, zones in crisis and post-conflict zones. Hirondelle USA was established in 2008.

Activities: Supports the development of the media, including radio stations in countries affected by war, or in post-conflict situations. Works in partnership with the UN and local journalists.

Geographical Area of Activity: International.

Restrictions: Does not make grants.

Finance: projects are primarily financed by governments and institutional donors. Annual budget 9,000,000 Swiss francs (2010).

Address: Ave du Temple 19c, 1012 Lausanne.

Telephone: 216542020; **Internet:** www.hirondelle.org; **e-mail:** info@hirondelle.org.

Fondation Internationale Florence Nightingale (Florence Nightingale International Foundation)

Founded in 1934 in memory of Florence Nightingale. The organization aims to assist nurses throughout the world and to improve standards of nursing.

Activities: Leading foundation of the International Council of Nurses (ICN), supporting and complementing the work and objectives of ICN. The Girl Child Education Fund, a signature initiative of the Foundation, supports the primary and secondary schooling of girls under the age of 18 in developing countries whose nurse parent or parents have died. The Foundation supports the International Centre for Human Resources in Nursing—an online resource to inform policy and strengthen the capacity of countries better to plan, manage and develop their nursing workforce. It recognizes the contributions of nurses who make a difference. The International Achievement Award is given biennially to a mid-career practising nurse who is currently influencing nursing internationally in two of nursing's four domains: direct care, education, research and management. The Award accords world-wide recognition of the recipient's achievements and contribution to nursing internationally.

Geographical Area of Activity: International.

Publications: Project publications.

Principal Staff: Pres. Rosemary Bryant; First Vice-Pres. Rudolph Cini.

Address: International Council of Nurses, 3 pl. Jean-Marteau, 1201 Geneva.

Telephone: 229080100; **Fax:** 229080101; **Internet:** www.fnif .org; **e-mail:** williamson@icn.ch.

Fondation ISREC (ISREC Foundation)

Formerly known as the Fondation Institut Suisse de Recherche Expérimentale sur le Cancer (Swiss Institute for Experimental Cancer Research/Schweizerisches Institut für experimentelle Krebsforschung). The Foundation was established by G. Candardjis, J.-L. de Coulon, H. Isliker, P. Mercier, A. de Muralt, A. Sauter, P. Schumacher, R. Stadler and F. Zumstein in 1964 to carry out experimental research on cancer.

Activities: The ISREC Foundation operates through research and teaching. It selects and supports cancer research projects that help the transfer of knowledge and collaboration between fundamental research and clinical research; and supports projects encouraging scientific and academic development in cancer research, in particular supporting PhD students in biology or medicine taking part in doctoral programmes.

Geographical Area of Activity: Switzerland.

Publications: Annual Report.

Board of Trustees: Y. J. Paternot (Pres.); Prof. F. Cavalli (Chair., Scientific Bd).

Principal Staff: Pres. Y. J. Paternot; Administrator Aylin Niederberger.

Address: Route de la Corniche 4, 1066 Epalinges/Lausanne.

Telephone: 216530716; **Fax:** 216526933; **Internet:** www.isrec .ch; **e-mail:** claudine.ravussin@isrec.ch.

Fondation Louis-Jeantet de Médecine (Louis-Jeantet Medical Foundation)

Established in 1982 to promote basic and clinical medical research, with additional support given for teaching and research at the Faculty of Medicine at the University of Geneva.

Activities: Within Switzerland, the Foundation awards the annual Prix Louis-Jeantet de Médecine at the Faculty of Medicine, University of Geneva; and within Europe, the Foundation awards prizes in recognition of medical research work.

Geographical Area of Activity: Switzerland and Europe.

Publications: Brochures, books, audio and video publications.

Board of Trustees: Prof. Jean-Louis Carpentier (Pres.); Prof. Bernard C. Rossier (Vice-Pres.).

Principal Staff: Admin. Inge-Marie Campana.

Address: Chemin Rieu 17, CP 270, 1211 Geneva 17.

Telephone: 227043636; **Fax:** 227043637; **Internet:** www .jeantet.ch; **e-mail:** info@jeantet.ch.

Fondation Latsis Internationale (International Latsis Foundation)

Established in 1975 by the Greek family Latsis in Geneva.

Activities: Operates in the field of science and technology. Annually awards four University Latsis Prizes (25,000 Swiss

francs each) and the National Latsis Prize (100,000 Swiss francs). The Fondation Européenne de la Science (q.v.) awards the annual European Latsis Prize (100,000 Swiss francs), funded by the Foundation, which is made in recognition of an individual under the age of 40 or an organization's contribution to research in a particular scientific field.

Geographical Area of Activity: Europe.

Board: Prof. Justin Thorens (Pres.).

Address: 3–5 chemin des Tuileries, 1293 Bellevue, Geneva.

Internet: www.fondationlatsis.org; **e-mail:** info@ fondationlatsis.org.

Fondation Charles Léopold Mayer pour le Progrès de l'Homme—FPH (Charles Léopold Mayer Foundation for Human Progress)

Founded in 1982 by Charles Léopold Mayer (1881–1971) to fund projects that would contribute to the progress of humanity.

Activities: The Foundation focuses on seven main areas: the promotion of peace; an end to exclusion; the future of the earth and its ecological systems; science, technology and society; peasant farming and modernization; promotion and exchange between cultures; and state and society. Set up a grants programme for young people with French newspaper *Le Monde*. Approximately two-thirds of the annual budget is allocated to grants and the remaining one-third spent on Foundation-initiated programmes. Maintains office in Paris, France.

Geographical Area of Activity: International.

Restrictions: Currently does not accept unsolicited individual applications for scholarships, fellowships or travel grants.

Publications: Newsletters; books and brochures.

Finance: Capital 300,000,000 Swiss francs.

Board of Trustees: Pierre Calame (Chair.); Françoise Astier (Vice-Pres.).

Principal Staff: Dir Matthieu Calame; Programme Man. Julien Woessner.

Address: 6 ave Charles Dickens, 1006 Lausanne.

Telephone: 213425010; **Fax:** 213425011; **Internet:** www.fph .ch.

Fondation Jean Monnet pour l'Europe (Jean Monnet Foundation for Europe)

Founded in 1978 by Jean Monnet, who gave the organization his archives. One of the aims is to bring a contribution to the construction of a united Europe in accordance with Jean Monnet's thoughts, methods and actions.

Activities: Maintains archives of several protagonists of European unification, conducts research and holds international conferences on topics related to European political and economic unity; publishes the results of research. Also awards the Jean Monnet Medal.

Geographical Area of Activity: Europe.

Publications: *Cahiers rouges* (series); books on European topics.

Finance: Funded through public and private sources.

Executive Council: José María Gil-Robles (Pres.); Pascal Fontaine (Vice-Pres.).

Principal Staff: Dir Patrick Piffaretti; Deputy Dir Gilles Grin.

Address: Ferme de Dorigny, 1015 Lausanne.

Telephone: 216922090; **Fax:** 216922095; **Internet:** www.jean -monnet.ch; **e-mail:** secr@fjme.unil.ch.

Fondation Nestlé pour l'Etude des Problèmes de l'Alimentation dans le Monde (Nestlé Foundation for the Study of the Problems of Nutrition in the World)

Founded in 1966 by Nestlé Alimentana SA, Vevey, to further the improvement of nutrition, particularly in those areas of the world suffering from malnutrition, by encouraging basic and applied research directly connected with human nutrition.

Activities: Operates internationally by developing and sponsoring nutrition-related research projects, awarding research grants to individuals and institutions, awarding scholarships for postgraduate studies in nutrition to candidates from selected nutrition units, organizing scientific conferences, and publishing and disseminating scientific literature.

Geographical Area of Activity: Low and lower-middle-income countries.

Publications: Annual Report; scientific publications.

Council: Prof. Susanne Suter (Pres.).

Principal Staff: Dir Prof. Paolo M. Suter; Asst to Dir Catherine Lieb.

Address: 4 pl. de la Gare, POB 581, 1001 Lausanne.

Telephone: 213203351; **Fax:** 213203392; **Internet:** www .nestlefoundation.org; **e-mail:** nf@nestlefoundation.org.

Fondation Simón I. Patiño (Simón I. Patiño Foundation)

Set up in 1958 in memory of the Bolivian industrialist, Simón I. Patiño, by his heirs. Its principal objective is to create and develop for South America and in particular Bolivia, research and application programmes in the spheres of education, culture, research, health, nutrition, hygiene, agriculture and ecology.

Activities: Operates internationally in the fields of education, culture, research, health, nutrition, hygiene, agriculture and ecology, through self-conducted programmes and publications, conducted at a number of operational centres. The Albina R. de Patiño Paediatric Centre, in Cochabamba, provides medical care, and carries out training and research; it also runs a nutritional centre for malnourished children. The Simón I. Patiño Pedagogical and Cultural Centre, also in Cochabamba, offers literacy programmes through a network of village-based libraries, a central library and cultural events. In Pairumani, the Foundation conducts agricultural research at its Phytoecogenetic Research Centre, and at its Seed Centre, and applied programmes at the Pairumani Model Farm. In Santa Cruz and Concepción, the Foundation develops applied agro-biological programmes aimed at sustainable agricultural and environmental development, at the Centre for Applied Ecology. A cultural centre is managed in La Paz, which also hosts the Documentation Centre for Latin American Arts and Literature. Internationally, in particular in Switzerland, the Foundation provides university scholarships for high-potential Bolivian students, who will return to help in Bolivian development. It is also active in the field of arts and culture, through organizing visual arts exhibitions and musical events and offering scholarships for young artists. The Foundation's publishing house publishes books on philosophy and Latin American culture, poetry and literature.

Geographical Area of Activity: Central and South America (with an emphasis on Bolivia), Europe.

Restrictions: Principally establishes and maintains its own programmes.

Publications: *Bolivia Ecológica* (monthly); *Revista Boliviana de Ecología y Conservación Ambiental* (quarterly); Annual Report; other publications.

Governing Board: hans-Ulrich Doerig (Pres.); Nicolas du Chastel (Vice-Pres.); Olivier Mach (Sec.).

Principal Staff: Exec. Dir Grégoire de Sartiges.

Address: rue Giovanni-Gambini 8, 1206 Geneva.

Telephone: 223470211; **Fax:** 227891829; **Internet:** www .fundacionpatino.org; **e-mail:** fondpatino@bluewin.ch.

Fondation Pro Victimis Genève (Pro Victimis Foundation)

Established in 1988, the Pro Victimis Foundation (PVF) is a private grant-making foundation which operates internationally to bring about lasting changes in the lives of the most disadvantaged and vulnerable communities in developing countries.

Activities: To promote the economic and social development of those most in need, PVF funds projects or programmes implemented by NGOs, community-based organizations or social entrepreneurs. Priority is given to population groups and issues that receive little or no attention.

Geographical Area of Activity: International.

Restrictions: Grants not awarded for: emergency relief activities in the immediate wake of a disaster (natural or manmade); projects related to disaster situations with a large media coverage; activities entirely and permanently dependent on international funding; projects with religious or political objectives; general fund-raising drives or events; individual cases; scholarships/fellowships. Applications are discouraged from organizations with no history of prior donor funding, unless the project is carried out in partnership with a more experienced organization or from organizations with an annual budget of more than €10m.

Board of Trustees: René Merkt (Hon. Chair.); Prof. Doris Schopper (Chair.); Jean Bonna (Vice-Chair.).

Principal Staff: Exec. Dir Nicolas Borsinger.

Address: rue St Ours 5, 1205 Geneva.

Fax: 227814261; **Internet:** www.provictimis.org; **e-mail:** contact@provictimis.org.

Fondation Denis de Rougemont pour l'Europe

Founded in 1987; named after Denis de Rougemont, the founder of the Centre Européen de la Culture (European Cultural Centre, q.v.).

Activities: Promotes the unification of Europe and an awareness of cultural solidarity among Europeans, mainly through publications. Awards the Denis de Rougemont Prize in Geneva.

Geographical Area of Activity: Europe.

Publications: *Denis de Rougemont et l'Europe des Régions*; *Denis de Rougemont: Introduction à sa vie et son œuvre*; *Denis de Rougemont: de la Personne à l'Europe* (2000).

Finance: Annual budget approx. 30,000 Swiss francs.

Administrative Council: Claude Haegi (Pres.); Eric Gabus (Vice-Pres.); Jean-Claude Veillon (Vice-Pres.); François Saint-Ouen (Sec.).

Address: 34 rue de la Synagogue, 1204 Geneva.

Telephone: 228002200; **Fax:** 228002201; **Internet:** www .fondationderougemont.org; **e-mail:** contact@ fondationderougemont.org.

Fondation Charles Veillon

Established in 1972 to promote dialogues in which opinion, experience and philosophy can be linked together.

Activities: Operates in the fields of international relations and culture, through promoting dialogue covering European culture, philosophy, federalism and interdisciplinary studies. Offers the prestigious Prix Européen de l'Essai Charles Veillon for an essay dealing with contemporary society. The award of 30,000 Swiss francs is given every year, in collaboration with Lausanne University, to a European writer.

Geographical Area of Activity: Europe.

Board of Directors: Pascal Veillon (Pres.).

Principal Staff: Sec. Cornelia Herrenkind.

Address: 1012 Lausanne.

Telephone: 788700092; **Internet:** www.fondation-veillon.ch; **e-mail:** info@fondation-veillon.ch.

Fondation Franz Weber—FFW (Franz Weber Foundation)

Founded in 1975 by Franz Weber.

Activities: Operates in the field of conservation and the environment. Promotes the protection of nature and wildlife and defence of animal rights. Runs a series of national and international campaigns fighting the destruction of natural habitats and campaigning for the rights of indigenous species. Campaigns to obtain legal status for animals.

Geographical Area of Activity: International.

Publications: *Journal Franz Weber.*

Finance: Funded by contributions, donations and legacies. Annual expenditure approx. 2,000,000 Swiss francs.

Address: Case Postale, 1820 Montreux 1.

Telephone: 219642424; **Fax:** 219645736; **Internet:** www.ffw .ch; **e-mail:** ffw@ffw.ch.

Fondation Hans Wilsdorf—Montres Rolex (Hans Wilsdorf Foundation)

Established in 1945 and the sole owner of the share capital of Montres Rolex SA.

Activities: The Foundation funds projects and organizations in the fields of social welfare, arts and culture, and scientific and medical research.

Geographical Area of Activity: Mainly Switzerland.

Finance: Total assets approx. €9,000,000,000.

Principal Staff: Pres. Pierre Mottu; Sec.-Gen. Serge Bednarczyk.

Address: 20 notaire place d'Arme, 1227 Carouge.

Telephone: 227373000; **Fax:** 227002956; **e-mail:** fhw@ swissonline.ch.

Fonds für Entwicklung und Partnerschaft in Africa—FEPA (Fund for Development and Partnership in Africa)

Founded in 1963 by Hans and Hedwig Meyer-Schneeberger to support self-help projects in Africa.

Activities: Operates in Zimbabwe, Tanzania, South Africa and Mozambique, providing grants to self-help projects, especially youth and women. Provides funding for local development NGOs to promote empowerment of marginalized groups through skills-training, workshops in life skills and advocacy.

Geographical Area of Activity: South Africa, Tanzania, Zimbabwe and Mozambique.

Restrictions: No grants to individuals.

Publications: *FEPA—Mitteilungsblatt* (twice a year).

Finance: Annual revenue and expenditure approx. 350,000 Swiss francs.

Principal Staff: Man. Dir Barbara Müller.

Address: Drahtzugstr. 28, POB 195, 4005 Basel.

Telephone: 616818084; **Fax:** 616834312; **Internet:** www .fepafrika.ch; **e-mail:** info@fepafrika.ch.

Foundation for Environmental Conservation

Founded in 1975 by the International Union for Conservation of Nature and Natural Resources—IUCN (now the World Conservation Union, q.v.), the World Wildlife Fund—WWF (now the WWF—World Wide Fund for Nature, q.v.) and the late Prof. Dr Nicholas Polunin to undertake, in co-operation with appropriate individuals, organizations and other groups, all possible activities to maintain the biosphere and further environmental conservation.

Activities: The Foundation promotes studies of environmental change and ecosystems; issues publications; organizes conferences (notably the International Conferences on Environmental Future), lectures (including the Baer-Huxley Memorial Lectures) and specialist workshops; awards prizes for achievement in environmental conservation; and supports such initiatives as the World Campaign for the Biosphere, Biospheric Day and Biospheric Club.

Geographical Area of Activity: International.

Publications: Reports of operations; proceedings of the International Conferences on Environmental Future; *Environmental Conservation* (quarterly journal); *Environmental Challenge; World Who is Who and Does What in Environment and Conservation.*

Principal Staff: Environmental Conservation Officer Lynn Curne.

Address: 1148 Moiry.

Fax: 2186666616; **Internet:** www.ncl.ac.uk/icef; **e-mail:** envcons@ncl.ac.uk.

Anne Frank-Fonds (Anne Frank Fund)

Founded in 1963 by Otto H. Frank, father of Anne Frank, to promote charitable, social and cultural activities and tolerance in the spirit of Anne Frank, and protect the literary heritage and rights of the author.

Activities: Operates in the fields of the arts and humanities and social welfare, support of 'righteous gentiles' through the Anne Frank Medical Fund for the Righteous, founded in 1987; sponsoring the Anne Frank-Shoah Library, which specializes in the Nazi Holocaust period; providing finance for exchange visits and meetings of young Israelis, Germans and Arabs; providing support to Israeli and Palestinian peace organizations; supporting educational projects; and other related organizations and projects. Also makes grants to the Anne Frank Museum in Amsterdam and financed a professorship in ethics at the University of Basel.

Geographical Area of Activity: International.

Publications: Annual Reports.

Finance: Total grants 300,000 Swiss francs (2010).

Board of Trustees: Buddy Elias (Pres.); John D. Goldsmith (Vice-Pres.).

Principal Staff: Exec. Sec. Barbara Eldridge.

Address: Steinengraben 18, 4051 Basel.

Telephone: 612741174; **Fax:** 612741175; **Internet:** www .annefrank.ch; **e-mail:** info@annefrank.ch.

Gebert Rüf Stiftung

Established by Heinrich Gebert in 1997.

Activities: Supports scientific research projects at institutions of higher education in Switzerland related to innovation and transfer of science.

Geographical Area of Activity: Mainly Switzerland.

Publications: Annual Report.

Finance: Total assets 180,000,000 Swiss francs (Nov. 2010); annual grant budget approx. 10,000,000 Swiss francs.

Board of Trustees: Prof. Dr Rudolf Marty (Chair.); Prof. Dr Peter Forstmoser (Deputy Chair.).

Principal Staff: Dir Dr Philipp Egger; Deputy Dir Dr Pascale Vonmont.

Address: Bäumleingasse 22/4, 4051 Basel.

Telephone: 612708822; **Fax:** 612708823; **Internet:** www .grstiftung.ch; **e-mail:** info@grstiftung.ch.

Fritz-Gerber-Stiftung für Begabte Junge Menschen (Fritz Gerber Foundation for Gifted Young People)

Established by Fritz Gerber in March 1999 to assist talented young people.

Activities: Offers grants to young gifted people between the ages of 10 and 25, in need of financial assistance to develop a specific talent. Grants are made in areas outside formal education, including sport, and the arts and culture.

Geographical Area of Activity: Switzerland.

Publications: Activity report.

Finance: A donation of €12,400,000 from Fritz Gerber to establish the foundation. Total funds disbursed 1,343,061 Swiss francs (2010).

Trustees: Dr Fritz Gerber (Hon. Pres.); Urs Lauffer (Pres.); Renate Gerber (Vice-Pres.).

Principal Staff: Stéphanie Ramel, Fritz Frischknecht.

Address: Kirchgasse 38, Postfach 373, 8024 Zürich.

Telephone: 442605383; **Fax:** 442546035; **Internet:** www.fritz -gerber-stiftung.ch; **e-mail:** lanffer@bluewin.ch.

Global Digital Solidarity Fund—DSF

Established to reduce the digital divide to assist in the creation of a fair and all-inclusive information society.

Activities: The Fund's objectives are to ensure affordable and fair access to information technology for all; to promote access as a basic right; and to guarantee such access for everyone.

Geographical Area of Activity: World-wide.

Publications: *DSF-news* (by e-mail, 6 a year).

Presidency: Alain Madelin (Pres.); John R. Gagain Jr (Vice-Pres.); Nnenna Nwakanma (Vice-Pres.).

Principal Staff: Exec. Sec. Alain Clerc.

Address: Villa La Concorde, ave de la Concorde 20, 1203 Geneva.

Telephone: 229793250; **Fax:** 229793251; **Internet:** www.dsf-fsn.org; **e-mail:** secretariat@dsf-fsn.org.

Global Harmony Foundation—GHF

Established in 1989 by B. Affolter, R. Boschi, N. Dajani, C. Pfluger, and the late Sir Peter Ustinov to promote sustainable development for underprivileged people, charitable work and conservation of the environment.

Activities: Operates in the fields of aid to less-developed countries, conservation of the environment and functional education, through self-conducted programmes, conferences, training courses and publications. The Foundation's programmes aim to foster greater self-efficiency, self-reliance and self-esteem using traditional practices and with regard for local cultural frameworks. Areas of interest include pre-schooling, nutritional and health care; improvement of nutrition, health and hygiene; education of women; and facilitation of the development of schools, institutions and communities.

Geographical Area of Activity: Programmes operate in Brazil, Costa Rica, Dominican Republic, India and Mexico.

Publications: Training booklets and documents; annual calendar.

Finance: Annual budget approx. 500,000 Swiss francs.

Trustees: N. Dajani (Chair.); Igor Ustinov (Hon. Pres.).

Address: World Trade Centre, 2 ave Gratta-Paille, 1018 Lausanne.

Telephone: 216411088; **Fax:** 216411089; **Internet:** www.global-harmony.org; **e-mail:** admin@global-harmony.org.

Gulf Research Center Foundation

Established in Geneva in 2007 by Abdulaziz Sager to gather and disseminate knowledge on the Gulf region.

Activities: Carries out research on political, economic, social and security issues. Organizes workshops and conferences; issues publications; and maintains a library. Associated with the Gulf Research Center in Dubai, United Arab Emirates (q.v.).

Finance: Total assets 3,439,055 AED; income 13,122,473 AED (2008).

Council: Dr Abdulaziz Sager (Founder and Chair.).

Principal Staff: Dir Prof. Christian Koch.

Address: 49 ave Blanc, 1202 Geneva.

Telephone: 227162730; **Fax:** 227162739; **Internet:** www.grc.ae/index.php?sec_code=FoundationCouncil; **e-mail:** info@grc.ae.

Helvetas Swiss Intercooperation

Established in July 2011 following merger of Helvetas (founded 1955) and Intercooperation (founded 1982).

Activities: Co-ordinates development projects, offers advisory services to governmental and NGOs, and raises awareness concerning the problems faced by people in developing countries. Operates in some 30 countries in Africa, Asia, Latin America and Eastern Europe.

Geographical Area of Activity: Africa, Asia, Latin America and Eastern Europe.

Restrictions: No grants to individuals.

Publications: Annual Report and financial statement; position papers and archives.

Board of Directors: Peter Arbenz (Pres.); Elmar Ledergerber (Vice-Pres.).

Principal Staff: Exec. Dir Melchior Lengsfeld.

Address: Weinbergstr. 22A, 8021 Zürich.

Telephone: 443686500; **Fax:** 443686580; **Internet:** www.helvetas.ch; **e-mail:** info@helvetas.org.

Hilfswerk der Evangelischen Kirchen Schweiz—HEKS (Swiss Interchurch Aid)

HEKS was set up in 1946 by the Federation of Swiss Protestant Churches (FSPC) to contribute to the reconciliation and reconstruction of Europe in co-operation with the Protestant churches of the respective partner countries.

Activities: HEKS gives humanitarian and emergency aid and fights the causes of hunger, injustice and social deprivation in more than 300 projects in Switzerland and other countries. The focus of its commitment on behalf of socially disadvantaged sections of the population is the dignity of each and every individual. HEKS concentrates on the following focal points in its work: internationally—the development of rural communities, the promotion of peace and conflict resolution, humanitarian aid and collaboration with church groups; in Switzerland—the social integration of disadvantaged people and advocacy for the socially disadvantaged. Maintains five regional offices in Switzerland and co-ordination offices in 21 key countries.

Geographical Area of Activity: Africa, Central and South America, Asia, Europe.

Publications: Annual Report (in French and German); *HEKS-Magazin handeln* (quarterly); *agir* (quarterly).

Finance: Annual income approx. 61,800,000 Swiss francs (2010).

Board of Trustees: Dr Claude Ruey (Pres.); Doris Amsler-Thalmann (Vice-Pres.).

Principal Staff: Dir Ueli Locher.

Address: Seminarstrasse 28, Postfach, 8042 Zürich.

Telephone: 443608800; **Fax:** 443608801; **Internet:** www.heks.ch; **e-mail:** info@heks.ch.

Helmut-Horten-Stiftung (Helmut Horten Foundation)

Founded by Helmut Horten in 1971 to support health-care research and related initiatives.

Activities: The Foundation provides support to the health-care system in Switzerland, through financial contributions to medical research facilities, hospitals, and other health-care institutions, as well as to individuals who are in need of medical care. Preference is given to funding large-scale research projects, particularly where the Foundation is the sole funder. Significant initiatives funded by the Foundation include the Horten Center for Applied Research and Science and the Institute for Research in Biomedicine in Bellinzona, Switzerland. Scholarships are also occasionally awarded.

Geographical Area of Activity: Mainly Switzerland.

Board of Directors: Arthur Decurtins (Pres.).

Principal Staff: Gen. Man. Stelio Pesciallo.

Address: World Trade Center, 6982 Agno/Lugano.

Telephone: 916102280; **Fax:** 916001212; **Internet:** www.helmut-horten-stiftung.org; **e-mail:** info@helmut-horten-stiftung.org.

Institut Universitaire de Hautes Etudes Internationales et du Développement (Graduate Institute of International Studies and Development Studies)

Founded in 1927 by Prof. W. Rappard and Prof. P. Mantoux to carry out teaching and research devoted to the scientific study of contemporary international relations, and to contribute to the advancement of international fellowship through the impartial observation and objective analysis of ideas and events. Merged with the Institut Universitaire du Développement in 2008.

Activities: Operates internationally, as a teaching and research institution, in the fields of history of international relations, international economics, international law, and political science. The Institute's curriculum enables students of any nationality to qualify for the Diploma and Doctor's degrees in international relations, both conferred by the University of Geneva, and a Certificate in international relations, conferred by the Institute. Scholarships are available only to students of the Institute. Maintains a library that owns the printed documents of the League of Nations and serves as a depository of the publications of the UN.

Geographical Area of Activity: International.

Publications: Books; working papers.

Foundation Board: Jacques Forster (Chair.); Isabelle Werenfels (Vice-Chair.).

Principal Staff: Dir Prof. Philippe Burrin; Deputy Dir Elisabeth Prügl.

Address: 132 rue de Lausanne, CP 136, 1211 Geneva 21.

Telephone: 229085700; **Fax:** 229085710; **Internet:** graduateinstitute.ch; **e-mail:** info@graduateinstitute.ch.

International Baccalaureate Organization—IBO

Founded in 1968 to promote international secondary education and administer an international examination giving access to higher education in all countries, and to undertake educational research in relation to this objective, as well as for other educational purposes.

Activities: Offers the Primary Years Programme for children between the ages of three and 11, the Middle Years Programme for those aged between 11 and 16 years, and the Diploma Programme for students aged between 16 and 19 years. Operates through four regional offices, serving North America; Central and South America; Africa, Europe and the Middle East; and the Asia-Pacific region.

Geographical Area of Activity: International.

Publications: *IB World; Statistical Bulletin;* Annual Review; curriculum support materials.

Board of Governors: Carol Bellamy (Chair.); Dr Robin Cooper (Vice-Chair.); Dr Kenneth Vedra (Treas.); Katy Ricks (Sec.).

Principal Staff: Dir-Gen. Jeffrey R. Beard.

Address: Route des Morillons 15, Grand-Saconnex, 1218 Geneva.

Telephone: 223092540; **Fax:** 227910277; **Internet:** www.ibo .org; **e-mail:** ibhq@ibo.org.

International Balzan Foundation—Fund

Founded in 1956 by Angela Lina Balzan to honour the memory of her father, Eugenio Balzan, a famous Italian journalist, who died in 1953. The Foundation acts jointly through two foundations, the International Balzan Foundation—Fund under Swiss law, and the International Balzan Foundation—Prize under Italian law.

Activities: The International Balzan Foundation—Fund manages Eugenio Balzan's estate.

Geographical Area of Activity: World-wide.

Publications: *Premi Balzan* (published each February with information on the winners and the Foundation, in English, French, German and Italian); *Balzan's One Hundred Prize Winners.*

Finance: Total prize money 3,000,000 Swiss francs (2011).

Board: Achille Casanova (Chair.).

Principal Staff: Sec.-Gen. Dr Suzanne Werder.

Address: Claridenstrasse 35, Postfach 2448, 8022 Zürich.

Telephone: 442014822; **Fax:** 442014829; **Internet:** www .balzan.org; **e-mail:** balzan@balzan.ch.

International Council on Alcohol and Addictions— ICAA

Founded in 1907 to reduce and prevent the harmful effects of the use of alcohol and other drugs.

Activities: Conducts training programmes for health professionals on drug and alcohol problems, with particular reference to basic health care, socio-cultural and other relevant factors, and studies methods of prevention, treatment and rehabilitation. There is an Annual International Congress on Alcohol, Drugs, Tobacco and Gambling, and other international conferences, symposia and study groups are also organized. The Council works with the World Health Organization and other international, regional and national bodies: there are member organizations and individual members in 90 countries. Maintains a library of approximately 6,000 volumes on drug dependence, approximately 12,000 pamphlets, reprints, etc., and 120 periodicals. Regional offices are maintained in Argentina, Azerbaijan and Egypt.

Geographical Area of Activity: International.

Publications: *ICAA News* (quarterly); *Book of Abstracts* (annually); *Report of Plenary Sessions* (annually).

Board of Directors: Dr Peter A. Vamos (Pres.); Prof. Salme Ahlström (Deputy Pres.); Keith Evans (Deputy Pres.); Dr Arthur Guerra de Andrade (Deputy Pres.); Jack Law (Treas.); Mark V. Tillman (Sec.).

Principal Staff: Chief Admin. Officer Rupert Schildböck.

Address: ave Louis-Ruchonnet 14, POB 870, 1001 Lausanne.

Telephone: 213209865; **Fax:** 213209817; **Internet:** www.icaa .ch; **e-mail:** secretariat@icaa.ch.

Institut international des Droits de l'Enfant (International Institute for the Rights of the Child)

Founded in 1995 by Dr Bernard Comby and Jean Zermatten for the promotion of children's rights at an international level.

Activities: Operates in the field of law and human rights, specifically for children. Holds international seminars, provides training nationally and internationally, publishes a number of books on the subject of children's rights in the law, and maintains an interactive website.

Geographical Area of Activity: International.

Publications: Newsletter; books; working reports; documentary films.

Finance: Funded by the Swiss Confederation and by individual companies.

Principal Staff: Dir Jean Zermatten; Deputy Director Paola Riva Gapany; Co-ordinator Alexandra Prince.

Address: CP 4176, 1950 Sion 4.

Telephone: 272057303; **Fax:** 272057302; **Internet:** www .childsrights.org; **e-mail:** info@childsrights.org.

International Red Cross and Red Crescent Movement—ICRC

The International Red Cross and Red Crescent Movement is composed of the National Red Cross and Red Crescent Societies, the International Committee of the Red Cross (ICRC), founded in 1863 to help wounded soldiers on the battlefield, and the International Federation of Red Cross and Red Crescent Societies (the Federation), founded in 1919 (as the League of Red Cross and Red Crescent Societies) to promote humanitarian activities in peacetime.

Activities: The ICRC is an impartial, neutral and independent organization whose exclusively humanitarian mission is to protect the lives and dignity of victims of war and internal violence, and to provide them with assistance. It directs and co-ordinates the international relief activities conducted by the Movement in situations of conflict. It also endeavours to prevent suffering by promoting and strengthening humanitarian law and universal humanitarian principles. The Federation comprises 176 National Red Cross and Red Crescent Societies; it acts as a permanent body for liaison, co-ordination and study, advising members on the development of their services to the community. It also organizes international emergency relief operations for the victims of natural disasters, and co-ordinates relief preparedness programmes.

Geographical Area of Activity: International.

Publications: ICRC: *International Review of the Red Cross* (quarterly); *Red Cross Red Crescent* (quarterly, magazine produced jointly with the Federation, in English, French and Spanish); *Forum* (annually); Annual Report; Federation: Annual Review; *Handbook of the International Red Cross and Red Crescent Movement* (with the ICRC); *Weekly News*; *World Disasters Report* (annually); newsletters, guides and manuals.

Finance: Annual budget 969,452,000 Swiss francs (2012).

International Committee: Jakob Kellenberger (Pres.); Olivier Vodoz (Vice-Pres.); Christine Beerli (Vice-Pres.).

Principal Staff: Dir-Gen. Yves Daccord; Dir of Operations Pierre Krähenbühl.

Address: 19 ave de la Paix, 1202 Geneva.

Telephone: 227346001; **Fax:** 227332057; **Internet:** www.icrc .org; **e-mail:** press.gva@icrc.org.

International Service for Human Rights—ISHR

The International Service for Human Rights (ISHR) was established in 1984. It supports and facilitates the work of human rights defenders with the UN human rights system and regional human rights systems. While building human rights defenders' capacity effectively to engage

with human rights systems, ISHR also advocates for the improvement of these systems. The organization works at national, regional and international levels. Maintains small branch office in New York. .

Activities: Operates world-wide with the aim of safeguarding human rights by publishing news updates and analytical reports on developments in key human rights systems; providing training for human rights defenders on international and regional human rights mechanisms; and providing information, support and advisory services. Offers internships to self-funded graduates or students.

Geographical Area of Activity: International.

Restrictions: Not a grant-making organization; does not campaign on individual cases.

Publications: *Human Rights Monitor Quarterly* (quarterly); *Simple Guide to the UN Treaty Bodies*; *Road map for civil society: State reporting procedure of the African Commission on Human and Peoples Rights*.

Board of Directors: Mehr Kahn Williams (Chair.); Rosemary McCreery; (Vice-Chair.); Jean-Marie Fakhouri (Treas.).

Principal Staff: Dir Bjorn Pettersson.

Address: 1 rue de Varembé, CP 16, 1211 Geneva 20.

Telephone: 229197100; **Fax:** 229197125; **Internet:** www.ishr .ch; **e-mail:** information@ishr.ch.

International Union Against Cancer—UICC

Founded in 1933 as a world federation of non-governmental agencies and organizations that combat cancer.

Activities: Together with its members and collaborating organizations, the Union conducts activities throughout the world promoting collaboration between cancer organizations, among cancer investigators, physicians and allied health professionals and experts. Work focuses on four priority areas: building and enhancing cancer control capacity; tobacco control; population-based cancer prevention and control; and transfer of cancer knowledge and dissemination. Research and information programmes covering: tumour biology; epidemiology and prevention; treatment and rehabilitation; detection and diagnosis; professional education; campaigns and public education; patient support; international collaborative activities; tobacco and cancer. It organizes international conferences, study groups and courses, and administers the following fellowships: UICC International Cancer Technology Transfer Fellowships; Yamagiwa-Yoshida Memorial International Cancer Study Grants; American Cancer Society UICC International Fellowships for Beginning Investigators; Astra-Zeneca and Novartis UICC Translational Cancer Research

Fellowship; UICC Trish Greene International Oncology Nursing Fellowships; UICC Asia-Pacific Cancer Society Training Grants; and UICC Latin America COPES Education and Training Fellowships. The Union manages GLOBALink, a computer communications system.

Geographical Area of Activity: International.

Publications: *UICC International Directory of Cancer Institutes and Organizations* (electronic); *International Journal of Cancer and Predictive Oncology* (30 a year); *UICC News* (quarterly); Annual Report; *International Calendar of Meetings on Cancer* (2 a year); manuals (most publications are available electronically).

Finance: Income from membership dues, national subscriptions, grants and donations. Total assets US $6,101,717 (2008); annual income $9,443,895, expenditure $9,556,086 (2008).

Board of Directors: Dr Eduardo Cazap (Pres.); Prof. Mary Gospodarowicz (Pres. elect).

Principal Staff: CEO Cary Adams; Deputy CEO Dr Julie Torode; COO Juerg Boller.

Address: 62 route de Frontenex, 1207 Geneva.

Telephone: 228091811; **Fax:** 228091810; **Internet:** www.uicc .org; **e-mail:** info@uicc.org.

Internationale Stiftung Hochalpine Forschungsstationen Jungfraujoch und Gornergrat (International Foundation of the High-Altitude Research Stations Jungfraujoch and Gornergrat)

Founded in 1930 by representatives of scientific institutions in Belgium, Germany, Austria, France, the United Kingdom and Switzerland to promote high-altitude research. Italy is also a member of the Foundation.

Activities: Supports the research station and Sphinx laboratory on the Jungfraujoch, and the two astronomical observatories, Gornergrat South and Gornergrat North. Research is undertaken in the fields of physiology, physics, environment, astronomy and astrophysics.

Geographical Area of Activity: International.

Publications: Annual Report.

Board: Prof. Dr Hans Balsiger (Hon. Pres.); Prof. Dr Erwin O. Flückiger (Pres.); Karl Martin Wyss (Treas.).

Principal Staff: Dir Prof. Dr Markus Leuenberger; Sec. Louise Wilson.

Address: Sidlerstr. 5, 3012 Berne.

Telephone: 316314052; **Fax:** 316314405; **Internet:** www .ifjungo.ch; **e-mail:** louise.wilson@space.unibe.ch.

IUCN/UICN (International Union for Conservation of Nature)

Founded in 1948, IUCN is the world's largest professional global environmental network, a democratic union with more than 1,000 government and NGO member organizations, and almost 11,000 volunteer scientists in more than 160 countries. IUCN's work is supported by more than 1,000 professional staff in 60 offices and hundreds of partners in public and private sector organizations and NGOs around the world.

Activities: IUCN works in the areas of biodiversity, climate change, livelihoods, energy and green markets. It supports scientific research; manages field projects all over the world; and brings governments, NGOs, businesses, the UN, international conventions and community organizations together to develop policy, legislation and best practice. IUCN members include many of the world's leading conservation organizations and more than 200 of the world's most influential government ministries and agencies. In addition, IUCN works closely with a wide range of leading companies in a variety of sectors, academic organizations, social and indigenous groups and UN organizations.

Geographical Area of Activity: International.

Publications: *World Conservation/Planète conservation/Conservacion mundial* (three times a year); *The Red List of Threatened Species*; *Best Practice Guidelines on Protected Areas series*; *Environmental Policy and Law Papers*; *Species*

Conservation and Action Plans; reports and other specialist publications.

Finance: Income from membership, framework agreements and project agreements. Annual expenditure approx. 106,000,000 Swiss francs.

Council: Ashok Khosla (Pres.); Kurt Ramin (Treas.).

Principal Staff: Dir-Gen. Julia Marton-Lefèvre.

Address: 28 rue Mauverney, 1196 Gland.

Telephone: 229990000; **Fax:** 229990002; **Internet:** www .iucn.org; **e-mail:** webmaster@iucn.org.

Jacobs Foundation

Jacobs Foundation was launched in 1988 by Klaus J. Jacobs to foster child and youth development.

Activities: The Foundation supports research and intervention projects in the field of child and youth development. It focuses on the value chain paradigm: innovative research, practical testing of the findings in pilot interventions and market introduction, which ensures the systematic application of tested models on a larger scale. The Foundation funds projects that stand a strong chance of delivering a positive outcome and demonstrate potential for implementation elsewhere, pursuing the majority of projects in close collaboration with established partners.

Geographical Area of Activity: International.

Restrictions: No support is given for endowments, regular operating budgets, religious organizations, construction projects, or for financial aid/tuition assistance or scholarships.

Publications: Annual Report; brochure.

Finance: Total assets 573,006,000 Swiss francs (31 Dec. 2010); annual income 60,954,000 Swiss francs. annual expenditure 17,292,000 Swiss francs (2010).

Board of Directors: Dr Joh. Christian Jacobs (Chair).

Principal Staff: CEO Dr Bernd Ebersold.

Address: Seefeldquai 17, POB, 8034 Zürich.

Telephone: 443886123; **Fax:** 443886137; **Internet:** www .jacobsfoundation.org; **e-mail:** jf@jacobsfoundation.org.

C. G. Jung-Institut Zürich

A training institute, founded in 1948 by Prof. C. G. Jung, C. A. Meier, K. Binswanger, L. Frey-Rohn and J. Jacobi, for education and research in its primary field: analytical psychology.

Activities: Operates internationally in the fields of analytical psychology, education, science and medicine, through research, courses and contacts with others interested in psychology and the publication of scientific works. Also maintains a library containing some 15,000 volumes.

Geographical Area of Activity: Training and classes are in German and English with the English Programme being entirely international. Iran, India, Ireland, South Africa, Brazil, the United Kingdom, the USA, as well as all of the Asian countries are currently represented.

Restrictions: Applicants are required to apply to study.

Publications: A number of lectures, most of Marie-Louise von Franz's work and transcripts of classes are held at the Jung Institute. Major authors are: Jung, von Franz, Neumann, Edinger, Harding, C.A. Meier, Kast, Leonard, Woodman, Estes, Frey-Rhon, Ulanov, Wilmer, van der Post and Guggenbühl-Craig.

Finance: Financed through tuition and endowments. The Institute is a non-profit educational foundation.

Curatorium: Daniel Baumann (Pres.); Robert Hinshaw (Vice-Pres.); Georg Elser (Treas.).

Principal Staff: Dir of Studies Ursula Weiss.

Address: Hornweg 28, 8700 Küsnacht.

Telephone: 449141040; **Fax:** 449141050; **Internet:** www .junginstitut.ch; **e-mail:** cg@junginstitut.ch.

Landis & Gyr Stiftung (Landis & Gyr Foundation)

Established in 1971, as the Zuger Kulturstiftung Landis & Gyr, by the firm Landis & Gyr Ltd to promote and develop activities in culture, science and social concerns.

Activities: Operates in the field of the arts and humanities, through project support, as well as through a studio programme in fine arts, literature and culture criticism, linked exclusively to accommodation in Berlin, London or Zug. The Foundation also lends support to specific scientific institutions such as Collegium Budapest, New Europe College, Bucharest, and Centre for Advanced Study, Sofiato strengthen scientific exchange with Eastern Europe.

Geographical Area of Activity: Switzerland, Europe.

Restrictions: No project support outside Switzerland; studio programme through official application only; no applications accepted from outside Switzerland.

Finance: Annual expenditure approx. 3,000,000 Swiss francs.

Trustees: Dr Hugo Bütler (Pres.); Dr Thomas Sprecher (Vice-Pres.).

Principal Staff: Man. Dir Regula Koch; Sec. Lilian Shepherd Mürschberger.

Address: Dammstr. 16, Postfach 4858, 6304 Zug.

Telephone: 417242312; **Fax:** 417245383; **Internet:** www.lg -stiftung.ch.

Limmat Stiftung (Limmat Foundation)

Founded in 1972 by Dr Arthur Wiederkehr to promote initiatives for the common good in Switzerland and abroad, especially by offering the necessary organizational infrastructure.

Activities: Operates nationally and internationally in the fields of education, health, advancement of the poor (especially women) and vocational training. Programmes are instruction-orientated and encourage self-help.

Geographical Area of Activity: International.

Publications: Annual Report; articles.

Finance: Total income for projects 3,723,000 Swiss francs, total project expenditure 11,199,000 Swiss francs (2010).

Board: Dr Hans Thomas (Pres.); Elisabeth András (Sec.).

Principal Staff: Exec. Dir François Geinoz; Project Dir Juan J. Alarcon; Financial Dir André Meier.

Address: Rosenbühlstr. 32, 8044 Zürich.

Telephone: 442662030; **Fax:** 442662031; **Internet:** www .limmat.org; **e-mail:** limmat@limmat.org.

The Lutheran World Federation (Lutherischer Weltbund/Fédération luthérienne mondiale)

Founded in 1947 to serve Lutheran churches as an instrument for humanitarian assistance, mission and development, ecumenism, communication and theological study. In 2011 the Federation comprised 145 member churches in 79 countries, representing more than 70m. Christians.

Activities: Operates internationally in the fields of humanitarian assistance, communication, mission and development, human rights, ecumenical and interfaith relations. The Federation offers annual scholarships (mainly at graduate level) in theology and other disciplines, and vocational courses for members of Lutheran churches throughout the world. It also organizes study programmes and seminars to advance its theological, ecumenical and development work in the different world contexts. Maintains a Peace Fund, supporting the human rights ministries of member churches with training, financial and other assistance. The Federation has an international news service in English and German, and publishes studies and specialized publications on development, human rights and theological issues.

Geographical Area of Activity: International.

Publications: *Lutheran World Information/Lutherische Welt-Information* (news bulletin); *LWF Annual Report*; *LWF Documentation/LWB Dokumentation*; *LWF Studies/LWB-Studien*; *LWF Women*; *LWF Youth*; departmental and office reports and working papers.

Finance: Annual income US $103,400,000, annual expenditure $103,900,000 (2009).

Principal Staff: Pres. Bishop Dr Munib A. Younan; Gen. Sec. Rev. Martin Junge.

Address: 150 route de Ferney, POB 2100, 1211 Geneva 2.

Telephone: 227916111; **Fax:** 227916630; **Internet:** www .lutheranworld.org; **e-mail:** info@lutheranworld.org.

MAVA Fondation pour la Nature

Established in 1994 by Dr Luc Hoffmann.

Activities: Aims to promote the protection of nature through the preservation of rare or threatened species and their habitats; the preservation of biodiversity and landscapes; and the sustainable management of natural resources.

Geographical Area of Activity: Mediterranean Basin, Switzerland and the Alpine Arc, West African coastal zone.

Board of Directors: André Hoffmann (Pres.); Hubert du Plessix (Treas.).

Principal Staff: Dir-Gen. Lynda Mansson; Head of Admin. and Finance Rachel Sturm.

Address: Rue Mauverney 28, 1196 Gland.

Telephone: 215441600; **Fax:** 215441616; **Internet:** www.mava -foundation.org; **e-mail:** info@fondationmava.org.

Médecins Sans Frontières—MSF (Doctors Without Borders)

Founded in 1971 in Paris to provide medical care to populations in times of crisis in any part of the world.

Activities: The organization works in the fields of medicine and health, aid to less-developed countries, and law and human rights, through self-conducted programmes, conferences, training courses and publications. It relies on volunteer health professionals, and provides medical aid to those in need world-wide, in countries at war or coping with disaster. It runs missions in refugee camps and long-term operations in countries where health structures have broken down; promotes human rights; helps to secure long-term rehabilitation of health structures; organizes the training of MSF and local staff; and operates two centres for surveillance and applied research in epidemiology and public health. The international MSF network comprises 23 operational sections and delegate offices in Europe, North America and Asia; there are missions in more than 70 countries and territories world-wide. MSF was awarded the Nobel Peace Prize in 1999.

Geographical Area of Activity: International.

Publications: *MSF International Newsletter*; *Développement durable: espace de démocratie et d'intégration citoyenne*; *Populations in Danger* (annually); bulletins; Annual Report; activity reports.

Finance: More than 90% of funding comes from private sources. Total assets €715,200,000 (31 Dec. 2010); annual income €943,300,000, expenditure €812,900,000 (2010).

Board of Directors (Switzerland): Abiy Tamrat (Pres.); Thomas Nierle (Vice-Pres.); Manica Balasegaram (Sec.); Gilles Carbonnier (Treas.).

Principal Staff: International Pres. Dr Unni Karunakara; Sec.-Gen. Kris Torgeson.

Address: Rue de Lausanne 78, CP 116, 1211 Geneva 21.

Telephone: 228498400; **Fax:** 228498404; **Internet:** www.msf .org; **e-mail:** webmaster@msf.org.

Christoph-Merian-Stiftung (Christoph Merian Foundation)

Established in 1886.

Activities: The Foundation aims to assist thoe in need and promote a healthy environment, quality of life and culture in Basle, Switzerland. The basis for its activities is provided by the assets bequeathed to it by Christoph Merian (1800–58) and Margaretha Merian-Burckhardt (1806–1886). Only the income from those assets may be used for the Foundation and its diverse activities; the capital itself must be left intact.

Geographical Area of Activity: Basel, Switzerland.

Restrictions: No grants to individuals and no grants to organizations outside Basel.

Publications: Annual Report.

Finance: Net assets 220,000,000 Swiss francs.

Foundation Commission: Dr Lukas Faesch (Chair.); Prof. Dr Leonhard Burckhardt (Gov.).

Principal Staff: Dir Christian Felber.

Address: St Alban-Vorstadt 5, Postfach, 4002 Basel.

Telephone: 612263333; **Fax:** 612263344; **Internet:** www .merianstiftung.ch; **e-mail:** info@merianstiftung.ch.

Novartis Foundation for Sustainable Development—NFSD

Began as a department within the Novartis company for relations with developing countries, then from 1979 known as the Ciba-Geigy Foundation for Co-operation with Developing Countries, this foundation has been working for the sustainable improvement in the living conditions of poor people in developing countries since 1973.

Activities: As a non-profit-based organization the Foundation forms part of the corporate responsibility portfolio of Novartis. It does not make grants, but participates actively in the implementation of the health initiatives that it supports by lending both financial and technical assistance. At present, the Foundation is engaged in eight large projects and programmes.

Geographical Area of Activity: Sub-Saharan Africa, Indian subcontinent.

Restrictions: No unsolicited applications normally accepted.

Publications: Annual Reports; symposium reports; *Project Management Handbook*; *Leisunger: On Corporate Responsibility for Human Rights*.

Finance: Total budget 10,410,000 Swiss francs (2012).

Principal Staff: Pres. and Man. Dir Prof. Dr Klaus Leisinger.

Address: Novartis Campus, WSJ-210.10.26, 4002 Basel.

Telephone: 616962300; **Fax:** 616962333; **Internet:** www .novartisfoundation.org; **e-mail:** info@novartisfoundation .org.

Oak Foundation

Formally established in 1998. Comprised of a group of charitable and philanthropic organizations.

Activities: Operates programmes in various areas of the world, including programmes on climate change, marine conservation, human rights, child abuse, women's issues, homelessness and learning differences. Runs special programmes in Denmark and Zimbabwe. Maintains offices in Belize, Bulgaria, Denmark, Ethiopia, the United Kingdom, the USA and Zimbabwe.

Geographical Area of Activity: International.

Restrictions: No grants are made to religious organizations, for general funding, or for supporting political candidates; no grants under US $25,000. Enquiries should only be made to Oak Foundation's office in Geneva.

Finance: Total grants disbursed 116,720,000 Swiss francs (2010).

Board of Trustees: Kristian Parker (Chair.); Natalie Shipton (Vice-Chair.); Caroline Turner (Vice-Chair.).

Principal Staff: Pres. Kathleen Cravero-Kristoffersson; Dir of Admin. Vinit Rishi.

Address: Ave Louis Casaï 58, CP 115, 1216 Cointrin, Geneva.

Internet: www.oakfnd.org; **e-mail:** info@oakfnd.ch.

The Parthenon Trust

Established in 1995 for general charitable purposes. Registered in the United Kingdom.

Activities: Awards grants for medical research, treatment and care; assistance to the disadvantaged; to international aid organizations; and for cultural and heritage purposes.

Geographical Area of Activity: United Kingdom, Kenya, Nepal, Philippines, Romania, Russia, Switzerland, Uganda, Zambia.

Restrictions: Grants are not made to individuals.

Finance: Total assets £164,700 (31 Dec. 2010); Annual income £1,125,329, annual expenditure £1,416,382 (2010).

Board of Trustees: John Whittaker (Sec.).

Address: Saint-Nicolas 9, 2000 Neuchatel.

Telephone: 327248130; **Fax:** 327248131.

Pro Helvetia (Swiss Arts Council)

Founded in 1939 to promote the arts and cultural exchange.

Activities: The Foundation promotes creative cultural activities and cultural works relating to Switzerland nationally and internationally. Maintains a network of liaison offices and partner institutes world-wide.

Geographical Area of Activity: International.

Publications: *Passages* (Swiss cultural magazine, 3 a year); information sheets; Swiss cultural policy glossary; information series on Swiss culture; newsletters.

Finance: Annual budget 34,000,000 Swiss francs (2010).

Principal Staff: Pres. Mario Annoni; Dir/Head of Admin. Pius Knüsel.

Address: Hirschengraben 22, 8024 Zürich.

Telephone: 442677171; **Fax:** 442677106; **Internet:** www.prohelvetia.ch; **e-mail:** info@prohelvetia.ch.

Pro Juventute

Established in 1912 by Dr Carl Horber for the promotion of children and youth in personal development.

Activities: Works to protect and improve the quality of life for children and adolescents in the family and in society as a whole. Operates in the areas of education, human rights, health care and social welfare. Funds projects, makes grants to individuals, organizes conferences, developes and operates own projects.

Geographical Area of Activity: Switzerland.

Publications: *Futura* (quarterly magazine); Annual Report; brochures and fact sheets.

Finance: Funded by donations and the sale of stamps, cards and other products, cooperation with businesses.

Board of Trustees: Josef Felder (Pres.); Jean Guinand (Vice-Pres.).

Principal Staff: Dir Stephan Oetiker.

Address: Thurgauerstrasse 39, CP 8050 Zurich.

Telephone: 442567777; **Fax:** 442567778; **Internet:** www.projuventute.ch; **e-mail:** info@projuventute.ch.

Ramsay Foundation

Set up in 1998 to support educational and cultural activities.

Activities: Aims to further and enhance education, through support for pedagogy, training and post-training initiatives, as well as through funding for art and cultural activities, in Switzerland and overseas. Outside of Switzerland grants have been made to projects in Africa, Brazil, Bulgaria, Croatia, Germany, India, Israel, the Russian Federation, the United Kingdom and Ukraine.

Geographical Area of Activity: Switzerland and international, including Africa, Brazil, Bulgaria, Croatia, Germany, India, Israel, the Russian Federation, the United Kingdom and Ukraine.

Restrictions: No grants made to individuals, target groups comprising people over the age of 20, commercial projects and events, film or musical recording productions or large-scale projects.

Board of Trustees: Michaela Geiger (Pres.); Donald Vollen (Vice-Pres.).

Principal Staff: Man. Dir Marianne Herrmann.

Address: Postfach, 4001 Basel.

Telephone: 615562574; **Internet:** www.ramsayfoundation.ch; **e-mail:** info@ramsayfoundation.ch.

Marc Rich Foundation for Education, Culture and Welfare

Founded by Marc and Denise Rich in Switzerland in 1988 to promote Jewish cultural, artistic, educational, social and scientific awareness within a broad humanitarian framework.

Activities: The Foundation offers support in the areas of education, culture and social welfare world-wide.

Geographical Area of Activity: International.

Finance: Over US \$150,000,000 has been donated over 30 years.

Board of Directors: Marc Rich (Chair.).

Principal Staff: Man. Dir Avner Azulay.

Internet: www.marcrich.ch.

Rroma Foundation

Established in 1993 to support the Roma in Central and Eastern Europe; the Foundation was part of the Soros network of foundations, but is now a fully independent foundation.

Activities: Supports programmes in the fields of culture, education, community development, and human rights, including the training of Roma as teachers, journalists and human rights advisers, support for schools and summer schools, grants for publishing projects, offering scholarships, supporting bilingual journals and newspapers, grants for arts projects, and providing legal advice and assistance; promotes liaison between majority populations and the Roma minority; established a Roma Social Bureau in Bulgaria, which offers advice on civil rights issues, and planned to establish a similar bureau in Ukraine. Currently providing support to Roma refugees in Switzerland.

Geographical Area of Activity: Mainly Central and Eastern Europe.

Publications: Background reports.

Board of Trustees: Cristina I. Kruck (Chair.).

Principal Staff: Exec. Dir Dr Stephane Laederich.

Address: Gladbachstr. 67, 8044 Zürich.

Telephone: 13836326; **Fax:** 13836302; **Internet:** www.rroma.org; **e-mail:** admin@rroma.org.

Sandoz Fondation de Famille (Sandoz Family Foundation)

Established in 1964 by Marcel Edouard Sandoz, the son of the founder of Sandoz SA of Basle (now Novartis SA), to hold the Sandoz family's company shareholding.

Activities: Seeks to encourage entrepreneurial commitment through its commercial shareholdings, as well as encouraging creativity and private initiative. In 1982 it established the Fondation Edouard et Maurice Sandoz (FEMS), which awards the annual FEMS Prize to support artistic development, as well as supporting a range of cultural events and organizations. In 1999 the Foundation launched a programme funding science professorships at Swiss universities.

Geographical Area of Activity: Mainly Switzerland.

Board of Directors: Pierre Landolt (Pres.).

Principal Staff: Media Contact Jörg Denzler.

Address: Sandoz Family Office SA, 85 ave Général-Guisan, 1009 Pully.

Telephone: 217211336; **Internet:** www.sandozfoundation.ch.

Max Schmidheiny-Stiftung (Max Schmidheiny Foundation)

Established in 1978 at the University of St Gallen by Max Schmidheiny to promote individual, social and economic freedom.

Activities: The Foundation promotes valuable endeavours towards the preservation and further development of a free market economy and society, especially initiatives safeguarding individual freedom, the responsibility of the individual for his own welfare and the guaranteed maintenance of social security. In 2005, refocused its work to concentrate on supporting projects in the field of entrepreneurship and risk and the analysis of business in the socio-economic context, including the promotion of exchanges and collaboration between the younger generation of entrepreneurs, business people and politicians.

Geographical Area of Activity: Switzerland and international.

Board of Trustees: Prof. Dr Peter Gomez (Chair.).

Address: Dufourstr. 83, CP 1045, 9001 St Gallen.

Telephone: 712272070; **Fax:** 712272075; **Internet:** www.ms-foundation.org; **e-mail:** msf@ms-foundation.org.

Schwab Foundation for Social Entrepreneurship

In 1998 Klaus Schwab and his wife Hilde decided to create an initial endowment for the Schwab Foundation for Social Entrepreneurship to promote entrepreneurial solutions and social commitment, with a clear impact at the grassroots level.

Activities: The Foundation works to provide social entrepreneurs with a platform to showcase their important role in today's society. Since its creation, the Foundation has financially supported the selected social entrepreneurs of its network to actively participate in the various events and initiatives of the World Economic Forum, providing them with an opportunity to draw on the support, knowledge and networks of its members and constituents. In addition, the Foundation has channelled more than 50 scholarships for executive education courses at leading universities to its social entrepreneurs and enabled pro bono consulting and legal support.

Geographical Area of Activity: Switzerland.

Publications: brochures and reports.

Board of Trustees: Hilde Schwab (Pres. and Co-Founder); Klaus Schwab (Co-Founder).

Principal Staff: Senior Dir Mirjam Schöning; Associate Dir Sándor Nagy.

Address: 91–93 route de la Capite, 1223 Cologny/Geneva.

Telephone: 228691212; **Fax:** 227862744; **Internet:** www.schwabfound.org; **e-mail:** info@schwabfound.org.

Schweizerisch-Liechtensteinische Stiftung für archäologische Forschungen im Ausland—SLSA (Swiss-Liechtenstein Foundation for Archaeological Research Abroad—SLFA)

Established in 1986 with the personal participation of HSH Prince Hans-Adam II of Liechtenstein to assist developing countries to preserve their national heritage and contribute to international solidarity in the field of archaeological research.

Activities: Carries out research in the areas of archaeological, ethnographical and cultural research in developing countries, including Bhutan, China, Ecuador, Indonesia, Jordan, Mali, Mongolia, Peru and Syria, in collaboration with local research organizations and universities.

Geographical Area of Activity: Croatia, Jordan, Mali, Peru, Syria, Switzerland.

Restrictions: Only supports its own research.

Publications: Annual Report; research publications; *Ergebnisse der Schweizerisch-Liechtensteinischen Ausgrabungen* (2000); *Sauvegarde et Conservation du Patrimoine Archéologique* (2000); *Ergebnisse der Schweizerisch-Liechtensteinischen Ausgrabungen* (2006); *Cinq mille ans d'histoire au pied des volcans en Equateur* (2008), and other publications.

Finance: Funding from Prince Hans-Adam II of Liechtenstein, private sponsors and the Swiss State.

Foundation Council: Dr Hans Heinrich Coninx (Pres.); Dr Egmond Frommelt (Vice-Pres.); Danielle Ritter (Vice-Pres.).

Principal Staff: Sec.-Gen. Dr Eberhard Fischer; Admin. Claudia Zürcher.

Address: c/o Museum Rietberg Zürich, Gablerstr. 15, 8002 Zürich.

Telephone: 442017669; **Fax:** 442010548; **Internet:** www.slsa.ch; **e-mail:** postfach@slsa.ch.

Schweizerische Akademie der Medizinischen Wissenschaften (Swiss Academy of Medical Sciences)

Founded in 1943 to promote medical research in Switzerland and research carried out by the Swiss in other countries; to promote medico-scientific co-operation in Switzerland; to issue ethical guidelines for the medical profession; and to award prizes for medical scholars.

Activities: Supports advanced medical research; awards a limited number of grants and scholarships for research; patronizes symposia on various medical topics; awards several prizes, including the Bing Prize and the Ott Prize; organizes scientific meetings; and produces medico-scientific publications.

Geographical Area of Activity: Switzerland.

Restrictions: Support restricted to Switzerland.

Publications: Annual Report (in French and German); *Ethical Guidelines for Physicians*; *SAMW Bulletin* (quarterly, in German and French); various information brochures.

Finance: Annual budget approx. 2,000,000 Swiss francs.

Executive Board: Prof. Peter Meier-Abt (Pres.); Prof. Peter Suter (Vice-Pres.); Prof. Walter Reinhart (Vice-Pres.); Dr Dieter Scholer (Treas.).

Principal Staff: Sec.-Gen. Dr Hermann Amstad; Deputy Sec.-Gen. Michelle Salathé.

Address: Petersplatz 13, 4051 Basel.

Telephone: 612699030; **Fax:** 612699039; **Internet:** www.samw.ch; **e-mail:** mail@samw.ch.

Schweizerische Herzstiftung (Swiss Heart Foundation)

Founded in 1967 to promote research and prevention in the field of cardiovascular disease and stroke; to support researchers and encourage co-ordinated research.

Activities: The Swiss Heart Foundation is the only foundation nationally active in the cardiovascular field in Switzerland. The Foundation is committed to reducing the number of people suffering from cardiovascular diseases or remaining disabled by them, and to helping those affected to cope. Main activities are promotion of scientific research, informing patients and the general public about cardiovascular diseases, diagnosis, treatment, life-saving (HELP programme), heart groups and prevention.

Geographical Area of Activity: Switzerland.

Publications: Annual Report; information brochures; magazine for donors.

Finance: Total assets 6,534,532 Swiss francs (31 Dec. 2010); Average annual expenditure on grants 1,500,000 Swiss francs.

Governing Board: Prof. L. von Segesser (Pres.); PD Dr R. Mordasini (Vice-Pres.); Prof. A. Gallino, Prof. H. Mattle, Prof. A. Hoffmann, D. Folletête, B. Flückiger.

Principal Staff: Chief Exec. Therese Junker.

Address: Schwarztorstr. 18, POB 368, 3000 Berne 14.

Telephone: 313888080; **Fax:** 313888088; **Internet:** www.swissheart.ch; www.helpbyswissheart.ch; www.swissheartgroups.ch; **e-mail:** info@swissheart.ch.

Schweizerische Stiftung für Alpine Forschungen (Swiss Foundation for Alpine Research)

Founded in 1939 to organize, finance and equip expeditions to mountains outside Europe and to the Arctic and Antarctic regions; and for Alpine research.

Activities: Operates internationally in the fields of science, mountaineering and alpine safety—high-altitude medicine, glaciology, geology, avalanches, ecological deterioration of high-altitude regions, etc., through self-conducted programmes and research, carried out both at home and abroad, and through publications and topographical maps. The Foundation's website operates as a resource on alpine research.

Geographical Area of Activity: International.

Publications: Annual Report; newsletter; maps; books; DVDs.

Principal Staff: Pres. Étienne Gross; Sec. Thomas Weber-Wegst.

Address: Stadelhoferstrasse 42, 8001 Zürich.

Telephone: 442531200; **Fax:** 442531201; **Internet:** www.alpinfo.ch; **e-mail:** mail@alpinfo.ch.

Schweizerischer Nationalfonds zur Förderung der wissenschaftlichen Forschung/Fonds National Suisse de la Recherche Scientifique—SNF (Swiss National Science Foundation—SNF)

Founded in 1952 by the Schweizerische Naturforschende Gesellschaft, the Akademie der Medizinischen Wissenschaften, the Schweizerische Geisteswissenschaftliche Gesellschaft, the Schweizerischer Juristenverein and the Schweizerische Gesellschaft für Statistik und Volkswirtschaft to grant financial support to basic research in all scientific disciplines, at Swiss universities and other scientific institutions.

Activities: Operates nationally and internationally in the fields of education, science and medicine, the arts and humanities, law and other professions, through grants to individuals and institutions, research, fellowships, scholarships, conferences, courses, publications and lectures. The Foundation is responsible for several national research programmes and implements the National Centres of Competence in Research (NCCR). Maintains a database of funded projects, containing approximately 3,500 entries.

Geographical Area of Activity: Mainly Switzerland.

Restrictions: To be eligible for a research grant, candidates must be resident in Switzerland (regardless of citizenship); candidates for fellowships must be resident in Switzerland or have Swiss or Liechtenstein nationality.

Publications: Annual Report; *SNSF Profile*; *Facts and Figures*; *Fellowship Programmes at a Glance*; *Horizonte/Horizons* (quarterly); *SNF/FNSinfo*; *Multi-annual programme*; NCCR Portrait: *Cutting-edge research made in Switzerland*; *Guide 2011—The NCCR at a glance*; *Gender Studies Switzerland*; *Scientific co-operation with Eastern Europe*; *Media Guide*; *NRP Portrait: Research for you*.

Finance: Total assets 400,000,000 Swiss francs (31 Dec. 2010); annual income 830,000,000 Swiss francs, expenditure 855,000,000 Swiss francs (2010).

Foundation Council: Gabriele Gendotti (Pres.); Prof. Anne-Claude Berthoud (Vice-Pres.).

Principal Staff: Dir Daniel Höchli; Deputy Dir Angelika Kalt.

Address: Wildhainweg 3, POB 8232, 3001 Berne.

Telephone: 313082222; **Fax:** 313013009; **Internet:** www.snf.ch; **e-mail:** com@snf.ch.

Secours Dentaire International (International Dental Rescue)

Founded in 1981 to support co-operation and development in medical dentistry in less-developed countries.

Activities: Operates in Africa and the Caribbean in the field of dentistry. Teaches and trains staff for dental clinics; provides technical skills and trains school teachers. Maintains clinics in Benin, Burkina Faso, Cameroon, the Congo, Gabon, Haiti, Madagascar, Tanzania and Zimbabwe.

Geographical Area of Activity: Africa and Haiti; Switzerland.

Restrictions: No grants to individuals.

Publications: *SDI News 1*; *SDI News 2*; *Prophylactic Lessons in SDI clinics*; *Outreach Work in Zimbabwe*; statistics; posters; leaflets.

Finance: Funded by donations.

Board of Directors: Dr Michael Willi (Pres.).

Principal Staff: Dirs Dr Francis Clément, Dr Marco Santini, Dr Jürg Jent.

Address: Chemin de Publoz 2E, 1070 Puidoux-Gare.

Telephone: 219462532; **Internet:** www.secoursdentaire.ch; **e-mail:** info@secoursdentaire.ch.

Stiftung zur Förderung der Ernährungsforschung in der Schweiz—SFEFS (Swiss Nutrition Foundation)

Founded in 1969 by Nestlé SA, Hoffmann-La Roche & Cie, AG, and Wander AG to further scientific research in the field of nutrition.

Activities: Operates mainly nationally in the field of human nutrition, with emphasis on its physiological, medical and social aspects, through support to research projects, grants to individuals and institutions, fellowships and scholarships, and through the sponsoring of publications. Grants are provided to Swiss nationals for postgraduate studies and research abroad or research projects in Switzerland.

Geographical Area of Activity: Switzerland.

Publications: Annual Report.

Principal Staff: Pres. Prof. Dr Caspar Wenk; Sec. Monique Dupuis.

Address: c/o Institute of Animal Sciences, Nutrition Biology, ETH Zentrum LFW B 57, 8092 Zurich.

Telephone: 446323269; **Fax:** 446321128; **Internet:** www.sfefs.ethz.ch; **e-mail:** sekretariat-nb@inw.agrl.ethz.ch.

Stiftung Kinderdorf Pestalozzi (Pestalozzi Children's Foundation)

Founded in 1946 by Walter Robert Corti to provide help for children in need and distress, and to be a place of meeting and co-operation, a centre of mutual understanding beyond all national, religious and linguistic barriers.

Activities: Operates in Central America, East Africa, Asia and South-Eastern Europe in the programme fields of access to education and inter-cultural living together; addressing the needs of disadvantaged children and young people. All programmes and projects are partner-based with the Foundation not operating and implementing projects directly, but co-operating with local structures (governmental and non-governmental organizations). Currently the Foundation is running co-operation projects in Eritrea, Ethiopia, El Salvador, Guatemala, Honduras, Laos, Macedonia, Moldova, Myanmar, Romania, Serbia, Thailand and Tanzania. The Foundation also operates a village in Trogen, Switzerland, providing a home for children and adolescents, who live in family-like groups and have access to general and vocational training and education in a range of schools and colleges. The village also serves as a facility for exchange projects, bringing together approximately 2,500 children and young people each year from around the world for inter-cultural activities.

Geographical Area of Activity: East Africa, Central America, South-East Asia, South-Eastern Europe and Switzerland.

Restrictions: Project proposals that are outside the Foundation's range of activities and supported countries will not be considered.

Publications: Annual Report (available in English, French and German); other publications; newsletter.

Finance: Main financial support comes from donations, sponsorships and legacies. Total assets 33,923,071 Swiss francs (2008); total income 17,843,739 Swiss francs, expenditure 19,179,771 Swiss francs (2008).

Foundation Council: Brigitta M. Gadient (Pres.); Raeto Conrad (Vice-Pres.); Arthur Bolliger (Treas.).

Principal Staff: Exec. Dir Dr Urs Karl Egger.

Address: Kinderdorfstr. 20, 9043 Trogen.

Telephone: 713437373; **Fax:** 713437300; **Internet:** www.pestalozzi.ch; **e-mail:** info@pestalozzi.ch.

Stiftung Klimarappen (Climate Cent Foundation)

Founded in October 2005, the Climate Cent Foundation is a voluntary initiative of four major Swiss business associations.

Activities: The Foundation aims significantly to contribute to Switzerland's fulfilment of its climate policy targets as set by the Swiss CO2 Law and the Kyoto Protocol. It will invest its annual revenues of 100m. Swiss francs, generated by a charge levied at a rate of 1.5 cents per litre on petrol and diesel imports, in effective and credible climate protection projects in Switzerland and abroad.

Geographical Area of Activity: Switzerland and international.

Publications: Newsletter.

Board of Trustees: Dr David Syz (Chair.).

Principal Staff: Man. Dir Dr Marco Berg; Dir of Communications Stephanie Tobler.

Address: Freiestrasse 167, 8032 Zürich.

Telephone: 443879900; **Fax:** 443879909; **Internet:** www .klimarappen.ch; **e-mail:** info@stiftungklimarappen.ch.

Stiftung 'Leben für Alle' (Foundation 'Life for All')

Established in 1989, an NGO formed to help alleviate suffering.

Activities: Operates in Africa, Asia, Eastern Europe and South America in the fields of aid to less-developed countries, education and social welfare, primarily for children and women, through direct help to those suffering, disaster relief, running children's homes and schools, and providing medical care. 'Sister' organizations have been established in Germany and India.

Geographical Area of Activity: Africa, South America, Asia, Eastern Europe.

Restrictions: Grants are made directly to projects, no grants are made to individuals.

Board: Sah Bhola Prasad (Pres.); Dr Ales Tilen (Vice-Pres.).

Address: Seestr. 23, POB 1458, 8610 Uster.

Telephone: 433990701; **Fax:** 433990703; **Internet:** www.lfa .ch; **e-mail:** info@lfa.ch.

Stiftung Szondi-Institut (Szondi Institute Foundation)

Founded in 1969 by Dr Leopold Szondi to promote in-depth research in psychology.

Activities: Conducts research on the influence of heredity and environment on neuroses, psychoses and criminality, and on psychological tests, in particular the Szondi test. The Institute trains future psychotherapists and collaborates with researchers from other countries.

Geographical Area of Activity: Switzerland.

Publications: Bücher von Leopold Szondi; Bücher anderer Autorinnen; szondiana; Sonderschriften aus dem Szondi-Institut; Studienausgaben.

Principal Staff: Pres. Dr Armin Krauer; Secs Manuela Eccher, Esther Dürr.

Address: Krähbühlstr. 30, 8044 Zürich.

Telephone: 442524655; **Fax:** 442529188; **Internet:** www .szondi.ch; **e-mail:** info@szondi.ch.

Stiftung Vivamos Mejor (Vivamos Mejor Foundation)

Established in 1981 to aid social groups in Central and South America.

Activities: Vivamos Mejor was founded by a doctor in 1981 and is a private Swiss foundation headquartered in Berne. Vivamos Mejor has a neutral background towards politics. It is certified by ZEWO and recognized as a non-profit organization. The foundation co-finances and supervises development projects in Guatemala, Nicaragua, Colombia and Brazil. Focal points are on the following fields of activity: education (pre-school and school advancement, fostering of caring, responsible and non-violent behaviour); formation (adult education, professional training and advancement, organizational development, gender); employment (nutritional safety, earnings promotion, sustainable handling of natural resources); health (hygiene, health care, pregnancy, AIDS, and combat of maternal and infant mortality, balanced diet).

Geographical Area of Activity: Central and South America, Switzerland.

Publications: Annual report, newsletter (bi-annual), several brochures and flyers.

Finance: Annual income 2,167,073 Swiss francs (2010).

Trustees: Dr Andreas Gubler (Pres.); Jean-Pierre Remund (Treas.).

Principal Staff: Man. Nicole Stejskal.

Address: Fabrikstrasse 31, POB 873, 3000 Berne 9.

Telephone: 313313929; **Fax:** 313320309; **Internet:** www .vivamosmejor.ch; **e-mail:** info@vivamosmejor.ch.

SWISSAID Foundation

Established in 1948 to work towards a peaceful world, free from violence, war, poverty and hunger.

Activities: Operates in collaboration with local partner organizations in Africa (Chad, Guinea-Bissau, Niger and Tanzania), Asia (India and Myanmar) and Central and South America (Colombia, Ecuador and Nicaragua) to assist in sustainable development. Maintains offices in 10 countries.

Geographical Area of Activity: Africa, Central and South America, Asia.

Publications: *SWISSAID Spiegel/Le Monde* (quarterly, in German and French).

Finance: Receives donations and government contributions; operating revenue 16,200,000 Swiss francs, expenditure 12,000,000 Swiss francs (2010).

Board of Trustees: Rudolf Rechsteiner (Chair.).

Principal Staff: Dir Caroline Morel.

Address: Lorystrasse 6A, Postfach, 3000 Bern 5.

Telephone: 313505353; **Fax:** 313512783; **Internet:** www .swissaid.ch; www.swissaid.org.co; **e-mail:** info@swissaid .ch.

Swisscontact—Swiss Foundation for Technical Co-operation

Founded in 1959 by personalities of the Swiss private sector and of Swiss universities to promote technical assistance in Asia, Africa, Central and South America and Eastern Europe.

Activities: Conducts its own projects in Asia, Africa, Central and South America, and Eastern Europe, with the collaboration of local organizations and by providing expert volunteers to offer technical support and assistance. Programmes include the organization of professional training centres in the technical field as well as the promotion of small-scale enterprises and ecology in Asia (Bangladesh, Indonesia, Nepal, Viet Nam and Sri Lanka), Africa (Benin, Burkina Faso, Mali, Niger, Kenya, Uganda, Tanzania and South Africa), Central and South America (Honduras, Nicaragua, El Salvador, Costa Rica, Ecuador, Peru, Guatemala, Panama and Bolivia), and Eastern Europe (Albania, Ukraine and Kosovo). A subsidiary organization operates in Germany and a fundraising organization operates in the USA.

Geographical Area of Activity: Asia, Central and South America, Africa and Eastern Europe.

Restrictions: No grants to individuals.

Publications: Annual Report (in English and German).

Finance: Annual revenue and expenditure 46,000,000 Swiss Francs (2009).

Principal Staff: Exec. Dir Samuel Bon.

Address: Döltschiweg 39, 8055 Zürich.

Telephone: 444541717; **Fax:** 444541797; **Internet:** www .swisscontact.ch; **e-mail:** info@swisscontact.ch.

Syngenta Foundation for Sustainable Agriculture

Established in 2001 by Syngenta AG to assist in the development of smallholders and rural communities, improving livelihoods through innovation in sustainable agriculture.

Activities: Operates in agricultural development in less-developed, often semi-arid areas of Africa, Latin America and Asia to reduce poverty. Runs projects with local partners to increase smallholder productivity through access to technologies and markets. Also contributes to the agricultural development debate world-wide.

Geographical Area of Activity: Africa, Latin America, Asia.

Finance: Annual budget approx. €9,000,000.

Board of Directors: Martin Taylor (Chair.); Dirk Seidel (Sec.).

Principal Staff: Exec. Dir Marco Ferroni; Office Man. Marisa de Faveri.

Address: WRO-1002.11.52, Postfach, 4002 Basel, Switzerland.

Telephone: 613235634; **Fax:** 613237200; **Internet:** www .syngentafoundation.org; **e-mail:** syngenta.foundation@ syngenta.com.

Terre des Hommes Foundation

Founded in 1960 by Edmond Kaiser to support children in distress.

Activities: Provides short-term and long-term direct help to children in need without racial or religious prejudices. Conducts projects in more than 30 countries all over the world in the following priority intervention areas: health, social work and children's rights. All projects have an emphasis on the protection and support of children in need. Also provides emergency humanitarian aid. It operates through self-conducted programmes and grants to institutions and individuals. Also maintains offices in Canada, Denmark, France, Germany, Italy, Luxembourg and Syria.

Geographical Area of Activity: Over 30 countries in Europe, Africa Central and South America and Asia.

Publications: Annual Report; *Triebfeder/L'Obstiné* (quarterly newsletter); general brochure; country information sheets; various publications on child trafficking, juvenile justice and street children.

Finance: Total assets 38,624,225 Swiss francs (31 Dec. 2010); Annual income 61,022,714 Swiss francs, expenditure 60,130,918 Swiss francs (2010).

Council: Beat Mumenthaler (Acting Pres.); Heinrich von Grünigen (Vice-Pres.).

Principal Staff: CEO Peter Brey; Dir (Operations) Philippe Buchs.

Address: ave de Montchoisi 15, 1006 Lausanne.

Telephone: 586110666; **Fax:** 586110677; **Internet:** www.tdh .ch; **e-mail:** info@tdh.org.

Tibet-Institut Rikon (Tibetan Monastic Institute in Rikon, Switzerland)

Founded in 1967 by Henri Kuhn-Ziegler and Jacques Kuhn to take care of the spiritual and religious needs of the Tibetans living in exile in Switzerland; to serve immediate teaching purposes by enabling Tibetan scholars and learned priests to teach their young compatriots and to convey to them the values of their ancient culture, as well as enabling Tibetan scholars and priests to learn Western sciences and languages to become informed about the Western way of living and thinking; to serve as a meeting-place of Tibetan and Western cultures.

Activities: Operates internationally in the fields of education, social welfare and studies, science and the arts, and humanities, through research carried out in Switzerland and in co-operation with European and American institutions, and conferences, courses, publications and lectures. Research is undertaken in the fields of history of religion, literature, cultural anthropology, linguistics and related disciplines. Courses are held on Tibetan religion, history, script and language, and basic instruction is given in the techniques of meditation. Formal opinions and reports on Tibetan affairs are prepared by the monks. Maintains a library with a Western and Tibetan section, and film and photograph archives.

Geographical Area of Activity: International.

Publications: Annual Report and financial statement; *Opuscula Tibetana* (series of publications); *A Waterdrop from the Glorious Sea*; *Textbook of Colloquial Tibetan Language*; *Testimonies of Tibetan Tulkus*; *Political Officers, Sikkim, and Heads of British Mission, Lhasa*; *Tibetan songs from Dingri*; *The Historical Kingdom of Mili*; *Five Tibetan Legends from the Avadana Kalpalata*; *Transformation into the Exalted State*; *Tibetan Ritual Music*; *Samatha*.

Governing Board: Dr Rudolf Högger (President).

Principal Staff: Man. Director and Curator Philip Hepp; Sec. Barbara Ziegler.

Address: Wildbergstr. 10, 8486 Rikon, Switzerland.

Telephone: 523831729; **Internet:** www.tibet-institut.ch; **e-mail:** info@tibet-institut.ch.

Volkart-Stiftung (Volkart Foundation)

Founded in 1951 on the 100th anniversary of the Volkart Group.

Activities: Supports selected ideas, projects and organizations in the fields of sustainability, civil society, ecology, education, health, youth, and the arts and culture, through grants to organizations based in Brazil, India, Portugal and Switzerland.

Geographical Area of Activity: Brazil, India, Portugal and Switzerland.

Restrictions: Does not accept applications for funding.

Publications: Annual Report.

Board of Directors: Andreas Reinhart (Pres.).

Principal Staff: Man. Dir Judith Forster.

Address: Volkart Haus, Postfach, 8401 Winterthur.

Telephone: 522686868; **Fax:** 522686889; **Internet:** www .volkartstiftung.ch; **e-mail:** stiftung@volkart.ch.

Welfare Association

Established in 1983 in Geneva to support Palestinian society in sustainable development. Registered under the name Welfare Association, it is also known in the region by its Arabic name, Ta'awoun, which means co-operation.

Activities: Supports sustainable development initiatives in the Palestinian Autonomous Areas, in the period up until the end of 2003 concentrating on vertical development, through support for high-impact projects. Operates within three core programmes: Institution Building; Human Resource Development; and Culture and Identity; as well as running special programmes in Lebanon, for the revitalization of the Old City of Jerusalem and the PNGO project, to assist NGOs in delivering services to poor and marginalized sectors of the community. Support since 2003 has also been given to Information Technology projects and the Palestinian Remembrance Museum, as well as funding for emergency relief and development programmes. Also has offices in Amman and Jerusalem and a sister organization operates in London.

Geographical Area of Activity: Palestinian Autonomous areas and Palestinian refugee camps in Lebanon, London.

Restrictions: No grants are made to individuals.

Publications: *Ta'awoun* (newsletter, in Arabic); *Tanmiya* (newsletter, in English); Annual Report; other publications.

Board of Trustees: Nabil Hani Qaddumi (Pres.); Riad Kamal (Vice-Pres.); Faisal Alami (Vice-Pres.); Marwan al-Sayeh (Vice-Pres.); Sawsan Jafar Fahoum (Chair.).

Principal Staff: Dir-Gen. Dr Atallah Kuttab.

Address: POB 3765, 1211 Geneva 3.

Internet: www.welfareassociation.org; **e-mail:** info@ welfareassociation.org.uk.

World Alliance of YMCAs—Young Men's Christian Associations

Founded in 1844 by George Williams and centred on the Christian faith, the organization works for the physical, emotional and spiritual welfare of women and men of all faiths and of none.

Activities: The YMCA runs programmes world-wide in the areas of youth, emergency aid, peace-building, education, food security, climate change, migration, leadership development, inter-faith dialogue, gender equality and globalization. It operates in 125 countries. There are more than 45m. members world-wide. The national associations of countries form the World Alliance, which holds consultative status with the UN.

Geographical Area of Activity: Africa, Americas, Asia, Europe, Middle East and the Pacific.

Restrictions: Does not make grants.

Publications: *YMCA World*; *World Week of Prayer*; *Living in Hope*; directory; reports.

Executive Committee: Ken Colloton (Pres.); Fernando Ondarza (Deputy Pres.); Helen McEwan (Treas.).

Principal Staff: Sec.-Gen. Rev. Johan Vilhelm Eltvik.

Address: 12 clos Belmont, 1208 Geneva.

Telephone: 228495100; **Fax:** 228495110; **Internet:** www.ymca.int; **e-mail:** office@ymca.int.

World Economic Forum

Founded in 1971 by Prof. Klaus M. Schwab to contribute to the growth of world-wide prosperity through economic co-operation and the promotion of enterprise. Supervised by the Swiss Federal Council, with consultative status with the UN.

Activities: Encourages the direct exchange of information between world leaders in business, politics and the academic sphere, to promote world-wide prosperity, particularly through engaging its corporate members in global citizenship. The organization holds an annual meeting, the World Business Summit, in Davos, Switzerland, and arranges Industry Summits and conferences geared to the requirements of the specific needs of individual countries or regions. The Trustees '21' Project seeks to improve the state of the world in the transition from the 20th to the 21st century, through networking of global decision-makers, creating task forces comprising people from all sections of humanity.

Geographical Area of Activity: International.

Publications: *Global Competitiveness Report* (annually, in collaboration with the International Monetary Fund—IMF); *World Link* (magazine, 6 a year); Annual Meeting and Summit Reports; annual reports; institutional brochure; newsletters (institutional publications).

Principal Staff: Founder and Exec. Chair. Prof. Klaus M. Schwab.

Address: 91–93 route de la Capite, 1223 Cologny/Geneva.

Telephone: 228691212; **Fax:** 227862744; **Internet:** www.weforum.org; **e-mail:** contact@weforum.org.

World Scout Foundation

Founded in 1969 to support the 28m. participants in some 160 countries in the world scout movement.

Activities: Finances scouting activities; provides support to the World Organization of the Scout Movement.

Geographical Area of Activity: International.

Publications: Annual Report; *One Promise, One Image*; *28 million young people are changing the world*; *The World Scouting Report*; copyrights; Baden-Powell's writings; catalogue.

World Committee: Simon Rhee (Pres.); John May (Vice-Pres.); Wahid Labidi (Vice-Pres.).

Principal Staff: Sec.-Gen. Luc Panissod.

Address: Rue du Pré-Jérôme 5, CP 91, 1211 Geneva 4 Plainpalais.

Telephone: 227051010; **Fax:** 227051020; **Internet:** www.scout.org; **e-mail:** worldbureau@scout.org.

World Wide Web Foundation

Established in 2008 by Tim Berners-Lee, inventor of the Web; an international non-profit organization that aims to promote use of the World Wide Web for progress.

Activities: Operates in the area of web technology, including training and tools to support content creation, community building, support of Web science and research, advancement of Web standards.

Geographical Area of Activity: International.

Publications: newsletters.

Board of Directors: Alberto Ibargüen (Chair.).

Principal Staff: Chief Exec. Steve Bratt; Programme Man. José M. Alonso.

Address: c/o Lenz & Staehelin, route de Chêne 30, 1208 Geneva.

Internet: www.webfoundation.org.

Worlddidac Foundation

Established in 1984 by Worlddidac—the World Association of Publishers, Manufacturers and Distributors of Educational Materials.

Activities: Awards the Worlddidac Award, presented to the manufacturers of the best educational materials to promote creativity and innovation in the production of educational materials.

Geographical Area of Activity: International.

Publications: *Worlddidac Award Booklet*; newsletter.

Presidium: Dominic Savage (Pres.); Reinhard Koslitz (Vice-Pres. and Treas.).

Principal Staff: Dir-Gen. Beat Jost; Head of Office/Project Man. Regula Müller.

Address: Bollwerk 21, POB 8866, 3001 Berne.

Telephone: 313117682; **Fax:** 313121744; **Internet:** www.worlddidac.org; www.worlddidacaward.org; **e-mail:** info@worlddidac.org.

WWF International

Founded in 1961 by Sir Peter Scott and others to promote the conservation of natural resources and the diversity of species and ecosystems world-wide; originally known as the World Wildlife Fund.

Activities: Aims to stop the degradation of natural environments, conserve biodiversity, ensure the sustainable use of renewable resources, and promote the reduction of both pollution and wasteful consumption. Addresses six priority issues: forests; freshwater and marine species; climate change and toxics. WWH has identified and focuses its activities on 200 'ecoregions' the ('Global 200'), believed to contain the world's remaining biological diversity and actively supports and operates conservation programmes in more than 90 countries. Maintains 54 offices world-wide, five associate organizations and has around 5m. individual members.

Geographical Area of Activity: World-wide.

Publications: *WWF News* (quarterly); *Living Planet Report* (periodically updated); *Wildlife of India* (CD-ROM); Annual Report.

Finance: Total assets €79,578,000 (31 Dec. 2010); annual income €524,963,000, expenditure €494,316,000 (2010).

Board of Trustees: Yolanda Kakabadse Navarro (Pres.); André Hoffmann (Vice-Pres.); Markus Joytak Shaw (Treas.).

Principal Staff: Dir-Gen. James P. Leape.

Address: ave du Mont-Blanc 27, 1196 Gland.

Telephone: 223649111; **Fax:** 223648836; **Internet:** www.panda.org.

WWSF—Women's World Summit Foundation (Frauen Weltgipfel Stiftung/Fondation Sommet Mondial des Femmes)

Founded in March 1991 in Geneva, Switzerland by Elly Pradervand after the 2000 UN Childrens' Summit in support of the implementation of women and childrens' rights and the UN Development Goals. WWSF informs, educates, trains, empowers and communicates with a growing network of more than 40,000 contacts.

Activities: Operates through two principal sections, the WWSF Women's Section and the WWSF Children-Youth Section. The Women's Section includes an annual Prize for women's creativity in rural life; the International Day of rural women -15 October (since 2007 a UN Resolution Day); the Micro-credit sheep project in Mali; the Numbers Must Change campaign, which advocated greater gender equality, and the White Ribbon- Campaign Switzerland, which aims to create community dialogues for the elimination of violence against women. The WWSF Children-Youth section concentrates on prevention of abuse and violence against children and youth, includes an international coalition of relevant actors around the world, an annual Prize for innovative prevention activities, an International Clearinghouse, the Yellow-Ribbon campaign, a TV spot and signature cards. In 2010 the Foundation launched a YouthEngage website for the empowerment of young people to become involved in prevention of violence against children and young people.

Geographical Area of Activity: International.

Publications: *Empowering Women and Children* (newsletter, 2 a year); Annual Reports; brochures, posters, fliers, postcards, TV spots, calls to action, etc.

Finance: public support, memberships and government contributions.

Board of Directors: Gulzar Samji (Pres.); Bunny McBride (Vice-Pres.).

Principal Staff: Exec. Dir and Founder Elly Pradervand.

Address: POB 143, 1211 Geneva 20.

Telephone: 227386619; **Fax:** 227388248; **Internet:** www .woman.ch; white-ribbon.ch; YouthEngage.com; **e-mail:** info@wwsf.ch.

Taiwan

FOUNDATION CENTRES AND CO-ORDINATING BODIES

Himalaya Foundation

Established in 1990, a corporate foundation that aims to enable capable people of Chinese ancestry to develop their talents and participate broadly in the world community.

Activities: Operates in the fields of Chinese studies, economic affairs and civil society, through research, grants, exchanges, publications and involvement in international philanthropic associations. Also involved in the development of civil society and the third sector, setting up the Taiwan Philanthropy Information Center (q.v.) that informs on the non-profit sector in Taiwan and elsewhere by maintaining a database of foundations, as well as a library on philanthropy and the third sector. The Foundation has established the NPO Development Center for not-for-profit organization IT capacity building and the NPO book website providing publications relating to the third sector or published by not-for-profit organizations.

Geographical Area of Activity: Taiwan, Asia and the USA.

Restrictions: Prefers to fund projects that have tangible and far-reaching benefits for society.

Publications: *Directory of Foundations in Taiwan*; *Handbook on Good Practices for Laws Relating to Non-Governmental Organizations* (Chinese translation); series of books on the non-profit sector.

Board of Trustees: S. Gong (Chair.).

Principal Staff: Exec. Dir S. Gong; Asst. Exec. Dir Andy Kao.

Address: 9F-1, 167 Fu Hsing North Rd, Taipei 105.

Telephone: (2) 2544-8296; **Fax:** (2) 2718-5850; **Internet:** www.himalaya.org.tw; **e-mail:** hmfdtion@himalaya.org.tw.

Taiwan Philanthropy Information Center

Established in 1999 by the Himalaya Foundation (q.v.) as a centre of information on the non-profit sector in Taiwan.

Activities: Informs on the non-profit sector in Taiwan and elsewhere by maintaining a database of not-for-profit organizations operating in Taiwan and a library on philanthropy and the third sector.

Geographical Area of Activity: Taiwan.

Publications: *Tpic Newsletter* (weekly).

Address: c/o Himalaya Foundation, 9F-1, 167 Fu Hsing North Rd, Taipei 105.

Telephone: (2) 2544-8296; **Fax:** (2) 2718-5850; **Internet:** www.himalaya.org.tw/EN/Page_ID=261; **e-mail:** hmfdtion@himalaya.org.tw.

FOUNDATIONS, TRUSTS AND NON-PROFIT ORGANIZATIONS

Advantech Foundation

Founded in 1977 by Advantech Corporation.

Activities: Provides support to educational research in Taiwan and overseas, aiming to put the results into practice at individual, social and corporate level to improve people's standard of living. Active in the areas of entrepreneurship education as well as running a thesis programme and a technology innovation competition (TiC100).

Geographical Area of Activity: Taiwan and Malaysia.

Board of Directors: K. C. Liu (Chair.).

Principal Staff: Contact Lina Chou.

Address: 1 Alley 20, Lane 26, Rui-Kuan Rd, Nai-Hou, Taipei.

Telephone: (2) 2792-7818; **Fax:** (2) 2794-7327; **Internet:** www.tic100.org.tw; **e-mail:** tic100@advantech.com.tw.

AVRDC—The World Vegetable Center

Founded in 1971 as the Asian Vegetable Research and Development Center to encourage research and development of safe vegetable farming in the tropics and subtropics; and to help improve nutrition, health, employment and income of small-scale farmers in developing countries. As the organization's scope of work expanded over time, the name was changed to AVRDC—The World Vegetable Center.

Activities: Conducts research into vegetable development; maintains the world's largest public-sector gene bank of vegetable germplasm, with more than 58,000 accessions; holds training workshops, seminars and conferences; operates regional vegetable research and development networks; maintains an information database and a library of about 45,000 books and periodicals.

Geographical Area of Activity: International, with an emphasis on developing countries. Headquarters are in Taiwan, with four regional centers in Thailand, Tanzania, India and Dubai, and offices or staff in many other developing countries in Africa and Asia.

Publications: AVRDC newsletter; seminar proceedings; technical bulletins; production manuals; field guides.

Finance: Annual budget approx. US $15,000,000 (2012).

Board: Dr Samsom Tsou (Chair.); Dr. Eugene Terry (Vice-Chair.).

Principal Staff: Dir-Gen. J.D.H. Keatinge; Deputy Dir-Gen. (Research) Dr Jackie Hughes; Deputy Dir-Gen. (Administration and Services) Dr Yin-Fu Chang.

Address: POB 42, Shanhua, Tainan 74199.

Telephone: (6) 583-7801; **Fax:** (6) 583-0009; **Internet:** www.avrdc.org; **e-mail:** info@worldveg.org.

Chia Hsin Foundation

Founded in 1963 by Dr Ming-Yu Chang and Ming-Chong Oung, Chairman of the Board of Directors and Managing Director respectively of the Chia Hsin Cement Corporation, for the promotion of culture in Taiwan.

Activities: Operates nationally in the fields of the arts and humanities, social studies, science and medicine, law and education, through research projects, courses, conferences, lectures, publications, fellowships and scholarships, and grants to individuals and institutions. Grants the Chia Hsin Technology Award, the Distinguished Contribution Award, the Chia Hsin Prize for Journalism and the Chia Hsin Athletics Award. Also facilitates and finances study abroad for a limited number of students, and provides universities with free copies of Master of Arts and doctoral theses.

Geographical Area of Activity: Taiwan.

Publications: Report of operations.

Board of Directors: Jen-Shieng Yian (Chair.); M. Y. Chang, Hwuan Li, Jen-Fwu Gu, Yiou-Li Wu, Tsuen Chian (Vice-Chair.).

Principal Staff: Dirs Sueng-Chiou Tsu, Yu-Ren Gau.

Address: 96 Section 2, Chung Shan North Rd, Taipei 10449.

Telephone: (2) 2523-1461; **Fax:** (2) 2511-4002; **Internet:** www.chcgroup.com.tw/eng/business_subsidiary_foundation.htm; **e-mail:** ch_found@chcgroup.com.tw.

Chiang Ching-Kuo Foundation for International Scholarly Exchange—CCKF

Founded in 1989 by the Government of Taiwan and the private sector to promote Chinese studies and scholarly exchange.

Activities: Operates internationally in the fields of the arts and humanities, economic affairs, education, international affairs, law and human rights, medicine and health, and social welfare and social studies, through research, grants to institutions and individuals, and awarding scholarships and fellowships. Programmes cover the American Region (including North, Central and South America), the Asian/Pacific Region, the European Region and the Republic of China. Maintains an office in the USA and the Chiang Ching-kuo International Sinological Center at Charles University in the Czech Republic.

Geographical Area of Activity: International.

Publications: Annual Report (in Chinese and English); newsletter (quarterly); *Building for the Future: the First Decade.*

Finance: Operational funds derive from interest generated by original endowment of US $86m.

Board of Directors: Kao-wen Mao (Chair.).

Principal Staff: Pres. Yun-han Chu; Vice-Pres Gang Shyy, Ayling Wang.

Address: 13F, 65 Tun-Hwa South Rd, Section 2, Taipei 106.

Telephone: (2) 2704-5333; **Fax:** (2) 2701-6762; **Internet:** www.cckf.org; **e-mail:** cckf@ms1.hinet.net.

Pacific Cultural Foundation

Founded in 1974 to promote international cultural exchange.

Activities: Operates through organizing and participating in international academic and cultural conferences; organizing international artists' or performing groups' visits to Taiwan; hosting exhibitions at the Foundation's Cultural Center in Taipei; and promoting international academic and cultural exchange initiatives.

Geographical Area of Activity: International.

Board of Trustees: Huan Lee (Chair.).

Principal Staff: Pres. Yu-Sheng Chang; Vice-Pres. Wu-Jian Guo.

Address: 38 Chungking South Rd, Section 3, Taipei.

Telephone: (2) 2337-7155; **Fax:** (2) 2337-7167; **Internet:** www.pcf.org.tw; **e-mail:** pcfarts@pcf.org.tw.

Syin-Lu Social Welfare Foundation

Founded in 1987.

Activities: Works through campaigning for the rights of physically and mentally disabled people to ensure their entitlement to social benefits; funds education, rehabilitation, housing, leisure and counselling services for physically and mentally disabled people; trains professionals to mobilize community services on behalf of people with disabilities; and publishes relevant information.

Geographical Area of Activity: Taiwan.

Finance: Total annual expenditure approx. NT $100,000,000.

Principal Staff: Exec. Dir Ching-I Tsung.

Address: 364 Chilin Rd, 4F, Taipei.

Telephone: (2) 2592-9778; **Fax:** (2) 2592-8514; **Internet:** www.syinlu.org.tw; **e-mail:** isyinlu@gmail.com.

Tajikistan

FOUNDATIONS, TRUSTS AND NON-PROFIT ORGANIZATIONS

OSIAF—Open Society Institute Assistance Foundation—Tajikistan

Founded in 1996 to promote the development of open society in Tajikistan. An independent foundation, part of the Soros foundations network, which aims to foster political and cultural pluralism and reform economic structures to encourage free enterprise and a market economy.

Activities: Operates principally in the fields of educational and electoral reform, human rights and legal reform, regional co-operation, information and the media, and arts and culture.

Geographical Area of Activity: Tajikistan.

Board of Directors: Oinhol Bobonazarova (Chair.).

Principal Staff: Exec. Dir Zuhra Halimova.

Address: 37/1 Bokhtar St, Vefa Business Centre, 4th Floor, 734002 Dushanbe.

Telephone: (372) 441-07-28; **Fax:** (372) 51-01-42; **Internet:** www.soros.org/about/foundations/tajikistan; **e-mail:** zuhra .halimova@osi.tajik.net.

Tanzania

FOUNDATIONS, TRUSTS AND NON-PROFIT ORGANIZATIONS

Mwalimu Nyerere Foundation—MNF

Established in 1996 as a permanent tribute to Mwalimu Julius Nyerere, the country's first President; it is an independent body not linked to any political party, and its aim is to promote 'peace, unity and people-centred development in Africa'.

Activities: Seeks to carry out its aims through encouraging and organizing dialogues within Africa, among and between governments, people, NGOs and local institutions; co-operating with other similar institutions within and outside Africa; collecting, analysing and disseminating information; and establishing a specialist library. Operates three programmes, the African Unity Programme, Institutional Capacity Building, and Justice for All. Also aims to promote the study of the principles adopted and practised by Nyerere, through collecting, analysing and cataloguing documents, letters, reports, etc. concerning him, and to make available to the public all such information. The Foundation took a leading role in facilitating Burundi peace talks in 1999. Maintains a Documentation Research Centre.

Geographical Area of Activity: Africa.

Publications: *The Work of the Mwalimu Nyerere Foundation* (Swahili version); *Africa Today and Tomorrow* (collection of speeches by Mwalimu Julius Nyerere); *South Bulletin*.

Principal Staff: Exec. Dir Joseph W. Butiku.

Address: 6 Sokoine Dr., POB 71000, Dar es Salaam.

Telephone: (22) 2118354; **Fax:** (22) 2119216; **Internet:** hot255.com/nyerere; **e-mail:** mnf-tanzania@raha.com.

Tanzania Millennium Hand Foundation—TAMIHA

Established in 2007 to further the Millennium Goals in Tanzania.

Activities: Operates HIV/AIDS awareness and prevention campaigns, and provides health care; promotes environmental conservation; runs community programmes in the areas of gender empowerment and poverty reduction, through the promotion of micro-enterprises.

Geographical Area of Activity: Tanzania.

Principal Staff: Pres. and Chair. Sebastian Ritte; CEO Crispin K. Mugarula; Sec.-Gen. Placid Msuri.

Address: POB 541, Usa River, Arusha.

Telephone: (732) 971394; **Fax:** (787) 474341; **Internet:** www.tamiha.org; **e-mail:** info@tamiha.org.

Thailand

FOUNDATION CENTRE AND CO-ORDINATING BODY

CPCS—Center for Philanthropy and Civil Society

Established in 1997 under the National Institute of Development Administration, for the support of the third sector.

Activities: Aims to encourage the development of philanthropy and the third sector in Thailand, through carrying out research; maintaining databases; training and advisory services; lobbying; co-ordinating the activities and programmes of third-sector organizations; and educational programmes. Maintains an information centre.

Geographical Area of Activity: Thailand.

Executive Board: Dr Juree Vichit-Vadakan (Chair.).

Principal Staff: Director Dr Kanokkan Anukansai.

Address: National Institute of Development Administration, 118 Seri Thai Rd, Klongchan Bangkapi, Bangkok 10240.

Telephone: (2) 727-3504-5; **Fax:** (2) 374-7399; **e-mail:** juree@ nida.nida.ac.th.

FOUNDATIONS, TRUSTS AND NON-PROFIT ORGANIZATIONS

AIT—Asian Institute of Technology

Founded in 1959 as the SEATO Graduate School of Engineering, the Institute became fully independent under its present title in 1967. It aims to help meet the growing need for advanced engineering education and research in Asia in engineering, technology, planning and management.

Activities: Provides advanced (postgraduate) education in engineering, science and allied fields, through academic programmes leading to higher degrees, through research by students, faculty and research staff directed towards the solution of technological problems relevant to Asia, and through special programmes, including conferences, seminars and short courses. The Institute provides scholarships and grants to assist well-qualified students from the region. The Institute comprises four schools: the School of Advanced Technologies, School of Civil Engineering, School of Environment, Resources and Development, School of Management, and an AIT extension. There are also a number of academic centres. Maintains databases and a library comprising more than 230,000 volumes.

Geographical Area of Activity: Africa, Asia, Europe, and USA.

Publications: *Annual Report on Research and Activities*; *AIT Review* (3 a year); Annual Report.

Board of Trustees: Dr Thanat Khoman (Chair. Emer.); Dr Tej Bunnag (Chair.); Prof. Shinichiro Ohgaki (Vice-Chair.); Jean-Pierre Verbiest (Vice-Chair.); Kulvimol Wasuntiwongse (Sec.).

Principal Staff: Pres. Prof. Said Irandoust.

Address: POB 4, Klong Luang, Pathumthani 12120.

Telephone: (2) 5160144; **Fax:** (2) 5162126; **Internet:** www.ait .ac.th; **e-mail:** helpdesk@ait.ac.th.

ECPAT International

ECPAT was originally established in 1991 as a three-year project to combat child prostitution. In 1996 became a NGO and is now a network of organizations and individuals around the world working together for the elimination of child prostitution, child pornography and trafficking of children for sexual purposes.

Activities: Carries out local, national and international activities aimed at protecting children in every part of the world, including the whole range of issues revolving around the commercial sexual exploitation of children. Organizes conferences, operates an information and resource centre, carries out research, develops models of prevention and disseminates information. The ECPAT Network comprises more than 80 independent groups in more than 70 different countries across Asia, Central, South and North America, Eastern and Western Europe, the Middle East, North Africa and the Pacific. Holds a General Assembly every three years.

Geographical Area of Activity: International.

Publications: *Implementation of the Agenda for Action Against the Commercial Sexual Exploitation of Children* (annual); *ECPAT Newsletter* (quarterly); *Questions and Answers About the Commercial Sexual Exploitation of Children*; *Protecting Children Online: An ECPAT Guide*; *Regional Situational Analysis Reports*; Annual Report; research reports.

Board: Maureen Crombie (Chair.); David Ould (Treas.); Maria Eugenia Villarreal (Sec.).

Principal Staff: Exec. Dir Kathleen Speake.

Address: 328/1 Phaya Thai Rd, Bangkok 10400.

Telephone: (2) 215-3388; **Fax:** (2) 215-8272; **Internet:** www .ecpat.net; **e-mail:** info@ecpat.net.

The Education for Development Foundation—EDF

Since its establishment in 1987, the EDF has been playing an active role in the socio-educational field, with an emphasis on poverty reduction, education development and international peace building. The EDF collaborates with local educational services and various international partners in the private sector to provide scholarship funds to disadvantage students and initiate educational development projects in rural schools in the 19 north-eastern provinces of Thailand.

Activities: Activities include the scholarship programme, which enables students to continue their education beyond primary school; educational development projects, which aim to improve students' technological skills, agricultural knowledge and health education; and school infrastructure and facilities improvement, such as library building and water-filter installation.

Geographical Area of Activity: 19 provinces in the north-eastern region of Thailand.

Restrictions: Scholarships mainly available for poor students living in the North-east.

Publications: Newsletter; videos; CD-ROMs and multimedia.

Finance: Total assets 78,975,359 Baht; annual income 51,186,945 Baht; annual expenditure 50,816,689 Baht (2010).

Board of Directors: Col Somkid Sreesangkom (Chair.); Nartrudee Nakornvacha (Sec.).

Principal Staff: Man. Dir Sunphet Nilrat.

Address: Kasetsart University Alumni Bldg, 3rd Floor, 50 Paholyothin Rd, Jatujak, Bangkok 10900.

Telephone: (2) 940-5265; **Fax:** (2) 940-5266; **Internet:** www .edfthai.org; **e-mail:** info@edfthai.org.

Empower Foundation

Founded in 1994.

Activities: Active within two main programme areas: women and prostitution, and AIDS prevention and problem solving.

Carries out educational activities in the fields of legal rights, social benefits and AIDS prevention; grants scholarships; and provides medical fees and emergency funds for prostitutes. Also provides leadership training.

Geographical Area of Activity: Thailand.

Restrictions: Applications from domestic organizations for projects seeking to combat prostitution are rarely approved.

Publications: *Life Leading.*

Finance: Annual revenue approx. 800,000 Baht.

Principal Staff: Founder and Sec.-Gen. Chantawipa Apisuk.

Address: 57/60 Tivanond Rd, Nontaburi 11000.

Telephone: (2) 5268311; **Fax:** (2) 5263294; **Internet:** www .empowerfoundation.org; **e-mail:** badgirls@ empowerfoundation.org.

Foundation for Children

Founded in 1978 to support the welfare of children in Thailand.

Activities: The prime focus of the Foundation is the welfare of children in Thailand. Activities are within three programme areas: Educational and Cultural Institute Programmes, including support for village schools and projects helping homeless children; Children's Welfare and Education Institute, meeting basic needs of children; and the Children's Institute, developing knowledge in the community. Promotes physical and mental development of children, co-ordinates educational activities, provides scholarships and works in partnership with other NGOs. Also provides humanitarian relief and supports environmental preservation activities. Runs its own publishing house.

Geographical Area of Activity: Thailand.

Restrictions: Projects must be practical, transparent and simple enough to be monitored and evaluated.

Executive Committee: Sobhon Subhaphong (Pres.); Prof. Aree Wanyasewi (Treas.); Piphop Dhongchai (Sec.).

Principal Staff: Pres. Prof. Prawase Wasi; Vice-Pres. Khun Ying Amporn Meesuk.

Address: 95/24 Moo 6, Soi Kiat Ruammitra, Buddha Monthon 4, Sampharn, Nakhon Pathom 73220.

Telephone: (2) 8141481; **Fax:** (2) 8140369; **Internet:** www.ffc .or.th; **e-mail:** children@ffc.or.th.

Foundation for Women

Founded in 1984 to support women's development, help women and children victimized by violence, and to promote and support women's rights and equality.

Activities: Provides grants to projects promoting women's rights and equality, and to organizations helping marginalized women, particularly in the north and north-east of Thailand. Also provides training for women and young people in the areas of violence against young people, women and their rights; provides technical assistance and temporary accommodation to women who have experienced violence; and carries out research and data collection activities on various kinds of problems affecting women, including female trafficking, as well as disseminating this information to government and private organizations.

Geographical Area of Activity: Thailand.

Publications: *Voices of Thai Women* (newsletter).

Finance: Annual income approx. 3,000,000 Baht.

Principal Staff: Dir Dr Chalermsri Tammaboot.

Address: POB 47 Bangkoknoi, Bangkok 10700.

Telephone: (2) 4335149; **Fax:** (2) 4346774; **Internet:** www .womenthai.org; **e-mail:** info@womenthai.org.

Sem Pringpuangkeo Foundation

Established in 1995 to assist those people who suffer from illness, in particular AIDS, and to ensure an adequate education for those children orphaned as a result of these illnesses through a comprehensive fostering programme; works with hill tribes and other lowland peoples of northern Thailand to preserve natural environment; and encourages and supports education and religious work, including preserving local culture, customs and traditions.

Activities: Operates in the areas of social welfare, conservation and the environment, and medicine and health, through operating programmes. The Foster Parents Programme provides education and training to children affected by HIV/ AIDS in the six upper northern provinces of Thailand to prevent them from entering the cycle of drug abuse, homelessness, crime and child prostitution; operates a scholarship scheme; and educates children in agricultural skills and introduces children to traditional Thai cultural values. The Environmental Programme promotes family planning in the hill tribes; encourages the use of biological agriculture; and develops mutual co-operation on environmental preservation by establishing a house-temple-school network. Maintains office in Chinagmai.

Geographical Area of Activity: Thailand.

Finance: Total assets 19,671,878 Baht (2007).

Board of Directors: Kasem Snidvongs (Chair.); Isara Vongkusolkit (Vice-Chair.); Achara Soontornvatin (Sec. and Treas.).

Principal Staff: Man. Uraiwan Pakkasem; Asst Man. Ridthirong Santhabut.

Address: 219/28-31 Asoke Towers Office Bldg, 9th Floor, Sukhumvit 21 Rd, Klongtoey Nua, Wattana, Bangkok 10110.

Telephone: (2) 2600229; **Fax:** (2) 2602506; **Internet:** www .semfoundation.org; **e-mail:** sembkk@anet.net.th.

Seub Nakhasathien Foundation

Founded in 1990 to promote the environment.

Activities: Operates in the field of conservation of forest and natural resources through providing youth training programmes, teacher training programmes, exhibitions on environmental issues, and campaigning on environmental and conservation issues.

Geographical Area of Activity: Thailand.

Publications: *Seub Journal*; leaflets; and strategy reports.

Finance: Annual revenue approx. 3,000,000 Baht.

Principal Staff: Man. Nittaya Wongsawat.

Address: Dept of Medical Science, 4th Bldg, 693 Bumrungmuang Rd, Pombrab District, Bangkok 10100.

Telephone: (2) 5612469; **Fax:** (2) 5612470; **Internet:** www .seub.or.th; **e-mail:** snf@seub.or.th.

Siam Society

Founded in 1904 to investigate and encourage the arts and sciences in relation to Thailand and its neighbouring countries.

Activities: Operates internationally in the fields of education, economic affairs, the arts and humanities, religion, international relations and the conservation of natural resources, through self-conducted programmes, research, grants to institutions and individuals, fellowships, scholarships, conferences, courses, publications and lectures. Maintains a library.

Geographical Area of Activity: South-East Asia.

Publications: *Journal of the Siam Society* (2 a year); *Natural History Bulletin of the Siam Society* (2 a year); books; monographs; report of operations and financial statement; *The Customs of Cambodia*; *The Royal Chronicles of Ayutthaya*; *Footprints of The Buddhas of This Era in Thailand*; *Witnesses to a Revolution: Siam 1688*; *The Society of Siam: Selected Articles for The Siam Society's Centenary*; *Art and Art-Industry in Siam*; *Thai Culture in Transition.*

Council: Bilaibhan Sampatisiri (Pres.); Dr Wissanu Kreangam, Dr Weerachai Nankorn, Eileen Deeley (Vice-Pres); Suraya Supanwanich (Hon. Treas.).

Principal Staff: Gen. Man. Kanitha Kasina-Ubol.

Address: 131 Asoke Montri Rd (Sukhumvit 21), Bangkok 10110.

Telephone: (2) 6616470; **Fax:** (2) 2583491; **Internet:** www .siam-society.org; **e-mail:** info@siam-society.org.

Thairath Newspaper Foundation

Originally founded in 1979 and approved as a public charity organization in 1999.

Activities: Oversees and supports 101 Thai-Rath Witthaya Schools, provides humanitarian relief and awards the Kampon Wacharapon prize for an outstanding journalistic thesis. Also carries out research, including research into the development of arithmetic studies for primary school children, as well as providing training to teachers.

Geographical Area of Activity: Thailand.

Finance: Total endowment approx. 25,000,000 Baht.

Board of Directors: Khun Ying Praneetsilp Vacharaphol (Chair.); Wimol Yimlamai (Vice-Chair.); Yinglak Vacharaphol (Vice-Chair. and Treas.); Somboon Woraphong (Sec.).

Address: 1 Viphavadirangsit Rd, Bangkok 10900.

Telephone: (2) 2721030; **Fax:** (2) 2721754; **Internet:** www .thairath.co.th; **e-mail:** postmaster@thairath.co.th.

TISCO Foundation

Founded by the Tisco Group in 1982.

Activities: Provides support for social and economic development activities, through the award of scholarships, medical funding for patients in need, and grants for employment activities and business start-ups by poor people. Also provides humanitarian relief.

Geographical Area of Activity: Thailand.

Finance: Net income aprox. 120,000,000 Baht.

Board of Directors: Sivaporn Dardarananda (Chair.); Pliu Mangkornkanok (Vice-Chair.); Vannee Uboldejpracharak (Sec.); Duangrat Kittivittayakul (Treas.).

Principal Staff: Man. Pattira Wattanawarangkul; Asst Man. Dusadee Rattanapapaschala.

Address: 5th Floor, TISCO Tower, 48/11 North Sathorn Rd, Bangkok 10500.

Telephone: (2) 6337501; **Fax:** (2) 6380554; **Internet:** www .tiscofoundation.org; **e-mail:** webmaster@tiscofoundation .org.

TTF—Toyota Thailand Foundation

Established by the Toyota Company in Thailand in 1992.

Activities: Active in the fields of education, social welfare and community development in Thailand, through funding NGOs and training schemes. Projects include an initiative to encourage children to eat more green vegetables, provision of scholarships in engineering at the Institute of Traffic and Transport Engineering at Chulalongkorn University, support for orphans whose parents have died from AIDS and a programme to empower young women.

Geographical Area of Activity: Thailand.

Finance: Total assets approx. 250,000,000 Baht.

Principal Staff: Pres. Police Gen. Pao Sarasin.

Address: 186/1 Moo 1, Old Railway Rd, Sumrongtai, Prapadang, Samutprakarn.

Telephone: (2) 3861590; **Fax:** (2) 3847350; **Internet:** www .toyota.co.th; **e-mail:** tff@toyota.co.th.

Timor-Leste

FOUNDATIONS, TRUSTS AND NON-PROFIT ORGANIZATIONS

Haburas Foundation

Founded in 1998 by Demetrio do Amaral de Carvalho to promote and protect the environment in Timor-Leste.

Activities: Initiates and funds a number of projects designed to help Timor-Leste develop sustainably. Promotes eco-tourism initiatives, reforestation and the establishment of the country's first national park.

Geographical Area of Activity: Timor-Leste.

Publications: *Verde* (monthly bulletin); brochures.

Principal Staff: Exec. Dir Demetrio do Amaral de Carvalho.

Address: POB 390, rua Celestino da Silva, Farol, Dili.

Telephone: 331-0103; **Internet:** haburas.org; **e-mail:** haburaslorosae@yahoo.com.

Turkey

FOUNDATION CENTRES AND CO-ORDINATING BODIES

Sivil Toplum Geliştirme Merkezi—STGM (Civil Society Development Centre)

Formed in 2004 to enable civil and participatory democracy in Turkey.

Activities: Maintains a library and a database of NGOs. Runs a support centre for NGOs to meet and exchange information and experiences, and holds events and conferences for Turkish NGOs. Regional offices in the provinces of Adana, Denizli, Diyarbakır and Eskişehir.

Geographical Area of Activity: Turkey.

Publications: *Siviliz* (bulletin, 2 a month, in Turkish and English); *Gender Guide for Non-governmental Organizations*; *Voluntary Participation and Volunteer Management Guide for NGOs*; *Advocacy Guide for NGOs*; *Communication and Campaigning Guide for NGOs*; *Social Entrepreneurship Guide for Social Change*; *Legal Handbook for Non-governmental Organizations*; *Guide for Civil Networks in the World, in Europe and in Turkey*; *Story of Civil Society in Turkey: An Oasis Amidst Constraints*; *Feeling of Always Starting as Loser-Discriminatory Practices in Turkey: Victims and Specialists Tell About it*; *Issues and Resolutions of Rights Based NGOs in Turkey* (in Turkish and English); *Project Stories from Civil Society*; *Civil Life in Turkey*; *Handbook of Civil Society Activist*; *Project Cycle Management: Logical Framework Approach, Informatics Guide for NGOs, Governance Guide for NGOs*.

Finance: Funded by the European Union.

Administrative Board: Levent Korkut (Chair.); Hülya Denizalp (Vice-Chair.).

Principal Staff: Gen. Man. Ayça Haykir.

Address: Tunus Caddesi 85/8 06680 Kavaklıdere, Ankara.

Telephone: (312) 4424262; **Fax:** (312) 4425755; **Internet:** www.stgm.org.tr; **e-mail:** bilgi@stgm.org.tr.

Third Sector Foundation of Turkey—TÜSEV

Established in 1993 to strengthen the non-profit sector in Turkey.

Activities: TUSEV was established in 1993 by Turkey's leading civil society organizations, and has now grown to a supporting network of some 107 associations and foundations that share a vision of strengthening the legal, fiscal and operational infrastructure of the third (non-profit) sector in Turkey. Our programmes include civil society, law reform, social investment, international relations and networking research.

Geographical Area of Activity: Turkey.

Publications: *Turkish Foundations During the Republican Period*; *Directory of Member Foundations and Associations of the Third Sector Foundation of Turkey*; *Philanthropy in Turkey: Citizens, Foundations and the Pursuit of Social Justice*; *The Landscape of Philanthropy and Civil Society in Turkey: Key Findings, Reflections and Recommendations*; periodicals; monographs; information brochures.

Executive Board: Prof. Dr Üstün Ergüder (Chair.); İnal Avcı, Timur Erk (Vice-Chair.).

Principal Staff: Sec.-Gen. Namik Ceylanoglu; Programme Dir Tevfik Başak Ersen; Communications Coordinator Derya Kaya.

Address: Bankalar Caddesi Minerva Han 2, Kat 5, 34420 Karakoy/Istanbul.

Telephone: (212) 2438307; **Fax:** (212) 2438305; **Internet:** www.tusev.org.tr; **e-mail:** info@tusev.org.tr.

FOUNDATIONS, TRUSTS AND NON-PROFIT ORGANIZATIONS

Açık Toplum Enstitüsü (Open Society Institute—Turkey)

Established in 2001 as a member of the Soros foundations network, with the purpose of acting as a liaison office enhancing partnerships with Turkish donors and facilitating collaboration between Turkish civil society and the Soros foundations network.

Activities: Provides direct support and acts as a liaison organization in the fields of social, economic and European Union membership research, human rights, educational reform and co-operation among NGOs. In its first year of operation support included a scholarship programme for graduate-level study of human rights law offered by the Human Rights Center at Bilgi University and, in collaboration with the Open Society Foundation—Sofia, the organization also co-sponsored competitions for joint projects between Bulgarian and Turkish NGOs.

Geographical Area of Activity: Turkey.

Publications: e-newsletter.

Finance: Total expenditure US $2,500,000 (2010).

Advisory Board: Hakan Altinay (Pres.).

Principal Staff: Sec.-Gen. Gokce Tüylüoglu.

Address: Cevdet Pasa Caddesi, Mercan Apt No. 85, D11, Bebek 34342, Istanbul.

Telephone: (212) 2879986; **Fax:** (212) 2879967; **Internet:** www.aciktoplumvakfi.org.tr; **e-mail:** info@aciktoplumvakfi.org.tr.

Beyaz Nokta Gelişim Vakfi (White Point Development Foundation)

Established in 1994 by Ishak Alaton, M. Tinaz Titiz, Faruk Ekinci, Yuksel Domaniç, Mümin Erkunt and Ibrahim Kocabas to promote problem-solving in society.

Activities: Operates throughout Turkey in the field of education, through self-conducted programmes, research, prizes, conferences, training courses and publications. Projects include non-formal education for children unable to remain in the education system, a civic education project, a campaign to encourage responsible driving and donations of science equipment to develop children's interest in science education.

Geographical Area of Activity: Turkey.

Restrictions: Grants to foundation members only.

Publications: *Beyaz Bülten* (newsletter).

Finance: Total assets 124,063 Turkish liras (31 Dec. 2010).

Board of Directors: M. Tinaz Titiz (Chair.); Kavi Husamettin (Vice-Chair.); Dr Duran Oktay (Sec.-Gen.); Cimsit Hussein (Treas.).

Principal Staff: Gen. Co-ordinator Güler Yüksel.

Address: Sedat Simavi Sokak, Çankaya Sitesi No 29/Z-1, 06550 Çankaya, Ankara.

Telephone: (312) 4420760; **Fax:** (312) 4420776; **Internet:** www.beyaznokta.org.tr; **e-mail:** bnv@beyaznokta.org.tr.

Çevre Koruma ve Ambalaj Atiklari Degerlendirme Vakfi—CEVKO (Environmental Protection and Packaging Waste Recovery and Recycling Trust)

Established in 1991 by a number of national and multinational companies to promote and organize economically efficient and environmentally friendly packaging, waste recovery and recycling based on the principle of co-responsibility.

Activities: Operates in the field of conservation and the environment, through research and training courses, public awareness raising activities, and organizing national and international conferences. Co-ordinates the Green Dot implementation in Turkey.

Publications: Bulletin; Annual Report.

Finance: Total assets approx. US $400,000.

Management Board: Okyar Yayalar (Chair.); Atila Usanmaz, Cihan Topçu, Hayrünnisa Aligil (Vice-Chair.).

Principal Staff: Gen. Sec. Mete Imer.

Address: Cenap Sehabettin Sok. 94 Kosuyolu 81020, Kadiköy, Istanbul.

Telephone: (216) 4287890; **Fax:** (216) 4287895; **Internet:** www .cevko.org.tr; **e-mail:** cevko@cevko.org.tr.

Anne Çocuk Eğitim Vakfi—AÇEV (Mother Child Education Foundation)

Founded in 1993 with a mission to empower people through family-based education. AÇEV's main focus area is early childhood education and family literacy programmes, which aim to provide equal opportunity in education to all by targeting pre-school children and their families in disadvantaged communities. AÇEV believes in the power of the family in shaping the individual: it tries to provide a 'fair start' for all children prior to enrolling in schools by enabling families to support the development of their children.

Activities: AÇEV conducts research and develops and implements programmes in two main areas of expertise: early childhood and adult education. It implements programmes using a variety of models and mediums including training courses, seminars and awareness raising programmes through the television and media. Programmes are free and aim to reach the most vulnerable families and disadvantaged communities in Turkey. Since 1993, ACEV has trained more than 7,000 trainers and reached nearly 700,000 beneficiaries through its education programmes. AÇEV programmes try to provide a 'fair start' to schooling for all children by empowering families to support the development of their children in pre-school years. AÇEV collaborates with governmental agencies, local and international NGOs and organizations, universities and private businesses to fund its programme activities. The main education programmes include the Mother and Child Education Programme, the Father Support Programme and the Functional Literacy and Women's Empowerment Programme.

Geographical Area of Activity: Turkey.

Publications: *An Evaluation of the Mother Support Programme in South-Eastern Turkey* (2008); *Girls' Access to Primary Education Best Practices from Turkey* (2008); *Girls' Access to Primary Education Best Practices from the World* (2008); *Providing Access to Basic Literacy Education with Educational TV* (2008); *Early Childhood Education in Turkey: Access, Equality and Quality* (2009); *Mothers from Five Countries Reporting: Mother-Child Education Program* (2009); and others.

Principal Staff: Pres. Ayşen Özyeğin; Gen. Man. Ayla Göksel.

Address: Büyükdere Cad., Stad Han. 85, Kat 2, 34387 Mecidiyeköy, Istanbul.

Telephone: (212) 2134220; **Fax:** (212) 2133660; **Internet:** www .acev.org; **e-mail:** acev@acev.org.

Aydın Doğan Vakfi (Aydın Doğan Foundation)

Established by Aydın Doğan in 1996 to contribute to the development of Turkey in the areas of education and culture.

Activities: Operates nationally in the fields of education and culture. The Foundation has built a number of schools and dormitories, and libraries, sports and cultural centres. Makes a number of awards, including the Aydın Doğan International Cartoon Prize, Young Communicators' awards, and various awards in the areas of architecture, social services, literature and music. Maintains an art gallery.

Geographical Area of Activity: Turkey.

Finance: Annual expenditure €1,962,000 (2010).

Board of Directors: Aydın Doğan (Chair.); Arzuhan Doğan Yalcindağ (Pres.); Vuslat Doğan Sabanci (Deputy Chair.).

Principal Staff: Exec. Dir Candan Fetvaci.

Address: Burhaniye Mahallesi Kisikli Cad. No. 65, 34676 Üsküdar, Istanbul.

Telephone: (216) 5569176; **Fax:** (216) 5569147; **Internet:** www .aydindoganvakfi.org.tr; **e-mail:** advakfi@advakfi.org.

Hisar Education Foundation—HEV

Established in December 1970 by a number of individuals to contribute to the implementation of advanced education systems in Turkey and to provide institutions of all levels with funds for grants, scholarships and equipment.

Activities: Operates nationally in the field of education, through self-conducted programmes, scholarships and fellowships, conferences, training courses and publications. As well as making educational grants to various schools, the Foundation runs its own primary school.

Geographical Area of Activity: Turkey.

Publications: *Educating Young Children*.

Board of Directors: Feyyaz Berker (Hon. Pres.); Hüsnü Özyeğin (Pres.); Hasan Subaşi (Vice-Pres.); Jak Baruh (Sec.).

Principal Staff: Gen. Dir Hasan Subaşı.

Address: Uzunkemer Göktürk Beldesi 34077, Kemerburgaz, Istanbul.

Telephone: (212) 3220300; **Fax:** (212) 3220307; **Internet:** www .hisarschools.com; **e-mail:** kurumsalgelistirme@ hisarokullari.com.

İktisadi Kalkınma Vakfı (Economic Development Foundation)

Founded in 1965 by the Istanbul Chamber of Commerce and the Istanbul Chamber of Industry to monitor and evaluate Turkey-European Union (EU) relations, to inform the public and to represent the Turkish business world vis-a-vis the EU.

Activities: Conducts research on Turkey-EU relations; formulates and expresses opinions and proposals on behalf of the Turkish private sector on EU and Turkey-EU relations; carries out projects that aim to address general and technical issues related to Turkey-EU integration and thus help inform and involve the business world, NGOs, media and the public. Organizes conferences, seminars and panels on EU and Turkey-EU relations in Turkey and in various EU member states. Ensures a regular flow of information, including activities undertaken by Turkey in the harmonization process, to the European Commission and Parliament as well as to European NGOs and media representatives and carries out lobbying activities promoting Turkey. Maintains a library that is the depository library of EU publications in Turkey and permanent representation in Brussels, the first representation of the Turkish private sector in the EU.

Geographical Area of Activity: Turkey, European Union countries.

Publications: Research studies on various EU policies, the effects of these policies on Turkey, the level of harmonization with these policies and other studies on all aspects of Turkey-EU relations; *IKV Bulletin* (2 a month); *E-Bulletin* (weekly); annual almanac; various reports.

Finance: Fully financed by the private sector; does not receive any financial support from the Government.

Board of Directors: Prof. Dr Haluk Kabaalioğlu (Pres.); Zeynep Bodur Okyay, Niyazi Önen (Vice-Chair.).

Principal Staff: Sec.-Gen. Assoc. Prof. Çiğdem Nas; Project Dir Çisel Ileri.

Address: Esentepe Mah. Harmann Sok. TOBB Plaza No: 10, K: 7–8 Sisli, Istanbul.

Telephone: (212) 2709300; **Fax:** (212) 2703022; **Internet:** www .ikv.org.tr; **e-mail:** ikv@ikv.org.tr.

İnsan Hak ve Hürriyetleri İnsani Yardım Vakfı (Humanitarian Relief Foundation)

Established in 1995 by Bulent Yildirim and Mehmet Kose to support people affected by conflict or disaster.

Activities: Operates in the areas of aid to less-developed countries, education, law and human rights, medicine and health, and social welfare, by making grants to individuals, offering scholarships, carrying out emergency relief, and defending human rights.

Geographical Area of Activity: South-Eastern Europe, Central and South Asia, the Middle East, Africa, the Far East and Central and South America.

Publications: Annual Report; booklets; periodicals: *Düşünce Gündem* and *İnsani Yardım*.

Board of Trustees: Fehmi Bulent Yildirim (Pres.); Huseyin Oruc (Deputy Pres.).

Address: Büyük Karaman Caddesi Taylasan sokak, No. 3 Pk, 34230 Fatih, Istanbul.

Telephone: (212) 6312121; **Fax:** (212) 6217051; **Internet:** www .ihh.org.tr; **e-mail:** info@ihh.org.tr.

İnsan Kaynağını Geliştirme Vakfı—IKGV (Human Resource Development Foundation)

Founded in 1988 by a group of academics and business people to contribute to the solution of health, education and employment problems, which have a negative impact on the economic, social and cultural development of society.

Activities: The Foundation works to empower people (women and children in particular), through advocacy, training and service provision in the areas of population and sustainable development.

Geographical Area of Activity: Turkey.

Publications: Books, bulletins, leaflets, newsletters and training manuals on reproductive health and sex education (in Turkish; some manuals are available in Azeri and Russian).

Governing Board: Turgut Tokuş (Chair.); Prof. Dr Ayşen Bulut (Deputy Chair.); Hasip Buldanhoğlu (Treas.).

Principal Staff: Exec. Dir Dr Berna Eren.

Address: Yeniçarşı Caddesi 34, Beyoğlu 34425, Istanbul.

Telephone: (212) 2931605; **Fax:** (212) 2931009; **Internet:** www .ikgv.org; **e-mail:** ikgv@ikgv.org.

Kadın Emeğini Değerlendirme Vakfı—KEDV (Foundation for the Support of Women's Work)

Established in 1986 to support low-income women's groups to improve the quality of their lives, their communities and their leadership.

Activities: Runs programmes in the areas of early childcare and education services for the poor, capacity building, economic empowerment and natural disasters. Maintains a craft shop.

Geographical Area of Activity: Turkey.

Publications: Books and manuals.

Address: Bekar Sokak No 17, Beyoglu, Istanbul.

Telephone: (212) 2922672; **Fax:** (212) 2491508; **Internet:** www .kedv.org.tr; **e-mail:** kedv@kedv.org.tr.

Open Society Foundation—Turkey

Established in August 2008.

Activities: Operates in Turkey in the areas of financial and technical assistance in the areas of political reform and the European Union, media, gender, public health, and minority rights. Supports research on issues including women's participation in the public sphere, the development of a local governance participation model, urban sustainability processes, and the use of information technology in democratization. Also promotes social inclusion and equality, including people with mental health problems, people living with HIV/AIDS, and women facing gender-based violence; the Foundation also promotes increasing access to education and political mobilization among Roma people.

Geographical Area of Activity: Turkey.

Restrictions: Only provides institutional support for scholarships on a project basis.

Principal Staff: Exec. Dir Gökce Tüylüoglu.

Address: Cevdet Pasa Caddesi, Mercan Apt, No. 85, D.11, Bebek 34342, Istanbul.

Telephone: (212) 287-9986; **Fax:** (212) 287-9967; **Internet:** www.aciktoplumvakfi.org.tr; **e-mail:** info@aciktoplumvakfi .org.tr.

Sabancı Vakfı—Hacı Ömer Sabancı Foundation (Sabancı Foundation)

Established by the Sabancı family in 1974 to further Turkey's social and economic development.

Activities: The Foundation's overall aim is 'to promote social development and social awareness among current and future generations by supporting initiatives that impact and bring change to people's lives by creating authentic, innovative and lasting values'. In addition to supporting institutions, arts and culture, and providing scholarships and awards, the Foundation supports civil society organizations in promoting equity and active participation for youth, women and persons with disability.

Geographical Area of Activity: Turkey.

Restrictions: Only organizations in Turkey are eligible for funding.

Finance: Total assets €542,189,938 (31 Dec. 2010).

Board of Trustees: Güler Sabanci (Chair.), Hüsnü Paçacıoğlu (Vice-Chair.).

Principal Staff: Gen. Man. Zerrin Koyunsağan, Dir of Programmes and International Relations Filiz Bikmen.

Address: Sabancı Centre 4. Levent, 34330 Istanbul.

Telephone: (212) 3858800; **Fax:** (212) 3858811; **Internet:** www .sabancivakfi.org; **e-mail:** info@sabancivakfi.org.

Tarih Vakfı (History Foundation of Turkey)

Established in 1991 as the Economic and Social History Foundation of Turkey, by 264 members of the scientific and cultural community to create an archival and library collection of sources relating to the economic and cultural heritage of Turkey, and to promote historical study.

Activities: Operates in the area of history and the preservation of historical heritage, and the development of NGOs, nationally and internationally, through self-conducted programmes, research, conferences and publications. Co-operates with similar national and international organizations. Maintains an information and documentation centre, a liaison office in Ankara and an online database of Turkish NGOs.

Geographical Area of Activity: Turkey.

Publications: Books; magazines; journals; newsletters; encyclopedia; Latin script; *Istanbul* (periodical, 2 a year); *Toplumsal Tarih* (Social, periodical, monthly); *Tarih Vakfı'ndan Haberler* (monthly bulletin); *Istanbul'u Gezerken (Strolling through Istanbul)*; illustrated scholarly books.

Board of Directors: Oktay Özel (Pres.); Suay Aksoy, Bülent Bilmez (Vice-Pres.); Deniz Unsal (Sec.-Gen.); Tunc Müstecaplioglu (Treas.).

Address: Zindankapi Degirmen Sokak No 15 Eminonu, Istanbul.

Telephone: (212) 5220202; **Fax:** (212) 5135400; **Internet:** www .tarihvakfi.org.tr; **e-mail:** tarihvakfi@tarihvakfi.org.tr.

Türkiye Aile Sağlığı ve Planlaması Vakfı—TAPV
(Turkish Family Health and Planning Foundation)

Established in 1985 by Vehbi Koç to increase the quality and accessibility of reproductive health-care information and services for women in Turkey.

Activities: Operates nationally in the fields of women's and children's health care, reproductive health and family planning, and the enhancement of women's status in society. Publishes information, holds conferences and engages in projects to carry out its mission.

Geographical Area of Activity: Turkey.

Publications: Various publications.

Board of Directors: Caroline Koç (Chair.); Prof. Dr Baran Tuncer (Vice-Chair.); Erdogan Karakoyunlu (Comptroller).

Principal Staff: Pres. Prof. Dr Baran Tuncer.

Address: Güzel Konutlar Sitesi, A Blok D3–4, Ulus Mahallesi, 34760 Etiler, Istanbul.

Telephone: (212) 2577941; **Fax:** (212) 2577943; **Internet:** www.tapv.org.tr; **e-mail:** info@tapv.org.tr.

Türkiye Çevre Vakfı (Environment Foundation of Turkey)

Founded in 1978 by Dr Cevdet Aykan, Serbülent Bingöl, Muslih Fer, Ertugrul Soysal, Prof. Dr Necmi Sönmez, Engin Ural and Altan Zeki Ünver to establish a documentation centre on the environmental problems of Turkey and of other countries; to prepare and release articles and programmes for the mass media; to sponsor, carry out and publish research on environmental issues; to co-operate with institutions in other countries dealing with environmental problems; and to play an advocacy role in promoting the quality of the environment.

Activities: Operates in the field of conservation and the environment, through research, organizing national and international conferences and seminars, publications, environmental advice, promoting public awareness of environmental issues, and co-operation with the media and with international organizations. Maintains a library. Grants scholarships to Turkish university students studying in Turkey.

Geographical Area of Activity: Turkey, Central Asia and the Black Sea region.

Restrictions: Grants made only to specific NGOs working in Central Asia and the Black Sea region.

Publications: Newsletter (quarterly, in Turkish); books on the environment.

Trustees: Turgut Tokuş (Chair.).

Principal Staff: Sec.-Gen. Engin Ural.

Address: Tunalı Hilmi Caddesi 50/20, 06660 Ankara.

Telephone: (312) 4255508; **Fax:** (312) 4185118; **Internet:** www.cevre.org.tr; **e-mail:** cevre@cevre.org.tr.

Türkiye Erozyonla Mücadele Ağaçlandırma ve Doğal Varlıkları Koruma Vakfı—TEMA (Turkish Foundation for Combating Soil Erosion, for Reforestation and the Protection of Natural Habitats)

Established in 1992 to draw attention to soil erosion, land degradation and their associated effects.

Activities: Operates in Turkey through supporting projects such as education programmes, local conservation and development, rural development and land rehabilitation, as well as lobbying for sustainable policies and collaborating with similar NGOs and government agencies.

Geographical Area of Activity: Turkey.

Publications: Annual Report.

Finance: Financed by membership subscriptions.

Board of Trustees: Hayrettin Karaca (Chair.).

Principal Staff: Gen. Dir Ümit Y. Gürses.

Address: Çayır Çimen Sokak Emlak Kredi Blokları A-2, Blok Kat:2 Daire:8, 34330 Levent-İstanbul.

Telephone: (212) 2837816; **Fax:** (212) 2811132; **Internet:** www.tema.org.tr; **e-mail:** tema@tema.org.tr.

Türkiye İnsan Haklari Vakfi (Human Rights Foundation of Turkey)

Established in 1990 to provide treatment and rehabilitation services for torture survivors and to document human rights violations in Turkey.

Activities: Operates in Turkey in the field of human rights, through supporting measures against torture; protecting the rights of refugees and asylum-seekers; running treatment and rehabilitation centres; and maintaining a documentation centre.

Geographical Area of Activity: Turkey.

Publications: Reports.

Executive Board: Şebnem Korur Fincanci (Pres.); Metin Bakkalci (Sec.-Gen.).

Address: Akbaş Mahallesi Sarıca Sokak No. 7, Altındağ, 06080 Ankara.

Telephone: (312) 310 66 36; **Fax:** (312) 310 64 63; **Internet:** www.tihv.org.tr.

Türkiye Kalkinma Vakfi (Development Foundation of Turkey)

Founded in 1969 to alleviate poverty and improve the quality of life among resource-poor rural families, through small-scale agricultural investment projects and agricultural vocational training.

Activities: The Foundation develops and manages a wide range of agricultural development programmes in five regions of rural Turkey. Two of its programmes, bee-keeping development and broiler production, have become national programmes. Others include dairy farming, introduction of fodder crops, work with fruit and vegetables, sericulture improvement, development of small-scale irrigation schemes, introduction of better-yielding varieties of wheat, combating internal and external parasites in sheep, and assistance to rural communities in cheese production. The Foundation manages centres for training young women in rug-weaving, and assists with the marketing of the rugs. Many of the projects involve supervision of credits provided by the Agricultural Bank to participating farmers. The Foundation maintains regional offices and has 32 centres for developing the social and economic status of women in the Eastern Anatolia region.

Geographical Area of Activity: Eastern and South-Eastern Turkey.

Publications: *Mellifera* (annually); books and reports on specific areas of activity.

Finance: Funds are derived from the Turkish Government, institutions and individuals in Turkey, Europe and the USA, bilateral technical assistance programmes with Germany and Switzerland, and loans from national and international agencies.

Board of Trustees: Cemal Kulahli (Chair.).

Principal Staff: Gen. Man. Mihrace Erdogan.

Address: Fatih Mahallesi Vakif Caddesi, No. 43/B Kazan, 06980 Ankara.

Telephone: (312) 8141119; **Fax:** (312) 8141590; **Internet:** www.tkv-dft.org; **e-mail:** teknik_aricilik@tkv-dft.org.

Uluslararası Mavi Hilal İnsani Yardım ve Kalkınma Vakfı (International Blue Crescent Relief and Development Foundation—IBC)

Established in 1999 to provide humanitarian relief in Turkey and world-wide to alleviate human suffering caused by war, hunger, natural disasters, environmental problems and disease.

Activities: Operates humanitarian relief programmes in Central and South-Eastern Europe, Central Asia, the Middle East and Africa, including the provision of food, medical supplies, educational materials and clothing; redevelopment projects in disaster areas; and infrastructure projects.

Geographical Area of Activity: Central and South-Eastern Europe, Central Asia, the Middle East and Africa.

Board of Directors: Recep Üker (Pres.); Muzaffer Baca (Vice-Pres.).

Principal Staff: Gen. Sec. Uğur Güngör.

Address: Bagdat Cad. Fistikli Sok. Dilek Apt. No. 3/5, Suadiye, Istanbul.

Telephone: (216) 3841486; **Fax:** (216) 3615745; **Internet:** www .ibc.org.tr; **e-mail:** ibc@bluecrescent.net.

Umut Vakfi (Umut Foundation)

Established in 1993 to promote conflict resolution and peace.

Activities: The Foundation operates in Europe (especially South-Eastern Europe), the Middle East and Turkey, promoting peaceful conflict resolution and individual disarmament, helping young people develop strong leadership skills, promoting the rule of law and co-operating with similar NGOs.

Geographical Area of Activity: Turkey, South-Eastern Europe and the Middle East.

Publications: *Who's Who in Europe in the Science and Art of Peace and Reconciliation; Terror and Struggle Against Organised Crime; Individual Disarmament; Criminology; Criminal Law Reform; To Be A Citizen: Teachers' Hand Manual; To Be A Citizen: Student Book; Individual Disarmament: Give life a chance!* (cartoons).

Principal Staff: Pres. Nazire Dedeman Cagatay.

Address: Yildiz Posta Caddesi 52, Esentepe 34340, Istanbul.

Telephone: (212) 3372993; **Fax:** (212) 2886675; **Internet:** www .umut.org.tr; **e-mail:** vakif@umut.org.tr.

Vehbi Koç Vakfı (Vehbi Koç Foundation)

Founded in 1969 by Vehbi Koç, and supported by Koç Holding SA, for the allocation of financial support in education, medicine, culture and related areas.

Activities: Operates nationally in the fields of education, social welfare, science, arts and culture, and medicine and health, through research, conferences, courses, seminars, lectures, awards, scholarships and travel grants. Provides grants for social welfare, buildings and medical equipment for hospitals in Turkey. Supports public museums, including the Sadberk Hanım Müzesi, which exhibits collections in the fields of ethnography, archaeology and artistic cultural traditions; the Rahim H. Koç Museum, the first Turkish museum to be devoted to the history of technology and industry; and the Suna-Inan Kiraç Research Institute on Mediterranean Civilisations, which researches archaeology and indigenous cultures. Also funds the building of schools, established the Koç University, as well as funding the Vehbi Koç Professorship of Turkish Studies at Harvard University's Faculty of Arts and Sciences. In 1990 the Tofas Fiat Fund was created in conjunction with the Turkey Fiat Group to provide scholarships to students in Italy and Turkey to support conservation work and to sponsor bilingual (Italian and Turkish) art publications.

Geographical Area of Activity: Mainly Turkey and Western Europe.

Finance: Receives donations from Koç group companies.

Board of Directors: Semahat Arsel (Chair.); Rahmi M. Koç (Vice-Chair.).

Principal Staff: CEO Suna Kiraç; Gen. Man. Erdal Yidirim.

Address: Nakkastepe, Azizbey Sokak No. 1, Kuzguncuk, 81207 Istanbul.

Telephone: (216) 5310000; **Fax:** (216) 5310099; **Internet:** www .vkv.org.tr; **e-mail:** info@vkv.org.tr.

Uganda

FOUNDATIONS, TRUSTS AND NON-PROFIT ORGANIZATIONS

Kulika Charitable Trust (Uganda)

Founded in the United Kingdom in 1981 for general charitable purposes. In 2005 the operational management of Kulika was transferred to the Ugandan office.

Activities: Operates in the fields of education, sustainable agriculture and development in Uganda. Currently concentrating on providing scholarships, running a training and awareness programme in sustainable agriculture, supporting poverty alleviation and development projects, and funding environment and conservation projects.

Geographical Area of Activity: East Africa, mainly Uganda.

Publications: newsletter.

Finance: Gross income £195,681, total expenditure £131,351 (Aug. 2008).

Board: Prof. Maria G. N. Musoke (Chair.).

Principal Staff: Chief Exec. Elijah Kyamuwendo.

Address: Plot 472, Nsambya Hospital Rd, POB 11330, Kampala.

Telephone: (414) 266 261; **Fax:** (414) 510 005; **Internet:** www.kulika.org; **e-mail:** uganda@kulika.org.

Ukraine

FOUNDATION CENTRES AND CO-ORDINATING BODIES

Centre for Philanthropy

Established in 1998 to support non-profit organizations in Ukraine.

Activities: Aims to develop Ukrainian philanthropy and to provide a supporting environment, through carrying out research, issuing publications, providing a library and information service to both philanthropists and NGOs, providing technical support, and organizing international fundraising workshops and conferences.

Geographical Area of Activity: Ukraine.

Publications: Handbooks and training materials.

Principal Staff: Dir Svitlana Kuts; Man. Alexander Polyakov.

Address: 01034 Kiev, 36-E Yaroslaviv Val Str, Office 33.

Telephone: (44) 231-26-77; **Fax:** (44) 212-31-50; **Internet:** www.philanthropy.org.ua; **e-mail:** bulletin@philanthropy .org.ua.

Ednannia: Initiative Centre to Support Social Action—ISAR Ednannia

Ednannia (Joining Forces) was launched in 1997 as a not-for-profit NGO aiming to strengthen civil society through social initiatives, and improve Ukranian quality of life.

Activities: Provides grants, consultations, training, information, networking, research and numerous other services to NGOs and other interested parties; maintains an online NGO database, a library and a database of NGO experts in Ukraine; runs an NGO support network of 15 Centres for NGO Expertise and nine regional NGO Support Centres.

Geographical Area of Activity: Ukraine.

Publications: *Bulletin for NGOs* (monthly); *NGO Success Stories*; Annual Report.

Finance: Total income US $313,801, expenditure $305,818 (2008).

Advisory Board: Iryna Belashova (Hon. Chair.).

Principal Staff: Exec. Dir Volodymyr Sheyhus; Financial Dir Svitlana Sharai.

Address: 03150 Kiev, POB 447.

Telephone: (44) 201-01-60; **Fax:** (44) 201-01-60; **Internet:** www.ednannia.kiev.ua; **e-mail:** ednannia@isar.kiev.ua.

GURT Resource Centre for NGO Development

National information and support centre established in 1995 to provide a range of services to strengthen civil society organizations of all types and sizes.

Activities: Operates through three main programmes: the Societal Information Programme, which includes the collection, processing and dissemination of information about different events, projects, programmes and other activities of Ukrainian NGOs; the Civil Society Organizations Sustainability Programme, which aims to provide training and consultancy support to civil society organizations, NGOs, charitable foundations, political parties, local governments, etc. and also assist in establishing contacts with organizations abroad; and the Social Partnership Programme, which aims to research information on and implement different schemes of social partnership, establishing co-operative relations between NGOs and local government and businesses.

Geographical Area of Activity: Ukraine.

Publications: *GURT Bulletin* (weekly e-mail newsletter); publications on volunteering, NGO governance, public relations and fundraising; Annual Report.

Finance: Total income US $322,250, total expenditure $297,610 (2009).

Board: Serhij Ivanyuk (Chair.).

Principal Staff: Exec. Dir Bohdan Maslych.

Address: 01025 Kiev, 52 Popudrenka Str., Rm 609, POB 126.

Telephone: (44) 296-10-52; **Fax:** (44) 296-10-52; **Internet:** www.gurt.org.ua; **e-mail:** info@gurt.org.ua.

Innovation and Development Centre—IDC

IDC is a Kiev-based, not-for-profit group comprising an international charitable fund that was founded in 2001 and a civic organization that was founded in 1996.

Activities: IDC serves as a source of information on third-sector development in Ukraine; the information sources include an e-mail service, publications issued by IDC, Ukrainian NGO Net, and a database of more than 40,000 Ukrainian NGOs. Publications issued render information on events organized, grants provided by local and international organizations, other NGO-related information-issuing publications, and charities and foundations active in Ukraine.

Geographical Area of Activity: Ukraine.

Publications: *Crossroads* (6 a year, in Ukrainian); *NPO Accountant* (6 a year, in Ukrainian); various books on non-profit management, and NGO directories.

Finance: Receives donations from individuals and corporations.

Board of Trustees: Mink Mullay (Chair.).

Principal Staff: Dir Oleksander Sydorenko.

Address: 01023 Kiev, Esplanadna St 28, Suite 7.

Telephone: (44) 248-72-39; **Fax:** (44) 246-72-05; **Internet:** www.idc.org.ua; **e-mail:** idc@idc.org.ua.

FOUNDATIONS, TRUSTS AND NON-PROFIT ORGANIZATIONS

Dr F. P. Haaz Social Assistance Foundation

Established in 1987 in memory of Dr F. P. Haaz to provide assistance to elderly and disabled people and all those in need of social assistance.

Activities: Involved in helping the development of legal reforms in Ukraine in support of elderly people, people with disabilities and others in need. Has also established the Mother Marie Mercy Center, the Janush Corchak Rehabilitation Institute for Children with Mental Handicaps, the Alexander Men's Philanthropical College, the Humanist Youth Charity Society, the Socio-psychological Assistance Center, and the Institute of Municipal Democracy and Human Rights.

Geographical Area of Activity: Ukraine.

Publications: *Charter of Odessa*; *Comments on the Constitution of Ukraine*; *A Legal Weapon for Ukrainian Civil Society*; other reports.

Board: Alexander G. Muchnik (Pres.).

Address: 65023 Odesa, Pushkinskaya Str. 68.

Telephone: (48) 222-67-46; **Fax:** (48) 234-62-08; **Internet:** www.haaz.com.od.ua; **e-mail:** fsp@ukrpost.net.

Information Society of Ukraine Foundation

The Foundation is a not-for-profit NGO dedicated to transforming Ukraine into an informational society by developing co-operation among all social sectors: public, government authorities, scientific and business communities. The Foundation commenced its activities in early July 2001.

Activities: The Foundation works in collaboration with private companies, state institutions and NGOs in the fields of IT business, Information Technology and society development. The Foundation, in addition to acting as a consultant to NGOs, provides material and technical support as well. Activities include training teachers in the use of IT, an expert council online and projects to equip all schools in Ukraine with new or used computers; organizes campaigns advocating free press promotion in Ukraine.

Geographical Area of Activity: Ukraine.

Publications: Articles.

Board of Trustees: Lesya Berezovets (Chair.); Volodymyr Masarik (Deputy Chair.).

Principal Staff: Chief Exec. Pavel Varbanets.

Address: 01034 Kiyiv, Patorzinskogo 6.

Telephone: (44) 502-00-53; **Fax:** (44) 502-00-53; **Internet:** isu.org.ua; **e-mail:** isu@isu.org.ua.

International Charitable Fund 'Ukraine 3000'

Established in 2001 to assist in the development of Ukrainian society.

Activities: Operates in three principal areas: Yesterday (heritage, archaeology, ethnography); Today (health, social welfare); and Tomorrow (development of Ukraine).

Geographical Area of Activity: Ukraine.

Finance: Annual revenue US $7,293,921, expenditure $8,087,211 (2009).

Board of Directors: Maryna Antonova (Chair.).

Principal Staff: Head of Supervisory Board Kateryna Yushchenko.

Address: 04070 Kyiv, 37 Spaska St.

Telephone: (44) 390-05-44; **Fax:** (44) 390-05-49; **Internet:** www.ukraine3000.org.ua; **e-mail:** info@ukraine3000.org.ua.

International Renaissance Foundation—IRF

International Renaissance Foundation (IRF) has been working since 1990 and is a part of the Open Society Institute network, founded by George Soros. The mission of the Foundation is to provide financial and efficient assistance to the development of an open, democratic society in Ukraine by supporting key civil initiatives. The foundation is also supported by international donors as well as by Ukrainian and foreign organizations. Throughout the period of its activity, the Foundation has offered grants to various Ukrainian NGOs, scientific research and educational institutions and publishing houses totalling more than US $95m.

Activities: The Foundation allocates approximately US $6m. to projects promoting European integration, strengthening civil society, the advocacy system and securing the principle of the rule of law in Ukraine, implementation of the judicial and penitentiary reforms, fostering freedom of speech and information, promoting the civil activism of ethnic minorities and tolerance, educational and public health reforms, the translation of important academic works, and the development of Ukrainian publishing. IRF traditionally supports public initiatives during elections such as national exit polls, monitoring and supporting independent coverage of election campaigns in the mass media.

Geographical Area of Activity: Primarily Ukraine.

Publications: Annual Report; IRF Newsletter; brochures and leaflets.

Finance: Grants awarded US $11,131 (2009).

Supervisory Board: Roman Szporluk (Chair.); **Executive Board:** Igor Burakovsky (Chair.).

Principal Staff: Exec. Dir Yevhen Bystrytsky; Finance Dir Natalia Sannikova.

Address: 04053 Kyiv, Artema St 46.

Telephone: (44) 461-97-09; **Fax:** (44) 486-76-29; **Internet:** www.irf.kiev.ua; **e-mail:** irf@irf.kiev.ua.

Victor Pinchuk Foundation

Established in 2006 to organize better Victor Pinchuk's philanthropic projects.

Activities: Aims to develop a new generation of leaders within Ukraine through strategic modernization projects.

Geographical Area of Activity: Ukraine.

Publications: Annual Report.

Finance: Annual income US $13,786,836, expenditure $13,782,004 (2009).

Board: Julia Chebotareva (Pres.); Thomas Weihe (Vice-Pres.); Valery Vakariuk (Vice-Pres.).

Principal Staff: Exec. Dir Victoria Chernyavska.

Address: 01601 Kiev, 2 Mechnikova Str.

Telephone: (44) 490-48-35; **Fax:** (44) 490-48-78; **Internet:** www.pinchukfund.org; **e-mail:** info@pinchukfund.org.

Ukrainian Women's Fund

Founded in 2000 to provide public organizations, particularly women's organizations, from Ukraine, Moldova and Belarus, with financial, informational and consultational support.

Activities: Works to facilitate the consolidation of the women's movement in Ukraine, Moldova and Belarus, to promote issues of gender and diversity, and to attract more resources to support women's initiatives by developing a culture of philanthropy in Ukraine. The Fund has made grants to projects for expanding economic opportunities for women, developing businesses run by women and reducing unemployment among women, increasing women's political participation and gender equality. Promotes information exchange between women's organizations, which can facilitate the establishment and development of networks of NGOs that work on women's and gender issues; aims to increase the activity of young women in the community life of Ukraine, preparing future female leaders, and promoting the formation of a women's movement among the younger generation.

Geographical Area of Activity: Belarus, Moldova and Ukraine.

Publications: *Directory of non-governmental organizations of Ukraine working on women's and gender issues; Basic strategies and methodologies of gender mainstreaming; Training manual for civil servants* (in Ukrainian).

Finance: Annual income US $192,743, expenditure $200,067 (2008).

Board of Directors: Natalia Karbowska (Chair.).

Principal Staff: Dir Olesya Bondar; Finance Man. Lyudmyla Bezsonova; Information Programme Man. Olena Zaytseva; Programme Asst Veronika Pedorych.

Address: 04050 Kiev, 79 Artema Str., Office 38.

Telephone: (44) 568-53-89; **Fax:** (44) 484-62-05; **Internet:** www.uwf.kiev.ua; **e-mail:** uwf@uwf.kiev.ua.

United Arab Emirates

FOUNDATIONS, TRUSTS AND NON-PROFIT ORGANIZATIONS

Emirates Foundation

Established in 2005, and funded by the United Arab Emirates government and the private sector in UAE, to improve the quality of life in the country.

Activities: Operates in the fields of education, science and technology, arts and culture, social development, the environment and public awareness.

Geographical Area of Activity: UAE.

Publications: Newsletter.

Board of Directors: HH Sheikh Abdullah bin Zayed al-Nahyan (Chair.).

Principal Staff: CEO Clare Woodcraft; Man. Dir H. E. Sheikh Sultan bin Tahnoon al-Nahyan; Finance Dir Tarek Dweik.

Address: POB 111445, Mezzanine Floor, Al Mamoura Building, 4th and 15th Sts, Abu Dhabi.

Telephone: (2) 404-2900; **Fax:** (2) 404-2901; **Internet:** www.emiratesfoundation.ae; **e-mail:** information@emiratesfoundation.ae.

Gulf Research Center

An independent research institute established in 2000 by Abdulaziz Sager to carry out politically neutral and academically sound research on the Gulf Co-operation Council countries and to disseminate information.

Activities: Carries out research on the Gulf region; promotes co-operation; issues publications. The Gulf Research Centre Foundation operates in Switzerland (q.v.).

Geographical Area of Activity: Gulf region.

Publications: Annual Report; research papers; *Araa magazine* (monthly).

Finance: Total assets 1,927,396 AED (31 Dec. 2010); annual revenue 5,227,349 AED (2010).

Board: Dr Abdulaziz Sager (Chair.).

Principal Staff: Man. Bhuvaneswari Kannan.

Address: POB 80758, 187 Oud Metha Tower, 11th Floor, 303 Sheikh Rashid Rd, Dubai.

Telephone: (4) 324-7770; **Fax:** (4) 324-7771; **Internet:** www.grc.ae; **e-mail:** info@kcorp.net.

Mohammed bin Rashid Al Maktoum Foundation

Established in 2007 by HH Sheikh Mohammed bin Rashid Al Maktoum, Vice-President and Prime Minister of the United Arab Emirates and Ruler of Dubai.

Activities: Operates in the areas of the arts and culture, business and education. Runs the Dubai International Poetry Festival and the Dubai International Children's Book Fair.

Geographical Area of Activity: UAE.

Publications: reports.

Finance: Launched with endowment of 37,000,000,000 AED (US $10,000,000,000).

Principal Staff: Chair. Sheikh Mohammed bin Rashid Al Maktoum.

Address: POB 214444, Bldg 7, Dubai Outsource Zone, Dubai.

Telephone: (14) 329-9999; **Fax:** (14) 368-7777; **Internet:** www.mbrfoundation.ae; **e-mail:** contactus@mbrfoundation.ae.

United Kingdom

FOUNDATION CENTRES AND CO-ORDINATING BODIES

Association of Charitable Foundations

Formed in September 1989, the Association is a membership organization for independent grant-making trusts and foundations in the United Kingdom, with more than 300 members varying in size from small and local grant-makers to some of the world's largest. The Association aims to support the work of charitable grant-making trusts by: seeking a constructive influence on the law and public policy affecting grant-making charities, and providing relevant information to the membership; enabling trusts and foundations to learn from each other's experience, to discuss matters of common concern, to confer with funders from other sectors, and to achieve good practice in grant-making; encouraging philanthropy and promoting the development of new grant-making foundations; seeking to improve understanding of trusts and foundations, among grant-seekers and the general public.

Activities: The Association is a membership organization, open to any charitable organization based in the United Kingdom whose principal function is grant-making, supported by income from property or another assured source (except for grants from government or other grant-making trusts). Associate membership is open to other grant-makers. The Association's activities include lobbying for public policy and legislation affecting grant-making charities; running a varied meeting programme; liaising with government departments concerned with grant-making and with other organizations of the voluntary sector; assisting individuals and corporations planning to set up new foundations; and research. Member foundations convene interest groups on areas such as the arts, education, the environment, penal affairs, children and young people, housing, and international funding. The Association also maintains contacts with a variety of relevant bodies in the USA, Europe, Australia and elsewhere, and with WINGS and the European Foundation Centre (qq.v.).

Geographical Area of Activity: United Kingdom.

Restrictions: Does not make grants, nor does it give individual advice to grant-seeking organizations or individuals.

Publications: *Trust & Foundation News* (quarterly).

Finance: Annual revenue £804,397, expenditure £822,855 (Dec. 2010).

Trustee Board: John Kingston (Chair.); Sara Llewellin (Vice-Chair.); James Brooke Turner (Treas.).

Address: Central House, 14 Upper Woburn Pl., London WC1H OAE.

Telephone: (20) 7255-4499; **Fax:** (20) 7255-4496; **Internet:** www.acf.org.uk; **e-mail:** acf@acf.org.uk.

Association of Medical Research Charities—AMRC

Formally established in 1987 to further medical research in the United Kingdom generally and in particular to advance the effectiveness of United Kingdom medical research charities.

Activities: AMRC aims to support the medical and health research charities sector's effectiveness and advance medical research by developing best practice, providing information and guidance, improving public dialogue about research and science, and influencing government. AMRC has more than 120 member charities that contribute more than £1,000m. annually to research aimed at tackling diseases such as heart disease, cancer and diabetes, as well as rarer conditions like cystic fibrosis and motor neurone disease.

Geographical Area of Activity: United Kingdom.

Restrictions: United Kingdom only. Does not fund medical research itself, or assist grant applicants with finding grants from member charities.

Finance: Annual revenue £676,593, expenditure £579,387 (March 2010).

Executive Council: Lord Willis of Knaresborough (Chair.); Simon Moore (Vice-Chair.).

Principal Staff: Chief Exec. Sharmila Nebhrajani.

Address: Charles Darwin House, 12 Roger St, London WC1N 2JU.

Telephone: (20) 7685-2620; **Fax:** (20) 7685-2621; **Internet:** www.amrc.org.uk; **e-mail:** info@amrc.org.uk.

CAF—Charities Aid Foundation

Established in its original form in 1924 as part of the National Council of Social Service; launched as an independent foundation in 1974, under a Declaration of Trust between the NCSS (now the National Council for Voluntary Organisations, q.v.) and the Trustees of the Foundation; aims to increase the resources available to the voluntary sector.

Activities: Operates the CAF Charity Account scheme for private and corporate donors, which gives them greater flexibility to donate tax-efficiently. Also manages Give As You Earn, a payroll deduction scheme. These services are used by more than 300,000 individuals and 6,500 companies. Services offered to charities include banking, investment and administration designed to meet the specific needs of charities. Publishes research findings and statistics concerning the voluntary sector. Organizes annual conferences on matters of current concern to charities and voluntary organizations. All CAF surpluses are distributed in grants, throughout the voluntary sector. CAF maintains a number of overseas offices.

Geographical Area of Activity: North and South America, Southern Africa, Australia, Europe, India and United Kingdom.

Restrictions: No grants to individuals.

Publications: *Charity Trends*; and numerous other publications on the non-profit sector.

Finance: Annual revenue £377,433,000, expenditure £307,838,000 (April 2010).

Trustees: Dominic Casserley (Chair.).

Principal Staff: Chief Exec. John Low; Finance Dir Mike Dixon.

Address: 25 Kings Hill Ave, Kings Hill, West Malling ME19 4TA.

Telephone: (3000) 123000; **Fax:** (3000) 123001; **Internet:** www.cafonline.org; **e-mail:** enquiries@cafonline.org.

Charities Advisory Trust

A registered charity, established in 1979 under the name The Charity Trading Advisory Group to render unbiased information on all aspects of charity trading.

Activities: The Trust aims to redress injustice and inequality through practical approaches. The Trust is self-financing, earning its income through self-devised activities; however, some activities may be sponsored by others; researches on all aspects of charity trading to provide authentic information on the sector; prints charity Christmas cards under the brand name Card Aid, which are sold to supporters of charity; donates around £500,000 annually; charitable donations are also made in numerous other areas including peace and reconciliation projects, medical research including diabetic prevention and control, prevention of blindness, and early detection of cancer; provides information on proposals made by governments as well as NGOs on third sector reform and income generation; had funded The Green Hotel venture in Mysore, in southern India, the proceeds of which are channelled to environmental and charitable projects in India; training courses for graduates interested in careers in international development are also hosted by the Hotel; also focuses on urban tree-planting and tackling homelessness; the Foundation's Good Gifts Catalogue is an outlet for purchasing gifts through charity donations.

Geographical Area of Activity: Mainly United Kingdom and India.

Restrictions: No grants to individuals, large fund-raising organizations or to missionary charities. Grants considered for any charitable purpose; unsolicited applications are rarely responded to.

Publications: *The Charity Shops Handbook*; *Charities, Trading and the Law*; *Trading by Charities: A Statistical Analysis*; and other publications.

Finance: Annual revenue £2,886,324, expenditure £2,684,748 (June 2009).

Trustees: Dr Cornelia Navari; Dr Carolyne Dennis; Dawn Stephanie Penso; Brij Bhushan.

Principal Staff: Dir Hilary Blume.

Address: Radius Works, Back Lane, London NW3 1HL.

Telephone: (20) 7794-9835; **Fax:** (20) 7431-3739; **Internet:** www.charitiesadvisorytrust.org.uk; **e-mail:** people@charitiesadvisorytrust.org.uk.

Community Foundation Network—CFN

Established in 1991 as the support organization for United Kingdom community foundations and formerly known as the Association of Community Trusts and Foundations.

Activities: Works to promote the concept of community foundations (as organizations that encourage philanthropy, identify local needs and make grants) to stimulate their growth and development, and provide information and practical support. All grant-making is done by individual community foundations, of which there are around 60 at various stages of development in the United Kingdom. Manages the Fair Share Trust programme, which distributes money from the Big Lottery Fund to disadvantaged areas of the United Kingdom.

Geographical Area of Activity: United Kingdom.

Restrictions: Members (community foundations) make grants to voluntary and community groups within their own areas.

Publications: *Changing the Future: Community foundations and grant-making*; *The Price of Giving: A Study of the Costs of Grant-Making*; magazine (quarterly); Annual Review; manuals; information sheets; publications list.

Finance: Total income £6,997,000; total expenditure £3,307,000 (2010).

Trustees: Matthew Bowcock (Chair.); Hamish Buchan (Treas.); Baroness Usha Prashar (Hon. Pres.).

Principal Staff: Chief Exec. Stephen Hammersley.

Address: 12 Angel Gate, 320–326 City Rd, London EC1V 2PT.

Telephone: (20) 7713-9326; **Fax:** (20) 7278-9068; **Internet:** www.communityfoundations.org.uk; **e-mail:** network@communityfoundations.org.uk.

DEC—Disasters Emergency Committee

Established in 1963 to provide support for relief sector charities in the United Kingdom dealing with the effects of major overseas disasters.

Activities: Operates through providing an accredited national forum for fund-raising and a focal point for public response, facilitating co-operation, co-ordination and communication, and ensuring that funds are used effectively and properly. The Committee has a Rapid Response Network of partners that provides free facilities as and when required, comprising television and radio, the banking sector, Royal Mail, regional and national telephone companies, and a range of organizations in the corporate sector. The aid agencies that meet the Committee's membership criteria are Actionaid, British Red Cross Society, CAFOD—Catholic Agency for Overseas Development, CARE International, Christian Aid, Concern Worldwide, Help the Aged, Islamic Relief, MERLIN—Medical Emergency Relief International, Oxfam, Save the Children, Tearfund and World Vision.

Geographical Area of Activity: United Kingdom.

Publications: *DEC Policy Handbook*; Annual Review.

Finance: Annual revenue £49,511,000, expenditure £59,070,000 (March 2011).

Trustees: Clive Jones (Chair.); Clare Thompson (Hon. Treas.).

Principal Staff: Chief Exec. Brendan Gormley.

Address: 43 Chalton St, 1st Floor, London NW1 1DU.

Telephone: (20) 7387-0200; **Internet:** www.dec.org.uk; **e-mail:** info@dec.org.uk.

Directory of Social Change

Founded in 1975; strives to be independent source of information and support of international recognition to voluntary and community sectors world-wide.

Activities: Promotes the voluntary sector by running conferences, conducting practical training courses, briefings and seminars on current issues influencing the sector, researching and publishing handbooks and reference guides, online information, CD-ROMs and journals, organizing Charityfair, encouraging voluntary groups to communicate and share information, and campaigning to nurture the interests of the voluntary sector. Also issues publications and conducts training courses on management, fund-raising, organizational and personal development, finance, law and communication.

Geographical Area of Activity: United Kingdom.

Publications: Annual Report; *A Guide to Grants for Individuals in need* (2007); *The Educational Grants Directory* (2007); books and information catalogue.

Finance: Annual revenue £2,755,547, expenditure £2,845,459 (Dec. 2010).

Trustees: Nick Seddon (Chair.).

Principal Staff: Chief Exec. Debra Allcock Tyler.

Address: 24 Stephenson Way, London NW1 2DP.

Telephone: (20) 7391-4800; **Fax:** (20) 7391-4808; **Internet:** www.dsc.org.uk; **e-mail:** info@dsc.org.uk.

The Hague Club

Established in 1971, the Club is an informal association of individuals. Its purpose is to facilitate discussion and co-operation between chief executives of important foundations in Europe and prominent persons involved with foundations.

Activities: Membership is restricted to the chief executives of selected foundations in Europe (and one foundation from Israel), and so-called Corresponding Members from different parts of the world. The members convene once a year. A Steering Committee, elected for a period of two years, conducts cay-to-day affairs. The members of the Club are the Chief Executives of: Fundação Calouste Gulbenkian; Fondation Roi Baudouin; Bernard van Leer Foundation; European Cultural Foundation; Ramón Areces Fundación; Nuffield Foundation; Finnish Cultural Foundation; Fritz-Thyssen-Stiftung; Bodossaki Foundation; Jenny and Antti Wihuri Foundation; Volkswagen-Stiftung; Leverhulme Trust; Oranje Fonds (formerly the Juliana Welzijn Fonds); Robert-Bosch-Stiftung GmbH; Novartis Foundation; Fondazione Adriano Olivetti; Bank of Sweden Tercentenary Foundation; Prince Bernhard Cultural Foundation; Compagnia di San Paolo; ZEIT-Stiftung Ebelin und Gerd Bucerius; Fundación Instituto de Empresa; Institusjonen Fitt ord; Nobel Foundation; the Wellcome Trust; Zuger Kulturstiftung Landis & Cyr (qq.v.), and the Velux Foundation. The Corresponding Members are the Chief Executives of: Consiglio Italiano per le Scienze Sociali, Italy; the Council on Foundations, USA; Fundacão Roberto Marinho, Brazil;

Japan Center for International Exchange, Japan; the Myer Foundation, Australia; the Jacobs Foundation, Switzerland; and the Van Leer Group Foundation, Netherlands.

Geographical Area of Activity: Mainly Europe.

Restrictions: Does not make grants.

Principal Staff: Pres. Sir Mark Walport, Wellcome Trust.

Address: c/o Wellcome Trust, Gibbs Bldg, 215 Euston Rd, London NW1 2BE.

International NGO Training and Research Centre— INTRAC

Established in 1991, carries out specialist training, and provides consultancy and research services to organizations executing international development and relief programmes.

Activities: Provides specially designed training, consultancy and research services to organizations involved in international development and relief. It aims to improve civil society performance by strengthening management and organizational effectiveness, and by exploring policy issues. Operates by promoting enhanced organizational and managerial capacity for NGOs and CSOs, researching global NGO trends and conducting analyses, and extends support for the advancement of the NGO sector.

Geographical Area of Activity: Central Asia, South America, countries of the former USSR, Africa, Cyprus, and Central and Eastern Europe.

Restrictions: Does not make grants.

Publications: *ONTRAC* (newsletter, 3 a year); Annual Report; notes and papers for practitioners on issues affecting NGOs in development; occasional papers; resource materials; policy briefing papers.

Finance: Annual revenue £1,613,174, expenditure £1,617,351 (March 2009).

Board of Trustees: Geof Wood (Chair.); Rosemary Preston (Vice-Chair.); Graham Nixey (Hon. Treas.).

Principal Staff: Exec. Dir Brian Pratt.

Address: Oxbridge Ct, Osney Mead, Oxford OX2 0ES.

Telephone: (1865) 201851; **Fax:** (1865) 201852; **Internet:** www.intrac.org; **e-mail:** info@intrac.org.

National Council for Voluntary Organisations— NCVO

NCVO started in 1919 as the National Council of Social Services, thanks to a £1,000 legacy from Edward Vivian Birchall who was killed during the Battle of the Somme in France in 1916 on his 32nd birthday.

Activities: NCVO is a lobbying organization and represents the views of its members, and the wider voluntary sector, to government, the European Union and other bodies. It also researches and analyses the voluntary sector. NCVO campaigns on generic issues affecting the voluntary sector, such as the role of voluntary organizations in public service delivery and the future of local government. It has several specialist teams that provide information, advice and support to others working in or with the voluntary sector. Runs networking and training events, manages and facilitates a wide range of forums and networks for staff and volunteers working in specific areas such as policy, planning, ICT, membership, publishing and public service delivery. Provides direct support to organizations through the NCVO Consultancy service. Runs a helpdesk providing information and support for NCVO members.

Geographical Area of Activity: United Kingdom.

Publications: Reports, toolkits, briefing papers and books.

Principal Staff: Chief Exec. Sir Stuart Etherington.

Address: Regent's Wharf, 8 All Saints St, London N1 9RL.

Telephone: (20) 7713-6161; **Fax:** (20) 7713-6300; **Internet:** www.ncvo-vol.org.uk; **e-mail:** ncvo@ncvo-vol.org.uk.

FOUNDATIONS, TRUSTS AND NON-PROFIT ORGANIZATIONS

Action for Children

Founded in 1869, and formerly known as NCH (National Children's Home), the charity changed its name to Action for Children in 2008. It aims to provide help for children and young people suffering as a result of poverty, disability, abuse, neglect and social exclusion.

Activities: Operates across the United Kingdom, through campaigning for policy changes to benefit children and young people. Operates in the following areas: ending child poverty and social exclusion; providing safeguards for children and young people at risk of abuse; promoting education and health; preventing youth crime and homelessness; improving the quality of life for children in care; foster care; family centres and residential homes; mediation services; and ensuring safe use of the Internet for children. Runs short-break projects, residential centres and community centres. Maintains additional offices in Wales, Scotland and Northern Ireland.

Geographical Area of Activity: United Kingdom.

Publications: *Adoption*; *Care leavers*; *Child migration*; *Children's rights*; *Children in care*; *Commissioning services*; *Education*; *Family support*; facts and statistics; complaints.

Finance: Annual revenue £200,429,000, expenditure £202,323,000 (March 2011).

Council of Trustees: Pamela Chesters (Chair.); Catherine Dugmore (Vice-Chair.).

Principal Staff: Chief Exec. Dame Clare Tickell.

Address: 3 The Boulevard, Ascot Rd, Watford WD18 8AG.

Telephone: (1923) 361500; **Internet:** www.actionforchildren.org.uk; **e-mail:** ask.us@actionforchildren.org.uk.

The Sylvia Adams Charitable Trust

Established in 1995 to make grants to charities working to alleviate poverty and disease, in particular among children, and to support charities working with the homeless, projects in developing countries and health education.

Activities: Provides start-up and time-limited funding for a wide variety of purposes and causes.

Geographical Area of Activity: Hertfordshire, United Kingdom; Africa, South Asia and South America.

Restrictions: No grants are made to individuals, projects specifically benefiting the elderly, animal charities or medical research.

Finance: Annual revenue £474,071, expenditure £625,753 (March 2008).

Trustees: Jerry Golland (Chair.).

Principal Staff: Dir Jane Young.

Address: Sylvia Adams House, 24 The Common, Hatfield AL10 0NB.

Telephone: (1707) 259259; **Fax:** (1707) 259268; **Internet:** www.sylvia-adams.org.uk; **e-mail:** info@sylvia-adams.org.uk.

Afghanaid

Established in 1981 to provide humanitarian relief to Afghans in hardship and distress, and to assist with the rehabilitation and development of Afghanistan.

Activities: Operates in Afghanistan through major infrastructure work such as building and maintaining roads and bridges; macro-irrigation structures; and sustainable community development projects, including agriculture, microfinance, income generation, animal health, health and basic literacy education and skills training for women.

Geographical Area of Activity: Afghanistan.

Restrictions: Currently funding its own projects only.

Publications: Annual Report; regular newsletters.

Finance: Annual revenue £3,420,089, expenditure £3,037,917 (March 2010).

Trustees: David Page (Chair.); Elizabeth Winter (Vice-Chair.); Gemma Parrott (Treas.).

Principal Staff: Man. Dir Farhana Faruqi Stocker.

Address: Development House, 56–64 Leonard St, London, EC2A 4LT.

Telephone: (20) 7065 0825; **Internet:** www.afghanaid.org.uk; **e-mail:** info@afghanaid.org.uk.

Africa Educational Trust

Founded in 1958 by Rev. Michael Scott to support education in and outside Africa, for persons who, in the opinion of the trustees, are wholly or partly of African descent, and to advise on educational immigration and welfare provisions for African students.

Activities: Operates in Africa in the field of education, especially non-formal education and skills training; primary and secondary education; and development of local NGOs. In the United Kingdom, the organization supports African community organizations through offering training, and offers scholarships and grants to African students in the United Kingdom. Maintains a regional office in Kenya.

Geographical Area of Activity: Africa, United Kingdom and Ireland.

Publications: Annual Report; *The Situation of AET Sponsored Namibians After their Return Home.*

Finance: Net assets £1,480,741 (Aug. 2007); annual revenue £2,369,837, expenditure £1,868,427 (2007).

Trustees: Dr Christopher Beer (Chair.); Sally Healy (Vice-Chair.); Prof. Richard Hodder-Williams (Treas.).

Principal Staff: Dir Dr Michael Brophy; Deputy Dir Jill Landymore.

Address: 18 Hand Ct, London WC1V 6JF.

Telephone: (20) 7831-3283; **Fax:** (20) 7242-3265; **Internet:** www.africaeducationaltrust.org; **e-mail:** info@africaeducationaltrust.org.

Africa Foundation (UK)

Founded in 1992 to facilitate the empowerment and development of individuals, living in, or adjacent to, protected areas in Africa, by forging unique partnerships between conservation initiatives and local communities. Formerly known as the Rural Investment Trust, an independent arm of CC Africa, a South Africa-based safari company,.

Activities: Supports projects in the fields of education, health care and small business development. In the field of education, support includes building classrooms, pre-schools, laboratories and media centres, and educational bursaries to community leaders; health-care activities include building medical clinics, AIDS prevention programmes, hosting educational workshops and providing family planning; and in the area of small business development, funding is given to promising entrepreneurs, supporting community centres and small businesses, and encouraging eco-tourism and community development initiatives. Conservation lessons are provided for local children to further knowledge of the environment and the value of conservation to the next generation. Projects are currently run in Kenya, Tanzania, Zanzibar, Zimbabwe, Namibia and Botswana. Also maintains an office in the USA.

Geographical Area of Activity: Southern and East Africa.

Board of Trustees: Robin James (Chair.).

Principal Staff: Chief Exec. Susannah Friend.

Address: c/o Sutton Pl. (UK) Ltd, 6 Chesterfield Gardens, London W1J 5BQ.

Telephone: (7884) 258616; **Internet:** www.africafoundation.org; **e-mail:** mike@africafoundation.org; susannah@africafoundation.org.

Aga Khan Foundation (UK)—AKF

Established in 1967 by HH the Aga Khan to promote social development in developing countries of Asia and Africa by funding health, education and rural development programmes, without regard to race, religion or background. An affiliate of the Aga Khan Foundation in Switzerland (q.v.).

Activities: Channels funds to support organizations and programmes principally in less-developed countries in Asia and Africa, and also in Canada, Portugal, Tajikistan, Switzerland, the United Kingdom and the USA. The Foundation is involved in conservation and the environment, education, medicine and health, and social welfare, through grants to institutions, promoting community self-help projects, scholarships and fellowships, conferences and publications. It operates programmes to aid child development and education, especially by improving the quality of formal education and early childhood education; family health and nutrition through community-orientated health development; and rural development through income-generation and the management of renewable resources. Promotes skills development, training and technical exchanges internationally.

Geographical Area of Activity: International.

Restrictions: The Foundation does not solicit applications for funding, nor will it respond positively to any such requests.

Publications: Project briefings; information sheets on Foundation activities; and evaluation reports on Foundation-supported projects; Annual Report.

Finance: Annual revenue £14,413,026, expenditure £11,758,512 (2007).

Board of Directors: HH Prince Karim Aga Khan (Founder and Chair.).

Principal Staff: Chief Exec. Aly-Raza Nazerali.

Address: 210 Euston Rd, London NW1 2DA.

Telephone: (20) 7383-9090; **Fax:** (20) 7589-0641; **Internet:** www.akdn.org/akf; **e-mail:** frontoffice@akdn.org.

Al Fayed Charitable Foundation

Established in 1987 for general charitable purposes.

Activities: Operates nationally in the fields of medicine, health and social welfare. Awards grants to children's hospitals and hospices.

Geographical Area of Activity: United Kingdom.

Publications: Press releases.

Trustees: Mohamed Al Fayed.

Principal Staff: Susie Mathis.

Address: c/o Susie Mathis, 60 Park Lane, London W1K 1QE.

Telephone: (20) 7225-6673; **Fax:** (20) 7225-6872; **Internet:** www.alfayed.com; **e-mail:** writetome@alfayed.com.

The Al-Khoei Benevolent Foundation

Established in August 1989; aims to advance the Islamic religion.

Activities: Operates schools and a mosque, and organizes religious and social meetings.

Geographical Area of Activity: USA, South-East Asia, Europe.

Publications: *Dialogue* (in English); *Al-Ghadeer* (in Arabic).

Finance: Gross income £1,290,12, expenditure £1,304,260 (Aug. 2006).

Trustees: Jawad Habib Ridha; Kadam Abdul Hosain Mohamad; Mohsin Ali Najafi; Sadigheh Khoei; Seyed Saheb Khoei; Yusuf Ali Nafsi.

Principal Staff: Finance Dir M. Mousavi; Public Relations Dir Y. A. Al-Khoei; Seyed Saheb Khoei.

Address: Stone Hall, Chevening Rd, London NW6 6TN.

Telephone: (20) 7372-4049; **Fax:** (20) 7372-0694; **Internet:** www.al-khoei.org; **e-mail:** comments@al-khoei.org.

Alchemy Foundation

Founded as the Starlight Foundation in 1985 by Richard and Annabel Stilgoe to support mental and physical health care of the elderly and children, and to assist in famine relief.

Activities: Operates world-wide in the fields of aid and development, arts and humanities, education, medicine and health, and social welfare. It promotes self-conducted programmes and aims in particular to aid people (especially children) suffering from mental or physical illness or disability, and people suffering from the effects of famine.

Geographical Area of Activity: International.

Restrictions: No grants to individuals.

Finance: Annual revenue £434,786, expenditure £256,356 (2009).

Trustees: Alexander Armitage; Andrew Murison; Annabel Stilgoe; Rev. Donald Reeves; Esther Rantzen; Holly Stilgoe; Jack Stilgoe; Dr Jemima Stilgoe; Joeseph Stilgoe; Richard Stilgoe; Rufus Stilgoe.

Principal Staff: Founder and Chair. Richard Stilgoe; Correspondent Annabel Stilgoe.

Address: Trevereux Manor, Limpsfield Chart, Oxted RH8 0TL.

Telephone: (1883) 730600; **Fax:** (1883) 730800.

All Saints Educational Trust

Founded in 1979 to promote the training of teachers and research and development in education.

Activities: The Trust aims to promote education, principally in schools—both maintained and independent—through: making awards to those undertaking professional teacher training and to teachers who wish to gain further qualifications; providing resources to encourage innovative classroom activity, libraries and other pedagogical initiatives; promoting research, particularly in home economics and religious education.

Geographical Area of Activity: Europe and all other countries.

Restrictions: Courses must lead to degrees awarded by United Kingdom institutions. Applications from citizens of non-United Kingdom/European Union countries must be for one year, full-time Master's programmes only.

Publications: Annual Report.

Finance: Net assets £9,739,229 (June 2011); annual revenue £382,155 expenditure £459,902 (June 2011).

Trustees: K. G. Riglin (Chair.); D. J. Trillo (Vice-Chair.).

Principal Staff: Clerk S. P. Harrow.

Address: Suite 8C, First Floor, VSC Charity Centre, Royal London House, 22–25 Finsbury Sq., London EC2A 1DX.

Telephone: (20) 7920-6465; **Internet:** www.aset.org.uk; **e-mail:** aset@aset.org.uk.

Amnesty International

Founded in 1961 by Peter Benenson and others to secure throughout the world the provisions of the UN Universal Declaration of Human Rights (1948) and other internationally recognized human rights instruments.

Activities: Operates internationally in the field of human rights. The organization works against the imprisonment, detention or other physical restrictions imposed on any person by reason of their political, religious or conscientiously held beliefs or by reason of their ethnic origin, gender, colour, language, national or social origin, economic status, birth or other status, provided that he or she has not used or advocated violence ('prisoners of conscience'), as well as working against the detention of any political prisoner without fair trial or any trial procedures that do not conform to internationally recognized norms; the death penalty, and the torture or other cruel, inhuman or degrading treatment or punishment of prisoners, whether or not they have used or advocated violence; and the extrajudicial execution of persons whether or not detained, and 'disappearances', whether or not the persons affected have used or advocated violence. Also seeks to co-operate with other not-for-profit organizations, the UN and regional inter-governmental organizations; ensure control of international military, security and police relations to prevent human rights abuses; and organizes human rights education and awareness-raising programmes. Amnesty International has more than 50 national sections and in excess of 2,800,000 members and subscribers in more than 150 countries and territories world-wide.

Geographical Area of Activity: International.

Publications: *Amnesty International Report* (annually); *The Wire* (2 a month); annual reports; thematic and regional reports on human rights issues.

Finance: Annual revenue £50,968,000, expenditure £43,606,000 (2011).

International Executive Committee: Pietro Antonioli (Chair.); Guadelupe Rivas (Vice-Chair.); Bernard Sintobin (Treas.).

Principal Staff: Sec.-Gen. Salil Shetty.

Address: International Secretariat, Peter Benenson House, 1 Easton St, London WC1X 0DW.

Telephone: (20) 7413-5500; **Fax:** (20) 7956-1157; **Internet:** www.amnesty.org; **e-mail:** amnestyis@amnesty.org.

Ancient India and Iran Trust

Established in July 1978 by Prof. Sir Harold Bailey, Prof. Joan van Lohuizen, Dr Raymond Allchin and Dr Bridget Allchin.

Activities: Promotes public and academic interest in the early cultures and languages of the Indo-Iranian world, through maintaining a library of more than 25,000 volumes open to the public, running courses and lectures, and organizing regular symposia and seminars on related subjects.

Geographical Area of Activity: Central and South Asia.

Restrictions: Small research grants only to researchers in the regions covered, when funds permit.

Publications: *The Crossroads of Asia: Transformation in Image and Symbol; Living Traditions: Studies in the Ethnoarchaeology of South Asia; Ghandharan Art in Context: East-West Exchanges at the Crossroads of Asia;* paper and online newsletter, INDIRAN.

Finance: Funded by interest from capital endowment, donations and grants from foundations; annual revenue £85,000, expenditure £74,600 (2008).

Trustees: Nicholas Sims-Williams (Chair.); Almut Hintze (Treas.); Christine van Ruymbeke (Sec.); Ursula Sims Williams (Hon. Librarian); Bridget Allchin (Chair. Emer.); Sir Nicholas Barrington; Mr T. Richard Blurton; Samuel Lieu; Neil Kreitman; Michael Petraglia; Cameron Petrie.

Principal Staff: Admin. Anna Collar; Custodian James Cormick; Asst Librarian Jose John.

Address: 23 Brooklands Ave, Cambridge CB2 8BG.

Telephone: (1223) 356841; **Fax:** (1223) 361125; **Internet:** www.indiran.org; indiairantrust.wordpress.com; **e-mail:** info@indiran.org.

Andrews Charitable Trust

Founded by C. Jackson-Cole in 1965 to alleviate suffering and to advance Christianity. Formerly known as the Phyllis Trust and later as World in Need. It is the majority shareholder of Andrews & Partners estate agency business, which was also set up by Jackson-Cole and which now has 100% charitable ownership. The minority shares are held by ACT's sister trusts, Christian Initiative Trust and Christian Book Promotion Trust.

Activities: ACT supports initiatives that are innovative, replicable and sustainable. The Trust looks for ideas that will make a significant difference on the world. Works with founders of new organizations or those organizations wanting to make a step change in how they deliver services. Supports innovation in partnership and collaboration and how resources can be used most effectively to address real needs. Provides pro-bono support in addition to grant funding and looks for applicants who are receptive to this approach.

Geographical Area of Activity: United Kingdom and international.

Restrictions: Supports the above activities only.

Finance: Total income £169,107, expenditure £434,101 (Dec. 2010).

Trustees: Andrew Radford (Chair.), Helen Battrick, Chris Chapman, Nicholas Colloff, Paul Heal, Liz Hughes, Tony Jackson, Alastair Page, Michael Robson, David Saint, David Westgate, Nick Wright (Treas.).

Principal Staff: Dir Siân Edwards.

Address: The Clockhouse, Bath Hill, Keynsham, Bristol BS31 1HL.

Telephone: (117) 9461834; **Internet:** www .andrewscharitabletrust.org.uk; **e-mail:** info@ andrewscharitabletrust.org.uk.

Anti-Slavery International

Founded in 1839 (known as the Anti-Slavery Society for the Protection of Human Rights until 1990); aims to eradicate slavery and forced labour in all their forms.

Activities: The organization seeks to attain its aims through: research and the publication of information about all forms of slavery throughout the world; generating greater awareness of such abuses; campaigning nationally and internationally; and working with local partners to help the victims of human rights injustices. The organization has consultative status with the UN Economic and Social Council (ECOSOC), and has members world-wide. Launched the annual Anti-Slavery Award in 1991.

Geographical Area of Activity: International.

Restrictions: Does not make grants.

Publications: *Anti-Slavery Reporter* (quarterly newsletter); various other publications on issues including bonded, forced and child labour; Annual Report and Accounts.

Finance: Sources of finance include trusts and foundations, the public, European Union and government funding, etc.; total income £2,175,571, expenditure £1,901,360 (2009).

Trustees: Andrew Clark (Chair.).

Principal Staff: Dir Aidan McQuade.

Address: Thomas Clarkson House, The Stableyard, Broomgrove Rd, London SW9 9TL.

Telephone: (20) 7501-8920; **Fax:** (20) 7738-4110; **Internet:** www.antislavery.org; **e-mail:** info@antislavery.org.

The Arab-British Chamber Charitable Foundation

Founded in 1980 by the Joint Arab British Chamber of Commerce for the advancement of science and education for needy young people and adults from Arab states, with particular emphasis on fields of relevance to Arab countries, for example industry, commerce, technology and the professions.

Activities: Awards scholarships and makes grants to Arab students for postgraduate study in the United Kingdom; makes donations to charities working on health and education projects in the Arab world.

Geographical Area of Activity: United Kingdom and the Middle East.

Finance: Total revenue £58,310 (2009).

Trustees: Baroness Symons of Vernham Dean (Chair.).

Principal Staff: Chief Exec. and Sec.-Gen. Dr Afnan Al-Shuaiby.

Address: Longmead, Benhall Green, Benhall, Saxmundham IP17 1HU.

Telephone: (1728) 603359; **Fax:** (1728) 603359; **Internet:** www .abcc.org.uk; **e-mail:** abccf@abcc.org.uk.

ARK—Absolute Return for Kids

Established as an international charity in 2002 to transform the lives of children.

Activities: Manages programmes that are efficient, accountable and that deliver measurable social returns in the following areas: HIV/AIDS (Southern Africa), helping prevent children from being orphaned or dying from AIDS; Education (United Kingdom and India), currently has a network of eight academy schools and aims to open a futher four by 2012, also runs programmes to develop leadership in UK inner-city schools and is piloting a programme to improve the educational opportunities of deprived children; and Children in Care (Romania) reforming child-care systems, and assisting in the closure of institutions and the placement of children with families or small group homes.

Geographical Area of Activity: Southern Africa, United Kingdom, India, Eastern Europe.

Publications: Annual Report.

Finance: Annual revenue £23,885,000, expenditure £19,120,000 (Aug. 2009).

Board of Trustees: Ian Wace (Chair.).

Principal Staff: CEO Nick Jenkins; Man. Dir Charles Abani.

Address: 65 Kingsway, London WC2B 6TD.

Telephone: (20) 3116-0700; **Fax:** (20) 7831-9469; **Internet:** www.arkonline.org; www.arkschools.org; **e-mail:** info@ arkonline.org.

Art Fund—National Art Collections Fund

Founded in 1903 to foster the visual arts and to help public museums, galleries and historic houses to acquire works of art.

Activities: Operates in the United Kingdom in the arts, through grants or bequests to regional and national institutions for the acquisition of works of art of national and historical importance. Campaigns on behalf of museums and galleries, particularly on issues such as free admission to national collections and funding for acquisitions, as well as promoting art to a wider audience.

Geographical Area of Activity: United Kingdom.

Publications: Annual Report and Accounts; *Review* (annually); *Art Quarterly*.

Finance: Annual revenue £10,036,000, expenditure £12,198,000 (Dec. 2010).

Board of Trustees: David Verey (Chair.); Paul Zuckerman (Treas.).

Principal Staff: Dir Dr Stephen Deuchar.

Address: Millais House, 7 Cromwell Pl., London SW7 2JN.

Telephone: (20) 7225-4800; **Fax:** (20) 7225-4848; **Internet:** www.artfund.org; **e-mail:** info@artfund.org.

Arthritis Research UK

Founded in 1936 as the Empire Rheumatism Council to promote medical research into the cause, treatment and cure of arthritis and musculoskeletal conditions. Previously known as Arthritis Research Campaign.

Activities: A leading authority on arthritis in the United Kingdom, which conducts scientific and medical research into all types of arthritis and musculoskeletal conditions. It is committed to funding high-quality research into the cause, treatment and cure of arthritis.

Geographical Area of Activity: United Kingdom.

Publications: Range of publications and resources aimed at general practitioners, hospital doctors, allied health professionals and medical students; over 90 patient information booklets on arthritis and musculoskeletal conditions; quarterly research magazine.

Finance: Annual revenue £37,519,000, expenditure £31,947,000 (2009).

Board of Trustees: Charles Maisey (Chair.).

Principal Staff: CEO Liam O'Toole.

Address: Copeman House, St Mary's Gate, Chesterfield, Derbyshire S41 7TD.

Telephone: (300) 790-0400; **Fax:** (300) 790-0401; **Internet:** www.arthritisresearchuk.org; **e-mail:** enquiries@ arthritisresearchuk.org.

Arts Council England

The national development agency for the arts in England, distributing public money from government and the national lottery.

Activities: Operates in England in the area of the arts. Distributes both National Lottery and Government funds to artists and arts organizations (see also Lottery Arts Fund for England, Scotland, Wales and Northern Ireland). Funding programmes seek to support the highest artistic achievements and to make these available to as many people as possible; to encourage new work and new audiences; to bring challenging art to all sectors of the community; and to celebrate the diversity of cultures contributing to artistic life in England. Currently working on the Creative Partnerships initiative, which will develop long-term partnerships between schools, cultural and creative organizations and artists; Decibel, a project funding culturally diverse projects and Artsmark, a national arts award for schools.

Geographical Area of Activity: England.

Publications: *Audience Development, and Resource Development*; Annual Review; publications on different arts activities; information sheets; newsletters.

Finance: Receives a grant-in-aid from the British Government and a portion of the National Lottery money for the arts; budget for arts expenditure £1,300,000,000 (2008–11).

National Council: Dame Liz Forgan (Chair.).

Principal Staff: Chief Exec. Alan Davey.

Address: 14 Great Peter St, London SW1P 3NQ.

Telephone: (845) 300-6200; **Fax:** (161) 934-4426; **Internet:** www.artscouncil.org.uk; **e-mail:** emma.russell@artscouncil.org.uk.

Ashden Charitable Trust

Established in 1990 for general charitable purposes. One of the Sainsbury Family Charitable Trusts, which share a common administration.

Activities: Operates the following projects: conservation and the environment overseas; environmental projects in the United Kingdom; sustainable regeneration; People at Risk; community arts; and Social Investment Fund. Offers small grants to organizations. Co-funds the Ashden Awards for sustainable energy, in association with other Sainsbury Family Charitable Trusts.

Geographical Area of Activity: United Kingdom, Africa, Asia and developing countries.

Restrictions: No grants are made to individuals.

Publications: Annual Report; *The Ashden Directory*; reports.

Finance: Annual revenue £2,400,546, expenditure £1,552,507 (2009) Total assets £26,728,330 2010).

Trustees: S. Butler-Sloss; R. Butler-Sloss; J. S. Portrait.

Principal Staff: Dir Alan Bookbinder.

Address: Allington House, 1st Floor, 150 Victoria St, London SW1E 5AE.

Telephone: (20) 7410-0330; **Internet:** www.ashdentrust.org.uk; **e-mail:** ashdentrust@sfct.org.uk.

Association for International Cancer Research—AICR

AICR was founded in 1979 as a branch of a US charity. It is now an independent United Kingdom-registered charity. In 1984 AICR moved from London to St Andrews.

Activities: AICR aims to save lives by investing in basic and translational research to improve the prevention, diagnosis and treatment of the disease. AICR invites applications for funding twice a year, in April and October. AICR funds 222 projects in 24 countries around the world.

Geographical Area of Activity: International.

Publications: Newsletters; leaflets; Annual Report.

Finance: Financed by donations, covenants, legacies, competitions and raffles. Annual revenue £17,486,571, expenditure £10,969,878 (Sept. 2010).

Board of Directors: J. C. Murray (Chair.).

Principal Staff: Chief Exec. Norman Barrett.

Address: Madras House, St Andrews, Fife KY16 9EH.

Telephone: (1334) 477910; **Fax:** (1334) 478667; **Internet:** www.aicr.org.uk; **e-mail:** enquiries@aicr.org.uk.

Asthma UK

In 1927 the Asthma Research Council (ARC) was founded to research into the 'cause and cure of asthma from a firm scientific foundation'. By 1972 the Friends of Asthma Research Council was set up to raise funds for the ARC. In 1989 the two merged to form the National Asthma Campaign. In May 2004 the name was changed to Asthma UK.

Activities: Funds scientific research; operates the Asthma UK Adviceline for people with asthma; runs activity holidays for children and produces publications for health professionals and people with asthma. Maintains offices in London, Edinburgh, Cardiff and Belfast.

Geographical Area of Activity: United Kingdom.

Publications: Annual Report; information booklets; posters; factsheets; and other publications.

Finance: Annual revenue £8,321,000, expenditure £8,411,000 (2009/10).

Trustees: Dr Rob Wilson (Chair.).

Principal Staff: Chief Exec. Neil Churchill.

Address: Summit House, 70 Wilson St, London EC2A 2DB.

Telephone: (20) 7786-4900; **Fax:** (20) 7256-6075; **Internet:** www.asthma.org.uk; **e-mail:** info@asthma.org.uk.

The Andrew Balint Charitable Trust

Founded in 1961 to provide funds for general charitable purposes.

Activities: The Trust awards grants to recognized charities, nationally and internationally, aiming to assist them with achieving their respective objectives. Linked to The George Balint Charitable Trust, The Paul Charitable Trust and The Trust for Former Employees of Balint Companies, which are jointly administered.

Geographical Area of Activity: International.

Restrictions: No grants are made to individuals.

Finance: Annual revenue £51,113, expenditure £71,108 (April 2010).

Trustees: Agnes Balint; Dr G. G. Balint-Kurti; Roy David Balint-Kurti; Daniel Balint-Kurti.

Principal Staff: Contact David Kramer.

Address: Enterprise House, 21 Buckle St, London E1 8NN.

Telephone: (20) 7309-3800.

Baring Foundation

The Baring Foundation was set up in 1969 to give money to charities and voluntary organizations pursing charitable purposes. In 41 years the Foundation has given almost £100m. in grants.

Activities: The Foundation has three core grant programmes: the Joint International Development Programme is run in collaboration with the John Ellerman Foundation, and aims to improve the effectiveness of non-govenmental organizations and community-based organizations in Sub-Saharan Africa, and to address problems arising from long-term forced migration. The Arts Programme theme is organizational development funding for arts organizations in the United Kingdom already producing and presenting arts made by older people. The Strengthening the Voluntary Sector Programme will not be open to applications in 2011, but it will continue to work on the theme of independence in the voluntary sector. The Foundation is working on three special initiatives: African

Diaspora-African Development, Climate Change and the Third Sector and Interculturality.

Geographical Area of Activity: United Kingdom and Sub-Saharan Africa.

Restrictions: No grants to individuals. Applicant organizations must be charities or voluntary sector not-for-profit organizations registered in the United Kingdom.

Publications: *Report on Activities* (annual); *Housing Associations in England and the Future of the Voluntary Sector*, by Andrew Purkis; *An Unexamined Truth*, by Matthew Smerdon.

Finance: Total grant budget £2,100,000 (2012).

Trustees: Amanda Jordan (Chair.).

Principal Staff: Dir David Cutler; Deputy Dir Matthew Smerdon.

Address: 60 London Wall, London EC2M 5TQ.

Telephone: (20) 7767-1348; **Fax:** (20) 7767-7121; **Internet:** www.baringfoundation.org.uk; **e-mail:** baring.foundation@ uk.ing.com.

Barnardo's

Established in 1867 to help children, young people and their families in the United Kingdom.

Activities: Provides guidance, support and care to young people and their families, including counselling for abused children, support for families with a disabled child, family centres, fostering and adoption schemes, help for homeless young people, schools and shared houses for those leaving care, support for children and families with HIV and AIDS, and research and lobbying activities. Maintains regional offices throughout the United Kingdom and international offices in Australia, Ireland and New Zealand.

Geographical Area of Activity: United Kingdom.

Publications: *What Works?* (series); *Counting the Cost of Child Poverty*; *Joined-Up Youth Research, Policy and Practice: A New Agenda for Change?*; and other publications.

Finance: Financed through Barnardo's shops, fund-raising, trusts and foundations, campaigns, etc. Total income £201,438,000, expenditure £203,784,000 (2011).

Trustees: Hilary A. Keenlyside (Chair.); Judy Clemets (Vice-Chair.); Ian Marshall (Hon. Treas.).

Principal Staff: Chief Exec. Anne Marie Carrie.

Address: Tanners Lane, Barkingside, Ilford IG6 1QG.

Telephone: (20) 8550-8822; **Fax:** (20) 8551-6870; **Internet:** www.barnardos.org.uk; **e-mail:** info@barnardos.org.uk.

The Batchworth Trust

Founded in 1965 for general charitable purposes world-wide.

Activities: Operates in the fields of the environment, education, medicine and health, and social welfare. Makes donations to institutions world-wide that are recognized as exclusively charitable.

Geographical Area of Activity: International, with an emphasis on England and Wales, Africa and Asia.

Restrictions: Unsolicited applications are not considered.

Finance: Annual revenue £267,000, expenditure £369,000 (April 2011).

Trustees: Lockwell Trustees Ltd.

Principal Staff: Admin. Exec. M. Neve.

Address: c/o CLB Gatwick LLP, Imperial Buildings, 68 Victoria Rd, Horley, Surrey RH6 7PZ.

Telephone: (1293) 776411; **Fax:** (1293) 820161; **e-mail:** mrn@ clbgatwick.co.uk.

BBC Children in Need Appeal

Charity established in 1980 (in its present form) by the BBC (British Broadcasting Corporation) to make a positive difference to the lives of disadvantaged children.

Activities: Operates nationally by distributing grants to registered charities and voluntary and community groups for projects that will improve the lives of children who are disadvantaged, including those experiencing poverty or deprivation, suffering from illness, abuse or neglect, with mental or physical disabilities, and children with behavioural and psychological disorders.

Geographical Area of Activity: United Kingdom.

Restrictions: No grants are made to individuals or businesses.

Publications: Annual Report; newsletters.

Finance: BBC Children in Need Appeal revenue approx. £40,000,000 (2010).

Trustees: Stevie Spring (Chair.).

Principal Staff: Chief Exec. David Ramsden.

Address: POB 1000, London W12 7WJ.

Telephone: (20) 8576-7788; **Internet:** www.bbc.co.uk/pudsey; **e-mail:** pudsey@bbc.co.uk.

BBC World Service Trust

Founded in November 1992 by the BBC (British Broadcasting Corporation) as the BBC Marshall Plan of the Mind Trust, present name since 1999. BBC Service Trust uses media to enable people in the developing world to have access to life-changing information that can help them survive, shape their lives and thrive.

Activities: The Trust operates in developing countries in the following principal areas: Education, through radio broadcasts and tutorials; Emergency Response, through broadcasting information; the Environment in partnership with local NGOs to offer information; Governance and Human Rights; Health; and Livelihoods. Works in partnerships with local NGOs and broadcasters.

Geographical Area of Activity: Africa, Asia, Eastern Europe and the Middle East.

Publications: Newsletter; Annual Report; fact sheets and workbooks to accompany programmes broadcast.

Finance: Annual revenue £28,200,000, expenditure £27,100,000 (March 2010).

Trustees: Peter Horrocks (Chair.).

Principal Staff: Exec. Dir Caroline Nursey.

Address: Room 301 NE, POB 76, Bush House, Strand, London WC2B 4PH.

Telephone: (20) 7557-2462; **Fax:** (20) 7379-1622; **Internet:** www.bbcworldservicetrust.org; **e-mail:** ws.trust@bbc.co.uk.

Beaverbrook Foundation

Founded in 1954 by Lord Beaverbrook for general charitable purposes.

Activities: Provides funds to charities.

Geographical Area of Activity: United Kingdom and Canada (New Brunswick and Nova Scotia).

Restrictions: Grants are not made to individuals.

Finance: Annual revenue £155,248, expenditure £3,328,908 (Sept. 2007).

Trustees: John Kidd; Lady Beaverbrook; Lady Violet Aitken; Hon. Laura Levi; Lord Maxwell Beaverbrook; Hon. Maxwell Aitken.

Principal Staff: CEO J. S. Ford.

Address: 11–12 Dover St, London W1S 4LJ.

Telephone: 020 7042 9435; **Internet:** www .beaverbrookfoundation.org; **e-mail:** jane@ beaverbrookfoundation.org.

Beit Trust

Founded in 1906 by Alfred Beit for charitable purposes of an educational or public nature that will best promote the welfare of the inhabitants of Zimbabwe, Zambia and Malawi.

Activities: Works in Zimbabwe, Zambia and Malawi in the fields of education and health and welfare, usually in the form of building grants. Operates a secondary school bursary scheme and also a Postgraduate Scholarships scheme for students from Zimbabwe, Zambia and Malawi at universities in the United Kingdom, Ireland and South Africa. The Beit Memorial Fellowships for Medical Research transferred all its undertakings to the Wellcome Trust on 1 October 2009.

Geographical Area of Activity: Malawi, Zambia and Zimbabwe.

Restrictions: Grants are not made to undergraduates.

Publications: Annual Report.

Finance: Annual revenue £2,819,366, expenditure £2,374,140 (2008).

Trustees: Sir Alan Munro (Chair.).

Principal Staff: Sec. Maj.-Gen. A. I. Ramsay; Rep. T. M. Johnson.

Address: Beit House, Grove Rd, Woking, Surrey GU21 5JB.

Telephone: (1483) 772575; **Fax:** (1483) 725833; **Internet:** www.beittrust.org.uk; **e-mail:** sec@beittrust.org.uk.

Benesco Charity Limited

Founded in 1970 to advance medical research and education.

Activities: Provides funds to registered charities to support medical research, education and welfare.

Geographical Area of Activity: World-wide.

Restrictions: No grants to individuals; grants made to United Kingdom-based charities only.

Publications: Annual Report.

Finance: Annual revenue £8,464,000, expenditure £8,107,000 (April 2011).

Trustees: Jonathan Ragol-Levy.

Principal Staff: Correspondent Cynthia Margaret Crawford.

Address: Russell Sq. House, 10–12 Russell Sq., London WC1B 5LF.

BibleLands

Founded in 1854 as the Turkish Missions Aid Society; also formerly known as the Bible Lands Society. Its original aim was to support existing Christian missions in the lands of the Bible; currently it supports local Christians serving the needs of the poor, vulnerable and disadvantaged in the lands of the Bible.

Activities: BibleLands supports overseas partners who provide health, education and community development programmes for the most disadvantaged people in the lands of the Bible, regardless of their faith or nationality. The organization aims to increase the working capacity and resources of local Christian partners so that they are able to respond strategically and effectively to the needs in the region.

Geographical Area of Activity: Egypt, Lebanon and Israel and Palestinian Autonomous Areas.

Restrictions: No grants are made to individuals.

Publications: *The Star in the East* (3 a year); *Life Lines*; *The Child Sponsor*; *The Care Sharer*; Annual Review.

Finance: Annual revenue £3,500,000, expenditure £3,700,000 (2009).

Council of Trustees: Hugh Bradley (Chair.); Rev. Brian Jolly (Vice-Chair.); Vicky Smith (Treas.).

Principal Staff: CEO Jeremy Moodey.

Address: 24 London Rd West, Amersham, Buckinghamshire HP7 0EZ.

Telephone: (1494) 897950; **Fax:** (1494) 897951; **Internet:** www.biblelands.org.uk; **e-mail:** info@biblelands.org.uk.

Big Lottery Fund

Founded in 1994, as the National Lottery Charities Board, to help meet the needs of the most disadvantaged in society and improve the quality of life of the community. Name changed in April 2001 to the Community Fund. In June 2004 the Fund merged with the New Opportunities Fund to become the Big Lottery Fund.

Activities: Operates nationally and internationally through capital grants and revenue funding. The principal grants programmes are: main grants (funding projects that help people or communities overcome problems that stop them from playing a full part in economic, social and community activities); grants for projects up to £60,000; international grants (for NGOs based in the United Kingdom to work in collaboration with NGOs abroad in the area of development education and addressing the causes of poverty and inequality); research grants (for social and medical research, in particular in the areas of young and old people, minority ethnic groups and people with learning disabilities); small grants; and Awards for All (for small groups involved in areas such as sports, heritage and the arts, and community and voluntary activities).

Geographical Area of Activity: International.

Restrictions: Only funds United Kingdom-based charities and voluntary groups.

Publications: Magazine *Big Times;* regional newsletters; corporate reports.

Finance: Revenue comes from the Board's share of 28% of the profits derived from the United Kingdom's National Lottery; total estimated budget £2,300,000,000 (2006–09).

Board: Peter Ainsworth (Chair.); Anna Southall (Vice-Chair.); Nat Sloane (England Chair.); Frank Hewitt (Northern Ireland Chair.); Maureen McGinn (Scotland Chair.); Sir Adrian Webb (Wales Chair.).

Principal Staff: Chief Exec. Peter Wanless.

Address: 1 Plough Pl., London EC4A 1DE.

Telephone: (20) 7211-1800; **Fax:** (20) 7211-1750; **Internet:** www.biglotteryfund.org.uk; **e-mail:** general.enquiries@biglotteryfund.org.uk.

Biotechnology and Biological Sciences Research Council—BBSRC

The BBSRC was established in 1994, one of the organizations formed by the splitting up of the Science and Engineering Research Council (SERC).

Activities: BBSRC is the United Kingdom funding agency for research in the life sciences. Sponsored by Government, BBSRC annually invests around £470m. in a wide range of research that makes a significant contribution to the quality of life for United Kingdom citizens and supports a number of important industrial stakeholders including the agriculture, food, chemical, health care and pharmaceutical sectors. BBSRC carries out its mission by funding internationally competitive research, providing training in the biosciences, fostering opportunities for knowledge transfer and innovation, and promoting interaction with the public and other stakeholders on issues of scientific interest in universities, centres and institutes. The Babraham Institute, Institute for Animal Health, Institute of Food Research, John Innes Centre and Rothamsted Research are Institutes of BBSRC. The Institutes conduct long-term, mission-orientated research using specialist facilities. They have strong interactions with industry, government departments and other end-users of their research.

Geographical Area of Activity: United Kingdom.

Publications: Annual Report and accounts; policy and planning documents; corporate brochures; business, knowledge transfer and innovation documents; *BBSRC Business* (quarterly magazine).

Finance: Financed by the British Government; annual expenditure on research funding £468,900,000 (2010).

Council: Prof. Sir Tom Blundell FRS (Chair.).

Principal Staff: Chief Exec. Prof. Douglas Kell; Deputy Chief Exec. Steve Visscher.

Address: Polaris House, North Star Ave, Swindon SN2 1UH.

Telephone: (1793) 413200; **Fax:** (1793) 413201; **Internet:** www.bbsrc.ac.uk; **e-mail:** external.relations@bbsrc.ac.uk.

BirdLife International

Founded in 1922 as the International Council for Bird Preservation, renamed BirdLife International in 1993; a world-wide partnership of organizations working for the diversity of all life through the conservation of birds and their habitats.

Activities: Operates internationally in the field of conservation, through programmes (e.g. bird surveys and studies; conservation programmes for particular species or areas and for the sustainable use of natural resources; public education campaigns; and provision of expert advice to governments on bird conservation issues); support for local societies and their projects; international conferences; conservation expeditions; compiling and disseminating information, including a computer databank, international data books and other publications. There are more than 300 member organizations and regional offices in Belgium, Ecuador, Fiji, Japan, Jordan and Kenya. Maintains a reference library of 5,000 volumes.

Geographical Area of Activity: International.

Publications: *Bird Red Data Book*; *Bird Conservation International* (quarterly); BirdLife Conservation Series; Annual Report; newsletter; technical publications; study reports; surveys; conference proceedings; *World Birdwatch* (quarterly magazine); *Rare Birds Yearbook*; partner journals.

Finance: Annual revenue £11,898,000, expenditure £11,152,000 (Dec. 2010).

Global Council: Peter Schei (Chair.); Benjamin Olewine IV (Treas.).

Principal Staff: Dir and Chief Exec. Dr Marco Lambertini.

Address: Wellbrook Ct, Girton Rd, Cambridge CB3 0NA.

Telephone: (1223) 277318; **Fax:** (1223) 277200; **Internet:** www.birdlife.org; **e-mail:** birdlife@birdlife.org.

Tony Blair Faith Foundation

Established by Tony Blair in 2008 to promote respect and understanding of and between the major religions and to make the case for faith as a force for good in the modern world. The Foundation aims to work with Christians, Muslims, Jews, Hindus, Sikhs and Buddhists.

Activities: The Foundation shows the good of faith in action by mobilizing faith communities to work together in pursuit of the UN Millennium Development Goals to tackle global poverty and conflict. The Foundation's first aim is the eradication of deaths from malaria through multi-faith action.

Geographical Area of Activity: International.

Trustees: Robert Clinton; Robert Coke; Jeremy Sinclair.

Principal Staff: Chief Exec. Ruth Turner.

Address: POB 60519, London W2 7JU.

Internet: www.tonyblairfaithfoundation.org; **e-mail:** info@tonyblairfaithfoundation.org.

The Body Shop Foundation

Established in 1990 to provide a means of gathering together funds raised by directors, employees, national and international franchisees and friends of The Body Shop to allocate these to social, human and environmental welfare.

Activities: The Foundation operates nationally and internationally in the fields of human and civil rights, and animal and environmental protection.

Geographical Area of Activity: International.

Restrictions: Does not accept unsolicited applications for funding.

Finance: Annual revenue £1,615,297, expenditure £1,736,051 (2010).

Trustees: Jan Buckingham; Paul McGreevy; Simon Henzell-Thomas; Joana Edwards; Vicki Rayment; Jonathan Staunton; Lady Jay of Ewelme; Paul Sanderson.

Principal Staff: CEO Lisa Jackson.

Address: Watersmead, Littlehampton BN17 6LS.

Telephone: (1903) 844039; **Fax:** (1903) 844202; **Internet:** www.thebodyshopfoundation.org; **e-mail:** bodyshopfoundation@thebodyshop.com.

Book Aid International—BAI

Founded as the Ranfurly Library by Hermione, Countess of Ranfurly, in 1954; present name adopted in 1994. Book Aid International's vision is of a world in which everyone enjoys access to the information they need, and every country has a lively book trade that reflects local values and culture. It works in partnership with organizations in developing countries to support local initiatives in literacy, education and publishing.

Activities: Provides more than 600,000 selected books and journals each year to support learning and skills development in 12 countries in Sub-Saharan Africa, Palestinian Autonomous Areas and Sri Lanka. Responds to requests from organizations that urgently need up-to-date information resources. Its partners include library networks, schools, universities, vocational colleges and hospitals. Launched the Books Change Lives campaign in 2008.

Geographical Area of Activity: America, primarily Sub-Saharan Africa, South-East Asia and the Caribbean.

Publications: *Book Mark* (newsletter); Annual Review; Report and Accounts.

Finance: Annual revenue £7,154,905, expenditure £7,018,933 (Dec. 2010).

Board of Trustees: Philip Walters (Chair.); Fergus Cass (Hon. Treas.).

Principal Staff: Dir Clive Nettleton.

Address: 39–41 Coldharbour Lane, Camberwell, London SE5 9NR.

Telephone: (20) 7733-3577; **Fax:** (20) 7978-8006; **Internet:** www.bookaid.org; **e-mail:** info@bookaid.org.

Born Free Foundation Limited

Founded by Bill Travers and Virginia McKenna to co-ordinate and develop effective campaigns to prevent animal suffering, protect endangered species and their habitats, and keep wildlife in the wild.

Activities: The Foundation's programmes include Zoo Check, to monitor conditions of wildlife in zoos, safari parks and circuses, with the aim of preventing the abuse of captive animals; ELEFRIENDS Elephant Protection Group, aiming to combat poachers and end trade in ivory; Big Cat Campaign, to rescue big cats in captivity and protect those in the wild; Wolf Campaign, to save Ethiopian wolves from extinction and provide information on the species; Dolphin Campaign, to bring about an end to the practice of holding dolphins and whales captive in marine parks, and to protect orca in the wild; Primate Campaign, to protect orphaned and abused baby chimpanzees at a sanctuary in Uganda, and to protect primates in the wild; and Bear Campaign, to return orphaned bears to the wild and campaign against the exploitation of bears. Maintains offices in Kenya and the USA.

Geographical Area of Activity: World-wide.

Publications: Newsletters; Annual Report.

Finance: Annual revenue £3,294,125, expenditure £3,496,675 (March 2011).

Trustees: Michael Reyner (Chair.).

Principal Staff: Founder Virginia McKenna; CEO Will Travers.

Address: 3 Grove House, Foundry Lane, Horsham, West Sussex RH13 5PL.

Telephone: (1403) 240170; **Internet:** www.bornfree.org.uk; **e-mail:** info@bornfree.org.uk.

Britain-Nepal Medical Trust

Founded in 1968 by Dr J. Cunningham to assist the people of Nepal to improve their health.

Activities: Operates in Nepal in the field of health and community development through self-conducted programmes, research, training and capacity building. Works in collaboration with the Government of Nepal's Ministry of Health, international and local NGOs, local committees and communities.

Geographical Area of Activity: Nepal and Europe.

Restrictions: Funds currently restricted to the Trust's own work.

Publications: Annual Report.

Finance: Net assets £563,184 (Dec. 2010); annual revenue £558,553, expenditure £898,048 (2010).

Trustees: Jeffrey W. Mecaskey (Chair.).

Principal Staff: Nepalese Dir Pradhan Gurung; Sec. and Admin. A. G. Peck.

Address: Export House, 130 Vale Rd, Tonbridge, Kent TN9 1SP.

Telephone: (1732) 360284; **Fax:** (1732) 363876; **Internet:** www.britainnepalmedicaltrust.org.uk; **e-mail:** info@britainnepalmedicaltrust.org.uk.

British Academy

Established in 1902 to promote the study of the humanities and social sciences.

Activities: The United Kingdom national academy for the humanities and social sciences. Operates nationally and internationally in the fields of academic research in the humanities and social sciences. Provides grants to British scholars for a wide range of personal research projects, for conference attendance, and for international collaboration. Supports research posts (post-doctoral and senior level) and a series of scholarly projects. Also funds a number of British institutes abroad and in the United Kingdom. Publishes monographs or serial publications relating to various aspects of the social sciences. Organizes and publishes papers from lectures, conferences and symposia. Maintains links with international partners (academies and research councils) and supports international scholarly collaboration. Member of international organizations including the European Science Foundation (q.v.), ALLEA and the Union Académique Internationale.

Geographical Area of Activity: International.

Restrictions: In most cases, awards offered only for post-doctoral research in the humanities and social sciences undertaken by scholars normally resident in the United Kingdom.

Publications: Monographs and other scholarly publications; annual proceedings; biannual review; editions; catalogues; conference proceedings, lectures and biographies.

Finance: Annual revenue £28,139,608, expenditure £27,669,921 (March 2010).

Council: Prof. Sir Adam Roberts (Pres.); Prof. Michael Fulford (Treas.); Prof. Duncan Gallie (Foreign Sec.); Dame Hazel Genn (Vice-Pres. Communications and External Relations); Prof. Susan Mendus (Vice-Pres. Social Sciences); Prof. Martin Millett (Vice-Pres. British Academy Sponsored Institutes and Societies); Prof. Nigel Vincent (Vice-Pres. Research and HE Policy); Prof. Albert Weale (Vice-Pres. Public Policy); Prof. Chris Wickham (Publications Sec.); Prof. Hugh Williamson (Vice-Pres. Humanities).

Principal Staff: Chief Exec. and Sec. Dr Robin Jackson.

Address: 10–11 Carlton House Terrace, London SW1Y 5AH.

Telephone: (20) 7969-5200; **Fax:** (20) 7969-5300; **Internet:** www.britac.ac.uk; **e-mail:** chiefexec@britac.ac.uk.

The British Council

Established to promote educational and cultural relations between the United Kingdom and other countries world-wide.

Activities: Operates internationally through cultural, educational, English language and information programmes. Maintains 227 offices and teaching centres in 110 countries.

Geographical Area of Activity: International.

Publications: Numerous publications in the fields of English language, education and the arts; Annual Report.

Finance: Financed by a grant-in-aid from the Government, and revenues from its teaching and examination activities. Annual revenue £692,963,000, expenditure £665,321,000 (March 2011).

Board of Trustees: Sir Vernon Ellis (Chair.); Alan Buckle (Deputy Chair.).

Principal Staff: Chief Exec. Martin Davidson.

Address: 10 Spring Gardens, London SW1A 2BN.

Telephone: (20) 7389-4385; **Fax:** (20) 7389-6347; **Internet:** www.britishcouncil.org; **e-mail:** general.enquiries@britishcouncil.org.

British Heart Foundation

Founded in 1961, the British Heart Foundation is the leading British medical research charity working in the field of cardiovascular disease.

Activities: The Foundation funds medical research into the causes, prevention, diagnosis and treatment of heart disease. It provides support and information to sufferers and their families, through British Heart Foundation nurses, rehabilitation programmes and support groups. The Foundation educates the public and health professionals about heart disease prevention and treatment. It promotes training in emergency life-support skills for the public and health professionals, and provides equipment to hospitals and other health providers.

Geographical Area of Activity: United Kingdom.

Publications: Leaflets and videos for members of the public, patients and their families, schools, hospitals and doctors' surgeries.

Finance: Annual revenue £233,398,000, expenditure £290,786,000 (March 2011).

Trustees: Phil Yea (Chair.).

Principal Staff: CEO Peter Hollins.

Address: Greater London House, 180 Hampstead Rd, London NW1 7AW.

Telephone: (20) 7554-0000; (300) 330-3311 (helpline, Mon–Fri, 0900–1800); **Fax:** (20) 7554-0100; **Internet:** www.bhf.org.uk; **e-mail:** supporterservices@bhf.org.uk.

British Institute at Ankara

Founded in 1948 to support, facilitate, promote and publish British research focused on Turkey and the Black Sea littoral in all academic disciplines within the arts, humanities and social sciences, and to maintain a centre of excellence in Ankara focused on the archaeology and related subjects of Turkey.

Activities: Supports, promotes and publishes British research focused on Turkey and the Black Sea littoral in all academic disciplines within the arts, humanities and social sciences, while maintaining a centre of excellence in Ankara focused on the archaeology and related subjects of Turkey. A small staff at the Institute's premises in Ankara conduct research, assist scholars and maintain the centre of excellence, which houses a library of more than 52,000 volumes, research collections of botanical, faunal, epigraphic and pottery material, together with collections of maps, photographs and fieldwork archives, and a laboratory and computer services. In 2011 the following initiatives were supported: the Climate History of Anatolia and the Black Sea; the Frontiers of the Ottoman world; and the Settlement History of Anatolia.

Geographical Area of Activity: United Kingdom, Turkey and the Black Sea region.

Publications: *Anatolian Studies* (annually); *Heritage Turkey* (previously *Anatolian Archaeology*) (annually); monograph series.

Finance: Annual revenue £587,747, expenditure £605,751 (2009/10).

Council of Management: Sir David Logan (Chair.); Prof. Stephen Mitchell (Hon. Sec.); Dr Nicholas Milner (Hon. Treas.).

Principal Staff: Dir Dr Lutgarde Vandeput; Man. Claire McCafferty.

Address: 10 Carlton House Terrace, London SW1Y 5AH; Tahran Caddesi 24, Kavaklıdere, 06700 Ankara, Turkey.

Telephone: (20) 7969-5204; **Fax:** (20) 7969-5401; **Internet:** www.biaa.ac.uk; **e-mail:** biaa@britac.ac.uk.

British Institute of International and Comparative Law

Founded in 1958 to provide an international centre for the study of the practical application to current problems of public international law, private international law, European Community (now European Union) law and comparative law.

Activities: The Institute carries out independent research, organizes lectures, seminars and conferences, and publishes books and periodicals in its fields of interest.

Geographical Area of Activity: International.

Publications: *International and Comparative Law Quarterly* and monographs.

Finance: Assets £1,131,277 (2009).

Trustees: Sir Franklin Berman (Chair.).

Principal Staff: Dir Prof. Robert McCorquodale.

Address: Charles Clore House, 17 Russell Sq., London WC1B 5JP.

Telephone: (20) 7862 5151; **Fax:** (20) 7862 5152; **Internet:** www.biicl.org; **e-mail:** info@biicl.org.

British Red Cross

The British Red Cross, founded in 1870 by Royal Charter and part of the International Red Cross and Red Crescent movement (q.v.), provides emergency services and skilled care for those in need and crisis in their local community and overseas.

Activities: In the United Kingdom, operates through local branches and centres to provide a full range of services in the community, which include: medical loans, home from hospital, therapeutic care, emergency response, fire and emergency support services, Event First Aid, Ambulance Support, International tracing and messaging, Refudee services, Youth and schools services and First Aid training. Funds are raised to enable the British Red Cross to send aid in the form of money, materials or personnel to disaster-stricken areas of the United Kingdom or abroad.

Geographical Area of Activity: International.

Restrictions: No grants are made to individuals.

Publications: Annual Report and Review.

Finance: Annual revenue £205,700,000, expenditure £199,200,000 (2010).

Elected Trustees: Sue Brown, Stella Cummings, Stan Fitches, Amy Foan, Chris Hedges, Gordon Low, Lady Lamport, Vicky Peterkin, Dr Kay Richmond.

Co-opted Trustees: David Fall CMG, Michael Herriot MBE, Mohammed Afzal Khan CBE, Dr Lise Llewellyn, Graham Stegmann CBE, Russell Walls, Steve John.

Principal Staff: CEO Sir Nick Young; Chair. James Cochrane.

Address: 44 Moorfields, London EC2Y 9AL.

Telephone: (20) 7138-7900; **Fax:** (20) 7562-2000; **Internet:** www.redcross.org.uk; **e-mail:** information@redcross.org.uk.

CABI

Established as the Commonwealth Agricultural Bureaux (CAB) in 1913, it became an international non-profit organization with a new constitution in 1986, called the Centre for Agricultural Bioscience International. Later known as CAB International, it adopted the name CABI in 2006. It aims to disseminate scientific knowledge to promote sustainable development and human welfare.

Activities: Operates in three principal areas: research and development, publishing, and microbial services, carrying out research into biodiversity, pest management and environmental issues; and publishing books on applied life sciences, journals and information in electronic forms. There are ten centres world-wide, in People's Republic of China, India, Malaysia, Pakistan, Switzerland, Kenya, Trinidad and Tobago, the USA and the United Kingdom.

Geographical Area of Activity: International.

Publications: Abstracts; Annual Review.

Finance: Annual revenue £21,681,000, expenditure £22,148,000 (Dec. 2009).

Executive Board: John Ripley (Chair.).

Principal Staff: Chief Exec. Dr Trevor Nicholls.

Address: Nosworthy Way, Wallingford, Oxfordshire OX10 8DE.

Telephone: (1491) 832111; **Fax:** (1491) 829292; **Internet:** www.cabi.org; **e-mail:** enquiries@cabi.org.

William Adlington Cadbury Charitable Trust

Founded by William C. Cadbury in 1923 to provide funds for general charitable purposes, with preference given to the West Midlands.

Activities: The Trust's main funding areas are: the West Midlands, the rest of the United Kingdom, as well as cross-community projects between Northern Ireland and the Republic of Ireland, and national charities working overseas (Africa). It operates in the fields of the Society of Friends and other religious organizations, social welfare, health and medicine, conservation of the environment, sustainable development, and education, through grants to registered charities.

Geographical Area of Activity: United Kingdom and Africa.

Restrictions: Grants only to charities registered in the United Kingdom; no funding for individuals. International grants currently to organizations known to the Trust.

Publications: Annual Report; grant policy and guidelines.

Finance: Annual revenue £784,280, expenditure £790,719 (March 2011).

Trustees: Sarah Stafford (Chair.), W. James, B. Taylor, Rupert A. Cadbury, Katherine M. van Hagen Cadbury, C. Margaret Salmon, John C. Penny, Adrian D. M. Thomas, Sophy J. Blandy, Janine E. Cobain.

Principal Staff: Sec. C. F. Bettis.

Address: Rokesley, Bristol Rd, Selly Oak, Birmingham B29 6QF.

Telephone: (121) 4721464; **Internet:** www.wa-cadbury.org.uk; **e-mail:** info@wa-cadbury.org.uk.

Edward Cadbury Charitable Trust, Inc

Founded in 1945 for general charitable purposes.

Activities: Principally supports the voluntary sector in the Midlands region. The main areas of grant giving focus on education, ecumenical mission and interfaith relations, the oppressed and disadvantaged, the arts and the environment.

Geographical Area of Activity: United Kingdom (Midlands).

Restrictions: Grants are made to registered charities only: grants are not made to students nor to individuals.

Finance: Annual revenue £829,967, expenditure £724,165 (April 2011).

Trustees: C. E. Gillett; N. R. Cadbury; C. R. Gillett; A. S. Littleboy; R. H. S. Marriott; Dr W. Southall.

Principal Staff: Trust Man. S. Anderson.

Address: Rokesley, Bristol Rd, Selly Oak, Birmingham B29 6QF.

Telephone: (121) 472-1838; **e-mail:** ecadburytrust@fsmail.net.

CAFOD—Catholic Agency for Overseas Development

Established in 1962 as the official organization of the Roman Catholic Bishops' Conference of England and Wales, through which the Catholic Church in those countries shares its resources with sister churches and other partners throughout the world to work with them to combat poverty, hunger, ignorance, disease and suffering.

Activities: Operates in partnership with local NGOs in more than 40 developing countries in Africa, Central and South America and the Caribbean, and Asia. The main work is in the funding of development projects in food production;

preventive health; vocational training; community development; non-formal education; and block grants made to Church development agencies. Specialized fields include emergency aid and projects concerned with AIDS. Campaigns are conducted in the United Kingdom to raise awareness of the causes of poverty and injustice world-wide. CAFOD also co-funds with the United Kingdom's Department for International Development and the European Union. Maintains offices in Bolivia, Democratic Republic of the Congo, Ethiopia, Kenya, Mozambique, Nicaragua, Nigeria, Sierra Leone and Sudan, with staff in a number of other countries world-wide.

Geographical Area of Activity: International.

Restrictions: Projects involving heavy construction costs are not undertaken, nor are funds provided for primary or secondary education.

Publications: Trustees' Report and Financial Statements; *Side by Side*; *CAFOD Bulletin*.

Finance: Grants from benefactors including the United Kingdom Government and the European Union. Total income £47,900,000, expenditure £45,500,000 (2007/08).

Trustees: Rt Rev. John Arnold (Chair.); Charles Reeve-Tucker (Treas.).

Principal Staff: Dir Chris Bain.

Address: Romero House, 55 Westminster Bridge Rd, London SE1 7JB.

Telephone: (20) 7733-7900; **Fax:** (20) 7274-9630; **Internet:** www.cafod.org.uk; **e-mail:** cafod@cafod.org.uk.

Cambridge Commonwealth Trust

Established in 1982 by the University of Cambridge to give financial support to outstanding students from within the Commonwealth who apply to study at the University of Cambridge.

Activities: Grants scholarships annually to graduates from Commonwealth countries to pursue their studies at the University of Cambridge. The Trust operates in collaboration with the Cambridge Overseas Trust (q.v.) and other agencies.

Geographical Area of Activity: Commonwealth countries.

Trustees: Sir Martin Harris (Chair.); Simon Lebus (Vice-Chair.).

Principal Staff: Dir Michael O'Sulivan.

Address: 53–54 Sidney St, Cambridge CB2 3HX.

Telephone: (1223) 338498; **Fax:** (1223) 760618; **Internet:** www.cambridgetrusts.org; **e-mail:** info@overseastrusts.cam.ac.uk.

Cambridge Overseas Trust

The Cambridge Overseas Trust was established in 1989 by the University of Cambridge, to give financial support to outstanding students from outside the Commonwealth who apply to study at the University of Cambridge.

Activities: Grants scholarships annually to students who are permanent residents or citizens of countries outside the Commonwealth to pursue their studies at the University of Cambridge. The Trust operates in collaboration with the Cambridge Commonwealth Trust and other agencies.

Geographical Area of Activity: International.

Trustees: Sir Martin Harris (Chair.); Simon Lebus (Vice-Chair.).

Principal Staff: Dir Michael O'Sullivan.

Address: 53–54 Sidney St, Cambridge CB2 3HX.

Telephone: (1223) 338498; **Fax:** (1223) 760618; **Internet:** www.cambridgetrusts.org; **e-mail:** info@overseastrusts.cam.ac.uk.

Cancer Research UK

Established in 2002, as a result of the merger of the Cancer Research Campaign and the Imperial Cancer Research Fund, to investigate all matters connected with or bearing on the causes, prevention, treatment and cure of cancer.

Activities: Supports and undertakes a comprehensive programme of research in institutes, hospitals, universities and medical schools throughout Britain and Northern Ireland. Works in anti-cancer drug development and to ensure cancer sufferers receive new treatments as quickly as possible; carries out research into the psychological impact of cancer and improving communication between doctor and patient; provides a wide range of authoritative cancer information publications and guidelines for general practitioners; and promotes cancer prevention through education and research. Also trains cancer scientists and doctors.

Geographical Area of Activity: United Kingdom.

Publications: Annual Report; scientific report; brochures; leaflets; factsheets; accounts.

Finance: Total revenue £483,000,000, total expenditure £493,000,000.

Trustees: Michael Pragnell (Chair.), Dr Keith F. Palmer (Treas.).

Principal Staff: Chief Exec. Harpal Kumar.

Address: Angel Building, 407 St John St, London EC1V 4AD.

Telephone: (20) 7242-0200; **Fax:** (20) 7121-6700; **Internet:** www.cancerresearchuk.org; **e-mail:** pressoffice@cancer.org.uk.

Carnegie Trust for the Universities of Scotland

Founded in 1901 to promote the development of Scottish universities.

Activities: Provides grants to Scottish undergraduates to help with university fees and to staff and graduates of Scottish universities to fund study and research. Also makes a number of larger grants to projects of interest to Scottish universities as a whole.

Geographical Area of Activity: Scotland.

Publications: Books.

Finance: Assets £51,581,543 (2011); grants disbursed £1,895,569 (2011).

Trustees: Sir David Edward (Chair.).

Principal Staff: Sec. and Treas. Prof. Andrew Miller.

Address: Andrew Carnegie House, Pittencrieff St, Dunfermline, Fife KY12 8AW.

Telephone: (1383) 724990; **Fax:** (1383) 749799; **Internet:** www.carnegie-trust.org; **e-mail:** jgray@carnegie-trust.org.

Carnegie UK Trust

Founded in 1913 by Andrew Carnegie and one of a network of 23 Carnegie foundations world-wide. The Trust is an independent not-for-profit foundation supporting action-research and public policy analysis and advocacy in the field of social action, democracy building, civil society, sustainable rural community development and youth participation.

Activities: Operates within the United Kingdom and the Republic of Ireland. The current emphasis is on supporting sustainable rural communities, and strengthening democracy and civil society. The Trust establishes independent Commissions and Inquires, supported by action-research and publication and dissemination programmes. From March 2005 the Trust ended its unsolicited grassroots grant programmes, replacing them with larger-scale funding for a more limited number of action-research programmes with selected partners. Limited funding is also available for international networking and exchange.

Geographical Area of Activity: Mainly United Kingdom and Ireland; also works with international partners on issues of a more global nature that affect the United Kingdom and Ireland.

Restrictions: No unsolicited requests accepted; advice available on tendering for the different funding programmes.

Publications: Annual Review; research reports; rural community development reports; other publications.

Finance: Annual revenue £1,938,749, expenditure £2,106,415 (Dec. 2009).

Trustees: William Thomson (Pres.); Melanie Leech (Chair.); Angus Hogg (Vice-Chair.).

Principal Staff: Chief Exec. Martyn Evans.

Address: Andrew Carnegie House, Pittencrieff St, Dunfermline, Fife KY12 8AW.

Telephone: (1383) 721445; **Fax:** (1383) 749799; **Internet:** www.carnegieuktrust.org.uk; **e-mail:** info@carnegieuk.org.

Sir Ernest Cassel Educational Trust

Founded in 1919 by Sir Ernest Cassel to promote adult education by voluntary bodies, and the higher education of women.

Activities: Awards Mountbatten Memorial Grants to Commonwealth students experiencing hardship in their final year of higher education. Overseas research grants administered by the British Academy. Mountbatten Memorial Award at Christ's College Cambs. Award of grants to organizations providing opportunities for young people to serve overseas and for adult education in the United Kingdom.

Geographical Area of Activity: United Kingdom.

Finance: Annual revenue £59,148, expenditure £60,015 (2010).

Trustees: Countess Mountbatten of Burma (Patron); Ann Sheila Kennedy; Anne Sofer; Amanda Ellingworth; Colin Lucas; Prof. Francis Robinson; Dr Gordon Johnson; Nicholas Allan; Kit Hunter Gordon.

Principal Staff: Sec. Kathryn Hodges.

Address: 5 Grimston Park Mews, Grimston Park, Tadcaster LS24 9DB.

Telephone: (1937) 834730; **Internet:** www.casseltrust.co.uk; **e-mail:** casseltrust@btinternet.com.

Charity Islamic Trust Elrahma

Established in 1993 to assist the needy in the Muslim community in the United Kingdom and internationally.

Activities: Operates in the fields of social welfare, education and religion nationally and internationally, through grants for the building of schools, mosques and institutions for orphans, and for the relief of poverty.

Geographical Area of Activity: International.

Finance: Annual revenue £1,693,000, expenditure £1,439,000 (2008).

Trustees: O. Megerisi; Patrick Daniels; Abubaker Megerisi; Hazem Megerisi; Otman Megerisi; Mohamed Megerisi.

Principal Staff: Contact M. Zamir.

Address: 3 The Ave, London NW6 7YG.

Telephone: (20) 8459-3244; **Fax:** (20) 8451-7993; **Internet:** www.elrahma.org.uk; **e-mail:** projects@elrahma.org.uk.

Leonard Cheshire Disability International

Founded in the United Kingdom in 1948 by Group Capt. Leonard Cheshire, the organization has undertaken international work since 1955. LCI's mission is to work with disabled people throughout the world by providing the environment necessary for each individual's physical, mental and spiritual well-being.

Activities: Provides support and guidance to more than 250 locally-run programmes for disabled people and their families, in 57 countries outside the United Kingdom; programmes include rehabilitation centres, skills training centres, community-based support services and residential homes. The organization also advises local communities on obtaining grants for new developments.

Geographical Area of Activity: International.

Restrictions: Grants only to Leonard Cheshire Services.

Publications: Annual Report; *Disability and Inclusive Development*; *Compass* (quarterly).

Finance: Annual revenue £149,655,000, expenditure £146,046,000 (March 2008).

Trustees: Dr Alan Elliott; Anthony Hughes; Col Shaun Longsdon; David Reed; Diane Ritherdon; Dr Graham Mitchell; George Miall; Jennifer Phillips; John Hemsley; John Standen; Patrick Salmon; Peter Bailey; Peter Kingdon; Ruth Grice;

Simon Leslie; Sir Edward Clay; Sir Nigel Broomfield; Dr Stephen Helliwell Large; Stewart Brown; Tom Bartlam; Vanessa Bourne.

Principal Staff: Chair. Richard Thomas; Int. Dir Tanya Barron; Deputy Int. Dir Mark O'Kelly, Asst Dir Sarah Dyer.

Address: 66 South Lambeth Rd, London SW8 1RL.

Telephone: (20) 3242-0200; **Fax:** (20) 3242-0250; **Internet:** www.lcint.org; **e-mail:** international@lcdisability.org.

Child Migrants Trust

Established in 1987 by Margaret Humphreys as an advisory and support organization for former child migrants who were sent abroad from the United Kingdom between the end of the Second World War and 1970.

Activities: Operates as a counselling and advisory organization in the United Kingdom, Australia, Canada, New Zealand, USA and Zimbabwe for former child migrants and their families. Maintains offices in Perth and Melbourne (Australia).

Geographical Area of Activity: Australia, Canada, New Zealand, United Kingdom, USA and Zimbabwe.

Publications: *Empty Cradles*; *Lost Children of the Empire*.

Finance: Annual revenue £307,600, expenditure £254,800 (2009).

Trustees: Joan Taylor; Mike Hoare; Patricia Higham.

Principal Staff: Dir Margaret Humphreys.

Address: 28a Musters Rd, West Bridgford, Nottingham NG2 7PL.

Telephone: (115) 982-2811; **Fax:** (115) 981-7168; **Internet:** www.childmigrantstrust.com; **e-mail:** enquiries@childmigrantstrust.com.

ChildHope

Established in 1990, ChildHope is dedicated to improving the rights and opportunities of young people around the world. It is linked to independent ChildHope (q.v.) organizations in Brazil and the Philippines.

Activities: Operates in the fields of human rights and social welfare, through financial support and providing training for projects helping children, in particular 'street children' in developing countries. Operates in partnership with local NGOs in Africa, South Asia and South America in three main areas: reducing child abuse and exploitation; improving child justice and participation; and promoting the rights of children affected by HIV and AIDS.

Geographical Area of Activity: Asia, Africa and Central and South America.

Publications: Annual Report; *Street Children – Resource Sheets for Project Management*; newsletter.

Finance: The Foundation receives funding from the British Government, European Union, various foundations, trusts and charities, individual supporters and members of the public. Annual revenue £1,770,332, expenditure £1,768,722 (Dec. 2010).

Trustees: Chris Mowles (Chair.); Helen Turnbull (Hon. Treas.).

Principal Staff: Exec. Dir Jill Healey.

Address: Development House, 56–64 Leonard St, London EC2A 4LT.

Telephone: (20) 7065-0950; **Fax:** (20) 7065-0951; **Internet:** www.childhope.org.uk; **e-mail:** info@childhope.org.uk.

Childwick Trust

Founded in 1985, the Trust operates in six main areas: to assist elderly people in need; charities connected with Thoroughbred horse breeding or racing; Jewish charities in the United Kingdom; charities involved in education and assistance for people who have worked in the mining industry in South Africa; and charities benefiting disabled people in the United Kingdom.

Activities: The Trust operates in the United Kingdom for the promotion of health and for the benefit of the elderly and disabled. The Trust also operates in South Africa in the field of pre school education and training.

Geographical Area of Activity: United Kingdom and South Africa.

Restrictions: No grants to individuals and grants are made to United Kingdom-based organizations only.

Finance: Annual revenue £3,102,757, expenditure £2,709,750 (April 2009).

Trustees: Peter Glossop; John Wood; Sarah Frost; Anthony Cane; Peter Anwyl-Harris.

Principal Staff: Trust Admin. Karen Groom.

Address: 9 The Green, Childwick Bury, St Albans, Hertfordshire AL3 6JJ.

Telephone: (1727) 844666; **Internet:** www.childwicktrust.org; **e-mail:** karen@childwicktrust.org.

Christian Aid

Christian Aid was founded by the British Council of Churches to finance practical programmes of aid, development and relief for the neediest people across the world, including disaster victims and refugees; and to improve understanding of poverty by carrying out educational work in the United Kingdom.

Activities: Christian Aid is active mainly in developing countries, through regional and local organizations involved in relief, resettlement, development (in spheres of health, urban welfare, agriculture and water resources) and education programmes. Some funds are granted to race relations, community and development education projects in the United Kingdom.

Geographical Area of Activity: International.

Publications: Annual Report; audited accounts; quarterly list of grants; *Christian Aid News*; catalogue of current publications and resources list.

Finance: Annual revenue £95,000,000, expenditure £90,100,000 (March 2011).

Trustees: Dame Anne Owers (Chair.).

Principal Staff: Dir Loretta Minghella.

Address: 35 Lower Marsh, Waterloo, London SE1 7RL.

Telephone: (20) 7620-4444; **Fax:** (20) 7620-0719; **Internet:** www.christianaid.org.uk; **e-mail:** info@christian-aid.org.

Winston Churchill Memorial Trust

Founded in 1965 to provide travelling fellowships.

Activities: About 100 fellowships are awarded annually to British citizens, resident in the United Kingdom, of any age, for a stay overseas of four to eight weeks.

Restrictions: Does not cover courses, academic studies, student grants or gap year projects.

Publications: Newsletter (1 a year); explanatory leaflet and brochure.

Finance: Annual revenue £866,851, expenditure £1,209,628 (Sept. 2010).

Board of Trustees: Rt Hon. The Lord Fellowes (Chair.).

Principal Staff: Dir-Gen. Maj.-Gen. James Balfour.

Address: South Door, 29 Great Smith St, London SW1P 3BL.

Telephone: (20) 7799-1660; **Fax:** (20) 7799-1667; **Internet:** www.wcmt.org.uk; **e-mail:** office@wcmt.org.uk.

Citizenship Foundation

Founded in 1989 to promote improved understanding of citizenship, political, social and legal systems, and participation in community and voluntary projects. The Foundation had as its predecessor the Law in Education Project, established in 1984 to develop teaching materials that introduce students to the notions of responsibilities and rights, and the role of law in democratic society.

Activities: Operates a wide range of educational programmes in the field of law and human rights, including public debates, competitions and training initiatives.

Geographical Area of Activity: International.

Publications: *Passport to Life*; Annual Report; educational resources and publications; newsletter; books; pamphlets; papers.

Finance: Net assets £544,200 (2011); annual revenue £1,930,825, expenditure £2,123,615 (March 2011).

Board of Trustees: Michael Maclay (Chair.); Andrew Phillips (Pres.); Martin Bostock (Deputy Chair.); Susan Simmonds (Deputy Chair.); Nick Johnson (Treas.).

Principal Staff: Chief Exec. Andy Thornton.

Address: 63 Gee St, London EC1V 3RS.

Telephone: (20) 7566-4141; **Fax:** (20) 7566-4131; **Internet:** www.citizenshipfoundation.org.uk; **e-mail:** info@citizenshipfoundation.org.uk.

The City Bridge Trust

The Trust, known until 2006 as Bridge House Trust, can trace its origins back as far as 1097 when a special tax was raised to help repair the wooden London Bridge. The Trust increased through administration of property assets in the City of London and in the surrounding countryside. It built Blackfriars Bridge and Tower Bridge, purchased Southwark Bridge and, most recently, took over the ownership of Millennium Bridge. Maintaining bridges in the City of London is still the main purpose of the Fund, although a Charitable Scheme was set up in 1995.

Activities: The Charitable Scheme enables the Trust to apply its surplus money for the benefit of Greater London. Any year's income which is above that required to support the City bridges the Trust maintains may be applied towards charitable aims to benefit Greater London and its inhabitants. Grants are made to organizations that do work that addresses at least one of the Trust's published priorities. In addition, the Trust also funds strategic work for the benefit of London and the wider charity sector in the form of research, learning events and feasibility studies.

Geographical Area of Activity: London, United Kingdom.

Restrictions: Grants are made in London only. They are not made to individuals, statutory bodies, political parties, for medical or academic research, to churches or religious bodies for religious purposes or maintenance of religious buildings, nor to educational establishments.

Publications: Annual Review; Annual Report and Financial Statements; *Working with Londoners—Programme Guidelines*; *The Knowledge—Learning from London*.

Finance: Annual revenue £40,000,000; expenditure £37,600,00, of which £16,300,000 was charitable grants (2010/11).

Trust Committee: William Harry Dove MBE JP (Chair.); Joyce Carruthers Nash OBE (Deputy Chair.).

Principal Staff: Chief Grants Officer Clare Thomas.

Address: City of London, POB 270, Guildhall, London EC2P 2EJ.

Telephone: (20) 7332-3710; **Fax:** (20) 7332-3127; **Internet:** www.citybridgetrust.org.uk; **e-mail:** citybridgetrust@cityoflondon.gov.uk.

CLIC Sargent

CLIC Sargent was formed in 2005 after a successful merger between CLIC (Cancer and Leukaemia in Childhood founded in 1976 by Bob Woodward following the death of his young son to cancer) and Sargent Cancer Care for Children (founded in 1968 by Sylvia Darley OBE in memory of conductor Sir Malcolm Sargent).

Activities: The United Kingdom's leading cancer charity for children and young people, and their families. Provides clinical, practical, financial and emotional support.

Geographical Area of Activity: United Kingdom.

Restrictions: Applications must be made through a hospital social worker.

Publications: Annual report; storybooks; guides; booklets; leaflets.

Finance: Annual revenue £26,490,000 ; expenditure £21,140,000 (31 March 2011).

Board of Trustees: Daphne Pullen (Chair.), Graham Clarke (Treas.-elect), Alison Arnfield, Rachel Billsberry-Grass, Jane Burt, Will Carter, Michael O'Connor, Keith Exford, Ian Gibson, Dominic Grainger, Tim Holley, Meriel Jenney, Jonathan Plumtree .

Principal Staff: Chief Exec. Lorraine Clifton.

Address: CLIC Sargent, Horatio House, 77–85 Fulham Palace Rd, London W6 8JA.

Telephone: 0300 330 0803; **Fax:** (20) 8752-2806; **Internet:** www.clicsargent.org.uk; **e-mail:** mediarelations@ clicsargent.org.uk.

Clore Duffield Foundation—CDF

Founded in 1964, as the Clore Foundation to provide financial assistance for general charitable purposes. Money is donated at the discretion of the trustees.

Activities: Donations are made to registered charities usually in the United Kingdom, with a particular focus on supporting children, young people and society's most vulnerable individuals, principally in the fields of museum and gallery education, art and design education, performing arts education, health, social welfare and disability. Operates a main grants programme, with grants ranging between £10,000 and £2,500,000, a small grants programme for museum and gallery education, an Artworks Programme making awards for high-quality art teaching and funding art research, and the Clore Cultural Leadership Programme, promoting the leadership and management of cultural organizations in the United Kingdom, launched in January 2004.

Geographical Area of Activity: Mainly United Kingdom.

Restrictions: No funding for individuals and only rarely for organizations working outside the United Kingdom.

Publications: Annual Report and Accounts; *Space for Learning: A Handbook for Education Spaces in Museums, Heritage Sites and Discovery Centres (2004)*; *The Clore Small Grants Programme for Museum*; *Gallery Eduction, 1999–2004*; *State of the Art*.

Finance: Total income £3,642,267, expenditure £3,642,267 (2008).

Trustees: Dame Vivien Duffield (Chair.).

Principal Staff: Exec. Dir Sally Bacon.

Address: Studio 3, Chelsea Manor Studios, Flood St, London SW3 5SR.

Telephone: (20) 7351-6061; **Fax:** (20) 7351-5308; **Internet:** www.cloreduffield.org.uk; **e-mail:** info@cloreduffield.org.uk.

Colt Foundation

Established in 1978; promotes research into social, medical and environmental problems created by commerce and industry, and supports the publication of the results of such research.

Activities: Finances research projects, especially concerning occupational health, carried out at universities and research establishments in the United Kingdom. The Foundation also awards Fellowships to PhD students whose subjects are relevant to occupational and environmental medicine, and also supports the MSc in Human and Applied Physiology at King's College London. Recent projects include: National Heart and Lung Institute with the Royal Brompton Hospital; research on particle toxicology at Edinburgh Napier University; work on nanoparticles and nanotubes at the University of Edinburgh; the Centre for Occupational and Environmental Health, University of Manchester; the University of Sheffield for an *Investigation of the effects of outdoor air pollution on stroke incidence, phenotypes and survival*; the University of Aberdeen for work entitled *The effects of metal particles on inflammatory response in welders and non-welders*; and the NHLI at Imperial College

for work entitled *Does FEV1 predict capacity to work in an ageing population?*.

Geographical Area of Activity: United Kingdom.

Restrictions: Grants are not made to individuals, to projects outside the United Kingdom, nor to the general funds of charities.

Publications: Annual Report.

Finance: Annual revenue £486,513, expenditure £629,182 (2010).

Trustees: Prof. Sir Anthony Newman Taylor (Chair.).

Principal Staff: Dir Jackie Douglas.

Address: New Lane, Havant, Hampshire PO9 2LY.

Telephone: (23) 9249-1400; **Fax:** (23) 9249-1363; **Internet:** www.coltfoundation.org.uk; **e-mail:** jackie.douglas@uk .coltgroup.com.

Comic Relief

Established in 1984, as Charity Projects, to provide aid for disadvantaged people in the United Kingdom and Africa.

Activities: Operates in the United Kingdom and internationally, principally in Africa (one-third of grants are made in the United Kingdom, and two-thirds in Africa, although a new International Grants programme has been established to make grants internationally). Grants programmes in the United Kingdom and in Africa focus on social welfare, giving grants to small organizations. International projects are run to support children, including those affected by conflict and orphans. The organization runs the Red Nose Day fund-raising campaign biennially and in 2002 launched the Sport Relief fund-raiser.

Geographical Area of Activity: International (mainly Africa and the United Kingdom).

Publications: Annual Report and accounts; information leaflet.

Finance: Annual income £121,510,000, expenditure £110,443,000 (July 2011).

Trustees: Peter Bennett-Jones (Chair.); Richard Curtis (Vice-Chair.); Mike Harris (Treas.).

Principal Staff: CEO Kevin Cahill.

Address: 89 Albert Embankment, London SE1 7TP.

Telephone: (20) 7820-5555; **Fax:** (20) 7820-5500; **Internet:** www.comicrelief.com; **e-mail:** info@comicrelief.com.

Commonwealth Foundation

An inter-governmental organization originally founded in 1965 to support the work of the non-governmental sector within the Commonwealth, in particular the strengthening of civil society, sustainable development and poverty eradication, and to facilitate pan-Commonwealth and inter-country connections between people, their associations and communities at all levels.

Activities: The Foundation's work is guided by Commonwealth values and programme priorities. These relate to democracy and good governance, respect for human rights and gender equality, poverty reduction, and sustainable, people-centred development. The Foundation supports civil society activities that contribute to the achievement of the Millennium Development Goals. It funds inter-country networking (particularly between developing countries), training, capacity building and information exchange. In particular, it targets activities that strengthen civil society organizations in their work on poverty eradication, good governance and sustainable development and it places emphasis and importance on using culture as a tool in development. Its four programme areas are: communities and livelihoods, culture, governance and democracy and human development.

Geographical Area of Activity: Commonwealth countries.

Publications: Annual Report; *Educating Girls: A foundation for development; Putting Culture First: Commonwealth perspectives on culture and development; Breaking the Taboo: Perspectives of African civil society on innovative sources of finance for* *development; The Implications of High Food and Energy Prices for Economic Management; Multi-Stakeholder Partnerships for Gender Equality—Perspectives from Government; Climate Change and Its Implications: Which Way Now?; Engaging with Faith: Report of the Foundation project on improving understanding and co-operation between different faith communities; Transforming Commonwealth Societies to Achieve Political, Economic and Human Development: Civil Society Perspectives.*

Finance: Annual revenue £3,484,458, expenditure £3,448,296 (June 2008).

Trustees: Simone de Comarmond (Chair.).

Principal Staff: Interim Dir Dr Dhananjayan Sriskandarajah.

Address: Marlborough House, Pall Mall, London SW1Y 5HX.

Telephone: (20) 7930-3783; **Fax:** (20) 7839-8157; **Internet:** www.commonwealthfoundation.com; **e-mail:** geninfo@commonwealth.int.

Community Foundation for Northern Ireland

Founded in 1979 to support voluntary and community projects in Northern Ireland; until 2003 known as the Northern Ireland Voluntary Trust.

Activities: The Foundation's main emphasis is on community empowerment and social justice, supporting projects that deal with social problems in urban and rural areas: young people, women's groups, unemployed people, community care, the arts, education, welfare rights and inter-community activity. Also maintains an office in Derry.

Geographical Area of Activity: Northern Ireland.

Publications: Annual Report and accounts; *Infonotes* (publication series); *In Brief* (report series).

Finance: Annual revenue £5,198,029, expenditure £5,516,246 (2011).

Trustees: Tony McCusker (Chair.); Les Allamby (Vice-Chair.).

Principal Staff: Dir Avila Kilmurray.

Address: Community House, Citylink Business Park, Albert St, Belfast BT12 4HQ.

Telephone: (28) 9024-5927; **Fax:** (28) 9032-9839; **Internet:** www.communityfoundationni.org; **e-mail:** info@communityfoundationni.org.

Concern Universal

Founded in 1976 to provide aid to less-developed countries.

Activities: Promotes development and improved living conditions in less-developed countries, particularly among refugees, victims of war, people with AIDS and their children. Supports environmental conservation efforts, adult literacy and basic education training, provides emergency humanitarian relief, promotes children's rights, and develops food security and sustainable agriculture initiatives. Currently working in Bangladesh, Brazil, Colombia, Gambia, Ghana, Guinea, India, Kenya, Malawi, Mozambique, Nigeria, Senegal and the United Kingdom.

Geographical Area of Activity: Sub-Saharan Africa, Central and South America, Asia and Europe.

Restrictions: Does not make grants.

Finance: Annual revenue £12,213,077, expenditure £12,967,232 (2010/11).

Governing Council: Peter Ayres (Acting Chair.); Dan Bishop (Vice-Chair.).

Principal Staff: Exec. Dir Dr Ian Williams.

Address: 21 King St, Hereford HR4 9BX.

Telephone: (1432) 355111; **Fax:** (1432) 355086; **Internet:** www.concern-universal.org; **e-mail:** cu.uk@concern-universal.org.

Conservation Foundation

Founded in 1982 by Prof. David Bellamy and David Shreeve to provide a means for interested parties—governments, corporations, institutions, organizations and associations—to collaborate on environmental causes in which common ground can be found.

Activities: The Foundation works nationally and internationally in the fields of conservation and the environment, working with commercial and environmental organizations to create award schemes, research and information programmes, conferences, educational materials, multimedia presentations and publications. Supports ethno-medical research by young scientists in rainforests, and local conservation projects in the United Kingdom and Europe.

Geographical Area of Activity: International.

Publications: *Network 21* (environmental news service); *Parish Pump* (newsletter).

Finance: Annual revenue £1,379,900, expenditure £978,765 (2009).

Council: Matthew Bennett (Chair.); William Moloney (Sec.).

Principal Staff: Pres. Prof. David Bellamy; Dir David Shreeve.

Address: 1 Kensington Gore, London SW7 2AR.

Telephone: (20) 7591-3111; **Fax:** (20) 7591-3110; **Internet:** www.conservationfoundation.co.uk; **e-mail:** info@conservationfoundation.co.uk.

Marjorie Coote Animal Charities Trust

Founded in 1954 for the benefit of all or any of five named charities and of any other charitable organization that has as its main purpose the care and protection of horses, dogs or other animals or birds.

Activities: The Trust concentrates on funding research into animal health problems and on the protection of species, while a small proportion of the grants expenditure goes towards general animal welfare, including sanctuaries.

Geographical Area of Activity: World-wide.

Restrictions: No grants are made to individuals; applications must be made in writing to the correspondent, to arrive during the month of September.

Finance: Assets £2,466,736 (2009); annual revenue £100,000, grants expenditure £111,000 (2010).

Trustees: Sir Hugh Neill; J. P. Holah; Lady Neill; S. E. Browne.

Principal Staff: Contact J. P. Holah.

Address: Dykelands Farm, Whenby, York YO61 4SF.

Telephone: (1909) 562806.

Marie Curie Cancer Care

Founded in 1948 by T. B. Robinson and four others to provide in-patient and community care for cancer patients. Previously known as the Marie Curie Memorial Foundation, Marie Curie Cancer Care is dedicated to the care of people affected by cancer and the enhancement of their quality of life, through its caring services, cancer research and education.

Activities: Operates Marie Curie hospices throughout the United Kingdom. Provides a network of Marie Curie nurses across the United Kingdom, giving practical nursing care at home to people with cancer, free of charge. The Foundation also has its own Marie Curie Research Institute at Oxted in Surrey, and runs education and training courses for health professionals involved in cancer care. Maintains an office in Scotland.

Geographical Area of Activity: England, Northern Ireland, Scotland, Wales.

Publications: Annual Report and accounts; other leaflets and brochures; e-newsletter; *Shine On* (magazine).

Finance: Annual revenue £132,530,000, expenditure £129,026,000 (March 2011).

Trustees: John Varley (Chair.); Anthony Doggart (Hon. Treas.).

Principal Staff: Chief Exec. Thomas Hughes-Hallett.

Address: 89 Albert Embankment, London SE1 7TP.

Telephone: (20) 7599-7777; **Fax:** (20) 7599-7788; **Internet:** www.mariecurie.org.uk; **e-mail:** supporter.services@ mariecurie.org.uk.

Cystic Fibrosis Trust

Founded in 1964 to finance medical and scientific research aimed at understanding, treating and curing cystic fibrosis and ensuring that people with cystic fibrosis receive the best possible care and support in all aspects of their lives.

Activities: The Trust's principal objectives are to fund research to find a cure for cystic fibrosis and to improve symptom control; ensure appropriate clinical care for those with cystic fibrosis; and to support those affected by cystic fibrosis by providing information, support and, where appropriate, financial assistance.

Geographical Area of Activity: Mainly United Kingdom.

Publications: Report of operations and financial statement; *CF Today* (5 a year); *CF Talk; Focus on Fundraising;* extensive booklet series; booklets; factsheets; consensus documents.

Finance: Annual revenue £8,180,000, expenditure £8,180,000 (March 2011).

Trustees: Allan Gormly (Chair.).

Principal Staff: Chief Exec. Matthew Reed.

Address: 11 London Rd, Bromley, Kent BR1 1BY.

Telephone: (20) 8464-7211; **Fax:** (20) 8313-0472; **Internet:** www.cftrust.org.uk; **e-mail:** enquiries@cftrust.org.uk.

Roald Dahl's Marvellous Children's Charity

Founded in 1991 as the Roald Dahl Foundation. Changed its name in 2010.

Activities: Provides funding in the United Kingdom to benefit children with specific haematological and neurological conditions. Priorities include serious blood disorders (excluding cancer), severe epilepsy, acquired brain injury and specific neuro-degenerative conditions. Funds are given for specialist paediatric nursing, medical equipment that allows patients to be cared for at home, and information and support provided by charities. Grants are also given to individual children with these medical conditions who experiencing financial hardship. The Charity aims to help organizations for which funds are not readily available, i.e. small or new organizations.

Geographical Area of Activity: United Kingdom.

Restrictions: Grants are made in the United Kingdom only to NHS hospitals and charitable organizations. Grant applications are not considered for general appeals from large, well-established charities, nor for education fees.

Finance: Annual revenue £576,810, expenditure £736,688 (March 2010).

Trustees: Felicity Dahl; Martin A. F. Goodwin; Roger E. Hills; Georgina Howson, Virginia Fisher.

Principal Staff: Chief Exec: James Fitzpatrick.

Address: 81A High St, Great Missenden, Buckinghamshire HP16 0AL.

Telephone: (1494) 890465; **Fax:** (1494) 890459; **Internet:** www .roalddahlcharity.org; **e-mail:** enquiries@roalddahlcharity .org.

Daiwa Anglo-Japanese Foundation

Established in 1988 with a benefaction from Daiwa Securities Co Ltd to support closer links between the United Kingdom and Japan; aims to enhance the United Kingdom's and Japan's understanding of each other's people and culture; to enable British and Japanese students and academics to further their education through exchanges and co-operation; and to make grants available to individuals and organizations to promote links between the United Kingdom and Japan at all levels.

Activities: The Foundation carries out its work principally through the awarding of Daiwa Scholarships, grant-giving and a year-round programme of events. For the Daiwa Scholarship programme, up to 10 talented British graduates are chosen each year to spend 19 months in Japan. The scholarship has

three elements: language study, homestay and work placement. Scholars come from diverse backgrounds and past participants are now forging careers in architecture, the arts, science, media, law, academia and medicine. Grants are awarded to a wide range of beneficiaries who have included artists, scientists, university academics, schoolchildren, community-based organizations, theatre groups, research institutes, and national and regional museums; further details of the Foundation's grant-giving programmes are available on its website. The Foundation's headquarters in central London acts as a centre for academic and cultural activities relating to Japan. It provides a forum for discussion and exchange, meeting rooms for Japan and United Kingdom-Japan-associated activities and a Centre for Visiting Academics. Cultural and academic events held throughout the year include seminars, lectures, book launches and exhibitions, and all are aimed at increasing understanding between the United Kingdom and Japan, and stimulating cross-cultural debate. All events organized by the Foundation are free of charge.

Geographical Area of Activity: United Kingdom and Japan.

Restrictions: Grants are made for United Kingdom-Japanese exchange only.

Finance: Annual revenue £1,772,706, expenditure £1,702,054 (March 2008).

Trustees: Sir John Whitehead (Chair.); Masahiro Dozen (Vice-Chair.).

Principal Staff: Dir-Gen. Jason James.

Address: Daiwa Foundation Japan House, 13–14 Cornwall Terrace, London NW1 4QP.

Telephone: (20) 7486-4348; **Fax:** (20) 7486-2914; **Internet:** www.dajf.org.uk; **e-mail:** office@dajf.org.uk.

Miriam Dean Fund

Founded in 1964 as the Miriam Dean Refugee Trust Fund to provide aid to victims of war or other disasters; later renamed the Miriam Dean Fund.

Activities: Awards grants to charitable organizations abroad, particularly in South India and increasingly in Africa.

Geographical Area of Activity: South India, Kenya, South Africa.

Restrictions: No grants to individuals; grants only to specific NGOs.

Publications: Annual Report; Bi-annual newsletter.

Finance: Annual revenue £199,000; expenditure £221,000 (of which, grants disbursed £216,000).

Trustees: Jenny Buchanan; Robert Buchanan; Sheila Moore; Andy Moore; Brian Tims; Christine Tims.

Principal Staff: All trustees are volunteers; no paid staff.

Address: Hidden House, 3 Ladwell Close, Newbury, Berkshire RG14 6PJ.

Telephone: (1635) 34979; **Internet:** www.miriamdeanfund .org.uk; **e-mail:** trustees@miriamdeanfund.org.uk.

The Delius Trust

Founded in 1935 according to the will of Jelka Delius to promote the music of Frederick Delius by providing financial aid for performances and recordings and by publishing a collected edition of his works.

Activities: Operates nationally and internationally in the field of the arts and humanities, through providing grants to individuals and institutions towards the cost of performances and to finance recordings.

Publications: *The Collected Edition of the works of Frederick Delius;* several other books on the life and works of Frederick Delius; collected works.

Finance: Total income £135,744, expenditure £321,648 (2008).

Trustees: William Parker; Martin Williams; David Lloyd-Jones.

Principal Staff: Sec. Helen Faulkner.

Address: 7–11 Britannia St, London WC1X 9JS.

Telephone: (20) 7239-9143; **Internet:** www.delius.org.uk; **e-mail:** secretary@thedeliussociety.org.uk.

Diabetes UK

Founded in 1934, and previously known as the British Diabetic Association, to fund research into the prevention, treatment and cure of diabetes; to provide information and support to people living with diabetes.

Activities: Funds and initiates research into the causes and treatment of diabetes (about 38% of expenditure); provides advice and information to people with diabetes, and to health care professionals; campaigns against discrimination and promotes improved services for people with diabetes.

Geographical Area of Activity: United Kingdom.

Publications: Annual Report and accounts; *Diabetes Update* (quarterly journal); *Balance* (magazine, 2 a month); publications and leaflets; newsletters.

Finance: Annual revenue £29,334,000, expenditure £26,332,000 (2010).

Trustees: Prof. Sir George Alberti (Chair.); John Grumitt (Vice-Chair.); Graham Spooner (Treas.).

Principal Staff: Chief Exec. Barbara Young; Pres. Richard Lane.

Address: Macleod House, 10 Parkway, London NW1 7AA.

Telephone: (20) 7424-1000; **Fax:** (20) 7424-1001; **Internet:** www.diabetes.org.uk; **e-mail:** info@diabetes.org.uk.

Diageo Foundation

Established in 1998 by Diageo PLC, which includes the brands Guinness and Burger King, with a commitment to contribute 1% of Diageo's world-wide trading profit, less interest, to the community; aims to act as a primary funding and support organization for social investment programmes and charitable giving.

Activities: Operates internationally, principally where Diageo PLC businesses operate, through the following main programmes: Local Citizens; Alcohol Education; Our People (i.e. employee involvement); and Water of Life. Aspects of former programmes Global Brands and Skills for Life are incorporated into the current programmes. Works in collaboration with community charitable groups.

Geographical Area of Activity: International.

Restrictions: Does not fund individuals, medical charities, religious or political organizations, or animal welfare charities.

Finance: Annual revenue £1,137,651, expenditure £1,086,590 (June 2008).

Trustees: G. T. Bush; I. Wright; W. Bullard; K. M. Harvey; J. White; K. Chapman; N. Cartwright; F. Erlandsson; L. Menuhin; J. Lloyd.

Principal Staff: Sec. Richard P. Brierley.

Address: 7 Lakeside Dr., Park Royal, London NW10 7HQ.

Telephone: (20) 7927-5276; **Internet:** www.diageo.com; **e-mail:** diageofoundation@diageo.com.

Diana, Princess of Wales Memorial Fund

Established in 1997 in memory of Diana, Princess of Wales (1961–97), by donations from the public and revenue from commemorative goods, including the sale of a music single by Sir Elton John, for charitable purposes.

Activities: Disburses funds to organizations working in the fields of medicine and health (HIV/AIDS), aid to less-developed countries (clearing landmines), social welfare and studies (refugees and asylum seekers).

Geographical Area of Activity: United Kingdom.

Restrictions: No demand-driven open grants rounds are envisaged, apart from a restricted amount of funding to be made available through an open grants process under the Refugee and Asylum-Seekers Initiative.

Publications: *Strategic Plan 2007–12*; Annual Report.

Finance: Annual revenue £903,000, expenditure £6,324,000 (Dec. 2009).

Directors: Lady Sarah McCorquodale (Pres.); Sir Roger Singleton (Chair.); Terry Hitchcock (Treas.).

Principal Staff: Chief Exec. Dr Astrid Bonfield.

Address: County Hall, Westminster Bridge Rd, London SE1 7PB.

Telephone: (20) 7902-5500; **Fax:** (20) 7902-5511; **Internet:** www.theworkcontinues.org; **e-mail:** memorial.fund@memfund.org.uk.

Ditchley Foundation

Founded in 1958 by Sir David Wills to promote, carry out or advance any charitable objects, and in particular any branches or aspects of education likely to be for the common benefit of British subjects and citizens of the USA.

Activities: Exclusively supports in-house activities; maintains Ditchley Park as a conference centre and supports the Ditchley conference programme. Facilities are available to other bodies on a fee-paying basis. Organizes invitation-only conferences on topics of international concern to the British and American peoples, with the participation of other nationalities, particularly from member states of the European Union. US and Canadian Ditchley Foundations exist with similar aims, and to assist in the work of the United Kingdom Ditchley Foundation.

Restrictions: No grants to individuals or groups unless at Ditchley.

Publications: Annual Report and financial statement; newsletters and conference reports.

Finance: Total income £1,076,627, total expenditure £1,273,801 (March 2007).

Council of Management: Lady Wills (Hon. Life Pres.); Lord Robertson (Chair.); Sir Richard Mottram (Vice-Chair.).

Principal Staff: Dir Sir John Holmes.

Address: Ditchley Park, Enstone, Chipping Norton OX7 4ER.

Telephone: (1608) 677346; **Fax:** (1608) 677399; **Internet:** www.ditchley.co.uk; **e-mail:** info@ditchley.co.uk.

Dulverton Trust

Founded in 1949 by the first Lord Dulverton for general charitable purposes at the discretion of the trustees.

Activities: Operates nationally and to a lesser extent in East Africa and Southern Africa in the fields of youth and education, conservation, general welfare, religion, preservation, peace and security.

Geographical Area of Activity: East Africa and Southern Africa, United Kingdom.

Restrictions: No grants in area of medicine and health, nor to organizations based in Greater London or Northern Ireland, nor to museums, arts organizations, expeditions, schools, colleges or universities. Grants only made to registered charities and never to individuals.

Publications: Annual Report.

Finance: Annual revenue £2,582,261, expenditure £3,171,820 (March 2011).

Trustees: Christopher Wills (Chair.); Sir John Kemp-Welch (Vice-Chair.).

Principal Staff: Dir Andrew Stafford.

Address: 5 St James's Pl., London SW1A 1NP.

Telephone: (20) 7629-9121; **Fax:** (20) 7495-6201; **Internet:** www.dulverton.org; **e-mail:** trust@dulverton.org.

John Ellerman Foundation

Formed in 1992 by the merger of the New Moorgate Trust Fund and the Moorgate Trust Fund, for general charitable purposes.

Activities: Works in the United Kingdom and, to a limited extent, in Sub-Saharan Africa. Grants given are based on merit and worthiness, and are made within five categories:

arts, social welfare, health and disability, conservation and overseas (the latter jointly with the Baring Foundation).

Geographical Area of Activity: Southern and East Africa, United Kingdom.

Restrictions: Grants are not made to individuals, nor for education; only supports organizations with an office in the United Kingdom.

Publications: Annual Report.

Finance: Annual revenue £1,340,000, expenditure £5,170,000 (March 2011).

Trustees: Lady Sarah Riddell (Chair.).

Principal Staff: Dir Tim Glass.

Address: Aria House, 23 Craven St, London WC2N 5NS.

Telephone: (20) 7930-8566; **Fax:** (20) 7839-3654; **Internet:** www.ellerman.org.uk; **e-mail:** enquiries@ellerman.org.uk.

EMI Music Sound Foundation

Established in 1997 as an independent charity dedicated to the improvement of music education; formerly known as the Music Sound Foundation.

Activities: Operates in the United Kingdom in the areas of primary, secondary and tertiary education in the field of music, through making grants to schools, to music students to pay for instruments, and to music teachers for training. Sponsors specialist performing arts colleges.

Geographical Area of Activity: United Kingdom and Ireland.

Restrictions: Does not currently fund community projects or music therapy.

Publications: Annual Review.

Finance: Annual revenue £384,000, expenditure £514,300 (July 2007).

Trustees: David Hughes (Chair.).

Principal Staff: Chief Exec. Janie Orr.

Address: 27 Wrights Lane, London W8 5SW.

Telephone: (20) 7795-7000; **Fax:** (20) 7795-7296; **Internet:** www.emimusicsoundfoundation.com; **e-mail:** enquiries@emimusicsoundfoundation.com.

EMUNAH (Faith)

Founded in 1933 to promote the welfare of underprivileged and vulnerable children in Israel, provide funds for education and therapy, and help dysfunctional families. EMUNAH UK funds 35 of the 225 EMUNAH projects in Israel and is part of World EMUNAH with more than 180,000 members in 30 countries. In recognition of the valuable contribution made to Israeli society more than 75 years, EMUNAH, along with two other organizations, was awarded the Israel Prize in 2008, coinciding with Israel's 60th Anniversary.

Activities: Operates in Israel in the above areas, providing funding for special needs centres, residential homes, schools, after-school activities, community centres, sports centres and day-care centres.

Geographical Area of Activity: Israel.

Publications: Newsletter (quarterly), legacy information leaflet plus other information showing various ways to support the charity.

Trustees: L. Brodie; G. Compton; R. Selby; G. Grahame. R. Cohen.

Principal Staff: Chair. Camille Compton; Dir Deborah Nathan.

Address: Shield House, Harmony Way, London NW4 2BZ.

Telephone: (20) 8203-6066; **Fax:** (20) 8203-6668; **Internet:** www.emunah.org.uk; **e-mail:** info@emunah.org.uk.

Engineering and Physical Sciences Research Council—EPSRC

The Science Research Council (SRC) was formed in 1965 to address issues highlighted by the Trend Committee to do with the organization of civil science in the United Kingdom.

In 1981 this became the Science and Engineering Research Council (SERC) to reflect the increased emphasis on engineering research, and was responsible for all publicly funded scientific engineering and research activities, including astronomy, biotechnology and biological sciences, space research and particle physics in the United Kingdom. In 1994 the SERC was split into discipline-specific areas, resulting in the formation of the Engineering and Physical Sciences Research Council (EPSRC).

Activities: The Council's mission is to: promote and support, by any means, high-quality, basic, strategic and applied research and related postgraduate training in engineering and the physical sciences; advance knowledge and technology (including the promotion and support of the exploitation of research outcomes), and provide trained scientists and engineers, which meet the needs of users and beneficiaries (including the chemical, communications, construction, electrical, electronic, energy, engineering, information technology, pharmaceutical, process and other industries), thereby contributing to the economic competitiveness of the United Kingdom and the quality of life. The Council may also: generate public awareness, communicate research outcomes, encourage public engagement and dialogue, disseminate knowledge and provide advice. The Council's vision is for the United Kingdom to be the most dynamic and stimulating environment in which to engage in research and innovation. In 2009/10-disbursed more than £800m. of funds on research and training in engineering and the physical sciences. In 2008/09 invested £3.3bn in more than 6,000 research projects, as well as supporting 23,400 researchers and students, and collaborating with more than 2,000 companies through programmes.

Geographical Area of Activity: United Kingdom.

Restrictions: Grants only to universities.

Publications: Annual Report and Accounts; Strategic Plan; Delivery Plan; Delivery Report; magazines and newsletters: Pioneer, Connect; brochures: *IDEAS Factory, Connecting with Business, Engaging Maths.*

Finance: Most funding comes from the Department for Business, Innovation and Skills. Total assets £97,076,000 (2009/10).

Principal Staff: Chair. John Armitt; Chief Exec. Prof. David Delpy.

Address: Polaris House, North Star Ave, Swindon SN2 1ET.

Telephone: (1793) 444000; **Internet:** www.epsrc.ac.uk; **e-mail:** infoline@epsrc.ac.uk.

English-Speaking Union

Founded in 1918 by Sir Evelyn Wrench to promote the mutual advancement of the education of the English-speaking peoples of the world.

Activities: Operates internationally through groups in more than 40 countries in the fields of education, the arts and humanities, science, environment, and international affairs, through self-conducted programmes and conferences. Provides scholarships and fellowships for British graduates and teachers to pursue research at US universities and institutions, for study trips to the USA, and awards for British graduates or holders of professional qualifications to work on projects in developing countries.

Geographical Area of Activity: International.

Publications: Annual Report; *Concord* (magazine, 2 a year); *ESU Newsletter* (6 a year).

Finance: Annual revenue £2,041,747, expenditure £2,056,816 (March 2010).

Trustees: Dame Mary Richardson (Chair.); Jonathan Dye (Deputy Chair.); Sir Peter Jennings (Deputy Chair.); Alan Cox (Hon. Treas.).

Principal Staff: Dir-Gen. Peter Kyle.

Address: Dartmouth House, 37 Charles St, London W1J 5ED.

Telephone: (20) 7529-1550; **Fax:** (20) 7495-6108; **Internet:** www.esu.org; **e-mail:** esu@esu.org.

Environmental Justice Foundation—EJF

Established in 2000 with the aim of empowering people most affected by environmental abuses to prevent such abuses.

Activities: Provides training to organizations in the southern hemisphere in finding solutions to environmental abuses; promotes environmental security; produces films; campaigns internationally on issues including illegal fishing, agricultural production, pesticide use and wildlife depletion. Works with partner organizations in Brazil, Indonesia, Mali, Mauritius, Sierra Leone, Uzbekistan and Viet Nam.

Geographical Area of Activity: International.

Trustees: Anne Burley; William Lana; Steve McIvor; Rachel Rossi; Steve Trent.

Address: 1 Amwell St, London EC1R 1UL.

Telephone: (20) 7239-3310; **Internet:** www.ejfoundation.org; **e-mail:** info@ejfoundation.org.

European Association for Cancer Research

Founded in 1968 to advance cancer research by facilitating communication between scientists. The mission is to advance cancer research, from basic research to prevention, treatment and care.

Activities: Operates internationally (mainly in Europe) in the field of medicine and science, by organizing conferences, sponsoring researchers, awarding fellowships and issuing publications. There are more than 8,000 members from more than 80 countries both within and outside Europe.

Geographical Area of Activity: International (mainly Europe).

Publications: *EACR Newsletter* (annually); *European Journal of Cancer* (18 a year).

Executive Committee: Julio Celis (Pres.); Moshe Oren (Pres. elect); Richard Marais (Sec.-Gen.); Christof von Kalle (Treas.).

Principal Staff: Exec. Dir Robert Kenney.

Address: School of Pharmacy, University of Nottingham, Nottingham NG7 2RD.

Telephone: (115) 951-5114; **Fax:** (115) 951-5115; **Internet:** www.eacr.org; **e-mail:** eacr@nottingham.ac.uk.

The Eveson Charitable Trust

Founded in 1994 according to the will of Violet Eveson for general charitable purposes.

Activities: Provides grants to organizations working in Herefordshire, Worcestershire and the West Midlands, including Birmingham and Coventry, in the fields of the physically or mentally disabled, hospitals and hospices, the elderly, blind and deaf people, children, the homeless and medical research.

Geographical Area of Activity: United Kingdom (Herefordshire, Worcestershire and the West Midlands).

Restrictions: Grants are made only in Herefordshire, Worcestershire and the West Midlands; no grants for individuals.

Finance: Annual revenue £587,151, expenditure £2,343,563 (March 2010).

Trustees: David Philip Pearson (Chair.).

Principal Staff: Admin. Alex D. Gay.

Address: 45 Park Rd, Gloucester GL1 1LP.

Telephone: (1452) 501352; **Fax:** (1452) 302195.

Esmée Fairbairn Foundation

Founded in 1961 as the Esmée Fairbairn Charitable Trust (name changed in 2001).

Activities: Funds the charitable activities of organizations that have the ideas and ability to achieve change for the better. Supports work that might otherwise be considered difficult to fund. Primary interests are in the arts, education and learning, the environment and social change.

Geographical Area of Activity: United Kingdom.

Restrictions: Guidance notes must be obtained from the Foundation website or office before an application is submitted.

Finance: Grant budget £28,746,000 (2010).

Trustees: Tom Chandos (Chair.).

Principal Staff: CEO Dawn Austwick.

Address: Kings Pl., 90 York Way, London N1 9AG.

Telephone: (20) 7812-3700; **Internet:** www.esmeefairbairn.org.uk; **e-mail:** info@esmeefairbairn.org.uk.

Farm Africa

Established in 1985 to assist African farming and forest communities to reduce poverty through the development of agriculture and the effective use of natural resources.

Activities: Promotes effective agricultural development in East Africa. Maintains regional offices in Ethiopia, Kenya, Sudan and Tanzania.

Geographical Area of Activity: East Africa.

Finance: Annual revenue £8,225,000, expenditure £7,522,000 (2010).

Board: Dr Martin Evans (Chair.); Richard Lackmann (Treas.); Victoria Rae (Sec.).

Principal Staff: Pres. Sir Martin Wood; CEO Nigel Harris.

Address: Clifford's Inn, Fetter Lane, London EC4A 1BZ.

Telephone: (20) 7430-0440; **Fax:** (20) 7430-0460; **Internet:** www.farmafrica.org.uk; **e-mail:** farmafrica@farmafrica.org.uk.

The Federal Trust for Education and Research

Founded in 1945 under the auspices of William Beveridge to explore, through research and education, the suitability of federal solutions to problems of governance at national, continental and global level.

Activities: Involved in carrying out and promoting research, nationally and internationally, in the fields of international citizenship, constitutional developments, good governance at European and global level, European Union (EU) enlargement and various aspects of EU policy, through self-conducted programmes, conferences and publications. The Trust currently conducts research into the issue of devolution in the United Kingdom, democracy and stakeholder participation in the United Kingdom, the United Kingdom's relationship with the countries of the EU, EU policy, the role of international organizations such as the International Monetary Fund, the UN, and the World Trade Organization in developing global governance.

Geographical Area of Activity: United Kingdom, Europe.

Publications: *Europe, Parliament and the Media*; *European Futures*; *The Euro Debate*; *Treaty of Nice Explained*; newsletter; books; reports; policy reports; papers; european policy briefs; catalogue.

Finance: Annual revenue £162,670, expenditure £159,670 (Dec. 2007).

Trustees: Sir Stephen Wall (Chair.); Peter Sutherland (Pres.).

Principal Staff: Dir Brendan Donnelly.

Address: 31 Jewry St, London EC3N 2EY.

Telephone: (20) 7320-3045; **Internet:** www.fedtrust.co.uk; **e-mail:** info@fedtrust.co.uk.

Feed the Minds

Founded by Lord Coggan in 1964 to support the development of Christian literature programmes in less-developed countries.

Activities: Feed the Minds is a United Kingdom-based Christian charity that supports literacy projects in developing countries, giving financial assistance and enabling the capacity development of grassroots organizations.

Geographical Area of Activity: Developing countries.

Finance: Annual revenue £732,948, expenditure £826,463 (April 2008).

Board of Trustees: David Goodbourn (Chair.).

Principal Staff: Chief Exec. Josephine Carlsson.

Address: Park Pl., 12 Lawn Lane, London SW8 1UD.

Telephone: (20) 7582-3535; **Internet:** www.feedtheminds .org; **e-mail:** info@feedtheminds.org.

Finnish Institute in London Trust

Founded in 1990, the mission of the Institute is to identify emerging issues in contemporary society and to facilitate social change.

Activities: The Institute works with artists, researchers, experts and policy-makers in Finland, the United Kingdom and Ireland to promote strong networks in the field of culture and social studies; encourages new, unexpected collaborations and supports artistic interventions and social innovation. There are two main programme strands: Culture and Society. Within the field of culture, the Institute works to facilitate cultural export, artist exchange and innovative collaborations across the arts and across borders. Within social studies it invites broad participation to focus on challenges and opportunities in contemporary society to turn research results into evidence for policy-makers.

Geographical Area of Activity: United Kingdom, Republic of Ireland, Finland.

Publications: E-newsletter.

Finance: Financed by the Finnish Ministry of Education, with projects funded from various sources.

Executive Board: Tapio Markkanen (Chair.); Marianna Kajantie (Vice-Chair.).

Principal Staff: Dir Raija Koli.

Address: Finnish Institute, 35–36 Eagle St, London WC1R 4AQ.

Telephone: (20) 7404-3309; **Fax:** (20) 7404-8893; **Internet:** www.finnish-institute.org.uk; **e-mail:** info@finnish -institute.org.uk.

FORWARD—Foundation for Women's Health, Research and Development

Founded by Efua Dorkenoo in 1983 to promote improved reproductive health among African women and their children, and education to counter traditional practices that are prejudicial to the health of women and children.

Activities: The primary objective of the Foundation since 1985 has been to campaign for the elimination of female genital mutilation through: sponsoring local health and education programmes; supporting community self-help groups; facilitating the development of co-ordinated policies on the issue within local authorities in the United Kingdom; disseminating information to professionals and students working on the issue; and providing training for professionals, including health workers to provide better services to affected women.

Geographical Area of Activity: United Kingdom and Africa.

Restrictions: Not a grant-making organization.

Publications: *Voices of Tarime girls: Views on Child Marriage, Health and Rights*; *Child Protection and Female Genital Mutilation*; *Holistic Care for Women: A Practical Guide for Midwives*; *Female Genital Mutilation: Proposals for Change*; *Out of Sight, Out of Mind*; *Another Form of Physical Abuse: Prevention of Female Genital Mutilation in the United Kingdom* (video); online newsletter and other publications; newsletters (annually); Annual Reports.

Finance: Annual revenue £499,680, expenditure £448,512 (March 2009).

Board of Trustees: Dr Soheil O'Neil (Chair.); Hanan Ibrahim (Vice-Chair.); Lisa Smith (Treas.).

Principal Staff: Exec. Dir Naana Otoo-Oyortey.

Address: Suite 2.1, Chandelier House, 8 Scrubs Lane, London NW10 6RB.

Telephone: (20) 8960-4000; **Fax:** (20) 8960-4014; **Internet:** www.forwarduk.org.uk; **e-mail:** forward@forwarduk.org.uk.

Foundation for International Environmental Law and Development—FIELD

Founded in 1989 by James Cameron and Philippe Sands to contribute to the progressive development of international law for the protection of the environment and the attainment of sustainable development.

Activities: An NGO that brings together public international lawyers committed to the promotion of environmental protection and sustainable development through law, promotes the development of the law through research, disseminates the law through teaching, training and publishing, and applies the law through advocacy, advice and assistance. There are three core programmes covering Biodiversity and Marine Resources; Climate Change and Energy; and Trade, Investment and Sustainable Development.

Geographical Area of Activity: International.

Restrictions: FIELD is not a grant-making organization.

Publications: *FIELD in Brief* (newsletter); Annual Report; and other publications.

Trustees: Kate Gilmore (Chair.).

Principal Staff: Dir Joy Hyvarinen.

Address: 3 Endsleigh St, London WC1H 0DD.

Telephone: (20) 7872-7200; **Fax:** (20) 7388-2826; **Internet:** www.field.org.uk; **e-mail:** field@field.org.uk.

Foundation for Management Education—FME

Founded in 1960 to support and make grants to colleges and other institutions at university level for the study of business management; to establish professorships, fellowships, lectureships and scholarships.

Activities: Operates nationally through grants to business schools, universities and colleges for specific projects.

Geographical Area of Activity: United Kingdom.

Restrictions: No grants are awarded to individuals.

Publications: Annual Report and financial statement.

Council: John Wybrew (Chair.); Sir Bob Reid (Pres.).

Principal Staff: Dir Mike Jones.

Address: TBAC Business Centre, Avenue Four, Station Lane, Witney OX28 4BN.

Telephone: (1993) 848722; **Internet:** www.management -education.org.uk; **e-mail:** fme@lineone.net.

Foundation for Sport and the Arts

Founded in 1991 by Littlewoods, Vernons and Zetters football pools companies to promote greater participation in, and enjoyment of, sport and the arts.

Activities: Operates nationally in the field of the arts and sports. Seeks to enhance the quality of life of the community in general. Its main objective is to help increase participation in, and enjoyment of, sport and the arts by the whole community. The Foundation is not accepting applications as of March 2009 and is to cease its activities in 2012. It has awarded grants worth £350m. since its establishment.

Geographical Area of Activity: United Kingdom (excluding the Isle of Man and the Channel Islands).

Restrictions: No applications were to be considered after March 2009.

Trustees: Lord Attenborough (Hon. Pres.); Sir Tim Rice (Chair.); Lord Brabazon of Tara (Deputy Chair.).

Principal Staff: Sec. Richard Boardley.

Address: Walton House, 55 Charnock Rd, Walton, Liverpool L67 1AA.

Telephone: (151) 259-5505; **Fax:** (151) 230-0664; **Internet:** www.thefsa.net; **e-mail:** contact@thefsa.net.

Foundation for the Study of Infant Deaths

Founded in 1971 by Mrs J. Hunter-Gray to raise funds for research into sudden infant death syndrome (cot death—SIDS), to support bereaved families and to act as an information centre.

Activities: Operates in England, Wales and Northern Ireland in the fields of medicine and health, and social welfare and studies, through self-conducted programmes, research, grants to institutions and individuals, conferences, training courses and publications. The Foundation supports research programmes in various areas concerning the sudden and unexplained death of infants, including epidemiology, immunology, pathology, statistics and infection. Research grants relevant to SIDS are offered to researchers in the United Kingdom and elsewhere. Also provides support to families whose babies have died suddenly and unexpectedly and disseminates information about cot death and baby care among professionals and the public.

Geographical Area of Activity: England, Wales and Northern Ireland.

Publications: E-newsletters and numerous leaflets.

Finance: Annual revenue £1,429,708, expenditure £1,511,347 (June 2007).

Council of Trustees: T. Hebden (Chair.).

Principal Staff: CEO Francine Bates.

Address: 11 Belgrave Rd, London SW1V 1RB.

Telephone: (20) 7802-3200; **Fax:** (20) 7802-3229; **Internet:** www.fsid.org.uk; **e-mail:** office@fsid.org.uk.

The Anne Frank Trust UK

Founded in 1991 to advance public education in the United Kingdom in the principles of racial and religious tolerance and democracy.

Activities: Organizes travelling exhibitions and educational workshops.

Geographical Area of Activity: Europe, United Kingdom.

Restrictions: Does not make grants.

Finance: Annual revenue £895,887, expenditure £869,766 (Dec. 2009).

Board of Trustees: Daniel Mendoza (Chair.); Lynne Berry (Vice-Chair.).

Principal Staff: Exec. Dir Gillian Walnes; COO Robert Posner.

Address: Star House, 104–108 Grafton Rd, London NW5 4BA.

Telephone: (20) 7284-5858; **Fax:** (20) 7428-2601; **Internet:** www.annefrank.org.uk; **e-mail:** info@annefrank.org.uk.

The Gaia Foundation

Founded in 1985 as the Gaia Foundation to demonstrate how human development and well-being are linked to the health and understanding of the living planet; began its work in the Amazon region.

Activities: Collaborates with projects in Europe, Central and South America, Africa and Asia to protect biodiversity and promote sustainable living. Co-ordinates information and seeks to create links between communities, individuals and organizations in the North and communities in the South, and to encourage financial collaboration in projects in developing countries.

Geographical Area of Activity: Central and South America, Africa, Asia and Europe.

Restrictions: Does not make grants to individuals.

Publications: *Cool Tobacco, Sweet Coca*; *Biopiracy–The Plunder of Nature and Knowledge*; *Indigenous Peoples of Colombia and the Law*; *The Forest Within*; *The Movement for Collective Intellectual Rights*; *Raiding the Future: Patent Truths or Patent Lies*; briefings; papers.

Finance: Annual revenue £1,614,648, expenditure £1,739,273 (Dec. 2007).

Trustees: Jules Cashford; Nic Marks; Edward Posey; Michael Shaw; Tracy Worcester.

Principal Staff: Dir Liz Hosken.

Address: 6 Heathgate Pl., Agincourt Rd, Hampstead, London NW3 2NU.

Telephone: (20) 7428-0055; **Fax:** (20) 7428-0056; **Internet:** www.gaiafoundation.org; **e-mail:** info@gaianet.org.

Garden Organic/Henry Doubleday Research Association—HDRA

Founded in 1958 by Lawrence Hills to research and promote organic gardening, farming and food; officially known as the Henry Doubleday Research Association; working name Garden Organic since 2005.

Activities: Operates in the fields of conservation and the environment and education, through self-conducting programmes nationally and internationally, research, conferences and training courses. The Association runs organic gardens, an education and conference centre, and a consultancy department on organic waste disposal. It collaborates with other organic research centres and groups in the United Kingdom and overseas. Also maintains a Heritage Seed Library and trades through Organic Enterprises Ltd; maintains the Vegetable Kingdom visitor centre.

Geographical Area of Activity: International.

Publications: *The Organic Way* (quarterly); step-by-step guides; organic gardening books; composting manuals.

Finance: Total income £3,574,838, expenditure £4,061,377 (Dec. 2008).

Board: M. Hitchins (Chair.).

Principal Staff: Chief Exec. M. Bremner.

Address: Garden Organic, Coventry, Warwickshire CV8 3LG.

Telephone: (24) 7630-3517; **Fax:** (24) 7663-9229; **Internet:** www.gardenorganic.org.uk; **e-mail:** enquiry@gardenorganic.org.uk.

The Gatsby Charitable Foundation

Founded in 1967 to provide funds for general charitable purposes. One of the Sainsbury Family Charitable Trusts, which share a common administration.

Activities: The Foundation gives grants for work in the following areas: aid to less-developed countries (Africa); economic and social research; mental health; plant science; technical education; cognitive neuroscience; disadvantaged children and young people; local economic renewal; and the arts. The Foundation also funds the Sainsbury Centre for Mental Health. Local trusts, directed by local trustees, have been established in Cameroon, Kenya, Tanzania and Uganda to fund development projects.

Geographical Area of Activity: Africa and United Kingdom.

Restrictions: Unsolicited applications are not normally considered for funding. Grants are not normally made to individuals.

Publications: *Gatsby Papers*; *Technology Transfer: Report on Six Pilot Projects*; Annual Report; newsletters.

Finance: Assets £334,239,000 (2006); annual revenue £64,407,000, expenditure £52,733,000 (April 2009).

Trustees: C. T. S. Stone (Chair.).

Principal Staff: Dir Michael Pattison; Deputy Dir P. Hesketh; Fin. Dir P. Spokes; Dir A. Bookbinder.

Address: Allington House, 1st Floor, 150 Victoria St, London SW1E 5AE.

Telephone: (20) 7410-0330; **Fax:** (20) 7410-0332; **Internet:** www.gatsby.org.uk; **e-mail:** contact@gatsby.org.uk.

J. Paul Getty Jnr Charitable Trust

Founded in 1985 to support general charitable purposes in areas of deprivation in the United Kingdom.

Activities: Involved in projects assisting the homeless, offenders and ex-offenders, the mentally ill, drug and alcohol addicts, community groups, self-help groups, and projects working with young people and ethnic minorities. Some support may also be given to conservation projects. Potential applicants are asked to visit the Trust's website and read the guidelines carefully before applying for a grant.

Geographical Area of Activity: United Kingdom.

Restrictions: Financial assistance is provided only to registered charities, not individuals. Charities already widely supported are unlikely to be considered. Preference is given to projects outside the South-East of the United Kingdom; no funds are offered outside the United Kingdom.

Publications: Annual Reports.

Finance: Annual revenue £1,086,079, expenditure £9,655,137 (2010).

Trustees: Christopher Gibbs (Chair.).

Principal Staff: Dir Elizabeth Rantzen.

Address: 1 Park Sq. West, London NW1 4LJ.

Telephone: (20) 7486-1859; **Internet:** www.jpgettytrust.org .uk.

The Glass-House Trust

Established in 1993 (as the Alex Sainsbury Charitable Trust) to work in the areas of parenting, family welfare and child development. One of the Sainsbury Family Charitable Trusts, which share a common administration.

Activities: Operates in the above areas through making grants to United Kingdom organizations working nationally and internationally. It also supports projects in the areas of child-care and family support, education and research/policy development. Co-funder of the Ashden Awards for Sustainable Energy.

Geographical Area of Activity: International.

Finance: Annual revenue £504,376, expenditure £540,611 (April 2010).

Trustees: Alex Sainsbury; Elinor Sainsbury; James Sainsbury; Jessica Sainsbury; Judith Portrait.

Principal Staff: Dir A. Bookbinder.

Address: Allington House, 1st Floor, 150 Victoria St, London SW1E 5AE.

Telephone: (20) 7410-0330; **Fax:** (20) 7410-0332; **Internet:** www.sfct.org.uk/glass_house.html; **e-mail:** sfct@sfct.org.uk.

Goodenough College

The College was founded in 1930 to improve international tolerance and understanding among people on the brink of their careers by providing a forum in which they could interact.

Activities: An independent college for international postgraduate students, organizes workshops, seminars, conferences and cultural, artistic and sporting activities.

Geographical Area of Activity: International.

Publications: Newsletter (2 a year); brochures; Yearbook.

Finance: Independently funded.

Board: Jonathan Hirst (Chair.).

Principal Staff: Pres. Advisory Council Lord Fellowes; Dir Andrew Ritchie.

Address: Mecklenburgh Sq., London WC1N 2AB.

Telephone: (20) 7837-8888; **Fax:** (20) 7833-5829; **Internet:** www.goodenough.ac.uk; **e-mail:** appointments@ goodenough.ac.uk.

Great Britain Sasakawa Foundation

Founded in 1985 to enhance mutual appreciation and understanding in the United Kingdom and Japan of each other's institutions, culture and achievements.

Activities: Operates principally in the United Kingdom and Japan, especially favouring projects involving reciprocal action between the two countries. Special awards include the Butterfield Awards for collaboration in medicine and health and the Programme for Japanese Studies, which seeks to promote the study of Japanese contemporary issues in British universities.

Geographical Area of Activity: Japan and United Kingdom.

Restrictions: Grants are made to citizens of either the United Kingdom or Japan or those working for institutions in those countries. Consideration may be given to projects dealing with matters concerning the two countries, from national and multinational organizations elsewhere.

Publications: Annual Report and accounts; brochures; books.

Finance: Annual revenue £1,244,174, expenditure £1,332,873 (2008).

Trustees: Prof. Peter Mathias (Pres.); Earl of St Andrews (Chair.); Jeremy Brown (Vice-Chair.); Michael French (Treas.).

Principal Staff: Chief Exec. Stephen McEnally.

Address: Dilke House, 1 Malet St, London WC1E 7JN.

Telephone: (20) 7436-9042; **Internet:** www.gbsf.org.uk; **e-mail:** gbsf@gbsf.org.uk.

HALO Trust

Established in 1989; specializes in the removal of the debris of war, particularly mine clearance.

Activities: Operates in countries of Africa, South-East and Central Asia, and the Caucasus and Balkans, through training local teams of managers, mine clearers, mechanics, medical staff, technicians and drivers. The Trust also uses teams of Mine Awareness trainers.

Geographical Area of Activity: Africa, South-East and Central Asia, and the Caucasus and Balkans.

Restrictions: No grants are disbursed.

Publications: Annual Report.

Finance: The Trust is financed by donations from private individuals, charities and foundations, and national governments. Total income £16,646,000, expenditure £15,727,000 (March 2007).

Trustees: Tom McMullen (Chair.).

Principal Staff: Chief Exec. Guy Willoughby.

Address: Carronfoot, Thornhill, Dumfries DG3 5BF.

Telephone: (1848) 331100; **Fax:** (1848) 331122; **Internet:** www .halotrust.org; **e-mail:** mail@halotrust.org.

Paul Hamlyn Foundation—PHF

Founded in 1987 (incorporating an earlier Paul Hamlyn Foundation, founded in 1972) to contribute to developments in the areas of the arts, education, social justice and overseas projects in India.

Activities: Currently operates three United Kingdom programmes: Arts, Education and Learning, and Social Justice, each of which runs an open grants scheme alongside special initiatives that focus on particular issues. PHF also operates a grants programme for NGOs in India. The Foundation is particularly concerned with children and young people, and disadvantaged people. It aims to help people fulfil their potential and improve their quality of life.

Geographical Area of Activity: United Kingdom and India.

Restrictions: Grants do not support: individuals or proposals for the benefit of one individual; funding for work that has already started; general circulars/appeals; proposals about property or which are mainly about equipment or other capital items; overseas travel, expeditions, adventure and residential courses; promotion of religion; animal welfare; medical/health/residential or day care; proposals from organizations outside the United Kingdom, except under the India programme; proposals that benefit people living outside the United Kingdom, except under the India programme.

Publications: *PHF Yearbook; PHF Strategic Plan 2006–12; PHF Awards Made.*

Finance: Annual revenue £11,239,000, expenditure £23,396,000 (March 2010).

Trustees: Jane Hamlyn (Chair.).

Principal Staff: Dir Robert Dufton.

Address: 18 Queen Anne's Gate, London SW1H 9AA.

Telephone: (20) 7227-3500; **Fax:** (20) 7222-0601; **Internet:** www.phf.org.uk; **e-mail:** information@phf.org.uk.

Headley Trust

Founded in 1973 for general charitable purposes. One of the Sainsbury Family Charitable Trusts, which share a common administration.

Activities: Operates nationally and internationally in a variety of fields, including arts and heritage (nationally and abroad), aid to less-developed countries, education, health and social welfare. Co-funder of the Ashden Awards for Sustainable Energy.

Geographical Area of Activity: International.

Restrictions: Unsolicited applications are not normally accepted. Grants are not normally made to individuals.

Publications: Annual report.

Finance: Annual revenue £2,420,000, expenditure £3,350,000 (2010).

Trustees: J. R. Benson; J. S. Portrait; Lady S. Sainsbury; Rt Hon. Sir T. Sainsbury; T. J. Sainsbury.

Principal Staff: Dir A. Bookbinder.

Address: Allington House, 1st Floor, 150 Victoria St, London SW1E 5AE.

Telephone: (20) 7410-0330; **Fax:** (20) 7410-0332; **Internet:** www.sfct.org.uk/headley.html; **e-mail:** sfct@sfct.org.uk.

Health Foundation

Established to improve standards in the provision of health care; to advance knowledge, skills and services in health care and public health; and to enhance the contributions of health-care practitioners to the quality of life of all the community; formerly known as the PPP Foundation, itself previously the PPP Healthcare Medical Trust.

Activities: The Health Foundation is an independent charitable foundation working to improve the quality of health care across the United Kingdom and beyond. Its endowment enables the Foundation to spend more than £20m. annually to develop leaders in health care, to test new ways of improving the quality of health services and to disseminate evidence for changing health policy and practice. Currently funds projects in five main areas: building and promoting knowledge on how to improve care; developing leadership for quality improvement; transforming organizations to deliver safer patient care; engaging with clinical communities to improve health care quality and value; and supporting patients' active contribution to better health and health care outcomes.

Geographical Area of Activity: Developing countries in Africa and Asia as part of specific grant programmes, and United Kingdom.

Restrictions: No grants for capital building.

Publications: Briefings; research reports; corporate publications; Annual Report.

Finance: Annual revenue £18,581,000, expenditure £16,436,000 (Dec. 2009).

Board of Governors: Sir Alan Langlands (Chair.); Adrienne Fresko (Vice-Chair.).

Principal Staff: Chief Exec. Stephen Thornton.

Address: 90 Long Acre, London WC2E 9RA.

Telephone: (20) 7257-8000; **Fax:** (20) 7257-8001; **Internet:** www.health.org.uk; **e-mail:** info@health.org.uk.

HelpAge International

Founded in 1983 by Help the Aged (Canada), HelpAge (India), HelpAge (Kenya), Help the Aged (United Kingdom) and Pro Vida Colombia; a global network of non-profit-making organizations with a mission to improve the lives of disadvantaged older people.

Activities: Provides expertise and grants to organizations serving the needs of older people in 80 developing countries, assisting them to help the most disadvantaged to lead independent lives. Promotes a positive image of old people world-wide, assisting them to achieve their full potential. Works in advocacy, training and research, disaster relief, refugee resettlement and rehabilitation. Develops and supports programmes designed to meet the financial, material, medical and social needs of older people world-wide. Maintains regional offices in Central and South America, the Caribbean, East and Central Europe, Africa and Asia, in Belgium, Bolivia, Kenya, South Africa, St Lucia and Thailand. Also runs country development programmes in Cambodia, Ethiopia, Mozambique, Rwanda, Sudan and Tanzania.

Geographical Area of Activity: International.

Restrictions: Grants only to older people and those working with them. Mainly funds own projects.

Publications: Newsletter; briefings; research papers on rights abuses, access to services, health and social protection; *The Madrid International Plan of Action on Ageing*; Annual Report.

Finance: Annual revenue £21,500,000, expenditure £19,700,000 (March 2010).

Governing Board: Tilak de Zoysa (Chair.); Cynthia Cox Roman (Vice-Chair.).

Principal Staff: CEO Richard Blewitt.

Address: POB 32832, London N1 9ZN.

Telephone: (20) 7278-7778; **Fax:** (20) 7713-7993; **Internet:** www.helpage.org; **e-mail:** info@helpage.org.

Heritage Lottery Fund—HLF

The HLF was set up by the United Kingdom Parliament in 1994 to give grants to a wide range of projects involving the local, regional and national heritage of the United Kingdom.

Activities: Grants are made for a wide range of heritage projects including countryside, parks and gardens; objects and sites that are linked to the United Kingdom's industrial, transport and maritime history; records such as local-history archives, photographic collections or oral history; historic buildings; and museum and gallery collections.

Geographical Area of Activity: United Kingdom.

Publications: *Heritage Matters*; *Strategic Plan*; *Research and Consultation*; *Broadening the Horizons of Heritage*; *Capturing the Public Value of Heritage*; *Equality Impact Assessment*; Annual Report; application packs; fact sheets; guidance notes.

Finance: Annual revenue £224,076,000, expenditure £249,241,000 (March 2011).

Trustees: Dame Jenny Abramsky (Chair.).

Principal Staff: Chief Exec. Carole Souter.

Address: 7 Holbein Pl., London SW1W 8NR.

Telephone: (20) 7591-6000; **Fax:** (20) 7591-6271; **Internet:** www.hlf.org.uk; **e-mail:** enquire@hlf.org.uk.

Terrence Higgins Trust—THT

In July 1982 Terry Higgins was one of the first people in the United Kingdom to die from AIDS. The Terrence Higgins Trust was established in 1982 by a group of his friends who wanted to prevent more people facing the same illness. Over the years, the organization has changed, but it has retained many of the overall aims: to reduce the spread of HIV and to promote good sexual health; to provide services and support for those affected to improve their quality of life; and to campaign for greater public understanding of HIV and AIDS and sexual health in general.

Activities: Operates in England, Wales and Scotland with people infected by HIV, people affected by HIV and those concerned about their sexual health. Runs a national helpline, THT Direct, which provides advice, information and support over the phone, by e-mail and through a web-based service called Sex Facts. Runs a network of local centres.

Geographical Area of Activity: United Kingdom.

Publications: Publications about living with HIV; publications which have a sexual health promotion function (i.e. about preventing HIV), and reports produced by the policy team, supporting campaigns; DVD aimed at people living with HIV, *Positively Living*.

Finance: Annual revenue £21,166,000, expenditure £22,084,000 (March 2011).

Trustees: Nick Hulme (Chair.).

Principal Staff: Chief Exec. Sir Nicholas Partridge; Deputy Chief Exec. Paul Ward.

Address: 314–320 Gray's Inn Rd, London WC1X 8DP.

Telephone: (20) 7812-1600; **Fax:** (20) 7812-1601; **Internet:** www.tht.org.uk; **e-mail:** info@tht.org.uk.

Hilden Charitable Fund

Founded in 1963 by Tony Rampton for general charitable purposes.

Activities: Principally involved in supporting projects in the United Kingdom in the areas of homelessness, asylum seekers and refugees, penal affairs and community based initiatives for disadvantaged young people; and in developing countries in the areas of community development, education and health.

Geographical Area of Activity: United Kingdom and developing countries.

Restrictions: No grants are made to individuals.

Publications: Annual Report.

Finance: Annual revenue £411,497, expenditure £594,395 (April 2011).

Trustees: J. R. A. Rampton; Prof. M. B. H. Rampton; A. J. M. Rampton; C. S. L. Rampton; Prof. D. S. Rampton; E. M. C. Rampton; Prof. C. H. Rodeck; E. K. Rodeck; E. J. Rodeck; C. H. Younger; M. E. Baxter.

Principal Staff: Sec. Rodney Hedley.

Address: 34 North End Rd, London W14 0SH.

Telephone: (20) 7603-1525; **Fax:** (20) 7603-1525; **Internet:** www.hildencharitablefund.org.uk; **e-mail:** hildencharity@hotmail.com.

Jane Hodge Foundation

Founded in 1962 to provide funds for the advancement of medical research and medical and surgical science, education and religion.

Activities: Provides grants to registered charities throughout the world, with particular emphasis on those supporting research into cancer, diseases affecting children, polio and tuberculosis.

Geographical Area of Activity: World-wide.

Restrictions: Grants only to exempt or registered charities.

Publications: *Annual Memorial Lecture*.

Finance: Annual revenue £559,000, expenditure £756,000 (Oct. 2010).

Trustees: D. L. Jones; E. M. Hammonds; I. H. Davies; J. Harrison; Lady Moira Hodge; M. Cason; R. J. Hodge.

Principal Staff: Contact Dianne Lydiard.

Address: Ty Gwyn, Lisvane Rd, Lisvane, Cardiff CF14 0SG.

Telephone: (29) 20766521; **Fax:** (29) 20757009.

Homeless International

Founded in 1989 for the relief of poverty following the 1987 UN International Year of Shelter for the Homeless. Initially formed as a trust, the organization later became Homeless International.

Activities: Operates internationally supporting community-led housing and infrastructure-related development, through grants to organizations, working in collaboration with local partners on long-term development. Also provides advisory and financial services, carries out research, and gives specialist technical assistance.

Geographical Area of Activity: Africa and Asia.

Publications: Annual Report; CLIFF Annual Report.

Finance: Total net assets £1,629,425; revenue £2,598,963, expenditure £3,182,594 (March 2010).

Council of Management: Simon Dow (Chair.); Tamson Stirling (Vice-Chair.); Suzanne Forster (Hon. Treas.).

Principal Staff: CEO Larry English.

Address: Queens House, 16 Queens Rd, Coventry CV1 3EG.

Telephone: (24) 7663-2802; **Fax:** (24) 7663-2911; **Internet:** www.homeless-international.org; **e-mail:** info@homeless-international.org.

A. S. Hornby Educational Trust

Founded in 1961 for the advancement of the English language, and its teaching and learning as a foreign language.

Activities: Provides scholarships (approx. 10 a year) and grants for foreign teachers to study teaching English as a foreign language in the United Kingdom. Awards include the English Speaking Union Summer School Bursary and British Council Summer School Scholarships. Works in collaboration with the British Council (q.v.).

Geographical Area of Activity: International.

Restrictions: Grants are made through the British Council; there are no direct grants.

Trustees: appointed by the British Council since 1978.

Address: c/o Bridgewater House, 58 Whitworth St, Manchester M1 6BB.

Telephone: (161) 9577755; **Fax:** (161) 9577762; **Internet:** www.britishcouncil.org/learning-elt-hornby.htm; **e-mail:** general.enquiries@britishcouncil.org.

Mo Ibrahim Foundation (Fondation Mo Ibrahim)

The Mo Ibrahim Foundation is committed to supporting great African leadership that will improve the economic and social prospects of the people of Africa.

Activities: The Mo Ibrahim Foundation was established to stimulate debate on governance in Africa. The Foundation offers the Ibrahim Prize for Achievement in African Leadership; the Ibrahim Index of African Governance; the Ibrahim Scholarship Programme; and the Ibrahim Fellowship Programme.

Geographical Area of Activity: Africa.

Publications: Ibrahim Index of African Governance.

Board: Mo Ibrahim (Chair.).

Address: 3rd Floor North, 35 Portman Sq., London W1H 6LR.

Telephone: (20) 7535-5063; **Internet:** www.moibrahimfoundation.org; **e-mail:** media@moibrahimfoundation.org.

Inclusion International—II

Inclusion International is a global federation of family-based organizations advocating for the human rights of people with intellectual disabilities world-wide. Established for more than 40 years, the organization now represents more than 200 member federations in 115 countries throughout five regions, including the Middle East and North Africa, Europe, Africa and the Indian Ocean, the Americas, and Asia Pacific.

Activities: The organization's implementation strategy for 2010–12 includes hosting a regional forum for families and self-advocates to learn from each other about initiatives in different countries that promote and implement aspects of the Convention. It will draw on the knowledge and expertise of its volunteers and member organizations to support country-level initiatives. It will work in partnership with the International Disability Alliance, and with UN agencies and development agencies to identify opportunities to include and promote the rights of people with intellectual disabilities in their work. It will launch a global campaign to promote the right to live in the community.

Geographical Area of Activity: International.

Publications: *Inclusion Around the World* (newsletter); *Global Report on Poverty and Disability—Hear Our Voices; Global Report on Education—Better Education for All, when we are included too; Priorities for People with Intellectual Disabilities in implementing the UNCRPD; The implication of the CRPD.*

Trustees and Officers: Klaus Lachwitz (Pres.); Ralph Jones (Sec.-Gen.).

Principal Staff: Exec. Dir Connie Laurin-Bowie.

Address: The Knowledge Dock, University of East London, Docklands Campus, 4–6 University Way, London E16 2RD.

Telephone: (20) 8223-7709; **Internet:** www.inclusion-international.org; **e-mail:** info@inclusion-international.org.

John Innes Foundation—JIF

John Innes Foundation (JIF) is an independent charity and a company limited by guarantee. It was formed in 1910 following a bequest from John Innes, a landowner in the City of London.

Activities: In 1910 the trustees of the Foundation founded the John Innes Horticultural Institution at Merton, London, John Innes's home. In 1945, finding those premises too restrictive, the Institution purchased an estate at Bayfordbury, Hertfordshire, and then, in 1967 moved to its present site in Colney, Norfolk. The Foundation provides grants to students for the advancement of education in agriculture, horticulture and biotechnology. It also provides land and buildings for research at the John Innes Centre in Norwich and supports a library there, containing material on the history of genetics and rare botanical books. It supports Emeritus Fellows and PhD studentships at JIC and the foundation also makes a contribution to a variety of on-site amenities including sport and environment.

Geographical Area of Activity: United Kingdom.

Finance: Annual revenue £1,114,467, expenditure £1,510,540 (2008).

Trustees: J. F. Oldfield (Chair.).

Principal Staff: Clerk to the Trustees J. P. Webster.

Address: 5 Nethergate St, Bungay.

Internet: www.johninnesfoundation.org.uk; **e-mail:** mail@jpwebster.co.uk.

Institute for European Environmental Policy—IEEP

Founded as an office of the European Cultural Foundation (q.v.), became independent in 1990.

Activities: The Institute carries out research and promotes strategies and alternatives for dealing with environmental problems in Europe, and proposes solutions to national governments, the European Parliament and other institutions. Research covers a number of areas, including agriculture, environmental governance, fisheries, marine conservation, nature conservation and biodiversity, climate change, rural development and transport. Also operates from Belgium and Finland.

Geographical Area of Activity: Europe.

Publications: *The Environment in Europe* (in English, French and German); *Manual of Environmental Policy: the EU and Britain* (updated twice yearly); Annual Reports.

Finance: Annual revenue £2,872,524, expenditure £2,775,196 (Dec. 2009).

Board of Trustees: Sir John Harman (Chair.).

Principal Staff: Exec. Dir David Baldock.

Address: 15 Queen Anne's Gate, London SW1H 9BU.

Telephone: (20) 7799-2244; **Fax:** (20) 7799-2600; **Internet:** www.ieep.eu; **e-mail:** aglynn@ieep.eu.

Interact Worldwide

The organization was established originally as the international branch of the Family Planning Association of the United Kingdom, and formerly known as Population Concern. It became fully independent in 1991.

Activities: Interact Worldwide is a United Kingdom-based international sexual and reproductive health and rights organization that has been working to promote family planning and reproductive health for more than 30 years. Maintains partnerships across Africa, Asia and Central and South America, and collaborative undertakings with organizations based in the United Kingdom, continental Europe, and the USA. Supports and implements programmes that enable marginalized people to fulfil their rights to sexual and reproductive health, including programmes that address the global HIV/Aids epidemic.

Geographical Area of Activity: International.

Publications: Annual Review; *Young People: Sexual and Reproductive Health* (booklet); *Partnerships in Action; Intimate Links: A call to action on HIV/AIDS and sexual and reproductive health and rights; Condom Shortage: Counting the Cost in Lives; Public Attitudes to HIV; Speaking Out—An expert opinion; Generating Gender Equity.*

Finance: Annual revenue £3,363,543, expenditure £2,837,816 (June 2011).

Trustees: Andrew Rogerson (Co-Chair.); Libby Cooper (Co-Chair.); Javaid Kahn (Accountant).

Principal Staff: Chief Exec. Marie Staunton; COO Alan Smith.

Address: Finsgate, 5–7 Cranwood St, London EC1V 9LH.

Telephone: (300) 777-8500; **Fax:** (300) 777-9778; **Internet:** www.interactworldwide.org; **e-mail:** programmes@interactworldwide.org.

International Alert—Alert

Founded in 1986 by Martin Ennals, Archbishop Desmond Tutu and other human rights advocates, on the simple belief that: 'Without peace, there is little hope for human rights'. International Alert is working towards a world where differences are resolved without resorting to violent conflict.

Activities: International Alert has three main aims: to work with people who live in areas affected or threatened by armed conflict to make a positive difference for peace; to work at government, European Union and UN levels to improve both the substance and implementation of international policies that affect prospects for peace; and to strengthen the peace-building sector through increasing its effectiveness and profile so that more people recognize the necessity of peace-building, what can be done to address violent conflict and the realities involved. Alert runs a body of programmes on conflict in the Great Lakes region of Africa, West Africa, Eurasia, South Asia and on peace-building issues including aid effectiveness, climate change, gender, security and economy/business.

Geographical Area of Activity: more than 20 countries and territories around the world, including West Africa (Guinea, São Tomé and Príncipe, Liberia, Sierra Leone), the Great Lakes region (Burundi, Rwanda, Uganda, Democratic Republic of Congo), Caucasus (Georgia, Armenia, Azerbaijan, Abkhazia and Nagorny Karabakh), Central Asia, the Philippines, Nepal and Sri Lanka.

Restrictions: Not a grant-making organization.

Publications: Annual Report, Annual Review, resource packs, research reports and other publications.

Finance: Annual revenue £10,510,000, expenditure £9,711,000 (2009).

Board of Trustees: Frida Nokken (Chair.); Pierre Schori (Vice-Chair.); Will Samuel (Hon. Treas.).

Principal Staff: Sec.-Gen. Dan Smith; COO Sue McCready.

Address: 346 Clapham Rd, London SW9 9AP.

Telephone: (20) 7627-6800; **Fax:** (20) 7627-6900; **Internet:** www.international-alert.org; **e-mail:** communications@international-alert.org.

International Association for the Exchange of Students for Technical Experience—IAESTE

Founded in 1948 by James Newby to provide students at institutions of higher education with technical experience abroad relative to their studies in the broadest sense, and to promote international understanding and goodwill among the students of all nations.

Activities: Arranges the exchange of training places among its 93 members and co-operating institutions in 85 countries world-wide, mainly for students of engineering and technology, but also for students of agriculture, applied arts, commerce, languages and science, enabling them to spend between two and 18 months gaining experience abroad as trainees of industrial and other organizations.

Geographical Area of Activity: International.

Restrictions: Not a grant-making organization.

Publications: Annual Report; Activity Report.

Finance: Funded by member subscriptions.

Board Members: Dr Pulat Pulatov; Gunter Muller-Graetschel; Thomas Faltner; Desanka Ichitrajkova.

Principal Staff: Gen. Sec. Pauline Ferguson; Pres. Goran Radnović.

Address: POB 102, Banbridge BT32 4WY.

Telephone: (28) 4062-5485; **Fax:** (28) 4062-5485; **Internet:** www.iaeste.org; **e-mail:** info@iaeste.org.

International Centre for the Legal Protection of Human Rights—Interights

Established in 1982 to support and promote the development of legal protection for human rights and freedoms world-wide through the effective use of international and comparative human rights law.

Activities: The Centre works in Africa, Commonwealth states of the Caribbean, Central and Eastern Europe and Southern Asia, providing technical advice and assistance to strengthen capacity and develop jurisprudence in each region and internationally. Programmes are developed in consultation with lawyers, judges, NGOs and others and generally combine casework, education and training, institutional development and provision of resources. The Centre also offers representation before regional and international tribunals; conducts workshops and seminars on the techniques associated with the use and interpretation of human rights law; publishes materials to ensure the dissemination of developments in human rights law; and maintains a specialized public library on international and comparative human rights law.

Geographical Area of Activity: Africa, Europe, South Asia and the Commonwealth.

Publications: *INTERIGHTS Bulletin* (quarterly journal); *Commonwealth Human Rights Law Digest* (journal, 3 a year); Annual Review; and other reports and publications.

Finance: Annual revenue £1,366,025, expenditure £1,341,552 (March 2008).

Board of Directors: Lord Lester of Herne Hill (Hon. Pres.); Prof. Jeremy McBride (Chair.); Priscilla Ashun-Sarpy (Treas.).

Principal Staff: Exec. Dir Danny Silverstone.

Address: Lancaster House, 33 Islington High St, London N1 9LH.

Telephone: (20) 7278-3230; **Fax:** (20) 7278-4334; **Internet:** www.interights.org; **e-mail:** ir@interights.org.

International Institute for Environment and Development—IIED

Founded in 1971 by economist and policy adviser Barbara Ward. The institute played key roles in the Stockholm Conference of 1972, the Brundtland Commission of 1987, the 1992 Earth Summit and the 2002 World Summit on Sustainable Development, and is now helping to shape the global debate on climate change. The Institute promotes sustainable world development through research, policy studies, networking and information dissemination.

Activities: The Institute seeks to change the world in partnership with others by providing leadership in researching and promoting sustainable development at a local, national and global level, with the aim of shaping a future that ends global poverty and sustains fair and sound management of the world's resources. Partnerships are key to the work of IIED. By forging alliances with individuals and organizations ranging from urban slum-dwellers to global institutions, IIED ensures that national and international policy reflects the agendas of marginalized people.

Geographical Area of Activity: Primarily Africa, Asia, and Central and South America.

Publications: IIED produces a range of books, journals, briefing papers, DVDs and CD ROMs. Publications include: *Environment and Urbanization (Human Settlements)*; *Participation, Learning and Action (Natural Resources)*; *Haramata (Climate Change)*; *Gatekeeper (Natural Resources)*; *Tiempo (Climate Change Group)*; *The Earthscan Reader in Rural-Urban Linkages*; *Reducing Poverty and Sustaining the Environment*; *Evidence for Hope*; *Words Into Action*; *Pelican Man—A Video Documentary*; *Sustainable Development Opinion Papers*.

Finance: Total revenue £20,188,018, expenditure £20,431,566 (March 2011).

Trustees: Maureen O'Neil (Chair.); Alan Jenkins (Vice-Chair.); Frank Kirwan (Treas.).

Principal Staff: Finance Officer Caroline Adebanjo.

Address: 80–86 Grays Inn Rd, London WC1X 8NH.

Telephone: (20) 7388-2117; **Fax:** (20) 7388-2826; **Internet:** www.iied.org; **e-mail:** info@iied.org.

The International Institute for Strategic Studies—IISS

Founded in 1958, its objective, amended in 1992, is to promote on a non-party basis the study and discussion of, and exchange of information on, military strategy, weapons control, regional security and conflict resolution.

Activities: Operates in the field of international affairs by providing an independent centre for research, debate and the dissemination of information. Most research is carried out by a team of Research Fellows and Research Associates and funded by various foundations. Most research is in three inter-related areas: the changing nature of international security; national and regional security; and arms control and demilitarization. The Institute, which is a membership organization, holds several conferences a year, including a major annual conference for members, and an annual memorial lecture (given by an important international figure) in memory of the first Director, Alastair Buchan, and discussion meetings and seminars. Maintains a library and information centre.

Geographical Area of Activity: USA, Asia, United Kingdom.

Publications: *The Military Balance* (annually); *Strategic Survey* (annually); *Survival* (quarterly); *Adelphi Papers* (monographs, 8–10 a year); *Strategic Comments* (10 a year); *Strategic Dossier*; newsletters.

Finance: Income from research grants, membership, publications, dialogues and conferences. Annual revenue £10,419,240, expenditure £7,856,707 (Sept. 2009).

Board of Trustees: Fleur de Villiers (Chair.).

Principal Staff: Dir-Gen. and Chief Exec. Dr John Chipman.

Address: Arundel House, 13–15 Arundel St, Temple Pl., London WC2R 3DX.

Telephone: (20) 7379-7676; **Fax:** (20) 7836-3108; **Internet:** www.iiss.org; **e-mail:** iiss@iiss.org.

International Maritime Rescue Foundation—IMRF

Founded in 1924 as the International Lifeboat Federation, to co-ordinate the activities of national non-government and government lifeboat organizations; formally incorporated in 2003.

Activities: Provides technical assistance to countries exploring how to start a marine search and rescue service to meet the International Maritime Organization's World Maritime Search and Rescue Regional Plan, through operating training programmes, search and rescue services, medical care, communications and finance; finances research into lifeboat design; and promotes exchange of information. Maintains a reference library.

Geographical Area of Activity: International.

Publications: *Conference Report* (every 4 years); ILF Newsletter (2 a year).

Finance: Annual revenue £98,289, expenditure £124,568 (Dec. 2007).

Trustees: Capt. Rolf Westerstrom; Michael Vlasto; Capt. Song Jiahui; Hamish McDonald; Sip Wiebenga; Udo Fox.

Address: The Old Pier, Stonehaven, Aberdeenshire AB39 2JU.

Telephone: (1202) 663398; **Fax:** (1202) 663399; **Internet:** www.international-maritime-rescue.org; **e-mail:** info@international-maritime-rescue.org.

International Planned Parenthood Federation—IPPF

Founded in 1952, the IPPF is a Federation of autonomous family planning associations. It links national member associations in more than 180 countries world-wide. It is the world's largest voluntary organization working in sexual and reproductive health, choice and rights. It promotes and defends the rights of women and men, including young people, to decide freely the number and spacing of their children, and the right to the highest possible level of sexual and reproductive health.

Activities: Initiates and supports the promotion of sexual and reproductive health world-wide, including family planning. Highlights these and related issues, including human rights, HIV/AIDS, gender, young people, refugees, violence against women, and poverty, to the media, governmental organizations, NGOs and the general public. Works to mobilize financial resources to fund programmes and materials, and provides training on issues relating to adolescents, HIV/AIDS, abortion, access to contraception and global advocacy. The International Medical Panel of the IPPF, comprising leading medical experts, provides guidelines and statements on current medical and scientific thinking and the best practices. The IPPF offers contraceptive services and equipment, ranging from clinical and office equipment to vehicles, for member associations and other public health bodies. A Youth Working Group exists to ensure programmes are accessible to young people and to promote young people's rights.

Geographical Area of Activity: Europe, Asia (South and South-East), Oceania, Africa, the Middle East, the USA, and Central and South America.

Restrictions: Only funds member family planning associations.

Publications: *Newsletter for Donors* (quarterly); *Family Planning Handbook for Health Professionals*; *IPPF Directory of Hormonal Contraceptives* (online publication); *IPPF Medical Bulletin* (6 a year, in English, French and Spanish); *News, News, News* (online publication); *Mezzo* (in English, French and Spanish); *Press* (2 a year, in English, French and Spanish); *Voice* (in English, French and Spanish); books, factsheets, audiovisual materials and cassettes.

Finance: Annual revenue £124,201,000, expenditure £126,760,000 (Dec. 2010).

Governing Council: Dr Naomi Seboni (Pres.); Sujatha Natarajan (Treas.).

Principal Staff: Dir-Gen. Tewodros Melesse.

Address: 4 Newhams Row, London SE1 3UZ.

Telephone: (20) 7939-8200; **Fax:** (20) 7939-8300; **Internet:** www.ippf.org; **e-mail:** info@ippf.org.

International Refugee Trust—IRT

The Trust, launched in 1989 to serve the objective of supporting refugees overseas, operates by funding small-scale projects.

Activities: The Trust lays emphasis on health, medicine, training, education and well-being of refugees; promotes projects operated by local people aimed at attaining self-sufficiency; supports two orphanages in Uganda, which help Sudanese refugee children; carries out development programmes in Sudan, which include a health clinic for the aged, children and mothers; operates a medical care programme in Jordan to provide medical aid to refugee mothers and infants from Palestinian Autonomous Areas and Iraq; and assists Myanma refugees residing on the Thai-Myanmar border by providing medical and food aid.

Geographical Area of Activity: Africa, Asia and the Middle East.

Restrictions: No grants to individuals; grants only made overseas.

Publications: Appeals; newsletter; Annual Report.

Finance: Net assets £185,9466 (2010); annual revenue £675,045, expenditure £632,381 (March 2010).

Trustees: Simon Whitfield (Chair.).

Principal Staff: Chief Exec. Adrian Hatch.

Address: POB 31452, Chiswick, London W4 4JG.

Telephone: (20) 8994-9120; **Fax:** (20) 8742-0315; **Internet:** www.irt.org.uk; **e-mail:** info@irt.org.uk.

International Tree Foundation—ITF

Formerly known as Men of the Trees, founded in 1924 by Dr Richard St Barbe Baker. Aims to sustain and enhance the environment through the planting and protection of trees.

Activities: Plants trees world-wide to increase land fertility; particularly active in desert areas and tropical rain forests. Supports sustainable projects in developing countries.

Geographical Area of Activity: International.

Publications: Annual Journals; e-bulletins.

Trustees: Mike Turnbull (Chair.); Roger Leakey (Vice-Chair.); Roger Mathers (Treas.).

Principal Staff: Dir Lorraine Dunk.

Address: Sandy Lane, Crawley Down RH10 4HS.

Telephone: (1342) 717300; **Fax:** (1342) 718282; **Internet:** www.internationaltreefoundation.org; **e-mail:** info@internationaltreefoundation.org.

Iran Heritage Foundation—IHF

Established in 1995, Iran Heritage Foundation is a non-political, United Kingdom-registered charity that seeks to promote and preserve the history, languages and cultures of Iran and the Persian world. Organizes activities of cultural or scholarly merit world-wide.

Activities: Engages in a variety of activities in the pursuit of its mission. These include involvement in the academic world through the organization of conferences, symposiums, seminars and workshops, as well as the publication of conference proceedings and monographs, and funding research and travel grants. The Foundation's Institutional Partnerships Programme (IPP) provides much needed support for fellowships, teaching positions, curatorial positions and centres dedicated to the Iranian studies at respected academic and cultural institutions based in the United Kingdom and abroad. IHF collaborates with institutional partners to help sustain posts in Iranian studies and culture that would otherwise be unsustainable. Current IPPs include the British Library, V&A Museum, Freer & Sackler Galleries and the universities of Oxford, Cambridge, Edinburgh and the School of Oriental and African Studies (SOAS) among others. Furthermore, IHF engages in and facilitates a multiplicity of cultural activities. Highlights include the first ever major exhibition of contemporary Iranian art in Europe in 2001; the 'Forgotten Empire: the World of Ancient Persia' and 'Shah 'Abbas: The Remaking of Iran' exhibitions at the British Museum in 2005 and 2009 respectively; 'Epic of the Persian Kings' at the Fitzwilliam Museum in 2010; and many others.

Geographical Area of Activity: Mainly in the United Kingdom.

Publications: *Forough Farrokhzad, Poet of Modern Iran: Iconic Woman and Feminine Pioneer of New Persian Poetry* (eds Dr P. Brookshaw and Dr. N. Rahimieh; *Iran's Constitutional Revolution: Popular Politics, Cultural Transformations amd Transnational Connections* (eds Prof. H. Chehabi and Prof. V. Martin).

Finance: Receives predominantly private donations from individuals and companies. Annual revenue £554,000, expenditure £422,400 (Dec. 2007).

Board of Directors: Sedigheh Rastegar (Hon. Pres.); Vahid Alaghband (Chair.); Hashem Arouzi; Manucher Azmudeh; Yousef Daneshvar; Roshanak Dwyer; Ali Gholi Hedayat; Dr Kimya Kamshad (Sec.); Ardeshir Naghshineh; Rouzbeh Pirouz; Ali Rashidian; Alireza Rastegar; Ali Sarikhani; Dr Ali Sattaripour.

Principal Staff: CEO Farad Azima.

Address: 5 Stanhope Gate, London W1K 1AH.

Telephone: (20) 7493-4766; **Fax:** (20) 7499-9293; **Internet:** www.iranheritage.org; **e-mail:** info@iranheritage.org.

Islamic Relief Worldwide

An international relief and development charity established in 1984 by Dr Hany El Banna.

Activities: Operates in the areas of social welfare, disaster management and sustainable development. Islamic Relief partner organizations operate in Australia, Belgium, Canada, France, Germany, Malaysia, Mauritius, Netherlands, Sweden, Switzerland, the USA and the Middle East.

Geographical Area of Activity: International.

Trustees: Dr Essam A. El Hadda (Chair.).

Principal Staff: CEO Dr Mohamed Ashmawey.

Address: 19 Rea St South, Digbeth, Birmingham B5 6LB.

Telephone: (121) 605-5555; **Internet:** www.islamic-relief.com.

IVS—International Voluntary Service

Founded in 1931 by Pierre Cérésole and Jean Inebnit as the British branch of Service Civil International (q.v.) to provide opportunities for men and women, young and old, irrespective of their race, nationality, creed or politics to join together in giving useful voluntary service to the community in a spirit of friendship and international understanding.

Activities: Provides volunteer help to local and global communities in more than 45 countries, and works to promote greater inter-cultural understanding by bringing people from different cultures and backgrounds to live and work together. Supported projects are within the areas of environment and conservation, children, people with disabilities, culture and peace, and solidarity.

Geographical Area of Activity: International.

Restrictions: This is not a grant-making organization.

Publications: Annual Report; *International Volunteer Projects Directory*; quarterly newsletter.

Finance: Annual revenue £158,513, expenditure £64,362 (2009).

Governing Board: Hilary Campbell (Chair.); Samantha Coope (Vice-Chair.); Kris von Wald (acting Treas.).

Principal Staff: Development Dir Helen Wass O'Donnell.

Address: Thorn House, 5 Rose St, Edinburgh EH2 2PR.

Telephone: (131) 243-2745; **Fax:** (131) 243-2747; **Internet:** www.ivs-gb.org.uk; **e-mail:** info@ivsgb.org.

Japan Foundation Endowment Committee—JFEC

Founded in 1974 by the University Grants Committee (UGC) to administer an endowment made by the Japanese Government through the Japan Foundation (q.v.) for the promotion of Japanese studies within universities in the United Kingdom.

Activities: Provides small grants to support academic research in Japanese studies by staff and doctoral research students in higher education institutions in the United Kingdom, covering research on any aspect of Japan within the humanities and social sciences (including comparative studies where Japan is a major element). Applications are considered for funding for fieldwork in Japan, other forms of research support, and the partial support of doctoral students.

Geographical Area of Activity: United Kingdom.

Restrictions: Applications must be made by staff of United Kingdom higher education institutions; applications may not be made directly by students. Funding is not available for coursework or master's dissertations.

Publications: Annual Report.

Finance: Grants disbursed approx. £50,000 per year.

Trustees: Prof Ian Neary (Chair.).

Principal Staff: Exec. Sec. Lynn Baird; Patron Sir Stephen Gomersall.

Address: c/o JFEC, Lynn Baird, University of Essex, Colchester CO4 3SQ.

Telephone: (1206) 872543; **Fax:** (1206) 873965; **Internet:** www.jfec.org.uk; **e-mail:** admin@jfec.org.uk.

JCA Charitable Foundation

Founded in 1891 as the Jewish Colonization Association by Baron Maurice de Hirsch to assist Jews in need, particularly in those countries where they were oppressed.

Activities: Provides funds to organizations involved in assisting Jewish refugees; finances agricultural institutions and research in Israel, and international school networks for Jewish students; encourages the formation of Jewish groups within institutions throughout the world.

Geographical Area of Activity: World-wide.

Restrictions: Does not make grants to individuals; nor does it usually accept applications from bodies not currently linked to the Foundation.

Publications: Annual Report; *Centenary Brochure*.

Finance: Annual revenue £2,603,000, expenditure £4,718,000 (Dec. 2008).

Council of Administration: Sir Stephen Waley Cohen, Bt (Pres.); Alain Philippson (Vice-Pres.).

Principal Staff: Timothy Martin.

Address: Victoria Palace Theatre, Victoria St, London SW1E 5EA.

Telephone: (20) 7828-0600; **Fax:** (20) 7828-6882; **Internet:** www.ica-is.org.il; **e-mail:** icaisra@netvision.net.il.

Jephcott Charitable Trust—JCT

Founded in 1965 by Sir Harry Jephcott for general charitable purposes.

Activities: Main current areas of interest are projects in developing countries to improve quality of life, especially in the fields of population control, education, health and the environment. Grants are mainly given to charities involved in smaller projects.

Geographical Area of Activity: World-wide.

Restrictions: No grants are made to large national organizations, nor to those concerned with education or alleviating poverty in the United Kingdom, nor individuals, for animal welfare, or heritage.

Publications: Annual Report.

Finance: Total income £205,009, total expenditure £224,296 (June 2010).

Trustees: Lady Jephcott (Chair.); District Judge A. North (Deputy Chair.).

Principal Staff: Pres. Sir Neil Jephcott.

Address: The Threshing Barn, Ford, Kingsbridge, Devon TQ7 2LN.

Internet: www.jephcottcharitabletrust.org.uk.

Jerusalem Trust

Founded in 1982 for the advancement of Christian religion; the advancement of Christian education and learning; and for the benefit of charitable purposes or charitable institutions determined by the trustees. One of the Sainsbury Family Charitable Trusts, which share a common administration.

Activities: Operates nationally and internationally in the areas of Christian evangelism and relief work overseas; Christian media; Christian education; Christian art; Christian evangelism and social responsibility work in the United Kingdom.

Geographical Area of Activity: World-wide.

Restrictions: Unsolicited applications are unlikely to be successful. No grants are made to individuals.

Finance: Annual revenue £2,664,000, expenditure £2,817,000 (Dec. 2010).

Trustees: V. E. Hartley Booth; Dr Peter Doimi de Frankopan; Phillida Goad; Lady Susan Sainsbury; Sir T. Sainsbury.

Principal Staff: Dir Alan Bookbinder.

Address: Allington House, 1st Floor, 150 Victoria St, London SW1E 5AE.

Telephone: (20) 7410-0330; **Fax:** (20) 7410-0332; **Internet:** www.sfct.org.uk/jerusalem.html; **e-mail:** sfct@sfct.org.uk.

JNF Charitable Trust—JNFCT

Founded in 1901, JNF is Israel's leading environmental and humanitarian charity, supporting the country's basic land, water and other environmental needs.

Activities: JNF raises funds in the United Kingdom to support a a range of environmental and humanitarian projects in Israel.

Geographical Area of Activity: Israel and the Middle East.

Restrictions: No grants are made to individuals.

Publications: Annual Report; books.

Finance: Annual revenue £12,157,000, expenditure £12,337,000 (2010).

Executive Board: Samuel Hayek (Chair.); Dr Michael Sinclair (Vice-Chair.).

Principal Staff: CEO: David Goodman.

Address: JNF House, Spring Villa Park, Spring Villa Rd, Edgware HA8 7ED.

Telephone: (20) 8732-6100; **Fax:** (20) 8732-6111; **Internet:** www.jnf.co.uk; **e-mail:** info@jnf.co.uk.

Elton John AIDS Foundation—EJAF

Founded in 1993 by Sir Elton John as an international non-profit organization funding direct patient care services that help to alleviate the physical, emotional and financial hardship of those living with HIV/AIDS, as well as AIDS prevention programmes. A sister organization with offices in Los Angeles, USA, was established in 1992 to fund programmes in North America.

Activities: The Elton John AIDS Foundation in the United Kingdom is an international non-profit organization funding programmes that help to alleviate the physical, emotional and financial hardship of those living with, affected by or at risk of HIV/AIDS. The Foundation was formed primarily to look after the needs of people with HIV/AIDS living in the United Kingdom. The Foundation has more recently extended the scope of its work and now funds in 15 countries more than four continents. To date it has raised more than £65m., which has been used to support more than 1,200 projects reaching millions of people infected, affected or at risk of HIV/AIDS, including: providing information about HIV/AIDS to more than 150m. people around the globe, including 5m. children; giving 185,000 people with AIDS in South Africa proper palliative care; providing 10,000 adults with antiretroviral treatment in Sub-Saharan Africa; supporting more than 57,000 people in need to access income generation programmes, vocational training, grants or loans; enabling more than 200,000 people living with HIV/AIDS to be supported through positive people's groups and networks.

Geographical Area of Activity: International.

Restrictions: Grants are restricted to selected countries in Africa, Asia and Europe.

Finance: Annual revenue £9,203,560, expenditure £9,334,934 (Dec. 2010).

Trustees: David Furnish (Chair.); Nigel Roberts (Treas.).

Principal Staff: Exec. Dir Anne Aslett.

Address: 1 Blythe Rd, London W14 0HG.

Telephone: (20) 7603-9996; **Fax:** (20) 7348-4848; **Internet:** www.ejaf.com; **e-mail:** admin@ejaf.com.

JPMorgan Educational Trust

Founded in 1974 to promote education in the United Kingdom.

Activities: The Trust supports schools, tertiary-level educational establishments, museums and research bodies; projects which provide education and training to young people with special needs, and to those in inner-city and rural areas and to ethnic minorities; arts education projects; and new methods of advancing education. Also provides scholarships and bursaries to organizations for education fees and maintenance.

Geographical Area of Activity: United Kingdom.

Restrictions: No grants are given to individuals. Grants are made exclusively in the United Kingdom.

Finance: Annual revenue £30,000, expenditure £30,000 (Dec. 2010).

Trustees: Swantje Conrad; Campbell Fleming; Carol Lake; Eva Lindholm; Jakob Stott.

Principal Staff: Dir Duncan Grant.

Address: 10 Aldermanbury, London EC2V 7RF.

Telephone: (20) 7325-1308; **Fax:** (20) 7325-8195; **e-mail:** duncan.grant@jpmorganfleming.com.

JPMorgan Foundation

Founded in 1985 for general charitable purposes, particularly in the field of education.

Activities: Funds recognized charitable organizations in the United Kingdom working with children and young people in the areas of education and training, education for those with special needs, education in the arts, and other charitable purposes.

Geographical Area of Activity: United Kingdom.

Restrictions: Grants are not awarded directly to individuals, and international activities are limited.

Finance: Total income £72,000, expenditure £995,000 (Dec. 2008).

Trustees: Swantje Conrad; Campbell Fleming; Carol Lake; Eva Lindholm; Jakob Stott.

Principal Staff: Dir Duncan Grant.

Address: 10 Aldermanbury, London EC2V 7RF.

Telephone: (20) 7325-1308; **Fax:** (20) 7325-8195; **e-mail:** duncan.grant@jpmorganfleming.com.

Karuna Trust/ Aid for India

Established in 1980 for the relief of poverty through educational, medical and skills projects, particularly in India.

Activities: Operates in India in the fields of aid to less-developed countries, education, and medicine and health, through self-conducted programmes and grants; also issues publications.

Geographical Area of Activity: India.

Publications: Annual Report.

Finance: Total income £1,584,462, total expenditure £1,518,680 (March 2011).

Trustees: Ulla Brown (Chair.).

Principal Staff: Dir Jonathan Clark.

Address: 72 Holloway Rd, London N7 8JG.

Telephone: (20) 7700-3434; **Fax:** (20) 7700-3535; **Internet:** www.karuna.org; **e-mail:** info@karuna.org.

Kennedy Memorial Trust

Founded in 1966 from the proceeds of a National Memorial Appeal launched by the Lord Mayor of London following the death of President Kennedy to enable graduates from the United Kingdom to spend one year studying at one of the faculties of Harvard University or the Massachusetts Institute of Technology.

Activities: Operates in the field of education, through granting about 10 scholarships annually tenable by British citizens ordinarily resident in the United Kingdom, and wholly or mainly educated there. Scholarships are tenable in all areas of the arts, sciences, social sciences and political studies. Awards for 2011 are tuition costs and a stipend of US $23,500.

Geographical Area of Activity: United Kingdom.

Restrictions: Fellowships to British citizens only.

Trustees: Prof. Tony Badger (Chair.).

Principal Staff: Sec. Annie Thomas.

Address: 3 Birdcage Walk, Westminster, London SW1H 9JJ.

Telephone: (20) 7222-1151; **Fax:** (20) 7222-7189; **Internet:** www.kennedytrust.org.uk; **e-mail:** annie@kennedytrust.org.uk.

The King's Fund

Founded in 1897 (as King Edward's Hospital Fund for London) by King Edward VII, then Prince of Wales, originally for the support, benefit and extension of the hospitals of London, now interpreted broadly to include all the health services in Greater London.

Activities: Supports the health of Londoners through policy analysis, service development and education. The Fund operates in seven main areas: health and social care; health-care policy; primary care; public health; leadership development; rehabilitation; and health systems. Activities include giving grants to innovative health projects in London, running leadership courses for National Health Service (NHS) managers, and producing frequent publications on key policy issues. Also provides conference and library facilities. Also distributes King's Fund Millennium Awards.

Geographical Area of Activity: London, United Kingdom.

Publications: Annual Report; *Funding Health Care: 2008 and beyond*; *An Anatomy of GP Referral Decisions: A qualitative study of GPs' views on their role in supporting patient choice*; *How to Regulate Health Care in England? An international perspective*; *NHS Reform: Getting back on track*; *Future Trends and Challenges for Cancer Services in England: A review of literature and policy*; *Grow Your Own: Creating the conditions for sustainable workforce development*; *Clearing the Air: Debating smoke-free policies in psychiatric units*; *Designing the 'new NHS: Ideas to make a supplier market in health care work*; *Assessing the New NHS Consultant Contract: A something for something deal?*.

Finance: Annual revenue £12,761,000, total expenditure £15,550,000 (Dec. 2008).

Trustees: Sir Christopher Kelly (Chair.); Dr Penny Dash (Vice-Chair.); Strone Macpherson (Treas.).

Principal Staff: Chief Exec. Chris Ham.

Address: 11–13 Cavendish Sq., London W1G 0AN.

Telephone: (20) 7307-2400; **Fax:** (20) 7307-2801; **Internet:** www.kingsfund.org.uk; **e-mail:** enquiry@kingsfund.org.uk.

Ernest Kleinwort Charitable Trust

Founded in 1963 for general charitable purposes.

Activities: The Trust principally operates internationally in the fields of wildlife, environmental conservation and family planning, and nationally in the fields of the disabled, medical research, elderly and youth welfare.

Geographical Area of Activity: International.

Restrictions: Preference is given to charities operating in Sussex.

Finance: Annual revenue £1,508,543, expenditure £1,288,001 (March 2009).

Trustees: Sir Simon Robertson (Chair.).

Principal Staff: Admin. Louise Marsden.

Address: 30 Gresham St, London EC2V 7PG.

Telephone: (20) 3207-7113; **Internet:** www.ekct.org.uk.

Frank Knox Memorial Fellowships

Founded in 1949 by Mrs Frank Knox to promote scholarly exchange between the USA, the United Kingdom and the dominions of the British Commonwealth.

Activities: Operates in the field of education, through fellowships, available to citizens of Australia, Canada, New Zealand and the United Kingdom. Awards are tuition costs and a stipend.

Geographical Area of Activity: United Kingdom.

Restrictions: Fellowships only to United Kingdom citizens.

Trustees: The President and Fellows of Harvard University.

Principal Staff: Sec. Annie Thomas.

Address: 3 Birdcage Walk, Westminster, London SW1H 9JJ.

Telephone: (20) 7222-1151; **Fax:** (20) 7222-7189; **Internet:** www.frankknox.harvard.edu.

Heinz, Anna and Carol Kroch Foundation

Founded in 1962 by Falk Heinz Kroch and Anna Kroch to further medical research, and relieve individuals suffering severe poverty and financial hardship who have ongoing medical problems.

Activities: Operates in the United Kingdom and Ireland. The Foundation's main concern is the assistance of individuals who suffer severe poverty and financial hardship. Applications must come through the social services or another recognized agency.

Geographical Area of Activity: United Kingdom and Ireland.

Restrictions: Grants are not made for projects, nor for medical research. No grants for holidays or education projects.

Finance: Annual revenue £146,000, expenditure £137,000 (April 2010).

Trustees: M. Cottam; Dr A. Kashti; D. Lang; X. Lang; A. Page; C. Rushbrook; J. Seagrim.

Principal Staff: Admin. H. Astle.

Address: POB 5, Bentham, Lancaster LA2 7XA.

Telephone: (01524) 263001; **Fax:** (01524) 262721; **e-mail:** hakf50@hotmail.com.

Maurice and Hilda Laing Charitable Trust

Established in 1996 as the Hilda Laing Charitable Trust.

Activities: The Trust supports organizations promoting Christianity throughout the world, through funding religious education as well as funding projects working to combat poverty and support people with physical and mental disabilities. Most overseas grants are channelled through United Kingdom-registered charities. Grants are co-ordinated with the Beatrice Laing Trust and the Kirby Laing Foundation (q.v.).

Geographical Area of Activity: International.

Restrictions: No grants to individuals.

Finance: Annual revenue £1,510,000, total expenditure £2,702,000 (Dec. 2010).

Board of Trustees: Sir Ewan Harper; Peter Harper; Andrea Jane Currie; Stephen Ludlow; Robert MacFarlane Harley; Donald Parr.

Principal Staff: Admin. Elizabeth Harley.

Address: 33 Bunns Lane, London NW7 2DX.

Telephone: (20) 8238-8890; **Fax:** (20) 8238-8897.

Kirby Laing Foundation

Founded in 1972 for general charitable purposes.

Activities: Operates nationally and internationally, making donations to registered charities. Most donations overseas are channelled through United Kingdom registered charities. Grants are co-ordinated with the Beatrice Laing Trust, and with the Maurice and Hilda Laing Charitable Trust (qq.v.).

Geographical Area of Activity: United Kingdom.

Restrictions: No grants to individuals.

Finance: Annual revenue £1,734,000, total expenditure £1,585,000 (Dec. 2010).

Trustees: Rev. Charles Burch; David Eric Laing; Lady Isobel Laing; Simon Webley.

Principal Staff: Admin. E. A. Harley.

Address: 33 Bunns Lane, Mill Hill, London NW7 2DX.

Telephone: (20) 8238-8890; **Fax:** (20) 8238-8897.

Beatrice Laing Trust

Founded in 1952 for the relief of poverty, and for the advancement of the evangelical faith internationally.

Activities: Grants are made to charities working in deprived sections of the community in the United Kingdom, to missionary societies and, less frequently, to individuals working in the field of missions, in the United Kingdom and abroad. Most donations overseas are channelled through United Kingdom registered charities. The Trust co-ordinates donations with the Kirby Laing Foundation and the Maurice and Hilda Laing Charitable Trust (qq.v.).

Geographical Area of Activity: Europe, United Kingdom.

Restrictions: No grants to individuals.

Finance: Annual revenue £2,121,027, expenditure £1,754,441 (April 2011).

Trustees: Charles William David Laing; Christopher Maurice Laing; David Eric Laing; Sir John Martin Kirby Laing; Paula Joan Stephanie Blacker; Alex Gregory.

Principal Staff: Admin. Elizabeth Anne Harley.

Address: 33 Bunns Lane, London NW7 2DX.

Telephone: (20) 8238-8890; **Fax:** (20) 8238-8897.

Allen Lane Foundation

Founded in 1966 by Sir Allen Lane to support general charitable purposes.

Activities: The Foundation funds a variety of projects in the United Kingdom. Current priorities include: refugees and asylum seekers; migrant workers; elderly people; those experiencing mental health problems; those experiencing violence or abuse; offenders and former offenders; gay, lesbian, bisexual or transgender people; and Gypsies and Travellers. Priority is given to projects that will make a long-term difference to the problems addressed.

Geographical Area of Activity: United Kingdom.

Restrictions: No grants are made to individuals or to organisations outside of the UK. There are a number of other restrictions and applicants should request the full guidelines before applying.

Finance: Net assets £16,731,112; annual revenue £461,454; expenditure £914,154 (to 31 March 2011).

Trustees: Guy Dehn; John Hughes; Clare Murpurgo; Lea Morpurgo; Christine Teale; Zoë Teale; Fredi Teale; Juliet Walker; Jane Walsh.

Principal Staff: Exec. Sec. Tim Cutts.

Address: 90 The Mount, York YO24 1AR.

Telephone: (1904) 613223; **Fax:** (1904) 613133; **Internet:** www.allenlane.org.uk; **e-mail:** enquiries@allenlane.org.uk.

Laureus Sport for Good Foundation

Established in 2000 by DaimlerChrysler and Richemont to promote sport world-wide in order to bring people together and effect social change.

Activities: Aims to fund and promote the use of sport as a tool for social change. Supports nearly 80 sporting projects world-wide that bring about social change. The key areas that projects focus on are: social exclusion; gun and gang violence; discrimination; community integration and cohesion; peace and reconciliation; education and health.

Geographical Area of Activity: World-wide.

Restrictions: Applicants must be community-based organizations or NGOs legally registered in country. The Foundation does not fund certain types of organizations or activities, including: statutory bodies or profit-making organizations; organizations working purely with elite sport or promoting specific sporting talent; individual athletes or professional sports teams; individuals for their sole benefit; major infrastructural projects or large capital grants; disaster or emergency humanitarian relief projects.

Publications: regular publications; magazine.

Founding Patron Board: Dr Johann Rupert (founder); Dr Dieter Zetsche.

Principal Staff: Co Sec. Dr Guy Sanan.

Address: 460 Fulham Rd, London SW6 1BZ.

Telephone: (20) 7514-2863; **Fax:** (20) 7514-2837; **Internet:** www.laureus.com; **e-mail:** foundation@laureus.com.

Law Society Charity

Established to offer support in the field of law and justice nationally and internationally.

Activities: Operates in the United Kingdom and abroad in the field of law, offering grants to organizations furthering law and justice, including support for legal education, the welfare of members of the profession and the promotion of human rights.

Geographical Area of Activity: England and Wales.

Restrictions: Grants are usually made only to United Kingdom organizations.

Publications: Annual Report.

Finance: Annual revenue £16,527, expenditure £491,139 (April 2010).

Trustees: J. N. W. Dodds (Chair.).

Principal Staff: Co Sec. Andrew Dobson.

Address: 113 Chancery Lane, London WC2A 1PL.

Telephone: (20) 7320-5736; **Internet:** www.lawsociety.org.uk/lscharity.pageaboutlawsociety/charity/; **e-mail:** lawsocietycharity@lawsociety.org.uk.

Leprosy Mission International

International Christian charity established in 1874 by Wellesley Bailey to provide ministry to people and communities affected by leprosy world-wide.

Activities: Works in co-operation with national governments and with other organizations to improve the quality of life of people affected by leprosy, by dealing with the detection, treatment, care, rehabilitation and reintegration of people and communities affected by leprosy. This includes raising awareness of leprosy in all areas, removing stigma attached to the disease, and reducing discrimination. Runs centres to provide suitable treatment and carries out surgery, engages in research into leprosy and its treatment, provides socio-economic assistance to patients in developing countries, and supports community-based rehabilitation and self-help initiatives.

Geographical Area of Activity: Leprosy-related projects in Africa, and South and South-East Asia. National support offices in Europe, South Africa, America, Canada, Australia and New Zealand.

Publications: *Ask Prayer Guide.*

Finance: Annual revenue £13,038,168, expenditure £13,969,510 (2008).

Board of Trustees: David Parry (Chair.).

Principal Staff: Pres. Prof. Cairns Smith; Vice-Pres. Silvano Perotti, Paul du Plessis, Grace Warren; Gen. Dir Geoff Warne.

Address: 80 Windmill Rd, Brentford TW8 0QH.

Telephone: (20) 8326-6767; **Fax:** (20) 8326-6777; **Internet:** www.leprosymission.org; **e-mail:** friends@tlmint.org.

Leukaemia and Lymphoma Research

Founded in 1960 as Leukaemia Research; changed name in 2010.

Activities: Leukaemia and Lymphoma Research is dedicated exclusively to researching blood cancers and disorders including leukaemia, Hodgkin's and other lymphomas, and myeloma. The Foundation's doctors work in more than 50 research centres across the United Kingdom, seeking to improve diagnosis of blood disorders and treatments for patients and to understand why and how cells become cancerous.

Geographical Area of Activity: United Kingdom.

Restrictions: Grants for research only.

Publications: Annual review; information for health professionals; patient information booklets; newsletters.

Finance: Total revenue £19,900,000, total expenditure £24,100,000 (March 2011).

Board of Trustees: Earl Cadogan (Chair.); Richard Delderfield (Vice-Chair.); Peter Burrell (Hon. Treas.).

Principal Staff: Pres. Sir Ian Botham; Chief Exec. Cathy Gilman.

Address: 39–40 Eagle St, London WC1R 4TH.

Telephone: (20) 7405-0101; **Fax:** (20) 7405-3139; **Internet:** www.beatbloodcancers.org; **e-mail:** info@beatbloodcancers .org.

Leverhulme Trust

Founded in 1925 under the provisions of the will of the first Viscount Leverhulme to provide scholarships for research and education.

Activities: Grants are made to institutions and charitable organizations in the United Kingdom and abroad for specific research projects, for educational innovations and for Trust-approved schemes of academic interchange between the United Kingdom and other countries. A number of smaller individual awards of research fellowships and grants, emeritus fellowships and studentships for study abroad are made under annually publicized schemes. Also provides grants to support artists' residencies. Grants to institutions are made by the Trust Board, meeting three times a year; awards to individuals are made annually on the recommendation of the Trust's Research Awards Advisory Committee.

Geographical Area of Activity: Mainly United Kingdom.

Restrictions: Does not give support in the areas of medicine or social policy. Grants for endowments, buildings, equipment or general funds are excluded.

Publications: Brochure; Guide for Applicants; Newsletter (3 a year); Annual Report; recently awarded and previously awarded grants; RAAC awards; major research fellowships; Philip Leverhulme Prize recipients.

Finance: Total revenue £59,115,000, expenditure £51,479,000 (2010).

Trustees: Sir Michael Perry (Chair.).

Principal Staff: Dir Prof. Richard Brook.

Address: 1 Pemberton Row, London EC4A 3BG.

Telephone: (20) 7042-9888; **Fax:** (20) 7042-9889; **Internet:** www.leverhulme.ac.uk; **e-mail:** enquiries@leverhulme.ac .uk.

Joseph Levy Foundation

Founded in 1965 for general charitable purposes; formerly known as the Joseph Levy Charitable Foundation.

Activities: Operates mainly in the areas of medicine, health, and children and young people.

Geographical Area of Activity: United Kingdom.

Restrictions: No grants are made to individuals.

Finance: Total income £841,750, expenditure £395,909 (April 2009).

Trustees: Peter Levy; Jane Jason; Silas Krendel; Melanie Levy; Claudia Giat; James Jason.

Principal Staff: Dir Sue Nyfield.

Address: 1 Bell St, London NW1 5BY.

Telephone: (20) 7616-1200; **Fax:** (20) 7616-1206; **Internet:** www.levyfoundation.org.uk; **e-mail:** info@jlcf.org.uk.

Lifeline Energy

Established in 1998 by Freeplay Energy Group, now Freeplay Energy Plc, to promote alternative energy sources in the developing world to assist the poor to access information sources. Changed its name from Freeplay Foundation in 2010.

Activities: Created and distributes the Lifeline wind-up or solar-powered radio. Offices in South Africa and the USA.

Geographical Area of Activity: Less-developed countries.

Finance: Annual revenue £353,890, expenditure £388,435 (Dec. 2009).

Principal Staff: Chief Exec. Kristine Pearson.

Address: 71 Gloucester Pl., London W1U 8JW.

Telephone: (20) 7935-5350; **Fax:** (20) 7487-1328; **Internet:** www.lifelineenergy.org; **e-mail:** enquiries@lifelineenergy .org.

Linbury Trust

Founded in 1973 for general charitable purposes. One of the Sainsbury Family Charitable Trusts, which share a common administration.

Activities: Operates nationally and internationally in the fields of aid to less-developed countries, the arts and humanities, conservation and the environment, education, medicine and health (in particular the aged and research into Chronic Fatigue Syndrome), and social welfare.

Geographical Area of Activity: International.

Restrictions: No grants are made directly to individuals.

Publications: Annual report; charity information.

Finance: Annual revenue £8,305,000, expenditure £7,441,000 (April 2011) Total grants disbursed £5,700,000 (2010/11).

Trustees: Sir Martin Jacomb; Lord Sainsbury of Preston Candover; Lady Sainsbury; Sir James Spooner.

Principal Staff: Dir A. Bookbinder.

Address: Allington House, 1st Floor, 150 Victoria St, London SW1E 5AE.

Telephone: (20) 7410-0330; **Fax:** (20) 7410-0332; **Internet:** www.linburytrust.org.uk; **e-mail:** info@sfct.org.uk.

Lloyd Foundation

Founded in 1972 to enable children of British citizens whose families are living by necessity overseas to obtain a British education.

Activities: Awards grants to enable the children of British citizens whose families are living by necessity abroad to attend the nearest English-language school; when there is no alternative, the Foundation assists with boarding fees for children to study in the United Kingdom.

Geographical Area of Activity: International.

Publications: Annual Report.

Board of Trustees: Brian William Howes (Chair.); Joan Heather Caesar (Vice-Chair.).

Principal Staff: Sec. M. E. Keyte.

Address: Fairway, Round Oak View, Tillington, Hereford HR4 8EQ.

Telephone: (1432) 760409; **Fax:** (1432) 760409; **e-mail:** lloymit@borderoffice.net.

Lloyds TSB Foundation for England and Wales

Established in 1986 to alleviate community and social need.

Activities: Operates in England and Wales in the area of social welfare. The Foundation makes grants to registered charities that work in England and Wales in the area of social welfare, and supports organizations helping people, especially those who are disadvantaged, play a fuller role in their communities. It runs three main grant-making programmes: the Community Open Programme; the Community Priority Programme and the Collaborative Programme. Grants are available for local, regional and national projects. Lloyds TSB Foundations also operate in Northern Ireland, Scotland and the Channel Islands.

Geographical Area of Activity: England and Wales.

Restrictions: See guidelines online.

Publications: Annual Review; guidelines; grants list.

Finance: Annual revenue £26,063,000, expenditure £27,013,000 (Dec. 2010).

Trustees: Prof. Ian Diamond (Chair.).

Principal Staff: CEO Linda Kelly.

Address: Pentagon House, 52–54 Southwark St, London SE1 1UN.

Telephone: (870) 411-1223; **Fax:** (870) 411-1224; **Internet:** www .lloydstsbfoundations.org.uk; **e-mail:** enquiries@ lloydstsbfoundations.org.uk.

The Mackintosh Foundation

Founded in 1988 by Sir Cameron Mackintosh, for general charitable purposes.

Activities: Operates in the fields of the arts and humanities (in particular the performing arts), education and medicine and health. Provides funding through grants to institutions and individuals.

Geographical Area of Activity: United Kingdom and overseas.

Restrictions: No grants for individual, politics or religion.

Publications: Information sheet.

Finance: Net assets £9,737,000 (March 2011); annual income £67,000, expenditure £368,000 (March 2011).

Trustees: Cameron Mackintosh (Chair.).

Principal Staff: Appeals Dir Nicholas Mackintosh; Company Sec. Richard Knibb; Admin. Amanda Parker.

Address: 1 Bedford Sq., London WC1B 3RB.

Telephone: (20) 7637-8866; **Fax:** (20) 7436-2683.

Macmillan Cancer Relief

Founded in 1911 by Douglas Macmillan for the purpose of engaging in any activities that may lessen the suffering of cancer patients, including the protection and preservation of the health of their families and carers.

Activities: Operates training courses for doctors and nurses in the care of patients, particularly pain control; funds specialist Macmillan nurses and doctors; provides care in the home and, through special units, within hospitals; provides cash grants to patients in need, grants and scholarships for relevant study, and academic appointments; provides a telephone helpline; and funds certain charities in the United Kingdom that offer support and information to cancer sufferers.

Geographical Area of Activity: East Anglia, London, Northern Ireland, Northern England, South East England, Scotland, Wales.

Restrictions: Activities are restricted to the United Kingdom and Ireland (where funds are provided for patient support only).

Publications: *Macmillan News* (quarterly); Annual Review; booklets; cancer publications; *Talking to children when an adult has cancer* (2004); *Macmillan spokespeople* (newsletter); *Resources and contacts for journalists* (newsletter); *Cancer Services and Campaigns* (newsletter); *Cancer Voice News* (newsletter).

Finance: Annual revenue £133,600,000, expenditure £96,000,000 (Dec. 2010).

Trustees: Julia Palca (Chair.); Simon Heale (Treas.).

Principal Staff: Chief Exec. Ciarán Devane.

Address: 89 Albert Embankment, London SE1 7UQ.

Telephone: (20) 7840-7840; **Fax:** (20) 7840-7841; **Internet:** www.macmillan.org.uk; **e-mail:** webmanager@macmillan .org.uk.

MAG—Mines Advisory Group

MAG was founded in 1989 after Soviet troops left Afghanistan to deal with the legacy of landmines and other unexploded ordnance.

Activities: MAG is an international humanitarian organization that has operated in more than 40 countries since 1989. MAG was co-laureate of the 1997 Nobel Peace Prize. Operates in countries left with landmines and unexploded ordnance. Assists by collecting and analysing information on incidents, and enlightening local communities on safe practices. MAG imparts training and provides employment to local communities, clears unexploded ordnance and landmines, aiming to restore a healthy land for the benefit of communities.

Geographical Area of Activity: World-wide, in particular Angola, Burundi, Cambodia, Chad, Colombia, Democratic Republic of Congo, Republic of Congo, Iraq, Laos, Lebanon, Pakistan, Rwanda, Somalia, Sri Lanka, Sudan and Viet Nam.

Publications: Country reports; Annual Report; grant list; news articles.

Finance: Annual revenue £33,827,629, expenditure £31,840,531 (June 2010).

Trustees: Rev. Prof. Michael Hugh Taylor (Chair.); Paul Nielsen (Treas.).

Principal Staff: Chief Exec. Lou McGrath.

Address: 68 Sackville St, Manchester M1 3NJ.

Telephone: (161) 2364311; **Fax:** (161) 2366244; **Internet:** www .maginternational.org; **e-mail:** info@maginternational.org.

Mayfair Charities Ltd

Founded in 1968 for the benefit of charitable organizations promoting orthodox Judaism.

Activities: Grants are made to charities nationally and internationally for educational and religious purposes in Israel, the United Kingdom and the USA.

Geographical Area of Activity: United Kingdom, Israel and the USA.

Finance: Annual revenue £5,227,000, total expenditure £6,309,000 (March 2011).

Trustees: Benzion Schalom Eliezer Freshwater; David Davis; Solomon Israel Freshwater.

Principal Staff: Dir Benzion Schalom Eliezer Freshwater.

Address: 158–162 Shaftesbury Ave, London WC2H 8HR.

Telephone: (20) 7836-1555; **Fax:** (20) 7379-6365.

Medical Foundation for the Care of Victims of Torture

Established in 1985 by Helen Bamber to provide medical and psychological care to victims of torture and their families, alongside practical support, welfare advice and forensic examination of injuries sustained under torture that can be used as documentary evidence in support of an individual's claim for refugee protection. A vital part of the MF's goal in protecting survivors and preventing torture is policy, advocacy and communications work.

Activities: Operates in the United Kingdom, aiming to provide survivors of torture with medical treatment, practical assistance and psychotherapeutic support; document evidence of torture; provide training for health professionals working with torture survivors; educate the public and decision-makers about torture and its consequences; and ensure that the United Kingdom offers support to asylum-seekers and refugees. The Foundation has in the past run a number of overseas projects. Maintains centres in London, Manchester (North West), Glasgow (Scotland), Newcastle (North East) and Birmingham (West Midlands).

Geographical Area of Activity: United Kingdom.

Restrictions: Services are for the victims of torture and organized violence, including individuals and their families.

Publications: Annual Review; *Supporter* (e-newsletter); country reports; thematic reports.

Finance: Annual revenue £7,964,000, expenditure £7,679,000 (2009).

Trustees: Alison Wetherfield (Chair.); Simon Erskine (Treas.).

Principal Staff: Chief Exec. Keith Best.

Address: 111 Isledon Rd, Islington, London N7 7JW.

Telephone: (20) 7697-7777; **Fax:** (20) 7697-7799; **Internet:** www.torturecare.org.uk.

MENCAP

Founded in 1946 to campaign for equal rights for people with learning difficulties, a membership organization with a local network of more than 400 affiliated groups.

Activities: Campaigns locally, nationally and in Europe to highlight learning disability issues; provides residential, education and employment services, leisure opportunities, and support and advice for those with learning disabilities and their families and carers. The Society's leisure division, Gateway, supports approx. 400 clubs and projects throughout the United Kingdom, which provide sport, music, dance and drama facilities. Runs a helpline to deal with issues relating to benefits, employment, housing and other issues.

Geographical Area of Activity: Mainly England, Northern Ireland and Wales.

Publications: *Viewpoint* (newspaper); campaign reports.

Finance: Annual revenue £189,116,000, expenditure £186,045,000 (March 2009).

Trustees: Jim Glover (Chair.).

Principal Staff: Pres. Lord Rix; CEO Mark Goldring.

Address: 123 Golden Lane, London EC1Y 0RT.

Telephone: (20) 7454-0454; **Fax:** (20) 7608-3254; **Internet:** www.mencap.org.uk; **e-mail:** information@mencap.org.uk.

Mental Health Foundation

Founded in 1949, the Foundation's purpose is to support research into learning disabilities and mental health problems. The Foundation incorporates the Foundation for People with Learning Disabilities.

Activities: The Mental Health Foundation takes an integrated approach to mental health and mental illness. The Foundation bases its activity on the understanding that social or biological factors are crucial in understanding mental health. Work topics include: nutrition; exercise; alcohol; family situations; parenting; schools; acute services; early intervention; and cultural diversity. It aims to help the general public to understand and manage their own mental health. It does its own research, and generates new findings that inform its policy, service development and campaigns work.

Geographical Area of Activity: United Kingdom.

Publications: *Fundamental facts: all the latest facts and figures on mental illness*; *Bright futures: promoting children and young people's mental health*; *Building expectations: opportunities and services for people with a learning disability*; information booklets; research and policy briefings.

Finance: Annual revenue £4,187,936, expenditure £5,131,722 (March 2009).

Trustees: Prof. Dinesh Bhugra (Chair.).

Principal Staff: CEO Dr Andrew McCulloch.

Address: 9th Floor, Sea Containers House, 20 Upper Ground, London SE1 9QB.

Telephone: (20) 7803-1100; **Fax:** (20) 7803-1111; **Internet:** www.mentalhealth.org.uk; **e-mail:** mhf@mhf.org.uk.

Mentor Foundation

Established in 1994 working in the field of drug misuse prevention at a global level, with a focus on identifying and disseminating best practice in drug prevention methods. The founding members were HM Queen of Sweden, HRH Grand Duke Henri of Luxembourg, HM Queen Noor of Jordan, HRH Prince Talal Bin Abdul Aziz as-Saud, Bertil Hult, Stefan Persson, Nino Cerruti, Corinne Schuler-Voith, Princess Anni-Frid Reuss and Ivan Pictet.

Activities: The Foundation operates through the Mentor Prevention Academy, the Mentor Prevention Awards and field-based projects, aiming to help practitioners, policy makers and those who care and have responsibility for children and young people to be more focused and effective in their drug prevention work, as well as to ensure young people are fully informed about the dangers of drugs and that they are better equipped to make responsible decisions. Support is given to drug prevention practitioners by identifying and sharing advice and information that will help them develop promising and effective practices in drug misuse prevention at a global level. Mentor also initiates and runs its own projects and supports other field-based work aimed at preventing drug use. Most of the project work is undertaken with support from the Foundation's network of national centres, based in the Arab world, Belgium (in development) Colombia, Germany, Lithuania, Sweden, United Kingdom and the USA.

Geographical Area of Activity: International.

Finance: Annual income €1,219,350, total expenditure €1,030,862 (March 2010).

Trustees: Yvonne Thunell (Chair.).

Principal Staff: Pres. HM Queen Silvia of Sweden; Exec. Dir Jeff Lee.

Address: 5 Forest Rd, Loughborough LE11 3NW.

Telephone: (1509) 221622; **Fax:** (1509) 808111; **Internet:** www.mentorfoundation.org; **e-mail:** secretariat@mentorfoundation.org.

Mercers' Charitable Foundation

Founded in 1983 by the Worshipful Company of Mercers (City of London) to make grants for charitable purposes according to English law.

Activities: Operates nationally in the fields of the arts, conservation, education, the advancement of religion, medicine and social welfare. The Foundation makes grants to education, heritage, arts, medical and social welfare projects. The co-administered Mercers' Educational Trust Fund provides grants to individuals for educational purposes, while welfare projects are funded by the Whittington Charity and the Earl of Northampton's Charity.

Geographical Area of Activity: United Kingdom.

Restrictions: No grants are made to individuals.

Finance: Annual revenue £6,488,000, expenditure £5,904,000 (March 2009). Total assets £516,529,000 (Dec. 2010).

Trustees: D. H. Hodson (Chair.).

Address: Mercers' Hall, Ironmonger Lane, London EC2V 8HE.

Telephone: (20) 7726-4991; **Fax:** (20) 7600-1158; **Internet:** www.mercers.co.uk; **e-mail:** mail@mercers.co.uk.

Mercury Phoenix Trust

Established in memory of Freddie Mercury, principal singer of the pop group Queen, by the remaining members of the group and the group's manager to assist people with AIDS and HIV world-wide.

Activities: Operates world-wide in the areas of medicine and health, and social welfare, through making grants to relieve the poverty and distress of people with HIV and AIDS, and to increase awareness of AIDS. Has funded projects in collaboration with the World Health Organization, and projects in various African countries, India and Nepal.

Geographical Area of Activity: International.

Finance: Annual revenue £403,883, expenditure £283,412 (March 2009).

Trustees: Brian May; Jim Beach; Mary Austin; Roger Taylor.

Principal Staff: Admin. Peter Chant.

Address: 22 Cottage Offices, Latimer Park, Latimer, Chesham, Bucks HP5 1TU.

Telephone: (1494) 766799; **Internet:** www.mercuryphoenixtrust.com; **e-mail:** info@mercuryphoenixtrust.com.

MERLIN—Medical Emergency Relief International

A charity established in 1993 by Merlin Board Ltd to provide health care in areas in crisis around the world.

Activities: Operates mostly in Africa, South-East Asia and the countries of the former USSR in the areas of aid to less-developed countries, and medicine and health, through international programmes and projects, including projects in emergency medical relief, health education and infrastructure, and strategic development. Projects are currently active in Afghanistan, Democratic Republic of the Congo, Ethiopia, Georgia, Iran, Iraq, Kenya, Liberia, Palestinian Autonomous Areas, Russia, Sierra Leone and Tajikistan. Assists the World Health Organization (WHO) to implement the Roll Back Malaria campaign, and promotes cost-effective treatment for tuberculosis, improved access to primary health care, and training for health professionals. A member of the Disasters Emergency Committee—DEC (q.v.).

Geographical Area of Activity: Africa, Middle East, South-East Asia and the countries of the former USSR.

Restrictions: Not a grant-making organization.

Publications: Annual Report; *Response Newsletter.*

Finance: Annual revenue £59,507,197, expenditure £59,898,593 (Dec. 2010).

Trustees: Lord Jay of Ewelme (Chair.); Steve Mirfin (Hon. Treas.).

Principal Staff: Chief Exec. Carolyn Miller.

Address: 12th Floor, 207 Old St, London EC1V 9NR.

Telephone: (20) 7014-1600; **Fax:** (20) 7014-1601; **Internet:** www.merlin.org.uk; **e-mail:** hq@merlin.org.uk.

Minority Rights Group International

Established to support the rights of ethnic, religious and linguistic minority groups world-wide.

Activities: Carries out research and publishes reports on minorities world-wide; lobbies the UN, international organizations and governments on behalf of the rights of minority groups; networks with similar organizations internationally; and educates on the rights of minority groups. Main programmes operate in Europe and Central Asia, Asia and the Pacific, and Africa and the Middle East. There are also specific programmes for Roma people and inter-regional programmes. Maintains a co-ordination office in Budapest.

Geographical Area of Activity: International.

Publications: *Outsider* (newsletter); *World Directory of Minorities;* Annual Report; reports; training manuals; workshop reports.

Finance: Annual revenue £2,920,171, expenditure £2,743,759 (Dec. 2009).

Council: Mukesh Kapila (Chair.); Arjan Buteijn (Treas.).

Principal Staff: Exec. Dir Mark Lattimer.

Address: 54 Commercial St, London E1 6LT.

Telephone: (20) 7422-4200; **Fax:** (20) 7422-4201; **Internet:** www.minorityrights.org; **e-mail:** minority.rights@mrgmail.org.

The Mission to Seafarers

Founded in 1856 as the Missions to Seamen, the charity's object was to care for the unseen and neglected workforce of merchant seafarers during the heydey of British maritime power. In 2000 the charity changed its name to The Mission to Seafarers to reflect the fact that a career at sea was now being taken up by women. Funded entirely by voluntary donations, the Mission seeks support and partnerships with shipping companies, which employ the seafarers whose welfare the charity promotes.

Activities: Operates in 250 ports around the world through a network of frontline staff and shipvisitors who act as first responders to offer emergency assistance and support to seafarers facing disaster or distress—shipwreck, piracy attack, abandonment, bullying, abuse or family problems. Offers trained counselling for post-trauma stress and bereavement, in addition to advocacy and practical assistance, such as transport, translation and referral, and advice. Provides recreational Flying Angel Clubs and communications centres in 100 ports where seafarers can contact their families by phone or Internet; has links with local parish clergy to provide support for seafarers.

Geographical Area of Activity: International.

Principal Staff: Pres. HRH The Princess Royal; Sec.-Gen. Rev Tom Heffer; Head of Communications JN Spence.

Address: St Michael Paternoster Royal, College Hill, London EC4R 2RL.

Telephone: (20) 7248-5202; **Fax:** (20) 7248-4761; **Internet:** www.missiontoseafarers.org; **e-mail:** pr@missiontoseafarers.org.

Monument Trust

Founded in 1965 for general charitable purposes. One of the Sainsbury Family Charitable Trusts, which share a common administration.

Activities: Operates nationally in the fields of the arts, the environment, health and community care, AIDS and social development.

Geographical Area of Activity: United Kingdom.

Restrictions: Unsolicited applications are unlikely to be successful. No grants are made directly to individuals.

Publications: Annual Report.

Finance: Annual revenue £7,034,000, expenditure £34,769,000 (April 2011).

Trustees: S. Grimshaw, L. Heathcoat-Amory, Sir Anthony Tennant.

Principal Staff: Dir Alan Bookbinder.

Address: Allington House, 1st Floor, 150 Victoria St, London SW1E 5AE.

Telephone: (20) 7410-0330; **Fax:** (20) 7410-0332; **Internet:** www.sfct.org.uk/monument.html; **e-mail:** sfct@sfct.org.uk.

The Henry Moore Foundation

Founded in 1977 by Henry Moore for the education of the public in the appreciation of the fine arts and the works of Henry Moore in particular.

Activities: Operates nationally and internationally through self-conducted programmes, and nationally through research, grants to institutions, scholarships, bursaries and fellowships, and publications.

Geographical Area of Activity: International.

Restrictions: No grants are made to individuals.

Publications: Bibliographies; catalogues; *Celebrating Moore;* books; *Henry Moore: Complete Sculpture;* essays on sculptors; The British Sculptors and Sculpture Series; *Henry Moore: War and Utility;* exhibition catalogues; Annual Report and financial statement.

Finance: Annual revenue £1,775,283, expenditure £5,413,858 (March 2010).

Trustees: Duncan Robinson (Chair.).

Principal Staff: Dir Richard Calvocoressi.

Address: Dane Tree House, Perry Green, Much Hadham SG10 6EE.

Telephone: (1279) 843333; **Fax:** (1279) 843647; **Internet:** www.henry-moore.org; **e-mail:** info@henry-moore.org.

John Moores Foundation

Founded in 1964 to provide funding for general charitable purposes.

Activities: Awards grants to voluntary organizations in Northern Ireland and on Merseyside working in the following areas: local community groups, women's groups; ethnic minorities; advice on welfare rights; second chance learning; and community work. On Merseyside, the Foundation also awards grants to voluntary organizations providing grassroots social health initiatives, family support, services for carers, homeless people, refugees and young people.

Geographical Area of Activity: Northern Ireland and Merseyside, United Kingdom.

Restrictions: No grants to individuals; grants to organizations only awarded on Merseyside and in Northern Ireland.

Finance: Annual expenditure £1,170,376 (2009).

Trustees: B. Moores; K. Moores; N. Eastwood; A. Navarro.

Principal Staff: Grants Dir Phil Godfrey.

Address: Gostins Bldg, 7th Floor, 32–36 Hanover St, Liverpool L1 4LN.

Telephone: (151) 707-6077; **Fax:** (151) 707-6066; **Internet:** www.jmf.org.uk; **e-mail:** info@johnmooresfoundation.com.

Multiple Sclerosis Society of Great Britain and Northern Ireland

Founded in 1953 by Sir Richard Cave to promote research into the cause and cure of multiple sclerosis (MS), and to provide a welfare and support service for people with MS and their friends, families and carers.

Activities: Conducts and supports research within the United Kingdom although due to limited research funds the MS Society is unable to fund research grant applications where the principal investigator is based outside the United Kingdom. However, collaborative applications (with United Kingdom-based research groups) are encouraged and, where there is genuine participation of research groups outside the United Kingdom, welcomed. The Society also holds international conferences, disseminates information and runs a national helpline for people affected by MS.

Geographical Area of Activity: United Kingdom.

Publications: *MS Matters* (member magazine, 6 a year); Annual Report; information booklets.

Finance: Annual revenue £29,532,000, expenditure £35,144,000 (Dec. 2009).

Board of Trustees: Hilary Sears (Chair.); Stuart Nixon (Vice-Chair.); Ian Douglas (Treas.).

Principal Staff: Chief Exec. Simon Gillespie.

Address: MS National Centre, 372 Edgware Rd, London NW2 6ND.

Telephone: (20) 8438-0700; **Fax:** (20) 8438-0701; **Internet:** www.mssociety.org.uk; **e-mail:** infoteam@mssociety.org.uk.

Gilbert Murray Trust

Founded in 1956 to promote the study of ancient Greek literature and thought, and the propagation of Hellenic culture; to promote, with the help of travelling fellowships, scholarships, grants or other means, the study of the purpose and work of the UN.

Activities: Operates internationally in the fields of international relations and Hellenic culture, through grants to institutions and organizations, and grants to individuals. The Trust has two committees: the Classical Committee, which awards annual grants for travel to Greece and for activities such as summer schools; and the International Committee, which offers awards of £300 to students under 25 years, who are or have been students at a university or similar institution in the United Kingdom to travel abroad to study international affairs.

Geographical Area of Activity: International.

Publications: Annual Report.

Finance: Annual revenue and expenditure about £6,500.

Trustees: Prof. Edith Hall (Chair.); Prof. Mike Edwards (Hon. Sec.); David Faulkner (Hon. Treas.).

Principal Staff: Correspondent David Faulkner.

Address: 99 Blacketts Wood Dr., Chorleywood, Rickmansworth WD3 5PS.

Telephone: (1923) 283373; **Fax:** (1923) 447814; **e-mail:** david.faulkner57@ntlworld.com.

Muscular Dystrophy Campaign

Founded as the Muscular Dystrophy Group of Great Britain and Northern Ireland in 1959 by Frederick Nattrass, John Walton and Joseph Patrick to fund medical research into muscular dystrophy and allied diseases, and to offer support to those affected and to their families. In 1999 changed its name to the Muscular Dystrophy Campaign to reflect its active role in lobbying and campaigning.

Activities: Finances research by means of grants to individuals and United Kingdom institutions, and organizes conferences. Member of the Founding Board of the European Neuromuscular Centre, and collaborates with and promotes the exchange of information between similar associations in other countries. Provides a range of information to people living with muscular dystrophy and related muscle diseases.

Geographical Area of Activity: United Kingdom.

Publications: *Target MD* (quarterly magazine); fact sheets and other publications.

Finance: Annual revenue £7,041,000, expenditure £6,470,000 (March 2007).

Trustees: Bill Ronald (Chair.); Keith Rushton (Vice-Chair.).

Principal Staff: Pres. Sue Barker; Chief Exec. Robert Meadowcroft.

Address: 61 Southwark St, London SE1 0HL.

Telephone: (20) 7803-4800; **Fax:** (20) 7401 3495; **Internet:** www.muscular-dystrophy.org; **e-mail:** info@muscular-dystrophy.org.

Muslim Aid

Established in 1985 to alleviate poverty.

Activities: Distributes grants through partner organizations in the fields of emergency relief, health care, education, water conservation, skills training, orphan care and shelter.

Geographical Area of Activity: Africa, Asia, Europe and South America, Middle east.

Restrictions: Aid distributed through partner and local community organization only.

Publications: Annual Review.

Finance: Receives donations from individuals and organizations in the United Kingdom and overseas. Annual revenue £25,162,479, expenditure £21,310,522 (Dec. 2010).

Board of Trustees: Sir Iqbal Sacranie (Chair.); Dr Manazir Ahsan (Vice-Chair.); S. M. T. Wasti (Sec.); Dr Zahid Ali Parvez (Treas.).

Principal Staff: CEO Syed Sharfuddin.

Address: POB 3, London E1 1WP.

Telephone: (20) 7377-4200; **Fax:** (20) 7377-4201; **Internet:** www.muslimaid.org; **e-mail:** mail@muslimaid.org.

National Foundation for Educational Research—NFER

Founded in 1946 as an independent education and children's services research body that aims to gather, analyse and disseminate research-based information to improve children's services, education and training.

Activities: Undertakes research on behalf of government, local authorities, professional associations and external clients in all areas of children's services and education, from pre-school and primary to further and higher education. Provides evaluation services on the impact of various education and training programmes at local and national levels. Develops and researches tests of all types, including those for the National Curriculum. Maintains a full range of support services including library, national and international information services, in-house publishing unit, computing and statistics, and survey administration. Also works internationally in co-operation with overseas partner organizations.

Geographical Area of Activity: International.

Publications: Research findings; *NFER News* (newsletter, 2 a year); practical research for education; *nferdirect* (monthly updates); CERUK Plus database; international education current awareness bulletin.

Finance: Annual revenue £12,542,000, expenditure £13,264,000 (March 2010).

Trustees: Richard Bunker (Chair.); David Whitbread (Vice-Chair. and Treas.).

Principal Staff: CEO Sue Rossiter.

Address: The Mere, Upton Park, Slough SL1 2DQ.

Telephone: (1753) 574123; **Fax:** (1753) 691632; **Internet:** www .nfer.ac.uk; **e-mail:** enquiries@nfer.ac.uk.

The National Trust for Places of Historic Interest or Natural Beauty

Founded in 1895 to support the preservation of historic buildings or sites of natural beauty in England, Wales and Northern Ireland.

Activities: Maintains historically or architecturally important buildings, as well as parks, gardens, coast and countryside to which it may provide public access; also conducts educational programmes. The Trust has 3m. members.

Geographical Area of Activity: England, Wales and Northern Ireland.

Restrictions: Does not normally make grants.

Publications: Annual Reports; magazine (3 a year); *National Trust Handbook for Members and Visitors* (annually); *Information for Visitors with Disabilities* (annually); more than 70 further publications promoting the work of the Trust.

Finance: Annual revenue £412,866,00, expenditure £441,566,000 (Feb. 2011).

Trustees: Simon Jenkins (Chair.); Sir Laurie Magnus (Deputy Chair.).

Principal Staff: Pres. HRH Prince Charles; Dir-Gen. Dame Fiona Reynolds.

Address: 32 Queen Anne's Gate, London SW1H 9AS.

Telephone: (1793) 817400; **Fax:** (1793) 817401; **Internet:** www .nationaltrust.org.uk; **e-mail:** enquiries@nationaltrust.org .uk.

Airey Neave Trust

Founded in 1979 in memory of Airey Neave, by Sir John Tilney, and the late Baroness Airey of Abingdon and Lord McAlpine of Moffat, for the furtherance of research into personal freedom under the law, and for financial help for the educational needs of refugees.

Activities: Funds research projects into all aspects of individual freedom under the law, of which approximately one-half are related to terrorism. Gives direct help to refugees by contributing towards their postgraduate fees so that they can qualify or requalify in their trades or professions.

Geographical Area of Activity: United Kingdom.

Restrictions: Grants to individuals are made to refugees and to Fellows attached to law faculties only.

Publications: *Children Enslaved*; *The Victims of Terrorism*; *The International Covenant on Civil and Political Rights and the UK*; *Study of the Operation and Impact of the Council of Europe Committee for the Prevention of Torture*; *Political Violence and Commercial Victims*; *The Position of Refugees in British and European Law and Practice*; *Terrorist Use of Weapons of Mass Destruction*; *Walking Away from Terrorism*.

Trustees: John Giffard (Chair.); Hugh Tilney (Vice-Chair.); Howard Dawson (Hon. Treas.).

Principal Staff: Pres. Lord Mayhew of Twysden; Admin. Sophie Butler.

Address: POB 36800, 40 Bernard St, London WC1N 1WJ.

Telephone: (20) 7833-4440; **Internet:** www.aireyneavetrust .org.uk.

NESTA—National Endowment for Science, Technology and the Arts

Established in July 1998 as a national endowment under the National Lottery Act 1998, NESTA's mission is to make the United Kingdom more innovative.

Activities: NESTA aims to be the strongest single catalyst for innovation in the United Kingdom, seeking to increase the country's capacity to fulfil its vast innovative potential. Through a blend of early-stage investment, practical programmes and policy and research, NESTA demonstrates how innovation can help solve some of the big economic and social challenges facing the United Kingdom.

Geographical Area of Activity: United Kingdom.

Restrictions: NESTA's remit is restricted to the United Kingdom.

Publications: Annual Report; research papers; policy briefings.

Finance: Annual revenue £18,797,000, expenditure £29,542,000 (March 2011).

Board of Trustees: Sir John Chisholm (Chair.).

Principal Staff: CEO Geoff Mulgan.

Address: 1 Plough Pl., London EC4A 1DE.

Telephone: (20) 7438-2500; **Fax:** (20) 7438-2501; **Internet:** www.nesta.org.uk; **e-mail:** information@nesta.org.uk.

Network for Social Change

Founded in 1986 as Network Foundation, for general charitable purposes. Changed name to Network for Social Change.

Activities: Seeks out projects to fund rather than responding to applications from charities or individuals; unsolicited applications are not accepted; operates nationally and internationally.

Geographical Area of Activity: United Kingdom and international.

Finance: Annual revenue £877,050, expenditure £874,220 (Aug. 2010).

Board of Trustees: T. Bragg, B. Gillet, S. Gillie, A. Stoll, C. Freeman, S. Robin, P. Boase, A. Robbins.

Principal Staff: Tish McCrory.

Address: BM Box 2063, London WC1N 3XX.

Telephone: (1647) 61106; **Internet:** http:// thenetworkforsocialchange.org.uk/; **e-mail:** thenetwork@gn .apc.org.

New Economics Foundation—NEF

Established in 1984 as a research organization ('think tank') aiming to develop practical and enterprising solutions to the social, environmental and economic challenges facing the local, regional, national and global economies.

Activities: Carries out research and policy work, principally focusing on participative democracy, local economic renewal, local works and reshaping the global economy. Involved in the development of the LETS alternative currency schemes, as well as developing community time banks, and introducing benchmark surveys on ethical consumption and corporate performance. The Foundation was also involved in forming the Institute for Social and Ethical Accountability and is the United Kingdom home of the Jubilee Campaign on debt.

Geographical Area of Activity: United Kingdom.

Publications: *Ghost Town Britain*; *Real World Economic Outlook*; *Profiting from Poverty*; *Radical Economics*; *Are You Happy? New economics past, present and future*; *Hooked on Oil: Breaking the habit with a windfall tax*; *A Long Row to Hoe: Family farming and rural poverty in developing countries*; *Aspects of Co-production: The implications for work, health and volunteering*; *Migration and the Remittance Euphoria: Development or dependency?*; *Odious Lending: Debt relief as if morals mattered*.

Finance: Annual revenue £2,505,069, total expenditure £2,652,116 (June 2011).

Board of Trustees: Sam Clarke (Chair.).

Principal Staff: Exec. Dir Stewart Wallis.

Address: 3 Jonathan St, London SE11 5NH.

Telephone: (20) 7820-6300; **Fax:** (20) 7820-6301; **Internet:** www.neweconomics.org; **e-mail:** info@neweconomics.org.

Northern Rock Foundation

Established in 1997 by the former Northern Rock Building Society to support disadvantaged people in the North-East of England and Cumbria.

Activities: Operates in the North-East of England and Cumbria to combat disadvantage and to improve quality of life, through making grants under four programmes: Changing Lives (personalized support for disadvantaged young people, substance misusers and people facing prejudice and discrimination); Enabling Independence and Choice (services for older people, learning-disabled people, people with mental health problems, and carers); Safety and Justice for Victims of Abuse (tackling domestic abuse, sexual violence and exploitation, child abuse and hate crimes); Managing Money (helps people who are in debt or have other financial problmes) and Having a Home (helps vulnerable people who are homeless or in danger of becoming homeless). Although Northern Rock was taken into temporary public ownership in 2008, it was announced by the Treasury that the company would provide the Foundation with a minimum of £15m. a year from 2008–10, and that the Board of the bank would consider the Foundation's longer-term future.

Geographical Area of Activity: North-East of England and Cumbria.

Restrictions: Only supports projects in the North East of England (Northumberland, Tyne and Wear, County Durham and the Tees Valley) and Cumbria, and organizations whose purposes are recognized as charitable in law.

Publications: *Rock Reports* (newsletter); *Think* (research series); *Insight* (learning from grants made); Annual Report; media guide.

Finance: Annual income £15,173,000, annual expenditure £13,443,000 (Dec. 2010).

Trustees: Alastair Balls (Chair.).

Principal Staff: Chief Exec. Penny Wilkinson.

Address: The Old Chapel, Woodbine Rd, Gosforth, Newcastle upon Tyne NE3 1DD.

Telephone: (191) 284-8412; **Fax:** (191) 284-8413; **Internet:** www.nr-foundation.org.uk; **e-mail:** generaloffice@nr-foundation.org.uk.

NSPCC—National Society for the Prevention of Cruelty to Children

The London Society of Prevention of Cruelty to Children was founded in 1884 by the Reverend Benjamin Waugh. Changed its name to the National Society of Prevention of Cruelty to Children in 1889.

Activities: Runs a national Helpline, which offers advice and support to anyone concerned about the welfare of a child, and ChildLine, a free helpline for children and young people in the United Kingdom. Also local services throughout the United Kingdom to help children and families recover from their experiences.

Geographical Area of Activity: United Kingdom.

Publications: Annual Report; Annual Review; parenting and information leaflets; and numerous other specialist publications.

Finance: Annual revenue £148.6m, expenditure £150.6m (2010/11).

Board of Trustees: Mark Wood (Chair.); Locksley Ryan (Vice-Chair.); Jonathan Bloomer (Hon. Treas.).

Principal Staff: Dir and Chief Exec. Andrew Flanagan.

Address: Weston House, 42 Curtain Rd, London EC2A 3NH.

Telephone: (20) 7825-2500; **Fax:** (20) 7825-2525; **Internet:** www.nspcc.org.uk; **e-mail:** info@nspcc.org.uk.

Nuffield Foundation

Founded in 1943 by Lord Nuffield for the advancement of social well-being, particularly through scientific research. The Commonwealth Relations Trust (founded in 1937) is now formally part of the Foundation.

Activities: Grants are awarded through institutions in the United Kingdom. Major grants are for experimental or development projects in education or social welfare. Small grants and fellowships in science and social science are also offered under research grant schemes, which are open to members of universities and other research institutions in the United Kingdom. The Foundation also runs its own initiatives, including the Nuffield Council on Bioethics and the Curriculum Programme. It sponsors the Africa Programme (formerly run by the Commonwealth Relations Trust, which has now formally merged with the Foundation).

Geographical Area of Activity: United Kingdom and countries of Eastern and Southern Africa.

Restrictions: No grants to individuals for financial assistance.

Publications: Annual Report; various publications produced by the Foundation, the Council on Bioethics and the Curriculum Programme.

Finance: Annual revenue £4,692,000, expenditure £12,044,000 (Dec. 2010).

Trustees: Prof. D. Rhind (Chair.).

Principal Staff: Dir Anthony Tomei; Deputy Dir Sharon Witherspoon.

Address: 28 Bedford Sq., London WC1B 3JS.

Telephone: (20) 7631-0566; **Fax:** (20) 7323-4877; **Internet:** www.nuffieldfoundation.org; **e-mail:** info@nuffieldfoundation.org.

The Officers' Association

Founded in 1919 by Admiral of the Fleet Earl Beatty, Field Marshal Earl Haig and Air Marshal Sir Hugh Montagu Trenchard, for the relief of financial distress among male or female ex-officers of HM Naval, Military or Air Forces, their widows and dependants, and to assist such persons in such ways as are legally charitable.

Activities: Operates in the United Kingdom and abroad in the field of social welfare, through grants to individuals; providing advice on finding accommodation in homes for the elderly; the running of a home for the elderly and an estate for disabled ex-officers; and through a Resettlement and Employment Department.

Geographical Area of Activity: International.

Publications: Report of operations and financial statement.

Finance: Annual revenue £3,224,000, expenditure £3,158,000 (Sept. 2009).

Executive and Finance Committee: Dominic Fisher (Chair. and Hon. Treas.).

Principal Staff: Gen. Sec. Maj.-Gen. John C. B. Sutherell.

Address: Mountbarrow House, First Floor, 6–20 Elizabeth St, London SW1W 9RB.

Telephone: (20) 7808-4166; **Internet:** www.officersassociation.org.uk; **e-mail:** info@officersassociation.org.uk.

OneWorld International Foundation

Founded in 1999 to promote sustainable use of resources and the protection of human rights and democratic structures, through operating as an online media gateway without regard to geographic or linguistic barriers.

Activities: The Foundation operates a network of 11 OneWorld Centres (in Austria, Canada, Costa Rica, Finland, India, Italy, the Netherlands, Spain, the United Kingdom, the USA and Zambia) dedicated to the promotion of human rights and sustainable development; the OneWorld network aims to utilize the potential of the Internet to achieve its objectives. OneWorld International Ltd, a not-for-profit company, carries out the day-to-day support and co-ordination of the network; the company also undertakes production contracts for like-minded organizations.

Geographical Area of Activity: Austria, Central and South America, Finland, India, Italy, the Netherlands, Spain, the USA and Zambia.

Publications: Annual Report; archive.

Finance: Annual revenue £804,457, expenditure £607,652 (March 2009).

Trustees: Larry Kirkman (Founder and Co-Chair.); Mike Yates (Co-Chair.).

Principal Staff: Exec. Dir Anuradha Vittachi; Innovations Dir Peter Armstrong.

Address: 2nd Floor, CAN Mezzanine, 32–36 Loman St, London SE1 0EH.

Telephone: (20) 7922-7846; **Fax:** (20) 7922-7706; **Internet:** www.oneworldgroup.org; **e-mail:** owuk@oneworld.net.

Open Society Foundation—London

An independent charity, part of the Soros foundations network.

Activities: The Foundation manages Soros initiative programmes, including Central Eurasia Project, Early Childhood Programme, Open Society Initiative for Eastern Africa, and scholarship, education and information programmes in collaboration with other Soros foundations and organizations in the UK.

Geographical Area of Activity: International.

Finance: Annual revenue £10,711,300, expenditure £10,968,700 (2010).

Principal Staff: Admin. Dir Margaret Wright.

Address: Cambridge House, 5th Floor, 100 Cambridge Grove, London W6 0LE.

Telephone: (20) 7031-0200; **Fax:** (20) 7031-0201; **Internet:** www.soros.org/about/locations/london.

Opportunity International UK

Founded as Opportunity Trust in 1992 to empower people and communities in developing countries, and to overcome poverty and secure sustainable improvement in the quality of life in these countries.

Activities: Operates in the fields of aid to less-developed countries, economic affairs and education, through self-conducted programmes, research, grants to institutions and publications. Works through 40 partner organizations world-wide, providing small business loans to those without access to the formal banking sector. Works in 27 countries in four continents: Africa, Asia, Eastern Europe, and Central and South America. In 2006 launched the Opportunity International Bank of Rwanda (OIBR).

Geographical Area of Activity: International.

Restrictions: Grants only to Opportunity International implementing partner organizations.

Publications: Annual Report; *Impact* (newsletter).

Finance: Annual revenue £5,000,000, expenditure £5,000,000 (2010).

Trustees: John Ford (Chair.).

Principal Staff: Chief Exec. Edward Fox.

Address: Angel Ct, 81 St Clements St, Oxford OX4 1AW.

Telephone: (1865) 725304; **Fax:** (1865) 295161; **Internet:** www.opportunity.org.uk; **e-mail:** info@opportunity.org.uk.

Our Spaces—Foundation for the Good Governance of International Spaces

Founded in 2009 to focus on the nearly 70% of the Earth's surface that lies outside national boundaries and thus outside national laws and governance, called international spaces.

Activities: Aims to stimulate discussion between disciplines and nationalities to further environmental protection or improvement. This is done by advancing education and raising awareness; and promoting research (the results of which will be publicly available) on the governance of international spaces. In 2010 initiated Antarctica Day on 1 December to celebrate the 1 December 1959 signing of the Antarctic Treaty

.

Geographical Area of Activity: World-wide, with particular emphasis on polar regions.

Board: John Dutton (Chair.).

Principal Staff: Admin. Dir Julie A. Hambrook Berkman.

Address: 20 Chishill Rd, Heydon, Herts SG8 8PW.

Internet: www.ourspaces.org.uk; **e-mail:** director@ourspaces.org.uk.

Overseas Development Institute—ODI

Founded in 1960 as an independent non-governmental centre for development research and a forum for discussion of the problems facing developing countries.

Activities: Operates nationally and internationally in the fields of economic affairs, development policy and social studies, through research, publications and the ODI Fellowship Scheme. The Institute's main research and policy programmes are: Poverty and Public Policy Group (which includes the Centre for Aid and Public Expenditure); International Economic Development Group; Humanitarian Policy Group; Rural Policy and Governance Group; and Research and Policy in Development Group. Manages international networks of practitioners, policy-makers and researchers, including: the Humanitarian Practice Network; Evidence-based Policy in Development Network; and Mwananchi – Strengthening Citizen Engagement. Also hosts the Secretariat of the Active Learning Network for Accountability and Performance in Humanitarian Action. Maintains a reference library and information centre and hosts public events.

Geographical Area of Activity: International.

Publications: *Briefing Papers; Development Policy Review* (quarterly); *Disasters* (quarterly); *Natural Resources Perspectives;* Annual Report; Working Papers; bookshop for purchases; network publications; humanitarian publications; practical toolkits; journals.

Finance: Annual revenue £17,145,602, expenditure £16,789,376 (March 2010).

Council: Dr Daleep Mukarji (Chair.).

Principal Staff: Dir Alison Evans.

Address: 111 Westminster Bridge Rd, London SE1 7JD.

Telephone: (20) 7922-0300; **Fax:** (20) 7922-0399; **Internet:** www.odi.org.uk; **e-mail:** odi@odi.org.uk.

Oxfam GB

Founded in 1942, as the Oxford Committee for Famine Relief, to relieve poverty, distress and suffering in any part of the world. Now Oxfam supports poor people, regardless of race or religion, in their struggle against hunger, disease, exploitation and poverty world-wide, particularly by tackling the impacts of climate change. Part of the Oxfam confederation of 15 organizations (qq.v.).

Activities: Oxfam works with others to overcome poverty in three ways. First, by providing relief in emergencies, especially through the fast provision of clean drinking water and sanitation facilities. Second, by working with local partners on sustainable development programmes that empower people to work their way out of poverty. Finally, through campaigning and educational programmes that help raise public awareness and tackle the underlying practices that create and sustain poverty.

Geographical Area of Activity: International.

Publications: Annual Report and accounts; *Change* (quarterly); *Inside Oxfam* (quarterly); general and technical publications; business papers; educational and audio-visual materials.

Finance: Funds are raised through volunteer-run shops, local and national fundraising events, and a wide range of donation schemes. Total net income £242,600,000, total expenditure £219,400,000 (April 2010).

Trustees: John Gaventa (Chair.); Vanessa Godfrey (Vice-Chair.); Gareth Davies (Treas.).

Principal Staff: Dir Barbara Stocking.

Address: Oxfam House, John Smith Dr., Cowley, Oxford OX4 2JY.

Telephone: (1865) 473727; **Internet:** www.oxfam.org.uk; **e-mail:** agornall@oxfam.org.uk.

Oxfam International

Established in 1995, Oxfam is an international confederation of 15 organizations (qq.v.) working world-wide to find lasting solutions to poverty and injustice.

Activities: Oxfam works in 92 countries to find lasting solutions to poverty and injustice. As well as helping people gain better access to opportunities to improve their livelihoods, Oxfam also assists those affected by humanitarian disasters, through preventive measures as well as emergency relief. Oxfam lobbies to change international policies and campaigns to raise awareness of humanitarian issues. The international secretariat is based in Oxford, with campaigning offices in Geneva, Brussels, New York, Washington, and a liason with the african union office in Addis Ababa.

Geographical Area of Activity: International.

Restrictions: Affiliate organizations make grants.

Publications: Annual Report; *Strategic Plan 2007–2012: Demanding Justice*; policy papers and reports.

Finance: Net assets £2,800,000 (March 2010); annual revenue £8,500,000, expenditure £9,000,000 (2010).

Board: Janet Mckinley; Raymond Offenheiser; Michael Henry; Andrew Hewett; Anton Reithinger; Stefan Declercq; Kelly Bruton; Robert Fox; Reynald Blion; Luc Lampriere; Matthias von Bismarck-Osten; Paul Bendix; John Gaventa; Barbara Stocking; Chi Kin Lo; John Sayer; Josep Miralles; Ariane Arpa; Tony McMullan; Jim Clarken; Cristina Safa; Carlos Zarco; Peter Conway; Barry Coates; Prof. Joris Voorhoeve; Farah Karimi; Monique Letourneau; Pierre Veronneau.

Principal Staff: Chair. Keith Johnston; Exec. Dir Jeremy Hobbs; Treas. Monique Letourneau.

Address: 266 Banbury Rd, Suite 20, Oxford OX2 7DL.

Telephone: (1865) 339100; **Fax:** (1865) 339101; **Internet:** www.oxfam.org; **e-mail:** information@oxfaminternational.org.

Peace Brigades International—PBI

Founded in 1981 to promote non-violence and protect human rights.

Activities: The organization works at local, regional and international levels to protect human rights defenders and communities whose lives and work are threatened by political violence. Physical accompaniment by trained international volunteers is backed up by an international political support network. This serves to deter attacks against human rights defenders by sending a powerful message that the world is watching. PBI has programmes in Guatemala, Mexico, Colombia, Indonesia and Nepal and country groups in Argentina, Australia, Belgium, Canada, France, Germany, Italy, Luxembourg, the Netherlands, Norway, Portugal, Spain, Sweden, Switzerland and the USA.

Geographical Area of Activity: World-wide.

Restrictions: No funding is given to groups or individuals.

Publications: Annual Review; *Special report: breaking cycles of repression, ending impunity;* project publications.

Finance: Annual revenue US $3,822,830, expenditure $3,457,006 (Dec. 2008).

Address: PBI International Office, Development House, 56–64 Leonard St, London EC2A 4LT.

Telephone: (20) 7065-0775; **Fax:** (20) 7065-0779; **Internet:** www.peacebrigades.org; **e-mail:** admin@peacebrigades.org.

Penal Reform International—PRI

Founded in 1989.

Activities: PRI is an NGO with Consultative Status at the the UN Economic and Social Council (ECOSOC) and the Council of Europe, and Observer Status with the African Commission on Human and Peoples' Rights. It aims to develop and promote international standards for the administration of justice, reduce the unnecessary use of imprisonment and promote the use of alternative sanctions that encourage reintegration while taking into account the interests of victims. It has programmes in Africa, the Middle East and the former USSR, and offices in Georgia, Jordan, Kazakhstan, Russia, Rwanda and the United Kingdom.

Geographical Area of Activity: World-wide.

Board: David Daubney (Chair.); Anthony Tang (Treas.).

Principal Staff: Sec.-Gen. Juliet Lyon.

Address: 60–62 Commercial St, London E1 6LT.

Telephone: (20) 7247 6515; **Fax:** (20) 7377-8711; **Internet:** www.penalreform.org; **e-mail:** info@penalreform.org.

Pesticide Action Network UK—PAN UK

An NGO, founded in 1987, and part of PAN International, to promote healthy food, sustainable agriculture and a safe environment without using hazardous pesticides.

Activities: Supports projects with partner organizations in developing countries, researches related issues, engages with retailers and producers on supply chain issues, and undertakes policy advocacy. Provides information through publishing briefings, books and journals.

Geographical Area of Activity: International.

Restrictions: Not a grant-making organization.

Publications: *Pesticides News*; *Current Research Monitor*; Annual Report.

Finance: Total income £1,044,216, expenditure £1,112,989 (Dec. 2008).

Board of Directors: Martin Tyler (Chair.); Natasha Clayton (Treas.).

Principal Staff: Dir Keith Tyrell.

Address: Development House, 56–64 Leonard St, London EC2A 4LT.

Telephone: (20) 7065-0905; **Fax:** (20) 7065-0907; **Internet:** www.pan-uk.org; **e-mail:** admin@pan-uk.org.

PHG Foundation

Established in 2007; an independent not-for-profit public health organization working in the field of science and biomedical innovation to improve health, especially genome-based science and technologies.

Activities: Carries out research in the areas of biomedical science.

Board: Baroness Onora O'Neill; Ian Peacock; Prof. Sir Brian Heap; Sir Keith Peters; Dr Ron Zimmern (Chair.); Prof. Patrick Sissons.

Principal Staff: Dir Dr Hilary Burton.

Address: 2 Worts Causeway, Cambridge CB1 8RN.

Telephone: (1223) 740-200; **Fax:** (1223) 740-892; **Internet:** www.phgfoundation.org.

Pilgrim Trust

Founded in 1930 by Edward Stephen Harkness for such charitable purposes within Great Britain and Northern Ireland as the trustees may from time to time determine.

Activities: Operates nationally in the fields of Art and Learning, through funding scholarships, academic research, cataloguing and conservation within museums, galleries, libraries and archives; Preservation, in particular architectural or historical features on historic buildings or the conservation of individual monuments or structures that are of importance to the surrounding environment; Records, encompassing the cataloguing and conservation of records associated with archaeology, marine archaeology, historic buildings and designed landscapes; and Places of Worship, through annual block grants for the repair of the fabric of historic churches of any denomination to the Historic Churches Preservation Trust for churches in England and Wales and to the Scottish Churches Architectural Heritage Trust.

Geographical Area of Activity: United Kingdom.

Restrictions: No grants to individuals or organizations outside the United Kingdom.

Publications: Annual Report and financial statement; guidelines.

Finance: Annual revenue £1,427,213, expenditure £2,636,954 (Dec. 2009).

Trustees: Lady Jay of Ewelme (Chair.).

Principal Staff: Dir Georgina Nayler.

Address: Clutha House, 10 Storeys Gate, London SW1P 3AY.

Telephone: (20) 7222-4723; **Fax:** (20) 7976-0461; **Internet:** www.thepilgrimtrust.org.uk; **e-mail:** info@thepilgrimtrust.org.uk.

PLAN International—PI

Established in 1937 by John Langdon-Davies and Eric Muggeridge; aims to create child-focused development programmes to aid communities world-wide.

Activities: Operates internationally in less-developed countries, through child sponsorship to assist in community development. PLAN operates programmes in five priority areas: health; education; habitat; livelihood; and building relationships. Health programmes include: safe motherhood and child survival, early childhood care and development, reproductive health and HIV/AIDS; education programmes include: access to quality education, out of school education, and adult literacy and vocational skills; habitat programmes include: land and housing tenure, sanitation, and managing natural resources; livelihood programmes include: improved agricultural production, credit and financial services, and vocational training; and building relationships programmes aim to ensure that children and their communities play a leading part in all development projects, and promote the relationships between sponsors and their sponsored children. Sister organizations operate in 15 other countries.

Geographical Area of Activity: World-wide.

Publications: Annual Report; *Count me in!*; *Tradition and Rights: Female genital cutting in West Africa*; *Plan's Global AIDS Framework*; *1-year on from the tsunami: the children's stories*; *Water and environmental sanitation*; *Improving schools*; *Gender Equality Report*; *Violence against teenagers*.

Finance: Annual revenue €591,418,000, expenditure €561,219,000 (2011).

International Board of Directors: Ellen Loj (Chair.); Dorota Keverian (Vice-Chair.); Peter Gross (Treas.).

Principal Staff: CEO Nigel Chapman.

Address: Chobham House, Christchurch Way, Woking, Surrey GU21 6JG.

Telephone: (1483) 755155; **Fax:** (1483) 756505; **Internet:** www.plan-international.org; **e-mail:** info@plan-international.org.

Plunkett Foundation

Founded in 1919 by Sir Horace Curzon Plunkett to promote and disseminate information regarding the principles of co-operative business systems. The Foundation's work is supported by members in the United Kingdom and overseas.

Activities: Undertakes training courses, consultancy projects and research studies on co-operative development and management in the United Kingdom and in developing countries. Assists rural communities to establish and run enterprises that provide essential services. Organizes study programmes for organizations and individuals. Maintains a library of more than 20,000 books, pamphlets, reports and periodicals on co-operation world-wide, with plans to make the collection available online.

Geographical Area of Activity: International, mainly United Kingdom.

Publications: Annual Report; *The Journal of Co-operative Studies*; *Directory and Statistics of Agricultural Co-operatives and Farmer Controlled Businesses in the UK*; *Rural Connections* (quarterly newsletter); *Plunkett Weekly News* (newsletter); *Village e-news* (newsletter); *Organisational Structures for Rural Social Enterprises*; *The Real Choice: How local foods can survive the supermarket onslaught*; *Enterprising Approaches to Rural Community Transport*; *Supporting Rural Enterprise in England*; *Rural Lifelines: Older People and Rural Social Enterprises*; *The Co-operative Opportunity*; *Farming Together for Profit*.

Finance: The Foundation's international work is supported by partners and agencies including the British Overseas Development Agency, the Government's Know-How Fund, the European Commission of the EU, the World Bank and the UN. Annual revenue £2,860,286, expenditure £2,856,930 (Dec. 2008).

Board of Trustees: Peter Cleasby (Chair.); Susan Knox (Vice-Chair.).

Principal Staff: CEO Peter Couchman.

Address: The Quadrangle, Woodstock, Oxfordshire OX20 1LH.

Telephone: (1993) 810730; **Fax:** (1993) 810849; **Internet:** www.plunkett.co.uk; **e-mail:** info@plunkett.co.uk.

Polden-Puckham Charitable Foundation—PPCF

Founded in 1991 for general charitable purposes.

Activities: The Foundation funds in two areas: peace and sustainable security, supporting the development of ways of resolving violent conflicts peacefully, and of addressing their underlying causes; environmental sustainability, supporting work that addresses the pressures and conditions leading towards global environmental breakdown, particularly national initiaitves in the United Kingdom that promote sustainable living. The Foundation is linked with the Society of Friends (Quakers).

Geographical Area of Activity: United Kingdom.

Restrictions: The Foundation does not fund: organizations that work outside the United Kingdom (unless they are of international focus); grants to individuals; travel bursaries (including overseas placements and expeditions); study; academic research; capital projects (e.g. building projects or purchase of nature reserves); community or local practical projects (except innovative projects for widespread application); environmental/ecological conservation; international agencies and overseas appeals; human rights work (except where it relates to peace and environmental sustainability).

Publications: Annual Report; Review of Grant Giving 2000-2010.

Finance: Annual revenue £459,334, expenditure £395,235 (April 2010).

Trustees: Daniel Barlow; Linda Batten; Val Ferguson; Benjamin Gillett; Martin Bevis Gillett; Harriet Jane Gillett; Suzy Gillett.

Principal Staff: Exec. Sec. Bryn Higgs.

Address: BM PPCF, London WC1N 3XX.

Telephone: (20) 7193-7364; **Internet:** www.polden-puckham.org.uk; **e-mail:** ppcf@polden-puckham.org.uk.

Policy Studies Institute—PSI

Founded in 1978 (formerly known as Political and Economic Planning—PEP, founded in 1931) as an independent research organization, undertaking studies of social, economic and cultural policy.

Activities: Operates nationally and internationally, carrying out research in the fields of the arts and humanities, education, training, economic affairs, and social and political studies, examining selected problems. Research areas include arts and culture, communications, criminal justice, disability, education and training, employment, ethnic minorities, evaluation, family life, health, household budgets, income and wealth, industrial relations, information, the legal system, local and regional studies, new technology, policing, social care, social security, women and young people. The Institute publishes the results of its research. In 1998 the Institute became a wholly-owned subsidiary of the University of Westminster.

Geographical Area of Activity: United Kingdom.

Publications: Annual Report; *Policy Studies* (quarterly journal); *Cultural Trends* (quarterly journal); *Changing priorities*; *Transformed opportunities*; *Why people work after state pension age*; *Green taxes and charges: Reducing their impact on low-income households*; *Job Satisfaction and Employer Behaviour*; *Climate change and fuel poverty*; *The Benefits of Public Arts*; *Amateur Arts in the UK*; *Research Discussion Series* (reports).

Council: Geoffery Petts; Charles Cox; Baroness Patricia Hollis; Barry Minton; Malcolm Rigg.

Principal Staff: Dir Malcolm Rigg.

Address: 50 Hanson St, London W1W 6UP.

Telephone: (20) 7911-7500; **Fax:** (20) 7911-7501; **Internet:** www.psi.org.uk; **e-mail:** website@psi.org.uk.

The Porter Foundation

Founded in 1970 by Sir Leslie Porter and Dame Shirley Porter to support projects in the fields of education, culture, conservation and the environment, and health and welfare.

Activities: Operates in the United Kingdom and Israel in the fields of the arts, conservation and the environment, education and medicine, through grants to institutions.

Geographical Area of Activity: Israel and United Kingdom.

Finance: Annual revenue £866,000, expenditure £1,710,000 (April 2011).

Trustees: Dame Shirley Porter (Chair.); Albert Castle; David John Brecher; John Robert Porter; Linda Hazel Streit; Sir Walter Bodmer; Steven Nigel Porter.

Principal Staff: Exec. Dir Paul Williams.

Address: Trust Dept, 12 York Gate, Regent's Park, London NW1 4QS.

Telephone: (20) 7544-8863; **e-mail:** theporterfoundation@btinternet.com.

Practical Action

Established in 1966 as the Intermediate Technology Development Group—ITDG by the economist Dr E. F. Schumacher and others to promote development.

Activities: An international development agency working with poor communities to help them choose and use technology to improve their lives.

Geographical Area of Activity: International.

Publications: Annual Reports (international and by region); *The State They're In: An Agenda for International Action on Poverty in Africa*; *The Aid Chain*; *Just One Planet: Poverty, Justice and Climate Change*; *Small-Scale Mining, Rural Subsistence and Poverty in West Africa*; *Aiding Peace? The Role of NGOs in Armed Conflict*; *Policy Entrepreneurship for Poverty Reduction: Bridging Research and Policy in International Development*; *Small Enterprise Development*; *Waterlines* (journal).

Finance: Annual revenue £27,357,000, expenditure £26,712,000 (March 2011).

Trustees: Prof. Stephen Watson (Chair.); Ruth McNeil (Vice-Chair.); John E. Heskett (Treas.).

Principal Staff: Chief Exec. Simon Trace.

Address: The Schumacher Centre for Technology and Development, Bourton on Dunsmore, Rugby CV23 9QZ.

Telephone: (1926) 634400; **Fax:** (1926) 634401; **Internet:** www.practicalaction.org.uk; **e-mail:** practicalaction@practicalaction.org.uk.

The Prince's Trust

The Trust was founded in 1976 by HRH The Prince of Wales to enable young people, in particular the most disadvantaged, to develop themselves and serve the community. Incorporates the Royal Jubilee Trusts comprising the Queen's Silver Jubilee Trust (founded in 1977) and King George's Jubilee Trust (founded in 1936); and has merged with The Prince's Youth Business Trust, The Prince's Trust for the Welsh Environment and The Prince's Trust Volunteers.

Activities: Operates in the United Kingdom, the Commonwealth, and Eastern and Western Europe to further the development of young people aged 14–30, through grants to organizations, groups and individuals, training courses and publications. Particular emphasis is placed on projects to aid the community, education, training and employment programmes, and helping young offenders and the homeless. Runs a business start-up programme for young people, the Prince's Trust Volunteers programmes, a European programme, a community grant initiative and a programme for young care leavers.

Geographical Area of Activity: United Kingdom, the Commonwealth, and Eastern and Western Europe.

Publications: Annual Report; *Trust* (magazine); *Update* (volunteers' newsletter); *Business* (magazine, quarterly); *Europe–A Manual, Partners in Europe*; *Study Support Resources Pack*; *A Place for Success* (Study Support Centre's Report); *Changing Inside* (Young Offenders Report); application forms and guidelines; information brochures; policy papers; research reports.

Finance: Annual income £33,900,000, expenditure £35,800,000 (March 2010).

Council: Charles Dunstone (Chair.).

Principal Staff: Pres. HRH The Prince of Wales; Chief Exec. Martina Milburn.

Address: 18 Park Sq. East, London NW1 4LH.

Telephone: (20) 7543-1234; **Fax:** (20) 7543-1200; **Internet:** www.princes-trust.org.uk; **e-mail:** info@princes-trust.org.uk.

Progressio

Established in 1940 as The Sword of the Spirit; changed its name to the Catholic Institute for International Relations in 1965; since 2006 known as Progressio. The organization now operates as an international development agency.

Activities: Operates programmes in Central America and the Caribbean, South America, Africa and the Middle East, and Asia. The Foundation provides skilled development workers to work with grassroots organizations in developing countries, to help improve the lives of poor people.

Geographical Area of Activity: South and Central America, Africa.

Finance: Annual expenditure £5,907,173 (2010/11).

Trustees: Martin McEnery (Chair.).

Principal Staff: Exec. Dir Christine Allen.

Address: Unit 3, Canonbury Yard, 190A New North Rd, London N1 7BJ.

Telephone: (20) 7354-0883; **Fax:** (20) 7359-0017; **Internet:** www.progressio.org.uk; **e-mail:** enquiries@progressio.org.uk.

Project Trust

Founded in 1967 to promote a broader education for young people through volunteer work-experience schemes abroad, and for general charitable purposes.

Activities: Sends European school leavers overseas to take part in voluntary work, usually in developing countries.

Geographical Area of Activity: Africa, South and Latin America, Asia.

Restrictions: Not a grant-making organization.

Publications: *Project Post* (quarterly newsletter).

Finance: Annual income £1,584,911, expenditure £1,256,054 (Sept. 2010).

Trustees: Ivor Dunbar (Chair.); Maggie Taylor (Vice-Chair.); Nicholas Maclean-Bristol (Founder and Pres.).

Principal Staff: Dir Ingrid Emerson.

Address: The Hebridean Centre, Isle of Coll, Argyll, PA78 6TE.

Telephone: (1879) 230444; **Fax:** (1879) 230357; **Internet:** www .projecttrust.org.uk; **e-mail:** info@projecttrust.org.uk.

PRS for Music Foundation

Established in 1999, previously PRS (Performing Rights Society) for Music since 1953.

Activities: Supports new music in the United Kingdom through grants to performers, composers and producers of new music; grants to music projects; and awards, including the New Music Award which in 2010 amounted to £50,000. Collaborates with music organizations internationally.

Geographical Area of Activity: United Kingdom.

Finance: Grants of £13,500,000 during 2000–10.

Trustees: Sally Taylor (Chair.).

Principal Staff: Exec. Dir Vanessa Reed.

Address: 29–33 Berners St, London W1T 3AB.

Telephone: (20) 7306-4044; **Fax:** (20) 7306-4814; **Internet:** www.prsformusicfoundation.com; **e-mail:** info@ prsformusicfoundation.com.

A. M. Qattan Foundation

Founded in 1993 by Abdul Mohsen and Leila Al-Qattan to advance education, cultural development and awareness; preserve the cultural values and heritage and enrich the social fabric of Palestinian communities world-wide.

Activities: Operates in the United Kingdom and the Middle East in the fields of culture and education, with offices in London, Ramallah and Gaza City. Projects include the Qattan Centre for Educational Research and Development; the Qattan Centre for the Child, Gaza City; the Culture and Arts Programme, including Palestinian Audio-Visual Project (recently renamed the Production Support Project); the Gaza Music School; and The Mosaic Rooms, an exhibition and events space in London.

Geographical Area of Activity: Palestinian Autonomous Areas, Lebanon, Jordan, Syria, United Kingdom.

Publications: *Flowers of Palestine*; *Young Artist of the Year Award* (catalogue); research reports; and numerous other publications; Educational quarterly *Rua Tarbawiyyah (Educational Outlooks)*.

Finance: Net assets £3,590,987 (2010); annual revenue £1,838,995, expenditure £1,927,426 (2010).

Trustees: Abdel Mohsin Al-Qattan (Chair.); Omar Al-Qattan (Sec.).

Principal Staff: Exec. Dir Ziad Khalaf; Dir of Finance Bashar Idkeidek; Dir Qattan Centre for Educational Research and Development Wasim Kurdi; Dir Qattan Centre for the Child Reem Abu Jabr; Dir Culture and Arts Programme Mahmoud Abu Hashhash.

Address: Tower House, 226 Cromwell Rd, London SW5 0SW.

Telephone: (20) 7370-9990; **Fax:** (20) 7370-1606; **Internet:** www.qattanfoundation.org; **e-mail:** omar@uk .qattanfoundation.org.

Quilliam Foundation

Established by Muslim scholars in 2008 as a 'think tank' to counter extremism.

Activities: Works in the field of civil society, community cohesion and Muslim integration, through research projects, media campaigns and other events, publications and training.

Geographical Area of Activity: United Kingdom.

Finance: Annual revenue £915,456, expenditure £928,893 (March 2009).

Advisory Board: Iqbal Wahhab (Chair.).

Principal Staff: Co-Founders Ed Husain, Maajid Nawaz.

Address: POB 60380, London WC1A 9AZ.

Telephone: (20) 7182-7280; **Fax:** (20) 7637-4944; **Internet:** www.quilliamfoundation.org; **e-mail:** information@ quilliamfoundation.org.

The Rainforest Foundation

Founded in 1989 by Gordon Sumner (Sting) and Trudie Styler; aims to support indigenous people and traditional populations of the world's rainforests in their efforts to protect their environment and fulfil their rights.

Activities: Aims to support indigenous peoples' efforts to protect the world's rainforests by assisting them in: securing and controlling the natural resources necessary for their long-term well-being and managing these resources in ways that do not harm their environment, violate their culture or compromise their future; and developing the means to protect their individual and collective rights and to obtain, shape and control basic services from the state. Currently funding projects and campaigns in Cameroon, Guyana, Madagascar, Peru, Thailand, the United Kingdom and Venezuela. Works in conjunction with affiliate foundations in Austria, Japan, Norway and the USA, and partner organizations in Brazil.

Geographical Area of Activity: International.

Publications: Annual Report; *The Myth and Reality of the Forest Stewardship Council*; *Life After Logging (report)*; *Out of Commission*; *Forest in Focus* (newsletter, 2 a year); *Conflict Timber—Africa Case Studies*; *Congo Basin Forests and the Law*; *Divided Forests—Towards Fairer Zoning*; *Forest Law Rights and Poverty*; *Strengthening the Rights of Pygmy Peoples*.

Finance: Annual revenue £1,484,737, expenditure £1,416,783 (Dec. 2011).

Board of Trustees: John Paul Davidson (Chair.); Dr John Hemming (Sec.); Mark Campanale (Treas.).

Principal Staff: Exec. Dir Simon Counsell.

Address: 2nd Floor, Imperial Works, Perren St, London NW5 3ED.

Telephone: (20) 7485-0193; **Fax:** (20) 7485-0315; **Internet:** www.rainforestfoundationuk.org; **e-mail:** info@ rainforestuk.com.

The Rank Foundation

Founded in 1953 by Lord and Lady Rank to promote the Christian religion, education and general charitable purposes in the United Kingdom and overseas.

Activities: Provides funds to organizations working in the promotion of Christianity (funds in this area are committed to an associated charity, the Foundation for Christian Communication Ltd). Also makes grants in the areas of education, including educational programmes for young offenders; youth; and other charitable projects, including the elderly and the disabled.

Geographical Area of Activity: United Kingdom.

Restrictions: No grants are made to individuals; only one unsolicited application in four is successful.

Publications: Annual Report.

Finance: Annual revenue £7,847,000, expenditure £7,058,000 (Dec. 2009).

Trustees: L. G. Fox (Chair.); J. R. Newton (Deputy Chair.).

Principal Staff: Sr Exec. David Sanderson.

Address: 12 Warwick Sq., London SW1V 2AA.

Telephone: (20) 7834-7731; **Internet:** www.rankfoundation .com; **e-mail:** jan.carter@rankfoundation.co.uk.

Sigrid Rausing Trust

Established in 1995 by Dr Sigrid Rausing.

Activities: The Trust's funding is divided between four programme areas: civil and political rights; women's rights; minority rights; and social justice. Support emphasises the promotion and protection of human rights, gender equality, self-reliance and sustainability, including research on the impact of aid on gender issues, and hands-on conservation projects, focusing on issues such as dam building, pesticides and toxic waste.

Geographical Area of Activity: International.

Restrictions: No grants to individuals; does not generally accept unsolicited applications.

Board of Trustees: Sigrid Rausing (Chair.).

Address: 12 Penzance Pl., London W11 4PA.

Telephone: (20) 7313-7720; **Fax:** (20) 7313-7721; **Internet:** www.sigrid-rausing-trust.org; **e-mail:** info@srtrust.org.

Rayne Foundation

Founded in 1962 by Lord Rayne for general charitable purposes.

Activities: Operates nationally, in the fields of the arts, education, health and medicine, and social welfare and development, through grants to charitable and voluntary organizations.

Geographical Area of Activity: United Kingdom.

Restrictions: No grants are made for work outside the United Kingdom or to individuals.

Publications: Annual Report.

Finance: Annual revenue £1,307,398, expenditure £1,655,404 (Nov. 2009).

Trustees: Robert A. Rayne (Chair.).

Principal Staff: Dir Tim Joss.

Address: Carlton House, 33 Robert Adam St, London W1U 3HR.

Telephone: (20) 7487-9650; **Fax:** (20) 7935-3737; **Internet:** www.raynefoundation.org.uk; **e-mail:** info@raynefoundation.org.uk.

RedR International

Established in 1979 by Peter Guthrie, and originally known as Registered Engineers for Disaster Relief, to train personnel to work for humanitarian aid agencies internationally; its members are mainly engineers, but other professions are represented.

Activities: Operates world-wide, selecting and training personnel to work for humanitarian aid agencies for short periods. Maintains a register of people who can be called on at short notice to spend up to three months on secondment from their usual employer to assist in disaster relief. Maintains offices in Australia, Canada, India, Kenya, New Zealand and the United Kingdom.

Geographical Area of Activity: International.

Board: Ian Smout (Chair.); Katharine Collett (Vice-Chair.); Robert Hodgson (Vice-Chair.); P.J. Greeves (Treas.).

Principal Staff: Sec. Barry Grear; Dir Koen Versavel.

Address: Lower Beer, Uplowman, Tiverton EX16 7PF.

Telephone: (1884) 821239; **Internet:** www.redr.org; **e-mail:** redr.international@redr.org.

RedR UK

An international disaster relief charity founded in 1980, following engineer Peter Guthrie's experiences working in a refugee camp during the Vietnamese Boat People crises. Oxfam (q.v.) provided RedR with a start-up fund.

Activities: Trains aid workers and provides skilled professionals to humanitarian programmes world-wide. Permanent humanitarian training programmes in Pakistan, Sudan, South Sudan, Kenya and the United Kingdom. Also delivers tailor-made humanitarian training to aid agencies worldwide. Has 1,700 members, experienced humanitarians with wide-ranging skills, who work in more than 80 countries each year and respond to disasters, wherever they occur.

Geographical Area of Activity: International.

Publications: RedAlert magazine (2 a year), Annual Report; handbooks, reports, aid-related materials and guides.

Finance: Annual revenue £3,525,133, expenditure £3,198,304 (31 March 2011).

Trustees: Ian Smout (Chair.); Katherine Collett (Vice-Chair.); Robert Hodgson (Vice-Chair.); P. J. Greeves (Treas.).

Principal Staff: Chief Exec. Martin McCann.

Address: 250A Kennington Lane, London SE11 5RD.

Telephone: (20) 7840-6000; **Fax:** (20) 7582-8669; **Internet:** www.redr.org.uk; **e-mail:** info@redr.org.uk.

Rhodes Trust

Founded in 1902 by Cecil John Rhodes, for educational and general purposes.

Activities: The Trust operates internationally in the field of education, by awarding 82 Rhodes Scholarships annually for overseas graduates (mainly from the Commonwealth, the USA and Germany) to study at the University of Oxford. Applicants must be between the ages of 19 and 25 (those applying from Kenya must be under the age of 27). Scholarships cover tuition fees, a maintenance allowance and travel costs.

Geographical Area of Activity: International.

Finance: Annual revenue £7,400,507, expenditure £8,731,069 (2011).

Board of Trustees: Dr John Hood (Chair.).

Principal Staff: Warden and Sec. Dr Donald Markwell.

Address: Rhodes House, South Parks Rd, Oxford OX1 3RG.

Telephone: (1865) 270902; **Fax:** (1865) 270914; **Internet:** www.rhodestrust.org; **e-mail:** admin@rhodeshouse.ox.ac.uk.

Rowan Charitable Trust

Founded in 1964 to promote humanitarian causes.

Activities: Operates nationally and internationally (in Africa, Middle and Far East, the Pacific Islands, Central America and the northern countries of South America) in the fields of aid to less-developed countries, development studies, conservation and the environment, conflict resolution, human rights, medicine and health, fair trade and social welfare, through grants to United Kingdom-registered charities. Within the United Kingdom the focus is on funding charitable activities on Greater Merseyside.

Geographical Area of Activity: United Kingdom, Africa, Asia and the Pacific, Central and South America, and the Middle East.

Restrictions: No grants available for individuals, expeditions, bursaries or scholarships, general office equipment including IT hardware, vehicles, buildings or building works, academic and medical research or equipment, or animal welfare charities.

Finance: Annual revenue £139,009, expenditure £1,482,174 (Oct. 2010).

Trustees: Christopher Jones; Celia Pilkington; Rev. John Pilkington.

Address: c/o Morley Tippett, White Park Barn, Loseley Park, Guildford GU3 1HS.

Telephone: (1483) 575193.

Joseph Rowntree Charitable Trust

Founded in 1904 by Joseph Rowntree, who placed particular emphasis on justice, equal opportunity and the unique value of each individual.

Activities: Operates by making grants, mainly in the United Kingdom, Ireland and South Africa, supporting work on peaceful resolution of international and other conflicts; racial justice; democratic process; human rights; corporate responsibility; and work connected with the Religious Society of Friends (Quakers).

Geographical Area of Activity: United Kingdom, Republic of Ireland, Europe and South Africa.

Restrictions: No grants for large established charities; general appeals; local work (except in Northern Ireland or parts of Yorkshire); building, buying or repairing buildings; providing care for elderly people, children, people with learning difficulties, people with physical disabilities, or people using mental health services; work in mainstream education, including schools and academic or medical research; work on housing and homelessness; travel or adventure projects; business development or job creation; paying off debts; work which the Trust believes should be funded by the State; educational bursaries; work outside the United Kingdom, Ireland and South Africa; and the arts.

Publications: Information leaflets; Triennial reports.

Finance: Annual revenue £4,375,000, expenditure £7,299,000 (Dec. 2010).

Trustees: Margaret Bryan (Chair.); Peter Coltman (Vice-Chair.); Christine Davis (Vice-Chair.).

Principal Staff: Trust Sec. Stephen Pittam.

Address: The Garden House, Water End, York YO30 6WQ.

Telephone: (1904) 627810; **Fax:** (1904) 651990; **Internet:** www.jrct.org.uk; **e-mail:** angela.forster@jrct.org.uk.

Joseph Rowntree Foundation

Founded in 1904 by Joseph Rowntree, and formerly known as the Joseph Rowntree Memorial Trust, to seek out the causes of social problems, and, by better understanding them, help improve policy and practice development in the United Kingdom.

Activities: Spends about £10m. a year on a research and development programme that seeks to better understand the causes of social difficulties and explore ways of overcoming them. Current research themes include: housing and neighbourhoods; poverty and disadvantage; practice and research; drugs and alcohol; governance; immigration and inclusion; and independent living and parenting. Runs the Joseph Rowntree Housing Trust (a registered housing association), a number of residential care homes, and the United Kingdom's first continuing care retirement community.

Geographical Area of Activity: United Kingdom.

Restrictions: No grants to individuals.

Publications: Research findings.

Finance: Annual revenue £6,918,000, expenditure £8,631,000 (Dec. 2010).

Trustees: Tony Stoller (Chair.); Prof. Dianne Willcocks (Deputy Chair.).

Principal Staff: Chief Exec. Julia Unwin.

Address: The Homestead, 40 Water End, York YO30 6WP.

Telephone: (1904) 629241; **Fax:** (1904) 620072; **Internet:** www.jrf.org.uk; **e-mail:** info@jrf.org.uk.

Joseph Rowntree Reform Trust Ltd (including the JRSST Charitable Trust)

Founded in 1904 by Joseph Rowntree to promote political reform, constitutional change and social justice.

Activities: Operates in the field of politics, campaigning activities, and pressure groups; through self-conducted programmes and through grants to organizations and individuals. Note: Although the Joseph Rowntree Reform Trust is not charitable in law, its subsidiary, the JRSST Charitable Trust, makes charitable grants for purposes closely related to those of the Joseph Rowntree Reform Trust.

Geographical Area of Activity: Mainly United Kingdom.

Restrictions: Does not provide funding for research; nor does it fund work that can be funded from charitable sources.

Finance: Grants disbursed approx. £1,000,000.

Directors: Dr Christopher Greenfield (Chair.); Tina Day (Vice-Chair.).

Principal Staff: Trust Sec. Tina Walker; Project Adviser Hanneke Hart; Admin. Sec. Gael Bayliss.

Address: The Garden House, Water End, York YO30 6WQ.

Telephone: (1904) 625744; **Fax:** (1904) 651502; **Internet:** www.jrrt.org.uk; **e-mail:** info@jrrt.org.uk.

Royal Aeronautical Society—RAES

Founded in 1866 for the general advancement of aeronautical art, science and engineering, the Royal Aeronautical Society is the global forum for the entire aerospace community.

Activities: Awards scholarships for study and research in aeronautics by citizens of the United Kingdom and the Commonwealth, in approved United Kingdom or foreign establishments; issues professional qualifications and medals; maintains a library and ensures the highest professional standards in all aerospace disciplines. It also plays a key role in influencing opinion on aviation matters.

Geographical Area of Activity: International.

Publications: *The Aeronautical Journal*; *Aerospace International*; *The Aerospace Professional* (all monthly).

Finance: Annual revenue £3,868,668, expenditure £3,706,651 (Dec. 2010).

Trustees: Lee Balthazor (Pres.); Phil Boyle (Pres.-elect); Philip Riley (Hon. Treas.).

Principal Staff: CEO Simon Luxmoore; Deputy CEO Paul Bailey; COO Jonathan Byrne.

Address: 4 Hamilton Pl., London W1J 7BQ.

Telephone: (20) 7670-4300; **Fax:** (20) 7670-4309; **Internet:** www.aerosociety.com; **e-mail:** society@aerosociety.com.

Royal Air Force Benevolent Fund

Founded in 1919 by Lord Trenchard for the relief of distress experienced by anyone who has entered productive service in the Royal Air Force, or any of its associated Forces, as well as their immediate dependants. The Fund also maintains the RAF Memorial on the Victoria Embankment, London.

Activities: Operates internationally, providing financial, practical and emotional support to all members of the RAF family, from childhood through to old age. The Fund owns homes in Sussex, offering short-term respite care, as well as jointly owning homes in Northumberland, Avon and Lancashire. It also manages the Royal Air Force Benevolent Fund Housing Trust.

Geographical Area of Activity: United Kingdom and international.

Restrictions: Only serving or former member of the RAF or their partners may be eligible.

Publications: Report of operations and financial statement; newsletters.

Finance: Annual revenue £18,400,000, expenditure £27,100,000 (2010).

Trustees: Viscount Trenchard of Wolfeton (Chair.).

Principal Staff: Controller Air Marshal Sir Robert Wright.

Address: 12 Park Crescent, London W1B 1PH.

Telephone: (20) 7580-8343; (800) 169-2942; **Fax:** (20) 7636-7005; **Internet:** www.rafbf.org; **e-mail:** mail@rafbf.org.uk.

Royal Anthropological Institute of Great Britain and Ireland—RAI

Founded in 1871 by the merger of the Ethnological Society and the Anthropological Society.

Activities: Operates nationally and internationally in anthropology, through publications, conferences and lectures, the provision of library facilities for research, the promotion of anthropological film, and grants and scholarships to individual researchers from trust funds. It also manages a photographic archive, and raises funds. Awards several international prizes, such as the Curl Essay Prize, the Wellcome Medal for Medical Anthropology, the Lucy Mair Medal for Applied Anthropology, and the J. B. Donne Essay Prize in the Anthropology of Art.

Geographical Area of Activity: International.

Restrictions: Grants and scholarships are open only to those replying to published advertisements.

Publications: Report of operations and financial statement; *The Journal of the Royal Anthropological Institute* (quarterly journal, incorporating *Man*); *Anthropology Today* (6 a year); *Anthropological Index Online* (internet service); *Discovering Anthropology;* occasional papers.

Finance: Annual revenue £880,248, expenditure £842,619 (2010).

Council: Prof. Clive Gamble (Pres.); Prof. Elizabeth Edwards, Prof. Andre Singer, Prof. Brian Street (Vice-Pres); Eric Hirsch (Sec.).

Principal Staff: Dir David Shankland; Asst Dir Christine M. R. Patel.

Address: 50 Fitzroy St, London W1T 5BT.

Telephone: (20) 7387-0455; **Fax:** (20) 7388-8817; **Internet:** www.therai.org.uk; **e-mail:** admin@therai.org.uk.

Royal Asiatic Society of Great Britain and Ireland

Founded in 1823 by Henry Thomas Colebrooke to promote the study of Asia.

Activities: Main activities are publishing journals and books, managing a library and collection, organizing lectures, seminars and exhibitions, and operating a fellowship programme. The Society has around 700 members, one-half of whom are based outside the United Kingdom.

Geographical Area of Activity: Asia.

Publications: *Journal of the Royal Asiatic Society Third Series* (quarterly); books; monographs.

Council of Management: Dr G. Johnson (Pres.).

Principal Staff: Dir Alison Ohta.

Address: 14 Stephenson Way, London NW1 2HD.

Telephone: (20) 7388-4539; **Fax:** (20) 7391-9429; **Internet:** www.royalasiaticsociety.org; **e-mail:** info@royalasiaticsociety.org.

Royal British Legion

Founded in 1921 by Field Marshal Earl Haig to promote the welfare of ex-service people and their dependants.

Activities: The Legion provides assistance to those serving, or who have served in the armed forces and to their dependants. Assists disabled and needy ex-servicemen and women, and their dependants, by running residential homes, providing sheltered employment and special housing, proving entitlement to pensions and assisting individual cases of hardship, advising on small businesses and providing resettlement training; it also arranges visits to war graves abroad. There are more than 3,000 branches in the United Kingdom and more than 50 overseas.

Geographical Area of Activity: International.

Publications: Annual Report and accounts; *Legion* (magazine); leaflets; fact sheets; newsletters.

Finance: Annual revenue £125,077,000, expenditure £112,150,000 (Sept. 2009).

Trustees: John Farmer (Chair.); John Crisford (Vice-Chair.).

Principal Staff: Pres. Lt Gen. Sir John Kiszely; Dir-Gen. Chris Simpkins.

Address: 199 Borough High St, London SE1 1AA.

Telephone: (20) 3207-2100; **Internet:** www.britishlegion.org.uk; **e-mail:** webmaster@britishlegion.org.uk.

Royal Commission for the Exhibition of 1851

Founded in 1850 to enquire into the promotion of the Great Exhibition; supplementary charter in 1851, to use surplus funds of the Exhibition to extend industrial education and the influence of science and art on productive industry.

Activities: Operates in the fields of the physical and biological sciences, pure and applied, and engineering and industrial design, principally through postgraduate research awards and fellowships. Some other special awards are made.

Publications: Annual Report; *Record of Award Holders in Science, Engineering and the Arts, 1891–2000*; *The Crystal Palace and the Great Exhibition, Art, Science and Productive Industry – A History of the Royal Commission for the Exhibition of 1851.*

Commission: HRH The Princess Royal (Pres.); Sir Alan Rudge (Chair.).

Principal Staff: Sec. Nigel Williams; Accountant Amahl Smith; Sr Admin. Jenifer Hewett; Archivist Angela Kenny.

Address: 453 Sherfield Bldg, Imperial College, London SW7 2AZ.

Telephone: (20) 7594-8790; **Fax:** (20) 7594-8794; **Internet:** www.royalcommission1851.org.uk; **e-mail:** royalcom1851@imperial.ac.uk.

The Royal Commonwealth Society—RCS

Founded in 1868 (adopted present name 1956); its aim is to promote the increase and spread of knowledge with respect to the people and countries of the Commonwealth.

Activities: Operates internationally in the fields of development studies, international affairs and education by holding conferences and other meetings, lectures and a major Commonwealth essay competition; maintains a library of 500,000 items on the Commonwealth (situated at the University of Cambridge Library), suitable for researchers and general readers; provides residential and conference facilities. There are more than 10,000 members world-wide, and branches, representatives and affiliated organizations in 39 countries.

Geographical Area of Activity: International.

Restrictions: Not a grant-making organization.

Publications: Annual Report; events guide; newsletters.

Finance: Total income £3,146,755, total expenditure £3,672,096 (Dec. 2008).

Council: Peter Kellner (Chair.); Chris Nonis (Deputy Chair.); Claire Whitaker (Deputy Chair.); Michael Bostelman (Treas.).

Principal Staff: Pres. Baroness Prashar.

Address: 25 Northumberland Ave, London WC2N 5AP.

Telephone: (20) 7930-6733; **Fax:** (20) 7930-9705; **Internet:** www.thercs.org; **e-mail:** info@thercs.org.

Royal Geographical Society (with The Institute of British Geographers)

Founded in 1830 by Sir John Barrow and others for the 'advancement of geographical science'.

Activities: The Royal Geographical Society (with The Institute of British Geographers) is the learned society and professional body for geography. Formed in 1830, its Royal Charter of 1859 is for 'the advancement of geographical science'. Today, it delivers this objective through developing, supporting and promoting geographical research, expeditions and fieldwork, education, public engagement, and geography input to policy. It aims to foster an understanding and informed enjoyment of our world. It holds the world's largest private geographical collection and provides public access to it. It has a thriving Fellowship and membership and offers the professional accreditation 'Chartered Geographer'.

Geographical Area of Activity: International.

Publications: *The Geographical Journal*; *Geographical Magazine; Area; Transactions; WIRES Climate Change (online).*

Finance: Annual revenue £6,510,000, expenditure £4,540,000 (2010).

Council: Michael Palin (Pres.).

Principal Staff: Dir and Sec. Dr Rita Gardner.

Address: 1 Kensington Gore, London SW7 2AR.

Telephone: (20) 7591-3000; **Fax:** (20) 7591-3001; **Internet:** www.rgs.org; **e-mail:** info@rgs.org.

Royal Institute of International Affairs—RIIA—Chatham House

Founded in 1920 to encourage and facilitate the scientific study of international questions. The Institute is precluded by its charter from expressing opinions of its own.

Activities: Operates as an independent centre for the study of international political and economic affairs, through self-conducted programmes of research, discussion, exposition and publication, designed to serve an informed public in general and the Institute's 3,000 members in particular. The Institute maintains a library and information service, and runs an active programme of meetings for its members. Its research programme includes work on Europe, the countries of the former USSR, South Asia, Japan and East Asia, Africa, the Middle East, international economic relations, international security questions and international energy and environmental issues. All research is directed towards publication; meetings, seminars and conferences related to research are organized at home and abroad.

Geographical Area of Activity: International.

Restrictions: The Institute is exclusively an operating body, and does not give grants.

Publications: *The World Today* (monthly); *International Affairs* (six a year); books; *Chatham House Reports*; briefing papers; programme papers; Annual Report.

Finance: Annual revenue £8,107,000, expenditure £7,890,000 (March 2011).

Board of Trustees: Dr DeAnne Julius (Chair.); Sir Roderic Lyne (Deputy Chair.); Ed Smith (Hon. Treas.).

Principal Staff: Dir Dr Robin Niblett.

Address: Chatham House, 10 St James's Sq., London SW1Y 4LE.

Telephone: (20) 7957-5700; **Fax:** (20) 7957-5710; **Internet:** www.chathamhouse.org.uk; **e-mail:** contact@chathamhouse.org.uk.

Royal National Institute of Blind People—RNIB

Founded in 1868, the purpose of the Institute is to provide advice, information and services to enable blind and partially sighted people to take charge of their own lives; and to challenge the underlying causes of blindness by helping to prevent, cure or alleviate it.

Activities: The Institute provides information, support and advice to people with sight problems, through access to Braille, large print, 'talking' books, computer training and seeking innovative and imaginative solutions to everyday challenges, as well as campaigning to change society's attitudes, actions and assumptions, so that people with sight problems can enjoy the same rights, freedoms and responsibilities as fully sighted people. Also funds pioneering research into the prevention and treatment of eye disease and promotes eye health by running public health awareness campaigns.

Geographical Area of Activity: United Kingdom.

Publications: *RNIB Hotel Guide 2006*; *Patient Focus*; *The Accessible Office*; *The See it Right pack*; *Vision Magazine*; *The See Change pack*; Annual Report.

Finance: Annual revenue £119,781,000, expenditure £116,311,000 (March 2011).

Board of Trustees: Kevin Carey (Chair.); Derek Child (Vice-Chair.); Terry Moody (Hon. Treas.).

Principal Staff: CEO Lesley-Anne Alexander.

Address: 105 Judd St, London WC1H 9NE.

Telephone: (20) 7388-1266; (303) 123-9999 (helpline); **Fax:** (20) 7388-2034; **Internet:** www.rnib.org.uk; **e-mail:** helpline@rnib.org.uk.

Royal Over-Seas League—ROSL

Founded in 1910 by Sir Evelyn Wrench to promote friendship and understanding; it is a self-funding, non-profit-making organization that operates under a Royal Charter, and is pledged to work for the service of others, the good of the Commonwealth, and humanity in general.

Activities: The League has more than 22,000 members worldwide. It encourages the arts, in particular among the young people of the Commonwealth, through staging an Annual Music Competition, an Annual Open Exhibition and a Literary Lecture programme. Also commissions works of art and musical compositions, and awards scholarships to artists and musicians for travel and study overseas. In 1995 the League initiated joint welfare projects including travelling eye camps in Sri Lanka, and projects in Namibia that support school bursaries and resource materials for bushmen and farm children.

Geographical Area of Activity: International.

Publications: *Overseas* (quarterly journal).

Principal Staff: Dir-Gen. Maj.-Gen. Roddy Porter.

Address: Over-Seas House, Park Pl., St James's St, London SW1A 1LR.

Telephone: (20) 7408-0214; **Fax:** (20) 7499-6738; **Internet:** www.rosl.org.uk; **e-mail:** info@rosl.org.uk.

Royal Society

Founded in 1660 to promote natural knowledge; granted a Royal Charter by King Charles II in 1662.

Activities: Operates nationally and internationally in the fields of education, natural and applied science (including mathematics, engineering and medicine), international scientific relations and the conservation of natural resources, through self-conducted programmes, research, grants to institutions and individuals, fellowships and scholarships, conferences, publications and lectures. The Society provides an independent source of advice on scientific matters, notably to the British Government.

Geographical Area of Activity: International.

Publications: *Proceedings of the Royal Society A: Mathematical, Physical & Engineering Sciences*; *Proceedings of the Royal Society B: Biological Sciences*; *Philosophical Transactions of the Royal Society A: Mathematical, Physical & Engineering Sciences*; *Philosophical Transactions of the Royal Society B: Biological Sciences*; *Biology Letters*; *Journal of the Royal Society Interface*; *Interface Focus*; *Notes & Records of the Royal Society*; *Biographical Memoirs of Fellows of the Royal Society*; *Year Book of the Royal Society*.

Finance: Annual revenue £72,863,000, expenditure £71,392,000 (March 2010).

Council: Sir Paul Nurse (Pres.); Sir Peter Williams (Treas.).

Principal Staff: Exec. Dir Dr Julie Maxton.

Address: 6–9 Carlton House Terrace, London SW1Y 5AG.

Telephone: (20) 7451-2500; **Fax:** (20) 7930-2170; **Internet:** royalsociety.org; **e-mail:** press@royalsociety.org.

Royal Society for the Encouragement of Arts, Manufactures and Commerce—RSA

Founded in 1754 by William Shipley for the encouragement of the arts, manufactures and commerce.

Activities: Operates nationally and internationally in the arts, manufactures, commerce, design, education and the environment. It works to remove the barriers to social progress. It drives ideas, innovation and social change through its ambitious programme of projects, events and lectures, and with the support of a 27,000-strong fellowship.

Geographical Area of Activity: International.

Restrictions: Not a grant-making organization.

Publications: *RSA Journal* (every quarter); other reports and publications.

Finance: Annual revenue £8,258,000, expenditure £6,966,000 (March 2010).

Trustee Board: Luke Johnson (Chair.); Suzy Walton (Deputy Chair.); Lord Best (Treas.); Vanessa Harrison (Treas.).

Principal Staff: Chief Exec. Matthew Taylor.

Address: 8 John Adam St, London WC2N 6EZ.

Telephone: (020) 7930-5115; **Fax:** (020) 7839-5805; **Internet:** www.thersa.org; **e-mail:** general@rsa.org.uk.

The Royal Society of Medicine—RSM

Founded in 1805 to promote the interests of medical science using its neutrality to encourage co-operation in medicine and provide education through a wide variety of means, including meetings, debates, conferences, publications and a library.

Activities: Operates nationally and internationally in medicine and science, through meetings, conferences, publications, e-learning, prizes for doctors and students across 58 specialties and providing members (those involved in medicine, science and health care-related professions) with access to the library, online journals and databases and use of club facilities in central London.

Geographical Area of Activity: United Kingdom.

Publications: *Journal of the RSM*; JRSM Short Reports, *Tropical Doctor*; *AIDS and Hepatitis Digest*; *International Journal of STD and AIDS*; *Journal of Medical Biography*; *Journal of Telemedicine and Telecare*; *Annals of Clinical Biochemistry*; *Clinical Risk*; *Handbook of Practice Management*; *Journal of Health Services Research and Policy*; *Journal of Integrated Care Pathways*; *Journal of Laryngology and Otology*.

Finance: Total income £15,393,000, expenditure £13,350,000 (Sept. 2010).

Council: Prof. Parveen Kumar (Pres.); Dr John Scadding (Vice-Pres.); Mr John Skuse (Vice-Pres.); B Sethia (Treas.); Prof. Nadey Hakim (Hon. Sec.); Dr W. R. Cattell (Hon. Librarian).

Principal Staff: CEO Ian Balmer; Marketing and Communications Dir Janice Liverseidge; Dir of Press Philip Manley; Dir of Education Caroline Langley; Dir of Library Services Wayne Sime.

Address: 1 Wimpole St, London W1G 0AE.

Telephone: (20) 7290-2900; **Fax:** (20) 7290-2989; **Internet:** www.rsm.ac.uk; **e-mail:** membership@rsm.ac.uk.

Royal Society for the Prevention of Cruelty to Animals—RSPCA

Founded as the Society for the Prevention of Cruelty to Animals in 1824, present name since 1840. The RSPCA as a charity will, by all lawful means, prevent cruelty, promote kindness to and alleviate suffering of all animals.

Activities: From endangered whales to fairground goldfish, from pet cats to circus lions, the RSPCA is on a mission to promote compassion for all creatures. The Society encourages responsible pet care, supports animal welfare projects and operates a 24-hour cruelty and advice line. It campaigns to improve the welfare of pets, improve the lives and reduce the suffering of farm animals, improve the welfare of wild animals and reduce the suffering of animals used in research. The Society educates in schools and through its network of educational professionals, and also carries out scientific and technical research on all aspects of farm, wild, laboratory and companion animal welfare.

Geographical Area of Activity: England and Wales, with some international activity.

Publications: *Science Review*; *Animal Life*; *Animal Action*; *The Welfare State: Measuring Animal Welfare in the UK;* Annual Review; Trustees' Report and Accounts.

Finance: Annual revenue £129,251,000, expenditure £119,339,000 (2009).

Governing Council: Michael Tomlinson (Chair.); Paul Draycott (Vice-Chair.) Barbara Gardner (Treas.).

Principal Staff: Chief Exec. Gavin Grant.

Address: Wilberforce Way, Southwater, Horsham, West Sussex RH13 9RS.

Telephone: (300) 123-0100 (switchboard); (300) 1234-555 (enquiries); **Fax:** (303) 123-0100; **Internet:** www.rspca.org.uk; **e-mail:** plittlefair@rspca.org.uk.

Royal Society for the Protection of Birds—RSPB

Founded as the Society for the Protection of Birds in 1889, became the Royal Society for the Protection of Birds 1904 to campaign against the slaughter of wild birds for their plumage for use in the millinery trade. The Society now promotes the conservation of birds and wildlife throughout the United Kingdom and world-wide.

Activities: The Society works to protect and recreate habitats for endangered birds and wildlife. It acquires land and manages many nature reserves; campaigns for better protection and management of wildlife sites not in conservation ownership; works in partnership with conservation organizations, including BirdLife International (q.v.), in Europe, Africa and Asia; and aims to develop awareness of conservation issues through education, and to influence education in agriculture, planning and other key professions. Programmes include birds and biodiversity, biodiversity and sustainability, and collaboration with local communities on issues of national importance. Also seeks to influence national and international government policy.

Geographical Area of Activity: United Kingdom, Europe, Africa, Asia and Middle East.

Publications: Annual Review and Annual Report; *Birds* (members' magazine).

Finance: Total revenue £122,519,000, expenditure £108,794,000 (March 2011).

Trustees: Kate Humble (Pres.); 13 Vice-Pres; Ian Darling (Chair.); Alan Martin (Treas.).

Principal Staff: Chief Exec. Mike Clarke.

Address: The Lodge, Sandy SG19 2DL.

Telephone: (1767) 680551; **Internet:** www.rspb.org.uk; **e-mail:** wildlife@rspb.org.uk.

The Rufford Foundation

Established in August 2003 as the Rufford Maurice Laing Foundation, as a result of a merger between the Maurice Laing Foundation, founded by Sir Maurice Laing in June 1972 and the Rufford Foundation founded in June 1982 by John Hedley Laing. Changed its name in 2010.

Activities: The Foundation has a special interest in conservation, the environment and sustainable development in developing countries, however, projects in the fields of medicine and health care, and social welfare (particularly those related to HIV/AIDS) are also supported. Operates a small grants programme in the field of nature conservation.

Geographical Area of Activity: Mainly less-developed countries.

Restrictions: Grants to registered charities only, no grants to individuals. No funding for building or construction projects.

Finance: Annual revenue £3,155,000, expenditure £5,742,000 (April 2009).

Board of Trustees: John H. Laing (Chair.).

Principal Staff: Dir Terry Kenny.

Address: 248 Tottenham Court Rd, 6th Floor, London W1T 7QZ.

Telephone: (20) 7436-8604; **Internet:** www.rufford.org; **e-mail:** admin@rufford.org.

Bertrand Russell Peace Foundation—BRPF

Founded in 1963 by Bertrand Russell to campaign for international disarmament, peace and social justice.

Activities: Organizes campaigns for peace and disarmament and for political prisoners, and the European Peace and Human Rights Conference.

Geographical Area of Activity: Europe.

Publications: *The Spokesman* (quarterly); leaflets, letters, books and pamphlets.

Trustees: Michael Barratt Brown; Ken Fleet; Regan Scott, Tony Simpson.

Principal Staff: Dir and Sec. Ken Fleet; Publisher Tony Simpson.

Address: Russell House, Bulwell Lane, Nottingham NG6 0BT.

Telephone: (115) 978-4504; **Fax:** (115) 942-0433; **Internet:** www.spokesmanbooks.com; www.russfound.org; **e-mail:** elfeuro@compuserve.com.

Said Foundation

Founded in 1982 to alleviate poverty and suffering among children and young people in the Middle East.

Activities: Operates in the fields of education and disability through grants to institutions working with disadvantaged children and young people. Grants are usually made to experienced NGOs in Jordan, Lebanon, the Palestinian Autonomous Areas and Syria. Awards scholarships to students from the Middle East for postgraduate study in the United Kingdom. Supports the Said Business School (at the University of Oxford) Strategic Development Fund. Encourages the development of Syria particularly in the areas of disability, health, education and culture.

Geographical Area of Activity: Middle East (in particular Syria, as well as Jordan, Lebanon and the Palestinian Autonomous Areas), and the United Kingdom.

Publications: e-newsletter; annual printed newsletter; brochure.

Finance: Annual revenue £1,860,000, expenditure £3,270,000 (Aug. 2009). Expenditure of £18,900,000 to Aug. 2010, with the major commitment to a second phase of construction at the Said Business School.

Trustees: Wafic Rida Said (Chair.).

Principal Staff: CEO Julian Gore-Booth.

Address: 4th Floor, 54 Bartholomew Close, London EC1A 7HP.

Telephone: (20) 7367 9910; **Fax:** (20) 7726 6837; **Internet:** www.saidfoundation.org; **e-mail:** admin@saidfoundation.org.

St John Ambulance

A foundation of the Order of St John that traces its roots back to the 11th-century Crusades. The St John Ambulance Association was founded in the United Kingdom in 1877 to provide care for the sick and organize classes in first aid.

Activities: Provides first aid and care training to almost 500,000 people every year in the United Kingdom. Care programmes include: primary health care for the homeless; training courses for those working with the homeless; conferences to promote healthy lifestyles, aimed at young people; care courses; care handbook; young carers support groups; young carers resource pack. Operates first aid courses for young people through co-operation with schools; develops new courses and course materials to meet the needs of communities and customers; provides first aid cover at sporting and entertainment events, at national and local levels. The organization is supported by more than 47,000 volunteer workers, more than half of whom are under the age of 18 years. Internationally, St John Ambulance has diversified its activities to meet the needs of different communities, in addition to first aid, it provides dental and ophthalmic care, relief and disaster planning, primary health care, operates youth programmes, and in some cases provides the statutory ambulance service. There are members in 42 countries world-wide. Maintains a reference library.

Geographical Area of Activity: World-wide.

Publications: Annual Review.

Finance: Funded entirely by donations from major corporate donors and members of the public. Annual revenue £87,472,000, expenditure £83,509,000 (2010).

Council of Trustees: Rodney Green (Chair.).

Principal Staff: CEO Sue A. Killen.

Address: 27 St John's Lane, London EC1M 4BU.

Telephone: (8700) 104950; **Fax:** (8700) 104065; **Internet:** www.sja.org.uk; **e-mail:** webteam@sja.org.uk.

The Salvation Army

Founded in 1865 by William Booth for the advancement of the Christian religion as promulgated in the religious doctrines that are professed, believed and taught by the Army and, pursuant thereto, the advancement of education, the relief of poverty and other charitable objects beneficial to society or the community of mankind as a whole. A quasi-military command structure was introduced in 1878. The organization operates in 119 countries.

Activities: Promotes the advancement of the Christian religion. Also organizes specific projects around the world, including emergency housing, feeding and clothing; medical and educational work; agricultural training and social welfare programmes.

Geographical Area of Activity: International.

Trustees: The Salvation Army Int. Trustee Co.

Principal Staff: General Commissioner Linda Bond; Chief of Staff Commissioner Barry C. Swanson.

Address: 101 Queen Victoria St, London EC4P 4EP.

Telephone: (20) 7332-0101; **Fax:** (20) 7236-4681; **Internet:** www.salvationarmy.org; **e-mail:** info@salvationarmy.org.uk.

Save the Children

Established in May 1919 by Eglantyne Jebb and her sister Dorothy Buxton, as the international arm of Save the Children (q.v.) to promote a world view that respects and values each child; listens to and learns from children; and where all children have hope and opportunity. In 2007 some 28 organizations world-wide were members. Formerly known as International Save the Children Alliance.

Activities: Operates internationally through its 27 member organizations in more than 110 countries, promoting children's rights, assisting children involved in war or natural disasters, and delivering immediate and lasting improvements to children's lives world-wide. Works through both domestic and international programmes. Promotes the International Convention on the Rights of the Child. Maintains a regional office in Brussels.

Geographical Area of Activity: International.

Publications: *Children's Rights: A Second Chance; UN study on violence against children; Forgotten Casualites of War; Child Protection Policy;* Annual Reports and other publications.

Finance: Total revenue £2,410,587 expenditure £2,407,397 (2010).

Board: Charles R. Perrin (Chair.).

Principal Staff: CEO Jasmine Whitbread.

Address: 2nd Floor, Cambridge House, 100 Cambridge Grove, London W6 0LE.

Telephone: (20) 8748-2554; **Fax:** (20) 8237-8000; **Internet:** www.savethechildren.net; **e-mail:** info@save-children-alliance.org.

Save the Children (UK)

Established in 1919 to assist disadvantaged and vulnerable children world-wide; has a commitment to the rights of children, as now enshrined in the UN Convention on the Rights of the Child.

Activities: Runs programmes nationally and internationally to help children in the areas of social protection, welfare and inclusion, education, health, food security and nutrition, HIV/AIDS and children, and work. Supports projects in around 70 countries. Provides emergency relief as well as long-term development and prevention work. Collaborates in its work with local, national and international organizations, and governments.

Geographical Area of Activity: International.

Restrictions: No grants to individuals; works in partnership with other NGOs, governments and local, national and international organizations.

Publications: Annual Report; financial accounts; subject-specific publications: *What makes me happy; The Right Not to Lose Hope; Safe Learning; Paying with their lives.*

Finance: Annual revenue £291,472,000, expenditure £266,552,000 (Dec. 2010).

Trustees: Alan Parker (Chair.); Richard Winter (Hon. Treas.).

Principal Staff: Chief Exec. Justin Forsyth.

Address: 1 St John's Lane, London EC1M 4AR.

Telephone: (20) 7012-6400; **Fax:** (20) 7012-6963; **Internet:** www.savethechildren.org.uk; **e-mail:** supporter.care@savethechildren.org.uk.

Science and Technology Facilities Council—STFC

The STFC was established in 2007, from a merger of the Council for the Central Laboratory of the Research Councils, the Particle Physics and Astronomy Research Council and the transfer of responsibility for nuclear physics from the Engineering and Physical Sciences Research Council.

Activities: STFC makes it possible for a broad range of scientists to do the highest quality research, tackling some of the most fundamental scientific questions. It funds researchers in universities directly through grants, particularly in astronomy, particle physics, space science and nuclear physics. It provides access to world-class facilities, including ISIS, the Central Laser Facility, and High-End Computing Terascale Resource (HECToR). It is also a major stakeholder in the Diamond Light Source, which started operations in 2007. STFC provides a broad range of scientific and technical expertise in space and ground-based astronomy technologies, microelectronics, wafer scale manufacturing, particle and nuclear physics, alternative energy production, radio communications and radar. It provides access to world-class facilities overseas, including through the European Organization for Nuclear Research (CERN), the European Space Agency, the European Southern Observatory, the European Synchrotron Radiation Facility, the Institut Laue-Langevin and telescope facilities in Chile, Hawaii, La Palma and the MERLIN/VLBI National Facility, which includes the Lovell Telescope at Jodrell Bank Observatory. Finally, it suppliesy highly skilled scientists and engineers, and generates ideas and technologies that have a much broader social and economic impact.

Geographical Area of Activity: United Kingdom; funding for telescopes in Australia, Chile, Hawaii and Canary Islands, international partnerships in world-leading research.

Finance: Funded by the United Kingdom Government.

Council: Prof. Michael Sterling (Chair.).

Principal Staff: Chief Exec. John Womersley; COO Prof. Richard Wade.

Address: Polaris House, North Star Ave, Swindon SN2 1SZ.

Telephone: (1793) 442000; **Fax:** (1793) 442125; **Internet:** www.stfc.ac.uk; **e-mail:** enquiries@stfc.ac.uk.

Scope

Scope, the cerebral palsy charity, was established in 1952 for the public benefit and for general charitable purposes according to the laws of England and Wales and in particular, but not exclusively, for the promotion of equality, diversity, independence and health of disabled people, especially those with cerebral palsy.

Activities: Scope is the United Kingdom's leading disability charity. Its focus is on children and adults with cerebral palsy and people living with other severe and complex impairments. Scope's vision is for disabled people to have the same opportunities to fulfill their life ambitions as non-disabled people.

Geographical Area of Activity: England and Wales.

Finance: Annual revenue £101,614,000, expenditure £94,928,000 (March 2010).

Trustees: Alice Maynard (Chair.); Ian Black (Hon. Treas.); John Corneille (Vice-Chair.).

Principal Staff: Chief Exec. Richard Hawkes.

Address: 6 Market Rd, London N7 9PW.

Telephone: (20) 7619-7100; **Fax:** (1908) 321051; **Internet:** www.scope.org.uk; **e-mail:** response@scope.org.uk.

Scottish Catholic International Aid Fund—SCIAF

Founded in 1965 as the overseas relief development agency of the Scottish Catholic Church.

Activities: Provides support to poor communities in developing countries, raises awareness of the underlying causes of poverty, and campaigns for a fairer world. Funding programmes include the development education mini-grant initiative.

Geographical Area of Activity: Developing countries.

Publications: Annual Report; mission statement; newsletter; *Review* magazine.

Finance: Annual revenue £6,385,430, expenditure £5,804,879 (2009).

Trustees: Cardinal Keith Patrick O'Brien (Chair.).

Principal Staff: Head of International Programmes Lorraine Currie.

Address: 19 Park Circus, Glasgow G3 6BE.

Telephone: (141) 3545555; **Fax:** (141) 3545533; **Internet:** www.sciaf.org.uk; **e-mail:** sciaf@sciaf.org.uk.

Scouloudi Foundation

Founded in 1962 by I. Scouloudi for general charitable purposes; formerly known as the Twenty-Seven Foundation.

Activities: Operates in the United Kingdom. Current policy is to distribute funds in the following areas: annual donations to the Institute of Historical Research of the University of London for research, publications and historical awards fellowships; regular donations to a selected list of national charities; and donations for special needs as they arise.

Geographical Area of Activity: United Kingdom.

Finance: Annual revenue £229,000, expenditure £300,000 (Feb. 2011).

Trustees: David Marnham; James Sewell; Sarah Stowell.

Address: c/o Haysmacintyre, Fairfax House, 15 Fulwood Pl., London WC1V 6AY.

Telephone: (20) 7969-5500; **Fax:** (20) 7969-5600; **e-mail:** service@haysmacintyre.com.

Seafarers UK

Founded in 1917 by HM King George V to raise funds to support Marine Benevolent and Welfare Institutions throughout the United Kingdom and the Commonwealth. Granted a Royal Charter in 1920. Formerly known as the King George's Fund for Sailors.

Activities: A national grant giving charity working to unite the maritime charity sector to address the specific needs of all seafarers and their families.

Geographical Area of Activity: United Kingdom and Commonwealth.

Restrictions: No grants to individuals.

Publications: *Flagship* (supporter magazine, 3 a year); *Nautical Welfare Guide* (every 2–3 years); Annual Report and accounts.

Finance: Annual revenue £3,358,000, expenditure £4,215,000 (Dec. 2009).

Principal Staff: Dir-Gen. Commander B. W. Bryant; Exec. Man. Kate Brown.

Address: 8 Hatherley St, London SW1P 2YY.

Telephone: (20) 7932-0000; **Fax:** (20) 7932-0095; **Internet:** www.seafarers-uk.org; **e-mail:** seafarers@seafarers-uk.org.

Samuel Sebba Charitable Trust

Founded in 1967 for general charitable purposes.

Activities: The Trust operates nationally and internationally, with a specific focus on supporting Jewish causes.

Geographical Area of Activity: United Kingdom and Israel.

Finance: Annual revenue £705,000, expenditure £3,103,000 (April 2010).

Trustees: Victor Klein; Clive Marks; Leigh Sebba; Leslie Sebba; Stanley Sebba.

Principal Staff: Clive Marks.

Address: 25–26 Enford St, London W1H 1DW.

Telephone: (20) 7388 3577; **Fax:** (20) 7388-3570.

Shackleton Foundation

Established in 2007 to support individuals of all ages, nationalities and backgrounds who exemplify the spirit of Sir Ernest Shackleton, i.e. who are inspirational leaders aiming to assist the disadvantaged.

Activities: Commemorates the life of Sir Ernest Shackleton. Also offers Leadership Awards.

Board of Trustees: Bill Shipton (Chair.).

Address: c/o 52 Mount St, London W1K 2SF.

Internet: www.shackletonfoundation.org; **e-mail:** info@shackletonfoundation.org.

Shell Foundation

Established by the Royal Dutch/Shell Group in June 2000 to support initiatives world-wide in the area of sustainable development.

Activities: Operates world-wide in the field of conservation and the environment, mainly through its Sustainable Energy Programme, but also through two further programmes, the Sustainable Communities and the Promoting Youth Enterprise Programmes, all of which offer grants for projects carried out by non-profit-making groups or organizations.

Geographical Area of Activity: World-wide.

Publications: Financial Report; newsletter.

Finance: Annual revenue £33,326,000, expenditure £13,287,000 (Dec. 2009).

Trustees: Malcolm Brinded (Chair.).

Principal Staff: Dir Chris West; Deputy Dir Jeroen Blum.

Address: Shell Centre, London SE1 7NA.

Telephone: (20) 7934-2727; **Fax:** (20) 7934-7348; **Internet:** www.shellfoundation.org; **e-mail:** info@shellfoundation.org.

Shelter—National Campaign for Homeless People

Founded to improve the quality of life of homeless people and those with inadequate housing.

Activities: The organization supports homeless people through the following programmes: Shelterline, a free national telephone helpline, which provides advice and information; Housing Aid Centres at 59 locations, which provide information, advice and advocacy; Homeless to Home Projects, which aim to resettle homeless families; the Street Homelessness Project, which works with local authorities and voluntary organizations to help reduce the number of people sleeping in the street; the National Homelessness Advice Service; and the Homework Project, which aims to prevent homelessness through educating children and providing educational materials to schools. In addition to these programme areas, Shelter runs Shelter Training, works with politicians at all levels on housing and welfare issues, and is closely involved with initiatives dealing with social exclusion.

Geographical Area of Activity: United Kingdom.

Publications: *Roof* (newsletter, 6 a year); policy reports, briefings and fact sheets; Annual Report; and other publications on housing-related subjects.

Finance: Annual revenue £53,026,000, expenditure £48,992,000 (March 2011).

Board of Trustees: Prof. A. D. H. Crook (Chair.); Hugh Norton (Vice-Chair.).

Principal Staff: Chief Exec. Campbell Robb.

Address: 88 Old St, London EC1V 9HU.

Telephone: (20) 7505-2162; (808) 800-4444 (helpline); **Fax:** (20) 7505-2030; **Internet:** www.shelter.org.uk; **e-mail:** info@shelter.org.uk.

Archie Sherman Charitable Trust

Founded in 1967 for general charitable purposes.

Activities: Operates nationally and internationally in the fields of health and education.

Geographical Area of Activity: International.

Finance: Total income £1,337,000, expenditure £1,304,000 (April 2010).

Board of Trustees: Eric Charles; Michael J. Gee; Allan Henry Simon Morgenthau.

Address: Flat 27, Berkeley House, 15 Hay Hill, London W1J 8NS.

Telephone: (20) 7493-1904; **e-mail:** trust@sherman.co.uk.

Sight Savers International

Founded in 1950 to prevent and cure blindness and promote the welfare, education and employment of blind people in developing countries.

Activities: Operates in 32 developing countries in the field of blindness prevention and cure. Works in co-operation with the the World Health Organization and major international NGOs. Projects are designed and delivered with the assistance of local and regional organizations and national agencies to bring services to the maximum number of people.

Geographical Area of Activity: Africa, Southern Asia, the Caribbean and Europe.

Publications: Annual Report; newsletter (monthly).

Finance: Annual revenue £32,792,000, expenditure £32,323,000 (2010).

Trustees: Lord Crisp (Chair.).

Principal Staff: Chief Exec. Dr Caroline Harper.

Address: Grosvenor Hall, Bolnore Rd, Haywards Heath RH16 4BX.

Telephone: (1444) 446600; **Fax:** (1444) 446688; **Internet:** www.sightsavers.org; **e-mail:** info@sightsavers.org.

Sino-British Fellowship Trust—SBFT

Founded in 1948 to provide educational scholarships dedicated to the advancement of human welfare.

Activities: Provides scholarships for postgraduate students from China, and for British postgraduate students proceeding to and from the Far East. The majority of grants are made to allied organizations; a small amount is available for individual grants in special circumstances.

Geographical Area of Activity: China and Europe.

Restrictions: Candidates must be over 27 years of age.

Publications: Annual Report.

Finance: Annual revenue £28,139,608, expenditure £27,669,921 (March 2010).

Council: Prof. Sir Adam Roberts (Pres.); Prof. Michael Fulford (Treas.).

Principal Staff: Chief Exec. Dr Robin Jackson.

Address: c/o The British Academy, 10 Carlton House Terrace, London SW1Y 5AH.

Telephone: (20) 7969-5200; **Fax:** (20) 7969-5300; **Internet:** www.britac.ac.uk/funding/guide/intl/sbft.cfm; **e-mail:** chiefexec@britac.ac.uk.

The Henry Smith Charity

Established in 1628 for the relief of the poor kindred of Henry Smith, the relief and maintenance of 'Godly preachers', and limited charitable purposes.

Activities: Operates in the United Kingdom (with local programmes in certain United Kingdom counties), in the areas of medicine and health, and social welfare, through making grants for projects in the fields of hospitals, hospices, young people, the elderly, disabled people, counselling and family advice, homelessness, drugs and alcohol, community service, general welfare and medical research.

Geographical Area of Activity: United Kingdom.

Restrictions: Grants are not made to individuals, except for the relief of the poor kindred of Henry Smith and clergy of the

Church of England; grants are made to charitable organizations only, and no grants are made for purposes outside the charity's objectives. Grants are usually made to small charities, not to other grant-making organizations.

Publications: Annual Report.

Finance: Annual revenue £14,264,000, expenditure £35,421,000 (Dec. 2010).

Trustees: J. D. Hambro (Chair.).

Principal Staff: Dir Richard Hopgood; Grants Head Virginia Graham; Sec. Alastair Marr.

Address: 6th Floor, 65 Leadenhall St, London EC3A 2AD.

Telephone: (20) 7264-4970; **Fax:** (20) 7488-9097; **Internet:** www.henrysmithcharity.org.uk.

Sobell Foundation

Founded in 1977 by the late Sir Michael Sobell for general charitable purposes.

Activities: The Foundation operates in the fields of medicine and health, and social welfare, through supporting projects that benefit children, the elderly, the poor, the ill and the disabled. Supports Jewish charities and non-Jewish charities in England, Wales, Israel and the Commonwealth of Independent States.

Geographical Area of Activity: England, Wales, Israel, Commonwealth of Independent States.

Restrictions: No grants to individuals; applicants must be United Kingdom registered charities.

Finance: Annual revenue £2,146,889, expenditure £2,657,124 (April 2009).

Trustees: Andrea Gaie Scouller; Roger Kingston Lewis; Susan Gina Lacroix.

Principal Staff: Admin. Penny Newton.

Address: POB 2137, Shepton Mallet, Somerset BA4 6YA.

Telephone: (1749) 813135; **Fax:** (1749) 813136; **Internet:** www.sobellfoundation.org.uk; **e-mail:** enquiries@sobellfoundation.org.uk.

Soroptimist International

An NGO established in 1921 to strive for human rights and advance the status of women.

Activities: The organization is an international NGO with more than 90,000 female members in 124 countries worldwide. Operates internationally in the areas of aid to less-developed countries, humanities, conservation, environment, education, international affairs, human rights, health, and through projects, grants and seminars. The organization consists of four federations: the Americas, Europe, Great Britain and Ireland, and the South-West Pacific.

Geographical Area of Activity: World-wide.

Publications: *The International Soroptimist* and *Federation* magazines.

Principal Staff: Int. Pres. Alice Wells; Int. Treas. Patricia Carruthers; Int. Programme Dir Reilly Anne Dempsey.

Address: 87 Glisson Rd, Cambridge CB1 2HG.

Telephone: (1223) 311833; **Fax:** (1223) 467951; **Internet:** www.soroptimistinternational.org; **e-mail:** hq@soroptimistinternational.org.

Spinal Research

Established in 1980 by Stewart Yesner to fund research nationally and internationally with the aim of ending permanent paralysis caused by spinal cord injury.

Activities: Operates nationally and internationally in the field of medical research into spinal cord injury, through funding laboratories in its research network.

Geographical Area of Activity: World-wide.

Publications: Newsletters; Annual Review; research updates; *Annual Research Review.*

Finance: Annual income £1,974,824, expenditure £2,217,281 (March 2011).

Board of Trustees: John Hick (Chair.); P. Herbert (Vice-Chair.); Martin Curtis (Hon. Treas.).

Principal Staff: CEO Jonathan Miall.

Address: Bramley Business Centre, Station Rd, Bramley, Guildford, Surrey GU5 0AZ.

Telephone: (1483) 898786; **Fax:** (1483) 898763; **Internet:** www.spinal-research.org; **e-mail:** info@spinal-research.org.

Staples Trust

Staples Trust is one of the Sainsbury Family Charitable Trusts, with a joint administration.

Activities: The objective of the Trust, as per the Trust deed, is general-purpose charity.

Geographical Area of Activity: United Kingdom.

Restrictions: No grants are made to individuals.

Publications: Annual Report.

Finance: Total income £442,813, expenditure £516,266 (April 2011).

Trustees: Alexander John Sainsbury; Judy Portrait.

Principal Staff: Dir Michael Pattison.

Address: Allington House, 1st Floor, 150 Victoria St, London SW1E 5AE.

Telephone: (20) 7410-0330; **Fax:** (20) 7410-0332; **Internet:** www.sfct.org.uk/staples.html; **e-mail:** info@sfct.org.uk.

Stewards Company Limited

Founded in 1922 for general charitable purposes.

Activities: Provides grants to religious charitable organizations throughout the world, particularly those involved in missionary work.

Geographical Area of Activity: International.

Finance: Annual revenue £4,339,009, expenditure £5,006,819 (June 2011).

Trustees: Dr Alexander Douglas Scott; Alexander Lindsay Mcilhinney; Andrew James Street; Brian John Chapman; Douglas Thomas Reid Spence; Dr John Henry Burness; Paul Young; William Brian Adams; William Ovenstone Wood; Ian Childs; Denis S Cooper; James Crookes; Glyn J Davies; John Gamble; Andrew B Griffiths; Philip Page; Alan Paterson; Philip Symonds; Arthur Williamson; Keith Bintley; John Aitken.

Principal Staff: Contact Brian John Chapman.

Address: 124 Wells Rd, Bath BA2 3AH.

Telephone: (1225) 427236; **e-mail:** stewardsco@stewards.co.uk.

Sir Halley Stewart Trust

Established in 1924 by Sir Halley Stewart to promote and support pioneering research in the medical, social, educational and religious fields, and help prevent human suffering.

Activities: Funds work in the United Kingdom and in parts of Africa through research and development grants. Approximately 44% of the Trust's grants are awarded to research workers for medical research, in particular in the areas of problems of the elderly, preventing disability in children and researching tropical diseases. The remaining 56% is awarded to social, educational and ecumenical religious projects, especially small, innovative grassroots projects, projects dealing with cultural and racial divides, projects to help people move beyond disadvantage, and exploring spiritual needs.

Geographical Area of Activity: United Kingdom, Burkina Faso, northern Ghana.

Restrictions: Only postal applications are accepted; no gap-year projects supported. Only grants to United Kingdom registered charities.

Finance: Grant expenditure £800,000 (2011).

Trustees: Lord Stewartby (Pres.); Prof. Phil Whitfield (Chair.); Dr Duncan Stewart (Vice-Chair.); Joanna Womack (Hon. Treas.).

Principal Staff: Admin. Mrs Susan West.

Address: 22 Earith Rd, Willingham, Cambridge CB24 5LS.

Telephone: (01954) 260707; **Fax:** (01954) 260707; **Internet:** www.sirhalleystewart.org.uk; **e-mail:** email@ sirhalleystewart.org.uk.

Marie Stopes International—MSI

Founded as the Mothers' Clinic in 1921, by Marie Stopes. The organization's mission is to support the right to have children by choice, not by chance, through the provision of information and services.

Activities: The organization lobbies governments and international organizations to influence policy and allocation of resources in the areas of family-planning services and reproductive health care. Provides information, and family-planning and health care services, in 37 countries world-wide, working in collaboration with local organizations. Each programme is managed and run by a local team, and meets the specific needs of the country with the focus on building the capacity of indigenous organizations.

Geographical Area of Activity: World-wide.

Publications: Annual Report; *First People* (newsletter); *Handbook on European Community Support*; *Abortion*; *Female sterilisation*; *Fees*; *Health screening*; *Sex education*; *Vasectomy*.

Finance: Annual revenue £129,860,000, expenditure £125,947,000 (Dec. 2010).

Board of Directors: Yasmin Ahmed; Cyprian Awiti; Pim Black; Philip Dow Harvey; Lady Flather; Timothy Morton Rutter; Bill Stanford.

Principal Staff: Chief Exec. Dana Hovig.

Address: 1 Conway St, Fitzroy Sq., London W1T 6LP.

Telephone: (20) 7636-6200; **Fax:** (20) 7034-2370; **Internet:** www.mariestopes.org.uk; **e-mail:** press@mariestopes.org .uk.

The Stroke Association

Established in 1899 as the National Association for the Prevention of Tuberculosis, becoming the Stroke Association in 1992; its purpose is to provide practical support to people who have had strokes, and their families; and to increase awareness of stroke in society.

Activities: Operates in England and Wales; provides community services; maintains a central information service and a network of regional information centres; offers support to families, and to those suffering from dysphasia; provides welfare grants; makes grants for stroke research.

Geographical Area of Activity: England and Wales.

Publications: *Stroke News* (quarterly); leaflets and booklets; Annual review and accounts.

Finance: Annual revenue £28,672,000, expenditure £26,950,000 (March 2010).

Council: Sir Charles George (Chair.); Michael Watts (Treas.).

Principal Staff: Chief Exec. John Barrick.

Address: Stroke House, 240 City Rd, London EC1V 2PR.

Telephone: (20) 7566-0300; **Fax:** (20) 7490-2686; **Internet:** www.stroke.org.uk; **e-mail:** info@stroke.org.uk.

The Bernard Sunley Charitable Foundation

Founded in 1960 to provide funds for general charitable purposes.

Activities: Seek to raise the quality of life, particularly for those who are young, disadvantaged, deprived, disabled or elderly. Provide financial assistance to charitable projects in the United Kingdom in areas including education for those with special needs, activities for young people to realise their potential, the arts and humanities, wildlife and the environment, hospices and medical research, encouraging community cohesion and youth training, and provision for the elderly.

Geographical Area of Activity: United Kingdom.

Restrictions: No grants made to individuals.

Publications: Annual Report.

Finance: Annual revenue £3,064,000, expenditure £3,082,000 (March 2011).

Trustees: Mrs Anabel Knight (Chair.).

Principal Staff: Dir John Rimington.

Address: 20 Berkeley Sq., London W1J 6LH.

Telephone: (20) 7408-2198; **Fax:** (20) 7499-8832; **e-mail:** office@sunleyfoundation.com.

Survival International

Founded in 1969, a world-wide organization supporting the rights of tribal peoples to decide their own future, and to protect their lives, lands and human rights.

Activities: The organization runs campaigns to attract international support for indigenous peoples under threat; provides information and educational materials; and supports health and educational projects that benefit indigenous peoples; it has members in more than 90 countries.

Geographical Area of Activity: World-wide.

Publications: News releases; background materials.

Finance: Annual revenue £1,039,760, expenditure £1,052,857 (Dec. 2010).

Board of Trustees: M. Davis (Treas.).

Principal Staff: Dir-Gen. Stephen Corry.

Address: 6 Charterhouse Bldgs, London EC1M 7ET.

Telephone: (20) 7687-8700; **Fax:** (20) 7687-8701; **Internet:** www.survivalinternational.org; **e-mail:** info@ survivalinternational.org.

John Swire 1989 Charitable Trust

Founded in 1989.

Activities: The Trust awards grants for general charitable purposes.

Geographical Area of Activity: International.

Restrictions: Individual applications are not accepted.

Finance: Annual revenue £1,825,000, expenditure £512,000 (Dec. 2010).

Trustees: John Samuel Swire; Barnaby Nicholas Swire; Lady Moira Cecilia Swire; Michael Cradock Robinson; Sir John Anthony Swire.

Principal Staff: Michael Todhunter.

Address: Swire House, 59 Buckingham Gate, London SW1E 6AJ.

Telephone: (20) 7834-7717; **Fax:** (20) 7630-5534.

Tearfund

Founded in 1968 by the Evangelical Alliance to serve churches in the United Kingdom and Ireland; a relief and development agency, working for the relief of poverty, suffering and distress among peoples of the world.

Activities: Tearfund facilitates, inspires and challenges local churches to help transform lives materially and spiritually. Our ten-year vision is to see 50m. people released from material and spiritual poverty through a world-wide network of 100,000 local churches. We are recognised for our professional expertise in development, disaster response, disaster risk reduction and advocacy.

Geographical Area of Activity: World-wide.

Publications: *Tear Times*; Annual Report.

Finance: Annual revenue £61,141,000, expenditure £64,525,000 (March 2010).

Board of Directors: Clive Mather (Chair.); David Todd (Treas.).

Principal Staff: Chief Exec. Matthew Frost.

Address: 100 Church Rd, Teddington, TW11 8QE.

Telephone: (20) 8977-9144; **Fax:** (20) 8943-3594; **Internet:** www.tearfund.org; **e-mail:** enquiries@tearfund.org.

Thomson Foundation

Founded in 1962 by Roy Thomson (later Lord Thomson of Fleet) to provide training facilities for journalism and television in developing countries.

Activities: Practical training is given in the United Kingdom for media management and senior journalists, and specialized training in television production and engineering by arrangement; training teams are provided to help overseas media and media institutions to raise professional standards. More recently, the emphasis has been on providing experienced trainers to supply in-country training. The Foundation works in collaboration with UNESCO and other organizations to provide training advisory services to developing countries.

Geographical Area of Activity: International.

Restrictions: Grants only for Thomson courses.

Publications: Training manuals for journalism; television engineering video tapes; news archive.

Finance: Total income £1,627,000, expenditure £1,966,000 (Dec. 2006).

Board of Trustees: Lord Fowler of Suttonfield (Chair.).

Principal Staff: CEO Nigel Baker.

Address: 37 Park Pl., Cardiff CF10 3BB.

Telephone: (29) 2035-3060; **Fax:** (29) 2035-3061; **Internet:** www.thomsonfoundation.org; **e-mail:** enquiries@thomfound.org.

Thomson Reuters Foundation

Founded in 1982 by Reuters, the international news and information organization to aid the media in developing countries, and to narrow the gap in information technology between developed and developing countries.

Activities: Organizes training courses for practising journalists from developing countries and Eastern Europe in subjects including international, environmental, HIV/AIDS and business news-writing, photo and television journalism. Reuters Foundation Fellowships are offered to journalists for study at the University of Oxford. The Foundation operates AlertNet, an Internet service aimed at providing news, field reports and forums to the international disaster relief community: www.alertnet.org, and AIDfund, a programme which provides funding to aid organizations dealing with large-scale natural disasters.

Geographical Area of Activity: International.

Restrictions: Reuters Foundation is not a grant giving organization. Local causes are supported by the giving of Reuters time, skills and talents through volunteering engagement.

Finance: Annual revenue £2,416,000, expenditure £3,419,000 (Dec. 2007).

Board of Trustees: David W. Binet (Chair.).

Principal Staff: CEO Monique Villa.

Address: Thomson Bldg, 30 South Colonnade, Canary Wharf, London E14 5EP.

Telephone: (20) 7542-7015; **Internet:** www.thomsonreutersfoundation.org; **e-mail:** foundation@reuters.com.

The Sir Jules Thorn Charitable Trust

Founded in 1964 by Sir Jules Thorn for general charitable purposes.

Activities: The founder hoped that through its grant-making the Trust would be able to improve the quality of life for the sick and disadvantaged. It does this through funding medical research in universities and National Health Service organizations, and humanitarian work undertaken by registered charities. In 2001 the Trust launched the annual Sir Jules Thorn Award for Biomedical Research. This provides a grant of up to £1.25m. over five years for a programme of translational research. Its humaniarian grants include an annual Special Project award or awards up to a maximum of approximately £500,000 linked to a theme, selected by the Trustees, and numerous small donations to a wide range of charities.

Geographical Area of Activity: United Kingdom.

Restrictions: Grants are not made to individuals, nor to applicants from countries other than the United Kingdom.

Finance: Annual revenue £3,032,453, expenditure £2,604,207 (Dec. 2009).

Trustees: Elizabeth Charal (Chair.).

Principal Staff: Dir David H. Richings; Senior Exec. Andrew Elliot.

Address: 24 Manchester Sq., London W1U 3TH.

Telephone: (20) 7487-5851; **Fax:** (20) 7224-3976; **Internet:** www.julesthorntrust.org.uk; **e-mail:** info@julesthorntrust.org.uk.

Trans-Antarctic Association—TAA

Founded in 1962 by the Committee of Management of the Trans-Antarctic Expedition to further research in subjects relating to the Antarctic.

Activities: Makes annual awards to individuals for research and exploration in the Antarctic regions, publication of results, cost of travel to Antarctica, or attendance at international meetings concerned with Antarctic science.

Geographical Area of Activity: Antarctica.

Restrictions: Awards are made to citizens of the United Kingdom, Australia, New Zealand and South Africa only.

Finance: Assets approx. £278,221; annual awards approx. £15,000.

Trustees: Dr P. D. Clarkson (Chair.).

Principal Staff: Sec. Dr Michael Curtis.

Address: c/o British Antarctic Survey, High Cross, Madingley Rd, Cambridge, CB3 0ET.

Telephone: (1223) 221429; **Fax:** (1223) 362616; **Internet:** www.transantarctic.org.uk; **e-mail:** taagrants@bas.ac.uk.

Trust for London

Founded in 1891 as the City Parochial Foundation (CPF) for general charitable purposes in the Metropolitan Police District of London and the City of London. Changed its name to Trust for London in July 2010, following the Foundation's amalgamation with Trust for London.

Activities: Operates within all London boroughs and the City of London; main priority areas are tackling poverty and inequality. Grants are made to organizations working in these areas.

Geographical Area of Activity: London Boroughs and City of London.

Restrictions: No grants are made to individuals, nor for medical research or equipment, trips abroad, one-off events, major capital appeals, the direct replacement of public funds, publications or endowment appeals.

Publications: *Capital Youth*; *Financial Fitness*; *London Prisons Link*; Annual Report; grant guidelines; grants review.

Finance: Annual revenue £8,299,513, expenditure £13,441,173 (2010).

Trustees: Peter Williams (Chair.).

Principal Staff: Chief Exec. Bharat Mehta.

Address: 6 Middle St, London EC1A 7PH.

Telephone: (20) 7606-6145; **Fax:** (20) 7600-1866; **Internet:** www.trustforlondon.org.uk; **e-mail:** info@trustforlondon.org.uk.

Trusthouse Charitable Foundation

Established in 1997 following the takeover of the Forte company by Granada (and superseding the non-charitable but grant-distributing Council of Forte, established in 1904 to promote temperance), for general charitable purposes.

Activities: The Council of Forte made grants mainly to medical projects and for the support of former members of the armed forces. Applications should specify the specific project and normally be for a small amount of funding.

Geographical Area of Activity: United Kingdom.

Restrictions: The Foundation will not normally support the following: small local charities; applications from individuals; foreign charities (although applications are considered from United Kingdom-based organizations that that operate overseas). No grants to other grant-making bodies; medical research projects; animal welfare; revenue funding for more than one year; social research; training professionals within the United Kingdom.

Publications: Annual Report.

Finance: Annual revenue £722,000, expenditure £2,723,000 (June 2011).

Board of Trustees: Olga Polizzi (Chair.).

Principal Staff: Prin. Officer Richard Hopgood.

Address: 6th Floor, 65 Leadenhall St, London EC3A 2AD.

Telephone: (20) 7264-4990; **Fax:** (20) 7488-9097; **Internet:** trusthousecharitablefoundation.org.uk.

Tudor Trust

Founded in 1955 for general charitable purposes, the Tudor Trust is a generalist social welfare funder.

Activities: The Tudor Trust is an independent grant-making trust that supports organizations working across the United Kingdom. The Trust does not focus its funding on specific themes or programmes but instead aims to fund a wide range of organizations that are working to achieve lasting change in their communities. Tudor is most interested in supporting smaller, under-resourced organizations that provide direct services to marginalized people, and which involve the people they work with in their planning.

Geographical Area of Activity: United Kingdom.

Restrictions: Applications for funding from outside the United Kingdom are not accepted. No grants are made to individuals, and demand for funding greatly exceeds the available finance. Check guidelines for exclusions which include organizations working primarily in the field of physical illness, physical disability, learning disability and sensory impairment. No applications accepted by either fax or e-mail.

Publications: *Funding Guidelines*; Annual Report.

Finance: Annual revenue £13,493,000, expenditure £18,572,000 (March 2009).

Trustees: Mary Graves; Helen Dunwell; Desmond Graves; Nell Buckler; Christopher Graves; Catherine Antcliff; Louise Collins; Elizabeth Crawshaw; Matt Dunwell; James Long; Ben Dunwell; Francis Runacres; Monica Barlow; Vanessa James.

Principal Staff: Dir Christopher Graves.

Address: 7 Ladbroke Grove, London W11 3BD.

Telephone: (20) 7727-8522; **Fax:** (20) 7221-8522; **Internet:** www.tudortrust.org.uk.

Turquoise Mountain Foundation

Established to promote the regeneration and preservation of old Kabul, Afghanistan.

Activities: Works to preserve historic buildings and culture in Kabul. Maintains an office in Kabul. A separate US foundation operates in the USA.

Geographical Area of Activity: Afghanistan.

Trustees: Sir Thomas Shebbeare; Joy de Menil; Sir John Tusa; Richard Keith; Edward Viscount Chelsea; Khaled Said; Tamim Samee; Shirazuddin Siddiqi.

Principal Staff: Pres HRH Prince of Wales, HE Hamid Karzai; Contact Shoshana Coburn.

Address: Broich, Crieff PH7 3RX.

Telephone: (1764) 650888; **Internet:** www.turquoisemountain.org; **e-mail:** contact@turquoisemountain.org.

Tutu Foundation UK

Established in 2007 to assist in peacebuilding in communities in the UK.

Board of Trustees: Lord Walker of Aldringham (acting Chair.); Peter King (Sec.); Malcolm Alexander (Treas.).

Principal Staff: Chief Exec. Alexandra Ankrah.

Address: Central Hall Westminster, Room 410, Storey's Gate, London SW1H 9NH
Room 410.

Telephone: (20) 7654-3822; **Internet:** www.tutufoundationuk.org; **e-mail:** info@tutufoundationuk.org.

TVE—Television Trust for the Environment

Founded in 1984 by Central Independent Television, WWF (q.v.) and the UN Environment Programme to advance the education of the public world-wide by the dissemination of information on the environment and resources of the world, using electronic communications.

Activities: TVE is editorially independent and functions as both producer and distributor, encouraging film-makers to make new programmes and promoting the distribution of finished films. Since 1985 TVE has produced and co-produced around 1,000 films on the environment and on development, human rights and health issues. It distributes programmes either free or on a subsidized basis to television stations in developing countries, has set up a distribution system to schools and colleges, runs environmental education projects, and has undertaken a feasibility study for a clearing-house to improve the distribution of environmental programmes. Also maintains offices in Beijing, Kolkata, Colombo, Seoul and Tokyo.

Geographical Area of Activity: World-wide.

Publications: *Snapshots of Change*; *Reel to Real: Women Broadcasting for Change*; *Last Plant Standing* (short film); news releases.

Finance: Total income £1,660,712, expenditure £1,891,630 (Dec. 2008).

Trustees: Richard Creasey (Chair.).

Principal Staff: Exec. Dir Cheryl Campbell.

Address: 21 Elizabeth St, London SW1W 9RP.

Telephone: (20) 7901-8855; **Fax:** (20) 7901-8856; **Internet:** www.tve.org; **e-mail:** tve@tve.org.uk.

Twenty-Ninth May 1961 Charity

Founded anonymously on 29 May 1961 for general charitable purposes.

Activities: Operates nationally in the fields of education, social welfare, science and medicine, and the arts and humanities, through grants to institutions.

Geographical Area of Activity: United Kingdom.

Restrictions: Grants are not made to individuals.

Publications: List of grants awarded.

Finance: Annual revenue £3,183,000, expenditure £4,699,000 (April 2011).

Trustees: A. C. Jones; A. Mead; V. E. Treves; P. Varney.

Principal Staff: Trustees' Sec. Amanda Davis.

Address: Ryder Ct, 14 Ryder St, London SW1Y 6QB.

Telephone: (20) 7312-3270; **Fax:** (20) 7312-3220; **e-mail:** enquiries@29may1961charity.org.uk.

UJIA—United Jewish Israel Appeal

Founded in 1968 to ensure a positive future for young people in the United Kingdom and Israel.

Activities: Operates numerous school and after-school programmes for pupils and teachers; runs Jewish youth movements and the UJIA Israel Experience; supports the Union of Jewish Students and young people in the United Kingdom; and educational initiatives for young people Israel.

Geographical Area of Activity: United Kingdom and the Galil, northern Israel.

Finance: Annual revenue £13,146,000, expenditure £8,319,000 (Sept. 2010).

Trustees: Mick Davis (Chair.); Michael Goldstein, Geoffrey Ognall (Vice-Chair.); Sam Clarke (Hon. Treas.).

Principal Staff: Chief Exec. Douglas Krikler.

Address: 37 Kentish Town Rd, London NW1 8NX.

Telephone: (20) 7424-6400; **Fax:** (20) 7424-6401; **Internet:** www.ujia.org; **e-mail:** central@ujia.org.

UNA Trust—United Nations Association Trust

The UNA Trust strives to make reality of the UN's aim to promote peace, justice and development for all. The UNA Trust is a registered charity, independent of the UN and not funded by it.

Activities: Operates nationally and internationally in the fields of education and international relations, through self-conducted programmes.

Geographical Area of Activity: International.

Restrictions: The funds are used almost exclusively to assist the educational work of the UN Association (UNA) and the work of UNA International Service (UNAIS).

Publications: *New World* (magazine).

Board of Directors: Sir Jeremy Greenstock (Chair.); Stephen Harrow (Vice-Chair.).

Principal Staff: Exec. Dir Philip Mulligan.

Address: 3 Whitehall Ct, London SW1A 2EL.

Telephone: (20) 7766-3444; **Fax:** (20) 7930-5893; **Internet:** www.una.org.uk; **e-mail:** membership@una.org.uk.

United Society for Christian Literature—USCL

Founded in 1799 (incorporated 1899) to disseminate the Christian message through the use of the printed word, and thus to serve the Churches at home and abroad.

Activities: Operates internationally in the fields of religion and education, by making grants to institutions for the production and dissemination of Christian literature in developing countries, principally through Feed the Minds (q.v., founded in 1964 to raise funds for literature and communication programmes in developing countries).

Geographical Area of Activity: International.

Restrictions: No grants are made to individuals.

Publications: Report of operations and financial statement.

Finance: Annual revenue £147,214, expenditure £193,530 (April 2007).

Committee: J. Clark (Chair.).

Principal Staff: Gen. Sec. Josephine Carlsson.

Address: Park Pl., 12 Lawn Lane, London SW8 1UD.

Telephone: (8451) 212102; **Fax:** (20) 7592-3939; **Internet:** www.uscl.org.uk; **e-mail:** info@feedtheminds.org.

United Society for the Propagation of the Gospel—USPG

Founded in 1701 by Dr Thomas Bray, DD, as the Society for the Propagation of the Gospel, it merged with the Universities' Mission to Central Africa (founded in 1857) in 1968. It exists to help churches work together to fulfil the mission of bringing the message of God to all parts of the world.

Activities: USPG, Anglicans in World Mission, works in direct partnership with Anglican and United Churches in more than 50 countries, helping to strengthen the Church and build communities. USPG provides the resources that partner organizations define as necessary to meet local needs in vital areas of work including healthcare, education, leadership training and action for social justice.

Geographical Area of Activity: International.

Publications: *Quarterly* newsletter; educational, promotional and prayer material, DVDs.

Finance: Annual revenue £4,209,310, expenditure £5,006,466 (Dec. 2010).

Trustees: Lay Canon Linda Ali (Chair.).

Principal Staff: Pres. Most Rev. and Rt Hon Dr Rowan Williams Archbishop of Canterbury; Gen. Sec. Janette O'Neill.

Address: 200 Great Dover St, London SE1 4YB.

Telephone: (20) 7378-5678; **Fax:** (20) 7378-5650; **Internet:** www.uspg.org.uk; **e-mail:** enquiries@uspg.org.uk.

Van Neste Foundation

Founded in 1959 for general charitable purposes.

Activities: Operates nationally and internationally, especially in developing countries and Eastern Europe, in the areas of assisting the disabled and the elderly, and the promotion of religion, the community and the family.

Geographical Area of Activity: International.

Finance: Annual revenue £228,000, expenditure £235,000 (April 2010).

Trustees: Martin Appleby; Tom Appleby; Benedict Appleby; Fergus Lyons; Jeremy Lyons; Gerald Walker; Michael Lyons.

Principal Staff: Sec. F. J. F. Lyons.

Address: 15 Alexandra Rd, Clifton, Bristol BS8 2DD.

Telephone: (117) 973-5167.

Victoria League for Commonwealth Friendship

Founded in 1901 to promote friendship and understanding among the peoples of the Commonwealth.

Activities: The League runs a hostel in London, provides student accommodation, and organizes trips and events for United Kingdom and Commonwealth members and guests in the United Kingdom. It established and supports HOST (Hosting for Overseas Students), which organizes weekends with British families for young overseas visitors. The League operates autonomously in Australia, New Zealand, Scotland, South Africa and Zimbabwe; there are affiliated organizations in Canada, the USA and Bermuda.

Geographical Area of Activity: International.

Publications: Report of operations and financial statement; Victoria League newsletter.

Finance: Total income £323,000, expenditure £328,000 (Dec. 2009).

Board of Trustees: Lyn D. Hopkins (Chair.).

Principal Staff: Gen. Man. Doreen Henry.

Address: Victoria League House, 55 Leinster Sq., London W2 4PW.

Telephone: (20) 7243-2633; **Fax:** (20) 7229-2994; **Internet:** www.victorialeague.co.uk; **e-mail:** victorialeaguehq@btconnect.com.

Vodafone Group Foundation

Established in 2001 to offer disaster relief, and to fund cultural and sports projects for disadvantaged young people and communities.

Activities: Operates in countries where the Vodafone companies operate, in a number of areas, including health, social welfare, the arts and culture, and conservation and the environment, through grants made via local Vodafone foundations. Twenty-four Vodafone foundations and social investment programmes operate, which distribute two-thirds of Foundation funding. One-third of grants are awarded for disaster relief and preparedness, and for sport and music projects for disadvantaged young people. It was announced in February 2008 that the Foundation would co-operate with the UN World Food Programme and the UN Foundation (q.v.) to establish an information technology training programme to help agencies respond to disasters and emergencies world-wide.

Geographical Area of Activity: International.

Finance: Annual revenue £21,186,391, expenditure £26,748,491 (March 2010).

Trustees: Nick Land (Chair.).

Principal Staff: Dir Andrew Dunnett.

Address: Vodafone House, The Connection, Newbury RG14 2FN.

Internet: www.vodafone.com; **e-mail:** groupfoundation@vodafone.com.

VSO

Founded in 1958, VSO is a leading independent international development charity that works through volunteers to fight poverty in developing countries.

Activities: VSO works in around 44 of the world's disadvantaged countries in Europe, Africa, Asia, the Pacific, Latin America and the Carribean, working with local organizations to tackle poverty. Volunteers share their skills in education, health, business, management, technical and natural resources placements to achieve specific goals in education, HIV and AIDS, disability, health and social well-being, secure livelihoods and participation and governance. The organization adopts three approaches in its work: empowerment, partnership and commitment to training through a range of approaches, including international volunteering, networking and alliance-building, awareness-raising and advocacy.

Geographical Area of Activity: Africa, Eastern Europe, South and South-East Asia, Latin America and the Pacific.

Restrictions: Does not make grants.

Publications: Annual Report and Financial Statements; education and development publications for development practitioners; advocacy papers; working papers.

Finance: Annual revenue £54,675,000, expenditure £53,846,000 (2011).

International Board: Sir Andrew Cubie (Chair.); John Bason (Treas.).

Principal Staff: Chief Exec. Marg Mayne; Deputy Chief Exec. Sarah Wilson.

Address: Carlton House, 27A Carlton Dr., Putney, London SW15 2BS.

Telephone: (20) 8780-7500; **Internet:** www.vso.org.uk; **e-mail:** enquiry@vso.org.uk.

Charles Wallace India Trust

Founded in 1981 to provide funds to enable citizens of India to undertake study or research, or to gain professional experience in the United Kingdom.

Activities: The Trust normally provides grants in the areas of the performing and visual arts, Indian artistic and cultural heritage, and the humanities.

Geographical Area of Activity: India and the United Kingdom.

Restrictions: Grants only made to Indian citizens normally resident and domiciled in that country.

Finance: Annual revenue £273,881, expenditure £200,959 (April 2008).

Trustees: Colin Perchard; Caroline Douglas; Ingval Maxwell; Dr Yasmin Khan.

Principal Staff: Sec. Richard Alford.

Address: 36 Lancaster Ave, London SE27 9DZ.

Telephone: (20) 8670-2825; **Internet:** www.britishcouncil.org/india-scholarships-cwit; **e-mail:** cwit@btinternet.com.

War on Want

Founded in 1951 by Harold Wilson and Victor Gollancz to campaign against world poverty.

Activities: Operates nationally and internationally in the fields of aid to less-developed countries and development studies, through grants to institutions, and organizing training courses and conferences. Current campaign programmes include: supermarkets and sweatshops; corporations and conflict; trade justice; fighting occupation in Palestinian Autonomous Areas, Iraq and Western Sahara; tax dodging; financial crisis.

Geographical Area of Activity: International.

Restrictions: No unsolicited applications accepted.

Publications: *Upfront* (magazine); reports; Annual Report.

Finance: Total income £1,879,648, expenditure £1,831,556 (March 2010).

Council: Steve Preston (Chair.); Polly Jones (Vice-Chair.): David Hillman (Vice-Chair.); Sue Branford (Treas.).

Principal Staff: Exec. Dir John Hilary; Co. Sec. Ben Birnberg.

Address: 44–48 Shepherdess Walk, London N1 7JP.

Telephone: (20) 7324-5040; **Fax:** (20) 7324-5041; **Internet:** www.waronwant.org; **e-mail:** mailroom@waronwant.org.

WaterAid

Founded in 1981 at the start of the UN decade for water to help ensure access to safe water and sanitation for the world's poorest people.

Activities: WaterAid enables the world's poorest people to gain access to safe water and sanitation. Together with improved hygiene, these basic human rights underpin health, education and livelihoods, forming the first essential step in overcoming poverty. Wateraid works with local partners who understand local issues, and provides them with the skills and support to help communities set up and manage practical and sustainable projects that meet their real needs. They also work locally and internationally to change policy and practice, and ensure that water, hygiene and sanitation's vital role in reducing poverty is recognized.

Geographical Area of Activity: Africa and southern Asia.

Restrictions: Grants only to specific (partner) organizations.

Publications: *Oasis* (journal, 2 a year); Annual Report; and a number of other resources, such as country information sheets and issue sheets.

Finance: Annual revenue £48,100,000, expenditure £50,800,000 (2011).

Trustees: Jeremy Pelczer (Chair.).

Principal Staff: Chief Exec. Barbara Frost.

Address: 47–49 Durham St, London SE11 5JD.

Telephone: (20) 7793-4500; **Fax:** (20) 7793-4545; **Internet:** www.wateraid.org; **e-mail:** wateraid@wateraid.org.

Wates Foundation

Founded in 1966 by Norman E. Wates, Ronald W. Wates and Allan C. Wates mainly for improvement of the quality of life, and to alleviate stress, particularly in the urban community.

Activities: Foundation grants are articulated in five broad programme areas, each of which has specific aims set by the trustees. These aims, which are reviewed regularly, are the criteria against which the trustees assess the relevance and potential impact of outcomes that a grant applicant proposes to achieve with the help of a Foundation grant. The five programme areas are: Community Support and Development; Aid to Ethnic and Immigrant Communities; Foundations of Society; Arts, Heritage and the Environment; and Areas of Special Focus. There is also an emphasis on the physical, mental and spiritual welfare of young and disadvantaged people aged between 8 and 25, and racial equality is addressed throughout. Grants are concentrated on projects in the Greater London area, particularly South London and South-East England. Preference is given to projects that seek to comply with recognized quality assurance and accreditation schemes.

Geographical Area of Activity: Greater London.

Restrictions: Grants are not made to individuals, and recipients must have charitable status. No funds are allocated to United Kingdom charities for projects overseas, nor to overseas organizations.

Publications: Annual Report.

Finance: Annual revenue £159,622, expenditure £3,460,353 (March 2010).

Trustees: William Wates (Chair.).

Principal Staff: Dir Brian Wheelwright.

Address: Wates House, Station Approach, Leatherhead, Surrey KT22 7SW.

Telephone: (1372) 861000; **Fax:** (1372) 861252; **Internet:** www.watesfoundation.org.uk; **e-mail:** director@watesfoundation.org.uk.

Webb Memorial Trust

Webb Memorial Trust was founded in 1947 in memory of Beatrice Webb.

Activities: The Trust finances projects furthering the cause of economic and social justice, in Eastern Europe and the United Kingdom, funds fellowships at Ruskin College, Oxford.

Geographical Area of Activity: Eastern Europe and the United Kingdom.

Board of Trustees: Richard Rawes (Chair.).

Principal Staff: Hon. Sec. Michael Parker.

Address: Mount Royal, Allendale Rd, Hexham NE46 2NJ.

Internet: www.webbmemorialtrust.org.uk.

Wellbeing of Women

Established in 1964 to support research concerned with better health of women and babies; formerly known as WellBeing and prior to that as Birthright.

Activities: Wellbeing of Women is a charity that raises money to improve women's health through research, training and education. It funds medical research to develop better treatments, supports specialist training to improve doctors' effectiveness, and provides education for women so that they can stay well.

Geographical Area of Activity: United Kingdom and the Republic of Ireland.

Publications: Fact sheets; pamphlets; booklets; *Wellbeing magazine.*

Finance: Annual revenue £1,936,900, expenditure £2,674,100 (Dec. 2010).

Trustees: Dr Tony Falconer (Pres.); Sir Victor Blank (Chair.); Eve Pollard (Vice-Chair.).

Principal Staff: Dir Liz Campbell.

Address: 27 Sussex Pl., Regent's Park, London NW1 4SP.

Telephone: (20) 7772-6400; **Fax:** (20) 7724-7725; **Internet:** www.wellbeingofwomen.org.uk; **e-mail:** wellbeingofwomen@rcog.org.uk.

Wellcome Trust

Founded in 1936 by the will of the late Sir Henry Wellcome to support clinical and basic scientific research into human and veterinary medicine.

Activities: Supports research in all branches of clinical medicine (except cancer research) and basic biomedical sciences, through the provision of clinical and non-clinical research fellowships and postgraduate studentships, and programme, travel, project, refurbishment and equipment grants. Special interests include support of research into tropical medicine, population issues and the history of medicine. Special initiative funding includes the Joint Infrastructure Fund, University Challenge Fund, functional genomics, pathogen genome sequencing, United Kingdom Population Biomedical Collections and the Cardiovascular Initiative; the Trust is currently providing a significant contribution to the Human Genome Project. In 2009 the Beit Memorial Fellowships for Medical Research transferred all their undertakings to the Wellcome Trust.

Geographical Area of Activity: International.

Publications: *Wellcome News* (quarterly magazine); Annual Report and accounts; grants information booklet.

Finance: Annual revenue £236,800,000, expenditure £672,100,000 (2011).

Board of Governors: Sir William Castell (Chair.); Peter Rigby (Deputy Chair.).

Principal Staff: Dir Sir Mark Walport.

Address: Gibbs Bldg, 215 Euston Rd, London NW1 2BE.

Telephone: (20) 7611-8888; **Fax:** (20) 7611-8545; **Internet:** www.wellcome.ac.uk; **e-mail:** contact@wellcome.ac.uk.

Westminster Foundation for Democracy—WFD

Founded in April 1992 to strengthen pluralist democratic development overseas.

Activities: The Foundation is an independent public body sponsored by the Foreign and Commonwealth Office, specializing in parliamentary strengthening and political party development. The Foundation is uniquely placed to draw directly on the expertise and involvement of all the Westminster political parties and works both on a party-to-party and cross-party basis to develop the capacity of local political parties and politicians to operate effectively in pluralistic and vibrant democracies. The Foundation's parliamentary work aims to strengthen good governance through developing sustainable capacity among parliamentarians, parliamentary staff and parliamentary structures to ensure transparency and accountability. The three main political parties in the United Kingdom are represented on the Governing Board, which also includes a representative of the smaller parties and independent members. WFD is currently delivering long-term parliamentary strengthening and cross-party programmes in 15 countries: Macedonia, Montenegro, Georgia, Ukraine, Democratic Republic of Congo, Ghana, Kenya, Mozambique, Sierra Leone, Uganda, Iraq (Kurdish region), Lebanon, Morocco, Bangladesh and Hong Kong. Together with political party development projects, WFD is working in more than 40 countries.

Geographical Area of Activity: Has traditionally worked in three key regions: Eastern Europe, Sub-Saharan Africa and the Middle East and North Africa. However, there is considerable potential and demand to expand further into Africa and Asia, in particular in Commonwealth countries.

Publications: Annual Report and Accounts; Annual Review, *Building Better Democracies*; *Handbook on Parliamentary Ethics and Conduct - A Guide for Parliamentarians.*

Finance: Receives core funding from the United Kingdom FCO, as well as funding for specific programmes from the United Kingdom Department for International Development, the European Union and the British Council.

Board of Governors: Gary Streeter (Chair.); Meg Munn (Vice-Chair.); Myles Wickstead (Vice-Chair.).

Principal Staff: CEO Linda Duffield.

Address: Artillery House, 11–19 Artillery Row, London SW1P 1RT.

Telephone: (20) 7799 1311; **Fax:** (20) 7799 1312; **Internet:** www.wfd.org; **e-mail:** wfd@wfd.org.

Garfield Weston Foundation

Founded in 1958 for general charitable purposes.

Activities: Grants are made for the support of activities in the areas of religion, conservation and the environment, education, the arts, medicine and health, and welfare, community and youth.

Geographical Area of Activity: Mainly United Kingdom, with limited funding available overseas.

Restrictions: Grants are made to registered charities only (with the exception of applications from churches). No grants are made for animal welfare projects.

Publications: Annual Report.

Finance: Annual revenue £60,052,000, expenditure £34,939,000 (April 2010).

Trustees: Guy H. Weston (Chair.).

Principal Staff: Sec. Janette Cattell.

Address: Weston Centre, 10 Grosvenor St, London W1K 4QY.

Telephone: (20) 7399-6565; **Fax:** (20) 7399-6580; **Internet:** www.garfieldweston.org; **e-mail:** fhare@garfieldweston.org.

Whitley Fund for Nature

Established in 1994 by Edward Whitley to offer awards in the area of conservation.

Activities: Offers awards and grants in the area of conservation to nature conservationists world-wide. Whitley Awards are worth £30,000 each; the Gold Award of an additional £30,000 is offered annually to one recipient.

Geographical Area of Activity: International.

Trustees: Edward Whitley (Chair.); Sir David Attenborough; Tim Dye; Catherine Faulks.

Principal Staff: Dir Georgina Domberger.

Address: 33 Drayson Mews, London W8 4LY.

Telephone: (20) 7368-6568; **Internet:** www.whitleyaward.org; **e-mail:** info@whitleyaward.org.

Harold Hyam Wingate Foundation

Founded in 1960 by Harold Hyam Wingate, the principal objective being the general advancement of Jewish and other charitable purposes.

Activities: The Foundation's main interests lie in supporting Jewish organizations, the performing arts, music, and problems associated with social exclusion. Grants are made to established charitable organizations.

Geographical Area of Activity: United Kingdom, Israel, developing countries.

Publications: Annual Accounts.

Finance: Annual revenue £378,196, expenditure £1,231,261 (April 2010).

Trustees: R. C. Wingate; Dr A. J. Wingate; Prof. R. H. Cassen; Prof. D. L. Wingate; Dr R. Wingate; Prof. J. Drori; D. Hyman; E. Kasriel.

Principal Staff: Admin. Karen C. Marshall.

Address: 20–22 Stukeley St, 2nd Floor, London WC2B 5LR.

Internet: www.wingatefoundation.org.uk.

The Wolfson Family Charitable Trust

Founded in 1958, and formerly known as the Edith and Isaac Wolfson Charitable Trust, for the advancement of health, education, the arts and humanities. The Trust has shared objectives and joint administration with the Wolfson Foundation.

Activities: Operates through grants to institutions, in the United Kingdom and Israel in the above areas.

Geographical Area of Activity: United Kingdom and Israel.

Restrictions: No grants to individuals.

Publications: Annual Report and accounts.

Finance: Assets £40,000,000 (2010); annual revenue approx. £1,500,000–£2,000,000.

Trustees: Janet Wolfson de Botton (Chair.).

Principal Staff: Chief Exec. Paul Ramsbottom.

Address: c/o The Wolfson Foundation, 8 Queen Anne St, London W1G 9LD.

Telephone: (20) 7323-5730; **Fax:** (20) 7323-3241; **Internet:** www.wolfson.org.uk/wfct/.

The Wolfson Foundation

Founded in 1955 for the support of science and medicine, health, education and the arts.

Activities: Supports excellence in science and medicine, health, education and the arts, usually through the provision of infrastructure.

Geographical Area of Activity: United Kingdom, the Commonwealth and Israel.

Restrictions: No grants to individuals.

Publications: Annual Report and accounts.

Finance: Total net assets £725,000,000 (2010); annual revenue £24,380,000, expenditure £28,847,000 (April 2010).

Trustees: Janet Wolfson de Botton (Chair.).

Principal Staff: Chief Exec. Paul Ramsbottom.

Address: 8 Queen Anne St, London W1G 9LD.

Telephone: (20) 7323-5730; **Fax:** (20) 7323-3241; **Internet:** www.wolfson.org.uk.

Wood Family Trust

Established in 2007.

Activities: Operates internationally in three main areas: making markets work for the poor in Sub-Saharan Africa; volunteering overseas and global citizenship; and developing young people in Scotland.

Geographical Area of Activity: International and domestic.

Restrictions: The Trust does not accept unsolicited applications.

Finance: Annual revenue £9,500,000, expenditure £1,200,000 (2010).

Trustees: Sir Ian Wood (Chair.).

Principal Staff: Chief Exec. Jo Mackie; Dir. Africa David Knopp; UK Investment Man. Alison MacLachlan.

Address: John Wood House, Greenwell Rd, Aberdeen AB12 3AX.

Telephone: (1224) 373516; **Fax:** (1224) 851211; **Internet:** www.woodfamilytrust.org; **e-mail:** info@woodfamilytrust.org.uk.

World Land Trust—WLT

Established in 1989 to purchase and protect critically threatened tropical forests and other endangered habitats.

Activities: The Trust is concerned with conservation initiatives, including land purchase and protection of threatened areas in partnership with overseas project partner organizations. WLT raises funds and public awareness to support its conservation aims and objectives. The Trust's Carbon Balanced programme delivers carbon offsets through restoration ecology and avoided deforestation. WLT runs outreach and training local to its office in East Anglia, United Kingdom.

Geographical Area of Activity: Central and South America, India, South-East Asia and Kenya.

Restrictions: No grants to individuals. All funds go directly to WLT projects.

Publications: *WLT News* (3 a year); monthly e-mail bulletins.

Finance: Individual, corporate and trust donations; annual revenue £2,958,555, expenditure £2,711,588 (2009).

Board of Trustees: Rohini Finch (Chair.); Mark Leaney (Hon. Treas.).

Principal Staff: Chief Exec. John A. Burton.

Address: Blyth House, Bridge St, Halesworth IP19 8AB.

Telephone: (1986) 874422; **Fax:** (1986) 874425; **Internet:** www.worldlandtrust.org; www.carbonbalanced.org; www.wildlifefocus.org; www.focusonforests.org; **e-mail:** info@worldlandtrust.org.

World Society for the Protection of Animals

Founded in January 1981 by the merger of the International Society for the Protection of Animals and the World Federation for the Protection of Animals. Its aim is to promote effective means for the protection of animals, for the prevention of cruelty to and the relief from suffering and exploitation of animals.

Activities: Operates internationally, with more than 900 member animal welfare societies in more than 150 countries, in the field of protection of animals and conservation of their environment, and in related areas of education, international relations and international law, through self-conducted programmes, education campaigns, research, conferences and courses, publications and lectures. Current projects include campaigns in the areas of whaling, disaster management, bullfighting, working horses, bears, stray animals and factory farming.

Geographical Area of Activity: International.

Publications: *Animals International*; Annual Report.

Finance: Annual revenue £19,714,000, expenditure £16,657,000 (Dec. 2009).

Trustees: Dr Ranald Munro (Pres.); Dr Hugh Wirth (Sr Vice-Pres.); Dominique Bellemare (Jr Vice-Pres.); Dr Andrew Rowan (Treas.); Hanja Maij-Weggen (Sec.).

Principal Staff: Dir-Gen. Maj.-Gen. Peter Davies.

Address: 5th Floor, 222 Grays Inn Rd, London WC1X 8HB.

Telephone: (20) 7239-0500; **Fax:** (20) 7239-0653; **Internet:** www.wspa.org.uk; **e-mail:** wspa@wspa.org.uk.

YMCA—Young Men's Christian Association

Founded in 1844 by George Williams, the YMCA's vision is of an inclusive Christian Movement, transforming communities so that all young people truly belong, contribute and thrive.

Activities: The YMCA works to empower young people with the right skills and education; support families; provide suitable accommodation for young people; and promote physical activity as a key part of the preventative health agenda. In England there are 135 YMCAs working in more than 250 communities, offering more than 7,000 bed spaces every night. The YMCA is an international movement with more than 45m. members and volunteers working in more than 125 countries world-wide.

Geographical Area of Activity: International.

Publications: Annual review and summary accounts.

Finance: Each of the 135 YMCAs is an independent charity. YMCA England (The National Council of YMCAs) had a total income of £23,390,000 and total expenditure of £22,320,000 in (2010/11).

Trustees: Most Rev. John Sentamu (Pres.).

Principal Staff: Chief Exec. Ian Green.

Address: YMCA England, 45 Beech St, London EC2Y 8AD.

Telephone: (20) 7070-2160; **Internet:** www.ymca.org.uk; **e-mail:** enquiries@ymca.org.uk.

Zochonis Charitable Trust

Founded in 1977 to provide funds for general charitable purposes.

Activities: Operates nationally and internationally in the fields of education, social welfare and the arts and humanities.

Geographical Area of Activity: England and Wales.

Restrictions: Awards grants to registered charities only.

Finance: Annual revenue £3,137,000, expenditure £3,600,000 (April 2011).

Trustees: Sir John Zochonis; Joseph Swift; Archibald Calder; Christopher Green.

Principal Staff: Contact Marie Gallagher.

Address: Manchester Business Park, 3500 Aviator Way, Manchester M22 5TG.

Telephone: (845) 165-5270.

Zurich Community Trust

Founded in 1973, and formerly known as the Allied Dunbar Charitable Trust, for general charitable purposes and to help the most disadvantaged in the community move from dependence to independence locally, nationally and in developing countries.

Activities: The Foundation operates nationally and in developing countries in the fields of law and human rights, and medicine and health. Current programmes include: the India Programme, which combines funding and management development opportunities; the Breaking the Cycle Programme, which is providing £1,200,000 to break the generational cycle of drug abuse; the Mental Health and Families Programme, which involves £1,100,000 in funding over five years; and the Older People programme, which is making grants of £2,200,000 over five years to tackle the issues facing older people. Incorporates Zurich Cares, a staff volunteering and payroll giving programme, and the Openwork Foundation, supported by more than 3,000 members of the financial advisers and employees of Openwork, and currently involved in the Cares Cares 4 Kids theme, which supports children and young people aged 0–18 years old who are disadvantaged in some way—socially, mentally or physically.

Geographical Area of Activity: International.

Restrictions: No grants to individuals, for research, animal welfare, emergency or disaster appeals, nor to political, religious or mainstream educational institutions (unless directly benefiting people with disabilities).

Finance: Grants disbursed approx. £2,594,000 (2011).

Trustees: Chris Gillies (Chair.).

Principal Staff: Contact Pam Webb.

Address: POB 1288, Swindon SN1 1FL.

Telephone: (1793) 502450; **Internet:** www.zurich.org.uk; **e-mail:** zct@zct.org.uk.

United States of America

FOUNDATION CENTRES AND CO-ORDINATING BODIES

Africa Grantmakers' Affinity Group—AGAG

Originally established in the 1980s as the South Africa Grant-makers Affinity Group (SAGAG); adopted current name in 2000 following expansion of remit.

Activities: Operates as a membership network of grant-makers currently funding in Africa or interested in funding in Africa, promoting greater foundation interest and more effective grant-making in Africa.

Geographical Area of Activity: Africa, USA, Europe.

Restrictions: No grants awarded.

Publications: Newsletter; research findings.

Steering Committee: Andrea Johnson (Chair.).

Principal Staff: Exec. Dir Niamani Mutima; Communications and Programme Man. Talaya Grimes.

Address: 1776 I St NW, Suite 900, Washington, DC 20006.

Telephone: (202) 756-4835; **Fax:** (202) 403-3207; **Internet:** www.africagrantmakers.org; **e-mail:** info@ africagrantmakers.org.

America's Development Foundation—ADF

Founded in 1980, ADF is a private non-profit organization that aims to help the development of democracy throughout the world.

Activities: Operates internationally in more than 35 countries, across Eastern and Central Europe, the Middle East, Central America and the Caribbean, and Africa. Provides training, assistance and grants to NGOs to strengthen democracy and democratic institutions, promote the development of civil society, and support fundamental human rights. Provides legal aid and advocacy services.

Geographical Area of Activity: International.

Restrictions: Grants made through in-country programmes in connection with donor-funded projects.

Finance: Annual turnover approx. US $17,000,000.

Board of Trustees: John Hardy (Chair.).

Principal Staff: Pres. Michael D. Miller; Vice-Pres. Chien Wendel.

Address: 101 North Union St, Suite 200, Alexandria, VA 22314.

Telephone: (703) 836-2717; **Fax:** (703) 836-3379; **Internet:** www.adfusa.org; **e-mail:** mmiller@adfusa.org.

Council on Foundations, Inc

Founded in 1949 and incorporated in 1957 as a publicly supported charitable organization.

Activities: The Council's members (more than 2,100 grant-makers) include private, community- and company-sponsored foundations and corporate contributors; regional associations of grant-makers are also affiliated with the Council and work closely with it in providing information and services. The Council provides a variety of technical and advisory services to guide its members on matters ranging from legal and tax issues to investment management, programme development and grant-making principles and practices. It maintains regular liaison with other parts of the philanthropic sector, including the Foundation Center (q.v.), through direct communication and participation in conferences and 'umbrella' organizations. The Council conducts an annual conference and other meetings throughout the year to assist its members in their grant-making activities; and sponsors research and educational programmes. Awards offered include the Wilmer Shields and Distinguished Grantmaker Awards.

Geographical Area of Activity: USA.

Publications: Annual Report; *Council Columns*; *Foundation News and Commentary Magazine*; *Principles and Practices for Effective Grantmaking*; and numerous other publications.

Finance: Total assets US $22,747,134 (31 Dec. 2008); annual revenue $20,798,530, expenditure $21,714,198 (2008); grants disbursed $263,835 (2008).

Board of Directors: Carol S. Larson (Chair.); Kevin Murphy (Vice-Chair.); Sherece West (Sec.); Will Ginsberg (Treas.).

Principal Staff: Interim Pres. and CEO Jeff Clarke; Exec. Vice-Pres. and COO Kisha Green Dimbo.

Address: 2121 Crystal Dr., Suite 700, Arlington, VA 22202.

Telephone: (800) 673-9036; **Internet:** www.cof.org; **e-mail:** webmaster@cof.org.

FHI 360

Established 2011 as a global development organization following the takeover of Academy for Educational Development (AED, founded 1961) by Family Health International (FHI, founded 1971).

Activities: Works in collaboration with local and national partner organizations; operates in some 125 countries.

Geographical Area of Activity: International.

Publications: Annual Report.

Board of Directors: Albert J. Siemens (Chair.); Edward W. Whitehorne (Vice-Chair.); Martin Mittag-Lenkheym (Treas.).

Principal Staff: CEO Albert J. Siemens; COO Marjorie Newman-Williams.

Address: 2224 E NC Highway 54, Durham, NC 27713.

Telephone: (919) 544-7040; **Fax:** (919) 544-7261; **Internet:** www.aed.org; **e-mail:** contact@fhi360.org.

Foundation Center

Opened as the Foundation Library Center in November 1956, with founding president F. Emerson Andrews of the Russell Sage Foundation and author of *Foundation Watcher*. To achieve its goal of providing broad, open access to foundation information, the Center began in 1959 to establish depositories of information in other libraries—now known as Cooperating Collections—nation-wide. In 1960 it published the first *Foundation Directory*, which is still being published annually. In 1968 the organization's name was officially changed to the Foundation Center, signifying expansion of its services and activities beyond that of a library.

Activities: Operates five library/learning centres in New York City; Washington, DC; Atlanta; Cleveland; and San Francisco. These offer free access to information resources and educational programmes. Access is also available internationally through more than 450 funding information centres. The Center maintains unique databases of information on the entire universe of foundations, corporate donors and grant-making public charities in the USA and their grants; conducts research and publishes reports on the growth of the foundation field and on trends in foundation support of the non-profit sector, including the annual *Foundations Today Series*; educates thousands of people each year through a full curriculum of training courses in the classroom and online.

Geographical Area of Activity: USA.

Restrictions: The Center does not direct applications for funds to particular foundations, nor does it arrange introductions to foundation officials or assist persons seeking positions in foundations.

Publications: *Foundation Directory Online*; *Philanthropy In/Sight*; *Map of Cross-Border Giving*.

Finance: Total assets US $27,212,322 (31 Dec. 2010); annual revenue $21,444,863, expenditure $19,887,795 (2010).

Board of Trustees: M. Christine DeVita (Chair.); Barron M. Tenny (Vice-Chair.).

Principal Staff: Pres. Bradford K. Smith.

Address: 79 Fifth Ave/16th St, New York, NY 10003.

Telephone: (212) 620-4230; **Fax:** (212) 807-3677; **Internet:** foundationcenter.org; **e-mail:** communications@foundationcenter.org.

Global Impact

Global Impact is dedicated to raising funds to support humanitarian relief and development programmes for the world's most vulnerable people. Since 1956 Global Impact has raised more than US $1,200m. for thousands of charitable organizations through a comprehensive set of programmes.

Activities: Global Impact adheres to a rigorous series of checks and balances that ensure transparency and sound financial management. In addition to supporting critical international programmes, Global Impact manages two of the largest workplace giving campaigns in the world: the Combined Federal Campaign of the National Capital Area, serving all Federal employees in the Washington DC area, and the Combined Federal Campaign—Overseas for civilian and military Department of Defense personnel stationed abroad. Comprises 62 member charities (2012).

Geographical Area of Activity: International.

Publications: Annual Report.

Finance: Total assets US $22,681,965 (30 June 2010); annual revenue $21,407,347, expenditure $20,987,256 (2009/10).

Board of Directors: Peter M. Grant (Chair.); Joseph A. Crupi (Vice-Chair); H. Kenneth Fleishman (Sec. and Treas.).

Principal Staff: Pres. and CEO Renée S. Acosta.

Address: 66 Canal Center Plaza, Suite 310, Alexandria, VA 22314.

Telephone: (703) 717-5200; **Fax:** (703) 717-5215; **Internet:** www.charity.org; **e-mail:** mail@charity.org.

Grantmakers Without Borders—Gw/oB

Operates as a network of trustees and staff of public and private foundations as well as individual donors who practise global social change philanthropy. Aims to improve the quantity and the quality of US grant-making.

Activities: Aims to develop and promote US global social change philanthropy through collaboration, debate and discussion, exchanging experiences, sharing best practices, and advocating progressive policies in the philanthropic community. Provides information for both grant-makers and grant-seekers.

Geographical Area of Activity: World-wide.

Publications: *Tax Planning for Cross-Border Philanthropy by US Donors*; *International Grantmaking Resource Packet; An Grantmaker's Guide to Microfinance*.

Board of Directors: Shalini Nataraj (Co-Chair.); Tanya Dawkins (Co-Chair.); Lourdes Inga (Sec.); Molly Singer (Treas.).

Principal Staff: Interim Exec. Dir Pete Stanga.

Address: 1009 General Kennedy Ave, Suite 2, San Francisco, CA 94129.

Telephone: (415) 264-4370; **Fax:** (415) 561-7651; **Internet:** www.gwob.net; **e-mail:** gwob@gwob.net.

Independent Sector

Founded in 1980, a national coalition of foundations, non-profit organizations and corporations that aims to strengthen philanthropy and citizen action in the USA.

Activities: Acts as a forum for member organizations, as a source of information and as a mediator between the grant-making and grant-seeking communities. Also works to encourage volunteer work and community action in society. Supports and engages in non-profit initiatives in areas such as public policy, research and communications.

Geographical Area of Activity: USA.

Publications: *Principles for Good Governance and Ethical Practice: A Guide for Charities and Foundations (2007)*; *Giving and Volunteering Signature Series*; *Giving and Volunteering in the United States*; *The New Nonprofit Almanac and Desk Reference*; *Outcome Measurement in Nonprofit Organizations: Current Practices and Recommendations*; *What You Should Know About Nonprofits*; *Facts and Finding Series* (series of research reports); Annual Report; numerous reports, papers and other publications.

Finance: Annual revenue US $10,146,448, expenditure $9,278,152 (2010).

Board of Directors: Stephen B. Heintz (Chair.); Ralph B. Everett (Vice-Chair.); Lorie A. Slutsky (Sec.); Kelvin H. Taketa (Treas.).

Principal Staff: Pres. and CEO Diana Aviv.

Address: 1602 L St NW, Suite 900, Washington, DC 20036.

Telephone: (202) 467-6100; **Fax:** (202) 467-6101; **Internet:** www.independentsector.org; **e-mail:** info@independentsector.org.

InterAction American Council for Voluntary International Action

Formed in 1984 by the merger of the American Council of Voluntary Agencies for Foreign Service and Private Agencies Collaborating Together, InterAction is a coalition of more than 190 US private and voluntary organizations dedicated to international humanitarian issues. Its main purpose is to enhance the effectiveness and professional capacities of its members while fostering partnership, collaboration and leadership within the voluntary organization community.

Activities: Member organizations' activities include disaster relief, refugee protection, assistance and resettlement, sustainable development, public policy and educating the American public on global development issues.

Geographical Area of Activity: USA.

Publications: *Gender Mainstreaming*; *Global Works*; *Foreign Assistance in Focus: Monday Developments* (2 a month); *InterAction Member Profiles* (biennially); newsletters and media guides.

Finance: Annual revenue US $5,686,250, expenditure $7,882,738 (2010).

Board of Directors: Kathy Spahn (Chair.); Tsehaye Teferra (Vice-Chair.); Jonathan Quick (Treas.).

Principal Staff: Pres. and CEO Samuel A. Worthington.

Address: 1400 16th St NW, Suite 210, Washington, DC 20036.

Telephone: (202) 667-8227; **Fax:** (202) 667-8236; **Internet:** www.interaction.org; **e-mail:** ia@interaction.org.

International Society for Third-Sector Research—ISTR

Founded in March 1992, ISTR is an international association promoting research and education in the fields of civil society, philanthropy and the non-profit sector. Committed to building a global community of scholars and interested others dedicated to the creation, discussion and advancement of knowledge relating to the third sector and its impact on human and global well-being and development internationally. The Society's mission is to promote the development of high-quality research and education internationally on third sector-related issues, theories and policies; and to enhance the dissemination and application of knowledge about the third sector as widely as possible throughout the world. ISTR strives to broaden the participation of researchers in all parts of the world and in all disciplines, with special emphasis given to expanding the number of third sector researchers in developing nations and Central and Eastern Europe.

Activities: Members come from 89 countries. Holds conferences biennially to promote the exchange of ideas and research findings in the voluntary sector, and promotes discussion and co-operation between researchers and scholars. ISTR has established a number of regional research networks: African Research Network, Asia/Pacific Research Network, European Research Network and Latin America and the Caribbean Research Network. Has one formal Affinity Group: Gender.

Geographical Area of Activity: International.

Publications: *Inside ISTR* (quarterly newsletter); *ISTR Report*; *Voluntas* (journal); membership directory (online); Annual Report; Working Papers.

Finance: Supported by membership dues, conference fees and grants.

Board of Directors: Brenda Gainer (Pres.); Wendy Earles (Pres. elect); Paul Dekker (Sec.); Hagai Katz (Treas.).

Principal Staff: Exec. Dir Margery B. Daniels.

Address: 559 Wyman Park Bldg, 3400 North Charles St, Baltimore, MD 21218-2688.

Telephone: (410) 516-4678; **Fax:** (410) 516-4870; **Internet:** www.istr.org; **e-mail:** istr@jhu.edu.

ISAR: Resources for Environmental Activists

Established in 1983 by Harriett Crosby and Nancy Graham as the Institute for Soviet and American Relations. Adopted the above name in 2009.

Activities: Works to assist the communities of the former USSR in resolving the environmental issues in the region by providing individuals and NGOs with training and informational resources. Three main programme areas are: environmental advocacy, environmental infrastructure and environmental media and information. Aims to strengthen advocacy skills, increase public participation in environmental campaigns and to help establish environmental networks in the region. Maintains field offices in Russia (Moscow, Novosibirsk, Vladivostok) and Belarus (Minsk).

Geographical Area of Activity: Countries of the former USSR.

Publications: *Give & Take: A Journal on Civil Society in Eurasia* (quarterly newsletter); *ISAR in Focus* (newsletter and annual report); *Surviving Together* (articles).

Finance: Funded by public and private sources.

Principal Staff: Pres. Harriett Crosby.

Address: POB 70029, Washington, DC 20024-0029.

Telephone: (202) 966-0880; **e-mail:** general@isar.org.

Synergos—The Synergos Institute

Established in 1986; aims to develop effective, sustainable and locally based solutions to poverty in Africa, Asia and Central and South America.

Activities: In partnership with other groups, Synergos aims to strengthen the capacity of civil society in less-developed countries and of leading philanthropists from around the world to deepen the effectiveness of their social investments and to forge partnerships to leverage their impact, through its projects, Global Philanthropy and Foundation Building, Bridging Leadership and Global Philanthropists Circle, which assist grassroots grant-making organizations to develop their skills and effectiveness to provide long-term solutions and sustainable development. Maintains an online database of foundations operating in Central and South America and South-East Asia and also works through a Country Office in Brazil.

Geographical Area of Activity: Africa, Asia and Central and South America.

Publications: Annual Reports; *Foundation Building Sourcebook: A Practitioner's Guide Based upon Experience from Africa, Asia and Latin America*; *Global Giving Matters* (online newsletter, 6 a year); case studies, conference reports and other publications.

Finance: Funded by private foundations, international agencies, corporations and individual donations. Annual revenue US \$4,469,237, expenditure \$9,199,794 (2009).

Board of Directors: Peggy Dulany (Chair.).

Principal Staff: Pres. and CEO Robert H. Dunn.

Address: 3 East 54th St, 14th Floor, New York, NY 10022.

Telephone: (646) 963-2100; **Fax:** (646) 201-5220; **Internet:** www.synergos.org; **e-mail:** synergos@synergos.org.

FOUNDATIONS, TRUSTS AND NON-PROFIT ORGANIZATIONS

ACCION International

Founded in 1961, an independent agency that aims to help local organizations reach small businesses in urban and rural areas of North, Central and South America, South and East Asia and Sub-Saharan Africa.

Activities: Advises on issues affecting small businesses; assists in employment and financial projects, small business development and micro-credit loan programmes; and provides management assistance for development agencies. Maintains a small reference library and publishes a monthly e-mail newsletter. In 2001 launched the Citi-ACCION Outstanding Microentrepreneur Prize with Citigroup and the Citigroup Foundation (q.v.). Also operates offices in Washington, DC, and Colombia and India.

Geographical Area of Activity: North, Central and South America, Sub-Saharan Africa, South and East Asia.

Restrictions: Does not lend to, nor fund, individuals directly.

Publications: *InSight* (bulletin); *ACCION International Publications* (annual); Annual Report; and other leaflets, manuals, discussion papers and publications on microfinance.

Finance: Total assets US \$427,063,042 (31 Dec. 2010); annual revenue \$20,128,396, expenditure \$31,992,602 (2010).

Board of Directors: Diana Taylor (Chair.); Gustavo Herrero (Vice-Chair.); Russell B. Faucett (Treas.); Anne Stetson (Sec.).

Principal Staff: Pres. and CEO Michael Schlein; COO Esteban A. Altschul.

Address: 56 Roland St, Suite 300, Boston, MA 02129.

Telephone: (617) 625-7080; **Fax:** (617) 625-7020; **Internet:** www.accion.org; **e-mail:** info@accion.org.

ACDI/VOCA

Established in 1997 by the merger of Agricultural Co-operative Development International (ACDI) and Volunteers in Overseas Co-operative Assistance (VOCA), as a development organization with the aim of promoting the liberalization of markets and democratic principles, alongside environmentally sound use of natural resources.

Activities: Aims to provide farmers with the necessary resources to succeed in the world economy. It does this through programmes that lend the technical expertise and experience of consultants to farmers and businesses in developing countries, enabling them to make use of the economic opportunities that are afforded to them, as well as creating international co-operative partnerships. The organization works on many long-term projects as well as short-term volunteer assignments; supports local environment groups; helps develop member-controlled businesses and associations; encourages sustainable agricultural methods; and works towards the protection of national parks and reserves. Members include agribusinesses and farm credit banks. Maintains offices in 41 countries.

Geographical Area of Activity: International.

Publications: *World Report* (quarterly newsletter); *Global Connections* (e-mail newsletter); Annual Report.

Finance: Total assets US $67,625,083 (31 Dec. 2010); annual revenue $140,022,817; expenditure $139,343,370 (2010).

Board of Directors: Mortimer H. Neufville (Chair.); Timothy J. Penny (Vice-Chair.).

Principal Staff: Pres. and CEO Carl H. Leonard; COO Bill Polidoro.

Address: 50 F St NW, Suite 1075, Washington, DC 20001.

Telephone: (202) 469-2000; **Fax:** (202) 469-6257; **Internet:** www.acdivoca.org; **e-mail:** webmaster@acdivoca.org.

Acumen Fund

Founded in April 2001 with seed money from the Rockefeller Foundation (q.v.), the Cisco Systems Foundation and a group of individual investors.

Activities: Acumen Fund invests patient capital in innovative businesses that serve the BOP and that have high potential to solve social and economic problems. Acumen provides both financial and technical support to these investments; develops talent and leaders through its Fellows programme; and serves as a leading organization in developing the social impact investing sector. Acumen seeks investment in five sectors: water, health, housing, energy and agriculture. Acumen maintains offices in New York (USA), New Delhi (India), Karachi (Pakistan) and Nairobi (Kenya).

Geographical Area of Activity: Africa, India, Pakistan.

Publications: Newsletter (quarterly).

Finance: Total assets US $95,300,000 (31 Dec. 2010); annual revenue $13,400,000, annual expenditure $10,100,000 (2010).

Board of Directors: Andrea Soros Colombel (Chair.).

Principal Staff: CEO Jacqueline Novogratz; Chief Investment Officer Brian Trelstad.

Address: 76 Ninth Ave, Suite 315, New York, NY 10011.

Telephone: (212) 566-8821; **Fax:** (212) 566-8817; **Internet:** www.acumenfund.org; **e-mail:** info@acumenfund.org.

Adventist Development and Relief Agency International—ADRA

Formed in 1956 by the Seventh-day Adventist Church as an independent humanitarian agency to provide disaster relief and individual and community development without prejudice to those in need, regardless of age, political or religious affiliation or ethnicity.

Activities: An independent NGO, ADRA works in disaster areas and parts of the developing world, providing aid and support. Its development programmes help to improve education, health care, food supplies and economic and social well-being for people in more than 120 countries and territories, helping to achieve sustainable change and long-term humanitarian solutions.

Geographical Area of Activity: International.

Publications: *ADRA Works* (quarterly newsletter); *ADRA News* (weekly e-mail newsletter); *ADRA World Update* (weekly 30-minute television programme); Annual Report.

Finance: Total assets US $41,150,314 (31 Dec. 2010); annual revenue $71,834,102, expenditure $72,405,155 (2010).

Principal Staff: Pres. Dr Rudi Maier.

Address: 12501 Old Columbia Pike, Silver Spring, MD 20904.

Telephone: (301) 680-6380; **Fax:** (301) 680-6370; **Internet:** www.adra.org; **e-mail:** media.inquiries@adra.org.

Advocacy Center at ISC

Formerly Advocacy Institute. Name changed in 2006 following its merger with the Institute for Sustainable Communities (ISC). Established to assist people to influence and change public policy world-wide.

Activities: Operates world-wide in the field of human rights, in areas including improving public health, fighting poverty, working towards sustainable development, protecting the environment and promoting gender equality. The Institute promotes political and social justice for all and strengthens world-wide movements working towards these goals. Its work also includes advocacy skills development, developing and analysing new strategies, and international networking of advocates. The Institute is linked with a number of NGOs dealing with critical human rights problems all over the world. The Advocacy Institute Fellows Program aims to strengthen the ability of social change leaders world-wide, while the Leadership for a Changing World programme is a national award scheme run in conjunction with the Ford Foundation (q.v.) and the Robert F. Wagner School of Public Service, New York University.

Geographical Area of Activity: International.

Publications: *The Quantum Leadership: Community in Motion; Advocacy for Social Justice: A Global Action and Reflection Guide; Justice Begins at Home: Strengthening Social Justice Advocacy in the US; Become a Leader for Social Justice*; Annual Report; resource guides; and other publications.

Finance: Annual revenue US $15,200,000, expenditure $14,700,000 (2009/10).

Board of Directors: Stephen D. Ramsey (Chair.); Janet Ballantyne (Vice-Chair.); Elizabeth Knup (Sec.); John A. Dooley (Treas.).

Principal Staff: Pres. George Hamilton.

Address: 535 Stone Cutters Way, Montpelier, VT 05602.

Telephone: (802) 229-2900; **Fax:** (802) 229-2919; **Internet:** www.advocacy.org; **e-mail:** isc@iscvt.org.

Africa-America Institute—AAI

Founded in 1953 to help further development in Africa, improve African-American understanding and inform Americans about Africa.

Activities: Engages in educational training, development assistance and informational activities in two areas: African Higher Education and Training and Educational Outreach and Policy. Sponsors African-American Conferences, media workshops and regional conferences and seminars. Maintains a presence in more than 50 countries in Africa, including offices in Mozambique and South Africa.

Geographical Area of Activity: Southern Africa and the USA.

Publications: *AAIONLINE* (quarterly newsletter); *African Perspectives; Africa Report* magazine; Biennial Report; also policy forum, symposium and conference reports; art exhibit catalogues, bulletins and educational materials.

Finance: Annual revenue US $5,292,850, expenditure $4,489,311 (Sept. 2007).

Board: Kofi Appenteng (Chair.); Joseph Moodhe (Sec.).

Principal Staff: Pres. and CEO Mora McLean; Programme Officer Tahnia Charles-Belle.

Address: 420 Lexington Ave, Suite 1706, New York, NY 10170-0002.

Telephone: (212) 949-5666; **Fax:** (212) 682-6174; **Internet:** www.aaionline.org; **e-mail:** aainy@aaionline.org.

African Development Institute, Inc

A public policy research institute set up in 1995 to promote the human and material development of Africa through education, research and policy analysis.

Activities: The Institute works to promote alternative development strategies by three methods: problem-orientated research; empowering education; and advocacy of self-reliant and endogenous development policies. Has special consultative status with the Economic and Social Council of the UN.

Geographical Area of Activity: Africa and the USA.

Publications: *Sankofa* (quarterly newsletter).

Principal Staff: Exec. Dir and Chair. Kwame Akonor; Pres. Enock Mensah.

Address: POB 1644, New York, NY 10185.

Telephone: (201) 838-7900; **Fax:** (908) 850-3016; **e-mail:** ca498@bfn.org.

African Wildlife Foundation—AWF

Founded in 1961 as the African Wildlife Leadership Foundation, Inc, adopting its present name in 1982.

Activities: Promotes wildlife management and conservation in Africa.

Geographical Area of Activity: Botswana, Democratic Republic of the Congo, Kenya, Mozambique, Namibia, Rwanda, South Africa, Tanzania, Uganda, Zambia and Zimbabwe.

Publications: Annual Report; *African Wildlife News* (quarterly newsletter); *African Heartland News* (newsletter); fact sheets, wall calendar; reports and periodic publishings in peer-reviewed journals.

Finance: Total assets US $38,605,613 (30 June 2011); annual revenue $28,060,154, expenditure $20,989,783 (2010/11).

Board of Trustees: David Thomson (Chair.).

Principal Staff: Chief Exec. Patrick J. Bergin; Pres. Helen W. Gichohi; Sec. Myma Belo-Osagie.

Address: 1400 16th St NW, Suite 120, Washington, DC 20036.

Telephone: (202) 939-3333; **Fax:** (202) 939-3332; **Internet:** www.awf.org; **e-mail:** africanwildlife@awf.org.

Africare

Founded in 1971, originally in response to severe droughts in West Africa, now aiming to help families and communities in every major region of Sub-Saharan Africa. Also operates in a number of countries in North Africa.

Activities: Has operated in some 36 countries in Africa. Supervises development and self-help programmes in aid, medicine and health, conservation and environment and social welfare and studies.

Geographical Area of Activity: Africa.

Publications: *Africare* (online newsletter); Annual Report.

Finance: Total assets US $47,627,669 (30 June 2010); annual revenue $61,957,670, expenditure $63,868,022 (2009/10).

Board of Directors: Nelson R. Mandela (Hon. Chair.); Maria Walker (Hon. Vice-Chair.); W. Frank Fountain (Chair.); Larry Bailey (Vice-Chair); Barbara McKinzie (Treas.); Josephy Kennedy (Sec.).

Principal Staff: Pres. Darius Mans; COO Diane White.

Address: Africare House, 440 R St NW, Washington, DC 20001-1935.

Telephone: (202) 462-3614; **Fax:** (202) 387-1034; **Internet:** www.africare.org; **e-mail:** info@africare.org.

Daniele Agostino Derossi Foundation

Founded in 1991 by Flavia Robinson to promote the well-being of Mayan women and children.

Activities: Aims to promote the well-being of Mayan women and children through grants to support projects active in the fields of education, health and women's co-operatives.

Geographical Area of Activity: primarily Guatemala.

Restrictions: No grants to individuals.

Finance: Total assets US $1,878,260 (31 Dec. 2009); grants disbursed $314,701 (2009).

Board of Directors: Daniele C. Derossi (Pres.); David J. Pollack (Vice-Pres. and Treas.); Flavia Derossi Robinson (Sec. and Pres. Emeritus).

Address: 40 Wachusett Dr., Lexington, MA 02421-6936.

Internet: www.dafound.org; **e-mail:** dafound@dafound.org.

The Ahmanson Foundation

Founded in 1952 by Howard F. Ahmanson, Dorothy G. Sullivan and others for general charitable services.

Activities: Operates mainly in Los Angeles, California, in the fields of education, arts and culture, medicine and health, and science and welfare. Types of support include programme support, capital, research, endowment and scholarships.

Geographical Area of Activity: USA (primarily Los Angeles).

Restrictions: No grants are made to individuals. Grants are made only to organizations that are tax-exempt.

Publications: Annual Report.

Finance: Assets US $774,170,000 (31 Oct. 2008); grants disbursed $57,337,000 (2007/08).

Principal Staff: Pres. William H. Ahmanson; Man. Dir Karen Ahmanson Hoffman; CFO and Treas. Kristen K. O'Connor.

Address: 9215 Wilshire Blvd, Beverly Hills, CA 09210.

Telephone: (310) 278-0770; **Internet:** www.theahmansonfoundation.org; **e-mail:** info@theahmansonfoundation.org.

Alavi Foundation

Founded in 1973, and formerly known as the Mostazafan Foundation of New York, with religious, philanthropic and educational aims.

Activities: Operates its own programmes emphasizing research into the Islamic religion; publishes and distributes educational and religious material. Contributes to educational centres and Sunday schools for the teaching of Middle Eastern languages and of the Islamic religion and culture. Contributes to disaster relief funds; provides student loans.

Geographical Area of Activity: USA.

Publications: *Fundamentals of Islamic Teachings*; *A Glance at the Life of Prophet Mohammed*.

Finance: Total assets US $40,358,767 (31 March 2010); annual revenue $5,926,061, annual expenditure $5,521,610 (2009/10).

Board of Trustees: Mohammad Geramian (Pres.); Alireza Ebrahimi (Sec.); Abbas Mirakhor (Treas.).

Address: 500 Fifth Ave, Suite 2320, New York, NY 10110-0397.

Telephone: (212) 944-8333; **Fax:** (212) 921-0325; **Internet:** www.alavifoundation.org; **e-mail:** info@alavifoundation.org.

Alcoa Foundation

Founded in 1952 by the Aluminum Company of America (Alcoa) to improve the quality of life for people in communities where Alcoa plants or offices are located, and for the public at large.

Activities: Operates nationally and internationally (in countries where Alcoa operates), principally in the fields of global education and workplace skills, conservation and sustainability, business and community partnerships, and safe and healthy children and families. Grants are given to educational institutions for equipment, improvement of facilities, and the provision of fellowships and scholarships. The Foundation also makes grants for cultural events and to health and welfare organizations, hospitals and medical centres, civic and community organizations, and youth organizations.

Geographical Area of Activity: International.

Restrictions: No grants are made to individuals, other than through the Sons and Daughters Scholarship programme for the children of Alcoa employees, and only certified charitable organizations are considered.

Publications: Annual Report.

Finance: Total assets approx. US $446,000,000 (2012); total funds disbursed $37,900,000 (2011).

Principal Staff: Pres. Paula Davis.

Address: Alcoa Corporate Center, 201 Isabella St, Pittsburgh, PA 15212-5858.

Telephone: (412) 553-4545; **Fax:** (412) 553-4498; **Internet:** www.alcoa.com/global/en/community/foundation.asp; **e-mail:** alcoa.foundation@alcoa.com.

The George I. Alden Trust

Founded in 1912 by George I. Alden for the promotion of education in schools, colleges or other educational institutes, with a preference for industrial, vocational or professional education; for the promotion of work carried out by the Young Men's Christian Association in Massachusetts; and for the benefit of the Worcester Trade Schools and the Worcester Polytechnic Institute.

Activities: Involved in the fields of higher and vocational education in the USA, through funding, research, conferences, scholarships and endowment funds.

Geographical Area of Activity: USA.

Publications: Annual Report; information brochure; Financial Report.

Finance: Annual revenue US $22,526,000, expenditure $7,606,000 (2010).

Board of Trustees: Warner S. Fletcher (Chair.); Douglas Q. Meystre (Clerk); James E. Collins (Treas.).

Address: 370 Main St, 11th Floor, Worcester, MA 01608.

Telephone: (508) 459-8005; **Fax:** (508) 459-8305; **Internet:** www.aldentrust.org; **e-mail:** trustees@aldentrust.org.

The Paul G. Allen Family Foundation

Established by Paul G. Allen and Jo Lynn Allen in 1990.

Activities: Operates in the areas of community development and social change; arts and culture; science and technology; education and youth engagement, and emergency relief.

Geographical Area of Activity: Primarily north-west USA.

Finance: Grants awarded US $438,000,000 (1990–2011).

Board of Directors: Paul G. Allen (Co-Founder and Chair.).

Principal Staff: Co-Founder and Pres. Jo Lynn Allen; Vice-Pres. Susan Coliton; Sr Program Officer Jim McDonald.

Address: 505 5th Ave South, Suite 900, Seattle, WA 98104.

Telephone: (206) 342-2030; **Fax:** (206) 342-3030; **Internet:** www.pgafoundations.com; **e-mail:** info@pgafamilyfoundation.org.

Isabel Allende Foundation

Established in 1996 to promote social and economic justice for women.

Activities: Operates in the San Francisco Bay area of the USA and in Chile to promote the empowerment of women and girls.

Finance: Grants are typically of US $1,000–$5,000.

Principal Staff: Exec. Dir Lori Barra.

Address: 116 Caledonia St, Sausalito, CA 94965.

Telephone: (415) 289-0992; **Fax:** (415) 298-1154; **Internet:** www.isabelallendefoundation.org; **e-mail:** lori@isabelallendefoundation.org.

Alliance for International Educational and Cultural Exchange

Formed in 1992 by a group of US international exchange organizations to create and promote public policies that facilitate international cultural exchanges between the USA and other countries around the world, so as to improve cultural understanding between people of different nations.

Activities: Supports the interests of 76 international exchange organizations in the USA, through advocacy, information services and networking. Also organizes a programme of government relations activities, and provides a place where the issues and concerns of leaders of international exchange groups can be discussed and addressed. It endeavours to inform the public about the importance of the role of international exchange globally, nationally and in terms of individuals.

Geographical Area of Activity: USA.

Publications: *The Policy Monitor* (quarterly journal); *News News News* (bulletin); *Action Alerts*; *International Exchange Locator: a Resource Directory for Educational and Cultural Exchange* (2005 edition).

Board of Directors: Christine Schulze (Chair.); Lynn Shotwell (Vice-Chair.); Goran Rannefors (Treas.).

Principal Staff: Exec. Dir Michael McCarry.

Address: 1828 L St NW, Suite 1150, Washington, DC 20036.

Telephone: (202) 293-6141; **Fax:** (202) 293-6144; **Internet:** www.alliance-exchange.org; **e-mail:** information@alliance-exchange.org.

Jenifer Altman Foundation—JAF

Founded in 1991 by Jenifer Altman.

Activities: Makes grants within the fields of environmental health and mind-body health, primarily supporting work on the impact of endocrine disrupting chemicals and other foetal contaminants on human health and on biodiversity. Also administers the Mitchell Kapor Foundation (q.v.). Grants range from US $1,000 to $10,000.

Geographical Area of Activity: Central and South America, USA, Europe, Asia.

Restrictions: No grants to individuals.

Publications: Annual report; grants list; programme policy statement; application guidelines.

Board of Directors: Michael Lerner (Pres.); Catherine Porter (Sec.); Albert Wells (Treas.).

Principal Staff: Exec. Dir Marni Rosen.

Address: Thoreau Center for Sustainability, Presidio Building 1016, First Floor, POB 29209, San Francisco, CA 04129.

Telephone: (415) 561-2182; **Fax:** (415) 561-6480; **Internet:** www.jaf.org; **e-mail:** info@jaf.org.

American Association of University Women Educational Foundation—AAUW

Founded in 1959 by the American Association of University Women to encourage, among the members of the AAUW and the community, the continuation of education beyond college; to enable women scholars to carry on advanced research, study and creative work; to engage in and promote studies and research in education; to provide for the diffusion of knowledge obtained thereby, and to foster intellectual and educational growth; to encourage standards of excellence in public school education and in higher education; and to co-operate with other organizations with similar purposes and activities.

Activities: Operates nationally and internationally in the field of education. Provides one-year, non-renewable fellowships to American women for dissertation writing and postdoctoral research, as well as short-term publications fellowships. Career Development Grants support women who hold a Bachelor's degree and who are preparing to advance or change their careers, or re-enter the workforce. Selected Professions Fellowships are awarded to women who are US citizens or permanent residents and who intend to pursue a full-time course of study (during the fellowship year) in designated degree programmes, where traditionally women's participation has been low. One-year non-renewable International Fellowships are awarded to women who are not US citizens or permanent residents of the USA for study in the USA at the master's, PhD or postdoctoral levels. Six fellowships are awarded annually to women who are members of organizations affiliated with the International Federation of University Women—IFUW for one year of graduate study anywhere in the world. The Foundation also makes several prestigious national awards recognizing excellence in achievement and the AAUW Legal Advocacy Fund supports women fighting sex discrimination cases in higher education.

Geographical Area of Activity: International.

Restrictions: Grants only to women.

Publications: Report of operations and financial statement; *Action Alert* (newsletter).

Finance: Total assets US $133,121,239 (June 2011); total revenue $13,483,252, total expenditure $16,347,890 (2010/11).

Board of Directors: Carolyn H. Garfein (Pres.); Patricia Ho (Vice-Pres.); Mildred Hoffler-Foushee (Finance Vice-Pres.); Connie Hildebrand (Sec.).

Principal Staff: Exec. Dir Linda D. Hallman.

Address: 1111 16th St NW, Washington, DC 20036.

Telephone: (202) 785-7700; **Fax:** (202) 872-1425; **Internet:** www.aauw.org; **e-mail:** connect@aauw.org.

American Council of Learned Societies—ACLS

Founded in 1919 (incorporated in 1924) for the advancement of humanistic studies in all fields of learning and the maintenance and strengthening of relations among the national societies devoted to such studies.

Activities: The Council comprises 71 American scholarly organizations concerned with the humanities and related social sciences. ACLS Fellowships are offered to US citizens or permanent residents to carry out post-doctoral research in the humanities. Internationally, the Council supports various research and planning activities to encourage research on specific countries or regions of the world, as well as comparative and transnational research projects.

Geographical Area of Activity: International.

Restrictions: No funding for fellowships or scholarships for undergraduate study and no grants for creative work.

Publications: Annual Report; occasional paper series; newsletter; *Recent Publications*; *ACLS History E-Book Project*; *National Endowment for the Humanities Reports;* and other publications.

Finance: Assets US $116,036,079 (30 June 2010); annual revenue $29,605,210, annual expenditure $21,783,365 (2009/10).

Board of Directors: Kwame Anthony Appiah (Chair.); Anand A. Yang (Vice-Chair.); James J. O'Donnell (Sec.); Nancy J. Vickers (Treas.).

Principal Staff: Pres. Pauline Yu; Vice-Pres. Steven C. Wheatley.

Address: 633 Third Ave, 8th Floor, New York, NY 10017-6795.

Telephone: (212) 697-1505; **Fax:** (212) 949-8058; **Internet:** www.acls.org; **e-mail:** grants@acls.org.

American Councils for International Education—ACTR/ACCELS

Established in 1974 as an international not-for-profit organization working to advance education, research, and mutual understanding across the USA and the nations of Eastern Europe, Eurasia, and South-Eastern Europe. Its mission is to foster democratic development and civil societies by advancing education and research, cultivating leadership, and empowering individuals and institutions through learning. With a staff of more than 370 professionals based in 24 countries, American Councils designs, implements and supports innovative programmes in education, community outreach and scholarly research.

Activities: Operates in the field of education, funding academic exchanges, professional training, institution building, research, materials development, technical assistance and consultation. Currently, ACTR (American Council of Teachers of Russian) is the professional association that focuses on educational, research and training programmes for citizens of the USA, while ACCELS (American Council for Collaboration in Education and Language Study) deals with exchanges, training and technical assistance programmes in Eastern Europe, Russia and Central Asia. ACCELS also runs more than 40 educational programmes in the countries of the former USSR.

Geographical Area of Activity: USA, Afghanistan, countries of the former USSR, South-Eastern Europe and South Asia.

Restrictions: Not a grant-maker in its own right, administers government funding.

Publications: Annual Report; specialist videos, papers, journals and books in fields of interest; *Predictors of Foreign Language Gain during Study Abroad; Journal of Eurasian Research*.

Finance: Net assets US $1,561,955 (30 June 2009); annual revenue $46,199,800, expenditure $45,344,390 (2008/09).

Board of Directors: Dr Richard D. Brecht (Chair.).

Principal Staff: Pres. Dr Dan E. Davidson; Vice-Pres David Patton, Lisa Choate.

Address: 1828 L St NW, Suite 1200, Washington, DC 20036.

Telephone: (202) 833-7522; **Fax:** (202) 833-7523; **Internet:** www.americancouncils.org; **e-mail:** general@americancouncils.org.

American Express Foundation

Founded in 1850 in New York by the American Express Co. and its subsidiaries for charitable purposes in the areas of community service, education and employment, cultural programmes, historic preservation and economic independence.

Activities: Supports projects world-wide within the themes of community service, cultural heritage and economic independence. Projects supported include those involved with the arts and humanities, education, historic conservation, community welfare, minorities, AIDS, drug abuse, child development and welfare, and the disabled. Involved in efforts to create partnerships between public and private organizations, especially in the fields of education, employment and training programmes; and programmes to promote understanding of the world's cultural diversity and heritage. The Foundation aims to promote the development of the tourism industry through its Academies of Travel and Tourism in the USA and its international Travel and Tourism Programme, currently operating in Brazil, Canada, Hong Kong, Hungary, Ireland, Mexico, Russia, South Africa and the United Kingdom. Its Economic Independence Fund supports community development and financial literacy programmes and the Performing Arts Fund assists performing arts organizations across the USA to attract broader audiences.

Geographical Area of Activity: International.

Restrictions: Grants made only to non-profit organizations.

Publications: *Philanthropy at American Express Report*.

Principal Staff: Pres. Tim McClimon.

Address: 3 World Financial Center, New York, NY 10285-4804.

Telephone: (212) 640-5661; **Fax:** (212) 693-1033; **e-mail:** judy.g.tenzer@aexp.com.

American Foundation for AIDS Research—amfAR

Founded in 1985 by the merger of the AIDS Medical Foundation and the National AIDS Research Foundation to prevent HIV infection and the death and disease associated with HIV/AIDS and to protect the human rights of all people threatened by HIV/AIDS.

Activities: Raises funds to provide grants and awards to support AIDS research, AIDS prevention and treatment education, and the advocacy of sound AIDS-related public policy. Awards grants to non-profit institutions for basic biomedical and clinical research in fields related to HIV/AIDS and for post-doctoral investigators to study at other institutions; office in Washington, DC.

Geographical Area of Activity: International.

Restrictions: Grants only to non-profit organizations.

Publications: *amfAR e-News* (e-mail newsletter); *amfAR News* (biannual newsletter); *Treat Asia Report* (quarterly); Annual Report; and other publications.

Finance: Total assets US $35,804,429 (30 September 2010); annual revenue $26,550,025, expenditure $22,878,649 (2009/10).

Board of Trustees: Kenneth Cole (Chair.); Patricia J. Matson (Vice-Chair.); John C. Simons (Vice-Chair.); Wallace Sheft (Treas.); Diana L. Taylor (Sec.).

Principal Staff: CEO Kevin R. Frost.

Address: 120 Wall St, 13th Floor, New York, NY 10005-3908.

Telephone: (212) 806-1600; **Fax:** (212) 806-1601; **Internet:** www.amfar.org; **e-mail:** information@amfar.org.

American Foundation for the Blind, Inc—AFB

Founded in 1921 to support visually impaired people and to educate the general public about blindness.

Activities: Provides educational, vocational, advisory and social services, and publications (including 'talking books') related to blindness; awards a number of scholarships for undergraduate and graduate visually impaired and blind students, including the Delta Gamma Foundation Florence Margaret Harvey Memorial Scholarship and the Rudolph Dillman Memorial Scholarship for students in the field of rehabilitation or education of blind or visually impaired people, the Gladys C. Anderson Memorial Scholarship and the R. L. Gillette Scholarship for female students studying religious music, classical music or literature, the Karen D. Carsel Memorial Scholarship and the Ferdinand Torres AFB Scholarship for full-time students in economic need, and the Paul W. Ruckes Scholarship for students pursuing a degree in engineering or in computer, physical or life sciences. Also distributes Helen Keller Achievement Awards promoting achievement of individuals who act as role models or improve the quality of life of individuals with visual impairment; maintains offices in Washington, DC, Atlanta, GA, Dallas, TX (the AFB Center on Vision Loss), Huntington, WV (AFB TECH, working with manufacturers to increase accessibility to technology for blind people) and San Francisco, CA.

Geographical Area of Activity: USA.

Publications: *Access World: Technology for Consumers with Visual Impairment* (6 a year); *AFB Directory of Services for Blind and Visually Impaired Persons in the US and Canada*; *Journal of Visual Impairment and Blindness* (10 a year); Annual Report.

Finance: Total assets US $47,502,000 (30 June 2011); annual revenue $16,251,000, expenditure $12,366,000 (2010/11).

Board of Trustees: Concetta F. Conkling (Chair.); Michael N. Gilliam (Vice-Chair.); Peter D. Tonks (Treas.); Elaine J. Pommells (Sec.).

Principal Staff: Pres. and CEO Carl R. Augusto.

Address: 2 Penn Plaza, Suite 1102, New York, NY 10121.

Telephone: (212) 502-7600; **Fax:** (212) 502-7777; **Internet:** www.afb.org; **e-mail:** afbinfo@afb.net.

American Foundation for Pharmaceutical Education—AFPE

Founded in 1942 to provide support for graduate study of pharmaceutical science.

Activities: Funds research and offers grants, fellowships and scholarships in the field of pharmaceutical sciences, particularly pharmaceutics, pharmacology, manufacturing pharmacy, pharmaco-economics and medicinal chemistry. Awards include Student Gateway Research Scholarships, First Year Graduate School Scholarships, Pre-Doctoral Graduate Scholarships in the Pharmaceutical Sciences, Clinical Pharmacy Post-Pharmaceutical Doctoral Fellowships in the Biomedical Research Sciences, and Pharmacy Faculty Investigator Grants.

Geographical Area of Activity: USA.

Restrictions: Grants are usually only open to those studying in the USA.

Finance: Total scholarships and grants US $750,000 (2007/08).

Board of Directors: Ernest Mario (Chair.); Alice E. Till (Vice-Chair.); Lonnie Hollingsworth (Treas.).

Principal Staff: Pres. Robert M. Bachman.

Address: 1 Church St, Suite 400, Rockville, MD 20850-4158.

Telephone: (301) 738-2160; **Fax:** (301) 738-2161; **Internet:** www.afpenet.org; **e-mail:** info@afpenet.org.

American Friends Service Committee—AFSC

Founded in 1917, AFSC is a Quaker organization that aims to overcome poverty, injustice and strife in the world through practical aid and non-violent means. The work is based on the belief in the good of every person, regardless of race or religion.

Activities: Operates in 17 countries in Africa, Asia, Central and South America and the Caribbean, Eastern Europe, the Middle East and the USA, in the areas of peace-building, conflict resolution, demilitarization, community development, economic and social justice, and supporting youth. It aims to address the root causes of poverty, injustice and conflict, working for relief both through immediate aid and long-term development projects.

Geographical Area of Activity: Africa, Asia, Central and South America and the Caribbean, Eastern Europe, the Middle East and the USA.

Publications: *Peacework* (periodical, 10 a year); *Quaker Action* (periodical, 3 a year); *Toward Peace and Justice, Faces of Hope, Project Voice, Wage Peace* (e-mail newsletters); and other regional and area newsletters.

Finance: Annual revenue US $27,585,741, expenditure $31,907,989 (2009/10).

Principal Staff: Presiding Clerk Arlene Kelly; Treas. Thomas P. Bennett; Gen. Sec. Shan Cretin.

Address: 1501 Cherry St, Philadelphia, PA 19102.

Telephone: (215) 241-7000; **Fax:** (215) 241-7275; **Internet:** www.afsc.org; **e-mail:** afscinfo@afsc.org.

American Health Assistance Foundation—AHAF

AHAF supports basic scientific investigations to better understand and find cures for Alzheimer's disease, glaucoma and macular degeneration, and has a strong public outreach mission to inform people about these age-related, degenerative diseases.

Activities: AHAF grants awards to peer-reviewed and selected researchers around the world through its three programmes, Alzheimer's Disease Research, National Glaucoma Research and Macular Degeneration Research. AHAF also provides vital information to the public, especially those affected by these three age-related, degenerative diseases.

Geographical Area of Activity: International.

Publications: Publications include booklets on all three diseases, shorter brochures, and newsletters with research updates.

Finance: Annual revenue US $32,813,000, expenditure $29,060,000 (March 2010).

Board of Directors: Brian K. Regan (Chair.); Grace Frisone (Vice-Chair.); Nicholas W. Raymond (Treas.); Michael H. Barnett (Sec.).

Principal Staff: Pres. and CEO Stacy Pagos Haller.

Address: 22512 Gateway Center Dr., Clarksburg, MD 20871.

Telephone: (301) 948-3244; **Fax:** (301) 258-9454; **Internet:** www.ahaf.org; **e-mail:** info@ahaf.org.

American Heart Association, Inc

Founded in 1948 with the aim of preventing premature strokes and cardiovascular disease.

Activities: The Association awards fellowships for US undergraduate research, and grants-in-aid to support research in the fields of cardiovascular disease and stroke. International Research Fellowships enable researchers who are US citizens or permanent residents to study in foreign institutions, or foreign citizens to study at US institutions. The Association also bestows awards aimed at encouraging clinically trained physicians to pursue careers in cardiovascular and stroke research, as well as supporting stroke survivors and their families; maintains eight affiliate offices in USA and Puerto Rico.

Geographical Area of Activity: International.

Restrictions: No grants to individuals working at private companies, nor to organizations receiving funding from a different source.

Publications: *Stroke Connection* (magazine, 2 a month); *Traditional Cookbooks*; *Health Information Publications*; *Heart and Stroke Facts*; *Magazine Cookbooks*.

Finance: Total assets US $1,009,842,000 (30 June 2011); annual revenue $690,818,000, expenditure $488,033,000 (2010/11).

Board of Directors: Bill Roach (Chair.); Ron Haddock (Chair. Elect).

Principal Staff: Pres. Gordon F. Tomaselli; CEO Nancy Brown.

Address: National Center, 7272 Greenville Ave, Dallas, TX 75231-4596.

Telephone: (214) 360-6106; **Fax:** (214) 360-6124; **Internet:** www.heart.org; **e-mail:** AHA.NSC.General@heart.org.

American Historical Association

Founded in 1884 for the promotion of historical studies, the collection and preservation of historical manuscripts, and the dissemination of historical research.

Activities: Operates mainly nationally in the field of education and historical studies, by supporting research, awarding more than 100 fellowships and grants for work on various aspects of history, and issuing publications.

Geographical Area of Activity: USA.

Restrictions: Research grants only made to AHA members.

Publications: *American Historical Review*; *Perspectives on History* (newsletter); *Directory of History Departments and Organizations in the United States and Canada*; Annual Report; essays, studies, doctoral dissertations, details of grants and fellowships for historians.

Finance: Fellowships total approx. US $30,000.

Council: William Cronon (Pres.);Kenneth Pomeranz (Pres. elect); Anthony Grafton (Immed. Past Pres.); Jacqueline Jones (Vice-Pres.); John R. McNeill (Vice-Pres.); Patricia Nelson Limerick (Vice-Pres.).

Principal Staff: Exec. Dir James Grossman.

Address: 400 A St SE, Washington, DC 20003-3889.

Telephone: (202) 544-2422; **Fax:** (202) 544-8307; **Internet:** www.historians.org; **e-mail:** info@historians.org.

American Hungarian Foundation

Founded in 1955 to further the understanding and appreciation of the Hungarian cultural and historical heritage in the USA.

Activities: Provides educational scholarships and grants, and conducts lectures, exhibitions and special events to further understanding of Hungarian heritage and culture; maintains a library containing more than 60,000 volumes, an exhibition space and a museum; has established several academic institutions as well as programmes promoting Hungarian studies, such as the Institute for Hungarian Studies at Rutgers, the State University of New Jersey.

Geographical Area of Activity: Hungary and the USA.

Board of Directors: Dr Zsolt Harsanyi (Chair.); August J. Molnar (Co-Chair.); Thomas G. Gaspar, Michael Kaufman, Laszlo Papp (Vice-Chair.); James F. Horvath (Sec.); John M. Kerekes (Asst Sec.); Scott B. Lukacs (Treas.).

Principal Staff: Exec. Dir Gergely Hajdu-Nemeth; Librarian/Archivist Margaret Papai.

Address: 300 Somerset St, POB 1084, New Brunswick, NJ 08903.

Telephone: (732) 846-5777; **Fax:** (732) 249-7033; **Internet:** www.ahfoundation.org; **e-mail:** info@ahfoundation.org.

American Institute of Pakistan Studies

Founded in 1973 by Dr Hafeez Malik, it aims to promote scholarly exchange between the USA and Pakistan and to support research on issues relevant to Pakistan.

Activities: Offers pre-doctoral and post-doctoral research fellowships to scholars who are US citizens and are engaged in research on Pakistan, in all fields of the humanities and social sciences. Also administers lectureships and organizes academic conferences. Maintains an office in Islamabad, Pakistan.

Geographical Area of Activity: USA.

Restrictions: Grants only made to US citizens.

Publications: *The Annual of Urdu Studies; Modern Asian Studies; Pakistan Studies News* (newsletter).

Principal Staff: Pres. Dr Kamran Asdar Ali; Vice-Pres. Anita Weiss; Sec. Andan Malik; Dir in Islamabad Nadeem Akbar.

Address: 203 Ingraham Hall, 1155 Observatory Dr., Madison, WI 53706.

Telephone: (608) 261-1194; **Fax:** (608) 265-3062; **Internet:** www.pakistanstudies-aips.org; **e-mail:** aips@pakistanstudies-aips.org.

American Jewish Joint Distribution Committee—JDC

Founded in 1914 to distribute funds raised by the Orthodox Central Committee for the Relief of Jews, the American Jewish Relief Committee and the People's Relief Committee; the organization aims to provide aid to Jews in need in a non-partisan and non-political way, in every continent outside North America.

Activities: JDC represents the American Jewish community overseas and works by funding programmes of relief, rescue and reconstruction in a number of countries. It works to ensure that all elderly survivors of the Holocaust are able to live out their lives in dignity; revives and strengthens Jewish communities; and endeavours to help social service concerns in Israel.

Geographical Area of Activity: International.

Publications: *American Jewry and The Holocaust; Archives of the Holocaust; A Continuing Task; I Seek My Brethren; My Brother's Keeper; Out of the Ashes; Renewal; The Saving Remnant; To Save a World; To the Rescue.*

Finance: Total assets US $607,549,972 (31 Dec. 2010); annual revenue $276,764,779, expenditure $246,707,571 (2010).

Board: Dr Irving A. Smokler (Chair.); Stanley A. Rabin (Treas.); Caryn Wolf Wechsler (Sec.).

Principal Staff: Pres. Penny Blumenstein; CEO Steven Schwager.

Address: POB 530, 132 East 43rd St, New York, NY 10017.

Telephone: (212) 687-6200; **Internet:** www.jdc.org; **e-mail:** info@jdc.org.

American Jewish World Service—AJWS

Founded in 1985, is an international development organization motivated by Judaism's imperative to pursue justice. AJWS is dedicated to alleviating poverty, hunger and disease among the people of the developing world regardless of race, religion or nationality. Through grants to grassroots organizations, volunteer service, advocacy and education, AJWS fosters civil society, sustainable development and human rights for all people, while promoting the values and responsibilities of global citizenship within the Jewish community.

Activities: AJWS funds hundreds of grassroots projects throughout Africa, Asia and Latin America that promote health, education, sustainable economic development, disaster relief, and social and political change. AJWS works with women, youth, ethnic, religious and sexual minorities, indigenous people, refugees and internally displaced people, and people living with HIV/AIDS. AJWS volunteer service programmes are designed to increase the impact of its grant making and to create a cadre of global social justice leaders. Each year, around 400 AJWS volunteers, ranging from high school students to retirees, travel to the developing world to work with AJWS's project partners. In partnership with grantees, AJWS advocates US engagement to help find peaceful and just resolutions to the world's worst conflicts and to provide support to rebuild societies devastated by crisis. AJWS's current advocacy work focuses on the genocide in Darfur, HIV/AIDS, debt relief, women's rights, and universal access to education. AJWS seeks to make the pursuit of global justice an integral part of American Jewish identity.

Geographical Area of Activity: International.

Publications: *AJWS Reports* (magazine); Annual Report.

Finance: Total assets US $31,003,443 (31 Dec. 2010); annual revenue $49,130,336, expenditure $44,422,776 (2010).

Board of Trustees: Barbara Dobkin (Chair.); Jolie Schwab (Vice-Chair.); Kathleen Levin (Vice-Chair.);James Dubey (Sec.); Michael Hirschhorn (Treas.).

Principal Staff: Pres. Ruth W. Messinger; Exec. Vice-Pres. Robert Bank.

Address: 45 West 36th St, New York, NY 10018-7904.

Telephone: (212) 792-2900; **Fax:** (212) 792-2930; **Internet:** www.ajws.org; **e-mail:** ajws@ajws.org.

American Near East Refugee Aid—ANERA

Established in 1968, ANERA works towards improving the lives of the people of the Middle East by reducing poverty and suffering. It aims to address long-term issues relating to Palestinian and Lebanese people, as well as providing emergency aid in time of war.

Activities: ANERA works in various fields in the Middle East, providing humanitarian aid and relief and partial funding to community, micro-credit and environmental services; working with local organizations to improve community services and health care; providing education for all; aiming to increase employment; providing sustainable agricultural solutions; developing infrastructure; and advancing information technology resources. Maintains additional offices in Gaza, Hebron, Nablus, Ramallah, Jerusalem, Amman and Beirut.

Geographical Area of Activity: Palestinian Autonomous Areas, Israel, Jordan, Lebanon.

Publications: Annual Report; newsletter (quarterly).

Finance: Total assets US $9,780,895 (31 May 2011); annual revenue US $74,338,942, expenditure $73,047,933 (2010/11).

Board of Directors: Edward Gnehm (Chair.); Judith Judd (Vice-Chair.); Randa Fahmy Hudome (Vice-Chair.); Tom Veblen (Treas.).

Principal Staff: Pres. and CEO William D. Corcoran; Vice-Pres. Philip Davies; CFO Donna Diane.

Address: 1111 14th St NW, Suite 400, Washington, DC 20005.

Telephone: (202) 266-9700; **Fax:** (202) 266-9701; **Internet:** www.anera.org; **e-mail:** anera@anera.org.

American Philosophical Society—APS

Founded in 1743 by Benjamin Franklin.

Activities: The Society promotes scholarly research in the sciences and humanities through grants and fellowships. Awards, about 185 of which are made each year, are open to US citizens, and to foreign nationals for research in the USA. The grant and fellowship programmes include: Franklin Research Grants; Daland Fellowships in Clinical Investigation; Lewis and Clark Fund for Exploration and Field Research; Lewis and Clark Fund for Exploration and Field Research in Astrobiology; Phillips Fund Grants for Native American Research; Sabbatical Fellowships in the Humanities and Social Sciences; and Library Resident Research Fellowships. The Society holds two annual conferences or symposia and has a library of 200,000 volumes and around 7m. manuscripts, specializing in the history of science.

Geographical Area of Activity: World-wide.

Restrictions: Institutions are not eligible to apply. Grants available to residents of the USA or to US citizens abroad. Foreign nationals whose research is to be carried out in the USA may also apply.

Publications: *Proceedings* (quarterly); *Transactions* (2 a month); *Mendel Newsletter* (annually); memoirs; yearbook; *News* (2 a year).

Finance: Grants disbursed approx. US $1,000,000 annually.

Principal Staff: Exec. Officer Mary Patterson McPherson.

Address: 104 South Fifth St, Philadelphia, PA 19106-3387.

Telephone: (215) 440-3400; **Fax:** (215) 440-3450; **Internet:** www.amphilsoc.org/grants; **e-mail:** mvignola@amphilsoc .org.

American Refugee Committee—ARC

Established in 1978 by Neal Ball; a non-profit, non-sectarian organization that aims to improve the quality of life of refugees, asylum-seekers and displaced persons, and to enable them to rebuild their lives with dignity and purpose.

Activities: ARC sends medical teams and other specialists to refugee camps in a number of countries to provide adequate health care and humanitarian assistance. It runs programmes to improve water and sanitation in refugee camps, teaches shelter repair and construction, gives resettlement advice and assistance, offers micro-credit and vocational training, provides psycho-social services, looks after primary health care concerns and works towards enabling refugees to return home. Works in collaboration with other international organizations, such as the UN High Commissioner for Refugees (UNHCR). Maintains field offices in Haiti, Liberia, Rwanda, South Sudan, Uganda, Pakistan, Somalia, Thailand, and Darfur, Sudan.

Geographical Area of Activity: World-wide.

Publications: Annual Report.

Finance: Total assets US $25,944,680 (31 Dec. 2010); annual revenue $44,084,995, expenditure $22,061,876 (2010).

Board of Directors: Peter Bell (Chair.); Neal Ball (Founder and Hon. Chair.); Sheila Leatherman (Vice-Chair.); Perry Witkin (Sec.); Ben Boyum (Treas.).

Principal Staff: Pres. and CEO Daniel Wordsworth; CFO Mike Zeitouny.

Address: 615 1st Ave NE, Suite 500, Minneapolis, MN 55413-2681.

Telephone: (612) 872-7060; **Fax:** (612) 607-6499; **Internet:** www.arcrelief.org; **e-mail:** info@archq.org.

American Scandinavian Foundation—ASF

Founded in 1910 (incorporated in the State of New York in 1911) to promote international understanding through educational and cultural exchange between the USA and Denmark, Finland, Iceland, Norway and Sweden.

Activities: Awards fellowships and grants; sponsors cultural programmes, sponsors trainee/internship placements, issues publications; operates Scandinavia House: the Nordic Center in America, which presents exhibitions, films, concerts, lectures, and has a library, children's centre, cafe, and shop. ASF makes several awards, including an annual Translation Prize.

Geographical Area of Activity: USA and Scandinavia.

Publications: *Scandinavian Review* (3 a year); *The Longboat* (newsletter); *Scan* (quarterly newsletter); *Directory of Fellows;* Annual Report.

Finance: Total assets US $43,584,774 (30 June 2009); annual revenue $3,369,369, expenditure $3,510,761 (2008/09).

Board: Richard E. Oldenburg (Co-Chair.); Bernt Reitan (Co-Chair.); Bente Svensen Frantz (Deputy Chair.); Lena Biörck Kaplan (Vice-Chair. for Sweden); Edward E. Elson (Vice-Chair. for Denmark); Robin Chandler Duke (Vice-Chair. for the USA); Linda Nordberg (Vice-Chair. for Finland); Kristján T. Ragnarsson (Vice-Chair. for Iceland); Christian R. Sonne (Treas.); Lynn Carter (Sec.).

Principal Staff: Pres. Edward P. Gallagher; Exec. Vice-Pres. Lynn Carter.

Address: Scandinavia House, 58 Park Ave, between 37th and 38th Sts, New York, NY 10016-3007.

Telephone: (212) 779-3587; **Fax:** (212) 686-1157; **Internet:** www.amscan.org; **e-mail:** info@amscan.org.

American Schools of Oriental Research—ASOR

Founded in 1900 by the Society of Biblical Literature, the Archaeological Institute of America and the American Oriental Society to support research into the peoples and cultures of the Near East.

Activities: Operates internationally in the fields of education and the humanities by conducting and supporting research into Middle Eastern culture, from earliest times to the present day, especially through archaeological, anthropological and historical projects; runs research institutes in the Near East (the W. F. Albright Institute of Archaeological Research, Jerusalem, the American Center of Oriental Research, Amman and the Cyprus American Archaeological Research Institute, Nicosia); awards research fellowships, publishes the results of research, and holds an Annual Meeting.

Geographical Area of Activity: USA and the Middle East.

Publications: *Bulletin of the American Schools of Oriental Research*; *ASOR Newsletter*; *Near Eastern Archaeology*; *Journal of Cuneiform Studies; Archaeological Report Series.*

Board of Trustees: P. E. MacAllister (Chair.); Jim Strange (Sec.); Sheldon Fox (Treas.).

Principal Staff: Pres. Timothy P. Harrison; Exec. Dir Andrew G. Vaughn.

Address: Boston University, 656 Beacon St, 5th Floor, Boston, MA 02215.

Telephone: (617) 353-6570; **Fax:** (617) 353-6575; **Internet:** www.asor.org; **e-mail:** asor@bu.edu.

AmeriCares Foundation, Inc

Initiated by Robert C. Macauley in 1975, and officially founded in 1982. A non-profit international organization that provides immediate response to emergency medical needs and supports long-term humanitarian assistance programmes for people around the world irrespective of race, creed or political persuasion.

Activities: Provides aid to people affected by famine, civil conflict and natural disasters internationally with emergency relief supplies, including medicines and medical supplies. It also operates nationally, responding to disaster and crisis as well as supports three community programmes that mobilize volunteers to deliver health care services to the uninsured.

Geographical Area of Activity: International.

Publications: Annual Report; financial statements.

Finance: Total assets US $148,865,783 (30 June 2011); annual revenue $688,678,354, expenditure $672,302,922 (2010/11).

Board of Directors: C. Dean Maglaris (Chair.); Alma Jane Macauley (Co-Founder and Vice-Chair.).

Principal Staff: Pres. and CEO Curtis R. Welling.

Address: 88 Hamilton Ave, Stamford, CT 06902.

Telephone: (203) 658-9500; **Fax:** (203) 327-5200; **Internet:** www.americares.org; **e-mail:** websiteteam@americares.org.

Amerind Foundation, Inc

Founded in 1937 by William Shirley Fulton to promote anthropological studies of the native peoples of America, the preservation and conservation of their material culture and the development of related educational programmes.

Activities: Organizes anthropological field research, collections study, seminars and visiting scholar programmes, and co-operates with organizations and individuals engaged in similar work. Maintains an anthropological research facility, archaeological, ethnographic and fine arts museum complex, archaeological site files, photographic collections and a library.

Geographical Area of Activity: USA, Mexico.

Restrictions: Grants are made only for advanced seminars.

Publications: *Amerind New World Studies Series*; and other publications.

Finance: Funded through endowment, donations and income earned.

Principal Staff: Exec. Dir Dr John A. Ware; Museum Curator Eric Kaldahl.

Address: 2100 North Amerind Rd, POB 400, Dragoon, AZ 85609.

Telephone: (520) 586-3666; **Fax:** (520) 586-4679; **Internet:** www.amerind.org; **e-mail:** amerind@amerind.org.

AMIDEAST—America-Mideast Educational and Training Services, Inc

International NGO founded in 1951 by Dorothy Thompson to strengthen mutual understanding and co-operation between Americans and peoples of the Middle East and North Africa.

Activities: Through a network of field offices in 11 Arab countries, AMIDEAST administers publicly and privately sponsored programmes in the Middle East and North Africa in the areas of professional training and development, English language training, institutional development, educational advising and testing, and international educational exchange. It also administers study abroad programmes for US citizens and develops and distributes educational resources on the Middle East and North Africa to US schools and libraries.

Geographical Area of Activity: North Africa, the Middle East and USA.

Restrictions: Not a grant-making organization.

Publications: *The Advising Quarterly*; Annual Report.

Finance: Total assets US $28,381,082 (30 September 2010); annual income $78,220,068, annual expenditure $77,223,517 (2009/10).

Board of Directors: Dr Mary W. Gray (Chair.); Nicholas Veliotes (Vice-Chair.); Robert H. Pelletreau (Treas.).

Principal Staff: CEO and Pres. Theodore H. Kattouf; Vice-Pres. and CFO Linda DeNicola.

Address: 1730 M St, NW, Suite 1100, Washington, DC 20036-4505.

Telephone: (202) 776-9600; **Fax:** (202) 776-7000; **Internet:** www.amideast.org; **e-mail:** inquiries@amideast.org.

Ananda Marga Universal Relief Team—AMURT

Founded in India in 1965, AMURT works towards improving the quality of life of the poor and underprivileged and offering long-term solutions to break the poverty cycle; it aims to provide opportunities for everyone regardless of race, religion, sex or social status. It also provides emergency supplies for victims of natural and man-made disasters.

Activities: Works towards mitigating the effects of poverty and developing local solutions in approximately 80 countries world-wide in the fields of education, health, micro-enterprise and community development. AMURT field officers are based in the area for which they work, helping to provide both short- and long-term solutions to poverty-related problems and assistance for disaster victims. A sister organization, AMURTEL, established in 1975, concentrates on the problems affecting women and children.

Geographical Area of Activity: International.

Principal Staff: Exec. Dir Peter Sage.

Address: 2502 Lindley Terrace, Rockville, MD 20850.

Telephone: (301) 738-7122; **Fax:** (301) 738-7123; **Internet:** www.amurt.net; **e-mail:** info@amurt.net.

The Annenberg Foundation

Founded in 1989 by Walter H. Annenberg, who died in 2002, for general charitable purposes.

Activities: Operates mainly in the fields of education, especially early childhood and pre-collegiate education and cultural programmes, primarily in the USA. Also supports other arts and cultural initiatives, health programmes, and civic and community projects.

Geographical Area of Activity: Primarily USA.

Restrictions: Unsolicited requests from organizations outside the USA are not accepted; no grants are made to individuals; no grants for scholarships or book publications.

Publications: Application Guidelines.

Finance: Total assets US $1,720,105,770 (30 June 2011); annual revenue $249,202,535, expenditure $113,123,167 (2010/11).

Principal Staff: Pres. and CEO Wallis Annenberg; Vice-Pres Gregory Annenberg Weingarten, Charles Annenberg Weingarten; Exec. Dir Leonard Aube.

Address: 2000 Ave of the Stars, Suite 1000 S, Los Angeles, CA 90067.

Telephone: (310) 209-4560; **Fax:** (310) 209-1631; **Internet:** www.annenbergfoundation.org; **e-mail:** info@ annenbergfoundation.org.

Anti-Defamation League of B'nai B'rith—ADL

Founded in 1913 to counter the defamation of Jewish people; aims to identify and combat anti-Semitic and bigoted sentiments, and promote democratic ideals and civil rights for all.

Activities: Operates internationally through carrying out research on and monitoring anti-Semitic and racist groups all over the world, and disseminating information. Also serves as a resource for governments, media and the public, runs courses educating people about the Holocaust and related issues, and works towards safeguarding religious liberty in the world. Carries out an annual audit of anti-Semitic incidents in the USA. Also supports peace talks in the Middle East. Maintains offices throughout the USA, and in Israel and Russia.

Geographical Area of Activity: International.

Publications: Annual Report, ADL on the Frontline, HeAD-Lines.

Finance: Total assets US $170,193,000 (31 Dec. 2009); annual revenue $53,797,000, expenditure $63,000,000 (2009).

Board of Directors: Robert B. Sugarman (Chair.).

Principal Staff: Nat. Dir Abraham Foxman; Deputy Nat. Dir Kenneth Jacobson.

Address: 605 Third Ave, New York, NY 10158.

Telephone: (212) 885-7700; **Fax:** (212) 867-9406; **Internet:** www.adl.org.

Arca Foundation

Founded in 1952 by Nancy S. Reynolds to promote the well-being of humanity throughout the world.

Activities: Addresses international and domestic issues. Seeks to influence public policy, especially economic and political issues in the USA. Supports projects in Central and South America and the Caribbean that promote a foreign policy based on respect for human rights, national sovereignty and international law. Currently focusing on US policy towards Cuba, reform of political party funding, education, fighting deterioration in conditions for working people, capital punishment, and the need for strong coalitions to create equality for all individuals in society.

Geographical Area of Activity: USA, and Central and South America and the Caribbean.

Restrictions: Does not extend grants to direct social services or research fellowships. No grants made to individuals, groups outside the USA, scholarship funds or scholarly research, government programmes, nor to capital projects/endowments.

Publications: Annual Report.

Finance: Total assets US $43,211,205 (31 Dec. 2008); annual revenue $14,066,721, expenditure $709,994 (2008).

Board of Directors: Nancy R. Bagley (Pres.); Nicole Bagley (Vice-Pres.); Mary E. King (Sec.).

Principal Staff: Exec. Dir Anna Lefer Kuhn.

Address: 1308 19th St NW, Washington, DC 20036.

Telephone: (202) 822-9193; **Fax:** (202) 785-1446; **Internet:** www.arcafoundation.org; **e-mail:** grants@arcafoundation .org.

Arcus Foundation

Established in 2000 to achieve social justice that is inclusive of sexual orientation, gender identity and race, and to secure conservation and respect for the great apes and their natural habitat.

Activities: Maintains offices in New York and Cambridge, United Kingdom.

Geographical Area of Activity: International.

Publications: newsletter; Annual Report.

Finance: Total assets US $179,187,817 (31 Dec. 2010); annual revenue $49,015,257, expenditure $34,275,602 (2010).

Board of Directors: John Stryker (Pres. and Founder).

Principal Staff: CEO Dr Yvette C. Burton.

Address: 402 East Michigan Ave, Kalamazoo, MI 49007.

Telephone: (269) 373-4373; **Fax:** (269) 373-0277; **Internet:** www.arcusfoundation.org; **e-mail:** contact@ arcusfoundation.org.

Lance Armstrong Foundation—Livestrong

Established in 1997 to support people with cancer.

Geographical Area of Activity: USA.

Publications: newsletter.

Finance: Expenditure on programmes US $31,200,000 (2009).

Address: 2201 E. Sixth St, Austin, TX 78702.

Telephone: (877) 236-8820; **Internet:** www.livestrong.org.

Arthritis Foundation

Founded in 1948 to improve lives through leadership in the prevention, control and cure of arthritis and related diseases.

Activities: Operates nationally in the fields of education, science and medicine, through self-conducted programmes, research, grants to institutions and individuals, fellowships, scholarships, conferences, courses, publications and lectures. Five key areas of work are: increasing funding to arthritis-related research; building awareness; empowering health actions, through involving everyone in healthy behaviour; influencing national health policy; and exploring all possible research angles. Awards the Russell L. Cecil Arthritis Medical Journalism Awards, the Arthritis Investigator Award and the Segal Clinical Scientist Grants for Osteoarthritis Biomarkers. Maintains 46 local offices around the USA.

Geographical Area of Activity: USA.

Publications: *Arthritis Today* (6 a year); Annual Report; consumer health magazine.

Finance: Total assets US $198,647,592 (31 Dec. 2010); annual revenue $111,597,303, expenditure $105,288,063 (2010).

Board of Trustees: David E. Shuey (Chair.); Daniel T. McGowan (Vice-Chair.); Frank Kelly, Jr (Vice-Chair. and Sec.); Kenneth G. Baltes (Treas.).

Principal Staff: Pres. and CEO John H. Klippel.

Address: POB 7669, Atlanta, GA 30357-0669.

Telephone: (800) 283-7800; **Internet:** www.arthritis.org.

Asia Foundation

Established in 1954, the Foundation is a private, non-profit NGO dedicated to advancing the mutual interests of the USA and the Asia-Pacific region.

Activities: Operates in four main areas: governance, law and civil society; economic reform and development; women's political participation; and international relations, through collaboration with partner organizations from the public and private sectors to support institutional development, exchanges and dialogue, technical assistance, research and policy engagement. Also makes grants to organizations based in Asia. The Foundation maintains a network of 17 offices throughout Asia, as well as an office in Washington, DC. In 2001 launched the Give2Asia fundraising initiative and since 1954 has been running its Books for Asia initiative, distributing books, software programmes, and other educational materials to educational institutions in 40 countries in Asia.

Geographical Area of Activity: USA and the Asia-Pacific region.

Restrictions: No grants to individuals.

Publications: Annual Report; *Asian Perspectives Series*; numerous reports and publications.

Finance: Total assets US $68,568,000 (30 September 2010); annual income $152,611,000, expenditure $152,213,000 (2009/10).

Board of Trustees: Michael H. Armacost (Chair.); Harry Harding (Vice-Chair.); Missie Rennie (Vice-Chair.); Susan J. Pharr (Sec.); Paul S. Slawson (Treas.).

Principal Staff: Pres. David D. Arnold; Exec. Vice-Pres. and COO Suzanne E. Siskel.

Address: 465 California St, 9th Floor, San Francisco, CA 94104.

Telephone: (415) 982-4640; **Fax:** (415) 392-8863; **Internet:** www.asiafoundation.org; **e-mail:** info@asiafound.org.

Asia Society

Asia Society is the leading global and pan-Asian organization working to strengthen relationships and promote understanding among the people, leaders, and institutions of the USA and Asia. We seek to increase knowledge and enhance dialogue, encourage creative expression, and generate new ideas across the fields of arts and culture, policy and business, and education.

Activities: Asia Society was founded in 1956 by John D. Rockefeller 3rd. Initially established to promote greater knowledge of Asia in the USA, the Society today is a global institution—with offices throughout the USA and Asia—that fulfills its educational mandate through a wide range of cross-disciplinary programming. As economies and cultures have become more interconnected, the Society's programmes have expanded to address Asian American issues, the effects of globalization, and pressing concerns in Asia, including human rights, the status of women, and environmental and global health issues such as HIV/AIDS.

Geographical Area of Activity: USA, South-East Asia and Australasia.

Finance: Total assets US $107,735,174 (30 June 2011); annual revenue $30,327,662, expenditure $26,010,461 (2010/11).

Board of Trustees: Ronnie C. Chan (Co-Chair.); Henrietta H. Fore (Co-Chair.).

Principal Staff: Pres. Vishakha N. Desai; CFO and Vice-Pres. (Operations) Don Nagle.

Address: 725 Park Ave/70th St, New York, NY 10021.

Telephone: (212) 288-6400; **Fax:** (212) 517-8315; **Internet:** www.asiasociety.org; **e-mail:** info@asiasociety.org.

Asian Cultural Council—ACC

Founded in 1963 by John D. Rockefeller, III, and originally known as the JDR 3rd Program, it has been formally affiliated to the Rockefeller Brothers Fund (q.v.) since 1991. It was established to support cultural exchange in the visual and performing arts between the USA and Asia. The Asian Cultural Council received some initial support for administrative expenses from the JDR 3rd Fund, but has to raise funds for grant programmes from other foundations, government agencies, corporations and individuals.

Activities: The emphasis of the grant programme of the Council is on providing individual fellowship awards to artists, scholars, students and specialists in the visual and performing arts for research, travel, study and creative work involving cultural exchange between Asia and the USA. A limited number of grants are also made to arts organizations and educational institutions for specific projects of Asian-American cultural exchange. As funds are limited, priority consideration is currently given to individuals in East and South-East Asia seeking grant assistance for research, travel, study, training or creative activity in the USA. The geographic purview of the Council comprises those countries of Asia extending from Pakistan eastwards to Japan. Has additional offices in Taiwan, Hong Kong and Japan.

Geographical Area of Activity: Mainly Asia.

Restrictions: No grants to individuals for lecture programmes, personal exhibitions, individual performance tours, undergraduate studies, nor for activities by individuals within their home countries. No grants to organizations for publications, film and video productions, capital campaigns or general programme or administrative costs.

Publications: Annual Report; information brochure.

Finance: Annual expenditure US $4,790,954 (2010).

Board of Trustees: Elizabeth J. McCormack (Chair.); Valerie Rockefeller Wayne (Vice-Chair.); Pauline R. Yu (Sec.); Robert S. Pirie (Treas.).

Principal Staff: Pres. Richard S. Lanier; Vice-Pres. Stephen B. Heintz.

Address: 6 West 48th St, 12th Floor, New York, NY 10036-1802.

Telephone: (212) 843-0403; **Fax:** (212) 843-0343; **Internet:** www.asianculturalcouncil.org; **e-mail:** acc@accny.org.

Asian Youth Center

The Asian Youth Center was established in 1989, and advocates and extends support for international laws that address local and regional issues of poverty and privation. AYC works towards the promotion of regional federation of development, peace and youth organizations. AYC conducts programmes to create awareness, and evolves new opportunities to uplift the deprived sections of society.

Activities: Focuses on youth empowerment by being a platform of information exchange for organizations all over Asia; works towards the cause of creating global awareness on issues of poverty in Asia, towards making social justice accessible to all, and promoting volunteerism and involvement of youngsters in welfare activities, and finances educational schemes.

Geographical Area of Activity: South-East Asia.

Publications: Annual Report; *Asian Youth News* (newsletter).

Board of Directors: Gay Q. Yuen (Pres.); Daniel H. Deng (Past Pres.); Jones Moy (Vice-Pres.); David Lawton (Sec.); Angela Chang (Treas.).

Principal Staff: Interim Exec. Dir Michelle L. Freridge.

Address: 100 West Clary Ave, San Gabriel, CA 91776.

Telephone: (626) 309-0622; **Fax:** (626) 309-0717; **Internet:** www.asianyouthcenter.org; **e-mail:** admin@ asianyouthcenter.org.

Aspen Institute

Founded in 1950 as a global forum for world leaders and policy-makers to discuss issues affecting the human condition.

Activities: Runs a series of Seminar Programs and Policy Programs aimed at encouraging corporate leaders to act responsibly and providing the forum for debates on domestic and international issues ranging from the growth of micro-enterprises to the control of nuclear weapons. Operates internationally through a network of partner organizations in Europe and Asia.

Geographical Area of Activity: International.

Restrictions: Not a grant-making organization.

Publications: *The Aspen Idea.*

Finance: Annual revenue US $71,935,800, expenditure $65,412,073 (Dec. 2009).

Board of Trustees: Robert K. Steel (Chair.).

Principal Staff: Pres. and CEO Walter Isaacson.

Address: One Dupont Circle NW, Suite 700, Washington, DC 20036-1133.

Telephone: (202) 736-5800; **Fax:** (202) 467-0790; **Internet:** www.aspeninstitute.org; **e-mail:** info@aspeninstitute.org.

Atkinson Foundation

Founded in 1939 by George H. Atkinson and Mildred M. Atkinson for general charitable purposes.

Activities: Priority areas of interest are: tax-exempt, not-for-profit organizations, mainly in San Mateo County, CA, working in the areas of the disadvantaged, the homeless, child welfare, family planning, the disabled, education, welfare and AIDS; and international development, technical assistance, population and health education projects in Mexico and Central America.

Geographical Area of Activity: USA, Central and South America.

Restrictions: The Foundation does not give directly to individuals, nor does it finance research; grants are only made to US charitable, tax-exempt organizations.

Publications: Annual Report.

Finance: Grants disbursed US $745,403 (2010).

Board of Directors: Ray N. Atkinson (Chair.); James C. Ingwersen (Sec.); John E. Herrell (Treas.).

Principal Staff: Admin. Elizabeth H. Curtis.

Address: 1720 S Amphlett Blvd, Suite 100, San Mateo, CA 94402-2710.

Telephone: (650) 357-1101; **Fax:** (650) 357-1101; **Internet:** atkinsonfdn.org; **e-mail:** atkinfdn@aol.com.

Atlantic Philanthropies

Established in 1982 by Charles F. Feeney to bring about lasting changes that will improve the lives of disadvantaged and vulnerable people. Consists of the Atlantic Foundation and the Atlantic Trust, both domiciled in Bermuda, several smaller foundations based in Bermuda, the United Kingdom, Ireland and the USA, and regional service companies that select and evaluate potential grant recipients, oversee grants once awarded, and manage the endowment.

Activities: Grants are made to projects in Bermuda, the United Kingdom (Northern Ireland), Ireland, South Africa, the USA and Viet Nam in the fields of ageing, disadvantaged children and young people, health of populations in developing countries, and reconciliation and human rights. Focuses on tackling the root causes of big and neglected problems that are amenable to solution and where where a grant can make a lasting contribution and achieve enduring change. In early 2002 the Board of Directors decided to reduce the endowment gradually over an expected 12–15 years.

Geographical Area of Activity: Bermuda, Northern Ireland and United Kingdom, Ireland, South Africa, USA, Viet Nam.

Restrictions: Proposals are considered by invitation only.

Publications: Annual Report; *Atlantic Reports.*

Finance: Net assets US $2,094,540,000 (31 Dec. 2010); annual revenue $285,848,000, expenditure $211,418,000 (2010).

Board of Directors: Peter Smitham (Chair.); Thomas N. Mitchell (Deputy Chair.); Sara Lawrence-Lightfoot (Deputy Chair.).

Principal Staff: Pres. and CEO Christopher G. Oechsli.

Address: 75 Varick St, New York, NY 10013-1917.

Telephone: (212) 916-7300; **Fax:** (212) 922-0360; **Internet:** www.atlanticphilanthropies.org; **e-mail:** USA@atlanticphilanthropies.org.

Atlas Economic Research Foundation

Founded in 1981 by the late Sir Antony Fisher to help develop and strengthen a global network of market-orientated think-tanks.

Activities: Aims to discover intellectual entrepreneurs, support the development and dissemination of their work to current and potential opinion leaders, and to support the development of think-tanks. Makes grants to think-tanks and similar institutions, funds international travel for young people wishing to develop the ideas of the free market, and through its Health and Welfare Program provides start-up grants to encourage and facilitate think-tank work on health and welfare issues, especially work concerning more 'vulnerable' sectors of society. Also funds workshops, teaching initiatives, makes prizes for publications, and operates the Templeton Freedom Awards and Program, which recognizes new institutes with exceptional future promise, as well as outstanding work by leading think-tanks in the areas of free-market solutions to poverty, ethics and values, social entrepreneurship, and outreach to students.

Geographical Area of Activity: International.

Publications: *Highlights* (newsletter); *Atlas Investor Reports* (newsletter); *AZAD Newsletter*; Annual Report.

Finance: Total assets US $2,812,151 (31 Dec. 2010); annual revenue $7,016,554, expenditure $7,701,798 (2010).

Board of Directors: Dan Grossman (Chair.).

Principal Staff: Pres. Alejandro Chafuen; CEO Brad Lips.

Address: 1201 L St NW, Washington, DC 20005.

Telephone: (202) 449-8449; **Fax:** (202) 280-1259; **Internet:** atlasnetwork.org; **e-mail:** info@atlasnetwork.org.

AT&T Foundation

Founded in 1984 by AT&T Corporation as a philanthropic organization dedicated to the support of education, arts and culture and civic and community services nationally and internationally.

Activities: Operates in the fields of education, arts and culture, and civic and community service, and provides 33% of its budget to a local grants initiative, operated by local offices supporting communities in their area. Within the field of education, support is given to projects focusing on the use of technology to enhance teaching and learning, and promoting family involvement in education, providing professional development opportunities for educators and promoting life-long learning and community collaboration. Civic and community service programme grants are given to health services for those in need, diversity in the workplace, environmental projects, national US organizations conducting public policy research, and projects enhancing the effectiveness of the voluntary sector. The arts and culture programme assists the production and creation of new artistic work, brings the work of women artists and artists of diverse cultures to a wider public, and mobilizes new technologies to promote artistic innovation and increase access to the arts. Local grants are given within areas where the company operates or has a significant presence.

Geographical Area of Activity: International, including Argentina, Australia, Brazil, Canada, Chile, China, Colombia, Denmark, France, Germany, Hong Kong, Japan, Mexico, Netherlands, New Zealand, Peru, Puerto Rico, South Africa, Spain, Sweden, Taiwan, the United Kingdom and the USA.

Restrictions: The AT&T Foundation prefers to work with charitable organizations that have clearly stated objectives, long-range planning, active participation of the governing board and strategies that incorporate diversified sources of support. The AT&T Foundation also considers grants to organizations that qualify as government instrumentalities.

Publications: Biennial Report; newsletters.

Finance: Total giving through AT&T Foundation and company programmes approx. US $148,000,000 (2010).

Board of Trustees: James W. Cicconi (Chair.).

Principal Staff: Pres. William F. Aldinger III; Exec. Dir John B. McCoy.

Address: 32 Ave of the Americas, 6th Floor, New York, NY 10013.

Telephone: (212) 387-6555; **Fax:** (212) 387-4882; **Internet:** www.att.com/gen/corporate-citizenship?pid=17884; **e-mail:** sustainability@attnews.us.

The Francis Bacon Foundation, Inc

Founded in 1937 by Walter Conrad Arensberg and Louise Stevens Arensberg to conduct and promote research in history, philosophy, science and literature, with special reference to the life and works of Francis Bacon, and his influence on his own and succeeding times; to make grants to colleges and universities; and to create and operate a library for those purposes.

Activities: Operates in the fields of education and the arts and humanities, nationally through self-conducted programmes, grants to institutions, particularly in southern California, conferences and courses, and nationally and internationally through publications and lectures. Awards Visiting Professorships and Lectureships in the Humanities to smaller colleges and universities to enable them to attract outstanding scholars, as well as the biennial Francis Bacon Award in the history of science, the history of technology, or historically engaged philosophy of science, in conjunction with the California Institute of Technology, worth US $20,000. Maintains the Huntington Library with a collection of almost 13,000 vols in San Marino, CA.

Geographical Area of Activity: USA.

Publications: Annual Report.

Finance: Total assets US $3,473,134 (31 Dec. 2009); total giving $156,593 (2010).

Trustees: Karl I. Swaidan (Sec.).

Address: 100 E Corson St, Suite 200, Pasadena, CA 91103-3841.

Telephone: (626) 795-5894; **Internet:** www.sirfrancisbacon.org.

Baltic-American Partnership Fund—BAPF

Established in 1998 by the US Agency for International Development (USAID) and the Open Society Institute (q.v.) to support the continued development of democratic institutions and market economies in the Baltic states by improving the sense of civic ownership and increasing individual capacity to participate effectively in political and economic decision-making.

Activities: Sub-grantees were selected to implement the Fund's programmes: the Open Estonia Foundation and the Soros Foundation–Latvia (q.v.), for their long-term track records in civil society development and the promotion of positive social change. Each foundation has established a Baltic-American Partnership Program—BAPP, advised by a local expert council, and managed by a local programme officer. Based on the Fund's overall strategy, set by its board and in dialogue with the Open Society Foundation boards, the BAPP local councils and staff develop the annual programme plans for their countries. Funds of US $15m. were to be used over a 10-year period to support projects in collaboration with other donors. Support is provided for the institutional development of non-profit organizations and for initiatives strengthening the legal and regulatory framework in which non-profit organizations function.

Geographical Area of Activity: Baltic countries (Estonia, Lithuania and Latvia).

Publications: Annual Report.

Board of Directors: Stephen J. Del Rosso, Jr (Chair.).

Principal Staff: Exec. Dir Rebecca Tolson.

Address: 400 W 59th St, 4th Floor, New York, NY 10019.

Telephone: (212) 548-0319; **Fax:** (212) 547-6901; **Internet:** www.bapf.org; **e-mail:** bapf@bapf.org.

Bank of America Foundation

Founded in 1998 by the Bank of America Corpn to fund private, non-profit, tax-exempt organizations providing services to communities nationally and internationally in areas where the company operates.

Activities: Support is given through grants, investments and loans within three main areas: providing educational opportunities; building inclusive communities and promoting cultural outreach, including economic development and environmental awareness; and arts and culture. A Volunteer Grants Program supports non-profit organizations where company associates volunteer their time; education grants are made to a variety of learning, educator development and literacy projects; and the Joe Martin Scholarship Program offers financial assistance to students who are dependants of company employees.

Geographical Area of Activity: USA and areas where the Bank of America Corpn operates.

Publications: Newsletter (quarterly); Annual Report.

Finance: Annual grants awarded around US $200,000,000.

Trustees: Kenneth D. Lewis (Chair.); Sandra Cohen (Sec.); John Fatheree (Treas.).

Principal Staff: CEO Kenneth D. Lewis; Pres. and Exec. Dir Lynn E. Drury; Vice-Pres. James S. Wagele.

Address: 10 Light St, 19th Floor, Baltimore, MD 21201.

Telephone: (888) 488-9802; **Internet:** www.bankofamerica.com/foundation; **e-mail:** nicole.nastacie@bankofamerica.com.

Baptist World Aid—BWAid

Established in 1905 to work in the field of international relief and development. It is a division of the Baptist World Alliance.

Activities: Operates, without regard to race or religion, in famine, disaster and refugee relief work. Funds long-term development programmes in the areas of training in self-sufficiency, agriculture, health and education in developing countries. It also offers fellowship assistance to Baptists across the world.

Geographical Area of Activity: International.

Restrictions: Works through member bodies of the Baptist World Alliance.

Publications: Newsletter; *Baptist World Centenary Congress: Official Report*; *Baptists Together in Christ 1905–2005*; numerous studies and research papers.

Finance: Funded by individuals and member churches.

Principal Staff: Pres. John Upton; Gen. Sec. Neville Callam.

Address: 405 North Washington St, Falls Church, VA 22046.

Telephone: (703) 790-8980; **Fax:** (703) 893-5160; **Internet:** www.bwanet.org; **e-mail:** bwa@bwanet.org.

Benton Foundation

Founded in 1981, following the principles of William Benton relating to the use of communications to benefit society and help solve social problems.

Activities: The Foundation works in three areas to achieve its objectives: it defines and advocates public policies that recognize new media's capacity for working in the public interest; helps NGOs use the media and communications technologies to best provide information for the public; and works to create Internet-based 'knowledge networks' that are accessible sources of information for non-profit action groups, journalists and educators. Established the Richard M. Neustadt Center for Communications in the Public Interest.

Geographical Area of Activity: USA.

Restrictions: No unsolicited or general grant applications accepted.

Publications: *Technology Literacy Benchmarks for Nonprofit Organizations*; *Benton Foundation 20 Year Report*; *Youth Activism and Global Engagement*; *Networking for Better Care: Health Care in the Information Age*; *Native Networking: Telecommunications and Information Technology in Indian Country*; *Losing Ground Bit by Bit: Low-Income Communities in the Information Age*; *Effective Language for Discussing Early Childhood Education and Policy*; *Universal Service: A Historical Perspective and Policies for the 21st Century*.

Finance: Annual revenue US $1,337,972, expenditure $3,288,742 (2009).

Board of Directors: Charles Benton (Chair.); Michael Smith (Treas.); Adrianne Benton Furniss (Sec.).

Principal Staff: Exec. Dir Cecilia Garcia.

Address: 1250 Connecticut Ave NW, Suite 200, Washington DC 20036.

Telephone: (202) 638-5770; **Fax:** (240) 235-5024; **Internet:** benton.org; **e-mail:** info@benton.org.

Better World Campaign—BWC

Established in 1997 as the Better World Fund along with its sister organization, the UN Foundation (q.v.), following the gift of US $1,000m. to the UN by R. E. (Ted) Turner; the Fund aims to promote the UN through supporting projects designed to inform the public world-wide about the organization's economic, social, environmental and humanitarian work.

Activities: Conducts and finances projects such as the Better World Campaign, aimed at educating the public about the work and role of the UN in addressing global issues, and building public support for the organization, in particular highlighting the UN's work to strengthen international security through global co-operation. In conjunction with the UN Foundation, the Fund sponsors the daily *UN Wire* news summary on UN and global affairs. In 2006 the Fund's projects also focused on encouraging US leadership on a constructive reform process that aims to strengthen the UN's ability to carry out its important responsibilities in the world.

Geographical Area of Activity: International.

Board of Directors: R. E. (Ted) Turner (Chair.).

Principal Staff: Exec. Dir Peter Yeo; Dir Mike Beard; Communications Dir Heather Wong.

Address: 1800 Massachusetts Ave NW, Suite 400, Washington, DC 20036.

Telephone: (202) 462-4900; **Fax:** (202) 462-2686; **Internet:** www.betterworldcampaign.org; **e-mail:** info_BWC@betterworldcampaign.org.

Blue Moon Fund, Inc

Founded in 2002 by Diane Edgerton Miller and Patricia Jones Edgerton, following the restructuring of the W. Alton Jones Foundation (founded in 1944 to promote environmental conservation and world peace).

Activities: The Foundation provides grants to organizations concerned with the protection and conservation of environmental resources. Funded initiatives include sustainable economic development projects in Brazil, promoting of green energy schemes in China, and the establishment of a carbon trading facility to finance small renewable energy and energy efficiency projects in developing countries, initially in India, China and the Americas. The Fund also sponsors an urban initiative and fellowship programme aimed at promoting cutting-edge approaches providing solutions to the questions of human consumption, the natural world, and economic advancement, placing fellows employed in the private or governmental sectors in non-profit organizations.

Geographical Area of Activity: Asia, North America, Central America and South America.

Restrictions: No grants are made to individuals, for building construction, endowment funds, basic research, scholarships, fellowships, international exchanges or conferences.

Principal Staff: Pres. and CEO Diane Edgerton Miller.

Address: 222 W South St, Charlottesville, VA 22902.

Telephone: (434) 295-5160; **Fax:** (434) 295-6894; **Internet:** www.bluemoonfund.org; **e-mail:** info@bluemoonfund.org.

Lynde and Harry Bradley Foundation, Inc

Founded in 1942 as the Allen-Bradley Foundation, Inc to support local and national initiatives. Converted to a private foundation and present name adopted in 1985.

Activities: The Foundation operates locally in the fields of the arts, education, social welfare and public policy. Support is given to US organizations involved in research into national and international public policy, and grants are made to institutes of higher education on a national level, especially in the field of the arts and humanities. Promotes citizenship and civil society.

Geographical Area of Activity: USA.

Publications: Annual Report; *Donor Intent Program*; *Intellectual Infrastructure*; *Improve Education*; *Revitalize Civil Society*; *Legacy of Milwaukee*; *Fifteen Years of Giving* (report).

Finance: Annual revenue US $78,818,000, expenditure $46,837,000 (2010).

Board of Directors: Terry Considine (Chair.); David V. Uihlein, Jr (Vice-Chair.).

Principal Staff: Pres. and CEO Michael W. Grebe.

Address: The Lion House, 1241 North Franklin Pl., Milwaukee, WI 53202-2901.

Telephone: (414) 291-9915; **Fax:** (414) 291-9991; **Internet:** www.bradleyfdn.org.

Bridge to Asia—BTA

Founded in 1987 by Jeffrey Smith to aid the modernization of education in China and other Asian countries.

Activities: The Foundation helps libraries at universities and research institutes upgrade their collections, through donations of books, journals and other materials in China, Viet Nam and other countries.

Geographical Area of Activity: China, South-East Asia and USA.

Board of Directors: Geraldine Kunstadter (Chair.).

Principal Staff: Pres. Jeff Smith; Vice-Pres. Newton Liu.

Address: 665 Grant Ave, San Francisco, CA 94108-2430.

Telephone: (415) 678-2990; **Fax:** (415) 678-2996; **Internet:** www.bridge.org; **e-mail:** asianet@bridge.org.

Bridges for Education, Inc—BFE

Founded in 1994 by J. Beth Ciesielski, in response to the increasing need for educational assistance in Central and Eastern Europe.

Activities: Aims to promote international education in Central and Eastern Europe, Turkey and China, through organizing education camps and recruiting and sending volunteer teachers from the USA and Canada. Also awards scholarships.

Geographical Area of Activity: Central, Eastern and Western Europe, Canada and the People's Republic of China.

Principal Staff: Exec. Dir and Founder Beth Ciesielski; Sr Programme Co-ordinators Don Orton, Shirley Orton; Applications Co-ordinator Margaret Dodge.

Address: 94 Lamarck Dr., Buffalo, NY 14226.

Telephone: (716) 839-0180; **Fax:** (716) 839-9493; **Internet:** www.bridges4edu.org; **e-mail:** jbc@bridges4edu.org.

Bristol-Myers Squibb Foundation

Established to fund and support projects that enhance and extend human lives around the world.

Activities: Supports a broad range of initiatives that deal with important health and social matters around the world, including women's health education and biomedical research. Support includes research grants and donations of medical supplies and pharmaceutical products. One of the foundation's largest projects is the US $115m. Secure the Future programme to address the HIV/AIDS problem in Southern and Western African countries, funding research, training, education and community outreach work to reduce the impact the epidemic has had in these countries. In 2010 the Foundation launched an initiative to help people with diabetes.

Geographical Area of Activity: International.

Restrictions: Does not award grants to individuals; political, social, fraternal or veterans' organizations; religious or sectarian organizations unless engaged in action significantly beneficial to the community; organizations in receipt of funds from United Way; endowments; advertising; conferences, videos or special events.

Publications: Annual Report.

Finance: Funded by the Bristol-Myers Squibb Company.

Board of Directors: Lamberto Andreotti (Chair.).

Principal Staff: Pres. John L. Damonti.

Address: 345 Park Ave, 43rd Floor, New York, NY 10154-0037.

Telephone: (212) 546-4000; **Fax:** (609) 252-6031; **Internet:** www.bms.com/foundation.

British Schools and Universities Foundation, Inc—BSUF

Founded in 1961 to promote closer relations between the USA and the British Commonwealth, through educational assistance.

Activities: A charitable foundation that makes grants to educational institutions in the United Kingdom and the British Commonwealth, and supports reciprocal Anglo-American education.

Geographical Area of Activity: United Kingdom, the Commonwealth and the USA.

Publications: Annual Report.

Finance: Cumulative grants US $36,000,000 (1965–2011).

Board of Directors: David Lipson (Chair.); Roger H. Martin (Deputy Chair.); Patrick M. Russell (Treas.); Allerton G. Smith (Vice-Pres. Investments); John G. Stiller (Vice-Pres. Institutions); Daniel O'Day, Jr (Vice-Pres. Scholarships); David W. Webber (Vice-Pres. Communications); Rosalind C. Benedict (Hon. Sec.); Jay H. McDowell (General Counsel).

Principal Staff: Exec. Dir James E. Marlow.

Address: 575 Madison Ave, Suite 1006, New York, NY 10022-2511.

Telephone: (212) 662-5576; **Internet:** www.bsuf.org; **e-mail:** info@bsuf.org.

The Broad Foundations

Established by Eli and Edythe Broad, the foundations include the Eli and Edythe Broad Foundation and the Broad Art Foundation.

Activities: The foundations operate in the fields of public education in the USA, scientific and medical research, contemporary arts world-wide, and civic projects in Los Angeles.

Geographical Area of Activity: USA and international.

Finance: Total assets US $2,200,058,000 (31 Dec. 2009); annual revenue $432,084,000, expenditure $150,454,000 (2010).

Principal Staff: Senior Dir Lydia Logan.

Address: 10900 Wilshire Blvd, 12th Floor, Los Angeles, CA 90024.

Telephone: (310) 954-5000; **Fax:** (310) 954-5051; **Internet:** www.broadfoundation.org; **e-mail:** info@broadfoundation .org.

Brookings Institution

Founded in 1927 by Robert S. Brookings and others to conduct and foster research, education, training and publication on public policy issues in the broad fields of economics, government administration, foreign policy and the social sciences.

Activities: Through its Economic Studies programme, the Institution carries out policy-orientated research involving analysis of issues pertinent to labor economics, social and urban economics, public finance, economic growth and stability, international economics, and industrial organization and regulation; the Governmental Studies programme focuses on social policy, political institutions and regulation and economic policy; issues related to international economic policy, national security policy and energy and regional studies, are dealt through its Foreign Policy Studies programme; organizes educational conferences for leaders in business, government professions on issues of public policy; research fellowships are granted in support of policy-orientated pre-doctoral research in national security policy, government and economics.

Geographical Area of Activity: USA.

Publications: *Brookings Papers on Economic Activity* (2 a year); *Brookings Review* (quarterly); Annual Report; periodic journals, policy briefs, analysis and commentary.

Finance: Annual revenue US $69,003,000, expenditure $78,869,000 (2009/10).

Board of Trustees: John L. Thornton (Chair.); Glenn Hutchins, Suzanne Nora Johnson, David M. Rubenstein (Vice-Chair.).

Principal Staff: Pres. Strobe Talbott.

Address: 1775 Massachusetts Ave NW, Washington, DC 20036-2188.

Telephone: (202) 797-6000; **Fax:** (202) 797-6004; **Internet:** www.brookings.edu; **e-mail:** communications@brookings .edu.

Brother's Brother Foundation

Founded in 1958 by Dr Robert Hingson to distribute donated educational, medical, agricultural and humanitarian aid to those in need internationally.

Activities: Requests and distributes donated aid shipments of medical, educational and humanitarian resources to those in need, whether because of war, or natural or man-made disasters, and without regard to race, religion or political affiliation.

Geographical Area of Activity: International.

Publications: Newsletters; Annual Report.

Finance: Total assets US $18,804,595 (31 Dec. 2010); annual revenue $272,712,158, expenditure $274,032,226 (2010).

Board of Trustees: Charles J. Stout (Chair.); B. J. Leber (Vice-Chair.); Rachel L. Allen (Sec.); Joseph T. Senko (Treas.).

Principal Staff: Pres. Luke L. Hingson.

Address: 1200 Galveston Ave, Pittsburgh, PA 15233-1604.

Telephone: (412) 321-3160; **Fax:** (412) 321-3325; **Internet:** www.brothersbrother.org; **e-mail:** mail@brothersbrother .org.

The Brush Foundation

Founded by Charles F. Brush in 1929; aims to ensure that family planning world-wide becomes acceptable, available, accessible, affordable, effective and safe.

Activities: Funds national and international innovative family planning projects which: protect and enhance people's ability to manage their reproductive health; carry out public policy analysis and/or public education in areas related to reproductive behaviour and its social implications; and advance the knowledge and purposeful behaviour of young people regarding sexuality within both a social and health context. Annual project grants generally range from US $5,000 to $25,000.

Geographical Area of Activity: International.

Restrictions: No unsolicited proposals accepted; no funding normally for videos, conferences, pre- or post-natal care, or youth theatre groups.

Finance: Total assets US $6,746,780 (31 Dec. 2010); total giving $297,500 (2010).

Board of Managers: Jacqueline E. Darroch (Pres.); Gita Gidwani (Vice-Pres.); Ellen Rome (Treas.); Elizabeth Stites (Sec.).

Principal Staff: Admin. Asst Jan Wolf.

Address: 25350 Rockside Rd, 3rd Floor, Bedford Heights, OH 44146-3704.

Telephone: (216) 334-2209; **Fax:** (216) 334-2211; **Internet:** foundationcenter.org/grantmaker/brush; **e-mail:** brushfoundation@hotmail.com.

Pearl S. Buck International

Established by Nobel and Pulitzer prize-winning author and humanitarian Pearl S. Buck, Pearl S. Buck International is an international development and humanitarian organization dedicated to helping children and promoting intercultural understanding.

Activities: Works to improve the quality of life and available opportunities for children who suffer discrimination related to the circumstances of their birth, by promoting tolerance and human rights, mitigating the effects of injustices suffered by children, and supporting many related programmes around the world, with a particular emphasis on projects working in South-East Asia.

Geographical Area of Activity: World-wide, with an emphasis on the People's Republic of China, the Philippines, the Republic of Korea, Taiwan, Thailand and Viet Nam.

Restrictions: Grants to affiliated and partner organizations.

Publications: Annual Report; *Connections* (biennial newsletter).

Finance: Total assets US $3,125,678 (30 June 2011) annual revenue $2,914,181, expenditure $3,020,381 (2010/11).

Board of Directors: David D. Yoder (Chair.); David R. Breidinger (Vice-Chair.); Sandy Weikel (Sec.); Sang Kim (Treas.).

Principal Staff: CEO Janet L. Mintzer.

Address: 520 Dublin Rd, Perkasie, PA 18944.

Telephone: (215) 249-0100; **Fax:** (215) 249-9657; **Internet:** www.psbi.org; **e-mail:** info@pearlsbuck.org.

Burroughs Wellcome Fund—BWF

Founded in 1955 by the Burroughs Wellcome Co, USA, as a private non-profit foundation to advance medical science by supporting research and other scientific and educational activities.

Activities: The Fund has two primary goals, to help outstanding scientists early in their career, and to advance fields in the basic medical sciences that are undervalued or in need of particular encouragement. The Fund makes grants primarily to institutions within the USA and Canada for research in the basic biomedical sciences through a series of competitive award programmes in: infectious diseases, interfaces in science, translational research, population and laboratory based sciences, reproductive sciences, biomedical sciences and science education. Most grants are made on a competitive basis, but they are also made to non-profit organizations conducting activities to improve the general environment for science.

Geographical Area of Activity: USA and Canada.

Restrictions: No grants are made to individuals.

Publications: Annual Report; *FOCUS* (e-newsletter); programme brochures; special reports.

Finance: Total grants disbursed US $19,950,000 (2009/10).

Board of Directors: Dr George Langford (Chair.).

Principal Staff: Pres. John E. Burris; Vice-Pres. (Finance) Scott Schoedler.

Address: POB 13901, 21 T. W. Alexander Dr., Research Triangle Park, NC 27709-3901.

Telephone: (919) 991-5100; **Fax:** (919) 991-5160; **Internet:** www.bwfund.org; **e-mail:** info@bwfund.org.

The Bydale Foundation

Founded in 1965 by James P. Warburg to support various charitable purposes.

Activities: The Foundation provides support for programmes in the areas of the environment, social justice, women's rights, human rights and poetry.

Geographical Area of Activity: USA.

Restrictions: No grants made to individuals. Unsolicited proposals for organizations outside the Foundation's areas of interest are unlikely to receive funding.

Finance: Total assets US $11,474,019 (31 Dec. 2010); grants disbursed $503,500 (2010).

Principal Staff: Agent Christine O'Donnell.

Address: 1 Bryant Park, NY1-100-28-05, New York, NY 10036-6715.

Telephone: (646) 855-1011; **Fax:** (646) 855-5463.

Carnegie Corporation of New York

Founded in 1911 by Andrew Carnegie to promote the advancement and diffusion of knowledge and understanding among the peoples of the USA, Russia and of certain countries that are, or have been, members of the British Commonwealth.

Activities: Current areas of interest are education; international peace and security; international development; and strengthening US democracy. Also operates a Carnegie Corporation Scholars Program, supporting research by outstanding young scholars, as well as a Special Opportunities Fund for projects falling outside the main areas of interest. Support is directed towards the development of children and youth, childhood health and development, educational achievement, science education and the reform of education; the development of human resources in less-developed countries; and co-operative security and the avoidance of conflict between nations. Grant programmes support: science-based analyses of the ways in which the risk of nuclear war can be diminished; projects linking educational reform to social and economic changes; research into the prevention of problems for children and young teenagers such as school failure, school-age pregnancy, childhood injury and substance abuse; and efforts to improve maternal and infant health in English-speaking countries of Africa and to strengthen indigenous scientific capacity to solve development problems. Most grants are made to organizations in the USA, but support is also given overseas with a current focus on Commonwealth Africa. Projects involving both Russian and American participants are also funded. Supports conferences and seminars, exchange programmes and publications.

Geographical Area of Activity: USA and countries that are, or have been, members of the British Commonwealth, with a current emphasis on Commonwealth Africa, and Russia.

Restrictions: No grants to individual schools.

Publications: Annual Report; *New Directions for Carnegie Corporation of New York*; *Carnegie Quarterly*; newsletters (quarterly); magazines (quarterly).

Finance: Total assets US $2,531,000,000 (2010).

Board of Trustees: Janet Robinson (Chair.); Kurt Schmoke (Vice-Chair.).

Principal Staff: Pres. Vartan Gregorian; Dir Grants Man. Nicole Howe Buggs.

Address: 437 Madison Ave, New York, NY 10022.

Telephone: (212) 371-3200; **Fax:** (212) 754-4073; **Internet:** www.carnegie.org.

Carnegie Endowment for International Peace

Private non-profit organization dedicated to advancing co-operation between nations and promoting active international engagement by the USA. Founded in 1910 by Andrew Carnegie, its work is non-partisan, and works to achieve practical results.

Activities: The Carnegie Endowment conducts research, publishes information, holds meetings, and occasionally creates new institutions and international networks. Activities operate in the following fields: the China Program, the Democracy and Rule of Law Program, the Energy and Climate Program, the Middle East Program, the Nonproliferation Program, the Russia and Eurasia Program, the Carnegie South Asia Program, and the Trade, Equity and Development Program. The interests of Endowment associates are international, and concentrate on relations between governments, businesses, international organizations and civil society, focusing on the economic, political and technological forces driving global change. Through the Carnegie Moscow Center, founded in 1992, the Endowment helps to develop a tradition of public policy analysis in the states of the former USSR, and to improve relations between Russia and the USA. The Endowment publishes *Foreign Policy*, one of the world's leading magazines about international politics and economics, which reaches readers in more than 120 countries.

Geographical Area of Activity: USA, China, Middle East, South Asia and Russian Federation.

Restrictions: Not a grant-making organization.

Publications: *Foreign Policy* (6 a year); monographs, books, newsletters, working papers, reports and other publications on international relations and foreign policy.

Finance: Key sources of funding are the endowment and grants.

Board of Trustees: Richard Giordano (Chair.); Stephen R. Lewis, Jr (Vice-Chair.).

Principal Staff: Pres. Jessica Tuchman Mathews.

Address: 1779 Massachusetts Ave NW, Washington, DC 20036-2103.

Telephone: (202) 483-7600; **Fax:** (202) 483-1840; **Internet:** www.carnegieendowment.org; **e-mail:** info@carnegieendowment.org.

Carnegie Hero Fund Commission

Founded in 1904 by Andrew Carnegie to recognize, with the award of medals and sums of money, heroism voluntarily performed by civilians in the USA and Canada, in saving, or attempting to save, the lives of others at extraordinary risk to the life of the rescuer.

Activities: Operates in the USA and Canada in the field of social welfare, through grants to individuals, including scholarship assistance and continuing aid to those disabled in their attempts to save others, and grants to the dependants of those who died in such attempts. National Carnegie Hero Fund Foundations were established in 1908 in the United Kingdom, 1909 in France and 1911 in Belgium, Denmark, Italy, the Netherlands, Norway, Sweden and Switzerland. These foundations also award medals and diplomas to individuals in those countries who have risked or lost their lives, as well as cash grants.

Geographical Area of Activity: USA and Canada.

Restrictions: Act of heroism must have occurred in the USA or Canada and the Commission must be notified within two years.

Publications: Annual Report; newsletter; leaflets.

Commission: Mark Laskow (Pres.); Priscilla J. McCrady (Vice-Pres.); Walter F. Rutkowski (Sec.); James M. Walton (Treas.).

Principal Staff: Exec. Dir Walter F. Rutkowski.

Address: 436 Seventh Ave, Suite 1101, Pittsburgh, PA 15219-1841.

Telephone: (412) 281-1302; **Fax:** (412) 281-5751; **Internet:** www.carnegiehero.org; **e-mail:** carnegiehero@carnegiehero.org.

The John W. Carson Foundation

Established by Johnny Carson in 1981 to support children, education and health services. On his death in 2005, US $156m. was left to the Foundation.

Activities: Supports non-profit organizations.

Geographical Area of Activity: Principally Los Angeles and Nebraska.

Finance: Total assets US $168,013,295 (30 June 2010); total giving $5,137,250 (2009/10).

Address: 9350 Wilshire Blvd, Suite 250, Beverly Hills, CA 90212-3219.

The Carter Center

Established to work in partnership with Emory University, with a fundamental commitment to human rights and the alleviation of human suffering; it seeks to prevent and resolve conflicts, enhance freedom and democracy, and improve health world-wide.

Activities: Operates peace programmes in the areas of democracy, human rights, conflict resolution, the Americas and China; and health programmes to fight six preventable diseases—Guinea worm, river blindness, trachoma, schistosomiasis, lymphatic filariasis, and malaria—by using health education and simple, low-cost methods.

Geographical Area of Activity: Less-developed countries world-wide.

Finance: Total assets US $475,815,106 (31 Aug. 2010); annual revenue $216,761,561, expenditure $216,046,505 (2009/10).

Board of Trustees: Jimmy Carter (Founder); Rosalynn Carter (Founder); Kent C. 'Oz' Nelson (Chair.).

Principal Staff: Pres. and CEO John Hardman.

Address: One Copenhill, 453 Freedom Parkway, Atlanta, GA 30307.

Telephone: (404) 420-5100; **Internet:** www.cartercenter.org; **e-mail:** carterweb@emory.edu.

Carthage Foundation

Founded in 1964 by Richard M. Scaife for general charitable purposes; shares administrative offices with the Allegheny Foundation, the Sarah Scaife Foundation and the Scaife Family Foundation (q.v.).

Activities: Operates mainly in the area of public policy research, especially in the fields of international affairs, government, the law and public policy, through grants for conferences, seminars and other purposes.

Geographical Area of Activity: USA.

Restrictions: No grants are made to individuals.

Publications: Annual Report.

Finance: Total assets US $26,371,835 (31 Dec. 2010); grants disbursed $602,500 (2010).

Officers and Trustees: Richard M. Scaife (Chair.); R. Daniel McMichael (Sec.); Michael W. Gleba (Treas.); Alexis J. Konkol (Asst Sec.); Roger W. Robinson, Jr (Asst Treas.).

Principal Staff: Treas. Michael W. Gleba.

Address: 1 Oxford Center, 301 Grant St, Suite 3900, Pittsburgh, PA 15219-6401.

Telephone: (412) 392-2900; **Internet:** www.scaife.com/carthage.html.

Caterpillar Foundation

Corporate foundation established in 1952 to make sustainable communities possible through advancing knowledge, protecting the environment and conserving resources, and promoting access to basic human needs.

Activities: Operates internationally in the areas of education, health and social welfare, and civic, cultural and environmental causes.

Geographical Area of Activity: International.

Finance: Total assets US $32,093,038 (31 Dec. 2009; grants disbursed $31,239,085 (2009).

Principal Staff: Man. Maryann Morrison.

Address: 100 NE Adams St, Peoria, IL 61629-1480.

Telephone: (309) 675-5941; **Internet:** www.caterpillar.com/sustainability/caterpillar-foundation; **e-mail:** foundation@cat.com.

Center for Citizen Initiatives—CCI

Founded in 1983, CCI works to support democracy in post-communist Russia and encourage economic reform; and to provide aid to disadvantaged people in the Russian Federation.

Activities: Funds a number of volunteer programmes in the Russian Federation, including a Productivity Enhancement Program (PEP), providing US-based management training for Russian entrepreneurs; the Advanced Business Management Program for Russian Executives and their Team of Top Managers (ABMP); the Entrepreneur-to-Entrepreneur Business Training (EEBT); and the Russian Youth Program (RYP). Operates six partner offices in the Russian Federation.

Geographical Area of Activity: Russian Federation.

Publications: *PEP Brochure 2000*; *PEP Profiles 2000;* newsletter (quarterly).

Board of Directors: Arlie Schardt (Chair.).

Principal Staff: Pres. Sharon Tennison; Program Officer Masha Maslova.

Address: Presidio of San Francisco, POB 29249, San Francisco, CA 94129-0249.

Telephone: (415) 561-7777; **Fax:** (415) 561-7778; **Internet:** www.ccisf.org; **e-mail:** info@ccisf.org.

Center for Communications, Health and the Environment—CECHE

Private, non-profit institution founded in 1990. Aims to assist underserved communities in the USA, Central and Eastern Europe, India and developing countries world-wide.

Activities: Operates in underserved communities world-wide supporting programmes that improve lifestyles and reduce health risks, and counteract the harmful effects of pollution. Main programme areas, with an emphasis on the use of mass media, focus on nutrition, tobacco control, public health, democracy and health, private voluntary action and environmental health.

Geographical Area of Activity: Developing countries, underserved communities in Europe, and the USA.

Restrictions: Grants only to non-profit organizations for joint projects.

Publications: *In Focus* (online periodical); fact sheets; project reports; Annual Report.

Finance: Funding from foundations, international organizations and local government. Total assets US $338,313 (31 Dec. 2009); annual income $132,021, expenditure $188,933 (2009).

Board of Directors: Dr Sushma Palmer (Chair.); Mark Palmer (Vice-Chair.).

Principal Staff: Dir Dr Leonard Silverstein.

Address: 4437 Reservoir Rd NW, Washington, DC 20007.

Telephone: (202) 965-5990; **Fax:** (202) 965-5996; **Internet:** www.ceche.org; **e-mail:** ceche@comcast.net.

The Center for International Humanitarian Cooperation—CIHC

Founded in 1992 by a group of physicians and diplomats to promote healing and peace in countries affected by conflict, ethnic violence or natural disaster.

Activities: The Center aims to professionalize training in the humanitarian field. By covering a variety of topics, including disaster management, mental health issues and negotiation, the CIHC programmes prepare members of international relief organizations and humanitarian workers to be effective in their work in conflict and post-conflict areas.

Geographical Area of Activity: International.

Publications: include *Technology for Humanitarian Action; Human Security for All; Emergency Relief Operations; Traditions, Values and Humanitarian Actions; Basics of International Humanitarian Missions; Preventive Diplomacy; Clearing the Fields; A Framework for Survival; The Pulse of Humanitarian Assistance; Even in Chaos: Education in Times of Emergency; The Open Door*; newsletters.

Board of Directors: Kevin M. Cahill (Pres.).

Principal Staff: Admin. Dir Brendan Cahill.

Address: 850 Fifth Ave, New York, NY 10065.

Telephone: (212) 636-6294; **Fax:** (212) 636-7060; **Internet:** www.cihc.org; **e-mail:** mail@cihc.org.

Center for Victims of Torture—CVT

Founded in 1985, CVT works locally, nationally and internationally to heal the wounds of torture on individuals, their families and their communities, and to stop torture worldwide.

Activities: Provides direct care for victims of politically motivated torture and their families in St Paul, MN, the Democratic Republic of Congo, Kenya and Jordan; evaluates and monitors the progress of survivors in its care programmes; runs training programmes for health care, education and social work professionals in the USA and abroad; and works towards the elimination of torture through public policy initiatives and education campaigns in collaboration with other human rights and civic organizations.

Geographical Area of Activity: International.

Publications: Annual Report; *Storycloth* (newsletter); training materials for social workers, physicians, health workers and educators.

Finance: Total assets US $3,618,356 (31 Dec. 2010); annual income $9,461,400, annual expenditure $9,183,432 (2010).

Directors: Patti Andreini Arnold (Chair.); Babette Apland (Vice-Chair.); John Cairns (Past Chair.); Connie Magnuson (Treas.).

Principal Staff: Interim Exec. Dir Ruth Barrett Rendler; CFO Diane Fisher.

Address: 649 Dayton Ave, St Paul, MN 55104.

Telephone: (612) 436-4800; **Fax:** (612) 436-2600; **Internet:** www.cvt.org; **e-mail:** cvt@cvt.org.

Centre for Development and Population Activities—CEDPA

Founded in 1975, a non-profit international organization that aims to help and empower women at all levels of society and to involve them in development work.

Activities: Operates internationally in collaboration with partner NGOs and networks, in the areas of gender equality and developing the role of women in society, through linking reproductive health care with women's empowerment; improving facilities and capabilities of development centres and networks; increasing women's involvement in policy-making; and promoting youth involvement in development agendas. Maintains country offices in India and Nigeria.

Geographical Area of Activity: International.

Publications: Project reports; fact sheets; newsletter (quarterly); booklets; Annual Report.

Finance: Total assets US $4,695,731 (31 Dec. 2010); annual income $10,103,284, expenditure $10,998,559 (2010).

Board of Directors: Ann Van Dusen (Chair.); Barie Carmichael (Sec.).

Principal Staff: Pres. and CEO Carol Peasley; Chief Financial and Admin. Officer Kristan Beck.

Address: 1120 20th St NW, Suite 720, Washington, DC 20036.

Telephone: (202) 667-1142; **Fax:** (202) 332-4496; **Internet:** www.cedpa.org; **e-mail:** info@cedpa.org.

The Century Foundation

Founded in 1919 by Edward A. Filene for research on major economic, political and social institutions and issues. Formerly known as the Twentieth Century Fund, Inc.

Activities: Research is conducted nationally and internationally in the fields of communications, international affairs and economic development, and on major political, economic and social institutions. Main programme areas are Economics and Inequality, Retirement Security, Education, Health Care, Homeland Security, Election Reform, Media and Politics and International Affairs. Research results are published in book form. Awards the Leonard Silk Journalism Fellowship to an established journalist producing a book on what the Foundation considers an important contemporary issue. Maintains office in Washington, DC.

Geographical Area of Activity: International, USA.

Restrictions: Not a grant-making foundation.

Publications: Annual Report; newsletter; studies and paperback series.

Trustees: Alan Brinkley (Chair.); Kathleen M. Sullivan (Vice-Chair.); Lewis B. Kaden (Treas.); Alicia H. Munnell (Sec. and Clerk).

Principal Staff: Pres. Janice Nittoli.

Address: 41 East 70th St, New York, NY 10021.

Telephone: (212) 535-4441; **Fax:** (212) 879-9197; **Internet:** www.tcf.org; **e-mail:** info@tcf.org.

Chatlos Foundation, Inc

Founded in 1953 by William F. Chatlos.

Activities: The Foundation operates nationally and internationally, providing funding in the fields of bible colleges and seminaries (amounting to 33% of funding), religious causes

(30% of funding), medicine and health, liberal arts colleges (principally private colleges) and social welfare.

Geographical Area of Activity: World-wide.

Restrictions: Only non-profit organizations that are tax exempt for US federal income tax purposes may apply. No grants directly to international organizations, to individual churches, secondary schools, arts or medical research organizations. No grants to individuals, endowment funds, medical research, conferences, bricks and mortar, or multi-year grants; no loans.

Publications: Information brochure; application guidelines.

Board of Directors: Kathryn A. Randle (Chair.); William J. Chatlos (Pres.); Carol J. Chatlos (Sec.); Charles O. Morgan, Jr; Cindee L. Randon; Esther J. Kemsey; Michele Chatlos Roach (Vice-Pres. and Treas.).

Principal Staff: Pres. William J. Chatlos; Vice-Pres and Treas. Michele Chatlos Roach.

Address: POB 915048, Longwood, FL 32791-5048.

Telephone: (407) 862-5077; **Internet:** www.chatlos.org; **e-mail:** info@chatlos.org.

CHF International

Founded in 1952, CHF International serves as a catalyst for long-lasting positive change in low- and moderate-income communities around the world, helping families and communities improve their economic circumstances, environment and infrastructure. The organization provides technical expertise and leadership in international development, including development finance, housing and entrepreneurship.

Activities: Operates internationally, and has worked in around 100 countries since its inception, in the area of housing and community development. Offers technical expertise in communities, habitat and finance, and serves as a catalyst for sustainable positive change in low- and moderate-income communities world-wide, helping to improve housing, economic circumstances and environments. Works in partnership with other organizations to develop systems, policies and practices that increase access to affordable housing, community services and finance.

Geographical Area of Activity: International.

Restrictions: No grants to individuals; grants are given only to project-specific local organizations. CHF International does not accept unsolicited proposals or requests for support.

Publications: *Building a Better World* (annual international programme report); factsheets; bulletins; booklets, including *International Development Matters*.

Finance: Annual revenue US $255,519,850, expenditure $246,899,984 (2009/10).

Board of Trustees: Robert A. Mosbacher, Jr (Chair.); Lauri Fitz-Pegado (Vice-Chair.); Caroline Blakely (Treas.).

Principal Staff: Pres. and CEO David A. Weiss; Exec. Vice-Pres. and COO Chris Sale.

Address: 8601 Georgia Ave, Suite 800, Silver Spring, MD 20910.

Telephone: (301) 587-4700; **Fax:** (301) 587-7315; **Internet:** www.chfinternational.org; **e-mail:** mailbox@chfinternational.org.

The Chicago Community Trust

Founded in 1915 for such charitable purposes as will best make for the mental, moral, intellectual and physical improvement, assistance and relief of the inhabitants of the County of Cook, State of Illinois.

Activities: Operates mainly in Greater Chicago in the fields of education, health, basic human needs, the arts and humanities, and community development, through grants for both general operating support and specific programmes.

Geographical Area of Activity: USA.

Restrictions: No grants are made to individuals.

Publications: Annual Report; *Trust News* (3 a year); grant guidelines; financial statement.

Finance: Total assets US $1,595,765,501 (30 Sept. 2010); grant commitments $136,161,206 (2009/10).

Executive Committee: Frank M. Clark (Chair.).

Principal Staff: Pres. and CEO Tony Mazany.

Address: 111 East Wacker Dr., Suite 1400, Chicago, IL 60601.

Telephone: (312) 616-8000; **Fax:** (312) 616-7955; **Internet:** www.cct.org; **e-mail:** info@cct.org.

Child Health Foundation—CHF

Founded in 1985 to promote better health of children and their mothers in developing countries and medically underserved populations.

Activities: Operates mainly in the area of diarrhoeal diseases, malnutrition and poverty, through the development of low-cost technologies, conducting health, educational and training programmes, promoting research capabilities in institutions in developing countries, and through charitable activities. Maintains a speaker's bureau and through its Innovative Small Grant Program awards grants of up to US $5,000 to research or service projects aiming to improve the health of children.

Geographical Area of Activity: International.

Publications: Annual Report; newsletter.

Finance: Net assets US $150,494 (31 Dec. 2010); annual revenue $268,644, expenditure $241,353 (2010).

Board of Directors: Maureen Black (Chair.); Pamela Johnson (Vice-Chair.); David A. Sack (Sec.); Nathaniel Pierce (Sec. and Treas.).

Principal Staff: Dir R. Bradley Sack; Dir of Admin. Rosario Davison.

Address: 10630 Little Patuxent Parkway, Century Plaza, Suite 126, Columbia, MD 21044.

Telephone: (410) 992-5512; **Fax:** (410) 992-5641; **Internet:** www.childhealthfoundation.org; **e-mail:** contact@childhealthfoundation.org.

ChildFund International

Founded in 1938 by a Presbyterian minister; aims to assist children world-wide; formerly known as Christian Children's Fund—CCF.

Activities: Operates in the USA and in more than 30 less-developed countries, including South-Eastern Europe, through child sponsorship, grants and contributions aiming to provide long-term solutions to help combat poverty, in order that children can grow up safely, healthy and educated. Through a number of programmes, funded by sponsors, donors, foundations and grant organizations, the Fund provides better access to health care, immunization, clean water, better nutrition, clothing, educational assistance and training for children in need, regardless of race, religion or gender. Also provides emergency assistance/relief, micro-enterprise activities for parents and assistance to AIDS orphans.

Geographical Area of Activity: Africa, America, Asia, the Caribbean, South-Eastern Europe.

Restrictions: No grants to individuals.

Publications: Annual Report; *When AIDS Hits Home* (special report); newsletters; *ChildWorld*; *ChildWire* (e-newsletter); booklets; studies; programme briefs.

Finance: Total assets US $101,401,580 (30 June 2011); annual revenue $237,647,089, expenditure $226,735,876 (2010/11).

Board of Directors: Maureen Denlea Massey (Chair.); A. Hugh Ewing, III (Vice-Chair.); Dr Charles Caravati (Past Chair.); John C. Purnell, Jr (Sec.).

Principal Staff: Pres. and CEO Anne Lynam Goddard; Chief Financial Officer James Tuite.

Address: 2821 Emerywood Parkway, POB 26484, Richmond, VA 23294.

Telephone: (804) 756-2700; **Fax:** (804) 756-2719; **Internet:** www.childfund.org; **e-mail:** questions@childfund.org.

Children of The Americas—COTA

Established in 1984 by Dr William and Judy Schwank as a national network of volunteers who provide free medical care to children world-wide, and especially in Guatemala.

Activities: Operates in the fields of medicine and health, and social welfare. Medical teams travel to Guatemala regularly to provide medical treatment. Children are also referred to the organization's medical team in Kentucky from throughout the world. Has established an orphanage and a surgical centre in Guatemala. Also provides educational services and scholarships in Mexico and Central America.

Geographical Area of Activity: International.

Publications: *One Child* (quarterly newsletter); Annual Report.

Finance: Total assets US $10,937 (31 Dec. 2010); annual revenue $1,011,626, expenditure $1,022,680 (2010).

Board of Directors: Dave Brisbin (Pres.); Terry Neville (Treas.); Marian Brisbin (Sec.).

Address: 67 Gingham St, Trabuco Canyon, CA 92679.

Telephone: (949) 709-0673; **Fax:** (949) 709-0674; **Internet:** www.americaschildren.org; **e-mail:** 4kids@ americaschildren.org.

Children International—CI

Established in 1936, Children International is a non-profit humanitarian organization that aims to help children around the world to overcome the effects of poverty to become healthy, well-educated, self-sustaining and integrated members of society.

Activities: Operates child sponsorship projects in Central and South America, Asia, Africa and the USA for the benefit of children, providing the opportunity for people to support children in the developing world. Sponsor contributions are used to assist children particularly in the fields of health and education, as well as buying basic provisions such as food and clothing.

Geographical Area of Activity: Central and South America, Asia, Africa and the USA.

Restrictions: Does not provide individual educational benefits to children who are not yet enrolled in school.

Publications: *Children International* (newsletter); Annual Report.

Finance: Total assets US $60,109,127 (30 Sept. 2011); annual revenue $156,422,279, expenditure $155,129,314 (2010/11).

Board of Directors: Larry Lee (Chair.); Charles Maahs (Treas.).

Principal Staff: Pres. and CEO James R. Cook; Sr Vice-Pres. and CFO David Houchen.

Address: 2000 East Red Bridge Rd, POB 219055, Kansas City, MO 64121.

Telephone: (816) 942-2000; **Fax:** (816) 942-3714; **Internet:** www.children.org; **e-mail:** children@children.org.

Children's Wish Foundation International—CWFI

Founded in 1985 by Linda Dozoretz, the Foundation aims to fulfil the wishes of terminally ill children who are not expected to reach the age of 18.

Activities: Regardless of religion, race or economic status, the Foundation provides children who have been diagnosed as being terminally ill with an experience, following their own personal wish, to enjoy with their family. Also runs a programme that donates entertainment and educational supplies and provides children's entertainers for hospitals; and supports summer camps for young people with terminal illnesses.

Geographical Area of Activity: International.

Restrictions: Unlike other wish granting organizations, there is no minimum age, however, if the child's health allows it, the Foundation tries to wait to fulfill the wish until the child is old enough to enjoy fully and remember the experience.

Publications: Newsletter.

Finance: Total assets US $2,690,758 (30 June 2009); annual revenue $10,919,215, expenditure $11,020,069 (2008/09); grants disbursed $2,272,518 (2008/09).

Principal Staff: Pres. and CEO Arthur Stein; Exec. Dir Linda Dozoretz; Chief Financial Officer Susan D. Sprague.

Address: 8615 Roswell Rd, POB 28785, Atlanta, GA 30358.

Telephone: (770) 393-9474; **Fax:** (770) 393-0683; **Internet:** www.childrenswish.org; **e-mail:** contact@childrenswish .org.

Jane Coffin Childs Memorial Fund for Medical Research

Founded in 1937 by Alice S. Coffin and Starling W. Childs to further research into the causes, origins and treatment of cancer.

Activities: Operates nationally and internationally in the field of cancer research, through post-doctoral fellowships; US citizens may hold fellowships in any country, foreigners must study in the USA.

Geographical Area of Activity: World-wide.

Publications: Newsletter.

Finance: Total net assets US $33,665,479 (30 June 2009).

Board of Scientific Advisers: Dr Randy Schekman (Chair.).

Principal Staff: Admin. Dir Kim Roberts.

Address: 333 Cedar St, SHM L300, New Haven, CT 06510.

Telephone: (203) 785-4612; **Fax:** (203) 785-3301; **Internet:** www.jccfund.org; **e-mail:** jccfund@yale.edu.

China Medical Board

Founded in 1928 by the Rockefeller Foundation (q.v.) to provide financial support to the Peking Union Medical College and similar institutions in the Far East.

Activities: The Board assists health profession educational institutions to enhance educational and research activities in medicine, nursing and public health. Grants are made to designated national medical, nursing and public health educational institutions in Hong Kong, Indonesia, Republic of Korea, Malaysia, the Philippines, Singapore, China (Taiwan), Laos, Myanmar, Thailand and the People's Republic of China (including Tibet).

Geographical Area of Activity: East and South-East Asia.

Restrictions: Unsolicited grant applications not accepted. No support for governments, professional societies, or research institutes not directly under medical school control. No grants to individuals (except for scholarships and fellowships), nor for capital funds, operating budgets for medical care, special projects, or the basic equipping of medical schools, nursing schools, or schools of public health that are the responsibility of various governments or universities; no loans.

Publications: include Annual Report; *The China Medical Board: 50 Years of Programs, Partnerships and Progress 1950– 2000;* numerous research papers and speeches.

Finance: Annual revenue US $7,183,228, expenditure $10,451,516 (2007/08).

Board: Mary Brown Bullock (Chair.).

Principal Staff: Pres. Lincoln C. Chen; Dir of Finance and Operations Sally Paquet.

Address: 2 Arrow St, Cambridge, MA 02138.

Telephone: (617) 979-8000; **Internet:** www.cmbfound.org; **e-mail:** info@chinamedicalboard.org.

Winston Churchill Foundation of the United States

The Foundation, authorized by Sir Winston Churchill and founded in 1959, is a charitable organization granting scholarships to American students of exceptional academic ability and outstanding achievement for studies at the University of Cambridge, United Kingdom.

Activities: Awards scholarships to students of outstanding calibre to pursue graduate studies in mathematics, engineering, or the sciences; offers at least 14 scholarships annually to postgraduates in engineering, sciences and mathematics at the University of Cambridge.

Geographical Area of Activity: USA.

Restrictions: Eligible candidates are those aged between 19 and 26 with US citizenship, holding a bachelors degree from a US university or college and enrolled at one of the more than 100 US institutions taking part in the programme.

Finance: Assets US $13,500,000 (2011); annual revenue $650,000, expenditure $750,000 (2008).

Board of Trustees: Hon. John L. Loeb, Jr (Chair.); David D. Burrows (Treas.); James A. FitzPatrick, Jr (Sec.).

Principal Staff: Pres. Patrick A. Gerschel; Exec. Dir Peter C. Patrikis.

Address: 600 Madison Ave, 16th Floor, New York, NY 10022-1737.

Telephone: (212) 752-3200; **Fax:** (212) 246-8330; **Internet:** www.winstonchurchillfoundation.org; **e-mail:** info@winstonchurchillfoundation.org.

Citi Foundation

Established to improve the quality of life of children, families and communities world-wide, through supporting organizations contributing to education, economic and community development, and quality of life. Formerly known as Citigroup Foundation.

Activities: Operates world-wide in the areas of education and community development, with a small amount of funding for arts education, and health and welfare. In the area of education, the Foundation operates through funding projects in early childhood, technology for the classroom, higher education for minority groups and women, and financial literacy. In community development, it supports organizations funding affordable housing, small business loans in the USA, microcredit in less-developed countries and welfare-to-work initiatives. In 2004 the Foundation committed US $200m. for the following 10 years to support financial education initiatives.

Geographical Area of Activity: International.

Restrictions: Grants are not made to individuals, to political causes, religious organizations, nor for fundraising events; prospective grantees are usually approached by the Foundation; unsolicited applications are less likely to succeed.

Publications: Annual Report.

Finance: Grants disbursed US $65,800,000 (2009).

Board of Directors: Lewis B. Kaden (Chair.).

Principal Staff: Pres. Pamela P. Flaherty.

Address: Citigroup Inc., 399 Park Ave, New York, NY 10022.

Telephone: (212) 793-8451; **Fax:** (212) 793-5944; **Internet:** www.citifoundation.com; **e-mail:** citizenship@citi.com.

Civitas International

An international consortium inaugurated in 1995, comprising individuals, governmental and non-governmental organizations, and international organizations, promoting civic education, aiming to support education for citizenship in new and established democracies world-wide.

Activities: Operates a world-wide network to promote civic education, through computer networking and international exchange of educators. Maintains the Civnet website for civic education practitioners, administrators, NGOs, etc., containing resources and other information on civic education and society.

Geographical Area of Activity: World-wide.

Publications: *Civnet Journal* (6 a year); Activity Report.

Board: Charles N. Quigley (Chair.); Murray Print (Vice-Chair.).

Address: c/o The Center for Civic Education, 5145 Douglas Fir Rd, Calabases, CA 91302-1467.

Telephone: (818) 591-9321; **Fax:** (818) 591-9330; **Internet:** www.civnet.org; **e-mail:** info@civnet.org.

Liz Claiborne and Art Ortenberg Foundation

Founded in 1984 by Arthur Ortenberg and Elizabeth Claiborne Ortenberg to foster natural resource and wildlife conservation and protection.

Activities: The Foundation's main programmes are: the mitigation of conflict between the land and the resource needs of local communities and the preservation of biological diversity; the implementation of scientific, technical and practical conservation of biological diversity in rural landscapes outside parks and reserves; and the implementation of relevant, field-based, scientific, technical and practical training programmes for local people. These programmes operate in the Rocky Mountain region of the USA and in developing countries in Africa, Central and South America and Asia, as well as the Russian Far East.

Geographical Area of Activity: Africa, Central and South America, USA (Rocky Mountains), Asia, and Russian Far East.

Restrictions: No grants are provided for general support for underwriting of overheads.

Principal Staff: Programme Dir Jim Murtaugh.

Address: 650 Fifth Ave, 15th Floor, New York, NY 10019.

Telephone: (212) 333-2536; **Fax:** (212) 956-3531; **Internet:** www.lcaof.org; **e-mail:** lcaof@lcaof.org.

Clean Water Fund—CWF

Established in 1978, it aims to help people campaign for clean, safe water, clean air and protection from pollution everywhere.

Activities: Involved in training, research and education intended to ensure safe drinking water and clean seas. Promotes safe solid waste management, control of workplace and community toxic hazards, conservation of natural resources and protects public health and environmental safety. Builds on and complements the work of Clean Water Action, a 700,000-member national organization that has helped develop, pass, strengthen and defend the nation's major water and toxics laws such as the Clean Water Act, Safe Drinking Water Act, Superfund and others.

Geographical Area of Activity: USA only.

Restrictions: No large grants available.

Publications: Reports; fact sheets.

Finance: Total assets US $2,124,232 (31 Dec. 2010); annual revenue $4,288,445, expenditure $3,824,040 (2010).

Principal Staff: Pres. Peter Lockwood; Exec. Vice-Pres. Robert Wendelgass; Sec. Dianne Akabli; Asst Sec. Kathy Aterno.

Address: 1010 Vermont Ave NW, Suite 400, Washington, DC 20005.

Telephone: (202) 895-0432; **Fax:** (202) 895-0438; **Internet:** www.cleanwaterfund.org; **e-mail:** cwf@cleanwater.org.

Cleveland Foundation

Founded in 1914 by Frederick Harris Goff as the world's first community foundation. The Foundation provides the means through which individuals can contribute most effectively to philanthropies in the Cleveland area, and provides leadership in dealing with community problems.

Activities: Operates principally for the benefit of citizens of the Greater Cleveland community with broad purposes in the fields of economic transformation, public school improvement, youth development, neighbourhoods and arts advancement, through scholarships and grants; grants are made primarily to tax-exempt private agencies, and in some cases to governmental agencies. Also administers the annual Anisfield-Wolf Book Awards, presented to books that address the issue of racism or expand appreciation of human diversity.

Geographical Area of Activity: USA.

Restrictions: No grants for religious purposes, and not normally for endowments, membership drives, fundraising projects, travel, publications and videos.

Publications: *Donor Connections* (quarterly newsletter); *Giving Voice* (quarterly newsletter); annual report; application guidelines; financial statement; informational brochures; information for donors, attorneys and financial planners; grant list.

Finance: Total assets US $1,888,630,534 (31 Dec. 2010); annual revenue $243,064,288, expenditure $114,935,701 (2010).

Board of Directors: Charles Bolton (Chair.); Frank C. Sullivan (Vice-Chair.).

Principal Staff: Pres. and CEO Ronald B. Richard.

Address: 1422 Euclid Ave, Suite 1300, Cleveland, OH 44115.

Telephone: (216) 861-3810; **Fax:** (216) 861-1729; **Internet:** www.clevelandfoundation.org; **e-mail:** contactus@clevefdn.org.

William J. Clinton Foundation

Founded in 2002.

Activities: Operates internationally in the areas of medicine and health (especially in the areas of HIV/AIDS), sustainable development, economic development, and ethnic, racial and religious reconciliation, through carrying out programmes in the USA and world-wide. Maintains offices in New York City, NY, Boston, MA, and Little Rock, AR.

Restrictions: Does not usually make grants to outside organizations.

Finance: Annual revenue US $321,772,692, expenditure $304,282,682 (2010).

Principal Staff: Chief Exec. Bruce R. Lindsey.

Address: 55 West 125th St, New York, NY 10027.

Internet: www.clintonfoundation.org.

The Coca-Cola Foundation, Inc

Founded in 1984 by the Coca-Cola Co to improve the quality of life in the community and support education.

Activities: Gives primarily to initiatives concerned with: HIV/AIDS, water stewardship, education, community recycling and healthy and active lifestyles; also provides emergency relief.

Geographical Area of Activity: International.

Restrictions: No grants are made to individuals.

Publications: Annual Report.

Finance: Total assets US $45,051,312 (31 Dec. 2008); grants disbursed $36,743,015 (2008).

Board of Directors: Ingrid Saunders Jones (Chair.); Gary P. Fayard (Treas.); William Hawkins (Asst Treas.); Melody Justice (Sec.).

Principal Staff: Exec. Dir Helen Smith Price.

Address: 1 Coca-Cola Plaza, Atlanta, GA 30313-2420.

Telephone: (404) 676-2568; **Fax:** (404) 676-8804; **Internet:** www.thecoca-colacompany.com/citizenship/foundation_coke.html; **e-mail:** cocacolacommunityrequest@na.ko.com.

Cogitare Foundation

Founded in 1998 as the Leonard and Charlotte S. Cooper Foundation by Peter Cooper and Elaine Scialo; renamed the Cogitare Foundation in 2000. Aims to provide assistance, mentoring, broad-based financial support, and creative educational and training programmes to the chronically unemployed.

Activities: Operates grant programmes to help the target population to develop the skills, education and training necessary to find meaningful and productive employment, including programmes targeting the under-educated, ill-trained, and unemployed. Currently funds initiatives in Africa. Types of support provided include direct payment of tuition and rent, and assistance in securing financing for self-employment. Maintains an office in Zambia.

Geographical Area of Activity: Africa.

Restrictions: Does not provide assistance to religious organizations.

Board: Randall Cooper (Chair.).

Principal Staff: Pres. Elaine Scialo; Vice-Pres. Peter D. Cooper.

Address: 9 Waccabuc River Lane, South Salem, NY 10590.

Telephone: (212) 362-2136; **Internet:** www.cogitarefoundation.org; **e-mail:** escialo@cogitarefoundation.org.

The Commonwealth Fund

Founded in 1918 by Anna M. Harkness and others to enhance the common good.

Activities: Major programme areas supported are as follows: to improve health insurance coverage and access to medical care; to improve the quality of health-care services; to promote ways for elderly Americans to participate more fully in community life; to develop the capacities of children and young people; and to improve the health of minorities. Also supports related projects in these areas. Promotes innovative health-care policy and practice in the USA and abroad. The Fund operates internationally in the field of education, through the Harkness Fellowships Program, which provides health policy fellowships to potential leaders from Australia, New Zealand and the United Kingdom for study and research in the USA. It also makes grants to enhance the quality of life in New York City.

Geographical Area of Activity: International.

Publications: Annual Report; grants list; newsletters.

Finance: Total assets US $604,524,965 (30 June 2010); annual revenue $7,919,985, expenditure $41,161,876 (2009/10).

Board of Directors: James R. Tallon, Jr (Chair.); Cristine Russell (Vice-Chair.).

Principal Staff: Pres. Karen Davis; Exec. Vice-Pres. and COO John Craig.

Address: 1 E 75th St, New York, NY 10021.

Telephone: (212) 606-3800; **Fax:** (212) 606-3500; **Internet:** www.commonwealthfund.org; **e-mail:** info@cmwf.org.

Compton Foundation, Inc

Founded in 1973 as the successor to the Compton Trust (founded 1946) by members of the Compton family to address community, national and international concerns in the areas of peace and world order, population and the environment.

Activities: Operates nationally and internationally in the fields of peace and world order, family planning, the environment, equal educational opportunity, community welfare and social justice, and culture and the arts.

Geographical Area of Activity: Sub-Saharan Africa, Central America, USA, Mexico.

Restrictions: The Foundation does not make grants to individuals.

Publications: Report (biennially); information brochure.

Finance: Total assets US $68,374,135 (31 Dec. 2010); annual revenue $7,856,161, expenditure $4,886,134 (2010).

Board of Directors: Rebecca DiDomenico (Pres.); Vanessa Compton (Vice-Pres.); W. Danforth Compton (Sec.); Marty Krasney (Treas.).

Principal Staff: Exec. Dir Ellen Friedman; Programme Dir Jennifer L. Sokolove.

Address: 255 Shoreline Dr., Suite 540, Redwood City, CA 94065.

Telephone: (650) 508-1181; **Fax:** (650) 508-1191; **Internet:** www.comptonfoundation.org.

Conservation International

Founded in 1987 for conservation and environmental purposes.

Activities: Active in more than 30 countries; collaborates with governments and other organizations to promote sustained biological diversity and ecosystems and prevent species extinction, along with basic economic and social requirements. Conducts programmes in North, Central and South

America, Africa, Asia and the Pacific; carries out research; promotes educational projects and eco-tourism; researches and markets rain forest products; and assists in the formulation of policy. Grants are made to individuals and to local not-for-profit organizations in all countries or regions that are hot spots or wilderness areas.

Geographical Area of Activity: International.

Publications: include Annual Report and newsletters; *A Climate for Life; A Perfect Storm in the Amazon Wilderness; Lemurs of Madagascar; Consuming Nature*.

Finance: Total assets US $287,281,000 (30 June 2010); annual revenue $140,927,000, expenditure $138,823,000 (2010).

Board of Directors: Peter A. Seligmann (Chair.); Harrison Ford (Vice-Chair.).

Principal Staff: CEO Peter A. Seligmann; Pres. Russell A. Mittermeier.

Address: 2011 Crystal Dr., Suite 500, Arlington, VA 22202.

Telephone: (703) 341-2400; **Internet:** www.conservation.org; **e-mail:** inquiry@conservation.org.

Consuelo Foundation, Inc—CFI

The Foundation, formerly known as the Children and Youth Foundation of the Philippines, was founded through an affiliation agreement between two USA-based organizations, the Consuelo Foundation and the International Youth Foundation (q.v.), which share a common mission to improve the conditions and prospects of youth by fostering their positive development. CFI, like the Consuelo Foundation, has been led by Consuelo Zobel Alger and Patti J. Lyons. In 1995, it became a full subsidiary of the Consuelo Foundation and now oversees children and youth programmes in the Philippines, specifically those below 25 years of age who are victims of abuse and neglect, street children, children of indigenous people, out-of-school youth, child labourers, and those exposed to violence and armed conflict. Also supports programmes on women, families and communities so they may attain dignity, self-esteem and self-sufficiency.

Activities: Together with more than 100 community-based partner organizations, the Foundation works to give hope to young people, supporting programmes for community development, reproductive health, prevention of child sexual exploitation, improvement of the lives of street children and out-of-school youth, promoting juvenile justice and alternative education for children of indigenous people. It also manages a Resource Center and conducts the annual Consuelo Awards to recognize outstanding NGOs in the Philippines that have made a significant difference to the lives of disadvantaged Philippine children, women and families. In Hawaii, promotes community development and self-help projects.

Geographical Area of Activity: Hawaii and the Philippines.

Restrictions: Contracts, financial and technical support are only given to partner organizations, which must maintain excellent levels of organizational and service delivery standards.

Publications: *Building Bridges: The Development of a Leadership Training Program for Indigenous Youth; Looking After Filipino Children: A Compendium of Philippine Laws and Policies on Youth and Children; A Profile Report of Child and Women Abuse in the Province of Albay 1994–1999; On Their Own Behalf: Case Studies of Child and Youth Participation in the Philippines*.

Board of Directors: Jeffrey N. Watanabe (Chair.); Constance H. Lau (Treas.); Patti J. Lyons (Sec.).

Principal Staff: Pres. and CEO Jon Kei Matsuoka; CFO Jonathan San Vuong.

Address: 110 N Hotel St, Honolulu, HI 96817.

Telephone: (808) 532-3939; **Fax:** (808) 532-3930; **Internet:** www.consuelo.org; **e-mail:** info@consuelo.org.

Consultative Group on International Agricultural Research—CGIAR

Founded in 1971 by the International Bank for Reconstruction and Development (World Bank) and other UN agencies to improve the quantity and quality of food in developing countries and eradicate poverty.

Activities: Comprises a network of 15 autonomous international agricultural research centres and organizations in Central and South America, Asia, Africa, the Middle East, Europe and the USA. Research programmes, which focus on increasing productivity, protecting the environment, saving biodiversity, improving policies and strengthening national research. Also makes the biennial King Baudouin Award aimed to recognize and stimulate agricultural research, Third World development and the agricultural production of ordinary farmers.

Geographical Area of Activity: International.

Publications: *CGIAR News*; Annual Report; study papers; research documents; and other publications.

Finance: Annual revenue US $553,000,000, expenditure $542,000,000 (2008).

Fund Council: Rachel Kyte (Chair.).

Principal Staff: Exec. Sec. Jonathan Wadsworth.

Address: The World Bank, MSN G6–601, 1818 H St NW, Washington, DC 20433.

Telephone: (202) 473-8951; **Fax:** (202) 473-8110; **Internet:** www.cgiar.org; **e-mail:** cgiarfund@cgiar.org.

Cottonwood Foundation

Established in 1992 to promote empowerment, cultural diversity, volunteerism, and to protect the environment.

Activities: Supports grassroots organizations in the USA and internationally that empower people to meet their basic needs, promote cultural diversity (including the survival of an endangered or threatened culture), protect the environment, and which rely on volunteer efforts.

Geographical Area of Activity: International.

Restrictions: No funding for political or religious organizations, governmental agencies, for-profit businesses, individuals or universities. Cottonwood Foundation does not typically provide grants for research purposes. Currently provides funding only to a preselected group of Cottonwood Partner organizations.

Publications: Annual Report; newsletter; electronic newsletter.

Finance: Total assets US $84,300 (31 Dec. 2010); annual revenue $33,426 (2010); total grants awarded $42,000 (2010).

Board of Directors: Laura Bray (Chair.), Craig Miller (Vice-Chair.); Prabhakar Karri (Treas.); Jamie Ford (Sec.).

Principal Staff: Exec. Dir Paul Moss.

Address: POB 10803, White Bear Lake, MN 55110.

Telephone: (651) 426-8797; **Fax:** (651) 294-1012; **Internet:** www.cottonwoodfdn.org; **e-mail:** info@cottonwoodfdn.org.

Council on International Educational Exchange—CIEE

Founded in 1947 by organizations active in the field of international education and student travel to improve understanding and co-operation between countries, and help re-establish student exchanges after the Second World War.

Activities: The Council represents educational institutions in developing educational exchange policy, provides consultation services and evaluation of exchange programmes, and acts as a clearing-house for information. Organizes conferences and seminars, and administers Study Abroad Programs in some 35 countries.

Geographical Area of Activity: International.

Publications: *Journal of Studies in International Education* (bi-annual); *Council–ISP News* (monthly newsletter); *Update* (monthly); *Work, Study, Travel Abroad: The Whole World Handbook; Volunteer! The Comprehensive Guide to Voluntary Service* *in the US and Abroad; Going Places; The High School Student's Guide to Study, Travel and Adventure Abroad; Basic Facts on Study Abroad; Where to Stay USA and Smart Vacations: The Traveler's Guide to Learning Adventures Abroad.*

Board of Directors: Robert E. Fallon (Chair.); Kenton Keith (Vice-Chair. and Sec.).

Principal Staff: Pres. and CEO James P. Pellow.

Address: 300 Fore St, Portland, ME 04101.

Telephone: (207) 553-4000; **Fax:** (207) 553-4299; **Internet:** www.ciee.org; **e-mail:** contact@ciee.org.

Council for International Exchange of Scholars— CIES

Founded in 1947 to assist the US Government in administering the Fulbright Scholar Program.

Activities: Aims to increase mutual understanding between the people of the USA and those of other nations; to strengthen the ties that unite the USA with other nations; and promote international co-operation for educational and cultural advancement. Awards about 800 Fulbright Scholar Awards for research and lecturing abroad annually, open to US citizens holding a doctorate or comparable professional qualification, along with university or college teaching experience, for research or teaching in any discipline, in more than 140 countries world-wide. Open also to nationals of those same 140 countries to conduct research or lecture within the USA.

Geographical Area of Activity: International.

Publications: *Fulbright Online Awards Catalog; Fulbright Scholar Program: Grants for Faculty and Professionals;* Annual Report.

Finance: Funded by the US Dept of State, Bureau of Educational and Cultural Affairs.

Address: 1400 K St NW, Suite 700, Washington, DC 20005.

Telephone: (202) 686-4000; **Fax:** (202) 686-4029; **Internet:** www.cies.org; **e-mail:** scholars@iie.org.

Counterpart

Founded in 1965, a diverse, non-profit, international development organization dedicated to helping people in need in the areas of civil society, food security, private enterprise, environmental resource management, humanitarian relief and health care. Counterpart does this by building the capacity of local partner NGOs, lenders, businesses, governments and other institutions to solve their own self-defined economic, ecological, political and social problems in ways that are sustainable, practical and independent.

Geographical Area of Activity: International.

Publications: Annual Report; newsletters.

Board of Directors: Jeffrey T. LaRiche (Chair.).

Principal Staff: Pres. and CEO Joan Parker; Sr Vice-Pres. Tim Ogborn.

Address: 2345 Crystal Dr., Suite 301, Arlington, VA 22202.

Telephone: (703) 236-1200; **Fax:** (703) 412-5035; **Internet:** www.counterpart.org; **e-mail:** communications@counterpart.org.

Covenant Foundation

Established in 1990, by the Crown Family Foundation in partnership with the Jewish Education Service of North America. Aims to build on strengths within the field of Jewish education in North America, and thus perpetuate the identity and cultural heritage of Jewish people.

Activities: Operates in the field of Jewish education in the USA and Canada. Supports innovative programmes in Jewish schools and institutions, and funds creative Jewish educators for the development and implementation of significant and cost-effective approaches to Jewish education. The maximum grant available over five years is US $250,000. Also distributes information about effective programmes through publications and conferences.

Geographical Area of Activity: USA and Canada.

Restrictions: No funding for endowments, building funds or tuition fees.

Publications: *A Covenant of Dreams: Realizing the Promise of Jewish Education; The Covenant Foundation:The First Ten Years 1990–2000.*

Board of Directors: Eli N. Evans (Chair.).

Principal Staff: Exec. Dir Harlene Winnick Appelman; Associate Dir Joni Blinderman.

Address: 1270 Ave of the Americas, Suite 304, New York, NY 10020-1702.

Telephone: (212) 245-3500; **Fax:** (212) 245-0619; **Internet:** www.covenantfn.org; **e-mail:** info@covenantfn.org.

CRDF Global

Established in 1995 by the National Science Foundation (q.v.), and formerly known as the US Civilian Research & Development Foundation, to promote international scientific and technical collaboration.

Activities: The Foundation's vision is to promote peace and prosperity through international science collaboration. The Foundation offers grants, technical resources and training to promote scientific and technical collaboration. Maintains offices in Russia, Ukraine, Kazakhstan and Jordan.

Geographical Area of Activity: International.

Publications: newsletter and fact sheets.

Finance: Net assets US $23,269,022 (31 Dec. 2009); annual revenue $16,882,774, expenditure $23,325,322 (2009).

Board of Directors: Dr William Wulf (Co-Chair.); Dona L. Crawford (Co-Chair.); Dr Rodney Nichols (Sec.); Paul Longsworth (Treas.).

Principal Staff: Pres. and Chief Exec. Cathleen A. Campbell; CFO Stephen Wolk.

Address: 1530 Wilson Blvd, 3rd Floor, Arlington, VA 22209.

Telephone: (703) 526-9720; **Fax:** (703) 526-9721; **Internet:** www.crdf.org; **e-mail:** information@crdf.org.

Creating Hope International—CHI

Founded in 1982; aims to help victims of war, political unrest and natural disasters through grassroots programmes so that they can rebuild their lives for a better future.

Activities: Provides technical and financial assistance to raise the level of education, health and economy throughout parts of the world where people, particularly women and children, are underprivileged, poor, oppressed or generally in need. Fosters world-wide interest in these causes to increase funding for those who lack basic health-care, educational and training opportunities. Currently concentrates on assisting women and children in Afghanistan, through the Afghan Institute of Learning, and Tibetan refugees in India.

Geographical Area of Activity: International, including Afghanistan, Pakistan and Tibet.

Finance: Assets US $900,000 (31 Dec. 2008); annual revenue $869,000 (2008).

Principal Staff: Exec. Dir Toc Dunlap; Vice-Pres. Dr Sakena Yacoobi.

Address: POB 1058, Dearborn, MI 48121.

Telephone: (313) 278-5806; **Internet:** www.creatinghope.org; **e-mail:** chi@creatinghope.org.

Crown Family Philanthropies

The Arie and Ida Crown Memorial was founded in 1947 by members of the Crown family for general charitable purposes. Name changed in 2009.

Activities: Operates primarily in the metropolitan Chicago area, with emphasis on Jewish welfare funds in the fields of social welfare, education, the arts and humanities, health care, community development, inner cities, youth, the elderly and the disabled.

Geographical Area of Activity: USA (Chicago area) and Israel.

Restrictions: No grants are made to individuals; no unsolicited applications accepted.

Finance: Annual revenue US $13,364,253 (loss), expenditure $14,978,079 (2009).

Principal Staff: Exec. Dir Caren Yanis; CFO Aaron Rappaport.

Address: 222 North LaSalle St, Suite 2000, Chicago, IL 60601-1109.

Telephone: (312) 750-6671; **Fax:** (312) 984-1499; **Internet:** www.crownmemorial.org; **e-mail:** aicm@crown-chicago.com.

Cystic Fibrosis Foundation

Established in 1955 to fund research into finding the means to cure and control systic fibrosis, and to assist those with the disease.

Activities: The Foundation funds research into cystic fibrosis, care centres for those with cystic fibrosis, and adult care programmes. There are more than 75 chapters and branch offices in the USA.

Geographical Area of Activity: USA.

Finance: Total assets US $272,534,810 (31 Dec. 2010); annual revenue $313,308,873, expenditure $261,300,507 (2010).

Board: Catherine C. McLoud (Chair.).

Principal Staff: Pres. and Chief Exec. Robert J. Beall.

Address: 6931 Arlington Rd, 2nd Floor, Bethesda, MD 20814.

Telephone: (301) 951-4422; **Fax:** (301) 951-6378; **Internet:** www.cff.org; **e-mail:** info@cff.org.

The Baron de Hirsch Fund

Founded in 1891 by Baron Maurice De Hirsch and Baroness Clara De Hirsch to assist in the economic assimilation of Jewish immigrants in the USA and Israel, and in providing them with vocational training in trade and agriculture.

Activities: Makes grants, primarily in the New York area and Israel, for the above purposes, and assists agencies helping to obtain education and employment for immigrants. Awards fellowships to Israeli agriculturalists.

Geographical Area of Activity: USA and Israel.

Finance: Total assets US $5,101,155 (30 June 2010); total giving $309,500 (2009/10).

Board of Trustees: Roni Rubenstein (Pres.); Ellen Merlo (Vice-Pres.); Stanley Baumblatt (Sec. and Treas.).

Principal Staff: Man. Dir Lauren Katzowitz Shenfield.

Address: 130 East 59th St, 12th Floor, New York, NY 10022-1302.

Telephone: (212) 836-1358; **Fax:** (212) 453-6512.

Charles Delmar Foundation

Founded in 1957 by Charles Delmar for general charitable purposes to be undertaken mainly in the Washington area and in Puerto Rico and Central and South America.

Activities: Operates nationally and internationally in the fields of education and social welfare, with emphasis on inter-American studies, higher education, literacy, the arts, hospitals, and youth and child welfare agencies.

Geographical Area of Activity: Central and South America, USA, India.

Restrictions: No grants are made to individuals.

Finance: Total aasets US $6,601,078 (31 Dec. 2009); annual revenue $25,884 (loss), expenditure $437,945 (2009).

Trustees: Mareen D. Hughes (Pres.); R. Bruce Hughes (Vice-Pres., Sec. and Treas.); Christopher Braddock (Asst Treas.).

Address: c/o Mareen Hughes, POB 1501, Pennington, NJ 08534-0671.

Arthur S. DeMoss Foundation

Founded in 1955 as the National Liberty Foundation of Valley Forge Inc to provide support for Christian agency and Church programmes in the USA and abroad, mainly in developing countries.

Activities: Offers financial support to set up and run Christian evangelical programmes in the USA and in developing countries; operates a fund matching programme.

Geographical Area of Activity: International.

Finance: Total assets US $243,731,792; total giving $27,625,178 (Dec. 2008).

Board of Directors: Nancy S. DeMoss (Chair.); Robert G. DeMoss (Pres., Sec. and Treas.); Charlotte A. DeMoss (Sec.).

Principal Staff: CFO Larry R. Nelson; Exec. Dir Ken Fuller.

Address: Phillips Point-W. Twr., 777 South Flagler Dr., Suite 1600W, West Palm Beach, FL 33401-6158.

Telephone: (561) 804-9000.

Deutsche Bank Americas Foundation and Community Development Group

The Foundation, formerly known by the name BT Foundation, was set up to realize the philanthropic aims of Deutsche Bank in Canada, South and Central America and the USA.

Activities: Is active all over America focusing on promoting education, arts and culture and community development by providing grants to local organizations in whose collaboration the Foundation works.

Geographical Area of Activity: Canada, Central and South America, USA.

Publications: Annual Report; guidelines; *Community Focus* (newsletter).

Finance: Over US $19,000,000 in grants disbursed (2009).

Trustees: Seth Waugh (Chair.).

Principal Staff: Pres. Gary Hattem.

Address: 60 Wall St, NYC60–2112, New York, NY 10005.

Telephone: (212) 250-0539; **Fax:** (212) 797-2255.

Development Gateway—DG

Development Gateway was established in 2001 in partnership with the International Bank for Reconstruction and Development (World Bank). DG is an international non-profit organization with dual expertise in information solutions and international development. To contribute to increased transparency and better governance, DG designs and provides information management solutions to manage aid more effectively, facilitate the interactive exchange of information and good practice, and improve tendering.

Activities: Development Gateway's global team of experts creates cost-effective Web-based information systems to enhance decision-making at the local, national and international level. DG's custom-designed aid management systems and services have been deployed world-wide, creating sustainable solutions by enhancing local capacity and leveraging a strong user network. DG's programmes include: the Aid Management Platform (AMP), a web-based software that enables recipient governments to manage foreign aid flows; AidData, an online portal for information on development finance; Zunia, an online platform for knowledge-exchange between development actors; dgMarket, an online tender information service; and Country Gateways, locally owned public-private partnerships that facilitate access to and use of ICT. DG also provides consulting services, and partners with development actors to generate custom technology solutions tailored to unique needs and problems.

Geographical Area of Activity: International.

Publications: DG Newsletter (quarterly); Annual Report.

Finance: Total assets US $5,037,000 (30 June 2010); annual revenue $7,765,000, expenditure $7,543,000 (2009/10).

Board of Directors: Mary O'Kane (Chair.).

Principal Staff: CEO Jean-Louis Sarbib; CFO Jennifer Cumiskey.

Address: 1889 F St, NW, 2nd Floor, Washington, DC 20006.

Telephone: (202) 572-9200; **Fax:** (202) 572-9290; **Internet:** www.developmentgateway.org; **e-mail:** info@developmentgateway.org.

Cleveland H. Dodge Foundation, Inc

Founded in 1917 by Cleveland H. Dodge to promote the well-being of mankind throughout the world.

Activities: Makes grants to selected international organizations active in the Middle East, to selected national agencies in the USA, and to organizations based in New York City. Grants in the USA are mainly for education, youth programmes, child welfare and cultural programmes.

Geographical Area of Activity: USA and the Middle East.

Restrictions: No grants are made to individuals.

Publications: Annual Report; programme policy statement.

Finance: Grants expenditure US $1,270,253 (2010).

Board of Directors: William D. Rueckert (Pres.); Bayard Dodge (Vice-Pres.); Louis E. Black (Sec.); Phyllis Criscuoli (Treas.).

Principal Staff: Exec. Dir Phyllis Criscuoli.

Address: 420 Lexington Ave, Suite 2331, New York, NY 10170.

Telephone: (212) 972-2800; **Fax:** (212) 972-1049; **Internet:** www.chdodgefoundation.org; **e-mail:** info@chdodgefoundation.org.

The William H. Donner Foundation, Inc

Founded in 1961 with funds originally donated by William Donner, the Foundation supports programmes concerned with US-Canadian affairs, international relations, education and public policy.

Activities: Operates nationally, through funding programmes to support the growth of undergraduate and graduate studies programmes in Canadian affairs at US universities; and to support experimental grants in fields such as education and public affairs.

Geographical Area of Activity: USA and Canada.

Restrictions: Does not accept or acknowledge unsolicited proposals for grants.

Publications: Annual Report.

Board: M. Hunter Spencer (Pres.); Timothy E. Donner (Vice-Pres. and Asst Treas.); Cristina Winsor (Sec.); Joseph W. Donner, III (Treas.).

Address: 60 East 42nd St, Suite 1560, New York, NY 10165.

Telephone: (212) 949-0404; **Fax:** (212) 949-6022; **Internet:** www.donner.org; **e-mail:** dfeeney@donner.org.

The Camille and Henry Dreyfus Foundation, Inc

Founded in 1946 by Camille E. Dreyfus to advance the sciences of chemistry, biochemistry, chemical engineering and related sciences as a means of improving human relations and circumstances throughout the world.

Activities: Assists academic institutions in fostering fundamental research and in training students for graduate study for the doctoral degree in chemistry. Other qualifying organizations, such as research institutes with similar goals, are also eligible for grant consideration. Sponsors the Post-doctoral Program in Environmental Chemistry, the Dreyfus Teacher-Scholar Awards Program, the Dreyfus Prize in the Chemical Sciences and the Special Grant Program in the Chemical Sciences. Also sponsors the ACS Awards administered by the American Chemical Society: the ACS Award for Encouraging Women into Careers in the Chemical Sciences and the ACS Award for Encouraging Disadvantaged Students into Careers in the Chemical Sciences.

Geographical Area of Activity: USA.

Restrictions: Grants are not made to individuals.

Publications: Annual Report; programme brochures.

Board of Directors: Henry C. Walter (Pres.); Dorothy Dinsmoor (Vice-Pres. and Sec.); John R. H. Blum (Treas.).

Principal Staff: Exec. Dir Mark J. Cardillo; Operations Man. Adam J. Lore.

Address: 555 Madison Ave, 20th Floor, New York, NY 10022-3301.

Telephone: (212) 753-1760; **Fax:** (212) 593-2256; **Internet:** www.dreyfus.org; **e-mail:** admin@dreyfus.org.

Dreyfus Health Foundation—DHF

Founded in 1965 as the Dreyfus Medical Foundation, renamed in 1988; it is a division of The Rogosin Institute, an independent, non-profit institution for scientific and medical research, treatment and education, which is affiliated with Cornell University Medical College and New York Presbyterian Hospital; the Foundation aims for better health world-wide through the optimization of the use of available resources.

Activities: Operates in Africa, Asia, Central and Eastern Europe, South America, Central America and the Caribbean, the Middle East and North America, supporting innovative scientific and health projects through its own programmes and through funding special projects. The Foundation operates through the following programmes: Problem Solving for Better Health, which aims to improve health at the local level and promote an international exchange of ideas; Problem Solving for Better Health—Nursing, raising the role of the nurse in global health provision; and Communications for Better Health, disseminating information through the Internet and CD-ROMs. Also maintains a workshop and project database.

Geographical Area of Activity: Africa, North, Central and South America, Asia, the Caribbean, Central and Eastern Europe and the Middle East.

Publications: Annual report; *Connections* (newsletter); health database; articles; special publications.

Board of Directors: Sidney R. Knafel (Chair.).

Principal Staff: Dir Barry H. Smith.

Address: 205 E 64th St, Suite 404, New York, NY 10065.

Telephone: (212) 750-5075; **Fax:** (212) 371-2776; **Internet:** www.dhfglobal.org; **e-mail:** info@dhfglobal.org.

Drug Policy Alliance—DPA

DPA was a result of the merger that took place in 2000, between the Lindesmith Center, a drug policy think tank set up in 1994 by Ethan Nadelmann, and Drug Policy Foundation, a grant-making and membership organization launched in 1987. DPA works towards promoting drug policy reforms in political discourse as well as the mainstream public.

Activities: Provides research fellowships and grants; analyses government drug policies and their ramifications; maintains an information center and a library; promotes reforms in drug policies; and conducts conference and seminars on topics of interest; is associated with the Open Society Institute's programme—International Harm Reduction Development which is aimed at reducing individual and social damage consequent to the use of drugs in the former USSR and Eastern Europe by offering grants to projects working on alleviation of drug impact.

Geographical Area of Activity: USA, Eastern Europe and the countries of the former USSR.

Publications: Journal articles; reports; testimonies; fact sheets; working papers; bibilographies; research briefs and monographs.

Finance: Annual revenue US $8,937,453, expenditure $8,364,938 (2010).

Board of Directors: Ira Glasser (Pres.); Richard B. Wolf (Treas.); Rev. Edwin Sanders (Sec.).

Principal Staff: Founder and Exec. Dir Ethan Nadelmann.

Address: 70 W 36th St, 16th Floor, New York, NY 10018.

Telephone: (212) 613-8020; **Fax:** (212) 613-8021; **Internet:** www.drugpolicy.org; **e-mail:** nyc@drugpolicy.org.

Duke Endowment

Founded in 1924 by James B. Duke to provide in some measure for the physical, mental and spiritual needs of mankind.

Activities: Operates four grant programmes in North and South Carolina: supporting education, health care, child care and rural church initiatives.

Geographical Area of Activity: USA (North and South Carolina).

Restrictions: No awards are made outside the states of North and South Carolina or outside the four established grant programmes.

Publications: *Issues* (newsletter); Annual Report; reports on foundation programmes; *Guidelines for Environmentally Friendly Structures; The Indenture of Trust; A New Effort.*

Finance: Total assets US $2,700,000,000 (31 Dec. 2010); annual revenue $929,396,136, expenditure $19,585,736 (2008).

Trustees: L. Neil Williams (Chair.); Mary D. T. Jones (Vice-Chair.); Minor M. Shaw (Vice-Chair.).

Principal Staff: Pres. Eugene W. Cochrane, Jr; Gen. Counsel Arthur E. Morehead IV.

Address: 100 North Tryon St, Suite 3500, Charlotte, NC 28202-4012.

Telephone: (704) 376-0291; **Fax:** (704) 376-9336; **Internet:** www.dukeendowment.org.

Dumbarton Oaks

Founded in 1940 by Mr and Mrs Robert Woods Bliss to promote research and study in the areas of Byzantine, Pre-Columbian and garden and landscape studies.

Activities: The Dumbarton Oaks Research Library and Collection houses important research and study collections in the above three fields. It offers residential summer fellowships, as well as one-year junior and post-doctoral fellowships. Dumbarton Oaks also makes grants to assist scholarly projects in the three fields with which it is concerned, and organizes conferences and symposia.

Geographical Area of Activity: USA and Canada.

Restrictions: Grants are limited to applicants holding a doctorate or the equivalent for research purposes or to fund a suitable project. Grants are not normally made for the purchase of computers or the salary of the principal investigator.

Publications: *Lighting in Early Byzantium; Three Byzantine Military Treatises; Byzantine Magic; Dumbarton Oaks Papers 61; Gardens and Imagination: Cultural History and Agency; Gardens, City Life and Culture: A World Tour; Palace of the Ancient New World; Script and Glyph: Pre-Hispanic History, Colonial Bookmaking, and the Historia Tolteca-Chichimeca.*

Trustees: Drew Gilpin Faust (Pres.); James F. Rothenberg (Treas.).

Principal Staff: Dir Jan M. Ziolkowski; Exec. Dir Yota Batsaki.

Address: 1703 32nd St NW, Washington, DC 20007.

Telephone: (202) 339-6401; **Fax:** (202) 339-6419; **Internet:** www.doaks.org; **e-mail:** museum@doaks.org.

Earhart Foundation

Founded in 1929 by Harry Boyd Earhart to support education and research.

Activities: The Foundation awards fellowships and grants for graduate study and research in the fields of history, economics, political science and international affairs. Grants are made to individuals and institutions.

Geographical Area of Activity: World-wide.

Restrictions: Not for general operating support, endowment or building programmes.

Publications: Annual Report.

Finance: Total assets US $35,723,529 (31 Dec. 2009); annual revenue $671,636, expenditure $6,154,181 (2009).

Board of Trustees: Dennis L. Bark (Chair.); John. H. Moore (Vice-Chair.); Montgomery B. Brown (Sec.); Kathleen B. Mason (Treas.).

Principal Staff: Pres. Ingrid Ann Gregg.

Address: 2200 Green Rd, Suite H, Ann Arbor, MI 48105-1569.

Telephone: (734) 761-8592; **Fax:** (734) 761-2722.

Earth Island Institute—EII

Established in 1982 by David Brower to develop conservation and environment projects.

Activities: Operates in the field of conservation, preservation and restoration of the environment, by promoting citizen action and incubating a diverse group of global projects. Provides mentoring, training and support for more than 40 projects doing work in more than 25 countries including Borneo, Russia, Taiwan and the USA. Supported projects include Baikal Watch; Bay Area Wilderness Training; the Fiji Organic Project; the International Marine Mammal Project; Global Services Corps; Reef Protection International; SAVE International and the Tibetan Plateau Project.

Geographical Area of Activity: International.

Publications: *Earth Island Journal;* Annual Report; *Island-Wire; Borneo Wire; ECO; Global Service Corps; INLAKECH!; Kids for the Bay; Late Friday* (newsletter); electronic publications.

Finance: Annual revenue US $11,297,096, expenditure $9,720,221 (2009).

Board of Directors: Martha Davis (Pres.); Kenneth Brower (Vice-Pres.); Michael Hathaway (Vice-Pres.); Jennifer Snyder (Sec.); Alex Geidt (Treas.).

Principal Staff: Exec. Dirs John A. Knox, Dave Phillips.

Address: 2150 Allston Way, Suite 460, Berkeley, CA 94704-1375.

Telephone: (510) 859-9100; **Fax:** (510) 859-9091; **Internet:** www.earthisland.org; **e-mail:** erin@earthisland.org.

Earthrights International—ERI

ERI was founded in 1995 along the Thai–Myanmar border, with a focus on using innovative legal strategies and mechanisms to bring justice to indigenous Myanmar communities abused by the military regime and its corporate partners in the name of development.

Activities: ERI both represents and partners with individuals and communities around the world that are victims, survivors, or at risk of human rights and environmental abuses which occur during natural resource extraction projects such as oil and gas development, water diversion projects, logging and mining. ERI uses legal actions, campaigns and training initiatives to fight earth rights abusers and change the way that governments and corporations conduct business. ERI has pioneered corporate accountability litigation in US courts, winning landmark judgments and successful settlements, most notably in its actions against Unocal and Shell. It also advocates for strong domestic and international legal mechanisms for corporate accountability. ERI's Advocacy and Campaigns programme uses media, public education and organizing strategies to hold corporate and government human rights and environmental offenders accountable in the 'court of public opinion'. Its goal is to build a broad constituency for the earth and its peoples, who will ensure that there are strong mechanisms for accountability with regard to human rights and environmental abuses, and to deter such abuses by highlighting the heavy costs associated with such violations. ERI's EarthRights Schools and training programmes equip the next generation of grassroots human rights and environmental defenders with the necessary skills, knowledge and networks to protect their rights and homelands. ERI has two EarthRights Schools and a Regional Legal Training Program and Mekong Legal Advocacy Institute.

Geographical Area of Activity: South-East Asia, South America and the USA.

Publications: publications include: *Gaining Ground: Earth Rights Abuses in Burma Exposed*; *Litigation Manual* (2nd edn); *Oil Impacts in the Territory of the Native Communities of Peru*; *Flooding the Future: Hydropower and Cultural Survival in the Salween River Basin*; *If We Dont Have Time to Take Care of Our Fields Our Rice Will Die*; *Shock and Law: George W. Bush's Attack on Law and Universal Human Rights*.

Finance: Funded by private foundations and individuals. Total assets US \$4,664,210 (31 Jan. 2011); annual revenue \$2,555,616, expenditure \$1,741,651 (2010/11).

Board of Directors: Neil Popovic (Co-Chair.); Rebecca Rockefeller (Co-Chair.).

Principal Staff: Co-Founder and Exec. Dir Ka Hsaw Wa; Man. Dir Marie Soveroski.

Address: 1612 K St NW, Suite 401, Washington, DC 20006.

Telephone: (202) 466-5188; **Fax:** (202) 466-5189; **Internet:** www.earthrights.org; **e-mail:** infousa@earthrights.org.

Earthtrust, Inc

Established in 1976 by Don White.

Activities: Conservation organization dedicated to the preservation of wildlife and the natural environment. Organizes international campaigns against whaling and damage to dolphin stocks through the use of drift nets. Other initiatives include the Endangered Wildlife Initiative, Dolphin Cognition Research and the Saving Whales with DNA Project. The organization is also involved in research and environmental education. Founding member of the Flipper Foundation.

Geographical Area of Activity: World-wide.

Publications: Annual Report; newsletter.

Advisory Board: Lloyd Bridges (Hon. Pres.).

Principal Staff: Pres. Don White.

Address: Windward Environmental Center, 1118 Maunawili Rd, Kailua, HI 96734.

Telephone: (808) 261-5339; **Fax:** (206) 202-3893; **Internet:** www.earthtrust.org; **e-mail:** info@earthtrust.us.

East-West Center—EWC

Founded in 1960 by the US Congress with a mandate 'to promote better relations and understanding between the USA and the nations of Asia and Pacific through co-operative study, training and research' the Center is a public, non-profit national and international research and education institution. The Center for Cultural and Technical Interchange between East and West is commonly known as the East-West Center.

Activities: The Center receives most of its financial support from the US Congress, but there are also contributions from Asian and Pacific governments, as well as from private agencies and corporations. Its staff regularly co-operate in study, research and training with research fellows, graduates and professionals in business and government in the areas of economic change, international co-operation, national economic development strategies, energy policy, politics and security, environmental issues, behaviour and health and Pacific islands development. Its facilities include administrative and research offices, three residential halls and an international conference centre equipped for simultaneous translation; maintains office in Washington, DC.

Geographical Area of Activity: South-East, East and Southern Asia, the Pacific and USA.

Restrictions: Grants only for degree and non-degree scholarships, workshop participants and visiting fellowships.

Publications: Annual Report; *International Production Networks in Asia: Rivalry or Riches?*; *Regional Dynamics and Future US Policy*; *Population Aging Raises Questions for Policymakers*; *AsiaPacific Issues*; *Asia-Pacific Population and Policy*; *East-West Center Observer* (quarterly newsletter); conference proceedings.

Finance: Receives funding from US Government, foundations, Asian and Pacific governments. Total assets US \$39,486,734 (30 Sept. 2010); annual revenue \$34,845,184, expenditure 33,487,276 (2009/10).

Board of Governors: Puongpun Sananikone (Chair.); Ricky Kubota (Treas.); Carleen G. Gumapac (Sec.).

Principal Staff: Pres. Dr Charles E. Morrison.

Address: 1601 East-West Rd, Honolulu, HI 96848.

Telephone: (808) 944-7111; **Fax:** (808) 944-7376; **Internet:** www.eastwestcenter.org; **e-mail:** fellowships@eastwestcenter.org.

Easter Island Foundation

Established in 1989 to promote the conservation and protection of the cultural heritage of Easter Island.

Activities: Created and helps to support the William Mulloy Library on Easter Island (Rapa Nui). Provides scholarships to academically promising students of Rapanui ancestry (under 30 years of age) for further education. Publishes books and a bi-annual journal and sponsors conferences on Easter Island and the Pacific. Assists with educational, archaeological and environmental research projects on Easter Island.

Geographical Area of Activity: Easter Island and Polynesia.

Publications: *Rapa Nui Journal*; series of books about Easter Island and other Polynesian islands.

Board of Directors: David Rose (Pres.); Kay Sanger (Vice-Pres.); Michael Chamberlain (Treas.); Elaine Dvorak (Sec.).

Address: POB 6774, Los Osos, CA 93412.

Telephone: (805) 528-8558; **Fax:** (805) 534-9301; **Internet:** www.islandheritage.org; **e-mail:** books@islandheritage.org.

eBay Foundation

Founded in 1998 to contribute to the economic and social well-being of local communities.

Activities: Makes grants to non-profit organizations and NGOs that strengthen the local communities where eBay employees live and work. Strategic grants have a focus in fostering economic opportunity.

Geographical Area of Activity: USA and international.

Restrictions: No grants for fundraising events; advertising; government agencies; sponsorships; individuals; organizations with a limited constituency (such as fraternities or veterans' groups); organizations that limit their services to members of one religious group; political organizations.

Finance: Annual revenue US \$1,384,151 (loss), expenditure \$2,621,855 (2009).

Board of Directors: Bill Barmeier (Chair.); Amyn Thawer (Sec.).

Principal Staff: Pres. Lauren Moore; CEO and Exec. Dir Irene Wong.

Address: 2440 W El Camino Real, No. 300, Mountain View, CA 94040.

Telephone: (650) 450-5400; **Internet:** www.ebayinc.com/profile/ebay_foundation; **e-mail:** ebayfdn@cfsv.org.

EcoHealth Alliance

Wildlife Trust was founded in 1971 by British naturalist Gerald M. Durrell, as a sister organization to the Jersey Wildlife Preservation Trust (now the Durrell Wildlife Conservation Trust); formerly known as Wildlife Preservation Trust International. Aims to protect endangered species, promote conservation and training for local scientists, and promote the development of conservation organizations. Adopted present name in 2010.

Activities: Makes grants to around 65 environmental projects in more than 20 countries in North, Central and South America and the Caribbean, Africa and Asia. Supports research in the field of captive breeding of endangered species, the reintroduction of captive-bred animals to the wild, conservation, and associated environmental education programmes. The Trust aims to train local conservation professionals. Jointly administers the Gerald Durrell Memorial Funds in conjunction with the Durrell Wildlife Conservation Trust and the Wildlife Preservation Trust Canada, supporting endangered species conservation projects by International Conservation Center graduates. Also makes small grants through the Species Survival Fund. Edge of the Sea Aquatic Conservation Program based in St Petersburg, Florida.

Geographical Area of Activity: North, Central and South America, the Caribbean, Africa and Asia.

Publications: *EcoHealth Journal*; *Wildlife Trust Magazine*; *Conservation Medicine-Ecological Health in Practice*; *Wildlife Trust* (e-newsletter); *Edge of the Sea* (brochure).

Board of Directors: Sandra E. Peterson (Chair.); Allen J. Model, Cynthia R. Stebbins (Vice-Chair.); Robert Hoguet (Treas.); Victoria Mars (Sec.).

Principal Staff: Pres. Peter Daszak.

Address: 460 W 34th St, 17th Floor, New York NY 10001-2320.

Telephone: (212) 380-4460; **Fax:** (212) 380-4465; **Internet:** www.ecohealthalliance.org; **e-mail:** homeoffice@ ecohealthalliance.org.

ECOLOGIA—Ecologists Linked for Organizing Grassroots Initiatives and Action

Founded in 1989, aims to provide technical advice and assistance in ecological matters to grassroots groups in Eastern Europe and the USSR.

Activities: Operates in the field of conservation and the environment by working with local environmental groups in the countries of the former USSR and Eastern Europe, providing training, information and technical assistance. Promotes the development of democratic and informed decision-making skills on environmental matters. Established the Virtual Foundation (q.v.), which supports grassroots community-based initiatives and provides funding support to organizations in the countries of the former USSR and Eastern Europe where ECOLOGIA acts as a full partner. Has extended its activities to China where it operates a number of programmes to promote sustainable development among local communities. Maintains offices in Moscow and Chengd.

Geographical Area of Activity: Eastern Europe and the People's Republic of China.

Restrictions: No grants to independent organizations or individuals except via the Virtual Foundation.

Board of Directors: Randy Kritkausky (Pres.); Carolyn Schmidt (Sec.); Ed Shoener (Treas.).

Address: POB 268, Middlebury, VT 05753.

Telephone: (802) 623-8075; **Fax:** (802) 623-8075; **Internet:** www.ecologia.org; **e-mail:** ecologia@ecologia.org.

Albert Einstein Institution

Founded in 1983 to promote the strategic use and study of non-violence as a means of achieving effective results in international conflicts and struggles.

Activities: Promotes the use of non-violent solutions to conflicts throughout the world. The Institute also advances the study of non-violence as a means of defending democratic freedoms and institutions, examining the past use of non-violent action and dedicating itself to finding how peace, freedom and justice can be achieved without the need for violence and war. It communicates the results of its research to the general public through the media, conferences and its own publications as well as running a policy and outreach programme advising groups involved in conflict about the potential effectiveness of non-violent action, through courses, workshops, consultations and dissemination of written materials.

Geographical Area of Activity: International.

Publications: Annual Report; *Nonviolent Action* (newsletter); monographs and handouts; papers, reports and publications on non-violent action.

Board: Cornelia Sargent (Chair.).

Principal Staff: Exec. Dir Jamila Raqib.

Address: POB 455, East Boston, MA 02128.

Telephone: (617) 247-4882; **Fax:** (617) 247-4035; **Internet:** www.aeinstein.org; **e-mail:** einstein@igc.org.

endPoverty.org

Established in 1985, Enterprise Development International, now endPoverty.org, is a faith-based organization dedicated to enabling the working poor in the developing world to lift themselves out of poverty.

Activities: Provides small loans to poor entrepreneurs with limited access to capital. Offers vocational training to individuals in impoverished communities expressing a desire to start and maintain their own businesses. Provides ongoing mentorship and community support networks to borrowers to help ensure their micro-business success and personal growth. Closely partnered with local microfinance and development institutions in 12 countries in Africa, Asia, South America and Eastern Europe.

Geographical Area of Activity: International.

Publications: Annual Report.

Finance: Annual revenue US $715,714, expenditure $784,778 (2009).

Board of Directors: Larry Roadman (Chair.); Laura Kent (Vice-Chair.); Charles W. Seale (Vice-Chair.); C. W. Gardner (Treas.); Colby M. May (Sec.).

Principal Staff: Interim Exec. Dir Larry Roadman.

Address: 7910 Woodmont Ave, Suite 800, Bethesda, MD 20814.

Telephone: (240) 396-1146; **Fax:** (240) 235-3550; **Internet:** www.endpoverty.org; **e-mail:** for-more-info@endpoverty .org.

EngenderHealth

Established in 1943 as a non-profit organization that aims to improve reproductive health services around the world and make them safe, reliable and available to everyone; known as AVSC International until March 2001.

Activities: Works in more than 20 countries in the area of health, improving family planning and reproductive health care, working with governments, health institutions and clinic staff to develop services where none currently exist, and improving care in already existing facilities. This is done through technical assistance and training; running training seminars and providing on-site help for health-care workers on safe medical techniques; management and supervision; research on family planning issues and attitudes; and through publications that make technical reference material and information accessible to those working in the area of reproductive health. The organization is also involved in women's general health care, including HIV/AIDS issues and maternity services.

Geographical Area of Activity: World-wide.

Publications: *EngenderHealth Update* (quarterly newsletter); *EngenderHealth Connect* (monthly electronic newsletter); *Client-Education Materials*; *Counselling, Informed Choice, and Informed Consent*; *Medical and Surgical Guidelines*; *Service Management/Quality of Care*; *About EngenderHealth*; Annual Report.

Finance: Annual revenue US $63,203,341, expenditure $62,342,293 (2009/10).

Board of Directors: Brenda J. Drake (Chair.); Cecily C. Williams (Interim Chair.); Janice Hansen Zakin (Vice-Chair.); Mary K. Stevens (Asst Sec.); Donald J. Abrams (Treas.); Robert D. Petty (Asst Treas.).

Principal Staff: Pres. and CEO Pamela W. Barnes; COO Daniel Doucette.

Address: 440 Ninth Ave, New York, NY 10001.

Telephone: (212) 561-8000; **Fax:** (212) 561-8067; **Internet:** www.engenderhealth.org; **e-mail:** info@engenderhealth.org.

EnterpriseWorks/VITA—EWV

Non-profit organization, formerly known as Appropriate Technology International, which aims to provide economic opportunity for all as a long-term solution to poverty in the developing world.

Activities: Operates in the field of economic development in more than 60 countries in Africa, Asia, and Central and South America, supporting small businesses to increase the earning power, income and quality of life of the world's 2,000m. small producers, with the aim of breaking the poverty cycle and enabling the underprivileged to provide their families with a better quality of life. EnterpriseWorks focuses on producers in the areas of small-scale irrigation, energy, oil-seeds and staple foods, tree crops, dairy and other livestock, and natural products. Merged with Relief International in 2009.

Geographical Area of Activity: World-wide.

Publications: e-newsletter; various manuals and proceedings.

Board of Directors: Simon Goodall (Chair.).

Principal Staff: Pres. Dr Farshad Rastegar.

Address: 1100 H St, NW, Suite 1200, Washington, DC 20005.

Telephone: (202) 639-8660; **Fax:** (202) 639-8664; **Internet:** www.enterpriseworks.org; **e-mail:** info@enterpriseworks.org.

Epilepsy Foundation

Founded in 1968 by merger of the Epilepsy Foundation (founded in 1954) and the Epilepsy Association of America (founded in 1965) as the national, voluntary health organization for the prevention and cure of seizure disorders, the alleviation of their effects, and improvement of the quality of life for people who have these disorders.

Activities: Operates mainly nationally in the field of medicine and health; conducts and supports research, awards fellowships for research and exchange of expertise (including the Fritz E. Dreyfuss International Travel Program); supports training programmes for sufferers from epilepsy; holds conferences; and disseminates information through its publications.

Geographical Area of Activity: Mainly USA.

Publications: Annual Report; *Between Us* (quarterly); *Epilepsy USA* (2 a month and online newsletter); *Kids News* (quarterly); brochures and specialist publications.

Board of Directors: Brien J. Smith (Chair.); Louis Testoni (Sr Vice-Chair.); Julie DesJardins (Treas.); Robert Pinkerton (Sec.).

Principal Staff: Pres. and CEO Richard P. Denness; Exec. Vice-Pres. Sandy Finucane.

Address: 8301 Professional Pl., Landover, MD 20785.

Telephone: (301) 459-3700; **Fax:** (301) 577-2684; **Internet:** www.epilepsyfoundation.org; **e-mail:** info@efa.org.

Esperança, Inc

Founded in 1970 to support the work of Fr Luke Tupper. The organization aims to provide adequate health care for children around the world.

Activities: Operates in the field of medicine and health in developing countries, working to improve health care, particularly focusing on reducing child mortality. Currently runs projects in Bolivia, Nicaragua and the USA, including training doctors and nurses so as to improve the quality of health services, informing mothers on disease-prevention methods, and funding health education.

Geographical Area of Activity: USA, Africa, Central and South America.

Restrictions: No grants available.

Publications: Annual Report; newsletters.

Finance: Total assets US $3,013,743 (30 Sept. 2011); annual revenue $5,066,279, expenditure $5,086,039 (2010/11).

Board of Directors: Sandra Erickson (Chair.); Rosary Hernandez (Vice-Chair.); Jerry Morgan (Sec.); Charlie Broucek (Treas.).

Principal Staff: Pres. and CEO Tom Egan; Finance and Admin. Dir Kevin Benney.

Address: 1911 West Earll Dr., Phoenix, AZ 85015.

Telephone: (602) 252-7772; **Fax:** (602) 340-9197; **Internet:** www.esperanca.org; **e-mail:** info@esperanca.org.

Etruscan Foundation

Founded in 1958 to support the work of students and scholars interested in classical archaeology, especially the history of ancient Etruscan civilization, and the preservation of the natural and cultural heritage of Tuscany, ancient land of the Etruscans.

Activities: The Foundation provides annual fellowships for conservation, fieldwork and research activities at Etruscan sites across Italy. The Cinelli Lecture Series provides annual lecture programmes on Etruscan and Italic archaeology through the Archaeological Institute of America. Etruscan Studies: Journal of the Etruscan Foundation is the leading scholarly publication on Etruscology and related disciplines in the English language.

Geographical Area of Activity: USA and Italy.

Publications: *Etruscan Studies: Journal of the Etruscan Foundation.*

Board of Directors: Kenneth B. Katz (Pres.); Elizabeth Renick Bracher (Sec.); Peter Cinelli (Treas.).

Principal Staff: Exec. Dir Richard String.

Address: POB 26, Fremont, MI 49412.

Telephone: (231) 519-0675; **Fax:** (231) 924-0777; **Internet:** www.etruscanfoundation.org; **e-mail:** office@etruscanfoundation.org.

Eurasia Foundation

Founded in 1992 with funds from the US Agency for International Development (USAID) to promote the advancement of democratic institutions and private enterprise in the countries of the former USSR.

Activities: Created to empower the people of the former USSR to guide the social and economic development of their countries. Since 2004, Eurasia Foundation has evolved from a US-based foundation with multiple field offices into the Eurasia Foundation Network – a constellation of affiliated, locally registered foundations in Russia, Central Asia, the South Caucasus, Ukraine and Moldova that works in partnership with the US foundation. Today, the Eurasia Foundation Network promotes stability and prosperity throughout the region by supporting institutions that advance open, pluralistic and entrepreneurial societies. Its programmes harness the energy and aspirations of ordinary citizens seeking to improve schools, businesses and government in their communities. Working with local partners and international experts and donors, it encourages co-operation across sectors and borders to address problems of mutual concern. As a network of six partner foundations rooted in local communities, yet linked to international donors and experts, the Eurasia Foundation Network channels resources and expertise to the region and connects its citizens to the wider world.

Geographical Area of Activity: Russia, Eastern Europe and Central Asia.

Restrictions: Funding is not provided to political parties or movements and activities of a religious nature.

Publications: Annual Report; information brochure; application guidelines; newsletter.

Finance: The Foundation has awarded a total of US $126,911,984 in grants since it was founded in 1992; Total assets $20,170,907 (30 Sept. 2010).

Board of Trustees: Jan Kalicki (Chair.); Daniel Witt (Vice-Chair.).

Principal Staff: Pres. William Horton Beebe-Center.

Address: 1350 Connecticut Ave NW, Suite 1000, Washington, DC 20036.

Telephone: (202) 234-7370; **Fax:** (202) 234-7377; **Internet:** www.eurasia.org; **e-mail:** eurasia@eurasia.org.

Feed the Children

Founded in 1979, Feed the Children is a Christian, non-profit charitable organization that aims to provide support and aid to children, families and people in need all over the world.

Activities: Works in the USA and internationally in four main fields: food supply; sustainable development; medical care; and emergency relief. Distributes food, and provides medical assistance and educational opportunities to children and supports orphanages, schools and other charities and NGOs financially. Sends medical teams and supplies to developing regions, and promotes self-sustaining development for families, so as to provide a long-term solution to poverty and hunger.

Geographical Area of Activity: International.

Publications: Financial statements.

Finance: Totral assets US $181,750,786 (30 June 2010); annual revenue $808,287,709, expenditure $901,881,944 (2009/10).

Board of Directors: Rick England (Chair.); Gregg Yeilding (Treas.).

Principal Staff: Interim Pres. Cass Wheeler; COO and Interim CEO Travis Arnold.

Address: POB 36, Oklahoma City, OK 73101-0036.

Telephone: (405) 942-0228; **Fax:** (405) 945-4177; **Internet:** www.feedthechildren.org; **e-mail:** ftc@feedthechildren.org.

Feed My Hungry People, Inc

Established as an international organization known as Feed My People International.

Activities: A charitable organization that aims to store, distribute food and commodities to thousands of the most impoverished people in northern Arizona and the South-West of the USA. Supports the Northern Arizona Food Bank (founded 1986). Also assists in food distribution on a national basis as required for disaster relief.

Geographical Area of Activity: USA.

Publications: newsletter.

Finance: Annual revenue US $34,610,084, expenditure $34,836,493 (2010).

Principal Staff: Dir Kerry Ketchum.

Address: 3805 East Huntington Dr., Flagstaff, AZ 86004.

Telephone: (928) 526-2211; **Fax:** (928) 526-9505; **Internet:** www.feedmypeople.org; **e-mail:** info@feedmypeople.org.

FINCA International

Founded in 1984 to support the economic and human development of families trapped in severe poverty to enable them to create their own jobs, raise household incomes and improve their standard of living. This is done through a global network of locally managed, self-supporting institutions.

Activities: Supports economic self-sufficiency in less-developed countries, through the creation of sustainable development projects, including village banks to provide loans of US $50–$1,000 to individuals and to initiate savings programmes. Operates in North, Central and South America, and the Caribbean, Africa, the Middle East, certain countries of the former USSR, and Kosovo and Metohija.

Geographical Area of Activity: North, Central and South America, and the Caribbean, Africa, the Middle East, Kosovo and Metohija and countries of the former USSR.

Publications: *Village Bank Notes* (quarterly newsletter).

Finance: Total assets US $496,025,630 (31 Dec. 2010).

Board of Directors: Robert W. Hatch (Chair.); John Hatch (Sec.).

Principal Staff: Pres. and CEO Rupert W. Scofield; Vice-Pres. and COO Volker Renner.

Address: 1101 14th St NW, 11th Floor, Washington, DC 20005.

Telephone: (202) 682-1510; **Fax:** (202) 682-1535; **Internet:** www.finca.org; **e-mail:** info@finca.org.

Firefly, Inc.

Established in 2000 by Jonathan and Julie Baker.

Activities: Works to help local governments in Russia develop programmes that will keep children in their birth families. Promotes the establishment of foster homes, small group homes, and domestic adoption when living with birth families is not an option. By offering technical assistance, best practices, and targeted capacity building to local leaders, Firefly assists local champions who are eager to create a Russia without orphanages.

Geographical Area of Activity: Russia.

Publications: *Firefly Newsletter*.

Board of Directors: Nicole Levine (Pres.); Diana England (Sec.); J. Jonathan F. Baker (Treas.).

Principal Staff: Programme Dir Melinda Richards.

Address: 8317 Woodhaven Blvd, Bethesda, MD 20817.

Telephone: (917) 359-7207; **Fax:** (240) 396-2107; **Internet:** www.fireflykids.org; **e-mail:** mrichards@fireflykids.org.

Firelight Foundation

Founded in 1999 by Kerry Olson and David Katz to support children in need, principally in Sub-Saharan Africa, with a focus on HIV/AIDS.

Activities: Aims to support children in need in Sub-Saharan Africa by funding community-based initiatives that work directly and effectively to support the fundamental needs and rights of children (from birth to 21 years of age) orphaned or otherwise affected by HIV/AIDS. Priority is given to grass-roots projects developed in direct response to local community needs, particularly organizations that raise resources from within the local community. Firelight provides initial one-year grants of US $1,000–$10,000, with subsequent grants of up to $15,000.

Geographical Area of Activity: Sub-Saharan Africa.

Restrictions: Priority countries for grantmaking are Lesotho, Malawi, Rwanda, South Africa, Tanzania, Zambia, and Zimbabwe. From Ethiopia, Kenya, and Uganda, Firelight accepts only renewal requests and solicited proposals.

Publications: Annual Report; *From Faith to Action*; *The Promise of a Future*.

Finance: Total assets US $5,485,034 (30 June 2011); annual revenue $9,052,484, expenditure $4,142,342 (2010/11).

Board of Directors: Kerry Olson (Founder and Pres.); David Katz (Vice-Pres.); Jonathan C. Lewis (Treas.).

Principal Staff: Exec. Dir Peter Laugharn; Finance Man. Jane Stokes.

Address: 740 Front St, Suite 380, Santa Cruz, CA 95060.

Telephone: (831) 429-8750; **Fax:** (831) 429-2036; **Internet:** www.firelightfoundation.org; **e-mail:** info@firelightfoundation.org.

First Peoples Worldwide—FPW

Established in 1997 by the First Nations Development Institute to work as an advocate for indigenous rights world-wide.

Activities: Operates world-wide in the field of human rights for indigenous peoples. Works to help sustain the land and culture of indigenous peoples in a number of ways, including encouraging and enabling indigenous peoples to take an active role in issues concerning the environment, the economy and the legal system; providing technical and financial support for culturally-appropriate development programmes; advocating self-governance; building and maintaining a database containing information on indigenous land rights and self-governance; and operating a fellowship programme for community leaders. It has been engaged in direct work in Southern Africa and Australia, and is currently operating projects in South America. Since 2007 financial and adminstrative support has been provided by the Tides Center.

Geographical Area of Activity: Africa, South America, Australia.

Publications: *Indigenous Peoples Funding and Resource Guide.*

Policy Board: Rebecca Adamson (Founder and Pres.).

Principal Staff: Man. Dir Neva Adamson.

Address: 857 Leeland Rd, Fredericksburg, VA 22405-6005.

Telephone: (540) 899-6545; **Fax:** (540) 899-6501; **Internet:** www.firstpeoplesworldwide.org; **e-mail:** info@firstpeoples.org.

Flight Safety Foundation

Founded in 1947 by R. Crane, H. DeHaven and J. Morrison to promote and foster improvements in international conditions of air safety.

Activities: Publishes, and distributes to members, bulletins on aviation safety and accident prevention. Conducts specialized research and carries out flight safety analyses for operators. Organizes annual business air safety seminars and annual awards. Has a membership of more than 1,200 organizations, individuals, companies, etc. from some 150 countries. Maintains a library of approximately 1,000 volumes and a regional office in Melbourne, Australia.

Geographical Area of Activity: World-wide.

Publications: *Annual Index*; *Accident Prevention* (monthly); *Airport Operations* (6 a year); *Aviation Mechanics Bulletin* (6 a year); *Cabin Crew Safety* (6 a year); *Flight Safety Digest* (monthly); *Helicopter Safety* (6 a year); *Human Factors and Aviation Medicine* (6 a year); seminar and workshop proceedings, special reports, technical manuals and studies, membership directory; Annual Report.

Finance: Annual budget approx. US $2,500,000.

Board of Governors: Lynn Brubaker (Chair.); Steven M. Atkins (Vice-Chair.); Kenneth P. Quinn (Gen. Counsel and Sec.); David Barger (Treas.).

Principal Staff: Pres. and CEO William R. Voss; COO Capt. Kevin L. Hiatt.

Address: 801 N Fairfax St, Suite 400, Alexandria, VA 22314-1774.

Telephone: (703) 739-6700; **Fax:** (703) 739-6708; **Internet:** www.flightsafety.org; **e-mail:** mcgee@flightsafety.org.

Food for the Hungry—FH

Founded in the USA in 1971 as a Christian organization with the purpose of relieving poverty world-wide.

Activities: Operates programmes in the fields of health care, community development, nutrition and emergency relief; provides an information and education service; organizes seminars and workshops; provides training for farmers; promotes child sponsorship; gives financial assistance to other development organizations.

Geographical Area of Activity: Asia, Africa and Latin America.

Publications: *Food for the Hungry Story* (newsletter); Annual Report.

Finance: Total assets US $26,657,000 (30 Sept. 2008); annual revenue $98,940,000, expenditure $97,706,000 (2009/10).

Board of Directors: Ken Wathome (Chair.).

Principal Staff: Pres. Dave Evans.

Address: 1224 East Washington St, Phoenix, AZ 85034-1102.

Telephone: (480) 998-3100; **Internet:** www.fh.org; **e-mail:** webquestions@fh.org.

Food for the Poor, Inc

Established in 1982 by Robin Mahfood, an NGO that seeks to link the Church in developed countries with that in less-developed areas and help the poor.

Activities: Works internationally to support the poor in developing countries. Has links with 12,000 primarily religious and indigenous NGOs world-wide, and works with them to raise funding and develop projects to improve conditions in Central and South America and the Caribbean, especially in the areas of food supplies, education, health care and social welfare.

Geographical Area of Activity: Central and South America and the Caribbean.

Restrictions: Operates only in Central and South American and Caribbean countries.

Publications: Annual Report; newsletters.

Finance: Total assets US $39,602,242 (31 Dec. 2010); annual revenue $1,047,498,583, expenditure $1,051,214,423 (2010).

Board of Directors: P. Todd Kennedy (Chair.); Bill Benson (Vice-Chair.); David T. Price (Sec. and Treas.).

Principal Staff: Pres. and CEO Robin G. Mahfood; Exec. Dir Angel Aloma.

Address: 6401 Lyons Rd, Coconut Creek, FL 33073.

Telephone: (954) 427-2222; **Fax:** (954) 570-7654; **Internet:** www.foodforthepoor.org; **e-mail:** donorservice@foodforthepoor.com.

Ford Foundation

Founded in 1936 by Henry Ford and his son Edsel B. Ford, the Foundation is a resource for innovative people and institutions world-wide, aiming to strengthen democratic values, reduce poverty and injustice, promote international co-operation and advance human achievement.

Activities: Grants are made primarily to institutions within the Foundation's three programme areas: Asset Building and Community Development, which incorporates Community and Resource Development and Economic Development; Peace and Social Justice, which comprises two units, Human Rights and Governance and Civil Society; and Knowledge, Creativity and Freedom, which also comprises two units, Education, Sexuality and Religion, and Media, Arts and Culture. The Foundation has field offices in Brazil, Chile, the People's Republic of China, Egypt, India, Indonesia, Kenya, Philippines, Mexico, Nigeria, the Russian Federation, South Africa and Viet Nam, and associations in Israel and Eastern Europe. Support is given for conferences and seminars, general purposes, matching funds, publications, research, programme-related investments, seed money, special projects, technical assistance, endowment funds, fellowships and individual grants.

Geographical Area of Activity: World-wide.

Restrictions: Support not given for personal needs, religious activities or building construction.

Publications: Annual Report; magazine (quarterly); *Current Interests* (biennially).

Finance: Total assets US $10,344,933 (30 Sept. 2011); annual revenue $138,547,000, expenditure $526,034,000 (2010/11).

Board of Trustees: Irene Hirano Inouye (Chair.).

Principal Staff: Pres. Luis A. Ubiñas; Vice-Pres., Treas. and CFO Nicholas M. Gabriel.

Address: 320 East 43rd St, New York, NY 10017.

Telephone: (212) 573-5000; **Fax:** (212) 351-3677; **Internet:** www.fordfoundation.org; **e-mail:** office-of-communications@fordfoundation.org.

Foreign Policy Association

Founded in 1918 to educate Americans about international events and issues and to encourage them to participate in the foreign policy process.

Activities: Seeks to educate Americans about US foreign policy and global affairs, principally through its Great Decisions programme, which consists of an annual impartial briefing of eight key foreign policy issues, discussed by groups, and at seminars and public forums aimed at both students and adults. Also publishes books, leaflets and produces other educational online resources.

Geographical Area of Activity: World-wide.

Restrictions: Not a grant-making organization.

Publications: *Great Decisions* (annual programme guide);- *Global Views*; *FPA Today*; *Great Decisions Online*; *Global Jobs*;

Foreign Policy Alert (online newsletters); Annual Report; and other publications.

Board of Directors: Archibald Cox, Jr. (Chair.); Mary L. Belknap (Vice-Chair.).

Principal Staff: Pres. and CEO Noel V. Lateef.

Address: 470 Park Ave S, New York, NY 10016.

Telephone: (212) 481-8100; **Fax:** (212) 481-9275; **Internet:** www.fpa.org; **e-mail:** info@fpa.org.

Foundation for a Civil Society—FCS

Founded in 1990 to act as a co-ordinating body to promote civil society, democracy and market economy. Formerly known as the Foundation for a Civil Society (Charter 77 Foundation-New York).

Activities: The Foundation has two main functions: to act as a catalyst, initiating and supporting projects; and to act as facilitator, connecting funding sources with institutions and individuals wishing to establish programmes and projects. The Foundation has an extensive network of high-level contacts in the USA and other parts of the world. The major programmes of the Foundation include the New Slovakia initiative designed to ensure that the new governments in the Slovak Republic move smoothly toward European integration. The Foundation's offices in the Czech Republic and Slovakia became independent NGOs known as VIA Foundation (q.v.) and Nadácia Pre Občiansku Spoločnost, respectively.

Geographical Area of Activity: International, with an emphasis on Central and Eastern Europe, Northern Ireland and Central America.

Publications: Annual Report.

Board of Directors: Catolyn Seely Wiener (Chair.); Wendy W. Luers (Pres.).

Principal Staff: Pres. Wendy W. Luers.

Address: 25 East End Ave, 1B, New York, NY 10028.

Telephone: (212) 980-4584; **Fax:** (212) 980-4583; **Internet:** www.fcsny.org; **e-mail:** info@fcsny.org.

Foundation for Deep Ecology

Established in 1990. Concerned with the environment, conservation and protection of biodiversity and wilderness, ecological agriculture and the environmental impact of economic globalization and the technological systems that serve it.

Activities: The Foundation focuses on fundamental ecological issues in three areas: Biodiversity and Wilderness, including protection of forests, aquatic ecosystems and other habitats, wildlands philanthropy (i.e. buying land to save it), wilderness recovery (supporting the design and implementation of large-scale wilderness recovery networks), funding for activists campaigning for full protection of species and ecosystems, and funding efforts to eliminate resource extraction on public lands; Ecological Agriculture, including support for alternative models of agriculture that support biodiversity, local self-reliance and healthy agrarian communities, support for efforts to combat industrialization of agriculture, and support for efforts to link conservationists with farmers and activists to integrate habitat preservation and restoration with diverse farming practices; and Education, including campaigns to educate the public about and to resist the growth of the new macro-economic trends and the technological systems that drive these trends (e.g. international free-trade agreements), and providing aid to groups working towards viable local economic systems (for example community-building, local currencies and defining new technological and economic systems). From 2003 the Foundation increased its focus on wildlands philanthropy, with a resulting reduction in available grants in the remaining grant programmes.

Geographical Area of Activity: USA, South America and Canada (primarily Chile and Argentina). Grants to some groups in the Netherlands, Spain, United Kingdom.

Restrictions: No new grant proposals accepted.

Publications: *Century of Failed Forest Policy; Fatal Harvest; The Tragedy of Industrial Agriculture.*

Board of Directors: Douglas R. Tompkins (Pres.); Quincey Imhoff (Vice-Pres.); Kristine McDivitt Tompkins (Vice-Pres.); Debra B. Ryker (Sec. and Treas.).

Principal Staff: Editorial Projects Dir Tom Butler.

Address: Building 1062, Fort Cronkhite, Sausalito, CA 94965.

Telephone: (415) 229-9339; **Fax:** (415) 229-9340; **Internet:** www.deepecology.org; **e-mail:** info@deepecology.org.

FLAAR—Foundation for Latin American Anthropological Research

Founded in 1969 by Dr Nicholas M. Hellmuth to engage in academic research in the fields of archaeology, art history and tropical flora and fauna.

Activities: Operates in the fields of the arts and humanities, with respect to ancient cultures of Central America, especially in the areas of archaeology, ethno-zoology, ethno-botany, ethno-history of sports, conservation and the environment, and education, through conferences and training courses, and field trips to Central America. Focuses on evaluation of digital camera equipment and wide-format inkjet printers of the above topics to assist museums, zoos, national parks, botanical gardens, and university research institutes with knowledge on digital imaging related to anthropology broadly defined. Most research is carried out in Mexico, Guatemala, Honduras and Belize, but the Foundation also carries out studies of Mesoamerican art in museums world-wide. Maintains libraries in Austria, and Guatemala, and a photographic archive.

Geographical Area of Activity: Mainly Central America, Mexico.

Publications: Electronic reports on archaeology, pre-Columbian art, ancient architecture and sports in Pre-Hispanic America, and on digital imaging to record and exhibit these subjects.

Finance: Annual revenue and expenditure approx. US $150,000.

Principal Staff: Dir Dr Nicholas M. Hellmuth; Man. Flor de Maria Setina.

Address: 12317 Inletridge Dr., Maryland Heights, MO 63043.

Telephone: (419) 823-9218; **Internet:** www.flaar.org; **e-mail:** readerservice@flaar.org.

Foundation for Middle East Peace—FMEP

Founded in 1979 by Merle Thorpe, Jr to assist in an understanding of Israeli-Palestinian relations, including the identification of US interests, and to contribute to a just and peaceful resolution.

Activities: Carries out research into Middle East peace, and supports elements in the Arab and Jewish communities that are working towards peace between Israelis and Palestinians. Grants have supported educational, humanitarian, public affairs, civil rights, and Palestinian-Israeli reconciliation activities, as well as small-scale economic projects that meet the needs of victims of the current conflict.

Geographical Area of Activity: Israel and Palestinian Autonomous Areas.

Restrictions: No grants are made to individuals; grants are made only to organizations and projects that contribute to Israeli-Palestinian peace.

Publications: *The West Bank: Hostage of History; Prescription for Conflict: Israel's West Bank Settlement Policy; Error and Betrayal in Lebanon; Facing the PLO Question; A Policy for the Moment of Truth; No Trumpets, No Drums; Report on Israeli Settlement in the Occupied Territories* (6 a year); settlement reports.

Finance: Funded by endowment and annual income.

Board of Trustees: Calvin H. Cobb, Jr (Chair.).

Principal Staff: Pres. Philip C. Wilcox, Jr.

Address: 1761 N St NW, Washington, DC 20036.

Telephone: (202) 835-3650; **Fax:** (202) 835-3651; **Internet:** www.fmep.org; **e-mail:** info@fmep.org.

Foundation for Russian-American Economic Co-operation—FRAEC

Established in 1989, the Foundation fosters expanded economic ties between Russia and the USA, with a special focus on building bridges between the Russian Far East and the US West Coast.

Activities: The Foundation works through building bilateral and multilateral relationships and serving as a hub through which grassroots organizations, the private sector, regional officials and federal decision-makers are interconnected. The Foundation activities reflect the contemporary realities of US-Russian relations in a range of areas including small and medium-sized enterprise development, nuclear cities, customs reform, sustainable development, legislative reform, good governance, law enforcement, public health and non-profit capacity building.

Geographical Area of Activity: USA and the Russian Federation (with an emphasis on the Russian Far East).

Publications: Annual Report; *Fast Facts* (monthly newsletter); *News Digest* (weekly Russia report).

Board of Directors: Michael Nunes (Chair.); John Schmidt (Vice-Chair.); Carol Kessler (Sec.); Lana Rich (Treas.).

Principal Staff: Founder and Pres. Carol Vipperman.

Address: 2601 Fourth Ave, Suite 600, Seattle, WA 98121.

Telephone: (206) 443-1935; **Fax:** (206) 443-0954; **Internet:** www.fraec.org; **e-mail:** fraec@fraec.org.

Michael J. Fox Foundation for Parkinson's Research

Established in 2000 to find a cure for Parkinson's disease.

Activities: Funds research into Parkinson's disease.

Publications: *Accelerating the Cure* (newsletter, 3 a year); *Fox-Flash* (e-newsletter).

Finance: Annual revenue US $57,630,995, expenditure $60,070,822 (2010).

Board of Directors: Michael J. Fox (Founder); Woody Shackleton (Chair.); George E. Prescott (Vice-Chair.).

Principal Staff: CEO Todd Sherer; Co-Founder and Exec. Vice-Chair. Deborah W. Brooks.

Address: Church St Station, POB 780, New York, NY 10008-0780.

Telephone: (800) 708-7644; **Internet:** www.michaeljfox.org; **e-mail:** info@michaeljfox.org.

Francis Family Foundation

Founded in 1989 as a result of the merger of the Parker B. Francis Foundation and the Parker B. Francis, III Foundation. The Foundation's purpose is to fund medical fellowships in pulmonary medicine and anaesthesiology and to support principal educational and cultural institutions within the Greater Kansas City metropolitan area.

Activities: Awards fellowships to citizens of the USA or Canada (or to foreign nationals intending to take up permanent residence in the USA or Canada) for post-doctoral research related to pulmonary disease. Also supports child and youth development programmes in the areas of life-long learning and arts and culture in the Greater Kansas City metropolitan area.

Geographical Area of Activity: North America.

Publications: Annual Report.

Finance: Grants disbursed more than US $600,000 (2009).

Board of Directors: David V. Francis (Chair.).

Principal Staff: Exec. Dir Jim Koeneman; Program Officer Lyn Knox.

Address: 800 West 47th St, Suite 717, Kansas City, MO 64112.

Telephone: (816) 531-0077; **Fax:** (816) 531-8810; **Internet:** www.francisfoundation.org; **e-mail:** webmaster@francisfoundation.org.

Franciscans International

Established in 1984.

Activities: Works in collaboration with other NGOs, the UN and Franciscans around the world on global issues, especially relating to peace-making and concern for the poor, including projects on religious intolerance, human rights, migration and development in Africa. Also runs an internship programme. Aims to represent the poor at the UN. Maintains offices in Geneva and Bangkok.

Geographical Area of Activity: World-wide.

Publications: include Annual Report; *Pax et Bonum* (newsletter); *West Papua Factsheet; World Poverty—Franciscan Reflections.*

Finance: Annual revenue US $1,346,690, expenditure $1,422,271 (2009).

Board of Directors: John Doctor (Pres.); Doug Clorey (Vice-Pres.); Regina Holz (Sec.); John Celischowski (Treas.).

Principal Staff: Exec. Dir Denise Boyle.

Address: 246 E 46th St, Suite 1F, New York, NY 10017-2937.

Telephone: (212) 490-4624; **Fax:** (212) 490-4626; **Internet:** www.franciscansinternational.org; **e-mail:** newyork@fiop.org.

The Freedom Forum

Non-partisan, international foundation established in 1991 under the direction of Allen H. Neuharth, as the successor to a foundation started in 1935 by newspaper publisher Frank E. Gannett. It is dedicated to free press, free speech and free spirit for all people.

Activities: An operating foundation, which focuses on four main priorities: the Newseum, First Amendment issues, newsroom diversity and world press freedom. The Newseum is an independent affiliate, funded by the Freedom Forum, an interactive museum of news, based in Arlington, VA. The Foundation also funds the First Amendment Center, another independent affiliate, with offices at Vanderbilt University in Nashville, TN, New York City and Arlington, which works to preserve and protect First Amendment freedoms through information and education. The Center serves as a forum for the study and exploration of free-expression issues, including freedom of speech, of the press and of religion, the right to assemble and to petition the government. Makes several annual awards in recognition of quality journalism and to promote freedom of speech. The Foundation has operating offices in Buenos Aires, Hong Kong, Johannesburg, London and Cocoa Beach, FL, but operates principally in the USA.

Geographical Area of Activity: Mainly USA.

Restrictions: This is an operating foundation, which does not accept unsolicited requests for funding.

Publications: Annual Report; information brochures; conference and seminar reports; video and audio tapes of programmes; *Media Ethics and Fairness; Media Studies Journal; World Press Freedom; Newsroom Diversity.*

Finance: Funded by income from an endowment of diversified assets. Net assets US $454,900,000 (2010).

Board of Trustees: Jan Neurath (Chair.); Howard Baker (Sec.).

Principal Staff: Pres. and CEO James C. Duff.

Address: 555 Pennsylvania Ave NW, Washington, DC 20001.

Telephone: (202) 292-6100; **Internet:** www.freedomforum.org; **e-mail:** news@freedomforum.org.

Freedom House, Inc

Founded by Eleanor Roosevelt, Wendell Willkie, and other Americans concerned with the mounting threats to peace and democracy to promote democratic values and oppose dictatorships of the far left and the far right. In 1997 incorporated the programmes of the National Forum Foundation.

Activities: Promotes the development of the world's young democracies, which are coping with the debilitating legacy of statism, dictatorship and political repression, through conducting US and overseas research, advocacy, education and training initiatives that promote human rights, democracy, free-market economics, the rule of law, independent media, and US engagement in international affairs. Regional programmes are developed concerning a range of issues, including raising the sustainability of independent local media, reducing violence against women, torture treatment and prevention, and human-rights training. Also maintains offices in Almaty, Amman, Belgrade, Bishkek, Bucharest, Budapest, Dushanbe, Kiev, Lagos, Mexico City, Tashkent, Warsaw and New York.

Geographical Area of Activity: World-wide.

Publications: *Freedom in the World* (annually); *Freedom of the Press*; special reports; *Nations in Transit* (annually); *Countries at the Crossroads* (annually); *Women's Rights Survey*; Annual Report.

Finance: Total assets US $8,730,855 (June 2008).

Board of Trustees: William H. Taft IV (Chair.); Ruth Wedgwood (Vice-Chair.); Thomas A. Dine (Vice-Chair.); David Nastro (Treas.); John Norton Moore (Sec.).

Principal Staff: Exec. Dir David J. Kramer; COO Jacquelyn J. Bennett.

Address: 1301 Connecticut Ave NW, 6th Floor, Washington, DC 20036.

Telephone: (202) 296-5101; **Fax:** (202) 293-2840; **Internet:** www.freedomhouse.org; **e-mail:** info@freedomhouse.org.

Freedom from Hunger

Founded in 1946, Freedom from Hunger brings innovative and sustainable self-help solutions to the fight against chronic hunger and poverty.

Activities: Collaborates with partner organizations that provide small cash loans and education to women's groups in poor rural villages of developing countries. Works with about 150 local partner organizations, including NGOs, rural banks and credit unions, in 19 developing nations.

Geographical Area of Activity: Latin America, Africa, Asia.

Publications: Annual Report; newsletters, white papers.

Finance: Annual revenue US $6,520,033, expenditure $6,550,757 (2010/11).

Board of Trustees: J. Grover Thomas, Jr (Chair.); Richard C. Auger (Vice-Chair.); Catherine C. Roth (Sec.); William B. Robinson (Treas.).

Principal Staff: Pres. Steve Hollingworth; Vice-Pres. Kathleen E. Stack.

Address: 1644 Da Vinci Ct, Davis, CA 95618.

Telephone: (530) 758-6200; **Fax:** (530) 758-6241; **Internet:** www.freedomfromhunger.org; **e-mail:** info@freedomfromhunger.org.

Freeman Foundation

The Foundation was set up in 1994 in memory of Mansfield Freeman, by Houghton Freeman and other Freeman family members.

Activities: The Foundation focuses on environment protection, conservation of natural resources and promoting international studies; utilizes education to deepen mutual appreciation and understanding of cultures, economies and histories, existing institutions and their purpose of establishment, between the USA and the East Asian countries; supports projects that are contributive to the development of an international free enterprise system; the Foundation runs an exchange programme, extends general support, and provides funds.

Geographical Area of Activity: International.

Finance: Annual revenue US $142,128,445, expenditure $31,560,112 (2009).

Principal Staff: Exec. Dir Graeme Freeman; Office Man. Andrea Robertson.

Address: 10 Rockefeller Plaza, 3rd Floor, New York, NY 10020.

Telephone: (212) 549-5270.

French-American Foundation—FAF

FAF was established in 1976 to enhance relationships between France and the USA and promote a mutual active dialogue.

Activities: The Foundation acts as a platform of communication for leaders, policy-makers and professionals of France and the USA where problems of concern to both countries are put forward for discussion, opinions are shared on common issues, productive relationships are created between people of both nations, and attempts are made to bring about a change through mutual harmony; FAF keeps devising various programmes that address cultural, business, social, political and educational issues through lectures, conferences, exchanges and study tours that are conducive to the adoption of innovative practices being implemented in both nations.

Geographical Area of Activity: USA and France.

Restrictions: No grants available.

Publications: Annual Report; project reports; newsletter.

Finance: Total assets US $3,177,762 (31 Dec. 2010); annual revenue $1,469,607, expenditure $1,737,679 (2010).

Board of Directors: Allan M. Chapin (Chair.); François Bujon de l'Estang (Vice-Chair.); Elizabeth Fondaras (Vice-Chair.).

Principal Staff: Pres. Antoine Treuille.

Address: 28 West 44th St, Suite 1420, New York, NY 10036.

Telephone: (212) 829-8800; **Fax:** (212) 829-8810; **Internet:** www.frenchamerican.org; **e-mail:** info@frenchamerican.org.

Freshwater Society

Freshwater Society is a not-for-profit organization working towards the promotion of protection and judicious utilization and management of fresh water resources.

Activities: The organization focuses on environment and conservation through educational programmes, research and demonstration projects to encourage protection of fresh water resources, and resource management; as part of fresh water resource protection, restores and conserves such resources together with the surrounding watersheds; also initiates programmes in surface water and groundwater stewardship activities, freshwater resource management, conducts conferences, carries out public education, and issues publications.

Geographical Area of Activity: World-wide.

Publications: Annual Report; *Minnesota Weatherguide Environment Calendar*; *Guide to Lake Protection and Management*; *ANS Digest* (quarterly); *Facets of Freshwater* (newsletter).

Board of Directors: Tom Skramstad (Chair.); Stuart E. Grubb (Vice-Chair.); Barbara Luikens (Sec.); Rick Bateson (Treas.).

Principal Staff: Pres. Gene Merriam; Exec. Dir Joan Nephew.

Address: 2500 Shadywood Rd, Excelsior, MN 55331.

Telephone: (952) 471-9773; **Fax:** (952) 471-7685; **Internet:** www.freshwater.org; **e-mail:** freshwater@freshwater.org.

Alfred Friendly Press Fellowships

Founded by the late Alfred Friendly in 1983 to promote a free press, and co-operation between the press and other institutions in the USA and abroad.

Activities: Provides work experience in the USA for foreign journalists through a fellowship programme. Applications are accepted from journalists from Eastern Europe and less-developed countries with an emerging free press.

Geographical Area of Activity: International.

Restrictions: Each applicant must have an excellent command of English, at least three years' experience as a print journalist, a demonstrated commitment to journalism in his or her home country, and be currently employed as a journalist.

Publications: Newsletter.

Foundation Board: Jonathan Friendly (Chair.); Patrick Stueve (Treas.); Susan Talalay (Sec.).

Principal Staff: Exec. Dir Kathleen Graham; Programme Man. Katie Rudolph.

Address: 1100 Connecticut Ave NW, Suite 440, Washington, DC 20036.

Telephone: (202) 429-3740; **Fax:** (202) 429-3741; **Internet:** www.pressfellowships.org; **e-mail:** info@pressfellowships.org.

FXB International—Association François-Xavier Bagnoud

Established in Switzerland in 1989 to commemorate François-Xavier Bagnoud, a helicopter pilot who died at the age of 24, by his mother Countess Albina du Boisrouvray, members of her family and friends. Formerly known as the François-Xavier Bagnoud Foundation, it promotes social welfare and studies, education, and science and technology.

Activities: The Association carries out its activities on a national as well as an international level in the fields of science and technology, education and health and welfare. In 1992 the François-Xavier Bagnoud Center for Health and Human Rights was launched at Harvard University School of Public Health. The Association has financed a Chair in Aerospace Engineering at the University of Michigan College of Engineering, awards the François-Xavier Bagnoud Aerospace Prize (US $250,000), and the Association also strives to defend childrens' rights, as well as health and human rights, and carries out some 100 projects supporting child HIV/AIDS victims and families subjected to social ostracism in 15 countries. FXB supports orphans and susceptible child victims of AIDS by voicing their concerns and extending direct assistance to communities and families who are involved in nurturing such victims. It carries out projects to support children exploited as prostitutes, soldiers or terrorists.

Geographical Area of Activity: International.

Restrictions: Grants are made only to pre-selected organizations, and no grants are made to individuals.

Publications: Annual Report; articles.

Finance: Annual revenue US $1,178,080, expenditure $1,077,010 (estimates, 2011).

Board: Albina du Boisrouvray (Pres.); Alejandro Haag (Treas.).

Principal Staff: CEO Sean Mayberry.

Address: 777 United Nations Plaza, New York, NY 10017.

Telephone: (212) 697-3566; **Fax:** (212) 697-2065; **Internet:** www.fxb.org; **e-mail:** info@fxb.org.

Bill and Melinda Gates Foundation

Established in 1994, by William (Bill) Gates and Melinda Gates to help improve the lives of people world-wide through health and learning; the Gates Learning Foundation (founded in 1997 as the successor to the Microsoft/American Library Association) and the William H. Gates Foundation (founded in 1994) were integrated into the Bill and Melinda Gates Foundation in 1999.

Activities: The Foundation integrates the operations of the Gates Learning Foundation, which operated in the USA, and the William H. Gates Foundation, which operated nationally and internationally. Works in the areas of medicine and health, education and community welfare, through three main projects: Global Health (especially projects in the areas of vaccine-preventable diseases, reproductive and child health, and conditions associated with poverty, including a US $100m. donation over 10 years to the Global Fund for AIDS and Health and the $1m. Gates Award for Global Health administered by the Global Health Council—q.v.), Global Development and the US Program. The Foundation established a scholarship programme in 2000, setting up the Gates Cambridge Trust, endowed with $210,000,000, to enable gifted graduate students from any country outside the United Kingdom to study at the University of Cambridge. In 2002 the Foundation announced that more than $40m. was to be used to establish a network of small schools in the USA offering college courses; and in 2003 launched the Grand Challenges in Global Health initiative, in partnership with the National Institutes of Health (NIH), with a grant of $200,000,000. It was announced in January 2008 that the Foundation was to give $14,700,000 for health improvement in Ethiopia.

Geographical Area of Activity: International.

Restrictions: Currently not accepting grant applications for Global Libraries and Education initiatives.

Publications: Annual Report; newsletters.

Finance: Total assets US $37,430,151,000; annual revenue $3,281,000, expenditure $2,639,113,000 (2010).

Board of Trustees: Bill Gates (Co-Chair.); Melinda French Gates (Co-Chair.); William Gates, Sr (Co-Chair.).

Principal Staff: CEO Jeff Raikes; CFO Richard Henriques.

Address: POB 23350, Seattle, WA 98102.

Telephone: (206) 709-3100; **Fax:** (206) 709-3180; **Internet:** www.gatesfoundation.org; **e-mail:** info@gatesfoundation.org.

GE Foundation

Founded in 1952 as the General Electric Foundation for the support of education in the USA. Adopted present name in 1994, as a result of the merger of the General Electric Foundation and the General Electric Foundation, Inc.

Activities: The Foundation provides financial assistance in the fields of the environment, education and public policy. Focuses primarily on the field of education and provides financial assistance to institutions for general education; graduate research and teaching; minority group education; physical science, engineering, computer science, mathematics, industrial management and business administration education; selected public schools; and arts and cultural centres. Grants are also awarded to other US organizations, including those concerned with international understanding and culture. Grants are made internationally to support higher education institutions and government-run schools and community organizations working to improve access to education for disadvantaged people, raise educational achievement and to test innovative solutions or implementing best practice that can be replicated.

Geographical Area of Activity: International.

Restrictions: Unlikely to make grants to unsolicited projects.

Publications: Annual Report; archives.

Finance: Grants disbursed more than US $100,000,000 (2009).

Board of Directors: Robert L. Corcoran (Chair.); Michael J. Cosgrove (Treas.); Paul Bueker (Sec.).

Principal Staff: Pres. Robert Corcoran.

Address: 3135 Easton Turnpike, Fairfield, CT 06431.

Telephone: (203) 373-3216; **Fax:** (203) 373-3029; **Internet:** www.gefoundation.com; **e-mail:** gefoundation@ge.com.

General Service Foundation

Founded in 1946 by Clifton R. Musser and Margaret Kulp Musser.

Activities: Makes grants to charitable organizations that operate in the following fields: International Peace, particularly in Central America, Mexico and the Caribbean; Reproductive Health and Rights in the USA and Mexico; and Western Water, in the interior west of the USA.

Geographical Area of Activity: North and Central America and the Caribbean.

Restrictions: Grants are not made to individuals, for annual campaigns, capital expenditures or relief.

Finance: Total assets US $46,725,738 (31 Dec. 2009); annual revenue $7,770,446 (loss), expenditure $3,804,512 (2009).

Board of Directors: Robin Snidow (Chair.); Zoe Estrin (Vice-Chair.); Marcie J. Musser (Sec.); Will Halby (Treas.).

Principal Staff: Exec. Dir Lani Shaw; CFO William M. Repplinger.

Address: 557 North Mill St, Suite 201, Aspen, CO 81611.

Telephone: (970) 920-6834; **Fax:** (970) 920-4578; **Internet:** www.generalservice.org; **e-mail:** info@generalservice.org.

German Marshall Fund of the United States—GMF

Created in 1972 by a gift from the German people as a permanent memorial to the Marshall Plan. The Fund is an American institution that promotes understanding and co-operation between the USA and Europe in the spirit of the post-war Marshall Plan.

Activities: The Fund's grant-making promotes the study of international and domestic policies, supports comparative research and debate on key issues, and assists policy and opinion leaders's understanding of these issues. Makes grants in the following areas: foreign policy; economics; the environment; civic participation and democratization; and immigration and integration. Projects must address issues important to European countries and the USA, and they must involve people or institutions on both sides of the Atlantic. GMF has a particular interest in leadership development. Programmes that involve political, media and other professionals who have a strong interest in transatlantic relations and leadership potential will be given special attention. Projects normally include the transfer of experience and innovations, preferably involving practitioners and policy-makers. In 2003 launched the Balkan Trust for Democracy, in a funding partnership with the US Agency for International Development (USAID) and the Charles Stewart Mott Foundation (q.v.). Maintains offices in Ankara, Belgrade, Berlin, Bratislava, Brussels, Bucharest and Paris.

Geographical Area of Activity: USA and Europe.

Publications: Annual Report; special reports.

Finance: Total assets US $208,861,537 (31 May 2010); annual revenue $37,031,008, expenditure $38,720,296 (2009/10).

Board of Trustees: Dr Guido Goldman (Co-Chair.); Marc Leland (Co-Chair.).

Principal Staff: Pres. Craig Kennedy.

Address: 1744 R St NW, Washington, DC 20009.

Telephone: (202) 683-2650; **Fax:** (202) 265-1662; **Internet:** www.gmfus.org; **e-mail:** info@gmfus.org.

J. Paul Getty Trust

Founded in 1953 by J. Paul Getty (as the J. Paul Getty Museum); a private operating foundation dedicated to the visual arts and the humanities. The Getty Grant Program was established in 1984.

Activities: Operates through four programmes: the J. Paul Getty Museum; the Getty Research Institute, which includes the Research Library; the Getty Conservation Institute; and the Getty Foundation, which provides grants to further the understanding and preservation of the visual arts throughout the world and, through the Leadership Institute, enables the professional development of museum leaders.

Geographical Area of Activity: International.

Publications: Annual Report; *The Getty Grant Program Funding Priorities*; *Grants Awarded* (booklet); various museum and conservation publications.

Finance: Total assets US $8,913,773,000 (30 June 2011); annual revenue $1,043,198,000, expenditure $269,815,000 (2010/11).

Board of Trustees: Mark S. Siegel (Chair.); Neil L. Rudenstine (Vice-Chair.).

Principal Staff: Pres. and CEO James Cuno.

Address: 1200 Getty Center Dr., Los Angeles, CA 90049-1679.

Telephone: (310) 440-7300; **Fax:** (310) 440-7703; **Internet:** www.getty.edu; **e-mail:** communications@getty.edu.

Howard Gilman Foundation, Inc

Established in 1981 by the Gilman Paper and Investment Corporation to nurture and conserve a vibrant natural and cultural environment.

Activities: Operates in the fields of the arts and humanities, conservation and the environment, and medicine and health, through research, offering grants to institutions and conferences.

Geographical Area of Activity: USA and the countries of the former USSR.

Restrictions: No grants are made to individuals.

Publications: Application guidelines.

Board of Directors: Mary C. Farrell (Pres.); Stephen W. Cropper (Vice-Pres., Sec. and Treas.).

Principal Staff: Pres. Mary C. Farrell; Vice-Pres. Stephen W. Cropper.

Address: 111 West 50th St, 40th Floor, New York, NY 10020.

Telephone: (212) 246-3300; **Fax:** (212) 262-4108; **Internet:** www.gilmanfoundation.org; **e-mail:** info@ howardgilmanfoundation.org.

Giving USA Foundation

Founded in 1985 by the American Association of Fund-Raising Counsel as the AAFRC Trust for Philanthropy.

Activities: Aims to increase public awareness and understanding of philanthropy through conducting programmes; funds and commissions research into philanthropy and promotes projects set up by other similar organizations. Develops and conducts college courses on philanthropy in conjunction with the American Association of Colleges; and sponsors the John Grenzebach awards for outstanding research in the field. Co-ordinates Giving USA, an annual analysis of all sources of philanthropic funding in the USA.

Geographical Area of Activity: USA.

Publications: *Giving USA* (annually); *Giving USA Update* (irregular); newsletters (quarterly).

Board of Directors: James D. Yunker (Chair.); L. Gregg Carlson (Vice-Chair.); Jennifer Furla (Sec.); W. Keith Curtis (Treas.).

Address: 303 West Madison St, Suite 2650, Chicago, IL 60606.

Telephone: (312) 981-6794; **Fax:** (312) 265-2911; **Internet:** www.givinginstitute.org; **e-mail:** info@givinginstitute.org.

Elizabeth Glaser Pediatric AIDS Foundation

Founded in 1988 to support pediatric AIDS research.

Activities: Aims to eradicate paediatric AIDS; provides care and treatment for people with HIV/AIDS and aims to accelerate the discovery of new treatments for other serious and life-threatening paediatric illnesses. The Foundation advocates for public policies that support children's health in the USA and world-wide, funds research and makes awards.

Geographical Area of Activity: World-wide.

Publications: Annual Reports.

Finance: Total assets US $36,506,742 (31 Dec. 2010); annual revenue $151,356,673, expenditure $129,162,911 (2010).

Board of Directors: Paul Glaser (Hon. Chair.); David Kessler (Chair.); Willow Bay (Vice-Chair.); Russ Hagey (Vice-Chair.).

Principal Staff: Pres. and CEO Charles Lyons.

Address: 1140 Connecticut Ave NW, Suite 200, Washington, DC 20036.

Telephone: (202) 296-9165; **Fax:** (202) 296-9185; **Internet:** www.pedaids.org; **e-mail:** info@pedaids.org.

Global Alliance for Women's Health—GAWH

Established in 1994 for the advancement of women's health world-wide.

Activities: Works in co-operation with national and international NGOs, women's groups and other organizations to advance women's health in all areas of the world. Promotes the implementation of improvements to health-care services and research into women's health. Distributes women's health care information and organizes health conferences and symposia on a variety of health policy issues.

Geographical Area of Activity: International.

Publications: Annual Report; newsletter; reports; seminar proceedings.

Executive Board: Elaine M. Wolfson (Founding Pres.); Fantaye Mekbeb (Vice-Pres.); Kenneth L. Brown (Treas.).

Address: 777 United Nations Plaza, 7th Floor, New York, NY 10017.

Telephone: (212) 286-0424; **Fax:** (212) 286-9561; **Internet:** www.gawh.org; **e-mail:** wolfson@gawh.org.

Global Fund for Women—GFW

Founded in 1987 by Anne Firth Murray to promote the growth of women's groups and links between groups world-wide.

Activities: The Fund operates in the fields of economic affairs, education, human rights, medicine and health, and social welfare and studies, by assisting grassroots women's organizations outside the USA. Maintains office in New York.

Geographical Area of Activity: International.

Restrictions: Operates internationally, but does not support individuals or groups based in the USA.

Publications: *Raising Our Voices* (newsletter); *Women's Fundraising Handbook; Caught in the Storm: The Impact of Natural Disasters; What Girls Need to Grow: Lessons for Social Change Philanthropy; More Than Money: Strategies to Build Women's Economic Power;* Annual Report; information brochure.

Finance: Total assets US $21,016,863 (30 June 2011) annual revenue $15,672,055, expenditure $15,685,439 (2010/11).

Board of Directors: Leila Hessini (Chair.); Marissa Wesely (Treas.); Dina Dublon (Sec.).

Principal Staff: Pres. and CEO Dr Musimbi Kanyoro; CFO Dale Needles.

Address: 222 Sutter St, Suite 500, San Francisco, CA 94108.

Telephone: (415) 248-4800; **Fax:** (415) 248-4801; **Internet:** www.globalfundforwomen.org; **e-mail:** gfw@globalfundforwomen.org.

Global Greengrants Fund

Established in 1993; aims to protect the global environment by strengthening grassroots movements in developing countries working on environmental sustainability and human rights issues.

Activities: Awards small grants, typically ranging from US $500 to $5,000, throughout the world to grassroots NGOs working for environmental and social justice causes.

Geographical Area of Activity: International, working in over 120 countries world-wide.

Restrictions: No unsolicited proposals accepted.

Publications: Annual Report; feature pieces on: Sustainability, Energy, Water, Indigenous Peoples and Women; e-newsletter.

Finance: Total assets US $5,694,976 (30 June 2010); annual revenue $8,414,193, expenditure $7,779,959 (2009/10).

Board of Directors: Mele Lau Smith (Chair.); Maxine A. Burkett (Vice-Chair.); Larry Kressley (Sec. and Treas.).

Principal Staff: Exec. Dir and CEO Terry Odendahl; Dir of Finance Jan Combs.

Address: 2840 Wilderness Pl., Suite A, Boulder, CO 80301.

Telephone: (303) 939-9866; **Fax:** (303) 939-9867; **Internet:** www.greengrants.org; **e-mail:** info@greengrants.org.

Global Health Council

Established in 1972, as the National Council for International Health, a membership organization of individuals, organizations and communities working in the field of health internationally. Changed its name to the Global Health Council in 1999.

Activities: Operates in the field of health world-wide by working in collaboration with local partner organizations; its main areas of activity are HIV/AIDS (the Global AIDS Program), reproductive and maternal health, infectious diseases, child health and nutrition, disaster and refugee health, and health systems. Holds an annual conference to promote human development. Administers the Gates Award for Global Health, funded by the Bill and Melinda Gates Foundation (q.v.) and the Jonathan Mann Award for Global Health and Human Rights in partnership with Doctors of the World and the Association François-Xavier Bagnoud (q.v.), as well as making other awards recognizing excellence in global health issues.

Geographical Area of Activity: International.

Restrictions: Not a funding organization.

Finance: Total assets US $5,482,409 (30 Sept. 2010).

Board of Directors: Joel Lamstein (Chair.); Alvaro Bermejo (Sec.); Elizabeth Furst Frank (Treas.).

Principal Staff: Interim Co-CEOs Smita Baruah, Susan Higman.

Address: 1111 19th St NW, Suite 1120, Washington, DC 20036.

Telephone: (202) 833-5900; **Fax:** (202) 833-0075; **Internet:** www.globalhealth.org; **e-mail:** webmaster@globalhealth.org.

Global Links

Established in 1989 to assist health-care institutions in developing countries regardless of nationality, or religious or political affiliation.

Activities: Collects donations of a wide variety of surplus medical supplies, including equipment, instruments, sutures and other supplies and hospital furnishings from the USA and distributes them to health care facilities in developing countries to improve the medical care received by those in need. Donations are currently sent to institutions in Bolivia, Cuba, Guyana, Honduras and Jamaica, although sutures are donated throughout the world.

Geographical Area of Activity: Mainly Central and South America and the Caribbean.

Publications: Annual Report; *Global Links News* (newsletter).

Finance: Total assets US $4,511,310 (31 Dec. 2010); annual revenue $5,053,109, expenditure $5,034,048 (2010).

Board of Directors: Mimi Falbo (Chair.); Jeffrey Ford (Vice-Chair.); Charles Vargo (Treas.); Rev. Eugene F. Lauer (Sec.).

Principal Staff: CEO Kathleen Hower; Dep. Dir Angela Garcia.

Address: 4809 Penn Ave, Suite 2, Pittsburgh, PA 15224.

Telephone: (412) 361-3424; **Fax:** (412) 361-4950; **Internet:** www.globallinks.org; **e-mail:** info@globallinks.org.

Richard and Rhoda Goldman Fund

Established in 1951 by San Francisco philanthropists and civic leaders Richard and Rhoda Goldman to promote protection of the environment and for general charitable purposes.

Activities: The Foundation awards the Goldman Environment Prize each year to one person from each of the six inhabited continents deemed to have made a significant contribution in the field of environmental protection; each prize carries a monetary award of US $125,000. Also operates in the areas of Jewish affairs, the prevention of violence, children and youth, the elderly, social and human services, population, health, education, democracy and civil society, and the arts and humanities. Apart from the environmental prize, grants are usually made within the San Francisco Bay area, CA. Grants are also paid from the Richard and Rhoda Goldman Foundation, a supporting foundation of the Jewish Community Endowment Fund of the Jewish Community Federation of San Francisco, the Peninsula, Marin and Sonoma Counties. The Fund will cease operations on 31 December 2012.

Geographical Area of Activity: International.

Restrictions: No unsolicited proposals currently in the areas of the arts, education or health; final grants have now been allocated.

Publications: Newsletter; occasional report; information brochure; *Benefit Magazine*; Annual Report.

Finance: Assets US $255,000,000 (31 Dec. 2009); grants disbursed $36,140,937 (2009).

Principal Staff: Exec. Dir Amy Lyons.

Address: 160 Pacific Ave, Suite 200, San Francisco, CA 94111.

Telephone: (415) 249-5888; **Fax:** (415) 772-9137; **Internet:** www.goldmanfund.org; **e-mail:** info@goldmanfund.org.

The Goldman Sachs Foundation

Established in December 1999 by the Goldman Sachs banking and securites firm to assist in the creation of partnerships in the public, private and non-profit sectors to promote innovation and excellence in education and youth development throughout the world. Formerly known as the Goldman Sachs Charitable Fund.

Activities: Operates nationally and internationally, supporting projects in the field of education through promoting partnerships between the public, private and non-profit sectors. Assistance is given to large projects that enhance academic outcomes and offer educational opportunities in the field of business and entrepreneurship. Major programme areas are Developing High Potential Youth, Promoting Entrepreneurship and Leadership, and Advancing Academic Achievement.

Geographical Area of Activity: International.

Publications: Annual Report; *Highlights of the Portfolio*; *Ideas into Action*.

Finance: A contribution of US $200,000,000 was made by the Goldman Sachs group to launch the Foundation. Annual revenue US $314,572,404, expenditure $25,302,602 (2009).

Board of Directors: Dina H. Powell (Pres.); John F. W. Rogers (Vice-Pres.); Kim Azzarelli (Vice-Pres.); Eileen M. Dillon (Vice-Pres.); Nancy D. Browne (Vice-Pres.); Russell A. Broome (Vice-Pres.); Noa Meyer (Vice-Pres.); Manda J. D'Agata (Treas.); Benjamin J. Rader (Sec.).

Principal Staff: CEO Lloyd C. Blankfein; Pres. and Co-COO Jon Winkelried, Gary D. Cohn.

Address: 85 Broad St, 22nd Floor, New York, NY 10004-2434.

Telephone: (212) 902-5402; **Internet:** www2.goldmansachs.com/citizenship/foundation.

Horace W. Goldsmith Foundation

Founded in 1955 by Horace W. Goldsmith to provide support for cultural activities, Jewish welfare funds and temple support, hospitals, particularly for the elderly, and education, especially higher education.

Activities: Operates in the USA and Israel to carry out its aims.

Geographical Area of Activity: USA and Israel.

Restrictions: No grants are made to individuals.

Finance: Total assets US $385,953,190 (31 Dec. 2010); total giving $17,460,666 (2010).

Principal Staff: CEO William A. Slaughter.

Address: 375 Park Ave, Suite 1602, New York, NY 10152-1600.

Telephone: (212) 319-8700.

Good360

Established in 1984, as Gifts in Kind International, to promote the donation of products from the private and commercial sectors to charitable causes around the world; name changed in April 2011.

Activities: A global network that co-ordinates and distributes donated products from the private sector, providing quality services and goods for poorer communities in different countries. These donations include computers for education, clothing for the homeless, products for disaster relief and construction materials for the rehabilitation of residential areas.

Geographical Area of Activity: International.

Publications: Annual Report; newsletter.

Finance: Total assets US $34,829,005 (31 Dec. 2010); annual revenue $290,066,003, expenditure $281,528,284 (2010).

Board of Directors: Gail Aldrich (Chair.); Mikel Durham (Vice-Chair.).

Principal Staff: Pres. and CEO Cindy Hallberlin; CFO Don Miller.

Address: 1330 Braddock Pl., Suite 600, Alexandria, VA 22314.

Telephone: (703) 836-2121; **Fax:** (703) 798-3192; **Internet:** www.good360.org; **e-mail:** serviceteam@good360.org.

Goodwill Industries International, Inc

Established in 1902 by Rev. Edgar Helms to assist in training and finding jobs for people who otherwise have difficulty in finding employment; with the long-term aim of helping ensure every person in the global community has the opportunity to achieve his/her fullest potential as an individual and to participate and contribute fully in all aspects of a productive life.

Activities: Operates internationally, running employment and training programmes to increase the self-sufficiency of people with barriers to work, for example people with disabilities, illiterate or homeless people. Seeks to create opportunities for vocational training and employment through its network of 165 autonomous, community-based agencies in the USA and Canada, and by creating alliances with other NGOs, foundations and companies. Affiliated with 14 organizations in countries around the world. Runs a chain of more than 1,900 Goodwill charity shops in the USA and Canada to raise funds. Goodwill Global, with an office in Washington, DC, seeks to foster Goodwill's entrepreneurial efforts outside the USA and Canada.

Geographical Area of Activity: International.

Publications: *Working!* (quarterly magazine); Annual Report.

Finance: Annual revenue US $39,708,989, expenditure $38,903,021 (Dec. 2009).

Principal Staff: Pres. and CEO Jim Gibbons.

Address: 15810 Indianola Dr., Rockville, MD 20855.

Telephone: (301) 530-6500; **Fax:** (301) 530-1516; **Internet:** www.goodwill.org; **e-mail:** contactus@goodwill.org.

Google.org

Activities: Google.org uses Google's strengths in information and technology to build products and advocate for policies that address global challenges. Manages the Google Foundation.

Geographical Area of Activity: World-wide.

Finance: Foundation assets total US $81,871,066 (31 Dec. 2008); annual revenue $1,625,222, expenditure $5,308,209 (2008); funding disbursed by the Foundation $900,000 (2008).

Board of Directors: Megan Smith (Pres.); Luis Arbulu (Sec. and Treas.).

Principal Staff: Pres. Megan Smith.

Address: 1600 Amphitheatre Parkway, Mountain View CA 94043-1351.

Internet: www.google.org; **e-mail:** press@google.com.

The Adolph and Esther Gottlieb Foundation, Inc

Founded in 1976 to assist artists in financial need.

Activities: Conducts two grant programmes to assist painters, sculptors and printmakers in a mature phase of their art who are in current financial need: the Emergency Assistance Programme available throughout the year; and the Individual Support Grant awarded on an annual basis.

Geographical Area of Activity: USA.

Restrictions: No grants to organizations, students, educational institutions, to those working in crafts, graphic artists or for projects.

Finance: Total assets US $28,778,366; total giving $461,505 (2007).

Principal Staff: Pres. Dr Dick Netzer; Exec. Dir Sanford Hirsch; Grants Man. Sheila Ross.

Address: 380 West Broadway, New York, NY 10012-5115.

Telephone: (212) 226-0581; **Fax:** (212) 226-0584; **Internet:** www.gottliebfoundation.org; **e-mail:** shirsch@gottliebfoundation.org.

Florence Gould Foundation

Founded in 1957 by Florence J. Gould to promote good relations between France and the USA, and for general charitable purposes.

Activities: Offers fellowships for research to be carried out in France; and a translation prize.

Geographical Area of Activity: USA and France.

Finance: Total assets US $74,028,098 (31 Dec. 2009); annual revenue $2,569,930 (loss), expenditure $8,106,217 (2009).

Board of Directors: John R. Young (Pres.); Daniel Davison (Vice-Pres. and Treas.); Walter C. Cliff (Sec.).

Address: 80 Pine St, Suite 1548, New York, NY 10005-1702.

Telephone: (212) 701-3400.

Graham Foundation for Advanced Studies in the Fine Arts

Founded in 1956, the Graham Foundation for Advanced Studies in the Fine Arts makes project-based grants to individuals and organizations and produces public programmes to foster the development and exchange of diverse and challenging ideas about architecture and its role in the arts, culture, and society.

Activities: Architecture and related spatial practices engage a wide range of cultural, social, political, technological, environmental, and aesthetic issues. The Foundation is interested in projects that investigate the contemporary condition, expand historical perspectives, or explore the future of architecture and the designed environment.

The Foundation supports innovative, thought-provoking investigations in architecture; architectural history, theory, and criticism; design; engineering; landscape architecture; urban planning; urban studies; visual arts; and related fields of inquiry. The Foundation's interest also extends to work being done in the fine arts, humanities, and sciences that expands the boundaries of thinking about architecture and space. In an effort to bridge communities and different fields of knowledge, the Foundation supports a wide range of practitioners (such as architects, scholars, critics, writers, artists, curators and educators) and organizations (such as non-profit galleries, colleges and universities, publishers and museums).

Open discourse is essential to advance study and understanding, therefore the Foundation's grant-making focuses on the public dissemination of ideas. With the Foundation's support, the work of individuals and organizations reaches new audiences, from specialized to general, and creates opportunities for critical dialogue between various publics.

Geographical Area of Activity: USA, international.

Finance: Annual revenue US $1,179,517, expenditure $2,183,333 (2009).

Board of Trustees: Linda Searl (Pres.); Hamza Walker (Vice-Pres.; Jeffrey Jahns (Treas.); Elizabeth Smith (Sec.)   .

Principal Staff: Dir Sarah Herda.

Address: Madlener House, 4 West Burton Pl., Chicago, IL 60610-1416.

Telephone: (312) 787-4071; **Internet:** www.grahamfoundation.org; **e-mail:** info@grahamfoundation.org.

Grameen Foundation—GF

Founded in 1997 by a group of friends who were inspired by the work of Grameen Bank in Bangladesh with the aim of combating poverty in the USA and world-wide; the organization grew from the Grameen Bank, offering small amounts of credit, and has now become a world-wide movement.

Activities: Supports the Grameen Bank in its anti-poverty programmes; these programmes include support for micro-credit institutions, projects in the areas of education and technical assistance, establishing joint ventures with the private sector, marketing products produced by small enterprises, and educating the public and government in the USA about poverty and its alleviation through micro-credit. Has established the Grameen Technology Center in Bangladesh.

Geographical Area of Activity: Middle East and North Africa, Sub-Saharan Africa, Latin America and the Caribbean, USA, East Asia, South Asia.

Publications: Papers; *Village Computing: A State of the Field, Reflections on the Village Computing Consultation; Measuring the Impact of Microfinance; Thinking About Microfinance Through a Commercial Lens; Banker to the Poor: Microlending and the Battle Against World Poverty; More Pathways Out of Poverty;* Annual Report; books.

Finance: Total assets US $29,714,993 (31 March 2011); annual revenue $24,609,497, expenditure $24,778,499 (2010/11).

Board of Directors: Paul Maritz (Chair.); Robert Eichfeld (Vice-Chair.); Si White (Treas.); Robert G. Ottenhoff (Sec.).

Principal Staff: Pres. and CEO Alex Counts.

Address: 1101 15th St NW, 3rd Floor, Washington, DC 20005.

Telephone: (202) 628-3560; **Fax:** (202) 628-3880; **Internet:** www.grameenfoundation.org; **e-mail:** development@grameenfoundation.org.

William T. Grant Foundation

Founded in 1936 by William T. Grant to promote the research capacity of promising scholars who investigate topics relevant to the understanding of and promoting the well-being and healthy development of children and adolescents, and generally helping young people reach their full potential.

Activities: The goal of the William T. Grant Foundation is to help create a society that values young people and enables them to reach their full potential. It pursues this goal by investing in research and in people and projects that use evidence-based approaches. Provides support to research on how contexts such as families, programmes, and policies affect youth, how these contexts can be improved, and how scientific evidence affects influential adults. Funded research outside the USA must clearly address an issue or question affecting a large number of young people aged 8 to 25 in the US or a particularly vulnerable subgroup of US young people.

Geographical Area of Activity: Mainly USA.

Restrictions: Funded to a limited number of communications activities.

Publications: Annual Report; brochures.

Finance: Annual research grant budget approx. US $7,500,000 (2010).

Board of Trustees: Henry E. Gooss (Chair.); Christine James-Brown (Vice-Chair.); Russell Pennoyer (Sec. and Treas.).

Principal Staff: Pres. Robert Granger.

Address: 570 Lexington Ave, 18th Floor, New York, NY 10022-6837.

Telephone: (212) 752-0071; **Fax:** (212) 752-1398; **Internet:** www.wtgrantfoundation.org; **e-mail:** info@wtgrantfdn.org.

The Grass Foundation

Founded in 1955 by Albert and Ellen Grass to support research and education in neuroscience.

Activities: Operates in the fields of medicine and science through a fellowship programme offering summer fellowships for young researchers conducting independent research at the Marine Biological Laboratory, Woods Hole, MA. Also supports several courses in neuroscience, provides annual funding of lectureships, awards prizes and organizes annual lectures.

Geographical Area of Activity: USA.

Restrictions: Applicants from overseas are eligible for fellowships, but work must be carried out at a North American institution. No support for ongoing research, full-time students, symposia or conferences.

Publications: Application guidelines; programme policy statement; information brochure.

Principal Staff: Pres. Janis C. Weeks.

Address: POB 241458, Los Angeles, CA 90024.

Telephone: (424) 832-4188; **Fax:** (310) 986-2252; **Internet:** www.grassfoundation.org; **e-mail:** info@grassfoundation.org.

Grassroots International—GRI

GRI was set up in 1983 as an autonomous, not-for-profit agency to attain positive social transformation.

Activities: The Organization carries out activities in the fields of social welfare and human rights in partnership with organizations in Latin America, Asia, Africa, the Caribbean and the Middle East; supports community development works by providing grants through partner NGOs to bring about a positive social change; carries out advocacy and educational activities on behalf of its partner organizations; and directs world attention to issues of power, social change and poverty through media.

Geographical Area of Activity: Africa (Horn), Asia, Middle East, Latin America and the Caribbean.

Restrictions: Grants are only made to specific organizations in specific regions.

Publications: *Insights* (newsletter); *GrassrootsONLINE*; fact sheets; reports and summaries; Annual Report.

Finance: Total assets US $2,313,939 (31 Oct. 2010); annual revenue $2,709,831, expenditure $2,868,184 (2009/10).

Board of Directors: Hayat Imam (Pres. and Chair.); David Holmstrom (Treas.); Soya Jung (Sec.).

Principal Staff: Exec. Dir Nikhil Aziz.

Address: 179 Boylston St, 4th Floor, Boston, MA 02130.

Telephone: (617) 524-1400; **Fax:** (617) 524-5525; **Internet:** www.grassrootsonline.org; **e-mail:** info@grassrootsonline.org.

William and Mary Greve Foundation, Inc

Founded in 1964 by Mary P. Greve.

Activities: The Foundation operates in the fields of education, international relations, especially between the USA and Eastern Europe, the environment and the performing arts, through grants to organizations.

Geographical Area of Activity: USA.

Restrictions: The Foundation does not generally accept unsolicited applications for grants. No grants are made to individuals, nor for scholarships or fellowships.

Principal Staff: Chair. John W. Kiser, III; Pres. Anthony C. M. Kiser.

Address: 665 Broadway, Suite 1001, New York, NY 10112.

Telephone: (212) 307-7850; **Internet:** www.wmgreve.org.

Solomon R. Guggenheim Foundation

Established in 1937 for the collection and preservation of, and research into, modern and contemporary art.

Activities: Funds the Solomon R. Guggenheim Museum, New York; the Peggy Guggenheim Collection, Venice, Italy; the Guggenheim Museum Bilbao, Spain and the Guggenheim Abu Dhabi, United Arab Emirates. Also supports international partnerships and the development of new museums in other regions of the world, special exhibitions, conservation efforts, educational initiatives, and research.

Geographical Area of Activity: International.

Finance: Annual revenue US $53,865,182, expenditure $65,515,442 (Dec. 2008).

Trustees: William L. Mack (Chair.); Jennifer Blei Stockman (Pres.); Wendy L-J. McNeil, Edward H. Meyer, Stephen C. Swid, Mark R. Walter (Vice-Pres); Robert C. Baker (Treas.); Edward F. Rover (Sec.).

Principal Staff: Dir Richard Armstrong; Sr Deputy Dir and COO Marc Steglitz.

Address: Solomon R. Guggenheim Museum, 1071 Fifth Ave (at 89th St), New York, NY 10128-0173.

Telephone: (212) 423-3500; **Internet:** www.guggenheim.org; **e-mail:** visitorinfo@guggenheim.org.

The Harry Frank Guggenheim Foundation

Founded in 1929 by Harry Frank Guggenheim to study and research 'Man's Relation to Man', the Foundation supports specific and innovative projects that seek to promote understanding of human social problems related to violence, aggression and dominance.

Activities: Operates nationally and internationally in the field of science, through research and grants to individuals for research; also makes awards for support during the writing of doctoral theses. Grants are available for holders of a doctorate or professional equivalent, and for doctoral candidates for the writing of their dissertation. Support is mainly given for basic research in the social, behavioural and biological sciences.

Geographical Area of Activity: International.

Restrictions: No grants to institutions, nor for programmes.

Publications: *HFG Review of Research;* Annual Report; research reports.

Finance: Total assets US $76,695,563 (31 Dec. 2009).

Board of Trustees: Peter Lawson-Johnston (Chair.); Deirdre Hamill (Sec. and Treas.).

Principal Staff: Pres. Josiah Bunting, III.

Address: 25 W 53rd St, 16th Floor, New York, NY 10019-5401.

Telephone: (646) 428-0971; **Fax:** (646) 428-0981; **Internet:** www.hfg.org; **e-mail:** info@hfg.org.

John Simon Guggenheim Memorial Foundation

Founded in 1925 by Senator and Mrs Simon Guggenheim to improve the quality of education and the practice of the arts and professions; to foster research; and to provide for the cause of better international understanding.

Activities: Operates nationally and internationally in all fields of science, the humanities and the creative arts, through fellowships and grants to individuals who have demonstrated exceptional capacity for productive scholarship or exceptional creative ability in the arts. Fellowships are open to all citizens and permanent residents of the USA, Canada, and Central and South America and the Caribbean.

Geographical Area of Activity: North, Central and South America and the Caribbean.

Restrictions: No grants to organizations or institutions, only to individuals. No grants for the performing arts.

Publications: Annual Report; brochures.

Finance: Annual revenue US $25,041,599, expenditure $12,622,709 (2010).

Board of Trustees: Joseph A. Rice (Chair.).

Principal Staff: Pres. Edward Hirsch.

Address: 90 Park Ave, New York, NY 10016.

Telephone: (212) 687-4470; **Fax:** (212) 697-3248; **Internet:** www.gf.org; **e-mail:** fellowships@gf.org.

Habitat for Humanity International

Founded in 1976 by Millard and Linda Fuller to provide affordable homes for families in need by building and rehabilitating simple housing.

Activities: Operates in the USA and less-developed countries in the field of social welfare, in particular housing, by providing volunteers to work alongside those in need of shelter to build adequate basic houses. Homes are then sold to families at no profit or interest. Also promotes sustainable building, providing education and training to local affiliates. Conducts programmes in more than 90 countries. Regional headquarters for Europe and Central Asia are located in Bratislava, Slovakia.

Geographical Area of Activity: International.

Publications: *Habitat World Magazine*; Annual Report.

Finance: Total assets US $253,154,816 (30 June 2011); annual revenue $322,634,707, expenditure $319,514,017 (2010/11).

Board of Directors: Elizabeth Crossman (Chair.); Fernando Zobel de Ayala (Vice-Chair.); Renee Glover (Vice-Chair.); Henry Cisneros (Sec.); Eduardo Tabush (Treas.).

Principal Staff: CEO Jonathan Reckford.

Address: 121 Habitat St, Americus, GA 31709.

Telephone: (229) 924-6935; **Fax:** (229) 924-6541; **Internet:** www.habitat.org; **e-mail:** publicinfo@habitat.org.

The John A. Hartford Foundation

Founded in 1929 by John A. Hartford for general charitable purposes.

Activities: Operates two programmes in the field of Ageing and Health: the Academic Geriatrics and Training Initiative and the Integrating and Improving Services Initiative. These programmes provide grants to US organizations aiming to improve the efficacy and affordability of health care for the increasingly ageing population in the USA.

Geographical Area of Activity: USA.

Restrictions: No grants are made directly to individuals.

Publications: Annual Report; E-newsletter; articles include *Decades of Focus: Grant Making at the John A. Hartford Foundation*; *Strategies to Advance Geriatric Nursing: The John A. Hartford Foundation Initiatives*; *The John A. Hartford Geriatric Social Work Initiatives*; *Views from Funding Agencies: The John A. Hartford Foundation*; *Foundation Funding for Geriatric Training*.

Finance: Annual revenue US $41,950,697, expenditure $11,199,206 (2010).

Board of Trustees: Norman H. Volk (Chair.); William T. Comfort (Sec.).

Principal Staff: Pres. Kathryn D. Wriston; Exec. Dir and Treas. Corinne H. Rieder.

Address: 55 E 59th St, 16th Floor, New York, NY 10022-1713.

Telephone: (212) 832-7788; **Fax:** (212) 593-4913; **Internet:** www.jhartfound.org; **e-mail:** mail@jhartfound.com.

Hasbro Children's Fund, Inc

Established in 2006 by Hasbro, Inc to improve quality of life for disadvantaged children aged 12 and under, their families and communities in the USA. The Fund includes giving formerly carried out by the Hasbro Children's Foundation (established 1984) and the Hasbro Charitable Trust.

Activities: Supports programmes in the USA and world-wide that assist disadvantaged and seriously ill children, and work in the areas of children's education and social welfare.

Geographical Area of Activity: USA and international.

Restrictions: No grants are made to individuals, to religious or political organizations, or to schools.

Publications: Annual Report.

Finance: Donated US $9,200,000 in financial support, $14,500,000 in toys and games (2010).

Board of Directors: Brian Goldner (Pres.); Barry Nagler (Sr Vice-Pres., Gen. Counsel and Sec.); David D. R. Hargreaves (Sr Vice-Pres.); Deborah Thomas (Sr Vice-Pres.); Karen Davis (Vice-Pres.); Martin R. Trueb (Treas.).

Principal Staff: Pres. and CEO Brian Goldner; CFO David D. R. Hargreaves.

Address: 1027 Newport Ave, Pawtucket, RI 02862.

Telephone: (401) 727-5429; **Fax:** (401) 727-5089; **Internet:** www.hasbro.com/corporate/community-relations/about.cfm; **e-mail:** hcfinfo@hasbro.com.

Health Alliance International—HAI

Established in 1987 as the Mozambique Health Committee, name changed in 1993 to reflect the expanding reach of its activities. Aims to improve the health and welfare of those in need around the world; and to educate North Americans about social, economic and political issues that affect those in Southern Africa.

Activities: Operates in the field of health care internationally in a number of ways in collaboration with local organizations: works to identify economic, social and political factors causing poor health care for marginalized peoples, and to raise public awareness of these matters; provides direct technical and material assistance in support of basic health services; engages in research and training in public health care in the USA and abroad (including parts of Sub-Saharan Africa, Central and South America, the Caribbean, Asia and the Middle East) and supports graduate training in public health at the University of Washington. Also tries to ensure the equal distribution and efficient delivery of quality health care world-wide and seeks to support policies that promote health, equality, social justice and self-sufficiency.

Geographical Area of Activity: International.

Publications: *Sickness and Wealth—The Corporate Assault on Global Health*; books; editorials; lectures; papers; presentations; newsletters (quarterly); Annual Report.

Finance: Annual revenue US $21,135,518, expenditure $21,033,492 (Dec. 2009).

Board of Directors: Aaron Katz (Pres.); Jo Anne Myers-Ciecko (Vice-Pres.); Kathy Hubenet (Sec.); Marlow Kee (Treas.).

Principal Staff: Exec. Dir Stephen S. Gloyd.

Address: 4534 11th Ave NE, Seattle WA 98105.

Telephone: (206) 543-8382; **Fax:** (206) 685-4184; **Internet:** www.healthallianceinternational.org; **e-mail:** info@ healthallianceinternational.org.

Health Volunteers Overseas—HVO

A private non-profit organization established in 1986 to improve health care in developing countries through training and education.

Activities: Operates in the field of health care and international development, working to improve the accessibility and quality of health care in developing countries in a number of ways. Volunteer professionals train local people in pathologies and medical problems they might encounter in their area, thus providing a self-sustaining, long-term medical presence in under-developed areas using local available supplies and equipment. Programmes specialize in child health, primary care, trauma and rehabilitation, essential surgical care, nursing education, oral health, blood disorders and cancer, infectious disease, and wound management.

Geographical Area of Activity: Africa, Central and South America, Asia.

Restrictions: Not a grant-making organization.

Publications: *The HVO Guide to Volunteering Overseas*; *The Volunteer Connection* (newsletter, biannual); The Net Connection (monthly e-newsletter); Annual Report.

Finance: Total assets US $1,225,324 (31 Dec. 2010); annual revenue $7,509,317, expenditure $7,245,393 (2010).

Board of Directors: Julia Plotnick (Chair.).

Principal Staff: Exec. Dir Nancy A. Kelly.

Address: 1900 L St NW, Suite 310, Washington, DC 20036.

Telephone: (202) 296-0928; **Fax:** (202) 296-8018; **Internet:** www.hvousa.org; **e-mail:** info@hvousa.org.

The Hearst Foundation, Inc

Founded in 1945 by William Randolph Hearst to support general charitable purposes in the USA. Shares an administration with The William Randolph Hearst Foundation (q.v.).

Activities: The Foundation supports programmes in the USA and its overseas dependencies in the fields of higher and private secondary education, health care, social welfare, and culture, through the provision of funds. Maintains an office in San Francisco, CA.

Geographical Area of Activity: USA and its dependencies.

Restrictions: Grants are not made to individuals.

Finance: Grants awarded US $34,165,000 (2011).

Board of Directors: George R. Hearst, Jr (Pres.).

Principal Staff: Dir George Irish; Dir of Grants Mason Granger.

Address: 300 West 57th St, 26th Floor, New York, NY 10019-3741.

Telephone: (212) 649-3750; **Fax:** (212) 586-1917; **Internet:** www.hearstfdn.org; **e-mail:** hearst.ny@hearstfdn.org.

The William Randolph Hearst Foundation

Established in 1948 by William Randolph Hearst to carry out general charitable activities. The Foundation shares a common administration with The Hearst Foundation, Inc (q.v.).

Activities: Extends financial support to organizations implementing projects in the areas of culture, social welfare, education and health care; makes miscellaneous grants, which are confined to the USA and its dependencies; offers scholarships through two programmes, the US Senate Youth Program and the Journalism Awards Program.

Geographical Area of Activity: USA and its dependencies.

Restrictions: No grants are made to individuals, for loans and programme-related investments, multi-year grants, start-up or seed funding, equipment of any kind, publishing projects, radio, film, television or other media-related projects, conferences, workshops or seminars, public policy research, special events, tickets, tables or advertising for fundraising events.

Finance: Grants disbursed US $34,165,000 (2011).

Board of Directors: William R. Hearst, III (Pres.).

Principal Staff: Dir George Irish.

Address: 300 West 57th St, 26th Floor, New York, NY 10019.

Telephone: (212) 586-5404; **Fax:** (212) 586-1917; **Internet:** www.hearstfdn.org; **e-mail:** hearst.ny@hearstfdn.org.

Heart to Heart International

Founded in 1992 by Dr Gary Morsch, an international development and relief organization that aims to alleviate human suffering.

Activities: Operates a number of programmes world-wide in the fields of international development and relief, including educational and medical supplies projects in developing countries, an international food programme, disaster relief for the victims of natural and man-made disasters, and ongoing domestic projects to help the poor, neglected and abused in the USA. Works in approximately 100 countries world-wide.

Geographical Area of Activity: International.

Publications: *The Link* (quarterly newletter); special reports.

Finance: Net assets US $25,715,126 (31 Dec. 2010); annual revenue $84,240,206, expenditure $82,636,637 (2010).

Board of Directors: Jim Kerr (Chair.).

Principal Staff: Founder and Pres. Gary Morsch; CEO André T. Butler.

Address: 401 S Clairborne Rd, Suite 302, Olathe, KS 66062.

Telephone: (913) 764-5200; **Fax:** (913) 764-0809; **Internet:** www.hearttoheart.org; **e-mail:** info@hearttoheart.org.

Hebrew Immigrant Aid Society—HIAS

Founded in 1881, HIAS aims to assist oppressed people (both Jews and non-Jews) world-wide and to resettle them in a safe country.

Activities: Assists refugees, mainly Jews, under threat internationally and helps to resettle them. The organization works to fulfill its mission in a number of ways, including providing information and services for refugees throughout the migration process; communicating between clients, resettlement communities and government authorities; acting as an advocate for better policies affecting refugees and immigrants; and providing advice and orientation for resettled people in the USA and elsewhere. In the USA, HIAS also assists immigrants with integration and acculturation to American society, and runs a scholarship programme for American and Israeli students. Maintains offices in New York, Latin America, Nairobi, Tel Aviv, Kiev and Vienna.

Geographical Area of Activity: International.

Publications: Annual Report; *Passages Magazine*; Policy Paper.

Finance: Total assets US $60,542,000 (31 Dec. 2009); annual revenue $31,547,000, expenditure $24,829,000 (2009).

Board of Directors: Marc Silberberg (Chair.); Suzette Brooks Masters (Sec.); Sanford K. Mozes (Treas.).

Principal Staff: Pres. and CEO Gideon Aronoff.

Address: 333 Seventh Ave, 16th Floor, New York, NY 10001.

Telephone: (212) 967-4100; **Fax:** (212) 967-4483; **Internet:** www.hias.org; **e-mail:** info@hias.org.

Heifer International

Founded in 1944 by Dan West, with the aim of providing long-term solutions to hunger and poverty.

Activities: Operates in the field of aid to less-developed countries and social welfare, by providing animals that can be a source of food and income to families in need (including heifers, goats, llamas, geese, sheep, buffalos, rabbits and pigs) and training. In this way, the family receives a nutritious long-term food source, a potential income to be used for better education, housing and health care, and learns sustainable agricultural techniques. Recipients pass on offspring of donated animals to others. Established the Heifer International Foundation in 1990 to provide an ongoing endowment for the Heifer International and to educate people about charitable giving and estate planning. Operates active projects in 23 US states and maintains 38 field offices around the world.

Geographical Area of Activity: Africa, America, Asia and Eastern Europe.

Publications: *The Exchange* (quarterly newsletter); Annual Report.

Finance: Annual revenue US $98,237,000, expenditure $125,234,000 (June 2009).

Board of Directors: Marcia E. Williams (Chair.); Norman Doll (Vice-Chair.).

Principal Staff: Interim CEO Ardyth Neill.

Address: 1 World Ave, Little Rock, AR 72202.

Telephone: (888) 422-1161; **Fax:** (501) 907-2606; **Internet:** www.heifer.org; **e-mail:** info@heifer.org.

Howard Heinz Endowment

Founded in 1941 as the Howard Heinz Endowment and incorporating the Vera Heinz Endowment, established in 1986.

Activities: Works through five programme areas seeking innovative ways of improving the quality of life in Pennsylvania, supporting organizations that are concerned with the arts and culture, education, the environment, innovation economy and children, youth and families.

Geographical Area of Activity: USA, Pennsylvania.

Restrictions: No grants to individuals; grants only to non-profit organizations with an emphasis on programmes either in south-western Pennsylvania or of clear benefit to the region.

Publications: Annual Report; programme policy statement.

Finance: Annual revenue US $172,748,000, expenditure $57,286,000 (2010).

Board of Directors: Teresa Heinz (Chair.); James M. Walton (Vice-Chair.).

Principal Staff: Pres. Robert F. Vagt.

Address: 30 Dominion Tower, 625 Liberty Ave, Pittsburgh, PA 15222.

Telephone: (412) 281-5777; **Fax:** (412) 281-5788; **Internet:** www.heinz.org; **e-mail:** info@heinz.org.

Heiser Program for Research in Leprosy and Tuberculosis

Founded in 1972 by Dr Victor G. Heiser to support biomedical research into leprosy (research into tuberculosis was added in 1992). Part of the New York Community Trust, a public non-profit organization.

Activities: Operates internationally, through post-doctoral research fellowships awarded to biomedical students beginning post-doctoral training in research in leprosy and/or tuberculosis at a stipend of US $30,000–$35,000 a year; and research grants for one year of up to $30,000 (the same amount to apply should application for a second year be approved) made to laboratories conducting leprosy researchto accelerate the World Health Organization's efforts to eliminate leprosy as a public health problem throughout the world. Has also funded a project to determine the DNA sequence of the entire genome of *Mycobacterium leprae*.

Geographical Area of Activity: International.

Restrictions: Grants for research fellowships only. In 2012 the Heiser Program is funding leprosy research only and will not support post-doctoral fellowships in tuberculosis research.

Publications: Annual Reports; grants newsletters; financial statements; guidelines for grant applicants; handbook; brochure; professional notes newsletters.

Board of Directors: Charlynn Goins (Chair.).

Principal Staff: Dir Len McNally.

Address: c/o The New York Community Trust, 909 Third Ave, New York, NY 10022.

Telephone: (212) 686-0010; **Fax:** (212) 532-8528; **Internet:** www.nycommunitytrust.org; **e-mail:** lm@nyct-cfi.org.

The Leona M. and Harry B. Helmsley Charitable Trust

Established by Leona Helmsley in 1999.

Activities: Leona Helmsley died in 2007 and bequeathed her estate, estimated at more than US $4,000,000,000, to the Foundation, which was to continue the Helmsleys' philanthropic legacy.

Geographical Area of Activity: USA.

Finance: Total assets US $4,143,881,000 (31 March 2011).

Principal Staff: CEO John R. Ettinger.

Address: 230 Park Ave, New York, NY 10169-0698.

Telephone: (212) 679-3600; **Internet:** helmsleytrust.org; **e-mail:** info@helmsleytrust.org.

HELP International

Founded in 1999 in reponse to the suffering caused by Hurricane Mitch in Honduras. An initial group of 46 volunteers raised more than US $115,000 and spent four months in Honduras conducting humanitarian aid work and administering micro-credit loans to those in need. These initial projects affected the lives of an estimated 4,000 people, providing relief to many people left homeless bythe hurricane.

Activities: A registered 501 (c) 3 non-profit organization serving in various projects, including earthquake relief, microfinance impact assessment, family gardening, adobe stoves, libraries, business training and teaching English as a second language. HELP currently operates in El Salvador, India, Uganda, Peru, Tanzania, Thailand, Belize and Fiji. Continues to focus on facilitating poverty elimination world-wide.

Geographical Area of Activity: Belize, El Salvador, Peru, Fiji, India, Thailand, Uganda, Tanzania.

Board of Directors: Warner P. Woodworth (Chair).

Principal Staff: Co-Exec. Dirs Matthew Colling (Operations), Mike Duthrie (Finance); Programme Dir Arturo Fuentes.

Address: 455 N University Ave, Suite 212, Provo, UT 84601.

Telephone: (801) 374-0556; **Fax:** (801) 374-0457; **Internet:** www.help-international.org; **e-mail:** humanresources@help-international.org.

The William and Flora Hewlett Foundation

Founded in 1966 by William R. Hewlett, Flora Lamson Hewlett and Walter B. Hewlett to promote the well-being of humanity by supporting selected activities of a charitable, religious, scientific, literary or educational nature as well as organizations or institutions engaged in such activities.

Activities: Operates primarily in the fields of education, environment, global development, performing arts, population and philanthropy, through the provision of grants to relevant institutions and regional grants. Activities are restricted to the USA. A proportion of the organization's funds are given to projects in the San Francisco Bay area, CA.

Geographical Area of Activity: USA.

Restrictions: The Foundation makes grants to non-profit charitable organizations. The Foundation normally does not make grants intended to support basic research, capital construction funds, endowment, general fundraising drives, or fundraising events; nor does it make grants intended to support candidates for political office, to influence legislation, or to support sectarian or religious purposes.

Publications: Annual Report; brochures and programme reports; newsletter.

Finance: Annual revenue US $889,652,000, expenditure $250,035,000 (2010).

Board: Walter B. Hewlett (Chair.); Harvey V. Fineberg (Vice-Chair.).

Principal Staff: Pres. Paul Brest; Vice-Pres. Susan Bell; Vice-Pres. and Co-Chief Investment Officer Laurance R. Hoagland, Jr.

Address: 2121 Sand Hill Rd, Menlo Park, CA 94025.

Telephone: (650) 234-4500; **Fax:** (650) 234-4501; **Internet:** www.hewlett.org; **e-mail:** ebrown@hewlett.org.

Conrad N. Hilton Foundation and Conrad N. Hilton Fund—CNHF

Founded in 1944 by Conrad N. Hilton, hotel entrepreneur, for the alleviation of the suffering of the world's most disadvantaged people, with a special emphasis on children and support for the work of the Roman Catholic Sisters.

Activities: In 1996 the Foundation established the annual Conrad N. Hilton Humanitarian Prize of US $1,000,000, which honours a charitable or NGO that has made extraordinary contributions toward alleviating human suffering anywhere in the world. Each year the award is presented at an international humanitarian conference sponsored by the Foundation. Also initiates and develops long-term projects and seeks out organizations to implement them, in the priority funding areas of: world-wide blindness prevention and treatment through the Perkins School for the Blind; potable water development and sanitation in Africa (Ghana, Niger and Mali) through the West Africa Water Initiative; early childhood development; substance abuse prevention through the BEST Foundation for a Drug-Free Tomorrow, and its Project ALERT curriculum; hospitality management education through sponsorship of the Conrad N. Hilton College of Hotel and Restaurant Management at the University of Houston; and homeless and mentally ill people through the launch of the initiative, Strengthening at Risk and Homeless Young Mothers and funding of the Corporation for Supportive Housing and the National Alliance to End Homelessness. The Conrad N. Hilton Fund's principal beneficiary is the Conrad N. Hilton Fund for Sisters, established in 1986 and administered separately, which supports projects operated by Roman Catholic Sisters serving the economically disadvantaged worldwide. It was announced in December 2007 that, under the terms of Barron Hilton's will, the Foundation would receive $1,200m.

Geographical Area of Activity: World-wide.

Restrictions: Does not accept unsolicited proposals; no grants to individuals.

Publications: Annual Report.

Finance: Total assets US $2,140,385,895 (31 Dec. 2010).

Board of Directors: Barron Hilton (Chair.).

Principal Staff: Pres. and CEO Steven M. Hilton.

Address: 10100 Santa Monica Blvd, Suite 1000, Los Angeles, CA 90067.

Telephone: (310) 556-4694; **Fax:** (310) 556-2301; **Internet:** www.hiltonfoundation.org; **e-mail:** prize@hiltonfoundation.org.

Hitachi Foundation

Founded in 1985 by Hitachi Ltd, Japan. This foundation is a non-profit philanthropic organization and contributes to strengthening communities in the USA.

Activities: The foundation has three major activities: a grant programme for business and communities; Yoshiyama Awards for exemplary services; and a community action partnership. Hitachi aims to support grassroots non-profit organizations throughout America, through its general grants programme; work with employees of the Hitachi companies in its Matching Funds Program; and makes 10 annual Yoshiyama Awards to senior school students in recognition of their community activities.

Geographical Area of Activity: USA.

Restrictions: The Foundation does not accept unsolicited proposals.

Finance: Total assets US $21,795,784 (31 Dec. 2010); annual revenue $2,797,524, expenditure $3,233,258 (2010).

Board of Directors: Bruce MacLaury (Chair.); Tsutomu Kanai (Hon. Chair.).

Principal Staff: Pres. and CEO Barbara Dyer; CFO Nalin Liyanamana.

Address: 1215 17th St NW, Washington, DC 20036.

Telephone: (202) 457-0588; **Fax:** (202) 296-1098; **Internet:** www.hitachifoundation.org; **e-mail:** info@hitachifoundation.org.

Holt International

Established in 1956 as Holt International Children's Services—HICS, serves as an international adoption agency, which has programmes in 10 countries.

Activities: Operates in the field of child welfare, specifically national and international adoption and family preservation. Has a network of its own offices, agencies and affiliated organizations around the world and is committed to successfully reuniting families and arranging adoptions, so that every child in their care is placed in a loving and secure family unit. Supports adopting families and funds staff training in child welfare and recommends policies related to children's rights and those of adoptive and birth parents to national governments and the UN.

Geographical Area of Activity: USA, Central America and Asia.

Publications: Annual Report; *Holt International Magazine*.

Finance: Total net assets US $7,683,558 (31 Dec. 2010); annual revenue $24,085,746, expenditure $23,940,959 (2010).

Board of Directors: Jeff Saddington (Chair.); Becca Brandt (Vice-Chair.).

Principal Staff: Pres. and CEO Phillip Littleton.

Address: POB 2880 (1195 City View), Eugene, OR 97402.

Telephone: (541) 687-2202; **Fax:** (541) 683-6175; **Internet:** www.holtinternational.org; **e-mail:** info@holtinternational.org.

J. Homer Butler Foundation, Inc

Founded in 1961 with donations from the late Mabel A. Tod to assist projects that care for sick people, especially leprosy patients and those with HIV/AIDS.

Activities: Funds projects helping seriously ill people, with a particular emphasis on the relief of people with leprosy and HIV/AIDS.

Geographical Area of Activity: Central and South America, Africa, Asia (the Philippines, India).

Restrictions: No grants to individuals, nor for education or construction.

Finance: Total assets US $4,786,860 (31 Dec. 2010); Total grants disbursed $168,500 (2010).

Principal Staff: Pres. James K. Yannare, Jr; Grants Admin. Dorothy Montalto.

Address: 30 West 16th St, New York, NY 10011.

Telephone: (718) 356-9293; **Fax:** (718) 442-5088.

Houston Endowment, Inc

Founded in 1937 by Mr and Mrs Jesse H. Jones for the support of any charitable, educational or religious undertaking.

Activities: Operates nationally, with greatest priority on local and state needs, in the fields of education and health institutions, through grants to institutions, scholarships and the construction and equipping of educational establishments and hospitals. Also makes grants in the areas of arts and culture, community enhancement and medical facilities and research.

Geographical Area of Activity: USA.

Restrictions: No grants to individuals; grants only to non-profit organizations.

Publications: Annual Report and financial statement.

Finance: Total assets US $1,349,331,842 (31 Dec. 2010); annual revenue $27,104,918, expenditure $19,634,889 (2010).

Board of Directors: Anthony W. Hall, Jr (Chair.).

Principal Staff: Pres. Ann B. Stern.

Address: 600 Travis, Suite 6400, Houston, TX 77002-3000.

Telephone: (713) 238-8100; **Fax:** (713) 238-8101; **Internet:** www.houstonendowment.org; **e-mail:** info@houstonendowment.org.

The George A. and Eliza Gardner Howard Foundation

Founded in 1952 by Nicea Howard to aid the personal development of promising individuals at the crucial middle stage of their careers.

Activities: Awards a limited number of one-year fellowships for independent projects in a five-year rotation of categories, as follows: creative non-fiction, literary translation into English, literary studies, film studies; photography, anthropology, archaeology; painting, sculpture, history of art and architecture; playwriting, music, musicology, theatre studies, history; and creative writing in English, including fiction and poetry, philosophy.

Geographical Area of Activity: USA.

Restrictions: The fellowships are tenable anywhere in the world, but are restricted to candidates who, regardless of their country of citizenship, are professionally based in the USA. Fellowships are not given to support degree candidates.

Principal Staff: Admin. Dir Prof. William C. Crossgrove; Co-ordinator Susan M. Clifford.

Address: Brown University, Box 1945, Providence, RI 02912.

Telephone: (401) 863-2640; **Fax:** (401) 863-6280; **Internet:** www.brown.edu/howard_foundation; **e-mail:** howard_foundation@brown.edu.

Howard Hughes Medical Institute—HHMI

Founded in 1953 by Howard R. Hughes to support the field of science, particularly medical research and education. Also interested in minority issues, notably Asian/Pacific islanders, African Americans, Latinos and Native Americans.

Activities: Operates a Medical Research Program conducting biomedical research in the USA in such fields as cell biology, genetics, immunology, neuroscience, structural biology and bioinformatics/computational biology. Makes grants to promote education in the biological sciences in the USA and supports research abroad, particularly in Central and South America, Canada, Europe (including the United Kingdom), Russia and Australia. Also assists scientists in the Czech Republic, Hungary and Poland through grants to the European Molecular Biology Organization. Fellowships are awarded for research training for medical students.

Geographical Area of Activity: World-wide.

Restrictions: Grants are made primarily within defined competitive programmes; rarely funds unsolicited proposals.

Publications: Annual Report; *HHMI Bulletin*; occasional reports; quarterly magazine; grant programme announcements.

Finance: Total assets US $18,237,794,000 (31 Aug. 2011); annual revenue $2,180,443,000, expenditure $870,121,000 (2010/11).

Trustees: Kurt L. Schmoke (Chair.).

Principal Staff: Pres. Robert Tjian; Exec. Vice-Pres. and COO Cheryl A. Moore.

Address: 4000 Jones Bridge Rd, Chevy Chase, MD 20815-6789.

Telephone: (301) 215-8500; **Fax:** (301) 215-8863; **Internet:** www.hhmi.org; **e-mail:** webmaster@hhmi.org.

Human Rights Watch—HRW

Established in 1978 as Helsinki Watch, with the aim of assisting in the protection of human rights world-wide; it does not accept direct or indirect funding from any government.

Activities: Operates in the field of human rights internationally in collaboration with other NGOs. Maintains five offices in the USA, and offices in London, Berlin, Toronto, Paris, Johannesburg, Moscow, Tokyo, Geneva and Brussels, which collect information on human rights, in areas such as executions, torture, restrictions on religious organizations, children's and women's rights, refugees, prisons, landmines and discrimination. Also carries out research; disseminates information; and lobbies national governments and international organizations.

Geographical Area of Activity: World-wide.

Publications: *World Report 2012 Arms; Business and Human Rights; Children's Rights; Emergencies; Health and Human Rights; International Justice; Lesbian, Gay, Bisexual & Transgender Rights; Refugee Policy; Terrorism/ Counterterrorism; Women's Rights*; and numerous other publications.

Finance: Annual revenue US $48,796,540, expenditure $44,152,639 (June 2010).

Board of Directors: James F. Hoge, Jr (Chair.); Susan Manilow (Vice-Chair.); Joel Motley (Vice-Chair.); Sid Sheinberg (Vice-Chair.); John J. Studzinski (Vice-Chair.); Hassan Elmasry (Treas.); Bruce Rabb (Sec.).

Principal Staff: Exec. Dir Kenneth Roth.

Address: 350 Fifth Ave, 34th Floor, New York, NY 10118-3299.

Telephone: (212) 290-4700; **Fax:** (212) 736-1300; **Internet:** www.hrw.org; **e-mail:** hrwpress@hrw.org.

The Humana Foundation, Inc

Founded in 1981 by Humana, Inc for general charitable purposes.

Activities: Operates mainly in Kentucky in the fields of the arts and culture, health and human services, education, community development and international projects; awards scholarships; operates institutes for medical research and training, and funds medical schools. Operates a wide-spread humanitarian aid project in Romania.

Geographical Area of Activity: Currently USA, Poland and Romania.

Restrictions: Focuses on organizations supporting communities where Humana, Inc has a business presence.

Board of Directors: Michael B. McCallister (Chair.).

Principal Staff: Pres. and CEO Michael B. McCallister; CFO James H. Bloem; Exec. Dir Virginia K. Judd.

Address: 500 W Main St, Suite 208, Louisville, KY 40202.

Telephone: (502) 580-4140; **Fax:** (502) 580-1256; **Internet:** www.humanafoundation.org; **e-mail:** humanafoundation@humana.com.

The Hunger Project

Non-profit organization dedicated to eliminating chronic hunger around the world by focusing on the human issues that cause it.

Activities: Operates in the fields of aid to less-developed countries and social welfare, through seeking to empower disadvantaged people in Africa, Asia and Central and South America to improve their own health, education, nutrition and income in collaboration with local grassroots organizations. Also committed to gender equality and the reduction of infant mortality. Awards the annual Africa Prize for Leadership for the Sustainable End of Hunger. Maintains offices in Australia, Bangladesh, Belgium, Benin, Bolivia, Burkina Faso, Canada, Ethiopia, Germany, Ghana, India, Japan, Malawi, Mexico, Mozambique, Netherlands, New Zealand, Peru, Senegal, Sweden, Switzerland, Uganda and United Kingdom.

Geographical Area of Activity: Africa, South Asia, and Central and South America, Latin America.

Publications: Newsletter (monthly); Annual Report.

Finance: Annual revenue US $14,404,782, expenditure $14,356,378 (2010).

Board of Directors: Steven J. Sherwood (Chair.).

Principal Staff: Pres. and CEO Mary Ellen McNish; CFO Lena Ariola.

Address: 5 Union Sq. West, New York, NY 10003.

Telephone: (212) 251-9100; **Fax:** (212) 532-9785; **Internet:** www.thp.org; **e-mail:** webmaster@thp.org.

IAPA Scholarship Fund

Founded in 1955 by the Inter American Press Association (IAPA) to support the exchange of journalists and journalism students between Western hemisphere countries.

Activities: Operates internationally (in the Western hemisphere) in the field of journalism, through exchange programmes and scholarships (at least 10 a year) awarded to residents of North, Central and South America and the Caribbean for study at university schools of journalism abroad.

Geographical Area of Activity: North, Central and South America and the Caribbean.

Board: Jorge Andrés Saieh (Pres.); Carlos Salinas (Vice-Pres.); Alfredo Jiménez de Sandi (Vice-Pres.); Silvia Miró Quesada (Treas.); Nélida Rajneri (Sec.).

Principal Staff: Co-ordinator Mauricio J. Montaldo.

Address: 1801 SW Third Ave, Miami, FL 33129.

Telephone: (305) 634-2465; **Fax:** (305) 635-2272; **Internet:** www.sipiapa.com/v4/index .php?page=area_becas&idioma=us **e-mail:** mmontaldo@sipiapa.org; .

IBM International Foundation

Founded in 1985 for general charitable purposes in South Africa; in 1992 its charter was amended to allow charitable giving world-wide.

Activities: Operates nationally and internationally, mainly in the field of education; projects also include: global initiatives in early learning and the arts and culture; and grants to organizations working in Africa, Asia and Europe. The Foundation launched the Smarter Cities Initiative in 2010 to assist in the technological development of 100 cities world-wide.

Geographical Area of Activity: World-wide.

Restrictions: Does not consider requests from individuals, or for individual endeavours.

Publications: Information brochure.

Finance: Funded by IBM Corporation.

Officers and Directors: Stanley S. Litow (Pres.); Paula W. Baker (Vice-Chair.).

Address: c/o IBM Corporation, New Orchard Rd, Armonk, NY 10504-1709.

Telephone: (914) 766-1900; **Fax:** (914) 499-7624; **Internet:** www.ibm.com/ibm/ibmgives; **e-mail:** kelly.sims@us.ibm .com.

IMA World Health—Interchurch Medical Assistance, Inc

Founded in 1960.

Activities: IMA World Health helps provide essential health care services and supplies, without bias, to people in need in developing countries. This is accomplished through direct provision to hospitals, clinics, programmes, and other health-care providers, and by strengthening health-care systems through training, education, and oversight. Faith-based organizations are key partners in the work.

Geographical Area of Activity: World-wide.

Restrictions: Not a grant-making organization; channels grant monies to identified local partners as appropriate.

Publications: Annual Report.

Finance: Annual revenue US $143,000,446, expenditure $172,425,072 (2008/09).

Board: Timothy McCully (Chair.); Kirsten Laursen Muth (Vice-Chair.); Lisa Rothenberger (Sec.); William Clark (Treas.).

Principal Staff: Pres. and CEO Richard L. Santos.

Address: POB 429, New Windsor, MD 21776.

Telephone: (410) 635-8720; **Fax:** (410) 635-8726; **Internet:** www.imaworldhealth.org; **e-mail:** imainfo@imaworldhealth .org.

India Partners

Founded in 1984 to support self-help ministry projects in India through partner organizations that are committed to providing long-term solutions to poverty for every individual, regardless of race, religion, caste or sex.

Activities: Supports work in the fields of development assistance, leadership training, disaster relief, education and health work. Also works on short-term projects (including programmes related to agriculture, construction and water resource management among others) and runs a child sponsorship programme.

Geographical Area of Activity: India.

Publications: Annual Report; newsletter.

Finance: Total assets US $275,418 (30 June 2010); annual revenue $851,874, expenditure $932,970 (2009/10).

Board of Directors: Susan Paiement (Chair.); Susan Cannon (Vice-Chair.); Maryanne Obersinner (Sec.); John Kalita (Treas.).

Principal Staff: Pres. and CEO Brent Hample.

Address: POB 5470, Eugene, OR 97405.

Telephone: (877) 874-6342; **Fax:** (541) 683-2773; **Internet:** www.indiapartners.org; **e-mail:** info@indiapartners.org.

INMED Partnerships for Children

Established in 1986 to rescue children from the immediate and irreversible harm of disease, hunger, abuse, neglect or violence, and to prepare them to shape a brighter future for themselves and the next generation.

Activities: Works through a broad range of health, social, education, violence prevention and community development programmes focused on: securing children's health, development and safety; developing skills, knowledge and opportunities for children and youth; and building family and community capacity to support and sustain positive change.

Geographical Area of Activity: USA, Brazil, Peru, Jamaica, Trinidad and Tobago, South Africa.

Publications: *Home Visitors Handbook*; *Women's Wellness Sourcebook*; *Curriculum Sourcebook*; Annual Report; newsletters.

Board of Directors: Paul C. Bosland (Chair.); James R. Rutherford (Treas.); Wendy Balter (Sec.).

Principal Staff: Pres. and CEO Dr Linda Pfeiffer.

Address: 20110 Ashbrook Pl., Suite 260, Ashburn, VA 20147.

Telephone: (703) 729-4951; **Fax:** (703) 858-7253; **Internet:** www.inmed.org; **e-mail:** contact@inmed.org.

Institute of Current World Affairs—ICWA

Founded in 1925 by Charles R. Crane and Walter S. Rogers (and also known as the Crane-Rogers Foundation) to provide opportunity and full financial support to a few persons of high character and unusual promise to enable them to observe and study at first hand particular areas and problems of contemporary significance outside the USA.

Activities: Operates through the granting of a limited number of long-term fellowships with the purpose of promoting a thorough and balanced knowledge of particular areas or problems outside the USA and the effective communication of this knowledge. Fellowships are for study in Eastern Europe, the Middle East and Sub-Saharan Africa and for outside these areas. Fellowships are not awarded to support work towards academic degrees, nor to underwrite specific studies or programmes of research as such, but for independent self-designed programmes of study.

Geographical Area of Activity: World-wide, excluding USA.

Restrictions: Fellowship candidates must be fluent in the English language; fellowships are awarded only to candidates under 36 years of age.

Publications: Information brochure.

Finance: Total assets US $12,492,602 (2010); annual revenue $95,597, expenditure $620,589 (2010).

Board of Trustees: Joseph Battat (Chair.); Virginia R. Foote (Treas.).

Principal Staff: Exec. Dir Steve Butler.

Address: 4545 42nd St NW, Suite 311, Washington, DC 20016.

Telephone: (202) 364-4068; **Fax:** (202) 364-0498; **Internet:** www.icwa.org; **e-mail:** icwa@icwa.org.

Institute of International Education—IIE

Founded in 1919, following the First World War, by Dr Stephen Duggan, Dr Nicholas Murray Butler and Elihu Root, and based on the belief that the sharing of knowledge and skills is the only road to lasting peace and international understanding.

Activities: An independent non-profit, IIE is dedicated to increasing the capacity of people to think and work on a global basis. IIE implements more than 250 international exchange programmes, benefiting more than 20,000 people from 175 countries. Foremost is the world-renowned Fulbright Program, which IIE has administered on behalf of the US Department of State since the programme's inception in 1947. The Institute also serves corporations, foundations and government agencies world-wide, making available testing and advisory services, scholarships, information on opportunities for international study, emergency assistance to students and scholars, and the IIE Network membership programme, which links colleges and universities around the globe.

Geographical Area of Activity: International.

Publications: Annual Report; *Open Doors* (annually); *Funding for U.S. Study* (annually); *IIE Passport Study Abroad Directory* (annually); *IIENetwork Membership Directory* (annually); studies, handbooks, surveys and leaflets on international education.

Finance: Total assets US $319,761,000 (30 Sept. 2010); annual revenue $327,208,000, expenditure $335,400,000 (2009/10).

Board of Trustees: Thomas S. Johnson (Chair.); Henry Kaufman (Chair. Emer.); Dr Allan E. Goodman (Pres. and CEO);

Thomas A. Russo (Chair., Exec. Cttee); Ruth Hinerfeld, Henry G. Jarecki (Vice-Chair.); Mark A. Angelson (Treas.).

Principal Staff: Pres. and CEO Allan E. Goodman.

Address: 809 United Nations Plaza, New York, NY 10017.

Telephone: (212) 883-8200; **Fax:** (212) 984-5452; **Internet:** www.iie.org; **e-mail:** info@iie.org.

Inter-American Foundation—IAF

Founded in 1969 by the US Congress (as an independent agency, so that its operations would not be affected by short-term US policy considerations) to support the self-help efforts of disadvantaged people in Central and South America and the Caribbean.

Activities: The IAF is an independent agency of the US government that provides grants to non-governmental and community-based organizations in Latin America and the Caribbean for innovative, sustainable and participatory self-help programmes. The IAF primarily funds partnerships among grassroots and non-profit organizations, businesses and local governments, directed at improving the quality of life of poor people and strengthening participation, accountability and democratic practices. To contribute to a better understanding of the development process, the IAF also shares its experiences and the lessons it has learned.

Geographical Area of Activity: Central and South America and the Caribbean.

Publications: *Grassroots Development* (journal, 2 a year in English, Spanish and Portuguese); annual review; fact sheets.

Finance: The Foundation receives about 60% of its annual budget from the US Congress (appropriation of US19,300,000 in 2007); it also receives funding from the Social Progress Trust Fund of the Inter-American Development Bank.

Board of Directors: John P. Salazar (Chair.); Thomas J. Dodd (Vice-Chair.).

Principal Staff: Pres. Robert N. Kaplan.

Address: 901 N Stuart St, 10th Floor, Arlington, VA 22203.

Telephone: (703) 306-4301; **Fax:** (703) 306-4365; **Internet:** www.iaf.gov; **e-mail:** info@iaf.gov.

International Aid, Inc—IA

Established in 1980, IA is a non-profit Christian relief and development agency that works globally to improve the health of the world's poorest people.

Activities: Programmes include the HydrAidTM BioSand Water Filter, which provides households throughout the developing world with safe drinking water, as well as the distribution of new and refurbished medical equipment and supplies to hospitals and clinics in developing countries. IA also partners with academia, corporations and NGOs to develop and implement training programmes for health professionals throughout the world. Has field staff in Central America, Africa and Asia.

Geographical Area of Activity: International.

Publications: Annual Report.

Finance: Total net assets US $1,601,335 (30 June 2011); annual revenue $133,291,853, expenditure $132,745,846 (2010/11).

Principal Staff: Pres. and CEO Myles D. Fish.

Address: 17011 Hickory St, Spring Lake, MI 49456-9712.

Telephone: (616) 846-7490; **Fax:** (616) 846-3842; **Internet:** www.internationalaid.org; **e-mail:** ia@internationalaid.org.

International Center for Not-for-Profit Law—ICNL

Established in 1992, ICNL strives to create a world where civil society can freely develop in all its forms and participate in public decisions. In pursuit of that goal, ICNL's programmes and research focus on promoting an enabling legal environment for civil society and public participation world-wide.

Activities: Operates in more than 90 countries, co-operating with national and international organizations in the area of third-sector law. Provides technical legal assistance, training and educational materials for legal professionals; organizes conferences; hosts senior research fellowships; and publishes research. Maintains an online library and resource centre with more than 2,300 materials. ICNL has offices in Washington DC, Budapest, Almaty, Kiev, Sofia, Ashgabat, Kabul, Moscow, Baku, Bishkek and Dushanbe.

Geographical Area of Activity: World-wide.

Publications: Annual Reports; *Defending Civil Society: A Report of the World Movement for Democracy*; *International Investment Treaty Protection of Not-for-Profit Organizations*; *Safeguarding Civil Society in Politically Complex Environments*; *Recent Laws and Legislative Proposals to Restrict Civil Society and Civil Society Organizations*; *Handbook on Freedom of Association under the European Convention of Human Rights and Fundamental Freedoms*;*The International Journal of Not-for-Profit Law*; *International Investment Treaty Protection of Not-for-Profit Organizations*; *NGO Laws in Select Arab States*; *Development of Noncommercial Law in Kazakhstan*; *Freedom of Association in Central Asia*; *Law and Civil Society in the South Pacific*.

Finance: Annual revenue US $5,218,446, expenditure $4,631,016 (2009).

Board of Directors: Lindsay Driscoll (Chair.); Filiz Bikmen Bugay (Vice-Chair.); W. Aubrey Webson (Sec. and Treas.).

Principal Staff: Pres. Douglas Rutzen.

Address: 1126 16th St NW, Suite 400, Washington, DC 20036.

Telephone: (202) 452-8600; **Fax:** (202) 452-8555; **Internet:** www.icnl.org; **e-mail:** infoicnl@icnl.org.

International Center for Research on Women—ICRW

ICRW was founded in 1976 and since inception it has been working in collaboration with governments and partner organizations world-wide towards attaining reduction in poverty, promoting development that is impartial to gender, and bettering the lives of the female population.

Activities: The Center extends support to issues influencing women everywhere, including HIV/AIDS, economic growth, poverty reduction, reproductive health and nutrition, policy and communications, population and social transition, social struggle and transformation, through research, direct action and advocacy. The Center's country office is located in New Delhi, India, and a project office is located at Secunderabad, also in India. Also maintains a project office in Kampala, Uganda.

Geographical Area of Activity: World-wide.

Publications: Annual Report; research reports; newsletters.

Finance: Total assets US $15,746,516 (30 Sept. 2010); annual revenue $14,260,282, expenditure $14,193,461 (2009/10).

Board of Directors: Jeanne L. Warner (Chair.).

Principal Staff: Pres. Sarah Degnan Kambou.

Address: 1120 20th St NW, Suite 500 North, Washington, DC 20036.

Telephone: (202) 797-0007; **Fax:** (202) 797-0020; **Internet:** www.icrw.org; **e-mail:** info@icrw.org.

International Child Art Foundation

A charity founded in 1997 by Ashfaq Ishaq to harness children's imagination for positive social change.

Activities: Operates the Arts Olympiad, World Children's Festival, Healing Arts Program and Peace Through Art Program.

Geographical Area of Activity: International.

Restrictions: Arts Olympiad restricted to children between the ages of eight and 12. No grants to individuals or non-profit organizations.

Publications: *ChildArt* (quarterly magazine); *Sketches* (newsletter).

Executive Board: Dr Ashfaq Ishaq (Chair.); Katty Guerami (Sec.).

Address: POB 58133, Washington, DC 20037.

Telephone: (202) 530-1000; **Fax:** (202) 530-1080; **Internet:** www.icaf.org; **e-mail:** childart@icaf.org.

International College of Surgeons—ICS

Founded in 1935 by Dr Max Thorek; a world-wide federation of organizations that aims to encourage world-wide surgical excellence through training, humanitarian work, education and fellowship.

Activities: Operates in the field of medicine and health, through the exchange of surgical knowledge and techniques, and assisting in surgical missions in developing countries around the world, including disaster relief work and providing surgical care alongside other humanitarian agencies. Offers scholarships for surgical training, funds surgical research and lectureships. There are 60 national sections, of which ICS–USA is the largest. Maintains the International Museum of Surgical Science, in Chicago, IL.

Geographical Area of Activity: World-wide.

Publications: *International Surgery* (bimonthly journal).

Principal Staff: Exec. Dir Max C. Downham.

Address: 1516 N Lakeshore Dr., Chicago, IL 60610.

Telephone: (312) 642-3555; **Fax:** (312) 787-1624; **Internet:** www.icsglobal.org; **e-mail:** info@icsglobal.org.

International Education Research Foundation, Inc—IERF

Founded in 1969 as a public-benefit, non-profit agency.

Activities: Evaluates international education credentials in terms of US equivalence for employment purposes, for colleges, universities, licensing agencies, professional organizations and the armed services. The Foundation also conducts workshops and research, maintains a library on international education, and operates a research grant programme.

Geographical Area of Activity: World-wide.

Board of Directors: Leo A. Van Cleve (Chair.); Ilan Haimoff (Treas.); Debra Bean (Sec.).

Principal Staff: Exec. Dir Susan J. Bedil.

Address: POB 3665, Culver City, CA 90231-3665.

Telephone: (310) 258-9451; **Fax:** (310) 342-7086; **Internet:** www.ierf.org; **e-mail:** info@ierf.org.

International Executive Service Corps— IESC

IESC is a private, not-for-profit organization founded in 1964 by David Rockefeller, that capitalizes on the skills of industry-expert volunteers, consultants, and professional staff to promote economic growth around the world.

Activities: Promotes economic development world-wide by providing technical or managerial experts to assist in enterprise projects in the developing world, thus ultimately increasing employment and standards of living. Skills Bank registry of more than 8,500 volunteer and consultant experts and alliances with more than 15 similar organizations world-wide.

Geographical Area of Activity: World-wide.

Publications: IESC Update Newsletter; mid-year reports.

Finance: Funded by USAID, other US Government agencies, corporations and foundations.

Board of Directors: John R. Torrell, III (Chair.).

Principal Staff: Pres. and CEO Thomas Miller.

Address: 1900 M St NW, Suite 500, Washington, DC 20036.

Telephone: (202) 589-2600; **Fax:** (202) 326-0289; **Internet:** www.iesc.org; **e-mail:** iesc@iesc.org.

International Eye Foundation—IEF

Founded in 1961 as the International Eye Bank by Dr John Harry King, Jr, to promote the prevention and cure of blindness in developing countries, through the provision of training; clinical, surgical and preventive services; equipment, supplies and medication; public education; and technical assistance in the development of health infrastructure. Present name adopted in 1969.

Activities: Operates internationally in the fields of medicine, public health and education, through co-operative programmes with health ministries and private indigenous organizations, as well as through fellowships for ophthalmic training and scientific conferences. Addresses the prevention and amelioration of conditions such as onchocerciasis (river blindness), xerophthalmia, glaucoma, cataracts and other major eye diseases, through projects in Africa, Asia, Central and South America, and Eastern Europe.

Geographical Area of Activity: World-wide.

Publications: *Eye to Eye*; *Eye Care in Developing Nations*; *IEF Fact Sheets*; Annual Report.

Finance: Total assets US $3,425,131 (30 June 2011); annual revenue $7,326,034, expenditure $7,153,969 (2010/11).

Board of Directors: Frank S. Ashburn, Jr (Chair.); Fran Legon (Vice-Chair.); Roger Jantio (Treas.); Kathryn D. Leckey (Sec.).

Principal Staff: Pres. and CEO Victoria M. Sheffield.

Address: 10801 Connecticut Ave, Kensington, MD 20895.

Telephone: (240) 290-0263; **Fax:** (240) 290-0269; **Internet:** www.iefusa.org; **e-mail:** ief@iefusa.org.

The International Foundation

Founded in 1948 to assist people of developing countries in their endeavours to attain a better standard of living and to obtain a reasonable degree of self-sufficiency.

Activities: Makes grants to US-based agencies or institutions engaged in aid to developing countries in Asia, Central and South America, the Caribbean, the Middle East, the South Pacific and Southern Africa, with priority given to agricultural research and production; medicine and health (including sanitation and nutrition); education and research; and social welfare and development (including the arts and humanities, business, refugees and population planning).

Geographical Area of Activity: Southern Africa, the Middle East, Central and South America, Asia and the South Pacific.

Restrictions: No grants to individuals, nor for scholarships, conferences, operating budgets or endowment funds.

Publications: Information brochure.

Board of Trustees: Frank H. Madden (Pres.); John D. Carrico (Sec. and Treas.).

Principal Staff: Grants Chair. Dr Edward A. Holmes.

Address: 1700 Route 23 North, Suite 300, Wayne, NJ 07470.

Telephone: (973) 406-3970; **Fax:** (973) 406-3969; **Internet:** www.intlfoundation.org; **e-mail:** info@intlfoundation.org.

International Foundation for Art Research—IFAR

Founded in 1969 by John de Menil, John Rewald and Harry Bober to research authentication problems and provide information to the art world.

Activities: Operates in the field of the arts and humanities, nationally through self-conducted programmes, and internationally through research, grants to institutions, publications and training courses. The Foundation has an Art Advisory Council and a Law Advisory Council. Provides an art authentication service.

Geographical Area of Activity: World-wide.

Publications: *IFAR Journal* (incorporating *Stolen Art Alert*, quarterly, in co-operation with the Art Loss Register, the art community, insurance companies, the police, the Federal Bureau of Investigation—FBI and Interpol); IFAR reports.

Board of Directors: Jack A. Josephson (Chair.).

Principal Staff: Exec. Dir Dr Sharon Flescher.

Address: 500 Fifth Ave, Suite 935, New York, NY 10110.

Telephone: (212) 391-6234; **Fax:** (212) 391-8794; **Internet:** www.ifar.org; **e-mail:** kferg@ifar.org.

International Foundation for Education and Self-Help—IFESH

Founded by the Rev. Leon H. Sullivan to reduce poverty and unemployment in Sub-Saharan Africa, and improve links between Africa and the USA.

Activities: Operates in the fields of agriculture, business and economic development, democracy and governance, education and health to improve the quality of life in developing countries, with a particular focus on Sub-Saharan Africa. Its programmes work in a number of areas including reducing hunger and poverty, increasing literacy levels through better education, providing training to the unemployed and unskilled, helping to reduce the spread of HIV/AIDS, providing basic health care, and encouraging cultural, social and economic relations between Africans and African-Americans.

Geographical Area of Activity: Sub-Saharan Africa.

Restrictions: Operates its own programmes.

Publications: Annual newsletter; Annual Report.

Finance: Total assets US $4,964,125 (30 Sept. 2010); annual revenue $13,139,980, expenditure $13,270,867 (2009/10).

Board of Directors: Dr Eamon M. Kelly (Chair.).

Principal Staff: Pres. and CEO Dr Julie H. Sullivan.

Address: 5040 East Shea Blvd, Suite 260, Scottsdale, AZ 85254.

Telephone: (480) 443-1800; **Fax:** (480) 443-1824; **Internet:** www.ifesh.org; **e-mail:** information@ifesh.org.

International Foundation for Electoral Systems—IFES

Established in 1987, a private non-profit organization that provides technical assistance in the promotion of democracy world-wide.

Activities: Operates world-wide in the fields of education, international affairs, law and human rights, politics and civil society, through self-conducted programmes, research, grants to institutions, scholarships and fellowships, conferences, training courses and publications. Also offers information about democratic development and elections. The Foundation has developed methodologies that promote the understanding of the political, social and economic background to international electoral events. It organizes training courses for election officials and NGOs; the Foundation supports civil society, rule of law and the strengthening of international governance. Has worked in more than 100 countries.

Geographical Area of Activity: World-wide.

Restrictions: Not a grant-making institution, however, public funds are expended to carry out programmes internationally, and sub-grants are made to in-country partners.

Publications: Annual Report; *Elections Today* (quarterly); *Money and Politics in Nigeria; The Resolution of Election Disputes: Legal Principles That Control Election Challenges* (2nd edn); *International Directory of Election Offices; Afro-Ecuadorians Strive for Political Rights; The Right Time for Re-engagement; Buyer's Guide to Election Suppliers.*

Finance: Total assets US $19,738,081 (2009).

Board of Directors: Peter G. Kelly (Chair.); William J. Hybl (Vice-Chair.); Lesley Israel (Treas.).

Principal Staff: Pres. and CEO Bill Sweeney.

Address: 1850 K St NW, 5th Floor, Washington, DC 20006.

Telephone: (202) 350-6700; **Fax:** (202) 350-6701; **Internet:** www.ifes.org; **e-mail:** info.communications@ifes.org.

International Foundation for Ethical Research

Founded in 1985 to support basic and applied research into valid alternatives to the use of live animals for research, testing and educational purposes.

Activities: Operates in the area of scientific research, through grants of up to US $15,000 per award and renewal postgraduate fellowships of up to $15,000. Grants are awarded to scientists who are developing credible alternatives to live animal research, and to postgraduate students seeking to incorporate animal welfare issues into their studies. The Foundation also disseminates information designed to increase awareness of alternatives through seminars, publications and workshops.

Geographical Area of Activity: International.

Publications: Newsletter; workshop proceedings.

Finance: Total expenditure US $1,050,000 (2007).

Principal Staff: Exec. Dir Peter O'Donovan.

Address: 53 West Jackson Blvd, Suite 1552, Chicago, IL 60604.

Telephone: (312) 427-6025; **Fax:** (312) 427-6524; **Internet:** www.ifer.org; **e-mail:** ifer@navs.org.

International Fund for Animal Welfare—IFAW

Founded in 1969 by Brian Davies to campaign for animal welfare.

Activities: Operates in the field of animal welfare, seeking to improve conditions for wild and domestic animals all over the world. Aims to reduce commercial exploitation of animals, protect natural habitats, and help animals in distress through campaigning and research. IFAW seeks to motivate the public to prevent cruelty to animals and promote animal welfare and conservation policies that advance the well-being of both animals and people. Works closely with a number of non-profit organizations, government leaders and volunteers to protect animals world-wide.

Geographical Area of Activity: World-wide.

Publications: Annual Report; *Our Shared World* (quarterly magazine); animal fact sheets; programme publications.

Finance: Total assets US $51,884,904 (30 June 2010); annual revenue US $29,438,853, expenditure $26,420,177 (2009/10).

Board of Directors: Thomas C. Ramey (Chair.).

Principal Staff: Pres. and CEO Fred O'Regan; CFO Thom Maul.

Address: 290 Summer St, Yarmouth Port, MA 02675.

Telephone: (508) 744-2000; **Fax:** (508) 744-2009; **Internet:** www.ifaw.org; **e-mail:** info@ifaw.org.

International League for Human Rights—ILHR

Established in 1942, a non-profit NGO aiming to defend individual human rights advocates.

Activities: Operates in the field of human rights, seeking to keep human rights at the forefront of international affairs, and working to ensure that laws and treaties relating to human rights are adhered to at all times. Holds consultative status with the UN and other international organizations, and raises issues and cases before the UN and other regional organizations to co-ordinate strategies for human rights protection, and to bring attention to particular causes. Conducts regular seminars for policy-makers, government officials and NGO representatives concerning prominent issues in the field of human rights. Presents a Human Rights Award annually. Maintains a representative office in Geneva, and has affiliates and partner organizations world-wide.

Geographical Area of Activity: International.

Publications: *League Reports*; newsletter.

Principal Staff: Pres. Robert Arsenault.

Address: 352 Seventh Ave, Suite 1234, New York, NY 10001.

Telephone: (212) 661-0480; **Fax:** (212) 661-0416; **Internet:** www.ilhr.org; **e-mail:** info@ilhr.org.

International Orthodox Christian Charities, Inc—IOCC

Established in 1992 as the official humanitarian arm of the Standing Conference of Canonical Orthodox Bishops in the Americas.

Activities: Operates in the field of international and humanitarian development, identifying priority needs in countries overseas and working on aid programmes through the Orthodox Church and local groups. Programmes include working with orphans, refugees and displaced persons, the elderly, children, single-parent families, the disabled and in hospitals and schools. It is currently working in Central and Eastern Europe, Palestinian Autonomous Areas, Africa, the Middle East, South Asia, the USA and Greece. International Orthodox Christian Charities is a member organization of InterAction (q.v.).

Geographical Area of Activity: Africa, USA and Central and South America, Central and Eastern Europe, the Middle East and Greece.

Restrictions: Does not support programmes of church mission.

Publications: *News and Needs* (newsletter); Annual Report.

Finance: Annual revenue US $37,760,024, expenditure $40,978,162 (2010).

Board of Directors: Michael S. Homsey (Chair.); Frank B. Cerra (Vice-Chair.); Mark D. Stavropoulos (Treas.); Maria Z. Mossaides (Sec.).

Principal Staff: Exec. Dir and CEO Constantine M. Triantafilou.

Address: 110 West Rd, Suite 360, Baltimore, MD 21024.

Telephone: (410) 243-9820; **Fax:** (410) 243-9824; **Internet:** www.iocc.org; **e-mail:** relief@iocc.org.

International Relief and Development—IRD

Aims to improve the quality of life of people living in developing countries throughout the world.

Activities: Operates in the fields of international aid and development, implementing programmes in less-developed countries with the support of other aid organizations, government agencies and private business sources. Works in more than 30 countries in Central and Eastern Europe and Central and South-East Asia in the areas of democracy and governance, economic growth, emergency response, food and agriculture, health and hygiene and rebuilding infrastructure. Maintains field offices in Armenia, Azerbaijan, Georgia, Indonesia, Montenegro, Serbia and Ukraine.

Geographical Area of Activity: USA (Gulf Coast), Central and South-East Asia and Central and Eastern Europe.

Restrictions: No grants are made.

Publications: Information bulletin; Annual Report and newsletters.

Finance: Annual revenue US $720,048,356, expenditure $714,221,508 (2010).

Board of Directors: Daniel L. Florea (Chair.); Roland Johnson (Vice-Chair.); Vera R. Silverman (Treas.); Rev. Dr John Deckenback (Sec.).

Principal Staff: CEO Rev. Dr Arthur B. Keys.

Address: 1621 North Kent St, Fourth Floor, Arlington, VA 22209.

Telephone: (703) 248-0161; **Fax:** (703) 248-0194; **Internet:** www.ird.org; **e-mail:** ird@ird-dc.org.

International Relief Teams

Established in 1988, a non-profit organization aiming to provide medical and non-medical relief to the victims of poverty and disaster around the world.

Activities: Organizes relief teams to travel to areas in which people are suffering through extreme poverty, or the effects of natural and man-made disasters. Much of the assistance lent is medical, including training programmes for doctors and medical staff in Central and Eastern Europe to improve quality of life and decrease infant mortality rates, the emergency provision of medical supplies, and surgical outreach programmes in Central and South America. However, the relief teams also work to bring clean water and improved sanitation to many, and provide disaster relief in the USA and in more than 50 countries abroad.

Geographical Area of Activity: International.

Publications: *TEAMNews* (newsletter); Annual Report.

Finance: Total revenue US $33,927,743, expenditure $33,816,519 (2010/11).

Board of Directors: Kay R. Gilbert (Chair.).

Principal Staff: Exec. Dir Barry La Forgia.

Address: 4560 Alvarado Canyon Rd, Suite 2G, San Diego, CA 92120-4309.

Telephone: (619) 284-7979; **Fax:** (619) 284-7938; **Internet:** www.irteams.org; **e-mail:** info@irteams.org.

International Rescue Committee, Inc—IRC

Voluntary organization founded in 1933 at the suggestion of Albert Einstein to help Germans suffering under the Nazi regime in Germany. Now works to provide relief, protection and assistance to refugees and victims of oppression or conflict internationally.

Activities: Works internationally to help those fleeing victimization, oppression and conflict. Resettles and rehouses refugees; and provides emergency shelter and supplies for homeless and displaced people, and health services and health care training in areas suffering the effects of violent conflict. Also awards the annual IRC Freedom Award.

Geographical Area of Activity: World-wide.

Publications: Annual Report.

Finance: Total assets US $195,269,000 (30 Sept. 2011); annual revenue $391,256,000, expenditure $355,623,000 (2010/11).

Board of Directors: Sarah O'Hagan (Co-Chair.); Tom Schick (Co-Chair.); Liv Ullmann (Vice-Chair.); Jean Kennedy Smith (Sec.); Tracy Wolstencroft (Treas.).

Principal Staff: Pres. and CEO George Rupp.

Address: 122 East 42nd St, New York, NY 10168.

Telephone: (212) 551-3000; **Fax:** (212) 551-3179; **Internet:** www.rescue.org; **e-mail:** donorservices@rescue.org.

International Rivers

Founded in 1985 as a non-profit organization aiming to protect river systems and the communities that depend on them, and to fight for world-wide environmental integrity, social justice and human rights.

Activities: Works with environmental and human rights organizations around the world to campaign for community-based river development, and with people who are directly affected by dams and other large-scale water intervention projects. Fosters greater understanding and respect for rivers and participates in research and project analyses. Makes recommendations for alternative solutions to international environmental problems caused by governments' environmental policies.

Geographical Area of Activity: World-wide.

Publications: *World Rivers Review* (2 a month); *River Revival Bulletin*; Annual Report; special reports; fact sheets; working papers; information resources.

Finance: Annual revenue US $2,271,431, expenditure $2,202,204 (2010).

Board of Directors: Marcia McNally (Co-Chair.); Deborah Moore (Co-Chair.).

Principal Staff: Exec. Dir Jason Rainey.

Address: 2150 Allston Way, Suite 300, Berkeley, CA 94704-1378.

Telephone: (510) 848-1155; **Fax:** (510) 848-1008; **Internet:** www.irn.org; **e-mail:** info@internationalrivers.org.

International Women's Health Coalition—IWHC

Founded in 1980 to improve reproductive and sexual education and health in the developing world.

Activities: Operates in the fields of medicine and health, and social welfare, in Bangladesh, Brazil, Cameroon, Chile, Nigeria and Peru to reduce preventable deaths and illnesses by providing better reproductive and sexual health information and services. Promotes women's rights; provides technical, practical and financial support to grassroots organizations that work in reproductive and sexual health care and women's rights; holds meetings and conferences; publishes books and information papers; raises awareness in the

USA of the problems facing women in these areas; acts as an advocate for new and improved health and population policies to benefit the lives of women and their communities; and provides grants for organizations engaging in innovative health care schemes, training, public education and advocacy.

Geographical Area of Activity: Selected countries in Africa, Asia and Central and South America.

Publications: *Positively Informed: Lesson Plans and Guidance for Sexuality Educators and Advocates*; *Twenty Years One Goal: 20th Anniversary Report 2004*; *Reproductive Health and Human Rights*; *My Father Didn't Think This Way*; *Nigerian Boys Contemplate Gender Equality*; Annual Report; and other publications.

Finance: Annual revenue US $6,019,818, expenditure $6,086,501 (2008/09).

Board of Directors: Brian A. Brink (Chair.); Debora Diniz (Vice-Chair.); Ann Unterberg (Vice-Chair.); Catherine A. Gellert (Sec. and Treas.).

Principal Staff: Pres. Françoise Girard.

Address: 333 Seventh Ave, 6th Floor, New York, NY 10001.

Telephone: (212) 979-8500; **Fax:** (212) 979-9009; **Internet:** www.iwhc.org; **e-mail:** info@iwhc.org.

International Women's Rights Action Watch—IWRAW

Established in 1985 at the World Conference on Women in Nairobi, Kenya.

Activities: A resource centre for activists, academics and organizations concerned with the advancement of women's human rights internationally. Supports NGOs throughout the globe in their work to improve women's status, advocating for positive change in government policy and law. Monitors the implementation of the Convention on the Elimination of All Forms of Discrimination Against Women—CEDAW—and implementation of women's human rights under the other human rights treaties.

Geographical Area of Activity: International.

Publications: Guides and tools for using international human rights principles and procedures to advance women's human rights; special projects.

Address: University of Minnesota, 229 19th Ave South, Minneapolis, MN 55455.

Telephone: (612) 625-4985; **Fax:** (612) 625-2011; **Internet:** www.iwraw.net; **e-mail:** mfreeman@umn.edu.

International Youth Foundation—IYF

Founded in 1990 by Richard R. Little, with funds provided by the W. K. Kellogg Foundation and the Rockefeller Foundation (qq.v.), to support programmes that help children and youth world-wide to develop skills in learning and living.

Activities: The Foundation is dedicated to the positive development of children and youth, between the ages of five and 20. It operates internationally in the fields of education, employability, leadership and engagement and health education and awareness. It identifies, strengthens and replicates effective programmes for young people, building a global network of independent, indigenous foundations committed to positive youth development, and increasing international philanthropy in support of such efforts. In 2010 there were 200 civil society organizations operating in around 73 countries.

Geographical Area of Activity: International.

Restrictions: Grants directed towards partner foundations only. The Foundation does not accept unsolicited proposals.

Publications: Annual Report; brochures; *What Works* series; country reports and studies; *Youth* magazine; articles; *Youth in Action*; *Our Time is Now*.

Finance: Annual revenue US $29,593,777, expenditure $22,198,485 (2010).

Board of Directors: Douglas L. Becker (Chair.).

Principal Staff: Pres. and CEO William S. Reese; CFO Samantha Barbee.

Address: 32 South St, Baltimore, MD 21202.

Telephone: (410) 951-1500; **Fax:** (410) 347-1188; **Internet:** www.iyfnet.org; **e-mail:** youth@iyfnet.org.

IREX—International Research & Exchanges Board

A non-profit organization established in 1968 and committed to international education in its broadest sense.

Activities: Operates in the field of education. Administers programmes in academic research, professional training, institution-building, technical assistance and policy-making, which operate collaboratively between the USA and the countries of Eastern Europe, the countries of the former USSR, Asia and the Middle East.

Geographical Area of Activity: USA, Middle East and North Africa, Asia, Central and Eastern Europe and Central Asia.

Publications: *Frontline* (newsletter); Annual Report; policy papers; online newsletter; conference reports.

Finance: Supported by public and private funds.

Board of Directors: Avis T. Bohlen (Chair.).

Principal Staff: Pres. W. Robert Pearson.

Address: 2121 K St NW, Suite 700, Washington, DC 20037.

Telephone: (202) 628-8188; **Fax:** (202) 628-8189; **Internet:** www.irex.org; **e-mail:** irex@irex.org.

The James Irvine Foundation

Founded in 1937 by James Irvine for charitable purposes.

Activities: Operates within California in the fields of arts, education, civic participation, culture and youth services not receiving government support, through grants to institutions; maintains office in Los Angeles.

Geographical Area of Activity: California, USA.

Restrictions: No grants are made to individuals, private secondary schools, for sectarian religious activities, normal operating expenses, nor for general support.

Publications: Annual Report; information brochure; publications relating to areas of interest; *Irvine Quarterly* online newsletter.

Finance: Annual revenue US $205,944,770, expenditure $72,722,127 (2010).

Board of Directors: Peter J. Taylor (Chair.); Gregory M. Avis (Vice-Chair.).

Principal Staff: Pres. and CEO James E. Canales.

Address: 575 Market St, Suite 3400, San Francisco, CA 94105.

Telephone: (415) 777-2244; **Fax:** (415) 777-0869; **Internet:** www.irvine.org; **e-mail:** communications@irvine.org.

Ittleson Foundation

Founded in 1932 by Henry Ittleson for the promotion of the well-being of humanity throughout the world, including, as means to that end, research, publication, the establishment and maintenance of charitable, religious and educational activities, agencies and institutions; and the aid of any such activities, agencies and institutions already established.

Activities: Operates nationally in the fields of the environment, health, welfare and education for health and welfare, with special emphasis on mental health and psychiatric research, through research grants to institutions, conferences, courses, publications and lectures. The Foundation's current main focus areas are AIDS, the environment and mental health.

Geographical Area of Activity: USA.

Restrictions: No fellowships or scholarships, travel grants or grants-in-aid to individuals; with a limited budget, the Foundation is unable to fund individuals, direct service programmes, continuing support or capital campaigns.

Publications: Annual Report.

Finance: Total assets US $15,820,845 (31 Dec. 2009); grants awarded $728,210 (2008).

Board of Directors: H. Anthony Ittleson (Chair. and Pres.); Anthony C. Wood (Sec. and Exec. Dir); Henry Davison (Treas.).

Principal Staff: Pres. H. Anthony Ittleson; Exec. Dir Anthony C. Wood.

Address: 15 East 67th St, New York, NY 10021.

Telephone: (212) 794-2008; **Fax:** (212) 794-0351; **Internet:** www.ittlesonfoundation.org.

Izumi Foundation

Established in 1998 to support and enhance the goals of Shinnyo-En USA, which are to address the root causes of human suffering, increase compassion and caring among all human beings, and promote a society that respects all living things. The Foundation focuses on the alleviation of human suffering through improved health care, in particular for the poorest and most vulnerable members of society.

Activities: Primarily operates through supporting efforts to reduce infectious diseases in less-developed and low-income countries in Sub-Saharan Africa and Central and South America, in particular projects that recognize the inter-relationship between disease and poverty; address the underlying causes of diseases and persistent health care problems; use innovative solutions to promote and help ensure sustainable outcomes; and increase collaboration and partnerships among local health care providers.

Geographical Area of Activity: Considers support for projects in Sub-Saharan Africa (Botswana, Burkina Faso, Ethiopia, Gambia, Ghana, Kenya, Lesotho, Madagascar, Malawi, Mali, Mozambique, Namibia, Niger, Nigeria, Rwanda, Senegal, South Africa, Swaziland, Tanzania, Uganda and Zambia) and Central and South America (Bolivia, El Salvador, Guatemala, Guyana, Haiti, Honduras, Nicaragua and Paraguay).

Restrictions: No unsolicited proposals accepted. No funding for medical research or other research-related activities; endowments, capital costs or fundraising activities; ongoing general operating expenses or existing deficits; lobbying of any kind; individuals; religious activities; or indirect costs.

Finance: Maximum grant available US $100,000.

Principal Staff: Programme Dir S. Eliza Petrow.

Address: One Financial Center, 28th Floor, Boston, MA 02111.

Telephone: (617) 292-2333; **Fax:** (617) 292-2315; **Internet:** www.izumi.org; **e-mail:** info@izumi.org.

Jewish Community Development Fund—JCDF

Established by the American Jewish World Service (q.v.) to support grassroots Jewish renewal and human rights programmes in Russia and Ukraine.

Activities: The Fund aims to revive Jewish religion, education and culture in Russia and Ukraine through supporting grassroots projects conceived and developed by local activists involved in community and leadership development, including youth groups, schools, child-care centres and inter-religious dialogue programmes.

Geographical Area of Activity: Russia and Ukraine.

Board of Trustees: Jim Meier (Chair.); Linda Heller Kamm (Vice-Chair); Ruth W. Messinger (Pres.); Nancy Schwartz Sternoff (Sec.); Marty Friedman (Treas.).

Principal Staff: Pres. Ruth R. Messinger; Dir Martin Horwitz; Deputy Dir Jon Orren.

Address: American Jewish World Service, 45 West 36th St, New York, NY 10018.

Telephone: (212) 792-2917; **Fax:** (212) 792-2932; **e-mail:** ajws@ajws.org.

Lyndon Baines Johnson Foundation

Founded in 1969, responsible for managing gifts that benefit two institutions at the University of Texas at Austin—the Lyndon B. Johnson Library and Museum and the Lyndon B. Johnson School of Public Affairs.

Activities: Makes grants for living and travel expenses incurred by researchers of any nationality while conducting research on the life and career of Lyndon B. Johnson at the Johnson Library; also awards fellowship for work to be done in National Archives facilities, including Presidential Libraries.

Geographical Area of Activity: USA.

Finance: Total assets US $157,507,011 (31 Aug. 2011); annual revenue $11,407,201, expenditure $7,294,538 (2010/11).

Board: Larry Temple (Chair.); Ben Barnes (Vice-Chair.); Lyndon Olson (Vice-Chair.).

Principal Staff: Pres. Elizabeth Christian; Exec. Dir Elizabeth Boone.

Address: LBJ Library and Museum, 2313 Red River St, Austin, TX 78705.

Telephone: (512) 232-2266; **Fax:** (512) 232-2285; **Internet:** www.lbjfoundation.org.

Robert Wood Johnson Foundation—RWJF

Founded in 1936 by Robert Wood Johnson for the improvement of health care in the USA.

Activities: The Foundation operates through grants to hospitals, medical, nursing and public schools, hospices, professional associations, research organizations, local and government agencies and community groups, and focuses on three primary concerns in its grant-giving: to ensure that Americans of all ages have access to basic health care at reasonable cost; to improve the organization and provision of services to people with chronic health conditions; and to promote health and reduce the personal, social and economic harm caused by substance abuse (tobacco, alcohol and illicit drugs).

Geographical Area of Activity: USA.

Publications: Annual Report; *Advance* (newsletter); books; occasional reports.

Finance: Annual revenue US $62,076,000, expenditure $342,843,000 (2010).

Board of Trustees: Thomas H. Kean (Chair.).

Principal Staff: Pres. and CEO Risa Lavizzo-Mourey.

Address: POB 2316, Route 1 and College Rd East, Princeton, NJ 08543-2316.

Telephone: (609) 452-8701; **Fax:** (609) 452-1865; **Internet:** www.rwjf.org; **e-mail:** mail@rwjf.org.

The Johnson Foundation at Wingspread

Founded in 1958 by Herbert F. Johnson to promote international understanding, educational excellence, intellectual and cultural growth, and improvement of the human environment.

Activities: The Foundation aims to serve as a catalyst for innovative public and private solutions to healthy environments and healthy local communities. Activities are carried out principally through planning and carrying out conferences at Wingspread, the Foundation's educational conference centre in Racine, WI.

Geographical Area of Activity: USA.

Restrictions: Supports conference-related activities by non-profit organizations.

Publications: *Wingspread Journal*; Annual Report; information brochure.

Finance: Assets US $54,654,000 (30 June 2007); annual revenue $9,372,000, expenditure $4,834,000 (2006/07).

Board: Helen Johnson-Leipold (Chair.).

Principal Staff: Pres. Roger C. Dower.

Address: 33 East Four Mile Rd, Racine, WI 53402-2621.

Telephone: (262) 639-3211; **Fax:** (262) 681-3327; **Internet:** www.johnsonfdn.org; **e-mail:** info@johnsonfdn.org.

Joyce Foundation

Independent private foundation established in 1948 by Beatrice Joyce Kean to promote conservation, culture, economic development, education, campaign finance reform and the prevention of gun violence in the Great Lakes area.

Activities: Awards grants to not-for-profit organizations whose aims are to improve public policies in the areas of education, employment, environment, gun violence, campaign finance and culture. Also works to reduce poverty, to protect the natural environment of the Great Lakes and to prevent political corruption. In 2003 initiated the Joyce Awards, an annual competition open to major and mid-size cultural organizations in mid-West cities. Operates in the mid-West states, and in Canada.

Geographical Area of Activity: USA and Canada.

Publications: Annual Report; newsletters; *Welfare to Work: What Have We Learned*.

Finance: Annual revenue US $100,592,000, expenditure $44,743,000 (2010).

Board of Directors: Roger R. Fross (Chair.); Charles U. Daly (Vice-Chair.).

Principal Staff: Pres. Ellen S. Alberding.

Address: 70 West Madison St, Suite 2750, Chicago, IL 60602.

Telephone: (312) 782-2464; **Fax:** (312) 782-4160; **Internet:** www.joycefdn.org; **e-mail:** info@joycefdn.org.

Juvenile Diabetes Research Foundation International—JDRF

Founded in 1970 to support research into the causes, treatment, prevention and cure of type 1 diabetes and its complications.

Activities: Promotes research and education in the area of medicine and health, as well as outreach to those affected by diabetes and the general public. Offers grants and awards including: the Career Development Award in diabetes research for post-doctoral study in any country; the New Training for Established Scientist Award to provide assistance for visiting scholars researching in any country, in a field different from, but related to, the diabetes-related area in which the applicant normally works; the Summer Student Program in diabetes research to assist colleges, universities, medical schools, etc., in supporting student research work; and fellowships and research awards tenable in any country for research into diabetes and its complications.

Geographical Area of Activity: International.

Publications: Annual Report; *Online Countdown*; *Emerging Technologies E-Newsletter*; *Life with Diabetes E-Newsletter*; fact sheets.

Finance: Annual revenue US $203,800,000, expenditure $220,300,000 (2010/11).

Board of Directors: Mary Tyler Moore (Int. Chair.); Robert Wood Johnson IV (Chair. of JDRF); Frank Ingrassia (Chair. Bd of Dirs); Mary Elizabeth Bunzel (Sec. and Chair. Nominating and Governance); David W. Nelms (Treas. and Chair. Finance); Susan Alberti (Int. Patron); Gail Pressberg (Chair. Bd of Chancellors).

Principal Staff: Pres. and CEO Jeffrey Brewer.

Address: 26 Broadway, 14th Floor, New York, NY 10004.

Telephone: (800) 533-2873; **Fax:** (212) 785-9595; **Internet:** www.jdrf.org; **e-mail:** info@jdrf.org.

Max Kade Foundation, Inc

Founded in 1944 by Max Kade for general charitable purposes.

Activities: Operates nationally and internationally in the field of education, by sponsoring post-doctoral research exchange programmes between the USA and Europe in medicine and in the natural and physical sciences. Particular focus on developing relations between Germany and America.

Geographical Area of Activity: USA and Europe.

Restrictions: No grants or loans are made to individuals.

Finance: Annual revenue US $1,298,420, expenditure $3,923,503 (2009).

Board of Directors: Lya Friedrich Pfeifer (Pres. and Treas.); Berteline Baier Dale (Sec.).

Address: 6 E 87th St, 5th Floor, New York, NY 10128-0505.

Telephone: (646) 672-4354.

The Henry J. Kaiser Family Foundation

Founded in 1948 by Henry J. Kaiser and his family members principally to support medical care programmes.

Activities: The Foundation operates in the areas of health policy, media and public education, and health and development in South Africa, through the provision of funds for research grants, special projects, fellowships, scholarships, professorships, seminars, conferences and technical assistance. Grants in the Community Grants Program are limited to California, other grants are made in the USA and Canada. Awards the annual Nelson Mandela Award for Health and Human Rights.

Geographical Area of Activity: North America and South Africa.

Restrictions: No grants are made to individuals and no unsolicited requests for funding accepted.

Publications: Annual Report; news releases; fact sheets.

Board of Trustees: Richard Schlosberg (Chair.).

Principal Staff: Pres. and CEO Drew Altman.

Address: 2400 Sand Hill Rd, Menlo Park, CA 94025.

Telephone: (650) 854-9400; **Fax:** (650) 854-4800; **Internet:** www.kff.org; **e-mail:** kffhelp@kff.org.

Mitchell Kapor Foundation

Founded in 1997 by Mitchell Kapor to protect the environment, improve quality of life for all people and help sustain healthy ecosystems. Administered by the Jenifer Altman Foundation (q.v.).

Activities: Operates in the area of the environment, and science and technology, through two main programmes, relating to environmental health and the impact of information technology on society, by awarding grants to organizations and individuals carrying out work or research in these areas. Also helped found the Level Playing Fields Institute, which administers a small grants programme funding innovative projects on behalf of the Foundation. The Foundation's environmental health programme activities are managed by the Jennifer Altman Foundation (q.v.).

Geographical Area of Activity: USA.

Publications: Biennial Report.

Finance: Annual revenue US $3,306,979, expenditure $5,413,570 (2010).

Board: Mitchell Kapor; Freada Kapor Klein.

Principal Staff: CEO Cedric Brown.

Address: 543 Howard St, 5th Floor, San Francisco, CA 94105.

Telephone: (415) 946-3025; **Fax:** (415) 561-6480; **Internet:** www.mkf.org; **e-mail:** cbrown@mkf.org.

Howard Karagheusian Commemorative Corporation—HKCC

Founded in 1921 by Mihran Karagheusian and others to promote child welfare, public health services and international relief programmes in the Armenian refugee communities of Lebanon and Syria, and, on a smaller scale, in native Muslim Arab groups in the same communities.

Activities: Operates through self-conducted programmes, in Lebanon, Syria and Armenia, including establishing a health centre in Lebanon and offering related social and community services.

Geographical Area of Activity: Armenia, Lebanon and Syria.

Restrictions: No grants are made to individuals or organizations.

Publications: Annual Report.

Finance: Total assets US $47,498,229 (31 Dec. 2010); total grants disbursed $2,500 (2010).

Board of Directors: Michael Haratunian (Pres.); H. Irma Der Stepanian (Vice-Pres.); Harry A. Dorian (Treas.); Edward Janjigian (Sec.).

Principal Staff: Exec. Dir Walter C. Bandazian.

Address: 386 Park Ave S, Suite 1601, New York, NY 10016-8804.

Telephone: (212) 725-0973; **Fax:** (212) 447-0378.

Helen Keller International—HKI

Founded in 1915, HKI has programmes in 22 countries that combat malnutrition, cataract, trachoma, onchocerciasis (river blindness) and refractive error.

Activities: Major areas of focus are eye health and nutrition. HKI works with governments and partners to create sustainable solutions for problems that threaten the sight and survival of children and adults. In eye health, HKI currently addresses: Onchocerciasis (river blindness) by distributing ivermectin and providing information, education and community assistance in nine countries throughout Africa; Trachoma, by implementing the World Health Organization-endorsed SAFE strategy, and offering school- and community-based education, training and activities throughout Africa and in Nepal; Cataract, by training surgeons, nurses and community health workers, setting up Direct Referral Services and providing surgeries in Niger, Nigeria, Senegal, Tanzania, People's Republic of China, Indonesia and Viet Nam; and Refractive Error, by offering ChildSight, which provides vision screenings, refractions, eyeglasses and referrals for students in the USA, China and Indonesia. In Nutrition, HKI's current programmes include: Vitamin A Supplementation, to prevent blindness, enhance child survival and promote healthy development throughout Africa and Asia; Nutritional Surveillance, the collection and analysis of critical nutritional data for governments and other development partners to influence policy and shape programme design in Bangladesh and Indonesia; Food Fortification, the enrichment of commonly used food products, such as wheat flour, cooking oil or soy sauce with essential vitamins and minerals, throughout Africa and in Indonesia; Multi-micronutrient Supplementation, the promotion and distribution of Vitalita sachets with 14 vitamins and minerals, which are sprinkled on food in Cambodia and Indonesia; Iron Supplementation, to avoid iron deficiency and control anaemia throughout Africa; Production and Consumption of Micronutrient-rich Food—Homestead Food Production, the creation of gardens and small poultry farms to simultaneously promote economic independence while providing a source of nutrient-rich foods in Bangladesh, Burkina Faso, Cambodia, Nepal and the Philippines; and Orange-fleshed Sweetpotato Cultivation, to improve food security and combat vitamin A deficiency in Burkina Faso and Mozambique.

Geographical Area of Activity: Africa, Asia, USA and Europe, encompassing 22 nations.

Restrictions: Does not distribute grants.

Publications: Key bulletins and reports; Annual Report; anaemia research and publications; food fortification research and publications; general health and nutrition research and publications; eye health research and publications; homestead food production resources and publications; micronutrient resources and publications; nutrition surveillance resources and publications; river blindness/onchocerciasis research and publications.

Finance: Net assets US $12,717,662 (30 June 2010); annual revenue $112,229,387, expenditure $114,235,232 (2009/10).

Board of Trustees: Henry C. Barkhorn III (Chair.); Desmond G. Fitzgerald (Vice-Chair.); Mary Crawford (Sec.); Robert M. Thomas, Jr (Treas.).

Principal Staff: Pres. and CEO Kathy Spahn.

Address: 352 Park Ave S, Suite 1200, New York, NY 10010.

Telephone: (212) 532-0544; **Fax:** (212) 532-6014; **Internet:** www.hki.org; **e-mail:** info@hki.org.

W. K. Kellogg Foundation

Founded in 1930 by W. K. Kellogg, the breakfast cereal pioneer, to build the capacity of individuals, communities and institutions to solve their own problems. Current aims are to support children, families and communities so as to allow vulnerable children to achieve success as individuals and as members of society.

Activities: Operates with the aim of improving human well-being in the USA, Central and South America, the Caribbean and Southern African countries (Botswana, Lesotho, Mozambique, South Africa, Swaziland and Zimbabwe). Support for the needs of young people is an area of major programming concentration. Limited world-wide involvement is achieved through Kellogg International Fellowship programmes. The Foundation also supports the needs of young people through its other areas for assistance: health; youth and education; rural development; food systems; philanthropy and volunteerism.

Geographical Area of Activity: USA, Central and South America and the Caribbean, and Southern Africa.

Restrictions: The Foundation does not support research or endowment projects, nor does it award grants for operational phases of established programmes, capital facilities, equipment, conferences, films, television or radio programmes (unless these are an integral phase of a project the Foundation is already supporting), planning and studies, religious purposes, nor to individuals except for fellowships in specific areas of Foundation programming.

Publications: Annual Report; newsletter; brochures and reports.

Finance: Annual revenue US $589,400,573, expenditure $433,560,917 (2010).

Board of Trustees: Roderick D. Gillum (Chair.).

Principal Staff: Pres. and CEO Sterling K. Speirn; COO and Treas. La June Montgomery Tabron.

Address: 1 Michigan Ave E, Battle Creek, MI 49017-4012.

Telephone: (269) 968-1611; **Fax:** (269) 968-0413; **Internet:** www.wkkf.org; **e-mail:** int@wkkf.org.

Kennan Institute

Established in 1974 to increase American understanding and knowledge of Russia and the former USSR.

Activities: The Institute hosts US-based scholars selected through a competition, so that they can conduct their individual research on the Newly Independent States (countries of the former USSR). Also provides scholarships to researchers from the Newly Independent States and also runs a public lecture series during the academic year. The Institute has a publication programme; and other activities include a junior scholar workshops series and a human rights fellowship in memory of former scholar Galina Starovoitova. Maintains offices in Moscow and Kiev.

Geographical Area of Activity: Russia and other countries of the former USSR (excluding the Baltic states).

Restrictions: Short-term grants only to individuals from the USA and former USSR.

Publications: Monthly calendar/meeting reports; occasional paper series; commercially published books.

Finance: Receives funding from the US Dept of State, Carnegie Corporation of New York and Woodrow Wilson International Center for Scholars (qq.v.), federal appropriation and income from endowment.

Council: Christopher Kennan (Chair.).

Principal Staff: Dir Blair A. Ruble; Deputy Dir William E. Pomeranz.

Address: Woodrow Wilson Center, 1 Woodrow Wilson Plaza, 1300 Pennsylvania Ave NW, Washington, DC 20004-3027.

Telephone: (202) 691-4100; **Fax:** (202) 691-4247; **Internet:** www.wilsoncenter.org/index.cfm?fuseaction=topics .home&topic_id=1424; **e-mail:** kennan@wilsoncenter.org.

Joseph P. Kennedy, Jr Foundation

Founded in 1946 by Mr and Mrs Joseph P. Kennedy for the prevention of mental disability by identifying its causes, and for the improvement of the means by which society deals with its mentally disabled citizens.

Activities: Makes grants for research, special projects, advisory services, conferences and seminars involving medicine and health, education and welfare of people with mental disability. Funds are limited to proposals in the field of mental disability. Awards scholarships for a one-week bioethics course held at the Kennedy Institute of Ethics at Georgetown University, and Public Policy Leadership Fellowships for professionals and parents involved in the field of mental disability.

Restrictions: Does not fund specialized, local projects; does not provide funds to individuals.

Publications: *The New Housing Choice Voucher Program*; *Improved Care for Neglected Population Must Be 'Rule Rather Than Exception'*; *Putting Mental Retardation and Mental Illness on Health Care Professionals' Radar Screen*.

Board of Trustees: Joseph E. Hakim (Treas.).

Address: 1133 19th St NW, 12th Floor, Washington, DC 20036-3604.

Telephone: (202) 393-1250; **Fax:** (202) 824-0351; **Internet:** www.jpkf.org.

Kerzner Marine Foundation—KMF

Established in 2005 as a private non-profit foundation by the Kerzner International group of companies to assist in the protection of marine habitats.

Activities: Operates in the field of conservation of tropical marine ecosystems, through scientific research, education and community projects. The Foundation especially favours projects in the areas of development and management of marine protected areas, and conservation of coral reefs and cetaceans, as well as research.

Geographical Area of Activity: Marine environments in the Caribbean, Indian Ocean and the Pacific.

Restrictions: KMF does not fund litigation, political activities, fund-raising, scholarships, endowment and university overhead costs.

Finance: Financed by Kerzner International.

Board of Directors: George Markantonis (Pres.); Dr Paul Dayton (Vice-Pres.); Tim Wise (Treas.).

Address: 1000 South Pine Island Rd, Suite 800, Plantation, FL 33324-3907.

Telephone: (954) 809-2179; **Fax:** (954) 809-2303; **Internet:** www.kerznermarinefoundation.org; **e-mail:** info@kerznermarinefoundation.org.

Kettering Foundation

Founded in 1927 by Charles F. Kettering, the Foundation deals with questions associated with governing, educating and science, all in relation to one another and in an international perspective, with attention to both formal and informal institutions to learn how democracy can work better.

Activities: Conducts projects that aim to find solutions to fundamental problems in the areas of governance, education and science. Carries out research in six inter-related areas: citizens and public choice; community politics and community leadership; the public and public schools; institutions, professionals and the public; the public-government relations; and the international and the civil. As an operating, rather than a grant-giving, foundation, it pursues its projects in collaboration with organizations sharing its interests. It maintains a publications programme and holds training workshops in the USA and abroad.

Geographical Area of Activity: Mainly USA.

Restrictions: Not a grant-making organization.

Publications: *Voices of Hope: The Story of the Jane Addams School for Democracy*; *Collective Decision Making Around the World*; *When Citizens Deliberate: Russian and American Citizens Consider Their Relationship*; *Reclaiming Public Education by Reclaiming Our Democracy*; *Citizens and Public Choice*; *Civil Investing*; *Community Politics and Leadership*; *International and the Civil*; *Journalism and Democracy*.

Board of Directors: Suzanne Morse (Chair.).

Principal Staff: Pres. and CEO David Mathews; Vice-Pres. and Treas. Brian T. Cobb.

Address: 200 Commons Rd, Dayton, OH 45459.

Telephone: (937) 434-7300; **Fax:** (937) 439-9804; **Internet:** www.kettering.org; **e-mail:** fogt@kettering.org.

Koch Foundation, Inc

Established in 1979 by Carl E. Koch and Paula Koch to promote Roman Catholicism.

Activities: Awards grants to Catholic organizations nationally and internationally, that propagate the Catholic faith. Grants are made for different evangelization programmes, educational and spiritual formation of evangelists, resource-poor Catholic schools that are the principal means of evangelization in the community, a Catholic presence in the media, and capital expenditures. Priority is given to situations involving financially distressed, underdeveloped areas.

Geographical Area of Activity: International.

Restrictions: No grants are made to individuals; no loans or scholarships.

Publications: Annual Report.

Finance: Net assets US $117,115,333 (31 March 2011); annual revenue $2,506,515, annual disbursements $11,107,286 (2010/11).

Officers and Directors: W. A. Bomberger (Pres.); I. L. Vraney (Vice-Pres.); C. L. Bomberger (Treas.); R. A. Bomberger (Sec.).

Principal Staff: Exec. Dir Carolyn A. Young.

Address: 4421 NW 39th Ave, Bldg 1, Suite 1, Gainesville, FL 32606.

Telephone: (352) 373-7491; **Internet:** www.thekochfoundation.org; **e-mail:** staff@thekochfoundation.org.

Susan G. Komen for the Cure

Established in 1982 by Nancy Brinker; aims to eradicate breast cancer as a life-threatening disease.

Activities: Funds breast cancer research, education, screening and treatment programmes, as well as operating a community-based grant programme, funding breast cancer health education and screening projects aimed at disadvantaged people. Funding is provided to non-profit organizations, educational institutions and government agencies. Also funds fellowships designed to improve the quality of care for breast cancer patients and operates an International Grant Fund. Operates a national telephone helpline.

Geographical Area of Activity: USA.

Publications: Annual Report.

Finance: Total assets US $458,030,000 (31 March 2010); annual revenue $400,895,000, expenditure $359,949,000 (2009/10).

Board of Directors: Dr LaSalle D. Leffall, Jr (Chair.).

Principal Staff: Founder and CEO Nancy K. Brinker.

Address: 5005 LBJ Freeway, Suite 250, Dallas, TX 75244.

Telephone: (972) 855-1600; **Fax:** (972) 855-1605; **Internet:** www.komen.org; **e-mail:** grants@komen.org.

Koret Foundation

Founded in 1966 by Joseph Koret and Stephanie Koret for general charitable purposes.

Activities: Operates in California, mainly in the San Francisco Bay area, and Israel, in the fields of community development and Jewish life and culture. Initiatives include the Koret Israel Economic Development Funds, the Koret Jewish Studies Publications Program, the Koret Jewish Book Awards, the

Koret Israel Emergency Fund, the Koret Synagogue Initiative, Routes to Learning, and the Koret Prize.

Geographical Area of Activity: USA and Israel.

Restrictions: No support is given to private foundations, nor to individuals.

Publications: *Catalyst* (newsletter); community reports; *Perspectives*.

Finance: Grants disbursed US $15,219,213 (2010).

Board of Directors: Susan Koret (Chair.).

Principal Staff: Pres. Tad Taube; CEO Jeffrey A. Farber.

Address: 33 New Montgomery St, Suite 1090, San Francisco, CA 94105.

Telephone: (415) 882-7740; **Fax:** (415) 882-7775; **Internet:** www.koretfoundation.org; **e-mail:** info@koretfoundation .org.

The Kosciuszko Foundation, Inc

Founded in 1925 by Stephen P. Mizwa, Dr Henry Noble Mac-Cracken, Willis H. Booth, Cedric E. Fauntleroy, Dr Robert H. Lord, Dr Paul Monroe and Samuel M. Vauclain to promote a better knowledge of their Polish heritage among Americans of Polish descent, and develop a sense of pride in the accomplishment of their ancestors which is basic to an appreciation of their American heritage; to promote understanding between the USA and Poland; to encourage younger generations of Americans of Polish descent into higher education and contribute to the educational level in the USA; and to promote the growth of Polish studies in the USA.

Activities: Operates nationally and internationally in the fields of education, science and medicine, and the arts and humanities, through grants to institutions and individuals, fellowships, scholarships, conferences, courses, publications and lectures. Grants are awarded to enable Polish Americans to enter medical schools in Poland, and to enable writers, artists and students to complete scholarly, artistic or literary projects that would serve to implement the purposes of the Kosciuszko Foundation. Scholarships are awarded to enable Polish Americans to go on to higher education, and to enable Americans of non-Polish background to undertake Polish studies. Chopin Piano Competition and Marcella Sembrich Competition in Voice are held annually, as well as the Metchie J. E. Budka Award for outstanding scholarly work.

Geographical Area of Activity: Poland and USA.

Publications: Newsletters; Annual Report; and other publications.

Finance: Annual revenue US $1,036,872, expenditure $2,954,632 (2007/08).

Board of Trustees: Joseph E. Gore (Chair.); William J. Nareski, II (Vice-Chair.); Wanda M. Senko (Vice-Chair.); Cynthia Rosicki (Vice-Chair.); Henry C. Walentowicz (Sec.).

Principal Staff: Pres. and Exec. Dir Alex Storozynski.

Address: 15 East 65th St, New York, NY 10065.

Telephone: (212) 734-2130; **Fax:** (212) 628-4552; **Internet:** www.thekf.org; **e-mail:** alex@thekf.org.

Kresge Foundation

Founded in 1924 by Sebastian S. Kresge for general charitable purposes.

Activities: Provides challenge grants only towards projects involving construction or renovation of facilities; purchase of major items of equipment or an integrated equipment at a cost of at least US $300,000 (which may include computer software expenses, if applicable); or the purchase of real estate. Those eligible to apply are well-established, financially sound, tax-exempt charitable organizations operating in the fields of higher education (awarding baccalaureate and/or graduate degrees), health and long-term care, human services, science and the environment, the arts and humanities, and public affairs. Full accreditation is required for higher education and hospital applicants. Also supporting development at historically black colleges and universities and makes local grants in Detroit and South-Eastern Michigan. Office in Detroit opened in early 2012.

Geographical Area of Activity: Canada, Mexico, South Africa, USA, United Kingdom.

Restrictions: Requests towards debt retirement or completed projects are not eligible.

Publications: Annual Report.

Finance: Total assets US $3,293,222,730 (31 Dec. 2010); annual revenue $412,329,513, expenditure $176,441,363 (2010).

Board of Trustees: Elaine D. Rosen (Chair.).

Principal Staff: Pres. and CEO Rip Rapson.

Address: 3215 West Big Beaver Rd, Troy, MI 48084.

Telephone: (248) 643-9630; **Fax:** (248) 643-0588; **Internet:** www.kresge.org; **e-mail:** info@kresge.org.

Samuel H. Kress Foundation

Founded in 1929 to promote education in the history of art and advanced training in fine arts conservation.

Activities: Provides grants for individuals and institutions to conduct research in European art from antiquity to 1850 and in the conservation of works of art; for the conservation and restoration of monuments in Western Europe; and for the development of scholarly resources in the areas of art history and conservation. Awards scholarships, fellowships for study and travel, and supports conferences and publications.

Geographical Area of Activity: USA, Europe.

Restrictions: No grants to artists or for the purchases of art. Grants only to organizations with US non-profit status.

Publications: Annual Report (annually); articles.

Finance: Total assets US $75,460,504 (30 June 2010); annual revenue $1,596,999, expenditure $3,831,865 (2009/10).

Board of Trustees: Frederick W. Beinecke (Chair.); David Rumsey (Sec. and Treas.).

Principal Staff: Pres. Max Marmor; Dep. Dir L. W. Schermerhorn.

Address: 174 East 80th St, New York, NY 10075.

Telephone: (212) 861-4993; **Fax:** (212) 628-3146; **Internet:** www.kressfoundation.org; **e-mail:** info@kressfoundation .org.

KRS Education and Rural Development Foundation, Inc

Established by the KRS Group in 1991 to support projects relating to the environment, education and development, mainly in India.

Activities: Aims to improve education and health conditions for women and children in rural parts of India. Sponsors activities in the USA to advance global awareness and human understanding. Runs the Centre for Environment, Education and Development, which carries out research and development, as well as providing consultancy and information and running training courses and seminars.

Geographical Area of Activity: India and USA.

Finance: Major source of funds is through individual contributions.

Address: POB 820932, Vicksburg, MS 39182.

Telephone: (601) 638-5459; **Internet:** www.krsfoundation .org; **e-mail:** info@krsfoundation.org.

La Leche League International—LLLI

Established in October 1956 to promote breastfeeding and to help breastfeeding mothers around the world.

Activities: Operates internationally in the area of health and social welfare. Provides encouragement, education and information on topics and issues related to breastfeeding and parenting help, shared knowledge and support. Raises awareness of breastfeeding as an important element in the healthy development of the baby, the mother and the relationship between them.

Geographical Area of Activity: World-wide.

Publications: Annual Report; *New Beginnings* (2 a month); *Leaven* (quarterly); *Abstracts* (quarterly); archives of breast-feeding information.

Finance: Annual revenue US $1,837,053, expenditure $2,114,026 (2010).

Board of Directors: Cynthia Garrison (Co-Chair.); Shera Lyn Parpia (Co-Chair.); Shirley Phillips (First Vice-Chair.); Lavinia Belli (Second Vice-Chair.); Villy Kaltsa (Treas.); Ann Calandro (Sec.).

Principal Staff: Exec. Dir Barbara Emanuel.

Address: POB 4079, Schaumburg, IL 60168-4079; 957 N. Plum Grove Rd, Schaumberg, IL 60173.

Telephone: (847) 519-7730; **Fax:** (847) 969-0460; **Internet:** www.llli.org; **e-mail:** fdassociate@llli.org.

Lannan Foundation

Founded in 1960 by J. Patrick Lannan Sr, supports the visual and literary arts and rural Native American communities.

Activities: The Foundation's visual arts programme makes awards, grants and fellowships with the aim of promoting, exhibiting, studying and discussing contemporary art. The literary programme fosters the writing of prose and poetry through grants and projects, and attempts to bring literature to a wider audience. The programme has awarded more than US $3,400,000 to 75 writers of fiction, non-fiction and poetry since 1989 through its annual literary awards, which include a $200,000 Lifetime Achievement Award. It also awards the Lannan Prize for Cultural Freedom. The Indigenous Communities Program supports the efforts of Native Americans to continue their traditions by funding projects that revive and preserve languages and culture.

Geographical Area of Activity: USA.

Publications: Audio and bookworm archives; programme statements.

Board of Directors: Patrick Lannan (Pres.); Frank C. Lawler (Vice-Pres.).

Principal Staff: Programme Dirs Laurie Betlach, Jo Chapman, Christie Mazuera Davis, Martha Jessup.

Address: 313 Read St, Santa Fe, NM 87501-2628.

Telephone: (505) 986-8160; **Fax:** (505) 986-8195; **Internet:** www.lannan.org; **e-mail:** info@lannan.org.

Latter-day Saint Charities—LDSC

Established in 1996 to provide life-sustaining resources to people in emergencies, help strengthen families to help them become self-reliant, and offer opportunities for giving and service.

Activities: Provides emergency relief response; builds self-reliance through health promotion and disease prevention initiatives; literacy, English language, and other training for teachers; gardening and food production; and assisting children to live within loving families, or in appropriate institutions when necessary.

Geographical Area of Activity: World-wide.

Restrictions: No grants to individuals.

Finance: Funded by public donations and by the Church of Jesus Christ of Latter-day Saints.

Principal Staff: Dir Brett V. Bass.

Address: 50 East North Temple St, Floor 7, Salt Lake City, UT 84150-6890.

Telephone: (801) 240-1201; **Fax:** (801) 240-1964; **Internet:** lds.org; **e-mail:** lds-charities@ldschurch.org.

Leakey Foundation

Founded in 1968 to increase scientific knowledge, education, and public understanding of human origins, evolution, behaviour and survival.

Activities: Supports postgraduate research (principally doctoral candidates and scientists with professional qualifications and demonstrated capability) in human origins and evolution, and human behaviour and survival, especially in the areas of: the ecology, archaeology and human paleontology of the Miocene, Pliocene and Pleistocene eras; great apes and primate behaviour; and the ecology of contemporary hunter-gatherer societies. Also awards the Franklin Mosher Baldwin Memorial Fellowships to students with citizenship in an African country who wish to obtain an advanced degree or carry out specialist training in an area of study related to human origins research.

Geographical Area of Activity: USA.

Publications: *AnthroQuest* (newsletter); news articles; press releases; podcast: DigDeeper.

Board of Trustees: Gordon P. Getty (Chair.); Donald E. Dana (Pres.); Dr Diana McSherry (Vice-Pres.); J. Michael Gallagher (Vice-Pres., Governance Chair.); Julie M. LaNasa (Development Chair.); Camilla Smith (Communications and Public Outreach Chair.); Owen P. O'Donnell (Grants Chair.); Joy Sterling (Nominations Chair.); Alice M. Corning (Sec.); William P. Richards, Jr (Treas., Investment Chair.); G. Robert Muehlhauser (Finance Chair.).

Principal Staff: Man. Dir Sharal Camisa; Grants Officer Paddy Moore; Communications Man. Beth Lawrie-Green.

Address: 1003B O'Reilly Ave, San Francisco, CA 94129-1359.

Telephone: (415) 561-4646; **Fax:** (415) 561-4647; **Internet:** www.leakeyfoundation.org; **e-mail:** info@leakeyfoundation.org.

Levi Strauss Foundation

Founded in 1952 by Levi Strauss & Co.

Activities: Since 1982 has contributed approximately US $45m. to HIV/AIDS service organizations in more than 40 countries. In 2010 it dedicated roughly $2,100,000 to this area. The Foundation has been committed to asset building programmes since 1997, and in 2010 it devoted approximately $1,600,000 of grant funds to advance its goals in asset building in the USA and abroad. The Foundation also supports programmes that reach approximately 300,000 apparel and textile workers annually in 15 countries where the company's products are made. Programmes range from asset building and financial literacy programmes to address the impact of the expiration of the Multi-Fiber Arrangement (MFA) in Latin America, to helping the significant female migrant labour force in the People's Republic of China. The Foundation aims to educate workers and factory management on labour rights and responsibilities; improve the health of workers (including hygiene, reproductive health and HIV/AIDS); provide asset-building opportunities for workers; and enhance oversight of labour laws through support for factory-level dispute resolution mechanisms, legal aid and arbitration channels.

Geographical Area of Activity: World-wide.

Restrictions: The Foundation does not accept unsolicited proposals. It does not make grants to individuals, nor does it fund capital or endowment campaigns or building funds; recreational activities, sporting events or athletic associations; advertising; sectarian or religious activities; political campaigns or causes; or organizations that do not comply with the Foundation's non-discrimination policy.

Publications: Annual Report.

Principal Staff: Exec. Dir Daniel Jae-Won Lee.

Address: 1155 Battery St, LS/5, San Francisco, CA 94111.

Internet: http://levistrauss.com/about/foundations/levi-strauss-foundation.

Liberty Fund, Inc

Founded in 1960 by Pierre F. Goodrich.

Activities: The Fund publishes print and electronic scholarly resources including new editions of classic works in American constitutional history, European history, law, political philosophy and theory, economics, and education. The organization also conducts around 165 conferences annually throughout the USA, Canada, Central and South America, and Europe.

Geographical Area of Activity: World-wide.

Restrictions: Not a grant-making organization.

Publications: *AMAGI* books (around 20 titles).

Board of Directors: T. Alan Russell (Chair.).

Principal Staff: Pres. and CEO Chris L. Talley; Exec. Vice-Pres. and COO Emilio J. Pacheco.

Address: 8335 Allison Pointe Trail, Suite 300, Indianapolis, IN 46250.

Telephone: (317) 842-0880; **Fax:** (317) 579-6060; **Internet:** www.libertyfund.org; **e-mail:** books@libertyfund.org.

Life Sciences Research Foundation—LSRF

Founded in 1981 by Dr Donald D. Brown to administer an international programme of post-doctoral fellowships in all areas of life sciences.

Activities: Operates nationally and internationally in the fields of conservation and the environment, education, medicine and health, and science and technology. Provides grants to institutions and individuals, and funding for research. The Foundation accepts applications from American and foreign candidates conducting their research in US laboratories.

Geographical Area of Activity: USA.

Restrictions: Applications from non-US citizens must be for study in the USA.

Publications: Financial statements; information brochure.

Finance: Annual revenue US $1,687,389, expenditure $1,612,773 (2009/10).

Principal Staff: Pres. Donald D. Brown; Vice-Pres. Douglas E. Koshland; Treas. Christine Pratt.

Address: 3520 San Martin Dr., Baltimore, ML 21218.

Telephone: (410) 467-2597; **Internet:** www.lsrf.org; **e-mail:** lsrf@ciwemb.edu.

Lifebridge Foundation, Inc

Established in 1992 to promote holistic life, and to support individuals and organizations working to develop deeper understanding among people regarding the wholeness of humanity and the interdependence of all life.

Activities: Finances organizations working in the following categories: community service, science, environment, youth and education, arts and culture and world goodwill. Although the grant-making programme has been reduced temporarily, grant amounts range from US $2,000 to $10,000.

Geographical Area of Activity: World-wide, but 95% of funded projects are in the USA.

Restrictions: Since 2005 the Foundation has been unable to accept any requests for funding because it is using funds to establish the Lifebridge Sanctuary.

Publications: *The Bridging Tree* (newsletter, 2 a year).

Principal Staff: Pres. Barbara L. Valocore; Sec. Dr Nancy B. Roof.

Address: POB 327, High Falls, NY 12440.

Telephone: (845) 658-3439; **Internet:** www.lifebridge.org; **e-mail:** info@lifebridge.org.

Lifewater International—LI

Non-profit Christian organization founded by William A. Ashe in 1979. Aims to help poor people living in rural areas around the world to obtain safe water, sanitation systems and hygiene education.

Activities: Operates in less-developed countries through providing volunteers to train local organizations and people in the technical skills necessary to improve water supplies and sanitation, and donating equipment and financial support to assist communities to become self-sufficient and to provide a long-term solution to the problems caused by unclean water.

Geographical Area of Activity: East Africa, West Africa, Latin America and Caribbean, North America, Asia Pacific.

Publications: *Lifewater International Newsletter* (quarterly).

Finance: Annual revenue US $3,130,744, expenditure $2,919,666 (2009/10).

Board of Directors: Josh Brown (Chair.); Lisa Wen (Vice-Chair.); Tim Geisse (Sec.).

Principal Staff: CEO Joe Harbison; CFO Mary Sanderson.

Address: POB 3131, San Luis Obispo, CA 93403.

Telephone: (805) 541-6634; **Fax:** (805) 541-6649; **Internet:** www.lifewater.org; **e-mail:** info@lifewater.org.

Lilly Endowment, Inc

Founded in 1937 by the Lilly family for the promotion and support of religious, educational or charitable programmes.

Activities: Operates mainly in the fields of religion, education and community development (including social welfare and the arts and humanities). Special attention is given to programmes in Indianapolis and Indiana. Emphasis is on projects that depend on private support, but a limited number of grants are made to governmental institutions and tax-supported programmes. International projects supported by the Endowment are limited to a small number of emergency relief efforts and public policy programmes, mostly in Canada and Mexico. Projects in health care, biological and physical science research, housing, transport, environment and population are usually not funded.

Geographical Area of Activity: Mainly Indiana, USA; some funding to Canada and Mexico.

Restrictions: Grants are not made to individuals.

Publications: Annual Report; occasional report; newsletter.

Board of Directors: Thomas M. Lofton (Chair.); David D. Biber (Sec.); Diane M. Stenson (Treas.).

Principal Staff: Pres. N. Clay Robbins.

Address: POB 88068, Indianapolis, IN 46208.

Telephone: (317) 924-5471; **Fax:** (317) 926-4431; **Internet:** www.lillyendowment.org; **e-mail:** webmaster@lei.org.

Charles A. and Anne Morrow Lindbergh Foundation

Founded in 1977 by members of the Explorers Club, including Gen. James H. Doolittle and astronaut Neil Armstrong, to further Charles and Anne Morrow Lindbergh's vision of a balance between the advance of technology and the preservation of the environment.

Activities: Operates nationally and internationally in the fields of conservation and the environment by funding grants and sponsoring other educational and motivational efforts designed to honour the legacy of Charles and Anne Lindbergh and advance their vision of balance, including grants, awards and educational programmes. Funds around 8–10 Lindbergh Grants each year of amounts up to US $10,580 each.

Geographical Area of Activity: International.

Restrictions: Grants to individuals whose work demonstrates a balance between the innovative use or advancement of technology with the preservation of the environment. In 2011 funding was to be focused on aviation-environmental projects only.

Publications: Newsletter (3 a year); Annual Report; financial statements.

Finance: Funded by private, corporate and non-profit contributions. Total assets US $731,387 (31 Dec. 2010); annual income $172,769, expenditure $390,994 (2010).

Governing Board of Directors: Larry Williams (Chair.); Gregg E. Maryniak (Vice-Chair.); David Treinis (Vice-Chair.); John L. Petersen (Sec.).

Principal Staff: Pres. and CEO. Larry E. Williams; Man. Dir/Grants Administrator Shelley L. Nehl.

Address: 2150 Third Ave N, Suite 310, Anoka, MN 55303-2200.

Telephone: (763) 576-1596; **Fax:** (763) 576-1664; **Internet:** www.lindberghfoundation.org; **e-mail:** info@lindberghfoundation.org.

Lucius N. Littauer Foundation, Inc

Founded in 1929 by Lucius N. Littauer to enlarge the realms of human knowledge and to promote the general moral, mental and physical improvement of society.

Activities: Provides grants to US institutions for study in the fields of the humanities, the environment, academic Jewish studies, Judaism and the Middle East, and medical ethics; establishes book funds at universities for the acquisition of Jewish collections.

Geographical Area of Activity: USA, South America, Israel, Europe.

Restrictions: No grants to individuals; grants only to non-profit organizations in the USA.

Publications: Guidelines.

Finance: Total assets US $40,823,826 (31 Dec. 2010); total giving $1,862,220 (2009).

Trustees: Geula R. Solomon (Treas.); Noah B. Perlman (Sec.).

Principal Staff: Pres. William Lee Frost; Vice-Pres. Peter J. Solomon.

Address: 60 East 42nd St, Suite 4600, New York, NY 10165-0009.

Telephone: (212) 697-2677.

The Long Now Foundation—LNF

Established in 1996 to develop the 10,000 Year Old Clock and Library projects, which aim to become the basis of a long-term cultural institution.

Activities: Organizes seminars about long-term thinking, which aim to build a coherent and compelling body of ideas to help promote the Foundation's goal of making long-term thinking automatic and common. The 10,000 Year Old Clock project, conceived by Danny Hillis, aims to be a monument to long-term thinking. The design development on the Clock began in 1997 and has generated an early prototype. The Rosetta Project website is currently the largest collection of linguistic data on the Internet, containing collected material in more than 2,300 languages.

Geographical Area of Activity: USA.

Publications: Audio downloads.

Finance: Membership, private donations, grants.

Board of Directors: Danny Hillis (Co-Chair.); Stewart Brand (Co-Chair.); Kevin Kelly (Sec.).

Principal Staff: Exec. Dir Alexander Rose.

Address: Fort Mason Center, Bldg A, San Francisco, CA 94123.

Telephone: (415) 561-6582; **Fax:** (415) 561-6297; **Internet:** www.longnow.org; **e-mail:** services@longnow.org.

Henry Luce Foundation, Inc

Founded in 1936 by Henry Robinson Luce to make grants for specific projects in the broad areas of Asian affairs, higher education and scholarship, theology, American arts and public affairs.

Activities: The Luce Scholars Program gives a select group of young Americans, who are not Asian specialists, a year's work/study experience in East and South-East Asia. Funding in the arts focuses on research, scholarship and exhibitions in American art; direct support for specific projects at major museums and service organizations; and dissertation support for topics in American art history through the American Council of Learned Societies (q.v.). The Clare Boothe Luce Program is designed to enhance the careers of women in science and engineering by offering scholarships, fellowships and professorships at invited institutions. Grants are also available in the fields of public policy, the environment and theology. The Henry R. Luce Professorship Program, which until 2004 provided six- to nine-year support for a limited number of integrative academic programmes in the humanities and social sciences at private colleges and universities, is currently on hold.

Geographical Area of Activity: USA.

Publications: American Art Press releases; financial reports.

Finance: Total assets US $762,603,542 (31 Dec. 2010); annual revenue $78,936,616, expenditure $34,324,264 (2010).

Board of Directors: Margaret Boles Fitzgerald (Chair.).

Principal Staff: Pres. Michael Gilligan.

Address: 51 Madison Ave, 30th Floor, New York, NY 10010.

Telephone: (212) 489-7700; **Fax:** (212) 581-9541; **Internet:** www.hluce.org; **e-mail:** hlfl@hluce.org.

Ludwig Institute for Cancer Research—LICR

The Ludwig Institute for Cancer Research (LICR) was set up in 1971 by Daniel K. Ludwig, a US business tycoon. LICR is now an international non-profit institute dedicated to understanding and controlling cancer.

Activities: Research on cancer is carried out by staff financed by and employed within the Institute in collaboration with medical centres and hospitals. In Europe, LICR branches are located within the University of Oxford (United Kingdom), the Karolinska Institute and Uppsala University (Sweden), the Louvain Catholic University (Belgium) and the University of Lausanne and Swiss Institute for Vaccine Research (Switzerland). The Institute has five other branches outside Europe.

Geographical Area of Activity: Australasia, Europe, North and South America.

Publications: Annual and financial reports; news archive.

Finance: Annual revenue US $110,318,092, expenditure $115,572,722 (2010).

Board of Directors: John L. Notter (Chair.); Richard D. J. Walker (Sec.).

Principal Staff: Pres. and CEO Edward A. McDermott, Jr.

Address: 666 Third Ave, 28th Floor, New York, NY 10017.

Telephone: (212) 450-1500; **Fax:** (212) 450-1565; **Internet:** www.licr.org.

Georges Lurcy Charitable and Educational Trust

Founded in 1985 by Georges Lurcy to support educational purposes.

Activities: The Trust provides grants to students of US and French universities and colleges for educational exchanges. Also supports cultural organizations and secondary education.

Geographical Area of Activity: France and USA.

Finance: Total assets US $22,814,060; grants disbursed $874,600 (June 2009).

Principal Staff: Contact Seth E. Frank.

Address: 1290 Ave of the Americas, 29th Floor, New York, NY 10104-0101.

Internet: www.lurcy.org.

LWR—Lutheran World Relief

Established to offer humanitarian aid around the world.

Activities: Operates in the fields of agriculture, health, housing, community work, gender equality, education and emergency aid, working to improve quality of life in communities in more than 50 countries. Engages in long-term programmes in partnership with local organizations to overcome poverty and injustice, and in short-term relief work, aiming to alleviate human suffering resulting from natural disasters, war or famine.

Geographical Area of Activity: Africa, Latin America, Asia and the Middle East.

Restrictions: No funding to US-based organizations.

Publications: Annual Report; *African Advocacy* (newsletter).

Board of Directors: Rev. Dr Richard A. Nelson (Chair.); Dr Gloria S. Edwards (Vice-Chair.); Jonathan D. Schultz (Sec.).

Principal Staff: Pres. and CEO John Arthur Nunes; Exec. Vice-Pres. Jeff Whisenant.

Address: 700 Light St, Baltimore, MD 21230.

Telephone: (410) 230-2800; **Fax:** (410) 230-2882; **Internet:** www.lwr.org; **e-mail:** lwr@lwr.org.

The John D. and Catherine T. MacArthur Foundation

Founded in 1978 by John D. and Catherine T. MacArthur. The MacArthur Foundation supports creative people and effective institutions committed to building a just and peaceful world.

Activities: Fosters the development of knowledge, nurtures individual creativity, strengthens institutions, helps improve public policy, and provides information to the public, primarily through support for public interest media. The Foundation makes grants and loans through four programmes: the Program on Global Security and Sustainability focuses on international issues, including human rights and international justice, peace and security, conservation and sustainable development, higher education in Nigeria and Russia, migration and human mobility, and population and reproductive health; the Program on Human and Community Development addresses issues in the USA, including community and economic development, housing, with a focus on the preservation of affordable rental housing, juvenile justice reform, education, with an emerging interest in digital media and learning, and policy research and analysis; the General Program supports public interest media, including public radio, documentary programming, and work to explore the use of digital technologies to reach and engage the public; the MacArthur Fellow Program awards five-year, unrestricted fellowships to individuals across all ages and fields who show exceptional merit and promise of continued creative work.

Geographical Area of Activity: USA and international, including India, Mexico, Nigeria and Russia.

Restrictions: The Foundation does not support political activities or attempts to influence action on specific legislation; nor provides scholarships or tuition assistance for undergraduate, graduate, or postgraduate studies.

Publications: Annual Report.

Finance: Total assets US $5,666,612,008 (31 Dec. 2010); total disbursements $243,800,000 (2010).

Board of Directors: Robert E. Denham (Chair.).

Principal Staff: Pres. Robert L. Gallucci; Sec. Elizabeth Kane.

Address: 140 S Dearborn St, Chicago, IL 60603-5285.

Telephone: (312) 726-8000; **Fax:** (312) 920-6258; **Internet:** www.macfound.org; **e-mail:** 4answers@macfound.org.

The Craig and Susan McCaw Foundation

The Craig and Susan McCaw Foundation was launched to undertake philanthropic activities in the areas of education, child development and environment. The Foundation focuses on poverty reduction, economic development, and helping people gain access to technology world-wide. The Foundation also contributes a significant amount of its grants to organizations that implement an entrepreneurial and innovative approach to realize their mission.

Activities: Provides aid to under-developed countries for health and welfare; offers grants to organizations serving in Africa including the Foundation for Community Development (qq.v.) and the Nelson Mandela Foundation; provides small-scale loans in support of technology development in Asia.

Geographical Area of Activity: Africa and South-East Asia.

Finance: Annual revenue US $5,217,582, expenditure $4,642,449 (2009).

Board of Directors: Craig O. McCaw (Pres.); Susan R. McCaw (Vice-Pres.); Amit Mehta (Vice-Pres.); Teresa Mason (Sec.); Cindy Hegge (Treas.).

Address: POB 2908, Kirkland, WA 98083-2908.

Telephone: (425) 828-8000.

The Edna McConnell Clark Foundation

Incorporated in New York in 1950 and in Delaware in 1969, the two organizations merged in 1974. The Foundation's aim is to improve conditions for persons who are poorly or unfairly served by the established institutions of society.

Activities: Operates nationally in the field of social welfare and internationally in the field of tropical disease research only, particularly in Sub-Saharan Africa. The Foundation's grant-making focuses on four distinct programmes: improving the efficacy of social welfare services in protecting children from abuse or neglect; providing funding for specific communities in New York City where poor housing and under-investment increase the risk of family homelessness; implementing reforms in middle schools in urban areas to improve the education offered to disadvantaged students in grades six to nine; and attempting to control or reduce the two major causes of infectious blindness in the developing world, onchocerciasis and trachoma. Programmes include the Tropical Disease Research Program, the Program for New York Neighborhoods, the Program for Children, the Program for Student Achievement, and the Program for Justice. The Foundation also maintains a small Special Projects fund to respond to important or interesting projects that relate to its basic mission, but fall outside the specific programme areas. In 1999 launched the International Trachoma Initiative in conjunction with pharmaceutical company Pfizer Inc.

Geographical Area of Activity: Mainly USA, but occasionally runs international programmes.

Restrictions: Grants are not made to individuals, nor for scholarship or capital purposes.

Publications: Annual Reports; evaluation reports; programme assessments and related materials.

Finance: Total assets US $813,159,608 (30 Sept. 2010); annual revenue $88,275,388, expenditure $42,750,973 (2009/10).

Board of Trustees: Theodore E. Martin (Chair.).

Principal Staff: Pres. Nancy Roob.

Address: 415 Madison Ave, 10th Floor, NY 10017.

Telephone: (212) 551-9100; **Fax:** (212) 421-9325; **Internet:** www.emcf.org; **e-mail:** info@emcf.org.

Robert R. McCormick Foundation

Established as the Robert R. McCormick Charitable Trust in 1955 by Robert R. McCormick; became a foundation in 1990.

Activities: Aims to improve the social and economic development, encourage a free and responsible discussion of issues affecting the nation, enhance the effectiveness of US education and to stimulate responsible citizenship. Operates mainly in the Chicago metropolitan area supporting work in the fields of communities, citizenship, education and journalism. Operates a Journalism Program nationally and in Central and South America.

Geographical Area of Activity: USA, and Central and South America.

Restrictions: No grants are made to individuals.

Publications: Annual Report; information brochure.

Finance: Annual revenue US $40,105,967, expenditure $32,120,066 (2010).

Board of Directors: Dennis J. FitzSimons (Chair.).

Principal Staff: Pres. and CEO David D. Hiller; Exec. Sec. Tonya Pitrof.

Address: 205 North Michigan Ave, Suite 4300, Chicago, IL 60601.

Telephone: (312) 445-5000; **Fax:** (312) 445-5001; **Internet:** www.rrmtf.org; **e-mail:** info@mccormickfoundation.org.

James S. McDonnell Foundation

Founded in 1950 by aerospace pioneer James S. McDonnell, the Foundation was established to 'improve the quality of life', and does so by contributing to the generation of new knowledge through its support of research and scholarship. The Foundation awards grants via the Foundation-initiated, peer-reviewed proposal processes described in the 21st Century Science Initiative.

Activities: Operates in the fields of biological and behavioural sciences. Runs the 21st Century Science Initiative supporting individual and collaborative research in two areas: Studying Complex Systems; and Brain Cancer Research. Individual grants are awarded over a three- to six-year period. International applications are invited.

Geographical Area of Activity: International.

Restrictions: Grants only to not-for-profit 501 (c)3 organizations or foreign equivalent.

Finance: Total assets US $433,226,256 (2008); grants disbursed $20,000,000 (2008).

Principal Staff: Pres. John T. Bruer; Vice-Pres. Susan M. Fitzpatrick.

Address: 1034 South Brentwood Blvd, Suite 1850, St Louis, MO 63117.

Telephone: (314) 721-1532; **Fax:** (314) 721-7421; **Internet:** www.jsmf.org; **e-mail:** info@jsmf.org.

McKnight Foundation

Founded in 1953 by William L. and Maude L. McKnight and Virginia M. and James M. Binger for general charitable purposes.

Activities: Gives funding in the fields of children and families; communities and regions; the arts; environment; research; and international funding. Scientific research is divided into two main areas: neuroscience, particularly diseases affecting the memory; and crop research, particularly in developing countries. Has interests in Tanzania, Uganda, Zimbabwe, Cambodia, Laos and Viet Nam, where the emphasis is on agricultural development, community development, health care, assistance for land-mine victims, and micro-enterprise development.

Geographical Area of Activity: Mainly USA (Minnesota); some grants in Cambodia, Laos, Tanzania, Uganda, Viet Nam and Zimbabwe.

Restrictions: Grants are rarely made outside the state of Minnesota.

Publications: Annual Report; grants list; occasional report; information brochure.

Finance: Annual revenue US $245,165,000, expenditure $159,990,000 (2010).

Board of Directors: Ted Staryk (Chair.); Richard D. McFarland (Treas.); Bill Gregg (Asst Treas.).

Principal Staff: Pres. Kate Wolford.

Address: 710 South Second St, Suite 400, Minneapolis, MN 55401.

Telephone: (612) 333-4220; **Fax:** (612) 332-3833; **Internet:** www.mcknight.org; **e-mail:** grants@mcknight.org.

Maclellan Foundation, Inc

Incorporated in 1945 by Robert J. Maclellan and family. Reincorporated in 1992. Provides funding for Christian ministries world-wide.

Activities: Invests in faith-based solutions throughout the world and encourages wise giving.

Geographical Area of Activity: World-wide.

Restrictions: No grants are made to individuals. All ministries must have a 501 (c) 3 tax-exempt status or be in a fiscal sponsor relationship with a US tax-exempt group.

Board of Trustees: Hugh O. Maclellan, Jr (Chair.).

Principal Staff: Exec. Dir David Denmark.

Address: 820 Broad St, Suite 300, Chattanooga, TN 37402.

Telephone: (423) 755-1366; **Fax:** (423) 755-1640; **Internet:** www.maclellan.net; **e-mail:** info@maclellan.net.

Josiah Macy, Jr Foundation

Founded in 1930 by Kate Macy Ladd to advance medicine and health in the USA and abroad; the Foundation's major interest is in medical education.

Activities: Operates nationally and internationally in the fields of science and medicine, through health programmes, grants to institutions, conferences and publications. Particularly concerned with African American, Latino and Native American health issues, and enhancing the representation of minorities in the health profession. Currently focused on improving health professional education, increasing teamwork between and among multiple health professions, educational strategies that increase access and use of health care facilities by underserved communities, and increasing diversity among health care professionals.

Geographical Area of Activity: Mainly USA.

Restrictions: No grants are given for building, endowment, annual fund appeals or individual travel.

Publications: Annual Report; *Continuing Education in the Health Professions: Improving Healthcare through Lifelong Learning*; *Women and Medicine*; *The Convergence of Neuroscience, Behavioral Science, Neurology, and Psychiatry*; *The Future of Pediatric Education in the 21st Century*; *Macy-Morehouse Conferences on Primary Care for the Underserved*; *Modern Psychiatry: Challenges in Educating Health Professionals to Meet New Needs*; *Education of Health Professionals in Complementary/Alternative Medicine*; *Enhancing Interactions Between Nursing and Medicine: Opportunities in Health Professional Education*; *Education for More Synergistic Practice of Medicine and Public Health*; *The Implications of Genetics for Health Professional Education*.

Finance: Total assets US $133,757,295 (30 June 2010); annual revenue $2,210,145, expenditure $7,676,084 (2009/10).

Board of Directors: William H. Wright, II (Chair.).

Principal Staff: Pres. George E. Thibault.

Address: 44 East 64th St, New York, NY 10065.

Telephone: (212) 486-2424; **Fax:** (212) 644-0765; **Internet:** www.josiahmacyfoundation.org; **e-mail:** info@macyfoundation.org.

MADRE

Founded in 1983 by a group of women with the aim of advancing women's human rights by meeting urgent needs in communities and building lasting solutions to the crises women face.

Activities: Operates in the field of international human rights by working with grassroots women's organizations in communities around the world, focusing on health, combating violence against women, peace building, economic and environmental justice and other basic human rights. Provides financial and technical support for these partner groups, while raising awareness of relevant issues within the USA. Programmes currently operate in Afghanistan, Colombia, Guatemala, Haiti, Iraq, Kenya, Mexico, Nicaragua, Palestine, Peru and Sudan.

Geographical Area of Activity: South America, Central America and the Caribbean, Asia, Africa and the Middle East.

Restrictions: Grants only to partner organizations.

Publications: Newsletter; position papers; articles.

Board of Directors: Anne H. Hess (Co-Chair.); Dr Zala Highsmith-Taylor (Co-Chair.); Margaret Ratner-Kunstler (Vice-Pres.); Linda Flores-Rodríguez (Sec.).

Principal Staff: Exec. Dir Yifat Susskind.

Address: 121 W 27th St, Suite 301, New York, NY 10001.

Telephone: (212) 627-0444; **Fax:** (212) 675-3704; **Internet:** www.madre.org; **e-mail:** madre@madre.org.

A. L. Mailman Family Foundation, Inc

Established by Abraham Mailman in 1980 to support communities and families in providing care and stability for young children.

Activities: Funds national projects in the USA to improve the quality of early child care and education, with a specific emphasis on advocacy projects. In 2000 the Foundation launched the Early Childhood Leadership Award, accompanied by a grant to support leadership development and mentorship activities.

Geographical Area of Activity: USA.

Restrictions: No grants for direct services, local programmes, individuals or scholarships, childcare centres and schools, capital campaigns and endowments, deficit reduction or general operating expenses.

Finance: Assets approx. US $17,000,000; total grants disbursed approx. $600,000 (2011).

Board of Directors: Richard D. Segal (Pres.); Betty S. Bardige (Vice-Pres.).

Principal Staff: Exec. Dir Luba Lynch.

Address: 707 Westchester Ave, White Plains, NY 10604.

Telephone: (914) 683-8089; **Fax:** (914) 686-5519; **Internet:** www.mailman.org; **e-mail:** info@mailman.org.

MAP International—Medical Assistance Programs

Established in 1954 by Dr J. Raymond Knighton, a non-profit Christian relief and development organization that aims to promote the health of people living in developing countries.

Activities: Operates in developing countries in Africa and Central and South America in the area of medicine and health, through works in partnership with other organizations to provide essential medicines to those in need, so as to prevent and eradicate diseases (particularly addressing the problem of HIV/AIDS) and to promote community health development in less-developed countries. Also provides emergency health care in areas suffering from the effects of natural and man-made disasters. Offers scholarships to medical students from North America to travel to developing countries to work at hospitals helping people in financial need. Maintains overseas offices in Bolivia, Ecuador, Indonesia, Cote d'Ivoire, Kenya and Uganda.

Geographical Area of Activity: Africa, Central and South America and South-East Asia.

Finance: Total assets US $65,959,990 (30 Sept. 2009); annual revenue $209,558,094, expenditure $261,890,398 (2009/10).

Board of Directors: Immanuel Thangaraj (Chair.); Ambassador Edwin G. Corr (Vice-Chair.); Chok-Pin Foo (Treas.); Ingrid Mason Mail (Sec.).

Principal Staff: CEO and Pres. Michael J. Nyenhuis.

Address: 4700 Glynco Parkway, Brunswick, GA 31525-6901.

Telephone: (912) 265-6010; **Fax:** (912) 265-6170; **Internet:** www.map.org; **e-mail:** map@map.org.

March of Dimes

Founded in 1938 by US President Franklin Roosevelt as the National Foundation for Infantile Paralysis to combat polio; later renamed March of Dimes Birth Defects Foundation. The Foundation's current aim is to help prevent birth defects and infant mortality through education and research.

Activities: Promotes the continuing education of professionals in the field of perinatal care, and the expansion of education programmes for the general public. Makes grants to organizations for research in aspects of birth defects; and various research awards for research in the USA, including Clinical Research Grants, Pre-doctoral Graduate Research Training Fellowships, Social and Behavioral Sciences Research Grants, the Summer Science Research Program for Medical Students, the Basil O'Connor Starter Scholar Research Award Program and the Research Support Program on Reproductive Hazards in the Workplace, Home, Community and Environment.

Geographical Area of Activity: Africa, Latin America, Asia, Central and Eastern Europe.

Publications: Annual Report; newsletter.

Finance: Total assets US $156,956,237 (31 Dec. 2009); annual revenue $214,716,000, expenditure $212,414,000 (2009).

Board of Trustees: LaVerne H. Council (Chair.); Carol Evans (Vice-Chair.); Gary Dixon (Vice-Chair.); Jonathan Spector (Vice-Chair.); David R. Smith (Sec.).

Principal Staff: Pres. Dr Jennifer L. Howse; Exec. Vice-Pres. Jane E. Massey.

Address: 1275 Mamaroneck Ave, White Plains, NY 10605.

Telephone: (914) 997-4488; **Fax:** (914) 997-4650; **Internet:** www.marchofdimes.com; **e-mail:** donorservice@marchofdimes.com.

Marisla Foundation

Founded in 1986 to provide funding to preserve individual rights to have a safe place to live to organizations that work to preserve the world's natural resources.

Activities: Operates in the field of environmental conservation and protection on the West Coast of the USA, Hawaii and the Pacific. The Foundation has a special interest in programmes promoting marine conservation. Also concerned with women's centres and services in Los Angeles County and Orange County in Southern California.

Geographical Area of Activity: USA, Hawaii and the Pacific.

Finance: Total assets US $61,912,925 (31 Dec. 2009); total giving $34,792,400 (2009).

Principal Staff: Admin. Glenda Menges.

Address: 668 North Coast Highway, PMB 1400, Laguna Beach, CA 92651.

Telephone: (949) 494-0365; **Fax:** (949) 494-8392; **e-mail:** glenda@marisla.org.

Markle Foundation

Founded in 1927 by John Markle and Mary Markle to promote the advancement and diffusion of knowledge and the general good of humanity. The Foundation is now concentrating on the potential of mass communications and information technology to enhance learning, and improving the mass media, including services growing out of new technologies for the processing and transfer of information.

Activities: Operates throughout the USA in the field of health and national security, through self-conducted programmes, research and grants to institutions. The Foundation has made substantial commitments to the following programme areas: developing policies for a networked society, promoting information technologies for better health, as well as operating an Opportunity Fund.

Geographical Area of Activity: USA.

Restrictions: No grants are made to individuals.

Publications: Financial documents; *Health; A Model for Remote Health Care in the Developing World: The Markle Foundation Telemedicine Clinic in Cambodia; Connecting for Health; Time Series Modeling for Syndromic Surveillance; It is about Health: Securing a National Health Information Infrastructure; The Quality Case for Information Technology in Healthcare; Creating a Trusted Information Network for Homeland Security.*

Board of Directors: Lewis B. Kaden (Chair.).

Principal Staff: Pres. Zoë Baird Budinger.

Address: 10 Rockefeller Plaza, 16th Floor, New York, NY 10020-1903.

Telephone: (212) 713-7600; **Fax:** (212) 765-9690; **Internet:** www.markle.org; **e-mail:** info@markle.org.

The Max Foundation

Established by Pedro José Rivarola in 1997, a non-profit organization that aims to improve the quality of life and the treatment of patients suffering from leukaemia and other blood diseases, especially children of Hispanic and Latino origin.

Activities: Operates in Asia, the USA and in Central and South America in the field of medicine and health. Provides information about treatment options; offers advice and emotional and financial support to sufferers of blood-related diseases; and raises awareness of the importance of becoming a bone marrow donor. Also working to establish the VidaMax-MaxLife Bone Marrow and Cord Blood Registry to increase patients' chances of survival and successful treatment; and operates the Max For Life community fundraising programme, encouraging individuals to donate small amounts of funds to support the improvement of the health-care system in some of the regions of the world most in need. Maintains satellite MaxStations in Argentina, Bolivia, Chile, India, Malaysia, Mexico, Pakistan, Paraguay, Peru, the Philippines, Russia, Singapore, South Africa, Thailand, Turkey and Uruguay.

Geographical Area of Activity: World-wide.

Publications: Newsletter.

Principal Staff: Founder and CEO Pedro Rivarola.

Address: 110 West Dayton St, Suite 205, Edmonds, WA 98020.

Telephone: (425) 778-8660; **Fax:** (425) 778-8760; **Internet:** www.themaxfoundation.org; **e-mail:** info@themaxfoundation.org.

MDA—Muscular Dystrophy Association

Founded in 1950 by a group of New York parents and relatives of young people affected by muscular dystrophy to fight the disease and related neuromuscular disorders, through world-wide research and a comprehensive programme of services available to residents of the USA, and a professional and public education programme.

Activities: Aims to combat neuromuscular disease through world-wide support of basic and clinical research directed at developing affective treatments for neuro-muscular disorders. Also operates a national programme of medical services and clinical care, including diagnostic services and rehabilitative follow-up care through a nationwide network of hospital-affiliated clinics; provides selected medical equipment; and offers support groups and summer camp programmes. It attempts to broaden public awareness of neuromuscular disease through its publications, video presentations and press releases and offer onion information services.

Geographical Area of Activity: Conducts research world-wide; services only available in the USA.

Restrictions: Grants to individual scientific investigators affiliated with academic institutions or qualified research facility.

Publications: Annual Report; brochures; *ALS Newsletter*; *Quest; Quest Magazine*; *MDA/ALS Newsmagazine*; *Facts About* (booklets); publications about MDA programmes; publications about daily living with neuromuscular diseases.

Finance: Annual revenue US $204,340,000, expenditure $118,625,000 (2010).

Board: R. Rodney Howell (Chair.); Suzanne Lowden (Treas.).

Principal Staff: Pres. and CEO Gerald C. Weinberg.

Address: 3300 East Sunrise Dr., Tucson, AZ 85718-3208.

Telephone: (520) 529-2000; **Fax:** (520) 529-5300; **Internet:** www.mdausa.org; **e-mail:** mda@mdausa.org.

Richard King Mellon Foundation

Founded in 1947 by Richard King Mellon for general charitable purposes. The major focus of the Foundation is on the quality of life in Pittsburgh and south-west Pennsylvania; however, it also promotes national conservation programmes.

Activities: Operates programmes in the fields of conservation; regional economic development; children, youth and young adults; education and human services; and non-profit capacity building.

Geographical Area of Activity: USA (particularly south-western Pennsylvania).

Restrictions: The Foundation will not consider requests on behalf of individuals or from outside the USA.

Publications: Annual Report and financial statement; information brochure.

Finance: Grants approved US $90,845,750 (2011).

Trustees: Seward Prosser Mellon (Chair. and CEO); Robert B. Burr, Jr (Treas.); Lisa Kuzma (Sec.).

Principal Staff: Pres. Bruce King Mellon Henderson; Vice-Pres. Douglas L. Sisson.

Address: BNY Mellon Center, 500 Grant St, Suite 4106, Pittsburgh, PA 15219.

Telephone: (412) 392-2800; **Fax:** (412) 392-2837; **Internet:** foundationcenter.org/grantmaker/rkmellon.

The Andrew W. Mellon Foundation

Founded in 1969 by the merger of the Avalon Foundation (founded in 1940 by Ailsa Mellon Bruce) and the Old Dominion Foundation (founded in 1941 by Paul Mellon) to furnish support for higher education and cultural institutions.

Activities: Operates nationally in the five programme areas of: higher education and scholarship; scholarly communications and information technology; art history, museums and art conservation; performing arts; and conservation and the environment. Offers Distinguished Achievement in the Humanities awards annually to academics holding tenured positions at US universities.

Geographical Area of Activity: Mainly USA.

Restrictions: The Foundation makes few grants to non-US organizations, and no grants to individuals.

Publications: Annual Report; *Equity and Excellence*; *Reclaiming the Game*; *JSTOR: A History*; *Stand and Prosper*; *The Game of Life*; *Library Automation in Transitional Societies*; *Promise and Dilemma*; *Technology and Scholarly Communication*; *The Shape of the River*; *Universities and Their Leadership*; *Crafting a Class*; *What's Happened to the Humanities*; *The New-York Historical Society*; *Managing Change in the Nonprofit Sector*; *Inside the Boardroom*; *The Charitable Nonprofits*; *University Libraries and Scholarly Communication*; *In Pursuit of the PHD*; *Prospects for Faculty in Arts and Sciences*.

Finance: Annual revenue US $692,374,000, expenditure $269,302,000 (2010).

Trustees: Anne M. Tatlock (Chair.).

Principal Staff: Pres. Don Michael Randel; Vice-Pres Philip E. Lewis, Mariët Westermann.

Address: 140 East 62nd St, New York, NY 10065.

Telephone: (212) 838-8400; **Fax:** (212) 888-4172; **Internet:** www.mellon.org; **e-mail:** inquiries@mellon.org.

Memorial Foundation for Jewish Culture

Founded in 1965 by Dr Nahum Goldmann with reparation funds from the Government of West Germany. Aims to encourage and assist Jewish scholarship and education; and to contribute to the preservation, enhancement and transmission of Jewish culture throughout the world.

Activities: Awards scholarships to prepare future scholars, researchers and rabbinical leaders, and fellowships to aid scholars, writers and artists. Supports special training programmes for rabbis, educators and Jewish communal workers for countries that do not have adequate training facilities. Also provides grants for Jewish research and publication, higher education and for programmes to commemorate and document the Holocaust.

Geographical Area of Activity: World-wide.

Principal Staff: Pres. Prof. Ismar Schorsch; Exec. Vice-Pres. Dr Jerry Hochbaum; Asst Dir Dr Marc G. Brandriss.

Address: 50 Broadway, 34th Floor, New York, NY 10004.

Telephone: (212) 425-6606; **Fax:** (212) 425-6602; **Internet:** www.mfjc.com; **e-mail:** office@mfjc.org.

The John Merck Fund

Founded in 1970 by the late Serena S. Merck for charitable purposes.

Activities: Operates nationally and internationally in the areas of developmental disabilities, the environment, reproductive health, providing job opportunities, and human rights, through awarding grants to medical teaching hospitals and small organizations; offers support for conferences, seminars and research, and fellowships. Also awards the annual Serena Merck Memorial Award to an exceptional individual who has demonstrated long-term, selfless dedication and compassion in the care or service to children who are mentally disabled and have significant mental health problems.

Geographical Area of Activity: International, mainly USA.

Restrictions: Endowment or capital-fund projects; large organizations with well-established funding sources (except those that need help launching promising new projects for which funding is not readily available); general support (except in the case of small organizations whose entire mission coincides with one of The Fund's areas of interest); individuals (except if his or her project is sponsored by a domestic or foreign educational, scientific or charitable organization).

Publications: Grant reports.

Finance: Annual revenue US $15,110,010, expenditure $11,769,775 (2009).

Board of Trustees: Dinah Buechner-Vischer (Co-Chair.); Whitney Hatch (Co-Chair.); Ruth Hennig (Sec.); Huyler C. Held (Treas.).

Principal Staff: Exec. Dir Ruth G. Hennig; Dep. Dir Nancy Stockford.

Address: 2 Oliver St, 8th Floor, Boston, MA 02109.

Telephone: (617) 556-4120; **Fax:** (617) 556-4130; **Internet:** www.jmfund.org; **e-mail:** info@jmfund.org.

Mercy Corps

Humanitarian organization founded in 1981 by Dan O'Neill and Ellsworth Culver to alleviate suffering around the world. Merged with NetAid (established 1999 to help alleviate poverty world-wide) in 2007.

Activities: Operates as a network of organizations with offices in around 35 countries working internationally in the fields of sustainable community development, civil society and emergency relief. Programmes are primarily targeted at providing long-term solutions for people suffering the effects of poverty, oppression and conflict, through health care, housing, education, economic and community development, material aid and micro-enterprise schemes. Provides emergency relief for those affected by natural and man-made disasters and also works to promote citizen participation, the accountability of governments, and conflict management.

Geographical Area of Activity: World-wide.

Publications: Annual Report.

Finance: Total net assets US $82,019,973 (30 June 2010); annual revenue $297,993,330, expenditure $302,044,912 (2009/10).

Board of Directors: Linda A. Mason (Chair.); Robert Newell (Treas.).

Principal Staff: CEO Neal Keny-Guyer.

Address: Dept W, POB 2669, Portland, OR 97208-2669.

Telephone: (503) 796-6800; **Internet:** www.mercycorps.org; **e-mail:** donorservices@mercycorps.org.

Mercy-USA for Aid and Development—M-USA

Incorporated in 1988, Mercy-USA is a non-profit international relief and development organization dedicated to alleviating human suffering and supporting individuals and their communities in their efforts to become more self-sufficient.

Activities: Operates in the areas of aid to less-developed countries, education, medicine and health, and social welfare, through a number of projects, including promoting economic and educational growth, disaster relief, reconstruction and rehabilitation, and international development projects.

Geographical Area of Activity: Africa, Central and South-Eastern Europe, Central and Southern Asia, and the USA.

Restrictions: No grants are made to individuals.

Publications: *Mercy News* (newsletter); Annual Report.

Finance: Funded by donations from private individuals, grants and gifts-in-kind from agencies of the US Government, the UN and from various NGOs, and investment revenue Annual revenue US5,902,090, expenditure $5,808,855 (Dec. 2009).

Board of Directors: Iman Elkadi (Chair.); Dr Ali el-Menshawi (Vice-Chair.); Naushad Virji (Treas.).

Principal Staff: Pres. and CEO Umar al-Qadi; CFO Anas Alhaidar.

Address: 44450 Pinetree Dr., Suite 201, Plymouth, MI 48170-3869.

Telephone: (734) 454-0011; **Fax:** (734) 454-0303; **Internet:** www.mercyusa.org; **e-mail:** info@mercyusa.org.

Mertz Gilmore Foundation

Founded in 1959 by Joyce Mertz-Gilmore for general charitable purposes.

Activities: Currently makes grants to non-profit organizations active in the following programme areas: Climate Change Solutions; Human Rights in the USA; New York City Communities; New York City Dance.

Geographical Area of Activity: USA.

Restrictions: No grants are made for individuals, sectarian religious concerns, conferences, film or media projects, endowments, publications or for single country projects.

Publications: Report (biennially); information brochure; grants list; staff departure.

Finance: Annual revenue US $13,906,943, expenditure $7,729,913 (2010).

Board of Directors: Mikki Shepard (Chair.); Andrew Park (Sec.); Rini Banerjee (Treas.).

Principal Staff: Pres. Jay Beckner.

Address: 218 East 18th St, New York, NY 10003-3694.

Telephone: (212) 475-1137; **Fax:** (212) 777-5226; **Internet:** www.mertzgilmore.org; **e-mail:** info@mertzgilmore.org.

The Michael Fund—International Foundation for Genetic Research

Founded in 1978 by Randy Engel and the late Dr Jerome Lejeune to promote cure and treatment research programmes for genetic disorders, including Down's Syndrome.

Activities: Operates in the area of medicine and health internationally, carrying out research and awarding grants to individuals for research and defending the rights of physically and mentally disabled people.

Geographical Area of Activity: World-wide.

Publications: *The Friends of the Michael Fund* (newsletter); *Non-Directive Counselling*; *Obstetric Genetic Counselling for Lethal Anomalies*; *Little David*; *A March of Dimes Primer*; *The A–Z of Eugenic Killing*.

Trustees: Fr Clifton Hill (Chair.).

Principal Staff: Exec. Dir Randy Engel.

Address: 4371 Northern Pike, Pittsburgh, PA 15146.

Telephone: (412) 374-1111; **Internet:** www.michaelfund.org; **e-mail:** randy@michaelfund.org.

Milbank Memorial Fund

Founded in 1905 by Elizabeth Milbank Anderson to improve the physical, mental and moral condition of humanity. The Fund's work in health policy now addresses three themes: improving health-care and related services for patients; protecting and improving the health of people in communities and workplaces; and improving the governance of public and private organizations so that they offer more effective care and health protection, as well as opportunities for health improvement.

Activities: The Fund is an endowed foundation that engages in non-partisan analysis, study, research and communication on significant issues in health policy. The results are made available in meetings with decision-makers and publications. Most of the Fund's work is collaborative, involving strategic relationships with decision makers in the public and private sectors. It uses its resources in ways that complement the resources of its partners, not making grants in the traditional sense.

Geographical Area of Activity: USA.

Publications: *The Milbank Quarterly*; reports and books.

Principal Staff: Pres. Carmen Hooker Odom; Vice-Pres. and COO Kathleen S. Andersen.

Address: 645 Madison Ave, 15th Floor, New York, NY 10022-1095.

Telephone: (212) 355-8400; **Fax:** (212) 355-8599; **Internet:** www.milbank.org; **e-mail:** mmf@milbank.org.

MIUSA—Mobility International USA

Founded in 1981 by Susan Sygall and Barbara Williams with the goal of empowering people with disabilities around the world to achieve their human rights through international exchange and international development.

Activities: Operates internationally to provide people with disabilities with equal opportunities, and promotes their inclusion in development programmes through international exchange, information, technical assistance and training. Also manages the National Clearinghouse on Disability and Exchange (NCDE).

Geographical Area of Activity: World-wide.

Publications: Books, fact sheets and videos including *A World Awaits You, A Practice of Yes, Survival Strategies for Going Abroad: A Guide for People with Disabilties, Building an Inclusive Development Community, Rights and Responsibilities, Building Bridges.*

Board of Trustees: Linda Phelps; David Evans; Shelley Snow; Patty Prather; Kim Leval; Linda Kessel; Heidi von Ravensberg; Molly Rogers.

Principal Staff: CEO Susan Sygall.

Address: 132 East Broadway, Suite 343, Eugene, OR 97401.

Telephone: (541) 343-1284; **Fax:** (541) 343-6812; **Internet:** www.miusa.org; **e-mail:** info@miusa.org.

The Ambrose Monell Foundation

Established to contribute to religious, charitable, scientific, literary and educational purposes in New York, the USA in general, and world-wide. Shares an administration with the G. Unger Vetlesen Foundation (q.v.).

Activities: Operates in New York, the USA in general and internationally; makes grants to organizations operating in the above fields.

Geographical Area of Activity: International.

Restrictions: No grants are made to individuals.

Finance: Annual revenue US $9,360,127, expenditure $10,348,216 (2010).

Principal Staff: Pres. George Rowe; Vice-Pres Ambrose K. Monell, Eugene P. Grisanti.

Address: 1 Rockefeller Plaza, Suite 301, New York, NY 10020-2002.

Telephone: (212) 586-0700; **Fax:** (212) 245-1863; **Internet:** www.monellvetlesen.org; **e-mail:** info@monellvetlesen.org.

Moody Foundation

Founded in 1942 by William Lewis Moody, Jr, and Libbie Shearn Moody.

Activities: Operates in Texas primarily in the fields of conservation and renovation, with organizations involved in social services, education, or the arts, through research, grants to institutions, fellowships, scholarships, publications, conferences and lectures. Currently, however, approximately 95% of the Foundation's grant-making is concentrated on the Moody Gardens in Galveston Island and the Transitional Learning Center, which offers facilities for the rehabilitation of people with brain injuries.

Geographical Area of Activity: USA (Texas).

Restrictions: No grants to individuals, except for scholarships to Galveston County students. Grants only to organizations in Texas.

Publications: Annual Report; application guidelines.

Finance: Annual revenue US $93,416,000, expenditure $66,386,000 (2009).

Board of Trustees: Robert L. Moody, Sr (Chair.).

Principal Staff: Exec. Dir Frances Moody-Dahlberg; Programme Officer Gerald J. Smith; CFO Garrik Addison.

Address: 2302 Post Office St, Suite 704, Galveston, TX 77550.

Telephone: (409) 797-1500; **Fax:** (409) 763-5564; **Internet:** www.moodyf.org; **e-mail:** info@moodyf.org.

Gordon and Betty Moore Foundation

Established in 2000. Seeks to improve the quality of life for future generations.

Activities: The Foundation operates in three specific areas of focus—environmental conservation, science, and the San Francisco Bay area, CA—where a significant and measurable impact can be achieved. Distinct initiatives have been created within these programme areas. An initiative employs a portfolio of grants that are expected to help achieve targeted, large-scale outcomes in a specific time frame.

Geographical Area of Activity: USA.

Restrictions: Does not accept unsolicited proposals. Instead, funds Foundation-generated initiatives, commitments and special opportunities within the areas of focus, and makes local grants through the San Francisco Bay area programme.

Publications: Annual Report; financial documents; data-sharing policy and guidelines.

Finance: Total assets US $5,585,288,763 (31 Dec. 2010); annual revenue $660,240,582, expenditure $253,719,457 (2010).

Board of Trustees: Gordon Moore (Chair.).

Principal Staff: Pres. Steven J. McCormick; Exec. Asst Linda Baron.

Address: 1661 Page Mill Rd, Palo Alto, CA 94304-1209.

Telephone: (650) 213-3000; **Fax:** (650) 213-3003; **Internet:** www.moore.org; **e-mail:** info@moore.org.

Morehead-Cain Foundation

Founded in 1945 by John Motley Morehead III, a prominent philanthropist and descendant of North Carolina Governor John Motley Morehead. As a graduate of the University of North Carolina at Chapel Hill, Morehead endowed the Foundation to administer the first merit scholarship in the USA. In 2007 the was renamed following a US $100m. grant from the Gordon and Mary Cain Foundation.

Activities: Awards merit scholarships for undergraduate study at the University of North Carolina at Chapel Hill. In addition to covering the full cost of attending UNC-CH, the scholarship includes four summer enrichment programmes across the country and around the world. Morehead-Cain Scholars are selected from North Carolina high schools, British and Canadian secondary schools, and selected high schools across the USA. Selected international secondary schools are also permitted to nominate candidates. Modeled on the Rhodes Scholarship at Oxford University, United Kingdom, the Morehead-Cain is the oldest merit scholarship in the USA.

Restrictions: Awards scholarships for undergraduate study at the University of North Carolina at Chapel Hill.

Publications: Annual Report, electronic newsletters, online multimedia resources for scholars, prospective scholars and program alumni.

Finance: Assets US $200,000,000 (30 June 2009); total giving $8,000,000 (2009).

Trustees: Lucy Hanes Chatham (Chair.); Timothy B. Burnett (Vice-Chair.).

Principal Staff: Exec. Dir Charles E. Lovelace, Jr.

Address: POB 690, Chapel Hill, North Carolina 27514-0690.

Telephone: (919) 962-1201; **Fax:** (919) 962-1615; **Internet:** www.moreheadcain.org; **e-mail:** moreheadcain@unc.edu.

The J. P. Morgan Chase Foundation

Established in 1956 as the Manufacturers Hanover Foundation, becoming the Chemical Bank Foundation in 1993. Merged with the J. P. Morgan Charitable Trust, following the merger of J. P. Morgan and Chase Manhattan Bank in 2000.

Activities: Operates in the fields of the arts and culture, community development and education (especially early childhood and youth). Grants are mainly given in the New York City area and parts of New York state where the Chemical Bank operates, but also internationally through US-based non-profit organizations.

Geographical Area of Activity: International.

Restrictions: Programmes outside the geographic markets served; individuals; fraternal organizations; athletic teams or social groups; public agencies; private schools; public schools (K-12), unless in partnership with a qualified not-for-profit organization; parent-teacher associations; scholarships or tuition assistance; fundraising events (e.g. golf outings, school events); advertising, including ads in event, performance or athletic programmes; volunteer-operated organizations; funds to pay down operating deficits; programmes designed to promote religious or political doctrines; endowments or capital campaigns (exceptions are made by invitation only). In general, also higher education; and organizations that discriminate on the basis of race, sex, sexual orientation, age or religion; health- or medical-related organizations.

Publications: *Community Development Group news* (Annual Report).

Principal Staff: Pres. Kimberly B. Davis.

Address: 1 Chase Manhattan Plaza, 5th Floor, New York, NY 10081.

Telephone: (212) 552-1112; **Internet:** www.jpmorganchase.com.

Mosaic Foundation

Established in 1997 by the spouses of Arab ambassadors to the USA to work towards better lives for women and children, and to promote awareness and understanding between the peoples of the Arab world and the USA.

Geographical Area of Activity: International.

Finance: Assets US $2,737,800 (30 Sept. 2008).

Board of Trustees: HRH Princess Haifa al-Faisal (Chair.); Kathleen el-Maaroufi (Treas.); Nicole Saba Chedid (Sec.).

Principal Staff: Pres. Maria Felice Mekouar; Exec. Dir Mona Hamdy.

Address: The Mosaic Foundation, Attn Jeri Pierre, 730 11th St NW, Suite 302, Washington, DC 20001.

Telephone: (202) 388-0000; **Fax:** (202) 388-0061; **Internet:** www.mosaicfound.org; **e-mail:** info@mosaicfound.org.

Charles Stewart Mott Foundation—CSMF

Founded in 1926 by Charles Stewart Mott for charitable purposes.

Activities: Operates nationally and (on a limited basis) internationally, in the fields of social welfare, education, the environment and civil society, through grants to institutions. Supports projects that lead to better community and family relations, more inter-agency co-operation, and the strengthening of the non-profit sector. The Foundation, a pioneer in the concept of community education, now supports limited programme development in Canada, the United Kingdom, South Africa, Eastern and Central Europe and the countries of the former USSR, and other countries, and maintains additional offices in South Africa and the United Kingdom, and has staff representatives in Hungary and Ireland. The four main programme areas of the Foundation are: Civil Society; the Environment; the town of Flint, MI; and Pathways out of Poverty. Also supports Exploratory and Special Projects. Maintains an online grants database on grants made by the Foundation since 1993.

Geographical Area of Activity: North America, Central and Eastern Europe, Western Europe, South Africa.

Restrictions: Grants are not made to individuals, nor to religious organizations for religious purposes.

Publications: Annual Report; occasional reports.

Finance: Total assets US $2,227,400,000 (31 Dec. 2010); annual revenue $275,500,000, expenditure $127,900,000 (2010).

Trustees: William S. White (Chair.); Frederick S. Kirkpatrick (Vice-Chair.).

Principal Staff: Pres. and CEO William S. White.

Address: Mott Foundation Bldg, 503 S Saginaw St, Suite 1200, Flint, MI 48502-1851.

Telephone: (810) 238-5651; **Fax:** (810) 766-1753; **Internet:** www.mott.org; **e-mail:** info@mott.org.

The Mountain Institute—TMI

Non-profit educational and scientific organization founded in 1972 that aims to help and protect mountain environments and cultures around the world.

Activities: Engages in conservation work in the Andes, the Himalayas and the Appalachians, protecting the habitat of mountain wildlife; funds programmes to improve the quality of life of people living in and around mountain parks and protected areas, including projects dedicated to economic development and the promotion of cultural heritage; established the Mountain Forum, an international alliance that acts as a base for information-sharing on issues that affect mountain environments; and founded the Spruce Knob Mountain Learning Center, which serves as the Institute's education, demonstration, conservation, research, and conference facility. Corporate Business Office located in Morgantown, WV. Also maintains offices in the People's Republic of China, India, Nepal and Peru.

Geographical Area of Activity: Asia, North and South America.

Publications: *TMI Teams up to Assist Survivors of Pakistan Earthquake* (newsletter); Annual Report.

Finance: Annual revenue US $3,195,653, expenditure $3,974,773 (2008/09).

Board of Trustees: C. William Carmean (Chair.); Ruth Greenspan Bell (Vice-Chair.); Jane M. Farmer (Sec.); Eliot Kalter (Treas.).

Principal Staff: Exec. Dir Andrew Taber; Dir for Special Projects Bob Davis.

Address: 3000 Connecticut Ave NW, Suite 138, Washington, DC 20008.

Telephone: (202) 234-4050; **Fax:** (202) 234-4054; **Internet:** www.mountain.org; **e-mail:** summit@mountain.org.

Ms Foundation for Women

Founded in 1972 to improve the lives of women and girls.

Activities: So as to achieve its aims, the Foundation operates in three project areas: Women's Economic Security; Women's Health and Safety; and Girls, Young Women and Leadership. It conducts advocacy and public education campaigns, provides technical assistance, and directs resources to organizations operating in these project areas. Also administers the Katrina Women's Response Fund. The Foundation established Take Our Daughters To Work Day.

Geographical Area of Activity: USA.

Restrictions: No grants to direct service organizations, individuals, for scholarships, university-based research, state agencies, religious institutions, cultural or media projects, publications or conferences, nor to applications not submitted in response to a request for proposals.

Publications: Annual Report; newsletter.

Finance: Total assets US $42,702,948 (30 June 2011); annual revenue $10,351,586, expenditure $8,676,800 (2010/11).

Board of Directors: Cathy Raphael (Chair.); Ashley Blanchard (Vice-Chair.); Elizabeth L. Bremner (Treas.); Verna L. Williams (Sec.).

Principal Staff: Pres. and CEO Anika Rahman; COO Susan Wefald.

Address: 12 MetroTech Center, 26th Floor, New York, NY 11201.

Telephone: (212) 742-2300; **Fax:** (212) 742-1653; **Internet:** www.ms.foundation.org; **e-mail:** info@ms.foundation.org.

National Fish and Wildlife Foundation

Founded in 1984 by the US Congress for the conservation of natural resources through grant-making to effective and innovative projects.

Activities: Runs projects concerned with habitat protection, environmental education, public policy development, natural resource management, ecosystem rehabilitation and leadership training for conservation workers. Operates nationally and internationally, although with a focus on the USA, through matching grant and special grant programmes for institutions and individuals.

Geographical Area of Activity: Mainly USA.

Restrictions: No awards for lobbying, political activism or litigation.

Publications: Annual Report.

Finance: Total assets US $228,200,000 (Sept. 2007).

Board of Directors: Carl Kuehner, III (Chair.); Max C. Chapman, Jr (Vice-Chair.); Paul Tudor Jones, II (Vice-Chair.); Amy Robbins (Vice-Chair.).

Principal Staff: Exec. Dir Jeff Trandahl.

Address: 1133 Fifteenth St NW, Suite 1100, Washington, DC 20005.

Telephone: (202) 857-0166; **Fax:** (202) 857-0162; **Internet:** www.nfwf.org; **e-mail:** info@nfwf.org.

National Humanities Center

Incorporated in 1978 by the American Academy of Arts and Sciences to support advanced post-doctoral scholarship in the humanities and to foster the influence of the humanities in the USA.

Activities: Awards up to 40 fellowships annually for post-doctoral scholars in the humanities, including history, philosophy, languages, literature, classics, religion, history of art, etc.; open to students of any nationality for study in the USA.

Geographical Area of Activity: USA.

Restrictions: Grants only for study in the USA.

Publications: *News of the National Humanities Center* (newsletter); *Ideas* (2 a year); Annual Report; conference reports; occasional papers.

Finance: Annual revenue US $5,496,447, expenditure $4,988,810 (2009/10).

Trustees: Alan Brinkley (Chair.); Peter A. Benoliel (Vice-Chair.); Steven Marcus (Vice-Chair.); Patricia Meyer Spacks (Vice-Chair.); John F. Adams (Sec.); Merril M. Halpern (Treas.).

Principal Staff: Pres. and Dir Geoffrey G. Harpham.

Address: 7 Alexander Dr., POB 12256, Research Triangle Park, NC 27709-2256.

Telephone: (919) 549-0661; **Fax:** (919) 990-8535; **Internet:** nationalhumanitiescenter.org; **e-mail:** lmorgan@nationalhumanitiescenter.org.

National Kidney Foundation, Inc

Established to prevent kidney and urinary tract diseases, improve the health and well-being of individuals and families affected by these diseases and increase the availability of all organs for transplantation.

Activities: Awards about 40 post-doctoral fellowships annually for kidney research in the USA by scholars of any nationality, who have not completed more than two years of research training at the start of the fellowship tenure; Young Investigator Grants in nephrology, urology and related disciplines, for students beginning a career in the faculty of a US medical school; and Clinical Scientist Awards to support investigators who have demonstrated outstanding research

potential. Also operates in the fields of patient services and public health education.

Geographical Area of Activity: USA.

Restrictions: Grants only for study in the USA.

Publications: Periodicals and specific publications; Annual Report (annually).

Finance: Assets US $19,579,123 (30 June 2011); Annual revenue $51,156,699, expenditure $53,912,285 (2010/11).

Scientific Advisory Board: Lynda A. Szczech (Chair.).

Principal Staff: CEO Bruce Skyer.

Address: 30 East 33rd St, New York, NY 10016.

Telephone: (212) 889-2210; **Fax:** (212) 689-9261; **Internet:** www.kidney.org; **e-mail:** info@kidney.org.

National Organization for Women Foundation, Inc—NOW Foundation

Established in 1986 to advance women's rights and promote equality in the USA and around the world.

Activities: Operates in the field of women's rights through education, advocacy, conferences, publications, training and leadership development. Runs projects in areas including women's reproductive rights, women with disabilities, prevention of violence against women, sexual harassment, lesbian rights, global feminism and other related issues. Affiliated with the National Organization for Women—NOW.

Geographical Area of Activity: World-wide.

Publications: Annual Report.

Governing Board: Terry O'Neill (Sec. and Treas.).

Principal Staff: Pres. Kim A. Gandy; Exec. Vice-Pres. Karen Johnson; Exec. Vice-Pres. Olga Vives.

Address: POB 1848, Merrifield, VA 22116-8048.

Telephone: (202) 628-8669; **Fax:** (202) 785-8576; **Internet:** www.nowfoundation.org; **e-mail:** now@now.org.

National Science Foundation

Founded as an independent US Government agency to facilitate and fund research into all areas of science and engineering except for human health and medical research.

Activities: Supports research in the areas of biological sciences, computers, information science and engineering, education, environmental research, geosciences, mathematics, physical sciences, polar research, social, behavioural and economic sciences. Also supports co-operative research between US scientists and those in other countries.

Geographical Area of Activity: Mainly USA.

Publications: *Frontiers* (monthly newsletter); directory of projects; forms; general information; news releases; newsletters; policies and procedures; programme announcements and information; reports; statistical reports on US science; summary of awards.

Finance: Funded at approx. US $6,800,000,000 for the 2011 fiscal year.

National Science Board: Dr Ray M. Bowen (Chair.); Dr esin Gulari (Vice-Chair.); Dr Michael L. Van Woert (Exec. Officer).

Principal Staff: Dir Dr Subra Suresh.

Address: 4201 Wilson Blvd, Arlington, VA 22230.

Telephone: (703) 292-5111; **Fax:** (703) 292-9041; **Internet:** www.nsf.gov; **e-mail:** info@nsf.gov.

National Wildlife Federation—NWF

Founded in 1936 to promote the study of wildlife, conservation and the environment, and to increase public awareness of such issues.

Activities: The organization provides fellowships, internships and awards. Environmental Conservation Fellowships are open to Canadian, Mexican and US citizens for advanced study in the USA or abroad. Internships are for work in the Resources Conservation Department in Washington, DC, and for research in the Institute for Wildlife Research. Environmental Publication Awards are offered to student publications in the field of environmental science. Runs various environmental educational programmes, including the Environmental Education Division Internships. Maintains the Institute for Wildlife Research.

Geographical Area of Activity: North America and Mexico.

Publications: Annual Report; books, directories and reports; *Conservation Directory* (annually); *Conservation Exchange* (quarterly); *EYAS* (newsletter, 3 a year); *International Wildlife* (6 a year); *National Wildlife* (6 a year); *Ranger Rick* (monthly); *Your Big Backyard* (monthly); *Animal Baby Magazine* (10 a year).

Finance: Annual revenue US $99,534,000, expenditure $96,946,000 (2009/10).

Board of Directors: Stephen K. Allinger (Chair.); Craig Thompson (Immediate Past Chair.); David Carruth (Central Vice-Chair.); Kathleen Hadley (Western Vice-Chair.); Deborah Spalding (Eastern Vice-Chair.).

Principal Staff: Pres. and CEO Larry J. Schweiger; Exec. Vice-Pres. and COO Jaime Matyas.

Address: 11100 Wildlife Center Dr., Reston, VA 20190-5362.

Telephone: (703) 438-6000; **Fax:** (703) 438-6045; **Internet:** www.nwf.org; **e-mail:** info@nwf.org.

The Nature Conservancy

Established in 1951 with the aim of saving the world's most beautiful areas for future generations.

Activities: Operates in the field of international conservation, working with governments, corporations and landowners as well as local people to help save and preserve land including forests, aquatic areas, prairies and deserts and the communities that support such areas.

Geographical Area of Activity: North, Central and South America and the Caribbean, USA, Asia and the Pacific.

Publications: *Nature Conservancy* (newsletter); Annual Report; financial statements.

Finance: Total assets US $6,029,014,000 (30 June 2011); annual revenue $1,172,365,000, expenditure $691,769,000 (2010/11).

Board of Directors: Teresa Beck (Co-Chair.); Steven A. Denning (Co-Chair.); Gordon Crawford (Vice-Chair.); Roberto Hernández Ramírez (Vice-Chair.); Muneer A. Satter (Treas.); Frank E. Loy (Sec.).

Principal Staff: Pres. and CEO Mark Tercek; COO Brian McPeek.

Address: 4245 North Fairfax Dr., Suite 100, Arlington, VA 22203-1606.

Telephone: (703) 841-5300; **Internet:** www.nature.org; **e-mail:** webmaster@tnc.org.

NCSJ—National Conference on Soviet Jewry

Created in 1971. Aims to safeguard the individual and communal political rights of Jews living in the former USSR, as well as working to secure their religious and political freedoms.

Activities: Advocates on behalf of Jews in Russia, Ukraine, the Baltic states and the republics of Central Asia, and represents the American Jewish community abroad. Monitors compliance by the governments of the former USSR in the areas of free emigration and religious and cultural rights, and also monitors developments related to anti-Semitism in the former USSR. Runs Operation Lifeline, which provides materials, kosher food, and religious and cultural objects to Jews in the countries of the former USSR. Holds conferences, seminars and special events.

Geographical Area of Activity: USA, the republics of Central Asia, Baltic states, Russia, Ukraine.

Restrictions: Not a grant-making organization.

Publications: *Newswatch*; country reports; weekly bulletin; resources: *History of Soviet Jewry* (March 1999); *Listen to Moscow Synagogue Choir*; *Russian Federal Law on Religion* (1997); state department documents: *Global Anti-Semitism Report*

(2005); *International Religious Freedom Report*; *US on Human Rights Abroad*; *Human Rights Report*.

Executive Committee: Richard Stone (Chair.); Alexander Smukler (Pres.).

Principal Staff: Exec. Dir Mark B. Levin.

Address: 2020 K St, NW, Suite 7800, Washington, DC 20006.

Telephone: (202) 898-2500; **Fax:** (202) 898-0822; **Internet:** www.ncsj.org; **e-mail:** ncsj@ncsj.org.

NDI—National Democratic Institute for International Affairs

Affiliated to the US Democratic Party and set up as an independent organization to expand and strengthen democracy world-wide; created as part of the 1984 statute that set up the National Endowment for Democracy.

Activities: Provides practical assistance to civic and political leaders in 79 countries advancing democratic values, practices and institutions. Provides support to build political and civic organizations, safeguard elections, and to promote citizen participation, openness and accountability in government through the provision of expert volunteers, technical resources and training. Programmes focus on citizen participation, civil-military relations, election and political processes, democratic governance, political party development and women's participation.

Geographical Area of Activity: World-wide.

Restrictions: Not a grant-making organization.

Publications: include *NDI Reports: A review of political developments in new democracies* (newsletter); *Consituent Relations Manual: a Guide to Best Practices*; *Assessing Women's Political Party Programs: Best Practices and Recommendations 2008*; *New Mandate, New Opportunities: Evaluation of the Work of the Assembly of Kosovo*.

Board of Directors: Madeleine K. Albright (Chair.); Thomas A. Daschle (Vice-Chair.); Harriet C. Babbitt (Vice-Chair.); Marc B. Nathanson (Vice-Chair.); Patrick J. Griffin (Sec.); Eugene Eidenberg (Treas.).

Principal Staff: Pres. Kenneth Wollack; Vice-Pres. Shari K. Bryan.

Address: 455 Massachusetts Ave, NW, 8th Floor, Washington, DC 20001-2621.

Telephone: (202) 728-5500; **Fax:** (888) 875-2887; **Internet:** www.ndi.org; **e-mail:** adudley@ndi.org.

NEF—Near East Foundation

Founded in 1915 by Cleveland E. Dodge, Thomas Jesse Jones, Paul Monroe, Edwin M. Bulkley and Otis W. Caldwell to offer people of developing nations technical assistance in the implementation of programmes of rural and community improvement.

Activities: Works in the Middle East and Africa on projects to increase food production, with related activities in rural and community development, and primary health care. The Foundation sends qualified technicians overseas to assist with technical-skills transfer and human-resource development. It provides start-up funds for projects until support is available from local sources, and often works in co-operation with other donor agencies. The Foundation has offices in Egypt, Jordan, Mali, Morocco, Sudan, and Palestinian Autonomous Areas.

Geographical Area of Activity: Africa and Middle East.

Restrictions: Operating rather than grant-making foundation.

Publications: Annual Report; brochures.

Finance: Total assets US $4,549,520 (30 June 2010); annual revenue $7,660,468, expenditure $5,357,594 (2009/10).

Board of Directors: Shant Mardirossian (Chair.); Johnson Garrett (Vice-Chair.); Haig Mardikian (Sec.).

Principal Staff: Pres. Dr Charles Benjamin; Vice-Pres. Lucy Berkowitz.

Address: 430–432 Crouse Hinds Hall, 900 S Crouse Ave, Syracuse, NY 13244-2130.

Telephone: (315) 428-8670; **Internet:** www.neareast.org; **e-mail:** info@neareast.org.

The New World Foundation

Founded in 1954 by Anita McCormick Blaine for the support of equal rights, public education, health care, community development and peaceful international relations.

Activities: The Foundation operates through four main programmes: The Global Environmental Health and Justice Fund; The Phoenix Fund for Workers and Communities; The New Majority Fund; and the Arts for Justice Program. Emphasis is placed on youth, the community, enfranchisement of voters and democracy.

Geographical Area of Activity: World-wide.

Restrictions: No grants are made to individuals; no unsolicited proposals.

Publications: Biennial Report; articles; books; reports.

Board of Directors: Nsombi Lambright (Chair.); Michael Leon Guerrero (Vice-Chair.); Jonathan Glionna (Treas.); Maria Rodríguez (Sec.).

Principal Staff: Pres. Dr Colin Greer; Sr Program Officer Ann Bastian.

Address: 666 West End Ave, New York, NY 10025.

Telephone: (212) 497-3470; **Fax:** (212) 472-0508; **Internet:** www.newwf.org; **e-mail:** recept@newwf.org.

Newberry Library

Founded in 1887 at the bequest of Walter Loomis Newberry to collect, preserve and make available to readers books, journals, newspapers, maps, manuscripts and other library materials in history and the humanities; and to foster the use of these materials by all available means, including fellowships, lectures, seminars, exhibitions and publications.

Activities: Offers fellowships for scholars proposing to work in residence, and sponsors conferences, courses, publications, lectures and four research centres. The Library comprises more than 1.5m. volumes, 5m. manuscripts and 500,000 historic maps, and has strong general collections embracing history and the humanities within Western Europe and the Americas from the late Middle Ages to the early 20th century, and a specialization in genealogy. Also operates research and education programmes.

Publications: Atlas of Historical County Boundaries.

Trustees: Victoria J. Herget (Chair.); David C. Hilliard (Vice-Chair.); David E. McNeel (Vice-Chair.); Paul J. Miller (Sec.); Norman Bobins (Treas.).

Principal Staff: Pres. and Librarian David Spadafora.

Address: 60 West Walton St, Chicago, IL 60610.

Telephone: (312) 255-3666; **Fax:** (312) 255-3680; **Internet:** www.newberry.org; **e-mail:** research@newberry.org.

NFCR—National Foundation for Cancer Research

Founded in 1973 by Nobel Prize winner Albert Szent-Gyorgyi to provide seed-funding for basic scientific research toward the better understanding of and cures for cancer.

Activities: Funds nearly 50 laboratories around the world in a variety of scientific disciplines. Holds conferences and symposia. Awards the annual Albert Szent Györgyi Prize for Progress in Cancer Research—an award of US $25,000 to a researcher who has made an outstanding contribution in the field of cancer research. Has provided more than $275m. toward basic science cancer research.

Geographical Area of Activity: USA, Europe and Asia.

Publications: Research for a Cure (newsletter); website, booklets and papers; newsletters and e-newsletter.

Finance: Annual revenue US $18,470,700, expenditure 15,782,224 (2010).

Board of Directors: Judith P. Barnhard (Chair.); Michael Burke (Treas.).

Principal Staff: Pres. Franklin C. Salisbury, Jr.

Address: 4600 East West Highway, Suite 525, Bethesda, MD 20814.

Telephone: (301) 654-1250; **Fax:** (301) 654-5824; **Internet:** www.nfcr.org; **e-mail:** info@nfcr.org.

Novartis US Foundation

Established in 1997 as part of Novartis Corporation's commitment to social investment in the USA. Aims to support social, health and education ventures initiated by communities and organizations.

Activities: Supports innovative biomedical science programmes and effective education to encourage the advancement of the life sciences. Also works to ensure that every young person in the USA has a good start in life with sufficient care and support for a healthy development.

Geographical Area of Activity: USA.

Restrictions: Grants only to US programmes.

Address: 608 5th Ave, New York, NY 10020.

Telephone: (212) 830-2408; **Fax:** (212) 830-2424; **Internet:** www.us.novartis.com/novartis-us-foundation/index.shtml; **e-mail:** us.foundation@novartis.com.

NoVo Foundation

Established to assist in the creation of a peaceful society through focusing on improving the status and well-being of girls and women world-wide.

Activities: Makes grants to USA-based charities carrying out projects in the areas of promoting gender equality, ending violence against women and girls, empowerment of girls in less-developed countries. Grants are also offered for projects advancing social and emotional learning in the USA. In May 2011 the Foundation announced that US $80m. was to be spent over the following 10 years to help end violence against women in the USA.

Geographical Area of Activity: International.

Restrictions: Does not currently accept unsolicited proposals or requests for funding.

Board of Directors: Jennifer Buffett (Pres. and Co-Chair.); Peter Buffett (Co-Chair.).

Principal Staff: Pres. Jennifer Buffett; Operations Man. Kelly Merryman.

Internet: http://novofoundation.org.

The Ocean Foundation

A community foundation with a mission to support, strengthen and promote those organizations working to reverse the destruction of ocean environments around the world.

Activities: Operates in four main areas: conserving marine habitats and special places; protecting species of concern; building the capacity of the marine conservation community; and expanding ocean literary and public awareness. This is done through field of interest funds, special initiatives, fiscal sponsorship and donor funds.

Geographical Area of Activity: International.

Publications: Annual Report; newsletter.

Finance: Total assets US $4,169,154 (30 June 2011); annual revenue $5,004,165, expenditure $5,638,045 (2010/11).

Board of Directors: Mark J. Spalding (Chair. and Pres.); Wolcott Henry (Founding Chair. and Sec.); .

Principal Staff: COO Karen Muir; Special Projects Dir Jeremy Linneman.

Address: 1990 M St NW, Suite 250, Washington, DC 20036.

Telephone: (202) 887-8992; **Internet:** www.oceanfdn.org; **e-mail:** info@oceanfdn.org.

Omidyar Network

Established in 2004 by Pam and Pierre Omidyar, the founder of eBay, based on the belief that every person has the potential to make a difference.

Activities: Funds for-profit and non-profit organizations to create opportunities for people, enabling them to improve their lives and make powerful contributions to their communities.

Geographical Area of Activity: International.

Finance: Annual revenue US $56,013,567, expenditure $34,811,734 (2010).

Board: Pierre Omidyar (Co-Founder); Pam Omidyar (Co-Founder).

Principal Staff: Dirs Paula Goldman, Joe Goldman; Vice-Pres Christopher Keefe, Amy Klement.

Address: 1991 Broadway St, Suite 200, Redwood City, CA 94063.

Telephone: (650) 482-2500; **Fax:** (650) 482-2525; **Internet:** www.omidyar.com; **e-mail:** info@omidyar.com.

Open Society Institute—New York

Founded in December 1993 by George Soros, the Open Society Institute assists the work of the national foundations in Central and Eastern Europe, promotes the development of open societies, encourages public debate on policy alternatives in controversial areas and manages many regional programmes conducted throughout Central and Eastern Europe and the countries of the former USSR. The New York office acts as the administrative, financial and communications headquarters of the Soros foundations network.

Activities: The Open Society Institute assists the network of Soros foundations world-wide by operating OSI initiatives which provide administrative, financial and technical support to the Soros foundations and also OSI initiatives, which address specific issues on a regional or network-wide basis, and other independent programmes. The Institute is also the home of a series of programmes that focus principally on the USA. In the American capital, the OSI Washington office engages in public education on a range of domestic and international issues, including criminal and civil justice reform, women's rights, US policy in Colombia, and Central Eurasia. The Open Society Policy Center, a separate organization that is incorporated as a 501 (c) 4 non-profit, undertakes lobbying efforts on these and other public policy issues. The Institute's initiatives address specific issue areas on a regional or network-wide basis around the world. Most of the initiatives are administered by OSI in New York or OSI–Budapest (q.v.) and implemented in co-operation with Soros foundations in various countries. The nearly 20 OSI initiatives cover a range of activities aimed at building free and open societies, including children and youth, the strengthening of civil society; economic reform; education at all levels; human rights; legal reform and public administration; media and communications; public health; women's rights; and arts and culture. In 2004 launched the US Justice Fund and the Strategic Opportunities Fund. Maintains additional offices in Baltimore, MD, Brussels, London and Paris.

Geographical Area of Activity: Europe, the countries of the former USSR, Africa, Latin America and the Caribbean, the Middle East, Asia and the USA.

Publications: Annual Report; *Open Society News* (quarterly newsletter); leaflets and directory of Soros foundations; articles; and other publications.

Trustees: George Soros (Chair.).

Principal Staff: Pres. Aryeh Neier (until July 2012), Prof. Christopher Stone (from July 2012).

Address: 400 West 59th St, New York, NY 10019.

Telephone: (212) 548-0600; **Fax:** (212) 548-4600; **Internet:** www.soros.org; **e-mail:** web@sorosny.org.

Open Society Institute—Washington, DC

Established to address civil liberties violations in the USA and expand the Open Society Institute's policy and advocacy work in the areas of criminal and civil justice reform. The Institute is part of the Open Society network of foundations and institutes established by George Soros.

Geographical Area of Activity: USA.

Address: 1730 Pennsylvania Ave, NW, 7th Floor, Washington, DC 20006.

Telephone: (202) 721-5600; **Fax:** (202) 530-0128; **Internet:** www.soros.org/about/locations/washington-dc.

Operation Rainbow, Inc

Founded in 1978 by Dr William B. Riley, Jr to provide free reconstructive surgery for underprivileged children in the USA and in developing countries around the world.

Activities: Operates in the field of medicine and health care, by raising money from individuals, foundations and corporations to fund reconstructive surgery (plastic and orthopaedic) to be performed by volunteer surgeons on children with medical problems primarily in Asia, Central and South America and the USA. Also provides teaching and training for local medical staff overseas, and runs a sponsorship programme, so that nurses and physicians from abroad are sponsored to come to the USA for additional training. Countries currently covered by programmes include Brazil, Mexico and Venezuela.

Geographical Area of Activity: Asia, Central and South America, and the USA.

Finance: Funded by donations and volunteer support.

Board: Dr William B. Riley (Founder).

Principal Staff: Dir Laura Escobosa; Man. Dir William B. Riley; Man. Dir Gus Gialamas; Man. Dir David Atkin.

Address: 4200 Park Blvd, PMB 157, Oakland, CA 94602.

Telephone: (510) 273-2485; **Internet:** www.operationrainbow.org; **e-mail:** laura@operationrainbow.org.

Operation USA

Established in 1979 as Operation California; aims to mitigate the effects of poverty and the results of natural and man-made disasters in the USA and abroad.

Activities: Provides emergency medical, nutritional and shelter supplies to victims of poverty and disaster throughout Asia, Africa, Central and South America and the Caribbean, Eastern Europe and the Balkans. Also runs a domestic disaster response programme, micro-enterprise initiatives, a community clinic support programme in the USA, and initiated Operation Landmine in 1995 to engage in de-mining activities around the world.

Geographical Area of Activity: International; USA.

Publications: Annual Report.

Finance: Total assets US $8,434,653 (30 June 2010); annual revenue $22,680,870, expenditure $20,317,746 (2009/10).

Board of Directors: Michael Mahdesian (Chair.); Gary Larsen (Vice-Chair.).

Principal Staff: CEO and Pres. Richard M. Walden.

Address: 7421 Beverly Blvd, Los Angeles, CA 90036.

Telephone: (323) 413-2353; **Fax:** (323) 931-5400; **Internet:** www.opusa.org; **e-mail:** info@opusa.org.

Opportunity International USA

Established with the aim of transforming the lives of those living in chronic poverty, through job creation, small business development and community support; a network of 45 autonomous affiliated implementing partners in developing countries world-wide and seven support partners in developed countries.

Activities: Operates internationally in collaboration with indigenous partner organizations in the areas of aid to less-developed countries and social welfare, through promoting micro-enterprise schemes to combat poverty and offering loans and basic business training. Founded the Women's Opportunity Network, and in 2003 launched the US $25m. Lending Hope to Africa Campaign. Other members of the network operate from Australia, Canada, Germany and the United Kingdom (q.v.).

Geographical Area of Activity: Africa, Asia, Central and South America, the Caribbean, Central and Eastern Europe.

Publications: *Impact* (newsletter, 2 a year); Annual Report.

Board of Directors: Betty Jane Hess (Chair.); Mark A. Thompson (Vice-Chair.); Mark Vaselkiv (Treas.); Jim Hamilton (Sec.).

Principal Staff: Interim CEO Jon Yasuda; Sr Vice-Pres. and CFO Richard C. John.

Address: 2122 York Rd, Suite 150, Oak Brook, IL 60523.

Telephone: (630) 242-4100; **Fax:** (630) 645-1458; **Internet:** www.opportunity.org.

Orbis International

Established in 1982 to reduce preventable blindness throughout the world through training, health education and improved access to eye care.

Activities: The organization started its work by building a mobile teaching eye hospital—a fully equipped aeroplane—to travel around the world training doctors and medical staff in developing countries, transferring knowledge and skills through lectures and training. Since then, Orbis has expanded to include specialized training programmes and community health projectsto further improve the standard of eye care in less-developed countries where a large percentage of blindness is because of preventable conditions. Currently operates projects in Africa (including Botswana, Burkina Faso, Cameroon, Ethiopia, Ghana, Kenya, Mali, Malawi, Nigeria,Tanzania and Uganda), Asia (Bangladesh, People's Republic of China, India and Viet Nam), and Latin America and the Caribbean (Jamaica and Peru).

Geographical Area of Activity: World-wide.

Publications: Annual Report; brochures; posters and advertisements; *Vision for the World* (brochure); *Aviation advertisement poster*; fact sheet; *Observer* (newsletter).

Finance: Annual revenue US $83,799,811, expenditure $80,952,131 (2010).

Board of Directors: Robert F. Walters (Chair.); James R. Parker (Vice-Chair.); Diana Wheeler (Sec.); Peter Hickson (Treas.).

Principal Staff: Interim Pres. and CEO Robert F. Walters.

Address: 520 Eighth Ave, 11th Floor, New York, NY 10018.

Telephone: (646) 674-5500; **Fax:** (646) 674-5599; **Internet:** www.orbis.org; **e-mail:** info@orbis.org.

Orentreich Foundation for the Advancement of Science, Inc—OFAS

Founded in 1961 and classified as an operating private foundation in 1972, the Foundation carries out its own research and/or collaborates with other institutions on projects that aim to prevent or reverse disorders decreasing length or quality of life.

Activities: Operates in the field of medicine and health, through conferences, seminars and research, which it carries out at its biomedical research centre in New York state. Also makes occasional grants to help fund joint or collaborative research in fields of substantial OFAS research interest, which it usually initiates.

Geographical Area of Activity: Mainly USA.

Restrictions: Recipients are typically at or above post-graduate level in science or medicine at accredited universities or research institutions in the USA.

Publications: Annual Directors' Report; *VitaLongevity News Letters*.

Principal Staff: Founder and Co-Dir Norman Orentreich; Co-Dir David Orentreich; Dep. Dir Bernardita Calinao.

Address: Biomedical Research Station, 855 Route 301, Cold Spring, NY 10516.

Fax: (845) 265-4210; **Internet:** www.orentreich.org; **e-mail:** library@orentreich.org.

Outreach International

Incorporated in April 1979; an international development organization that aims to alleviate suffering in the world.

Activities: Works to eliminate the poverty, hunger and disease suffered by people around the world by providing long-term solutions, through Participatory Human Development, a non-directive process designed to involve the poor in the decisions that affect them in order that they can learn to sustain themselves. Focuses on three main areas: Human and Community Development; Literacy and Child Survival; Civil Society. Currently operates programmes in 13 countries around the world.

Geographical Area of Activity: North, Central and South America, Africa, Asia and the Caribbean.

Publications: *Outreach Developments* (quarterly newsletter); Annual Report.

Finance: Total net assets US $2,012,883 (30 Sept. 2010); annual revenue $3,498,413, expenditure $3,360,631 (2009/10).

Board of Directors: Harry Ashenhurst (Chair.); Randall Pratt (Vice-Chair.); Constance L. Thatcher (Sec.); Karen Mercer (Treas.).

Principal Staff: Pres. and CEO Kevin Prine; Dir of Finance and Admin. Orval Fisher.

Address: 129 W Lexington, Independence, MO 64050.

Telephone: (816) 833-0883; **Fax:** (816) 833-0103; **Internet:** www.outreach-international.org; **e-mail:** info@outreach-international.org.

Oxfam America

Established in 1970; part of the Oxfam confederation of organizations (qq.v.).

Activities: Assists people affected by emergencies, conflicts and natural disasters world-wide; campaigns on issues including food security and aid.

Geographical Area of Activity: International.

Publications: Annual Report; OXFAM Exchange (magazine, 3 a year); factsheets, papers,etc.

Finance: Total assets US $98,856,000 (31 Oct. 2010); annual revenue $86,526,000, expenditure $78,198,000 (2009/10).

Board of Directors: Barry Gaberman (Acting Chair.); Joe H. Hamilton (Treas. and Sec.).

Principal Staff: Pres. Raymond C. Offenheiser; Exec. Vice-Pres. Manish Bapna.

Address: 226 Causeway St., 5th Floor, Boston, MA 02114-2206.

Internet: www.oxfamamerica.org; **e-mail:** info@oxfamamerica.org.

David and Lucile Packard Foundation

Founded in 1964 by David and Lucile Packard to support projects in the areas of child development and health, family planning, education, the environment and conservation, marine sciences and global population studies.

Activities: Primarily concerned with supporting local projects; however, the Foundation also offers support in the fields of conservation and science, population studies, children, family and communities, and capacity building in Central and South America, particularly Mexico and Colombia. Also operates a Local Area Fund.

Geographical Area of Activity: North, Central and South America.

Restrictions: No grants are made to individuals.

Publications: Annual Report and financial statement; grants list; occasional report; information brochure; programme policy statement; programme area publications; Foundation e-newsletter.

Finance: Total assets US $6,100,000,000 (31 Dec. 2010); total grant awards $234,000,000 (2010).

Board of Trustees: Susan Packard Orr (Chair.); Julie E. Packard (Vice-Chair.); Nancy Packard Burnett (Vice-Chair.); Mary Anne Rodgers (Sec. and Gen. Counsel).

Principal Staff: Pres. and CEO Carol S. Larson; Exec. Asst to CEO Cathy Winter.

Address: 300 Second St, Los Altos, CA 94022.

Telephone: (650) 948-7658; **Fax:** (650) 948-2957; **Internet:** www.packard.org; **e-mail:** inquiries@packard.org.

Pact

Established in 1971 to assist indigenous organizations working for development.

Activities: Runs its own development programmes throughout Africa, Asia, and South America alongside partner organizations and local NGOs. Projects deal with areas including food security, education, health (HIV/AIDS), micro-credit and small enterprise, capacity building, women's empowerment, increasing the effectiveness of grassroots civil society organizations, and rural development. Maintains 24 field offices.

Geographical Area of Activity: World-wide.

Restrictions: This is not a grant-making organization, although does provide financial resources to local partner organizations.

Publications: Annual Report; and a number of books related to the areas in which Pact works.

Finance: Total assets US $102,928,568 (30 Sept. 2010); annual revenue $204,705,859, expenditure $204,812,392 (2009/10).

Board of Directors: Stephen H. Oleskey (Chair.); Dr Lyndon Haviland (Vice-Chair.).

Principal Staff: Pres. and CEO Mark Viso; COO Will Warshauer.

Address: 1828 L St NW, Suite 300, Washington, DC 20036.

Telephone: (202) 466-5666; **Fax:** (202) 466-5669; **Internet:** www.pactworld.org; **e-mail:** info@pactworld.org.

PADF—Pan American Development Foundation

Founded in 1962 to promote social and economic development of the Americas.

Activities: The Foundation's primary objective is to assist in bringing technical expertise and resources to Central and South America and the Caribbean, as well as providing disaster assistance. Main project areas are the strengthening of local civic institutions, sustainable agricultural production, increasing family incomes, and family health promotion. The Foundation operates in partnership with local organizations, with multinational corporations, private businesses and NGOs in the region, along with the US Government and non-governmental inter-American organizations. Maintains offices in Colombia and Haiti.

Geographical Area of Activity: Central and South America and the Caribbean.

Publications: Annual Report; *PADF Newsletter*; technical publications.

Finance: Total assets US $15,302,872 (30 Sept. 2010); annual revenue $55,670,340, expenditure $55,324,421 (2009/10).

Board of Trustees: José Miguel Insulza (Chair.); Albert R. Ramdin (Vice-Chair.); Frank Gómez (Pres.); Frank Kanayet Yépes (First Vice-Pres.); Gladys Coupet (Second Vice-Pres.); Maston N. Cunningham (Treas.); Kathleen C. Barclay (Sec.).

Principal Staff: Exec. Dir John Sanbrailo; Dep. Exec. Dir and COO Dr Judith Hermanson.

Address: 1889 F St NW, Washington, DC 20006.

Telephone: (202) 458-3969; **Fax:** (202) 458-6316; **Internet:** www.padf.org; **e-mail:** info@padf.org.

PAHEF—Pan American Health and Education Foundation (Fundación Panamericana de la Salud y Educación)

Founded in 1968 to promote and stimulate efforts to combat disease, lengthen life, improve health care services, foster health research, and enhance the capabilities of health workers in the Americas through grant-making and direct programme implementation. Enjoys a unique relationship with the Pan American Health Organization, the Regional Office for the Americas of the World Health Organization (WHO), and shares the vision of health for all. In pursuit of this vision, PAHEF's targeted efforts help to promote healthy living (prevention of chronic disease, healthy ageing, prevention of childhood obesity) and enhance the training of medical professionals and health workers.

Activities: Operates, mainly in Latin America and the Caribbean, in the field of public health, through self-conducted programmes, awarding prizes, and issuing publications. Programmes include: Expanded Textbook and Instructional Materials Program (PALTEX); Awards for Excellence in Inter-American Public Health Program; and PAHEF Grants Program.

Geographical Area of Activity: Latin America and the Caribbean.

Restrictions: The Foundation only accepts proposals that respond to its annual call for proposals.

Publications: Numerous publications and manuals; brochures; other promotional materials.

Finance: Grants disbursed US $6,000,000 (2007).

Board of Directors: Benjamin Caballero (Chair.); Rafael Pérez-Escamilla (Vice-Chair.); Sally Shelton-Colby (Treas.); Fernando Mendoza (Sec.).

Principal Staff: Pres. Edward L. Kadunc; Dir of Programs Pilar M. Torres.

Address: 1889 F St, NW, Suite 312, Washington, DC 20006.

Telephone: (202) 974-3416; **Fax:** (202) 974-3636; **Internet:** www.pahef.org; **e-mail:** info@pahef.org.

PAI—Population Action International

An independent policy advocacy group working to strengthen political and financial support world-wide for population programmes grounded in individual rights. PAI is committed to advancing universal access to family planning and related health services and to educational and economic opportunities, especially for girls and women. Founded in 1965, PAI is a private, non-profit group and accepts no government funds.

Activities: PAI fosters the development of US and international policy on urgent population and reproductive health issues through an integrated programme of research, advocacy and communications. PAI seeks to make clear the linkages between population, reproductive health, the environment and development. Serving as a bridge between the academic and policy-making communities, PAI disseminates strategic, action-orientated research publications; participates in and sponsors conferences, meetings and seminars; and works to educate and inform policy-makers and international colleagues in related fields.

Geographical Area of Activity: International.

Publications: *Progress & Promises: Trends in International Assistance for Reproductive Health and Population; Countdown 2015: Sexual & Reproductive Health & Rights For All; What You Need to Know About the Global Gag Rule and US HIV/AIDS Assistance: An Unofficial Guide; The Security Demographic: Population and Civil Conflict After the Cold War; Access Denied: US Restrictions on International Family Planning; Condoms Count: Meeting the Need in the Era of HIV/AIDS; In This Generation: Sexual & Reproductive Health Policies for a Youthful World*; newsletter; other fact sheets, books and charts; Annual Report.

Finance: Annual revenue US $7,457,378, expenditure $7,457,378 (2009).

Board of Directors: Moises Naim (Chair.); Harriet C. Babbitt (Vice-Chair.); Dr Pouru Bhiwandi (Treas.); Vicki Sant (Sec.).

Principal Staff: Pres. and CEO Suzanne Ehlers; COO Carolyn Gibb Vogel.

Address: 1300 19th St NW, Suite 200, Washington, DC 20036.

Telephone: (202) 557-3400; **Fax:** (202) 728-4177; **Internet:** www.populationaction.org; **e-mail:** pai@popact.org.

Panasonic Foundation

Established in 1984 by Matsushita Electrical Corporation of America (MECA), and formerly known as the Matsushita

Foundation, a subsidiary company of the Japan-based Matsushita Electrical Industrial Co Ltd.

Activities: The Foundation operates in the field of education through partnerships with a small number of school districts, which are provided with direct technical assistance to bring about school reform.

Geographical Area of Activity: USA.

Restrictions: Does not award grants.

Publications: Newsletter; articles and books; *The Panasonic Foundation and School Reform: 20 Years of Corporate Commitment*; *The Panasonic Foundation 25 Years*; *Learning by Doing: Panasonic Partnerships and Systemic School Reform.*

Officers and Trustees: Milton Chen (Chair.); Michael Riccio (Treas.); Robert Ohme (Asst Treas.): Sandra Karriem (Sec.).

Principal Staff: Exec. Dir Larry Leverett; Asst Exec. Dir Scott Thompson.

Address: 3 Panasonic Way, 21-1, Secaucus, NJ 07094.

Telephone: (201) 392-4132; **Fax:** (201) 392-4126; **Internet:** www.panasonic.com/meca/foundation/foundation.html; **e-mail:** info@foundation.us.panasonic.com.

Parkinson's Disease Foundation, Inc—PDF

Founded in 1957 by William Black to raise funds to plan, undertake, support and promote investigation into the cause and cure of Parkinson's disease and related disorders, and to provide patients suffering from the disease with a better quality of life. Merged with the United Parkinson Foundation, Chicago in 1999.

Activities: Operates nationally and internationally in the fields of research, education and advocacy. Makes grants to institutions and individuals, awards scholarships and fellowships, holds conferences, runs advisory services and issues publications. Programmes include an International Research Grants Program; H. Houston Merritt Fellowship Program; and Summer Fellowship Program; and a post-doctoral programme.

Geographical Area of Activity: Mainly USA, although international grants are available.

Publications: Annual Report; *PDF Newsletter*; *PDF Science Bulletin*; *Progress, Promise and Hope!*; *Exercises for the Parkinson Patient*; *The Parkinson Patient at Home*; leaflets and brochures.

Finance: Total assets US $13,675,022 (30 June 2010); annual revenue $9,526,410, expenditure $9,500,399 (2009/10).

Board of Directors: Page Morton Black (Chair.); Lewis P. Rowland (Pres.); Timothy A. Pedley (Vice-Pres.); Stephen Ackerman (Treas.); Isobel Robins Konecky (Sec.); Stanley Fahn (Scientific Dir).

Principal Staff: Exec. Dir Robin Anthony Elliot.

Address: 1359 Broadway, Suite 1509, New York, NY 10018.

Telephone: (212) 923-4700; **Fax:** (212) 923-4778; **Internet:** www.pdf.org; **e-mail:** info@pdf.org.

PATH—Program for Appropriate Technology in Health

PATH was founded in 1977 as PIACT, or the Program for the Introduction and Adaptation of Contraceptive Technology. The organization has been known as PATH since 1981.

Activities: PATH is an international non-profit organization that creates sustainable, culturally relevant solutions, enabling communities world-wide to break longstanding cycles of poor health. By collaborating with diverse public- and private-sector partners, PATH helps provide appropriate health technologies and vital strategies that change the way people think and act. PATH's work improves global health and well-being. Headquartered in Seattle, Washington, PATH has offices in 34 cities in 23 countries. PATH currently works in more than 70 countries in the areas of health technologies, maternal and child health, reproductive health, vaccines and immunization, and emerging and epidemic diseases.

Geographical Area of Activity: International.

Restrictions: Not a grant-making organization.

Publications: More than 800 publications, including: *Directions in Global Health*; *Outlook* (on reproductive health issues); *PATH Today* (newsletter); Annual Report; other resources.

Finance: Annual revenue US $283,277,000; expenditure $282,605,000 (2010).

Board of Directors: Molly Joel Coye (Chair); Vincent McGee (Vice-Chair.); Dean Allen (Treas.); Jay Satia (Sec.).

Principal Staff: Pres. and CEO Christopher J. Elias.

Address: 2201 Westlake Ave, Suite 200 Seattle WA 98121.

Telephone: (206) 285-3500; **Fax:** (206) 285-6619; **Internet:** www.path.org; **e-mail:** info@path.org.

Pathfinder International

Incorporated as the Pathfinder Fund in 1957 by Dr Clarence Gamble to introduce better family planning information and facilities around the world.

Activities: Works to improve reproductive health services in the developing world, aiming thereby to improve the lives of women and their families, particularly in the areas of improving access to services, advocacy work, AIDS and abortion services. Funds and participates in national family planning programmes in Africa, Central and South America, Asia and the Caribbean.

Geographical Area of Activity: Africa, Central and South America, Asia and the Caribbean.

Publications: Annual Report, *Reproductive Health Resources, Guides and Tools*; technical guidelines, training curricula, articles, working papers, reports, *Pathways* (newsletter).

Finance: Net assets US $33,505,948 (30 June 2011); annual revenue $100,042,923, expenditure $99,717,439 (2010/11).

Directors: Cynthia A. Fields (Chair.); James M. Schwartz (Vice-Chair.); Manuel Urbina (Sec.); Benjamin R. Kahrl (Treas.).

Principal Staff: Pres. Purnima Mane; Sr Vice-Pres. Caroline Crosbie; CFO Thomas Downing.

Address: 9 Galen St, Suite 217, Watertown, MA 02472.

Telephone: (617) 924-7200; **Fax:** (617) 924-3833; **Internet:** www.pathfind.org; **e-mail:** information@pathfind.org.

Alicia Patterson Foundation—APF

Founded in 1965 by members of the Albright and Patterson families to support print journalists.

Activities: Awards one-year and six-month fellowships to print journalists with at least five years' experience who are US citizens. Fellowship recipients pursue independent projects of significant interest in the USA or overseas.

Geographical Area of Activity: USA.

Restrictions: Fellowships only open to US citizens, or non-US citizens who work on US print publications. No grants are made for academic study.

Publications: *APF Reporter* (quarterly); web magazine; Annual Report; information brochure.

Board of Directors: Alice Arlen (Chair.); Adam Albright (Treas.); Margaret Engel (Sec.).

Principal Staff: Pres. Robert Lee Hotz.

Address: 1090 Vermont Ave NW, Suite 1000, Washington, DC 20005.

Telephone: (202) 393-5995; **Fax:** (301) 951-8512; **Internet:** www.aliciapatterson.org; **e-mail:** director@aliciapatterson.org.

PCI-Media Impact

Founded in 1985, as Population Communications International (PCI), aims to work creatively with the media and other organizations to influence population trends.

Activities: Promotes sustainable development through the research, production and broadcast of locally run and culturally appropriate radio and television serial dramas. These productions inform and educate local communities in Africa, Asia, Central and South America, and the USA about population and development issues through popular entertainment, and work to enhance communications between NGOs. Issues covered include reproductive health and family planning, HIV prevention, gender equality, social welfare and the protection of the environment. Also acts as the Secretariat for the NGO Committee on Population and Development, which encourages co-operation between the UN and NGOs.

Geographical Area of Activity: International.

Restrictions: Does not make grants.

Publications: *Mónica en busca de amor*; *Jam Packed*; *Time to Act*; *The Cost of Cool*; *Telling Stories, Saving Lives;* Annual Report; research papers; *PCI Strengthens HIV/AIDS Initiative in Peru; PCI partner stays on the air despite violence in Oaxaca, Mexico.*

Finance: Annual revenue US $747,810, expenditure $1,396,999 (2009).

Board of Directors: Fred Cohen (Chair.); Rita Fredricks Salzman (Vice-Chair.); Alexander F. Watson (Treas.); Dr Lynne Yeannakis (Sec.).

Principal Staff: Exec. Dir Sean Southey; CFO Anthony M. Scala.

Address: 777 United Nations Plaza, 5th Floor, New York, NY 10017.

Telephone: (212) 687-3366; **Fax:** (212) 661-4188; **Internet:** www.population.org; **e-mail:** info@mediaimpact.org.

PepsiCo Foundation, Inc

Founded in 1962 by PepsiCo, Inc, and Frito-Lay, Inc.

Activities: The Foundation provides financial support to non-profit organizations primarily where employees of PepsiCo are involved as volunteers. Priority is given to organizations concerned with Nutrition and Activity, Safe Water and Usage Efficiencies and Education and Empowerment. Also involved in disaster response.

Geographical Area of Activity: World-wide.

Restrictions: The Foundation will only consider grant applications made online. No grants are made to individuals.

Finance: Grants disbursed US $27,900,000 (2009).

Board of Directors: Indra Nooyi (Chair.); Christine C. Griff (Sec.).

Principal Staff: Pres. Joseph F. McCann.

Address: c/o PepsiCo, Inc, 700 Anderson Hill Rd, Purchase, NY 10577.

Telephone: (914) 253-3153; **Internet:** www.pepsico.com/Purpose/PepsiCo-Foundation.html; **e-mail:** gale.quint@pepsico.com.

Pesticide Action Network North America—PANNA

Founded in 1982 as a regional centre of the PAN International network to campaign for safer forms of pest control in Canada, Mexico and the USA.

Activities: Promotes healthier and more effective methods of pest-control to replace harmful pesticides, through research, policy development, media coverage, education and international advocacy campaigns. Provides activists, researchers and policy-makers with technical information, analysis, training, campaign support and policy guidance. Enlists the support of numerous health, consumer, agricultural and environmental groups throughout North America to eliminate harmful pesticide use.

Geographical Area of Activity: North and Central America.

Publications: *PAN Magazine.*

Finance: Total assets US $1,246,478 (30 June 2011); annual revenue $2,050,003, expenditure $2,380,370 (2010/11).

Board of Directors: Judy Hatcher (Pres.); Polly Hoppin (Vice-Pres.); Jennifer Sokolove (Treas.); Lucia Sayre (Sec.).

Principal Staff: Co-Dirs Kathryn Gilje, Heather Pilatic and Steve Scholl-Buckwald.

Address: 49 Powell St, Suite 500, San Francisco, CA 94102.

Telephone: (415) 981-1771; **Fax:** (415) 981-1991; **Internet:** www.panna.org; **e-mail:** panna@panna.org.

Peter G. Peterson Foundation

Established by Peter G. Peterson in 2008 to support all forms of sustainability in the USA.

Activities: The Foundation operates in the USA to draw attention to future problems in the areas of social welfare, medicine and health, and conservation and the environment, including costs of welfare and health care, energy consumption, global warming and nuclear and biological weapons.

Geographical Area of Activity: USA.

Restrictions: Proposals are currently by invitation only.

Board of Directors: Peter G. Peterson (Founder and Chair.); Michael A. Peterson (Vice-Chair.).

Principal Staff: CfO Paul Newman; Vice-Pres Susan Tanaka, Loretta Ucelli.

Address: 888-C 8th Ave, Box 144, New York, NY 10019.

Internet: www.pgpf.org; **e-mail:** comments@pgpf.org.

The Pew Charitable Trusts

The Pew Charitable Trusts include the Pew Memorial Trust (founded in 1948), the J. N. Pew, Jr Charitable Trust (founded in 1956), the J. Howard Pew Freedom Trust, the Mabel Pew Myrin Trust and the Mary Anderson Trust (all founded in 1957), the Knollbrook Trust (founded in 1965) and the Medical Trust (founded in 1979).

Activities: The Trusts support non-profit activities in three main areas: informing the public, through the Pew Research Center, based in Washington, DC, which explores important issues and trends that affect public opinion; improving public policy nationally and globally by helping to find non-partisan solutions for the problems affecting communities; stimulating civic life including by supporting organizations in Philadelphia concerned with encouraging the participation of local citizens in the city's arts and culture community.

Geographical Area of Activity: USA, with a special emphasis on the Philadelphia area.

Restrictions: No grants are made to individuals, for scholarships, nor for endowment funds; non-applied research; land acquisition; equipment purchases; capital projects; debt reduction.

Publications: *Program Resource Guide*; *Trust* (quarterly magazine); strategy papers; reports; and other publications.

Finance: Annual revenue US $390,308,664, expenditure $243,860,115 (2009).

Principal Staff: Pres. and CEO Rebecca W. Rimel.

Address: 1 Commerce Sq., 2005 Market St, Suite 1700, Philadelphia, PA 19103-7077.

Telephone: (215) 575-9050; **Fax:** (215) 575-4939; **Internet:** www.pewtrusts.org; **e-mail:** info@pewtrusts.org.

Pfizer Foundation

Independent charitable organization founded in 1953 by Pfizer Inc.

Activities: Operates in areas where the Pfizer company has offices. Promotes access to health care and education, encourages and develops innovation, and supports the community involvement of Pfizer workers. Internationally programmes focus on the donation of medicines and providing support to train health care workers in diagnosis and treatment, and help patients understand how to live healthier lives to prevent the spread of preventable diseases. A world-wide programme with a budget of US $33m. to improve the diagnosis and treatment of cancer and to support tobacco control was announced in February 2008. Also provides disaster relief in the form of funding and gifts-in-kind.

Geographical Area of Activity: World-wide.

Restrictions: Unsolicited proposals are discouraged, but not refused.

Finance: Total assets US $209,307,790 (31 Dec. 2010); total giving $19,126,855 (2010).

Board: William C. Steere (Chair.).

Principal Staff: Pres. Caroline T. Roan.

Address: Philanthropy Programs, Pfizer Inc, 235 East 42nd St, New York, NY 10017-5703.

Telephone: (212) 733-4250; **Internet:** www.pfizer.com/responsibility.

The Carl and Lily Pforzheimer Foundation, Inc

Founded in 1942 by members of the Pforzheimer family for general charitable purposes.

Activities: Operates primarily in the field of American and English literature, in collaboration with libraries and educational institutions, through publications and through the Carl H. Pforzheimer Library. Support is given to certain selected institutions active in the fields of education, medicine, social welfare and the arts.

Geographical Area of Activity: USA.

Finance: Total assets US $4,997,015 (31 Dec. 2010); grants disbursed $1,986,824 (2010).

Board of Directors: Carl H Pforzheimer, III (Pres. and Treas.); Nancy P. Aronson (Vice-Pres.); George L. K. Frelinghuysen (Asst Treas.); Martin F. Richman (Sec.); Jennifer Lui (Asst Sec.).

Principal Staff: Comptroller Anthony L. Ferranti.

Address: 950 3rd Ave, 30th Floor, New York, NY 10022-2705.

Telephone: (212) 223-6500.

PH International

Founded in 1985 as Project Harmony, with the aim creating a stronger global community. Rebranded as PH International in 2009.

Activities: Co-ordinates cultural, educational and professional exchanges to enhance international understanding, strengthen communities and nurture personal friendships. Also carries out programmes in youth leadership, civic participation, combatting domestic violence, reparative justice, media literacy, economic development and projects that use information technology for these purposes. Offices in the USA, Armenia, Georgia, Russia and Ukraine, with additional projects in Turkey and Kazakhstan.

Geographical Area of Activity: World-wide, with special focus on Eurasia, Middle East, People's Republic of China and USA.

Restrictions: None.

Publications: E-newsletter; Annual Report; financial summary.

Finance: Total assets US $780,000 (31 Dec. 2010); annual revenue $4,952,000, expenditure $4,952,000 (2010).

Board of Directors: Charles Hosford (Founder).

Principal Staff: Exec. Dir Ann Martin.

Address: 5197 Main St, Unit 6, Waitsfield, VT 05673.

Telephone: (802) 496-4545; **Fax:** (802) 496-4548; **Internet:** www.ph-int.org; **e-mail:** ph-vt@ph-int.org.

Philippine Development Foundation—PhilDev

Established in 2000 as the Ayala Foundation USA to build links between Filipino communities in the USA and the Philippines. Linked to the Ayala Foundation in the Philippines (q.v.). Renamed in 2010.

Activities: Assists the development of philanthropic giving for the Philippines in partnership with individuals and organizations/networks of Filipinos in the USA. Aims to increase awareness of socio-economic issues affecting poverty, hunger, illiteracy, environmental degradation and homelessness. Raises funds to support projects in the Philippines including assistance to poor communities; education, technological and business skills development to help economically disadvantaged young people and adults to find employment; and enhancing cultural, historical and environmental conservation awareness through communication, publication and governance. Maintains a database on donor opportunities in the Philippines.

Geographical Area of Activity: USA and the Philippines.

Restrictions: Grants are made in the Philippines to non-profit organizations engaged in social development.

Publications: Annual Report; newsletter; e-bulletin (monthly).

Finance: Annual revenue US $1,467,000, expenditure $1,574,000 (2009).

Board of Trustees: Diosdado Banatao (Chair.); Fernando Zobel de Ayala (Vice-Chair.); Victoria P. Garchitorena (Pres.).

Principal Staff: Pres. Victoria P. Garchitorena; Dep. Dir Rene Encarnacion.

Address: 1065 E Hillsdale Blvd, Suite 105, Foster City, CA 94404.

Telephone: (650) 288-3937; **Fax:** (650) 288-3916; **Internet:** www.phildev.org; **e-mail:** info@phildev.org.

Physicians for Human Rights—PHR

Founded in 1986, PHR aims to mobilize members of the medical profession to encourage public support for global human rights issues.

Activities: Uses medical and scientific methods to research and expose human rights violations around the world and campaigns to stop such violations. Educates health professionals about these issues and encourages them to become active in the fight against human rights abuses. Focus issues include youth justice, HIV/AIDS, landmines and Afghanistan. Maintains office in Washington, DC.

Geographical Area of Activity: World-wide.

Publications: *Measuring Landmine Incidents and Injuries*; *War Crimes in Kosovo: A Population Based Assessment of Human Rights Violations Against Kosovar Albanians*; *Endless Brutality: War Crimes in Chechnya*; *Women's Health and Human Rights in Afghanistan*; *The Record* (newsletter); Annual Report; audio tapes; journals.

Finance: Total assets US $6,707,542 (30 June 2011); annual revenue $5,041,393, expenditure $5,098,333 (2010/11).

Board of Directors: Robert S. Lawrence (Chair.); Deborah D. Ascheim (Vice-Chair.); David Dantzker (Treas.); Troy A. Brennan (Sec.).

Principal Staff: Exec. Dir Donna McKay.

Address: 2 Arrow St, Suite 301, Cambridge, MA 02138.

Telephone: (617) 301-4200; **Fax:** (617) 301-4250; **Internet:** www.phrusa.org; **e-mail:** phrusa@phrusa.org.

Plenty International

Established in 1974 by The Farm community, a non-government alternative organization aiming to help share the world's resources and knowledge.

Activities: Facilitates the exchange of technology, skills, information and friendship between communities and cultures by sending volunteers to areas of need around the world, who work on sustainable development projects relating to health care, education, food and nutrition (particularly soya nutrition), alternative energy, protection of the environment and disaster relief. Works on long-term projects in Central America, West Africa and the USA, especially with Native Americans.

Geographical Area of Activity: North and Central America, Mexico, the Caribbean and West Africa.

Publications: *The Plenty Bulletin* (quarterly newsletter).

Board of Directors: Peter Schweitzer; Lisa Wartinger; Bruce Curtis; Tom Kanatakeniate Cook; Karen Heikkala; William Meeker; Patricia O'Bannon; Carol Nelson; Mary Ellen Bowen; Jake Frohman.

Principal Staff: Exec. Dir Peter Schweitzer; Associate Dir Lisa Wartinger.

Address: POB 394, Summertown, TN 38483.

Telephone: (931) 964-4323; **Fax:** (931) 964-4864; **Internet:** www.plenty.org; **e-mail:** plenty@plenty.org.

Ploughshares Fund

Public foundation founded in 1981 to help prevent the spread of nuclear weapons, control the sale of conventional weapons, take steps toward preventing armed conflict, and to build global and regional security.

Activities: Operates on an international basis in the fields of weapons control and international conflict resolution, particularly in the USA, Europe, Asia, the Middle East, the Russian Federation, the Democratic People's Republic of Korea and Japan. Grants are made for projects, research, conferences and to individuals.

Geographical Area of Activity: World-wide.

Publications: Annual Report; newsletter.

Finance: Net assets US $35,549,869 (30 June 2011); annual revenue $10,850,272, expenditure $9,605,989 (2010/11).

Board of Directors: Roger Hale (Chair.); Joseph Cirincione (Pres.); Doug Carlston (Treas.); Brooks Walker, III (Sec.).

Principal Staff: Exec. Dir and COO Philip Yun.

Address: 1808 Wedemeyer St, Suite 200, The Presidio of San Francisco, San Francisco, CA 94129.

Telephone: (415) 668-2244; **Fax:** (415) 668-2214; **Internet:** www.ploughshares.org; **e-mail:** ploughshares@ploughshares.org.

Pollock–Krasner Foundation, Inc

Founded in 1985 by Lee Krasner to support artists.

Activities: The Foundation awards grants to professional, working artists in the fields of sculpture, painting, works on paper and printmaking. Since 1985 the Foundation has awarded more than 3,500 grants totalling more than US $54m. to artists in 72 countries.

Geographical Area of Activity: World-wide.

Restrictions: No grants are made for academic study, nor to commercial artists, photographers, performance artists, video artists, film-makers or artisans.

Publications: Grant Report.

Finance: Total grants US $1,545,000 (2010/11).

Board of Directors: Charles C. Bergman (Chair.).

Principal Staff: Pres. Samuel Sachs II; Exec. Vice-Pres. Kerrie Buitrago.

Address: 863 Park Ave, New York, NY 10021.

Telephone: (212) 517-5400; **Fax:** (212) 288-2836; **Internet:** www.pkf.org; **e-mail:** grants@pkf.org.

Wladyslaw Poniecki Foundation, Inc

Founded in 1990 by W. I. Poniecki and previously known as the Wladyslaw Poniecki Charitable Foundation. Aims to enhance education through technology, and support activities in developing countries, especially emerging market economies.

Activities: Operates in the fields of education and technology. Its main programmes concentrate on Internet training for librarians, but other work includes the translation of workbooks relating to technology and software, publishing educational books in the areas of medicine, business, the environment and education, and the stimulation of grassroots, professional, non-profit associations. Work is principally centred on Central and Eastern Europe, but the foundation is not restricted to this area and its expertise is also applicable to other parts of the developing world.

Geographical Area of Activity: Mainly Central and Eastern Europe.

Finance: Funded by private donations, corporate and government grants, and support from other foundations.

Board of Directors: Wandzia Rose; Andrzej Witkowski; Marvin Rose; Ewa Witkowska; Monica Dodds Grycz.

Principal Staff: Pres. Wandzia Rose; CFO Andrzej Witkowski.

Address: 3020 El Cerrito Plaza, Suite 311, El Cerrito, CA 94530-2728.

Telephone: (510) 621-3498; **Fax:** (510) 588-4670; **Internet:** www.poniecki.org; **e-mail:** info@poniecki.org.

Population Council

International, non-profit NGO, founded in 1952 by John D. Rockefeller, III; seeks to improve the well-being and reproductive health of current and future generations around the world, and to help achieve a humane, equitable and sustainable balance between people and resources.

Activities: The Council conducts research in three areas: HIV and AIDS; poverty, gender, and youth; and reproductive health. Established in 1952, the Council is governed by an international board of trustees. Its New York headquarters supports a global network of regional and country offices. The Population Council's work ranges over the broad field of population: from research to improve services and products that respond to people's reproductive health needs to designing interventions to treat and prevent HIV/AIDS and other sexually transmitted diseases; from studies of the effects of population factors on a country's ability to provide a better life for its citizens to research that investigates the influence of education and livelihood opportunities on young girls and women. The Council is also concerned with the reproductive health and well-being of the 1,000m. adolescents in the developing world who are about to enter their reproductive years and whose behaviour will shape the future of their countries. These are some of the global issues that engage the Council and its scientists. Leads research on a broad range of population issues. The Council is unique in combining excellence in demographic studies, operations research, technical assistance, basic research on reproductive physiology, and the development of new contraceptives. In addition, the Council helps to improve the research capacity of reproductive and population scientists in developing countries through grants, fellowships, and support of research centres.

Geographical Area of Activity: Africa, Asia, Middle East, North and South America and the Caribbean.

Restrictions: Grants only in the form of doctoral and post-doctoral fellowships in the biomedical, health and social sciences.

Publications: *Studies in Family Planning* (quarterly); *Population and Development Review* (quarterly); Annual Report; books; newsletters; regional monographs; *Poverty, Gender and Youth Working Papers*.

Finance: Annual revenue US $99,807,830, expenditure $90,034,542 (2010).

Trustees: Mark A. Walker (Chair.).

Principal Staff: Pres. Peter J. Donaldson; Vice-Pres. and Distinguished Scholar John Bongaarts; Vice-Pres. and Dir of Corporate Affairs James E. Sailer.

Address: 1 Dag Hammarskjöld Plaza, New York, NY 10017.

Telephone: (212) 339-0500; **Fax:** (212) 755-6052; **Internet:** www.popcouncil.org; **e-mail:** pubinfo@popcouncil.org.

Pro Mujer International (Pro Women International)

Established in 1990 by Lynne Patterson and Carmen Velasco, a private non-profit charitable organization that aims to help women in Central and South America to play a more effective role in their own personal development and that of their children, families and society.

Activities: Works in Argentina, Bolivia, Mexico, Nicaragua and Peru, providing loans and micro-enterprise training for women to start or improve businesses, empowering them to develop their business skills and to support their families. Also informs and trains women in health, family planning and child development. Maintains office in Bolivia.

Geographical Area of Activity: USA, Argentina, Bolivia, Mexico, Nicaragua and Peru.

Publications: Newsletter; Annual Report and financial statement.

Finance: Annual revenue US $23,135,557, expenditure $18,944,809 (2009).

Board of Directors: Gail Landis (Chair.); Ruth B. Cowan (Interim Vice-Chair.); Mary McCaffrey (Treas.).

Principal Staff: CEO Rosario Pérez; CFO Jenny Hourihan.

Address: 253 West 35th St, 11th Floor South, New York, NY 10001.

Telephone: (646) 626-7000; **Fax:** (212) 904-1038; **Internet:** www.promujer.org; **e-mail:** promujer@promujer.org.

Project Concern International—PCI

Established in 1961 by Dr James Turpin to help the world's vulnerable children, families and communities, provide access to health resources, prevent disease and promote development through dynamic partnerships that build local capacity in efficient and measurable ways.

Activities: Works in four key areas; Women and Children's Health, including child survival interventions (immunizations, breastfeeding, control of diarrhoeal disease and acute respiratory infections, integrated management of childhood illnesses, provision of Vitamin A) as well as family planning, reproductive health, prenatal care and men's health education; Food Security, improving access, availability and utilization of food resources, promoting home gardens, nutritional education programmes, community infrastructure development, school feeding programmes and food aid for households affected by HIV/AIDS; Disease Prevention and Mitigation, preventing the spread of communicable and vector-borne diseases, as well as the activities that mitigate their impact, home-based care for people with AIDS, community-based programmes that address the needs of orphans and vulnerable children, tuberculosis and leprosy screening and treatment; and Water and Sanitation, improving access to potable water and sanitation facilities, including the construction and training in community management of wells, gravity-fed arrangements and rainwater catchment systems, small-scale municipal sewerage systems and solid waste disposal systems.

Geographical Area of Activity: International, with an emphasis on Bolivia, Central America, Ghana, India, Indonesia, Romania, the USA and Zambia.

Restrictions: No grants to individuals.

Publications: *CONCERNews* (quarterly newsletter); Annual Report.

Finance: Total assets US $19,165,110 (30 Sept. 2009); annual revenue $29,701,154, expenditure $30,687,533 (2008/09).

Board of Directors: Anne Otterson (Chair.); Judith A. Ettinger (Man. Dir); Kevin E. Moley (Chair. Emeritus).

Principal Staff: CEO and Pres. George Guimaraes; CFO George Gates.

Address: 5151 Murphy Canyon Rd, Suite 320, San Diego, CA 92123.

Telephone: (858) 279-9690; **Fax:** (858) 694-0294; **Internet:** www.projectconcern.org; **e-mail:** postmaster@ projectconcern.org.

Project HOPE

Project HOPE (Health Opportunity for People Everywhere) is the principal activity of the People-to-People Health Foundation, founded in 1958 by William B. Walsh.

Activities: Promotes the development of health system infrastructure, the training of local health workers in modern medical techniques in developing countries world-wide, and assists in the development of medical facilities. Distributes medical textbooks and journals to institutions throughout the world. Holds conferences. The Foundation's Center for Health Affairs carries out research in health policy. Has established national organizations in Germany, Hong Kong, Japan, Switzerland, the United Kingdom and the USA.

Geographical Area of Activity: Africa, Asia, Central and Eastern Europe, the Russian Federation and Central Asia, the Americas and the Caribbean, and the Middle East.

Publications: Annual Report; newsletter; brochures.

Finance: Total assets US $64,025,000 (30 June 2011); annual revenue $206,847,000, expenditure $205,797,000 (2010/11).

Board of Directors: Richard T. Clark (Chair.); Charles A. Sanders (Chair. Emeritus); George B. Abercrombie (Vice-Chair.); William F. Brandt, Jr (Treas.); Dayton Ogden (Sec.).

Principal Staff: Pres. and CEO John P. Howe, III; Exec. Vice-Pres. Michael D. Maves.

Address: 255 Carter Hall Lane, Millwood, VA 22646.

Telephone: (540) 837-2100; **Fax:** (540) 837-1813; **Internet:** www.projecthope.org; **e-mail:** hope@projecthope.org.

ProLiteracy

Formed by the 2002 merger of Laubach Literacy International and Literacy Volunteers of America.

Activities: Monitors public policy and legislation concerning adult learners and literacy providers. Projects in the USA concerned with: Performance Accountability; Volunteers in Adult Basic Education; National Referral Service; Increasing Intensity of Instruction; Literacy and Home Safety; and Reducing Student Waiting Lists. Operates a Literacy for Social Change project, training projects, initiatives and partner programmes in more than 50 developing countries. Runs credentialling programmes. Administers the National Book Fund and the Charles Evans Book Fund. Holds an annual conference.

Geographical Area of Activity: World-wide.

Publications: Books; educational materials; documentaries.

Finance: Annual revenue US $9,880,369, expenditure $10,050,781 (2009/10).

Board of Directors: Kevin Morgan (Chair.); John Ward (Vice-Chair.); Anne DuPrey (Sec.); Thomas Fiscoe (Treas.).

Principal Staff: Pres. and CEO David C. Harvey.

Address: 1320 Jamesville Ave, Syracuse, NY 13210.

Telephone: (315) 422-9121; **Fax:** (315) 422-6369; **Internet:** www.proliteracy.org; **e-mail:** info@proliteracy.org.

Prudential Foundation

Founded in 1977 by the Prudential Insurance Co of America and the Prudential Property & Casualty Co for general charitable purposes.

Activities: Involved in the fields of education, economic development and civic infrastructure, mainly in areas of company operations.

Geographical Area of Activity: USA, Brazil, Mexico, Japan, Republic of Korea, India, Taiwan and People's Republic of China.

Restrictions: No grants are made to individuals; generally no funding for capital campaigns or endowments.

Publications: Annual Report.

Finance: Grants disbursed exceed US $25,000,000 annually.

Board of Trustees: Sharon C. Taylor (Chair.).

Principal Staff: Pres. Gabriella Morris.

Address: 751 Broad St, 15th Floor, Newark, NJ 07102-3777.

Telephone: (973) 802-4791; **Internet:** www.prudential.com/ view/page/public/12373; **e-mail:** community.resources@ prudential.com.

Public Welfare Foundation, Inc

Established in 1947 by Charles Edward Marsh, a newspaper publisher, and his wife Claudia.

Activities: Operates in the USA in three programme areas: criminal and juvenile justice; health reform and workers' rights. The Foundation provides grants to organizations.

Geographical Area of Activity: USA.

Restrictions: No grants to individuals, nor for scholarships, graduate work, government projects, research or capital projects or foreign study.

Publications: Annual Report; guidelines.

Finance: Total assets US $468,539,762 (31 Oct. 2010); annual revenue $11,947,246 (loss), expenditure $27,779,389 (2009/10).

Board of Directors: Peter B. Edelman (Chair.); Myrtis H. Powell (Vice-Chair.); Lydia Micheaux Marshall (Sec. and Treas.).

Principal Staff: Pres. Mary E. McClymont; Chief Financial and Admin. Officer Phillipa Taylor.

Address: 1200 U St NW, Washington, DC 20009.

Telephone: (202) 965-1800; **Fax:** (202) 265-8851; **Internet:** www.publicwelfare.org; **e-mail:** info@publicwelfare.org.

Rainforest Action Network—RAN

Founded in 1985 by Randy Hayes to protect the Earth's rainforests and support the rights of their inhabitants through education, local community organization and non-violent direct action.

Activities: A non-profit organization working nationally and internationally with other environmental and human rights organizations to protect rain forests. There are four primary campaigns: Freedom from Oil; Global Finance; Old Growth; and Rainforest Agribusiness. The Protect-an-Acre programme provides grant funding directly to organizations and communities in rain forest regions. The Network is also involved in negotiation, research, conferences and seminars, and education. Issues publications and maintains a speakers' bureau and library. In 2007 the Network launched Action Tank, a project designed to provide training for activists and develop effective techniques for grassroots action. There are some 25,000 active members, and more than 175 Rainforest Action Groups world-wide.

Geographical Area of Activity: International.

Publications: *Cut Waste, Not Trees: a wood use reduction guide*; *Importing Destruction*; *Drilling to the Ends of the Earth*; *500 Year Plan*; *Action Alerts* (2 a month); Annual Report; fact sheets and information packs.

Finance: Net assets US $1,517,101 (30 June 2011); annual revenue $4,064,571, expenditure $3,954,750 (2010/11).

Board of Directors: André Carothers (Chair.); Anna Hawken McKay (Development Co-Chair.); Jodie Evans (Development Co-Chair.); Stephen Stevick (Governance Chair.); Michael Klein (Sec. and Program Chair.); Scott B. Price (Treas. and Finance Chair.); Randall Hayes (Founder).

Principal Staff: Pres. James D. Gollin.

Address: 221 Pine St, 5th Floor, San Francisco, CA 94104.

Telephone: (415) 398-4404; **Fax:** (415) 398-2732; **Internet:** www.ran.org; **e-mail:** answers@ran.org.

Rainforest Foundation US

Established in 1989; part of the Rainforest Foundation group of organizations (qq.v.) established to conserve rainforests and their indigenous peoples.

Activities: Operates in Central and South America, working in partnership with indigenous groups and local organizations to help secure land rights, advocate for policies to protect resources and build community leadership.

Geographical Area of Activity: Brazil, Guyana, Panama and Peru.

Finance: Annual revenue US $1,043,211, expenditure $1,183,505 (2010).

Board of Directors: S. Todd Crider (Chair.).

Principal Staff: Exec. Dir Suzanne Pelletier; Financial Dir Athos Gontijo.

Address: 180 Varick St, Suite 528, New York, NY 10014.

Telephone: (212) 431-9098; **Internet:** www.rainforestfoundation.org.

Reef Ball Foundation

A non-profit public international environment organization established in 1993 by Todd Barber to support ocean reef systems through the use of designed artificial reefs and related technologies for betterment of marine ecosystems.

Activities: Operates internationally through the use of artificial reefs designed by the Foundation to assist in the rehabilitation of natural reef systems. To date, the Foundation has placed around 500,000 artificial reefs in more than 59 countries. The Foundation is also involved in conservation projects including coral reefs, mangrove plantings and oyster reef conservation and development, erosion control, and collaborates with other organizations.

Geographical Area of Activity: International.

Publications: *Step by Step Guide to Reef Rehabilitation for Grassroots Organization*.

Board of Directors: Todd Barber (Chair.).

Principal Staff: Exec. Dir Katherine Kirbo.

Address: 890 Hill St, Athens, GA 30606.

Telephone: (706) 714-4399; **Fax:** (509) 357-2722; **Internet:** www.reefball.org; **e-mail:** reefball@reefball.com.

Christopher and Dana Reeve Foundation

Established in 1999 following the merger of the American Paralysis Association (formed in 1982) and the Christopher Reeve Paralysis Foundation.

Activities: Operates in the field of medical research, especially in the area of spinal cord injury research. The Foundation offers two-year research awards of a maximum of US $75,000 per award: to encourage new research on regeneration and recovery, in particular with regard to spinal cord injuries; to encourage established researchers to transfer their research efforts onto spinal cord research; and to assist researchers with new ideas to seek awards from other sources of funding. Funds activities that hold promise of identifying therapies for paralysis and other sequelae of spinal cord injury. Development of effective therapies for chronic injury is a priority for the organization, although funding is also provided for studies more relevant to the acute phase of injury. Basic research is supported if it has clear potential to accelerate progress at the applied end of the continuum and/or if it reflects a research change in direction. The Quality of Life Program includes health promotion programmes for people with paralysis-related disabilities; these programmes aim to remove societal and environmental barriers that limit an individual's ability to participate in life's activities; grants are made to regional and local organizations. Maintains a Paralysis Resource Center and offices in Westlake Village, CA and Washington, DC.

Geographical Area of Activity: USA.

Restrictions: Cannot make grants to individuals.

Publications: Annual Report; *The Spinal Cord: A Christopher and Dana Reeve Foundation Text and Atlas*; Annual Reports, informational brochures including the Reeve Report and Progress in Research.

Finance: Total assets US $10,039,063 (31 Dec. 2010); annual revenue $14,344,259, expenditure $14,540,650 (2010).

Board of Directors: John M. Hughes (Chair.); Arnold H. Snider (Vice-Chair.); Henry G. Stifel, III (Vice-Chair.); Michael W. Blair (Sec.); Robert L. Guyett (Treas.).

Principal Staff: Pres. and CEO Peter T. Wilderotter.

Address: 636 Morris Turnpike, Suite 3A, Short Hills, NJ 07078.

Telephone: (973) 225-0292; **Fax:** (973) 912-9433; **Internet:** www.christopherreeve.org; **e-mail:** media@christopherreeve.org.

Refugees International—RI

Established in 1979 to act as an independent voice for humanitarian action on behalf of the least-known and most vulnerable victims of war, famine and disaster.

Activities: Operates in areas of war and crisis, providing direct aid to refugees and people who have been displaced from their homes, including emergency relief, repatriation and protection. Also provides on-site field assessments and reports to policy and opinion makers world-wide to mobilize help for the victims. Since 2000, the organization has been working towards reforms in six areas designed to help avoid or alleviate chronic, continuing refugee crises: improvement of the UN peace-keeping capability through the creation of an established rapid-reaction peace and security force; new protection for internally displaced people; increased attention to the needs of refugee women; an end to the recruitment and use of child soldiers; more attention to the transition between relief operations and economic development; and building local capacity and institutions.

Geographical Area of Activity: International.

Publications: Newsletter (monthly); Annual Report; bulletins; articles; videos.

Finance: Annual revenue US $4,249,687, expenditure $4,136,051 (2009).

Board of Directors: Eileen Shields-West (Chair.); Sam Waterston (Vice-Chair.); Michael Hawkins (Sec.); Michael Berkman (Treas.).

Principal Staff: Pres. Michael Gabaudan; Dir of Finance Solomon David.

Address: 2001 S St NW, Suite 700, Washington, DC 20009.

Telephone: (202) 828-0110; **Fax:** (202) 828-0819; **Internet:** www.refugeesinternational.org; **e-mail:** ri@refugeesinternational.org.

Rehabilitation International—RI

Founded in 1922 to assist and act as an advocate for disabled people around the world.

Activities: A federation of more than 1,000 organizations in 96 countries, RI is a global network promoting and implementing the rights and inclusion of people with disabilities. Acts as an open forum for the exchange of information and experience on research and practice. Maintains regional offices in Africa, Arab, Asia, Europe, North America, South America and Central America.

Geographical Area of Activity: International.

Publications: *Rehabilitation Review* (annually); *One in Ten*; bulletins; reviews; catalogues.

Executive Committee: Anne Hawker (Pres.); Jan A. Monsbakken (Pres. Elect); Prof. Martin Grabois (Treas.).

Principal Staff: Sec.-Gen. Venus Ilagan; Development and Program Officer Megan Brinster.

Address: 25 East 21st St, New York, NY 10010.

Telephone: (212) 420-1500; **Fax:** (212) 505-0871; **Internet:** www.riglobal.org; **e-mail:** ri@riglobal.org.

Relief International

Non-profit humanitarian organization founded in 1990 to reduce suffering world-wide.

Activities: Provides humanitarian assistance in the form of emergency relief, rehabilitation, development assistance and more long-term services to communities around the world, including health, shelter, reconstruction, education, community development, agriculture, food, income generation and conflict resolution. Promotes self-reliance in developing countries and empowers communities by maximizing local resources.

Geographical Area of Activity: Afghanistan, Azerbaijan, Bangladesh, Ghana, Indonesia, Iran, Iraq, Jordan, Lebanon, Myanmar, Niger, Pakistan, Palestinian Autonomous Areas, Senegal, Somalia, Sri Lanka, Sudan (Darfur and South Sudan) and Tajikistan.

Publications: Annual Report.

Finance: Annual revenue US $44,992,738 (2008).

Board of Directors: Simon Goodall (Chair.).

Principal Staff: CEO Farshad Rastegar.

Address: 5455 Wilshire Blvd, Suite 1280, Los Angeles, CA 90036.

Telephone: (323) 932-7888; **Fax:** (323) 932-7878; **Internet:** www.ri.org; **e-mail:** info@ri.org.

Research Corporation for Science Advancement—RCSA

Founded in 1912 by Frederick Gardner Cottrell and others to receive and acquire inventions, patent rights and letters patent, and to render the latter more available and effective in the useful arts and manufactures; to provide means for the advancement of technical and scientific investigation, research and experimentation, by contributing the net earnings of the Corporation to scientific and educational institutions and societies.

Activities: The Foundation's programmes, operating in the USA and Canada, aid research proposed by college and university faculty members. These programmes include the Cottrell College Science Awards (physics, chemistry and astronomy at undergraduate institutions); Research Opportunity Awards (to assist mid-career chemists, astronomers and physicists in doctoral departments to pursue new areas of research); Research Innovation Awards (to assist highly original research by faculty members at research universities); Cottrell Scholars Awards (research and teaching in physics, chemistry and astronomy at graduate institutions); and Special Opportunities in Science Awards (to assist projects with potential for advancing science that do not fall under other programme guidelines).

Geographical Area of Activity: USA and Canada.

Publications: Newsletter; Annual Report; occasional reports; books.

Finance: Annual revenue US $17,911,482, expenditure $8,265,577 (2010).

Board of Directors: Patricia C. Barron (Chair.).

Principal Staff: Pres. James M. Gentile; Vice-Pres. Martha Gilliland; CFO Daniel Gasch.

Address: 4703 East Camp Lowell Dr., Suite 201, Tuscon, AZ 85712.

Telephone: (520) 571-1111; **Fax:** (520) 571-1119; **Internet:** www.rescorp.org; **e-mail:** awards@rescorp.org.

Christopher Reynolds Foundation, Inc

Founded by Libby Holman Reynolds in 1952 to support initiatives in the field of international relations.

Activities: The Foundation supports projects dealing with injustice in social, economic and environmental matters, provides funds to humanitarian organizations in the USA and in Cuba, and seeks to promote improved relations between the two countries.

Geographical Area of Activity: USA and Cuba.

Restrictions: Does not support individuals, capital or endowment funds, deficit financing, scholarships, or matching gifts.

Publications: Report (every 5 years); Annual Report.

Board of Directors: John R. Boettiger (Chair.); Suzanne Derrer (Vice-Chair.).

Principal Staff: Exec. Dir Andrea Panaritis.

Address: 267 Fifth Ave, Suite 1001, New York, NY 10016.

Telephone: (212) 532-1606; **Fax:** (212) 532-1403; **Internet:** www.creynolds.org; **e-mail:** inquiries@creynolds.org.

Righteous Persons Foundation

Established in 1994 by filmmaker Steven Spielberg, initially with his profits from the film Schindler's List. Since then, the Foundation has invested in organizations and efforts working to: revitalize Jewish arts, culture, and identity; engage the next generation; strengthen a commitment to social justice; and promote understanding between Jews and those of other faiths and backgrounds.

Activities: The Righteous Persons Foundation is dedicated to supporting efforts that build a vibrant, just and inclusive Jewish community in the USA.

Geographical Area of Activity: Mainly USA.

Restrictions: No grants are made to individuals.

Publications: Application guidelines.

Finance: Grants totalling US $765,000 awarded in 2008.

Board of Directors: Gerald Breslauer (Pres.); Steven Spielberg (Chair.).

Principal Staff: Exec. Dir Margery Tabankin; Assoc. Dir Rachel Levin.

Address: 2800 28th St, Suite 105, Santa Monica, CA 90405.

Telephone: (310) 314-8393; **Fax:** (310) 314-8396; **Internet:** www.righteouspersons.org; **e-mail:** grants@righteouspersons.org.

RNRF—Renewable Natural Resources Foundation

Founded in 1972 to advance scientific and public education in renewable natural resources; to promote the application of sound scientific practices in managing and conserving renewable natural resources; and to foster co-operation among professional, scientific and educational organizations having leadership responsibilities for renewable natural resources.

Activities: Operates in the field of conservation and the environment, nationally through self-conducted programmes, and nationally and internationally by awarding prizes, organizing conferences and through publications.

Geographical Area of Activity: International.

Restrictions: Funds own activities and solicits grants from public and private entities.

Publications: *Renewable Resources Journal* (quarterly); reports include *Environmental Impacts of Emerging Contaminants; Building Capacity for Coastal Solutions; Federal Natural Resources Agencies Confront an Aging Workforce and Challenges to Their Future Roles; Assessing America's Renewable Energy Future.*

Board of Directors: Howard N. Rosen (Chair.); Richard A. Engberg (Vice-Chair).

Principal Staff: Exec. Dir Robert D. Day.

Address: 5430 Grosvenor Lane, Bethesda, MD 20814.

Telephone: (301) 493-9101; **Fax:** (301) 493-6148; **Internet:** www.rnrf.org; **e-mail:** info@rnrf.org.

Robertson Foundation for Government—RFFG

A non-profit family foundation, established in 2010 by the family of the late Charles and Marie Robertson, that aims to identify, educate and motivate US graduate students to pursue careers in the federal government in the areas of foreign policy, national security and international affairs.

Activities: The first programme was the Robertson Fellows Program, offering scholarships and stipends to students at four universities. Other programmes were to be introduced from 2011.

Geographical Area of Activity: USA.

Principal Staff: Exec. Dir Timothy Kemper.

Address: 14255 US Highway 1, Juno Beach, FL 33408.

Telephone: (561) 721-6700; **Fax:** (561) 627-7021; **Internet:** www.rffg.org; **e-mail:** info@rffg.org.

Rockefeller Brothers Fund

Founded in 1940 as a vehicle through which the five sons and daughter of John D. Rockefeller, Jr, could share advice and research on charitable activities and combine philanthropies to better effect. John D. Rockefeller, Jr, made a substantial gift to the Fund in 1951, and in 1960 the Fund received a major bequest from his estate. Together, these constitute the original endowment of the Fund. The Fund merged with the Charles E. Culpeper Foundation in July 1999.

Activities: Encourages social change that contributes to a more just, sustainable, and peaceful world. Grantmaking is organized around three themes: Democratic Practice, Sustainable Development and Peace and Security. Operates worldwide but concentrates cross-programmatic attention on 'RBF pivotal places': sub-national areas, nation-states, or cross-border regions that have special importance with regard to the Fund's substantive concerns and whose future will have disproportionate significance for the future of a surrounding region, an ecosystem or the planet. The Fund currently works in four such pivotal places: New York City, South Africa, Western Balkans, and southern China.

Geographical Area of Activity: International.

Restrictions: No programmes operate in Central or South America.

Publications: Annual Report; *Statistical Review*; various other publications.

Finance: Annual revenue US $2,345,877, expenditure $43,764,155 (2010).

Principal Staff: Pres. Stephen B. Heintz; Vice-Pres. for Finance and Operations Geraldine Watson.

Address: 475 Riverside Dr., Suite 900, New York, NY 10115.

Telephone: (212) 812-4200; **Fax:** (212) 812-4299; **Internet:** www.rbf.org; **e-mail:** communications@rbf.org.

Rockefeller Foundation

Founded in 1913 by John D. Rockefeller, Sr to promote the well-being of mankind throughout the world.

Activities: Operates nationally and internationally through offering grants. Maintains the Bellagio Study and Conference Center in Italy, for international conferences and residencies for artists and scholars. The Foundation maintains offices in Bangkok, Nairobi and San Francisco.

Geographical Area of Activity: International.

Restrictions: No grants are made for personal aid to individuals, nor for general institutional support or fund endowments, nor for building or operating funds.

Publications: Annual Report.

Finance: Annual revenue US $21,000,000, expenditure $173,000,000 (2009).

Board of Trustees: David Rockefeller, Jr (Chair.).

Principal Staff: Pres. Judith Rodin; COO Peter Madonia.

Address: 420 Fifth Ave, New York, NY 10018.

Telephone: (212) 869-8500; **Fax:** (212) 764-3468; **Internet:** www.rockefellerfoundation.org; **e-mail:** cmmocommon@rockfound.org.

The Rotary Foundation

Founded in 1917 by Rotary International to further understanding and friendly relations between peoples of different nations.

Activities: Operates internationally in financing scholarships, grants for charitable and educational projects, cultural and educational exchanges of business and professional leaders, and grants for major health, hunger relief and humanitarian projects. Awards and grants are open to men and women with no restriction on race or creed. Programmes include: PolioPlus Grants; Disaster Recovery; District Simplified Grants; Health, Hunger and Humanity Grants; Matching Grants; Volunteer Service Grants; Ambassadorial Scholarships; Group Study Exchange; Rotary Grants for University Teachers; Rotary World Peace Fellowships.

Geographical Area of Activity: International.

Publications: Annual Report; programme brochures.

Finance: Annual revenue US $268,500,000, expenditure $226,600,000 (2010).

Board of Trustees: Carl-Wilhelm Stenhammar (Chair.); William B. Boyd (Chair. elect); John F. Germ (Vice-Chair.).

Principal Staff: Gen. Sec. John Hewko.

Address: 1 Rotary Center, 1560 Sherman Ave, Evanston, IL 60201.

Telephone: (847) 866-3000; **Fax:** (847) 328-8554; **Internet:** www.rotary.org/foundation; **e-mail:** contact.center@rotary .org.

The Judith Rothschild Foundation

Founded in 1993 with the purpose of promoting, presenting and interpreting the work of lesser-known American artists who had died since 12 September 1976. In 2009 the Foundation was evaluating the most effective way to re-focus the activities of the grant programme.

Activities: Promotes lesser-known artists through support for exhibitions, the acquisition of their work by museums and the safe-keeping of paintings; cataloguing of works of art; scholarly research; operates programmes for study and inter-pretation of works of art.

Geographical Area of Activity: USA.

Publications: Annual Report.

Finance: Total grants US $100,000 (2009).

Address: POB 223, Flourtown, PA 19031.

Telephone: (215) 540-8400; **Fax:** (215) 540-8401; **Internet:** www.judithrothschildfdn.org; **e-mail:** slatereliz@aol.com.

The Edmond de Rothschild Foundations

Founded in 1963 by Edmond de Rothschild for general charita-ble purposes.

Activities: Operate primarily in New York and in France, but also make grants in Israel, in the fields of Jewish social wel-fare, education, including business administration and reli-gious education, science and medicine, and the arts and humanities, through grants to institutions.

Geographical Area of Activity: USA, France and Israel.

Restrictions: The Foundations make grants only to pre-selected organizations. Unsolicited applications are not accepted.

Finance: Total assets US $59,152,415 (31 Dec. 2010); total giv-ing $2,277,572 (2010).

Board of Directors: Benjamin de Rothschild (Chair.); Firoz Ladak (Treas.); Philip M. Susswein (Sec. and Asst Treas.).

Principal Staff: Pres. Ariane de Rothschild.

Address: 1585 Broadway, 24th Floor, New York, NY 10036-8204.

Telephone: (212) 969-3250.

Samuel Rubin Foundation

Founded in 1958 to promote peace and justice.

Activities: The Foundation provides grants to organizations concerned with human rights, justice, peace and the redistri-bution of resources in the world; promotes social, economic, political, civil and cultural rights. Operates in the fields of edu-cation, human rights and social welfare.

Geographical Area of Activity: World-wide.

Restrictions: No grants to individuals, for building funds or scholarships.

Publications: Programme policy statement.

Finance: Assets US $10,898,638 (30 June 2011); total annual expenditure $730,231 (2011).

Board of Directors: Cora Weiss (Pres.); Daniel Weiss (Vice-Pres.); Judy Weiss (Vice Pres.); Tamara Weiss (Vice-Pres.); Peter Weiss (Sec. and Treas.).

Principal Staff: Grants Admin. Lauranne Jones.

Address: 777 United Nations Plaza, New York, NY 10017-3521.

Telephone: (212) 697-8945; **Fax:** (212) 682-0886; **Internet:** www.samuelrubinfoundation.org; **e-mail:** lauranne@igc.org.

Damon Runyon Cancer Research Foundation

Founded in 1946 to support all theoretical and experimental research relevant to the study of cancer, and the search for its causes, mechanisms, treatment and prevention.

Activities: Awards up to 60 post-doctoral research fellow-ships a year for basic scientists and physician scientists, allow-ing scientists and medical practitioners beginning full-time post-doctoral research to carry out cancer research.

Geographical Area of Activity: USA.

Restrictions: US citizens may study in any country; foreign researchers' study must be carried out in the USA.

Publications: Annual Report.

Finance: Total assets US $106,487,205 (30 June 2011); annual revenue $15,110,764, expenditure $13,750,711 (2010/11).

Board of Directors: Alan M. Leventhal (Chair.); David M. Livingston (Vice-Chair.); Leon G. Cooperman (Vice-Chair. and Treas.); Sanford W. Morhouse (Vice-Chair.); Michael L. Gordon (Vice-Chair.); David M. Beirne (Vice-Chair.).

Principal Staff: Pres. and CEO Lorraine W. Egan; CFO Travis Carey.

Address: 1 Exchange Plaza, 55 Broadway, Suite 302, New York, NY 10006.

Telephone: (212) 455-0500; **Fax:** (212) 455-0509; **Internet:** www.drcrf.org; **e-mail:** info@damonrunyon.org.

Russell Sage Foundation—RSF

Founded in 1907 by Margaret Olivia Sage for the improvement of social and living conditions in the USA: now devoted exclu-sively to research in the social sciences, as a means to improve social policies.

Activities: The Foundation's professional staff of about 21 social scientists (Resident Scholars, Visiting Scholars, Visiting Post-doctoral Fellows and part-time advisers and consultants) conduct research on selected topics (including basic research in improvements in methodology, data and theory). The Foun-dation also provides support for the work of scholars at other academic and research institutions; sponsors special semi-nars; and publishes books and monographs. Research grants are made in the main programme areas of: the future of work; immigration; cultural contact; and social inequality. Other special projects and research initiatives include the Septem-ber 11 Initiative and the Behavioral Economics Roundtable.

Geographical Area of Activity: USA.

Restrictions: No grants are made internationally; no grants for pre-doctoral study or research; no scholarships or other types of grants for support of college funding.

Publications: Biennial Report; books and monographs.

Board of Trustees: Robert E. Denham (Chair.); Shelley E. Taylor (Treas.).

Principal Staff: Pres. Eric Wanner; CFO Christopher Brogna.

Address: 112 East 64th St, New York, NY 10065.

Telephone: (212) 750-6000; **Fax:** (212) 371-4761; **Internet:** www.russellsage.org; **e-mail:** info@rsage.org.

Rutherford Institute

Non-profit organization founded by John Whitehead in 1982. It is dedicated to the defence of civil and human rights.

Activities: Provides lawyers to help people whose civil rights or human rights have been violated. Also provides educational opportunities to improve standards of social justice in the USA.

Geographical Area of Activity: International.

Publications: *Insider* (e-mail newsletter); various pamphlets, books and videos.

Finance: Assets US $1,014,251 (30 June 2008); annual revenue $2,909,473, expenditure $3,001,179 (2007/08).

Board of Directors: John W. Whitehead (Chair.); Michael Masters (Vice-Chair.); Thomas S. Neuberger (Sec. and Treas.).

Principal Staff: Pres. John W. Whitehead.

Address: POB 7482, Charlottesville, VA 22906.

Telephone: (434) 978-3888; **Fax:** (434) 978-1789; **Internet:** www.rutherford.org; **e-mail:** staff@rutherford.org.

Sabre Foundation, Inc

Founded by Josiah Lee Auspitz in 1969 to promote the philosophy and practice of free institutions.

Activities: Primary activities include donating large quantities of new books and other educational materials to needy individuals in developing regions of the world, and assisting organizations to take advantage of Internet and related information technologies through conducting training workshops. The Foundation operates through NGO partner organizations, libraries, universities, schools, research institutes and other similar organizations.

Geographical Area of Activity: Africa, Asia, Central and Eastern Europe, the countries of the former USSR, and Central and South America and the Caribbean.

Restrictions: Not a grant-making organization.

Publications: Annual Report; *Foundation Update* (2 a year).

Finance: Annual revenue US $12,238,136, expenditure $12,226,905 (2009).

Board of Directors: Franz Colloredo-Mansfeld (Pres.); Kenneth G. Bartels (Vice-Pres.); John L. G. Archibald (Treas.); Charles Getchell (Sec.).

Principal Staff: Exec. Dir Tania Vitvitsky.

Address: 872 Massachusetts Ave, Suite 2–1, Cambridge, MA 02139.

Telephone: (617) 868-3510; **Fax:** (617) 868-7916; **Internet:** www.sabre.org; **e-mail:** inquiries@sabre.org.

Samaritan's Purse

International non-denominational Christian organization founded in 1970 by Dr Robert Pierce. Aims to help people suffering around the world.

Activities: Provides aid and assistance to victims of war, disasters, disease, famine and poverty, as well as promoting the Gospel world-wide. The organization is active in many countries, engaging in a number of programmes, including emergency health care and improving existing medical facilities, providing emergency supplies including food and clothing, funding community development projects, and providing shelters for abandoned children. Also organizes evangelical festivals throughout the world. Has offices in Australia, Canada, Germany, Ireland, the Netherlands and the United Kingdom.

Geographical Area of Activity: International.

Publications: Newsletter; Annual Report.

Finance: Net assets US $203,107,265 (31 Dec. 2008); annual revenue $313,256,181, expenditure $302,969,135 (2008).

Board of Directors: Franklin Graham (Chair. and Pres.); James Furman (Vice-Chair.); Sterling Carroll (Treas.); Phyllis Payne (Sec.).

Principal Staff: Pres. and CEO Franklin Graham.

Address: POB 3000, Boone, NC 28607.

Telephone: (828) 262-1980; **Fax:** (828) 266-1056; **Internet:** www.samaritanspurse.org; **e-mail:** info@samaritan.org.

San Diego Foundation

Charitable endowment, established in 1975, which aims to improve the human condition in San Diego.

Activities: Supports communities and individuals in San Diego, and increases effective philanthropy. The Foundation awards grants to individuals and organizations, in areas including the arts and culture, economic development, education, the environment, health care and human service, and religious endeavours; contributes to charitable causes; awards scholarships; lends organizational support to projects; and acts as centre of communication for San Diego's communities, raising and discussing issues that effect people in the area.

Geographical Area of Activity: USA.

Finance: Total assets US $560,136,000 (30 June 2011); annual revenue $131,819,000, expenditure $48,339,000 (2010/11).

Board of Governors: Jennifer Adams-Brooks (Chair.); Robert Dynes (Vice-Chair.); Garry Ridge (Vice-Chair.); Steven R. Smith (Vice-Chair. and Sec.); John D. Wylie (Vice-Chair.).

Principal Staff: Pres. and CEO Bob Kelly; Chief Financial and Investment Officer Hal Orr.

Address: 2508 Historic Decatur Rd, Suite 200, San Diego, CA 92106.

Telephone: (619) 235-2300; **Fax:** (619) 239-1710; **Internet:** www.sdfoundation.org; **e-mail:** info@sdfoundation.org.

San Francisco Foundation

Founded in 1948 for the support of philanthropic undertakings in the San Francisco Bay area, CA.

Activities: Makes grants to organizations in the San Francisco Bay area in the fields of arts, education, environment, community health and community development to mobilize resources, act as a catalyst for change, foster civic leadership, and promote philanthropy in the area. Initiatives include leadership programmes, such as the Koshland Program, which makes awards to grassroots social innovators, and the Community Leadership Awards, which recognize outstanding individuals and organizations.

Geographical Area of Activity: San Francisco Bay area, USA.

Restrictions: Serves the Alameda, Contra Costa, Marin, San Francisco, and San Mateo counties only.

Publications: include Annual Report (annually); *Enews*; *Koshland Connect* (annually).

Finance: Total assets US $1,101,069,000 (30 June 2010); annual revenue $223,639,000, expenditure $95,338,000 (2010/11).

Trustees: David Friedman (Chair.); Stephanie DiMarco (Vice-Chair.).

Principal Staff: CEO Sandra R. Hernández.

Address: 225 Bush St, Suite 500, San Francisco, CA 94104.

Telephone: (415) 733-8500; **Fax:** (415) 477-2783; **Internet:** www.sff.org; **e-mail:** info@sff.org.

Scaife Family Foundation

Established by the Scaife family; shares administrative offices with the Carthage Foundation and the Sarah Scaife Foundation (qq.v.).

Activities: The Foundation supports projects that aim to strengthen families, address issues surrounding the health and welfare of women and children, promote animal welfare, demonstrate the beneficial interaction between humans and animals, and encourage private conservation. Grants are also made to organizations working in the area of early intervention and prevention efforts in the area of drug and alcohol addiction.

Geographical Area of Activity: USA (emphasis on Florida and Pennsylvania).

Restrictions: No grants for events, capital campaigns nor renovations, nor for government agencies. No grants for individuals.

Publications: Annual Report (annually).

Finance: Annual revenue US $1,582,812, expenditure $2,655,028 (2009).

Trustees: Jennie K. Scaife (Chair.); Barbara M. Sloan (Sec. and Treas.).

Principal Staff: Pres. Barbara M. Sloan; Vice-Pres Beth H. Genter, Mary T. Walton.

Address: Phillips Point, 777 South Flagler Dr., West Tower, Suite 903, West Palm Beach, FL 33401.

Telephone: (561) 659-1188; **Internet:** www.scaifefamily.org.

Sarah Scaife Foundation, Inc

Founded in 1941 by Sarah Mellon Scaife for broad charitable purposes; present name adopted in 1974.

Activities: Supports public policy programmes that address major domestic and international issues, in areas such as education, government, economics, international law, crime and law enforcement, international affairs, etc. Makes grants for fellowships, research, projects, conferences and publications.

Geographical Area of Activity: World-wide.

Restrictions: No grants are made to individuals nor to nationally-organized fundraising groups.

Publications: Annual Report (annually).

Finance: Annual revenue US $7,696,265, expenditure $15,696,838 (2009).

Trustees: Richard M. Scaife (Chair.); Barbara L. Slaney (Vice-Pres. and Treas.); R. Daniel McMichael (Sec.); Yvonne Marie Bly (Asst Treas.).

Principal Staff: Pres. Michael W. Gleba.

Address: 1 Oxford Center, 301 Grant St, Suite 3900, Pittsburgh, PA 15219-6401.

Telephone: (412) 392-2900; **Internet:** www.scaife.com/sarah.html.

Robert Schalkenbach Foundation, Inc—RSF

Founded in 1925 by Robert Schalkenbach to promote the social and economic philosophy of Henry George, especially his views concerning the single tax on land values and international free trade. Also promotes sustainable economic development, human rights, the resolution of conflicts regarding land rights, wealth redistribution, ecological use of the earth's resources and the public sharing of land values (including electromagnetic, oceanic, mineral, forest, agricultural and urban location values).

Activities: Operates through research, publications, seminars and conferences, and grants to educational institutions.

Geographical Area of Activity: USA, People's Republic of China, Europe and Russian Federation.

Restrictions: No grants are made to individuals; grants are made only to specific organizations.

Publications: *Progress and Poverty* (by Henry George); *Land Value Taxation Around the World* (by R.V. Andelson); *The American Journal of Economics and Sociology* (quarterly); numerous monographs.

Board of Directors: Francis K. Peddle (Pres.); Gilbert Herman (Vice-Pres.); William Peirce (Treas.); Mark A. Sullivan (Sec.).

Principal Staff: Admin. Dir Mark A. Sullivan; Program Dir Damon J. Gross.

Address: 90 John St, Suite 501, New York, NY 10038.

Telephone: (212) 683-6424; **Fax:** (212) 683-6454; **Internet:** www.schalkenbach.org; **e-mail:** info@schalkenbach.org.

Dr Scholl Foundation

Founded in 1947 by William M. Scholl, and formerly known as the William M. Scholl Foundation, for general charitable purposes.

Activities: Operates in the fields of culture, social welfare and economic affairs, through awarding grants and providing support primarily for private education, medical and nursing institutions; medical and scientific research; programmes for children, young people, the developmentally disabled and older people; civic, cultural, social services, environmental and religious institutions; and for conferences and seminars.

Geographical Area of Activity: USA and Canada.

Restrictions: No grants are made to individuals, endowments or capital campaigns, political organizations, political action committees, and for operating deficit reduction, loans, general support, liquidation of a debt, event sponsorships; only one request from the same organization in the same year.

Finance: Annual revenue US $1,431,421 (loss), expenditure $8,865,259 (2009).

Board of Directors: Pamela Scholl (Chair.); Jeanne M. Scholl (Sec.); John A. Nitschke (Treas.).

Principal Staff: Pres. Pamela Scholl; Vice-Pres. Anne Moseley.

Address: 1033 Skokie Blvd, Suite 230, Northbrook, IL 60062.

Telephone: (847) 559-7430; **Internet:** www.drschollfoundation.com.

Charles and Lynn Schusterman Family Foundation—CLSFF

Founded in 1987, exclusively for charitable, religious, literacy, scientific and educational purposes.

Activities: Operates nationally and internationally, in Israel and the former USSR, to support and expand Jewish communities; gives grants to institutions, offers scholarships and fellowships, runs conferences and training courses, all with the aim of promoting education, child development and community service; maintains office in Washington, DC.

Geographical Area of Activity: USA, Israel and the former USSR.

Restrictions: No grants to individuals, non-sectarian groups outside Tulsa, local Jewish programmes in communities outside Tulsa, endowments, deficits, programmes appropriately funded by government, nor for permanent financing.

Board of Trustees: Lynn Schusterman (Chair.).

Principal Staff: Pres. Sanford R. Cardin; Dir Stacy H. Schusterman; COO Alana Hughes.

Address: 2 West 2nd St, Tulsa, OK 74103-3101.

Telephone: (918) 591-1090; **Fax:** (918) 591-1758; **Internet:** www.schusterman.org; **e-mail:** ahughes@schusterman.org.

Seeds of Peace

Founded by John Wallach in 1993 to empower young leaders from regions of conflict with the leadership skills required to advance reconciliation and co-existence.

Activities: Seeks to develop the leadership skills of young people in regions of conflict, with a particular emphasis on the Middle East, as well as South Asia, Cyprus and the Balkans. In the Middle East, Seeds of Peace focuses on training young people in conflict-resolution skills, which had been used in other conflict regions, including Cyprus, Albania, Bosnia-Herzegovina, Bulgaria, Croatia, Macedonia, the former Yugoslavia (including Montenegro, Serbia and Kosovo) and Romania, and Afghanistan, India and Pakistan. Also runs a domestic programme called Maine Seeds to address ethnic and racial tensions between the diverse communities that have settled in the organization's home state of Maine, and through its Beyond Borders programme the organization brings teenagers from additional Middle East countries including Iraq, Saudi Arabia and Kuwait to Maine to participate in a cultural exchange programme between American and Arab young people. Maintains offices in Otisfield, ME and Washington, DC, as well as Kabul, Lahore, Mumbai, Amman, Cairo, Gaza, Jerusalem, Ramallah and Tel-Aviv.

Geographical Area of Activity: USA, Middle East, South Asia, Cyprus and the Balkans.

Publications: e-Newsletters (monthly); Annual Report.

Finance: Total assets US $2,423,601 (31 Dec. 2010); annual revenue $4,845,726, expenditure $4,200,957 (2010).

Board of Directors: Richard Berman (Chair.); Joseph Gantz (Chair. of the Exec. Committee); Samuel L. Samelson (Treas.); Christine R. Covey (Sec.).

Principal Staff: Exec. Dir Leslie Adelson Lewin.

Address: 370 Lexington Ave, Suite 2103, New York, NY 10017.

Telephone: (212) 573-8040; **Fax:** (212) 573-8047; **Internet:** www.seedsofpeace.org; **e-mail:** info@seedsofpeace.org.

William G. and Marie Selby Foundation

Established by William G. Selby and Marie Selby in 1955 to carry out philanthropic activities, especially in the area of education in the Sarasota County area.

Activities: The Foundation is active in Florida, focusing on social welfare, education, community development, health and culture; realizes objectives through scholarships and grants for students and organizations in Florida.

Geographical Area of Activity: Florida, USA only.

Restrictions: No grants are made to individuals, nor generally for endowments, deficit financing, debt reduction, or ordinary operating expenses; conferences, seminars, workshops, travel, surveys, advertising, fundraising costs or research; annual giving campaigns; or projects that have already been completed.

Publications: Commemorative publications.

Principal Staff: Pres. and CEO Dr Sarah H. Pappas; Grants Man. Evan G. Jones.

Address: 1800 Second St, Suite 750, Sarasota, FL 34236.

Telephone: (941) 957-0442; **Fax:** (941) 957-3135; **Internet:** www.selbyfdn.org; **e-mail:** secretary@mccurry.com.

SERRV International, Inc

Established in 1949 by the Church of the Brethren to help refugees in Europe after the Second World War; became SERRV International in 1999, aiming to promote the economic and social progress of people living in developing countries and to alleviate poverty through fair trade.

Activities: Acts as a fair trade, non-profit organization, through advancing money to low-income artisans in developing countries so they can buy raw materials to make crafts. SERRV then purchases and markets the finished items, selling them through more than 3,000 churches, non-profit groups and retail outlets.

Geographical Area of Activity: World-wide.

Publications: *SERRV Catalogue*; newsletters (quarterly).

Finance: Annual revenue US $5,882,797, expenditure $5,355,688 (2010).

Board of Directors: Marsha Hoover (Chair.); Ann Engelman (Vice-Chair.); Brad J. Hamrlik (Treas.); Pushpika Freitas (Sec.).

Principal Staff: Pres. and CEO Robert Chase.

Address: 122 State St, Suite 600, Madison, WI 53701.

Telephone: (608) 251-3766; **Fax:** (608) 255-0451; **Internet:** www.serrv.org; **e-mail:** orders@serrv.org.

Seva Foundation

Founded to help relieve and prevent suffering in the world and to generate hope through compassionate action.

Activities: Operates internationally to promote health, including eye care, nutrition, education, economic development and self help, native Americans, community development and social and economic justice. The Foundation works in partnership with organizations in the USA and in Cambodia, Guatemala, India, Mexico, Nepal, Tanzania and Tibet.

Geographical Area of Activity: USA, Asia and Africa.

Restrictions: No unsolicited grant requests accepted.

Publications: Annual Report; newsletters; special programme reports; *25th Anniversary Report; Spirit of Service* (newsletters).

Finance: Total assets US $3,515,121 (30 June 2011); annual revenue $3,874,460, expenditure $3,748,286 (2010/11).

Board of Directors: Gary Hahn (Chair.); Stephen Miller (Treas. and Chair.-elect); Jahanara Romney (Sec.).

Principal Staff: Exec. Dir Jack Blanks; Finance Dir Deborah Moses.

Address: 1786 Fifth St, Berkeley, CA 94710.

Telephone: (510) 845-7382; **Fax:** (510) 845-7410; **Internet:** www.seva.org; **e-mail:** admin@seva.org.

The Sierra Club Foundation

Founded in 1960 to advance the preservation and protection of the natural environment.

Activities: Promotes environmental protection through support for education, litigation and training activities. Active at grassroots level, providing funding for more than 900 volunteer environmental organizations nationally and internationally.

Geographical Area of Activity: Mainly USA.

Restrictions: Does not accept unsolicited proposals.

Publications: *Foundation News* (quarterly supporters newsletter); Annual Report; information brochure; financial statement.

Finance: Annual revenue US $47,758,187, expenditure $45,981,871 (2009).

Board of Directors: Loren Blackford (Chair.); Nels Leutwiler (Vice-Chair.); Paul Farr (Treas.); Larry Keeshan (Sec.); Chuck Frank (Fifth Officer).

Principal Staff: Exec. Dir Peter Martin.

Address: 85 Second St, Suite 750, San Francisco, CA 94105.

Telephone: (415) 995-1780; **Fax:** (415) 995-1791; **Internet:** www.sierraclub.org/foundation; **e-mail:** foundation@ sierraclub.org.

L. J. Skaggs and Mary C. Skaggs Foundation

Founded in 1967 by L. J. Skaggs and Mary C. Skaggs for general charitable purposes; the Foundation's interest is in the alleviation of social problems and concerns, and the enrichment and preservation of cultural and historic heritages, in the USA and abroad.

Activities: Operates nationally and internationally, making grants under four main programme categories: Performing Arts, Projects of Historic Interest, Environment/Ecology and Special Projects. Emphasis is given to projects proposing unusual and untried solutions or innovative processes. Also awards discretionary grants to projects relating to the Foundation's interests.

Geographical Area of Activity: United Kingdom and USA.

Restrictions: No grants are made to individuals.

Publications: Report of operations and financial statements.

Finance: Total assets US $409,034 (31 Dec. 2009); grants disbursed $38,800 (2009).

Board of Directors: Philip M. Jelley (Pres.); Jayne C. Davis (Vice-Pres.); Georgia A. Fulstone (Vice-Pres.); Joseph W. Martin, Jr (Sec. and Treas.).

Principal Staff: Dir Robert N. Janopaul.

Address: 1221 Broadway, 21st Floor, Oakland, CA 94612-1837.

Telephone: (510) 451-3300; **Fax:** (510) 451-1527; **Internet:** www.skaggs.org; **e-mail:** skaggs@fablaw.com.

Skoll Foundation

Established by Jeff Skoll in 1999 and based on the belief that small investments can lead to significant social change; incorporates the Skoll Fund, associated with Community Foundation Silicon Valley.

Activities: The Foundation invests in mid- to late-stage social entrepreneurs and their initiatives around the world, including supporting microfinance projects, and the development of mass-market, low-cost technologies to help create new businesses. Also aims to connect social change agents through Social Edge, an online community it has created for social entrepreneurs and other members of the social sector to promote networking and resource sharing. Established the Skoll Awards for Social Entrepreneurship. Also supports conferences, and in 2003 funded the launch of the Skoll Centre for Social Entrepreneurship at the Said Business School, Oxford University, United Kingdom, with a donation of US $7,500,000.

Geographical Area of Activity: USA.

Publications: Annual Report.

Finance: Total assets US $515,484,831 (31 Dec. 2010); annual revenue $62,016,774, expenditure $18,959,740 (2010).

Board of Directors: Jeffrey S. Skoll (Founder and Chair.).

Principal Staff: Pres. and CEO Sally Osberg; COO Richard Fahey.

Address: 250 University Ave, Suite 200, Palo Alto, CA 94301.

Telephone: (650) 331-1031; **Fax:** (650) 331-1033; **Internet:** www.skollfoundation.org; **e-mail:** info@skollfoundation.org.

Alfred P. Sloan Foundation

Established in 1934 by Alfred Pritchard Sloan Jr, then-President and Chief Executive Officer of the General Motors Corporation, the Foundation makes grants in support of original research and education in science, technology, engineering, mathematics and economic performance.

Activities: Operates through self-conducted programmes and grants to institutions within six areas: basic research, science education, public understanding of science and technology, economic performance and quality of life, select national issues, and civic initiatives. The Foundation sponsors the Sloan Fellowships for Basic Research for young chemists, physicists, mathematicians, neuroscientists and economists in institutions in the USA and Canada.

Geographical Area of Activity: USA.

Restrictions: Only rarely supports activities outside the USA and does not normally support projects in areas of religion, creative or performing arts, elementary or secondary education, the humanities, medical research or health care. No grants for endowments, buildings or equipment.

Publications: Annual Report; information brochure.

Finance: Total assets US $1,703,820,396 (Dec. 2010).

Board of Trustees: Stephen L. Brown (Chair.).

Principal Staff: Pres. Paul Joskow.

Address: 630 Fifth Ave, Suite 2550, New York, NY 10111-0242.

Telephone: (212) 649-1649; **Fax:** (212) 757-5117; **Internet:** www.sloan.org.

Smith Richardson Foundation, Inc

Founded in 1935 by H. S. Richardson, Sr and Grace Jones Richardson for the support of research relating to government operations; and for programmes promoting a better understanding of American society and the economy.

Activities: The Foundation aims to inform important public policy debates through supporting pragmatic, policy-relevant research, analysis and writing. Grants are provided in two main programme areas: the International Security and Foreign Policy Program, which supports research and policy projects on issues central to the strategic interests of the USA; and the Domestic Public Policy Program, researching the development of US economic, social and governmental institutions.

Geographical Area of Activity: USA.

Restrictions: The majority of unsolicited applications are rejected. No grants are made for projects in the arts and humanities, physical sciences or historic restoration, nor are grants made to individuals.

Publications: Annual Report.

Finance: Annual revenue US $7,898,329, expenditure $25,885,832 (2009).

Trustees: Peter L. Richardson (Chair.).

Principal Staff: Pres. Peter L. Richardson; Sr Vice-Pres. Dr Marin Strmecki.

Address: 60 Jesup Rd, Westport, CT 06880.

Telephone: (203) 222-6222; **Fax:** (203) 222-6282; **Internet:** www.srf.org; **e-mail:** jhollings@srf.org.

Smithsonian Institution

Created in 1846 by Act of Congress in accordance with the terms of the will of James Smithson of England, who in 1826 bequeathed his property to the USA to found at Washington, under the name of the Smithsonian Institution, an establishment for the increase and diffusion of knowledge among men.

Activities: Operates nationally and internationally in the fields of education, science, the arts and humanities, and the conservation of natural resources. The Institution performs basic research, publishes results of studies, explorations and investigations, maintains study and reference collections in the sciences, culture and history, and exhibitions in the arts, American history, technology, aeronautics, space exploration and natural history. It administers various museums, art galleries and other institutions including the Anacostia Museum and Center for African American History and Culture; Archives of American Art; Arts and Industries Building; Cooper-Hewitt, National Design Museum; Freer Gallery of Art; Hirshhorn Museum and Sculpture Garden; National Air and Space Museum, including the Steven F. Udvar-Hazy Center; National Museum of African Art; Smithsonian American Art Museum; National Museum of American History; National Museum of the American Indian; National Museum of Natural History/Museum of Man; National Portrait Gallery; National Postal Museum; National Zoological Park; Renwick Gallery; Arthur M. Sackler Gallery; Smithsonian Astrophysical Observatory; Smithsonian Environmental Research Center; Smithsonian Institution Building; Smithsonian Tropical Research Institute. Fellowships are offered to students of all nationalities to study at Smithsonian Institution facilities. Through the National Museum Act, grants are made to museum professionals for museum studies. The Smithsonian Institution Travelling Exhibition Service organizes exhibitions that circulate to museums around the USA, while the Smithsonian Affiliates Program establishes links and affiliations across the country.

Geographical Area of Activity: USA.

Publications: Annual Report and financial statement; *Smithsonian Opportunities for Research and Study*; *Smithsonian Magazine*; various scholarly and popular publications; *Air and Space Magazine*; *American Art*; *Zooger*; museum publications; Research Center publications and books.

Finance: Annual revenue US $1,139,000,000, expenditure $980,000,000 (2010).

Board of Regents: Patty Stonesifer (Chair.).

Principal Staff: Sec. G. Wayne Clough; Chief of Staff to Sec. Patricia Bartlett.

Address: POB 37012, SI Bldg, Rm 153, MRC 010, Washington, DC 20013.

Telephone: (202) 357-1729; **Internet:** www.si.edu; **e-mail:** info@si.edu.

Snow Leopard Trust

Established in 1981 by Helen Freeman, Stan Freeman, Douglas Fleming and Kathleen Braden.

Activities: The Trust is a non-profit organization, operating in Central Asia, dedicated to the conservation of the snow leopard and its mountain ecosystem, through conservation, research, education and information exchange, symposia, running projects in collaboration with local organizations, and publications. Certain environmental education, captive breeding and research programmes are carried out outside Central Asia.

Geographical Area of Activity: Mainly Central Asia.

Publications: *Conservation Handbook*; symposia proceedings; scholarly articles; pamphlets; annual reports; annual conservation reports; newsletters (monthly).

Finance: Annual revenue US $1,296,000, expenditure $1,222,000 (2010).

Board of Directors: Carol Hosford (Pres.); Rhetick Sengupta (Vice-Pres.); Andrea Gates Sanford (Vice-Pres.); Steven Kearsley (Sec. and Treas.).

Principal Staff: Exec. Dir Brad Rutherford.

Address: 4649 Sunnyside Ave North, Suite 325, Seattle, WA 98103.

Telephone: (206) 632-2421; **Fax:** (206) 632-3967; **Internet:** www.snowleopard.org; **e-mail:** info@snowleopard.org.

Sorenson Legacy Foundation

A non-profit corporation established by the James LeVoy Sorenson family to offer support in the areas of welfare, religion, education, the arts and science.

Activities: Operates in the USA in the fields of social welfare, education, the arts and humanities, science and religion. It was announced in 2008 that James LeVoy Sorenson had left his entire fortune, estimated at some US $4,500m. to the Foundation.

Geographical Area of Activity: USA.

Principal Staff: Contact Lisa Meiling.

Address: 2511 South West Temple, Salt Lake City, UT 84115.

Telephone: (801) 461-9700; **Internet:** sorensonlegacyfoundation.org; **e-mail:** lisa@sorensoncompanies.com.

Soros Economic Development Fund

Established in 1997; a non-profit private foundation, part of the Soros foundations network, which aims to alleviate poverty through making investments in banks, microfinance institutions, co-operatives and other such organizations world-wide.

Activities: Operates mainly in Eastern and Central Europe, although also in Africa, Central and South America, the Caribbean and South Asia, through offering loans, equity, guarantees and deposits, to selected financial institutions.

Geographical Area of Activity: International.

Finance: Annual revenue US $51,673,502, expenditure $5,539,436 (2009).

Board of Directors: Jonathan Soros (Acting Chair.).

Principal Staff: Pres. Stewart J. Paperin.

Address: 1700 Broadway, 17th Floor, New York, NY 10019.

Telephone: (212) 548-0111; **Fax:** (646) 557-2551; **Internet:** www.sedfny.org; **e-mail:** sedf@sorosny.org.

Spencer Foundation

Founded in 1962 by Lyle M. Spencer to support research leading to the improvement of education.

Activities: Supports research into all aspects of education, in the USA and abroad. The Foundation is interested in a wide variety of disciplinary and interdisciplinary approaches, though by direction of its charter it gives emphasis to the behavioural sciences; it defines education broadly to include all the situations and institutions in which education proceeds, regardless of age. The Foundation is interested in a wide variety of research formats, from relatively low-cost efforts extending over a few months to more expensive collaborative efforts extending over several years.

Geographical Area of Activity: World-wide.

Publications: Annual Report; conference reports; influential research; usable knowledge in education; grantee books; *On the Edge of Commitment: Educational Attainment and Race in the United States* (2005); *Intelligent and Effective Direction: The Fisk University Race Relations Institute and the Struggle for Civil Rights, 1944–1969* (2005); *Diversity and Citizenship Education: Global Perspectives* (2004); *The Almighty Latin King and Queen Nation: Street Politics and the Transformation of a New York City Gang* (2004); *School Sense: How to Help Your Child Succeed in Elementary School* (2004); and other books.

Finance: Total assets US $431,615,000 (31 March 2011); annual revenue $7,237,000, expenditure $7,142,000 (2010/11).

Board of Directors: Deborah Loewenberg Ball (Chair.); Michael S. McPherson (Pres.); Pamela Grossman (Vice-Chair.).

Principal Staff: Pres. Michael S. McPherson; Sr Vice-Pres. Diana Hess; CFO Julie Hubbard.

Address: 625 North Michigan Ave, Suite 1600, Chicago, IL 60611.

Telephone: (312) 337-7000; **Fax:** (312) 337-0282; **Internet:** www.spencer.org.

The Stanley Foundation

Founded in 1956 by C. Maxwell and Elizabeth M. Stanley to encourage study, research and education in the field of international policy that contributes to secure peace with freedom and justice. Emphasis is placed on activities related to international institutions and US foreign policy.

Activities: Operates the following initiatives: UN and Global Institutions; US and Global Security; US and Middle East Security; US and Asian Security; Rising Powers; Nonproliferation, Arms Control and Disarmament; and Community Partnerships. Also organizes off-the-record conferences for policy-makers to discuss global issues and global security. Reports from conferences and seminars are published periodically and distributed free.

Geographical Area of Activity: World-wide.

Restrictions: The Foundation is not a grant-making organization.

Publications: *Courier* (newsletter, 3 a year); conference reports; books on global change, the UN, security and disarmament, human rights and global education; policy briefs; analytical articles; reports; and other publications.

Board of Directors: Richard H. Stanley (Chair.); Brian T. Hanson (Vice-Chair.); Sarah C. Stanley (Vice-Chair.); Betty J. Anders (Sec.); Dana W. Pittman (Treas.).

Principal Staff: Pres. Vladimir P. Sambaiew.

Address: 209 Iowa Ave, Muscatine, IA 52761.

Telephone: (563) 264-1500; **Fax:** (563) 264-0864; **Internet:** www.stanleyfdn.org; **e-mail:** info@stanleyfoundation.org.

Star of Hope International

Since 1966 Star of Hope organizations have cared for people who are suffering or in need around the world. Today Star of Hope USA, Sweden, Norway and Finland bring hope to children and their families in 18 countries.

Activities: Operates internationally in the fields of aid to less-developed countries, through assisting local organizations in areas of greatest need, and particularly through helping children. Maintains offices in Argentina, Brazil, Finland, Ghana, Haiti, Kenya, Latvia, Norway, Philippines, Romania, Belarus, Sweden, Trinidad.

Geographical Area of Activity: International.

Publications: Newsletters; Annual Report.

Principal Staff: Pres. and CEO Barry W. Borror.

Address: POB 427, Ellinwood, KS 67526-0427.

Telephone: (866) 653-0321; **Internet:** www.starofhope.org; **e-mail:** usa@starofhopeusa.org.

The Starr Foundation

Founded in 1955 by Cornelius V. Starr. The Foundation currently has assets of approximately US $3,500,000,000, making it one of the largest private foundations in the USA. It makes grants in a number of areas, including education, medicine and health care, human needs, public policy, culture and the environment.

Activities: Makes grants largely in the area of education, particularly higher education. Also active in culture, medicine and health, human needs, public policy in international relations, welfare and social services. Offers funding for scholarships, professorships, fellowships and endowment funds.

Geographical Area of Activity: USA.

Restrictions: No grants are made to individuals. Does not accept unsolicited applications for grants.

Publications: Annual report; *Biography of Cornelius Vander Starr (1892–1968)*; *Introduction: The Gentle Laopan*; *A Family Album*; *A Man for Many Seasons*; *Citizen of the World*; *The World of Business*; *The Opera*; *Fine Art*; *Places He Loved*; *A Sense of Common Humanity*; *Architecture*; *Thirst for Knowledge*; *An Interest in People*; and other books.

Finance: Annual revenue US $73,565,084 (loss), expenditure $197,580,394 (2008).

Board of Directors: Maurice R. Greenberg (Chair.).

Principal Staff: Pres. Florence A. Davis; Vice-Pres. Paula Lawrence.

Address: 399 Park Ave, 17th Floor, New York, NY 10022.

Telephone: (212) 909-3600; **Fax:** (212) 750-3536; **Internet:** www.starrfoundation.org.

Stewardship Foundation

Founded in 1962 by the C. Davis Weyerhaeuser Irrevocable Trust to contribute to the propagation of religious organizations.

Activities: Concerned with funding evangelical religious organizations whose ministries operate over a wide area. Areas of involvement include education, mental health, youth development, international economic development and peace and reconciliation. Grants are made to international development organizations, foreign missions and youth ministries.

Geographical Area of Activity: World-wide.

Restrictions: No grants are made to individuals; grants are made only to US public non-profit organizations.

Finance: Grants disbursed US $5,947,754 (2011).

Board of Trustees: William T. Weyerhaeuser (Chair.); Gail T. Weyerhaeuser (Vice-Chair. and Treas.).

Principal Staff: Exec. Dir Cary A. Paine; Grants Man. Amy Alva.

Address: POB 1278, Tacoma, WA 98401-1278; 1145 Broadway, Suite 1500, Tacoma, WA 98402.

Telephone: (253) 620-1340; **Fax:** (253) 572-2721; **Internet:** www.stewardshipfdn.org; **e-mail:** info@stewardshipfdn.org.

The Streisand Foundation

Founded in 1986 by Barbra Streisand to provide funding in the fields of civil rights, voter outreach, the environment, women's issues, AIDS, and programmes for the disadvantaged youth of Los Angeles, CA.

Activities: Makes grants to US-based organizations working on a national level to promote and support: environmental issues; women's issues including reproductive choice and health-related concerns; civil liberties and democratic values; civil rights and race relations; children's and youth-related issues with a focus on the economically disadvantaged; nuclear disarmament; and AIDS research, advocacy, service and litigation. Awards are in the range of US $1,000–25,000.

Geographical Area of Activity: USA.

Restrictions: No grants are made to individuals, nor to local organizations, except for programmes for disadvantaged youth in Los Angeles.

Publications: Application guidelines.

Trustees: Barbra Streisand (Pres.).

Principal Staff: Exec. Dir Margery Tabankin.

Address: 2800 28th St, Suite 105, Santa Monica, CA 90405.

Telephone: (310) 535-3767; **Fax:** (310) 314-8396; **Internet:** www.barbrastreisand.com.

Surdna Foundation, Inc

Founded in 1917 by John E. Andrus for general charitable purposes.

Activities: Operates in the following areas: the environment (in particular energy, transportation, urban and suburban land use, human systems, and biological and cultural diversity); community revitalization (taking a comprehensive and holistic approach to restoring communities in the USA, in particular through entrepreneurial programmes offering solutions to difficult systemic problems); building an effective citizenry (promoting a civil society through character development, ethical behaviour, social and emotional learning, and conflict resolution); and the arts, focusing on arts education and young people. Also provides funding to support the development of the non-profit sector in the US, grants for organizational capacity building, and commissions reports in its areas of interest.

Geographical Area of Activity: USA.

Restrictions: No grants are made to individuals.

Publications: Annual Report; reports; announcements; commissioned reports.

Finance: Assets US $754,986,525 (30 June 2010); total revenue $91,103,251, expenditure $42,503,146 (2009/10).

Board of Directors: Josephine Lowman (Chair.); Peter B. Benedict, II (Vice-Chair.).

Principal Staff: Pres. Phillip Henderson; Chief Financial and Admin. Officer Marc de Venoge.

Address: 330 Madison Ave, 30th Floor, New York, NY 10017-5001.

Telephone: (212) 557-0010; **Fax:** (212) 557-0003; **Internet:** www.surdna.org; **e-mail:** questions@surdna.org.

TechnoServe

Founded in 1968 to help increase the income of rural farmers and businesspeople in developing countries; has helped to create or improve more than 1,500 businesses, benefiting millions of people in 30 countries. TechnoServe is currently working to build and expand businesses in Mozambique, South Africa, Tanzania, Kenya, Swaziland, Uganda, Ghana, Côte d'Ivoire, India, El Salvador, Honduras, Nicaragua, Guatemala, Peru and Colombia.

Activities: Runs its own projects to help rural families to create their own local businesses, giving them advice, sharing technical expertise, and providing the marketing and capital needed to create prosperity and a long-term sustainable solution to poverty.

Geographical Area of Activity: Central and South America, and Africa.

Restrictions: Runs own projects. No unsolicited applications for grants accepted. Not a grant-making foundation.

Publications: Annual report.

Board of Directors: Paul E. Tierney, Jr (Chair.); John B. Caron (Vice-Chair.); Peter A. Flaherty (Vice-Chair.); Suzanne Nora Johnson (Treas.); Jennifer Bullard Broggini (Sec.).

Principal Staff: Pres. and CEO Bruce McNamer; CFO George Schutter.

Address: 1120 19th St NW, 8th Floor, Washington, DC 20036.

Telephone: (202) 785-4515; **Fax:** (202) 785-4544; **Internet:** www.technoserve.org; **e-mail:** technoserve@tns.org.

John Templeton Foundation

Founded in 1987 by Sir John Templeton.

Activities: Encourages civil, informed dialogue among scientists, philosophers and theologians, on subjects including complexity, evolution, infinity, creativity, forgiveness, love and free will. Awards the Templeton Prize, established in 1972, to a living person who has made an exceptional contribution to affirming life's spiritual dimension.

Geographical Area of Activity: International.

Publications: *The Templeton Report* (e-newsletter, twice a month); *Big Questions Online* (magazine); books.

Finance: Endowment US $1,500,000,000 (2009); grant disbursements $60,000,000 (2009).

Board of Trustees: Dr Jack Templeton (Chair.); Harvey M. Templeton, III (Sec.).

Principal Staff: Pres. Dr Jack Templeton.

Address: 300 Conshohocken State Rd, Suite 500, West Conshohocken, PA 19428.

Telephone: (610) 941-2828; **Fax:** (610) 825-1730; **Internet:** www.templeton.org; **e-mail:** info@templeton.org.

Thiel Foundation

Aims to defend and promote freedom in all its dimensions: political, personal and economic.

Activities: Runs programmes in the areas of freedom, antiviolence and science. Offers 20 scholarships to people under the age of 20 to pursue innovative scientific and technical projects. The Breakout Labs programme was initiated in 2011 to support entrepreneurial research in science.

Geographical Area of Activity: International.

Address: 1 Letterman Dr., Bldg C, Suite 400, San Francisco, CA 94117.

Internet: http://thielfoundation.org; **e-mail:** info@ thielfoundation.org.

Thrasher Research Fund

Founded in 1977 by E. W. Thrasher to support meritorious, innovative research projects that seek to improve child health and well-being.

Activities: Grants are made to institutions in any country for medical research, without restriction as to geographical location, ethnicity, gender, creed or nationality. The Fund gives priority to practical applied research with the potential to benefit large numbers of children and find sustainable solutions to major problems of child health and well-being. The main focus is currently on gaps in paediatric medical research most likely to have an impact on the treatment of children with critical illnesses and major health problems. Grants range from US $10,000 to $400,000 and generally run for one to three years.

Geographical Area of Activity: International.

Restrictions: No grants for research on human foetal tissue; behavioural science research; educational programmes; general operating expenses; construction or renovation of buildings or facilities; general donations; loans, student aid, scholarships; nor to other funding organizations.

Publications: Biennial Report and application brochure.

Finance: Annual revenue US $21,541,336 (loss), expenditure $7,219,305 (2008).

Principal Staff: Pres. A. Dean Byrd; Admin. Asst Allison F. Martínez.

Address: 68 S. Main St, Suite 400, Salt Lake City, UT 84101.

Telephone: (801) 240-4753; **Fax:** (801) 240-1625; **Internet:** www.thrasherresearch.org; **e-mail:** ByrdAD@ thrasherresearch.org.

Tibet Fund

Established in 1981 to assist the educational, social and economic development of Tibetans living inside and outside Tibet.

Activities: Provides assistance to the Tibetan community through supporting community and economic development projects in refugee communities in India and Nepal; providing emergency relief and resettling new refugees who have fled Tibet; improving health conditions in the refugee communities, providing scholarships to Tibetan students and professionals; preserving Tibetan culture and promoting cultural exchange; and providing assistance for health, education and economic development projects in Tibet.

Geographical Area of Activity: People's Republic of China, India, Nepal, Tibet and the USA.

Publications: brochures.

Finance: Annual revenue US $5,579,044, expenditure $8,070,907 (2010).

Board of Directors: Mickey Lemle (Chair.); Jessica Brackman (Sec.); Susan M. Holgate (Treas.).

Principal Staff: Pres. Rinchen Dharlo; Exec. Dir Robyn Brentano.

Address: 241 East 32nd St, New York, NY 10016.

Telephone: (212) 213-5011; **Fax:** (212) 213-1219; **Internet:** www.tibetfund.org; **e-mail:** info@tibetfund.org.

Tides

Founded in 1976, a grant-making organization dedicated to positive social change.

Activities: Acts as a mediator between donors and charitable organizations in need of resources, promoting human rights, social justice and a healthy environment. Strengthens community non-profit organizations, and awards grants in a large number of areas, including progressive media, arts and culture; economic development; the environment; gay and lesbian issues; HIV/AIDS; Native American communities; women's empowerment; violence prevention; reproductive health; and youth. Current programmes include the Death Penalty Mobilization Fund, Bridging the Economic Divide, Rapid Response Initiative and a Democracy Fund. Offers a number of services to donors to ensure that their money makes a lasting social impact. These include: flexible and personalized grant-making programmes; expert advice; and the opportunity to network.

Geographical Area of Activity: USA.

Publications: Donor guides.

Finance: Annual revenue US $218,500,000, expenditure $244,100,000 (2010).

Board of Directors: Maya Wiley (Chair.); Stephanie J. Clohesy (Vice-Chair.).

Principal Staff: CEO Melissa L. Bradley.

Address: POB 29198, San Francisco, CA 94129-0198.

Telephone: (415) 561-6400; **Fax:** (415) 561-6401; **Internet:** www.tides.org; **e-mail:** info@tides.org.

Tiffany & Co. Foundation

Established in 2000.

Activities: Operates nationally and internationally in the fields of art and culture, and preservation of the environment, specifically promotion of responsible mining.

Board: Anisa Kamadoli Costa (Pres.).

Principal Staff: Program Officer Samara Rudolph; Treas. Michael W. Connolly.

Address: 200 Fifth Ave, New York, NY 10010.

Telephone: (212) 230 6591; **Internet:** www .tiffanyandcofoundation.org; **e-mail:** foundation@tiffany .com.

Tinker Foundation, Inc

Founded in 1959 by Edward Larocque Tinker to promote better understanding between the peoples of the Americas and for the support of work in, or directly related to, Antarctica.

Activities: Operates in the following fields: social sciences, with particular emphasis on economic and political matters having strong public policy implications; and environmental policy. The Foundation supports research projects, conferences and workshops. The Foundation also promotes collaboration between organizations in the USA and Central and South America, and Antarctica, and among institutions in those regions.

Geographical Area of Activity: Central and South America, Mexico, and Antarctica.

Restrictions: No grants are made to individuals.

Publications: Annual Report.

Finance: Assets US $75,750,000 (31 Dec. 2009); annual grants expenditure $2,775,650 (2009).

Board of Directors: Renate Rennie (Chair); Kathleen Waldron (Treas.); Richard de J. Osborne (Sec.).

Principal Staff: Pres. Renate Rennie; Dir of Finance and Admin. Jessica S. Tomb.

Address: 55 East 59th St, New York, NY 10022.

Telephone: (212) 421-6858; **Internet:** www.tinker.org; **e-mail:** tinker@tinker.org.

The Trull Foundation

Founded in 1967 by R. B. Trull, Florence M. Trull, Gladys T. Brooking, Jean T. Herlin and Laura Shiflett for general charitable purposes.

Activities: Focuses its grants on four priority areas: Matagorda County area, Texas, where the Foundation has its roots; children and families, directing them from abuse, neglect, hunger; those dealing with substance abuse; coastal environment of Texas, including farming, ranching, aquaculture and birds.

Geographical Area of Activity: USA (mainly Texas).

Restrictions: The foundation does not provide grants for long-term commitments, buildings, endowments, or research.

Publications: Report (biennially).

Trustees: Colleen Claybourn (Chair.); Cara P. Herlin (Vice-Chair.); R. Scott Trull (Sec. and Treas.).

Principal Staff: Exec. Dir E. Gail Purvis.

Address: 404 Fourth St, Palacios, TX 77465.

Telephone: (361) 972-5241; **Fax:** (361) 972-1109; **Internet:** www.trullfoundation.org; **e-mail:** info@trullfoundation.org.

Trust for Mutual Understanding

Founded in 1984 to provide support to American non-profit cultural and environmental organizations for professional exchanges between the USA and Central and Eastern Europe and the countries of the former USSR.

Activities: Some three-quarters of funds are directed at cultural exchanges, with the remaining one-quarter allocated to environmental projects. Grants are made for exchange programmes that include a significant amount of professional interaction and collaboration between the two countries involved.

Geographical Area of Activity: USA, Central Asia, Eastern and Central Europe and the countries of the former USSR.

Restrictions: Grants only to American non-profit organizations for international travel, and related expenses of Russian, Eastern and Central European, and American exchange participants.

Publications: Annual Report.

Finance: Total grants US $3,520,350 (2009).

Principal Staff: Exec. Dir Jennifer P. Goodale; Assoc. Dir Barbara Lanciers.

Address: 6 West 48th St, 12th Floor, New York, NY 10036-1802.

Telephone: (212) 843-0404; **Fax:** (212) 843-0344; **Internet:** www.tmuny.org; **e-mail:** tmu@tmuny.org.

Turner Foundation, Inc

Founded in 1990 to prevent damage to the environment and to support those institutions working to protect the environment and promote sustainable practices.

Activities: The Foundation focuses on the areas of conservation and protection of natural resources, preservation of the environment, protection of wildlife and population management, and supports education and activism in these areas. The primary environmental concerns of the foundation are: protection of the atmosphere through promotion of energy efficiency and renewables; the protection of biodiversity through habitat preservation; the protection of water from toxic pollution; and the development and implementation of sound, equitable practices and policies designed to reduce population growth rates.

Geographical Area of Activity: International.

Restrictions: No funding for buildings, land acquisition, endowments, or start-up funds, nor to fund films, books, magazines, or other specific media projects. No support for individuals. Some programmes are restricted to certain states of the USA.

Publications: Annual Report.

Finance: Total assets US $4,000,000 (31 Dec. 2008); grants disbursed $10,700,000 (2008).

Board of Trustees: R. E. (Ted) Turner, III (Chair.); J. Rutherford Seydel (Sec.); Mike Finley (Treas.).

Principal Staff: Pres. Mike Finley; Sr Program Officer Judy Adler.

Address: 133 Luckie St NW, 2nd Floor, Atlanta, GA 30303.

Telephone: (404) 681-9900; **Fax:** (404) 681-0172; **Internet:** www.turnerfoundation.org; **e-mail:** turnerfi@turnerfoundation.org.

Desmond Tutu Peace Foundation—DTPF

Established in 2000 to advance the philosophy and practices of Archbishop Desmond Tutu.

Activities: Establishes leadership academies in the USA and Africa. The academies focus on developing emerging leaders who act for peace, reconciliation and restorative justice, and human rights.

Geographical Area of Activity: South Africa and the USA.

Publications: Grant list; annual reports; news.

Board of Directors: Robert V. Taylor (Chair.); David Caitlin Pierce (Sec.); Barry H. Smith (Treas.).

Address: 205 East 64th St, Suite 503, New York, NY 10066.

Telephone: (212) 750-5504; **Fax:** (212) 371-2776; **Internet:** www.tutufoundationusa.org; **e-mail:** info@tutfoundation-usa.org.

G. Unger Vetlesen Foundation

Founded in 1955 by Georg Unger Vetlesen to contribute to religious, charitable, scientific, literary and educational causes world-wide. Shares an administration with the Ambrose Monell Foundation (q.v.).

Activities: Operates in New York, the USA in general and internationally in education and other fields; grants are mainly made in the areas of oceanographies, climate studies and other earth sciences; offers an international science award biennially for discoveries in the earth sciences; and makes grants for biological, geophysical and environmental scientific research, higher education and cultural activities, with an emphasis on Norwegian-US relations and maritime issues. Also supports public policy research and libraries.

Geographical Area of Activity: International.

Restrictions: No grants are made to individuals.

Publications: Annual Report.

Finance: Net assets US $42,993,597 (31 Dec. 2010); annual revenue $2,840,283, expenditure $4,895,249 (2010).

Board of Directors: George Rowe, Jr (Pres. and Treas.); Ambrose K. Monell (Vice-Pres.); Eugene P. Grisanti (Vice-Pres.); Maurizio J. Morello (Sec. and Asst Treas.).

Address: 1 Rockefeller Plaza, Suite 301, New York, NY 10020.

Telephone: (212) 586-0700; **Fax:** (212) 245-1863; **Internet:** www.monellvetlesen.org/vetlesen/default.htm; **e-mail:** info@monellvetlesen.org.

Unitarian Universalist Service Committee

Established in 1940, a non-sectarian organization committed to human rights and social justice.

Activities: Works in the field of human rights internationally, through advocacy, education and partnerships with grassroots organizations. Maintains partnerships in the USA, South and South-East Asia, Central Africa, and Central and South America and the Caribbean, and sponsors programmes related to the rights of children, indigenous people, oppressed groups and the empowerment of women. Also provides financial and technical support to areas suffering the effects of disaster, especially where human rights are threatened.

Geographical Area of Activity: International.

Publications: Newsletter; Annual Report.

Finance: Annual revenue US $8,644,031, expenditure $5,639,883 (2009/10).

Board of Trustees: Chuck Spence (Chair.); Dave Madan (Vice-Chair.); Charles Sandmel (Treas.); Lucia Santini-Field (Sec.).

Principal Staff: Pres. and CEO Rev. Dr William F. Schulz.

Address: 689 Massachusetts Ave, Cambridge, MA 02139-3302.

Telephone: (617) 868-6600; **Fax:** (617) 868-7102; **Internet:** www.uusc.org; **e-mail:** info@uusc.org.

United Nations Foundation

Established in 1997 along with its sister organization, the Better World Fund (q.v.), following a gift of US $1,000m. to the UN by R. E. (Ted) Turner; the Foundation seeks to support the goals and objectives of the UN and its Charter to promote a more peaceful, prosperous and just world, with special emphasis on the work of the UN, especially on behalf of economic, social, environmental and humanitarian causes.

Activities: Invests in UN-sponsored agencies and programmes. Its main campaigns and initiatives include: the Better World Campaign; the Energy Future Coalition; Friends of World Heritage; Nothing But Nets (grassroots campaign to prevent malaria); and The People Speak (international co-operation). The Foundation also funds campaigns and projects in the fields of renewable energy, education, health (AIDS, tuberculosis, malaria and polio), and land-mine clearance.

Geographical Area of Activity: International.

Restrictions: Grants are made only in support of UN programmes.

Publications: Annual Report; campaign reports; *UN Wire* (e-mail news briefing).

Finance: Annual revenue US $135,853,781, expenditure $106,625,013 (2010).

Board of Directors: R. E. (Ted) Turner (Founder and Chair.).

Principal Staff: Pres. Timothy E. Wirth; CEO Kathy Calvin; COO Richard Parnell.

Address: 1800 Massachusetts Ave NW, Suite 400, Washington, DC 20036.

Telephone: (202) 887-9040; **Fax:** (202) 887-9021; **Internet:** www.unfoundation.org; **e-mail:** unf@unfoundation.org.

United States African Development Foundation—USADF

Established by the US Congress in 1980 as an independent agency to provide economic assistance to grassroots communities in Africa.

Activities: Operates in Africa through providing economic development assistance and capacity building resources in the areas of: agricultural production; micro- and small enterprises; micro-credit; education and training; community grassroots empowerment; HIV prevention; natural resource management and conservation; travel grants; research; institutional strengthening; and educational outreach, through publications and electronic media. Currently funds projects in 20 countries in Africa. Grants are available for up to US $250,000.

Geographical Area of Activity: Sub-Saharan Africa (Benin, Botswana, Burundi, Cape Verde, Democratic Republic of Congo, Ghana, Guinea, Liberia, Mali, Namibia, Niger, Nigeria, Rwanda, Senegal, Swaziland, Tanzania, Uganda and Zambia).

Restrictions: Grants only in those sub-Saharan African countries where the Foundation is active; grants only to registered African NGOs and community-based organizations; does not provide funding for individuals.

Publications: *USADF Messenger* (online); *USADF e-news*; *USADF Approach* (online); issue papers; project briefs; Annual Report; reports.

Finance: Annual revenue US $30,320,055, expenditure $29,821,561 (2008/09).

Board of Directors: Jack Leslie (Chair.); Dr John O. Agwunobi (Vice-Chair.).

Principal Staff: Pres. Lloyd O. Pierson.

Address: 1400 I St NW, Suite 1000, Washington, DC 20005-2248.

Telephone: (202) 673-3916; **Fax:** (202) 673-3810; **Internet:** www.adf.gov; **e-mail:** info@adf.gov.

United States-Japan Foundation

Founded in 1980 by Ryoichi Sasakawa to strengthen co-operation and understanding between the people of the USA and Japan.

Activities: The Foundation supports grants in the areas of pre-college education, communications/public opinion, and policy in the USA and Japan.

Geographical Area of Activity: USA and Japan.

Restrictions: No grants to individuals or for-profit organizations.

Publications: Annual Report.

Finance: Annual revenue US $1,184,720, expenditure $3,391,095 (2010).

Board of Trustees: Thomas S. Johnson (Chair.); Shinji Fukukawa (Vice-Chair.); Yusuke Saraya (Sec.).

Principal Staff: Pres. Dr George R. Packard; Vice-Pres. and Dir, Tokyo Office Takeo Takuma.

Address: 145 East 32nd St, 12th Floor, New York, NY 10016.

Telephone: (212) 481-8753; **Fax:** (212) 481-8762; **Internet:** www.us-jf.org; **e-mail:** info@us-jf.org.

United Way Worldwide

Established in 1974 as a support organization, helping to build community capacity for a better quality of life world-wide, through voluntary giving and action. Formerly known as United Way International—UWI.

Activities: Operates in the area of community development, working with corporations, foundations and other donors to assist them with their global philanthropic needs.

Geographical Area of Activity: International.

Publications: Annual Report; UWI campaign brochure; newsletter; financial statements.

Finance: Total assets US $26,033,613 (31 Dec. 2007); annual revenue $34,800,602, expenditure $29,008,011 (2007).

Board of Directors: John Dooner, Jr (Chair. Emeritus); Sunil Wadhwani (Treas.); Peggy Conlon (Sec.).

Principal Staff: Pres. and CEO Brian A. Gallagher; CFO Robert Berdelle.

Address: 701 North Fairfax St, Alexandria, VA 22314-2045.

Telephone: (703) 836-7112; **Fax:** (703) 519-0097; **Internet:** www.uwint.org; **e-mail:** worldwide@unitedway.org.

University of Southern California Shoah Foundation Institute for Visual History and Education

Established by Steven Spielberg in 1994 to record and preserve the testimonies of Holocaust survivors and other witnesses, and to overcome prejudice, ignorance and bigotry, and the suffering they cause, through the educational use of visual history testimonies. The Shoah Foundation has collected nearly 52,000 recorded testimonies of Holocaust survivors and other witnesses in 56 countries.

Activities: The Foundation works to develop partnerships to support three main strategic goals: to use the archive to create educational projects for classrooms and broader dissemination; to build and support educational programmes; and to preserve the archive and provide access to it.

Geographical Area of Activity: World-wide.

Restrictions: Does not make grants.

Publications: *Past Forward* (newsletter, 2 a year); documentary films; CD-ROMs; study guides; and books.

Board of Councilors: Robert J. Katz (Chair.); Susan Crown (Vice-Chair.); Harry Robinson (Vice-Chair.).

Principal Staff: Exec. Dir Dr Stephen D. Smith.

Address: Leavey Library, 650 West 35th St, Suite 114, Los Angeles, CA 90089-2571.

Telephone: (213) 740-6001; **Fax:** (213) 740-6044; **Internet:** college.usc.edu/vhi; **e-mail:** vhi-web@usc.edu.

UPS Foundation

Established by United Parcel Service in 1951 to support higher education and social welfare projects and charities.

Activities: Operates nationally and internationally, making grants in areas including economic and global literacy, environmental sustainability, non-profit effectiveness, strength from diversity and community safety.

Geographical Area of Activity: USA and international.

Restrictions: Unsolicited requests for funding are not accepted.

Publications: Annual Report.

Finance: Grants disbursed US $43,000,000 (2009).

Board of Trustees: D. Scott Davis (Chair.).

Principal Staff: Pres. Ken Sternad; CEO D. Scott Davis.

Address: 55 Glenlake Parkway NE, Atlanta, GA 30328.

Telephone: (404) 828-7123; **Internet:** www.community.ups.com/UPS+Foundation; **e-mail:** community@ups.com.

US-Baltic Foundation—USBF

Established in 1990 to promote the social, democratic and economic development of the Baltic states.

Activities: Operates in the Baltic states in the areas of education and trainingto fulfil its aims. Established offices in Estonia, Latvia and Lithuania, which now operate as independent foundations. Programmes support the development of democracy and an independent media. The Foundation has also funded three Schools of Public Administration in Estonia, Latvia and Lithuania.

Geographical Area of Activity: Estonia, Latvia and Lithuania.

Finance: Annual revenue US $142,405, expenditure $221,203 (June 2009).

Board of Directors: Maria Kivisild Ogrydziak (Chair.); Hamid Ladjevardi (Co-Chair., Baltics); Krista Bard (Sec.); George Ramonas (Treas.).

Principal Staff: Office Man. Trevor Dane.

Address: 1025 Connecticut Ave NW, Suite 1000, Washington, DC 20036.

Telephone: (202) 785-5056; **Fax:** (202) 785-5058; **Internet:** www.usbaltic.org; **e-mail:** info@usbaltic.org.

US-Ukraine Foundation

The Foundation was established in 1991 to support democracy, a free market, and human rights in Ukraine.

Activities: Supports democratic development in Ukraine through its own projects, in the areas of public policy, economic development and education. Established the Pylyp Orlyk Institute for Democracy in Ukraine to carry out policy research. Activities include sponsoring workshops and seminars, providing support, training and technical resources, publishing and disseminating information; and providing emergency and development relief to certain sectors of the population in Ukraine. Maintains an office in Kyiv, Ukraine.

Geographical Area of Activity: Ukraine.

Restrictions: Does not make grants.

Finance: Annual revenue US $812,365, expenditure $812,229 (2009/10).

Board of Directors: Nadia K. McConnell (Pres.).

Principal Staff: Pres. Nadia K. McConnell; Vice-Pres. and COO John A. Kun.

Address: 1 Thomas Circle NW, 10th Floor Caplin Mailroom, Washington, DC 20005.

Telephone: (202) 223-2228; **Fax:** (202) 223-1224; **Internet:** www.usukraine.org; **e-mail:** info@usukraine.org.

Lawson Valentine Foundation

Founded in 1989 for general charitable purposes.

Activities: Primarily concerned with the fields of sustainable agriculture and food systems, environment, human rights, race relations and community programmes.

Geographical Area of Activity: Africa, Asia and Latin America.

Restrictions: No funds granted to groups with annual budgets of several million dollars. Maximum grant US $25,000.

Publications: Application guidelines.

Finance: Total assets US $12,498,963 (31 Dec. 2009); total grants $543,685 (2009).

Principal Staff: Programme Officer Valentine Doyle.

Address: 1000 Farmington Ave, West Hartford, CT 06107.

Telephone: (860) 570-0728; **Fax:** (860) 570-0728; **e-mail:** valentinedoyle@sbcglobal.net.

Virtual Foundation

Founded in 1996 by ECOLOGIA (q.v.), an international non-profit organization, to support community-based projects in the areas of the environment, sustainable development and health; and to encourage philanthropy by fostering partnerships between local groups and online donors.

Activities: The Foundation works in collaboration with NGOs world-wide to fund projects in the fields of the environment; health; community building and sustainable economic activity; and increasing capacity of grassroots NGOs. Project proposals submitted to the Virtual Foundation are posted on the Virtual Foundation's website for evaluation by visitors to the site, who may make a donation to the project of their choice.

Geographical Area of Activity: International.

Restrictions: No grants for emergency crisis aid or research.

Board of Directors: Randy Kritkausky (Pres.); Carolyn Schmidt (Sec.); Ed Shoener (Treas.).

Principal Staff: Programme Man. Carolyn Schmidt.

Address: POB 268, Middlebury, VT 05753.

Telephone: (802) 623-8075; **Fax:** (802) 623-8069; **Internet:** www.virtualfoundation.org; **e-mail:** cschmidt@ecologia.org.

Alberto Vollmer Foundation, Inc

Founded in 1965 by Alberto F. Vollmer for general charitable purposes; incorporated in 1987.

Activities: Operates in the fields of medicine and health, education and social welfare, through grants to hospitals and institutions of higher education in Venezuela. Also supports the Catholic Church in Venezuela.

Geographical Area of Activity: South America.

Restrictions: No grants are made to individuals.

Principal Staff: Asst Sec. Albert L. Ennist.

Address: POB 704, Butler, NJ 07405-0704.

Telephone: (201) 492-2309; **Internet:** www.fundavollmer.com; **e-mail:** fundavollmer@gmail.com.

The Wallace Foundation

The DeWitt Wallace—Reader's Digest Fund, Inc and the Lila Wallace—Reader's Digest Fund, Inc were founded in the 1950s by the founders of the Reader's Digest Association to provide support to arts and cultural organizations, and promote educational and youth development opportunities. The two foundations merged in 2003.

Activities: The Foundation operates within the USA. It seeks to enable institutions to expand learning and enrichment opportunities for all people. Current objectives are to strengthen education leadership to improve student achievement; improve after-school learning opportunities; and expand participation in the arts and culture.

Geographical Area of Activity: USA only.

Restrictions: Grants are rarely made for unsolicited projects; no grants are made to individuals.

Publications: Annual Report; education reports.

Finance: Annual revenue US $9,457,349, expenditure $30,003,410 (2010).

Board of Directors: Rob D. Nagel (Treas.).

Principal Staff: Pres. Will Miller; CFO Mary Geras.

Address: 5 Penn Plaza, 7th Floor, New York, NY 10001.

Telephone: (212) 251-9700; **Fax:** (212) 679-6990; **Internet:** www.wallacefoundation.org; **e-mail:** info@wallacefoundation.org.

Miriam G. and Ira D. Wallach Foundation

Founded in 1956 to support general charitable purposes, mainly in New York.

Activities: The Foundation provides financial assistance in the fields of international affairs, education, the humanities, social welfare and Jewish organizations.

Restrictions: Grants are made to pre-selected organizations only, applications are not accepted.

Finance: Total assets US $130,662,000 (31 Oct. 2009); total giving $8,014,117 (2008/09).

Board of Directors: Ira D. Wallach (Chair.); Kenneth L. Wallach (Vice-Chair.); Miriam G. Wallach (Vice-Chair.); Edgar Wachenheim, III (Vice-Pres.); Peter C. Siegfried (Sec.); Reginald Reinhardt (Treas.).

Principal Staff: Pres. Kenneth L. Wallach.

Address: 3 Manhattanville Rd, Purchase, NY 10577-2110.

Telephone: (914) 696-9060; **Fax:** (914) 696-1066; **e-mail:** purchase@cng-inc.com.

Walmart Foundation

Activities: Operates in four main areas: education; workforce development and economic opportunity; environmental sustainability; and health and well-being.

Finance: Grants disbursed US $110,896,000 (2008).

Principal Staff: Pres. Sylvia Mathews Burwell.

Address: Walmart, 702 SW 8th St, Walmart, Bentonville, AK 72716-8611.

Internet: walmartstores.com/CommunityGiving/203.aspx.

The Andy Warhol Foundation for the Visual Arts, Inc

Founded in 1987 by Andy Warhol for the promotion of the visual arts.

Activities: Operates nationally and (on a limited scale) internationally in the areas of the visual arts, aspects of performing arts incorporating the plastic arts, education and historic preservation and urban development. Gives grants for curatorial programmes in museums, universities and other organizations to assist in the presentation of the visual arts in innovative ways and to support artists themselves and their work; and to organizations assisting in the preservation of historic properties and parks, and promoting public participation in urban planning.

Geographical Area of Activity: Mainly USA, but organizations elsewhere are eligible to apply.

Restrictions: Unable to make grants directly to individuals.

Publications: Annual Report.

Board of Directors: Michael Straus (Chair.).

Principal Staff: Pres. Joel Wachs; CFO and Treas. K. C. Maurer.

Address: 65 Bleecker St, 7th Floor, New York, NY 10012.

Telephone: (212) 387-7555; **Fax:** (212) 387-7560; **Internet:** www.warholfoundation.org; **e-mail:** info@warholfoundation.org.

Water.org, Inc

Established by Matt Damon and Gary White in 2009 through a merger between Water Partners and H2O Africa to help provide access to clean drinking water and sanitation.

Activities: Operates in Africa, South Asia and Central America to help provide access to safe water and sanitation. Maintains offices in India and Kenya.

Geographical Area of Activity: Africa, South Asia and Central America.

Publications: newsletter.

Finance: Total assets US $6,728,148 (30 Sept. 2011); annual revenue $8,951,134, expenditure $6,540,525 (2010/11).

Principal Staff: CEO and Co-Founder Gary White; Dir of Finance and Admin. Yvonne Kean.

Address: 920 Main St, Suite 1800, Kansas City, MO 64105.

Internet: http://water.org.

Web Lab—Digital Innovations, Inc

Established in 1997 by Marc N. Weiss as a not-for-profit think tank that encourages and supports innovation on the Web, with a special emphasis on developing the potential of the medium to bring people together to explore both personal and public issues in powerful, transforming ways.

Activities: The organization's principal projects include Small Group Dialogues, which aims to provide an innovative alternative to conventional online dialogue models; Crossover, which aims to stimulate collaboration and experimentation across communications disciplines and develop groundbreaking ideas for new projects through convening filmmakers, interactive artists, designers, animators, writers, technologists, game designers, web producers and cultural theorists; and the Web Development Fund, which provides funding to committed new media innovators to create groundbreaking Web projects addressing public and/or private issues.

Geographical Area of Activity: International.

Restrictions: Proposals are not currently accepted.

Publications: Newsletter.

Principal Staff: Exec. Producer Marc N. Weiss; Dir, Collaboration and Community Jed Miller; Dir of Special Projects Suzanne Seggerman.

Address: 174 Fifth Ave, Suite 401, New York, NY 10010.

Telephone: (212) 353-0080; **Fax:** (212) 353-0572; **Internet:** www.weblab.org; **e-mail:** suzanne@weblab.org.

Weeden Foundation

Founded in 1963 by Frank Weeden to address concerns about the destruction of natural resources and the problems associated with a growing global population.

Activities: Operates nationally and internationally in the field of conservation and the environment through running programmes: Domestic Bio-diversity; International Bio-diversity (30%–40% of annual grants expenditure, with projects based in Chile and the Russian Federation); Land Acquisition (acquisition of threatened natural areas of biodiversity, with projects in Africa and Central and South America); Population; and Consumption (promoting sustainability).

Geographical Area of Activity: International.

Restrictions: No grants for individuals, nor for endowment or capital fund projects, for large organizations unless for new projects, or for general support.

Finance: Total assets US $34,157,742 (30 June 2008); annual revenue $4,140,048, expenditure $3,070,626 (2007/08).

Board of Directors: Norman Weeden (Pres.); Tina Roux (Vice-Pres.); Leslie Weeden (Sec.); Bob Weeden (Treas.).

Principal Staff: Exec. Dir Donald A. Weeden; Research Asst Charmayne S. Palomba.

Address: 747 Third Ave, 34th Floor, New York, NY 10017.

Telephone: (212) 888-1672; **Fax:** (212) 888-1354; **Internet:** www.weedenfdn.org; **e-mail:** weedenfdn@weedenfdn.org.

Harry and Jeanette Weinberg Foundation, Inc

Established in 1959 to assist the poor.

Activities: Operates in the areas of social welfare and health, particularly in housing, nutrition and socialization, through grants to organizations located in Hawaii, Pennsylvania, New York, Israel and the countries of the former USSR. An emphasis is places on the elderly and the Jewish community.

Geographical Area of Activity: USA, former USSR and Israel.

Restrictions: No grants are made to individuals.

Finance: Annual revenue US $12,734,820, expenditure $117,458,948 (2010).

Trustees: Donn Weinberg (Chair.); Alvin Awaya (Vice-Pres.); Barry I. Schloss (Treas.).

Principal Staff: Pres. Rachel Garbow Monroe.

Address: 7 Park Center Ct, Owings Mills, MD 21117-4200.

Telephone: (410) 654-8500; **Fax:** (410) 654-4900; **Internet:** hjweinbergfoundation.org; **e-mail:** rmonroe@hjweinberg .org.

The Welch Foundation

Founded in 1954 by Robert A. Welch for basic chemical research.

Activities: Supports a programme of basic research in chemistry with grants to faculty members at colleges and universities in Texas. Also sponsors a conference, a lectureship series yearly and scholarships and professorships in chemistry. Awards the Welch Award in Chemistry and the Norman Hackerman Award in Chemical Research.

Geographical Area of Activity: USA.

Publications: Annual Report; newsletters.

Finance: Annual revenue US $9,965,469, expenditure $5,531,454 (2009/10).

Board of Directors: Wilhelmina E. Robertson (Chair.); Charles W. Tate (Vice-Chair.); James T. Hackett (Treas.); Ernest H. Cockrell (Sec.).

Principal Staff: Pres. Norbert Dittrich.

Address: 5555 San Felipe, Suite 1900, Houston, TX 77056.

Telephone: (713) 961-9884; **Fax:** (713) 961-5168; **Internet:** www.welch1.org; **e-mail:** dittrich@welch1.org.

Rob and Bessie Welder Wildlife Foundation

Founded in 1954 by Mr and Mrs R. H. Welder and others to promote graduate-level education in wildlife conservation, and to support research into wildlife and methods for increasing wildlife populations.

Activities: Operates in the field of conservation and the environment, through funding research, fellowships and internships, open to US citizens or to foreigners registered at a US university for a graduate degree; and the operation of the Welder Foundation Refuge.

Geographical Area of Activity: USA, particularly Texas.

Restrictions: No grants for work outside continental USA.

Publications: Report (biennially).

Principal Staff: Dir Dr Terry L. Blankenship; Asst Dir Dr Selma Glasscock.

Address: POB 1400, Sinton, TX 78387.

Telephone: (361) 364-2643; **Fax:** (361) 364-2650; **Internet:** www.welderwildlife.org; **e-mail:** welderfoundation@ welderwildlife.org.

Wenner-Gren Foundation

Founded in 1941 as the Viking Fund, Inc, by Dr Axel L. Wenner-Gren to support research in all branches of anthropology, including cultural and social anthropology, ethnology, biological and physical anthropology, archaeology, anthropological linguistics, and in closely related disciplines concerned with human origins, development and variation.

Activities: Operates an individual research grants programme, awarding up to approximately US $25,000 for basic research in anthropology to holders of a doctorate degree and doctoral candidates undertaking dissertation projects; and offers a number of awards and scholarships, including: Richard Carley Hunt Post-doctoral Fellowships for applicants who have had a PhD for 10 years or less, and up to a maximum of approximately $40,000 is available to aid the writing up of research results for publication; Professional Development International Fellowships for training in anthropology at PhD level and for post-doctoral scholars and advanced students from developing countries; Conference Grants, of up to approximately $15,000, to organizers of conferences; and International Collaborative Research Grants, of up to approximately $30,000, to assist anthropological research projects undertaken jointly by two or more investigators from different countries, with priority given to projects involving at least one principal investigator from outside the countries of North

America and Western Europe. Sponsors the publication of *Current Anthropology* journal.

Geographical Area of Activity: International.

Restrictions: No scholarships.

Publications: Annual Report.

Finance: Annual revenue US $34,003,000, expenditure $5,707,000 (2009).

Trustees: Seth Masters (Chair.); Dr John Immerwahr (Vice-Chair.); William Cobb (Treas.); Maugha Kenny (Sec.).

Principal Staff: Pres. Dr Leslie C. Aiello; Maugha Kenny (Vice-Pres. for Finance).

Address: 470 Park Ave S, 8th Floor, New York, NY 10001.

Telephone: (212) 683-5000; **Fax:** (212) 683-9151; **Internet:** www.wennergren.org; **e-mail:** inquiries@wennergren.org.

Weyerhaeuser Family Foundation, Inc

Founded in 1950, and formerly known as the Weyerhaeuser Foundation, by F. K. Weyerhaeuser, E. W. Davis, Margaret W. Driscoll, Sarah-Maud W. Rosenberry, Frederick Weyerhaeuser, G. F. Jewett, Elizabeth W. Titcomb, Carl A. Weyerhaeuser, C. Davis Weyerhaeuser and John P. Weyerhaeuser, Jr, for the relief of the poor, the advancement of the Christian religion, the advancement of education and science, including medical science, and the application of the same through hospitals, clinics and research institutions. Since the 1960s emphasis has been placed on the support of programmes of national and international significance that attempt to identify and correct the causes of maladjustment in society.

Activities: Operates nationally and internationally in the fields of the arts and humanities (through programmes that assist the public to understand various art forms), education (opportunities for minority groups, religious training, youth development projects and private higher education), health (mental health, alcoholism, psychiatry), social welfare, international activities, religion and the environment, science and technology (environmental preservation, utilization of scarce resources and forestry), through grants to institutions. The Foundation supports international projects that enable people to help themselves via population planning, agricultural improvements, self-government and peace education.

Geographical Area of Activity: International.

Restrictions: The Foundation does not normally make grants for projects with limited geographical emphasis, operating budgets, annual campaigns, building and equipment, elementary and secondary education, lobbying or propaganda. Nor does it make grants to individuals, for scholarships, fellowships or for travel.

Publications: Annual Report.

Finance: Grants disbursed US $657,254 (2010).

Principal Staff: Grants Admin. Gayle Roth; Programme Consultant Peter A. Konrad.

Address: 2000 Wells Fargo Pl., 30 East Seventh St, St Paul, MN 55101-4930.

Telephone: (651) 215-4408; **Internet:** www .wfamilyfoundation.org; **e-mail:** dlc@fidcouns.com.

Whirlpool Foundation

Founded in 1951 by Louis and Frederick Upton (Co-Founders of the Whirlpool Corporation) to improve the quality of life in the communities where the corporation operates.

Activities: Operates world-wide, particularly in the USA and Canada, Western and Eastern Europe, and Asia, within three programme areas: the quality of family life; cultural diversity; and life-long learning. Principally aimed at projects likely to have an impact in communities where the company has a presence. Also runs a programme of citizenship grants within the USA, aimed at organizations supporting general education, health and human services, arts and culture and civic and community; and employee-directed programmes.

Geographical Area of Activity: International.

Restrictions: No grants are given to religious or labour organizations.

Trustees: D. Jeff Noel (Chair.); John Geddes (Sec. and Treas.).

Principal Staff: Pres. D. Jeff Noel; Vice-Pres. Dave Binkley; Man. Candy Garman.

Address: 2000 North M-63, Benton Harbor, MI 49022.

Telephone: (269) 923-5580; **Fax:** (269) 925-0154; **Internet:** www.whirlpoolcorp.com/responsibility/building_communities/whirlpool_foundation.aspx; **e-mail:** whirlpool_foundation@whirlpool.com.

Whitehall Foundation, Inc

Founded in 1937 by George M. Moffett, Jeremiah Milbank, Willis D. Wood, Frederick T. Fisher, Morris Sayre, Frank H. Hall and Linus C. Coggan to give financial aid to charitable, benevolent or educational work through such agencies or institutions as the Trustees may determine.

Activities: Assists scholarly work in the life sciences, through a programme of grants and grants-in-aid primarily targeting dynamic areas of basic biological research that are not generally supported by Federal agencies or other foundations with specialized missions. Currently interested in basic research in neurobiology: invertebrate and vertebrate neurobiology, exclusive of human beings, including investigation into the neural mechanisms involved in sensory, motor and other complex functions of the whole organism as these relate to behaviour. Research grants are for up to three years, awarded to established scientists working at accredited institutions in the USA. Grants-in-aid are for a one year period and are designed especially for young postgraduate investigators who have not yet established themselves, as well as to senior scientists.

Geographical Area of Activity: USA.

Restrictions: Funds are not awarded to investigators who have substantial existing or potential support, for construction projects, office expenses, nor for research focused primarily on disease(s) unless it will also provide insights into normal functioning. The Foundation does not consider grant applications from outside the USA.

Publications: Report of operations and financial statement.

Finance: Research grants range from US $30,000–$75,000 per year; grants-in-aid do not exceed $30,000.

Principal Staff: Pres. George M. Moffett, II.

Address: POB 3423, Palm Beach, FL 33480; 125 Worth Ave, Suite 220, Palm Beach, FL 33480.

Telephone: (561) 655-4474; **Fax:** (561) 655-1296; **Internet:** www.whitehall.org; **e-mail:** email@whitehall.org.

The Elie Wiesel Foundation for Humanity

Founded in 1986 by Elie Wiesel, winner of the Nobel Peace Prize, for the promotion of human rights and peace worldwide, and to combat indifference to injustice, particularly in parts of the world where those rights are repeatedly ignored, abused or denied, to preserve memory by encouraging an understanding or appreciation of history to create a more humane and hopeful future.

Activities: Seeks to promote human rights and peace through the creation of a new forum for the discussion of the ethical and moral issues confronting the world. Holds international conferences. Established a Humanitarian Award, and the Elie Wiesel Prize in Ethics (an essay competition). Operates also in Israel, in the area of education.

Geographical Area of Activity: World-wide.

Finance: Total assets US $754,274 (31 Dec. 2008); annual revenue $5,623,747, expenditure $1,357,369 (2008).

Board of Directors: Prof. Elie Wiesel (Pres.); Marion Wiesel (Vice-Pres.); Marc Winkelman (Sec. and Treas.).

Principal Staff: Exec. Dir Daniel Schwartz; Programme Coordinator Leslie Myers.

Address: 555 Madison Ave, 20th Floor, New York, NY 10022.

Fax: (212) 490-6006; **Internet:** www.eliewieselfoundation.org; **e-mail:** info@eliewieselfoundation.org.

Wikimedia Foundation

Established in 2003 by Jimmy Wales, Co-Founder of the Wikipedia online encyclopedia, to disseminate information worldwide through the Internet, in multi-lingual format.

Activities: Operates Internet information sites, including Wikipedia, dictionaries and e-books.

Finance: Total assets US $26,165,567 (30 June 2011); annual revenue $24,785,092, expenditure $17,889,794 (2010/11).

Board of Trustees: Ting Chen (Chair.); Jimmy Wales (Founder); Stu West (Vice-Chair. and Treas.); Jan-Bart de Vreede (Vice-Chair.); Samuel Klein (Exec. Sec.).

Principal Staff: Exec. Dir Sue Gardner; Deputy Dir Erik Möller.

Address: 149 New Montgomery St, 3rd Floor, San Francisco, CA 94105.

Telephone: (415) 839-6885; **Fax:** (415) 882-0495; **Internet:** wikimediafoundation.org; **e-mail:** info@wikimedia.org.

Wilbur Foundation

Established in 1975 by Marguerite Eyer Wilbur.

Activities: Operates in the field of the humanities, particularly history, literature, religion and philosophy, supporting institutions and projects that are calculated to uphold or carry on the 'permanent things of society'. Support includes funding for a resident fellowship scheme at the Russell Kirk Center in Mecosta, Michigan.

Geographical Area of Activity: USA.

Restrictions: No grants are made to individuals, with the exception of Residential Writing Grants fellowships at the Russell Kirk Center, Mecosta, MI.

Finance: Total assets US $2,163,560 (31 Dec. 2010); total giving $140,341 (2010).

Officers and Trustees: Gary R. Ricks (Pres.); Annette Y. Kirk (Vice-Pres.); Gleaves Whitney (Treas.).

Address: POB 3370, Santa Barbara, CA 93130-3370.

Telephone: (805) 884-9538; **Fax:** (805) 563-1082; **e-mail:** info@wilburfoundation.org.

The WILD Foundation—International Wilderness Leadership Foundation

Founded in 1974 by Ian Player as the International Wilderness Leadership Foundation to protect and sustain critical wild areas, wilderness values and endangered wildlife throughout the world, with a special emphasis on Southern Africa, by initiating or assisting environmental education, experiential projects and programmes.

Activities: Operates internationally in the field of conservation and the environment. Runs programmes on wilderness and wildlife, eco-tourism and education and training; projects are conducted in Southern Africa and elsewhere. Promotes the wise use of wildland resources and provides environmental education and training. Works in partnership with other organizations world-wide. WILD's flagship programme is the World Wilderness Congress.

Geographical Area of Activity: International, with an emphasis on southern Africa.

Publications: include Annual Report; *The White Rhino Saga*; *Climate for Life: Meeting the Global Challenge*; *Protecting Wild Nature on Native Lands*; *When Elephants Fly*; *International Journal of Wilderness*; *A Handbook on International Wilderness Law and Policy*.

Finance: Net assets US $1,334,250 (31 Dec. 2008); annual revenue $2,972,177, expenditure $3,042,905 (2008).

Board of Directors: Charlotte Baron (Chair.).

Principal Staff: Pres. Vance G. Martin.

Address: 717 Poplar Ave, Boulder, CO 80304 USA.

Telephone: (303) 442-8811; **Fax:** (303) 442-8877; **Internet:** www.wild.org; **e-mail:** info@wild.org.

WILPF—Women's International League for Peace and Freedom

Founded in 1915 to create an environment of political, economic, social and psychological freedom for all members of humanity.

Activities: Operates campaigns and advocacy projects worldwide on a variety of issues including peace and disarmament, empowerment of women and racial justice. WILPF has an international office located in Geneva, Switzerland, a UN office in New York City, and sections in 37 countries world-wide.

Geographical Area of Activity: International.

Restrictions: Not a grant-making organization.

Finance: Total assets US $271,395; annual revenue $599,952, expenditure $414,449 (2008).

National Board: Laura Roskos (Pres.); Barbara Reed (Sec.); Eva Havlicsek (Treas.); Randa Solick (Program Cttee Co-Chair.); Georgia Pinkel (Program Cttee Co-Chair.); Robin Lloyd (Development Chair.); Joan Bazar (Personnel Cttee Chair.); Darien Delu (Nominating Cttee Chair.).

Principal Staff: Dir of Operations Laurie Belton.

Address: 11 Arlington St, Boston, MA 02116.

Telephone: (617) 266-0999; **Fax:** (617) 266-1688; **Internet:** www.wilpf.org; **e-mail:** lbelton@wilpf.org.

E. O. Wilson Biodiversity Foundation

Founded with the aim of fostering the appropriate business and educational strategies to maintain environmental biodiversity.

Principal Staff: Pres. Morgan Ryan.

Address: POB 1356, Carrboro, NC 27510.

Telephone: (919) 933-1195; **Internet:** www .eowilsonfoundation.org; **e-mail:** info@eowilsonfoundation .org.

Woodrow Wilson International Center for Scholars

Founded in 1968 as a memorial to President Woodrow Wilson to symbolize and strengthen the fruitful relation between the world of learning and the world of public affairs. The Center is part of the Smithsonian Institution (q.v.), but is administered by its own Board of Trustees.

Activities: Awards 20–25 annual post-doctoral fellowships for full-time research to be conducted at the Center by scholars from any country. Fellowships are awarded within the broad themes of governance, including the key issues of the development of democratic institutions, democratic society, civil society and citizen participation; the US role in the world and issues of partnership and leadership; and key long-term future challenges confronting the USA and the world.

Geographical Area of Activity: World-wide.

Publications: Annual Report; *Centerpoint* (monthly newsletter); *The Wilson Quarterly*; books; conference reports.

Finance: Total assets US $114,340,759 (30 Sept. 2010); annual revenue $35,756,231, expenditure $35,498,938 (2009/10).

Trustees: Joseph B. Gildenhorn (Chair.); Sander R. Gerber (Vice-Chair.).

Principal Staff: Dir, Pres. and CEO Jane Harman; Exec. Vice-Pres. Michael Van Dusen.

Address: Ronald Reagan Building and International Trade Center, 1 Woodrow Wilson Plaza, 1300 Pennsylvania Ave NW, Washington, DC 20004-3027.

Telephone: (202) 691-4000; **Fax:** (202) 691-4001; **Internet:** www.wilsoncenter.org; **e-mail:** sharon.mccarter@ wilsoncenter.org.

Woodrow Wilson National Fellowship Foundation

Founded in 1945 to respond to a shortage of college faculty at the conclusion of World War II by offering talented students the opportunity to attend doctoral programmes and begin college teaching careers. Today's 20,000 Fellows include 13 Nobel Laureates, 35 MacArthur 'genius grant' recipients, 11 Pulitzer Prize winners, two Fields Medalists in mathematics and many other noted scholars and leaders.

Activities: The Foundation has a suite of Fellowships that support the development of future leaders at a variety of career stages in several critical fields: teaching; foreign affairs; conservation; women and gender; religion and ethics; access and opportunity.

Geographical Area of Activity: USA.

Publications: Annual Report; newsletter (2 a year); policy reports; news releases.

Finance: Assets US $34,277,435; annual revenue $27,846,482, expenditure $14,266,439 (2008).

Board of Trustees: Frederick L.A. Grauer (Chair.); Walter W. Buckley, Jr (Chair.-Elect).

Principal Staff: Pres. Arthur Levine.

Address: POB 5281, Princeton, NJ 08543-5281; 5 Vaughn Dr., Suite 300, Princeton, NJ 08540-6313.

Telephone: (609) 452-7007; **Fax:** (609) 452-0066; **Internet:** www.woodrow.org; **e-mail:** marrow@woodrow.org.

Windstar Foundation

Founded by John Denver and Tom Crum in 1976 to promote an holistic approach to global issues through encouraging people to make responsible choices and take responsibility for a peaceful and environmentally sustainable future.

Activities: The Foundation aims to raise environmental awareness and develop leadership potential in all people. Programmes include the Environmental Studies Scholarship awarded to first-year university students in the fields of environmental studies or environmental engineering; the Trees from Grass-Roots project, which raises funds for the Foundation, re-forests areas damaged by natural disasters, erosion or excessive logging in the USA and abroad, and aims to involve all its members in a common project; and EarthCamps, summer camps for children.

Geographical Area of Activity: World-wide.

Restrictions: Does not make grants.

Publications: *Vision* (newsletter).

Finance: Annual revenue US $51,266,640, expenditure $47,102,400 (2008/09).

Board of Trustees: Ron Deutschendorf (Chair.); JoLynn Long (Treas.).

Principal Staff: Pres. Ron Deutschendorf; Vice-Pres. JoLynn Long; Exec. Dir Pam Peterson.

Address: 2317 Snowmass Creek Rd, Snowmass, CO 81654.

Telephone: (970) 927-5430; **Internet:** www.wstar.org; **e-mail:** windstarco@wstar.org.

Winrock International

Formed in 1985 by the merger of the Agricultural Development Council (founded in 1953 by John D. Rockefeller, III), the International Agricultural Development Service (founded in 1975 by the Rockefeller Foundation, q.v.) and the Winrock International Livestock Research and Training Center (founded in 1975 by the bequest of Winthrop Rockefeller). Aims to reduce poverty and hunger through sustainable agricultural and rural development.

Activities: Offers sustainable solutions through comprehensive, integrated programmes in more than 100 countries, responding to changing economic, environmental and social conditions. Technical assistance and development services are grouped into three programmes: Empowerment and Civic Engagement aimed at strengthening capacity of women, children, youth and civil society organizations; Enterprise and Agriculture to support establishment and growth of small and medium-sized enterprises and agricultural initiatives targeting sustainable production driven by market demand; Environment—Forestry, Energy and Ecosystem Services— promoting sustainable use and management of natural resources to support the food and income needs of growing populations and the health of the planet. Maintains an office in Arlington, Virginia.

Geographical Area of Activity: Asia, Africa, the Middle East, North, Central and South America, the Caribbean, Eastern Europe.

Publications: *Innovations* (e-mail newsletter); global projects and financial statement report; project fact sheets; development education series books; research papers.

Finance: Total assets US $74,666,089 (2008); annual revenue $43,563,769, expenditure $67,355,011 (2008).

Board of Directors: Brooks Browne (Chair.); Elizabeth Campbell (Vice-Chair.).

Principal Staff: Pres. and CEO Frank Tugwell; Vice-Pres., Operations Ron Hubbard.

Address: 2101 Riverfront Dr., Little Rock, AR 72202.

Telephone: (501) 280-3000; **Fax:** (501) 280-3090; **Internet:** www.winrock.org; **e-mail:** information@winrock.org.

WMF—World Monuments Fund

Established in 1965 for the preservation of historic structures.

Activities: Works to preserve historic structures at sites in more than 90 countries. Headquarters in New York City and offices in Paris, London, Madrid and Lisbon. Issues World Monuments Watch, a list of 100 most endangered sites, biennially.

Geographical Area of Activity: World-wide.

Publications: Project reports; Annual Report.

Finance: total assets US $57,268,443 (30 June 2011); annual revenue US $24,046,709, expenditure $17,742,783 (2010/11).

Board of Trustees: Christopher Ohrstrom (Chair.); James E. Jordan (Vice-Chair.); Robert W. Wilson (Vice-Chair. and Treas.); Robert J. Geniesse (Sec.).

Principal Staff: Pres. Bonnie Burnham; Exec. Vice-Pres. and COO Lisa Ackerman.

Address: 350 Fifth Ave, Suite 2412, New York, NY 10118.

Telephone: (646) 424-9594; **Fax:** (646) 424-9593; **Internet:** www.wmf.org; **e-mail:** wmf@wmf.org.

Women for International Peace and Arbitration—WIPA

Founded in 1985, non-profit, public benefit organization that aims to promote the peaceful settlement of international disputes, and gender equality.

Activities: Acts as an advocate for peace and non-violence, and supports programmes that work to eliminate human rights abuses, especially those affecting the rights of women and children. Recent projects have included building schools and funding university education for girls in the People's Republic of China. Affiliate organizations are based in Canada, Sierra Leone and Switzerland.

Geographical Area of Activity: World-wide.

Principal Staff: Pres. Juana Conrad.

Address: POB 9619, Glendale, CA 91226-0619.

Telephone: (818) 240-7014; **Fax:** (818) 240-7014; **e-mail:** information@wipa.org.

Women's Environment and Development Organization—WEDO

An international advocacy network established in 1990 by Bella Abzug and Mim Kelber to increase the power of women world-wide as policy-makers in governance and policy-making institutions.

Activities: Works in three programme areas: Climate Change; Corporate Accountability and Governance. Established the Women's Caucus, an advocacy organization participating at UN and other inter-governmental conferences.

Geographical Area of Activity: International.

Restrictions: Not a grant-making organization; carries out its own projects.

Publications: Newsletters.

Board of Directors: Monique Essed Fernandes (Chair.).

Principal Staff: Exec. Dir Cate Owren; Finance Man. Ugoagha Jessica Awa.

Address: 355 Lexington Ave, 3rd Floor, New York, NY 10017.

Telephone: (212) 973-0325; **Fax:** (212) 973-0335; **Internet:** www.wedo.org; **e-mail:** cate@wedo.org.

World Concern

International relief and development organization founded in 1955 to alleviate human suffering in the world.

Activities: Operates in the field of aid to less-developed countries, through emergency relief, rehabilitation and long-term development programmes. Projects have included vocational training to equip people with the skills to support themselves; providing emergency food supplies to famine victims; training farmers in improved agricultural methods of food production; supplying survivors of disasters with food, clothing and critical aid.

Geographical Area of Activity: Africa, Asia, and North, Central and South America.

Restrictions: Not a grant-making organization.

Publications: Annual Report.

Finance: Annual revenue US $81,453,000, expenditure $81,987,000 (2009/10).

Board: Deborah Limb (Chair.); Kirsten Miller (Vice-Chair.); Kevin Gabelein (Treas.); Stephen Grey (Sec.).

Principal Staff: Pres. David Eller.

Address: 19303 Fremont Ave North, Seattle, WA 98133.

Telephone: (206) 546-7201; **Fax:** (206) 546-7269; **Internet:** www.worldconcern.org; **e-mail:** info@worldconcern.org.

World Education, Inc

Non-profit organization dedicated to improving the lives of the poor through economic and social development. Founded in 1951 to meet the needs of the educationally disadvantaged, World Education provides training and technical assistance in nonformal education across a wide array of sectors.

Activities: Operates in the field of development aid, with an emphasis on education and capacity building, with projects in areas including child labour and trafficking, skills training, literacy, civil society development, support for refugees, and sustainable agriculture. Provides training and technical assistance for adults and children who are not in formal education to help generate an income for themselves and their families; provides relief and assistance to refugees and displaced people; runs an enterprise development programme; and educates people about the environment, reproductive and family health, including HIV/AIDS prevention. Projects aim to develop individual growth as well as contributing to the community and the nation.

Geographical Area of Activity: Africa, Asia, North, Central and South America, and Eastern Europe.

Restrictions: Not a grant-making organization.

Publications: *IDR Reports*; training manuals; development resources; Annual Report; newsletter.

Finance: Total assets US $4,389,150 (30 June 2007); annual revenue $32,459,272, expenditure on programmes $32,269,283 (2006/07).

Board of Trustees: Leland B. Goldberg (Chair.); Fred O'Regan (Treas.).

Principal Staff: Pres. Joel H. Lamstein.

Address: 44 Farnsworth St, Boston, MA 02210.

Telephone: (617) 482-9485; **Fax:** (617) 482-0617; **Internet:** www.worlded.org; **e-mail:** wei@worlded.org.

World Emergency Relief—WER

Established in 1985, a Christian-founded, public-benefit, non-profit organization aiming to help people in need around the world, especially children and families.

Activities: Responds to aid requests from around the world, delivering emergency supplies to people in need, including food, clothing, medical care, shelter, education and emotional and spiritual support. Assistance is particularly directed towards children: the organization has supported many orphanages and child refugees. Runs domestic programmes focusing on the needs of Native Americans, and to provide basic needs to severely wounded returning service members . Currently prefers to direct its work towards its own projects or to partner projects in the areas supported. Maintains offices in Honduras, Asia, France the Netherlands, and the United Kingdom.

Geographical Area of Activity: Africa, Asia, North, Central and South America and the Caribbean, South-Eastern Europe, Russian Federation.

Restrictions: Does not accept unsolicited requests for support. No grants are made to individuals.

Publications: Annual Reports; financial statements.

Finance: Annual expenditure US $23,813,382 (2010).

Board of Directors: Gary Becks (Chair.); W. Foster Rich (Vice-Chair.); Lawrence E. Cutting (Sec.).

Principal Staff: CEO Kristy Scott; CFO Michael Batarseh.

Address: POB 1760, Temecula, CA 92593; 27715 Jefferson Ave, Suite 205, Temecula, CA 92590.

Telephone: (951) 225-6700; **Fax:** (951) 225-6799; **Internet:** www.wer-us.org; **e-mail:** info@wer-us.org.

World Federation for Mental Health—WFMH

Non-profit organization founded in 1948 to advance the prevention of mental illnesses around the world, promote the cause of mental health and raise public awareness, and improve the treatment and care of mental and emotional disorders.

Activities: Works through public education programmes. Holds a World Congress biennially, alternating with a smaller conference on evidence-based prevention of mental and behavioural disorders and promotion of mental health. Works through nine regional vice-presidents (Africa, Eastern Mediterranean, Europe, Mexico and Central America, North America and the Caribbean, Oceania, South America, South-East Asia and Western Pacific) to promote regional and local programmes and activities. Eight academic collaborating centres at universities provide advice. Established annual project—World Mental Health Day—in 1992.

Geographical Area of Activity: International.

Restrictions: Does not make grants.

Publications: Newsletter; Annual Report; World Mental Health Day campaign packet (distributed internationally); mental health/illness related educational material.

Finance: Annual expenditure US $606,475 (2008).

Executive Committee: Deborah Wan (Pres.); George Christodolou (Pres.-Elect); Anthony Fowke (Immediate Past Pres.); Mohammed Abou-Saleh (Vice-Pres. Constituency Development); Ellen R. Mercer (Vice-Pres. Program Development); John Bowis (Vice-Pres. Government); Helen Miller (Treas.); Larry Cimino (Sec.).

Principal Staff: Sec.-Gen. and CEO Dr Vijay K. Ganju; Dir of Admin. Deborah Maguire.

Address: POB 807, Occoquan, VA 22125.

Internet: www.wfmh.org; **e-mail:** info@wfmh.com.

World Learning

Founded in 1932 as The Experiment in International Living to promote inter-cultural understanding and community development.

Activities: Operates in the fields of education, training, international exchange and international development, through projects including: World Learning for International Development; the School for International Training; and the Experiment in International Living. Administers social and economic projects in international development and training world-wide under US government and international contracts and grants, specializing in developing the skills and potential of individuals and institutions. Active in five broad sectors: democracy and governance, education, training and exchange, institutional capacity building, and societies in transition.

Geographical Area of Activity: World-wide.

Publications: Annual Reports; *SIT Occasional Papers Series*; *World Learning Odyssey*; and others.

Finance: Total assets US $75,160,920 (30 June 2011); annual revenue $127,973,603, expenditure $125,962,585 (2010/11).

Board of Trustees: Rosamond Delori (Chair.); Robert W. Adams (Vice-Chair.); Thomas Hiatt (Vice-Chair.); Dana Kull (Vice-Chair.).

Principal Staff: Pres. and CEO Adam Weinberg; Sr Vice-Pres. and CFO Nancy Rowden Brock.

Address: Kipling Rd, POB 676, Brattleboro, VT 05302-0676.

Telephone: (802) 257-7751; **Fax:** (802) 258-3248; **Internet:** www.worldlearning.org; **e-mail:** info@worldlearning.org.

World Lung Foundation

Established in 2004 with the aim of assisting communities around the world in preventing and and managing lung disease.

Activities: The projects supported by the Foundation include: research and scientific exchanges; pilot projects in treatment and control of tuberculosis and lung disease; training of health personnel in Sub-Saharan Africa.

Geographical Area of Activity: World-wide.

Publications: Annual report; economic reports.

Finance: Annual revenue US $58,893,652, expenditure $50,268,019 (2009).

Board of Directors: Louis James de Viel Castel (Pres.); Marc Sznajderman (Vice-Pres.); Andrew S. Rendeiro (Treas.); Nils W. Billo (Sec.).

Principal Staff: CEO Peter A. Baldini; Vice-Pres. of Operations Joanna Thomas.

Address: 61 Broadway, Suite 2800, New York, NY 10006.

Telephone: (212) 542-8870; **Internet:** www .worldlungfoundation.org; **e-mail:** info@ worldlungfoundation.org.

World Neighbors

Founded in 1951 by Dr John L. Peters. Aims to improve the lives of those living in rural communities in developing countries through long-term development.

Activities: World Neighbors works to improve agriculture, health care and family planning, conservation, water and sanitation, and small business development through programmes in 15 countries in Asia, Africa and Latin America and the Caribbean. The organization's programmes focus on helping individuals and communities determine their own solutions to poverty, through long-term sustainable development projects.

Geographical Area of Activity: Africa, Latin America and the Caribbean, Asia.

Restrictions: Not a grant-making organization. Works directly with selected partners in the regions in which it operates.

Publications: Books; videos; papers; financial statements; Annual Report; monthly e-newsletter; *Neighbors* magazine.

Finance: Annual revenue US $5,706,505, expenditure $6,266,719 (2009/10).

Board of Trustees: Steve Schomberg (Chair.); David Bearden (Vice-Chair.); Carl James (Treas.); Marnie Taylor (Sec.).

Principal Staff: Pres. and CEO Melanie Macdonald.

Address: 4127 NW 122nd St, Oklahoma City, OK 73120.

Telephone: (405) 752-9700; **Fax:** (405) 752-9393; **Internet:** www.wn.org; **e-mail:** eengelke@wn.org.

World Peace Foundation—WPF

Founded in 1910 by Edwin Ginn to encourage international peace and co-operation.

Activities: Seeks to advance the cause of world peace through study, analysis and the advocacy of wise action. The Foundation, through a series of interrelated projects, aims to examine how the forces of world order may most effectively engage in preventive diplomacy, create early warning systems leading to early preventive action, engage in regional conflict avoidance and attack the underlying causes of enmity and war. The Foundation is active in Burma, Cyprus, Haiti, Sri Lanka, and the whole of Africa. It focuses on failed states and global governance.

Geographical Area of Activity: Africa, Central Asia, South-East Asia, Cyprus.

Restrictions: Support only for its self-initiated projects.

Publications: *World Peace Foundation Reports*; books.

Board of Trustees: Philip S. Khoury (Chair.); Thomas M. O'Reilly (Treas.); Richard D. Allen (Counsel).

Principal Staff: Exec. Dir Alex de Waal.

Address: POB 382144, Cambridge, MA 02238-2144.

Telephone: (617) 823-1461; **Fax:** (617) 491-8588; **Internet:** www.worldpeacefoundation.org; **e-mail:** worldpeace1910@gmail.com.

World Research Foundation

Founded in 1984 to work in the fields of medicine and health.

Activities: Makes information available to the public on the latest developments in health and environmental issues; informs the public and health-care professionals about technology unavailable in the USA; maintains a library; provides consultancy services to governmental, medical, and scientific organizations throughout the world; organizes International Health Congresses; and conducts data searches in the fields of health and the environment. Maintains European headquarters in Stuttgart, Germany, and offices in the Far East.

Geographical Area of Activity: International.

Publications: Newsletter.

Address: 41 Bell Rock Plaza, Sedona, AZ 86351.

Telephone: (928) 284-3300; **Fax:** (928) 284-3530; **Internet:** www.wrf.org; **e-mail:** info@wrf.org.

World Resources Institute

Founded in 1982 with a grant from the John D. and Catherine T. MacArthur Foundation (q.v.) as a centre for policy research seeking to discover how the world's people and nations can meet their basic needs and economic requirements without at the same time undermining the earth's ability to provide the natural resources and environmental quality on which life, growth and security depend.

Activities: Carries out specific policy research in four major areas: Climate, Energy and Transport; Governance and Access; Markets and Enterprise; and People and Ecosystems. In developing countries the Institute's Center for International Development and Environment provides policy advice, technical assistance and other supporting services to governments, NGOs and local groups charged with managing natural resources and economic development. Research is conducted by the Institute's own staff or by visiting fellows, or may be undertaken in collaboration with other institutions and affiliated groups throughout the USA and abroad. The Institute organizes conferences and seminars, issues publications and offers material for use in the media.

Geographical Area of Activity: International.

Publications: Annual Report; *WRI Digest;* books; reports; studies; papers; handbooks; videos and CD-ROMs.

Finance: Annual revenue US $37,376,000, expenditure $37,376,000 (2009/10).

Board of Directors: James A. Harmon (Chair.); Harriet Babbitt (Vice-Chair.).

Principal Staff: Interim Pres. Manish Bapna; CFO and Vice-Pres. for Finance and Admin. Steve Barker.

Address: 10 G St NE, Suite 800, Washington, DC 20002.

Telephone: (202) 729-7600; **Fax:** (202) 729-7610; **Internet:** www.wri.org; **e-mail:** moko@wri.org.

World Vision Inc

International Christian organization founded in 1950 that aims to help the poor through humanitarian programmes and relief.

Activities: Engages in emergency relief, providing aid for victims of disaster, including food, clothing and shelter; and long-term development and advocacy work. Programmes are carried out in the areas of community development, child sponsorship, education, health care, agriculture, micro-enterprise and clean water and sanitation. The majority of World Vision's work is child-focused.

Geographical Area of Activity: International.

Publications: Annual Report; *World Vision Magazine* (quarterly); *World Vision News* (quarterly); *World Vision eNews* (monthly); reports; research papers; books.

Finance: Total assets US $287,843,000 (30 Sept. 2011); annual revenue $1,058,347,000, expenditure $1,079,055,000 (2010/11).

Principal Staff: Pres. Richard E. Stearns; Sr Vice-Pres. and CFO Larry Probus.

Address: POB 9716, Department W, Federal Way, WA 98063-9716.

Telephone: (253) 815-1000; **Internet:** www.worldvision.org; **e-mail:** info@worldvision.org.

Worldwatch Institute

Founded in 1974 as a non-profit research organization that aims to inform policy-makers and the public about emerging global problems, and the implications of links between the world economy and its environmental support systems.

Activities: Works to foster an environmentally sustainable society, through the provision of information. Disseminates the results of research regarding global environmental issues through a number of publications, thus raising public awareness of environmental threats. Focuses on issues such as climate change, depletion of the ozone layer, pollution of the oceans, population growth, biodiversity, ecosystems, sustainable agriculture and economics, the impact of globalization on the environment, and energy.

Geographical Area of Activity: International and USA.

Restrictions: Does not make grants to individuals or organizations.

Publications: include *State of the World* (annually); *Vital Signs* (annually); *World Watch* (magazine, 6 a year); Annual Report; books; papers.

Finance: Annual revenue US $3,417,104, expenditure $3,321,080 (2010/11).

Board of Directors: Ed Groark (Chair.); Robert Charles Friese (Vice-Chair.); Nancy Hitz (Sec.).

Principal Staff: Pres. Robert Engelman; Dir of Finance and Admin. Barbara Fallin.

Address: 1776 Massachusetts Ave NW, Suite 800, Washington, DC 20036-1904.

Telephone: (202) 452-1999; **Fax:** (202) 296-7365; **Internet:** www.worldwatch.org; **e-mail:** worldwatch@worldwatch.org.

The Helene Wurlitzer Foundation of New Mexico

Founded in 1954 by Mrs Howard E. Wurlitzer to promote the arts and humanities.

Activities: Provides artist residencies in Taos, New Mexico to national and international artists in the literary and visual arts, and to musicians and composers.

Geographical Area of Activity: South-Western USA.

Restrictions: Artist residencies offered to individuals only.

Finance: Assets US $2,471,247 (March 2009); total giving $51,306 (2009).

Board of Directors: Rena Rosequist (Pres.); P. Nelson (Vice-Pres.); E. Ebie (Treas.); Harold Hahn (Sec.).

Principal Staff: Exec. Dir Michael A. Knight.

Address: POB 1891, Taos, NM 87571.

Telephone: (505) 758-2413; **Fax:** (505) 758-2559; **Internet:** www.wurlitzerfoundation.org; **e-mail:** hwf@taosnet.com.

X Prize Foundation

Established to promote innovation that will benefit humanity.

Activities: Awards prizes of US $10m. to first team to achieve a specific goal in areas that include Exploration (Space and Underwater); Life Sciences; Energy and Environment; Education; and Global Development. In 2011 it was announced that the prize would be offered for the development of a medical diagnostic device similar to the 'tricorder' that appeared in television science fiction series Star Trek.

Geographical Area of Activity: World-wide.

Board of Trustees: Dr Peter H. Diamandis (Founder and Chair.); Robert K. Weiss (Vice-Chair.); Gregg E. Maryniak (Sec.); J. Barry Thompson (Treas.).

Principal Staff: Pres. Robert K. Weiss.

Address: 5510 Lincoln Blvd, Suite 100, Playa Vista, CA 90094-2034.

Telephone: (310) 741-4880; **Fax:** (310) 741-4974; **Internet:** www.xprize.org.

Zonta International Foundation—ZIF

Founded in 1984, Zonta International is a world-wide service organization of executives in business and the professions working together to advance the status of women. There are more than 30,000 members in more than 1,200 clubs in 63 countries and geographic areas, supporting women's advancement, rights, education and leadership.

Activities: The mission of the Zonta International Foundation is to support the charitable and educational programmes of Zonta International through effective fund-raising, investment of funds, and the distribution of proceeds. Through its financial support of Zonta International programmes, the Foundation becomes the catalyst for greater service to women throughout the world.

Geographical Area of Activity: International.

Restrictions: No grants to individuals except for established scholarships; international development projects for women primarily through UN agencies.

Finance: Total assets US $14,231,897 (31 May 2011); annual revenue $6,240,493, expenditure $5,843,440 (2010/11).

Principal Staff: Pres. Dianne Curtis.

Address: 1211 West 22nd St, Suite 900, Oak Brook, IL 60523.

Telephone: (630) 928-1400; **Fax:** (630) 928-1559; **Internet:** www.zonta.org; **e-mail:** zontaintl@zonta.org.

Uruguay

FOUNDATION CENTRE AND CO-ORDINATING BODY

Instituto del Tercer Mundo—ITeM (Third World Institute)

Established in 1989 to promote civil society internationally, in particular with the aim of building democratic and environmentally sustainable societies.

Activities: Aims to promote the development of civil society nationally and internationally, through communication, information, research and education. Encourages networking between organizations, through the promotion of electronic information networks. Publishes books on the subject of the third sector. Has consultative status at the UN.

Geographical Area of Activity: International.

Restrictions: No grants to individuals; grants made only in specific countries or regions.

Publications: *The World Guide* (biennially); *Social Watch Report* (annual); *Revista del Sur*; *Tercer Mundo Económico*; books and magazines and CD-ROMs.

Finance: Financed by grants from international organizations, and from the sale of its own products and services.

Executive Board: Celia Eccher (Pres.); Álvaro Padrón (Sec.).

Principal Staff: Exec. Dir Roberto Bissio.

Address: 18 de julio 1077/903, Montevideo 11100.

Telephone: (2) 9020490; **Fax:** (2) 9020113; **Internet:** www.item.org.uy; **e-mail:** item@item.org.uy.

FOUNDATIONS, TRUSTS AND NON-PROFIT ORGANIZATIONS

Foro Juvenil (Youth Forum)

Established in 1981 to promote opportunities for young people in Uruguay.

Activities: Promotes programmes and policies that expand social, cultural and economic opportunities for all young people in Uruguay, through managing programmes, raising awareness, and influencing national public institutions and policies. Since 1985 it has been experimenting with alternative approaches to combating the problem of youth unemployment and under-employment, working to have the best practices adapted and replicated in the formal education system. Also provides support to small and medium-sized companies run by young people; space for youth cultural exhibitions; services for the defence of young people's civil rights; programmes for young people living in poverty, without homes, and in disadvantageous situations; and programmes focusing on young women, domestic violence and sexual abuse.

Geographical Area of Activity: Uruguay.

Publications: *Participación* (e-newsletter).

Board of Directors: Daniel Espíndola (Pres.); Álvaro Aadiego (Sec.).

Principal Staff: Exec. Dir Dr Magdalena Ejectuva Montero.

Address: Rodó 1836 esquina Frugoni, Montevideo.

Telephone: (2) 4003743; **Internet:** www.forojuvenil.org.uy; **e-mail:** direccionforojuvenil@gmail.com.

Uzbekistan

FOUNDATIONS, TRUSTS AND NON-PROFIT ORGANIZATIONS

Sog'lom Avlod Uchun (For a Healthy Generation)

Founded in 1993 by I. A. Karimov to promote improved health for future generations.

Activities: Conducts programmes and carries out research in the following areas: medical, humanitarian, educational, cultural and sports. Operates a network of more than 180 branch offices throughout Uzbekistan for the distribution of donated medicines and humanitarian assistance and conducts health and other programmes, including health, humanitarian and educational programmes. Works in co-operation with AmeriCares, SitiHope, Peace Village International, Procter & Gamble and Nestlé. Also owns two journals and three newspapers.

Geographical Area of Activity: Uzbekistan.

Finance: Owns five commercial companies. Net assets US $70,000,000; annual revenue approx. $20,000,000.

Board of Directors: Svetlana Tursunovna (Chair.).

Principal Staff: Exec. Dir Muminov Nazimjan Ergashevich; Sec. Rahimnazarova Sarvinoz Bokijon Qizi.

Address: Istiqbol str. 15, 100047 Tashkent.

Telephone: (71) 232-00-82; **Fax:** (71) 233-89-49; **Internet:** www.sau.uz/welcome.html; **e-mail:** fondsau@yahoo.com.

Vatican City

FOUNDATION CENTRE AND CO-ORDINATING BODY

Caritas Internationalis—CI

Established in 1950, in Rome, Italy, as International Caritas Conference (ICC) to respond to the need for a high-level global umbrella organization for the various national Catholic humanitarian assistance, social service, and and development organizations world-wide, many of which, but not all, used the name 'Caritas'. Incorporated the already-existing Caritas Internationalis based in Lucerne, Switzerland. Statutes were approved and adopted on an *ad experimentum* basis in September 1950 and a Constitutional Assembly took place in December 1951, in Rome, attended by delegates from national organizations in 13 countries. Current name was adopted in November 1954. The full title of the organization is Caritas Internationalis—International Confederation of Catholic Organizations for Charitable and Social Action (Confédération internationale d'organismes catholiques d'action charitable et sociale—Confederación Internacional de Organizaciones Católicas de Acción Caritativa y Social).

Activities: As an international Catholic Organization, CI stimulates and aids national Caritas organizations to facilitate the assistance, advancement, and integral development of the most underprivileged, by means of active charity in keeping with the teaching and tradition of the Catholic Church. The organization studies, when possible with other international organizations, the problems arising from poverty, investigates causes and proposes solutions conforming to justice and the dignity of the human person; encourages national Caritas organizations to undertake collaborative study and research; with the approval of the local hierarchy, fosters the foundation of national Catholic charitable organizations where none exists, and, if necessary, contributes to their development; promotes collaboration among member organizations and co-ordinates their international activities, without infringing on their autonomy; participates in efforts of all people to better their individual and collective living standards, so as to achieve full human development; encourages and co-ordinates humanitarian assistance work by member organizations in cases of disaster as and when emergency intervention is required; represents member organizations conforming to current statutes at inter-denominational and international levels; promotes maximal co-operation with other international aid and development organizations. Caritas has consultative status with a number of international organizations, including the UN Economic and Social Council (ECOSOC), the Office of the UN High Commissioner for Refugees (UNHCR), FAO, the World Food Programme, the World Health Organization, the UN Children s Fund (UNICEF), ILO. Caritas had 165 member organizations in 2011. It maintains offices at the UN in New York and Geneva.

Geographical Area of Activity: International.

Publications: Blog; annual report; information sheets, reports and monographs.

Bureau: Cardinal Oscar Rodríguez Maradiaga (Pres.); Michel Roy (Sec.-Gen.); Dr Juerg Krummenacher (Treas.).

Address: Palazzo San Calisto 16, 00120 Vatican City.

Telephone: (06) 69879799; **Fax:** (06) 69887237; **Internet:** www.caritas.org; **e-mail:** caritas.internationalis@caritas.va.

FOUNDATIONS, TRUSTS AND NON-PROFIT ORGANIZATIONS

Foundation 'Populorum Progressio'

Established in February 1992 by Pope John Paul II to promote solidarity with the poor in the developing countries of Central and South America, and the Caribbean, support the work of other charities working in the region, and contribute to the development of populations that are marginalized, especially indigenous and mixed-race peoples, in accordance with the social teachings of the Church.

Activities: Operates in the field of aid to less-developed countries through financing projects nominated by national sociopastoral institutions, and which conform to the aims of the Foundation. Maintains an Administration Council in Colombia.

Geographical Area of Activity: Central and South America and the Caribbean.

Restrictions: Grants only to projects approved by the local ecclesiastical authority.

Finance: Grants awarded US $2,102,500 (2011).

Board of Directors: Cardinal Juan Sandoval Íñiguez (Pres.); Most Rev. Edmundo Luis Flavio Abastoflor Montero (Vice-Pres.); Dr Juan Vicente Isaza Ocampo (Sec.).

Address: Pontificio Consiglio Cor Unum, Palazzo San Pio X, 00120 Vatican City.

Telephone: (06) 69887331; **Fax:** (06) 69887301; **Internet:** www.corunum.va; **e-mail:** corunum@corunum.va.

Venezuela

FOUNDATION CENTRES AND CO-ORDINATING BODIES

Fundación Eugenio Mendoza (Eugenio Mendoza Foundation)

Founded in 1951 by Eugenio Mendoza and Luisa R. de Mendoza to promote social development, education, agriculture and culture.

Activities: Provides microfinance for community development programmes and entrepreneurial training for low-income families. In co-operation with other organizations, the Foundation has created Bangente, the first private Venezuelan Bank in microfinances and in 2005, with Grupo Santander, it created Bancrecer development bank.

Geographical Area of Activity: Venezuela.

Restrictions: No grants are made to individuals or organizations.

Publications: Operations and financial reports, publications in the arts and regarding children.

Board of Directors: Luisa Elena Mendoza de Pulido (Pres.); Mariana Pulido de Sucre (Exec. Vice-Pres.).

Address: Av. Ppal. de Las Mercedes, Edificio Ávila, 3°, Urb. Las Mercedes, Caracas 1060.

Telephone: (212) 993-0555; **Internet:** www .fundacioneugeniomendoza.org.ve; **e-mail:** contacto@ fundacioneugeniomendoza.org.ve.

Sinergia—Asociación Nacional de Organizaciones de la Sociedad Civil (National Association of Civil Society Organizations)

Founded in 1996 to support the development of civil society organizations in Venezuela.

Activities: Provides and publishes information on civil society organizations in Venezuela; provides technical assistance for establishing civil society organizations; and promotes philanthropy in Venezuela.

Geographical Area of Activity: Venezuela.

Restrictions: No grants available.

Publications: *Monthly Information Bulletin*; *Las Redes y el Cambio Social* (*Networks and social change*, 2000); online articles on civil society and NGO development.

Finance: Income is based on projects financed by such institutions as the Konrad Adenauer Foundation (q.v.), Thalita Koum and the US Agency for International Development (USAID).

Operating Committee: Feliciano Reyna (Pres.); Déborah Van Berkel (Vice-Pres.); Diana Vegas (Treas.).

Principal Staff: Exec. Dir Meneses Wileyma.

Address: Centro Rental de la Universidad Metropolitana, Edificio Andrés Germán Otero, 2°, Urb. Terrazas del Ávila, Caracas 1071.

Telephone: (212) 242-0101; **Fax:** (212) 243-9133; **Internet:** www.sinergia.org.ve; **e-mail:** acsinergia@gmail.com.

FOUNDATIONS, TRUSTS AND NON-PROFIT ORGANIZATIONS

Fundación de Apoyo a las Iniciativas Locales de Desarrollo—FUNDAPILDE (Foundation in Support of Local Development Initiatives)

Founded in 1997 to promote economic development and improved standards of living in Venezuela and the countries of Central and South America, especially in the areas of providing support for local development initiatives and projects that benefit women and young people in rural areas.

Activities: Programmes include a training programme for people running small businesses and a Skills Promotion Plan for craftspeople in the Simón Bolívar del Estado Miranda municipality. These programmes are intended to help small businesses in the area improve the quality of their work and develop new markets. Also operates a programme of short courses for local children during their summer holidays.

Geographical Area of Activity: Venezuela.

Principal Staff: Contact Carola Blanco.

Address: POB 14852, Caracas 1011-A.

Telephone: (212) 481-8303; **Internet:** www.members.tripod .com/~handmade/index.html; **e-mail:** cablanco@zeus.ucab .edu.ve.

Fundación para la Defensa de la Naturaleza—FUDENA (Foundation for the Protection of Nature)

Founded in 1975 to promote the conservation of the environment through the preservation of natural resources and sustainable development.

Activities: The Foundation conducts research; organizes the planning and management of protected areas and endangered species; runs environmental education and community participation projects; promotes co-operation between environmental groups; and disseminates information to the public.

Geographical Area of Activity: Venezuela.

Publications: newsletters; research reports; technical reports.

Board of Directors: Carolina Stone (Pres.); Edgar Díaz (Vice-Pres.); Enrique Sánchez (Treas.).

Principal Staff: Exec. Dir Déborah Bigio.

Address: Edif. Centro Empresarial Senderos, 5°, Oficina 505, Avda Principal de Los Cortijos de Lourdes con 2°, Apdo 77076, Caracas 1071.

Telephone: (212) 238-2930; **Fax:** (212) 239-6547; **Internet:** www.fudena.org.ve; **e-mail:** dbigio@fudena.org.ve.

Fundación Empresas Polar (Polar Companies Foundation)

Founded in 1977 by Empresas Polar to contribute to the social development of Venezuela.

Activities: Collaborates with other public and private development institutions; conducts projects in the fields of education, community development and health. Develops its own projects and works in partnership with other organizations.

Geographical Area of Activity: Venezuela.

Publications: Environmental publications; science magazine; and publications within other interest areas.

Board of Directors: Leonor Giménez de Mendoza (Pres.); Morella Pacheco Ramella (Vice-Pres.).

Principal Staff: Gen. Man. Graciela Pantín.

Address: Segunda avenida, Los Cortijos de Lourdes, edif. Fundación Polar, 1°, Los Ruices Municipio Sucre, 1071-A Caracas.

Telephone: (212) 202-7530; **Fax:** (212) 202-7522; **Internet:** www.fundacionempresaspolar.org; **e-mail:** institucional@fundacionempresaspolar.org.

Fundación La Salle de Ciencias Naturales—FLASA
(La Salle Foundation for Natural Sciences)

Founded in 1957 by Pablo Mandazen Soto to develop scientific research on natural resources and technical training of the young; to disseminate the knowledge acquired by means of specialized publications, lectures, seminars and museums; to assist the marginal population, mainly workers, peasants, tribal Indians and fishermen, by direct action such as the setting up of co-operatives and assisted projects.

Activities: Promotes national development in science and technology, education, social welfare, conservation and the environment, through self-conducted programmes, environmental and social impact services for the industry and the State, conferences, courses, publications and lectures. Maintains a Marine Research Station at Isla de Margarita, on the eastern coast, to increase knowledge of the Venezuelan sea and its resources and to help to establish an education system adapted to the needs of the fishing industry. The Foundation has also pioneered the development of technical schools whose programmes combine academic preparation with technical training—courses are of six years' duration, and embrace a wide range of subjects from mechanics and refrigeration to fishing and marine biology. The Foundation established three schools at Isla de Margarita, Ciudad Guayana and San Carlos (Edo. Cojedes); also at Isla de Margarita the Instituto Universitario de Tecnología del Mar (IUTEMAR) was created, devoted to research on marine ecosystems and resources, emphasizing fisheries management. Other specialist institutes established by the Foundation are the La Salle Museum of Natural History, whose long-term commitment is producing an inventory of Venezuela's biodiversity, the Station of Hydrobiological research, and the Instituto Caribe de Antropología y Sociología (Caribbean Institute of Anthropology and Sociology), which houses projects of applied anthropological research, aimed at reducing the shock of cultural transition and providing Indian communities with a basic training that will enable them to raise their standard of living. Maintains offices in Cojedes, Isla de Margarita and Trujillo, and in Guyana.

Geographical Area of Activity: Venezuela.

Publications: Report of operations and financial statement; *Antropológica* (review); *Memoria* (monographic series); *Natura;* books on science and technology.

Finance: Funded by the Ministry of Education and corporate donations.

Board of Directors: Francer Goenaga (Pres.).

Principal Staff: Research Dir Daniel Lew.

Address: Edif. Fundación La Salle, Avda Boyacá, Cota Mil, Apdo 1930, Caracas 1010-A.

Telephone: (2) 793-4255; **Fax:** (2) 793-7493; **Internet:** www.fundacionlasalle.org.ve; **e-mail:** alba.clamens@fundacionlasalle.org.ve.

Fundación de la Vivienda Popular (Foundation for Low-Cost Housing)

Founded in 1958 by Eugenio Mendoza, with the support and participation of 41 public figures, 59 companies and four foundations, to contribute to the solution of the housing problem facing low-income sections of the community.

Activities: Operates nationally in the field of housing in two areas: Social Action; and Research and Development. The Social Action programme aims to stimulate community self-management, supporting low-income families and motivating them to take part in improving their housing and environment through the creation of a housing association (Asociación Civil de Vivienda); it also advises businesses wishing to contribute a solution to housing problems experienced by their workers, and trains public and private institutions interested in setting up housing associations. The Research and Development programme aims to carry out research in areas associated with housing, especially families with few economic resources; its support programmes seek to advance knowledge of housing and the environment, and it promotes the Eugenio Mendoza Chair in Housing at national universities, and the Eugenio Mendoza Prize for Research in Housing. The Foundation also maintains a documentation and information centre, which offers information on housing and the environment.

Geographical Area of Activity: Venezuela.

Publications: The Foundation is the main publisher of housing literature in Venezuela.

Board: Eugenio A. Mendoza (Pres.); Dr Pablo A. Pulido M. (Vice-Pres.); Dr Manuel Azpúrua Arreaza (Vice-Pres.); Omar Feaugas Guédez (Vice-Pres.).

Principal Staff: Dir-Gen. Oswaldo Carrillo Jiménez.

Address: Avda Diego Cisneros (Principal de Los Ruices), Edif. Centro Empresarial Autana, 1°, Urb. Los Ruices, Municipio Sucre, Estado Maranda, Caracas.

Telephone: (212) 238-47-08; **Fax:** (212) 234-65-13; **Internet:** www.viviendaenred.com; **e-mail:** viviendaenred@cantv.net.

Viet Nam

FOUNDATIONS, TRUSTS AND NON-PROFIT ORGANIZATIONS

Toyota Vietnam Foundation—TVF

Established in September 2005 by Toyota Motor Vietnam Co Ltd in recognition of the company's 10th anniversary of operations in Viet Nam.

Activities: Aims to contribute to the development of Vietnamese society, primarily through supporting educational initiatives. The Foundation's first two main programmes were a traffic-safety education programme for primary school pupils and a Monozukuri course at Hanoi University of Technology. Other activities include the provision of scholarships for Vietnamese students and sponsorship of the Vietnam National Symphony Orchestra.

Geographical Area of Activity: Viet Nam.

Finance: Established with an initial donation from Toyota Motor Vietnam Co Ltd of US $4,000,000.

Principal Staff: Pres. Akito Tachibana.

Address: c/o Toyota Motor Vietnam Co Ltd, Phuc Thang Ward, Phuc Yen Town, Vinh Phuc Province.

Telephone: (3) 868100112; **Fax:** (3) 868117; **Internet:** www.toyotavn.com.vn/templates/views/38/203; **e-mail:** veamcorp@hn.vnn.vn.

Unilever Vietnam Foundation—UVF

Established in 2004 by Unilever Vietnam to co-ordinate the company's social and community programmes.

Activities: Funding is directed to projects providing support to children and women, especially those living in rural areas, including initiatives focusing on community health care and hygiene, education, environmental protection, and supporting people in need.

Geographical Area of Activity: Viet Nam.

Finance: Committed to investing some 70,000,000,000 VND every year to social and community projects.

Address: 156 Nguyen Luong Bang Ave, Tan Phu Ward, District 7, Ho Chi Minh City.

Telephone: (8) 5 4135686; **Fax:** (8) 5 4135626; **Internet:** www.unilever.com.vn; **e-mail:** enquiry.uvn@unilever.com.

Zambia

FOUNDATIONS, TRUSTS AND NON-PROFIT ORGANIZATIONS

Mindolo Ecumenical Foundation—MEF

Founded in 1958 by Rev. Peter Mathews to promote, develop and train lay and ordained church leaders.

Activities: The Foundation serves as an ecumenical training centre, organizing courses for African churches, church-related organizations and NGOs; programmes operated by the Foundation include: women's training; youth leadership; ecumenical church ministries; pre-school teachers and trainers; peace building and conflict transformation; and community development; awards scholarships, organizes conferences and training courses, and issues publications; maintains a library of 30,000 books.

Geographical Area of Activity: Africa.

Publications: *Mindolo World* (two a year); conference reports.

Principal Staff: Dir Dr William Temu.

Address: POB 21493, Kitwe.

Telephone: (2) 214572; **Fax:** (2) 211001; **e-mail:** mef@zamnet.zm.

Zimbabwe

FOUNDATIONS, TRUSTS AND NON-PROFIT ORGANIZATIONS

African Capacity Building Foundation—ACBF

Founded in 1991 through a collaboration between the African Development Bank, the World Bank and the UN Development Programme to help the countries and regional organizations of Africa build and strengthen indigenous capacity to reduce poverty.

Activities: The Foundation promotes and supports the improvement of human and institutional capacities in the areas of policy analysis and development management in Sub-Saharan Africa. It awards fellowships to improve research and training skills and to expand in-service training for professionals. The ACB Fund has been established to provide direct funding for capacity building projects. The Partnership for Capacity Building in Africa (PACT) initiative aims to provide an integrated framework for capacity building, good governance and sustainable development in Africa; to promote a partnership between African governments, the private sector, civil society and development partners to strengthen Africa's ownership, leadership and responsibility in the capacity building process; and to provide a forum for sharing experiences and best practices, and discussing issues and problems.

Geographical Area of Activity: Sub-Saharan Africa.

Publications: *ACBF Newsletter* (quarterly); *ACBF Working Paper Series (AWPS)*; *Challenges in the Building of Public Service Capacity in Africa*; *Beating Occupational Fraud through Awareness and Prevention*; *The Role of Agriculture in Strengthening Regional Integration in Africa*; Annual Reports; books; workshop reports; occasional reports.

Finance: Total disbursements US $32,800,000 (2010); Resources pledged for 2012–16 US $124,600,000.

Board of Governors: Dr Ngozi Okonjo-Iweala (Chair.).

Principal Staff: Chair. of Exec. Board Paul Baloyi; Exec. Sec. Dr Frannie A. Léautier.

Address: ZB Life Towers, 7th Floor, cnr Jason Moyo ave/Sam Nujoma St, POB 1562, Harare.

Telephone: (4) 702931; **Fax:** (4) 702915; **Internet:** www.acbf-pact.org; **e-mail:** root@acbf-pact.org.

African Forum and Network on Debt and Development—AFRODAD

Established with the aim of securing lasting solutions to Africa's mounting debt problem and to promote the continent's development.

Activities: Network of African NGOs, organizations, churches and individuals that promotes debt relief, and raises awareness of debt and development issues within Africa; takes part in conferences in the Northern hemisphere to promote empathy with the African position regarding international debt; main areas of research include: The Poverty Reduction Growth Facility (PGRF) and Fiscal Space in Africa, with country case studies on Malawi, Mozambique and Uganda; and The Challenges of Debt Sustainability in Africa.

Geographical Area of Activity: Africa.

Publications: Occasional papers; articles; newsletter (2 a month).

Board of Trustees: Opa Kapijimpanga (Chair.).

Principal Staff: Exec. Dir Collins Magalasi.

Address: 31 Atkinson Dr., Hillside, Harare.

Telephone: (4) 778531; **Fax:** (4) 747878; **Internet:** www.afrodad.org; **e-mail:** mercyln@afrodad.co.zw.

The J. F. Kapnek Trust Zimbabwe

Established by the estate of James F. Kapnek, the Trust aims to support excellence in medical and health-related education and research in Zimbabwe.

Activities: Aims to promote medical and health-related education and research in Zimbabwe, in a variety of areas, including reducing the transmission of HIV from mother to child; supporting maternal and infant health; educating and training young women in Zimbabwe for leadership positions, especially those who wish to pursue medicine and related healthcare professions; promotes collaboration between the medical, research, academic, service and donor communities of Zimbabwe, the USA, the United Kingdom and countries of Sub-Saharan Africa; and encouraging research into environmental issues and the impact of environmental problems on health; programmes include Strengthening Science for Women; Pediatric AIDS Fund Zimbabwe; a Visiting Scholars Programme; a pre-school programme for Orphans and other Vunerable Children, and a Small Grants Programme. A sister organization operates in the USA.

Geographical Area of Activity: USA, Zimbabwe.

Publications: Annual Report.

Finance: Annual revenue US $2,468,130, expenditure $2,303,918 (2009/2010).

Board of Directors: Tsungai Chipato (Chair.).

Principal Staff: Man. Dir Greg Powell; Admin. Man. Gail Downey.

Address: 33 Lawson Ave., Milton Park, Harare.

Telephone: (4) 792153; **Internet:** www.jfkapnektrust.org; **e-mail:** gdowney@ctazim.co.zw.

Self Help Development Foundation

Established in 1963 by Francis Waddelove for the reduction of poverty through food security.

Activities: Operates in Zimbabwe and Southern Africa in the areas of economic affairs, education and social welfare, through providing credit; education for self-survival; mobilization of savings; civic education; and social welfare in the area of food security. The Foundation makes grants and loans to groups and individual members, and carries out projects.

Geographical Area of Activity: Zimbabwe and Southern Africa.

Principal Staff: Exec. Dir Wadzanayi Vere.

Address: 17 Nirvana Rd, Hatfield, POB 4576, Harare.

Telephone: (4) 570611; **Fax:** (4) 570139; **Internet:** www.shdf-tas.org.zw; **e-mail:** shdftas@africaonline.co.zw.

Select Bibliography

ALLIANCE PUBLISHING TRUST. *Alliance* (quarterly journal).

ANHEIER, H. K. *Civil Society: Measurement, Evaluation, Policy.* Earthscan, London, 2004.
Non-Profit Organizations: Theory, Management, Policy. Routledge, Abingdon, 2005.

ANHEIER, H. K. and S. DALY. *The Roles and Visions of Foundations in Europe.* London School of Economics, London, 2004.
(Editors) *The Politics of Foundations: Comparative Perspectives from Europe and Beyond.* Routledge, Abingdon, 2006.

ANHEIER, H. K., M. GLASIUS and PROF. M. H. KALDOR. (Editors). *Global Civil Society Yearbook 2009: Global Civil Society and Poverty Alleviation.* London, Sage Publications, 2009.

ANHEIER, H. K. and HAMMACK, DAVID. American Foundations: Roles and Contributions. Brookings Institution, Washington, DC, 2010.

ANHEIER, H. K. and JEREMY KENDALL. *Third Sector Policy at the Crossroads: An International Non-Profit Analysis.* Routledge, London, 2001.

ANHEIER, H. K. and D. LEAT. *From Charity to Creativity: Philanthropic Foundations in the 21st Century: Perspectives from Britain and Beyond.* Comedia, Stroud, 2002.
Creative Philanthropy: Toward a New Philanthropy for the Twenty-First Century. Routledge, Abingdon, 2006.

ANHEIER, H. K. and REGINA A. LIST. *A Dictionary of Civil Society. Philanthropy and the Non-Profit Sector.* Routledge, London, 2005.

ANHEIER, H. K. and S. TOEPLER. (Editors). *Private Funds, Public Purpose: Philanthropic foundations in international perspective.* Kluwer Academic/Plenum Publishers, USA, 1999.

ARMSTRONG, D., V. BELLO, J. GILSON and D. SPINI. *Civil Society and International Governance: The role of non-state actors in the EU, Africa, Asia and Middle East.* Routledge, Abingdon, 2010.

BAKER, G. and D. CHANDLER. *Global Civil Society: Contested Futures.* Routledge, Abingdon, 2006.

BEBBINGTON, A. J., S. HICKEY and D. MITLIN. (Editors). *Can NGOs Make a Difference? The Challenge of Development Alternatives.* Zed Books, London, 2007.

BREMNER, ROBERT H. *Giving: Charity and Philanthropy in History.* Rutgers University Press, New Brunswick, NJ, 1995.

BUNDESVERBAND DEUTSCHER STIFTUNGEN E.V. (Editor). *Verzeichnis Deutscher Stiftungen.* Verlag Deutscher Stiftungen, 2011.

CAVATORTA, F. and V. DURAC. *Civil Society and Democratization in the Arab World.* Routledge, Abingdon, 2010.

CENTRO MEXICANO PARA LA FILANTROPÍA, AC. *Directorio de Instituciones Filantrópicas,* México.

CENTRO PORGUGUÊS DE FUNDAÇÕES. *Guia das Fundações Portuguesas/Portuguese Foundations Guide,* 1996.

CHEW, CELINE. *Strategic Positioning in Voluntary and Charitable Organizations.* Routledge, Abingdon, 2009.

CLARK, J., D. KANE, K. WILDING and P. BASS. *UK Civil Society Almanac 2012.* London, NCVO, 2012.

CREATE (Editor). *The Irish Funding Handbook.* Sixth edn, Dublin, 2007.

CUNNINGGIM, MERRIMON. *Private Money and Public Service: The Role of Foundations in American Society.* Herder & Herder, New York, 1972.

DIRECTORY OF SOCIAL CHANGE. *The Directory of Grant Making Trusts 2012–13* (London, 2012); *A Guide to the Major Trusts* (2 vols, London, 2012).

EDITIONS RUYANT. *GAFA—Guide Annuaire des Fondations et des Associations.* Cosne sur Loire, 2009.

EDWARDS, M. *Civil Society.* Polity, Cambridge, 2004.

ELLSWORTH, F. K. and J. JUMARDA. (Editors). *From Grantmaker to Leader: Emerging Strategies for Twenty-First Century Foundations.* John Wiley & Sons, Hoboken, NJ, 2003.

ENJOLRAS, BERNARD. *Voluntas: International Journal of Voluntary and Nonprofit Organizatiaons* (official quarterly journal of the International Society for Third-Sector Research). Springer.

EUROPA PUBLICATIONS. *European Foundations and Grant-making NGOs* (London, 2004).

EUROPEAN FOUNDATION CENTRE (EFC). *Selected Bibliography on Foundations and Corporate Funders in Europe* (1994); *Typology of Foundations in Europe* (1994–95); *European Foundation Fundaments* (1999); *Working With Foundations: Why and How?* (2001); *Foundations for Europe: Rethinking our Legal and Fiscal Environments* (2003); *Disaster Grantmaking: A Practical Guide for Foundations and Corporations* (2002); *Foundations in the European Union: Profiling Legal and Fiscal Environments* (2002); *Funding Vocational Training and Employment for People with Disabilities: Guidelines for Good Grantmaking Practice* (2002); *Foundation Facts and Figures across the EU* (2005); *Foundations' Legal and Fiscal Environments: Mapping the European Union of 27* (2007); *Comparative Highlights of Foundation Laws: The European Union of 27* (2007); *EFC Principles of Good Practice* (2007); *Comparative Map of the Foundation Sector in the EU* (2008); *efc bookshelf* (quarterly newsletter, updating the bibliography); *efc newsline* (newsletter); *efc partners europe* (newsletter); *efc alerts* (information bulletins); *EFFECT Magazine* (3 a year); other books, conference and meeting reports and annual reports.

FLEISHMAN, J. *The Foundation: A Great American Secret—How Private Weath is Changing the World.* PublicAffairs, New York, 2007.

FOUNDATION CENTER. *The Foundation Directory* (annually); *Philanthropy News Digest* (weekly, by e-mail); *RFP Bulletin*; *FC Stats*; *The Foundation Grants Index* (quarterly and annually); *Guide to US Foundations, their Trustees, Officers, and Donors*; *The Foundation 1000*; *Foundation Fundamentals*; *Foundation Giving*; *The Foundation Grants Index Quarterly*; *National Directory of Corporate Giving*; *Foundation Grants for Individuals.*

FREEMAN, DAVID F. and the COUNCIL ON FOUNDATIONS. *Handbook on Private Foundations.* Foundation Center, New York 1991.

FUNDACIÓN JOSÉ MARÍA ARAGÓN. *Primer Directorio de Fundaciones de la República Argentina.* Buenos Aires, 1980; *Guía de Becas de Postgraduado 1991–92.* Buenos Aires, 7th edn, 1991.

FUNDACIÓN ARIAS PARA LA PAZ Y EL PROGRESO HUMANO. *Directorio de organizaciones para la promoción de la micro, pequeña y mediana empresa en Centroamérica.* San José, 2006.

GALE CENGAGE LEARNING. *Encyclopedia of Associations, International Organizations.* Detroit, MI, 50th edn, 2011.

GERMAIN, R. and M. KENNY. *The Idea of Global Civil Society: Ethics and Politics in a Globalizing Era.* Routledge, Abingdon, 2006.

GLASIUS, M., D. LEWIS and HAKAN SECKINELGIN (Editors). *Exploring Civil Society: Political and Cultural Contexts.* Routledge, Abingdon, 2004.

HOLLY, KARINA (Editor). *Philanthropy in Europe.* Philanthropy in Europe Ltd, www.philanthropyineurope.com (3 a year).

IMAGINE CANADA. *Canadian Directory to Foundations and Corporations.*

INFORMATION TODAY. *Annual Register of Grant Support.* Medford, NJ, 45th edn, 2011.

INTERNATIONAL SOCIETY FOR THIRD-SECTOR RESEARCH—ISTR. *Inside ISTR* (quarterly newsletter); *ISTR Report; Voluntas.*

JAMES, H. (Editor). *Civil Society, Religion and Global Governance.* Routledge, Abingdon, 2007.

JAPAN FOUNDATION CENTER. *JFC Views* (in Japanese); *Directory of Grantmaking Foundations* (in Japanese).

JEGERS, MARC. *Managerial Economics of Non-Profit Organizations.* Routledge, Abingdon, 2009.

JOBERT, B. and B. KOHLER-KOCH. (Editors). *Changing Images of Civil Society.* Routledge, Abingdon, 2008.

JOSEPH JAMES A. (Editor). *The Charitable Impulse: Wealth and Social Conscience in Communities and Cultures Outside the United States.* Foundation Center, New York, 1989.

MAGAT, RICHARD (Editor). *An Agile Servant: Community Leadership by Community Foundations.* Foundation Center, New York, 1989.

MARTIN, MIKE W. *Virtuous Giving: Philanthropy, Voluntary Service, and Caring.* Indiana University Press, Bloomington, IN, 1995.

MARTIN, SAMUEL A. *An Essential Grace: Funding Canada's Health Care, Education, Welfare, Religion and Culture.* McClelland and Stewart, Toronto, 1984.

NAGAI, A., R. LERNER and R. ROTHMAN. (Editors). *Giving for Social Change: Foundations, Public Policy, and the American Political Agenda.* Praeger Publishers, Westport, CT, 1994.

O'CONNELL, BRIAN (Editor). *America's Voluntary Spirit: A Book of Readings.* Foundation Center, New York, 1983.

ODENDAHL, TERESA, ELIZABETH BORIS and ARLENE DANIELS. *Working in Foundations: Career Patterns of Women and Men.* Foundation Center, New York, 1985.

OSBORNE, STEPHEN P. *The Third Sector in Europe: Prospects and Challenges.* Routledge, Abingdon, 2008.

PALGRAVE MACMILLAN. *The Grants Register 2012.* London, 30th edn, 2011.

PHILANTHROPY AUSTRALIA INC. *Australian Philanthropy* (journal, 3 a year); *The Australian Directory of Philanthropy* (biennially).

PIFER, ALAN. *Philanthropy in an Age of Transition.* Foundation Center, New York, 1984.

POMEY, MICHEL. *Traité des Fondations d'Utilité Publique.* Presse Universitaire de France, 1980.

ROUTLEDGE. *Journal of Civil Society.* (journal, 3 a year). Routledge, Abingdon.

SALAMON, LESTER M. *The Global Associational Revolution: The Rise of the Third Sector on the World Scene.* Johns Hopkins University, Institute for Policy Studies, Baltimore, MD, 1993.

SALAMON, LESTER M. and ANHEIER, H. K. *The Emerging Nonprofit Sector: An Overview.* Manchester University Press, Manchester, 1996.

SALAMON, LESTER M. and H. K. ANHEIER. *The Emerging Sector: The Nonprofit Sector in Comparative Perspective: An Overview.* John Hopkins University, Institute for Policy Studies, Baltimore, MD, 1994.

SALAMON, LESTER M. and H. K. ANHEIER (Editors). *Defining the Nonprofit Sector: A Cross-National Analysis.* Manchester University Press, Manchester, 1997.

SALAMON, LESTER M., H. K. ANHEIER, S. TOEPLER, S. W. SOKOLOWSKI, R. LIST, et al. *Global Civil Society: Dimensions of the Nonprofit Sector.* Kumarian Press, 2006.

SALAMON, LESTER M., S. W. SOKOLOWSKI and R. LIST. *Global Civil Society: An Overview.* John Hopkins University, Institute for Policy Studies, Baltimore, MD, 2003.

SCHOOLHOUSE PARTNERS. *Directory of Research Grants; Directory of Grants in the Humanities; Directory of Biomedical and Health Care Grants; Operating Grants for Nonprofit Organizations; Directory of Environmental Grants; Funding Sources for Faith-Based Programs.* Nashville, IN.

SIEGEL, DANIEL and JENNY YANCEY. *The Rebirth of Civil Society: The Development of the Nonprofit Sector in East Central Europe and the Role of Western Assistance.* Rockefeller Brothers Fund, New York, 1992.

SIEVERS, BRUCE R. *Civil Society, Philanthropy, and the Fate of the Commons.* Tufts, 2010.

SUNDAR, PUSHPA. *Foreign Aid for Indian NGOs: Problem or Solution?* Routledge, Abingdon, 2009

TAYLOR, RUPERT. *Third Sector Research.* Springer, 2010.

THOMAS, RALPH LINGO. *Policies Underlying Corporate Giving.* Prentice-Hall, Inc, Englewood Cliffs, NJ, 1966.

UNION OF INTERNATIONAL ASSOCIATIONS. *Transnational Associations* (quarterly, in English and French); *International Congress Calendar* (quarterly); *Yearbook of International Organizations* (annually).

URAL, ENGIN (Editor). *Foundations in Turkey.* Development Foundation of Turkey, Ankara, 1978.

VERENIGING VAN FONDSEN IN NEDERLAND. *Fondsenboek* (biennially); *Fondsendisk* (annually).

VINCENT, JEREMY and CATHY PHAROAH. *Patterns of independent grantmaking in the UK.* CAF Publications, CAF (Charities Aid Foundation), West Malling, 2000.

WEAVER, WARREN. *U.S. Philanthropic Foundations: Their History, Structure, Management and Record.* Harper & Row, New York, 1967.

PART THREE

Indexes

Index of Foundations

1818 Fund Foundation, Netherlands, 280
1945 Foundation, Canada, 90
30 Million Friends Foundation, France, 151

A. G. Leventis Foundation, Cyprus, 111
A. G. Leventis Foundation Nigeria, Nigeria, 290
A. L. Mailman Family Foundation, Inc, USA, 521
A. M. M. Sahabdeen Trust Foundation, Sri Lanka, 350
A. M. Qattan Foundation, UK, 440
The A. P. Møller and Chastine Mc-Kinney Møller Foundation, Denmark, 120
A. P. Møller og Hustru Chastine Mc-Kinney Møllers Fond til almene Formaal, Denmark, 120
A. S. Hornby Educational Trust, UK, 421
AARDO—Afro-Asian Rural Development Organization, India, 199
AAUW—American Association of University Women Educational Foundation, USA, 463
AbaF—Australia Business Arts Foundation, Australia, 37
Abdul Hameed Shoman Foundation, Jordan, 242
Abegg Foundation, Switzerland, 360
Abegg-Stiftung, Switzerland, 360
Abrinq Foundation for the Rights of Children and Adolescents, Brazil, 70
Absolute Return for Kids—ARK, UK, 401
Académie Goncourt—Société des Gens de Lettres, France, 136
Academy for the Development of Philanthropy in Poland, Poland, 305
Academy of European Law, Germany, 167
Accademia Musicale Chigiana, Italy, 216
Acceso, Costa Rica, 106
Access Foundation, Costa Rica, 106
ACCION International, USA, 460
ACCU—Asian Cultural Centre for UNESCO, Japan, 231
ACDI/VOCA, USA, 460
Açık Toplum Enstitüsü, Turkey, 387
Acíndar Foundation, Argentina, 31
ACLS—American Council of Learned Societies, USA, 464
ACORD—Agency for Co-operation and Research in Development, Kenya, 245
ACRI—Associazione di Fondazioni e di Casse di Risparmio Spa, Italy, 216
Acting for Life, France, 136
Action for Children, UK, 398
Action Children Aid, Denmark, 117
Action in Development—AID, Bangladesh, 52
Action contre la Faim, France, 136
Action Group for Justice and Social Equality, Benin, 65
Action against Hunger, France, 136
Action Solidarité Tiers Monde—ASTM, Luxembourg, 257
Action d'Urgence Internationale—AUI, France, 136
ActionAid, South Africa, 331
Activ Foundation, Australia, 36
ACTR/ACCELS—American Councils for International Education, USA, 464
Acumen Fund, USA, 461
Adams (Sylvia) Charitable Trust, UK, 398
Adenauer (Konrad) Stiftung eV, Germany, 160
Adessium Foundation, Netherlands, 272
ADF—America's Development Foundation, USA, 458
ADI—Association for Democratic Initiatives, Macedonia, 258
ADL—Anti-Defamation League of B'nai B'rith, USA, 469
The Adolph and Esther Gottlieb Foundation, Inc, USA, 498
ADRA—Adventist Development and Relief Agency International, USA, 461
Adriano Olivetti Foundation, Italy, 223
Advantech Foundation, Taiwan, 379

Adventist Development and Relief Agency International—ADRA, USA, 461
Advocacy Center at ISC, USA, 461
AF—Association of Foundations, Philippines, 301
AFAP—Australian Foundation for the Peoples of Asia and the Pacific, Australia, 38
Afghanaid, UK, 398
AFPE—American Foundation for Pharmaceutical Education, USA, 465
Africa-America Institute—AAI, USA, 461
Africa Educational Trust, UK, 399
Africa Foundation (UK), UK, 399
Africa Grantmakers' Affinity Group—AGAG, USA, 458
Africa Humanitarian Action, Ethiopia, 130
The African Agricultural Technology Foundation—AATF, Kenya, 245
African Association for Literacy and Adult Education, Senegal, 323
African Capacity Building Foundation—ACBF, Zimbabwe, 567
African Development Institute, Inc, USA, 461
African Forum and Network on Debt and Development—AFRODAD, Zimbabwe, 567
African Medical and Research Foundation—AMREF, Kenya, 245
African NGOs Environment Network—ANEN, Kenya, 244
African Refugees Foundation—AREF, Nigeria, 289
African Wildlife Foundation—AWF, USA, 462
African Women's Development Fund—AWDF, Ghana, 185
African Youth Network for Sustainable Development, Algeria, 30
Africare, USA, 462
Afro-Asian Institute in Vienna, Austria, 46
Afro-Asian Rural Development Organization—AARDO, India, 199
Afro-Asiatisches Institut in Wien, Austria, 46
AFRODAD—African Forum and Network on Debt and Development, Zimbabwe, 567
AFSC—American Friends Service Committee, USA, 465
AFTAAC—Arab Fund for Technical Assistance to African Countries, Egypt, 127
Aga Khan Agency for Microfinance, Switzerland, 360
Aga Khan Development Network—AKDN, Switzerland, 360
Aga Khan Foundation (UK)—AKF, UK, 399
Aga Khan Foundation—AKF, Switzerland, 360
Aga Khan Foundation Canada, Canada, 80
Aga Khan Fund for Economic Development, Switzerland, 361
Aga Khan Trust for Culture—AKTC, Switzerland, 361
AGAG—Africa Grantmakers' Affinity Group, USA, 458
Agence Internationale pour le Développement Fédération—AIDE, France, 140
Agency for Co-operation and Research in Development, Kenya, 245
Agency for the Non-profit Sector, Czech Republic, 112
Agnelli (Giovanni), Fondazione, Italy, 218
AGNES—Vzdělávací Organizace, Czech Republic, 112
Agora Foundation, Poland, 306
Agostino (Daniele Derossi) Foundation, USA, 462
Agriculteurs Français et Développement International—AFDI, France, 136
Agromart Foundation, Sri Lanka, 350
Agromisa Foundation, Netherlands, 280
Agronomes et vétérinaires sans frontières—AVSF, France, 136
Agrupació Mutual Foundation, Spain, 338
The Ahmanson Foundation, USA, 462
AIC—Association internationale des charités, Belgium, 57

Aid to the Church in Need—ACN, Germany, 160
Aid for Development Club, Austria, 46
Aid for India/ Karuna Trust, UK, 426
Aide et Action, France, 137
Aide Médicale Internationale, France, 137
AIIT—Ancient India and Iran Trust, UK, 400
AINA—Arctic Institute of North America, Canada, 81
Air France Corporate Foundation, France, 144
Air Pollution and Climate Secretariat—AirClim, Sweden, 352
AirClim—Air Pollution and Climate Secretariat, Sweden, 352
Airey Neave Trust, UK, 434
AISA—Africa Institute of South Africa, South Africa, 332
AIT—Asian Institute of Technology, Thailand, 383
AIV—Asia-Africa International Voluntary Foundation, Japan, 231
AJWS—American Jewish World Service, USA, 466
Akademia Rozwoju Filantropii w Polsce, Poland, 305
AKNS—Asociácia komunitných nadácií Slovenska, Slovakia, 327
Aktion Børnehjælp, Denmark, 117
Al Fayed Charitable Foundation, UK, 399
The Al-Khoei Benevolent Foundation, UK, 399
Alamire Foundation, Belgium, 56
Åland Fund for the Future of the Baltic Sea, Finland, 131
Alavi Foundation, USA, 462
Albanian Civil Society Foundation, Albania, 29
Albanian Disability Rights Foundation, Albania, 29
Albéniz (Isaac), Fundación, Spain, 339
Albéniz Foundation, Spain, 339
Albert Einstein Institution, USA, 488
Albert Schweitzer Ecological Centre, Switzerland, 362
Alberta Innovates Health Solutions, Canada, 81
Alberto Vollmer Foundation, Inc, USA, 551
Alchemy Foundation, UK, 399
Alcoa Foundation, USA, 462
Alden (George I) Trust, USA, 463
Alemán (Miguel), Fundación, Mexico, 262
Alert—International Alert, UK, 422
Alessio Pezcoller Foundation, Italy, 223
Alexander von Humboldt Foundation, Germany, 170
Alexander von Humboldt Stiftung, Germany, 170
Alexander S. Onassis Public Benefit Foundation, Greece, 189
Alfred Benzon Foundation, Denmark, 117
Alfred Benzons Fond, Denmark, 117
Alfred Friendly Press Fellowships, USA, 494
Alfred Heineken Fondsen Foundation, Netherlands, 281
Alfred P. Sloan Foundation, USA, 545
Alfred Toepfer Foundation F.V.S., Germany, 183
Alfred Toepfer Stiftung F.V.S., Germany, 183
Alfried Krupp von Bohlen und Halbach Foundation, Germany, 173
Alfried Krupp von Bohlen und Halbach-Stiftung, Germany, 173
Alicia Patterson Foundation—APF, USA, 533
ALIDE—Asociación Latinoamericana de Instituciones Financieras para el Desarrollo, Peru, 299
All India Disaster Mitigation Institute, India, 199
All Saints Educational Trust, UK, 400
Allavida—Alliances for Voluntary Initiatives and Development, Kenya, 244
Allen (Paul G.) Family Foundation, USA, 463
Allen Lane Foundation, UK, 428
Alliance for International Educational and Cultural Exchange, USA, 463
Alliance Israélite Universelle, France, 137
Alliance Sud—Swiss Alliance of Development Organisations, Switzerland, 359

Alliances for Voluntary Initiatives and
Development—Allavida, Kenya, 244
Allianz Cultural Foundation, Germany, 160
Allianz Foundation for Sustainability,
Germany, 160
Allianz Kulturstiftung, Germany, 160
Allianz Umweltstiftung, Germany, 160
Almeida (Eng. António de), Fundação,
Portugal, 310
Alternatives for Development Foundation,
Ecuador, 124
Altman (Jenifer) Foundation, USA, 463
The Alva Foundation, Canada, 81
Alvares Penteado (Armando), Fundação,
Brazil, 71
Alzheimer Spain Foundation, Spain, 339
AMADE Mondiale—Association Mondiale des
Amis de l'Enfance, Monaco, 265
Amancio Ortega Foundation, Spain, 346
Amberes (Carlos de), Fundación, Spain, 339
Ambiente y Recursos Naturales, Fundación,
Argentina, 31
The Ambrose Monell Foundation, USA, 525
Ambrosiana Paolo VI Foundation, Italy, 218
Ambuja Cement Foundation, India, 199
America for Bulgaria Foundation, Bulgaria, 75
America–Mideast Educational and Training
Services Inc, USA, 468
American Association of University Women
Educational Foundation—AAUW, USA, 463
American Council of Learned Societies—ACLS,
USA, 464
American Council for Voluntary International
Action—InterAction, USA, 459
American Councils for International
Education—ACTR/ACCELS, USA, 464
American Express Foundation, USA, 464
American Foundation for AIDS Research—
amfAR, USA, 464
American Foundation for the Blind, Inc—AFB,
USA, 465
American Foundation for Pharmaceutical
Education—AFPE, USA, 465
American Friends Service Committee—AFSC,
USA, 465
American Health Assistance Foundation—
AHAF, USA, 465
American Heart Association, Inc, USA, 465
American Historical Association, USA, 466
American Hungarian Foundation, USA, 466
American Institute of Pakistan Studies, USA, 466
American Jewish Joint Distribution
Committee—JDC, USA, 466
American Jewish World Service—AJWS,
USA, 466
American Near East Refugee Aid—ANERA,
USA, 467
American Philosophical Society—APS, USA, 467
American Refugee Committee—ARC, USA, 467
American Scandinavian Foundation—ASF,
USA, 467
American Schools of Oriental Research—ASOR,
USA, 467
AmeriCares Foundation, Inc, USA, 468
America's Development Foundation—ADF,
USA, 458
Amerind Foundation, Inc, USA, 468
amfAR—American Foundation for AIDS
Research, USA, 464
AMI—Fundação Assistência Médica
International, Portugal, 310
AMIDEAST—America-Mideast Educational and
Training Services, Inc, USA, 468
Amigos de la Tierra, Netherlands, 275
Les Amis de la Terre, Netherlands, 275
Amnesty International, UK, 400
Dell'Amore (Giordano) Foundation, Italy, 220
AMP Foundation, Australia, 36
AMREF—African Medical and Research
Foundation, Kenya, 245
AMURT—Ananda Marga Universal Relief
Team, USA, 468
AMURT International, Austria, 46
Ana Mata Manzanedo Foundation, Spain, 345
Ananda Marga Universal Relief Team—AMURT,
USA, 468
Ancient India and Iran Trust, UK, 400
Anders Jahre's Foundation for Humanitarian
Purposes, Norway, 291
Anders Jahres Humanitære Stiftelse,
Norway, 291
The Andrew Balint Charitable Trust, UK, 402
The Andrew W. Mellon Foundation, USA, 523
Andrews Charitable Trust, UK, 400
The Andy Warhol Foundation for the Visual Arts,
Inc, USA, 552
ANERA—American Near East Refugee Aid,
USA, 467

ANESVAD, Spain, 337
Angaja Foundation, India, 199
Angelo Della Riccia Foundation, Italy, 221
ANGOC—Asian NGO Coalition for Agrarian
Reform and Rural Development,
Philippines, 301
Anna Lindh Euro-Mediterranean Foundation for
Dialogue between Cultures, Egypt, 127
ANND—Arab NGO Network for Development,
Lebanon, 252
Anne Çocuk Eğitim Vakfı—AÇEV, Turkey, 388
Anne Frank-Fonds, Switzerland, 366
Anne Frank Foundation, Netherlands, 274
Anne Frank Fund, Switzerland, 366
Anne Frank Stichting, Netherlands, 274
The Anne Frank Trust UK, UK, 418
The Annenberg Foundation, USA, 468
Anti-Defamation League of B'nai B'rith—ADL,
USA, 469
Anti-Slavery International, UK, 401
AOHR—Arab Organization for Human Rights,
Egypt, 127
AOYE—Arab Office for Youth and Environment,
Egypt, 127
APACE Village First Electrification Group—
APACE VFEG, Australia, 36
APAN—Asian Philanthropy Advisory Network,
Philippines, 301
APC—Association for Progressive
Communications, South Africa, 331
Apex Foundation, Australia, 36
APHEDA—Union Aid Abroad, Australia, 45
APMN—Asia Pacific Mountain Network,
Nepal, 271
Appropriate Technology for Community and
Environment—APACE, Australia, 36
The Arab-British Chamber Charitable
Foundation, UK, 401
Arab Fund for Technical Assistance to African
Countries—AFTAAC, Egypt, 127
Arab Image Foundation, Lebanon, 252
Arab Office for Youth and Environment—AOYE,
Egypt, 127
Arab Organization for Human Rights, Egypt, 127
Arab Thought Foundation, Lebanon, 252
Aragón (José María), Fundación, Argentina, 31
Arbeiterwohlfahrt Bundesverband eV—AWO,
Germany, 160
ARC—American Refugee Committee, USA, 467
Arca Foundation, USA, 469
ArcelorMittal Acesita Foundation, Brazil, 71
Archie Sherman Charitable Trust, UK, 448
Arctic Institute of North America—AINA,
Canada, 81
Arcus Foundation, USA, 469
Areces (Ramón), Fundación, Spain, 340
AREF—African Refugees Foundation,
Nigeria, 289
AREGAK—Sun/Soleil, Armenia, 35
ARGUS, Belgium, 56
Arias Foundation for Peace and Human Progress,
Costa Rica, 106
Arie and Ida Crown Memorial, USA, 483
ARK—Absolute Return for Kids, UK, 401
Armand-Frappier Foundation, Canada, 88
Armando Alvares Penteado Foundation,
Brazil, 71
Armstrong (Lance) Foundation, USA, 469
Arpad Szenes–Vieira da Silva Foundation,
Portugal, 313
Art Fund—National Art Collections Fund,
UK, 401
Arthritis Australia, Australia, 37
Arthritis Foundation, USA, 469
Arthritis Foundation of Australia, Australia, 37
Arthritis Research Campaign, UK, 401
Arthritis Research UK, UK, 401
Arthritis and Rheumatism Council for Research
in Great Britain and the Commonwealth,
UK, 401
Arthur Rubinstein International Music Society,
Israel, 215
Arthur S. DeMoss Foundation, USA, 484
Arts Council England, UK, 402
Arts Council Korea, Korea (Republic), 246
The Arts Grants Committee, Sweden, 354
Asahi Beer Arts Foundation, Japan, 230
Asahi Biiru Geijutsu Bunka Zaidan, Japan, 230
Asahi Glass Foundation, Japan, 230
ASEAN Foundation, Indonesia, 207
Ashden Charitable Trust, UK, 402
Asia-Africa International Voluntary
Foundation—AIV, Japan, 231
Asia Crime Prevention Foundation—ACPF,
Japan, 231
Asia Foundation, USA, 469
Asia/Pacific Cultural Centre for UNESCO—
ACCU, Japan, 231

Asia Pacific Foundation of Canada, Canada, 81
Asia-Pacific Mountain Network—APMN,
Nepal, 271
Asia Society, USA, 470
Asian Community Trust—ACT, Japan, 231
Asian Cultural Council—ACC, USA, 470
Asian Development Research Institute—ADRI,
India, 200
Asian Health Institute—AHI, Japan, 231
Asian Institute for Rural Development,
India, 200
Asian NGO Coalition for Agrarian Reform and
Rural Development—ANGOC,
Philippines, 301
Asian Philanthropy Advisory Network—APAN,
Philippines, 301
Asian Youth Center, USA, 470
ASKO Europa-Stiftung, Germany, 161
ASKO Europe Foundation, Germany, 161
ASMAE—Association de coopération et
d'éducation aux développements, Belgium, 56
Asociácia komunitných nadácií Slovenska—
AKNS, Slovakia, 327
Asociación Española de Fundaciones, Spain, 337
Asociación Latinoamericana de Instituciones
Financieras para el Desarrollo—ALIDE,
Peru, 299
Asociación Latinoamericana de Organizaciones
de Promoción al Desarrollo—ALOP,
Mexico, 262
Asociación Nacional de Organizaciones Sociedad
Civil, Venezuela, 563
ASOR—American Schools of Oriental Research,
USA, 467
Aspen Institute, USA, 470
Assembly of Belarusian Pro-democratic Non-
governmental Organizations, Belarus, 54
Association of Charitable Foundations, UK, 396
Association for Civil Society Development—
SMART, Croatia, 109
Association of Community Trusts and
Foundations, UK, 397
Association de coopération et d'éducation aux
développements—ASMAE, Belgium, 56
Association for Democratic Initiatives—ADI,
Macedonia, 258
Association for Development Co-operation and
Education, Belgium, 56
Association Egyptologique Reine Elisabeth,
Belgium, 57
Association des fondations donatrices suisses,
Switzerland, 360
Association of Foundations and Businesses,
Argentina, 31
Association of Foundations in the Netherlands,
Netherlands, 272
Association of the Friends of the Swedish
Institute at Athens, Sweden, 353
Association of German Foundations,
Germany, 159
Association of Grantmaking Foundations in
Switzerland, Switzerland, 360
Association for International Cancer Research—
AICR, UK, 402
Association Internationale des Charités—AIC,
Belgium, 57
Association of Italian Foundations and Savings
Banks, Italy, 216
Association of Medical Research Charities—
AMRC, UK, 396
Association Mondiale des Amis de l'Enfance,
Monaco, 265
Association of Non-Governmental Organizations
in The Gambia—TANGO, Gambia, 156
Association for Progressive Communications—
APC, South Africa, 331
Association of Slovakian Community
Foundations, Slovakia, 327
Association for the Study of the World Refugee
Problem, Germany, 168
Association of Voluntary Agencies for Rural
Development—AVARD, India, 198
Association of Voluntary Service
Organisations—AVSO, Belgium, 57
Associazione Donatella Flick, Switzerland, 361
Associazione di Fondazioni e di Casse di
Risparmio Spa—ACRI, Italy, 216
Asthma UK, UK, 402
ASTM—Action Solidarité Tiers Monde,
Luxembourg, 257
AT&T Foundation, USA, 471
ATD Fourth World, France, 137
ATD Quart-Monde, France, 137
Atkinson Foundation, USA, 470
Atlantic Philanthropies, USA, 471
Atlas Charity Foundation, Poland, 306
Atlas Economic Research Foundation, USA, 471
Atlas Network, USA, 471

ATSE Clunies Ross Foundation, Australia, 37
Auchan Foundation for Youth, France, 140
Augusto César Sandino Foundation, Nicaragua, 288
Auschwitz-Birkenau Foundation, Poland, 306
Auschwitz Foundation, Belgium, 60
Australasian Spinal Research, Australia, 44
Australia Business Arts Foundation—AbaF, Australia, 37
Australia Foundation for Culture and the Humanities Ltd, Australia, 37
Australia-Japan Foundation, Australia, 37
Australian Academy of the Humanities, Australia, 37
Australian Academy of Science, Australia, 37
Australian-American Fulbright Commission, Australia, 37
Australian Association of Philanthropy, Australia, 36
Australian Cancer Research Foundation, Australia, 38
Australian Conservation Foundation, Australia, 38
Australian Council for International Development, Australia, 38
The Australian Elizabethan Theatre Trust, Australia, 38
Australian Foundation for the Peoples of Asia and the Pacific—AFAP, Australia, 38
Australian Institute of International Affairs, Australia, 39
Australian Multicultural Foundation—AMF, Australia, 39
Australian People Health Education, Australia, 45
Australian Spinal Research Foundation, Australia, 39
Australian Volunteers International, Australia, 39
Australian Youth Foundation, Australia, 41
Austrian Research Foundation for International Development, Austria, 48
Austrian Science Fund, Austria, 47
Austrian Society for Environment and Technology, Austria, 48
Autonómia Foundation, Hungary, 195
Auxilia Foundation, Czech Republic, 112
AVARD—Association of Voluntary Agencies for Rural Development, India, 198
Aventis Foundation, Germany, 161
Aviation Sans Frontières—ASF, France, 137
Aviation Without Frontiers, France, 137
AVINA Foundation, Panama, 297
AVRDC—The World Vegetable Center, Taiwan, 379
AWDF—African Women's Development Fund, Ghana, 185
AWHRC—Asian Women's Human Rights Council, India, 200
AWO—Arbeiterwohlfahrt Bundesverband, Germany, 160
Axel Springer Foundation, Germany, 179
Axel-Springer-Stiftung, Germany, 179
Axel Wenner-Gren Foundation for International Exchange of Scientists, Sweden, 358
Ayala Foundation, Inc—AFI, Philippines, 301
Ayala Foundation USA—AF-USA, USA, 535
Aydın Doğan Foundation, Turkey, 388
Aydın Doğan Vakfı, Turkey, 388
Ayrton Senna Institute, Brazil, 73
Azim Premji Foundation, India, 204

BaBe—Budi aktivna, Budi emancipirana, Croatia, 109
Bacon (Francis) Foundation, Inc, USA, 471
BAFROW—Foundation for Research on Women's Health, Productivity and the Environment, Gambia, 156
Bagnoud (François-Xavier) Association, USA, 495
Baker (E. A.) Foundation for the Prevention of Blindness, Canada, 85
Baker Heart Research Institute, Australia, 39
Baker IDI Heart & Diabetes Institute, Australia, 39
Balint (Andrew) Charitable Trust, UK, 402
Baltic-American Partnership Fund—BAPF, USA, 472
Baltic Sea Foundation, Finland, 131
Balzan Fonds, Internationale Stiftung, Switzerland, 368
Bangladesh Freedom Foundation, Bangladesh, 52
Bangladesh Rural Advancement Committee—BRAC, Bangladesh, 52
BANHCAFE Foundation, Honduras, 193
Bank of America Foundation, USA, 472
Bank of Brazil Foundation, Brazil, 71
Bank of Cyprus Cultural Foundation, Cyprus, 111

Baptist World Aid—BWAid, USA, 472
Barceló Foundation, Spain, 340
Barenboim-Said Foundation, Spain, 340
Bariloche Foundation, Argentina, 32
Baring Foundation, UK, 402
Barka Foundation, Poland, 308
Barnardo's, UK, 403
The Baron de Hirsch Fund, USA, 484
The Barretstown Camp Fund Ltd, Ireland, 210
Barrié de la Maza (Pedro, Conde de Fenosa), Fundación, Spain, 340
The Batchworth Trust, UK, 403
BBC Children in Need Appeal, UK, 403
BBC World Service Trust, UK, 403
BBVA Foundation, Spain, 340
BCAF—Bulgarian Charities Aid Foundation, Bulgaria, 74
Be Active, Be Emancipated, Croatia, 109
Beatrice Laing Trust, UK, 428
The Beautiful Foundation, Korea (Republic), 246
Beaverbrook Foundation, UK, 403
Beinum (Eduard Van) Stichting, Netherlands, 272
Beisheim (Professor Otto) Stiftung, Germany, 161
Beit Trust, UK, 403
Belarusian Charitable Fund 'For the Children of Chornobyl', Belarus, 57
Belém Cultural Centre Foundation, Portugal, 310
Belgian Foundation Network, Belgium, 55
Bell (Max) Foundation, Canada, 81
Bellagio Forum for Sustainable Development, Germany, 161
Benecke (Otto) Stiftung eV, Germany, 161
Benesco Charity Limited, UK, 404
Benetton Foundation for Study and Research, Italy, 219
Benton Foundation, USA, 472
Benzon (Alfred) Foundation, Denmark, 117
Berghof Foundation for Conflict Research, Germany, 161
Berghof Stiftung für Konfliktforschung GmbH, Germany, 161
Bernadottes (Folke) Minnesfond, Sweden, 352
Bernard van Leer Foundation, Netherlands, 277
The Bernard Sunley Charitable Foundation, UK, 450
Bernheim Foundation, Belgium, 60
Bertelsmann Foundation, Germany, 162
Bertelsmann Stiftung, Germany, 162
Bertoni (Moisés) Foundation, Paraguay, 298
Bertrand Russell Peace Foundation—BRPF, UK, 445
Beth (Evert Willem) Foundation, Netherlands, 272
Bettencourt Schueller Foundation, France, 141
Better World Campaign—BWC, USA, 472
Beyaz Nokta Gelişim Vakfı, Turkey, 387
BibleLands, UK, 404
Biblioteca dell'Accademia Nazionale dei Lincei, Italy, 216
BID-INTAL—Instituto para la Integración de America Latina y el Caribe, Argentina, 34
Big Lottery Fund, UK, 404
Bill and Melinda Gates Foundation, USA, 495
Binding (Sophie und Karl) Stiftung, Switzerland, 361
Biotechnology and Biological Sciences Research Council—BBSRC, UK, 404
BirdLife International, UK, 404
Birthright, UK, 455
Bischöfliches Hilfswerk Misereor eV, Germany, 162
Black Sea NGO Network—BSNN, Bulgaria, 75
Black Sea University Foundation—BSUF, Romania, 316
Blanc (José María), Fundación, Spain, 341
Blanceflor Boncompagni-Ludovisi, née Bildt Foundation, Sweden, 356
Bleustein-Blanchet (Marcel), Fondation pour la Vocation, France, 141
Blue Moon Fund, Inc, USA, 473
BMW Foundation Herbert Quandt, Germany, 162
BMW Stiftung Herbert Quandt, Germany, 162
BNP Paribas Foundation, France, 141
BOCONGO—Botswana Council of NGOs, Botswana, 69
Bodossaki Foundation, Greece, 186
The Body Shop Foundation, UK, 405
Boehringer Ingelheim Fonds—Stiftung für Medizinische Grundlagenforschung, Germany, 162
Bofill (Jaume), Fundació, Spain, 338
Boghossian Foundation, Belgium, 60
Böll (Heinrich) Stiftung, Germany, 162
Boltzmann (Ludwig) Gesellschaft, Austria, 46
Book Aid International—BAI, UK, 405
Borchardt (Ludwig) Stiftung, Switzerland, 361
Borderland Foundation, Poland, 307
Bordoni (Ugo), Fondazione, Italy, 219

Born Free Foundation Limited, UK, 405
Bosch (Robert) Stiftung GmbH, Germany, 163
BOTA Foundation, Kazakhstan, 243
Bóthar, Ireland, 210
Boticário Group Foundation, Brazil, 71
Botín (Marcelino) Fundación, Spain, 341
Botswana Council of Non-Governmental Organisations—BOCONGO, Botswana, 69
BRAC—Building Resources Across Communities, Bangladesh, 52
Bradley (Lynde and Harry) Foundation, Inc, USA, 473
Brandt (Bundeskanzler Willy), Stiftung, Germany, 163
Brazil Foundation, Brazil, 70
Brazilian Foundation for Nature Conservation, Brazil, 71
Bread for the World, Germany, 163
Bridge to Asia—BTA, USA, 473
Bridge Asia Japan—BAJ, Japan, 232
The Bridge Foundation, India, 200
The Bridge Foundation—TBF, Ghana, 185
Bridge House Estates Trust Fund, UK, 410
Bridges for Education, Inc—BFE, USA, 473
Brigitte Bardot Foundation, France, 141
Bristol-Myers Squibb Foundation, USA, 473
Britain-Nepal Medical Trust, UK, 405
British Academy, UK, 406
The British Council, UK, 406
British Heart Foundation, UK, 406
British Institute at Ankara, UK, 406
British Institute of International and Comparative Law, UK, 407
British Red Cross, UK, 407
British Schools and Universities Foundation, Inc—BSUF, USA, 473
The Broad Foundations, USA, 474
Brockhoff (Jack) Foundation, Australia, 39
Brookings Institution, USA, 474
Brot für die Welt, Germany, 163
Brother's Brother Foundation, USA, 474
Bruno Kreisky Forum for International Dialogue, Austria, 47
Bruno Kreisky Forum für internationalen Dialog, Austria, 47
The Brush Foundation, USA, 474
Buck (Pearl S. Buck) International, USA, 474
Budi aktivna, Budi emancipiran—BaBe!, Croatia, 109
Building Resources Across Communities—BRAC, Bangladesh, 52
Bulgarian Donors' Forum, Bulgaria, 74
Bulgarian Fund for Women, Bulgaria, 75
Bundeskanzler-Willy-Brandt-Stiftung, Germany, 163
Bundesverband Deutscher Stiftungen eV, Germany, 159
Bunge y Born Foundation, Argentina, 32
Burroughs Wellcome Fund—BWF, USA, 475
Business Formation Foundation, Guatemala, 190
Business Institute Foundation, Spain, 344
Business and Society Foundation, Spain, 342
Butler (J. Homer) Foundation, USA, 504
The Bydale Foundation, USA, 475

C. G. Jung-Institut Zürich, Switzerland, 370
C. P. Ramaswami Aiyar Foundation, India, 204
CAB International, UK, 407
CABI, UK, 407
Cadbury (Edward) Charitable Trust, Inc, UK, 407
Cadbury (William Adlington) Charitable Trust, UK, 407
Caetani (Leone), Fondazione, Italy, 216
CAF—Charities Aid Foundation, UK, 396
CAF Russia—Charities Aid Foundation Russia, Russian Federation, 318
CAFOD—Catholic Agency for Overseas Development, UK, 407
Caisses d'Epargne Foundation for Social Solidarity, France, 141
Caja Madrid Foundation, Spain, 341
Calouste Gulbenkian Foundation, Portugal, 311
The Camargo Foundation, France, 138
Cambridge Commonwealth Trust, UK, 408
Cambridge Overseas Trust, UK, 408
The Camille and Henry Dreyfus Foundation, Inc, USA, 485
Campaign Against Exclusion Foundation, France, 140
The Canada Council for the Arts/Conseil des Arts du Canada, Canada, 82
Canada Foundation for Innovation/Fondation canadienne pour l'innovation, Canada, 82
Canada Israel Cultural Foundation, Canada, 82
Canada World Youth/Jeunesse Canada Monde, Canada, 82
Canadian Baptist Ministries, Canada, 97
Canadian Cancer Society, Canada, 83

Canadian Catholic Organization for Development and Peace, Canada, 83
Canadian Centre for International Studies and Co-operation/Centre d'études et de coopération internationale—CECI, Canada, 83
Canadian Centre for Philanthropy, Canada, 80
Canadian Co-operative Association, Canada, 80
Canadian Council for International Co-operation—CCIC/Conseil canadien pour la coopération internationale—CCCI, Canada, 80
Canadian Crossroads International/Carrefour Canadien International—CCI, Canada, 83
Canadian Executive Service Organization—CESO/Service d'assistance canadienne aux organismes—SACO, Canada, 83
Canadian Feed the Children, Canada, 84
Canadian Foodgrains Bank, Canada, 84
Canadian Friends of the Hebrew University, Canada, 84
Canadian Hunger Foundation, Canada, 84
Canadian International Council/Conseil International du Canada—CIC, Canada, 84
Canadian Liver Foundation/Fondation Canadienne du Foie, Canada, 85
Canadian Organization for Development through Education—CODE, Canada, 85
Canadian Physicians for Aid and Relief—CPAR, Canada, 86
Canadian Urban Institute, Canada, 85
Cancer Council Australia, Australia, 40
Cancer Relief Macmillan Fund, UK, 430
Cancer Research Fund of the Damon Runyon-Walter Winchell Foundation, USA, 541
Cancer Research UK, UK, 408
Cancer Society of New Zealand, Inc, New Zealand, 284
Cancerfonden, Sweden, 352
Canon Foundation in Europe, Netherlands, 272
Capacity Building International, Germany, 172
CARE International—CI, Switzerland, 361
Caribbean Marine Biology Institute Foundation, Curaçao, 110
Caribbean Policy Development Centre, Barbados, 53
Cariplo Foundation, Italy, 219
Caritas de France—Secours Catholique, France, 154
Caritas Internationalis—CI, Vatican City, 562
Carl Duisberg Gesellschaft eV, Germany, 172
The Carl and Lily Pforzheimer Foundation, Inc, USA, 535
Carl-Zeiss Foundation, Germany, 184
Carl-Zeiss-Stiftung, Germany, 184
Carlo Cattaneo Institute, Italy, 227
Carlo Collodi National Foundation, Italy, 223
Carlos de Amberes Foundation, Spain, 339
Carlsberg Foundation, Denmark, 117
Carlsbergfondet, Denmark, 117
CARMABI Foundation, Curaçao, 110
Carnegie Corporation of New York, USA, 475
Carnegie Endowment for International Peace, USA, 475
Carnegie Foundation, Wateler Fund, Netherlands, 272
Carnegie Hero Fund Commission, USA, 476
Carnegie-Stichting, Watelerfonds, Netherlands, 272
Carnegie Trust for the Universities of Scotland, UK, 408
Carnegie UK Trust, UK, 408
Carpathian Foundation, Hungary, 195
Carson (John W.) Foundation, USA, 476
The Carter Center, USA, 476
Carthage Foundation, USA, 476
Cartier Foundation for Contemporary Art, France, 141
Cassel (Sir Ernest) Educational Trust, UK, 409
Caterpillar Foundation, USA, 476
Catholic Agency for Overseas Development—CAFOD, UK, 407
Catholic Agency for World Development—Trócaire, Ireland, 213
Catholic Fund for Overseas Development—CAFOD, UK, 407
Catholic Help—Caritas France, France, 154
Cattaneo (Carlo), Istituto, Italy, 227
Caucasus Institute for Peace, Democracy and Development—CIPDD, Georgia, 157
CBM, Germany, 163
CCCI—Conseil canadien pour la coopération internationale, Canada, 80
CCF—Christian Children's Fund, USA, 478
CCI—Carrefour Canadien International, Canada, 83
CCI—Center for Citizen Initiatives, USA, 476

CCIC—Canadian Council for International Co-operation, Canada, 80
CCK Foundation—Chiang Ching-Kuo Foundation for International Scholarly Exchange, Taiwan, 380
CDCS—Centre for Development of Civil Society, Armenia, 35
CEAAL—Consejo de Educación de Adultos de América Latina, Panama, 297
CEAS—Centre Ecologique Albert Schweitzer, Switzerland, 362
CECHE—Center for Communications, Health and the Environment, USA, 477
CECI—Canadian Centre for International Studies and Co-operation/Centre d'études et de coopération internationale, Canada, 83
CEDPA—Centre for Development and Population Activities, USA, 477
CEDRO—Centro de Información y Educación para la Prevención del Abuso de Drogas, Peru, 299
CEGA—Creating Effective Grassroots Alternatives, Bulgaria, 75
CenDHRRA—Center for the Development of Human Resources in Rural Asia, Philippines, 302
CENSIS—Fondazione Centro Studi Investimenti Sociali, Italy, 216
Centar za razvoj neprofitnih organizacija—CERANEO, Croatia, 109
Centar za Razvoj Nevladinih Organizacija—CRNVO, Montenegro, 267
Center for Citizen Initiatives—CCI, USA, 476
Center for Communications, Health and the Environment—CECHE, USA, 477
Center for Cultural and Technical Interchange between East and West—East-West Center, USA, 487
Center for the Development of Human Resources in Rural Asia—CenDHRRA, Philippines, 302
Center for Human Research and Social Development—CHRSD, Palestinian Autonomous Areas, 296
The Center for International Humanitarian Cooperation—CIHC, USA, 477
Center for Victims of Torture—CVT, USA, 477
Central and Eastern European Media Centre Foundation, Poland, 307
CENTRAS—Assistance Centre for NGOs, Romania, 316
Centre of Advanced European Studies and Research, Germany, 179
Centre for Advancement of Philanthropy—CAP, India, 198
Centre for Civil Society, India, 198
Centre for the Development of Civil Society—CDCS, Armenia, 35
Centre for the Development of Non-Governmental Organizations, Montenegro, 267
Centre for Development of Non-Profit Organizations, Croatia, 109
Centre for Development of Non-Profit Sector, Serbia, 324
Centre for Development and Population Activities—CEDPA, USA, 477
Centre Ecologique Albert Schweitzer—CEAS, Switzerland, 362
Centre for Environment, Education and Development, USA, 516
Centre d'Études, de Documentation, d'Information et d'Action Sociales—CÉDIAS—Musée Social, France, 138
Centre Européen de la Culture—CEC, Switzerland, 362
Centre Français de Droit Comparé, France, 138
Centre Français des Fondations—CFF, France, 135
Centre for the Information Service, Co-operation and Development of NGOs, Slovenia, 330
Centre International de Coopération pour le Développement Agricole—CICDA, France, 136
Centre International de Développement et de Recherche—CIDR, France, 138
Centre International de Recherche sur le Cancer—CIRC, France, 138
Centre Pan-Africain de Prospective Sociale, Benin, 65
Centre for Philanthropy, Ukraine, 393
Centre for Philanthropy and Social Responsibility—Ufadhili, Kenya, 244
Centre for Promotion and Development of Civil Initiatives—OPUS, Poland, 305
Centre for Social Studies, Documentation, Information and Action, France, 138
Centre for Training and Consultancy, Georgia, 157

Centro di Cultura e Civiltà Contadina, Italy, 216
Centro de Información y Educación para la Prevención del Abuso de Drogas—CEDRO, Peru, 299
Centro Internacional de Agricultura Tropical—CIAT, Colombia, 104
Centro Internacional de Mejoramiento de Maíz y Trigo—CIMMYT, Mexico, 262
Centro de Investigación para la Paz, CIP—FUHEM, Spain, 338
Centro Mexicano para la Filantropía—CEMEFI, Mexico, 262
Centro Português de Fundações—CPF, Portugal, 310
Centro Studi e Ricerca Sociale Fondazione Emanuela Zancan Onlus, Italy, 217
Centrul Naţional de Asistenţă şi Informare a Organizaţiilor Neguvernamentale din Republica Moldova, Moldova, 264
The Century Foundation, USA, 477
CEPH—Centre d'Étude du Polymorphisme Humain, France, 142
Cera, Belgium, 57
CERANEO—Centar za razvoj neprofitnih organizacija, Croatia, 109
CERES—Ecuadorean Consortium for Social Responsibility, Ecuador, 124
Česko-německý fond budoucnosti, Czech Republic, 113
CESO—Canadian Executive Service Organization, Canada, 83
Çevre Koruma ve Ambalaj Atiklari Degerlendirme Vakfi—CEVKO, Turkey, 388
CFI—Consuelo Foundation, Inc, USA, 482
CFPA—China Foundation for Poverty Alleviation, China (People's Republic), 102
CGIAR—Consultative Group on International Agricultural Research, USA, 482
CGP—Japan Foundation Centre Global Partnership, Japan, 236
Champalimaud Foundation, Portugal, 310
Chandana Art Foundation International, India, 200
Chardin (Teilhard de), Fondation, France, 150
Charities Advisory Trust, UK, 396
Charities Aid Foundation Bulgaria, Bulgaria, 74
Charities Aid Foundation—CAF, UK, 396
Charity Islamic Trust Elrahma, UK, 409
Charity Projects, UK, 411
Charles A. and Anne Morrow Lindbergh Foundation, USA, 518
Charles Darwin Foundation for the Galapagos Islands—CDF, Ecuador, 124
Charles Delmar Foundation, USA, 484
Charles F. Kettering Foundation, USA, 515
Charles Léopold Mayer Foundation for Human Progress, Switzerland, 364
Charles and Lynn Schusterman Family Foundation—CLSFF, USA, 543
Charles Stewart Mott Foundation—CSMF, USA, 526
Charles Wallace India Trust, UK, 454
Charter 77 Foundation, Czech Republic, 114
Charter 77 Foundation, New York—Foundation for a Civil Society, USA, 492
Chastell Foundation, Canada, 85
Chatham House, UK, 443
Chatlos Foundation, Inc, USA, 477
Chemical Bank Foundation, USA, 526
Chemistry Centre Foundation, France, 147
Chemtech Foundation, India, 201
Cheshire (Leonard) Foundation, UK, 409
CHF International, USA, 478
Chia Hsin Foundation, Taiwan, 379
Chiang Ching-Kuo Foundation for International Scholarly Exchange—CCKF, Taiwan, 380
The Chicago Community Trust, USA, 478
Child Health Foundation—CHF, USA, 478
Child Migrants Trust, UK, 409
ChildFund International, USA, 478
ChildFund Korea, Korea (Republic), 246
ChildHope, UK, 409
ChildHope Asia Philippines, Inc, Philippines, 302
ChildHope Brasil, Brazil, 70
ChildHope—Hope for the Children Foundation, Guatemala, 190
Children in Africa Foundation, Germany, 181
Children of The Americas—COTA, USA, 479
Children International—CI, USA, 479
Children of the Mekong, France, 139
Children and Sharing, France, 139
Children of Slovakia Foundation, Slovakia, 328
Children's Foundation of China, China (People's Republic), 102
Children's Medical Research Institute, Australia, 40
Children's Wish Foundation International—CWFI, USA, 479

Childs (Jane Coffin) Memorial Fund for Medical Research, USA, 479
Childwick Trust, UK, 409
Chile Foundation, Chile, 100
China Environmental Protection Foundation, China (People's Republic), 102
China Foundation Center, China (People's Republic), 102
China Foundation for Poverty Alleviation—CFPA, China (People's Republic), 102
China Medical Board, USA, 479
China NPO Network, China (People's Republic), 102
China Soong Ching Ling Foundation, China (People's Republic), 102
China Youth Development Foundation, China (People's Republic), 103
Chirac Foundation, France, 142
Chobe Wildlife Trust, Botswana, 69
Chr. Michelsen Institute—CMI, Norway, 291
Christian Aid, UK, 410
Christian Blind Mission International, Germany, 163
Christoffel Blindenmission, Germany, 163
Christoph Merian Foundation, Switzerland, 371
Christoph-Merian-Stiftung, Switzerland, 371
Christopher and Dana Reeve Foundation, USA, 538
Christopher Reynolds Foundation, Inc, USA, 539
Christos Stelios Ioannou Foundation, Cyprus, 111
Churches' Commission for Migrants in Europe, Belgium, 57
Churchill (Winston) Foundation of the United States, USA, 479
Churchill (Winston) Memorial Trust, UK, 410
CIAT—Centro Internacional de Agricultura Tropical, Colombia, 104
CIC—Canadian International Council/Conseil International du Canada, Canada, 84
CIDOB Foundation, Spain, 338
CIDR—Centre International de Développement et de Recherche, France, 138
CIDSE—Together for Global Justice, Belgium, 58
CIMADE—Service Oecuménique d'Entraide, France, 138
Cindi Foundation, Czech Republic, 113
Cini (Giorgio), Fondazione, Italy, 220
Cité Internationale des Arts, France, 139
Cité Internationale Universitaire de Paris, France, 139
Citi Foundation, USA, 480
Citizenship Foundation, UK, 410
Città Italia Foundation, Italy, 220
The City Bridge Trust, UK, 410
City of Lisbon Foundation, Portugal, 311
Civic Forum Foundation, Czech Republic, 113
Civic Initiatives, Serbia, 324
Civic Responsibility Foundation, Lithuania, 256
CIVICUS—World Alliance for Citizen Participation, South Africa, 331
Civil Society Development Centre, Turkey, 387
Civil Society Development Foundation, Romania, 316
Civil Society Development Foundation–Hungary, Hungary, 195
Civil Society Support Centre, Georgia, 157
CIVITAS Foundation for Civil Society, Romania, 316
Civitas International, USA, 480
CLADEM—Comité de América Latina y el Caribe para la Defensa de los Derechos de la Mujer, Peru, 299
Claiborne (Liz) and Ortenberg (Art) Foundation, USA, 480
Claude Pompidou Foundation, France, 148
Clean Up the World Pty Ltd, Australia, 40
Clean Water Foundation, Netherlands, 282
Clean Water Fund—CWF, USA, 480
Cleveland Foundation, USA, 480
Cleveland H. Dodge Foundation, Inc, USA, 485
CLIC Sargent, UK, 410
Climate Cent Foundation, Switzerland, 375
Clive and Vera Ramaciotti Foundations, Australia, 43
Clore Duffield Foundation—CDF, UK, 411
Clovek v tisni—spolecnost pri Ceske televizi, o.p.s., Czech Republic, 113
Club 2/3, Canada, 85
Clunies Ross (Ian) Memorial Foundation, Australia, 37
CMI—Chr. Michelsens Institutt, Norway, 291
CNIB/INCA, Canada, 85
CNVOS—Zavod Center za Informiranje, Sodelovanje in Razvoj Nevladnih Organizacije, Slovenia, 330
Co-operation Committee for Cambodia, Cambodia, 79

Co-operation for the Promotion and Development of Welfare Activities, Spain, 342
Co-operative Housing Foundation, USA, 478
Coady International Institute, Canada, 86
Coalition of National Voluntary Organizations, Canada, 80
The Coca-Cola Foundation, Inc, USA, 481
CODE—Canadian Organization for Development through Education, Canada, 85
Cogitare Foundation, USA, 481
the cogito foundation, Switzerland, 362
Collier Charitable Fund, Australia, 40
Collodi (Carlo), Fondazione Nazionale, Italy, 223
Colombian Habitat Foundation, Colombia, 105
Colt Foundation, UK, 411
Columbia Foundation, Canada, 86
Comic Relief, UK, 411
Comité de América Latina y el Caribe para la Defensa de los Derechos de la Mujer—CLADEM, Peru, 299
Commission des Eglises auprès des Migrants en Europe/Kommission der Kirchen für Migranten in Europa, Belgium, 57
Committee of Good Will—Olga Havel Foundation, Czech Republic, 115
Commonwealth Foundation, UK, 411
The Commonwealth Fund, USA, 481
Communication Foundation for Asia, Philippines, 302
Community Aid Abroad—Oxfam Australia, Australia, 43
Community Development Foundation, Mozambique, 269
Community Foundation Network—CFN, UK, 397
Community Foundation for Northern Ireland, UK, 412
Community Foundations Initiative, Germany, 159
Community Fund, UK, 404
Compagnia di San Paolo, Italy, 217
Comprehensive Rural Foundation, Costa Rica, 107
Compton Foundation, Inc, USA, 481
CONCAWE—Oil Companies' European Association for Environment, Health and Safety in Refining and Distribution, Belgium, 58
Concern India Foundation, India, 201
Concern Universal, UK, 412
Concern Worldwide, Ireland, 210
Conrad N. Hilton Foundation and Conrad N. Hilton Fund—CNHF, USA, 503
Conseil des Arts du Canada, Canada, 82
Consejo de Educación de Adultos de América Latina—CEAAL, Panama, 297
Consejo de Fundaciones Americanas de Desarrollo—Solidarios, Dominican Republic, 123
Consejo de Fundaciones Privadas de Guatemala—CFPG, Guatemala, 190
Conservation Foundation, UK, 412
Conservation International, USA, 481
Consuelo Foundation, Inc—CFI, USA, 482
Consultants on Gender and Development, Netherlands, 274
Consultative Group on International Agricultural Research—CGIAR, USA, 482
CONTACT—National Assistance and Information Centre for NGOs in Moldova, Moldova, 264
Cooperación Internacional para el Desarrollo y la Solidaridad, Belgium, 58
Cooperazione Internazionale—COOPI, Italy, 217
COOPI—Cooperazione Internazionale, Italy, 217
Coote (Marjorie) Animal Charities Trust, UK, 412
Le Corbusier Foundation, France, 142
COSIS, Italy, 221
Costa Rican Foundation for Development, Costa Rica, 106
Costopoulos (J. F.) Foundation, Greece, 186
Cottonwood Foundation, USA, 482
Coubertin Foundation, France, 142
Council of American Development Foundations, Dominican Republic, 123
Council for the Education of Adults in Latin America, Panama, 297
Council of Finnish Foundations, Finland, 131
Council on Foundations, Inc, USA, 458
Council of Humanitarian Associations, Czech Republic, 112
Council on International Educational Exchange—CIEE, USA, 482
Council for International Exchange of Scholars—CIES, USA, 483
Council of Private Foundations of Guatemala, Guatemala, 190
Counterpart, USA, 483
Coutu (Marcelle et Jean), Fondation, Canada, 88

Covenant Foundation, USA, 483
CPAR—Canadian Physicians for Aid and Relief, Canada, 86
CPCS—Center for Philanthropy and Civil Society, Thailand, 383
The Craafoord Foundation, Sweden, 352
Crafoordska stiftelsen, Sweden, 352
The Craig and Susan McCaw Foundation, USA, 520
Crane-Rogers Foundation, USA, 506
The CRB Foundation/La Fondation CRB, Canada, 86
CRDF Global, USA, 483
Creating Effective Grassroots Alternatives—CEGA, Bulgaria, 75
Creating Hope International—CHI, USA, 483
Credit Union Foundation Australia—CUFA, Australia, 40
CReDO—Resource Centre for the Human Rights NGOs of Moldova, Moldova, 264
Croucher Foundation, Hong Kong, 194
Crown (Arie and Ida) Memorial, USA, 483
Crown Family Philanthropies, USA, 483
CRT Foundation, Italy, 220
CUFA—Credit Union Foundation Australia, Australia, 40
Cultural Center of the Philippines—CCP, Philippines, 302
Cultural Foundation of the German Länder, Germany, 174
CUSO-VSO, Canada, 86
CVT—Center for Victims of Torture, USA, 477
Cystic Fibrosis Canada, Canada, 87
Cystic Fibrosis Foundation, USA, 484
Cystic Fibrosis Trust, UK, 413
Czech Donors Forum, Czech Republic, 112
Czech-German Fund for the Future, Czech Republic, 113
Czech Literary Fund, Czech Republic, 113
Czech Music Fund Foundation, Czech Republic, 113
Czech TV Foundation, Czech Republic, 113
Czegei Wass Foundation, Hungary, 196

DAAD—Deutscher Akademischer Austauschdienst, Germany, 166
Dag Hammarskjöld Foundation, Sweden, 356
Dahl (Roald) Foundation, UK, 413
Daimler and Benz Foundation, Germany, 164
Daimler und Benz Stiftung, Germany, 164
Daiwa Anglo-Japanese Foundation, UK, 413
Damien Foundation, Belgium, 58
Damon Runyon Cancer Research Foundation, USA, 541
Daniel Langlois Foundation/Fondation Daniel Langlois, Canada, 92
Daniele Agostino Derossi Foundation, USA, 462
Danielle Mitterrand France-Liberty Foundation, France, 151
The Danish Cultural Institute, Denmark, 117
Danish Institute for Human Rights, Denmark, 118
Danish Outdoor Council, Denmark, 118
Danish Peace Foundation, Denmark, 118
Danmark-Amerika Fondet, Denmark, 117
Danske Kulturinstitut, Denmark, 117
Darwin (Charles) Foundation for the Galapagos Islands, Ecuador, 124
Dasra, India, 198
David and Lucile Packard Foundation, USA, 531
Davis (Lady) Fellowship Trust, Israel, 214
DEC—Disasters Emergency Committee, UK, 397
Defence for Children International—DCI, Switzerland, 362
Defense of Green Earth Foundation—DGEF, Japan, 232
The Delius Trust, UK, 413
Delmar (Charles) Foundation, USA, 484
Demokratikus Atalakulásért Intézet, Hungary, 196
DeMoss (Arthur S.) Foundation, USA, 484
DEMUCA—Fundación para el Desarrollo Local y el Fortalecimiento Municipal e Institucional de Centroamérica y el Caribe, Costa Rica, 106
Denmark-America Foundation, Denmark, 117
The Desmond Tutu Educational Trust, South Africa, 335
Desmond Tutu Peace Foundation—DTPF, USA, 549
Deutsch-Russischer Austausch eV—DRA, Germany, 164
Deutsch-Tschechischer Zukunftsfonds, Czech Republic, 113
Deutsche AIDS-Stiftung, Germany, 164
Deutsche Bank Americas Foundation and Community Development Group, USA, 484

Deutsche Bank Endowment Fund for the
  Promotion of Science in Research and
  Teaching, Germany, 182
Deutsche Bank Foundation, Germany, 164
Deutsche Bank Stiftung, Germany, 164
Deutsche Bundesstiftung Umwelt—DBU,
  Germany, 164
Deutsche Gesellschaft für Auswärtige Politik—
  DGAP, Germany, 164
Deutsche Krebshilfe eV, Germany, 165
Deutsche Nationalstiftung, Germany, 165
Deutsche Orient-Stiftung, Germany, 165
Deutsche Stiftung für internationale
  Entwicklung, Germany, 172
Deutsche Stiftung für internationale rechtliche
  Zusammenarbeit eV, Germany, 165
Deutsche Stiftung Weltbevölkerung—DSW,
  Germany, 165
Deutsche Telekom Foundation, Germany, 166
Deutsche Telekom Stiftung, Germany, 166
Deutscher Akademischer Austauschdienst—
  DAAD, Germany, 166
Deutsches Institut für Internationale
  Pädagogische Forschung, Germany, 166
Deutsches Institut für internationale Politik und
  Sicherheit—Stiftung Wissenschaft und
  Politik, Germany, 182
Deutsches Rheuma-Forschungszentrum Berlin,
  Germany, 166
Development Foundation, Guatemala, 190
Development Foundation of Turkey, Turkey, 390
Development Gateway—DG, USA, 484
Development and Peace Foundation,
  Germany, 180
DEVI—Dignity, Education, Vision International,
  India, 201
DeWitt Wallace—Reader's Digest Fund, Inc,
  USA, 551
DGEF—Defense of Green Earth Foundation,
  Japan, 232
DGIA—Stiftung Deutsche
  Geisteswissenschaftliche Institute im
  Ausland, Germany, 179
Diabetes UK, UK, 414
Diageo Foundation, UK, 414
Diakonia, Sweden, 352
Dian Desa Foundation, Indonesia, 207
Diana, Princess of Wales Memorial Fund,
  UK, 414
Dietmar Hopp Foundation, Germany, 170
Dietmar-Hopp-Stiftung, Germany, 170
Dignity, Education, Vision International—DEVI,
  India, 201
Dinu Patriciu Foundation, Romania, 317
Directory of Social Change, UK, 397
Disabled People's International, Canada, 87
Disasters Emergency Committee—DEC, UK, 397
Ditchley Foundation, UK, 414
Dmitry Zimin Dynasty Foundation, Russian
  Federation, 319
Dobbo Yala Foundation, Panama, 297
Dóchas, Ireland, 210
Doctors Without Borders, Switzerland, 371
Doctors of the World International, France, 153
Dodge (Cleveland H.) Foundation, Inc, USA, 485
DOEN Foundation, Netherlands, 280
Doğan (Aydın) Vakfı, Turkey, 388
Dom Manuel II Foundation, Portugal, 311
Dominican Development Foundation, Dominican
  Republic, 123
Don Bosco Foundation of Cambodia—DBFC,
  Cambodia, 79
Donegani (Guido), Fondazione, Italy, 221
Donner (William H.) Foundation, Inc, USA, 485
Donors' Association for the Promotion of Sciences
  and Humanities, Germany, 159
Dr Antonio Esteve Foundation, Spain, 343
Dr Barnardo's, UK, 403
Dr F. P. Haaz Social Assistance Foundation,
  Ukraine, 393
Dr H. P. Heineken Foundation, Netherlands, 275
Dr H. P. Heineken Stichting, Netherlands, 275
Dr J. R. Villavicencio Foundation, Argentina, 33
Dr Marcus Wallenberg Foundation for Further
  Education in International Industry,
  Sweden, 358
Dr Marcus Wallenbergs Stiftelse för Utbildning i
  Internationellt Industriellt Företagande,
  Sweden, 358
Dr Rainer Wild Foundation for Healthy
  Nutrition, Germany, 184
Dr Rainer Wild-Stiftung—Stiftung für gesunde
  Ernährung, Germany, 184
Dr Scholl Foundation, USA, 543
Dräger Foundation, Germany, 166
Dräger-Stiftung, Germany, 166
Dreyfus (Camille and Henry) Foundation, Inc,
  USA, 485

Dreyfus Health Foundation—DHF, USA, 485
DRFN—Desert Research Foundation of Namibia,
  Namibia, 270
Droits et Démocratie, Canada, 96
Drug Policy Alliance—DPA, USA, 485
DSW—Deutsche Stiftung Weltbevölkerung,
  Germany, 165
del Duca (Simone et Cino), Fondation, France, 143
Duke Endowment, USA, 486
Dulverton Trust, UK, 414
Dumbarton Oaks, USA, 486
Dutch Cancer Society, Netherlands, 276

E. O. Wilson Biodiversity Foundation, USA, 555
EABL Foundation, Kenya, 245
Earhart Foundation, USA, 486
Earth Island Institute—EII, USA, 486
Earthrights International—ERI, USA, 486
Earthtrust, Inc, USA, 487
Earthwatch—United Nations System-wide
  Earthwatch, Switzerland, 362
East African Association of Grantmakers,
  Kenya, 244
East-West Center—EWC, USA, 487
Easter Island Foundation, USA, 487
eBay Foundation, USA, 487
Ebelin and Gerd Bucerius ZEIT Foundation,
  Germany, 184
Eberhard Schöck Foundation, Germany, 178
Eberhard-Schöck-Stiftung, Germany, 178
Ebert (Friedrich) Stiftung, Germany, 167
Eça de Queiroz Foundation, Portugal, 312
EcoCiencia—Fundación Ecuatoriana de
  Estudios Ecologicos, Ecuador, 124
EcoHealth Alliance, USA, 487
Écoles Sans Frontières—ESF, France, 139
ECOLOGIA—Ecologists Linked for Organizing
  Grassroots Initiatives and Action, USA, 488
Ecológica Universal, Fundación, Argentina, 32
Ecological Library Foundation, Poland, 307
Ecologists Linked for Organizing Grassroots
  Initiatives and Action—ECOLOGIA,
  USA, 488
Ecology and Agriculture Foundation,
  Germany, 181
Economic Development Foundation, Turkey, 388
Economic Foundation, Poland, 307
ECPAT International, Thailand, 383
ECPD—European Centre for Peace and
  Development, Serbia, 324
Ecuadorean Consortium for Social
  Responsibility—CERES, Ecuador, 124
Ecuadorean Development Foundation,
  Ecuador, 125
Ecuadorian Foundation of Ecological Studies,
  Ecuador, 124
Ecumenical Service for Mutual Help, France, 138
Eden Foundation, Sweden, 353
EDF Foundation, France, 143
The Edmond de Rothschild Foundations,
  USA, 541
The Edna McConnell Clark Foundation,
  USA, 520
Ednannia: Initiative Centre to Support Social
  Action—ISAR Ednannia, Ukraine, 393
EDP Foundation, Portugal, 311
Eduard Van Beinum Foundation,
  Netherlands, 272
Eduard Van Beinum Stichting, Netherlands, 272
Eduardo Capa Foundation, Spain, 341
The Education for Development Foundation—
  EDF, Thailand, 383
Edward Cadbury Charitable Trust, Inc, UK, 407
Eesti Mittetulundusühingute ja Sihtasutuste
  Liit, Estonia, 129
Eestimaa Looduse Fond—ELF, Estonia, 129
EFC—European Foundation Centre, Belgium, 55
EFQM—European Foundation for Quality
  Management, Belgium, 60
Egmont Fonden, Denmark, 118
Egmont Foundation, Denmark, 118
EGMONT—Institut royal des relations
  internationales, Belgium, 58
Einaudi (Luigi), Fondazione, Italy, 221
Einstein (Albert) Institution, USA, 488
Eisai Foundation, France, 143
EJLB Foundation, Canada, 87
Ekhaga Foundation, Sweden, 353
Ekhagastiftelsen, Sweden, 353
Ekopolis Foundation, Slovakia, 327
ELCI—Environment Liaison Centre
  International, Kenya, 244
Eldee Foundation, Canada, 87
ELIAMEP—Hellenic Foundation for European
  and Foreign Policy, Greece, 187
The Elie Wiesel Foundation for Humanity,
  USA, 554

Elizabeth Glaser Pediatric AIDS Foundation,
  USA, 496
Elizabeth Kostova Foundation for Creative
  Writing, Bulgaria, 76
Ellerman (John) Foundation, UK, 414
Else Kröner-Fresenius Foundation, Germany, 173
Else Kröner-Fresenius-Stiftung, Germany, 173
Elton John AIDS Foundation—EJAF, UK, 426
Emanuela Zancan Onlus Foundation Centre for
  Social Studies and Research, Italy, 217
EMERGENCY, Italy, 217
EMI Music Sound Foundation, UK, 415
Emile Chanoux Foundation—Institute for
  Federalism and Regionalist Studies, Italy, 218
Emirates Foundation, United Arab Emirates, 395
Emmaüs International, France, 139
EMonument, Belgium, 58
Empower Foundation, Thailand, 383
EMUNAH, UK, 415
ENCOD—European NGO Council on Drugs and
  Development, Belgium, 59
End Child Prostitution, Child Pornography and
  Trafficking of Children for Sexual Purposes,
  Thailand, 383
Enda Third World—Environment and
  Development Action in the Third World,
  Senegal, 322
Enda Tiers Monde—Environnement et
  Développement du Tiers-Monde, Senegal, 322
endPoverty.org, USA, 488
Energies for the World Foundation, France, 143
EnerGreen Foundation, Canada, 87
Enfance et Partage, France, 139
Enfants du Mekong, France, 139
Enfants Réfugiés du Monde—ERM, France, 140
Eng. António de Almeida Foundation,
  Portugal, 310
EngenderHealth, USA, 488
Engineering and Physical Sciences Research
  Council—EPSRC, UK, 415
English-Speaking Union, UK, 415
Eni Foundation, Italy, 217
Enrico Mattei Eni Foundation, Italy, 218
Ente Cassa di Risparmio di Firenze, Italy, 217
Enterprise Development International, USA, 488
Enterprise Foundation of Benin, Benin, 65
EnterpriseWorks/VITA—EWV, USA, 488
Entraide Protestante Suisse, Switzerland, 367
Entwicklungshilfe-Klub, Austria, 46
Environment Foundation of Turkey, Turkey, 390
Environment and Natural Resources Foundation,
  Argentina, 31
Environmental Foundation Bellona, Norway, 291
Environmental Foundation of Jamaica,
  Jamaica, 229
Environmental Justice Foundation—EJF,
  UK, 416
Environmental Protection and Packaging Waste
  Recovery and Recycling Trust, Turkey, 388
Environmental Protection Research Foundation,
  India, 201
Environnement et Développement du Tiers-
  Monde—Enda, Senegal, 322
Epilepsy Foundation, USA, 489
ERA—Europäische Rechtsakademie,
  Germany, 167
Erik Philip-Sörensen Foundation, Sweden, 356
Erik Philip-Sörensen Foundation for the
  Promotion of Genetic and Humanistic
  Research, Sweden, 356
Erik Philip-Sörensens Stiftelse, Sweden, 356
Erinnerung, Verantwortung und Zukunft,
  Germany, 167
ERM—Enfants Réfugiés du Monde, France, 140
The Ernest C. Manning Awards Foundation,
  Canada, 93
Ernest Kleinwort Charitable Trust, UK, 427
Ernst Schering Foundation, Germany, 177
Ernst-Schering-Stiftung, Germany, 177
ERRC—Europako Rromano Čačimasko Centro,
  Hungary, 196
ERSTE Foundation, Austria, 46
ERSTE Stiftung—Die ERSTE Österreichische
  Spar-Casse Privatstiftung, Austria, 46
Eskom Development Foundation, South
  Africa, 332
Esmée Fairbairn Foundation, UK, 416
Espejo (Eugenio), Fundación, Ecuador, 125
Esperança, Inc, USA, 489
Esquel Group Foundation—Ecuador,
  Ecuador, 125
Estonian Foundation Centre, Estonia, 129
Estonian Fund for Nature, Estonia, 129
Estonian National Culture Foundation,
  Estonia, 129
ETC Group—Action Group on Erosion,
  Technology and Concentration, Canada, 88
Etruscan Foundation, USA, 489

Eugenio Espejo Foundation, Ecuador, 125
Eugenio Mendoza Foundation, Venezuela, 563
Eurasia Foundation, USA, 489
Euris Foundation, France, 144
EURODAD—European Network on Debt and
  Development, Belgium, 59
EURONATUR—Stiftung Europäisches
  Naturerbe, Germany, 180
Euronisa Foundation, Czech Republic, 114
Europa Employment Foundation—Enterprise
  and Solidarity, Italy, 221
Europa Nostra, Netherlands, 273
Europäische Rechtsakademie—ERA,
  Germany, 167
Europako Rromano Čačimasko Centro—ERRC,
  Hungary, 196
European Anti-Poverty Network—EAPN,
  Belgium, 59
European Association for Cancer Research,
  UK, 416
European Centre of Culture, Switzerland, 362
European Centre for Peace and Development—
  ECPD, Serbia, 324
European Centre for Social Welfare Policy and
  Research, Austria, 47
European Climate Foundation, Netherlands, 273
European Coalition for Just and Effective Drug
  Policies—ENCOD, Belgium, 59
European Cultural Foundation—ECF,
  Netherlands, 273
European Environmental Bureau, Belgium, 59
European Federation of National Organizations
  Working with the Homeless, Belgium, 55
European Foundation Centre—EFC, Belgium, 55
European Foundation for the Improvement of
  Living and Working Conditions, Ireland, 211
European Foundation for Management
  Development, Belgium, 59
European Foundation for Quality Management—
  EFQM, Belgium, 60
European Foundation for Street Children—
  EFSC, Luxembourg, 257
European Foundation for the Sustainable
  Development of the Regions—FEDRE,
  Switzerland, 363
European Institute of Health and Social Welfare,
  Spain, 349
European Institute of Progressive Cultural
  Policies, Austria, 47
European Mediterranean Institute, Spain, 349
European Nature Heritage Fund, Germany, 180
European Network on Debt and Development—
  EURODAD, Belgium, 59
European Network of Foundations for Social
  Economy, Belgium, 56
European NGOs on Agriculture, Food, Trade and
  Development, France, 135
European Roma Rights Centre, Hungary, 196
European Science Foundation, France, 144
European Training Foundation—ETF, Italy, 218
European Venture Philanthropy Association—
  EVPA, Belgium, 55
European Youth For Action—EYFA,
  Netherlands, 273
European Youth Foundation—EYF, France, 151
Europese Culterele Stichting, Netherlands, 273
Eurostep—European Solidarity Towards Equal
  Participation of People, Belgium, 60
Eurotransplant International Foundation,
  Netherlands, 274
Evangelisches Studienwerk eV, Germany, 167
Evens Foundation, Belgium, 61
Evert Willem Beth Foundation, Netherlands, 272
Eveson (Violet) Charitable Trust, UK, 416
The Eveson Charitable Trust, UK, 416
The Evian Group at IMD, Switzerland, 363
EVPA—European Venture Philanthropy
  Association, Belgium, 55
Evrika Foundation, Bulgaria, 75
EWC—East-West Center, USA, 487
EWT—Endangered Wildlife Trust, South
  Africa, 332
EYFA—European Youth For Action,
  Netherlands, 273

F. C. Flick Foundation against Xenophobia,
  Racism and Intolerance, Germany, 168
F. C. Flick-Stiftung gegen Fremdenfeindlichkeit,
  Rassismus und Intoleranz, Germany, 168
The F. K. Morrow Foundation, Canada, 94
FAF—French-American Foundation, USA, 494
FAFIDESS—Fundación de Asesoría Financiera a
  Instituciones de Desarrollo y Servicio Social,
  Guatemala, 190
Fairbairn (Esmée) Foundation, UK, 416
Faith, UK, 415
FAL—France Amérique Latine, France, 151
The Family Federation of Finland, Finland, 133

Family Planning, New Zealand, 284
Farm Africa, UK, 416
FARM Foundation— Foundation for World
  Agriculture and Rural Life, France, 145
FARN—Fundación Ambiente y Recursos
  Naturales, Argentina, 31
Fate Foundation, Nigeria, 289
De Faunabescherming, Netherlands, 274
FAVDO—Forum for African Voluntary
  Development Organizations, Senegal, 322
FDC—Fundação para o Desenvolvimento da
  Comunidade, Mozambique, 269
FDD—Fundación Dominicana de Desarrollo,
  Dominican Republic, 123
FDH—Frères des Hommes, France, 152
FEANTSA—Fédération Européenne des
  Associations Nationales Travaillant avec les
  Sans-Abri, Belgium, 55
Federação Democrática Internacional de
  Mulheres, Brazil, 70
Federación Argentina de Apoyo Familiar—FAAF,
  Argentina, 31
Federal Association of Social Welfare
  Organizations, Germany, 160
Federal Chancellor Willy Brandt Foundation,
  Germany, 163
The Federal Trust for Education and Research,
  UK, 416
Fédération des Agences Internationales pour le
  Développement—AIDE, France, 140
Fédération Démocratique Internationale des
  Femmes, Brazil, 70
Fédération Européenne des Associations
  Nationales Travaillant avec les Sans-Abri—
  FEANTSA, Belgium, 55
Federation of International Agencies for
  International Development, France, 140
Fédération Internationale des Ligues des Droits
  de L'Homme—FIDH, France, 135
Fédération Panafricaine des Cinéastes—
  FEPACI, Burkina Faso, 78
Fedesarrollo—Fundación para la Educación
  Superior y el Desarrollo, Colombia, 104
FEDRE—European Foundation for the
  Sustainable Development of the Regions,
  Switzerland, 363
FEE—Foundation for Environmental Education,
  Denmark, 118
Feed the Children, USA, 490
Feed the Minds, UK, 416
Feed My Hungry People, Inc, USA, 490
FEEM—Fondazione ENI Enrico Mattei,
  Italy, 218
FEIM—Fundación para Estudio e Investigación
  de la Mujer, Argentina, 32
Feltrinelli (Giangiacomo), Fondazione, Italy,
  Italy, 221
FEMCONSULT, Netherlands, 274
FEPP—Fondo Ecuatoriano Populorum
  Progressio, Ecuador, 124
Fernand Lazard Foundation, Belgium, 63
Fernand Lazard Stichting, Belgium, 63
Fernando Rielo Foundation, Spain, 347
Ferrero (Piera, Pietro e Giovanni), Fondazione,
  Italy, 221
FEU—Fundación Ecológica Universal,
  Argentina, 32
FFL—Fondation Follereau Luxembourg,
  Luxembourg, 257
FH—Food for the Hungry, USA, 491
FHI 360, USA, 458
FIDH—Fédération Internationale des Ligues des
  Droits de L'Homme, France, 135
FIELD—Foundation for International
  Environmental Law and Development,
  UK, 417
filia.die frauenstiftung, Germany, 168
filia—the Women's Foundation, Germany, 168
Finafrica Foundation—Giordano Dell'Amore
  Foundation, Italy, 220
Financiera FAMA, Nicaragua, 288
FINCA—Fundación Integral Campesina, Costa
  Rica, 107
FINCA International, USA, 490
Finnish Cultural Foundation, Finland, 132
Finnish Foundation for Technology Promotion,
  Finland, 133
Finnish Institute in London Trust, UK, 417
Finnish NGO Foundation for Human Rights—
  KIOS, Finland, 132
FIP—Forum Inicjatyw Pozarzadowych,
  Poland, 305
FIPP—Fondation Internationale Pénale et
  Pénitentiaire, Netherlands, 276
Firefly, Inc., USA, 490
Firelight Foundation, USA, 490
First Peoples Worldwide—FPW, USA, 490
FirstRand Foundation, South Africa, 332

FLAAR—Foundation for Latin American
  Anthropological Research, USA, 492
Flight Safety Foundation, USA, 491
Florence Gould Foundation, USA, 499
Florence Nightingale International Foundation,
  Switzerland, 363
Florence Savings Bank Foundation, Italy, 217
Focus on Hope—Nana Mouskouri Foundation,
  Switzerland, 363
Focus Humanitarian Assistance, Canada, 88
FOKAL—Fondation Connaissance et Liberté
  (Haiti), Haiti, 192
Folke Bernadotte Memorial Foundation,
  Sweden, 352
Folke Bernadottes Minnesfond, Sweden, 352
Follereau Foundation Luxembourg,
  Luxembourg, 257
Folmer Wisti Fonden, Denmark, 122
Folmer Wisti Foundation, Denmark, 122
FOM—Stichting voor Fundamenteel Onderzoek
  der Materie, Netherlands, 281
FONADES—Fondation Nationale pour le
  Développement et la Solidarité, Burkina
  Faso, 78
Fondaccioni per Iniciative Demokratike,
  Kosovo, 248
Fondacioni Shoqeria e Hapur per Shqiperine,
  Albania, 29
Fondacioni Shqiptar per te Drejtat e Paaftesise,
  Albania, 29
FONDAD—Forum on Debt and Development,
  Netherlands, 274
Fondation 30 Millions d'Amis, France, 151
Fondation Abbé Pierre pour le logement des
  défavorisés, France, 140
Fondation Abri International, Canada, 97
Fondation Africaine pour les Technologies
  Agricoles, Kenya, 245
Fondation Agir Contre l'Exclusion—FACE,
  France, 140
Fondation pour l'Agriculture et la Ruralité dans
  le Monde—Fondation FARM, France, 145
Fondation Albert 1er, Prince de Monaco—
  Institut Océanographique, France, 152
Fondation Arabe pour l'Image, Lebanon, 252
Fondation pour l'Architecture, Belgium, 60
Fondation Armand-Frappier, Canada, 88
Fondation Auchan pour la Jeunesse, France, 140
Fondation Auschwitz, Belgium, 60
Fondation de l'Avenir, France, 140
Fondation Baxter and Alma Ricard, Canada, 88
Fondation Bernheim, Belgium, 60
Fondation Bettencourt-Schueller, France, 141
Fondation BNP Paribas, France, 141
Fondation Boghossian, Belgium, 60
Fondation Brigitte Bardot, France, 141
Fondation Caisses d'Epargne pour la solidarité—
  FCES, France, 141
Fondation canadienne contre la faim, Canada, 84
Fondation Cartier pour l'Art Contemporain,
  France, 141
Fondation Casip-Cojasor, France, 142
Fondation Charles Léopold Mayer pour le
  Progrès de l'Homme—FPH, Switzerland, 364
Fondation Charles Veillon, Switzerland, 365
Fondation Chirac, France, 142
Fondation Claude Pompidou, France, 148
Fondation Connaissance et Liberté (Haiti)—
  FOKAL, Haiti, 192
Fondation Le Corbusier—FLC, France, 142
Fondation de Coubertin, France, 142
Fondation Denis de Rougemont pour l'Europe,
  Switzerland, 365
Fondation pour le Développement de la
  Psychothérapie Médicale, spécialement de la
  psychothérapie de groupe, Switzerland, 363
Fondation Eisai, France, 143
Fondation EJLB, Canada, 87
Fondation Electricité de France, France, 143
Fondation Emile Chanoux—Institut d'Etudes
  Fédéralistes et Régionalistes, Italy, 218
Fondation Energies pour le Monde, France, 143
Fondation Ensemble, France, 143
Fondation 'Entente Franco-Allemande',
  France, 143
Fondation de l'Entrepreneurship du Bénin,
  Benin, 65
Fondation d'Entreprise Air France, France, 144
Fondation d'Entreprise France Telecom,
  France, 148
Fondation d'Entreprise Gaz de France,
  France, 144
Fondation d'Entreprise La Poste, France, 144
Fondation d'Entreprise Renault, France, 144
Fondation d'Entreprise VINCI pour la Cité,
  France, 144
Fondation Euris, France, 144

Fondation Européenne de la Culture/Europese Culturele Stichting, Netherlands, 273
Fondation Européenne de la Science, France, 144
Fondation Evens Stichting, Belgium, 61
Fondation FACE—Fondation Agir Contre l'Exclusion, France, 140
Fondation contre la Faim, USA, 491
Fondation FARM—Fondation pour l'Agriculture et la Ruralité dans le Monde, France, 145
Fondation Follereau Luxembourg—FFL, Luxembourg, 257
Fondation pour la formation internationale, Canada, 88
Fondation de France, France, 135
Fondation France-Israel, France, 145
Fondation Franco-Japonaise Sasakawa, France, 145
Fondation Francqui, Belgium, 61
Fondation Franz Weber—FFW, Switzerland, 365
Fondation Fyssen, France, 145
Fondation Groupama Gan pour le Cinéma, France, 145
Fondation Hans Wilsdorf—Montres Rolex, Switzerland, 366
Fondation Henri Cartier-Bresson, France, 142
Fondation Hindemith, Switzerland, 363
Fondation Hirondelle: Media for Peace and Human Dignity, Switzerland, 363
Fondation Hugot du Collège de France, France, 145
Fondation Institut Suisse de Recherche Expérimentale sur le Cancer, Switzerland, 364
Fondation Internationale Florence Nightingale, Switzerland, 363
Fondation Internationale pour la Gestion de la Faune—IGF, France, 146
Fondation Internationale Léon Mba—Institut de Médecine et d'Epidémiologie Appliquée, France, 146
Fondation Internationale Pénale et Pénitentiaire—FIPP, Netherlands, 276
Fondation ISREC, Switzerland, 364
Fondation Jean Dausset—Centre d'Étude du Polymorphisme Humain—CEPH, France, 142
Fondation Jean-Louis Lévesque, Canada, 88
Fondation Jean Monnet pour l'Europe, Switzerland, 364
Fondation Jean-Paul II pour le sahel, Burkina Faso, 78
Fondation Langlois pour l'Art, la Science et la Technologie, Canada, 92
Fondation Latsis Internationale, Switzerland, 364
Fondation Léopold Sédar Senghor, Senegal, 322
Fondation Louis-Jeantet de Médecine, Switzerland, 364
Fondation de Lourmarin Laurent-Vibert, France, 146
Fondation MACIF, France, 146
Fondation MAIF, France, 147
Fondation de la Maison de la Chimie, France, 147
Fondation Maison des Sciences de l'Homme—FMSH, France, 147
Fondation Marc de Montalembert, France, 148
Fondation Marcel Bleustein-Blanchet pour la Vocation, France, 141
Fondation Marcel Hicter, Belgium, 61
Fondation Marcelle et Jean Coutu, Canada, 88
Fondation Marguerite et Aimé Maeght, France, 145
Fondation Méditerranéenne d'Etudes Stratégiques—FMES, France, 147
Fondation Mérieux, France, 147
Fondation Mo Ibrahim, UK, 421
Fondation Mondiale Recherche et Prévention SIDA, France, 148
Fondation Nationale pour le Développement et la Solidarité—FONADES, Burkina Faso, 78
Fondation Nationale pour l'Enseignement de la Gestion des Entreprises, France, 148
Fondation Nationale des Sciences Politiques, France, 148
Fondation Nestlé pour l'Etude des Problèmes de l'Alimentation dans le Monde, Switzerland, 364
Fondation Nicolas Hulot pour la Nature et l'Homme, France, 146
Fondation Orange, France, 148
Fondation des Organisations Rurales pour l'Agriculture et la Gestion Ecologique—FORAGE, Senegal, 322
Fondation Orient-Occident, Morocco, 268
Fondation P&V, Belgium, 61
Fondation du Patrimoine, France, 148
Fondation Paul-Henri Spaak—Stichting Paul-Henri Spaak, Belgium, 61
Fondation Philias, Switzerland, 359

Fondation 'Pour la Science'—Centre International de Synthèse, France, 149
Fondation Prince Albert II de Monaco, Monaco, 265
Fondation Princesse Grace, Monaco, 265
Fondation Pro Victimis Genève, Switzerland, 365
Fondation pour la Recherche Médicale, France, 149
Fondation pour la Recherche Stratégique, France, 149
Fondation René Seydoux pour le Monde Méditerranéen, France, 150
Fondation pour le Renforcement des Capacités en Afrique, Zimbabwe, 567
Fondation Ripaille, France, 149
Fondation Robert Schuman, France, 150
Fondation du Roi Abdul-Aziz al-Saoud pour les Etudes Islamiques et les Sciences Humaines, Morocco, 268
Fondation Roi Baudouin, Belgium, 62
Fondation Rurale pour l'Afrique de l'Ouest, Senegal, 322
Fondation Scelles, France, 149
Fondation Schneider Electric, France, 149
Fondation Simón I. Patiño, Switzerland, 365
Fondation Simone et Cino del Duca, France, 143
Fondation Singer-Polignac, France, 150
Fondation Sommet Mondial des Femmes, Switzerland, 378
Fondation Suisse-Liechtenstein pour les Recherches Archéologiques à l'Etranger, Switzerland, 373
Fondation Syngenta pour une Agriculture Durable, Switzerland, 376
Fondation Teilhard de Chardin, France, 150
Fondation Total, France, 150
Fondation Ushuaia, France, 146
Fondazione Adriano Olivetti, Italy, 223
Fondazione Alessio Pezcoller, Italy, 221
Fondazione Ambrosiana Paolo VI, Italy, 218
Fondazione Angelo Della Riccia, Italy, 221
Fondazione per l'Arte, Italy, 219
Fondazione Benetton Studi Ricerche, Italy, 219
Fondazione Cariplo, Italy, 219
Fondazione Cassa di Risparmio delle Provincie Lombarde—Fondazione Cariplo, Italy, 219
Fondazione Cassa di Risparmio di Padova e Rovigo, Italy, 219
Fondazione Cassa di Risparmio di Torino, Italy, 220
Fondazione Centro Studi Investimenti Sociali—CENSIS, Italy, 216
Fondazione Cittàltalia, Italy, 220
Fondazione Edoardo Garrone, Italy, 222
Fondazione Europa Occupazione—Impresa e Solidarietà, Italy, 221
Fondazione Giangiacomo Feltrinelli, Italy, 221
Fondazione Giordano Dell'Amore, Italy, 220
Fondazione Giorgio Cini, Italy, 220
Fondazione Giovanni Agnelli, Italy, 218
Fondazione Giovanni Lorenzini, Italy, 222
Fondazione Giulio Pastore—FGP, Italy, 223
Fondazione Guido Donegani, Italy, 221
Fondazione Ing. Carlo M. Lerici—FL, Italy, 222
Fondazione Internazionale Menarini, Italy, 222
Fondazione ISMU—Iniziative e Studi sulla Multietnicità, Italy, 222
Fondazione per l'Istituto Svizzero di Roma, Italy, 222
Fondazione Italcementi Cavaliere del Lavoro Carlo Presenti, Italy, 222
Fondazione Lelio e Lisli Basso Issoco—Sezione Internazionale, Italy, 219
Fondazione Leone Caetani, Italy, 216
Fondazione Luigi Einaudi, Italy, 221
Fondazione Nazionale Carlo Collodi, Italy, 223
Fondazione Piera, Pietro e Giovanni Ferrero—ONLUS, Italy, 221
Fondazione Prada, Italy, 224
Fondazione Querini Stampalia, Italy, 224
Fondazione Ricci Onlus, Italy, 224
Fondazione Rodolfo Debenedetti—FRDB, Italy, 220
Fondazione Roma, Italy, 224
Fondazione Roma-Mediterraneo, Italy, 224
Fondazione Romaeuropa, Italy, 224
Fondazione RUI, Italy, 225
Fondazione Salvatore Maugeri—Clinica del Lavoro e della Riabilitazione, Italy, 223
Fondazione di Studi di Storia dell'Arte 'Roberto Longhi', Italy, 225
Fondazione Ugo Bordoni, Italy, 219
Fondazione Umana Mente, Italy, 225
Fondazione Unipolis, Italy, 225
Fondazione di Venezia, Italy, 225
Fondazzjoni Patrimonju Malti, Malta, 261
Fondo per l'Ambiente Italiano—FAI, Italy, 225

Fondo Ecuatoriano Populorum Progressio—FEPP, Ecuador, 124
Fondo Latinoamericano de Desarrollo, Costa Rica, 106
Fonds für Entwicklung und Partnerschaft in Africa—FEPA, Switzerland, 366
Fonds Européen pour la Jeunesse—FEJ, France, 151
Fonds zur Förderung der Wissenschaftlichen Forschung—FWF, Austria, 47
Fonds InBev-Baillet Latour, Belgium, 61
Fonds National de la Recherche Scientifique—FNRS, Belgium, 61
Fonds National Suisse de la Recherche Scientifique, Switzerland, 376
Fonds Wetenschappelijk Onderzoek—Vlaanderen, Belgium, 62
FOOD—Foundation of Occupational Development, India, 201
Food for the Hungry—FH, USA, 491
Food for the Poor, Inc, USA, 491
FOPERDA—Fondation Royale Père Damien pour la Lutte Contre la Lèpre, Belgium, 58
Ford Foundation, USA, 491
Foreign Policy Association, USA, 491
Foreign Policy and United Nations Association of Austria—UNA-AUSTRIA, Austria, 48
Föreningen Svenska Atheninstitutets Vänner, Sweden, 353
Foro Juvenil, Uruguay, 560
Forschungsgesellschaft für das Weltflüchtlingsproblem—AWR, Germany, 168
Forum for African Voluntary Development Organizations—FAVDO, Senegal, 322
Forum on Debt and Development—FONDAD, Netherlands, 274
Forum Inicjatyw Pozarzadowych—FIP, Poland, 305
Forum International de l'Innovation Sociale—FIIS, France, 151
Forum for Non-Governmental Initiatives, Poland, 305
Forumul Donatorilor din România, Romania, 316
FORWARD—Foundation for Women's Health, Research and Development, UK, 417
FOSIM—Foundation Open Society Institute Macedonia, Macedonia, 258
Foundation for Agricultural Development, Ecuador, 125
Foundation for Agricultural Research in the Province of Almería, Spain, 344
Foundation for the Arts, Italy, 219
Foundation for Assistance, Training and Integration of Disadvantaged People, Spain, 339
Foundation for Basic Development, Costa Rica, 107
Foundation for Basic Research in Biomedicine, Germany, 162
Foundation Cassa di Risparmio di Padova e Rovigo, Italy, 219
Foundation Center, USA, 458
Foundation Centre for the Study of Social Investment, Italy, 216
Foundation for Children, Germany, 181
Foundation for a Civil Society—FCS, USA, 492
Foundation for Commercial and Technical Sciences—KAUTE, Finland, 131
Foundation for the Comparative Study of European Dictatorships and their Democratic Transition, Germany, 180
Foundation for the Conservation of the Atlantic Rainforest, Brazil, 72
Foundation Czech Art Fund, Czech Republic, 114
Foundation for Deep Ecology, USA, 492
Foundation for Democratic Initiatives—FDI, Kosovo, 248
Foundation for the Development of Medical Psychotherapy, especially Group Psychotherapy, Switzerland, 363
Foundation for Development and Partnership in Africa, Switzerland, 366
Foundation for Ecodevelopment, Netherlands, 281
Foundation for Environmental Conservation, Switzerland, 366
Foundation for Environmental Education—FEE, Denmark, 118
Foundation for the Financial Assessment of Social Service and Development Institutions, Guatemala, 190
Foundation for Franco-German Co-operation, France, 143
Foundation for Fundamental Research on Matter, Netherlands, 281
Foundation of the Future, France, 140
Foundation for German Humanities Institutes Abroad, Germany, 179

Foundation for German–Polish Co-operation, Poland, 308
Foundation for the Good Governance of International Spaces—Our Spaces, UK, 436
Foundation of the Hellenic World, Greece, 186
Foundation for Higher Education and Development, Colombia, 104
Foundation House of the Social Sciences, France, 147
Foundation for Human Rights and Humanitarian Relief, Turkey, 389
Foundation for International Community Assistance, USA, 490
Foundation for International Environmental Law and Development—FIELD, UK, 417
Foundation for International Scientific Co-ordination, France, 149
Foundation for International Studies—FIS, Malta, 261
Foundation for International Training—FIT, Canada, 88
Foundation for International Understanding, Denmark, 122
Foundation for the Investment and Development of Exports, Honduras, 193
Foundation for Knowledge and Liberty, Haiti, 192
Foundation for Latin American Anthropological Research, USA, 492
Foundation for Latin American Economic Research, Argentina, 32
Foundation Library Center of Japan, Japan, 230
Foundation 'Life for All', Switzerland, 375
Foundation for Local Development and the Municipal and Institutional Support of Central America and the Caribbean, Costa Rica, 106
Foundation for Low-Cost Housing, Venezuela, 564
Foundation for Management Education—FME, UK, 417
Foundation for Medical Research, France, 149
Foundation for Middle East Peace—FMEP, USA, 492
Foundation Museum of American Man, Brazil, 72
Foundation Nicolas Hulot for Nature and Humankind, France, 146
Foundation of Occupational Development—FOOD, India, 201
Foundation Open Society Institute Macedonia—FOSIM, Macedonia, 258
Foundation Open Society Institute—Pakistan, Pakistan, 294
Foundation Open Society Institute—Representative Office Montenegro—FOSI ROM, Montenegro, 267
Foundation for Peace, Ecology and the Arts, Argentina, 33
Foundation for the People's Economy, Costa Rica, 107
Foundation for the Peoples of the South Pacific, Australia, 38
Foundation for the Peoples of the South Pacific—Counterpart, USA, 483
Foundation 'Populorum Progressio', Vatican City, 562
Foundation to Promote Health, Liechtenstein, 255
Foundation for the Promotion of the German Rectors' Conference, Germany, 180
Foundation for the Protection of Nature, Venezuela, 563
Foundation for the Qualification and Consultancy in Microfinance, El Salvador, 128
Foundation for Reading, Germany, 181
Foundation for Research on Women's Health, Productivity and the Environment—BAFROW, Gambia, 156
Foundation for Revitalization of Local Health Traditions—FRLHT, India, 201
Foundation Robert Laurent-Vibert, France, 146
Foundation Rodolfo Debenedetti, Italy, 220
Foundation of Rural Organizations for Agriculture and Economic Management, Senegal, 322
Foundation for Russian-American Economic Co-operation—FRAEC, USA, 493
Foundation of Savings Banks, Spain, 341
Foundation of Spanish Commercial Agents, Spain, 339
Foundation for Sport and the Arts, UK, 417
Foundation for Strategic Research, France, 149
Foundation for the Study of Infant Deaths, UK, 417
Foundation in Support of Local Democracy, Poland, 308
Foundation in Support of Local Development Initiatives, Venezuela, 563
Foundation for the Support of Women's Work, Turkey, 389

Foundation for Sustainable Development, Spain, 348
Foundation for the Sustainable Development of Small and Medium-sized Enterprises—FUNDES International, Costa Rica, 107
Foundation for Swedish Culture in Finland, Finland, 133
Foundation for the Swiss Institute of Rome, Italy, 222
Foundation for the Unity and Development of Rural Communities, Costa Rica, 107
Foundation of Village Community Development, Indonesia, 208
Foundation of Weimar Classics, Germany, 173
Foundation for Women, Spain, 345
Foundation for Women's Health, Research and Development—FORWARD, UK, 417
Foundation for Women's Research and Studies, Argentina, 32
Foundation for Young Australians, Australia, 41
Foundation for Youth Research, Germany, 180
France Amérique Latine—FAL, France, 151
France-Israel Foundation, France, 145
France-Libertés Fondation Danielle Mitterrand, France, 151
France Nature Environnement, France, 151
The Francis Bacon Foundation, Inc, USA, 471
Francis Family Foundation, USA, 493
Franciscans International, USA, 493
Franco-Japanese Sasakawa Foundation, France, 145
Francqui Foundation, Belgium, 61
Frank (Anne) Stichting, Netherlands, 274
Frank Knox Memorial Fellowships, UK, 427
Frankfurt Foundation for German-Italian Studies, Germany, 168
Frankfurter Stiftung für Deutsch-Italienische Studien, Germany, 168
Franz Weber Foundation, Switzerland, 365
Frappier (Armand), Fondation, Canada, 88
Frauen Weltgipfel Stiftung/Fondation Sommet Mondial des Femmes, Switzerland, 378
The Fred Hollows Foundation, Australia, 41
Fredsfonden, Denmark, 118
Freedom of Expression Foundation, Norway, 291
The Freedom Forum, USA, 493
Freedom from Hunger, USA, 494
Freedom from Hunger Council of Ireland—Gorta, Ireland, 211
Freedom House, Inc, USA, 493
Freeman Foundation, USA, 494
Freeplay Foundation, UK, 429
French Agriculturalists and International Development, France, 136
French-American Foundation—FAF, USA, 494
French Centre of Comparative Law, France, 138
French Foundation Centre, France, 135
French National Foundation for Management Education, France, 148
Frères des Hommes—FDH, France, 152
Freshwater Society, USA, 494
Freudenberg Stiftung, Germany, 168
FRIDE—A European Think Tank for Global Action, Spain, 338
FRIDE—Fundación para las Relaciones Internacionales y el Diálogo Exterior, Spain, 338
Fridtjof Nansen Institute—FNI, Norway, 291
Friede Springer Foundation, Germany, 179
Friede Springer Heart Foundation, Germany, 179
Friede Springer Herz Stiftung, Germany, 179
Friede Springer Stiftung, Germany, 179
Friedensdorf International, Germany, 169
Friedrich Ebert Foundation, Germany, 167
Friedrich-Ebert-Stiftung eV, Germany, 167
Friedrich Naumann Foundation, Germany, 175
Friedrich-Naumann-Stiftung, Germany, 175
Friendly (Alfred) Foundation, USA, 494
Friends of the Earth International, Netherlands, 275
Friends of Nature Foundation, Bolivia, 67
Friluftsraadet, Denmark, 118
Fritz Gerber Foundation for Gifted Young People, Switzerland, 366
Fritz-Gerber-Stiftung für Begabte Junge Menschen, Switzerland, 366
Fritz Thyssen Foundation, Germany, 183
Fritz Thyssen Stiftung, Germany, 183
FRLHT—Foundation Revitalization Local Health, India, 201
Frontiers Foundation Inc/Fondation Frontière Inc, Canada, 89
FSLD—Foundation in Support of Local Democracy, Poland, 308
FUHEM—Fundación Hogar del Empleado, Spain, 343
FUNBANHCAFE—Fundación BANHCAFE, Honduras, 193

Fund for the Development of the Carpathian Euroregion, Hungary, 195
Fund for Development and Partnership in Africa, Switzerland, 366
Fund for the Italian Environment, Italy, 225
Fund for an Open Society—Serbia, Serbia, 324
Fundação Abrinq pelos Direitos da Criança e do Adolescente, Brazil, 70
Fundação ArcelorMittal Acesita, Brazil, 71
Fundação Armando Alvares Penteado—FAAP, Brazil, 71
Fundação Arpad Szenes–Vieira da Silva, Portugal, 313
Fundação Assistência Médica Internacional—AMI, Portugal, 310
Fundação de Atendimento à Criança e ao Adolescente Professor Hélio Augusto de Souza—Fundhas, Brazil, 73
Fundação Banco do Brasil, Brazil, 71
Fundação O Boticário de Proteção à Natureza, Brazil, 71
Fundação Brasileira para a Conservação da Natureza, Brazil, 71
Fundação Calouste Gulbenkian, Portugal, 311
Fundação da Casa de Mateus, Portugal, 310
Fundação Centro Cultural de Belém, Portugal, 310
Fundação Champalimaud, Portugal, 310
Fundação Cidade de Lisboa, Portugal, 311
Fundação das Descobertas, Portugal, 310
Fundação para o Desenvolvimento da Comunidade, Mozambique, 269
Fundação Dom Manuel II, Portugal, 311
Fundação Eça de Queiroz, Portugal, 312
Fundação EDP, Portugal, 311
Fundação Eng. António de Almeida, Portugal, 310
Fundação Gaia, Brazil, 71
Fundação Gulbenkian (Calouste), Portugal, 311
Fundação Hélio Augusto de Souza—Fundhas, Brazil, 73
Fundação Iochpe, Brazil, 72
Fundação Luso-Americana para o Desenvolvimento, Portugal, 312
Fundação Maria Cecilia Souto Vidigal, Brazil, 73
Fundação Mário Soares, Portugal, 313
Fundação Maurício Sirotsky Sobrinho, Brazil, 72
Fundação Museu do Homem Americano—FUMDHAM, Brazil, 72
Fundação Oriente, Portugal, 312
Fundação Ricardo do Espírito Santo Silva, Portugal, 311
Fundação Roberto Marinho, Brazil, 72
Fundação Romi, Brazil, 72
Fundação de Serralves, Portugal, 312
Fundação SOS Mata Atlântica, Brazil, 72
Fundació Agrupació Mútua, Spain, 338
Fundació CIDOB, Spain, 338
Fundació Jaume Bofill, Spain, 338
Fundació 'La Caixa', Spain, 338
Fundación Acceso, Costa Rica, 106
Fundación Acíndar, Argentina, 31
Fundación Actilibre, Spain, 339
Fundación AFIM—Ayuda, Formación e Integración del Minusválido, Spain, 339
Fundación de los Agentes Comerciales de España, Spain, 339
Fundación Albéniz, Spain, 339
Fundación Alberto Vollmer, USA, 551
Fundación Alternativas para el Desarrollo, Ecuador, 124
Fundación Alzheimer España—FAE, Spain, 339
Fundación Amancio Ortega, Spain, 346
Fundación Amanecer, Colombia, 104
Fundación Ambiente y Recursos Naturales—FARN, Argentina, 31
Fundación Amigos de la Naturaleza, Bolivia, 67
Fundación Ana Mata Manzanedo, Spain, 345
Fundación Antonio Restrepo Barco, Colombia, 104
Fundación de Apoyo a las Iniciativas Locales de Desarrollo—FUNDAPILDE, Venezuela, 563
Fundación para el Apoyo a la Microempresa—Financiera FAMA, Nicaragua, 288
Fundación Arias para la Paz y el Progreso Humano, Costa Rica, 106
Fundación de Asesoría Financiera a Instituciones de Desarrollo y Servicio Social—FAFIDESS, Guatemala, 190
Fundación de Asistencia para la Pequeña Empresa, Guatemala, 190
Fundación Augusto César Sandino—FACS, Nicaragua, 288
Fundación AVINA, Panama, 297
Fundación Banco Bilbao Vizcaya Argentaria—Fundación BBVA, Spain, 340
Fundación BANHCAFE—FUNBANHCAFE, Honduras, 193

Fundación Barceló, Spain, 340
Fundación Barenboim-Said, Spain, 340
Fundación Bariloche, Argentina, 32
Fundación BBVA—Fundación Banco Bilbao
　Vizcaya Argentaria, Spain, 340
Fundación Bunge y Born, Argentina, 32
Fundación Caja Madrid, Spain, 341
Fundación de las Cajas de Ahorros—FUNCAS,
　Spain, 341
Fundación de Capacitación y Asesoría en
　Microfinanzas, El Salvador, 128
Fundación Carlos de Amberes, Spain, 339
Fundación Charles Darwin para las Islas
　Galápagos—FCD, Ecuador, 124
Fundación Chile, Chile, 100
Fundación Científica de la Asociación Española
　Contra el Cáncer—AECC, Spain, 342
Fundación CODESPA—Futuro en Marcha,
　Spain, 342
Fundación Comunitaria de Puerto Rico—FCPR,
　Puerto Rico, 314
Fundación Corona, Colombia, 104
Fundación Costarricense de Desarrollo—
　FUCODES, Costa Rica, 106
Fundación para la Defensa de la Naturaleza—
　FUDENA, Venezuela, 563
Fundación para el Desarrollo Agropecuario—
　FUNDAGRO, Ecuador, 125
Fundación para el Desarrollo de Base—
　FUNDEBASE, Costa Rica, 107
Fundación para el Desarrollo—FUNDAP,
　Guatemala, 190
Fundación para el Desarrollo Local y el
　Fortalecimiento Municipal e Institucional de
　Centroamérica y el Caribe, Costa Rica, 106
Fundación para el Desarrollo de la
　Microempresa, Guatemala, 191
Fundación para el Desarrollo Regional de Aysen,
　Chile, 100
Fundación para el Desarrollo Sostenible de la
　Pequeña y Mediana Empresa—FUNDES
　Internacional, Costa Rica, 107
Fundación Desarrollo Sostenido—FUNDESO,
　Spain, 348
Fundación Dobbo Yala, Panama, 297
Fundación Dominicana de Desarrollo—FDD,
　Dominican Republic, 123
Fundación Dr Antonio Esteve, Spain, 343
Fundación Dr J. Roberto Villavicencio,
　Argentina, 33
Fundación EAES, Spain, 342
Fundación Ecológica Universal—FEU,
　Argentina, 32
Fundación para la Economía Popular—
　FUNDECO, Costa Rica, 107
Fundación Ecuatoriana de Desarrollo—FED,
　Ecuador, 125
Fundación Ecuatoriana de Estudios Ecologicos—
　EcoCiencia, Ecuador, 124
Fundación Eduardo Capa, Spain, 341
Fundación para la Educación Superior y el
　Desarrollo—Fedesarrollo, Colombia, 104
Fundación EFE, Spain, 342
Fundación Empresa y Sociedad, Spain, 342
Fundación Empresa-Universidad de Zaragoza—
　FEUZ, Spain, 342
Fundación Empresas Polar, Venezuela, 563
Fundación Entorno, Empresara y Desarrollo
　Sostenible, Spain, 343
Fundaciòn Escuela Andaluza de Economía
　Social, Spain, 342
Fundación Esperanza de los Niños,
　Guatemala, 190
Fundación para Estudio e Investigación de la
　Mujer—FEIM, Argentina, 32
Fundación Eugenio Espejo, Ecuador, 125
Fundación Eugenio Mendoza, Venezuela, 563
Fundación Fernando Rielo, Spain, 347
Fundación Gala–Salvador Dalí, Spain, 343
Fundación General Ecuatoriana, Ecuador, 125
Fundación Génesis Empresarial, Guatemala, 190
Fundación Grupo Esquel—Ecuador, Ecuador, 125
Fundación Hábitat Colombia—FHC,
　Colombia, 105
Fundación Herencia Verde, Colombia, 105
Fundación Hogar del Empleado—FUHEM,
　Spain, 343
Fundación Innovación de la Economía Social—
　INNOVES, Spain, 343
Fundación Instituto de Empresa, Spain, 344
Fundación Integral Campesina—FINCA, Costa
　Rica, 107
Fundación Intervida, Spain, 344
Fundación para la Inversión y Desarrollo de
　Exportaciones—FIDE, Honduras, 193
Fundación para la Investigación Agraria de la
　Provincia de Almería—FIAPA, Spain, 344

Fundación de Investigaciones Económicas
　Latinoamericanas—FIEL, Argentina, 32
Fundación Invica, Chile, 100
Fundación Jiménez Díaz, Spain, 344
Fundación José María Aragón, Argentina, 31
Fundación José María Blanc, Spain, 341
Fundación José Miguel de Barandiarán,
　Spain, 340
Fundación José Ortega y Gasset, Spain, 346
Fundación Juan March, Spain, 345
Fundación Juanelo Turriano, Spain, 348
Fundación Laboral Sonsoles Ballvé Lantero,
　Spain, 344
Fundación Lealtad, Spain, 337
Fundación Loewe, Spain, 345
Fundación Luis Vives, Spain, 348
Fundación MAPFRE, Spain, 345
Fundación Marcelino Botín, Spain, 341
Fundación María Francisca de Roviralta,
　Spain, 347
Fundación Mediterránea—IERAL,
　Argentina, 33
Fundación México Unido—FMU, Mexico, 263
Fundación MICROS—Fundación para el
　Desarrollo de la Microempresa,
　Guatemala, 191
Fundación Miguel Alemán AC, Mexico, 262
Fundación Moisés Bertoni—FMB, Paraguay, 298
Fundación Mujer, Costa Rica, 107
Fundación Mujeres, Spain, 345
Fundación Mujeres en Igualdad, Argentina, 33
Fundación Nacional para el Desarrollo, El
　Salvador, 128
Fundación Nacional para el Desarrollo de
　Honduras—FUNADEH, Honduras, 193
Fundación Nantik Lum, Spain, 345
Fundación Natura, Ecuador, 126
Fundación ONCE, Spain, 346
Fundación Pablo Neruda, Chile, 100
Fundación Paideia Galiza, Spain, 346
Fundación Panamericana de la Salud y
　Educación, USA, 532
Fundación Paz, Ecología y Arte—Fundación
　PEA, Argentina, 33
Fundación Paz y Solidaridad Serafín Aliaga—
　FPyS, Spain, 346
Fundación PEA—Fundación Paz, Ecología y
　Arte, Argentina, 33
Fundación Pedro Barrié de la Maza, Spain, 340
Fundación Príncipe de Asturias, Spain, 347
Fundación Promi, Spain, 347
Fundación Rafael del Pino, Spain, 347
Fundación Ramón Areces, Spain, 340
Fundación para las Relaciones Internacionales y
　el Diálogo Exterior—FRIDE, Spain, 338
Fundación La Salle de Ciencias Naturales—
　FLASA, Venezuela, 564
Fundación Salvadoreña para el Desarrollo
　Económico y Social, El Salvador, 128
Fundación Santa María, Spain, 348
Fundación Santillana, Spain, 348
Fundación Sartawi, Bolivia, 67
Fundación Schcolnik, Argentina, 33
Fundación SERVIVIENDA, Colombia, 105
Fundación SES—Sustentabilidad, Educación,
　Solidaridad, Argentina, 33
Fundación Solidaridad, Dominican Republic, 123
Fundación Soros Guatemala, Guatemala, 191
Fundación Unión y Desarrollo de Comunidades
　Campesinas, Costa Rica, 107
Fundación Universidad-Empresa—UE,
　Spain, 348
Fundación de la Vivienda Popular, Venezuela, 564
Fundación de Viviendas Hogar de Cristo,
　Chile, 100
Fundación Yannick y Ben Jakober, Spain, 344
Fundacja Agory, Poland, 306
Fundacja Auschwitz-Birkenau, Poland, 306
Fundacja Bankowa im. Leopolda Kronenberga,
　Poland, 306
Fundacja Biblioteka Ekologiczna, Poland, 307
Fundacja Centrum Prasowe, Poland, 307
Fundacja Gospodarcza, Poland, 307
Fundacja im. Stefana Batorego, Poland, 307
Fundacja Partnerstwo dla Środowiska,
　Poland, 307
Fundacja Pogranicze, Poland, 307
Fundacja Pomocy Wzajemnej Barka, Poland, 308
Fundacja Pro Bono II, Poland, 308
Fundacja Rozwoju Demokracji Loaklnej,
　Poland, 308
Fundacja Solidarności Polsko-Czesko-
　Słowackiej, Poland, 308
Fundacja Współpracy Polsko-Niemieckiej/
　Stiftung für Deutsch-Polnische
　Zusammenarbeit, Poland, 308
Fundacja Wspomagania Wsi, Poland, 308

FUNDAGRO—Fundación para el Desarrollo
　Agropecuario, Ecuador, 125
FUNDAP—Fundación para el Desarrollo,
　Guatemala, 190
Fundatia Dinu Patriciu, Romania, 317
Fundatia pentru Dezvoltarea Societatii Civile—
　FDSC, Romania, 316
FUNDEBASE—Fundación para el Desarrollo de
　Base, Costa Rica, 107
FUNDESO—Fundación Desarrollo Sostenido,
　Spain, 348
Fundhas—Fundação Hélio Augusto de Souza,
　Brazil, 73
FWF—Fonds zur Förderung der
　Wissenschaftlichen Forschung, Austria, 47
FXB International—Association François-
　Xavier Bagnoud, USA, 495
Fyssen Foundation, France, 145

G. Unger Vetlesen Foundation, USA, 549
Gaia Foundation, Brazil, 71
GAIA—Groupe d'Action dans l'Intérêt des
　Animaux, Belgium, 62
Gairdner Foundation, Canada, 89
GAJES—Groupe d'Action pour la Justice et
　l'Egalité Sociale, Benin, 65
Gandhi (Mahatma) Foundation for World Peace,
　Canada, 89
Gandhi Peace Foundation, India, 202
Gannett Foundation, USA, 493
Garden Organic/Henry Doubleday Research
　Association—HDRA, UK, 418
Garfield Weston Foundation, UK, 455
Gates (Bill and Melinda) Foundation, USA, 495
Gates Learning Foundation, USA, 495
The Gatsby Charitable Foundation, UK, 418
Gaudeamus Foundation, Netherlands, 281
Gaz de France Foundation, France, 144
GE Foundation, USA, 495
GEA—Global Environmental Action, Japan, 232
Gebert Rüf Stiftung, Switzerland, 366
Gemeinnützige Hertie Foundation, Germany, 169
Gemeinnützige Hertie-Stiftung, Germany, 169
General Ecuadorean Foundation, Ecuador, 125
General Service Foundation, USA, 495
The George A. and Eliza Gardner Howard
　Foundation, USA, 504
George Cedric Metcalf Charitable Foundation,
　Canada, 94
The George I. Alden Trust, USA, 463
George and Thelma Paraskevaides Foundation,
　Cyprus, 111
Georges Lurcy Charitable and Educational
　Trust, USA, 519
Gerber (Fritz) Stiftung für begabte junge
　Menschen, Switzerland, 366
Gerda Henkel Foundation, Germany, 170
Gerda Henkel Stiftung, Germany, 170
German Academic Exchange Service,
　Germany, 166
German AIDS Foundation, Germany, 164
German Cancer Assistance, Germany, 165
German Catholic Bishops' Organization for
　Development Co-operation, Germany, 162
German Council on Foreign Relations,
　Germany, 164
German Federal Foundation for the
　Environment, Germany, 164
German Foundation for International Legal Co-
　operation, Germany, 165
German Foundation for World Population,
　Germany, 165
German Institute of Global and Area Studies—
　GIGA, Germany, 169
German Institute for International Educational
　Research, Germany, 166
German Institute for International and Security
　Affairs, Germany, 182
German Marshall Fund of the United States—
　GMF, USA, 496
German National Academic Foundation,
　Germany, 182
German National Trust, Germany, 165
German Orient Foundation, Germany, 165
German Rheumatism Research Centre Berlin,
　Germany, 166
German-Russian Exchange, Germany, 164
Getty (J. Paul) Jnr Charitable Trust, UK, 418
Getty (J. Paul) Trust, USA, 496
Giangiacomo Feltrinelli Foundation, Italy, 221
GIFE—Grupo de Institutos, Fundações e
　Empresas, Brazil, 70
Gift of the Givers Foundation, South Africa, 332
Gifts in Kind International—GIKI, USA, 498
GIGA—German Institute of Global and Area
　Studies, Germany, 169
Gilbert Murray Trust, UK, 433
Gilman (Howard) Foundation, USA, 496

Giordano Dell'Amore Foundation, Italy, 220
Giorgio Cini Foundation, Italy, 220
Giovanni Agnelli Foundation, Italy, 218
Giovanni Lorenzini Foundation, Italy, 222
Giulio Pastore Foundation, Italy, 223
Giving USA Foundation, USA, 496
GLARP—Grupo Latinoamericano de
    Rehabilitación Profesional, Colombia, 105
Glasnost Defence Foundation—GDF, Russian
    Federation, 319
The Glass-House Trust, UK, 419
Global Action in the Interest of Animals,
    Belgium, 62
Global Alliance for Women's Health—GAWH,
    USA, 496
Global Digital Solidarity Fund—DSF,
    Switzerland, 366
Global Ethic Foundation, Germany, 181
Global Ethic Foundation Czech Republic, Czech
    Republic, 114
Global Fund for Community Foundations—
    GFCF, South Africa, 331
Global Fund for Women—GFW, USA, 497
Global Greengrants Fund, USA, 497
Global Harmony Foundation—GHF,
    Switzerland, 367
Global Health Council, USA, 497
Global Impact, USA, 459
Global Links, USA, 497
Global Voluntary Service—GVS, Japan, 232
Global Water Foundation, South Africa, 333
Globe Foundation of Canada—GLOBE,
    Canada, 89
Globetree Association, Sweden, 353
GMF—German Marshall Fund of the United
    States, USA, 496
GOAL, Ireland, 211
Gobabeb Training and Research Centre,
    Namibia, 270
Goethe Institut, Germany, 169
Goethe-Institut Inter Nationes, Germany, 169
Goldman (Richard and Rhoda) Fund, USA, 497
Goldman Environmental Foundation, USA, 497
The Goldman Sachs Foundation, USA, 498
Goldsmith (Horace W.) Foundation, USA, 498
Goncourt Academy—Literary Society,
    France, 136
Good Neighbors International, Korea
    (Republic), 246
Good360, USA, 498
Goodenough College, UK, 419
Goodwill Industries International, Inc, USA, 498
Google.org, USA, 498
Gorbachev Foundation, Russian Federation, 319
Gordon (Walter and Duncan) Charitable
    Foundation, Canada, 89
Gordon and Betty Moore Foundation, USA, 525
Gorta—Freedom from Hunger Council of
    Ireland, Ireland, 211
Gottlieb (Adolph and Esther) Foundation, Inc,
    USA, 498
Gould (Florence) Foundation, USA, 499
Gradjanske inicijative—GI, Serbia, 324
Graduate Institute of International Studies and
    Development Studies, Switzerland, 367
Graham Foundation for Advanced Studies in the
    Fine Arts, USA, 499
Grameen Foundation—GF, USA, 499
Grant (William T.) Foundation, USA, 499
Grantmakers Without Borders—Gw/oB,
    USA, 459
The Grass Foundation, USA, 499
Grassroots International—GRI, USA, 500
Great Britain Sasakawa Foundation, UK, 419
Green Heritage Foundation, Colombia, 105
Green Perspective Foundation, Slovakia, 328
Greve (William and Mary) Foundation, Inc,
    USA, 500
Group of Institutes, Foundations and
    Enterprises, Brazil, 70
Groupama Gan Foundation for the Cinema,
    France, 145
Groupe d'Action dans l'Intérêt des Animaux—
    GAIA, Belgium, 62
Groupe d'Action pour la Justice et l'Egalité
    Sociale—GAJES, Benin, 65
GRUMIN—Grupo Mulher-Educação Indigena,
    Brazil, 73
Grupa Zagranica, Poland, 305
Grupo de Fundaciones y Empresas, Argentina, 31
Grupo Latinoamericano para la Participación, la
    Integración y la Inclusión de Personas con
    Discapacidad—GLARP-IIPD, Colombia, 105
Grupo Mulher-Educação Indigena—GRUMIN,
    Brazil, 73
Gruss (Joseph S. and Caroline) Life Monument
    Fund, Israel, 214

Guggenheim (Harry Frank) Foundation,
    USA, 500
Guggenheim (John Simon) Memorial Foundation,
    USA, 500
Guggenheim (Solomon R.) Foundation, USA, 500
Guido Donegani Foundation, Italy, 221
Gulf Research Center, United Arab Emirates, 395
Gulf Research Center Foundation,
    Switzerland, 367
GURT Resource Centre for NGO Development,
    Ukraine, 393
Guttman Center of Applied Social Research,
    Israel, 214
Gyllenbergs (Signe och Ane) stiftelse,
    Finland, 131

H. W. and J. Hector Foundation, Germany, 169
H. W. und J. Hector-Stiftung, Germany, 169
Haaz (Dr F. P.) Social Assistance Foundation,
    Ukraine, 393
Habitat for Humanity International, USA, 500
Haburas Foundation, Timor-Leste, 386
The Hague Club, UK, 397
HAI—Health Alliance International, USA, 501
Haitian Economic Development Foundation,
    Haiti, 192
HALO Trust, UK, 419
Hamdard Foundation Pakistan, Pakistan, 294
Hamlyn (Paul) Foundation, UK, 419
Hammarskjölds (Dag), Minnesfond, Stiftelsen,
    Sweden, 356
Handicap International, France, 152
Haniel Foundation, Germany, 169
Haniel-Stiftung, Germany, 169
Hanns Seidel Foundation, Germany, 178
Hanns-Seidel-Stiftung eV, Germany, 178
Hans Wilsdorf Foundation, Switzerland, 366
Haribon Foundation, Philippines, 302
Haribon Foundation for the Conservation of
    Natural Resources, Inc, Philippines, 302
Harold Hyam Wingate Foundation, UK, 456
The Harry Frank Guggenheim Foundation,
    USA, 500
Harry and Jeanette Weinberg Foundation, Inc,
    USA, 552
Hartford (John A.) Foundation, Inc, USA, 501
Hasbro Children's Fund, Inc, USA, 501
Havelaar (Max) Foundation, Netherlands, 281
Headley Trust, UK, 420
Health Action International, Netherlands, 275
Health Alliance International—HAI, USA, 501
Health Foundation, UK, 420
Health Volunteers Overseas—HVO, USA, 501
For a Healthy Generation, Uzbekistan, 561
Hearst (William Randolph) Foundation, USA, 502
The Hearst Foundation, Inc, USA, 501
Heart Foundation, Australia, 42
Heart to Heart International, USA, 502
Hebrew Immigrant Aid Society—HIAS, USA, 502
Hedwig and Robert Samuel Foundation,
    Germany, 177
Hedwig und Robert Samuel-Stiftung,
    Germany, 177
Heifer International, USA, 502
Heine (Heinrich) Stiftung für Philosophie und
    Kritische Wissenschaft, Germany, 170
Heineken (Alfred) Fondsen Foundation,
    Netherlands, 281
Heineken (Dr H. P.) Stichting, Netherlands, 275
Heineman (Minna James) Stiftung, Germany, 170
Heinrich Böll Foundation, Germany, 162
Heinrich-Böll-Stiftung, Germany, 162
Heinrich Heine Foundation for Philosophy and
    Critical Theory, Germany, 170
Heinrich-Heine-Stiftung für Philosophie und
    Kritische Wissenschaft, Germany, 170
Heinz (Howard) Endowment, USA, 502
Heinz, Anna and Carol Kroch Foundation,
    UK, 427
Heiser Program for Research in Leprosy and
    Tuberculosis, USA, 503
HEKS—Hilfswerk Evangelischen Kirchen
    Schweiz, Switzerland, 367
Helen Keller International—HKI, USA, 514
The Helen Suzman Foundation, South Africa, 335
The Helene Wurlitzer Foundation of New Mexico,
    USA, 558
Hélio Augusto de Souza Foundation, Brazil, 73
Hellenic Foundation for Culture, Greece, 186
Hellenic Foundation for European and Foreign
    Policy—ELIAMEP, Greece, 187
Hellenic Society for Disabled Children,
    Greece, 187
Helmich (Janson Johan og Marcia) Legat,
    Norway, 291
Helmsley (Leona M. and Harry B.) Charitable
    Trust, USA, 503
Helmut Horten Foundation, Switzerland, 367

Helmut-Horten-Stiftung, Switzerland, 367
HELP International, USA, 503
HelpAge International, UK, 420
Helsingin Sanomain Säätiö, Finland, 131
Helsingin Sanomat Foundation, Finland, 131
Helvetas Swiss Intercooperation,
    Switzerland, 367
Henie Onstad Art Centre, Norway, 292
Henie Onstad kunstsenter, Norway, 292
Henkel (Gerda) Stiftung, Germany, 170
Henri Cartier-Bresson Foundation, France, 142
Henrietta Szold Institute—National Institute for
    Research in the Behavioural Sciences,
    Israel, 215
Henry Doubleday Research Association, UK, 418
The Henry J. Kaiser Family Foundation, USA, 513
Henry Luce Foundation, Inc, USA, 519
The Henry Moore Foundation, UK, 432
The Henry Smith Charity, UK, 448
HER Fund, Hong Kong, 194
Heritage Foundation, France, 148
Heritage Lottery Fund—HLF, UK, 420
Hesse and Thuringia Savings Banks Cultural
    Foundation, Germany, 178
Hestia—The National Volunteer Centre, Czech
    Republic, 114
Hewlett (William and Flora) Foundation,
    USA, 503
Heydar Aliyev Foundation, Azerbaijan, 50
HIAS—Hebrew Immigrant Aid Society, USA, 502
Hicter (Marcel), Fondation, Belgium, 61
Higgins (Terrence) Trust, UK, 420
Hilden Charitable Fund, UK, 421
Hilfswerk der Evangelischen Kirchen Schweiz—
    HEKS, Switzerland, 367
Hilton (Conrad N.) Foundation, USA, 503
Hilton (Conrad N.) Fund, USA, 503
Himalaya Foundation, Taiwan, 379
Himalayan Light Foundation—HLF, Nepal, 271
Hindemith Foundation, Switzerland, 363
Hirsch (Baron de) Fund, USA, 484
Hirschfeld-Eddy Foundation, Germany, 170
Hirschfeld-Eddy-Stiftung, Germany, 170
Hisar Education Foundation—HEV, Turkey, 388
History Foundation of Turkey, Turkey, 389
Hitachi Foundation, USA, 504
The Hitachi Scholarship Foundation, Japan, 232
HIVOS—Humanistisch Institut voor
    Ontwikkelings Samenwerking,
    Netherlands, 275
Hjärt-Lungfonden, Sweden, 353
HLF—Himalayan Light Foundation, Nepal, 271
Hodge (Jane) Foundation, UK, 421
Hogar de Cristo, Chile, 100
Hollows (Fred) Foundation, Australia, 41
Holt International, USA, 504
Holt International Children's Services—HICS,
    USA, 504
Home of Christ, Chile, 100
Homeland Foundation, USA, 522
Homeless International, UK, 421
Honda Foundation, Japan, 233
Hong Kong Society for the Blind, Hong Kong, 194
Hope for the Children Foundation,
    Guatemala, 190
HOPE International Development Agency—
    HOPE, Canada, 90
Hopp (Dietmar) Stiftung, Germany, 170
Horace W. Goldsmith Foundation, USA, 498
Horizons of Friendship, Canada, 90
Horizonti, the Foundation for the Third Sector,
    Georgia, 157
Hornby (A. S.) Educational Trust, UK, 421
Horten (Helmut) Stiftung, Switzerland, 367
Hoso Bunka Foundation, Inc—HBF, Japan, 233
Hospital for Sick Children Foundation,
    Canada, 97
House of Europe Cultural Foundation,
    Germany, 174
Housing Services Foundation, Colombia, 105
Houston Endowment, Inc, USA, 504
Howard (George A. and Eliza Gardner)
    Foundation, USA, 504
Howard (Katharine) Foundation, Ireland, 211
Howard Gilman Foundation, Inc, USA, 496
Howard Heinz Endowment, USA, 502
Howard Hughes Medical Institute—HHMI,
    USA, 504
Howard Karagheusian Commemorative
    Corporation—HKCC, USA, 513
Hugot Foundation of the Collège of France,
    France, 145
Human Resource Development Foundation,
    Turkey, 389
Human Rights Foundation of Turkey, Turkey, 390
Human Rights Watch—HRW, USA, 505
The Humana Foundation, Inc, USA, 505

Humanistic Institute for Co-operation with
Developing Countries, Netherlands, 275
Humanistisch Instituut voor Ontwikkelings
Samenwerking—HIVOS, Netherlands, 275
Humanitarian Relief Foundation, Turkey, 389
von Humboldt (Alexander) Stiftung, Germany, 170
Hungarian Foundation for Self-Reliance—HFSR,
Hungary, 195
Hungarian Interchurch Aid—HIA, Hungary, 196
The Hunger Project, USA, 505

IACD—Institute of Asian Culture and
Development, Korea (Republic), 246
IAESTE—International Association for the
Exchange of Students for Technical
Experience, UK, 422
IAI—Istituto Affari Internazionali, Italy, 226
Ian Potter Foundation, Australia, 43
IAPA Scholarship Fund, USA, 505
IARC—International Agency for Research on
Cancer, France, 138
IASC—International Arctic Science Committee,
Germany, 171
IATSS—International Association of Traffic and
Safety Sciences, Japan, 233
IBIS, Denmark, 118
IBM International Foundation, USA, 505
IBON Foundation, Philippines, 303
ICAA—International Council on Alcohol and
Addictions, Switzerland, 368
ICAF—International Child Art Foundation,
USA, 507
Icelandic Human Rights Centre, Iceland, 197
ICLARM—The World Fish Center, Malaysia, 260
ICN Foundation, Czech Republic, 112
ICN—Information Centre for Non-profit
Organizations, Czech Republic, 112
ICNL—International Center for Not-for-Profit
Law, USA, 507
ICSSR—Indian Council of Social Science
Research, India, 202
ICVA—International Council of Voluntary
Agencies, Switzerland, 359
IDC—Innovation and Development Centre,
Ukraine, 393
IDLO—International Development Law
Organization, Italy, 226
IEIAS—Institut Européen Interuniversitaire de
l'Action Sociale, Belgium, 62
IEMed—Institut Europeu de la Mediterrània,
Spain, 349
IERAL—Fundación Mediterránea,
Argentina, 33
IFAD—International Fund for Agricultural
Development, Italy, 226
IFAW—International Fund for Animal Welfare,
USA, 509
IFES—International Foundation for Electoral
Systems, USA, 509
IFHD—International Foundation for Human
Development, India, 203
IHCF—Stiftung zur Förderung der Gesundheit,
Liechtenstein, 255
IHE—International Health Exchange, UK, 441
IIEE—Indian Institute of Ecology and
Environment, India, 202
IISD—International Institute for Sustainable
Development, Canada, 91
IKEA Foundation, Netherlands, 275
IKGV—İnsan Kaynağını Geliştirme Vakfı,
Turkey, 389
İktisadi Kalkınma Vakfı, Turkey, 388
Îles de Paix, Belgium, 62
IMA World Health—Interchurch Medical
Assistance, Inc, USA, 506
IMADR—International Movement against All
Forms of Discrimination and Racism,
Japan, 234
Imagine Canada, Canada, 80
Impact First International, Canada, 89
Imperial Cancer Research Fund, UK, 408
Imperial Oil Foundation, Canada, 90
InBev-Baillet Latour Fund, Belgium, 61
Inclusion International—II, UK, 421
Independent Sector, USA, 459
India Assistance, Germany, 171
India Partners, USA, 506
Indian Centre for Philanthropy, India, 198
Indian Council for Child Welfare, India, 202
Indian Council for Cultural Relations, India, 202
Indian Council of Social Science Research—
ICSSR, India, 202
Indian National Trust for Art and Cultural
Heritage—INTACH, India, 203
IndianNGOs.com Pvt Ltd, India, 198
Indienhilfe eV, Germany, 171
Indigenous Women's Education Group, Brazil, 73

Indonesia Biodiversity Foundation,
Indonesia, 208
Indonesian Forum for the Environment—Friends
of the Earth Indonesia, Indonesia, 207
Indonesian Foundation for Rural Progress,
Indonesia, 207
Indonesian Prosperity Foundation,
Indonesia, 208
INFID—International NGO Forum on
Indonesian Development, Indonesia, 207
Information Centre for Foundations and other
Non-profit Organizations—ICN, Czech
Republic, 112
Information and Education Centre for the
Prevention of Drug Abuse, Peru, 299
Information Society of Ukraine Foundation,
Ukraine, 394
Ing. Carlo M. Lerici Foundation, Italy, 222
INHURED International—International
Institute for Human Rights, Environment and
Development, Nepal, 271
Initiative and Achievement, Foundation of the
Nassauische Sparkasse for Culture, Sport and
Society, Germany, 171
Initiative Bürgerstiftungen, Germany, 159
Initiative und Leistung, Stiftung der
Nassauischen Sparkasse für Kultur, Sport
und Gesellschaft, Germany, 171
Inlaks Foundation, India, 203
INMED Partnerships for Children, USA, 506
Innes (John) Foundation, UK, 422
Innovation and Development Centre—IDC,
Ukraine, 393
INNOVES—Fundación Innovación de la
Economía Social, Spain, 343
İnsan Hak ve Hürriyetleri İnsani Yardım Vakfı,
Turkey, 389
İnsan Kaynağını Geliştirme Vakfı—IKGV,
Turkey, 389
Institusjonen Fritt Ord, Norway, 291
Institut für Agrarentwicklung in Mittel- und
Osteuropa—IAMO, Germany, 171
Institut Arctique de l'Amérique du Nord—IAAN,
Canada, 81
Institut Català Mediterrània, Spain, 349
Institut Européen Interuniversitaire de l'Action
Sociale—IEIAS, Belgium, 62
Institut Europeu de la Mediterrània—IEMed,
Spain, 349
Institut international des Droits de l'Enfant,
Switzerland, 368
Institut de Médecine et d'Épidémiologie
Africaines—Fondation Léon Mba,
France, 146
Institut for Menneskerettigheder, Denmark, 118
Institut Mittag-Leffler, Sweden, 353
Institut Néerlandais, France, 152
Institut Nord-Sud, Canada, 95
Institut Océanographique—Fondation Albert 1er,
Prince de Monaco, France, 152
Institut Pasteur, France, 152
Institut Pasteur de Lille, France, 153
Institut royal des relations internationales—
EGMONT, Belgium, 58
Institut Universitaire de Hautes Etudes
Internationales et du Développement,
Switzerland, 367
Institut urbain du Canada, Canada, 85
Institute for Agricultural Development in
Central and Eastern Europe, Germany, 171
Institute of Asian Culture and Development—
IACD, Korea (Republic), 246
Institute of British Geographers, UK, 443
Institute of Cultural Affairs International,
Canada, 90
Institute of Current World Affairs—ICWA,
USA, 506
Institute of Developing Economies/Japan
External Trade Organization—IDE-JETRO,
Japan, 233
Institute for Development Research, USA, 556
The Institute of Energy Economics, Japan—
IEEJ, Japan, 233
Institute for European Environmental Policy—
IEEP, UK, 422
Institute of Human Rights and Humanitarian
Law, Nigeria, 289
Institute of International Affairs, Italy, 226
Institute of International Education—IIE,
USA, 506
Institute for Latin American and Caribbean
Integration, Argentina, 34
Institute for Palestine Studies, Publishing and
Research Organization—IPS, Lebanon, 252
Institute for Private Enterprise and
Democracy—IPED, Poland, 309
Institute for Scientific Interchange Foundation—
ISI, Italy, 225

Institute of Social Studies—ISS,
Netherlands, 276
Instituto Ayrton Senna, Brazil, 73
Instituto Europeo de Salud y Bienestar Social,
Spain, 349
Instituto para la Integración de América Latina y
el Caribe—BID-INTAL, Argentina, 34
Instituto Interamericano de Derechos
Humanos—IIHR, Costa Rica, 107
Instituto Senna (Ayrton), Brazil, 73
Instituto del Tercer Mundo—ITeM, Uruguay, 560
Instituto Torcuato di Tella, Argentina, 34
Institutul Cultural Român, Romania, 317
INTACH (UK) Trust, India, 203
INTACH—Indian National Trust for Art and
Cultural Heritage, India, 203
INTEGRATA Foundation, Germany, 171
INTEGRATA—Stiftung für Humane Nutzung
der Informationstechnologie, Germany, 171
Integrated Rural Development Foundation,
Philippines, 303
Inter-American Foundation—IAF, USA, 507
Inter-American Institute of Human Rights, Costa
Rica, 107
Inter American Press Association Scholarship
Fund, USA, 505
Inter Pares, Canada, 90
Interact Worldwide, UK, 422
InterAction American Council for Voluntary
International Action, USA, 459
Interchurch Medical Assistance, Inc, USA, 506
Intermediate Technology Development Group—
ITDG, UK, 439
Intermón Oxfam, Spain, 349
Internationaal Instituut voor Sociale
Geschiedenis—IISG, Netherlands, 276
International Agency for Research on Cancer—
IARC, France, 138
International Aid, Inc—IA, USA, 507
International Alert—Alert, UK, 422
International Arctic Science Committee—IASC,
Germany, 171
International Association of Charities,
Belgium, 57
International Association for the Exchange of
Students for Technical Experience—IAESTE,
UK, 422
International Association of Traffic and Safety
Sciences, Japan, 233
International Baccalaureate Organization—IBO,
Switzerland, 368
International Balzan Foundation—Fund,
Switzerland, 368
International Balzan Foundation—Prize,
Italy, 226
International Bank of Ideas, Russian
Federation, 318
International Blue Crescent Relief and
Development Foundation—IBC, Turkey, 390
International Center for Not-for-Profit Law—
ICNL, USA, 507
International Center for Research on Women—
ICRW, USA, 507
International Centre for the Arts, France, 139
International Centre for Democratic
Transition—ICDT, Hungary, 196
International Centre for Development and
Research, France, 138
International Centre for Human Rights and
Democratic Development, Canada, 96
International Centre for the Legal Protection of
Human Rights—Interights, UK, 423
International Centre for Living Aquatic
Resources—ICLARM, Malaysia, 260
International Centre for Tropical Agriculture,
Colombia, 104
International Charitable Fund of Bermuda—
ICFB, Bermuda, 66
International Charitable Fund 'Ukraine 3000',
Ukraine, 394
International Child Art Foundation, USA, 507
International Co-operation, Italy, 217
International Co-operation for Development and
Solidarity, Belgium, 58
International College of Surgeons—ICS,
USA, 508
International Confederation of Catholic
Organizations for Charitable and Social
Action, Vatican City, 562
International Confederation of Family Support,
Argentina, 31
International Council on Alcohol and
Addictions—ICAA, Switzerland, 368
International Council for Bird Preservation,
UK, 404
International Council of Voluntary Agencies—
ICVA, Switzerland, 359
International Dental Rescue, Switzerland, 374

International Development Center of Japan, Japan, 234
International Development Law Organization—IDLO, Italy, 226
International Development and Relief Foundation, Canada, 91
International Diabetes Institute, Australia, 39
International Education Research Foundation, Inc—IERF, USA, 508
International Emergency Action, France, 136
International Environmental Foundation of the Kommunale Umwelt-AktioN UAN—IntEF-UAN, Germany, 172
International Executive Service Corps— IESC, USA, 508
International Eye Foundation—IEF, USA, 508
International Federation of Human Rights, France, 135
International Forum for Social Innovation—IFSI, France, 151
The International Foundation, USA, 508
International Foundation for Art Research—IFAR, USA, 508
International Foundation for the Conservation of Wildlife, France, 146
International Foundation for Culture and Civilization, Germany, 172
International Foundation for Education and Self-Help—IFESH, USA, 509
International Foundation for Electoral Systems—IFES, USA, 509
International Foundation for Ethical Research, USA, 509
International Foundation for Genetic Research—The Michael Fund, USA, 524
International Foundation of the High-Altitude Research Stations Jungfraujoch and Gornergrat, Switzerland, 369
International Foundation for Human Development—IFHD, India, 203
International Foundation Léon Mba—Institute of Applied Medicine and Epidemiology, France, 146
International Foundation for Science—IFS, Sweden, 354
International Foundation for Social, Economic, and Political Research—Gorbachev Foundation, Russian Federation, 319
The International Foundation for Socio-Economic and Political Studies, Russian Federation, 319
International Fund for Agricultural Development—IFAD, Italy, 226
International Fund for Animal Welfare—IFAW, USA, 509
International Fund for Ireland, Ireland, 211
International Health Exchange—IHE, UK, 441
International Humanitarian Assistance—IHA, Albania, 29
International Institute for Applied Systems Analysis—IIASA, Austria, 47
International Institute for Environment and Development—IIED, UK, 423
International Institute for Human Rights, Environment and Development—INHURED International, Nepal, 271
International Institute for the Rights of the Child, Switzerland, 368
International Institute of Rural Reconstruction—IIRR, Philippines, 303
International Institute of Social History—IISH, Netherlands, 276
International Institute of Social Studies (ISS), Netherlands, 276
The International Institute for Strategic Studies—IISS, UK, 423
International Institute for Sustainable Development—IISD, Canada, 91
International Institute of Tropical Agriculture—IITA, Nigeria, 289
International Islamic Relief Organization of Saudi Arabia—IIROSA, Saudi Arabia, 321
International Lake Environment Committee Foundation, Japan, 234
International Latsis Foundation, Switzerland, 364
International League for Human Rights—ILHR, USA, 509
The International Maize and Wheat Improvement Center, Mexico, 262
International Maritime Rescue Foundation—IMRF, UK, 423
International Medical Assistance Foundation, Portugal, 310
International Medical Services for Health—INMED, USA, 506

The International Movement against All Forms of Discrimination and Racism—IMADR, Japan, 234
International Music and Art Foundation, Liechtenstein, 255
International NGO Forum on Indonesian Development—INFID, Indonesia, 207
International NGO Training and Research Centre—INTRAC, UK, 398
International Office for Water, France, 153
International Orthodox Christian Charities, Inc—IOCC, USA, 509
International Penal and Penitentiary Foundation—IPPF, Netherlands, 276
International Planned Parenthood Federation—IPPF, UK, 424
International Press Institute—IPI, Austria, 47
International Red Cross and Red Crescent Movement—ICRC, Switzerland, 368
International Refugee Trust—IRT, UK, 424
International Relief and Development—IRD, USA, 510
International Relief Teams, USA, 510
International Renaissance Foundation—IRF, Ukraine, 394
International Rescue Committee, Inc—IRC, USA, 510
International Research & Exchanges Board—IREX, USA, 511
International Research Institute for Media, Communication and Cultural Development—MEDIACULT, Austria, 48
International Rivers, USA, 510
International Save the Children Alliance, UK, 446
International Service for Human Rights—ISHR, Switzerland, 369
International Society for Human Rights—ISHR, Germany, 172
International Society for Third-Sector Research—ISTR, USA, 459
International Solidarity Foundation—ISF, Finland, 132
International Standing Conference on Philanthropy—Interphil, Switzerland, 359
International Tree Foundation—ITF, UK, 424
International Union Against Cancer—UICC, Switzerland, 369
International Union for Conservation of Nature, Switzerland, 369
International Union for Health Promotion and Education—IUHPE, France, 153
International University Centre of Paris, France, 139
International Visegrad Fund—IVF, Slovakia, 328
International Water Management Institute—IWMI, Sri Lanka, 350
International Wilderness Leadership Foundation, USA, 554
International Women's Health Coalition—IWHC, USA, 510
International Women's Rights Action Watch—IWRAW, USA, 511
International Work Group for Indigenous Affairs—IWGIA, Denmark, 119
International Workers Aid, Belgium, 64
International Yehudi Menuhin Foundation—IYMF, Belgium, 62
International Youth Foundation—IYF, USA, 511
International Youth Library Foundation, Germany, 172
Internationale Bachakademie Stuttgart, Germany, 172
Internationale Jugendbibliothek, Germany, 172
Internationale Stiftung zur Förderung von Kultur und Zivilisation, Germany, 172
Internationale Stiftung Hochalpine Forschungsstationen Jungfraujoch und Gornergrat, Switzerland, 369
Internationale Vrijwilligersprojecten—SIW, Netherlands, 276
Interphil—International Standing Conference on Philanthropy, Switzerland, 359
Intervida Foundation, Spain, 344
INTRAC—International NGO Training and Research Centre, UK, 398
Investigaciones Económicas Latinoamericanas, Fundación, Argentina, 32
Invica Foundation, Chile, 100
InWEnt—Internationale Weiterbildung und Entwicklung gemeinnützige GmbH, Germany, 172
Ioannou (Christos Stelios) Foundation, Cyprus, 111
IOMS—Islamic Organization for Medical Sciences, Kuwait, 249
IPI—International Press Institute, Austria, 47

IPPF—International Planned Parenthood Federation, UK, 424
Iran Heritage Foundation—IHF, UK, 424
IRC—International Rescue Committee, Inc, USA, 510
IREX—International Research & Exchanges Board, USA, 511
Irish Association of Non-Governmental Development Organizations—DOCHAS, Ireland, 210
Irish Funders Forum, Ireland, 210
Irish Youth Foundation, Ireland, 212
Irvine (James) Foundation, USA, 511
Isabel Allende Foundation, USA, 463
ISAR: Resources for Environmental Activists, USA, 460
Ishizaka Foundation, Japan, 234
Isis Internacional, Chile, 100
Isis International, Chile, 100
Islamic Relief Worldwide, UK, 425
Islamic Thought Foundation, Iran, 209
Islands of Peace, Belgium, 62
ISMU—Fondazione Cariplo per le Iniziative e lo Studio sulla Multietnicità, Italy, 222
ISMU Foundation—Initiatives and Studies on Multi-ethnicity, Italy, 222
Israel Institute Applied Social Research, Israel, 214
ISREC Foundation, Switzerland, 364
Istituto Affari Internazionali—IAI, Italy, 226
Istituto Auxologico Italiano, Italy, 227
Istituto Carlo Cattaneo, Italy, 227
Istituto Luigi Sturzo, Italy, 227
Istituto di Ricerche Farmacologiche Mario Negri, Italy, 227
Istituto Svedese di Studi Classici, Italy, 228
ISTR—International Society for Third-Sector Research, USA, 459
Italcementi Carlo Presenti Foundation, Italy, 222
Italian Institute for Auxology, Italy, 227
ITeM—Instituto del Tercer Mundo, Uruguay, 560
Ittleson Foundation, USA, 511
IUC-Europe International Education Centre, Denmark, 119
IUC-Europe Internationalt Uddanneless Center, Denmark, 119
IUCN/UICN, Switzerland, 369
IUHPE—International Union for Health Promotion and Education, France, 153
Ivey (Richard) Foundation, Canada, 91
Ivey Foundation, Canada, 91
IVS—International Voluntary Service, UK, 425
Iwatani Naoji Foundation, Japan, 235
Izumi Foundation, USA, 512

The J. F. Costopoulos Foundation, Greece, 186
The J. F. Kapnek Trust Zimbabwe, Zimbabwe, 567
J. Homer Butler Foundation, Inc, USA, 504
The J. P. Morgan Chase Foundation, USA, 526
J. Paul Getty Jnr Charitable Trust, UK, 418
J. Paul Getty Trust, USA, 496
J. R. McKenzie Trust, New Zealand, 284
The J.W. McConnell Family Foundation, Canada, 92
J&S Pro Bono Poloniae Foundation, Poland, 309
Jack Brockhoff Foundation—JBF, Australia, 39
JACO—Japan Association of Charitable Organizations, Japan, 230
Jacobs Foundation, Switzerland, 370
Jahnsson (Yrjö) Foundation, Finland, 131
The James Irvine Foundation, USA, 511
James S. McDonnell Foundation, USA, 520
Jan Hus Educational Foundation, Slovakia, 329
Jane Coffin Childs Memorial Fund for Medical Research, USA, 479
Jane Hodge Foundation, UK, 421
JANIC—Japanese NGO Center for International Co-operation, Japan, 230
Janson Johan Helmich and Marcia Jansons Foundation, Norway, 291
Janson Johan Helmich og Marcia Jansons Legat, Norway, 291
Japan Association of Charitable Organizations—JACO, Japan, 230
Japan Center for Economic Research—JCER, Japan, 235
Japan Economic Research Institute Inc—JERI, Japan, 235
The Japan Foundation, Japan, 235
Japan Foundation Center, Japan, 230
The Japan Foundation Centre for Global Partnership—CGP, Japan, 236
Japan Foundation Endowment Committee—JFEC, UK, 425
Japan Heart Foundation, Japan, 236
Japan International Volunteer Center—JVC, Japan, 236

Japan Shipbuilding Industry Foundation, Japan, 238
Japan Society for the Promotion of Science—JSPS, Japan, 236
Japanese-German Center Berlin, Germany, 173
Japanisch-Deutsches Zentrum Berlin, Germany, 173
Jaume Bofill Foundation, Spain, 338
JCA Charitable Foundation, UK, 425
JCIE—Japan Center for International Exchange, Japan, 236
JDC—American Jewish Joint Distribution Committee, USA, 466
Jean-Louis Lévesque Foundation, Canada, 88
Jean Monnet Foundation for Europe, Switzerland, 364
JEN, Japan, 237
Jenifer Altman Foundation—JAF, USA, 463
Jenny and Antti Wihuri Foundation, Finland, 134
Jenny ja Antti Wihurin Rahasto, Finland, 134
Jephcott Charitable Trust—JCT, UK, 425
JERI—Japan Economic Research Institute Inc, Japan, 235
Jerusalem Foundation, Israel, 214
Jerusalem Trust, UK, 425
Jeunesse Canada Monde, Canada, 82
Jewish Agency for Israel Allocations Program, Israel, 214
Jewish Colonization Association, UK, 425
Jewish Community Development Fund—JCDF, USA, 512
Jewish Philanthropic Association, UK, 452
JFEC—Japan Foundation Endowment Committee, UK, 425
JIIA—Japan Institute of International Affairs, Japan, 237
Jiménez Díaz Foundation, Spain, 344
JNF Charitable Trust—JNFCT, UK, 426
Johanna-Quandt-Stiftung, Germany, 177
The John A. Hartford Foundation, USA, 501
The John D. and Catherine T. MacArthur Foundation, USA, 520
John Ellerman Foundation, UK, 414
John Innes Foundation—JIF, UK, 422
The John Merck Fund, USA, 523
John Moores Foundation, UK, 432
John Motley Morehead Foundation, USA, 525
John Paul II Foundation for the Sahel, Burkina Faso, 78
John Simon Guggenheim Memorial Foundation, USA, 500
John Swire 1989 Charitable Trust, UK, 450
John Templeton Foundation, USA, 547
The John W. Carson Foundation, USA, 476
Johnson (Lyndon Baines) Foundation, USA, 512
Johnson (Robert Wood) Foundation, USA, 512
The Johnson Foundation at Wingspread, USA, 512
JOHUD—Jordanian Hashemite Fund for Human Development, Jordan, 241
Jones (W. Alton) Foundation, USA, 473
Jordan River Foundation, Jordan, 241
Jordanian Hashemite Fund for Human Development, Jordan, 241
José María Aragón Foundation, Argentina, 31
José María Blanc Foundation, Spain, 341
José Miguel de Barandiaran Foundation, Spain, 340
José Ortega y Gasset Foundation, Spain, 346
Joseph Levy Charitable Foundation, UK, 429
Joseph Levy Foundation, UK, 429
Joseph P. Kennedy, Jr Foundation, USA, 515
Joseph Rowntree Charitable Trust, UK, 441
Joseph Rowntree Foundation, UK, 442
Joseph Rowntree Reform Trust Ltd (including the JRSST Charitable Trust), UK, 442
Joseph S. and Caroline Gruss Life Monument Fund, Israel, 214
Joseph Tanenbaum Charitable Foundation, Canada, 98
Josiah Macy, Jr Foundation, USA, 521
Joyce Foundation, USA, 512
JPMorgan Educational Trust, UK, 426
JPMorgan Fleming Foundation, UK, 426
JPMorgan Foundation, UK, 426
JRSST Charitable Trust, UK, 442
Juan March Foundation, Spain, 345
Juanelo Turriano Foundation, Spain, 348
The Judith Rothschild Foundation, USA, 541
Jung (C. G.) Institut Zürich, Switzerland, 370
Jusélius (Sigrid) Säätiö, Finland, 132
Jusélius (Sigrid) Stiftelse, Finland, 132
Juvenile Diabetes Research Foundation International—JDRF, USA, 513

Kade (Max) Foundation, Inc, USA, 513
Kadın Emeğini Değerlendirme Vakfı—KEDV, Turkey, 389

Kahanoff Foundation, Canada, 91
Kaiser (Henry J.) Family Foundation, USA, 513
Kajima Foundation, Japan, 237
Kansainvälinen solidaarisuussäätiö, Finland, 132
Kapnek (J. F.) Charitable Trust Zimbabwe, Zimbabwe, 567
Kapor (Mitchell) Foundation, USA, 513
Karagheusian (Howard) Commemorative Corporation, USA, 513
Karić fondacija, Serbia, 325
Karić Foundation, Serbia, 325
Karl Kübel Foundation for Child and Family, Germany, 174
Karl-Kübel-Stiftung für Kind und Familie, Germany, 174
Karuna Trust/Aid for India, UK, 426
Katharine Howard Foundation, Ireland, 211
KAUTE—Foundation for Commercial and Technical Sciences, Finland, 131
KCDF—Kenya Community Development Foundation, Kenya, 245
KDDI Foundation, Japan, 237
KEHATI—Yayasan Keanekaragaman Hayati Indonesia, Indonesia, 208
Keidanren Ishizaka Memorial Foundation, Japan, 234
Keller (Helen) International, USA, 514
Kellogg (W. K.) Foundation, USA, 514
Kennan Institute, USA, 514
Kennedy (Joseph P.), Jr Foundation, USA, 515
Kennedy Memorial Trust, UK, 426
Kensington Estate—Henry Smith Charity, UK, 448
Kerzner Marine Foundation—KMF, USA, 515
Kettering Foundation, USA, 515
KFAS—Kuwait Foundation for the Advancement of Sciences, Kuwait, 249
Khemka (Nand and Jeet) Foundation, India, 203
KIEDF—Koret Israel Economic Development Funds, Israel, 214
Kinder in Afrika, Stiftung, Germany, 181
King Abdul-Aziz al-Saoud Foundation for Islamic Study and the Humanities, Morocco, 268
King Baudouin Foundation, Belgium, 62
King Faisal Foundation—KFF, Saudi Arabia, 321
King George's Fund for Sailors, UK, 447
King Gustaf V 90th Birthday Foundation, Sweden, 354
King Hussein Foundation—KHF, Jordan, 241
The King's Fund, UK, 427
KIOS—Finnish NGO Foundation for Human Rights, Finland, 132
Kirby Laing Foundation, UK, 427
Kirk (Norman) Memorial Trust, New Zealand, 284
KK-stiftelsen, Sweden, 354
Klassik Stiftung Weimar, Germany, 173
Klaus Tschira Foundation, Germany, 183
Klaus Tschira Stiftung GmbH, Germany, 183
Kleinwort (Ernest) Charitable Trust, UK, 427
Klon/Jawor Association, Poland, 306
Knowledge Foundation, Sweden, 354
Knox (Frank) Memorial Fellowships, UK, 427
Knut and Alice Wallenberg Foundation, Sweden, 358
Knut och Alice Wallenbergs Stiftelse, Sweden, 358
Koç (Vehbi), Vakfı, Turkey, 391
Koch Foundation, Inc, USA, 515
Kofi Annan Foundation, Switzerland, 361
Kokkalis Foundation, Greece, 187
Komen (Susan G.) Breast Cancer Foundation, USA, 515
Köning Boudewijnstichting/Fondation Roi Baudouin, Belgium, 62
Koningin Wilhelmina Fonds—Nederlandse Kankerbestrijding, Netherlands, 276
Koninklijke Hollandsche Maatschappij der Wetenschappen, Netherlands, 276
Konrad Adenauer Foundation, Germany, 160
Konrad-Adenauer-Stiftung eV—KAS, Germany, 160
Konstnärsnämnden, Sweden, 354
Konung Gustaf V's 90-Årsfond, Sweden, 354
Körber Foundation, Germany, 173
Körber-Stiftung, Germany, 173
The Korea Foundation, Korea (Republic), 246
Korean Culture and Arts Foundation, Korea (Republic), 246
Koret Foundation, USA, 515
Koret Israel Economic Development Funds—KIEDF, Israel, 214
The Kosciuszko Foundation, Inc, USA, 516
Kosovar Civil Society Foundation, Kosovo, 248
Kosovo Foundation for Open Society—KFOS, Kosovo, 248
Kostova (Elizabeth) Foundation for Creative Writing, Bulgaria, 76

Kresge Foundation, USA, 516
Kress (Samuel H.) Foundation, USA, 516
Kroch (Heinz, Anna and Carol) Foundation, UK, 427
Kroch (Heinz and Anna) Foundation, UK, 427
Kronenberga (Leopolda), Fundacja Bankowa, Poland, 306
Kröner-Fresenius (Else) Stiftung, Germany, 173
KRS Education and Rural Development Foundation, Inc, USA, 516
Krupp von Bohlen und Halbach (Alfried) Stiftung, Germany, 173
Kübel (Karl) Stiftung für Kind und Familie, Germany, 174
Kulika Charitable Trust (Uganda), Uganda, 392
The Kulika Charitable Trust 1981, Uganda, 392
Kulturfonder for Sverige och Finland, Sweden, 354
KulturKontakt Austria—KKA, Austria, 48
Kulturstiftung Haus Europa, Germany, 174
Kulturstiftung der Länder—KSL, Germany, 174
Kurt Tucholsky Foundation, Germany, 183
Kurt-Tucholsky-Stiftung, Germany, 183
Kuwait Awqaf Public Foundation, Kuwait, 249
Kuwait Foundation for the Advancement of Sciences—KFAS, Kuwait, 249
Kuwait Institute for Scientific Research—KISR, Kuwait, 249
Kvinna till Kvinna Foundation, Sweden, 354
KWF Kankerbestrijding, Netherlands, 276

L. J. Skaggs and Mary C. Skaggs Foundation, USA, 544
'La Caixa' Foundation, Spain, 338
La Salle Foundation for Natural Sciences, Venezuela, 564
LACWHN—Latin American and Caribbean Women's Health Network, Chile, 101
Lady Davis Fellowship Trust, Israel, 214
Lady Tata Memorial Trust—LTMT, India, 205
Laidlaw Foundation, Canada, 91
Laing (Beatrice) Trust, UK, 428
Laing (J. W.) Trust, UK, 449
Laing (Kirby) Foundation, UK, 427
Laing (Maurice and Hilda) Charitable Trust, UK, 427
Lama Gangchen World Peace Foundation, Italy, 227
Lambrakis Foundation, Greece, 187
Lambrakis Research Foundation, Greece, 187
Lance Armstrong Foundation—Livestrong, USA, 469
Landis & Gyr Foundation, Switzerland, 370
Landis & Gyr Stiftung, Switzerland, 370
Lane (Allen) Foundation, UK, 428
Langlois (Daniel) Foundation for Art, Science and Technology, Canada, 92
Lannan Foundation, USA, 517
Lateinamerika-Zentrum eV—LAZ, Germany, 174
Latin America Centre, Germany, 174
Latin America France, France, 151
Latin American, African and Asian Social Housing Service, Chile, 101
Latin American Association of Development Financing Institutions, Peru, 299
Latin American Association of Development Organizations, Mexico, 262
Latin American and Caribbean Women's Health Network—LACWHN, Chile, 101
Latin American Committee for the Defence of Women's Rights, Peru, 299
Latin American Fund for Development, Costa Rica, 106
Latin American Group for the Participation, Integration and Inclusion of People with Disability, Colombia, 105
Latter-day Saint Charities—LDSC, USA, 517
Latvia Children's Fund, Latvia, 251
Latvian Cultural Foundation, Latvia, 251
Latvijas Bērnu fonds, Latvia, 251
Latvijas Kultūras Fonds—LKF, Latvia, 251
Lauder (Ronald S.) Foundation, Germany, 174
Laureus Sport for Good Foundation, UK, 428
Lauritzen Fonden, Denmark, 119
Lauritzen Foundation, Denmark, 119
Law Foundation of New South Wales, Australia, 41
Law and Justice Foundation of New South Wales, Australia, 41
Law Society Charity, UK, 428
The Lawson Foundation, Canada, 92
Lawson Valentine Foundation, USA, 551
LBJ Foundation, USA, 512
Leakey (L. S. B.) Foundation, USA, 517
Leakey Foundation, USA, 517
La Leche League International—LLLI, USA, 516
van Leer (Bernard) Foundation, Netherlands, 277
Van Leer Jerusalem Institute, Israel, 215

Lego Fonden, Denmark, 119
The Lego Foundation, Denmark, 119
Leibniz-Institut für Globale und Regionale
  Studien, Germany, 169
Lelio and Lisli Basso Issoco Foundation—
  International Section, Italy, 219
The Leona M. and Harry B. Helmsley Charitable
  Trust, USA, 503
Leonard Cheshire Disability International,
  UK, 409
Léonie Sonning Music Foundation, Denmark, 121
Léonie Sonnings Musikfond, Denmark, 121
Leopold Kronenberg Foundation, Poland, 306
Léopold Sédar Senghor Foundation, Senegal, 322
Leprosy Mission International, UK, 428
Lerici (Ing. Carlo M.), Fondazione presso il
  Politecnico di Milano, Italy, 222
Lesotho Council of Non-Governmental
  Organisations, Lesotho, 254
Leukaemia and Lymphoma Research, UK, 428
Leventis (A. G.) Foundation, Cyprus, 111
Leventis (A. G.) Foundation Nigeria, Nigeria, 290
Leverhulme Trust, UK, 429
Levesque (Jean-Louis), Fondation, Canada, 88
Levi Strauss Foundation, USA, 517
Levy (Joseph) Foundation, UK, 429
Li Ka-shing Foundation, Hong Kong, 194
Liberty Fund, Inc, USA, 517
Library of the National Academy of Lincei,
  Italy, 216
Lietuvos vaikų fondas, Lithuania, 256
Life Sciences Research Foundation—LSRF,
  USA, 518
Lifebridge Foundation, Inc, USA, 518
Lifeforce Foundation, Canada, 92
Lifeline Energy, UK, 429
Lifewater International—LI, USA, 518
Lila Wallace—Reader's Digest Fund, Inc,
  USA, 551
Liliane Foundation, Netherlands, 281
Lilly Endowment, Inc, USA, 518
Limmat Foundation, Switzerland, 370
Limmat Stiftung, Switzerland, 370
Linbury Trust, UK, 429
Lindbergh (Charles A.) Fund, Inc, USA, 518
Lithuanian Children's Fund, Lithuania, 256
Littauer (Lucius N.) Foundation, Inc, USA, 519
Livestrong, USA, 469
Liz Claiborne and Art Ortenberg Foundation,
  USA, 480
Lloyd Foundation, UK, 429
Lloyds TSB Foundation for England and Wales,
  UK, 429
Loewe Foundation, Spain, 345
London Goodenough Trust Overseas Graduates,
  UK, 419
The Long Now Foundation—LNF, USA, 519
Longhi (Roberto), Fondazione di Studi di Storia
  dell'Arte, Italy, 225
Lorenzini (Giovanni), Fondazione, Italy, 222
The Lotte and John Hecht Memorial Foundation,
  Canada, 90
Louis-Jeantet Medical Foundation,
  Switzerland, 364
Lower Saxony Savings Bank Foundation,
  Germany, 175
Loyalty Foundation, Spain, 337
Luce (Henry) Foundation, Inc, USA, 519
Lucie and André Chagnon Foundation/
  Fondation Lucie et André Chagnon,
  Canada, 85
Lucius N. Littauer Foundation, Inc, USA, 519
Ludwig Boltzmann Gesellschaft, Austria, 46
Ludwig Borchardt Foundation, Switzerland, 361
Ludwig-Borchardt-Stiftung, Switzerland, 361
Ludwig Institute for Cancer Research—LICR,
  USA, 519
Luigi Einaudi Foundation, Italy, 221
Luigi Sturzo Institute, Italy, 227
Luis Vives Foundation, Spain, 348
Lundbeck Foundation, Denmark, 120
Lundbeckfonden, Denmark, 120
Lurcy (Georges) Charitable and Educational
  Trust, USA, 519
Luso-American Development Foundation,
  Portugal, 312
The Lutheran World Federation, Switzerland, 370
Lutherischer Weltbund/Fédération luthérienne
  mondiale, Switzerland, 370
Luxemburg (Rosa) Stiftung, Germany, 174
LWR—Lutheran World Relief, USA, 519
Lynde and Harry Bradley Foundation, Inc,
  USA, 473
Lyndon Baines Johnson Foundation, USA, 512

M. S. Swaminathan Research Foundation—
  MSSRF, India, 205

M-USA—Mercy-USA for Aid and Development,
  USA, 524
M. Venkatarangaiya Foundation, India, 206
MacArthur (John D. and Catherine T.)
  Foundation, USA, 520
McCaw (Craig and Susan) Foundation, USA, 520
McConnell (J. W.) Family Foundation, Canada, 92
McConnell Clark (Edna) Foundation, USA, 520
McCormick (Robert R.) Foundation, USA, 520
Macdonald Stewart Foundation, Canada, 92
McDonnell (James S.) Foundation, USA, 520
Macedonian Centre for International Co-
  operation—MCIC, Macedonia, 258
MACIF Foundation, France, 146
McKenzie (J. R.) Trust, New Zealand, 284
The Mackintosh Foundation, UK, 430
McKnight Foundation, USA, 521
The McLean Foundation, Canada, 93
Maclellan Foundation, Inc, USA, 521
Macmillan Cancer Relief, UK, 430
Macquarie Charitable Foundation, Australia, 41
Macquarie Group Foundation, Australia, 41
Macy (Josiah), Jr Foundation, USA, 521
Madariaga European Foundation, Belgium, 63
MADRE, USA, 521
Maecenata Foundation, Germany, 159
Maecenata Management GmbH, Germany, 159
Maecenata Stiftung, Germany, 159
Maeght (Marguerite et Aimé), Fondation,
  France, France, 147
MAG—Mines Advisory Group, UK, 430
Magyar Ökumenikus Segélyszervezet,
  Hungary, 196
Mahatma Gandhi Canadian Foundation for
  World Peace, Canada, 89
MAIF Foundation, France, 147
Mailman (A. L.) Family Foundation, USA, 521
Maison Franco-Japonaise, Japan, 237
Maj and Tor Nessling Foundation, Finland, 132
Makarna Mittag-Lefflers Matematiska Stiftelse,
  Sweden, 353
Malcolm Sargent Cancer Fund for Children,
  UK, 410
Malta Ecological Foundation, Malta, 261
Maltese Heritage Foundation, Malta, 261
Mama Cash, Netherlands, 277
Management Development Foundation,
  Netherlands, 277
Mandela (Nelson) Children's Fund, South
  Africa, 333
Mandela (Nelson) Foundation, South Africa, 333
The Mandela Rhodes Foundation, South
  Africa, 333
Manfred Woerner Foundation, Bulgaria, 74
Mani Tese, Italy, 227
Manning (Ernest C.) Awards Foundation,
  Canada, 93
Mannréttindaskrifstofa Íslands, Iceland, 197
Manzanedo (Ana Mata), Fundación, Spain, 345
MAP International—Medical Assistance
  Programs, USA, 522
MAPFRE Foundation, Spain, 345
Marangopoulos Foundation for Human Rights,
  Greece, 188
Marc de Montalembert Foundation, France, 148
Marc Rich Foundation for Education, Culture
  and Welfare, Switzerland, 372
Marcel Bleustein-Blanchet Vocation Foundation,
  France, 141
Marcel Hicter Foundation, Belgium, 61
Marcelino Botín Foundation, Spain, 341
Marcelle et Jean Coutu Foundation, Canada, 88
March (Juan), Fundación, Spain, 345
March of Dimes, USA, 522
Marguerite and Aimé Maeght Foundation,
  France, 147
María Francisca de Roviralta Foundation,
  Spain, 347
Marie Curie Cancer Care, UK, 412
Marie Stopes International—MSI, UK, 450
Marinho (Roberto), Fundação, Brazil, 72
Mario Negri Pharmacological Research
  Institute, Italy, 227
Mário Soares Foundation, Portugal, 313
Marisla Foundation, USA, 522
Marjorie Coote Animal Charities Trust, UK, 412
Markle (John and Mary R.) Foundation, USA, 522
Markle Foundation, USA, 522
The MasterCard Foundation, Canada, 93
Match International Centre, Canada, 93
Mateus House Foundation, Portugal, 310
The Matsumae International Foundation,
  Japan, 238
Matsushita Foundation, USA, 532
Mattei (Enrico), Fondazione ENI, Italy, 218
Maurice and Hilda Laing Charitable Trust,
  UK, 427
Maurício Sirotsky Nephew Foundation, Brazil, 72

MAVA Fondation pour la Nature,
  Switzerland, 371
Max Bell Foundation, Canada, 81
The Max Foundation, USA, 522
Max Havelaar Foundation, Netherlands, 281
Max Kade Foundation, Inc, USA, 513
Max-Planck-Gesellschaft zur Förderung der
  Wissenschaften eV, Germany, 176
Max Planck Society for the Advancement of
  Science, Germany, 176
Max Schmidheiny Foundation, Switzerland, 372
Max Schmidheiny-Stiftung, Switzerland, 372
Maxová (Tereza) Foundation, Czech Republic, 115
Mayfair Charities Ltd, UK, 430
The Maytree Foundation, Canada, 93
Mba (Léon), Fondation—Institut de Médecine et
  d'Épidémiologie Africaines, France, 146
MCIC—Macedonian Centre for International Co-
  operation, Macedonia, 258
MDA—Muscular Dystrophy Association,
  USA, 523
MDF Training & Consultancy, Netherlands, 277
Médecins du Monde International, France, 153
Médecins Sans Frontières—MSF,
  Switzerland, 371
MEDIACULT—International Research Institute
  for Media, Communication and Cultural
  Development, Austria, 48
medica mondiale e.V., Germany, 175
Medical Assistance Programs, USA, 522
Medical Emergency Relief International—
  MERLIN, UK, 432
Medical Foundation for the Care of Victims of
  Torture, UK, 430
Medical Women's International Association—
  MWIA, Canada, 94
Medico International, Germany, 175
Mediterranean Foundation, Argentina, 33
Mediterranean Foundation of Strategic Studies,
  France, 147
Mellon (Andrew W.) Foundation, USA, 523
Mellon (Richard King) Foundation, USA, 523
Memorial Foundation for Jewish Culture,
  USA, 523
Menarini International Foundation, Italy, 222
MENCAP, UK, 431
Mendoza (Eugenio) Fundación, Venezuela, 563
Mental Health Foundation, UK, 431
Mentor Foundation, UK, 431
Menzies (R. G.) Scholarship Fund, Australia, 42
Menzies (Sir Robert) Foundation Ltd,
  Australia, 41
Mercers' Charitable Foundation, UK, 431
Merck (John) Fund, USA, 523
Mercury Phoenix Trust, UK, 431
Mercy Corps, USA, 524
Mercy-USA for Aid and Development—M-USA,
  USA, 524
Merian (Christoph) Stiftung, Switzerland, 371
Mérieux Foundation, France, 147
MERLIN—Medical Emergency Relief
  International, UK, 432
Mertz Gilmore Foundation, USA, 524
Messerschmitt Foundation, Germany, 175
Messerschmitt-Stiftung, Germany, 175
Metcalf (George Cedric) Charitable Foundation,
  Canada, 94
Mexican Centre for Philanthropy, Mexico, 262
The Michael Fund—International Foundation
  for Genetic Research, USA, 524
Michael J. Fox Foundation for Parkinson's
  Research, USA, 493
Michael Otto Foundation for Environmental
  Protection, Germany, 176
Michael-Otto-Stiftung für Umweltschutz,
  Germany, 176
Microenterprise Development Foundation,
  Guatemala, 191
Microfinance Centre—MFC, Poland, 309
Miguel Alemán Foundation, Mexico, 262
Milan Simecka Foundation, Slovakia, 329
Milbank Memorial Fund, USA, 524
Milieukontakt International, Netherlands, 277
Milieukontakt Oost-Europa, Netherlands, 277
Mindolo Ecumenical Foundation—MEF,
  Zambia, 566
Mines Advisory Group—MAG, UK, 430
Minna James Heineman Foundation,
  Germany, 170
Minna-James-Heineman-Stiftung, Germany, 170
Minor Foundation for Major Challenges,
  Norway, 291
Minority Rights Group International, UK, 432
Miriam Dean Fund, UK, 413
Miriam Dean Refugee Trust Fund, UK, 413
Miriam G. and Ira D. Wallach Foundation,
  USA, 552

MISEREOR—Bischöfliches Hilfswerk, eV, Germany, 162
The Mission to Seafarers, UK, 432
Mitchell Kapor Foundation, USA, 513
Mittag-Leffler Foundation of the Royal Swedish Academy of Science, Sweden, 353
Mittag-Leffler Foundation of the Royal Swedish Academy of Sciences, Sweden, 353
Mitterrand (Danielle), Fondation, France, 151
MIUSA—Mobility International USA, USA, 525
Mo Ibrahim Foundation, UK, 421
Moawad (René) Foundation, Lebanon, 253
Mobility International USA—MIUSA, USA, 525
Mohammed bin Rashid Al Maktoum Foundation, United Arab Emirates, 395
Moisés Bertoni Foundation, Paraguay, 298
Møller (A.P.) and Chastine Mc-Kinney Møller Foundation, Denmark, 120
Molson Donations Fund/Fonds de bienfaisance Molson, Canada, 94
Molson Family Foundation, Canada, 94
Molson Foundation, Canada, 94
Monell (Ambrose) Foundation, USA, 525
Mongolian Women's Fund—MONES, Mongolia, 266
Monnet (Jean), Fondation pour l'Europe, Switzerland, 364
Mønsteds (Otto) Fond, Denmark, 120
Montres Rolex, Fondation, Switzerland, 366
Monument Trust, UK, 432
Moody Foundation, USA, 525
Moore (Henry) Foundation, UK, 432
Moores (John) Foundation, UK, 432
Morehead-Cain Foundation, USA, 525
Morfotiko Idryma Ethnikis Trapezis—MIET, Greece, 188
Moriya Foundation, Japan, 238
Morrow (The F. K.) Foundation, Canada, 94
Mosaic Foundation, USA, 526
Mostazafan Foundation of New York, USA, 462
Mother Child Education Foundation, Turkey, 388
Mott (Charles Stewart) Foundation, USA, 526
The Mountain Institute—TMI, USA, 526
Mouskouri (Nana) Foundation, Switzerland, 363
MS ActionAid Denmark, Denmark, 120
Ms Foundation for Women, USA, 526
MS—Mellemfolkeligt Samvirke, Denmark, 120
Mukti Lawrence Foundation, Bangladesh, 52
Multiple Sclerosis Society of Great Britain and Northern Ireland, UK, 433
Mum and Dad Foundation, Czech Republic, 115
Murdoch Children's Research Institute, Australia, 42
Murray (Gilbert) Trust, UK, 433
Muscular Dystrophy Campaign, UK, 433
Music Sound Foundation, UK, 415
Muslim Aid, UK, 433
The Muttart Foundation, Canada, 94
Mutual Aid and Liaison Service, France, 154
Mwalimu Nyerere Foundation—MNF, Tanzania, 382
Myer (Sidney) Fund, Australia, 42
The Myer Foundation, Australia, 42

Naandi Foundation—A New Beginning, India, 203
Nacionalne Zaklade za Razvoj Civilnoga Drustva, Croatia, 109
Nadace Auxilia, Czech Republic, 112
Nadace cesky hudebni fond, Czech Republic, 113
Nadace Charty 77, Czech Republic, 114
Nadace ICN, Czech Republic, 112
Nadace SLUNÍČKO, Czech Republic, 114
Nadace Táta a Máma, Czech Republic, 115
Nadácia Ekopolis, Slovakia, 327
Nadácia Milana Šimečku, Slovakia, 329
Nadácia Pontis, Slovakia, 327
Nadácia pre deti Slovenska, Slovakia, 328
Nadácia Zelená Nádej, Slovakia, 328
Naito Foundation, Japan, 238
Nana Mouskouri Foundation, Switzerland, 363
Nand and Jeet Khemka Foundation, India, 203
Nansen (Fridtjof) Institute, Norway, 291
Nantik Lum Foundation, Spain, 345
Nathan Steinberg Family Foundation, Canada, 98
National Art Collections Fund—Art Fund, UK, 401
National Assistance and Information Centre for NGOs in Moldova—CONTACT, Moldova, 264
National Association of Civil Society Organizations, Venezuela, 563
National Asthma Campaign, UK, 402
National Bank of Greece Cultural Foundation, Greece, 188
National Conference on Soviet Jewry, USA, 528
National Council for Voluntary Organisations—NCVO, UK, 398

National Democratic Institute for International Affairs—NDI, USA, 528
National Endowment for Science, Technology and the Arts—NESTA, UK, 434
National Fish and Wildlife Foundation, USA, 527
National Foundation for Civil Society Development, Croatia, 109
National Foundation for Development, El Salvador, 128
National Foundation for the Development of Honduras, Honduras, 193
National Foundation for Educational Research—NFER, UK, 433
National Foundation for Political Sciences, France, 148
National Foundation for Solidarity and Development, Burkina Faso, 78
National Fund for Scientific Research, Belgium, 61
National Heart Foundation of Australia, Australia, 42
National Heart Foundation of New Zealand, New Zealand, 285
National Heritage Memorial Fund, UK, 420
National Humanities Center, USA, 527
National Institute for Research in the Behavioural Sciences—Szold (Henrietta) Institute, Israel, 215
National Institute for Sustainable Development—NISD, India, 204
National Kidney Foundation, Inc, USA, 527
National Lottery Charities Board, UK, 404
National Organization for Women Foundation, Inc—NOW Foundation, USA, 527
National Science Foundation, USA, 527
National Society for the Prevention of Cruelty to Children, UK, 435
National Trust EcoFund, Bulgaria, 76
The National Trust for Places of Historic Interest or Natural Beauty, UK, 434
National Volunteer Centre—Hestia, Czech Republic, 114
National Wildlife Federation—NWF, USA, 527
National Youth Foundation, Greece, 188
The Nature Conservancy, USA, 528
Nature Foundation, Ecuador, 126
Naumann (Friedrich) Stiftung, Germany, 175
NCH—National Children's Home, UK, 398
NCSJ—National Conference on Soviet Jewry, USA, 528
NCVO—National Council for Voluntary Organisations, UK, 398
NDI—National Democratic Institute for International Affairs, USA, 528
Nederlands instituut voor Zuidelijk Afrika—NiZA, Netherlands, 278
Nederlandsche Maatschappij voor Nijverheid en Handel—NMNH, Netherlands, 278
Nederlandse Organisatie voor Internationale Ontwikkelingssamenwerking—Stichting NOVIB, Netherlands, 279
Nederlandse organisatie voor internationale samenwerking in het hoger onderwijs, Netherlands, 278
NEF—Near East Foundation, USA, 528
NEF—New Economics Foundation, UK, 434
Negri (Mario), Istituto di Ricerche Farmacologiche, Italy, 227
Nelson Mandela Children's Fund, South Africa, 333
Nelson Mandela Children's Fund—Canada, Canada, 93
Nelson Mandela Foundation, South Africa, 333
Nepal Forward Foundation, Nepal, 271
Neruda (Pablo), Fundación, Chile, 100
Nessling (Maj and Tor) Foundation, Finland, 132
NESsT—Nonprofit Enterprise and Self-sustainability Team, Chile, 101
NESTA—National Endowment for Science, Technology and the Arts, UK, 434
Van Neste Foundation, UK, 453
Nestlé Foundation for the Study of the Problems of Nutrition in the World, Switzerland, 364
Netherlands Institute, France, 152
Netherlands Institute for Southern Africa, Netherlands, 278
Netherlands Organization for International Co-operation in Higher Education—NUFFIC, Netherlands, 278
Netherlands Society for Industry and Trade, Netherlands, 278
Network of Estonian Non-profit Organizations, Estonia, 129
Network of European Foundations—NEF, Belgium, 66
Network for Human Development, Brazil, 73
Network of Information and Support for Non-Governmental Organizations, Poland, 306

Network for Social Change, UK, 434
New Carlsberg Foundation, Denmark, 121
New Economics Foundation—NEF, UK, 434
New Eurasia Foundation, Russian Federation, 319
New Perspectives Foundation, Russian Federation, 319
The New World Foundation, USA, 529
New Zealand Association of Philanthropic Trusts, New Zealand, 284
New Zealand Winston Churchill Memorial Trust, New Zealand, 285
Newberry Library, USA, 529
NFCR—National Foundation for Cancer Research, USA, 529
NFER—National Foundation for Educational Research, UK, 433
NFI—National Foundation for India, India, 204
NGDO—Non-Governmental Development Organizations Platform, Slovakia, 327
NGO Centre—NGOC, Armenia, 35
NGO Development Centre, Russian Federation, 318
NGO Development Centre/United Way–Belarus, Belarus, 54
NGO Information and Support Centre—NISC, Lithuania, 256
NGO Rural and Social Initiative, Moldova, 264
Niarchos (Stavros) Foundation, Greece, 188
Niedersächsische Sparkassenstiftung, Germany, 175
Nigerian Conservation Foundation—NCF, Nigeria, 290
Nigerian Institute of International Affairs—NIIA, Nigeria, 290
Nightingale (Florence), Fondation Internationale, Switzerland, 363
Nihon Enerugi Keizai Kenkyu-Sho, Japan, 233
Nihon Kokusai Mondai Kenkyusho, Japan, 237
NIOK—Nonprofit Információs és Oktató Központ Alapítvány, Hungary, 195
Nippon Foundation, Japan, 238
Nirnaya, India, 204
NISC—NGO Information and Support Centre, Lithuania, 256
Niwano Peace Foundation, Japan, 238
Nobel Foundation, Sweden, 355
Nobelstiftelsen, Sweden, 355
Non-Governmental Ecological Vernadsky Foundation, Russian Federation, 320
Non-Governmental Organization JEN, Japan, 237
Non-Profit Information and Training Centre Foundation, Hungary, 195
Nonprofit Enterprise and Self-sustainability Team—NESsT, Chile, 101
Nonprofit Információs és Oktató Központ Alapítvány—NIOK, Hungary, 195
Noor al-Hussein Foundation—NHF, Jordan, 241
Nordic Africa Institute Scholarships, Sweden, 355
Nordic Culture Fund, Denmark, 120
Nordic Institute for Theoretical Physics, Sweden, 355
Nordisk Institut for Teoretisk Fysik—NORDITA, Sweden, 355
Nordisk Kulturfond, Denmark, 120
Nordiska Afrikainstitutets Stipendier, Sweden, 355
NORDITA—Nordisk Institut for Teoretisk Fysik, Sweden, 355
Norman Kirk Memorial Trust, New Zealand, 284
Norsk Utenrikspolitisk Institutt—NUPI, Norway, 292
North-South-Bridge Foundation, Germany, 181
North-South Institute/Institut Nord-Sud, Canada, 95
Northern Ireland Voluntary Trust, UK, 412
Northern Rock Foundation, UK, 435
Norwegian Institute of International Affairs—NUPI, Norway, 292
Novartis Foundation for Sustainable Development—NFSD, Switzerland, 371
Novartis Foundation for Therapeutical Research, Germany, 175
Novartis Stiftung für Nachhaltige Entwicklung, Switzerland, 371
Novartis-Stiftung für therapeutische Forschung, Germany, 175
Novartis US Foundation, USA, 529
NOVIB (Oxfam Netherlands), Netherlands, 279
NoVo Foundation, USA, 529
Novo Nordisk Foundation, Denmark, 120
NOW Foundation—National Organization for Women Foundation, USA, 527
NRF—National Research Foundation, South Africa, 333

NSPCC—National Society for the Prevention of Cruelty to Children, UK, 435
NUFFIC—Netherlands organization for international co-operation in higher education, Netherlands, 278
Nuffield Foundation, UK, 435
Ny Carlsbergfondet, Denmark, 121
NZIIA—New Zealand Institute of International Affairs, New Zealand, 285

Oak Foundation, Switzerland, 371
The Ocean Foundation, USA, 529
Oceanographic Institute—Albert 1st, Prince of Monaco Foundation, France, 152
ODI—Overseas Development Institute, UK, 436
Office du Baccalauréat International—OBI, Switzerland, 368
Office International de l'Eau, France, 153
The Officers' Association, UK, 435
Oil Companies' European Association for Environment, Health and Safety in Refining and Distribution—CONCAWE, Belgium, 58
OISCA International, Japan, 239
Olivetti (Adriano), Fondazione, Italy, Italy, 223
Olof Palme Memorial Foundation, Sweden, 355
Olof Palmes Minnesfond, Sweden, 355
Omidyar (Pierre) Family Foundation, USA, 529
Omidyar Foundation, USA, 529
Omidyar Network, USA, 529
Onassis (Alexander S.) Public Benefit Foundation, Greece, 189
ONCE—Spanish National Organization for the Blind—Foundation, Spain, 346
The One Foundation, Ireland, 212
OneWorld International Foundation, UK, 435
OPALS—Organisation Panafricaine de Lutte Contre le SIDA, France, 153
Open Estonia Foundation, Estonia, 129
Open Society Forum (Mongolia), Mongolia, 266
Open Society Foundation, Romania, 317
Open Society Foundation for Albania—OSFA, Albania, 29
Open Society Foundation—Bratislava, Slovakia, 328
Open Society Foundation—London, UK, 436
Open Society Foundation for South Africa—OSF-SA, South Africa, 334
Open Society Foundation—Turkey, Turkey, 389
Open Society Fund—Bosnia-Herzegovina, Bosnia and Herzegovina, 68
Open Society Fund Prague—OSF Prague, Czech Republic, 115
Open Society Georgia Foundation, Georgia, 157
Open Society Initiative for Southern Africa—OSISA, South Africa, 334
Open Society Initiative for West Africa, Senegal, 322
Open Society Institute—Assistance Foundation (Azerbaijan), Azerbaijan, 50
Open Society Institute Assistance Foundation, Armenia—OSIAFA, Armenia, 35
Open Society Institute Assistance Foundation—Tajikistan, Tajikistan, 381
Open Society Institute—Brussels, Belgium, 63
Open Society Institute Montenegro, Montenegro, 267
Open Society Institute—New York, USA, 530
Open Society Institute—Paris (Soros Foundations), France, 135
Open Society Institute—Sofia (Bulgaria), Bulgaria, 76
Open Society Institute—Turkey, Turkey, 387
Open Society Institute—Washington, DC, USA, 530
Operation Beaver—Frontiers Foundation Inc, Canada, 89
Operation Eyesight Universal/Action universelle de la vue, Canada, 95
Operation Rainbow, Inc, USA, 530
Operation USA, USA, 530
Opportunity International UK, UK, 436
Opportunity International USA, USA, 530
OPUS—Centre for Promotion and Development of Civil Initiatives, Poland, 305
Orange Foundation, France, 148
Oranje Fonds, Netherlands, 278
Orbis International, USA, 531
Orentreich Foundation for the Advancement of Science, Inc—OFAS, USA, 531
Organisation Afro-Asiatique Pour Le Developpement Rural, India, 199
Organisation internationale de droit du développement—OIDD, Italy, 226
Organisation Panafricaine de Lutte Contre le SIDA—OPALS, France, 153
Organization for Industrial, Spiritual and Cultural Advancement (OISCA) International, Japan, 239

Orient Foundation, Portugal, 312
The Orient-Occident Foundation, Morocco, 268
Ortega (Amancio) Fundación, Spain, 346
OSGF—Open Society Georgia Foundation, Georgia, 157
OSIAF—Open Society Institute Assistance Foundation—Tajikistan, Tajikistan, 381
OSIWA—Open Society Initiative for West Africa, Senegal, 322
Österreichische Forschungsstiftung für Internationale Entwicklung—ÖFSE, Austria, 48
Österreichische Gesellschaft für Außenpolitik und Internationale Beziehungen, Austria, 48
Österreichische Gesellschaft für Umwelt und Technik—ÖGUT, Austria, 48
Otto (Michael) Stiftung, Germany, 176
Otto Benecke Foundation, Germany, 161
Otto-Benecke-Stiftung eV, Germany, 161
Otto Mønsteds Fond, Denmark, 120
Otto Mønsteds Foundation, Denmark, 120
Our Spaces—Foundation for the Good Governance of International Spaces, UK, 436
Outreach International, USA, 531
Overseas Development Institute—ODI, UK, 436
Oxfam America, USA, 531
Oxfam Australia, Australia, 43
Oxfam Canada, Canada, 95
Oxfam Deutschland e.V., Germany, 176
Oxfam-en-Belgique, Belgium, 63
Oxfam France, France, 153
Oxfam GB, UK, 436
Oxfam Hong Kong, Hong Kong, 194
Oxfam India, India, 204
Oxfam International, UK, 437
Oxfam Ireland, Ireland, 212
Oxfam Mexico, Mexico, 263
Oxfam New Zealand, New Zealand, 285
Oxfam NOVIB—Nederlandse Organisatie voor Internationale Ontwikkelingssamenwerking, Netherlands, 279
Oxfam NOVIB—Netherlands Organization for International Development Co-operation, Netherlands, 279
Oxfam-Québec, Canada, 95
OzChild, Australia, 43

PAALAE—Pan African Association for Literacy and Adult Education, Senegal, 323
Paavo Nurmen Säätiö, Finland, 132
Paavo Nurmi Foundation, Finland, 132
Pablo Neruda Foundation, Chile, 100
PAC—Partnership Africa Canada, Canada, 95
Pacific Cultural Foundation, Taiwan, 380
Pacific Development and Conservation Trust, New Zealand, 285
Pacific Leprosy Foundation, New Zealand, 286
Pacific Peoples' Partnership, Canada, 95
Packard (David and Lucile) Foundation, USA, 531
Pact, USA, 532
PADF—Pan American Development Foundation, USA, 532
PAHEF—Pan American Health and Education Foundation, USA, 532
PAI—Population Action International, USA, 532
Paideia Galiza Foundation, Spain, 346
Pakistan Centre for Philanthropy—PCP, Pakistan, 294
Pakistan Institute of International Affairs—PIIA, Pakistan, 294
Palme (Olof) Minnesfond för Internationell Förståelse och Gemensam Säkerhet, Sweden, 355
PAN Africa—Pesticide Action Network Africa, Senegal, 323
Pan-African Centre for Social Prospects, Benin, 65
Pan-African Federation of Film-makers, Burkina Faso, 78
Pan-African Organization for AIDS Prevention, France, 153
PAN Asia and the Pacific—Pesticide Action Network Asia and the Pacific, Malaysia, 260
PAN Europe—Pesticides Action Network Europe, Germany, 176
Pan-European Federation for Cultural Heritage, Netherlands, 273
PAN UK—Pesticide Action Network UK, UK, 437
Panasonic Foundation, USA, 532
Paraskevaides (George and Thelma) Foundation, Cyprus, 111
Parkinson's Disease Foundation, Inc—PDF, USA, 533
Partage, France, 154
The Parthenon Trust, Switzerland, 371
Partners in Rural Development, Canada, 84
Partnership Africa Canada—PAC, Canada, 95

PASOS—Policy Association for an Open Society, Czech Republic, 113
Pasteur Institute, France, 152
Pasteur Institute of Lille, France, 153
Pastore (Giulio), Fondazione, Italy, 223
PATH—Program for Appropriate Technology in Health, USA, 533
Pathfinder International, USA, 533
Patiño (Simón I.), Fondation, Switzerland, 365
Patrimoine mondial, France, 154
Patterson (Alicia) Foundation, USA, 533
The Paul G. Allen Family Foundation, USA, 463
Paul Hamlyn Foundation—PHF, UK, 419
Paul-Henri Spaak Foundation, Belgium, 61
Paulo Foundation, Finland, 132
Paulon Säätiö, Finland, 132
Paz y Cooperación, Spain, 349
PBI—Peace Brigades International, UK, 437
PCI-Media Impact, USA, 533
PCI—Population Communications International, USA, 533
Peace Brigades International—PBI, UK, 437
Peace and Co-operation, Spain, 349
Peace and Disarmament Education Trust—PADET, New Zealand, 286
Peace, Health and Human Development Foundation—PHD Foundation, Japan, 239
Peace Research Center, Spain, 338
Peace Research Institute Oslo—PRIO, Norway, 292
Peace Village International, Germany, 169
Peace Winds Japan—PWJ, Japan, 239
Pearl S. Buck International, USA, 474
Pearson Peacekeeping Centre—PPC, Canada, 95
Pediatric AIDS Foundation, USA, 496
Pedro Barrié de la Maza Foundation, Spain, 340
PEF Israel Endowment Funds, Inc, Israel, 215
Penal Reform International—PRI, UK, 437
People in Need, Czech Republic, 113
People-to-People Health Foundation, Inc—Project Hope, USA, 537
People's Harmonious Development Society, Georgia, 158
PepsiCo Foundation, Inc, USA, 534
Peres Center for Peace, Israel, 215
Perpetual Foundation, Australia, 43
Perpetual Trustees Australia, Australia, 43
Pertubuhan Pertolongan Wanita, Malaysia, 260
Pestalozzi Children's Foundation, Switzerland, 374
Pesticide Action Network Asia and the Pacific—PAN AP, Malaysia, 260
Pesticide Action Network—Europe, Belgium, 63
Pesticide Action Network North America—PAN, USA, 534
Pesticide Action Network North America—PANNA, USA, 534
Pesticide Action Network UK—PAN UK, UK, 437
Pesticides Action Network Europe—PAN Europe, Germany, 176
Peter G. Peterson Foundation, USA, 534
Peterson (Peter G.) Foundation, USA, 534
The Pew Charitable Trusts, USA, 534
Pezcoller (Alessio), Fondazione, Italy, 223
Pfizer Foundation, USA, 534
Pforzheimer (Carl and Lily) Foundation, Inc, USA, 535
PH International, USA, 535
The PHD Foundation—Peace, Health and Human Development Foundation, Japan, 239
PHF—Paul Hamlyn Foundation, UK, 419
PHG Foundation, UK, 437
Philanthropy Australia, Australia, 36
Philanthropy Ireland, Ireland, 210
Philanthropy New Zealand, New Zealand, 284
PhilDev—Philippine Development Foundation, USA, 535
Philias Foundation, Switzerland, 359
Philippine-American Educational Foundation—PAEF, Philippines, 303
Philippine Development Foundation—PhilDev, USA, 535
Philippine Foundation Center—PFC, Philippines, 301
PHR—Physicians for Human Rights, USA, 535
Physicians for Human Rights—PHR, USA, 535
Piera, Pietro and Giovanni Ferrero Foundation, Italy, 221
Pilgrim Trust, UK, 437
Pilietinės Atsakomybés Fondas, Lithuania, 256
Pinchuk (Victor) Foundation, Ukraine, 394
Pire (Dominique) Foundation, Belgium, 62
Pitseng Trust, South Africa, 334
PLAN International—PI, UK, 438
Plan Ireland, Ireland, 212
Planck (Max) Gesellschaft zur Förderung der Wissenschaften eV, Germany, 176

Platforma Mimovládnych Rozvojovych Organizáchií—MVRO, Slovakia, 327
Plenty International, USA, 535
Ploughshares Fund, USA, 536
Plunkett Foundation, UK, 438
Polar Companies Foundation, Venezuela, 563
Polden-Puckham Charitable Foundation—PPCF, UK, 438
Pôle européen des fondations de l'économie sociale, Belgium, 56
Policy Studies Institute—PSI, UK, 438
Polish-American Freedom Foundation, Poland, 305
Polish-Czech-Slovak Solidarity Foundation, Poland, 308
Polish Environmental Partnership Foundation, Poland, 307
Polish Foundation for Science Advancement—PFSA, Poland, 309
Pollock–Krasner Foundation, Inc, USA, 536
POLSAT Foundation, Poland, 309
Polska Fundacja Upowszechniania Nauki—PFUN, Poland, 309
Polsko-Amerykańska Fundacja Wolności, Poland, 305
Poniecki (Wladyslaw) Foundation, Inc, USA, 536
Pontis Foundation, Slovakia, 327
Population Concern, UK, 422
Population Council, USA, 536
The Porter Foundation, UK, 439
Portuguese Foundation Centre, Portugal, 310
Post Office Foundation, France, 144
Potanin (Vladimir) Foundation, Russian Federation, 320
Potter (Ian) Foundation, Australia, 43
PPP Foundation, UK, 420
Practical Action, UK, 439
Prada Foundation, Italy, 224
Praemium Erasmianum Foundation, Netherlands, 282
Praemium Erasmianum, Stichting, Netherlands, 282
Pratt Foundation, Australia, 43
Preciosa Foundation, Czech Republic, 115
Premji (Azim) Foundation, India, 204
Presbyterian World Service and Development, Canada, 96
Press Foundation of Asia—PFA, Philippines, 303
Primate's World Relief and Development Fund, Canada, 96
Prince Albert II of Monaco Foundation, Monaco, 265
Prince of Asturias Foundation, Spain, 347
Prince Bernhard Cultural Foundation, Netherlands, 282
Prince Claus Fund for Culture and Development, Netherlands, 279
The Prince's Trust, UK, 439
Princess Grace Foundation, Monaco, 265
Prins Bernhard Culturfonds, Stichting, Netherlands, 282
Prins Claus Fonds Voor Cultuur en Ontwikkeling, Netherlands, 279
PRIO—Peace Research Institute Oslo, Norway, 292
Prix Jeunesse Foundation, Germany, 176
Pro Bono Foundation, Poland, 308
Pro Helvetia, Switzerland, 372
Pro Juventute, Switzerland, 372
Pro Mujer International, USA, 536
Pro Nature—Peruvian Foundation for Nature Conservation, Peru, 299
Pro Victimis Foundation, Switzerland, 365
Pro Women International, USA, 536
PRODESSA—Proyecto de Desarrollo Santiago, Guatemala, 191
Professor Otto Beisheim Foundation, Germany, 161
Professor Otto Beisheim Stiftung, Germany, 161
proFonds, Switzerland, 359
Program for Appropriate Technology in Health—PATH, USA, 533
Progressio, UK, 439
Project Concern International—PCI, USA, 537
Project Harmony, USA, 535
Project HOPE, USA, 537
Project Trust, UK, 439
ProLiteracy, USA, 537
Promi Foundation, Spain, 347
ProNaturaleza—Fundación Peruana para la Conservación de la Naturaleza, Peru, 299
PROTERRA, Peru, 299
Protestant Study Foundation, Germany, 167
PROVICOOP—Fundación Invica, Chile, 100
PRS for Music Foundation, UK, 440
Prudential Foundation, USA, 537
PSI—Policy Studies Institute, UK, 438
Public Welfare Foundation, Inc, USA, 537

Puerto Rico Community Foundation, Puerto Rico, 314

Qatar Foundation, Qatar, 315
Qattan (A. M.) Foundation, UK, 440
Quaid-i-Azam Academy, Pakistan, 294
Quandt (Herbert) Stiftung, Germany, 162
Queen Alia Fund for Social Development, Jordan, 241
Queen Elisabeth Egyptological Association, Belgium, 57
Queen's Silver Jubilee Trust, UK, 439
Queen's Trust for Young Australians, Australia, 41
Querini Stampalia Foundation, Italy, 224
Quilliam Foundation, UK, 440

R. E. Ross Trust, Australia, 44
R. G. Menzies Scholarship Fund, Australia, 42
R. Howard Webster Foundation, Canada, 99
Rabobank Foundation, Netherlands, 279
Rafael del Pino Foundation, Spain, 347
Rafik Hariri Foundation, Lebanon, 252
The Rafto Foundation, Norway, 292
Rainforest Action Network—RAN, USA, 538
The Rainforest Foundation, UK, 440
Rainforest Foundation Norway, Norway, 293
Rainforest Foundation US, USA, 538
Rajiv Gandhi Foundation, India, 201
Ramaciotti (Clive and Vera) Foundation, Australia, 43
Ramaswami Aiyar (C. P.) Foundation, India, 204
Ramón Areces Foundation, Spain, 340
Ramon Magsaysay Award Foundation, Philippines, 303
Ramsay Foundation, Switzerland, 372
The Rank Foundation, UK, 440
Rausing (Ruben and Elisabeth) Trust, UK, 440
Rayne Foundation, UK, 441
RBC Foundation, Canada, 96
Realdania, Denmark, 121
Red de Acción en Plaguicidas y sus Alternativas de América Latina—RAP-AL, Argentina, 34
Red Mujeres Afrolatinoamericanas Afrocaribeñas, Costa Rica, 107
Red de Mujeres para el Desarrollo, Costa Rica, 107
RED—Ruralité-environnement-développement, Belgium, Belgium, 63
Red de Salud de las Mujeres Latinoamericanas y del Caribe, Chile, 101
Rede de Desenvolvimento Humano—REDEH, Brazil, 73
REDEH—Rede de Desenvolvimento Humano, Brazil, 73
RedR International, UK, 441
RedR UK, UK, 441
Reef Ball Foundation, USA, 538
Reeve (Christopher and Dana) Foundation, USA, 538
Refugee Foundation, Netherlands, 282
Refugee Trust International, Ireland, 213
Refugees International Japan—RIJ, Japan, 239
Refugees International—RI, USA, 538
Regional Centre for Strategic Studies—RCSS, Sri Lanka, 350
Regional Development Foundation of Aysen, Chile, 100
Regional Environmental Center for Central and Eastern Europe—REC, Hungary, 196
Regnskogfondet, Norway, 293
Rehabilitation International—RI, USA, 539
Reichstein Foundation, Australia, 44
Reimers (Werner) Stiftung, Germany, 177
Reine Elisabeth, Association Égyptologique, Belgium, 57
Relief International, USA, 539
Remembrance, Responsibility and the Future, Germany, 167
Renault Foundation, France, 144
René Moawad Foundation, Lebanon, 253
René Seydoux Foundation for the Mediterranean World, France, 150
Renewable Natural Resources Foundation—RNRF, USA, 540
Research Corporation for Science Advancement—RCSA, USA, 539
Research Foundation—Flanders, Belgium, 62
Réseau Africain de la Jeunesse pour le Développement Durable, Algeria, 30
Réseau des ONG Africaines sur l'Environnement, Kenya, 244
Réseau d'ONG Européennes sur l'Agro-alimentaire, le Commerce, l'Environnement et le Développement—RONGEAD, France, 135
Resource Center Foundation, Bulgaria, 74

Resource Centre for the Human Rights Nongovernmental Organizations of Moldova—CReDO, Moldova, 264
Reumatikerförbundet, Sweden, 355
Reynolds (Christopher) Foundation, USA, 539
Rhodes Trust, UK, 441
RIA—Royal Irish Academy, Ireland, 212
Ricardo do Espírito Santo Silva Foundation, Portugal, 311
Ricci Onlus Foundation, Italy, 224
Della Riccia (Angelo), Fondazione, Italy, 221
Richard King Mellon Foundation, USA, 523
Richard and Rhoda Goldman Fund, USA, 497
Richelieu International, Canada, 96
Rielo (Fernando), Fundación, Spain, 347
Right Livelihood Awards Foundation, Sweden, 356
Righteous Persons Foundation, USA, 539
Rights and Democracy/Droits et Démocratie, Canada, 96
RIIA—Royal Institute of International Affairs, UK, 443
Ripaille Foundation, France, 149
RNIB—Royal National Institute of Blind People, UK, 444
RNRF—Renewable Natural Resources Foundation, USA, 540
Roald Dahl's Marvellous Children's Charity, UK, 413
Rob and Bessie Welder Wildlife Foundation, USA, 553
Robert A. Welch Foundation, USA, 553
Robert Bosch Foundation, Germany, 163
Robert-Bosch-Stiftung GmbH, Germany, 163
Robert Marinho Foundation, Brazil, 72
Robert R. McCormick Foundation, USA, 520
Robert Schalkenbach Foundation, Inc—RSF, USA, 543
Robert Schuman Foundation, France, 150
Robert Wood Johnson Foundation—RWJF, USA, 512
Roberto Longhi Foundation for the Study of the History of Art, Italy, 225
Robertson Foundation for Government—RFFG, USA, 540
Rockefeller Brothers Fund, USA, 540
Rockefeller Foundation, USA, 540
Rockwool Fonden, Denmark, 121
Rockwool Foundation, Denmark, 121
Rohm Music Foundation, Japan, 239
Roma Lom Foundation, Bulgaria, 76
Romaeuropa Foundation, Italy, 224
Romanian Cultural Foundation, Romania, 317
Romanian Cultural Institute, Romania, 317
Romanian Donors' Forum, Romania, 316
Rome Foundation, Italy, 224
Romi Foundation, Brazil, 72
The Ronald S. Lauder Foundation, Germany, 174
RONGEAD—Réseau d'ONG Européennes sur l'Agro-alimentaire, le Commerce, l'Environnement et le Développement, France, 135
Rooftops Canada Foundation, Canada, 97
Rosa Luxemburg Foundation, Germany, 174
Rosa-Luxemburg-Stiftung, Germany, 174
Ross (R. E.) Trust, Australia, 44
Rössing Foundation, Namibia, 270
The Rotary Foundation, USA, 540
Rotary Yoneyama Memorial Foundation, Inc, Japan, 239
Rothschild (Edmond de) Foundations, USA, 541
Rothschild (Judith) Foundation, USA, 541
Roviralta (María Francisca de), Fundación, Spain, 347
Rowan Charitable Trust, UK, 441
Rowntree (Joseph) Charitable Trust, UK, 441
Rowntree (Joseph) Foundation, UK, 442
Rowntree (Joseph) Reform Trust, UK, 442
Royal Aeronautical Society—RAES, UK, 442
Royal Air Force Benevolent Fund, UK, 442
Royal Anthropological Institute of Great Britain and Ireland—RAI, UK, 442
Royal Asiatic Society of Great Britain and Ireland, UK, 443
The Royal Australasian College of Physicians—RACP, Australia, 44
Royal Bank of Canada Charitable Foundation, Canada, 96
Royal Bank Financial Group Foundation, Canada, 96
Royal British Legion, UK, 443
Royal Children's Hospital Research Institute, Australia, 42
Royal Commission for the Exhibition of 1851, UK, 443
Royal Commonwealth Society for the Blind—Sight Savers International, UK, 448

The Royal Commonwealth Society—RCS, UK, 443
Royal Flying Doctor Service of Australia—RFDS, Australia, 44
Royal Forest and Bird Protection Society of New Zealand, New Zealand, 286
Royal Geographical Society (with The Institute of British Geographers), UK, 443
Royal Holland Society of Sciences and Humanities, Netherlands, 276
Royal Institute of International Affairs—RIIA—Chatham House, UK, 443
Royal Institute of International Relations, Belgium, 58
Royal Jubilee Trusts, UK, 439
Royal National Institute of Blind People—RNIB, UK, 444
Royal Over-Seas League—ROSL, UK, 444
Royal Society, UK, 444
Royal Society for the Encouragement of Arts, Manufactures and Commerce—RSA, UK, 444
The Royal Society of Medicine—RSM, UK, 444
Royal Society for Mentally Handicapped Children and Adults—MENCAP, UK, 431
Royal Society for the Prevention of Cruelty to Animals—RSPCA, UK, 445
Royal Society for the Protection of Birds—RSPB, UK, 445
Rroma Foundation, Switzerland, 372
RSA—Royal Society for the encouragement of Arts, Manufactures and Commerce, UK, 444
RSPB—Royal Society for the Protection of Birds, UK, 445
RSPCA—Royal Society for the Prevention of Cruelty to Animals, UK, 445
Ruben and Elisabeth Rausing Trust, UK, 440
Rubin (Samuel) Foundation, Inc, USA, 541
Rubinstein (Arthur) International Music Society, Israel, 215
The Rufford Foundation, UK, 445
Rufford Maurice Laing Foundation, UK, 445
RUI Foundation, Italy, 225
Runyon (Damon)–Winchell (Walter) Foundation, Cancer Research Fund, USA, 541
Rural Advancement Foundation International—RAFI, Canada, 88
Rural Culture and Civilization Centre, Italy, 216
Rural Development Foundation, Poland, 308
Ruralité Environnement Développement—RED, Belgium, 63
Rurality Environment Development, Belgium, 63
Russell (Bertrand) Peace Foundation, UK, 445
Russell Sage Foundation—RSF, USA, 541
Russian Cultural Foundation, Russian Federation, 320
Russian Donors Forum, Russian Federation, 318
Rutgers WPF, Netherlands, 279
Rutherford Institute, USA, 541
RWJF—Robert Wood Johnson Foundation, USA, 512
Ryan Foundation International, India, 205

SA ASTA—South African Agency for Science and Technology Advancement, South Africa, 334
Säätiöiden ja rahastojen neuvottelukunta ry, Finland, 131
Sabancı (Hacı Ömer) Foundation, Turkey, 389
Sabancı Foundation, Turkey, 389
Sabancı Vakfı—Hacı Ömer Sabancı Foundation, Turkey, 389
Sabera Foundation, India, 205
Sabera Foundation India, India, 205
Sabre Foundation, Inc, USA, 542
SACO—Service d'assistance canadienne aux organismes, Canada, 83
Safe Internet Foundation—SIF, Netherlands, 279
Sahabdeen (A. M. M.) Trust Foundation, Sri Lanka, 350
SAIA—Slovak Academic Information Agency, Slovakia, 327
Said Foundation, UK, 446
Saint Cyril and Saint Methodius International Foundation, Bulgaria, 76
The Saison Foundation, Japan, 240
Salamander Foundation, Canada, 97
Sales Exchange for Refugee Rehabilitation Vocation, USA, 544
Salvador Dalí Foundation, Spain, 343
El Salvador Foundation for Economic and Social Development, El Salvador, 128
The Salvation Army, UK, 446
Salvatore Maugeri Foundation—Occupational Health and Rehabilitation Clinic, Italy, 223
Samaritan's Purse, USA, 542
Sampradaan Indian Centre for Philanthropy, India, 198
Samuel (Hedwig und Robert) Stiftung, Germany, 177

Samuel H. Kress Foundation, USA, 516
Samuel Lunenfeld Charitable Foundation, Canada, 92
Samuel Rubin Foundation, USA, 541
Samuel and Saidye Bronfman Family Foundation, Canada, 92
Samuel Sebba Charitable Trust, UK, 447
San Diego Foundation, USA, 542
San Francisco Foundation, USA, 542
Sander (Wilhelm) Stiftung, Germany, 177
Sandino (Augusto César), Fundación, Nicaragua, 288
Sandoz Family Foundation, Switzerland, 372
Sandoz Fondation de Famille, Switzerland, 372
Santa María Foundation, Spain, 348
Santé Sud, France, 154
Santiago Development Project, Guatemala, 191
Santillana Foundation, Spain, 348
Sarah Scaife Foundation, Inc, USA, 542
Sartawi Foundation, Bolivia, 67
Sasakawa, Fondation Franco-Japonaise, France, 145
Sasakawa Foundation, Japan, 238
Sasakawa Peace Foundation—SPF, Japan, 240
Save & Prosper Foundation, UK, 426
Save the Children, UK, 446
Save the Children (UK), UK, 446
Save Our Future Environmental Foundation, Germany, 177
Save Our Future Umweltstiftung—SOF, Germany, 177
Savings Bank Foundation DnB NOR, Norway, 293
Savings Banks Foundation for International Cooperation, Germany, 179
Scaife (Sarah) Foundation, Inc, USA, 542
Scaife Family Foundation, USA, 542
Scelles Foundation, France, 149
Schalkenbach (Robert) Foundation, Inc, USA, 543
Schcolnik Foundation, Argentina, 33
Schering (Ernst) Stiftung, Germany, 177
Schlumberger Foundation, France, 154
Schneider Electric Foundation, France, 149
Schools Without Frontiers, France, 139
Schuman (Robert), Fondation, France, 150
Schusterman (Charles and Lynn) Family Foundation, USA, 543
Schwab Foundation for Social Entrepreneurship, Switzerland, 373
Schwarzkopf Foundation Young Europe, Germany, 178
Schwarzkopf Stiftung Junges Europa, Germany, 178
Schweisfurth Foundation, Germany, 178
Schweisfurth-Stiftung, Germany, 178
Schweizerisch-Liechtensteinische Stiftung für archäologische Forschungen im Ausland—SLSA, Switzerland, 373
Schweizerische Akademie der Medizinischen Wissenschaften, Switzerland, 373
Schweizerische Herzstiftung, Switzerland, 373
Schweizerische Stiftung für Alpine Forschungen, Switzerland, 373
Schweizerische Stiftung Kardiologie, Switzerland, 373
Schweizerischer Nationalfonds zur Förderung der wissenschaftlichen Forschung/Fonds National Suisse de la Recherche Scientifique—SNF, Switzerland, 374
SCIAF—Scottish Catholic International Aid Fund, UK, 447
Science and Technology Facilities Council—STFC, UK, 447
Scientific Foundation of Hisham Adeeb Hijjawi, Jordan, 241
Scientific Foundation of the Spanish Cancer Association, Spain, 342
Scope, UK, 447
Scottish Catholic International Aid Fund—SCIAF, UK, 447
Scouloudi Foundation, UK, 447
ScriptumLibre Foundation, Netherlands, 279
Seafarers UK, UK, 447
Secours Catholique—Caritas de France, France, 154
Secours Dentaire International, Switzerland, 374
Seeds of Peace, USA, 543
SEEENN—South East European Environmental NGOs Network, Macedonia, 258
SEEMO—IPI—South East Europe Media Organisation, Austria, 49
Seidel (Hanns) Stiftung, Germany, 178
SEL—Service d'Entraide et de Liaison, France, 154
SELAVIP International—Service de Promotion de l'Habitation Populaire en Amérique Latine, Afrique et Asie, Chile, 101

Selby (William G. and Marie) Foundation, USA, 543
Self Help Development Foundation, Zimbabwe, 567
Self Help Development International, Ireland, 213
Sem Pringpuangkeo Foundation, Thailand, 384
Semmelweis Alapítvány Magyarországi Ortopédia Fejlesztéséért, Hungary, 195
Semmelweis Foundation for the Development of Orthopaedics in Hungary, Hungary, 195
Seoam Scholarship Foundation, Korea (Republic), 247
Serafín Aliaga Foundation for Peace and Solidarity, Spain, 346
Sergiu Celibidache Foundation, Germany, 163
Sergiu-Celibidache-Stiftung, Germany, 163
Serralves Foundation, Portugal, 312
SERRV International, Inc, USA, 544
Service Civil International—SCI, Belgium, 63
Service d'Entraide et de Liaison—SEL, France, 154
Service International pour les Droits de l'Homme, Switzerland, 369
SES Foundation—Sustainability, Education, Solidarity, Argentina, 33
Seub Nakhasathien Foundation, Thailand, 384
Seva Foundation, USA, 544
Seydoux (René), Fondation pour le Monde Méditerranéen, France, 150
Shackleton Foundation, UK, 448
Share, France, 154
The Sharing Way, Canada, 97
Shastri Indo-Canadian Institute, Canada, 97
Shell Foundation, UK, 448
Shelter—National Campaign for Homeless People, UK, 448
Sherman (Archie) Charitable Trust, UK, 448
Shoman (Abdul Hameed) Foundation, Jordan, 242
Shuttleworth Foundation, South Africa, 334
Siam Society, Thailand, 384
SickKids Foundation, Canada, 97
SID—Society for International Development, Italy, 228
Sidney Myer Fund, Australia, 42
Sieć SPLOT, Poland, 306
Sieć Wspierania Organizacji Pozarządowych—SPLOT, Poland, 306
The Sierra Club Foundation, USA, 544
Sight Savers International, UK, 448
Signe and Ane Gyllenberg Foundation, Finland, 131
Signe och Ane Gyllenbergs stiftelse, Finland, 131
Sigrid Jusélius Foundation, Finland, 132
Sigrid Jusélius Säätiö, Finland, 132
Sigrid Rausing Trust, UK, 440
Sihtasutus Eesti Rahvuskultuuri Fond, Estonia, 129
Silva (Ricardo do Espírito Santo), Fundação, Portugal, 311
Simón I. Patiño Foundation, Switzerland, 365
Simone and Cino del Duca Foundation, France, 143
Sinergia—Asociación Nacional de Organizaciones de la Sociedad Civil, Venezuela, 563
Singapore International Foundation—SIF, Singapore, 326
Singer-Polignac Foundation, France, 150
Sino-British Fellowship Trust—SBFT, UK, 448
SIPRI—Stockholm International Peace Research Institute, Sweden, 357
Sir Ahmadu Bello Foundation, Nigeria, 289
Sir Ahmadu Bello Memorial Foundation, Nigeria, 289
Sir Dorabji Tata Trust, India, 205
Sir Ernest Cassel Educational Trust, UK, 409
Sir Halley Stewart Trust, UK, 449
The Sir Jules Thorn Charitable Trust, UK, 451
The Sir Robert Menzies Memorial Foundation Ltd, Australia, 41
Sivil Toplum Geliştirme Merkezi—STGM, Turkey, 387
SIW International Volunteer Projects, Netherlands, 280
SIW Internationale Vrijwilligersprojecten, Netherlands, 280
Skaggs (L. J.) and Skaggs (Mary C.) Foundation, USA, 544
Skoll Foundation, USA, 544
Sloan (Alfred P.) Foundation, USA, 545
Slovak Academic Information Agency–Service Center for the Third Sector—SAIA-SCTS, Slovakia, 327
Slovak-Czech Women's Fund, Czech Republic, 115
Slovak Donors' Forum—SDF, Slovakia, 328
Slovak Humanitarian Council, Slovakia, 328
Slovak NGDOs Platform, Slovakia, 327

Slovenian Science Foundation, Slovenia, 330
Slovenská Humanitná Rada, Slovakia, 328
SLSA—Schweizerisch Liechtensteinische Stiftung, Switzerland, 373
Slunicko Foundation, Czech Republic, 114
Small Business Assistance Foundation, Guatemala, 190
SMART—Association for Civil Society Development, Croatia, 109
Smith Richardson Foundation, Inc, USA, 545
Smithsonian Institution, USA, 545
SNF—Swedish Nutrition Foundation, Sweden, 356
Snow Leopard Trust, USA, 545
Soares (Mário), Fundação, Portugal, 313
Sobell Foundation, UK, 449
Société Littéraire des Goncourt—Académie Goncourt, France, 136
Software AG Foundation, Germany, 178
Sog'lom Avlod Uchun, Uzbekistan, 561
Solidar, Belgium, 64
Solidarios—Consejo de Fundaciones Americanas de Desarrollo, Dominican Republic, 123
Solidarité, France, 155
Solidarity, France, 155
Solidarity Foundation, Dominican Republic, 123
Solidarity National Commission—Economic Foundation, Poland, 307
Solidarity Overseas Service Malta—SOS Malta, Malta, 261
Solidarność NSZZ—Economic Foundation, Poland, 307
Solomon R. Guggenheim Foundation, USA, 500
Song Qingling Foundation, China (People's Republic), 102
Sonning (Léonie) Musikfond, Denmark, 121
Sonning Foundation, Denmark, 121
Sonnings-Fonden, Denmark, 121
Sonsoles Ballvé Lantero Labour Foundation, Spain, 344
Sophie and Karl Binding Foundation, Switzerland, 361
Sophie und Karl Binding-Stiftung, Switzerland, 361
Sorenson Legacy Foundation, USA, 545
Soroptimist International, UK, 449
Soros Economic Development Fund, USA, 546
Soros Foundation (Czech Republic), Czech Republic, 115
Soros Foundation (Estonia), Estonia, 129
Soros Foundation (Georgia), Georgia, 157
Soros Foundation (Slovakia), Slovakia, 328
Soros Foundation (South Africa), South Africa, 334
Soros Foundation (Tajikistan), Tajikistan, 381
Soros Foundation (USA), USA, 530
Soros Foundation Guatemala, Guatemala, 191
Soros Foundation—Kazakhstan, Kazakhstan, 243
Soros Foundation–Kyrgyzstan, Kyrgyzstan, 250
Soros Foundation Latvia, Latvia, 251
Soros Foundation Macedonia, Macedonia, 258
Soros Foundation—Moldova, Moldova, 264
Soros Foundation Romania, Romania, 317
Soros Serbia Foundation, Serbia, 324
SOS Atlantic Forest Foundation, Brazil, 72
SOSNA Foundation, Slovakia, 329
SOTA—Research Centre for Turkestan and Azerbaijan, Netherlands, 280
South African Agency for Science and Technology Advancement—SAASTA, South Africa, 334
South African Institute of International Affairs, South Africa, 335
South African Institute of Race Relations, South Africa, 335
South East Europe Media Organisation, Austria, 49
South East Europe Media Organisation—SEEMO—IPI, Austria, 49
South East European Environmental NGOs Network—SEEENN, Macedonia, 258
South-East Institute—Foundation for Academic Research into South-Eastern Europe, Germany, 182
South Pacific Peoples Foundation Canada, Canada, 95
Southern African Nature Foundation, South Africa, 336
Southern Health, France, 154
Spaak (Paul-Henri), Fondation, Belgium, 61
Spanish Association of Foundations, Spain, 337
Sparebankstiftelsen DnB NOR, Norway, 293
Sparkassen-Kulturstiftung Hessen-Thüringen, Germany, 178
Sparkassenstiftung für internationale Kooperation eV, Germany, 179
Spencer Foundation, USA, 546

Spinal Research, UK, 449
SpinalCure Australia, Australia, 44
Springer (Axel) Stiftung, Germany, 179
St John Ambulance, UK, 446
Standing International Forum on Ethnic Conflict, Genocide and Human Rights—International Alert, UK, 422
The Stanley Foundation, USA, 546
Staples Trust, UK, 449
Star of Hope International, USA, 546
The Starr Foundation, USA, 546
State Scholarships Foundation, Greece, 189
Stavros Niarchos Foundation, Greece, 188
Steelworkers Humanity Fund, Canada, 98
Stefan Batory Foundation, Poland, 307
Steinberg (Nathan) Family Foundation, Canada, 98
Stewards Company Limited, UK, 449
Stewardship Foundation, USA, 547
Stewart (Sir Halley) Trust, UK, 449
Stichting Agromisa, Netherlands, 280
Stichting Alfred Heineken Fondsen, Netherlands, 281
Stichting Caraïbisch Marien Biologisch Instituut—CARMABI, Curaçao, 110
Stichting DOEN, Netherlands, 280
Stichting Fonds 1818, Netherlands, 280
Stichting voor Fundamenteel Onderzoek der Materie —FOM, Netherlands, 281
Stichting Gaudeamus, Netherlands, 281
Stichting Liliane Fonds, Netherlands, 281
Stichting Max Havelaar, Netherlands, 281
Stichting Mondiaal Alternatief, Netherlands, 281
Stichting Praemium Erasmianum, Netherlands, 282
Stichting Prins Bernhard Cultuurfonds, Netherlands, 282
Stichting Reinwater, Netherlands, 282
Stichting Spaak (Paul-Henri), Belgium, 61
Stichting voor de Technische Wetenschappen, Netherlands, 283
Stichting Triodos Foundation, Netherlands, 282
Stichting Vluchteling, Netherlands, 282
Stichting VSB Fonds, Netherlands, 280
Stiftelsen Blanceflor Boncompagni-Ludovisi, född Bildt, Sweden, 356
Stiftelsen Dag Hammarskjölds Minnesfond, Sweden, 356
Stiftelsen för Miljöstrategisk Forskning—Mistra, Sweden, 356
Stiftelsen Riksbankens Jubileumsfond, Sweden, 357
Stiftelsen Teknikens Främjande—Tekniikan Edistämissäätiö, Finland, 133
Stifterverband für die Deutsche Wissenschaft eV, Germany, 159
Stiftung CAESAR, Germany, 179
Stiftung Deutsche Geisteswissenschaftliche Institute im Ausland—DGIA, Germany, 179
Stiftung Entwicklung und Frieden—SEF, Germany, 180
Stiftung Ettersberg, Germany, 180
Stiftung Europäisches Naturerbe—EURONATUR, Germany, 180
Stiftung zur Förderung der Ernährungsforschung in der Schweiz—SFEFS, Switzerland, 374
Stiftung zur Förderung der Hochschulrektorenkonferenz, Germany, 180
Stiftung FVS, Germany, 183
Stiftung Jugend forscht e.V., Germany, 180
Stiftung für Kinder, Germany, 181
Stiftung Kinder in Afrika, Germany, 181
Stiftung Kinderdorf Pestalozzi, Switzerland, 374
Stiftung Klimarappen, Switzerland, 375
Stiftung 'Leben für Alle', Switzerland, 375
Stiftung Lesen, Germany, 181
Stiftung für Medizinische Grundlagenforschung—Boehringer Ingelheim Fonds, Germany, 162
Stiftung Nord-Süd-Brücken, Germany, 181
Stiftung Ökologie & Landbau, Germany, 181
Stiftung Prix Jeunesse, Germany, 176
Stiftung Szondi-Institut, Switzerland, 375
Stiftung Vivamos Mejor, Switzerland, 375
Stiftung Weimarer Klassik Kunstsammlungen, Germany, 173
Stiftung Weltethos, Germany, 181
Stiftung West-Östliche Begegnungen, Germany, 182
Stiftung Wissenschaft und Politik—Deutsches Institut für internationale Politik und Sicherheit—SWP, Germany, 182
Stiftung für wissenschaftliche Südosteuropaforschung—Südost-Institut, Germany, 182

Stiftungsfonds Deutsche Bank zur Förderung der Wissenschaft in Forschung und Lehre, Germany, 182
Stockholm Environment Institute, Sweden, 357
Stockholm International Peace Research Institute—SIPRI, Sweden, 357
Stowarzyszenie Klon/Jawor, Poland, 306
Street Kids International, Canada, 98
The Streisand Foundation, USA, 547
Stretched Hands, Italy, 227
Strickland Foundation, Malta, 261
The Stroke Association, UK, 450
Studienstiftung des deutschen Volkes, Germany, 182
Sturzo (Luigi), Istituto, Italy, 227
Stuttgart International Bach Academy, Germany, 172
Südost-Institut—Stiftung für wissenschaftliche Südosteuropaforschung, Germany, 182
Suider-Afrikaanse Natuurstigting, South Africa, 336
Sultan bin Abdulaziz al-Saud Foundation, Saudi Arabia, 321
Sun/Soleil—AREGAK, Armenia, 35
Sunley (Bernard) Charitable Foundation, UK, 450
Suomen Kulttuurirahasto, Finland, 132
Support Centre for Associations and Foundations—SCAF, Belarus, 54
Surdna Foundation, Inc, USA, 547
Survival, UK, 450
Survival International, UK, 450
Susan G. Komen for the Cure, USA, 515
Sutherland Self Help Trust, New Zealand, 286
Suzman (Helen) Foundation, South Africa, 335
Svenska Institutet i Rom/Istituto Svedese di Studi Classici a Roma, Italy, 228
Svenska Kulturfonden, Finland, 133
Sverige-Amerika Stiftelsen, Sweden, 357
Sweden-America Foundation, Sweden, 357
Sweden-Japan Foundation—SJF, Sweden, 357
Swedish Cancer Society, Sweden, 352
Swedish and Finnish Cultural Foundation, Sweden, 354
Swedish Foundation for Strategic Environmental Research, Sweden, 356
The Swedish Heart-Lung Foundation, Sweden, 353
Swedish Institute at Athens, Greece, 189
Swedish Institute in Rome, Italy, 228
Swedish NGO Secretariat on Acid Rain, Sweden, 352
Swedish Nutrition Foundation—SNF, Sweden, 356
Swedish Rheumatism Association, Sweden, 355
Swiss Academy of Medical Sciences, Switzerland, 373
Swiss Alliance of Development Organisations, Switzerland, 359
Swiss Arts Council, Switzerland, 372
Swiss Coalition of Development Organisations, Switzerland, 359
Swiss Foundation for Alpine Research, Switzerland, 373
Swiss Foundation for Technical Co-operation, Switzerland, 375
Swiss Heart Foundation, Switzerland, 373
Swiss Interchurch Aid, Switzerland, 367
Swiss-Liechtenstein Foundation for Archaeological Research Abroad—SLFA, Switzerland, 373
Swiss National Science Foundation—SNF, Switzerland, 374
Swiss Nutrition Foundation, Switzerland, 374
SWISSAID Foundation, Switzerland, 375
Swisscontact—Swiss Foundation for Technical Co-operation, Switzerland, 375
SwissFoundations—Verband der Schweizer Förderstiftungen/Association des fondations donatrices suisses, Switzerland, 360
Syin-Lu Social Welfare Foundation, Taiwan, 380
The Sylvia Adams Charitable Trust, UK, 398
Sylvia and Charles Viertel Charitable Foundation, Australia, 45
Synergos—The Synergos Institute, USA, 460
Syngenta Foundation for Sustainable Agriculture, Switzerland, 376
Syngenta Stiftung für Nachhaltige Landwirtschaft, Switzerland, 376
Szenes (Arpad)–Vieira da Silva, Fundação, Portugal, 313
Szondi Institute Foundation, Switzerland, 375

Taiga Rescue Network—TRN, Finland, 133
Taiwan Philanthropy Information Center, Taiwan, 379
Tanenbaum (Joseph) Charitable Foundation, Canada, 98

TANGO—Association of NGOs in the Gambia, Gambia, 156
TANZ—Trade Aid NZ Inc, New Zealand, 287
Tanzania Millennium Hand Foundation—TAMIHA, Tanzania, 382
Tarih Vakfı, Turkey, 389
Tea Research Foundation of Central Africa, Malawi, 259
TEAR Australia, Australia, 45
Tearfund, UK, 450
Tebtebba Foundation, Philippines, 304
Technologiestichting—STW, Netherlands, 283
Technology Foundation, Netherlands, 283
TechnoServe, USA, 547
Teilhard de Chardin Foundation, France, 150
Tekniikan Edistämissäätiö-Stiftelsen för teknikens främjande—TES, Finland, 133
Television Trust for the Environment, UK, 452
di Tella (Torcuato), Instituto, Argentina, 34
Terre des Hommes Foundation, Switzerland, 376
Terre Sans Frontières—TSF, Canada, 98
Terrence Higgins Trust—THT, UK, 420
Tewa, Nepal, 271
TFF—Transnationella Stiftelsen för Freds- och Framtidsforskning, Sweden, 358
Thairath Newspaper Foundation, Thailand, 385
Thiel Foundation, USA, 547
Third Sector Foundation of Turkey—TÜSEV, Turkey, 387
Third World Institute, Uruguay, 560
Third World Network—TWN, Malaysia, 260
Third World Solidarity Action, Luxembourg, 257
Thomas B. Thrige Foundation, Denmark, 121
Thomas B. Thriges Fond, Denmark, 121
Thomson Foundation, UK, 451
Thomson Reuters Foundation, UK, 451
Thorn (The Sir Jules) Charitable Trust, UK, 451
Thrasher Research Fund, USA, 548
Thriges (Thomas B.) Fond, Denmark, 121
Thyssen (Fritz) Stiftung, Germany, 183
TI—Transparency International, Germany, 183
Tibet Fund, USA, 548
Tibet-Institut Rikon, Switzerland, 376
Tibetan Monastic Institute in Rikon, Switzerland, Switzerland, 376
Tides, USA, 548
Tides Foundation, USA, 548
Tifa Foundation—Indonesia, Indonesia, 207
Tiffany & Co. Foundation, USA, 548
Tilapia International Foundation, Netherlands, 283
Tindall Foundation, New Zealand, 286
Tinker Foundation, Inc, USA, 548
TISCO Foundation, Thailand, 385
TK Foundation, Bahamas, 51
The Todd Foundation, New Zealand, 287
Toepfer (Alfred) Stiftung, Germany, 183
Together Foundation, France, 143
Tokyu Foundation for Inbound Students, Japan, 240
Tony Blair Faith Foundation, UK, 405
Torcuato di Tella Institute, Argentina, 34
Toshiba International Foundation—TIFO, Japan, 240
Total Foundation, France, 150
The Toyota Foundation, Japan, 240
Toyota Vietnam Foundation—TVF, Viet Nam, 565
Trade Aid NZ Inc—TANZ, New Zealand, 287
Trans-Antarctic Association—TAA, UK, 451
Transnational Foundation for Peace and Future Research, Sweden, 358
Transnationella Stiftelsen för Freds- och Framtidsforskning—TFF, Sweden, 358
Transnet Foundation, South Africa, 335
Transparency International—TI, Germany, 183
Triodos Foundation, Netherlands, 282
TRN—Taiga Rescue Network, Finland, 133
Trócaire—Catholic Agency for World Development, Ireland, 213
The Trull Foundation, USA, 548
Trust for Civil Society in Central and Eastern Europe, Bulgaria, 76
Trust for London, UK, 451
Trust for Mutual Understanding, USA, 549
Trusthouse Charitable Foundation, UK, 451
Tschira (Klaus) Stiftung, Germany, 183
TTF—Toyota Thailand Foundation, Thailand, 385
Tucholsky (Kurt) Stiftung, Germany, 183
Tudor Trust, UK, 452
Turin Savings Bank Foundation, Italy, 220
Turkish Family Health and Planning Foundation, Turkey, 390
Turkish Foundation for Combating Soil Erosion, for Reforestation and the Protection of Natural Habitats, Turkey, 390
Türkiye Aile Sağlığı ve Planlaması Vakfı—TAPV, Turkey, 390

Türkiye Çevre Vakfi, Turkey, 390
Türkiye Erozyonla Mücadele Ağaçlandırma ve Doğal Varlıkları Koruma Vakfı—TEMA, Turkey, 390
Türkiye İnsan Haklari Vakfi, Turkey, 390
Türkiye Kalkinma Vakfi, Turkey, 390
Turner Foundation, Inc, USA, 549
Turquoise Mountain Foundation, UK, 452
Turriano (Juanelo) Fundación, Spain, 348
Tutu (Desmond) Peace Foundation, USA, 549
Tutu Foundation UK, UK, 452
TVE—Television Trust for the Environment, UK, 452
Twenty-Ninth May 1961 Charity, UK, 452

UAI—Union des associations internationales, Belgium, 56
Ufadhili Trust, Kenya, 244
Ugo Bordoni Foundation, Italy, 219
UICC—International Union Agains Cancer, Switzerland, 369
UICN—Union mondiale pour la nature, Switzerland, 369
UICN—Unión Mundial para la Naturaleza, Switzerland, 369
UJIA—United Jewish Israel Appeal, UK, 452
Ukraine 3000, Ukraine, 394
Ukrainian Women's Fund, Ukraine, 394
Uluslararası Mavi Hilal İnsani Yardım ve Kalkınma Vakfı, Turkey, 390
Umana Mente Foundation, Italy, 225
Umut Foundation, Turkey, 391
Umut Vakfi, Turkey, 391
UNA Trust—United Nations Association Trust, UK, 453
UniCredit Foundation—Unidea, Italy, 228
Unilever Vietnam Foundation—UVF, Viet Nam, 565
Union Aid Abroad—APHEDA, Australia, 45
Union des associations internationales—UAI, Belgium, 56
Union of Bulgarian Foundations and Associations, Bulgaria, 74
Union of Charitable Organizations of Russia, Russian Federation, 318
Union of International Associations—UIA/Unie van de Internationale Vereinigingen—UIV, Belgium, 56
Union Internationale de Promotion de la Santé et de l'Education pour la Santé, France, 153
Unitarian Universalist Service Committee, USA, 549
United Mexico Foundation, Mexico, 263
United Nations Foundation, USA, 549
United Service Committee of Canada, Canada, 98
United Society for Christian Literature—USCL, UK, 453
United Society for the Propagation of the Gospel—USPG, UK, 453
United States African Development Foundation—USADF, USA, 550
United States-Israel Educational Foundation—USIEF, Israel, 215
United States-Japan Foundation, USA, 550
United Way—Belarus/NGO Development Centre, Belarus, 54
United Way International—UWI, USA, 550
United Way Worldwide, USA, 550
Unity Foundation, Luxembourg, 257
Universal Ecological Foundation, Argentina, 32
Universal Education Foundation—UEF, France, 155
Universal Jewish Alliance, France, 137
Universitaire Stichting, Belgium, 64
University Foundation, Belgium, 64
University-Industry Foundation, Spain, 348
University of Southern California Shoah Foundation Institute for Visual History and Education, USA, 550
University of Zaragoza Business Foundation, Spain, 342
UPS Foundation, USA, 550
US-Baltic Foundation—USBF, USA, 551
US-Ukraine Foundation, USA, 551
USC Canada, Canada, 98
USIEF—United States-Israel Educational Foundation, Israel, 215

Väestöliitto, Finland, 133
Valentine (Lawson) Foundation, USA, 551
Values Foundation, Bulgaria, 77
Vanarai, India, 206
Vancouver Foundation, Canada, 99
Vehbi Koç Foundation, Turkey, 391
Vehbi Koç Vakfı, Turkey, 391
Venice Foundation, Italy, 225
Venkatarangaiya (M.) Foundation, India, 206

Verband der Schweizer Förderstiftungen, Switzerland, 360
Vereniging van Fondsen in Nederland—FIN, Netherlands, 272
Vetlesen (G. Unger) Foundation, USA, 549
VIA Foundation, Czech Republic, 115
Victor Pinchuk Foundation, Ukraine, 394
Victoria Children Foundation, Russian Federation, 320
Victoria League for Commonwealth Friendship, UK, 453
Vienna Institute for International Dialogue and Co-operation, Austria, 49
Viertel (Sylvia and Charles) Charitable Foundation, Australia, 45
Villar Foundation, Inc., Philippines, 304
Villavicencio (Dr J. Roberto), Fundación, Argentina, 33
VINCI Corporate Foundation for the City, France, 144
Virtual Foundation, USA, 551
Vita, Ireland, 213
Vivamos Mejor Foundation, Switzerland, 375
The Vladimir Potanin Foundation, Russian Federation, 320
Vodafone Foundation Germany, Germany, 183
Vodafone Group Foundation, UK, 453
Vodafone Stiftung Deutschland, Germany, 183
Volkart Foundation, Switzerland, 376
Volkart-Stiftung, Switzerland, 376
Volkswagen Foundation, Germany, 183
VolkswagenStiftung, Germany, 183
Vollmer (Alberto) Foundation, Inc, USA, 551
Voluntary Action Network India—VANI, India, 206
Voluntary Service Overseas, UK, 454
Volunteer Service Abroad—VSA, New Zealand, 287
VSA—Volunteer Service Abroad, New Zealand, 287
VSO, UK, 454
Výbor dobré vule—Nadace Olgy Havlové, Czech Republic, 115
Vzdělávací nadace Jana Husa, Czech Republic, 116
Vzdelávacia nadácia Jana Husa, Slovakia, 329

W. K. Kellogg Foundation, USA, 514
Wahana Lingkungan Hidup Indonesia—WALHI, Indonesia, 207
WAHF—World Animal Handicap Foundation, Belgium, 64
WALHI—Wahana Lingkungan Hidup Indonesia, Indonesia, 207
Wallace (Charles) India Trust, UK, 454
The Wallace Foundation, USA, 551
Wallach (Miriam G. and Ira D.) Foundation, USA, 552
Wallenberg (Knut och Alice) Stiftelse, Sweden, 358
Walmart Foundation, USA, 552
Walter and Duncan Gordon Charitable Foundation, Canada, 89
War on Want, UK, 454
Warhol (Andy) Foundation for the Visual Arts, USA, 552
WasserStiftung, Germany, 184
Water Foundation, Germany, 184
Water.org, Inc, USA, 552
WaterAid, UK, 454
Wates Foundation, UK, 454
Web Development Fund, USA, 552
Web Lab—Digital Innovations, Inc, USA, 552
Webb Memorial Trust, UK, 455
Weber (Franz), Fondation, Switzerland, 365
Webster (R. Howard) Foundation, Canada, 99
Weeden Foundation, USA, 552
Weinberg (Harry and Jeanette) Foundation, USA, 552
The Welch Foundation, USA, 553
Welder (Rob and Bessie) Wildlife Foundation, USA, 553
Welfare Association, Switzerland, 376
WellBeing, UK, 455
Wellbeing of Women, UK, 455
Wellcome Trust, UK, 455
Welzijn Juliana Fonds, Netherlands, 278
Wenner-Gren Centre Foundation for Scientific Research, Sweden, 358
Wenner-Gren Foundation, USA, 553
Wenner-Gren Foundations, Sweden, 358
Werner Reimers Foundation, Germany, 177
Werner-Reimers-Stiftung, Germany, 177
West African Rural Foundation, Senegal, 322
West-East Foundation, Germany, 182
West-Nordic Foundation, Iceland, 197
Westminster Foundation for Democracy—WFD, UK, 455

Weston (Garfield) Foundation, UK, 455
Weyerhaeuser Family Foundation, Inc, USA, 553
WHEAT Trust—Women's Hope Education and Training Trust, South Africa, 336
Whirlpool Foundation, USA, 553
White Point Development Foundation, Turkey, 387
Whitehall Foundation, Inc, USA, 554
Whitley Fund for Nature, UK, 456
Wiener Institut für Internationalen Dialog und Zusammenarbeit, Austria, 49
Wiesel (Elie) Foundation for Humanity, USA, 554
Wihuri (Jenny and Antti) Foundation, Finland, 134
Wihuri Foundation for International Prizes, Finland, 133
Wihurin kansainvälisten palkintojen rahasto, Finland, 133
Wikimedia Foundation, USA, 554
Wilbur Foundation, USA, 554
Wild (Dr Rainer) Stiftung, Germany, 184
The WILD Foundation—International Wilderness Leadership Foundation, USA, 554
Wildlife Preservation Trust International, USA, 487
Wildlife Protection, Netherlands, 274
Wildlife Trust, USA, 487
Wilhelm Sander Foundation, Germany, 177
Wilhelm-Sander-Stiftung, Germany, 177
William Adlington Cadbury Charitable Trust, UK, 407
The William and Flora Hewlett Foundation, USA, 503
William G. and Marie Selby Foundation, USA, 543
The William H. Donner Foundation, Inc, USA, 485
William J. Clinton Foundation, USA, 481
William and Mary Greve Foundation, Inc, USA, 500
The William Randolph Hearst Foundation, USA, 502
William T. Grant Foundation, USA, 499
WILPF—Women's International League Peace Freedom, USA, 555
Wilson (E. O.) Biodiversity Foundation, USA, 555
Wilson (Woodrow) International Center for Scholars, USA, 555
Windstar Foundation, USA, 555
Wingate (Harold Hyam) Foundation, UK, 456
WINGS—Worldwide Initiatives for Grantmaker Support, Brazil, 70
Winrock International, USA, 555
Winston Churchill Foundation of the United States, USA, 479
Winston Churchill Memorial Trust, UK, 410
Wisti (Folmer) Foundation for International Understanding, Denmark, 122
Wladyslaw Poniecki Foundation, Inc, USA, 536
WMF—World Monuments Fund, USA, 556
Woerner (Manfred) Foundation, Bulgaria, 74
The Wolfson Family Charitable Trust, UK, 456
The Wolfson Foundation, UK, 456

Women in Equality Foundation, Argentina, 33
Women for International Peace and Arbitration—WIPA, USA, 556
Women's Aid, Ireland, 213
Women's Aid Organisation—WAO, Malaysia, 260
Women's Development Network, Costa Rica, 107
Women's Environment and Development Organization—WEDO, USA, 556
Women's Foundation, Costa Rica, 107
Women's Hope Education and Training Trust—Wheat Trust, South Africa, 336
Women's International Democratic Federation, Brazil, 70
Wood Family Trust, UK, 456
Woodrow Wilson International Center for Scholars, USA, 555
Woodrow Wilson National Fellowship Foundation, USA, 555
Workers' Centre Foundation, Spain, 343
World Accord, Canada, 99
World Alliance for Citizen Participation—CIVICUS, South Africa, 331
World Alliance of YMCAs—Young Men's Christian Associations, Switzerland, 377
World Animal Handicap Foundation—WAHF, Belgium, 64
World Association of Children's Friends, Monaco, 265
World Concern, USA, 556
World Economic Forum, Switzerland, 377
World Education, Inc, USA, 556
World Emergency Relief—WER, USA, 556
World Federation for Mental Health—WFMH, USA, 557
World Forum of Civil Society Networks—UBUNTU, Spain, 337
World Foundation for AIDS Research and Prevention, France, 148
World Heritage, France, 154
World Land Trust—WLT, UK, 456
World Learning, USA, 557
World Literacy of Canada—WLC, Canada, 99
World Lung Foundation, USA, 557
World Mercy Fund (Ireland) Ltd, Ireland, 213
World in Need—Andrews Charitable Trust, UK, 400
World Neighbors, USA, 557
The World of NGOs, Austria, 46
World Peace Foundation—WPF, USA, 557
World Population Foundation, Netherlands, 279
World Research Foundation, USA, 558
World Resources Institute, USA, 558
World Scout Foundation, Switzerland, 377
World Society for the Protection of Animals, UK, 456
World Teacher Trust, India, 206
World University Service of Canada/Entraide universitaire mondiale du Canada, Canada, 99
World Vision Inc, USA, 558
World Wide Fund for Nature, Switzerland, 377
World Wide Web Foundation, Switzerland, 377
Worlddidac Foundation, Switzerland, 377

The WorldFish Center, Malaysia, 260
Worldwatch Institute, USA, 558
Worldwide Initiatives for Grantmaker Support—WINGS, Brazil, 70
Wurlitzer (Helene) Foundation of New Mexico, USA, 558
WWF International, Switzerland, 377
WWF South Africa, South Africa, 336
WWSF—Women's World Summit Foundation, Switzerland, 378

X Prize Foundation, USA, 559
XminusY Solidarity Fund, Netherlands, 283

YADESA—Yayasan Pengembangan Masyarakat Desa, Indonesia, 208
Yannick and Ben Jakober Foundation, Spain, 344
YASIKA—Yayasan Indonesia untuk Kemajuan Desa, Indonesia, 207
Yayasan Dian Desa, Indonesia, 207
Yayasan Indonesia Sejahtera, Indonesia, 208
Yayasan Indonesia untuk Kemajuan Desa (YASIKA), Indonesia, 207
Yayasan Keanekaragaman Hayati Indonesia—KEHATI, Indonesia, 208
Yayasan Pengembangan Masyarakat Desa—YADESA, Indonesia, 208
YMCA—Young Men's Christian Association, UK, 457
Youth for Development and Co-operation—YDC, Netherlands, 283
Youth Forum, Uruguay, 560
Yrjö Jahnsson Foundation, Finland, 131
Yrjö Jahnssonin säätiö, Finland, 131

Z. V. M. G. Rangoonwala Trust, Pakistan, 295
Zagranica Group, Poland, 305
Zakat House, Kuwait, 249
Zancan Onlus (Emanuela), Fondazione Centro Studi e Ricerca Sociale, Italy, 217
Zavod Center za Informiranje, Sodelovanje in Razvoj Nevladnih Organizacije—CNVOS, Slovenia, 330
Zeiss (Carl) Stiftung, Germany, 184
ZEIT-Stiftung Ebelin und Gerd Bucerius, Germany, 184
Zero-Kap Foundation, Netherlands, 283
Zimin (Dmitry) Dynasty Foundation, Russian Federation, 319
ZOA, Netherlands, 283
Zochonis Charitable Trust, UK, 457
Zonta International Amelia Earhart Fellowship Fund, USA, 559
Zonta International Foundation—ZIF, USA, 559
Zorig Foundation, Mongolia, 266
Zuleikhabai Valy Mohammad Gany (Z. V. M. G.) Rangoonwala Trust, Pakistan, 295
Zurich Community Trust, UK, 457
Zurich Financial Services (UKISA) Community Trust Ltd, UK, 457

Index of Main Activities

Foundation centres and co-ordinating bodies	595
Aid to less-developed countries	596
Arts and humanities	600
Conservation and the environment	605
Economic affairs	608
Education	611
International affairs	618
Law, civil society and human rights	620
Medicine and health	623
Science and technology	628
Social welfare	631

FOUNDATION CENTRES AND CO-ORDINATING BODIES

Academy for the Development of Philanthropy in Poland, Poland, 305
ACRI—Associazione di Fondazioni e di Casse di Risparmio Spa, Italy, 216
ADI—Association for Democratic Initiatives, Macedonia, 258
AF—Association of Foundations, Philippines, 301
Africa Grantmakers' Affinity Group—AGAG, USA, 458
African NGOs Environment Network—ANEN, Kenya, 244
AGAG—Africa Grantmakers' Affinity Group, USA, 458
Agency for the Non-profit Sector, Czech Republic, 112
AGNES—Vzdělávací Organizace, Czech Republic, 112
Akademia Rozwoju Filantropii w Polsce, Poland, 305
AKNS—Asociácia komunitných nadácií Slovenska, Slovakia, 327
Albanian Civil Society Foundation, Albania, 29
ALIDE—Asociación Latinoamericana de Instituciones Financieras para el Desarrollo, Peru, 299
Allavida—Alliances for Voluntary Initiatives and Development, Kenya, 244
Alliances for Voluntary Initiatives and Development—Allavida, Kenya, 244
American Council for Voluntary International Action—InterAction, USA, 459
AMP Foundation, Australia, 36
ANGOC—Asian NGO Coalition for Agrarian Reform and Rural Development, Philippines, 301
ANND—Arab NGO Network for Development, Lebanon, 252
APAN—Asian Philanthropy Advisory Network, Philippines, 301
Asian NGO Coalition for Agrarian Reform and Rural Development—ANGOC, Philippines, 301
Asian Philanthropy Advisory Network—APAN, Philippines, 301
Asociácia komunitných nadácií Slovenska—AKNS, Slovakia, 327
Asociación Española de Fundaciones, Spain, 337
Asociación Latinoamericana de Instituciones Financieras para el Desarrollo—ALIDE, Peru, 299
Asociación Latinoamericana de Organizaciones de Promoción al Desarrollo—ALOP, Mexico, 262
Asociación Nacional de Organizaciones Sociedad Civil, Venezuela, 563
Assembly of Belarusian Pro-democratic Non-governmental Organizations, Belarus, 54
Association of Charitable Foundations, UK, 396
Association for Civil Society Development—SMART, Croatia, 109
Association of Community Trusts and Foundations, UK, 397
Association for Democratic Initiatives—ADI, Macedonia, 258

Association des fondations donatrices suisses, Switzerland, 360
Association of Foundations and Businesses, Argentina, 31
Association of Foundations in the Netherlands, Netherlands, 272
Association of German Foundations, Germany, 159
Association of Grantmaking Foundations in Switzerland, Switzerland, 360
Association of Italian Foundations and Savings Banks, Italy, 216
Association of Medical Research Charities—AMRC, UK, 396
Association of Non-Governmental Organizations in The Gambia—TANGO, Gambia, 156
Association of Slovakian Community Foundations, Slovakia, 327
Association of Voluntary Agencies for Rural Development—AVARD, India, 198
Associazione di Fondazioni e di Casse di Risparmio Spa—ACRI, Italy, 216
Australian Association of Philanthropy, Australia, 36
Autonómia Foundation, Hungary, 195
Auxilia Foundation, Czech Republic, 112
AVARD—Association of Voluntary Agencies for Rural Development, India, 198
AVINA Foundation, Panama, 297
BCAF—Bulgarian Charities Aid Foundation, Bulgaria, 74
Belgian Foundation Network, Belgium, 55
BOCONGO—Botswana Council of NGOs, Botswana, 69
Botswana Council of Non-Governmental Organisations—BOCONGO, Botswana, 69
Bulgarian Donors' Forum, Bulgaria, 74
Bundesverband Deutscher Stiftungen eV, Germany, 159
CAF—Charities Aid Foundation, UK, 396
CAF Russia—Charities Aid Foundation Russia, Russian Federation, 318
Canadian Centre for Philanthropy, Canada, 80
Canadian Co-operative Association, Canada, 80
Canadian Council for International Co-operation—CCIC/Conseil canadien pour la coopération internationale—CCCI, Canada, 80
Caribbean Policy Development Centre, Barbados, 53
CCCI—Conseil canadien pour la coopération internationale, Canada, 80
CCIC—Canadian Council for International Co-operation, Canada, 80
CDCS—Centre for Development of Civil Society, Armenia, 35
Centar za razvoj neprofitnih organizacija—CERANEO, Croatia, 109
Centar za Razvoj Nevladinih Organizacija—CRNVO, Montenegro, 267
CENTRAS—Assistance Centre for NGOs, Romania, 316
Centre for Advancement of Philanthropy—CAP, India, 198
Centre for Civil Society, India, 198
Centre for the Development of Civil Society—CDCS, Armenia, 35

Centre for the Development of Non-Governmental Organizations, Montenegro, 267
Centre for Development of Non-Profit Organizations, Croatia, 109
Centre for Development of Non-Profit Sector, Serbia, 324
Centre Français des Fondations—CFF, France, 135
Centre for the Information Service, Co-operation and Development of NGOs, Slovenia, 330
Centre for Philanthropy, Ukraine, 393
Centre for Philanthropy and Social Responsibility—Ufadhili, Kenya, 244
Centre for Promotion and Development of Civil Initiatives—OPUS, Poland, 305
Centre for Training and Consultancy, Georgia, 157
Centro Mexicano para la Filantropía—CEMEFI, Mexico, 262
Centro Português de Fundações—CPF, Portugal, 310
Centrul Naţional de Asistenţă şi Informare a Organizaţiilor Neguvernamentale din Republica Moldova, Moldova, 264
CERANEO—Centar za razvoj neprofitnih organizacija, Croatia, 109
CERES—Ecuadorean Consortium for Social Responsibility, Ecuador, 124
Charities Advisory Trust, UK, 396
Charities Aid Foundation Bulgaria, Bulgaria, 74
Charities Aid Foundation—CAF, UK, 396
China Foundation Center, China (People's Republic), 102
China NPO Network, China (People's Republic), 102
Civic Initiatives, Serbia, 324
Civil Society Development Centre, Turkey, 387
Civil Society Development Foundation, Romania, 316
Civil Society Development Foundation–Hungary, Hungary, 195
Civil Society Support Centre, Georgia, 157
CIVITAS Foundation for Civil Society, Romania, 316
CNVOS—Zavod Center za Informiranje, Sodelovanje in Razvoj Nevladnih Organizacije, Slovenia, 330
Co-operation Committee for Cambodia, Cambodia, 79
Coalition of National Voluntary Organizations, Canada, 80
Community Foundation Network—CFN, UK, 397
Community Foundations Initiative, Germany, 159
Consejo de Fundaciones Americanas de Desarrollo—Solidarios, Dominican Republic, 123
Consejo de Fundaciones Privadas de Guatemala—CFPG, Guatemala, 190
CONTACT—National Assistance and Information Centre for NGOs in Moldova, Moldova, 264
Council of American Development Foundations, Dominican Republic, 123
Council of Finnish Foundations, Finland, 131
Council on Foundations, Inc, USA, 458
Council of Humanitarian Associations, Czech Republic, 112

Council of Private Foundations of Guatemala, Guatemala, 190
CPCS—Center for Philanthropy and Civil Society, Thailand, 383
CReDO—Resource Centre for the Human Rights NGOs of Moldova, Moldova, 264
Czech Donors Forum, Czech Republic, 112
Dasra, India, 198
Directory of Social Change, UK, 397
Dóchas, Ireland, 210
Donors' Association for the Promotion of Sciences and Humanities, Germany, 159
East African Association of Grantmakers, Kenya, 244
Ecuadorean Consortium for Social Responsibility—CERES, Ecuador, 124
Ednannia: Initiative Centre to Support Social Action—ISAR Ednannia, Ukraine, 393
Eesti Mittetulundusühingute ja Sihtasutuste Liit, Estonia, 129
Ekopolis Foundation, Slovakia, 327
Estonian Foundation Centre, Estonia, 129
Eugenio Mendoza Foundation, Venezuela, 563
European Federation of National Organizations Working with the Homeless, Belgium, 55
European Network of Foundations for Social Economy, Belgium, 56
European NGOs on Agriculture, Food, Trade and Development, France, 135
European Venture Philanthropy Association—EVPA, Belgium, 55
EVPA—European Venture Philanthropy Association, Belgium, 55
FAVDO—Forum for African Voluntary Development Organizations, Senegal, 322
FEANTSA—Fédération Européenne des Associations Nationales Travaillant avec les Sans-Abri, Belgium, 55
Fédération Européenne des Associations Nationales Travaillant avec les Sans-Abri—FEANTSA, Belgium, 55
FIP—Forum Inicjatyw Pozarzadowych, Poland, 305
Fondation de France, France, 135
Fondation Philias, Switzerland, 359
Forum for African Voluntary Development Organizations—FAVDO, Senegal, 322
Forum Inicjatyw Pozarzadowych—FIP, Poland, 305
Forum for Non-Governmental Initiatives, Poland, 305
Forumul Donatorilor din România, Romania, 316
Foundation Center, USA, 458
Foundation Library Center of Japan, Japan, 230
French Foundation Centre, France, 135
Fundación AVINA, Panama, 297
Fundación Eugenio Mendoza, Venezuela, 563
Fundación Lealtad, Spain, 337
Fundatia pentru Dezvoltarea Societatii Civile—FDSC, Romania, 316
GIFE—Grupo de Institutos, Fundações e Empresas, Brazil, 70
Global Fund for Community Foundations—GFCF, South Africa, 331
Gradjanske inicijative—GI, Serbia, 324
Group of Institutes, Foundations and Enterprises, Brazil, 70
Grupa Zagranica, Poland, 305
Grupo de Fundaciones y Empresas, Argentina, 31
GURT Resource Centre for NGO Development, Ukraine, 393
The Hague Club, UK, 397
Himalaya Foundation, Taiwan, 379
Horizonti, the Foundation for the Third Sector, Georgia, 157
Hungarian Foundation for Self-Reliance—HFSR, Hungary, 195
ICN Foundation, Czech Republic, 112
ICN—Information Centre for Non-profit Organizations, Czech Republic, 112
IDC—Innovation and Development Centre, Ukraine, 393
Imagine Canada, Canada, 80
Independent Sector, USA, 459
Indian Centre for Philanthropy, India, 198
IndianNGOs.com Pvt Ltd, India, 198
INFID—International NGO Forum on Indonesian Development, Indonesia, 207
Information Centre for Foundations and other Non-profit Organizations—ICN, Czech Republic, 112
Initiative Bürgerstiftungen, Germany, 159
Innovation and Development Centre—IDC, Ukraine, 393
InterAction American Council for Voluntary International Action, USA, 459
International Bank of Ideas, Russian Federation, 318

International NGO Forum on Indonesian Development—INFID, Indonesia, 207
Irish Association of Non-Governmental Development Organizations—DOCHAS, Ireland, 210
Irish Funders Forum, Ireland, 210
ISAR: Resources for Environmental Activists, USA, 460
JACO—Japan Association of Charitable Organizations, Japan, 230
JANIC—Japanese NGO Center for International Co-operation, Japan, 230
Japan Association of Charitable Organizations—JACO, Japan, 230
Japan Foundation Center, Japan, 230
Klon/Jawor Association, Poland, 306
Latin American Association of Development Financing Institutions, Peru, 299
Latin American Association of Development Organizations, Mexico, 262
Lesotho Council of Non-Governmental Organisations, Lesotho, 254
Loyalty Foundation, Spain, 337
Macedonian Centre for International Co-operation—MCIC, Macedonia, 258
Maecenata Management GmbH, Germany, 159
Manfred Woerner Foundation, Bulgaria, 74
MCIC—Macedonian Centre for International Co-operation, Macedonia, 258
Mendoza (Eugenio) Fundación, Venezuela, 563
Mexican Centre for Philanthropy, Mexico, 262
Mongolian Women's Fund—MONES, Mongolia, 266
Nacionalne Zaklade za Razvoj Civilnoga Drustva, Croatia, 109
Nadace Auxilia, Czech Republic, 112
Nadace ICN, Czech Republic, 112
Nadácia Ekopolis, Slovakia, 327
Nadácia Pontis, Slovakia, 327
National Assistance and Information Centre for NGOs in Moldova—CONTACT, Moldova, 264
National Association of Civil Society Organizations, Venezuela, 563
National Council for Voluntary Organisations—NCVO, UK, 398
National Foundation for Civil Society Development, Croatia, 109
NCVO—National Council for Voluntary Organisations, UK, 398
Network of Estonian Non-profit Organizations, Estonia, 129
Network of European Foundations—NEF, Belgium, 56
Network of Information and Support for Non-Governmental Organizations, Poland, 306
New Zealand Association of Philanthropic Trusts, New Zealand, 284
NGDO—Non-Governmental Development Organizations Platform, Slovakia, 327
NGO Centre—NGOC, Armenia, 35
NGO Development Centre, Russian Federation, 318
NGO Development Centre/United Way–Belarus, Belarus, 54
NGO Information and Support Centre—NISC, Lithuania, 256
NGO Rural and Social Initiative, Moldova, 264
NIOK—Nonprofit Információs és Oktató Központ Alapítvány, Hungary, 195
NISC—NGO Information and Support Centre, Lithuania, 256
Non-Profit Information and Training Centre Foundation, Hungary, 195
Nonprofit Információs és Oktató Központ Alapítvány—NIOK, Hungary, 195
Open Society Institute—Paris (Soros Foundations), France, 135
OPUS—Centre for Promotion and Development of Civil Initiatives, Poland, 305
Pakistan Centre for Philanthropy—PCP, Pakistan, 294
PASOS—Policy Association for an Open Society, Czech Republic, 113
Philanthropy Australia, Australia, 36
Philanthropy Ireland, Ireland, 210
Philanthropy New Zealand, New Zealand, 284
Philias Foundation, Switzerland, 359
Philippine Foundation Center—PFC, Philippines, 301
Platforma Mimovládnych Rozvojovych Organizáchií—MVRO, Slovakia, 327
Pôle européen des fondations de l'économie sociale, Belgium, 56
Polish-American Freedom Foundation, Poland, 305
Polsko-Amerykańska Fundacja Wolności, Poland, 305
Pontis Foundation, Slovakia, 327

Portuguese Foundation Centre, Portugal, 310
proFonds, Switzerland, 359
Réseau des ONG Africaines sur l'Environnement, Kenya, 244
Réseau d'ONG Européennes sur l'Agro-alimentaire, le Commerce, l'Environnement et le Développement—RONGEAD, France, 135
Resource Center Foundation, Bulgaria, 74
Resource Centre for the Human Rights Nongovernmental Organizations of Moldova—CReDO, Moldova, 264
Romanian Donors' Forum, Romania, 316
RONGEAD—Réseau d'ONG Européennes sur l'Agro-alimentaire, le Commerce, l'Environnement et le Développement, France, 135
Russian Donors Forum, Russian Federation, 318
Säätiöiden ja rahastojen neuvottelukunta ry, Finland, 131
SAIA—Slovak Academic Information Agency, Slovakia, 327
Sampradaan Indian Centre for Philanthropy, India, 198
SEEENN—South East European Environmental NGOs Network, Macedonia, 258
Semmelweis Alapítvány Magyarországi Ortopédia Fejlesztéséért, Hungary, 195
Semmelweis Foundation for the Development of Orthopaedics in Hungary, Hungary, 195
Sieć SPLOT, Poland, 306
Sieć Wspierania Organizacji Pozarzadowych—SPLOT, Poland, 306
Sinergia—Asociación Nacional de Organizaciones de la Sociedad Civil, Venezuela, 563
Sivil Toplum Geliştirme Merkezi—STGM, Turkey, 387
Slovak Academic Information Agency–Service Center for the Third Sector—SAIA-SCTS, Slovakia, 327
Slovak Donors' Forum—SDF, Slovakia, 328
Slovak Humanitarian Council, Slovakia, 328
Slovak NGDOs Platform, Slovakia, 327
Slovenská Humanitná Rada, Slovakia, 328
SMART—Association for Civil Society Development, Croatia, 109
Solidarios—Consejo de Fundaciones Americanas de Desarrollo, Dominican Republic, 123
South East European Environmental NGOs Network—SEEENN, Macedonia, 258
Spanish Association of Foundations, Spain, 337
Stifterverband für die Deutsche Wissenschaft eV, Germany, 159
Stowarzyszenie Klon/Jawor, Poland, 306
Support Centre for Associations and Foundations—SCAF, Belarus, 54
SwissFoundations—Verband der Schweizer Förderstiftungen/Association des fondations donatrices suisses, Switzerland, 360
Synergos—The Synergos Institute, USA, 460
Taiwan Philanthropy Information Center, Taiwan, 379
TANGO—Association of NGOs in the Gambia, Gambia, 156
Third Sector Foundation of Turkey—TÜSEV, Turkey, 387
Trust for Civil Society in Central and Eastern Europe, Poland, 306
Ufadhili Trust, Kenya, 244
Union of Bulgarian Foundations and Associations, Bulgaria, 74
Union of Charitable Organizations of Russia, Russian Federation, 318
United Way—Belarus/NGO Development Centre, Belarus, 54
Verband der Schweizer Förderstiftungen, Switzerland, 360
Vereniging van Fondsen in Nederland—FIN, Netherlands, 272
Woerner (Manfred) Foundation, Bulgaria, 74
The World of NGOs, Austria, 46
Zagranica Group, Poland, 305
Zavod Center za Informiranje, Sodelovanje in Razvoj Nevladnih Organizacije—CNVOS, Slovenia, 330

AID TO LESS-DEVELOPED COUNTRIES

AARDO—Afro-Asian Rural Development Organization, India, 199
Absolute Return for Kids—ARK, UK, 401
Acceso, Costa Rica, 106
Access Foundation, Costa Rica, 106
ACCION International, USA, 460
ACCU—Asian Cultural Centre for UNESCO, Japan, 231

ACORD—Agency for Co-operation and Research in Development, Kenya, 245
Acting for Life, France, 136
Action contre la Faim, France, 136
Action against Hunger, France, 136
Action Solidarité Tiers Monde—ASTM, Luxembourg, 257
Acumen Fund, USA, 461
Adams (Sylvia) Charitable Trust, UK, 398
Afghanaid, UK, 398
Africa-America Institute—AAI, USA, 461
Africa Educational Trust, UK, 399
Africa Foundation (UK), UK, 399
African Capacity Building Foundation—ACBF, Zimbabwe, 567
African Development Institute, Inc, USA, 461
African Forum and Network on Debt and Development—AFRODAD, Zimbabwe, 567
African Medical and Research Foundation—AMREF, Kenya, 245
African Women's Development Fund—AWDF, Ghana, 185
African Youth Network for Sustainable Development, Algeria, 30
Africare, USA, 462
Afro-Asian Institute in Vienna, Austria, 46
Afro-Asian Rural Development Organization—AARDO, India, 199
Afro-Asiatisches Institut in Wien, Austria, 46
AFRODAD—African Forum and Network on Debt and Development, Zimbabwe, 567
AFSC—American Friends Service Committee, USA, 465
AFTAAC—Arab Fund for Technical Assistance to African Countries, Egypt, 127
Aga Khan Agency for Microfinance, Switzerland, 360
Aga Khan Foundation—AKF, Switzerland, 360
Aga Khan Foundation Canada, Canada, 80
Aga Khan Fund for Economic Development, Switzerland, 361
Agency for Co-operation and Research in Development, Kenya, 245
Agostino (Daniele Derossi) Foundation, USA, 462
Agriculteurs Français et Développement International—AFDI, France, 136
Agromisa Foundation, Netherlands, 280
Agronomes et vétérinaires sans frontières—AVSF, France, 136
Aid for Development Club, Austria, 46
Aid for India/ Karuna Trust, UK, 426
Aide et Action, France, 137
AISA—Africa Institute of South Africa, South Africa, 332
AIV—Asia-Africa International Voluntary Foundation, Japan, 231
AJWS—American Jewish World Service, USA, 466
Albert Schweitzer Ecological Centre, Switzerland, 362
Alberto Vollmer Foundation, Inc, USA, 551
Alchemy Foundation, UK, 399
ALIDE—Asociación Latinoamericana de Instituciones Financieras para el Desarrollo, Peru, 299
All India Disaster Mitigation Institute, India, 199
Allavida—Alliances for Voluntary Initiatives and Development, Kenya, 244
Alliances for Voluntary Initiatives and Development—Allavida, Kenya, 244
Alternatives for Development Foundation, Ecuador, 124
AMADE Mondiale—Association Mondiale des Amis de l'Enfance, Monaco, 265
American Friends Service Committee—AFSC, USA, 465
American Jewish World Service—AJWS, USA, 466
American Near East Refugee Aid—ANERA, USA, 467
Dell'Amore (Giordano) Foundation, Italy, 220
AMREF—African Medical and Research Foundation, Kenya, 245
ANERA—American Near East Refugee Aid, USA, 467
ANESVAD, Spain, 337
ANGOC—Asian NGO Coalition for Agrarian Reform and Rural Development, Philippines, 301
APACE Village First Electrification Group—APACE VFEG, Australia, 36
APHEDA—Union Aid Abroad, Australia, 45
Appropriate Technology for Community and Environment—APACE, Australia, 36
Arab Fund for Technical Assistance to African Countries—AFTAAC, Egypt, 127
ARK—Absolute Return for Kids, UK, 401

Asia-Africa International Voluntary Foundation—AIV, Japan, 231
Asia Foundation, USA, 469
Asia/Pacific Cultural Centre for UNESCO—ACCU, Japan, 231
Asian Community Trust—ACT, Japan, 231
Asian NGO Coalition for Agrarian Reform and Rural Development—ANGOC, Philippines, 301
Asian Youth Center, USA, 470
ASMAE—Association de coopération et d'éducation aux développements, Belgium, 56
Asociación Latinoamericana de Instituciones Financieras para el Desarrollo—ALIDE, Peru, 299
Asociación Latinoamericana de Organizaciones de Promoción al Desarrollo—ALOP, Mexico, 262
Association de coopération et d'éducation aux développements—ASMAE, Belgium, 56
Association for Development Co-operation and Education, Belgium, 56
Association Mondiale des Amis de l'Enfance, Monaco, 265
ASTM—Action Solidarité Tiers Monde, Luxembourg, 257
Atkinson Foundation, USA, 470
Atlantic Philanthropies, USA, 471
Australian People Health Education, Australia, 45
Australian Volunteers International, Australia, 39
Austrian Research Foundation for International Development, Austria, 48
AVINA Foundation, Panama, 297
AVRDC—The World Vegetable Center, Taiwan, 379
AWDF—African Women's Development Fund, Ghana, 185
Bangladesh Rural Advancement Committee—BRAC, Bangladesh, 52
Bariloche Foundation, Argentina, 32
BCAF—Bulgarian Charities Aid Foundation, Bulgaria, 74
Beit Trust, UK, 403
Benecke (Otto) Stiftung eV, Germany, 161
Bettencourt Schueller Foundation, France, 141
Book Aid International—BAI, UK, 405
Bóthar, Ireland, 210
BRAC—Building Resources Across Communities, Bangladesh, 52
Bread for the World, Germany, 163
Bridge to Asia—BTA, USA, 473
Bridge Asia Japan—BAJ, Japan, 232
The Bridge Foundation, India, 200
Britain-Nepal Medical Trust, UK, 405
Brot für die Welt, Germany, 163
Brother's Brother Foundation, USA, 474
Buck (Pearl S. Buck) International, USA, 474
Building Resources Across Communities—BRAC, Bangladesh, 52
CAF Russia—Charities Aid Foundation Russia, Russian Federation, 318
Canadian Catholic Organization for Development and Peace, Canada, 83
Canadian Centre for International Studies and Co-operation/Centre d'études et de coopération internationale—CECI, Canada, 83
Canadian Co-operative Association, Canada, 80
Canadian Council for International Co-operation—CCIC/Conseil canadien pour la coopération internationale—CCCI, Canada, 80
Canadian Crossroads International/Carrefour Canadien International—CCI, Canada, 83
Canadian Executive Service Organization—CESO/Service d'assistance canadienne aux organismes—SACO, Canada, 83
Canadian Foodgrains Bank, Canada, 84
Canadian Hunger Foundation, Canada, 84
Canadian Organization for Development through Education—CODE, Canada, 85
Canadian Physicians for Aid and Relief—CPAR, Canada, 86
Canadian Urban Institute, Canada, 85
CARE International—CI, Switzerland, 361
Cariplo Foundation, Italy, 219
Carnegie Corporation of New York, USA, 475
Carpathian Foundation, Hungary, 195
The Carter Center, USA, 476
Catholic Agency for World Development—Trócaire, Ireland, 213
CCCI—Conseil canadien pour la coopération internationale, Canada, 80
CCF—Christian Children's Fund, USA, 478
CCI—Carrefour Canadien International, Canada, 83

CCIC—Canadian Council for International Co-operation, Canada, 80
CEAS—Centre Ecologique Albert Schweitzer, Switzerland, 362
CECHE—Center for Communications, Health and the Environment, USA, 477
CECI—Canadian Centre for International Studies and Co-operation/Centre d'études et de coopération internationale, Canada, 83
CEGA—Creating Effective Grassroots Alternatives, Bulgaria, 75
CenDHRRA—Center for the Development of Human Resources in Rural Asia, Philippines, 302
Center for Communications, Health and the Environment—CECHE, USA, 477
Center for the Development of Human Resources in Rural Asia—CenDHRRA, Philippines, 302
CENTRAS—Assistance Centre for NGOs, Romania, 316
Centre Ecologique Albert Schweitzer—CEAS, Switzerland, 362
Centre International de Coopération pour le Développement Agricole—CICDA, France, 136
Centre International de Développement et de Recherche—CIDR, France, 138
Centre Pan-Africain de Prospective Sociale, Benin, 65
Centro Internacional de Agricultura Tropical—CIAT, Colombia, 104
CESO—Canadian Executive Service Organization, Canada, 83
Charities Advisory Trust, UK, 396
Charities Aid Foundation Bulgaria, Bulgaria, 74
Charity Projects, UK, 411
Charles Stewart Mott Foundation—CSMF, USA, 526
ChildFund International, USA, 478
ChildFund Korea, Korea (Republic), 246
ChildHope—Hope for the Children Foundation, Guatemala, 190
Children in Africa Foundation, Germany, 181
Children International—CI, USA, 479
Children of the Mekong, France, 139
Christopher Reynolds Foundation, Inc, USA, 539
CIAT—Centro Internacional de Agricultura Tropical, Colombia, 104
CIDR—Centre International de Développement et de Recherche, France, 138
City of Lisbon Foundation, Portugal, 311
Civil Society Development Foundation–Hungary, Hungary, 195
Clovek v tisni—spolecnost pri Ceske televizi, o.p.s., Czech Republic, 113
Club 2/3, Canada, 85
Co-operation for the Promotion and Development of Welfare Activities, Spain, 342
CODE—Canadian Organization for Development through Education, Canada, 85
Comic Relief, UK, 411
Commonwealth Foundation, UK, 411
Community Aid Abroad—Oxfam Australia, Australia, 43
Community Development Foundation, Mozambique, 269
Concern Universal, UK, 412
Consejo de Fundaciones Americanas de Desarrollo—Solidarios, Dominican Republic, 123
Cooperazione Internazionale—COOPI, Italy, 217
COOPI—Cooperazione Internazionale, Italy, 217
Costa Rican Foundation for Development, Costa Rica, 106
Council of American Development Foundations, Dominican Republic, 123
Coutu (Marcelle et Jean), Fondation, Canada, 88
CPAR—Canadian Physicians for Aid and Relief, Canada, 86
The Craig and Susan McCaw Foundation, USA, 520
Creating Effective Grassroots Alternatives—CEGA, Bulgaria, 75
Credit Union Foundation Australia—CUFA, Australia, 40
CUFA—Credit Union Foundation Australia, Australia, 40
CUSO-VSO, Canada, 86
Czech TV Foundation, Czech Republic, 113
Damien Foundation, Belgium, 58
Daniele Agostino Derossi Foundation, USA, 462
Demokratikus Átalakulásért Intézet, Hungary, 196
DEMUCA—Fundación para el Desarrollo Local y el Fortalecimiento Municipal e Institucional de Centroamérica y el Caribe, Costa Rica, 106
Deutsche AIDS-Stiftung, Germany, 164

Deutsche Bank Americas Foundation and
 Community Development Group, USA, 484
Deutsche Stiftung Weltbevölkerung—DSW,
 Germany, 165
Development Foundation of Turkey, Turkey, 390
DEVI—Dignity, Education, Vision International,
 India, 201
Diakonia, Sweden, 352
Dian Desa Foundation, Indonesia, 207
Diana, Princess of Wales Memorial Fund,
 UK, 414
Dignity, Education, Vision International—DEVI,
 India, 201
DOEN Foundation, Netherlands, 280
Dom Manuel II Foundation, Portugal, 311
Don Bosco Foundation of Cambodia—DBFC,
 Cambodia, 79
Dreyfus Health Foundation—DHF, USA, 485
DSW—Deutsche Stiftung Weltbevölkerung,
 Germany, 165
Dulverton Trust, UK, 414
Écoles Sans Frontières—ESF, France, 139
Ecuadorean Development Foundation,
 Ecuador, 125
Eden Foundation, Sweden, 353
ENCOD—European NGO Council on Drugs and
 Development, Belgium, 59
Enda Third World—Environment and
 Development Action in the Third World,
 Senegal, 322
Enda Tiers Monde—Environnement et
 Développement du Tiers-Monde, Senegal, 322
endPoverty.org, USA, 488
Enfants du Mekong, France, 139
Enfants Réfugiés du Monde—ERM, France, 140
Enterprise Development International, USA, 488
Entraide Protestante Suisse, Switzerland, 367
Entwicklungshilfe-Klub, Austria, 46
Environnement et Développement du Tiers-
 Monde—Enda, Senegal, 322
ERM—Enfants Réfugiés du Monde, France, 140
Esperança, Inc, USA, 489
Esquel Group Foundation—Ecuador,
 Ecuador, 125
Eugenio Mendoza Foundation, Venezuela, 563
Eurasia Foundation, USA, 489
European Coalition for Just and Effective Drug
 Policies—ENCOD, Belgium, 59
European NGOs on Agriculture, Food, Trade and
 Development, France, 135
Eurostep—European Solidarity Towards Equal
 Participation of People, Belgium, 60
FAL—France Amérique Latine, France, 151
The Family Federation of Finland, Finland, 133
Family Planning, New Zealand, 284
Farm Africa, UK, 416
FARM Foundation— Foundation for World
 Agriculture and Rural Life, France, 145
FAVDO—Forum for African Voluntary
 Development Organizations, Senegal, 322
FDC—Fundação para o Desenvolvimento da
 Comunidade, Mozambique, 269
FDH—Frères des Hommes, France, 152
Feed the Children, USA, 490
FEIM—Fundación para Estudio e Investigación
 de la Mujer, Argentina, 32
FEPP—Fondo Ecuatoriano Populorum
 Progressio, Ecuador, 124
FFL—Fondation Follereau Luxembourg,
 Luxembourg, 257
FH—Food for the Hungry, USA, 491
filia.die frauenstiftung, Germany, 168
filia—the Women's Foundation, Germany, 168
Finafrica Foundation—Giordano Dell'Amore
 Foundation, Italy, 220
FINCA International, USA, 490
Follereau Foundation Luxembourg,
 Luxembourg, 257
FONADES—Fondation Nationale pour le
 Développement et la Solidarité, Burkina
 Faso, 78
Fondation Abri International, Canada, 97
Fondation pour l'Agriculture et la Ruralité dans
 le Monde—Fondation FARM, France, 145
Fondation Bettencourt-Schueller, France, 141
Fondation canadienne contre la faim, Canada, 84
Fondation Ensemble, France, 143
Fondation contre la Faim, USA, 491
Fondation FARM—Fondation pour l'Agriculture
 et la Ruralité dans le Monde, France, 145
Fondation Follereau Luxembourg—FFL,
 Luxembourg, 257
Fondation de France, France, 135
Fondation Internationale Léon Mba—Institut de
 Médecine et d'Epidémiologie Appliquée,
 France, 146
Fondation Jean-Paul II pour le sahel, Burkina
 Faso, 78

Fondation Marc de Montalembert, France, 148
Fondation Marcelle et Jean Coutu, Canada, 88
Fondation Nationale pour le Développement et la
 Solidarité—FONADES, Burkina Faso, 78
Fondation Pro Victimis Genève, Switzerland, 365
Fondation pour le Renforcement des Capacités en
 Afrique, Zimbabwe, 567
Fondation Rurale pour l'Afrique de l'Ouest,
 Senegal, 322
Fondation Simón I. Patiño, Switzerland, 365
Fondation Syngenta pour une Agriculture
 Durable, Switzerland, 376
Fondazione Cariplo, Italy, 219
Fondazione Cassa di Risparmio delle Provincie
 Lombarde—Fondazione Cariplo, Italy, 219
Fondazione Cassa di Risparmio di Padova e
 Rovigo, Italy, 219
Fondazione Giordano Dell'Amore, Italy, 220
Fondazione Ing. Carlo M. Lerici—FL, Italy, 222
Fondazione RUI, Italy, 225
Fondo Ecuatoriano Populorum Progressio—
 FEPP, Ecuador, 124
Fonds für Entwicklung und Partnerschaft in
 Africa—FEPA, Switzerland, 366
Food for the Hungry—FH, USA, 491
Food for the Poor, Inc, USA, 491
FOPERDA—Fondation Royale Père Damien pour
 la Lutte Contre la Lèpre, Belgium, 58
Forum for African Voluntary Development
 Organizations—FAVDO, Senegal, 322
Foundation Cassa di Risparmio di Padova e
 Rovigo, Italy, 219
Foundation for Children, Germany, 181
Foundation for Deep Ecology, USA, 492
Foundation for Development and Partnership in
 Africa, Switzerland, 366
Foundation for Human Rights and Humanitarian
 Relief, Turkey, 389
Foundation for International Community
 Assistance, USA, 490
Foundation 'Life for All', Switzerland, 375
Foundation for Local Development and the
 Municipal and Institutional Support of
 Central America and the Caribbean, Costa
 Rica, 106
Foundation 'Populorum Progressio', Vatican
 City, 562
Foundation in Support of Local Democracy,
 Poland, 308
Foundation in Support of Local Development
 Initiatives, Venezuela, 563
Foundation for Sustainable Development,
 Spain, 348
Foundation of Village Community Development,
 Indonesia, 208
Foundation for Women, Spain, 345
Foundation for Women's Research and Studies,
 Argentina, 32
France Amérique Latine—FAL, France, 151
Freedom from Hunger, USA, 494
Freedom from Hunger Council of Ireland—
 Gorta, Ireland, 211
Freeplay Foundation, UK, 429
French Agriculturalists and International
 Development, France, 136
Frères des Hommes—FDH, France, 152
Frontiers Foundation Inc/Fondation Frontière
 Inc, Canada, 89
FSLD—Foundation in Support of Local
 Democracy, Poland, 308
Fund for the Development of the Carpathian
 Euroregion, Hungary, 195
Fund for Development and Partnership in Africa,
 Switzerland, 366
Fundação Cidade de Lisboa, Portugal, 311
Fundação para o Desenvolvimento da
 Comunidade, Mozambique, 269
Fundação Dom Manuel II, Portugal, 311
Fundación Acceso, Costa Rica, 106
Fundación Alberto Vollmer, USA, 551
Fundación Alternativas para el Desarrollo,
 Ecuador, 124
Fundación Amanecer, Colombia, 104
Fundación de Apoyo a las Iniciativas Locales de
 Desarrollo—FUNDAPILDE, Venezuela, 563
Fundación AVINA, Panama, 297
Fundación Bariloche, Argentina, 32
Fundación CODESPA—Futuro en Marcha,
 Spain, 342
Fundación Comunitaria de Puerto Rico—FCPR,
 Puerto Rico, 314
Fundación Costarricense de Desarrollo—
 FUCODES, Costa Rica, 106
Fundación para el Desarrollo Local y el
 Fortalecimiento Municipal e Institucional de
 Centroamérica y el Caribe, Costa Rica, 106
Fundación para el Desarrollo Regional de Aysen,
 Chile, 100

Fundación Desarrollo Sostenido—FUNDESO,
 Spain, 348
Fundación Ecuatoriana de Desarrollo—FED,
 Ecuador, 125
Fundación Empresa-Universidad de Zaragoza—
 FEUZ, Spain, 342
Fundación Esperanza de los Niños,
 Guatemala, 190
Fundación para Estudio e Investigación de la
 Mujer—FEIM, Argentina, 32
Fundación Eugenio Mendoza, Venezuela, 563
Fundación Grupo Esquel—Ecuador, Ecuador, 125
Fundación Invica, Chile, 100
Fundación María Francisca de Roviralta,
 Spain, 347
Fundación Mujeres, Spain, 345
Fundación Nantik Lum, Spain, 345
Fundación Panamericana de la Salud y
 Educación, USA, 532
Fundación Paz y Solidaridad Serafín Aliaga—
 FPyS, Spain, 346
Fundación Sartawi, Bolivia, 67
Fundación de Viviendas Hogar de Cristo,
 Chile, 100
Fundacja Rozwoju Demokracji Loaklnej,
 Poland, 308
Fundacja Solidarności Polsko-Czesko-
 Słowackiej, Poland, 308
FUNDESO—Fundación Desarrollo Sostenido,
 Spain, 348
The Gaia Foundation, UK, 418
The Gatsby Charitable Foundation, UK, 418
German AIDS Foundation, Germany, 164
German Foundation for World Population,
 Germany, 165
Gilman (Howard) Foundation, USA, 496
Giordano Dell'Amore Foundation, Italy, 220
Global Fund for Community Foundations—
 GFCF, South Africa, 331
Global Harmony Foundation—GHF,
 Switzerland, 367
Global Voluntary Service—GVS, Japan, 232
Global Water Foundation, South Africa, 333
Good Neighbors International, Korea
 (Republic), 246
Gorta—Freedom from Hunger Council of
 Ireland, Ireland, 211
Grameen Foundation—GF, USA, 499
Grassroots International—GRI, USA, 500
Grupa Zagranica, Poland, 305
HALO Trust, UK, 419
Hamlyn (Paul) Foundation, UK, 419
Harry and Jeanette Weinberg Foundation, Inc,
 USA, 552
Health Volunteers Overseas—HVO, USA, 501
Hedwig and Robert Samuel Foundation,
 Germany, 177
Hedwig und Robert Samuel-Stiftung,
 Germany, 177
HEKS—Hilfswerk Evangelischen Kirchen
 Schweiz, Switzerland, 367
HELP International, USA, 503
Helvetas Swiss Intercooperation,
 Switzerland, 367
Hilden Charitable Fund, UK, 421
Hilfswerk der Evangelischen Kirchen Schweiz—
 HEKS, Switzerland, 367
HIVOS—Humanistisch Instituut voor
 Ontwikkelings Samenwerking,
 Netherlands, 275
Hogar de Cristo, Chile, 100
Home of Christ, Chile, 100
Hope for the Children Foundation,
 Guatemala, 190
Horizons of Friendship, Canada, 90
Howard Gilman Foundation, Inc, USA, 496
Howard Karagheusian Commemorative
 Corporation—HKCC, USA, 513
Humanistic Institute for Co-operation with
 Developing Countries, Netherlands, 275
Humanistisch Instituut voor Ontwikkelings
 Samenwerking—HIVOS, Netherlands, 275
Humanitarian Relief Foundation, Turkey, 389
Hungarian Interchurch Aid—HIA, Hungary, 196
IACD—Institute of Asian Culture and
 Development, Korea (Republic), 246
IBIS, Denmark, 118
ICLARM—The WorldFish Center, Malaysia, 260
IFAD—International Fund for Agricultural
 Development, Italy, 226
IFHD—International Foundation for Human
 Development, India, 203
IKEA Foundation, Netherlands, 275
Îles de Paix, Belgium, 62
Impact First International, Canada, 89
India Assistance, Germany, 171
India Partners, USA, 506
IndianNGOs.com Pvt Ltd, India, 198

Indienhilfe eV, Germany, 171
Indonesia Biodiversity Foundation,
    Indonesia, 208
Indonesian Foundation for Rural Progress,
    Indonesia, 207
Indonesian Prosperity Foundation,
    Indonesia, 208
INFID—International NGO Forum on
    Indonesian Development, Indonesia, 207
Ing. Carlo M. Lerici Foundation, Italy, 222
INMED Partnerships for Children, USA, 506
İnsan Hak ve Hürriyetleri İnsani Yardım Vakfı,
    Turkey, 389
Institut de Médecine et d'Épidémiologie
    Africaines—Fondation Léon Mba,
    France, 146
Institut Nord-Sud, Canada, 95
Institut urbain du Canada, Canada, 85
Institute of Asian Culture and Development—
    IACD, Korea (Republic), 246
Institute for Development Research, USA, 556
Integrated Rural Development Foundation,
    Philippines, 303
Inter-American Foundation—IAF, USA, 507
Inter Pares, Canada, 90
International Blue Crescent Relief and
    Development Foundation—IBC, Turkey, 390
International Centre for Democratic
    Transition—ICDT, Hungary, 196
International Centre for Development and
    Research, France, 138
International Centre for Living Aquatic
    Resources—ICLARM, Malaysia, 260
International Centre for Tropical Agriculture,
    Colombia, 104
International Co-operation, Italy, 217
International Development and Relief
    Foundation, Canada, 91
International Executive Service Corps— IESC,
    USA, 508
The International Foundation, USA, 508
International Foundation for Education and Self-
    Help—IFESH, USA, 509
International Foundation for Human
    Development—IFHD, India, 203
International Foundation Léon Mba—Institute
    of Applied Medicine and Epidemiology,
    France, 146
International Fund for Agricultural
    Development—IFAD, Italy, 226
International Fund for Ireland, Ireland, 211
International Institute for Environment and
    Development—IIED, UK, 423
International Institute of Rural
    Reconstruction—IIRR, Philippines, 303
International Medical Services for Health—
    INMED, USA, 506
International NGO Forum on Indonesian
    Development—INFID, Indonesia, 207
International Orthodox Christian Charities,
    Inc—IOCC, USA, 509
International Refugee Trust—IRT, UK, 424
International Relief and Development—IRD,
    USA, 510
International Relief Teams, USA, 510
International Solidarity Foundation—ISF,
    Finland, 132
International Water Management Institute—
    IWMI, Sri Lanka, 350
Invica Foundation, Chile, 100
Islamic Relief Worldwide, UK, 425
Islands of Peace, Belgium, 62
Japan International Volunteer Center—JVC,
    Japan, 236
JCIE—Japan Center for International Exchange,
    Japan, 236
JEN, Japan, 237
John Paul II Foundation for the Sahel, Burkina
    Faso, 78
Kansainvälinen solidaarisuussäätiö, Finland, 132
Karagheusian (Howard) Commemorative
    Corporation, USA, 513
Karl Kübel Foundation for Child and Family,
    Germany, 174
Karl-Kübel-Stiftung für Kind und Familie,
    Germany, 174
Karuna Trust/ Aid for India, UK, 426
KEHATI—Yayasan Keanekaragaman Hayati
    Indonesia, Indonesia, 208
Kinder in Afrika, Stiftung, Germany, 181
Kirk (Norman) Memorial Trust, New
    Zealand, 284
Kübel (Karl) Stiftung für Kind und Familie,
    Germany, 174
Kulika Charitable Trust (Uganda), Uganda, 392
The Kulika Charitable Trust 1981, Uganda, 392
Kvinna till Kvinna Foundation, Sweden, 354

Lama Gangchen World Peace Foundation,
    Italy, 227
Lateinamerika-Zentrum eV—LAZ, Germany, 174
Latin America Centre, Germany, 174
Latin America France, France, 151
Latin American, African and Asian Social
    Housing Service, Chile, 101
Latin American Association of Development
    Financing Institutions, Peru, 299
Latin American Association of Development
    Organizations, Mexico, 262
Lerici (Ing. Carlo M.), Fondazione presso il
    Politecnico di Milano, Italy, 222
Lifeline Energy, UK, 429
Lifewater International—LI, USA, 518
Liliane Foundation, Netherlands, 281
Lilly Endowment, Inc, USA, 518
LWR—Lutheran World Relief, USA, 519
M. S. Swaminathan Research Foundation—
    MSSRF, India, 205
M-USA—Mercy-USA for Aid and Development,
    USA, 524
McCaw (Craig and Susan) Foundation, USA, 520
Macedonian Centre for International Co-
    operation—MCIC, Macedonia, 258
Maecenata Management GmbH, Germany, 159
Magyar Ökumenikus Segélyszervezet,
    Hungary, 196
Mani Tese, Italy, 227
MAP International—Medical Assistance
    Programs, USA, 522
Marc de Montalembert Foundation, France, 148
Marcelle et Jean Coutu Foundation, Canada, 88
María Francisca de Roviralta Foundation,
    Spain, 347
Match International Centre, Canada, 93
Mba (Léon), Fondation—Institut de Médecine et
    d'Épidémiologie Africaines, France, 146
MCIC—Macedonian Centre for International Co-
    operation, Macedonia, 258
Medical Assistance Programs, USA, 522
Medical Emergency Relief International—
    MERLIN, UK, 432
Mendoza (Eugenio) Fundación, Venezuela, 563
Mercy-USA for Aid and Development—M-USA,
    USA, 524
MERLIN—Medical Emergency Relief
    International, UK, 432
Mindolo Ecumenical Foundation—MEF,
    Zambia, 566
Miriam Dean Fund, UK, 413
Miriam Dean Refugee Trust Fund, UK, 413
Mott (Charles Stewart) Foundation, USA, 526
MS ActionAid Denmark, Denmark, 120
MS—Mellemfolkeligt Samvirke, Denmark, 120
Mutual Aid and Liaison Service, France, 154
Nadácia Pontis, Slovakia, 327
Nantik Lum Foundation, Spain, 345
National Foundation for Solidarity and
    Development, Burkina Faso, 78
Nederlands instituut voor Zuidelijk Afrika—
    NiZA, Netherlands, 278
Nederlandse Organisatie voor Internationale
    Ontwikkelingssamenwerking—Stichting
    NOVIB, Netherlands, 279
NEF—Near East Foundation, USA, 528
Nelson Mandela Children's Fund—Canada,
    Canada, 93
Nepal Forward Foundation, Nepal, 271
Van Neste Foundation, UK, 453
Netherlands Institute for Southern Africa,
    Netherlands, 278
NFI—National Foundation for India, India, 204
NGDO—Non-Governmental Development
    Organizations Platform, Slovakia, 327
NGO Rural and Social Initiative, Moldova, 264
Nigerian Conservation Foundation—NCF,
    Nigeria, 290
Non-Governmental Organization JEN,
    Japan, 237
Nordic Africa Institute Scholarships,
    Sweden, 355
Nordiska Afrikainstitutets Stipendier,
    Sweden, 355
Norman Kirk Memorial Trust, New Zealand, 284
North-South-Bridge Foundation, Germany, 181
North-South Institute/Institut Nord-Sud,
    Canada, 95
Novartis Foundation for Sustainable
    Development—NFSD, Switzerland, 371
Novartis Stiftung für Nachhaltige Entwicklung,
    Switzerland, 371
NOVIB (Oxfam Netherlands), Netherlands, 279
NoVo Foundation, USA, 529
Nuffield Foundation, UK, 435
OneWorld International Foundation, UK, 435
OPALS—Organisation Panafricaine de Lutte
    Contre le SIDA, France, 153

Open Society Initiative for Southern Africa—
    OSISA, South Africa, 334
Operation Beaver—Frontiers Foundation Inc,
    Canada, 89
Operation Eyesight Universal/Action universelle
    de la vue, Canada, 95
Operation USA, USA, 530
Opportunity International USA, USA, 530
Organisation Afro-Asiatique Pour Le
    Developpement Rural, India, 199
Organisation Panafricaine de Lutte Contre le
    SIDA—OPALS, France, 153
Österreichische Forschungsstiftung für
    Internationale Entwicklung—ÖFSE,
    Austria, 48
Otto Benecke Foundation, Germany, 161
Otto-Benecke-Stiftung eV, Germany, 161
Outreach International, USA, 531
Oxfam Australia, Australia, 43
Oxfam Canada, Canada, 95
Oxfam Deutschland e.V., Germany, 176
Oxfam Hong Kong, Hong Kong, 194
Oxfam India, India, 204
Oxfam Ireland, Ireland, 212
Oxfam Mexico, Mexico, 263
Oxfam New Zealand, New Zealand, 285
Oxfam NOVIB—Nederlandse Organisatie voor
    Internationale Ontwikkelingssamenwerking,
    Netherlands, 279
Oxfam NOVIB—Netherlands Organization for
    International Development Co-operation,
    Netherlands, 279
Oxfam-Québec, Canada, 95
PAC—Partnership Africa Canada, Canada, 95
PADF—Pan American Development Foundation,
    USA, 532
PAHEF—Pan American Health and Education
    Foundation, USA, 532
Pan-African Centre for Social Prospects,
    Benin, 65
Pan-African Organization for AIDS Prevention,
    France, 153
The Parthenon Trust, Switzerland, 371
Partners in Rural Development, Canada, 84
Partnership Africa Canada—PAC, Canada, 95
Pathfinder International, USA, 533
Patiño (Simón I.), Fondation, Switzerland, 365
Paul Hamlyn Foundation—PHF, UK, 419
Peace, Health and Human Development
    Foundation—PHD Foundation, Japan, 239
Pearl S. Buck International, USA, 474
People in Need, Czech Republic, 113
People-to-People Health Foundation, Inc—
    Project Hope, USA, 537
Peres Center for Peace, Israel, 215
Perpetual Foundation, Australia, 43
Perpetual Trustees Australia, Australia, 43
Pestalozzi Children's Foundation,
    Switzerland, 374
The PHD Foundation—Peace, Health and Human
    Development Foundation, Japan, 239
PHF—Paul Hamlyn Foundation, UK, 419
Pire (Dominique) Foundation, Belgium, 62
Plan Ireland, Ireland, 212
Platforma Mimovládnych Rozvojových
    Organizáchií—MVRO, Slovakia, 327
Plenty International, USA, 535
Plunkett Foundation, UK, 438
Polish-Czech-Slovak Solidarity Foundation,
    Poland, 308
Poniecki (Wladyslaw) Foundation, Inc, USA, 536
Pontis Foundation, Slovakia, 327
Population Council, USA, 536
Press Foundation of Asia—PFA, Philippines, 303
Prince Claus Fund for Culture and Development,
    Netherlands, 279
Prins Claus Fonds Voor Cultuur en Ontwikkeling,
    Netherlands, 279
Pro Mujer International, USA, 536
Pro Victimis Foundation, Switzerland, 365
Pro Women International, USA, 536
PRODESSA—Proyecto de Desarrollo Santiago,
    Guatemala, 191
Progressio, UK, 439
Project HOPE, USA, 537
Project Trust, UK, 439
PROVICOOP—Fundación Invica, Chile, 100
Puerto Rico Community Foundation, Puerto
    Rico, 314
Rabobank Foundation, Netherlands, 279
Refugee Trust International, Ireland, 213
Regional Development Foundation of Aysen,
    Chile, 100
Relief International, USA, 539
Réseau Africain de la Jeunesse pour le
    Développement Durable, Algeria, 30
Réseau d'ONG Européennes sur l'Agro-
    alimentaire, le Commerce, l'Environnement

et le Développement—RONGEAD,
France, 135
Reynolds (Christopher) Foundation, USA, 539
Rockefeller Brothers Fund, USA, 540
Rockwool Fonden, Denmark, 121
Rockwool Foundation, Denmark, 121
RONGEAD—Réseau d'ONG Européennes sur
l'Agro-alimentaire, le Commerce,
l'Environnement et le Développement,
France, 135
Rooftops Canada Foundation, Canada, 97
Roviralta (María Francisca de), Fundación,
Spain, 347
Rowan Charitable Trust, UK, 441
Royal Commonwealth Society for the Blind—
Sight Savers International, UK, 448
The Rufford Foundation, UK, 445
Rufford Maurice Laing Foundation, UK, 445
RUI Foundation, Italy, 225
Rutgers WPF, Netherlands, 279
Sabera Foundation, India, 205
Sabera Foundation India, India, 205
SACO—Service d'assistance canadienne aux
organismes, Canada, 83
Said Foundation, UK, 446
Samuel (Hedwig und Robert) Stiftung,
Germany, 177
Santé Sud, France, 154
Santiago Development Project, Guatemala, 191
Sartawi Foundation, Bolivia, 67
Savings Banks Foundation for International
Cooperation, Germany, 179
Schools Without Frontiers, France, 139
SCIAF—Scottish Catholic International Aid
Fund, UK, 447
Scottish Catholic International Aid Fund—
SCIAF, UK, 447
SEEMO—IPI—South East Europe Media
Organisation, Austria, 49
SEL—Service d'Entraide et de Liaison,
France, 154
SELAVIP International—Service de Promotion
de l'Habitation Populaire en Amérique Latine,
Afrique et Asie, Chile, 101
Self Help Development International, Ireland, 213
Semmelweis Alapítvány Magyarországi
Ortopédia Fejlesztéséért, Hungary, 195
Semmelweis Foundation for the Development of
Orthopaedics in Hungary, Hungary, 195
Serafín Aliaga Foundation for Peace and
Solidarity, Spain, 346
Service d'Entraide et de Liaison—SEL,
France, 154
Seva Foundation, USA, 544
Shastri Indo-Canadian Institute, Canada, 97
Sight Savers International, UK, 448
Simón I. Patiño Foundation, Switzerland, 365
Skoll Foundation, USA, 544
Slovak NGDOs Platform, Slovakia, 327
SNF—Swedish Nutrition Foundation,
Sweden, 356
Solidarios—Consejo de Fundaciones Americanas
de Desarrollo, Dominican Republic, 123
Solidarité, France, 155
Solidarity, France, 155
South East Europe Media Organisation,
Austria, 49
South East Europe Media Organisation—
SEEMO—IPI, Austria, 49
Southern African Nature Foundation, South
Africa, 336
Southern Health, France, 154
Sparkassenstiftung für internationale
Kooperation eV, Germany, 179
Staples Trust, UK, 449
Steelworkers Humanity Fund, Canada, 98
Stichting Agromisa, Netherlands, 280
Stichting DOEN, Netherlands, 280
Stichting Liliane Fonds, Netherlands, 281
Stichting Triodos Foundation, Netherlands, 282
Stiftung für Kinder, Germany, 181
Stiftung Kinder in Afrika, Germany, 181
Stiftung Kinderdorf Pestalozzi, Switzerland, 374
Stiftung 'Leben für Alle', Switzerland, 375
Stiftung Nord-Süd-Brücken, Germany, 181
Stiftung Vivamos Mejor, Switzerland, 375
Street Kids International, Canada, 98
Stretched Hands, Italy, 227
Suider-Afrikaanse Natuurstigting, South
Africa, 336
Swedish Nutrition Foundation—SNF,
Sweden, 356
Swiss Foundation for Technical Co-operation,
Switzerland, 375
Swiss Interchurch Aid, Switzerland, 367
SWISSAID Foundation, Switzerland, 375
Swisscontact—Swiss Foundation for Technical
Co-operation, Switzerland, 375

The Sylvia Adams Charitable Trust, UK, 398
Synergos—The Synergos Institute, USA, 460
Syngenta Foundation for Sustainable
Agriculture, Switzerland, 376
Syngenta Stiftung für Nachhaltige
Landwirtschaft, Switzerland, 376
TANZ—Trade Aid NZ Inc, New Zealand, 287
TEAR Australia, Australia, 45
Terre des Hommes Foundation, Switzerland, 376
Terre Sans Frontières—TSF, Canada, 98
Tewa, Nepal, 271
Third World Network—TWN, Malaysia, 260
Third World Solidarity Action, Luxembourg, 257
Thomson Foundation, UK, 451
The Todd Foundation, New Zealand, 287
Together Foundation, France, 143
Trade Aid NZ Inc—TANZ, New Zealand, 287
Triodos Foundation, Netherlands, 282
Trócaire—Catholic Agency for World
Development, Ireland, 213
Türkiye Kalkinma Vakfi, Turkey, 390
Uluslararası Mavi Hilal İnsani Yardım ve
Kalkınma Vakfı, Turkey, 390
UniCredit Foundation—Unidea, Italy, 228
Union Aid Abroad—APHEDA, Australia, 45
United Service Committee of Canada, Canada, 98
United Society for the Propagation of the
Gospel—USPG, UK, 453
United States African Development
Foundation—USADF, USA, 550
Unity Foundation, Luxembourg, 257
University of Zaragoza Business Foundation,
Spain, 342
USC Canada, Canada, 98
Väestöliitto, Finland, 133
Vita, Ireland, 213
Vivamos Mejor Foundation, Switzerland, 375
Vodafone Group Foundation, UK, 453
Volkart Foundation, Switzerland, 376
Volkart-Stiftung, Switzerland, 376
Vollmer (Alberto) Foundation, Inc, USA, 551
Voluntary Service Overseas, UK, 454
Volunteer Service Abroad—VSA, New
Zealand, 287
VSA—Volunteer Service Abroad, New
Zealand, 287
VSO, UK, 454
War on Want, UK, 454
WasserStiftung, Germany, 184
Water Foundation, Germany, 184
Water.org, Inc, USA, 552
WaterAid, UK, 454
Webb Memorial Trust, UK, 455
Weinberg (Harry and Jeanette) Foundation,
USA, 552
Welfare Association, Switzerland, 376
West African Rural Foundation, Senegal, 322
Westminster Foundation for Democracy—WFD,
UK, 455
Winrock International, USA, 555
Wladyslaw Poniecki Foundation, Inc, USA, 536
World Accord, Canada, 99
World Association of Children's Friends,
Monaco, 265
World Education, Inc, USA, 556
World Literacy of Canada—WLC, Canada, 99
World Neighbors, USA, 557
World Population Foundation, Netherlands, 279
The WorldFish Center, Malaysia, 260
WWF South Africa, South Africa, 336
YADESA—Yayasan Pengembangan Masyarakat
Desa, Indonesia, 208
YASIKA—Yayasan Indonesia untuk Kemajuan
Desa, Indonesia, 207
Yayasan Dian Desa, Indonesia, 207
Yayasan Indonesia Sejahtera, Indonesia, 208
Yayasan Indonesia untuk Kemajuan Desa
(YASIKA), Indonesia, 207
Yayasan Keanekaragaman Hayati Indonesia—
KEHATI, Indonesia, 208
Yayasan Pengembangan Masyarakat Desa—
YADESA, Indonesia, 208
Youth for Development and Co-operation—YDC,
Netherlands, 283
Zagranica Group, Poland, 305
Zakat House, Kuwait, 249
Zero-Kap Foundation, Netherlands, 283
ZOA, Netherlands, 283

ARTS AND HUMANITIES

1818 Fund Foundation, Netherlands, 280
A. G. Leventis Foundation, Cyprus, 111
A. G. Leventis Foundation Nigeria, Nigeria, 290
A. M. Qattan Foundation, UK, 440
The A. P. Møller and Chastine Mc-Kinney Møller
Foundation, Denmark, 120

A. P. Møller og Hustru Chastine Mc-Kinney
Møllers Fond til almene Formaal,
Denmark, 120
AbaF—Australia Business Arts Foundation,
Australia, 37
Abdul Hameed Shoman Foundation, Jordan, 242
Abegg Foundation, Switzerland, 360
Abegg-Stiftung, Switzerland, 360
Académie Goncourt—Société des Gens de
Lettres, France, 136
ACCU—Asian Cultural Centre for UNESCO,
Japan, 231
Açık Toplum Enstitüsü, Turkey, 387
The Adolph and Esther Gottlieb Foundation, Inc,
USA, 498
Adriano Olivetti Foundation, Italy, 223
Africa-America Institute—AAI, USA, 461
African Youth Network for Sustainable
Development, Algeria, 30
Agora Foundation, Poland, 306
The Ahmanson Foundation, USA, 462
AIIT—Ancient India and Iran Trust, UK, 400
AINA—Arctic Institute of North America,
Canada, 81
The Al-Khoei Benevolent Foundation, UK, 399
Alamire Foundation, Belgium, 56
Alavi Foundation, USA, 462
Albéniz (Isaac), Fundación, Spain, 339
Albéniz Foundation, Spain, 339
Alchemy Foundation, UK, 399
Alemán (Miguel), Fundación, Mexico, 262
Alfred Toepfer Foundation F.V.S., Germany, 183
Alfred Toepfer Stiftung F.V.S., Germany, 183
Alicia Patterson Foundation—APF, USA, 533
Allen (Paul G.) Family Foundation, USA, 463
Allianz Cultural Foundation, Germany, 160
Allianz Kulturstiftung, Germany, 160
Almeida (Eng. António de), Fundação,
Portugal, 310
Alvares Penteado (Armando), Fundação,
Brazil, 71
Amberes (Carlos de), Fundación, Spain, 339
Ambrosiana Paolo VI Foundation, Italy, 218
American Foundation for the Blind, Inc—AFB,
USA, 465
American Historical Association, USA, 466
American Hungarian Foundation, USA, 466
American Scandinavian Foundation—ASF,
USA, 467
American Schools of Oriental Research—ASOR,
USA, 467
Amerind Foundation, Inc, USA, 468
Ancient India and Iran Trust, UK, 400
Anders Jahre's Foundation for Humanitarian
Purposes, Norway, 291
Anders Jahres Humanitære Stiftelse,
Norway, 291
The Andrew W. Mellon Foundation, USA, 523
The Andy Warhol Foundation for the Visual Arts,
Inc, USA, 552
Anna Lindh Euro-Mediterranean Foundation for
Dialogue between Cultures, Egypt, 127
The Annenberg Foundation, USA, 468
Apex Foundation, Australia, 36
Arab Image Foundation, Lebanon, 252
Arab Thought Foundation, Lebanon, 252
ArcelorMittal Acesita Foundation, Brazil, 71
Arctic Institute of North America—AINA,
Canada, 81
Areces (Ramón), Fundación, Spain, 340
Arie and Ida Crown Memorial, USA, 483
Armando Alvares Penteado Foundation,
Brazil, 71
Arpad Szenes–Vieira da Silva Foundation,
Portugal, 313
Art Fund—National Art Collections Fund,
UK, 401
Arthur Rubinstein International Music Society,
Israel, 215
Arts Council England, UK, 402
Arts Council of Korea, Korea (Republic), 246
Asahi Beer Arts Foundation, Japan, 230
Asahi Biiru Geijutsu Bunka Zaidan, Japan, 230
Ashden Charitable Trust, UK, 402
Asia/Pacific Cultural Centre for UNESCO—
ACCU, Japan, 231
Asia Pacific Foundation of Canada, Canada, 81
Asia Society, USA, 470
Asian Cultural Council—ACC, USA, 470
ASOR—American Schools of Oriental Research,
USA, 467
Association Égyptologique Reine Elisabeth,
Belgium, 57
Association of the Friends of the Swedish
Institute at Athens, Sweden, 353
Associazione Donatella Flick, Switzerland, 361
Auschwitz-Birkenau Foundation, Poland, 306
Auschwitz Foundation, Belgium, 60

Australia Business Arts Foundation—AbaF, Australia, 37
Australia Foundation for Culture and the Humanities Ltd, Australia, 37
Australia-Japan Foundation, Australia, 37
Australian Academy of the Humanities, Australia, 37
The Australian Elizabethan Theatre Trust, Australia, 38
Australian Multicultural Foundation—AMF, Australia, 39
Axel Springer Foundation, Germany, 179
Axel-Springer-Stiftung, Germany, 179
Ayala Foundation, Inc—AFI, Philippines, 301
Ayala Foundation USA—AF-USA, USA, 535
Aydın Doğan Foundation, Turkey, 388
Aydın Doğan Vakfi, Turkey, 388
Bacon (Francis) Foundation, Inc, USA, 471
BANHCAFE Foundation, Honduras, 193
Bank of America Foundation, USA, 472
Bank of Brazil Foundation, Brazil, 71
Bank of Cyprus Cultural Foundation, Cyprus, 111
Barceló Foundation, Spain, 340
Barenboim-Said Foundation, Spain, 340
Baring Foundation, UK, 402
Barrié de la Maza (Pedro, Conde de Fenosa), Fundación, Spain, 340
BBC World Service Trust, UK, 403
BBVA Foundation, Spain, 340
Beaverbrook Foundation, UK, 403
Beisheim (Professor Otto) Stiftung, Germany, 161
Belém Cultural Centre Foundation, Portugal, 310
Benetton Foundation for Study and Research, Italy, 219
The Bernard Sunley Charitable Foundation, UK, 450
Bernheim Foundation, Belgium, 60
Bertelsmann Foundation, Germany, 162
Bertelsmann Stiftung, Germany, 162
Beth (Evert Willem) Foundation, Netherlands, 272
Bettencourt Schueller Foundation, France, 141
Biblioteca dell'Accademia Nazionale dei Lincei, Italy, 216
Binding (Sophie und Karl) Stiftung, Switzerland, 361
Bleustein-Blanchet (Marcel), Fondation pour la Vocation, France, 141
Bofill (Jaume), Fundació, Spain, 338
Boghossian Foundation, Belgium, 60
Boltzmann (Ludwig) Gesellschaft, Austria, 46
Book Aid International—BAI, UK, 405
Borchardt (Ludwig) Stiftung, Switzerland, 361
Borderland Foundation, Poland, 307
Bosch (Robert) Stiftung GmbH, Germany, 163
Botín (Marcelino) Fundación, Spain, 341
Bradley (Lynde and Harry) Foundation, Inc, USA, 473
Brazil Foundation, Brazil, 70
Bridge to Asia—BTA, USA, 473
Bridge House Estates Trust Fund, UK, 410
British Institute at Ankara, UK, 406
The Broad Foundations, USA, 474
Buck (Pearl S. Buck) International, USA, 474
Bunge y Born Foundation, Argentina, 32
The Bydale Foundation, USA, 475
C. P. Ramaswami Aiyar Foundation, India, 204
Cadbury (Edward) Charitable Trust, Inc, UK, 407
Caetani (Leone), Fondazione, Italy, 216
Caja Madrid Foundation, Spain, 341
The Camargo Foundation, France, 138
The Canada Council for the Arts/Conseil des Arts du Canada, Canada, 82
Canada Israel Cultural Foundation, Canada, 82
Canadian Urban Institute, Canada, 85
Canon Foundation in Europe, Netherlands, 272
Cariplo Foundation, Italy, 219
The Carl and Lily Pforzheimer Foundation, Inc, USA, 535
Carlo Cattaneo Institute, Italy, 227
Carlo Collodi National Foundation, Italy, 223
Carlos de Amberes Foundation, Spain, 339
Carlsberg Foundation, Denmark, 117
Carlsbergfondet, Denmark, 117
Cartier Foundation for Contemporary Art, France, 141
Cattaneo (Carlo), Istituto, Italy, 227
CENSIS—Fondazione Centro Studi Investimenti Sociali, Italy, 216
Center for Cultural and Technical Interchange between East and West—East-West Center, USA, 487
Center for Human Research and Social Development—CHRSD, Palestinian Autonomous Areas, 296
Central and Eastern European Media Centre Foundation, Poland, 307

Centre Européen de la Culture—CEC, Switzerland, 362
Centro di Cultura e Civiltà Contadina, Italy, 216
Cera, Belgium, 57
Chandana Art Foundation International, India, 200
Charles and Lynn Schusterman Family Foundation—CLSFF, USA, 543
Charles Wallace India Trust, UK, 454
Charter 77 Foundation, Czech Republic, 114
Chia Hsin Foundation, Taiwan, 379
The Chicago Community Trust, USA, 478
Children's Foundation of China, China (People's Republic), 102
China Soong Ching Ling Foundation, China (People's Republic), 102
Christoph Merian Foundation, Switzerland, 371
Christoph-Merian-Stiftung, Switzerland, 371
Cini (Giorgio), Fondazione, Italy, 220
Cité Internationale des Arts, France, 139
CittàItalia Foundation, Italy, 220
The City Bridge Trust, UK, 410
Civic Forum Foundation, Czech Republic, 113
Cleveland Foundation, USA, 480
Cleveland H. Dodge Foundation, Inc, USA, 485
Collodi (Carlo), Fondazione Nazionale, Italy, 223
Commonwealth Foundation, UK, 411
Communication Foundation for Asia, Philippines, 302
Community Foundation for Northern Ireland, UK, 412
Compagnia di San Paolo, Italy, 217
Compton Foundation, Inc, USA, 481
Conseil des Arts du Canada, Canada, 82
Consejo de Fundaciones Privadas de Guatemala—CFPG, Guatemala, 190
Le Corbusier Foundation, France, 142
Costopoulos (J. F.) Foundation, Greece, 186
Council of Private Foundations of Guatemala, Guatemala, 190
The CRB Foundation/La Fondation CRB, Canada, 86
Crown (Arie and Ida) Memorial, USA, 483
Crown Family Philanthropies, USA, 483
CRT Foundation, Italy, 220
Cultural Center of the Philippines—CCP, Philippines, 302
Cultural Foundation of the German Länder, Germany, 174
Czech Literary Fund, Czech Republic, 113
Czech Music Fund Foundation, Czech Republic, 113
Daiwa Anglo-Japanese Foundation, UK, 413
The Danish Cultural Institute, Denmark, 117
Danske Kulturinstitut, Denmark, 117
David and Lucile Packard Foundation, USA, 531
Davis (Lady) Fellowship Trust, Israel, 214
The Delius Trust, UK, 413
Deutsche Bank Americas Foundation and Community Development Group, USA, 484
Deutsche Bank Foundation, Germany, 164
Deutsche Bank Stiftung, Germany, 164
Deutsche Nationalstiftung, Germany, 165
Deutsche Orient-Stiftung, Germany, 165
DeWitt Wallace—Reader's Digest Fund, Inc, USA, 551
Dodge (Cleveland H.) Foundation, Inc, USA, 485
DOEN Foundation, Netherlands, 280
Doğan (Aydın) Vakfi, Turkey, 388
Donors' Association for the Promotion of Sciences and Humanities, Germany, 159
Dr Scholl Foundation, USA, 543
Dulverton Trust, UK, 414
Dumbarton Oaks, USA, 486
East-West Center—EWC, USA, 487
Easter Island Foundation, USA, 487
Ebelin and Gerd Bucerius ZEIT Foundation, Germany, 184
Eça de Queiroz Foundation, Portugal, 312
The Edmond de Rothschild Foundations, USA, 541
EDP Foundation, Portugal, 311
Eduardo Capa Foundation, Spain, 341
Edward Cadbury Charitable Trust, Inc, UK, 407
Egmont Fonden, Denmark, 118
Egmont Foundation, Denmark, 118
Einaudi (Luigi), Fondazione, Italy, 221
Elizabeth Kostova Foundation for Creative Writing, Bulgaria, 76
Ellerman (John) Foundation, UK, 414
EMI Music Sound Foundation, UK, 415
Emirates Foundation, United Arab Emirates, 395
Eng. António de Almeida Foundation, Portugal, 310
Ente Cassa di Risparmio di Firenze, Italy, 217
Erik Philip-Sörensen Foundation, Sweden, 356

Erik Philip-Sörensen Foundation for the Promotion of Genetic and Humanistic Research, Sweden, 356
Erik Philip-Sörensens Stiftelse, Sweden, 356
ERSTE Foundation, Austria, 46
ERSTE Stiftung—Die ERSTE Österreichische Spar-Casse Privatstiftung, Austria, 46
Esmée Fairbairn Foundation, UK, 416
Estonian National Culture Foundation, Estonia, 129
Etruscan Foundation, USA, 489
Eugenio Mendoza Foundation, Venezuela, 563
Euronisa Foundation, Czech Republic, 114
Europa Nostra, Netherlands, 273
European Centre of Culture, Switzerland, 362
European Cultural Foundation—ECF, Netherlands, 273
European Institute of Health and Social Welfare, Spain, 349
European Institute of Progressive Cultural Policies, Austria, 47
European Mediterranean Institute, Spain, 349
European Science Foundation, France, 144
European Youth For Action—EYFA, Netherlands, 273
European Youth Foundation—EYF, France, 151
Europese Culerele Stichting, Netherlands, 273
Evangelisches Studienwerk eV, Germany, 167
Evens Foundation, Belgium, 61
Evert Willem Beth Foundation, Netherlands, 272
EWC—East-West Center, USA, 487
EYFA—European Youth For Action, Netherlands, 273
The F. K. Morrow Foundation, Canada, 94
FAF—French-American Foundation, USA, 494
Fairbairn (Esmée) Foundation, UK, 416
Fédération Panafricaine des Cinéastes—FEPACI, Burkina Faso, 78
Feltrinelli (Giangiacomo), Fondazione, Italy, 221
Ferrero (Piera, Pietro e Giovanni), Fondazione, Italy, 221
Finnish Cultural Foundation, Finland, 132
Finnish Institute in London Trust, UK, 417
FLAAR—Foundation for Latin American Anthropological Research, USA, 492
Florence Gould Foundation, USA, 499
Florence Savings Bank Foundation, Italy, 217
FOKAL—Fondation Connaissance et Liberte (Haiti), Haiti, 192
Fondation Arabe pour l'Image, Lebanon, 252
Fondation Auschwitz, Belgium, 60
Fondation Bernheim, Belgium, 60
Fondation Bettencourt-Schueller, France, 141
Fondation Boghossian, Belgium, 60
Fondation Cartier pour l'Art Contemporain, France, 141
Fondation Connaissance et Liberté (Haiti)—FOKAL, Haiti, 192
Fondation Le Corbusier—FLC, France, 142
Fondation d'Entreprise La Poste, France, 142
Fondation Européenne de la Culture/Europese Culerele Stichting, Netherlands, 273
Fondation Européenne de la Science, France, 144
Fondation Evens Stichting, Belgium, 61
Fondation de France, France, 135
Fondation France-Israel, France, 145
Fondation Franco-Japonaise Sasakawa, France, 145
Fondation Groupama Gan pour le Cinéma, France, 145
Fondation Hans Wilsdorf—Montres Rolex, Switzerland, 366
Fondation Henri Cartier-Bresson, France, 142
Fondation Hindemith, Switzerland, 363
Fondation Hirondelle: Media for Peace and Human Dignity, Switzerland, 363
Fondation Hugot du Collège de France, France, 145
Fondation Jean Monnet pour l'Europe, Switzerland, 364
Fondation Léopold Sédar Senghor, Senegal, 322
Fondation de Lourmarin Laurent-Vibert, France, 146
Fondation Marc de Montalembert, France, 148
Fondation Marcel Bleustein-Blanchet pour la Vocation, France, 141
Fondation Marcel Hicter, Belgium, 61
Fondation Marguerite et Aimé Maeght, France, 147
Fondation Orient-Occident, Morocco, 268
Fondation du Patrimoine, France, 148
Fondation Princesse Grace, Monaco, 265
Fondation René Seydoux pour le Monde Méditerranéen, France, 150
Fondation du Roi Abdul-Aziz al-Saoud pour les Etudes Islamiques et les Sciences Humaines, Morocco, 268

Fondation Roi Baudouin, Belgium, 62
Fondation Simón I. Patiño, Switzerland, 365
Fondation Singer-Polignac, France, 150
Fondazione Adriano Olivetti, Italy, 223
Fondazione Ambrosiana Paolo VI, Italy, 218
Fondazione per l'Arte, Italy, 219
Fondazione Benetton Studi Ricerche, Italy, 219
Fondazione Cariplo, Italy, 219
Fondazione Cassa di Risparmio delle Provincie
  Lombarde—Fondazione Cariplo, Italy, 219
Fondazione Cassa di Risparmio di Padova e
  Rovigo, Italy, 219
Fondazione Cassa di Risparmio di Torino,
  Italy, 220
Fondazione Centro Studi Investimenti Sociali—
  CENSIS, Italy, 216
Fondazione CittàItalia, Italy, 220
Fondazione Edoardo Garrone, Italy, 222
Fondazione Giangiacomo Feltrinelli, Italy, 221
Fondazione Giorgio Cini, Italy, 220
Fondazione Ing. Carlo M. Lerici—FL, Italy, 222
Fondazione per l'Istituto Svizzero di Roma,
  Italy, 222
Fondazione Leone Caetani, Italy, 216
Fondazione Luigi Einaudi, Italy, 221
Fondazione Nazionale Carlo Collodi, Italy, 223
Fondazione Piera, Pietro e Giovanni Ferrero—
  ONLUS, Italy, 221
Fondazione Prada, Italy, 224
Fondazione Querini Stampalia, Italy, 224
Fondazione Ricci Onlus, Italy, 224
Fondazione Roma, Italy, 224
Fondazione Roma-Mediterraneo, Italy, 224
Fondazione Romaeuropa, Italy, 224
Fondazione RUI, Italy, 225
Fondazione di Studi di Storia dell'Arte 'Roberto
  Longhi', Italy, 225
Fondazione di Venezia, Italy, 225
Fondazzjoni Patrimonju Malti, Malta, 261
Fondo per l'Ambiente Italiano—FAI, Italy, 225
Fonds Européen pour la Jeunesse—FEJ,
  France, 151
Fonds National Suisse de la Recherche
  Scientifique, Switzerland, 374
Fonds Wetenschappelijk Onderzoek—
  Vlaanderen, Belgium, 62
Föreningen Svenska Atheninstitutets Vänner,
  Sweden, 353
FOSIM—Foundation Open Society Institute
  Macedonia, Macedonia, 258
Foundation for the Arts, Italy, 219
Foundation Cassa di Risparmio di Padova e
  Rovigo, Italy, 219
Foundation Centre for the Study of Social
  Investment, Italy, 216
Foundation Czech Art Fund, Czech Republic, 114
Foundation for German–Polish Co-operation,
  Poland, 308
Foundation of the Hellenic World, Greece, 186
Foundation for International Studies—FIS,
  Malta, 261
Foundation for Knowledge and Liberty, Haiti, 192
Foundation for Latin American Anthropological
  Research, USA, 492
Foundation Open Society Institute Macedonia—
  FOSIM, Macedonia, 258
Foundation for Peace, Ecology and the Arts,
  Argentina, 33
Foundation for Reading, Germany, 181
Foundation Robert Laurent-Vibert, France, 146
Foundation for Sport and the Arts, UK, 417
Foundation for Swedish Culture in Finland,
  Finland, 133
Foundation for the Swiss Institute of Rome,
  Italy, 222
Foundation of Weimar Classics, Germany, 173
France-Israel Foundation, France, 145
The Francis Bacon Foundation, Inc, USA, 471
Franco-Japanese Sasakawa Foundation,
  France, 145
Frankfurt Foundation for German-Italian
  Studies, Germany, 168
Frankfurter Stiftung für Deutsch-Italienische
  Studien, Germany, 168
Freedom of Expression Foundation, Norway, 291
The Freedom Forum, USA, 493
French-American Foundation—FAF, USA, 494
Friede Springer Foundation, Germany, 179
Friede Springer Stiftung, Germany, 179
Fritz Gerber Foundation for Gifted Young People,
  Switzerland, 366
Fritz-Gerber-Stiftung für Begabte Junge
  Menschen, Switzerland, 366
Fritz Thyssen Foundation, Germany, 183
Fritz Thyssen Stiftung, Germany, 183
FUHEM—Fundación Hogar del Empleado,
  Spain, 343

FUNBANHCAFE—Fundación BANHCAFE,
  Honduras, 193
Fund for the Italian Environment, Italy, 225
Fund for an Open Society—Serbia, Serbia, 324
Fundação ArcelorMittal Acesita, Brazil, 71
Fundação Armando Alvares Penteado—FAAP,
  Brazil, 71
Fundação Arpad Szenes–Vieira da Silva,
  Portugal, 313
Fundação Banco do Brasil, Brazil, 71
Fundação da Casa de Mateus, Portugal, 310
Fundação Centro Cultural de Belém,
  Portugal, 310
Fundação das Descobertas, Portugal, 310
Fundação Eça de Queiroz, Portugal, 312
Fundação EDP, Portugal, 311
Fundação Eng. António de Almeida,
  Portugal, 310
Fundação Iochpe, Brazil, 72
Fundação Luso-Americana para o
  Desenvolvimento, Portugal, 312
Fundação Mário Soares, Portugal, 313
Fundação Oriente, Portugal, 312
Fundação Ricardo do Espírito Santo Silva,
  Portugal, 311
Fundação Roberto Marinho, Brazil, 72
Fundação de Serralves, Portugal, 312
Fundació Jaume Bofill, Spain, 338
Fundació 'La Caixa', Spain, 338
Fundación Actilibre, Spain, 339
Fundación Albéniz, Spain, 339
Fundación Banco Bilbao Vizcaya Argentaria—
  Fundación BBVA, Spain, 340
Fundación BANHCAFE—FUNBANHCAFE,
  Honduras, 193
Fundación Barceló, Spain, 340
Fundación Barenboim-Said, Spain, 340
Fundación BBVA—Fundación Banco Bilbao
  Vizcaya Argentaria, Spain, 340
Fundación Bunge y Born, Argentina, 32
Fundación Caja Madrid, Spain, 341
Fundación Carlos de Amberes, Spain, 339
Fundación Comunitaria de Puerto Rico—FCPR,
  Puerto Rico, 314
Fundación Eduardo Capa, Spain, 341
Fundación EFE, Spain, 342
Fundación Empresa-Universidad de Zaragoza—
  FEUZ, Spain, 342
Fundación Empresas Polar, Venezuela, 563
Fundación Eugenio Mendoza, Venezuela, 563
Fundación Gala–Salvador Dalí, Spain, 343
Fundación Hogar del Empleado—FUHEM,
  Spain, 343
Fundación José Miguel de Barandiarán,
  Spain, 340
Fundación José Ortega y Gasset, Spain, 346
Fundación Juan March, Spain, 345
Fundación Juanelo Turriano, Spain, 348
Fundación Laboral Sonsoles Ballvé Lantero,
  Spain, 344
Fundación Loewe, Spain, 345
Fundación MAPFRE, Spain, 345
Fundación Marcelino Botín, Spain, 341
Fundación María Francisca de Roviralta,
  Spain, 347
Fundación Miguel Alemán AC, Mexico, 262
Fundación Pablo Neruda, Chile, 100
Fundación Paz, Ecología y Arte—Fundación
  PEA, Argentina, 33
Fundación Paz y Solidaridad Serafín Aliaga—
  FPyS, Spain, 346
Fundación PEA—Fundación Paz, Ecología y
  Arte, Argentina, 33
Fundación Pedro Barrié de la Maza, Spain, 340
Fundación Ramón Areces, Spain, 340
Fundación Santa María, Spain, 348
Fundación Santillana, Spain, 348
Fundación Yannick y Ben Jakober, Spain, 344
Fundacja Agory, Poland, 306
Fundacja Auschwitz-Birkenau, Poland, 306
Fundacja Bankowa im. Leopolda Kronenberga,
  Poland, 306
Fundacja Centrum Prasowe, Poland, 307
Fundacja Pogranicze, Poland, 307
Fundacja Pro Bono II, Poland, 308
Fundacja Solidarności Polsko-Czesko-
  Słowackiej, Poland, 308
Fundacja Współpracy Polsko-Niemieckiej/
  Stiftung für Deutsch–Polnische
  Zusammenarbeit, Poland, 308
Gandhi (Mahatma) Foundation for World Peace,
  Canada, 89
Gandhi Peace Foundation, India, 202
Gannett Foundation, USA, 493
Garfield Weston Foundation, UK, 455
The Gatsby Charitable Foundation, UK, 418
The George A. and Eliza Gardner Howard
  Foundation, USA, 504

George Cedric Metcalf Charitable Foundation,
  Canada, 94
Georges Lurcy Charitable and Educational
  Trust, USA, 519
Gerber (Fritz) Stiftung für begabte junge
  Menschen, Switzerland, 366
German National Academic Foundation,
  Germany, 182
German National Trust, Germany, 165
German Orient Foundation, Germany, 165
Getty (J. Paul) Jnr Charitable Trust, UK, 418
Giangiacomo Feltrinelli Foundation, Italy, 221
Gilbert Murray Trust, UK, 433
Giorgio Cini Foundation, Italy, 220
Glasnost Defence Foundation—GDF, Russian
  Federation, 319
Global Harmony Foundation—GHF,
  Switzerland, 367
Goldsmith (Horace W.) Foundation, USA, 498
Goncourt Academy—Literary Society,
  France, 136
Gottlieb (Adolph and Esther) Foundation, Inc,
  USA, 498
Gould (Florence) Foundation, USA, 499
Great Britain Sasakawa Foundation, UK, 419
Greve (William and Mary) Foundation, Inc,
  USA, 500
Groupama Gan Foundation for the Cinema,
  France, 145
Guggenheim (John Simon) Memorial Foundation,
  USA, 500
Hamlyn (Paul) Foundation, UK, 419
Hans Wilsdorf Foundation, Switzerland, 366
Harold Hyam Wingate Foundation, UK, 456
Hearst (William Randolph) Foundation, USA, 502
The Hearst Foundation, Inc, USA, 501
Heinz (Howard) Endowment, USA, 502
The Helene Wurlitzer Foundation of New Mexico,
  USA, 558
Hellenic Foundation for Culture, Greece, 186
Helsingin Sanomain Säätiö, Finland, 131
Helsingin Sanomat Foundation, Finland, 131
Henie Onstad Art Centre, Norway, 292
Henie Onstad kunstsenter, Norway, 292
Henri Cartier-Bresson Foundation, France, 142
The Henry J. Kaiser Family Foundation, USA, 513
Henry Luce Foundation, Inc, USA, 519
Heritage Foundation, France, 148
Hesse and Thuringia Savings Banks Cultural
  Foundation, Germany, 178
Hewlett (William and Flora) Foundation,
  USA, 503
Heydar Aliyev Foundation, Azerbaijan, 50
Hicter (Marcel), Fondation, Belgium, 61
Hindemith Foundation, Switzerland, 363
History Foundation of Turkey, Turkey, 389
HIVOS—Humanistisch Institut voor
  Ontwikkelings Samenwerking,
  Netherlands, 275
Horace W. Goldsmith Foundation, USA, 498
House of Europe Cultural Foundation,
  Germany, 174
Howard (George A. and Eliza Gardner)
  Foundation, USA, 504
Howard (Katharine) Foundation, Ireland, 211
Howard Heinz Endowment, USA, 502
Hugot Foundation of the Collège of France,
  France, 145
The Humana Foundation, Inc, USA, 505
Humanistic Institute for Co-operation with
  Developing Countries, Netherlands, 275
Humanistisch Instituut voor Ontwikkelings
  Samenwerking—HIVOS, Netherlands, 275
IACD—Institute of Asian Culture and
  Development, Korea (Republic), 246
Ian Potter Foundation, Australia, 43
IAPA Scholarship Fund, USA, 505
IEMed—Institut Europeu de la Mediterrània,
  Spain, 349
Imperial Oil Foundation, Canada, 90
Indian National Trust for Art and Cultural
  Heritage—INTACH, India, 203
Ing. Carlo M. Lerici Foundation, Italy, 222
Initiative and Achievement, Foundation of the
  Nassauische Sparkasse for Culture, Sport and
  Society, Germany, 171
Initiative und Leistung, Stiftung der
  Nassauische Sparkasse für Kultur, Sport
  und Gesellschaft, Germany, 171
Institusjonen Fritt Ord, Norway, 291
Institut Arctique de l'Amérique du Nord—IAAN,
  Canada, 81
Institut Català Mediterrània, Spain, 349
Institut Europeu de la Mediterrània—IEMed,
  Spain, 349
Institut Néerlandais, France, 152
Institut urbain du Canada, Canada, 85

Institute of Asian Culture and Development—IACD, Korea (Republic), 246
Instituto Europeo de Salud y Bienestar Social, Spain, 349
Institutul Cultural Român, Romania, 317
INTACH (UK) Trust, India, 203
INTACH—Indian National Trust for Art and Cultural Heritage, India, 203
Inter American Press Association Scholarship Fund, USA, 505
International Bank of Ideas, Russian Federation, 318
International Centre for the Arts, France, 139
International Charitable Fund 'Ukraine 3000', Ukraine, 394
International Renaissance Foundation—IRF, Ukraine, 394
International Visegrad Fund—IVF, Slovakia, 328
Irvine (James) Foundation, USA, 511
Ishizaka Foundation, Japan, 234
Istituto Carlo Cattaneo, Italy, 227
Istituto Luigi Sturzo, Italy, 227
Istituto Svedese di Studi Classici, Italy, 228
IUC-Europe International Education Centre, Denmark, 119
IUC-Europe Internationalt Uddanneless Center, Denmark, 119
The J. F. Costopoulos Foundation, Greece, 186
J. Paul Getty Jnr Charitable Trust, UK, 418
J&S Pro Bono Poloniae Foundation, Poland, 309
The James Irvine Foundation, USA, 511
Jan Hus Educational Foundation, Slovakia, 329
Japanese-German Center Berlin, Germany, 173
Japanisch-Deutsches Zentrum Berlin, Germany, 173
Jaume Bofill Foundation, Spain, 338
Jean Monnet Foundation for Europe, Switzerland, 364
Jenny and Antti Wihuri Foundation, Finland, 134
Jenny ja Antti Wihurin Rahasto, Finland, 134
Jerusalem Foundation, Israel, 214
John Ellerman Foundation, UK, 414
John Simon Guggenheim Memorial Foundation, USA, 500
Jordan River Foundation, Jordan, 241
José Miguel de Barandiaran Foundation, Spain, 340
José Ortega y Gasset Foundation, Spain, 346
Joyce Foundation, USA, 512
Juan March Foundation, Spain, 345
Juanelo Turriano Foundation, Spain, 348
The Judith Rothschild Foundation, USA, 541
Kahanoff Foundation, Canada, 91
Kaiser (Henry J.) Family Foundation, USA, 513
Karić fondacija, Serbia, 325
Karić Foundation, Serbia, 325
Katharine Howard Foundation, Ireland, 211
KCDF—Kenya Community Development Foundation, Kenya, 245
Keidanren Ishizaka Memorial Foundation, Japan, 234
KFAS—Kuwait Foundation for the Advancement of Sciences, Kuwait, 249
Khemka (Nand and Jeet) Foundation, India, 203
King Abdul-Aziz al-Saoud Foundation for Islamic Study and the Humanities, Morocco, 268
King Baudouin Foundation, Belgium, 62
Klassik Stiftung Weimar, Germany, 173
Knut and Alice Wallenberg Foundation, Sweden, 358
Knut och Alice Wallenbergs Stiftelse, Sweden, 358
Koç (Vehbi), Vakfı, Turkey, 391
Köning Boudewijnstichting/Fondation Roi Baudouin, Belgium, 62
Korean Culture and Arts Foundation, Korea (Republic), 246
Koret Foundation, USA, 515
The Kosciuszko Foundation, Inc, USA, 516
Kosovo Foundation for Open Society—KFOS, Kosovo, 248
Kostova (Elizabeth) Foundation for Creative Writing, Bulgaria, 76
Kresge Foundation, USA, 516
Kress (Samuel H.) Foundation, USA, 516
Kronenberga (Leopolda), Fundacja Bankowa, Poland, 306
Kulturfonder for Sverige och Finland, Sweden, 354
KulturKontakt Austria—KKA, Austria, 48
Kulturstiftung Haus Europa, Germany, 174
Kulturstiftung der Länder—KSL, Germany, 174
Kuwait Awqaf Public Foundation, Kuwait, 249
Kuwait Foundation for the Advancement of Sciences—KFAS, Kuwait, 249
L. J. Skaggs and Mary C. Skaggs Foundation, USA, 544
'La Caixa' Foundation, Spain, 338

Lady Davis Fellowship Trust, Israel, 214
Laidlaw Foundation, Canada, 91
Lama Gangchen World Peace Foundation, Italy, 227
Lambrakis Foundation, Greece, 187
Lambrakis Research Foundation, Greece, 187
Landis & Gyr Foundation, Switzerland, 370
Landis & Gyr Stiftung, Switzerland, 370
Lannan Foundation, USA, 517
Latvian Cultural Foundation, Latvia, 251
Latvijas Kultūras Fonds—LKF, Latvia, 251
Lauder (Ronald S.) Foundation, Germany, 174
Van Leer Jerusalem Institute, Israel, 215
Léonie Sonning Music Foundation, Denmark, 121
Léonie Sonnings Musikfond, Denmark, 121
Leopold Kronenberg Foundation, Poland, 306
Léopold Sédar Senghor Foundation, Senegal, 322
Lerici (Ing. Carlo M.), Fondazione presso il Politecnico di Milano, Italy, 222
Leventis (A. G.) Foundation, Cyprus, 111
Leventis (A. G.) Foundation Nigeria, Nigeria, 290
Leverhulme Trust, UK, 429
Library of the National Academy of Lincei, Italy, 216
Lila Wallace—Reader's Digest Fund, Inc, USA, 551
Lilly Endowment, Inc, USA, 518
Littauer (Lucius N.) Foundation, Inc, USA, 519
Loewe Foundation, Spain, 345
The Long Now Foundation—LNF, USA, 519
Longhi (Roberto), Fondazione di Studi di Storia dell'Arte, Italy, 225
Lower Saxony Savings Bank Foundation, Germany, 175
Luce (Henry) Foundation, Inc, USA, 519
Lucius N. Littauer Foundation, Inc, USA, 519
Ludwig Boltzmann Gesellschaft, Austria, 46
Ludwig Borchardt Foundation, Switzerland, 361
Ludwig-Borchardt-Stiftung, Switzerland, 361
Luigi Einaudi Foundation, Italy, 221
Luigi Sturzo Institute, Italy, 227
Lurcy (Georges) Charitable and Educational Trust, USA, 519
Luso-American Development Foundation, Portugal, 312
Luxemburg (Rosa) Stiftung, Germany, 174
Lynde and Harry Bradley Foundation, Inc, USA, 473
McCormick (Robert R.) Foundation, USA, 520
Macdonald Stewart Foundation, Canada, 92
The Mackintosh Foundation, UK, 430
McKnight Foundation, USA, 521
The McLean Foundation, Canada, 93
Maecenata Management GmbH, Germany, 159
Maeght (Marguerite et Aimé), Fondation, France, France, 147
Mahatma Gandhi Canadian Foundation for World Peace, Canada, 89
Maison Franco-Japonaise, Japan, 237
Maltese Heritage Foundation, Malta, 261
Mandela (Nelson) Foundation, South Africa, 333
MAPFRE Foundation, Spain, 345
Marc de Montalembert Foundation, France, 148
Marcel Bleustein-Blanchet Vocation Foundation, France, 141
Marcel Hicter Foundation, Belgium, 61
Marcelino Botín Foundation, Spain, 341
March (Juan), Fundación, Spain, 345
Marguerite and Aimé Maeght Foundation, France, 147
María Francisca de Roviralta Foundation, Spain, 347
Marinho (Roberto), Fundação, Brazil, 72
Mário Soares Foundation, Portugal, 313
Mateus House Foundation, Portugal, 310
Mellon (Andrew W.) Foundation, USA, 523
Mendoza (Eugenio) Fundación, Venezuela, 563
Menzies (R. G.) Scholarship Fund, Australia, 42
Mercers' Charitable Foundation, UK, 431
Merian (Christoph) Stiftung, Switzerland, 371
Mertz Gilmore Foundation, USA, 524
Messerschmitt Foundation, Germany, 175
Messerschmitt-Stiftung, Germany, 175
Metcalf (George Cedric) Charitable Foundation, Canada, 94
Miguel Alemán Foundation, Mexico, 262
Mindolo Ecumenical Foundation—MEF, Zambia, 566
Miriam G. and Ira D. Wallach Foundation, USA, 552
Mohammed bin Rashid Al Maktoum Foundation, United Arab Emirates, 395
Møller (A.P.) and Chastine Mc-Kinney Møller Foundation, Denmark, 120
Monnet (Jean), Fondation pour l'Europe, Switzerland, 364
Montres Rolex, Fondation, Switzerland, 366
Monument Trust, UK, 432

Moody Foundation, USA, 525
Morfotiko Idryma Ethnikis Trapezis—MIET, Greece, 188
Morrow (The F. K.) Foundation, Canada, 94
Mosaic Foundation, USA, 526
Mostazafan Foundation of New York, USA, 462
Murray (Gilbert) Trust, UK, 433
Music Sound Foundation, UK, 415
Mwalimu Nyerere Foundation—MNF, Tanzania, 382
Myer (Sidney) Fund, Australia, 42
The Myer Foundation, Australia, 42
Nadace cesky hudebni fond, Czech Republic, 113
Nadace Charty 77, Czech Republic, 114
Nand and Jeet Khemka Foundation, India, 203
Nathan Steinberg Family Foundation, Canada, 98
National Art Collections Fund—Art Fund, UK, 401
National Bank of Greece Cultural Foundation, Greece, 188
National Conference on Soviet Jewry, USA, 528
National Endowment for Science, Technology and the Arts—NESTA, UK, 434
National Humanities Center, USA, 527
The National Trust for Places of Historic Interest or Natural Beauty, UK, 434
National Youth Foundation, Greece, 188
NCSJ—National Conference on Soviet Jewry, USA, 528
Nederlands instituut voor Zuidelijk Afrika—NiZA, Netherlands, 278
Nelson Mandela Children's Fund—Canada, Canada, 93
Nelson Mandela Foundation, South Africa, 333
Neruda (Pablo), Fundación, Chile, 100
NESsT—Nonprofit Enterprise and Self-sustainability Team, Chile, 101
NESTA—National Endowment for Science, Technology and the Arts, UK, 434
Netherlands Institute, France, 152
Netherlands Institute for Southern Africa, Netherlands, 278
New Carlsberg Foundation, Denmark, 121
New Zealand Winston Churchill Memorial Trust, New Zealand, 285
Newberry Library, USA, 529
Niedersächsische Sparkassenstiftung, Germany, 175
Nonprofit Enterprise and Self-sustainability Team—NESsT, Chile, 101
Nordic Africa Institute Scholarships, Sweden, 355
Nordiska Afrikainstitutets Stipendier, Sweden, 355
Northern Ireland Voluntary Trust, UK, 412
Ny Carlsbergfondet, Denmark, 121
Olivetti (Adriano), Fondazione, Italy, Italy, 223
Open Society Forum (Mongolia), Mongolia, 266
Open Society Foundation, Romania, 317
Open Society Foundation—Bratislava, Slovakia, 328
Open Society Fund—Bosnia-Herzegovina, Bosnia and Herzegovina, 68
Open Society Fund Prague—OSF Prague, Czech Republic, 115
Open Society Georgia Foundation, Georgia, 157
Open Society Initiative for Southern Africa—OSISA, South Africa, 334
Open Society Initiative for West Africa, Senegal, 322
Open Society Institute—Assistance Foundation (Azerbaijan), Azerbaijan, 50
Open Society Institute Assistance Foundation, Armenia—OSIAFA, Armenia, 35
Open Society Institute Assistance Foundation—Tajikistan, Tajikistan, 381
Open Society Institute—Paris (Soros Foundations), France, 135
Open Society Institute—Sofia (Bulgaria), Bulgaria, 76
Open Society Institute—Turkey, Turkey, 387
Orient Foundation, Portugal, 312
The Orient-Occident Foundation, Morocco, 268
OSGF—Open Society Georgia Foundation, Georgia, 157
OSIAF—Open Society Institute Assistance Foundation—Tajikistan, Tajikistan, 381
OSIWA—Open Society Initiative for West Africa, Senegal, 322
Pablo Neruda Foundation, Chile, 100
Pacific Peoples' Partnership, Canada, 95
Packard (David and Lucile) Foundation, USA, 531
PADF—Pan American Development Foundation, USA, 532
Pan-African Federation of Film-makers, Burkina Faso, 78
Pan-European Federation for Cultural Heritage, Netherlands, 273

The Parthenon Trust, Switzerland, 371
Patiño (Simón I.), Fondation, Switzerland, 365
Patterson (Alicia) Foundation, USA, 533
The Paul G. Allen Family Foundation, USA, 463
Paul Hamlyn Foundation—PHF, UK, 419
Paulo Foundation, Finland, 132
Paulon Säätiö, Finland, 132
Pearl S. Buck International, USA, 474
Pedro Barrié de la Maza Foundation, Spain, 340
People's Harmonious Development Society,
    Georgia, 158
Perpetual Foundation, Australia, 43
Perpetual Trustees Australia, Australia, 43
The Pew Charitable Trusts, USA, 534
Pforzheimer (Carl and Lily) Foundation, Inc,
    USA, 535
PHF—Paul Hamlyn Foundation, UK, 419
PhilDev—Philippine Development Foundation,
    USA, 535
Philippine-American Educational Foundation—
    PAEF, Philippines, 303
Philippine Development Foundation—PhilDev,
    USA, 535
Piera, Pietro and Giovanni Ferrero Foundation,
    Italy, 221
Pilgrim Trust, UK, 437
Pinchuk (Victor) Foundation, Ukraine, 394
Polar Companies Foundation, Venezuela, 563
Polish-Czech-Slovak Solidarity Foundation,
    Poland, 308
The Porter Foundation, UK, 439
Post Office Foundation, France, 144
Potanin (Vladimir) Foundation, Russian
    Federation, 320
Potter (Ian) Foundation, Australia, 43
Prada Foundation, Italy, 224
Preciosa Foundation, Czech Republic, 115
Press Foundation of Asia—PFA, Philippines, 303
Prince Bernhard Cultural Foundation,
    Netherlands, 282
Prince Claus Fund for Culture and Development,
    Netherlands, 279
Princess Grace Foundation, Monaco, 265
Prins Bernhard Culturfonds, Stichting,
    Netherlands, 282
Prins Claus Fonds Voor Cultuur en Ontwikkeling,
    Netherlands, 279
Pro Bono Foundation, Poland, 308
Professor Otto Beisheim Foundation,
    Germany, 161
Professor Otto Beisheim Stiftung, Germany, 161
Protestant Study Foundation, Germany, 167
PRS for Music Foundation, UK, 440
Prudential Foundation, USA, 537
Puerto Rico Community Foundation, Puerto
    Rico, 314
Qattan (A. M.) Foundation, UK, 440
Quaid-i-Azam Academy, Pakistan, 294
Queen Elisabeth Egyptological Association,
    Belgium, 57
Querini Stampalia Foundation, Italy, 224
R. G. Menzies Scholarship Fund, Australia, 42
R. Howard Webster Foundation, Canada, 99
Rafik Hariri Foundation, Lebanon, 252
Rajiv Gandhi Foundation, India, 201
Ramaswami Aiyar (C. P.) Foundation, India, 204
Ramón Areces Foundation, Spain, 340
Ramon Magsaysay Award Foundation,
    Philippines, 303
Rayne Foundation, UK, 441
RBC Foundation, Canada, 96
Reimers (Werner) Stiftung, Germany, 177
Reine Elisabeth, Association Égyptologique,
    Belgium, 57
René Seydoux Foundation for the Mediterranean
    World, France, 150
Research Foundation—Flanders, Belgium, 62
Réseau Africain de la Jeunesse pour le
    Développement Durable, Algeria, 30
RIA—Royal Irish Academy, Ireland, 212
Ricardo do Espírito Santo Silva Foundation,
    Portugal, 311
Ricci Onlus Foundation, Italy, 224
Richelieu International, Canada, 96
Righteous Persons Foundation, USA, 539
Robert Bosch Foundation, Germany, 163
Robert-Bosch-Stiftung GmbH, Germany, 163
Robert Marinho Foundation, Brazil, 72
Robert R. McCormick Foundation, USA, 520
Roberto Longhi Foundation for the Study of the
    History of Art, Italy, 225
Rohm Music Foundation, Japan, 239
Roma Lom Foundation, Bulgaria, 76
Romaeuropa Foundation, Italy, 224
Romanian Cultural Foundation, Romania, 317
Romanian Cultural Institute, Romania, 317
Rome Foundation, Italy, 224
The Ronald S. Lauder Foundation, Germany, 174

Rosa Luxemburg Foundation, Germany, 174
Rosa-Luxemburg-Stiftung, Germany, 174
Rothschild (Edmond de) Foundations, USA, 541
Rothschild (Judith) Foundation, USA, 541
Roviralta (María Francisca de), Fundación,
    Spain, 347
Royal Asiatic Society of Great Britain and
    Ireland, UK, 443
Royal Bank of Canada Charitable Foundation,
    Canada, 96
Royal Bank Financial Group Foundation,
    Canada, 96
Rroma Foundation, Switzerland, 372
Rubinstein (Arthur) International Music Society,
    Israel, 215
RUI Foundation, Italy, 225
Rural Culture and Civilization Centre, Italy, 216
Russian Cultural Foundation, Russian
    Federation, 320
Sabancı (Hacı Ömer) Foundation, Turkey, 389
Sabancı Foundation, Turkey, 389
Sabancı Vakfı—Hacı Ömer Sabancı Foundation,
    Turkey, 389
Said Foundation, UK, 446
Saint Cyril and Saint Methodius International
    Foundation, Bulgaria, 76
Salamander Foundation, Canada, 97
Salvador Dalí Foundation, Spain, 343
Samuel H. Kress Foundation, USA, 516
Samuel and Saidye Bronfman Family Foundation,
    Canada, 82
San Francisco Foundation, USA, 542
Sandoz Family Foundation, Switzerland, 372
Sandoz Fondation de Famille, Switzerland, 372
Santa María Foundation, Spain, 348
Santillana Foundation, Spain, 348
Sasakawa, Fondation Franco-Japonaise,
    France, 145
Savings Bank Foundation DnB NOR, Norway, 293
Schusterman (Charles and Lynn) Family
    Foundation, USA, 543
Schweizerischer Nationalfonds zur Förderung
    der wissenschaftlichen Forschung/Fonds
    National Suisse de la Recherche
    Scientifique—SNF, Switzerland, 374
Scouloudi Foundation, UK, 447
SEEMO—IPI—South East Europe Media
    Organisation, Austria, 49
Selby (William G. and Marie) Foundation,
    USA, 543
Serafín Aliaga Foundation for Peace and
    Solidarity, Spain, 346
Serralves Foundation, Portugal, 312
Seydoux (René), Fondation pour le Monde
    Méditerranéen, France, 150
Shastri Indo-Canadian Institute, Canada, 97
Shoman (Abdul Hameed) Foundation,
    Jordan, 242
Siam Society, Thailand, 384
Sidney Myer Fund, Australia, 42
Sihtasutus Eesti Rahvuskultuuri Fond,
    Estonia, 129
Silva (Ricardo do Espírito Santo), Fundação,
    Portugal, 311
Simón I. Patiño Foundation, Switzerland, 365
Singapore International Foundation—SIF,
    Singapore, 326
Singer-Polignac Foundation, France, 150
Sino-British Fellowship Trust—SBFT, UK, 448
Sir Dorabji Tata Trust, India, 205
Skaggs (L. J.) and Skaggs (Mary C.) Foundation,
    USA, 544
Slovak Humanitarian Council, Slovakia, 328
Slovenská Humanitná Rada, Slovakia, 328
Smithsonian Institution, USA, 545
Soares (Mário), Fundação, Portugal, 313
Société Littéraire des Goncourt—Académie
    Goncourt, France, 136
Song Qingling Foundation, China (People's
    Republic), 102
Sonning (Léonie) Musikfond, Denmark, 121
Sonning Foundation, Denmark, 121
Sonnings-Fonden, Denmark, 121
Sonsoles Ballvé Lantero Labour Foundation,
    Spain, 344
Sophie and Karl Binding Foundation,
    Switzerland, 361
Sophie und Karl Binding-Stiftung,
    Switzerland, 361
Sorenson Legacy Foundation, USA, 545
Soros Foundation (Czech Republic), Czech
    Republic, 115
Soros Foundation (Georgia), Georgia, 157
Soros Foundation (Slovakia), Slovakia, 328
Soros Foundation (Tajikistan), Tajikistan, 381
Soros Foundation–Kyrgyzstan, Kyrgyzstan, 250
Soros Foundation Latvia, Latvia, 251
Soros Foundation Macedonia, Macedonia, 258

Soros Foundation—Moldova, Moldova, 264
Soros Foundation Romania, Romania, 317
Soros Serbia Foundation, Serbia, 324
South East Europe Media Organisation,
    Austria, 49
South East Europe Media Organisation—
    SEEMO—IPI, Austria, 49
South-East Institute—Foundation for Academic
    Research into South-Eastern Europe,
    Germany, 182
South Pacific Peoples Foundation Canada,
    Canada, 95
Sparebankstiftelsen DnB NOR, Norway, 293
Sparkassen-Kulturstiftung Hessen-Thüringen,
    Germany, 178
Springer (Axel) Stiftung, Germany, 179
The Starr Foundation, USA, 546
Steinberg (Nathan) Family Foundation,
    Canada, 98
Stichting DOEN, Netherlands, 280
Stichting Fonds 1818, Netherlands, 280
Stichting Prins Bernhard Cultuurfonds,
    Netherlands, 282
Stichting Triodos Foundation, Netherlands, 282
Stichting VSB Fonds, Netherlands, 280
Stiftelsen Riksbankens Jubileumsfond,
    Sweden, 357
Stifterverband für die Deutsche Wissenschaft eV,
    Germany, 159
Stiftung FVS, Germany, 183
Stiftung Lesen, Germany, 181
Stiftung Weimarer Klassik Kunstsammlungen,
    Germany, 173
Stiftung West-Östliche Begegnungen,
    Germany, 182
Stiftung für wissenschaftliche
    Südosteuropaforschung—Südost-Institut,
    Germany, 182
Strickland Foundation, Malta, 261
Studienstiftung des deutschen Volkes,
    Germany, 182
Sturzo (Luigi), Istituto, Italy, 227
Südost-Institut—Stiftung für wissenschaftliche
    Südosteuropaforschung, Germany, 182
Sunley (Bernard) Charitable Foundation,
    UK, 450
Suomen Kulttuurirahasto, Finland, 132
Support Centre for Associations and
    Foundations—SCAF, Belarus, 54
Surdna Foundation, Inc, USA, 547
Svenska Institutet i Rom/Istituto Svedese di
    Studi Classici a Roma, Italy, 228
Svenska Kulturfonden, Finland, 133
Sweden-Japan Foundation—SJF, Sweden, 357
Swedish and Finnish Cultural Foundation,
    Sweden, 354
Swedish Institute at Athens, Greece, 189
Swedish Institute in Rome, Italy, 228
Swiss National Science Foundation—SNF,
    Switzerland, 374
Szenes (Arpad)-Vieira da Silva, Fundação,
    Portugal, 313
Tarih Vakfı, Turkey, 389
Thomson Foundation, UK, 451
Thyssen (Fritz) Stiftung, Germany, 183
Tides, USA, 548
Tides Foundation, USA, 548
The Todd Foundation, New Zealand, 287
Toepfer (Alfred) Stiftung, Germany, 183
The Toyota Foundation, Japan, 240
Toyota Vietnam Foundation—TVF, Viet Nam, 565
Triodos Foundation, Netherlands, 282
The Trull Foundation, USA, 548
Trust for Mutual Understanding, USA, 549
Turin Savings Bank Foundation, Italy, 220
Turquoise Mountain Foundation, UK, 452
Turriano (Juanelo) Fundación, Spain, 348
Twenty-Ninth May 1961 Charity, UK, 452
Ukraine 3000, Ukraine, 394
University of Zaragoza Business Foundation,
    Spain, 342
Values Foundation, Bulgaria, 77
Vehbi Koç Foundation, Turkey, 391
Vehbi Koç Vakfı, Turkey, 391
Venice Foundation, Italy, 225
Victor Pinchuk Foundation, Ukraine, 394
Villar Foundation, Inc., Philippines, 304
The Vladimir Potanin Foundation, Russian
    Federation, 320
Vodafone Foundation Germany, Germany, 183
Vodafone Group Foundation, UK, 453
Vodafone Stiftung Deutschland, Germany, 183
Vzdelávacia nadácia Jana Husa, Slovakia, 329
Wallace (Charles) India Trust, UK, 454
The Wallace Foundation, USA, 551
Wallach (Miriam G. and Ira D.) Foundation,
    USA, 552

Wallenberg (Knut och Alice) Stiftelse,
    Sweden, 358
Warhol (Andy) Foundation for the Visual Arts,
    USA, 552
Wates Foundation, UK, 454
Webster (R. Howard) Foundation, Canada, 99
Welfare Association, Switzerland, 376
Werner Reimers Foundation, Germany, 177
Werner-Reimers-Stiftung, Germany, 177
West-East Foundation, Germany, 182
Weston (Garfield) Foundation, UK, 455
Whirlpool Foundation, USA, 553
Wihuri (Jenny and Antti) Foundation,
    Finland, 134
Wilbur Foundation, USA, 554
The William and Flora Hewlett Foundation,
    USA, 503
William G. and Marie Selby Foundation,
    USA, 543
William and Mary Greve Foundation, Inc,
    USA, 500
The William Randolph Hearst Foundation,
    USA, 502
Wingate (Harold Hyam) Foundation, UK, 456
The Wolfson Family Charitable Trust, UK, 456
Woodrow Wilson National Fellowship
    Foundation, USA, 555
Workers' Centre Foundation, Spain, 343
World Literacy of Canada—WLC, Canada, 99
Wurlitzer (Helene) Foundation of New Mexico,
    USA, 558
Yannick and Ben Jakober Foundation, Spain, 344
ZEIT-Stiftung Ebelin und Gerd Bucerius,
    Germany, 184
Zochonis Charitable Trust, UK, 457

CONSERVATION AND THE ENVIRONMENT

1818 Fund Foundation, Netherlands, 280
A. G. Leventis Foundation, Cyprus, 111
A. G. Leventis Foundation Nigeria, Nigeria, 290
Acíndar Foundation, Argentina, 31
Action in Development—AID, Bangladesh, 52
Adriano Olivetti Foundation, Italy, 223
Africa Foundation (UK), UK, 399
African NGOs Environment Network—ANEN,
    Kenya, 244
African Wildlife Foundation—AWF, USA, 462
African Youth Network for Sustainable
    Development, Algeria, 30
Africare, USA, 462
AFSC—American Friends Service Committee,
    USA, 465
Aga Khan Foundation—AKF, Switzerland, 360
Agromisa Foundation, Netherlands, 280
AIIT—Ancient India and Iran Trust, UK, 400
AINA—Arctic Institute of North America,
    Canada, 81
AISA—Africa Institute of South Africa, South
    Africa, 332
AJWS—American Jewish World Service,
    USA, 466
Åland Fund for the Future of the Baltic Sea,
    Finland, 131
Albert Schweitzer Ecological Centre,
    Switzerland, 362
Alchemy Foundation, UK, 399
Alemán (Miguel), Fundación, Mexico, 262
Alfred Toepfer Foundation F.V.S., Germany, 183
Alfred Toepfer Stiftung F.V.S., Germany, 183
Alicia Patterson Foundation—APF, USA, 533
Allianz Foundation for Sustainability,
    Germany, 160
Allianz Umweltstiftung, Germany, 160
Altman (Jenifer) Foundation, USA, 463
Ambiente y Recursos Naturales, Fundación,
    Argentina, 31
Ambuja Cement Foundation, India, 199
America for Bulgaria Foundation, Bulgaria, 75
American Friends Service Committee—AFSC,
    USA, 465
American Jewish World Service—AJWS,
    USA, 466
Ana Mata Manzanedo Foundation, Spain, 345
Ancient India and Iran Trust, UK, 400
The Andrew W. Mellon Foundation, USA, 523
ANGOC—Asian NGO Coalition for Agrarian
    Reform and Rural Development,
    Philippines, 301
AOYE—Arab Office for Youth and Environment,
    Egypt, 127
APACE Village First Electrification Group—
    APACE VFEG, Australia, 36
APHEDA—Union Aid Abroad, Australia, 45
APMN—Asia Pacific Mountain Network,
    Nepal, 271

Appropriate Technology for Community and
    Environment—APACE, Australia, 36
Arab Office for Youth and Environment—AOYE,
    Egypt, 127
ArcelorMittal Acesita Foundation, Brazil, 71
Arctic Institute of North America—AINA,
    Canada, 81
Arcus Foundation, USA, 469
ARGUS, Belgium, 56
ASEAN Foundation, Indonesia, 207
Ashden Charitable Trust, UK, 402
Asia-Pacific Mountain Network—APMN,
    Nepal, 271
Asia Society, USA, 470
Asian Institute for Rural Development,
    India, 200
Asian NGO Coalition for Agrarian Reform and
    Rural Development—ANGOC,
    Philippines, 301
Association of Voluntary Agencies for Rural
    Development—AVARD, India, 198
Augusto César Sandino Foundation,
    Nicaragua, 288
Australian Academy of Science, Australia, 37
Australian Conservation Foundation,
    Australia, 38
Australian People Health Education,
    Australia, 45
Austrian Society for Environment and
    Technology, Austria, 48
AVARD—Association of Voluntary Agencies for
    Rural Development, India, 198
Ayala Foundation, Inc—AFI, Philippines, 301
BAFROW—Foundation for Research on Women's
    Health, Productivity and the Environment,
    Gambia, 156
Baltic Sea Foundation, Finland, 131
Bangladesh Freedom Foundation, Bangladesh, 52
Bangladesh Rural Advancement Committee—
    BRAC, Bangladesh, 52
BANHCAFE Foundation, Honduras, 193
Bariloche Foundation, Argentina, 32
The Batchworth Trust, UK, 403
Beaverbrook Foundation, UK, 403
Beit Trust, UK, 403
Benetton Foundation for Study and Research,
    Italy, 219
The Bernard Sunley Charitable Foundation,
    UK, 450
Bertoni (Moisés) Foundation, Paraguay, 298
Bettencourt Schueller Foundation, France, 141
Binding (Sophie und Karl) Stiftung,
    Switzerland, 361
Black Sea NGO Network—BSNN, Bulgaria, 75
Blanc (José María), Fundación, Spain, 341
Blue Moon Fund, Inc, USA, 473
Bodossaki Foundation, Greece, 186
Boticário Group Foundation, Brazil, 71
Botín (Marcelino) Fundación, Spain, 341
BRAC—Building Resources Across
    Communities, Bangladesh, 52
Brazilian Foundation for Nature Conservation,
    Brazil, 71
Bridge House Estates Trust Fund, UK, 410
British Institute at Ankara, UK, 406
Building Resources Across Communities—
    BRAC, Bangladesh, 52
The Bydale Foundation, USA, 475
Cadbury (Edward) Charitable Trust, Inc, UK, 407
Cadbury (William Adlingon) Charitable Trust,
    UK, 407
Canadian Physicians for Aid and Relief—CPAR,
    Canada, 86
Canadian Urban Institute, Canada, 85
Canon Foundation in Europe, Netherlands, 272
Caribbean Marine Biology Institute Foundation,
    Curaçao, 110
Cariplo Foundation, Italy, 219
CARMABI Foundation, Curaçao, 110
Carnegie UK Trust, UK, 408
Carpathian Foundation, Hungary, 195
CEAS—Centre Ecologique Albert Schweitzer,
    Switzerland, 362
CENSIS—Fondazione Centro Studi Investimenti
    Sociali, Italy, 216
Centre Ecologique Albert Schweitzer—CEAS,
    Switzerland, 362
Centre for Environment, Education and
    Development, USA, 516
Centro Internacional de Agricultura Tropical—
    CIAT, Colombia, 104
Cera, Belgium, 57
Çevre Koruma ve Ambalaj Atiklari
    Degerlendirme Vakfi—CEVKO, Turkey, 388
CGP—Japan Foundation Centre Global
    Partnership, Japan, 236
Charles Darwin Foundation for the Galapagos
    Islands—CDF, Ecuador, 124

Charles Stewart Mott Foundation—CSMF,
    USA, 526
Chemtech Foundation, India, 201
Chile Foundation, Chile, 100
China Environmental Protection Foundation,
    China (People's Republic), 102
Chobe Wildlife Trust, Botswana, 69
Christoph Merian Foundation, Switzerland, 371
Christoph-Merian-Stiftung, Switzerland, 371
Christopher Reynolds Foundation, Inc, USA, 539
CIAT—Centro Internacional de Agricultura
    Tropical, Colombia, 104
Cini (Giorgio), Fondazione, Italy, 220
The City Bridge Trust, UK, 410
Civic Forum Foundation, Czech Republic, 113
Claiborne (Liz) and Ortenberg (Art) Foundation,
    USA, 480
Clean Water Foundation, Netherlands, 282
Clean Water Fund—CWF, USA, 480
Climate Cent Foundation, Switzerland, 375
Colombian Habitat Foundation, Colombia, 105
Commonwealth Foundation, UK, 411
Communication Foundation for Asia,
    Philippines, 302
Compagnia di San Paolo, Italy, 217
Compton Foundation, Inc, USA, 481
CONCAWE—Oil Companies' European
    Association for Environment, Health and
    Safety in Refining and Distribution,
    Belgium, 58
Consejo de Fundaciones Americanas de
    Desarrollo—Solidarios, Dominican
    Republic, 123
Cooperazione Internazionale—COOPI, Italy, 217
COOPI—Cooperazione Internazionale, Italy, 217
Coote (Marjorie) Animal Charities Trust,
    UK, 412
Council of American Development Foundations,
    Dominican Republic, 123
CPAR—Canadian Physicians for Aid and Relief,
    Canada, 86
CUSO-VSO, Canada, 86
Danish Outdoor Council, Denmark, 118
Darwin (Charles) Foundation for the Galapagos
    Islands, Ecuador, 124
David and Lucile Packard Foundation, USA, 531
Defense of Green Earth Foundation—DGEF,
    Japan, 232
Deutsch-Russischer Austausch eV—DRA,
    Germany, 164
DGEF—Defense of Green Earth Foundation,
    Japan, 232
Diakonia, Sweden, 352
Dian Desa Foundation, Indonesia, 207
Dobbo Yala Foundation, Panama, 297
DOEN Foundation, Netherlands, 280
Dom Manuel II Foundation, Portugal, 311
Dr Scholl Foundation, USA, 543
Dräger Foundation, Germany, 166
Dräger-Stiftung, Germany, 166
DRFN—Desert Research Foundation of Namibia,
    Namibia, 270
Dulverton Trust, UK, 414
E. O. Wilson Biodiversity Foundation, USA, 555
EABL Foundation, Kenya, 245
Earthrights International—ERI, USA, 486
Easter Island Foundation, USA, 487
Eça de Queiroz Foundation, Portugal, 312
EcoCiencia—Fundación Ecuatoriana de
    Estudios Ecologicos, Ecuador, 124
EcoHealth Alliance, USA, 487
ECOLOGIA—Ecologists Linked for Organizing
    Grassroots Initiatives and Action, USA, 488
Ecológica Universal, Fundación, Argentina, 32
Ecological Library Foundation, Poland, 307
Ecologists Linked for Organizing Grassroots
    Initiatives and Action—ECOLOGIA,
    USA, 488
Ecology and Agriculture Foundation,
    Germany, 181
Ecuadorian Foundation of Ecological Studies,
    Ecuador, 124
Eden Foundation, Sweden, 353
Ednannia: Initiative Centre to Support Social
    Action—ISAR Ednannia, Ukraine, 393
EDP Foundation, Portugal, 311
Edward Cadbury Charitable Trust, Inc, UK, 407
Eestimaa Looduse Fond—ELF, Estonia, 129
EJLB Foundation, Canada, 87
Ekopolis Foundation, Slovakia, 327
Eldee Foundation, Canada, 87
ELIAMEP—Hellenic Foundation for European
    and Foreign Policy, Greece, 187
Ellerman (John) Foundation, UK, 414
Emirates Foundation, United Arab Emirates, 395
Enda Third World—Environment and
    Development Action in the Third World,
    Senegal, 322

Enda Tiers Monde—Environnement et Développement du Tiers-Monde, Senegal, 322

Environment Foundation of Turkey, Turkey, 390

Environment and Natural Resources Foundation, Argentina, 31

Environmental Foundation of Jamaica, Jamaica, 229

Environmental Justice Foundation—EJF, UK, 416

Environmental Protection and Packaging Waste Recovery and Recycling Trust, Turkey, 388

Environmental Protection Research Foundation, India, 201

Environnement et Développement du Tiers-Monde—Enda, Senegal, 322

Ernest Kleinwort Charitable Trust, UK, 427

Esmée Fairbairn Foundation, UK, 416

Estonian Fund for Nature, Estonia, 129

Etruscan Foundation, USA, 489

EURONATUR—Stiftung Europäisches Naturerbe, Germany, 180

Europa Nostra, Netherlands, 273

European Climate Foundation, Netherlands, 273

European Cultural Foundation—ECF, Netherlands, 273

European Environmental Bureau, Belgium, 59

European Foundation for the Sustainable Development of the Regions—FEDRE, Switzerland, 363

European Institute of Health and Social Welfare, Spain, 349

European Nature Heritage Fund, Germany, 180

European Network of Foundations for Social Economy, Belgium, 56

European Science Foundation, France, 144

European Youth For Action—EYFA, Netherlands, 273

Europese Culterele Stichting, Netherlands, 273

EWT—Endangered Wildlife Trust, South Africa, 332

EYFA—European Youth For Action, Netherlands, 273

Fairbairn (Esmée) Foundation, UK, 416

Farm Africa, UK, 416

FARN—Fundación Ambiente y Recursos Naturales, Argentina, 31

De Faunabescherming, Netherlands, 274

FEDRE—European Foundation for the Sustainable Development of the Regions, Switzerland, 363

FEIM—Fundación para Estudio e Investigación de la Mujer, Argentina, 32

FEPP—Fondo Ecuatoriano Populorum Progressio, Ecuador, 124

FEU—Fundación Ecológica Universal, Argentina, 32

Finnish Cultural Foundation, Finland, 132

Finnish Foundation for Technology Promotion, Finland, 133

FOKAL—Fondation Connaissance et Liberte (Haiti), Haiti, 192

Fondaccioni per Iniciative Demokratike, Kosovo, 248

Fondation Albert 1er, Prince de Monaco—Institut Océanographique, France, 152

Fondation Bettencourt-Schueller, France, 141

Fondation Connaissance et Liberté (Haiti)—FOKAL, Haiti, 192

Fondation EJLB, Canada, 87

Fondation Ensemble, France, 143

Fondation Européenne de la Culture/Europese Culturele Stichting, Netherlands, 273

Fondation Européenne de la Science, France, 144

Fondation de France, France, 135

Fondation Nicolas Hulot pour la Nature et l'Homme, France, 146

Fondation des Organisations Rurales pour l'Agriculture et la Gestion Ecologique—FORAGE, Senegal, 322

Fondation du Patrimoine, France, 148

Fondation Ripaille, France, 149

Fondation Rurale pour l'Afrique de l'Ouest, Senegal, 322

Fondation Simón I. Patiño, Switzerland, 365

Fondation Singer-Polignac, France, 150

Fondation Suisse-Liechtenstein pour les Recherches Archéologiques à l'Etranger, Switzerland, 373

Fondation Syngenta pour une Agriculture Durable, Switzerland, 376

Fondation Ushuaia, France, 146

Fondazione Adriano Olivetti, Italy, 223

Fondazione Benetton Studi Ricerche, Italy, 219

Fondazione Cariplo, Italy, 219

Fondazione Cassa di Risparmio delle Provincie Lombarde—Fondazione Cariplo, Italy, 219

Fondazione Cassa di Risparmio di Padova e Rovigo, Italy, 219

Fondazione Centro Studi Investimenti Sociali—CENSIS, Italy, 216

Fondazione Giorgio Cini, Italy, 220

Fondazione Ing. Carlo M. Lerici—FL, Italy, 222

Fondazione Ricci Onlus, Italy, 224

Fondo per l'Ambiente Italiano—FAI, Italy, 225

Fondo Ecuatoriano Populorum Progressio—FEPP, Ecuador, 124

Fonds Wetenschappelijk Onderzoek—Vlaanderen, Belgium, 62

FOOD—Foundation of Occupational Development, India, 201

Foundation Cassa di Risparmio di Padova e Rovigo, Italy, 219

Foundation Centre for the Study of Social Investment, Italy, 216

Foundation for the Conservation of the Atlantic Rainforest, Brazil, 72

Foundation for Deep Ecology, USA, 492

Foundation for Democratic Initiatives—FDI, Kosovo, 248

Foundation for German–Polish Co-operation, Poland, 308

Foundation for International Studies—FIS, Malta, 261

Foundation for Knowledge and Liberty, Haiti, 192

Foundation Museum of American Man, Brazil, 72

Foundation Nicolas Hulot for Nature and Humankind, France, 146

Foundation of Occupational Development—FOOD, India, 201

Foundation for Peace, Ecology and the Arts, Argentina, 33

Foundation for the Protection of Nature, Venezuela, 563

Foundation for Research on Women's Health, Productivity and the Environment—BAFROW, Gambia, 156

Foundation for Revitalization of Local Health Traditions—FRLHT, India, 201

Foundation of Rural Organizations for Agriculture and Economic Management, Senegal, 322

Foundation in Support of Local Democracy, Poland, 308

Foundation of Village Community Development, Indonesia, 208

Foundation for Women's Research and Studies, Argentina, 32

Freshwater Society, USA, 494

Fridtjof Nansen Institute—FNI, Norway, 291

Friends of Nature Foundation, Bolivia, 67

Friluftsraadet, Denmark, 118

FRLHT—Foundation Revitalization Local Health, India, 201

FSLD—Foundation in Support of Local Democracy, Poland, 308

FUHEM—Fundación Hogar del Empleado, Spain, 343

FUNBANHCAFE—Fundación BANHCAFE, Honduras, 193

Fund for the Development of the Carpathian Euroregion, Hungary, 195

Fund for the Italian Environment, Italy, 225

Fundação ArcelorMittal Acesita, Brazil, 71

Fundação O Boticário de Proteção à Natureza, Brazil, 71

Fundação Brasileira para a Conservação da Natureza, Brazil, 71

Fundação Dom Manuel II, Portugal, 311

Fundação Eça de Queiroz, Portugal, 312

Fundação EDP, Portugal, 311

Fundação Gaia, Brazil, 71

Fundação Luso-Americana para o Desenvolvimento, Portugal, 312

Fundação Museu do Homem Americano—FUMDHAM, Brazil, 72

Fundação Roberto Marinho, Brazil, 72

Fundação de Serralves, Portugal, 312

Fundação SOS Mata Atlântica, Brazil, 72

Fundació 'La Caixa', Spain, 338

Fundación Acíndar, Argentina, 31

Fundación Amanecer, Colombia, 104

Fundación Ambiente y Recursos Naturales—FARN, Argentina, 31

Fundación Amigos de la Naturaleza, Bolivia, 67

Fundación Ana Mata Manzanedo, Spain, 345

Fundación Augusto César Sandino—FACS, Nicaragua, 288

Fundación BANHCAFE—FUNBANHCAFE, Honduras, 193

Fundación Bariloche, Argentina, 32

Fundación Charles Darwin para las Islas Galápagos—FCD, Ecuador, 124

Fundación Chile, Chile, 100

Fundación para la Defensa de la Naturaleza—FUDENA, Venezuela, 563

Fundación Dobbo Yala, Panama, 297

Fundación Ecológica Universal—FEU, Argentina, 32

Fundación Ecuatoriana de Estudios Ecologicos—EcoCiencia, Ecuador, 124

Fundación Empresa-Universidad de Zaragoza—FEUZ, Spain, 342

Fundación Empresas Polar, Venezuela, 563

Fundación Entorno, Empresara y Desarrollo Sostenible, Spain, 343

Fundación para Estudio e Investigación de la Mujer—FEIM, Argentina, 32

Fundación Hábitat Colombia—FHC, Colombia, 105

Fundación Herencia Verde, Colombia, 105

Fundación Hogar del Empleado—FUHEM, Spain, 343

Fundación José María Blanc, Spain, 341

Fundación MAPFRE, Spain, 345

Fundación Marcelino Botín, Spain, 341

Fundación María Francisca de Roviralta, Spain, 347

Fundación Miguel Alemán AC, Mexico, 262

Fundación Moisés Bertoni—FMB, Paraguay, 298

Fundación Nacional para el Desarrollo, El Salvador, 128

Fundación Natura, Ecuador, 126

Fundación Paz, Ecología y Arte—Fundación PEA, Argentina, 33

Fundación Paz y Solidaridad Serafín Aliaga—FPyS, Spain, 346

Fundación PEA—Fundación Paz, Ecología y Arte, Argentina, 33

Fundación La Salle de Ciencias Naturales—FLASA, Venezuela, 564

Fundacja Bankowa im. Leopolda Kronenberga, Poland, 306

Fundacja Biblioteka Ekologiczna, Poland, 307

Fundacja Partnerstwo dla Srodowiska, Poland, 307

Fundacja Rozwoju Demokracji Loaklnej, Poland, 308

Fundacja Współpracy Polsko-Niemieckiej/Stiftung für Deutsch–Polnische Zusammenarbeit, Poland, 308

Gaia Foundation, Brazil, 71

GAIA—Groupe d'Action dans l'Intérêt des Animaux, Belgium, 62

Garfield Weston Foundation, UK, 455

General Service Foundation, USA, 495

George Cedric Metcalf Charitable Foundation, Canada, 94

George and Thelma Paraskevaides Foundation, Cyprus, 111

German Marshall Fund of the United States—GMF, USA, 496

German-Russian Exchange, Germany, 164

Getty (J. Paul) Jnr Charitable Trust, UK, 418

Gilman (Howard) Foundation, USA, 496

Giorgio Cini Foundation, Italy, 220

Global Action in the Interest of Animals, Belgium, 62

Global Ethic Foundation Czech Republic, Czech Republic, 114

Global Harmony Foundation—GHF, Switzerland, 367

Global Voluntary Service—GVS, Japan, 232

Globe Foundation of Canada—GLOBE, Canada, 89

GMF—German Marshall Fund of the United States, USA, 496

Gobabeb Training and Research Centre, Namibia, 270

Gordon and Betty Moore Foundation, USA, 525

Great Britain Sasakawa Foundation, UK, 419

Green Heritage Foundation, Colombia, 105

Green Perspective Foundation, Slovakia, 328

Greve (William and Mary) Foundation, Inc, USA, 500

Groupe d'Action dans l'Intérêt des Animaux—GAIA, Belgium, 62

Haburas Foundation, Timor-Leste, 386

Haribon Foundation, Philippines, 302

Haribon Foundation for the Conservation of Natural Resources, Inc, Philippines, 302

Havelaar (Max) Foundation, Netherlands, 281

Hellenic Foundation for European and Foreign Policy—ELIAMEP, Greece, 187

Heritage Foundation, France, 148

Heritage Lottery Fund—HLF, UK, 420

Hesse and Thuringia Savings Banks Cultural Foundation, Germany, 178

Hewlett (William and Flora) Foundation, USA, 503

Heydar Aliyev Foundation, Azerbaijan, 50

Himalayan Light Foundation—HLF, Nepal, 271

HIVOS—Humanistisch Instituut voor Ontwikkelings Samenwerking, Netherlands, 275

HLF—Himalayan Light Foundation, Nepal, 271
Homeland Foundation, USA, 522
Howard Gilman Foundation, Inc, USA, 496
Humanistic Institute for Co-operation with
    Developing Countries, Netherlands, 275
Humanistisch Instituut voor Ontwikkelings
    Samenwerking—HIVOS, Netherlands, 275
IACD—Institute of Asian Culture and
    Development, Korea (Republic), 246
Ian Potter Foundation, Australia, 43
IASC—International Arctic Science Committee,
    Germany, 171
IBIS, Denmark, 118
ICLARM—The WorldFish Center, Malaysia, 260
ICSSR—Indian Council of Social Science
    Research, India, 202
IIEE—Indian Institute of Ecology and
    Environment, India, 202
India Assistance, Germany, 171
India Partners, USA, 506
Indian Council of Social Science Research—
    ICSSR, India, 202
Indian National Trust for Art and Cultural
    Heritage—INTACH, India, 203
Indienhilfe eV, Germany, 171
Indonesia Biodiversity Foundation,
    Indonesia, 208
Indonesian Forum for the Environment—Friends
    of the Earth Indonesia, Indonesia, 207
Ing. Carlo M. Lerici Foundation, Italy, 222
INHURED International—International
    Institute for Human Rights, Environment and
    Development, Nepal, 271
Initiative and Achievement, Foundation of the
    Nassauische Sparkasse for Culture, Sport and
    Society, Germany, 171
Initiative und Leistung, Stiftung der
    Nassauische Sparkasse für Kultur, Sport
    und Gesellschaft, Germany, 171
INMED Partnerships for Children, USA, 506
Institut Arctique de l'Amérique du Nord—IAAN,
    Canada, 81
Institut Océanographique—Fondation Albert 1er,
    Prince de Monaco, France, 152
Institut urbain du Canada, Canada, 85
Institute of Asian Culture and Development—
    IACD, Korea (Republic), 246
Institute for European Environmental Policy—
    IEEP, UK, 422
Instituto Europeo de Salud y Bienestar Social,
    Spain, 349
INTACH (UK) Trust, India, 203
INTACH—Indian National Trust for Art and
    Cultural Heritage, India, 203
Integrated Rural Development Foundation,
    Philippines, 303
International Arctic Science Committee—IASC,
    Germany, 171
International Bank of Ideas, Russian
    Federation, 318
International Centre for Living Aquatic
    Resources—ICLARM, Malaysia, 260
International Centre for Tropical Agriculture,
    Colombia, 104
International Co-operation, Italy, 217
International Environmental Foundation of the
    Kommunale Umwelt-AktioN UAN—IntEF-
    UAN, Germany, 172
International Foundation of the High-Altitude
    Research Stations Jungfraujoch and
    Gornergrat, Switzerland, 369
International Institute for Environment and
    Development—IIED, UK, 423
International Institute for Human Rights,
    Environment and Development—INHURED
    International, Nepal, 271
International Institute of Rural
    Reconstruction—IIRR, Philippines, 303
International Medical Services for Health—
    INMED, USA, 506
International Water Management Institute—
    IWMI, Sri Lanka, 350
Internationale Stiftung Hochalpine
    Forschungsstationen Jungfraujoch und
    Gornergrat, Switzerland, 369
ISAR: Resources for Environmental Activists,
    USA, 460
Islamic Relief Worldwide, UK, 425
Islamic Thought Foundation, Iran, 209
Ivey (Richard) Foundation, Canada, 91
Ivey Foundation, Canada, 91
Iwatani Naoji Foundation, Japan, 235
J. Paul Getty Jnr Charitable Trust, UK, 418
The Japan Foundation Centre for Global
    Partnership—CGP, Japan, 236
Japan International Volunteer Center—JVC,
    Japan, 236
Japanese-German Center Berlin, Germany, 173

Japanisch-Deutsches Zentrum Berlin,
    Germany, 173
Jenifer Altman Foundation—JAF, USA, 463
Jerusalem Foundation, Israel, 214
JNF Charitable Trust—JNFCT, UK, 426
The John D. and Catherine T. MacArthur
    Foundation, USA, 520
John Ellerman Foundation, UK, 414
The Johnson Foundation at Wingspread,
    USA, 512
Jones (W. Alton) Foundation, USA, 473
José María Blanc Foundation, Spain, 341
Joyce Foundation, USA, 512
Kapor (Mitchell) Foundation, USA, 513
KCDF—Kenya Community Development
    Foundation, Kenya, 245
KEHATI—Yayasan Keanekaragaman Hayati
    Indonesia, Indonesia, 208
Kerzner Marine Foundation—KMF, USA, 515
Khemka (Nand and Jeet) Foundation, India, 203
King Hussein Foundation—KHF, Jordan, 241
Kleinwort (Ernest) Charitable Trust, UK, 427
Kress (Samuel H.) Foundation, USA, 516
Kronenberga (Leopolda), Fundacja Bankowa,
    Poland, 306
KRS Education and Rural Development
    Foundation, Inc, USA, 516
Kuwait Institute for Scientific Research—KISR,
    Kuwait, 249
L. J. Skaggs and Mary C. Skaggs Foundation,
    USA, 544
'La Caixa' Foundation, Spain, 338
La Salle Foundation for Natural Sciences,
    Venezuela, 564
Laidlaw Foundation, Canada, 91
Lama Gangchen World Peace Foundation,
    Italy, 227
Lambrakis Foundation, Greece, 187
Lambrakis Research Foundation, Greece, 187
Lateinamerika-Zentrum eV—LAZ, Germany, 174
Latin America Centre, Germany, 174
Lauder (Ronald S.) Foundation, Germany, 174
Lawson Valentine Foundation, USA, 551
Van Leer Jerusalem Institute, Israel, 215
Leopold Kronenberg Foundation, Poland, 306
Lerici (Ing. Carlo M.), Fondazione presso il
    Politecnico di Milano, Italy, 222
Leventis (A. G.) Foundation, Cyprus, 111
Leventis (A. G.) Foundation Nigeria, Nigeria, 290
Leverhulme Trust, UK, 429
Life Sciences Research Foundation—LSRF,
    USA, 518
Lifewater International—LI, USA, 518
Littauer (Lucius N.) Foundation, Inc, USA, 519
Liz Claiborne and Art Ortenberg Foundation,
    USA, 480
The Long Now Foundation—LNF, USA, 519
Lucius N. Littauer Foundation, Inc, USA, 519
Luso-American Development Foundation,
    Portugal, 312
M. S. Swaminathan Research Foundation—
    MSSRF, India, 205
M. Venkatarangaiya Foundation, India, 206
MacArthur (John D. and Catherine T.)
    Foundation, USA, 520
The Mackintosh Foundation, UK, 430
The McLean Foundation, Canada, 93
MADRE, USA, 521
Maecenata Management GmbH, Germany, 159
Maj and Tor Nessling Foundation, Finland, 132
Malta Ecological Foundation, Malta, 261
Manzanedo (Ana Mata), Fundación, Spain, 345
MAPFRE Foundation, Spain, 345
Marcelino Botín Foundation, Spain, 341
María Francisca de Roviralta Foundation,
    Spain, 347
Marinho (Roberto), Fundação, Brazil, 72
Marisla Foundation, USA, 522
Marjorie Coote Animal Charities Trust, UK, 412
MAVA Fondation pour la Nature,
    Switzerland, 371
Max Havelaar Foundation, Netherlands, 281
Mellon (Andrew W.) Foundation, USA, 523
Mellon (Richard King) Foundation, USA, 523
Mercers' Charitable Foundation, UK, 431
Merian (Christoph) Stiftung, Switzerland, 371
Mertz Gilmore Foundation, USA, 524
Metcalf (George Cedric) Charitable Foundation,
    Canada, 94
Michael Otto Foundation for Environmental
    Protection, Germany, 176
Michael-Otto-Stiftung für Umweltschutz,
    Germany, 176
Miguel Alemán Foundation, Mexico, 262
Milieukontakt International, Netherlands, 277
Milieukontakt Oost-Europa, Netherlands, 277
Minor Foundation for Major Challenges,
    Norway, 291

Mitchell Kapor Foundation, USA, 513
Moisés Bertoni Foundation, Paraguay, 298
Monument Trust, UK, 432
Moody Foundation, USA, 525
Mott (Charles Stewart) Foundation, USA, 526
The Mountain Institute—TMI, USA, 526
Muslim Aid, UK, 433
Myer (Sidney) Fund, Australia, 42
The Myer Foundation, Australia, 42
Naandi Foundation—A New Beginning,
    India, 203
Nadace SLUNÍČKO, Czech Republic, 114
Nadácia Ekopolis, Slovakia, 327
Nadácia Zelená Nádej, Slovakia, 328
Nand and Jeet Khemka Foundation, India, 203
Nansen (Fridtjof) Institute, Norway, 291
National Endowment for Science, Technology and
    the Arts—NESTA, UK, 434
National Fish and Wildlife Foundation, USA, 527
National Foundation for Development, El
    Salvador, 128
National Heritage Memorial Fund, UK, 420
National Institute for Sustainable
    Development—NISD, India, 204
National Trust EcoFund, Bulgaria, 76
The National Trust for Places of Historic Interest
    or Natural Beauty, UK, 434
National Wildlife Federation—NWF, USA, 527
The Nature Conservancy, USA, 528
Nature Foundation, Ecuador, 126
Nederlandsche Maatschappij voor Nijverheid en
    Handel—NMNH, Netherlands, 278
Nederlandse Organisatie voor Internationale
    Ontwikkelingssamenwerking—Stichting
    NOVIB, Netherlands, 279
Nepal Forward Foundation, Nepal, 271
Nessling (Maj and Tor) Foundation, Finland, 132
NESsT—Nonprofit Enterprise and Self-
    sustainability Team, Chile, 101
NESTA—National Endowment for Science,
    Technology and the Arts, UK, 434
Netherlands Society for Industry and Trade,
    Netherlands, 278
Network for Human Development, Brazil, 73
New Zealand Winston Churchill Memorial Trust,
    New Zealand, 285
Nigerian Conservation Foundation—NCF,
    Nigeria, 290
Non-Governmental Ecological Vernadsky
    Foundation, Russian Federation, 320
Nonprofit Enterprise and Self-sustainability
    Team—NESsT, Chile, 101
NOVIB (Oxfam Netherlands), Netherlands, 279
Oak Foundation, Switzerland, 371
Oceanographic Institute—Albert 1st, Prince of
    Monaco Foundation, France, 152
Oil Companies' European Association for
    Environment, Health and Safety in Refining
    and Distribution—CONCAWE, Belgium, 58
Olivetti (Adriano), Fondazione, Italy, Italy, 223
Österreichische Gesellschaft für Umwelt und
    Technik—ÖGUT, Austria, 48
Otto (Michael) Stiftung, Germany, 176
Oxfam NOVIB—Nederlandse Organisatie voor
    Internationale Ontwikkelingssamenwerking,
    Netherlands, 279
Oxfam NOVIB—Netherlands Organization for
    International Development Co-operation,
    Netherlands, 279
Pacific Development and Conservation Trust,
    New Zealand, 285
Pacific Peoples' Partnership, Canada, 95
Packard (David and Lucile) Foundation, USA, 531
PAN Africa—Pesticide Action Network Africa,
    Senegal, 323
PAN Asia and the Pacific—Pesticide Action
    Network Asia and the Pacific, Malaysia, 260
PAN Europe—Pesticides Action Network
    Europe, Germany, 176
Pan-European Federation for Cultural Heritage,
    Netherlands, 273
Paraskevaides (George and Thelma) Foundation,
    Cyprus, 111
Patiño (Simón I.), Fondation, Switzerland, 365
Patterson (Alicia) Foundation, USA, 533
Perpetual Foundation, Australia, 43
Perpetual Trustees Australia, Australia, 43
Pesticide Action Network Asia and the Pacific—
    PAN AP, Malaysia, 260
Pesticide Action Network—Europe, Belgium, 63
Pesticide Action Network North America—PAN,
    USA, 534
Pesticide Action Network North America—
    PANNA, USA, 534
Pesticides Action Network Europe—PAN
    Europe, Germany, 176
Peter G. Peterson Foundation, USA, 534
Peterson (Peter G.) Foundation, USA, 534

The Pew Charitable Trusts, USA, 534
Pilgrim Trust, UK, 437
Plenty International, USA, 535
Polar Companies Foundation, Venezuela, 563
Polden-Puckham Charitable Foundation—PPCF,
    UK, 438
Pôle européen des fondations de l'économie
    sociale, Belgium, 56
Polish Environmental Partnership Foundation,
    Poland, 307
The Porter Foundation, UK, 439
Potter (Ian) Foundation, Australia, 43
Preciosa Foundation, Czech Republic, 115
Prince Bernhard Cultural Foundation,
    Netherlands, 282
Prins Bernhard Culturfonds, Stichting,
    Netherlands, 282
Pro Nature—Peruvian Foundation for Nature
    Conservation, Peru, 299
PRODESSA—Proyecto de Desarrollo Santiago,
    Guatemala, 191
Progressio, UK, 439
ProNaturaleza—Fundación Peruana para la
    Conservación de la Naturaleza, Peru, 299
PROTERRA, Peru, 299
R. E. Ross Trust, Australia, 44
Rainforest Foundation Norway, Norway, 293
Rainforest Foundation US, USA, 538
Rajiv Gandhi Foundation, India, 201
Ramsay Foundation, Switzerland, 372
RBC Foundation, Canada, 96
Realdania, Denmark, 121
Red de Acción en Plaguicidas y sus Alternativas
    de América Latina—RAP-AL, Argentina, 34
RED—Ruralité-environnement-développement,
    Belgium, Belgium, 63
Rede de Desenvolvimento Humano—REDEH,
    Brazil, 73
REDEH—Rede de Desenvolvimento Humano,
    Brazil, 73
Refugee Trust International, Ireland, 213
Refugees International Japan—RIJ, Japan, 239
Regional Environmental Center for Central and
    Eastern Europe—REC, Hungary, 196
Regnskogfondet, Norway, 293
Research Foundation—Flanders, Belgium, 62
Réseau Africain de la Jeunesse pour le
    Développement Durable, Algeria, 30
Réseau des ONG Africaines sur l'Environnement,
    Kenya, 244
Reynolds (Christopher) Foundation, USA, 539
Ricci Onlus Foundation, Italy, 224
Richard King Mellon Foundation, USA, 523
Ripaille Foundation, France, 149
Rob and Bessie Welder Wildlife Foundation,
    USA, 553
Robert Marinho Foundation, Brazil, 72
Rockefeller Brothers Fund, USA, 540
The Ronald S. Lauder Foundation, Germany, 174
Ross (R. E.) Trust, Australia, 44
Rössing Foundation, Namibia, 270
Roviralta (María Francisca de), Fundación,
    Spain, 347
Rowan Charitable Trust, UK, 441
Royal Bank of Canada Charitable Foundation,
    Canada, 96
Royal Bank Financial Group Foundation,
    Canada, 96
Royal Forest and Bird Protection Society of New
    Zealand, New Zealand, 286
Royal Society for the Protection of Birds—RSPB,
    UK, 445
RSPB—Royal Society for the Protection of Birds,
    UK, 445
The Rufford Foundation, UK, 445
Rufford Maurice Laing Foundation, UK, 445
Ruralité Environnement Développement—RED,
    Belgium, 63
Rurality Environment Development, Belgium, 63
Salamander Foundation, Canada, 97
Samuel H. Kress Foundation, USA, 516
Samuel and Saidye Bronfman Family Foundation,
    Canada, 82
San Francisco Foundation, USA, 542
Sandino (Augusto César), Fundación,
    Nicaragua, 288
Santiago Development Project, Guatemala, 191
Savings Bank Foundation DnB NOR, Norway, 293
Scaife Family Foundation, USA, 542
Schweisfurth Foundation, Germany, 178
Schweisfurth-Stiftung, Germany, 178
Schweizerisch-Liechtensteinische Stiftung für
    archäologische Forschungen im Ausland—
    SLSA, Switzerland, 373
Scouloudi Foundation, UK, 447
SEEENN—South East European Environmental
    NGOs Network, Macedonia, 258
Self Help Development International, Ireland, 213

Sem Pringpuangkeo Foundation, Thailand, 384
Serafín Aliaga Foundation for Peace and
    Solidarity, Spain, 346
Serralves Foundation, Portugal, 312
Seub Nakhasathien Foundation, Thailand, 384
Seva Foundation, USA, 544
Siam Society, Thailand, 384
Sidney Myer Fund, Australia, 42
The Sierra Club Foundation, USA, 544
Simón I. Patiño Foundation, Switzerland, 365
Singer-Polignac Foundation, France, 150
Sino-British Fellowship Trust—SBFT, UK, 448
Sir Ahmadu Bello Foundation, Nigeria, 289
Sir Ahmadu Bello Memorial Foundation,
    Nigeria, 289
Skaggs (L. J.) and Skaggs (Mary C.) Foundation,
    USA, 544
Skoll Foundation, USA, 544
SLSA—Schweizerisch Liechtensteinische
    Stiftung, Switzerland, 373
Slunicko Foundation, Czech Republic, 114
Smithsonian Institution, USA, 545
Snow Leopard Trust, USA, 545
Software AG Foundation, Germany, 178
Solidarios—Consejo de Fundaciones Americanas
    de Desarrollo, Dominican Republic, 123
Sophie and Karl Binding Foundation,
    Switzerland, 361
Sophie und Karl Binding-Stiftung,
    Switzerland, 361
SOS Atlantic Forest Foundation, Brazil, 72
SOSNA Foundation, Slovakia, 329
South East European Environmental NGOs
    Network—SEEENN, Macedonia, 258
South Pacific Peoples Foundation Canada,
    Canada, 95
Southern African Nature Foundation, South
    Africa, 336
Sparebankstiftelsen DnB NOR, Norway, 293
Sparkassen-Kulturstiftung Hessen-Thüringen,
    Germany, 178
Staples Trust, UK, 449
Stichting Agromisa, Netherlands, 280
Stichting Caraïbisch Marien Biologisch
    Instituut—CARMABI, Curaçao, 110
Stichting DOEN, Netherlands, 280
Stichting Fonds 1818, Netherlands, 280
Stichting Max Havelaar, Netherlands, 281
Stichting Prins Bernhard Cultuurfonds,
    Netherlands, 282
Stichting Reinwater, Netherlands, 282
Stichting Triodos Foundation, Netherlands, 282
Stichting VSB Fonds, Netherlands, 282
Stiftelsen för Miljöstrategisk Forskning—
    Mistra, Sweden, 356
Stiftelsen Teknikens Främjande—Tekniikan
    Edistämissäätiö, Finland, 133
Stiftung Europäisches Naturerbe—
    EURONATUR, Germany, 180
Stiftung FVS, Germany, 183
Stiftung Klimarappen, Switzerland, 375
Stiftung Ökologie & Landbau, Germany, 181
Stiftung Vivamos Mejor, Switzerland, 375
Suider-Afrikaanse Natuurstigting, South
    Africa, 336
Sunley (Bernard) Charitable Foundation,
    UK, 450
Suomen Kulttuurirahasto, Finland, 132
Surdna Foundation, Inc, USA, 547
Swedish Foundation for Strategic Environmental
    Research, Sweden, 356
Swiss Foundation for Technical Co-operation,
    Switzerland, 375
Swiss-Liechtenstein Foundation for
    Archaeological Research Abroad—SLFA,
    Switzerland, 373
Swisscontact—Swiss Foundation for Technical
    Co-operation, Switzerland, 375
Syngenta Foundation for Sustainable
    Agriculture, Switzerland, 376
Syngenta Stiftung für Nachhaltige
    Landwirtschaft, Switzerland, 376
Taiga Rescue Network—TRN, Finland, 133
Tanzania Millennium Hand Foundation—
    TAMIHA, Tanzania, 382
Tekniikan Edistämissäätiö-Stiftelsen för
    teknikens främjande—TES, Finland, 133
Third World Network—TWN, Malaysia, 260
Tides, USA, 548
Tides Foundation, USA, 548
Tindall Foundation, New Zealand, 286
Tinker Foundation, Inc, USA, 548
Toepfer (Alfred) Stiftung, Germany, 183
Together Foundation, France, 143
The Toyota Foundation, Japan, 240
Triodos Foundation, Netherlands, 282
TRN—Taiga Rescue Network, Finland, 133
The Trull Foundation, USA, 548

Trust for Mutual Understanding, USA, 549
Turkish Foundation for Combating Soil Erosion,
    for Reforestation and the Protection of
    Natural Habitats, Turkey, 390
Türkiye Çevre Vakfı, Turkey, 390
Türkiye Erozyonla Mücadele Ağaçlandırma ve
    Doğal Varlıkları Koruma Vakfı—TEMA,
    Turkey, 390
Twenty-Ninth May 1961 Charity, UK, 452
UniCredit Foundation—Unidea, Italy, 228
Union Aid Abroad—APHEDA, Australia, 45
United States African Development
    Foundation—USADF, USA, 550
Universal Ecological Foundation, Argentina, 32
University of Zaragoza Business Foundation,
    Spain, 342
Valentine (Lawson) Foundation, USA, 551
Vanarai, India, 206
Venkatarangaiya (M.) Foundation, India, 206
VIA Foundation, Czech Republic, 115
Villar Foundation, Inc., Philippines, 304
Vita, Ireland, 213
Vivamos Mejor Foundation, Switzerland, 375
Vodafone Group Foundation, UK, 453
Volkart Foundation, Switzerland, 376
Volkart-Stiftung, Switzerland, 376
Wahana Lingkungan Hidup Indonesia—WALHI,
    Indonesia, 207
WALHI—Wahana Lingkungan Hidup Indonesia,
    Indonesia, 207
WasserStiftung, Germany, 184
Water Foundation, Germany, 184
Wates Foundation, UK, 454
Welder (Rob and Bessie) Wildlife Foundation,
    USA, 553
West African Rural Foundation, Senegal, 322
Weston (Garfield) Foundation, UK, 455
Wildlife Preservation Trust International,
    USA, 487
Wildlife Protection, Netherlands, 274
Wildlife Trust, USA, 487
William Adlington Cadbury Charitable Trust,
    UK, 407
The William and Flora Hewlett Foundation,
    USA, 503
William and Mary Greve Foundation, Inc,
    USA, 500
Wilson (E. O.) Biodiversity Foundation, USA, 555
Winrock International, USA, 555
Workers' Centre Foundation, Spain, 343
World Land Trust—WLT, UK, 456
The WorldFish Center, Malaysia, 260
WWF South Africa, South Africa, 336
YADESA—Yayasan Pengembangan Masyarakat
    Desa, Indonesia, 208
Yayasan Dian Desa, Indonesia, 207
Yayasan Keanekaragaman Hayati Indonesia—
    KEHATI, Indonesia, 208
Yayasan Pengembangan Masyarakat Desa—
    YADESA, Indonesia, 208
Youth for Development and Co-operation—YDC,
    Netherlands, 283

ECONOMIC AFFAIRS

1818 Fund Foundation, Netherlands, 280
1945 Foundation, Canada, 90
ACCION International, USA, 460
Action in Development—AID, Bangladesh, 52
Acumen Fund, USA, 461
ADI—Association for Democratic Initiatives,
    Macedonia, 258
Africa-America Institute—AAI, USA, 461
Africa Foundation (UK), UK, 399
African Capacity Building Foundation—ACBF,
    Zimbabwe, 567
African Forum and Network on Debt and
    Development—AFRODAD, Zimbabwe, 567
AFRODAD—African Forum and Network on
    Debt and Development, Zimbabwe, 567
Aga Khan Agency for Microfinance,
    Switzerland, 360
Aga Khan Fund for Economic Development,
    Switzerland, 361
Agromart Foundation, Sri Lanka, 350
AINA—Arctic Institute of North America,
    Canada, 81
AISA—Africa Institute of South Africa, South
    Africa, 332
Alemán (Miguel), Fundación, Mexico, 262
Alfred P. Sloan Foundation, USA, 545
ALIDE—Asociación Latinoamericana de
    Instituciones Financieras para el Desarrollo,
    Peru, 299
Alternatives for Development Foundation,
    Ecuador, 124
Altman (Jenifer) Foundation, USA, 463

America for Bulgaria Foundation, Bulgaria, 75
Dell'Amore (Giordano) Foundation, Italy, 220
ANGOC—Asian NGO Coalition for Agrarian Reform and Rural Development, Philippines, 301
Arctic Institute of North America—AINA, Canada, 81
AREGAK—Sun/Soleil, Armenia, 35
Asia Pacific Foundation of Canada, Canada, 81
Asia Society, USA, 470
Asian NGO Coalition for Agrarian Reform and Rural Development—ANGOC, Philippines, 301
Asociación Latinoamericana de Instituciones Financieras para el Desarrollo—ALIDE, Peru, 299
Asociación Latinoamericana de Organizaciones de Promoción al Desarrollo—ALOP, Mexico, 262
Association for Democratic Initiatives—ADI, Macedonia, 258
Association of Voluntary Agencies for Rural Development—AVARD, India, 198
Augusto César Sandino Foundation, Nicaragua, 288
Austrian Research Foundation for International Development, Austria, 48
AVARD—Association of Voluntary Agencies for Rural Development, India, 198
AVINA Foundation, Panama, 297
BaBe—Budi aktivna, Budi emancipirana, Croatia, 109
BAFROW—Foundation for Research on Women's Health, Productivity and the Environment, Gambia, 156
Baltic-American Partnership Fund—BAPF, USA, 472
Bangladesh Rural Advancement Committee—BRAC, Bangladesh, 52
BANHCAFE Foundation, Honduras, 193
BBC World Service Trust, UK, 403
BBVA Foundation, Spain, 340
Be Active, Be Emancipated, Croatia, 109
The Beautiful Foundation, Korea (Republic), 246
Bertelsmann Foundation, Germany, 162
Bertelsmann Stiftung, Germany, 162
BID-INTAL—Instituto para la Integración de America Latina y el Caribe, Argentina, 34
BRAC—Building Resources Across Communities, Bangladesh, 52
The Bridge Foundation, India, 200
Brookings Institution, USA, 474
Bruno Kreisky Forum for International Dialogue, Austria, 47
Bruno Kreisky Forum für internationalen Dialog, Austria, 47
Budi aktivna, Budi emancipiran—BaBe!, Croatia, 109
Building Resources Across Communities—BRAC, Bangladesh, 52
Bulgarian Fund for Women, Bulgaria, 75
Business Formation Foundation, Guatemala, 190
Business Institute Foundation, Spain, 344
Business and Society Foundation, Spain, 342
Canadian Co-operative Association, Canada, 80
Canadian Executive Service Organization—CESO/Service d'assistance canadienne aux organismes—SACO, Canada, 83
Canadian International Council/Conseil International du Canada—CIC, Canada, 84
Canadian Urban Institute, Canada, 85
Canon Foundation in Europe, Netherlands, 272
Carl-Zeiss Foundation, Germany, 184
Carl-Zeiss-Stiftung, Germany, 184
Catholic Agency for World Development—Trócaire, Ireland, 213
CCI—Center for Citizen Initiatives, USA, 476
CENSIS—Fondazione Centro Studi Investimenti Sociali, Italy, 216
Center for Citizen Initiatives—CCI, USA, 476
Center for Cultural and Technical Interchange between East and West—East-West Center, USA, 487
Centre for Environment, Education and Development, USA, 516
Centre d'Études, de Documentation, d'Information et d'Action Sociales—CEDIAS—Musée Social, France, 138
Centre International de Développement et de Recherche—CIDR, France, 138
Centre for Social Studies, Documentation, Information and Action, France, 138
CESO—Canadian Executive Service Organization, Canada, 83
CGP—Japan Foundation Centre Global Partnership, Japan, 236
Chr. Michelsen Institute—CMI, Norway, 291
Christopher Reynolds Foundation, Inc, USA, 539

CIC—Canadian International Council/Conseil International du Canada, Canada, 84
CIDR—Centre International de Développement et de Recherche, France, 138
Civil Society Support Centre, Georgia, 157
Cleveland Foundation, USA, 480
CMI—Chr. Michelsens Institutt, Norway, 291
Co-operation for the Promotion and Development of Welfare Activities, Spain, 342
Commonwealth Foundation, UK, 411
Community Development Foundation, Mozambique, 269
Comprehensive Rural Foundation, Costa Rica, 107
COSIS, Italy, 221
Costa Rican Foundation for Development, Costa Rica, 106
Credit Union Foundation Australia—CUFA, Australia, 40
CUFA—Credit Union Foundation Australia, Australia, 40
Czegei Wass Foundation, Hungary, 196
Deutsche Bank Americas Foundation and Community Development Group, USA, 484
Deutsche Bank Foundation, Germany, 164
Deutsche Bank Stiftung, Germany, 164
Development Foundation, Guatemala, 190
Ditchley Foundation, UK, 414
Dominican Development Foundation, Dominican Republic, 123
Dr Marcus Wallenberg Foundation for Further Education in International Industry, Sweden, 358
Dr Marcus Wallenbergs Stiftelse för Utbildning i Internationellt Industriellt Företagande, Sweden, 358
Dr Scholl Foundation, USA, 543
Dräger Foundation, Germany, 166
Dräger-Stiftung, Germany, 166
East-West Center—EWC, USA, 487
Eberhard Schöck Foundation, Germany, 178
Eberhard-Schöck-Stiftung, Germany, 178
Ecological Library Foundation, Poland, 307
Economic Development Foundation, Turkey, 388
Economic Foundation, Poland, 307
ECPD—European Centre for Peace and Development, Serbia, 324
Ecuadorean Development Foundation, Ecuador, 125
Einaudi (Luigi), Fondazione, Italy, 221
ELIAMEP—Hellenic Foundation for European and Foreign Policy, Greece, 187
Emile Chanoux Foundation—Institute for Federalist and Regionalist Studies, Italy, 218
endPoverty.org, USA, 488
Enrico Mattei Eni Foundation, Italy, 218
Enterprise Development International, USA, 488
Enterprise Foundation of Benin, Benin, 65
Espejo (Eugenio), Fundación, Ecuador, 125
Eugenio Espejo Foundation, Ecuador, 125
Eugenio Mendoza Foundation, Venezuela, 563
Eurasia Foundation, USA, 489
Europa Employment Foundation—Enterprise and Solidarity, Italy, 221
European Centre for Peace and Development—ECPD, Serbia, 324
European Mediterranean Institute, Spain, 349
European Network of Foundations for Social Economy, Belgium, 56
Evangelisches Studienwerk eV, Germany, 167
The Evian Group at IMD, Switzerland, 363
Evrika Foundation, Bulgaria, 75
EWC—East-West Center, USA, 487
FAFIDESS—Fundación de Asesoría Financiera a Instituciones de Desarrollo y Servicio Social, Guatemala, 190
Fate Foundation, Nigeria, 289
FDC—Fundação para o Desenvolvimento da Comunidade, Mozambique, 269
FDD—Fundación Dominicana de Desarrollo, Dominican Republic, 123
The Federal Trust for Education and Research, UK, 416
Fedesarrollo—Fundación para la Educación Superior y el Desarrollo, Colombia, 104
FEEM—Fondazione ENI Enrico Mattei, Italy, 218
Feltrinelli (Giangiacomo), Fondazione, Italy, 221
FEPP—Fondo Ecuatoriano Populorum Progressio, Ecuador, 124
Finafrica Foundation—Giordano Dell'Amore Foundation, Italy, 220
Financiera FAMA, Nicaragua, 288
FINCA—Fundación Integral Campesina, Costa Rica, 107

FONADES—Fondation Nationale pour le Développement et la Solidarité, Burkina Faso, 78
Fondation Emile Chanoux—Institut d'Etudes Fédéralistes et Régionalistes, Italy, 218
Fondation de l'Entrepreneurship du Bénin, Benin, 65
Fondation MACIF, France, 146
Fondation Méditerranéenne d'Etudes Stratégiques—FMES, France, 147
Fondation Nationale pour le Développement et la Solidarité—FONADES, Burkina Faso, 78
Fondation Nationale pour l'Enseignement de la Gestion des Entreprises, France, 148
Fondation Nationale des Sciences Politiques, France, 148
Fondation Paul-Henri Spaak—Stichting Paul-Henri Spaak, Belgium, 61
Fondation pour le Renforcement des Capacités en Afrique, Zimbabwe, 567
Fondation Robert Schuman, France, 150
Fondazione Centro Studi Investimenti Sociali—CENSIS, Italy, 216
Fondazione Europa Occupazione—Impresa e Solidarietà, Italy, 221
Fondazione Giangiacomo Feltrinelli, Italy, 221
Fondazione Giordano Dell'Amore, Italy, 220
Fondazione Luigi Einaudi, Italy, 221
Fondazione Rodolfo Debenedetti—FRDB, Italy, 220
Fondo Ecuatoriano Populorum Progressio—FEPP, Ecuador, 124
Fondo Latinoamericano de Desarrollo, Costa Rica, 106
FOOD—Foundation of Occupational Development, India, 201
Foreign Policy and United Nations Association of Austria—UNA-AUSTRIA, Austria, 48
Foro Juvenil, Uruguay, 560
FOSIM—Foundation Open Society Institute Macedonia, Macedonia, 258
Foundation for Basic Development, Costa Rica, 107
Foundation Centre for the Study of Social Investment, Italy, 216
Foundation for Commercial and Technical Sciences—KAUTE, Finland, 131
Foundation for the Financial Assessment of Social Service and Development Institutions, Guatemala, 190
Foundation for Higher Education and Development, Colombia, 104
Foundation for International Studies—FIS, Malta, 261
Foundation for the Investment and Development of Exports, Honduras, 193
Foundation for Latin American Economic Research, Argentina, 32
Foundation of Occupational Development—FOOD, India, 201
Foundation Open Society Institute Macedonia—FOSIM, Macedonia, 258
Foundation for the People's Economy, Costa Rica, 107
Foundation for the Qualification and Consultancy in Microfinance, El Salvador, 128
Foundation for Research on Women's Health, Productivity and the Environment—BAFROW, Gambia, 156
Foundation Rodolfo Debenedetti, Italy, 220
Foundation for Russian-American Economic Co-operation—FRAEC, USA, 493
Foundation of Savings Banks, Spain, 341
Foundation of Spanish Commercial Agents, Spain, 339
Foundation in Support of Local Democracy, Poland, 308
Foundation in Support of Local Development Initiatives, Venezuela, 563
Foundation for the Sustainable Development of Small and Medium-sized Enterprises—FUNDES International, Costa Rica, 107
Foundation of Village Community Development, Indonesia, 208
French National Foundation for Management Education, France, 148
FSLD—Foundation in Support of Local Democracy, Poland, 308
FUNBANHCAFE—Fundación BANHCAFE, Honduras, 193
Fundação para o Desenvolvimento da Comunidade, Mozambique, 269
Fundação Luso-Americana para o Desenvolvimento, Portugal, 312
Fundação Romì, Brazil, 72
Fundación de los Agentes Comerciales de España, Spain, 339

Fundación Alternativas para el Desarrollo, Ecuador, 124
Fundación de Apoyo a las Iniciativas Locales de Desarrollo—FUNDAPILDE, Venezuela, 563
Fundación para el Apoyo a la Microempresa—Financiera FAMA, Nicaragua, 288
Fundación de Asesoría Financiera a Instituciones de Desarrollo y Servicio Social—FAFIDESS, Guatemala, 190
Fundación de Asistencia para la Pequeña Empresa, Guatemala, 190
Fundación Augusto César Sandino—FACS, Nicaragua, 288
Fundación AVINA, Panama, 297
Fundación Banco Bilbao Vizcaya Argentaria—Fundación BBVA, Spain, 340
Fundación BANCHAFE—FUNBANHCAFE, Honduras, 193
Fundación BBVA—Fundación Banco Bilbao Vizcaya Argentaria, Spain, 340
Fundación de las Cajas de Ahorros—FUNCAS, Spain, 341
Fundación de Capacitación y Asesoría en Microfinanzas, El Salvador, 128
Fundación CODESPA—Futuro en Marcha, Spain, 342
Fundación Costarricense de Desarrollo—FUCODES, Costa Rica, 106
Fundación para el Desarrollo de Base—FUNDEBASE, Costa Rica, 107
Fundación para el Desarrollo—FUNDAP, Guatemala, 190
Fundación para el Desarrollo de la Microempresa, Guatemala, 191
Fundación para el Desarrollo Sostenible de la Pequeña y Mediana Empresa—FUNDES Internacional, Costa Rica, 107
Fundación Dominicana de Desarrollo—FDD, Dominican Republic, 123
Fundación para la Economía Popular—FUNDECO, Costa Rica, 107
Fundación Ecuatoriana de Desarrollo—FED, Ecuador, 125
Fundación para la Educación Superior y el Desarrollo—Fedesarrollo, Colombia, 104
Fundación Empresa y Sociedad, Spain, 342
Fundación Empresa-Universidad de Zaragoza—FEUZ, Spain, 342
Fundación Eugenio Espejo, Ecuador, 125
Fundación Eugenio Mendoza, Venezuela, 563
Fundación Génesis Empresarial, Guatemala, 190
Fundación Innovación de la Economía Social—INNOVES, Spain, 343
Fundación Instituto de Empresa, Spain, 344
Fundación Integral Campesina—FINCA, Costa Rica, 107
Fundación para la Inversión y Desarrollo de Exportaciones—FIDE, Honduras, 193
Fundación de Investigaciones Económicas Latinoamericanas—FIEL, Argentina, 32
Fundación Mediterránea—IERAL, Argentina, 33
Fundación MICROS—Fundación para el Desarrollo de la Microempresa, Guatemala, 191
Fundación Miguel Alemán AC, Mexico, 262
Fundación Mujer, Costa Rica, 107
Fundación Nacional para el Desarrollo, El Salvador, 128
Fundación Nacional para el Desarrollo de Honduras—FUNADEH, Honduras, 193
Fundación Nantik Lum, Spain, 345
Fundación Paideia Galiza, Spain, 346
Fundación Rafael del Pino, Spain, 347
Fundación Salvadoreña para el Desarrollo Económico y Social, El Salvador, 128
Fundación Sartawi, Bolivia, 67
Fundación Soros Guatemala, Guatemala, 191
Fundacja Biblioteka Ekologiczna, Poland, 307
Fundacja Gospodarcza, Poland, 307
Fundacja Rozwoju Demokracji Loaklnej, Poland, 308
Fundacja Wspomagania Wsi, Poland, 308
FUNDAP—Fundación para el Desarrollo, Guatemala, 190
FUNDEBASE—Fundación para el Desarrollo de Base, Costa Rica, 107
Garfield Weston Foundation, UK, 455
German Marshall Fund of the United States—GMF, USA, 496
Giangiacomo Feltrinelli Foundation, Italy, 221
Giordano Dell'Amore Foundation, Italy, 220
Globe Foundation of Canada—GLOBE, Canada, 89
GMF—German Marshall Fund of the United States, USA, 496
Great Britain Sasakawa Foundation, UK, 419

Guggenheim (John Simon) Memorial Foundation, USA, 500
Haitian Economic Development Foundation, Haiti, 192
The Helen Suzman Foundation, South Africa, 335
Hellenic Foundation for European and Foreign Policy—ELIAMEP, Greece, 187
HELP International, USA, 503
Helvetas Swiss Intercooperation, Switzerland, 367
Himalaya Foundation, Taiwan, 379
History Foundation of Turkey, Turkey, 389
ICSSR—Indian Council of Social Science Research, India, 202
IEMed—Institut Europeu de la Mediterrània, Spain, 349
IERAL—Fundación Mediterránea, Argentina, 33
İktisadi Kalkınma Vakfı, Turkey, 388
Impact First International, Canada, 89
Indian Council of Social Science Research—ICSSR, India, 202
INFID—International NGO Forum on Indonesian Development, Indonesia, 207
INNOVES—Fundación Innovación de la Economía Social, Spain, 343
Institut Arctique de l'Amérique du Nord—IAAN, Canada, 81
Institut Català Mediterrània, Spain, 349
Institut Europeu de la Mediterrània—IEMed, Spain, 349
Institut Nord-Sud, Canada, 95
Institut urbain du Canada, Canada, 85
Institute for Latin American and Caribbean Integration, Argentina, 34
Institute for Private Enterprise and Democracy—IPED, Poland, 309
Instituto para la Integración de América Latina y el Caribe—BID-INTAL, Argentina, 34
Instituto Torcuato di Tella, Argentina, 34
International Bank of Ideas, Russian Federation, 318
International Centre for Development and Research, France, 138
International Executive Service Corps—IESC, USA, 508
International Fund for Ireland, Ireland, 211
International Institute for Environment and Development—IIED, UK, 423
International NGO Forum on Indonesian Development—INFID, Indonesia, 207
Investigaciones Económicas Latinoamericanas, Fundación, Argentina, 32
Jahnsson (Yrjö) Foundation, Finland, 131
The Japan Foundation Centre for Global Partnership—CGP, Japan, 236
Japanese-German Center Berlin, Germany, 173
Japanisch-Deutsches Zentrum Berlin, Germany, 173
Jenifer Altman Foundation—JAF, USA, 463
Jenny and Antti Wihuri Foundation, Finland, 134
Jenny ja Antti Wihurin Rahasto, Finland, 134
John Simon Guggenheim Memorial Foundation, USA, 500
Jordan River Foundation, Jordan, 241
Joyce Foundation, USA, 512
KAUTE—Foundation for Commercial and Technical Sciences, Finland, 131
KCDF—Kenya Community Development Foundation, Kenya, 245
Khemka (Nand and Jeet) Foundation, India, 203
KIEDF—Koret Israel Economic Development Funds, Israel, 214
KK-stiftelsen, Sweden, 354
Knowledge Foundation, Sweden, 354
Koret Foundation, USA, 515
Koret Israel Economic Development Funds—KIEDF, Israel, 214
KRS Education and Rural Development Foundation, Inc, USA, 516
Latin American Association of Development Financing Institutions, Peru, 299
Latin American Association of Development Organizations, Mexico, 262
Latin American Fund for Development, Costa Rica, 106
Van Leer Jerusalem Institute, Israel, 215
Leverhulme Trust, UK, 429
Lifewater International—LI, USA, 518
The Lotte and John Hecht Memorial Foundation, Canada, 90
Luigi Einaudi Foundation, Italy, 221
Luso-American Development Foundation, Portugal, 312
Luxemburg (Rosa) Stiftung, Germany, 174
MACIF Foundation, France, 146
Maison Franco-Japonaise, Japan, 237
Match International Centre, Canada, 93

Mattei (Enrico), Fondazione ENI, Italy, 218
Mediterranean Foundation, Argentina, 33
Mediterranean Foundation of Strategic Studies, France, 147
Mellon (Richard King) Foundation, USA, 523
Mendoza (Eugenio) Fundación, Venezuela, 563
Menzies (R. G.) Scholarship Fund, Australia, 42
Microenterprise Development Foundation, Guatemala, 191
Microfinance Centre—MFC, Poland, 309
Miguel Alemán Foundation, Mexico, 262
Moawad (René) Foundation, Lebanon, 253
Mongolian Women's Fund—MONES, Mongolia, 266
Mønsteds (Otto) Fond, Denmark, 120
Ms Foundation for Women, USA, 526
Nand and Jeet Khemka Foundation, India, 203
Nantik Lum Foundation, Spain, 345
National Endowment for Science, Technology and the Arts—NESTA, UK, 434
National Foundation for Development, El Salvador, 128
National Foundation for the Development of Honduras, Honduras, 193
National Foundation for Political Sciences, France, 148
National Foundation for Solidarity and Development, Burkina Faso, 78
Nederlandsche Maatschappij voor Nijverheid en Handel—NMNH, Netherlands, 278
NESsT—Nonprofit Enterprise and Self-sustainability Team, Chile, 101
NESTA—National Endowment for Science, Technology and the Arts, UK, 434
Netherlands Society for Industry and Trade, Netherlands, 278
New Eurasia Foundation, Russian Federation, 319
New Zealand Winston Churchill Memorial Trust, New Zealand, 285
Nigerian Institute of International Affairs—NIIA, Nigeria, 290
Nonprofit Enterprise and Self-sustainability Team—NESsT, Chile, 101
Noor al-Hussein Foundation—NHF, Jordan, 241
Nordic Africa Institute Scholarships, Sweden, 355
Nordiska Afrikainstitutets Stipendier, Sweden, 355
Norsk Utenrikspolitisk Institutt—NUPI, Norway, 292
North-South Institute/Institut Nord-Sud, Canada, 95
Northern Rock Foundation, UK, 435
Norwegian Institute of International Affairs—NUPI, Norway, 292
Nuffield Foundation, UK, 435
Open Society Forum (Mongolia), Mongolia, 266
Open Society Foundation—Bratislava, Slovakia, 328
Open Society Foundation for South Africa—OSF-SA, South Africa, 334
Open Society Initiative for Southern Africa—OSISA, South Africa, 334
Opportunity International USA, USA, 530
Österreichische Forschungsstiftung für Internationale Entwicklung—ÖFSE, Austria, 48
Österreichische Gesellschaft für Außenpolitik und Internationale Beziehungen, Austria, 48
Otto Mønsteds Fond, Denmark, 120
Otto Mønsteds Foundation, Denmark, 120
Paideia Galiza Foundation, Spain, 346
Pakistan Institute of International Affairs—PIIA, Pakistan, 294
Paul-Henri Spaak Foundation, Belgium, 61
Paulo Foundation, Finland, 132
Paulon Säätiö, Finland, 132
Peres Center for Peace, Israel, 215
Plunkett Foundation, UK, 438
Pôle européen des fondations de l'économie sociale, Belgium, 56
Protestant Study Foundation, Germany, 167
Prudential Foundation, USA, 537
R. G. Menzies Scholarship Fund, Australia, 42
Rabobank Foundation, Netherlands, 279
Rafael del Pino Foundation, Spain, 347
RED—Ruralité-environnement-développement, Belgium, 63
René Moawad Foundation, Lebanon, 253
Resource Center Foundation, Bulgaria, 74
Reynolds (Christopher) Foundation, USA, 539
Richard King Mellon Foundation, USA, 523
Robert Schalkenbach Foundation, Inc—RSF, USA, 543
Robert Schuman Foundation, France, 150
Romi Foundation, Brazil, 72
Rosa Luxemburg Foundation, Germany, 174

Rosa-Luxemburg-Stiftung, Germany, 174
Rural Development Foundation, Poland, 308
Ruralité Environnement Développement—RED, Belgium, 63
Rurality Environment Development, Belgium, 63
SACO—Service d'assistance canadienne aux organismes, Canada, 83
El Salvador Foundation for Economic and Social Development, El Salvador, 128
Sandino (Augusto César), Fundación, Nicaragua, 288
Sandoz Family Foundation, Switzerland, 372
Sandoz Fondation de Famille, Switzerland, 372
Sartawi Foundation, Bolivia, 67
Savings Banks Foundation for International Cooperation, Germany, 179
Schalkenbach (Robert) Foundation, Inc, USA, 543
Schuman (Robert), Fondation, France, 150
Schwarzkopf Foundation Young Europe, Germany, 178
Schwarzkopf Stiftung Junges Europa, Germany, 178
Schweisfurth Foundation, Germany, 178
Schweisfurth-Stiftung, Germany, 178
SEEMO—IPI—South East Europe Media Organisation, Austria, 49
Self Help Development Foundation, Zimbabwe, 567
Seva Foundation, USA, 544
Siam Society, Thailand, 384
Sir Ahmadu Bello Foundation, Nigeria, 289
Sir Ahmadu Bello Memorial Foundation, Nigeria, 289
Skoll Foundation, USA, 544
Sloan (Alfred P.) Foundation, USA, 545
Small Business Assistance Foundation, Guatemala, 190
Smith Richardson Foundation, Inc, USA, 545
Solidarity National Commission—Economic Foundation, Poland, 307
Solidarność NSZZ—Economic Foundation, Poland, 307
Soros Foundation (Slovakia), Slovakia, 328
Soros Foundation (South Africa), South Africa, 334
Soros Foundation Guatemala, Guatemala, 191
Soros Foundation—Kazakhstan, Kazakhstan, 243
Soros Foundation–Kyrgyzstan, Kyrgyzstan, 250
Soros Foundation Latvia, Latvia, 251
Soros Foundation Macedonia, Macedonia, 258
South African Institute of Race Relations, South Africa, 335
South East Europe Media Organisation, Austria, 49
South East Europe Media Organisation—SEEMO—IPI, Austria, 49
Spaak (Paul-Henri), Fondation, Belgium, 61
Sparkassenstiftung für internationale Kooperation eV, Germany, 179
Stichting Fonds 1818, Netherlands, 280
Stichting Spaak (Paul-Henri), Belgium, 61
Stichting Triodos Foundation, Netherlands, 282
Stichting VSB Fonds, Netherlands, 280
Stiftelsen Riksbankens Jubileumsfond, Sweden, 357
Sun/Soleil—AREGAK, Armenia, 35
Suzman (Helen) Foundation, South Africa, 335
Sweden-Japan Foundation—SJF, Sweden, 357
TANZ—Trade Aid NZ Inc, New Zealand, 287
Tanzania Millennium Hand Foundation—TAMIHA, Tanzania, 382
Tarih Vakfı, Turkey, 389
TEAR Australia, Australia, 45
di Tella (Torcuato), Instituto, Argentina, 34
Third World Network—TWN, Malaysia, 260
Tides, USA, 548
Tides Foundation, USA, 548
Tinker Foundation, Inc, USA, 548
Torcuato di Tella Institute, Argentina, 34
Trade Aid NZ Inc—TANZ, New Zealand, 287
Triodos Foundation, Netherlands, 282
Trócaire—Catholic Agency for World Development, Ireland, 213
Ukrainian Women's Fund, Ukraine, 394
United Service Committee of Canada, Canada, 98
United States African Development Foundation—USADF, USA, 550
University of Zaragoza Business Foundation, Spain, 342
US-Baltic Foundation—USBF, USA, 551
US-Ukraine Foundation, USA, 551
USC Canada, Canada, 98
Villar Foundation, Inc., Philippines, 304
West-Nordic Foundation, Iceland, 197
Weston (Garfield) Foundation, UK, 455

Wihuri (Jenny and Antti) Foundation, Finland, 134
Women's Foundation, Costa Rica, 107
Wood Family Trust, UK, 456
YADESA—Yayasan Pengembangan Masyarakat Desa, Indonesia, 208
Yayasan Pengembangan Masyarakat Desa—YADESA, Indonesia, 208
Youth Forum, Uruguay, 560
Yrjö Jahnsson Foundation, Finland, 131
Yrjö Jahnssonin säätiö, Finland, 131
Zeiss (Carl) Stiftung, Germany, 184

EDUCATION

A. G. Leventis Foundation, Cyprus, 111
A. G. Leventis Foundation Nigeria, Nigeria, 290
A. L. Mailman Family Foundation, Inc, USA, 521
A. M. M. Sahabdeen Trust Foundation, Sri Lanka, 350
A. M. Qattan Foundation, UK, 440
The A. P. Møller and Chastine Mc-Kinney Møller Foundation, Denmark, 120
A. P. Møller og Hustru Chastine Mc-Kinney Møllers Fond til almene Formaal, Denmark, 120
Absolute Return for Kids—ARK, UK, 401
Academy for the Development of Philanthropy in Poland, Poland, 305
Academy of European Law, Germany, 167
ACCU—Asian Cultural Centre for UNESCO, Japan, 231
Açık Toplum Enstitüsü, Turkey, 387
Acíndar Foundation, Argentina, 31
ACORD—Agency for Co-operation and Research in Development, Kenya, 245
Action in Development—AID, Bangladesh, 52
Activ Foundation, Australia, 36
ACTR/ACCELS—American Councils for International Education, USA, 464
Adams (Sylvia) Charitable Trust, UK, 398
ADI—Association for Democratic Initiatives, Macedonia, 258
Advantech Foundation, Taiwan, 379
AFAP—Australian Foundation for the Peoples of Asia and the Pacific, Australia, 38
Africa-America Institute—AAI, USA, 461
Africa Educational Trust, UK, 399
Africa Foundation (UK), UK, 399
African Association for Literacy and Adult Education, Senegal, 323
African Capacity Building Foundation—ACBF, Zimbabwe, 567
African Youth Network for Sustainable Development, Algeria, 30
Afro-Asian Institute in Vienna, Austria, 46
Afro-Asiatisches Institut in Wien, Austria, 46
Aga Khan Foundation—AKF, Switzerland, 360
Aga Khan Fund for Economic Development, Switzerland, 361
Agency for Co-operation and Research in Development, Kenya, 245
Agency for the Non-profit Sector, Czech Republic, 112
Agnelli (Giovanni), Fondazione, Italy, 218
AGNES—Vzdělávací Organizace, Czech Republic, 112
Agora Foundation, Poland, 306
Agostino (Daniele Derossi) Foundation, USA, 462
Agromart Foundation, Sri Lanka, 350
The Ahmanson Foundation, USA, 462
Aid for India/ Karuna Trust, UK, 426
Aide et Action, France, 137
AIIT—Ancient India and Iran Trust, UK, 400
AINA—Arctic Institute of North America, Canada, 81
Air France Corporate Foundation, France, 144
AIT—Asian Institute of Technology, Thailand, 383
AIV—Asia-Africa International Voluntary Foundation, Japan, 231
AJWS—American Jewish World Service, USA, 466
Akademia Rozwoju Filantropii w Polsce, Poland, 305
Alavi Foundation, USA, 462
Albéniz (Isaac), Fundación, Spain, 339
Albéniz Foundation, Spain, 339
Alberto Vollmer Foundation, Inc, USA, 551
Alden (George I.) Trust, USA, 463
Alemán (Miguel), Fundación, Mexico, 262
Alfred P. Sloan Foundation, USA, 545
Alfred Toepfer Foundation F.V.S., Germany, 183
Alfred Toepfer Stiftung F.V.S., Germany, 183
Allen (Paul G.) Family Foundation, USA, 463
Alliance for International Educational and Cultural Exchange, USA, 463

Allianz Cultural Foundation, Germany, 160
Allianz Kulturstiftung, Germany, 160
Almeida (Eng. António de), Fundação, Portugal, 310
Alternatives for Development Foundation, Ecuador, 124
Alvares Penteado (Armando), Fundação, Brazil, 71
AMADE Mondiale—Association Mondiale des Amis de l'Enfance, Monaco, 265
Amancio Ortega Foundation, Spain, 346
Amberes (Carlos de), Fundación, Spain, 339
Ambiente y Recursos Naturales, Fundación, Argentina, 31
Ambuja Cement Foundation, India, 199
America for Bulgaria Foundation, Bulgaria, 75
America–Mideast Educational and Training Services Inc, USA, 468
American Councils for International Education—ACTR/ACCELS, USA, 464
American Foundation for the Blind, Inc—AFB, USA, 465
American Historical Association, USA, 466
American Jewish World Service—AJWS, USA, 466
American Near East Refugee Aid—ANERA, USA, 467
American Scandinavian Foundation—ASF, USA, 467
American Schools of Oriental Research—ASOR, USA, 467
Amerind Foundation, Inc, USA, 468
AMIDEAST—America-Mideast Educational and Training Services, Inc, USA, 468
AMP Foundation, Australia, 36
Ana Mata Manzanedo Foundation, Spain, 345
Ancient India and Iran Trust, UK, 400
The Andrew Balint Charitable Trust, UK, 402
The Andrew W. Mellon Foundation, USA, 523
ANERA—American Near East Refugee Aid, USA, 467
ANESVAD, Spain, 337
Angelo Della Riccia Foundation, Italy, 221
Anna Lindh Euro-Mediterranean Foundation for Dialogue between Cultures, Egypt, 127
Anne Çocuk Eğitim Vakfı—AÇEV, Turkey, 388
The Anne Frank Trust UK, UK, 418
The Annenberg Foundation, USA, 468
APHEDA—Union Aid Abroad, Australia, 45
APMN—Asia Pacific Mountain Network, Nepal, 271
The Arab-British Chamber Charitable Foundation, UK, 401
Arab Thought Foundation, Lebanon, 252
ArcelorMittal Acesita Foundation, Brazil, 71
Archie Sherman Charitable Trust, UK, 448
Arctic Institute of North America—AINA, Canada, 81
AREGAK—Sun/Soleil, Armenia, 35
Arias Foundation for Peace and Human Progress, Costa Rica, 106
Arie and Ida Crown Memorial, USA, 483
ARK—Absolute Return for Kids, UK, 401
Armand-Frappier Foundation, Canada, 88
Armando Alvares Penteado Foundation, Brazil, 71
Arthritis Foundation, USA, 469
Arthritis Research Campaign, UK, 401
Arthritis Research UK, UK, 401
Arthritis and Rheumatism Council for Research in Great Britain and the Commonwealth, UK, 401
Arthur Rubinstein International Music Society, Israel, 215
Asahi Beer Arts Foundation, Japan, 230
Asahi Biiru Geijutsu Bunka Zaidan, Japan, 230
ASEAN Foundation, Indonesia, 207
Asia-Africa International Voluntary Foundation—AIV, Japan, 231
Asia/Pacific Cultural Centre for UNESCO—ACCU, Japan, 231
Asia-Pacific Mountain Network—APMN, Nepal, 271
Asia Society, USA, 470
Asian Community Trust—ACT, Japan, 231
Asian Cultural Council—ACC, USA, 470
Asian Development Research Institute—ADRI, India, 200
Asian Health Institute—AHI, Japan, 231
Asian Youth Center, USA, 470
ASMAE—Association de coopération et d'éducation aux développements, Belgium, 56
Asociación Española de Fundaciones, Spain, 337
ASOR—American Schools of Oriental Research, USA, 467
Association de coopération et d'éducation aux développements—ASMAE, Belgium, 56

Association for Democratic Initiatives—ADI, Macedonia, 258
Association for Development Co-operation and Education, Belgium, 56
Association Mondiale des Amis de l'Enfance, Monaco, 265
Association of Voluntary Agencies for Rural Development—AVARD, India, 198
Atkinson Foundation, USA, 470
Augusto César Sandino Foundation, Nicaragua, 288
Auschwitz Foundation, Belgium, 60
Australia-Japan Foundation, Australia, 37
Australian Academy of the Humanities, Australia, 37
Australian Academy of Science, Australia, 37
Australian-American Fulbright Commission, Australia, 37
Australian Foundation for the Peoples of Asia and the Pacific—AFAP, Australia, 38
Australian Multicultural Foundation—AMF, Australia, 39
Australian People Health Education, Australia, 45
Australian Youth Foundation, Australia, 41
Austrian Research Foundation for International Development, Austria, 48
Austrian Science Fund, Austria, 47
Auxilia Foundation, Czech Republic, 112
AVARD—Association of Voluntary Agencies for Rural Development, India, 198
AWHRC—Asian Women's Human Rights Council, India, 200
Axel Springer Foundation, Germany, 179
Axel-Springer-Stiftung, Germany, 179
Ayala Foundation, Inc—AFI, Philippines, 301
Ayala Foundation USA—AF-USA, USA, 535
Aydın Doğan Foundation, Turkey, 388
Aydın Doğan Vakfı, Turkey, 388
Ayrton Senna Institute, Brazil, 73
Azim Premji Foundation, India, 204
Bacon (Francis) Foundation, Inc, USA, 471
BAFROW—Foundation for Research on Women's Health, Productivity and the Environment, Gambia, 156
Baker (E. A.) Foundation for the Prevention of Blindness, Canada, 85
Balint (Andrew) Charitable Trust, UK, 402
Baltic-American Partnership Fund—BAPF, USA, 472
Bangladesh Rural Advancement Committee—BRAC, Bangladesh, 52
Bank of America Foundation, USA, 472
Bank of Brazil Foundation, Brazil, 71
Barceló Foundation, Spain, 340
The Baron de Hirsch Fund, USA, 484
Barrié de la Maza (Pedro, Conde de Fenosa), Fundación, Spain, 340
The Batchworth Trust, UK, 403
BBC World Service Trust, UK, 403
Beaverbrook Foundation, UK, 403
Beisheim (Professor Otto) Stiftung, Germany, 161
Beit Trust, UK, 403
Belarusian Charitable Fund 'For the Children of Chornobyl', Belarus, 54
Benecke (Otto) Stiftung eV, Germany, 161
Benesco Charity Limited, UK, 404
The Bernard Sunley Charitable Foundation, UK, 450
Bernheim Foundation, Belgium, 60
Bertelsmann Foundation, Germany, 162
Bertelsmann Stiftung, Germany, 162
Beyaz Nokta Gelişim Vakfı, Turkey, 387
BibleLands, UK, 404
Binding (Sophie und Karl) Stiftung, Switzerland, 361
Black Sea University Foundation—BSUF, Romania, 316
Blanceflor Boncompagni-Ludovisi, née Bildt Foundation, Sweden, 356
Bleustein-Blanchet (Marcel), Fondation pour la Vocation, France, 141
Bodossaki Foundation, Greece, 186
Bofill (Jaume), Fundació, Spain, 338
Boghossian Foundation, Belgium, 60
Borderland Foundation, Poland, 307
BOTA Foundation, Kazakhstan, 243
Botín (Marcelino) Fundación, Spain, 341
BRAC—Building Resources Across Communities, Bangladesh, 52
Bradley (Lynde and Harry) Foundation, Inc, USA, 473
Brazil Foundation, Brazil, 70
Bread for the World, Germany, 163
Bridge to Asia—BTA, USA, 473
The Bridge Foundation—TBF, Ghana, 185
Bridge House Estates Trust Fund, UK, 410
Bridges for Education, Inc—BFE, USA, 473

British Schools and Universities Foundation, Inc—BSUF, USA, 473
The Broad Foundations, USA, 474
Brockhoff (Jack) Foundation, Australia, 39
Brookings Institution, USA, 474
Brot für die Welt, Germany, 163
Brother's Brother Foundation, USA, 474
Buck (Pearl S. Buck) International, USA, 474
Building Resources Across Communities—BRAC, Bangladesh, 52
Bulgarian Fund for Women, Bulgaria, 75
Bunge y Born Foundation, Argentina, 32
Burroughs Wellcome Fund—BWF, USA, 475
Business Institute Foundation, Spain, 344
C. P. Ramaswami Aiyar Foundation, India, 204
Cadbury (Edward) Charitable Trust, Inc, UK, 407
Cadbury (William Adlington) Charitable Trust, UK, 407
Caisses d'Epargne Foundation for Social Solidarity, France, 141
Caja Madrid Foundation, Spain, 341
The Camille and Henry Dreyfus Foundation, Inc, USA, 485
Canadian Co-operative Association, Canada, 80
Canadian Friends of the Hebrew University, Canada, 84
Canadian International Council/Conseil International du Canada—CIC, Canada, 84
Canadian Organization for Development through Education—CODE, Canada, 85
Canadian Urban Institute, Canada, 85
Cancer Relief Macmillan Fund, UK, 430
Canon Foundation in Europe, Netherlands, 272
CARE International—CI, Switzerland, 361
Cariplo Foundation, Italy, 219
The Carl and Lily Pforzheimer Foundation, Inc, USA, 535
Carlos de Amberes Foundation, Spain, 339
Carnegie Corporation of New York, USA, 475
Carnegie Trust for the Universities of Scotland, UK, 408
Carnegie UK Trust, UK, 408
Carpathian Foundation, Hungary, 195
Carson (John W.) Foundation, USA, 476
Carthage Foundation, USA, 476
Catholic Agency for World Development—Trócaire, Ireland, 213
CCF—Christian Children's Fund, USA, 478
CDCS—Centre for Development of Civil Society, Armenia, 35
CEAAL—Consejo de Educación de Adultos de América Latina, Panama, 297
CECHE—Center for Communications, Health and the Environment, USA, 477
Centar za razvoj neprofitnih organizacija—CERANEO, Croatia, 109
Center for Communications, Health and the Environment—CECHE, USA, 477
Center for Cultural and Technical Interchange between East and West—East-West Center, USA, 487
Center for Human Research and Social Development—CHRSD, Palestinian Autonomous Areas, 296
CENTRAS—Assistance Centre for NGOs, Romania, 316
Centre of Advanced European Studies and Research, Germany, 179
Centre for the Development of Civil Society—CDCS, Armenia, 35
Centre for Development of Non-Profit Organizations, Croatia, 109
Centre for Environment, Education and Development, USA, 516
Centre d'Etudes, de Documentation, d'Information et d'Action Sociales—CEDIAS—Musée Social, France, 138
Centre Européen de la Culture—CEC, Switzerland, 362
Centre for the Information Service, Co-operation and Development of NGOs, Slovenia, 330
Centre Pan-Africain de Prospective Sociale, Benin, 65
Centre for Social Studies, Documentation, Information and Action, France, 138
Centre for Training and Consultancy, Georgia, 157
Cera, Belgium, 57
CERANEO—Centar za razvoj neprofitnih organizacija, Croatia, 109
Česko-německý fond budoucnosti, Czech Republic, 113
CGP—Japan Foundation Centre Global Partnership, Japan, 236
Charles Delmar Foundation, USA, 484
Charles F. Kettering Foundation, USA, 515
Charles and Lynn Schusterman Family Foundation—CLSFF, USA, 543

Charles Stewart Mott Foundation—CSMF, USA, 526
Charles Wallace India Trust, UK, 454
Charter 77 Foundation, Czech Republic, 114
Chastell Foundation, Canada, 85
Chia Hsin Foundation, Taiwan, 379
The Chicago Community Trust, USA, 478
ChildFund International, USA, 478
ChildHope Asia Philippines, Inc, Philippines, 302
Children in Africa Foundation, Germany, 181
Children of The Americas—COTA, USA, 479
Children International—CI, USA, 479
Children of Slovakia Foundation, Slovakia, 328
Children's Foundation of China, China (People's Republic), 102
Childwick Trust, UK, 409
Chile Foundation, Chile, 100
China Medical Board, USA, 479
China Soong Ching Ling Foundation, China (People's Republic), 102
China Youth Development Foundation, China (People's Republic), 103
Churchill (Winston) Foundation of the United States, USA, 479
CIC—Canadian International Council/Conseil International du Canada, Canada, 84
Cini (Giorgio), Fondazione, Italy, 220
Cité Internationale Universitaire de Paris, France, 139
The City Bridge Trust, UK, 410
City of Lisbon Foundation, Portugal, 311
Civic Initiatives, Serbia, 324
CIVITAS Foundation for Civil Society, Romania, 316
Clean Water Foundation, Netherlands, 282
Cleveland Foundation, USA, 480
Cleveland H. Dodge Foundation, Inc, USA, 485
Clive and Vera Ramaciotti Foundations, Australia, 43
Clore Duffield Foundation—CDF, UK, 411
Clovek v tisni—spolecnost pri Ceske televizi, o.p.s., Czech Republic, 113
CNIB/INCA, Canada, 85
CNVOS—Zavod Center za Informiranje, Sodelovanje in Razvoj Nevladnih Organizacije, Slovenia, 330
Co-operation for the Promotion and Development of Welfare Activities, Spain, 342
CODE—Canadian Organization for Development through Education, Canada, 85
Cogitare Foundation, USA, 481
the cogito foundation, Switzerland, 362
Collier Charitable Fund, Australia, 40
Colt Foundation, UK, 411
Committee of Good Will—Olga Havel Foundation, Czech Republic, 115
Commonwealth Foundation, UK, 411
Communication Foundation for Asia, Philippines, 302
Community Aid Abroad—Oxfam Australia, Australia, 43
Community Foundation for Northern Ireland, UK, 412
Compagnia di San Paolo, Italy, 217
Compton Foundation, Inc, USA, 481
Concern India Foundation, India, 201
Consejo de Educación de Adultos de América Latina—CEAAL, Panama, 297
Consejo de Fundaciones Americanas de Desarrollo—Solidarios, Dominican Republic, 123
Consejo de Fundaciones Privadas de Guatemala—CFPG, Guatemala, 190
Cooperazione Internazionale—COOPI, Italy, 217
COOPI—Cooperazione Internazionale, Italy, 217
Costopoulos (J. F.) Foundation, Greece, 186
Coubertin Foundation, France, 142
Council of American Development Foundations, Dominican Republic, 123
Council for the Education of Adults in Latin America, Panama, 297
Council of Private Foundations of Guatemala, Guatemala, 190
Covenant Foundation, USA, 483
CPCS—Center for Philanthropy and Civil Society, Thailand, 383
The CRB Foundation/La Fondation CRB, Canada, 86
Croucher Foundation, Hong Kong, 194
Crown (Arie and Ida) Memorial, USA, 483
Crown Family Philanthropies, USA, 483
CRT Foundation, Italy, 220
CUSO-VSO, Canada, 86
Czech-German Fund for the Future, Czech Republic, 113
Czech TV Foundation, Czech Republic, 113
Czegei Wass Foundation, Hungary, 196
Daiwa Anglo-Japanese Foundation, UK, 413

Daniele Agostino Derossi Foundation, USA, 462
The Danish Cultural Institute, Denmark, 117
Danmark-Amerika Fondet, Denmark, 117
Danske Kulturinstitut, Denmark, 117
David and Lucile Packard Foundation, USA, 531
Davis (Lady) Fellowship Trust, Israel, 214
Delmar (Charles) Foundation, USA, 484
Denmark-America Foundation, Denmark, 117
The Desmond Tutu Educational Trust, South
    Africa, 335
Desmond Tutu Peace Foundation—DTPF,
    USA, 549
Deutsch-Tschechischer Zukunftsfonds, Czech
    Republic, 113
Deutsche Bank Americas Foundation and
    Community Development Group, USA, 484
Deutsche Bank Endowment Fund for the
    Promotion of Science in Research and
    Teaching, Germany, 182
Deutsche Krebshilfe eV, Germany, 165
Deutsche Stiftung Weltbevölkerung—DSW,
    Germany, 165
Deutsche Telekom Foundation, Germany, 166
Deutsche Telekom Stiftung, Germany, 166
Deutsches Institut für Internationale
    Pädagogische Forschung, Germany, 166
DEVI—Dignity, Education, Vision International,
    India, 201
DeWitt Wallace—Reader's Digest Fund, Inc,
    USA, 551
Dian Desa Foundation, Indonesia, 207
Dietmar Hopp Foundation, Germany, 170
Dietmar-Hopp-Stiftung, Germany, 170
Dignity, Education, Vision International—DEVI,
    India, 201
Dinu Patriciu Foundation, Romania, 317
Ditchley Foundation, UK, 414
Dmitry Zimin Dynasty Foundation, Russian
    Federation, 319
Dóchas, Ireland, 210
Dodge (Cleveland H.) Foundation, Inc, USA, 485
Doğan (Aydın) Vakfı, Turkey, 388
Dom Manuel II Foundation, Portugal, 311
Dominican Development Foundation, Dominican
    Republic, 123
Don Bosco Foundation of Cambodia—DBFC,
    Cambodia, 79
Donner (William H.) Foundation, Inc, USA, 485
Donors' Association for the Promotion of Sciences
    and Humanities, Germany, 159
Dr J. R. Villavicencio Foundation, Argentina, 33
Dr Marcus Wallenberg Foundation for Further
    Education in International Industry,
    Sweden, 358
Dr Marcus Wallenbergs Stiftelse för Utbildning i
    Internationellt Industriellt Företagande,
    Sweden, 358
Dr Rainer Wild Foundation for Healthy
    Nutrition, Germany, 184
Dr Rainer Wild-Stiftung—Stiftung für gesunde
    Ernährung, Germany, 184
Dr Scholl Foundation, USA, 543
Dreyfus (Camille and Henry) Foundation, Inc,
    USA, 485
Dreyfus Health Foundation—DHF, USA, 485
Drug Policy Alliance—DPA, USA, 485
DSW—Deutsche Stiftung Weltbevölkerung,
    Germany, 165
Duke Endowment, USA, 486
Dulverton Trust, UK, 414
Dumbarton Oaks, USA, 486
E. O. Wilson Biodiversity Foundation, USA, 555
EABL Foundation, Kenya, 245
East-West Center—EWC, USA, 487
Easter Island Foundation, USA, 487
Ebelin and Gerd Bucerius ZEIT Foundation,
    Germany, 184
Eça de Queiroz Foundation, Portugal, 312
EcoCiencia—Fundación Ecuatoriana de
    Estudios Ecologicos, Ecuador, 124
Écoles Sans Frontières—ESF, France, 139
Economic Foundation, Poland, 307
ECPD—European Centre for Peace and
    Development, Serbia, 324
Ecuadorean Development Foundation,
    Ecuador, 125
Ecuadorian Foundation of Ecological Studies,
    Ecuador, 124
The Edmond de Rothschild Foundations,
    USA, 541
Ednannia: Initiative Centre to Support Social
    Action—ISAR Ednannia, Ukraine, 393
Eduardo Capa Foundation, Spain, 341
The Education for Development Foundation—
    EDF, Thailand, 383
Edward Cadbury Charitable Trust, Inc, UK, 407
Eesti Mittetulundusühingute ja Sihtasutuste
    Liit, Estonia, 129

Eestimaa Looduse Fond—ELF, Estonia, 129
Egmont Fonden, Denmark, 118
Egmont Foundation, Denmark, 118
ELIAMEP—Hellenic Foundation for European
    and Foreign Policy, Greece, 187
Emile Chanoux Foundation—Institute for
    Federalist and Regionalist Studies, Italy, 218
Emirates Foundation, United Arab Emirates, 395
Empower Foundation, Thailand, 383
ENCOD—European NGO Council on Drugs and
    Development, Belgium, 59
Enda Third World—Environment and
    Development Action in the Third World,
    Senegal, 322
Enda Tiers Monde—Environnement et
    Développement du Tiers-Monde, Senegal, 322
endPoverty.org, USA, 488
Eng. António de Almeida Foundation,
    Portugal, 310
Enterprise Development International, USA, 488
Entraide Protestante Suisse, Switzerland, 367
Environment and Natural Resources Foundation,
    Argentina, 31
Environmental Protection Research Foundation,
    India, 201
Environnement et Développement du Tiers-
    Monde—Enda, Senegal, 322
ERA—Europäische Rechtsakademie,
    Germany, 167
Esmée Fairbairn Foundation, UK, 416
Espejo (Eugenio), Fundación, Ecuador, 125
Estonian Foundation Centre, Estonia, 129
Estonian Fund for Nature, Estonia, 129
Estonian National Culture Foundation,
    Estonia, 129
Etruscan Foundation, USA, 489
Eugenio Espejo Foundation, Ecuador, 125
Eugenio Mendoza Foundation, Venezuela, 563
Eurasia Foundation, USA, 489
Euris Foundation, France, 144
Euronisa Foundation, Czech Republic, 114
Europäische Rechtsakademie—ERA,
    Germany, 167
European Centre of Culture, Switzerland, 362
European Centre for Peace and Development—
    ECPD, Serbia, 324
European Coalition for Just and Effective Drug
    Policies—ENCOD, Belgium, 59
European Cultural Foundation—ECF,
    Netherlands, 273
European Institute of Health and Social Welfare,
    Spain, 349
European Mediterranean Institute, Spain, 349
European Network of Foundations for Social
    Economy, Belgium, 56
European Science Foundation, France, 144
European Youth Foundation—EYF, France, 151
Europese Culterele Stichting, Netherlands, 273
Evangelisches Studienwerk eV, Germany, 167
Evens Foundation, Belgium, 61
Evrika Foundation, Bulgaria, 75
EWC—East-West Center, USA, 487
The F. K. Morrow Foundation, Canada, 94
FAF—French-American Foundation, USA, 494
Fairbairn (Esmée) Foundation, UK, 416
Family Planning, New Zealand, 284
FARN—Fundación Ambiente y Recursos
    Naturales, Argentina, 31
FDD—Fundación Dominicana de Desarrollo,
    Dominican Republic, 123
Federación Argentina de Apoyo Familiar—FAAF,
    Argentina, 31
The Federal Trust for Education and Research,
    UK, 416
FEIM—Fundación para Estudio e Investigación
    de la Mujer, Argentina, 32
FEPP—Fondo Ecuatoriano Populorum
    Progressio, Ecuador, 124
Fernand Lazard Foundation, Belgium, 63
Fernand Lazard Stichting, Belgium, 63
filia.die frauenstiftung, Germany, 168
filia—the Women's Foundation, Germany, 168
Finnish Cultural Foundation, Finland, 132
Finnish Foundation for Technology Promotion,
    Finland, 133
Finnish Institute in London Trust, UK, 417
Firefly, Inc., USA, 490
FirstRand Foundation, South Africa, 332
FLAAR—Foundation for Latin American
    Anthropological Research, USA, 492
Florence Gould Foundation, USA, 499
FOKAL—Fondation Connaissance et Liberte
    (Haiti), Haiti, 192
Folmer Wisti Fonden, Denmark, 122
Folmer Wisti Foundation, Denmark, 122
Fondaccioni per Iniciative Demokratike,
    Kosovo, 248

Fondacioni Shoqeria e Hapur per Shqiperine,
    Albania, 29
Fondation Abri International, Canada, 97
Fondation Armand-Frappier, Canada, 88
Fondation Auschwitz, Belgium, 60
Fondation Baxter and Alma Ricard, Canada, 88
Fondation Bernheim, Belgium, 60
Fondation Boghossian, Belgium, 60
Fondation Caisses d'Epargne pour la solidarité—
    FCES, France, 141
Fondation Charles Veillon, Switzerland, 365
Fondation Connaissance et Liberté (Haiti)—
    FOKAL, Haiti, 192
Fondation de Coubertin, France, 142
Fondation Emile Chanoux—Institut d'Etudes
    Fédéralistes et Régionalistes, Italy, 218
Fondation d'Entreprise Air France, France, 144
Fondation d'Entreprise Renault, France, 144
Fondation Euris, France, 144
Fondation Européenne de la Culture/Europese
    Culturele Stichting, Netherlands, 273
Fondation Européenne de la Science, France, 144
Fondation Evens Stichting, Belgium, 61
Fondation France-Israel, France, 145
Fondation Franco-Japonaise Sasakawa,
    France, 145
Fondation Francqui, Belgium, 61
Fondation Hugot du Collège de France,
    France, 145
Fondation Institut Suisse de Recherche
    Expérimentale sur le Cancer, Switzerland, 364
Fondation ISREC, Switzerland, 364
Fondation Jean-Louis Lévesque, Canada, 88
Fondation Léopold Sédar Senghor, Senegal, 322
Fondation Marcel Bleustein-Blanchet pour la
    Vocation, France, 141
Fondation Méditerranéenne d'Etudes
    Stratégiques—FMES, France, 147
Fondation Mo Ibrahim, UK, 421
Fondation Nationale pour l'Enseignement de la
    Gestion des Entreprises, France, 148
Fondation Nationale des Sciences Politiques,
    France, 148
Fondation des Organisations Rurales pour
    l'Agriculture et la Gestion Ecologique—
    FORAGE, Senegal, 322
Fondation Orient-Occident, Morocco, 268
Fondation Paul-Henri Spaak—Stichting Paul-
    Henri Spaak, Belgium, 61
Fondation Pro Victimis Genève, Switzerland, 365
Fondation René Seydoux pour le Monde
    Méditerranéen, France, 150
Fondation pour le Renforcement des Capacités en
    Afrique, Zimbabwe, 567
Fondation Simón I. Patiño, Switzerland, 365
Fondation Syngenta pour une Agriculture
    Durable, Switzerland, 376
Fondazione Angelo Della Riccia, Italy, 221
Fondazione per l'Arte, Italy, 219
Fondazione Cariplo, Italy, 219
Fondazione Cassa di Risparmio delle Provincie
    Lombarde—Fondazione Cariplo, Italy, 219
Fondazione Cassa di Risparmio di Padova e
    Rovigo, Italy, 219
Fondazione Cassa di Risparmio di Torino,
    Italy, 220
Fondazione Giorgio Cini, Italy, 220
Fondazione Giovanni Agnelli, Italy, 218
Fondazione Giovanni Lorenzini, Italy, 222
Fondazione Ing. Carlo M. Lerici—FL, Italy, 222
Fondazione per l'Istituto Svizzero di Roma,
    Italy, 222
Fondazione Roma, Italy, 224
Fondazione RUI, Italy, 225
Fondazione di Venezia, Italy, 225
Fondazzjoni Patrimonju Malti, Malta, 261
Fondo Ecuatoriano Populorum Progressio—
    FEPP, Ecuador, 124
Fonds Européen pour la Jeunesse—FEJ,
    France, 151
Fonds zur Förderung der Wissenschaftlichen
    Forschung—FWF, Austria, 47
Fonds National Suisse de la Recherche
    Scientifique, Switzerland, 374
Fonds Wetenschappelijk Onderzoek—
    Vlaanderen, Belgium, 62
FOOD—Foundation of Occupational
    Development, India, 201
Food for the Poor, Inc, USA, 491
Foro Juvenil, Uruguay, 560
FOSIM—Foundation Open Society Institute
    Macedonia, Macedonia, 258
Foundation for the Arts, Italy, 219
Foundation Cassa di Risparmio di Padova e
    Rovigo, Italy, 219
Foundation for Children, Germany, 181
Foundation for Commercial and Technical
    Sciences—KAUTE, Finland, 131

Foundation for Democratic Initiatives—FDI, Kosovo, 248
Foundation for German–Polish Co-operation, Poland, 308
Foundation of the Hellenic World, Greece, 186
Foundation for Human Rights and Humanitarian Relief, Turkey, 389
Foundation for International Understanding, Denmark, 122
Foundation for Knowledge and Liberty, Haiti, 192
Foundation for Latin American Anthropological Research, USA, 492
Foundation for Latin American Economic Research, Argentina, 32
Foundation 'Life for All', Switzerland, 375
Foundation for Management Education—FME, UK, 417
Foundation of Occupational Development—FOOD, India, 201
Foundation Open Society Institute Macedonia—FOSIM, Macedonia, 258
Foundation Open Society Institute—Pakistan, Pakistan, 294
Foundation Open Society Institute—Representative Office Montenegro—FOSI ROM, Montenegro, 267
Foundation for the Peoples of the South Pacific, Australia, 38
Foundation to Promote Health, Liechtenstein, 255
Foundation for the Promotion of the German Rectors' Conference, Germany, 180
Foundation for Reading, Germany, 181
Foundation for Research on Women's Health, Productivity and the Environment—BAFROW, Gambia, 156
Foundation of Rural Organizations for Agriculture and Economic Management, Senegal, 322
Foundation of Spanish Commercial Agents, Spain, 339
Foundation for Sustainable Development, Spain, 348
Foundation for Swedish Culture in Finland, Finland, 133
Foundation for the Swiss Institute of Rome, Italy, 222
Foundation of Village Community Development, Indonesia, 208
Foundation for Women, Spain, 345
Foundation for Women's Research and Studies, Argentina, 32
Foundation for Young Australians, Australia, 41
Foundation for Youth Research, Germany, 180
France-Israel Foundation, France, 145
The Francis Bacon Foundation, Inc, USA, 471
Franco-Japanese Sasakawa Foundation, France, 145
Francqui Foundation, Belgium, 61
Frank Knox Memorial Fellowships, UK, 427
Frankfurt Foundation for German-Italian Studies, Germany, 168
Frankfurter Stiftung für Deutsch-Italienische Studien, Germany, 168
Frappier (Armand), Fondation, Canada, 88
The Freedom Forum, USA, 493
Freeman Foundation, USA, 494
French-American Foundation—FAF, USA, 494
French National Foundation for Management Education, France, 148
Freshwater Society, USA, 494
Freudenberg Stiftung, Germany, 168
Friede Springer Foundation, Germany, 179
Friede Springer Stiftung, Germany, 179
Fritz Thyssen Foundation, Germany, 183
Fritz Thyssen Stiftung, Germany, 183
Frontiers Foundation Inc/Fondation Frontière Inc, Canada, 89
FUHEM—Fundación Hogar del Empleado, Spain, 343
Fund for the Development of the Carpathian Euroregion, Hungary, 195
Fund for an Open Society—Serbia, Serbia, 324
Fundação ArcelorMittal Acesita, Brazil, 71
Fundação Armando Alvares Penteado—FAAP, Brazil, 71
Fundação de Atendimento à Criança e ao Adolescente Professor Hélio Augusto de Souza—Fundhas, Brazil, 73
Fundação Banco do Brasil, Brazil, 71
Fundação da Casa de Mateus, Portugal, 310
Fundação Cidade de Lisboa, Portugal, 311
Fundação Dom Manuel II, Portugal, 311
Fundação Eça de Queiroz, Portugal, 312
Fundação Eng. António de Almeida, Portugal, 310
Fundação Hélio Augusto de Souza—Fundhas, Brazil, 73

Fundação Iochpe, Brazil, 72
Fundação Luso-Americana para o Desenvolvimento, Portugal, 312
Fundação Maria Cecilia Souto Vidigal, Brazil, 73
Fundação Mário Soares, Portugal, 313
Fundação Oriente, Portugal, 312
Fundação Ricardo do Espírito Santo Silva, Portugal, 311
Fundação Roberto Marinho, Brazil, 72
Fundação Romi, Brazil, 72
Fundação de Serralves, Portugal, 312
Fundació Jaume Bofill, Spain, 338
Fundació 'La Caixa', Spain, 338
Fundación Acíndar, Argentina, 31
Fundación Actilibre, Spain, 339
Fundación de los Agentes Comerciales de España, Spain, 339
Fundación Albéniz, Spain, 339
Fundación Alberto Vollmer, USA, 551
Fundación Alternativas para el Desarrollo, Ecuador, 124
Fundación Amancio Ortega, Spain, 346
Fundación Amanecer, Colombia, 104
Fundación Ambiente y Recursos Naturales—FARN, Argentina, 31
Fundación Ana Mata Manzanedo, Spain, 345
Fundación Arias para la Paz y el Progreso Humano, Costa Rica, 106
Fundación Augusto César Sandino—FACS, Nicaragua, 288
Fundación Barceló, Spain, 340
Fundación Bunge y Born, Argentina, 32
Fundación Caja Madrid, Spain, 341
Fundación Carlos de Amberes, Spain, 339
Fundación Chile, Chile, 100
Fundación Científica de la Asociación Española Contra el Cáncer—AECC, Spain, 342
Fundación CODESPA—Futuro en Marcha, Spain, 342
Fundación Comunitaria de Puerto Rico—FCPR, Puerto Rico, 314
Fundación Corona, Colombia, 104
Fundación Desarrollo Sostenido—FUNDESO, Spain, 348
Fundación Dominicana de Desarrollo—FDD, Dominican Republic, 123
Fundación Dr J. Roberto Villavicencio, Argentina, 33
Fundación EAES, Spain, 342
Fundación Ecuatoriana de Desarrollo—FED, Ecuador, 125
Fundación Ecuatoriana de Estudios Ecologicos—EcoCiencia, Ecuador, 124
Fundación Eduardo Capa, Spain, 341
Fundación EFE, Spain, 342
Fundación Empresa-Universidad de Zaragoza—FEUZ, Spain, 342
Fundación Empresas Polar, Venezuela, 563
Fundación Escuela Andaluza de Economía Social, Spain, 342
Fundación para Estudio e Investigación de la Mujer—FEIM, Argentina, 32
Fundación Eugenio Espejo, Ecuador, 125
Fundación Eugenio Mendoza, Venezuela, 563
Fundación Gala–Salvador Dalí, Spain, 343
Fundación General Ecuatoriana, Ecuador, 125
Fundación Hogar del Empleado—FUHEM, Spain, 343
Fundación Instituto de Empresa, Spain, 344
Fundación de Investigaciones Económicas Latinoamericanas—FIEL, Argentina, 32
Fundación Jiménez Díaz, Spain, 344
Fundación Laboral Sonsoles Ballvé Lantero, Spain, 344
Fundación MAPFRE, Spain, 345
Fundación Marcelino Botín, Spain, 341
Fundación María Francisca de Roviralta, Spain, 347
Fundación Mediterránea—IERAL, Argentina, 32
Fundación Miguel Alemán AC, Mexico, 262
Fundación Mujeres, Spain, 33
Fundación Mujeres en Igualdad, Argentina, 33
Fundación Nacional para el Desarrollo de Honduras—FUNADEH, Honduras, 193
Fundación Nantik Lum, Spain, 345
Fundación Natura, Ecuador, 126
Fundación Pablo Neruda, Chile, 100
Fundación Paideia Galiza, Spain, 346
Fundación Paz y Solidaridad Serafín Aliaga—FPyS, Spain, 346
Fundación Pedro Barrié de la Maza, Spain, 340
Fundación Rafael del Pino, Spain, 347
Fundación La Salle de Ciencias Naturales—FLASA, Venezuela, 564
Fundación Santa María, Spain, 348
Fundación Santillana, Spain, 348
Fundación Schcolnik, Argentina, 33

Fundación SES—Sustentabilidad, Educación, Solidaridad, Argentina, 33
Fundación de Viviendas Hogar de Cristo, Chile, 100
Fundacja Agory, Poland, 306
Fundacja Gospodarcza, Poland, 307
Fundacja im. Stefana Batorego, Poland, 307
Fundacja Pogranicze, Poland, 307
Fundacja Pro Bono II, Poland, 308
Fundacja Solidarności Polsko-Czesko-Słowackiej, Poland, 308
Fundacja Współpracy Polsko-Niemieckiej/ Stiftung für Deutsch–Polnische Zusammenarbeit, Poland, 308
Fundacja Wspomagania Wsi, Poland, 308
Fundatia Dinu Patriciu, Romania, 317
FUNDESO—Fundación Desarrollo Sostenido, Spain, 348
Fundhas—Fundação Hélio Augusto de Souza, Brazil, 73
FWF—Fonds zur Förderung der Wissenschaftlichen Forschung, Austria, 47
Gannett Foundation, USA, 493
Garfield Weston Foundation, UK, 455
The Gatsby Charitable Foundation, UK, 418
Gebert Rüf Stiftung, Switzerland, 366
Gemeinnützige Hertie Foundation, Germany, 169
Gemeinnützige Hertie-Stiftung, Germany, 169
General Ecuadorean Foundation, Ecuador, 125
General Service Foundation, USA, 495
George Cedric Metcalf Charitable Foundation, Canada, 94
The George I. Alden Trust, USA, 463
George and Thelma Paraskevaides Foundation, Cyprus, 111
Georges Lurcy Charitable and Educational Trust, USA, 519
German Cancer Assistance, Germany, 165
German Foundation for World Population, Germany, 165
German Institute for International Educational Research, Germany, 166
German Marshall Fund of the United States—GMF, USA, 496
Gift of the Givers Foundation, South Africa, 332
Giorgio Cini Foundation, Italy, 220
Giovanni Agnelli Foundation, Italy, 218
Giovanni Lorenzini Foundation, Italy, 222
Giving USA Foundation, USA, 496
GLARP—Grupo Latinoamericano de Rehabilitación Profesional, Colombia, 105
Global Ethic Foundation Czech Republic, Czech Republic, 114
Global Harmony Foundation—GHF, Switzerland, 367
Global Voluntary Service—GVS, Japan, 232
GMF—German Marshall Fund of the United States, USA, 496
Gobabeb Training and Research Centre, Namibia, 270
Goldsmith (Horace W.) Foundation, USA, 498
Good Neighbors International, Korea (Republic), 246
Gordon (Walter and Duncan) Charitable Foundation, Canada, 89
Gould (Florence) Foundation, USA, 499
Gradjanske inicijative—GI, Serbia, 324
Graduate Institute of International Studies and Development Studies, Switzerland, 367
Grameen Foundation—GF, USA, 499
The Grass Foundation, USA, 499
Great Britain Sasakawa Foundation, UK, 419
Greve (William and Mary) Foundation, Inc, USA, 500
Grupo Latinoamericano para la Participación, la Integración y la Inclusión de Personas con Discapacidad—GLARP-IIPD, Colombia, 105
Guggenheim (John Simon) Memorial Foundation, USA, 500
Gulf Research Center, United Arab Emirates, 395
Gulf Research Center Foundation, Switzerland, 367
Hamdard Foundation Pakistan, Pakistan, 294
Hamlyn (Paul) Foundation, UK, 419
Haniel Foundation, Germany, 169
Haniel-Stiftung, Germany, 169
Harold Hyam Wingate Foundation, UK, 456
Health Volunteers Overseas—HVO, USA, 501
Hearst (William Randolph) Foundation, USA, 502
The Hearst Foundation, Inc, USA, 501
Hedwig and Robert Samuel Foundation, Germany, 177
Hedwig und Robert Samuel-Stiftung, Germany, 177
Heinz (Howard) Endowment, USA, 502
HEKS—Hilfswerk Evangelischen Kirchen Schweiz, Switzerland, 367
The Helen Suzman Foundation, South Africa, 335

Hélio Augusto de Souza Foundation, Brazil, 73
Hellenic Foundation for Culture, Greece, 186
Hellenic Foundation for European and Foreign
    Policy—ELIAMEP, Greece, 187
Hellenic Society for Disabled Children,
    Greece, 187
HELP International, USA, 503
Henrietta Szold Institute—National Institute for
    Research in the Behavioural Sciences,
    Israel, 215
Henry Luce Foundation, Inc, USA, 519
HER Fund, Hong Kong, 194
Hestia—The National Volunteer Centre, Czech
    Republic, 114
Hewlett (William and Flora) Foundation,
    USA, 503
Heydar Aliyev Foundation, Azerbaijan, 50
Hilden Charitable Fund, UK, 421
Hilfswerk der Evangelischen Kirchen Schweiz—
    HEKS, Switzerland, 367
Himalayan Light Foundation—HLF, Nepal, 271
Hirsch (Baron de) Fund, USA, 484
Hisar Education Foundation—HEV, Turkey, 388
Hitachi Foundation, USA, 504
The Hitachi Scholarship Foundation, Japan, 232
HIVOS—Humanistisch Instituut voor
    Ontwikkelings Samenwerking,
    Netherlands, 275
HLF—Himalayan Light Foundation, Nepal, 271
Hogar de Cristo, Chile, 100
Home of Christ, Chile, 100
Hopp (Dietmar) Stiftung, Germany, 170
Horace W. Goldsmith Foundation, USA, 498
Horizonti, the Foundation for the Third Sector,
    Georgia, 157
Houston Endowment, Inc, USA, 504
Howard Heinz Endowment, USA, 502
Hugot Foundation of the Collège of France,
    France, 145
Human Resource Development Foundation,
    Turkey, 389
The Humana Foundation, Inc, USA, 505
Humanistic Institute for Co-operation with
    Developing Countries, Netherlands, 275
Humanistisch Instituut voor Ontwikkelings
    Samenwerking—HIVOS, Netherlands, 275
Humanitarian Relief Foundation, Turkey, 389
IACD—Institute of Asian Culture and
    Development, Korea (Republic), 246
Ian Potter Foundation, Australia, 43
IAPA Scholarship Fund, USA, 505
IBON Foundation, Philippines, 303
ICN Foundation, Czech Republic, 112
ICN—Information Centre for Non-profit
    Organizations, Czech Republic, 112
ICSSR—Indian Council of Social Science
    Research, India, 202
IEIAS—Institut Européen Interuniversitaire de
    l'Action Sociale, Belgium, 62
IEMed—Institut Europeu de la Mediterrània,
    Spain, 349
IERAL—Fundación Mediterránea,
    Argentina, 33
IFHD—International Foundation for Human
    Development, India, 203
IHCF—Stiftung zur Förderung der Gesundheit,
    Liechtenstein, 255
IKEA Foundation, Netherlands, 275
IKGV—İnsan Kaynağını Geliştirme Vakfı,
    Turkey, 389
Imperial Oil Foundation, Canada, 90
India Assistance, Germany, 171
Indian Council for Child Welfare, India, 202
Indian Council of Social Science Research—
    ICSSR, India, 202
Indienhilfe eV, Germany, 171
Indonesia Biodiversity Foundation,
    Indonesia, 208
Indonesian Prosperity Foundation,
    Indonesia, 208
Information Centre for Foundations and other
    Non-profit Organizations—ICN, Czech
    Republic, 112
Ing. Carlo M. Lerici Foundation, Italy, 222
Inlaks Foundation, India, 203
INMED Partnerships for Children, USA, 506
Innes (John) Foundation, UK, 422
İnsan Hak ve Hürriyetleri İnsani Yardım Vakfı,
    Turkey, 389
İnsan Kaynağını Geliştirme Vakfı—IKGV,
    Turkey, 389
Institut Arctique de l'Amérique du Nord—IAAN,
    Canada, 81
Institut Català Mediterrània, Spain, 349
Institut Européen Interuniversitaire de l'Action
    Sociale—IEIAS, Belgium, 62
Institut Europeu de la Mediterrània—IEMed,
    Spain, 349

Institut Universitaire de Hautes Etudes
    Internationales et du Développement,
    Switzerland, 367
Institut urbain du Canada, Canada, 85
Institute of Asian Culture and Development—
    IACD, Korea (Republic), 246
Institute for Development Research, USA, 556
Instituto Ayrton Senna, Brazil, 73
Instituto Europeo de Salud y Bienestar Social,
    Spain, 349
Instituto Interamericano de Derechos
    Humanos—IIHR, Costa Rica, 107
Instituto Senna (Ayrton), Brazil, 73
Instituto Torcuato di Tella, Argentina, 34
Institutul Cultural Român, Romania, 317
Inter-American Foundation—IAF, USA, 507
Inter-American Institute of Human Rights, Costa
    Rica, 107
Inter American Press Association Scholarship
    Fund, USA, 505
International Blue Crescent Relief and
    Development Foundation—IBC, Turkey, 390
International Charitable Fund of Bermuda—
    ICFB, Bermuda, 66
International Co-operation, Italy, 217
International Confederation of Family Support,
    Argentina, 31
International Development and Relief
    Foundation, Canada, 91
The International Foundation, USA, 508
International Foundation for Education and Self-
    Help—IFESH, USA, 509
International Foundation for Human
    Development—IFHD, India, 203
International Institute of Rural
    Reconstruction—IIRR, Philippines, 303
International Medical Services for Health—
    INMED, USA, 506
International Orthodox Christian Charities,
    Inc—IOCC, USA, 509
International Refugee Trust—IRT, UK, 424
International Renaissance Foundation—IRF,
    Ukraine, 394
International Research & Exchanges Board—
    IREX, USA, 511
International University Centre of Paris,
    France, 139
International Visegrad Fund—IVF, Slovakia, 328
Investigaciones Económicas Latinoamericanas,
    Fundación, Argentina, 32
IREX—International Research & Exchanges
    Board, USA, 511
Irish Association of Non-Governmental
    Development Organizations—DOCHAS,
    Ireland, 210
Irvine (James) Foundation, USA, 511
ISAR: Resources for Environmental Activists,
    USA, 460
Ishizaka Foundation, Japan, 234
Islamic Thought Foundation, Iran, 209
ISREC Foundation, Switzerland, 364
Istituto Svedese di Studi Classici, Italy, 228
IUC-Europe International Education Centre,
    Denmark, 119
IUC-Europe Internationalt Uddanneless Center,
    Denmark, 119
The J. F. Costopoulos Foundation, Greece, 186
The J. F. Kapnek Trust Zimbabwe, Zimbabwe, 567
J&S Pro Bono Poloniae Foundation, Poland, 309
Jack Brockhoff Foundation—JBF, Australia, 39
Jahnsson (Yrjö) Foundation, Finland, 131
The James Irvine Foundation, USA, 511
Jan Hus Educational Foundation, Slovakia, 329
The Japan Foundation Centre for Global
    Partnership—CGP, Japan, 236
Japan Foundation Endowment Committee—
    JFEC, UK, 425
Japan International Volunteer Center—JVC,
    Japan, 236
Japanese-German Center Berlin, Germany, 173
Japanisch-Deutsches Zentrum Berlin,
    Germany, 173
Jaume Bofill Foundation, Spain, 338
JCA Charitable Foundation, UK, 425
JCIE—Japan Center for International Exchange,
    Japan, 236
Jean-Louis Lévesque Foundation, Canada, 88
JEN, Japan, 237
Jenny and Antti Wihuri Foundation, Finland, 134
Jenny ja Antti Wihurin Rahasto, Finland, 134
Jerusalem Foundation, Israel, 214
Jewish Agency for Israel Allocations Program,
    Israel, 214
Jewish Colonization Association, UK, 425
Jewish Community Development Fund—JCDF,
    USA, 512
Jewish Philanthropic Association, UK, 452

JFEC—Japan Foundation Endowment
    Committee, UK, 425
Jiménez Díaz Foundation, Spain, 344
Johanna-Quandt-Stiftung, Germany, 177
The John D. and Catherine T. MacArthur
    Foundation, USA, 520
John Innes Foundation—JIF, UK, 422
John Simon Guggenheim Memorial Foundation,
    USA, 500
John Swire 1989 Charitable Trust, UK, 450
The John W. Carson Foundation, USA, 476
Johnson (Lyndon Baines) Foundation, USA, 512
JOHUD—Jordanian Hashemite Fund for Human
    Development, Jordan, 241
Jordanian Hashemite Fund for Human
    Development, Jordan, 241
Joseph Rowntree Charitable Trust, UK, 441
Joyce Foundation, USA, 512
JPMorgan Educational Trust, UK, 426
JPMorgan Fleming Foundation, UK, 426
JPMorgan Foundation, UK, 426
Kade (Max) Foundation, Inc, USA, 513
Kahanoff Foundation, Canada, 91
Kapnek (J. F.) Charitable Trust Zimbabwe,
    Zimbabwe, 567
Karić fondacija, Serbia, 325
Karić Foundation, Serbia, 325
Karl Kübel Foundation for Child and Family,
    Germany, 174
Karl-Kübel-Stiftung für Kind und Familie,
    Germany, 174
Karuna Trust/ Aid for India, UK, 426
KAUTE—Foundation for Commercial and
    Technical Sciences, Finland, 131
KCDF—Kenya Community Development
    Foundation, Kenya, 245
KEHATI—Yayasan Keanekaragaman Hayati
    Indonesia, Indonesia, 208
Keidanren Ishizaka Memorial Foundation,
    Japan, 234
Kennan Institute, USA, 514
Kennedy Memorial Trust, UK, 426
Kettering Foundation, USA, 515
Khemka (Nand and Jeet) Foundation, India, 203
Kinder in Afrika, Stiftung, Germany, 181
King Hussein Foundation—KHF, Jordan, 241
The King's Fund, UK, 427
Kirk (Norman) Memorial Trust, New
    Zealand, 284
KK-stiftelsen, Sweden, 354
Knowledge Foundation, Sweden, 354
Knox (Frank) Memorial Fellowships, UK, 427
Knut and Alice Wallenberg Foundation,
    Sweden, 358
Knut och Alice Wallenbergs Stiftelse,
    Sweden, 358
Koç (Vehbi), Vakfı, Turkey, 391
Kokkalis Foundation, Greece, 187
Koret Foundation, USA, 515
The Kosciuszko Foundation, Inc, USA, 516
Kosovo Foundation for Open Society—KFOS,
    Kosovo, 248
KRS Education and Rural Development
    Foundation, Inc, USA, 516
Kübel (Karl) Stiftung für Kind und Familie,
    Germany, 174
Kulika Charitable Trust (Uganda), Uganda, 392
The Kulika Charitable Trust 1981, Uganda, 392
'La Caixa' Foundation, Spain, 338
La Salle Foundation for Natural Sciences,
    Venezuela, 564
Lady Davis Fellowship Trust, Israel, 214
Lama Gangchen World Peace Foundation,
    Italy, 227
Lambrakis Foundation, Greece, 187
Lambrakis Research Foundation, Greece, 187
Lannan Foundation, USA, 517
Latin American Group for the Participation,
    Integration and Inclusion of People with
    Disability, Colombia, 105
Latvia Children's Fund, Latvia, 251
Latvijas Bērnu fonds, Latvia, 251
Lauder (Ronald S.) Foundation, Germany, 174
LBJ Foundation, USA, 512
Van Leer Jerusalem Institute, Israel, 215
Léopold Sédar Senghor Foundation, Senegal, 322
Leprosy Mission International, UK, 428
Lerici (Ing. Carlo M.), Fondazione presso il
    Politecnico di Milano, Italy, 222
Leventis (A. G.) Foundation, Cyprus, 111
Leventis (A. G.) Foundation Nigeria, Nigeria, 290
Leverhulme Trust, UK, 429
Levesque (Jean-Louis), Fondation, Canada, 88
Lifewater International—LI, USA, 518
Lila Wallace—Reader's Digest Fund, Inc,
    USA, 551
Lilly Endowment, Inc, USA, 518
The Long Now Foundation—LNF, USA, 519

Lorenzini (Giovanni), Fondazione, Italy, 222
Luce (Henry) Foundation, Inc, USA, 519
Lucie and André Chagnon Foundation/
 Fondation Lucie et André Chagnon,
 Canada, 85
Lurcy (Georges) Charitable and Educational
 Trust, USA, 519
Luso-American Development Foundation,
 Portugal, 312
LWR—Lutheran World Relief, USA, 519
Lynde and Harry Bradley Foundation, Inc,
 USA, 473
Lyndon Baines Johnson Foundation, USA, 512
M-USA—Mercy-USA for Aid and Development,
 USA, 524
M. Venkatarangaiya Foundation, India, 206
MacArthur (John D. and Catherine T.)
 Foundation, USA, 520
McCormick (Robert R.) Foundation, USA, 520
Macdonald Stewart Foundation, Canada, 92
The Mackintosh Foundation, UK, 430
The McLean Foundation, Canada, 93
Macmillan Cancer Relief, UK, 430
MADRE, USA, 521
Maecenata Management GmbH, Germany, 159
Mailman (A. L.) Family Foundation, USA, 521
Maison Franco-Japonaise, Japan, 237
Maltese Heritage Foundation, Malta, 261
Mama Cash, Netherlands, 277
Mandela (Nelson) Foundation, South Africa, 333
The Mandela Rhodes Foundation, South
 Africa, 333
Manfred Woerner Foundation, Bulgaria, 74
Manzanedo (Ana Mata), Fundación, Spain, 345
MAPFRE Foundation, Spain, 345
Marcel Bleustein-Blanchet Vocation Foundation,
 France, 141
Marcelino Botín Foundation, Spain, 341
María Francisca de Roviralta Foundation,
 Spain, 347
Marinho (Roberto), Fundação, Brazil, 72
Mário Soares Foundation, Portugal, 313
Match International Centre, Canada, 93
Mateus House Foundation, Portugal, 310
Matsushita Foundation, Japan, 532
Max Kade Foundation, Inc, USA, 513
Mayfair Charities Ltd, UK, 430
Mediterranean Foundation, Argentina, 33
Mediterranean Foundation of Strategic Studies,
 France, 147
Mellon (Andrew W.) Foundation, USA, 523
Mellon (Richard King) Foundation, USA, 523
MENCAP, UK, 431
Mendoza (Eugenio) Fundación, Venezuela, 563
Menzies (R. G.) Scholarship Fund, Australia, 42
Menzies (Sir Robert) Foundation Ltd,
 Australia, 41
Mercers' Charitable Foundation, UK, 431
Mercy-USA for Aid and Development—M-USA,
 USA, 524
Metcalf (George Cedric) Charitable Foundation,
 Canada, 94
Michael Otto Foundation for Environmental
 Protection, Germany, 176
Michael-Otto-Stiftung für Umweltschutz,
 Germany, 176
Miguel Alemán Foundation, Mexico, 262
Milan Simecka Foundation, Slovakia, 329
Milieukontakt International, Netherlands, 277
Milieukontakt Oost-Europa, Netherlands, 277
Mindolo Ecumenical Foundation—MEF,
 Zambia, 566
Miriam Dean Fund, UK, 413
Miriam Dean Refugee Trust Fund, UK, 413
Miriam G. and Ira D. Wallach Foundation,
 USA, 552
Mo Ibrahim Foundation, UK, 421
Moawad (René) Foundation, Lebanon, 253
Møller (A.P.) and Chastine Mc-Kinney Møller
 Foundation, Denmark, 120
Molson Donations Fund/Fonds de bienfaisance
 Molson, Canada, 94
Molson Family Foundation, Canada, 94
Molson Foundation, Canada, 94
Mongolian Women's Fund—MONES,
 Mongolia, 266
Mønsteds (Otto) Fond, Denmark, 120
Moody Foundation, USA, 525
Moriya Foundation, Japan, 238
Morrow (The F. K.) Foundation, Canada, 94
Mostazafan Foundation of New York, USA, 462
Mother Child Education Foundation, Turkey, 388
Mott (Charles Stewart) Foundation, USA, 526
Muslim Aid, UK, 433
The Muttart Foundation, Canada, 94
Myer (Sidney) Fund, Australia, 42
The Myer Foundation, Australia, 42

Naandi Foundation—A New Beginning,
 India, 203
Nadace Auxilia, Czech Republic, 112
Nadace Charty 77, Czech Republic, 114
Nadace ICN, Czech Republic, 112
Nadácia Milana Šimečku, Slovakia, 329
Nadácia Pontis, Slovakia, 327
Nadácia pre deti Slovenska, Slovakia, 328
Nand and Jeet Khemka Foundation, India, 203
Nantik Lum Foundation, Spain, 345
Nathan Steinberg Family Foundation, Canada, 98
National Endowment for Science, Technology and
 the Arts—NESTA, UK, 434
National Foundation for the Development of
 Honduras, Honduras, 193
National Foundation for Political Sciences,
 France, 148
National Humanities Center, USA, 527
National Institute for Research in the
 Behavioural Sciences—Szold (Henrietta)
 Institute, Israel, 215
National Institute for Sustainable
 Development—NISD, India, 204
National Science Foundation, USA, 527
National Volunteer Centre—Hestia, Czech
 Republic, 114
National Youth Foundation, Greece, 188
Nature Foundation, Ecuador, 126
Nelson Mandela Children's Fund—Canada,
 Canada, 93
Nelson Mandela Foundation, South Africa, 333
Neruda (Pablo), Fundación, Chile, 100
NESsT—Nonprofit Enterprise and Self-
 sustainability Team, Chile, 101
NESTA—National Endowment for Science,
 Technology and the Arts, UK, 434
Network of Estonian Non-profit Organizations,
 Estonia, 129
Network of Information and Support for Non-
 Governmental Organizations, Poland, 306
New Eurasia Foundation, Russian
 Federation, 319
New Perspectives Foundation, Russian
 Federation, 319
New Zealand Winston Churchill Memorial Trust,
 New Zealand, 285
NGO Rural and Social Initiative, Moldova, 264
NIOK—Nonprofit Információs és Oktató
 Központ Alapítvány, Hungary, 195
Nirnaya, India, 204
Non-Governmental Organization JEN,
 Japan, 237
Non-Profit Information and Training Centre
 Foundation, Hungary, 195
Nonprofit Enterprise and Self-sustainability
 Team—NESsT, Chile, 101
Nonprofit Információs és Oktató Központ
 Alapítvány—NIOK, Hungary, 195
Nordic Africa Institute Scholarships,
 Sweden, 355
Nordiska Afrikainstitutets Stipendier,
 Sweden, 355
Norman Kirk Memorial Trust, New Zealand, 284
Norsk Utenrikspolitisk Institutt—NUPI,
 Norway, 292
Northern Ireland Voluntary Trust, UK, 412
Norwegian Institute of International Affairs—
 NUPI, Norway, 292
NRF—National Research Foundation, South
 Africa, 333
Nuffield Foundation, UK, 435
Oak Foundation, Switzerland, 371
Open Estonia Foundation, Estonia, 129
Open Society Forum (Mongolia), Mongolia, 266
Open Society Foundation, Romania, 317
Open Society Foundation for Albania—OSFA,
 Albania, 29
Open Society Foundation—Bratislava,
 Slovakia, 328
Open Society Fund—Bosnia-Herzegovina,
 Bosnia and Herzegovina, 68
Open Society Fund Prague—OSF Prague, Czech
 Republic, 115
Open Society Georgia Foundation, Georgia, 157
Open Society Initiative for Southern Africa—
 OSISA, South Africa, 334
Open Society Institute—Assistance Foundation
 (Azerbaijan), Azerbaijan, 50
Open Society Institute Assistance Foundation,
 Armenia—OSIAFA, Armenia, 35
Open Society Institute Assistance Foundation—
 Tajikistan, Tajikistan, 381
Open Society Institute Montenegro,
 Montenegro, 267
Open Society Institute—Paris (Soros
 Foundations), France, 135
Open Society Institute—Sofia (Bulgaria),
 Bulgaria, 76

Open Society Institute—Turkey, Turkey, 387
Operation Beaver—Frontiers Foundation Inc,
 Canada, 89
Orient Foundation, Portugal, 312
The Orient-Occident Foundation, Morocco, 268
Ortega (Amancio) Fundación, Spain, 346
OSGF—Open Society Georgia Foundation,
 Georgia, 157
OSIAF—Open Society Institute Assistance
 Foundation—Tajikistan, Tajikistan, 381
Österreichische Forschungsstiftung für
 Internationale Entwicklung—ÖFSE,
 Austria, 48
Otto (Michael) Stiftung, Germany, 176
Otto Benecke Foundation, Germany, 161
Otto-Benecke-Stiftung eV, Germany, 161
Otto Mønsteds Fond, Denmark, 120
Otto Mønsteds Foundation, Denmark, 120
Oxfam Australia, Australia, 43
Oxfam-Québec, Canada, 95
OzChild, Australia, 43
PAALAE—Pan African Association for Literacy
 and Adult Education, Senegal, 323
Pablo Neruda Foundation, Chile, 100
Pacific Peoples' Partnership, Canada, 95
Packard (David and Lucile) Foundation, USA, 531
Paideia Galiza Foundation, Spain, 346
Pan-African Centre for Social Prospects,
 Benin, 65
Panasonic Foundation, USA, 532
Paraskevaides (George and Thelma) Foundation,
 Cyprus, 111
Patiño (Simón I.), Fondation, Switzerland, 365
The Paul G. Allen Family Foundation, USA, 463
Paul Hamlyn Foundation—PHF, UK, 419
Paul-Henri Spaak Foundation, Belgium, 61
Peace and Disarmament Education Trust—
 PADET, New Zealand, 286
Pearl S. Buck International, USA, 474
Pedro Barrié de la Maza Foundation, Spain, 340
PEF Israel Endowment Funds, Inc, Israel, 215
People in Need, Czech Republic, 113
People's Harmonious Development Society,
 Georgia, 158
Perpetual Foundation, Australia, 43
Perpetual Trustees Australia, Australia, 43
Pestalozzi Children's Foundation,
 Switzerland, 374
The Pew Charitable Trusts, USA, 534
Pforzheimer (Carl and Lily) Foundation, Inc,
 USA, 535
PHF—Paul Hamlyn Foundation, UK, 419
PhilDev—Philippine Development Foundation,
 USA, 535
Philippine-American Educational Foundation—
 PAEF, Philippines, 303
Philippine Development Foundation—PhilDev,
 USA, 535
Pinchuk (Victor) Foundation, Ukraine, 394
Pitseng Trust, South Africa, 334
Plan International, Ireland, 212
Plenty International, USA, 535
Plunkett Foundation, UK, 438
Polar Companies Foundation, Venezuela, 563
Pôle européen des fondations de l'économie
 sociale, Belgium, 56
Polish-American Freedom Foundation,
 Poland, 305
Polish-Czech-Slovak Solidarity Foundation,
 Poland, 308
POLSAT Foundation, Poland, 309
Polsko-Amerykańska Fundacja Wolności,
 Poland, 305
Poniecki (Wladyslaw) Foundation, Inc, USA, 536
Pontis Foundation, Slovakia, 327
The Porter Foundation, UK, 439
Potanin (Vladimir) Foundation, Russian
 Federation, 320
Potter (Ian) Foundation, Australia, 43
Preciosa Foundation, Czech Republic, 115
Premji (Azim) Foundation, India, 204
Press Foundation of Asia—PFA, Philippines, 303
Prince Bernhard Cultural Foundation,
 Netherlands, 282
Prins Bernhard Cultuurfonds, Stichting,
 Netherlands, 282
Pro Bono Foundation, Poland, 308
Pro Juventute, Switzerland, 372
Pro Victimis Foundation, Switzerland, 365
PRODESSA—Proyecto de Desarrollo Santiago,
 Guatemala, 191
Professor Otto Beisheim Foundation,
 Germany, 161
Professor Otto Beisheim Stiftung, Germany, 161
Project Trust, UK, 439
Protestant Study Foundation, Germany, 167
Prudential Foundation, USA, 537

Puerto Rico Community Foundation, Puerto Rico, 314
Qatar Foundation, Qatar, 315
Qattan (A. M.) Foundation, UK, 440
Quaid-i-Azam Academy, Pakistan, 294
Queen Alia Fund for Social Development, Jordan, 241
Queen's Trust for Young Australians, Australia, 41
R. E. Ross Trust, Australia, 44
R. G. Menzies Scholarship Fund, Australia, 42
R. Howard Webster Foundation, Canada, 99
Rafael del Pino Foundation, Spain, 347
Rafik Hariri Foundation, Lebanon, 252
Rajiv Gandhi Foundation, India, 201
Ramaciotti (Clive and Vera) Foundation, Australia, 43
Ramaswami Aiyar (C. P.) Foundation, India, 204
Ramsay Foundation, Switzerland, 372
The Rank Foundation, UK, 440
Rayne Foundation, UK, 441
RBC Foundation, Canada, 96
Refugees International Japan—RIJ, Japan, 239
Relief International, USA, 539
Renault Foundation, France, 144
René Moawad Foundation, Lebanon, 253
René Seydoux Foundation for the Mediterranean World, France, 150
Research Corporation for Science Advancement—RCSA, USA, 539
Research Foundation—Flanders, Belgium, 62
Réseau Africain de la Jeunesse pour le Développement Durable, Algeria, 30
Rhodes Trust, UK, 441
RIA—Royal Irish Academy, Ireland, 212
Ricardo do Espírito Santo Silva Foundation, Portugal, 311
Della Riccia (Angelo), Fondazione, Italy, 221
Richard King Mellon Foundation, USA, 523
Richelieu International, Canada, 96
Robert A. Welch Foundation, USA, 553
Robert Marinho Foundation, Brazil, 72
Robert R. McCormick Foundation, USA, 520
Robertson Foundation for Government—RFFG, USA, 540
Rockefeller Brothers Fund, USA, 540
Roma Lom Foundation, Bulgaria, 76
Romanian Cultural Foundation, Romania, 317
Romanian Cultural Institute, Romania, 317
Rome Foundation, Italy, 224
Romi Foundation, Brazil, 72
The Ronald S. Lauder Foundation, Germany, 174
Rooftops Canada Foundation, Canada, 97
Ross (R. E.) Trust, Australia, 44
Rössing Foundation, Namibia, 270
Rothschild (Edmond de) Foundations, USA, 541
Roviralta (María Francisca de), Fundación, Spain, 347
Rowan Charitable Trust, UK, 441
Rowntree (Joseph) Charitable Trust, UK, 441
Royal Air Force Benevolent Fund, UK, 442
Royal Bank of Canada Charitable Foundation, Canada, 96
Royal Bank Financial Group Foundation, Canada, 96
Royal Commonwealth Society for the Blind—Sight Savers International, UK, 448
Royal Society for Mentally Handicapped Children and Adults—MENCAP, UK, 431
Rroma Foundation, Switzerland, 372
Rubinstein (Arthur) International Music Society, Israel, 215
RUI Foundation, Italy, 225
Rural Development Foundation, Poland, 308
SAASTA—South African Agency for Science and Technology Advancement, South Africa, 334
Sabancı (Hacı Ömer) Foundation, Turkey, 389
Sabancı Foundation, Turkey, 389
Sabancı Vakfı—Hacı Ömer Sabancı Foundation, Turkey, 389
Sabera Foundation, India, 205
Sabera Foundation India, India, 205
Sabre Foundation, Inc, USA, 542
Sahabdeen (A. M. M.) Trust Foundation, Sri Lanka, 350
SAIA—Slovak Academic Information Agency, Slovakia, 327
Said Foundation, UK, 446
Saint Cyril and Saint Methodius International Foundation, Bulgaria, 76
Salvador Dalí Foundation, Spain, 343
Samuel (Hedwig und Robert) Stiftung, Germany, 177
Samuel and Saidye Bronfman Family Foundation, Canada, 82
Samuel Sebba Charitable Trust, UK, 447
San Diego Foundation, USA, 542
San Francisco Foundation, USA, 542

Sandino (Augusto César), Fundación, Nicaragua, 288
Santa María Foundation, Spain, 348
Santiago Development Project, Guatemala, 191
Santillana Foundation, Spain, 348
Sasakawa, Fondation Franco-Japonaise, France, 145
Save & Prosper Foundation, UK, 426
Savings Banks Foundation for International Cooperation, Germany, 179
Schcolnik Foundation, Argentina, 33
Schools Without Frontiers, France, 139
Schusterman (Charles and Lynn) Family Foundation, USA, 543
Schwarzkopf Foundation Young Europe, Germany, 178
Schwarzkopf Stiftung Junges Europa, Germany, 178
Schweisfurth Foundation, Germany, 178
Schweisfurth-Stiftung, Germany, 178
Schweizerischer Nationalfonds zur Förderung der wissenschaftlichen Forschung/Fonds National Suisse de la Recherche Scientifique—SNF, Switzerland, 374
Scientific Foundation of Hisham Adeeb Hijjawi, Jordan, 241
Scientific Foundation of the Spanish Cancer Association, Spain, 342
Scouloudi Foundation, UK, 447
Seeds of Peace, USA, 543
SEEMO—IPI—South East Europe Media Organisation, Austria, 49
Selby (William G. and Marie) Foundation, USA, 543
Sem Pringpuangkeo Foundation, Thailand, 384
Semmelweis Alapítvány Magyarországi Ortopédia Fejlesztéséért, Hungary, 195
Semmelweis Foundation for the Development of Orthopaedics in Hungary, Hungary, 195
Seoam Scholarship Foundation, Korea (Republic), 247
Serafín Aliaga Foundation for Peace and Solidarity, Spain, 346
Serralves Foundation, Portugal, 312
SES Foundation—Sustainability, Education, Solidarity, Argentina, 33
Seva Foundation, USA, 544
Seydoux (René), Fondation pour le Monde Méditerranéen, France, 150
Shackleton Foundation, UK, 448
Shastri Indo-Canadian Institute, Canada, 97
Sherman (Archie) Charitable Trust, UK, 448
Siam Society, Thailand, 384
Sidney Myer Fund, Australia, 42
Sieć SPLOT, Poland, 306
Sieć Wspierania Organizacji Pozarządowych—SPLOT, Poland, 306
Sight Savers International, UK, 448
Sihtasutus Eesti Rahvuskultuuri Fond, Estonia, 129
Silva (Ricardo do Espírito Santo), Fundação, Portugal, 311
Simón I. Patiño Foundation, Switzerland, 365
Sino-British Fellowship Trust—SBFT, UK, 448
Sir Ahmadu Bello Foundation, Nigeria, 289
Sir Ahmadu Bello Memorial Foundation, Nigeria, 289
Sir Dorabji Tata Trust, India, 205
The Sir Robert Menzies Memorial Foundation Ltd, Australia, 41
Skoll Foundation, USA, 544
Sloan (Alfred P.) Foundation, USA, 545
Slovak Academic Information Agency–Service Center for the Third Sector—SAIA-SCTS, Slovakia, 327
Slovak-Czech Women's Fund, Czech Republic, 115
Slovak Humanitarian Council, Slovakia, 328
Slovenian Science Foundation, Slovenia, 330
Slovenská Humanitná Rada, Slovakia, 328
Smithsonian Institution, USA, 545
Soares (Mário), Fundação, Portugal, 313
Software AG Foundation, Germany, 178
Solidarios—Consejo de Fundaciones Americanas de Desarrollo, Dominican Republic, 123
Solidarity National Commission—Economic Foundation, Poland, 307
Solidarność NSZZ—Economic Foundation, Poland, 307
Song Qingling Foundation, China (People's Republic), 102
Sonsoles Ballvé Lantero Labour Foundation, Spain, 344
Sophie and Karl Binding Foundation, Switzerland, 361
Sophie und Karl Binding-Stiftung, Switzerland, 361
Sorenson Legacy Foundation, USA, 545

Soros Foundation (Czech Republic), Czech Republic, 115
Soros Foundation (Estonia), Estonia, 129
Soros Foundation (Georgia), Georgia, 157
Soros Foundation (Slovakia), Slovakia, 328
Soros Foundation (Tajikistan), Tajikistan, 381
Soros Foundation–Kyrgyzstan, Kyrgyzstan, 250
Soros Foundation Latvia, Latvia, 251
Soros Foundation Macedonia, Macedonia, 258
Soros Foundation Romania, Romania, 317
Soros Serbia Foundation, Serbia, 324
South African Agency for Science and Technology Advancement—SAASTA, South Africa, 334
South African Institute of Race Relations, South Africa, 335
South East Europe Media Organisation, Austria, 49
South East Europe Media Organisation—SEEMO—IPI, Austria, 49
South Pacific Peoples Foundation Canada, Canada, 95
Spaak (Paul-Henri), Fondation, Belgium, 61
Spanish Association of Foundations, Spain, 337
Sparkassenstiftung für internationale Kooperation eV, Germany, 179
Springer (Axel) Stiftung, Germany, 179
The Starr Foundation, USA, 546
Stefan Batory Foundation, Poland, 307
Steinberg (Nathan) Family Foundation, Canada, 98
Stichting Prins Bernhard Cultuurfonds, Netherlands, 282
Stichting Reinwater, Netherlands, 282
Stichting Spaak (Paul-Henri), Belgium, 61
Stichting Triodos Foundation, Netherlands, 282
Stiftelsen Blanceflor Boncompagni-Ludovisi, född Bildt, Sweden, 356
Stiftelsen Riksbankens Jubileumsfond, Sweden, 357
Stiftelsen Teknikens Främjande—Tekniikan Edistämissäätiö, Finland, 133
Stifterverband für die Deutsche Wissenschaft eV, Germany, 159
Stiftung CAESAR, Germany, 179
Stiftung zur Förderung der Hochschulrektorenkonferenz, Germany, 180
Stiftung FVS, Germany, 183
Stiftung Jugend forscht e. V., Germany, 180
Stiftung für Kinder, Germany, 181
Stiftung Kinder in Afrika, Germany, 181
Stiftung Kinderdorf Pestalozzi, Switzerland, 374
Stiftung 'Leben für Alle', Switzerland, 375
Stiftung Lesen, Germany, 181
Stiftung Vivamos Mejor, Switzerland, 375
Stiftung West-Östliche Begegnungen, Germany, 182
Stiftungsfonds Deutsche Bank zur Förderung der Wissenschaft in Forschung und Lehre, Germany, 182
Street Kids International, Canada, 98
Sultan bin Abdulaziz al-Saud Foundation, Saudi Arabia, 321
Sun/Soleil—AREGAK, Armenia, 35
Sunley (Bernard) Charitable Foundation, UK, 450
Suomen Kulttuurirahasto, Finland, 132
Support Centre for Associations and Foundations—SCAF, Belarus, 54
Sutherland Self Help Trust, New Zealand, 286
Suzman (Helen) Foundation, South Africa, 335
Svenska Institutet i Rom/Istituto Svedese di Studi Classici a Roma, Italy, 228
Svenska Kulturfonden, Finland, 133
Sverige-Amerika Stiftelsen, Sweden, 357
Sweden-America Foundation, Sweden, 357
Sweden-Japan Foundation—SJF, Sweden, 357
Swedish Institute at Athens, Greece, 189
Swedish Institute in Rome, Italy, 228
Swiss Foundation for Technical Co-operation, Switzerland, 375
Swiss Interchurch Aid, Switzerland, 367
Swiss National Science Foundation—SNF, Switzerland, 374
Swisscontact—Swiss Foundation for Technical Co-operation, Switzerland, 375
The Sylvia Adams Charitable Trust, UK, 398
Syngenta Foundation for Sustainable Agriculture, Switzerland, 376
Syngenta Stiftung für Nachhaltige Landwirtschaft, Switzerland, 376
TEAR Australia, Australia, 45
Tekniikan Edistämissäätiö–Stiftelsen för teknikens främjande—TES, Finland, 133
di Tella (Torcuato), Instituto, Argentina, 34
Terre des Hommes Foundation, Switzerland, 376
Terre Sans Frontières—TSF, Canada, 98
Tewa, Nepal, 271

Thairath Newspaper Foundation, Thailand, 385
Thomas B. Thrige Foundation, Denmark, 121
Thomas B. Thriges Fond, Denmark, 121
Thomson Foundation, UK, 451
Thriges (Thomas B.) Fond, Denmark, 121
Thyssen (Fritz) Stiftung, Germany, 183
Tides, USA, 548
Tides Foundation, USA, 548
Tinker Foundation, Inc, USA, 548
TISCO Foundation, Thailand, 385
The Todd Foundation, New Zealand, 287
Toepfer (Alfred) Stiftung, Germany, 183
Tokyu Foundation for Inbound Students,
    Japan, 240
Torcuato di Tella Institute, Argentina, 34
The Toyota Foundation, Japan, 240
Toyota Vietnam Foundation—TVF, Viet Nam, 565
Transnet Foundation, South Africa, 335
Triodos Foundation, Netherlands, 282
Trócaire—Catholic Agency for World
    Development, Ireland, 213
The Trull Foundation, USA, 548
Trust for Civil Society in Central and Eastern
    Europe, Bulgaria, 76
TTF—Toyota Thailand Foundation,
    Thailand, 385
Turin Savings Bank Foundation, Italy, 220
Tutu (Desmond) Peace Foundation, USA, 549
Twenty-Ninth May 1961 Charity, UK, 452
UJIA—United Jewish Israel Appeal, UK, 452
Uluslararası Mavi Hilal İnsani Yardım ve
    Kalkınma Vakfı, Turkey, 390
Umut Foundation, Turkey, 391
Umut Vakfı, Turkey, 391
UniCredit Foundation—Unidea, Italy, 228
Unilever Vietnam Foundation—UVF, Viet
    Nam, 565
Union Aid Abroad—APHEDA, Australia, 45
United Society for the Propagation of the
    Gospel—USPG, UK, 453
United States African Development
    Foundation—USADF, USA, 550
United States-Israel Educational Foundation—
    USIEF, Israel, 215
United States-Japan Foundation, USA, 550
Unity Foundation, Luxembourg, 257
Universitaire Stichting, Belgium, 64
University Foundation, Belgium, 64
University of Zaragoza Business Foundation,
    Spain, 342
US-Baltic Foundation—USBF, USA, 551
US-Ukraine Foundation, USA, 551
USIEF—United States-Israel Educational
    Foundation, Israel, 215
Values Foundation, Bulgaria, 77
Vehbi Koç Foundation, Turkey, 391
Vehbi Koç Vakfı, Turkey, 391
Venice Foundation, Italy, 225
Venkatarangaiya (M.) Foundation, India, 206
Victor Pinchuk Foundation, Ukraine, 394
Villar Foundation, Inc., Philippines, 304
Villavicencio (Dr J. Roberto), Fundación,
    Argentina, 33
Vivamos Mejor Foundation, Switzerland, 375
The Vladimir Potanin Foundation, Russian
    Federation, 320
Volkart Foundation, Switzerland, 376
Volkart-Stiftung, Switzerland, 376
Vollmer (Alberto) Foundation, Inc, USA, 551
Voluntary Service Overseas, UK, 454
Volunteer Service Abroad—VSA, New
    Zealand, 287
VSA—Volunteer Service Abroad, New
    Zealand, 287
VSO, UK, 454
Výbor dobré vule—Nadace Olgy Havlové, Czech
    Republic, 115
Vzdělávací nadace Jana Husa, Czech
    Republic, 116
Vzdelávacia nadácia Jana Husa, Slovakia, 329
Wallace (Charles) India Trust, UK, 454
The Wallace Foundation, USA, 551
Wallach (Miriam G. and Ira D.) Foundation,
    USA, 552
Wallenberg (Knut och Alice) Stiftelse,
    Sweden, 358
Walmart Foundation, USA, 552
Walter and Duncan Gordon Charitable
    Foundation, Canada, 89
WaterAid, UK, 454
Wates Foundation, UK, 454
Webb Memorial Trust, UK, 455
Webster (R. Howard) Foundation, Canada, 99
The Welch Foundation, USA, 553
West-East Foundation, Germany, 182
Weston (Garfield) Foundation, UK, 455
WHEAT Trust—Women's Hope Education and
    Training Trust, South Africa, 336

Whirlpool Foundation, USA, 553
White Point Development Foundation,
    Turkey, 387
Wihuri (Jenny and Antti) Foundation,
    Finland, 134
Wilbur Foundation, USA, 554
Wild (Dr Rainer) Stiftung, Germany, 184
William Adlington Cadbury Charitable Trust,
    UK, 407
The William and Flora Hewlett Foundation,
    USA, 503
William G. and Marie Selby Foundation,
    USA, 543
The William H. Donner Foundation, Inc,
    USA, 485
William and Mary Greve Foundation, Inc,
    USA, 500
The William Randolph Hearst Foundation,
    USA, 502
Wilson (E. O.) Biodiversity Foundation, USA, 555
Wingate (Harold Hyam) Foundation, UK, 456
Winrock International, USA, 555
Winston Churchill Foundation of the United
    States, USA, 479
Wisti (Folmer) Foundation for International
    Understanding, Denmark, 122
Wladyslaw Poniecki Foundation, Inc, USA, 536
Woerner (Manfred) Foundation, Bulgaria, 74
The Wolfson Family Charitable Trust, UK, 456
Women in Equality Foundation, Argentina, 33
Women's Hope Education and Training Trust—
    Wheat Trust, South Africa, 336
Wood Family Trust, UK, 456
Woodrow Wilson National Fellowship
    Foundation, USA, 555
Workers' Centre Foundation, Spain, 343
World Association of Children's Friends,
    Monaco, 265
World Education, Inc, USA, 556
World Literacy of Canada—WLC, Canada, 99
The World of NGOs, Austria, 46
World Teacher Trust, India, 206
YADESA—Yayasan Pengembangan Masyarakat
    Desa, Indonesia, 208
Yayasan Dian Desa, Indonesia, 207
Yayasan Indonesia Sejahtera, Indonesia, 208
Yayasan Keanekaragaman Hayati Indonesia—
    KEHATI, Indonesia, 208
Yayasan Pengembangan Masyarakat Desa—
    YADESA, Indonesia, 208
Youth Forum, Uruguay, 560
Yrjö Jahnsson Foundation, Finland, 131
Yrjö Jahnssonin säätiö, Finland, 131
Zavod Center za Informiranje, Sodelovanje in
    Razvoj Nevladnih Organizacije—CNVOS,
    Slovenia, 330
ZEIT-Stiftung Ebelin und Gerd Bucerius,
    Germany, 184
Zimin (Dmitry) Dynasty Foundation, Russian
    Federation, 319
ZOA, Netherlands, 283
Zochonis Charitable Trust, UK, 457
Zorig Foundation, Mongolia, 266

INTERNATIONAL AFFAIRS

Academy of European Law, Germany, 167
ACCU—Asian Cultural Centre for UNESCO,
    Japan, 231
ADI—Association for Democratic Initiatives,
    Macedonia, 258
Africa-America Institute—AAI, USA, 461
African Forum and Network on Debt and
    Development—AFRODAD, Zimbabwe, 567
Afro-Asian Institute in Vienna, Austria, 46
Afro-Asiatisches Institut in Wien, Austria, 46
AFRODAD—African Forum and Network on
    Debt and Development, Zimbabwe, 567
AINA—Arctic Institute of North America,
    Canada, 81
Airey Neave Trust, UK, 434
AISA—Africa Institute of South Africa, South
    Africa, 332
Alert—International Alert, UK, 422
Alfred Toepfer Foundation F.V.S., Germany, 183
Alfred Toepfer Stiftung F.V.S., Germany, 183
Alliance for International Educational and
    Cultural Exchange, USA, 463
Allianz Cultural Foundation, Germany, 160
Allianz Kulturstiftung, Germany, 160
America-Mideast Educational and Training
    Services Inc, USA, 468
American Institute of Pakistan Studies, USA, 466
American Schools of Oriental Research—ASOR,
    USA, 467
AMIDEAST—America-Mideast Educational and
    Training Services, Inc, USA, 468

ANGOC—Asian NGO Coalition for Agrarian
    Reform and Rural Development,
    Philippines, 301
Anna Lindh Euro-Mediterranean Foundation for
    Dialogue between Cultures, Egypt, 127
APACE Village First Electrification Group—
    APACE VFEG, Australia, 36
APHEDA—Union Aid Abroad, Australia, 45
Appropriate Technology for Community and
    Environment—APACE, Australia, 36
Arca Foundation, USA, 469
Arctic Institute of North America—AINA,
    Canada, 81
AREGAK—Sun/Soleil, Armenia, 35
Asia Foundation, USA, 469
Asia/Pacific Cultural Centre for UNESCO—
    ACCU, Japan, 231
Asia Pacific Foundation of Canada, Canada, 81
Asia Society, USA, 470
Asian NGO Coalition for Agrarian Reform and
    Rural Development—ANGOC,
    Philippines, 301
ASKO Europa-Stiftung, Germany, 161
ASKO Europe Foundation, Germany, 161
Asociación Latinoamericana de Organizaciones
    de Promoción al Desarrollo—ALOP,
    Mexico, 262
ASOR—American Schools of Oriental Research,
    USA, 467
Aspen Institute, USA, 470
Association for Democratic Initiatives—ADI,
    Macedonia, 258
Association of Voluntary Service
    Organisations—AVSO, Belgium, 57
Augusto César Sandino Foundation,
    Nicaragua, 288
Australia-Japan Foundation, Australia, 37
Australian Institute of International Affairs,
    Australia, 39
Australian People Health Education,
    Australia, 45
Baring Foundation, UK, 402
BBVA Foundation, Spain, 340
Berghof Foundation for Conflict Research,
    Germany, 161
Berghof Stiftung für Konfliktforschung GmbH,
    Germany, 161
Bertelsmann Foundation, Germany, 162
Bertelsmann Stiftung, Germany, 162
BID-INTAL—Instituto para la Integración de
    America Latina y el Caribe, Argentina, 34
Bosch (Robert) Stiftung GmbH, Germany, 163
Bradley (Lynde and Harry) Foundation, Inc,
    USA, 473
Brookings Institution, USA, 474
Bruno Kreisky Forum for International
    Dialogue, Austria, 47
Bruno Kreisky Forum für internationalen
    Dialog, Austria, 47
Buck (Pearl S. Buck) International, USA, 474
Bulgarian Donors' Forum, Bulgaria, 74
The Camargo Foundation, France, 138
The Canada Council for the Arts/Conseil des
    Arts du Canada, Canada, 82
Canadian Co-operative Association, Canada, 80
Canadian International Council/Conseil
    International du Canada—CIC, Canada, 84
Canadian Urban Institute, Canada, 85
Canon Foundation in Europe, Netherlands, 272
Carnegie Corporation of New York, USA, 475
Carthage Foundation, USA, 476
Caucasus Institute for Peace, Democracy and
    Development—CIPDD, Georgia, 157
Centar za razvoj neprofitnih organizacija—
    CERANEO, Croatia, 109
Center for Human Research and Social
    Development—CHRSD, Palestinian
    Autonomous Areas, 296
CENTRAS—Assistance Centre for NGOs,
    Romania, 316
Centre for Development of Non-Profit
    Organizations, Croatia, 109
Centre Européen de la Culture—CEC,
    Switzerland, 362
Centro de Investigación para la Paz, CIP—
    FUHEM, Spain, 338
CERANEO—Centar za razvoj neprofitnih
    organizacija, Croatia, 109
CGP—Japan Foundation Centre Global
    Partnership, Japan, 236
Charles F. Kettering Foundation, USA, 515
Chr. Michelsen Institute—CMI, Norway, 291
CIC—Canadian International Council/Conseil
    International du Canada, Canada, 84
CIDOB Foundation, Spain, 338
Civic Initiatives, Serbia, 324
Clean Water Foundation, Netherlands, 282
CMI—Chr. Michelsens Institutt, Norway, 291

Colombian Habitat Foundation, Colombia, 105
Commonwealth Foundation, UK, 411
Conseil des Arts du Canada, Canada, 82
Daiwa Anglo-Japanese Foundation, UK, 413
Danish Peace Foundation, Denmark, 118
Demokratikus Átalakulásért Intézet,
    Hungary, 196
Deutsch-Russischer Austausch eV—DRA,
    Germany, 164
Deutsche Gesellschaft für Auswärtige Politik—
    DGAP, Germany, 164
Deutsche Nationalstiftung, Germany, 165
Deutsche Stiftung für internationale rechtliche
    Zusammenarbeit eV, Germany, 165
Development and Peace Foundation,
    Germany, 180
Diakonia, Sweden, 352
Ditchley Foundation, UK, 414
Dóchas, Ireland, 210
DOEN Foundation, Netherlands, 280
Donner (William H.) Foundation, Inc, USA, 485
Dräger Foundation, Germany, 166
Dräger-Stiftung, Germany, 166
Economic Development Foundation, Turkey, 388
ECPD—European Centre for Peace and
    Development, Serbia, 324
Eesti Mittetulundusühingute ja Sihtasutuste
    Liit, Estonia, 129
ELIAMEP—Hellenic Foundation for European
    and Foreign Policy, Greece, 187
Emile Chanoux Foundation—Institute for
    Federalist and Regionalist Studies, Italy, 218
ENCOD—European NGO Council on Drugs and
    Development, Belgium, 59
endPoverty.org, USA, 488
Enterprise Development International, USA, 488
ERA—Europäische Rechtsakademie,
    Germany, 167
Estonian Foundation Centre, Estonia, 129
Eugenio Mendoza Foundation, Venezuela, 563
Europäische Rechtsakademie—ERA,
    Germany, 167
European Centre of Culture, Switzerland, 362
European Centre for Peace and Development—
    ECPD, Serbia, 324
European Coalition for Just and Effective Drug
    Policies—ENCOD, Belgium, 59
European Cultural Foundation—ECF,
    Netherlands, 273
European Mediterranean Institute, Spain, 349
European Network of Foundations for Social
    Economy, Belgium, 56
European Youth Foundation—EYF, France, 151
Europese Culterele Stichting, Netherlands, 273
Eurostep—European Solidarity Towards Equal
    Participation of People, Belgium, 60
The Evian Group at IMD, Switzerland, 363
Evrika Foundation, Bulgaria, 75
FAF—French-American Foundation, USA, 494
The Federal Trust for Education and Research,
    UK, 416
Fédération Panafricaine des Cinéastes—
    FEPACI, Burkina Faso, 78
Fedesarrollo—Fundación para la Educación
    Superior y el Desarrollo, Colombia, 104
Feltrinelli (Giangiacomo), Fondazione, Italy,
    221
Folmer Wisti Fonden, Denmark, 122
Folmer Wisti Foundation, Denmark, 122
Fondation Charles Veillon, Switzerland, 365
Fondation Denis de Rougemont pour l'Europe,
    Switzerland, 365
Fondation Emile Chanoux—Institut d'Etudes
    Fédéralistes et Régionalistes, Italy, 218
Fondation 'Entente Franco-Allemande',
    France, 143
Fondation Européenne de la Culture/Europese
    Culterele Stichting, Netherlands, 273
Fondation Hugot du Collège de France,
    France, 145
Fondation Jean Monnet pour l'Europe,
    Switzerland, 364
Fondation Léopold Sédar Senghor, Senegal, 322
Fondation Méditerranéenne d'Etudes
    Stratégiques—FMES, France, 147
Fondation Nationale des Sciences Politiques,
    France, 148
Fondation Paul-Henri Spaak—Stichting Paul-
    Henri Spaak, Belgium, 61
Fondation pour la Recherche Stratégique,
    France, 149
Fondation Robert Schuman, France, 150
Fondazione Giangiacomo Feltrinelli, Italy, 221
Fondazione RUI, Italy, 225
Fonds Européen pour la Jeunesse—FEJ,
    France, 151
Fonds National Suisse de la Recherche
    Scientifique, Switzerland, 374

FOOD—Foundation of Occupational
    Development, India, 201
Foreign Policy and United Nations Association of
    Austria—UNA-AUSTRIA, Austria, 48
Foundation for Franco-German Co-operation,
    France, 143
Foundation for German–Polish Co-operation,
    Poland, 308
Foundation for Higher Education and
    Development, Colombia, 104
Foundation for International Studies—FIS,
    Malta, 261
Foundation for International Understanding,
    Denmark, 122
Foundation for Middle East Peace—FMEP,
    USA, 492
Foundation of Occupational Development—
    FOOD, India, 201
Foundation of Savings Banks, Spain, 341
Foundation of Spanish Commercial Agents,
    Spain, 339
Foundation for Strategic Research, France, 149
Foundation for Women, Spain, 345
Fredsfonden, Denmark, 118
Freeman Foundation, USA, 494
French-American Foundation—FAF, USA, 494
Fridtjof Nansen Institute—FNI, Norway, 291
Friede Springer Foundation, Germany, 179
Friede Springer Stiftung, Germany, 179
Fritz Thyssen Foundation, Germany, 183
Fritz Thyssen Stiftung, Germany, 183
Fundação Luso-Americana para o
    Desenvolvimento, Portugal, 312
Fundação Mário Soares, Portugal, 313
Fundació CIDOB, Spain, 338
Fundación de los Agentes Comerciales de
    España, Spain, 339
Fundación Augusto César Sandino—FACS,
    Nicaragua, 288
Fundación Banco Bilbao Vizcaya Argentaria—
    Fundación BBVA, Spain, 340
Fundación BBVA—Fundación Banco Bilbao
    Vizcaya Argentaria, Spain, 340
Fundación de las Cajas de Ahorros—FUNCAS,
    Spain, 341
Fundación para la Educación Superior y el
    Desarrollo—Fedesarrollo, Colombia, 104
Fundación Empresa-Universidad de Zaragoza—
    FEUZ, Spain, 342
Fundación Eugenio Mendoza, Venezuela, 563
Fundación Hábitat Colombia—FHC,
    Colombia, 105
Fundación Juan March, Spain, 345
Fundación Mujeres, Spain, 345
Fundación Mujeres en Igualdad, Argentina, 33
Fundación Nacional para el Desarrollo, El
    Salvador, 128
Fundación Paz y Solidaridad Serafín Aliaga—
    FPyS, Spain, 346
Fundación Rafael del Pino, Spain, 347
Fundacja im. Stefana Batorego, Poland, 307
Fundacja Solidarności Polsko-Czesko-
    Słowackiej, Poland, 308
Fundacja Współpracy Polsko-Niemieckiej/
    Stiftung für Deutsch-Polnische
    Zusammenarbeit, Poland, 308
Gandhi (Mahatma) Foundation for World Peace,
    Canada, 89
Gandhi Peace Foundation, India, 202
Gemeinnützige Hertie Foundation, Germany, 169
Gemeinnützige Hertie-Stiftung, Germany, 169
German Council on Foreign Relations,
    Germany, 164
German Foundation for International Legal Co-
    operation, Germany, 165
German Marshall Fund of the United States—
    GMF, 496
German National Trust, Germany, 165
German-Russian Exchange, Germany, 164
Giangiacomo Feltrinelli Foundation, Italy, 221
Gilbert Murray Trust, UK, 433
GMF—German Marshall Fund of the United
    States, USA, 496
Gradjanske inicijative—GI, Serbia, 324
Graduate Institute of International Studies and
    Development Studies, Switzerland, 367
Great Britain Sasakawa Foundation, UK, 419
Greve (William and Mary) Foundation, Inc,
    USA, 500
Guggenheim (John Simon) Memorial Foundation,
    USA, 500
Gulf Research Center, United Arab Emirates, 395
Gulf Research Center Foundation,
    Switzerland, 367
Haniel Foundation, Germany, 169
Haniel-Stiftung, Germany, 169
Havelaar (Max) Foundation, Netherlands, 281
The Helen Suzman Foundation, South Africa, 335

Hellenic Foundation for European and Foreign
    Policy—ELIAMEP, Greece, 187
HELP International, USA, 503
Henry Luce Foundation, Inc, USA, 519
Hitachi Foundation, USA, 504
House of Europe Cultural Foundation,
    Germany, 174
Hugot Foundation of the Collège of France,
    France, 145
ICSSR—Indian Council of Social Science
    Research, India, 202
IEMed—Institut Europeu de la Mediterrània,
    Spain, 349
İktisadi Kalkınma Vakfı, Turkey, 388
Indian Council of Social Science Research—
    ICSSR, India, 202
INFID—International NGO Forum on
    Indonesian Development, Indonesia, 207
Institut Arctique de l'Amérique du Nord—IAAN,
    Canada, 81
Institut Català Mediterrània, Spain, 349
Institut Europeu de la Mediterrània—IEMed,
    Spain, 349
Institut Nord-Sud, Canada, 95
Institut Universitaire de Hautes Etudes
    Internationales et du Développement,
    Switzerland, 367
Institut urbain du Canada, Canada, 85
Institute for Latin American and Caribbean
    Integration, Argentina, 34
Institute for Palestine Studies, Publishing and
    Research Organization—IPS, Lebanon, 252
Instituto para la Integración de América Latina y
    el Caribe—BID-INTAL, Argentina, 34
International Alert—Alert, UK, 422
International Centre for Democratic
    Transition—ICDT, Hungary, 196
International Institute for Environment and
    Development—IIED, UK, 423
International NGO Forum on Indonesian
    Development—INFID, Indonesia, 207
International Renaissance Foundation—IRF,
    Ukraine, 394
International Research & Exchanges Board—
    IREX, USA, 511
IREX—International Research & Exchanges
    Board, USA, 511
Irish Association of Non-Governmental
    Development Organizations—DOCHAS,
    Ireland, 210
Islamic Thought Foundation, Iran, 209
IUC-Europe International Education Centre,
    Denmark, 119
IUC-Europe Internationalt Uddanneless Center,
    Denmark, 119
The Japan Foundation Centre for Global
    Partnership—CGP, Japan, 236
Japanese-German Center Berlin, Germany, 173
Japanisch-Deutsches Zentrum Berlin,
    Germany, 173
JCIE—Japan Center for International Exchange,
    Japan, 236
Jean Monnet Foundation for Europe,
    Switzerland, 364
JIIA—Japan Institute of International Affairs,
    Japan, 237
The John D. and Catherine T. MacArthur
    Foundation, USA, 520
John Simon Guggenheim Memorial Foundation,
    USA, 500
Joseph Rowntree Charitable Trust, UK, 441
Juan March Foundation, Spain, 345
Karić fondacija, Serbia, 325
Karić Foundation, Serbia, 325
Kettering Foundation, USA, 515
Kirk (Norman) Memorial Trust, New
    Zealand, 284
Kosovar Civil Society Foundation, Kosovo, 248
Kulturfonder for Sverige och Finland,
    Sweden, 354
Kulturstiftung Haus Europa, Germany, 174
Lambrakis Foundation, Greece, 187
Lambrakis Research Foundation, Greece, 187
Latin American Association of Development
    Organizations, Mexico, 262
Léopold Sédar Senghor Foundation, Senegal, 322
Leverhulme Trust, UK, 429
Luce (Henry) Foundation, Inc, USA, 519
Luso-American Development Foundation,
    Portugal, 312
Luxemburg (Rosa) Stiftung, Germany, 174
Lynde and Harry Bradley Foundation, Inc,
    USA, 473
MacArthur (John D. and Catherine T.)
    Foundation, USA, 520
Macedonian Centre for International Co-
    operation—MCIC, Macedonia, 258
Madariaga European Foundation, Belgium, 63

Maecenata Management GmbH, Germany, 159
Mahatma Gandhi Canadian Foundation for
World Peace, Canada, 89
Maison Franco-Japonaise, Japan, 237
Manfred Woerner Foundation, Bulgaria, 74
March (Juan), Fundación, Spain, 345
Mário Soares Foundation, Portugal, 313
Max Havelaar Foundation, Netherlands, 281
MCIC—Macedonian Centre for International Co-
operation, Macedonia, 258
Mediterranean Foundation of Strategic Studies,
France, 147
Mendoza (Eugenio) Fundación, Venezuela, 563
Menzies (R. G.) Scholarship Fund, Australia, 42
Miriam G. and Ira D. Wallach Foundation,
USA, 552
Monnet (Jean), Fondation pour l'Europe,
Switzerland, 364
Mosaic Foundation, USA, 526
Murray (Gilbert) Trust, UK, 433
Mwalimu Nyerere Foundation—MNF,
Tanzania, 382
Nansen (Fridtjof) Institute, Norway, 291
National Foundation for Development, El
Salvador, 128
National Foundation for Political Sciences,
France, 148
Network of Estonian Non-profit Organizations,
Estonia, 129
New Eurasia Foundation, Russian
Federation, 319
New Perspectives Foundation, Russian
Federation, 319
New Zealand Winston Churchill Memorial Trust,
New Zealand, 285
NGO Rural and Social Initiative, Moldova, 264
Nigerian Institute of International Affairs—
NIIA, Nigeria, 290
Nihon Kokusai Mondai Kenkyusho, Japan, 237
Nordic Africa Institute Scholarships,
Sweden, 355
Nordiska Afrikainstitutets Stipendier,
Sweden, 355
Norman Kirk Memorial Trust, New Zealand, 284
Norsk Utenrikspolitisk Institutt—NUPI,
Norway, 292
North-South Institute/Institut Nord-Sud,
Canada, 95
Norwegian Institute of International Affairs—
NUPI, Norway, 292
Open Society Foundation, Romania, 317
Open Society Fund Prague—OSF Prague, Czech
Republic, 115
Open Society Initiative for Southern Africa—
OSISA, South Africa, 334
Open Society Institute—Brussels, Belgium, 63
Österreichische Gesellschaft für Außenpolitik
und Internationale Beziehungen, Austria, 48
Pacific Peoples' Partnership, Canada, 95
Pakistan Institute of International Affairs—
PIIA, Pakistan, 294
Pan-African Federation of Film-makers, Burkina
Faso, 78
Pathfinder International, USA, 533
Paul-Henri Spaak Foundation, Belgium, 61
Peace and Disarmament Education Trust—
PADET, New Zealand, 286
Peace Research Center, Spain, 338
Pearl S. Buck International, USA, 474
People's Harmonious Development Society,
Georgia, 158
Peres Center for Peace, Israel, 215
The Pew Charitable Trusts, USA, 534
Philippine-American Educational Foundation—
PAEF, Philippines, 303
Ploughshares Fund, USA, 536
Polden-Puckham Charitable Foundation—PPCF,
UK, 438
Pôle européen des fondations de l'économie
sociale, Belgium, 56
Polish-Czech-Slovak Solidarity Foundation,
Poland, 308
R. G. Menzies Scholarship Fund, Australia, 42
Rafael del Pino Foundation, Spain, 347
Rajiv Gandhi Foundation, India, 201
Ramon Magsaysay Award Foundation,
Philippines, 303
RED—Ruralité-environnement-développement,
Belgium, Belgium, 63
Regional Centre for Strategic Studies—RCSS, Sri
Lanka, 350
Robert Bosch Foundation, Germany, 163
Robert-Bosch-Stiftung GmbH, Germany, 163
Robert Schuman Foundation, France, 150
Rockefeller Brothers Fund, USA, 540
Rosa Luxemburg Foundation, Germany, 174
Rosa-Luxemburg-Stiftung, Germany, 174
Rowntree (Joseph) Charitable Trust, UK, 441

RUI Foundation, Italy, 225
Ruralité Environnement Développement—RED,
Belgium, 63
Rurality Environment Development, Belgium, 63
Sandino (Augusto César), Fundación,
Nicaragua, 288
Schuman (Robert), Fondation, France, 150
Schwarzkopf Foundation Young Europe,
Germany, 178
Schwarzkopf Stiftung Junges Europa,
Germany, 178
Schweizerischer Nationalfonds zur Förderung
der wissenschaftlichen Forschung/Fonds
National Suisse de la Recherche
Scientifique—SNF, Switzerland, 374
Seeds of Peace, USA, 543
Semmelweis Alapítvány Magyarországi
Ortopédia Fejlesztéséért, Hungary, 195
Semmelweis Foundation for the Development of
Orthopaedics in Hungary, Hungary, 195
Serafín Aliaga Foundation for Peace and
Solidarity, Spain, 346
Siam Society, Thailand, 384
Singapore International Foundation—SIF,
Singapore, 326
Smith Richardson Foundation, Inc, USA, 545
Soares (Mário), Fundação, Portugal, 313
Soros Foundation (Czech Republic), Czech
Republic, 115
Soros Foundation Romania, Romania, 317
SOTA—Research Centre for Turkestan and
Azerbaijan, Netherlands, 280
South African Institute of International Affairs,
South Africa, 335
South African Institute of Race Relations, South
Africa, 335
South-East Institute—Foundation for Academic
Research into South-Eastern Europe,
Germany, 182
South Pacific Peoples Foundation Canada,
Canada, 95
Spaak (Paul-Henri), Fondation, Belgium, 61
Standing International Forum on Ethnic
Conflict, Genocide and Human Rights—
International Alert, UK, 422
Steelworkers Humanity Fund, Canada, 98
Stefan Batory Foundation, Poland, 307
Stichting DOEN, Netherlands, 280
Stichting Max Havelaar, Netherlands, 281
Stichting Reinwater, Netherlands, 282
Stichting Spaak (Paul-Henri), Belgium, 61
Stichting Triodos Foundation, Netherlands, 282
Stiftelsen Riksbankens Jubileumsfond,
Sweden, 357
Stiftung Entwicklung und Frieden—SEF,
Germany, 180
Stiftung FVS, Germany, 183
Stiftung West-Östliche Begegnungen,
Germany, 182
Stiftung für wissenschaftliche
Südosteuropaforschung—Südost-Institut,
Germany, 182
Südost-Institut—Stiftung für wissenschaftliche
Südosteuropaforschung, Germany, 182
Sun/Soleil—AREGAK, Armenia, 35
Support Centre for Associations and
Foundations—SCAF, Belarus, 54
Suzman (Helen) Foundation, South Africa, 335
Swedish and Finnish Cultural Foundation,
Sweden, 354
Swedish Institute at Athens, Greece, 189
Swiss National Science Foundation—SNF,
Switzerland, 374
TFF—Transnationella Stiftelsen för Freds- och
Framtidsforskning, Sweden, 358
Third World Network—TWN, Malaysia, 260
Thyssen (Fritz) Stiftung, Germany, 183
Tinker Foundation, Inc, USA, 548
Toepfer (Alfred) Stiftung, Germany, 183
Transnational Foundation for Peace and Future
Research, Sweden, 358
Transnationella Stiftelsen för Freds- och
Framtidsforskning—TFF, Sweden, 358
Triodos Foundation, Netherlands, 282
Umut Foundation, Turkey, 391
Umut Vakfi, Turkey, 391
Union Aid Abroad—APHEDA, Australia, 45
United States-Japan Foundation, USA, 550
University of Zaragoza Business Foundation,
Spain, 342
Wallach (Miriam G. and Ira D.) Foundation,
USA, 552
West-East Foundation, Germany, 182
The William H. Donner Foundation, Inc,
USA, 485
William and Mary Greve Foundation, Inc,
USA, 500

Wisti (Folmer) Foundation for International
Understanding, Denmark, 122
Woerner (Manfred) Foundation, Bulgaria, 74
Women in Equality Foundation, Argentina, 33
World Peace Foundation—WPF, USA, 557

LAW, CIVIL SOCIETY AND HUMAN RIGHTS

Academy of European Law, Germany, 167
Açık Toplum Enstitüsü, Turkey, 387
Acting for Life, France, 136
Action for Children, UK, 398
Action in Development—AID, Bangladesh, 52
Action Group for Justice and Social Equality,
Benin, 65
Action Solidarité Tiers Monde—ASTM,
Luxembourg, 257
ADI—Association for Democratic Initiatives,
Macedonia, 258
AFSC—American Friends Service Committee,
USA, 465
AINA—Arctic Institute of North America,
Canada, 81
Airey Neave Trust, UK, 434
AJWS—American Jewish World Service,
USA, 466
Alert—International Alert, UK, 422
Alicia Patterson Foundation—APF, USA, 533
Allavida—Alliances for Voluntary Initiatives and
Development, Kenya, 244
Alliances for Voluntary Initiatives and
Development—Allavida, Kenya, 244
AMADE Mondiale—Association Mondiale des
Amis de l'Enfance, Monaco, 265
Ambiente y Recursos Naturales, Fundación,
Argentina, 31
Ambuja Cement Foundation, India, 199
America for Bulgaria Foundation, Bulgaria, 75
America–Mideast Educational and Training
Services Inc, USA, 468
American Friends Service Committee—AFSC,
USA, 465
American Jewish World Service—AJWS,
USA, 466
AMIDEAST—America-Mideast Educational and
Training Services, Inc, USA, 468
ANESVAD, Spain, 337
Angaja Foundation, India, 199
ANGOC—Asian NGO Coalition for Agrarian
Reform and Rural Development,
Philippines, 301
AOHR—Arab Organization for Human Rights,
Egypt, 127
APHEDA—Union Aid Abroad, Australia, 45
Arab Organization for Human Rights, Egypt, 127
Arca Foundation, USA, 469
Arctic Institute of North America—AINA,
Canada, 81
Arcus Foundation, USA, 469
AREGAK—Sun/Soleil, Armenia, 35
Arias Foundation for Peace and Human Progress,
Costa Rica, 106
Asia Foundation, USA, 469
Asian NGO Coalition for Agrarian Reform and
Rural Development—ANGOC,
Philippines, 301
Asociación Latinoamericana de Organizaciones
de Promoción al Desarrollo—ALOP,
Mexico, 262
Assembly of Belarusian Pro-democratic Non-
governmental Organizations, Belarus, 54
Association for Democratic Initiatives—ADI,
Macedonia, 258
Association Mondiale des Amis de l'Enfance,
Monaco, 265
Association of Voluntary Agencies for Rural
Development—AVARD, India, 198
ASTM—Action Solidarité Tiers Monde,
Luxembourg, 257
Auschwitz-Birkenau Foundation, Poland, 306
Auschwitz Foundation, Belgium, 60
Australian Multicultural Foundation—AMF,
Australia, 39
Australian People Health Education,
Australia, 45
Australian Youth Foundation, Australia, 41
Autonómia Foundation, Hungary, 195
AVARD—Association of Voluntary Agencies for
Rural Development, India, 198
AWHRC—Asian Women's Human Rights
Council, India, 200
BaBe—Budi aktivna, Budi emancipirana,
Croatia, 109
Baltic-American Partnership Fund—BAPF,
USA, 472
Bangladesh Freedom Foundation, Bangladesh, 52

Baring Foundation, UK, 402
BBC World Service Trust, UK, 403
BBVA Foundation, Spain, 340
Be Active, Be Emancipated, Croatia, 109
Borderland Foundation, Poland, 307
Brazil Foundation, Brazil, 70
Buck (Pearl S. Buck) International, USA, 474
Budi aktivna, Budi emancipiran—BaBe!,
    Croatia, 109
Bulgarian Fund for Women, Bulgaria, 75
The Bydale Foundation, USA, 475
Cadbury (William Adlingon) Charitable Trust,
    UK, 407
Canadian Catholic Organization for Development
    and Peace, Canada, 83
Canadian Centre for International Studies and
    Co-operation/Centre d'études et de
    coopération internationale—CECI,
    Canada, 83
Canadian Council for International Co-
    operation—CCIC/Conseil canadien pour la
    coopération internationale—CCCI,
    Canada, 80
Canadian Physicians for Aid and Relief—CPAR,
    Canada, 86
Canon Foundation in Europe, Netherlands, 272
The Carter Center, USA, 476
Carthage Foundation, USA, 476
Catholic Agency for World Development—
    Trócaire, Ireland, 213
CCCI—Conseil canadien pour la coopération
    internationale, Canada, 80
CCIC—Canadian Council for International Co-
    operation, Canada, 80
CDCS—Centre for Development of Civil Society,
    Armenia, 35
CECI—Canadian Centre for International
    Studies and Co-operation/Centre d'études et
    de coopération internationale, Canada, 83
Centar za razvoj neprofitnih organizacija—
    CERANEO, Croatia, 109
Centre for the Development of Civil Society—
    CDCS, Armenia, 35
Centre for Development of Non-Profit
    Organjzations, Croatia, 109
Centre d'Études, de Documentation,
    d'Information et d'Action Sociales—
    CÉDIAS—Musée Social, France, 138
Centre for Social Studies, Documentation,
    Information and Action, France, 138
Centro de Investigación para la Paz, CIP—
    FUHEM, Spain, 338
CERANEO—Centar za razvoj neprofitnih
    organizacija, Croatia, 109
Charter 77 Foundation, Czech Republic, 114
Chia Hsin Foundation, Taiwan, 379
Child Migrants Trust, UK, 409
ChildHope Asia Philippines, Inc, Philippines, 302
ChildHope Brasil, Brazil, 70
ChildHope—Hope for the Children Foundation,
    Guatemala, 190
Children and Sharing, France, 139
Chr. Michelsen Institute—CMI, Norway, 291
Churches' Commission for Migrants in Europe,
    Belgium, 57
CIMADE—Service Oecuménique d'Entraide,
    France, 138
Civic Initiatives, Serbia, 324
Civil Society Development Centre, Turkey, 387
Civil Society Development Foundation,
    Bulgaria, 74
CLADEM—Comité de América Latina y el
    Caribe para la Defensa de los Derechos de la
    Mujer, Peru, 299
Clovek v tisni—spolecnost pri Ceske televizi,
    o.p.s., Czech Republic, 113
CMI—Chr. Michelsens Institutt, Norway, 291
Comité de América Latina y el Caribe para la
    Defensa de los Derechos de la Mujer—
    CLADEM, Peru, 299
Commission des Eglises auprès des Migrants en
    Europe/Kommission der Kirchen für
    Migranten in Europa, Belgium, 57
Commonwealth Foundation, UK, 411
Communication Foundation for Asia,
    Philippines, 302
Consejo de Fundaciones Privadas de
    Guatemala—CFPG, Guatemala, 190
Cooperazione Internazionale—COOPI, Italy, 217
COOPI—Cooperazione Internazionale, Italy, 217
Council of Humanitarian Associations, Czech
    Republic, 112
Council of Private Foundations of Guatemala,
    Guatemala, 190
CPAR—Canadian Physicians for Aid and Relief,
    Canada, 86
CReDO—Resource Centre for the Human Rights
    NGOs of Moldova, Moldova, 264

CUSO-VSO, Canada, 86
Czech TV Foundation, Czech Republic, 113
Danish Peace Foundation, Denmark, 118
Demokratikus Átalakulásért Intézet,
    Hungary, 196
Desmond Tutu Peace Foundation—DTPF,
    USA, 549
Deutsch-Russischer Austausch eV—DRA,
    Germany, 164
Deutsche Stiftung für internationale rechtliche
    Zusammenarbeit eV, Germany, 165
Diakonia, Sweden, 352
Dóchas, Ireland, 210
DOEN Foundation, Netherlands, 280
Dr F. P. Haaz Social Assistance Foundation,
    Ukraine, 393
Dräger Foundation, Germany, 166
Dräger-Stiftung, Germany, 166
Drug Policy Alliance—DPA, USA, 485
Earthrights International—ERI, USA, 486
Ebelin and Gerd Bucerius ZEIT Foundation,
    Germany, 184
Écoles Sans Frontières—ESF, France, 139
ECPD—European Centre for Peace and
    Development, Serbia, 324
Ecumenical Service for Mutual Help, France, 138
The Edna McConnell Clark Foundation,
    USA, 520
Ednannia: Initiative Centre to Support Social
    Action—ISAR Ednannia, Ukraine, 393
Eesti Mittetulundusühingute ja Sihtasutuste
    Liit, Estonia, 129
Ekopolis Foundation, Slovakia, 327
ELIAMEP—Hellenic Foundation for European
    and Foreign Policy, Greece, 187
Emile Chanoux Foundation—Institute for
    Federalist and Regionalist Studies, Italy, 218
ENCOD—European NGO Council on Drugs and
    Development, Belgium, 59
Enfance et Partage, France, 139
Entraide Protestante Suisse, Switzerland, 367
Environment and Natural Resources Foundation,
    Argentina, 31
Environmental Justice Foundation—EJF,
    UK, 416
ERA—Europäische Rechtsakademie,
    Germany, 167
ERRC—Europako Rromano Čačimasko Centro,
    Hungary, 196
Esmée Fairbairn Foundation, UK, 416
Esquel Group Foundation—Ecuador,
    Ecuador, 125
Estonian Foundation Centre, Estonia, 129
Eurasia Foundation, USA, 489
Europäische Rechtsakademie—ERA,
    Germany, 167
Europako Rromano Čačimasko Centro—ERRC,
    Hungary, 196
European Centre for Peace and Development—
    ECPD, Serbia, 324
European Coalition for Just and Effective Drug
    Policies—ENCOD, Belgium, 59
European Federation of National Organizations
    Working with the Homeless, Belgium, 55
European Foundation for the Improvement of
    Living and Working Conditions, Ireland, 211
European Network of Foundations for Social
    Economy, Belgium, 56
European Roma Rights Centre, Hungary, 196
European Youth For Action—EYFA,
    Netherlands, 273
The Evian Group at IMD, Switzerland, 363
EYFA—European Youth For Action,
    Netherlands, 273
F. C. Flick Foundation against Xenophobia,
    Racism and Intolerance, Germany, 168
F. C. Flick-Stiftung gegen Fremdenfeindlichkeit,
    Rassismus und Intoleranz, Germany, 168
Fairbairn (Esmée) Foundation, UK, 416
FAL—France Amérique Latine, France, 151
FARN—Fundación Ambiente y Recursos
    Naturales, Argentina, 31
FDH—Frères des Hommes, France, 152
FEANTSA—Fédération Européenne des
    Associations Nationales Travaillant avec les
    Sans-Abri, Belgium, 55
The Federal Trust for Education and Research,
    UK, 416
Fédération Européenne des Associations
    Nationales Travaillant avec les Sans-Abri—
    FEANTSA, Belgium, 55
Feltrinelli (Giangiacomo), Fondazione, Italy,
    Italy, 221
FEPP—Fondo Ecuatoriano Populorum
    Progressio, Ecuador, 124
filia.die frauenstiftung, Germany, 168
filia—the Women's Foundation, Germany, 168

Finnish NGO Foundation for Human Rights—
    KIOS, Finland, 132
First Peoples Worldwide—FPW, USA, 490
FirstRand Foundation, South Africa, 332
Fondaccioni per Iniciative Demokratike,
    Kosovo, 248
Fondacioni Shoqeria e Hapur per Shqiperine,
    Albania, 29
Fondation Auschwitz, Belgium, 60
Fondation Charles Veillon, Switzerland, 365
Fondation Emile Chanoux—Institut d'Etudes
    Fédéralistes et Régionalistes, Italy, 218
Fondation 'Entente Franco-Allemande',
    France, 143
Fondation Hirondelle: Media for Peace and
    Human Dignity, Switzerland, 363
Fondation Léopold Sédar Senghor, Senegal, 322
Fondation Mo Ibrahim, UK, 421
Fondation Orient-Occident, Morocco, 268
Fondation Robert Schuman, France, 150
Fondation Roi Baudouin, Belgium, 62
Fondation Rurale pour l'Afrique de l'Ouest,
    Senegal, 322
Fondazione Giangiacomo Feltrinelli, Italy, 221
Fondo Ecuatoriano Populorum Progressio—
    FEPP, Ecuador, 124
Fonds für Entwicklung und Partnerschaft in
    Africa—FEPA, Switzerland, 366
Fonds National Suisse de la Recherche
    Scientifique, Switzerland, 374
FORWARD—Foundation for Women's Health,
    Research and Development, UK, 417
FOSIM—Foundation Open Society Institute
    Macedonia, Macedonia, 258
Foundation for Children, Germany, 181
Foundation for the Comparative Study of
    European Dictatorships and their Democratic
    Transition, Germany, 180
Foundation for Democratic Initiatives—FDI,
    Kosovo, 248
Foundation for Development and Partnership in
    Africa, Switzerland, 366
Foundation for Franco-German Co-operation,
    France, 143
Foundation for Human Rights and Humanitarian
    Relief, Turkey, 389
Foundation for International Studies—FIS,
    Malta, 261
Foundation for Middle East Peace—FMEP,
    USA, 492
Foundation Open Society Institute Macedonia—
    FOSIM, Macedonia, 258
Foundation Open Society Institute—Pakistan,
    Pakistan, 294
Foundation Open Society Institute—
    Representative Office Montenegro—FOSI
    ROM, Montenegro, 267
Foundation for Peace, Ecology and the Arts,
    Argentina, 33
Foundation in Support of Local Democracy,
    Poland, 308
Foundation of Village Community Development,
    Indonesia, 208
Foundation for Women, Spain, 345
Foundation for Women's Health, Research and
    Development—FORWARD, UK, 417
Foundation for Young Australians, Australia, 41
France Amérique Latine—FAL, France, 151
Fredsfonden, Denmark, 118
Freedom of Expression Foundation, Norway, 291
Frères des Hommes—FDH, France, 152
Freudenberg Stiftung, Germany, 168
Fridtjof Nansen Institute—FNI, Norway, 291
Friede Springer Foundation, Germany, 179
Friede Springer Stiftung, Germany, 179
Fritz Thyssen Foundation, Germany, 183
Fritz Thyssen Stiftung, Germany, 183
FSLD—Foundation in Support of Local
    Democracy, Poland, 308
Fund for Development and Partnership in Africa,
    Switzerland, 366
Fund for an Open Society—Serbia, Serbia, 324
Fundação Mário Soares, Portugal, 313
Fundación Ambiente y Recursos Naturales—
    FARN, Argentina, 31
Fundación Arias para la Paz y el Progreso
    Humano, Costa Rica, 106
Fundación Banco Bilbao Vizcaya Argentaria—
    Fundación BBVA, Spain, 340
Fundación BBVA—Fundación Banco Bilbao
    Vizcaya Argentaria, Spain, 340
Fundación Esperanza de los Niños,
    Guatemala, 190
Fundación Grupo Esquel—Ecuador, Ecuador, 125
Fundación MAPFRE, Spain, 345
Fundación Mujeres, Spain, 345
Fundación Mujeres en Igualdad, Argentina, 33

Fundación Nacional para el Desarrollo, El Salvador, 128
Fundación Paz, Ecología y Arte—Fundación PEA, Argentina, 33
Fundación Paz y Solidaridad Serafín Aliaga—FPyS, Spain, 346
Fundación PEA—Fundación Paz, Ecología y Arte, Argentina, 33
Fundación Salvadoreña para el Desarrollo Económico y Social, El Salvador, 128
Fundación Solidaridad, Dominican Republic, 123
Fundación Soros Guatemala, Guatemala, 191
Fundacja Auschwitz-Birkenau, Poland, 306
Fundacja im. Stefana Batorego, Poland, 307
Fundacja Pogranicze, Poland, 307
Fundacja Rozwoju Demokracji Loaklnej, Poland, 308
GAJES—Groupe d'Action pour la Justice et l'Egalité Sociale, Benin, 65
Gandhi Peace Foundation, India, 202
George Cedric Metcalf Charitable Foundation, Canada, 94
German Foundation for International Legal Co-operation, Germany, 165
German National Academic Foundation, Germany, 182
German-Russian Exchange, Germany, 164
Giangiacomo Feltrinelli Foundation, Italy, 221
GLARP—Grupo Latinoamericano de Rehabilitación Profesional, Colombia, 105
Glasnost Defence Foundation—GDF, Russian Federation, 319
Gordon (Walter and Duncan) Charitable Foundation, Canada, 89
Gradjanske inicijative—GI, Serbia, 324
Graduate Institute of International Studies and Development Studies, Switzerland, 367
Grassroots International—GRI, USA, 500
Groupe d'Action pour la Justice et l'Egalité Sociale—GAJES, Benin, 65
GRUMIN—Grupo Mulher-Educação Indigena, Brazil, 73
Grupo Latinoamericano para la Participación, la Integración y la Inclusión de Personas con Discapacidad—GLARP-IIPD, Colombia, 105
Grupo Mulher-Educação Indigena—GRUMIN, Brazil, 73
Haaz (Dr F. P.) Social Assistance Foundation, Ukraine, 393
HEKS—Hilfswerk Evangelischen Kirchen Schweiz, Switzerland, 367
The Helen Suzman Foundation, South Africa, 335
Hellenic Foundation for European and Foreign Policy—ELIAMEP, Greece, 187
HER Fund, Hong Kong, 194
Hilfswerk der Evangelischen Kirchen Schweiz—HEKS, Switzerland, 367
HIVOS—Humanistisch Instituut voor Ontwikkelings Samenwerking, Netherlands, 275
Hope for the Children Foundation, Guatemala, 190
Horizons of Friendship, Canada, 90
Howard (Katharine) Foundation, Ireland, 211
Human Resource Development Foundation, Turkey, 389
Human Rights Foundation of Turkey, Turkey, 390
Humanistic Institute for Co-operation with Developing Countries, Netherlands, 275
Humanistisch Instituut voor Ontwikkelings Samenwerking—HIVOS, Netherlands, 275
Humanitarian Relief Foundation, Turkey, 389
Hungarian Foundation for Self-Reliance—HFSR, Hungary, 195
IACD—Institute of Asian Culture and Development, Korea (Republic), 246
IBON Foundation, Philippines, 303
Icelandic Human Rights Centre, Iceland, 197
ICSSR—Indian Council of Social Science Research, India, 202
IKGV—İnsan Kaynağını Geliştirme Vakfı, Turkey, 389
Indian Centre for Philanthropy, India, 198
Indian Council of Social Science Research—ICSSR, India, 202
Indigenous Women's Education Group, Brazil, 73
Indonesian Forum for the Environment—Friends of the Earth Indonesia, Indonesia, 207
INFID—International NGO Forum on Indonesian Development, Indonesia, 207
INHURED International—International Institute for Human Rights, Environment and Development, Nepal, 271
İnsan Hak ve Hürriyetleri İnsani Yardım Vakfı, Turkey, 389
İnsan Kaynağını Geliştirme Vakfı—IKGV, Turkey, 389
Institusjonen Fritt Ord, Norway, 291

Institut Arctique de l'Amérique du Nord—IAAN, Canada, 81
Institut international des Droits de l'Enfant, Switzerland, 368
Institut Nord-Sud, Canada, 95
Institut Universitaire de Hautes Etudes Internationales et du Développement, Switzerland, 367
Institute of Asian Culture and Development—IACD, Korea (Republic), 246
Institute of Human Rights and Humanitarian Law, Nigeria, 289
Instituto Interamericano de Derechos Humanos—IIHR, Costa Rica, 107
Inter-American Institute of Human Rights, Costa Rica, 107
International Alert—Alert, UK, 422
International Centre for Democratic Transition—ICDT, Hungary, 196
International Centre for the Legal Protection of Human Rights—Interights, UK, 423
International Co-operation, Italy, 217
International Institute for Human Rights, Environment and Development—INHURED International, Nepal, 271
International Institute for the Rights of the Child, Switzerland, 368
International NGO Forum on Indonesian Development—INFID, Indonesia, 207
International Renaissance Foundation—IRF, Ukraine, 394
International Women's Health Coalition—IWHC, USA, 510
Irish Association of Non-Governmental Development Organizations—DOCHAS, Ireland, 210
Isabel Allende Foundation, USA, 463
ISAR: Resources for Environmental Activists, USA, 460
Isis Internacional, Chile, 100
Isis International, Chile, 100
Islamic Thought Foundation, Iran, 209
Jan Hus Educational Foundation, Slovakia, 329
Japanese-German Center Berlin, Germany, 173
Japanisch-Deutsches Zentrum Berlin, Germany, 173
Jenny and Antti Wihuri Foundation, Finland, 134
Jenny ja Antti Wihurin Rahasto, Finland, 134
Jewish Community Development Fund—JCDF, USA, 512
The John D. and Catherine T. MacArthur Foundation, USA, 520
The Johnson Foundation at Wingspread, USA, 512
JOHUD—Jordanian Hashemite Fund for Human Development, Jordan, 241
Jordanian Hashemite Fund for Human Development, Jordan, 241
Joseph Rowntree Reform Trust Ltd (including the JRSST Charitable Trust), UK, 442
JRSST Charitable Trust, UK, 442
Katharine Howard Foundation, Ireland, 211
Kennan Institute, USA, 514
King Baudouin Foundation, Belgium, 62
King Hussein Foundation—KHF, Jordan, 241
KIOS—Finnish NGO Foundation for Human Rights, Finland, 132
Köning Boudewijnstichting/Fondation Roi Baudouin, Belgium, 62
Koret Foundation, USA, 515
Kosovar Civil Society Foundation, Kosovo, 248
Kosovo Foundation for Open Society—KFOS, Kosovo, 248
Kvinna till Kvinna Foundation, Sweden, 354
LACWHN—Latin American and Caribbean Women's Health Network, Chile, 101
Lateinamerika-Zentrum eV—LAZ, Germany, 174
Latin America Centre, Germany, 174
Latin America France, France, 151
Latin American Association of Development Organizations, Mexico, 262
Latin American and Caribbean Women's Health Network—LACWHN, Chile, 101
Latin American Committee for the Defence of Women's Rights, Peru, 299
Latin American Group for the Participation, Integration and Inclusion of People with Disability, Colombia, 105
Latvia Children's Fund, Latvia, 251
Latvijas Bērnu fonds, Latvia, 251
Law Foundation of New South Wales, Australia, 41
Law and Justice Foundation of New South Wales, Australia, 41
Law Society Charity, UK, 428
Van Leer Jerusalem Institute, Israel, 215
Léopold Sédar Senghor Foundation, Senegal, 322
Leprosy Mission International, UK, 428

Leverhulme Trust, UK, 429
Littauer (Lucius N.) Foundation, Inc, USA, 519
Lucius N. Littauer Foundation, Inc, USA, 519
Luxemburg (Rosa) Stiftung, Germany, 174
MacArthur (John D. and Catherine T.) Foundation, USA, 520
McConnell Clark (Edna) Foundation, USA, 520
MADRE, USA, 521
Maison Franco-Japonaise, Japan, 237
Mama Cash, Netherlands, 277
Manfred Woerner Foundation, Bulgaria, 74
Mannréttindaskrifstofa Íslands, Iceland, 197
MAPFRE Foundation, Spain, 345
Marangopoulos Foundation for Human Rights, Greece, 188
Mário Soares Foundation, Portugal, 313
Match International Centre, Canada, 93
Max Schmidheiny Foundation, Switzerland, 372
Max Schmidheiny-Stiftung, Switzerland, 372
medica mondiale e.V., Germany, 175
Medical Foundation for the Care of Victims of Torture, UK, 430
MENCAP, UK, 431
Menzies (R. G.) Scholarship Fund, Australia, 42
Mertz Gilmore Foundation, USA, 524
Metcalf (George Cedric) Charitable Foundation, Canada, 94
Milan Simecka Foundation, Slovakia, 329
Mo Ibrahim Foundation, UK, 421
Moawad (René) Foundation, Lebanon, 253
Mongolian Women's Fund—MONES, Mongolia, 266
Ms Foundation for Women, USA, 526
Myer (Sidney) Fund, Australia, 42
Nadace Charty 77, Czech Republic, 114
Nadácia Ekopolis, Slovakia, 327
Nadácia Milana Šimečku, Slovakia, 329
Nansen (Fridtjof) Institute, Norway, 291
National Conference on Soviet Jewry, USA, 528
National Foundation for Development, El Salvador, 128
National Institute for Sustainable Development—NISD, India, 204
NCH—National Children's Home, UK, 398
NCSJ—National Conference on Soviet Jewry, USA, 528
Nederlands instituut voor Zuidelijk Afrika—NiZA, Netherlands, 278
Nederlandse Organisatie voor Internationale Ontwikkelingssamenwerking—Stichting NOVIB, Netherlands, 279
Nepal Forward Foundation, Nepal, 271
NESsT—Nonprofit Enterprise and Self-sustainability Team, Chile, 101
Netherlands Institute for Southern Africa, Netherlands, 278
Network of Estonian Non-profit Organizations, Estonia, 129
New Perspectives Foundation, Russian Federation, 319
New Zealand Winston Churchill Memorial Trust, New Zealand, 285
NGO Rural and Social Initiative, Moldova, 264
NIOK—Nonprofit Információs és Oktató Központ Alapítvány, Hungary, 195
Nirnaya, India, 204
Non-Profit Information and Training Centre Foundation, Hungary, 195
Nonprofit Enterprise and Self-sustainability Team—NESsT, Chile, 101
Nonprofit Információs és Oktató Központ Alapítvány—NIOK, Hungary, 195
Nordic Africa Institute Scholarships, Sweden, 355
Nordiska Afrikainstitutets Stipendier, Sweden, 355
North-South Institute/Institut Nord-Sud, Canada, 95
Northern Rock Foundation, UK, 435
Novartis Foundation for Sustainable Development—NFSD, Switzerland, 371
Novartis Stiftung für Nachhaltige Entwicklung, Switzerland, 371
NOVIB (Oxfam Netherlands), Netherlands, 279
NoVo Foundation, USA, 529
Nuffield Foundation, UK, 435
Oak Foundation, Switzerland, 371
OneWorld International Foundation, UK, 435
Open Estonia Foundation, Estonia, 129
Open Society Forum (Mongolia), Mongolia, 266
Open Society Foundation, Romania, 317
Open Society Foundation for Albania—OSFA, Albania, 29
Open Society Foundation—Bratislava, Slovakia, 329
Open Society Foundation for South Africa—OSF-SA, South Africa, 334
Open Society Foundation—Turkey, Turkey, 389

Open Society Fund—Bosnia-Herzegovina, Bosnia and Herzegovina, 68
Open Society Fund Prague—OSF Prague, Czech Republic, 115
Open Society Georgia Foundation, Georgia, 157
Open Society Initiative for Southern Africa—OSISA, South Africa, 334
Open Society Initiative for West Africa, Senegal, 322
Open Society Institute—Assistance Foundation (Azerbaijan), Azerbaijan, 50
Open Society Institute Assistance Foundation, Armenia—OSIAFA, Armenia, 35
Open Society Institute Assistance Foundation—Tajikistan, Tajikistan, 381
Open Society Institute—Brussels, Belgium, 63
Open Society Institute Montenegro, Montenegro, 267
Open Society Institute—Sofia (Bulgaria), Bulgaria, 76
Open Society Institute—Turkey, Turkey, 387
Open Society Institute—Washington, DC, USA, 530
The Orient-Occident Foundation, Morocco, 268
OSGF—Open Society Georgia Foundation, Georgia, 157
OSIAF—Open Society Institute Assistance Foundation—Tajikistan, Tajikistan, 381
OSIWA—Open Society Initiative for West Africa, Senegal, 322
Oxfam Canada, Canada, 95
Oxfam India, India, 204
Oxfam Ireland, Ireland, 212
Oxfam Mexico, Mexico, 263
Oxfam New Zealand, New Zealand, 285
Oxfam NOVIB—Nederlandse Organisatie voor Internationale Ontwikkelingssamenwerking, Netherlands, 279
Oxfam NOVIB—Netherlands Organization for International Development Co-operation, Netherlands, 279
Oxfam-Québec, Canada, 95
PAC—Partnership Africa Canada, Canada, 95
Pacific Peoples' Partnership, Canada, 95
Pakistan Institute of International Affairs—PIIA, Pakistan, 294
Partnership Africa Canada—PAC, Canada, 95
PASOS—Policy Association for an Open Society, Czech Republic, 113
Patterson (Alicia) Foundation, USA, 533
PBI—Peace Brigades International, UK, 437
Peace Brigades International—PBI, UK, 437
Peace and Disarmament Education Trust—PADET, New Zealand, 286
Peace Research Center, Spain, 338
Pearl S. Buck International, USA, 474
People in Need, Czech Republic, 113
People's Harmonious Development Society, Georgia, 158
Pertubuhan Pertolongan Wanita, Malaysia, 260
Pinchuk (Victor) Foundation, Ukraine, 394
Pitseng Trust, South Africa, 334
Polden-Puckham Charitable Foundation—PPCF, UK, 438
Pôle européen des fondations de l'économie sociale, Belgium, 56
Polish-American Freedom Foundation, Poland, 305
Polsko-Amerykańska Fundacja Wolności, Poland, 305
Pro Juventute, Switzerland, 372
Public Welfare Foundation, Inc, USA, 537
Quaid-i-Azam Academy, Pakistan, 294
Queen Alia Fund for Social Development, Jordan, 241
Queen's Trust for Young Australians, Australia, 41
Quilliam Foundation, UK, 440
R. G. Menzies Scholarship Fund, Australia, 42
Rajiv Gandhi Foundation, India, 201
Red Mujeres Afrolatinoamericanas Afrocaribeñas, Costa Rica, 107
Red de Mujeres para el Desarrollo, Costa Rica, 107
Red de Salud de las Mujeres Latinoamericanas y del Caribe, Chile, 101
Refugee Trust International, Ireland, 213
Refugees International Japan—RIJ, Japan, 239
René Moawad Foundation, Lebanon, 253
Resource Centre for the Human Rights Nongovernmental Organizations of Moldova—CReDO, Moldova, 264
Robert Schuman Foundation, France, 150
Rosa Luxemburg Foundation, Germany, 174
Rosa-Luxemburg-Stiftung, Germany, 174
Rowan Charitable Trust, UK, 441
Rowntree (Joseph) Reform Trust, UK, 442

Royal Society for Mentally Handicapped Children and Adults—MENCAP, UK, 431
Rroma Foundation, Switzerland, 372
Rutgers WPF, Netherlands, 279
Sabancı (Hacı Ömer) Foundation, Turkey, 389
Sabancı Foundation, Turkey, 389
Sabancı Vakfı—Hacı Ömer Sabancı Foundation, Turkey, 389
Sabre Foundation, Inc, USA, 542
El Salvador Foundation for Economic and Social Development, El Salvador, 128
Sampradaan Indian Centre for Philanthropy, India, 198
Samuel and Saidye Bronfman Family Foundation, Canada, 82
Schools Without Frontiers, France, 139
Schuman (Robert), Fondation, France, 150
Schweizerischer Nationalfonds zur Förderung der wissenschaftlichen Forschung/Fonds National Suisse de la Recherche Scientifique—SNF, Switzerland, 374
SEEMO—IPI—South East Europe Media Organisation, Austria, 49
Self Help Development Foundation, Zimbabwe, 567
Serafín Aliaga Foundation for Peace and Solidarity, Spain, 346
Seva Foundation, USA, 544
Sidney Myer Fund, Australia, 42
Sir Ahmadu Bello Foundation, Nigeria, 289
Sir Ahmadu Bello Memorial Foundation, Nigeria, 289
Sivil Toplum Geliştirme Merkezi—STGM, Turkey, 387
Skoll Foundation, USA, 544
Slovak-Czech Women's Fund, Czech Republic, 115
Slovak Humanitarian Council, Slovakia, 328
Slovenská Humanitná Rada, Slovakia, 328
Soares (Mário), Fundação, Portugal, 313
Solidarity Foundation, Dominican Republic, 123
Soros Foundation (Czech Republic), Czech Republic, 115
Soros Foundation (Estonia), Estonia, 129
Soros Foundation (Georgia), Georgia, 157
Soros Foundation (Slovakia), Slovakia, 328
Soros Foundation (South Africa), South Africa, 334
Soros Foundation (Tajikistan), Tajikistan, 381
Soros Foundation Guatemala, Guatemala, 191
Soros Foundation—Kazakhstan, Kazakhstan, 243
Soros Foundation Latvia, Latvia, 251
Soros Foundation Macedonia, Macedonia, 258
Soros Foundation—Moldova, Moldova, 264
Soros Foundation Romania, Romania, 317
Soros Serbia Foundation, Serbia, 324
SOTA—Research Centre for Turkestan and Azerbaijan, Netherlands, 283
South African Institute of Race Relations, South Africa, 335
South East Europe Media Organisation, Austria, 49
South East Europe Media Organisation—SEEMO—IPI, Austria, 49
South Pacific Peoples Foundation Canada, Canada, 95
Standing International Forum on Ethnic Conflict, Genocide and Human Rights—International Alert, UK, 422
Staples Trust, UK, 449
Steelworkers Humanity Fund, Canada, 98
Stefan Batory Foundation, Poland, 307
Stichting DOEN, Netherlands, 280
Stichting Triodos Foundation, Netherlands, 282
Stiftelsen Riksbankens Jubileumsfond, Sweden, 357
Stiftung Ettersberg, Germany, 180
Stiftung für Kinder, Germany, 181
The Streisand Foundation, USA, 547
Strickland Foundation, Malta, 261
Studienstiftung des deutschen Volkes, Germany, 182
Sun/Soleil—AREGAK, Armenia, 35
Support Centre for Associations and Foundations—SCAF, Belarus, 54
Suzman (Helen) Foundation, South Africa, 335
Swiss Interchurch Aid, Switzerland, 367
Swiss National Science Foundation—SNF, Switzerland, 374
SWISSAID Foundation, Switzerland, 375
Taiga Rescue Network—TRN, Finland, 133
TEAR Australia, Australia, 45
Terre des Hommes Foundation, Switzerland, 376
Tewa, Nepal, 271
TFF—Transnationella Stiftelsen för Freds- och Framtidsforskning, Sweden, 358
Thiel Foundation, USA, 547

Third Sector Foundation of Turkey—TÜSEV, Turkey, 387
Third World Network—TWN, Malaysia, 260
Third World Solidarity Action, Luxembourg, 257
Thyssen (Fritz) Stiftung, Germany, 183
Tides, USA, 548
Tides Foundation, USA, 548
Tifa Foundation—Indonesia, Indonesia, 207
Tinker Foundation, Inc, USA, 548
Transnational Foundation for Peace and Future Research, Sweden, 358
Transnationella Stiftelsen för Freds- och Framtidsforskning—TFF, Sweden, 358
Triodos Foundation, Netherlands, 282
TRN—Taiga Rescue Network, Finland, 133
Trócaire—Catholic Agency for World Development, Ireland, 213
Trust for Civil Society in Central and Eastern Europe, Bulgaria, 76
Türkiye İnsan Hakları Vakfı, Turkey, 390
Tutu (Desmond) Peace Foundation, USA, 549
Tutu Foundation UK, UK, 452
Ukrainian Women's Fund, Ukraine, 394
Umut Foundation, Turkey, 391
Umut Vakfı, Turkey, 391
Union Aid Abroad—APHEDA, Australia, 45
US-Ukraine Foundation, USA, 551
Values Foundation, Bulgaria, 77
VIA Foundation, Czech Republic, 115
Victor Pinchuk Foundation, Ukraine, 394
Vita, Ireland, 213
Voluntary Action Network India—VANI, India, 206
Vzdelávacia nadácia Jana Husa, Slovakia, 329
Wahana Lingkungan Hidup Indonesia—WALHI, Indonesia, 207
WALHI—Wahana Lingkungan Hidup Indonesia, Indonesia, 207
Walter and Duncan Gordon Charitable Foundation, Canada, 89
WaterAid, UK, 454
West African Rural Foundation, Senegal, 322
Westminster Foundation for Democracy—WFD, UK, 455
WHEAT Trust—Women's Hope Education and Training Trust, South Africa, 336
Wihuri (Jenny and Antti) Foundation, Finland, 134
William Adlington Cadbury Charitable Trust, UK, 407
Woerner (Manfred) Foundation, Bulgaria, 74
Women in Equality Foundation, Argentina, 33
Women's Aid, Ireland, 213
Women's Aid Organisation—WAO, Malaysia, 260
Women's Development Network, Costa Rica, 107
Women's Hope Education and Training Trust—Wheat Trust, South Africa, 336
World Association of Children's Friends, Monaco, 265
The World of NGOs, Austria, 46
World Peace Foundation—WPF, USA, 557
World Population Foundation, Netherlands, 279
YADESA—Yayasan Pengembangan Masyarakat Desa, Indonesia, 208
Yayasan Pengembangan Masyarakat Desa—YADESA, Indonesia, 208
Youth for Development and Co-operation—YDC, Netherlands, 283
ZEIT-Stiftung Ebelin und Gerd Bucerius, Germany, 184
ZOA, Netherlands, 283
Zorig Foundation, Mongolia, 266
Zurich Community Trust, UK, 457
Zurich Financial Services (UKISA) Community Trust Ltd, UK, 457

MEDICINE AND HEALTH

1818 Fund Foundation, Netherlands, 280
1945 Foundation, Canada, 90
A. G. Leventis Foundation, Greece, 188
A. G. Leventis Foundation Nigeria, Nigeria, 290
A. M. M. Sahabdeen Trust Foundation, Sri Lanka, 350
The A. P. Møller and Chastine Mc-Kinney Møller Foundation, Denmark, 120
A. P. Møller og Hustru Chastine Mc-Kinney Møllers Fond til almene Formaal, Denmark, 120
Absolute Return for Kids—ARK, UK, 401
Açık Toplum Enstitüsü, Turkey, 387
Acíndar Foundation, Argentina, 31
ACORD—Agency for Co-operation and Research in Development, Kenya, 245
Action contre la Faim, France, 136
Action against Hunger, France, 136

Action Solidarité Tiers Monde—ASTM, Luxembourg, 257
Activ Foundation, Australia, 36
Acumen Fund, USA, 461
Adams (Sylvia) Charitable Trust, UK, 398
AFAP—Australian Foundation for the Peoples of Asia and the Pacific, Australia, 38
AFPE—American Foundation for Pharmaceutical Education, USA, 465
Africa Foundation (UK), UK, 399
Africa Humanitarian Action, Ethiopia, 130
African Medical and Research Foundation—AMREF, Kenya, 245
African Refugees Foundation—AREF, Nigeria, 289
Africare, USA, 462
Aga Khan Foundation—AKF, Switzerland, 360
Aga Khan Fund for Economic Development, Switzerland, 361
Agency for Co-operation and Research in Development, Kenya, 245
Agostino (Daniele Derossi) Foundation, USA, 462
The Ahmanson Foundation, USA, 462
Aid for India/ Karuna Trust, UK, 426
Aide Médicale Internationale, France, 137
AINA—Arctic Institute of North America, Canada, 81
Air France Corporate Foundation, France, 144
AIV—Asia-Africa International Voluntary Foundation, Japan, 231
AJWS—American Jewish World Service, USA, 466
Al Fayed Charitable Foundation, UK, 399
Albanian Disability Rights Foundation, Albania, 29
Alberta Innovates Health Solutions, Canada, 81
Alberto Vollmer Foundation, Inc, USA, 551
Alchemy Foundation, UK, 399
Alemán (Miguel), Fundación, Mexico, 262
Alfred Benzon Foundation, Denmark, 117
Alfred Benzons Fond, Denmark, 117
Alfred P. Sloan Foundation, USA, 545
Alicia Patterson Foundation—APF, USA, 533
Allavida—Alliances for Voluntary Initiatives and Development, Kenya, 244
Alliances for Voluntary Initiatives and Development—Allavida, Kenya, 244
The Alva Foundation, Canada, 81
Alzheimer Spain Foundation, Spain, 339
AMADE Mondiale—Association Mondiale des Amis de l'Enfance, Monaco, 265
Ambuja Cement Foundation, India, 199
American Foundation for the Blind, Inc—AFB, USA, 465
American Foundation for Pharmaceutical Education—AFPE, USA, 465
American Heart Association, Inc, USA, 465
American Jewish World Service—AJWS, USA, 466
American Near East Refugee Aid—ANERA, USA, 467
AMREF—African Medical and Research Foundation, Kenya, 245
ANERA—American Near East Refugee Aid, USA, 467
ANESVAD, Spain, 337
The Annenberg Foundation, USA, 468
Apex Foundation, Australia, 36
APHEDA—Union Aid Abroad, Australia, 45
Archie Sherman Charitable Trust, UK, 448
Arctic Institute of North America—AINA, Canada, 81
AREF—African Refugees Foundation, Nigeria, 289
AREGAK—Sun/Soleil, Armenia, 35
Arie and Ida Crown Memorial, USA, 483
ARK—Absolute Return for Kids, UK, 401
Armand-Frappier Foundation, Canada, 88
Armstrong (Lance) Foundation, USA, 469
Arthritis Australia, Australia, 37
Arthritis Foundation, USA, 469
Arthritis Foundation of Australia, Australia, 37
Arthritis Research Campaign, UK, 401
Arthritis Research UK, UK, 401
Arthritis and Rheumatism Council for Research in Great Britain and the Commonwealth, UK, 401
Asia-Africa International Voluntary Foundation—AIV, Japan, 231
Asian Community Trust—ACT, Japan, 231
Asian Health Institute—AHI, Japan, 231
Association of Medical Research Charities—AMRC, UK, 396
Association Mondiale des Amis de l'Enfance, Monaco, 265
Association of Voluntary Agencies for Rural Development—AVARD, India, 198
Associazione Donatella Flick, Switzerland, 361

Asthma UK, UK, 402
ASTM—Action Solidarité Tiers Monde, Luxembourg, 257
Atlantic Philanthropies, USA, 471
Augusto César Sandino Foundation, Nicaragua, 288
Australasian Spinal Research, Australia, 44
Australian Cancer Research Foundation, Australia, 38
Australian Foundation for the Peoples of Asia and the Pacific—AFAP, Australia, 38
Australian People Health Education, Australia, 45
Australian Spinal Research Foundation, Australia, 39
Australian Youth Foundation, Australia, 41
AVARD—Association of Voluntary Agencies for Rural Development, India, 198
AVRDC—The World Vegetable Center, Taiwan, 379
Ayala Foundation USA—AF-USA, USA, 535
Aydın Doğan Foundation, Turkey, 388
Aydın Doğan Vakfı, Turkey, 388
Ayrton Senna Institute, Brazil, 73
BAFROW—Foundation for Research on Women's Health, Productivity and the Environment, Gambia, 156
Baker (E. A.) Foundation for the Prevention of Blindness, Canada, 85
Baker Heart Research Institute, Australia, 39
Baker IDI Heart & Diabetes Institute, Australia, 39
Bank of America Foundation, USA, 472
Barceló Foundation, Spain, 340
The Barretstown Camp Fund Ltd, Ireland, 210
Barrié de la Maza (Pedro, Conde de Fenosa), Fundación, Spain, 340
The Batchworth Trust, UK, 403
BBC World Service Trust, UK, 403
Beaverbrook Foundation, UK, 403
Beit Trust, UK, 403
Belarusian Charitable Fund 'For the Children of Chornobyl', Belarus, 54
Bell (Max) Foundation, Canada, 81
Benesco Charity Limited, UK, 404
Benzon (Alfred) Foundation, Denmark, 117
The Bernard Sunley Charitable Foundation, UK, 450
Bertelsmann Foundation, Germany, 162
Bertelsmann Stiftung, Germany, 162
Bettencourt Schueller Foundation, France, 141
BibleLands, UK, 404
Birthright, UK, 455
Bleustein-Blanchet (Marcel), Fondation pour la Vocation, France, 141
Bodossaki Foundation, Greece, 186
Boghossian Foundation, Belgium, 60
Boltzmann (Ludwig) Gesellschaft, Austria, 46
Bosch (Robert) Stiftung GmbH, Germany, 163
Brazil Foundation, Brazil, 70
Bread for the World, Germany, 163
Bridge to Asia—BTA, USA, 473
Britain-Nepal Medical Trust, UK, 405
British Heart Foundation, UK, 406
The Broad Foundations, USA, 474
Brockhoff (Jack) Foundation, Australia, 39
Brot für die Welt, Germany, 163
Brother's Brother Foundation, USA, 474
Buck (Pearl S. Buck) International, USA, 474
Bunge y Born Foundation, Argentina, 32
Burroughs Wellcome Fund—BWF, USA, 475
Butler (J. Homer) Foundation, USA, 504
C. P. Ramaswami Aiyar Foundation, India, 204
Cadbury (William Adlington) Charitable Trust, UK, 407
Canadian Cancer Society, Canada, 83
Canadian Liver Foundation/Fondation Canadienne du Foie, Canada, 85
Canadian Physicians for Aid and Relief—CPAR, Canada, 86
Cancer Council Australia, Australia, 40
Cancer Relief Macmillan Fund, UK, 430
Cancer Research Fund of the Damon Runyon-Walter Winchell Foundation, USA, 541
Cancer Research UK, UK, 408
Cancer Society of New Zealand, Inc, New Zealand, 284
Cancerfonden, Sweden, 352
Canon Foundation in Europe, Netherlands, 272
CARE International—CI, Switzerland, 361
Cariplo Foundation, Italy, 219
Carnegie Corporation of New York, USA, 475
Carson (John W.) Foundation, USA, 476
The Carter Center, USA, 476
Catholic Agency for World Development—Trócaire, Ireland, 213
CCF—Christian Children's Fund, USA, 478

CECHE—Center for Communications, Health and the Environment, USA, 477
Center for Communications, Health and the Environment—CECHE, USA, 477
Centre for Environment, Education and Development, USA, 516
Centre International de Développement et de Recherche—CIDR, France, 138
CEPH—Centre d'Étude du Polymorphisme Humain, France, 142
Cera, Belgium, 57
Charity Projects, UK, 411
Charles and Lynn Schusterman Family Foundation—CLSFF, USA, 543
Charter 77 Foundation, Czech Republic, 114
Chastell Foundation, Canada, 85
Chia Hsin Foundation, Taiwan, 379
The Chicago Community Trust, USA, 478
ChildFund International, USA, 478
ChildFund Korea, Korea (Republic), 246
Children in Africa Foundation, Germany, 181
Children of The Americas—COTA, USA, 479
Children International—CI, USA, 479
Children of the Mekong, France, 139
Children and Sharing, France, 139
Children's Medical Research Institute, Australia, 40
Childwick Trust, UK, 409
China Medical Board, USA, 479
Christopher and Dana Reeve Foundation, USA, 538
Christos Stelios Ioannou Foundation, Cyprus, 111
CIDR—Centre International de Développement et de Recherche, France, 138
Cindi Foundation, Czech Republic, 113
Claude Pompidou Foundation, France, 148
CLIC Sargent, UK, 410
Clive and Vera Ramaciotti Foundations, Australia, 43
Clore Duffield Foundation—CDF, UK, 411
CNIB/INCA, Canada, 85
Collier Charitable Fund, Australia, 40
Colt Foundation, UK, 411
Comic Relief, UK, 411
Committee of Good Will—Olga Havel Foundation, Czech Republic, 115
Community Aid Abroad—Oxfam Australia, Australia, 43
Community Development Foundation, Mozambique, 269
Community Foundation for Northern Ireland, UK, 412
Compagnia di San Paolo, Italy, 217
Concern India Foundation, India, 201
Consejo de Fundaciones Americanas de Desarrollo—Solidarios, Dominican Republic, 123
Cooperazione Internazionale—COOPI, Italy, 217
COOPI—Cooperazione Internazionale, Italy, 217
Council of American Development Foundations, Dominican Republic, 123
CPAR—Canadian Physicians for Aid and Relief, Canada, 86
The CRB Foundation/La Fondation CRB, Canada, 86
Croucher Foundation, Hong Kong, 194
Crown (Arie and Ida) Memorial, USA, 483
Crown Family Philanthropies, USA, 483
CRT Foundation, Italy, 220
CUSO-VSO, Canada, 86
Cystic Fibrosis Canada, Canada, 87
Cystic Fibrosis Foundation, USA, 484
Cystic Fibrosis Trust, UK, 413
Dahl (Roald) Foundation, UK, 413
Damien Foundation, Belgium, 58
Damon Runyon Cancer Research Foundation, USA, 541
Daniele Agostino Derossi Foundation, USA, 462
Deutsche AIDS-Stiftung, Germany, 164
Deutsche Bank Foundation, Germany, 164
Deutsche Bank Stiftung, Germany, 164
Deutsche Krebshilfe eV, Germany, 165
Deutsche Stiftung Weltbevölkerung—DSW, Germany, 165
Deutsches Rheuma-Forschungszentrum Berlin, Germany, 166
Diabetes UK, UK, 414
Dian Desa Foundation, Indonesia, 207
Diana, Princess of Wales Memorial Fund, UK, 414
Dietmar Hopp Foundation, Germany, 170
Dietmar-Hopp-Stiftung, Germany, 170
Dóchas, Ireland, 210
Doğan (Aydın) Vakfı, Turkey, 388
Donors' Association for the Promotion of Sciences and Humanities, Germany, 159
Dr Antonio Esteve Foundation, Spain, 343
Dr J. R. Villavicencio Foundation, Argentina, 33

Dr Rainer Wild Foundation for Healthy
Nutrition, Germany, 184
Dr Rainer Wild-Stiftung—Stiftung für gesunde
Ernährung, Germany, 184
Dr Scholl Foundation, USA, 543
Dräger Foundation, Germany, 166
Dräger-Stiftung, Germany, 166
Dreyfus Health Foundation—DHF, USA, 485
Drug Policy Alliance—DPA, USA, 485
DSW—Deutsche Stiftung Weltbevölkerung,
Germany, 165
Duke Endowment, USA, 486
Dutch Cancer Society, Netherlands, 276
EcoHealth Alliance, USA, 487
ECPD—European Centre for Peace and
Development, Serbia, 324
Eden Foundation, Sweden, 353
The Edmond de Rothschild Foundations,
USA, 541
The Edna McConnell Clark Foundation,
USA, 520
Egmont Fonden, Denmark, 118
Egmont Foundation, Denmark, 118
Eisai Foundation, France, 143
EJLB Foundation, Canada, 87
Eldee Foundation, Canada, 87
Ellerman (John) Foundation, UK, 414
Else Kröner-Fresenius Foundation, Germany, 173
Else Kröner-Fresenius-Stiftung, Germany, 173
Empower Foundation, Thailand, 383
EMUNAH, UK, 415
ENCOD—European NGO Council on Drugs and
Development, Belgium, 59
Enda Third World—Environment and
Development Action in the Third World,
Senegal, 322
Enda Tiers Monde—Environnement et
Développement du Tiers-Monde, Senegal, 322
endPoverty.org, USA, 488
Enfance et Partage, France, 139
Enfants du Mekong, France, 139
Ente Cassa di Risparmio di Firenze, Italy, 217
Enterprise Development International, USA, 488
Entraide Protestante Suisse, Switzerland, 367
Environnement et Développement du Tiers-
Monde—Enda, Senegal, 322
Epilepsy Foundation, USA, 489
Eskom Development Foundation, South
Africa, 332
Espejo (Eugenio), Fundación, Ecuador, 125
Esperança, Inc, USA, 489
Estonian National Culture Foundation,
Estonia, 129
Eugenio Espejo Foundation, Ecuador, 125
European Centre for Peace and Development—
ECPD, Serbia, 324
European Coalition for Just and Effective Drug
Policies—ENCOD, Belgium, 59
European Federation of National Organizations
Working with the Homeless, Belgium, 55
European Institute of Health and Social Welfare,
Spain, 349
European Network of Foundations for Social
Economy, Belgium, 56
European Science Foundation, France, 144
Eurotransplant International Foundation,
Netherlands, 274
Evangelisches Studienwerk eV, Germany, 167
Eveson (Violet) Charitable Trust, UK, 416
The Eveson Charitable Trust, UK, 416
Evrika Foundation, Bulgaria, 75
Faith, UK, 415
The Family Federation of Finland, Finland, 133
Family Planning, New Zealand, 284
FDC—Fundação para o Desenvolvimento da
Comunidade, Mozambique, 269
FEANTSA—Fédération Européenne des
Associations Nationales Travaillant avec les
Sans-Abri, Belgium, 55
Fédération Européenne des Associations
Nationales Travaillant avec les Sans-Abri—
FEANTSA, Belgium, 55
FEPP—Fondo Ecuatoriano Populorum
Progressio, Ecuador, 124
Ferrero (Piera, Pietro e Giovanni), Fondazione,
Italy, 221
FFL—Fondation Follereau Luxembourg,
Luxembourg, 257
FH—Food for the Hungry, USA, 491
Finnish Cultural Foundation, Finland, 132
Firefly, Inc., USA, 490
Firelight Foundation, USA, 490
FirstRand Foundation, South Africa, 332
Florence Gould Foundation, USA, 499
Florence Savings Bank Foundation, Italy, 217
Follereau Foundation Luxembourg,
Luxembourg, 257

Fondacioni Shqiptar per te Drejtat e Paaftesise,
Albania, 29
Fondation Armand-Frappier, Canada, 88
Fondation de l'Avenir, France, 140
Fondation Bettencourt-Schueller, France, 141
Fondation Boghossian, Belgium, 60
Fondation Claude Pompidou, France, 148
Fondation pour le Développement de la
Psychothérapie Médicale, spécialement de la
psychothérapie de groupe, Switzerland, 363
Fondation Eisai, France, 143
Fondation EJLB, Canada, 87
Fondation d'Entreprise Air France, France, 144
Fondation Européenne de la Science, France, 144
Fondation contre la Faim, USA, 491
Fondation Follereau Luxembourg—FFL,
Luxembourg, 257
Fondation de France, France, 135
Fondation Hans Wilsdorf—Montres Rolex,
Switzerland, 366
Fondation Hugot du Collège de France,
France, 145
Fondation Institut Suisse de Recherche
Expérimentale sur le Cancer, Switzerland, 364
Fondation Internationale Léon Mba—Institut de
Médecine et d'Epidémiologie Appliquée,
France, 146
Fondation ISREC, Switzerland, 364
Fondation Jean Dausset—Centre d'Étude du
Polymorphisme Humain—CEPH, France, 142
Fondation Jean-Louis Lévesque, Canada, 88
Fondation Louis-Jeantet de Médecine,
Switzerland, 364
Fondation Marcel Bleustein-Blanchet pour la
Vocation, France, 141
Fondation Princesse Grace, Monaco, 265
Fondation Pro Victimis Genève, Switzerland, 365
Fondation pour la Recherche Médicale,
France, 149
Fondation Roi Baudouin, Belgium, 62
Fondation Simón I. Patiño, Switzerland, 365
Fondazione Cariplo, Italy, 219
Fondazione Cassa di Risparmio delle Provincie
Lombarde—Fondazione Cariplo, Italy, 219
Fondazione Cassa di Risparmio di Padova e
Rovigo, Italy, 219
Fondazione Cassa di Risparmio di Torino,
Italy, 220
Fondazione Giovanni Lorenzini, Italy, 222
Fondazione Internazionale Menarini, Italy, 222
Fondazione Piera, Pietro e Giovanni Ferrero—
ONLUS, Italy, 221
Fondazione Roma, Italy, 224
Fondazione Salvatore Maugeri—Clinica del
Lavoro e della Riabilitazione, Italy, 223
Fondo Ecuatoriano Populorum Progressio—
FEPP, Ecuador, 124
Fonds für Entwicklung und Partnerschaft in
Afrika—FEPA, Switzerland, 366
Fonds National de la Recherche Scientifique—
FNRS, Belgium, 61
Fonds National Suisse de la Recherche
Scientifique, Switzerland, 374
Fonds Wetenschappelijk Onderzoek—
Vlaanderen, Belgium, 62
FOOD—Foundation of Occupational
Development, India, 201
Food for the Hungry—FH, USA, 491
Food for the Poor, Inc, USA, 491
FOPERDA—Fondation Royale Père Damien pour
la Lutte Contre la Lèpre, Belgium, 58
FORWARD—Foundation for Women's Health,
Research and Development, UK, 417
FOSIM—Foundation Open Society Institute
Macedonia, Macedonia, 258
Foundation Cassa di Risparmio di Padova e
Rovigo, Italy, 219
Foundation for Children, Germany, 181
Foundation for the Development of Medical
Psychotherapy, especially Group
Psychotherapy, Switzerland, 363
Foundation for Development and Partnership in
Africa, Switzerland, 366
Foundation of the Future, France, 140
Foundation for Human Rights and Humanitarian
Relief, Turkey, 389
Foundation for Medical Research, France, 149
Foundation of Occupational Development—
FOOD, India, 201
Foundation Open Society Institute Macedonia—
FOSIM, Macedonia, 258
Foundation for the Peoples of the South Pacific,
Australia, 38
Foundation to Promote Health,
Liechtenstein, 255
Foundation for Research on Women's Health,
Productivity and the Environment—
BAFROW, Gambia, 156

Foundation for Revitalization of Local Health
Traditions—FRLHT, India, 201
Foundation for the Study of Infant Deaths,
UK, 417
Foundation for Women's Health, Research and
Development—FORWARD, UK, 417
Foundation for Young Australians, Australia, 41
Francis Family Foundation, USA, 493
Frappier (Armand), Fondation, Canada, 88
The Fred Hollows Foundation, Australia, 41
Freedom from Hunger, USA, 494
Friede Springer Heart Foundation, Germany, 179
Friede Springer Herz Stiftung, Germany, 179
Fritz Thyssen Foundation, Germany, 183
Fritz Thyssen Stiftung, Germany, 183
FRLHT—Foundation Revitalization Local
Health, India, 201
FUHEM—Fundación Hogar del Empleado,
Spain, 343
Fund for Development and Partnership in Africa,
Switzerland, 366
Fund for an Open Society—Serbia, Serbia, 324
Fundação para o Desenvolvimento da
Comunidade, Mozambique, 269
Fundação Maria Cecilia Souto Vidigal, Brazil, 73
Fundació 'La Caixa', Spain, 338
Fundación Acíndar, Argentina, 31
Fundación Alberto Vollmer, USA, 551
Fundación Alzheimer España—FAE, Spain, 339
Fundación Antonio Restrepo Barco,
Colombia, 104
Fundación Augusto César Sandino—FACS,
Nicaragua, 288
Fundación Barceló, Spain, 340
Fundación Bunge y Born, Argentina, 32
Fundación Científica de la Asociación Española
Contra el Cáncer—AECC, Spain, 342
Fundación Corona, Colombia, 104
Fundación Dr Antonio Esteve, Spain, 343
Fundación Dr J. Roberto Villavicencio,
Argentina, 33
Fundación Empresa-Universidad de Zaragoza—
FEUZ, Spain, 342
Fundación Empresas Polar, Venezuela, 563
Fundación Eugenio Espejo, Ecuador, 125
Fundación General Ecuatoriana, Ecuador, 125
Fundación Hogar del Empleado—FUHEM,
Spain, 343
Fundación Jiménez Díaz, Spain, 344
Fundación MAPFRE, Spain, 345
Fundación María Francisca de Roviralta,
Spain, 347
Fundación Miguel Alemán AC, Mexico, 262
Fundación ONCE, Spain, 346
Fundación Panamericana de la Salud y
Educación, USA, 532
Fundación Pedro Barrié de la Maza, Spain, 340
Fundación Rafael del Pino, Spain, 347
Fundación de Viviendas Hogar de Cristo,
Chile, 100
Fundacja Bankowa im. Leopolda Kronenberga,
Poland, 306
Fundacja im. Stefana Batorego, Poland, 307
Fundacja Pro Bono II, Poland, 308
Garfield Weston Foundation, UK, 455
The Gatsby Charitable Foundation, UK, 418
Gemeinnützige Hertie Foundation, Germany, 169
Gemeinnützige Hertie-Stiftung, Germany, 169
General Ecuadorean Foundation, Ecuador, 125
George Cedric Metcalf Charitable Foundation,
Canada, 94
George and Thelma Paraskevaides Foundation,
Cyprus, 111
German AIDS Foundation, Germany, 164
German Cancer Assistance, Germany, 165
German Foundation for World Population,
Germany, 165
German National Academic Foundation,
Germany, 182
German Rheumatism Research Centre Berlin,
Germany, 166
Gift of the Givers Foundation, South Africa, 332
Gilman (Howard) Foundation, USA, 496
Giovanni Lorenzini Foundation, Italy, 222
The Glass-House Trust, UK, 419
Global Ethic Foundation Czech Republic, Czech
Republic, 114
Global Harmony Foundation—GHF,
Switzerland, 367
Global Voluntary Service—GVS, Japan, 232
Global Water Foundation, South Africa, 333
Goldsmith (Horace W.) Foundation, USA, 498
Good Neighbors International, Korea
(Republic), 246
Gould (Florence) Foundation, USA, 499
Grant (William T.) Foundation, USA, 499
The Grass Foundation, USA, 499
Great Britain Sasakawa Foundation, UK, 419

Guggenheim (John Simon) Memorial Foundation, USA, 500
H. W. and J. Hector Foundation, Germany, 169
H. W. und J. Hector-Stiftung, Germany, 169
HALO Trust, UK, 419
Hamdard Foundation Pakistan, Pakistan, 294
Hans Wilsdorf Foundation, Switzerland, 366
Harry and Jeanette Weinberg Foundation, Inc, USA, 552
Hartford (John A.) Foundation, Inc, USA, 501
Health Action International, Netherlands, 275
Health Volunteers Overseas—HVO, USA, 501
For a Healthy Generation, Uzbekistan, 561
Hearst (William Randolph) Foundation, USA, 502
The Hearst Foundation, Inc, USA, 501
Heart Foundation, Australia, 42
Heinz (Howard) Endowment, USA, 502
HEKS—Hilfswerk Evangelischen Kirchen Schweiz, Switzerland, 367
Hellenic Society for Disabled Children, Greece, 187
Helmsley (Leona M. and Harry B.) Charitable Trust, USA, 503
Helmut Horten Foundation, Switzerland, 367
Helmut-Horten-Stiftung, Switzerland, 367
The Henry J. Kaiser Family Foundation, USA, 513
The Henry Smith Charity, UK, 448
Hesse and Thuringia Savings Banks Cultural Foundation, Germany, 178
Heydar Aliyev Foundation, Azerbaijan, 50
Higgins (Terrence) Trust, UK, 420
Hilden Charitable Fund, UK, 421
Hilfswerk der Evangelischen Kirchen Schweiz—HEKS, Switzerland, 367
Hjärt-Lungfonden, Sweden, 353
Hogar de Cristo, Chile, 100
Hollows (Fred) Foundation, Australia, 41
Home of Christ, Chile, 100
Hong Kong Society for the Blind, Hong Kong, 194
Hopp (Dietmar) Stiftung, Germany, 170
Horace W. Goldsmith Foundation, USA, 498
Horizons of Friendship, Canada, 90
Horten (Helmut) Stiftung, Switzerland, 367
Hospital for Sick Children Foundation, Canada, 97
Houston Endowment, Inc, USA, 504
Howard Gilman Foundation, Inc, USA, 496
Howard Heinz Endowment, USA, 502
Hugot Foundation of the Collège of France, France, 145
Human Resource Development Foundation, Turkey, 389
The Humana Foundation, Inc, USA, 505
Humanitarian Relief Foundation, Turkey, 389
IACD—Institute of Asian Culture and Development, Korea (Republic), 246
Ian Potter Foundation, Australia, 43
IASC—International Arctic Science Committee, Germany, 171
ICSSR—Indian Council of Social Science Research, India, 202
IHCF—Stiftung zur Förderung der Gesundheit, Liechtenstein, 255
IKEA Foundation, Netherlands, 275
IKGV—İnsan Kaynağını Geliştirme Vakfı, Turkey, 389
Imperial Cancer Research Fund, UK, 408
Imperial Oil Foundation, Canada, 90
India Assistance, Germany, 171
Indian Council of Social Science Research—ICSSR, India, 202
Indienhilfe eV, Germany, 171
Inlaks Foundation, India, 203
INMED Partnerships for Children, USA, 506
İnsan Hak ve Hürriyetleri İnsani Yardım Vakfı, Turkey, 389
İnsan Kaynağını Geliştirme Vakfı—IKGV, Turkey, 389
Institut Arctique de l'Amérique du Nord—IAAN, Canada, 81
Institut de Médecine et d'Épidémiologie Africaines—Fondation Léon Mba, France, 146
Institut Pasteur de Lille, France, 153
Institute of Asian Culture and Development—IACD, Korea (Republic), 246
Institute for Development Research, USA, 556
Instituto Ayrton Senna, Brazil, 73
Instituto Europeo de Salud y Bienestar Social, Spain, 349
Instituto Senna (Ayrton), Brazil, 73
International Arctic Science Committee—IASC, Germany, 171
International Blue Crescent Relief and Development Foundation—IBC, Turkey, 390
International Centre for Development and Research, France, 138

International Charitable Fund 'Ukraine 3000', Ukraine, 394
International Co-operation, Italy, 217
International Dental Rescue, Switzerland, 374
International Development and Relief Foundation, Canada, 91
International Diabetes Institute, Australia, 39
The International Foundation, USA, 508
International Foundation for Education and Self-Help—IFESH, USA, 509
International Foundation Léon Mba—Institute of Applied Medicine and Epidemiology, France, 146
International Medical Services for Health—INMED, USA, 506
International Orthodox Christian Charities, Inc—IOCC, USA, 509
International Refugee Trust—IRT, UK, 424
International Relief and Development—IRD, USA, 510
International Relief Teams, USA, 510
International Renaissance Foundation—IRF, Ukraine, 394
International Visegrad Fund—IVF, Slovakia, 328
International Women's Health Coalition—IWHC, USA, 510
Ioannou (Christos Stelios) Foundation, Cyprus, 111
IOMS—Islamic Organization for Medical Sciences, Kuwait, 249
Irish Association of Non-Governmental Development Organizations—DOCHAS, Ireland, 210
Islamic Thought Foundation, Iran, 209
ISREC Foundation, Switzerland, 364
Istituto Auxologico Italiano, Italy, 227
Italian Institute for Auxology, Italy, 227
Ittleson Foundation, USA, 511
Ivey (Richard) Foundation, Canada, 91
Ivey Foundation, Canada, 91
Izumi Foundation, USA, 512
The J. F. Kapnek Trust Zimbabwe, Zimbabwe, 567
J. Homer Butler Foundation, Inc, USA, 504
J. R. McKenzie Trust, New Zealand, 284
Jack Brockhoff Foundation—JBF, Australia, 39
Jahnsson (Yrjö) Foundation, Finland, 131
Japan Heart Foundation, Japan, 236
Japanese-German Center Berlin, Germany, 173
Japanisch-Deutsches Zentrum Berlin, Germany, 173
Jean-Louis Lévesque Foundation, Canada, 88
JEN, Japan, 237
Jenny and Antti Wihuri Foundation, Finland, 134
Jenny ja Antti Wihurin Rahasto, Finland, 134
Jerusalem Foundation, Israel, 214
Jiménez Díaz Foundation, Spain, 344
The John A. Hartford Foundation, USA, 501
John Ellerman Foundation, UK, 414
John Simon Guggenheim Memorial Foundation, USA, 500
The John W. Carson Foundation, USA, 476
Johnson (Robert Wood) Foundation, USA, 512
Joseph Levy Charitable Foundation, UK, 429
Joseph Levy Foundation, UK, 429
Joseph P. Kennedy, Jr Foundation, USA, 515
Josiah Macy, Jr Foundation, USA, 521
Kade (Max) Foundation, Inc, USA, 513
Kahanoff Foundation, Canada, 91
Kaiser (Henry J.) Family Foundation, USA, 513
Kapnek (J. F.) Charitable Trust Zimbabwe, Zimbabwe, 567
Karuna Trust/ Aid for India, UK, 426
Kennedy (Joseph P.), Jr Foundation, USA, 515
Kensington Estate—Henry Smith Charity, UK, 448
KFAS—Kuwait Foundation for the Advancement of Sciences, Kuwait, 249
Kinder in Afrika, Stiftung, Germany, 181
King Baudouin Foundation, Belgium, 62
King Hussein Foundation—KHF, Jordan, 241
The King's Fund, UK, 427
Knut and Alice Wallenberg Foundation, Sweden, 358
Knut och Alice Wallenbergs Stiftelse, Sweden, 358
Koç (Vehbi), Vakfı, Turkey, 391
Kokkalis Foundation, Greece, 187
Komen (Susan G.) Breast Cancer Foundation, USA, 515
Köning Boudewijnstichting/Fondation Roi Baudouin, Belgium, 62
Koningin Wilhelmina Fonds—Nederlandse Kankerbestrijding, Netherlands, 276
Kronenberga (Leopolda), Fundacja Bankowa, Poland, 306
Kröner-Fresenius (Else) Stiftung, Germany, 173
KRS Education and Rural Development Foundation, Inc, USA, 516

Kuwait Foundation for the Advancement of Sciences—KFAS, Kuwait, 249
Kvinna till Kvinna Foundation, Sweden, 354
KWF Kankerbestrijding, Netherlands, 276
'La Caixa' Foundation, Spain, 338
LACWHN—Latin American and Caribbean Women's Health Network, Chile, 101
Lama Gangchen World Peace Foundation, Italy, 227
Lance Armstrong Foundation—Livestrong, USA, 469
Lateinamerika-Zentrum eV—LAZ, Germany, 174
Latin America Centre, Germany, 174
Latin American and Caribbean Women's Health Network—LACWHN, Chile, 101
Latvia Children's Fund, Latvia, 251
Latvijas Bērnu fonds, Latvia, 251
The Lawson Foundation, Canada, 92
The Leona M. and Harry B. Helmsley Charitable Trust, USA, 503
Leopold Kronenberg Foundation, Poland, 306
Leprosy Mission International, UK, 428
Leukaemia and Lymphoma Research, UK, 428
Leventis (A. G.) Foundation, Greece, 188
Leventis (A. G.) Foundation Nigeria, Nigeria, 290
Levesque (Jean-Louis), Fondation, Canada, 88
Levy (Joseph) Foundation, UK, 429
Lietuvos vaikų fondas, Lithuania, 256
Life Sciences Research Foundation—LSRF, USA, 518
Lifewater International—LI, USA, 518
Liliane Foundation, Netherlands, 281
Lithuanian Children's Fund, Lithuania, 256
Livestrong, USA, 469
Lorenzini (Giovanni), Fondazione, Italy, 222
The Lotte and John Hecht Memorial Foundation, Canada, 90
Louis-Jeantet Medical Foundation, Switzerland, 364
Lucie and André Chagnon Foundation/ Fondation Lucie et André Chagnon, Canada, 85
Ludwig Boltzmann Gesellschaft, Austria, 46
Ludwig Institute for Cancer Research—LICR, USA, 519
Lundbeck Foundation, Denmark, 120
Lundbeckfonden, Denmark, 120
LWR—Lutheran World Relief, USA, 519
M-USA—Mercy-USA for Aid and Development, USA, 524
McConnell Clark (Edna) Foundation, USA, 520
McCormick (Robert R.) Foundation, USA, 520
Macdonald Stewart Foundation, Canada, 92
McKenzie (J. R.) Trust, New Zealand, 284
The Mackintosh Foundation, UK, 430
McKnight Foundation, USA, 521
The McLean Foundation, Canada, 93
Macmillan Cancer Relief, UK, 430
Macy (Josiah), Jr Foundation, USA, 521
MADRE, USA, 521
Malcolm Sargent Cancer Fund for Children, UK, 410
Mandela (Nelson) Children's Fund, South Africa, 333
MAP International—Medical Assistance Programs, USA, 522
MAPFRE Foundation, Spain, 345
Marcel Bleustein-Blanchet Vocation Foundation, France, 141
March of Dimes, USA, 522
María Francisca de Roviralta Foundation, Spain, 347
Marie Curie Cancer Care, UK, 412
Markle (John and Mary R.) Foundation, USA, 522
Markle Foundation, USA, 522
Match International Centre, Canada, 93
Max Bell Foundation, Canada, 81
The Max Foundation, USA, 522
Max Kade Foundation, Inc, USA, 513
Mba (Léon), Fondation—Institut de Médecine et d'Épidémiologie Africaines, France, 146
medica mondiale e.V., Germany, 175
Medical Assistance Programs, USA, 522
Medical Emergency Relief International—MERLIN, UK, 432
Medical Foundation for the Care of Victims of Torture, UK, 430
Mellon (Richard King) Foundation, USA, 523
Menarini International Foundation, Italy, 222
Mental Health Foundation, UK, 431
Menzies (R. G.) Scholarship Fund, Australia, 42
Menzies (Sir Robert) Foundation Ltd, Australia, 41
Mercy-USA for Aid and Development—M-USA, USA, 524
MERLIN—Medical Emergency Relief International, UK, 432

Metcalf (George Cedric) Charitable Foundation, Canada, 94
Michael J. Fox Foundation for Parkinson's Research, USA, 493
Miguel Alemán Foundation, Mexico, 262
Milbank Memorial Fund, USA, 524
Miriam Dean Fund, UK, 413
Miriam Dean Refugee Trust Fund, UK, 413
Moawad (René) Foundation, Lebanon, 253
Møller (A.P.) and Chastine Mc-Kinney Møller Foundation, Denmark, 120
Molson Family Foundation, Canada, 94
Molson Foundation, Canada, 94
Montres Rolex, Fondation, Switzerland, 366
Monument Trust, UK, 432
Moody Foundation, USA, 525
Ms Foundation for Women, USA, 526
Mukti Lawrence Foundation, Bangladesh, 52
Multiple Sclerosis Society of Great Britain and Northern Ireland, UK, 433
Muscular Dystrophy Campaign, UK, 433
Muslim Aid, UK, 433
Myer (Sidney) Fund, Australia, 42
Nadace Charty 77, Czech Republic, 114
Naito Foundation, Japan, 238
Nathan Steinberg Family Foundation, Canada, 98
National Asthma Campaign, UK, 402
National Endowment for Science, Technology and the Arts—NESTA, UK, 434
National Fund for Scientific Research, Belgium, 61
National Heart Foundation of Australia, Australia, 42
National Heart Foundation of New Zealand, New Zealand, 285
National Institute for Sustainable Development—NISD, India, 204
National Kidney Foundation, Inc, USA, 527
Nelson Mandela Children's Fund, South Africa, 333
Nelson Mandela Children's Fund—Canada, Canada, 93
NESsT—Nonprofit Enterprise and Self-sustainability Team, Chile, 101
NESTA—National Endowment for Science, Technology and the Arts, UK, 434
New Zealand Winston Churchill Memorial Trust, New Zealand, 285
NFCR—National Foundation for Cancer Research, USA, 529
NGO Rural and Social Initiative, Moldova, 264
Non-Governmental Organization JEN, Japan, 237
Nonprofit Enterprise and Self-sustainability Team—NESsT, Chile, 101
Noor al-Hussein Foundation—NHF, Jordan, 241
Northern Ireland Voluntary Trust, UK, 412
Novartis Foundation for Sustainable Development—NFSD, Switzerland, 371
Novartis Foundation for Therapeutical Research, Germany, 175
Novartis Stiftung für Nachhaltige Entwicklung, Switzerland, 371
Novartis-Stiftung für therapeutische Forschung, Germany, 175
Novo Nordisk Foundation, Denmark, 120
ONCE—Spanish National Organization for the Blind—Foundation, Spain, 346
OPALS—Organisation Panafricaine de Lutte Contre le SIDA, France, 153
Open Society Foundation for South Africa—OSF-SA, South Africa, 334
Open Society Initiative for Southern Africa—OSISA, South Africa, 334
Open Society Initiative for West Africa, Senegal, 322
Open Society Institute—Assistance Foundation (Azerbaijan), Azerbaijan, 50
Open Society Institute Assistance Foundation, Armenia—OSIAFA, Armenia, 35
Open Society Institute Assistance Foundation—Tajikistan, Tajikistan, 381
Open Society Institute—Sofia (Bulgaria), Bulgaria, 76
Open Society Institute—Turkey, Turkey, 387
Operation Eyesight Universal/Action universelle de la vue, Canada, 95
Operation Rainbow, Inc, USA, 530
Orentreich Foundation for the Advancement of Science, Inc—OFAS, USA, 531
Organisation Panafricaine de Lutte Contre le SIDA—OPALS, France, 153
OSIAF—Open Society Institute Assistance Foundation—Tajikistan, Tajikistan, 381
OSIWA—Open Society Initiative for West Africa, Senegal, 322
Oxfam Australia, Australia, 43
Oxfam Canada, Canada, 95

Oxfam-Québec, Canada, 95
Paavo Nurmen Säätiö, Finland, 132
Paavo Nurmi Foundation, Finland, 132
Pacific Leprosy Foundation, New Zealand, 286
Pacific Peoples' Partnership, Canada, 95
PAHEF—Pan American Health and Education Foundation, USA, 532
Pan-African Organization for AIDS Prevention, France, 153
Paraskevaides (George and Thelma) Foundation, Cyprus, 111
Parkinson's Disease Foundation, Inc—PDF, USA, 533
The Parthenon Trust, Switzerland, 371
Pasteur Institute of Lille, France, 153
Pathfinder International, USA, 533
Patiño (Simón I.), Fondation, Switzerland, 365
Patterson (Alicia) Foundation, USA, 533
Paulo Foundation, Finland, 132
Paulon Säätiö, Finland, 132
Peace, Health and Human Development Foundation—PHD Foundation, Japan, 239
Pearl S. Buck International, USA, 474
Pedro Barrié de la Maza Foundation, Spain, 340
PEF Israel Endowment Funds, Inc, Israel, 215
People-to-People Health Foundation, Inc—Project Hope, USA, 537
Perpetual Foundation, Australia, 43
Perpetual Trustees Australia, Australia, 43
Peter G. Peterson Foundation, USA, 534
Peterson (Peter G.) Foundation, USA, 534
The Pew Charitable Trusts, USA, 534
The PHD Foundation—Peace, Health and Human Development Foundation, Japan, 239
PHG Foundation, UK, 437
PhilDev—Philippine Development Foundation, USA, 535
Philippine-American Educational Foundation—PAEF, Philippines, 303
Philippine Development Foundation—PhilDev, USA, 535
Piera, Pietro and Giovanni Ferrero Foundation, Italy, 221
Pinchuk (Victor) Foundation, Ukraine, 394
Plan Ireland, Ireland, 212
Plenty International, USA, 535
Polar Companies Foundation, Venezuela, 563
Pôle européen des fondations de l'économie sociale, Belgium, 56
POLSAT Foundation, Poland, 309
Population Council, USA, 536
The Porter Foundation, UK, 439
Potter (Ian) Foundation, Australia, 43
Preciosa Foundation, Czech Republic, 115
Princess Grace Foundation, Monaco, 265
Pro Bono Foundation, Poland, 308
Pro Juventute, Switzerland, 372
Pro Victimis Foundation, Switzerland, 365
Project HOPE, USA, 537
Protestant Study Foundation, Germany, 167
Public Welfare Foundation, Inc, USA, 537
Queen's Trust for Young Australians, Australia, 41
R. E. Ross Trust, Australia, 44
R. G. Menzies Scholarship Fund, Australia, 42
R. Howard Webster Foundation, Canada, 99
Rafael del Pino Foundation, Spain, 347
Rajiv Gandhi Foundation, India, 201
Ramaciotti (Clive and Vera) Foundation, Australia, 43
Ramaswami Aiyar (C. P.) Foundation, India, 204
Rayne Foundation, UK, 441
RBC Foundation, Canada, 96
Red de Salud de las Mujeres Latinoamericanas y del Caribe, Chile, 101
Reeve (Christopher and Dana) Foundation, USA, 538
Refugees International Japan—RIJ, Japan, 239
Reimers (Werner) Stiftung, Germany, 177
Relief International, USA, 539
René Moawad Foundation, Lebanon, 253
Research Foundation—Flanders, Belgium, 62
Reumatikerförbundet, Sweden, 355
Richard King Mellon Foundation, USA, 523
Richelieu International, Canada, 96
RNIB—Royal National Institute of Blind People, UK, 444
Roald Dahl's Marvellous Children's Charity, UK, 413
Robert Bosch Foundation, Germany, 163
Robert-Bosch-Stiftung GmbH, Germany, 163
Robert R. McCormick Foundation, USA, 520
Robert Wood Johnson Foundation—RWJF, USA, 512
Rome Foundation, Italy, 224
Ross (R. E.) Trust, Australia, 44
Rothschild (Edmond de) Foundations, USA, 541

Roviralta (María Francisca de), Fundación, Spain, 347
Rowan Charitable Trust, UK, 441
Royal Air Force Benevolent Fund, UK, 442
The Royal Australasian College of Physicians—RACP, Australia, 44
Royal Bank of Canada Charitable Foundation, Canada, 96
Royal Bank Financial Group Foundation, Canada, 96
Royal Commonwealth Society for the Blind—Sight Savers International, UK, 448
Royal Flying Doctor Service of Australia—RFDS, Australia, 44
Royal National Institute of Blind People—RNIB, UK, 444
The Rufford Foundation, UK, 445
Rufford Maurice Laing Foundation, UK, 445
Runyon (Damon)–Winchell (Walter) Foundation, Cancer Research Fund, USA, 541
Rutgers WPF, Netherlands, 279
RWJF—Robert Wood Johnson Foundation, USA, 512
Sahabdeen (A. M. M.) Trust Foundation, Sri Lanka, 350
Said Foundation, UK, 446
Salvatore Maugeri Foundation—Occupational Health and Rehabilitation Clinic, Italy, 223
Samuel Lunenfeld Charitable Foundation, Canada, 92
San Francisco Foundation, USA, 542
Sander (Wilhelm) Stiftung, Germany, 177
Sandino (Augusto César), Fundación, Nicaragua, 288
Santé Sud, France, 154
Schusterman (Charles and Lynn) Family Foundation, USA, 543
Schweizerische Akademie der Medizinischen Wissenschaften, Switzerland, 373
Schweizerische Herzstiftung, Switzerland, 373
Schweizerische Stiftung Kardiologie, Switzerland, 373
Schweizerischer Nationalfonds zur Förderung der wissenschaftlichen Forschung/Fonds National Suisse de la Recherche Scientifique—SNF, Switzerland, 374
Scientific Foundation of the Spanish Cancer Association, Spain, 342
Scope, UK, 447
Secours Dentaire International, Switzerland, 374
Selby (William G. and Marie) Foundation, USA, 543
Sem Pringpuangkeo Foundation, Thailand, 384
Semmelweis Alapítvány Magyarországi Ortopédia Fejlesztéséért, Hungary, 195
Semmelweis Foundation for the Development of Orthopaedics in Hungary, Hungary, 195
Seva Foundation, USA, 544
Sherman (Archie) Charitable Trust, UK, 448
SickKids Foundation, Canada, 97
Sidney Myer Fund, Australia, 42
Sight Savers International, UK, 448
Sihtasutus Eesti Rahvuskultuuri Fond, Estonia, 129
Simón I. Patiño Foundation, Switzerland, 365
Sino-British Fellowship Trust—SBFT, UK, 448
Sir Ahmadu Bello Foundation, Nigeria, 289
Sir Ahmadu Bello Memorial Foundation, Nigeria, 289
Sir Dorabji Tata Trust, India, 205
Sir Halley Stewart Trust, UK, 449
The Sir Jules Thorn Charitable Trust, UK, 451
The Sir Robert Menzies Memorial Foundation Ltd, Australia, 41
Skoll Foundation, USA, 544
Sloan (Alfred P.) Foundation, USA, 545
Slovak Humanitarian Council, Slovakia, 328
Slovenská Humanitná Rada, Slovakia, 328
Smithsonian Institution, USA, 545
SNF—Swedish Nutrition Foundation, Sweden, 356
Sobell Foundation, UK, 449
Software AG Foundation, Germany, 178
Sog'lom Avlod Uchun, Uzbekistan, 561
Solidarios—Consejo de Fundaciones Americanas de Desarrollo, Dominican Republic, 123
Soros Foundation (South Africa), South Africa, 334
Soros Foundation (Tajikistan), Tajikistan, 381
Soros Foundation—Kazakhstan, Kazakhstan, 243
Soros Foundation–Kyrgyzstan, Kyrgyzstan, 250
Soros Foundation Latvia, Latvia, 251
Soros Foundation Macedonia, Macedonia, 258
Soros Foundation—Moldova, Moldova, 264
Soros Serbia Foundation, Serbia, 324
South African Institute of Race Relations, South Africa, 335

South Pacific Peoples Foundation Canada, Canada, 95
Southern Health, France, 154
Sparkassen-Kulturstiftung Hessen-Thüringen, Germany, 178
SpinalCure Australia, Australia, 44
St John Ambulance, UK, 446
The Starr Foundation, USA, 546
Stefan Batory Foundation, Poland, 307
Steinberg (Nathan) Family Foundation, Canada, 98
Stewart (Sir Halley) Trust, UK, 449
Stichting Fonds 1818, Netherlands, 280
Stichting Liliane Fonds, Netherlands, 281
Stichting Triodos Foundation, Netherlands, 282
Stichting VSB Fonds, Netherlands, 280
Stifterverband für die Deutsche Wissenschaft eV, Germany, 159
Stiftung zur Förderung der Ernährungsforschung in der Schweiz—SFEFS, Switzerland, 374
Stiftung für Kinder, Germany, 181
Stiftung Kinder in Afrika, Germany, 181
Stiftung Szondi-Institut, Switzerland, 375
Stiftung Vivamos Mejor, Switzerland, 375
The Streisand Foundation, USA, 547
The Stroke Association, UK, 450
Studienstiftung des deutschen Volkes, Germany, 182
Sun/Soleil—AREGAK, Armenia, 35
Sunley (Bernard) Charitable Foundation, UK, 450
Suomen Kulttuurirahasto, Finland, 132
Susan G. Komen for the Cure, USA, 515
Sutherland Self Help Trust, New Zealand, 286
Swedish Cancer Society, Sweden, 352
The Swedish Heart-Lung Foundation, Sweden, 353
Swedish Nutrition Foundation—SNF, Sweden, 356
Swedish Rheumatism Association, Sweden, 355
Swiss Academy of Medical Sciences, Switzerland, 373
Swiss Heart Foundation, Switzerland, 373
Swiss Interchurch Aid, Switzerland, 367
Swiss National Science Foundation—SNF, Switzerland, 374
Swiss Nutrition Foundation, Switzerland, 374
The Sylvia Adams Charitable Trust, UK, 398
Sylvia and Charles Viertel Charitable Foundation, Australia, 45
Szondi Institute Foundation, Switzerland, 375
Tanzania Millennium Hand Foundation—TAMIHA, Tanzania, 382
TEAR Australia, Australia, 45
Terre des Hommes Foundation, Switzerland, 376
Terrence Higgins Trust—THT, UK, 420
Third World Network—TWN, Malaysia, 260
Third World Solidarity Action, Luxembourg, 257
Thorn (The Sir Jules) Charitable Trust, UK, 451
Thyssen (Fritz) Stiftung, Germany, 183
TISCO Foundation, Thailand, 385
The Todd Foundation, New Zealand, 287
Transnet Foundation, South Africa, 335
Triodos Foundation, Netherlands, 282
Trócaire—Catholic Agency for World Development, Ireland, 213
Trusthouse Charitable Foundation, UK, 451
Turin Savings Bank Foundation, Italy, 220
Turkish Family Health and Planning Foundation, Turkey, 390
Türkiye Aile Sağlığı ve Planlaması Vakfı—TAPV, Turkey, 390
Twenty-Ninth May 1961 Charity, UK, 452
Ukraine 3000, Ukraine, 394
Uluslararası Mavi Hilal İnsani Yardım ve Kalkınma Vakfı, Turkey, 390
UniCredit Foundation—Unidea, Italy, 228
Unilever Vietnam Foundation—UVF, Viet Nam, 565
Union Aid Abroad—APHEDA, Australia, 45
United Society for the Propagation of the Gospel—USPG, UK, 453
Unity Foundation, Luxembourg, 257
University of Zaragoza Business Foundation, Spain, 342
Väestöliitto, Finland, 133
Vehbi Koç Foundation, Turkey, 391
Vehbi Koç Vakfı, Turkey, 391
Victor Pinchuk Foundation, Ukraine, 394
Viertel (Sylvia and Charles) Charitable Foundation, Australia, 45
Villar Foundation, Inc., Philippines, 304
Villavicencio (Dr J. Roberto), Fundación, Argentina, 33
Vivamos Mejor Foundation, Switzerland, 375
Vodafone Foundation Germany, Germany, 183
Vodafone Group Foundation, UK, 453

Vodafone Stiftung Deutschland, Germany, 183
Volkart Foundation, Switzerland, 376
Volkart-Stiftung, Switzerland, 376
Vollmer (Alberto) Foundation, Inc, USA, 551
Voluntary Service Overseas, UK, 454
Volunteer Service Abroad—VSA, New Zealand, 287
VSA—Volunteer Service Abroad, New Zealand, 287
VSO, UK, 454
Výbor dobré vule—Nadace Olgy Havlové, Czech Republic, 115
Wallenberg (Knut och Alice) Stiftelse, Sweden, 358
Walmart Foundation, USA, 552
WasserStiftung, Germany, 184
Water Foundation, Germany, 184
Water.org, Inc, USA, 552
WaterAid, UK, 454
Wates Foundation, UK, 454
Webster (R. Howard) Foundation, Canada, 99
Weinberg (Harry and Jeanette) Foundation, USA, 552
WellBeing, UK, 455
Wellbeing of Women, UK, 455
Werner Reimers Foundation, Germany, 177
Werner-Reimers-Stiftung, Germany, 177
Weston (Garfield) Foundation, UK, 455
WHEAT Trust—Women's Hope Education and Training Trust, South Africa, 336
Wihuri (Jenny and Antti) Foundation, Finland, 134
Wild (Dr Rainer) Stiftung, Germany, 184
Wildlife Preservation Trust International, USA, 487
Wildlife Trust, USA, 487
Wilhelm Sander Foundation, Germany, 177
Wilhelm-Sander-Stiftung, Germany, 177
William Adlington Cadbury Charitable Trust, UK, 407
William G. and Marie Selby Foundation, USA, 543
The William Randolph Hearst Foundation, USA, 502
William T. Grant Foundation, USA, 499
The Wolfson Family Charitable Trust, UK, 456
Women's Hope Education and Training Trust—Wheat Trust, South Africa, 336
Workers' Centre Foundation, Spain, 343
World Association of Children's Friends, Monaco, 265
World Education, Inc, USA, 556
World Neighbors, USA, 557
World Population Foundation, Netherlands, 279
World Teacher Trust, India, 206
Yayasan Dian Desa, Indonesia, 207
Yrjö Jahnsson Foundation, Finland, 131
Yrjö Jahnssonin säätiö, Finland, 131
Zurich Community Trust, UK, 457
Zurich Financial Services (UKISA) Community Trust Ltd, UK, 457

SCIENCE AND TECHNOLOGY

A. M. Qattan Foundation, UK, 440
The A. P. Møller and Chastine Mc-Kinney Møller Foundation, Denmark, 120
A. P. Møller og Hustru Chastine Mc-Kinney Møllers Fond til almene Formaal, Denmark, 120
Abdul Hameed Shoman Foundation, Jordan, 242
AFPE—American Foundation for Pharmaceutical Education, USA, 465
The African Agricultural Technology Foundation—AATF, Kenya, 245
African Youth Network for Sustainable Development, Algeria, 30
AFTAAC—Arab Fund for Technical Assistance to African Countries, Egypt, 127
Agromisa Foundation, Netherlands, 280
AINA—Arctic Institute of North America, Canada, 81
AIT—Asian Institute of Technology, Thailand, 383
Albert Schweitzer Ecological Centre, Switzerland, 362
Alemán (Miguel), Fundación, Mexico, 262
Alfred Benzon Foundation, Denmark, 117
Alfred Benzons Fond, Denmark, 117
Alfred P. Sloan Foundation, USA, 545
Alfred Toepfer Foundation F.V.S., Germany, 183
Alfred Toepfer Stiftung F.V.S., Germany, 183
Alicia Patterson Foundation—APF, USA, 533
Allen (Paul G.) Family Foundation, USA, 463
Allianz Foundation for Sustainability, Germany, 160
Allianz Umweltstiftung, Germany, 160

Alvares Penteado (Armando), Fundação, Brazil, 71
Amancio Ortega Foundation, Spain, 346
American Foundation for the Blind, Inc—AFB, USA, 465
American Foundation for Pharmaceutical Education—AFPE, USA, 465
American Near East Refugee Aid—ANERA, USA, 467
ANERA—American Near East Refugee Aid, USA, 467
Angelo Della Riccia Foundation, Italy, 221
Anna Lindh Euro-Mediterranean Foundation for Dialogue between Cultures, Egypt, 127
APACE Village First Electrification Group—APACE VFEG, Australia, 36
APMN—Asia Pacific Mountain Network, Nepal, 271
Appropriate Technology for Community and Environment—APACE, Australia, 36
Arab Fund for Technical Assistance to African Countries—AFTAAC, Egypt, 127
Arctic Institute of North America—AINA, Canada, 81
Areces (Ramón), Fundación, Spain, 340
ARGUS, Belgium, 56
Armand-Frappier Foundation, Canada, 88
Armando Alvares Penteado Foundation, Brazil, 71
Arthritis Research Campaign, UK, 401
Arthritis Research UK, UK, 401
Arthritis and Rheumatism Council for Research in Great Britain and the Commonwealth, UK, 401
ASEAN Foundation, Indonesia, 207
Asia-Pacific Mountain Network—APMN, Nepal, 271
Asian Institute for Rural Development, India, 200
Association of Medical Research Charities—AMRC, UK, 396
Association of Voluntary Agencies for Rural Development—AVARD, India, 198
Australia-Japan Foundation, Australia, 37
Australian Academy of Science, Australia, 37
Austrian Science Fund, Austria, 47
Austrian Society for Environment and Technology, Austria, 48
AVARD—Association of Voluntary Agencies for Rural Development, India, 198
AVRDC—The World Vegetable Center, Taiwan, 379
Axel Springer Foundation, Germany, 179
Axel-Springer-Stiftung, Germany, 179
Axel Wenner-Gren Foundation for International Exchange of Scientists, Sweden, 358
Ayala Foundation, Inc—AFI, Philippines, 301
Ayala Foundation USA—AF-USA, USA, 535
Bank of Brazil Foundation, Brazil, 71
Bariloche Foundation, Argentina, 32
Barrié de la Maza (Pedro, Conde de Fenosa), Fundación, Spain, 340
BBVA Foundation, Spain, 340
Benton Foundation, USA, 472
Benzon (Alfred) Foundation, Denmark, 117
Beth (Evert Willem) Foundation, Netherlands, 272
Bettencourt Schueller Foundation, France, 141
Biotechnology and Biological Sciences Research Council—BBSRC, UK, 404
Blanceflor Boncompagni-Ludovisi, née Bildt Foundation, Sweden, 359
Bleustein-Blanchet (Marcel), Fondation pour la Vocation, France, 141
Bodossaki Foundation, Greece, 186
Bofill (Jaume), Fundació, Spain, 338
Boltzmann (Ludwig) Gesellschaft, Austria, 46
Bordoni (Ugo), Fondazione, Italy, 219
Botín (Marcelino) Fundación, Spain, 341
Bridge to Asia—BTA, USA, 473
Brockhoff (Jack) Foundation, Australia, 39
Bunge y Born Foundation, Argentina, 32
Burroughs Wellcome Fund—BWF, USA, 475
Caja Madrid Foundation, Spain, 341
The Camille and Henry Dreyfus Foundation, Inc, USA, 485
Canada Foundation for Innovation/Fondation canadienne pour l'innovation, Canada, 82
Canadian Urban Institute, Canada, 85
Cancer Research Fund of the Damon Runyon-Walter Winchell Foundation, USA, 541
Canon Foundation in Europe, Netherlands, 272
Caribbean Marine Biology Institute Foundation, Curaçao, 110
Cariplo Foundation, Italy, 219
Carl-Zeiss Foundation, Germany, 184
Carl-Zeiss-Stiftung, Germany, 184
Carlsberg Foundation, Denmark, 117

Carlsbergfondet, Denmark, 117
CARMABI Foundation, Curaçao, 110
Carnegie Corporation of New York, USA, 475
CEAS—Centre Ecologique Albert Schweitzer, Switzerland, 362
CECHE—Center for Communications, Health and the Environment, USA, 477
Centar za razvoj neprofitnih organizacija—CERANEO, Croatia, 109
Center for Communications, Health and the Environment—CECHE, USA, 477
Centre of Advanced European Studies and Research, Germany, 179
Centre for Development of Non-Profit Organizations, Croatia, 109
Centre Ecologique Albert Schweitzer—CEAS, Switzerland, 362
Centro Internacional de Agricultura Tropical—CIAT, Colombia, 104
CEPH—Centre d'Étude du Polymorphisme Humain, France, 142
CERANEO—Centar za razvoj neprofitnih organizacija, Croatia, 109
Charles Darwin Foundation for the Galapagos Islands—CDF, Ecuador, 124
Charles F. Kettering Foundation, USA, 515
Charter 77 Foundation, Czech Republic, 114
Chemistry Centre Foundation, France, 147
Chia Hsin Foundation, Taiwan, 379
Chile Foundation, Chile, 100
Chr. Michelsen Institute—CMI, Norway, 291
Churchill (Winston) Foundation of the United States, USA, 479
CIAT—Centro Internacional de Agricultura Tropical, Colombia, 104
CMI—Chr. Michelsens Institutt, Norway, 291
the cogito foundation, Switzerland, 362
Colt Foundation, UK, 411
CONCAWE—Oil Companies' European Association for Environment, Health and Safety in Refining and Distribution, Belgium, 58
The Craig and Susan McCaw Foundation, USA, 520
CRDF Global, USA, 483
Croucher Foundation, Hong Kong, 194
CRT Foundation, Italy, 220
CUSO-VSO, Canada, 86
Czech Literary Fund, Czech Republic, 113
Damon Runyon Cancer Research Foundation, USA, 541
Darwin (Charles) Foundation for the Galapagos Islands, Ecuador, 124
David and Lucile Packard Foundation, USA, 531
Deutsche Bank Endowment Fund for the Promotion of Science in Research and Teaching, Germany, 182
Deutsche Orient-Stiftung, Germany, 165
Deutsche Telekom Foundation, Germany, 166
Deutsche Telekom Stiftung, Germany, 166
Deutsches Rheuma-Forschungszentrum Berlin, Germany, 166
Dietmar Hopp Foundation, Germany, 170
Dietmar-Hopp-Stiftung, Germany, 170
Dmitry Zimin Dynasty Foundation, Russian Federation, 319
Don Bosco Foundation of Cambodia—DBFC, Cambodia, 79
Donani (Guido), Fondazione, Italy, 221
Donors' Association for the Promotion of Sciences and Humanities, Germany, 159
Dr J. R. Villavicencio Foundation, Argentina, 33
Dr Rainer Wild Foundation for Healthy Nutrition, Germany, 184
Dr Rainer Wild-Stiftung—Stiftung für gesunde Ernährung, Germany, 184
Dräger Foundation, Germany, 166
Dräger-Stiftung, Germany, 166
Dreyfus (Camille and Henry) Foundation, Inc, USA, 485
Drug Policy Alliance—DPA, USA, 485
E. O. Wilson Biodiversity Foundation, USA, 555
Easter Island Foundation, USA, 487
Ebelin and Gerd Bucerius ZEIT Foundation, Germany, 184
Eberhard Schöck Foundation, Germany, 178
Eberhard-Schöck-Stiftung, Germany, 178
EcoHealth Alliance, USA, 487
ECPD—European Centre for Peace and Development, Serbia, 324
The Edmond de Rothschild Foundations, USA, 541
Eestimaa Looduse Fond—ELF, Estonia, 129
EJLB Foundation, Canada, 87
Else Kröner-Fresenius Foundation, Germany, 173
Else Kröner-Fresenius-Stiftung, Germany, 173
Emirates Foundation, United Arab Emirates, 395

Engineering and Physical Sciences Research Council—EPSRC, UK, 415
Enrico Mattei Eni Foundation, Italy, 218
Erik Philip-Sörensen Foundation, Sweden, 356
Erik Philip-Sörensen Foundation for the Promotion of Genetic and Humanistic Research, Sweden, 356
Erik Philip-Sörensens Stiftelse, Sweden, 356
Estonian Fund for Nature, Estonia, 129
Estonian National Culture Foundation, Estonia, 129
Etruscan Foundation, USA, 489
European Centre for Peace and Development—ECPD, Serbia, 324
European Science Foundation, France, 144
Evens Foundation, Belgium, 61
Evert Willem Beth Foundation, Netherlands, 272
Evrika Foundation, Bulgaria, 75
Farm Africa, UK, 416
FEEM—Fondazione ENI Enrico Mattei, Italy, 218
Finnish Cultural Foundation, Finland, 132
Finnish Foundation for Technology Promotion, Finland, 133
FOKAL—Fondation Connaissance et Liberte (Haiti), Haiti, 192
FOM—Stichting voor Fundamenteel Onderzoek der Materie, Netherlands, 281
Fondation Africaine pour les Technologies Agricoles, Kenya, 245
Fondation Albert 1er, Prince de Monaco—Institut Océanographique, France, 152
Fondation Armand-Frappier, Canada, 88
Fondation Bettencourt-Schueller, France, 141
Fondation Connaissance et Liberté (Haiti)—FOKAL, Haiti, 192
Fondation EJLB, Canada, 87
Fondation Européenne de la Science, France, 144
Fondation Evens Stichting, Belgium, 61
Fondation de France, France, 135
Fondation France-Israel, France, 145
Fondation Franco-Japonaise Sasakawa, France, 145
Fondation Hugot du Collège de France, France, 145
Fondation Jean Dausset—Centre d'Étude du Polymorphisme Humain—CEPH, France, 142
Fondation Latsis Internationale, Switzerland, 364
Fondation Léopold Sédar Senghor, Senegal, 322
Fondation de Lourmarin Laurent-Vibert, France, 146
Fondation de la Maison de la Chimie, France, 147
Fondation Marcel Bleustein-Blanchet pour la Vocation, France, 141
Fondation 'Pour la Science'—Centre International de Synthèse, France, 149
Fondation Ripaille, France, 149
Fondation Simón I. Patiño, Switzerland, 365
Fondation Singer-Polignac, France, 150
Fondation Syngenta pour une Agriculture Durable, Switzerland, 376
Fondazione Angelo Della Riccia, Italy, 221
Fondazione per l'Arte, Italy, 219
Fondazione Cariplo, Italy, 219
Fondazione Cassa di Risparmio delle Provincie Lombarde—Fondazione Cariplo, Italy, 219
Fondazione Cassa di Risparmio di Padova e Rovigo, Italy, 219
Fondazione Cassa di Risparmio di Torino, Italy, 220
Fondazione Giovanni Lorenzini, Italy, 222
Fondazione Guido Donegani, Italy, 221
Fondazione Roma, Italy, 224
Fondazione Ugo Bordoni, Italy, 219
Fondazione di Venezia, Italy, 225
Fonds zur Förderung der Wissenschaftlichen Forschung—FWF, Austria, 47
Fonds National de la Recherche Scientifique—FNRS, Belgium, 61
Fonds National Suisse de la Recherche Scientifique, Switzerland, 374
Fonds Wetenschappelijk Onderzoek—Vlaanderen, Belgium, 62
FOOD—Foundation of Occupational Development, India, 201
Foundation for Agricultural Development, Ecuador, 125
Foundation for Agricultural Research in the Province of Almería, Spain, 344
Foundation for the Arts, Italy, 219
Foundation Cassa di Risparmio di Padova e Rovigo, Italy, 219
Foundation for Commercial and Technical Sciences—KAUTE, Finland, 131
Foundation for Fundamental Research on Matter, Netherlands, 281

Foundation for German–Polish Co-operation, Poland, 308
Foundation of the Hellenic World, Greece, 186
Foundation for International Scientific Co-ordination, France, 149
Foundation for Knowledge and Liberty, Haiti, 192
Foundation Museum of American Man, Brazil, 72
Foundation of Occupational Development—FOOD, India, 201
Foundation for the Protection of Nature, Venezuela, 563
Foundation Robert Laurent-Vibert, France, 146
Foundation for Swedish Culture in Finland, Finland, 133
Foundation for Youth Research, Germany, 180
France-Israel Foundation, France, 145
Franco-Japanese Sasakawa Foundation, France, 145
Frappier (Armand), Fondation, Canada, 88
Freeplay Foundation, UK, 429
Freshwater Society, USA, 494
Friede Springer Foundation, Germany, 179
Friede Springer Stiftung, Germany, 179
Fritz Thyssen Foundation, Germany, 183
Fritz Thyssen Stiftung, Germany, 183
Fundação Armando Alvares Penteado—FAAP, Brazil, 71
Fundação Banco do Brasil, Brazil, 71
Fundação da Casa de Mateus, Portugal, 310
Fundação Luso-Americana para o Desenvolvimento, Portugal, 312
Fundação Mário Soares, Portugal, 313
Fundação Museu do Homem Americano—FUMDHAM, Brazil, 72
Fundação Oriente, Portugal, 312
Fundació Jaume Bofill, Spain, 338
Fundación Amancio Ortega, Spain, 346
Fundación Banco Bilbao Vizcaya Argentaria—Fundación BBVA, Spain, 340
Fundación Bariloche, Argentina, 32
Fundación BBVA—Fundación Banco Bilbao Vizcaya Argentaria, Spain, 340
Fundación Bunge y Born, Argentina, 32
Fundación Caja Madrid, Spain, 341
Fundación Charles Darwin para las Islas Galápagos—FCD, Ecuador, 124
Fundación Chile, Chile, 100
Fundación para la Defensa de la Naturaleza—FUDENA, Venezuela, 563
Fundación para el Desarrollo Agropecuario—FUNDAGRO, Ecuador, 125
Fundación Dr J. Roberto Villavicencio, Argentina, 33
Fundación para la Investigación Agraria de la Provincia de Almería—FIAPA, Spain, 344
Fundación Jiménez Díaz, Spain, 344
Fundación José Miguel de Barandiarán, Spain, 340
Fundación Juan March, Spain, 345
Fundación Juanelo Turriano, Spain, 348
Fundación MAPFRE, Spain, 345
Fundación Marcelino Botín, Spain, 341
Fundación Miguel Alemán AC, Mexico, 262
Fundación Paideia Galiza, Spain, 346
Fundación Paz y Solidaridad Serafín Aliaga—FPyS, Spain, 346
Fundación Pedro Barrié de la Maza, Spain, 340
Fundación Ramón Areces, Spain, 340
Fundación La Salle de Ciencias Naturales—FLASA, Venezuela, 564
Fundacja Bankowa im. Leopolda Kronenberga, Poland, 306
Fundacja Współpracy Polsko-Niemieckiej/Stiftung für Deutsch–Polnische Zusammenarbeit, Poland, 308
FUNDAGRO—Fundación para el Desarrollo Agropecuario, Ecuador, 125
FWF—Fonds zur Förderung der Wissenschaftlichen Forschung, Austria, 47
Garfield Weston Foundation, UK, 455
The Gatsby Charitable Foundation, UK, 418
Gebert Rüf Stiftung, Switzerland, 366
German National Academic Foundation, Germany, 182
German Orient Foundation, Germany, 165
German Rheumatism Research Centre Berlin, Germany, 166
Giovanni Lorenzini Foundation, Italy, 222
Gordon and Betty Moore Foundation, USA, 525
The Grass Foundation, USA, 499
Great Britain Sasakawa Foundation, UK, 419
Guggenheim (John Simon) Memorial Foundation, USA, 500
Guido Donegani Foundation, Italy, 221
HALO Trust, UK, 419
Hamdard Foundation Pakistan, Pakistan, 294
Heineman (Minna James) Stiftung, Germany, 170

Helmsley (Leona M. and Harry B.) Charitable Trust, USA, 503
Helmut Horten Foundation, Switzerland, 367
Helmut-Horten-Stiftung, Switzerland, 367
Helsingin Sanomain Säätiö, Finland, 131
Helsingin Sanomat Foundation, Finland, 131
Helvetas Swiss Intercooperation, Switzerland, 367
Hopp (Dietmar) Stiftung, Germany, 170
Horten (Helmut) Stiftung, Switzerland, 367
Hugot Foundation of the Collège of France, France, 145
IACD—Institute of Asian Culture and Development, Korea (Republic), 246
Ian Potter Foundation, Australia, 43
IASC—International Arctic Science Committee, Germany, 171
ICLARM—The WorldFish Center, Malaysia, 260
Information Society of Ukraine Foundation, Ukraine, 394
Innes (John) Foundation, UK, 422
Institut für Agrarentwicklung in Mittel- und Osteuropa—IAMO, Germany, 171
Institut Arctique de l'Amérique du Nord—IAAN, Canada, 81
Institut Océanographique—Fondation Albert 1er, Prince de Monaco, France, 152
Institut urbain du Canada, Canada, 85
Institute for Agricultural Development in Central and Eastern Europe, Germany, 171
Institute of Asian Culture and Development—IACD, Korea (Republic), 246
Institutul Cultural Român, Romania, 317
International Arctic Science Committee—IASC, Germany, 171
International Centre for Living Aquatic Resources—ICLARM, Malaysia, 260
International Centre for Tropical Agriculture, Colombia, 104
International Charitable Fund of Bermuda—ICFB, Bermuda, 66
International Foundation of the High-Altitude Research Stations Jungfraujoch and Gornergrat, Switzerland, 369
International Latsis Foundation, Switzerland, 364
Internationale Stiftung Hochalpine Forschungsstationen Jungfraujoch und Gornergrat, Switzerland, 369
Islamic Thought Foundation, Iran, 209
Iwatani Naoji Foundation, Japan, 235
Jack Brockhoff Foundation—JBF, Australia, 39
Japanese-German Center Berlin, Germany, 173
Japanisch-Deutsches Zentrum Berlin, Germany, 173
Jaume Bofill Foundation, Spain, 338
Jenny and Antti Wihuri Foundation, Finland, 134
Jenny ja Antti Wihurin Rahasto, Finland, 134
Jewish Community Development Fund—JCDF, USA, 512
Jiménez Díaz Foundation, Spain, 344
John Innes Foundation—JIF, UK, 422
John Simon Guggenheim Memorial Foundation, USA, 500
José Miguel de Barandiaran Foundation, Spain, 340
Juan March Foundation, Spain, 345
Juanelo Turriano Foundation, Spain, 348
Kade (Max) Foundation, Inc, USA, 513
Kajima Foundation, Japan, 237
Kapor (Mitchell) Foundation, USA, 513
KAUTE—Foundation for Commercial and Technical Sciences, Finland, 131
Kettering Foundation, USA, 515
KFAS—Kuwait Foundation for the Advancement of Sciences, Kuwait, 249
Knut and Alice Wallenberg Foundation, Sweden, 358
Knut och Alice Wallenbergs Stiftelse, Sweden, 358
Kokkalis Foundation, Greece, 187
Koninklijke Hollandsche Maatschappij der Wetenschappen, Netherlands, 276
The Kosciuszko Foundation, Inc, USA, 516
Kronenberga (Leopolda), Fundacja Bankowa, Poland, 306
Kröner-Fresenius (Else) Stiftung, Germany, 173
Kulika Charitable Trust (Uganda), Uganda, 392
The Kulika Charitable Trust 1981, Uganda, 392
Kuwait Awqaf Public Foundation, Kuwait, 249
Kuwait Foundation for the Advancement of Sciences—KFAS, Kuwait, 249
Kuwait Institute for Scientific Research—KISR, Kuwait, 249
La Salle Foundation for Natural Sciences, Venezuela, 564
Lambrakis Foundation, Greece, 187
Lambrakis Research Foundation, Greece, 187

Landis & Gyr Foundation, Switzerland, 370
Landis & Gyr Stiftung, Switzerland, 370
The Leona M. and Harry B. Helmsley Charitable Trust, USA, 503
Leopold Kronenberg Foundation, Poland, 306
Léopold Sédar Senghor Foundation, Senegal, 322
Leverhulme Trust, UK, 429
Life Sciences Research Foundation—LSRF, USA, 518
Lifeline Energy, UK, 429
Lifewater International—LI, USA, 518
The Long Now Foundation—LNF, USA, 519
Lorenzini (Giovanni), Fondazione, Italy, 222
Ludwig Boltzmann Gesellschaft, Austria, 46
Lundbeck Foundation, Denmark, 120
Lundbeckfonden, Denmark, 120
Luso-American Development Foundation, Portugal, 312
M. S. Swaminathan Research Foundation—MSSRF, India, 205
McCaw (Craig and Susan) Foundation, USA, 520
McKnight Foundation, USA, 521
Maecenata Management GmbH, Germany, 159
Maj and Tor Nessling Foundation, Finland, 132
MAPFRE Foundation, Spain, 345
Marcel Bleustein-Blanchet Vocation Foundation, France, 141
Marcelino Botín Foundation, Spain, 341
March (Juan), Fundación, Spain, 345
Mário Soares Foundation, Portugal, 313
Markle (John and Mary R.) Foundation, USA, 522
Markle Foundation, USA, 522
Mateus House Foundation, Portugal, 310
Mattei (Enrico), Fondazione ENI, Italy, 218
Max Kade Foundation, Inc, USA, 513
Menzies (R. G.) Scholarship Fund, Australia, 42
Messerschmitt Foundation, Germany, 175
Messerschmitt-Stiftung, Germany, 175
Michael J. Fox Foundation for Parkinson's Research, USA, 493
Miguel Alemán Foundation, Mexico, 262
Milieukontakt International, Netherlands, 277
Milieukontakt Oost-Europa, Netherlands, 277
Minna James Heineman Foundation, Germany, 170
Minna-James-Heineman-Stiftung, Germany, 170
Mitchell Kapor Foundation, USA, 513
Møller (A.P.) and Chastine Mc-Kinney Møller Foundation, Denmark, 120
Mongolian Women's Fund—MONES, Mongolia, 266
Moody Foundation, USA, 525
Nadace Charty 77, Czech Republic, 114
Naito Foundation, Japan, 238
National Endowment for Science, Technology and the Arts—NESTA, UK, 434
National Fund for Scientific Research, Belgium, 61
National Science Foundation, USA, 527
Nessling (Maj and Tor) Foundation, Finland, 132
NESsT—Nonprofit Enterprise and Self-sustainability Team, Chile, 101
NESTA—National Endowment for Science, Technology and the Arts, UK, 434
New Perspectives Foundation, Russian Federation, 319
New Zealand Winston Churchill Memorial Trust, New Zealand, 285
NFCR—National Foundation for Cancer Research, USA, 529
Nonprofit Enterprise and Self-sustainability Team—NESsT, Chile, 101
Nordic Institute for Theoretical Physics, Sweden, 355
Nordisk Institut for Teoretisk Fysik—NORDITA, Sweden, 355
NORDITA—Nordisk Institut for Teoretisk Fysik, Sweden, 355
Novartis US Foundation, USA, 529
NRF—National Research Foundation, South Africa, 333
Oceanographic Institute—Albert 1st, Prince of Monaco Foundation, France, 152
Oil Companies' European Association for Environment, Health and Safety in Refining and Distribution—CONCAWE, Belgium, 58
Open Society Fund—Bosnia-Herzegovina, Bosnia and Herzegovina, 68
Open Society Initiative for Southern Africa—OSISA, South Africa, 334
Open Society Initiative for West Africa, Senegal, 322
Orentreich Foundation for the Advancement of Science, Inc—OFAS, USA, 531
Orient Foundation, Portugal, 312
Ortega (Amancio) Fundación, Spain, 346
OSIWA—Open Society Initiative for West Africa, Senegal, 322

Österreichische Gesellschaft für Umwelt und Technik—ÖGUT, Austria, 48
Packard (David and Lucile) Foundation, USA, 531
Paideia Galiza Foundation, Spain, 346
PAN Asia and the Pacific—Pesticide Action Network Asia and the Pacific, Malaysia, 260
Patiño (Simón I.), Fondation, Switzerland, 365
Patterson (Alicia) Foundation, USA, 533
The Paul G. Allen Family Foundation, USA, 463
Pedro Barrié de la Maza Foundation, Spain, 340
Pesticide Action Network Asia and the Pacific—PAN AP, Malaysia, 260
PhilDev—Philippine Development Foundation, USA, 535
Philippine Development Foundation—PhilDev, USA, 535
Poniecki (Wladyslaw) Foundation, Inc, USA, 536
Potter (Ian) Foundation, Australia, 43
Preciosa Foundation, Czech Republic, 115
Qatar Foundation, Qatar, 315
Qattan (A. M.) Foundation, UK, 440
R. G. Menzies Scholarship Fund, Australia, 42
Ramón Areces Foundation, Spain, 340
Reimers (Werner) Stiftung, Germany, 177
Research Corporation for Science Advancement—RCSA, USA, 539
Research Foundation—Flanders, Belgium, 62
Réseau Africain de la Jeunesse pour le Développement Durable, Algeria, 30
RIA—Royal Irish Academy, Ireland, 210
Della Riccia (Angelo), Fondazione, Italy, 221
Ripaille Foundation, France, 149
Robert A. Welch Foundation, USA, 553
Rockwool Fonden, Denmark, 121
Rockwool Foundation, Denmark, 121
Romanian Cultural Foundation, Romania, 317
Romanian Cultural Institute, Romania, 317
Rome Foundation, Italy, 224
Rössing Foundation, Namibia, 270
Rothschild (Edmond de) Foundations, USA, 541
Royal Holland Society of Sciences and Humanities, Netherlands, 276
Runyon (Damon)–Winchell (Walter) Foundation, Cancer Research Fund, USA, 541
SAASTA—South African Agency for Science and Technology Advancement, South Africa, 334
Safe Internet Foundation—SIF, Netherlands, 279
Sandoz Family Foundation, Switzerland, 372
Sandoz Fondation de Famille, Switzerland, 372
Sasakawa, Fondation Franco-Japonaise, France, 145
Schweisfurth Foundation, Germany, 178
Schweisfurth-Stiftung, Germany, 178
Schweizerischer Nationalfonds zur Förderung der wissenschaftlichen Forschung/Fonds National Suisse de la Recherche Scientifique—SNF, Switzerland, 374
Science and Technology Facilities Council—STFC, UK, 447
Scientific Foundation of Hisham Adeeb Hijjawi, Jordan, 241
Semmelweis Alapítvány Magyarországi Ortopédia Fejlesztéséért, Hungary, 195
Semmelweis Foundation for the Development of Orthopaedics in Hungary, Hungary, 195
Serafín Aliaga Foundation for Peace and Solidarity, Spain, 346
Shackleton Foundation, UK, 448
Shoman (Abdul Hameed) Foundation, Jordan, 242
Sihtasutus Eesti Rahvuskultuuri Fond, Estonia, 129
Simón I. Patiño Foundation, Switzerland, 365
Singer-Polignac Foundation, France, 150
Sino-British Fellowship Trust—SBFT, UK, 448
Sloan (Alfred P.) Foundation, USA, 545
Slovenian Science Foundation, Slovenia, 330
Smithsonian Institution, USA, 545
Soares (Mário), Fundação, Portugal, 313
Software AG Foundation, Germany, 178
Sorenson Legacy Foundation, USA, 545
South African Agency for Science and Technology Advancement—SAASTA, South Africa, 334
Springer (Axel) Stiftung, Germany, 179
Stichting Agromisa, Netherlands, 280
Stichting Caraïbisch Marien Biologisch Instituut—CARMABI, Curaçao, 110
Stichting voor Fundamenteel Onderzoek der Materie—FOM, Netherlands, 281
Stichting voor de Technische Wetenschappen, Netherlands, 283
Stichting Triodos Foundation, Netherlands, 282
Stiftelsen Blanceflor Boncompagni-Ludovisi, född Bildt, Sweden, 356
Stiftelsen Riksbankens Jubileumsfond, Sweden, 357

Stiftelsen Teknikens Främjande—Tekniikan Edistämissäätiö, Finland, 133
Stifterverband für die Deutsche Wissenschaft eV, Germany, 159
Stiftung CAESAR, Germany, 179
Stiftung FVS, Germany, 183
Stiftung Jugend forscht e. V., Germany, 180
Stiftungsfonds Deutsche Bank zur Förderung der Wissenschaft in Forschung und Lehre, Germany, 182
Studienstiftung des deutschen Volkes, Germany, 182
Suomen Kulttuurirahasto, Finland, 132
Sutherland Self Help Trust, New Zealand, 286
Svenska Kulturfonden, Finland, 133
Sweden-Japan Foundation—SJF, Sweden, 357
Swiss Foundation for Technical Co-operation, Switzerland, 375
Swiss National Science Foundation—SNF, Switzerland, 374
Swisscontact—Swiss Foundation for Technical Co-operation, Switzerland, 375
Syngenta Foundation for Sustainable Agriculture, Switzerland, 376
Syngenta Stiftung für Nachhaltige Landwirtschaft, Switzerland, 376
Tea Research Foundation of Central Africa, Malawi, 259
Technologiestichting—STW, Netherlands, 283
Technology Foundation, Netherlands, 283
Tekniikan Edistämissäätiö–Stiftelsen för teknikens främjande—TES, Finland, 133
Thiel Foundation, USA, 547
Thomas B. Thrige Foundation, Denmark, 121
Thomas B. Thriges Fond, Denmark, 121
Thriges (Thomas B.) Fond, Denmark, 121
Thyssen (Fritz) Stiftung, Germany, 183
Tinker Foundation, Inc, USA, 548
Toepfer (Alfred) Stiftung, Germany, 183
Trans-Antarctic Association—TAA, UK, 451
Triodos Foundation, Netherlands, 282
Turin Savings Bank Foundation, Italy, 220
Turriano (Juanelo) Fundación, Spain, 348
Twenty-Ninth May 1961 Charity, UK, 452
Ugo Bordoni Foundation, Italy, 219
United States African Development Foundation—USADF, USA, 550
Universitaire Stichting, Belgium, 64
University Foundation, Belgium, 64
Venice Foundation, Italy, 225
Villavicencio (Dr J. Roberto), Fundación, Argentina, 33
Voluntary Service Overseas, UK, 454
VSO, UK, 454
Wallenberg (Knut och Alice) Stiftelse, Sweden, 358
The Welch Foundation, USA, 553
Welfare Association, Switzerland, 376
Wenner-Gren Centre Foundation for Scientific Research, Sweden, 358
Wenner-Gren Foundations, Sweden, 358
Werner Reimers Foundation, Germany, 177
Werner-Reimers-Stiftung, Germany, 177
Weston (Garfield) Foundation, UK, 455
Whitehall Foundation, Inc, USA, 554
Wihuri (Jenny and Antti) Foundation, Finland, 134
Wild (Dr Rainer) Stiftung, Germany, 184
Wildlife Preservation Trust International, USA, 487
Wildlife Trust, USA, 487
Wilson (E. O.) Biodiversity Foundation, USA, 555
Winston Churchill Foundation of the United States, USA, 479
Wladyslaw Poniecki Foundation, Inc, USA, 536
The Wolfson Family Charitable Trust, UK, 456
The WorldFish Center, Malaysia, 260
Zeiss (Carl) Stiftung, Germany, 184
ZEIT-Stiftung Ebelin und Gerd Bucerius, Germany, 184
Zimin (Dmitry) Dynasty Foundation, Russian Federation, 319

SOCIAL WELFARE

1818 Fund Foundation, Netherlands, 280
A. G. Leventis Foundation, Greece, 188
A. L. Mailman Family Foundation, Inc, USA, 521
A. M. M. Sahabdeen Trust Foundation, Sri Lanka, 350
The A. P. Møller and Chastine Mc-Kinney Møller Foundation, Denmark, 120
A. P. Møller og Hustru Chastine Mc-Kinney Møllers Fond til almene Formaal, Denmark, 120
Abrinq Foundation for the Rights of Children and Adolescents, Brazil, 70

Absolute Return for Kids—ARK, UK, 401
Academy for the Development of Philanthropy in Poland, Poland, 305
ACCU—Asian Cultural Centre for UNESCO, Japan, 231
Açık Toplum Enstitüsü, Turkey, 387
ACORD—Agency for Co-operation and Research in Development, Kenya, 245
Acting for Life, France, 136
Action for Children, UK, 398
Action Children Aid, Denmark, 117
Action in Development—AID, Bangladesh, 52
Action contre la Faim, France, 136
Action against Hunger, France, 136
Action Solidarité Tiers Monde—ASTM, Luxembourg, 257
Activ Foundation, Australia, 36
Adams (Sylvia) Charitable Trust, UK, 398
ADI—Association for Democratic Initiatives, Macedonia, 258
AFAP—Australian Foundation for the Peoples of Asia and the Pacific, Australia, 38
Afghanaid, UK, 398
Africa Humanitarian Action, Ethiopia, 130
African Refugees Foundation—AREF, Nigeria, 289
African Women's Development Fund—AWDF, Ghana, 185
African Youth Network for Sustainable Development, Algeria, 30
Africare, USA, 462
Afro-Asian Institute in Vienna, Austria, 46
Afro-Asiatisches Institut in Wien, Austria, 46
AFSC—American Friends Service Committee, USA, 465
Aga Khan Agency for Microfinance, Switzerland, 360
Aga Khan Fund for Economic Development, Switzerland, 361
Agency for Co-operation and Research in Development, Kenya, 245
Agora Foundation, Poland, 306
Agromart Foundation, Sri Lanka, 350
Agrupació Mutual Foundation, Spain, 338
The Ahmanson Foundation, USA, 462
Aid for Development Club, Austria, 46
Aide et Action, France, 137
AINA—Arctic Institute of North America, Canada, 81
Air France Corporate Foundation, France, 144
Airey Neave Trust, UK, 434
AISA—Africa Institute of South Africa, South Africa, 332
AJWS—American Jewish World Service, USA, 466
Akademia Rozwoju Filantropii w Polsce, Poland, 305
Aktion Børnehjælp, Denmark, 117
Al Fayed Charitable Foundation, UK, 399
Albanian Disability Rights Foundation, Albania, 29
Alberto Vollmer Foundation, Inc, USA, 551
Alchemy Foundation, UK, 399
Alemán (Miguel), Fundación, Mexico, 262
Alicia Patterson Foundation—APF, USA, 533
All India Disaster Mitigation Institute, India, 199
Allavida—Alliances for Voluntary Initiatives and Development, Kenya, 244
Allen (Paul G.) Family Foundation, USA, 463
Allen Lane Foundation, UK, 428
Alliances for Voluntary Initiatives and Development—Allavida, Kenya, 244
Altman (Jenifer) Foundation, USA, 463
The Alva Foundation, Canada, 81
Alzheimer Spain Foundation, Spain, 339
Amancio Ortega Foundation, Spain, 346
Ambuja Cement Foundation, India, 199
America for Bulgaria Foundation, Bulgaria, 75
American Foundation for the Blind, Inc—AFB, USA, 465
American Friends Service Committee—AFSC, USA, 465
American Jewish World Service—AJWS, USA, 466
American Near East Refugee Aid—ANERA, USA, 467
Ana Mata Manzanedo Foundation, Spain, 345
The Andrew Balint Charitable Trust, UK, 402
The Andrew W. Mellon Foundation, USA, 523
ANERA—American Near East Refugee Aid, USA, 467
Apex Foundation, Australia, 36
The Arab-British Chamber Charitable Foundation, UK, 401
Arbeiterwohlfahrt Bundesverband eV—AWO, Germany, 160
ArcelorMittal Acesita Foundation, Brazil, 71

Arctic Institute of North America—AINA, Canada, 81
Arcus Foundation, USA, 469
AREF—African Refugees Foundation, Nigeria, 289
AREGAK—Sun/Soleil, Armenia, 35
Arias Foundation for Peace and Human Progress, Costa Rica, 106
Arie and Ida Crown Memorial, USA, 483
ARK—Absolute Return for Kids, UK, 401
ASEAN Foundation, Indonesia, 207
Ashden Charitable Trust, UK, 402
Asia Foundation, USA, 469
Asia/Pacific Cultural Centre for UNESCO—ACCU, Japan, 231
Asian Community Trust—ACT, Japan, 231
Asian Development Research Institute—ADRI, India, 200
Asian Institute for Rural Development, India, 200
Asian Youth Center, USA, 470
Association for Democratic Initiatives—ADI, Macedonia, 258
Association of Voluntary Agencies for Rural Development—AVARD, India, 198
Association of Voluntary Service Organisations—AVSO, Belgium, 57
ASTM—Action Solidarité Tiers Monde, Luxembourg, 257
Atkinson Foundation, USA, 470
Atlantic Philanthropies, USA, 471
Atlas Charity Foundation, Poland, 306
Auchan Foundation for Youth, France, 140
Australian Foundation for the Peoples of Asia and the Pacific—AFAP, Australia, 38
Australian Multicultural Foundation—AMF, Australia, 39
Australian Youth Foundation, Australia, 41
Austrian Research Foundation for International Development, Austria, 48
Autonómia Foundation, Hungary, 195
AVARD—Association of Voluntary Agencies for Rural Development, India, 198
AVINA Foundation, Panama, 297
AVRDC—The World Vegetable Center, Taiwan, 379
AWDF—African Women's Development Fund, Ghana, 185
AWO—Arbeiterwohlfahrt Bundesverband, Germany, 160
Axel Springer Foundation, Germany, 179
Axel-Springer-Stiftung, Germany, 179
Ayala Foundation, Inc—AFI, Philippines, 301
Ayala Foundation USA—AF-USA, USA, 535
Ayrton Senna Institute, Brazil, 73
BaBe—Budi aktivna, Budi emancipirana, Croatia, 109
Balint (Andrew) Charitable Trust, UK, 402
Bangladesh Freedom Foundation, Bangladesh, 52
BANHCAFE Foundation, Honduras, 193
Bank of Brazil Foundation, Brazil, 71
Bariloche Foundation, Argentina, 32
Baring Foundation, UK, 402
Barka Foundation, Poland, 308
Barnardo's, UK, 403
The Baron de Hirsch Fund, USA, 484
The Barretstown Camp Fund Ltd, Ireland, 210
Barrié de la Maza (Pedro, Conde de Fenosa), Fundación, Spain, 340
The Batchworth Trust, UK, 403
BBC Children in Need Appeal, UK, 403
Be Active, Be Emancipated, Croatia, 109
Beatrice Laing Trust, UK, 428
The Beautiful Foundation, Korea (Republic), 246
Beit Trust, UK, 403
Belarusian Charitable Fund 'For the Children of Chornobyl', Belarus, 54
Benton Foundation, USA, 472
The Bernard Sunley Charitable Foundation, UK, 450
Bernheim Foundation, Belgium, 60
Bertelsmann Foundation, Germany, 162
Bertelsmann Stiftung, Germany, 162
Bettencourt Schueller Foundation, France, 141
BibleLands, UK, 404
Binding (Sophie und Karl) Stiftung, Switzerland, 361
Bodossaki Foundation, Greece, 186
Boghossian Foundation, Belgium, 60
Bosch (Robert) Stiftung GmbH, Germany, 163
BOTA Foundation, Kazakhstan, 243
Botín (Marcelino) Fundación, Spain, 341
Bradley (Lynde and Harry) Foundation, Inc, USA, 473
Bread for the World, Germany, 163
Bridge Asia Japan—BAJ, Japan, 232
The Bridge Foundation, India, 200
The Bridge Foundation—TBF, Ghana, 185

Bridge House Estates Trust Fund, UK, 410
Brockhoff (Jack) Foundation, Australia, 39
Brot für die Welt, Germany, 163
Buck (Pearl S. Buck) International, USA, 474
Budi aktivna, Budi emancipiran—BaBe!,
    Croatia, 109
Bunge y Born Foundation, Argentina, 32
Business Formation Foundation, Guatemala, 190
Business and Society Foundation, Spain, 342
Cadbury (Edward) Charitable Trust, Inc, UK, 407
Cadbury (William Adlingon) Charitable Trust,
    UK, 407
CAF—Charities Aid Foundation, UK, 396
Caisses d'Epargne Foundation for Social
    Solidarity, France, 141
Campaign Against Exclusion Foundation,
    France, 140
Canadian Catholic Organization for Development
    and Peace, Canada, 83
Canadian Physicians for Aid and Relief—CPAR,
    Canada, 86
Canadian Urban Institute, Canada, 85
Cancer Council Australia, Australia, 40
Canon Foundation in Europe, Netherlands, 272
CARE International—CI, Switzerland, 361
Cariplo Foundation, Italy, 219
The Carl and Lily Pforzheimer Foundation, Inc,
    USA, 535
Carlo Cattaneo Institute, Italy, 227
Carnegie Corporation of New York, USA, 475
Carnegie Hero Fund Commission, USA, 476
Carnegie UK Trust, UK, 408
Carpathian Foundation, Hungary, 195
Carson (John W.) Foundation, USA, 476
Catholic Agency for World Development—
    Trócaire, Ireland, 213
Cattaneo (Carlo), Istituto, Italy, 227
CCI—Center for Citizen Initiatives, USA, 476
CDCS—Centre for Development of Civil Society,
    Armenia, 35
CEDRO—Centro de Información y Educación
    para la Prevención del Abuso de Drogas,
    Peru, 299
CEGA—Creating Effective Grassroots
    Alternatives, Bulgaria, 75
CENSIS—Fondazione Centro Studi Investimenti
    Sociali, Italy, 216
Centar za razvoj neprofitnih organizacija—
    CERANEO, Croatia, 109
Center for Citizen Initiatives—CCI, USA, 476
Center for Cultural and Technical Interchange
    between East and West—East-West Center,
    USA, 487
Center for Human Research and Social
    Development—CHRSD, Palestinian
    Autonomous Areas, 296
CENTRAS—Assistance Centre for NGOs,
    Romania, 316
Centre for the Development of Civil Society—
    CDCS, Armenia, 35
Centre for Development of Non-Profit
    Organizations, Croatia, 109
Centre for Development of Non-Profit Sector,
    Serbia, 324
Centre for Environment, Education and
    Development, USA, 516
Centre d'Études, de Documentation,
    d'Information et d'Action Sociales—
    CEDIAS—Musée Social, France, 138
Centre Pan-Africain de Prospective Sociale,
    Benin, 65
Centre for Social Studies, Documentation,
    Information and Action, France, 138
Centro de Información y Educación para la
    Prevención del Abuso de Drogas—CEDRO,
    Peru, 299
Cera, Belgium, 57
CERANEO—Centar za razvoj neprofitnih
    organizacija, Croatia, 109
Česko-německý fond budoucnosti, Czech
    Republic, 113
CFI—Consuelo Foundation, Inc, USA, 482
CFPA—China Foundation for Poverty
    Alleviation, China (People's Republic), 102
CGP—Japan Foundation Centre Global
    Partnership, Japan, 236
Charities Advisory Trust, UK, 396
Charities Aid Foundation—CAF, UK, 396
Charity Islamic Trust Elrahma, UK, 409
Charity Projects, UK, 411
Charles Delmar Foundation, USA, 484
Charles and Lynn Schusterman Family
    Foundation—CLSFF, USA, 543
Charles Stewart Mott Foundation—CSMF,
    USA, 526
Charter 77 Foundation, Czech Republic, 114
Chastell Foundation, Canada, 85
Chia Hsin Foundation, Taiwan, 379

The Chicago Community Trust, USA, 478
Child Migrants Trust, UK, 409
ChildFund Korea, Korea (Republic), 246
ChildHope Asia Philippines, Inc, Philippines, 302
ChildHope Brasil, Brazil, 70
ChildHope—Hope for the Children Foundation,
    Guatemala, 190
Children in Africa Foundation, Germany, 181
Children of The Americas—COTA, USA, 479
Children of the Mekong, France, 139
Children of Slovakia Foundation, Slovakia, 328
Children's Foundation of China, China (People's
    Republic), 102
Childwick Trust, UK, 409
China Foundation for Poverty Alleviation—
    CFPA, China (People's Republic), 102
China Soong Ching Ling Foundation, China
    (People's Republic), 102
China Youth Development Foundation, China
    (People's Republic), 103
Chr. Michelsen Institute—CMI, Norway, 291
Christopher and Dana Reeve Foundation,
    USA, 538
Christopher Reynolds Foundation, Inc, USA, 539
Christos Stelios Ioannou Foundation, Cyprus, 111
CIMADE—Service Oecuménique d'Entraide,
    France, 138
The City Bridge Trust, UK, 410
Civic Initiatives, Serbia, 324
Civic Responsibility Foundation, Lithuania, 256
Civil Society Development Foundation,
    Bulgaria, 74
Claude Pompidou Foundation, France, 148
Clean Water Fund—CWF, USA, 480
Cleveland Foundation, USA, 480
Cleveland H. Dodge Foundation, Inc, USA, 485
CLIC Sargent, UK, 410
Clore Duffield Foundation—CDF, UK, 411
Clovek v tisni—spolecnost pri Ceske televizi,
    o.p.s., Czech Republic, 113
CMI—Chr. Michelsens Institutt, Norway, 291
Co-operation for the Promotion and Development
    of Welfare Activities, Spain, 342
Cogitare Foundation, USA, 481
Collier Charitable Fund, Australia, 40
Colombian Habitat Foundation, Colombia, 105
Columbia Foundation, Canada, 86
Comic Relief, UK, 411
Committee of Good Will—Olga Havel
    Foundation, Czech Republic, 115
Commonwealth Foundation, UK, 411
Communication Foundation for Asia,
    Philippines, 302
Community Development Foundation,
    Mozambique, 269
Community Foundation for Northern Ireland,
    UK, 412
Compagnia di San Paolo, Italy, 217
Comprehensive Rural Foundation, Costa
    Rica, 107
Compton Foundation, Inc, USA, 481
Concern India Foundation, India, 201
Concern Universal, UK, 412
Consejo de Fundaciones Americanas de
    Desarrollo—Solidarios, Dominican
    Republic, 123
Consejo de Fundaciones Privadas de
    Guatemala—CFPG, Guatemala, 190
Consuelo Foundation, Inc—CFI, USA, 482
Cooperazione Internazionale—COOPI, Italy, 217
COOPI—Cooperazione Internazionale, Italy, 217
COSIS, Italy, 221
Costa Rican Foundation for Development, Costa
    Rica, 106
Council of American Development Foundations,
    Dominican Republic, 123
Council of Humanitarian Associations, Czech
    Republic, 114
Council of Private Foundations of Guatemala,
    Guatemala, 190
Coutu (Marcelle et Jean), Fondation, Canada, 88
CPAR—Canadian Physicians for Aid and Relief,
    Canada, 86
Creating Effective Grassroots Alternatives—
    CEGA, Bulgaria, 75
Credit Union Foundation Australia—CUFA,
    Australia, 40
Crown (Arie and Ida) Memorial, USA, 483
Crown Family Philanthropies, USA, 483
CRT Foundation, Italy, 220
CUFA—Credit Union Foundation Australia,
    Australia, 40
CUSO-VSO, Canada, 86
Cystic Fibrosis Canada, Canada, 87
Cystic Fibrosis Trust, UK, 413
Czech-German Fund for the Future, Czech
    Republic, 113
Czech TV Foundation, Czech Republic, 113

Czegei Wass Foundation, Hungary, 196
Dahl (Roald) Foundation, UK, 413
The Danish Cultural Institute, Denmark, 117
Danske Kulturinstitut, Denmark, 117
Dasra, India, 198
David and Lucile Packard Foundation, USA, 531
Delmar (Charles) Foundation, USA, 484
Deutsch-Tschechischer Zukunftsfonds, Czech
    Republic, 113
Deutsche AIDS-Stiftung, Germany, 164
Deutsche Bank Americas Foundation and
    Community Development Group, USA, 484
Deutsche Bank Foundation, Germany, 164
Deutsche Bank Stiftung, Germany, 164
Deutsche Stiftung Weltbevölkerung—DSW,
    Germany, 165
Development Foundation, Guatemala, 190
Development Foundation of Turkey, Turkey, 390
Dian Desa Foundation, Indonesia, 207
Diana, Princess of Wales Memorial Fund,
    UK, 414
Dodge (Cleveland H.) Foundation, Inc, USA, 485
DOEN Foundation, Netherlands, 280
Dom Manuel II Foundation, Portugal, 311
Dominican Development Foundation, Dominican
    Republic, 123
Don Bosco Foundation of Cambodia—DBFC,
    Cambodia, 79
Dr Barnardo's, UK, 403
Dr F. P. Haaz Social Assistance Foundation,
    Ukraine, 393
Dr Scholl Foundation, USA, 543
Dreyfus Health Foundation—DHF, USA, 485
Drug Policy Alliance—DPA, USA, 485
DSW—Deutsche Stiftung Weltbevölkerung,
    Germany, 165
Duke Endowment, USA, 486
Dulverton Trust, UK, 414
EABL Foundation, Kenya, 245
East-West Center—EWC, USA, 487
Economic Development Foundation, Turkey, 388
Economic Foundation, Poland, 307
ECPD—European Centre for Peace and
    Development, Serbia, 324
Ecuadorean Development Foundation,
    Ecuador, 125
Ecumenical Service for Mutual Help, France, 138
Eden Foundation, Sweden, 353
The Edmond de Rothschild Foundations,
    USA, 541
The Edna McConnell Clark Foundation,
    USA, 520
Ednannia: Initiative Centre to Support Social
    Action—ISAR Ednannia, Ukraine, 393
Edward Cadbury Charitable Trust, Inc, UK, 407
Egmont Fonden, Denmark, 118
Egmont Foundation, Denmark, 118
Einaudi (Luigi), Fondazione, Italy, 221
Ellerman (John) Foundation, UK, 414
Emirates Foundation, United Arab Emirates, 395
EMUNAH, UK, 415
ENCOD—European NGO Council on Drugs and
    Development, Belgium, 59
endPoverty.org, USA, 488
Enfants du Mekong, France, 139
Ente Cassa di Risparmio di Firenze, Italy, 217
Enterprise Development International, USA, 488
Entraide Protestante Suisse, Switzerland, 367
Entwicklungshilfe-Klub, Austria, 46
Environmental Foundation of Jamaica,
    Jamaica, 229
Environmental Justice Foundation—EJF,
    UK, 416
The Ernest C. Manning Awards Foundation,
    Canada, 93
Ernest Kleinwort Charitable Trust, UK, 427
Eskom Development Foundation, South
    Africa, 332
Esmée Fairbairn Foundation, UK, 416
Espejo (Eugenio), Fundación, Ecuador, 125
Eugenio Espejo Foundation, Ecuador, 125
Eugenio Mendoza Foundation, Venezuela, 563
Eurasia Foundation, USA, 489
Euronisa Foundation, Czech Republic, 114
Europa Employment Foundation—Enterprise
    and Solidarity, Italy, 221
European Anti-Poverty Network—EAPN,
    Belgium, 59
European Centre for Peace and Development—
    ECPD, Serbia, 324
European Centre for Social Welfare Policy and
    Research, Austria, 47
European Coalition for Just and Effective Drug
    Policies—ENCOD, Belgium, 59
European Federation of National Organizations
    Working with the Homeless, Belgium, 55
European Foundation for the Improvement of
    Living and Working Conditions, Ireland, 211

European Institute of Health and Social Welfare, Spain, 349
European Network of Foundations for Social Economy, Belgium, 56
European Youth Foundation—EYF, France, 151
Evangelisches Studienwerk eV, Germany, 167
Eveson (Violet) Charitable Trust, UK, 416
The Eveson Charitable Trust, UK, 416
EWC—East-West Center, USA, 487
The F. K. Morrow Foundation, Canada, 94
FAFIDESS—Fundación de Asesoría Financiera a Instituciones de Desarrollo y Servicio Social, Guatemala, 190
Fairbairn (Esmée) Foundation, UK, 416
Faith, UK, 415
FAL—France Amérique Latine, France, 151
The Family Federation of Finland, Finland, 133
Fate Foundation, Nigeria, 289
FDC—Fundação para o Desenvolvimento da Comunidade, Mozambique, 269
FDD—Fundación Dominicana de Desarrollo, Dominican Republic, 123
FEANTSA—Fédération Européenne des Associations Nationales Travaillant avec les Sans-Abri, Belgium, 55
Federación Argentina de Apoyo Familiar—FAAF, Argentina, 31
Federal Association of Social Welfare Organizations, Germany, 160
Fédération Européenne des Associations Nationales Travaillant avec les Sans-Abri—FEANTSA, Belgium, 55
Fedesarrollo—Fundación para la Educación Superior y el Desarrollo, Colombia, 104
Feed My Hungry People, Inc, USA, 490
FEIM—Fundación para Estudio e Investigación de la Mujer, Argentina, 32
Feltrinelli (Giangiacomo), Fondazione, Italy, 221
FEPP—Fondo Ecuatoriano Populorum Progressio, Ecuador, 124
Ferrero (Piera, Pietro e Giovanni), Fondazione, Italy, 221
FFL—Fondation Follereau Luxembourg, Luxembourg, 257
FH—Food for the Hungry, USA, 491
filia.die frauenstiftung, Germany, 168
filia—the Women's Foundation, Germany, 168
FINCA—Fundación Integral Campesina, Costa Rica, 107
Finnish Institute in London Trust, UK, 417
Firefly, Inc., USA, 490
Firelight Foundation, USA, 490
First Peoples Worldwide—FPW, USA, 490
FirstRand Foundation, South Africa, 332
Florence Savings Bank Foundation, Italy, 217
FOKAL—Fondation Connaissance et Liberté (Haiti), Haiti, 192
Follereau Foundation Luxembourg, Luxembourg, 257
Fondaccioni per Iniciative Demokratike, Kosovo, 248
Fondacioni Shoqeria e Hapur per Shqiperine, Albania, 29
Fondacioni Shqiptar per te Drejtat e Paaftesise, Albania, 29
Fondation Abbé Pierre pour le logement des défavorisés, France, 140
Fondation Agir Contre l'Exclusion—FACE, France, 140
Fondation Auchan pour la Jeunesse, France, 140
Fondation Bernheim, Belgium, 60
Fondation Bettencourt-Schueller, France, 141
Fondation Boghossian, Belgium, 60
Fondation Caisses d'Epargne pour la solidarité—FCES, France, 141
Fondation Casip-Cojasor, France, 142
Fondation Claude Pompidou, France, 148
Fondation Connaissance et Liberté (Haiti)—FOKAL, Haiti, 192
Fondation 'Entente Franco-Allemande', France, 143
Fondation d'Entreprise Air France, France, 144
Fondation d'Entreprise VINCI pour la Cité, France, 144
Fondation FACE—Fondation Agir Contre l'Exclusion, France, 140
Fondation contre la Faim, USA, 491
Fondation Follereau Luxembourg—FFL, Luxembourg, 257
Fondation de France, France, 135
Fondation Hans Wilsdorf—Montres Rolex, Switzerland, 366
Fondation Jean-Louis Lévesque, Canada, 88
Fondation MAIF, France, 147
Fondation Marcelle et Jean Coutu, Canada, 88
Fondation Orient-Occident, Morocco, 268
Fondation P&V, Belgium, 61

Fondation Pro Victimis Genève, Switzerland, 365
Fondation Roi Baudouin, Belgium, 62
Fondazione per l'Arte, Italy, 219
Fondazione Cariplo, Italy, 219
Fondazione Cassa di Risparmio delle Provincie Lombarde—Fondazione Cariplo, Italy, 219
Fondazione Cassa di Risparmio di Padova e Rovigo, Italy, 219
Fondazione Cassa di Risparmio di Torino, Italy, 220
Fondazione Centro Studi Investimenti Sociali—CENSIS, Italy, 216
Fondazione Europa Occupazione—Impresa e Solidarietà, Italy, 221
Fondazione Giangiacomo Feltrinelli, Italy, 221
Fondazione Giovanni Lorenzini, Italy, 222
Fondazione Luigi Einaudi, Italy, 221
Fondazione Piera, Pietro e Giovanni Ferrero—ONLUS, Italy, 221
Fondazione Roma, Italy, 224
Fondazione RUI, Italy, 225
Fondazione Umana Mente, Italy, 225
Fondazione Unipolis, Italy, 225
Fondo Ecuatoriano Populorum Progressio—FEPP, Ecuador, 124
Fondo Latinoamericano de Desarrollo, Costa Rica, 106
Fonds für Entwicklung und Partnerschaft in Africa—FEPA, Switzerland, 366
Fonds Européen pour la Jeunesse—FEJ, France, 151
Fonds Wetenschappelijk Onderzoek—Vlaanderen, Belgium, 62
FOOD—Foundation of Occupational Development, India, 201
Food for the Hungry—FH, USA, 491
Food for the Poor, Inc, USA, 491
Foro Juvenil, Uruguay, 560
FORWARD—Foundation for Women's Health, Research and Development, UK, 417
FOSIM—Foundation Open Society Institute Macedonia, Macedonia, 258
Foundation for Agricultural Development, Ecuador, 125
Foundation for the Arts, Italy, 219
Foundation for Assistance, Training and Integration of Disadvantaged People, Spain, 339
Foundation Cassa di Risparmio di Padova e Rovigo, Italy, 219
Foundation Centre for the Study of Social Investment, Italy, 216
Foundation for Children, Germany, 181
Foundation for Democratic Initiatives—FDI, Kosovo, 248
Foundation for Development and Partnership in Africa, Switzerland, 366
Foundation for the Financial Assessment of Social Service and Development Institutions, Guatemala, 190
Foundation for Franco-German Co-operation, France, 143
Foundation for Higher Education and Development, Colombia, 104
Foundation for Human Rights and Humanitarian Relief, Turkey, 389
Foundation for Knowledge and Liberty, Haiti, 192
Foundation 'Life for All', Switzerland, 375
Foundation for Low-Cost Housing, Venezuela, 564
Foundation of Occupational Development—FOOD, India, 201
Foundation Open Society Institute Macedonia—FOSIM, Macedonia, 258
Foundation Open Society Institute—Representative Office Montenegro—FOSI ROM, Montenegro, 267
Foundation for the People's Economy, Costa Rica, 107
Foundation for the Peoples of the South Pacific, Australia, 38
Foundation of Savings Banks, Spain, 341
Foundation of Spanish Commercial Agents, Spain, 339
Foundation for Sport and the Arts, UK, 417
Foundation for the Study of Infant Deaths, UK, 417
Foundation for the Support of Women's Work, Turkey, 389
Foundation for Sustainable Development, Spain, 348
Foundation for Swedish Culture in Finland, Finland, 133
Foundation for the Unity and Development of Rural Communities, Costa Rica, 107
Foundation of Village Community Development, Indonesia, 208
Foundation for Women, Spain, 345

Foundation for Women's Health, Research and Development—FORWARD, UK, 417
Foundation for Women's Research and Studies, Argentina, 32
Foundation for Young Australians, Australia, 41
France Amérique Latine—FAL, France, 151
Freedom from Hunger, USA, 494
Freudenberg Stiftung, Germany, 168
Fritz Gerber Foundation for Gifted Young People, Switzerland, 366
Fritz-Gerber-Stiftung für Begabte Junge Menschen, Switzerland, 366
Frontiers Foundation Inc/Fondation Frontière Inc, Canada, 89
FUHEM—Fundación Hogar del Empleado, Spain, 343
FUNBANHCAFE—Fundación BANHCAFE, Honduras, 193
Fund for the Development of the Carpathian Euroregion, Hungary, 195
Fund for Development and Partnership in Africa, Switzerland, 366
Fund for an Open Society—Serbia, Serbia, 324
Fundação Abrinq pelos Direitos da Criança e do Adolescente, Brazil, 70
Fundação ArcelorMittal Acesita, Brazil, 71
Fundação de Atendimento à Criança e ao Adolescente Professor Hélio Augusto de Souza—Fundhas, Brazil, 73
Fundação Banco do Brasil, Brazil, 71
Fundação para o Desenvolvimento da Comunidade, Mozambique, 269
Fundação Dom Manuel II, Portugal, 311
Fundação Hélio Augusto de Souza—Fundhas, Brazil, 73
Fundação Iochpe, Brazil, 72
Fundação Maria Cecilia Souto Vidigal, Brazil, 73
Fundação Maurício Sirotsky Sobrinho, Brazil, 72
Fundação Oriente, Portugal, 312
Fundação Romi, Brazil, 72
Fundació Agrupació Mútua, Spain, 338
Fundació 'La Caixa', Spain, 338
Fundación AFIM—Ayuda, Formación e Integración del Minusválido, Spain, 339
Fundación de los Agentes Comerciales de España, Spain, 339
Fundación Alberto Vollmer, USA, 551
Fundación Alzheimer España—FAE, Spain, 339
Fundación Amancio Ortega, Spain, 346
Fundación Ana Mata Manzanedo, Spain, 345
Fundación Antonio Restrepo Barco, Colombia, 104
Fundación Arias para la Paz y el Progreso Humano, Costa Rica, 106
Fundación de Asesoría Financiera a Instituciones de Desarrollo y Servicio Social—FAFIDESS, Guatemala, 190
Fundación de Asistencia para la Pequeña Empresa, Guatemala, 190
Fundación AVINA, Panama, 297
Fundación BANHCAFE—FUNBANHCAFE, Honduras, 193
Fundación Bariloche, Argentina, 32
Fundación Bunge y Born, Argentina, 32
Fundación de las Cajas de Ahorros—FUNCAS, Spain, 341
Fundación CODESPA—Futuro en Marcha, Spain, 342
Fundación Comunitaria de Puerto Rico—FCPR, Puerto Rico, 314
Fundación Corona, Colombia, 104
Fundación Costarricense de Desarrollo—FUCODES, Costa Rica, 106
Fundación para el Desarrollo Agropecuario—FUNDAGRO, Ecuador, 125
Fundación para el Desarrollo—FUNDAP, Guatemala, 191
Fundación para el Desarrollo de la Microempresa, Guatemala, 191
Fundación Desarrollo Sostenido—FUNDESO, Spain, 348
Fundación Dominicana de Desarrollo—FDD, Dominican Republic, 123
Fundación para la Economía Popular—FUNDECO, Costa Rica, 107
Fundación Ecuatoriana de Desarrollo—FED, Ecuador, 125
Fundación para la Educación Superior y el Desarrollo—Fedesarrollo, Colombia, 104
Fundación Empresa y Sociedad, Spain, 342
Fundación Empresa-Universidad de Zaragoza—FEUZ, Spain, 342
Fundación Esperanza de los Niños, Guatemala, 190
Fundación para Estudio e Investigación de la Mujer—FEIM, Argentina, 32
Fundación Eugenio Espejo, Ecuador, 125
Fundación Eugenio Mendoza, Venezuela, 563

Fundación General Ecuatoriana, Ecuador, 125
Fundación Génesis Empresarial, Guatemala, 190
Fundación Hábitat Colombia—FHC, Colombia, 105
Fundación Hogar del Empleado—FUHEM, Spain, 343
Fundación Innovación de la Economía Social—INNOVES, Spain, 343
Fundación Integral Campesina—FINCA, Costa Rica, 107
Fundación Intervida, Spain, 344
Fundación Invica, Chile, 100
Fundación Juan March, Spain, 345
Fundación Laboral Sonsoles Ballvé Lantero, Spain, 344
Fundación Luis Vives, Spain, 348
Fundación MAPFRE, Spain, 345
Fundación Marcelino Botín, Spain, 341
Fundación María Francisca de Roviralta, Spain, 347
Fundación México Unido—FMU, Mexico, 263
Fundación MICROS—Fundación para el Desarrollo de la Microempresa, Guatemala, 191
Fundación Miguel Alemán AC, Mexico, 262
Fundación Mujeres, Spain, 345
Fundación Nacional para el Desarrollo, El Salvador, 128
Fundación Nacional para el Desarrollo de Honduras—FUNADEH, Honduras, 193
Fundación Nantik Lum, Spain, 345
Fundación ONCE, Spain, 346
Fundación Paideia Galiza, Spain, 346
Fundación Paz y Solidaridad Serafín Aliaga—FPyS, Spain, 346
Fundación Pedro Barrié de la Maza, Spain, 340
Fundación Promi, Spain, 347
Fundación Rafael del Pino, Spain, 347
Fundación La Salle de Ciencias Naturales—FLASA, Venezuela, 564
Fundación Salvadoreña para el Desarrollo Económico y Social, El Salvador, 128
Fundación Santa María, Spain, 348
Fundación Schcolnik, Argentina, 33
Fundación SERVIVIENDA, Colombia, 105
Fundación SES—Sustentabilidad, Educación, Solidaridad, Argentina, 33
Fundación Solidaridad, Dominican Republic, 123
Fundación Soros Guatemala, Guatemala, 191
Fundación Unión y Desarrollo de Comunidades Campesinas, Costa Rica, 107
Fundación de la Vivienda Popular, Venezuela, 564
Fundación de Viviendas Hogar de Cristo, Chile, 100
Fundacja Agory, Poland, 306
Fundacja Bankowa im. Leopolda Kronenberga, Poland, 306
Fundacja Gospodarcza, Poland, 307
Fundacja im. Stefana Batorego, Poland, 307
Fundacja Pomocy Wzajemnej Barka, Poland, 308
Fundacja Pro Bono II, Poland, 308
FUNDAGRO—Fundación para el Desarrollo Agropecuario, Ecuador, 125
FUNDAP—Fundación para el Desarrollo, Guatemala, 190
FUNDESO—Fundación Desarrollo Sostenido, Spain, 348
Fundhas—Fundação Hélio Augusto de Souza, Brazil, 73
The Gaia Foundation, UK, 418
Garfield Weston Foundation, UK, 455
The Gatsby Charitable Foundation, UK, 418
Gemeinnützige Hertie Foundation, Germany, 169
Gemeinnützige Hertie-Stiftung, Germany, 169
General Ecuadorean Foundation, Ecuador, 125
General Service Foundation, USA, 495
George Cedric Metcalf Charitable Foundation, Canada, 94
Gerber (Fritz) Stiftung für begabte junge Menschen, Switzerland, 366
German AIDS Foundation, Germany, 164
German Foundation for World Population, Germany, 165
German Marshall Fund of the United States—GMF, USA, 496
Getty (J. Paul) Jnr Charitable Trust, UK, 418
Giangiacomo Feltrinelli Foundation, Italy, 221
Gift of the Givers Foundation, South Africa, 332
Giovanni Lorenzini Foundation, Italy, 222
Giving USA Foundation, USA, 496
GLARP—Grupo Latinoamericano de Rehabilitación Profesional, Colombia, 105
The Glass-House Trust, UK, 419
Global Harmony Foundation—GHF, Switzerland, 367
Global Voluntary Service—GVS, Japan, 232
GMF—German Marshall Fund of the United States, USA, 496

Goldsmith (Horace W.) Foundation, USA, 498
Good Neighbors International, Korea (Republic), 246
Gordon (Walter and Duncan) Charitable Foundation, Canada, 89
Gordon and Betty Moore Foundation, USA, 525
Gradjanske inicijative—GI, Serbia, 324
Grameen Foundation—GF, USA, 499
Grant (William T.) Foundation, USA, 499
Grassroots International—GRI, USA, 500
Great Britain Sasakawa Foundation, UK, 419
GRUMIN—Grupo Mulher-Educação Indigena, Brazil, 73
Grupo Latinoamericano para la Participación, la Integración y la Inclusión de Personas con Discapacidad—GLARP-IIPD, Colombia, 105
Grupo Mulher-Educação Indigena—GRUMIN, Brazil, 73
Gruss (Joseph S. and Caroline) Life Monument Fund, Israel, 214
Guggenheim (John Simon) Memorial Foundation, USA, 500
Guttman Center of Applied Social Research, Israel, 214
Haaz (Dr F. P.) Social Assistance Foundation, Ukraine, 393
Hamdard Foundation Pakistan, Pakistan, 294
Hamlyn (Paul) Foundation, UK, 419
Hans Wilsdorf Foundation, Switzerland, 366
Harold Hyam Wingate Foundation, UK, 456
Harry and Jeanette Weinberg Foundation, Inc, USA, 552
Hearst (William Randolph) Foundation, USA, 502
The Hearst Foundation, Inc, USA, 501
Hedwig and Robert Samuel Foundation, Germany, 177
Hedwig und Robert Samuel-Stiftung, Germany, 177
Heifer International, USA, 502
Heinz (Howard) Endowment, USA, 502
Heinz, Anna and Carol Kroch Foundation, UK, 427
HEKS—Hilfswerk Evangelischen Kirchen Schweiz, Switzerland, 367
The Helen Suzman Foundation, South Africa, 335
Hélio Augusto de Souza Foundation, Brazil, 73
Hellenic Society for Disabled Children, Greece, 187
Helmsley (Leona M. and Harry B.) Charitable Trust, USA, 503
HELP International, USA, 503
Helvetas Swiss Intercooperation, Switzerland, 367
Henrietta Szold Institute—National Institute for Research in the Behavioural Sciences, Israel, 215
The Henry J. Kaiser Family Foundation, USA, 513
The Henry Smith Charity, UK, 448
HER Fund, Hong Kong, 194
Heritage Lottery Fund—HLF, UK, 420
Hesse and Thuringia Savings Banks Cultural Foundation, Germany, 178
Hestia—The National Volunteer Centre, Czech Republic, 114
Hewlett (William and Flora) Foundation, USA, 503
Higgins (Terrence) Trust, UK, 420
Hilden Charitable Fund, UK, 421
Hilfswerk der Evangelischen Kirchen Schweiz—HEKS, Switzerland, 367
Himalayan Light Foundation—HLF, Nepal, 271
Hirsch (Baron de) Fund, USA, 484
History Foundation of Turkey, Turkey, 389
Hitachi Foundation, USA, 504
HLF—Himalayan Light Foundation, Nepal, 271
Hogar de Cristo, Chile, 100
Holt International, USA, 504
Holt International Children's Services—HICS, USA, 504
Home of Christ, Chile, 100
Homeland Foundation, USA, 522
Hope for the Children Foundation, Guatemala, 190
Horace W. Goldsmith Foundation, USA, 498
Housing Services Foundation, Colombia, 105
Howard (Katharine) Foundation, Ireland, 211
Howard Heinz Endowment, USA, 502
Howard Karagheusian Commemorative Corporation—HKCC, USA, 513
Human Resource Development Foundation, Turkey, 389
Humanitarian Relief Foundation, Turkey, 389
Hungarian Foundation for Self-Reliance—HFSR, Hungary, 195
Hungarian Interchurch Aid—HIA, Hungary, 196
IACD—Institute of Asian Culture and Development, Korea (Republic), 246
Ian Potter Foundation, Australia, 43

ICSSR—Indian Council of Social Science Research, India, 202
IEIAS—Institut Européen Interuniversitaire de l'Action Sociale, Belgium, 62
IFAD—International Fund for Agricultural Development, Italy, 226
IKEA Foundation, Netherlands, 275
IKGV—İnsan Kaynağını Geliştirme Vakfı, Turkey, 389
İktisadi Kalkınma Vakfı, Turkey, 388
Imperial Oil Foundation, Canada, 90
India Assistance, Germany, 171
India Partners, USA, 506
Indian Centre for Philanthropy, India, 198
Indian Council for Child Welfare, India, 202
Indian Council of Social Science Research—ICSSR, India, 202
Indienhilfe eV, Germany, 171
Indigenous Women's Education Group, Brazil, 73
INFID—International NGO Forum on Indonesian Development, Indonesia, 207
Information and Education Centre for the Prevention of Drug Abuse, Peru, 299
Initiative and Achievement, Foundation of the Nassauische Sparkasse for Culture, Sport and Society, Germany, 171
Initiative und Leistung, Stiftung der Nassauischen Sparkasse für Kultur, Sport und Gesellschaft, Germany, 171
INMED Partnerships for Children, USA, 506
INNOVES—Fundación Innovación de la Economía Social, Spain, 343
İnsan Hak ve Hürriyetleri İnsani Yardım Vakfı, Turkey, 389
İnsan Kaynağını Geliştirme Vakfı—IKGV, Turkey, 389
Institut Arctique de l'Amérique du Nord—IAAN, Canada, 81
Institut Européen Interuniversitaire de l'Action Sociale—IEIAS, Belgium, 62
Institut urbain du Canada, Canada, 85
Institute of Asian Culture and Development—IACD, Korea (Republic), 246
Institute for Development Research, USA, 556
Institute for Private Enterprise and Democracy—IPED, Poland, 309
Instituto Ayrton Senna, Brazil, 73
Instituto Europeo de Salud y Bienestar Social, Spain, 349
Instituto Senna (Ayrton), Brazil, 73
Istituto Torcuato di Tella, Argentina, 34
Integrated Rural Development Foundation, Philippines, 303
Inter-American Foundation—IAF, USA, 507
Inter Pares, Canada, 90
International Blue Crescent Relief and Development Foundation—IBC, Turkey, 390
International Charitable Fund of Bermuda—ICFB, Bermuda, 66
International Charitable Fund 'Ukraine 3000', Ukraine, 394
International Co-operation, Italy, 217
International Confederation of Family Support, Argentina, 31
International Development and Relief Foundation, Canada, 91
The International Foundation, USA, 508
International Foundation for Education and Self-Help—IFESH, USA, 509
International Fund for Agricultural Development—IFAD, Italy, 226
International Fund for Ireland, Ireland, 211
International Medical Services for Health—INMED, USA, 506
International NGO Forum on Indonesian Development—INFID, Indonesia, 207
International Refugee Trust—IRT, UK, 424
International Relief and Development—IRD, USA, 510
International Renaissance Foundation—IRF, Ukraine, 394
International Women's Health Coalition—IWHC, USA, 510
Intervida Foundation, Spain, 344
Invica Foundation, Chile, 100
Ioannou (Christos Stelios) Foundation, Cyprus, 111
Irish Youth Foundation, Ireland, 212
Irvine (James) Foundation, USA, 511
Isabel Allende Foundation, USA, 463
Islamic Relief Worldwide, UK, 425
Islamic Thought Foundation, Iran, 209
Israel Institute Applied Social Research, Israel, 214
Istituto Carlo Cattaneo, Italy, 227
Istituto Luigi Sturzo, Italy, 227
Ittleson Foundation, USA, 511
Ivey (Richard) Foundation, Canada, 91

Ivey Foundation, Canada, 91
J. Paul Getty Jnr Charitable Trust, UK, 418
J. R. McKenzie Trust, New Zealand, 284
Jack Brockhoff Foundation—JBF, Australia, 39
The James Irvine Foundation, USA, 511
Jan Hus Educational Foundation, Slovakia, 329
The Japan Foundation Centre for Global
    Partnership—CGP, Japan, 236
Japan International Volunteer Center—JVC,
    Japan, 236
Japanese-German Center Berlin, Germany, 173
Japanisch-Deutsches Zentrum Berlin,
    Germany, 173
JCA Charitable Foundation, UK, 425
Jean-Louis Lévesque Foundation, Canada, 88
JEN, Japan, 237
Jenifer Altman Foundation—JAF, USA, 463
Jerusalem Foundation, Israel, 214
Jewish Agency for Israel Allocations Program,
    Israel, 214
Jewish Colonization Association, UK, 425
Jewish Community Development Fund—JCDF,
    USA, 512
Jewish Philanthropic Association, UK, 452
JNF Charitable Trust—JNFCT, UK, 426
The John D. and Catherine T. MacArthur
    Foundation, USA, 520
John Ellerman Foundation, UK, 414
John Moores Foundation, UK, 432
John Simon Guggenheim Memorial Foundation,
    USA, 500
John Swire 1989 Charitable Trust, UK, 450
The John W. Carson Foundation, USA, 476
The Johnson Foundation at Wingspread,
    USA, 512
JOHUD—Jordanian Hashemite Fund for Human
    Development, Jordan, 241
Jordan River Foundation, Jordan, 241
Jordanian Hashemite Fund for Human
    Development, Jordan, 241
Joseph Levy Charitable Foundation, UK, 429
Joseph Levy Foundation, UK, 429
Joseph P. Kennedy, Jr Foundation, USA, 515
Joseph Rowntree Charitable Trust, UK, 441
Joseph Rowntree Foundation, UK, 442
Joseph S. and Caroline Gruss Life Monument
    Fund, Israel, 214
JPMorgan Fleming Foundation, UK, 426
JPMorgan Foundation, UK, 426
Juan March Foundation, Spain, 345
Kadın Emeğini Değerlendirme Vakfı—KEDV,
    Turkey, 389
Kahanoff Foundation, Canada, 91
Kaiser (Henry J.) Family Foundation, USA, 513
Karagheusian (Howard) Commemorative
    Corporation, USA, 513
Karić fondacija, Serbia, 325
Karić Foundation, Serbia, 325
Karl Kübel Foundation for Child and Family,
    Germany, 174
Karl-Kübel-Stiftung für Kind und Familie,
    Germany, 174
Katharine Howard Foundation, Ireland, 211
KCDF—Kenya Community Development
    Foundation, Kenya, 245
Kennedy (Joseph P.), Jr Foundation, USA, 515
Kensington Estate—Henry Smith Charity,
    UK, 448
Khemka (Nand and Jeet) Foundation, India, 203
Kinder in Afrika, Stiftung, Germany, 181
King Baudouin Foundation, Belgium, 62
King George's Fund for Sailors, UK, 447
King Gustaf V 90th Birthday Foundation,
    Sweden, 354
King Hussein Foundation—KHF, Jordan, 241
Kirby Laing Foundation, UK, 427
Kirk (Norman) Memorial Trust, New
    Zealand, 284
Kleinwort (Ernest) Charitable Trust, UK, 427
Koç (Vehbi), Vakfı, Turkey, 391
Köning Boudewijnstichting/Fondation Roi
    Baudouin, Belgium, 62
Konung Gustaf V's 90-Årsfond, Sweden, 354
Koret Foundation, USA, 515
Kosovo Foundation for Open Society—KFOS,
    Kosovo, 248
Kresge Foundation, USA, 516
Kroch (Heinz, Anna and Carol) Foundation,
    UK, 427
Kroch (Heinz and Anna) Foundation, UK, 427
Kronenberga (Leopolda), Fundacja Bankowa,
    Poland, 306
KRS Education and Rural Development
    Foundation, Inc, USA, 516
Kübel (Karl) Stiftung für Kind und Familie,
    Germany, 174
Kuwait Awqaf Public Foundation, Kuwait, 249
'La Caixa' Foundation, Spain, 338

La Salle Foundation for Natural Sciences,
    Venezuela, 564
Laidlaw Foundation, Canada, 91
Laing (Beatrice) Trust, UK, 428
Laing (Kirby) Foundation, UK, 427
Lama Gangchen World Peace Foundation,
    Italy, 227
Lambrakis Foundation, Greece, 187
Lambrakis Research Foundation, Greece, 187
Lane (Allen) Foundation, UK, 428
Lateinamerika-Zentrum eV—LAZ, Germany, 174
Latin America Centre, Germany, 174
Latin America France, France, 151
Latin American, African and Asian Social
    Housing Service, Chile, 101
Latin American Fund for Development, Costa
    Rica, 106
Latin American Group for the Participation,
    Integration and Inclusion of People with
    Disability, Colombia, 105
Latvia Children's Fund, Latvia, 251
Latvijas Bērnu fonds, Latvia, 251
Lauder (Ronald S.) Foundation, Germany, 174
The Lawson Foundation, Canada, 92
The Leona M. and Harry B. Helmsley Charitable
    Trust, USA, 503
Leopold Kronenberg Foundation, Poland, 306
Leprosy Mission International, UK, 428
Leventis (A. G.) Foundation, Greece, 188
Levesque (Jean-Louis), Fondation, Canada, 88
Levy (Joseph) Foundation, UK, 429
Lietuvos vaikų fondas, Lithuania, 256
Lifewater International—LI, USA, 518
Lilly Endowment, Inc, USA, 518
Lithuanian Children's Fund, Lithuania, 256
Littauer (Lucius N.) Foundation, Inc, USA, 519
Lloyds TSB Foundation for England and Wales,
    UK, 429
The Long Now Foundation—LNF, USA, 519
Lorenzini (Giovanni), Fondazione, Italy, 222
Lucie and André Chagnon Foundation/
    Fondation Lucie et André Chagnon,
    Canada, 85
Lucius N. Littauer Foundation, Inc, USA, 519
Luigi Einaudi Foundation, Italy, 221
Luigi Sturzo Institute, Italy, 227
Luis Vives Foundation, Spain, 348
LWR—Lutheran World Relief, USA, 519
Lynde and Harry Bradley Foundation, Inc,
    USA, 473
M-USA—Mercy-USA for Aid and Development,
    USA, 524
M. Venkatarangaiya Foundation, India, 206
MacArthur (John D. and Catherine T.)
    Foundation, USA, 520
McConnell Clark (Edna) Foundation, USA, 520
McCormick (Robert R.) Foundation, USA, 520
McKenzie (J. R.) Trust, New Zealand, 284
McKnight Foundation, USA, 521
The McLean Foundation, Canada, 93
Magyar Ökumenikus Segélyszervezet,
    Hungary, 196
MAIF Foundation, France, 147
Mailman (A. L.) Family Foundation, USA, 521
Maison Franco-Japonaise, Japan, 237
Malcolm Sargent Cancer Fund for Children,
    UK, 410
Mama Cash, Netherlands, 277
Mandela (Nelson) Children's Fund, South
    Africa, 333
Manfred Woerner Foundation, Bulgaria, 74
Manning (Ernest C.) Awards Foundation,
    Canada, 93
Manzaneo (Ana Mata), Fundación, Spain, 345
MAPFRE Foundation, Spain, 345
Marcelino Botín Foundation, Spain, 341
Marcelle et Jean Coutu Foundation, Canada, 88
March (Juan), Fundación, Spain, 345
March of Dimes, USA, 522
María Francisca de Roviralta Foundation,
    Spain, 347
Marie Curie Cancer Care, UK, 412
Marisla Foundation, USA, 522
Match International Centre, Canada, 93
Maurício Sirotsky Nephew Foundation, Brazil, 72
Maxová (Tereza) Foundation, Czech Republic, 115
The Maytree Foundation, Canada, 93
medica mondiale e.V., Germany, 175
Medical Foundation for the Care of Victims of
    Torture, UK, 430
Mellon (Andrew W.) Foundation, USA, 523
Mellon (Richard King) Foundation, USA, 523
MENCAP, UK, 431
Mendoza (Eugenio) Fundación, Venezuela, 563
Mental Health Foundation, UK, 431
Mercy-USA for Aid and Development—M-USA,
    USA, 524
Mertz Gilmore Foundation, USA, 524

Metcalf (George Cedric) Charitable Foundation,
    Canada, 94
Microenterprise Development Foundation,
    Guatemala, 191
Miguel Alemán Foundation, Mexico, 262
Milan Simecka Foundation, Slovakia, 329
Miriam Dean Fund, UK, 413
Miriam Dean Refugee Trust Fund, UK, 413
Miriam G. and Ira D. Wallach Foundation,
    USA, 552
Moawad (René) Foundation, Lebanon, 253
Møller (A.P.) and Chastine Mc-Kinney Møller
    Foundation, Denmark, 120
Molson Donations Fund/Fonds de bienfaisance
    Molson, Canada, 94
Molson Family Foundation, Canada, 94
Molson Foundation, Canada, 94
Mongolian Women's Fund—MONES,
    Mongolia, 266
Montres Rolex, Fondation, Switzerland, 366
Monument Trust, UK, 432
Moody Foundation, USA, 525
Moores (John) Foundation, UK, 432
Morrow (The F. K.) Foundation, Canada, 94
Mott (Charles Stewart) Foundation, USA, 526
The Mountain Institute—TMI, USA, 526
Ms Foundation for Women, USA, 526
Mukti Lawrence Foundation, Bangladesh, 52
Mum and Dad Foundation, Czech Republic, 115
Muslim Aid, UK, 433
The Muttart Foundation, Canada, 94
Myer (Sidney) Fund, Australia, 42
The Myer Foundation, Australia, 42
Nadace Charty 77, Czech Republic, 114
Nadace Táta a Máma, Czech Republic, 115
Nadácia Milana Šimečku, Slovakia, 329
Nadácia pre deti Slovenska, Slovakia, 328
Nand and Jeet Khemka Foundation, India, 203
Nantik Lum Foundation, Spain, 345
Nathan Steinberg Family Foundation, Canada, 98
National Council for Voluntary Organisations—
    NCVO, UK, 398
National Endowment for Science, Technology and
    the Arts—NESTA, UK, 434
National Foundation for Development, El
    Salvador, 128
National Foundation for the Development of
    Honduras, Honduras, 193
National Heritage Memorial Fund, UK, 420
National Institute for Research in the
    Behavioural Sciences—Szold (Henrietta)
    Institute, Israel, 215
National Institute for Sustainable
    Development—NISD, India, 204
National Society for the Prevention of Cruelty to
    Children, UK, 435
National Volunteer Centre—Hestia, Czech
    Republic, 114
NCH—National Children's Home, UK, 398
NCVO—National Council for Voluntary
    Organisations, UK, 398
Nederlands instituut voor Zuidelijk Afrika—
    NiZA, Netherlands, 278
Nederlandsche Maatschappij voor Nijverheid en
    Handel—NMNH, Netherlands, 278
NEF—Near East Foundation, USA, 528
Nelson Mandela Children's Fund, South
    Africa, 333
Nelson Mandela Children's Fund—Canada,
    Canada, 93
Nepal Forward Foundation, Nepal, 271
NESsT—Nonprofit Enterprise and Self-
    sustainability Team, Chile, 101
NESTA—National Endowment for Science,
    Technology and the Arts, UK, 434
Van Neste Foundation, UK, 453
Netherlands Institute for Southern Africa,
    Netherlands, 278
Netherlands Society for Industry and Trade,
    Netherlands, 278
Network of Information and Support for Non-
    Governmental Organizations, Poland, 306
New Perspectives Foundation, Russian
    Federation, 319
New Zealand Winston Churchill Memorial Trust,
    New Zealand, 285
NGO Rural and Social Initiative, Moldova, 264
Nirnaya, India, 204
Non-Governmental Organization JEN,
    Japan, 237
Nonprofit Enterprise and Self-sustainability
    Team—NESsT, Chile, 101
Noor al-Hussein Foundation—NHF, Jordan, 241
Nordic Africa Institute Scholarships,
    Sweden, 355
Nordiska Afrikainstitutets Stipendier,
    Sweden, 355
Norman Kirk Memorial Trust, New Zealand, 284

Northern Ireland Voluntary Trust, UK, 412
Northern Rock Foundation, UK, 435
Novartis Foundation for Sustainable
  Development—NFSD, Switzerland, 371
Novartis Stiftung für Nachhaltige Entwicklung,
  Switzerland, 371
Novartis US Foundation, USA, 529
NoVo Foundation, USA, 529
NSPCC—National Society for the Prevention of
  Cruelty to Children, UK, 435
Nuffield Foundation, UK, 435
Oak Foundation, Switzerland, 371
The Officers' Association, UK, 435
ONCE—Spanish National Organization for the
  Blind—Foundation, Spain, 346
The One Foundation, Ireland, 212
OneWorld International Foundation, UK, 435
OPALS—Organisation Panafricaine de Lutte
  Contre le SIDA, France, 153
Open Society Forum (Mongolia), Mongolia, 266
Open Society Foundation, Romania, 317
Open Society Foundation for Albania—OSFA,
  Albania, 29
Open Society Foundation—Bratislava,
  Slovakia, 328
Open Society Foundation for South Africa—OSF-
  SA, South Africa, 334
Open Society Fund—Bosnia-Herzegovina,
  Bosnia and Herzegovina, 68
Open Society Initiative for Southern Africa—
  OSISA, South Africa, 334
Open Society Institute—Assistance Foundation
  (Azerbaijan), Azerbaijan, 50
Open Society Institute Assistance Foundation,
  Armenia—OSIAFA, Armenia, 35
Open Society Institute Assistance Foundation—
  Tajikistan, Tajikistan, 381
Open Society Institute Montenegro,
  Montenegro, 267
Open Society Institute—Paris (Soros
  Foundations), France, 135
Open Society Institute—Sofia (Bulgaria),
  Bulgaria, 76
Open Society Institute—Turkey, Turkey, 387
Operation Beaver—Frontiers Foundation Inc,
  Canada, 89
Opportunity International USA, USA, 530
Oranje Fonds, Netherlands, 278
Organisation Panafricaine de Lutte Contre le
  SIDA—OPALS, France, 153
Orient Foundation, Portugal, 312
The Orient-Occident Foundation, Morocco, 268
Ortega (Amancio) Fundación, Spain, 346
OSIAF—Open Society Institute Assistance
  Foundation—Tajikistan, Tajikistan, 381
Österreichische Forschungsstiftung für
  Internationale Entwicklung—ÖFSE,
  Austria, 48
Oxfam Canada, Canada, 95
Oxfam Deutschland e.V., Germany, 176
Oxfam Hong Kong, Hong Kong, 194
Oxfam India, India, 204
Oxfam Ireland, Ireland, 212
Oxfam Mexico, Mexico, 263
Oxfam New Zealand, New Zealand, 285
Oxfam-Québec, Canada, 95
OzChild, Australia, 43
Pacific Leprosy Foundation, New Zealand, 286
Pacific Peoples' Partnership, Canada, 95
Packard (David and Lucile) Foundation, USA, 531
PADF—Pan American Development Foundation,
  USA, 532
Paideia Galiza Foundation, Spain, 346
Pan-African Centre for Social Prospects,
  Benin, 65
Pan-African Organization for AIDS Prevention,
  France, 153
The Parthenon Trust, Switzerland, 371
Patterson (Alicia) Foundation, USA, 533
The Paul G. Allen Family Foundation, USA, 463
Paul Hamlyn Foundation—PHF, UK, 419
Peace and Disarmament Education Trust—
  PADET, New Zealand, 286
Peace, Health and Human Development
  Foundation—PHD Foundation, Japan, 239
Pearl S. Buck International, USA, 474
Pedro Barrié de la Maza Foundation, Spain, 340
PEF Israel Endowment Funds, Inc, Israel, 215
People in Need, Czech Republic, 113
People-to-People Health Foundation, Inc—
  Project Hope, USA, 537
People's Harmonious Development Society,
  Georgia, 158
Peres Center for Peace, Israel, 215
Perpetual Foundation, Australia, 43
Perpetual Trustees Australia, Australia, 43
Pertubuhan Pertolongan Wanita, Malaysia, 260

Pestalozzi Children's Foundation,
  Switzerland, 374
Peter G. Peterson Foundation, USA, 534
Peterson (Peter G.) Foundation, USA, 534
Pforzheimer (Carl and Lily) Foundation, Inc,
  USA, 535
The PHD Foundation—Peace, Health and Human
  Development Foundation, Japan, 239
PHF—Paul Hamlyn Foundation, UK, 419
PhilDev—Philippine Development Foundation,
  USA, 535
Philippine Development Foundation—PhilDev,
  USA, 535
Piera, Pietro and Giovanni Ferrero Foundation,
  Italy, 221
Pilgrim Trust, UK, 437
Pilietinés Atsakomybés Fondas, Lithuania, 256
Pinchuk (Victor) Foundation, Ukraine, 394
Pitseng Trust, South Africa, 334
Plan Ireland, Ireland, 212
Plenty International, USA, 535
Plunkett Foundation, UK, 438
Pôle européen des fondations de l'économie
  sociale, Belgium, 56
Population Council, USA, 536
Potter (Ian) Foundation, Australia, 43
Preciosa Foundation, Czech Republic, 115
Pro Bono Foundation, Poland, 308
Pro Juventute, Switzerland, 372
Pro Victimis Foundation, Switzerland, 365
Progressio, UK, 439
Project HOPE, USA, 537
Project Trust, UK, 439
Promi Foundation, Spain, 347
Protestant Study Foundation, Germany, 167
PROVICOOP—Fundación Invica, Chile, 100
Prudential Foundation, USA, 537
Public Welfare Foundation, Inc, USA, 537
Puerto Rico Community Foundation, Puerto
  Rico, 314
Qatar Foundation, Qatar, 315
Queen Alia Fund for Social Development,
  Jordan, 241
Queen's Trust for Young Australians,
  Australia, 41
R. E. Ross Trust, Australia, 44
R. Howard Webster Foundation, Canada, 99
Rafael del Pino Foundation, Spain, 347
Rajiv Gandhi Foundation, India, 201
The Rank Foundation, UK, 440
Rayne Foundation, UK, 441
RBC Foundation, Canada, 96
Reeve (Christopher and Dana) Foundation,
  USA, 538
Refugee Trust International, Ireland, 213
Refugees International Japan—RIJ, Japan, 239
Reichstein Foundation, Australia, 44
Reimers (Werner) Stiftung, Germany, 177
Relief International, USA, 539
René Moawad Foundation, Lebanon, 253
Research Foundation—Flanders, Belgium, 62
Réseau Africain de la Jeunesse pour le
  Développement Durable, Algeria, 30
Reumatikerförbundet, Sweden, 355
Reynolds (Christopher) Foundation, USA, 539
RIA—Royal Irish Academy, Ireland, 212
Richard King Mellon Foundation, USA, 523
Righteous Persons Foundation, USA, 539
RNIB—Royal National Institute of Blind People,
  UK, 444
Roald Dahl's Marvellous Children's Charity,
  UK, 413
Robert Bosch Foundation, Germany, 163
Robert-Bosch-Stiftung GmbH, Germany, 163
Robert R. McCormick Foundation, USA, 520
Rockefeller Brothers Fund, USA, 540
Rockwool Fonden, Denmark, 121
Rockwool Foundation, Denmark, 121
Roma Lom Foundation, Bulgaria, 76
Rome Foundation, Italy, 224
Romi Foundation, Brazil, 72
The Ronald S. Lauder Foundation, Germany, 174
Ross (R. E.) Trust, Australia, 44
Rothschild (Edmond de) Foundations, USA, 541
Roviralta (María Francisca de), Fundación,
  Spain, 347
Rowan Charitable Trust, UK, 441
Rowntree (Joseph) Charitable Trust, UK, 441
Rowntree (Joseph) Foundation, UK, 442
Royal Air Force Benevolent Fund, UK, 442
Royal Bank of Canada Charitable Foundation,
  Canada, 96
Royal Bank Financial Group Foundation,
  Canada, 96
Royal Commonwealth Society for the Blind—
  Sight Savers International, UK, 448
Royal National Institute of Blind People—RNIB,
  UK, 444

Royal Society for Mentally Handicapped
  Children and Adults—MENCAP, UK, 431
Royal Society for the Prevention of Cruelty to
  Animals—RSPCA, UK, 445
RSPCA—Royal Society for the Prevention of
  Cruelty to Animals, UK, 445
The Rufford Foundation, UK, 445
Rufford Maurice Laing Foundation, UK, 445
RUI Foundation, Italy, 225
Russell Sage Foundation—RSF, USA, 541
Rutgers WPF, Netherlands, 279
Sabancı (Hacı Ömer) Foundation, Turkey, 389
Sabancı Foundation, Turkey, 389
Sabancı Vakfi—Hacı Ömer Sabancı Foundation,
  Turkey, 389
Sabera Foundation, India, 205
Sabera Foundation India, India, 205
Sahabdeen (A. M. M.) Trust Foundation, Sri
  Lanka, 350
Said Foundation, UK, 446
El Salvador Foundation for Economic and Social
  Development, El Salvador, 128
Sampradaan Indian Centre for Philanthropy,
  India, 198
Samuel (Hedwig und Robert) Stiftung,
  Germany, 177
Samuel Lunenfeld Charitable Foundation,
  Canada, 92
Samuel and Saidye Bronfman Family Foundation,
  Canada, 82
Samuel Sebba Charitable Trust, UK, 447
San Diego Foundation, USA, 542
San Francisco Foundation, USA, 542
Santa María Foundation, Spain, 348
Save & Prosper Foundation, UK, 426
Scaife Family Foundation, USA, 542
Schcolnik Foundation, Argentina, 33
Schusterman (Charles and Lynn) Family
  Foundation, USA, 543
SCIAF—Scottish Catholic International Aid
  Fund, UK, 447
Scientific Foundation of Hisham Adeeb Hijjawi,
  Jordan, 241
Scope, UK, 447
Scottish Catholic International Aid Fund—
  SCIAF, UK, 447
Scouloudi Foundation, UK, 447
Seafarers UK, UK, 447
SELAVIP International—Service de Promotion
  de l'Habitation Populaire en Amérique Latine,
  Afrique et Asie, Chile, 101
Selby (William G. and Marie) Foundation,
  USA, 543
Self Help Development Foundation,
  Zimbabwe, 567
Self Help Development International, Ireland, 213
Sem Pringpuangkeo Foundation, Thailand, 384
Semmelweis Alapítvány Magyarországi
  Ortopédia Fejlesztéséért, Hungary, 195
Semmelweis Foundation for the Development of
  Orthopaedics in Hungary, Hungary, 195
Serafín Aliaga Foundation for Peace and
  Solidarity, Spain, 346
SES Foundation—Sustainability, Education,
  Solidarity, Argentina, 33
Seva Foundation, USA, 544
Shackleton Foundation, UK, 448
Shelter—National Campaign for Homeless
  People, UK, 448
Sidney Myer Fund, Australia, 42
Sieć SPLOT, Poland, 306
Sieć Wspierania Organizacji Pozarządowych—
  SPLOT, Poland, 306
Sight Savers International, UK, 448
Singapore International Foundation—SIF,
  Singapore, 326
Sino-British Fellowship Trust—SBFT, UK, 448
Sir Ahmadu Bello Foundation, Nigeria, 289
Sir Ahmadu Bello Memorial Foundation,
  Nigeria, 289
Sir Dorabji Tata Trust, India, 205
Sir Halley Stewart Trust, UK, 449
The Sir Jules Thorn Charitable Trust, UK, 451
Skoll Foundation, USA, 544
Slovak-Czech Women's Fund, Czech Republic, 115
Slovak Humanitarian Council, Slovakia, 328
Slovenská Humanitná Rada, Slovakia, 328
Small Business Assistance Foundation,
  Guatemala, 190
Smith Richardson Foundation, Inc, USA, 545
Sobell Foundation, UK, 449
Software AG Foundation, Germany, 178
Solidarios—Consejo de Fundaciones Americanas
  de Desarrollo, Dominican Republic, 123
Solidarity Foundation, Dominican Republic, 123
Solidarity National Commission—Economic
  Foundation, Poland, 307

Solidarność NSZZ—Economic Foundation, Poland, 307
Song Qingling Foundation, China (People's Republic), 102
Sonsoles Ballvé Lantero Labour Foundation, Spain, 344
Sophie and Karl Binding Foundation, Switzerland, 361
Sophie und Karl Binding-Stiftung, Switzerland, 361
Sorenson Legacy Foundation, USA, 545
Soros Foundation (Slovakia), Slovakia, 328
Soros Foundation (South Africa), South Africa, 334
Soros Foundation (Tajikistan), Tajikistan, 381
Soros Foundation Guatemala, Guatemala, 191
Soros Foundation–Kyrgyzstan, Kyrgyzstan, 250
Soros Foundation Macedonia, Macedonia, 258
Soros Foundation Romania, Romania, 317
Soros Serbia Foundation, Serbia, 324
South African Institute of Race Relations, South Africa, 335
South Pacific Peoples Foundation Canada, Canada, 95
Sparkassen-Kulturstiftung Hessen-Thüringen, Germany, 178
Springer (Axel) Stiftung, Germany, 179
The Starr Foundation, USA, 546
Stefan Batory Foundation, Poland, 307
Steinberg (Nathan) Family Foundation, Canada, 98
Stewart (Sir Halley) Trust, UK, 449
Stichting DOEN, Netherlands, 280
Stichting Fonds 1818, Netherlands, 280
Stichting Triodos Foundation, Netherlands, 282
Stichting VSB Fonds, Netherlands, 280
Stiftelsen Riksbankens Jubileumsfond, Sweden, 357
Stiftung für Kinder, Germany, 181
Stiftung Kinder in Afrika, Germany, 181
Stiftung Kinderdorf Pestalozzi, Switzerland, 374
Stiftung 'Leben für Alle', Switzerland, 375
Stiftung Vivamos Mejor, Switzerland, 375
Street Kids International, Canada, 98
The Streisand Foundation, USA, 547
The Stroke Association, UK, 450
Sturzo (Luigi), Istituto, Italy, 227
Sultan bin Abdulaziz al-Saud Foundation, Saudi Arabia, 321
Sun/Soleil—AREGAK, Armenia, 35
Sunley (Bernard) Charitable Foundation, UK, 450
Support Centre for Associations and Foundations—SCAF, Belarus, 54
Surdna Foundation, Inc, USA, 547
Sutherland Self Help Trust, New Zealand, 286
Suzman (Helen) Foundation, South Africa, 335
Svenska Kulturfonden, Finland, 133
Swedish Rheumatism Association, Sweden, 355
Swiss Interchurch Aid, Switzerland, 367
SWISSAID Foundation, Switzerland, 375
Syin-Lu Social Welfare Foundation, Taiwan, 380
The Sylvia Adams Charitable Trust, UK, 398
Sylvia and Charles Viertel Charitable Foundation, Australia, 45
Tanzania Millennium Hand Foundation—TAMIHA, Tanzania, 382
Tarih Vakfı, Turkey, 389
TEAR Australia, Australia, 45
di Tella (Torcuato), Instituto, Argentina, 34

Terre des Hommes Foundation, Switzerland, 376
Terrence Higgins Trust—THT, UK, 420
Tewa, Nepal, 271
TFF—Transnationella Stiftelsen för Freds- och Framtidsforskning, Sweden, 358
Third World Solidarity Action, Luxembourg, 257
Thorn (The Sir Jules) Charitable Trust, UK, 451
Tibet Fund, USA, 548
Tides, USA, 548
Tides Foundation, USA, 548
Tindall Foundation, New Zealand, 286
Tinker Foundation, Inc, USA, 548
TISCO Foundation, Thailand, 385
The Todd Foundation, New Zealand, 287
Torcuato di Tella Institute, Argentina, 34
The Toyota Foundation, Japan, 240
Transnational Foundation for Peace and Future Research, Sweden, 358
Transnationella Stiftelsen för Freds- och Framtidsforskning—TFF, Sweden, 358
Triodos Foundation, Netherlands, 282
Trócaire—Catholic Agency for World Development, Ireland, 213
The Trull Foundation, USA, 548
Trust for Civil Society in Central and Eastern Europe, Bulgaria, 76
Trust for London, UK, 451
Trusthouse Charitable Foundation, UK, 451
TTF—Toyota Thailand Foundation, Thailand, 385
Tudor Trust, UK, 452
Turin Savings Bank Foundation, Italy, 220
Turkish Family Health and Planning Foundation, Turkey, 390
Türkiye Aile Sağlığı ve Planlaması Vakfı—TAPV, Turkey, 390
Türkiye Kalkınma Vakfı, Turkey, 390
Twenty-Ninth May 1961 Charity, UK, 452
UJIA—United Jewish Israel Appeal, UK, 452
Ukraine 3000, Ukraine, 394
Ukrainian Women's Fund, Ukraine, 394
Uluslararası Mavi Hilal İnsani Yardım ve Kalkınma Vakfı, Turkey, 390
Umana Mente Foundation, Italy, 225
UniCredit Foundation—Unidea, Italy, 228
Unilever Vietnam Foundation—UVF, Viet Nam, 565
United Mexico Foundation, Mexico, 263
United Service Committee of Canada, Canada, 98
United Society for the Propagation of the Gospel—USPG, UK, 453
United States African Development Foundation—USADF, USA, 550
University of Zaragoza Business Foundation, Spain, 342
US-Ukraine Foundation, USA, 551
USC Canada, Canada, 98
Väestöliitto, Finland, 133
Vanarai, India, 206
Vancouver Foundation, Canada, 99
Vehbi Koç Foundation, Turkey, 391
Vehbi Koç Vakfı, Turkey, 391
Venkatarangaiya (M.) Foundation, India, 206
VIA Foundation, Czech Republic, 115
Victor Pinchuk Foundation, Ukraine, 394
Victoria Children Foundation, Russian Federation, 320
Viertel (Sylvia and Charles) Charitable Foundation, Australia, 45
Villar Foundation, Inc., Philippines, 304

VINCI Corporate Foundation for the City, France, 144
Vita, Ireland, 213
Vivamos Mejor Foundation, Switzerland, 375
Vodafone Foundation Germany, Germany, 183
Vodafone Group Foundation, UK, 453
Vodafone Stiftung Deutschland, Germany, 183
Vollmer (Alberto) Foundation, Inc, USA, 551
Voluntary Service Overseas, UK, 454
VSO, UK, 454
Výbor dobré vule—Nadace Olgy Havlové, Czech Republic, 115
Vzdelávacia nadácia Jana Husa, Slovakia, 329
Wallach (Miriam G. and Ira D.) Foundation, USA, 552
Walmart Foundation, USA, 552
Walter and Duncan Gordon Charitable Foundation, Canada, 89
War on Want, UK, 454
Wates Foundation, UK, 454
Webster (R. Howard) Foundation, Canada, 99
Weinberg (Harry and Jeanette) Foundation, USA, 552
Welfare Association, Switzerland, 376
Welzijn Juliana Fonds, Netherlands, 278
Werner Reimers Foundation, Germany, 177
Werner-Reimers-Stiftung, Germany, 177
West-Nordic Foundation, Iceland, 197
Weston (Garfield) Foundation, UK, 455
WHEAT Trust—Women's Hope Education and Training Trust, South Africa, 336
Whirlpool Foundation, USA, 553
Wilbur Foundation, USA, 554
William Adlington Cadbury Charitable Trust, UK, 407
The William and Flora Hewlett Foundation, USA, 503
William G. and Marie Selby Foundation, USA, 543
The William Randolph Hearst Foundation, USA, 502
William T. Grant Foundation, USA, 499
Wingate (Harold Hyam) Foundation, UK, 456
Winrock International, USA, 555
Woerner (Manfred) Foundation, Bulgaria, 74
The Wolfson Family Charitable Trust, UK, 456
Women's Aid, Ireland, 213
Women's Aid Organisation—WAO, Malaysia, 260
Women's Hope Education and Training Trust—Wheat Trust, South Africa, 336
Workers' Centre Foundation, Spain, 343
World Education, Inc, USA, 556
World Literacy of Canada—WLC, Canada, 99
World Neighbors, USA, 557
The World of NGOs, Austria, 46
World Population Foundation, Netherlands, 279
World Teacher Trust, India, 206
YADESA—Yayasan Pengembangan Masyarakat Desa, Indonesia, 208
Yayasan Dian Desa, Indonesia, 207
Yayasan Pengembangan Masyarakat Desa—YADESA, Indonesia, 208
Youth Forum, Uruguay, 560
Zakat House, Kuwait, 249
ZOA, Netherlands, 283
Zochonis Charitable Trust, UK, 457
Zorig Foundation, Mongolia, 266

Index by Area of Activity

Note: organizations will appear either in the All Regions index or in one or more of the regions listed below. All Regions means an organization is active in every region of the world. If an organization is listed under All Regions, it will not appear under any other region heading.

All Regions	639
Africa South of the Sahara	644
Australasia	647
Central and South-Eastern Europe	649
East and South-East Asia	652
Eastern Europe and the Republics of Central Asia	655
Middle East and North Africa	658
South America, Central America and the Caribbean	660
South Asia	664
USA and Canada	666
Western Europe	669

ALL REGIONS

30 Million Friends Foundation, France, 151
A. S. Hornby Educational Trust, UK, 421
AAUW—American Association of University Women Educational Foundation, USA, 463
Accademia Musicale Chigiana, Italy, 216
ACDI/VOCA, USA, 460
ACLS—American Council of Learned Societies, USA, 464
Action d'Urgence Internationale—AUI, France, 136
ActionAid, South Africa, 331
Adenauer (Konrad) Stiftung eV, Germany, 160
Adessium Foundation, Netherlands, 272
ADF—America's Development Foundation, USA, 458
ADL—Anti-Defamation League of B'nai B'rith, USA, 469
ADRA—Adventist Development and Relief Agency International, USA, 461
Adventist Development and Relief Agency International—ADRA, USA, 461
Advocacy Center at ISC, USA, 461
Aga Khan Development Network—AKDN, Switzerland, 360
Aga Khan Foundation (UK)—AKF, UK, 399
Aga Khan Trust for Culture—AKTC, Switzerland, 361
Agence Internationale pour le Développement Fédération—AIDE, France, 140
AIC—Association internationale des charités, Belgium, 57
Aid to the Church in Need—ACN, Germany, 160
Air Pollution and Climate Secretariat—AirClim, Sweden, 352
AirClim—Air Pollution and Climate Secretariat, Sweden, 352
Albert Einstein Institution, USA, 488
Alcoa Foundation, USA, 462
Alessio Pezcoller Foundation, Italy, 223
Alexander von Humboldt Foundation, Germany, 170
Alexander von Humboldt Stiftung, Germany, 170
Alexander S. Onassis Public Benefit Foundation, Greece, 189
Alfred Friendly Press Fellowships, USA, 494
Alfred Heineken Fondsen Foundation, Netherlands, 281
Alfried Krupp von Bohlen und Halbach Foundation, Germany, 173
Alfried Krupp von Bohlen und Halbach-Stiftung, Germany, 173
All Saints Educational Trust, UK, 400
Alliance Israélite Universelle, France, 137
Alliance Sud—Swiss Alliance of Development Organisations, Switzerland, 359
The Ambrose Monell Foundation, USA, 525
American Association of University Women Educational Foundation—AAUW, USA, 463
American Council of Learned Societies—ACLS, USA, 464

American Express Foundation, USA, 464
American Foundation for AIDS Research—amfAR, USA, 464
American Health Assistance Foundation—AHAF, USA, 465
American Jewish Joint Distribution Committee—JDC, USA, 466
American Philosophical Society—APS, USA, 467
American Refugee Committee—ARC, USA, 467
AmeriCares Foundation, Inc, USA, 468
America's Development Foundation—ADF, USA, 458
amfAR—American Foundation for AIDS Research, USA, 464
AMI—Fundação Assistência Médica International, Portugal, 310
Amigos de la Tierra, Netherlands, 275
Les Amis de la Terre, Netherlands, 275
Amnesty International, UK, 400
AMURT—Ananda Marga Universal Relief Team, USA, 468
AMURT International, Austria, 46
Ananda Marga Universal Relief Team—AMURT, USA, 468
Andrews Charitable Trust, UK, 400
Anne Frank-Fonds, Switzerland, 366
Anne Frank Foundation, Netherlands, 274
Anne Frank Fund, Switzerland, 366
Anne Frank Stichting, Netherlands, 274
Anti-Defamation League of B'nai B'rith—ADL, USA, 469
Anti-Slavery International, UK, 401
APC—Association for Progressive Communications, South Africa, 331
Aragón (José María), Fundación, Argentina, 31
ARC—American Refugee Committee, USA, 467
Arthur S. DeMoss Foundation, USA, 484
The Arts Grants Committee, Sweden, 354
Asahi Glass Foundation, Japan, 230
Asia Crime Prevention Foundation—ACPF, Japan, 231
Association for International Cancer Research—AICR, UK, 402
Association Internationale des Charités—AIC, Belgium, 57
Association for Progressive Communications—APC, South Africa, 331
Association for the Study of the World Refugee Problem, Germany, 168
AT&T Foundation, USA, 471
ATD Fourth World, France, 137
ATD Quart-Monde, France, 137
Atlas Economic Research Foundation, USA, 471
Atlas Network, USA, 471
Australian Council for International Development, Australia, 38
Aventis Foundation, Germany, 161
Aviation Sans Frontières—ASF, France, 137
Aviation Without Frontiers, France, 137
Bagnoud (François-Xavier) Association, USA, 495

Balzan Fonds, Internationale Stiftung, Switzerland, 368
Baptist World Aid—BWAid, USA, 472
Beinum (Eduard Van) Stichting, Netherlands, 272
Bellagio Forum for Sustainable Development, Germany, 161
Bernadottes (Folke) Minnesfond, Sweden, 352
Bernard van Leer Foundation, Netherlands, 277
Bertrand Russell Peace Foundation—BRPF, UK, 445
Better World Campaign—BWC, USA, 472
Big Lottery Fund, UK, 404
Bill and Melinda Gates Foundation, USA, 495
BirdLife International, UK, 404
Bischöfliches Hilfswerk Misereor eV, Germany, 162
BMW Foundation Herbert Quandt, Germany, 162
BMW Stiftung Herbert Quandt, Germany, 162
BNP Paribas Foundation, France, 141
The Body Shop Foundation, UK, 405
Boehringer Ingelheim Fonds—Stiftung für Medizinische Grundlagenforschung, Germany, 162
Böll (Heinrich) Stiftung, Germany, 162
Born Free Foundation Limited, UK, 405
Brandt (Bundeskanzler Willy), Stiftung, Germany, 163
Brigitte Bardot Foundation, France, 141
Bristol-Myers Squibb Foundation, USA, 473
British Academy, UK, 406
The British Council, UK, 406
British Institute of International and Comparative Law, UK, 407
British Red Cross, UK, 407
The Brush Foundation, USA, 474
Bundeskanzler-Willy-Brandt-Stiftung, Germany, 163
C. G. Jung-Institut Zürich, Switzerland, 370
CAB International, UK, 407
CABI, UK, 407
CAFOD—Catholic Agency for Overseas Development, UK, 407
Calouste Gulbenkian Foundation, Portugal, 311
Cambridge Commonwealth Trust, UK, 408
Cambridge Overseas Trust, UK, 408
Canada World Youth/Jeunesse Canada Monde, Canada, 82
Canadian Baptist Ministries, Canada, 97
Canadian Feed the Children, Canada, 84
Capacity Building International, Germany, 172
Caritas de France—Secours Catholique, France, 154
Caritas Internationalis—CI, Vatican City, 562
Carl Duisberg Gesellschaft eV, Germany, 172
Carnegie Endowment for International Peace, USA, 475
Carnegie Foundation, Wateler Fund, Netherlands, 272
Carnegie-Stichting, Watelerfonds, Netherlands, 272
Cassel (Sir Ernest) Educational Trust, UK, 409
Caterpillar Foundation, USA, 476

Catholic Agency for Overseas Development—
CAFOD, UK, 407
Catholic Fund for Overseas Development—
CAFOD, UK, 407
Catholic Help—Caritas France, France, 154
CBM, Germany, 163
CCK Foundation—Chiang Ching-Kuo
Foundation for International Scholarly
Exchange, Taiwan, 380
CEDPA—Centre for Development and Population
Activities, USA, 477
The Center for International Humanitarian
Cooperation—CIHC, USA, 477
Center for Victims of Torture—CVT, USA, 477
Centre for Development and Population
Activities—CEDPA, USA, 477
Centre Français de Droit Comparé, France, 138
Centre International de Recherche sur le
Cancer—CIRC, France, 138
Centro Internacional de Mejoramiento de Maíz y
Trigo—CIMMYT, Mexico, 262
Centro Studi e Ricerca Sociale Fondazione
Emanuela Zancan Onlus, Italy, 217
The Century Foundation, USA, 477
CGIAR—Consultative Group on International
Agricultural Research, USA, 482
Champalimaud Foundation, Portugal, 310
Chardin (Teilhard de), Fondation, France, 150
Charles A. and Anne Morrow Lindbergh
Foundation, USA, 518
Charles Léopold Mayer Foundation for Human
Progress, Switzerland, 364
Charter 77 Foundation, New York—Foundation
for a Civil Society, USA, 492
Chatham House, UK, 443
Chatlos Foundation, Inc, USA, 477
Chemical Bank Foundation, USA, 526
Cheshire (Leonard) Foundation, UK, 409
CHF International, USA, 478
Chiang Ching-Kuo Foundation for International
Scholarly Exchange—CCKF, Taiwan, 380
Child Health Foundation—CHF, USA, 478
ChildHope, UK, 409
Children's Wish Foundation International—
CWFI, USA, 479
Childs (Jane Coffin) Memorial Fund for Medical
Research, USA, 479
Chirac Foundation, France, 142
Christian Aid, UK, 410
Christian Blind Mission International,
Germany, 163
Christoffel Blindenmission, Germany, 163
Churchill (Winston) Memorial Trust, UK, 410
CIDSE—Together for Global Justice, Belgium, 58
Citi Foundation, USA, 480
Citizenship Foundation, UK, 410
CIVICUS—World Alliance for Citizen
Participation, South Africa, 331
Civitas International, USA, 480
Clean Up the World Pty Ltd, Australia, 40
Co-operative Housing Foundation, USA, 478
Coady International Institute, Canada, 86
The Coca-Cola Foundation, Inc, USA, 481
The Commonwealth Fund, USA, 481
Community Fund, UK, 404
Concern Worldwide, Ireland, 210
Conrad N. Hilton Foundation and Conrad N.
Hilton Fund—CNHF, USA, 503
Conservation Foundation, UK, 412
Conservation International, USA, 481
Consultants on Gender and Development,
Netherlands, 274
Consultative Group on International
Agricultural Research—CGIAR, USA, 482
Cooperación Internacional para el Desarrollo y la
Solidaridad, Belgium, 58
Cottonwood Foundation, USA, 482
Council on International Educational
Exchange—CIEE, USA, 482
Council for International Exchange of
Scholars—CIES, USA, 483
Counterpart, USA, 483
The Craoford Foundation, Sweden, 352
Crafoordska stiftelsen, Sweden, 352
Crane–Rogers Foundation, USA, 506
Creating Hope International—CHI, USA, 483
CVT—Center for Victims of Torture, USA, 477
DAAD—Deutscher Akademischer
Austauschdienst, Germany, 166
Dag Hammarskjöld Foundation, Sweden, 356
Daimler and Benz Foundation, Germany, 164
Daimler und Benz Stiftung, Germany, 163
Daniel Langlois Foundation/Fondation Daniel
Langlois, Canada, 92
Danielle Mitterrand France-Liberty Foundation,
France, 151
Danish Institute for Human Rights,
Denmark, 118

DEC—Disasters Emergency Committee, UK, 397
Defence for Children International—DCI,
Switzerland, 362
DeMoss (Arthur S.) Foundation, USA, 484
Deutsche Bundesstiftung Umwelt—DBU,
Germany, 164
Deutsche Stiftung für internationale
Entwicklung, Germany, 172
Deutscher Akademischer Austauschdienst—
DAAD, Germany, 166
Deutsches Institut für internationale Politik und
Sicherheit—Stiftung Wissenschaft und
Politik, Germany, 182
Development Gateway—DG, USA, 484
DGIA—Stiftung Deutsche
Geisteswissenschaftliche Institute im
Ausland, Germany, 179
Diageo Foundation, UK, 414
Disabled People's International, Canada, 87
Disasters Emergency Committee—DEC, UK, 397
Doctors Without Borders, Switzerland, 371
Doctors of the World International, France, 153
Dr H. P. Heineken Foundation, Netherlands, 275
Dr H. P. Heineken Stichting, Netherlands, 275
Droits et Démocratie, Canada, 96
del Duca (Simone et Cino), Fondation, France, 143
Earhart Foundation, USA, 486
Earth Island Institute—EII, USA, 486
Earthtrust, Inc, USA, 487
Earthwatch—United Nations System-wide
Earthwatch, Switzerland, 362
eBay Foundation, USA, 487
Ebert (Friedrich) Stiftung, Germany, 167
ECPAT International, Thailand, 383
EDF Foundation, France, 143
Eduard Van Beinum Foundation,
Netherlands, 272
Eduard Van Beinum Stichting, Netherlands, 272
EFC—European Foundation Centre, Belgium, 55
EFQM—European Foundation for Quality
Management, Belgium, 60
EGMONT—Institut royal des relations
internationales, Belgium, 58
Einstein (Albert) Institution, USA, 488
Ekhaga Foundation, Sweden, 353
Ekhagastiftelsen, Sweden, 353
ELCI—Environment Liaison Centre
International, Kenya, 244
The Elie Wiesel Foundation for Humanity,
USA, 554
Elizabeth Glaser Pediatric AIDS Foundation,
USA, 496
Elton John AIDS Foundation—EJAF, UK, 426
Emanuela Zancan Onlus Foundation Centre for
Social Studies and Research, Italy, 217
EMERGENCY, Italy, 217
Emmaüs International, France, 139
EMonument, Belgium, 58
End Child Prostitution, Child Pornography and
Trafficking of Children for Sexual Purposes,
Thailand, 383
Energies for the World Foundation, France, 143
EnerGreen Foundation, Canada, 87
EngenderHealth, USA, 488
English-Speaking Union, UK, 415
Eni Foundation, Italy, 217
EnterpriseWorks/VITA—EWV, USA, 488
Environmental Foundation Bellona, Norway, 291
Erinnerung, Verantwortung und Zukunft,
Germany, 167
Ernst-Schering Foundation, Germany, 177
Ernst-Schering-Stiftung, Germany, 177
ETC Group—Action Group on Erosion,
Technology and Concentration, Canada, 88
EURODAD—European Network on Debt and
Development, Belgium, 59
European Association for Cancer Research,
UK, 416
European Foundation Centre—EFC, Belgium, 55
European Foundation for Management
Development, Belgium, 59
European Foundation for Quality Management—
EFQM, Belgium, 60
European Foundation for Street Children—
EFSC, Luxembourg, 257
European Network on Debt and Development—
EURODAD, Belgium, 59
European Training Foundation—ETF, Italy, 218
Federação Democrática Internacional de
Mulheres, Brazil, 70
Federal Chancellor Willy Brandt Foundation,
Germany, 162
Fédération des Agences Internationales pour le
Développement—AIDE, France, 140
Fédération Démocratique Internationale des
Femmes, Brazil, 70
Federation of International Agencies for
International Development, France, 140

Fédération Internationale des Ligues des Droits
de L'Homme—FIDH, France, 135
FEE—Foundation for Environmental Education,
Denmark, 118
Feed the Minds, UK, 416
FEMCONSULT, Netherlands, 274
Fernando Rielo Foundation, Spain, 347
FHI 360, USA, 458
FIDH—Fédération Internationale des Ligues des
Droits de L'Homme, France, 135
FIELD—Foundation for International
Environmental Law and Development,
UK, 417
FIPP—Fondation Internationale Pénale et
Pénitentiaire, Netherlands, 276
Flight Safety Foundation, USA, 491
Florence Nightingale International Foundation,
Switzerland, 363
Focus on Hope—Nana Mouskouri Foundation,
Switzerland, 363
Focus Humanitarian Assistance, Canada, 88
Folke Bernadotte Memorial Foundation,
Sweden, 352
Folke Bernadottes Minnesfond, Sweden, 352
FONDAD—Forum on Debt and Development,
Netherlands, 274
Fondation 30 Millions d'Amis, France, 151
Fondation pour l'Architecture, Belgium, 60
Fondation BNP Paribas, France, 141
Fondation Brigitte Bardot, France, 141
Fondation Charles Léopold Mayer pour le
Progrès de l'Homme—FPH, Switzerland, 364
Fondation Chirac, France, 142
Fondation Électricité de France, France, 143
Fondation Énergies pour le Monde, France, 143
Fondation d'Entreprise France Telecom,
France, 148
Fondation d'Entreprise Gaz de France,
France, 144
Fondation pour la formation internationale,
Canada, 88
Fondation Franz Weber—FFW, Switzerland, 365
Fondation Fyssen, France, 145
Fondation Internationale Florence Nightingale,
Switzerland, 363
Fondation Internationale pour la Gestion de la
Faune—IGF, France, 146
Fondation Internationale Pénale et
Pénitentiaire—FIPP, Netherlands, 276
Fondation Langlois pour l'Art, la Science et la
Technologie, Canada, 92
Fondation Maison des Sciences de l'Homme—
FMSH, France, 147
Fondation Mérieux, France, 147
Fondation Mondiale Recherche et Prévention
SIDA, France, 148
Fondation Nestlé pour l'Etude des Problèmes de
l'Alimentation dans le Monde,
Switzerland, 364
Fondation Orange, France, 148
Fondation Prince Albert II de Monaco,
Monaco, 265
Fondation Scelles, France, 149
Fondation Schneider Electric, France, 149
Fondation Simone et Cino del Duca, France, 143
Fondation Sommet Mondial des Femmes,
Switzerland, 378
Fondation Teilhard de Chardin, France, 150
Fondation Total, France, 150
Fondazione Alessio Pezcoller, Italy, 223
Fondazione Giulio Pastore—FGP, Italy, 223
Fondazione ISMU—Iniziative e Studi sulla
Multietnicità, Italy, 222
Fondazione Italcementi Cavaliere del Lavoro
Carlo Presenti, Italy, 222
Fondazione Lelio e Lisli Basso Issoco—Sezione
Internazionale, Italy, 219
Fonds InBev-Baillet Latour, Belgium, 61
Ford Foundation, USA, 491
Foreign Policy Association, USA, 491
Forschungsgesellschaft für das
Weltflüchtlingsproblem—AWR, Germany, 168
Forum on Debt and Development—FONDAD,
Netherlands, 274
Forum International de l'Innovation Sociale—
FIIS, France, 151
Foundation for Basic Research in Biomedicine,
Germany, 162
Foundation for a Civil Society—FCS, USA, 492
Foundation for Ecodevelopment,
Netherlands, 281
Foundation for Environmental Conservation,
Switzerland, 366
Foundation for Environmental Education—FEE,
Denmark, 118
Foundation for German Humanities Institutes
Abroad, Germany, 179

Foundation for the Good Governance of International Spaces—Our Spaces, UK, 436
Foundation House of the Social Sciences, France, 147
Foundation for International Environmental Law and Development—FIELD, UK, 417
Foundation for International Training—FIT, Canada, 88
Foundation for the Peoples of the South Pacific—Counterpart, USA, 483
France-Libertés Fondation Danielle Mitterrand, France, 151
France Nature Environnement, France, 151
Franciscans International, USA, 493
Frank (Anne) Stichting, Netherlands, 274
Franz Weber Foundation, Switzerland, 365
Frauen Weltgipfel Stiftung/Fondation Sommet Mondial des Femmes, Switzerland, 378
Freedom House, Inc, USA, 493
French Centre of Comparative Law, France, 138
FRIDE—A European Think Tank for Global Action, Spain, 338
FRIDE—Fundación para las Relaciones Internacionales y el Diálogo Exterior, Spain, 338
Friedensdorf International, Germany, 169
Friedrich Ebert Foundation, Germany, 167
Friedrich-Ebert-Stiftung eV, Germany, 167
Friedrich Naumann Foundation, Germany, 175
Friedrich-Naumann-Stiftung, Germany, 175
Friendly (Alfred) Foundation, USA, 494
Friends of the Earth International, Netherlands, 275
Fundação Assistência Médica International—AMI, Portugal, 310
Fundação Calouste Gulbenkian, Portugal, 311
Fundação Champalimaud, Portugal, 310
Fundação Gulbenkian (Calouste), Portugal, 311
Fundación Fernando Rielo, Spain, 347
Fundación José María Aragón, Argentina, 31
Fundación Príncipe de Asturias, Spain, 347
Fundación para las Relaciones Internacionales y el Diálogo Exterior—FRIDE, Spain, 338
Fundación Universidad-Empresa—UE, Spain, 348
FXB International—Association François-Xavier Bagnoud, USA, 495
Fyssen Foundation, France, 145
G. Unger Vetlesen Foundation, USA, 549
Gairdner Foundation, Canada, 89
Garden Organic/Henry Doubleday Research Association—HDRA, UK, 418
Gates (Bill and Melinda) Foundation, USA, 495
Gates Learning Foundation, USA, 495
Gaudeamus Foundation, Netherlands, 281
Gaz de France Foundation, France, 144
GE Foundation, USA, 495
GEA—Global Environmental Action, Japan, 232
Gerda Henkel Foundation, Germany, 170
Gerda Henkel Stiftung, Germany, 170
German Academic Exchange Service, Germany, 166
German Catholic Bishops' Organization for Development Co-operation, Germany, 162
German Federal Foundation for the Environment, Germany, 164
German Institute of Global and Area Studies—GIGA, Germany, 169
German Institute for International and Security Affairs, Germany, 182
Getty (J. Paul) Trust, USA, 496
Gifts in Kind International—GIKI, USA, 498
GIGA—German Institute of Global and Area Studies, Germany, 169
Giulio Pastore Foundation, Italy, 223
Global Alliance for Women's Health—GAWH, USA, 496
Global Digital Solidarity Fund—DSF, Switzerland, 366
Global Ethic Foundation, Germany, 181
Global Fund for Women—GFW, USA, 497
Global Greengrants Fund, USA, 497
Global Health Council, USA, 497
Global Impact, USA, 459
Global Links, USA, 497
Globetree Association, Sweden, 353
GOAL, Ireland, 211
Goethe Institut, Germany, 169
Goethe-Institut Inter Nationes, Germany, 169
Goldman (Richard and Rhoda) Fund, USA, 497
Goldman Environmental Foundation, USA, 497
The Goldman Sachs Foundation, USA, 498
Good360, USA, 498
Goodenough College, UK, 419
Goodwill Industries International, Inc, USA, 498
Google.org, USA, 498
Gorbachev Foundation, Russian Federation, 319

Graham Foundation for Advanced Studies in the Fine Arts, USA, 499
Grantmakers Without Borders—Gw/oB, USA, 459
Guggenheim (Harry Frank) Foundation, USA, 500
Guggenheim (Solomon R.) Foundation, USA, 500
Gyllenbergs (Signe och Ane) stiftelse, Finland, 131
Habitat for Humanity International, USA, 500
HAI—Health Alliance International, USA, 501
Hammarskjölds (Dag), Minnesfond, Stiftelsen, Sweden, 356
Handicap International, France, 152
Hanns Seidel Foundation, Germany, 178
Hanns-Seidel-Stiftung eV, Germany, 178
The Harry Frank Guggenheim Foundation, USA, 500
Hasbro Children's Fund, Inc, USA, 501
Headley Trust, UK, 420
Health Alliance International—HAI, USA, 501
Health Foundation, UK, 420
Heart to Heart International, USA, 502
Hebrew Immigrant Aid Society—HIAS, USA, 502
Heine (Heinrich) Stiftung für Philosophie und Kritische Wissenschaft, Germany, 170
Heineken (Alfred) Fondsen Foundation, Netherlands, 281
Heineken (Dr H. P.) Stichting, Netherlands, 275
Heinrich Böll Foundation, Germany, 162
Heinrich-Böll-Stiftung, Germany, 162
Heinrich Heine Foundation for Philosophy and Critical Theory, Germany, 170
Heinrich-Heine-Stiftung für Philosophie und Kritische Wissenschaft, Germany, 170
Heiser Program for Research in Leprosy and Tuberculosis, USA, 503
Helen Keller International—HKI, USA, 514
Helmich (Janson Johan og Marcia) Legat, Norway, 291
HelpAge International, UK, 420
Henkel (Gerda) Stiftung, Germany, 170
Henry Doubleday Research Association, UK, 418
The Henry Moore Foundation, UK, 432
HIAS—Hebrew Immigrant Aid Society, USA, 502
Hilton (Conrad N.) Foundation, USA, 503
Hilton (Conrad N.) Fund, USA, 503
Hirschfeld-Eddy Foundation, Germany, 170
Hirschfeld-Eddy-Stiftung, Germany, 170
Hodge (Jane) Foundation, UK, 421
Homeless International, UK, 421
Honda Foundation, Japan, 233
HOPE International Development Agency—HOPE, Canada, 90
Hornby (A. S.) Educational Trust, UK, 421
Hoso Bunka Foundation, Inc—HBF, Japan, 233
Howard Hughes Medical Institute—HHMI, USA, 504
Human Rights Watch—HRW, USA, 505
von Humboldt (Alexander) Stiftung, Germany, 170
The Hunger Project, USA, 505
IAESTE—International Association for the Exchange of Students for Technical Experience, UK, 422
IAI—Istituto Affari Internazionali, Italy, 226
IARC—International Agency for Research on Cancer, France, 138
IATSS—International Association of Traffic and Safety Sciences, Japan, 233
IBM International Foundation, USA, 505
ICAA—International Council on Alcohol and Addictions, Switzerland, 368
ICAF—International Child Art Foundation, USA, 507
ICNL—International Center for Not-for-Profit Law, USA, 507
ICVA—International Council of Voluntary Agencies, Switzerland, 359
IDLO—International Development Law Organization, Italy, 226
IFAW—International Fund for Animal Welfare, USA, 509
IFES—International Foundation for Electoral Systems, USA, 509
IHE—International Health Exchange, UK, 441
IISD—International Institute for Sustainable Development, Canada, 91
IMA World Health—Interchurch Medical Assistance, Inc, USA, 506
IMADR—International Movement against All Forms of Discrimination and Racism, Japan, 234
InBev-Baillet Latour Fund, Belgium, 61
Inclusion International—II, UK, 421
Indian Council for Cultural Relations, India, 202
Institut for Menneskerettigheder, Denmark, 118
Institut Mittag-Leffler, Sweden, 353
Institut Pasteur, France, 152

Institut royal des relations internationales—EGMONT, Belgium, 58
Institute of British Geographers, UK, 443
Institute of Cultural Affairs International, Canada, 90
Institute of Current World Affairs—ICWA, USA, 506
Institute of Developing Economies/Japan External Trade Organization—IDE-JETRO, Japan, 233
The Institute of Energy Economics, Japan—IEEJ, Japan, 233
Institute of International Affairs, Italy, 226
Institute of International Education—IIE, USA, 506
Institute for Scientific Interchange Foundation—ISI, Italy, 225
Institute of Social Studies—ISS, Netherlands, 276
Instituto del Tercer Mundo—ITeM, Uruguay, 560
INTEGRATA Foundation, Germany, 171
INTEGRATA—Stiftung für Humane Nutzung der Informationstechnologie, Germany, 171
Interact Worldwide, UK, 422
Interchurch Medical Assistance, Inc, USA, 506
Intermediate Technology Development Group—ITDG, UK, 439
Intermón Oxfam, Spain, 349
Internationaal Instituut voor Sociale Geschiedenis—IISG, Netherlands, 276
International Agency for Research on Cancer—IARC, France, 138
International Aid, Inc—IA, USA, 507
International Association of Charities, Belgium, 57
International Association for the Exchange of Students for Technical Experience—IAESTE, UK, 422
International Association of Traffic and Safety Sciences, Japan, 233
International Baccalaureate Organization—IBO, Switzerland, 368
International Balzan Foundation—Fund, Switzerland, 368
International Balzan Foundation—Prize, Italy, 226
International Center for Not-for-Profit Law—ICNL, USA, 507
International Center for Research on Women—ICRW, USA, 507
International Centre for Human Rights and Democratic Development, Canada, 96
International Child Art Foundation, USA, 507
International Co-operation for Development and Solidarity, Belgium, 58
International College of Surgeons—ICS, USA, 508
International Confederation of Catholic Organizations for Charitable and Social Action, Vatican City, 562
International Council on Alcohol and Addictions—ICAA, Switzerland, 368
International Council for Bird Preservation, UK, 404
International Council of Voluntary Agencies—ICVA, Switzerland, 359
International Development Center of Japan, Japan, 234
International Development Law Organization—IDLO, Italy, 226
International Education Research Foundation, Inc—IERF, USA, 508
International Emergency Action, France, 136
International Eye Foundation—IEF, USA, 508
International Federation of Human Rights, France, 135
International Forum for Social Innovation—IFSI, France, 151
International Foundation for Art Research—IFAR, USA, 508
International Foundation for the Conservation of Wildlife, France, 146
International Foundation for Culture and Civilization, Germany, 172
International Foundation for Electoral Systems—IFES, USA, 509
International Foundation for Ethical Research, USA, 509
International Foundation for Genetic Research—The Michael Fund, USA, 524
International Foundation for Science—IFS, Sweden, 354
International Foundation for Social, Economic, and Political Research—Gorbachev Foundation, Russian Federation, 319
The International Foundation for Socio-Economic and Political Studies, Russian Federation, 319

International Fund for Animal Welfare—IFAW, USA, 509
International Health Exchange—IHE, UK, 441
International Humanitarian Assistance—IHA, Albania, 29
International Institute for Applied Systems Analysis—IIASA, Austria, 47
International Institute of Social History—IISH, Netherlands, 276
International Institute of Social Studies (ISS), Netherlands, 276
The International Institute for Strategic Studies—IISS, UK, 423
International Institute for Sustainable Development—IISD, Canada, 91
International Institute of Tropical Agriculture—IITA, Nigeria, 289
International Islamic Relief Organization of Saudi Arabia—IIROSA, Saudi Arabia, 321
International Lake Environment Committee Foundation, Japan, 234
International League for Human Rights—ILHR, USA, 509
The International Maize and Wheat Improvement Center, Mexico, 262
International Maritime Rescue Foundation—IMRF, UK, 423
International Medical Assistance Foundation, Portugal, 310
The International Movement against All Forms of Discrimination and Racism—IMADR, Japan, 234
International Music and Art Foundation, Liechtenstein, 255
International NGO Training and Research Centre—INTRAC, UK, 398
International Office for Water, France, 153
International Penal and Penitentiary Foundation—IPPF, Netherlands, 276
International Planned Parenthood Federation—IPPF, UK, 424
International Press Institute—IPI, Austria, 47
International Red Cross and Red Crescent Movement—ICRC, Switzerland, 368
International Rescue Committee, Inc—IRC, USA, 510
International Research Institute for Media, Communication and Cultural Development—MEDIACULT, Austria, 48
International Rivers, USA, 510
International Save the Children Alliance, UK, 446
International Service for Human Rights—ISHR, Switzerland, 369
International Society for Human Rights—ISHR, Germany, 172
International Society for Third-Sector Research—ISTR, USA, 459
International Standing Conference on Philanthropy—Interphil, Switzerland, 359
International Tree Foundation—ITF, UK, 424
International Union Against Cancer—UICC, Switzerland, 369
International Union for Conservation of Nature, Switzerland, 369
International Union for Health Promotion and Education—IUHPE, France, 153
International Wilderness Leadership Foundation, USA, 554
International Women's Rights Action Watch—IWRAW, USA, 511
International Work Group for Indigenous Affairs—IWGIA, Denmark, 119
International Workers Aid, Belgium, 64
International Yehudi Menuhin Foundation—IYMF, Belgium, 62
International Youth Foundation—IYF, USA, 511
International Youth Library Foundation, Germany, 172
Internationale Bachakademie Stuttgart, Germany, 172
Internationale Jugendbibliothek, Germany, 172
Internationale Stiftung zur Förderung von Kultur und Zivilisation, Germany, 172
Internationale Vrijwilligersprojecten—SIW, Netherlands, 280
Interphil—International Standing Conference on Philanthropy, Switzerland, 359
INTRAC—International NGO Training and Research Centre, UK, 398
InWEnt—Internationale Weiterbildung und Entwicklung gemeinnützige GmbH, Germany, 172
IPI—International Press Institute, Austria, 47
IPPF—International Planned Parenthood Federation, UK, 424
Iran Heritage Foundation—IHF, UK, 424

IRC—International Rescue Committee, Inc, USA, 510
ISMU—Fondazione Cariplo per le Iniziative e lo Studio sulla Multietnicità, Italy, 222
ISMU Foundation—Initiatives and Studies on Multi-ethnicity, Italy, 222
Istituto Affari Internazionali—IAI, Italy, 226
Istituto di Ricerche Farmacologiche Mario Negri, Italy, 227
ISTR—International Society for Third-Sector Research, USA, 459
Italcementi Carlo Presenti Foundation, Italy, 222
ITeM—Instituto del Tercer Mundo, Uruguay, 560
IUCN/UICN, Switzerland, 369
IUHPE—International Union for Health Promotion and Education, France, 153
IVS—International Voluntary Service, UK, 425
The J. P. Morgan Chase Foundation, USA, 526
J. Paul Getty Trust, USA, 496
Jacobs Foundation, Switzerland, 370
James S. McDonnell Foundation, USA, 520
Jane Coffin Childs Memorial Fund for Medical Research, USA, 479
Jane Hodge Foundation, UK, 421
Janson Johan Helmich and Marcia Jansons Foundation, Norway, 291
Janson Johan Helmich og Marcia Jansons Legat, Norway, 291
Japan Center for Economic Research—JCER, Japan, 235
Japan Economic Research Institute Inc—JERI, Japan, 235
The Japan Foundation, Japan, 235
Japan Shipbuilding Industry Foundation, Japan, 238
Japan Society for the Promotion of Science—JSPS, Japan, 236
JDC—American Jewish Joint Distribution Committee, USA, 466
Jephcott Charitable Trust—JCT, UK, 425
JERI—Japan Economic Research Institute Inc, Japan, 235
Jerusalem Trust, UK, 425
Jeunesse Canada Monde, Canada, 82
The John Merck Fund, USA, 523
John Motley Morehead Foundation, USA, 525
John Templeton Foundation, USA, 547
José María Aragón Foundation, Argentina, 31
Joseph Tanenbaum Charitable Foundation, Canada, 98
Jung (C. G.) Institut Zürich, Switzerland, 370
Jusélius (Sigrid) Säätiö, Finland, 132
Jusélius (Sigrid) Stiftelse, Finland, 132
Juvenile Diabetes Research Foundation International—JDRF, USA, 513
KDDI Foundation, Japan, 237
Keller (Helen) International, USA, 514
Kellogg (W. K.) Foundation, USA, 514
King Faisal Foundation—KFF, Saudi Arabia, 321
Klaus Tschira Foundation, Germany, 183
Klaus Tschira Stiftung GmbH, Germany, 183
Koch Foundation, Inc, USA, 515
Kofi Annan Foundation, Switzerland, 361
Konrad Adenauer Foundation, Germany, 160
Konrad-Adenauer-Stiftung eV—KAS, Germany, 160
Konstnärsnämnden, Sweden, 354
Körber Foundation, Germany, 173
Körber-Stiftung, Germany, 173
The Korea Foundation, Korea (Republic), 246
Krupp von Bohlen und Halbach (Alfried) Stiftung, Germany, 173
Kurt Tucholsky Foundation, Germany, 183
Kurt-Tucholsky-Stiftung, Germany, 183
Lady Tata Memorial Trust—LTMT, India, 205
Laing (J. W.) Trust, UK, 449
Laing (Maurice and Hilda) Charitable Trust, UK, 427
Langlois (Daniel) Foundation for Art, Science and Technology, Canada, 92
Latter-day Saint Charities—LDSC, USA, 517
Laureus Sport for Good Foundation, UK, 428
Lauritzen Fonden, Denmark, 119
Lauritzen Foundation, Denmark, 119
Leakey (L. S. B.) Foundation, USA, 517
Leakey Foundation, USA, 517
La Leche League International—LLLI, USA, 516
van Leer (Bernard) Foundation, Netherlands, 277
Lego Fonden, Denmark, 119
The Lego Foundation, Denmark, 119
Leibniz-Institut für Globale und Regionale Studien, Germany, 169
Lelio and Lisli Basso Issoco Foundation—International Section, Italy, 219
Leonard Cheshire Disability International, UK, 409
Levi Strauss Foundation, USA, 517
Li Ka-shing Foundation, Hong Kong, 194

Liberty Fund, Inc, USA, 517
Lifebridge Foundation, Inc, USA, 518
Lifeforce Foundation, Canada, 92
Limmat Foundation, Switzerland, 370
Limmat Stiftung, Switzerland, 370
Linbury Trust, UK, 429
Lindbergh (Charles A.) Fund, Inc, USA, 518
Lloyd Foundation, UK, 429
London Goodenough Trust Overseas Graduates, UK, 419
The Lutheran World Federation, Switzerland, 370
Lutherischer Weltbund/Fédération luthérienne mondiale, Switzerland, 370
McDonnell (James S.) Foundation, USA, 520
Maclellan Foundation, Inc, USA, 521
Macquarie Charitable Foundation, Australia, 41
Macquarie Group Foundation, Australia, 41
Maecenas Foundation, Germany, 159
Maecenas Stiftung, Germany, 159
MAG—Mines Advisory Group, UK, 430
Makarna Mittag-Lefflers Matematiska Stiftelse, Sweden, 353
Management Development Foundation, Netherlands, 277
Marc Rich Foundation for Education, Culture and Welfare, Switzerland, 372
Marie Stopes International—MSI, UK, 450
Mario Negri Pharmacological Research Institute, Italy, 227
The MasterCard Foundation, Canada, 93
The Matsumae International Foundation, Japan, 238
Maurice and Hilda Laing Charitable Trust, UK, 427
Max-Planck-Gesellschaft zur Förderung der Wissenschaften eV, Germany, 176
Max Planck Society for the Advancement of Science, Germany, 176
MDA—Muscular Dystrophy Association, USA, 523
MDF Training & Consultancy, Netherlands, 277
Médecins du Monde International, France, 153
Médecins Sans Frontières—MSF, Switzerland, 371
MEDIACULT—International Research Institute for Media, Communication and Cultural Development, Austria, 48
Medical Women's International Association—MWIA, Canada, 94
Medico International, Germany, 175
Memorial Foundation for Jewish Culture, USA, 523
Mentor Foundation, UK, 431
Merck (John) Fund, USA, 523
Mercury Phoenix Trust, UK, 431
Mercy Corps, USA, 524
Mérieux Foundation, France, 147
The Michael Fund—International Foundation for Genetic Research, USA, 524
Mines Advisory Group—MAG, UK, 430
Minority Rights Group International, UK, 432
MISEREOR—Bischöfliches Hilfswerk, eV, Germany, 162
The Mission to Seafarers, UK, 432
Mittag-Leffler Foundation of the Royal Swedish Academy of Science, Sweden, 353
Mittag-Leffler Foundation of the Royal Swedish Academy of Sciences, Sweden, 353
Mitterrand (Danielle), Fondation, France, 151
MIUSA—Mobility International USA, USA, 525
Mobility International USA—MIUSA, USA, 525
Monell (Ambrose) Foundation, USA, 525
Moore (Henry) Foundation, UK, 432
Morehead-Cain Foundation, USA, 525
Mouskouri (Nana) Foundation, Switzerland, 363
Murdoch Children's Research Institute, Australia, 42
Nana Mouskouri Foundation, Switzerland, 363
National Democratic Institute for International Affairs—NDI, USA, 528
National Foundation for Educational Research—NFER, UK, 433
National Lottery Charities Board, UK, 404
National Organization for Women Foundation, Inc—NOW Foundation, USA, 527
Naumann (Friedrich) Stiftung, Germany, 175
NDI—National Democratic Institute for International Affairs, USA, 528
Nederlandse organisatie voor internationale samenwerking in het hoger onderwijs, Netherlands, 278
NEF—New Economics Foundation, UK, 434
Negri (Mario), Istituto di Ricerche Farmacologiche, Italy, 227
Nestlé Foundation for the Study of the Problems of Nutrition in the World, Switzerland, 364

Netherlands Organization for International Co-operation in Higher Education—NUFFIC, Netherlands, 278
Network for Social Change, UK, 434
New Economics Foundation—NEF, UK, 434
The New World Foundation, USA, 529
NFER—National Foundation for Educational Research, UK, 433
Niarchos (Stavros) Foundation, Greece, 188
Nightingale (Florence), Fondation Internationale, Switzerland, 363
Nihon Energi Keizai Kenkyu-Sho, Japan, 233
Nippon Foundation, Japan, 238
Niwano Peace Foundation, Japan, 238
Nobel Foundation, Sweden, 355
Nobelstiftelsen, Sweden, 355
Nordic Culture Fund, Denmark, 120
Nordisk Kulturfond, Denmark, 120
NOW Foundation—National Organization for Women Foundation, USA, 527
NUFFIC—Netherlands organization for international co-operation in higher education, Netherlands, 278
NZIIA—New Zealand Institute of International Affairs, New Zealand, 285
The Ocean Foundation, USA, 529
ODI—Overseas Development Institute, UK, 436
Office du Baccalauréat International—OBI, Switzerland, 368
Office International de l'Eau, France, 153
OISCA International, Japan, 239
Olof Palme Memorial Foundation, Sweden, 355
Olof Palmes Minnesfond, Sweden, 355
Omidyar (Pierre) Family Foundation, USA, 529
Omidyar Foundation, USA, 529
Omidyar Network, USA, 529
Onassis (Alexander S.) Public Benefit Foundation, Greece, 189
Open Society Foundation—London, UK, 436
Open Society Institute—New York, USA, 530
Opportunity International UK, UK, 436
Orange Foundation, France, 148
Orbis International, USA, 531
Organisation internationale de droit du développement—OIDD, Italy, 226
Organization for Industrial, Spiritual and Cultural Advancement (OISCA) International, Japan, 239
Our Spaces—Foundation for the Good Governance of International Spaces, UK, 436
Overseas Development Institute—ODI, UK, 436
Oxfam America, USA, 531
Oxfam-en-Belgique, Belgium, 63
Oxfam France, France, 153
Oxfam GB, UK, 436
Oxfam International, UK, 437
Pacific Cultural Foundation, Taiwan, 380
Pact, USA, 532
PAI—Population Action International, USA, 532
Palme (Olof) Minnesfond för Internationell Förståelse och Gemensam Säkerhet, Sweden, 355
PAN UK—Pesticide Action Network UK, UK, 437
Partage, France, 154
Pasteur Institute, France, 152
Pastore (Giulio), Fondazione, Italy, 223
PATH—Program for Appropriate Technology in Health, USA, 533
Patrimoine mondial, France, 154
Paz y Cooperación, Spain, 349
PCI-Media Impact, USA, 533
PCI—Population Communications International, USA, 533
Peace and Co-operation, Spain, 349
Peace Research Institute Oslo—PRIO, Norway, 292
Peace Village International, Germany, 169
Peace Winds Japan—PWJ, Japan, 239
Pearson Peacekeeping Centre—PPC, Canada, 95
Pediatric AIDS Foundation, USA, 496
Penal Reform International—PRI, UK, 437
PepsiCo Foundation, Inc, USA, 534
Pesticide Action Network UK—PAN UK, UK, 437
Pezcoller (Alessio), Fondazione, Italy, 223
Pfizer Foundation, USA, 534
PH International, USA, 535
PHR—Physicians for Human Rights, USA, 535
Physicians for Human Rights—PHR, USA, 535
PLAN International—PI, UK, 438
Planck (Max) Gesellschaft zur Förderung der Wissenschaften eV, Germany, 176
Policy Studies Institute—PSI, UK, 438
Polish Foundation for Science Advancement—PFSA, Poland, 309
Pollock–Krasner Foundation, Inc, USA, 536

Polska Fundacja Upowszechniania Nauki—PFUN, Poland, 309
Population Concern, UK, 422
PPP Foundation, UK, 420
Practical Action, UK, 439
Praemium Erasmianum Foundation, Netherlands, 282
Praemium Erasmianum, Stichting, Netherlands, 282
Pratt Foundation, Australia, 43
Presbyterian World Service and Development, Canada, 96
Primate's World Relief and Development Fund, Canada, 96
Prince Albert II of Monaco Foundation, Monaco, 265
Prince of Asturias Foundation, Spain, 347
The Prince's Trust, UK, 439
PRIO—Peace Research Institute Oslo, Norway, 292
Prix Jeunesse Foundation, Germany, 176
Pro Helvetia, Switzerland, 372
Program for Appropriate Technology in Health—PATH, USA, 533
Project Concern International—PCI, USA, 537
Project Harmony, USA, 535
ProLiteracy, USA, 537
PSI—Policy Studies Institute, UK, 438
Quandt (Herbert) Stiftung, Germany, 162
Queen's Silver Jubilee Trust, UK, 439
The Rafto Foundation, Norway, 292
Rainforest Action Network—RAN, USA, 538
The Rainforest Foundation, UK, 440
Rausing (Ruben and Elisabeth) Trust, UK, 440
RedR International, UK, 441
RedR UK, UK, 441
Reef Ball Foundation, USA, 538
Refugee Foundation, Netherlands, 282
Refugees International—RI, USA, 538
Rehabilitation International—RI, USA, 539
Remembrance, Responsibility and the Future, Germany, 167
Renewable Natural Resources Foundation—RNRF, USA, 540
Richard and Rhoda Goldman Fund, USA, 497
Rielo (Fernando), Fundación, Spain, 347
Right Livelihood Awards Foundation, Sweden, 356
Rights and Democracy/Droits et Démocratie, Canada, 96
RIIA—Royal Institute of International Affairs, UK, 443
RNRF—Renewable Natural Resources Foundation, USA, 540
Rockefeller Foundation, USA, 540
The Rotary Foundation, USA, 540
Rotary Yoneyama Memorial Foundation, Inc, Japan, 239
Royal Aeronautical Society—RAES, UK, 442
Royal Anthropological Institute of Great Britain and Ireland—RAI, UK, 442
Royal British Legion, UK, 443
Royal Children's Hospital Research Institute, Australia, 42
Royal Commission for the Exhibition of 1851, UK, 443
The Royal Commonwealth Society—RCS, UK, 443
Royal Geographical Society (with The Institute of British Geographers), UK, 443
Royal Institute of International Affairs—RIIA—Chatham House, UK, 443
Royal Institute of International Relations, Belgium, 58
Royal Jubilee Trusts, UK, 439
Royal Over-Seas League—ROSL, UK, 444
Royal Society, UK, 444
Royal Society for the Encouragement of Arts, Manufactures and Commerce—RSA, UK, 444
The Royal Society of Medicine—RSM, UK, 444
RSA—Royal Society for the encouragement of Arts, Manufactures and Commerce, UK, 444
Ruben and Elisabeth Rausing Trust, UK, 440
Rubin (Samuel) Foundation, Inc, USA, 541
Rural Advancement Foundation International—RAFI, Canada, 88
Russell (Bertrand) Peace Foundation, UK, 445
Rutherford Institute, USA, 541
Ryan Foundation International, India, 205
The Saison Foundation, Japan, 240
Sales Exchange for Refugee Rehabilitation Vocation, USA, 544
The Salvation Army, UK, 446
Samaritan's Purse, USA, 542
Samuel Rubin Foundation, USA, 541
Sarah Scaife Foundation, Inc, USA, 542
Sasakawa Foundation, Japan, 238
Sasakawa Peace Foundation—SPF, Japan, 240

Save the Children, UK, 446
Save the Children (UK), UK, 446
Save Our Future Environmental Foundation, Germany, 177
Save Our Future Umweltstiftung—SOF, Germany, 177
Scaife (Sarah) Foundation, Inc, USA, 542
Scelles Foundation, France, 149
Schering (Ernst) Stiftung, Germany, 177
Schlumberger Foundation, France, 154
Schneider Electric Foundation, France, 149
Schwab Foundation for Social Entrepreneurship, Switzerland, 373
Schweizerische Stiftung für Alpine Forschungen, Switzerland, 373
ScriptumLibre Foundation, Netherlands, 279
Secours Catholique—Caritas de France, France, 154
Seidel (Hanns) Stiftung, Germany, 178
Sergiu Celibidache Foundation, Germany, 163
Sergiu-Celibidache-Stiftung, Germany, 163
SERRV International, Inc, USA, 544
Service Civil International—SCI, Belgium, 63
Service International pour les Droits de l'Homme, Switzerland, 369
Share, France, 154
The Sharing Way, Canada, 97
Shell Foundation, UK, 448
Shuttleworth Foundation, South Africa, 334
SID—Society for International Development, Italy, 228
Signe and Ane Gyllenberg Foundation, Finland, 131
Signe och Ane Gyllenbergs stiftelse, Finland, 131
Sigrid Jusélius Foundation, Finland, 132
Sigrid Jusélius Säätiö, Finland, 132
Sigrid Rausing Trust, UK, 440
Simone and Cino del Duca Foundation, France, 143
SIPRI—Stockholm International Peace Research Institute, Sweden, 357
Sir Ernest Cassel Educational Trust, UK, 409
SIW International Volunteer Projects, Netherlands, 280
SIW Internationale Vrijwilligersprojecten, Netherlands, 280
Solidar, Belgium, 64
Solidarity Overseas Service Malta—SOS Malta, Malta, 261
Solomon R. Guggenheim Foundation, USA, 500
Soroptimist International, UK, 449
Soros Economic Development Fund, USA, 546
Soros Foundation (USA), USA, 530
Spencer Foundation, USA, 546
Spinal Research, UK, 449
The Stanley Foundation, USA, 546
Star of Hope International, USA, 546
State Scholarships Foundation, Greece, 189
Stavros Niarchos Foundation, Greece, 188
Stewards Company Limited, UK, 449
Stewardship Foundation, USA, 547
Stichting Alfred Heineken Fondsen, Netherlands, 281
Stichting Gaudeamus, Netherlands, 281
Stichting Mondiaal Alternatief, Netherlands, 281
Stichting Praemium Erasmianum, Netherlands, 282
Stichting Vluchteling, Netherlands, 282
Stiftelsen Dag Hammarskjölds Minnesfond, Sweden, 356
Stiftung Deutsche Geisteswissenschaftliche Institute im Ausland—DGIA, Germany, 179
Stiftung für Medizinische Grundlagenforschung—Boehringer Ingelheim Fonds, Germany, 162
Stiftung Prix Jeunesse, Germany, 176
Stiftung Weltethos, Germany, 181
Stiftung Wissenschaft und Politik—Deutsches Institut für internationale Politik und Sicherheit—SWP, Germany, 182
Stockholm Environment Institute, Sweden, 357
Stockholm International Peace Research Institute—SIPRI, Sweden, 357
Stuttgart International Bach Academy, Germany, 172
Survival, UK, 450
Survival International, UK, 450
Swedish NGO Secretariat on Acid Rain, Sweden, 352
Swiss Alliance of Development Organisations, Switzerland, 359
Swiss Arts Council, Switzerland, 372
Swiss Coalition of Development Organisations, Switzerland, 359
Swiss Foundation for Alpine Research, Switzerland, 373
Tanenbaum (Joseph) Charitable Foundation, Canada, 98

Tearfund, UK, 450
Tebtebba Foundation, Philippines, 304
TechnoServe, USA, 547
Teilhard de Chardin Foundation, France, 150
Television Trust for the Environment, UK, 452
Third World Institute, Uruguay, 560
Thomson Reuters Foundation, UK, 451
Thrasher Research Fund, USA, 548
TI—Transparency International, Germany, 183
Tibet-Institut Rikon, Switzerland, 376
Tibetan Monastic Institute in Rikon, Switzerland, Switzerland, 376
Tiffany & Co. Foundation, USA, 548
Tilapia International Foundation, Netherlands, 283
TK Foundation, Bahamas, 51
Tony Blair Faith Foundation, UK, 405
Toshiba International Foundation—TIFO, Japan, 240
Total Foundation, France, 150
Transparency International—TI, Germany, 183
Tschira (Klaus) Stiftung, Germany, 183
Tucholsky (Kurt) Stiftung, Germany, 183
Turner Foundation, Inc, USA, 549
TVE—Television Trust for the Environment, UK, 452
UAI—Union des associations internationales, Belgium, 56
UICC—International Union Agains Cancer, Switzerland, 369
UICN—Union mondiale pour la nature, Switzerland, 369
UICN—Unión Mundial para la Naturaleza, Switzerland, 369
UNA Trust—United Nations Association Trust, UK, 453
Union des associations internationales—UAI, Belgium, 56
Union of International Associations—UIA/Unie van de Internationale Vereinigingen—UIV, Belgium, 56
Union Internationale de Promotion de la Santé et de l'Education pour la Santé, France, 153
Unitarian Universalist Service Committee, USA, 549
United Nations Foundation, USA, 549
United Society for Christian Literature—USCL, UK, 453
United Way International—UWI, USA, 550
United Way Worldwide, USA, 550
Universal Education Foundation—UEF, France, 155
Universal Jewish Alliance, France, 137
University-Industry Foundation, Spain, 348
University of Southern California Shoah Foundation Institute for Visual History and Education, USA, 550
UPS Foundation, USA, 550
Vetlesen (G. Unger) Foundation, USA, 549
Victoria League for Commonwealth Friendship, UK, 453
Vienna Institute for International Dialogue and Co-operation, Austria, 49
Virtual Foundation, USA, 551
Volkswagen Foundation, Germany, 183
VolkswagenStiftung, Germany, 183
W. K. Kellogg Foundation, USA, 514
WAHF—World Animal Handicap Foundation, Belgium, 64
Web Development Fund, USA, 552
Web Lab—Digital Innovations, Inc, USA, 552
Weber (Franz), Fondation, Switzerland, 365
Weeden Foundation, USA, 552
Wellcome Trust, UK, 455
Wenner-Gren Foundation, USA, 553
Weyerhaeuser Family Foundation, Inc, USA, 553
Whitley Fund for Nature, UK, 456
Wiener Institut für Internationalen Dialog und Zusammenarbeit, Austria, 49
Wiesel (Elie) Foundation for Humanity, USA, 554
Wihuri Foundation for International Prizes, Finland, 133
Wihuri kansainvälisten palkintojen rahasto, Finland, 133
Wikimedia Foundation, USA, 554
The WILD Foundation—International Wilderness Leadership Foundation, USA, 554
William J. Clinton Foundation, USA, 481
WILPF—Women's International League Peace Freedom, USA, 555
Wilson (Woodrow) International Center for Scholars, USA, 555
Windstar Foundation, USA, 555
WINGS—Worldwide Initiatives for Grantmaker Support, Brazil, 70
Winston Churchill Memorial Trust, UK, 410
WMF—World Monuments Fund, USA, 556
The Wolfson Foundation, UK, 456

Women for International Peace and Arbitration—WIPA, USA, 556
Women's Environment and Development Organization—WEDO, USA, 556
Women's International Democratic Federation, Brazil, 70
Woodrow Wilson International Center for Scholars, USA, 555
World Alliance for Citizen Participation—CIVICUS, South Africa, 331
World Alliance of YMCAs—Young Men's Christian Associations, Switzerland, 377
World Animal Handicap Foundation—WAHF, Belgium, 64
World Concern, USA, 556
World Economic Forum, Switzerland, 377
World Emergency Relief—WER, USA, 556
World Federation for Mental Health—WFMH, USA, 557
World Forum of Civil Society Networks—UBUNTU, Spain, 337
World Foundation for AIDS Research and Prevention, France, 148
World Heritage, France, 154
World Learning, USA, 557
World Lung Foundation, USA, 557
World Mercy Fund (Ireland) Ltd, Ireland, 213
World in Need—Andrews Charitable Trust, UK, 400
World Research Foundation, USA, 558
World Resources Institute, USA, 558
World Scout Foundation, Switzerland, 377
World Society for the Protection of Animals, UK, 456
World University Service of Canada/Entraide universitaire mondiale du Canada, Canada, 99
World Vision Inc, USA, 558
World Wide Fund for Nature, Switzerland, 377
World Wide Web Foundation, Switzerland, 377
Worlddidac Foundation, Switzerland, 377
Worldwatch Institute, USA, 558
Worldwide Initiatives for Grantmaker Support—WINGS, Brazil, 70
WWF International, Switzerland, 377
WWSF—Women's World Summit Foundation, Switzerland, 378
X Prize Foundation, USA, 559
XminusY Solidarity Fund, Netherlands, 283
YMCA—Young Men's Christian Association, UK, 457
Z. V. M. G. Rangoonwala Trust, Pakistan, 295
Zancan Onlus (Emanuela), Fondazione Centro Studi e Ricerca Sociale, Italy, 217
Zonta International Amelia Earhart Fellowship Fund, USA, 559
Zonta International Foundation—ZIF, USA, 559
Zuleikhabai Valy Mohammad Gany (Z. V. M. G.) Rangoonwala Trust, Pakistan, 295

AFRICA SOUTH OF THE SAHARA

A. G. Leventis Foundation, Greece, 188
A. G. Leventis Foundation Nigeria, Nigeria, 290
AARDO—Afro-Asian Rural Development Organization, India, 199
Absolute Return for Kids—ARK, UK, 401
ACCION International, USA, 460
ACORD—Agency for Co-operation and Research in Development, Kenya, 245
Acting for Life, France, 136
Action contre la Faim, France, 136
Action Group for Justice and Social Equality, Benin, 65
Action against Hunger, France, 136
Action Solidarité Tiers Monde—ASTM, Luxembourg, 257
Acumen Fund, USA, 461
Adams (Sylvia) Charitable Trust, UK, 398
AFAP—Australian Foundation for the Peoples of Asia and the Pacific, Australia, 38
Africa-America Institute—AAI, USA, 461
Africa Educational Trust, UK, 399
Africa Foundation (UK), UK, 399
Africa Grantmakers' Affinity Group—AGAG, USA, 458
Africa Humanitarian Action, Ethiopia, 130
The African Agricultural Technology Foundation—AATF, Kenya, 245
African Association for Literacy and Adult Education, Senegal, 323
African Capacity Building Foundation—ACBF, Zimbabwe, 567
African Development Institute, Inc, USA, 461
African Forum and Network on Debt and Development—AFRODAD, Zimbabwe, 567

African Medical and Research Foundation—AMREF, Kenya, 245
African NGOs Environment Network—ANEN, Kenya, 244
African Refugees Foundation—AREF, Nigeria, 289
African Wildlife Foundation—AWF, USA, 462
African Women's Development Fund—AWDF, Ghana, 185
African Youth Network for Sustainable Development, Algeria, 30
Africare, USA, 462
Afro-Asian Institute in Vienna, Austria, 46
Afro-Asian Rural Development Organization—AARDO, India, 199
Afro-Asiatisches Institut in Wien, Austria, 46
AFRODAD—African Forum and Network on Debt and Development, Zimbabwe, 567
AFSC—American Friends Service Committee, USA, 465
AFTAAC—Arab Fund for Technical Assistance to African Countries, Egypt, 127
Aga Khan Agency for Microfinance, Switzerland, 360
Aga Khan Foundation—AKF, Switzerland, 360
Aga Khan Foundation Canada, Canada, 80
Aga Khan Fund for Economic Development, Switzerland, 361
AGAG—Africa Grantmakers' Affinity Group, USA, 458
Agency for Co-operation and Research in Development, Kenya, 245
Agriculteurs Français et Développement International—AFDI, France, 136
Agromisa Foundation, Netherlands, 280
Agronomes et vétérinaires sans frontières—AVSF, France, 136
Aide et Action, France, 137
Aide Médicale Internationale, France, 137
Air France Corporate Foundation, France, 144
AISA—Africa Institute of South Africa, South Africa, 332
AIV—Asia-Africa International Voluntary Foundation, Japan, 231
AJWS—American Jewish World Service, USA, 466
Albert Schweitzer Ecological Centre, Switzerland, 362
Alchemy Foundation, UK, 399
Alert—International Alert, UK, 422
Allavida—Alliances for Voluntary Initiatives and Development, Kenya, 244
Alliances for Voluntary Initiatives and Development—Allavida, Kenya, 244
AMADE Mondiale—Association Mondiale des Amis de l'Enfance, Monaco, 265
American Friends Service Committee—AFSC, USA, 465
American Jewish World Service—AJWS, USA, 466
AMREF—African Medical and Research Foundation, Kenya, 245
The Andrew W. Mellon Foundation, USA, 523
ANESVAD, Spain, 337
APHEDA—Union Aid Abroad, Australia, 45
Arab Fund for Technical Assistance to African Countries—AFTAAC, Egypt, 127
Arab Image Foundation, Lebanon, 252
Arcus Foundation, USA, 469
AREF—African Refugees Foundation, Nigeria, 289
ARK—Absolute Return for Kids, UK, 401
Ashden Charitable Trust, UK, 402
Asia-Africa International Voluntary Foundation—AIV, Japan, 231
Asian Institute for Rural Development, India, 200
ASMAE—Association de coopération et d'éducation aux développements, Belgium, 56
Association de coopération et d'éducation aux développements—ASMAE, Belgium, 56
Association for Development Co-operation and Education, Belgium, 56
Association Mondiale des Amis de l'Enfance, Monaco, 265
Association of Non-Governmental Organizations in The Gambia—TANGO, Gambia, 156
ASTM—Action Solidarité Tiers Monde, Luxembourg, 257
Atlantic Philanthropies, USA, 471
Australian Foundation for the Peoples of Asia and the Pacific—AFAP, Australia, 38
Australian People Health Education, Australia, 45
Australian Volunteers International, Australia, 39
AVRDC—The World Vegetable Center, Taiwan, 379

AWDF—African Women's Development Fund, Ghana, 185
BAFROW—Foundation for Research on Women's Health, Productivity and the Environment, Gambia, 156
Barceló Foundation, Spain, 340
Baring Foundation, UK, 402
The Batchworth Trust, UK, 403
BBC World Service Trust, UK, 403
Beit Trust, UK, 403
Benecke (Otto) Stiftung eV, Germany, 161
BOCONGO—Botswana Council of NGOs, Botswana, 69
Book Aid International—BAI, UK, 405
Bóthar, Ireland, 210
Botswana Council of Non-Governmental Organisations—BOCONGO, Botswana, 69
Bread for the World, Germany, 163
The Bridge Foundation—TBF, Ghana, 185
Brot für die Welt, Germany, 163
Brother's Brother Foundation, USA, 474
Butler (J. Homer) Foundation, USA, 504
Cadbury (William Adlingon) Charitable Trust, UK, 407
Canadian Catholic Organization for Development and Peace, Canada, 83
Canadian Centre for International Studies and Co-operation/Centre d'études et de coopération internationale—CECI, Canada, 83
Canadian Co-operative Association, Canada, 80
Canadian Crossroads International/Carrefour Canadien International—CCI, Canada, 83
Canadian Executive Service Organization—CESO/Service d'assistance canadienne aux organismes—SACO, Canada, 83
Canadian Foodgrains Bank, Canada, 84
Canadian Hunger Foundation, Canada, 84
Canadian Organization for Development through Education—CODE, Canada, 85
Canadian Physicians for Aid and Relief—CPAR, Canada, 86
CARE International—CI, Switzerland, 361
Cariplo Foundation, Italy, 219
Carnegie Corporation of New York, USA, 475
The Carter Center, USA, 476
Catholic Agency for World Development—Trócaire, Ireland, 213
CCF—Christian Children's Fund, USA, 478
CCI—Carrefour Canadien International, Canada, 83
CEAS—Centre Ecologique Albert Schweitzer, Switzerland, 362
CECI—Canadian Centre for International Studies and Co-operation/Centre d'études et de coopération internationale, Canada, 83
Centre Ecologique Albert Schweitzer—CEAS, Switzerland, 362
Centre International de Coopération pour le Développement Agricole—CICDA, France, 136
Centre International de Développement et de Recherche—CIDR, France, 138
Centre Pan-Africain de Prospective Sociale, Benin, 65
Centre for Philanthropy and Social Responsibility—Ufadhili, Kenya, 244
Centro Internacional de Agricultura Tropical—CIAT, Colombia, 104
CESO—Canadian Executive Service Organization, Canada, 83
Charity Projects, UK, 411
Charles Stewart Mott Foundation—CSMF, USA, 526
Child Migrants Trust, UK, 409
ChildFund International, USA, 478
ChildFund Korea, Korea (Republic), 246
Children in Africa Foundation, Germany, 181
Children International—CI, USA, 479
Children and Sharing, France, 139
Childwick Trust, UK, 409
China Youth Development Foundation, China (People's Republic), 103
Chobe Wildlife Trust, Botswana, 69
Chr. Michelsen Institute—CMI, Norway, 291
CIAT—Centro Internacional de Agricultura Tropical, Colombia, 104
CIDOB Foundation, Spain, 338
CIDR—Centre International de Développement et de Recherche, France, 138
CIMADE—Service Oecuménique d'Entraide, France, 138
City of Lisbon Foundation, Portugal, 311
Claiborne (Liz) and Ortenberg (Art) Foundation, USA, 480
Clovek v tisni—spolecnost pri Ceske televizi, o.p.s., Czech Republic, 113
Club 2/3, Canada, 85

CMI—Chr. Michelsens Institutt, Norway, 291
Co-operation for the Promotion and Development of Welfare Activities, Spain, 342
CODE—Canadian Organization for Development through Education, Canada, 85
Cogitare Foundation, USA, 481
Comic Relief, UK, 411
Commonwealth Foundation, UK, 411
Community Aid Abroad—Oxfam Australia, Australia, 43
Community Development Foundation, Mozambique, 269
Compton Foundation, Inc, USA, 481
Concern Universal, UK, 412
Cooperazione Internazionale—COOPI, Italy, 217
COOPI—Cooperazione Internazionale, Italy, 217
CPAR—Canadian Physicians for Aid and Relief, Canada, 86
The Craig and Susan McCaw Foundation, USA, 520
CRDF Global, USA, 483
CUSO-VSO, Canada, 86
Czech TV Foundation, Czech Republic, 113
Damien Foundation, Belgium, 58
Defense of Green Earth Foundation—DGEF, Japan, 232
The Desmond Tutu Educational Trust, South Africa, 335
Desmond Tutu Peace Foundation—DTPF, USA, 549
Deutsche AIDS-Stiftung, Germany, 164
Deutsche Stiftung Weltbevölkerung—DSW, Germany, 165
DGEF—Defense of Green Earth Foundation, Japan, 232
Diakonia, Sweden, 352
Diana, Princess of Wales Memorial Fund, UK, 414
DOEN Foundation, Netherlands, 280
Dom Manuel II Foundation, Portugal, 311
Dreyfus Health Foundation—DHF, USA, 485
DRFN—Desert Research Foundation of Namibia, Namibia, 270
DSW—Deutsche Stiftung Weltbevölkerung, Germany, 165
Dulverton Trust, UK, 414
EABL Foundation, Kenya, 245
Earthrights International—ERI, USA, 486
East African Association of Grantmakers, Kenya, 244
EcoHealth Alliance, USA, 487
Écoles Sans Frontières—ESF, France, 139
Ecumenical Service for Mutual Help, France, 138
Eden Foundation, Sweden, 353
Ellerman (John) Foundation, UK, 414
Else Kröner-Fresenius Foundation, Germany, 173
Else Kröner-Fresenius-Stiftung, Germany, 173
Enda Third World—Environment and Development Action in the Third World, Senegal, 322
Enda Tiers Monde—Environnement et Développement du Tiers-Monde, Senegal, 322
endPoverty.org, USA, 488
Enfance et Partage, France, 139
Enfants Réfugiés du Monde—ERM, France, 140
Enterprise Development International, USA, 488
Enterprise Foundation of Benin, Benin, 65
Entraide Protestante Suisse, Switzerland, 367
Environmental Justice Foundation—EJF, UK, 416
Environnement et Développement du Tiers-Monde—Enda, Senegal, 322
ERM—Enfants Réfugiés du Monde, France, 140
Eskom Development Foundation, South Africa, 332
European NGOs on Agriculture, Food, Trade and Development, France, 135
Eurostep—European Solidarity Towards Equal Participation of People, Belgium, 60
EWT—Endangered Wildlife Trust, South Africa, 332
The Family Federation of Finland, Finland, 133
Farm Africa, UK, 416
FARM Foundation— Foundation for World Agriculture and Rural Life, France, 145
Fate Foundation, Nigeria, 289
FAVDO—Forum for African Voluntary Development Organizations, Senegal, 322
FDC—Fundação para o Desenvolvimento da Comunidade, Mozambique, 269
FDH—Frères des Hommes, France, 152
Federación Argentina de Apoyo Familiar—FAAF, Argentina, 31
Fédération Panafricaine des Cinéastes—FEPACI, Burkina Faso, 78
Feed the Children, USA, 490
FFL—Fondation Follereau Luxembourg, Luxembourg, 257

FH—Food for the Hungry, USA, 491
FINCA International, USA, 490
Finnish NGO Foundation for Human Rights—KIOS, Finland, 132
Firelight Foundation, USA, 490
First Peoples Worldwide—FPW, USA, 490
FirstRand Foundation, South Africa, 332
Follereau Foundation Luxembourg, Luxembourg, 257
FONADES—Fondation Nationale pour le Développement et la Solidarité, Burkina Faso, 78
Fondation Abri International, Canada, 97
Fondation Africaine pour les Technologies Agricoles, Kenya, 245
Fondation pour l'Agriculture et la Ruralité dans le Monde—Fondation FARM, France, 145
Fondation Arabe pour l'Image, Lebanon, 252
Fondation canadienne contre la faim, Canada, 84
Fondation Ensemble, France, 143
Fondation de l'Entrepreneurship du Bénin, Benin, 65
Fondation d'Entreprise Air France, France, 144
Fondation contre la Faim, USA, 491
Fondation FARM—Fondation pour l'Agriculture et la Ruralité dans le Monde, France, 145
Fondation Follereau Luxembourg—FFL, Luxembourg, 257
Fondation Internationale Léon Mba—Institut de Médecine et d'Epidémiologie Appliquée, France, 146
Fondation Jean-Paul II pour le sahel, Burkina Faso, 78
Fondation Léopold Sédar Senghor, Senegal, 322
Fondation Marcel Hicter, Belgium, 61
Fondation Mo Ibrahim, UK, 421
Fondation Nationale pour le Développement et la Solidarité—FONADES, Burkina Faso, 78
Fondation Nicolas Hulot pour la Nature et l'Homme, France, 146
Fondation des Organisations Rurales pour l'Agriculture et la Gestion Ecologique—FORAGE, Senegal, 322
Fondation Pro Victimis Genève, Switzerland, 365
Fondation pour le Renforcement des Capacités en Afrique, Zimbabwe, 567
Fondation Rurale pour l'Afrique de l'Ouest, Senegal, 322
Fondation Suisse-Liechtenstein pour les Recherches Archéologiques à l'Etranger, Switzerland, 373
Fondation Syngenta pour une Agriculture Durable, Switzerland, 376
Fondation Ushuaia, France, 146
Fondazione Cariplo, Italy, 219
Fondazione Cassa di Risparmio delle Provincie Lombarde—Fondazione Cariplo, Italy, 219
Fonds für Entwicklung und Partnerschaft in Africa—FEPA, Switzerland, 366
Food for the Hungry—FH, USA, 491
FOPERDA—Fondation Royale Père Damien pour la Lutte Contre la Lèpre, Belgium, 58
Forum for African Voluntary Development Organizations—FAVDO, Senegal, 322
FORWARD—Foundation for Women's Health, Research and Development, UK, 417
Foundation for Development and Partnership in Africa, Switzerland, 366
Foundation for Human Rights and Humanitarian Relief, Turkey, 389
Foundation for International Community Assistance, USA, 490
Foundation 'Life for All', Switzerland, 375
Foundation Nicolas Hulot for Nature and Humankind, France, 146
Foundation for the Peoples of the South Pacific, Australia, 38
Foundation for Research on Women's Health, Productivity and the Environment—BAFROW, Gambia, 156
Foundation of Rural Organizations for Agriculture and Economic Management, Senegal, 322
Foundation for Sustainable Development, Spain, 348
Foundation for Women, Spain, 345
Foundation for Women's Health, Research and Development—FORWARD, UK, 417
The Fred Hollows Foundation, Australia, 41
Freedom from Hunger, USA, 494
Freedom from Hunger Council of Ireland—Gorta, Ireland, 211
Freeplay Foundation, UK, 429
French Agriculturalists and International Development, France, 136
Frères des Hommes—FDH, France, 152
Fund for Development and Partnership in Africa, Switzerland, 366

Fundação Cidade de Lisboa, Portugal, 311
Fundação para o Desenvolvimento da
    Comunidade, Mozambique, 269
Fundação Dom Manuel II, Portugal, 311
Fundação Luso-Americana para o
    Desenvolvimento, Portugal, 312
Fundació CIDOB, Spain, 338
Fundación Barceló, Spain, 340
Fundación CODESPA—Futuro en Marcha,
    Spain, 342
Fundación Desarrollo Sostenido—FUNDESO,
    Spain, 348
Fundación Intervida, Spain, 344
Fundación María Francisca de Roviralta,
    Spain, 347
Fundación Mujeres, Spain, 345
Fundación Paz y Solidaridad Serafín Aliaga—
    FPyS, Spain, 346
FUNDESO—Fundación Desarrollo Sostenido,
    Spain, 348
The Gaia Foundation, UK, 418
GAJES—Groupe d'Action pour la Justice et
    l'Egalité Sociale, Benin, 65
The Gatsby Charitable Foundation, UK, 418
German AIDS Foundation, Germany, 164
German Foundation for World Population,
    Germany, 165
Gift of the Givers Foundation, South Africa, 332
Global Fund for Community Foundations—
    GFCF, South Africa, 331
Global Voluntary Service—GVS, Japan, 232
Global Water Foundation, South Africa, 333
Gobabeb Training and Research Centre,
    Namibia, 270
Good Neighbors International, Korea
    (Republic), 246
Gorta—Freedom from Hunger Council of
    Ireland, Ireland, 211
Grameen Foundation—GF, USA, 499
Grassroots International—GRI, USA, 500
Groupe d'Action pour la Justice et l'Egalité
    Sociale—GAJES, Benin, 65
HALO Trust, UK, 419
Harold Hyam Wingate Foundation, UK, 456
Havelaar (Max) Foundation, Netherlands, 281
Health Action International, Netherlands, 275
Health Volunteers Overseas—HVO, USA, 501
Heifer International, USA, 502
HEKS—Hilfswerk Evangelischen Kirchen
    Schweiz, Switzerland, 367
The Helen Suzman Foundation, South Africa, 335
HELP International, USA, 503
Helvetas Swiss Intercooperation,
    Switzerland, 367
The Henry J. Kaiser Family Foundation, USA, 513
Hicter (Marcel), Fondation, Belgium, 61
Hilden Charitable Fund, UK, 421
Hilfswerk der Evangelischen Kirchen Schweiz—
    HEKS, Switzerland, 367
HIVOS—Humanistisch Instituut voor
    Ontwikkelings Samenwerking,
    Netherlands, 275
Hollows (Fred) Foundation, Australia, 41
Humanistic Institute for Co-operation with
    Developing Countries, Netherlands, 275
Humanistisch Instituut voor Ontwikkelings
    Samenwerking—HIVOS, Netherlands, 275
Humanitarian Relief Foundation, Turkey, 389
Hungarian Interchurch Aid—HIA, Hungary, 196
IBIS, Denmark, 118
ICLARM—The WorldFish Center, Malaysia, 260
IFAD—International Fund for Agricultural
    Development, Italy, 226
IFHD—International Foundation for Human
    Development, India, 203
IKEA Foundation, Netherlands, 275
Îles de Paix, Belgium, 62
INMED Partnerships for Children, USA, 506
İnsan Hak ve Hürriyetleri İnsani Yardım Vakfı,
    Turkey, 389
Institut international des Droits de l'Enfant,
    Switzerland, 368
Institut de Médecine et d'Épidémiologie
    Africaines—Fondation Léon Mba,
    France, 146
Institut Nord-Sud, Canada, 95
Institute for Development Research, USA, 556
Institute of Human Rights and Humanitarian
    Law, Nigeria, 289
Inter Pares, Canada, 90
International Alert—Alert, UK, 422
International Blue Crescent Relief and
    Development Foundation—IBC, Turkey, 390
International Centre for Development and
    Research, France, 138
International Centre for the Legal Protection of
    Human Rights—Interights, UK, 423

International Centre for Living Aquatic
    Resources—ICLARM, Malaysia, 260
International Centre for Tropical Agriculture,
    Colombia, 104
International Co-operation, Italy, 217
International Confederation of Family Support,
    Argentina, 31
International Dental Rescue, Switzerland, 374
International Development and Relief
    Foundation, Canada, 91
International Executive Service Corps— IESC,
    USA, 508
The International Foundation, USA, 508
International Foundation for Education and Self-
    Help—IFESH, USA, 509
International Foundation for Human
    Development—IFHD, India, 203
International Foundation Léon Mba—Institute
    of Applied Medicine and Epidemiology,
    France, 146
International Fund for Agricultural
    Development—IFAD, Italy, 226
International Institute for Environment and
    Development—IIED, UK, 423
International Institute for the Rights of the
    Child, Switzerland, 368
International Institute of Rural
    Reconstruction—IIRR, Philippines, 303
International Medical Services for Health—
    INMED, USA, 506
International Orthodox Christian Charities,
    Inc—IOCC, USA, 509
International Refugee Trust—IRT, UK, 424
International Relief Teams, USA, 510
International Solidarity Foundation—ISF,
    Finland, 132
International Water Management Institute—
    IWMI, Sri Lanka, 310
International Women's Health Coalition—IWHC,
    USA, 510
Intervida Foundation, Spain, 344
Islands of Peace, Belgium, 62
Izumi Foundation, USA, 512
The J. F. Kapnek Trust Zimbabwe, Zimbabwe, 567
J. Homer Butler Foundation, Inc, USA, 504
Japan International Volunteer Center—JVC,
    Japan, 236
JEN, Japan, 237
The John D. and Catherine T. MacArthur
    Foundation, USA, 520
John Ellerman Foundation, UK, 414
John Paul II Foundation for the Sahel, Burkina
    Faso, 78
Joseph Rowntree Charitable Trust, UK, 441
Kaiser (Henry J.) Family Foundation, USA, 513
Kansainvälinen solidaarisuussäätiö, Finland, 132
Kapnek (J. F.) Charitable Trust Zimbabwe,
    Zimbabwe, 567
KCDF—Kenya Community Development
    Foundation, Kenya, 245
Kinder in Afrika, Stiftung, Germany, 181
KIOS—Finnish NGO Foundation for Human
    Rights, Finland, 132
Kresge Foundation, USA, 516
Kröner-Fresenius (Else) Stiftung, Germany, 173
Kulika Charitable Trust (Uganda), Uganda, 392
The Kulika Charitable Trust 1981, Uganda, 392
Kvinna till Kvinna Foundation, Sweden, 354
Latin American, African and Asian Social
    Housing Service, Chile, 101
Léopold Sédar Senghor Foundation, Senegal, 322
Leprosy Mission International, UK, 428
Lesotho Council of Non-Governmental
    Organisations, Lesotho, 254
Leventis (A. G.) Foundation, Greece, 188
Leventis (A. G.) Foundation Nigeria, Nigeria, 290
Leverhulme Trust, UK, 429
Lifeline Energy, UK, 429
Lifewater International—LI, USA, 518
Liliane Foundation, Netherlands, 281
Liz Claiborne and Art Ortenberg Foundation,
    USA, 480
Luso-American Development Foundation,
    Portugal, 312
Luxemburg (Rosa) Stiftung, Germany, 174
LWR—Lutheran World Relief, USA, 519
M-USA—Mercy-USA for Aid and Development,
    USA, 524
MacArthur (John D. and Catherine T.)
    Foundation, USA, 520
McCaw (Craig and Susan) Foundation, USA, 520
McKnight Foundation, USA, 521
MADRE, USA, 521
Magyar Ökumenikus Segélyszervezet,
    Hungary, 196
Mama Cash, Netherlands, 277
Mandela (Nelson) Children's Fund, South
    Africa, 333

Mandela (Nelson) Foundation, South Africa, 333
The Mandela Rhodes Foundation, South
    Africa, 333
Mani Tese, Italy, 227
MAP International—Medical Assistance
    Programs, USA, 522
Marcel Hicter Foundation, Belgium, 61
March of Dimes, USA, 522
María Francisca de Roviralta Foundation,
    Spain, 347
Match International Centre, Canada, 93
MAVA Fondation pour la Nature,
    Switzerland, 371
The Max Foundation, USA, 522
Max Havelaar Foundation, Netherlands, 281
Mba (Léon), Fondation—Institut de Médecine et
    d'Épidémiologie Africaines, France, 146
medica mondiale e.V., Germany, 175
Medical Assistance Programs, USA, 522
Medical Emergency Relief International—
    MERLIN, UK, 432
Mellon (Andrew W.) Foundation, USA, 523
Mercy-USA for Aid and Development—M-USA,
    USA, 524
MERLIN—Medical Emergency Relief
    International, UK, 432
Milieukontakt International, Netherlands, 277
Milieukontakt Oost-Europa, Netherlands, 277
Mindolo Ecumenical Foundation—MEF,
    Zambia, 566
Miriam Dean Fund, UK, 413
Miriam Dean Refugee Trust Fund, UK, 413
Mo Ibrahim Foundation, UK, 421
Mott (Charles Stewart) Foundation, USA, 526
MS ActionAid Denmark, Denmark, 120
MS—Mellemfolkeligt Samvirke, Denmark, 120
Muslim Aid, UK, 433
Mutual Aid and Liaison Service, France, 154
Mwalimu Nyerere Foundation—MNF,
    Tanzania, 382
Nadácia Pontis, Slovakia, 327
National Foundation for Solidarity and
    Development, Burkina Faso, 78
Nederlands instituut voor Zuidelijk Afrika—
    NiZA, Netherlands, 278
Nederlandse Organisatie voor Internationale
    Ontwikkelingssamenwerking—Stichting
    NOVIB, Netherlands, 279
NEF—Near East Foundation, USA, 528
Nelson Mandela Children's Fund, South
    Africa, 333
Nelson Mandela Children's Fund—Canada,
    Canada, 93
Nelson Mandela Foundation, South Africa, 333
Van Neste Foundation, UK, 453
Netherlands Institute for Southern Africa,
    Netherlands, 278
Nigerian Conservation Foundation—NCF,
    Nigeria, 290
Nigerian Institute of International Affairs—
    NIIA, Nigeria, 290
Non-Governmental Organization JEN,
    Japan, 237
Nordic Africa Institute Scholarships,
    Sweden, 355
Nordiska Afrikainstitutets Stipendier,
    Sweden, 355
North-South-Bridge Foundation, Germany, 181
North-South Institute/Institut Nord-Sud,
    Canada, 95
Novartis Foundation for Sustainable
    Development—NFSD, Switzerland, 371
Novartis Stiftung für Nachhaltige Entwicklung,
    Switzerland, 371
NOVIB (Oxfam Netherlands), Netherlands, 279
NRF—National Research Foundation, South
    Africa, 333
Nuffield Foundation, UK, 435
Oak Foundation, Switzerland, 371
OneWorld International Foundation, UK, 435
OPALS—Organisation Panafricaine de Lutte
    Contre le SIDA, France, 153
Open Society Foundation for South Africa—OSF-
    SA, South Africa, 334
Open Society Initiative for Southern Africa—
    OSISA, South Africa, 334
Open Society Initiative for West Africa,
    Senegal, 322
Operation Eyesight Universal/Action universelle
    de la vue, Canada, 95
Operation USA, USA, 530
Opportunity International USA, USA, 530
Organisation Afro-Asiatique Pour Le
    Developpement Rural, India, 199
Organisation Panafricaine de Lutte Contre le
    SIDA—OPALS, France, 153
OSIWA—Open Society Initiative for West Africa,
    Senegal, 322

Otto Benecke Foundation, Germany, 161
Otto-Benecke-Stiftung eV, Germany, 161
Outreach International, USA, 531
Oxfam Australia, Australia, 43
Oxfam Canada, Canada, 95
Oxfam Deutschland e.V., Germany, 176
Oxfam Hong Kong, Hong Kong, 194
Oxfam Ireland, Ireland, 212
Oxfam Mexico, Mexico, 263
Oxfam NOVIB—Nederlandse Organisatie voor Internationale Ontwikkelingssamenwerking, Netherlands, 279
Oxfam NOVIB—Netherlands Organization for International Development Co-operation, Netherlands, 279
Oxfam-Québec, Canada, 95
PAALAE—Pan African Association for Literacy and Adult Education, Senegal, 323
PAC—Partnership Africa Canada, Canada, 95
PAN Africa—Pesticide Action Network Africa, Senegal, 323
Pan-African Centre for Social Prospects, Benin, 65
Pan-African Federation of Film-makers, Burkina Faso, 78
Pan-African Organization for AIDS Prevention, France, 153
The Parthenon Trust, Switzerland, 371
Partners in Rural Development, Canada, 84
Partnership Africa Canada—PAC, Canada, 95
Pathfinder International, USA, 533
People in Need, Czech Republic, 113
People-to-People Health Foundation, Inc—Project Hope, USA, 537
Pestalozzi Children's Foundation, Switzerland, 374
Pire (Dominique) Foundation, Belgium, 62
Pitseng Trust, South Africa, 334
Plan Ireland, Ireland, 212
Plenty International, USA, 535
Pontis Foundation, Slovakia, 327
Population Council, USA, 536
Prince Claus Fund for Culture and Development, Netherlands, 279
Prins Claus Fonds Voor Cultuur en Ontwikkeling, Netherlands, 279
Pro Victimis Foundation, Switzerland, 365
Progressio, UK, 439
Project HOPE, USA, 537
Project Trust, UK, 439
Rabobank Foundation, Netherlands, 279
Rainforest Foundation Norway, Norway, 293
Ramsay Foundation, Switzerland, 372
Refugee Trust International, Ireland, 213
Refugees International Japan—RIJ, Japan, 239
Regnskogfondet, Norway, 293
Relief International, USA, 539
Réseau Africain de la Jeunesse pour le Développement Durable, Algeria, 30
Réseau des ONG Africaines sur l'Environnement, Kenya, 244
Réseau d'ONG Européennes sur l'Agro-alimentaire, le Commerce, l'Environnement et le Développement—RONGEAD, France, 135
Rhodes Trust, UK, 441
Richelieu International, Canada, 96
Rockefeller Brothers Fund, USA, 540
Rockwool Fonden, Denmark, 121
Rockwool Foundation, Denmark, 121
RONGEAD—Réseau d'ONG Européennes sur l'Agro-alimentaire, le Commerce, l'Environnement et le Développement, France, 135
Rooftops Canada Foundation, Canada, 97
Rosa Luxemburg Foundation, Germany, 174
Rosa-Luxemburg-Stiftung, Germany, 174
Rössing Foundation, Namibia, 270
Roviralta (María Francisca de), Fundación, Spain, 347
Rowan Charitable Trust, UK, 441
Rowntree (Joseph) Charitable Trust, UK, 441
Royal Commonwealth Society for the Blind—Sight Savers International, UK, 448
Royal Society for the Protection of Birds—RSPB, UK, 445
RSPB—Royal Society for the Protection of Birds, UK, 445
The Rufford Foundation, UK, 445
Rufford Maurice Laing Foundation, UK, 445
Rutgers WPF, Netherlands, 279
SAASTA—South African Agency for Science and Technology Advancement, South Africa, 334
Sabre Foundation, Inc, USA, 542
SACO—Service d'assistance canadienne aux organismes, Canada, 83
Santé Sud, France, 154

Savings Banks Foundation for International Cooperation, Germany, 179
Schools Without Frontiers, France, 139
Schweisfurth Foundation, Germany, 178
Schweisfurth-Stiftung, Germany, 178
Schweizerisch-Liechtensteinische Stiftung für archäologische Forschungen im Ausland—SLSA, Switzerland, 373
SCIAF—Scottish Catholic International Aid Fund, UK, 447
Scottish Catholic International Aid Fund—SCIAF, UK, 447
Secours Dentaire International, Switzerland, 374
SEL—Service d'Entraide et de Liaison, France, 154
SELAVIP International—Service de Promotion de l'Habitation Populaire en Amérique Latine, Afrique et Asie, Chile, 101
Self Help Development Foundation, Zimbabwe, 567
Self Help Development International, Ireland, 213
Serafín Aliaga Foundation for Peace and Solidarity, Spain, 346
Service d'Entraide et de Liaison—SEL, France, 154
Seva Foundation, USA, 544
Sight Savers International, UK, 448
Sir Ahmadu Bello Foundation, Nigeria, 289
Sir Ahmadu Bello Memorial Foundation, Nigeria, 289
Sir Halley Stewart Trust, UK, 449
SLSA—Schweizerisch Liechtensteinische Stiftung, Switzerland, 373
Solidarité, France, 155
Solidarity, France, 155
Soros Foundation (South Africa), South Africa, 334
South African Agency for Science and Technology Advancement—SAASTA, South Africa, 334
South African Institute of International Affairs, South Africa, 335
South African Institute of Race Relations, South Africa, 335
Southern African Nature Foundation, South Africa, 336
Southern Health, France, 154
Sparkassenstiftung für internationale Kooperation eV, Germany, 179
St John Ambulance, UK, 446
Standing International Forum on Ethnic Conflict, Genocide and Human Rights—International Alert, UK, 422
Steelworkers Humanity Fund, Canada, 98
Stewart (Sir Halley) Trust, UK, 449
Stichting Agromisa, Netherlands, 280
Stichting DOEN, Netherlands, 280
Stichting Liliane Fonds, Netherlands, 281
Stichting Max Havelaar, Netherlands, 281
Stichting Triodos Foundation, Netherlands, 282
Stiftelsen Riksbankens Jubileumsfond, Sweden, 357
Stiftung Kinder in Afrika, Germany, 181
Stiftung Kinderdorf Pestalozzi, Switzerland, 374
Stiftung 'Leben für Alle', Switzerland, 375
Stiftung Nord-Süd-Brücken, Germany, 181
Street Kids International, Canada, 98
Stretched Hands, Italy, 227
Suider-Afrikaanse Natuurstigting, South Africa, 336
Suzman (Helen) Foundation, South Africa, 335
Swiss Foundation for Technical Co-operation, Switzerland, 375
Swiss Interchurch Aid, Switzerland, 367
Swiss-Liechtenstein Foundation for Archaeological Research Abroad—SLFA, Switzerland, 373
SWISSAID Foundation, Switzerland, 375
Swisscontact—Swiss Foundation for Technical Co-operation, Switzerland, 375
The Sylvia Adams Charitable Trust, UK, 398
Synergos—The Synergos Institute, USA, 460
Syngenta Foundation for Sustainable Agriculture, Switzerland, 376
Syngenta Stiftung für Nachhaltige Landwirtschaft, Switzerland, 376
TANGO—Association of NGOs in the Gambia, Gambia, 156
TANZ—Trade Aid NZ Inc, New Zealand, 287
Tanzania Millennium Hand Foundation—TAMIHA, Tanzania, 382
Tea Research Foundation of Central Africa, Malawi, 259
TEAR Australia, Australia, 45
Terre des Hommes Foundation, Switzerland, 376
Terre Sans Frontières—TSF, Canada, 98
Third World Network—TWN, Malaysia, 260
Third World Solidarity Action, Luxembourg, 257

Thomson Foundation, UK, 451
Together Foundation, France, 143
Trade Aid NZ Inc—TANZ, New Zealand, 287
Trans-Antarctic Association—TAA, UK, 451
Transnet Foundation, South Africa, 335
Triodos Foundation, Netherlands, 282
Trócaire—Catholic Agency for World Development, Ireland, 212
Tutu (Desmond) Peace Foundation, USA, 549
Ufadhili Trust, Kenya, 244
Uluslararası Mavi Hilal İnsani Yardım ve Kalkınma Vakfı, Turkey, 390
UniCredit Foundation—Unidea, Italy, 228
Union Aid Abroad—APHEDA, Australia, 45
United Service Committee of Canada, Canada, 98
United Society for the Propagation of the Gospel—USPG, UK, 453
United States African Development Foundation—USADF, USA, 550
Unity Foundation, Luxembourg, 257
USC Canada, Canada, 98
Väestöliitto, Finland, 133
Vita, Ireland, 213
Voluntary Service Overseas, UK, 454
Volunteer Service Abroad—VSA, New Zealand, 287
VSA—Volunteer Service Abroad, New Zealand, 287
VSO, UK, 454
War on Want, UK, 454
WasserStiftung, Germany, 184
Water Foundation, Germany, 184
Water.org, Inc, USA, 552
WaterAid, UK, 454
West African Rural Foundation, Senegal, 322
Westminster Foundation for Democracy—WFD, UK, 455
WHEAT Trust—Women's Hope Education and Training Trust, South Africa, 336
Wildlife Preservation Trust International, USA, 487
Wildlife Trust, USA, 487
William Adlington Cadbury Charitable Trust, UK, 407
Wingate (Harold Hyam) Foundation, UK, 456
Winrock International, USA, 555
Women's Hope Education and Training Trust—Wheat Trust, South Africa, 336
Wood Family Trust, UK, 456
World Association of Children's Friends, Monaco, 265
World Education, Inc, USA, 556
World Land Trust—WLT, UK, 456
World Neighbors, USA, 557
World Peace Foundation—WPF, USA, 557
World Population Foundation, Netherlands, 279
The WorldFish Center, Malaysia, 260
WWF South Africa, South Africa, 336
Youth for Development and Co-operation—YDC, Netherlands, 283
Zakat House, Kuwait, 249
Zero-Kap Foundation, Netherlands, 283
ZOA, Netherlands, 283

AUSTRALASIA

A. M. M. Sahabdeen Trust Foundation, Sri Lanka, 350
AbaF—Australia Business Arts Foundation, Australia, 37
ACCU—Asian Cultural Centre for UNESCO, Japan, 231
Action contre la Faim, France, 136
Action against Hunger, France, 136
Action Solidarité Tiers Monde—ASTM, Luxembourg, 257
Activ Foundation, Australia, 36
AFAP—Australian Foundation for the Peoples of Asia and the Pacific, Australia, 38
AFSC—American Friends Service Committee, USA, 465
AJWS—American Jewish World Service, USA, 466
Alert—International Alert, UK, 422
Altman (Jenifer) Foundation, USA, 463
American Friends Service Committee—AFSC, USA, 465
American Jewish World Service—AJWS, USA, 466
AMP Foundation, Australia, 36
ANESVAD, Spain, 337
APACE Village First Electrification Group—APACE VFEG, Australia, 36
APAN—Asian Philanthropy Advisory Network, Philippines, 301
Apex Foundation, Australia, 36

APMN—Asia Pacific Mountain Network, Nepal, 271
Appropriate Technology for Community and Environment—APACE, Australia, 36
Arthritis Australia, Australia, 37
Arthritis Foundation of Australia, Australia, 37
Asia Foundation, USA, 469
Asia/Pacific Cultural Centre for UNESCO—ACCU, Japan, 231
Asia Pacific Foundation of Canada, Canada, 81
Asia-Pacific Mountain Network—APMN, Nepal, 271
Asia Society, USA, 470
Asian Philanthropy Advisory Network—APAN, Philippines, 301
Aspen Institute, USA, 470
ASTM—Action Solidarité Tiers Monde, Luxembourg, 257
Australasian Spinal Research, Australia, 44
Australia Business Arts Foundation—AbaF, Australia, 37
Australia Foundation for Culture and the Humanities Ltd, Australia, 37
Australia-Japan Foundation, Australia, 37
Australian Academy of the Humanities, Australia, 37
Australian Academy of Science, Australia, 37
Australian-American Fulbright Commission, Australia, 37
Australian Association of Philanthropy, Australia, 36
Australian Cancer Research Foundation, Australia, 38
Australian Conservation Foundation, Australia, 38
Australian Foundation for the Peoples of Asia and the Pacific—AFAP, Australia, 38
Australian Institute of International Affairs, Australia, 39
Australian Multicultural Foundation—AMF, Australia, 39
Australian Spinal Research Foundation, Australia, 39
Australian Volunteers International, Australia, 39
Australian Youth Foundation, Australia, 41
AWHRC—Asian Women's Human Rights Council, India, 200
Baker Heart Research Institute, Australia, 39
Baker IDI Heart & Diabetes Institute, Australia, 39
BBC World Service Trust, UK, 403
Bell (Max) Foundation, Canada, 81
BID-INTAL—Instituto para la Integración de America Latina y el Caribe, Argentina, 34
British Schools and Universities Foundation, Inc—BSUF, USA, 473
Brockhoff (Jack) Foundation, Australia, 39
Brother's Brother Foundation, USA, 474
Butler (J. Homer) Foundation, USA, 504
Canadian Catholic Organization for Development and Peace, Canada, 83
Canadian Centre for International Studies and Co-operation/Centre d'études et de coopération internationale—CECI, Canada, 83
Cancer Council Australia, Australia, 40
Cancer Society of New Zealand, Inc, New Zealand, 284
CARE International—CI, Switzerland, 361
Catholic Agency for World Development—Trócaire, Ireland, 213
CECHE—Center for Communications, Health and the Environment, USA, 477
CECI—Canadian Centre for International Studies and Co-operation/Centre d'études et de coopération internationale, Canada, 83
Center for Communications, Health and the Environment—CECHE, USA, 477
Center for Cultural and Technical Interchange between East and West—East-West Center, USA, 487
Centro Internacional de Agricultura Tropical—CIAT, Colombia, 104
CFI—Consuelo Foundation, Inc, USA, 482
Charity Projects, UK, 411
Child Migrants Trust, UK, 409
Children's Medical Research Institute, Australia, 40
CIAT—Centro Internacional de Agricultura Tropical, Colombia, 104
Climate Cent Foundation, Switzerland, 375
Clive and Vera Ramaciotti Foundations, Australia, 43
Collier Charitable Fund, Australia, 40
Comic Relief, UK, 411
Commonwealth Foundation, UK, 411

Community Aid Abroad—Oxfam Australia, Australia, 43
Concern Universal, UK, 412
Consuelo Foundation, Inc—CFI, USA, 482
Credit Union Foundation Australia—CUFA, Australia, 40
CUFA—Credit Union Foundation Australia, Australia, 40
CUSO-VSO, Canada, 86
Damien Foundation, Belgium, 58
DOEN Foundation, Netherlands, 280
Dreyfus Health Foundation—DHF, USA, 485
East-West Center—EWC, USA, 487
Easter Island Foundation, USA, 487
EcoHealth Alliance, USA, 487
Écoles Sans Frontières—ESF, France, 139
endPoverty.org, USA, 488
Enterprise Development International, USA, 488
European NGOs on Agriculture, Food, Trade and Development, France, 135
EWC—East-West Center, USA, 487
The Family Federation of Finland, Finland, 133
Family Planning, New Zealand, 284
FDH—Frères des Hommes, France, 152
FH—Food for the Hungry, USA, 491
filia.die frauenstiftung, Germany, 168
filia—the Women's Foundation, Germany, 168
First Peoples Worldwide—FPW, USA, 490
Fondation d'Entreprise Renault, France, 144
Fondation contre la Faim, USA, 491
Fondation Marguerite et Aimé Maeght, France, 147
Food for the Hungry—FH, USA, 491
FOPERDA—Fondation Royale Père Damien pour la Lutte Contre la Lèpre, Belgium, 58
Foundation for Human Rights and Humanitarian Relief, Turkey, 389
Foundation 'Life for All', Switzerland, 375
Foundation for the Peoples of the South Pacific, Australia, 38
Foundation to Promote Health, Liechtenstein, 255
Foundation for Young Australians, Australia, 41
The Fred Hollows Foundation, Australia, 41
Freeplay Foundation, UK, 429
Frères des Hommes—FDH, France, 152
The Gaia Foundation, UK, 418
Global Fund for Community Foundations—GFCF, South Africa, 331
Globe Foundation of Canada—GLOBE, Canada, 89
Haribon Foundation, Philippines, 302
Haribon Foundation for the Conservation of Natural Resources, Inc, Philippines, 302
Havelaar (Max) Foundation, Netherlands, 281
Health Action International, Netherlands, 275
Health Volunteers Overseas—HVO, USA, 501
Heart Foundation, Australia, 42
Hellenic Foundation for Culture, Greece, 186
Hollows (Fred) Foundation, Australia, 41
Homeland Foundation, USA, 522
Humanitarian Relief Foundation, Turkey, 389
Ian Potter Foundation, Australia, 43
ICLARM—The WorldFish Center, Malaysia, 260
IFAD—International Fund for Agricultural Development, Italy, 226
IFHD—International Foundation for Human Development, India, 203
IHCF—Stiftung zur Förderung der Gesundheit, Liechtenstein, 255
Impact First International, Canada, 89
INFID—International NGO Forum on Indonesian Development, Indonesia, 207
INHURED International—International Institute for Human Rights, Environment and Development, Nepal, 271
İnsan Hak ve Hürriyetleri İnsani Yardım Vakfı, Turkey, 389
Institut international des Droits de l'Enfant, Switzerland, 368
Institut Nord-Sud, Canada, 95
Institute for Development Research, USA, 556
Institute for Latin American and Caribbean Integration, Argentina, 34
Instituto para la Integración de América Latina y el Caribe—BID-INTAL, Argentina, 34
Inter Pares, Canada, 90
International Alert—Alert, UK, 422
International Centre for the Legal Protection of Human Rights—Interights, UK, 423
International Centre for Living Aquatic Resources—ICLARM, Malaysia, 260
International Centre for Tropical Agriculture, Colombia, 104
International Diabetes Institute, Australia, 39
International Executive Service Corps—IESC, USA, 508
The International Foundation, USA, 508

International Foundation for Human Development—IFHD, India, 203
International Fund for Agricultural Development—IFAD, Italy, 226
International Institute for Human Rights, Environment and Development—INHURED International, Nepal, 271
International Institute for the Rights of the Child, Switzerland, 368
International NGO Forum on Indonesian Development—INFID, Indonesia, 207
International Refugee Trust—IRT, UK, 424
International Relief and Development—IRD, USA, 510
International Relief Teams, USA, 510
International Research & Exchanges Board—IREX, USA, 511
International Water Management Institute—IWMI, Sri Lanka, 350
International Women's Health Coalition—IWHC, USA, 510
IREX—International Research & Exchanges Board, USA, 511
Isis Internacional, Chile, 100
Isis International, Chile, 100
Islamic Relief Worldwide, UK, 425
J. Homer Butler Foundation, Inc, USA, 504
J. R. McKenzie Trust, New Zealand, 284
Jack Brockhoff Foundation—JBF, Australia, 39
JCIE—Japan Center for International Exchange, Japan, 236
Jenifer Altman Foundation—JAF, USA, 463
Kerzner Marine Foundation—KMF, USA, 515
Kirk (Norman) Memorial Trust, New Zealand, 284
Lama Gangchen World Peace Foundation, Italy, 227
Law Foundation of New South Wales, Australia, 41
Law and Justice Foundation of New South Wales, Australia, 41
Leprosy Mission International, UK, 428
Lifeline Energy, UK, 429
Lifewater International—LI, USA, 518
Liliane Foundation, Netherlands, 281
The Long Now Foundation—LNF, USA, 519
Ludwig Institute for Cancer Research—LICR, USA, 519
LWR—Lutheran World Relief, USA, 519
M-USA—Mercy-USA for Aid and Development, USA, 524
McKenzie (J. R.) Trust, New Zealand, 284
Maeght (Marguerite et Aimé), Fondation, France, France, 147
Mama Cash, Netherlands, 277
Manfred Woerner Foundation, Bulgaria, 74
March of Dimes, USA, 522
Marguerite and Aimé Maeght Foundation, France, 147
Marisla Foundation, USA, 522
Match International Centre, Canada, 93
Max Bell Foundation, Canada, 81
Max Havelaar Foundation, Netherlands, 281
Medical Emergency Relief International—MERLIN, UK, 432
Menzies (R. G.) Scholarship Fund, Australia, 42
Menzies (Sir Robert) Foundation Ltd, Australia, 41
Mercy-USA for Aid and Development—M-USA, USA, 524
MERLIN—Medical Emergency Relief International, UK, 432
Moriya Foundation, Japan, 238
Myer (Sidney) Fund, Australia, 42
The Myer Foundation, Australia, 42
National Heart Foundation of Australia, Australia, 42
National Heart Foundation of New Zealand, New Zealand, 285
The Nature Conservancy, USA, 528
New Zealand Association of Philanthropic Trusts, New Zealand, 284
New Zealand Winston Churchill Memorial Trust, New Zealand, 285
NFCR—National Foundation for Cancer Research, USA, 529
Norman Kirk Memorial Trust, New Zealand, 284
North-South-Bridge Foundation, Germany, 181
North-South Institute/Institut Nord-Sud, Canada, 95
Operation Rainbow, Inc, USA, 530
Operation USA, USA, 530
Opportunity International USA, USA, 530
Oxfam Australia, Australia, 43
Oxfam New Zealand, New Zealand, 285
OzChild, Australia, 43
Pacific Development and Conservation Trust, New Zealand, 285

Pacific Leprosy Foundation, New Zealand, 286
Pacific Peoples' Partnership, Canada, 95
PAN Asia and the Pacific—Pesticide Action
    Network Asia and the Pacific, Malaysia, 260
Pathfinder International, USA, 533
PBI—Peace Brigades International, UK, 437
Peace Brigades International—PBI, UK, 437
Peace and Disarmament Education Trust—
    PADET, New Zealand, 286
Peace, Health and Human Development
    Foundation—PHD Foundation, Japan, 239
Perpetual Foundation, Australia, 43
Perpetual Trustees Australia, Australia, 43
Pesticide Action Network Asia and the Pacific—
    PAN AP, Malaysia, 260
The PHD Foundation—Peace, Health and Human
    Development Foundation, Japan, 239
Philanthropy Australia, Australia, 36
Philanthropy New Zealand, New Zealand, 284
Population Council, USA, 536
Potter (Ian) Foundation, Australia, 43
Press Foundation of Asia—PFA, Philippines, 303
Project Trust, UK, 439
Queen's Trust for Young Australians,
    Australia, 41
R. E. Ross Trust, Australia, 44
R. G. Menzies Scholarship Fund, Australia, 42
Ramaciotti (Clive and Vera) Foundation,
    Australia, 43
Reichstein Foundation, Australia, 44
Renault Foundation, France, 144
Réseau d'ONG Européennes sur l'Agro-
    alimentaire, le Commerce, l'Environnement
    et le Développement—RONGEAD,
    France, 135
Rhodes Trust, UK, 441
RONGEAD—Réseau d'ONG Européennes sur
    l'Agro-alimentaire, le Commerce,
    l'Environnement et le Développement,
    France, 135
Ross (R. E.) Trust, Australia, 44
Rowan Charitable Trust, UK, 441
Royal Asiatic Society of Great Britain and
    Ireland, UK, 443
Royal Flying Doctor Service of Australia—
    RFDS, Australia, 44
Royal Forest and Bird Protection Society of New
    Zealand, New Zealand, 286
Royal Society for the Protection of Birds—RSPB,
    UK, 445
RSPB—Royal Society for the Protection of Birds,
    UK, 445
Rutgers WPF, Netherlands, 279
Sabre Foundation, Inc, USA, 542
Sahabdeen (A. M. M.) Trust Foundation, Sri
    Lanka, 350
Schools Without Frontiers, France, 139
SCIAF—Scottish Catholic International Aid
    Fund, UK, 447
Science and Technology Facilities Council—
    STFC, UK, 447
Scottish Catholic International Aid Fund—
    SCIAF, UK, 447
Seva Foundation, USA, 544
Sidney Myer Fund, Australia, 42
The Sir Robert Menzies Memorial Foundation
    Ltd, Australia, 41
South Pacific Peoples Foundation Canada,
    Canada, 95
SpinalCure Australia, Australia, 44
St John Ambulance, UK, 446
Standing International Forum on Ethnic
    Conflict, Genocide and Human Rights—
    International Alert, UK, 422
Stichting DOEN, Netherlands, 280
Stichting Liliane Fonds, Netherlands, 281
Stichting Max Havelaar, Netherlands, 281
Stiftung Klimarappen, Switzerland, 375
Stiftung 'Leben für Alle', Switzerland, 375
Stiftung Nord-Süd-Brücken, Germany, 181
Sutherland Self Help Trust, New Zealand, 286
Sylvia and Charles Viertel Charitable
    Foundation, Australia, 45
TANZ—Trade Aid NZ Inc, New Zealand, 287
TEAR Australia, Australia, 45
Terre des Hommes Foundation, Switzerland, 376
Third World Solidarity Action, Luxembourg, 257
Tindall Foundation, New Zealand, 286
The Todd Foundation, New Zealand, 287
Tokyu Foundation for Inbound Students,
    Japan, 240
The Toyota Foundation, Japan, 240
Trade Aid NZ Inc—TANZ, New Zealand, 287
Trans-Antarctic Association—TAA, UK, 451
Trócaire—Catholic Agency for World
    Development, Ireland, 213
United Society for the Propagation of the
    Gospel—USPG, UK, 453

Unity Foundation, Luxembourg, 257
Väestöliitto, Finland, 133
Viertel (Sylvia and Charles) Charitable
    Foundation, Australia, 45
Voluntary Service Overseas, UK, 454
Volunteer Service Abroad—VSA, New
    Zealand, 287
VSA—Volunteer Service Abroad, New
    Zealand, 287
VSO, UK, 454
Wildlife Preservation Trust International,
    USA, 487
Wildlife Trust, USA, 487
Winrock International, USA, 555
Woerner (Manfred) Foundation, Bulgaria, 74
World Education, Inc, USA, 556
World Neighbors, USA, 557
World Population Foundation, Netherlands, 279
World Teacher Trust, India, 206
The WorldFish Center, Malaysia, 260
Youth for Development and Co-operation—YDC,
    Netherlands, 283
Zurich Community Trust, UK, 457
Zurich Financial Services (UKISA) Community
    Trust Ltd, UK, 457

CENTRAL AND SOUTH-EASTERN EUROPE

A. G. Leventis Foundation, Cyprus, 111
Absolute Return for Kids—ARK, UK, 401
Academy for the Development of Philanthropy in
    Poland, Poland, 305
Academy of European Law, Germany, 167
Açık Toplum Enstitüsü, Turkey, 387
Action contre la Faim, France, 136
Action against Hunger, France, 136
ACTR/ACCELS—American Councils for
    International Education, USA, 464
ADI—Association for Democratic Initiatives,
    Macedonia, 258
Adriano Olivetti Foundation, Italy, 223
AFSC—American Friends Service Committee,
    USA, 465
Agora Foundation, Poland, 306
Agronomes et vétérinaires sans frontières—
    AVSF, France, 136
Air France Corporate Foundation, France, 144
AIT—Asian Institute of Technology,
    Thailand, 383
Akademia Rozwoju Filantropii w Polsce,
    Poland, 305
AKNS—Asociácia komunitných nadácií
    Slovenska, Slovakia, 327
Åland Fund for the Future of the Baltic Sea,
    Finland, 131
Albanian Civil Society Foundation, Albania, 29
Albanian Disability Rights Foundation,
    Albania, 29
Alfred Toepfer Foundation F.V.S., Germany, 183
Alfred Toepfer Stiftung F.V.S., Germany, 183
Allianz Cultural Foundation, Germany, 160
Allianz Kulturstiftung, Germany, 160
AMADE Mondiale—Association Mondiale des
    Amis de l'Enfance, Monaco, 265
America for Bulgaria Foundation, Bulgaria, 75
American Councils for International
    Education—ACTR/ACCELS, USA, 464
American Friends Service Committee—AFSC,
    USA, 465
ANESVAD, Spain, 337
Anne Çocuk Eğitim Vakfi—AÇEV, Turkey, 388
The Anne Frank Trust UK, UK, 418
ARK—Absolute Return for Kids, UK, 401
Arthur Rubinstein International Music Society,
    Israel, 215
Asociácia komunitných nadácií Slovenska—
    AKNS, Slovakia, 327
Association for Civil Society Development—
    SMART, Croatia, 109
Association for Democratic Initiatives—ADI,
    Macedonia, 258
Association Mondiale des Amis de l'Enfance,
    Monaco, 265
Association of Slovakian Community
    Foundations, Slovakia, 327
Atlas Charity Foundation, Poland, 306
Auschwitz-Birkenau Foundation, Poland, 306
Auschwitz Foundation, Belgium, 60
Austrian Society for Environment and
    Technology, Austria, 48
Autonómia Foundation, Hungary, 195
Auxilia Foundation, Czech Republic, 112
Axel Springer Foundation, Germany, 179
Axel-Springer-Stiftung, Germany, 179
BaBe—Budi aktivna, Budi emancipirana,
    Croatia, 109

Baltic Sea Foundation, Finland, 131
Barka Foundation, Poland, 308
The Barretstown Camp Fund Ltd, Ireland, 210
BCAF—Bulgarian Charities Aid Foundation,
    Bulgaria, 74
Be Active, Be Emancipated, Croatia, 109
Beatrice Laing Trust, UK, 428
Berghof Foundation for Conflict Research,
    Germany, 161
Berghof Stiftung für Konfliktforschung GmbH,
    Germany, 161
Beyaz Nokta Gelişim Vakfi, Turkey, 387
Black Sea NGO Network—BSNN, Bulgaria, 75
Black Sea University Foundation—BSUF,
    Romania, 316
Bleustein-Blanchet (Marcel), Fondation pour la
    Vocation, France, 141
Bodossaki Foundation, Greece, 186
Boghossian Foundation, Belgium, 60
Book Aid International—BAI, UK, 405
Borderland Foundation, Poland, 307
Bosch (Robert) Stiftung GmbH, Germany, 163
Bridges for Education, Inc—BFE, USA, 473
Brother's Brother Foundation, USA, 474
Bruno Kreisky Forum for International
    Dialogue, Austria, 47
Bruno Kreisky Forum für internationalen
    Dialog, Austria, 47
Budi aktivna, Budi emancipiran—BaBe!,
    Croatia, 109
Bulgarian Donors' Forum, Bulgaria, 74
Bulgarian Fund for Women, Bulgaria, 75
Canadian Executive Service Organization—
    CESO/Service d'assistance canadienne aux
    organismes—SACO, Canada, 83
Cancer Relief Macmillan Fund, UK, 430
CARE International—CI, Switzerland, 361
Carpathian Foundation, Hungary, 195
Cartier Foundation for Contemporary Art,
    France, 141
Catholic Agency for World Development—
    Trócaire, Ireland, 213
CCF—Christian Children's Fund, USA, 478
CEGA—Creating Effective Grassroots
    Alternatives, Bulgaria, 75
Centar za razvoj neprofitnih organizacija—
    CERANEO, Croatia, 109
Centar za Razvoj Nevladinih Organizacija—
    CRNVO, Montenegro, 267
Central and Eastern European Media Centre
    Foundation, Poland, 307
CENTRAS—Assistance Centre for NGOs,
    Romania, 316
Centre for the Development of Non-
    Governmental Organizations,
    Montenegro, 267
Centre for Development of Non-Profit
    Organizations, Croatia, 109
Centre for Development of Non-Profit Sector,
    Serbia, 324
Centre Européen de la Culture—CEC,
    Switzerland, 362
Centre for the Information Service, Co-operation
    and Development of NGOs, Slovenia, 330
Centre International de Coopération pour le
    Développement Agricole—CICDA,
    France, 136
Centre for Promotion and Development of Civil
    Initiatives—OPUS, Poland, 305
CERANEO—Centar za razvoj neprofitnih
    organizacija, Croatia, 109
Česko-německý fond budoucnosti, Czech
    Republic, 113
CESO—Canadian Executive Service
    Organization, Canada, 83
Charities Aid Foundation Bulgaria, Bulgaria, 74
Charity Projects, UK, 411
Charles Stewart Mott Foundation—CSMF,
    USA, 526
Charter 77 Foundation, Czech Republic, 114
ChildFund International, USA, 478
Children of Slovakia Foundation, Slovakia, 328
Churches' Commission for Migrants in Europe,
    Belgium, 57
CIMADE—Service Oecuménique d'Entraide,
    France, 138
Cindi Foundation, Czech Republic, 113
Civic Forum Foundation, Czech Republic, 113
Civic Initiatives, Serbia, 324
Civic Responsibility Foundation, Lithuania, 256
Civil Society Development Centre, Turkey, 387
Civil Society Development Foundation,
    Romania, 316
Civil Society Development Foundation–Hungary,
    Hungary, 195
CIVITAS Foundation for Civil Society,
    Romania, 316

Clovek v tisni—spolecnost pri Ceske televizi,
o.p.s., Czech Republic, 113
CNVOS—Zavod Center za Informiranje,
Sodelovanje in Razvoj Nevladnih
Organizacije, Slovenia, 330
Comic Relief, UK, 411
Commission des Eglises auprès des Migrants en
Europe/Kommission der Kirchen für
Migranten in Europa, Belgium, 57
Committee of Good Will—Olga Havel
Foundation, Czech Republic, 115
CONCAWE—Oil Companies' European
Association for Environment, Health and
Safety in Refining and Distribution,
Belgium, 58
Cooperazione Internazionale—COOPI, Italy, 217
COOPI—Cooperazione Internazionale, Italy, 217
COSIS, Italy, 221
Costopoulos (J. F.) Foundation, Greece, 186
Council of Humanitarian Associations, Czech
Republic, 112
CRDF Global, USA, 483
Creating Effective Grassroots Alternatives—
CEGA, Bulgaria, 75
Cultural Foundation of the German Länder,
Germany, 174
Czech Donors Forum, Czech Republic, 112
Czech-German Fund for the Future, Czech
Republic, 113
Czech Literary Fund, Czech Republic, 113
Czech Music Fund Foundation, Czech
Republic, 113
Czech TV Foundation, Czech Republic, 113
Czegei Wass Foundation, Hungary, 196
The Danish Cultural Institute, Denmark, 117
Danish Outdoor Council, Denmark, 118
Danske Kulturinstitut, Denmark, 117
Demokratikus Atalakulásért Intézet,
Hungary, 196
Deutsch-Tschechischer Zukunftsfonds, Czech
Republic, 113
Deutsche Gesellschaft für Auswärtige Politik—
DGAP, Germany, 164
Deutsche Stiftung für internationale rechtliche
Zusammenarbeit eV, Germany, 165
Dinu Patriciu Foundation, Romania, 317
Donegani (Guido), Fondazione, Italy, 221
Dreyfus Health Foundation—DHF, USA, 485
Drug Policy Alliance—DPA, USA, 485
Ebelin and Gerd Bucerius ZEIT Foundation,
Germany, 184
Eberhard Schöck Foundation, Germany, 178
Eberhard-Schöck-Stiftung, Germany, 178
Écoles Sans Frontières—ESF, France, 139
ECOLOGIA—Ecologists Linked for Organizing
Grassroots Initiatives and Action, USA, 488
Ecological Library Foundation, Poland, 307
Ecologists Linked for Organizing Grassroots
Initiatives and Action—ECOLOGIA,
USA, 488
Economic Development Foundation, Turkey, 388
Economic Foundation, Poland, 307
ECPD—European Centre for Peace and
Development, Serbia, 324
Ecumenical Service for Mutual Help, France, 138
Eesti Mittetulundusühingute ja Sihtasutuste
Liit, Estonia, 129
Eestimaa Looduse Fond—ELF, Estonia, 129
Einaudi (Luigi), Fondazione, Italy, 221
Ekopolis Foundation, Slovakia, 327
ELIAMEP—Hellenic Foundation for European
and Foreign Policy, Greece, 187
Emile Chanoux Foundation—Institute for
Federalist and Regionalist Studies, Italy, 218
ENCOD—European NGO Council on Drugs and
Development, Belgium, 59
endPoverty.org, USA, 488
Enfants Réfugiés du Monde—ERM, France, 140
Enterprise Development International, USA, 488
Entraide Protestante Suisse, Switzerland, 367
Environment Foundation of Turkey, Turkey, 390
ERA—Europäische Rechtsakademie,
Germany, 167
ERM—Enfants Réfugiés du Monde, France, 140
ERRC—Europako Rromano Čačimasko Centro,
Hungary, 196
ERSTE Foundation, Austria, 46
ERSTE Stiftung—Die ERSTE Österreichische
Spar-Casse Privatstiftung, Austria, 46
Estonian Foundation Centre, Estonia, 129
Estonian Fund for Nature, Estonia, 129
Estonian National Culture Foundation,
Estonia, 129
EURONATUR—Stiftung Europäisches
Naturerbe, Germany, 180
Euronisa Foundation, Czech Republic, 114
Europa Employment Foundation—Enterprise
and Solidarity, Italy, 221

Europa Nostra, Netherlands, 273
Europäische Rechtsakademie—ERA,
Germany, 167
Europako Rromano Čačimasko Centro—ERRC,
Hungary, 196
European Anti-Poverty Network—EAPN,
Belgium, 59
European Centre of Culture, Switzerland, 362
European Centre for Peace and Development—
ECPD, Serbia, 324
European Centre for Social Welfare Policy and
Research, Austria, 47
European Climate Foundation, Netherlands, 273
European Coalition for Just and Effective Drug
Policies—ENCOD, Belgium, 59
European Cultural Foundation—ECF,
Netherlands, 273
European Environmental Bureau, Belgium, 59
European Federation of National Organizations
Working with the Homeless, Belgium, 55
European Foundation for the Improvement of
Living and Working Conditions, Ireland, 211
European Foundation for the Sustainable
Development of the Regions—FEDRE,
Switzerland, 363
European Institute of Progressive Cultural
Policies, Austria, 47
European Mediterranean Institute, Spain, 349
European Nature Heritage Fund, Germany, 180
European Network of Foundations for Social
Economy, Belgium, 56
European NGOs on Agriculture, Food, Trade and
Development, France, 135
European Roma Rights Centre, Hungary, 196
European Science Foundation, France, 144
European Venture Philanthropy Association—
EVPA, Belgium, 55
European Youth For Action—EYFA,
Netherlands, 273
European Youth Foundation—EYF, France, 151
Europese Culterele Stichting, Netherlands, 273
Eurostep—European Solidarity Towards Equal
Participation of People, Belgium, 60
Eurotransplant International Foundation,
Netherlands, 274
Evens Foundation, Belgium, 61
EVPA—European Venture Philanthropy
Association, Belgium, 55
Evrika Foundation, Bulgaria, 75
EYFA—European Youth For Action,
Netherlands, 273
FEANTSA—Fédération Européenne des
Associations Nationales Travaillant avec les
Sans-Abri, Belgium, 55
Fédération Européenne des Associations
Nationales Travaillant avec les Sans-Abri—
FEANTSA, Belgium, 55
FEDRE—European Foundation for the
Sustainable Development of the Regions,
Switzerland, 363
Fernand Lazard Foundation, Belgium, 63
Fernand Lazard Stichting, Belgium, 63
filia.die frauenstiftung, Germany, 168
filia—the Women's Foundation, Germany, 168
FINCA International, USA, 490
FIP—Forum Inicjatyw Pozarzadowych,
Poland, 305
Folmer Wisti Fonden, Denmark, 122
Folmer Wisti Foundation, Denmark, 122
Fondaccioni per Iniciative Demokratike,
Kosovo, 248
Fondacioni Shoqeria e Hapur per Shqiperine,
Albania, 29
Fondacioni Shqiptar per te Drejtat e Paaftesise,
Albania, 29
Fondation Auschwitz, Belgium, 60
Fondation Boghossian, Belgium, 60
Fondation Cartier pour l'Art Contemporain,
France, 141
Fondation Charles Veillon, Switzerland, 365
Fondation Denis de Rougemont pour l'Europe,
Switzerland, 365
Fondation Emile Chanoux—Institut d'Etudes
Fédéralistes et Régionalistes, Italy, 218
Fondation Ensemble, France, 143
Fondation d'Entreprise Air France, France, 144
Fondation Européenne de la Culture/Europese
Culturele Stichting, Netherlands, 273
Fondation Européenne de la Science, France, 144
Fondation Evens Stichting, Belgium, 61
Fondation Jean Monnet pour l'Europe,
Switzerland, 364
Fondation Marcel Bleustein-Blanchet pour la
Vocation, France, 141
Fondation Marcel Hicter, Belgium, 61
Fondation Marguerite et Aimé Maeght,
France, 147

Fondation Nicolas Hulot pour la Nature et
l'Homme, France, 146
Fondation Paul-Henri Spaak—Stichting Paul-
Henri Spaak, Belgium, 61
Fondation Robert Schuman, France, 150
Fondation Roi Baudouin, Belgium, 62
Fondation Ushuaia, France, 146
Fondazione Adriano Olivetti, Italy, 223
Fondazione Europa Occupazione—Impresa e
Solidarietà, Italy, 221
Fondazione Giovanni Lorenzini, Italy, 222
Fondazione Guido Donegani, Italy, 221
Fondazione Ing. Carlo M. Lerici—FL, Italy, 222
Fondazione Internazionale Menarini, Italy, 222
Fondazione Luigi Einaudi, Italy, 221
Fondazione di Studi di Storia dell'Arte 'Roberto
Longhi', Italy, 225
Fonds Européen pour la Jeunesse—FEJ,
France, 151
Forum Inicjatyw Pozarzadowych—FIP,
Poland, 305
Forum for Non-Governmental Initiatives,
Poland, 305
Forumul Donatorilor din România, Romania, 316
FOSIM—Foundation Open Society Institute
Macedonia, Macedonia, 258
Foundation Czech Art Fund, Czech Republic, 114
Foundation for Democratic Initiatives—FDI,
Kosovo, 248
Foundation for German–Polish Co-operation,
Poland, 308
Foundation of the Hellenic World, Greece, 186
Foundation for Human Rights and Humanitarian
Relief, Turkey, 389
Foundation for International Community
Assistance, USA, 490
Foundation for International Studies—FIS,
Malta, 261
Foundation for International Understanding,
Denmark, 122
Foundation 'Life for All', Switzerland, 375
Foundation Nicolas Hulot for Nature and
Humankind, France, 146
Foundation Open Society Institute Macedonia—
FOSIM, Macedonia, 258
Foundation Open Society Institute—
Representative Office Montenegro—FOSI
ROM, Montenegro, 267
Foundation in Support of Local Democracy,
Poland, 308
Foundation for Women, Spain, 345
Freedom of Expression Foundation, Norway, 291
Friluftsraadet, Denmark, 118
FSLD—Foundation in Support of Local
Democracy, Poland, 308
Fund for the Development of the Carpathian
Euroregion, Hungary, 195
Fund for an Open Society—Serbia, Serbia, 324
Fundación Empresa-Universidad de Zaragoza—
FEUZ, Spain, 342
Fundación Juanelo Turriano, Spain, 348
Fundación Mujeres, Spain, 345
Fundación Paz y Solidaridad Serafín Aliaga—
FPyS, Spain, 346
Fundacja Agory, Poland, 306
Fundacja Auschwitz-Birkenau, Poland, 306
Fundacja Bankowa im. Leopolda Kronenberga,
Poland, 306
Fundacja Biblioteka Ekologiczna, Poland, 307
Fundacja Centrum Prasowe, Poland, 307
Fundacja Gospodarcza, Poland, 307
Fundacja im. Stefana Batorego, Poland, 307
Fundacja Partnerstwo dla Srodowiska,
Poland, 307
Fundacja Pogranicze, Poland, 307
Fundacja Pomocy Wzajemnej Barka, Poland, 308
Fundacja Pro Bono II, Poland, 308
Fundacja Rozwoju Demokracji Loaklnej,
Poland, 308
Fundacja Solidarności Polsko-Czesko-
Słowackiej, Poland, 308
Fundacja Współpracy Polsko-Niemieckiej/
Stiftung für Deutsch–Polnische
Zusammenarbeit, Poland, 308
Fundacja Wspomagania Wsi, Poland, 308
Fundatia Dinu Patriciu, Romania, 317
Fundatia pentru Dezvoltarea Societatii Civile—
FDSC, Romania, 316
The Gaia Foundation, UK, 418
Gemeinnützige Hertie Foundation, Germany, 169
Gemeinnützige Hertie-Stiftung, Germany, 169
German Council on Foreign Relations,
Germany, 164
German Foundation for International Legal Co-
operation, Germany, 165
German Marshall Fund of the United States—
GMF, USA, 496
Gift of the Givers Foundation, South Africa, 332

Giovanni Lorenzini Foundation, Italy, 222
Global Ethic Foundation Czech Republic, Czech Republic, 114
Global Fund for Community Foundations—GFCF, South Africa, 331
Globe Foundation of Canada—GLOBE, Canada, 89
GMF—German Marshall Fund of the United States, USA, 496
Gradjanske inicijative—GI, Serbia, 324
Green Perspective Foundation, Slovakia, 328
Grupa Zagranica, Poland, 305
Guido Donegani Foundation, Italy, 221
HALO Trust, UK, 419
Health Action International, Netherlands, 275
Heifer International, USA, 502
HEKS—Hilfswerk Evangelischen Kirchen Schweiz, Switzerland, 367
Hellenic Foundation for Culture, Greece, 186
Hellenic Foundation for European and Foreign Policy—ELIAMEP, Greece, 187
Hellenic Society for Disabled Children, Greece, 187
The Henry Smith Charity, UK, 448
Hestia—The National Volunteer Centre, Czech Republic, 114
Hicter (Marcel), Fondation, Belgium, 61
Hilfswerk der Evangelischen Kirchen Schweiz—HEKS, Switzerland, 367
Hisar Education Foundation—HEV, Turkey, 388
HIVOS—Humanistisch Instituut voor Ontwikkelings Samenwerking, Netherlands, 275
Human Resource Development Foundation, Turkey, 389
The Humana Foundation, Inc, USA, 505
Humanistic Institute for Co-operation with Developing Countries, Netherlands, 275
Humanistisch Instituut voor Ontwikkelings Samenwerking—HIVOS, Netherlands, 275
Humanitarian Relief Foundation, Turkey, 389
Hungarian Foundation for Self-Reliance—HFSR, Hungary, 195
Hungarian Interchurch Aid—HIA, Hungary, 196
ICN Foundation, Czech Republic, 112
ICN—Information Centre for Non-profit Organizations, Czech Republic, 112
IEIAS—Institut Européen Interuniversitaire de l'Action Sociale, Belgium, 62
IEMed—Institut Europeu de la Mediterrània, Spain, 349
IKEA Foundation, Netherlands, 275
IKGV—İnsan Kaynağını Geliştirme Vakfı, Turkey, 389
İktisadi Kalkınma Vakfı, Turkey, 388
Information Centre for Foundations and other Non-profit Organizations—ICN, Czech Republic, 112
Ing. Carlo M. Lerici Foundation, Italy, 222
İnsan Hak ve Hürriyetleri İnsani Yardım Vakfı, Turkey, 389
İnsan Kaynağını Geliştirme Vakfı—IKGV, Turkey, 389
Institusjonen Fritt Ord, Norway, 291
Institut für Agrarentwicklung in Mittel- und Osteuropa—IAMO, Germany, 171
Institut Català Mediterrània, Spain, 349
Institut Européen Interuniversitaire de l'Action Sociale—IEIAS, Belgium, 62
Institut Europeu de la Mediterrània—IEMed, Spain, 349
Institute for Agricultural Development in Central and Eastern Europe, Germany, 171
Institute for Development Research, USA, 556
Institute for European Environmental Policy—IEEP, UK, 422
Institute for Private Enterprise and Democracy—IPED, Poland, 309
Institutul Cultural Român, Romania, 317
International Blue Crescent Relief and Development Foundation—IBC, Turkey, 390
International Centre for Democratic Transition—ICDT, Hungary, 196
International Centre for the Legal Protection of Human Rights—Interights, UK, 423
International Co-operation, Italy, 217
International Development and Relief Foundation, Canada, 91
International Orthodox Christian Charities, Inc—IOCC, USA, 509
International Relief and Development—IRD, USA, 510
International Relief Teams, USA, 510
International Research & Exchanges Board—IREX, USA, 511
International Visegrad Fund—IVF, Slovakia, 328
IREX—International Research & Exchanges Board, USA, 511

Istituto Luigi Sturzo, Italy, 227
IUC-Europe International Education Centre, Denmark, 119
IUC-Europe Internationalt Uddanneless Center, Denmark, 119
The J. F. Costopoulos Foundation, Greece, 186
J&S Pro Bono Poloniae Foundation, Poland, 309
Jan Hus Educational Foundation, Slovakia, 329
Jean Monnet Foundation for Europe, Switzerland, 364
Juanelo Turriano Foundation, Spain, 348
Kade (Max) Foundation, Inc, USA, 513
Karić fondacija, Serbia, 325
Karić Foundation, Serbia, 325
Karl Kübel Foundation for Child and Family, Germany, 174
Karl-Kübel-Stiftung für Kind und Familie, Germany, 174
Kennan Institute, USA, 514
Kensington Estate—Henry Smith Charity, UK, 448
King Baudouin Foundation, Belgium, 62
King Gustaf V 90th Birthday Foundation, Sweden, 354
Klon/Jawor Association, Poland, 306
Kokkalis Foundation, Greece, 187
Köning Boudewijnstichting/Fondation Roi Baudouin, Belgium, 62
Konung Gustaf V's 90-Årsfond, Sweden, 354
The Kosciuszko Foundation, Inc, USA, 516
Kosovar Civil Society Foundation, Kosovo, 248
Kosovo Foundation for Open Society—KFOS, Kosovo, 248
Kronenberga (Leopolda), Fundacja Bankowa, Poland, 306
Kübel (Karl) Stiftung für Kind und Familie, Germany, 174
KulturKontakt Austria—KKA, Austria, 48
Kulturstiftung der Länder—KSL, Germany, 174
Kvinna till Kvinna Foundation, Sweden, 354
Laing (Beatrice) Trust, UK, 428
Lama Gangchen World Peace Foundation, Italy, 227
Lambrakis Foundation, Greece, 187
Lambrakis Research Foundation, Greece, 187
Landis & Gyr Foundation, Switzerland, 370
Landis & Gyr Stiftung, Switzerland, 370
Latvia Children's Fund, Latvia, 251
Latvian Cultural Foundation, Latvia, 251
Latvijas Bērnu fonds, Latvia, 251
Latvijas Kultūras Fonds—LKF, Latvia, 251
Lauder (Ronald S.) Foundation, Germany, 174
Leopold Kronenberg Foundation, Poland, 306
Lerici (Ing. Carlo M.), Fondazione presso il Politecnico di Milano, Italy, 222
Leventis (A. G.) Foundation, Cyprus, 111
Leverhulme Trust, UK, 429
Lietuvos vaikų fondas, Lithuania, 256
Lithuanian Children's Fund, Lithuania, 256
Littauer (Lucius N.) Foundation, Inc, USA, 519
Longhi (Roberto), Fondazione di Studi di Storia dell'Arte, Italy, 225
Lorenzini (Giovanni), Fondazione, Italy, 222
Lucius N. Littauer Foundation, Inc, USA, 519
Luigi Einaudi Foundation, Italy, 221
Luigi Sturzo Institute, Italy, 227
Luxemburg (Rosa) Stiftung, Germany, 174
M-USA—Mercy-USA for Aid and Development, USA, 524
Macedonian Centre for International Co-operation—MCIC, Macedonia, 258
Macmillan Cancer Relief, UK, 430
Madariaga European Foundation, Belgium, 63
Maecenata Management GmbH, Germany, 159
Maeght (Marguerite et Aimé), Fondation, France, France, 147
Magyar Ökumenikus Segélyszervezet, Hungary, 196
Mama Cash, Netherlands, 277
Manfred Woerner Foundation, Bulgaria, 74
Marangopoulos Foundation for Human Rights, Greece, 188
Marcel Bleustein-Blanchet Vocation Foundation, France, 141
Marcel Hicter Foundation, Belgium, 61
March of Dimes, USA, 522
Marguerite and Aimé Maeght Foundation, France, 147
Max Kade Foundation, Inc, USA, 513
Maxová (Tereza) Foundation, Czech Republic, 115
MCIC—Macedonian Centre for International Co-operation, Macedonia, 258
medica mondiale e.V., Germany, 175
Menarini International Foundation, Italy, 222
Mercy-USA for Aid and Development—M-USA, USA, 524
Microfinance Centre—MFC, Poland, 309
Milan Simecka Foundation, Slovakia, 329

Milieukontakt International, Netherlands, 277
Milieukontakt Oost-Europa, Netherlands, 277
Monnet (Jean), Fondation pour l'Europe, Switzerland, 364
Mother Child Education Foundation, Turkey, 388
Mott (Charles Stewart) Foundation, USA, 526
Mum and Dad Foundation, Czech Republic, 115
Muslim Aid, UK, 433
Nacionalne Zaklade za Razvoj Civilnoga Drustva, Croatia, 109
Nadace Auxilia, Czech Republic, 112
Nadace cesky hudebni fond, Czech Republic, 113
Nadace Charty 77, Czech Republic, 114
Nadace ICN, Czech Republic, 112
Nadace SLUNÍČKO, Czech Republic, 114
Nadace Táta a Máma, Czech Republic, 115
Nadácia Ekopolis, Slovakia, 327
Nadácia Milana Šimečku, Slovakia, 329
Nadácia Pontis, Slovakia, 327
Nadácia pre deti Slovenska, Slovakia, 328
Nadácia Zelená Nádej, Slovakia, 328
National Conference on Soviet Jewry, USA, 528
National Foundation for Civil Society Development, Croatia, 109
National Trust EcoFund, Bulgaria, 76
National Volunteer Centre—Hestia, Czech Republic, 114
NCSJ—National Conference on Soviet Jewry, USA, 528
Nederlandse Organisatie voor Internationale Ontwikkelingssamenwerking—Stichting NOVIB, Netherlands, 279
NESsT—Nonprofit Enterprise and Self-sustainability Team, Chile, 101
Van Neste Foundation, UK, 453
Network of Estonian Non-profit Organizations, Estonia, 129
Network of Information and Support for Non-Governmental Organizations, Poland, 306
NGDO—Non-Governmental Development Organizations Platform, Slovakia, 327
NGO Information and Support Centre—NISC, Lithuania, 256
NGO Rural and Social Initiative, Moldova, 264
NIOK—Nonprofit Információs és Oktató Központ Alapítvány, Hungary, 195
NISC—NGO Information and Support Centre, Lithuania, 256
Non-Profit Information and Training Centre Foundation, Hungary, 195
Nonprofit Enterprise and Self-sustainability Team—NESsT, Chile, 101
Nonprofit Információs és Oktató Központ Alapítvány—NIOK, Hungary, 195
NOVIB (Oxfam Netherlands), Netherlands, 279
Oak Foundation, Switzerland, 371
Oil Companies' European Association for Environment, Health and Safety in Refining and Distribution—CONCAWE, Belgium, 58
Olivetti (Adriano), Fondazione, Italy, Italy, 223
Open Society Foundation, Romania, 317
Open Society Foundation for Albania—OSFA, Albania, 29
Open Society Foundation—Bratislava, Slovakia, 328
Open Society Fund—Bosnia-Herzegovina, Bosnia and Herzegovina, 68
Open Society Fund Prague—OSF Prague, Czech Republic, 115
Open Society Institute—Brussels, Belgium, 63
Open Society Institute Montenegro, Montenegro, 267
Open Society Institute—Paris (Soros Foundations), France, 135
Open Society Institute—Sofia (Bulgaria), Bulgaria, 76
Open Society Institute—Turkey, Turkey, 387
Operation USA, USA, 530
Opportunity International USA, USA, 530
OPUS—Centre for Promotion and Development of Civil Initiatives, Poland, 305
Oranje Fonds, Netherlands, 278
Österreichische Gesellschaft für Umwelt und Technik—ÖGUT, Austria, 48
Oxfam NOVIB—Nederlandse Organisatie voor Internationale Ontwikkelingssamenwerking, Netherlands, 279
Oxfam NOVIB—Netherlands Organization for International Development Co-operation, Netherlands, 279
PAN Europe—Pesticides Action Network Europe, Germany, 176
Pan-European Federation for Cultural Heritage, Netherlands, 273
The Parthenon Trust, Switzerland, 371
PASOS—Policy Association for an Open Society, Czech Republic, 113
Paul-Henri Spaak Foundation, Belgium, 61

People in Need, Czech Republic, 113
People-to-People Health Foundation, Inc—
    Project Hope, USA, 537
People's Harmonious Development Society,
    Georgia, 158
Pestalozzi Children's Foundation,
    Switzerland, 374
Pesticide Action Network—Europe, Belgium, 63
Pesticides Action Network Europe—PAN
    Europe, Germany, 176
Pilietinés Atsakomybés Fondas, Lithuania, 256
Pinchuk (Victor) Foundation, Ukraine, 394
Plan Ireland, Ireland, 212
Platforma Mimovládnych Rozvojových
    Organizáchií—MVRO, Slovakia, 327
Ploughshares Fund, USA, 536
Pôle européen des fondations de l'économie
    sociale, Belgium, 56
Polish-American Freedom Foundation,
    Poland, 305
Polish-Czech-Slovak Solidarity Foundation,
    Poland, 308
Polish Environmental Partnership Foundation,
    Poland, 307
POLSAT Foundation, Poland, 309
Polsko-Amerykańska Fundacja Wolności,
    Poland, 305
Poniecki (Wladyslaw) Foundation, Inc, USA, 536
Pontis Foundation, Slovakia, 327
Preciosa Foundation, Czech Republic, 115
Pro Bono Foundation, Poland, 308
Project HOPE, USA, 537
Ramsay Foundation, Switzerland, 372
RED—Ruralité-environnement-développement,
    Belgium, Belgium, 63
Regional Environmental Center for Central and
    Eastern Europe—REC, Hungary, 196
Réseau d'ONG Européennes sur l'Agro-
    alimentaire, le Commerce, l'Environnement
    et le Développement—RONGEAD,
    France, 135
Resource Center Foundation, Bulgaria, 74
Robert Bosch Foundation, Germany, 163
Robert-Bosch-Stiftung GmbH, Germany, 163
Robert Schalkenbach Foundation, Inc—RSF,
    USA, 543
Robert Schuman Foundation, France, 150
Roberto Longhi Foundation for the Study of the
    History of Art, Italy, 225
Rockefeller Brothers Fund, USA, 540
Roma Lom Foundation, Bulgaria, 76
Romanian Cultural Foundation, Romania, 317
Romanian Cultural Institute, Romania, 317
Romanian Donors' Forum, Romania, 316
The Ronald S. Lauder Foundation, Germany, 174
RONGEAD—Réseau d'ONG Européennes sur
    l'Agro-alimentaire, le Commerce,
    l'Environnement et le Développement,
    France, 135
Rosa Luxemburg Foundation, Germany, 174
Rosa-Luxemburg-Stiftung, Germany, 174
Rroma Foundation, Switzerland, 372
Rubinstein (Arthur) International Music Society,
    Israel, 215
Rural Development Foundation, Poland, 308
Ruralité Environnement Développement—RED,
    Belgium, 63
Rurality Environment Development, Belgium, 63
Sabre Foundation, Inc, USA, 542
SACO—Service d'assistance canadienne aux
    organismes, Canada, 83
SAIA—Slovak Academic Information Agency,
    Slovakia, 327
Saint Cyril and Saint Methodius International
    Foundation, Bulgaria, 76
Savings Banks Foundation for International
    Cooperation, Germany, 179
Schalkenbach (Robert) Foundation, Inc,
    USA, 543
Schools Without Frontiers, France, 139
Schuman (Robert), Fondation, France, 150
Schwarzkopf Foundation Young Europe,
    Germany, 178
Schwarzkopf Stiftung Junges Europa,
    Germany, 178
SCIAF—Scottish Catholic International Aid
    Fund, UK, 447
Scottish Catholic International Aid Fund—
    SCIAF, UK, 447
Seeds of Peace, USA, 543
SEEENN—South East European Environmental
    NGOs Network, Macedonia, 258
SEEMO—IPI—South East Europe Media
    Organisation, Austria, 49
Semmelweis Alapítvány Magyarországi
    Ortopédia Fejlesztéséért, Hungary, 195
Semmelweis Foundation for the Development of
    Orthopaedics in Hungary, Hungary, 195

Serafín Aliaga Foundation for Peace and
    Solidarity, Spain, 346
Sieć SPLOT, Poland, 306
Sieć Wspierania Organizacji Pozarządowych—
    SPLOT, Poland, 306
Sihtasutus Eesti Rahvuskultuuri Fond,
    Estonia, 129
Sivil Toplum Geliştirme Merkezi—STGM,
    Turkey, 387
Slovak Academic Information Agency–Service
    Center for the Third Sector—SAIA-SCTS,
    Slovakia, 327
Slovak-Czech Women's Fund, Czech Republic, 115
Slovak Donors' Forum—SDF, Slovakia, 328
Slovak Humanitarian Council, Slovakia, 328
Slovak NGDOs Platform, Slovakia, 327
Slovenian Science Foundation, Slovenia, 330
Slovenská Humanitná Rada, Slovakia, 328
Slunicko Foundation, Czech Republic, 114
SMART—Association for Civil Society
    Development, Croatia, 109
Software AG Foundation, Germany, 178
Solidarity National Commission—Economic
    Foundation, Poland, 307
Solidarność NSZZ—Economic Foundation,
    Poland, 307
Soros Foundation (Czech Republic), Czech
    Republic, 115
Soros Foundation (Slovakia), Slovakia, 328
Soros Foundation Macedonia, Macedonia, 258
Soros Foundation—Moldova, Moldova, 264
Soros Foundation Romania, Romania, 317
Soros Serbia Foundation, Serbia, 324
SOSNA Foundation, Slovakia, 329
South East Europe Media Organisation,
    Austria, 49
South East Europe Media Organisation—
    SEEMO—IPI, Austria, 49
South East European Environmental NGOs
    Network—SEEENN, Macedonia, 258
South-East Institute—Foundation for Academic
    Research into South-Eastern Europe,
    Germany, 182
Spaak (Paul-Henri), Fondation, Belgium, 61
Sparkassenstiftung für internationale
    Kooperation eV, Germany, 179
Springer (Axel) Stiftung, Germany, 179
Stefan Batory Foundation, Poland, 307
Stichting Spaak (Paul-Henri), Belgium, 61
Stichting Triodos Foundation, Netherlands, 282
Stiftelsen Riksbankens Jubileumsfond,
    Sweden, 357
Stiftung Europäisches Naturerbe—
    EURONATUR, Germany, 180
Stiftung FVS, Germany, 183
Stiftung Kinderdorf Pestalozzi, Switzerland, 374
Stiftung 'Leben für Alle', Switzerland, 375
Stiftung für wissenschaftliche
    Südosteuropaforschung—Südost-Institut,
    Germany, 182
Stowarzyszenie Klon/Jawor, Poland, 306
Sturzo (Luigi), Istituto, Italy, 227
Südost-Institut—Stiftung für wissenschaftliche
    Südosteuropaforschung, Germany, 182
Swiss Foundation for Technical Co-operation,
    Switzerland, 375
Swiss Interchurch Aid, Switzerland, 367
Swisscontact—Swiss Foundation for Technical
    Co-operation, Switzerland, 375
Terre des Hommes Foundation, Switzerland, 376
Third Sector Foundation of Turkey—TÜSEV,
    Turkey, 387
Thomson Foundation, UK, 451
Toepfer (Alfred) Stiftung, Germany, 183
Together Foundation, France, 143
Triodos Foundation, Netherlands, 282
Trócaire—Catholic Agency for World
    Development, Ireland, 213
Trust for Civil Society in Central and Eastern
    Europe, Bulgaria, 76
Trust for Mutual Understanding, USA, 549
Turkish Family Health and Planning
    Foundation, Turkey, 390
Turkish Foundation for Combating Soil Erosion,
    for Reforestation and the Protection of
    Natural Habitats, Turkey, 390
Türkiye Aile Sağlığı ve Planlaması Vakfı—TAPV,
    Turkey, 390
Türkiye Çevre Vakfi, Turkey, 390
Türkiye Erozyonla Mücadele Ağaçlandırma ve
    Doğal Varlıkları Koruma Vakfı—TEMA,
    Turkey, 390
Turriano (Juanelo) Fundación, Spain, 348
Uluslararası Mavi Hilal İnsani Yardım ve
    Kalkınma Vakfı, Turkey, 390
Umut Foundation, Turkey, 391
Umut Vakfi, Turkey, 391
UniCredit Foundation—Unidea, Italy, 228

Union of Bulgarian Foundations and
    Associations, Bulgaria, 74
University of Zaragoza Business Foundation,
    Spain, 342
Values Foundation, Bulgaria, 77
VIA Foundation, Czech Republic, 115
Victor Pinchuk Foundation, Ukraine, 394
Voluntary Service Overseas, UK, 454
VSO, UK, 454
Výbor dobré vule—Nadace Olgy Havlové, Czech
    Republic, 115
Vzdělávací nadace Jana Husa, Czech
    Republic, 116
Vzdelávacia nadácia Jana Husa, Slovakia, 329
Webb Memorial Trust, UK, 455
Welzijn Juliana Fonds, Netherlands, 278
Westminster Foundation for Democracy—WFD,
    UK, 455
Whirlpool Foundation, USA, 553
White Point Development Foundation,
    Turkey, 387
Winrock International, USA, 555
Wisti (Folmer) Foundation for International
    Understanding, Denmark, 122
Wladyslaw Poniecki Foundation, Inc, USA, 536
Woerner (Manfred) Foundation, Bulgaria, 74
World Association of Children's Friends,
    Monaco, 265
World Education, Inc, USA, 556
Zagranica Group, Poland, 305
Zavod Center za Informiranje, Sodelovanje in
    Razvoj Nevladnih Organizacije—CNVOS,
    Slovenia, 330
ZEIT-Stiftung Ebelin und Gerd Bucerius,
    Germany, 184

EAST AND SOUTH-EAST ASIA

A. M. M. Sahabdeen Trust Foundation, Sri
    Lanka, 350
AARDO—Afro-Asian Rural Development
    Organization, India, 199
ACCION International, USA, 460
ACCU—Asian Cultural Centre for UNESCO,
    Japan, 231
Acting for Life, France, 136
Action contre la Faim, France, 136
Action against Hunger, France, 136
Action Solidarité Tiers Monde—ASTM,
    Luxembourg, 257
Advantech Foundation, Taiwan, 379
AF—Association of Foundations,
    Philippines, 301
Afro-Asian Institute in Vienna, Austria, 46
Afro-Asian Rural Development Organization—
    AARDO, India, 199
Afro-Asiatisches Institut in Wien, Austria, 46
AFSC—American Friends Service Committee,
    USA, 465
Aga Khan Agency for Microfinance,
    Switzerland, 360
Agriculteurs Français et Développement
    International—AFDI, France, 136
Agromisa Foundation, Netherlands, 280
Agronomes et vétérinaires sans frontières—
    AVSF, France, 136
Aide et Action, France, 137
Aide Médicale Internationale, France, 137
Air France Corporate Foundation, France, 144
AIT—Asian Institute of Technology,
    Thailand, 383
AIV—Asia-Africa International Voluntary
    Foundation, Japan, 231
AJWS—American Jewish World Service,
    USA, 466
The Al-Khoei Benevolent Foundation, UK, 399
Alert—International Alert, UK, 422
Altman (Jenifer) Foundation, USA, 463
AMADE Mondiale—Association Mondiale des
    Amis de l'Enfance, Monaco, 265
American Friends Service Committee—AFSC,
    USA, 465
American Jewish World Service—AJWS,
    USA, 466
ANESVAD, Spain, 337
ANGOC—Asian NGO Coalition for Agrarian
    Reform and Rural Development,
    Philippines, 301
APACE Village First Electrification Group—
    APACE VFEG, Australia, 36
APAN—Asian Philanthropy Advisory Network,
    Philippines, 301
APHEDA—Union Aid Abroad, Australia, 45
APMN—Asia Pacific Mountain Network,
    Nepal, 271
Appropriate Technology for Community and
    Environment—APACE, Australia, 36

Arts Council Korea, Korea (Republic), 246
Asahi Beer Arts Foundation, Japan, 230
Asahi Biiru Geijutsu Bunka Zaidan, Japan, 230
ASEAN Foundation, Indonesia, 207
Ashden Charitable Trust, UK, 402
Asia-Africa International Voluntary
 Foundation—AIV, Japan, 231
Asia Foundation, USA, 469
Asia/Pacific Cultural Centre for UNESCO—
 ACCU, Japan, 231
Asia Pacific Foundation of Canada, Canada, 81
Asia-Pacific Mountain Network—APMN,
 Nepal, 271
Asia Society, USA, 470
Asian Community Trust—ACT, Japan, 231
Asian Cultural Council—ACC, USA, 470
Asian Health Institute—AHI, Japan, 231
Asian Institute for Rural Development,
 India, 200
Asian NGO Coalition for Agrarian Reform and
 Rural Development—ANGOC,
 Philippines, 301
Asian Philanthropy Advisory Network—APAN,
 Philippines, 301
Asian Youth Center, USA, 470
Aspen Institute, USA, 470
Association Mondiale des Amis de l'Enfance,
 Monaco, 265
ASTM—Action Solidarité Tiers Monde,
 Luxembourg, 257
Atlantic Philanthropies, USA, 471
Australia-Japan Foundation, Australia, 37
Australian People Health Education,
 Australia, 45
Australian Volunteers International,
 Australia, 39
AVRDC—The World Vegetable Center,
 Taiwan, 379
AWHRC—Asian Women's Human Rights
 Council, India, 200
Ayala Foundation, Inc—AFI, Philippines, 301
Ayala Foundation USA—AF-USA, USA, 535
The Batchworth Trust, UK, 403
BBC World Service Trust, UK, 403
The Beautiful Foundation, Korea (Republic), 246
Bell (Max) Foundation, Canada, 81
Bettencourt Schueller Foundation, France, 141
BID-INTAL—Instituto para la Integración de
 America Latina y el Caribe, Argentina, 34
Blue Moon Fund, Inc, USA, 473
Book Aid International—BAI, UK, 405
Bóthar, Ireland, 210
Bread for the World, Germany, 163
Bridge to Asia—BTA, USA, 473
Bridge Asia Japan—BAJ, Japan, 232
Bridges for Education, Inc—BFE, USA, 473
British Schools and Universities Foundation,
 Inc—BSUF, USA, 473
Brot für die Welt, Germany, 163
Brother's Brother Foundation, USA, 474
Buck (Pearl S. Buck) International, USA, 474
Butler (J. Homer) Foundation, USA, 504
Canadian Catholic Organization for Development
 and Peace, Canada, 83
Canadian Centre for International Studies and
 Co-operation/Centre d'études et de
 coopération internationale—CECI,
 Canada, 83
Canadian Executive Service Organization—
 CESO/Service d'assistance canadienne aux
 organismes—SACO, Canada, 83
Canadian Foodgrains Bank, Canada, 84
Canadian Hunger Foundation, Canada, 84
Canon Foundation in Europe, Netherlands, 272
CARE International—CI, Switzerland, 361
The Carter Center, USA, 476
Cartier Foundation for Contemporary Art,
 France, 141
Catholic Agency for World Development—
 Trócaire, Ireland, 213
CCF—Christian Children's Fund, USA, 478
CECHE—Center for Communications, Health
 and the Environment, USA, 477
CECI—Canadian Centre for International
 Studies and Co-operation/Centre d'études et
 de coopération internationale, Canada, 83
CenDHRRA—Center for the Development of
 Human Resources in Rural Asia,
 Philippines, 302
Center for Communications, Health and the
 Environment—CECHE, USA, 477
Center for Cultural and Technical Interchange
 between East and West—East-West Center,
 USA, 487
Center for the Development of Human Resources
 in Rural Asia—CenDHRRA, Philippines, 302

Centre International de Coopération pour le
 Développement Agricole—CICDA,
 France, 136
Centro Internacional de Agricultura Tropical—
 CIAT, Colombia, 104
CESO—Canadian Executive Service
 Organization, Canada, 83
CFI—Consuelo Foundation, Inc, USA, 482
CFPA—China Foundation for Poverty
 Alleviation, China (People's Republic), 102
CGP—Japan Foundation Centre Global
 Partnership, Japan, 236
Chandana Art Foundation International,
 India, 200
Charity Projects, UK, 411
Chia Hsin Foundation, Taiwan, 379
ChildFund International, USA, 478
ChildFund Korea, Korea (Republic), 246
ChildHope Asia Philippines, Inc, Philippines, 302
Children International—CI, USA, 479
Children of the Mekong, France, 139
Children and Sharing, France, 139
Children's Foundation of China, China (People's
 Republic), 102
China Environmental Protection Foundation,
 China (People's Republic), 102
China Foundation Center, China (People's
 Republic), 102
China Foundation for Poverty Alleviation—
 CFPA, China (People's Republic), 102
China Medical Board, USA, 479
China NPO Network, China (People's
 Republic), 102
China Soong Ching Ling Foundation, China
 (People's Republic), 102
China Youth Development Foundation, China
 (People's Republic), 103
Chr. Michelsen Institute—CMI, Norway, 291
CIAT—Centro Internacional de Agricultura
 Tropical, Colombia, 104
Claiborne (Liz) and Ortenberg (Art) Foundation,
 USA, 480
Climate Cent Foundation, Switzerland, 375
Clovek v tisni—spolecnost pri Ceske televizi,
 o.p.s., Czech Republic, 113
Club 2/3, Canada, 85
CMI—Chr. Michelsens Institutt, Norway, 291
Co-operation Committee for Cambodia,
 Cambodia, 79
Co-operation for the Promotion and Development
 of Welfare Activities, Spain, 342
Comic Relief, UK, 411
Commonwealth Foundation, UK, 411
Communication Foundation for Asia,
 Philippines, 302
Community Aid Abroad—Oxfam Australia,
 Australia, 43
Concern Universal, UK, 412
Consuelo Foundation, Inc—CFI, USA, 482
CPCS—Center for Philanthropy and Civil
 Society, Thailand, 383
The Craig and Susan McCaw Foundation,
 USA, 520
CRDF Global, USA, 483
Credit Union Foundation Australia—CUFA,
 Australia, 40
Croucher Foundation, Hong Kong, 194
CUFA—Credit Union Foundation Australia,
 Australia, 40
Cultural Center of the Philippines—CCP,
 Philippines, 302
CUSO-VSO, Canada, 86
Czech TV Foundation, Czech Republic, 113
Daiwa Anglo-Japanese Foundation, UK, 413
Damien Foundation, Belgium, 58
Defense of Green Earth Foundation—DGEF,
 Japan, 232
Demokratikus Átalakulásért Intézet,
 Hungary, 196
Deutsche Gesellschaft für Auswärtige Politik—
 DGAP, Germany, 164
Deutsche Stiftung für internationale rechtliche
 Zusammenarbeit eV, Germany, 165
DGEF—Defense of Green Earth Foundation,
 Japan, 232
Diakonia, Sweden, 352
Dian Desa Foundation, Indonesia, 207
DOEN Foundation, Netherlands, 280
Dom Manuel II Foundation, Portugal, 311
Don Bosco Foundation of Cambodia—DBFC,
 Cambodia, 79
Dreyfus Health Foundation—DHF, USA, 485
Earthrights International—ERI, USA, 486
East-West Center—EWC, USA, 487
EcoHealth Alliance, USA, 487
Écoles Sans Frontières—ESF, France, 139
ECOLOGIA—Ecologists Linked for Organizing
 Grassroots Initiatives and Action, USA, 488

Ecologists Linked for Organizing Grassroots
 Initiatives and Action—ECOLOGIA,
 USA, 488
The Education for Development Foundation—
 EDF, Thailand, 383
Else Kröner-Fresenius Foundation, Germany, 173
Else Kröner-Fresenius-Stiftung, Germany, 173
Empower Foundation, Thailand, 383
Enda Third World—Environment and
 Development Action in the Third World,
 Senegal, 322
Enda Tiers Monde—Environnement et
 Développement du Tiers-Monde, Senegal, 322
endPoverty.org, USA, 488
Enfance et Partage, France, 139
Enfants du Mekong, France, 139
Enterprise Development International, USA, 488
Entraide Protestante Suisse, Switzerland, 367
Environmental Justice Foundation—EJF,
 UK, 416
Environnement et Développement du Tiers-
 Monde—Enda, Senegal, 322
European NGOs on Agriculture, Food, Trade and
 Development, France, 135
The Evian Group at IMD, Switzerland, 363
EWC—East-West Center, USA, 487
The Family Federation of Finland, Finland, 133
Family Planning, New Zealand, 284
FARM Foundation— Foundation for World
 Agriculture and Rural Life, France, 145
FDH—Frères des Hommes, France, 152
Feed the Children, USA, 490
FH—Food for the Hungry, USA, 491
filia.die frauenstiftung, Germany, 168
filia—the Women's Foundation, Germany, 168
First Peoples Worldwide—FPW, USA, 490
Fondation Abri International, Canada, 97
Fondation pour l'Agriculture et la Ruralité dans
 le Monde—Fondation FARM, France, 145
Fondation Bettencourt-Schueller, France, 141
Fondation canadienne contre la faim, Canada, 84
Fondation Cartier pour l'Art Contemporain,
 France, 141
Fondation Ensemble, France, 143
Fondation d'Entreprise Air France, France, 144
Fondation d'Entreprise Renault, France, 144
Fondation contre la Faim, USA, 491
Fondation FARM—Fondation pour l'Agriculture
 et la Ruralité dans le Monde, France, 145
Fondation Franco-Japonaise Sasakawa,
 France, 145
Fondation Marguerite et Aimé Maeght,
 France, 147
Fondation Pro Victimis Genève, Switzerland, 365
Fondation Syngenta pour une Agriculture
 Durable, Switzerland, 376
Fondazione Ing. Carlo M. Lerici—FL, Italy, 222
Food for the Hungry—FH, USA, 491
FOPERDA—Fondation Royale Père Damien pour
 la Lutte Contre la Lèpre, Belgium, 58
Foundation for Children, Germany, 181
Foundation for Human Rights and Humanitarian
 Relief, Turkey, 389
Foundation Library Center of Japan, Japan, 230
Foundation 'Life for All', Switzerland, 375
Foundation to Promote Health,
 Liechtenstein, 255
Foundation for Sustainable Development,
 Spain, 348
Foundation of Village Community Development,
 Indonesia, 208
Foundation for Women, Thailand, 384
Franco-Japanese Sasakawa Foundation,
 France, 145
The Fred Hollows Foundation, Australia, 41
Freedom from Hunger, USA, 494
Freedom from Hunger Council of Ireland—
 Gorta, Ireland, 211
Freeman Foundation, USA, 494
Freeplay Foundation, UK, 429
French Agriculturalists and International
 Development, France, 136
Frères des Hommes—FDH, France, 152
Fundação Dom Manuel II, Portugal, 311
Fundação Oriente, Portugal, 311
Fundación CODESPA—Futuro en Marcha,
 Spain, 342
Fundación Desarrollo Sostenido—FUNDESO,
 Spain, 348
Fundación Intervida, Spain, 344
FUNDESO—Fundación Desarrollo Sostenido,
 Spain, 348
The Gaia Foundation, UK, 418
German Council on Foreign Relations,
 Germany, 164
German Foundation for International Legal Co-
 operation, Germany, 165
Gift of the Givers Foundation, South Africa, 332

Global Fund for Community Foundations—
GFCF, South Africa, 331
Global Voluntary Service—GVS, Japan, 232
Globe Foundation of Canada—GLOBE,
Canada, 89
Good Neighbors International, Korea
(Republic), 246
Gorta—Freedom from Hunger Council of
Ireland, Ireland, 211
Grameen Foundation—GF, USA, 499
Grassroots International—GRI, USA, 500
Great Britain Sasakawa Foundation, UK, 419
Haburas Foundation, Timor-Leste, 386
HALO Trust, UK, 419
Haribon Foundation, Philippines, 302
Haribon Foundation for the Conservation of
Natural Resources, Inc, Philippines, 302
Havelaar (Max) Foundation, Netherlands, 281
Health Action International, Netherlands, 275
Health Volunteers Overseas—HVO, USA, 501
Hedwig and Robert Samuel Foundation,
Germany, 177
Hedwig und Robert Samuel-Stiftung,
Germany, 177
Heifer International, USA, 502
HEKS—Hilfswerk Evangelischen Kirchen
Schweiz, Switzerland, 367
HELP International, USA, 503
Helvetas Swiss Intercooperation,
Switzerland, 367
HER Fund, Hong Kong, 194
Hilden Charitable Fund, UK, 421
Hilfswerk der Evangelischen Kirchen Schweiz—
HEKS, Switzerland, 367
Himalaya Foundation, Taiwan, 379
The Hitachi Scholarship Foundation, Japan, 232
HIVOS—Humanistisch Institut voor
Ontwikkelings Samenwerking,
Netherlands, 275
Hollows (Fred) Foundation, Australia, 41
Holt International, USA, 504
Holt International Children's Services—HICS,
USA, 504
Hong Kong Society for the Blind, Hong Kong, 194
Humanistic Institute for Co-operation with
Developing Countries, Netherlands, 275
Humanistisch Instituut voor Ontwikkelings
Samenwerking—HIVOS, Netherlands, 275
Humanitarian Relief Foundation, Turkey, 389
IACD—Institute of Asian Culture and
Development, Korea (Republic), 246
IBON Foundation, Philippines, 303
ICLARM—The WorldFish Center, Malaysia, 260
IFAD—International Fund for Agricultural
Development, Italy, 226
IFHD—International Foundation for Human
Development, India, 203
IHCF—Stiftung zur Förderung der Gesundheit,
Liechtenstein, 255
IKEA Foundation, Netherlands, 275
Impact First International, Canada, 89
Indonesia Biodiversity Foundation,
Indonesia, 208
Indonesian Forum for the Environment—Friends
of the Earth Indonesia, Indonesia, 207
Indonesian Foundation for Rural Progress,
Indonesia, 207
Indonesian Prosperity Foundation,
Indonesia, 208
INFID—International NGO Forum on
Indonesian Development, Indonesia, 207
Ing. Carlo M. Lerici Foundation, Italy, 222
INHURED International—International
Institute for Human Rights, Environment and
Development, Nepal, 271
İnsan Hak ve Hürriyetleri İnsani Yardım Vakfı,
Turkey, 389
Institut international des Droits de l'Enfant,
Switzerland, 368
Institut Nord-Sud, Canada, 95
Institute of Asian Culture and Development—
IACD, Korea (Republic), 246
Institute for Development Research, USA, 556
Institute for Latin American and Caribbean
Integration, Argentina, 34
Instituto para la Integración de América Latina y
el Caribe—BID-INTAL, Argentina, 34
Integrated Rural Development Foundation,
Philippines, 303
Inter Pares, Canada, 90
International Alert—Alert, UK, 422
International Centre for Democratic
Transition—ICDT, Hungary, 196
International Centre for the Legal Protection of
Human Rights—Interights, UK, 423
International Centre for Living Aquatic
Resources—ICLARM, Malaysia, 260

International Centre for Tropical Agriculture,
Colombia, 104
International Development and Relief
Foundation, Canada, 91
International Executive Service Corps— IESC,
USA, 508
The International Foundation, USA, 508
International Foundation for Human
Development—IFHD, India, 203
International Fund for Agricultural
Development—IFAD, Italy, 226
International Institute for Environment and
Development—IIED, UK, 423
International Institute for Human Rights,
Environment and Development—INHURED
International, Nepal, 271
International Institute for the Rights of the
Child, Switzerland, 368
International Institute of Rural
Reconstruction—IIRR, Philippines, 303
International NGO Forum on Indonesian
Development—INFID, Indonesia, 207
International Refugee Trust—IRT, UK, 424
International Relief and Development—IRD,
USA, 510
International Relief Teams, USA, 510
International Research & Exchanges Board—
IREX, USA, 511
International Water Management Institute—
IWMI, Sri Lanka, 350
International Women's Health Coalition—IWHC,
USA, 510
Intervida Foundation, Spain, 344
IREX—International Research & Exchanges
Board, USA, 511
Ishizaka Foundation, Japan, 234
Isis Internacional, Chile, 100
Isis International, Chile, 100
Islamic Relief Worldwide, UK, 425
Iwatani Naoji Foundation, Japan, 235
J. Homer Butler Foundation, Inc, USA, 504
JACO—Japan Association of Charitable
Organizations, Japan, 230
JANIC—Japanese NGO Center for International
Co-operation, Japan, 230
Japan Association of Charitable Organizations—
JACO, Japan, 230
Japan Foundation Center, Japan, 230
The Japan Foundation Centre for Global
Partnership—CGP, Japan, 236
Japan Heart Foundation, Japan, 236
Japan International Volunteer Center—JVC,
Japan, 236
Japanese-German Center Berlin, Germany, 173
Japanisch-Deutsches Zentrum Berlin,
Germany, 173
JCIE—Japan Center for International Exchange,
Japan, 236
JEN, Japan, 237
Jenifer Altman Foundation—JAF, USA, 463
JIIA—Japan Institute of International Affairs,
Japan, 237
Jones (W. Alton) Foundation, USA, 473
Kajima Foundation, Japan, 237
Karl Kübel Foundation for Child and Family,
Germany, 174
Karl-Kübel-Stiftung für Kind und Familie,
Germany, 174
KEHATI—Yayasan Keanekaragaman Hayati
Indonesia, Indonesia, 208
Keidanren Ishizaka Memorial Foundation,
Japan, 234
Kerzner Marine Foundation—KMF, USA, 515
Korean Culture and Arts Foundation, Korea
(Republic), 246
Kröner-Fresenius (Else) Stiftung, Germany, 173
Kübel (Karl) Stiftung für Kind und Familie,
Germany, 174
Lama Gangchen World Peace Foundation,
Italy, 227
Latin American, African and Asian Social
Housing Service, Chile, 101
Leprosy Mission International, UK, 428
Lerici (Ing. Carlo M.), Fondazione presso il
Politecnico di Milano, Italy, 222
Lifeline Energy, UK, 429
Lifewater International—LI, USA, 518
Liliane Foundation, Netherlands, 281
Liz Claiborne and Art Ortenberg Foundation,
USA, 480
The Long Now Foundation—LNF, USA, 519
Luxemburg (Rosa) Stiftung, Germany, 174
LWR—Lutheran World Relief, USA, 519
M-USA—Mercy-USA for Aid and Development,
USA, 524
McCaw (Craig and Susan) Foundation, USA, 520
McKnight Foundation, USA, 521

Maeght (Marguerite et Aimé), Fondation,
France, France, 147
Maison Franco-Japonaise, Japan, 237
Mama Cash, Netherlands, 277
Manfred Woerner Foundation, Bulgaria, 74
Mani Tese, Italy, 227
MAP International—Medical Assistance
Programs, USA, 522
March of Dimes, USA, 522
Marguerite and Aimé Maeght Foundation,
France, 147
Match International Centre, Canada, 93
Max Bell Foundation, Canada, 81
The Max Foundation, USA, 522
Max Havelaar Foundation, Netherlands, 281
medica mondiale e.V., Germany, 175
Medical Assistance Programs, USA, 522
Medical Emergency Relief International—
MERLIN, UK, 432
Mercy-USA for Aid and Development—M-USA,
USA, 524
MERLIN—Medical Emergency Relief
International, UK, 432
Moriya Foundation, Japan, 238
Muslim Aid, UK, 433
Mutual Aid and Liaison Service, France, 154
The Myer Foundation, Australia, 42
Naito Foundation, Japan, 238
The Nature Conservancy, USA, 528
Nederlandse Organisatie voor Internationale
Ontwikkelingssamenwerking—Stichting
NOVIB, Netherlands, 279
NFCR—National Foundation for Cancer
Research, USA, 529
Nihon Kokusai Mondai Kenkyusho, Japan, 237
Non-Governmental Organization JEN,
Japan, 237
North-South-Bridge Foundation, Germany, 181
North-South Institute/Institut Nord-Sud,
Canada, 95
NOVIB (Oxfam Netherlands), Netherlands, 279
The One Foundation, Ireland, 212
Operation Rainbow, Inc, USA, 530
Operation USA, USA, 530
Opportunity International USA, USA, 530
Organisation Afro-Asiatique Pour Le
Developpement Rural, India, 199
Orient Foundation, Portugal, 312
Outreach International, USA, 531
Oxfam Australia, Australia, 43
Oxfam Hong Kong, Hong Kong, 194
Oxfam New Zealand, New Zealand, 285
Oxfam NOVIB—Nederlandse Organisatie voor
Internationale Ontwikkelingssamenwerking,
Netherlands, 279
Oxfam NOVIB—Netherlands Organization for
International Development Co-operation,
Netherlands, 279
Oxfam-Québec, Canada, 95
PAN Asia and the Pacific—Pesticide Action
Network Asia and the Pacific, Malaysia, 260
The Parthenon Trust, Switzerland, 371
Partners in Rural Development, Canada, 84
Pathfinder International, USA, 533
PBI—Peace Brigades International, UK, 437
Peace Brigades International—PBI, UK, 437
Peace, Health and Human Development
Foundation—PHD Foundation, Japan, 239
Pearl S. Buck International, USA, 474
People in Need, Czech Republic, 113
People-to-People Health Foundation, Inc—
Project Hope, USA, 537
Pertubuhan Pertolongan Wanita, Malaysia, 260
Pestalozzi Children's Foundation,
Switzerland, 374
Pesticide Action Network Asia and the Pacific—
PAN AP, Malaysia, 260
The PHD Foundation—Peace, Health and Human
Development Foundation, Japan, 239
PhilDev—Philippine Development Foundation,
USA, 535
Philippine-American Educational Foundation—
PAEF, Philippines, 303
Philippine Development Foundation—PhilDev,
USA, 535
Philippine Foundation Center—PFC,
Philippines, 301
Plan Ireland, Ireland, 212
Ploughshares Fund, USA, 536
Population Council, USA, 536
Press Foundation of Asia—PFA, Philippines, 303
Prince Claus Fund for Culture and Development,
Netherlands, 279
Prins Claus Fonds Voor Cultuur en Ontwikkeling,
Netherlands, 279
Pro Victimis Foundation, Switzerland, 365
Project HOPE, USA, 537
Project Trust, UK, 439

Prudential Foundation, USA, 537
Rabobank Foundation, Netherlands, 279
Rainforest Foundation Norway, Norway, 293
Ramon Magsaysay Award Foundation, Philippines, 303
Ramsay Foundation, Switzerland, 372
Refugees International Japan—RIJ, Japan, 239
Regnskogfondet, Norway, 293
Relief International, USA, 539
Renault Foundation, France, 144
Réseau d'ONG Européennes sur l'Agro-alimentaire, le Commerce, l'Environnement et le Développement—RONGEAD, France, 135
Rhodes Trust, UK, 441
Robert Schalkenbach Foundation, Inc—RSF, USA, 543
Rockefeller Brothers Fund, USA, 540
Rohm Music Foundation, Japan, 239
RONGEAD—Réseau d'ONG Européennes sur l'Agro-alimentaire, le Commerce, l'Environnement et le Développement, France, 135
Rooftops Canada Foundation, Canada, 97
Rosa Luxemburg Foundation, Germany, 174
Rosa-Luxemburg-Stiftung, Germany, 174
Rowan Charitable Trust, UK, 441
Royal Asiatic Society of Great Britain and Ireland, UK, 443
Royal Society for the Protection of Birds—RSPB, UK, 445
RSPB—Royal Society for the Protection of Birds, UK, 445
The Rufford Foundation, UK, 445
Rufford Maurice Laing Foundation, UK, 445
Rutgers WPF, Netherlands, 279
Sabre Foundation, Inc, USA, 542
SACO—Service d'assistance canadienne aux organismes, Canada, 83
Sahabdeen (A. M. M.) Trust Foundation, Sri Lanka, 350
Samuel (Hedwig und Robert) Stiftung, Germany, 177
Sasakawa, Fondation Franco-Japonaise, France, 145
Savings Banks Foundation for International Cooperation, Germany, 179
Schalkenbach (Robert) Foundation, Inc, USA, 543
Schools Without Frontiers, France, 139
Schweisfurth Foundation, Germany, 178
Schweisfurth-Stiftung, Germany, 178
SCIAF—Scottish Catholic International Aid Fund, UK, 447
Science and Technology Facilities Council—STFC, UK, 447
Scottish Catholic International Aid Fund—SCIAF, UK, 447
SEL—Service d'Entraide et de Liaison, France, 154
SELAVIP International—Service de Promotion de l'Habitation Populaire en Amérique Latine, Afrique et Asie, Chile, 101
Sem Pringpuangkeo Foundation, Thailand, 384
Seoam Scholarship Foundation, Korea (Republic), 247
Service d'Entraide et de Liaison—SEL, France, 154
Seub Nakhasathien Foundation, Thailand, 384
Seva Foundation, USA, 544
Siam Society, Thailand, 384
Singapore International Foundation—SIF, Singapore, 326
Sino-British Fellowship Trust—SBFT, UK, 448
Solidarité, France, 155
Solidarity, France, 155
Song Qingling Foundation, China (People's Republic), 102
Sparkassenstiftung für internationale Kooperation eV, Germany, 179
St John Ambulance, UK, 446
Standing International Forum on Ethnic Conflict, Genocide and Human Rights—International Alert, UK, 422
Stichting Agromisa, Netherlands, 280
Stichting DOEN, Netherlands, 280
Stichting Liliane Fonds, Netherlands, 281
Stichting Max Havelaar, Netherlands, 281
Stiftelsen Riksbankens Jubileumsfond, Sweden, 357
Stiftung für Kinder, Germany, 181
Stiftung Kinderdorf Pestalozzi, Switzerland, 374
Stiftung Klimarappen, Switzerland, 375
Stiftung 'Leben für Alle', Switzerland, 375
Stiftung Nord-Süd-Brücken, Germany, 181
Stretched Hands, Italy, 227
Sweden-Japan Foundation—SJF, Sweden, 357

Swiss Foundation for Technical Co-operation, Switzerland, 375
Swiss Interchurch Aid, Switzerland, 367
SWISSAID Foundation, Switzerland, 375
Swisscontact—Swiss Foundation for Technical Co-operation, Switzerland, 375
Syin-Lu Social Welfare Foundation, Taiwan, 380
Synergos—The Synergos Institute, USA, 460
Syngenta Foundation for Sustainable Agriculture, Switzerland, 376
Syngenta Stiftung für Nachhaltige Landwirtschaft, Switzerland, 376
Taiwan Philanthropy Information Center, Taiwan, 379
TANZ—Trade Aid NZ Inc, New Zealand, 287
TEAR Australia, Australia, 45
Terre des Hommes Foundation, Switzerland, 376
Thairath Newspaper Foundation, Thailand, 385
Third World Network—TWN, Malaysia, 260
Third World Solidarity Action, Luxembourg, 257
Thomson Foundation, UK, 451
Tibet Fund, USA, 548
Tifa Foundation—Indonesia, Indonesia, 207
Tindall Foundation, New Zealand, 286
TISCO Foundation, Thailand, 385
Together Foundation, France, 143
Tokyu Foundation for Inbound Students, Japan, 240
The Toyota Foundation, Japan, 240
Toyota Vietnam Foundation—TVF, Viet Nam, 565
Trade Aid NZ Inc—TANZ, New Zealand, 287
Trócaire—Catholic Agency for World Development, Ireland, 213
TTF—Toyota Thailand Foundation, Thailand, 385
Unilever Vietnam Foundation—UVF, Viet Nam, 565
Union Aid Abroad—APHEDA, Australia, 45
United Service Committee of Canada, Canada, 98
United Society for the Propagation of the Gospel—USPG, UK, 453
United States-Japan Foundation, USA, 550
Unity Foundation, Luxembourg, 257
USC Canada, Canada, 98
Väestöliitto, Finland, 133
Villar Foundation, Inc., Philippines, 304
Voluntary Service Overseas, UK, 454
Volunteer Service Abroad—VSA, New Zealand, 287
VSA—Volunteer Service Abroad, New Zealand, 287
VSO, UK, 454
Wahana Lingkungan Hidup Indonesia—WALHI, Indonesia, 207
WALHI—Wahana Lingkungan Hidup Indonesia, Indonesia, 207
War on Want, UK, 454
Westminster Foundation for Democracy—WFD, UK, 455
Whirlpool Foundation, USA, 553
Wildlife Preservation Trust International, USA, 487
Wildlife Trust, USA, 487
Winrock International, USA, 555
Woerner (Manfred) Foundation, Bulgaria, 74
Women's Aid Organisation—WAO, Malaysia, 260
World Accord, Canada, 99
World Association of Children's Friends, Monaco, 265
World Education, Inc, USA, 556
World Land Trust—WLT, UK, 456
World Neighbors, USA, 557
World Peace Foundation—WPF, USA, 557
World Population Foundation, Netherlands, 279
World Teacher Trust, India, 206
The WorldFish Center, Malaysia, 260
YADESA—Yayasan Pengembangan Masyarakat Desa, Indonesia, 208
YASIKA—Yayasan Indonesia untuk Kemajuan Desa, Indonesia, 207
Yayasan Dian Desa, Indonesia, 207
Yayasan Indonesia Sejahtera, Indonesia, 208
Yayasan Indonesia untuk Kemajuan Desa (YASIKA), Indonesia, 207
Yayasan Keanekaragaman Hayati Indonesia—KEHATI, Indonesia, 208
Yayasan Pengembangan Masyarakat Desa—YADESA, Indonesia, 208
Youth for Development and Co-operation—YDC, Netherlands, 283
Zakat House, Kuwait, 249
Zero-Kap Foundation, Netherlands, 283
ZOA, Netherlands, 283
Zorig Foundation, Mongolia, 266
Zurich Community Trust, UK, 457
Zurich Financial Services (UKISA) Community Trust Ltd, UK, 457

EASTERN EUROPE AND THE REPUBLICS OF CENTRAL ASIA

A. G. Leventis Foundation, Cyprus, 111
Academy of European Law, Germany, 167
Action contre la Faim, France, 136
Action against Hunger, France, 136
ACTR/ACCELS—American Councils for International Education, USA, 464
Adriano Olivetti Foundation, Italy, 223
Aga Khan Agency for Microfinance, Switzerland, 360
Aga Khan Foundation—AKF, Switzerland, 360
Aga Khan Fund for Economic Development, Switzerland, 361
Agency for the Non-profit Sector, Czech Republic, 112
AGNES—Vzdělávací Organizace, Czech Republic, 112
Agronomes et vétérinaires sans frontières—AVSF, France, 136
AIIT—Ancient India and Iran Trust, UK, 400
Air France Corporate Foundation, France, 144
Åland Fund for the Future of the Baltic Sea, Finland, 131
Alert—International Alert, UK, 422
Allianz Cultural Foundation, Germany, 160
Allianz Kulturstiftung, Germany, 160
AMADE Mondiale—Association Mondiale des Amis de l'Enfance, Monaco, 265
American Councils for International Education—ACTR/ACCELS, USA, 464
Ancient India and Iran Trust, UK, 400
Anne Çocuk Eğitim Vakfı—AÇEV, Turkey, 388
AREGAK—Sun/Soleil, Armenia, 35
Arthur Rubinstein International Music Society, Israel, 215
Aspen Institute, USA, 470
Assembly of Belarusian Pro-democratic Non-governmental Organizations, Belarus, 54
Association Mondiale des Amis de l'Enfance, Monaco, 265
Atlas Charity Foundation, Poland, 306
Auschwitz Foundation, Belgium, 60
AVRDC—The World Vegetable Center, Taiwan, 379
Baltic-American Partnership Fund—BAPF, USA, 472
Baltic Sea Foundation, Finland, 131
The Barretstown Camp Fund Ltd, Ireland, 210
BBC World Service Trust, UK, 403
Beatrice Laing Trust, UK, 428
Belarusian Charitable Fund 'For the Children of Chornobyl', Belarus, 54
Berghof Foundation for Conflict Research, Germany, 161
Berghof Stiftung für Konfliktforschung GmbH, Germany, 161
Bertelsmann Foundation, Germany, 162
Bertelsmann Stiftung, Germany, 162
Black Sea NGO Network—BSNN, Bulgaria, 75
Blue Moon Fund, Inc, USA, 473
Borderland Foundation, Poland, 307
BOTA Foundation, Kazakhstan, 243
Bóthar, Ireland, 210
Bread for the World, Germany, 163
Bridges for Education, Inc—BFE, USA, 473
Brot für die Welt, Germany, 163
Brother's Brother Foundation, USA, 474
CAF—Charities Aid Foundation, UK, 396
CAF Russia—Charities Aid Foundation Russia, Russian Federation, 318
Canadian Executive Service Organization—CESO/Service d'assistance canadienne aux organismes—SACO, Canada, 83
Canadian Foodgrains Bank, Canada, 84
CARE International—CI, Switzerland, 361
Carnegie Corporation of New York, USA, 475
Catholic Agency for World Development—Trócaire, Ireland, 213
Caucasus Institute for Peace, Democracy and Development—CIPDD, Georgia, 157
CCF—Christian Children's Fund, USA, 478
CCI—Center for Citizen Initiatives, USA, 476
CDCS—Centre for Development of Civil Society, Armenia, 35
CECHE—Center for Communications, Health and the Environment, USA, 477
Center for Citizen Initiatives—CCI, USA, 476
Center for Communications, Health and the Environment—CECHE, USA, 477
Central and Eastern European Media Centre Foundation, Poland, 307
Centre for the Development of Civil Society—CDCS, Armenia, 35
Centre International de Coopération pour le Développement Agricole—CICDA, France, 136

Centre for Philanthropy, Ukraine, 393
Centre for Training and Consultancy,
    Georgia, 157
Centrul Naţional de Asistenţă şi Informare a
    Organizaţiilor Neguvernamentale din
    Republica Moldova, Moldova, 264
CESO—Canadian Executive Service
    Organization, Canada, 83
Chandana Art Foundation International,
    India, 200
Charities Aid Foundation—CAF, UK, 396
Charity Projects, UK, 411
Charles and Lynn Schusterman Family
    Foundation—CLSFF, USA, 543
Charles Stewart Mott Foundation—CSMF,
    USA, 526
ChildFund International, USA, 478
Churches' Commission for Migrants in Europe,
    Belgium, 57
CIDOB Foundation, Spain, 338
Civil Society Support Centre, Georgia, 157
Claiborne (Liz) and Ortenberg (Art) Foundation,
    USA, 480
Clovek v tisni—spolecnost pri Ceske televizi,
    o.p.s., Czech Republic, 113
Comic Relief, UK, 411
Commission des Eglises auprès des Migrants en
    Europe/Kommission der Kirchen für
    Migranten in Europa, Belgium, 57
CONTACT—National Assistance and
    Information Centre for NGOs in Moldova,
    Moldova, 264
Costopoulos (J. F.) Foundation, Greece, 186
CRDF Global, USA, 483
CReDO—Resource Centre for the Human Rights
    NGOs of Moldova, Moldova, 264
Czech Donors Forum, Czech Republic, 112
Czech TV Foundation, Czech Republic, 113
The Danish Cultural Institute, Denmark, 117
Danish Outdoor Council, Denmark, 118
Danske Kulturinstitut, Denmark, 117
Demokratikus Átalakulásért Intézet,
    Hungary, 196
Deutsch-Russischer Austausch eV—DRA,
    Germany, 164
Deutsche Bank Foundation, Germany, 164
Deutsche Bank Stiftung, Germany, 164
Deutsche Gesellschaft für Auswärtige Politik—
    DGAP, Germany, 164
Deutsche Stiftung für internationale rechtliche
    Zusammenarbeit eV, Germany, 165
Development Foundation of Turkey, Turkey, 390
Diakonia, Sweden, 352
Diana, Princess of Wales Memorial Fund,
    UK, 414
Directory of Social Change, UK, 397
Dmitry Zimin Dynasty Foundation, Russian
    Federation, 319
Dr F. P. Haaz Social Assistance Foundation,
    Ukraine, 393
Dräger Foundation, Germany, 166
Dräger-Stiftung, Germany, 166
Dreyfus Health Foundation—DHF, USA, 485
Drug Policy Alliance—DPA, USA, 485
Ebelin and Gerd Bucerius ZEIT Foundation,
    Germany, 184
Eberhard Schöck Foundation, Germany, 178
Eberhard-Schöck-Stiftung, Germany, 178
Eça de Queiroz Foundation, Portugal, 312
ECOLOGIA—Ecologists Linked for Organizing
    Grassroots Initiatives and Action, USA, 488
Ecologists Linked for Organizing Grassroots
    Initiatives and Action—ECOLOGIA,
    USA, 488
Economic Development Foundation, Turkey, 388
ECPD—European Centre for Peace and
    Development, Serbia, 324
Ednannia: Initiative Centre to Support Social
    Action—ISAR Ednannia, Ukraine, 393
EDP Foundation, Portugal, 311
Eesti Mittetulundusühingute ja Sihtasutuste
    Liit, Estonia, 129
Eestimaa Looduse Fond—ELF, Estonia, 129
ELIAMEP—Hellenic Foundation for European
    and Foreign Policy, Greece, 187
Elizabeth Kostova Foundation for Creative
    Writing, Bulgaria, 76
Emile Chanoux Foundation—Institute for
    Federalist and Regionalist Studies, Italy, 218
Enda Third World—Environment and
    Development Action in the Third World,
    Senegal, 322
Enda Tiers Monde—Environnement et
    Développement du Tiers-Monde, Senegal, 322
endPoverty.org, USA, 488
Enterprise Development International, USA, 488
Entraide Protestante Suisse, Switzerland, 367
Environment Foundation of Turkey, Turkey, 390

Environmental Justice Foundation—EJF,
    UK, 416
Environnement et Développement du Tiers-
    Monde—Enda, Senegal, 322
ERA—Europäische Rechtsakademie,
    Germany, 167
Estonian Foundation Centre, Estonia, 129
Estonian Fund for Nature, Estonia, 129
Estonian National Culture Foundation,
    Estonia, 129
Eurasia Foundation, USA, 489
Europa Nostra, Netherlands, 273
Europäische Rechtsakademie—ERA,
    Germany, 167
European Anti-Poverty Network—EAPN,
    Belgium, 59
European Centre for Peace and Development—
    ECPD, Serbia, 324
European Centre for Social Welfare Policy and
    Research, Austria, 47
European Cultural Foundation—ECF,
    Netherlands, 273
European Environmental Bureau, Belgium, 59
European Federation of National Organizations
    Working with the Homeless, Belgium, 55
European Network of Foundations for Social
    Economy, Belgium, 56
European NGOs on Agriculture, Food, Trade and
    Development, France, 135
European Science Foundation, France, 144
European Venture Philanthropy Association—
    EVPA, Belgium, 55
European Youth For Action—EYFA,
    Netherlands, 273
European Youth Foundation—EYF, France, 151
Europese Culterele Stichting, Netherlands, 273
Eurostep—European Solidarity Towards Equal
    Participation of People, Belgium, 60
Evangelisches Studienwerk eV, Germany, 167
EVPA—European Venture Philanthropy
    Association, Belgium, 55
EYFA—European Youth For Action,
    Netherlands, 273
The Family Federation of Finland, Finland, 133
FARM Foundation— Foundation for World
    Agriculture and Rural Life, France, 145
FEANTSA—Fédération Européenne des
    Associations Nationales Travaillant avec les
    Sans-Abri, Belgium, 55
The Federal Trust for Education and Research,
    UK, 416
Fédération Européenne des Associations
    Nationales Travaillant avec les Sans-Abri—
    FEANTSA, Belgium, 55
Fernand Lazard Foundation, Belgium, 63
Fernand Lazard Stichting, Belgium, 63
filia.die frauenstiftung, Germany, 168
filia—the Women's Foundation, Germany, 168
FINCA International, USA, 490
Firefly, Inc., USA, 490
Fondation pour l'Agriculture et la Ruralité dans
    le Monde—Fondation FARM, France, 145
Fondation Auschwitz, Belgium, 60
Fondation Emile Chanoux—Institut d'Etudes
    Fédéralistes et Régionalistes, Italy, 218
Fondation d'Entreprise Air France, France, 144
Fondation d'Entreprise Renault, France, 144
Fondation Européenne de la Culture/Europese
    Culturele Stichting, Netherlands, 273
Fondation Européenne de la Science, France, 144
Fondation FARM—Fondation pour l'Agriculture
    et la Ruralité dans le Monde, France, 145
Fondation Marcel Hicter, Belgium, 61
Fondation Marguerite et Aimé Maeght,
    France, 147
Fondation Pro Victimis Genève, Switzerland, 365
Fondation Robert Schuman, France, 150
Fondazione Adriano Olivetti, Italy, 223
Fondazione Prada, Italy, 224
Fonds Européen pour la Jeunesse—FEJ,
    France, 151
Foundation for Human Rights and Humanitarian
    Relief, Turkey, 389
Foundation for International Community
    Assistance, USA, 490
Foundation 'Life for All', Switzerland, 375
Foundation for Russian-American Economic Co-
    operation—FRAEC, USA, 493
Foundation in Support of Local Democracy,
    Poland, 308
Friluftsraadet, Denmark, 118
FSLD—Foundation in Support of Local
    Democracy, Poland, 308
Fundação Eça de Queiroz, Portugal, 312
Fundação EDP, Portugal, 311
Fundació CIDOB, Spain, 338
Fundación Paideia Galiza, Spain, 346
Fundacja Centrum Prasowe, Poland, 307

Fundacja Pogranicze, Poland, 307
Fundacja Rozwoju Demokracji Loaklnej,
    Poland, 308
German Council on Foreign Relations,
    Germany, 164
German Foundation for International Legal Co-
    operation, Germany, 165
German-Russian Exchange, Germany, 164
Gift of the Givers Foundation, South Africa, 332
Gilman (Howard) Foundation, USA, 496
Glasnost Defence Foundation—GDF, Russian
    Federation, 319
Global Fund for Community Foundations—
    GFCF, South Africa, 331
Globe Foundation of Canada—GLOBE,
    Canada, 89
GURT Resource Centre for NGO Development,
    Ukraine, 393
Haaz (Dr F. P.) Social Assistance Foundation,
    Ukraine, 393
HALO Trust, UK, 419
Harry and Jeanette Weinberg Foundation, Inc,
    USA, 552
Havelaar (Max) Foundation, Netherlands, 281
Health Action International, Netherlands, 275
For a Healthy Generation, Uzbekistan, 561
Heifer International, USA, 502
HEKS—Hilfswerk Evangelischen Kirchen
    Schweiz, Switzerland, 367
Hellenic Foundation for European and Foreign
    Policy—ELIAMEP, Greece, 187
Helvetas Swiss Intercooperation,
    Switzerland, 367
Heydar Aliyev Foundation, Azerbaijan, 50
Hicter (Marcel), Fondation, Belgium, 61
Hilfswerk der Evangelischen Kirchen Schweiz—
    HEKS, Switzerland, 367
Horizonti, the Foundation for the Third Sector,
    Georgia, 157
House of Europe Cultural Foundation,
    Germany, 174
Howard Gilman Foundation, Inc, USA, 496
Howard Karagheusian Commemorative
    Corporation—HKCC, USA, 513
Human Resource Development Foundation,
    Turkey, 389
Humanitarian Relief Foundation, Turkey, 389
Hungarian Interchurch Aid—HIA, Hungary, 196
IACD—Institute of Asian Culture and
    Development, Korea (Republic), 246
IDC—Innovation and Development Centre,
    Ukraine, 393
IEIAS—Institut Européen Interuniversitaire de
    l'Action Sociale, Belgium, 62
IKGV—İnsan Kaynağını Geliştirme Vakfı,
    Turkey, 389
İktisadi Kalkınma Vakfı, Turkey, 388
Information Society of Ukraine Foundation,
    Ukraine, 394
Innovation and Development Centre—IDC,
    Ukraine, 393
İnsan Hak ve Hürriyetleri İnsani Yardım Vakfı,
    Turkey, 389
İnsan Kaynağını Geliştirme Vakfı—IKGV,
    Turkey, 389
Institut für Agrarentwicklung in Mittel- und
    Osteuropa—IAMO, Germany, 171
Institut Européen Interuniversitaire de l'Action
    Sociale—IEIAS, Belgium, 62
Institut international des Droits de l'Enfant,
    Switzerland, 368
Institute for Agricultural Development in
    Central and Eastern Europe, Germany, 171
Institute of Asian Culture and Development—
    IACD, Korea (Republic), 246
Institute for Development Research, USA, 556
Institute for European Environmental Policy—
    IEEP, UK, 422
International Alert—Alert, UK, 422
International Bank of Ideas, Russian
    Federation, 318
International Blue Crescent Relief and
    Development Foundation—IBC, Turkey, 390
International Centre for Democratic
    Transition—ICDT, Hungary, 196
International Centre for the Legal Protection of
    Human Rights—Interights, UK, 423
International Charitable Fund 'Ukraine 3000',
    Ukraine, 394
International Development and Relief
    Foundation, Canada, 91
International Environmental Foundation of the
    Kommunale Umwelt-AktioN UAN—IntEF-
    UAN, Germany, 172
International Executive Service Corps— IESC,
    USA, 508
International Institute for the Rights of the
    Child, Switzerland, 368

International Orthodox Christian Charities, Inc—IOCC, USA, 509
International Relief and Development—IRD, USA, 510
International Relief Teams, USA, 510
International Renaissance Foundation—IRF, Ukraine, 394
International Research & Exchanges Board—IREX, USA, 511
International Solidarity Foundation—ISF, Finland, 132
International Water Management Institute—IWMI, Sri Lanka, 350
IREX—International Research & Exchanges Board, USA, 511
ISAR: Resources for Environmental Activists, USA, 460
IUC-Europe International Education Centre, Denmark, 119
IUC-Europe Internationalt Uddanneless Center, Denmark, 119
The J. F. Costopoulos Foundation, Greece, 186
Japanese-German Center Berlin, Germany, 173
Japanisch-Deutsches Zentrum Berlin, Germany, 173
JEN, Japan, 237
Jewish Community Development Fund—JCDF, USA, 512
The John D. and Catherine T. MacArthur Foundation, USA, 520
Jones (W. Alton) Foundation, USA, 473
Kansainvälinen solidaarisuussäätiö, Finland, 132
Karagheusian (Howard) Commemorative Corporation, USA, 513
Kennan Institute, USA, 514
King Gustaf V 90th Birthday Foundation, Sweden, 354
Konung Gustaf V's 90-Årsfond, Sweden, 354
Kostova (Elizabeth) Foundation for Creative Writing, Bulgaria, 76
Kulturstiftung Haus Europa, Germany, 174
Kvinna till Kvinna Foundation, Sweden, 354
Laing (Beatrice) Trust, UK, 428
Lambrakis Foundation, Greece, 187
Lambrakis Research Foundation, Greece, 187
Latin American, African and Asian Social Housing Service, Chile, 101
Latvia Children's Fund, Latvia, 251
Latvijas Bērnu fonds, Latvia, 251
Lauder (Ronald S.) Foundation, Germany, 174
Leventis (A. G.) Foundation, Cyprus, 111
Littauer (Lucius N.) Foundation, Inc, USA, 519
Liz Claiborne and Art Ortenberg Foundation, USA, 480
Lucius N. Littauer Foundation, Inc, USA, 519
Luxembourg (Rosa) Stiftung, Germany, 174
LWR—Lutheran World Relief, USA, 519
MacArthur (John D. and Catherine T.) Foundation, USA, 520
The Mackintosh Foundation, UK, 430
Maecenata Management GmbH, Germany, 159
Maeght (Marguerite et Aimé), Fondation, France, France, 147
Magyar Ökumenikus Segélyszervezet, Hungary, 196
Maj and Tor Nessling Foundation, Finland, 132
Mama Cash, Netherlands, 277
Marangopoulos Foundation for Human Rights, Greece, 188
Marcel Hicter Foundation, Belgium, 61
Marguerite and Aimé Maeght Foundation, France, 147
Max Havelaar Foundation, Netherlands, 281
Medical Emergency Relief International—MERLIN, UK, 432
MERLIN—Medical Emergency Relief International, UK, 432
Michael Otto Foundation for Environmental Protection, Germany, 176
Michael-Otto-Stiftung für Umweltschutz, Germany, 176
Microfinance Centre—MFC, Poland, 309
Milieukontakt International, Netherlands, 277
Milieukontakt Oost-Europa, Netherlands, 277
Mongolian Women's Fund—MONES, Mongolia, 266
Mother Child Education Foundation, Turkey, 388
Mott (Charles Stewart) Foundation, USA, 526
Muslim Aid, UK, 433
National Assistance and Information Centre for NGOs in Moldova—CONTACT, Moldova, 264
National Conference on Soviet Jewry, USA, 528
National Youth Foundation, Greece, 188
NCSJ—National Conference on Soviet Jewry, USA, 528
Nederlandse Organisatie voor Internationale Ontwikkelingssamenwerking—Stichting NOVIB, Netherlands, 279

Nessling (Maj and Tor) Foundation, Finland, 132
Van Neste Foundation, UK, 453
Network of Estonian Non-profit Organizations, Estonia, 129
Network of Information and Support for Non-Governmental Organizations, Poland, 306
New Eurasia Foundation, Russian Federation, 319
New Perspectives Foundation, Russian Federation, 319
NGO Centre—NGOC, Armenia, 35
NGO Development Centre, Russian Federation, 318
NGO Development Centre/United Way–Belarus, Belarus, 54
Non-Governmental Ecological Vernadsky Foundation, Russian Federation, 320
Non-Governmental Organization JEN, Japan, 237
Norsk Utenrikspolitisk Institutt—NUPI, Norway, 292
Norwegian Institute of International Affairs—NUPI, Norway, 292
NOVIB (Oxfam Netherlands), Netherlands, 279
Olivetti (Adriano), Fondazione, Italy, Italy, 223
Open Estonia Foundation, Estonia, 129
Open Society Georgia Foundation, Georgia, 157
Open Society Institute—Assistance Foundation (Azerbaijan), Azerbaijan, 50
Open Society Institute Assistance Foundation, Armenia—OSIAFA, Armenia, 35
Open Society Institute Assistance Foundation—Tajikistan, Tajikistan, 381
Open Society Institute—Paris (Soros Foundations), France, 135
Operation USA, USA, 530
Opportunity International USA, USA, 530
OSGF—Open Society Georgia Foundation, Georgia, 157
OSIAF—Open Society Institute Assistance Foundation—Tajikistan, Tajikistan, 381
Otto (Michael) Stiftung, Germany, 176
Oxfam NOVIB—Nederlandse Organisatie voor Internationale Ontwikkelingssamenwerking, Netherlands, 279
Oxfam NOVIB—Netherlands Organization for International Development Co-operation, Netherlands, 279
Paavo Nurmen Säätiö, Finland, 132
Paavo Nurmi Foundation, Finland, 132
Paideia Galiza Foundation, Spain, 346
PAN Europe—Pesticides Action Network Europe, Germany, 176
Pan-European Federation for Cultural Heritage, Netherlands, 273
The Parthenon Trust, Switzerland, 371
People in Need, Czech Republic, 113
People-to-People Health Foundation, Inc—Project Hope, USA, 537
People's Harmonious Development Society, Georgia, 158
Pesticides Action Network Europe—PAN Europe, Germany, 176
Ploughshares Fund, USA, 536
Pôle européen des fondations de l'économie sociale, Belgium, 56
Poniecki (Wladyslaw) Foundation, Inc, USA, 536
Potanin (Vladimir) Foundation, Russian Federation, 320
Prada Foundation, Italy, 224
Pro Victimis Foundation, Switzerland, 365
Project HOPE, USA, 537
Protestant Study Foundation, Germany, 167
Ramsay Foundation, Switzerland, 372
RED—Ruralité-environnement-développement, Belgium, Belgium, 63
Refugees International Japan—RIJ, Japan, 239
Regional Environmental Center for Central and Eastern Europe—REC, Hungary, 196
Relief International, USA, 539
Renault Foundation, France, 144
Réseau d'ONG Européennes sur l'Agro-alimentaire, le Commerce, l'Environnement et le Développement—RONGEAD, France, 135
Resource Centre for the Human Rights Nongovernmental Organizations of Moldova—CReDO, Moldova, 264
Rhodes Trust, UK, 441
Robert Schalkenbach Foundation, Inc—RSF, USA, 543
Robert Schuman Foundation, France, 150
Rockefeller Brothers Fund, USA, 540
Rockwool Fonden, Denmark, 121
Rockwool Foundation, Denmark, 121
The Ronald S. Lauder Foundation, Germany, 174
RONGEAD—Réseau d'ONG Européennes sur l'Agro-alimentaire, le Commerce,

l'Environnement et le Développement, France, 135
Rosa Luxemburg Foundation, Germany, 174
Rosa-Luxemburg-Stiftung, Germany, 174
Rroma Foundation, Switzerland, 372
Rubinstein (Arthur) International Music Society, Israel, 215
Ruralité Environnement Développement—RED, Belgium, 63
Rurality Environment Development, Belgium, 63
Russian Cultural Foundation, Russian Federation, 320
Russian Donors Forum, Russian Federation, 318
Sabre Foundation, Inc, USA, 542
SACO—Service d'assistance canadienne aux organismes, Canada, 83
Savings Banks Foundation for International Cooperation, Germany, 179
Schalkenbach (Robert) Foundation, Inc, USA, 543
Schuman (Robert), Fondation, France, 150
Schusterman (Charles and Lynn) Family Foundation, USA, 543
Schwarzkopf Foundation Young Europe, Germany, 178
Schwarzkopf Stiftung Junges Europa, Germany, 178
SCIAF—Scottish Catholic International Aid Fund, UK, 447
Scottish Catholic International Aid Fund—SCIAF, UK, 447
Seeds of Peace, USA, 543
SELAVIP International—Service de Promotion de l'Habitation Populaire en Amérique Latine, Afrique et Asie, Chile, 101
Semmelweis Alapítvány Magyarországi Ortopédia Fejlesztéséért, Hungary, 195
Semmelweis Foundation for the Development of Orthopaedics in Hungary, Hungary, 195
Sieć SPLOT, Poland, 306
Sieć Wspierania Organizacji Pozarządowych—SPLOT, Poland, 306
Sihtasutus Eesti Rahvuskultuuri Fond, Estonia, 129
Snow Leopard Trust, USA, 545
Sobell Foundation, UK, 449
Sog'lom Avlod Uchun, Uzbekistan, 561
Solidarité, France, 155
Solidarity, France, 155
Soros Foundation (Estonia), Estonia, 129
Soros Foundation (Georgia), Georgia, 157
Soros Foundation (Tajikistan), Tajikistan, 381
Soros Foundation—Kazakhstan, Kazakhstan, 243
Soros Foundation–Kyrgyzstan, Kyrgyzstan, 250
Soros Foundation Latvia, Latvia, 251
SOTA—Research Centre for Turkestan and Azerbaijan, Netherlands, 280
Sparkassenstiftung für internationale Kooperation eV, Germany, 179
Standing International Forum on Ethnic Conflict, Genocide and Human Rights—International Alert, UK, 422
Stichting Max Havelaar, Netherlands, 281
Stiftelsen Riksbankens Jubileumsfond, Sweden, 357
Stiftung 'Leben für Alle', Switzerland, 375
Stiftung West-Östliche Begegnungen, Germany, 182
Street Kids International, Canada, 98
Sun/Soleil—AREGAK, Armenia, 35
Support Centre for Associations and Foundations—SCAF, Belarus, 54
Swedish Institute at Athens, Greece, 189
Swiss Foundation for Technical Co-operation, Switzerland, 375
Swiss Interchurch Aid, Switzerland, 367
Swisscontact—Swiss Foundation for Technical Co-operation, Switzerland, 375
Taiga Rescue Network—TRN, Finland, 133
Terre des Hommes Foundation, Switzerland, 376
TRN—Taiga Rescue Network, Finland, 133
Trócaire—Catholic Agency for World Development, Ireland, 213
Trust for Civil Society in Central and Eastern Europe, Poland, 306
Trust for Mutual Understanding, USA, 549
Türkiye Çevre Vakfı, Turkey, 390
Türkiye Kalkınma Vakfı, Turkey, 390
Ukraine 3000, Ukraine, 394
Ukrainian Women's Fund, Ukraine, 394
Uluslararası Mavi Hilal İnsani Yardım ve Kalkınma Vakfı, Turkey, 390
Union of Charitable Organizations of Russia, Russian Federation, 318
United Way—Belarus/NGO Development Centre, Belarus, 54
US-Baltic Foundation—USBF, USA, 551

US-Ukraine Foundation, USA, 551
Väestöliitto, Finland, 133
Victoria Children Foundation, Russian
Federation, 320
The Vladimir Potanin Foundation, Russian
Federation, 320
Voluntary Service Overseas, UK, 454
VSO, UK, 454
Weinberg (Harry and Jeanette) Foundation,
USA, 552
Welfare Association, Switzerland, 376
West-East Foundation, Germany, 182
Westminster Foundation for Democracy—WFD,
UK, 455
Whirlpool Foundation, USA, 553
Winrock International, USA, 555
Wladyslaw Poniecki Foundation, Inc, USA, 536
World Association of Children's Friends,
Monaco, 265
World Education, Inc, USA, 556
World Land Trust—WLT, UK, 456
World Peace Foundation—WPF, USA, 557
Youth for Development and Co-operation—YDC,
Netherlands, 283
ZEIT-Stiftung Ebelin und Gerd Bucerius,
Germany, 184
Zimin (Dmitry) Dynasty Foundation, Russian
Federation, 319

MIDDLE EAST AND NORTH AFRICA

A. G. Leventis Foundation, Cyprus, 111
A. M. Qattan Foundation, UK, 440
AARDO—Afro-Asian Rural Development
Organization, India, 199
Abdul Hameed Shoman Foundation, Jordan, 242
Acting for Life, France, 136
Action Solidarité Tiers Monde—ASTM,
Luxembourg, 257
Africa Grantmakers' Affinity Group—AGAG,
USA, 458
African NGOs Environment Network—ANEN,
Kenya, 244
African Refugees Foundation—AREF,
Nigeria, 289
African Youth Network for Sustainable
Development, Algeria, 30
Africare, USA, 462
Afro-Asian Institute in Vienna, Austria, 46
Afro-Asian Rural Development Organization—
AARDO, India, 199
Afro-Asiatisches Institut in Wien, Austria, 46
AFSC—American Friends Service Committee,
USA, 465
AFTAAC—Arab Fund for Technical Assistance
to African Countries, Egypt, 127
Aga Khan Agency for Microfinance,
Switzerland, 360
AGAG—Africa Grantmakers' Affinity Group,
USA, 458
Aid for Development Club, Austria, 46
Aide Médicale Internationale, France, 137
Air France Corporate Foundation, France, 144
AISA—Africa Institute of South Africa, South
Africa, 332
The Al-Khoei Benevolent Foundation, UK, 399
Allianz Cultural Foundation, Germany, 160
Allianz Kulturstiftung, Germany, 160
AMADE Mondiale—Association Mondiale des
Amis de l'Enfance, Monaco, 265
America–Mideast Educational and Training
Services Inc, USA, 468
American Friends Service Committee—AFSC,
USA, 465
American Near East Refugee Aid—ANERA,
USA, 467
American Schools of Oriental Research—ASOR,
USA, 467
AMIDEAST—America-Mideast Educational and
Training Services, Inc, USA, 468
ANERA—American Near East Refugee Aid,
USA, 467
ANND—Arab NGO Network for Development,
Lebanon, 252
Anne Çocuk Eğitim Vakfı—AÇEV, Turkey, 388
AOHR—Arab Organization for Human Rights,
Egypt, 127
AOYE—Arab Office for Youth and Environment,
Egypt, 127
APHEDA—Union Aid Abroad, Australia, 45
The Arab-British Chamber Charitable
Foundation, UK, 401
Arab Fund for Technical Assistance to African
Countries—AFTAAC, Egypt, 127
Arab Image Foundation, Lebanon, 252
Arab Office for Youth and Environment—AOYE,
Egypt, 127

Arab Organization for Human Rights, Egypt, 127
Arab Thought Foundation, Lebanon, 252
Archie Sherman Charitable Trust, UK, 448
Arcus Foundation, USA, 469
AREF—African Refugees Foundation,
Nigeria, 289
ASMAE—Association de coopération et
d'éducation aux développements, Belgium, 56
ASOR—American Schools of Oriental Research,
USA, 467
Association de coopération et d'éducation aux
développements—ASMAE, Belgium, 56
Association for Development Co-operation and
Education, Belgium, 56
Association Égyptologique Reine Elisabeth,
Belgium, 57
Association Mondiale des Amis de l'Enfance,
Monaco, 265
ASTM—Action Solidarité Tiers Monde,
Luxembourg, 257
Australian People Health Education,
Australia, 45
Australian Volunteers International,
Australia, 39
AVRDC—The World Vegetable Center,
Taiwan, 379
Axel Springer Foundation, Germany, 179
Axel-Springer-Stiftung, Germany, 179
Aydın Doğan Foundation, Turkey, 388
Aydın Doğan Vakfı, Turkey, 388
Bank of Cyprus Cultural Foundation, Cyprus, 111
Barenboim-Said Foundation, Spain, 340
The Baron de Hirsch Fund, USA, 484
BBC World Service Trust, UK, 403
BibleLands, UK, 404
Boghossian Foundation, Belgium, 60
Borchardt (Ludwig) Stiftung, Switzerland, 361
Bóthar, Ireland, 210
Bread for the World, Germany, 163
British Institute at Ankara, UK, 406
Brot für die Welt, Germany, 163
Brother's Brother Foundation, USA, 474
Business Institute Foundation, Spain, 344
Cadbury (William Adlingon) Charitable Trust,
UK, 407
Canada Israel Cultural Foundation, Canada, 82
Canadian Catholic Organization for Development
and Peace, Canada, 83
Canadian Foodgrains Bank, Canada, 84
CARE International—CI, Switzerland, 361
Cariplo Foundation, Italy, 219
The Carter Center, USA, 476
Catholic Agency for World Development—
Trócaire, Ireland, 213
Center for Human Research and Social
Development—CHRSD, Palestinian
Autonomous Areas, 296
Centro de Investigación para la Paz, CIP—
FUHEM, Spain, 338
Çevre Koruma ve Ambalaj Atiklari
Degerlendirme Vakfı—CEVKO, Turkey, 388
Charity Projects, UK, 411
Charles and Lynn Schusterman Family
Foundation—CLSFF, USA, 543
Children in Africa Foundation, Germany, 181
Chr. Michelsen Institute—CMI, Norway, 291
Christos Stelios Ioannou Foundation, Cyprus, 111
CIMADE—Service Oecuménique d'Entraide,
France, 138
Cleveland H. Dodge Foundation, Inc, USA, 485
Climate Cent Foundation, Switzerland, 375
Clovek v tisni—spolecnost pri Ceske televizi,
o.p.s., Czech Republic, 113
CMI—Chr. Michelsens Institutt, Norway, 291
Co-operation for the Promotion and Development
of Welfare Activities, Spain, 342
Comic Relief, UK, 411
Commonwealth Foundation, UK, 411
Cooperazione Internazionale—COOPI, Italy, 217
COOPI—Cooperazione Internazionale, Italy, 217
CRDF Global, USA, 483
Czech TV Foundation, Czech Republic, 113
Damien Foundation, Belgium, 58
Davis (Lady) Fellowship Trust, Israel, 214
Demokratikus Atalakulásért Intézet,
Hungary, 196
Deutsche Orient-Stiftung, Germany, 165
Deutsche Stiftung für internationale rechtliche
Zusammenarbeit eV, Germany, 165
Diakonia, Sweden, 352
Dodge (Cleveland H.) Foundation, Inc, USA, 485
Doğan (Aydın) Vakfı, Turkey, 388
Dreyfus Health Foundation—DHF, USA, 485
Ebelin and Gerd Bucerius ZEIT Foundation,
Germany, 184
Ecumenical Service for Mutual Help, France, 138
The Edmond de Rothschild Foundations,
USA, 541

Eldee Foundation, Canada, 87
ELIAMEP—Hellenic Foundation for European
and Foreign Policy, Greece, 187
Emirates Foundation, United Arab Emirates, 395
EMUNAH, UK, 415
Enda Third World—Environment and
Development Action in the Third World,
Senegal, 322
Enda Tiers Monde—Environnement et
Développement du Tiers-Monde, Senegal, 322
endPoverty.org, USA, 488
Enfants Réfugiés du Monde—ERM, France, 140
Enterprise Development International, USA, 488
Entraide Protestante Suisse, Switzerland, 367
Entwicklungshilfe-Klub, Austria, 46
Environment Foundation of Turkey, Turkey, 390
Environmental Protection and Packaging Waste
Recovery and Recycling Trust, Turkey, 388
Environnement et Développement du Tiers-
Monde—Enda, Senegal, 322
ERM—Enfants Réfugiés du Monde, France, 140
EURONATUR—Stiftung Europäisches
Naturerbe, Germany, 180
European Mediterranean Institute, Spain, 349
European Nature Heritage Fund, Germany, 180
European Network of Foundations for Social
Economy, Belgium, 56
European NGOs on Agriculture, Food, Trade and
Development, France, 135
Eurostep—European Solidarity Towards Equal
Participation of People, Belgium, 60
The Evian Group at IMD, Switzerland, 363
Faith, UK, 415
Feed the Children, USA, 490
FH—Food for the Hungry, USA, 491
FINCA International, USA, 490
Fondation Abri International, Canada, 97
Fondation Arabe pour l'Image, Lebanon, 252
Fondation Boghossian, Belgium, 60
Fondation Ensemble, France, 143
Fondation d'Entreprise Air France, France, 144
Fondation contre la Faim, USA, 491
Fondation France-Israel, France, 145
Fondation Marguerite et Aimé Maeght,
France, 147
Fondation Méditerranéenne d'Etudes
Stratégiques—FMES, France, 147
Fondation Mo Ibrahim, UK, 421
Fondation Nicolas Hulot pour la Nature et
l'Homme, France, 146
Fondation Orient-Occident, Morocco, 268
Fondation Pro Victimis Genève, Switzerland, 365
Fondation René Seydoux pour le Monde
Méditerranéen, France, 150
Fondation du Roi Abdul-Aziz al-Saoud pour les
Etudes Islamiques et les Sciences Humaines,
Morocco, 268
Fondation Suisse-Liechtenstein pour les
Recherches Archéologiques à l'Etranger,
Switzerland, 373
Fondation Ushuaia, France, 146
Fondazione Cariplo, Italy, 219
Fondazione Cassa di Risparmio delle Provincie
Lombarde—Fondazione Cariplo, Italy, 219
Fondazione Roma-Mediterraneo, Italy, 224
Food for the Hungry—FH, USA, 491
FOPERDA—Fondation Royale Père Damien pour
la Lutte Contre la Lèpre, Belgium, 58
Foundation for Agricultural Research in the
Province of Almería, Spain, 344
Foundation for Human Rights and Humanitarian
Relief, Turkey, 389
Foundation for International Community
Assistance, USA, 490
Foundation for International Studies—FIS,
Malta, 261
Foundation 'Life for All', Switzerland, 375
Foundation for Middle East Peace—FMEP,
USA, 492
Foundation Nicolas Hulot for Nature and
Humankind, France, 146
Foundation for the Support of Women's Work,
Turkey, 389
France-Israel Foundation, France, 145
Freedom from Hunger, USA, 494
Fundación Barenboim-Said, Spain, 340
Fundación CODESPA—Futuro en Marcha,
Spain, 342
Fundación Instituto de Empresa, Spain, 344
Fundación para la Investigación Agraria de la
Provincia de Almería—FIAPA, Spain, 344
Fundación María Francisca de Roviralta,
Spain, 347
Fundación Paz y Solidaridad Serafín Aliaga—
FPyS, Spain, 346
The Gaia Foundation, UK, 418
George and Thelma Paraskevaides Foundation,
Cyprus, 111

German Foundation for International Legal Co-operation, Germany, 165
German Orient Foundation, Germany, 165
Gift of the Givers Foundation, South Africa, 332
Global Fund for Community Foundations—GFCF, South Africa, 331
Globe Foundation of Canada—GLOBE, Canada, 89
Goldsmith (Horace W.) Foundation, USA, 498
Grameen Foundation—GF, USA, 499
Grassroots International—GRI, USA, 500
Gruss (Joseph S. and Caroline) Life Monument Fund, Israel, 214
Gulf Research Center, United Arab Emirates, 395
Gulf Research Center Foundation, Switzerland, 367
Guttman Center of Applied Social Research, Israel, 214
Harold Hyam Wingate Foundation, UK, 456
Harry and Jeanette Weinberg Foundation, Inc, USA, 552
Heifer International, USA, 502
Heineman (Minna James) Stiftung, Germany, 170
HEKS—Hilfswerk Evangelischen Kirchen Schweiz, Switzerland, 367
Hellenic Foundation for Culture, Greece, 186
Hellenic Foundation for European and Foreign Policy—ELIAMEP, Greece, 187
Henrietta Szold Institute—National Institute for Research in the Behavioural Sciences, Israel, 215
Hilfswerk der Evangelischen Kirchen Schweiz—HEKS, Switzerland, 367
Hirsch (Baron de) Fund, USA, 484
Hisar Education Foundation—HEV, Turkey, 388
History Foundation of Turkey, Turkey, 389
HIVOS—Humanistisch Instituut voor Ontwikkelings Samenwerking, Netherlands, 275
Horace W. Goldsmith Foundation, USA, 498
Howard Karagheusian Commemorative Corporation—HKCC, USA, 513
Human Resource Development Foundation, Turkey, 389
Human Rights Foundation of Turkey, Turkey, 390
Humanistic Institute for Co-operation with Developing Countries, Netherlands, 275
Humanistisch Instituut voor Ontwikkelings Samenwerking—HIVOS, Netherlands, 275
Humanitarian Relief Foundation, Turkey, 389
IACD—Institute of Asian Culture and Development, Korea (Republic), 246
ICLARM—The WorldFish Center, Malaysia, 260
IEMed—Institut Europeu de la Mediterrània, Spain, 349
IFAD—International Fund for Agricultural Development, Italy, 226
IFHD—International Foundation for Human Development, India, 203
IKEA Foundation, Netherlands, 275
IKGV—İnsan Kaynağını Geliştirme Vakfı, Turkey, 389
İnsan Hak ve Hürriyetleri İnsani Yardım Vakfı, Turkey, 389
İnsan Kaynağını Geliştirme Vakfı—IKGV, Turkey, 389
Institut Català Mediterrània, Spain, 349
Institut Europeu de la Mediterrània—IEMed, Spain, 349
Institut Nord-Sud, Canada, 95
Institute of Asian Culture and Development—IACD, Korea (Republic), 246
Institute for Palestine Studies, Publishing and Research Organization—IPS, Lebanon, 252
International Blue Crescent Relief and Development Foundation—IBC, Turkey, 390
International Centre for Democratic Transition—ICDT, Hungary, 196
International Centre for Living Aquatic Resources—ICLARM, Malaysia, 260
International Co-operation, Italy, 217
International Development and Relief Foundation, Canada, 91
International Executive Service Corps—IESC, USA, 508
The International Foundation, USA, 508
International Foundation for Human Development—IFHD, India, 203
International Fund for Agricultural Development—IFAD, Italy, 226
International Orthodox Christian Charities, Inc—IOCC, USA, 509
International Refugee Trust—IRT, UK, 424
International Relief Teams, USA, 510
International Research & Exchanges Board—IREX, USA, 511
International Water Management Institute—IWMI, Sri Lanka, 350

International Women's Health Coalition—IWHC, USA, 510
Ioannou (Christos Stelios) Foundation, Cyprus, 111
IOMS—Islamic Organization for Medical Sciences, Kuwait, 249
IREX—International Research & Exchanges Board, USA, 511
Islamic Relief Worldwide, UK, 425
Islamic Thought Foundation, Iran, 209
Israel Institute Applied Social Research, Israel, 214
Japan International Volunteer Center—JVC, Japan, 236
JCA Charitable Foundation, UK, 425
JEN, Japan, 237
Jerusalem Foundation, Israel, 214
Jewish Agency for Israel Allocations Program, Israel, 214
Jewish Colonization Association, UK, 425
Jewish Philanthropic Association, UK, 452
JNF Charitable Trust—JNFCT, UK, 426
JOHUD—Jordanian Hashemite Fund for Human Development, Jordan, 241
Jordan River Foundation, Jordan, 241
Jordanian Hashemite Fund for Human Development, Jordan, 241
Joseph S. and Caroline Gruss Life Monument Fund, Israel, 214
Kadın Emeğini Değerlendirme Vakfı—KEDV, Turkey, 389
Karagheusian (Howard) Commemorative Corporation, USA, 513
Kerzner Marine Foundation—KMF, USA, 515
KFAS—Kuwait Foundation for the Advancement of Sciences, Kuwait, 249
KIEDF—Koret Israel Economic Development Funds, Israel, 214
Kinder in Afrika, Stiftung, Germany, 181
King Abdul-Aziz al-Saoud Foundation for Islamic Study and the Humanities, Morocco, 268
King Hussein Foundation—KHF, Jordan, 241
Koç (Vehbi), Vakfı, Turkey, 391
Koret Foundation, USA, 515
Koret Israel Economic Development Funds—KIEDF, Israel, 214
Kuwait Awqaf Public Foundation, Kuwait, 249
Kuwait Foundation for the Advancement of Sciences—KFAS, Kuwait, 249
Kuwait Institute for Scientific Research—KISR, Kuwait, 249
Kvinna till Kvinna Foundation, Sweden, 354
Lady Davis Fellowship Trust, Israel, 214
Latin American, African and Asian Social Housing Service, Chile, 101
Van Leer Jerusalem Institute, Israel, 215
Leprosy Mission International, UK, 428
Leventis (A. G.) Foundation, Cyprus, 111
Lifewater International—LI, USA, 518
Liliane Foundation, Netherlands, 281
Littauer (Lucius N.) Foundation, Inc, USA, 519
Lucius N. Littauer Foundation, Inc, USA, 519
Ludwig Borchardt Foundation, Switzerland, 361
Ludwig-Borchardt-Stiftung, Switzerland, 361
LWR—Lutheran World Relief, USA, 519
M-USA—Mercy-USA for Aid and Development, USA, 524
MADRE, USA, 521
Maeght (Marguerite et Aimé), Fondation, France, France, 147
Mama Cash, Netherlands, 277
The Mandela Rhodes Foundation, South Africa, 333
Manfred Woerner Foundation, Bulgaria, 74
Marangopoulos Foundation for Human Rights, Greece, 188
March of Dimes, USA, 522
Marguerite and Aimé Maeght Foundation, France, 147
María Francisca de Roviralta Foundation, Spain, 347
The Max Foundation, USA, 522
Mayfair Charities Ltd, UK, 430
medica mondiale e.V., Germany, 175
Medical Emergency Relief International—MERLIN, UK, 432
Mediterranean Foundation of Strategic Studies, France, 147
Mercy-USA for Aid and Development—M-USA, USA, 524
MERLIN—Medical Emergency Relief International, UK, 432
Mindolo Ecumenical Foundation—MEF, Zambia, 566
Minna James Heineman Foundation, Germany, 170
Minna-James-Heineman-Stiftung, Germany, 170

Mo Ibrahim Foundation, UK, 421
Moawad (René) Foundation, Lebanon, 253
Mohammed bin Rashid Al Maktoum Foundation, United Arab Emirates, 395
Mosaic Foundation, USA, 526
Mother Child Education Foundation, Turkey, 388
Muslim Aid, UK, 433
Nadácia Pontis, Slovakia, 327
Nathan Steinberg Family Foundation, Canada, 98
National Institute for Research in the Behavioural Sciences—Szold (Henrietta) Institute, Israel, 215
Nederlandse Organisatie voor Internationale Ontwikkelingssamenwerking—Stichting NOVIB, Netherlands, 279
NEF—Near East Foundation, USA, 528
Non-Governmental Organization JEN, Japan, 237
Noor al-Hussein Foundation—NHF, Jordan, 241
North-South Institute/Institut Nord-Sud, Canada, 95
Novartis Foundation for Sustainable Development—NFSD, Switzerland, 371
Novartis Stiftung für Nachhaltige Entwicklung, Switzerland, 371
NOVIB (Oxfam Netherlands), Netherlands, 279
Open Society Foundation—Turkey, Turkey, 389
Organisation Afro-Asiatique Pour Le Developpement Rural, India, 199
The Orient-Occident Foundation, Morocco, 268
Oxfam NOVIB—Nederlandse Organisatie voor Internationale Ontwikkelingssamenwerking, Netherlands, 279
Oxfam NOVIB—Netherlands Organization for International Development Co-operation, Netherlands, 279
Oxfam-Québec, Canada, 95
Paraskevaides (George and Thelma) Foundation, Cyprus, 111
Pathfinder International, USA, 533
Peace Research Center, Spain, 338
PEF Israel Endowment Funds, Inc, Israel, 215
People in Need, Czech Republic, 113
People-to-People Health Foundation, Inc—Project Hope, USA, 537
Peres Center for Peace, Israel, 215
Ploughshares Fund, USA, 536
Pôle européen des fondations de l'économie sociale, Belgium, 56
Pontis Foundation, Slovakia, 327
Population Council, USA, 536
Pro Victimis Foundation, Switzerland, 365
Project HOPE, USA, 537
Project Trust, UK, 439
Qatar Foundation, Qatar, 315
Qattan (A. M.) Foundation, UK, 440
Queen Alia Fund for Social Development, Jordan, 241
Queen Elisabeth Egyptological Association, Belgium, 57
Rafik Hariri Foundation, Lebanon, 252
Ramsay Foundation, Switzerland, 372
Refugees International Japan—RIJ, Japan, 239
Reine Elisabeth, Association Égyptologique, Belgium, 57
Relief International, USA, 539
René Moawad Foundation, Lebanon, 253
René Seydoux Foundation for the Mediterranean World, France, 150
Réseau Africain de la Jeunesse pour le Développement Durable, Algeria, 30
Réseau des ONG Africaines sur l'Environnement, Kenya, 244
Réseau d'ONG Européennes sur l'Agro-alimentaire, le Commerce, l'Environnement et le Développement—RONGEAD, France, 135
Richelieu International, Canada, 96
Rockefeller Brothers Fund, USA, 540
Rockwool Fonden, Denmark, 121
Rockwool Foundation, Denmark, 121
RONGEAD—Réseau d'ONG Européennes sur l'Agro-alimentaire, le Commerce, l'Environnement et le Développement, France, 135
Rooftops Canada Foundation, Canada, 97
Rothschild (Edmond de) Foundations, USA, 541
Roviralta (María Francisca de), Fundación, Spain, 347
Rowan Charitable Trust, UK, 441
Royal Society for the Protection of Birds—RSPB, UK, 445
RSPB—Royal Society for the Protection of Birds, UK, 445
Sabancı (Hacı Ömer) Foundation, Turkey, 389
Sabancı Foundation, Turkey, 389
Sabancı Vakfı—Hacı Ömer Sabancı Foundation, Turkey, 389

Said Foundation, UK, 446
Samuel Sebba Charitable Trust, UK, 447
Santé Sud, France, 154
Savings Banks Foundation for International
 Cooperation, Germany, 179
Schusterman (Charles and Lynn) Family
 Foundation, USA, 543
Schweizerisch-Liechtensteinische Stiftung für
 archäologische Forschungen im Ausland—
 SLSA, Switzerland, 373
SCIAF—Scottish Catholic International Aid
 Fund, UK, 447
Scientific Foundation of Hisham Adeeb Hijjawi,
 Jordan, 241
Scottish Catholic International Aid Fund—
 SCIAF, UK, 447
Seeds of Peace, USA, 543
SELAVIP International—Service de Promotion
 de l'Habitation Populaire en Amérique Latine,
 Afrique et Asie, Chile, 101
Serafín Aliaga Foundation for Peace and
 Solidarity, Spain, 346
Seydoux (René), Fondation pour le Monde
 Méditerranéen, France, 150
Sherman (Archie) Charitable Trust, UK, 448
Shoman (Abdul Hameed) Foundation,
 Jordan, 242
SLSA—Schweizerisch Liechtensteinische
 Stiftung, Switzerland, 373
Sobell Foundation, UK, 449
SOTA—Research Centre for Turkestan and
 Azerbaijan, Netherlands, 280
Southern Health, France, 154
Sparkassenstiftung für internationale
 Kooperation eV, Germany, 179
Springer (Axel) Stiftung, Germany, 179
Steinberg (Nathan) Family Foundation,
 Canada, 98
Stichting Liliane Fonds, Netherlands, 281
Stichting Triodos Foundation, Netherlands, 282
Stiftelsen Riksbankens Jubileumsfond,
 Sweden, 357
Stiftung Europäisches Naturerbe—
 EURONATUR, Germany, 180
Stiftung Kinder in Afrika, Germany, 181
Stiftung Klimarappen, Switzerland, 375
Stiftung 'Leben für Alle', Switzerland, 375
Street Kids International, Canada, 98
Sultan bin Abdulaziz al-Saud Foundation, Saudi
 Arabia, 321
Swiss Interchurch Aid, Switzerland, 367
Swiss-Liechtenstein Foundation for
 Archaeological Research Abroad—SLFA,
 Switzerland, 373
Tarih Vakfı, Turkey, 389
Terre des Hommes Foundation, Switzerland, 376
Third World Solidarity Action, Luxembourg, 257
Thomson Foundation, UK, 451
Together Foundation, France, 143
Triodos Foundation, Netherlands, 282
Trócaire—Catholic Agency for World
 Development, Ireland, 213
Turkish Family Health and Planning
 Foundation, Turkey, 390
Turkish Foundation for Combating Soil Erosion,
 for Reforestation and the Protection of
 Natural Habitats, Turkey, 390
Türkiye Aile Sağlığı ve Planlaması Vakfı—TAPV,
 Turkey, 390
Türkiye Çevre Vakfı, Turkey, 390
Türkiye Erozyonla Mücadele Ağaçlandırma ve
 Doğal Varlıkları Koruma Vakfı—TEMA,
 Turkey, 390
Türkiye İnsan Hakları Vakfı, Turkey, 390
UJIA—United Jewish Israel Appeal, UK, 452
Uluslararası Mavi Hilal İnsani Yardım ve
 Kalkınma Vakfı, Turkey, 390
Umut Foundation, Turkey, 391
Umut Vakfı, Turkey, 391
Union Aid Abroad—APHEDA, Australia, 45
United Society for the Propagation of the
 Gospel—USPG, UK, 453
United States-Israel Educational Foundation—
 USIEF, Israel, 215
USIEF—United States-Israel Educational
 Foundation, Israel, 215
Vehbi Koç Foundation, Turkey, 391
Vehbi Koç Vakfı, Turkey, 391
War on Want, UK, 454
WasserStiftung, Germany, 184
Water Foundation, Germany, 184
Weinberg (Harry and Jeanette) Foundation,
 USA, 552
Welfare Association, Switzerland, 376
Westminster Foundation for Democracy—WFD,
 UK, 455
William Adlington Cadbury Charitable Trust,
 UK, 407

Wingate (Harold Hyam) Foundation, UK, 456
Winrock International, USA, 555
Woerner (Manfred) Foundation, Bulgaria, 74
The Wolfson Family Charitable Trust, UK, 456
World Association of Children's Friends,
 Monaco, 265
World Peace Foundation—WPF, USA, 557
The WorldFish Center, Malaysia, 260
Youth for Development and Co-operation—YDC,
 Netherlands, 283
Zakat House, Kuwait, 249
ZEIT-Stiftung Ebelin und Gerd Bucerius,
 Germany, 184
Zero-Kap Foundation, Netherlands, 283

SOUTH AMERICA, CENTRAL AMERICA AND THE CARIBBEAN

Abrinq Foundation for the Rights of Children and
 Adolescents, Brazil, 70
Acceso, Costa Rica, 106
Access Foundation, Costa Rica, 106
ACCION International, USA, 460
Acíndar Foundation, Argentina, 31
Acting for Life, France, 136
Action contre la Faim, France, 136
Action against Hunger, France, 136
Action Solidarité Tiers Monde—ASTM,
 Luxembourg, 257
Adams (Sylvia) Charitable Trust, UK, 398
Afro-Asian Institute in Vienna, Austria, 46
Afro-Asiatisches Institut in Wien, Austria, 46
AFSC—American Friends Service Committee,
 USA, 465
Agostino (Daniele Derossi) Foundation, USA, 462
Agriculteurs Français et Développement
 International—AFDI, France, 136
Agromisa Foundation, Netherlands, 280
Agronomes et vétérinaires sans frontières—
 AVSF, France, 136
Aid for Development Club, Austria, 46
Aide et Action, France, 137
Aide Médicale Internationale, France, 137
Air France Corporate Foundation, France, 144
AJWS—American Jewish World Service,
 USA, 466
Alberto Vollmer Foundation, Inc, USA, 551
Alchemy Foundation, UK, 399
Alemán (Miguel), Fundación, Mexico, 262
Alert—International Alert, UK, 422
ALIDE—Asociación Latinoamericana de
 Instituciones Financieras para el Desarrollo,
 Peru, 299
Alternatives for Development Foundation,
 Ecuador, 124
Altman (Jenifer) Foundation, USA, 463
Alvares Penteado (Armando), Fundação,
 Brazil, 71
AMADE Mondiale—Association Mondiale des
 Amis de l'Enfance, Monaco, 265
Ambiente y Recursos Naturales, Fundación,
 Argentina, 31
American Friends Service Committee—AFSC,
 USA, 465
American Jewish World Service—AJWS,
 USA, 466
Amerind Foundation, Inc, USA, 468
ANESVAD, Spain, 337
Anne Çocuk Eğitim Vakfı—AÇEV, Turkey, 388
APHEDA—Union Aid Abroad, Australia, 45
Arab Image Foundation, Lebanon, 252
Arca Foundation, USA, 469
ArcelorMittal Acesita Foundation, Brazil, 71
Arias Foundation for Peace and Human Progress,
 Costa Rica, 106
Armando Alvares Penteado Foundation,
 Brazil, 71
Arpad Szenes-Vieira da Silva Foundation,
 Portugal, 313
Asociación Latinoamericana de Instituciones
 Financieras para el Desarrollo—ALIDE,
 Peru, 299
Asociación Latinoamericana de Organizaciones
 de Promoción al Desarrollo—ALOP,
 Mexico, 262
Asociación Nacional de Organizaciones Sociedad
 Civil, Venezuela, 563
Association of Foundations and Businesses,
 Argentina, 31
Association Mondiale des Amis de l'Enfance,
 Monaco, 265
ASTM—Action Solidarité Tiers Monde,
 Luxembourg, 257
Atkinson Foundation, USA, 470
Augusto César Sandino Foundation,
 Nicaragua, 288

Australian People Health Education,
 Australia, 45
Australian Volunteers International,
 Australia, 39
AVINA Foundation, Panama, 297
Ayrton Senna Institute, Brazil, 73
BANHCAFE Foundation, Honduras, 193
Bank of Brazil Foundation, Brazil, 71
Barceló Foundation, Spain, 340
Bariloche Foundation, Argentina, 32
BBC World Service Trust, UK, 403
BBVA Foundation, Spain, 340
Bertoni (Moisés) Foundation, Paraguay, 298
BID-INTAL—Instituto para la Integración de
 America Latina y el Caribe, Argentina, 34
Blue Moon Fund, Inc, USA, 473
Book Aid International—BAI, UK, 405
Bóthar, Ireland, 210
Boticário Group Foundation, Brazil, 71
Brazil Foundation, Brazil, 70
Brazilian Foundation for Nature Conservation,
 Brazil, 71
Bread for the World, Germany, 163
Brot für die Welt, Germany, 163
Brother's Brother Foundation, USA, 474
Bunge y Born Foundation, Argentina, 32
Business Formation Foundation, Guatemala, 190
Business Institute Foundation, Spain, 344
Butler (J. Homer) Foundation, USA, 504
Canadian Catholic Organization for Development
 and Peace, Canada, 83
Canadian Centre for International Studies and
 Co-operation/Centre d'études et de
 coopération internationale—CECI,
 Canada, 83
Canadian Co-operative Association, Canada, 80
Canadian Crossroads International/Carrefour
 Canadien International—CCI, Canada, 83
Canadian Foodgrains Bank, Canada, 84
Canadian Hunger Foundation, Canada, 84
Canadian Organization for Development through
 Education—CODE, Canada, 85
CARE International—CI, Switzerland, 361
Caribbean Marine Biology Institute Foundation,
 Curaçao, 110
Caribbean Policy Development Centre,
 Barbados, 53
CARMABI Foundation, Curaçao, 110
Carnegie Corporation of New York, USA, 475
The Carter Center, USA, 476
Catholic Agency for World Development—
 Trócaire, Ireland, 213
CCF—Christian Children's Fund, USA, 478
CCI—Carrefour Canadien International,
 Canada, 83
CEAAL—Consejo de Educación de Adultos de
 América Latina, Panama, 297
CECI—Canadian Centre for International
 Studies and Co-operation/Centre d'études et
 de coopération internationale, Canada, 83
CEDRO—Centro de Información y Educación
 para la Prevención del Abuso de Drogas,
 Peru, 299
Centre International de Coopération pour le
 Développement Agricole—CICDA,
 France, 136
Centre on Philanthropy, Bermuda, 66
Centro de Información y Educación para la
 Prevención del Abuso de Drogas—CEDRO,
 Peru, 299
Centro Internacional de Agricultura Tropical—
 CIAT, Colombia, 104
Centro de Investigación para la Paz, CIP—
 FUHEM, Spain, 338
Centro Mexicano para la Filantropía—CEMEFI,
 Mexico, 262
CERES—Ecuadorean Consortium for Social
 Responsibility, Ecuador, 124
Charity Projects, UK, 411
Charles Darwin Foundation for the Galapagos
 Islands—CDF, Ecuador, 124
Charles Delmar Foundation, USA, 484
ChildFund International, USA, 478
ChildFund Korea, Korea (Republic), 246
ChildHope Brasil, Brazil, 70
ChildHope—Hope for the Children Foundation,
 Guatemala, 190
Children of The Americas—COTA, USA, 479
Children International—CI, USA, 479
Children and Sharing, France, 139
Chile Foundation, Chile, 100
Chr. Michelsen Institute—CMI, Norway, 291
Christopher Reynolds Foundation, Inc, USA, 539
CIAT—Centro Internacional de Agricultura
 Tropical, Colombia, 104
CIDOB Foundation, Spain, 338

CLADEM—Comité de América Latina y el Caribe para la Defensa de los Derechos de la Mujer, Peru, 299
Claiborne (Liz) and Ortenberg (Art) Foundation, USA, 480
Climate Cent Foundation, Switzerland, 375
Club 2/3, Canada, 85
CMI—Chr. Michelsens Institutt, Norway, 291
Co-operation for the Promotion and Development of Welfare Activities, Spain, 342
CODE—Canadian Organization for Development through Education, Canada, 85
Colombian Habitat Foundation, Colombia, 105
Comic Relief, UK, 411
Comité de América Latina y el Caribe para la Defensa de los Derechos de la Mujer—CLADEM, Peru, 299
Commonwealth Foundation, UK, 411
Comprehensive Rural Foundation, Costa Rica, 107
Compton Foundation, Inc, USA, 481
Concern Universal, UK, 412
Consejo de Educación de Adultos de América Latina—CEAAL, Panama, 297
Consejo de Fundaciones Americanas de Desarrollo—Solidarios, Dominican Republic, 123
Consejo de Fundaciones Privadas de Guatemala—CFPG, Guatemala, 190
Cooperazione Internazionale—COOPI, Italy, 217
COOPI—Cooperazione Internazionale, Italy, 217
Costa Rican Foundation for Development, Costa Rica, 106
Council of American Development Foundations, Dominican Republic, 123
Council for the Education of Adults in Latin America, Panama, 297
Council of Private Foundations of Guatemala, Guatemala, 190
CUSO-VSO, Canada, 86
Damien Foundation, Belgium, 58
Daniele Agostino Derossi Foundation, USA, 462
The Danish Cultural Institute, Denmark, 117
Danske Kulturinstitut, Denmark, 117
Darwin (Charles) Foundation for the Galapagos Islands, Ecuador, 124
David and Lucile Packard Foundation, USA, 531
Delmar (Charles) Foundation, USA, 484
Demokratikus Átalakulásért Intézet, Hungary, 196
DEMUCA—Fundación para el Desarrollo Local y el Fortalecimiento Municipal e Institucional de Centroamérica y el Caribe, Costa Rica, 106
Deutsche Bank Americas Foundation and Community Development Group, USA, 484
Deutsche Stiftung für internationale rechtliche Zusammenarbeit eV, Germany, 165
Development Foundation, Guatemala, 190
Diakonia, Sweden, 352
Dobbo Yala Foundation, Panama, 297
DOEN Foundation, Netherlands, 280
Dom Manuel II Foundation, Portugal, 311
Dominican Development Foundation, Dominican Republic, 123
Dr J. R. Villavicencio Foundation, Argentina, 33
Dreyfus Health Foundation—DHF, USA, 485
Dutch Cancer Society, Netherlands, 276
Earthrights International—ERI, USA, 486
Easter Island Foundation, USA, 487
Eça de Queiroz Foundation, Portugal, 312
EcoCiencia—Fundación Ecuatoriana de Estudios Ecologicos, Ecuador, 124
EcoHealth Alliance, USA, 487
Ecoles Sans Frontières—ESF, France, 139
Ecológica Universal, Fundación, Argentina, 32
Ecuadorean Consortium for Social Responsibility—CERES, Ecuador, 124
Ecuadorean Development Foundation, Ecuador, 125
Ecuadorian Foundation of Ecological Studies, Ecuador, 124
Else Kröner-Fresenius Foundation, Germany, 173
Else Kröner-Fresenius-Stiftung, Germany, 173
Enda Third World—Environment and Development Action in the Third World, Senegal, 322
Enda Tiers Monde—Environnement et Développement du Tiers-Monde, Senegal, 322
endPoverty.org, USA, 488
Enfance et Partage, France, 139
Enfants Réfugiés du Monde—ERM, France, 140
Enterprise Development International, USA, 488
Entraide Protestante Suisse, Switzerland, 367
Entwicklungshilfe-Klub, Austria, 46
Environment and Natural Resources Foundation, Argentina, 31
Environmental Foundation of Jamaica, Jamaica, 229

Environmental Justice Foundation—EJF, UK, 416
Environnement et Développement du Tiers-Monde—Enda, Senegal, 322
ERM—Enfants Réfugiés du Monde, France, 140
Espejo (Eugenio), Fundación, Ecuador, 125
Esperança, Inc, USA, 489
Esquel Group Foundation—Ecuador, Ecuador, 125
Eugenio Espejo Foundation, Ecuador, 125
Eugenio Mendoza Foundation, Venezuela, 563
European NGOs on Agriculture, Food, Trade and Development, France, 135
FAFIDESS—Fundación de Asesoría Financiera a Instituciones de Desarrollo y Servicio Social, Guatemala, 190
FAL—France Amérique Latine, France, 151
FARM Foundation— Foundation for World Agriculture and Rural Life, France, 145
FARN—Fundación Ambiente y Recursos Naturales, Argentina, 31
FDD—Fundación Dominicana de Desarrollo, Dominican Republic, 123
FDH—Frères des Hommes, France, 152
Federación Argentina de Apoyo Familiar—FAAF, Argentina, 31
Fedesarrollo—Fundación para la Educación Superior y el Desarrollo, Colombia, 104
Feed the Children, USA, 490
FEIM—Fundación para Estudio e Investigación de la Mujer, Argentina, 32
FEPP—Fondo Ecuatoriano Populorum Progressio, Ecuador, 124
FEU—Fundación Ecológica Universal, Argentina, 32
FH—Food for the Hungry, USA, 491
Financiera FAMA, Nicaragua, 288
FINCA—Fundación Integral Campesina, Costa Rica, 107
FINCA International, USA, 490
First Peoples Worldwide—FPW, USA, 490
FLAAR—Foundation for Latin American Anthropological Research, USA, 492
FOKAL—Fondation Connaissance et Liberte (Haiti), Haiti, 192
Fondation Abri International, Canada, 97
Fondation pour l'Agriculture et la Ruralité dans le Monde—Fondation FARM, France, 145
Fondation Arabe pour l'Image, Lebanon, 252
Fondation canadienne contre la faim, Canada, 84
Fondation Connaissance et Liberté (Haiti)—FOKAL, Haiti, 192
Fondation d'Entreprise Air France, France, 144
Fondation d'Entreprise Renault, France, 144
Fondation contre la Faim, USA, 491
Fondation FARM—Fondation pour l'Agriculture et la Ruralité dans le Monde, France, 145
Fondation Pro Victimis Genève, Switzerland, 365
Fondation Simón I. Patiño, Switzerland, 365
Fondation Syngenta pour une Agriculture Durable, Switzerland, 376
Fondazione Ing. Carlo M. Lerici—FL, Italy, 222
Fondo Ecuatoriano Populorum Progressio—FEPP, Ecuador, 124
Fondo Latinoamericano de Desarrollo, Costa Rica, 106
Food for the Hungry—FH, USA, 491
Food for the Poor, Inc, USA, 491
FOPERDA—Fondation Royale Père Damien pour la Lutte Contre la Lèpre, Belgium, 58
Foro Juvenil, Uruguay, 560
Foundation for Agricultural Development, Ecuador, 125
Foundation for Agricultural Research in the Province of Almería, Spain, 344
Foundation for Basic Development, Costa Rica, 107
Foundation for the Conservation of the Atlantic Rainforest, Brazil, 72
Foundation for Deep Ecology, USA, 492
Foundation for the Financial Assessment of Social Service and Development Institutions, Guatemala, 190
Foundation for Higher Education and Development, Colombia, 104
Foundation for Human Rights and Humanitarian Relief, Turkey, 389
Foundation for International Community Assistance, USA, 490
Foundation for the Investment and Development of Exports, Honduras, 193
Foundation for Knowledge and Liberty, Haiti, 192
Foundation for Latin American Anthropological Research, USA, 492
Foundation for Latin American Economic Research, Argentina, 32
Foundation 'Life for All', Switzerland, 375

Foundation for Local Development and the Municipal and Institutional Support of Central America and the Caribbean, Costa Rica, 106
Foundation for Low-Cost Housing, Venezuela, 564
Foundation Museum of American Man, Brazil, 72
Foundation for Peace, Ecology and the Arts, Argentina, 33
Foundation for the People's Economy, Costa Rica, 107
Foundation 'Populorum Progressio', Vatican City, 562
Foundation for the Protection of Nature, Venezuela, 563
Foundation for the Qualification and Consultancy in Microfinance, El Salvador, 128
Foundation in Support of Local Development Initiatives, Venezuela, 563
Foundation for Sustainable Development, Spain, 348
Foundation for the Sustainable Development of Small and Medium-sized Enterprises—FUNDES International, Costa Rica, 107
Foundation for the Unity and Development of Rural Communities, Costa Rica, 107
Foundation for Women, Spain, 345
Foundation for Women's Research and Studies, Argentina, 32
France Amérique Latine—FAL, France, 151
Freedom from Hunger, USA, 494
Freedom from Hunger Council of Ireland—Gorta, Ireland, 211
French Agriculturalists and International Development, France, 136
Frères des Hommes—FDH, France, 152
Friends of Nature Foundation, Bolivia, 67
Frontiers Foundation Inc/Fondation Frontière Inc, Canada, 89
FUNBANHCAFE—Fundación BANHCAFE, Honduras, 193
Fundação Abrinq pelos Direitos da Criança e do Adolescente, Brazil, 70
Fundação ArcelorMittal Acesita, Brazil, 71
Fundação Armando Alvares Penteado—FAAP, Brazil, 71
Fundação Arpad Szenes–Vieira da Silva, Portugal, 313
Fundação de Atendimento à Criança e ao Adolescente Professor Hélio Augusto de Souza—Fundhas, Brazil, 73
Fundação Banco do Brasil, Brazil, 71
Fundação O Boticário de Proteção à Natureza, Brazil, 71
Fundação Brasileira para a Conservação da Natureza, Brazil, 71
Fundação Dom Manuel II, Portugal, 311
Fundação Eça de Queiroz, Portugal, 312
Fundação Gaia, Brazil, 71
Fundação Hélio Augusto de Souza—Fundhas, Brazil, 73
Fundação Iochpe, Brazil, 72
Fundação Maria Cecilia Souto Vidigal, Brazil, 73
Fundação Maurício Sirotsky Sobrinho, Brazil, 72
Fundação Museu do Homem Americano—FUMDHAM, Brazil, 72
Fundação Roberto Marinho, Brazil, 72
Fundação Romi, Brazil, 72
Fundação SOS Mata Atlântica, Brazil, 72
Fundació CIDOB, Spain, 338
Fundación Acceso, Costa Rica, 106
Fundación Acíndar, Argentina, 31
Fundación Alberto Vollmer, USA, 551
Fundación Alternativas para el Desarrollo, Ecuador, 124
Fundación Amanecer, Colombia, 104
Fundación Ambiente y Recursos Naturales—FARN, Argentina, 31
Fundación Amigos de la Naturaleza, Bolivia, 67
Fundación Antonio Restrepo Barco, Colombia, 104
Fundación de Apoyo a las Iniciativas Locales de Desarrollo—FUNDAPILDE, Venezuela, 563
Fundación para el Apoyo a la Microempresa—Financiera FAMA, Nicaragua, 288
Fundación Arias para la Paz y el Progreso Humano, Costa Rica, 106
Fundación de Asesoría Financiera a Instituciones de Desarrollo y Servicio Social—FAFIDESS, Guatemala, 190
Fundación de Asistencia para la Pequeña Empresa, Guatemala, 190
Fundación Augusto César Sandino—FACS, Nicaragua, 288
Fundación AVINA, Panama, 297
Fundación Banco Bilbao Vizcaya Argentaria—Fundación BBVA, Spain, 340
Fundación BANHCAFE—FUNBANHCAFE, Honduras, 193

Fundación Barceló, Spain, 340
Fundación Bariloche, Argentina, 32
Fundación BBVA—Fundación Banco Bilbao
 Vizcaya Argentaria, Spain, 340
Fundación Bunge y Born, Argentina, 32
Fundación de Capacitación y Asesoría en
 Microfinanzas, El Salvador, 128
Fundación Charles Darwin para las Islas
 Galápagos—FCD, Ecuador, 124
Fundación Chile, Chile, 100
Fundación CODESPA—Futuro en Marcha,
 Spain, 342
Fundación Comunitaria de Puerto Rico—FCPR,
 Puerto Rico, 314
Fundación Corona, Colombia, 104
Fundación Costarricense de Desarrollo—
 FUCODES, Costa Rica, 106
Fundación para la Defensa de la Naturaleza—
 FUDENA, Venezuela, 563
Fundación para el Desarrollo Agropecuario—
 FUNDAGRO, Ecuador, 125
Fundación para el Desarrollo de Base—
 FUNDEBASE, Costa Rica, 107
Fundación para el Desarrollo—FUNDAP,
 Guatemala, 190
Fundación para el Desarrollo Local y el
 Fortalecimiento Municipal e Institucional de
 Centroamérica y el Caribe, Costa Rica, 106
Fundación para el Desarrollo de la
 Microempresa, Guatemala, 191
Fundación para el Desarrollo Regional de Aysen,
 Chile, 100
Fundación para el Desarrollo Sostenible de la
 Pequeña y Mediana Empresa—FUNDES
 Internacional, Costa Rica, 107
Fundación Desarrollo Sostenido—FUNDESO,
 Spain, 348
Fundación Dobbo Yala, Panama, 297
Fundación Dominicana de Desarrollo—FDD,
 Dominican Republic, 123
Fundación Dr J. Roberto Villavicencio,
 Argentina, 33
Fundación Ecológica Universal—FEU,
 Argentina, 32
Fundación para la Economía Popular—
 FUNDECO, Costa Rica, 107
Fundación Ecuatoriana de Desarrollo—FED,
 Ecuador, 125
Fundación Ecuatoriana de Estudios Ecologicos—
 EcoCiencia, Ecuador, 124
Fundación para la Educación Superior y el
 Desarrollo—Fedesarrollo, Colombia, 104
Fundación Empresa-Universidad de Zaragoza—
 FEUZ, Spain, 342
Fundación Empresas Polar, Venezuela, 563
Fundación Entorno, Empresara y Desarrollo
 Sostenible, Spain, 343
Fundación Esperanza de los Niños,
 Guatemala, 190
Fundación para Estudio e Investigación de la
 Mujer—FEIM, Argentina, 32
Fundación Eugenio Espejo, Ecuador, 125
Fundación Eugenio Mendoza, Venezuela, 563
Fundación General Ecuatoriana, Ecuador, 125
Fundación Génesis Empresarial, Guatemala, 190
Fundación Grupo Esquel—Ecuador, Ecuador, 125
Fundación Hábitat Colombia—FHC,
 Colombia, 105
Fundación Herencia Verde, Colombia, 105
Fundación Instituto de Empresa, Spain, 344
Fundación Integral Campesina—FINCA, Costa
 Rica, 107
Fundación Intervida, Spain, 344
Fundación para la Inversión y Desarrollo de
 Exportaciones—FIDE, Honduras, 193
Fundación para la Investigación Agraria de la
 Provincia de Almería—FIAPA, Spain, 344
Fundación de Investigaciones Económicas
 Latinoamericanas—FIEL, Argentina, 32
Fundación Invica, Chile, 100
Fundación Lealtad, Spain, 337
Fundación MAPFRE, Spain, 345
Fundación María Francisca de Roviralta,
 Spain, 347
Fundación Mediterránea—IERAL,
 Argentina, 33
Fundación México Unido—FMU, Mexico, 263
Fundación MICROS—Fundación para el
 Desarrollo de la Microempresa,
 Guatemala, 191
Fundación Miguel Alemán AC, Mexico, 262
Fundación Moisés Bertoni—FMB, Paraguay, 298
Fundación Mujer, Costa Rica, 107
Fundación Mujeres, Spain, 345
Fundación Mujeres en Igualdad, Argentina, 33
Fundación Nacional para el Desarrollo, El
 Salvador, 128

Fundación Nacional para el Desarrollo de
 Honduras—FUNADEH, Honduras, 193
Fundación Nantik Lum, Spain, 345
Fundación Natura, Ecuador, 126
Fundación Pablo Neruda, Chile, 100
Fundación Panamericana de la Salud y
 Educación, USA, 532
Fundación Paz, Ecología y Arte—Fundación
 PEA, Argentina, 33
Fundación Paz y Solidaridad Serafín Aliaga—
 FPyS, Spain, 346
Fundación PEA—Fundación Paz, Ecología y
 Arte, Argentina, 33
Fundación La Salle de Ciencias Naturales—
 FLASA, Venezuela, 564
Fundación Salvadoreña para el Desarrollo
 Económico y Social, El Salvador, 128
Fundación Santa María, Spain, 348
Fundación Santillana, Spain, 348
Fundación Sartawi, Bolivia, 67
Fundación Schcolnik, Argentina, 33
Fundación SERVIVIENDA, Colombia, 105
Fundación SES—Sustentabilidad, Educación,
 Solidaridad, Argentina, 33
Fundación Solidaridad, Dominican Republic, 123
Fundación Soros Guatemala, Guatemala, 191
Fundación Unión y Desarrollo de Comunidades
 Campesinas, Costa Rica, 107
Fundación de la Vivienda Popular, Venezuela, 564
Fundación de Viviendas Hogar de Cristo,
 Chile, 100
FUNDAGRO—Fundación para el Desarrollo
 Agropecuario, Ecuador, 125
FUNDAP—Fundación para el Desarrollo,
 Guatemala, 190
FUNDEBASE—Fundación para el Desarrollo de
 Base, Costa Rica, 107
FUNDESO—Fundación Desarrollo Sostenido,
 Spain, 348
Fundhas—Fundação Hélio Augusto de Souza,
 Brazil, 73
Gaia Foundation, Brazil, 71
General Ecuadorean Foundation, Ecuador, 125
General Service Foundation, USA, 495
German Foundation for International Legal Co-
 operation, Germany, 165
GIFE—Grupo de Institutos, Fundações e
 Empresas, Brazil, 70
Gift of the Givers Foundation, South Africa, 332
GLARP—Grupo Latinoamericano de
 Rehabilitación Profesional, Colombia, 105
Global Fund for Community Foundations—
 GFCF, South Africa, 331
Global Harmony Foundation—GHF,
 Switzerland, 367
Global Voluntary Service—GVS, Japan, 232
Globe Foundation of Canada—GLOBE,
 Canada, 89
Good Neighbors International, Korea
 (Republic), 246
Gorta—Freedom from Hunger Council of
 Ireland, Ireland, 211
Grameen Foundation—GF, USA, 499
Grassroots International—GRI, USA, 500
Green Heritage Foundation, Colombia, 105
Group of Institutes, Foundations and
 Enterprises, Brazil, 70
GRUMIN—Grupo Mulher-Educação Indigena,
 Brazil, 73
Grupo de Fundaciones y Empresas, Argentina, 31
Grupo Latinoamericano para la Participación, la
 Integración y la Inclusión de Personas con
 Discapacidad—GLARP-IIPD, Colombia, 105
Grupo Mulher-Educação Indigena—GRUMIN,
 Brazil, 73
Guggenheim (John Simon) Memorial Foundation,
 USA, 500
Haitian Economic Development Foundation,
 Haiti, 192
Havelaar (Max) Foundation, Netherlands, 281
Health Action International, Netherlands, 275
Health Volunteers Overseas—HVO, USA, 501
Hearst (William Randolph) Foundation, USA, 502
The Hearst Foundation, Inc, USA, 501
Hedwig and Robert Samuel Foundation,
 Germany, 177
Hedwig und Robert Samuel-Stiftung,
 Germany, 177
Heifer International, USA, 502
HEKS—Hilfswerk Evangelischen Kirchen
 Schweiz, Switzerland, 367
Hélio Augusto de Souza Foundation, Brazil, 73
HELP International, USA, 503
Helvetas Swiss Intercooperation,
 Switzerland, 367
Hilden Charitable Fund, UK, 421
Hilfswerk der Evangelischen Kirchen Schweiz—
 HEKS, Switzerland, 367

HIVOS—Humanistisch Instituut voor
 Ontwikkelings Samenwerking,
 Netherlands, 275
Hogar de Cristo, Chile, 100
Holt International, USA, 504
Holt International Children's Services—HICS,
 USA, 504
Home of Christ, Chile, 100
Hope for the Children Foundation,
 Guatemala, 190
Horizons of Friendship, Canada, 90
Housing Services Foundation, Colombia, 105
Humanistic Institute for Co-operation with
 Developing Countries, Netherlands, 275
Humanistisch Instituut voor Ontwikkelings
 Samenwerking—HIVOS, Netherlands, 275
Humanitarian Relief Foundation, Turkey, 389
IAPA Scholarship Fund, USA, 505
IBIS, Denmark, 118
IERAL—Fundación Mediterránea,
 Argentina, 33
IFAD—International Fund for Agricultural
 Development, Italy, 226
IKEA Foundation, Netherlands, 275
Îles de Paix, Belgium, 62
Impact First International, Canada, 89
Indigenous Women's Education Group, Brazil, 73
Information and Education Centre for the
 Prevention of Drug Abuse, Peru, 299
Ing. Carlo M. Lerici Foundation, Italy, 222
INMED Partnerships for Children, USA, 506
Insan Hak ve Hürriyetleri İnsani Yardım Vakfı,
 Turkey, 389
Institut Nord-Sud, Canada, 95
Institute for Development Research, USA, 556
Institute for Latin American and Caribbean
 Integration, Argentina, 34
Instituto Ayrton Senna, Brazil, 73
Instituto para la Integración de América Latina y
 el Caribe—BID-INTAL, Argentina, 34
Instituto Interamericano de Derechos
 Humanos—IIHR, Costa Rica, 107
Instituto Senna (Ayrton), Brazil, 73
Instituto Torcuato di Tella, Argentina, 34
Inter-American Foundation—IAF, USA, 507
Inter-American Institute of Human Rights, Costa
 Rica, 107
Inter American Press Association Scholarship
 Fund, USA, 505
Inter Pares, Canada, 90
International Alert—Alert, UK, 422
International Centre for Democratic
 Transition—ICDT, Hungary, 196
International Centre for the Legal Protection of
 Human Rights—Interights, UK, 423
International Centre for Tropical Agriculture,
 Colombia, 104
International Charitable Fund of Bermuda—
 ICFB, Bermuda, 66
International Co-operation, Italy, 217
International Confederation of Family Support,
 Argentina, 31
International Executive Service Corps— IESC,
 USA, 508
The International Foundation, USA, 508
International Fund for Agricultural
 Development—IFAD, Italy, 226
International Institute for Environment and
 Development—IIED, UK, 423
International Medical Services for Health—
 INMED, USA, 506
International Orthodox Christian Charities,
 Inc—IOCC, USA, 509
International Relief Teams, USA, 510
International Solidarity Foundation—ISF,
 Finland, 132
International Women's Health Coalition—IWHC,
 USA, 510
Intervida Foundation, Spain, 344
Investigaciones Económicas Latinoamericanas,
 Fundación, Argentina, 32
Invica Foundation, Chile, 100
Isabel Allende Foundation, USA, 463
Isis Internacional, Chile, 100
Isis International, Chile, 100
Islands of Peace, Belgium, 62
Izumi Foundation, USA, 512
J. Homer Butler Foundation, Inc, USA, 504
JEN, Japan, 237
Jenifer Altman Foundation—JAF, USA, 463
The John D. and Catherine T. MacArthur
 Foundation, USA, 520
John Simon Guggenheim Memorial Foundation,
 USA, 500
Jones (W. Alton) Foundation, USA, 473
Kansainvälinen solidaarisuussäätiö, Finland, 132
Kerzner Marine Foundation—KMF, USA, 515

Koningin Wilhelmina Fonds—Nederlandse Kankerbestrijding, Netherlands, 276
Kröner-Fresenius (Else) Stiftung, Germany, 173
KWF Kankerbestrijding, Netherlands, 276
La Salle Foundation for Natural Sciences, Venezuela, 564
LACWHN—Latin American and Caribbean Women's Health Network, Chile, 101
Lama Gangchen World Peace Foundation, Italy, 227
Lateinamerika-Zentrum eV—LAZ, Germany, 174
Latin America Centre, Germany, 174
Latin America France, France, 151
Latin American, African and Asian Social Housing Service, Chile, 101
Latin American Association of Development Financing Institutions, Peru, 299
Latin American Association of Development Organizations, Mexico, 262
Latin American and Caribbean Women's Health Network—LACWHN, Chile, 101
Latin American Committee for the Defence of Women's Rights, Peru, 299
Latin American Fund for Development, Costa Rica, 106
Latin American Group for the Participation, Integration and Inclusion of People with Disability, Colombia, 105
Leprosy Mission International, UK, 428
Lerici (Ing. Carlo M.), Fondazione presso il Politecnico di Milano, Italy, 222
Leverhulme Trust, UK, 429
Lifewater International—LI, USA, 518
Liliane Foundation, Netherlands, 281
Lilly Endowment, Inc, USA, 518
Littauer (Lucius N.) Foundation, Inc, USA, 519
Liz Claiborne and Art Ortenberg Foundation, USA, 480
Loyalty Foundation, Spain, 337
Lucius N. Littauer Foundation, Inc, USA, 519
Ludwig Institute for Cancer Research—LICR, USA, 519
Luxemburg (Rosa) Stiftung, Germany, 174
LWR—Lutheran World Relief, USA, 519
MacArthur (John D. and Catherine T.) Foundation, USA, 520
McCormick (Robert R.) Foundation, USA, 520
MADRE, USA, 521
Mama Cash, Netherlands, 277
Mani Tese, Italy, 227
MAP International—Medical Assistance Programs, USA, 522
MAPFRE Foundation, Spain, 345
March of Dimes, USA, 522
María Francisca de Roviralta Foundation, Spain, 347
Marinho (Roberto), Fundação, Brazil, 72
Match International Centre, Canada, 93
Maurício Sirotsky Nephew Foundation, Brazil, 72
The Max Foundation, USA, 522
Max Havelaar Foundation, Netherlands, 281
medica mondiale e.V., Germany, 175
Medical Assistance Programs, USA, 522
Mediterranean Foundation, Argentina, 33
Mendoza (Eugenio) Fundación, Venezuela, 563
Mexican Centre for Philanthropy, Mexico, 262
Microenterprise Development Foundation, Guatemala, 191
Miguel Alemán Foundation, Mexico, 262
Milieukontakt International, Netherlands, 277
Milieukontakt Oost-Europa, Netherlands, 277
Moisés Bertoni Foundation, Paraguay, 298
Mother Child Education Foundation, Turkey, 388
The Mountain Institute—TMI, USA, 526
MS ActionAid Denmark, Denmark, 120
MS—Mellemfolkeligt Samvirke, Denmark, 120
Muslim Aid, UK, 433
Mutual Aid and Liaison Service, France, 154
Nadácia Pontis, Slovakia, 327
Nantik Lum Foundation, Spain, 345
National Association of Civil Society Organizations, Venezuela, 563
National Foundation for Development, El Salvador, 128
National Foundation for the Development of Honduras, Honduras, 193
National Wildlife Federation—NWF, USA, 527
The Nature Conservancy, USA, 528
Nature Foundation, Ecuador, 126
Nederlandsche Maatschappij voor Nijverheid en Handel—NMNH, Netherlands, 278
Nederlandse Organisatie voor Internationale Ontwikkelingssamenwerking—Stichting NOVIB, Netherlands, 279
Neruda (Pablo), Fundación, Chile, 100
NESsT—Nonprofit Enterprise and Self-sustainability Team, Chile, 101

Netherlands Society for Industry and Trade, Netherlands, 278
Network for Human Development, Brazil, 73
Non-Governmental Organization JEN, Japan, 237
Nonprofit Enterprise and Self-sustainability Team—NESsT, Chile, 101
North-South Institute/Institut Nord-Sud, Canada, 95
NOVIB (Oxfam Netherlands), Netherlands, 279
Oak Foundation, Switzerland, 371
OneWorld International Foundation, UK, 435
Operation Beaver—Frontiers Foundation Inc, Canada, 89
Operation Rainbow, Inc, USA, 530
Operation USA, USA, 530
Opportunity International USA, USA, 530
Outreach International, USA, 531
Oxfam Canada, Canada, 95
Oxfam Mexico, Mexico, 263
Oxfam NOVIB—Nederlandse Organisatie voor Internationale Ontwikkelingssamenwerking, Netherlands, 279
Oxfam NOVIB—Netherlands Organization for International Development Co-operation, Netherlands, 279
Oxfam-Québec, Canada, 95
Pablo Neruda Foundation, Chile, 100
PADF—Pan American Development Foundation, USA, 532
PAHEF—Pan American Health and Education Foundation, USA, 532
Partners in Rural Development, Canada, 84
Pathfinder International, USA, 533
Patiño (Simón I.), Fondation, Switzerland, 365
PBI—Peace Brigades International, UK, 437
Peace Brigades International—PBI, UK, 437
Peace Research Center, Spain, 338
People-to-People Health Foundation, Inc—Project Hope, USA, 537
Pestalozzi Children's Foundation, Switzerland, 374
Pesticide Action Network North America—PAN, USA, 534
Pesticide Action Network North America—PANNA, USA, 534
Pire (Dominique) Foundation, Belgium, 62
Plan Ireland, Ireland, 212
Plenty International, USA, 535
Polar Companies Foundation, Venezuela, 563
Pontis Foundation, Slovakia, 327
Population Council, USA, 536
Prince Bernhard Cultural Foundation, Netherlands, 282
Prince Claus Fund for Culture and Development, Netherlands, 279
Prins Bernhard Culturfonds, Stichting, Netherlands, 282
Prins Claus Fonds Voor Cultuur en Ontwikkeling, Netherlands, 279
Pro Mujer International, USA, 536
Pro Nature—Peruvian Foundation for Nature Conservation, Peru, 299
Pro Victimis Foundation, Switzerland, 365
Pro Women International, USA, 536
PRODESSA—Proyecto de Desarrollo Santiago, Guatemala, 191
Progressio, UK, 439
Project HOPE, USA, 537
Project Trust, UK, 439
ProNaturaleza—Fundación Peruana para la Conservación de la Naturaleza, Peru, 299
PROTERRA, Peru, 299
PROVICOOP—Fundación Invica, Chile, 100
Prudential Foundation, USA, 537
Puerto Rico Community Foundation, Puerto Rico, 314
Rabobank Foundation, Netherlands, 279
Rainforest Foundation Norway, Norway, 293
Rainforest Foundation US, USA, 538
Ramsay Foundation, Switzerland, 372
Red de Acción en Plaguicidas y sus Alternativas de América Latina—RAP-AL, Argentina, 34
Red Mujeres Afrolatinoamericanas Afrocaribeñas, Costa Rica, 107
Red de Mujeres para el Desarrollo, Costa Rica, 107
Red de Salud de las Mujeres Latinoamericanas y del Caribe, Chile, 101
Rede de Desenvolvimento Humano—REDEH, Brazil, 73
REDEH—Rede de Desenvolvimento Humano, Brazil, 73
Refugees International Japan—RIJ, Japan, 239
Regional Development Foundation of Aysen, Chile, 100
Regnskogfondet, Norway, 293

Relief International, USA, 539
Renault Foundation, France, 144
Réseau d'ONG Européennes sur l'Agro-alimentaire, le Commerce, l'Environnement et le Développement—RONGEAD, France, 135
Reynolds (Christopher) Foundation, USA, 539
Richelieu International, Canada, 96
Robert Marinho Foundation, Brazil, 72
Robert R. McCormick Foundation, USA, 520
Romi Foundation, Brazil, 72
RONGEAD—Réseau d'ONG Européennes sur l'Agro-alimentaire, le Commerce, l'Environnement et le Développement, France, 135
Rooftops Canada Foundation, Canada, 97
Rosa Luxemburg Foundation, Germany, 174
Rosa-Luxemburg-Stiftung, Germany, 174
Roviralta (María Francisca de), Fundación, Spain, 347
Rowan Charitable Trust, UK, 441
Royal Commonwealth Society for the Blind—Sight Savers International, UK, 448
The Rufford Foundation, UK, 445
Rufford Maurice Laing Foundation, UK, 445
Rutgers WPF, Netherlands, 279
Sabre Foundation, Inc, USA, 542
El Salvador Foundation for Economic and Social Development, El Salvador, 128
Samuel (Hedwig und Robert) Stiftung, Germany, 177
Sandino (Augusto César), Fundación, Nicaragua, 288
Santa María Foundation, Spain, 348
Santiago Development Project, Guatemala, 191
Santillana Foundation, Spain, 348
Sartawi Foundation, Bolivia, 67
Savings Banks Foundation for International Cooperation, Germany, 179
Schcolnik Foundation, Argentina, 33
Schools Without Frontiers, France, 139
SCIAF—Scottish Catholic International Aid Fund, UK, 447
Science and Technology Facilities Council—STFC, UK, 447
Scottish Catholic International Aid Fund—SCIAF, UK, 447
SEL—Service d'Entraide et de Liaison, France, 154
SELAVIP International—Service de Promotion de l'Habitation Populaire en Amérique Latine, Afrique et Asie, Chile, 101
Serafín Aliaga Foundation for Peace and Solidarity, Spain, 346
Service d'Entraide et de Liaison—SEL, France, 154
SES Foundation—Sustainability, Education, Solidarity, Argentina, 33
Seva Foundation, USA, 544
Sight Savers International, UK, 448
Simón I. Patiño Foundation, Switzerland, 365
Sinergia—Asociación Nacional de Organizaciones de la Sociedad Civil, Venezuela, 563
Small Business Assistance Foundation, Guatemala, 190
Software AG Foundation, Germany, 178
Solidarios—Consejo de Fundaciones Americanas de Desarrollo, Dominican Republic, 123
Solidarité, France, 155
Solidarity, France, 155
Solidarity Foundation, Dominican Republic, 123
Soros Foundation Guatemala, Guatemala, 191
SOS Atlantic Forest Foundation, Brazil, 72
Sparkassenstiftung für internationale Kooperation eV, Germany, 179
St John Ambulance, UK, 446
Standing International Forum on Ethnic Conflict, Genocide and Human Rights—International Alert, UK, 422
Steelworkers Humanity Fund, Canada, 98
Stichting Agromisa, Netherlands, 280
Stichting Caraïbisch Marien Biologisch Instituut—CARMABI, Curaçao, 110
Stichting DOEN, Netherlands, 280
Stichting Liliane Fonds, Netherlands, 281
Stichting Max Havelaar, Netherlands, 281
Stichting Prins Bernhard Cultuurfonds, Netherlands, 282
Stichting Triodos Foundation, Netherlands, 282
Stiftung Kinderdorf Pestalozzi, Switzerland, 374
Stiftung Klimarappen, Switzerland, 375
Stiftung 'Leben für Alle', Switzerland, 375
Stiftung Vivamos Mejor, Switzerland, 375
Street Kids International, Canada, 98
Stretched Hands, Italy, 227
Swiss Foundation for Technical Co-operation, Switzerland, 375

Swiss Interchurch Aid, Switzerland, 367
SWISSAID Foundation, Switzerland, 375
Swisscontact—Swiss Foundation for Technical
 Co-operation, Switzerland, 375
The Sylvia Adams Charitable Trust, UK, 398
Synergos—The Synergos Institute, USA, 460
Syngenta Foundation for Sustainable
 Agriculture, Switzerland, 376
Syngenta Stiftung für Nachhaltige
 Landwirtschaft, Switzerland, 376
Szenes (Arpad)–Vieira da Silva, Fundação,
 Portugal, 313
TANZ—Trade Aid NZ Inc, New Zealand, 287
di Tella (Torcuato), Instituto, Argentina, 34
Terre des Hommes Foundation, Switzerland, 376
Terre Sans Frontières—TSF, Canada, 98
Third World Network—TWN, Malaysia, 260
Third World Solidarity Action, Luxembourg, 257
Tinker Foundation, Inc, USA, 548
Torcuato di Tella Institute, Argentina, 34
Trade Aid NZ Inc—TANZ, New Zealand, 287
Triodos Foundation, Netherlands, 282
Trócaire—Catholic Agency for World
 Development, Ireland, 213
Union Aid Abroad—APHEDA, Australia, 45
United Mexico Foundation, Mexico, 263
United Service Committee of Canada, Canada, 98
United Society for the Propagation of the
 Gospel—USPG, UK, 453
Unity Foundation, Luxembourg, 257
Universal Ecological Foundation, Argentina, 32
University of Zaragoza Business Foundation,
 Spain, 342
USC Canada, Canada, 98
Villavicencio (Dr J. Roberto), Fundación,
 Argentina, 33
Vivamos Mejor Foundation, Switzerland, 375
Volkart Foundation, Switzerland, 376
Volkart-Stiftung, Switzerland, 376
Vollmer (Alberto) Foundation, Inc, USA, 551
Voluntary Service Overseas, UK, 454
VSO, UK, 454
War on Want, UK, 454
WasserStiftung, Germany, 184
Water Foundation, Germany, 184
Water.org, Inc, USA, 552
Westminster Foundation for Democracy—WFD,
 UK, 455
Wildlife Preservation Trust International,
 USA, 487
Wildlife Trust, USA, 487
The William Randolph Hearst Foundation,
 USA, 502
Winrock International, USA, 555
Women in Equality Foundation, Argentina, 33
Women's Development Network, Costa Rica, 107
Women's Foundation, Costa Rica, 107
World Accord, Canada, 99
World Association of Children's Friends,
 Monaco, 265
World Education, Inc, USA, 556
World Land Trust—WLT, UK, 456
World Neighbors, USA, 557
World Population Foundation, Netherlands, 279
World Teacher Trust, India, 206
Youth for Development and Co-operation—YDC,
 Netherlands, 283
Youth Forum, Uruguay, 560
Zakat House, Kuwait, 249
Zero-Kap Foundation, Netherlands, 283
ZOA, Netherlands, 283

SOUTH ASIA

A. M. M. Sahabdeen Trust Foundation, Sri
 Lanka, 350
AARDO—Afro-Asian Rural Development
 Organization, India, 199
Absolute Return for Kids—ARK, UK, 401
ACCION International, USA, 460
ACCU—Asian Cultural Centre for UNESCO,
 Japan, 231
Acting for Life, France, 136
Action Children Aid, Denmark, 117
Action in Development—AID, Bangladesh, 52
Action contre la Faim, France, 136
Action against Hunger, France, 136
Action Solidarité Tiers Monde—ASTM,
 Luxembourg, 257
Acumen Fund, USA, 461
Adams (Sylvia) Charitable Trust, UK, 398
Afghanaid, UK, 398
Afro-Asian Institute in Vienna, Austria, 46
Afro-Asian Rural Development Organization—
 AARDO, India, 199
Afro-Asiatisches Institut in Wien, Austria, 46

AFSC—American Friends Service Committee,
 USA, 465
Aga Khan Agency for Microfinance,
 Switzerland, 360
Aga Khan Foundation—AKF, Switzerland, 360
Aga Khan Foundation Canada, Canada, 80
Aga Khan Fund for Economic Development,
 Switzerland, 361
Agriculteurs Français et Développement
 International—AFDI, France, 136
Agromart Foundation, Sri Lanka, 350
Agromisa Foundation, Netherlands, 280
Agronomes et vétérinaires sans frontières—
 AVSF, France, 136
Aid for India/ Karuna Trust, UK, 426
Aide et Action, France, 137
Aide Médicale Internationale, France, 137
AIIT—Ancient India and Iran Trust, UK, 400
Air France Corporate Foundation, France, 144
AIT—Asian Institute of Technology,
 Thailand, 383
AIV—Asia-Africa International Voluntary
 Foundation, Japan, 231
AJWS—American Jewish World Service,
 USA, 466
Aktion Børnehjælp, Denmark, 117
Alchemy Foundation, UK, 399
Alert—International Alert, UK, 422
All India Disaster Mitigation Institute, India, 199
Altman (Jenifer) Foundation, USA, 463
AMADE Mondiale—Association Mondiale des
 Amis de l'Enfance, Monaco, 265
Ambuja Cement Foundation, India, 199
American Friends Service Committee—AFSC,
 USA, 465
American Jewish World Service—AJWS,
 USA, 466
Ancient India and Iran Trust, UK, 400
ANESVAD, Spain, 337
Angaja Foundation, India, 199
ANGOC—Asian NGO Coalition for Agrarian
 Reform and Rural Development,
 Philippines, 301
APAN—Asian Philanthropy Advisory Network,
 Philippines, 301
APMN—Asia Pacific Mountain Network,
 Nepal, 271
ARK—Absolute Return for Kids, UK, 401
Ashden Charitable Trust, UK, 402
Asia-Africa International Voluntary
 Foundation—AIV, Japan, 231
Asia Foundation, USA, 469
Asia/Pacific Cultural Centre for UNESCO—
 ACCU, Japan, 231
Asia Pacific Foundation of Canada, Canada, 81
Asia-Pacific Mountain Network—APMN,
 Nepal, 271
Asia Society, USA, 470
Asian Community Trust—ACT, Japan, 231
Asian Development Research Institute—ADRI,
 India, 200
Asian Health Institute—AHI, Japan, 231
Asian Institute for Rural Development,
 India, 200
Asian NGO Coalition for Agrarian Reform and
 Rural Development—ANGOC,
 Philippines, 301
Asian Philanthropy Advisory Network—APAN,
 Philippines, 301
Aspen Institute, USA, 470
Association Mondiale des Amis de l'Enfance,
 Monaco, 265
Association of Voluntary Agencies for Rural
 Development—AVARD, India, 198
ASTM—Action Solidarité Tiers Monde,
 Luxembourg, 257
The Australian Elizabethan Theatre Trust,
 Australia, 38
Australian Volunteers International,
 Australia, 39
AVARD—Association of Voluntary Agencies for
 Rural Development, India, 198
AVRDC—The World Vegetable Center,
 Taiwan, 379
AWHRC—Asian Women's Human Rights
 Council, India, 200
Azim Premji Foundation, India, 204
Bangladesh Freedom Foundation, Bangladesh, 52
Bangladesh Rural Advancement Committee—
 BRAC, Bangladesh, 52
The Batchworth Trust, UK, 403
BBC World Service Trust, UK, 403
Bell (Max) Foundation, Canada, 81
Berghof Foundation for Conflict Research,
 Germany, 161
Berghof Stiftung für Konfliktforschung GmbH,
 Germany, 161
Bettencourt Schueller Foundation, France, 141

BID-INTAL—Instituto para la Integración de
 América Latina y el Caribe, Argentina, 34
Blue Moon Fund, Inc, USA, 473
Bóthar, Ireland, 210
BRAC—Building Resources Across
 Communities, Bangladesh, 52
Bread for the World, Germany, 163
The Bridge Foundation, India, 200
Britain-Nepal Medical Trust, UK, 405
British Schools and Universities Foundation,
 Inc—BSUF, USA, 473
Brot für die Welt, Germany, 163
Brother's Brother Foundation, USA, 474
Building Resources Across Communities—
 BRAC, Bangladesh, 52
Butler (J. Homer) Foundation, USA, 504
C. P. Ramaswami Aiyar Foundation, India, 204
CAF—Charities Aid Foundation, UK, 396
Canadian Catholic Organization for Development
 and Peace, Canada, 83
Canadian Centre for International Studies and
 Co-operation/Centre d'études et de
 coopération internationale—CECI,
 Canada, 83
Canadian Co-operative Association, Canada, 80
Canadian Executive Service Organization—
 CESO/Service d'assistance canadienne aux
 organismes—SACO, Canada, 83
Canadian Foodgrains Bank, Canada, 84
Canadian Hunger Foundation, Canada, 84
CARE International—CI, Switzerland, 361
The Carter Center, USA, 476
Cartier Foundation for Contemporary Art,
 France, 141
Catholic Agency for World Development—
 Trócaire, Ireland, 213
CCF—Christian Children's Fund, USA, 478
CECHE—Center for Communications, Health
 and the Environment, USA, 477
CECI—Canadian Centre for International
 Studies and Co-operation/Centre d'études et
 de coopération internationale, Canada, 83
CenDHRRA—Center for the Development of
 Human Resources in Rural Asia,
 Philippines, 302
Center for Communications, Health and the
 Environment—CECHE, USA, 477
Center for Cultural and Technical Interchange
 between East and West—East-West Center,
 USA, 487
Center for the Development of Human Resources
 in Rural Asia—CenDHRRA, Philippines, 302
Centre for Advancement of Philanthropy—CAP,
 India, 198
Centre for Environment, Education and
 Development, USA, 516
Centre International de Coopération pour le
 Développement Agricole—CICDA,
 France, 136
Centro Internacional de Agricultura Tropical—
 CIAT, Colombia, 104
CESO—Canadian Executive Service
 Organization, Canada, 83
Chandana Art Foundation International,
 India, 200
Charities Advisory Trust, UK, 396
Charities Aid Foundation—CAF, UK, 396
Charity Projects, UK, 411
Charles Delmar Foundation, USA, 484
Charles Wallace India Trust, UK, 454
Chemtech Foundation, India, 201
ChildFund International, USA, 478
ChildFund Korea, Korea (Republic), 246
Children International—CI, USA, 479
Children of the Mekong, France, 139
CIAT—Centro Internacional de Agricultura
 Tropical, Colombia, 104
Claiborne (Liz) and Ortenberg (Art) Foundation,
 USA, 480
Climate Cent Foundation, Switzerland, 375
Clovek v tisni—spolecnost pri Ceske televizi,
 o.p.s., Czech Republic, 113
Co-operation for the Promotion and Development
 of Welfare Activities, Spain, 342
Comic Relief, UK, 411
Commonwealth Foundation, UK, 411
Community Aid Abroad—Oxfam Australia,
 Australia, 43
Concern India Foundation, India, 201
Concern Universal, UK, 412
CUSO-VSO, Canada, 86
Czech TV Foundation, Czech Republic, 113
Damien Foundation, Belgium, 58
Dasra, India, 198
Delmar (Charles) Foundation, USA, 484
Demokratikus Átalakulásért Intézet,
 Hungary, 196

Deutsche Gesellschaft für Auswärtige Politik—DGAP, Germany, 164
DEVI—Dignity, Education, Vision International, India, 201
Dignity, Education, Vision International—DEVI, India, 201
DOEN Foundation, Netherlands, 280
Dreyfus Health Foundation—DHF, USA, 485
East-West Center—EWC, USA, 487
EcoHealth Alliance, USA, 487
Écoles Sans Frontières—ESF, France, 139
Else Kröner-Fresenius Foundation, Germany, 173
Else Kröner-Fresenius-Stiftung, Germany, 173
Enda Third World—Environment and Development Action in the Third World, Senegal, 322
Enda Tiers Monde—Environnement et Développement du Tiers-Monde, Senegal, 322
endPoverty.org, USA, 488
Enfants du Mekong, France, 139
Enterprise Development International, USA, 488
Entraide Protestante Suisse, Switzerland, 367
Environmental Protection Research Foundation, India, 201
Environnement et Développement du Tiers-Monde—Enda, Senegal, 322
European NGOs on Agriculture, Food, Trade and Development, France, 135
The Evian Group at IMD, Switzerland, 363
EWC—East-West Center, USA, 487
The Family Federation of Finland, Finland, 133
FARM Foundation— Foundation for World Agriculture and Rural Life, France, 145
FDH—Frères des Hommes, France, 152
Federación Argentina de Apoyo Familiar—FAAF, Argentina, 31
Feed the Children, USA, 490
FH—Food for the Hungry, USA, 491
filia.die frauenstiftung, Germany, 168
filia—the Women's Foundation, Germany, 168
Finnish NGO Foundation for Human Rights—KIOS, Finland, 132
First Peoples Worldwide—FPW, USA, 490
Fondation Abri International, Canada, 97
Fondation pour l'Agriculture et la Ruralité dans le Monde—Fondation FARM, France, 145
Fondation Bettencourt-Schueller, France, 141
Fondation canadienne contre la faim, Canada, 84
Fondation Cartier pour l'Art Contemporain, France, 141
Fondation Ensemble, France, 143
Fondation d'Entreprise Air France, France, 144
Fondation d'Entreprise Renault, France, 144
Fondation contre la Faim, USA, 491
Fondation FARM—Fondation pour l'Agriculture et la Ruralité dans le Monde, France, 145
Fondation Marguerite et Aimé Maeght, France, 147
Fondation Pro Victimis Genève, Switzerland, 365
Fondation Syngenta pour une Agriculture Durable, Switzerland, 376
FOOD—Foundation of Occupational Development, India, 201
Food for the Hungry—FH, USA, 491
FOPERDA—Fondation Royale Père Damien pour la Lutte Contre la Lèpre, Belgium, 58
Foundation for Human Rights and Humanitarian Relief, Turkey, 389
Foundation 'Life for All', Switzerland, 375
Foundation of Occupational Development—FOOD, India, 201
Foundation Open Society Institute—Pakistan, Pakistan, 294
Foundation to Promote Health, Liechtenstein, 255
Foundation for Revitalization of Local Health Traditions—FRLHT, India, 201
The Fred Hollows Foundation, Australia, 41
Freedom from Hunger, USA, 494
Freedom from Hunger Council of Ireland—Gorta, Ireland, 211
Freeplay Foundation, UK, 429
French Agriculturalists and International Development, France, 136
Frères des Hommes—FDH, France, 152
FRLHT—Foundation Revitalization Local Health, India, 201
Fundación CODESPA—Futuro en Marcha, Spain, 342
Fundación Intervida, Spain, 344
Fundación María Francisca de Roviralta, Spain, 347
The Gaia Foundation, UK, 418
Gandhi Peace Foundation, India, 202
German Council on Foreign Relations, Germany, 164
Gift of the Givers Foundation, South Africa, 332

Global Fund for Community Foundations—GFCF, South Africa, 331
Global Harmony Foundation—GHF, Switzerland, 367
Global Voluntary Service—GVS, Japan, 232
Globe Foundation of Canada—GLOBE, Canada, 89
Good Neighbors International, Korea (Republic), 246
Gorta—Freedom from Hunger Council of Ireland, Ireland, 211
Grameen Foundation—GF, USA, 499
Grassroots International—GRI, USA, 500
HALO Trust, UK, 419
Hamdard Foundation Pakistan, Pakistan, 294
Hamlyn (Paul) Foundation, UK, 419
Havelaar (Max) Foundation, Netherlands, 281
Health Action International, Netherlands, 275
Health Volunteers Overseas—HVO, USA, 501
Hedwig and Robert Samuel Foundation, Germany, 177
Hedwig und Robert Samuel-Stiftung, Germany, 177
Heifer International, USA, 502
HEKS—Hilfswerk Evangelischen Kirchen Schweiz, Switzerland, 367
HELP International, USA, 503
Helvetas Swiss Intercooperation, Switzerland, 367
Hilden Charitable Fund, UK, 421
Hilfswerk der Evangelischen Kirchen Schweiz—HEKS, Switzerland, 367
Himalayan Light Foundation—HLF, Nepal, 271
HIVOS—Humanistisch Institut voor Ontwikkelings Samenwerking, Netherlands, 275
HLF—Himalayan Light Foundation, Nepal, 271
Hollows (Fred) Foundation, Australia, 41
Holt International, USA, 504
Holt International Children's Services—HICS, USA, 504
Humanistic Institute for Co-operation with Developing Countries, Netherlands, 275
Humanistisch Instituut voor Ontwikkelings Samenwerking—HIVOS, Netherlands, 275
Humanitarian Relief Foundation, Turkey, 389
IACD—Institute of Asian Culture and Development, Korea (Republic), 246
ICLARM—The WorldFish Center, Malaysia, 260
ICSSR—Indian Council of Social Science Research, India, 202
IFAD—International Fund for Agricultural Development, Italy, 226
IFHD—International Foundation for Human Development, India, 203
IHCF—Stiftung zur Förderung der Gesundheit, Liechtenstein, 255
IIEE—Indian Institute of Ecology and Environment, India, 202
IKEA Foundation, Netherlands, 275
Impact First International, Canada, 89
India Assistance, Germany, 171
India Partners, USA, 506
Indian Centre for Philanthropy, India, 198
Indian Council for Child Welfare, India, 202
Indian Council of Social Science Research—ICSSR, India, 202
Indian National Trust for Art and Cultural Heritage—INTACH, India, 203
IndianNGOs.com Pvt Ltd, India, 198
Indienhilfe eV, Germany, 171
INFID—International NGO Forum on Indonesian Development, Indonesia, 207
INHURED International—International Institute for Human Rights, Environment and Development, Nepal, 271
Inlaks Foundation, India, 203
İnsan Hak ve Hürriyetleri İnsani Yardım Vakfı, Turkey, 389
Institut international des Droits de l'Enfant, Switzerland, 368
Institut Nord-Sud, Canada, 95
Institute of Asian Culture and Development—IACD, Korea (Republic), 246
Institute for Development Research, USA, 556
Institute for Latin American and Caribbean Integration, Argentina, 34
Instituto para la Integración de América Latina y el Caribe—BID-INTAL, Argentina, 34
INTACH (UK) Trust, India, 203
INTACH—Indian National Trust for Art and Cultural Heritage, India, 203
Inter Pares, Canada, 90
International Alert—Alert, UK, 422
International Centre for Democratic Transition—ICDT, Hungary, 196
International Centre for the Legal Protection of Human Rights—Interights, UK, 423

International Centre for Living Aquatic Resources—ICLARM, Malaysia, 260
International Centre for Tropical Agriculture, Colombia, 104
International Confederation of Family Support, Argentina, 31
International Development and Relief Foundation, Canada, 91
International Executive Service Corps— IESC, USA, 508
The International Foundation, USA, 508
International Foundation for Human Development—IFHD, India, 203
International Fund for Agricultural Development—IFAD, Italy, 226
International Institute for Environment and Development—IIED, UK, 423
International Institute for Human Rights, Environment and Development—INHURED International, Nepal, 271
International Institute for the Rights of the Child, Switzerland, 368
International Institute of Rural Reconstruction—IIRR, Philippines, 303
International NGO Forum on Indonesian Development—INFID, Indonesia, 207
International Refugee Trust—IRT, UK, 424
International Relief and Development—IRD, USA, 510
International Relief Teams, USA, 510
International Research & Exchanges Board—IREX, USA, 511
International Water Management Institute—IWMI, Sri Lanka, 350
International Women's Health Coalition—IWHC, USA, 510
Intervida Foundation, Spain, 344
IREX—International Research & Exchanges Board, USA, 511
Ishizaka Foundation, Japan, 234
Isis Internacional, Chile, 100
Isis International, Chile, 100
J. Homer Butler Foundation, Inc, USA, 504
Japan International Volunteer Center—JVC, Japan, 236
JEN, Japan, 237
Jenifer Altman Foundation—JAF, USA, 463
The John D. and Catherine T. MacArthur Foundation, USA, 520
Jones (W. Alton) Foundation, USA, 473
Karl Kübel Foundation for Child and Family, Germany, 174
Karl-Kübel-Stiftung für Kind und Familie, Germany, 174
Karuna Trust/ Aid for India, UK, 426
Keidanren Ishizaka Memorial Foundation, Japan, 234
Kerzner Marine Foundation—KMF, USA, 515
Khemka (Nand and Jeet) Foundation, India, 203
KIOS—Finnish NGO Foundation for Human Rights, Finland, 132
Kröner-Fresenius (Else) Stiftung, Germany, 173
KRS Education and Rural Development Foundation, Inc, USA, 516
Kübel (Karl) Stiftung für Kind und Familie, Germany, 174
Lama Gangchen World Peace Foundation, Italy, 227
Latin American, African and Asian Social Housing Service, Chile, 101
Leprosy Mission International, UK, 428
Lifeline Energy, UK, 429
Lifewater International—LI, USA, 518
Liliane Foundation, Netherlands, 281
Liz Claiborne and Art Ortenberg Foundation, USA, 480
The Long Now Foundation—LNF, USA, 519
Luxemburg (Rosa) Stiftung, Germany, 174
LWR—Lutheran World Relief, USA, 519
M. S. Swaminathan Research Foundation—MSSRF, India, 205
M-USA—Mercy-USA for Aid and Development, USA, 524
M. Venkatarangaiya Foundation, India, 206
MacArthur (John D. and Catherine T.) Foundation, USA, 520
MADRE, USA, 521
Maeght (Marguerite et Aimé), Fondation, France, France, 147
Mama Cash, Netherlands, 277
Manfred Woerner Foundation, Bulgaria, 74
Mani Tese, Italy, 227
MAP International—Medical Assistance Programs, USA, 522
March of Dimes, USA, 522
Marguerite and Aimé Maeght Foundation, France, 147

María Francisca de Roviralta Foundation,
Spain, 347
Match International Centre, Canada, 93
Max Bell Foundation, Canada, 81
The Max Foundation, USA, 522
Max Havelaar Foundation, Netherlands, 281
Medical Assistance Programs, USA, 522
Medical Emergency Relief International—
MERLIN, UK, 432
Mercy-USA for Aid and Development—M-USA,
USA, 524
MERLIN—Medical Emergency Relief
International, UK, 432
Miriam Dean Fund, UK, 413
Miriam Dean Refugee Trust Fund, UK, 413
Moriya Foundation, Japan, 238
The Mountain Institute—TMI, USA, 526
Mukti Lawrence Foundation, Bangladesh, 52
Muslim Aid, UK, 433
Mutual Aid and Liaison Service, France, 154
Naandi Foundation—A New Beginning,
India, 203
Nand and Jeet Khemka Foundation, India, 203
National Institute for Sustainable
Development—NISD, India, 204
The Nature Conservancy, USA, 528
Nederlandse Organisatie voor Internationale
Ontwikkelingssamenwerking—Stichting
NOVIB, Netherlands, 279
Nepal Forward Foundation, Nepal, 271
Van Neste Foundation, UK, 453
NFCR—National Foundation for Cancer
Research, USA, 529
NFI—National Foundation for India, India, 204
Nirnaya, India, 204
Non-Governmental Organization JEN,
Japan, 237
North-South-Bridge Foundation, Germany, 181
North-South Institute/Institut Nord-Sud,
Canada, 95
Novartis Foundation for Sustainable
Development—NFSD, Switzerland, 371
Novartis Stiftung für Nachhaltige Entwicklung,
Switzerland, 371
NOVIB (Oxfam Netherlands), Netherlands, 279
OneWorld International Foundation, UK, 435
Open Society Forum (Mongolia), Mongolia, 266
Operation Eyesight Universal/Action universelle
de la vue, Canada, 95
Operation Rainbow, Inc, USA, 530
Operation USA, USA, 530
Opportunity International USA, USA, 530
Organisation Afro-Asiatique Pour Le
Developpement Rural, India, 199
Outreach International, USA, 531
Oxfam Australia, Australia, 43
Oxfam Canada, Canada, 95
Oxfam Deutschland e.V., Germany, 176
Oxfam Hong Kong, Hong Kong, 194
Oxfam India, India, 204
Oxfam NOVIB—Nederlandse Organisatie voor
Internationale Ontwikkelingssamenwerking,
Netherlands, 279
Oxfam NOVIB—Netherlands Organization for
International Development Co-operation,
Netherlands, 279
Pacific Peoples' Partnership, Canada, 95
Pakistan Centre for Philanthropy—PCP,
Pakistan, 294
Pakistan Institute of International Affairs—
PIIA, Pakistan, 294
PAN Asia and the Pacific—Pesticide Action
Network Asia and the Pacific, Malaysia, 260
The Parthenon Trust, Switzerland, 371
Partners in Rural Development, Canada, 84
Pathfinder International, USA, 533
Paul Hamlyn Foundation—PHF, UK, 419
Peace, Health and Human Development
Foundation—PHD Foundation, Japan, 239
People in Need, Czech Republic, 113
People-to-People Health Foundation, Inc—
Project Hope, USA, 537
Pestalozzi Children's Foundation,
Switzerland, 374
Pesticide Action Network Asia and the Pacific—
PAN AP, Malaysia, 260
The PHD Foundation—Peace, Health and Human
Development Foundation, Japan, 239
PHF—Paul Hamlyn Foundation, UK, 419
Plan Ireland, Ireland, 212
Ploughshares Fund, USA, 536
Population Council, USA, 536
Premji (Azim) Foundation, India, 204
Press Foundation of Asia—PFA, Philippines, 303
Prince Claus Fund for Culture and Development,
Netherlands, 279
Prins Claus Fonds Voor Cultuur en Ontwikkeling,
Netherlands, 279

Pro Victimis Foundation, Switzerland, 365
Project HOPE, USA, 537
Project Trust, UK, 439
Prudential Foundation, USA, 537
Quaid-i-Azam Academy, Pakistan, 294
Rajiv Gandhi Foundation, India, 201
Ramaswami Aiyar (C. P.) Foundation, India, 204
Ramon Magsaysay Award Foundation,
Philippines, 303
Ramsay Foundation, Switzerland, 372
Refugees International Japan—RIJ, Japan, 239
Regional Centre for Strategic Studies—RCSS, Sri
Lanka, 350
Relief International, USA, 539
Renault Foundation, France, 144
Réseau d'ONG Européennes sur l'Agro-
alimentaire, le Commerce, l'Environnement
et le Développement—RONGEAD,
France, 135
Rhodes Trust, UK, 441
RONGEAD—Réseau d'ONG Européennes sur
l'Agro-alimentaire, le Commerce,
l'Environnement et le Développement,
France, 135
Rooftops Canada Foundation, Canada, 97
Rosa Luxemburg Foundation, Germany, 174
Rosa-Luxemburg-Stiftung, Germany, 174
Roviralta (María Francisca de), Fundación,
Spain, 347
Rowan Charitable Trust, UK, 441
Royal Asiatic Society of Great Britain and
Ireland, UK, 443
The Royal Australasian College of Physicians—
RACP, Australia, 44
Royal Commonwealth Society for the Blind—
Sight Savers International, UK, 448
Royal Society for the Protection of Birds—RSPB,
UK, 445
RSPB—Royal Society for the Protection of Birds,
UK, 445
The Rufford Foundation, UK, 445
Rufford Maurice Laing Foundation, UK, 445
Rutgers WPF, Netherlands, 279
Sabera Foundation, India, 205
Sabera Foundation India, India, 205
Sabre Foundation, Inc, USA, 542
SACO—Service d'assistance canadienne aux
organismes, Canada, 83
Sahabdeen (A. M. M.) Trust Foundation, Sri
Lanka, 350
Sampradaan Indian Centre for Philanthropy,
India, 198
Samuel (Hedwig und Robert) Stiftung,
Germany, 177
Santé Sud, France, 154
Savings Banks Foundation for International
Cooperation, Germany, 179
Schools Without Frontiers, France, 139
Schweisfurth Foundation, Germany, 178
Schweisfurth-Stiftung, Germany, 178
SCIAF—Scottish Catholic International Aid
Fund, UK, 447
Scottish Catholic International Aid Fund—
SCIAF, UK, 447
Seeds of Peace, USA, 543
SEL—Service d'Entraide et de Liaison,
France, 154
SELAVIP International—Service de Promotion
de l'Habitation Populaire en Amérique Latine,
Afrique et Asie, Chile, 101
Service d'Entraide et de Liaison—SEL,
France, 154
Seva Foundation, USA, 544
Shastri Indo-Canadian Institute, Canada, 97
Sight Savers International, UK, 448
Sir Dorabji Tata Trust, India, 205
Solidarité, France, 155
Solidarity, France, 155
South Pacific Peoples Foundation Canada,
Canada, 95
Southern Health, France, 154
Sparkassenstiftung für internationale
Kooperation eV, Germany, 179
St John Ambulance, UK, 446
Standing International Forum on Ethnic
Conflict, Genocide and Human Rights—
International Alert, UK, 422
Stichting Agromisa, Netherlands, 280
Stichting DOEN, Netherlands, 280
Stichting Liliane Fonds, Netherlands, 281
Stichting Max Havelaar, Netherlands, 281
Stichting Triodos Foundation, Netherlands, 282
Stiftung Kinderdorf Pestalozzi, Switzerland, 374
Stiftung Klimarappen, Switzerland, 375
Stiftung 'Leben für Alle', Switzerland, 375
Stiftung Nord-Süd-Brücken, Germany, 181
Street Kids International, Canada, 98
Stretched Hands, Italy, 227

Swiss Foundation for Technical Co-operation,
Switzerland, 375
Swiss Interchurch Aid, Switzerland, 367
SWISSAID Foundation, Switzerland, 375
Swisscontact—Swiss Foundation for Technical
Co-operation, Switzerland, 375
The Sylvia Adams Charitable Trust, UK, 398
Synergos—The Synergos Institute, USA, 460
Syngenta Foundation for Sustainable
Agriculture, Switzerland, 376
Syngenta Stiftung für Nachhaltige
Landwirtschaft, Switzerland, 376
TANZ—Trade Aid NZ Inc, New Zealand, 287
TEAR Australia, Australia, 45
Terre des Hommes Foundation, Switzerland, 376
Tewa, Nepal, 271
Third World Network—TWN, Malaysia, 260
Third World Solidarity Action, Luxembourg, 257
Together Foundation, France, 143
Tokyu Foundation for Inbound Students,
Japan, 240
The Toyota Foundation, Japan, 240
Trade Aid NZ Inc—TANZ, New Zealand, 287
Triodos Foundation, Netherlands, 282
Trócaire—Catholic Agency for World
Development, Ireland, 213
Turquoise Mountain Foundation, UK, 452
United Service Committee of Canada, Canada, 98
United Society for the Propagation of the
Gospel—USPG, UK, 453
Unity Foundation, Luxembourg, 257
USC Canada, Canada, 98
Väestöliitto, Finland, 133
Vanarai, India, 206
Venkatarangaiya (M.) Foundation, India, 206
Volkart Foundation, Switzerland, 376
Volkart-Stiftung, Switzerland, 376
Voluntary Action Network India—VANI,
India, 206
Voluntary Service Overseas, UK, 454
Volunteer Service Abroad—VSA, New
Zealand, 287
VSA—Volunteer Service Abroad, New
Zealand, 287
VSO, UK, 454
Wallace (Charles) India Trust, UK, 454
War on Want, UK, 454
WasserStiftung, Germany, 184
Water Foundation, Germany, 184
Water.org, Inc, USA, 552
WaterAid, UK, 454
Westminster Foundation for Democracy—WFD,
UK, 455
Whirlpool Foundation, USA, 553
Wildlife Preservation Trust International,
USA, 487
Wildlife Trust, USA, 487
Winrock International, USA, 555
Woerner (Manfred) Foundation, Bulgaria, 74
World Accord, Canada, 99
World Association of Children's Friends,
Monaco, 265
World Education, Inc, USA, 556
World Land Trust—WLT, UK, 456
World Literacy of Canada—WLC, Canada, 99
World Neighbors, USA, 557
World Peace Foundation—WPF, USA, 557
World Population Foundation, Netherlands, 279
World Teacher Trust, India, 206
The WorldFish Center, Malaysia, 260
Youth for Development and Co-operation—YDC,
Netherlands, 283
Zakat House, Kuwait, 249
Zero-Kap Foundation, Netherlands, 283
ZOA, Netherlands, 283
Zurich Community Trust, UK, 457
Zurich Financial Services (UKISA) Community
Trust Ltd, UK, 457

USA AND CANADA

1945 Foundation, Canada, 90
A. L. Mailman Family Foundation, Inc, USA, 521
ACCION International, USA, 460
ACTR/ACCELS—American Councils for
International Education, USA, 464
The Adolph and Esther Gottlieb Foundation, Inc,
USA, 498
Adriano Olivetti Foundation, Italy, 223
AFPE—American Foundation for
Pharmaceutical Education, USA, 465
Africa-America Institute—AAI, USA, 461
Africa Grantmakers' Affinity Group—AGAG,
USA, 458
African Development Institute, Inc, USA, 461
African Wildlife Foundation—AWF, USA, 462

AFSC—American Friends Service Committee, USA, 465
Aga Khan Foundation—AKF, Switzerland, 360
Aga Khan Foundation Canada, Canada, 80
AGAG—Africa Grantmakers' Affinity Group, USA, 458
Agromart Foundation, Sri Lanka, 350
The Ahmanson Foundation, USA, 462
AINA—Arctic Institute of North America, Canada, 81
AIT—Asian Institute of Technology, Thailand, 383
Alamire Foundation, Belgium, 56
Alavi Foundation, USA, 462
Alberta Innovates Health Solutions, Canada, 81
Alden (George I.) Trust, USA, 463
Alfred P. Sloan Foundation, USA, 545
Alicia Patterson Foundation—APF, USA, 533
Allen (Paul G.) Family Foundation, USA, 463
Alliance for International Educational and Cultural Exchange, USA, 463
Altman (Jenifer) Foundation, USA, 463
The Alva Foundation, Canada, 81
America–Mideast Educational and Training Services Inc, USA, 468
American Council for Voluntary International Action—InterAction, USA, 459
American Councils for International Education—ACTR/ACCELS, USA, 464
American Foundation for the Blind, Inc—AFB, USA, 465
American Foundation for Pharmaceutical Education—AFPE, USA, 465
American Friends Service Committee—AFSC, USA, 465
American Heart Association, Inc, USA, 465
American Historical Association, USA, 466
American Hungarian Foundation, USA, 466
American Institute of Pakistan Studies, USA, 466
American Scandinavian Foundation—ASF, USA, 467
American Schools of Oriental Research—ASOR, USA, 467
Amerind Foundation, Inc, USA, 468
AMIDEAST—America-Mideast Educational and Training Services, Inc, USA, 468
The Andrew W. Mellon Foundation, USA, 523
The Andy Warhol Foundation for the Visual Arts, Inc, USA, 552
The Annenberg Foundation, USA, 468
Arca Foundation, USA, 469
Arctic Institute of North America—AINA, Canada, 81
Arcus Foundation, USA, 469
AREGAK—Sun/Soleil, Armenia, 35
Arie and Ida Crown Memorial, USA, 483
Armand-Frappier Foundation, Canada, 88
Armstrong (Lance) Foundation, USA, 469
Arthritis Australia, Australia, 37
Arthritis Foundation, USA, 469
Arthritis Foundation of Australia, Australia, 37
Arthur Rubinstein International Music Society, Israel, 215
Asia Foundation, USA, 469
Asia Pacific Foundation of Canada, Canada, 81
Asia Society, USA, 470
Asian Cultural Council—ACC, USA, 470
Asian Youth Center, USA, 470
ASOR—American Schools of Oriental Research, USA, 467
Aspen Institute, USA, 470
Association of Voluntary Service Organisations—AVSO, Belgium, 57
Atkinson Foundation, USA, 470
Atlantic Philanthropies, USA, 471
Australian-American Fulbright Commission, Australia, 37
Ayala Foundation USA—AF-USA, USA, 535
Bacon (Francis) Foundation, Inc, USA, 471
Baker (E. A.) Foundation for the Prevention of Blindness, Canada, 85
Bank of America Foundation, USA, 472
The Baron de Hirsch Fund, USA, 484
BBVA Foundation, Spain, 340
Beaverbrook Foundation, UK, 403
Bell (Max) Foundation, Canada, 81
Benton Foundation, USA, 472
Bertelsmann Foundation, Germany, 162
Bertelsmann Stiftung, Germany, 162
BID-INTAL—Instituto para la Integración de América Latina y el Caribe, Argentina, 34
Blue Moon Fund, Inc, USA, 473
Bosch (Robert) Stiftung GmbH, Germany, 163
Bradley (Lynde and Harry) Foundation, Inc, USA, 473
Bridge to Asia—BTA, USA, 473
Bridges for Education, Inc—BFE, USA, 473

British Schools and Universities Foundation, Inc—BSUF, USA, 473
The Broad Foundations, USA, 474
Brookings Institution, USA, 474
Buck (Pearl S. Buck) International, USA, 474
Burroughs Wellcome Fund—BWF, USA, 475
The Bydale Foundation, USA, 475
CAF—Charities Aid Foundation, UK, 396
The Camargo Foundation, France, 138
The Camille and Henry Dreyfus Foundation, Inc, USA, 485
The Canada Council for the Arts/Conseil des Arts du Canada, Canada, 82
Canada Foundation for Innovation/Fondation canadienne pour l'innovation, Canada, 82
Canada Israel Cultural Foundation, Canada, 82
Canadian Cancer Society, Canada, 83
Canadian Catholic Organization for Development and Peace, Canada, 83
Canadian Centre for International Studies and Co-operation/Centre d'études et de coopération internationale—CECI, Canada, 83
Canadian Centre for Philanthropy, Canada, 80
Canadian Co-operative Association, Canada, 80
Canadian Council for International Co-operation—CCIC/Conseil canadien pour la coopération internationale—CCCI, Canada, 80
Canadian Crossroads International/Carrefour Canadien International—CCI, Canada, 83
Canadian Executive Service Organization—CESO/Service d'assistance canadienne aux organismes—SACO, Canada, 83
Canadian Friends of the Hebrew University, Canada, 84
Canadian International Council/Conseil International du Canada—CIC, Canada, 84
Canadian Liver Foundation/Fondation Canadienne du Foie, Canada, 85
Canadian Urban Institute, Canada, 85
Cancer Research Fund of the Damon Runyon-Walter Winchell Foundation, USA, 541
The Carl and Lily Pforzheimer Foundation, Inc, USA, 535
Carnegie Corporation of New York, USA, 475
Carnegie Hero Fund Commission, USA, 476
Carson (John W.) Foundation, USA, 476
The Carter Center, USA, 476
Carthage Foundation, USA, 476
Cartier Foundation for Contemporary Art, France, 141
CCCI—Conseil canadien pour la coopération internationale, Canada, 80
CCF—Christian Children's Fund, USA, 478
CCI—Carrefour Canadien International, Canada, 83
CCI—Center for Citizen Initiatives, USA, 476
CCIC—Canadian Council for International Co-operation, Canada, 80
CECHE—Center for Communications, Health and the Environment, USA, 477
CECI—Canadian Centre for International Studies and Co-operation/Centre d'études et de coopération internationale, Canada, 83
Center for Citizen Initiatives—CCI, USA, 476
Center for Communications, Health and the Environment—CECHE, USA, 477
Center for Cultural and Technical Interchange between East and West—East-West Center, USA, 487
Centre for Environment, Education and Development, USA, 516
CESO—Canadian Executive Service Organization, Canada, 83
CGP—Japan Foundation Centre Global Partnership, Japan, 236
Chandana Art Foundation International, India, 200
Charities Aid Foundation—CAF, UK, 396
Charles Delmar Foundation, USA, 484
Charles F. Kettering Foundation, USA, 515
Charles and Lynn Schusterman Family Foundation—CLSFF, USA, 543
Charles Stewart Mott Foundation—CSMF, USA, 526
Chastell Foundation, Canada, 85
The Chicago Community Trust, USA, 478
ChildFund International, USA, 478
Children of The Americas—COTA, USA, 479
Children International—CI, USA, 479
Christopher and Dana Reeve Foundation, USA, 538
Christopher Reynolds Foundation, Inc, USA, 539
Churchill (Winston) Foundation of the United States, USA, 479
CIC—Canadian International Council/Conseil International du Canada, Canada, 84

Claiborne (Liz) and Ortenberg (Art) Foundation, USA, 480
Clean Water Fund—CWF, USA, 480
Cleveland Foundation, USA, 480
Cleveland H. Dodge Foundation, Inc, USA, 485
CNIB/INCA, Canada, 85
Coalition of National Voluntary Organizations, Canada, 80
Columbia Foundation, Canada, 86
Commonwealth Foundation, UK, 411
Compton Foundation, Inc, USA, 481
Conseil des Arts du Canada, Canada, 82
Costopoulos (J. F.) Foundation, Greece, 186
Council on Foundations, USA, 458
Coutu (Marcelle et Jean), Fondation, Canada, 88
Covenant Foundation, USA, 483
The Craig and Susan McCaw Foundation, USA, 520
The CRB Foundation/La Fondation CRB, Canada, 86
Crown (Arie and Ida) Memorial, USA, 483
Crown Family Philanthropies, USA, 483
CUSO-VSO, Canada, 86
Cystic Fibrosis Canada, Canada, 87
Cystic Fibrosis Foundation, USA, 484
Damon Runyon Cancer Research Foundation, USA, 541
Danmark-Amerika Fondet, Denmark, 117
David and Lucile Packard Foundation, USA, 531
Delmar (Charles) Foundation, USA, 484
Denmark-America Foundation, Denmark, 117
Desmond Tutu Peace Foundation—DTPF, USA, 549
Deutsche Bank Americas Foundation and Community Development Group, USA, 484
Deutsche Gesellschaft für Auswärtige Politik—DGAP, Germany, 164
DeWitt Wallace—Reader's Digest Fund, Inc, USA, 551
Diakonia, Sweden, 352
Dodge (Cleveland H.) Foundation, Inc, USA, 485
Donner (William H.) Foundation, Inc, USA, 485
Dr Scholl Foundation, USA, 543
Dräger Foundation, Germany, 166
Dräger-Stiftung, Germany, 166
Dreyfus (Camille and Henry) Foundation, Inc, USA, 485
Dreyfus Health Foundation—DHF, USA, 485
Drug Policy Alliance—DPA, USA, 485
Duke Endowment, USA, 486
Dumbarton Oaks, USA, 486
Earthrights International—ERI, USA, 486
East-West Center—EWC, USA, 487
Eça de Queiroz Foundation, Portugal, 312
EcoHealth Alliance, USA, 487
ECPD—European Centre for Peace and Development, Serbia, 324
The Edmond de Rothschild Foundations, USA, 541
The Edna McConnell Clark Foundation, USA, 520
EJLB Foundation, Canada, 87
Eldee Foundation, Canada, 87
ELIAMEP—Hellenic Foundation for European and Foreign Policy, Greece, 187
Elizabeth Kostova Foundation for Creative Writing, Bulgaria, 76
Emile Chanoux Foundation—Institute for Federalist and Regionalist Studies, Italy, 218
endPoverty.org, USA, 488
Enterprise Development International, USA, 488
Epilepsy Foundation, USA, 489
The Ernest C. Manning Awards Foundation, Canada, 93
Esperança, Inc, USA, 489
Etruscan Foundation, USA, 489
European Centre for Peace and Development—ECPD, Serbia, 324
EWC—East-West Center, USA, 487
The F. K. Morrow Foundation, Canada, 94
FAF—French-American Foundation, USA, 494
Feed My Hungry People, Inc, USA, 490
FINCA International, USA, 490
FLAAR—Foundation for Latin American Anthropological Research, USA, 492
Florence Gould Foundation, USA, 499
FOKAL—Fondation Connaissance et Liberté (Haiti), Haiti, 192
Fondation Armand-Frappier, Canada, 88
Fondation Baxter and Alma Ricard, Canada, 88
Fondation Cartier pour l'Art Contemporain, France, 141
Fondation Connaissance et Liberté (Haiti)—FOKAL, Haiti, 192
Fondation EJLB, Canada, 87
Fondation Emile Chanoux—Institut d'Etudes Fédéralistes et Régionalistes, Italy, 218
Fondation Jean-Louis Lévesque, Canada, 88

Fondation Jean Monnet pour l'Europe, Switzerland, 364
Fondation Marcelle et Jean Coutu, Canada, 88
Fondation Marguerite et Aimé Maeght, France, 147
Fondazione Adriano Olivetti, Italy, 223
Fondazione Giovanni Lorenzini, Italy, 222
Foundation Center, USA, 458
Foundation for Deep Ecology, USA, 492
Foundation for International Community Assistance, USA, 490
Foundation for Knowledge and Liberty, Haiti, 192
Foundation for Latin American Anthropological Research, USA, 492
Foundation for Middle East Peace—FMEP, USA, 492
Foundation for Russian-American Economic Co-operation—FRAEC, USA, 493
The Francis Bacon Foundation, Inc, USA, 471
Francis Family Foundation, USA, 493
Frappier (Armand), Fondation, Canada, 88
The Freedom Forum, USA, 493
Freeman Foundation, USA, 494
French-American Foundation—FAF, USA, 494
Freshwater Society, USA, 494
Frontiers Foundation Inc/Fondation Frontière Inc, Canada, 89
Fundação Eça de Queiroz, Portugal, 312
Fundação Luso-Americana para o Desenvolvimento, Portugal, 312
Fundación Banco Bilbao Vizcaya Argentaria—Fundación BBVA, Spain, 340
Fundación BBVA—Fundación Banco Bilbao Vizcaya Argentaria, Spain, 340
Gandhi (Mahatma) Foundation for World Peace, Canada, 89
Gannett Foundation, USA, 493
General Service Foundation, USA, 495
The George A. and Eliza Gardner Howard Foundation, USA, 504
George Cedric Metcalf Charitable Foundation, Canada, 94
The George I. Alden Trust, USA, 463
Georges Lurcy Charitable and Educational Trust, USA, 519
German Council on Foreign Relations, Germany, 164
German Marshall Fund of the United States—GMF, USA, 496
Gilman (Howard) Foundation, USA, 496
Giovanni Lorenzini Foundation, Italy, 222
Giving USA Foundation, USA, 496
Globe Foundation of Canada—GLOBE, Canada, 89
GMF—German Marshall Fund of the United States, USA, 496
Goldsmith (Horace W.) Foundation, USA, 498
Gordon (Walter and Duncan) Charitable Foundation, Canada, 89
Gordon and Betty Moore Foundation, USA, 525
Gottlieb (Adolph and Esther) Foundation, Inc, USA, 498
Gould (Florence) Foundation, USA, 499
Grameen Foundation—GF, USA, 499
Grant (William T.) Foundation, USA, 499
The Grass Foundation, USA, 499
Grassroots International—GRI, USA, 500
Greve (William and Mary) Foundation, Inc, USA, 500
Guggenheim (John Simon) Memorial Foundation, USA, 500
Harry and Jeanette Weinberg Foundation, Inc, USA, 552
Hartford (John A.) Foundation, Inc, USA, 501
Health Action International, Netherlands, 275
Hearst (William Randolph) Foundation, USA, 502
The Hearst Foundation, Inc, USA, 501
Heifer International, USA, 502
Heineman (Minna James) Stiftung, Germany, 170
Heinz (Howard) Endowment, USA, 502
The Helene Wurlitzer Foundation of New Mexico, USA, 558
Hellenic Foundation for Culture, Greece, 186
Hellenic Foundation for European and Foreign Policy—ELIAMEP, Greece, 187
Helmsley (Leona M. and Harry B.) Charitable Trust, USA, 503
HELP International, USA, 503
The Henry J. Kaiser Family Foundation, USA, 513
Henry Luce Foundation, Inc, USA, 519
Hewlett (William and Flora) Foundation, USA, 503
Hirsch (Baron de) Fund, USA, 484
Hitachi Foundation, USA, 504
Holt International, USA, 504
Holt International Children's Services—HICS, USA, 504
Homeland Foundation, USA, 522

Horace W. Goldsmith Foundation, USA, 498
Horizons of Friendship, Canada, 90
Hospital for Sick Children Foundation, Canada, 97
Houston Endowment, Inc, USA, 504
Howard (George A. and Eliza Gardner) Foundation, USA, 504
Howard Gilman Foundation, Inc, USA, 496
Howard Heinz Endowment, USA, 502
The Humana Foundation, Inc, USA, 505
IAPA Scholarship Fund, USA, 505
Imagine Canada, Canada, 80
Impact First International, Canada, 89
Imperial Oil Foundation, Canada, 90
Independent Sector, USA, 459
Indian National Trust for Art and Cultural Heritage—INTACH, India, 203
INMED Partnerships for Children, USA, 506
Institut Arctique de l'Amérique du Nord—IAAN, Canada, 81
Institut Nord-Sud, Canada, 95
Institut urbain du Canada, Canada, 85
Institute for Development Research, USA, 556
Institute for Latin American and Caribbean Integration, Argentina, 34
Institute for Palestine Studies, Publishing and Research Organization—IPS, Lebanon, 252
Instituto para la Integración de América Latina y el Caribe—BID-INTAL, Argentina, 34
INTACH (UK) Trust, India, 203
INTACH—Indian National Trust for Art and Cultural Heritage, India, 203
Inter American Press Association Scholarship Fund, USA, 505
Inter Pares, Canada, 90
InterAction American Council for Voluntary International Action, USA, 459
International Development and Relief Foundation, Canada, 91
International Medical Services for Health—INMED, USA, 506
International Orthodox Christian Charities, Inc—IOCC, USA, 509
International Relief Teams, USA, 510
International Research & Exchanges Board—IREX, USA, 511
International Women's Health Coalition—IWHC, USA, 510
IREX—International Research & Exchanges Board, USA, 511
Irvine (James) Foundation, USA, 511
Isabel Allende Foundation, USA, 463
Islamic Relief Worldwide, UK, 425
Ittleson Foundation, USA, 511
IUC-Europe International Education Centre, Denmark, 119
IUC-Europe Internationalt Uddanneless Center, Denmark, 119
Ivey (Richard) Foundation, Canada, 91
Ivey Foundation, Canada, 91
The J. F. Costopoulos Foundation, Greece, 186
The J. F. Kapnek Trust Zimbabwe, Zimbabwe, 567
The James Irvine Foundation, USA, 511
The Japan Foundation Centre for Global Partnership—CGP, Japan, 236
Japanese-German Center Berlin, Germany, 173
Japanisch-Deutsches Zentrum Berlin, Germany, 173
JCIE—Japan Center for International Exchange, Japan, 236
Jean-Louis Lévesque Foundation, Canada, 88
Jean Monnet Foundation for Europe, Switzerland, 364
Jenifer Altman Foundation—JAF, USA, 463
The John A. Hartford Foundation, USA, 501
The John D. and Catherine T. MacArthur Foundation, USA, 520
John Simon Guggenheim Memorial Foundation, USA, 500
The John W. Carson Foundation, USA, 476
Johnson (Lyndon Baines) Foundation, USA, 512
Johnson (Robert Wood) Foundation, USA, 512
The Johnson Foundation at Wingspread, USA, 512
Jones (W. Alton) Foundation, USA, 473
Joseph P. Kennedy, Jr Foundation, USA, 515
Josiah Macy, Jr Foundation, USA, 521
Joyce Foundation, USA, 512
The Judith Rothschild Foundation, USA, 541
Kade (Max) Foundation, Inc, USA, 513
Kahanoff Foundation, Canada, 91
Kaiser (Henry J.) Family Foundation, USA, 513
Kapnek (J. F.) Charitable Trust Zimbabwe, Zimbabwe, 567
Kapor (Mitchell) Foundation, USA, 513
Karić fondacija, Serbia, 325
Karić Foundation, Serbia, 325
Kennan Institute, USA, 514

Kennedy (Joseph P.), Jr Foundation, USA, 515
Kennedy Memorial Trust, UK, 426
Kettering Foundation, USA, 515
King Hussein Foundation—KHF, Jordan, 241
Kokkalis Foundation, Greece, 187
Komen (Susan G.) Breast Cancer Foundation, USA, 515
Koret Foundation, USA, 515
The Kosciuszko Foundation, Inc, USA, 516
Kostova (Elizabeth) Foundation for Creative Writing, Bulgaria, 76
Kresge Foundation, USA, 516
Kress (Samuel H.) Foundation, USA, 516
KRS Education and Rural Development Foundation, Inc, USA, 516
L. J. Skaggs and Mary C. Skaggs Foundation, USA, 544
Laidlaw Foundation, Canada, 91
Lama Gangchen World Peace Foundation, Italy, 227
Lance Armstrong Foundation—Livestrong, USA, 469
Lannan Foundation, USA, 517
The Lawson Foundation, Canada, 92
Lawson Valentine Foundation, USA, 551
LBJ Foundation, USA, 512
The Leona M. and Harry B. Helmsley Charitable Trust, USA, 503
Leprosy Mission International, UK, 428
Levesque (Jean-Louis), Fondation, Canada, 88
Life Sciences Research Foundation—LSRF, USA, 518
Lila Wallace—Reader's Digest Fund, Inc, USA, 551
Lilly Endowment, Inc, USA, 518
Littauer (Lucius N.) Foundation, Inc, USA, 519
Livestrong, USA, 469
Liz Claiborne and Art Ortenberg Foundation, USA, 480
The Long Now Foundation—LNF, USA, 519
Lorenzini (Giovanni), Fondazione, Italy, 222
The Lotte and John Hecht Memorial Foundation, Canada, 90
Luce (Henry) Foundation, Inc, USA, 519
Lucie and André Chagnon Foundation/Fondation Lucie et André Chagnon, Canada, 85
Lucius N. Littauer Foundation, Inc, USA, 519
Ludwig Institute for Cancer Research—LICR, USA, 519
Lurcy (Georges) Charitable and Educational Trust, USA, 519
Luso-American Development Foundation, Portugal, 312
Lynde and Harry Bradley Foundation, Inc, USA, 473
Lyndon Baines Johnson Foundation, USA, 512
M-USA—Mercy-USA for Aid and Development, USA, 524
MacArthur (John D. and Catherine T.) Foundation, USA, 520
McCaw (Craig and Susan) Foundation, USA, 520
McConnell Clark (Edna) Foundation, USA, 520
McCormick (Robert R.) Foundation, USA, 520
Macdonald Stewart Foundation, Canada, 92
The Mackintosh Foundation, UK, 430
McKnight Foundation, USA, 521
The McLean Foundation, Canada, 93
Macy (Josiah), Jr Foundation, USA, 521
Maecenata Management GmbH, Germany, 159
Maeght (Marguerite et Aimé), Fondation, France, France, 147
Mahatma Gandhi Canadian Foundation for World Peace, Canada, 89
Mailman (A. L.) Family Foundation, USA, 521
Manfred Woerner Foundation, Bulgaria, 74
Manning (Ernest C.) Awards Foundation, Canada, 93
MAP International—Medical Assistance Programs, USA, 522
Marangopoulos Foundation for Human Rights, Greece, 188
Marcelle et Jean Coutu Foundation, Canada, 88
March of Dimes, USA, 522
Marguerite and Aimé Maeght Foundation, France, 147
Marisla Foundation, USA, 522
Markle (John and Mary R.) Foundation, USA, 522
Markle Foundation, USA, 522
Match International Centre, Canada, 93
Matsushita Foundation, USA, 532
Max Bell Foundation, Canada, 81
The Max Foundation, USA, 522
Max Kade Foundation, Inc, USA, 513
Mayfair Charities Ltd, UK, 430
The Maytree Foundation, Canada, 93
Medical Assistance Programs, USA, 522
Mellon (Andrew W.) Foundation, USA, 523

Mellon (Richard King) Foundation, USA, 523
Menzies (R. G.) Scholarship Fund, Australia, 42
Mercy-USA for Aid and Development—M-USA, USA, 524
Mertz Gilmore Foundation, USA, 524
Metcalf (George Cedric) Charitable Foundation, Canada, 94
Michael J. Fox Foundation for Parkinson's Research, USA, 493
Milbank Memorial Fund, USA, 524
Minna James Heineman Foundation, Germany, 170
Minna-James-Heineman-Stiftung, Germany, 170
Miriam G. and Ira D. Wallach Foundation, USA, 552
Mitchell Kapor Foundation, USA, 513
Molson Donations Fund/Fonds de bienfaisance Molson, Canada, 94
Molson Family Foundation, Canada, 94
Molson Foundation, Canada, 94
Monnet (Jean), Fondation pour l'Europe, Switzerland, 364
Moody Foundation, USA, 525
Morrow (The F. K.) Foundation, Canada, 94
Mosaic Foundation, USA, 526
Mostazafan Foundation of New York, USA, 462
Mott (Charles Stewart) Foundation, USA, 526
The Mountain Institute—TMI, USA, 526
Ms Foundation for Women, USA, 526
The Muttart Foundation, Canada, 94
Nathan Steinberg Family Foundation, Canada, 98
National Conference on Soviet Jewry, USA, 528
National Fish and Wildlife Foundation, USA, 527
National Humanities Center, USA, 527
National Kidney Foundation, Inc, USA, 527
National Science Foundation, USA, 527
National Wildlife Federation—NWF, USA, 527
The Nature Conservancy, USA, 528
NCSJ—National Conference on Soviet Jewry, USA, 528
Nelson Mandela Children's Fund—Canada, Canada, 93
Newberry Library, USA, 529
NFCR—National Foundation for Cancer Research, USA, 529
North-South Institute/Institut Nord-Sud, Canada, 95
Novartis US Foundation, USA, 529
NoVo Foundation, USA, 529
Oak Foundation, Switzerland, 371
Olivetti (Adriano), Fondazione, Italy, Italy, 223
OneWorld International Foundation, UK, 435
Open Society Institute—Washington, DC, USA, 530
Operation Beaver—Frontiers Foundation Inc, Canada, 89
Operation Rainbow, Inc, USA, 530
Operation USA, USA, 530
Orentreich Foundation for the Advancement of Science, Inc—OFAS, USA, 531
Outreach International, USA, 531
Oxfam Canada, Canada, 95
Pacific Peoples' Partnership, Canada, 95
Packard (David and Lucile) Foundation, USA, 531
Panasonic Foundation, USA, 532
Parkinson's Disease Foundation, Inc—PDF, USA, 533
Patterson (Alicia) Foundation, USA, 533
The Paul G. Allen Family Foundation, USA, 463
PBI—Peace Brigades International, UK, 437
Peace Brigades International—PBI, UK, 437
Pearl S. Buck International, USA, 474
Pesticide Action Network North America—PAN, USA, 534
Pesticide Action Network North America—PANNA, USA, 534
Peter G. Peterson Foundation, USA, 534
Peterson (Peter G.) Foundation, USA, 534
The Pew Charitable Trusts, USA, 534
Pforzheimer (Carl and Lily) Foundation, Inc, USA, 535
PhilDev—Philippine Development Foundation, USA, 535
Philippine-American Educational Foundation—PAEF, Philippines, 303
Philippine Development Foundation—PhilDev, USA, 535
Plenty International, USA, 535
Ploughshares Fund, USA, 536
Population Council, USA, 536
Pro Mujer International, USA, 536
Pro Women International, USA, 536
Prudential Foundation, USA, 537
Public Welfare Foundation, Inc, USA, 537
R. G. Menzies Scholarship Fund, Australia, 42
R. Howard Webster Foundation, Canada, 99
RBC Foundation, Canada, 96

Red Mujeres Afrolatinoamericanas Afrocaribeñas, Costa Rica, 107
Red de Mujeres para el Desarrollo, Costa Rica, 107
Reeve (Christopher and Dana) Foundation, USA, 538
Relief International, USA, 539
Research Corporation for Science Advancement—RCSA, USA, 539
Reynolds (Christopher) Foundation, USA, 539
Rhodes Trust, UK, 441
Richard King Mellon Foundation, USA, 523
Richelieu International, Canada, 96
Righteous Persons Foundation, USA, 539
Rob and Bessie Welder Wildlife Foundation, USA, 553
Robert A. Welch Foundation, USA, 553
Robert Bosch Foundation, Germany, 163
Robert-Bosch-Stiftung GmbH, Germany, 163
Robert R. McCormick Foundation, USA, 520
Robert Schalkenbach Foundation, Inc—RSF, USA, 543
Robert Wood Johnson Foundation—RWJF, USA, 512
Robertson Foundation for Government—RFFG, USA, 540
Rockefeller Brothers Fund, USA, 540
Rothschild (Edmond de) Foundations, USA, 541
Rothschild (Judith) Foundation, USA, 541
Royal Bank of Canada Charitable Foundation, Canada, 96
Royal Bank Financial Group Foundation, Canada, 96
Rubinstein (Arthur) International Music Society, Israel, 215
Runyon (Damon)–Winchell (Walter) Foundation, Cancer Research Fund, USA, 541
Russell Sage Foundation—RSF, USA, 541
RWJF—Robert Wood Johnson Foundation, USA, 512
SACO—Service d'assistance canadienne aux organismes, Canada, 83
Salamander Foundation, Canada, 97
Samuel H. Kress Foundation, USA, 516
Samuel Lunenfeld Charitable Foundation, Canada, 92
Samuel and Saidye Bronfman Family Foundation, Canada, 82
San Diego Foundation, USA, 542
San Francisco Foundation, USA, 542
Scaife Family Foundation, USA, 542
Schalkenbach (Robert) Foundation, Inc, USA, 543
Schusterman (Charles and Lynn) Family Foundation, USA, 543
Science and Technology Facilities Council—STFC, UK, 447
Seeds of Peace, USA, 543
Selby (William G. and Marie) Foundation, USA, 543
Seva Foundation, USA, 544
Shastri Indo-Canadian Institute, Canada, 97
SickKids Foundation, Canada, 97
The Sierra Club Foundation, USA, 544
Skaggs (L. J.) and Skaggs (Mary C.) Foundation, USA, 544
Skoll Foundation, USA, 544
Sloan (Alfred P.) Foundation, USA, 545
Smith Richardson Foundation, Inc, USA, 545
Smithsonian Institution, USA, 545
Sorenson Legacy Foundation, USA, 545
South Pacific Peoples Foundation Canada, Canada, 95
The Starr Foundation, USA, 546
Steelworkers Humanity Fund, Canada, 98
Steinberg (Nathan) Family Foundation, Canada, 98
Stichting Triodos Foundation, Netherlands, 282
Stiftelsen Riksbankens Jubileumsfond, Sweden, 357
Street Kids International, Canada, 98
The Streisand Foundation, USA, 547
Sun/Soleil—AREGAK, Armenia, 35
Surdna Foundation, Inc, USA, 547
Susan G. Komen for the Cure, USA, 515
Sverige-Amerika Stiftelsen, Sweden, 357
Sweden-America Foundation, Sweden, 357
Synergos—The Synergos Institute, USA, 460
Taiga Rescue Network—TRN, Finland, 133
Thiel Foundation, USA, 547
Third World Network—TWN, Malaysia, 260
Tibet Fund, USA, 548
Tides, USA, 548
Tides Foundation, USA, 548
Tinker Foundation, Inc, USA, 548
Triodos Foundation, Netherlands, 282
TRN—Taiga Rescue Network, Finland, 133
The Trull Foundation, USA, 548

Trust for Mutual Understanding, USA, 549
Tutu (Desmond) Peace Foundation, USA, 549
United Service Committee of Canada, Canada, 98
United States African Development Foundation—USADF, USA, 550
United States-Israel Educational Foundation—USIEF, Israel, 215
United States-Japan Foundation, USA, 550
USC Canada, Canada, 98
USIEF—United States-Israel Educational Foundation, Israel, 215
Valentine (Lawson) Foundation, USA, 551
Vancouver Foundation, Canada, 99
The Wallace Foundation, USA, 551
Wallach (Miriam G. and Ira D.) Foundation, USA, 552
Walmart Foundation, USA, 552
Walter and Duncan Gordon Charitable Foundation, Canada, 89
Warhol (Andy) Foundation for the Visual Arts, USA, 552
Webster (R. Howard) Foundation, Canada, 99
Weinberg (Harry and Jeanette) Foundation, USA, 552
The Welch Foundation, USA, 553
Welder (Rob and Bessie) Wildlife Foundation, USA, 553
Whirlpool Foundation, USA, 553
Whitehall Foundation, Inc, USA, 554
Wilbur Foundation, USA, 554
Wildlife Preservation Trust International, USA, 487
Wildlife Trust, USA, 487
The William and Flora Hewlett Foundation, USA, 503
William G. and Marie Selby Foundation, USA, 543
The William H. Donner Foundation, Inc, USA, 485
William and Mary Greve Foundation, Inc, USA, 500
The William Randolph Hearst Foundation, USA, 502
William T. Grant Foundation, USA, 499
Winrock International, USA, 555
Winston Churchill Foundation of the United States, USA, 479
Woerner (Manfred) Foundation, Bulgaria, 74
Women's Development Network, Costa Rica, 107
Woodrow Wilson National Fellowship Foundation, USA, 555
World Accord, Canada, 99
World Education, Inc, USA, 556
World Literacy of Canada—WLC, Canada, 99
World Teacher Trust, India, 206
Wurlitzer (Helene) Foundation of New Mexico, USA, 558

WESTERN EUROPE

1818 Fund Foundation, Netherlands, 280
A. G. Leventis Foundation, Cyprus, 111
A. M. Qattan Foundation, UK, 440
The A. P. Møller and Chastine Mc-Kinney Møller Foundation, Denmark, 120
A. P. Møller og Hustru Chastine Mc-Kinney Møllers Fond til almene Formaal, Denmark, 120
Abegg Foundation, Switzerland, 360
Abegg-Stiftung, Switzerland, 360
Absolute Return for Kids—ARK, UK, 401
Académie Goncourt—Société des Gens de Lettres, France, 136
Academy of European Law, Germany, 167
ACRI—Associazione di Fondazioni e di Casse di Risparmio Spa, Italy, 216
Action for Children, UK, 398
Adriano Olivetti Foundation, Italy, 223
Africa Educational Trust, UK, 399
Africa Grantmakers' Affinity Group—AGAG, USA, 458
Afro-Asian Institute in Vienna, Austria, 46
Afro-Asiatisches Institut in Wien, Austria, 46
Aga Khan Foundation—AKF, Switzerland, 360
AGAG—Africa Grantmakers' Affinity Group, USA, 458
Agnelli (Giovanni), Fondazione, Italy, 218
Agrupació Mutual Foundation, Spain, 338
Aid for Development Club, Austria, 46
Air France Corporate Foundation, France, 144
Airey Neave Trust, UK, 434
Al Fayed Charitable Foundation, UK, 399
The Al-Khoei Benevolent Foundation, UK, 399
Alamire Foundation, Belgium, 56
Åland Fund for the Future of the Baltic Sea, Finland, 131
Albéniz (Isaac), Fundación, Spain, 339

Albéniz Foundation, Spain, 339
Alfred Benzon Foundation, Denmark, 117
Alfred Benzons Fond, Denmark, 117
Alfred Toepfer Foundation F.V.S., Germany, 183
Alfred Toepfer Stiftung F.V.S., Germany, 183
Allen Lane Foundation, UK, 428
Allianz Cultural Foundation, Germany, 160
Allianz Foundation for Sustainability,
  Germany, 160
Allianz Kulturstiftung, Germany, 160
Allianz Umweltstiftung, Germany, 160
Almeida (Eng. António de), Fundação,
  Portugal, 310
Altman (Jenifer) Foundation, USA, 463
Alzheimer Spain Foundation, Spain, 339
AMADE Mondiale—Association Mondiale des
  Amis de l'Enfance, Monaco, 265
Amancio Ortega Foundation, Spain, 346
Amberes (Carlos de), Fundación, Spain, 339
Ambrosiana Paolo VI Foundation, Italy, 218
American Hungarian Foundation, USA, 466
American Scandinavian Foundation—ASF,
  USA, 467
Dell'Amore (Giordano) Foundation, Italy, 220
Ana Mata Manzanedo Foundation, Spain, 345
Anders Jahre's Foundation for Humanitarian
  Purposes, Norway, 291
Anders Jahres Humanitære Stiftelse,
  Norway, 291
The Andrew Balint Charitable Trust, UK, 402
The Andrew W. Mellon Foundation, USA, 523
ANESVAD, Spain, 337
Angelo Della Riccia Foundation, Italy, 221
Anna Lindh Euro-Mediterranean Foundation for
  Dialogue between Cultures, Egypt, 127
Anne Çocuk Eğitim Vakfı—AÇEV, Turkey, 388
The Anne Frank Trust UK, UK, 418
The Arab-British Chamber Charitable
  Foundation, UK, 401
Arbeiterwohlfahrt Bundesverband eV—AWO,
  Germany, 160
Archie Sherman Charitable Trust, UK, 448
Areces (Ramón), Fundación, Spain, 340
ARGUS, Belgium, 56
ARK—Absolute Return for Kids, UK, 401
Arpad Szenes–Vieira da Silva Foundation,
  Portugal, 313
Art Fund—National Art Collections Fund,
  UK, 401
Arthritis Australia, Australia, 37
Arthritis Foundation of Australia, Australia, 37
Arthritis Research Campaign, UK, 401
Arthritis Research UK, UK, 401
Arthritis and Rheumatism Council for Research
  in Great Britain and the Commonwealth,
  UK, 401
Arthur Rubinstein International Music Society,
  Israel, 215
Arts Council England, UK, 402
Ashden Charitable Trust, UK, 402
ASKO Europa-Stiftung, Germany, 161
ASKO Europe Foundation, Germany, 161
Asociación Española de Fundaciones, Spain, 337
Aspen Institute, USA, 470
Association of Charitable Foundations, UK, 396
Association of Community Trusts and
  Foundations, UK, 397
Association Égyptologique Reine Elisabeth,
  Belgium, 57
Association des fondations donatrices suisses,
  Switzerland, 360
Association of Foundations in the Netherlands,
  Netherlands, 272
Association of the Friends of the Swedish
  Institute at Athens, Sweden, 353
Association of German Foundations,
  Germany, 159
Association of Grantmaking Foundations in
  Switzerland, Switzerland, 360
Association of Italian Foundations and Savings
  Banks, Italy, 216
Association of Medical Research Charities—
  AMRC, UK, 396
Association Mondiale des Amis de l'Enfance,
  Monaco, 265
Association of Voluntary Service
  Organisations—AVSO, Belgium, 57
Associazione Donatella Flick, Switzerland, 361
Associazione di Fondazioni e di Casse di
  Risparmio Spa—ACRI, Italy, 216
Asthma UK, UK, 402
Atlantic Philanthropies, USA, 471
Auchan Foundation for Youth, France, 140
Auschwitz Foundation, Belgium, 60
Austrian Research Foundation for International
  Development, Austria, 48
Austrian Science Fund, Austria, 47

Austrian Society for Environment and
  Technology, Austria, 48
AVINA Foundation, Panama, 297
AWO—Arbeiterwohlfahrt Bundesverband,
  Germany, 160
Axel Springer Foundation, Germany, 179
Axel-Springer-Stiftung, Germany, 179
Axel Wenner-Gren Foundation for International
  Exchange of Scientists, Sweden, 358
Ayrton Senna Institute, Brazil, 73
Balint (Andrew) Charitable Trust, UK, 402
Baltic Sea Foundation, Finland, 131
Barceló Foundation, Spain, 340
Barenboim-Said Foundation, Spain, 340
Baring Foundation, UK, 402
Barka Foundation, Poland, 308
Barnardo's, UK, 403
The Barretstown Camp Fund Ltd, Ireland, 210
Barrié de la Maza (Pedro, Conde de Fenosa),
  Fundación, Spain, 340
The Batchworth Trust, UK, 403
BBC Children in Need Appeal, UK, 403
BBC World Service Trust, UK, 403
BBVA Foundation, Spain, 340
Beatrice Laing Trust, UK, 428
Beaverbrook Foundation, UK, 403
Beisheim (Professor Otto) Stiftung, Germany, 161
Belém Cultural Centre Foundation, Portugal, 310
Belgian Foundation Network, Belgium, 55
Benecke (Otto) Stiftung eV, Germany, 161
Benesco Charity Limited, UK, 404
Benetton Foundation for Study and Research,
  Italy, 219
Benzon (Alfred) Foundation, Denmark, 117
Berghof Foundation for Conflict Research,
  Germany, 161
Berghof Stiftung für Konfliktforschung GmbH,
  Germany, 161
Bernheim Foundation, Belgium, 60
Bertelsmann Foundation, Germany, 162
Bertelsmann Stiftung, Germany, 162
Beth (Evert Willem) Foundation,
  Netherlands, 272
Bettencourt Schueller Foundation, France, 141
Biblioteca dell'Accademia Nazionale dei Lincei,
  Italy, 216
BID-INTAL—Instituto para la Integración de
  America Latina y el Caribe, Argentina, 34
Binding (Sophie und Karl) Stiftung,
  Switzerland, 361
Biotechnology and Biological Sciences Research
  Council—BBSRC, UK, 404
Birthright, UK, 455
Blanc (José María), Fundación, Spain, 341
Blanceflor Boncompagni-Ludovisi, née Bildt
  Foundation, Sweden, 356
Bleustein-Blanchet (Marcel), Fondation pour la
  Vocation, France, 141
Bofill (Jaume), Fundació, Spain, 338
Boltzmann (Ludwig) Gesellschaft, Austria, 46
Bordoni (Ugo), Fondazione, Italy, 219
Bosch (Robert) Stiftung GmbH, Germany, 163
Botín (Marcelino) Fundación, Spain, 341
Bridge House Estates Trust Fund, UK, 410
Britain-Nepal Medical Trust, UK, 405
British Heart Foundation, UK, 406
British Institute at Ankara, UK, 406
British Schools and Universities Foundation,
  Inc—BSUF, USA, 473
Bundesverband Deutscher Stiftungen eV,
  Germany, 159
Business Institute Foundation, Spain, 344
Business and Society Foundation, Spain, 342
Cadbury (Edward) Charitable Trust, Inc, UK, 407
Cadbury (William Adlingon) Charitable Trust,
  UK, 407
Caetani (Leone), Fondazione, Italy, 216
CAF—Charities Aid Foundation, UK, 396
Caisses d'Epargne Foundation for Social
  Solidarity, France, 141
Caja Madrid Foundation, Spain, 341
The Camargo Foundation, France, 138
Campaign Against Exclusion Foundation,
  France, 140
Cancer Relief Macmillan Fund, UK, 430
Cancer Research UK, UK, 408
Cancerfonden, Sweden, 352
Canon Foundation in Europe, Netherlands, 272
CARE International—CI, Switzerland, 361
Cariplo Foundation, Italy, 219
Carl-Zeiss Foundation, Germany, 184
Carl-Zeiss-Stiftung, Germany, 184
Carlo Cattaneo Institute, Italy, 227
Carlo Collodi National Foundation, Italy, 223
Carlos de Amberes Foundation, Spain, 339
Carlsberg Foundation, Denmark, 117
Carlsbergfondet, Denmark, 117

Carnegie Trust for the Universities of Scotland,
  UK, 408
Carnegie UK Trust, UK, 408
Cartier Foundation for Contemporary Art,
  France, 141
Catholic Agency for World Development—
  Trócaire, Ireland, 213
Cattaneo (Carlo), Istituto, Italy, 227
CENSIS—Fondazione Centro Studi Investimenti
  Sociali, Italy, 216
Centre of Advanced European Studies and
  Research, Germany, 179
Centre d'Études, de Documentation,
  d'Information et d'Action Sociales—
  CEDIAS—Musée Social, France, 138
Centre Européen de la Culture—CEC,
  Switzerland, 362
Centre Français des Fondations—CFF,
  France, 135
Centre International de Développement et de
  Recherche—CIDR, France, 138
Centre for Social Studies, Documentation,
  Information and Action, France, 138
Centro di Cultura e Civiltà Contadina, Italy, 216
Centro de Investigación para la Paz, CIP—
  FUHEM, Spain, 338
Centro Português de Fundações—CPF,
  Portugal, 310
CEPH—Centre d'Étude du Polymorphisme
  Humain, France, 142
Cera, Belgium, 57
Charities Advisory Trust, UK, 396
Charities Aid Foundation—CAF, UK, 396
Charity Islamic Trust Elrahma, UK, 409
Charles Stewart Mott Foundation—CSMF,
  USA, 526
Chemistry Centre Foundation, France, 147
Child Migrants Trust, UK, 409
Children of the Mekong, France, 139
Children and Sharing, France, 139
Childwick Trust, UK, 409
Christoph Merian Foundation, Switzerland, 371
Christoph-Merian-Stiftung, Switzerland, 371
Churches' Commission for Migrants in Europe,
  Belgium, 57
Churchill (Winston) Foundation of the United
  States, USA, 479
CIDOB Foundation, Spain, 338
CIDR—Centre International de Développement
  et de Recherche, France, 138
CIMADE—Service Oecuménique d'Entraide,
  France, 138
Cini (Giorgio), Fondazione, Italy, 220
Cité Internationale des Arts, France, 139
Cité Internationale Universitaire de Paris,
  France, 139
Cittàltalia Foundation, Italy, 220
The City Bridge Trust, UK, 410
City of Lisbon Foundation, Portugal, 311
Claude Pompidou Foundation, France, 148
Clean Water Foundation, Netherlands, 282
CLIC Sargent, UK, 410
Climate Cent Foundation, Switzerland, 375
Clore Duffield Foundation—CDF, UK, 411
Co-operation for the Promotion and Development
  of Welfare Activities, Spain, 342
the cogito foundation, Switzerland, 362
Collodi (Carlo), Fondazione Nazionale, Italy, 223
Colt Foundation, UK, 411
Commission des Eglises auprès des Migrants en
  Europe/Kommission der Kirchen für
  Migranten in Europa, Belgium, 57
Commonwealth Foundation, UK, 411
Community Foundation Network—CFN, UK, 397
Community Foundation for Northern Ireland,
  UK, 412
Community Foundations Initiative, Germany, 159
Compagnia di San Paolo, Italy, 217
CONCAWE—Oil Companies' European
  Association for Environment, Health and
  Safety in Refining and Distribution,
  Belgium, 58
Concern Universal, UK, 412
Coote (Marjorie) Animal Charities Trust,
  UK, 412
Le Corbusier Foundation, France, 142
Costopoulos (J. F.) Foundation, Greece, 186
Coubertin Foundation, France, 142
Council of Finnish Foundations, Finland, 131
CRT Foundation, Italy, 220
Cultural Foundation of the German Länder,
  Germany, 174
Cystic Fibrosis Trust, UK, 413
Czech Donors Forum, Czech Republic, 112
Dahl (Roald) Foundation, UK, 413
Daiwa Anglo-Japanese Foundation, UK, 413
The Danish Cultural Institute, Denmark, 117
Danish Outdoor Council, Denmark, 118

Danish Peace Foundation, Denmark, 118
Danmark-Amerika Fondet, Denmark, 117
Danske Kulturinstitut, Denmark, 117
The Delius Trust, UK, 413
Demokratikus Átalakulásért Intézet,
  Hungary, 196
Denmark-America Foundation, Denmark, 117
Deutsch-Russischer Austausch eV—DRA,
  Germany, 164
Deutsche AIDS-Stiftung, Germany, 164
Deutsche Bank Endowment Fund for the
  Promotion of Science in Research and
  Teaching, Germany, 182
Deutsche Bank Foundation, Germany, 164
Deutsche Bank Stiftung, Germany, 164
Deutsche Gesellschaft für Auswärtige Politik—
  DGAP, Germany, 164
Deutsche Krebshilfe eV, Germany, 165
Deutsche Nationalstiftung, Germany, 165
Deutsche Orient-Stiftung, Germany, 165
Deutsche Telekom Foundation, Germany, 166
Deutsche Telekom Stiftung, Germany, 166
Deutsches Institut für Internationale
  Pädagogische Forschung, Germany, 166
Deutsches Rheuma-Forschungszentrum Berlin,
  Germany, 166
Development and Peace Foundation,
  Germany, 180
Diabetes UK, UK, 414
Dietmar Hopp Foundation, Germany, 170
Dietmar-Hopp-Stiftung, Germany, 170
Ditchley Foundation, UK, 414
Dóchas, Ireland, 210
DOEN Foundation, Netherlands, 280
Dom Manuel II Foundation, Portugal, 311
Donegani (Guido), Fondazione, Italy, 221
Donors' Association for the Promotion of Sciences
  and Humanities, Germany, 159
Dr Antonio Esteve Foundation, Spain, 343
Dr Barnardo's, UK, 403
Dr Marcus Wallenberg Foundation for Further
  Education in International Industry,
  Sweden, 358
Dr Marcus Wallenbergs Stiftelse för Utbildning i
  Internationellt Industriellt Företagande,
  Sweden, 358
Dr Rainer Wild Foundation for Healthy
  Nutrition, Germany, 184
Dr Rainer Wild-Stiftung—Stiftung für gesunde
  Ernährung, Germany, 184
Dräger Foundation, Germany, 166
Dräger-Stiftung, Germany, 166
Dulverton Trust, UK, 414
Dutch Cancer Society, Netherlands, 276
Ebelin and Gerd Bucerius ZEIT Foundation,
  Germany, 184
Eça de Queiroz Foundation, Portugal, 312
Ecology and Agriculture Foundation,
  Germany, 181
Economic Development Foundation, Turkey, 388
ECPD—European Centre for Peace and
  Development, Serbia, 324
Ecumenical Service for Mutual Help, France, 138
The Edmond de Rothschild Foundations,
  USA, 541
Eduardo Capa Foundation, Spain, 341
Edward Cadbury Charitable Trust, Inc, UK, 407
Eesti Mittetulundusühingute ja Sihtasutuste
  Liit, Estonia, 129
Egmont Fonden, Denmark, 118
Egmont Foundation, Denmark, 118
Einaudi (Luigi), Fondazione, Italy, 221
Eisai Foundation, France, 143
ELIAMEP—Hellenic Foundation for European
  and Foreign Policy, Greece, 187
Elizabeth Kostova Foundation for Creative
  Writing, Bulgaria, 76
Ellerman (John) Foundation, UK, 414
Else Kröner-Fresenius Foundation, Germany, 173
Else Kröner-Fresenius-Stiftung, Germany, 173
EMI Music Sound Foundation, UK, 415
Emile Chanoux Foundation—Institute for
  Federalist and Regionalist Studies, Italy, 218
ENCOD—European NGO Council on Drugs and
  Development, Belgium, 59
Enfance et Partage, France, 139
Enfants du Mekong, France, 139
Eng. António de Almeida Foundation,
  Portugal, 310
Engineering and Physical Sciences Research
  Council—EPSRC, UK, 415
Enrico Mattei Eni Foundation, Italy, 218
Ente Cassa di Risparmio di Firenze, Italy, 217
Entraide Protestante Suisse, Switzerland, 367
Entwicklungshilfe-Klub, Austria, 46
ERA—Europäische Rechtsakademie,
  Germany, 167
Erik Philip-Sörensen Foundation, Sweden, 356

Erik Philip-Sörensen Foundation for the
  Promotion of Genetic and Humanistic
  Research, Sweden, 356
Erik Philip-Sörensens Stiftelse, Sweden, 356
Ernest Kleinwort Charitable Trust, UK, 427
ERRC—Europako Rromano Čačimasko Centro,
  Hungary, 196
ERSTE Foundation, Austria, 46
ERSTE Stiftung—Die ERSTE Österreichische
  Spar-Casse Privatstiftung, Austria, 46
Esmée Fairbairn Foundation, UK, 416
Estonian Foundation Centre, Estonia, 129
Etruscan Foundation, USA, 489
Euris Foundation, France, 144
EURONATUR—Stiftung Europäisches
  Naturerbe, Germany, 180
Europa Nostra, Netherlands, 273
Europäische Rechtsakademie—ERA,
  Germany, 167
Europako Rromano Čačimasko Centro—ERRC,
  Hungary, 196
European Anti-Poverty Network—EAPN,
  Belgium, 59
European Centre of Culture, Switzerland, 362
European Centre for Peace and Development—
  ECPD, Serbia, 324
European Centre for Social Welfare Policy and
  Research, Austria, 47
European Climate Foundation, Netherlands, 273
European Coalition for Just and Effective Drug
  Policies—ENCOD, Belgium, 59
European Cultural Foundation—ECF,
  Netherlands, 273
European Environmental Bureau, Belgium, 59
European Federation of National Organizations
  Working with the Homeless, Belgium, 55
European Foundation for the Improvement of
  Living and Working Conditions, Ireland, 211
European Foundation for the Sustainable
  Development of the Regions—FEDRE,
  Switzerland, 363
European Institute of Health and Social Welfare,
  Spain, 349
European Institute of Progressive Cultural
  Policies, Austria, 47
European Mediterranean Institute, Spain, 349
European Nature Heritage Fund, Germany, 180
European Network of Foundations for Social
  Economy, Belgium, 56
European NGOs on Agriculture, Food, Trade and
  Development, France, 135
European Roma Rights Centre, Hungary, 196
European Science Foundation, France, 144
European Venture Philanthropy Association—
  EVPA, Belgium, 55
European Youth For Action—EYFA,
  Netherlands, 273
European Youth Foundation—EYF, France, 151
Europese Culerele Stichting, Netherlands, 273
Eurostep—European Solidarity Towards Equal
  Participation of People, Belgium, 60
Eurotransplant International Foundation,
  Netherlands, 274
Evens Foundation, Belgium, 61
Evert Willem Beth Foundation, Netherlands, 272
Eveson (Violet) Charitable Trust, UK, 416
The Eveson Charitable Trust, UK, 416
The Evian Group at IMD, Switzerland, 363
EVPA—European Venture Philanthropy
  Association, Belgium, 55
Evrika Foundation, Bulgaria, 75
EYFA—European Youth For Action,
  Netherlands, 273
F. C. Flick Foundation against Xenophobia,
  Racism and Intolerance, Germany, 168
F. C. Flick-Stiftung gegen Fremdenfeindlichkeit,
  Rassismus und Intoleranz, Germany, 168
FAF—French-American Foundation, USA, 494
Fairbairn (Esmée) Foundation, UK, 416
FAL—France Amérique Latine, France, 151
De Faunabescherming, Netherlands, 274
FDH—Frères des Hommes, France, 152
FEANTSA—Fédération Européenne des
  Associations Nationales Travaillant avec les
  Sans-Abri, Belgium, 55
Federal Association of Social Welfare
  Organizations, Germany, 160
The Federal Trust for Education and Research,
  UK, 416
Fédération Européenne des Associations
  Nationales Travaillant avec les Sans-Abri—
  FEANTSA, Belgium, 55
FEDRE—European Foundation for the
  Sustainable Development of the Regions,
  Switzerland, 363
FEEM—Fondazione ENI Enrico Mattei,
  Italy, 218

Feltrinelli (Giangiacomo), Fondazione, Italy,
  Italy, 221
Fernand Lazard Foundation, Belgium, 63
Fernand Lazard Stichting, Belgium, 63
Ferrero (Piera, Pietro e Giovanni), Fondazione,
  Italy, 221
FFL—Fondation Follereau Luxembourg,
  Luxembourg, 257
Finafrica Foundation—Giordano Dell'Amore
  Foundation, Italy, 220
Finnish Cultural Foundation, Finland, 132
Finnish Foundation for Technology Promotion,
  Finland, 133
Finnish Institute in London Trust, UK, 417
Florence Gould Foundation, USA, 499
Florence Savings Bank Foundation, Italy, 217
Follereau Foundation Luxembourg,
  Luxembourg, 257
Folmer Wisti Fonden, Denmark, 122
Folmer Wisti Foundation, Denmark, 122
FOM—Stichting voor Fundamenteel Onderzoek
  der Materie, Netherlands, 281
Fondation Abbé Pierre pour le logement des
  défavorisés, France, 140
Fondation Agir Contre l'Exclusion—FACE,
  France, 140
Fondation Albert 1er, Prince de Monaco—
  Institut Océanographique, France, 152
Fondation Auchan pour la Jeunesse, France, 140
Fondation Auschwitz, Belgium, 60
Fondation de l'Avenir, France, 140
Fondation Bernheim, Belgium, 60
Fondation Bettencourt-Schueller, France, 141
Fondation Caisses d'Epargne pour la solidarité—
  FCES, France, 141
Fondation Cartier pour l'Art Contemporain,
  France, 141
Fondation Casip-Cojasor, France, 142
Fondation Charles Veillon, Switzerland, 365
Fondation Claude Pompidou, France, 148
Fondation Le Corbusier—FLC, France, 142
Fondation de Coubertin, France, 142
Fondation Denis de Rougemont pour l'Europe,
  Switzerland, 365
Fondation pour le Développement de la
  Psychothérapie Médicale, spécialement de la
  psychothérapie de groupe, Switzerland, 363
Fondation Eisai, France, 143
Fondation Emile Chanoux—Institut d'Etudes
  Fédéralistes et Régionalistes, Italy, 218
Fondation 'Entente Franco-Allemande',
  France, 143
Fondation d'Entreprise Air France, France, 144
Fondation d'Entreprise La Poste, France, 144
Fondation d'Entreprise VINCI pour la Cité,
  France, 144
Fondation Euris, France, 144
Fondation Européenne de la Culture/Europese
  Culturele Stichting, Netherlands, 273
Fondation Européenne de la Science, France, 144
Fondation Evens Stichting, Belgium, 61
Fondation FACE—Fondation Agir Contre
  l'Exclusion, France, 140
Fondation Follereau Luxembourg—FFL,
  Luxembourg, 257
Fondation de France, France, 135
Fondation France-Israel, France, 145
Fondation Franco-Japonaise Sasakawa,
  France, 145
Fondation Francqui, Belgium, 61
Fondation Groupama Gan pour le Cinéma,
  France, 145
Fondation Hans Wilsdorf—Montres Rolex,
  Switzerland, 366
Fondation Henri Cartier-Bresson, France, 142
Fondation Hindemith, Switzerland, 363
Fondation Hugot du Collège de France,
  France, 145
Fondation Institut Suisse de Recherche
  Expérimentale sur le Cancer, Switzerland, 364
Fondation Internationale Léon Mba—Institut de
  Médecine et d'Epidémiologie Appliquée,
  France, 146
Fondation ISREC, Switzerland, 364
Fondation Jean Dausset—Centre d'Étude du
  Polymorphisme Humain—CEPH, France, 142
Fondation Jean Monnet pour l'Europe,
  Switzerland, 364
Fondation Latsis Internationale,
  Switzerland, 364
Fondation Louis-Jeantet de Médecine,
  Switzerland, 364
Fondation de Lourmarin Laurent-Vibert,
  France, 146
Fondation MACIF, France, 146
Fondation MAIF, France, 147
Fondation de la Maison de la Chimie, France, 147
Fondation Marc de Montalembert, France, 148

Fondation Marcel Bleustein-Blanchet pour la Vocation, France, 141
Fondation Marcel Hicter, Belgium, 61
Fondation Marguerite et Aimé Maeght, France, 147
Fondation Méditerranéenne d'Etudes Stratégiques—FMES, France, 147
Fondation Nationale pour l'Enseignement de la Gestion des Entreprises, France, 148
Fondation Nationale des Sciences Politiques, France, 148
Fondation Nicolas Hulot pour la Nature et l'Homme, France, 146
Fondation P&V, Belgium, 61
Fondation Paul-Henri Spaak—Stichting Paul-Henri Spaak, Belgium, 61
Fondation Philias, Switzerland, 359
Fondation 'Pour la Science'—Centre International de Synthèse, France, 149
Fondation Princesse Grace, Monaco, 265
Fondation pour la Recherche Médicale, France, 149
Fondation pour la Recherche Stratégique, France, 149
Fondation René Seydoux pour le Monde Méditerranéen, France, 150
Fondation Ripaille, France, 149
Fondation Robert Schuman, France, 150
Fondation Roi Baudouin, Belgium, 62
Fondation Simón I. Patiño, Switzerland, 365
Fondation Singer-Polignac, France, 150
Fondation Suisse-Liechtenstein pour les Recherches Archéologiques à l'Etranger, Switzerland, 373
Fondation Ushuaia, France, 146
Fondazione Adriano Olivetti, Italy, 223
Fondazione Ambrosiana Paolo VI, Italy, 218
Fondazione Angelo Della Riccia, Italy, 221
Fondazione per l'Arte, Italy, 219
Fondazione Benetton Studi Ricerche, Italy, 219
Fondazione Cariplo, Italy, 219
Fondazione Cassa di Risparmio delle Provincie Lombarde—Fondazione Cariplo, Italy, 219
Fondazione Cassa di Risparmio di Padova e Rovigo, Italy, 219
Fondazione Cassa di Risparmio di Torino, Italy, 220
Fondazione Centro Studi Investimenti Sociali—CENSIS, Italy, 216
Fondazione CittàItalia, Italy, 220
Fondazione Edoardo Garrone, Italy, 222
Fondazione Giangiacomo Feltrinelli, Italy, 221
Fondazione Giordano Dell'Amore, Italy, 220
Fondazione Giorgio Cini, Italy, 220
Fondazione Giovanni Agnelli, Italy, 218
Fondazione Giovanni Lorenzini, Italy, 222
Fondazione Guido Donegani, Italy, 221
Fondazione Ing. Carlo M. Lerici—FL, Italy, 222
Fondazione Internazionale Menarini, Italy, 222
Fondazione per l'Istituto Svizzero di Roma, Italy, 222
Fondazione Leone Caetani, Italy, 216
Fondazione Luigi Einaudi, Italy, 221
Fondazione Nazionale Carlo Collodi, Italy, 223
Fondazione Piera, Pietro e Giovanni Ferrero—ONLUS, Italy, 221
Fondazione Prada, Italy, 224
Fondazione Querini Stampalia, Italy, 224
Fondazione Ricci Onlus, Italy, 224
Fondazione Rodolfo Debenedetti—FRDB, Italy, 220
Fondazione Roma, Italy, 224
Fondazione Roma-Mediterraneo, Italy, 224
Fondazione Romaeuropa, Italy, 224
Fondazione RUI, Italy, 225
Fondazione Salvatore Maugeri—Clinica del Lavoro e della Riabilitazione, Italy, 223
Fondazione Ugo Bordoni, Italy, 219
Fondazione Umana Mente, Italy, 225
Fondazione Unipolis, Italy, 225
Fondazione di Venezia, Italy, 225
Fondazzjoni Patrimonju Malti, Malta, 261
Fondo per l'Ambiente Italiano—FAI, Italy, 225
Fonds Européen pour la Jeunesse—FEJ, France, 151
Fonds zur Förderung der Wissenschaftlichen Forschung—FWF, Austria, 47
Fonds National de la Recherche Scientifique—FNRS, Belgium, 61
Fonds National Suisse de la Recherche Scientifique, Switzerland, 374
Fonds Wetenschappelijk Onderzoek—Vlaanderen, Belgium, 62
Foreign Policy and United Nations Association of Austria—UNA-AUSTRIA, Austria, 48
Föreningen Svenska Atheninstitutets Vänner, Sweden, 353

FORWARD—Foundation for Women's Health, Research and Development, UK, 417
Foundation for Agricultural Research in the Province of Almería, Spain, 344
Foundation for the Arts, Italy, 219
Foundation for Assistance, Training and Integration of Disadvantaged People, Spain, 339
Foundation Cassa di Risparmio di Padova e Rovigo, Italy, 219
Foundation Centre for the Study of Social Investment, Italy, 216
Foundation for Children, Germany, 181
Foundation for Commercial and Technical Sciences—KAUTE, Finland, 131
Foundation for the Comparative Study of European Dictatorships and their Democratic Transition, Germany, 180
Foundation for Deep Ecology, USA, 492
Foundation for the Development of Medical Psychotherapy, especially Group Psychotherapy, Switzerland, 363
Foundation for Franco-German Co-operation, France, 143
Foundation for Fundamental Research on Matter, Netherlands, 281
Foundation of the Future, France, 140
Foundation for German–Polish Co-operation, Poland, 308
Foundation of the Hellenic World, Greece, 186
Foundation for International Scientific Co-ordination, France, 149
Foundation for International Studies—FIS, Malta, 261
Foundation for International Understanding, Denmark, 122
Foundation for Management Education—FME, UK, 417
Foundation for Medical Research, France, 149
Foundation Nicolas Hulot for Nature and Humankind, France, 146
Foundation to Promote Health, Liechtenstein, 255
Foundation for the Promotion of the German Rectors' Conference, Germany, 180
Foundation for Reading, Germany, 181
Foundation Robert Laurent-Vibert, France, 146
Foundation Rodolfo Debenedetti, Italy, 220
Foundation of Savings Banks, Spain, 341
Foundation of Spanish Commercial Agents, Spain, 339
Foundation for Sport and the Arts, UK, 417
Foundation for Strategic Research, France, 149
Foundation for the Study of Infant Deaths, UK, 417
Foundation in Support of Local Democracy, Poland, 308
Foundation for Swedish Culture in Finland, Finland, 133
Foundation for the Swiss Institute of Rome, Italy, 222
Foundation of Weimar Classics, Germany, 173
Foundation for Women, Spain, 345
Foundation for Women's Health, Research and Development—FORWARD, UK, 417
Foundation for Youth Research, Germany, 180
France Amérique Latine—FAL, France, 151
France-Israel Foundation, France, 145
Franco-Japanese Sasakawa Foundation, France, 145
Francqui Foundation, Belgium, 61
Frank Knox Memorial Fellowships, UK, 427
Frankfurt Foundation for German-Italian Studies, Germany, 168
Frankfurter Stiftung für Deutsch-Italienische Studien, Germany, 168
Fredsfonden, Denmark, 118
Freedom of Expression Foundation, Norway, 291
French-American Foundation—FAF, USA, 494
French Foundation Centre, France, 135
French National Foundation for Management Education, France, 148
Frères des Hommes—FDH, France, 152
Fridtjof Nansen Institute—FNI, Norway, 291
Friede Springer Foundation, Germany, 179
Friede Springer Heart Foundation, Germany, 179
Friede Springer Herz Stiftung, Germany, 179
Friede Springer Stiftung, Germany, 179
Friluftsraadet, Denmark, 118
Fritz Gerber Foundation for Gifted Young People, Switzerland, 366
Fritz-Gerber-Stiftung für Begabte Junge Menschen, Switzerland, 366
Fritz Thyssen Foundation, Germany, 183
Fritz Thyssen Stiftung, Germany, 183
FSLD—Foundation in Support of Local Democracy, Poland, 308

FUHEM—Fundación Hogar del Empleado, Spain, 343
Fund for the Italian Environment, Italy, 225
Fundação Arpad Szenes–Vieira da Silva, Portugal, 313
Fundação da Casa de Mateus, Portugal, 310
Fundação Centro Cultural de Belém, Portugal, 310
Fundação Cidade de Lisboa, Portugal, 311
Fundação das Descobertas, Portugal, 310
Fundação Dom Manuel II, Portugal, 311
Fundação Eça de Queiroz, Portugal, 312
Fundação Eng. António de Almeida, Portugal, 310
Fundação Luso-Americana para o Desenvolvimento, Portugal, 312
Fundação Mário Soares, Portugal, 313
Fundação Oriente, Portugal, 312
Fundação Ricardo do Espírito Santo Silva, Portugal, 311
Fundação de Serralves, Portugal, 312
Fundació Agrupació Mútua, Spain, 338
Fundació CIDOB, Spain, 338
Fundació Jaume Bofill, Spain, 338
Fundació 'La Caixa', Spain, 338
Fundación Actilibre, Spain, 339
Fundación AFIM—Ayuda, Formación e Integración del Minusválido, Spain, 339
Fundación de los Agentes Comerciales de España, Spain, 339
Fundación Albéniz, Spain, 339
Fundación Alzheimer España—FAE, Spain, 339
Fundación Amancio Ortega, Spain, 346
Fundación Ana Mata Manzanedo, Spain, 345
Fundación AVINA, Panama, 297
Fundación Banco Bilbao Vizcaya Argentaria—Fundación BBVA, Spain, 340
Fundación Barceló, Spain, 340
Fundación Barenboim-Said, Spain, 340
Fundación BBVA—Fundación Banco Bilbao Vizcaya Argentaria, Spain, 340
Fundación Caja Madrid, Spain, 341
Fundación de las Cajas de Ahorros—FUNCAS, Spain, 341
Fundación Carlos de Amberes, Spain, 339
Fundación Científica de la Asociación Española Contra el Cáncer—AECC, Spain, 342
Fundación CODESPA—Futuro en Marcha, Spain, 342
Fundación Dr Antonio Esteve, Spain, 343
Fundación EAES, Spain, 342
Fundación Eduardo Capa, Spain, 341
Fundación EFE, Spain, 342
Fundación Empresa y Sociedad, Spain, 342
Fundación Empresa-Universidad de Zaragoza—FEUZ, Spain, 342
Fundación Entorno, Empresara y Desarrollo Sostenible, Spain, 343
Fundación Escuela Andaluza de Economía Social, Spain, 342
Fundación Gala–Salvador Dalí, Spain, 343
Fundación Hogar del Empleado—FUHEM, Spain, 343
Fundación Innovación de la Economía Social—INNOVES, Spain, 343
Fundación Instituto de Empresa, Spain, 344
Fundación para la Investigación Agraria de la Provincia de Almería—FIAPA, Spain, 344
Fundación Jiménez Díaz, Spain, 344
Fundación José María Blanc, Spain, 341
Fundación José Miguel de Barandiarán, Spain, 341
Fundación José Ortega y Gasset, Spain, 346
Fundación Juan March, Spain, 345
Fundación Juanelo Turriano, Spain, 348
Fundación Laboral Sonsoles Ballvé Lantero, Spain, 344
Fundación Lealtad, Spain, 337
Fundación Loewe, Spain, 345
Fundación Luis Vives, Spain, 348
Fundación MAPFRE, Spain, 345
Fundación Marcelino Botín, Spain, 341
Fundación María Francisca de Roviralta, Spain, 341
Fundación Mujeres, Spain, 345
Fundación Nantik Lum, Spain, 345
Fundación ONCE, Spain, 346
Fundación Paideia Galiza, Spain, 346
Fundación Pedro Barrié de la Maza, Spain, 340
Fundación Promi, Spain, 347
Fundación Rafael del Pino, Spain, 347
Fundación Ramón Areces, Spain, 340
Fundación Santa María, Spain, 348
Fundación Santillana, Spain, 348
Fundación Yannick y Ben Jakober, Spain, 344
Fundacja Pomocy Wzajemnej Barka, Poland, 308
Fundacja Rozwoju Demokracji Loaklnej, Poland, 308

Fundacja Współpracy Polsko-Niemieckiej/ Stiftung für Deutsch–Polnische Zusammenarbeit, Poland, 308
Fundaja Wspomagania Wsi, Poland, 308
FWF—Fonds zur Förderung der Wissenschaftlichen Forschung, Austria, 47
The Gaia Foundation, UK, 418
GAIA—Groupe d'Action dans l'Intérêt des Animaux, Belgium, 62
Garfield Weston Foundation, UK, 455
The Gatsby Charitable Foundation, UK, 418
Gebert Rüf Stiftung, Switzerland, 366
Gemeinnützige Hertie Foundation, Germany, 169
Gemeinnützige Hertie-Stiftung, Germany, 169
Georges Lurcy Charitable and Educational Trust, USA, 519
Gerber (Fritz) Stiftung für begabte junge Menschen, Switzerland, 366
German AIDS Foundation, Germany, 164
German Cancer Assistance, Germany, 165
German Council on Foreign Relations, Germany, 164
German Institute for International Educational Research, Germany, 166
German Marshall Fund of the United States— GMF, USA, 496
German National Academic Foundation, Germany, 182
German National Trust, Germany, 165
German Orient Foundation, Germany, 165
German Rheumatism Research Centre Berlin, Germany, 166
German-Russian Exchange, Germany, 164
Getty (J. Paul) Jnr Charitable Trust, UK, 418
Giangiacomo Feltrinelli Foundation, Italy, 221
Gift of the Givers Foundation, South Africa, 332
Gilbert Murray Trust, UK, 433
Giordano Dell'Amore Foundation, Italy, 220
Giorgio Cini Foundation, Italy, 220
Giovanni Agnelli Foundation, Italy, 218
Giovanni Lorenzini Foundation, Italy, 222
The Glass-House Trust, UK, 419
Global Action in the Interest of Animals, Belgium, 62
Globe Foundation of Canada—GLOBE, Canada, 89
GMF—German Marshall Fund of the United States, USA, 496
Goncourt Academy—Literary Society, France, 136
Gould (Florence) Foundation, USA, 499
Graduate Institute of International Studies and Development Studies, Switzerland, 367
Great Britain Sasakawa Foundation, UK, 419
Groupama Gan Foundation for the Cinema, France, 145
Groupe d'Action dans l'Intérêt des Animaux— GAIA, Belgium, 62
Guido Donegani Foundation, Italy, 221
H. W. and J. Hector Foundation, Germany, 169
H. W. und J. Hector-Stiftung, Germany, 169
The Hague Club, UK, 397
Hamlyn (Paul) Foundation, UK, 419
Haniel Foundation, Germany, 169
Haniel-Stiftung, Germany, 169
Hans Wilsdorf Foundation, Switzerland, 366
Harold Hyam Wingate Foundation, UK, 456
Health Action International, Netherlands, 275
Heineman (Minna James) Stiftung, Germany, 170
Heinz, Anna and Carol Kroch Foundation, UK, 427
HEKS—Hilfswerk Evangelischen Kirchen Schweiz, Switzerland, 367
Hellenic Foundation for Culture, Greece, 186
Hellenic Foundation for European and Foreign Policy—ELIAMEP, Greece, 187
Hellenic Society for Disabled Children, Greece, 187
Helmut Horten Foundation, Switzerland, 367
Helmut-Horten-Stiftung, Switzerland, 367
Helsingin Sanomain Säätiö, Finland, 131
Helsingin Sanomat Foundation, Finland, 131
Henie Onstad Art Centre, Norway, 292
Henie Onstad kunstsenter, Norway, 292
Henri Cartier-Bresson Foundation, France, 142
The Henry Smith Charity, UK, 448
Heritage Foundation, France, 148
Heritage Lottery Fund—HLF, UK, 420
Hesse and Thuringia Savings Banks Cultural Foundation, Germany, 178
Hicter (Marcel), Fondation, Belgium, 61
Higgins (Terrence) Trust, UK, 420
Hilden Charitable Fund, UK, 421
Hilfswerk der Evangelischen Kirchen Schweiz— HEKS, Switzerland, 367
Hindemith Foundation, Switzerland, 363

HIVOS—Humanistisch Institut voor Ontwikkelings Samenwerking, Netherlands, 275
Hjärt-Lungfonden, Sweden, 353
Hopp (Dietmar) Stiftung, Germany, 170
Horten (Helmut) Stiftung, Switzerland, 367
Howard (Katharine) Foundation, Ireland, 211
Hugot Foundation of the Collège of France, France, 145
Humanistic Institute for Co-operation with Developing Countries, Netherlands, 275
Humanistisch Instituut voor Ontwikkelings Samenwerking—HIVOS, Netherlands, 275
IASC—International Arctic Science Committee, Germany, 171
Icelandic Human Rights Centre, Iceland, 197
IEIAS—Institut Européen Interuniversitaire de l'Action Sociale, Belgium, 62
IEMed—Institut Europeu de la Mediterrània, Spain, 349
IHCF—Stiftung zur Förderung der Gesundheit, Liechtenstein, 255
İktisadi Kalkınma Vakfı, Turkey, 388
Imperial Cancer Research Fund, UK, 408
Indian National Trust for Art and Cultural Heritage—INTACH, India, 203
Ing. Carlo M. Lerici Foundation, Italy, 222
Initiative and Achievement, Foundation of the Nassauische Sparkasse for Culture, Sport and Society, Germany, 171
Initiative Bürgerstiftungen, Germany, 159
Initiative und Leistung, Stiftung der Nassauischen Sparkasse für Kultur, Sport und Gesellschaft, Germany, 171
Innes (John) Foundation, UK, 422
INNOVES—Fundación Innovación de la Economía Social, Spain, 343
Institusjonen Fritt Ord, Norway, 291
Institut Català Mediterrània, Spain, 349
Institut Européen Interuniversitaire de l'Action Sociale—IEIAS, Belgium, 62
Institut Europeu de la Mediterrània—IEMed, Spain, 349
Institut international des Droits de l'Enfant, Switzerland, 368
Institut de Médecine et d'Épidémiologie Africaines—Fondation Léon Mba, France, 146
Institut Néerlandais, France, 152
Institut Océanographique—Fondation Albert 1er, Prince de Monaco, France, 152
Institut Pasteur de Lille, France, 153
Institut Universitaire de Hautes Etudes Internationales et du Développement, Switzerland, 367
Institute for European Environmental Policy— IEEP, UK, 422
Institute for Latin American and Caribbean Integration, Argentina, 34
Instituto Ayrton Senna, Brazil, 73
Instituto Europeo de Salud y Bienestar Social, Spain, 349
Instituto para la Integración de América Latina y el Caribe—BID-INTAL, Argentina, 34
Instituto Senna (Ayrton), Brazil, 73
INTACH (UK) Trust, India, 203
INTACH—Indian National Trust for Art and Cultural Heritage, India, 203
International Arctic Science Committee—IASC, Germany, 171
International Centre for the Arts, France, 139
International Centre for Democratic Transition—ICDT, Hungary, 196
International Centre for Development and Research, France, 138
International Centre for the Legal Protection of Human Rights—Interights, UK, 423
International Dental Rescue, Switzerland, 374
International Executive Service Corps— IESC, USA, 508
International Foundation of the High-Altitude Research Stations Jungfraujoch and Gornergrat, Switzerland, 369
International Foundation Léon Mba—Institute of Applied Medicine and Epidemiology, France, 146
International Fund for Ireland, Ireland, 211
International Institute for the Rights of the Child, Switzerland, 368
International Latsis Foundation, Switzerland, 364
International University Centre of Paris, France, 139
Internationale Stiftung Hochalpine Forschungsstationen Jungfraujoch und Gornergrat, Switzerland, 369

Irish Association of Non-Governmental Development Organizations—DOCHAS, Ireland, 210
Irish Funders Forum, Ireland, 210
Irish Youth Foundation, Ireland, 212
Islamic Relief Worldwide, UK, 425
ISREC Foundation, Switzerland, 364
Istituto Auxologico Italiano, Italy, 227
Istituto Carlo Cattaneo, Italy, 227
Istituto Luigi Sturzo, Italy, 227
Istituto Svedese di Studi Classici, Italy, 228
Italian Institute for Auxology, Italy, 227
IUC-Europe International Education Centre, Denmark, 119
IUC-Europe Internationalt Uddanneless Center, Denmark, 119
The J. F. Costopoulos Foundation, Greece, 186
J. Paul Getty Jnr Charitable Trust, UK, 418
Jahnsson (Yrjö) Foundation, Finland, 131
Japan Foundation Endowment Committee— JFEC, UK, 425
Japanese-German Center Berlin, Germany, 173
Japanisch-Deutsches Zentrum Berlin, Germany, 173
Jaume Bofill Foundation, Spain, 338
JCA Charitable Foundation, UK, 425
JCIE—Japan Center for International Exchange, Japan, 236
Jean Monnet Foundation for Europe, Switzerland, 364
Jenifer Altman Foundation—JAF, USA, 463
Jenny and Antti Wihuri Foundation, Finland, 134
Jenny ja Antti Wihurin Rahasto, Finland, 134
Jewish Colonization Association, UK, 425
JFEC—Japan Foundation Endowment Committee, UK, 425
Jiménez Díaz Foundation, Spain, 344
Johanna-Quandt-Stiftung, Germany, 177
John Ellerman Foundation, UK, 414
John Innes Foundation—JIF, UK, 422
John Moores Foundation, UK, 432
John Swire 1989 Charitable Trust, UK, 450
José María Blanc Foundation, Spain, 341
José Miguel de Barandiaran Foundation, Spain, 340
José Ortega y Gasset Foundation, Spain, 346
Joseph Levy Charitable Foundation, UK, 429
Joseph Levy Foundation, UK, 429
Joseph Rowntree Charitable Trust, UK, 441
Joseph Rowntree Foundation, UK, 442
Joseph Rowntree Reform Trust Ltd (including the JRSST Charitable Trust), UK, 442
JPMorgan Educational Trust, UK, 426
JPMorgan Fleming Foundation, UK, 426
JPMorgan Foundation, UK, 426
JRSST Charitable Trust, UK, 442
Juan March Foundation, Spain, 345
Juanelo Turriano Foundation, Spain, 348
Kade (Max) Foundation, Inc, USA, 513
Karić fondacija, Serbia, 325
Karić Foundation, Serbia, 325
Karl Kübel Foundation for Child and Family, Germany, 174
Karl-Kübel-Stiftung für Kind und Familie, Germany, 174
Katharine Howard Foundation, Ireland, 211
KAUTE—Foundation for Commercial and Technical Sciences, Finland, 131
Kennedy Memorial Trust, UK, 426
Kensington Estate—Henry Smith Charity, UK, 448
King Baudouin Foundation, Belgium, 62
King George's Fund for Sailors, UK, 447
King Gustaf V 90th Birthday Foundation, Sweden, 354
The King's Fund, UK, 427
Kirby Laing Foundation, UK, 427
KK-stiftelsen, Sweden, 354
Klassik Stiftung Weimar, Germany, 173
Kleinwort (Ernest) Charitable Trust, UK, 427
Knowledge Foundation, Sweden, 354
Knox (Frank) Memorial Fellowships, UK, 427
Knut and Alice Wallenberg Foundation, Sweden, 358
Knut och Alice Wallenbergs Stiftelse, Sweden, 358
Koç (Vehbi), Vakfı, Turkey, 391
Kokkalis Foundation, Greece, 187
Köning Boudewijnstichting/Fondation Roi Baudouin, Belgium, 62
Koningin Wilhelmina Fonds—Nederlandse Kankerbestryding, Netherlands, 276
Koninklijke Hollandsche Maatschappij der Wetenschappen, Netherlands, 276
Konung Gustaf V's 90-Årsfond, Sweden, 354
Kostova (Elizabeth) Foundation for Creative Writing, Bulgaria, 76
Kresge Foundation, USA, 516

Kress (Samuel H.) Foundation, USA, 516
Kroch (Heinz, Anna and Carol) Foundation, UK, 427
Kroch (Heinz and Anna) Foundation, UK, 427
Kröner-Fresenius (Else) Stiftung, Germany, 173
Kübel (Karl) Stiftung für Kind und Familie, Germany, 174
Kulturfonder for Sverige och Finland, Sweden, 354
KulturKontakt Austria–KKA, Austria, 48
Kulturstiftung der Länder—KSL, Germany, 174
Kvinna till Kvinna Foundation, Sweden, 354
KWF Kankerbestrijding, Netherlands, 276
L. J. Skaggs and Mary C. Skaggs Foundation, USA, 544
'La Caixa' Foundation, Spain, 338
Laing (Beatrice) Trust, UK, 428
Laing (Kirby) Foundation, UK, 427
Lama Gangchen World Peace Foundation, Italy, 227
Lambrakis Foundation, Greece, 187
Lambrakis Research Foundation, Greece, 187
Landis & Gyr Foundation, Switzerland, 370
Landis & Gyr Stiftung, Switzerland, 370
Lane (Allen) Foundation, UK, 428
Latin America France, France, 151
Lauder (Ronald S.) Foundation, Germany, 174
Law Society Charity, UK, 428
Léonie Sonning Music Foundation, Denmark, 121
Léonie Sonnings Musikfond, Denmark, 121
Leprosy Mission International, UK, 428
Lerici (Ing. Carlo M.), Fondazione presso il Politecnico di Milano, Italy, 222
Leukaemia and Lymphoma Research, UK, 428
Leventis (A. G.) Foundation, Cyprus, 111
Leverhulme Trust, UK, 429
Levy (Joseph) Foundation, UK, 429
Library of the National Academy of Lincei, Italy, 216
Littauer (Lucius N.) Foundation, Inc, USA, 519
Lloyds TSB Foundation for England and Wales, UK, 429
Loewe Foundation, Spain, 345
The Long Now Foundation—LNF, USA, 519
Lorenzini (Giovanni), Fondazione, Italy, 222
Louis-Jeantet Medical Foundation, Switzerland, 364
Lower Saxony Savings Bank Foundation, Germany, 175
Loyalty Foundation, Spain, 337
Lucius N. Littauer Foundation, Inc, USA, 519
Ludwig Boltzmann Gesellschaft, Austria, 46
Ludwig Institute for Cancer Research—LICR, USA, 519
Luigi Einaudi Foundation, Italy, 221
Luigi Sturzo Institute, Italy, 227
Luis Vives Foundation, Spain, 348
Lundbeck Foundation, Denmark, 120
Lundbeckfonden, Denmark, 120
Lurcy (Georges) Charitable and Educational Trust, USA, 519
Luso-American Development Foundation, Portugal, 312
Luxemburg (Rosa) Stiftung, Germany, 174
MACIF Foundation, France, 146
The Mackintosh Foundation, UK, 430
Macmillan Cancer Relief, UK, 430
Madariaga European Foundation, Belgium, 63
Maecenata Management GmbH, Germany, 159
Maeght (Marguerite et Aimé), Fondation, France, France, 147
MAIF Foundation, France, 147
Maison Franco-Japonaise, Japan, 237
Maj and Tor Nessling Foundation, Finland, 132
Malcolm Sargent Cancer Fund for Children, UK, 410
Malta Ecological Foundation, Malta, 261
Maltese Heritage Foundation, Malta, 261
Mama Cash, Netherlands, 277
Manfred Woerner Foundation, Bulgaria, 74
Mannréttindaskrifstofa Íslands, Iceland, 197
Manzanedo (Ana Mata), Fundación, Spain, 345
MAPFRE Foundation, Spain, 345
Marangopoulos Foundation for Human Rights, Greece, 188
Marc de Montalembert Foundation, France, 148
Marcel Bleustein-Blanchet Vocation Foundation, France, 141
Marcel Hicter Foundation, Belgium, 61
Marcelino Botín Foundation, Spain, 341
March (Juan), Fundación, Spain, 345
Marguerite and Aimé Maeght Foundation, France, 147
María Francisca de Roviralta Foundation, Spain, 347
Marie Curie Cancer Care, UK, 412
Mário Soares Foundation, Portugal, 313
Marjorie Coote Animal Charities Trust, UK, 412

Mateus House Foundation, Portugal, 310
Mattei (Enrico), Fondazione ENI, Italy, 218
MAVA Fondation pour la Nature, Switzerland, 371
Max Kade Foundation, Inc, USA, 513
Max Schmidheiny Foundation, Switzerland, 372
Max Schmidheiny-Stiftung, Switzerland, 372
Mayfair Charities Ltd, UK, 430
Mba (Léon), Fondation—Institut de Médecine et d'Épidémiologie Africaines, France, 146
Medical Foundation for the Care of Victims of Torture, UK, 430
Mediterranean Foundation of Strategic Studies, France, 147
Mellon (Andrew W.) Foundation, USA, 523
Menarini International Foundation, Italy, 222
MENCAP, UK, 431
Mental Health Foundation, UK, 431
Mercers' Charitable Foundation, UK, 431
Merian (Christoph) Stiftung, Switzerland, 371
Messerschmitt Foundation, Germany, 175
Messerschmitt-Stiftung, Germany, 175
Michael Otto Foundation for Environmental Protection, Germany, 176
Michael-Otto-Stiftung für Umweltschutz, Germany, 176
Milieukontakt International, Netherlands, 277
Milieukontakt Oost-Europa, Netherlands, 277
Minna James Heineman Foundation, Germany, 170
Minna-James-Heineman-Stiftung, Germany, 170
Minor Foundation for Major Challenges, Norway, 291
Møller (A.P.) and Chastine Mc-Kinney Møller Foundation, Denmark, 120
Monnet (Jean), Fondation pour l'Europe, Switzerland, 364
Mønsteds (Otto) Fond, Denmark, 120
Montres Rolex, Fondation, Switzerland, 366
Monument Trust, UK, 432
Moores (John) Foundation, UK, 432
Morfotiko Idryma Ethnikis Trapezis—MIET, Greece, 188
Mother Child Education Foundation, Turkey, 388
Mott (Charles Stewart) Foundation, USA, 526
Mukti Lawrence Foundation, Bangladesh, 52
Multiple Sclerosis Society of Great Britain and Northern Ireland, UK, 433
Murray (Gilbert) Trust, UK, 433
Muscular Dystrophy Campaign, UK, 433
Music Sound Foundation, UK, 415
Muslim Aid, UK, 433
Nansen (Fridtjof) Institute, Norway, 291
Nantik Lum Foundation, Spain, 345
National Art Collections Fund—Art Fund, UK, 401
National Asthma Campaign, UK, 402
National Bank of Greece Cultural Foundation, Greece, 188
National Council for Voluntary Organisations—NCVO, UK, 398
National Endowment for Science, Technology and the Arts—NESTA, UK, 434
National Foundation for Political Sciences, France, 148
National Fund for Scientific Research, Belgium, 61
National Heritage Memorial Fund, UK, 420
National Society for the Prevention of Cruelty to Children, UK, 435
The National Trust for Places of Historic Interest or Natural Beauty, UK, 434
NCH—National Children's Home, UK, 398
NCVO—National Council for Voluntary Organisations, UK, 398
Nederlands instituut voor Zuidelijk Afrika—NiZA, Netherlands, 278
Nederlandsche Maatschappij voor Nijverheid en Handel—NMNH, Netherlands, 278
Nederlandse Organisatie voor Internationale Ontwikkelingssamenwerking—Stichting NOVIB, Netherlands, 279
Nessling (Maj and Tor) Foundation, Finland, 132
NESTA—National Endowment for Science, Technology and the Arts, UK, 434
Van Neste Foundation, UK, 453
Netherlands Institute, France, 152
Netherlands Institute for Southern Africa, Netherlands, 278
Netherlands Society for Industry and Trade, Netherlands, 278
Network of Estonian Non-profit Organizations, Estonia, 129
Network of European Foundations—NEF, Belgium, 56
New Carlsberg Foundation, Denmark, 121
NFCR—National Foundation for Cancer Research, USA, 529

Niedersächsische Sparkassenstiftung, Germany, 175
Non-Governmental Ecological Vernadsky Foundation, Russian Federation, 320
Nordic Africa Institute Scholarships, Sweden, 355
Nordic Institute for Theoretical Physics, Sweden, 355
Nordisk Institut for Teoretisk Fysik—NORDITA, Sweden, 355
Nordiska Afrikainstitutets Stipendier, Sweden, 355
NORDITA—Nordisk Institut for Teoretisk Fysik, Sweden, 355
Norsk Utenrikspolitisk Institutt—NUPI, Norway, 292
Northern Ireland Voluntary Trust, UK, 412
Northern Rock Foundation, UK, 435
Norwegian Institute of International Affairs—NUPI, Norway, 292
Novartis Foundation for Therapeutical Research, Germany, 175
Novartis-Stiftung für therapeutische Forschung, Germany, 175
NOVIB (Oxfam Netherlands), Netherlands, 279
Novo Nordisk Foundation, Denmark, 120
NSPCC—National Society for the Prevention of Cruelty to Children, UK, 435
Nuffield Foundation, UK, 435
Ny Carlsbergfondet, Denmark, 121
Oak Foundation, Switzerland, 371
Oceanographic Institute—Albert 1st, Prince of Monaco Foundation, France, 152
The Officers' Association, UK, 435
Oil Companies' European Association for Environment, Health and Safety in Refining and Distribution—CONCAWE, Belgium, 58
Olivetti (Adriano), Fondazione, Italy, Italy, 223
ONCE—Spanish National Organization for the Blind—Foundation, Spain, 346
The One Foundation, Ireland, 212
OneWorld International Foundation, UK, 435
OPALS—Organisation Panafricaine de Lutte Contre le SIDA, France, 153
Open Society Institute—Brussels, Belgium, 63
Oranje Fonds, Netherlands, 278
Organisation Panafricaine de Lutte Contre le SIDA—OPALS, France, 153
Orient Foundation, Portugal, 312
Ortega (Amancio) Fundación, Spain, 346
Österreichische Forschungsstiftung für Internationale Entwicklung—ÖFSE, Austria, 48
Österreichische Gesellschaft für Außenpolitik und Internationale Beziehungen, Austria, 48
Österreichische Gesellschaft für Umwelt und Technik—ÖGUT, Austria, 48
Otto (Michael) Stiftung, Germany, 176
Otto Benecke Foundation, Germany, 161
Otto-Benecke-Stiftung eV, Germany, 161
Otto Mønsteds Fond, Denmark, 120
Otto Mønsteds Foundation, Denmark, 120
Oxfam NOVIB—Nederlandse Organisatie voor Internationale Ontwikkelingssamenwerking, Netherlands, 279
Oxfam NOVIB—Netherlands Organization for International Development Co-operation, Netherlands, 279
Paideia Galiza Foundation, Spain, 346
Pan-African Organization for AIDS Prevention, France, 153
PAN Europe—Pesticides Action Network Europe, Germany, 176
Pan-European Federation for Cultural Heritage, Netherlands, 273
The Parthenon Trust, Switzerland, 371
Pasteur Institute of Lille, France, 153
Patiño (Simón I.), Fondation, Switzerland, 365
Paul Hamlyn Foundation—PHF, UK, 419
Paul-Henri Spaak Foundation, Belgium, 61
PBI—Peace Brigades International, UK, 437
Peace Brigades International—PBI, UK, 437
Peace Research Center, Spain, 338
Pedro Barrié de la Maza Foundation, Spain, 340
Pestalozzi Children's Foundation, Switzerland, 374
Pesticide Action Network—Europe, Belgium, 63
Pesticides Action Network Europe—PAN Europe, Germany, 176
PHF—Paul Hamlyn Foundation, UK, 419
PHG Foundation, UK, 437
Philanthropy Ireland, Ireland, 210
Philias Foundation, Switzerland, 359
Piera, Pietro and Giovanni Ferrero Foundation, Italy, 221
Pilgrim Trust, UK, 437
Ploughshares Fund, USA, 536
Plunkett Foundation, UK, 438

Polden-Puckham Charitable Foundation—PPCF, UK, 438
Pôle européen des fondations de l'économie sociale, Belgium, 56
The Porter Foundation, UK, 439
Portuguese Foundation Centre, Portugal, 310
Post Office Foundation, France, 144
Prada Foundation, Italy, 224
Prince Bernhard Cultural Foundation, Netherlands, 282
Princess Grace Foundation, Monaco, 265
Prins Bernhard Culturfonds, Stichting, Netherlands, 282
Pro Juventute, Switzerland, 372
Professor Otto Beisheim Foundation, Germany, 161
Professor Otto Beisheim Stiftung, Germany, 161
proFonds, Switzerland, 359
Promi Foundation, Spain, 347
PRS for Music Foundation, UK, 440
Qattan (A. M.) Foundation, UK, 440
Queen Elisabeth Egyptological Association, Belgium, 57
Querini Stampalia Foundation, Italy, 224
Quilliam Foundation, UK, 440
Rafael del Pino Foundation, Spain, 347
Ramón Areces Foundation, Spain, 340
Ramsay Foundation, Switzerland, 372
The Rank Foundation, UK, 440
Rayne Foundation, UK, 441
Realdania, Denmark, 121
RED—Ruralité-environnement-développement, Belgium, 63
Reimers (Werner) Stiftung, Germany, 177
Reine Elisabeth, Association Égyptologique, Belgium, 57
Relief International, USA, 539
René Seydoux Foundation for the Mediterranean World, France, 150
Research Foundation—Flanders, Belgium, 62
Réseau d'ONG Européennes sur l'Agro-alimentaire, le Commerce, l'Environnement et le Développement—RONGEAD, France, 135
Reumatikerförbundet, Sweden, 355
Rhodes Trust, UK, 441
RIA—Royal Irish Academy, Ireland, 212
Ricardo do Espírito Santo Silva Foundation, Portugal, 311
Ricci Onlus Foundation, Italy, 224
Della Riccia (Angelo), Fondazione, Italy, 221
Richelieu International, Canada, 96
Ripaille Foundation, France, 149
RNIB—Royal National Institute of Blind People, UK, 444
Roald Dahl's Marvellous Children's Charity, UK, 413
Robert Bosch Foundation, Germany, 163
Robert-Bosch-Stiftung GmbH, Germany, 163
Robert Schalkenbach Foundation, Inc—RSF, USA, 543
Robert Schuman Foundation, France, 150
Rockefeller Brothers Fund, USA, 540
Rockwool Fonden, Denmark, 121
Rockwool Foundation, Denmark, 121
Romaeuropa Foundation, Italy, 224
Rome Foundation, Italy, 224
The Ronald S. Lauder Foundation, Germany, 174
RONGEAD—Réseau d'ONG Européennes sur l'Agro-alimentaire, le Commerce, l'Environnement et le Développement, France, 135
Rosa Luxemburg Foundation, Germany, 174
Rosa-Luxemburg-Stiftung, Germany, 174
Rothschild (Edmond de) Foundations, USA, 541
Roviralta (María Francisca de), Fundación, Spain, 347
Rowan Charitable Trust, UK, 441
Rowntree (Joseph) Charitable Trust, UK, 441
Rowntree (Joseph) Foundation, UK, 442
Rowntree (Joseph) Reform Trust, UK, 442
Royal Air Force Benevolent Fund, UK, 442
Royal Commonwealth Society for the Blind—Sight Savers International, UK, 448
Royal Holland Society of Sciences and Humanities, Netherlands, 276
Royal National Institute of Blind People—RNIB, UK, 444
Royal Society for Mentally Handicapped Children and Adults—MENCAP, UK, 431
Royal Society for the Prevention of Cruelty to Animals—RSPCA, UK, 445
Royal Society for the Protection of Birds—RSPB, UK, 445
RSPB—Royal Society for the Protection of Birds, UK, 445
RSPCA—Royal Society for the Prevention of Cruelty to Animals, UK, 445

Rubinstein (Arthur) International Music Society, Israel, 215
The Rufford Foundation, UK, 445
Rufford Maurice Laing Foundation, UK, 445
RUI Foundation, Italy, 225
Rural Culture and Civilization Centre, Italy, 216
Rural Development Foundation, Poland, 308
Ruralité Environnement Développement—RED, Belgium, 63
Rurality Environment Development, Belgium, 63
Rutgers WPF, Netherlands, 279
Säätiöiden ja rahastojen neuvottelukunta ry, Finland, 131
Safe Internet Foundation—SIF, Netherlands, 279
Said Foundation, UK, 446
Salvador Dalí Foundation, Spain, 343
Salvatore Maugeri Foundation—Occupational Health and Rehabilitation Clinic, Italy, 223
Samuel H. Kress Foundation, USA, 516
Samuel Sebba Charitable Trust, UK, 447
Sander (Wilhelm) Stiftung, Germany, 177
Sandoz Family Foundation, Switzerland, 372
Sandoz Fondation de Famille, Switzerland, 372
Santa María Foundation, Spain, 348
Santillana Foundation, Spain, 348
Sasakawa, Fondation Franco-Japonaise, France, 145
Save & Prosper Foundation, UK, 426
Savings Bank Foundation DnB NOR, Norway, 293
Schalkenbach (Robert) Foundation, Inc, USA, 543
Schuman (Robert), Fondation, France, 150
Schwarzkopf Foundation Young Europe, Germany, 178
Schwarzkopf Stiftung Junges Europa, Germany, 178
Schweisfurth Foundation, Germany, 178
Schweisfurth-Stiftung, Germany, 178
Schweizerisch-Liechtensteinische Stiftung für archäologische Forschungen im Ausland—SLSA, Switzerland, 373
Schweizerische Akademie der Medizinischen Wissenschaften, Switzerland, 373
Schweizerische Herzstiftung, Switzerland, 373
Schweizerische Stiftung Kardiologie, Switzerland, 373
Schweizerischer Nationalfonds zur Förderung der wissenschaftlichen Forschung/Fonds National Suisse de la Recherche Scientifique—SNF, Switzerland, 374
Science and Technology Facilities Council—STFC, UK, 447
Scientific Foundation of the Spanish Cancer Association, Spain, 342
Scope, UK, 447
Scouloudi Foundation, UK, 447
Seafarers UK, UK, 447
Secours Dentaire International, Switzerland, 374
Semmelweis Alapítvány Magyarországi Ortopédia Fejlesztéséért, Hungary, 195
Semmelweis Foundation for the Development of Orthopaedics in Hungary, Hungary, 195
Serralves Foundation, Portugal, 312
Seydoux (René), Fondation pour le Monde Méditerranéen, France, 150
Shackleton Foundation, UK, 448
Shelter—National Campaign for Homeless People, UK, 448
Sherman (Archie) Charitable Trust, UK, 448
Sight Savers International, UK, 448
Silva (Ricardo do Espírito Santo), Fundação, Portugal, 311
Simón I. Patiño Foundation, Switzerland, 365
Singer-Polignac Foundation, France, 150
Sino-British Fellowship Trust—SBFT, UK, 448
The Sir Jules Thorn Charitable Trust, UK, 451
Skaggs (L. J.) and Skaggs (Mary C.) Foundation, USA, 544
SLSA—Schweizerisch Liechtensteinische Stiftung, Switzerland, 373
SNF—Swedish Nutrition Foundation, Sweden, 356
Soares (Mário), Fundação, Portugal, 313
Sobell Foundation, UK, 449
Société Littéraire des Goncourt—Académie Goncourt, France, 136
Software AG Foundation, Germany, 178
Solidarité, France, 155
Solidarity, France, 155
Sonning (Léonie) Musikfond, Denmark, 121
Sonning Foundation, Denmark, 121
Sonnings-Fonden, Denmark, 121
Sonsoles Ballvé Lantero Labour Foundation, Spain, 344
Sophie and Karl Binding Foundation, Switzerland, 361
Sophie und Karl Binding-Stiftung, Switzerland, 361

South-East Institute—Foundation for Academic Research into South-Eastern Europe, Germany, 182
Spaak (Paul-Henri), Fondation, Belgium, 61
Spanish Association of Foundations, Spain, 337
Sparebankstiftelsen DnB NOR, Norway, 293
Sparkassen-Kulturstiftung Hessen-Thüringen, Germany, 178
Springer (Axel) Stiftung, Germany, 179
St John Ambulance, UK, 446
Staples Trust, UK, 449
Stichting DOEN, Netherlands, 280
Stichting Fonds 1818, Netherlands, 280
Stichting voor Fundamenteel Onderzoek der Materie—FOM, Netherlands, 281
Stichting Prins Bernhard Cultuurfonds, Netherlands, 282
Stichting Reinwater, Netherlands, 282
Stichting Spaak (Paul-Henri), Belgium, 61
Stichting voor de Technische Wetenschappen, Netherlands, 283
Stichting Triodos Foundation, Netherlands, 282
Stichting VSB Fonds, Netherlands, 283
Stiftelsen Blanceflor Boncompagni-Ludovisi, född Bildt, Sweden, 356
Stiftelsen för Miljöstrategisk Forskning—Mistra, Sweden, 356
Stiftelsen Riksbankens Jubileumsfond, Sweden, 357
Stiftelsen Teknikens Främjande—Tekniikan Edistämissäätiö, Finland, 133
Stifterverband für die Deutsche Wissenschaft eV, Germany, 159
Stiftung CAESAR, Germany, 179
Stiftung Entwicklung und Frieden—SEF, Germany, 180
Stiftung Ettersberg, Germany, 180
Stiftung Europäisches Naturerbe—EURONATUR, Germany, 180
Stiftung zur Förderung der Ernährungsforschung in der Schweiz—SFEFS, Switzerland, 374
Stiftung zur Förderung der Hochschulrektorenkonferenz, Germany, 180
Stiftung FVS, Germany, 183
Stiftung Jugend forscht e. V., Germany, 180
Stiftung für Kinder, Germany, 181
Stiftung Kinderdorf Pestalozzi, Switzerland, 374
Stiftung Klimarappen, Switzerland, 375
Stiftung Lesen, Germany, 181
Stiftung Ökologie & Landbau, Germany, 181
Stiftung Szondi-Institut, Switzerland, 375
Stiftung Vivamos Mejor, Switzerland, 375
Stiftung Weimarer Klassik Kunstsammlungen, Germany, 173
Stiftung West-Östliche Begegnungen, Germany, 182
Stiftung für wissenschaftliche Südosteuropaforschung—Südost-Institut, Germany, 182
Stiftungsfonds Deutsche Bank zur Förderung der Wissenschaft in Forschung und Lehre, Germany, 182
Strickland Foundation, Malta, 261
The Stroke Association, UK, 450
Studienstiftung des deutschen Volkes, Germany, 182
Sturzo (Luigi), Istituto, Italy, 227
Südost-Institut—Stiftung für wissenschaftliche Südosteuropaforschung, Germany, 182
Svenska Institutet i Rom/Istituto Svedese di Studi Classici a Roma, Italy, 228
Svenska Kulturfonden, Finland, 133
Sverige-Amerika Stiftelsen, Sweden, 357
Sweden-America Foundation, Sweden, 357
Sweden-Japan Foundation—SJF, Sweden, 357
Swedish Cancer Society, Sweden, 352
Swedish and Finnish Cultural Foundation, Sweden, 354
Swedish Foundation for Strategic Environmental Research, Sweden, 356
The Swedish Heart-Lung Foundation, Sweden, 353
Swedish Institute in Rome, Italy, 228
Swedish Nutrition Foundation—SNF, Sweden, 356
Swedish Rheumatism Association, Sweden, 355
Swiss Academy of Medical Sciences, Switzerland, 373
Swiss Heart Foundation, Switzerland, 373
Swiss Interchurch Aid, Switzerland, 367
Swiss-Liechtenstein Foundation for Archaeological Research Abroad—SLFA, Switzerland, 373
Swiss National Science Foundation—SNF, Switzerland, 374
Swiss Nutrition Foundation, Switzerland, 374

SwissFoundations—Verband der Schweizer
Förderstiftungen/Association des fondations
donatrices suisses, Switzerland, 360
Szenes (Arpad)–Vieira da Silva, Fundação,
Portugal, 313
Szondi Institute Foundation, Switzerland, 375
Taiga Rescue Network—TRN, Finland, 133
Technologiestichting—STW, Netherlands, 283
Technology Foundation, Netherlands, 283
Tekniikan Edistämissäätiö–Stiftelsen för
teknikens främjande—TES, Finland, 133
Terre des Hommes Foundation, Switzerland, 376
Terrence Higgins Trust—THT, UK, 420
TFF—Transnationella Stiftelsen för Freds- och
Framtidsforskning, Sweden, 358
Third World Network—TWN, Malaysia, 260
Thomas B. Thrige Foundation, Denmark, 121
Thomas B. Thriges Fond, Denmark, 121
Thomson Foundation, UK, 451
Thorn (The Sir Jules) Charitable Trust, UK, 451
Thriges (Thomas B.) Fond, Denmark, 121
Thyssen (Fritz) Stiftung, Germany, 183
Toepfer (Alfred) Stiftung, Germany, 183
Trans-Antarctic Association—TAA, UK, 451
Transnational Foundation for Peace and Future
Research, Sweden, 358
Transnationella Stiftelsen för Freds- och
Framtidsforskning—TFF, Sweden, 358
Triodos Foundation, Netherlands, 282
TRN—Taiga Rescue Network, Finland, 133
Trócaire—Catholic Agency for World
Development, Ireland, 213
Trust for London, UK, 451
Trusthouse Charitable Foundation, UK, 451
Tudor Trust, UK, 452
Turin Savings Bank Foundation, Italy, 220
Turriano (Juanelo) Fundación, Spain, 348

Tutu Foundation UK, UK, 452
Twenty-Ninth May 1961 Charity, UK, 452
Ugo Bordoni Foundation, Italy, 219
Umana Mente Foundation, Italy, 225
Umut Foundation, Turkey, 391
Umut Vakfı, Turkey, 391
Universitaire Stichting, Belgium, 64
University Foundation, Belgium, 64
University of Zaragoza Business Foundation,
Spain, 342
Vehbi Koç Foundation, Turkey, 391
Vehbi Koç Vakfı, Turkey, 391
Venice Foundation, Italy, 225
Verband der Schweizer Förderstiftungen,
Switzerland, 360
Vereniging van Fondsen in Nederland—FIN,
Netherlands, 272
VINCI Corporate Foundation for the City,
France, 144
Vivamos Mejor Foundation, Switzerland, 375
Vodafone Foundation Germany, Germany, 183
Vodafone Stiftung Deutschland, Germany, 183
Volkart Foundation, Switzerland, 376
Volkart-Stiftung, Switzerland, 376
Wallenberg (Knut och Alice) Stiftelse,
Sweden, 358
War on Want, UK, 454
Wates Foundation, UK, 454
Webb Memorial Trust, UK, 455
WellBeing, UK, 455
Wellbeing of Women, UK, 455
Welzijn Juliana Fonds, Netherlands, 278
Wenner-Gren Centre Foundation for Scientific
Research, Sweden, 358
Wenner-Gren Foundations, Sweden, 358
Werner Reimers Foundation, Germany, 177
Werner-Reimers-Stiftung, Germany, 177

West-East Foundation, Germany, 182
West-Nordic Foundation, Iceland, 197
Weston (Garfield) Foundation, UK, 455
Whirlpool Foundation, USA, 553
Wihuri (Jenny and Antti) Foundation,
Finland, 134
Wild (Dr Rainer) Stiftung, Germany, 184
Wildlife Protection, Netherlands, 274
Wilhelm Sander Foundation, Germany, 177
Wilhelm-Sander-Stiftung, Germany, 177
William Adlington Cadbury Charitable Trust,
UK, 407
Wingate (Harold Hyam) Foundation, UK, 456
Winston Churchill Foundation of the United
States, USA, 479
Wisti (Folmer) Foundation for International
Understanding, Denmark, 122
Woerner (Manfred) Foundation, Bulgaria, 74
The Wolfson Family Charitable Trust, UK, 456
Women's Aid, Ireland, 213
Workers' Centre Foundation, Spain, 343
World Association of Children's Friends,
Monaco, 265
The World of NGOs, Austria, 46
World Population Foundation, Netherlands, 279
World Teacher Trust, India, 206
Yannick and Ben Jakober Foundation, Spain, 344
Yrjö Jahnsson Foundation, Finland, 131
Yrjö Jahnssonin säätiö, Finland, 131
Zeiss (Carl) Stiftung, Germany, 184
ZEIT-Stiftung Ebelin und Gerd Bucerius,
Germany, 184
Zochonis Charitable Trust, UK, 457
Zurich Community Trust, UK, 457
Zurich Financial Services (UKISA) Community
Trust Ltd, UK, 457